DICTIONARY OF MING BIOGRAPHY
Volume I
A-L

There is properly no History: only Biography.
—Ralph Waldo Emerson
Essays, first series (1841)

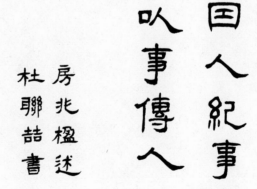

Dictionary
of
MING BIOGRAPHY
1368-1644

明代名人傳

THE MING BIOGRAPHICAL HISTORY PROJECT
OF THE
ASSOCIATION FOR ASIAN STUDIES

L. Carrington Goodrich, EDITOR
Chaoying Fang, ASSOCIATE EDITOR

Volume I
A-L

1976
COLUMBIA UNIVERSITY PRESS
New York and London

Library of Congress Cataloging in Publication Data

Association for Asian Studies. Ming Biographical
  History Project Committee.
    Dictionary of Ming biography, 1368–1644.

    Added title: Ming tai ming jen chuan.
    Bibliography: p. 1695.
    Includes index.
    1. China—History—Ming dynasty, 1368–1644—
Biography. 2. China—Biography. I. Goodrich,
Luther Carrington, 1894–   II. Fang, Chao-ying,
1908–   III. Title.
DS753.5.A84 1976   951′.026′0922 [B]   75-26938
ISBN 0-231-03801-1 (v. 1)
ISBN 0-231-03833-X (v. 2)

List of Contributors

Heinrich Busch
James F. Cahill
Cha Chuwhan 車柱環
Albert Chan 陳綸緒
David Chan 陳少岳
Hok-lam Chan 陳學霖
Chan Wing-tsit 陳榮捷
Chang Kuei-sheng 張桂生
Peter Chang 昌彼得
Ch'en Chih-mai 陳之邁
Toyoko Y. Chen 陳豐子
Chiang Yee 蔣彝
Julia Ching 秦家懿
Chiu Ling-yeong 趙令揚
Chou Ju-hsi 周汝禧
Chou Tao-chi 周道濟
Yung-deh Richard Chu 朱永德
Chun Hae-jong 全海宗
Jon Carter Covell
Robert Crawford
John W. Dardess
A. R. Davis
Ronald G. Dimburg
Edward L. Dreyer
George H. Dunne
Yu-ho Tseng Ecke 曾幼荷
Richard Edwards
Søren Egerod
Chaoying Fang 房兆楹
Lienche Tu Fang 杜聯喆
Edward L. Farmer
Eugen Feifel
Herbert Franke
Wolfgang Franke
Emile Gaspardone
Else Glahn
L. Carrington Goodrich
Tilemann Grimm
Dell R. Hales
Hŏ Sŏn-do 許善道
Angela Hsi 奚孫凝芝
K. C. Hsiao 蕭公權
Huang P'ei 黃培
Ray Huang 黃仁宇

Huang Yang-chih 黃養志
Arthur W. Hummel
Mingshui Hung 洪銘水
Charles O. Hucker
Jan Yün-hua 冉雲華
Jen Ch'ing-hwa Ho 任何慶華
D. R. Jonker
Edward Kelly
Barbara Krafft
D. W. Y. Kwok 郭穎頤
Ellen J. Laing
John D. Langlois, Jr.
Thomas Lawton
Lee Hwa-chou 李華宙
Peter H. Lee 李鶴洙
Donald D. Leslie
Li Chu-tsing 李鑄晉
Li T'ien-yi 李田意
I-cheng Liang 梁一成
Liu Chia-chü 劉家駒
James J. Y. Liu 劉若愚
Liu Lin-sheng 劉麟生
Liu Ts'un-yan 柳存仁
W. P. Liu 劉渭平
Lo Chin-tang 羅錦堂
Lo Jung-pang 羅榮邦
Ulrich Mammitzsch
Andrew L. March
John T. Meskill
Roy Andrew Miller
James F. Millinger
Min Du-gi 閔斗基
Frederick W. Mote
Mou Jun-sun 牟潤孫
W. Pachow 巴宙
James B. Parsons
Luciano Petech
T. Pokora
Donald L. Potter
Earl H. Pritchard
Hugh Richardson
K. G. Robinson
Morris Rossabi
Antonio Sisto Rosso

Anna Seidel

Henry Serruys

Nathan Sivin

Kwan-wai So 蘇均煒

Song Czetong 宋在東

E-tu Zen Sun 孫任以都

Sun Yüan-king 孫婉敬

Boleslaw Szczesniak

C. N. Tay 鄭僧一

Romeyn Taylor

Teng Ssu-yü 鄧嗣禹

T. H. Tsien 錢存訓

Tu Ching-i 涂敬詒

Tu Wei-ming 杜維明

Harrie Vanderstappen

Fritz Vos

Benjamin E. Wallacker

Wang Gung-wu 王賡武

Wang Yi-t'ung 王伊同

Alex Wayman

Hugh C. Wass

T. W. Weng 翁同文

John K. Whitmore

Bodo Wiethoff

B. H. Willeke

George H. C. Wong 黃道章

Edmund Worthy

Chi-hua Wu 吳緝華

K. T. Wu 吳光清

Nelson Wu 吳訥孫

Wu Pei-yi 吳百益

Yang Chin-yi 楊慶儀

Yang Tsung-han 楊宗翰

Winston L. Y. Yang 楊力宇

Martie W. Young

Chun-fang Yü 于君方

Leon Zolbrod

Introduction and Acknowledgments

These volumes grew out of a need, more and more urgently expressed during the 1950s in various circles of the Association for Asian Studies, for a work as fundamental for the nearly three hundred years of the Ming as for the almost equally long period of the Ch'ing. Our academic institutions in the west had many of the basic sources for research, could undoubtedly acquire or borrow more, and we were hopeful that sufficient specialized talent might be drawn upon to prepare material that would open up the riches of the centuries in question. The first formal proposal came in 1958 at a meeting of the Association held in New York, chaired by John K. Fairbank. It was agreed then and confirmed in 1959 at a meeting in Washington that a project to launch such a work was an enterprise eminently worthy of the best efforts of the Association.

In many ways the decision was a timely one. In 1959-60 William Theodore de Bary was able to enlist the services of Yukio Yamane of the Toyo Bunko in drawing up a bibliography of recent articles in Chinese and Japanese on personalities of the Ming epoch. (To this Dr. Yamane subsequently added several other valuable aids.) At the same time P. K. Yü (Yü Ping-ch'üan) was preparing independently his *Chinese History: Index to Learned Articles, 1902-1962*, vol. I (Hong Kong, 1963), which covered some of the same ground. Mr. de Bary's next signal service to the Project was to persuade Chaoying Fang and his able wife Lienche Tu Fang to leave Australia to join the editorial staff in New York (1963). In the meantime the National Central Library in Taipei was on the point of completing a condensed biographical dictionary of Ming figures, complete with dates and bibliographical references (published 1965/66 with help from the Asia Foundation), and the Academia Sinica (Taiwan) was about to bring out a carefully edited reproduction of the *Ming shih-lu* (The veritable records of the dynasty), published in Taipei during the years 1962-67. Shortly before, in 1958, a publishing house in Peking printed the almost indispensable private history of the Ming, the *Kuo-ch'üeh*, by T'an Ch'ien (*q. v.*), and the University of Kyoto was making available not only a microfilm copy of a valuable biographical collection, entitled the *Huang Ming wen-hai*, known only in manuscript, but also an index to it in three fascicles.

Several other significant aids appeared in these same early years. First let us mention an index of most of the biographies of Ming worthies contained in the vast corpus of the *Ku-chin T'u-shu chi-ch'eng*. Though this is acknowledgedly a secondary source, it includes thousands of sketches of people drawn verbatim from works that are often either obscure or lost; and it proved its usefulness time and again. This index was prepared under the supervision of Professor Mou Jun-sun of New Asia College in 1963, again with the help of the Asia Foundation. Second, there is Wolfgang Franke's *Introduction to the Sources of Ming History* (Kuala Lumpur and Singapore, 1968). Fortunately, the author shared a copy of his manuscript with the Project several years before publication; so it had the benefit of his research into the holdings of East Asian libraries almost from the start. Third, there is the recently edited *Ming-shih* (Taipei, 1963); its editors have redeemed their mistakes in punctuation by including a highly useful index of all personal names. Fourth, there is the valuable "Index of terms and titles in 'Governmental Organization of the Ming Dynasty,'" by Charles O. Hucker (Cambridge, Mass., 1961). These and numerous other books: library catalogues, lists of gazetteer holdings, collections of *ts'ung-shu*, reproductions of paintings and calligraphy, catalogues of artists, and the like, have lightened our work and made it more effective.

Through the generous cooperation of Columbia University, and with modest grants from a number of universities and colleges[1] and the Rockefeller Foundation, we started in the autumn of 1962 to lay the groundwork for the enterprise in two rooms (later expanded to three) in Kent Hall. As these rooms are but a short remove from the East Asian Library, our staff was able to make full use of that excellent depository, and even received permission to transfer many rare Ming books to locked cabinets in our own quarters. Throughout the decade of our tenancy we enjoyed the library's unfailing collaboration even to the extent of persuading it to acquire the entire set of microfilms of the rare books of the National Library of Peiping. Later, thanks to the assistance of the Asia Foundation in Taiwan, we succeeded in helping the National Central Library in Taipei to train a technician and set up a laboratory for the microfilming of many rare Chinese volumes printed during the Ming; the purchase of these, with grants from the American Council of Learned Societies and the China International Foundation, has constituted a major supplement to the microfilm materials previously acquired, and furnished a base for research of major usefulness.

[1]Australian National, California, Chicago, Columbia, Cornell, Dartmouth, Duke, Florida State, Harvard, Illinois, Indiana, Michigan, Pennsylvania, Princeton, Smith, Stanford, Texas, Washington (at Seattle), Wisconsin, Yale.

One of our initial activities was to solicit biographies from scholars all over the world.[2] The response was heart-warming. Their number includes contributors from Europe, India, Ceylon (Sri Lanka), Australia, Malaysia, Hong Kong, Korea, Taiwan (Republic of China), Japan, and, of course, the United States and Canada. In acknowledging their assistance I must at the same time give thanks to those in academic halls and libraries who have responded to requests for information and other favors. In addition to the mature scholars who have written biographies we have had the benefit over several summers of several younger men and women, generally candidates for the doctorate in Chinese. The American Council of Learned Societies has provided modest stipends, and our staff has had the pleasure and responsibility of introducing them to the literature and the techniques of research. This collaboration has worked both to our advantage and, hopefully, to theirs.

During the entire period of our labors we have had the unfailing support of the Association for Asian Studies, its Committee on the Ming Biographical History Project[3]—in particular its patient chairman, Charles O. Hucker, and executive secretary, William Theodore de Bary— and the Association's successive officers, especially the efficient comptroller, Victoria Spang. It is they who have been largely responsible for raising funds necessary to keep us solvent, from foundations (the Ford chiefly), universities and colleges, and from the United States government. Finally, a word of gratitude to the late Miss Elisabeth Shoemaker for reviewing our manuscript and readying it for publication, and to Nora C. (Mrs. Arthur) Buckley who has assisted the editor in tasks too numerous to mention.

L. Carrington Goodrich

Editor

[2]Certain individuals whose activities fell within our period have not been included as their biographies are in ECCP. For a list, see "Names arranged in chronological order," ECCP, pp. 983, 984.

[3]Robert B. Crawford, Wm. Theodore de Bary, Richard Edwards, John K. Fairbank, L. Carrington Goodrich, Ping-ti Ho, Charles O. Hucker, Arthur W. Hummel, Charles W. MacSherry, John Meskill, Frederick W. Mote, James B. Parsons, Earl H. Pritchard, Ssu-yu Teng, Hellmut Wilhelm, Arthur F. Wright, Lien-sheng Yang.

Explanatory Notes

Proper Names

The romanization systems employed are the Wade-Giles for Chinese (certain diacritical marks excepted), the Rōmaji for Japanese, and the McCune-Reischauer for Korean. Characters are generally supplied for less known place names, but widely known islands, rivers, lakes, mountains, cities, and the thirteen provinces of Ming times are given according to conventional English spellings. Anhwei, not a province until the beginning of the Ch'ing, is often mentioned in brackets to indicate the location of a district or prefecture. Personal names are written in the Chinese order, *hsing* then *ming*, followed (where known) by courtesy, *tzu* (=T.), pen, or *hao* (=H.), and posthumous (=Pth.) names. In a few cases, where a scholar may be better known by his *tzu*, this is cited after his *hsing*, his *ming* following in brackets.

The Calendar

Dates are calculated according to the western calendar. Occasionally the word *sui* (meaning years since conception) is employed when the exact year of birth is unknown, or when someone's birthday is celebrated at an advanced age.

Weights and Measures

Standard units include the following, with approximate English equivalents:

里 *li* = 1/3 English mile
畝 *mou* = 1/7 acre
石 *shih* (measure of grain) = picul = 133.3 pounds
頃 *ch'ing* = 100 *mou*
斤 *chin* = 1⅓ pounds
兩 *liang* = 1/16 *chin* = 1 tael
錢 *ch'ien* = 1/10 *liang*
貫 *kuan* = 1,000 cash

Civil Service Degrees or Ranks

監生 *chien-sheng* = student in one of the national universities
貢生 *kung-sheng* = tribute student to one of the national universities
生員 *sheng-yüan* (or *hsiu-ts'ai*) = bachelor (first degree), including students in the local

government school

舉人 *chü-jen* (cj) = provincial graduate (second degree)

進士 *chin-shih* (cs) = metropolitan graduate (third and highest degree)

狀元 *chuang-yüan* = optimus among the *chin-shih* in any given triennium

Certain Standard Terms

chüan (ch.) 卷 = chapter. In Korean *kwŏn*, in Japanese *kan*.

hua-pen 話本 = colloquial short story

nien-p'u 年譜 = chronological biography

pa-ku 八股 = eight-legged essay, required in civil examinations

pai-hua 白話 = colloquial or vulgate

tsa-chü 雜劇 = miscellaneous essays

ts'e 冊 = volume

tsung-mu 總目 = catalogue

ts'ung-shu 叢書 = collection of writings of one or more authors

tz'u 詞 = kind of poetry

wei-so 衞所 = guard or garrison system

wo-k'ou 倭寇 = initially referring to the Japanese pirates, but latterly to pirates in general

Libraries or Library Catalogues Frequently Cited by Initials

L. of C. = Library of Congress

L. of C. Catalogue of Rare Books = *A Descriptive Catalog of Rare Chinese Books in the Library of Congress*, 2 vols. (Washington, D.C., 1957)

NCL = National Central Library 國立中央圖書館

NCL Catalogue = 善本書目, 4 vols. (Taipei, 1967)

NLP = National Library of Peiping 國立北平圖書館

Naikaku Bunko Catalogue = 內閣文庫漢籍分類目錄 (Tokyo, 1956)

Seikado Bunko = 靜嘉堂文庫

Sonkeikaku Bunko = 尊經閣文庫

Ssu-k'u ch'üan-shu = 四庫全書, or Imperial Library of the Ch'ien-lung period

SK = *Ssu-k'u ch'üan-shu tsung-mu t'i-yao* 總目提要, published by the Ta-tung shu-chü (Shanghai, 1930)

Toyo Bunko = 東洋文庫

Important Sources and Reference Works

MSL = *Ming shih-lu* (Taiwan edition, published 1962–66). In addition to the parts described by Wolfgang Franke in *Sources* 1.1.1–1.1.15, there are the MSL *fu-lu* 附錄 which involves, *inter alia*, the *pao-hsün* 寶訓 of T'ai-tsu to Hsi-tsung inclusive.

Ming Index = *Ming-jen chuan-chi tzu-liao so-yin* 明人傳記資料索引 (2 vols., Taipei, 1965–66)

Harvard-Yenching Institute Sinological Index Series, nos. 7, 9, 24, and 35. They include the following Indexes, or *Yin-te:*

#7   Catalogue of the SK

#9   Thirty-three Collections of Ch'ing Dynasty Biographies

#24 Eighty-nine Collections of Ming Dynasty Biographies

#35 Thirty Collections of Liao, Chin, and Yüan Biographies (For the convenience of our readers we are listing *Yin-te* #24 at the beginning of each volume. The slashes found in the bibliographies stand for source number/*chüan*/page or folio.)

KC (1958) = *Kuo-ch'üeh* by T'an Ch'ien (*q.v.*) published in Peking in 1958.

TSCC (1885–88) = *Ku-chin T'u-shu chi-ch'eng* 古今圖書集成, edition published by Major Brothers in Shanghai in 1885–88.

TsSCC = *Ts'ung-shu chi-ch'eng* 叢書集成 (Shanghai, 1935–37)

SPPY = *Ssu-pu pei-yao* 四部備要 (Shanghai, 1927–35)

SPTK = *Ssu-pu ts'ung-k'an* 四部叢刊 (Shanghai, 1920–22), *hsü-pien* 續編 (Shanghai, 1934–35)

WMSCK = *Wan Ming shih-chi k'ao* 晚明史籍考 (Peiping, 1932)

CSL = *Ch'ing shih-lu* 清實錄

W. Franke, *Sources* = Wolfgang Franke, *An Introduction to the Sources of Ming History* (Kuala Lumpur and Singapore, 1968)

Pfister = Louis Pfister, *Notices Biographiques et Bibliographiques sur les Jésuites de l'ancienne mission de Chine, 1552–1773* (Shanghai, 1932)

Sommervogel = Carlos Sommervogel, *Bibliothèque des écrivains de la Compagnie de Jésus* (Paris, 1890–1960)

Sun Tien-ch'i (1957) = Sun Tien-ch'i 孫殿起, *Ch'ing-tai chin-shu chih-chien lu* 清代禁書知見錄 (Shanghai, 1957)

Yao Chin-yüan (1957) = Yao Chin-yüan 姚覲元, *Ch'ing-tai chin-hui shu-mu (pu-i)* 清代禁燬書目（補遺）(Shanghai, 1957)

BDRC   =Howard L. Boorman, editor, and Richard C. Howard, associate editor, *Biographical Dictionary of Republican China*, 4 vols. (New York, 1967–1971)

ECCP   =Arthur W. Hummel, editor, *Eminent Chinese of the Ch'ing Period*, 2 vols. (Washington, 1943–44)

Hsü Pang-ta =Hsü Pang-ta 徐邦達, *Li-tai liu-ch'uan shu-hua tso-p'in pien-nien piao* 歷代流傳書畫作品編年表 (Shanghai, 1963)

Ferguson   =Fu K'ai-sen 福開森 and Shang Ch'eng-tso 商承祚, *Li-tai chu-lu hua-mu* 歷代箸錄畫目 (Nanking, 1934)

Sirén   =Osvald Sirén, *Chinese Painting, Leading Masters and Principles* (New York, 1956–58)

KKSWC   =*Ku-kung shu-hua chi (yüeh k'an)* 故宮書畫集 (月刊), nos. 1–45 (Peking, October, 1930–June, 1934)

For abbreviations of titles of journals, see *Journal of Asian Studies*, Vol. XXII: 5, Bibliography (September, 1963), v-vi; *Harvard Journal of Asiatic Studies*, Vol. XXIV (1962–63), inside cover; and *Revue Bibliographique de Sinologie*, Vol. VII(1961), p. 24.

The Two Capitals

When Chu Yüan-chang took over the area in the lower Yangtze, he made his capital at Chin-ling 金陵 which he captured in 1356, and he named the prefecture Ying t'ien-fu 應天府. A few months after his enthronement (September, 1368) he decided to call it the southern capital, Nan-ching 南京, as he had determined on Kaifeng as the northern capital, Pei-ching 北京. Ying-t'ien was retained as the name for the prefecture at Chin-ling. Early in 1378 the name Nan-ching was dropped in favor of Ching-shih 京師 (capital city), as he had now concluded that it should be his main seat. When Chu Ti seized power and became emperor (1403), he discarded the term Ching-shih in favor of Nanking, for he was already planning to establish his capital at his princely residence in the north.

Under the Yüan, the capital of China was known as Ta-tu 大都. On the ousting of the Mongols in 1368, Chu Yüan-chang called the area Pei-p'ing-fu 北平府. In 1403 it was changed to Shun-t'ien-fu 順天府 when Chu Ti gave the city the name Pei-ching 北京. During the next eighteen years, whenever the emperor resided there, it was called a temporary capital (hsing-tsai 行在). In 1421, on the completion of the palaces, Peking received the name it was to hold for the rest of the dynasty. (For a vivid description of the ceremonies on the night of February 1 and morning of February 2, 1421, see the account of Hāfiz-i Abrū referred to in the biography of Chu

Ti.) The term hsing-tsai fell into disuse but not for long. The succeeding emperor, Chu Kao-chih, determined to restore Nanking as capital, decreed that all Peking offices be designated hsing-tsai (temporary or auxiliary). This practice persisted until the end of 1441, when the names Nanking and Peking were permanently adopted without further embellishment. In each of the two capitals a central government was established. The one in Peking, where the emperor resided, functioned with full power for over two centuries. Meanwhile the Nanking central government was headed by a triumvirate consisting of a eunuch, a general, and a civilian (usually the minister of War), whose function, besides serving as custodian of the imperial palaces and tombs, was to be prepared, at least in theory, to meet any military emergency in the southern provinces too critical to wait for a decision from Peking. Each central government was charged with the administration of a national capital area equivalent to a province. The prefectures and sub-prefectures in both areas had the prefix chih-li 直 隸 (directly controlled by the central government), and further differentiated by Pei 北 (north) and Nan 南 (south).

Because of the confusion likely to arise in the minds of our readers if we adhere to the names used contemporaneously, we are employing for the southern capital the term Nanking, and for the northern Peiping for the early decades and Peking (after 1421) throughout.

Illustrations

(following page 258)

(following page 802)

MAPS

Eighty-nine Collections of Ming Dynasty Biographies

(yin-te #24)

種數	書名	纂輯者	種數	書名	纂輯者
1	明史（列傳之部）	張廷玉等	46	皇明將略	李同芳
2	明史（列傳之部）	萬斯同	47	造邦賢勳錄略	王禕
3	明史稿（列傳之部）	王鴻緒	48	靖難功臣錄	朱當㵆
4	皇明通紀直解	張嘉和	49	勝朝粵東遺民錄	陳伯陶
5	國朝獻徵錄	焦竑	50	甲申後亡臣表	彭孫貽
6	國朝名世類苑	凌迪知	51	建文忠節錄	張芹
7	今獻備遺	項篤壽	52	熹朝忠節死臣列傳	吳應箕
8	明名臣言行錄	徐開江	53	前明忠義別傳	汪有典
9	皇明名臣琬琰錄	徐紘	54	崇禎忠節錄	高承埏
10	皇明名臣言行錄	王宗沐	55	勝朝殉節諸臣錄	舒赫德等
11	國朝名臣言行略	劉廷元	56	南都死難紀略	顧苓
12	皇明名臣言行錄	沈應魁	57	明季南都殉難記	屈大均
13	昭代明良錄	童時明	58	天問閣集	李長祥
14	皇明人物考	焦竑	59	小腆紀傳	徐鼒
15	皇明應諡名臣備攷錄	林之盛	60	小腆紀傳補遺	徐鼒
16	國朝列卿記	雷禮	61	明書	傅維鱗
17	嘉靖以來首輔傳	王世貞	62	明史分稿殘編	方象瑛
18	國朝內閣名臣事略	吳伯與	63	續藏書	李贄
19	內閣行實	雷禮	64	明詩紀事	陳田
20	皇明開國功臣錄	黃金	65	明畫錄	徐沁
21	蘭臺法鑒錄	何出光等	66	遜國記	未詳
22	皇明詞林人物考	王兆雲	67	滄江野史	未詳
23	明名人傳	未詳	68	海上紀聞	未詳
24	明人小傳	曹溶	69	沂陽日記	未詳

25	明儒言行錄續編	沈 佳	70	澤山雜記	未 詳
26	崇禎閣臣行略	陳 盟	71	溶溪雜記	未 詳
27	崇禎五十宰相傳	曹 溶	72	郊外農談	未 詳
28	掾曹名臣錄	王 凝齋	73	金石契	祝 肇
29	明末忠烈紀實	徐 秉義	74	畜德錄	陳 沂
30	續表忠記	趙 吉士	75	新倩籍	徐 禎卿
31	東林同難錄	繆 敬持	76	國寶新編	顧 璘
32	本朝分省人物攷	過 廷訓	77	啓禎野乘二集	鄒 漪
33	皇朝中州人物志	朱 睦㮮	78	江人事	章 于今
34	續吳先賢讚	劉 鳳	79	備遺錄	張 芹
35	南疆繹史	溫 睿臨	80	藩獻記	朱 謀㙔
36	南疆繹史撫遺	李 瑤	81	彤史拾遺記	毛 奇齡
37	續名賢小紀	徐 晟	82	恩邮諸公志略	孫 愼行
38	梅花草堂集	張 大復	83	明儒學案	黃 宗羲
39	東林列傳	陳 鼎	84	列朝詩集小傳	錢 謙益
40	明詩綜	朱 彝尊	85	盛明百家詩	俞 憲
41	小腆紀年	徐 鼒	86	靜志居詩話	朱 彝尊
42	明史竊	尹 守衡	87	煙艇永懷	龔 立本
43	明詞綜	朱 彝尊 王 昶	88	開國臣傳	朱 國楨
44	皇朝名臣言行錄	楊 廉 徐 咸	89	遜國諸臣傳	朱 國楨
45	明良錄略	沈 士謙			

Emperors of the Ming Dynasty

Name	Temple Name	Birth	Death	Enthroned	Reign title and dates in effect
Chu Yüan-chang	T'ai-tsu	10/21/1328	6/24/1398	1/23/1368	Hung-wu (1/23/1368-2/5/1399)
Chu Yün-wen	(Hui-tsung)	12/5/1377	7/13/1402?	6/30/1398	Chien-wen (2/6/1399-7/13/1402)
Chu Ti	T'ai-tsung / Ch'eng-tsu (conferred 10/3/1538)	5/2/1360	8/12/1424	7/17/1402	Yung-lo (1/23/1403-1/19/1425)
Chu Kao-chih	Jen-tsung	8/16/1378	5/29/1425	9/7/1424	Hung-hsi (1/20/1425-2/7/1426)
Chu Chan-chi	Hsüan-tsung	3/16/1399	1/31/1435	6/27/1425	Hsüan-te (2/8/1426-1/17/1436)
Chu Ch'i-chen	Ying-tsung (captive 9/1/1449-9/20/1450)	11/29/1427	2/23/1464	2/7/1435 / restored 2/11/1457	Cheng-t'ung (1/18/1436-1/13/1450) / T'ien-shun (2/11/1457-1/26/1465)
Chu Ch'i-yü	(Tai-tsung)	9/11/1428	3/14/1457	9/22/1449	Ching-t'ai (1/14/1450-2/11/1457)
Chu Chien-shen	Hsien-tsung	12/9/1447	9/9/1487	2/28/1464	Ch'eng-hua (1/27/1465-1/13/1488)
Chu Yu-t'ang	Hsiao-tsung	7/30/1470	6/8/1505	9/22/1487	Hung-chih (1/14/1488-1/23/1506)
Chu Hou-chao	Wu-tsung	10/26/1491	4/20/1521	6/19/1505	Cheng-te (1/24/1506-1/27/1522)
Chu Hou-ts'ung	Shih-tsung	9/16/1507	1/23/1567	5/27/1521	Chia-ching (1/28/1522-2/8/1567)
Chu Tsai-hou	Mu-tsung	2/4/1537	7/5/1572	2/4/1567	Lung-ch'ing (2/9/1567-2/1/1573)
Chu I-chün	Shen-tsung	9/4/1563	8/18/1620	7/19/1572	Wan-li (2/2/1573-1620)
Chu Ch'ang-lo	Kuang-tsung	9/29/1582	9/26/1620	8/28/1620	T'ai-ch'ang (8/28/1620-1/21/1621)
Chu Yu-chiao	Hsi-tsung	12/23/1605	9/30/1627	10/1/1620	T'ien-ch'i (1/22/1621-2/4/1628)
Chu Yu-chien	Ssu-tsung	2/6/1611	4/24/1644	10/2/1627	Ch'ung-chen (2/5/1628-1/27/1645)
Chu Yu-sung	(An-tsung)	12/12/1607	5/?/1646	6/7/1644	Hung-kuang (1645)
Chu Yü-chien	(Shao-tsung)	5/25/1602	10/?/1646	7/29/1645	Lung-wu (1646)
Chu Yu-lang		11/?/1623	6/?/1662	11/20/1646	Yung-li (2/5/1647-1661)

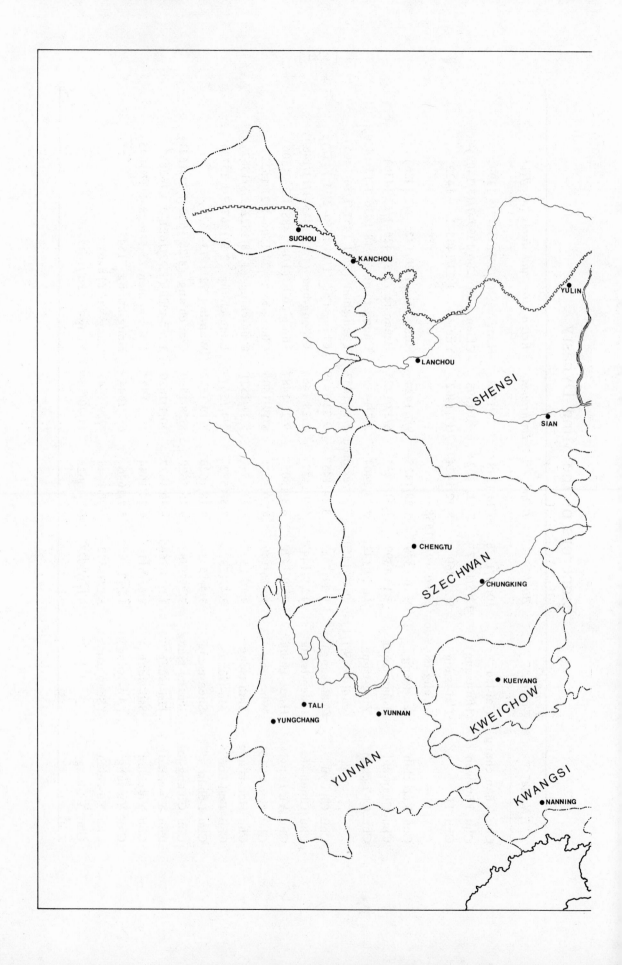

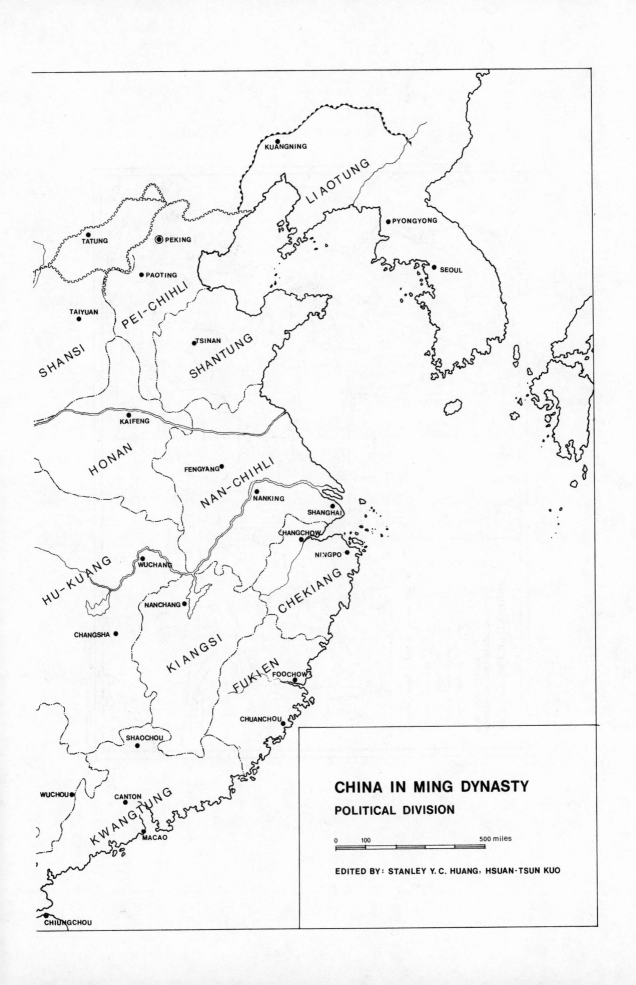

KUANGNING

LIAOTUNG

PYONGYONG

TATUNG ● PEKING

SEOUL

PAOTING

PEI-CHIHLI

TAIYUAN

SHANSI

TSINAN

SHANTUNG

KAIFENG

HONAN

FENGYANG

NAN-CHIHLI

NANKING

SHANGHAI

CHANGCHOW

NINGPO

HU-KUANG

WUCHANG

NANCHANG

CHEKIANG

CHANGSHA

KIANGSI

FUKIEN

FOOCHOW

CHUANCHOU

SHAOCHOU

WUCHOU

CANTON

MACAO

KWANGTUNG

CHIUNGCHOU

CHINA IN MING DYNASTY

POLITICAL DIVISION

0   100   500 miles

EDITED BY: STANLEY Y. C. HUANG, HSUAN-TSUN KUO

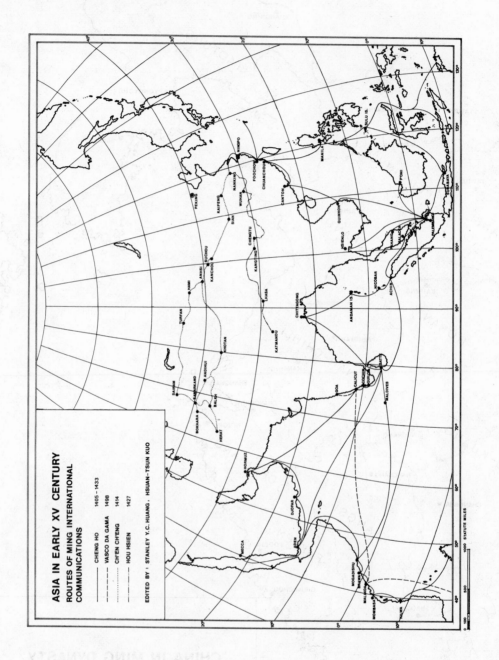

ASIA IN EARLY XV CENTURY

ROUTES OF MING INTERNATIONAL
COMMUNICATIONS

CHENG HO   1405 - 1433
VASCO DA GAMA   1498
CH'EN CH'ENG   1414
HOU HSIEN   1427

EDITED BY : STANLEY Y.C. HUANG . HSUAN-TSUN KUO

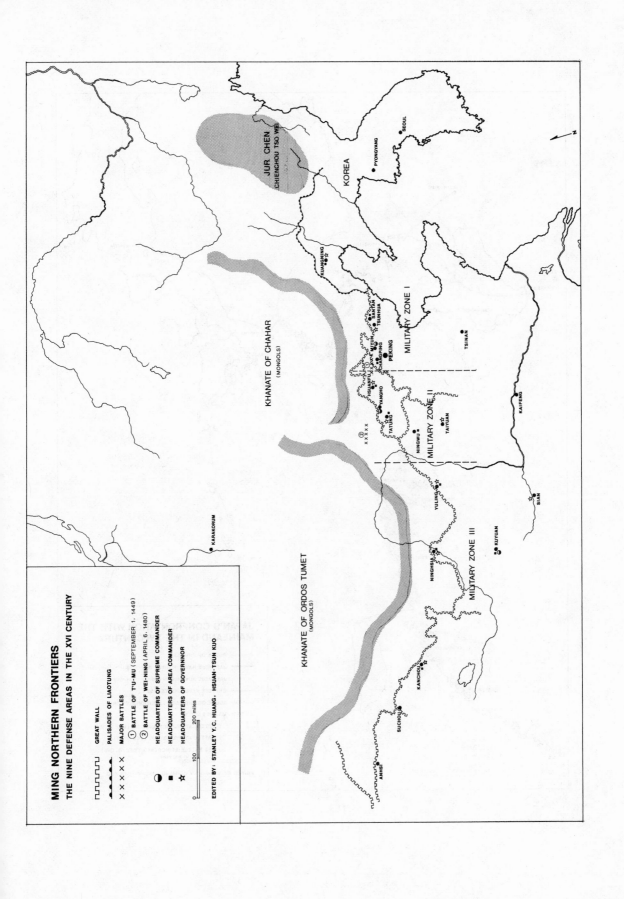

MING NORTHERN FRONTIERS
THE NINE DEFENSE AREAS IN THE XVI CENTURY

⊓⊔⊓⊔⊓⊔   GREAT WALL

▪▪▪▪▪   PALISADES OF LIAOTUNG

X X X X X   MAJOR BATTLES

① BATTLE OF T'U-MU (SEPTEMBER 1, 1449)

② BATTLE OF WEI-NING (APRIL 6, 1480)

◑   HEADQUARTERS OF SUPREME COMMANDER

▪   HEADQUARTERS OF AREA COMMANDER

☆   HEADQUARTERS OF GOVERNOR

EDITED BY: STANLEY Y.C. HUANG, HSUAN-TSUN KUO

0   100   200 miles

JUR CHEN
CHIENCHOU TSO WEI

KOREA

SEOUL

PYONGYANG

KUANGNING

KHANATE OF CHAHAR
(MONGOLS)

MILITARY ZONE I

SANTAN
TSUNHUA
WUHUAN
CHANGPING
PEKING
HSUANFU ①
YANGHO
MILITARY ZONE II
TATUNG
TAIYUAN
NINGWU

TSINAN

KAIFENG

② x x x x x

YULING

SIAN

MILITARY ZONE III

KUYUAN

NINGHSIA

KHANATE OF ORDOS TUMET
(MONGOLS)

KARAKORUM

KANCHOU

SUCHOU

ANHSI

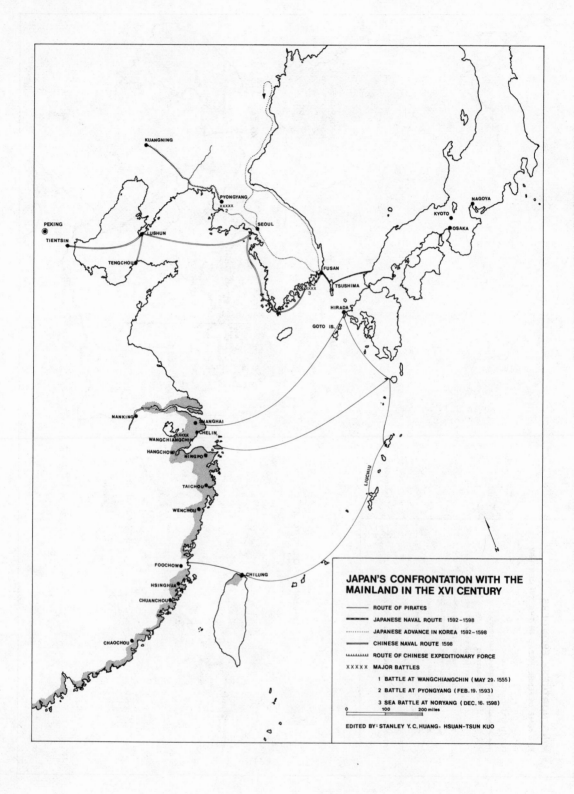

KUANGNING

PYONGYANG
XXXXX
2

PEKING

TIENTSIN   LUSHUN   SEOUL

TENGCHOU

FUSAN

TSUSHIMA

XXXXX
3

HIRADA

GOTO IS.

NAGOYA

KYOTO

OSAKA

NANKING

SHANGHAI

WANGCHIANGCHIN   CHELIN
1
XXXXX

HANGCHOW   NINGPO

TAICHOU

WENCHOU

LIUCHIU

N

FOOCHOW   CHILUNG

HSINGHUA

CHUANCHOU

CHAOCHOU

JAPAN'S CONFRONTATION WITH THE MAINLAND IN THE XVI CENTURY

——————— ROUTE OF PIRATES

▬▬▬▬▬ JAPANESE NAVAL ROUTE 1592–1598

················ JAPANESE ADVANCE IN KOREA 1592–1598

▬▬▬▬▬ CHINESE NAVAL ROUTE 1598

⊥⊥⊥⊥⊥⊥⊥ ROUTE OF CHINESE EXPEDITIONARY FORCE

X X X X X   MAJOR BATTLES

     1 BATTLE AT WANGCHIANGCHIN (MAY 29. 1555)

     2 BATTLE AT PYONGYANG (FEB. 19. 1593)

     3 SEA BATTLE AT NORYANG (DEC. 16. 1598)

0   100   200 miles

EDITED BY: STANLEY Y. C. HUANG; HSUAN-TSUN KUO

DICTIONARY OF MING BIOGRAPHY
Volume I
A-L

There is properly no History: only Biography.
—Ralph Waldo Emerson
Essays, first series (1841)

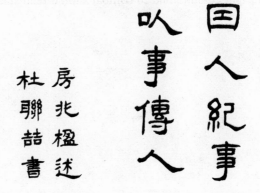

ERRATA ET CORRIGENDA

Page 291, right column, line 5, add (Mongol sources indicate that the Mongol who was in charge of the emperor during his captivity called him contemptuously "White Servant," and suggests that he may have been pockmarked. There is no confirmation of the last in the Chinese records. *See* H. Serruys, *Acta Orient. Hung.*, 28: 3[1974], 321.)

Page 648, left column, line 38, add: In addition to the books printed with movable type in 1497 by Hua Sui known to survive, there is the *Chiao-cheng yin-shih shih ching* 詩經, 20 *chüan*, in the David Eugene Smith Collection, Columbia University,

Page 809, right column, line 34 (*q.v.*) should read (*see* Yüan Hung-tao)

Page 903, left column, line 23 Tsai-hou should read Ch'en-hao

Page 946, left column, line 23 (*q.v.*) should read ECCP

Page 1199, right column, line 20 combat should read smaller

AḤMAD (A-hei-ma 阿黑馬), 1465/66–1503
/4, ruler of eastern Moghulistan in the
late 15th century, maintained consistently
poor relations with China, which occasionally resulted in armed conflict. His unfortunate dealings with the Chinese are not
surprising since his father, Ḥajjī ʿAlī (q.v.),
was also hostile. Unlike his father, Aḥmad
spent his boyhood among the nomads of
the steppe, rather than in the sophisticated centers of Persian civilization. As a
result, the description of him by his nephew, Babur, as "a true son of the steppe
—a man of powerful physique, a stern and
brave soldier, who preferred the sword to
any other weapon," is undoubtedly apt.
Aḥmad's "rudeness in his manner—and
harshness in his speech" also amazed the
future Moghul emperor of India.

On his father's death in 1487, Aḥmad
and his older brother Maḥmud divided
the territory bequeathed to them. Maḥmud
became the nominal ruler of all of Moghulistan, but in actual practice reigned in
the west while Aḥmad controlled the east.
Aḥmad was renowned for his military skill,
and the Oirat nicknamed him the "killer"
because of his exploits. He launched several
successful campaigns against both the Oirat
and the Kazakh, which made him the strongest ruler on China's northwestern border.

His disputes with China focused on
the state of Hami. After Ḥajjī Alī's departure to the west, Han-shen 罕慎, a Uighur
chieftain from Hami, defeated the small
Turfanese garrison in Hami and regained
control of his native land. Emperor Chu
Chien-shen (q.v.) rewarded him but, perhaps fearing to antagonize Turfan's rulers,
repeatedly rejected his entreaties for a
royal title. Emperor Chu Yu-t'ang (q.v.),
however, was less circumspect, and in 1488
enfeoffed Han-shen as the Chung-shun
wang 忠順王 of Hami. Aḥmad, who had
earlier tolerated Han-shen's de facto
supervision of Hami, now refused to accept
his assumption of a ceremonial title, as
well as actual jurisdiction over this important town on the route to central Asia.
He quickly moved his forces to the out-

skirts of Hami and sent a message to Han-
shen proposing a marriage alliance. Han-
shen permitted him and his troops to enter.
Taking advantage of the Uighur chieftain's
gullibility, Aḥmad killed him and plundered the city, but reported to the Chinese
court that he had died of natural causes
and asked to be enfeoffed as the new
prince of Hami. Instead the emperor sent a
letter rebuking Aḥmad for his raid and
insisting that he return Hami's seal.

In the ensuing years his relations with
China deteriorated even further. The ministry of Rites frequently criticized him
for sending too many envoys on his embassies and for offering tribute at improper
times. In 1489 the court learned that an
envoy from Turfan, while on his way to
the capital, bought prohibited goods including tea and colored satin. Again it chided
Aḥmad for the reprehensible behavior of
his ambassadors. Because of these abuses,
the court refused to permit several of
Aḥmad's tribute embassies to enter China.
These refusals may have prompted him to
return Hami's seal in 1492. The emperor,
on the recommendation of Minister of
War Ma Wen-sheng (q.v.), immediately
appointed Shan-pa (see Ma Wen-sheng),
a descendant of the original Hami royal
family, as the new ruler, but he was unable
to restrain Shan-pa and a few of his
subordinates from raiding the borders of
Turfan. In 1493 Aḥmad retaliated by un-
leashing an attack on Hami, killing over a
hundred people and capturing Shan-pa.

The court responded cautiously to Aḥmad's second invasion of Hami. Though
some officials sought a punitive expedition
against Turfan, the emperor merely dispatched a vice minister of War, Chang
Hai 張海 (T. 文淵, 1436–98, cs 1466), and
Kou Ch'ien 緱謙 (a regional commander),
to investigate and hopefully resolve the
dispute. Having reached the northwestern
frontier of China, Chang sent a memorial
urging that the tribute road from central
Asia be closed. He explained that China's
other tributary states, which desired and
in some cases urgently needed Chinese

products, would pressure Aḥmad into retreating from Hami. His plan was adopted but was not immediately successful, and the emperor opted for a more forceful policy. In 1495, with the encouragement of the emperor and Ma Wen-sheng, Hsü Chin (*q.v.*), governor of Kansu, gathered troops for an invasion of Hami. Unfortunately Aḥmad learned of Hsü's expedition and quickly evacuated Hami, leaving only a token force to meet him. Hsü easily overwhelmed this small contingent and recaptured Hami, but he failed to recover Hami's seal and Shan-pa. Ma, disappointed by Hsü's failure to rescue Shan-pa, now advocated a readoption of Chang Hai's policy. He decided that pacification of Aḥmad would succeed only through strict economic pressure; he then closed all the tribute routes across central Asia. He hoped other states and tribes in the Tarim basin, which relied on Chinese goods, would make Aḥmad relent. Undoubtedly feeling the effects of their pressure, Aḥmad finally gave in (November, 1497). His envoys returned Shan-pa and Hami's seal and requested the resumption of tribute relations. The emperor accepted the offering of the embassy and rewarded the envoys.

The emperor also sought to assist Shan-pa, awarding him lavish gifts, including a four-clawed dragon robe, and helping him to reestablish himself in Hami. His efforts were in vain, however; Shan-pa was apparently a despotic and unpopular ruler who, according to the *Ming-shih*, was a heavy drinker. His excesses upset many of the chiefs; so in 1503 they invited Aḥmad's thirteen-year-old son, Chen 眞 Timür, to Hami to wait until Shan-pa's actions led to his own undoing. The emperor, fearing another Turfanese conquest of Hami, sent a force to dissuade the dissident chieftains.

Aḥmad, unable to help his son and the rebellious chiefs of Hami, marched westward (*ca.* 1502) to assist his brother Maḥmūd in repelling the incursions of the Uzbeg ruler Muhammad Shibani. In the following year the Uzbegs captured both brothers. Though he was well treated, Aḥmad died of a stroke in Aksu at less than forty years of age.

Bibliography

1/329/7a, 21b; MSL (1964), Hsiao-tsung, 446, 811, 884, 1056, 1221, 1379, 1392, 1642, 1660, 2312; Hsü Chin, *P'ing-fan shih-mo*; Ma Wen-sheng, *Hsing-fu Ha-mi chi*; Fu Wei-lin, *Ming shu* (Shanghai, 1937), 3294; Lung Wen-pin 龍文彬 (1821-93), *Ming hui yao* (Peking-Shanghai, 1956), 1551; F. G. Talbot (ed.), *Memoirs of Baber, Emperor of India* (London, 1909), 69, 80; *Ajia Rekishi Daijiten*, Vol. 9, 54, includes a genealogy of the rulers of Moghulistan.

Morris Rossabi

ALENI, Giulio (Alenio, Jules, 艾儒略, T. 思及), 1582-August 3, 1649, was an Italian Jesuit missionary, who became an effective evangelist, a voluminous author in Chinese, and a contributor in the fields of mathematics and geography. He was born at Brescia at the foot of the Alps, studied mathematics and philosophy at Venice, taught literature for two years, and entered the Society of Jesus in 1600. Following his ordination for the priesthood, he asked to be sent to the East, and was dispatched in 1609, arriving in Macao in 1610. Together with Pierre Van Spiere (or Pieter de Spira), 史惟貞, T. 一覽, 1584-December 20, 1627, born at Douai, France, who became a member of the Society in 1603 and reached Macao in 1610 after a period of study in Goa, he tried the next year to penetrate China via Canton. They were frustrated by bandits, however, and forced to pay a heavy ransom before release. While waiting for another opportunity, he taught mathematics for two years in Macao and also made an observation of an eclipse of the moon on November 8, 1612. It began at 8:30 in the morning and ended at 11:45. It is worth remarking that in Nagasaki the Jesuit missionary and mathematician, Carlo Spinola (1564-September 10, 1622, who was to lose his life in the anti-Christian persecution), made an observation of the same eclipse, which began there at 9:30 a.m. When the two observations were brought together, it was noted that the difference between the meridians at Macao and Nagasaki was exactly one hour.

Conditions for travel being more favorable in 1613, the Society ordered Aleni, as one familiar with Hebrew, to make his way to Kaifeng, and inquire about the Scriptures used by the Jews in their synagogue (*see* Chao Ch'eng). He was rebuffed, however, so he continued on to Peking where he met Hsü Kuang-ch'i (ECCP), and shortly after accompanied him to the Hsü ancestral home in Shanghai. During the critical period 1616–17, when Shen Ch'üeh (*q.v.*) was endeavoring to banish all missionaries from China, Aleni and several other Jesuits sought refuge in Hangchow under the protective custody of Yang T'ing-yün (ECCP). In these months of forced inactivity Aleni markedly improved his knowledge of Chinese, becoming possibly as adept as any in his order at the time. He remained in the Shanghai-Hangchow sector for some years, in 1620 assisting at the obsequies of the mother of Li Chih-tsao (ECCP).

Early in this same year, or late in 1619, when Hsü Kuang-ch'i was asked by an official named Ma at Yangchow to send a Jesuit to tutor him in scientific subjects, he selected Aleni. [Editors' note: This Ma (variously called "Peter" Ma, Ma San-qui, and Ma San-chih 馬三芝) of Yangchow, according to Jesuit accounts, served about 1615 as an important official in Shensi and about 1620 as "viceroy" of Fukien. From a study of the gazetteers, however (cf. *Yang-chou-fu chih* of 1874, 47/57b, *Chiang-nan t'ung-chih* of 1736, 123/19a, *Ta-t'ung-hsien chih* of 1830, 16/74a, and *Yen-an-fu chih* of 1802, 18/7b; also the TSCC [1885–88] XI: 605/7a, which quotes the *Yang-chou-fu chih* of 1685 or earlier), we find that a Ma Ch'eng-hsiu 馬呈秀 (T. 君實, cs 1604) closely answers that description. The first point in favor of identifying

him as the convert Ma is that he was a *chin-shih* of the same year (1604) as (Paul) Hsü Kuang-ch'i, the disciple of Matteo Ricci. After serving as a judge and then a chief judge in the Grand Court of Revision, Ma was appointed prefect of Yen-an, Shensi, a post he held for four or five years. He was next promoted to be intendant at Shang-chou in the same province. His last appointment was that of surveillance vice commissioner of Fukien. Thus the sequence of his career fits the Jesuit accounts except in the case of his final position which is much lower than that of a viceroy—the kind of mistake often made by writers unfamiliar with official titles and their equivalents. Hence we may with some reason assert that Aleni's convert is Ma Ch'eng-hsiu.

The father of Ma Ch'eng-hsiu, Ma Feng 馬鳳, who hailed from Tatung, Shansi, became a salt merchant in Yangchow and established his home there. As a consequence the family is recorded in the gazetteers of both places. There is also a possibility that a Ma family of Tatung had a central Asian origin and tradition, although this is unprovable.

The local records fail to give a definite date for Ma Ch'eng-hsiu's incumbency in any of the offices to be held. It seems that he was in Yen-an from about 1616 to 1620 and in Yangchow early in 1620 where he was baptized by Aleni. Later in 1620 he went to his intendancy at Shang-chou accompanied by Aleni, and in 1621 was transferred to Fukien.]

Soon after joining Ma in Yangchow Aleni succeeded in converting the latter (already persuaded in his Peking days) to Christianity, baptizing him on March 25, 1620, giving him the name Peter. Aleni then accompanied Ma to Shang-chou 商州, his official post in Shensi. After five months of continuing instruction in religion and mathematics he moved on to Chiang-chou 絳州, Shansi. Here he discovered a good quality grape wine, which proved a boon to his fellow missioners, until then dependent for sacramental purposes on wine shipped from Portugal to Macao. Making his residence in the home of the convert Han Lin (ECCP), he succeeded in baptizing all the members of the Han family. In 1621 Aleni went south to Cheng-chou, Honan, where, in April, apparently on prearranged plans, he joined "Peter" Ma who was on his way to Fukien to a new and higher post. At Yangchow they parted, Ma continuing on to the south.

Around the end of 1621 Aleni found himself again in Hangchow, where he baptized Chang Keng 張賡 (T. 賡虞, H. 夏詹, 明皋, christened Matthew, cj 1597, native of Chin-chiang 晉江, Fukien, who met Ricci in 1607, and who later, early in 1625, was probably the first Christian to appreciate the significance of the Nestorian monument of 781), and where he collaborated with Yang T'ing-yün on a descriptive atlas of the world. The following year, at the invitation of Ch'ü Shih-ku (*see* Ch'ü Shih-ssu, ECCP), he moved on to Ch'ang-shu 常熟, in the Yangtze delta, for a few months, where he founded a church. In 1624, on the retirement of Yeh Hsiang-kao (*q. v.*) to his native province of Fukien, Aleni met the grand secretary in his stopover at Hangchow, and was invited to join Yeh in Foochow—an invitation which he promply accepted. He thus became (1625) the first Jesuit missionary in Fukien. The initial months were not easy. Wei Chung-hsien (ECCP) had spies everywhere looking out for political opponents, and at the same time the depredations of the Dutch on the coast (*see* Nan Chü-i) filled the local population with alarm against all foreigners. In due course, however, Aleni quietly made friends with scholars in the city, and was even persuaded to expound a text on the Confucian canon at the insistence of the president of the local academy. Among his acquaintances in Fukien, some of whom even indited poems in his honor, were Chang Jui-t'u, Ho Ch'iao-yüan (*qq.v.*), and Tseng Ch'u-ch'ing 曾楚卿 (T. 元贊, cs

1613, native of P'u-t'ien 莆田, who became a Hanlin academician and high official in the last years of the Ming). These pieces were published in the collection *Hsi-ch'ao ch'ung-cheng chi* 熙朝崇正集. Another, by Yeh Hsiang-kao, has been published in *Fonti Ricciane* by P. M. d'Elia together with translation into Italian. Aleni also traveled widely about the province, lingering for several days in each locality in an effort to make converts. It is reported that he was particularly successful in Ch'üan-chou 泉州 and Hsing-hua 興化. This would seem to argue a remarkable facility in the spoken language, that Aleni was able to make himself equally understood in Macao, Shansi, the lower Yangtze valley, and Fukien.

Persecution struck again in 1637. Along with other missionaries Aleni was ordered arrested. He was driven away, but returned secretly, certain scholars intervening on his behalf. In 1638, a chance discovery in the prefecture of Ch'üan-chou of several stone slabs bearing the cross in relief (the first being brought to light by Chang Keng) increased the interest of a number of people in the religion he preached. In 1641 he was appointed vice provincial of Jesuit missions in south China, and served until 1648. The years of Manchu conquest of the area (1647–48) Aleni spent in retirement at Yen-p'ing 延平 -fu, in a mountainous retreat. Here he died. His body was borne subsequently to Foochow and laid to rest at Shih-tzu shan 十字山 outside the north gate of the city.

Aleni's writings include thirty or more works of varying length, mostly in Chinese; see the bibliographies of Louis Pfister and Carlos Sommervogel. The best known of these works is the World Atlas which he compiled in collaboration with Yang T'ing-yün; it was based on the map of the world of Matteo Ricci (*q.v.*) and some manuscript notes by Diego de Pantoja and Sabatino de Ursis (*qq.v.*). The compilation seems to have been undertaken at the same time as a terrestrial globe, made in 1623 by Nicolo Longobardi and Manuel

Dias (*qq.v.*) now in the British Museum. (For an illustration of the globe *see* Joseph Needham). Both are more up-to-date than the last of Ricci's maps, and differ from each other only in small degree. The Atlas was engraved in 1623 in Hangchow under the title *Chih-fang wai-chi* 職方外紀, 5 *chüan*, and later (*ca.* 1640) divided into 6 *chüan*. The first edition was included in the seventeenth-century *T'ien-hsüeh ch'u-han* (see Li Chih-tsao, ECCP), copied into the eighteenth-century Imperial Library, and reprinted in no fewer than three nineteenth-century *ts'ung-shu*. Aleni's representation of European knowledge and scholarship in the work *Hsi-hsüeh fan* 西學凡 (Hangchow 1623, Foochow 1629), to which was appended the text of the Nestorian inscription of 781, received unfavorable criticism by the editors of the *Ssu-k'u* catalogue, but their comments, based on irrelevant information, show rather misapplied erudition. He was responsible also for a work in 2 *chüan* entitled *Hsi-fang ta-wen* 西方答問 (Questions and answers regarding the West), published in 1637 and 1644, and edited by Chiang Te-ching 蔣德璟 (T. 申葆, 若柳, H. 八公, a native of Chin-chiang 晉江, Fukien, cs 1622, d. 1646), whom he doubtless met in south China, and who in 1642–44 served in the cabinet. The earlier edition, a copy of which is in the Vatican Library, has been translated into English by John L. Mish. Among his other works, besides those devoted to theology, are the lives of Matteo Ricci, Yang T'ing-yün, and Chang Mi-k'o, or Michael, 張彌克 (i.e., Chang Shih 識, T. 見伯, 1605-August 5, 1622, son of Chang Keng). His life of Ricci, entitled *Ta-hsi Hsi-t'ai Li hsien-sheng hsing-chi* 大西西泰利先生行蹟, was engraved about 1630, and reprinted in 1919. A collated copy was edited by Hsiang Ta 向達 and printed in Peking in 1947. The life of Yang T'ing-yün, entitled *Yang Ch'i-yüan hsien-sheng ch'ao-hsing shih-chi* 楊淇園先生超性事蹟, was written in Chinese by Ting Chih-lin 丁志麟 from the dictation of Aleni.

A portrait of Aleni, engraved on wood,

black on white, is among the holdings of the Bibliothèque Nationale. It represents him as a man with a long beard, and wearing a Confucian scholar's hat. Another, possibly the same, is illustrated in *Shang-chih pien-i-kuan kuan-k'an* 上智編譯館館刊 (*Bulletin of the Institutum S. Thomae*) 2 (May-June, 1947), frontispiece. [Editors' note: Thanks to the collaboration of Professor Robert Ruhlmann, we learn that the biography of Aleni, preserved in manuscript in the Bibliothèque Nationale, gives certain data which are at variance with more official accounts. According to Li Ssu-hsüan 李嗣玄, the year of his arrival in China was 1609, the day of death June 10, 1649, and the name of his master 師 was 瑪瑟勒達 Macerata (?). It happens that this is not a surname, but the name of a city and place of origin of Matteo Ricci; it is situated a long way from Brescia. There may be some misunderstanding here. Unfortunately he makes no mention of the official and convert named Ma.]

Bibliography

Fang Hao 方豪, *Chung-kuo T'ien-chu-chiao shih jen-wu chuan* 中國天主教史人物傳 I (Hong Kong, 1967), 185; Pfister, 131; d'Elia, *Fonti Ricciane*, I (Rome, 1942), 182, II (1949), 42, n. l; *id.*, *Il mappamondo cinese del P. Matteo Ricci* (1938), 49; *id.*, "Le generalita sulle scienze occidentali 西學凡 di Giulio Aleni 艾儒略, RSO, XXV (1960), 58; Henri Havret, *La Stèle chrétienne de Si-ngan-fou*, II (Shanghai, 1895), 95; A. C. Moule, *Christians in China: Before the Year 1550* (London, 1930), fig. 9 & 10; Fortunato Margiotti, *Il cattolicismo nello Shansi dalle origini al 1738* (Rome, 1958), 61, 82; George H. Dunne, *Generation of Giants*, Notre Dame, 1962; *Enciclopedia Italiana*, II (1929), 294; Léon Wieger, *Textes Historiques*, II (Hsienhsien, 3d. ed., 1929), 1775; L. of C. *Catalogue of Rare Books*, I, 396; Helen M. Wallis and E. D. Grunstead, "A Chinese Terrestrial Globe, A. D. 1623," *British Museum Quarterly*, XXV (1962), 83; Joseph Needham, *Science and Civilization in China*, IV: 3 (Cambridge, England, 1971), fig. 1001; *Mémoires de l'Académie Royale des Sciences*, VII, pt. 2 (Paris, 1729), 706; Henri Cordier, TP, IX (1898), 110, 113; Liang Tzu-han 梁子涵, "Pa 跋 Hsi-ch'ao ch'ung-cheng chi" in

Ta-lu tsa-chih, 21: 8 (October 31, 1960), 17; Taga Akigoro 多賀秋五郎, "The position of Giulio Aleni on [sic] in the history of the Chinese education" (in Japanese), *Tōyō shigaku ronshū* 東洋史學論集, 1953; K. Enoki, "The geography of central Asia as described in *Chih-fang wai-chi*" (in Japanese) in *Festschrift Honoring Prof. S. Wada on his 70th Birthday* (*1960*), 211; id., "Editions of *Chih-fang wai-chi*" (in Japanese) in *Festschrift Honoring Dr. H. Iwai on his 70th Birthday* (1963), 136; Sommervogel, I, cols. 157-60; *Bulletin of the Institutum S. Thomas*, II (July-October, 1947), 361; Li Ssu-hsüan, *Ngai Siencheng hing chou* 艾先生行述, 1689/90; *Ch'üan-chou-fu-chih* (1927), 49/86a; John L. Mish, "Creating an Image of Europe for China: Aleni's *Hsi-fang ta-wen*,"MS, 23 (1964), 1.

L. Carrington Goodrich

ALTAN-qaɣan, 1507–82, the most powerful Mongol prince of his day on the Chinese border, is referred to in Chinese sources as An-ta 俺答, or An-ta a-pu-hai (阿不孩 Altan-abuɣai, i.e., Prince Altan). He was the second of seven sons of Bars-bolod-sayin-alaɣ 巴爾斯博羅特賽因阿拉克 (known in Chinese sources also as Sai-na-la 塞那喇, Sai-a-lang 諰阿郎, or A-chu 阿著, 1484–1531), who was the third son of Batu Möngke (*q.v.*) and *jinong* prince in command of the Three Western Tümen [Ten-thousand man unit] from 1512 to 1531. When Bars-bolod died his eldest son, Gün-bilig-mergen (*see* Qutuɣtai-sečen), inherited the *jinong* title and the ownership of the Ordos Tümen north of the Shensi border. He was referred to as Chi-nang 吉囊 by the Chinese. Altan-qaɣan was given the Twelve Tümed north of the Shansi border. Like their Mongol predecessors in these border regions for the past century or so, the two brothers led their men on sporadic raids into China chiefly to replenish their supplies of silk, clothes, and food. For about forty years, until 1570, the Chinese chronicles record lengthy accounts of raids led by the Tü-med and the Ordos. They were active on the entire northern Chinese borders but rarely invaded Liaotung on the north-eastern flank, the preserve of the great qaɣan Tümen, who claimed to be successor and heir of the Yüan emperors.

Altan-qaɣan preferred obtaining Chinese goods by peaceful means, such as through tribute trade, either in Peking or at specified border towns. But his overtures for peace prior to 1570 were repeatedly treated with suspicion, and rejected. In 1541 he and his elder brother asked for tribute privileges and, when the request was refused, conducted a terrifying raid into Shansi. In 1542 the sequence of request, refusal, and raid was repeated and a large part of Shansi was again ransacked. This time it was reported that a great number of Chinese were killed or captured and that Chi-nang died shortly after the raid. For some forty years thereafter Altan-qaɣan was recognized as the most powerful leader of the Mongols.

Some Chinese officials who had served on the border advised the throne to consent to the Mongol request for the tribute trade arrangement, but their suggestions were disregarded when court officials came up with patriotic-sounding but unrealistic arguments. After the military defenses on the border proved to be ineffective against the nomadic invaders and the Chinese people had suffered serious losses in property and lives, the court put the blame on the military commanders (*see* Ch'iu Luan and Yang Chi-sheng). There was a short period in 1551 when his proposals for trading Mongol horses for Chinese silk were acceded to. Two fairs were actually held, but when the Mongols requested grain as an additional article of trade, the market was abruptly abolished and was not reopened for twenty years.

The main reason advanced by the courtiers against selling grain to the Mongols was that the grain would be used to sustain the large number of Chinese settled in Altan-qaɣan's territory. Many were plain immigrants; some were prisoners captured by the Mongols during their raids; others were escaped criminals, army deserters, or fugitives from justice or injustice. All were regarded as "traitors" by Ming officials and so should receive no benefits from the grain trade. As grain was denied the Mongols, the entire border trade was interrupted, and Mongol raids were resumed.

On October 18, 1570, a grandson of Altan-qaɣan came to Tatung and asked for asylum. This was the Daičing Taiji (ca. 1552–83), better known in Chinese sources as Pa-han-na-chi 把漢那吉 from Baɣa-ači (Little grandson). He held a grudge against his grandfather for giving a girl he was going to marry to another man. When his grandfather went away on a campaign against the Tibetans, Baɣa-ači seized the opportunity to defect. It happened that the Chinese governor-general at Tatung, Wang Ch'ung-ku (q.v.), was an able commander who understood the Mongol situation. He at once gave the young Mongol prince shelter and advised the court in Peking to effect a peace by exploiting Altan-qaɣan's concern for his grandson. The grand secretaries at this time, Kao Kung and Chang Chü-cheng (q.v.), overriding much irrelevant opposition, gave support to Wang's proposal. The result was the conclusion of a peace agreement with Altan-qaɣan. One of the terms exacted by the Chinese was for the Mongols to hand over to China the leaders of the Chinese "traitors" living in Mongolia. Nine of these Chinese "traitors" were arrested and turned over to the Chinese authorities, who promptly executed them in Peking. Baɣa-ači returned to Mongolia with proper guarantees that he would not be molested for what he had done. On April 21, 1571, Altan-qaɣan was granted the rank of Shun-i Wang 順義王 (Obedient and righteous prince) and a number of princes received honorary ranks. Arrangements were made, moreover, for Altan-qaɣan and his relatives to present a yearly tribute of 500 horses and for the opening of fairs in several places along the border. Further arrangements

were made to include the Ordos in this plan; they were to present a yearly tribute of 200 horses and have their own markets to exchange horses and cattle for Chinese goods. Altan-qaɣan delivered his first tribute on July 15, 1571. Shortly afterwards the Ordos, too, offered theirs. From then on, it was presented fairly regularly, but Mongol tribute missions were never allowed to proceed to Peking as was the custom from other countries. The tribute was delivered at the border at the time of the annual fairs. The 1571 agreements included provisions whereby the Ming would no longer allow Mongols to cross into China and enter the Ming service, and Chinese officials decided not to press too hard for the return of other Chinese immigrants in Mongolia so as not to disrupt the economic life of the Mongols and bring about new causes of friction.

As Wang Ch'ung-ku had warned from the very beginning, it could not be expected that all difficulties would disappear overnight. He advised firmness, but also patience. Pressure was put on Altan-qaɣan to keep his subjects in check; on the other hand, Mongol noblemen who misbehaved lost tribute and trade privileges. On the whole, the plan worked rather well. After decades of insecurity, the northern borders knew peace until the Mongols of that region were conquered by the Manchus in 1634–35. Wang Ch'ung-ku had hoped that Baɣa-ači would one day succeed the qaɣan and China would thus have a friend in a position of power in Mongolia. Baɣa-ači was given the rank of a general in 1576, with the title Chao-yung chiang-chün 昭勇將軍. Around 1580 a translator from the Ssu-i kuan taught him the essentials of the *Chung-ching* 忠經 and the *Hsiao-ching* 孝經 (Classics of Loyalty and Filial Piety) but he hardly survived Altan-qaɣan, for he met his death in an accident in 1583. His first wife, Baɣabeyiji (the little princess), or Dayičing beyiji, later played a certain role in Sino-Mongol relations and in 1613 was granted the title of Chung-i fu-jen 忠義夫人 (Lady loyal and righteous).

Altan-qaɣan had direct control only over his own subjects, generally known as the Twelve Tümed, but comprising representatives of many other tribes and clans as well. His personal prestige no doubt made him influential in other areas of Mongolia, especially the Ordos, whose princely family was so closely related to him. But he did not rule the Ordos. Both Mongol and Ming sources inform us that he conducted a number of campaigns in northern and northwestern Mongolia and in central Asia. It does not seem, however, that these campaigns resulted in conquest and permanent occupation. He never attempted to unify all of Mongolia as Esen (*q.v.*) had done around 1450, and Batu Möngke towards the end of the 15th century.

After 1570, Altan-qaɣan called himself a vassal of the Ming, but this is a literary cliché. He remained absolutely independent and the Ming court satisfied itself that the border raids had come to an end. After his death his second or third wife was known as the Third Qatun, or San-niang-tzu 三娘子. Her Mongol name was Erketü Qatun. She must have been very young when she married him, for after his death, his son Sengge-dügüreng qung-tayiǰi (known in Chinese as Hsin-ai 辛愛) and later his grandson, Cürüke 撦力克) took her as wife according to the age-long central Asiatic custom. She always remained in favor of good relations with China. In 1586 she was granted the title of Chung-shun fu-jen 忠順夫人 (Lady loyal and obedient). She died in July, 1612.

Altan-qaɣan's name is associated with the revival of Lamaism of the Yellow Sect in Mongolia. Here, together with his grandnephew, Qutuɣtai-sečen qung-tayiǰi (*q.v.*) of the Ordos, he played a considerable role, but it was a revival not a reintroduction of Lamaism in Mongolia. Throughout the Ming period we find clear evidences, though sporadic and fragmentary, of Lamaism in Mongolia. At times lamas were sent by Mongol princes as envoys to China, or at least were members of tribute or other embassies.

It should be noted in this connection that Tibetan Lamaism was also well represented in Peking; around 1500, Tibetan lamas wielded considerable influence at the court. Members of the Mongol nobility were more or less familiar with Lamaism and had some knowledge of the role played by Tibetan dignitaries at the Yüan court. Altan-qaɣan, as well as the Ordos princes, had conducted several campaigns in such areas as Amdo and Köke-nuur, which had a strong Tibetan population and where they met lamas and certainly made new contacts. The memory of this cooperation of Lamaism with the court of the Yüan and the "need" for a religion with a written literature, with more cultural background, more ceremonial than native Mongol shamanism was able to provide, persuaded Altan-qaɣan and the other princes, especially Qutuɣtai-sečen, to promote Lamaism in Mongolia. In 1571, no sooner had negotiations been started with Wang Ch'ung-ku, than Altan-qaɣan requested dye-stuffs to paint images of the Buddha, and in the following years he repeatedly requested sūtras and Tibetan lamas from Peking. As there were always numerous Tibetans in the capital, on several occasions a few of them were sent to Mongolia with sūtras and other religious objects. From around 1575 on, Mongol princes had Lamaist temples constructed by Chinese laborers and craftsmen both in southern Mongolia and in Köke-nuur. The Ming seem to have been willing and even eager to promote the Mongols' interest in Lamaism.

It was this desire for Lamaism and Qutuɣtai-sečen's suggestion which in 1577 prompted Altan-qaɣan to invite bSod-nams-rgya-mts'o (*q.v.*), head of the 'Bras-spuns monastery of the Yellow Sect dGe-lugs-pa in Lhasa. Direct contact between the Mongols and Tibet was one thing the Ming were rather supicious of, but were unable to prevent. To what extent the invitation and subsequent visit of bSod-nams-rgya-mts'o was due to Mongol or to Tibetan initiative is not clear. At any rate bSod-nams-rgya-mts'o set out on the northward journey and met Altan-qaɣan with a considerable delegation of Mongol princes in 1578 in a temple built not long before on the banks of the Köke-nuur. It was on this occasion that Altan-qaɣan gave the title of Vajra-dhara Dalai-lama (Oceanic, or Universal, Lama, Holder of the Thunderbolt) to the Tibetan dignitary; and the latter declared Altan-qaɣan to be the reincarnation of Emperor Qubilai who had invited the monk hP'ags-pa, of whom he was the reincarnation. bSod-nams-rgya-mts'o thus became known as the third Dalai-lama, and his two predecessors. the first and the second successors of Tsong-kha-pa (q.v.), became retrospectively the first and the second Dalai-lama. His immediate successor, the fourth, was Altan-qaɣan's own great-grandson, Yon-tan-rgya-mts'o (q.v.).

After the meeting of 1578 in Köke-nuur, the Dalai-lama returned southward for an inspection trip through eastern Tibet, but sent a representative with Altan-qaɣan to Mongolia. Upon their return towards the end of 1579, both the qaɣan and the Dalai-lama's representative presented a tribute to the Ming court. The Dalai-lama himself was to come to Mongolia in 1585, after the qaɣan's death, and to die in Mongolia in 1588.

The most important immediate result of this meeting of the Dalai-lama with Altan-qaɣan and the representatives of the Mongol nobility was the intense interest of the Mongols in having Buddhist works translated, mostly from Tibetan, into Mongol. As early as 1572, Altan-qaɣan let it be known to the Chinese that he could read neither Tibetan nor Chinese sūtras, and requested sūtras in "Tatar" script. It does not appear that he obtained any sūtras in Mongol at that time, but this request of 1572 shows where his interest lay. He seems to have taken the initiative in this translation activity in 1579 by ordering a translation of the *Suvarṇaprabhāsa sūtra* (Altan Gerel: "Golden Light"); a Tibetan or more probably a Chinese version of this sūtra was sent to him by the Ming in 1574. From then on scores of translators, both Mongols and Tibetans, kept working indefatigably and brought out a large number of Buddhist works in Mongol.

Bibliography

1/327; Saɣang-sečen, *Erdeni-yin tobči*; *Mindai Mammō shiryō. Minjitsuroku-shō Mōkōhen*, VI-VIII; *Wan-li wu-kung lu*, ch. 7, 8; Wada Sei, "Mindai no Mōko to Manshū" in his *Tōa-shi ronsō* (1942), 334; H. Serruys, "Early Lamaism in Mongolia," OE, 10 (October 1963), 181.

Henry Serruys

AN Ch'eng, *see* **CHAO Ch'eng**

AN Kuo 安國 (T. 民泰, H. 桂坡), November 18, 1481–March 30, 1534, wealthy merchant, art connoisseur, book collector, and printer, was a native of Wusih, prefecture of Ch'ang-chou 常州. His ancestors are said to have been originally a Huang family of nearby Soochow. In the early Ming period a certain Huang Mao 黃茂 (T. 叔英) married a daughter of An Ming-shan 安明善 (T. 汝德, fl. 1350–1400) and was adopted by that family. An Ming-shan, originally from Hsiang-fu 祥符, Honan, later settled in Hou-ts'un 堠村, at the foot of Chiao-shan 膠山, Wusih. An Kuo, born into a family which had become prosperous over the years, was a fourth-generation descendant of this adopted son.

Shrewd in business, An Kuo is said to have stocked at little cost various commodities neglected by others and sold them at the right time for a good profit. Thus he accumulated a considerable fortune. He was, however, generous with his money towards members of his clan, contributed to the welfare of his native town and village, and spent much on his gardens and collections. He contributed to the repair of the city wall of Ch'ang-chou, famine relief in 1519, the deepening of the Pai-mao River 白茅河 in 1521, the campaign against Japanese pirates in 1525, and the rebuilding of the shrine of the Sung patriot Li Kang (1083–1140), who fought against the Chin Tatars. To support this shrine he also allocated a piece of land to it. He made numerous friends through personal favors and various acts of benevolence. His popularity is evidenced by the fact that some five thousand persons are said to have attended the funeral of his father, An Tsu 祚 (T. 友菊).

An Kuo cultivated the mountain slope near his home at Chiao-shan, making a spacious garden and planting thousands of cassias. He called his residence Kuei-p'o-kuan 桂坡館 (House of the cassia slope), and his studio T'ien-hsiang-t'ang 天香堂 (Hall of heavenly fragrance). He also built a garden, Chü-lo-yüan 菊樂園 (Garden for the enjoyment of chrysanthemums). Later he constructed in the garden an artificial lake covering several hundred *mou* by recruiting thousands of famine refugees for the project and paying them with food from his granaries. Two eminences standing in the lake he named after the famous Chin 金 and Chiao 焦 peaks in Chinkiang nearby. This garden, one of the most scenic spots in the area, came to be known later as Hsi-lin 西林 (West grove), about which many poems were written; these were included in the *Hsi-lin ch'üan-chi*, 20 ch. (1619), by his grandson, An Shao-fang 紹芳 (T. 懋卿. H. 研亭居士, 1511–79), who rebuilt the garden.

An Kuo was an enthusiastic traveler, making visits to many famous scenic mountains and rivers, including those in Shantung, Shansi, and Pei-Chihli to the north, Kiangsi and Hukuang to the west, Fukien to the south, and Chekiang to the east. His observations were expressed in poems and illustrations in his *Ssu-yu chi* 四遊記 (Accounts of four travels) and *Yu-yin kao* 遊吟藁, a collection of poems on his wanderings, with prefaces by several notables of his time. Neither title is known to have been published.

An Kuo was a noted collector of antiques and art objects, including paintings, rare books, and rubbings. The most famous pieces in his collection were several sets of the earliest extant rubbings of the inscriptions on the ten Stone Drums, dated variously from the 8th to 4th century B.C. [Editors' note: T'ang Lan 唐蘭 has recently advocated the plausible date of 374 B.C. for these Drums; *see* Bibliography.] These rubbings, made in the Northern Sung dynasty (960–1126), preserved the most nearly complete text of the entire ten stones then extant, and were of such rarity that he spent some twenty years and thousands of taels of silver for their acquisition. For the three rarest copies, rated by him as of equal importance, he employed such military terms as hsien-feng 先鋒 (vanguard), chung-ch'üan 中權 (center), and hou-ching 後勁 (rear guard) to avoid numbering them in order. The "vanguard" copy, made *ca*. 1050 as an imperial gift, is the oldest. The "center" copy made in 1114 with hemp paper and fine ink containing most of the text—almost 500 out of some 700 characters on the stone, as compared with only some 300 left today—he acquired in 1534 for one thousand taels of silver. The "rearguard" copy made around 1085 was acquired through exchange in 1523 for fifty *mou* of rice land. He expressed his joy and pride on the occasion of the completion of the collection of the ten rarest editions of the rubbings by naming the east chamber of his T'ien-hsiang-t'ang the Shih-ku-chai 十鼓齋 (Studio of Ten Stone Drums).

In his postscripts to the rubbings he repeatedly admonished his descendants to treasure these copies and never to sell, pawn, give, or lend them to others. It is said that he put these rubbings in a shrine and concealed them over the beam of his studio. They were discovered in the middle of the 19th century when the house was demolished. In the early part of this century, heedless of An's warnings that such an act would be unfilial, all three copies were successively sold to a Japanese collector. Four of the ten copies in the former An collection have been reproduced from photographic copies of the original rubbings by interested scholars and publishers. An unnamed copy and the "center" copy were published by the Shanghai Art Appreciation Society 上海藝苑珍賞社 in 1919 and 1935 respectively; the "vanguard" copy by Kuo Mo-jo (BDRC)—Commercial Press, 1940; and the "rearguard" copy by T'ang Lan—Chung Hua Book Co., 1937, by the Mitsui family—Nigensha, Tokyo, 1958, and by Chang Kuang-yüan 張光遠—Taipei, 1966.

An Kuo is also noted for his fine quality reprinting of many books, especially with bronze movable type. Apparently he reproduced, beginning about 1512, a great variety of titles, including encyclopedias, geographical works, and literary writings, based on the rare editions in his own or others' collections, but only a few survive. Among those extant or known, the *Tung-kuang-hsien chih* 東光縣志, a local gazetteer of the Tung-kuang district, Pei-Chihli, 6 ch., printed in 1521, was probably the earliest such work printed with bronze movable type in his font. Other works he similarly reprinted include the *Wei Hao-shan hsien-sheng ta ch'üan-chi* 魏鶴山先生大全集, the complete works of Wei Liao-weng (1178–1237), 109 ch. (published in 1523); the *Wu chung shui-li t'ung-chih* 吳中水利通志, an eleventh-century work with charts on the water facilities of the lower Yangtze valley, 17 ch. (appeared 1524); *Ku-chin ho-pi shih-lei pei-yao* 古今合璧事類備要, a thirteenth-century encyclopedia in five series, 359 ch.; the *Ch'un-ch'iu fan-lu* 春秋繁露, 17 ch., a work attributed to Tung Chung-shu (d. *ca.* 140 B.C.); *Wu ching shuo* 五經說, 7 ch., a discussion of the five Classics; *Hsiung P'eng-lai chi* 熊朋來集, the collected works of the Yüan scholar and musical historian; and *Shih-t'ien shih hsüan* 石田詩選, 10 ch., selected poems by the noted artist Shen Chou (*q.v.*). The last five titles he printed in the final decade of his life. Some of the books are known to have been printed twice, first by bronze movable type and later by block-print, apparently because reprints from the movable type edition could not be made without resetting the types when the first printing was exhausted, while the blocks could be used again. For example, the *Yen Lu-kung wen-chi* 顏魯公文集, the literary collection of Yen Chen-ch'ing (709–85), 15 ch., plus a supplement, was first printed with bronze movable type and later in facsimile of a Sung edition with blocks in 1523 (reprinted in the *Ssu-pu ts'ung-k'an*); and the *Ch'u-hsüeh chi* 初學記, 30 ch., a T'ang classified encyclopedia by Hsü Chien (659–729), was also first printed with bronze movable type and later in 1531 with blocks. Most of the books which An Kuo printed bore the notation Hsi-shan An-shih kuan 錫山安氏館 or Hsi-shan An Kuei-p'o kuan, and are noted both for craftsmanship and for careful collation.

An Kuo did not serve the government but was granted by imperial order the honorary title of vice director of a bureau in the ministry of Revenue in Nanking, because of contributions made by his elder son, An Ju-shan 如山 (b. 1505, cs 1529). The latter served as a magistrate of Yü-chou 裕州 (Honan) and was later promoted to be an assistant surveillance commissioner of Szechwan; at the age of almost sixty, he took a fifteen-year-old concubine, née Wu 吳, who gave birth to a son, An Hsi-fan 希范 (T. 小范, H. 我素, 1564–1621, cs 1586), a noted official and scholar. Early in 1594, while serving as the director of the office of appointments in the ministry of Personnel, An Hsi-fan submitted a memorial attacking the senior grand secretary, Wang Hsi-chüeh (*q.v.*), and was dismissed from office. After returning home, he participated in the establishment of the Tung-lin shu-yüan (*see* Ku Hsien-ch'eng). He occupied a separate room in the academy where he taught and wrote expositions of neo-Confucian thought. After his death his two sons, An Kuang-yü 廣譽 (T.

无咎), painter, calligrapher, and poet, and
An Kuang-chü 廣居 (T. 無曠), son-in-law
of the eminent scholar and official Kao
P'an-lung (*q.v.*), memorialized the throne,
presenting a plea on behalf of their father's
memory. An Hsi-fan was then granted
posthumous honors by imperial order as a
vice minister of the Court of Imperial Entertainments and celebrated in the temple to
the local worthies, and a shrine was built
for him in his native Hou-ts'un in 1740.

An Kuo of Wusih should not be confused with An Kuo 安國 (T. 良臣, Pth.
武敏, military *chü-jen* 1508, from Sui-te
綏德, prefecture of Yen-an), a military
commander of the Ning-hsia region during
the Cheng-te period, whose biography
appears in *Ming-shih*, 174ʲ19b.

Bibliography

MSL (1940), Shen-tsung, 268/11a; *Chiao-shan An
Huang shih tsung-p'u* 胶山安黃氏宗譜 (1922);
An O-su hsien-sheng nien-p'u 安我素先生年譜
(Ch'ien-lung ed.); Lü Nan 呂柟, *Ching-yeh hsien-
sheng wen-chi* 涇野先生文集 (1535), 34/20a; Wang
T'ing-hsiang, *Nei t'ai chi* (1539), 5/17a; Chan
Jo-shui, *Ch'üan-weng ta ch'üan-chi* (1540, reprint
1593), 60/2; *Huang Ming wen-hai* (microfilm),
18/5/24; *Ch'ang-chou-fu chih* (1695), 25/10a;
Wu-hsi Chin-kuei-hsien chih 金匱縣志 (1881),
25/6b, 27/15a, 29/13b, 33/39b, 40/20b; Yeh
Te-hui (BDRC), *Shu-lin ch'ing-hua* (1920),
8/10b; *T'ien-lu lin-lang shu-mu* 天祿琳瑯書目
(1775), 10/11b; Wang Ch'ung-min 王重民, "An
Kuo chuan 傳," *T'u-shu chi-k'an* 圖書季刊, n. s.
9, nos. 1-2 (1948), 22; Chang Hsiu-min 張秀民,
"Ming-tai te t'ung-huo-tzu" 明代的銅活字, *T'u-
shu kuan* 圖書館 (1961): 4, 55; Liang Tzu-han
梁子涵, "Ming-tai te huo-tzu yin-shu" 明代的活
字印書, *Ta-lu tsa-chih* 大陸雜誌, 33 (1966), nos.
6-7; T. H. Tsien 錢存訓, "Lun Ming-tai t'ung-
huo-tzu-pan wen-t'i" 論明代銅活字版問題, *Ch'ing-
chu Chiang Wei-t'ang hsien-sheng ch'i-shih jung-
ch'ing lun-wen-chi* 慶祝蔣慰堂先生七十榮慶論文集
(Taipei, 1969), 129; Kuo Mo-jo, *Shih-ku-wen
yen-chiu* 石鼓文研究 (1940), 2 vols.; T'ang Lan,
"Shih-ku-wen nien-tai k'ao" 年代考, *Ku-kung po-
wu-yüan yüan-k'an* 故宮博物院院刊, no. 1 (1958),
4; Na Chih-liang 那志良, *Shih-ku t'ung-k'ao* 通考
(1958), 213, portrait of An Kuo following p.
213; Chang Kuang-yüan, *Hsien-Ch'in shih-ku ts'un
shih k'ao* 先秦石鼓存詩考, 1966; Akatsuka Kiyoshi.
/A New Study of the *Shih-ku-wen*," *Acta
Asiatica*, 4 (Tokyo, 1963), 80; *Shoseki meihin
sōkan* 書跡名品叢刊, ser. 1. Tokyo, 1958; K. T.
Wu, "Ming Printing and Printers," HJAS
(1943), 218.

Tsuen-hsuin Tsien

ARUɣTAI (A-lu-t'ai 阿魯台), died 1434,
Eastern Mongol chieftain, was the main
target in the famous campaigns of Emperor Chu Ti (*q.v.*) against the Mongols.
Though H. H. Howorth mistakenly identifies him as Adai Khan, it is clear that
he never adopted the title khan and remained content with his position as chief
minister. During the three decades in
which his name appears in the Chinese
sources, they characterize him as generally
hostile. Neither the Chinese nor the Mongol
records, which scarcely refer to him, offer
a plausible explanation for his hostility.
Whether disputes over trade and tribute
relations or territory were involved are
unknown. We are afforded few glimpses
of his motivations, so that his biography
becomes merely a catalogue of his military adventures.

When Chu Ti became emperor in
1403, relations between China and the
Eastern Mongols were strained. Kuei-li-
ch'ih 鬼力赤, the Mongol khan, had not
made peace with China and, in fact, had
earned the emperor's wrath by poisoning
Engke-Temür (An-k'o T'ieh-mu-er 安克帖
木兒), the prince of Hami whom the court
had enfeoffed. During Kuei-li-ch'ih's lifetime little progress was made. But when
Aruɣtai (the chief minister) killed Kuei-
li-ch'ih in 1408 and recalled Bunyaširi
(Pen-ya-shih-li 本雅失里, also known as
Öljei Temür and a descendant of the
imperial Yüan house) from Bishbalik,
proclaiming him khan, Chu Ti sought a
reconciliation. In 1409 he dispatched the
supervising secretary Kuo Chi 郭驥 to
effect an agreement with the Mongols.
Instead, Bunyaširi and Aruɣtai killed the
unfortunate envoy, thus issuing a challenge
to the Chinese. They responded first by

presenting the title Shun-ning wang to the Oirat chief Maḥmūd (*q.v.*), the Eastern Mongols' principal rival, who administered a severe defeat to the armies of Bunyaširi and Aruγtai and forced them to migrate to the area of the Kerülen River 臚朐. Then, hoping to take advantage of their plight, the emperor sent Ch'iu Fu (*see* Qorγočin) with a hundred thousand troops on a punitive expedition against the Mongols, warning him repeatedly to be cautious and not to underestimate the enemy. Ch'iu ignored the warning, and, as a result, his campaign ended disastrously. He crossed the Kerülen where a captured Mongol prisoner told him that the armies of Bunyaširi and Aruγtai were demoralized and in retreat. Overruling his generals and advisers, Ch'iu decided to pursue them with a small force of a thousand men. Bunyaširi and Aruγtai continued to retreat and enticed him farther and farther into Mongolia, finally springing a surprise attack that decimated his forces and led to his death.

This defeat prompted Chu Ti to lead his own first campaign against the rebellious "barbarians." In the winter of 1409 his army started to prepare and by March of 1410 it consisted of over a hundred thousand men with more than thirty thousand carts of supplies. He marched his troops to the northern shores of the Kerülen where he had two short inscriptions proclaiming the glory of his armies carved into the rocks. The first read: "Victory rock, The Great Ming, 8th year, 4th month, 21st day of Yung-lo" (May 24, 1410), and the second: "8th year of Yung-lo keng-yin (year), 4th month ting-yu (month), 16th day jen-tzu (May 19, 1410), the Emperor of the Great Ming passed here with six armies during the punitive expedition against the barbarian robbers." In 1696 the Jesuit, Jean-François Gerbillon, who accompanied the K'ang-hsi emperor on his expedition against the Dzungar chief Galdan (ECCP), noticed these inscriptions, and in 1927 the Russian scholar V. M. Kasakevich made rubbings and translated them.

Chu Ti found the armies of Bunyaširi and Aruγtai in a state of disarray. On learning of the size and strength of the Chinese expedition, Aruγtai, ignoring Bunyaširi's plea for united action, fled to the east, while Bunyaširi moved west. Chu Ti first pursued Bunyaširi's forces, inflicting several defeats on them which culminated in a decisive battle at the Onon (Wo-nan 斡難) River on June 15, 1410. Bunyaširi escaped with a small escort, but his military might was smashed. The Chinese troops then followed Aruγtai's trail along the Khalka River, catching up to him a month later on the upper course of the Taor River at Ching-lu-chen 靜虜鎮. The emperor dispatched an envoy asking Aruγtai to surrender, and, according to the Chinese sources, the Mongol chief wished to submit, but his soldiers refused. Aruγtai lost the ensuing battle and barely escaped with a remnant of his battered army.

The Chinese historians imply that Aruγtai learned his lesson and sought good relations with the Ming. During the winter of that year he presented a tribute offering of horses to the emperor and was well compensated. In the following year he suggested an unusual covenant with China. He proposed to surrender and in return requested that China accept him as overlord of all foreign "barbarians"; the text of this agreement would be carved in metal, and he would place it in wine and order his vassal chiefs to drink the wine. The Chinese denied his request, but he was not offended and continued to send tribute and perform services for China. For example, in 1413 he reported that Maḥmūd had killed Bunyaširi and was planning incursions into Chinese territory. But initially using illness as an excuse, he did not take part in the Chinese counteroffensive of 1414 against Maḥmūd, the second of the emperor's Mongol campaigns. Nevertheless Chu Ti, as a sign of gratitude, released Aruγtai's relatives captured during the first campaign, and bestowed the title

Ho-ning wang 和寧王 on him, wang t'ai-fu-jen 王太夫人 on his mother, and wang fu-jen 王夫人 on his wife.

After Chu Ti's decisive defeat of Maḥmūd, Aruɣtai's influence and power grew and his relations with China deteriorated. Throughout this time he tightened his control over the Uriyangqad guards on China's northeastern border. Early in 1416 he took advantage of the Oirat temporary weakness to plunder their territory. The death of their chief, Maḥmūd, in the same year permitted him to pursue an even more aggressive policy. He pillaged several caravans on their way to and from Peking and harassed and robbed Chinese envoys to Mongolia and central Asia. Grand Secretary Yang Jung (q.v.) also accused him of spying on China, presumably with the intention of selecting the best time and place for an invasion.

Early in 1422 Aruɣtai overran the Hsing-ho 興和, an outpost fortress north of Kalgan, and killed its chiliarch, Wang Huan 王喚. The emperor responded by organizing his largest expedition to date— according to the Chinese sources, it comprised 235,146 men, 117,753 carts, and 340,000 animals. When Aruɣtai's agents informed him about the Chinese force, he panicked and hastily fled, leaving behind his supplies, horses, and cattle. The Chinese seized this booty, but did not pursue him, fearing that their supply lines were already too fragile. Instead, they pounced on the Uriyangqad guards, which Aruɣtai had coerced into aiding him, at the Ch'ü-lieh River 屈烈河 west of the Hsing-an mountains, inflicting heavy losses on these unfortunate tribes.

Following the conclusion of Chu Ti's third Mongol campaign, Aruɣtai, undaunted, continued to raid Chinese border settlements. On the other hand, Chu Ti now appeared weary of organizing yet another punitive expedition. H. Serruys explains the source of his frustration in this way: "The extreme elusiveness of the Mongol cavalry made real contact with the enemy all but impossible." But Aruɣtai's provo-

cations finally induced Chu Ti to initiate his fourth war against the Mongols in the autumn of 1423. Aruɣtai's forces again eluded him, but one of the important Mongol chieftains, Esen Tügel (q.v.), surrendered to the Ming troops. Chu Ti, who already lacked enthusiasm for this campaign, used Esen Tügel's submission as a pretext to proclaim a victory. When he also learned that the Oirat had just defeated Aruɣtai, he felt vindicated and returned immediately to Peking. But Aruɣtai was still not pacified. Early in 1424, he launched several attacks on Tatung and K'ai-p'ing 開平, and again Chu Ti responded with an offensive. As usual Aruɣtai seemed to vanish, and Chu Ti's fruitless efforts to find him ended at Ta-lan-na-mu-er 答蘭納木兒, a tributary of the upper Khalka. Perhaps depressed by his failure, Chu Ti fell sick and finally died while on campaign.

After the emperor's death, Aruɣtai no longer harassed the Chinese. He found himself in an increasingly precarious position, as the rejuvenated Oirat, under the leadership of Toɣon (see Esen), penetrated his territory, forcing him to move eastward. The Oirat also named Toɣto-buqa as khan (see Esen) to compete with his nomination of A-t'ai 阿台 (d. 1438), whom Toɣon later killed. In addition, the Uriyangqad guards grew restive under his control and apparently sought Chinese assistance against him. But the Chinese failed to support them, and in 1425 he easily crushed their rebellious chiefs. Faced with all of these threats, he wished to pursue harmonious relations with China. He sent annual tribute missions with horses and other gifts for the court. The Chinese responded with precious silks, satins, and other presents, probably hoping that he might assist them in case of Oirat attacks. But the Chinese effort proved worthless, as the Oirat continued to harass Aruɣtai. They defeated him in 1431, thus encouraging the Uriyangqad to rebel, albeit unsuccessfully. In 1434 the Oirat finally killed him in a battle at Mu-na-shan 母納山.

A-pu-chih-an 阿不只俺   (?Abuji'an), one of Aruγtai's sons, surrendered to the Ming on October 21, 1434. The court granted him a military title and gave him a house and furnishings in the capital. He died in 1435 without making any remarkable contributions to China, but his son T'o-t'o Po-lo-chi 脫脫孛羅吉 (Toγto Bolod, also known as Ho Yung 和勇) was a successful military commander. In 1465 he suppressed a rebellion of non-Chinese tribes in Kwangsi and was granted the title of earl of Ching-an 靖安伯. He died in 1474, the court giving him the posthumous name Wu-min 武敏 (military and energetic).

Several works describing Chu Ti's campaigns against Aruγtai and the Oirat are extant. The *Pei-cheng lu* 北征錄, 1 ch., and the *Hou* 後 *Pei-cheng lu*, 1 ch., by Chin Yu-tzu (*see* Empress Hsü), deal with the first and second expeditions. The former has been partially translated into German by W. Franke. Both works are found in the *Chi-lu hui-pien* edited by Shen Chieh-fu (*q.v.*). A shorter account of the fifth campaign of 1424, also found in the *Chi-lu hui-pien*, is the *Pei-cheng chi* by Yang Jung.

Bibliography

1/146/4a, 156/2a, 13a, ch. 327; MSL (1963), T'ai-tsung, ch. 104, 105, 250, 261, 267; Ku Ying-t'ai (ECCP), *Ming-ch'ao chi-shih pen-mo* (1658), ch. 21; Fu Wei-lin (ECCP), *Ming shu* (Shanghai, 1937), 3328; Hsia Hsieh (1799-1875?), *Ming t'ung-chien* (Peking-Shanghai, 1959), 671, 682, 689, 700, 708, 744, 750, 752, 760, 773, 826; Louis Hambis, *Documents sur l'histoire des Mongols à l'époque des Ming* (Paris, 1969), 18, 94; C. Y. Wu, "Who Were the Oirats?", *Yenching Journal of Social Studies*, III: 2 (1941), 187; E. Bretschneider, *Mediaeval Researches from Eastern Asiatic Sources*, II (London, 1910), 163; H. H. Howorth, *History of the Mongols* (London, 1876), pt. 1, 355; D. Pokotilov, *History of the Eastern Mongols during the Ming Dynasty from 1368 to 1634*, tr. by R. Loewenthal, *Studia Serica*, ser. A, no. 1 (Chengtu, 1947), pt. 1, 25; W. Franke, "Yunglo's Mongolei-Feldzüge," *Sinologische Arbeiten*, III (1945), 1; *id.*, "Addenda and Corrigenda," *Studia Serica*, ser. A, no. 3 (1949), pt. 2, 21; *id.*, "Chinesische Feldzüge durch die Mongolei im frühen 15. Jahrhundert," *Sinologica*, III (1951–53), 81; *id.*, *Sources*, 7. 3. 2, 3; V. M. Kasakevich, "Sources to the History of the Chinese Military Expeditions into Mongolia," MS, 8 (1943), 328; H. Serruys, "Mongols Ennobled during the Early Ming," HJAS, 22 (1959), 228, 245; *id.*, *Sino-Jürced Relations during the Yung-lo Period (1403-1424)*, (Weisbaden, 1955), 17; *id.*, *The Mongols in China during the Hung-wu Period (1368-1398)*, (Bruges, 1959), 244, 260; *id.*, "Sino-Mongol Relations with the Ming; The Tribute System and Diplomatic Missions (1400-1600)," MCB, XIV (1967), 6, 32, 51, 103, 126, 237, 267, 339, 350, 545, 562; Wada Sei 和田清, "Urianghai sanei ni kansuru kenkyū" 兀良哈三衞に關する研究, *Tōa shi kenkyū Mōkohen* 東亞史研究蒙古篇 (Tokyo, 1959), 215.

Morris Rossabi

AYUŠIRIDARA 愛猷識里達臘, 1338/9-78, son of Emperor Toγon Temür (*q.v.*) and a Korean concubine, née Ki 奇 (later empress), succeeded his father as ruler of the northern Yüan court two years after the expulsion of the Mongols from China in 1368. Ayuširidara received a formal and vigorous education during his boyhood. He started to learn Chinese at the age of ten, shortly after he had been taught Uighur writing, under the Confucian tutor Li Hao-wen (cs 1321), in a studio established for him, called Tuan-pen-t'ang 端本堂. He maintained his interest in Chinese studies after being designated heir apparent in 1353, and had friendly relations with a number of renowned Confucian scholars, including Ou-yang Hsüan (1283-1357); but he also flirted with Tibetan Buddhism. Besides being proficient in the Chinese Classics and literature, he is said to have been accomplished in calligraphy.

During the seventeen years of his heir apparency, Ayuširidara lived under the shadow of his mother, a shrewd, ambitious woman; she twice (1359, 1365) attempted to depose her feeble husband in favor of her son. When these plots were revealed, the emperor forgave her. During the same period, Ayuširidara was competing with Bolod Temür and Kökö Temür (*q.v.*) for political hegemony. He led a campaign against the former in 1364 as a consequence of an internal quarrel, and maintained an uneasy relationship with the latter. In the wake of the menace of the rebel Chinese forces in September, 1368, Toγon Temür entrusted Ayuširidara with the command of all armed units, but the Mongols, unable to resist the army of Chu Yüan-chang, fled from Ta-tu to their homeland. When Toγon Temür died at Ying-ch'ang 應昌, Jehol, in May, 1370, Ayuširidara succeeded to the Yüan imperial authority. He changed the reign title to Hsüan-kuang 宣光, and ruled over Mongolia for eight years until his death. Following his accession, Ayuširidara was increasingly under the influence of Kökö Temür, who proved himself the most effective leader of the Mongol resistance against the expanding Ming state. During Ayuširidara's rule the Mongols were under constant pressure from the Chinese, but they maintained their influence over Korea, whose king acknowledged the reign title of the Yüan court instead of that of the Ming.

Scarcely a fortnight after his enthronement, Ayuširidara's temporary capital at Ying-ch'ang was attacked (June 10) by Ming troops under the command of General Li Wen-chung (*q.v.*). The Mongol defenders were taken by surprise and overpowered, allegedly losing fifty thousand prisoners, including Ayuširidara's wife and young son, Maidiribala 買的里八剌, members of the nobility, and high officials. Ayuširidara himself escaped with a small force. The Ming army pursued him as far as Ch'ing-chou 慶州 (Jehol), after which he made his way unhindered across the Gobi to Qaraqorum, where he was joined by the rest of the Mongol army under Kökö Temür, who was returning after suffering defeat at Ting-hsi 定西 in Kansu. Meanwhile, the Mongol prisoners were sent to Nanking. Receiving Maidiribala in an audience on July 11, Chu Yüan-chang awarded him the title of marquis of Ch'ung-li 崇禮侯, and granted his

followers provisions and residences in the capital. The emperor, however, restrained his generals from too ebulliently celebrating their victories, and twice (July 13 and November 14) sent a letter urging Ayuširidara to submit. The latter did not respond, but as the year wore on many Mongol princes defected to the Ming. Late in December Chu Yüan-chang sent another letter, this one addressed to the remaining Mongol leaders as well as to Ayuširidara himself, but without effect. Early in 1371 the Yüan governor of Liaotung surrendered to the Ming, and the northern frontier of China became quiet, further reducing the authority of the Mongol ruler.

In 1372 the Ming made a major attempt to subdue the remaining Mongols by military force, and Li Wen-chung, Hsü Ta, Feng Sheng, and T'ang Ho (*qq.v.*) all led armies north of the Great Wall. Li Wen-chung and Feng Sheng won victories, but these were offset by the disaster to Hsü Ta's army at Qaraqorum (June) and by the defeat of T'ang Ho in Inner Mongolia (August). These reverses were followed by Mongol raids into Shansi. Late in January, 1373, Chu Yüan-chang once again wrote Ayuširidara to induce him to surrender voluntarily, but without success. Mongol raids on the border continued, resulting in the Ming government policy of evacuating the peasants to the interior, but late in November Kökö Temür suffered defeat at Huai-jou 懷柔. In May, 1374, Lan Yü (*q.v.*) overcame the Mongols and captured Hsing-ho 興和. These successes prompted Chu Yüan-chang to offer peace once again, and on October 20 he sent Maidiribala back to Mongolia with another summons to his father to accept his authority. That the emperor granted this special favor to Maidiribala was apparently because he believed that his courteous treatment had converted the prince to his side and hoped that the heir to the Mongol throne would persuade his people to submit. Ayuširidara, however, once more ignored the Ming offer, but the death of Kökö Temür in September of the following year dealt a serious blow to Mongol military effectiveness. Nevertheless, during the last years of Ayuširidara's reign, the Ming remained essentially on the defensive, responding with forceful counterattacks to Mongol raids on the border. Ayušuridara died in April/May 1378. Chu Yüan-chang then sent a special messenger to attend the mourning ceremonies and deliver a personal eulogy. This was apparently intended to gain the friendship of the Mongols. Ayuširidara was posthumously canonized as Chao-tsung 昭宗 and as Biligtü Qaγan 必里克圖汗. He was succeeded by his younger brother Toγus Temür (*q.v.*), rather than by his son, Maidiribala, presumably because the latter had been discredited by the court for his friendliness towards the Chinese emperor.

Bibliography

1/327/1a; *Yüan-shih*, 41/15a, 42/2a, 46/14b, 47/13a, 114/10b, 183/11a; T'ao Tsung-i, *Ch'o-keng lu*, 2/2b; MSL (1962), T'ai-tsu, 1021, 1040, 1119, 1150, 1417, 1621, 1927, 1935; K'o Shao-min (BDRC), *Hsin Yüan-shih*, 25/8a, 26/16b; Sun Yüeh-pan 孫岳頒 (ed.), *P'ei-wen-chai shu-hua p'u* 佩文齋書畫譜 (1883), 20/7b; Huang Chang-chien 黃彰健, "Lun Ming-ch'u Pei Yüan chün-chu shih-hsi" 論明初北元君主世系, CYYY, 37, pt. 1 (1967), 314; *Koryŏ-sa* 高麗史, Vol. 3 (1908), 690; H. H. Howorth, *History of the Mongols* (London, 1876), pt. I, 340; H. Franke, "Could the Mongol Emperors Read and Write Chinese?" AM, n. s. 3 (1952), 40; Henry Serruys, *The Mongols in China during the Hung-wu Period*, MCB, 11 (1959), 60, 154, 185, 289; L. Hambis, *Documents sur l'histoire des Mongols à l'époque des Ming* (Paris, 1969), 7.

Edward L. Dreyer and Hok-Lam Chan

BADAI, *see* **ESEN Tügel**

BATU Möngke 巴圖蒙克, *ca.* 1464-*ca.* 1532, unifier of the Eastern Mongols, led their incursions for several decades into Ming territory, and was the progenitor of most of the Mongol chiefs in the Ch'ing dynasty. After the death of Mandaγul-qaγan in 1467, the Mongols were soon divided into two hostile camps; one headed by Ismaïl 亦思馬因 (d. 1486?) and the other by Batu Möngke, known to history under his royal style of Dayan-qaγan or Ta-yen-han 達延汗. Batu's career can be reconstructed only in fragmentary fashion from often contradictory notices in the Chinese, Mongol, and other sources, which often copy each other and which cannot be reconciled chronologically. "All in all," wrote Henry Serruys in 1958, "the historical material concerning [him] is extremely confused, and it seems well-nigh impossible to clarify all aspects, and reconcile satisfactorily the Mongol sources with the Chinese records." These historiographical difficulties arise in part because the Chinese notice him only with relation to the continual Mongol incursions of Chinese territory in this period; the leadership of these campaigns was not always clear to the Chinese authorities, and, even when it was, such actions were almost always reported inaccurately or falsely to the court. When the military reports were not simply falsified, the identity of the leaders of the enemy forces was often less than clear. As a result, the Chinese sources confuse his activities with those of several other Mongol leaders. The Mongol sources, for their part, are more concerned with his role as a hero, particularly with his work of tribal unification and his establishment of the future lines of Mongol leadership. Later claims to succession within the khanate by reason of lineal descent from Jenghiz were in reality set largely by virtue of descent from Batu.

Batu was probably born sometime around 1464, and was elevated to the khanate about 1482. He married the widow of Mandaγul-qaγan at an extremely early age, probably when only six. His royal style, Dayan-qaγan, is a loanword version of Chinese ta-yüan 大元, which elsewhere appears as Middle Mongol dai-ön; his name is given in some of the Mongol sources as dayun, which seems to be the older and probably better reading, but the later assimilated form dayan is that used in a majority of the records and also the form under which he is known to history. The title was intended to emphasize both his ultimate genealogical connection with the Yüan imperial house and his mission as unifier of all the Mongols, as well as to express the hope that he would be able once more to bring them together into a single force such as they had presented to the world in Yüan times. In this he very nearly succeeded.

Ismaïl, leader of the Western Mongols and Oirat, came into contact and inevitable conflict with Batu in the course of his own eastward migrations. The direction of successful raids on Chinese territory was a sure road to popularity for any aspiring Mongol leader, and Ismaïl was not at all reluctant to press his advantage in this connection. He participated in successful raids on Liaotung and Tatung in 1480, and continued to exert military pressure on the Mongols of Urianghai 兀良哈 (east of the Hsingan Mountains). Ismaïl appears to have been killed sometime before 1488, perhaps in 1483, and with this removal of his chief rival from the scene, Batu quickly became the paramount leader of the Mongols and the effective director of their increasingly unified efforts against Ming China. From this time on he is the Hsiao-wang-tzu 小王子 (little prince) in the Chinese sources.

From about 1480 not a single year passed without some major Mongol raid across the Chinese northwestern frontier. Chinese military leadership proved itself almost completely incompetent to deal with these incursions. Most often their forces were quickly routed, and the Mongols advanced to pillage and loot almost at will, while the court was lulled into a false sense of security by totally misleading intelligence reports of Chinese victories. In 1500 a particularly incompetent triumvirate, Chu Hui 朱暉 (T. 東陽, 1448-1511), Shih Lin 史琳 (T. 天瑞, 1438-1506, cs 1466), and the eunuch Miao K'uei 苗逵, was put in command of Chinese military resistance to these Mongol incursions; by this time

Batu's unified forces had learned to shift their technique from scattered border raids to well-organized attacks, mounted from secure bases in new Mongol settlements in the Ordos and in Liaotung. Wang Ao 王鏊 (q.v.) summed up the responsibilities of the corrupt court officials in the matter in a celebrated memorial which concluded, "[Dayan-qaγan and his Mongols] are not as bad as the imperial favorites, who create confusion in matters of state." The military farce reached its nadir in two campaigns in 1501 in which a total of fifteen Mongols were killed; the reports to the court were so completely falsified that as a result Chu Hui's engagements were taken to be a triumph, and two hundred ten Chinese officers were advanced in rank.

By the time of the death of Emperor Chu Yu-t'ang (q. v.), Batu's forces had become increasingly efficient and a major concern of the Ming government. In 1506 Emperor Chu Hou-chao (q. v.) appointed Yang I-ch'ing (q. v.) supreme commander of the western defense areas, but eunuch intrigues hamstrung his attempts to salvage the situation by building a line of defensive fortifications. It seemed inevitable that Mongol military prowess would soon be able to reach into the heart of imperial China itself, and it would undoubtedly have done so had it not been for a breakdown in Mongol unity, probably set off around 1509 by a minor Chinese victory in the field. Batu's attempt to establish one of his sons, Ulus-bolod (b.1482), as a vice regent over portions of his Mongol hegemony was also unpopular and a source of internal dissension. By the winter of 1509/10 Batu became occupied in a struggle with two powerful adversaries, Ibrahim (q. v.), a principal chieftain in the region near modern Kalgan, and Ordos, i. e., the Ordos chieftain Mandulai Aγolqo.

Inter-tribal difficulties of this sort certainly weakened the impact of the Mongol force that could be brought to bear against the Ming, but nevertheless from about 1513 the Mongols were able to construct fortified camps as bases for their attacks, and to organize and train a highly mobile cavalry force estimated at fifteen thousand men. Their attacks approached Peking ever more closely until in 1517, in a forty-eight-hour battle directed (from a distance) by the emperor himself, the Mongols were forced to retreat; this was the high-water mark of Mongol power in the Ming dynasty and their last major engagement with Chinese forces. The sporadic raids into border areas continued but at a slackened pace, due in large measure to discord within their own ranks, set off by the murder of Ulus-bolod and the necessity to avenge his slaying.

In 1523 the apparent lull was broken by another major attack by Mongol forces directed by Batu, which pressed close to Peking and which continued to threaten the capital off and on until 1526. In 1532 Batu apparently sued the Chinese court for peace and the "right to offer tribute"; these demands were refused, and Chinese forces were for once, after fifty years, successful in repelling the attacks with which Batu replied to this calculated rebuff. From 1528 to the time of Batu's death, the date and circumstances of which are obscure, he appears to have begun to lose his control over the unified Mongol nation which he had led. He was succeeded as qaγan by Bodi-alaγ, his grandson by his second son, Törö-bolod, and from the 1520s on the term hsiao-wang-tzu in the Chinese sources refers to Bodi-alaγ, rather than to Batu.

For the Mongols, Batu was and is a figure of almost heroic importance. His great accomplishments were the unification of the Mongol forces and his division of Inner Mongolia into left and right wings (i 翼) subdivided into six tümen (wan-hu 萬戶), or three tümen for each wing. By defeating Ismaïl he became master of Chahar; he then destroyed opposition to his rule among the Oirat; he next proceeded to capture the region west of Chahar; and eventually came to rule over all Inner Mongolia and part of the eastern border of Outer Mongolia. He was probably ambitious to reestablish Mongol rule over China when he conducted sporadic raids and later large-scale, well organized invasions. When he approached old age, however, he was unable to control his forces, dissension developed, and his urge for conquest ebbed. On the other hand, he may well have been deterred from pressing his advantage by his own ideological acceptance of the traditional relationship between the Chinese court and its neighboring foreign peoples; certainly at several critical points in his military career he shows himself somewhat hesitant to push on to a final and irremediable severing of this relationship. If this was indeed the case, then in hampering Batu in his genius for tribal organization and military strategy in this way, the Ming state's Confucian ideology of proper ruler-vassal relationships seems to have proved to have been a far more powerful deterrent against foreign incursions than all the Chinese military forces together. At the same time one must bear in mind the marked differences in the style of frontier warfare between Mongol and Chinese; here we find light mounted bowmen fighting against walled fortifications defended with firearms.

Bibliography

1/327/14a; MSL (1964), Hsiao-tsung, 0349; KC (1958), 2567 [calls him 把禿猛可]; Wada Sei 和田清, "Tatsuenkan ni tsuite 達延汗いついて," 國際キリスト大學 [アジア文化研究論叢], 1 (October, 1958); id., "A Study of Dayan Khan," MTB, 19 (1960), 1; D. Pokotilov, "History of the Eastern Mongols during the Ming Dynasty from 1368 to 1634," tr. by R. Loewenthal, *Studia Serica*, ser. A, no. 1 (Chengtu, 1947), part 1, 79, 81, 98; W. Franke, "Addenda and Corrigenda," *Studia Serica*, ser. A, no. 3 (1949), part 2, 49, 52; H. Serruys, *Genealogical Tables of the Descendants of Dayan-Qan* ('s Gravenhage, 1958), 12; id., *The Mongols in China during the Hung-wu Period (Bruges, 1959)*, 289; B. Vladimirtsov, "O prozvische Dayan qaγan," *Doklad Akad. Nauk*, V (1924), 119; C. R. Bowden, tr., *The Mongol Chronicle Altan Tobči* (Wiesbaden, 1955), 181; H. H. Howorth, *History of the Mongols from the 9th to the 19th Century*, part 1 (London, 1876), 369; L. Hambis, *Documents sur l'histoire des Mongols à l'époque des Ming* (Paris, 1969), 212.

Roy Andrew Miller

BOYM, Michał Piotr (Chinese name: Pu-mi-ko 卜彌格, T. 致遠), 1612-August 22, 1659, a Polish Jesuit missionary, was born in Lwów, the son of the physician-royal to Sigismond III of Poland (r. 1587-1632). He might have followed in the same profession as his father—indeed, his later writings reveal a considerable knowledge of botany and medicine; instead, however, he decided on a religious vocation, entered the novitiate in Krakow in 1631, sojourned in Rome for a time, then embarked for the east from Lisbon in 1642, reaching Macao in 1643. He moved on to Tongking *ca.* 1645, and two years later was assigned to Ting-an 定安, Hainan. Probably in 1648 Boym received orders to abandon Hainan for Tongking, doubtless because of a Manchu invasion of the island, and after over a year there, to repair to Macao. Some time in 1649 Álvarō Semedo (*q.v.*), as vice provincial of the China mission, asked Boym to join Andreas Koffler (*q.v.*) at the court of Chu Yu-lang (EC CP), then resident at Chao-ch'ing 肇慶, Kwangtung. By February 7, 1650, however, Manchu pressure forced the emperor to move by boat to Wu-chou 梧州, and thence to Nan-ning 南寧, both in Kwangsi. As several members of Chu's immediate entourage had fallen under the influence of Christianity, it was not unnatural for them, as a last forlorn hope, to request outside aid (or possibly for the Jesuits to put the idea into their heads, as Paul Pelliot suggests), and Boym was asked to take letters addressed to Pope Innocent X and the general of the Jesuits. The empress dowager, née Wang 王, baptized as Helena, wrote to each of them on November 4, 1650; three days earlier the eunuch P'ang T'ien-shou, baptized as Achilleus (*see* EC-CP, p. 195), did likewise. (For a repro-duction of the letter of the empress dowager, and a partial translation, see Nigel Cameron.) P'ang also assigned two Chinese to accompany Boym: Kuo Jo-hsi 郭若習 (known as Joseph) and Cheng An-te-lo 鄭安德肋 (known as Andreas). While in Macao both confirmed by oath, before an ecclesiastical notary (November 23, 1650), Boym's mission and the authenticity of the letters delivered to Boym. These were anxious days for the authorities at Macao. The Manchus were close by, occupying Canton on November 25. If they were to become aware of the character of Boym's mission, anything might happen both to the Portuguese settlement and to the church in China. The Portuguese civil officials tried to prevent Boym's departure, but the Portuguese governor, threatened with excommunication by the Jesuit visitor, gave in.

Boym and his party left Macao probably on January 1, 1651. Kuo fell ill en route and did not continue. Cheng, a Chinese Christian convert of nineteen, with the rank of commander, accompanied him all the way to Rome and back, a journey which was to take eight and a half years. They reached Goa in May, but it was not until two years later that they finally arrived in Rome (November, 1652) via Golconda, Ispahan, Tauris, Smyrna, Venice, and Lorette, after a series of misadventures. In the meantime Innocent X had died and it fell finally to Pope Alexander VII to respond to the letters (December, 1655). Girard de Rialle characterizes those written to the princesses as "d'une grande banalité." Only the letter to the empress-dowager shows some understanding; the pontiff expresses the hope that her disunited empire may once more recover its one-time integrity. Boym carried the missives with him when he sailed once more from Lisbon in 1656.

Held up for a year in Goa, then besieged by the Dutch, Boym and Andreas finally reached Siam early in 1658, and after some delay—the Portuguese authorities in Macao refused them permission to return for fear of Manchu reprisals—they voyaged by a Chinese junk to Tongking. There were more delays as Boym sought for guides. At last in 1659 he penetrated Kwangsi to find all passes blocked by Manchu guards. He tried to reenter Tongking but authorization was denied. Completely discouraged, his letters undelivered, Boym fell ill and died, aged forty-seven. The ever faithful Andreas attended to his burial, set up a cross and tombstone with an inscription by the side of the road, then took flight into the mountains.

In spite of frequent travel and other claims on his time and energy, Boym was a voluminous writer, making contributions to European understanding of Chinese botany, medicine, language, and geography. The first work published in his lifetime was his report as envoy of the Ming court to the Holy See. Originally penned in Latin, it appeared in three German editions (1653), one in Latin (1653), and one in French (1654). The last published in Paris is known by the title *Briefve Relation De La Notable Conversion des Personnes Royales, & de l'estat de la Religion Chrestienne en la Chine.* Next is his *Flora Sinensis* (Vienna, 1656), a book of 77 pages of which 3 are blank and 23 have plates colored by hand. Seventeen of the illustrations are of cultivated plants of southeast Asia, five of animals, and one of the inscription on the Nestorian monument of A.D. 781, of which he was to make the first Latin translation of the Chinese text (published in Athanasius Kircher's *China Illustrata*). His work on medicine is *Clavis Medica ad Chinarum Doctrinam de Pulsibus.* It has two prefaces, both dated 1658 and written in Siam; it was not published, however, until 1686 in Belgium, and then only after certain alterations made by the editor (Chinese characters deleted, plates removed—only 5 out of 29 described therein appearing,—etc.). What is Boym's contribution is the description and use of 289 Chinese drugs, with Chinese names in romanized form. (It is not without interest that in 1825 Adrien de Jussieu assigned

Boym's name to a plant of the family Rutaceae, calling it "Boymiarutaecarpa." Unfortunately it was later discovered that the genus had already [1776] been described by J. R. and G. Forster, who called it "Evodia"; so Boym's name is known botanically only in a cross reference.) The section on the doctrine of the pulse attributed to Wang Shu-ho (fl. A.D. 300) is also Boym's translation. The Prussian Library in Berlin has preserved Boym's Chinese medical books with marginal notes.

In the field of language Boym was responsible, as noted above, for a translation of the Chinese text on the Nestorian tablet, with romanization of all the characters. These, 1604 in all, are numbered, the romanization with tone marks (first devised by L. Cattaneo, *q.v.*), and literal translation (not always accurate), presented in 29 columns, following the numbered order. Kircher's work also includes a short Chinese-French dictionary attributed by Pelliot and Boleslaw Szczesniak to Boym, but Walter Simon considers it to be possibly a collective work by other hands.

While waiting for action on his mission to the Vatican, Boym took time to prepare an atlas of China and several more specialized maps as well. Some have been described by Robert Chabrié, and others more recently discovered have been treated by Szczesniak. Of them the best known is the atlas preserved in the library of the Vatican, entitled *Magni Catay, Quod olim Serica, et modo Sinarum est Monarchia.* It is believed that this was based on the *Ti-t'u tsung-yao* 地圖綜要, 3 ch., compiled by Wu Hsüeh-yen 吳學儼 (T. 敬勝), Chu Shao-pen 朱紹本 (T. 支百), Chu Kuo-kan 朱國幹 (T. 大年, cs 1634), and Chu Kuo-ta 達 (T. 咸受), published 1643, a copy of which with Boym's marginal notes is preserved in the same library (Fondo Borgia Cinese). Besides the general map of China, which is colored and adorned with many picturesque illustrations, and is supplied with inaccurate indications of latitude and longitude, statistics of population, taxes, mining resources, and place names, written both in romanized form and in Chinese, there are maps of the fifteen provinces, also of Liaotung and Hainan. These have all remained in manuscript. One general map of China, previously unknown, was published by Szczesniak in *Imago mundi*, and another rare one by Nicolas Sanson.

There is little doubt but that the above and other writings of Boym played a considerable part in adding to Europe's fund of knowledge about China. His contemporary, Athanasius Kircher, wrote of them as "admiranda et posterorum memoria dignissima."

Bibliography

Yang Sen-fu 楊森富, *Chung-kuo chi-tu-chiao shih* 中國基督教史 (Taipei, 1968), 147; Fang Hao 方豪, *Chung-kuo T'ien-chu-chiao shih jen-wu chuan* 天主教史人物傳 (Hong Kong, 1967), 305; Ignatius Ying-ki, "The Last Emperor of the Ming Dynasty and Catholicity," *Bull. of the Catholic University of Peking*, no. 1 (September, 1926), 23; Robert Chabrié, *Michel Boym jésuite polonais et la fin des Ming en Chine (1646-1662), Contribution à l'histoire des missions d'Extrême-Orient* (Paris, 1933); H. Bernard, review in MS, 1 (1935), 215; Paul Pelliot, "Michel Boym," TP, 31 (1935), 95; Boleslaw Szczesniak, "The Beginnings of Chinese Lexicography in Europe with Particular Reference to the Work of Michael Boym (1612-1659)," JAOS, 67 (1947), 160; *id.*, "The Atlas and Geographic Description of China: a Manuscript of Michael Boym (1612-1659)," JAOS, 73 (1953), 65; *id.*, "Athanasius Kircher's *China Illustrata* and M. Boym," *Osiris*, 10 (1952), 385; *id.*, "John Floyer and the Art of the Pulse," *Osiris*, 10 (1954), 127; *id.*, "The Writings of Michael Boym," MS, 14 (1949-55), 481; *id.*, "The Seventeenth Century Maps of China: an Inquiry into the Compilations of European Cartographers," *Imago mundi*, 13 (1956), 116; *id.*, "The First Chinese Dictionary Published in Europe," Semi-centennial volume, AOS mid-west branch (1969) 2, 17; *id.*, "Mappa Imperii Sinarum of Michael Boym," *Imago mundi*, 19 (1965), 113; Pfister, 269; Walter Simon, "The Attribution to Michael Boym of Two Early Achievements of Western Sinology," AM, VII (1959), 165; *id.*, "The China Illustrata Romanization of João Soeiro's (Soerio's) *Sanctae Legis Compendium* and Michael Boym," *Studia Serica Bernhard Karlgren Dedicata* (Copenhagen, 1959), 265; Girard de Rialle, "Une mission chinoise à Venise au XVIIe siècle," TP, 1 (1890), 99; A. Kircher, *China Illustrata* (Amsterdam, 1667), 4; L. Carrington Goodrich, "Boym and Boymiae," TP, 57 (1971), 135; Adrien de Jussieu, in *Mémoires du Muséum d'Histoire Naturelle* (Paris, 1825), 507; J. D. Hooker, *The Flora of British India*, I (London, 1875), 490; Nigel Cameron, *Barbarians and Mandarins* (Tokyo, 1970), 223.

L. Carrington Goodrich and B. Szczesniak

bSOD-NAMS-RGYA-MTS'O 鎖南堅錯, March 1543-April 1588, reckoned as the third Dalai Lama of Tibet, was actually the first whom the Mongols called by this title. He was born at mDa'-rtse dGa'-k'aṅ-gsar-goṅ in the sTod-luṅ valley west of Lhasa, into a noble family. In 1545 the child was recognized as the incarnation of the deceased dGe-'dun-rgya-mts'o (*q. v.*) and was solemnly brought to 'Bras-spuṅs monastery, where he received his education and was formally installed as abbot.

In the 1560s he began his independent activity in politics. The chief characteristic of his comparatively short period as head of the Yellow Church was the search for supporters and allies outside Tibet. On one hand, the suspicion and hostility against the Red Sects had grown apace with the increasing influence of the Yellow Church on the popular masses; the more so as, during the years just preceding, many empty or decayed monasteries had been appropriated by the dGe-lugs-pa. On the other, the power of the ministers of the Rin-spuṅs rulers, staunch supporters of the Karma-pa, was increasing; in 1565 they occupied gŽis-ka-rtse (Shigatse), the capital of gTsaṅ, and the Rin-spuṅs chiefs lost all control. bSod-nams-rgya-mts'o thus found himself confronted with a difficult situation; no Tibetan supporter of his sect was strong enough to resist the new and vigorous rulers of south central Tibet. In vain his tutors, during his boyhood, had made him travel widely in gTsaṅ, and as a grown man he extended his travels to the regions on the Indian border, and above all to central Tibet; after 1569 he even resided for some years in bKra-śis-lhun-po, in the very heart of enemy country. But the petty chiefs of the south were no match for the powerful state of gTsaṅ; and the former rulers of Tibet, the P'ag-mo-gru-pa, although whole-heartedly devoted to the Yellow Sect, were but a shadow of their onetime selves, especially after an inner feud (1563 and 1564) had completely sapped their strength. In 1575 the army of gTsaṅ almost reached Lhasa.

This was the political background of the famous journey of bSod-nams-rgya-mts'o to Mongolia. He was invited there by Altan-qaγan (*q. v.*), who already in 1573, during a raid in northeastern Tibet, had entered into contact with lamas of the Yellow Sect. The latter advised him to invite their highest leader. A correspondence started, and in 1577 bSod-nams-rgya-mts'o accepted the invitation. On the 15th day of the fifth month (June 19) of 1578 he met Altan-qaγan at his camp in Inner Mongolia. This historic meeting resulted in the official acceptance of dGe-lugs-pa Buddhism by Altan-qaγan and his family, soon to be followed by almost all the Mongol princes. Altan-qaγan gave to bSod-nams-rgya-mts'o the title of Dalai Lama (Oceanic Teacher), by which he and his successors were henceforth known to the Mongols, and later to the Chinese and eventually to Westerners. Soon afterward bSod-nams-rgya-mts'o left Köke-nuur for eastern Tibet, traveling as far as Li-t'ang 裏塘. Before leaving he had sent a letter and gifts to the Chinese minister, Chang Chü-cheng (*q. v.*), delivered on March 12; and a little later (August-September, 1579), during his absence, the sToṅ-k'or C'os-rje, his representative with Altan-qaγan, received a letter sent by the Wan-li emperor granting to bSod-nams-rgya-mts'o (So-nan-chien-ts'o) a title and complimentary gifts. This was the first official contact between a Dalai Lama and the Chinese government.

bSod-nams-rgya-mts'o's journey to K'ams (eastern Tibet) brought a strengthening of the Yellow Sect's influence in that region; especially important was the entry of the prince of lJaṅ (Li-chiang, *see* Mu Tseng) into close relations with the Dalai Lama, from whom he received a title. In the meantime Altan-qaγan had died(1582), but his successors once more sent an invitation to bSod-nams-rgya-mts'o. On his way, at 'P'ags-śiṅ-kun (Lin-t'ao 臨桃), he mediated peace between the Chinese and local tribes. In 1584 he met Qutuγtai-sečen qungtayiji (*q. v.*) in the Ordos and several Mongol princes became his spiritual disciples. In 1586 he visited Altan-qaγan's son Senggedügüreng in Köke-qoto; but the prince died soon afterwards, the Dalai Lama conducting his funeral ceremonies. This journey had as a result the conversion and spiritual allegiance of the right wing of the Tümed; also the Qalqa and the Qaračin sent him presents.

According to his biography, in 1588 he received messengers from the Wan-li emperor conferring upon him the title Kuan-ting ta-kuo-shih 灌頂大國師 and inviting him tᴏ Peking; but the embassy is apparently not registered in the Chinese texts. bSod-nams-rgya-mts'o accepted the invitation, but before he could start the journey he died in the same year in Mongolia.

Bibliography

Ṅag-dban-blo-bzaṅ-rgya-mts'o (fifth Dalai Lama), *rJe-btsun t'ams-cad-mk'yen-pa bSod-nams-rgya-mts'o'i rnam-t'ar dṅos-grub-rgya-mts'o'i śiṅ-rta* (composed 1646), vol. Ña of his collected works; 1/31/5b; MSL (1940), Shen-tsung, 84/6b; KC (1958), 4342; *Meng-ku yüan-liu chien-cheng* 蒙古源流箋證 (1934), 6/30a, 7/15a; Saγang Sečen, *Erdeni-yin tobči*, tr. I. J. Schmidt (St. Petersburg, 1829), 237; G. Tucci, *Tibetan Painted Scrolls* (Rome, 1949), 41; G. Schulemann, *Die Geschichte der Dalai-Lamas*, 2nd ed. (Leipzig, 1958), 203; L. Petech, "The Dalai-Lamas and Regents of Tibet: A Chronological Study," TP, 47 (1959), 371.

Luciano Petech

CABALLERO, Antonio de (Santa Maria) 利安當, H. 克敦, April, 1602–May 13, 1669, founder of the second wave of Franciscan missions in China, was born in the province of Palencia, Spain. Completing his primary education at home, for his humanities he entered the University of Salamanca, where, on March 24, 1618, he became a Friar Minor at the Calvario convent of the San Pablo province. After professing his vows (March 25, 1619), he volunteered for the Franciscan Japanese mission, and, following his ordination as a priest, was assigned to Castroverde, whence in 1628 he left for the Philippines with twenty-nine other friars, reaching Manila the following year. His first appointment was as a professor of arts and theology (August, 1630) at the San Francisco convent of Manila; here he ministered also to the Japanese lepers at Balete and studied Japanese.

When Angelo Cocchi (*q. v.*), who had established a mission in 1632 at Fu-an 福安, Fukien, sent an appeal for help (December, 1632), Juan de Morales (*q.v.*), a Dominican, volunteered, and the Franciscan provincial allowed Caballero and Francisco Bermúdez to join him. The three sailed from Cavite on March 9, 1633, landing at T'an-shui 淡水, Taiwan, on April 2. Informed of their arrival Cocchi sent a boat for them manned by his catechist-scholar, Joachin Kuo, and three other converts, which entered the port (June 20), flying a red-crossed flag. Leaving Bermúdez behind, Caballero and Morales and the four Chinese sailed to the mainland. On July 2 Cocchi met them at Fu-an, escorted them into the city, and let them resume the study of Chinese. In September Cocchi informed the Jesuit Bento de Matos by letter of their presence in China, and expressed the wish that they might collaborate in their missionary endeavor. Matos replied that they should have come by way of Macao with permission from the bishop or the Jesuit vice-provincial; in other words, that they should serve under Portuguese patronage, a condition which the Holy See held no longer valid.

Wishing to relieve the Dominicans of his liability and to arrive at an understanding with the Jesuit vice-provincial, Manuel Dias (*q.v.*), Caballero started out November 2, hoping to find a place (perhaps Nanking) where he might pursue independent mission work and at the same time improve his knowledge of Chinese. Stopping at Chien-ch'ang 建昌, Kiangsi, he was welcomed on December 16 by the Jesuit, Gaspar Ferreira (*q.v.*), but the next day was told to seek permission from Dias, then at Nanchang, for a longer stay. So he went there to confer with Dias, who invited him to spend Christmas with him; a few days later, however, Dias advised him to look for larger mission fields. As Caballero's porter had left him, Dias replaced him with one of his own, a certain Andrew Siao Leu, and, pretending that there was no church in Nanking, wrote converts there a note of introduction, entrusting it to Siao. Late in January, 1634, the two arrived at the southern capital. Siao then began to harass Caballero, taking him from one house to another, alleging fear of detection and persecution, and at the end leaving him in the home of Chinese Christians outside the city, where he remained confined for forty-five days. When Francesco Sambiasi (*q.v.*), the resident Jesuit missionary, visited the place to hear confessions and anoint a man who was sick, Caballero was kept hidden. Upon Dias' arrival and obviously on his order, three Jesuit domestics bound Caballero and forced him into a boat destined for Fu-an. So it was that on April 8 his wandering of six months came to an end. At this point Caballero accepted the invitation of Morales, left alone by Cocchi's death, to help him care for the mission of Fu-an and Ting-t'ou 頂頭. In November, 1634, the Dominican, Francisco Díez 蘇芳積, and Bermúdez, joined them at Fu-an, and there by agreement the Dominicans kept Fu-an and the Franciscans took Ting-t'ou, where Caballero soon baptized his first convert, Lo Wen-tsao (ECCP, p. 876), who was to become the first Chinese Dominican priest and bishop.

Studying written Chinese with a scholar known as Thaddaeus Wang, Caballero one day came across the character chi祭. Wang explained that the word meant sacrifice, and was comparable to the Mass; on further questioning he admitted that Chinese Catholics also practiced worship of ancestors, of Confucius, and of city gods. Startled by learning this, Caballero informed Morales and urged him to inquire further. Tipped off and led by Francis Mieu, Caballero and Morales at dawn one day surprised members of the Mieu family, both Catholic and non-Catholic, worshiping their ancestors in their ancestral temple at Mu-yang 穆洋. Convinced of the superstitious nature of the rites, the friars refused to let their adherents perform or attend them or even keep the ancestral tablets. The prohibition caused a sensation among Catholics. So John Mieu wrote the Jesuit, Giulio Aleni (q.v.), who had baptized him, for instructions on the matter. The permissive attitude revealed in Aleni's reply did not satisfy Caballero. In answer to the latter's questions, Matos expressed the opinion that obeisance to Confucius was political and therefore permissible, and the same could be said of the respect paid to the ancestors; if, however, the rites were performed in sacrificial form with petitions to the dead, they should be considered sacrilegious. In his reply of September 19, Ignacio Lobo 盧納爵 (T. 亮貴, b. 1603) expressed deep concern over the superstitious nature of the rites and agreed with the attitude of the friars. The situation was novel only for the latter, for the Jesuits had debated the same problems beginning in 1610, especially at their meeting in 1628, at Chia-ting 嘉定, northwest of Shanghai (see Nicolas Longobardi). To clarify the subject and create a uniform procedure Morales and Bermúdez proceeded to Foochow in November to interview vice-provincial Francisco Furtado (q.v.) and Lobo, placing before them thirteen questions.

The inconclusive result of the meeting made the friars examine the entire problem and question their converts in order to refer the matter to the competent authorities. After two long sessions at Ting-t'ou (December 22, 1635, to January 9, 1636, and January 21, to February 10), Caballero and Díez were chosen to carry the minutes of the proceedings, studded with Chinese quotations, to their superiors in Manila. En route, it was decided that Díez should wait at T'an-shui, with a copy of the minutes and return to China if Caballero reached his destination. Assuming that all was going well with him, Díez was persuaded to return to the mainland at the head of five recruits, two Dominicans and three Franciscans. They sailed on September 1, 1636, landing at Ting-t'ou on the 7th. It happens, however, that Caballero had suffered shipwreck in the Taiwan strait, been captured by the Dutch at their newly built Castle Zeelandia, and sent in fetters to labor camps in Batavia and Ternate; only after eight months was he finally freed at Malacca, whence he reached Manila in June, 1637.

Caballero's first act was to hand the minutes of the Ting-t'ou proceedings to the Franciscan commissary visitor and to the Dominican provincial. On July 24 they petitioned the Manila archbishop to convene a meeting of theologians and jurists to discuss the Chinese pastoral problems. In preparation for it, the Dominicans offered an extract of the Ting-t'ou proceedings, while Caballero outlined fifteen questions and answers as agenda for the proposed meeting. His manuscript in forty-five pages is dated Manila, August 20, 1637. Two months later he supplemented this with other documents. The Jesuits were opposed to any such meeting, but members of other religious orders handed their papers to the archbishop. Feeling the need to present their case to higher authority, Caballero and Morales finally sailed (May, 1640) from Cavite for Macao. Realizing the hazards of the journey, especially from the Dutch corsairs, Caballero tried to dissuade Morales from going on to Rome, but finally let him depart in October, 1640. Stranded in Macao, Caballero undertook the spiritual direction of the Poor Clares (a convent founded in 1634), and began annotating the six-tome mystical work "Floresta franciscana" and writing philosophical and juridical papers. In 1642 Caballero sent word to the Spanish governor of the Philippines, advising him to try to prevent the Dutch mastery of Taiwan; his words were ignored, however, and eventually the Spanish had to abandon the northern tip of the island.

While Morales was in Rome he obtained from Urban VIII support for his cause, the study of mission documents by a Holy Office commission, and decrees appointing him and Caballero prefects apostolic of their respective missions (March and April, 1641). Meanwhile Caballero was facing an order calling for the expulsion of all Spaniards from Macao (signed at Goa on May 4, 1643). His last appeal of September 6, 1644, going unheeded, Caballero and seven nuns embarked for Manila on October 9, but contrary winds took them to Danang, Cochinchina, where they were brought to court and sentenced to death; the magistrate changed his mind, however, and the boy king, known posthumously as Thuân Hoang Đê 順皇帝 (b. 1629, reigned 1643-49), allowed them to stay and preach. Caballero baptized some two thousand people, including the king's brother, a monk in the mountains of Cham province, who shortly afterward was stoned to death. With royal permission, Caballero and the nuns (April, 1645) again embarked for Manila where they arrived five weeks later.

Always active, Caballero distinguished himself by aiding the victims of earthquakes in the Manila area of September 10 and November 30, 1645. In February, 1648, he roused the ire of the Spanish governor by preaching in the cathedral against vices in public life, and was punished by confinement in a mountain fastness. While there he received two sets of dispatches from Rome including word of his promotion to prefect apostolic. One set reached him in February by way of the Indian Ocean, the other in July, brought via Mexico and the Pacific by the returning Morales. While Morales announced the papal decree of 1645 to his superior in Manila, Caballero addressed acknowledgments to Rome of the dispatches he had received, requesting at the same time that the Holy See also send notifications of the decree to Japan, Korea, Tatary, and adjacent regions. He even went so far as to ask the Pope to confirm it to make sure that there should be no misunderstanding on the part of other missionaries.

Meanwhile, acting on a plea of Juan García de León 施若翰 for additional missionaries, the Dominican provincial secured from the irascible governor permission to send them to China. The captain of a junk owned by Cheng Chih-kuan (uncle of Cheng Ch'eng-kung, ECCP) agreed to take them to Fukien and eventually, on their third attempt, a composite mission band of Franciscans (Caballero, Buenaventura Ibáñez [文度辣, H. 道濟], José Casanova, and Brother, Diego), a Sangley from Ting-t'ou, and Dominicans (Morales, Francisco Varo, Timoteo Bottigli, and Manuel Rodríquez) sailed on July 21, 1649, and landed two weeks later near the seaport town of Anhai 安海, south of Ch'üan-chou 泉州, Fukien. The captain of the junk went immediately to see his master, Cheng Chih-kuan, whose brother, Cheng Chih-lung (ECCP) had left him in charge of the port, and handed him a letter introducing the missionaries. Eager to establish profitable commercial relations with Manila, Cheng Chih-kuan offered them one of his houses next door to his residence. In the beginning he and his brother and superior, Cheng Hung-k'uei (ECCP), saw the guests only through a peephole. On landing, the missionaries had met Lo Wen-tsao who was there chartering a junk for Manila to get the help requested by García de León. Lo told them that Governor Liu Chung-tsao (ECCP, p.

180), the Dominicans' friend, had committed suicide on May 22, 1649, the day before the Manchus took Foochow; that the scholar John Mieu had been beheaded by the Manchus entering Fu-an on the same day; and that Admiral Joachin Kuo, deserted by his marines, had fled from Ting-t'ou to a port near Fu-ning 福寧 where he was soon recognized and beheaded.

A few days later the missionaries were visited by the Portuguese-Chinese Antonio Rodriguez of Macao, grandson of Cheng Chih-lung. Rodriguez recognized Caballero as the friar who used to visit him at Macao, and told him that because of the precarious situation in Macao and the entire south coast he, his father (Manuel Vello, or Bello) and families, all Catholics, had moved in 1645, on the insistence of his father-in-law, to An-hai. The latter had promised that he would build them a church and invite a Franciscan priest, for the Franciscans lived (he said) frugally and asked for no money. When Cheng Chih-lung went to Peking with the Manchu army, he left his step-mother, Tai Fuje (太夫人？), with full authority to govern the area. So the Vellos and Rodriguez settled at An-hai in a spacious house where they set up a chapel. For two years the Jesuit Pietro Canevari had attended them, but he came to feel scruples about confining his activity there, and had left. Now Rodriguez invited Caballero and his companions to move in with them, ministering to them and all Catholics in town, including the Moorish bodyguard of Cheng Chih-lung. Caballero gladly accepted the offer for a number of reasons. He could not join the Dominicans at Fu-an because of the troubled conditions there, and such shelter would prevent tangles with local missionaries (Canevari and others). Then at the earliest opportunity he would found a mission of his own, possibly in Korea, where the people were said to be well disposed and to lead a simple life. Despite financial difficulties, the newcomers studied Chinese and helped in the ministry. On July 14, 1650, Caballero left An-hai bound for Korea. At Tientsin he learned that some merchants from Korea went twice a year to Peking to trade. So he traveled to the capital looking for the merchants, but they had already gone home. Uneasy about keeping an unreported and unknown foreigner in his house, Caballero's Manchu host told him that he would denounce him to the ministry of Rites unless someone would vouch for him. Whereupon Caballero mentioned Johann Adam Schall von Bell (q.v.) of the calendrical bureau. Schall advised Caballero to go to Tsinan, which had been abandoned by the Jesuits for lack of a following, and wrote a warm letter of introduction to his close friend, the "Xeu Tao" (Shou-tao 守道, circuit intendant). [Editors' note: This is presumably Liu Ta 劉達 (cs 1637), a native of Ta-ming-fu 大名府, who was serving as intendant at the time.] At the end of October, 1650, Caballero went there, settled at the house left by the Jesuits, and was welcomed by the intendant who, in returning Caballero's visit, saw how miserable the house was and, together with two friends who were administration commissioners, offered to contribute to the purchase of a better place. The three officials did give (August, 1651) 130 of the 150 taels needed. Caballero furnished it appropriately and opened a St. Francis church there. On September 9, Ibáñez left An-hai for Tsinan to hand Caballero the provincial order to quit and return to Manila. Arriving in December, 1651, he gave Caballero the dismal news of recall and no financial aid. But Caballero knew that he was there by order of the Holy See, and as prefect apostolic was exempt from provincial jurisdiction. So in January, 1652, he visited the mission stations in T'ai-an 泰安, where over a thousand converts had been without a priest for eight years. Early in 1652 he returned to Tsinan and wrote to his provincial to send no missionaries for the time being except possibly a companion for Casanova at An-hai and a brother surgeon. In February he revisited T'ai-an and baptized five hundred people. On Schall's invitation he spent Holy Week in Peking, helping in the rites. In September he sent Ibáñez to the capital to secure loans and explore the prospects for Korea. Chagrined by the Jesuits' failure to comply with the 1645 decree and by relative lack of success in mission work, Caballero had reverted to his first intention of proceeding to Korea and asked (January, 1653) the provincial to extend the original mission license. He entrusted the missive to Ibáñez who again went to Peking and there met Rodriguez, who had spent two years with Cheng Chih-lung trying to extricate him from the Manchu web. Upon reaching An-hai in March, 1653, Ibáñez forwarded Caballero's letters to Manila, while his new provincial was ordering him and Casanova to leave China and return to the Philippines. The letters were lost en route, and so Caballero wrote again asking for unrestricted license to travel to Korea, Japan, and adjacent islands with any companions he would think fit. He also described the three books in Chinese he had composed: 1) Basic truths about the Creator; 2) Falsity of worship of spirits as proved by the Chinese Classics; 3) Exposition of the virtues of faith, hope, and charity. In a subsequent letter (December 15) he repeated the information, adding that he could not engrave the said books for lack of funds, and requested that in his license the provincial mention Korea specifically, for he was eager to work there. In a follow-up letter (January, 1654), he insisted that the provincial send over the subsidy, which was supposed to be annual, enabling him and his two companions, Ibáñez and Casanova, to move to the peninsular kingdom. At long last the subsidy came, but, having no one to whom to entrust it, Ibáñez left An-hai with it himself; passing by Hangchow where he fell sick and was attended by the Jesuit vice-provincial Simon da Cunha (瞿西滿, T. 弗溢, 1590–September, 1660) and Manuel Dias, he finally reached Tsinan

after Christmas. The subsidy was barely enough to pay the debts incurred over the years. By this time Caballero had registered a number of conversions at Tsinan, T'ai-an, and Hsin-ch'eng 新城 (in Tsinan prefecture).

Caballero spent Easter week of 1655 at Peking, again helping Schall in the rites. For the occasion Caballero donated a small but beautiful monstrance which enabled Schall to make the first exposition of the Eucharist ever recorded in China. In the summer Caballero repeated his attempt to enter Korea, this time by way of Teng-chou 登州 (Shantung), but lack of boats, danger of pirates, and a severe attack of dysentery prevented him from realizing his dream, and he had to be taken back to Tsinan on a litter. The only way ever to enter Korea would be by royal permission, but Schall made Caballero understand that the king of Korea had wanted a priest who was also a qualified mathematician to regulate the royal calendar. So that project failed.

On June 18, 1656, Caballero reported to his provincial on the mission situation. He was now glad that he had not joined the Dominicans in his reentry to China as they were in deep trouble on account of war and other upheavals. Having found Korea closed he was content to settle in Shantung and spread his mission work among the poor. He recorded baptizing 738 people, most of them from Tsinan, but he failed to baptize a single member of the scholar-gentry class though many had come to converse and argue with him. In March, 1659, he reported a thousand baptisms that he had thus far administered in various towns and hamlets of the province and that he enjoyed the fraternal amity and complete agreement, even in the matter of Chinese rites, with Jean Valat (汪儒望, T. 聖同, 1599–1696), the new Jesuit missionary residing at his Hsi-t'ang 西堂 (western church), Caballero remaining at his Tung-t'ang 東堂 (eastern church). For the Easter rites (1659) Caballero sent Ibáñez to Peking to help

Schall, and entrusted him with the letters for the provincial to be routed via Macao. Leaving Ibáñez in charge of the mission (July), Caballero undertook a long journey to Lan-ch'i 蘭谿, Chekiang, to retrieve the provincial subsidy which the Dominican Vittorio Ricci had forwarded from Ssu-ming 思明, near Amoy. While en route he was detained at Yangchow because of Cheng Ch'eng-kung's attack on Nanking, and for fifteen days was a guest of prefect Yao（姚？）and his family, all Jesuit converts. Then, probably on Valat's secret information, he went straight to Hangchow to interview the Jesuit Martino Martini（衛匡國, T. 濟泰, 1614–61) about the permissive 1656 decree the latter had elicited from the Holy Office. He cited passages from Chinese publications by Jesuits and their converts, maintained the opposite of what Martini had presented to the Holy Office as facts about the superstitions connected with the rites to the dead, Confucius, and city gods. Martini was non committal. By September 21, Caballero was at Lan-ch'i where he met Morales and Domingo Coronado, and where they brought each other up-to-date on what had transpired. In his letters from Lan-ch'i Caballero asked his provincial to aid his mission in spite of the bad impression given by the Sangleys in the Philippines, and to send two qualified missionaries and a couple of young Philippinos as domestics. He urged him also to break all connection with the pirates operating out of Amoy (i. e., Cheng Ch'eng-kung) lest the emperor should learn about it and put the missionaries to death. At the end of September, he was on his way back and, passing by Yangchow, was again the guest of Prefect Yao, who donated 300 taels to be equally divided among Caballero, Ibáñez, and Valat.

On January 12, 1660, Caballero wrote to the governor of the Philippines that Cheng Ch'eng-kung would try to invade the Islands, with the support of those Sangleys who refused allegiance to the Ch'ing and that they could be recognized by their uncut hair (a piece of intelligence that he possibly picked up at Lan-ch'i as coming from Vittorio Ricci). Now Caballero turned all his attention to the rites issue. On September 4, 1660, he addressed to the Propaganda cardinals a memorandum in 28 paragraphs on the controversial points in Martini's questions and answers, citing or quoting from *Ta-k'o wen* 答客問 by Cosmas Chu Tsung-yüan 朱宗元, *Chu Wen-kung chia hsün* 朱文公家訓（*sic*) by Chu Yung-ch'un 朱用純（T. 致一, H. 柏廬, 1617, –89), *T'ien-chu shih-i* by Matteo Ricci (*q.v.*), and others, arguing that at least for the previous two hundred years such rites had been mingled with superstitious practices. A few days later Caballero sent Ibáñez off to Lan-ch'i to have this memorial forwarded to the Propaganda cardinals, as well as other dispatches to Manila, and to retrieve the subsidy and the letters from Manila that Morales might have brought up from the south. Meanwhile he prepared a more extensive and documented statement addressed to the cardinals of the Propaganda and to the Pope. This disquisition comprises 88 paragraphs, and compares each and every statement of the decree of 1645 with that of 1656, concluding with his own appraisal. The memorial was dated Tsinan, August 20, 1661, the very day the Dominicans meeting at Lan-ch'i were engaged in similar work; it was signed also by Ibáñez.

In March, 1662, Caballero wrote Clement VII a letter accompanying the said "Declaratio", and wrote also a supporting letter to the Propaganda cardinals, and asked them to secure a papal bull approving the Confraternity of the Crucifix 愛敬十字架會, which he had founded for the adherents of both sexes. Caballero wished that he might go to Rome himself to submit his communications in person, recruit new missionaries, and secure financial support for the mission; age, health, and mission work, however, persuaded him instead to dispatch Ibáñez, who left Tsinan in April, 1662.

Meanwhile other events were occupying

the center of the stage. Having expelled the Dutch from Taiwan (February 12, 1662) after an eight months' siege of Castle Zeelandia, Cheng Ch'eng-kung sent a kind of ultimatum to the governor-general of the Philippines (April 24, 1662), proving the accuracy of Caballero's warning. The threat did not materialize because Cheng died suddenly two months later.

In a major effort to inform and orient the Holy See about the rites and a final decision on them, Caballero composed in October, 1662, an important work, "Relatio Sinae Sectarum", divided into three parts: 1) The school of Chinese philosophers ancient and modern (18 chapters), 2) The sects of spirits prevalent among the common people (9 chapters and epilogue), 3) The entry of the Jesuits and other Roman Catholics into China, and the ancient vestiges of our faith (7 chapters).

In 1664, the state of Caballero's finances finally allowed him to have two of his Chinese books printed, namely: 1) *Wanwu pen-mo yüeh-yen* 萬物本末約言 (Compendium on the beginning and end of all things), the original edition of which is unknown to bibliographers, while its reprint, edited by Ibáñez, was published about 1680 in Chu-chiang (Canton) at Yang-jen-li Fu-yin t'ang 楊仁里福音堂 and includes an undated author's preface; 2) *T'ien ju yin* 天儒印 (Christianity and Confucianism compared) by Wei Hsüeh-ch'ü 魏學渠 (T. 子存, H. 青城, cj 1648), dated summer of 1664 and preface by the editor Shang Hu-ch'ing 尚祜卿 of Huai-yin 淮陰 (Nan-Chihli) dated Hsi-t'ang, Tsinan, 1664. Each of 37 paragraphs of the text explains a passage of the Four Books and compares it with points of Catholic doctrine. Caballero's mission seemed to prosper, and he could report two thousand more baptisms.

But the ink on these books was barely dry when a persecution of the missionaries at Peking, fomented by the Muslim Chinese court astronomers (*see* Schall von Bell), broke out in September, 1664. Later Cantonese officials submitted one of their periodical memorials against sects and heretics that brought about a general persecution entraining the destruction or closing of churches. Caballero and Valat were seized on January 20, 1665, just four days before Ibáñez sailed for Europe. On this occasion, Caballero lost all his Chinese books, his papers, manuscripts, and documents, which the militia burned, while they confiscated his European books. This fact explains the rarity of copies of Caballero's Chinese works, and there is no known copy of the original edition of his first book. On March 11 Caballero and Valat were taken to Peking, arriving on the 18th, and on September 13, were escorted, along with all the other missionaries, except a few hidden Dominicans, to Canton. En route Caballero wrote a Chinese refutation of the libel of Yang Kuang-hsien (ECCP), only to learn on his arrival, on March 25, 1666, that the Jesuit Luigi Buglio (ECCP, p. 547) had already published an excellent one. He then composed a detailed "Relación de la persecución" and other minor writings.

The missionaries of various orders, all confined to the old Jesuit residence and church, took the opportunity to discuss their pastoral problems in a meeting that lasted forty days. They reached an agreement on all forty-two questions propounded, but the ones dealing with the cult of the dead and of Confucius. Then on October 8, 1668, Caballero answered a letter of May 11, 1668, written by Luis da Gama, Jesuit visitor for China and Japan, with a learned tract in 67 pages. He held forth on three of the questions raised at the meeting, quoting from Chinese works. That was his last major effort. Seven months later he died at Canton and was buried outside the city on the Ho-nan Island at Pao-kang 河南寶崗, before he could benefit from the decree of restoration of the missions issued September 5, 1669. In 1685, Caballero's first convert Lo Wen-tsao, now Bishop Gregory Lo, composed a Latin and Chinese epitaph and had it engraved on a stone as a token of gratitude.

Caballero left a great number of books, essays, reports, and letters in Spanish, Latin, Portuguese, and Chinese. Scarcely one third of them have been published to date. A third Chinese book, *Cheng hsüeh liu shih* 正學鏐石 (True science's touchstone), was published posthumously with a preface by Shang Shih-chi 尙識己 as editor, dated Tsinan, 1698. In its eight chapters it deals with God and the ultimate; God and Shang-ti; God and the physical heaven; the ultimate and the primordial form and matter; heaven and earth, animate and inanimate beings; spirits and sacrifices; human life and death; and the soul. Surely this is not the third Chinese book Caballero described in his November, 1653, letter as dealing with faith, hope, and charity. Its publication occurred before Pedro de la Pinuela (石鐸琭, H. 振鐸) compiled Caballero's biographical sketch for his *Catalogus religiosorum S. P. N. S. Francisci* (Mexico, 1700) and Juan Martí Clement could enter it into his "Relación muy importante," dated Lumbáng, April 10, 1702.

Bibliography

Anastasius Van den Wyngaert (ed.), *Sinica Franciscana*, Vol. 2 (1933), 317, Vol. 3, 75, Vol. 4 (1942), 326; Georgius Mensaert (ed.), *Sinica Franciscana*, Vol. 7, 3; Otto Maas, *Cartas de China* (Sevilla, 1917), Vol. 1, 7, Vol. 2, 204; id., *Die Wiedereröffnung der Franziskanermission in China in der Neuzeit* (Münster i. W., 1926), 47; Lorenzo Pérez, "Los Franciscanos en el Extremo Oriente," *Archivum Franciscanum, Historicum* Vol. 2 (1909), 548, Vol. 3 (1910), 39, Vol. 4 (1911), 50, 482; id., *Origen de la misiones franciscanas en la provincia de Kwang-tung (China)*, Madrid, 1918; Antonio Sisto Rosso, *Apostolic Legations to China of the Eighteenth Century* (South Pasadena, 1948), 105; Paul Pelliot, "Inventaire sommaire des manuscrits et imprimés chinois de la Bibliothèque Vaticane" (typescript, 1922), 34, 50, 103; Maurice Courant, *Catalogue des livres chinois* (Paris, 1902-12), nos. 6971, 7148, 7154; William C. Hunter, *Bits of Old China* (London, 1885), 68; Edmond Noyé, "Notes pour l'histoire des missions catholiques du Shantong," *Echo de la Mission du Chan-tong Oriental (Chine)*, Vol. 19 (Chefoo, 1922) 41; Georgius Mensaert, "Sinae II. Tempore hodierno (1579-1957)," *Historia Missionum Ordinis Fratrum Minorum*, Vol. 1 (Rome, 1967), 131; Basilio Pandžić, "Quinque nondum editae P. Antonii Caballero, O. F. M. de Sinarum missionibus litterae," *Archivum Franciscanum Historicum*, Vol. 61 (1968), 176; Fang Hao 方豪, *Chung-kuo T'ien-chu-chiao shih jen-wu chuan* 中國天主教史人物傳, II (Hong Kong, 1970), 108.

Antonio Sisto Rosso

CATTANEO, Lazzaro (Lazare, 郭居靜, T. 仰鳳), 1560-January 19, 1640, Roman Catholic missionary, was born into a noble family at Sarzana near Genoa, in 1560, pursued studies privately in literature, philosophy, and theology, and entered his novitiate in the Society of Jesus near Rome on February 27, 1581. In 1585 he was dispatched first to Lisbon and thence to Goa, along with certain Japanese ambassadors (Itō Manshu [Mancio] 伊藤滿所 and others) who had been sent to Rome in 1582 and were now on the return voyage. There he remained for a while, and in 1589 became superior of the fishing coast of Malabar, where he served for two years before going to Macao (1593) for the study of the Chinese language. As a result of the deaths in Shao-chou 韶州, Kwangtung, of Antonio d'Almeida (麥安東, T. 立修, 1556-October 17, 1591) and Francesco de Petris (石方西, T. 鎭宇, 1563-November 5, 1593), he was ordered (1594) to join Matteo Ricci (*q.v.*), who was now alone in that not over-friendly city. It was at this juncture that the Jesuits decided to change their dress and tonsure (copied from the Buddhists) and pattern themselves after the scholar class. The following year Ricci departed for Nanchang, leaving Cattaneo in charge. His two years there were not easy ones. On one occasion ruffians attacked his residence, laid an accusation against two of his domestics who were duly whipped, and succeeded in persuading a magistrate to subject a lay brother, Chung Ming-jen 鍾銘 (or 鳴) 仁 (T. 念江, baptismal name 巴相, known to the Jesuits as Sebastian, 1562-1622), to a beating and a day's punishment by the cangue. Finally

Cattaneo fell ill, and was forced to return to Macao to recover his health. But his stay in Shao-chou was not fruitless. One of the acquaintances he made was Hsü Kuang-ch'i (ECCP), then tutoring in a private family in Shao-chou, who had seen a copy of the first edition of Ricci's world map. It was Cattaneo who first aroused his interest in the strange religion.

In 1597, accompanied by Nicolo Longobardi (*q.v.*), Cattaneo resumed his mission at Shao-chou. But his second stay was brief. At the suggestion of Wang Hung-hui 王弘誨 (T. 忠銘, 紹傳, cs 1565), minister of Rites in Nanking, 1589–90 and 1595–99 (d. May 27, 1615), he went north (1598) to join Ricci at Nanchang; together they journeyed on to Nanking, and thence to Peking via the Grand Canal. They arrived at the capital on September 7, 1598. The visit, however, was ill-timed. Peking was inhospitable to foreigners, as the war in Korea against the Japanese invaders had taken another unfavorable turn, and all non-Chinese were suspect; their host, Wang Hung-hui, was passed over in his bid for high office and so was in no position to use any influence; and the eunuchs were unwilling to arrange an audience with the throne. Further, the missionaries' funds were running low. Regretfully they retraced their steps, Ricci to Soochow, and Cattaneo to Nanking and Macao.

Their journey together was not wholly devoid of value. In their leisure hours they, along with Chung Ming-jen, worked on a Chinese vocabulary, arranged in European alphabetical order, in which the five tones and aspiration of all words in the official language (called by Ricci Quonhoa) were indicated. Ricci, writing later of this cooperative enterprise (in the words of Niklaas Trigault [*q.v.*], put into English by Louis J. Gallagher), relates: "Father Cattaneo contributed greatly to this work. He was an excellent musician, with a discriminating ear for delicate variations of sound and he readily discerned the variety of tones." This work, entitled *Vocabularium sinicum, ordine alphabetico europaeorum more con-* *cinnatum et per accentus suos digestum*, was referred to by Trigault in his compilation *Hsi-ju er-mu-tzu* 西儒耳目資 (1626), but seems to be no longer extant. They had also on their way north calculated the latitudes of the cities through which they passed on the basis of observations of the sun, at the same time setting down the distances between each successive city. They recorded the total distance from Canton to Peking as 7,065 *li*, or 1,413 Italian miles. The latitudes were Yangchow 32°, Huai-an approximately 34°, Hsü-chou 34 1/2°, Chi-ning 35 2/3°, Lin-ch'ing 37 2/3°, Tientsin 39 1/2°, and Peking 40°. The last gave them some satisfaction, for earlier calculations had placed Peking at 50° latitude. The suspicion grew on them, moreover, that "the Kingdom of China is one and identical with what some writers call the Great Cathay, and that Pekin is the seat of the Great Can, the present King of China." The Augustinian monk Martín de Rada (*q.v.*) had reached the same conclusion in 1575.

After a brief sojourn in Macao Cattaneo returned to Nanking early in 1600, along with a new recruit for Ricci, Diego de Pantoja (*q.v.*), and a new lot of gifts for possible presentation to the emperor. Ricci set out in May of the same year on his second trip to Peking, leaving Cattaneo in charge of the Catholic stations in Nanking, Nanchang, and Shao-chou. In 1604 Cattaneo returned once more to Macao, and made a brief trip to Malacca in the interests of the church. He came back to find himself in the midst of another disturbing situation. This was the time (1606) when the Dutch were commencing their raids in eastern waters and eyeing the Portuguese outpost in Macao covetously. The latter in their turn began to fortify the area. This alarmed the Chinese, who assumed that the Portuguese were scheming to take over the whole country and make Cattaneo emperor. He was even mentioned by name in a public proclamation, according to the journals of Ricci, as the leader of the conspiracy against the throne, being called Cotienieu (郭天佑?). This, as Gallagher translates the passage, "is the Chinese interpretation of his first name, Lazzaro, meaning divine assistance." Certain disaffected converts, led on by an ex-Jesuit, who had become an Augustinian, spread excited rumors about the Jesuits, which resulted in the burning and pillaging of the Portuguese church. The population, much disturbed, fled from the peninsula, and in Canton preparations were made for war. For the Portuguese the situation was grave. Not only military action but famine also stared them in the face. Fortunately the official sent from Canton to study the problem was a man of sensibility and quickly saw that there was no cause for alarm, that Cattaneo was a man of peace. So the latter was allowed to return (in 1606) to Nanchang and Nanking. Hsü Kuang-ch'i visited him at the southern capital in 1608 and persuaded him to establish a mission in Shanghai, where he remained for two years, converting the entire Hsü family, and several others besides. At the suggestion of Li Chih-tsao (ECCP) he moved on to Hangchow (1611) along with Trigault and Chung Ming-jen. Their great achievement in this city was the conversion in 1613 of Yang T'ing-yün (ECCP), one of the three scholar-officials most helpful to the cause of the church in the early years of the Jesuit mission.

During the troublous times of 1616–17 Cattaneo, Giulio Aleni (q.v.), and others, remained quietly in Hangchow under the protection of Yang T'ing-yün. Cattaneo employed his time in furthering his acquaintance with the Chinese language and literature. Later he strengthened the churches in Hangchow and Shanghai and on January 15, 1620, opened another in the nearby town of Chia-ting 嘉定, the native place of Sun Yüan-hua (ECCP), which became as well a center for the study of Chinese by such newcomers to the mission as Johann Terenz (q.v.). Cattaneo's last years (after 1627) were spent at Hangchow. He was not a well man, but continued his evangelistic labors until stricken with paralysis (1638). He died two years later at the age of eighty, and was buried in the same cemetery as Trigault, João da Rocha, Manuel Dias (qq.v.), and other Jesuits.

With the exception of the Vocabulary mentioned above, the few writings he left were generally in Chinese. One memoir was written to explain away the crimes of which he had been accused in 1606 by the Chinese officials.

Bibliography

MSL (1940), Shen-tsung, 532/2b; KC (1958), 5081; Fang Hao 方豪, *Chung-kuo t'ien-chu-chiao shih jen-wu chuan* 中國天主教史人物傳(1967), 93; *id.*, *Chung-hsi chiao-t'ung shih* 中西交通史 (1953), 3/89; *Ch'iung-chou-fu chih* (1841), 26/7a, 34/15a; Pfister (1932), 51; d'Elia, P. M., *Fonti Ricciane*, I (Rome, 1942), 159, 256, 331, 381, II (Rome, 1949), 33 ff., 316; Jean Crasset, *Histoire de l'église du Japon* (1715), 440; George H. Dunne, *Generation of Giants*, Notre Dame, 1962; Louis J. Gallagher, *China in the Sixteenth Century, The Journals of Matthew Ricci, 1583–1610*, New York, 1953; *Enciclopedie Italiana*, IX (Rome, 1931), 472; Boleslaw B. Szczesniak, "The Beginnings of Chinese Lexicography in Europe ...," JAOS, 67 (1947), 160; Sommervogel (Brussels, 1891), cols. 896, 897.

L. Carrington Goodrich

CHA Nai 查鼐 (T. 延和, H. 八十), musician and merchant, who lived in the early decades of the 16th century, was a native of Hsiu-ning 休寧, Nan-Chihli. His grandfather, Cha Hua 華, built a fortune through interregional trade, and his father, Cha K'o 珂, and elder brother were also merchants. At the time of his birth, his grandfather, who happened to be eighty *sui*, named the boy Pa-shih (Eighty). From then on he was known by his contemporaries as Cha Pa-shih. In his youth, he helped his father and brother in business and apparently became successful, for a contemporary reports that he had a large fortune.

Like many successful merchants of the Ming period, who took delight in cultivating expensive hobbies, Cha Nai made music his special interest. For a while he was proud of his technique in playing the p'i-pa 琵琶 (balloon guitar); then one day during a feast he felt greatly humiliated when a female entertainer (similar to a Japanese geisha) bettered him with her own p'i-pa playing. Cha Nai, a resolute young man who always determined to surpass others, swore at the party that he would someday excel in the art. He paid a thousand taels as fee to learn the technique from Chung Shan 鍾山 (T. 秀之), currently the best p'i-pa player in the country. Cha not only accomplished his goal, but far surpassed his teacher. In his first public performances, the listeners were so moved by his music that they regarded him as one blessed with a talent that was divine.

After he had earned fame as a superior instrumentalist, he began to learn other skills, such as swordsmanship from Li Kuei 李貴 of Hua-hsien 滑縣, Honan, horseback riding and archery from Wu Ch'i 吳奇 of Hsiang-yang 襄陽, Hukuang, football from Sun Ching 孫景 of Yü-chang 豫章, Kiangsi, the flute from Ma Ch'ing 馬清 of Nanking, and the ch'in 琴 (Chinese lute) from Chang Nan 張楠 (T. 大木) of Soochow, each one best in his own specialty. Upon the advice of a guest who told him one could not be an expert in all things, he concentrated on p'i-pa playing, becoming known eventually as the best player of his day. Wang Yin 王寅 (T. 仲房), a poet from She 歙 -hsien (Anhwei), wrote a poem declaring that none of the p'i-pa players of the north could be compared with Cha, and Huang Chi-shui, poet and son of Huang Hsing-tseng (q.v.), wrote a longer one describing the expert techniques of Cha Nai who, with his p'i-pa, could evoke scenes of nature and arouse the deepest feelings of man.

It is interesting to note that, although the best p'i-pa player, he did not commercialize this art, probably because a professional musician was looked down on by society. Instead, he continued his business which still seems to have prospered, and entertained only his friends, among them the famous poets and artists, Chu Yün-ming, Yang Shen, Wang Ch'ung, T'ang Yin, and Wen Cheng-ming (qq.v.). At one time, when he was at Ta-liang 大梁 (Kaifeng), Honan, the prince of Chou 周, possibly Chu Ch'ao-kang 朱朝堈 (enf. 1538, d. 1551), summoned him to play, but he did not go until the prince agreed to treat him as a guest of honor. He declined the invitation of other princes, and refused to have Li Ts'ung-yao 李從堯, a wealthy merchant of Yangchow, as his student, saying that his technique was not for sale.

When he retired, his second wife wanted him to accept concubines since he had no heir; but he refused on the ground that Heaven had already bestowed on him many blessings, such as fame, friends, and long life, and that he should not ask for more. Instead, he spent the rest of his days with young people in sparrow fighting, and in planting trees and flowers.

Bibliography

Wang Tao-k'un, *Fu mo* (NLP microfilm, roll 1046), 4/18a; Ho Liang-chün, *Ssu-yu-chai ts'ung-shuo* (Peking, *1959*), *37/343*; Wang Ch'ung, *Ya-i-shan-jen chi* (NLP microfilm, roll 918), 10/15b; TSCC (1885–88), XXIX: 113/2/5a.

Angela Hsi

CHA Shih-piao 查士標 (T. 二瞻, H. 梅壑散人, 嬾老), 1615-98, painter, calligrapher, art connoisseur, and poet, was a native of Hsiu-ning 休寧 in Hui-chou 徽州 prefecture, but he spent most of his life in Yangchow where he died. He became a student in the local school; after the fall of the Ming dynasty, however, he gave up further study for the examinations and devoted himself to calligraphy and painting. As a member of a wealthy family, probably one engaged in the salt business, he possessed a good collection of bronzes and authentic works of Sung and Yüan artists. In painting he first followed the style of Ni Tsan (q. v.), and later studied the brushwork of other masters, especially that of Tung Ch'i-ch'ang (ECCP). As he was born sixty years after the latter, whose birth year (1555) also had the cyclical designation i-mao, Cha carved a seal reading Hou i-mao sheng 後乙卯生 (born in the later i-mao) to show his admiration. In his late years he came to be respected as an outstanding painter, one who had penetrated the secrets of the Yüan artists. His copy of Ni Tsan's painting of the "Shih-tzu lin" 獅子林 (Lion Grove) was greatly admired by Sung Lao (ECCP) who, after Cha's death, wrote his biography and published his poetry.

Cha Shih-piao's paintings give an impression of effortlessness and detachment, presented with an economy of brush strokes. He was known as one of the "Four Masters of Hsin-an" 新安四大家 (*see* Hung-jen), Hsin-an being an older name for Hui-chou. Among his prominent students was Ho Wen-huang 何文煌 (T. 昭夏, H. 竹坡). [Editors' note: Toward his last years Cha Shih-piao seems to have painted chiefly in the style of Ni Tsan, sometimes even copying Tung Ch'i-ch'ang's imitation of Ni Tsan, as shown in the two albums *Cha Mei-ho shan-shui ts'e* 梅壑山水册 (Shanghai, 1921) and *Cha Mei-ho shan-shui hua* 畫 *ts'e* (Shanghai, 1939)].

Bibliography

Ch'ing-shih kao 清史稿 (1927), 510/5b; Chang Keng 張庚 (1685–1760), *Kuo-ch'ao hua-cheng lu*, 國朝畫徵錄, 上/15a (*Hua-shih* 畫史 *ts'ung-shu* ed., Shanghai, 1963); *T'u-hui pao chien hsü-tsuan* 圖繪寶鑑續纂 (*Hua-shih ts'ung-shu*), 2/36b; Hsü Pang-ta, *Li-tai... shu-hua... nien-piao* (Shanghai, 1963), 146; V. Contag and C. C. Wang, *Seals of Chinese Painters and Collectors of the Ming and Ch'ing period* (rev. ed., Hong Kong, 1966), 213, 667; E. J. Laing, *Chinese Paintings in Chinese Publications, 1956–1968* (Ann Arbor, 1969), 26; Osvald Sirén, *Chinese Paintings*, Vol. V, 117.

Wei-ping Liu

CHAN Hui 詹徽 (T. 資善), died 1393, a son of Chan T'ung (*q. v.*) who, like his father, rose to be minister of Personnel, was a native of Wu-yüan 婺源 (Anhwei). He was one of the thirty-seven hundred *hsiu-ts'ai* who passed a special examination held in Nanking in October, 1382. A month later he was appointed one of the first eight senior censors then jointly heading the newly established Censorate. In July, 1383, when the office was reorganized, Chan became an assistant censor-in-chief and early in 1384, after another reorganization of the central government, received promotion to censor-in-chief. In that capacity he served in the middle of June, 1390, as a judge during the trial of Li Shan-ch'ang (*q.v.*) who was falsely accused of treason by the emperor, Chu Yüan-chang. Apparently Chan pleased the emperor by his part in Li's prosecution and conviction; only a month later he was given another important office to run concurrently with the first—that of minister of Personnel. The significance of his holding two positions of such trust has not heretofore been pointed out by historians; this meant that he was in control of both appointment and supervision of all government officials. Chan's enjoyment of that power proved to be of short duration. In 1393, when he was in charge of a similar trial, that of Lan Yü (*q. v.*) accused of treason on trumped-up charges, he threatened Lan, probably in the same way that he had previously threatened Li. This time, however, Lan fought back at his tormentor and in a fit of fury named him as a fellow "conspirator." As a result Chan himself, as well as Lan, was put to death; others who met a similar fate were Chan's son, Chan Fu 紱, and some twenty thousand people, most of whom were either the emperor's former subordinates or their families. Chan is reported as having apprehended his fate for some time, for he had sensed the emperor's growing coolness and was as aware as any man of his time of the emperor's methods.

It is worth taking note of the fact that the names of neither Chan T'ung nor Chan Hui are included in the 24 *chüan* genealogy of the Chan clan of their area, the *Wu-yüan Ch'ing-yüan Chan-shih tsung-p'u* 婺源慶源詹氏宗譜 (published 1785). In spite of their early distinction, the compilers apparently saw fit to ignore them entirely, because of their sorry end.

Chan Hui had a relative (the grandson of an uncle), Chan Hsi-yüan 希源 (also written 希元, T. 孟舉), who served during the Hung-wu period as a drafter in the Central Drafting Office and was a celebrated calligrapher. It is said that he wrote most of the huge inscriptions on the Nanking city gates and arches, and on tablets bearing the names of the palaces and government offices. Joseph Needham draws attention to the fact that it was Chan who, *circa* 1370, suggested that, since water clocks would not function in the dead of winter, the water be replaced by sand. But, the *Ming-shih* reports (as translated by Needham), "this ran too fast to agree with the heavenly revolution, so to the (main driving) wheel with scoops, he added four wheels each having 36 teeth."

Bibliography

1/73/5a, 111/3a, 136/4a; 3/124/4b; 5/24/6b; 6/46/8a; 42/38/1a; 61/156/4a; 63/2/29b, 38b; MSL (1963), T'ai-tsu, 2456, 3031, 3161, 3296; KC (1958), 626, 639, 736, 739; *Wu-yüan-hsien chih* (1925), 42/4a; Joseph Needham, *Science and Civilization in China*, IV: 2 (Cambridge, England, 1965), 510, 3 (1971), 569.

Chou Tao-chi

CHAN Jo-shui 湛若水 (T. 民澤, 元明), November 20, 1466–May 16, 1560, thinker, official, educator, came from a wealthy family of Tseng-ch'eng 增城, northeast of Canton, Kwangtung. His home was situated in the southwestern section of the district, in a community known as Kan-ch'üan tu 甘泉都, from which he took his sobriquet Kan-ch'üan tzu 子. It is said that his grandfather (1410–75) greatly increased the family holdings in land, but his father, having been involved in a robbery case, suffered some kind of punishment at the local court and left the dying wish (*ca.* 1475) that his son would see to the family's rehabilitation. So Chan Jo-shui studied hard and, under his original name, Chan Lu 露,

passed the *chü-jen* examination in 1492. The following year, after failing in the metropolitan examinations in Peking, he returned home feeling dejected. For some reason he decided not to compete again and burned the pass that permitted him as a *chü-jen* to travel to Peking at government expense in order to take the higher examinations. In 1494 he became a disciple of the great Cantonese teacher, Ch'en Hsien-chang (*q.v.*), from whom he learned the principle of personal realization wherever one might be. About this time he changed his name to Chan Yü 雨. He was so devoted to Master Ch'en that, on the latter's death in 1500, he observed the three year mourning rites as if for a parent. On his part, Ch'en considered Chan to have the deepest understanding of his teachings and, predicting that this student was going to have a brilliant career, willed to him the Tiao-t'ai 釣臺, a luxuriously built lecture hall near Hsin-hui 新會. The two men are described as contrasting in appearance. While Ch'en was elegant and tall and spoke clearly with a carrying voice, Chan is portrayed as "bulky as the earth and as heavy as a mountain, and exhaled soft rain in a breeze."

In 1504 Chan changed his mind about going into public service, explaining his decision as due to the persuasion of his mother (1437–1515). First he took a new name, Chan Jo-shui, and then secured another pass to use on the long journey to Peking for the examinations. On the way he stopped in Nanking and registered in the National University under the chancellor, Chang Mou (*q.v.*). In 1505 Chan passed the *chin-shih* examination, ranking sixth on the list. On the same list were Yen Sung, Lu Shen (*qq. v.*), and Fang Hsien-k'o 科 who later changed his name to Fang Hsien-fu (*see* Kuei O). Fang, a fellow Cantonese and student of Ch'en Hsien-chang, was one of Chan's close friends. All four were selected to be bachelors in the Hanlin Academy. At this time Chan became acquainted with the great scholar Wang Shou-jen (*q. v.*), who was serving as a secretary in the ministry of War. Both were even then noted among officials in Peking for their lectures on philosophical subjects. In November, 1507, Chan was appointed a Hanlin compiler and named to the editorial board of the *Hsiao-tsung shih-lu* (*see* Chu Yu-t'ang). In March, 1508, he served as an assistant examiner in the metropolitan examinations; one of the candidates he recommended was Lü Nan (*q.v.*), who turned out to be the optimus of that year. A month later Chan obtained the assignment to serve on the mission for the investiture of an imperial prince. Such a mission was coveted by junior officials for it entitled one to a pass to travel by government post. After completing the mission he continued on south to his home in Kwangtung, and on the return journey to Peking took his mother with him. Late in 1511, when he was sent as envoy to represent the Ming court in the investiture of the king of Annam, she accompanied him as far as Canton, waited there until he returned, and went back to Peking with him in 1514. Late that year she suffered a stroke and died the following February. He took her coffin to Kwangtung for burial. On the way he made a short stop at the National University in Nanking, where he held some conversations with the students. These discussions were later brought together under the title *Chin-ling wen-ta* 金陵問答.

In 1517, after the mourning period, he purchased a scenic site on Mt. Hsi-ch'iao 西樵山, about forty miles southwest of Canton city, and built a luxurious residence on a plateau below the Ta-k'o 大科 peak. On the lower slope near the entrance to his house he constructed several school buildings which came to be known as the Ta-k'o Academy 書院. Students flocked there to study with him, for he provided free lodging and meals. He subjected them, however, to a strict regimen. Rising at 3 a.m., a student followed the schedule of six hours of intensive study, four hours of individual reading, two hours of writing compositions, four hours of meditative sitting, and four hours reviewing the day's work, leaving four hours for sleep. Chan is said to have kept such a schedule himself.

After Chu Hou-ts'ung (*q.v.*) ascended the throne in 1521, Chan had high hopes for the young emperor and thought of exerting some influence on his education. In 1522 he returned to Peking to his post of Hanlin compiler. A year later he was promoted to sub-reader and appointed an editor of the *Wu-tsung shih-lu* (*see* Chu Hou-chao). During these years he submitted several memorials, one on the selection of worthy eunuchs as attendants, another to warn against relaxation, and a third on the importance of frequent consultations with trusted advisers. The emperor received these admonitions with courtesy, but probably considered him somewhat pedantic. On the *Ta-li i* controversy he at first took the side of the majority in opposing the emperor's wish (*see* Chang Fu-ching), and his name appears in most of the memorials between March 5 and August 9, 1524, taking issue with the emperor's orders. He did not, however, take part in the demonstration of August 11 (*see* Yang Shen and Feng Hsi). This probably indicates a change of attitude on the matter. In any case, on September 25 he was promoted to chancellor of the National University in Nanking. There he established a hall, Kuan-kuang kuan 觀光館, where a number of special students attended his lectures on mind and nature, and where he printed for them his treatise on this subject, entitled *Hsin-hsing t'u shuo* 心性圖說, later expanded to *Hsin-hsing shu* 書.

In March, 1527, the emperor commented on the frailty of personal friendship in encountering the realities of political life, saying that Chan had broken off with Fang Hsien-fu because of the latter's sudden rise in office after gaining imperial favor. Meanwhile, Chan continued to give lectures after he was promoted in April, 1528, to junior vice minister of Personnel in Nanking. With his own funds he established two residences in the suburbs, which served also as school buildings. These were known as the Hsin-ch'üan 新泉 and San-shan 三山 academies, each with a granary to supply the needs of the students. On his way to Peking that year to make a report, he was detained at Yangchow by some salt merchants who asked him to give a lecture at a building which became known as the Kan-ch'üan hsing-wo 行窩. Here Kan-ch'üan refers to Chan's sobriquet and also commemorates a hill in the area.

In July, 1529, the court summoned him to Peking to serve as the junior vice minister of Rites. The emperor had recently (perhaps with a sense of smug satisfaction) published the account of his victory over the majority of the court in the *Ta-li i* controversy, and was embarking on a revision of the rites of the dynasty to accord with his own ideas of imperial supremacy. Chan's predecessor, Ho T'ang (*q.v.*), known for his orthodox views, was removed after only a month in office. Chan took the lesson to heart, followed orders, and remained. He was advanced two years later (November, 1531) to senior vice minister of Rites, in which capacity he served two years, cooperating with Hsia Yen (*q.v.*) in catering to the whims of the emperor in the performance of Taoist liturgy. Late that same year, when the emperor prayed for a son and heir, Chan was one of the seven officials who assisted in the ceremony. He apparently considered it an honor to be so favored by the emperor. For a teacher of Confucianism to compromise himself in such matters he was called a hypocrite by historians Hsü Hsüeh-mo and T'an Ch'ien (*qq.v.*). When the emperor carried the matter too far and began to send officials to select girls for his harem, to confer extraordinary favors on charlatans, and to order celebrations on the capture of some albinic hares [as an omen of fecundity?], Chan memorialized that desire for a son might be better helped by practicing self-restraint. This advice on continence was rejected by the emperor with the ill-humored reply that,

if Chan sincerely wanted him to practice self-control, he should not have presented such a memorial to irritate him. When in November, 1532, a censor called Chan an impractical pedant (*see* Feng En), the emperor probably concurred in the characterization.

Some months later (August, 1533), Chan was once more sent to serve in Nanking. During the following seven years in the southern capital he headed successively, first the ministry of Rites (to 1536), then the ministry of Personnel (to 1539), and finally that of War (to 1540). In the last capacity he had the concurrent duty of serving on the triumvirate in charge of the defense of the southern capital. On assuming that office in 1539 he issued a proclamation of twenty-seven articles in an attempt to give some relief to the common people and soldiers who were suffering from excessive taxation and illegal demands imposed by bureaucrats and eunuchs. The first article in this proclamation was a denunciation of the practice by Nanking office holders who used government vouchers to purchase goods for personal needs. The local merchants who had the duty to fill government orders without charge were thus illegally overtaxed. Chan announced that in the previous ten years he had not issued such a voucher, for he had paid directly for all personal purchases. Huo T'ao (*q.v.*), who served as minister of Rites in Nanking about the same time (1536-39), made a similar declaration. Huo happened also to be from a wealthy Cantonese family.

It seems that Chan never gave up hope of influencing Emperor Chu Hou-ts'ung through memorials and books. In 1528 he had presented to the throne a symposium in 100 *chüan* on sovereignty and statecraft, entitled *Sheng-hsüeh ko-wu t'ung* 聖學格物通, which the emperor accepted graciously. Five years later Chan submitted a smaller compilation, entitled *Ku-wen hsiao-hsüeh* 古文小學, 9 ch. *Hsiao-hsüeh* is a textbook for young men, generally attributed to Chu Hsi (1130-1200) as the editor and known as "Chu-tzu 朱子 hsiao-hsüeh." After finding the text different in many places from what Chu projected in his preface, Chan Jo-shui compiled a new one, following Chu's outline but making it consist only of quotations from the *Li-chi* 禮記, which in Chan's opinion contains many passages from the original text of the ancient *Hsiao-hsüeh*. He selected these passages, arranged them under seven headings, and asserted that he had restored the book to a close facsimile of the original text. Although his *Ku-wen hsiao-hsüeh* gained imperial sanction, it was evidently not accepted by the public and soon became extremely rare. A century later the bibliographer Huang Yü-chi (ECCP) gave it the wrong title of "Ku-chin hsiao-hsüeh" and the number of *chüan* as six instead of nine. The same mistakes appear in the bibliography section of the *Ming-shih*. Even the compilers of the *Kuang-tung t'ung-chih* of 1822 describe it as unavailable (*wei-chien* 未見). The only recorded extant copy seems to be the one in the Library of Congress.

In November, 1536, Chan submitted to the emperor another work of restoration. This time he attempted to recreate the ancient text of the Classics on rites, entitled *Er-li ching chuan ts'e* 二禮經傳測, 68 ch. In his opinion "Ch'ü-li" 曲禮 and "Shao-i" 少儀, the first and fifteenth chapters in the *Li-chi* and the entire book of the *I-li*, formed the original classic of rites and the rest of the *Li-chi* should be regarded as a commentary. This time the emperor rejected it as contrary to the teaching of Confucius. Possibly the emperor found some passages in the book which might be considered as a basis for criticizing or contradicting his own attempt to revise the rites of the dynasty. In any case, half a year later the inspecting censor of Nanking, Yu Chü-ching 游居敬 (T. 行簡, H. 可齋, 1506–71, cs 1532), denounced Chan for spreading fallacious teachings, and proposed the prohibition of all his books as well as those written by Wang Shou-jen. Yu also suggested the closing of all the academies

founded by the two men or by their disciples. Although the emperor did not proscribe the books, he did order the destruction of those academies established without first having secured imperial approval. This does not seem to have had much effect on Chan, for most of his academies continued to function and some were even started afterward. In July, 1540, he suddenly received the order to retire on account of his advanced age. He was then seventy-four but quite healthy and energetic, and took a leisurely tour of the scenic places in Chekiang and Fukien before returning to Kwangtung.

His admirers in Canton established an academy in his honor, naming it T'ien-kuan 天關 shu-yüan. By this time he had founded at least thirty-six academies, nineteen in Kwangtung, thirteen in the Nanking area, three in Fukien, and one in Hukuang, each with a shrine to his master, Ch'en Hsien-chang. It happened that Ch'en had once expressed a wish to retire to the sacred mountain of the south, Mt. Heng 衡 in Hukuang, but died before that could be realized. So in 1544 Chan took the long journey from Canton to Mt. Heng where he built a shrine to Ch'en with an endowed academy for its safekeeping. In this venture he was joined by several disciples, including Chiang Hsin (*q.v.*). To this shrine Chan paid at least two more visits, in 1553, when he was eighty-seven, and three years later at ninety. He was described as still keen of eyesight and capable of writing in small script for a considerable length of time. In 1558, when the students of Kwangtung came to Canton to take the provincial examination, his disciples assembled at the T'ien-kuan Academy to honor him. He wrote an account of the meeting describing how he sat quietly by to listen to the talks on mind, nature, and innate knowledge. Early in 1560 he felt so vigorous that he even invited a disciple, Hung Yüan 洪垣 (T. 峻之, H. 覺山, cs 1532, d. *ca.* 1590), to meet him on Mt. Heng. While on the way Hung received the report of the nonagenarian's death. Hung himself is said to have lived to almost ninety.

It seems that Emperor Chu Hou-ts'ung held some kind of a grudge against Chan beginning about 1536. In 1554 the officials in Kwangtung, representing the gentry of that province, requested the emperor to issue a congratulatory message to Chan on his up-coming ninetieth birthday. The request was ignored. A year after Chan died, a memorial submitted by his great-grandson, Chan Shou-lu 壽魯, entreating posthumous honors, was referred to the ministry of Personnel for scrutiny. When the ministry reported favorably on Chan Jo-shui as "orthodox and upright in scholarship and behavior" (學行醇正), the emperor commented impatiently that Chan "corrupted orthodoxy with fallacious teachings" (僞學亂正). Ordered to make a reexamination, the minister of Personnel, Ou-yang Pi-chin 歐陽必進 (T. 任夫, H. 約庵, cs 1517, 1491–1567), and his subordinates admitted their mistake and were punished. This happened late in November, 1561. Chan was thus denied posthumous honors due him during the lifetime of the Chia-ching emperor. After the death of the emperor in January, 1567, there followed a period of rehabilitation of those whom he had unjustly punished or flagrantly slighted (see Hsü Chieh).

In June Chan was raised to the honorary rank of a junior guardian of the heir apparent. About a year later he had conferred on him the posthumous name Wen-chien 文簡 "learned and consistent," which neatly sums up his lifelong activities as a teacher.

In the middle of the Ming period the world of eastern thought was chiefly represented by the two schools, Kan-ch'üan hsüeh-p'ai 學派 of Chan Jo-shui and Yang-ming 陽明 hsüeh-p'ai of Wang Shou-jen. Both stemmed more or less from the teaching of Ch'en Hsien-chang but, while Wang stressed reaching for the innate knowledge in one's own mind, thus relegating book learning to lesser importance, Chan taught the realization of the principle of nature wherever one might be and whatever one might be doing, including learning from books. In a letter to Wang (ca. 1522) Chan enumerated four reasons why he objected to Wang's interpretation of the term, ko-wu 格物 (from the Great Learning) "to investigate things," as cheng nien-t'ou chih fa 正念頭之發, "to rectify one's thought at its very beginning." Chan defended his own interpretation of the same term as "to reach the principle," which Wang had criticized as looking for the principle in outside things instead of in one's own mind. According to Chan, to reach the principle meant to realize the principle of nature anywhere, including both understanding and practice, and concerning everything, be it one's mind or body or one's family, country, or the universe. But one had to go through the process of learning, questioning, thinking, distinguishing, and practicing, for even Confucius had to reach seventy years before he could follow his own mind and do no wrong. It was this stress on learning that prompted Chan to establish endowed academies and to have thousands of disciples. Among his prominent followers, in addition to Lü Nan, Hung Yüan, and Chiang Hsin, may be mentioned Li Ch'un-fang (q.v.), Lü Huai 呂懷 (T. 汝德, H. 巾石, cs 1532), and T'ang Shu (see T'an Ch'ien), and the latter's disciple, Hsü Fu-yüan (see Hsü Chieh).

Among Chan's writings ten are described in the Ssu-k'u catalogue. Two of the ten were included in the Imperial Library, namely the Sheng-hsüeh ko-wu t'ung, already mentioned and a Ch'un-ch'iu cheng-chuan 春秋正傳, 37 ch., in which he pointed out the misconceptions of some earlier commentators. Among the rest may be mentioned the Hsin-hsing shu, the Er-li ching chuan ts'e, and the commentary on the philosophical poems of his master, Ch'en Hsien-chang, entitled Pai-sha shih-chiao chieh 白沙詩教解, 10 ch., to which was appended Chan's further expositions, Shih-chiao wai-chuan 外傳, 5 ch.

Chan's literary collection, mostly on

philosophical matters, was first printed in 1530 under the title *Kan-ch'üan hsien-sheng wen-lu lei-hsüan* 文錄類選, 21 *ch.*, of which the Naikaku Bunko seems to have the only extant copy. A new edition, entitled *Kan-ch'üan hsien-sheng wen-chi* 文集, 40 *ch.*, was printed in Yangchow in 1536. Again only one copy seems to be extant, as described by Wu Han (*see* Hai Jui) in the Yenching University Library *Bulletin*. Chan is known to have edited his "complete" works, *Ch'üan-weng ta-ch'üan chi* 泉翁大全集, variously described as 60 or 66 *ch.*, perhaps printed in Kwangtung in the 1540s during the early years of his retirement. In 1555, when he was almost ninety, there appeared in print a supplementary collection, known as *Kan-ch'üan hsien-sheng hsü-pien* 續編 *ta-ch'üan*, 33 *ch.*, a copy of which is preserved in the National Central Library in Taipei. Another collection printed about this time, *Chan-tzu shih-nan chi* 湛子使南集, 12 *ch.*, probably containing his writings during the mission to Annam in 1512, does not seem to be extant. In 1580 his disciples, with Hung Yüan as editor, published a new edition of Chan's collected works, entitled *Chan Kan-ch'üan wen-chi*, 35 *ch.*, consisting chiefly of sayings, letters, and works on philosophical topics. A copy of this edition is preserved in the Gest Oriental Library, Princeton University. Also recorded is an edition in 32 *chüan*, printed in 1681, and reprinted in 1866.

Bibliography

1/283/6a; 5/42/61a; 42/75/9b, 63/22/1b, 83/37; *Chin-shih lu* 進士錄 for the year 1505 (NCL microfilm); Ho Ch'iao-yüan, *Ming-shan ts'ang* (1971), 4644; *Chan Kan-ch'üan wen-chi* (1580), ch. 35; *MSL* (1965), Shih-tsung, 0490, 0861, 4191, 8307; KC (1958); 3281, 3294, 3308, 3348, 3377, 3401, 3453, 3455, 3473, 3479, 3482, 3485, 3529, 3535, 3545, 3579, 3586, 3593, 3840, 3940, 4057, 4085; Jung Chao-tsu 容肇祖, *Ming-tai ssu-hsiang shih* 明代思想史 (1941), 51; Huang Yü-chi, *Ch'ien-ch'ing-t'ang shu-mu* (1913 ed.), 2/14a, 3/43a; *Kwang-tung t'ung-chih* (1934), 3536; L. of C. *Catalogue of Rare Books* (1957), 465; Wu Ch'un-han, "Pa 跋 Ming Chia-ching Kan-ch'üan hsien-sheng chi" in Yenching University Library *Bulletin* (January 15, 1931), no. 1, 4; SK (1930), 25/1b, 28/6a, 39/2a, 93/5b, 96/1a, 175/11a, 176/5b; Lü Nan, *Lü Ching-ye wen-chi* (1832), 2/66a, 5/55b, 67a, 8/59a, 18/12a; Chang Pang-ch'i 張邦奇, *Mi-hui hsüan-chi* 靡悔軒集 (NCL microfilm), 12/14a; Chiang Hsin, *Chiang Tao-lin wen-ts'ui* 道林文粹 (NCL microfilm), 1/36a, 4/11b, 52b; Tilemann Grimm, "Some Remarks on the Suppression of Shu-yüan in Ming China," in *The Transactions of the International Conference of Orientalists in Japan*, no. 2 (1957); manuscript biography by Huang P'ei.

Chaoying Fang

A Contribution on Chan's Thought,
by Julia Ching

The philosophy of Chan Jo-shui can be best understood through comparison and contrast with that of Ch'en Hsien-chang and Wang Shou-jen. According to Chan, Ch'en's teaching emphasized the concept of tzu-jan 自然—what is so of itself, or "the natural." To live in accord with the natural was to live in harmony with the universe, participating in its creative activity. This could be best done in solitary meditation, through an effort aimed at emptying the mind-and-heart of all its distractions and obstructions, and at recovering its original goodness. Chan was Ch'en's most famous disciple. He transformed Ch'en's concept of the "natural" into that of "T'ien-li" 天理, or "principle of Heaven," the fullness of being and goodness, using the vocabulary of Ch'eng Hao (1032–85) while emphasizing also the "principle" or li of Chu Hsi. He objected to the excessive importance which Ch'en gave to "quiescence," developing rather the teaching of "realizing T'ien-li everywhere," in both activity and tranquillity. He also sought to unify the "inner" and "outer" spheres of reality by explaining that T'ien-li was none other than the mind-and-heart, in its "pre-stirred" (wei-fa 未發) state. The unity, or identification, between the self and the non-self could therefore be recovered through a moral process of ascesis. The goal—the recapture of the pristine condition of existence—was the mystical realization of the unity between man and all things, achieved especially through the rectification of the mind-and-heart.

Chan went on to identify the mind-and-heart with human nature and with nature at large, or all things. Human nature, he says, is that which forms "one body with Heaven and Earth and all things," since it is filled with the same ch'i 氣 (ether) as is the universe of time and space. The mind-and-heart is that which "experiences Heaven and Earth and all things without leaving anything out." In other words, the mind-and-heart is the dynamic principle of human nature, and contains within itself such "life-giving qualities" as the four beginnings of virtue, which, when developed, enable man to participate in the creative transformations of Heaven-and-Earth and all things. In a diagram entitled *Hsin-hsing t'u* 心性圖 (The mind-and-heart and human nature), he gives his explanation of the interaction which takes place between mind-and-heart, human nature, and nature at large or all things. It consists of a big circle, enclosing within itself three small circles. The big circle represents the mind-and-heart and human nature as "embracing" all things. The small ones signify their "penetration" of all things. This is done through the practice of ching 敬 or reverence, through vigilance over self when one is alone, achieving the state of harmony or equilibrium of emotions, which permits the development of the virtues and so attains unity with all things, again in an attitude of reverence. Thus, the diagram represents the totality of reality, and the participation of mind-and-heart and human nature in that reality.

The chief difference between Chan's teaching and that of Wang Shou-jen is in practical ascesis. For Wang, the quest for sagehood is purely moral and mystical. In his view, the Unity of Knowledge and Action implies that moral knowledge and moral action are almost indistinguishable, that the former lies in the latter. His overwhelming emphasis was therefore upon moral and spiritual ascesis, through the individual's continual responses to the movements of his own mind-and-heart and to the events of life which act upon it. Chan, however, insisted upon the necessity of intellectual effort, of the study of Classics. He considered it too difficult to ascertain the "correctness" or "orthodoxy" of one's thoughts and intentions without making intellectual efforts. He explained ko-wu, the "investigation of things," in terms of "the realization of T'ien-li." He was to publish, in 1533, a one hundred *chüan* work entitled *Sheng-hsüeh ko-wu t'ung* (A pentrating presentation of the doctrine of investigating things according to the school of sages), which was addressed to Emperor Chu Hou-ts'ung. There, he developed thoroughly his own understanding of ko-wu, making of it an all-reaching formula, extending from the practice of "making the intention sincere" to that of "governing the country" and "giving peace to the world."

Probably it is the closeness of Chan Jo-shui's thought to that of already dominant Ch'eng-Chu philosophy which kept it in relative obscurity, while allowing it to exert a moderating influence on the development of the Wang Yang-ming school, which was to experience a general popularization, as well as a gradual degeneration during the last hundred years of the Ming dynasty. Such men as Hsü Fu-yüan and his disciple, Feng Ts'ung-wu (*q.v.*), who inherited the mantle of Chan Jo-shui, combated the teachings of certain latter-day disciples of Wang: Lo Ju-fang and Chou Ju-teng (*qq.v.*), who were reducing Wang's teaching to Ch'an Buddhism. Their efforts eventually merged with those of the scholars of the Tung-lin Academy (*see* Ku Hsien-ch'eng), drawing more and more from the philosophy of Chu Hsi to mend that of Wang Shou-jen. In this way, the philosophy of Chan Jo-shui blended with that of Wang to produce a more moderate form of neo-Confucianism, which was essentially that which survived until the 20th century.

CHAN Shu, *see* **CHAN T'ung**

CHAN T'ung 詹同 (T. 同文, original *ming* Shu 書), fl. 1350-74, official and writer, was a native of Wu-yüan 婺源 (Anhwei). His grandfather and father served as minor officials in the Yüan government. He became a *chü-jen* and received an assignment as instructor in the school of Ch'en-chou 郴州, Hukuang. In the early 1350s he entered the service of the rebel contender Ch'en Yu-liang (*q.v.*) as censor and concurrently chancellor of the Hanlin Academy. When Chu Yüan-chang took over Wuchang (1364), he summoned Chan to become an erudite in the National University, and changed his name from Shu to T'ung. In the following decade, Chan became a chief counsellor of the future emperor on the Confucian principles of government and on rites and music, and was responsible for several major official compilations.

Shortly after Chu Yüan-chang claimed the imperial title Chan was appointed a director of the bureau of evaluations, then a diarist attached to the Hanlin Academy. In January of the following year he became a bachelor of the Hanlin and in April was promoted to be a senior expositor. His assignments included a special mission to recruit men of talent for government services (December, 1368), tutoring the imperial princes, and conducting public examinations (September, 1370). In 1371 he served in the ministry of Personnel, becoming minister in 1373, and again concurrently chancellor of the Hanlin, a position which he held until his retirement in 1374.

In October, 1373, Chan memorialized the court on the expediency of compiling the *jih-li* 日曆 (daily records of the court) as basic materials in preparation for the compilation of the veritable records (*see* Hsü I-k'uei). Acting on his recommedation, the emperor appointed him and Sung Lien (*q.v.*) supervisors of the compilation. When this was completed in June of the following year, it became known as the *Ta Ming jih-li*, 100 ch. (long lost), encompassing the events of the years from Chu's rise to power in early 1353 to the end of 1373. Following this, they submitted another memorial proposing the compilation of a manual of the imperial instructions for posterity to be modeled on the *Chen-kuan cheng-yao* 貞觀政要 of the T'ang. The reason was that the *jih-li*, being stored in the office of historiography, was not accessible to outsiders; hence it seemed advisable to compile another chronicle for public dissemination. The recommendation approved, on completion it came to be known as the *Huang Ming pao-hsün* 皇明寶訓, 5 ch. From then on it became a practice to produce an edition of the *pao-hsün* as a supplement to the *shih-lu*. A later version of the (Ming) *T'ai-tsu pao-hsün*, 6 ch., compiled in 1602 and recently reprinted(1967), was based probably on this work.

After the completion of his assignment, Chan begged for permission to retire. His request was granted, but a month later he was recalled to office to help in the preparation of a code of sacrificial rites. This done he was allowed relief from further duties. It is said that he died shortly after his retirement, survived by his son Chan Hui (*q. v.*). In October, 1644, Chan T'ung received the posthumous name Wen-hsien 文獻.

Chan was a scholar and a popular figure in the early years of the first emperor. Together with Sung Lien, Yüeh Shao-feng (*q.v.*), and Wu Ch'en 吳沈 (T. 濬仲, d. 1386), Chan became known as one of the ssu hsüeh-shih 四學士 (four scholars) of his time. Sung Lien, who contributed a preface to his collected works, highly praised his prose and poetry. Apart from official compilations, Chan was the author of two other works, neither of which seems to have survived: *T'ien-ch'ü yin-hsiao chi* 天衢吟嘯集, 1 ch. (the preface by Sung Lien being preserved in Sung's collected works), and *Hai-chüan* 海湞 *chi* (also known as *Hai-yüeh* 岳 *chüan ai* 埃 *chi*), 2 ch.

Bibliography

1/136/3b; 5/24/3a; 8/4/13a; 40/3/10b; 61/144/11a; 64/甲 5/2b; Ch'ien Ch'ien-i (ECCP), *Lieh ch'ao shih-chi*, 甲 14/2b; MSL (1962), T'ai-tsu, 1507, 1573, 1579; KC (1958), 386, 488, 504, 6148; *Wu-yüan-*

hsien chih (1925), 22/4a, 64/ 藝文 3/3a; Hsü I-k'uei, *Shih-feng kao*, 5/24b; Sung Lien, *Sung hsüeh-shih chi* (*SPTK ed.*), 7/16a; Li Chin-hua 李晉華, *Ming-tai ch'ih-chuan shu k'ao* 明代勅撰書考 (Peiping, 1932), 8, 9.

L. Carrington Goodrich and
Hok-lam Chan

CHANG Cheng-ch'ang 張正常 (T. 仲紀, H. 冲虛子), 1335-January 4, 1378, a reputed descendant of Chang Ling 陵 (or Chang Tao-ling 道陵), the founder of religious Taoism in the first and second centuries A. D., was the forty-second Taoist patriarch on Lung-hu shan 龍虎山 (Dragon Tiger Mountain) in Kiangsi. When his father, Chang Ssu-ch'eng 嗣成 (T. 次望, H. 太玄子), the thirty-ninth patriarch, died in 1344, his uncle, Chang Ssu-te 嗣德 (T. 太乙, H. 青黎散人, d. 1352), succeeded to the Taoist patriarchate as the fortieth in line. On the latter's demise, his son, Chang Cheng-yen 正言 (T. 仲詢, H. 東華子, d. 1359), became the forty-first patriarch. It was only after the death of his cousin (Chang Cheng-yen) that Chang Cheng-ch'ang succeeded to the patriarchate.

At this time the Yüan dynasty was nearing its end. Unrest prevailed throughout the empire. The Yangtze region found itself in turmoil, and Kiangsi was fought over by various insurgent leaders. Finally by 1361 Chu Yüan-chang led his victorious army into Kiangsi. Chang thereupon sent a messenger to the future Ming emperor declaring his allegiance. Even before Chu ascended the throne, Chang made two visits to Nanking, in 1365 and again in 1366. During his stay in Nanking in the latter year, thousands of people came to him for charms, hoping for providential protection against every ill and hazard. Because of the tremendous number of demands, it was impossible for him to supply and dispense charms individually, so he made an extremely large charm and threw it into the well of the Taoist temple Ch'ao-t'ien-kung 朝天宮. The people were so eager to receive divine benefits that they drank the water until the well went dry. When the future emperor heard of this, he ordered an arbor built over the well, and gave it the name T'ai-i ch'üan 太乙泉.

In 1368, when Chu Yüan-chang became emperor, Chang once more went to the capital to pay homage. He was formally installed as the Cheng-i chiao chu 正一教主 and called Chen-jen with the long title 護國闡祖通誠崇道弘德大眞人. Formerly the Taoist patriarchs were all known as T'ien-shih 天師 but under the Ming T'ien-shih was officially changed to Chen-jen 眞人. The change was made when Chu Yüan-chang questioned whether heaven had any teachers; hence the T'ien-shih title, which might mean "Heaven's teacher," was abolished. From 1368 to 1378, Chang visited the capital six times, performing various religious duties. When his mother, née Hu 胡, reached eighty *sui* in 1370, the emperor awarded honorific titles to her and her deceased husband. In 1377, at the time that officials were sent out to worship and offer sacrifices to the deities of the mountains and waters throughout the empire, Chang was ordered to accompany Li Shan-ch'ang (*q.v.*) to Sung shan 嵩山, the sacred mountain in Honan. Soon after his return from this trip, he died. He was survived by his wife, née Pao 包, four sons, and two daughters. Both his eldest son, Chang Yü-ch'u (*q.v.*), and his second son Chang Yü-ch'ing (see Chang Yü-ch'u) in turn became Taoist patriarchs.

For the whole span of nearly three centuries of the Ming dynasty, there were eleven Taoist patriarchs on Dragon Tiger Mountain, from the forty-second to the fifty-second. Neither in the promotion of Taoism nor in religious miracles did the Chang family accomplish anything of distinction. It is with justice that the editors of the *Ming-shih* commented that, other than dispensing charms and praying for rain or snow, the successive patriarchs could boast of very little.

Bibliography

1/299/21a; 3/281/8b; 5/118/104a; 61/160/19b; TSCC

(1885-88), XIV: 248/16/3b, XVIII: 291/2/13a; *Lung-hu-shan chih* 龍虎山志 (1740); *Kao-huang-ti yü-chih wen-chi* 高皇帝御製文集 (1582).

Lienche Tu Fang

CHANG Chia-yin 張佳胤 (T. 肖甫, H. 瀘山), 1527-88, statesman and man of letters, who rose in the official hierarchy to be minister of War, was a native of T'ung-liang 銅梁, Szechwan. Following his success in the examinations (cj 1549, cs 1550), he became magistrate of Hua 滑-hsien, Honan, in 1552. Here he demonstrated his tact and courage when he captured a local bandit (who had gained admittance to his official quarters) by posing as an officer of the Embroidered-uniform Guard. In the famine during this period he saved the lives of thousands of people by providing gruel made from government grain. For this he received a promotion to secretary of a bureau in the ministry of Revenue, where he proved his integrity while in charge of customs in Fukien and Kwangtung. Next came his transfer to secretary of the bureau of operations in the ministry of War; then, following his father's death and a period of mourning, he was shifted to director of a bureau in the ministry of Rites. His association with Wang Shih-chen and Li P'an-lung (*qq. v.*) incurred the displeasure of Yen Shih-fan, son of Yen Sung (*q.v.*); so he was sent out as vice prefect of Ch'en-chou 陳州, Honan. Subsequently he moved up successively to the magistracy of P'u-chou 蒲州, Shansi, assistant surveillance commissioner of Honan, education intendant of Yunnan, assistant administration commissioner of Kwangsi, and, after several promotions, surveillance commissioner of Shansi.

In the winter of 1571 came his appointment to the governorship of the Nanking area. In this post he became involved in settling a mutiny at Anking, for which he was criticized. In spite of this criticism Chang Chü-cheng (*q. v.*) recommended his appointment as chief minister of the Court of State Ceremonial in Nanking; soon thereafter he was shifted to the Court of Imperial Entertainment, and appointed governor of Paoting—a post he was unable to fill because of his mother's passing. In 1579, following the period of mourning, notice came of Chang's assignment as governor of Shensi, but before he took up his duties he was reassigned as governor of Hsüan-fu north of Peking. Here again he demonstrated his ability and recognition of the requirements of the situation by putting an end to border raids and by building fortifications at a minimum of expense. The court brought him back (in 1581) to the capital to take the office of right vice minister of War.

Two companies of government troops mutinied in Hangchow in the spring of 1582 because of an announced reduction in pay from nine to six ch'ien 錢of silver a month. In their wrath, the soldiers set upon and thrashed the governor of the province, Wu Shan-yen 吳善言 (cs 1562). On word of this outbreak, and concerned about the prevalence of insubordinate soldiers throughout the south (so much so that some governors even dug holes in the walls of their yamen for eventual escape), Chang Chü-cheng rushed Chang Chia-yin down to Hangchow to replace Wu as governor with full powers to deal with the mutiny. His arrival in Chekiang coincided with popular riots. As a consequence he succeeded in playing one group against the other and settling both disorders. For this achievement the emperor himself expressed satisfaction, and in 1583 Chang was recalled as left vice minister of War. On the way to the capital he was promoted to be minister of War (October 13, 1583), and in the following month he was made supreme commander of the Chi 薊 and Liao 遼 defense areas. Here again he proved himself by achieving military success in the field. The court gratefully named him junior guardian (March 5, 1584), then grand guardian of the heir apparent, and he returned to Peking in his capacity as minister of War (November 9, 1585).

Discouraged by arrogant eunuchs and by critical censors, Chang submitted repeated requests to retire on account of illness. Permission was finally granted early in 1587. Announcement of his passing came to the throne on August 7, 1588, and the court named him posthumously Hsiang-hsien 襄憲.

Chang Chia-yin was the author of the *Chü-lai shan-fang chi* 崌崍山房集 (or *Chü-lai wen* 文 *chi*), 65 *chüan*, published 1594, which includes 1 *chüan* of *fu* 賦, 28 of *shih* 詩, 35 of miscellaneous essays, and one which contains a eulogy and his own epitaph together with 11 prefaces and other writings by his contemporaries. This work received partial condemnation in the 18th century but a few copies have survived.

During the later years of the Chia-ching period, Wang Shih-chen and Li P'an-lung founded a poetry society first of five members, and then of seven, of whom Chang was one. Of the seven, he appears to have achieved the most success in governmental life. Even when at the frontier he continued to exchange poems with the others, and wherever he was he encouraged the pursuit of literature, and patronized men of letters. His own poetry is regarded as showing unquestioned talent, but lacking in depth and elegance.

Bibliography

1/222/26b; 3/205/18a; 61/134/16a; 84/439; MSL (1940), Shen-tsung, 122/2a, 124/11a, 140/13a, 166/4a, 181/6b; KC (1958), 4465, 4583; TSCC (1885-88), XI: 582/34/14b; SK (1930), 178/1b; *Hua-hsien chih* (1930), 11/21a; Wang Shih-chen, *Yen-chou shan-jen ssu pu kao*, 95/1a, *Chang Ssu-ma ting Che er luan chih* 張司馬定浙二亂志 (Ts SCC ed.); Ch'en Tzu-lung (ECCP), *Huang Ming ching-shih wen-pien*, 339/1a; SunTien-ch'i (1957), 96, 160.

L. Carrington Goodrich and
C. N. Tay

CHANG Ching 張經 (T. 廷彝, H. 半淵, Pth. 襄敏), died November 12, 1555, a high official, was a native of Hou-kuan 侯官, Fukien. His *chin-shih* degree of 1517 was awarded under the name of Ts'ai Ching 蔡經, which he retained for the next quarter of a century. He served (1521-25) as magistrate of Chia-hsing, Chekiang, and then was promoted to be a supervisory censor in the office of scrutiny. In the spring of 1525 Emperor Chu Hou-ts'ung (*q.v.*) realigned the personnel of the latter office by appointing nine supervising secretaries in one day, Ts'ai Ching's name topping the list. Favored by the emperor, he rose rapidly in official life, becoming vice minister of the Court of the Imperial Stud, chief minister of the Court of Revision, governor of Shantung in 1535, and two years later promoted to be governor-general of Kwangtung and Kwangsi, with the rank of a vice minister of War.

In 1538 the court decided to launch a punitive expedition against Mac Dăng-dung (*q.v.*) in Annam. Ts'ai Ching questioned the wisdom of such an operation. He argued that the manpower and supply capabilities of his territorial command could never adequately support the campaign as conceived. His memorial caused the emperor to call off the expedition. The next year, however, the war plan was brought up again. Ts'ai advised Mao Po-wen (*q.v.*), commander-in-chief of the expeditionary forces, to concentrate troops on the border but not to engage them in battle hastily. Consequently the threat was enough to induce Mac to come to terms; a major war was averted.

As governor-general Ts'ai Ching did his utmost to pacify his territory. At Tuan-t'eng Gorges 斷藤峽 near Kweilin, several thousand native brigands had for decades used the jungle-covered ravines as a sanctuary. In his campaign of suppression of 1539 Ts'ai committed fifty-one thousand troops. Once having dislodged the insurgents, Ts'ai ordered a vigorous pursuit, killing and capturing nearly five thousand. The operation rivaled that directed by Wang Shou-jen (*q.v.*) in 1528. Ts'ai went on to subdue the aboriginal tribes in western Kwangsi and on Hainan

Island. For his services the emperor advanced him in both his ministerial and censorial ranks. By the time he had relinquished his governor-generalship to mourn his father in early 1544, he held the ranks of minister of War and right censor-in-chief.

Historians have yet to unravel the complicated details that clouded his life and official career in the next nine years. Under the name Chang Ching he was appointed governor-general in Shensi(1546), but a charge against him for irregularities in handling military funds in Kwangtung caused the emperor to withdraw the appointment. In 1551, however, he received another appointment, that of minister of Revenue in Nanking in charge of granaries, but apparently was unable to assume the post because of the death of his mother. In the autumn of 1553 he was reasssigned to the ministry of Revenue in Nanking, two months later being transferred to be minister of War in the southern capital. In the spring of that year the *wo-k'ou* launched their full-scale invasion of the southeast seaboard. Government forces were no match for the marauders, who penetrated inland areas at will, neutralizing fortresses and taking walled cities. After three months' rampage they sailed away with their loot. Chang's transfer at this point was a part of the arrangement whereby the court sought to anticipate the next onslaught.

The invasion of 1554 took a different turn. In April the pirates seized the town of Che-lin柘林城on the coast southeast of Shanghai, fortified it as a permanent land base, and stationed twenty thousand of their men there. Their warships controlled a great length of the Whangpoo 黃浦. Sometimes their raiding columns converged and they besieged cities with artillery. Sometimes they dispersed into foray parties, sacking villages and victimizing inland boatmen. On June 17, 1554, the emperor made Chang Ching supreme commander of the armed forces in Nan-Chihli, Chekiang, Shantung, Kwangtung, Kwangsi, and

Fukien, with unspecified powers. At Chang's request he was relieved of his ministerial duty (November 8), so that he might devote his entire attention to the military command.

At this time the existing troops were unable to cope with the situation. Generals, such as Yü Ta-yu, Lu T'ang (*qq.v.*), and T'ang K'o-k'uan (*see* Lu T'ang), following their recent defeats, were all ordered "to achieve merit under suspended penalty." Reinforcements, largely mercenaries hastily recruited, were no longer reliable. That summer some six thousand recruits had arrived from Shantung, but after suffering a single defeat their *esprit de corps* evaporated. Their commanders under arrest, the soldiers deserted en masse. Before the winter was over the unit had to be disbanded. In the summer Chang Ching decided to call in volunteers from the aboriginal tribes in the southwestern provinces. With the emperor's approval recruiting agents were sent to Kwangsi and Hukuang. The recruiting took place before the end of the year. According to Chang Ching, five thousand *lang-ping* 狼兵 were dispatched from Kwangsi and six thousand native troops were made available from Hukuang. The volunteers were recruited as organized formations, commanded by their own chieftains and governed by tribal rules, although those from Hukuang were captained by militia officers. These aboriginal troops were transported to the front by inland waterway. The voyage from Kwangsi to Soochow took about seventy days, the forward echelon arriving either in late March or in early April of 1555. Those from Hukuang arrived on or about May 10. Meanwhile the military situation had been deteriorating rapidly. The pirates based at Che-lin, aided by seaborne reinforcements, intensified their activities. They penetrated Chekiang, wedged into the area south of the Yangtze and north of the Grand Canal, and raided the salterns on the coast, threatening Yangchow and Huai-an. The court agreed that the pirates' base

of operation, Che-lin, must first be eliminated. But how to do it developed into a
controversy which eventually cost Chang
Ching his life.

Chao Wen-hua (*q.v.*), vice minister of
Works, suggested to the emperor in the
early part of the year that sacrificing to
the sea god might help pacify the coast.
On March 13 the emperor dispatched Chao
to Nan-Chihli to perform the sacrifice, and
to inspect the military situation. Upon
arriving at Sung-chiang 松江 in April Chao
rushed the army commanders to attack,
in the hope of adding kudos to his own
mission. As imperial commissioner he
directed military operations without Chang's
approval. When the two met, further
personal clashes developed. Chao believed
that the government forces, reinforced by
lang-ping, were adequate to launch an
offensive. Chang on the other hand wanted
to delay the attack until the arrival of
the Hukuang troops. An account given by
Yü Ta-yu indicates that eventually the
pirates at Che-lin were maneuvered into
leaving their fortified positions because of
Chang's effort to starve them out. Probably
Chang never disclosed his plan to Chao,
as several sources have suggested. An
unconfirmed report indicates that Chao,
ostensibly for the expenses of the sacrificial ceremony, demanded thirty thousand
taels of silver from Chang, which the
latter failed to give. Infuriated, Chao
memorialized the throne, charging Chang
with deliberately delaying the operation
for personal reasons. Soon after the report
arrived in the capital word came that
Chang's troops had achieved a major
victory, annihilating nearly two thousand
pirates. (Chang's memorial gives the date
of the campaign as May 10, 1555, but it
is entered in the *shih-lu* under date of
May 20.) The military success, as it turned
out, did the supreme commander no good.
It convinced the emperor that Chang truly
had the capability of striking earlier but
had chosen to remain inactive, and that
only after hearing about Chao Wen-hua's
report had he rushed to take the field. On

the advice of Yen Sung (*q.v.*), the monarch ordered Chang's arrest on June 4.
Despite his pleading, Chang was given
the death sentence. That year more than
a hundred cases involving the same penalty
were brought up for imperial review; Chu
Hou-ts'ung directed that the execution of
nine persons, among them Chang Ching,
Li T'ien-ch'ung (*see* Hu Tseng-hsien), and
Yang Chi-sheng (*q.v.*) be carried out. These
three officials all died on the same day in
Peking. Chang's official titles were restored
posthumously on July 5, 1600.

Various accounts have described Chang
as tall in stature, possessed of a taste for
luxury, and lacking in courtesy toward his
subordinates. The charges against him in
1546 seem to suggest that he was not
strictly honest, but he was accepted by
his contemporaries as a sound strategist.
His favorite scheme of maneuver was to
trap the enemy with converging columns,
which usually required a considerable numerical superiority.

After his death, numerous commentators traced his tragic end to the conspiracy of Chao Wen-hua and Yen Sung.
Chang's own lack of tact has also been
deplored. Contemporary sources, however,
point out that Chang Ching was, to no
small extent, a victim of circumstances
and public opinion. By the time he became
supreme commander, the military unpreparedness on the seaboard was alarming.
Many wei-so 衞所 units had barely one
tenth of their prescribed strength. The
remaining soldiers were employed as boatmen, laborers, supernumerary guards, and
messengers. Their pay was frequently in
arrears from three months to half a year.
When Yü Ta-yu arrived in Chekiang, he
had only three hundred "personal troops"
under his command. In fact, Yü disobeyed
an order of attack issued by Chang Ching
on the ground that it was like "tossing
meat" at the enemy. The navy was in an
even more lamentable state. The majority
of the government craft were actually
civilian vessels converted to meet the
emergency. In 1554 forty such vessels saw

action on the Whangpoo, only to be seized, destroyed, or repulsed by the pirates. An undated report by Yü Ta-yu testifies that no more than eight such ships were serviceable on the Whangpoo. The pirates had more than three hundred seafaring vessels, plus many river craft which they commandeered.

After the build-up the total fighting strength of Chang's command was estimated by several authorities as between thirty and forty thousand. Aside from the aboriginal troops, the main body of his force was made up of local militia and mercenaries, the latter including professional salt-smugglers and Buddhist boxers. Their training was inadequate, the command chaotic, discipline a constant problem. Above all, no adequate services and supplies were available. Funds had been scraped together from a variety of sources to finance the military operation; but their receipt was uncertain and unscheduled, a great portion being eventually embezzled by the commanders. When detachments of government troops were ordered to defend a city, the officers demanded lump sums of money from the local population before ordering the soldiers to their posts. The militiamen, according to Kuei Yu-kuang (*q.v.*), were issued two wheat cakes per man per day, yet each of them had to provide his own candles (seven at least) when on night duty.

The indignation of the southern population over the military unpreparedness was vehement. Kuei Yu-kuang, for instance, who seems to have known Chang Ching personally, wrote that the situation caused him to "look up at the sky and sigh again and again, knock his chest, and weep." At the time that the emperor discussed the situation with Yen Sung, the latter told him that Chang Ching must be eliminated because of public opinion, citing in his support Hsü Chieh (*q.v.*) and Li Pen 李本 (also known as Lü 呂 Pen, 1504-July 10, 1587, cs 1532), his fellow grand secretaries from the south. The emperor, always ready to use his officials as scape-

goats on unpopular issues, acted accordingly.

One work left by Chang Ching, variously entitled *Pan-chou chi* 半洲集, 7 *ch.*, or *Pan-chou kao* 稿, 4 *ch.*, seems not to be extant; but the collection of his poems, *Pan-chou shih-chi* 詩集, 5 *ch.*, has partially survived.

Bibliography

1/198/17a, 205/4a, 308/12b, 18b; 3/188/16b; 64/戊13/3b; MSL (1965), Shih-tsung, 4210, 4350, 5197, 5824, 5845, 6642, 7024, 7057, 7151, 7178, 7216, 7307, 7321, 7354, Shen-tsung (1966), 6486, 6526; *Chia-hsing-hsien chih* (1896), 17/11b; Ku Ying-t'ai (ECCP), *Ming-ch'ao chi-shih-pen-mo*, 39/11a; *Min-hou* 閩侯-*hsien chih* (1933), 67/6a; *Fukien t'ung-chih* (1938), 34/14b; *Chekiang t'ung-chih* (1934), 2637; Ch'en Tzu-lung (ECCP), *Ming ching-shih wen-pien* (1964), 3/2260, 4/2720, 2724, 2810, 5/3554; Yü Ta-yu, *Cheng-ch'i-t'ang chi* (repr. of 1567 ed.), ix, 7/1a, *hsü-chi*, 7/1a; Kuei Yu-kuang, *Ch'üan-chi* (Hong Kong, 1959), 94, 96, 98; Li Kuang-ming 黎光明, *Chia-ching yü Wo Chiang-Che chu-k'o-chün k'ao* 嘉靖禦倭江浙主客軍考 (Peking, 1933); Hsü Wei-nan 徐蔚南, "Shanghai-ti wo-k'ou" 上海的倭寇, *I-ching* 逸經 (1936), 8/6, 9/7; Ch'en Mou-heng 陳懋恒, *Ming-tai wo-k'ou k'ao-lüeh* 明代倭寇考略 (Peking, 1934); *Pan-chou shih-chi* (NLP microfilm), roll no. 1005.

Ray Huang

CHANG Ching 張鯨, who became a eunuch, and died in June, 1608, was a native of Hsin-ch'eng 新城, Pei-Chihli, and a leading figure in palace intrigues during the early years of the Wan-li reign (1573-1620). Our knowledge of his career is limited. He was chosen in 1547 to serve in the palace under the eunuch Chang Hung 張宏 (H. 容齋, d. 1584). Later he was privileged to attend the heir apparent, and was promoted to the position of secretary in the directorate of ceremonial sometime before 1582. In this year he was twice sent (April 7 and June 7) on behalf of the emperor to visit the ailing grand secretary Chang Chü-cheng (*q.v.*), who died on June 9.

The most significant political experience in Cheng Ching's life was perhaps the role he played in the demotion of Feng Pao (*see* Chang Chü-cheng), the chief eunuch at the beginning of the Wan-li period. Feng Pao derived his political power from the support of the two empresses-dowager, Jen-sheng and Tz'u-sheng (*see* Li-shih), and later from his close alliance with Chang Chü-cheng. Chang Ching, however, represented the rising influence of the young emperor. On January 1, 1583, the censor Li Chih 李植 (*see* Shen Shih-hsing), accused Feng Pao of twelve serious crimes; Feng Pao was then shifted to a lower post in Nanking. His own contemporaries interpreted Feng's demotion variously. One frequently voiced opinion had it that it was because Feng treated the emperor as a little boy even after the latter reached his majority, an attitude which greatly annoyed the young ruler. Against this background Chang Ching plotted to get rid of Feng. He succeeded Feng as superintendent of the Eastern Depot and was named the acting head of the palace treasury. (About the same time, his mentor, Chang Hung, became the director of ceremonial.) On February 22 of the same year (1583), Chang Ching received orders to carry out the confiscation of Feng's properties after further accusation had been filed against him.

Following Feng's demotion, however, Chang Ching found a new competitor in Chang Ch'eng 張誠, who succeeded Chang Hung in 1584 as the director of ceremonial, the highest position in the eunuch hierarchy. In 1585, when a relative of Chang Ch'eng was granted the position of a chiliarch in the Embroidered-uniform Guard, Chang Ching's relative was awarded only the rank of centurion. In the spring of 1587 Chang Ch'eng, not Chang Ching, was sent on behalf of the emperor to make the annual inspection of the ministry of War.

The eclipse of Chang Ching began on December 30, 1588, when the censor of the Kweichow circuit, Ho Ch'u-kuang 何出光 (T. 兆文, cs 1583), accused him and

his clique of eight crimes which deserve the death penalty. Several of Chang's political associates received punishment, but Chang himself received none. This special imperial favor stirred several court officials to a chorus of accusations and attacks against Chang Ching. The sharpest ones came from Li I 李沂 (T. 景魯, cs 1586), the supervising secretary of the office of scrutiny for Personnel. In his accusation he cited the rumor that the emperor had received bribes from Chang Ching. This enraged the emperor. As a result, Li I and others were clapped into prison. This action led to more accusations and protests to the extent that even Grand Secretary Shen Shih-hsing submitted his resignation. Under such mounting pressure the emperor yielded and removed Chang from his position as the superintendent of the Eastern Depot, and sent him back to his native place.

Many believed that officialdom dared to voice its opposition to Chang Ching because of Chang Ch'eng's support behind the scene. It is worth noting that, after Chang Ching's removal, Chang Ch'eng succeeded him as the superindent of the Eastern Depot while still holding his post as director of ceremonial. It was further held that Chang Ch'eng and Li I, who tried so hard to oust Chang Ching, were actually taking revenge for the demotion of Feng Pao. On September 16, 1589, less than a year after Chang Ching's dismissal, he was recalled to serve in the palace. This time he held no significant position, but what bothered his opponents was his constant close association with the emperor. As a result they protested again. Attacks came from both the southern and the northern courts. These continued for four months but met no response from the throne. Finally, on January 26, 1590, a judge of the Grand Court of Revision, Lo Yü-jen (*see* Shen Shih-hsing), submitted a memorial which included four warnings. In one of them Lo mentioned the rumor that the emperor had received bribes from Chang Ching, as Li I had maintained the previous year.

This time, instead of getting furious, the emperor summoned Grand Secretary Shen Shih-hsing and a few others to reproach Chang Ching in his presence. They did as instructed but moderately. At this point Chang Ching's end had come.

During his period of ascendancy in the palace Chang Ching succeeded in bringing his younger brother, Chang Shu-shen 書紳 into the bureaucracy. First awarded a hereditary rank of guard officer, he rose to be vice commissioner-in-chief of a military commission, but lost his post in 1588 when Chang Ching was disgraced. Chang Ching's significance in his time, perhaps, can be seen from the fact that the editors of the *Ming-shih* accorded him a separate biography but did not do the same for either Chang Hung or Chang Ch'eng.

Bibliography

Ming-shih (Taiwan ed.), 305/3427; 3/179/6b, 7b; 40/54/20a; MSL(1966), Shen-tsung, ch. 128, 149, 157, 160, 171, 172, 206, 214, 219; KC(1958), ch. 71-75; Liu Jo-yü, *Cho-chung chih*, 5/2a; Shen Te-fu, *Wan-li yeh-hu pien*, 6/169; Wang Shih-chen, *Yen-shan-t'ang pieh-chi*, 100/30b.

Yung-deh Richard Chu

CHANG Ch'ou 張丑 (T. 青甫, 廣德, H. 米庵), 1577-1643?, was one of the celebrated art critics of his day. He was born in K'un-shan 崑山 (east of Soochow) where his family, members of the artisan category, had settled for several generations. His grandfather, Chang Ch'ing 情 (T. 約之, cs 1538), served at one time as prefect of Kiukiang, later rising to surveillance vice commissioner in Fukien. Chang Ch'ing's younger brother, Chang I 意 (T. 誠之, cs 1529), rose to the same rank in Shantung. Chang Ch'ou's father, Chang Ying-wen 應文 (T. 茂實, H. 彝甫, fl. 1530-94), failed to pass the higher civil examinations and led the life of a wealthy scholar, collecting antiques and indulging in the study of alchemical arts. In 1588 he moved his family to Soochow and changed their register to the district of Ch'ang-chou 長洲. Like his friends, Wang Shih-chen and

Wen Cheng-ming (*qq.v.*), Chang Ying-wen was a connoisseur and left a work on collecting objects of art, the *Ch'ing-mi-ts'ang* 清祕藏, 2 *ch.*

Chang Ch'ou edited and published his father's book and wrote a preface to it in 1595 when he was still using his original name, Chang Ch'ien-te 謙德 (T. 叔益). The change of name to Ch'ou probably took place shortly thereafter. He facetiously gave the reason for the change as the fact that he was born in the ch'ou year (the year of the cow, hence his infrequently used sobriquet, niu-lang 牛郎, "the cowboy"), and to his ownership of a seal of the 3d century B. C. which had belonged to a man whose name consisted of the same two characters. The word ch'ou, however, also means a clown, which seems to indicate the real reason for his choosing it. He never was on good terms with his elder half-brother, Chang Hou-te 厚德 (T. 坤甫, H. 寧宇), who passed the *chü-jen* examination in 1567, ten years before Chang Ch'ou was born, hence possibly was as many as thirty years his senior. As a *chü-jen*, and perhaps as the eldest son of the main wife, Chang Hou-te was favored by their father, especially during the division of property in 1594, shortly before the father's death. In later years Chang Ch'ou recorded that during the division of the estate he was given some less desirable land and when, in a pique, he showed his resentment, his father consoled him by handing him a scroll entitled "Yeh-wang min-yen" 野望憫言, painted by T'ang Yin (*q.v.*). He changed his name, however, as if to say that he had been made a clown. Meanwhile his half-brother also changed his name to Chang Te-ch'eng 德程 (T. 以繩), possibly as a way of emphasizing the break in the family. Chang Ch'ou once remarked that his half-brother was a collector of thousands of objects of which ninety-nine percent were fakes.

To compensate for his failure in the civil examination Chang Ch'ou tried first to be a writer; it is said that he named one of his studios Chien-shih-t'ang 鑴史堂

(Hall for the printing of historical works) and took pains to write annotations and commentaries on the *Shih-chi* by Ssu-ma Ch'ien (*ca.* 145–86 B.C.). He also compiled a 200 *chüan* history (of the Ming dynasty?) entitled *Ming-shan ts'ang* 名山藏 (not to be confused with the work of the same title, but in 100 *chüan*, by Ho Ch'iao-yüan [*q.v.*]). Neither of Chang's works is extant. It is doubtful that they were ever printed or even completed. In any case he turned to the study of painting and calligraphy, and found that he could take pride in his expertise as an art critic. He reminded others that his great-great-grandfather was a protégé of the calligrapher Shen Tu (*q.v.*), that his great-grandfather had a painting by Shen Chou (*q.v.*), that his grandfather and granduncle owned a large collection of paintings, and that his father was related by marriage to the sons of Wen Cheng-ming. Unfortunately, while the family treasures were in the possession of his half-brother, they were lost due to pillaging and a fire set by an enemy (1618?). He himself, in spite of his meager assets, was able to collect some genuine articles and had the good fortune to examine several important collections. In 1616 he completed a work entitled *Ch'ing-ho shu-hua fang* 清河書畫舫, 12 *ch.*, in which he commented on more than eighty of China's foremost artists and their works, which he either owned or had seen. Among his contributions were such discussions as the place in calligraphic history of Ts'ai Ching (1046-1126) and the age at death of Mi Fu (1051-1107). Generally in his day the four great calligraphers of the Northern Sung were held to be Su Shih (1037-1101), Huang T'ing-chien (1045-1105), Mi Fu, and Ts'ai Hsiang (1012-67). But Chang Ch'ou advanced the theory that the one first named was not Ts'ai Hsiang but Ts'ai Ching, pointing to the chronological order in which they were named. Had Ts'ai Hsiang been one of the four, his name would have appeared first. Chang Ch'ou suggested that the reason for the later substitution was the low esteem in which historians held Ts'ai Ching, sometimes called 六賊之首 (Chief of the six traitors), in spite of the excellence of his calligraphy. Wang Tsung-yen (ECCP, p. 39), a noted scholar and art critic of two centuries later, voiced the same opinion. "Ts'ai Ching's calligraphy," he wrote, "is decidedly superior to that of Ts'ai Hsiang." At the end of the book Chang included 101 verses of his own, eulogizing ancient and contemporary poets and artists. As the owner of one of Mi Fu's finest literary remains, entitled *Pao chang tai-fang lu* 寶章待訪錄 (Comments on calligraphy), Chang Ch'ou named his study Pao-Mi hsüan 寶米軒. The *Ch'ing-ho shu-hua fang*, in the opinion of Chiang Ch'ao-po 蔣超伯 (cs 1845), is the best work of its genre written during the Ming and Ch'ing dynasties. As soon as it was completed in 1616 people flocked to Chang Ch'ou to show him their treasured possessions. Recording only the genuine items, he wrote the *Chen-chi jih-lu* 眞蹟日錄, 3 *ch.*, which contains colophons dated as late as 1630. He also compiled four lists: the *Ch'ing-ho shu-hua piao* 表, recording eight members of his own family (including himself) and the items each had collected; the *Fa-shu ming-hua chien-wen piao* 法書名畫見聞表 on the items he had either seen or known of; and two on the collections of a Han family of Soochow, particularly those belonging to Han Shih-neng 韓世能 (T. 存良, cs 1568). Collectors highly valued all these works on art by Chang Ch'ou; they existed, however, only in manuscript until 1763 when a wealthy salt merchant of Soochow, Wu Ch'ang-yüan 吳長元 (T. 麗煌), in cooperation with another salt merchant, Pao T'ing-po (ECCP), edited and printed the *Ch'ing-ho shu-hua-fang*, which came to be known by the name of Wu's studio as the Ch'ih-pei ts'ao-t'ang 池北草堂 edition. It seems that this book was published in 1764, and that the *Chen-chi jih-lu* and its appendices (the four lists) were brought out with the same imprint. Pao T'ing-po later, however, produced his own edition of the *Chen-chi jih-lu* in a smaller format (20 characters to a column instead of the 22 in Wu's edition). This was the time when Pao began to publish his famous series of rare books, the *Chih-pu-tsu-chai ts'ung-shu*. Columbia University library possesses a copy of the *Chen-chi jih-lu* which has the Chih-pu-tsu-chai imprint. Yet for some reason it was not included in the series and was apparently sold as a separate item.

All these works by Chang Ch'ou were copied (from manuscripts submitted by the Pao family) into the Imperial Library in the 1780s. Also copied were the *P'ing-hua p'u* 瓶花譜, a work on cut flowers attributed to him, and the *Ch'ing-mi-ts'ang* by his father. The former has recently been rendered into English by Li Hui-lin and published in 1956 as *Chinese Flower Arrangement*. Chang Ch'ou is also the author of three more short works: one on tea, *Ch'a-ching* 茶經, one on ink sticks, *Lun-mo* 論墨 (probably an odd item from a quartet of the so-called wen-fang ssu-yu 文房四友 "four companions in a studio"), and one on goldfish, *Chu-sha yü-p'u* 硃砂魚譜. The last named has been translated by A. C. Moule.

There is an interesting story in connection with the names of Chang Ch'ou's grandfather, Chang Ch'ing, and granduncle Chang I, for the character *ch'ing* means grace or love and *i* means thoughtfulness, both rarely chosen as given names for males. That the two brothers retained their odd names even after they became important officials is explained in the following anecdote. It happened that their father, an indigent teacher in a country school, lived in a one-room hut by the Grand Canal. One night his wife complained about their being childless and pointed out that, for the sake of the family line, he should take a concubine while still in his early fifties. Their arguments were overheard by a merchant who, after mooring his boat for the night, took a walk past the hut. Wealthy but old, the merchant had several young women at home whom he was about to send away. So he presented one

to the teacher, adding a sizable dowry as inducement, much to the delight of the teacher's wife. The two boys born to this woman were consequently given these names as a way of commemorating the graciousness and thoughtfulness of the benefactor.

Bibliography

4/67/19b; 86/19/7a; Chang Ta-fu 張大復 (1554-1630), *K'un-shan jen-wu chuan* 人物傳, 7/29; Chang Ch'ou, *Chang-shih ssu-piao (Ts'ui-lang kan kuan ts'ung-shu* 翠琅玕館叢書 ed.); *Su-chou-fu chih* (1881), 87/12; SK (1930), 113/4a, 123/2a; Chiang Chao-po 蔣超伯, cs1845, *Nan-hsün hu-yü* 南滸楛語, 3/11; *K'un Hsin liang-hsien hsü-hsiu ho-chih* 新兩縣續修合志 (1880), 23/31, 30/20, 49/15, 21, and supplement (1922), 19/5; Wang Tsung-yen (1755-1826), *Wan-wen-chü-shih i-chi* 晚聞居士遺集, 5/19; *Seikai bunka-shi taikei* 世界文化史大系, Vol. 17, 69; A. C. Moule, "The Book of Vermilion Fish," TP, 39 (1950), 2, 53; Sir Percival David, *Transactions of the Oriental Ceramic Society*, 14 (1936-37), 38; L. S. Yang, rev. of H. L. Li, *Chinese Flower Arrangement*, CHHP, n. s. I (1958), 273.

Liu Lin-sheng and Chaoying Fang

CHANG Chü-cheng 張居正 (T. 叔大, H. 太岳), May 24, 1525–July 9, 1582, grand secretary and leading minister during the Lung-ch'ing and first years of the Wan-li eras, was a native of Chiang-ling 江陵 (Hukuang), on the Yangtze River about 290 miles west of Hankow. Chiang-ling was also the fief of the prince of Liao 遼 since 1404. His family belonged to the military category. His grandfather served as a guard in the palace of the prince of Liao. Chang Chü-cheng proved to be an able student, graduating as *chü-jen* in 1540 and *chin-shih* in 1547, and receiving an appointment as bachelor in the Hanlin. Hsü Chieh (*q.v.*), then grand secretary, recognizing his talent, was possibly responsible for Chang's promotion to Hanlin compiler. In these early years Chang was sensitive to politics at court and, while studying the institutions and regulations of the government, he established relations with Yen Sung (*q.v.*), then a rising star. In the spring of

1550 he returned home to bury his wife, and may well have come back to the capital just in time to be present at the siege of the city by the army of Altan-qaɣan (*q.v.*) during the early autumn. Seeing Yen Sung in action on this occasion may have persuaded him that Yen was hardly to be preferred to his old mentor Hsü Chieh. He also seems to have become discouraged over his failure to advance in the Academy, and possibly over the national crises— encroachments by the *wo-k'ou* on the southeast coast and by Mongols in the northwest—and the use made of these issues in power struggles at court. Whatever the reason, pleading illness, he received leave (1554) to return home to recuperate. During the next few years (to 1559) Chang was either convalescing at his native place or recuperating his strength through travel. This release from official duties gave him the opportunity to read and reflect. He resolved in the end on complete devotion to the state, on rejecting the customary rules of morality in serving it, and on a fundamental concern for the peasantry.

Returning to Peking, he received a promotion (1560) to be an instructor in and acting director of studies of the National University. While in this post he gained the friendship of Kao Kung 高拱 (T. 肅卿, 1512-78, cs 1541, Pth. 文襄), then chancellor of the University. In September, 1562, both Chang and Kao were appointed to take charge of making the second copy of the compendium, *Yung-lo ta-tien* (*see* Yao Kuang-hsiao), a task that was completed six years later. Meanwhile he was made reader in the Hanlin Academy and an associate editor of the *Ch'eng-t'ien ta-chih* 承天大誌 (May, 1563). Later he also served as a tutor of the heir apparent, the future Emperor Chu Tsai-hou (*q.v.*). This augured well for the future, for the prince esteemed him, and the eunuchs in the prince's household found him agreeable. One of them, Li Fang 李方 (d. 1570+), later promoted to chief eunuch, frequently sought him out for advice on books and on court problems.

In May, 1566, Chang was raised to reader-in-waiting in charge of the Hanlin Academy. Hsü Chieh had succeeded Yen Sung as chief grand secretary (1562), and Chang was one of the inner circle whom Hsü occasionally consulted. On the old emperor's death (January, 1567) Hsü even asked for Chang's advice in the drafting of the imperial will (遺詔) — a signal opportunity to correct abuses and introduce reforms.

Promotions and new responsibilities came rapidly. On March 6, 1567, Chang was promoted to a vice minister of Rites and concurrently chancellor of the Hanlin, whence, within a fortnight, he entered the Grand Secretariat, holding concurrently the office of senior vice minister of Personnel. By the beginning of May he was appointed one of the editors of the *Shih-tsung shih-lu*, and on May 23 his name appears, along with those of Hsü Chieh, Li Ch'un-fang (*q.v.*), Kao Kung, and others as responsible for the reproduction of the *Yung-lo ta-tien*, for which he was made concurrently minister of Rites and grand secretary of the Wu-ying pavilion. In February, 1568, Chang was given the higher honorary titles of junior guardian of the emperor, and grand guardian of the heir apparent. So, as the editors of the *Ming-shih* exclaim, it took him less than two years to rise from grade 5A to 1B.

At this time there was a good deal of in-fighting in the Grand Secretariat, especially between Hsü Chieh and Kao Kung. In June, 1567, Kao was forced to resign because of criticisms from certain censors, probably with Hsü's connivance. A year later Hsü himself also had to resign. Shortly thereafter, in September, 1568, Chang submitted his famous memorial of six points, in which he spelled out his proposed program of reform: 1) lessening of discussion, 2) enforcement of law and order, 3) emphasis on the follow-up of edicts and commands, 4) making names correspond with reality, 5) improving the livelihood of the people, 6) strengthening military preparedness; in short, advocating a strong but benevolent autocracy. Although junior to the other grand secretaries, he was already assuming leadership, determined to regenerate the country and permit no further deterioration of imperial control. The editors of the *Ming-shih* note that his bearing at this point was that of a chief grand secretary, haughty towards the ministers, intimate with none. Perhaps Chang himself thought that the emperor might entrust him with a program of reforms based on these points. The emperor, however, treated the memorial indifferently while listening to his favorite eunuchs. Then in January, 1570, Kao Kung was recalled to the Grand Secretariat and given concurrently the powerful position of minister of Personnel. According to Shen Te-fu (*q.v.*), Kao's unusual rise from retirement was through the machinations of a professional middleman, Shao Fang 邵芳 (H. 樗朽), who used large sums of money to persuade the emperor's favorite eunuchs to put in the right word for Kao. Apparently Chang Chü-cheng took this as a lesson, and began to cultivate friendship with the powerful eunuch, Feng Pao 馮保 (T. 永亭, H. 雙林, fl. 1530–82). By mid 1571 only Kao Kung, Chang, and Yin Shih-tan 殷士儋 (T. 正夫, H. 棠川, 1522– June 27, 1582, cs 1547) were members of the Secretariat, and the last was dismissed on November 27, possibly through the manipulations of Chang, with the approval of Kao.

It was at this juncture that the problem of making a settlement with Altan-qaγan arose. The able governor-general Wang Ch'ung-ku (*q.v.*) received the surrender in October, 1571, of Altan's grandson, who, together with a few followers, had deserted their chief. When the news reached Peking a long debate ensued as to the proper action to take. The two grand secretaries, after considerable correspondence with Wang, agreed with his detailed proposals for a settlement with Altan, who had crossed into Chinese territory with twenty thousand mounts, and was threatening Tatung. Altan proved amenable to Wang's proposals, promising not to invade China, but at the same time demanding a title, and the establishment of tribute and trade relations. This led Wang to memorialize once more, urging the approval of Altan's demands. Chang vigorously supported Wang's memorial writing in one of his letters to the governor-general: "This is a great opportunity and a fine plan for controlling the enemy and pacifying the frontier." In the end the emperor, though hesitant, gave his approval after prodding by both Kao Kung and Chang. The latter saw in this affair a chance to give China a period of respite, during which it might recoup its financial strength, fortify its border, train men, and reclaim frontier waste land. He recognized also that by restoring the horse markets, forbidden in the previous reign, China had a means of eliminating one of the primary causes of outbreaks across the Great Wall.

While engaged in trying to resolve this crisis, Chang was also busy with domestic affairs. In April, 1571, when put in charge of the metropolitan examination, he took great care in drawing up questions appropriate for the times. They demonstrate his belief in proper ruler-minister relationships, in laws suitable to the age that must be obeyed, in making names agree with reality. For this service as well as for his part in the capital evaluation the previous November he was given fresh honors including the title of Pillar of State. But all was not easy for him as associate grand secretary. Hsü Chieh, on his dismissal from high office in 1568, had entrusted his three sons to Chang's care. Now Kao Kung had built up an animosity against Hsü, and saw to the imprisonment of the sons on various grounds. Naturally, following an appeal from the father, Chang tried to intervene, and this led to estrangement between Kao and Chang. As the emperor died on July 5, 1572, and the eunuch Feng Pao, who was not on good terms with Kao, tried (with the aid of Chang ?) to draft the "imperial will," a function belonging to the chief grand secretary, Kao was incensed. Eventually, with the connivance of the empresses, Feng Pao won out. Kao was dismissed (July 25, 1572), Chang succeeding him (August 4). On this matter Kao never forgave Chang and wrote derogatory accounts about him. As Chang was out of the capital part of the time when these events were taking place—he was looking for a proper site for the tomb of the emperor, and on his return was on sick leave—it is difficult to determine what part, if any, he played in Kao's dismissal. That it was his ambition to reach the top, however, is not in doubt. On instruction from his mother, Li-shih (q.v.), the new emperor, Chu I-chün (q.v.), then a boy of nine, is said to have rewarded Chang handsomely, and delegated all authority to him. One of Chang's first acts, following an examination of their records, was to dismiss those in high office whom he considered incompetent, or those who had been in Kao's clique. The court became cowed. Even before this (in 1570) an example of the authority and awe Chang commanded came with the arrest of Mu Ch'ao-pi 沐朝弼, a descendant of Mu Ying (q.v.), who inherited the title of duke of Ch'ien-kuo (April 14, 1554). Mu, an almost independent satrap in Yunnan, was accused of several violations of the law, and it was popularly thought that no court official would dare to attempt to bring him to book, possibly because it might have a deleterious effect on the loyalty of his troops. But Chang sent men to arrest Mu, and escort him to Nanking. Mu meekly submitted, without any outcry from his men, and died in prison. His son, Mu Ch'ang-tso (see Chou Chia-mu), then succeeded to his title (June 27, 1570).

Possibly at the prompting of Feng Pao, Chu I-chün ordered that proper honors be accorded the two empresses, the widow of his father, and his own mother the imperial concubine, Li-shih. Feng proposed to Chang that both be given equal status. By rights Li-shih should have received lesser

rank, but Chang seems to have been willing to acquiesce in the eunuch's proposal, and approved his suggestion (August 24). Other problems pressed for solution. There was the matter of grain transport to the capital, whether to use the unpredictable sea route, with the dangers incident to piracy and to storm in rounding the Shantung peninsula, or to make extensive improvements in the route of the Grand Canal. Chang opted for the latter (see Liang Meng-lung, Wang Tsung-mu, and P'an Chi-hsün). There was the question of supply of horses, neatly solved when, with the improvement in the Grand Canal system, there resulted an abundance of grain which could be exchanged for horses as tribute relations with the Mongols commenced. There was the breakdown in the chain of command with officials in distant parts of the empire failing to act on orders from the capital. For this Chang introduced the evaluating-achievement regulation 考成法 (July 26, 1573) which required that all reports be made within time limits, according to their importance and urgency, those bureaucrats who failed to comply being subject to punishment. This order affected not only officials in the provinces but also ministers and supervising censors, and incidentally placed far more power in the hands of the Grand Secretary. Besides increasing efficiency in state business, it also had an effect on taxation and corvées, helped to eliminate corruption, and struck at the increasing power of major landowners. Chang's regulation was not without its critics, sharpest of whom may have been Liu T'ai (see Wang Tsung-tsai), first a censor and then regional inspector of Liaotung, who had received his *chin-shih* the year that Chang Chü-cheng directed the examination. It was, Liu declared (February 22, 1576), a violation of laws laid down by the founding emperor, anything the senior grand secretary might say to the contrary notwithstanding. Up till this time Chang had favored the younger man, reprimanding him only for sending out of turn the report about a victory in Liaotung. Now he saw to Liu's dismissal and the removal of his name from the rolls. Later Liu was exiled, dying on the way.

A fourth problem concerned the relationships between eunuchs and the bureaucracy and their relations among themselves. It arose forcibly in December, 1574, when intoxicated eunuchs in Nanking insulted the supervising secretary Chao Ts'an-lu 趙參魯 (T. 宗傳, H. 心堂, d. May 1, 1609, cs 1571, Pth. 端簡), who had graduated the same year as Liu T'ai. The censors petitioned for an investigation and punishment of the offenders. To please Feng Pao, Chang had Chao banished, at the same time urging the grand eunuch to restrain his followers. It appears that there were cliques among the eunuchs, some pro-Feng, some anti-(representing possibly the two capitals). So Feng himself had to walk a tight rope. On Chang Chü-cheng's part, he gave in to Feng in matters of ceremonial, but virtually eliminated eunuch interference in matters involving the six ministries. Part of his tactic was to cultivate the friendship of Empress-dowager Tz'u-sheng (Li-shih), with whom Feng Pao was on the best of terms.

Another point raised by the editors of the *Ming-shih* was Chang's effort to keep the censors from abusing their authority over provincial officials. If he learned of any impropriety on the part of the censors his sharply worded criticism was immediately forthcoming, and he saw that orders were issued for an investigation by their superiors. When Supervising Censor Yü Mou-hsüeh 余懋學 (T. 行之, cs 1568, Pth. 恭穆) urged more magnanimity, Chang took this as a personal affront, and saw to his dismissal. Other censorial critics were more violently punished with flogging, exile, and imprisonment, Chang even penalizing censors who visited their colleagues in prison. His fellow grand secretaries, Lü T'iao-yang and (later 1575) Chang Ssu-wei (*qq.v.*), bore this all in silence.

Chang Chü-cheng's exercise of power led inevitably to presents and bribes from the affluent. For the construction of a mansion in his native place, he received reportedly ninety percent of the cost (some 200,000 taels) from such friends as the emperor (2,000) and from officials in Hukuang and elsewhere. Elegant clothes came his way too, together with choice paintings, examples of calligraphy, and other objets d'art.

A continuing problem was the defense of the frontier. Altan-qaγan was quiet in the northwest, but not Tümen Jasaγtu qaγan 圖們 （土蠻） 札薩克圖汗, 1539–92) in the north. In the spring of 1578 Tümen made several probing attacks against Chinese strongholds, only to be beaten off by Li Ch'eng-liang (ECCP). Other successful defenders were Liang Meng-lung and Ch'i Chi-kuang (*q.v.*). The Chinese generals even made sorties beyond the Wall into enemy territory, so that for a time peace reigned on the border. In appreciation of his leadership and valor an earldom was created for Li (Ning-yüan po) in 1579. In the south too civil disorders were quickly suppressed. When word came of government troops mutinying in Hangchow early in 1582, Chang Chü-cheng promptly dispatched Chang Chia-yin (*q.v.*) to the scene to deal with the mutiny and to stop the rioting in the city, eventually bringing him back to the capital to take charge of the War ministry. Chang Chü-cheng clearly believed in stern measures, and picked the leaders of his military well. The resultant years of comparative peace obviously benefited the state financially, making possible the considerable expenditures on the Grand Canal, the military training program under Ch'i Chi-kuang, and other state enterprises.

The courier system, the over-supply of officials, the educational structure all came within Chang's purview. To utilize government facilities by land or water a man on official business needed a tally. Initially their issuance and use were strictly regulated; over the years, however, the regulations were relaxed, some people holding the tallies for a lifetime and passing them on to their heirs, others giving them to a friend (and changing the name). Chang's new rules limited the use of a tally to official business, reduced the number of reasons for which tallies could be issued, and made provisions for their surrender. As to the bureaucracy, its numbers were clearly inflated. Men waiting for assignment sometimes received no appointment, and advancement became even more difficult. Unhappy, they blamed the senior grand secretary for their lot. Chang saw to the curtailment of openings in the larger urban centers. This did not enhance his popularity. His next effort was to try to improve the educational system in the provinces where the students, on obtaining the initial degree, were exempted from the corvée, thereby becoming a privileged class, exploiting their status. In 1575 Chang obtained an edict which attempted to correct the situation; he instructed provincial educational officials to make sure 1) that the principles of the Classics were thoroughly taught and practiced; 2) that students be forbidden to interfere with the business of government; 3) that examiners be strict in tests given to keep the numbers down (from fifty in the larger prefectures to four or five in those "deficient in talent"; and 4) that certain other qualified students be utilized as functionaries either in their own localities or in neighboring prefectures. None of this was new, but previously no senior minister had the authority or could command the obedience to enforce the rules.

Ancillary to Chang's actions in repect to excess officials and troublesome students was the decree he succeeded in having pronounced, banning all private academies (February 17, 1579). Efforts of a similar sort had been made in the 1530s, but they had flourished nonetheless throughout the Chia-ching and Lung-ch'ing eras. Chang regarded them as possible centers of political opposition, as places where officials whiled away the time that should have been given to state business, as corporate owners of considerable blocks of land that he wished to see returned to the villages to which they belonged and which could be made subject to taxation, as social meeting places for "empty discussions," whereas he regarded the laws, institutions, and decrees of the dynasty as the sole object of study. This order was followed up with some vigor, both in 1580 and 1581, but actually, according to the *shih-lu* out of the hundreds then in existence, only the more prosperous in the urban centers of the Yangtze valley were affected, and some of these were restored after Chang's death.

On October 23, 1577, Chang's father, Chang Wen-ming 文明 (T. 治卿, H. 觀瀾, b. 1504), died, the news reaching the grand secretary on November 4. This came at an awkward moment. Chang Chü-cheng was at the height of his power, and his program of reforms was beginning to take hold. Empress-dowager Tz'u-sheng had just asked him to pay special attention to the young emperor, a charge which she was finding burdensome; furthermore, the emperor's wedding date had been set for the coming spring. Numerous people at court, from the emperor, both empress dowagers, and the eunuch Feng Pao on down besought him to remain, while a like number considered this impermissible in the light of time-worn precedent. When Minister of Personnel Chang Han (*q.v.*), whom Chang Chü-cheng had long favored and protected from slanderous attacks, agreed with the latter, he was immediately dismissed. Others, such as Tsou Yüan-piao (*q.v.*), who went so far as to criticize Chang for narrow-minded scholarship, intolerance of other views, and being not indispensable, were flogged severely, and either demoted or exiled. The emperor decreed that all criticism should now cease on pain of condign punishment. This pronouncement seems to have silenced the opposition. In the end, Chang's son and a eunuch were dispatched to represent the grand secretary at the funeral, while he remained in Peking and continued his functions, both as head of the government and as tutor to the emperor. His one concession was to wear mourning clothes, except on the occasion of the imperial wedding, when he appeared in a garb appropriate for the occasion. This drew a rebuke from a censor and he too was sent packing.

The great ceremony over, Chang begged for permission to leave; this the emperor gave, with the proviso that he return within a specified time. Chang took his departure on April 19, 1578, after arranging for the appointment of two officials for the Grand Secretariat, both of whom he felt he could trust in his absence: Ma Tzu-ch'iang 馬自強 (T. 體乾, H. 乾菴, 1513-November, 1578, cs 1553, Pth. 文莊) and Shen Shih-hsing (q.v.). The trip to and from Chiang-ling must have been one of continuous magnificence, as the emperor and both empresses-dowager issued orders that every comfort and facility be granted. Officials turned out in droves, and two imperial princes greeted him when he passed through their territories. Eunuchs and courtiers welcomed him on his return (July 19, 1578), the imperial family loaded him with more gifts, and the emperor ordered him to rest for ten days. Chang's mother followed a few months later, and received equal ceremony.

In spite of the effusiveness of the young emperor's attentions to his chief minister and tutor, he must have found his sermonizing wearisome and turned enthusiastically to indulgence in the extravagances for which his reign was to become noted. Chang found it necessary to remind His Majesty of the need for economy. When the emperor ordered the coinage of more money, or required more silk from Soochow, or wished to repair the palaces, or wanted more and more gifts for his kin or court favorites, the grand secretary had to make direct appeals, to which the emperor listened grudgingly. At a certain tutoring lesson (in May, 1581), Chang took the opportunity to tell him of a famine in Honan and the lower Yangtze valley, and requested relief measures and concurrent reduction of expenditures in the palace;

His Majesty again agreed. Meanwhile, for his part, Chang had become aware of the need to bolster the state's income. He did this by collecting tax arrears, by conducting a fresh land survey, and by introducing (1581) on a nation-wide scale the single-whip method of taxation. In the last he drew upon the successful experiences of Hai Jui in Chekiang and of P'ang Shang-p'eng (qq. v.) in Chekiang and Fukien. For the first he appointed officials he could trust to bear down on the wealthy, particularly in Nan-Chihli and Chekiang. And for the second he instituted, at the close of 1577, the collection of statistics on land. The figures are in doubt, but they seem to show that, up to the time of his death over four years later, there was an increase of land available for taxation over the results shown in the Hung-chih period, some seventy-five years earlier. Unfortunately the survey died with him. These policies may have been welcomed by the common folk, but (says the *Ming-shih*) they made him highly unpopular with the well-to-do and the powerful.

On April 13, 1582, Chang fell ill. His Majesty dutifully inquired after his health and sent gifts to help defray medical expenses. Numerous functionaries throughout the land, with certain conspicuous exceptions, such as Ku Hsien-ch'eng (q.v.), joined in Buddhist services, praying for his recovery. At the same time the emperor ordered Chang Ssu-wei, now a member of the Grand Secretariat, to take care of minor matters of state business, but to refer important ones to Chang Chü-cheng. This situation did not last long. Chang soon became so incapacitated that he could not function properly. Three months later he passed away. The emperor continued his acts of solicitude by giving him posthumous honors, naming him Superior Pillar of State 上柱國 and Wen-chung 文忠 (cultured and loyal), and by ordering a number of people at court to accompany the body to Chiang-ling.

As a consequence of the numerous unpopular measures of Chang Chü-cheng, certain officials promptly launched accusations against him, and the emperor, who disliked him for his strictness, ordered the cancellation of Chang's posthumous honors. In the end many of the people in office whom Chang had appointed were dismissed, most of his estate was confiscated, and his titles were all voided. In 1582, when someone falsely accused Chang of having had treasonous plans, the emperor believed him. Then the case of the eighth prince of Liao came up for review. Prince Chu Hsien-chieh 朱憲㸅 (b. 1525, enfeoffed 1540) was condemned in 1568 on the accusation of attempting a rebellion, deprived of his princedom, and imprisoned until he died. Now his widow blamed the condemnation of the prince on Chang Chü-cheng, attributing the motivation of Chang to his coveting of the land and other properties of the prince. The emperor, who was looking for an excuse to mete out severe punishments to Chang's family, took pleasure in acting on the princess' irrational accusations, and ordered the confiscation of Chang's properties, sending a eunuch and a vice minister to supervise the matter. It is said that all members of Chang's family were locked up for days without supplies, resulting in several starving to death. Chang's sons were tortured to reveal hidden treasures. The eldest son, Chang Ching-hsiu 敬修 (T. 炎州, cs 1580), a secretary of a bureau in the ministry of Rites, after severe torture, falsely confessed that he had entrusted 300,000 taels of gold to others, and then he committed suicide. Two younger sons, Chang Ssu嗣-hsiu(who placed second in the palace examinations of 1577) and Chang Mou 懋-hsiu (T. 斗樞, optimus of 1580, 1555–1634), suffered banishment to guard the frontiers, along with their paternal uncle Chang Chü-i 易, a regional commissioner. Chang Mou-hsiu, who also tried to commit suicide, was pardoned. He lived on to the age of eighty *sui* and was responsible for assembling much of his father's writings and the family papers. For the remainder of the Wan-li reign

the name of Chang Chü-cheng was held officially in disrepute but in high respect by people of understanding. In 1622 an effort was made to clear it, and the censor-in-chief Tsou Yüan-piao of all people was the one responsible. An imperial edict then restored all of Chang's titles and saw to his receiving an appropriate funeral and sacrifices. Chang Ching-hsiu too was rehabilitated in 1640 at the instance of his grandson, Chang T'ung-ch'ang 同敞 (T. 別山, Pth. 文烈), who died a martyr to the Ming cause in 1649 at Kueilin, Kwangsi (*see* Ch'ü Shih-su in ECCP).

Chang Chü-cheng, besides having a hand in several official publications, such as the *Shih-tsung shih-lu*, 566 *ch.*, *Pao-hsün*寶訓, 24 *ch.*, the *Mu-tsung shih-lu*, 70 *ch.*, and accompanying *Pao-hsün*, 8 *ch.*, also left works on the Confucian canon, collections of poetry and prose, and a considerable body of official and semi-official correspondence, together with some one hundred eighty memorials. One work which he and Lü T'iao-yang jointly produced for the young monarch at the onset of his reign (January 20, 1573) was an illustrated book, written in colloquial Chinese, entitled *Ti-chien t'u-shuo* 帝鑑圖說, 6 *ch.;* it contained eighty-one examples of good and thirty-six examples of evil deeds from legendary times on. The last, along with three other titles, is listed in the Imperial Catalogue, but not one was copied into the *Ssu-k'u ch'üan-shu*. Two of his writings, *T'ai-yüeh chi* 太岳集, 46 *ch.*, and *T'ung-chien ching-yen chi* 通鑑經筵集, were listed two centuries later to be banned. The latter may be lost, but the first, printed in 1612, was reprinted in 1828, and several times more. In some editions of the *T'ai-yüeh chi* there is a life of Chang Chü-cheng, entitled *Chang Wen-chung-kung hsing-shih* 行實, 1 *ch.*, written by Chang Ching-hsiu.

Bibliography (selective)

1/213/14a; 3/197/9b; 5/17/60a; 8/63/19a; 17/1/1a; 32/79/20b; 40/43/18a; 61/150/1a; 64/己9/1a; 84/丁中/59a; 86/13/1a; MSL (1965), Mu-tsung, ch. 1–70, Shen-tsung (1966), ch. 1–126; KC (1958),

4044-4414; *Chiang-ling-hsien chih* (1876), 26/6b, 7b, 27/44b, 45a, 49/5b; Shen Te-fu, *Wan-li yeh-hu-pien* (1959), 212, 218, 227; SK (1930), 13/5a, 90/1a, 127/7a, 177/18a; T'eng Shan 藤山, *Chang Chü-cheng nien-p'u* 年譜 (Chungking, 1940); Chu Tung-jun 朱東潤, *Chang Chü-cheng ta chuan* 大傳 (1947); T'ang Hsin 唐新, *Chang Chiang-ling hsin-chuan* 新傳 (Taipei, 1968); Sun Tien-ch'i (1957), 149; Naikaku Bunko *Catalogue*, 100; L. of C. *Catalogue of Rare Chinese Books*, 46, 141, 171, 441, 972; Robert B. Crawford, unpublished dissertation on Chang Chü-cheng (Univ. of Washington); E-tu Zen Sun and John De Francis, eds., *Chinese Social History* (Washington, D. C., 1956), 309; Tilemann Grimm, "Some Remarks on the Suppression of *Shu-yüan* in Ming China," *Tr. of the Int'l Confce of Orientalists in Japan*, 11 (1957), 8; P. Pokotilov, *History of the Eastern Mongols during the Ming Dynasty from 1368 to 1634*, tr. by R. Loewenthal (Chengtu, 1947), 125; W. Franke, *Sources* p. 12, 1.1.9, 1.1.10, 5.6.2.

Robert B. Crawford and L. Carrington Goodrich

CHANG Chung 張中 (T. 景華, 景和, better known by his sobriquet, T'ieh-kuan tao-jen 鐵冠道人), fl. 1362-70, was a Taoist physiognomist and diviner, who hailed from Lin-ch'uan 臨川, Kiangsi. He and Chang San-feng 張三峯, Leng Ch'ien (*q.v.*), and Chou Tien 周顛 were known as the "Four Taoists" of the early years of the Ming. Their role in the establishment of the dynasty has been subjected to extensive alteration by fictional writers to dramatize the events of their times. In the case of Chang Chung, there are few ascertainable facts left to reconstruct his biography, yet the imaginative anecdotes about him and the resultant transformation of the man into myth are of interest as a study in folklore.

Many of the later writings about Chang Chung are derived from the account written by Sung Lien (*q.v.*), who based himself partly on a file of notes compiled by Emperor Chu Yüan-chang. Sung relates that he began to keep a record about Chang Chung in 1364 when he was amazed by his predictions, and drafted his biography by imperial order in 1370 (when Chang was still alive). Sung knew Chang personally and describes him as haughty and taciturn but prone to sudden fits of disorderly speech which nobody could understand; also as a timid but irritable eccentric with a strange gift for inspired prophecy. Some of the dramatic episodes in his account, subsequently copied into the *T'ai-tsu shih-lu*, however, may very well have been the invention of the emperor himself.

According to Sung Lien, Chang Chung failed in the *chin-shih* examinations toward the end of the Yüan and on his subsequent travels he met a mysterious stranger who taught him the art of divination. In this capacity he was recommended to the future emperor in February, 1362, by General Teng Yü (*q.v.*). His predictions impressed Chu, who subsequently recruited him as one of his advisers. He is said to have foretold the uprising of Commander K'ang T'ai (*see* Teng Yü) at Nanchang and to have made a prediction which led to the discovery of a plot by Shao Jung 邵榮 and Chao Chi-tsu 趙繼祖 to assassinate Chu. Both were executed in August of that year. In 1363 he prophesied the outcome of Chu's struggle against his rival Ch'en Yu-liang (*q.v.*), and later, while accompanying the expedition, caused the winds to advance the fleet, and, as the legend goes, contributed to the final victory.

The last years of Chang Chung are developed by Lu Ts'an (*see* Kuei O) in his miscellany *Keng-ssu pien* 庚巳編 (*ca.* 1520); this supplements Sung's account and provides another source for later biographers. Lu reports that the Taoist dramatically ended his life by throwing himself from Ta-chung 大中 bridge at Nanking. On the same day, however, according to hearsay, he was seen walking through the T'ung 潼 Pass in Shensi, never to be seen again.

Chang Chung's story, exciting and fanciful as it was, inspired writers of later periods to dramatize his abilities and perpetuate the legend. Some of the bizarre accounts about the Taoist flourished in the Chia-ching and Wan-li periods, during which popular Taoism and fictional literature became an obsession. These stories were in part incorporated into the revised edition of the late Ming historical romance *Ying-lieh chuan* 英烈傳, preface 1616 (*see* Kuo Hsün), and reached a larger audience through its spread in various forms.

The first mention of Chang Chung's prophetic gift occurs in the *Ch'an-hsüan hsien-chiao pien* 禪玄顯教編 by Yang P'u (1373–1446, *see* Yang Shih-ch'i) which reports that the Taoist, after his first meeting with the emperor, left behind a text called *T'ieh-kuan tao-jen ko* 歌. Its contents, however, are not revealed. Endowing Chang with the gift of prophecy probably derives from stories about the usurpation of Chu Ti (*q.v.*) and the subsequent mysterious disappearance of Chu Yün-wen (*q.v.*). This reached a more or less definite shape in the fictional literature of the Chia-ching period. In the *Chin-yen* (preface 1566) of Cheng Hsiao (*q.v.*), the author relates a story of the Taoist prophesying to Chu Yüan-chang. Upon learning the accuracy of his earlier predictions, Chu summoned Chang, and, sharing a piece of hot roll with him, asked the Taoist to foretell the future of his dynasty. He then prophesied in veiled language the events of the years wu-yin 戊寅 and jen-wu 壬午. Later writers point out that these dates (1398 and 1402) allude to the reign of Emperor Chu Yün-wen and the rebellion of Chu Ti. The story of the emperor sharing a piece of hot roll with Chang Chung was transmitted in subsequent writings, and these supplied much of the background of a book of prophecy which is first mentioned in the miscellany *K'o-tso chui-yü*, preface 1617, by Ku Ch'i-yüan (*q.v.*). This adds to Cheng Hsiao's version the story that, after making the prediction, the Taoist left the *Cheng-ping* 蒸餅 *ko* (Steamed roll ballad) for the emperor and then vanished. The two lines of prophecy reported by Ku predicted the coup of Chu Ti and the capitulation of Emperor Chu Ch'i-chen (*q.v.*) in the battle of T'u-mu (1449). The story was also reported later in the *Tsui-wei lu* by Cha Chi-tso (ECCP), where the title of

the prophecy book is changed to *Ch'üeh* 缺-*ping ko* (Cracked roll ballad).

This *Cheng-ping ko* appears to be the prompt-book of the most publicized book of prophecy in modern China called *Shao* 燒-*ping ko* (The hot roll ballad) attributed to Liu Chi (*q.v.*), the chief adviser to Chu Yüan-chang, who was similarly regarded as a prophet in popular literature. In this book Liu reportedly divulged to Chu Yüan-chang the events of the next five hundred years. His prediction, made in a dialogue with the emperor in language subject to various interpretations, is said to have foretold the major upheavals in China from the Ming through the Ch'ing. In fact, most of Liu's predictions about the Ming, such as those of the usurpation of Chu Ti and the rebellion of Li Tzu-ch'eng (ECCP), originated as popular stories in Ming fictional works; only in the *Shao-ping ko* were they knit together into a continuous work. All the modern editions of the *Shao-ping ko*, beginning with the 1912 version, the earliest so far discovered (in the British Museum), mention Liu Chi as the author. But, according to a Wang Liu-men 王柳門 of Nanking (fl. 1850–1912), some of the manuscript copies of the *Shao-ping ko* circulating during his day were attributed to Chang Chung. The real author of this book may never be known, but its background story is obviously derived from the prevailing legend about Chang Chung in Ming times. The anecdote of Chu Yüan-chang sharing a piece of hot roll with Chang, for example, is repeated in the opening paragraph of the *Shao-ping ko*; but in this case, the man receiving the roll is Liu Chi, not Chang Chung. It is quite likely that Chang was first assigned the authorship; but for unknown reasons, at least from the last years of the Ch'ing onward, the text came to be transmitted in the name of Liu Chi.

In modern times Chang Chung's prophecies were continued in yet another similar book, known as *T'ieh-kuan tao-jen hsüan-chi shu* 玄機數 or *T'ui-t'ien* 透天 *hsüan-chi*, bearing his name as the author and appearing in at least two slightly different versions. In format and style, the *Hsüan-chi shu* resembles the *Shao-ping ko*, though the content is less detailed. It was probably written by astrologists of the 1920s when the uncertainties of the civil wars caused a resurgence of interest in prophecies and a market for books of this sort. The same situation prevailed after the fall of the Ming dynasty when the Chinese people tried to ascertain the reason for the disasters and how long the Manchus could maintain their rule.

There is also the Ch'ing novel on the insurrection of Li Tzu-ch'eng and Chang Hsien-chung (ECCP), entitled *T'ieh-kuan t'u ch'üan chuan* 圖全傳 by a Sung-tzu shan-jen 松滋山人 (one edition is dated 1890), which relates that Chang Chung predicted the end of the dynasty by a popular uprising and left in a sealed box three drawings depicting the event. This box, when opened by the last Ming emperor in 1644, revealed drawings portraying the triumph of the rebels and the suicide of the emperor by hanging. The story is extracted from contemporary writings, such as the late Ming miscellany *Ming-chi i-wen* 明季遺聞 (1657) by Tsou I 鄒漪 (T. 流綺), which attributed it to Liu Chi. The *T'ieh-kuan t'u* enjoyed a considerable vogue in Ch'ing times; it was adapted for the stage and became the theme of a popular song. These further enhanced the image of Chang Chung.

Bibliography

1/299/7b; 3/281/7a; 61/160/13b; MSL (1961), T'ai-tsu, 165, 168, 1521; KC (1958), 305, 744; TSCC (1880–85), XVIII/256/33/11a; *Fu-chou-fu chih* 撫州府志 (1876), 83/10a; Sung Lien, *Sung hsüeh-shih wen-chi* (SPTK), 9/2a; Yang P'u, *Chan-hsüan hsien-chiao pien* (TsSCC), 10b; Lu Ts'an, *Keng-ssu pien*, in *Chi-lu hui-pien*, 170/1a; Cheng Hsiao, *Chin-yen*, in *Chi-lu hui-pien*, 147/33a; Ku Ch'i-yüan, *K'o-tso chui-yü* (1617), 2/3a; Ho Ch'iao-yüan, *Ming-shan ts'ang* (*Fang-wai chi* 方外紀), 6a; Wang Ch'i, *Pai-shih hui-pien* (preface *1607*), 63/8b; Cha Chi-tso, *Tsui-wei lu* (SPTK), ch. 26, *Fang-wai*; Chai Hao 翟灝 (cs 1754), *T'ung-su pien* 通俗編 (TsSCC), 238; *T'ieh-kuan tao-jen hsüan-chi shu*, in *Chung-kuo yü-yen wu-chung* 中國預言五種 (1967 ed.), 23; Wang Liu-men, *Chien-ch'ing-shih sui-pi* 劍青室隨筆, in *Nan-ching wen-hsien* 南京文獻 (1947) , II, 14; Ch'ien Ching-fang 錢靜方, *Hsiao-shuo ts'ung-k'ao* 小說叢考 (1957), 226; Yüan Fou 袁阜, *Chung-kuo li-tai pu-jen chuan* 歷代卜人傳 (1948), 14/19; Liu Fu 劉復 and Li Chia-jui 李家瑞, eds., *Chung-kuo su-ch'ü tsung-mu kao* 俗曲總目稿(1932), 361; Chan Hok-lam, "Tu Liu Po-wen *Shao-ping ko*" 讀劉伯溫燒餅歌, in *Essays on Chinese Studies Presented to Professor Lo Hsiang-lin* (Hong Kong, 1970), 163; Nakano Kōkan 中野江漢, *Shina no yogen* 支那の豫言 (1925), 125, 134; Anna Seidel, "A Taoist Immortal of the Ming Dynasty: Chang San-feng," in *Self and Society in Ming Thought*, W. T. de Bary, ed. (1970), 488.

Hok-lam Chan and Anna Seidel

CHANG Feng-i 張鳳翼 (T. 伯起, H. 凌虛, 靈虛先生, 冷然居士), 1527–1613, poet, playwright, and calligrapher, was a native of Ch'ang-chou (Soochow). He became a *chü-jen* in 1564. His two younger brothers, Chang Hsien-i 獻翼 (T. 幼于, H. 百花山人, later changed his name to Mi 敉, d. 1604) and Chang Yen-i 燕翼 (T. 叔貽, also a *chü-jen* of 1564), were likewise known for their literary attainments; so the three were given the sobriquet in Soochow of the "Three Chang." After qualifying for the *chü-jen*, Chang Feng-i tried four times to pass the examinations for the advanced degree, but failed. Thereafter he gave up the pursuit of an official career and maintained a life of leisure in Soochow by selling specimens of his calligraphy and by other literary activities. In front of his gate he placed a bulletin board with the superscription: "This house is short of stationery. It is requested that applicants for my calligraphy pay a small fee as per list." It was said that he never approached prominent officials for favor, although few of the persons of note passing through Soochow failed to pay courtesy calls upon him. Some of his old friends rose to high rank in Peking and urged him to enter the public service, but he steadfastly refused. For relaxation he played the lute.

Chang was responsible for seven operas:

Hung-fu chi 紅拂記, *Chu-fa chi* 祝髮記, *Ch'ieh-fu chi* 窃符記, *Kuan-yüan chi* 灌園記, *Yen-i chi* 屍屢記, *Hu-fu chi* 虎符記, and *P'ing-po chi* 平播記. The first six were published under the general title *Yang-ch'un liu-chi* 陽春六集. The most popular of these operas, frequently performed on the stage, is the *Hung-fu chi*. This work, which Chang wrote at the time of his marriage, is based on a famous romance of the T'ang dynasty. The *Chu-fa chi* was written in celebration of his mother's eightieth birthday. (She lived on to the age of ninety *sui*.) Chu I-tsun (ECCP) in his *Ching-chih-chü shih-hua* characterized Chang's dramatic poetry as undistinguished.

On Chang's calligraphy Wang Shih-chen (*q.v.*) in *I-yüan chih-yen* made the comment: "Feng-i took pains to imitate Wang Hsi-chih (321-79) and Wang Hsien-chih (344-88), the most celebrated of Chinese calligraphers. His discarded brushes formed several heaps of rubbish which were then buried as a memorial. His style lacks naturalness, but the structure of his characters is excellent."

Chang also took part in dramatic performances. Once he and his son acted on stage in the well-known Yüan drama *P'i-pa chi* (*see* Kao Ming) and attracted a considerable crowd. He was most composed throughout. Besides his operatic contributions, he left the following works: *Ch'u-shih-t'ang chi* 處實堂集, *Meng-chan lei-k'ao* 夢占類考, *Wen-hsüan tsuan-chu* 文選纂註, *Hai-nei ming-chia kung-hua neng-shih* 海內名家工畫能事, and *T'an lu* 譚輅. The first of these works, which included poems (4 *ch.*), essays (3 *ch.*), and a short sketch book (1 *ch.*), suffered expunction in the following century. [Editors' note: Chang Feng-i was one of the first scholars to write a preface to the fictional work, *Shui-hu chuan* (*see* Shih Nai-an) and the only one to point out that certain officials are the actual robbers and that the readers of the work are thrilled whenever the commoner-bandits are victorious over the robber-officials. He also was critical of the publishers who appended "Wang Ch'ing"

and other irrelevant stories to the *Shui-hu chuan*. It is unknown which of its editions contained his preface, written *ca.* 1588-89. The edition he liked was the one published by Kuo Hsün (*q.v.*), *see* "Wen-hsüeh i-ch'an" in *Kuang-ming jih-pao*, May 9, 1965.]

There are at least two more individuals named Chang Feng-i with identical characters in the early 17th century, and the three are mistakenly taken to be one person in *Combined Indices to Eighty-nine Collections of Ming Dynasty Biographies*. The entries 1/257/15a and 3/240/15a refer to the Chang Feng-i of Tai-chou 代州, Shansi, who was a *chin-shih* of 1613, served as minister of War in 1630 and again in 1632-36, dying in office September 30. The entry 55/8/9b refers to the Chang Feng-i (T. 異羽) of T'ang-i 堂邑, Shantung, who was a *chin-shih* of 1625 and, while serving as governor of northern Shensi, died a martyr to the Ming cause in 1643 in a battle not far from Yen-an 延安 against the rebel, Li Tzu-ch'eng (ECCP).

Bibliography

37/x/26a; 40/45/30b; 43/4/5a; 64/己7/11a; 84/丁中/12a; 86/13/27a; *Tai-chou chih* 代州志 (1882), 8/33a; *Shantung t'ung-chih* (1934), 4852; Chu Chia 祝嘉, *Shu-hsüeh shih* 書學史, 13/369; Ma Tsung-huo 馬宗霍, *Shu-lin tsao-chien* 書林藻鑑, 11/323b; Aoki Masaru 青木正兒, *Shina kinsei gikyoku shi* 支那近世戲曲史, translated by Wang Ku-lu 王古魯 into Chinese (1936), 9/197; Fu Hsi-hua 傅惜華, *Ming-tai ch'uan-ch'i shu-mu* 明代傳奇書目 (1959), 44; Ch'en Nai-ch'ien 陳乃乾, *Chin-shu tsung-lu* 禁書總錄 (1932), ch. 下/21.

Liu Lin-sheng

CHANG Fu 張輔 (T. 文弼), 1375-September 1, 1449, commander in Annam wars between 1406 and 1416, was a native of Hsiang-fu 祥符 (Kaifeng), Honan. He was the son of Chang Yü 玉 (T. 世美, 1343-January 9, 1401), a military official of the Yüan, who remained loyal to the Mongol cause until 1385 before returning from Mongolia to submit to Chu Yüan-chang. Chang Yü later entered the service of Chu

Ti (*q. v.*) when the latter was prince of Yen at Peking. In 1399, when the prince challenged his nephew's rule, Chang Yü was one of his trusted officers and helped to plan the first of the campaigns which led to Chu Ti's eventual victory. Early in 1401, however, he was killed at the battle of Tung-ch'ang 東昌, Shantung. For his brilliant help, his son Chang Fu succeeded to his post as guard vice commander. After the final victory, Chang Yü was posthumouly enfeoffed as duke. He was further enfeoffed in 1425 as prince of Ho-chien 河間. His two other sons, Chang Ni 輗 (d. 1462) and Chang Yüeh (*see* Chu Ch'i-yü) were both enfeoffed by Chu Ch'i-chen (*q. v.*) for their help in recovering the throne for him in 1457, but they had otherwise undistinguished careers. Of greater distinction was Chang Yü's nephew, Chang Hsin 信 (a *chü-jen* of 1400), who rose to be vice minister of War and was then rewarded with a hereditary appointment in the imperial guards because of his cousin Chang Fu; in 1431 he went to Szechwan as assistant military commissioner and served there for fifteen years. It was also of importance to the family that Chang Yü's daughter (Chang Fu's sister) became one of Chu Ti's concubines.

Chang Fu himself fought well in Chu Ti's cause and, in 1402, was made an earl and in 1405 a marquis. Then in July, 1406, when Chang was thirty-one, Chu Ti decided to send an expeditionary army to invade Annam (in 1407 called Chiao-chih 交趾, *i.e.*, Tongking, and the northern parts of Annam in modern Vietnam) with Chang as deputy expeditionary commander to support the fallen Trần dynasty against the usurper Lê Quí-ly (*q.v.*). The commander, Chu Neng 朱能 (T. 士弘, 1370–November 12, 1406), who was one of Chu Ti's most trusted generals in the 1399–1402 campaigns, died unexpectedly while the army was still in Kwangsi. Chang Fu took command on December 1, 1406. By this time he had led the army through the passes south of P'ing-hsiang 憑祥 district into northern Annam. By the middle of

January, 1407, he was joined by the forces of the deputy commander, Mu Sheng (*see* Mu Ying), which had arrived by way of the Red River from Yunnan. On January 19 the two forces attacked the Annamite defenders at the fort of Đa-bang 多邦, west of the eastern capital at Thăng-long 昇龍 (modern Hanoi). Soon after the fort fell and Thăng-long was occupied. Chang then sent two of his generals to attack the western capital at Thanh-hoá 清化. Lê Quí-ly burned the palaces and granaries and abandoned it.

Chang also pursued the Annamite forces into the Red River delta region and the coast and defeated them in a number of river engagements during February. In early May Lê Quí-ly counter-attacked up the Red River towards Thăng-long. Chang Fu and Mu Sheng were prepared and waited for him at Ham-tu-quan 鹹子關, southeast of Thăng-long. Lê Quí-ly was decisively beaten and barely escaped with a few ships. Chang Fu's forces pursued him for another month until both he and his son Lê Han-thu'o'ng (*see* Lê Quí-ly) were trapped in the south near Mt. Hà-tỉnh 高望山. The first Annam campaign thus ended on June 17, 1407.

Even before Lê Quí-ly's rout, Chang had, on March 10, 1407, ordered an imperial proclamation to be read, asking everyone to remain calm while efforts were being made to find a virtuous descendant of the Trần royal house to be sent to Nanking for recognition as the king of Annam. A little more than a month later, he reported that over eleven hundred Annamite officials affirmed that all members of the Trần house had been killed by Lê Quí-ly and that there was no one to carry on the Trần line. Chang also reported that these officials asked that Annam be incorporated into the imperial administration as a *chün-hsien* 郡縣. After the victory in May, Chang followed up his report with a memorial asking the emperor to set up a military commission and provincial administration and surveillance offices. This received strong support from all officials at court, but the emperor decided to wait until Lê Quí-ly was captured before acting on it. When this news reached the court on July 5, the emperor agreed to incorporate Annam into the empire as the province of Chiao-chih. Military affairs were placed in the care of Lü I 呂毅 (d. January 9, 1409), who was assisted by Huang Chung 黃中 (d. *ca.* 1413), a deputy commander at Kwangsi who accompanied Lü I to Annam; Huang was later executed by Chang Fu, and this was held against Chang and became the subject of a minor historical controversy. Huang Fu (*q. v.*) was appointed both administration and surveillance commissioner. The prefectures, subprefectures, departments, and districts were mostly renamed and reorganized under the new provincial government.

Chang Fu still had over-all responsibility for establishing peace and order in Chiao-chih for another year, during which time his troops cleaned up local resistance, and he selected, in all, over nine thousand able scholars and officials to be sent to Nanking for appointment to office. Part of his army also was sent to quell tribal revolts in Kwangsi. Finally he led his men back to Nanking where he arrived in July, 1408. For his victories Chang Fu was rewarded with the dukedom of Ying 英國公 and his annual salary more than doubled to three thousand piculs.

Less than two months after Chang returned, a descendant of the Trần house appeared as the new leader of the Annamite resistance and loyalist forces. He was Trần Nguy 陳頠 also, known as Emperor Gian-dinh 簡定 (d. 1410, a son of Emperor Nghệ-tông 藝宗, r. 1370–72, who abdicated, lived on to influence the succession till his death in 1394 opened the way for Lê Quí-ly's usurpation). To deal with him, Mu Sheng was sent from Yunnan as commander, but his army suffered a disastrous defeat in January, 1409, Lü I being slain along with several of his senior staff. Chang was then ordered to lead an army to save Chiao-chih; he left on the same day as the emperor, Chu Ti, who

took off for Peking (February 23, 1409). Chang planned his campaign with care and by the end of September was able to defeat Trần Nguy south of Thăng-long. By this time another Annamite "emperor" appeared, Trần Quí-khoáng 陳季擴, a grandson of Nghệ-tông, who joined forces with his uncle, Trần Nguy, near Thănh-hoá. Chang rejected both their claims to legitimacy and pursued them south of Thănh-hoá where, on December 16, 1409, he captured Trần Nguy. This left Trần Quí-khoáng as leader of the Annamite resistance until 1414.

Early in 1410 Chang was recalled to join the emperor north of the Great Wall. He probably left Chiao-chih in February, putting Mu Sheng again in command. Two months later Chang was with Chu Ti, training troops in the Hsing-ho 興和 region (in modern Chahar) and presumably remained in the north until the emperor returned to Nanking in December, 1410. In the meantime Mu Sheng was faring badly against Trần Quí-khoáng and almost immediately after his return to Nanking, Chang was sent again to Chiao-chih as expeditionary commander. The Annamites practiced guerrilla tactics and avoided pitched battles with the Chinese forces. They harassed the Chinese and tied them down in the garrison towns. Only occasionally in the years 1411 to 1413 was Chang able to get the Annamites to fight in the Thanh-hoá area. When he could, he pursued them south towards Hà-tĩnh. Finally, at the end of December, 1413, he and Mu Sheng followed the Annamite forces as far south as Thuân-hoá and defeated them decisively. The remnants escaped inland. Chang pursued on foot into the mountain valleys and captured most of the resistance generals and officials. Trần escaped to Laos 老撾, and Chang had to send troops after him before he succeeded in his demand for the surrender of Trần. This happened on March 30, 1414, five years after the rebellion started. It had taken much longer to quell the rebellion than to conquer Annam.

Chang Fu stayed almost another year to help the military commissioner, Han Kuan 韓觀 (T. 彥賓, d. October 9, 1414), complete the work of pacification; he then returned to Nanking in March, 1415. But again he was needed in Chiao-chih, and less than two months later he was on his way. This time he met with little Annamite resistance and his stay of one and a half years was comparatively uneventful. By the end of 1416 we find him back in Peking.

Out of over ten years, between July, 1406, and December, 1416, Chang Fu had spent eight and a half on campaigns in Annam. He was still only forty-one and lived another thirty-three years. Yet, despite his military skill and experience, he was never given another command. This has led to speculation that his execution of Huang Chung displeased the emperor and his successors. It is interesting to note that he was one of the directors of the commission which compiled the *shih-lu* of Chu Ti's reign and that it excludes mention of Huang Chung's execution. The whole affair was later reconstructed mainly from *Shui-tung jih-chi* by Yeh Sheng (*q. v.*) and especially from *P'ing-ting Chiao-nan lu*, a work written about 1486 by Ch'iu Chün (*q. v.*) who based himself on documents supplied by the Chang family.

Chang Fu was spared the increasingly difficult task of holding down Chiao-chih after 1418 when another Annamite resistance leader emerged. This was Lê Lọ'i, the guerrilla fighter who finally forced the Chinese to abandon Annam in 1428. Chang was helpless in Peking, and his arguments for continuing the fight for Annam were made in vain.

From 1417, when he followed the emperor to Peking, until the latter's death in 1424, Chang remained at the emperor's side as the senior general and the trusted relation as well as one of Chu Ti's most intimate advisers. He accompanied the emperor on the last three campaigns against the Mongols in 1422, 1423, and 1424. And when the emperor was dying at Yü-mu ch'uan 榆木川 in August, he called Chang to hear his last testament and entrusted him with the succession of the heir apparent.

Chang Fu lived long enough to serve three other emperors, Chu Kao-chih, Chu Chan-chi (*qq. v.*), and Chu Ch'i-chen. In 1426 he played a key role in helping Chu Chan-chi crush the revolt of the emperor's uncle, the prince of Han, Chu Kao-hsü (*q. v.*). On the whole, however, he lived quietly and was content to be an influential member of the administration. When the eunuch Wang Chen (*q. v.*) began to dominate affairs after 1435, Chang was as helpless as all the other senior ministers and grand secretaries. When Chu Ch'i-chen was persuaded by Wang Chen to take personal leadership of an expeditionary army against the Mongols in 1449, Chang was apparently silent. He did accompany the emperor on the campaign and at the disastrous battle of T'u-mu 土木 he lost his life. He was posthumously enfeoffed as prince of Ting-hsing 定興. A collection of his writings, entitled *Chang Fu chi* 集, 2 *ch.*, is no longer extant.

His son Chang Mou 懋 (1441–1515) succeeded him as duke of Ying at the age of eight, held his dukedom for sixty-six years and the highest military ranks for forty, and was grand preceptor for twenty-five. As a senior general and imperial adviser, he made no notable contributions to the empire but gained the reputation of being an extravagant man.

Bibliography

1/154/1a, 145/4a, 321/1a; 3/136/1a; 5/5/63a; 61/97/6b; 63/9/19a.

Wang Gungwu

CHANG Fu-ching 張孚敬, originally named Ts'ung 璁 (T. 東用, 茂恭, H. 羅峯, 羅山), 1475–February 24, 1539, son of Chang Sheng 張昇, an official, was a native of Yung-chia 永嘉, Chekiang, and rose to be a grand secretary. He qualified for the *chü-*

jen in 1498. After failing seven times in the *chin-shih* examinations he finally passed in 1521, directly after the young prince, Chu Hou-ts'ung (*q.v.*), ascended the throne (May 27); he was then forty-six years of age. It was at this time that the emperor ordered the people at court to discuss the titles his parents should be given. As the senior grand secretary, Yang T'ing-ho (*q.v.*) made certain proposals which met with wide approval. Chang Ts'ung, however, was the first to oppose Yang. He addressed a memorial to the throne on August 4 insisting that due to His Majesty's station, certain changes should be made. The emperor agreed with Chang rather than with Yang; still a number of officials accused Chang of hetero-doxy, even going so far as to say that he spoke as he did for the purpose of seeking official advancement. This dispute created much dissension and for three years it raged and became known as the *Ta-li i* (*see* Chu Hou-ts'ung). Finally, on October 1, 1524, the emperor made his decision. He approved of the titles proposed by Chang.

Chang's first appointment, made in January, 1522, was as secretary of a bureau in the ministry of Justice in Nanking. Two and a half years later he became Hanlin chancellor. From then on his rise was rapid. He received promotions in January, 1526, to the post of grand supervisor of instruction, and in August of the same year to the office of right vice minister of War. Subsequently he was transferred to be left vice minister of War, all the while remaining as chancellor of the Hanlin. By this time he had become eager to take part in the direction of the whole administration, but his ambition was thwarted by Grand Secretary Fei Hung (*q.v.*); so Chang and his associate, Kuei O (*q.v.*), then vice minister of Rites, often attacked Fei. As a result, early in 1527 Fei was removed from office; simultaneously Grand Secretary Shih Pao 石珤 (T. 邦彥, d. 1529) resigned.

In September of the same year, Chang became became left censor-in-chief, Kuei minister of Justice, and Fang Hsien-fu (*see*

Kuei O) minister of the Grand Court of Revision; all three were ordered to investigate the case of Li Fu-ta 李福達 (also named Li Wu 午 or 五, native of Kuo-hsien 崞縣, Shansi), who had led a seditious society known as the White Lotus sect 白蓮教, in an uprising in Shensi. As Li Fu-ta had long gone under the name of Chang Yin 張寅, when he was seized in 1526 some said that he was not the rebel. Chang, Kuei, and Fang also came to the conclusion that the man detained (Chang Yin) was falsely accused, in the face of opposition of most of the court who insisted that Li Fu-ta and Chang Yin were one and the same person. The emperor preferred to consider the man innocent. As a consequence, Chang Yin was released, while many officials, suspected of associating with him for nefarious purposes, were punished, among them the previous minister of Justice, Yen I-shou 顏頤壽 (T. 天和, H. 梅田, 1462–1538, cs 1490), and the regional inspector of Shansi province, Ma Lu 馬錄 (T. 君卿, cs 1508), both of whom had proposed to the throne that Chang Yin be put to death. (As a matter of fact Chang Yin was Li Fu-ta. This mystery was cleared up when Li's grandson, Li T'ung 同, was arrested, found guilty, and executed in 1566. The judgment that Chang Ts'ung, Kuei O, and Fang Hsien-fu had rendered in Chang Yin's case in 1527 was perhaps made only to achieve their political ends.) On October 28, 1527, in recognition of his services, Chang was appointed titular minister of Rites and concurrently grand secretary, while still holding the post of left censor-in-chief. So, within six years after achieving the *chin-shih*, he finally came to share in the administration of the central government.

Early in 1528 Chang received further honors, and in June of the same year, when the *Ming lun ta-tien*, 24 ch. (*see* Yang I-ch'ing), a kind of white book containing many documents issued to justify the emperor's action in bestowing imperial honors upon his parents, was completed, he as one of its compilers was made titular minister of Personnel and shown other signs of imperial favor.

During these years the emperor held Chang in the highest confidence even though Yang I-ch'ing (*q.v.*) was the senior grand secretary. On the other hand, because Yang I-ch'ing's appointment as grand secretary in 1526 was partly due to the fact that Chang and Kuei had supported him, Yang allowed himself to be led by Chang. As time went on, however, Chang's envy of Yang got the better of him and he began to attack Yang. In retaliation the latter also criticized Chang. In September, 1529, accused of abuse of official authority by certain supervising secrearies, Chang Ts'ung was removed from office and left Peking for Chekiang. Nevertheless, about one month later, when he arrived at Tientsin, he was recalled to the capital to resume his office as his associate, Grand Supervisor of Instruction Huo T'ao (*q.v.*), had come to his defense in a memorial to the throne and had attacked Yang I-ch'ing severely. He even contended that the accusations against Chang had been instigated by Yang. Consequently, in October of the same year, Yang I-ch'ing was cashiered and Chang returned as senior secretary. One of his first concerns (November, 1530) as grand secretary was the revision of the ritual regulations. In this he was sharply opposed by Hsü Chieh (*q.v.*). The emperor sided with Chang, however, and Hsü was demoted.

Since his name Ts'ung 璁, and the character Ts'ung 熜 of the emperor's name were homophonous, he repeatedly requested the latter to change his name so that he might avoid breaking the taboo. On March 15, 1531, the emperor complied, giving him the name Fu-ching and the *tzu* 茂恭, the emperor personally writing out these four characters.

His relations at that time with the left vice minister of Rites and concurrently Hanlin chancellor, Hsia Yen (*q.v.*), had begun to deteriorate badly. By August of the same year, as his scheme to have Hsia falsely accused was revealed, he was re-moved from office and left for home. At the end of 1531, however, because of the concern of the empress dowager, née Chiang (*see* Chu Hou-ts'ung) on his behalf, the emperor summoned him back to court. In April, 1532, he returned once more as grand secretary. During these days Li Shih (*q.v.*) and Chai Luan (*see* Yen Sung) were serving in the same capacity and were joined a few week later by Fang Hsien-fu. Hsia Yen had been minister of Rites for almost one year. Although Chang Fu-ching was the senior grand secretary, he was not as powerful as before. On the night of September 2, 1532, when a comet appeared, the emperor thought that a certain minister must be to blame; accordingly Chang Fu-ching resigned from office.

Early in 1533 the emperor once more summoned Chang Fu-ching to court and reappointed him as grand secretary. In the following year his rank was elevated to that of titular minister of Personnel and concurrently senior grand secretary. In the spring of 1535 he became ill and begged to be retired; shortly afterwards the emperor granted his request. In 1536 the emperor sent off messengers to inquire after his health and recall him to the capital but he could not accept because his physical condition would not permit. He died three years later aged sixty-four, and was buried at Huang-ao 黃墺 in his native place. He was posthumously given the official title of T'ai-shih 太師 and canonized as Wen-chung 文忠.

Contemporaries describe Chang as a man with a long beard and commanding appearance. He is said to have been courageous, intelligent, and able to bear responsibility and blame. During his service in the court he often gave advice to the emperor, including among other things the support of Confucian ideas and institutions and the observance of certain ritual rules. Besides, he was incorruptible; he detested avaricious officials so strongly that when he was grand secretary few men dared to accept or offer bribes. His defect in character was that he was uncompromising, jealous of his rivals for power, and headstrong. His attacks against Fei Hung and Yang I-ch'ing successively were also considered improper.

Chang Fu-ching had four sons. The first, Chang Hsün-chih 遜志 (T. 伯懷, H. 靜修) was known for his filial piety. In the course of more than one year, when his mother, née Ts'ai 蔡, was ill and had taken to her bed, he attended her in person constantly. Grieving greatly over his mother's death around 1534, he too passed away soon afterwards. The second son, Chang Hsün-yeh業 (T. 有功, H. 甌江), was made a student of the National University by imperial favor, then served as drafter of the central drafting office, later rising to be executive assistant of the seal office. He died at the age of thirty-five. The other sons also passed away at an early age.

Chang Fu-ching was the author of several books, mostly collections of memorials, reports, and imperial edicts. W. Franke writes that the *T'ai-shih Chang Wen-chung kung chi, tsou-shu* 太師 張文忠公集, 奏疏, 8 *ch.*, contains some 180 memorials which he wrote during his years in office. A copy is preserved in the Sonkeikaku, Tokyo. The Library of Congress has copies of his three other books: *Loshan tsou-shu* 奏疏, 7 *ch.*, a collection of his memorials; *Tsou-tui kao* 奏對稿, 12 *ch.*, another collection of his memorials; and *Yü-tui lu* 諭對錄, 34+3 *ch.*, a collection of secret imperial edicts and his reports and memorials on them, written during the years from 1527 to 1536, and published in 1608.

Bibliography

1/196/1a; 3/182/1a; 4/9/29b; 5/16/1a; 6/2/21b, 15/ 37b, 27/1b, 29b, 28/26b, 35/7b, 38/9b, 15b, 18b, 42/17b; 7/41/13a; 8/45/10a; 11/4/65a; 14/3/11b; 18 /5/1a, 6/1a; 40/37/2a; 42/70/1a; 61/155/6b; 63/12/ 41a; 86/11/5b; MSL (1965), Shih-tsung, 1769, 2005, 2443, 2471, 2934, 3206, 4575; KC (1958), 3360, 3568; *Yung-chia-hsien chih* (1882), 14/31a, 16/9b, 35a; *Chekiang t'ung-chih* (1934), 2870, 4096 ; *Ming-shih i-wen-chih pu-pien fu-pien*, 37; SK (1930), 56/1b, 4b; L. of C. *Catalogue of Rare Books*, 166, 168; W. Franke, *Sources*, 5. 5.2, 7.1.

Chou Tao-chi

CHANG Fu-hua 張敷華 (T. 公實, H. 介庵, Pth. 簡肅), 1439–1508, a native of An-fu 安福, Kiangsi, left a name as one of the most incorruptible civil administrators in Ming history. Because his father, a censor, had died at T'u-mu in 1449 while participating in the ill-fated campaign (*see* Wang Chen) he received imperial protection. Enrolled in the National University, Chang subsequently took the metropolitan examination and qualified as *chin-shih* in 1464. Together with Liu Tahsia, Ni Yüeh, and Chiao Fang (*qq.v.*), he was selected to be a Hanlin bachelor. The following year he and Liu requested reassignment to ministerial offices in order to gain experience. Both received appointments as secretaries in the ministry of War. Thereafter Chang's rise up the civil service ladder was slow but steady with no rank skipped and no shortening of his appointments in any office. He remained in the ministry of War for ten years, receiving promotion first to vice director and then to director of a bureau. In 1475 he was appointed an assistant administration commissioner of Chekiang, thenceforth serving in the same province for another decade, and, following the regular sequence, becoming vice commissioner before his elevation to right commissioner. In 1488 he became left administration commissioner of Hukuang and three years later advanced to the governorship of Shansi, with the rank of right censor-in-chief.

In 1491, however, Chang was unable to accept the new appointment as his mother's death temporarily interrupted his official career. After the prescribed period of mourning, he reported for duty in 1493. As the governorship of Shansi was vacant, he was posted there again. In 1495 he was transferred to Shensi, and a year later became right vice minister of War in Nanking.

After 1499 his advancement was less regular. His appointment to be commissioner of the Grand Canal with the rank of right censor-in-chief in the autumn of that year followed the death of a predecessor. Late in 1501 with the same rank he was put in charge of the censorate in Nanking to succeed an official who had been shifted elsewhere. This time he remained in office for more than four years. At the end of December, 1505, he became minister of Justice in the southern capital. Less than two months later, he received orders to proceed to Peking to become censor-in-chief.

Chang is described by his contemporaries as austere and reserved. He insisted on living on his official salary and allowances, an extremely difficult task then as later. His family food budget was such that his elder son, a heavy eater, is said to have frequently left the dining table unsatisfied. A popular anecdote relates that once a highwayman intercepted Chang's luggage; upon discovering only seven taels of silver, however, he felt ashamed to take it from him. After completion of the term as administration commissioner of Hukuang, Chang achieved a treasury surplus of twenty thousand taels of silver which he meticulously registered in the ledger and handed on to his successor. His biographers point this out as an exceptional example of integrity. Ni Yüeh, a man with a reputation for honesty himself, lived, after his transfer to Peking as minister of Personnel in 1500, in a house belonging to an officer of the Embroidered-uniform Guard. This officer declined Ni's rent but begged him to write a letter to Chang Fu-hua, then canal commissioner residing at Huai-an 淮安 requesting the latter to let an unspecified amount of salt, owned by no other than the landlord, himself, pass without interception. But when the letter arrived, to Ni's chagrin, Chang refused to oblige, declaring that it was not his practice to break the law even to grant a favor to a friend.

It is said that on one occasion Liu Ta-hsia spoke very highly of Chang to Emperor Chu Yu-t'ang (q.v.). The latter, while conceding Chang's reputation for uprightness, commented that he was "too strict." There are only six entries in the shih-lu mentioning memorials or suggestions which he made to the throne, beginning with his appointment as canal commissioner in 1499; his arguments supporting his proposals are unhappily completely absent. In spite of his long-time occupation of the censorial office, not a single impeachment action which he may have initiated against any fellow official is recorded in the state chronicle. Despite his own strict rule of conduct there is no evidence that he demanded of others the same standards. Once, however, when he did suggest that the emperor check the prevailing graft and corruption within officialdom, he was speaking in a broad and general sense.

In dealing with those under his control, he was uniformly understanding and benevolent. One memorial of his resulted in an imperial order authorizing the army personnel engaged in grain transportation duty to carry salt on their return trips, duty free, to the amount of fifty piculs (about 1/3 of a ton) per ship, which enabled the soldiers to make a small profit to supplement their inadequate pay and allowances. Another petition, also approved by the emperor, permitted a consignment of about six hundred thousand piculs of grain to be delivered at the canal terminal near T'ung-chou 通州 instead of to the designated granaries in Peking; this saved the delivery personnel from paying the exorbitant vehicular charges for the fifteen mile overland trip. When he was administration commissioner in Chekiang, he was once called upon to deal with a riot of miners which flared up in open rebellion. While many officials urged suppression by force, he appealed to the rioters to surrender, subsequently arresting twelve leaders and setting the rest free.

His last service to the Ming court had to do with the attempt to eliminate the eunuch Liu Chin (q.v.). About October 1506, he submitted a memorial to Emperor Chu Hou-chao (*q.v.*), which, as quoted, makes no mention of Liu by name but does specifically point out the danger of trusting eunuchs. In this paper he criticizes the sovereign in plain language, charging that his deeds were incompatible with his own proclamations and contrary to the established laws and orders of preceding emperors. He further details unbefitting acts as ones which allow those close to the throne to violate the regulations on the salt gabelle, misappropriate state funds, grant imperial estates to favorites, organize a corps of "braves" of six- and seven-year old boys, and encourage eunuchs to interfere with the civil and military administration. In conclusion he warns the emperor, "What hundreds of ministerial officials strive to achieve can easily be destroyed by a handful of rogues." The petition created no positive results, nor did it cause any harm to the memorialist just then. In the latter part of the year, when minister of Revenue Han Wen (*q.v.*) pressed the issue further and the whole attempt backfired, many key officials including Han being forced to retire, Chang Fu-hua still retained his position as head of the censorate. At the close of the year, however, he was abruptly told that the emperor had ordered his retirement. The dismissal was undoubtedly directed by Liu Chin; nevertheless, the circumstances under which the order was released are not clear. Neither the command for Chang to retire nor his outspoken memorial is registered in the *shih-lu*. Three months after his removal his name was included in the list of "evil partisans" announced by Liu Chin in the name of the emperor.

Upon receiving his order of dismissal Chang started home that very day, knowing perhaps that Liu was plotting against his life as the eunuch had against his other antagonists. On his way south he found that no official dared to receive him or give him comfort. Over the rapids at Hsü-chou 徐州, his boat hit a rock and capsized. Chang survived and went to the nearby branch office of the ministry of Works for help. Arriving at midnight, he left before daybreak lest he might inconvenience his benefactor. The official in charge of the branch office was the grandfather of Lo Hung-hsien (*q.v.*). Lo later related the episode in his biography of Chang. Chang's tombstone inscriptions indicate that his memorials and other writings were collected in a manuscript entitled *Chieh-hsien chi* 介軒集. It is doubtful that it was ever published.

Bibliography

1/186/6a; 5/54/67a; KC (1958), 2879; Cheng Hsiao, *Wu-hsüeh-pien* (1572), 43/19a; MSL (1963), Hsien-tsung, 4517, Hsiao-tsung, 0252, 0952, 1471, 2096, 2732, 2941, 3041, 3301, 3363, 3595, 3863, 3929, *chiao-k'an-chi* 校勘記, 544, Wu-tsung, 0235, 0279, 0662, 0925; *An-fu-hsien chih* (1885), 10/12a; Ho Liang-chün, *Ssu-yu-chai ts'ung-shuo* (1957), 83.

Ray Huang

CHANG Han 張瀚 (T. 子文, H. 元洲, 虎林山人, Pth. 恭懿), 1511–93, official, scholar, calligrapher, and painter, was a native of Jen-ho 仁和 (Hangchow), a descendant of a silk weaver. After passing the provincial examinations in 1534, he became a *chin-shih* in the following year. As a bureau secretary in the Nanking ministry of Works, appointed in 1536, Chang was given the specific duty of supervising the Lung-chiang 龍江 shipyard. In preparation for the excursion of Emperor Chu Hou-ts'ung (*q.v.*) to the south, and the transportation of his mother's remains to Hukuang (1539) the supervisors of the shipyard found themselves faced with unusual demands, although the imperial trip finally took the route by land. Chang Han stayed at his post for three years, until late in 1539, when his mother died. His experience in this work prompted a very real interest in ship construction. Later when he officiated in Fukien (1561), it was his duty to entertain and send off two envoys to the Liu-ch'iu (Ryukyu) Islands. After visiting their ship, Chang Han wrote an informative account of it: "The ship is 160 *ch'ih* (200 feet) long and 36 *ch'ih* (45 feet) wide. Its mast is as tall as the ship is long. On the top of the mast is a structure shaped like a bushel measure, inside which sit four men facing the four directions to take note of wind currents. They stay there day and night. These men climb up and down the ropes as easily as though walking on level ground. The ship has four decks; in the hold spring water is stored, because the sea water is bitter and salty, not fit to drink; above that are provisions, utensils, and tools; and people live on the top level, where the two envoys and their retinue also stay. Tables and cots are suspended by means of ropes, because the hull of the ship has a keel, and the ocean waves rock the vessel without ceasing. One can neither sit nor lie down in comfort. There are about five hundred men on board, a number of them being skilled artisans. In a favorable wind this trip takes seven days. The ship always sails on the summer solstice, and arrives seven days later, during which time it is driven south by the wind the whole way. It returns on the winter solstice, setting out seven days prior to that day, for during this period the north wind prevails. Climatically this has always proved correct."

Resuming his official career in 1542, Chang first served as bureau vice director, and then as director in the ministry of Justice. In 1544 he became prefect of Lu-chou 盧州, Nan-Chihli, where he administered relief after a drought, prayed for rain and snow, and worked energetically for the welfare of the people. In 1546 he again had to leave office, this time on account of the death of his father. Fom 1550 to 1565 he held offices in Ta-ming-fu 大名府 (Pei-Chihli), in Shensi and Shansi, and then in southern and western China, Fukien, Kwangtung, and Szechwan. By 1565 he had risen to be governor and had gone back to Shensi. In 1566 he returned to Peking to head the Grand Court of Revision, and then served successively as vice minister of Justice and vice minister of

War. Later in the same year he left Peking to be director-general of the transportation of tribute grain. After a short term as governor-general of Kwangtung and Kwangsi where both banditry and piracy were rife, he returned home (1567). After another term as governor of Shensi, he was recalled in 1572 to Nanking to be right chief censor. In 1573, at the begining of the new reign when the post of minister of Personnel became vacant, Chang Han, with the backing of Chang Chü-cheng (*q.v.*), was elevated to that post, although he was not the most qualified. Thus other officials regarded him as one of Chang Chü-cheng's clique, even criticizing him for this reason. When Chang Chü-cheng stayed on in office after his father's death in 1577, however, Chang Han refused to endorse his action because he did not approve of to-ch'ing 奪情 (failure to observe the period of mourning for one's parent on an emperor's command). At this he was forced to retire. Only then did the court officials change their opinion and stop labeling him Chang Chü-cheng's lackey.

This reminds one of a similar case, that of Hsü Hsüeh-mo (*q.v.*). Both Hsü and Chang were able administrators with broad experience in the provinces. Both received extraordinary promotions backed by Chang Chü-cheng. It was therefore natural for others to accuse both of being his followers. While Chang Chü-cheng may have counted on their loyalty, he was also sincere in his recruitment for the central government of men of proven ability.

The collected literary works of Chang Han are entitled *Hsi-nang tu-yü* 奚囊蠹餘, 20 *ch.*, first printed in 1569, later reprinted in 1907 in the collection of *Wu-lin wang-che i-chu* 武林往哲遺著. His own memorials may be found in the *T'ai-sheng tsou-i* 臺省奏議, 8 *ch.* In the years from 1550 to 1553, when he was prefect of Ta-ming, he also compiled a collection of memorials by Ming officials, entitled the *Ming shu-i chi-lüeh* 明疏議輯畧, 37 *ch.* To all three, editors of the *Ssu-k'u* catalogue allotted notices, although the books were not included in the Imperial Library. Another compilation by him is a thin volume of portraits of and poems by a group of senior retired scholar-officials of the Hangchow area, bearing the title *Wu-lin i-lao-hui shih-chi* 怡老會詩集, first printed about 1588, and later reprinted in the seventh series of the *Wu-lin chang-ku ts'ung-pien* 掌故叢編 in 1882. There are sixteen portraits each with a short biographical note, and poems by nineteen authors (three without portraits), their age ranging from seventy-one to ninety *sui*. The I-lao-hui (association for the enjoyment of old age) was supposed to meet four times a year, in the middle month of each season, the exact time and place to be decided by the host of a particular meeting. Plenty of food and drink was provided. The members were free to write poems or not, and complete their poems if they wished. Conversations of good taste were acceptable on all topics except politics. Apparently this thin volume was the product of a few of their meetings. Years earlier in 1542, when Chang Han was a bureau secretary in the ministry of Justice, he had also formed a club of six members, and had their portraits made in six copies for commemorative purposes. Besides he had painted a series of pictures depicting his own life with colophons on each written in his own hand on the side, entitled *Huan-chi t'u* 宦蹟圖. He evidently valued illustrations as well as calligraphy.

The most interesting of all his works is perhaps the *Sung-ch'uang meng-yü* 松窗夢語, a memoir in 8 *chüan*, dealing with thirty-three topics. His own preface is dated 1593, which indicates that it was his last work. For three centuries, it seems, this work circulated only in hand-written copies, until 1896, when the renowned Hangchow bibliophile Ting Ping (ECCP) printed it in the *Wu-lin wang-che i-chu*. The topics cover many phases of his life and times, his travels and his dreams, the foreign lands and peoples close to China, government and social institutions, and contemporary personalities, crafts, commerce, and various professions. One topic concerns flora and another fauna together with vivid descriptions giving color, shape, and species. As he had traveled widely in China, he had seen a great deal more than many Chinese of his time. In his collected prose he has also an essay on goldfish. His interest, keen observation, and descriptive ability may have been derived from his artistic sensitivity and painter's eye. It is said that he gave up painting in his later life; yet we can find in his writings a number of essays and poems dedicated to paintings. Be that as it may, in the *Sung-ch'uang meng-yü* something rare, or rather something more is revealed than may be found in the writings of most scholars of his time.

Bibliography

1/225/1a; 5/25/67a; SK(1930), 56/5a, 11b, 177/12a; *Hsi-nang tu-yü fu-lu* 附錄; *Kwang-tung t'ung-chih*, 通志 (1934), 346, 4239; W. Franke, *Sources*, 4. 6.4, 5.1.2.

Lienche Tu Fang

CHANG Ho-ling 張鶴齡 (d. 1537?) and CHANG Yen-ling 延齡 (d. November 3, 1546), natives of Hsing-chi 興濟, a district which later came under the jurisdiction of Ch'ing-hsien 青縣, south of Tientsin, were the two younger brothers of Empress Hsiao-k'ang, consort of Emperor Chu Yu-t'ang (*q. v.*). Among people on the distaff side of the imperial family during the Ming dynasty, none enjoyed so much favor as the Chang and none met more unhappy ends. In marital relations Chu Yu-t'ang, unlike most emperors in Chinese history, was a devoted husband. As a consequence, during his reign the empress' family and relatives were given unparalleled privileges, material wealth, and social prerogatives. It is said that the two brothers and their mother, née Chin 金, often accompanied the emperor and empress, and went in and out of the palace freely, a practice uncommon in other reigns. Their father, Chang Luan 巒 (T. 來瞻, H. 秀峯, 1445-92), in his early years became a *kung-sheng* and was enrolled in the National University in Peking. In 1487, when his daughter was selected to marry the heir apparent, he received the honorary title of minister of the Court of State Ceremonial. When, on the enthronement of Chu Yu-t'ang his daughter became empress, Chang Luan was elevated to be vice commissioner-in-chief of the central military commission. Two years later he was made earl of Shou-ning 壽寧伯. In1491, following the birth of the heir apparent, Chu Hou-chao (*q. v.*), the maternal grandfather was raised in rank to marquis of Shou-ning, with an annual stipend of 1,200 *shih* of grain. Titles were bestowed on his ancestors of three generations, and the marquisate was made hereditary. As a clear sign of esteem and distinction, his biography and epitaphs after his death were prepared by three grand secretaries, namely, Hsü P'u, Ch'iu Chün, and Li Tung-yang (*qq. v.*). Posthumously Chang Luan was elevated to be duke of Ch'ang-kuo 昌國公 and given the name Chuang-su 莊肅.

At the time of their father's demise, both sons were still young. Chang Ho-ling was engaged to a daughter of Princess Chia-shan 嘉善公主 (1447-99, daughter of Emperor Chu Ch'i-chen [*q. v.*] and wife of Wang Tseng 王增, a grandson of Wang Chi 驥 [*q. v.*]). A few months later he, as the elder son, succeeded to the marquisate of Shou-ning, while Chang Yen-ling received the rank of vice commissioner-in-chief, and sometime afterwards became earl of Chien-ch'ang 建昌伯. A number of Chang Luan's relatives, cousins, nephews, adopted sons, sworn-brothers, and the husband of his wife's sister received military ranks. His widow received various honors, patents, and finally the title of Ch'ang-kuo fu-jen 夫人. Land was given for Chang's interment in the Western Hills, and his tomb was elaborately built. Structures in his memory were erected in his native place, Hsing-chi, with apparent disregard for expense. Throughout the Hung-chih period the Chang brothers received ever more honors, land, and stipends.

Young, overprivileged, and surrounded by hosts of servants and hangers-on, the brothers received everything they wanted and more besides. Sycophants even acted in their names. The brothers are said to have become involved in illegal dealings in land, in salt, and in merchandizing, and as usurers often forced people in default to hand over their young boys and girls. They found numberless ways of amassing wealth and oppressing the people. Many officials (such as Liu Lin, *q. v.*) tried to bring their iniquities to the attention of the emperor, either explicitly or implicitly, but, except for some mild reproofs, he made no effort to put a brake on their activities. On the contrary, it was usually the accusers who suffered the consequences. The imprisonment of Li Meng-yang (*q. v.*) early in 1505 is an outstanding example. Li likened Chang Ho-ling to a tiger with wings, feared and hated by the people. He advised the emperor to check his brother-in-law in time so that his action might not lead to an unhappy ending. As one might have foreseen, Li's prediction proved true some thirty years later.

In 1503 Chang Ho-ling received the additional honor of grand guardian and Chang Yen-ling became marquis of Chien-ch'ang. Soon after their nephew, Chu Hou-chao, ascended the throne in June, 1505, the former was made grand tutor and the latter grand guardian, and each received an increase in stipend. The new emperor, however, expressed no special feeling toward his maternal uncles. In 1515 a man named Ts'ao Tsu 曹祖 accused the Chang brothers of sedition, and committed suicide while in prison. It is said that Ts'ao, in accusing the Chang brothers, was in reality angered at his own son, then a servant of Chang Ho-ling, and showed his feelings by accusing his son's master. Be that as it may, the emperor took the accusation quite seriously; so the two brothers became frightened. As the empress-dowager spoke on their behalf, and numerous expensive gifts found their way to the young emperor (as the *shih-lu* records), the incident concluded without further ado. The emperor, however, never rescinded the order forbidding them to take part in the daily ceremonial audiences.

When Chu Hou-chao died in 1521 without an heir, Chu Hou-ts'ung (*q. v.*), a cousin, was brought in from the princedom of Hsing 興 in Chung-hsiang 鍾祥, northwest of Wuchang, to be the successor. According to reports Chang Ho-ling served on the mission sent from Peking to welcome the young prince. When Chang fell off his horse, he had the groom whipped to death; this made an extremely unfavorable impression on the future emperor. Yet in the first few years of his reign he treated the Chang brothers with proper decorum. For their support in 1522 Chang Ho-ling was elevated to grand preceptor and Chang Yen-ling to grand tutor. In the following year the former was raised to his father's rank as duke of Ch'ang-kuo. As time went on enmity began to develop between Empress-dowager Chang and the new emperor's mother, Chiang. It is said that the former did not accord the latter the respect due her in her new position. In the emperor's eyes, his mother was not only more important, but also deserved the honors that were rightfully hers. For this reason, Emperor Chu Hou-ts'ung for years did not visit his paternal aunt, and even refused to give her any audience. This situation, of course, did not help the Chang brothers when they found themselves in difficulty.

In 1533 disaster struck. The main culprit this time was the younger brother, whose crime involved killing three persons and acquiring illegal property. He was arrested and imprisoned in the jail of the ministry of Justice. His elder brother was demoted to be a vice-commander of the Embroidered-uniform Guard in Nanking. As a member of the family of Empress-dowager Hsiao-k'ang, Chang Yen-ling was treated with consideration, living in special quarters, and enjoying many luxuries. Probably intentionally he chose a quotation

from the *Sheng-hsüeh hsin-fa* of Emperor Chu Ti (*q. v.*) to practice his calligraphy on a panel. The quotation was one that might have been construed as insinuating that the emperor was inept. A notorious character, Liu Tung-shan 劉東山, was also imprisoned in the same jail in 1536. Because of his desire for attention and to satisfy a personal grudge, Liu collected all the accusations throughout the years against his celebrated fellow-prisoner, including the quotation just mentioned, and submitted them to the throne. The emperor was incensed, and sentenced Chang Yen-ling to death. His elder brother was recalled from Nanking in 1537 and died in prison soon afterwards. While the brothers were in serious trouble, some people took the opportunity to revenge themselves, others to blackmail them. Accusations both justified and unjustified were heaped upon them. In 1538 Chang Yen-ling was accused of using sorcery against the emperor. The Chang properties were confiscated. More than once the emperor wanted to have Chang Yen-ling executed, but Chang Fu-ching (*q. v.*) advised against the death penalty in consideration for the aged Empress-dowager Chang, who begged the emperor repeatedly and unsuccessfully for an audience. Finally she died in 1541. Chang Yen-ling was executed five years later. The brothers' sons, Chang Tsung-yüeh 宗說 and Chang Tsung-chien 簡, with their families were moved to Nanking.

Wang Shih-chen (*q. v.*) in his *Yüeh-fu-pien* 樂府變, a series of poems on the political events of the Chia-ching period, contributed one on the Chang family under the title "Shou-ning-ch'i" 泣; this depicted their corrupt tragic story. One also may recall the extreme caution of Wang Ao 鏊 (*q. v.*), who made every effort to disavow his relationship to the Chang family so as to avoid any involvement. The connection is so vaguely indicated in surviving documents that one cannot be sure whether the woman from the Chang family whom he married was a sister or an aunt of the empress.

Bibliography

1/114/1b, 300/17a; 5/3/3a, 32b; Hsü P'u, *Hsü Wen-ching kung chien-chai chi* (NCL microfilm), 7/47b; MSL (1964), Hsien-tsung, ch. 50, Hsiao-tsung, ch. 51–59, Wu-tsung (1965), 0117, 2587, Shih-tsung, 3502, 4055, 4318, 5043, 5906; KC (1958), 1959, 3490, 3534, 3553, 3615; Shen Te-fu, *Wan-li yeh-hu pien* (1959), 中/464; Wang Shih-chen, *Yen-chou shan-jen ssu pu kao* (1577), 6/16a; Hsü Hsüeh-mo, *Shih-miao chih-yü lu*, 7/12b, 8/8a; Chu Kuo-chen (ECCP), *Ta-shih chi*, 321/18a.

Lienche Tu Fang

CHANG Hsieh 張燮 (T. 紹和, H. 汰沃, 海濱逸史, 蜚遯老人, and 石戶主人), 1574–1640, author of a maritime geography of south Asia, *Tung-hsi-yang k'ao* 東西洋考, was a native of Lung-ch'i 龍溪, Fukien. His great-grandfather, Chang Ch'o 張綽 (T. 本寬), a *chin-shih* of 1493, served as a bureau director in the ministry of Justice. Both his father, Chang T'ing-pang 張廷榜 (T. 登材, 春宇, *ca.* 1545–1609), and his uncle, Chang T'ing-tung 張廷棟 (T. 國材), also became *chin-shih*, the former in 1574 and the latter six years later. Chang T'ing-pang served meritoriously as magistrate of T'ai-p'ing 太平, Chekiang, but was cashiered about 1580 while holding the post of vice prefect of Chinkiang. Chang Hsieh's closest friend, Huang Tao-chou (ECCP), the Ming loyalist, philosopher, and artist, in one of his memorials to the throne (1637), said that, in respect to high ideals and erudition, he could not compare with Chang Hsieh. Chang's other friends included Hsü Hung-tsu (ECCP), the well-known traveler and diarist, and Chou Ch'i-yüan 周起元 (T. 仲先, H. 綿貞, 1572–1626, cs 1601), whose attacks against the eunuchs and the political corruption of his day resulted in his death in prison.

Chang Hsieh never held a government office. After he became a *chü-jen* in 1594 he continued to take examinations for some thirty years. In 1637 he was recommended by Ho Ch'iao-yüan (*q.v.*) to share in the compilation of the *shih-lu*, but the court ignored the recommendation. In addition to a number of essays and poems transcribed in the local histories, he is credited with the authorship and editorship of fifteen books, most of which, especially several large works, have been lost. He is known to have collaborated with Ho Ch'iao-yüan in the compilation of *Huang Ming wen-cheng*, and with Hsü Luan 徐鑾 in *Chang-chou-fu hsin-chih* 漳州府新志, 20 *ch*. He served likewise as editor of *Liang Chien-wen-ti yü-chih chi* 梁簡文帝御製集, 16 *ch*., a copy of which is still extant in Peking, and compiled collections of the poetry of Wang P'o (648–75) and Lu Chao-lin (*ca.* 641–*ca.* 680), which too are extant. An incomplete copy of his collected literary works, entitled *Ch'ün-yü-lou chi* 羣玉樓集, 84 *ch*., printed 1638 (*chüan* 26–30 and 41 are missing), a microfilm of which is available, is preserved in the National Central Library, Taipei. Among the poems in the collection is one entitled "Hung-i hsing" 紅夷行, which describes the Dutch at the time of their occupation of the Pescadores (1622–24), their arrogance in demanding trade, and the disturbances they caused along the southeast coast. The work by which he is best remembered, however, is a short book entitled *Tung-hsi-yang k'ao*, 12 *ch*. This deals (in *chüan* 1–6), with the history, topography, products, and trade of the lands of southeast Asia, those on the east including the Philippine Islands, the Moluccas, and Brunei (on the north coast of Borneo), those on the west including the countries of Indo-China, the Malay peninsula, Sumatra, Java, and the southwest coast of Borneo, a total of thirty-eight countries; the book in addition discusses China's relations with Japan and the Dutch 紅毛番. The remaining *chüan* (7–12) are devoted to revenue, navigation (with compass directions and distances and rhymed rules for weather prediction), and to a certain eunuch revenue collector Kao Ts'ai (*see* Shen Yu-jung), who exacted tribute from merchants and overrode local officials until his recall to Peking in 1615 in face of popular riots, and impeachments by Chou Ch'i-yüan and others. Finally it includes documents and official communications between the Chinese court and various countries including Japan. He himself never went abroad, gaining his information from a wide range of historical and literary works and from conversations with merchants and sailors at his home town which was then a maritime center. His book has a preface dated 1617 by Hsiao Chi 蕭基, then acting prefectural registrar of Chang-chou, who was instrumental in persuading Wang Ch'i-tsung 王起宗, the assistant prefect (who also contributed the third preface dated 1618), to engage Chang to finish the work started some time earlier under the auspices of T'ao Jung 陶瑢 (cs 1610), former magistrate of Hai-ch'eng 海澄, the port city of Chang-chou. The second preface, undated, was written by Chou Ch'i-yüan. The book was completed in four months, from late autumn to the end of winter, and was immediately printed. His work quite naturally has been laid under contribution by a number of modern scholars such as W. P. Groeneveldt, P. Pelliot, Sei Wada, Joseph Needham, and Wang Yung 王庸; it was included in the *Ssu-k'u* library and reprinted twice in 1936.

He had a number of children but all appear to have died either in their infancy or in their youth. One son, Chang Yü-t'ang 于堂, passed away before reaching the age of twenty, another, Chang Yü-t'an 壇 (T. 升甫, 1601-22), died soon after marriage, and Chang Yü-lei 壘 (T. 凱甫, 1610-27), perhaps the most precocious, lived only long enough to achieve the *hsiu-ts'ai* and show promise as a poet. Their untimely deaths, as well as the loss of his wife, née Liu 劉 (1576-1621), greatly saddened Chang Hsieh. His poems reflect his grief as do the biographies he wrote of his wife and the last named son.

Bibliography

1/97/29b, 99/19b, 255/23b; SK (1930), 71/4a, 149/1b; *Chang-chou-fu chih* (1877), 29/6a, 41/7a, 42/26b, 46/7b, 49/21a; Huang Yü-chi (ECCP), *Ch'ien-ch'ing-t'ang shu-mu*, 7/21a, 25/26a, 31/13b; *Ch'ien-k'un cheng-ch'i chi* 乾坤正氣集 (1848), 518/12a, 521/42a, 522/28b, 523/31b; Sun T'ien-ch'i (1957), 219; Hsüeh Ch'eng-ch'ing 薛澄清, "Ming Chang Hsieh chi ch'i chu-shu k'ao" 及其著述考, *Ling-nan hsüeh-pao* 嶺南學報 4, no. 2 (1935), 28; W. P. Groeneveldt, "Notes on the Malay Archipelago and Malacca Compiled from Chinese Sources," (1880, reprinted Djakarta, 1960); P. Pelliot, *Mémoires sur les coutumes du Cambodge de Tcheou Ta-kouan* (Paris, 1951), 75; Sei Wada, "The Philippine Islands as known to the Chinese before the Ming Dynasty," MTB, 4 (1929), 121; Joseph Needham, *Science and Civilization in China*, III (Cambridge, England, 1965), 470, 512, IV: 3 (1971), 581; W. Franke, *Sources*, 7.7.4.

L. Carrington Goodrich and C. N. Tay

CHANG Hsüan 張萱 (T. 孟 [夢] 奇, H. 九岳, 西園), 1558-1641, scholar and historian, was a native of Po-lo 博羅, Kwangtung. His father Chang Cheng-hsi 張政熙 (T. 道亨, d. probably in the middle or late 1580's) was a *chü-jen* of 1555 who rose to the magistracy of Lu-ch'uan 陸川, Kwangsi. Both Chang Hsüan and his younger brother, Chang Ts'ui 張萃 (T. 仲蔚, d. *ca.* 1601), passed the provincial examinations and obtained the *chü-jen* degree in 1582. It seems that both brothers lived and pursued their studies for a period in Nanking, where they met some of the prominent scholars of the time, such as Wang Shih-chen and Wang Tao-k'un (*qq. v.*). It was either here in Nanking, or later in Peking, that Chang Hsüan met Matteo Ricci (*q.v.*), whom he mentions twice in his collection of study notes, the *I-yüeh* 疑耀. Chang was one of five scholars who later collaborated (1607) in the "checking" of the translation of Euclid's *Geometry* by Ricci and Hsü Kuang-ch'i (ECCP).

After failing repeatedly in the metropolitan examinations he took a secretarial post in the central drafting office of the Grand Secretariat (1598). Four years previously, under the guidance of Ch'en Yü-pi (*q.v.*), a Ming history project was launched in the capital. Although after Ch'en's death in 1597 the project unfortunately was discontinued, no official declaration of its formal termination was ever issued. It seems likely therefore that it was still nominally functioning in 1598, and that Chang Hsüan served with it in the Wen-yüan ko 文淵閣 Imperial Library. He was elated over the opportunity to examine the books and documents not available to the outside world. He made selections from the *shih-lu* and had these passages copied. Later he edited this material, entitling it *Hsi-Sheng chih-hsiao lu* 西省識小錄, 100 *ch.* By 1605 the Imperial Library was apparently put in good order, and a catalogue, the *Nei-ko shu-mu* 內閣書目, 8 *ch.*, completed; it bore Chang Hsüan's name., as well as those of his four coworkers. This catalogue may be found in the first series of the *Shih-yüan* 適園 *ts'ung-shu*, printed in 1913.

Probably it was in reward for his labors that he was appointed (1606) inspector of the Hu-shu customs 滸墅關 in the prefecture of Soochow. He left Peking with fifteen crates of notes and materials, largely on Ming history. As he had to go home to Kwangtung to escort his aged mother to his new post, he stored the crates in Nanking. Before he could return for them, however, to his horror and grief all were lost in a fire. He held the lucrative post at Hu-shu for almost five years until he retired in 1611 and returned to his home in Po-lo.

In retirement Chang Hsüan started anew to collect materials for his private Ming history project. The result was the *Hsi-yüan wen-chien lu* 西園聞見錄, a collection of notes covering the period from Hung-wu through Wan-li (1368–1620). To this work he first wrote a preface in 1627, and then added another in 1632, acknowledging certain contributions from his friends toward its printing, but expressing regret that, due to the lack of funds, the work was only partially printed. The *Hsi-yüan wen-chien lu* remained in manuscript and generally unavailable until 1940, when the Harvard-Yenching Institute printed it from a 106 *chüan* Ming hand-copied edition. These notes consist chiefly of quotations from works by or about an author or a man of action and are arranged under some 260 topics, each topic being divided into two categories, utterances 前言 and deeds 往行. A rough estimate places the number of entries as high as ten thousand, and the names of persons involved may run to as many as a thousand. While some names appear only once, others appear many times under different topics. For example, Ch'iu Chün (*q.v.*) appears in some fifty entries. As a reference work the book is rather clumsy, but it is rich in information and may also lead one to original sources. The Ming Biographical History Project has recently made a card index of the personal names. Another index is said to be under preparation at Kyoto University.

The authorship of the other collection of notes, the *I-yüeh*, is in dispute. According to consensus, however, together with Chang's testimony, the collection clearly shows it to be his and not the work of Li Chih (*q.v.*), as one Ming edition indicates. In 1845 the *I-yüeh* in 7 *chüan* was printed in the second series of *Ling-nan i-shu* 嶺南遺書; this same edition was later included in the *Ts'ung shu chi-ch'eng* in 1939. In the "new preface" to this work, Chang Hsüan narrates that it was in Nanking in 1608, when Chiao Hung (ECCP) and Huang Ju-heng 黃汝亨 (T. 貞公, cs 1598) saw his unfinished manuscript in 27 *chüan*, that they expressed their admiration and arranged for the printing of a 7 *chüan* edition. As years went by he made additional entries, and the number of *chüan* increased to 40. Some twenty years after this, when he was at home in retirement, he first heard of and then saw a 7 *chüan* edition of *I-yüeh* printed under the name of Li Chih. Not only was Li Chih named as the author, but also a preface, allegedly written by Chang Hsüan and in the calligraphy of Wang Chih-teng (*q.v.*), was included. Chang Hsüan was rightly indignant over this, for he was no follower of Li Chih, and was critical of both Buddhism and Taoism. In his opinion it must have been a trick played by Wang Chih-teng, because first, Wang advocated Li's teachings, and second, Wang took offense over Chang Hsüan's refusing to ask him for a preface to the *I-yüeh* at the time of its printing in 1608. No proof exists, however, for Chang's assumption. Probably the notice of the *I-yüeh* in the *Ssu-k'u* catalogue offers a sounder explanation of this dispute; it suggests that since works appearing under Li Chih's name had proved to be popular, some enterprising book dealer may have reprinted the *I-yüeh* in Li's name purely for the sake of gain.

In his retirement Chang Hsüan also prepared a compilation of materials on a general history of China prior to the Ming dynasty, entitled *Hsi-yüan hui-shih* 彙史. In a similar vein he tried to put together a compilation of materials on the Classics, *Hsi-yüan hui-ching* 經, and a compilation of materials for an etymological study, *Hsi-yüan hui-ya* 雅. It seems that the first two were not finished and are probably no longer extant, but the *Hsi-yüan hui-ya*, 20 *ch.*, and *hsü pien*, 28 *ch.*, survived and received unfavorable notice by the editors of the *Ssu-k'u* catalogue. Whether or not his collection of prose, the *Hsi-yüan ku-wen* 古文, 6 *ch.*, has survived has not been ascertained.

Another Kwangtung historian, Yin Shou-heng (*q.v.*), the author of the (*Ming*) *Shih-ch'ieh*, was not only a friend of Chang Hsüan but also received the *chü-jen* in the same year, 1582. Chang Hsüan's encouragement played no small part in bringing the *Shih-ch'ieh* to a successful conclusion. In 1638, on the printing of the *Shih-ch'ieh*, Chang Hsüan wrote a preface to the work of his friend to whom he had given such moral support. In writing this preface Chang took the opportunity to outline his philosophy of history. He held that a history must show evidences and must be factual and that the historian must be cautious and critical. Was he sounding a warning to his contemporaries, most of whom, following the general trend of the times, often wrote too freely, and

often insinuated their personal likes and dislikes?

Chang Hsüan is also known as an accomplished calligrapher and painter. One of his landscapes, known as "Gazing at a waterfall" (dated 1586), is in the National Museum, Stockholm. In 1656 he was commemorated in the shrine of local notables. He was said to have been generous in giving financial help to his clansmen and people of his home district. When at his post in Hu-shu, he also helped in many relief works.

The Combined Indices to Eighty-nine Collections of Ming Dynasty Biographies (Harvard-Yenching Institute Sinological Index Series, No. 24, 1935) has confused two men of the same name. The other Chang Hsüan 張萱 (T. 德暉, H. 頤拙, d. 1527) was a native of Shanghai and a *chin-shih* of 1502.

Bibliography

40/53/33a; 64/ 庚 13/11a; 65/8/4a; 86/15/28b, *Hui-chou-fu chih* 惠州府志 (Kuang-hsü ed.), 27/3b, 34/19a; *Kuang-tung t'ung-chih* (1934), 5011, 5017; TSCC (1885-88), XVII, 787/10a, XXIII, 100/12a; XXIV, 124/30a; SK (1930), 43/1b, 119/2a; Jung Chao-tsu 容肇祖, *I-yüeh k'ao-pien* "疑耀" 考辨, appendix I, in *Li Chih nien-p'u* 李贄年譜 (Peking, 1957), 115; P. M. d'Elia, *Fonti Ricciane*, II (1949), 358n.; O. Sirén, *Chinese Painting*, VII (1958), 154.

Lienche Tu Fang

CHANG Hsüeh-yen 張學顏 (T. 子愚, H. 心齋), d. 1598, minister of Revenue under Chang Chü-cheng (*q.v.*) for four years, and the one most responsible for realizing the latter's fiscal policies, was a native of Fei-hsiang 肥鄉, Pei-Chihli. After qualifying for the *chin-shih* degree in 1553 he served as the magistrate of Ch'ü-wo 曲沃, Shansi; then after several promotions he became assistant administration commissioner of Shansi, and next vice intendant of the military defense circuit of Yung-p'ing 永平 and Chi-chou 薊州 before his appointment in 1571 as governor of Liaotung and right assistant censor-in-chief.

Chang assumed the governorship just at the time that the Ming empire's frontier problem shifted from the north to the northeast. Altan-Qaγan (*q.v.*) had been enfeoffed only months before. The Tümed Mongols were pouring into Liaotung; the Jurchen tribes were also becoming restless. Their leaders, with Altan-Qaγan's example in mind, believed that by carrying out warlike acts they could wrest concessions from the imperial government. The territory of Liaotung was fortunate in having a capable army commander in Li Ch'eng-liang (ECCP), but its defenses were far from satisfactory. Following the famine of 1558 the government had not been able adequately to support the garrison forces. Desertion had greatly thinned the army ranks. Even after the strengthening of the garrisons by Chang's predecessors, the entire terrritorial command as of 1571 consisted probably of no more than thirty-five thousand men, or about one half of its prescribed strength. Upon his arrival Chang at first concentrated on the rehabilitation of the army. He filled its vacancies by recruiting, renewed its equipment, repaired old fortresses, a nd constructed new ones. Six years later, when he relinquished the governor's post, the territory boasted more than eighty thousand men at arms.

In dealing with the tribesmen Chang was both firm and flexible. He pointed out that the Jurchen were genuinely suffering from population pressure and many of them had already turned from hunting, fishing, and herding to a more settled life. These facts, he averred, must be given due consideration. At one time he petitioned Peking to allow him to hand out thirty thousand taels of silver as subsidies to several tribes. Trade between the cattle-raising folk and the Chinese, during Chang's administration, was in general liberalized, though the trading posts were under vigilant surveillance. When all these measures failed to bring about the cooperation of the non-Chinese groups, Chang did not hesitate to use force: he wanted

them to realize that lawlessness did not pay. In carrying out these policies he maintained close contact with Chang Chü-cheng and the latter's associate, Chang Ssu-wei (*q.v.*). The campaign against Wang Kao 王杲 (d. 1575) in 1574, for instance, was launched only after lengthy discussion by correspondence between the governor and the grand secretary. Chang Hsüeh-yen always carried out Chang Chü-cheng's orders faithfully; the latter, in turn, repeatedly rewarded him and promoted him in the name of the boy emperor Chu I-chün (*q.v.*).

In November, 1577, Chang Hsüeh-yen was called to Peking to become left vice minister of War in charge of the garrison troops around the capital. Two months later (January 6, 1578), he was given the title of right censor-in-chief. On August 4 he became minister of Revenue.

As the nation's chief fiscal administrator, Chang became known for his persistent efforts to revise the existing tax structure. On July 10, 1579, he initiated the program of investigating the landholdings of imperial clansmen and saw to the return to the imperial government of the income from their estates which exceeded the original grants or authorizations. On December 16, 1580, an edict issued in the name of the emperor authorized a nationwide land survey. (The above date is based on the *shih-lu*; other sources put the authorization as early as 1577.) Each local magistrate was responsible for conducting the survey in his territory. The purpose of the land reregistration was not to increase tax revenue, but to curb tax evasion and by this means to equalize the tax burden on the population. With few exceptions, the lump-sum tax quotas charged to the various districts and prefectures remained unchanged after the survey; only individual taxpayers were made to pay the prevailing rates according to their actual landholdings, these rates varying from one hsien to another. The result of the program apparently fell short of its goal, as it involved too many technical difficulties that could not all be resolved. Also too little time was allowed for so ambitious a program. While some provincial officials made a conscientious effort to carry out the court order, others acted only perfunctorily. Nevertheless by mid-1582, when the survey returns began to arrive in Peking, many territorial units reported substantial increases in their taxable acreages, Kweichow's increase being close to eighty percent, Shantung's nearly fifty percent. (Previously the latter province used a different yardstick in land assessment, its reported acreage being much smaller than the actual one.) The complete result of the survey, however, does not seem to be extant.

About the same time that the national land survey was in progress, Chang Hsüeh-yen proceeded to audit the tax income which fell into the category of ch'ai-i 差役 (service levy). The major items included in the category were palace supplies, military requirements such as bows and arrows, corvée labor, postal and militia services, and office expenses from the level of the district government to that of the provincial. Until the 15th century, the supplies had as a rule been requisitioned from the local communities and the services performed by the male adults registered in the Yellow Book. By the latter part of the 16th century silver payments instead of actual supplies and services were generally required of the local governments; but the accounts were administered by local officials, the central government not intervening. When Chang was in office, the ministry of Revenue not only reviewed these accounts, but also, in the name of the emperor, on many occasions directed that the various items be reduced, sometimes by as much as ten percent. Many of the annual accounts, after the ministerial review, were later published in book form. Called the *Fu-i ch'üan-shu* 賦役全書 (Comprehensive book on taxation and service levy [of a province or a prefecture]), the first appeared either in 1582 on 1583.

The most complete record of fiscal administration left by Chang was the *Wan-li k'uai-chi lu* 萬曆會計錄, 43 *ch*. The work contains the total taxable acreage of each prefecture, the annual land-tax quota, the income and expenditure of every frontier post, the receivables of the service agencies, stipends of imperial clansmen, and assorted data on the salt gabelle, the inland custom duty, land reclamation, etc. The project of compiling these data was initiated by a previous minister of Revenue, Wang Kuo-kuang 王國光 (T. 汝觀, H. 疎菴, cs 1544, minister of Revenue 1572-76). When Wang left office, a rough draft was already on hand. Chang Hsüeh-yen followed the outline and extended the scope much further. The numerical figures were checked in many sources. The historical background of each fiscal institution was added, sometimes including extracts from original documents. Under Chang's direction, fourteen staff members worked on the project for two years until the final draft was presented to the emperor on May 22, 1581. Three junior members who participated in the work, Ku Hsien-ch'eng, Li San-ts'ai, and Chao Nan-hsing (*qq.v.*), eventually rose to prominence early in the 17th century.

The cultivated land data in the *K'uai-chi lu*, however, are dated as of 1578; they therefore did not incorporate the returns of the national land survey. The units and measurements cited in the work are not always consistent. The receivables in silver, copper cash, government notes, and commodities of all kinds are not converted into a common standard and consolidated. Yet, despite all these weaknesses, the work is the most comprehensive and methodical of its kind throughout the Ming period. Its contents were later either reproduced or summarized in the Wan-li edition of the *Ta-Ming hui-tien* (*see* Shen Shih-hsing). In 1618, when the Ming court was forced to increase land taxes to deal with the Liaotung crisis, the land data from this book were used as the basis for apportioning the increase. (Microfilm copies of it are available at the libraries of Columbia University and the University of Chicago.)

Chang's critics charged him with being compliant in his relations with the emperor. They pointed out that, while as the minister of Revenue he was tightening governmental expenses, he had in 1578 permitted the emperor to enlarge his privy annual expense account by two hundred thousand taels of silver. But the evidence shows that the increase was ordered by the emperor during Chang Chü-cheng's leave of absence and two months before Chang Hsüeh-yen's appointment to his portfolio. Later Chang Hsüeh-yen did argue against the increase but without success. Nevertheless the criticism that Chang was overly submissive toward his superiors was not completely groundless. When Chang Chü-cheng was disposed to punish Liu T'ai because of a personal grudge (see Wang Tsung-tsai), Chang Hsüeh-yen also accused Liu of corruption. The charges on very slim evidence were based on something Liu had done about four years previously.

Chang Chü-cheng's death inevitably weakened Chang Hsüeh-yen's position. He remained as minister of Revenue, however, for almost another year until his transfer to be minister of War on May 21, 1583. Continually favored by Emperor Chu I-chün, he survived many impeachment actions against him. The emperor repeatedly banished his critics and gave him support. But the situation was too uncomfortable for him to linger on, and his resignation was finally accepted on April 18, 1585. His death was acknowledged by the emperor on September 28, 1598.

Chang's tombstone inscription cites four works which he either wrote or edited. Aside from the *Wan-li k'uai-chi lu*, the collection of his memorials, entitled *Chang Hsin-chai tsou-i* 張心齋奏議, seems to have disappeared. But ten memorials rom the collection have survived and are included in the current edition of the *Ming ching-shih wen-pien*. There is no evidence that the other two works, *Ching-shih pu-i* 經史補遺 and *Chang-shih chia-hsün* 張氏家

訓, are extant.

Bibliography

1/213/22a, 222/22b, 229/4b; MSL (1940), Shen-tsung, 3/23a, 41/2a, 7b, 51/20b, 69/11a, 77/1b, 78/2a, 85/11a, 106/2b, 6b, 111/10b, 123/9b, 143/9a, 157/4a, 159/6a, 325/9b; TSCC (1885–88), XI: 582/13b; *Chi-fu t'ung-chih* (1934), 6399, 7875; Chang Chü-cheng, *Chang-t'ai-yüeh wen-chi* (1612), 28/17a, 25b, 29/12b, 30/2a; Chu Tung-jun, *Chang Chü-cheng ta-chüan* (Shanghai, 1945), 216, 224, 239, 249; Chang Ssu-wei, *T'iao-lu-t'ang chi* (NLP microfilm roll no. 1048), 4/12a; *Ming ching-shih wen-pien* (1964), 3906.

Ray Huang

CHANG Huang 章潢 (T. 本清, H. 斗津), 1527–1608, an industrious scholar and devoted teacher who in 1592 became president of the Pai-lu-tung shu-yüan 白鹿洞書院 (White Deer Grotto Academy), was born in Nanchang, Kiangsi, and lived there most of his life teaching and writing. He built the Tz'u-hsi t'ang 此洗堂 (Purification hall) in 1567 on the bank of Tung-hu 東湖 (East Lake) where his students assembled to "encourage one another in moral behavior," and where he published a number of monographs on the Five Classics and the Four Books. He also compiled between the years 1562 and 1577 (with certain modifications later) an encyclopedic work in 127 *chüan* entitled *T'u-shu pien* 圖書編.

This compilation remained in manuscript for over three decades as the cost of engraving its seven thousand leaves was difficult to meet. Its publication was finally undertaken by a fellow townsman and disciple, Wan Shang-lieh 萬尚烈 (T. 思文, H. 恒 [or 衡] 麓, d. ca. 1640, aged 95 *sui*), who financed it with his own salary when he held the post of vice prefect of Shao-wu 邵武, Fukien (ca. 1606–ca. 1611). In 1613, while serving as a secretary in the ministry of Justice, Wan wrote a foreword reporting the completion of the engraving of the blocks with the financial assistance of two men, one contributing ten taels and the other fifty. In the foreword Wan also solicited the contribution of a preface, which was written in 1623 by Yüeh Yüan-sheng 岳元聲 (T. 之初, H. 石帆, 潛初子, 1557-1628, cs 1583), vice minister of War in Nanking. By this time the book had already been circulating for a decade.

Basing himself heavily upon two hundred thirteen earlier publications, Chang deals with the interpretation of the canon (*chüan* 1-15), the constitution of the universe, the movements of heavenly bodies, and calendrical calculations (*chüan* 16-28), historical and physical geography—touching on countries stretching from the Liu-ch'iu (Ryukyu) to Arabia and from Mongolia to Ceylon—and frontier defense both on the coast and on the northern border (*chüan* 29-67), the life of man—his moral and physical self, including possible cures for certain ills, and his political, social, and religious institutions (*chüan* 68-125). Most of these 125 *chüan* contain illustrative matter. *Chüan* 126 and 127, which seem to be appendices, contain a kind of concordance to the Book of Changes and the Book of Odes. In a number of places in his section on geography, Chang alludes to Matteo Ricci (*q. v.*), whom he met in Nanchang in 1595, and was the first of his people to include a representation of the Jesuit's *mappa mundi* of 1584. This is of some consequence as no copy of the original edition has survived. It shows the Northwest Passage extending across the continent of North America which Ricci eliminated from the maps of 1602 and later. Besides this he included, together with a description of a spherical world, two other world maps entitled Yü-ti t'u 輿地圖 *A* and *B*, which are both zenithal projections centered on the north and south poles, divided into 360 degrees of longitude. These two maps appear in the top and bottom left-hand corners of Ricci's map of 1602, and presumably were features of his original map of 1584. Rather inconsistently the Northwest Passage in Map *A* is shown as running from the St. Lawrence River through the Hudson Bay; also the North and South

American continents are depicted as separate entities rather than connected with an isthmus, as in the World Map. Another entry worth signaling is the author's resumé of information on human anatomy gleaned in the 12th century (1106). Possibly due to Chang's discussion of frontier affairs in *chüan* 43 and 44, a suggestion that the book be banned was forwarded to the throne in the 1780s; this apparently did not receive the court's approval for it was incorporated in the *Ssu-k'u* library, the editors considering it better documented than the *San-ts'ai t'u-hui* of Wang Ch'i (*q. v.*). The latter work, however, is of a much wider scope.

Some notion of Chang's thoroughness may be seen in an anecdote about his writing of the monograph on the Book of Changes, *Chou-i hsiang-i* 周易象義, 10 ch. It was his practice to paste a hexagram on the wall and its inscriptions beside it, then gaze at them and ponder their meaning for several days and nights before changing to another hexagram. This he started at the age of thirty-two and did not conclude until he was forty-seven. Only then was he content with his comprehension of this puzzling Classic. In contrast to some of his contemporaries he seems to have taken a more orthodox stand on the philosophical and ethical issues of his day.

At the age of seventy-nine *sui* (1605) the court summoned Chang to the post of prefectural assistant instructor at the capital. He did not proceed, but received his remuneration nonetheless. After his death his friends and students privately conferred on him the posthumous name Wen-te 文德 and his memory was preserved in the prefectural shrine for Nanchang's men of note. He came to be known as one of the four chün-tzu 君子 of Kiangsi, the others being Wu Yü-pi, Teng Yüan-hsi (*qq. v.*). and Liu Yüan-ch'ing 劉元卿 (T. 調父, 1544-1609, cj 1570).

Bibliography

1/283/29b; 3/265/18a; 83/24/13b; SK (1930), 8/4b,

136/3b; Chang Huang, *T'u-shu pien*, 29/33b, 43, 50, 68/33b, appendices; *Nan-ch'ang-fu chih* (1873), 43/19a, 22b; *Hsin-chien* 新建 *-hsien chih* (1871), 47/16b; *Pai-lu shu-yüan chih*, 5/4a; Sun Tien-ch'i (1957), 200; L. of C. *Catalogue of Rare Books*, 716; P. M. d'Elia, *Fonti Ricciane*, I (Rome, 1942), 371, n. 5; *id.*, *Il mappamondo cinese del P. Matteo Ricci, S. I.* (3d ed., Pechino, 1602, Citta del Vaticano, 1938), Tavola I.; A. W. Hummel, *Report of the Librarian of Congress* (1935), 188.

L. Carrington Goodrich and C. N. Tay

CHANG Hung 張洪 (T. 宗海, H. 止菴), February 14, 1364-December 14, 1447, official and author, who served as envoy to Japan and Burma, was a native of Ch'ang-shu 常熟 in the prefecture of Soochow. Chang Hung was born into the family of a tradesman by the name of Hou 侯. His mother having died only five days after his birth and his father having been away on business in Peking, he was adopted by a neighbor, a certain Chang Chiung 炯; hence he bore the surname Chang. A precocious child, Chang entered the district school at the age of ten but abandoned schooling five years later to go into business in order to support his foster parents. In 1385 Chang Hung, in mourning for his father, received a visitor, a convicted offender; this being a violation of the law, he was banished to Yunnan. Before long, a local military commander by the name of Ch'ü 瞿, impressed by his learning, employed him as the family tutor. Through the commander's recommendation, Chang Hung gained the recognition of Mu Ch'un, second prince of Ch'ien-ning (*see* Mu Ying), then overlord of Yunnan.

In October, 1397, an uprising occurred in Lu-ch'uan 麓川 in what is now the upper Shweli valley of northern Burma. A band of tribesmen from Mu-pang 木邦 (Mongkawng), led by Tao-kan-meng 刀干孟, rebelled, and defeated the ruling chieftain Ssu-lun-fa (*see* Ssu-jen-fa), who subsequently fled to Kunming. When the news reached Yunnan, Chang is said to have urged the authorities to take im-

mediate action. Chang reportedly pointed out to Mu Ch'un that, since Ssu-lun-fa had been causing trouble, they should take advantage of this to intervene and break up his domain into separate protectorates to undermine his authority. In June of the following year, after failing to force Tao-kan-meng to surrender, the court charged Mu Ch'un with the suppression of the rebels. Mu died unexpectedly during the expedition, but his deputy carried on, and before long succeeded in crushing the rebellion and capturing the ringleader. Ssu-lun-fa then returned to Lu-ch'uan under Chinese protection, having lost control of both Mu-pang and Meng-yang 孟養, an adjacent tribal settlement, which became protectorates directly under the Chinese, as Chang Hung had proposed. In 1399, through the recommendation of the local authorities, Chang Hung obtained an appointment as instructor in the Classics in the princely fief of Ching-chiang 靖江, but failed to assume the charge because of illness.

Following the enthronement of Chu Ti (*q.v.*), Chang Hung was appointed a messenger and received a summons (August, 1403) to join a mission to Japan headed by a transmission commissioner, Chao Chü-jen 趙居任 (d. March, 1419), and by the monk Tao-ch'eng 道成 (T. 鷟峯, H. 雪軒, 1352-1432), a deputy patriarch in the central Buddhist registry. The emperor apparently had two purposes in mind in dispatching the embassy: to make the Japanese cease their piratical depredations on the China coast, and to bring them back to the regular tributary system. The departure of the embassy, however, was delayed until December in order to escort the return of a Japanese mission which had come to congratulate Chu Ti on his accession to the throne and to submit tribute gifts. The Chinese envoys, being greeted in person upon arrival by the Ashikaga shōgun, Yoshimitsu (1358-1408) entered Kyoto in June, 1404. They presented to Yoshimitsu the imperial rescript and a seal designating him as "king of

Japan"; and concluded a commercial agreement with the shōgun. This set forth the provisions of the "tally system" (k'an-ho 勘合 or kangō), which enabled the Japanese to send trading missions to China in the form of tribute-bearing embassies once in every ten years, with each mission limited to two ships and two hundred persons. This accomplished, they departed a month later and arrived home late that year. Following this, Chang Hung received an assignment to proceed to Turfan to inspect the trade in Chinese tea for central Asian horses. Early in 1406 the court sent him to Liaotung to offer sacrifice to the deceased tribesmen who had lately submitted to the Chinese. A month after Chang's return (August 26), he was charged with a mission to Mien-tien 緬甸 (Ava-Burma) to persuade its chieftain Na-lo-t'a 那羅塔 to return the territory of Meng-yang and the hostages whom he had seized during a raid; Na-lo-t'a had also killed the pacification commissioner Tao-mu-tan 刀木旦 and his son. Before his departure, Chang took time to compile an historical account of the envoys sent to foreign lands from antiquity down to his own time, taking note of their character, intelligence, courage, speech, diplomatic skills, and other accomplishments. This collection, known as Shih-kuei 使規 (Instructions for envoys), grouped under sixteen categories, became a useful guidebook for envoys on missions to countries abroad in later times.

According to his reminiscences, Chang Hung arrived in the capital of Mien-tien in October with a party of seventy persons. Before this he had learned that many previous envoys, frightened by the tropical climate and the death rate among visitors, easily succumbed to the demands of the local ruler in return for a quick, safe passage home. He also heard that the native chieftain put poison in the meat served to guests and used women to distract the envoys from performing their duties. Accordingly he proceeded with great caution. Upon his arrival, he insisted

that the native chieftain honor him with Chinese rites and ceremonies, that the natives stay away from their procession as it passed through, and that the chieftain greet him in the manner of a subordinate. Na-lo-t'a acceded to all his demands. During the meeting Chang Hung upbraided Na-lo-t'a for his invasion of Meng-yang and commanded him to return the land to its lawful owner, or he would be liable to punishment. Na-lo-t'a, however, demurred. Chang is said to have composed six consecutive letters to convince him to come to an agreement. Na-lo-t'a finally gave in; whereupon Chang Hung took his departure. During his stay in Mien-tien, Chang admonished his men to abstain from rare meat, stay away from women, and keep their living quarters clean. Thus, when they returned to Yunnan, only one member of his mission took ill. Even the Burmese considered this to be a miracle. Shortly after his return, Chang Hung composed an account of his mission entitled Shih Mien lu 使緬錄, which, together with the six letters he sent to the Burmese chief, were included as appendices to his previous work, Shih-kuei. In May of the following year, making good his promise, Na-lo-t'a dispatched a special embassy to Peking to convey his apologies and submit tribute gifts. The emperor then decreed that Mien-tien be allowed to send envoys to China to pay tribute once every three years.

Not long afterwards, Chang Hung was recommended to the Wen-yüan 文淵 Hall to take part in editing the imperially sponsored compilation later known as Yung-lo ta-tien (see Yao Kuang-hsiao). This accomplished, he assumed temporary charge of a relief agency in Nanking (1412), and then served as vice director of the messenger office to the end of the reign of Chu Ti. In April, 1424, he received an appointment to be a compiler of the Hanlin Academy, where he officiated for the next five years and participated in the compilation of the veritable records of both Chu Ti and Chu Kao-chih (q.v.), completed in February, 1430. Three years later he obtained permission to retire. As a tribute to his service, Cheng K'o-hsiu 鄭克修, a skillful painter from Ch'ing-chiang 清江, Kiangsi, presented him a long scroll called "Tai-lou t'u" 待漏圖, signifying his service at court. Chang then composed an account of his career in two thousand words, and copied eight of the colophons to his commentaries on the Classical canon to serve as an appendix, which also contained a postscript by his fellow townsman Wu No (*q.v.*). The scroll does not seem to have survived, but the autobiographical account is preserved in Chang's collected works. This essay, together with the tomb-inscription composed by another fellow townsman Ch'ü Ju-chi (*see* Kao P'an-lung) in 1598, provides the basic sources for Chang Hung's biography. During his retirement Chang Hung devoted himself to scholarly activities. He compiled a gazetteer of his native place called *Ch'in-ch'uan hsin-chih* 琴川新志 (Ch'in-ch'uan being the ancient name of Ch'ang-shu), which is no longer extant. The local officials on various occasions invited him to compose commemorative essays for the locality, for which they gave him handsome honoraria—one source says they paid him up to 500 strings of cash per essay. He died late in 1447, at the advanced age of eighty-three. In 1486, together with Wu No, his tablet was housed in the shrine honoring Confucius' disciple Yen-tzu-yu 言子游 in Ch'ang-shu. Three years later (1489), the local magitrate erected a separate shrine in his memory.

A learned scholar and prolific writer, Chang Hung was the author of numerous works on subjects ranging from commentaries on the major Classics to reminiscences of his visits to foreign lands. Few of his works in the first category, with the exception of a treatise on the Four Books, entitled *Ssu-shu chieh-i* 四書解義, seem to have survived. A 2 *chüan* fragment of this work (out of an original 20 *ch.*), containing the section on Mencius, is preserved in the former National Library of Peiping and is available on microfilm (no. 230).

Many of his writings on other countries are extant. The most imprtant of these is *Shih Mien lu*, first quoted in the *Huang Ming yung-hua lei-pien hsü-pien* 皇明泳化類編續編 by Teng Ch'iu 鄧球 (cs 1535) and later in several gazetteers of Yunnan. This work also exists in manuscript either as an appendix to the *Shih-kuei* or as an independent essay in his collected works. It was later included in the *Ti-hsiang-chai* 棣香齋 *ts'ung-shu* (subtitle: *Lou-tung tsa-chu* 婁東雜著), edited by Shao T'ing-lieh 邵廷烈 in 1833. The French scholar Edouard Huber published a translation in 1904 on the basis of this edition, but he mistakenly identified the author with a contemporary of the same name Chang Hung (T. 敬軒. cs 1445), a censor who perished in the battle of T'u-mu in 1449. Our Chang Hung was, moreover, the author of *Nan-i chi* 南夷記, 1 *ch.*, a narrative about the aboriginal tribesmen on the China-Burma border based on personal observation. A manuscript copy of this work, listed as rare, is included in a collection known as *Ming-jen chi shih ch'i chung* 明人記事七種 preserved in the National Central Library, Taipei.

Chang Hung's collected literary works appear in two different versions, both of which survive in manuscript of the Ch'ing period. The first, entitled *Kuei-t'ien kao* 歸田稿, 3 *ch.*, with 1 *ch.* appendix, is available in the Toyo Bunko, Tokyo. The other, known as *Chang hsiu chuan i-chi* 修撰遺集, 4 *ch.* and 8 *ch.* respectively, with the same appendix, is preserved in the Peking Library. The latter is an enlarged version compiled and edited by scholars of a much later date. This collection contains a number of essays on the granaries, relief centers, and similar communal facilities in Ch'ang-shu; they are important additions to the source materials on the financial administration of this locality under the governorship of Chou Ch'en 周忱 (T. 恂如, H. 雙崖, 1381-1453, cs 1404, Pth. 文襄) and K'uang Chung (*q.v.*).

Bibliography

1/96/2b, 99/23b, 315/2b, 322/4b; 5/21/23a; 40/17/

30a; 84/2/16b; 86/6/16a; MSL (1963), T'ai-tsung, 410, 838, 925, Jen-tsung, 247, Hsüan-tsung, 1456; (*Chia-ching*) *Ch'ang-shu-hsien chih* (1539, 1965 repr.), 8/30b, 13/21a; *Ch'ang-Ch'ao ho-chih kao* 常昭合志稿 (1904), 14/11a, 15/42a, 24/9a, 43/12b, 45/14a; *Yunnan t'ung-chih* (1736), 241/25a; *Teng-Yüeh-chou chih* 騰越州志 (1838, 1931 repr.), 8/18a; SK 1930), 78/4a, 131/4a; Yang Jung, *Yang Wen-min kung chi* (NCL microfilm), 9/16a; Ch'ü Ju-ch'i, *Ch'ü Ch'iung-ch'ing chi* 冏卿集 (NCL microfilm), 11/43a; Feng Fu-ching 馮復京 (1578-1622), *Kuo-ch'ao* 國朝 *Ch'ang-shu hsien-hsien shih-lüeh* 先賢事略 (NCL microfilm), 1/1a; Teng Ch'iu, *Huang Ming yung-hua lei-pien hsü-pien* (1967 ed.), 14/1a; Wang Pao-jen 王寶仁, *Lou-shui wen-cheng* 婁水文徵 (1832), 9/12a; Huang T'ing-chien 黃廷鑑, *Ch'in-ch'uan san-chih pu-chi* 三志補記 (1898), 8/9b; Tōyō Bunko *Catalogue*, 105; NCL *Catalogue* (1967), 189, 382; Kanda Nobuo 神田信夫, "Chō Kō no Shi Men-rokū ni tsuite" 張洪の使緬錄について, *Iwai hakushi koki kinen rombonshū* 岩井博士古稀紀念論文集 (1963), 192; E. Huber, "Une ambassade Chinoise en Birmanie en 1406," BEFEO, vol. IV (1904), 429; Wang Yi-t'ung, *Official Relations between China and Japan* (1953), 24.

Hok-lam Chan

CHANG Hung 張宏 (T. 君度, H. 鶴澗), 1577-1668+, was an artist from Wu 吳-hsien (Soochow) who painted mainly landscapes, sometimes figures, and occasionally water buffaloes. Nothing is known of Chang's life except the little that can be garnered from his inscriptions on his own paintings. He like many other artists, made excursions, often with friends, to famous sites and then produced paintings depicting the scenes. Judging from the inscriptions both extant and recorded, Chang's travels were largely confined to the area between Soochow and Nanking. He visited Mt. Shih-hsieh in 1613 as shown by his "Shih-hsieh-shan t'u" 石屑山圖, in the National Palace Museum, Taipei. In 1618 he was at the Peach-leaf Ford 桃葉渡 located at the confluence of the Ch'in-huai 秦淮 and Ch'ing 青 Rivers, near Nanking; in 1634 he went to Mt. Ch'i-hsia, a mountain noted for its rock-cut Buddhist shrines and its difficult ascent. "Ch'i-hsia-shan 棲霞山 t'u" is a result of this trip and is in the same museum. In 1638 he

was in Ch'ang-chou 常州, and in 1650 journeyed to Mt. Chü-ch'ü 句曲, famous for its grottoes and Taoist associations, and painted the "Chü-ch'ü sung-feng 松風 t'u" (The wind in the pines of Mt. Chü-ch'ü), now in the Boston Museum of Fine Arts. Chang embarked on an extended tour through eastern Chekiang in the spring of 1639 and, upon his return in the autumn of the same year, produced an album of eight leaves entitled "Yüeh-chung ming-sheng" 越中名勝 (Famous scenes of Yüeh), depicting some of the scenery he had observed on his trip. At the end of his inscription on the last leaf of this album, he made the following significant comment, "Hearing about these places is not as good as seeing them."

Among his other artistic accomplishments are paintings on fans presented to friends and acquaintances, as well as paintings of Soochow gardens, local scenic spots (the nearby hills and lakes), and snowscapes. (For an example of the latter, *see Ku-kung* 故宮, no. 13.) In 1641 he collaborated with the portrait artist Shu Ku-ch'ing 舒固卿 in making a likeness of the literatus, Wang Hsin-i 王心一 (T. 純甫, H. 元珠, 1572-1645, cs 1613), for which Chang contributed the landscape setting.

Interestingly, for a period of four years, from 1644 until 1648, there is not a single painting by Chang Hung recorded or extant. Perhaps the Manchu take-over of China affected his artistic career. In any case he was painting again in 1648, but after 1652, when he was seventy-five years of age, he was forced to cease his artistic pursuits. It is said that students of painting looked up to Chang for some eighty years. This, plus the fact that his travels often took him to the Nanking area, helps explain his contact with the artist Tsou Che 鄒喆 (T. 方魯, 1636-1708?), a native of Soochow who lived in Nanking and who in the winter (tenth month) of 1668 dedicated a landscape painting to Chang when the latter was ninety-one years of age. From Chang's extant paintings, and from records of his other paintings, it is clear that he not only interpreted the styles of Yüan dynasty artists, but he also painted studies after both Northern and Southern Sung artists. He further executed paintings after such Ming dynasty masters as Shen Chou and Lu Chih (*qq.v.*). One of these by Chang is the "Fang Lu Chih ch'a-hua shui-hsien 仿陸治茶花水仙 t'u" (Camellia and narcissus after Lu Chih), now in the National Palace Museum. Besides those landscapes done after old masters, Chang's landscape technique is partially based upon the late Wu school style of Wen Cheng-ming(*q.v.*) and his associates. Beyond this, one major characteristic of Chang's art is a sense of a realistic scene conveyed through descriptive details and color. Chang sometimes uses extremely tall and narrow formats; for example, the painting of Mt. Ch'i-hsia measures one hundred thirty-five inches in height and forty inches in width. In this painting, the complex composition occupies nearly the entire space; the impressively rugged terrain is replete with an incredible amount of realistic detail: pavilions, stone walls, pagodas, halls, rock-cut shrines, paths, figures; multitudes of pines, other trees, and vegetation fill the steep ravine and cling to the cliff-tops. In the painting of Mt. Chü-ch'ü, the artist uses a minimum of ink strokes and instead constructs the major mountain forms by means of extensive areas of muted buff and green tones, in places covered with patches of grey wash. Sometimes the colors merge imperceptibly with each other, sometimes they dissolve into mists or outline winding paths. The colored mountain slopes and the inclusion of pertinent descriptive details suggest the reality of a scene more spacious and airy, if somewhat more barren, than that of Mt. Ch'i-hsia.

Chang's particular sensitivity to color in nature and the translation of it into painting through the use of extensive areas of color wash enabled him to produce the extremely evocative and softly poetic, moonlight-suffused landscape hand-scroll, "Hua-tzu kang yeh-yu 華子岡夜遊 t'u," which depicts the evening wanderings of the T'ang dynasty poet, Wang Wei (701–61), in the Hua-tzu hills. This hand scroll is now in the National Palace Museum. Very few of Chang's figure paintings have survived. What is perhaps the earliest one extant (undated, but bearing a colophon by Wang Chih-teng [*q.v.*]), is the hanging scroll in the National Palace Museum, entitled "Pu-tai lo-han 布袋羅漢 t'u" (Arhat Pu-tai, d. *ca.* 917), executed in broad strokes of fluid monochrome ink wash. Totally different in style is an album of figure studies, some with landscape backgrounds, painted in 1649 and now in a private collection. With neat, if sometimes mannered, ink outlines and light color washes, he realistically portrays the characteristic poses and gestures of such diverse subjects as fishermen and their families, woodcutters burdened with loads of kindling, gentlemen with servants in their gardens and studios, or school children at their classroom lessons. An example of Chang's depiction of water buffaloes and herdboys is reproduced by Sirén.

Bibliography

Chang Keng 張庚, *Kuo-ch'ao hua-cheng lu* 國朝畫徵錄 (*Hua-shih* 畫史 *ts'ung-shu* ed.), 1/6; Chiang Shao-shu 姜紹書, *Wu-sheng shih-shih* 無聲詩史, (*ibid.*), 4/76; Lan Ying 藍瑛 and Hsieh Pin 謝彬, *T'u-hui pao-chien hsü-tsuan* 圖繪寶鑑續纂 (*ibid.*), 2/15; Ch'in Tsu-yung 秦祖永, *T'ung-yin lun-hua* 桐陰論畫 (1918), 上, 8a; Hsü Pang-ta, *Li-tai···shu-hua···nien-piao* (Shanghai, 1963), 111; Kuan Mien-chün 關晃鈞, *San-ch'iu-ko shu-hua lu*, 三秋閣書畫錄 (1928), 上, 80b; Li Tso-hsien 李佐賢, *Shu-hua chien-ying* 書畫鑑影, 22/21b; KKSHC, nos. 9, 13, 24, 27, 40; Kuo Wei-ch'ü 郭味蕖, *Sung Yüan Ming Ch'ing shu-hua-chia nien-piao* 宋元明清書畫家年表 (Peking, 1962); 0. Sirén, *Chinese Painting: Leading Masters and Principles* (New York, 1956-58), Vol. V: 30, *VI:* pl.281, 283, 360, VII: 154; E. J. Laing, *Chinese Paintings in Chinese Publications, 1956-1968* (Ann Arbor, 1969), 151; John C. Ferguson, *Index of Artists* (Nanking, 1934), 264b; Kokka, no. 819; *The Famous Chinese Painting and Calligraphy of Tsin, T'ang, Five Dynasties, Sung, Yüan, Ming, and Ch'ing Dynasties*(1943), pl. 238; *Shina nanga taisei* 支那南畫大成, Vol. XI

(Tokyo, 1935-37), pls. 79-86; *T'ien-chin-shih i-shu po-wu-kuan ts'ang-hua hsü chi* 天津市藝術博物館藏畫續集 (Peking, 1963), pl. 70; K. Tomita and Hsien-chi Tseng, *Portfolio of Chinese Paintings in the Museum, Yüan to Ch'ing Periods* (Boston, 1961), pl. 83.

E. J. Laing

CHANG I 章溢 (T. 三益, H. 匡山居士), *ca.* 1314-July 2, 1369, a native of Lung-ch'üan 龍泉, Chekiang, supported Yüan authority from 1352 to 1359 in fighting the rebels, but after a brief period of retirement gave his allegiance to Chu Yüan-chang whom he served during the next decade. His civil and military skills and the confidence he enjoyed among the people of his region made him valuable to both regimes. He is primarily known from a long and affectionate biography written by his friend and official colleague, Sung Lien (*q. v.*). He came from a substantial family. His ancestors had lived in the same district for sixteen generations before Chang I's birth and his eighth-generation ancestor had been a *chin-shih*. In his youth Chang I is said to have been earnest and showed qualities of leadership. He once chided his older brothers for having allowed themselves to be taken advantage of while doing their corvée service; later, as a young clerk in the magistrate's office, he gained stature in the community by his ability "to find the correct principle and set matters straight." Although respected as a scholar he appears to have left no writing.

Early in life Chang I became an accomplished and well-connected scholar in the tradition of Sung learning. Before he reached his majority he studied under the retired Yüan official, Wang I 王毅 (T. 剛叔, 1303-54). His conversation on the subject of exemplary men in history was, according to Sung Lien, a delight to his hearers. He gave his scholarship a practical turn, carefully basing his decisions upon principle. As a writer, he was impatient with stylistic mannerisms and addressed himself to significant issues.

Chang in due course left Wang I for the nearby city of Chin-hua 金華, to which he had been drawn by its reputation as a center of learning. Here he obtained an interview with a Yüan official and won a place in his entourage. He then set out for Shensi, where his new patron had been appointed to another post, when a sudden premonition turned him back. On his return home he found that his father had fallen ill. After his father's death and before he could be buried bandits made a sudden attack and put the village to the torch. Chang was unable to check the flames before they consumed his father's coffin. Following this macabre incident he built a new home not far away in Lung-yüan 龍淵 and persuaded his long separated older brothers to live with him and help care for their mother.

During the years 1348-60, Yüan officials in Chekiang tried to maintain their authority against increasingly hopeless odds. Most of the seacoast had passed under the control of the personal regime of Fang Kuo-chen (*q. v.*). In the interior, the wooded hillsides afforded cover to indigenous rebel forces that struck without warning at towns and villages in the narrow valleys. At the same time the region was subject to invasion by rebel armies from the west, north, and south. Defense was made more difficult by the fact that most of the cities had been stripped of their defensive walls by the Yüan, and troops of the main regular army unit in the province, the Yen-hai 沿海 myriarch, had to be moved north to meet even greater threats by Chu Yüan-chang and Chang Shih-ch'eng (*q. v.*). The local officials, therefore, had at their disposal only those local militia they were able to recruit and train themselves.

The disorders in Chang I's own neighborhood were but a local manifestation of the persistent social unrest that had become general throughout the empire. If only to guard the interests of his family and his community, he found it necessary to join in the armed struggle on the side of the established authority and against the rebels and bandits. At the same time he entered the service of a new patron. In 1352 the messianic agents of Hsü Shou-hui (*q. v.*) entered Chekiang. One army raided Hangchow from the west, while a second invaded Ch'u-chou 處州 from the south. The defense of the city was then entrusted to Shih-mo I-sun 石抹宜孫 (d. 1360). The Shih-mo family in Chekiang claimed descent from a Ch'i-tan adherent of Jenghis Khan. They continued to serve the Mongols and were rewarded with hereditary command over the Yen-hai myriarch at T'ai-chou 台州. Shih-mo I-sun was inclined towards scholarship and when his younger brother, Shih-mo Hou-sun 厚孫, came of age, he turned the command over to him. After being called out of retirement (1352), Shih-mo I-sun got together a brilliant group of Chekiang scholars, including Chang I, Wang I, Liu Chi (*q. v.*), Sung Lien, Yeh Ch'en 葉琛 (T. 景淵, Pth. 貞肅), and Hu Ch'en 胡琛 (T. 仲淵, 1314–65). At the head of this cluster, Shih-mo achieved such a reputation among the common people of Ch'u-chou that, according to Liu Chi, they came to regard him as a god.

The specific occasion for Chang's entering Shih-mo's service was his nephew's capture during the invasion of Ch'u-chou. Chang's offer to serve as hostage for his nephew was readily accepted because the rebels knew of his reputation and wanted him to join their cause. After night had fallen, he tricked his guards and escaped. When he returned to Lung-ch'üan, he proceeded to organize a militia to attack the rebels. Shih-mo then arrived on the scene and Chang became a member of his staff. Successful campaigns against the enemy occupied the remainder of the year; then both men retired once more, Chang to Lung-ch'üan and Shih-mo to T'ai-chou.

In 1354 rebel forces besieged T'ai-chou and Shih-mo I-sun was ordered to take command there. When this was reported to Chang I, he quickly reassembled his militiamen and helped to lift the siege.

From T'ai-chou Shih-mo sent him to deal with a famine in the district of Ning-hai 寧海, not far away. When he found that rich families were hoarding rice, he compelled them to surrender a part of their stores for relief purposes. He also enlisted the aid of a number of monks who made rice gruel and fed it to those who were too weak to feed themselves. This done, Chang returned to Ch'u-chou (about the same time as Shih-mo) only to find a famine there as well and once again the suffering was exacerbated by hoarding. He set an example for others to follow by exchanging some of his lands for grain, which he then distributed to those in need.

By this time the armed uprisings had spread until every district in the prefecture of Ch'u-chou was under attack. The Lung-ch'üan magistrate, Pao-hu-ting 寶忽丁, however, carried avarice and brutality to such lengths that he drove the people to seek the help of a local rebel leader, who obliged them by driving him out. Chang I and Wang I dutifully took the field with their militiamen and recovered the district seat. For this they were rewarded with gifts of gold and silk from the provincial administration. The embarrassed Pao-hu-ting, fearing punishment for his incompetence, turned against the Yüan and had Wang I killed by a hired assassin.

In 1357 Shih-mo (now serving in a newly created sub-branch military commission), returned to Ch'u-chou, and his younger brother, Shih-mo Hou-sun, commanded the garrison at Chin-hua. Meanwhile Chang I continued to support his cause. He fought with bandits in the prefecture's central district of Li-shui 麗水, pursued them to their lairs, and destroyed their palisade forts. When the eastern districts of Chin-hua were raided by rebels, Shih-mo I-sun sent Chang I and Hu Ch'en to deal with them. In January 1359, however, Chin-hua fell to Chu Yüan-chang's invading army and Shih-mo was captured there, despite an ill-fated relief expedition sent from Ch'u-chou. Now the heart of

Chekiang province was under Chu's control and his armies advanced by land and sea into Ch'u-chou. Chang I at last abandoned the struggle, turned the command of his militiamen over to his son Chang Ts'un-tao 存道, and retired to K'uang-shan 匡山 (in Lung-ch'üan). When the prefectural seat was captured in December, however, Chang I joined Shih-mo in flight into Fukien. Here Shih-mo gathered a new force in a vain effort to recapture Ch'u-chou, but was killed the following summer. Chang and Hu escaped that fate because they had not joined Shih-mo.

During his years of military service against the rebels and bandits before 1360, Chang avoided an official commitment to the Yüan. On one hand, the forces he commanded were militiamen whom he had recruited in his own prefecture. On the other, he continued in an informal relationship with Shih-mo as a staff member without regular appointment. His good work had long been recognized by the authorities, and he had been offered progressively higher appointments, including an important post in the Che-tung chief commandery 都元帥府 which he persistently refused to accept. Now in exile in Fukien, he was visited by an emissary of Chu Yüan-chang and, although Shih-mo was still in the field at that time, he agreed in the month of March, 1360, to go to Nanking with Liu Chi, Sung Lien, and Yeh Ch'en to be received in audience. His first official appointment from Chu was as assistant agricultural commissioner. In this capacity he toured the war-ravaged farmlands of Chekiang and the Huai valley, where he was to assist in the redistribution of abandoned lands and in the reestablishment of agricultural taxes at appropriate levels. When the Chekiang surveillance office was established in 1363, Chang I was appointed an assistant commissioner. Here he once again found among his colleagues Hu Ch'en, who had already been appointed to an office in the provincial administration. As he had done

earlier under the Yüan, Chang now resumed his quest for social order by sending his militiamen against the bandits and rebels who still infested the hills and, at the same time, by trying to ameliorate the hardships among the peasantry and eliminate the causes of unrest.

Chang I's duties soon took him back to his native Ch'u-chou. Hu Ch'en, who had been charged with general civil and military responsibility for that prefecture, was called away for an audience at the capital, and in 1364 he took part in an expedition against Fang Kuo-chen's stronghold at Wen-chou. On both occasions, Chang served as Hu's replacement. He made the most of these opportunities to improve morale by distributing food and filling vacancies among the local irrigation managers. At the end of 1364, however, he was transferred to the newly established Hukuang surveillance office. Here he made a survey of local conditions and persuaded Chu Yüan-chang to expand military agriculture as a contribution to the security of the province, which still adjoined Yüan-controlled territory in the north.

In the summer of 1365 new trouble in Chekiang required Chang's presence once more. Hu Ch'en was killed in July while conducting an expedition against Ch'en Yu-ting (see Fang Kuo-chen) in Fukien. This defeat and the loss of their protector troubled the people of Ch'u-chou, who feared an invasion by Yüan forces in the south. Chang I was reappointed as assistant surveillance commissioner in Chekiang and was sent to Ch'u-chou to restore confidence and prepare the defenses there. The change of assignment came at an opportune time for him, because he had recently been the subject of corruption charges both in Hukuang and in Chekiang. His friend Liu Chi defended him to Chu Yüan-chang, and his own evident indispensability presumably served him well. On his return, he found that bandit stockades had already reappeared and he had his militiamen destroy them and capture and kill their leaders. In March, 1366, the southwestern districts of Lung-ch'üan and Ch'ing-yüan came under attack by a mixed force of local bandits and Yüan troops from Fukien. The regular army units of the province were already committed in northwest Fukien; so once again the burden of defense fell to Chang's militiamen, who rapidly constructed a chain of palisade forts at strategic points. The district seat of Lung-ch'üan also provided for its own defense by throwing up a wooden wall around the city. Deterred by these measures, the attackers withdrew.

Having made a successful defense of Ch'u-chou, Chang I now turned his attention to the suppression of banditry elsewhere in southeastern Chekiang. His services were then rewarded once more by promotion to the office of vice censor-in-chief (November 1, 1367). Meanwhile he was credited with many benefactions to his Ch'u-chou people. In the interest of better administration he investigated and exposed corruption in the collection of taxes. He successfully resisted several requisitions for the supply of troops in Fukien and for the construction of sea-going junks for the navy. On another occasion he bravely and successfully opposed Chu Yüan-chang's intention to move some Ch'u-chou militiamen commanded by Chang Ts'un-tao from a completed mission in Fukien to the northern campaign, in violation of a promise that they were to be allowed to go home. His alternative suggestion, which was adopted, was that civilians who had at some time been in rebellion (presumably against the new regime) should now be registered as military families and required to provide the needed men. His greatest contribution to the welfare of his prefecture, however, may well have been his successful campaign to restore the old agricultural tax quota for Ch'u-chou of 13,000 *tan*. As a matter of military necessity it had been increased tenfold, but by 1367 the local military emergency seemed to be at an end. In his own district he constructed a

new temple in honor of Wang I and Shih-mo I-sun, founded an endowed academy, and donated some of his land for use as a free cemetery. On behalf of his clan he completely rebuilt the ancestral temple and added more land to its endowment.

When Chang I and certain of his official colleagues were between assignments or held central government office, they were maintained near Chu's headquarters. In May or June, 1363, a Li-hsien kuan 禮賢館 (Savants' residence hall) was constructed to house them. Among those quareered there, in addition to Chang I, were T'ao An, Su Po-heng (*qq.v.*), Chang's old friends in Shih-mo I-sun's service, Liu Chi and Sung Lien, and several others. These gentlemen, when in residence, were expected to offer their patron instruction in classics and history as well as advice in practical affairs. It is also possible that Chu's holding them there was partly in the interests of security. They represented a major asset to his regime and he was careful to keep them employed or within his sight. Once, when he granted Chang I leave to visit his ailing mother, for example, he detained his youngest son, Chang Ts'un-hou 存厚, as hostage for his timely return.

In his relations with Chu Yüan-chang, Chang held his own. His demonstrated ability to protect and manage his unruly prefecture without help from regular military forces enabled him to be firm and outspoken without being made to suffer for it. He was also in a position to turn away his ruler's wrath. On the occasion of Chu's first imperial sacrifice to the gods of soil and grain in February, 1368, the participants were drenched by a sudden downpour. The emperor, believing that Heaven had thus signified that the ceremony had been improperly conducted, was prepared to execute certain officials for their part in the fiasco. Chang petitioned him, saying, "It has been raining for days, so this is nothing to wonder at. Granted, the officials responsible for the rites have not yet perfected them, but your Majesty's perfect sincerity will be enough in itself to move the gods. I hope that you may moderate your wrath." The emperor was then somewhat mollified. On another occasion the emperor paid him a characteristically grudging compliment when he said that he and his son, Chang Ts'un-tao, despite the fact that they were only scholars, had made a record not inferior to that of his generals.

In 1368 or 1369, on returning home after a few months in the capital, Chang learned that his mother had died. He now resigned himself to his own imminent end. Over the objections of his family, he insisted on carrying stones for the construction of his mother's tomb. He was in frail health at the time and the effort may have caused his death. At the end of the dynasty, in August, 1644, Emperor Chu Yu-sung (ECCP) gave Chang the posthumous name Chuang-min 莊敏. Of Chang I's three sons, the eldest, Chang Ts'un-tao became vice commander of the Ch'u-chou guard and the youngest, Chang Ts'un-hou, had an honorary office in the palace of the heir apparent and married a daughter of Hu Ch'en.

Bibliography

1/128/13b, 180/10a; 5/54/1a; 61/116/1b; *Yüan-shih* 元史, ch. 42–47, 188/9b; MSL (1962), T'ai-tsu, 0072, 0523, 0833; Wang Hsing-i 王馨一, *Liu Po-wen nien-p'u* 劉伯溫年譜 (Shanghai, 1936); Liu Chi, *Ch'eng-i po wen-chi*, 5/24b; Chi Liu-ch'i 計六奇, *Ming-chi nan-lüeh* 明季南略 (1936), 109; Wang I, *Mu-no-chai wen-chi* 木訥齋文集 (1949), 3/12a, 14a.

Romeyn Taylor

CHANG Jui-t'u 張瑞圖 (T. 長公, 果亭, H. 二水, 白毫庵主), 1570?- April/May 1641, one-time grand secretary and artist, came from a family in Chin-chiang 晉江, Ch'üan-chou prefecture 泉州府, Fukien, involved in the production of salt. After qualifying as a *chü-jen* in 1603 he achieved third place in the palace examination of 1607, and was made a compiler in the Hanlin, then junior supervisor of instruction, and eventually vice minister of Rites. In Sep-

tember, 1626, the grand eunuch Wei Chung-hsien (ECCP), now at the height of his power, saw to his becoming a member of the Grand Secretariat—one of the first Fukien men, along with his contemporary Yeh Hsiang-kao (q.v.), as the *Ming-shih* editors point out, to receive such high responsibility since the days of Yang Jung (q.v.), two centruies earlier. One of the ways in which he held Wei's favor was to serve as calligrapher of inscriptions to be carved on tablets in shrines erected in the eunuch's honor throughout China. His term in the Secretariat was brief. In April, 1628, he asked for leave for reasons of health, and the following year (April 12) his name came to be included on the list of the supporters of Wei Chung-hsien, and he was reduced to the status of a commoner. Chang spent the last years of his life at home indulging in his favorite occupations, writing, painting, and calligraphy.

The *Ch'üan-chou-fu chih* mentions several titles of books which Chang wrote. One included three hundred poems penned in 1629 and 1630, but does not seem to have survived. The only one published, and that is rare, is the *Pai-hao-an nei-p'ien* 白毫庵內篇, 4 *ch.*, with a preface of 1639. A copy is in the Naikaku Bunko. He is especially remembered for his skill as painter and calligrapher, in his own day being classed along with Hsing T'ung 邢侗 (T. 子愿, 1551-1612, cs 1574), Mi Wan-chung, and Tung Ch'i-ch'ang (both in ECCP). One critic, Y. Yanezawa (cited by Osvald Sirén), wrote in 1956: "He must be recognized as one of the most outstanding [painters] of the Ming." A number of Chang's paintings still survive, particularly in collections in Japan where his political associations at the court have not been held against him. Sirén has reproduced four examples of his handicraft, which he describes as mountains in mist (dated 1631), view over a distant valley (1636), and two album leaves which he entitles: "a rocky island in the open sea," and "mountains in mist on a moon-lit night." Bo Gyllensvärd has reproduced another large painting (dated 1635), now in a private collection in New York, which he describes as mountains with trees on cliffs, and Mrs. Ecke has reproduced examples of his calligraphy.

In the short Lung-wu period (1645–46) Chang's rank was posthumously restored, and he was given the name Wen-yin 文隱. He had one son, Chang Ch'ien-fu 潛夫, who qualified for the *chin-shih* in 1640, and who became a corrector in the Hanlin Academy.

Bibliography

1/110/21a, 306/14b; 3/225/2a; 27/x/19b; *Ming-shih* (Taiwan ed.), 3239; MSL (1966), Hsi-tsung, 3598, 3791, 3991; KC (1958), 5405, 5425, 5471, 5474; *Ch'ung-chen ch'ang-pien* 長編 (1967), 0054, 0165, 0325; *Chin-chiang-hsien chih* (1765, repr. 1967), 182; *Ch'üan-chou-fu chih* (1870), 34/18a, 35/40b, 54/67b, 74/44a; Wang Chuang-wei 王壯爲, "Chang Er-shui yü ch'i shu" 二水與其書 in *Shu-fa ts'ung t'an* 書法叢談 (Taipei, 1966), 147; Naikaku Bunko *Catalogue*, 367; V. Contag and C. C. Wang, *Seals of Chinese Painters and Collectors*, rev. ed. (Hong Kong, 1966), #242; O. Sirén, *Chinese Painting*, V (London, 1958), 47, VI, pl. 296, VII, 155; B. Gyllensvärd, "Some Chinese Paintings in the Ernest Erickson Collection," BMFEA, 36 (1964), pl. 13; E. J. Laing, *Chinese Paintings in Chinese Publications 1956–1968*, (Ann Arbor, 1969), 152; Tseng Yu-ho Ecke, *Chinese Calligraphy* (Philadelphia, 1971), #64, 65, 66.

L. Carrington Goodrich

CHANG Lien 張璉 (H. 石琚), died 1562, bandit chief, was a native of Jao-p'ing 饒平, Ch'ao-chou 潮州, Kwangtung. After beating a headman of his clan to death in a dispute and fearing punishment, Chang fled from the village early in his career and sought refuge among the bandits led by Cheng Pa 鄭八 and Hsiao Wan 蕭晚 (H. 雪峯, d. 1562). To elevate his standing he conjured up an omen and invoked it to achieve his purpose. The story goes that one day he secretly carved on a stone the words Fei-lung ch'uan-kuo chih-pao 飛龍傳國之寶 (precious seal of the "Flying Dragon" dynastic succession)

and dropped it in a pond. Then he dove into the water, picked up the stone, and showed it to his fellow bandits. Astonished, they said that it must be an omen proclaiming a change of mandate. Whereupon the bandits swore a blood-smearing oath, and pressed Chang to become their new chief. After Cheng Pa's death, most of his men submitted to Chang's command. When the district magistrate of Jao-p'ing became suspicious that sedition was brewing, he went to Chang's camp in person and tried to induce him to surrender with the offer of an official title, but was rebuffed. From 1559 Chang's forces steadily increased, drawing strength from villagers whose means of livelihood had been disrupted by the sporadic raids of the *wo-k'ou*; in time, they became a menace to the local communities. In this same year Chang is said to have aided the pirates by showing them how to raid Ch'ao-chou on the northeast coast. In 1560 Chang and Hsiao Wan and their forces pillaged several districts bordering southern Fukien, southeastern Kiangsi, and northeastern Kwangtung. In the same year Chang invested himself as Fei-lung jen-chu 人主 (Master of the "Flying Dragon" regime) and adopted Fei-lung as his reign title. He changed the calendrical name and even organized civil service examinations. At the same time he constructed two forts in Jao-p'ing as the stronghold of his embryonic kingdom. Several provincial forces were sent against Chang, but none succeeded in curbing his activities.

Alarmed by Chang's insurgency, Chang Nieh 張臬 (T. 正野, H. 百川, cs 1526), governor-general of Kwangtung and Kwangsi, memorialized the court in March, 1562, recommending the formation of a punitive expedition of about a hundred thousand men, to be recruited from the Lang-ping 狼兵 (soldiers from the Thai tribes of southwest China), with auxiliary units drawn from local forces in Fukien and Kiangsi. The court appointed Commissioner Liu Hsien 劉顯 (a native of Nanchang, d. 1581) and the area assistant commander Yü Ta-yu (*q. v.*) to head the expedition. By strategic maneuvering the government troops captured the bandit headquarters in Jao-p'ing and put a reward on the heads of Chang and Hsiao. Subsequently they secured the defection of a bandit headman; with the information he supplied, the punitive party captured both Chang and Hsiao in June. The bandits suffered heavy losses: a death toll of over twelve hundred is recorded, and some twenty thousand men who were forced to join the insurgents were released. Chang and Hsiao were executed on the spot. According to the genealogical record of the Chang family, Chang had privately accorded himself the posthumous title of Ying-lieh 英烈. Remnants of the band sought refuge among the Japanese pirates and aided them in harassing the coast of Kwangtung. In commemoration of the successful expedition, two administrative units were established in Chia-ying 嘉應 chou, formerly a rebel-infested region northwest of Ch'ao-chou. One was called P'ing-yüan 平遠 hsien, and the other Shen-wei ying 伸威 營.

Certain accounts such as the *Ming-shih*, however, confuse Chang's capture and execution with the story that he fled to Sumatra after his defeat by government troops. It is said that he operated a factory in Chiu-kang 舊港 (Palembang) where he had under his control many people from southern Fukien; like a superintendent of trade in China, he became master of all the native craft and at times was a ruthless pirate. Some contemporary writings, on the other hand, have identified him with the notorious buccaneer Chang Ssu-lao 張四老 whose pillaging was a threat to Portuguese shipping in the South China Sea. Substantial documentation, however, has ruled out all these claims, and lends support to the assertion that Chang was captured and executed by government troops in 1562.

Bibliography

1/212/6a, 324/27a; *MSL* (1965), Shih-tsung, 8228, 8274, 8351, 8382; *Ming-shu* 明書 (1937), 3226; Mao Ch'i-ling (ECCP), *Hou-chien lu* 後鑒錄, 4/3a (*Hsi-ho hsien-sheng ho-chi* [1761], bk. 40); *Ch'ao-chou-fu chih* (1893), 38/29a, 40/73a; *Jao-p'ing-hsien chih* (1883), 13; Fujita Toyohachi 藤田豐八, *Tōzai kosho-shi no kenkyū, nankai hen* 東西交涉史の研究, 南海篇, (Tokyo, 1932), 483; Chang Wei-hua 張維華, *Ming-shih Fo-lang-chi Lü-sung Ho-lan I-ta-li-ya ssu chuan chu-shih* 明史佛朗機呂宋和蘭意大利亞四傳注釋 (Peking, 1934), 58; Jao Tsung-i 饒宗頤, "Lun *Ming-shih* wai-kuo chuan chi Chang Lien t'ao wang San-fo-ch'i chih e" 論明史外國傳記張璉逃往三佛齊之訛, *History Society Annals* (University of Hong Kong, 1961), 6.

Hok-lam Chan

CHANG Mou 章懋 (T. 德懋, H. 闇然子), 1437-June 28, 1522, official, educator, thinker, was a native of Lan-hsi 蘭谿, Chekiang. He became a *chin-shih* in 1466, and was named a Hanlin bachelor. In November, 1467, he was appointed Hanlin compiler. Two months later, when Emperor Chu Chien-shen (*q.v.*), following the instruction of his mother, ordered the Hanlin members to prepare poems for the coming celebration of the feast of lanterns, Chang Mou, together with two other Hanlin compilers, Huang Chung-chao 黃仲昭 (*ming* 潛, but known by his tzu; H. 未軒先生, 退巖居士, cs 1466; 1435–1508), and Chuang Ch'ang 莊昶 (T. 孔暘, H. 定山, cs 1466, 1437–99), submitted memorials rebuking the sovereign for his preoccupation with sensual pleasures. All three were flogged and put in prison. Around the same time, another Hanlin compiler, Lo Lun (*q.v.*), also incurred the emperor's displeasure for the opinions he expressed regarding Li Hsien (*q.v.*), the grand secretary, who, after the death of his father, did not retire but continued in office. The four men became known as the four Hanlin remonstrators and were acclaimed for their courage. Many officials came to their rescue, petitioning for their release. In view of these circumstances, Chang Mou, although demoted to be magistrate of Lin-wu 臨武-hsien, Hukuang, was eventually pardoned before he assumed that office; instead he was promoted to be a judge in the Grand Court of Revision in Nanking, in which post he gained renown for his legal acumen and impartiality. Three years later he was elevated to be assistant surveillance commissioner for Fukien, where his policy of promoting trade with foreigners, and allowing the residents to engage in silver mining, improved the lot of the people, and lessened the urge to live ontside the law. He was transferred to the ministry of Personnel, but resigned from office (1478) to care for his parents, and to teach. After twenty-three years he was named chancellor of the National University in Nanking (1501), but, having just entered the period of mourning for his father, he did not assume the duties of office until 1504. In the meantime, the government enjoined Lo Ch'in-shun (q.v.), as director of studies, to act in his place. When he reached Nanking, Chang twice submitted memorials against misconduct in education and administration, but both were ignored. After eight requests, he was finally (1507) allowed to retire from official life. In 1510 and 1511 he declined successive promotions to be chief minister of the Court of Imperial Sacrifices and vice minister of the ministry of Rites, both in Nanking. In the end he was promoted to be minister of Rites there over his own protests, but was permitted to retire June 6, 1521. The next year he died at the age of eighty-five. He was posthumously designated grand guardian of the heir apparent, and honored with the name Wen-i 文懿. His disciples and friends called him the Master of Feng-shan 楓山.

Chang Mou's life reflects the trend among certain scholars and officials of Ming times towards a life of retreat rather than an official career. It is said that, in the more than fifty years following his appointment to the Hanlin Academy, Chang served at court only forty days, holding actual office in various capacities elsewhere for about nine years, during which he submitted more than twenty memorials requesting permission to retire. Sharing in the common notion of keng-tu 耕讀—that plowing and studying should go together—he was content to labor for his own sustenance and his sons with him, although his 20 mou of land could not produce half the quantity of rice to feed his family of ten. On occasions, he had to rely on the generosity of fellow-clansmen to provide meals fit for the guests who came to visit him. It is also said that in the small house in Lan-hsi, to which he later moved, the ceiling was so low that his hat rubbed against it whenever he paced up and down.

Chang Mou left few writings. When urged to write, he argued that he could add nothing to what the Sung thinkers had already said. There are two known extant collections bearing his name, both entitled Feng-shan Chang hsien-sheng wen-chi 先生文集. One in 9 chüan was published in 1531; the other in 4 chüan in 1545.

Chang Mou had four sons, the first three preceding him in death. The youngest, born in Chang's eighty-first year, was granted admission to the National University. Chang had also a nephew, Chang Cheng 拯 (T. 以道, H. 札菴, cs 1502, d. February 21, 1548, Pth. 恭惠), who was also his disciple. He was an able scholar, and served briefly as minister of Works (September-December 1529).

Bibliography

1/179/4b; 3/162/5b; 5/36/39a; 16/42/27a, 160/2b, 21a; 32/53/1a; 40/24/8b; 61/113/11a; 63/21/13a; 83/45/4b; MSL (1940), Hsien-tsung, 49/4a, Shih-tsung, 2/3b; KC (1958), 2205, 2210, 2243, 3223, 3261, 3712; Feng Shih-k'o 馮時可 (cs 1571), "Chang Wen-i kung Feng-shan Chang hsien-sheng hsing-chuang" 行狀, Huang Ming wen-hai (microfilm), ch. 47; Lin Chün 林俊 (1452-1527), "Ming Wen-i kung Feng-shan Chang hsien-sheng hsing-chuang," ibid., ch. 47; T'ang Lung 唐龍, "Feng-shan hsien-sheng hsing-chuang," ibid., ch. 47; Liu Ts'un-yan, "The Penetration of Taoism," TP, 57 (1971), 58; Ping-ti Ho, The Ladder of Success in Imperial China (New York, 1962), 75.

Ronald G. Dimburg and Julia Ching

CHANG Pi 張弼 (T. 汝弼, H. 東海居士),
1425-July 4, 1487, official, poet, and calligrapher, was a native of Hua-t'ing 華亭,
Sung-chiang prefecture 松江府, in the
lower Yangtze valley. Following his graduation as *chü-jen* in 1453 and *chin-shih* in
1466, he received an appointment first as
secretary, and then as vice director, of a
bureau in the ministry of War. Being
naturally outspoken, he irritated certain
high officials in the capital, especially his
superiors in the ministry of War, with the
consequence that in 1478 he was transferred to Kiangsi as prefect of Nan-an 南安,
near the southern border of the province.
This was a mountainous area, and at the
time infested with robbers. Chang's first
task was to eliminate them; that done, the
people began to enjoy a sense of security.
He next turned to the rehabilitation of
the poverty-stricken in the prefecture, instituting various relief measures by stimulating employment and promoting public
construction, such as the building of roads
and bridges.

He discovered too that the region
abounded in unorthodox temples; so he
took the drastic measure of destroying
more than a hundred of these (*ca.* 1479),
establishing schools in their place, and
erecting new shrines to such notable thinkers and writers as Chang Chiu-ling (673?-
740), Chou Tun-i (1017-73), Ch'eng Hao
(1032-85), and Ch'eng I (1033-1107). One
such structure bore the name Yin-feng
nung-yüeh t'ai 吟風弄月台 (Wind and
moon terrace). He also encouraged the
greater use of medicine among the diseas-
ed. After six years of conscientious administration, he retired from public life on
the pretext of failing health. Following
his departure, the people put up a temple
in his honor. He died at home at the age
of sixty-two.

Chang Pi's main avocations were
poetry and calligraphy. He published his
prose and poetry under five titles, but
only one of these—the *Tung-hai wen-chi* 文
集, 5 *ch.*—is listed in the Imperial Catalogue; the editors, however, did not include

it in the *Ssu-k'u ch'üan-shu*. The National
Central Library, Taipei, lists a defective
copy of this edition, but the Seikado Library reports a copy of his collected writings (全集), divided into prose, 4 *chüan*,
poetry, 4 *chüan*, and supplement, 1 *chüan*.

In calligraphy he made a genuine name
for himself. His running hand found particular favor. He wrote rapidly with bold
and forceful strokes, delighting the cog-
noscenti. Actually he was well versed in
other forms of calligraphy too. A contemporary calligrapher and poet, Li Tung-
yang (*q.v.*), was a cherished friend. In his
Lu-t'ang shih-hua, Li made the following
comment: "Chang Pi often told friends
that his calligraphy was not as good
as his poetry and his poetry not as good
as his prose. In calligraphy his large
characters were better than his small ones.
I don't agree with his pronouncement.
Yet I submit that his large characters are
really fine." (For examples of his calligraphy, see Wang Shih-chieh [BDRC], *et al.*,
A Garland of Chinese Calligraphy, II
[Hong Kong, 1967], ♯ 7, and Tseng Yu-ho
Ecke, *Chinese Calligraphy* [Philadelphia,
1971], ♯ 39).

Chang's bluntness, revealed in Peking
and elsewhere, indicates a man of strong
personality and unquestioned courage.
These characteristics appear too both in his
writings and in his calligraphy. Unlike
many of the literati of his time, however,
he never indulged in licentiousness. Careful
in his own deportment, he yet often made
sarcastic comments.

His second son, Chang Hung-i 弘宜 (T.
時措, H. 後樂, cs 1481), who rose from
the magistracy of Ning-hai 寧海, Chekiang,
to be surveillance vice commissioner of
Kwangsi (where he died in office), followed in his father's footsteps as an
accomplished calligrapher. Another son,
Chang Hung-chih 至 (T. 時行, cs 1496),
became first a Hanlin bachelor and then
supervising secretary in the office of scrutiny. [Editors' note: The conversion of the
"unorthodox temples" to schools by Confucianists like Chang Pi, an act considered

praiseworthy by the traditional Chinese historiographer, should serve as a clue to anthropologists that in the mountainous area of southern Kiangsi there probably existed customs and folklore representing non-Chinese or ancient Chinese cultures.]

Bibliography

1/286/7a; 5/87/17a; 6/2/43b, 27/24b; 14/5/16b; 22/3/28a; 32/25/31a; 40/24/9a; 64/丙5/10b; 84/丙/22b; 86/8/15b; SK(1930), 175/15a; Wang Ch'ang-shih 王昌時(cs 1631), *Huang Ming chün-mu Lien-p'ing chuan* 皇明郡牧廉平傳 (*ca.* 1960), ch. 4; Chi Yün (ECCP), *P'ei-wen-chai shu-hua p'u*, 80/17a; Ma Tsung-ho 馬宗霍, *Shu-lin tsao-chien* 書林藻鑑, 11/304a; *id.*, *Shu-lin chi-shih* 紀事, 11/68; Kiangsu Library *Catalogue*, 34/15b; Seikado Library *Catalogue*, 720.

Liu Lin-sheng

CHANG Shih-ch'eng 張士誠, 1321-October 9, 1367, also known as Chang Chiu-ssu 九四, was a native of Po-chü-ch'ang 白駒場, a village located in the eastern Huai salt fields about fifty miles northeast of Kao-yu 高郵 (Nan-Chihli). He and his brothers, Chang Shih-hsin 信, Chang Shih-i 義, and Chang Shih-te 德, were boatmen for the government salt monopoly. Oppressed by excessive corvée duties imposed by the Yüan authorities and frequently cheated by the influential people to whom they sold their smuggled salt at cut-rate prices, the Chang brothers and fourteen other salt workers formed a band for self-protection. Chang Shih-ch'eng, by virtue of his taciturnity, physical strength, and generosity was made its leader. Early in 1353, the band decided to take revenge against some of the powerful families by burning their houses; but when the conflagration spread farther than they had intended, Chang and his men were left with no recourse other than open rebellion. Visiting the local market places in order to recruit youths, Chang and his followers won a victory over forces led by a local gentryman at Ting-ch'i-ch'ang 丁溪場 (about twenty miles east of Hsing-hua 興

化); from there they moved southwest and reduced the city of T'ai-chou 泰州 (Nan-Chihli). Here the Yüan officials momentarily interested Chang in surrendering by offering him a civil office, but upon observing the weakness of their position Chang decided not to accept. Instead, he overran Hsing-hua, and then joined forces with another group of rebels on Lake Te-sheng 得勝. When these rebels were about to accept the terms of surrender proffered by attacking Yüan forces, Chang murdered their leaders and incorporated the men into his own army. He then abandoned Lake Te-sheng and on June 30, 1353, captured the city of Kao-yu on the Grand Canal.

After failing to dislodge Chang by military means, the Yüan sent envoys four times to try to get him to give up; when Chang arrested or murdered most of them, the Yüan once more turned to force. An expedition carried out in the summer of 1353, featuring an attack by a thousand Mongol cavalry upon the city, ended in complete rout. By the time a huge force of Chinese, Koreans, Tibetans, and central Asians under the command of the Yüan Chancellor of the Right, Toɤto (1313–55), converged on Kao-yu in the autumn of 1354, Chang Shih-ch'eng was in control of an arc of territory north of the Huai-nan provincial capital of Yangchow, which stretched to Liu-ho 六合 on the west, An-tung 安東 on the north, and T'ung-chou 通州 (Nan-t'ung) on the east. It was only by a miracle that Chang Shih-ch'eng survived this onslaught, for, just as Kao-yu was about to go under, Toɤto was cashiered by the emperor and the whole expedition disintegrated. Most of the loyalist troops mutinied and either joined existing rebel movements or went out on their own to plunder the countryside.

Chang, who had set himself up as Prince Ch'eng 誠王 under the reign-title T'ien-yu 天佑 (祐, Heaven protected) early in 1354, let his rebellion lie dormant for a year after his survival of the siege of Kao-yu. In 1356, because of a famine, he joined the general exodus of rebels from the Huai region after accepting an invitation from a former salt peddler and bandit whom the Yüan had put in charge of the strategic lower Yangtze city of Chiang-yin 江陰 to move south and take over the Yangtze delta area. Leaving troops to hold Kao-yu, Chang crossed the Yangtze in the early spring of 1356 and overran most of the country east of Lake T'ai with little difficulty. He made his capital at P'ing-chiang 平江 which he renamed Lung-p'ing-fu 隆平府 (=Soochow).

Daš Temür 達識帖睦邇, the chief Yüan provincial official in the area Chang had overrun, made an attempt to counter him and recover this economically vital region. He ordered Yang Wan-che (Öljei) 楊完者, commander of an army of Miao 苗 tribesmen, to attack Soochow from Chia-hsing 嘉興, and had the pirate Fang Kuo-chen (q.v.) assault the same point from K'un-shan 崑山 near the sea. The plan was spoiled by one Wang Yü-ching 王與敬, a disaffected loyalist, who chose this moment to rebel in Sung-chiang 松江 and go over to the enemy. By late 1357, Chang was in possession of Hangchow, which he had failed to take from Miao defenders the year before, and in December he moved unopposed into Shao-hsing after a civil war among Yüan officials in that city.

When Chang entered Soochow in 1356, he made his headquarters in a former Buddhist monastery and proceeded at once to set up a bureaucracy closely patterned on the Yüan model, but featuring some archaic nomenclature. Besides a central government, a military affairs bureau, and the six ministries, Chang established an academy to which he appointed scholars. His army commanders requisitioned the homes of the wealthy for their own private use. Among Chang's officials were Li Hsing-su 李行素, an occultist who served as prime minister, and Chou Jen 周仁 (also known as Chou Chen 辰 and Chou T'ieh-hsing 鐵星), a blacksmith's son and an avowed legalist who was hated by the common people for his tyranical tax-collecting methods. Chou was a close aide of Chang Shih-te, his elder brother's chief recruiter, planner, and military commander. The P'an 潘 family of T'ung-chou rose to great power under Chang's regime, largely through the efforts of the wife, who urged her husband and two sons to join Chang in 1353. Not only did she manage the family, but she also gave out rations, made uniforms, and treated the soldiers as her own sons. She was instrumental in getting Lü Chen 呂珍, later an outstanding general, introduced to Chang Shih-te, and she married her son, P'an Yüan-shao 元紹, to Chang Shih-ch'eng's daughter.

In 1357 Chang sent a letter to Daš Temür offering to surrender to the Yüan in return for the grant of the title of prince, but was finally prevailed upon to accept the less prestigious title of t'ai-wei 太尉 (Grand Commandant). Considering his earlier attitude, Chang must have wanted to surrender badly. He had just lost four cities—Ch'ang-hsing 長興, Ch'ang-chou 常州 (Wu-chin), Chiang-yin, and Ch'ang-shu 常熟—to Chu Yüan-chang. He had tried in October of the preceding year to buy peace from Chu, offering to send him two hundred thousand *shih* of grain and eight hundred *liang* of precious metals yearly. But Chu, who blamed Chang for starting the fighting, demanded five hundred thousand *shih* and the return of the prisoners Chang had captured. Chang did not reply. In addition to his troubles with Chu, Fang Kuo-chen was still threatening at K'un-shan, and under these cirumstances Chang could no longer afford to have the Yüan officials and their fierce Miao auxiliaries as enemies. It was also around this time that Chu captured the indispensable Chang Shih-te; the latter's functions then went to another brother, Chang Shih-hsin, who had much less talent. The price which the Yüan extracted for permitting the surrender was the resumption of the maritime grain shipments to Ta-tu (Peking).

In 1358 Daš Temür, who had come to

resent Yang Öljei's overbearing attitude, made a secret agreement with Chang to dispose of the Miao commander, who had lost his usefulness after Chang's surrender. Yang, suddenly surrounded in his camp near Hangchow, committed suicide as did his younger brother, Yang Bayan 楊伯顏. Part of Yang's tribal forces surrendered to Chang, but some thirty thousand of them went over to Chu Yüan-chang. In 1363 these Miao staged an attack on Chu's eastern border in Chekiang and went back to Chang, provoking a short-lived but serious crisis (see Li Wen-chung).

During the years that Chang acted nominally as a Yüan official, he retained full personal control over all matters within his domain. He maintained regular diplomatic relations with Korea; although he expressed in a letter of 1358 to the Korean king his intent to clean out the "western bandits," meaning Chu Yüan-chang's forces, his main reason for opening contacts seems to have been commercial. From 1359 to 1362 he sent yearly token shipments of grain to the Yüan capital. It took delicate negotiations by the Yüan officials to get the shipments started, for although the grain was grown in Chang's territory, the boats were provided by Fang Kuo-chen, and each warlord was suspicious of the other. Over a hundred thousand *shih* were shipped annually from 1359 to 1361. The Yüan authorities tried to get a million *shih* shipped in 1362, but were able to obtain only a fraction of that. In 1363 Chang sent in a total of only one hundred thirty thousand, and thereafter ceased the grain shipments altogether. Chang also monopolized some sixty percent of China's output of salt; Chu Yüan-chang was obliged to carry on a surreptitious trade with him in order to obtain this vital commodity.

Early in 1363, after four years of relative inaction, Chang began again to extend his realm, this time into the *terra nullius* of the eastern Huai. Chang's general, Lü Chen, allied with the rebel Tso Chün-pi 左君弼, a former follower of P'eng Ying-yü (see Hsü Shou-hui) who held the city of Lu-chou 盧州 (Anhwei), launched an attack on the capital of the Sung Red Turban emperor, Han Lin-er (q.v.), at An-feng 安豐 (Anhwei). Chu Yüan-chang's men beat off Lü and Tso, but after the Sung imperial entourage was evacuated, the city fell to Yüan elements friendly to Chang. By the autumn of 1363, Chang's territory reached its greatest extent: north to Hsü-chou 徐州, west to the upper Huai area formerly occupied by the Sung Red Turbans, south as far as Shao-hsing, and east to the sea. Chu was off fighting in Kiangsi, leaving his eastern front shaky; the Miao had recently rebelled there, and one of Chu's generals, posted on the border, defected to Chang. The Yüan court in addition was dominated by a faction friendly to Bolod Temür (see Kökö Temür) at the time; Bolod was engaged in a bitter struggle with Kökö whose territory bordered on Chang's. Under these circumstances, Chang may have considered it wise to disassociate himself from the court and Kökö's enemy. Rebuffed in an attempt to get the Yüan to promote him to prince, Chang assumed for himself the title of prince of Wu 吳王, just as Chu Yüan-chang was to do in 1367, and, also like Chu, adopted no special reign-title but merely used "first year of Wu," etc. In 1364 the hapless Daš Temür was put in confinement and compelled to cede his position to Chang Shih-hsin. From 1364 to 1366, Chang made attacks on Chu's eastern flank, but none of these succeeded. Additional funds for the fighting were procured by, among other means, doubling the fee for monks' ordination certificates.

From 1357 until late in 1365, Chang and Chu were locked in a virtual stalemate, each building defense works and launching intermittent attacks upon one another's positions. After disposing of the Kiangsi warlord Ch'en Yu-liang (q.v.) late in 1363, Chu decided to make an all-out assault against Chang. During 1365 and 1366, Chu seized Chang's territory north of the Yangtze in order to make impossible any alliance between him and the northern warlord Kökö Temür. On June 29, 1366, still using Han Lin-er's reign-title of Lung-feng, Chu issued a public indictment of Chang, listing eight of his supposed "crimes" in psychological preparation for the coming attack. Some two hundred thousand troops led by Hsü Ta and Ch'ang Yü-ch'un (*qq.v.*) set out on September 6; on December 2 they won a key victory at Chiu-kuan 舊館, about ten miles east of Wu-hsing, after which most of Chang's cities surrendered without a fight. Chang's capital, besieged on December 27, 1366, fell on October 1, 1367. All attempts to get Chang to surrender voluntarily had failed: perhaps he was expecting another miracle such as the one at Kao-yu twelve years before. Chang's wife drove all of the concubines and serving girls into a tower, had it set on fire, and then strangled herself. Chang was brought prisoner to Nanking where he was apparently beaten to death a week later. His capital was then renamed Su-chou-fu (Soochow).

Some of Chang Shih-ch'eng's chief officials and advisors (including Chou Jen) were put to death, as were a number of men formerly with Chu who had defected to Chang, but Chang's military arm seems to have been incorporated almost *en bloc* into Chu's forces. In a speech he gave to Chang's men, Chu admitted that most of his commanders were, like himself, from the area of Hao-chou 濠州 and Ssu-chou 泗州, but emphasized that there were good prospects for advancement for men of other regions if they were from poor families and if they renounced any desire they might have for soft living. Chu undoubtedly needed these troops for the forthcoming conquest of the north. In addition, Chu immediately began moving rich families out of Soochow and into the depopulated Huai area, especially around Hao-chou.

Chang Shih-ch'eng occupied China's richest agricultural and commercial area, and, largely because of the generous privileges and emoluments he was able to bestow, he never had the defection problem among his men that Chu Yüan-chang did. In fact, Chu had difficulty keeping officers, soldiers, and common people from going over to Chang. Chang also provided a congenial atmosphere for literary men. Yet a number of public works projects undertaken under Chang's rule were highly unpopular with the commoners, especially the rebuilding of the Hangchow wall in 1359 and the drainage operation near Lake T'ai in 1364.

Yang Wei-chen (*q.v.*) in a letter to Chang summed up what he saw as strong and weak points of the regime. The strong points were that the troops were not given to slaughter, officials received adequate salaries, corruption was vigorously checked, and Chang himself was personally modest and receptive to good advice. On the other hand, corvée assignments and tax-collecting were badly handled, loyal officials were suspect while defectors from the other side were trusted too openly, and too many incompetents were given high positions— indeed, there was a current joke that oil-pressers, noodle-makers, and laborers could become erudites, barbers compilers, servants and slaves directors of departments, and clerks ministers or dukes. Chu Yüan-chang thought Chang Shih-ch'eng too out of touch with reality and deceived by those around him. The traditional historians emphasize the refined sloth into which Chang and his generals fell after surrendering to the Yüan in 1357; the military men preferred high living and art-collecting to fighting, and were never punished for losing battles. A tradition favorable to Chang Shih-ch'eng seems to persist in Soochow to the present day. In June, 1964, the tomb of his parents, which Chu Yüan-chang gave strict orders to his troops in 1367 to honor and protect, was excavated by the local authorities.

Bibliography

1/123/6a; 5/119/7a; 61/90/1a; Cha Chi-tso (ECCP),

Tsui-wei lu 傳 6/24a; *Yüan-shih*, *chüan* 43, 97, 138, 142, 144, 187, 194; MSL (1940), T'ai-tsu; *Koryō-sa*, I (Tokyo, 1908-9), 584; Ch'ang-ku chen-i 長谷眞逸 (pseud.), *Nung-t'ien yü-hua* 農田餘話 (*Pao-yen-t'ang mi-chi* 寶顏堂秘笈 *ed.*); Liu Ch'en 劉辰, *Kuo-ch'u shih-chi* 國初事蹟; Wu K'uan, *P'ing Wu lu*; T'ao Tsung-i, *Cho keng lu* (TsSCC ed.), 127, 439, 466; Chu Yün-ming, *Chiu-ch'ao yeh-chi*, 6a; Hsü Mien-chih 徐勉之, *Pao Yüeh lu* 保越錄; Yao T'ung-shou 姚桐壽, *Lo-chiao ssu-yü* 樂郊私語; Yeh Tzu-ch'i, *Ts'ao-mu tzu*; Ch'ien Ch'ien-i (ECCP), *Kuo-ch'u ch'ün-hsiung shih-lüeh*; Chih Wei-ch'eng 支偉成, *Wu-wang Chang Shih-ch'eng tsai-chi*, Shanghai, 1932; *Kaogu* 考古 (Peking, 1965), no. 6, 285; Otagi Matsuo 愛岩松男, "Shu Go-koku to Chō Go-koku: shoki Min ōchō no seikaku ni kansuru ichi kōsatsu," 朱吳國と張吳國：初期明王朝の性格に關する一考察, *Bunka* 文化 XVII, no. 6(1953).

John Dardess

CHANG Ssu-wei 張四維 (T. 子維, H. 鳳磐), 1526-December 6, 1585, a native of P'u-chou 蒲州, Shansi, served as grand secretary from 1575 to 1583. As his distant ancestors came from the salt-producing district of Hsieh-chou 解州, it seems that most members of the family were in the salt trade, and this naturally was the source of their wealth. His father, Chang Yün-ling 允齡 (T. 伯延, H. 嵋川, 1506-83), a successful business man, married an elder sister of Wang Ch'ung-ku (*q. v.*). A younger brother, Chang Ssu-chiao 四教 (T. 子淑, H. 歷磐, 1530-84), who was said to have a gift for mathematics, was a salt merchant in Tientsin for over twenty years and occasionally made a tenfold profit.

The scholastic talents of Chang Ssu-wei were recognized early by his teachers, examiners, and local officials. He became a *chü-jen* in 1549, and a *chin-shih* selected to further his studies in the Hanlin Academy in 1553. Soon after he received his promotion to be a Hanlin Compiler in 1555 his mother died; so he retired to observe the mourning period. In 1558 he returned to the capital to resume his official career. His ability was noticed at

different times by Hsü Chieh, Chang Chü-cheng (*qq.v.*), and Kao Kung (*see* Chang Chü-cheng). In 1570, on the recommendation of Kao Kung, he became Hanlin chancellor. In this year, when the government was confronted with the delicate Mongol situation (*see* Altan-qaγan), Chang Ssu-wei contributed to its peaceful solution, not so much by any move made in his official capacity, as by his personal relationship with the three central figures, Wang Ch'ung-ku, Kao Kung, and Chang Chü-cheng. A record of these negotiations is to be found in twenty-three letters written to Wang, which are included in his literary works. Later that year he was also appointed right vice minister of Personnel, while still holding the post of Hanlin chancellor; shortly afterward he was transferred to be left vice minister. In 1571, as a result of attacks by certain critics, he resigned from office under pretext of illness and returned home.

On July 5, 1572, Emperor Chu Tsaihou (*q. v.*) died. As soon as Chu I-chün (*q. v.*) ascended the throne (July 19) Kao Kung was dismissed; Lü T'iao-yang (*q.v.*), recommended by Chang Chü-cheng, became grand secretary in his place, and Chang Chü-cheng, who had entered the Grand Secretariat in 1567, became senior grand secretary. Since the family of Chang Ssu-wei was rich, he often made presents to Chang Chü-cheng, especially on the occasion of festivals. In 1574 Chang Ssu-wei was recalled to Peking and put in charge of the supervisorate of imperial instruction. The following year Chang Chü-cheng requested the emperor to enlarge the Grand Secretariat; a little later Chang Ssu-wei, on the recommendation of Chang Chü-cheng and with the support of the eunuch Feng Pao (*see* Chang Chü-cheng), then the head of the directorate of ceremonial, was appointed titular minister of Rites and Grand Secretary. At this time Chang Chü-cheng dominated the whole government. He took it for granted that the national affairs should be under his sole direction and he regarded the other two grand secretaries as his subordinates. As a matter of fact, the appointments of both Lü T'iao-yang and Chang Ssu-wei were due to him; the former, moreover, was broken in health, and timid besides.

In 1577, when the *Shih-tsung shih-lu* was completed, Chang Ssu-wei, who had been vice director-general of the compilation, received a promotion; in the next few years other honors, concluding with the title of chu-kuo 柱國 (pillar of state) in 1581, and the rank of grand preceptor of the heir apparent in 1582, were heaped upon him.

At first Chang Ssu-wei allowed himself to be led by Chang Chü-cheng—often modifying his own ideas to conform to the latter's wishes. In due course, however, he refused to submit tamely to Chang Chü-cheng; the result was a gradual estrangement. For this reason, there was disharmony in the Grand Secretariat. On the death of Chang Chü-cheng in July 1582, Chang Ssu-wei became senior grand secretary. A month later, following the birth of the emperor's first son, Chu Ch'ang-lo (ECCP), Chang addressed a memorial to the throne which ran in part: "Although our nation is now enjoying peace, there are a number of high officials who do not understand the true intention of the Court. They often adopt measures which are so severe that they prove vexatious to the people. I beg Your Majesty to abolish all harsh laws and regulations, and establish immediately a lenient policy to express our joy over the prince's birth." The emperor approved. From that time on, the government changed its administrative procedures, and those officials who were charged with the responsibility of criticism were also able to function freely. As many censors and critics had sharply attacked the actions of Chang Chü-cheng, fear came over the latter's adherents.

In the face of this situation, left vice Minister of Personnel Wang Chuan 王篆 (T. 紹芳, cs 1562) and Minister of Works Tseng Sheng-wu 曾省吾 (T. 三甫, b. 1532,

cs 1556), both of whom were Chang Chü-cheng's followers, sought the aid of Grand Secretary Shen Shih-hsing (*q. v.*), with whom they were also closely associated. Just at this time the powerful eunuch Feng Pao became displeased with Chang Ssu-wei because Chang refused his request for the title of earl. Accordingly, in November, 1582, Investigating Censor Ts'ao I-k'uei 曹一夔 (T. 子韶, 雙華, cs 1574), at the instigation of Wang and Tseng, accused minister of Personnel Wang Kuo-kuang (*see* Chang Hsüeh-yen) of improprieties, in which Chang Ssu-wei was also involved. About the same time, Tseng Sheng-wu resigned from office and Wang Chuan was also dismissed. Then, as senior grand secretary, Chang Ssu-wei recommended to the government many men who had opposed Chang Chü-cheng and as a result had lost their posts. Although not all were given appointments, these measures put Chang Ssu-wei in good repute with the other grand secretaries (*see* Shen Shih-hsing).

A little later both Chang Ssu-wei's eldest son, Chang Chia-cheng 甲徵, and Shen Shih-hsing's son, Shen Yung-mou (*see* Shen Shih-hsing), qualified for the *chin-shih*. At this juncture, Censor Wei Yün-chen (*see* Ku Hsien-ch'eng) offered a memorial to the throne, saying among other things: "Chang Chü-cheng's three sons having successively received the *chin-shih* degree has brought some evil practices into the examination system. To do full justice, may I suggest that from now on those grand secretaries' sons who successfully pass the metropolitan examination (*hui-shih*) shall not be allowed to participate in a palace examination (*t'ing-shih* or *tien-shih*) until the grand secretary concerned is permitted to resign from office." This proposal angered Chang Ssu-wei and he made every effort to defend his son from any wrongdoing. Meanwhile Shen Shih-hsing also memorialized the throne to exonerate himself and his son. Shen, supported by Feng Pao, drafted a rescript proposing the dismissal of Wang Kuo-kuang; and this was carried out. In the course of these developments Chang Ssu-wei asked several times for retirement but his petition was denied.

A week later Censor Chang Wen-ta (*see* Li Chih) accused Chang Ssu-wei of a possible affront to the throne. Upset by this accusation, Chang Ssu-wei offered large bribes to Feng Pao to mollify him. As a consequence Feng became less antagonistic, and Chang Wen-ta was degraded and transferred to a distant province—the rescript for his transfer being drafted by Shen Shih-hsing, who wished by this means to save Chang Ssu-wei's face. The latter, however, secretly suspected Shen because he assumed that the accusations made by Ts'ao I-kuei and Chang Wen-ta were all instigated by Shen and were of a piece with his political maneuvering.

Soon afterward, accused by certain eunuchs, Feng Pao lost his close relationship to the throne. Whereupon Chang Ssu-wei bade his student, Li Chih (*see* Shen Shih-hsing), present to the emperor a memorial exposing the eunuch's misdeeds. On January 1, 1583, Feng was reduced to attendant of a eunuch agency in Nanking, and his property confiscated. The end result was that Chang and Shen were both absolved, and were retained in office by the emperor; Wei Yün-chen was demoted and transferred to a distant place on the ground that his insinuations that there had been some impropriety were uncalled for. It is worth mentioning, however, that, from then on, no one whose father was holding the post of grand secretary was granted the *chin-shih* degree.

After Chang Chü-cheng died, his followers often plotted to exclude Chang Ssu-wei from the Grand Secretariat and supported Shen Shih-hsing for the post of senior grand secretary. This made Chang Ssu-wei very unhappy. Once he asked Shen: "The replacement of a senior grand secretary is just like the rotation of the four seasons; why do you force me to yield?" Shen was greatly embarrassed by these words. Immediately before

Chang's return home, he and his one-time students, who were then censors or critics, planned secretly to censure Shen. When they had completed their memorial and were ready to present it to the throne, Chang received news of his father's death and left for his native place (May 26, 1583). Thus their plan was aborted. Chang Ssu-wei died in December when his period of mourning for his father was nearly at an end. Accorded various honors, he was posthumously canonized as Wen-i 文毅 (literary and resolute).

The collected literary works of Chang Ssu-wei, entitled the *T'iao-lu-t'ang chi* 條麓堂集 were first printed in 1586. Later the book was reedited by his second son, Chang T'ai-cheng 泰徵 (cs 1580), in 34 *chüan*, by adding 2 *chüan* of biographical materials (*chüan* 33 and 34), and printed in 1595 in Honan. In 1604 this 34 *chüan* edition, now beautifully engraved, was brought out in Soochow at the instance of his third son, Chang Ting-cheng 定徵, Shih Ch'ung-kuang 施重光 (T. 慶徵), then supervisor of the Soochow tariff, financing the publication. The microfilm copy of the 1604 edition in the collection of rare books of the Peiping National Library is unfortunately incomplete (lacking *chüan* 13 to 22); it is a fine specimen of good printing of the late Ming era.

During the Ming dynasty there were several people by the name of Chang Ssu-wei, one of whom was the dramatist Chang Ssu-wei (*see* Ch'en Yü-chiao).

Bibliography

1/219/1a; 5/17/134a; 84/己11/4a; TSCC (1885–88), XIV: 250/15a; *Huang Ming wen-hai* (microfilm), 2/2/9, 10; NLP microfilm, roll 1448; *P'u-chou-fu chih* 蒲州府志 (1754), 12下/36b; Fu Hsi-hua 傅惜華, *Ming-tai chuan-ch'i ch'üan-mu* 明代傳奇全目 (Peking, 1959), 106.

Chou Tao-chi and Lienche Tu Fang

CHANG Ts'ung, *see* **CHANG Fu-ching**

CHANG Yü 張羽, also known as Chang Lai-i 來儀 (T. 附鳳, H. 靜居, 清晏子), 1333-85, poet, painter, and official, was a native of Kiukiang, Kiangsi. At the time that his father was serving as an official in Chekiang around 1350, Chang Yü studied in Hangchow and later distinguished himself in literary circles. He is said to have made his home in Hu-chou 湖州, and succeeded in the Chekiang provincial examination. Some time later he was principal of the An-ting Academy 安定書院, newly established at Hu-chou which was dedicated to the Sung scholar Hu Yüan (993-1059).

After the rebel leader Chang Shih-ch'eng (q.v.) made Soochow the capital of his occupied territory (1356), Chang Yü moved to that city and stayed in the quarter outside the north wall. There he and nine other young men-of-letters were later called "Ten friends of the north wall" by the prominent poet Kao Ch'i (q.v.). Kao Ch'i, Hsü Pen, Yang Chi (qq.v.), and he were known also as the "Four outstanding figures of Soochow" for their skill in poetry. With the exception of Kao, they were painters as well. Although personally on good terms with officials in the service of Chang Shih-ch'eng's government, such as Jao Chieh (see Hsü Pen), he himself contrived never to accept any post. Around 1363 he even succeeded in persuading Hsü Pen to retire and lead the life of a recluse with him at Hu-chou. They lived on separate hilltops not far from each other. Chang Yü's rural dwelling named Ch'ing-yen-t'ang 清晏堂 being on Mt. Tai 戴 and Hsü Pen's on Mt. Shu 蜀. Their lives and excursions to neighboring regions are known from their poems, some of which also deal with their paintings representing the landscape there. Chang's praise of the superior artistry of Hsü's painting is also known from his prose.

Before Wu-hsing was taken by the armies of the rebel leader Chu Yüan-chang in October, 1366, both Chang and Hsü went to join their friends in Soochow. As Soochow was in its turn attacked a few months later, they shared the tribulations of the population in this besieged city during the ten months prior to its capture by Chu's armies the following year. Unlike some of his friends who were banished to Feng-yang 鳳陽, for having served Chang Shih-ch'eng, Chang Yü went to stay in Hangchow, and later returned to his old residence on Mt. Tai. He was summoned to an imperial audience by the Ming court in May, 1371, but was not given an appointment as a result of a divergence of opinion between the emperor and himself. During these years on Mt. Tai, he wrote many poems nostalgically thinking of his friends in general and Hsü Pen in particular, for they were all released from banishment in 1369, and each was given an official post elsewhere.

In 1373 Chang Yü was summoned again, and appointed assistant minister of the Court of Imperial Sacrifices. In January, 1375, he was charged with the mission of offering sacrifices at the mausoleum of the emperor's ancestors at their native place, Feng-yang. Later he recounted his trip vividly in a series of ten poems entitled "Chi hsing" 紀行. After this mission, he stayed on at his post for the next ten years, during which he also served concurrently in the Hanlin Academy. Little is known otherwise, however, of his official career. Among his writings of this period, there are the poems deploring the deaths of Kao Ch'i, Hsü Pen, and Yang Chi. Chang Yü was famous for his prose and also for his calligraphy. When a stone tablet was to be erected in December, 1383, in the temple dedicated to Kuo Tzu-hsing (q.v.) at Ch'u-chou 滁州, he was ordered to write an epigraph on Kuo's deeds and accomplishments in chronological order, which had been drafted by the emperor himself. This epigraph, entitled Ch'ih-tz'u Ch'u-yang wang miao-pei 勅賜滁陽王廟碑, is still extant.

In the summer of 1385, Chang Yü was banished to Kwangtung for having offended the emperor. While only half way to his destination, he was called back by an imperial order. Exactly one night after arriving at the capital in July, he drowned himself in the river in the west suburb, where he had composed a poem when he passed by during his journey to Fengyang in 1375. Since his friends, such as Kao Ch'i, had already been among the victims of the emperor's intolerance, and thousands had been implicated in the alleged conspiracy of Hu Wei-yung (*q.v.*) in 1380, the reason for his suicide may have been the fear of possible recrimination. His body, later transported to his native place, was buried there by his son. His friend T'ung Chi 童冀 (T. 中州), a pedagogue at the Hu-chou prefectural school, later composed an epitaph in his memory.

Chang Yü's poetic work entitled *Chingchü chi* 靜居集, 6 *ch.*, including the epitaph by T'ung Chi, was first edited by Chang Hsi (*see* Hsü Pen) in 1491. In 1603, on the basis of this edition, Ch'en Pang-chan (*q.v.*) made a new edition in four *chüan* without adding any new poems. This 1603 edition was copied into the *Ssu-k'u* and later reprinted in the *Yü-chang ts'ung-shu* (1915, see ECCP, p. 949). The 1491 edition discovered by Fu Tsenghsiang (BDRC) was later reproduced in the third series of the *Ssu-pu ts'ung-k'an*. In his colophon Fu made a comparison between these two editions, noting some textual differences. In the *Yü-chang ts'ungshu*, there is also one *chüan* of Chang Yü's essays entitled *Chang Lai-i hsien-sheng wen-chi* 文集, with a colophon by Huang P'ei-lieh (ECCP).

Chang Yü's paintings are said to be after the style of the Sung painter Mi Yu-jen (1074–1153). From the synthetical catalogue of John C. Ferguson we learn that seven paintings by Chang Yü figure in ancient catalogues. Mrs. Laing reports one depicting a cloudy mountain ravine and temple, dated 1367, now in a private collection in Hong Kong.

Bibliography:

1/285/21a; 3/266/17a; 5/70/44a; 84/甲/11a; MSL (1962), T'ai-tsu, 1219; Chang Yü, *Ching-chü chi* (SPTK 3d series), 1/27b, 34a, 52b, 2/11b, 3/6b, 4/4b, 5/13b, 6/18b; SK (1930) , 169/9b; Chang Yü, *Chang Lai-i hsien-sheng wen-chi* (*Yü-chang ts'ung-shu*), 1a, 16a, 35a, 39, 52b, *pu-i*, 1; *Chin-chiang-fu chih* (1874), 36/2a; J. C. Ferguson, *Index of Artists*, 264b; E. J. Laing, *Chinese Paintings in Chinese Publications, 1956–1968* (Ann Arbor, 1969), 152; F. W. Mote, *The Poet Kao Ch'i* (Princeton, 1962), 95, 97, 103, 193, 213.

Tung-wen Weng

CHANG Yü-ch'u 張宇初 (T. 子璿, H. 耆山, 無爲子), 1361–1410, eldest son of Chang Cheng-ch'ang (*q.v.*), was the forty-third Taoist patriarch on Lung-hu shan 龍虎山 in Kuei-hsi 貴溪, Kiangsi. When he went to Nanking for his first imperial audience after his succession to the hereditary patriarchate in 1378, Emperor Chu Yüan-chang remarked on his strong resemblance to his father. He was described as distinguished in appearance with big round eyes, which were regarded as signs of Taoist nobility. He was given the official Taoist title of Cheng-i Ta-chen-jen 正一大眞人 (senior true man of the Cheng-i sect). In 1383 he held a special service on Tzu-chin Mountain 紫金山 near Nanking, and two years later prayed for rain in the Temple of Divine Music, or Shen-yüeh kuan 神樂觀. By imperial order, his residence on Lung-hu shan was rebuilt. When an imperial edict prohibited making counterfeit charms in 1391, he was given a special seal to signify the authenticity of the charms which he issued.

During the short Chien-wen reign, for some reason Chang Yü-ch'u was castigated, and stripped of the Ta-chen-jen title. On the enthronement of Chu Ti (*q. v.*), however, he was reinstated. By 1406 he was ordered to head a project for the compilation of Taoist literature (*see* Chu Ch'i-chen). He received acclaim the following year for his service conducted in the Ch'ao-t'ien kung 朝天宮 in Nanking. Then in 1408 the emperor sent him to search for the famed and long-sought-for immortal Chang San-feng (*see*

Chang Chung) on Wu-tang 武當 Mountain in Hukuang. One day, early in 1410, he handed over his official seal and swords, symbols of Taoist authority, to his younger brother, Chang Yü-ch'ing 清 (T. 彥誠, H. 西壁, d. 1426), wrote a poem, and expired.

Chang Yü-ch'u was the most learned of all the Taoist patriarchs of the Ming period. Well versed in Confucian Classics and literature, he was also a calligrapher and painter. Even in his younger days, he was known for his scholarship, and esteemed by Sung Lien (*q.v.*) as a "Confucian Taoist Immortal" (列仙之儒). He left a literary collection, the *Hsien-ch'üan chi* 峴泉集, 12 *ch*. A four *chüan* edition of this work received a notice in the eighteenth century Imperial Catalogue in which the editors complimented Chang Yü-ch'u on his literary ability and his understanding of Confucian and neo-Confucian teachings.

Religious Taoism was dominated by two main sects in the Ming dynasty: the Cheng-i sect headed by the Chang family on Lung-hu shan, and the Ch'üan-chen (全眞) sect, founded by Wang Che (1112-70) in Shensi during the difficult times after the Sung court had moved south. The latter sect flourished in north China under the conquest dynasties of Chin and Yüan and it afforded a refuge for the Chinese educated class. It propounded the doctrine of uniting and harmonizing the "Three Religions," namely Confucianism, Taoism, and Buddhism. By the 14th century this doctrine was widespread and espoused by many, irrespective of their beliefs and leanings. Even the Taoist priests of the older Cheng-i sect took it up rather naturally. In Chang Yü-ch'u we find a good example. Therefore, although the Ch'üan-chen sect had ceased to hold strictly to its early tenets and produced no well-known leader, by the later years of the 14th century, its influence was great and universal.

Chang Yü-ch'u also left a short work on Taoist regulations, the *Tao-men shih-kuei* 道門十規, 1 *ch*. He annotated some Taoist classics and compiled two works: seven *chüan* of sayings of his ancestor, the thirtieth Taoist patriarch, Chang Chi-hsien (1092-1126), and a gazetteer, the *Lung-hu-shan chih*, 10 *ch*. Except for the gazetteer, all the others were printed in the *Tao-tsang* 道藏 of 1447 and may also be found in the reprinted edition of 1926.

His brother Chang Yü-ch'ing, the forty-fourth Taoist patriarch, was a scholar, painter, and calligrapher of some note. He was later succeeded by a nephew Chang Mou-ch'eng 懋丞 (T. 文開, H. 澹然, 九陽, 1387-1445), a son of Chang Yü-ch'eng 珵, the third brother of Chang Yü-ch'u and Chang Yü-ch'ing.

Bibliography

40/89/1a; 84/閏/17a; 86/23/44a; SK (1930), 170/1a; TSCC (1885-88), XIV: 248/16/12a, 249/17/1a, XVII: 788/22/10a; *Lung-hu-shan chih* (1740).

Lienche Tu Fang

CHANG Yüan-chi 張元吉 (T. 孟陽), 1435-ca.85, the forty-sixth Taoist patriarch on Lung-hu shan 龍虎山 (Dragon Tiger Mountain) in Kiangsi, was the grandson of Chang Mou-ch'eng (*see* Chang Yü-ch'u), the forty-fifth patriarch. As his father Chang Liu-kang 張留綱 died young, he succeeded to his grandfather's official Taoist post. At his grandfather's death in 1445, he came into the office but, as he was not yet of age, his grandmother née Tung 董 was appointed as regent. Chang Yüan-chi was summoned to Peking for an audience with the emperor in 1445. In 1446 both his mother née Kao 高 and his deceased father were given honorific titles. In another later audience a special hat and robe were bestowed on him as an imperial favor. During the reigns of Chu Ch'i-chen and Chu Ch'i-yü (*qq.v.*) he repeatedly performed services appreciated by both emperors. Twice he asked permission to be granted more ordination certificates, so that he might have a greater number of young novices in his establishment —420 more in the year 1454 and 350 more in 1463. His request was granted in the first instance, but in the second the government cut the number to 150.

That Chang Yüan-chi was spoiled in his childhood is a strong possibility. In any case all accounts agree that he had an unruly nature and was notorious for this both in his native place and among the members of the Chang clan. Perhaps because he was acquisitive as well, he was also lax in his responsibility in respect to the prohibition of counterfeit charms. Early in the Ch'eng-hua years (1465–87), through a regional inspector, all the grievances against him came to light and were reported to the emperor. Among his crimes and evil deeds were such serious ones as capturing young girls and boys and appropriating money and property by force, and beating or whipping people to death when they displeased him. It was said that as many as forty people died at his hand, and that he kept a private jail. He was also accused of using certain vehicles and articles exceeding those permitted his rank. In 1469 he was brought to Peking and thrown into prison. At a court hearing he was sentenced to death. Nevertheless, by his resourcefulness and skill in the ways of bribery, he succeeded in escaping execution. Instead he received one hundred strokes of the bastinado, and was banished to Su-chow 肅州 in northwest China, to be pardoned later.

For some ten years after the downfall of Chang Yüan-chi, the official post of Taoist patriarch on Dragon Tiger Mountain remained vacant. A family dispute between two candidates, Chang Kuang-fan 張光範 and Chang Yüan-ch'ing 張元慶 (T. 天錫, H. 貞一, 七一丈人, d. 1509), ensued. By 1478 Chang Yüan-ch'ing gained official support, won out, and succeeded as the forty-seventh patriarch. On his retirement, his son Chang Yen-yü 張彥頵 (T. 士瞻, H. 湛然, d. 1550) became the forty-eighth in line. Then, on Chang Yen-yü's retirement in 1549, his son Chang Yung-hsü 張永緒 (T. 允承, H. 三陽, d. 1565) succeeded to the post. During the Chia-ching

period, although the emperor was a devout Taoist, his two foremost Taoist favorites were Shao Yüan-chieh and T'ao Chung-wen (qq.v.), the Chang family of Dragon Tiger Mountain receiving no more than its traditional share.

At Chang Yung-hsü's death, his son Chang T'ien-yu 天佑 was still an infant. Before it was possible for him to be invested by the emperor as the successor of his father, he also died. Thus a nephew. Chang Kuo-hsiang 張國祥 (T. 心湛, d. 1623), became the successor, and the fiftieth Taoist patriarch in 1577. In 1585 he received the commission to collect and edit an additional group of Taoist works to supplement the Cheng-t'ung Taoist corpus. This was completed and printed in 1607, and became known as the *Wan-li hsü Tao-tsang* 萬曆續道藏. The *Cheng-t'ung Tao-tsang* (1421 titles, printed in 1447) and the *Wan-li hsü Tao-tsang* (55 titles) were both photolithographically reproduced by the Commercial Press in 1926.

Among the works included in the *Hsü Tao-tsang* are two relating to the history of the Chang patriarchs in the Ming dynasty, namely, the *Huang Ming en-ming shih-lu* 皇明恩命世錄, 9 ch., a collection of imperial edicts, instructions, and patents, dating from 1360 to 1605, and the *Han t'ien-shih shih-chia* 漢天師世家, 4 ch., containing biographical sketches of the Chang patriarchs, from the first to the forty-ninth, ending with the year 1565. Apparently both were edited by Chang Kuo-hsiang, and both works in abridged form were later incorporated in the *Lung-hu-shan chih* of 1740.

After Chang Kuo-hsiang, his son Chang Hsien-yung 張顯庸 (T. 九功, original name 顯祖, H. 浴梧散人) became the fifty-first patriarch. Then Chang Ying-ching 張應京 (T. 翊辰), most likely a son of Chang Hsien-yung, succeeded him as the fifty-second patriarch in 1636. After the Manchus conquered China, he went to Peking in 1651 to pay homage to the emperor of the new dynasty, whereupon he was reinvested as the Cheng-i ssu-chiao ta-chen-jen 正一嗣教大眞人 and remained as the Taoist patriarch. Thus dynasties came and went, but the Taoist institution on Dragon Tiger Moutain maintained its unbroken course.

Bibliography

TSCC (1885-8), XIV: 249/17/5a, XVIII: 291/2/13a; KC (1958), 2269; *Lung-hu-shan chih* (1740).
Lienche Tu Fang

CHANG Yüan-pien 張元忭 (T. 子蓋, H. 陽和), 1538-April 20, 1588, who was born in Shan-yin 山陰, Chekiang, and who became a student of Wang Chi (*q. v.*), was both a writer and an official. He graduated as optimus in 1571 after several unsuccessful attempts following his achievement of the *chü-jen* in 1558. His initial appointment was as a compiler in the Hanlin Academy. Much later he became reader-in-waiting in the Hanlin and an instructor of the heir apparent. His father, Chang T'ien-fu 張天復 (T. 復亨, H. 內山, d. 1578, cs 1547), author of *Huang-yü k'ao* 皇輿考, 12 *ch.*, served as surveillance vice commissioner of Yunnan (4a) and director of the Kansu branch of the Court of the Imperial Stud (3b).

A glimpse into the character of Chang Yüan-pien may be seen from the fact that, in his eighteenth year, he wrote a moving eulogy of Yang Chi-sheng (*q.v.*) on learning of the latter's execution in Peking. When in 1568 Chang T'ien-fu was compelled to return to Yunnan as a prisoner to stand trial for the defeat of government troops by tribal insurgents in Wu-ting 武定, the son accompanied him all the way, then hurried to the capital to lodge an appeal, rushing home when his father, deprived of rank, was released.

Following his father's death in 1578 and a period of mourning, Chang Yüan-pien was commissioned to teach in the palace school for eunuchs, then to take charge of imperial patents and to participate in the recording of the emperor's daily activities. On the birth of the heir apparent (1582) Chang was ordered to carry the news to Chu Hua-k'uei (*see* Kuo Cheng-yü) at Wuchang. This gave him an opportunity to travel on the rivers of Hunan and in the Wu-i mountains 武夷山 of Fukien; also to visit his mother just before her death. After the mourning period and a long stay at home, Chang returned to the court (1587) to assume the posts of reader-in-waiting in the Hanlin and instructor of the heir apparent; soon thereafter he became an expositor of the Classics to the emperor.

Earlier, on the occasion of the enthronement of Chu I-chün (*q.v.*) in 1572, Chang made an effort to clear his father's name and to restore his rank, at the same time offering to relinquish his own. This failing, much later he made another appeal. When this too was denied he fell ill and died. In the early 1620s he received the posthumous name of Wen-kung 文恭, and his fellow townsmen elected to keep his memory alive by enshrining him among Shao-hsing's men of note.

Although a protégé of Chang Chücheng (*q.v.*) Chang Yüan-pien did not join the ranks of his sycophants. He was a follower of Wang Shou-jen (*q.v.*), but saw no fundamental difference between the schools of Chu Hsi (1130–1200) and Lu Chiu-yüan (1139–93). To support this view he compiled an extract of those words of Chu Hsi which agreed with the pronouncements of Wang Shou-jen. Among other writings ascribed to him, in part or in whole, are the local histories of his native district, *Shan-yin-hsien chih* 縣志, 12 *ch.* (started by his father, and left unpublished?), of his own prefecture, *Shao-hsing-fu chih*, 50 *ch.* (printed 1586/87), and of a neighboring district, *K'uai-chi-hsien chih* 會稽縣志, 16 *ch.* The editors of the *Ssu-k'u* catalogue consider the last unique in that the final chapter describes all preceding local histories of the area beginning with the *Yüeh chüeh shu* 越絕書 and *Wu Yüeh ch'un-ch'iu* 吳越春秋, both of which date from the first century A.D. Other works include a study

of a mountain in his native district, the
Yün-men chih lüeh 雲門志略, 5 *ch.*, its
ancient sites, famous people, and the
literature they composed; the *Kuan-ko man-
lu* 館閣漫錄, 10 *ch.*, an annalistic record
of the appointment and transfer of
members of the Hanlin from 1402 to 1521
with occasional comments; the *Hanlin chu-
shu hsüan-ts'ui* 翰林諸書選粹, 4 *ch.*, which
deals with the words of certain philosophers divided into 25 categories; the *Pu-er-
chai wen-hsüan* 不二齋文選 [or 稿], 7 *ch.*,
a collection of his own pieces, essays, 6 *ch.*,
poems, 1 *ch.*, and the *Kuang* 廣 *huang-yü
k'ao*, 20 *ch.*, an extension of his father's
historio-geographical work. The last was
proscribed in the 18th century for remarks
on the frontier and on the Jurchen, but
it has been preserved.

Chang's son, Chang Ju-lin 張汝霖 (T.
蕭之, cs 1595), assistant administration
commissioner of Kiangsi, was the author
of at least three works. Another son,
Chang Ju-mou 汝懋 (cs 1613), rose to be
assistant minister of the Grand Court of
Revision. A great-grandson, Chang Tai
(ECCP), was noted for his literary and
historical writings.

Bibliography

1/110/1a, 283/26a; 5/19/27a; 61/115/1a; *Shan-
yin-hsien chih* (1803), 14/27a, 31b; SK (1930),
72/2a, 74/4a, 76/3a, 80/3b, 138/2b, 179/3a; KC
(1958), 4578; Huang Yü-chi (ECCP), *Chien-
ch'ing-tang shu-mu*, 7/22a; Chu Shih-chia, *Catalogue of local histories* (1957), 153, 154; Toyo
Bunko *Catalogue of local histories* (1964), 114;
Taiwan *Catalogue of local histories* (1957),
11, 14; Sun Tien-ch'i (1957), 208.

L. Carrington Goodrich and C. N. Tay

CHANG Yung 張永 (T. 德延, H. 守菴),
August 17, 1465-February 8, 1529, a
native of Hsin-ch'eng新城, about fifty miles
south of Peking, was a eunuch during the
Cheng-te period, known for his military
ability. Chang entered the palace at the
age of ten. Not until a dozen years later
did he begin to hold a relatively significant position, first as junior assistant-

director of the nei-kuan chien 內官監
(directorate of palace builders). In 1487,
on the accession of Chu Yu-t'ang (*q.v.*),
Chang was sent to serve at the tomb of
Emperor Chu Chien-shen (*q.v.*). This service lasted until 1496 when Chang was
recalled to wait on the young prince, Chu
Hou-chao (*q.v.*). It was in this assignment
that Chang quickly made himself known
along with Liu Chin and Ku Ta-yung
(*qq. v.*) as one of the "Eight Tigers". He
was on good terms with Liu, but after
the prince became emperor (June, 1505)
conflicts developed, and eventually Chang
served as the instrument of Liu Chin's
fall.

The emperor must have discovered his
military talent quite early, for Chang's
first assignment was as senior assistant-
director of the imperial stables, the
routine work of which was partly a
concern of the ministry of War. Shortly
afterwards, Chang was made director of
the Yü-yung chien 御用監 (directorate of
furniture supplies). On February 7, 1506,
he received command of the firearms
division, and soon became chief of the
capital garrison. By September 27, 1508,
he had assumed the responsibility for the
imperial military training corps. His
work must have given satisfaction, for
several of his close relatives had begun to
receive imperial favors. On February 4,
1507, his younger brother, Chang Jung 容,
was granted the position of centurion in
the Embroided-uniform Guard and within
a few months was promoted to chiliarch,
then to assistant commander. In October
of the same year, his father Chang Yu 友
was appointed Guard commander.

Chang's experience in military matters
was also tested by service in actual campaigns. The first of the sort came in 1510
when the prince of An-hua, Chu Chih-fan
(*see* Yang T'ing-ho), rose in rebellion.
Chang and Yang I-ch'ing (*q.v.*) received
orders to suppress the revolt. Before they
reached the disturbed area, however, the
rebel leader had been captured by General
Ch'iu Yüeh (*see* Ch'iu Luan). Having

assisted in restoring order, Chang Yung accompanied the captive back to the capital. This mission helped to bring Chang and Yang together. On their way to Peking the bond between them was further strengthened by their joint plot to oust Liu Chin, their common rival (see Yang I-ch'ing). From then on the two became life-long political allies.

Liu Chin's fall from power (1510) was a major event. Though the plot was conceived by both Chang and Yang, it was Chang who went to the emperor to convince him that Liu Chin had evil designs. On the night of their return from Ninghsia Liu was arrested. A few days later the emperor himself, it is said, discovered seals and weapons in Liu Chin's house, and ordered his execution. Then Chang Yung succeeded Liu as director of Ceremonial, and again other members of his family were rewarded. On October 8 his elder brother Chang Fu 富 was given the hereditary title of earl of T'ai-an 泰安 伯 and his younger brother, Chang Jung, became earl of An-ting 安定伯. Four days later his adopted son Chu Te 朱德 (who had been honored with the imperial surname) was made vice commander of the Guard with the title of earl of Yung-shou 永壽伯. Because of the success of his plot and the numerous imperial favors accorded him, Chang Yung overreached himself. On July 28, 1511, he arrested a certain Wang Ch'ai 王豸 who had tattooed dragon designs and the character for king on his body. Chang denounced him as a heretic and saw to his execution. For this deed Chang proposed that he himself be awarded the hereditary title of marquis; owing to strong opposition, however, his wish was frustrated. Following this disappointment Chang turned to other schemes. He embezzled some seven thousand ounces of silver from the palace treasury in order to make various kinds of amusing things for his own pleasure. When this illegal practice was revealed by his long-time colleague Ch'iu Chü (see Chu Hou-chao), Chang was demoted (December 15,

1512) to be an ordinary eunuch, deprived of all responsibilities. But this enforced retirement lasted less than two years, when again his talents came into demand.

In August, 1514, the Ning-hsia and Shansi front was again threatened by an invasion from the northwest. As an expert on the border region Chang Yung was summoned from seclusion, and appointed chief supervising officer, with twenty thousand imperial troops under his command. Recalled shortly afterwards to the capital, Chang was restored to his previous position as director of the Yü-yung chien, and in 1515 was ordered to share the command of the Shen-chi Garrison and the military training corps with Ku Ta-yung. In October of the same year, Chang and Ku were told to supervise the rebuilding of the Ch'ien-ch'ing palace 乾清 宮 (burned down on February 10, 1514). On February 24, 1517, Chang resumed full control of the firearms division, and on October 19, of the military training corps. He was then asked to accompany the emperor on his tour of the Ning-hsia, Shansi, and Shensi region to inspect defense preparations. In the spring of 1518 another of Chang's close relatives was favored with the position of chiliarch in the Embroidered-uniform Guard.

Chang's last role in military affairs came during the rebellion in Kiangsi (July, 1519) of the prince of Ning, Chu Ch'en-hao (see Wang Shou-jen). The emperor decided that he would take the field himself. Before the imperial forces reached Kiangsi, however, Wang Shou-jen had already captured the prince. When Chang, as commander of the vanguard, arrived at Hangchow, Wang turned his captive over to the eunuch. Wang also requested him to suggest the return of the imperial force to Peking in order to avoid disturbing the people in Kiangsi. The emperor did not move farther south, nor did his party return to Peking immediately. By January, 1521, however, the emperor was back at the capital, and only a few months later he was dead. This also marked the culmination of Chang Yung's influence.

Like many favored persons at court during the Ming, as soon as a new emperor succeeded to the throne, Chang Yung became the target of accusations. On June 1, 1521, a censor accused him and several other eunuchs of malpractices. So he was demoted once more to be an ordinary eunuch with no special responsibility. Within the month the same censor again attacked him. This time he was sent to serve the imperial tombs in Nanking. Fortunately his political ally, Grand Secretary Yang I-ch'ing, was still influential, and saw to his eventual return to Peking (1526).

By this time his health was in serious condition. On December 27, 1527, Yang I-ch'ing memorialized on his behalf requesting that Chang Yung be restored to responsible positions because of his service to the imperial house in the preceding reign. The emperor accepted the recommendation, and again made Chang the director of the Yü-yung chien, charged as well with the military training corps. When Chang was back in office he realized that the situation was different from what it had been six years earlier: the garrison forces had become weak, the number of soldiers and horses had decreased, the equipment had deteriorated, and morale was at a low ebb. Chang wasted no time and proposed necessary steps to revitalize the imperial forces. His proposal received imperial approval, but before he saw any of his suggestions carried out, he passed away.

Bibliography

5/117/26a; MSL (1965), Shih-tsung, 0049, 0101, 1862, 1899; KC (1958), ch. 46–54; *Ming-shih* (Taiwan ed.), 112b, 710a, 940a, 1514a, 2124a, 2128a, 2130a, 2174a, 2216b, 2275a, 3415a, 3421b; Wang Shih-chen, *Yen-shan-t'ang pieh-chi*, 95/2b, 28a, 31a; Ho Liang-chün, *Ssu-yu-chai ts'ung-shuo*, 8/66a; Shen Te-fu, *Wan-li yeh-hu pien*, 6/164a; *Hsin-ch'eng-hsien chih* (1895), 9/17a; Robert B. Crawford, "Eunuch Power in the Ming Dynasty," TP, 49 (1961), 121, n. 7.

Yung-deh Richard Chu

CH'ANG Lun 常倫 (T. 明卿, H. 樓居子), November 30, 1492–1525, poet, official, minor painter, and calligrapher, was a native of Ch'in-shui 沁水, Tse-chou 澤州 prefecture, Shansi, the grandnephew of Ch'ang Yüeh 軏 (cs 1481) and son of Ch'ang Tz'u 賜 (cs 1493, d. 1517). The latter rose successively from magistrate to censor and then to surveillance vice commissioner of Shensi, where he died in office. From childhood on Ch'ang Lun showed that he had natural gifts, but his family found him hard to control. His father spoiled him and let him have his own way. During his youth his poems and essays were sent for appraisal to such well-known writers as Li Meng-yang and Ho Ching-ming (*qq.v.*); their approbation led to his becoming proud and cocksure. At the age of eighteen he took second place in the provincial examination (his father having placed first in the same test in 1489). His pride hurt, Ch'ang Lun challenged the one adjudged to be his superior at the official banquet of celebration. A scene was avoided, however, when friends succeeded in calming him. The following year (1511) he achieved the *chin-shih*, and received an appointment as a judge (評事) in the Grand Court of Revision. His conduct, however, seems to have been hardly consistent with his duties, for he continued his carefree ways. As an accomplished horseman he competed in archery with scions of the nobility at the capital, who toasted him when he won. He loved to compose lyric poetry, drink wine, and sing his odes with girls of the gay quarters, with whom he would often spend the night. At times he was late in reaching his office. When scolded for his negligence, he replied contemptuously, "Even before receiving my official appointment, I slept with barbarian women (胡姬). Why should I cease my enjoyment of this life now?" On another occasion, because of his careless speech at a banquet when in his cups, he displeased certain officials, and was demoted to be a provincial official in the national scrutiny of 1515. Rather than accept this humiliation, however, he asked for sick leave and returned home.

With the assumption of power by Chu Hou-ts'ung (*q.v.*) in May, 1521, Ch'ang was posted to Shou-chou 壽州 in the prefecture of Feng-yang 鳳陽 as assistant magistrate. Here in the following year he made something of a name for himself in his defense of the region when it was invaded by bandits from Shantung by way of Honan. When the inspecting censor treated him discourteously, he left his office (1524) and returned home without informing his superiors. Not long afterwards word came that he had been given a promotion, but he declined it.

His end came in a dramatic way. One account has it that one day, tiring of his idle existence, he decided to seek another official appointment. He set out for Peking on horseback. Dressing himself in bright red garb, he rode off, waving his sword while at a gallop. When the horse became thirsty, it stopped for a drink at a stream near Lu-an 潞安, Shansi. Seeing his extraordinarily accoutered master's likeness mirrored in the water, the startled horse reared and fell into the river. So Ch'ang Lun died, his sword having pierced his abdomen. Another account has a somewhat different version; it relates that before his drowning he had first visited his ancestors' tombs and next had imbibed heavily at the residence of his maternal uncle. Then, dressed in red, he had galloped toward home, meeting his death on the way. He was only thirty-three years of age.

As Ch'ang had no close relatives who could manage proper funeral arrangements, the surveillance vice commissioner of Shansi, Han Pang-ch'i (*q.v.*), had the coffin transported to his home. Two other friends, both fellow *chin-shih* of 1511, also helped: Wang Ts'ou 王漆 (T. 公濟, H. 玉

溪子), then prefect of P'ing-yang-fu 平陽府 in the same province, provided for his burial, and Nan Ta-chi (*see* Wang Shou-jen) published two anthologies of his works, *Ch'ang P'ing-shih chi* 常評事集, 4 *ch.* (miscellaneous poems and essays), and *Ch'ang P'ing-shih hsieh-ch'ing chi* 寫情集, 2 *ch.* These are available in at least three collectanea. (One of them—the *Shan-yu* 山右 *ts'ung-shu*—is an official publication of the province of Shansi, sponsored by its last republican governor, Yen Hsi-shan [BDRC]). It is interesting to find in the additional notes printed at the end of *Ch'ang P'ing-shih chi* the contribution of a fellow townsman, Chang Ch'üan (ECCP), who supplies biographical data, and writes in praise of Ch'ang. Another short book which Ch'ang wrote on calligraphy, *Chiao-cheng tzu-fa* 校正字法, 1*ch.*, seems to have disappeared along with examples of his calligraphy and his painting. It is said that Ch'ang Lun's songs were so popular in Shansi that the prostitutes used to sing them. He also admired warrior heroes and doted on Taoist immortals. Besides his literary activities and his association with demimondaines, he devoted some of his time to alchemy in the hope of concocting potions which would give sexual pleasure and also bring about immortality. As the immortals are thought to inhabit dwellings high in the firmament, he gave himself the style (*hao*) Lou-chü-tzu 樓居子 (one who lives in a tower). In short, he was a romantic seeking a colorful but impractical life.

Bibliography

22/6/13a; 32/101/48b; 40/34/20a; 64/戊11/3a; 84/丙/101a; 85/1/28; TSCC (1885–88), XIV: 305/11b, 12a, XVII: 786/12a, XXIII: 99/21a, XXIV: 122/2b; Ho Liang-chün, *Ssu-yu-chai ts'ung-shuo* (1959), 235; *Shansi t'ung-chih* (1892), 17/24b, 31a, 18/3a, 129/12b, 148/26a, 155/32b; *Ch'in-shui-hsien chih* (1881), 6/5a, 10b, 8/23b, 28b, 11/1b, 17b; *Shou-chou chih* (1890), 13/25a; *Ch'ang P'ing-shih chi*; *Ch'ang P'ing-shih hsieh-ch'ing-chi* (in *Shan-yu ts'ung-shu*, Vols. 87 and 88).

Yang Chin-yi

CH'ANG Yü-ch'un 常遇春 (T. 伯仁), 1330–
August 9, 1369, eminent military leader
during the Ming founding, was a native
of Huai-yüan 懷遠, Hao-chou 濠州 prefecture, in the troubled Huai 淮 River
region, that, from the 1340s onward was
beset by disorder, famine, and banditry.
Here Chu Yüan-chang also began his
rebellious activities. Ch'ang Yü-ch'un came
from a peasant family about which nothing is known; it may be assumed that the
unsettled circumstances drove him into
banditry as they did so many others. At
the age of twenty-two he joined a local
bandit leader named Liu Chü 劉聚 and
quickly rose in the ranks. Ch'ang was tall
and powerfully built, skilled in the use of
all weapons but particularly with the bow
and arrow. During the spring of 1355
Ch'ang deserted Liu; leading a band of
several dozen personal followers, he asked
Chu Yüan-chang to accept him.

In was the moment in Chu Yüan-
chang's rise to power when he decided to
strike out from Ho-chou 和州 and cross
the Yangtze River; so he invited Ch'ang
to join him in this ambitious adventure.
On July 10, 1355, Chu set out upon the
dangerous exploit and gained a foothold
on the east bank. During the crucial two
or three days of fighting, Ch'ang Yü-ch'un
established himself as a warrior of great
courage and intelligence. On the first day
Ch'ang sped to the bank, leaped ashore
with a shout, and brandishing his spear
so menaced the defenders that they gave
ground, permitting Chu's forces to land.
These then fought their way directly into
the town of Ts'ai-shih 采石. Other adjacent
forts along the river surrendered. From
this beachhead Chu's army immediately
followed with an attack on T'ai-p'ing 太
平, a walled city and the prefectural seat.
It was garrisoned, but after a brief struggle its defenders fled in retreat north to
Chin-ling 金陵 (Nanking). Thus within
the day Chu had gained both Ts'ai-shih
and T'ai-p'ing. The following day Chu's
forces routed a government fleet and
maintained access to their families and

supplies still at the bases across the river.

In recognition of his contributions,
Ch'ang was given appointments within
Chu's command, first as vanguard regional
commander, and then commander. He
participated in attacks which followed,
first an unsuccessful storming of the walls
of Chin-ling in the middle of August, and
then successful attacks to seize Li-shui 溧水
and other nearby points. Early in 1356 in
a naval battle he displayed both aggressive
leadership in the field and great personal courage. The defeat of the government's
river forces paved the way for a new
attack on Chin-ling. It fell to Chu Yüan-
chang in April, and immediate follow-up
campaigns extended Chu's base area to
include Chinkiang downriver, as well as
other points controlling the land routes
to the east. As a result of the military
prowess displayed in these battles throughout 1355 and 1356, Ch'ang Yü-ch'un
gained a secure position within Chu Yüan-
chang's top command. Soon he was second
in reputation and in trust only to Hsü Ta
(q. v.). Throughout the next thirteen
years, from the capture of Chin-ling in
1356 until Ch'ang's death in Liao-tung,
Hsü as commander-in-chief and Ch'ang
as his vice-commander campaigned successfully against Chu's rivals in the central
and lower Yangtze region, and finally
against the Yüan forces in the north, virtually conquering the empire for Chu.

In the autumn of 1356 Chu's forces
were active on the eastern front against
a rival rebel leader, Chang Shih-ch'eng
(q. v.), based on Soochow. In October the
two opponents fought over the intermed-
iate prefectural city of Ch'ang 常-chou.
When Hsü Ta's attacking column was
surrounded, Ch'ang led the attack which
broke that encirclement, freed Hsü from
the trap, and destroyed a large enemy
force. After the capture of Ch'ang-chou
in March, 1357, Ch'ang Yü-ch'un was
promoted to general of the armies of the
center. Hsü and Ch'ang then turned southwestward against Yüan forces, capturing
Ning-kuo 寧國 prefecture in April. The

campaign got off to a slow start, but became a victorious one after Chu Yüan-chang joined his armies in the field and stayed with them as they pushed on, with Ch'ang busy fighting along the south bank of the Yangtze. In March, 1358, he was promoted to commander-in-chief of foot, horse, and naval forces of the Chiang-nan 江南 branch secretariat. At the end of the year and early in 1359, Ch'ang was one of the field commanders accompanying Chu Yüan-chang on the campaign into central Chekiang, still held by Yüan forces. They took Wu婺-chou (modern Chin-hua 金華) in January. Chu subsequently renamed it Ning-yüeh 寧越 -fu, where he set up a new branch of the chief military commission with Ch'ang as its assistant chief, and made it the base for further military penetration. Shortly afterwards Ch'ang was assigned to storm the next prefectural center to the southwest, Ch'ü 衢 chou, which he succeeded in capturing late in the autumn. Then, at the very end of the year and in the first months of 1360, he led the attempt to wrest Hang-chow from Chang Shih-ch'eng's grasp. In this campaign Ch'ang failed, although he was not defeated in the field. After suffering some losses, Ch'ang was recalled to Chin-ling (April) and Chu admonished him to be more cautious. Despite the failure to capture Hangchow, however, other points had been secured along the eastern front.

In mid-1360 Ch'ang was sent upriver to assist Hsü Ta in the continuing struggle against Ch'en Yu-liang (q.v.) on the western front. The objective was Anking, and one of Ch'en's major bastions on the Yangtze. Guessing that a lightly garrisoned Ch'ih-chou (modern Kuei-ch'ih 貴池, Anhwei), captured the previous year, would tempt Ch'en Yu-liang to attack, Ch'ang and Hsü Ta arranged an ambush. Once Ch'en had surrounded Ch'ih-chou, Ch'ang's and Hsü's forces, concealed in the surrounding hills, attacked and badly mauled Ch'en's army. Instead of withdrawing to the west, however, Ch'en assembled a large ground and naval force and turned downriver to attack and seize T'ai-p'ing, which had been Chu Yüan-chang's gateway to Chin-ling in 1355. There Ch'en murdered his nominal overlord, Hsü Shou-hui (q.v.), assumed the title of emperor in a new rebel dynasty which he called the Han, and moved against Chin-ling.

In this grave emergency, Chu Yüan-chang again took the field and charged Ch'ang Yü-ch'un with the rear-line defense of Chin-ling. That was only a temporary assignment, however, and in the elaborate ambush which was set up for Ch'en's advancing forces, Ch'ang and all the principal generals played important parts. Ch'en's advance units fell into the ambush and were destroyed; Ch'en gave up the attack and withdrew to the west. Ch'ang was among the commanders who accompanied Chu in pursuing Ch'en Yu-liang back towards Anking. At the end of 1361 Ch'ang was dispatched from the Anking front to return in haste to the eastern front. Chang Shih-ch'eng took this opportunity to send a major force to besiege Ch'ang-hsing 長興 on the west shore of Lake T'ai, astride the route into central Chekiang. On hearing that Ch'ang Yü-ch'un was coming to relieve the city, Chang's general abandoned the attack.

Ch'ang then again joined the forces upriver. Throughout 1362 he was engaged in the struggle that centered first on Anking and then on driving Ch'en Yu-liang west. Early in 1363 the eastern front produced another emergency. Chang Shih-ch'eng sent his best general, Lü Chen (see Chang Shih-ch'eng) with a large army to attack the rebel Sung capital at An-feng 安豐 (in northern Anhwei). Against the advice of strategists such as Liu Chi (q.v.), Chu Yüan-chang decided that he had an obligation to go to the rescue of his imperial master, the Lung-feng emperor, Han Lin-er (q.v.), even though he had become "the tail that wagged the dog." Taking Hsü Ta and Ch'ang Yü-ch'un, Chu moved quickly in late March, surrounded the enemy at An-feng, and, after furious attacks in which Ch'ang again distinguished himself, captured the city and broke the enemy force. Han Lin-er's court was removed to Ch'u-chou.

Meanwhile Chu learned that Ch'en Yu-liang had assembled his great fleet and sailed down the Yangtze to Kiukiang in Kiangsi, and then turned south into the vast Poyang Lake so as to besiege Nanchang. Chu quickly drew together his fleet of fewer and mostly much smaller vessels and sailed upriver to engage Ch'en; his ground forces went overland to rendezvous there. It was the middle of August. The battle zigzagged across the lake and around its shores through a series of engagements until the end of September. Ch'ang Yü-ch'un throughout the campaign bore a special title indicating that his task was to stay close to and protect Chu Yüan-chang; he saved his life on a number of occasions. Throughout twenty days of battle, Ch'en Yu-liang's superior forces held the advantage. Ch'en, however, was notably impatient, and this protracted struggle was wearing on his nerves. On October 3, after an engagement which left Chu's forces exhausted and inattentive, he tried to force the opening northward leading back to the Yangtze. The major portion of his fleet, more than one hundred of his largest ships, massed for the breakthrough. It was Ch'ang Yü-ch'un who anticipated this move and advised Chu Yüan-chang to prepare for it. After a bitter battle Ch'ang set fire to a number of small boats and freed them to drift downwind into the massed fleet of Ch'en's big ships. Ch'en's fleet soon was enveloped in flames and thousands perished. Again it was due to Ch'ang's insistence that he was permitted to head a fleet to follow up the success in the first engagement by pursuing Ch'en back to the lake. When the battle continued Ch'en happened to be killed in a flight of arrows, and as many of his command also had died in battle his forces broke and fled. Ch'ang then pursued remnants of Ch'en's army to Wuchang and

laid siege to that city until March, 1364. On this occasion, besides being awarded lavish gifts, Ch'ang and Yü T'ung-hai(q.v.) received appointments as chief administrators of the central Secretariat. Meanwhile, along with Teng Yü (q.v.), Ch'ang was kept busy in Hukuang, bringing the former territories of Ch'en entirely under Chu's control, and further extending his boundaries in Kiangsi and on the eastern front in Chekiang.

During 1366 Chu began to draw a noose around Chang Shih-ch'eng. Ch'ang Yü-ch'un and Hsü Ta were sent to campaign north of the Yangtze in the first two-thirds of that year, during which they eliminated Chang's holdings. The attention then turned to those south of the river. In September an army, estimated at two hundred thousand was formed with Hsü Ta in command and Ch'ang his lieutenant. After long strategy seessions in which Ch'ang undoubtedly was overruled, the officers decided on a cautious approach through Chang's southwest border. After cutting off all his possible retreat areas, they would attack his isolated capital at Soochow. Hu 湖-chou, Chang's principal base on the south shore of Lake T'ai, was the starting place. Hsü and Ch'ang besieged Hu-chou from September 29 until December 8, when its defenders surrendered. Throughout the siege Ch'ang Yü-ch'un's exploits were noteworthy. His forces then moved against several other important prefectural and district seats, took Hangchow, and turned northward to besiege Soochow itself. That campign lasted through most of 1367, causing great hardship to the defenders. The city finally fell to Hsü and Ch'ang in October. On the 21st, Ch'ang was given the honorary title and rank of duke of O-kuo 鄂國公, but he had scant leisure to enjoy the award. Weeks later a new field army was formed, a quarter of a million strong, with Hsü and Ch'ang in their familiar roles as commander and vice commander. This time the objective was the ultimate one—Ta-tu, the Yüan capital.

Ch'ang Yü-ch'un spent the last two years of his life in the field fighting against the Mongols and their supporters in the north. When the strategy sessions were held to determine the plans for the campaign, Ch'ang with his usual rashness and daring suggested a lightning strike directly against Ta-tu. Hsü Ta, always the more cautious and foresighted planner, suggested that the army divide forces and move carefully northward, cleaning up the resistance as they went. Ch'ang was to advance along the Grand Canal route into Shantung, while Hsü would take a parallel course somewhat to the west. Chu gave the nod to Hsü's plan, but expressed his admiration for Ch'ang's daring. The armies left Chin-ling on November 12 for what was to be a rather routine campaign. Ch'ang took all of Shantung by the following late spring, somewhat ahead of schedule, and turned west to meet Hsü Ta in Kaifeng. Chu, now emperor, joined them in the summer of 1368, and councils were held to plan the final attack on Ta-tu. The march to the north was uneventful, and the Ming armies entered the Yüan capital without a fight on September 14. The monarch and his court had fled into Mongolia, but the principal military force loyal to his cause, led by Kökö Temür (*q.v.*), was threateningly poised at Taiyuan, controlling Shansi to the west. The north was not secure while this situation obtained. Therefore they turned immediately to the conquest of Shansi. As they approached Taiyuan in January, 1369, with other branches of the field army active in supporting advances, Hsü Ta and Ch'ang consulted on how to deal with Kökö Temür. If they tried to encircle Taiyuan, that would require speed, and the infantry could not keep up with the cavalry. Yet in any full scale attack, both would be needed. Ch'ang then submitted a daring plan: take a picked force of the best horsemen and make a lightning attack, surprising the enemy. His forces would be unprepared, would fall in disarray, and be vulnerable. This time

Hsü accepted Ch'ang's typically brilliant but rash plan, and it succeeded. Kökö Temür was reading by lamplight in his tent when the attackers descended; he was wounded and had to withdraw in haste and confusion. All of Shansi came under Ming control.

Throughout the spring of 1369 Hsü and Ch'ang campaigned to the west along the Great Wall as far as central Kansu. Then in the summer they moved to attack the Mongols' summer capital at Shang-tu 上都 (Dolon-nor, called by the Ming K'ai-p'ing 開平), where the fugitive Mongol emperor had taken refuge. After investing that place and pursuing him still farther north, they captured three Mongol princes, immense supplies, and herds of animals. Then the entire field force returned to Ta-tu, now renamed Peiping. While on a brief excursion from Peiping to settle a dispute in western Manchuria, Ch'ang contracted some unidentified disease and died suddenly at Liu-ho-ch'uan 柳河川, at the age of thirty-nine. (His forces subsequently came under the command of Li Wenchung[*q.v.*].) Certain Muslims in China have claimed him as one of their own but this is not verified in any official source.

Chu Yüan-chang was deeply shaken when the news of Ch'ang's death reached Nanking on August 25. He is said to have been so overcome with sorrow that he dismissed a grieving court and secluded himself. On September 2, when the cortege bearing the body reached the capital, he went in person to meet it and conduct sacrifices. He personally selected a burial site on Mt. Chung 鍾山 in the northeastern suburb of Nanking and arranged for the building of a mausoleum and a state funeral. Hsü Ta was summoned from the north to attend the funeral. The emperor composed a memorial essay, but ordered Sung Lien (*q.v.*) to write a more detailed funerary inscription containing a full record of Ch'ang's contributions to the success in founding the new dynasty; in instructing Sung about how to write this, he gave

Ch'ang "seventy or eighty percent of the credit for the boundaries of the realm having reached their present extent." While that was not meant to be taken literally, it expressed the measure of the emperor's indebtedness. Early in November Ch'ang was awarded the posthumous name Chung-wu 忠武 and title prince of K'ai-p'ing, commemorating his last campaign. Titles and honors were awarded both to his ancestors and to his descendants. Few associates of the Ming founder were dealt with so generously.

Ch'ang Yü-ch'un had three sons and three daughters. His eldest daughter became principal consort of Chu Piao (q.v.). His sons were given names chosen by Chu Yüan-chang. The eldest, Ch'ang Mao 茂, although not born to Ch'ang's principal wife, was allowed to inherit, according to Wang Ch'ung-wu 王崇武, perhaps the unique exception to the Ming founder's strict rules governing inheritance. Ch'ang Mao was very young when his father died, and grew up a spoiled and lazy youth; he is described as arrogant, petulant, and unrestrained. Late in 1370 he was given his father's estates and income and the title of duke of Cheng-kuo 鄭國公. Chu Yüan-chang gave him no important tasks, but in 1387 assigned him to the staff of his father-in-law, General Feng Sheng (q.v.). Because of Ch'ang Mao's serious misbehavior during the campaign, he was deprived of his rank and placed under restraints in Kwangsi, a form of exile. He died in October, 1391. In November, 1388, Chu had the inheritance transferred to the second son, Ch'ang Sheng 昇, whose good qualities are recorded. He was given the honorary rank of duke of K'ai-kuo 開國, later exiled to Yunnan for resisting the usurpation in 1402, and was stripped of his title. Nothing is known about Ch'ang's third son, Ch'ang Sen 森. Ch'ang Yü-ch'un's line, therefore, continued through the descendants of Ch'ang Sheng. Few of them, however, achieved any distinction. In May. 1532, Emperor Chu Hou-ts'ung (q.v.) re-stored the title of the Ch'ang family by appointing Ch'ang Hsüan-chen 玄振 (d. 1549), Ch'ang Yü-ch'un's descendant in the eighth generation, to the rank of marquis of Huai-yüan. This title continued in the family to the end of the dynasty.

Ch'ang Yü-ch'un and Hsü Ta usually are mentioned together as the two greatest military leaders at the founding of the Ming. Some writers have said that Ch'ang had all the qualities of a great general 將, but Hsü had all those of a great commander-in-chief 帥. There was no shortage of military leadership in Chu Yüan-chang's camp, or indeed in the service of his opponents in the mid-fourteenth century. This is striking testimony to the fact that from among the illiterate peasantry in regions like the Huai basin there emerged several men who not only grew up familiar with weapons, but who also understood military organization, tactics, and strategic problems. Ch'ang seems to have remained almost illiterate, but he gained the ultimate accolade of the Chinese literati when mid- and late Ming historians universally agreed that, despite his educational limitations, his tactics "fully accorded with ancient models." The effectiveness of the generalship in Ch'ang's and Hsü's generation probably is more accurately to be ascribed to the fact that it was one of those unusual times in Chinese history when all the officers understood and could communicate naturally with the subordinate technician group within the Chinese military. In addition, however, Ch'ang had to a remarkable degree the quality of shrewd courage; he never retreated from a battlefield in defeat, and his impetuous daring was coupled with perceptive tactical sense. He was attentive to the needs and the concerns of his soldiers and close to them in spirit. The one serious charge against him is that he was ruthless in his treatment of the enemy. Chu Yüan-chang on a number of occasions criticized him for excessive killing, and tried to restrain him. In 1361, for example, he overruled Ch'ang's plan to exterminate captives at Ch'ih-chou considered to be still loyal to Ch'en Yu-liang. Ch'ang's action was based on his assessment of the military situation, and he did not delight in cruelty from the evidence available to us. He apparently was ambitious for success in the field, and subject to dejection when temporarily thwarted, but withal a person of great discipline and a cooperative leader. Although two years older than Hsü Ta, and always held subordinate to him in command, in honors, and in rank, the two remained on the most cordial terms, and Ch'ang is said never to have displayed any resentment or jealousy.

Bibliography

1/105/3a, 125/11a; 5/5/79a; 61/91/20b; 63/3/20a; MSL(1962), T'ai-tsu, ch. 3-44, Chia-ching(1965), 3226; *Huai-yüan-hsien chih* (1819), 18/9b, 4/34a; Wang Shih-chen, *Yen-chou shan-jen hsü-kao*, 81/1a; KC (1958), ch. 1-3; Fang Chüeh-hui 方覺慧, *Ming T'ai-tsu ko-ming wu-kung chi* 革命武功記 (preface dated 1940); Wang Ch'ung-wu, *Ming Ching-nan shih-shih k'ao-cheng kao* 明靖難史事考證稿 (1948), 106; ChinT'ien-chu 金天柱, *Ch'ing-chen shih-i pu chi* 清眞釋疑補輯 (preface 1738), 101; Fu T'ung-hsien 傅統先, *Chung-kuo hui-chiao shih* 回教史 (Shanghai, 1940), 102.

                                    F. W. Mote

CHAO Chen-chi 趙貞吉 (T. 孟靜, H. 大洲), 1508–April 13, 1576, official, scholar, and philosopher, was a native of Nei-chiang 內江, Szechwan. Known for his precocity, the youth at the age of fourteen is said to have read the *Ch'uan-hsi lu*, and generated such an admiration for its author, Wang Shou-jen (*q. v.*), that he wanted to meet the master to become his disciple. His parents refused to let him go; so he devoted himself to the study of the Classics in a search for the source of Wang's inspiration. After becoming a *chü-jen* in 1528, he visited the ex-grand secretary, Yang T'ing-ho (*q.v.*), who reportedly predicted that Chao was destined for a responsible position. In 1535 he became a *chin-shih*, was selected personally by

Emperor Chu Hou-ts'ung (*q. v.*), to enter the Hanlin Academy, and two years later received the appointment of compiler. During the following thirteen years, except on three occasions (1539-41, 1542-44, 1547-50) when he was on leave at his home in Szechwan, he officiated in various posts in Peking. He served in 1544 as a teacher of the eunuchs and in 1547 as an assistant examiner in the m etropolitan examination.

In April, 1550, he was appointed an instructor in th e supervisorate of instruction and concurrently the director of studies in the National Univ ersity. Six months later, when the Mongol marauders threatened the capital, he caught the attention of the emperor by his courageous and forthright pronouncements against capitulation, and received a promotion to left director of instruction and concurrently a censor. The emperor turned over to him 50,000 taels of silver to distribute to the troops assembled for the defense. As Chao was not among the partisans of Yen Sung (*q. v.*), his mission was handicapped, for Yen, in writing the traveling orders, withheld transportation facilities and military protection. As a result Chao could not go far, and returned to Peking in one day after distributing only part of the money. The emperor, not knowing the facts, was furious, ordered him flogged, imprisoned, and finally demoted to be a prison warden of Li-po 荔波, Kwangsi, on the border of Kweichow. On his way there he received a letter of welcome from the director of education, Wang Tsung-mu (*q. v.*), who, like many others of that day, admired him for his straightforward character and felt he had received an unjust sentence. Shortly thereafter Chang Yüeh 張岳 (T.維喬, H. 淨峯, 1492-January 8, 1553, cs 1517, Pth. 襄惠), supreme commander of Hukuang, Szechwan, and Kweichow, summoned Chao for a consultation, and then granted him leave to return home.

In 1553 he again started up the official ladder, first to assistant prefect of Hui-chou 徽州 (Anhwei), then to a secretary in the ministry of Personnel in Nanking. After several promotions he was appointed in April, 1559, a vice minister of Works in Nanking, but he had already left there on hearing of his father's death. Following the mourning period, he was recalled to serve as a vice minister of Revenue in Peking, but trouble again broke out between him and Yen Sung. Before long he was once more dismissed (November, 1561).

In 1567 under the new emperor, Chu Tsai-hou (*q. v.*), Chao Chen-chi became a vice minister of Rites, concurrently heading the supervisorate of imperial instruction in Peking and serving also as acting chancellor of the National University. Promoted to be minister of Rites in Nanking in the following year, he was immediately ordered back to Peking, because the emperor had enjoyed a lecture he gave in September, 1567. In October, 1569, he received a promotion to be grand secretary of the Wen-yüan ko 文淵閣. Later, when Kao Kung(*see* Chang Chü-cheng) assumed office as the senior grand secretary, he served concurrently as minister of Personnel. As this seemed to put too much power in the hands of one person, the emperor, to balance that power, gave Chao the concurrent post of acting head of the Censorate. Unable to get along with Kao Kung, Chao retired for good.

In his last years Chao held lecture gatherings and prepared a grand scheme for a philosophical work in two parts, the *Ching-shih t'ung* 經世通 and the *Ch'u* (出) *-shih t'ung*. The former was to reflect the teachings of Confucius, and the latter those of Buddhism and Taoism. His desire was to bring about an amalgamation of these three schools of thought. The work was not finished at his death; only a few introductory pieces are to be found in his collected literary works, the *Chao Wen-su kung chi* 文肅公集, 23 *ch.*, first printed in 1586. Wen-su was the posthumous name accorded him by imperial order. In regard to his own personal thinking, Chao has often been characterized as leaning towards Buddhism. It is said that when he taught in the Hanlin Academy (1568), he asked the academicians to read the famous Buddhist *Sūraṅ-gama-sūtra*.

A younger brother by two years, Chao Meng-chi 蒙吉 (T. 仲通, H. 圭洲, 小洲, 1510-74), was a *chü-jen* of 1531. The two brothers enjoyed each other's company throughout their lives. In writing his brother's epitaph, Chao Chen-chi narrates this story about their birth. Before his own, he reported, his mother (née Yü 余) dreamed of two little monks, one in a black robe, the other in white, both pulling the mother's sleeves, begging her to give them lodging. The one in black hung on more tenaciously, whereupon he was born. When, later, his mother dreamed of the little monk in a white robe, his younger brother was born. He also said that even in childhood they used to sit like Buddhists, and always played together in great harmony. Chao Chen-chi's son, Chao T'ai-ting 台鼎 (T. 長玄), showed even greater interest than his father in Taoist practices, especially that of breath circulation, as his treatise, *Mai-wang* 脈望, testifies.

Bibliography

1/193/15b; 5/17/48a; 8/63/13a; 42/71/7a; 83/33/1a; 84/丁文/58a; *Huang Ming wen-hai* (microfilm), 2/1/3; TSCC (1885-88), XI: 246/66/17a, XIV: 432/6/14b; MSL (1965), Shih-tsung, 6505, Mu-tsung, 0369, 0922, 1279; KC (1958), 3920, 3925, 3968, 4115, 4149; *Nei-chiang-hsien chih* (1905), 3/10a, 23b, 6/23a, 26a, also ch. 10-12; P'eng Shao-sheng (ECCP), *Chü-shih chuan*, 39/1a; SK (1930), 177/11b; Chao T'ai-ting, *Mai-wang* (TsSCC ed.), 1; Liu Ts'un-yan, "The Penetration of Taoism into the Ming Neo-Confucian Elite," TP, LVII (1971), 93.

Lienche Tu Fang

CHAO Ch'eng 趙誠, original name An San 俺三, later referred to also as An Ch'eng, fl. early 15th century, was a leading member of the Jewish community founded during the Sung period at the then capital, Pien

汴 or Kaifeng, by immigrants from Persia. This community as such is not mentioned in Chinese historical sources; it is only from the synagogue inscriptions in Chinese of the years 1489, 1512, 1663, and 1679 that we have any information about its early history and development.

According to the inscription of 1489 the first synagogue was built in Kaifeng in 1163 by a certain An-tu-la 俺都喇 (Abdullah? Hamdullah?) when Lieh-wei Wu-ssu-ta 列爲五思達 (Levi the Ustad?) was the religious head of the community. It was repaired in 1279 by another leader called simply Wu-ssu-ta. After the founding of the Ming dynasty land was granted to the synagogue and fourteen men were designated Man-la 滿剌 (Mullah) to manage its affairs. One of them, An P'ing-t'u 俺平徒 was perhaps descended from An-tu-la.

An Ch'eng came from this family and, a physician by profession, became a leading member of the community. In 1421 he undertook the reconstrution of the synagogue, called Ch'ing-chen-ssu 清眞寺, a generic name of Islamic mosques in China. At the ceremony of commemoration even the resident prince of Kaifeng, the first prince of Chou, Chu Su (*q. v.*), was obliged to send a present of incense, probably for the ceremony at the imperial tablet. Barely two years later (1423) An Ch'eng was awarded the high military rank of a commander of the Embroidered-uniform Guard for rendering conspicuous service to the emperor. His name was changed from An San to Chao Ch'eng. As Chao Ch'eng he later served as an assistant commander in the Chekiang regional military commission. The entrance of Chao Ch'eng and his family into Ming officialdom, with all the attendant implications of social prestige, power, and influence, undoubtedly accelerated the process of sinicization of the Kaifeng Jews. [Editors' note: The award of the rank of a commander (major or higher) in the Embroidered-uniform Guard is generally granted to a commoner only when he has

rendered unusual service to the throne. In the case of An Ch'eng he was further awarded, according to the inscription of 1489, a change of surname. The reason for these extraordinary honors is covered in the inscription by the vague statement "tsou-wen yu-kung" 奏聞有功, which could be interpreted either as "reported as meritorious" or as "adjudged meritorious for submitting information to the throne." Reported by whom and meritorious for what? Information on what or on whom and at what time? The vagueness of the statement and the lack of any documentary evidence to support it one way or the other makes it questionable to say the least. On the other hand, many unusual things happened in the first decades of the Ming, which were ignored or misrepresented in the *shih-lu* of the early Ming reigns. Hence some speculation may be ventured in the case of Chao Ch'eng if we accept the inscription as a reliable account. Many services, such as those rendered in the practice of medicine, must be ruled out, for the award was too high. If the statement meant that he was reported meritorious, one possibility was becuse of some service during a military campaign. But in such an event the service would have been an honorable one and proudly specified. The merit, therefore, was more likely given for rendering information, and it might have been for the revelation of a traitorous plot. There was such a case of treason in the fifth moon of 1423 which involved several guard commanders plotting to assassinate Emperor Chu Ti (*q. v.*), and to remove the heir apparent in favor of the emperor's youngest son, the prince of Chao 趙, Chu Kao-sui (*see* Empress Hsü). Only one man is recorded as the informer of the plot. He was a sergeant in one of the Guards, who, however, was promoted only to chiliarch commander (captain) in return for informing on such a serious matter. May the plot have really been discovered by An Ch'eng, who revealed it to the sergeant? Did the award of the surname Chao to An Ch'eng have any association with the title of the prince of Chao? This prince was finally exonerated at the trial conducted by the emperor himself, but the account of the event in the *shih-lu* is a scant summary that leaves many questions unanswered. Speculations of this kind can be justified only on the ground that they may serve as leads to further research.]

Following the restoration of the synagogue under Chao Ch'eng's leadership, a new building was added in 1445 by Li Jung 李榮 and Li Liang 良, apparently men of wealth, but all buildings were destroyed by a flood in 1461. At least three scrolls of the Torah on parchment were saved and, when the synagogue was rebuilt by Li Jung and others, there were not only more structures but also an additional Torah sent by the Jews of Ningpo, Chekiang. In 1489 the various buildings were renovated and more land added to the grounds, purchased with the contributions made by Chin Ying 金瑛, a Jew from Ning-hsia 寧夏, who is prominently cited in the inscription on the monument erected in that year. The inscription also mentions with pride two of the Kaifeng men, namely Kao Nien 高年, a scholar of the National University appointed magistrate of She-hsien 歙縣 (Anhwei) in 1439, who helped build the Confucian school during his term of office, and Ai Chün 艾俊 (cj 1447), one-time subdirector of studies of Ch'ung-ming 崇明 hsien in the Yangtze delta, who served as administrator of the household of the first prince of Te, Chu Chien-lin (*see* Li P'an-lung). Chin Chung 鍾, the composer of the inscription, is mentioned as a student of the prefectural school. Twenty-three yearslater, when the synagogue was again repaired and a new inscription composed, Chin Chung's name appeared also on that inscription.

During the mid-seventeenth century three members of the Chao family, all presumably descendants of Chao Ch'eng, enjoyed the status of leadership in the community, namely: Chao Ying-ch'eng 映乘 (T. 涵章, cs 1646, 1619-*ca*. 1657, probably the Moses of the Chinese genealogical register, no. 273); his brother Chao Ying-tou 映斗 (*kung-sheng* of 1653); and Chao Ch'eng-chi 承基 (fl. 1642-63), a military officer very likely their cousin. It happened that the synagogue was again destroyed by flood in 1642 when Kaifeng was inundated by the diversion of the Yellow River in the siege of the city. The Chao brothers and other leaders of the day managed to save some of the scrolls of the Law. In 1653 they took an active part in rebuilding the synagogue and in completing the restoration of the manuscripts. The work was concluded in 1663 and celebrated by the erection of another stone tablet. Chao Ch'eng-chi, who held the rank of captain-adjutant to the Kaifeng intendant in 1653 (appointed some time after 1642), was promoted in 1657, under the new dynasty to a majority and then lieutenant-colonelcy at Ku-yüan 固原, Shensi (at present in Kansu). He was back in Kaifeng in 1663. Chao Ying-ch'eng, after becoming a *chin-shih*, served in the ministry of Justice, rising to a department directorship. In 1650 he was appointed intendant of the Chang-nan circuit 漳南道, Fukien, with the rank of surveillance vice-commissioner with headquarters at Shang-hang 上杭. There he suppressed some armed brigands, built a cultural hall 講藝堂 (1653), cleared up judicial cases, and won the praise of the people. He was replaced that year and returned to Kaifeng for a period of mourning. In 1656 he was appointed military intendant of the Lower River circuit 下江道 in Hukuang with his headquarters at Ch'i-chou 蘄州 where, it is reported, he died in office, probably the following year. A Hebrew scholar, he wrote a work entitled *Sheng-ching chi-pien* 聖經記變 (The vicissitudes of the Holy Scriptures), about the recovery and restoration of the Kaifeng Torah. Another book of his, illustrating the sufferings endured by the population as a result of brigandage, is the

Chieh-nan t'u 刦難圖 in 30 *ts'e* (?), composed in 1651; it was submitted to Chang Hsüeh-sheng 張學聖 (T. 直隸), governor of Fukien from 1648 to 1653. He is also credited with a work entitled *Ssu-chu-t'ang chi-i* 四竹堂記異 (240 *ch.*?). None of these works has survived. What have come down are two small pieces entitled *Hang-ch'uan she-hsüeh chi* 杭川社學記 and *Lung-wen-hui hsü* 龍文會序 included in the section on literature of the Shang-hang district history. Chao Ying-tou, the younger brother, served from 1663 to 1669 or later as magistrate first of Kunming and then of I-liang 宜良, both in Yunnan. He is credited with a work in ten chapters on the Hebrew religion, entitled *Ming-tao hsü* 明道序. He and his brother were each permitted to honor their father, Chao Kuang-yü 光裕, with their own official titles and ranks. The preeminence in the Kaifeng community of Chao Kuang-yü and his two sons is evidenced by a memorial archway erected in 1678 at the entrance to the courtyard of the synagogue, with their names prominently displayed. It commemorated the contributions to the synagogue chiefly by members of the Chao family descended from Chao Ch'eng. It seems that by that time, of the three only Chao Ying-tou was still alive, for he was named in 1679 as responsible, together with another brother, Chao Ying-kun 映袞, for the erection of the stone tablet celebrating the completion of the Chao family archway. Apparently the tablet was placed in the Chao ancestral hall to the south of the synagogue. It was found around 1900 partly defaced, and, together with the stone tablet bearing the inscriptions of both 1489 and of 1512, was transferred to the compound of the Trinity Cathedral of Kaifeng. Some scrolls of the Torah from Kaifeng, other books of the Bible, prayers, and a Hebrew-Chinese Memorial Book and Register of the Dead of the seven Jewish clans, are now preserved in the Hebrew Union College, Cincinnati, and elsewhere.

The affluence of the Jewish community in the 1660s may be deduced from the fact that the tablet of 1663 bore an inscription composed by a retired minister of Works, and partly inscribed in the handwriting of two directors of provincial education. There were also smaller tablets presented to the synagogue by several officials. Most of these sponsors of the synagogue were friends or colleagues of the Chao brothers. Even in the early twentieth century the head of the community was a descendant of the Chao family, indicating that the influence of Chao Ch'eng and his line lasted some five hundred years.

Bibliography

Ch'en Yüan (BDRC), *K'ai-feng I-tz'u-lo-yeh chiao k'ao* 開封一賜樂業敎考 (1923); Fang Hao 方豪, *Chung-wai wen-hua chiao-t'ung-shih lun-ts'ung* 中外文化交通史論叢 (1944), 113; *Hsiang-fu-hsien chih* 祥符縣志 (1661, 1739, 1898); *K'ai-feng-fu chih* 府志 (1695), 38a/14b; *Yün-nan-fu chih* 雲南府志 (1696), 11b/10a, 12a; *She-hsien chih* 歙縣志 (1937), 2/ 官司志 2b; *Fu-chien t'ung-chih* (1737), 32/33b; *Huang-chou-fu chih* 黃州府志 (1884), 11b/21b; *Hsü Ho-nan t'ung-chih* (1767), 54/1b; *T'ing-chou-fu chih* 汀州府志 (1752), 18/1a, 20/32a; *Shang-hang-hsien chih* (1760), 3/53a, 4/20ʰ, 5/17a, 7/9a, 10 (2) /2a; *Kansu t'ung-chih* (1909), 53/13a; Jerome Tobar, *Inscriptions juives de K'ai-fong-fou*, Shanghai, 1912; R. Löwenthal, "The Nomenclature of Jews in China," MS, XII (1947), 97; *id.*, "The Early Jews in China: a Supplementary Bibliography," *Folklore Studies*, V (1946), 353; W. C. White, *Chinese Jews*, 3 parts, Toronto, 1942; D. Leslie, "Some Notes on the Jewish Inscriptions of K'aifeng," JAOS, 82 (1962), 346; *id.*, "The Kaifeng Jew Chao Ying-ch'eng and His Family," TP, 53 (1967), 147; *id.*, *The Survival of the Chinese Jews*, Leiden, 1972; Chaoying Fang, "Notes on the Jews of Kaifeng," JAOS, 85 (1965), 126.

Donald Leslie

CHAO Ch'ien 趙謙 (also known by his *tzu* Hui-ch'ien 撝謙), 1351-December 13, 1395, was originally named Chao Ku-tse 古則. A scholar and teacher, he was a native of Yü-yao 餘姚 -hsien, Chekiang, and reportedly a descendant of the imperial family of the Sung dynasty. Orphaned in youth, he was raised in a Buddhist monastery, but succeeded in acquiring an orthodox classical education, in the course of which he traveled arounh Chekiang to study under various masters. Among his fellow students at this time was Hsü I-k'uei (q.v.). Chao's reputation as a master of the Classics, especially in the field of phonetics, was such that in 1379 he received the position of registrar (典簿) in the National University at Chung-tu 中都 (Feng-yang 鳳陽 -fu, Nan Chih-li), but soon afterwards he resigned because of disagreements with Sung Lien (q. v.). In 1389, through the influence of friends at court, he was offered the post of instructor of Ch'iung-shan 瓊山 -hsien on Hainan Island in Kwangtung. There beside his school he constructed a studio called the K'ao-ku-t'ai 考古臺 (Hall for studying antiquity); as a result he came to be known as K'ao-ku hsien-sheng. He died in P'an-yü 番禺 (Canton) leaving his heirs too poor to return his body to Chekiang; the family consequently changed its legal residence to Canton.

A collection of Chao's poems and occasional pieces, entitled K'ao-ku wen-chi 文集, 2 ch. (manuscript copy edited by his great-grandson, Chao Hu 護, with a preface dated 1657), is available on microfilm (NLP no. 979). His other works were all used as school textbooks. The most extensive of these, entitled Sheng-yin wen-tzu t'ung 聲音文字通 (variously described as 100 and as 32 ch., is evidently lost, but three others, the Liu-shu pen-i 六書本義, 12 ch., the T'ung-meng hsi-chü 童蒙習句, 2 ch. (printed in a combined edition in 1610 with a preface by Chiao Hung, ECCP), and the Hsüeh-fan 學範, 2 ch., are said to be available in Japan. All five of these works are described in the Ssu-k'u Catalogue, but only the K'ao-ku wen-chi and the Liu-shu pen-i were copied in their entirety into the Imperial Library.

The survival of Chao Ch'ien's name does not rest alone on this meager literary output or on the existence of a line of scholars descended from him; it rests also on his coming to be considered an exemplary respresentative of the whole class of officials who ended their careers as hsien instructors. He gained this reputation because of the self-sacrifice he showed in taking up his position on Hainan Island, despite his poverty. Chiao Hung included him as one of only two examples of such instructors in his Kuo-ch'ao hsien-cheng lu, and his inclusion in the Ming-ju hsüeh-an of Huang Tsung-hsi (ECCP) stems from the same reason.

Bibliography

1/285/16b; 5/100/73a; 83/43/5b; Chu I-tsun (ECCP), P'u-shu-t'ing chi (SPTK), 64/10a; SK (1930), 41/10a, 43/4a, 44/2a, 131/4a, 169/7b; Naikaku Bunko Catalogue, 47, 274.

Edward L. Dreyer

CHAO Fang 趙汸 (T. 子常, H. 東山), March 29, 1319-November 29, 1369, scholar, was a native of Hsiu-ning 休寧 in the prefecture of Hui-chou 徽州 (Anhwei), where his family had lived for fifteen generations. During the Mongol conquest of that area (about 1276), his grandfather, Chao Hsiang-yüan 象元 (H. 可齋), joined the invaders and was commissioned an assistant magistrate of Hsiu-ning by the Yüan commander. It is said that on the plea of Chao Hsiang-yüan, the commander spared the local people from massacre. It is also said that he was later named a jail warden in a Kiangsi city, but declined on the excuse of illness, and that he then went north to the Yüan capital (Peking), was appointed a magistate, but died before assuming office. In any case, his son lived the life of a member of the gentry, and his grandson, Chao Fang, in his youth had the means to travel from place to place seeking a competent teacher of the Classics.

Chao Fang probably had in mind a career as an exponent of the Confucian teachings, like the great scholar, Chu Hsi (1130-1200), who was also a native of

Hui-chou prefecture, and whose works he had read. In the year 1337 he succeeded in becoming the disciple of the scholar Huang Tse (1260–1346) in Kiukiang. Huang's approach to the Classics stressed self-enlightenment through a process of cumulative meditation. He taught his students by encouraging them to make their own discoveries. Chao studied the six Classics with Huang, and copied some one thousand items which he took home to mull over. In the autumn of 1341 Chao returned to Huang's studio, this time to remain two years. During this period he received oral instruction on the 64 hexagrams of the Book of Changes, and became convinced of the critical importance of the Spring and Autumn Annals. Three years later he met the second great scholar who influenced him significantly. This was Yü Chi (1272–1348), a native of Szechwan who resided in Kiangsi. Yü Chi became a Hanlin academician under the Mongol rulers, and was a major contributor to the sinicization of Yüan institutions. He was well acquainted with Wu Ch'eng (1249–1333), the Confucian philosopher and classical scholar who served at the Yüan court on several occasions and wrote Wu's record of conduct (行狀).

Chao stayed at Yü's house as a student for over a year. A letter Chao wrote to his mentor in that year (quoted in the record of conduct) reveals his serious sense of duty to self-cultivation through study and introspective meditation. He expresses deep gratitude to Yü for having passed on to him and others the nature of Wu Ch'eng's intellectual pursuits, and also for having taught him how to "enter the gate of virtue" without losing his way by seeking and finding the truth within himself. Chao returned to Kiukiang in 1346 to see Huang Tse, but Huang had by then already died. Soon afterwards, Chao became acquainted with Yüan Ming-shan 袁明善 (T. 誠夫), a disciple of Wu Ch'eng who had compiled his master's teachings on the Four Books into the work Ssu-shu jih-lu 四書日錄. Chao

and Yüan engaged in discussions on the different approaches to the Four Books by Chu Hsi and Wu Ch'eng. Chao also knew Su T'ien-chüeh (1294–1352), a follower of Yü Chi and a Yüan official. On several occasions Su tried to get Chao to accompany him on official business to the capital, but Chao refused, preferring to look after his aging mother and to devote himself to study.

When in the early 1350s the Yüan peace was interrupted by rebel disturbances in southeast China, Chao took his mother into the remote hills of Nan-Chihli to seek refuge from the flames of war. Four years afterward (in 1356) the region was reconquered by Yüan troops. The author of Chao's record of conduct notes that the Yüan general who directed the victory sought to enlist Chao's services on his civil staff, but to no avail. Chao continued to reside in secluded areas until 1362 when he returned to his native district at Tung-shan 東山. By this time the future Ming emperor, Chu Yüan-chang, had already put the area under his control. Chu's officers repeatedly sent gifts to win Chao's support for the new regime, but without success.

In 1369 Chu Yüan-chang, now emperor, undertook to put Yüan loyalists into useful government employ by ordering them to compile the Yüan-shih. Chao Fang was among those who complied. When the work was completed, Chao went home, and died shortly afterwards. His major writings on the Spring and Autumn Annals were copied into the Ssu-k'u Library. These included Ch'un-ch'iu chi-chuan 春秋集傳, 15 ch., Ch'un-ch'iu shih-shuo 師說, 3 ch., Ch'un-ch'iu shu-tz'u 屬辭, 15 ch., Ch'un-ch'iu chin so-shih 金鎖匙, and Ch'un-ch'iu Tso-shih chuan pu-chu 左氏傳補注, 10 ch. There is a Japanese edition of the last mentioned work, printed in 1801.

The Ssu-k'u editors also included his Chou I wen-ch'üan 周易文詮, 4 ch., Chao's only work on the Book of Changes. They describe it as relatively shallow in comparison with his work on the Spring and

Autumn Annals. In their view the *Chou I wen-ch'üan* shows the influence of Ch'eng-Chu thought, as well as that of Shao Yung (1011-77). Chao's collected works—*Tung-shan ts'un-kao* 存稿, 7 *ch.*, plus *fu-lu* 附錄, 1 *ch.*—were likewise copied into the Imperial Library. He did not finish the *Ch'un-ch'iu chi-chuan* as he died having completed it only through the twenty-seventh year of Duke Chao 昭公 (614 B. C.). His follower Ni Shang-i 倪尚誼 brought it to conclusion on the basis of the principles worked out by Chao. The preface of this work is quoted in the *Sung Yüan hsüeh-an* and in the biography of Chao by Shao Yüan-p'ing (ECCP, p. 851) in *Yüan-shih lei-pien*. This, together with the prefaces to *Ch'un-ch'iu shu-tz'u* and *Ch'un-ch'iu Tso-shih chuan pu-chu*, reveals the nature of Chao's approach to the Spring and Autumn Annals.

Chao generally followed the lead of his master Huang Tse in taking the *Tso chuan* as the primary commentary on the Spring and Autumn Annals, and the *Ch'un-ch'iu Tso-shih ching-chuan chi-chieh* 經傳集解 by Tu Yü (222-84) as the best annotation of the *Tso chuan*. To supplement the deficiencies of Tu, Chao, in culling passages from the *Ku-liang chuan* and *Kung-yang chuan* and from the *Tso chuan chang-chih* 章旨 now only partially extant, sometimes entitled *Tso-shih chang-chih* and *Ch'un-ch'iu hou-chuan* by Ch'en Fu-liang (1137-1203), was also remaining true to the teachings of Huang Tse. The central problem Chao deals with in his works on the Spring and Autumn Annals concerns the principles by which Confucius, the alleged compiler of the work, determined which events to record, which to omit, and which language form to use when recording different types of event. This is the problem of pi-hsiao 筆削 (to transcribe and delete), the editorial technique supposedly employed by Confucius when he compiled the *Ch'un-ch'iu* on the basis of the ts'e-shu 策書 (bamboo slips) of the kingdom of Lu that had been assembled by the official historiographers.

Chao's purpose is to elucidate the principles (i 義) behind Confucius' pi-hsiao. In so doing Chao argues that only Mencius understood the true nature of the composition of the Annals; Confucius edited original records in order to record the dispersal of rebellion (志存撥亂), and, as Mencius noted, "The subject of the Ch'un-ch'iu concerned the affairs of Huan of Ch'i (684-42 B. C.) and Wen of Chin (635-28 B. C.), and its style was the historical. Confucius said, 'Its righteous decisions I ventured to make'." Chao criticizes Tso's commentary for failure to recognize that Confucius' pi-hsiao was motivated by a higher value structure (i. e., the making of "righteous decisions"), rather than simply by the desire faithfully to record "historical precedent" (史例). Tso's work, Chao holds, is unbalanced in that it focuses attention only on the historical aspect of the Spring and Autumn Annals. On the other hand, however, Chao also holds that the Kung-yang and Ku-liang commentaries, in their attempt to elucidate Confucius' pi-hsiao principles, are seriously deficient in that they failed to understand the historical nature of the text. Mencius understood, but his clue was not read correctly, Chao argues. Hence in his works on the Annals, Chao seeks "to take what is long in the one (commentary) to supplement what is short in the other" (Legge's translation of words by Chao). Chao's *Tung-shan ts'un kao* was reprinted in 1971 in Taiwan as part of the *Ssu-k'u chen-pen*, second series, 珍本二集, published by the National Palace Museum.

Bibliography

Yin-te #35: 22/236/11a; 23/34/23b; 25/88/19a; 29/二辛; *Yin-te* #24: 1/282/6a; 3/263/4b; 5/114/1a; 8/5/1a; 24/1/26a; 32/36/9a; 40/5/1a; 61/111/3a; 84/甲/25a; 86/2/19b; 89/9/42b; Chu Sheng, *Chi yu Chao Tung-shan wen* 祭友趙東山文, *Chu Feng-lin chi* (1616), 8/7; SK (1930), 4/7a, 28/3b, 168/11b; Huang Tsung-hsi (ECCP), *Sung Yüan hsüeh-an*, ch. 92; Wang Tzu-ts'ai 王梓材 and Feng Yün-hao 馮雲濠, *Sung Yüan hsüeh-an pu-i* 補遺, 92/80b; Sung Lien, *Ch'un-ch'iu shu-tzu hsü* 序, *Sung Wen-hsien kung ch'üan-chi* (SPPY ed.), 43/12b;

James Legge, *The Ch'un Ts'ew, with the Tso Chuen* (Hong Kong, 1872), prolegomena, 139.

John D. Langlois, Jr.

CHAO Nan-hsing 趙南星 (T. 夢白, H. 儕鶴, 清都散客), April 19, 1550-January 23, 1628, official, was a native of Kao-i 高邑 in the prefecture Chen-ting-fu 眞定府, southwest of Peking. His grandfather and his father, both one-time students of the National University, served as district magistrates, the former at Wu-kung 武功, Shensi, and the latter at Kuan-t'ao 館陶, Shantung. As a child Chao Nan-hsing was known for his precocity and as a youth for his witticisms. In 1569, while attending the academy, Heng-yang shu-yüan 恒陽書院 in Chen-ting city, he came under the influence of the head of that institution, Ai Mu 艾穆 (T. 和甫, H. 純卿, cj 1558, governor of Szechwan, 1591-93), and began to study both for self-cultivation and for government service. He became a *chü-jen* in 1570, a student in the National University in 1571, and a *chin-shih* in 1574. His first appointment was as prefectural judge of Ju-ning-fu 汝寧府, Honan, where he stayed six years (1575-81). While there he developed a strong aversion to Chang Chü-cheng (*q.v.*), especially after Chang had Ai Mu as well as Chao Yung-hsien and Tsou Yüan-piao (*qq. v.*) flogged at court in 1577.

In 1581 Chao Nan-hsing was promoted to the post of secretary in the ministry of Revenue in which capacity he served for several months in 1583 as inspector of the granaries at Tientsin. Late in 1583 he received a transfer to the ministry of Personnel, the powerful agency in charge of selection and evaluation of all civil officials, and came to be involved in the factional strife of that period(*see* Chu I-chün). It is said that when his superior, Yang Wei 楊巍 (T. 伯謙, H. 夢山, 1514-1605, cs 1547), was attacked by several supervising secretaries and censors in May, 1584, Chao was suspected of having supplied one of them, Wang Shih-hsing (*q.v.*),

with secrets of the ministry. For this Chao was forced to take sick leave. Late in 1588 the court recalled him to serve in the ministry, where during one year he acted as vice director in each of the four bureaus. In 1589 he took part in the metropolitan examination as an assistant examiner; one of the candidates whom he passed was Kao P'an-lung (*q. v*). Late in 1589 Chao submitted a memorial on four evils, namely, the unethical struggle for coveted posts, the use of falsification and hyperbole to remove men of character, the irresponsible selection of local officials for appointment or promotion, and the failure to restrict the local gentry from abusing their special privileges. In this one memorial he offended many officials and made himself the target of attack. Early in 1590 he again left on sick leave.

After living at home for two years he was once more called to service. Appointed director of the bureau of evaluations, he took part in the preparations for the sexennial evaluation of the central government officials which was to take place early in 1593. He and his superior, the minister of Personnel Sun Lung (*see* Ku Hsien-ch'eng), decided to do a thorough house-cleaning, keeping to themselves all decisions without even consulting their colleagues in the ministry. To show their impartiality they cashiered at the outset a nephew of Sun and a relative of Chao, and then proceeded to list for removal all officials adjudged unworthy on the strength of their records in office and of verified reports about their conduct at home. Reversing the practice of the past decades, Chao and Sun did not consult even the grand secretaries for approval of their actions, pointedly ignoring their private recommendations. When the list was published, it was hailed by the fair-minded as the most just evaluation in decades. A few malcontents, however, accused Sun and Chao of unjustifiably favoring their own protégés. The grand secretaries, especially Wang Hsi-chüeh (*q. v.*) and Chang Wei (*see* Ch'en Yü-pi, intent on preserving the power of supervision of the Grand Secretariat over the ministry of Personnel, took the opportunity to advise the emperor to condemn Chao and Sun as arrogating the power of evaluation to themselves and playing favorites in the case of three officials, Yüan Huang (*q. v.*), Yü Ch'un-hsi, and Yang Yü-t'ing (for both *see* Ku Hsien-ch'eng). Sun protested against the unfair charges and was permitted to retire. Chao was at first demoted but a few days later, on April 29, 1593, was deprived of all ranks and made a commoner. Several of those who protested in his favor were downgraded or cashiered (*see* Kao P'an-lung). Within about a year's time most officials whom Chao regarded as upright and incorruptible had left the court.

Chao returned home in 1593 and remained there for almost three decades; during this time there were many appeals for his recall, all ignored at court. He remained in Kao-i teaching students, editing textbooks, reading, and writing. He built a garden called Fang-ju-yüan 芳茹園 where he attended to the plants himself. He corresponded with men of like mind, sometimes criticizing the government for its faults, and came to be recognized as one of the three worthies in forced retirement, the others being Ku Hsien-ch'eng and Tsou Yüan-piao. Ku was the founder of the Tung-lin Academy and Tsou was in close contact with Ku and other Tung-lin men, but Chao had never been there in person and so, strictly speaking, was not a member of that political group. His sympathies, however, were on the side of the Tung-lin members, whom he called the cheng-jen 正人 (upright men). His name appears prominently on almost all Tung-lin lists prepared by enemies of the party.

While teaching the Classics and the way to write expository essays on classical questions as required at the examination halls, he found that often he could make simpler and more sensible explanations than those given in standard works. As a

consequence he compiled, wrote, or edited a number of books for his students, including two primers, the *San-tzu ching* 三字經 and the *Nü-er* 女兒 *ching*, the latter for the education of girls. Another was on the Great Learning and the Doctrine of the Mean, *Hsüeh Yung cheng-shuo* 學庸正說, later included in the *Ssu-k'u* manuscript library. Of particular interest are his extracts from the herbal of Li Shih-chen (*q. v.*), *Pen-ts'ao kang-mu*, entitled *Shang-i pen-ts'ao* 上醫本草, 4 *ch*. In the preface to this work Chao tells about his illness from 1616 to 1619, the symptoms indicating a severe case of despondency rather than any physical disorder, and about how he finally in 1618 began to cure himself by following and experimenting with the formulae and recommendations contained in Li's book, but he selected only common herbs and grains for his own treatment. As he observed in a cynical way, in the humorous but often incisive language of the common people, one who cures oneself without taking any medicine has the designation chung-i 中醫, or a middle grade physician. It was his conclusion that proper diet and temperance constituted a superior kind of medicine (shang-i).

Sometime before 1617 he had published a collection of his letters and perhaps some of his essays. In that year a student of his began to print his collected prose writings under the title *Meng-po hsien-sheng wen-chi* 夢白先生文集, but it seems that only three *chüan* of letters were printed at this time. Later other students, especially those who had taken part in a literary society, Cheng-hsin hui 正心會, under Chao's guidance, printed some of the texts edited by Chao and a few samples of Chao's pa-ku 八股 essays.

In May, 1620, after Chu Yu-chiao (ECCP) came to the throne, Chao received orders to resume government service, being enticed by a series of promotions, but each time he pleaded illness so that he might remain in retirement. Finally, late in 1622, persuaded by Yeh Hsiang-kao (*q. v.*) and other friends, he answered the call to serve as a vice minister of Works. As soon as he arrived in Peking he was made head of the Censorate. At this time the central government was almost under the complete control of the Tung-lin faction, with Yeh Hsiang-kao heading the Grand Secretariat and Chang Wen-ta (*see* Li Chih) in charge of the ministry of Personnel. Chao's predecessor, Tsou Yüan-piao, was also a stalwart Tung-lin partisan. The eunuch in power, Wei Chung-hsien(ECCP), was still mindful of public opinion and trying to cooperate with Yeh in the management of national affairs. Wei, moreover. came from a region less than a hundred miles from Chao's home and had long been aware of the elder statesman's reputation. Hence, during the eleven months when Chao headed the Censorate, each of his proposals received a favorable response. Soon after he assumed office Chao took part in the sexennial examination of central officials of 1623, during which a large number of them were cashiered, or their names were stricken from the official register; most of these had been active in the ousting of Tung-lin men in the previous evaluation of 1617. It was a period of national disasters, with defeats on the northeastern frontier and rebellions in the southwest—a time when the people, suffering from increased taxes, famine, exaction, and oppression, were already beginning to stage uprisings. Chao was appalled to find the court deep in its old ways of laxity and corruption. He and his associates had probably made an agreement to introduce reforms in the government, each to make the best effort possible in his own office. As head of the Censorate, Chao believed that if every censor inspecting a provincial government performed his duties well, he had it in his power to stop all abuses. Yet there were evidences that some censor inspectors at the end of their one year term of office were recommending only those local officials who had paid large sums as bribes. In

April, 1623, he submitted a memorial requesting permission to conduct a strict investigation of the records of each censor inspector returning to Peking and to punish those who had knowingly made unjustifiable recommendations. The memorial received imperial approval with the stipulation that Chao's proposal be written up and included in the regulations of the Censorate.

That November Chao was made minister of Personnel. He immediately launched an attack on certain improper practices, saying that officials returning from a provincial post used to bear gifts to the Personnel officers to the amount of twelve taels, which was acceptable. Now, however, gifts had risen ten or twenty times, each gift being accompanied by the demand for a desired position. This practice he intended to stamp out. He also paid attention to office hours. In one of his memorials of 1624 he said that, while lower officials in his ministry kept office in the mornings, the ministers and vice ministers stayed home until noon to receive visitors, and arrived at the ministry in the afternoons exhausted. This would no longer do. Ministers must keep early office hours too. Especially on a day scheduled for joint conference to fill a strategic post, he suggested that the conference be held at court early in the morning so that the ministers might return to their own offices by the period of ch'en (7-9 a. m.). Another practice which Chao advocated at this time was to avoid the use of parallel style in letter writing which he found a waste of time and energy.

Most of Chao's memorials of 1623 and 1626 happen to include the dates of presentation and reply. The imperial response came generally within one to three days, indicating an attentiveness to business and regularity in procedure markedly different from the laxity and indifference of the previous two decades (*see* Chu I-chün). As the emperor, Chu Yu-chiao, was known to be neglectful of duty and showed signs of immaturity, the credit perhaps should be attributed to the co-operation between Wei Chung-hsien and Yeh Hsiang-kao. That delicate relationship, however, was interrupted in July, 1624, when the less tolerant of the Tung-lin group, headed by Yang Lien (ECCP), tried to remove Wei by accusing him of various crimes. It is said that Wei was at first panic stricken but, after being assured of the support of the emperor, he fought back by joining up with a number of unscrupulous officials, themselves holding grudges against the Tung-lin group. By November the conflict became irreconcilable. Yeh and Chao were forced to resign and Kao P'an-lung, the censor-in-chief of less than a month, was dismissed. The purge of Tung-lin members went on for more than two years.

After his resignation Chao Nan-hsing was repeatedly attacked on various charges. In May, 1625, he and twenty other officials were prosecuted on the manufactured charge of having received large sums as bribes (see Hsiung T'ing-pi, ECCP). Each was fined the amount of the bribe he had allegedly accepted, and several were tortured to death while in prison. Chao, with the help of his friends, was able to pay the fine of fifteen thousand taels and received (January, 1626) the light sentence of exile as a common soldier to the Chen-wu 振武 guard, at Tai-chou 代州, Shansi, a post only about one hundred fifty miles from his home. His son, Chao Ch'ing-heng 清衡 (T. 公甫), received a heavier sentence, being exiled to the frontier guard, Chuang-lang-wei 莊浪衞 (present Yung-teng 永登 district, northwest of Lanchow, Kansu).

The septuagenarian took his unjust punishment courageously. At the place of exile he renovated an adobe house and named it Wei-po-chai 味檗齋 (Studio of Tasting the Yellow Bark, bitter medicine). There he spent the remainder of his life. It is said that after Emperor Chu Yu-chiao ascended the throne in October, 1627, an order for Chao's pardon was issued, but the governor held up his release awaiting a document from the ministry of War. In the meantime Chao died. In 1628 he was given the posthumous name Chung-i 忠毅. There is a work entitled Wei-po-chai i-pi 遺筆, containing seven historical essays which he wrote shortly before his death.

The collected essays and poems of Chao were edited and printed by Fan Ching-wen (ECCP) in 1628, under the title Chao Chung-i kung wen-chi 文集, 24 ch. which, though ordered destroyed in the 18th century, may be found in several libraries including the Library of Congress. Another edition, in 18 chüan of prose, without the 6 chüan of poems, is included in the Ch'ien-k'un cheng-ch'i chi (early 19th century, see ECCP, p. 347). The Chi-fu ts'ung-shu (ECCP, p. 776) of the late 19th century contains a smaller edition under the title Wei-po-chai wen-chi, 15 ch. It seems that the blocks for the printing of Chao's shorter works were kept in the family for centuries. About 1840 these were repaired for the issuing of a collection entitled Wei-po-chai i-shu 遺書, containing eighteen titles. It includes, in addition to some already mentioned, a biography of Chao Nan-hsing by his son, Chao Ch'ing-heng, a collection of notes, Hsien-chü tse-yen 閒居擇言, one of humorous tales, Hsiao-tsan 笑贊, and one of his songs, Fang-ju-yüan yüeh-fu 樂府. The last two were reprinted in 1936 by Lu Ch'ien, 盧前 under the title Ch'ing-tu san-k'o er chung 清都散客二種. The poet Cheng Ch'ien 鄭騫, ca. 1940, discovered a manuscript collection of Chao's songs in a light vein, entitled Chao Chung-i kung ch'ü 曲. Some of them are ribald, in a style apparently prevalent in the early 17th century, the days of Chin P'ing Mei and the like.

The Columbia University Library has a collection of Chao's works with the supplied title of Meng-po hsien-sheng ch'üan-chi 全集, apparently adapted from the title of the first item, the above-mentioned Meng-po hsien-sheng wen-chi. This collection contains eight of Chao's works, namely:

Meng-po hsien-sheng wen-chi, 3 *ch.*; *Cheng-hsin-hui liang Han-shu hsüan* 兩漢書選, 2 *ch*, (lacking the selections from *Hou Han-shu*), preface dated 1621; *Li-sao ching ting-chu* 離騷經訂註, preface of 1613; *Hsiao-ching ting-chu* 孝經訂註, preface of 1626; *Chao chin-shih wen-lun* 趙進士文論, pa-ku essays printed in 1580 with a preface by Wang Shih-hsing (*q.v.*); *Cheng-hsin hui-kao*, pa-ku essays of later days; *Wei-po-chai i-pi*; and *Hsien-chü tse-yen*. A comparison with the contents of the *Wei-po-chai i-shu* shows that all were included in the latter except the *Chao chin-shih wen-lun* and the *Cheng-hsin hui-kao*. The style of engraving and paper of the Columbia copy show that it is from original blocks and probably printed before 1644.

Bibliography

1/243/1a; 40/52/13a; 43/4/6b; 52/x/3a; 61/135/16b; Ch'ien Ch'ien-i (ECCP), *Lieh-ch'ao shih-chi*, 11/50b; Ch'en Ting 陳鼎 (b. 1651), *Tung-lin lieh-chuan* 列傳, 13/7b; *Huang Ming wen-hai* (microfilm) 3/9/8-11; *T'ien-chien-lu* 天鑒錄 in *Ming-chi pei-lüeh* 明季北略, *chüan* 2; Chin Jih-sheng 金日昇, *Sung-t'ien lu-pi* 頌天臚筆 (1629), 11/1a; Cheng Ch'ien, "Tu-ch'ü ts'ung-lu" 讀曲叢錄, in *Wen-hsüeh nien-pao* (1941), 80.

Chaoying Fang and Lee Hwa-chou

CHAO Wen-hua 趙文華, (T. 原實, 榮崗), died 1557, an official associated with Grand Secretary Yen Sung (*q.v.*), was a native of Tz'u-ch'i 慈谿, Chekiang. In 1529, he achieved the *chin-shih* and received an appointment as a secretary in the ministry of Justice. He established something of a reputation for his competence in essay writing. On account of neglect of duty he was demoted to the post of vice prefect of Tung-p'ing 東平, Shantung. In the course of time, however, he worked his way up to be transmission commissioner. His promotion to the latter position is generally ascribed to the influence of Yen Sung. Chao had studied in the National University, then under Yen's chancellorship. This brought him to the attention of Yen who thenceforth patronized him. In order to foil any impeachment moves by his opponents, Yen conceived the scheme of planting one of his faithful supporters in the office of transmission. The relation between the two became close and, according to contemporary accounts, Chao was considered to be one of Yen's adopted sons and therefore shared the notoriety accorded to Yen and his clique. For his proposal to build the southern city wall of the metropolis, Chao was made minister of Works.

During the 1550s the southeastern coast became plagued by the *wo-k'ou* (Japanese pirates). At the end of 1554, or beginning of 1555, he memorialized the throne recommending 1) sacrifice to the spirit of the sea to entreat its blessing; 2) conferment of imperial favor both on the dead by giving them a decent burial and on the living by reducing their tax burdens; 3) increase of the number of recruits for the maritime forces; 4) the imposition of extra levies on the cultivated land in the lower Yangtze delta in excess of one hundred *mou* owned by any one household and the collection of levies a year or two in advance; 5) encouragement of the wealthy to contribute to the cause with the promise of reward at the end of the crisis; 6) the dispatch of a high-ranking official with proper authorization to take command of all the armed forces dealing with the situation; and 7) the utilization of those people who had contacts with the barbarians and of salt smugglers on the coast so that they mighht spy on the pirates or play one group off against the other. The minister of War, Nieh Pao (*q.v.*), took no action on these recommendations and offered no positive plans himself to cope with the situation. The emperor, infuriated, first meted out punishment to the responsible officials of the ministry of War, and then, upon the suggestion of Yen Sung, ordered the dispatch of Chao to offer sacrifice to the spirit of the sea (a mission which he duly performed south of the city wall of Sung-chiang

松江, near Soochow), to express imperial concern about the welfare of the people, to gather information on the *wo-k'ou*, and to formulate appropriate measures for the suppression of piracy. Later, the court authorized Chao to take charge of the armed forces in the area.

While there Chao was confronted with a difficult situation. After a long period of peace, coastal and land defense had deteriorated deplorably. The high-ranking officials and officers were more concerned with preserving their own interests than risking a fight against the pirates. But Chao was a daring and ambitious man. He demanded action from all those under him and accordingly must have antagonized a great number of people, among them Chang Ching 張經 (*q.v.*) who, having been minister of War in Nanking and now serving as commander-in-chief, slighted the upstart Chao and refused to share with him his strategy in dealing with the pirates. Furthermore, after having sustained some losses in an engagement, Chang became so overcautious that, in spite of Chao's repeated urging, he refused to give battle. Chao then memorialized the throne denouncing Chang. At this juncture the government forces converged at Wang-chiang-ching 王江涇 and inflicted a smashing defeat on the pirates, taking more than one thousand nine hundred lives. A controversy thereupon arose: the pro-Chang critics ascribed the success to the tactics of Chang while the anti-Chang critics felt that Chang fought the pirates only after Chao had impeached him. Later Chang Ching, Li T'ien-ch'ung (*see* Hu Tsung-hsien), governor of Chekiang, and other officials whom Chao had impeached for allowing piracy to spread in the lower Yangtze area, were sentenced to death (November 12, 1555); for this conventional historians have blamed Chao and Yen Sung.

To do him justice one must mention that it was Chao who later strongly recommended such competent officials as Hu Tsung-hsien and T'ang Shun-chih (*qq. v.*)

for responsible positions and that it was these people who succeeded in bringing the situation under control. In fact, the ideas he had conceived in his 1555 memorial gradually materialized and were instrumental in the later successes. Yet the editors of the Veritable Records and the Ming history excoriated him for taking inordinate bribes, failing to discriminate between merit and demerit, disrupting military operations, violating military discipline, demoralizing the rank and file, and, what is worse, contributing to the spread of piracy despite the fact that soldiers had been recruited from half the empire.

At the end of 1555 Chao returned to the capital with imperial permission. But the pirates were not yet under control, for there had been only some initial successes and the government forces were to sustain further losses. Chao proposed the reclamation of a million *mou* of cultivable land to be garrisoned by soldiers for the purpose of defending the coastal area and bringing in more revenue, and suggested that the gentry residents of the affected area assume defense assignments. These ideas, however, were turned down by the ministry of War. In addition, the leading commanders of the local forces who succeeded those degraded or disgraced were not sufficiently competent. As to the quality of the troops, the officials soon learned that the tribal forces from such frontier areas as Kweichow and special groups of braves summoned from southern and northern provinces were not effective at all; sometimes they even caused more damage than the pirates. The local inhabitants might make better soldiers but it would take a long time to train them. When repeated news of defeat reached the capital, this no doubt reflected on Chao, for he had been overly optimistic in his early reports to the emperor, who became suspicious. He consulted Yen Sung several times and the latter tried to put in some good words for his favorite, but the emperor remained unconvinced.

Naturally Chao became much concerned.

In order to find favor with the emperor and to improve his position with respect to the situation in the southeast, Chao made a bold move. Once he had recommended that Hu Tsung-hsien, the regional inspector of Chekiang, be appointed governor-general of the area in command of the armed forces, but the minister of Personnel, Li Mo 李默 (T. 時言, d. 1556, cs 1521), rejected his recommendation. Li at this time was not on good terms with Yen Sung. Thinking that his friendship with the emperor's favorite officer, Lu Ping (*q.v.*), would stand him in good stead, and that his reappointment as minister of Personnel had been made by the emperor, Li made no effort to placate Yen and won his resentment and that of his clique by being unfriendly to Yen's supporters in the matter of appointment. Chao therefore attacked Li in a memorial, 1) for his failure to find the right people to handle the piracy problem, 2) for his hostility towards Chao for impeaching Chang Ching, who had come from the same district as Li, and, what is more, 3) for his unintended slight of the emperor as seen in an essay theme in an examination. Angered, the emperor ordered Li thrown into prison and punished. On the other hand, the emperor later found Chao to be loyal and promoted him (May 3, 1556) to be minister of Works, conferring on him as well the title of grand guardian of the heir apparent. Reportedly Yen, fearing that harm might come to his family after his death, even recommended that Chao serve the emperor in the composition of the Taoist offering prayers (ch'ing-tz'u 青詞) and be appointed to the Grand Secretariat; the last recommendation, however, was not accepted.

When more alarms were sounded on the southeastern coast, the authorities decided once more to dispatch an official with plenipotentiary powers. Even though the vice minister of War, Shen Liang-ts'ai 沈良才 (T. 德夫, 鳳岡, 1506-67, cs 1535) had already been appointed, Yen Sung still wanted Chao to offer his services and told the emperor that people in the affected region had been eagerly waiting for him to return. The emperor consented and gave Chao the concurrent title of junior vice censor-in-chief in command of military operations in the lower Yangtze region. At that time, upon Chao's recommendation, Hu Tsung-hsien was already holding the post of governor-general. The two men cooperated well. In August, 1556, they succeeded in capturing and executing a number pf pirate leaders such as Hsü Hai 徐海, and Ch'en Tung 陳東. After this, the court summoned Chao back to the capital and conferred on him the title of junior guardian and the privilege of having one of his sons appointed a chiliarch in the Embroidered-uniform Guard. Chao had now reached the apex of his career.

Not long afterwards, Chao began his swift decline from power, for he made the mistake of antagonizing too many people, even his patrons Yen Sung and his son Yen Shih-fan. In order to strengthen his own position, he tried to establish close relations with the emperor. Knowing that the latter was much interested in learning the art of longevity, he presented him a special kind of wine brewed by one of his Taoist aides. He falsely told the emperor that it was the same kind that had enabled his teacher-patron Yen Sung to prolong his life. The emperor liked the wine and asked Yen about it. Taken by surprise, Yen confessed his ignorance, saying that he did not know the cause of his advanced age. Naturally, Yen was much put out by Chao's self-seeking action and considered severing their relations. Later, through the good offices of Yen's wife, Chao patched up his differences. At the same time, Chao antagonized Yen Shih-fan, and also the eunuchs close to the emperor. Convinced of his own importance, Chao no longer showed the same respect to these people. According to some sources, Yen Shih-fan resented him because he did not present gifts of sufficient size and quality. But one can hardly be surprised over the development of some rivalry between these two, both of them ambitious and hungry for power.

The eunuchs whom he had slighted also contributed to the deterioration of his relations with the emperor. Once the latter sent a messenger to give him a present. It happened that Chao was intoxicated and could not receive the imperial gift according to the required etiquette. Upon hearing this report, the emperor was annoyed. On another occasion, when the emperor had finished some Taoist medicine Chao had presented, he sent for more, but the latter was unable to produce a fresh supply. Then Chao failed to complete on time a new storied building in the western garden of the palace. One day when the emperor went up to a high point in the palace grounds to look around, he noticed a high-raftered mansion on Ch'ang-an Street, and asked to whom it belonged. Someone said that it was Minister Chao's new mansion and one even remarked that the reason why Chao had been unable to finish the new storied building in the palace garden on time was because most of the lumber had been used for his own place. The emperor was furious. Then a fire burned down three palace halls. The emperor wanted to have a tower on Cheng-yang gate 正陽門樓 built as soon as possible, but Chao demurred. For all these reasons, the emperor lost all faith in the man. At the same time he also heard rumors that, while serving as commander-in-chief of the armed forces, Chao had taken large bribes and exaggerated his reports of victory. The emperor therefore made up his mind to dismiss him. He told Yen Sung that, being so slow in the construction of the tower on the gate, Chao did not act like his old self. Yen did not catch on to what the emperor meant and endeavored to cover up for Chao, remarking that, having braved the heat in his southern campaign, he had been taken ill; Yen recommended the appointment of a vice minister to take charge of the construction job (this man was Lei Li, *q. v.*); the emperor approved. Thereupon Chao memorialized the throne saying that, having taken ill, he begged for a short leave of absence for rest and recovery, The emperor personally wrote on the memorial the imperial decree that, now that important construction was under way, the minister of Works should undertake the task and that since Chao was ill he should go back to his native district for convalescence.

Having rid the court of Chao (September 13, 1557), the emperor was still not satisfied. In his view Chao had been treated too lightly, yet no censors made any moves for impeachment. It happened that Chao's son, Chao I-ssu 趙懌思, chiliarch guard, petitioned the throne for a leave of absence to escort his father home. He did this, however, at a time of imperial ceremonial fasting when no petition might be presented. This gave the emperor an excuse: he ordered Chao Wen-hua downgraded to the status of a commoner and his son banished to a frontier garrison (September 23). He also ordered an investigation of the supervising secretaries on rites for their failure to impeach the officials concerned. As a result, from the chief supervising secretary on down, six people were flogged and dismissed from office.

For some time Chao had been suffering from ku 蠱 (a swelling disease; a type of hernia?). Not long after his disgrace he died. Later, when censors checked the books of military operations finance, Chao was accused of misappropriating government funds to the extent of over one hundred thousand taels. A decree ordered that the money should be recovered from his family. Up to 1583 not even half of thesum had been refunded. When the authorities requested imperial permission to drop the case, the emperor, Chu I-chün (*q.v.*), refused, and banished Chao's son, Chao Shen-ssu 趙慎思, to the malarial frontier.

Chao Wen-hua is credited with the

authorship of several works. One is a history of Chia-hsing 嘉興 prefecture, 20 *ch.* (published in 1549); two others are collections of his memorials: *Chia-ching p'ing-wo chih-i chi-lüeh* 嘉靖平倭祇役紀略, 6 *ch.*, and a rare untitled work also dealing with pirate suppression (which includes two imperial edicts of 1555 and twenty-eight memorials of 1555-56), probably published in 1556; also several other items, such as his collected writings, *Shih-ching-t'ang-chi* 世敬堂集, an anthology of ancient prose, and two on coastal defense. [Editors' note: While a re-evaulation of the case of Yen Sung may be deemed justifiable to a degree, the charges against Chao Wen-hua by conventional historians such as T'an Ch'ien (*q.v.*) and by the compilers of *Ming shih-lu* and *Ming-shih* seem to be warranted.]

Bibliography

1/308/17b; 3/286/22a; KC (1958), 3845, 3880, 3897; MSL (1963), Shih-tsung, *chüan* 419-51; Cha Chi-tso (ECCP), *Tsui-wei lu*, 30/24a; Chao Wen-hua, *Chia-ching P'ing-wo chih-i chi-lüeh*, Hsü Hsüeh-mu, *Shih-miao shih-yü lu*; Hu Tsung-hsien, *Ch'ou-hai t'u-pien*; Ku Ying-t'ai (ECCP), *Ming-ch'ao chi-shih pen-mo*; Yen Sung, *Chia-ching tsou-tu-lu*; Chih Ta-lun支大綸, *Shih-Mu liang-ch'ao pien nien shih* 世穆兩朝編年史 (1956 ed.), 4/21b; R. Tsunoda (tr.) and L. Carrington Goodrich (ed.), *Japan in the Chinese Dynastic Histories* (South Pasadena, 1951), 130; A. W. Hummel, *Report of the Librarian of Congress, Div. of Orientalia* (1937), 184; L. of C. *Catalogue*, 177; L. Carrington Goodrich (tr.), "A Study of Literary Persecution during the Ming by Ku Chieh-kang," HJAS, III (1938), 287.

Kwan-wai So

CHAO Yüan 趙元 or 原 (T. 善長, H. 丹林懷長子), died after 1376, was usually known as an artist of Soochow. In many paintings, however, he signed his name as "Chao Yüan of Chü-ch'eng" 莒城, a town located in the southeastern part of Shantung province. In some references, he is mentioned as a man of "eastern Ch'i 齊 (Shantung), who lived in Wu" 吳. This can be interpreted as that he was either a native of Shantung but like many other prominent men of culture in late Yüan went to live in Soochow, or that he was actually born and raised in Soochow although his ancestors had moved from Shantung to that great city. A famous scholar-painter in Soochow during the period of transition from Yüan to Ming, he was described by a contemporary poet, Wang Feng 王逢 (T. 原吉, 元吉, H. 席帽山人, etc., 1319-88), as "unmatched by anyone in eastern Wu"—high praise indeed considering the fact that a number of well-known painters were active in the Soochow area during that time, such as his friend Ni Tsan (*q. v.*). In the last years of the Yüan, Chao seems to have remained a commoner, but in the early years of the Ming, he was summoned by Emperor Chu Yüan-chang to serve with other painters in the Secretariat in Nanking. Report has it that when ordered to paint portraits of the worthies of the past dynasties, he either failed to follow instructions or incurred the wrath of the new emperor to such a degree that he suffered execution.

Although the style of Chao's painting is said to have derived from a number of earlier masters, the most important influence came from Tung Yüan (d. 962). It was his paintings which seem to have inspired Chao to express in his works a "deep and mysterious feeling" which critics found in his portrayal of mountains and forests; his free and individualistic brushwork is perhaps another sign of indebtedness to the 10th century painter.

Among his extant works, the earliest dated one is the "Ho-hsi ts'ao-t'ang" 合溪草堂 (Thatched hut of Ho-hsi), now in the Shanghai museum, with a colophon written by Ku Ying (*see* Ch'en Yu-jen) in 1363. The painting depicts the scene around the latter's favorite retreat. A typical late Yüan composition showing pavilions and trees in the foreground and mountains in the background separated by a broad stretch of river or lake in between, it is close to the works of Wu Chen

(1280–1354) and Ni Tsan. The brushwork combines the finer strokes for figures and boats and the broader strokes for trees and rocks. This appears to be an indication of Chao's earlier style. Another painting, done in somewhat tighter brushwork and thus belonging to about the same time, is the short handscroll of landscape 山水小幅 formerly in the Fritz Low-Beer collection, New York. The fact that both brushwork and composition of this painting are different from most of his other works suggests that it may have been based on a model, probably of the Northern Sung period (960–1126). A third painting possibly of earlier date is the "Lin Tung Pei-yüan hsi shan hsing-lü t'u" 臨董北苑溪山行旅圖 (Travelers on streams and mountains, copying Tung Yüan), now in a private collection in Taipei. In both composition and brushwork the painting is obviously based on an earlier one, here mentioned as a work of Tung Yüan. Certain archaic elements, such as the disproportionate scale between the trees and houses and the very different treatment of the buildings and figures in finer brushwork) and the mountains (depicted more boldly) are still retained. The painting reflects the new interest in Tung Yüan among late Yüan painters.

Several other extant paintings show a very clear individual style. Although none of them is dated, each probably belongs to the early Ming period and shows his mature style. Two of them are in the National Palace Museum, Taipei: "Hsi-t'ing ch'iu se" 溪亭秋色 (Autumn colors on a pavilion by a stream), a hanging scroll, and "Lu Yü p'eng ch'a t'u" 陸羽烹茶圖 (Lu Yü [d. 804, author Ch'a-ching of, tea classic] brewing tea), a short handscroll mounted together with several other paintings by Yüan painters. A third painting is "Hsia shan tu-shu t'u" 夏山讀書圖 (Reading in the Hsia Hills), a hanging scroll after Tung Yüan, now in the Honolulu Academy of Arts. A fourth is the "Ch'ing-ch'uan sung-k'o t'u" 晴川送客圖 (Saying farewell at Ch'ing-ch'uan), once in the C. C. Wang

collection, New York. In all four of these, he shows a much freer brushstroke, which is spontaneous and expressionistic, with a strong nervous energy.

Another painting often associated with his name is "Shih-tzu-lin t'u" 獅子林圖 (The lion grove), a short handscroll depicting one of the famous scenic sights of Soochow. An inscription by Ni Tsan, saying that he had discussed the idea of the painting with Chao Yüan before its execution, has often led connoisseurs to the conclusion that the work was one of collaboration between the two artists. In some catalogues, such as the *Shu-hua chi* 書畫記 of Wu Ch'i-chen 吳其貞 (written before 1677), the author speculates that the painting was probably done by Chao while Ni was responsible only for the inscription. In style, however, the painting comes closer to Ni Tsan than to Chao Yüan. The date of Ni's inscription, 1373, would place this scroll among Chao's later works, but it is not in his later style. The painting is at least a good indication of the friendship between these two artists. There is a painting "Pan ch'uang su yü t'u" 半窗疏雨圖 (Bamboos in rain), a hanging scroll on silk, now in Nanzenji, Kyoto, unsigned, but bearing two seals, one of which is Chao Yüan's; its brushwork differs greatly from his authenticated paintings and seems to be the work of another artist.

Like his contemporaries, Ni Tsan and Wang Meng (*q. v.*), Chao Yüan was a scholar-painter who developed an individual style with very impulsive and energetic brushwork. Though not so wide-ranging and profound as the Four Masters of late Yüan, he had his place in the circle of literati of his time. The manner of his death is one of the main reasons that prevented his influence from spreading. Another is that, even in the late Ming period, some critics were already complaining about the scarcity of his works. He was a representative painter nonetheless of the late 14th century.

Bibliography

34/13/3a; 65/2/2b; Hsia Wen-yen 夏文彦 (fl. 1365), *T'u-hui pao-chien* 圖繪寶鑑, 5/106, 6/164; Yang Chi, *Mei-an chi* (SPTK ed.), 2/4b; Wang Feng, *Wu hsi chi* 梧溪集, 5/18b; *Cheng-te ku Su chih* 正德姑蘇志, 56/9b; Wang Ch'ih-teng, *Wu Chün tan ch'ing chih* (1563), 6; Li Jih-hua, *Liu-yen-chai pi-chi*, 2/39a; Chang Ch'ou, *Ch'ing-ho shu-hua fang* (1616), 7/25; Wu Ch'i-chen, *Shu-hua chi*, 1/270; Chiang Shao-shu 姜紹書 (16th century), *Wu-sheng shih shih* 無聲詩史, 1/6, 6/99; Lu Shih-hua 陸時化 (1714-79), *Wu Yüeh so chien shu-hua lu* 吳越所見書畫錄 (1910), 3/20a; Chang Ta-yung 張大鏞, *Tzu-i-yüeh-chai shu-hua lu* 自怡悅齋書畫錄 (1832), 1/15b; Li Tso-hsien 李佐賢 (cs 1835), *Shu-hua chien ying* 書畫鑑影 (1871), 12/2b, 20/23a; O. Sirén, *Chinese Painting, Leading Masters and Principles*, Vol. IV (1958), 94; Harada Kinjiro, *Shina Meigo hokan* (Tokyo, 1936), 392; *Toyo Bijutsu Taikan*, Vol. IX, Tokyo, 1912; *Exhibition of Chinese Art*, no. 789, Venice, 1954; Wen Fong, "The Problem of Forgeries in Chinese Painting," AA, XXV (1962), 110; Gustav Ecke, *Chinese Painting in Hawaii* (Honolulu, 1965), pl. XLIII and Fig. 79; V. Contag and C. C. Wang, *Seals of Chinese Painters and Collectors* (rev. ed., Hong Kong, 1966), 526; Wang Shih-chieh, *et al.*, *A Garland of Chinese Paintings*, II (Hong Kong, 1967), pls. 34 and 35; E. J. Laing, *Chinese Paintings in Chinese Publications, 1956-1968* (Ann Arbor, 1969), 116.

Chu-tsing Li

CHAO Yung-hsien 趙用賢 (T. 汝師. H. 定宇), 1535-April 12, 1596, scholar-official, was a native of Ch'ang-shu 常熟 in the prefecture of Soochow. His father, Chao Ch'eng-ch'ien 趙承謙 (T. 德光, H. 益齋, 1487-1568, cs 1538), served for a term as assistant administration commissioner of Kwangtung.

Following Chao Yung-hsien's own success in the examinations (cs 1571), he received an appointment in the Hanlin Academy. In 1576 he took part in the compilation of the *Ta Ming hui-tien* (*see* Shen Shih-hsing), and in the following year officiated in the metropolitan examination. On November 5, 1577, Chang Chü-cheng (*q. v.*) heard of his own father's death, and, fearing that his absence from the court might jeopardize his paramount position, connived with the eunuch Feng Pao (*see* Chang Chü-cheng) to set the stage for him to remain in office while he proceeded with an application for leave to observe the period of mourning. The other ministers took the hint, petitioning the throne as one that he be forbidden to leave. When the young emperor too told Chang he could not be spared, Chao Yung-hsien and his Hanlin colleague, Wu Chung-hsing 吳中行 (T. 子道, H. 復庵, 1540-*ca*. 1598, cs 1571), as well as two officials in the ministry of Justice, remonstrated against this breach of the ethical code, and begged the throne to insist that the son do his duty. All four were beaten severely (December 1, 1577), Chao and Wu each undergoing sixty blows of the bamboo, and cashiered, while the other two men received eighty apiece and were banished. On December 3, a fifth man, Tsou Yüan-piao (*q. v.*), who had just graduated as *chin-shih* and was serving as observer in the ministry of Justice, joined in the protest despite the emperor's solemn warning. He was subjected to the maximum of one hundred blows and banished. After Chao's ordeal, a palm-sized heap of pulverized flesh was collected from his body alone. (He was known to be tall and stout.) His wife treated and preserved it for his offspring as a memento of his exemplary conduct.

After the passing of Chang Chü-cheng (1582), Chao was recalled to office along with the others, and began again to work on the *Ming hui-tien*. He rose steadily in the ranks from deputy secretary of the supervisorate of instruction of the heir apparent to right vice minister of Rites in Nanking (1588). Then came his transfer to Peking as right vice minister of Rites and concurrent reader-in-waiting in the Hanlin (1591), and finally his appointment to left vice minister of Personnel with the same Hanlin affiliation (1593). This put him in a position to make good selections for bureaucratic posts, at the same time eliminating the unfit. In that year Chao was forced to step down from office because of a cabal of his enemies at court; with his departure and the exodus of his sympathizers, according to Ch'ien Ch'ien-i (ECCP), the Ming court was emptied of all worthy men.

Chao passed away at home in 1596. There is a story that he became the king of Hades. According to that story, at the time of Chao's death, a chin-shih of his own year, named Ch'en Yung-pin (q. v.), then serving as governor of Yunnan, who knew nothing of Chao's passing, held a session with the planchette (扶乩) for his own ailing wife. The seance resulted in the assertion that she was doomed to die, and Chao, having just taken office as Yen-wang 閻王 (king of Hades), was too upright to make any compromises even on behalf of the wife of a friend. In 1626 he received the posthumous name of Wen-i 文毅and was accorded the titles of junior guardian of the heir apparent, minister of Rites, and chancellor of the Hanlin Academy. His memory was preserved in Ch'ang-shu's shrine for local men of note.

During his six-year period at home (after his dismissal in 1577) Chao observed the poverty of the people living south of the Yangtze estuary, despite the region's resources which constituted a major fraction of the entire country. When he became deputy supervisor of instruction in 1586, he and the recently graduated Yüan Huang (q. v.), a man from a neighboring district pondered the situation for forty-seven consecutive days. Their deliberations resulted in a fourteen-point proposal for reform in which they emphasized the necessity to improve the revenue collecting system. The court rejected this on the ground that a local man should refrain from touching on matters concerning his native region.

Chao Yung-hsien was the author of the Sung-shih-chai chi 松石齋集., 30 ch., essays (five of them being his memorials), and poetry, 6 ch., published in 1618, a book which came to be listed on the 18th-century index expurgatorius. (The original is available on microfilm.) The memorials and poetry were reprinted in 1896; the essays, some of which had been lost, were not reprinted until 1902 after a copy of the complete text was discovered in 1899 in a bookshop by Chao's ninth generation descendant. This 1902 edition includes the original preface by Tsou Yüan-piao (undated, solicited by Chao's sons, Chao Ch'i-mei 琦美[T. 元度, H. 清常道人, 1563–1624] and Chao Lung-mei 隆美 [T. 季昌]), another preface by Huang Tao-chou (ECCP) dated 1637, and a portrait of Chao with an inscription by his grandson, Chao Shih-ch'un 士春 (T. 景之), dated 1657. Chao Yung-hsien also worked on two books in his advanced years, which he left unfinished (?), San Wu wen-hsien chih 三吳文獻志 and Kuo-ch'ao tien-chang yin-ko lu 國朝典章因革錄. Chao was a bibliophile and left a handwritten catalogue of his library which was reproduced in 1957 under the title Chao Ting-yü shu-mu 書目. This contains the only known listing of the 244 ts'e 冊 (volumes) in the miscellaneous collection Pai-t'ung 稗統 which is no longer extant. Chao Ch'i-mei like his father collected books; his catalogue, known as Mo-wang-kuan 脈望館 shu-mu, being engraved in 1910 by Lo Chen-yü (BDRC) in Yü-chien-chai 玉簡齋 ts'ung-shu, and also reproduced from the original manuscript in Han-fen-lou pi-chi 涵芬樓祕笈. Besides this he collected and collated, mainly in manuscript, 242 Yüan and Ming dramas, Ku-chin tsa-chü 古今雜劇, published in facsimile in Ku-pen hsi-ch'ü ts'ung-k'an 古本戲曲叢刊 (Peking, 1958). The original Ming copy is now in the Peking Library.

Chao Lung-mei's sons, Chao Shih-ch'un and Chao Shih-chin 士錦 (T. 前之), both achieved the chin-shih in 1637. Chao Shih-chin ended his career as vice director of a bureau in the ministry of Works. Chao Shih-ch'un, who placed third on the chin-shih list, was appointed a Hanlin compiler. When Yang Ssu-ch'ang (q. v.), then minister, also refrained from taking leave to mourn his father's passing, and Huang Tao-chou was cast into prison for making a protest to the throne, Chao Shih-ch'un remonstrated as his grandfather had done and was demoted and sent to Kwangtung as a recorder in the provincial administration office. Eventually restored to his original post, he ended his career as a secretary of the supervisorate of instruction, and died at the age of seventy-nine.

Bibliography

1/229/12a; 3/213/13a: 5/26/63a; 61/109/2185; MSL (1940), Shen-tsung, 67/9a, 68/6a, 9a; *Ch'ang Chao ho-chih* 常昭合志 (1785), 8/114b; KC (1958), 4320, 4324; Ch'ien Ch'ien-i, *Ch'u-hsüeh chi*, 62/1a; Sun Tien-ch'i (1957), 95; *Sung-shih-chai wen-chi* (1902); Chu-hung, *Chu-ch'uang san-pi* in *Yün-ch'i fa-hui* (1897), Vol. 26, 75a; *Yünnan t'ung-chih* (1894), 235/28a.

L. Carrington Goodrich and C. N. Tay

CHEN-k'o 眞可 (T. 達觀, H. 紫柏), July 2, 1544–January 18, 1604, Buddhist monk and poet, was a native of Wu-chiang 吳江, south of Soochow, where he was born into the Shen 沈 family. It is said that even at the age of four Chen-k'o could not speak. One day a strange monk came to the Shen family, laid his hand upon the child's head, and told the father that the boy would become a teacher of both mundane and heavenly things if he would enter the monastery. Then the monk disappeared, and Chen-k'o began to speak. During his boyhood he showed an unusual strength of will and character; he did not enjoy playing with other children and when he grew older he took a dislike to the sight of women. He never allowed a female to enter the bath before him and when one day his elder sister inadvertently came there, he made such a scene that afterwards no female member of the house dared to come near him at this time.

At the age of sixteen (1560) he took his sword, left the house, and wandered north to the Great Wall. On his way back he was stopped by rain at Soochow, where he met a monk, Ming-chüeh 明覺, who gave him shelter at Hu-ch'iu (Tiger Hill). ssu 虎丘寺. During the night he listened to Ming-chüeh reciting the 88 names of the Buddha; this impressed him so much that the next morning he asked to have his head shaven and be admitted as the latter's disciple. After some time Chen-k'o locked himself up in his cell, studied for six months, and was at last formally ordained at the age of nineteen (1563). The next few years he spent traveling from monastery to monastery and studying the doctrine with famous monks. He forced himself to walk until his calloused feet could take him sixty miles a day. He spent some time on Mt. Lu 廬山 (Kiangsi) where he tried to explore the hidden meaning of the dharmalakṣaṇa (fa-hsiang 法相). When he went to Peking, his teacher was for a while the monk Pien-yung 徧融. Chen-k'o wanted above all, however, to become acquainted with Te-ch'ing (*q. v.*), who, he thought, would be able to resolve all his doubts and scruples. After a visit to Mt. Wu-t'ai he returned to the Soochow region, having been away eight years. There he succeeded in establishing friendly relations with the influential official Lu Kuang-tsu (*see* Lu Nan), a devout Buddhist, whose protection became important for Chen-k'o's further activities. The Lu family helped him with financial contributions to restore the Leng-yen 楞嚴 ssu in Chia-hsing 嘉興, Chekiang, which had been appropriated by a rich family of the neighborhood and converted into a private garden. When the building was finished, Chen-k'o wrote a parallel verse with his own blood. These religious eccentricities and his successful missionary work among the gentry of the region earned him a more than local reputation, and pupils began to gather. One of these, whose religious name was Tao-k'ai 道開, became his faithful assistant for many years. Tao-k'ai was also his companion on his next journey to north China in 1586. This time Chen-k'o succeeded in meeting Te-ch'ing, who in the meantime had become a favorite of the empress dowager Li-shih (*q. v.*), a fervent patron of Buddhism. Chen-k'o met Te ch'-ing in the latter's hermitage on Lao 勞 shan in Shantung. It was the seventh month of the year and the autumn floods made travel difficult but Chen-k'o overcame all hardships bravely, and the two renowned Buddhists were able to spend ten days together and establish a spiritual friend-ship. Te-ch'ing also was to become even-tually his slightly older friend's biographer. It seems too that Te-ch'ing was instru-mental in introducing Chen-k'o to the court in Peking, although the chronology of Chen-k'o's extended travels cannot be established beyond doubt because of the scarcity of dates in the sources.

After his meeting, with Te-ch'ing in 1586, Chen-k'o seems to have visited famous Buddhist centers throughout the whole empire. His itinerary included Mt. O-mei in Szechwan, the Ch'ü-t'ang Gorge 瞿唐峽 in the same province, Wu-tang 武 當 shan in Hukuang, and again Lu shan in Kiangsi. It may have been about 1586 that Chen-k'o also spent some time on Shih-ching 石經 Mountain in Fang 房-shan-hsien near Peking. During his visit he noticed that the early T'ang monk, Ching-wan (d. 639), had deposited a relic of the Buddha in one of the caves; he then organized the transfer of the relic to the imperial palace for three days. For this the empress dowager presented him with a purple cassock. Ching-wan had also engraved the text of sūtras on stone, which gave Chen-k'o the idea of a simi-lar enterprise in order to achieve reli-gious merit. He decided to start the printing of a new version of the Buddhist canon, that is, the early Ming version augmented by forty-one additional texts. This too was promoted by the empress dowager. It was Chen-k'o's original idea, however, to have this version printed not in the traditional pothi format but in square volumes (fang-ts'e 方册) like ordi-nary Chinese books. The carving of the printing blocks was started on Wu-t'ai shan in 1589, supervised in part by Chen-k'o himself. After 1592 the work was continued in the Ching 徑 shan monastery west of Hangchow, which remained a center for many years to come. In the Soochow-Hangchow region too blocks were carved. All of them were transported, however, to the Leng-yen monastery in Chia-hsing for printing. The whole enter-prise was not finished until long after Chen-k'o's death. [Editors' note: The Bud-dhist texts from this edition, stored in the National Central Library in Taipei, con-stitute apparently the largest surviving collection known.]

After Chen-k'o had resided for a while on Mt. Wu-t'ai he went south again, took up his former residence on Lu shan and also traveled extensively in the Yangtze region. In 1591 (1592, according to one source) we find him again in the capital. In 1592 he met Te-ch'ing for the second time; they spent forty days together on Shih-ching shan where they agreed to com-pile a continuation of the history of Ch'an Buddhism, *Ch'uan-teng lu* 傳燈錄, bringing it down to their own time. They also planned to make a pilgrimage to Ts'ao-ch'i 曹溪, Kwangtung, where Hui-neng (638–713), the famous Sixth Patriarch of the Ch'an school, had lived. This trip had to be made by Chen-k'o alone, however, because Te-ch'ing had in the meantime been thrown into jail and later banished to Lei-chou, Kwangtung. Chen-k'o did, however, manage to meet him when he was on his way to his place of banish-ment. The two monks had a brief encoun-ter in Nanking in November of 1595. Chen-k'o also recited the Lotus Sūtra in order to obtain supernatural protection for Te-ch'ing, who was facing an uncertain fate. But whereas Te-ch'ing's banishment was for five years only, Chen-k'o himself a few years later became entangled in the web of court politics, and died as a victim of the judiciary system of his time.

The story is quite involved. In 1601 Chen-k'o decided to go to Peking for, if we are to believe his biographer Te-ch'ing, purely humanitarian reasons. He is said to have stated his purpose in the following way: "If Te-ch'ing does not return, I shall have greatly failed in religion; if the mining taxes are not canceled, I shall have greatly failed in helping the world; and if the *Ch'uan-teng lu* is not continued, I shall have greatly failed in my personal endeavors." This would show that his plan to go to Peking was occasioned by Te-ch'ing's exile and that he wanted to use his influence in court circles, especially with the empress dowager, to obtain his release. Chen-k'o's protest against the mining taxes goes back to the widespread discontent that had followed the introduction (*ca.* 1600) of new mining taxes, when the notoriously extravagant emperor needed additional money for his building enterprises. The palace eunuchs were largely in charge of this new taxation and exercised pressure on the local bureaucracy (*see* Wang Ying-chiao). Chen-k'o seems to have become active in this case on behalf of the prefect of Nan-k'ang 南康 (Kiangsi), Wu Pao-hsiu 吳寶秀 (T. 汝珍, cs 1589), a native of P'ing-yang 平陽 (Chekiang), and probably an earlier acquaintance of his. Wu Pao-hsiu was imprisoned and his wife, née Ch'en 陳, committed suicide when she was forbidden to accompany her husband. Wu was later released, possibly through Chen-k'o's intervention.

All this, though leading to hostility in the circle of eunuchs, was not necessarily fatal. What brought about Chen-k'o's ruin was the weird pamphlet case (*see* Lü K'un and Kuo Cheng-yü). When the emperor, Chu I-chün (*q. v.*), learned about the pamphlet, he flew into a rage and ordered a thorough investigation. A wave of arrests and raids followed, and Chen-k'o, who had been in and out of many of the suspected officials' houses, was detained as a potential accomplice. One source relates that the reason for his arrest, however, was not connected directly with the pamphlet case. During the investigation the house of the physician, Shen Ling-yü 沈令譽, was raided. (He was also a native of Wu-chiang and perhaps a clansman of Chen-k'o.) In Shen's house the police found letters written by several individuals implicated in the case and also a letter from Chen-k'o in which a passage read:"The empress dowager had wanted to build a monastery but the emperor would not assist her. How can this be called filial piety?" The discovery of this letter may after all have been the actual reason for his arrest. The emperor was angry, but it does not seem that he wished Chen-k'o executed, particularly because Chen-k'o had on an earlier occasion gratified the emperor by writing a complimentary poem on the ruler's Buddhist activities. Chen-k'o, however, was thrown into prison and received thirty blows with the bamboo cane, a torture which the monk, then in his sixtieth year, did not survive. His remains were taken away and buried temporarily. The final funeral, to which some high-ranking officials donated money, took place several years after his death; his body was cremated in December, 1616.

Te-ch'ing collected the essays and poetry by Chen-k'o and printed them together with his necrology under the title of *Tzu-po tsun-che ch'üan-chi* 紫柏尊者全集, 30 *ch.* Ch'ien Ch'ien-i (ECCP), a leading lay Buddhist who had never met Chen-k'o but revered him, compiled a *pieh-chi* 別集, 4 *ch.*, and a *fu-lu* 附錄, 1 *ch.* Some of Chen-k'o's religious conversations (yü-lu 語錄) were also edited separately under the title of *Ch'ang sung ju-t'ui* 長松茹退, 2 *ch.* (a work listed by the *Ssu-k'u* editors, but not copied into the Imperial Library), and incorporated into the continuation of *Pao-yen-t'ang pi-chi* 寶顏堂祕笈. The *Zoku Zōkyō* 續藏經 contains several works by Chen-k'o, all of them shorter treatises on the exegesis of *Pan-jo hsin-ching* 般若心經 (the Heart Sūtra), taken from *chüan* 6 of his collected works. Volume 39 of the same collection has an equally short treatise on *Chin-kang ching* 金剛經 (Diamond Sūtra) and Volume 98, an explanation of the pa-shih 八識 (Eight Modes of Perception).

Chen-k'o must be regarded as one of the spiritual leaders in late Ming Buddhism. In contrast to the more pietistic attitudes of Chu-hung (*q. v.*) and his insistence on enlightenment by meditation, he stressed the way of salvation through intellectual reasoning. At the same time he was a paragon of the syncretism fashionable in his day, in that he tried to combine a neo-Confucianism tainted by the ideas of Wang Shou-jen (*q. v.*) with Buddhistic scholastic philosophy. It is not easy to pin him down to any of the established schools of Buddhist thought. He is sometimes described as trying to combine Pure Land doctrine with Ch'an Buddhism; in the eyes of Te ch'ing, he was a follower of the Lin-chi 臨濟 school of Ch'an and going back to the teachings of I-hsing (683-727). Chen-k'o was also a student of the Book of Changes and one of his pupils Kuan Chihtao (*see* Ku Hsien-ch'eng), even tried to achieve a synthesis of that Classic with the *Avataṃsaka-sūtra*. On the other hand Chen-k'o may be regarded as a follower of the Invocation of Buddha school (nien-Fo 念佛), at least during his earlier years. One thing, however, is certain: he must have impressed his contemporaries with his personality. All sources, whether those influenced by Buddhist hagiography or "secular" ones, agree that he was highly respected among the literati and the officials, among them Tung Ch'i-ch'ang (ECCP) and Li Chih (*q.v.*). One of his closer friends was the poet, T'ang Hsien-tsu (ECCP), whom, it seems, he converted to Buddhism. T'ang gives him the epithet hsiung 雄 (heroic), and after his death wrote three poems to commemorate him. The two met several times, first in 1590 in Nanking and again in 1598 in Lin-ch'uan 臨川 (Kiangsi), T'ang's native place. In the beginning of the next year they traveled together to Nanchang by boat, a voyage documented by several poems.

Chen-k'o is described as a man of stern appearance, with bushy eyebrows and a royal bearing. He was uncompromising in all matters concerning monastic discipline and once even said: "A monk who eats meat and drinks wine ought to be killed." And when he learned that his first teacher, Ming-chüeh, had left the clergy and become a physician with a flourishing practice, he feigned illness and surprised him with a visit. It is said that Chen-k'o was able to persuade Ming-chüeh to resume monastic life. Another feature of his personality was a marked asceticism. For many years he never stretched out on a mat but spent the night sleeping seated in an upright position. He used to meditate in the open air regardless of wind and frost. In prison and under torture he was able to keep his serenity and even preached to his co-prisoner Ts'ao Hsüehch'eng (*see* Ch'en Chü) who was a victim too of court intrigue but, unlike Chenk'o, was later released. There are a number of stories on Chen-k'o's ability to foretell future events, and after his death he appeared to several of his former acquaintances in their dreams. All this points to the impression he made on his contemporaries, which was strengthened by the fact that he could, in a way, be regarded as a martyr.

Biblibgraphy

24/5/65b; 40/92/6b; 84/700 (Taipei, 1965); 86/23/37a; Te-ch'ing, "Ching-shan Ta-kuan k'o ch'anshih t'a-ming" 徑山達觀可禪師塔銘 (*Lu-shan chinshih hui-k'ao* 廬山金石匯考 in *Lu-shan chih fuk'an* 志副刊), ch. 上 (1933), 126a; *Ming-chi* 明紀 (SPPY ed.), 45, 19b; T'an Ch'ien, *Tsao-lin tsatsu* (*Pi-chi hsiao-shuo ta-kuan ed.*), ch. *i-chi* 義集, 20b; Chu Kuo-chen, *Yung-ch'uang hsiao-p'in*, *ibid*, 28/15a; Shen Te-fu, *Wan-li yeh-hu pien* (1959), 27/688; T'ang Hsien-tsu, *T'ang Hsien-tsu chi*, 298, 528, 543, 595; *Hsü teng-ts'un kao* 續燈存稿 (*Zoku Zōkyō* ed.), 12/143a; *Wu-teng yent'ung* 五燈嚴統, *ibid.*, ch. 16; SK (1930), 145/5b; *Bukkyō Daijiten*, Vol. 3, 2007, Vol. 10, 673; Ryuchi Kiyoshi 龍池清, "Mindai Kokuzōkō" 明代刻藏考, *Tōhō Gakuhō 8* (Tokyo, 1938), 319; Makita Tairyō 牧田諦亮, "Shihaku Shinga to sono Jōdokyō" 紫柏眞可とその浄土教, *Indogaku Bukkyōgaku Kenkyū*, 8 (1960), 645; Mochizuki

CH'EN Ch'eng

Shinkō 望月信亨, *Chūgoku Jōdokyō-rishi* 中國淨土数理史 (1964), 478; Araki Kengō 荒木見悟, "Minmatsu ni okeru Jubutsu Chōwaron no Seikaku" 明末における儒佛調和論の性格, *Nihon Chūgoku gakkai hō* 日本中國學會報, Vol. 15 (1966), 210; Kenneth K. S. Ch'en, *Buddhism in China* (1964), 445; C. T. Hsia, "The Plays of T'ang Hsien-tsu," *Self and Society in Ming Thought*, W. T. de Bary, ed. (1970), 250; Nelson I. Wu in *Confucian Personalities*, Arthur F. Wright and Denis Twitchett, eds. (Stanford, 1962), 280.

Herbert Franke

Ch'en Ch'eng 陳誠 (T. 子實, or 子魯, H. 竹山), died 1457+, envoy and author of a report on lands in central and western Asia, the *Hsi-yü fan-kuo chih* 西域蕃國志, was a native of Chi-shui 吉水, Kiangsi. Following his graduation as *chin-shih* in 1394 he received appointment to the messenger office, and on May 2, 1396, was dispatched on an embassy to the Sari Uighur to reestablish the An-ting 安定 and other guards (衛) south of Tun-huang. On December 31, 1396, he set out for Annam with his colleague, Lü Jang 呂讓 (T. 克遜, cj 1384, cs 1391), to settle a border dispute between that country and the tributary prefecture of Ssu-ming 思明 in Kwangsi (*see* Lê Quí-ly). The ruler of Annam tried to bribe him with two ingots of gold, four ingots of silver, garu-wood and sandalwood, but Ch'en refused them all. When he returned to the capital, he entered the Hanlin as a corrector. One source reports that during the Chien-wen period (1399–1402) he became assistant administration commissioner of Kwangtung. After the take-over of the government by Chu Ti (*q. v.*) in 1402, Ch'en Ch'eng was forced to live under surveillance at Fu-chou 撫州, Kiangsi. A year later he was restored to favor, becoming first a secretary and subsequently a vice director of the bureau of honors in the ministry of Personnel.

During the early years of the Yung-lo period, the emperor made a considerable effort to establish contact with countries abroad, both by sea and by land, Cheng Ho (*q. v.*) and Ch'en Ch'eng becoming among his most trusted lieutenants. The opportunity to dispatch the latter across Asia came in 1413 when missions from Herat, Samarkand, Shiraz, Andekan, Andkhui, Turfan, Karakhojo, Lukchak, and Kashgar arrived in Nanking bearing gifts of horses, lions, and leopards. Ch'en together with the eunuch Li Ta 李達 and another official, Li Hsien 李暹 (T. 賓暘, 1376–1445, cj 1399), received orders on October 12 to serve as their escorts on the return trip. Starting on February 3, 1414, and armed with such prospective gifts as plain and patterned silk, gauze, and fabrics, Ch'en and his party—going by way of Su-chou 肅州 in west China—reached Herat in present-day Afghanistan on October 27. During their embassy they paid official visits to seventeen states: Herat, Samarkand, Andkhui, Badakhshan, Termed, Shahrukhia, Tashkent, Bokhara, Sairam, Kez, Yanghikend, Bishbaliq, Karakhojō, Lukchak, Turfan, Yen-tse (Salt marsh), and Hami. On their return (November 30, 1415), he and Li Hsien submitted both a record of their travels, *Hsi-yü hsing-ch'eng chi* 西域行程記 (1 *ch.*), and the above mentioned report (1 *ch.*), on the places visited, including data on topography, products, and customs, a report that has been characterized as the "most important source for the situation in central Asia during the early Ming period." For his services Ch'en was made director of the bureau of honors.

This was not Ch'en's only excursion into the western regions. On the occasion of another submission of gifts to the court by missions from Herat, Samarkand, Shiraz, and Andkhui (July 13, 1416), he and a different envoy, the eunuch Lu An 魯安, received orders to accompany the foreign emissaries on their return journey, bearing gifts of silver, hemp, gauze, and silk fabrics to the prince of Herat, Shahrukh (son of Timur), and the ruler of Samarkand, Ulugh-beg, son of Shahrukh, and the heads of other states. The visit in Herat is recorded by Khorasanian historians who report that the Chinese spent the months of April and May, 1417, in Herat, Ulugh-beg himself (who frequently visited his father) arranging festivities in their honor on May 11, on the occasion of the royal audience. Ch'en and Lu returned to the capital (January 21, 1418) accompanied by ambassadors from Herat and Samarkand. The emperor then appointed Ch'en right assistant administration commissioner of Kwangtung.

On July 22, 1420, the emperor made Ch'en associate administration commissioner and dispatched him with the eunuch Kuo Ching 郭敬 to Herat and Samarkand, also to Badakhshan and Khotan (?), with presents of variegated silk for their rulers in return for gifts of horses. This was his final embassy. He retired in 1425, and remained at home until his death over thirty years later. The last time his name appears in the *shih-lu* is under date of February 19, 1457, when his title of vice minister of the Court of Imperial Entertainments (rank 5a) is changed to associate transmission commissioner (rank 4a).

His essays and poems were published in the collection *Ch'en Chu-shan wen-chi* 陳竹山文集, 4 *ch.* (which the editors of the *Ssu-k'u* catalogue mention by title only).

The report, known to the editors of the *Ssu-k'u* as *Shih* 使 *hsi-yü chi*, is not identical with the *Hsi-yü fan-kuo chih*, which is more detailed. The former was lifted from the *T'ai-tsung shih-lu*. Both of Ch'en's original works, long thought lost, were located in Ming manuscript copies in a private collection in Tientsin and acquired in 1934 by the National Library of Peiping. Subsequently the library published both of them photolithographically (1937) in its collection of rare books, the *Shan-pen ts'ung-shu* 善本叢書. It remains to add that Ch'en Ch'eng's report of his visits to Herat, Samarkand, and other lands passed not only into the *shih-lu* but also into the imperial geographical compilations *Huan-yü t'ung-chih*, edited by Ch'en

Hsün (*see* Lü Yüan) and others and *Ta Ming i-t'ung-chih* (90 *ch.*) edited by Li Hsien (*q. v.*) *et al.*, and into the section on foreign countries of the *Ming-shih*. It is from the last works that Emil Bretschneider drew much of his information for China's "intercourse with the countries of central and western Asia during the 15th and 16th centuries."

Bibliography

1/330/12b, 318/6b, 332/8b; 3/128/8a; MSL (1962), T'ai-tsu, 3556, 3600, T'ai-tsung (1963), 1690, 1706, 1884, 1934, 2049, 2216, Ying-tsung, 5820; KC (1958), 768, 2027; SK(1930), 64/2a, 175/3b; Matsumura Jun 松村潤, "Minshi saiiki-den Uten ko"明史西域傳于闐考, TG, 37 (March, 1955), 78, 500; *Shantung t'ung-chih* 山東通志 (1934), 2727, 2759; *Chi-an-fu chih* 吉安府志 (1875), 28/16a; *Chi-shui-hsien chih* 吉水縣志 (1875), 34/24b; E. Bretschneider, *Mediaeval Researches from Eastern Asiatic Sources*, II(London 1888, 1910), 137-294; V. V. Barthold, *Four Studies on the History of Central Asia*, II (Leiden, 1958, tr. by V. and T. Minorsky), 110; Henry Yule, *Cathay and the Way Thither*, I, rev. by H. Cordier (London, 1915), 271; L. Carrington Goodrich, "Geographical Additions of the XIV and XV Centuries," MS, 15 (1956), 203; W. Franke, *Sources*, 7.4.1; Henry Serruys, "Additional Note on the Origin of Lamaism in Mongolia," OE, 13 (December, 1966), 169.

L. Carrington Goodrich and C. N. Tay

CH'EN Ch'ia 陳洽 (T. 叔遠), February 2, 1370-December 5 (6), 1426, an officer who served for twenty years in Annam, was a native of Wu-chin 武進 in the prefecture of Ch'ang-chou 常州, Nan-Chihli. He was the son of a military officer, who served in the Wu-k'ai 五開 guard, Kweichow. Ch'en Ch'ia's elder brother, Ch'en Chi濟 (T. 伯載, 1364–1424), was a scholar who became one of the editors of the *Yung-lo ta-tien* (*see* Yao Kuang-hsiao). A serious boy, Ch'en Ch'ia impressed his teacher by his intelligence and industry. In the late 1380s, as a *hsiu-ts'ai* skilled in calligraphy, Ch'en entered government service through the recommendation of the local authorities, and received an appointment as a supervising secretary in the ministry of War. Chu Yüan-chang took note of his exceptional performance, particularly his retentive memory. One story relates that once, when reviewing a parade, Ch'en proved capable of recognizing the face and memorizing the name of every soldier passing before him. On learning of his father's death at his distant post in 1396, Ch'en Ch'ia made the long journey to Kweichow to escort his body home for burial. Before the mourning period was over, however, acting on the recommendation of Ju Ch'ang (*q. v.*), the minister of War, the emperor waived the ruling (which required one to spend the full twenty-seven months at home before accepting another post), and appointed him the director of the bureau of appointments in the ministry of Personnel.

When Chu Ti (*q. v.*) entered Nanking in July, 1402, as the victor in the rebellion against his nephew Chu Yün-wen (*q. v.*), Ch'en Ch'ia was among the scores of officials who came to the city gate to offer their submission. The following month he received the office of vice minister of Personnel and was transferred in October, 1405, to be the minister of the Grand Court of Revision. Ch'en's career, however, took an unexpected turn in 1406 when Chu Ti decided to invade Annam in support of the claimant to the fallen Trăn dynasty against the usurper Lê Quí-ly (*q. v.*). In July the emperor put Chu Neng and Chang Fu (for both *see* Chang Fu) in command of the expeditionary army, then dispatched Ch'en to Kwangsi to oversee the supply of rations. In September, under Ch'en's guidance, an auxiliary unit of thirty thousand local tribesmen was formed in support of the task force. This began Ch'en's connection with Annam which continued intermittently for two decades until his death. The Chinese forces scored several victories over the rebels, and succeeded in routing Lê Quí-ly, bringing to a conclusion the first Annam campaign in June, 1407, and the establishment of the Chiao-chih province. In the following month Ch'en

became vice minister of Personnel, with the special assignment to select people of caliber, Chinese and Annamite alike, to staff the administrative posts in the newly created Chinese province. A year later he returned to his former position in the ministry of Personnel, concurrently serving in the ministries of Rites and Works.

Late in February, 1409, Ch'en Ch'ia again accompanied Chang Fu to Chiao-chih when the latter was ordered to head an expeditionary army to suppress the uprising of Trăn Nguy (*see* Chang Fu), a descendant of the Trăn house who had won over the Chinese forces earlier in the year. Chang planned his campaign carefully, defeated the insurgents in September, and captured Trăn in December, thus temporarily suppressing the Annamite insurrection. Early in 1410, Chang was recalled to serve Chu Ti north of the Great Wall; Ch'en again joined his service, leaving Chiao-chih in February. Two months later they were with the emperor, training troops in the Hsing-ho 興和 region (north of Kalgan) and presumably remained there until the emperor returned to Nanking in December.

Following the completion of this assignment, Ch'en Ch'ia returned to Chiao-chih for the third time as Chang Fu's deputy, when the latter was reappointed commander of the expeditionary force to deal with the uprisings of Trăn Quí-khoáng (*see* Chang Fu) who had succeeded Trăn Nguy as leader of the Annamite resistance. Ch'en stayed with Chang Fu in Chiao-chih until the rebellion was quashed in March, 1414. In May, 1415, shortly after his return to Nanking, Ch'en was appointed minister of War, but was immediately dispatched to Chiao-chih in charge of the military operation. In the following decade he shared the new responsibility with Li Pin (*see* Lê Lọi), who succeeded Chang Fu as commander of the expeditionary force (1417–22). During this time the king of Champa, exploiting the chaotic situation, allied himself with the princes of the Trăn house, and made depredations on Chiao-chih, pillaging the villages and carrying away the spoils. Thus in December, taking a hard-line approach, Ch'en proposed to the court that an offensive be launched against Champa to remove the source of trouble. The court, however, rejected his suggestion for fear that such action would complicate the situation; instead it sent a rescript reprimanding the king of Champa and warned him of the consequence of such action. Meanwhile, the Chinese faced a continuous Annamite resistance spurred on by the leadership of Lê Lọi who had defeated Chinese forces several times. In October, 1424, Ch'en was ordered to take over the post of administrator and surveillance commissioner from Huang Fu (*q. v.*), recalled after seventeen years of service in Chiao-chih (1407-24).

In the next two years, Ch'en Ch'ia shouldered heavy responsibilities in his combined role as military adviser and administrative official. By this time the situation in Chiao-chih had further deteriorated due to the incompetence of the military commanders and the abuses of eunuchs in charge of the administration. An instance of the former may be seen in Ch'en's memorial of April, 1424, impeaching Ch'en Chih (*see* Lê Lọi) and Fang Cheng (*see* Ssu Jen-fa), who, because of their personal differences and refusal to cooperate, had led the Chinese forces to a humiliating defeat by Lê Lọi in Trà-long 茶隆州 (Nghê-an). Huang Fu's departure must have been a considerable loss to the Chinese cause, for, when the situation in Chiao-chih became desperate in 1426, Ch'en memorialized asking for Huang's return, but the latter arrived too late in 1427. In May, 1426, the court appointed Wang T'ung (*see* Huang Fu) as the new commander, with Ch'en remaining at his post to advise on military affairs.

It seems that Ch'en Ch'ia had a less cordial relation with Wang T'ung than with his predecessors since Wang was an officer of mediocre caliber, rash, willful,

and heedless of the advice of his more experienced counselors. This probably contributed to his humiliating defeat and the death of Ch'en Ch'ia. The disaster came in December, 1426, when Wang T'ung, after nullifying the rebels' attempt at Đông-quan 東關 (Đông-dô 東都), the capital of Chiao-chih, pursued Lê Lọi to the northwest. The battlefield lay in a secondary branch of the Red River, at Ninh-giang 寧江 to the west of the Đay, and from Sơn-tây 山西 to Hà-đồng 河東. According to the Chinese account, on December 5/6, Wang T'ung took his forces across the river against the counsel of Ch'en Ch'ia who, being familiar with the lay of the land feared an ambush and proposed instead to assemble in Thach-thât 石室 on the other side to observe the enemy's movement before taking action. As it turned out, the Ming forces were mired in Ninh-kiêu 寧橋 (south of Hà-đồng), and were badly defeated in Tôt-đồng 萃洞 and nearby places. Ch'en suffered a wound and died shortly afterwards. This debacle sealed the fate of Wang T'ung who was forced to negotiate peace with Lê Lọi, and end the presence of the Chinese in Annam.

Informed of the disaster, the court was stunned. In September, 1429, Emperor Chu Chan-chi (*q. v.*) awarded Ch'en the canonized name Chieh-min 簡愍 (Chaste and mournful), and appointed his son Ch'en Shu 樞 as a supervising secretary. Ch'en was later buried in effigy in his native place, where a shrine was erected (1527) in his honor; this housed a memorial stele engraved in November, 1531. In 1603 his name was entered in the Wu-chin shrine of local worthies.

Bibliography

1/154/1a, 321/15a, 324/4a; 5/38/19a; 61/106/7b; MSL (1963), T'ai-tsung, 170, 205, 710, 805, 814, 955, 1088, 1846, 1900, 1984, Jen-tsung, 43, Hsüan-tsung, 395, 408, 419, 546, 593, 1362, Shin-tsung (1965), 1806; KC (1958), 845, 1309; Chin Yu-tzu (*see* Empress Hsü), *Chin Wen-ching kung chi* 金文靖公集 (1969 ed.), 7/19b, 10/60a; Yen Ts'ung-chien 嚴從簡, *Shu yü chou-chih lu* 殊域周知錄 (1930), ch. 2; Chang Ching-hsin 張鏡心 *et al.*, *Yü chiao chi* 馭交記 (Kuang-hsü ed.), ch. 5, 6; *Wu-chin Yang-hu* 陽湖 *-hsien chih* (1879), 4/11b, 15a, 20/4a, 24/9b, 28/57b, 29/14b; TSCC (1885-88), XIV: 126/10/4a; Yamamoto Tatsurō 山本達郎, *Annam shi kenkyū* 安南史研究 (Tokyo, 1950), ch. 3, 4.

Hok-lam Chan

CH'EN Chien 陳建 (T. 廷肇, H. 清瀾釣叟, 粵濱逸史), September 16, 1497-1567, scholar and historian, came from a family that settled in Tung-kuan 東莞, Kwangtung, in the 12th century. His father Ch'en En 恩 (T. 宏濟, H. 理庵, 1450-1515), a *chü-jen* of 1489, served meritoriously as assistant instructor in Nan-an 南安, Fukien (*ca.* 1591-*ca.* 1599) and later as prefect of Kuang-nan-fu 廣南府, Yunnan, where he died in office. All of his four sons passed the provincial examinations successfully: Ch'en Yüeh 越 (T. 廷卓) in 1495, Ch'en Ch'ao 超 (T. 廷英) in 1504, Ch'en Fu 赴 (T. 廷獻) in 1510, and Ch'en Chien, the youngest, in 1528.

Failing twice in the metropolitan examinations, Ch'en Chien chose in 1532 to take an educational post and was appointed instructor in the district school of Hou-kuan 侯官, Fukien. About 1539 he received a promotion to be instructor of the prefectural school of Lin-chiang 臨江 in Kiangsi. While serving in both these capacities he was also called upon to assist in the provincial examinations of Kiangsi, Kwangsi, Hukuang, and Yunnan. His last post was as magistrate of Yang-hsin 陽信, Shantung. In 1544 he retired from official life and returned to Tung-kuan to be with his aged mother, née Ku 顧 (d. 1546, *ae.* 88). In retirement Ch'en Chien devoted his time and energy to teaching and writing.

Among the many titles recorded in catalogues and bibliographies under Ch'en's authorship, there are two that had an especial influence on later times, one on thought and the other on history. Both are the fruit of many years' labor, and their development and stages of progress are traceable.

First, the *Hsüeh-p'ou t'ung-pien* 學蔀通辨 (or 辯), 12 *ch.*, completed in 1548, is a documentary study of the differences between the philosophical approaches of Chu Hsi (1130-1200) and Lu Chiu-yüan (1139-93). Ch'en did this with two purposes in mind, one to prove that Lu was but a Buddhist in Confucian disguise, the other to expose the chronological manipulations by Wang Shou-jen (*q. v.*) in his *Chu-tzu wan-nien ting-lun* in an effort to reconcile the Chu-Lu differences. As a loyal and strict follower of Chu Hsi, Ch'en by attacking Lu indicated the possible corrupting effects of Wang's philosophy.

In 1530 by imperial order certain changes were effected in Confucian temples: wooden tablets took the place of images and the names of other scholars substituted for those no longer considered worthy to be celebrated therein. A disciple of Wang Shou-jen at this juncture proposed in a memorial that the name of Lu Chiu-yüan be among those to be entered and this was approved. As a student of the Chu Hsi school, Ch'en launched his study of the question.

In the late 1530s, while serving as an instructor at Hou-kuan and stimulated by a discussion with P'an Huang 潘潢 (T. 鷹叔, H. 朴溪, cs 1521, d. 1555), then commissioner of education in Fukien, Ch'en compiled a comparative chronology of Chu Hsi and Lu Chiu-yüan, the *Chu Lu pien-nien* 朱陸編年. Later at his post in Kiangsi he had the occasion to edit both the works of Chou Tun-i (1017-73), the *Chou-tzu ch'üan-shu* 周子全書, and of Ch'eng Hao (1032-85) and his brother Ch'eng I (1033-1107), the *Ch'eng-shih i-shu lei pien* 程氏遺書類編. Such studies further strengthened his position as an early defender of the Ch'eng-Chu school against the Lu-Wang teachings.

For almost six decades the *Hsüeh-p'ou t'ung-pien* remained unpublished. The only Ming printed edition, bearing an introduction by Ku Hsien-cheng (*q. v.*), appeared in 1606. The reason for this, observed a later scholar, was a kind of undeclared suppression imposed by the strength of Wang's influence. Be that as it may, throughout the Ch'ing dynasty this work became far more popular than during the author's own era. Scholars such as Ku Yen-wu, Chang Li-hsiang, and Lu Lung-chi (all in ECCP) took laudatory notice of it. In 1688 Ku T'ien-t'ing 顧天挺 (T. 蒼巖, cs 1670), recognizing its value, reprinted it in Honan. When Chang Po-hsing (ECCP) edited and published the *Cheng-i-t'ang ch'üan-shu* in the years 1707 to 1713, he included the *Hsüeh-p'ou t'ung-pien*. In 1718 Ch'en Chien's own great-great-grandson Ch'en Chang 璋 reprinted it, together with two more of his works. Over a century later in 1828, when some Kwangtung scholars planned to bring out another edition of this work, the famous official and scholar Juan Yüan (ECCP) contributed a preface and a postscript, and made suggestions for certain deletions in order to bring it into accord with the critique given in the Imperial Catalogue. Still later, in 1929, when another Kwangtung scholar from the same district, Ch'en Po-t'ao 陳伯陶 (cs 1892), printed the *Chü-te-t'ang* 聚德堂 *ts'ung-shu* (a compilation of works by authors all bearing the surname Ch'en and all from Tung-kuan), the *Hsüeh-p'ou t'ung-pien* was again included.

The second work of significance by Ch'en is an annalistic history of the Ming dynasty from its beginning to the end of the Cheng-te reign (1521), the *Huang Ming t'ung-chi* 皇明通紀. At first he wrote a chronology of the pre-Ming and Hung-wu periods, emphasizing the founding of the dynasty, which appeared under the title *Huang Ming ch'i-yün lu* 啓運錄; this was highly regarded by another Kwangtung scholar, Huang Tso (*q. v.*). Huang also encouraged him to continue it into the later reigns so that it would fill the need of a general history covering nearly two centuries of the Ming. In retirement

Ch'en labored on this work for some ten years, completing it in 1555. In the same year the *Huang Ming t'ung-chi* was printed in 27 *chüan*, the first ten being the original *Huang Ming ch'i-yün lu*, and the rest dealing with the reigns from Yung-lo to Cheng-te inclusively. It became so popular that numerous reprintings and editions, with supplements in different numbers of *chüan* and varying titles, appeared in the following century. One explanation for the book's great demand was surely its use as a handy reference by students in their preparation for the examinations. This fact led to fierce competition among publishing concerns, each trying to surpass the other in new editions and constantly bringing out further up-dated supplements. For example, in the Kiangsu provincial Kuo-hsüeh library of Nanking there is an edition of this work under the title *Huang Ming tzu-chih* 資治 *t'ung-chi* in 10 *chüan*, of which the first three consist of the entire *Huang Ming ch'i-yün lu* (originally in 10 *chüan*). The best known edition, probably the most available today, is the *Huang Ming t'ung-chi ts'ung-hsin lu* 從信錄, 40 *ch.*, printed in 1620 by Shen Kuo-yüan 沈國元 (T. 飛中), a *kung-sheng* from Hsiu-shui 秀水, Chekiang. The first part, 27 *ch.*, is by Ch'en Chien; *chüan* 28 to 33, covering the two periods of Chia-ching (1522–66) and Lung-ch'ing (1567–72), are by an anonymous author; *chüan* 34 to 40, treating the Wan-li period (1573–1620), are by Shen Kuo-yüan. After the death of Chu Yu-chiao (ECCP), Shen Kuo-yüan collected data on the two periods of T'ai-ch'ang and T'ien-ch'i (1620 to 1627) and compiled another annalistic work entitled *Liang-ch'ao* 兩朝 *ts'ung-hsin lu* in 35 *chüan*, printed in 1628 or thereabouts. Shen apparently lived through the last days of the Ming dynasty, for he is also known to have left a chronological record of the fateful year 1644, the *Chia-shen ta-shih chi* 甲申大事記.

Four years after Ch'en Chien's death, the *Huang Ming t'ung-chi* was banned by imperial decree. This came about as a

result of a memorial by Li Kuei-ho 李貴
和 (cs 1565, a native of Kaifeng, Honan)
a supervising secretary in the office of
scrutiny for Works. He condemned the
book for its fallacies, comments based on
hearsay, license in criticizing prominent
personalities, etc. Other sources, however,
reveal that Li's censure was mainly because
of Ch'en Chien's derogatory remarks about
the famous poet Li Meng-yang (q. v.), in
which he reproved Li for his compromise
with the rebel prince Chu Ch'en-hao (see
Wang Shou-jen). Li Meng-yang, although
a registered native of Shensi, lived in
Kaifeng, and therefore came to be considered a celebrity of the latter province as
well. Obviously Li Kuei-ho was showing
partiality toward a fellow provincial. On
account of the great popularity of the
work, with its many editions, supplements,
and variant titles, the ban was ineffective.
By the Ch'ien-lung period, two centuries
later, it appeared again on the proscribed
list. As a matter of fact, since Ch'en's
original work ends with the year 1521,
relations between the Jurchen and the
Ming had not reached a serious stage; so
to prohibit it was pointless. Nevertheless,
since it had almost always been printed
with one supplement or another, the ban
was unavoidable. Strangely enough, such
an imperially sponsored publication as the
T'u-shu chi-ch'eng (printed in 1728) made
extensive use of it. It is ironical that what
made its ban ineffective in 1571 furnished
the reason for its prohibition in the
following dynasty. Ch'en Chien's work
circulated not only throughout China, but
also in Korea. The Korean scholar, Yi
Hyŏn-sŏk 李玄錫, in compiling the general
Ming history, the Myŏngsa Kangmok 明史
綱目, 24 kwŏn (1704), cited Ch'en's work
as one of his sources. And the Tung-hua
lu 東華錄 records, under the date of
September 26, 1771, a complaint registered
by the Korean king, Yi Kŭm 李昑 (r. 1725-
76), protesting the historical treatment
of his ancestor, Yi Chong倧 (r. 1623–49),
in a supplement of the Huang Ming t'ung-
chi.

From his experience as an official and
his careful study of Ming history, Ch'en
Chien formulated definite opinions on
certain political issues of his day. He held
that reforms and changes were necessary,
as some laws and regulations good for
the early years of the dynasty were no
longer appropriate during the mid-sixteenth
century. These were written down in the
Chih-an yao-i 治安要議, 6 ch., 6 treatises
on 6 topics: 1) the imperial clan, 2) the
rewards for military merit, 3) the selection for government service, 4) the
appointment of officials, 5) the military
system, 6)border defense. The publication
date of the book (completed in 1548) is
not clear. His direct descendant Ch'en
Chang reprinted it in 1718, and in 1929
it was included in the Chü-te-t'ang ts'ung-
shu. His contemporaries valued these
treatises, some of his ideas reportedly
even being incorporated administratively.

Ch'en Chien's knowledge of general
history is shown in his careful note
to the hundred renowned poems on
historic topics by Li Tung-yang (q. v.).
The work entitled Ni-ku yüeh-fu t'ung-k'ao
擬古樂府通考, 2 ch., was first printed in
Fukien in the late 1530s, reprinted by
Ch'en Chang in 1718, and again reprinted
in the Chü-te-t'ang ts'ung-shu in 1929.
According to Ch'en Po-t'ao, the compiler
of the aforementioned ts'ung-shu, Ch'en
Chien's notes excel the more popularly
known annotations of those poems by Ho
Meng-ch'un (see Li Tung-yang).

In composing a biography of Ch'en
Chien for the Tung-kuan local history
Ch'en Po-t'ao included an interesting comment. He reports that in a letter from Lu
Lung-chi to Hsü Ch'ien-hsüeh (both in
ECCP) on the compilation of the Ming-
shih, Lu recommended the inclusion of a
biography of Ch'en Chien, as Ch'en was a
strong defender of the Chu Hsi school.
But no biography of Ch'en Chien is to be
found in the Ming-shih kao. In Ch'en Po-
t'ao's opinion it may have been deleted
by Wan Ssu-t'ung (ECCP) who, being a
native of Chekiang and a pupil directly

or indirectly of scholars of the Wang Yang-ming school, might have carried on the old quarrel by excluding Ch'en Chien from the official history.

Bibliography

Kwangtung t'ung-chih (1934), 4784, 4829; *Tung-kuan-hsien chih* (1911), 57/10a, 58/6a, *chüan* 83-88, 96/9a; MSL (1965), Mu-tsung, 1491; SK (1930), 96/5b; TSCC (1885-88), XXIII: 104/92/5a; Shen Te-fu, *Wan-li yeh-hu pien* (1959), 638; Hsieh Kuo-chen 謝國楨, *Wan-Ming shih-chi k'ao* 晚明史籍考 (1932), 1/16b; Ch'en Po-t'ao, *Chü-te-t'ang ts'ung-shu* (1929); Juan Yüan, *Yen-ching-t'ang hsü-chi*, 3/5a, 7a; Chou Ch'üeh 周愨,"Kuan-ts'ang Ch'ing-tai chin-shu shu-lüeh" 館藏清代禁書述略 in *Chiang-su sheng-li Kuo-hsüeh t'u-shu-kuan ti-ssu nien-k'an* 江蘇省立國學圖書館第四年刊, Nanking, 1930; *Ch'ing-tai wen-tzu-yü tang* 清代文字獄檔, Peiping Palace Museum (1931), 21b; L. Carrington Goodrich, "Korean Interference with Chinese Historical Records," JNCBRAS, 68 (1937), 32.

Lienche Tu Fang

CH'EN Chü 陳矩 (T. 萬化, H. 麟岡), July 14, 1539–January 29, 1608, an influential eunuch during the middle of the Wan-li reign, was a native of An-su 安肅, Pei-Chihli. He came from a family of military registry in the Mao-shan guard 茂山衛 at I-chou 易州, southwest of Peking. His father, Ch'en Hu 虎, was a farmer. Ch'en Chü had a younger brother, Ch'en Wan-ts'e 萬策 (T. 嘉謨), who became a *chin-shih* in 1592, but the highest post he held was that of an erudite in the National Academy; he was denied positions of influence by Ch'en Chü who shrank from any suggestion of nepotism.

It was the father's decision that led to the castration of Ch'en Chü at the age of eight; in the winter of 1547/48 he was selected to serve in the palace, and sent to study in the palace school for eunuchs. He achieved no prominence, however, until 1582, when the emperor chose him to be the recorder of the directorate of ceremonial. In the following year he was promoted first to be a junior assistant director, then successively made a senior assistant director, a senior eunuch, and an associate director. After fourteen years of routine assignments, he was advanced to be superintendent of the Eastern Depot, and finally, in 1605, made the keeper of the seal of the directorate of ceremonial 司禮掌印太監, the highest possible post for a eunuch.

Ch'en Chü's influence in court affairs first came to be felt in 1594 when he recommended a junior eunuch, Wang An (*see* Kao P'an-lung), to study with the eldest son of the emperor. The recommendation was accepted. As superintendent of the Eastern Depot, one of Ch'en's earliest assignments was to collect books. Among them was one entitled *Kuei-fan t'u-shuo* by Lü K'un (*q.v.*). The emperor presented a copy to the Consort Cheng Kuei-fei (*q.v.*). Evidently she liked it as she wrote a preface for it, but, before the official edition was printed, someone wrote a circular which appeared under the title Yu-wei hung-i. This reported that Lady Cheng was planning to make her own son heir apparent. It further suggested that her plan was supported by Lü K'un and other officials secretly. A few years later, in the autumn of 1603, the charge was further elaborated and was printed in the form of a circular entitled Hsü yu-wei hung-i. In this the author declared that plans were completed for the appointment of a new heir apparent. It revealed that many high officials were involved, among them Grand Secretary Chu Keng (*see* Shen I-kuan); the minister of military affairs in charge of the Peking Garrison (Jung-cheng shang-shu 戎政尚書), Wang Shih-yang 王世揚 (T. 孝甫, H. 懷棘, cs 1577); the supreme commander of the three border regions, Li Wen 李汶 (T. 宗齊, H. 次溪, 1536–1609, cs 1562); the commissioner-in-chief of the Embroidered-uniform Guard, Wang Chih-chen 王之楨; and Ch'en Chü. As a consequence the emperor ordered all his secret agencies to make a thorough investigation and find the author. Hundreds were arrested for interrogation and some men in power tried to prolong the case in order to involve their own adversaries. It was Ch'en Chü and his Eastern Depot agents who, within only a few days, apprehended a suspect, Chiao Sheng-kuang 皦生光, and saw to his trial, sentencing, and execution in the market place (May 20, 1604). In handling this case Ch'en Chü won praise from his contemporaries.

Ch'en obviously enjoyed the confidence of the emperor, for he often defended innocent victims courageously before the throne. In 1605 he rescued an assistant administrator, Chiang Shih-ch'ang (see Ku Hsien-ch'eng), from physical punishment; in 1606 he saw to the release from jail of the censor Ts'ao Hsüeh-ch'eng 曹學程 (T. 希明, cs 1583). It was his effort and sense of responsibility that led to the elimination of many false charges often made by secret agencies. To eradicate injustice seems to have been a marked characteristic of the Eastern Depot during Ch'en's tenure. It is no wonder that the editors of the *Ming-shih* characterize him as one of the few good eunuchs in the Ming period. Throughout his careeer Ch'en received many imperial gifts, including emoluments, a ceremonial robe, a jade girdle, etc. Besides, he was granted special privileges such as riding horseback in the palace area. On the conclusion of the Hsü yu-wei hung-i case (June 12, 1604), Ch'en's nephew, Ch'en Chü-kung 居恭 (T. 元禮), was granted the position of centurion in the Embroidered-uniform Guard, and on January 3, 1605, the rank was raised to that of a commissioner. On June 3 of that year, his grandnephew, Ch'en Ssu-chung 嗣忠, was also granted the position of centurion in the Embroidered-uniform Guard.

Ch'en Chü was honored after his death with a shrine, named Ch'ing-chung tz'u 清忠祠.

Bibliography

1/305/15b; 3/284/16b; MSL(1966), Shen-tsung, ch. 390-441; KC (1958), ch. 79, 80; *Pao-ting-fu chih* (1886), 54/6a, 23a; Shen Te-fu, *Wan-li yeh-hu pien*, 172, 173; "Ch'en-kung shen-tao pei" 公神道碑, *Li-wen chieh-chi* 李文節集 (NCL microfilm), 24/15; Liu Jo-yü, *Cho-chung chih*, ch. 7; *Shun-t'ien-fu chih* (1886), 107/13; P. M. d'Elia, *Fonti Ricciane*, II (Rome, 1949), 189.

Yung-deh Richard Chu

CH'EN Feng 陳奉 (*ca.* 1565-1615), was a eunuch of unknown origin who emerged briefly in March, 1599, from the obscurity of a career in the imperial stables, when he received an appointment by Emperor Chu I-chün (*q. v.*) as commercial tax collector in the Ching 荊 district, and mining and minting supervisor of the Hsing-kuo 興國 district in the rich Hukuang area. His ruthless and apparently effective way of handling his assignments endeared him to the emperor but created considerable resentment among the local populace. Ch'en ran into powerful opposition from gentry members and their allies in the local and central administrations and was repeatedly the target of violent outbursts in the city of Wuchang and the districts under his supervision, but he always managed to escape personal harm. On several occasions local officials and members of the bureaucracy in Nanking and Peking accused Ch'en of a variety of crimes ranging from oppressing and maltreating the people and their officials with the inevitably ensuing riots, and displays of improper conduct (he was charged with referring to himself as *ch'ien-sui* 千歲—a form of address reserved for princes of imperial blood), to jeopardizing the river and land-borne commercial activities in the Wuchang area. Officials who attempted to protect Ch'en against rioters, notably the governor of Hukuang, Chih K'o-ta 支可大 (T. 有功, cs 1574), were accused of hiding the facts of the eunuch's nefarious deeds from the emperor and of aiding Ch'en in his crimes. The emperor, apparently pleased with Ch'en's performance in rounding up revenue, not only ignored all attacks on the eunuch, including a request by the prestigious grand secretary, Shen I-kuan (*q. v.*), for Ch'en's removal, but even punished some of his most virulent critics, among them the assistant commissioner of the military defense circuit in Wuchang, Feng Ying-ching (*see* Matteo Ricci), and the two supervising secretaries, Ch'en Wei-ch'un 陳維春 (cs 1592) and Kuo Ju-hsing 郭如星 (cs 1589). They were reduced in rank and transferred to lower positions. One of those whose loss was especially to be regretted was the able and upright official Chao K'o-huai (*see* Matteo Ricci) who was sent in 1601 to Wuchang as governor to help quell the disturbances created by Ch'en Feng. Three years later Chao was slain in Wuchang by an imperial clansman, Chu Yün-chen 朱蘊鈜. Ch'en apparently survived all attacks and continued to serve his imperial master. His fate, after this flurry of impeachments, and the circumstances of his death, however, are unknown.

Bibliography

1/21/5a, 305/8b; 3/284/10a; 61/159/24a; MSL (1966), Shen-tsung, 6125, 7514; KC(1958), 4923, 4932; TSCC (1885-88), XIV: 41/4a; Ting I 丁易, *Ming-tai t'e-wu cheng-chih* 明代特務政治 (Peking, 1950), 213; P. M. d'Elia, *Fonti Ricciane*, II (Rome, 1949), 13, n. 4, 82, n. 1, 162.

Ulrich Mammitzsch

CH'EN Hsien-chang 陳獻章(T. 公甫, H. 石齋, 白沙), November 27, 1428–March 10, 1500), thinker, educator, and calligrapher, was born in the village of Tu-hui 都會 in the district of Hsin-hui 新會, Kwangtung. His name, however, was to become associated especially with the village of Po-sha 白沙, also of Hsin-hui, to which the family moved some time during his own life. According to one source, his ancestors were originally from north China, but had fled south in the 13th century to escape the Mongol invaders. Ch'en's family belonged to the land-owning local gentry of Hsin-hui. His father died about a month before the birth of Ch'en Hsien-chang. The younger of two sons, Ch'en grew up under the care of his mother and his grandparents. He described himself as having been a sickly child, very attached to his mother, who, for reasons of his health, fed him on milk until he was eight. But he grew to be quite tall, and the seven black spots on his right cheek—his birthmarks—calling to mind the stars of he Great Dipper, added to his impressive tappearance. He was a good student and evinced an unusual memory. At nineteen he succeeded in passing the provincial examinations. The following year (1448) he went to Peking for the metropolitan examinations, which he failed to pass. His name, however, appeared on the secondary list, thus allowing him to be enrolled in the National University, where he studied for some time. Those were difficult days, as the Ming dynasty suffered a severe setback after the defeat of Emperor Chu Ch'i-chen (*q. v.*) in 1449. Ch'en Hsien-chang attempted the metropolitan examinations once more in 1451, again without success. Some sime after that, he became very interested in the Sung thinkers.

In 1454, at the age of twenty-six, Ch'en Hsien-chang traveled to Lin-ch'uan 臨川, Kiangsi, to study under Wu Yü-pi (*q.v.*), and remained with him for several months, in the company of other disciples of Wu, including Lou Liang (*q. v.*). It is said that Wu Yü-pi employed him in menial tasks, and once reprimanded him for staying in bed in the morning at a time when Wu himself was already up and sieving rice. Ch'en Hsien-chang declared that Wu taught him many things, but that he was unable to find "the entrance gate" to truth. He was much stimulated by Wu's example, however, and soon returned to Hsin-hui with the determination to seek sagehood. He attempted at first to give himself over to assiduous study and extensive reading of Confucian as well as non-Confucian texts, staying up late at night, and pouring cold water on his feet to keep awake. After a few years of such activity, near he realized that he was nowhere near his desired goal. Convinced now that learning consists primarily of personal insights, he built himself a small dwelling, in which he led an isolated existence, seeing little even of his family members, who had to pass food to him through a hole in the wall. There, in his hermitage, Ch'en devoted himself for years to the practice of quiet sitting (ching-tso 靜坐), during which he experienced the beginnings of wisdom in the new vision of an inner world of peace and tranquillity. But such strenuous efforts were injurious to his health, and Ch'en learned from hard experience that personal cultivation could not be forced, not even by exercises in meditation. Thereupon he modified his way of life, taking frequent walks in the woods, singing to his heart's content, and boating and fishing at nearby streams. He acquired consciousness of the oneness of all things, and of his own participation in the dynamic transformation of the universe. His peaceful existence was interrupted in 1462 when Hsin-hui was raided by roving bandits. The following year Ch'en lost his first wife.

Probably about this time, around ten years after his return home from Lin-ch'uan, Ch'en Hsien-chang acquired the enlightenment experience he desired, which was the result of the accumulation of his many insights, as well as their culmination. His interior life became rooted in freedom and spontaneity. He had discovered and developed the self-determining quality of the mind and heart, source and goal of wisdom and perfection. His reputation had already attracted to Hsin-hui a number of disciples, including Chan Jo-shui (q. v.), who came to him in 1466. He passed his time in their company, discussing questions of learning and life, and adding to their program the practice of archery, as a physical exercise beneficial to health. This last interest caused him some difficulty, and he was warned that it might appear to the government as though he were attempting to surround himself with men trained in warlike skills for the sake of preparing a rebellion. Perhaps partly to avert such an opinion, and, besides, persuaded by his friends and disciples, Ch'en decided to try again for public office. He went to Peking in 1466, and reenrolled in the National University, where his poems drew praise from the chancellor, Hsing Jang 邢讓 (T. 遜之, 1427-77, cs 1448), who considered Ch'en's talents to be superior to those of the Sung philosopher, Yang Shih (1053-1135). Ch'en was sent by the University to the ministry of Personnel to gain experience. In the meantime, he became good friends with many scholars at the capital, including Lo Lun, Ho Ch'in, Chang Mou (qq.v.), and Hsüeh Ching-chih (see Hsüeh Hsüan). He returned south in 1467, and then went back north a year later. In 1469 he took the metropolitan examinations for the third time, again without success. After this, Ch'en returned to Hsin-hui to live in retirement. According to reports his health was declining. He married for the second time in 1472. During the ensuing years several of his disciples succeeded in the *chin-shih* examinations. Ch'en's own reputation as a teacher and thinker, as well as a man of virtue, steadily increased.

Finally, in 1482, on the recommendation of P'eng Shao (q.v.), vice administration commissioner of Kwangtung, and Governor Chu Ying 朱英 (T. 時傑, H. 誠菴, 1417-85, cs 1445), Ch'en was summoned to Peking, not by direct imperial order, but by the ministry of Personnel, because of his status as a scholar of the National University. Instead of receiving an immediate appointment, however, Ch'en was instructed to take an examination at that ministry. He declined to do so, pleading illness, and then addressed a petition to the emperor, requesting permission to return home to care for his aged mother. The emperor graciously bestowed on him the title of a Hanlin corrector, after which Ch'en finally took his leave. The death of his mother in 1485 brought him great sorrow. Ch'en observed the customary mourning and, even after its termination, never put on silk robes, as a token of perpetual mourning. Besides, as he explained to his friends, he had formerly worn silk only to please his mother. He died a few years later, at the age of seventy-two, reportedly after composing a last poem. His two sons, both by his first wife, had died before him. But he was survived by two married daughters. He had married again but his second wife was childless. Several thousands of his friends and disciples gathered for his funeral. His best-known disciple, Chan Jo-shui (q. v.), observed the three-year mourning as for a parent. In 1584 Ch'en Hsien-chang's memory was further honored when his tablet was placed in the Confucian temple. He was the first and only native of Kwangtung to receive this honor. He also acquired the posthumous name Wen-kung 文恭.

As a thinker, Ch'en Hsien-chang emphasized the importance of acquiring insights for oneself (tzu-te 自得). He definitely achieved a real independence of mind and spirit, being aided in so doing probably because he was a native of Kwangtung, the province freer than other provinces of the influence of older intellectual traditions. Besides, even more than Wang Shou-jen (q.v.), his younger contemporary, Ch'en had plenty of time to reflect. Where his one-time master, Wu Yü-pi, had been a faithful follower of the Ch'eng-Chu school of thought, with its dual emphasis on tranquil self-cultivation and the pursuit of study and intellectual inquiry, Ch'en Hsien-chang preferred to seek the truth in himself, through cultivation of his mind and heart alone, where he also discovered the presence of truth and moral principles (li 理). His own philosophy, which matured only after a long period of searching—in his own words, after twenty years of solitary study— was based especially on the principle of being natural (tzu-jan 自然). To this end, Ch'en Hsien-chang held that an empty and unobstructed mind, acquired by tranquil meditation, is essential for the realization

of truth. He recommended that one be always attentive, and yet remain free from artifice and anxiety. Ch'en maintained also that man and Heaven and Earth formed one body. Ch'en's penetration into man's oneness with the universe was such that (according to Jen Yu-wen) he cherished the thought that human life itself would continue even after death in the company of Heaven and Earth. In other words, he gave expression to his personal faith in an eternal life, which was beyond the usual Confucian conception.

Ch'en's idea of tranquillity can be traced to Chou Tun-i (1017-73) and his doctrine of quiet sitting to Ch'eng I (1033-1107). He has also been accused of Ch'an Buddhist sympathies, even by his fellow disciple Hu Chü-jen (q.v.). He is sometimes said to have exercised an influence on the development of the philosophy of Wang Shou-jen. In 1482, the year Ch'en Hsien-chang went for the last time to Peking, the boy Wang Shou-jen, then ten years old, also went to the capital in the company of his father. We have no evidence, however, that the two ever met. While their ideas have something in common, as Wang Shou-jen's disciple, Wang Chi (q.v.), readily admitted, Wang Shou-jen's recorded dialogues and writings make no mention of Ch'en Hsien-chang. Nevertheless, through his friendship with Chan Jo-shui, Wang Shou-jen must have acquired some awareness of Ch'en Hsien-chang and his thought. Besides Chan Jo-shui himself, Ch'en Hsien-chang's other important disciples included Ho Ch'in, Li Ch'eng-chi 李承箕 (T. 世卿, H. 大崖, 1452-1505, cj 1486), and Chang Hsü 張詡 (T. 廷實, H. 東所, 1455-1514, cs 1484). The school of Ch'en Hsien-chang is frequently referred to as that of Po-sha, or of Chiang-men 江門, the latter being the name of the town close to the Po-sha village.

Ch'en was a good calligrapher, and was also interested in painting. He left few writings. The Ming historian, Wang Shih-chen (q.v.), said of Ch'en's prose and poems that neither conformed to the known literary norms of his time, nor did they treat the usual themes, but that, in spite of all this, they reveal a certain marvelous quality, which went beyond the orthodox. This could have been due to Ch'en's superior spiritual perceptivity, as well as to the result of long meditations. Some of Ch'en's poems appear to have been published during his life time; for example, a certain collection bears a pre-face dated 1496. It is entitled *Po-sha shih chin-kao* 詩近藁, and was published by Wu T'ing-chü 吳廷舉 (T. 獻臣, H. 東湖, cs 1487). According to Jen Yu-wen, there were at least two collections of Ch'en's poems, different from each other, printed shortly after his death. Efforts were later made to print his collected writings. These include the 20 *chüan* edition, published in Kwangtung in 1505, entitled *Po-sha hsien-sheng* 先生 *ch'üan-chi*, which was revised and republished in Fukien in 1508, and appeared again in 21 *chüan*, with prefaces by Chan Jo-shui, Chang Hsü, and Lo Lun. This version, dated 1551, includes Ch'en's memorials, 1 *ch.*, prefaces, 1 *ch.*, other essays, 1 *ch.*, correspondence, 2 *ch.*, epigraphs and sacrificial essays, 2 *ch.*, and his poems, 14 *ch.* There have also been 8, 9, 6, and 10 *chüan* editions, printed in different provinces, between 1533 and 1771. The 1533 edition was edited by Kao Chien 高簡, a disciple of Chan Jo-shui, who amended the earlier versions and changed the title to *Po-sha tzu* 子. The 1710 edition, printed by Ho Chiu-ch'ou 何九疇, a grandson of Ho Hsiung-hsiang 熊祥 (T. 乾宰, Pth. 文懿, cs 1592), contains some 221 poems and prose not included in the previous edi-tions, and is entitled *Po-sha tzu ch'üan-chi*. The 1771 edition was edited by Ch'en Yü-neng 陳俞能, a descendant of the philoso-pher. It is entitled *Po-sha tzu ch'üan-chi*, 9 *ch.*, and is based on the 1710 edition but with the addition of one volume of Chan Jo-shui's *Po-sha tzu ku-shih chiao chieh* 古詩教解, and another volume of appen-dices. The 1505, 1508, and 1601 editions appear to be no longer extant. The 1710

edition is very rare. The 1533 edition has been reprinted by the Commercial Press, Shanghai. But the 1771 edition, reprinted several times, remains the most compre-hensive and most accessible. According to Jen Yu-wen, the original printing blocks for this edition are still preserved in the shrine honoring Ch'en Hsien-chang in the village of Po-sha. Jen reports too that certain of Ch'en's poems, not included in the earlier editions, have been recovered recently from some of his handwritten scrolls in private collections, and that a new edition of his works is being prepared by the Po-sha Cultural and Educational Association of Hong Kong (1970). This Association is also responsible for the publication of the journal, *Po-sha hsüeh-k'an* 學刊. To date, the only book length study of Ch'en Hsien-chang is that of Jen, entitled *Po-sha tzu yen-chiu* 研究, which was published in 1970.

Bibliography

1/283/1b; 3/265/1a; 5/22/20a; 6/45/36a; 14/5/18b; 22/2/30a; 32/110/31a; 40/20/17a; 44/4/84b; 84/丙/21b; 85/5/3a; MSL (1940), Hsien-tsung, 244/1b; KC (1958), 2480, 4492; SK (1930), 170/9a, 175/11a; Ch'en Hsien-chang, *Po-sha hsien-sheng ch'üan-chi* (1551), NLP microfilm no. 979-980; id., *Po-sha shih chin-kao* (1496), 10 ch., NLP microfilm no. 979; id., *Po-sha hsien-sheng i-chi* 遺蹟, ed. by Ch'en Ying-yao 陳應耀 (Hong Kong, 1959); Chang Hsü, "Po-sha hsien-sheng hsing-chuang," 行狀 in *Po-sha hsien-sheng chi-nien* 紀念 *chi*, comp. by Ch'en Ying-yao (Hong Kong, 1949); Juan Jung-ling 阮榕齡, "Ch'en Po-sha hsien-sheng nien-p'u," in *Po-sha hsien-sheng chi-nien chi* (Hong Kong, 1952); id., *Po-sha men-jen k'ao* 門人考 (Hong Kong, 1965); Keng Ting-hsiang, "Po-sha Ch'en hsien-sheng chuan," 傳 in *Keng T'ien-t'ai hsien-sheng wen-chi* (1598 ed., Taipei reprint, 1970), 13/12a; Li Ch'eng-ch'i, "Shih-weng 石翁 Ch'en hsien-sheng Hsien-chang mu-chih-ming" 墓誌銘, *Huang Ming wen-hai* microfilm, ch. 159; L. of C. *Catalogue of Rare Books*, 903, 1193; NCL *Catalogue of Rare Books*, 中, 111; Kuo-hsüeh 國學 *Library Cata-logue*, 19/29a, 34/12a; Jen Yu-wen, "Ch'en Hsien-chang's Philosophy of the Natural," in W. T. de Bary, ed., *Self and Society in Ming Thought* (New York, 1971), 53.

Huang P'ei and Julia Ching

CH'EN Hsüan 陳瑄 (T. 彥純), 1365–November 22, 1433, soldier and canal builder, was a native of Ho-fei (present Anhwei). His father, Ch'en Wen 聞, an officer of the volunteers under the Yüan, probably joined the founder of the Ming dynasty in the 1360s, and in 1371 served under Fu Yu-te (q.v.) in the conquest of Szechwan, where he was awarded the hereditary post of vice commander of the right Guard of Chengtu. It was here that Ch'en Hsüan grew up as the son of an officer and was tutored in the military arts. He distinguished himself in horsemanship and archery. In 1382 the Chengtu Guards were ordered to build the palace for the emperor's eleventh son, Chu Ch'un (see Chu Yüan-chang). The transporting of timber from the mountains was at first slow and costly until it was entrusted to Ch'en Hsüan who, then in his early twenties, showed his skill in management by finding a shorter route, by keeping the men healthy, and by delivering lumber of correct dimensions. The palace was completed in 1390. About this time his father retired and he inherited the rank of vice commander of the Chengtu Guard. In 1394, or thereabouts, his father was involved in the case of a former superior (probably Fu Yu-te, who was forced to commit suicide in that year) and was sentenced to banishment in Liaotung, but the sentence was revoked when Ch'en pleaded that he might take the place of his aged father.

During the Hung-wu and Chien-wen periods (1368–1402), Ch'en took part in campaigns in Yunnan and Szechwan against tribal uprisings, where his ability as a field officer was put to the test. In this capacity he was soon able to distinguish himself by achieving victory through bravery and superior strategy; in return he received the appointment of vice commissioner of the branch regional military commission of Szechwan.

Toward the end of the Chien-wen reign, Ch'en was promoted to assistant commissioner-in-chief of the central right military commission in Nanking; as such he was charged with river defense around the then capital in the critical year 1402, when the armies of the prince of Yen (Chu Ti, q. v.) were marching south to depose his nephew. But instead of fighting them, Ch'en, together with the men and boats under his command, greeted the rebels and joined the northern army upon its arrival at P'u-k'ou 浦口 on the northern bank of the Yangtze opposite Nanking. This enabled the prince to cross the river and enter Nanking against minimum opposition. After the establishment of the new reign, Ch'en was included in the list of the Ching-nan 靖難 meritorious officers (see Chu Ti) and given the title earl of P'ing-chiang 平江伯, with an annual stipend of 1,000 tan of rice. He received also the hereditary rank of a guard commander.

In 1403 Ch'en entered upon the second phase of his career which was to become his chief concern for the next thirty years. He became the field commander-in-chief in charge of the rice transport system. This meant that he and his deputy, Hsüan Hsin 宣信, were responsible for the delivery of some 490,000 to 600,000 tan (approximately thirty to forty thousand tons) of rice from the Yangtze region to the garrisons stationed at Peking and Liaotung. At this time the rice from the south was transported via the coastal route, a system inherited from the Yüan dynasty, and it was the practice in early Ming to entrust to the same officials the supervision of rice transport and the defense of the coast against Japanese pirates. Ch'en's military background stood him in good stead: in 1406, on his return voyage, after escorting a shipment of grain to the north, his flotilla encountered a group of pirates, whom he engaged and defeated, pursuing them to the coast of Korea where he burned all their ships. In 1411 he and Li Pin (see Lê Lợi) were ordered to fight pirates off the Chekiang-Fukien coast.

The military element in rice transportation did not continue to occupy him for long. As administrator of the vast grain transport system, Ch'en was called upon to demonstrate still another facet of his talents: working in harmony with the trend of the time, he modernized the inland waterways and reorganized the method of delivery of tribute rice, all of which had profound effect on the transport system for the next four hundred years. The first of his reforms was the construction at Tientsin of a large granary with a capacity of 1,000,000 *tan* of rice to serve as storage at the northern terminal of the sea route; this made it possible for the sailors to return south quickly and to leave the delivery of the grain destined for Peking to the local garrisons. Later, more granaries were built along the Canal route to be used as storage points. Secondly, he succeeded in creating normal relations between the crews of the transport vessels and the inhabitants of the coastal islands by requiring them to deal fairly with the islanders in their transactions—to pay a just price for everything bought from the local people; both benefited from this improvement. Thirdly, he began to direct his attention to the factor of topography as related to the problems of rice transport, and this led him to his major achievement, the reopening of the southern section of the Canal route. In this same year (1411) he was ordered to rebuild sea walls on the coast north of the Yangtze River that had been badly eroded by the sea; he is reported to have mobilized 400,000 laborers for this task, the total length of sea walls constructed being 18,000 *chang* (about 30 miles). The following year he proposed and received permission to construct an artificial hill at Chia-ting 嘉定 (where the terrain is low and flat) to serve as shelter for the sea-going rice boats moored there. This was an eminence some 100 *chang* square and over thirty *chang* high with a signal and lookout post on top. On its completion the emperor was so pleased that he commemorated the occasion with an essay from the imperial pen. It became known as Pao-shan 寶山 (Treasure Hill), after which the present district was named.

Meanwhile (1411) in north China, Sung Li (*q. v.*) and his colleagues had succeeded in restoring the northern section of the Grand Canal, or Hui-t'ung-ho 會通河, thus enabling boats to bypass the sea route north of the Yellow River estuary. Talk of abandoning this route completely and adopting an inland waterway was in the air. The problems faced by Ch'en Hsüan in the Yangtze-Huai River complex consisted chiefly of eliminating the lengthy portages between stretches of navigable waterways, controlling the flow of water to provide a proper and constant depth for navigation, and linking all usable waterways into one unbroken stream so that, when connected with the northern section, the Grand Canal in its entirety would become the artery of economic life in the country. This was achieved in 1415. Relying partly on the views of local inhabitants, Ch'en designed and supervised the building of a system of canals and locks that enabled the grain boats to sail directly from the Yangtze River northward to the Huai 淮 at Ch'ing-chiang-p'u 清江浦, thence continuing west up the Yellow River, then north on the reopened Canal to Lin-ch'ing 臨清 (Shantung), and finally down the Wei 渭 River to Tientsin. The water level was controlled along the southern route by a series of forty-seven locks; it was watched over by a contingent of troops stationed in 568 guard houses, whose special duty was to direct the boat traffic away from shallow spots in the channel and to pull the boats when necessary; and the channel was dredged regularly by men recruited from the countryside. To prevent erosion of the soil, trees were planted along the dykes on either side of the Canal, and wells were dug. By the shore of Kao-yu Lake 高郵湖 a special dyke was built, which formed a lagoon forty *li* long that could be used by boats for shelter in stormy weather. From this time on the sea route was discontinued, and rice transport was conducted entirely via the Grand Canal.

With his headquarters at Huai-an 淮安 (Nan-Chihli), Ch'en was now responsible for the construction of some 2,000 shallow draft boats to replace the seagoing vessels as suggested by the minister of Revenue, Yü Hsin 郁新 (T. 敦本, d. 1405), as early as 1403. The first year these grain boats brought two million *tan* of rice from the southern provinces to the Peking area, which amount was increased to five million in a few years. In 1421, six years after Ch'en had finished the Canal work, the capital was officially moved from Nanking to Peking.

In 1425 he proposed to the new emperor (Chu Kao-chih, *q. v.*) seven items of governmental reform, of which two dealt with the rice transport system: first, that the rice be delivered to collecting points, such as Huai-an, and then transported from there to Peking by grain transport troops, so as not to rob the people of too much agricultural time, and the government of taxes; second, that the grain transport troops not be overburdened with miscellaneous tasks at their garrisons, since they had enough to do in transporting the grain and repairing the boats after each voyage. The proposals were approved by the throne, but apparently were not given a chance for implementation as the emperor died after ruling for less than a year. In the same year Ch'en's earldom was made hereditary by special decree.

Upon the accession of the next emperor (Chu Chan-chi, *q. v.*) in 1426, Ch'en repeated his request that the people themselves be spared the task of sending the rice to Peking, which involved a round-trip journey that often took more than a year. This time the proposal was discussed by the chief minister and put into effect in 1431. Henceforth the system of exchange delivery (兌運) replaced that of people's delivery (民運); that is, the people who paid for the tribute rice brought it to a designated collecting station nearest to their locality, where the rice was loaded on grain boats by the transport troops who took it to Peking. Due to this improvement

the people were relieved of an onerous duty, while the concentration of grain transportation in the hands of the transport corps must have, one would imagine, greatly facilitated the administration's planning and control over the entire procedure.

After serving for thirty years as supervisor of the rice transport system, Ch'en died in 1433 at his post and was interred in the family's ancestral burial ground south of Nanking. He was posthumously advanced in title to marquis of P'ing-chiang, also given the title of grand guardian, and granted the honorific title of Kung-hsiang 恭襄. His associates regarded him highly. Historical records describe him as a man of decision with the ability to make long-range plans, an eloquent conversationalist, and an ardent reader of works on history. His descendants inherited the earldom of P'ing-chiang nine times until the end of the dynasty. The third, fourth, fifth, and seventh earls all served, each for some time in his day, as commander-in-chief at Huai-an in charge of grain transport. There is a shrine to the memory of Ch'en Hsüan at Huai-an and another at Lin-ch'ing.

Bibliography

1/79/2a, 85/16a, 106/19b, 153/4a; 3/80/1a, 142/4b; 5/9/21a; 8/20/8; 61/97/1956; Sung Ying-hsing (E CCP), *Chinese Technology in the Seventeenth Century*, tr. by E-tu Zen Sun and Shiou-chuan Sun (University Park, 1966), 172; Wu Chi-hua, 吳緝華, *Ming-tai hai-yün chi Yün-ho ti yen-chiu* 明代海運及運河的研究 (Taipei, 1961), 17, 76, 88; Fu Tse-hung (ECCP, p. 936), *Hsing-shui chin-chien*.

E-tu Zen Sun

CH'EN Hsüan 陳選 (T. 士賢, H. 克菴, Pth. 恭愍), 1429-86, left a name in Ming history mainly because of the circumstances connected with his death. This so touched the hearts of his fellow officials that they tended to see in him a man of blameless character. He was a native of Lin-hai 臨海, Chekiang. During the metropolitan examinations of 1460 he ranked first in the preliminary contest, but because "his appearance was unimpressive," he was placed fourteenth in the palace competition. Appointed an investigating censor, he subsequently served as education intendant, first in Nan-Chihli and then in Honan, later becoming surveillance commissioner in the same province. About 1482 he was promoted to right administration commissioner of Kwangtung and two years later advanced to left commissioner.

His biographers describe him as quiet, thrifty, diligent, honest, and fearless. It is said that while serving as investigating censor, Ch'en brought impeachment action against Ma Ang (see Chu Chien-shen), the empire's top strategist, and criticized Li Hsien (q.v.), the most trusted grand secretary of Emperor Chu Chien-shen (q.v.). Actually it was a group of censors who forced Ma, unpopular at court, to retire in 1468. The reason for criticism of Li was that in 1466 the emperor permitted him to dispense with the traditional custom of quitting office to mourn his mother. Lo Lun (q.v.), the optimus of that year and Hanlin compiler, protested, calling the dispensation unjustified. Only when the emperor, angered by Lo's memorial, demoted him did Ch'en Hsüan speak up on the latter's behalf. His argument was not a direct attack on the grand secretary, and his action, though taken with certain personal risk on his part, was by no means exceptional. Ch'en is also credited with blocking the appointment (1466) of Ni Ch'ien (q.v.), to the Grand Secretariat. According to the shih-lu, however, the petition for Ni's removal was signed by all supervising secretaries and censors, not by Ch'en alone. Only this overwhelming vote of non-confidence caused the emperor to withdraw the appointment.

As an educator, Ch'en Hsüan placed emphasis on decorum and philology. He made state students practice various kinds of ritual. He issued his own book, Hsiao-hsüeh chü-tou 小學句讀, 6 ch., also known as Hsiao-hsüeh chi-chu 集註, a work on phon-

etics and semantics, as a text. As a civil administrator, Ch'en became known for his leniency. He dismissed those who were brought to trial on minor charges and gave only light sentences to the more serious offenders. Still others he declared innocent. A man of integrity himself, he is said never to have dismissed anyone convicted of bribery, and the fines he meted out after such convictions were merely nominal, often only a small fraction of the bribes received. "Wherever he went," one biographer declares, "prisons were empty." Another mentions that he never flogged a servant.

In Kwangtung Ch'en's official function brought him into contact with maritime trade. In 1485 the tributary mission from Samarkand on its return trip went by way of Canton. Upon hearing that the head of the mission intended to purchase lions in Malacca as tribute for the emperor on his next journey to Peking, Ch'en reported it to the court and subsequently, by order of the emperor, the envoy received instructions to return home without carrying out the transaction. (Actually, late in 1489, an envoy from Samarkand was back in Peking, having come via Malacca, and did present a lion or lions to the court.) Circumstances suggest that the eunuch in charge of tributary trade at Canton, Wei Chüan, 韋眷, was involved in the attempted venture, as Wei was then cloaking private trade under tributary traffic and making enormous profit therefrom.

Ch'en Hsüan had the courage to stand firm against the eunuchs. While education intendant in Honan, he merely gave a perfunctory greeting to Wang Chih 汪直 (q.v.), the eunuch commissioner dispatched by Chu Chien-shen to inspect the province. This was at a time when all other officials saluted Wang much more obsequiously. On Wang's demand for a greater show of courtesy, Ch'en answered that as education intendant he must set a good example to the students. He therefore refused to humble himself and yet came through this confrontation unscathed probably because of the support of a crowd of students surrounding the office building. His encounter with Wei Chüan, however, ended differently.

Until 1485 sixty households from the district of P'an-yü 番禺 (in which the city of Canton was located) were assigned to Wei to provide him with supplies for his office. In that year Ch'en succeeded in obtaining the emperor's approval to reduce to thirty the number of households. Wei Chüan regarded this as an insult. Furthermore, the magistrate of P'an-yü, Kao Yao 高瑤 (T. 庭堅appointed 1483) had confiscated an immense amount of property from the merchants engaged in maritime trade, then illegal, in which Wei Chüan apparently had an interest. Ch'en, as administration commissioner, issued a circular letter commending the confiscation. The relationship between the eunuch commissioner and the two civil officials thus reached the breaking point. In the following year Wei accused Kao of receiving bribes and Ch'en of protecting Kao. He also charged Ch'en with falsely reporting the flood situation in Kwangtung and with distributing relief without imperial authorization. Wei tried as well to persuade a clerk, whom Ch'en had demoted, to testify against him. The clerk, however, not only refused, he even made his way to the capital where he submitted a lengthy memorial to the emperor in which he proclaimed Ch'en's innocence. The investigators of Wei's charges, nevertheless, all leaned to the side of the eunuch. The two accused officials were arrested, convicted, and ordered escorted to Peking for punishment. The day they left Canton thousands of people blocked the road, and the party had to take a side path to avoid a riot. In Kiangsi Ch'en fell ill. The escorts, on orders from Wei Chüan, saw to it that no medicine was administered. He died in a Buddhist temple in Nanchang, the death being entered in the *shih-lu* under the date of October 3. 1486. Ch'en's tombstone inscription indicates that he left a manuscript entitled *Tan-yai chi* 丹崖集,

but there is no indication that it was ever published.

Bibliography

1/161/14b, 304/18b; 5/99/8a; 64/丙4/5a; 83/45/10a; MSL (1963), Hsien-tsung, 3356, 4501, 4505, 4755, Hsiao-tsung, 0717; *Kwangtung t'ung-chih* (1934), 4250; *T'ai-chou* 臺州*-fu chih* (1936), 69/28b; Cheng Hsiao, *Wu-hsüeh-pien* (1572), 35/10b; Hsieh To 謝鐸 (d. Dec. 30, 1510), *T'ao-hsi ching-kao* 桃溪淨稿 (NLP microfilm, roll no. 953), 文12/1a; Hsüeh Ying-ch'i薛應旂 (cs 1535), *Fang-shan hsien-sheng wen-lu*方山先生文錄 (NLP microfilm, roll no. 927), 14/8b.

Ray Huang

CH'EN Jen-hsi 陳仁錫 (T. 明卿, H. 芝臺, 澹退居士, Pth. 文莊), 1579–1634, government official and scholar, was a native of Ch'ang-chou 長洲, Nan-Chihli. His father, Ch'en Yün-chien 允堅 (H. 毅軒 cs 1595), served as magistrate of Chu-chi 諸暨 and Ch'ung-te 崇德 districts (1595–97) in Chekiang. Ch'en Jen-hsi passed the *chü-jen* examinations in 1597 at the age of nineteen *sui*, but did not succeed in obtaining the *chin-shih* degree until 1622. In the palace examination he came out third in the first group and was given the rank of a compiler in the Hanlin Academy. In 1626 he served as an expositor of the Classics to the emperor and often seized the opportunity to admonish him about bad influences; he urged him to employ only the virtuous, thus covertly attacking the notorious eunuch, Wei Chung-hsien (ECCP). The eunuch succeeded in venting his spite; Ch'en soon found himself involved in a criminal case, and though able to escape punishment, he was reduced to the status of commoner in 1627. A few months later, however, the succession to the throne of Chu Yu-chien (ECCP) was followed by the suicide of Wei Chung-hsien and destruction of his faction. Ch'en Jen-hsi was reinstated as compiler and in the same year (1628) served as chief official of the military examination. In 1629 Ch'en was sent as special envoy to Liaotung where he made a study of the region and submitted to the throne a memorandum, Ch'ou-pien t'u shuo 籌邊圖說, part of which seems to be included in his works. In 1630 he served for some time as director of studies of the National University. In the same year he was named as one of the officials of the metropolitan examination. Later (1631) he went to Kaifeng as envoy to confer nobility on the Prince of Chou 周 Chu, Kung-hsiao (see Chu Su), descendant in the 11th generation of Emperor Chu Yüan-chang, enfeoffed in 1588, who was still living when Kaifeng was attacked in 1642. Upon his return he sought permission to resign from office. His petition, however, was not granted and in 1633 he was appointed chancellor of the National University in Nanking, but died before assuming office. He was given the posthumous title Wen-chuang 文莊 in October, 1644. [Editors'note: Ch'en's dates are erroneously given by Chiang Liang-fu 姜亮夫 as 1581–1636. According to the preface to his Wu-meng-yüan chi (see below) of 1635, he died one year before its publication, in 1634, which tallies with Kuei Chuang's statement that he was nineteen sui when he passed the provincial examination in 1597.]

Ch'en wrote a number of books on the Classics which were obviously intended for those preparing for civil examinations. It seems that he had a large establishment for the printing of books. As a literary critic he compiled the following anthologies of prose: Ku-wen ch'i-shang 古文奇賞, first series in 22 ch., second series in 24 ch., third series in 26 ch., and fourth series in 53 ch.; Ming-wen 明文ch'i-shang (40 ch.); I-p'in i han逸品繹函 (2 ch.); Wen-p'in fei han芾函 (3 ch.); Su-wen 蘇文ch'i-shang (5 ch.); and Ku-wen hui-pien古文彙編 (236 ch.). He also wrote or compiled works of a practical type: Fu-i 賦役ch'üan-shu on government taxes and Ts'ao-cheng k'ao 漕政考 (2 ch.) on transportation of grain. The Ching-chi pa-pien lei-tsuan經濟八編類纂 in 225 chüan is a collection of contributions by Ming authors on government and current affairs.

Ch'en is perhaps best known as a historian. His edition of the Tzu-chih t'ung-chien 資治通鑑 was printed in 1625 and presented to the throne. The Library of Congress has a copy of his Ching-k'ou san-shan chih 京口三山志 (20 ch.), and the National Central Library of Taipei possesses another of his writings, Ch'üan Wu ch'ou-huan yü-fang lu 全吳籌患預防錄. He was also responsible for the compilation of a general history of the Ming dynasty under the title Huang Ming er-tsu shih-ssu tsung tseng-pu piao-t'i p'ing-tuan shih-chi 皇明二祖十四宗增補標題評斷實記 (27 ch.). A similar work—shorter and written in five word rhymes—the Ming-chi-lüeh ting-luan 明紀略鼎欒 is also credited to him. This book was commented on by Ni Yüan-lu (ECCP); it speaks of the Manchus offensively in the fourth chüan. The Jen-wu shu 壬午書 (2 ch.), also written by Ch'en, deals with the Chien-wen period (1399–1402).

A very important work compiled by Ch'en is the Huang Ming shih-fa lu 皇明世法錄 in 92 chüan, a collection of government documents of the Ming period from important sources as well as from the author's own writings. It covers a wide range of subjects and some of the sources quoted no longer exist. Liu Tsung-chou (ECCP) in his biography of Ch'en says that this is Ch'en's magnum opus, one on which he labored up to the time of his death. Under the Manchus it was listed among the prohibited books and for a long time was considered rare, but in 1965 it was reprinted in Taipei in a photographic edition taken from the Ming copy now kept in the National Central Library.

Another work of importance is the Ch'ien-ch'üeh lei-shu 潛確類書 in 120 chüan, blocks cut in 1630—divided into thirteen classifications with over fourteen hundred sub-divisions. The eleventh chüan on the northern frontier and the fourteenth chüan containing data on barbarian tribes were considered seditious by the Manchus and the Ch'ien-lung commissioners ordered that they be excised from the text. The Columbia University Library owns an unexpurgated copy. The *Wu-meng-yüan chi* 無夢園集, a miscellaneous work by Ch'en, printed by his younger brother, Ch'en Li-hsi 禮錫 in 1635, was also listed among the prohibited books. A complete set is preserved in the Library of Congress.

Ch'en Jen-hsi's son, Ch'en Chi-sheng 濟生 (T. 皇士, H. 定叔, Pth. 節孝先生, fl. 1620-60), held the office of acting assistant minister of the Court of the Imperial Stud. In his early days, Ch'en Chi-sheng studied under Huang Tao-chou (ECCP) and Liu Tsung-chou and was reputed to have imbibed deeply of their learning. He wrote the *Tsai-sheng chi-lüeh* 再生記略 (1 *ch.*), a record of his experiences after the fall of Peking in 1644, when he was forced to go south. The account, however is not always reliable, as some of it depended on rumors he picked up on his journey. The *Kuang lien-chu* 廣連珠 (1 *ch.*) and *Yüeh-fu* 樂府 are his poetical works. He remained faithful to the Ming up to his last days and as an expression of his devotion he once had portraits painted of loyal ministers and heroes of the Ming.

Ch'en Chi-sheng did not live to see the disaster caused by his anthology, the *Ch'i Chen liang-ch'ao i-shih* 啓禎兩朝遺詩, which he compiled during the Shun-chih period (1644-61). The book was supposed to be a supplement to the *Lieh-ch'ao shih-chi* of Ch'ien Ch'ien-i (ECCP), but with stress on men of moral integrity whose biographies are given at the end of the book. Some of the poems selected refer to the political situation of the late Ming period and contain criticism of the Manchus. The printing of the book was not completed when in 1666, according to the account of Kuei Chuang (ECCP), it was used by several blackmailers to exact money from some of the persons involved; finally the matter was brought to the attention of the authorities in 1667. By imperial order the case was thoroughly investigated. Several of the blackmailers

were found guilty of calumny and sentenced to capital punishment; some were exiled. The trouble caused by the anthology, however, did not end with this case but continued into the following decades. In March, 1688, Chiang Yüan-heng 姜元衡 (also known as Huang 黃 Yüan-heng, a native of Chi-mo 卽墨, Shantung), a slave's son who had passed the *chin-shih* examinations (1649) and been appointed to serve in the Hanlin Academy, accused his master of having kept a copy of the *Chung-chieh lu* 忠節錄 (another title for the *Ch'i Chen liang-ch'ao i-shih*) in which were found passages offensive to the Manchus and hence actionable. One of the scholars involved was Ku Yen-wu (ECCP) whose elder sister was married to Ch'en Chi-sheng. Ku was imprisoned for more than six months in Tsinan, Shantung.

Bibliography

1/288/10a; 3/269/12b; 40/66/1b; 64 辛 18/3a; 86/18/27a; Chang Tai, *Shih-kuei-shu hou-chi* 石匱書後集 (Shanghai, 1959), 331; Ch'en Ho 陳鶴, *Ming chi* 明紀 (Shanghai, 1935), 51/522a; Ch'en Chi-sheng, *T'ien-ch'i Ch'ung-chen liang-ch'ao i-shih* (Shanghai, 1958), 2043, 2097; Huang Tao-chou (ECCP), *Chang-p'u chi* 漳浦集 (Tao-kuang ed.), 95/6a; Kuei Chuang (ECCP), *Kuei Chuang chi* 集 (Shanghai, 1962), 10/518; T'an Ch'ien, *Tsao-lin tsa-tsu* (Shanghai, 1935), 50b; Sun Tien-ch'i (1957), 15, 23, 45, 47, 48, 106, 121, 127, 174, 205.

Albert Chan

CH'EN Ju-yen 陳汝言 (T. 惟允, H, 秋水, 清癯生), *ca.* 1331-71, painter, poet, official, was a native of Soochow where his father, Ch'en Cheng 陳徵 (T. 明善, H. 天倪), born in Ch'ing-chiang 清江, Kiangsi, had settled. Probably like many learned Chinese under Mongol rule Ch'en Cheng served for some time as a government employee and in later life made his living as a teacher. Both Ch'en Ju-yen and his elder brother, Ch'en Ju-chih 秩 (T. 惟寅, 1329-85), were quite young when their father died. They studied diligently and distinguished themselves as students in the Soochow area. While Ch'en Ju-chih remained at home leading the quiet life of a teacher and a poet, Ch'en Ju-yen pursued an active career. Shortly after the age of twenty, Ch'en Ju-yen, while a guest of a wealthy poet of K'un-shan 崑山, Ku Ying顧瑛 (also known as Ku Te-hui 德輝, T. 仲瑛, H. 金粟道人, 1310–69), began to associate with illustrious men of letters. During a gathering at Ku's villa, Yü-shan ts'ao-t'ang 玉山草堂, on the 28th of January, 1353, he played the lute for his host and the assembled guests. Soon after this, his skill in pictorial art made his paintings the favorite subjects of some of the poets of his time. Later he became military adviser to P'an Yüan-ming 潘原明 (T. 友石, d. 1382), an official in the service of Chang Shih-ch'eng (q. v.), after Chang made Soochow his capital (1356). P'an's headquarters were first at Hu-chou 湖州 and later at Hangchow. In September, 1367, before Soochow was taken by Chu Yüan-chang, P'an negotiated the surrender of Hangchow to Chu's armies and consequently was allowed to remain at his post.

Shortly after the founding of the Ming dynasty in 1368, Ch'en went to the capital, Nanking, and was appointed registrar in the Shantung provincial administration office. At approximately the same time, Wang Meng (q. v.) was serving as prefect of T'ai-an 泰安 nearby. During the winter of 1370, Ch'en occasionally visited Wang. The latter had painted a landscape of Mount T'ai and as it happened to be snowing at the time, Ch'en changed Wang's painting into one of snow, spattering white powder on it by striking a small bow to which a brush had been attached. Since the white powder applied by this means vividly resembled falling snowflakes, Wang greatly appreciated the ingenious contrivance and entitled the painting "Tai-tsung mi-hsüeh t'u" 岱宗密雪圖.

Because of some blunder which he committed during his term of office, Ch'en was sentenced to death in the autumn of 1371. According to a poem by Chang Yü (q.v.) on the subject of the picture which

Ch'en painted just before his execution, he manifested self-control and handled his brush in a relaxed manner. Impressed by the record of his extraordinary coolness, Ch'ien Ch'ien-i (ECCP) later compared him with men of ancient times who showed similar fortitude.

Ch'en's collection of poems entitled *Ch'iu-shui-hsüan shih-chi* 秋水軒詩集 is no longer extant. As for paintings attributed to him, nine are listed in Osvald Sirén's *Chinese Painting*, which includes a reproduction of one of them. According to Sirén, they are in the style of Chao Meng-fu (1254–1322), but the first of these reproduced in the *Bunjin Gasen* 文人畫選 (edited by Ōmura Seigai 大村西崖), seems to be spurious because it is dated 1341 when the painter was still a child. The same is true of two other paintings not included in Sirén's list. One is also dated 1341, and is reproduced in the *Shina meiga hōkan* 支那名畫寶鑑; the other bears a date equivalent to 1342, and is reproduced in the *Chung-hua mei-shu t'u-chi* 中華美術圖集. Reproductions of two other paintings attributed to him are to be found in *Kokka* 國華 and in *Chinese Landscape Painting* by Sherman E. Lee.

After Ch'en's death, his widow, née Wu 吳, took his son Ch'en Chi 陳繼 (T. 嗣初, H. 怡庵, 1370–1434) back to Soochow; she was honored in 1406 as a noteworthy example of widowhood and motherhood. Approximately twenty thousand *chüan* of his father's library remained in Ch'en Chi's possession. He became well versed in the Classics and eventually achieved a high place in the Hanlin Academy. The father and uncle of Shen Chou (q.v.) studied the Classics under him, just as Shen Chou himself later was a disciple of his son, Ch'en K'uan 陳寬 (T. 孟賢, H. 醒庵).

There was another Ch'en Ju-yen (*see* Keng Chiu-ch'ou); he was a native of T'ung-kuan 潼關, Shansi, and became a *chin-shih* in 1442. As a member of the clique of Shih Heng (q.v.), he served for half a year as minister of War (1457–58);

imprisoned on the charge of accepting bribes, he died on January 22, 1462.

Bibliography

84/甲前8/23a, 10/26a, 乙 6/12a, 7/38a; Wang Chih-teng, *Tan-ch'ing-chih* (TsSCC ed.), 5; Feng Ts'ung-wu, *Yüan-ju k'ao-lüeh* (*Ying-fu-chai*英服齋*ts'ung-shu*, ed.), 3/2a; Ku Ssu-li顧嗣立(1669-1722), *Yüan shih-hsüan kuei-chi* 元詩選癸集 (*Sao-yeh shan-fang* 掃葉山房, ed. of 1888), 己下/30b, 辛上/22b; Chu Ts'un-li, *Shan-hu mu-nan*, 7/10b; *Ku-su chih* 姑蘇志 (1506), 52/18a, 57/16b, 38a; Ku Ying, *Yü-shan ts'ao-t'ang i-kao* 玉山草堂逸稿 (TsSCC ed.), 2/35, 39, 3/50, 4/70; Chang Yü張羽 (1333-85), *Ching-chü chi* 靜居集 (SPTK, 3d series), 1/26b; Ni Tsan, *Ni Yün-lin hsien-sheng shih-chi* (SPTK, 1st series), 1/27a; *Ku-kung shu-hua lu* 故宮書畫錄 (Taipei, 1959), 4/149, 5/255, 258, 6/228, no. 6; TSCC (1885-88), XIV: 125/9/4b, 126/10/10b, XVII: 783/17/5b, 785/19/3b, XXIII: 93/81/25b, 96/84/1b; *Chung-hua mei-shu t'u-chi* (Taipei, 1955); Osvald Sirén, *Chinese Painting*, VI, pl. 112, VII, 165; Ōmura Séigai, *Bunjin Gasen* (1921–22); Harada Kinjirō 原田謹次郎 (comp.), *Shina meiga hōkan* 支那名畫寶鑑 (Tokyo, 1936); *Kokka* (1942), no. 622, p. 210; Sherman E. Lee, *Chinese Landscape Painting* (Cleveland, 1954); E. J. Laing, *Chinese Paintings in Chinese Publications, 1956-1968* (Ann Arbor, 1969), 157. For the 2d Ch'en Ju-yen: 5/38/51a; KC (1958), 2130.

                                                T. W. Weng

CH'EN K'an 陳侃 (T. 應和, H. 思齊), 1489-1538, envoy to the Liu-ch'iu (Ryūkyū) Islands in 1534, was descended from one of the wealthy, landowning families which had settled in Yin 鄞-hsien (modern Ning-po), Chekiang. His great-great-grandfather was apparently a prosperous member of the gentry, his grandfather, Ch'en Ch'un 淳 (T. 德溫, cj 1453), the first in the family to acquire a literary degree, served as a magistrate, and his father, Ch'en Jui 瑞 (T. 鳳儀, cs 1487) concluded his career as a vice director of a bureau in the ministry of Justice.

Following his acquisition of the *chin-shih* in 1526, Ch'en K'an received an appointment in the messenger office. He then became a supervising secretary for three years (1529–32). During his term of office,

he submitted several memorials on state affairs and political matters, through which he established his reputation as an observant and courageous critic, particularly when he dared to attack the powerful grand secretary Chang Fu-ching (*q. v.*) late in 1531. He denounced Chang's false accusation against his rival, the Hanlin chancellor Hsia Yen (*q. v.*), and, after Chang's resignation, proposed the banishment of members of his clique. It appears, however, that his attack on the grand secretary produced little effect, as Chang Fu-ching and his protégés soon returned to power.

Ch'en K'an's career took a new turn when, in June, 1532, he was delegated chief envoy to head a special mission to the Liu-ch'iu Islands to conduct the investiture of the new ruler of the Chung-shan 中山 (Chuzan) kingdom. The appointment followed the arrival in May of the embassy of the Liu-ch'iu prince, Shang Ch'ing 尚清 (Shō Sei, d. 1555), who informed the court of the death of his father Shang Chen眞 (Shō Shin, d. 1526), and requested a formal investiture to legalize his succession. The mission's departure, however, was delayed by the preparation of a code of rites for the ceremony, as the files for Liu-ch'iu had lately been destroyed by fire, and also by time needed for the construction of a new vessel for the voyage. Ch'en went to Fukien in June of the following year to supervise the ship-building; this task was completed in May, 1534, at the official cost of 2,500 taels of silver. Finally, on June 19, Ch'en set sail from the port of Ch'ang-lo 長樂, leading a delegation that included as his deputy Kao Ch'eng 高澄 (T. 肅卿, H. 東玉, cs 1529, 1494-1552), and a retinue of over two hundred personnel; he took besides a shipload of gifts for presentation.

After seventeen days at sea, on a trip marred by occasional rough winds and a change of course, the party reached its destination, and landed at the port of Na-pa 那霸 (Naha) on July 6. Ch'en and his retinue received warm greetings from the Liu-ch'iu prince, after which they visited various parts of the kingdom and conducted a sacrificial offering to the late king, but had to wait until August 11 to invest Shang Ch'ing as king in an elaborate ceremony. Due to the monsoon season, however, their departure was postponed until October 26, after they had spent a total of 150 days on the island. As they were about to leave, the king presented forty taels of gold to Ch'en and Kao, but they declined the gift as its acceptance was in violation of the rules governing the conduct of envoys. Their return journey was even more hazardous than the first. On the second they encountered a hurricane so turbulent that it almost engulfed their vessel; in desperation the crew prayed to the Goddess of the Sea for deliverance. A few days later the wind, as if responding to their plea, miraculously subsided; they continued their voyage, landing safely on November 7 at Fort Ting-hai 定海, east of Foochow. On his arrival at Peking, Ch'en petitioned the court for permission to erect a memorial tablet in honor of the Goddess on the cliff overlooking the port from which they set sail. His request was approved. Shortly afterwards, Ch'en composed an account of his mission entitled Shih Liu-ch'iu lu使琉球錄, 1 ch., which, upon presentation to the court early in the following year, was well received.

In August, 1535, the court promoted Ch'en K'an to the rank of assistant minister in the Court of Imperial Entertainments, and Kao Ch'eng from a messenger to the post of bureau director of the Seal Office. Early in January of the following year the Liu-ch'iu king returned with a delegation to express his gratitude, and instructed his envoy to offer Ch'en the forty taels of gold which he had declined earlier, insisting that he accept the gift. With the approval of the court, Ch'en shared the gold with his partner. He later used his share to purchase tracts of land in his native village to provide income for sacrifices to his ancestors and for other communal services. Over two years later (September, 1538), Ch'en was further advanced to be an assistant minister in the Court of the Imperial Stud. He died late that year at the age of forty-nine.

Ch'en K'an is chiefly known for the report on his mission, the Shih Liu-ch'iu lu. Its value lies in the fact that it is not only the earliest extant eyewitness account by a Ming visitor to the Islands, but it is also one of the best informed and vividly written journals of its kind of that age. It supplies information not only on the Liu-ch'iu of his day but also on the organization of the Chinese missions sent overseas during this period. The original edition of this work, engraved late in 1534, with a preface by Ch'en himself and a postface by Kao Ch'eng, was reproduced in photolithographic form in 1937 by the Commercial Press. A slightly shorter version, without the prefatory materials and the postface appears in the Chi-lu hui-pien by Shen Chieh-fu (q. v.). There exist also several Japanese manuscript transcriptions and a Korean edition.

The full version of the Shih Liu-ch'iu lu consists of four parts. The first contains a collection of official documents on the appointment of the mission, including imperial edicts addressed to the Liu-ch'iu king, and lists of gifts to be presented. The second, dealing with the mission proper, gives a vivid account of the preparation for the journey, the construction of the vessel, the arrival in Liu-ch'iu, the investiture, and the hazards of the return voyage. Here some of Ch'en's comments are of particular interest and value to historians. He observed, for example, the splendor of the Liu-ch'iu palace, the local topography, and customs such as the observance of the Chinese mid-autumn moon festival and the dragon-boat race, and the Japanese influence on the island kingdom. The last observation reveals the fact that, despite his subservience to the Ming court, the Liu-ch'iu king also paid lip-service to the Japanese fief of Satsuma, maintaining a secret relationship with his powerful neighbor. The third is a compendium of earlier accounts on the Liu-ch'iu Islands culled from T'ang and early Ming literature (including the *Hsing-ch'a sheng-lan* of Fei Hsin (*q.v.*), some of which are no longer extant. Ch'en presents these materials both for the sake of reference and to correct certain erroneous impressions in China about the Liu-ch'iu. He refuted, for example, certain mistakes in the *Ta Ming i-t'ung chih*, such as that on the sea route to the Liu-ch'iu, and the report about the primitive nature of the Liu-ch'iu palace, which was said to have been decorated with human skulls. The fourth presents, in fifteen groups, a list of 407 words and expressions used by the Liu-ch'iu inhabitants, with indications of native pronunciations. This is followed by an appendix of crude approximations of the 48 Japanese (hiragana) symbols. It concludes with a compendium of documents submitted by Ch'en and his deputy concerning their mission and the presentationer of the journal, with the official replies.

Because of its value, the *Shih Lin-ch'iu lu* became a guide for later envoys sent to Liu-ch'iu, such as Kuo Ju-lin 郭汝霖 (T. 時望, H. 一厓, cs 1553) in 1558, Hsiao Ch'ung-yeh 蕭崇業 (T. 允修, H. 養乾, cs 1571), Hsieh Chieh (*see* Hsieh Chao-che) in 1576, and others; it also served as the main source for their own reports, all of which bear similar titles.

Bibliography

1/323/7b; 16/132/4a; MSL (1965), Shih-tsung, 2496, 2668, 2679, 3235, 3245, 3826, 3877, 4401; *Yin-hsien chih*(1877), 33/23b, 30a, 36/14a; Chang Pang-ch'i 張邦奇 (cs 1505), *Hsü-yü-lou chi* 紆玉樓集 (NCL microfilm), 3/19b; T'u Ying-chün (*see* T'u Shu-fang), *T'u Chien-shan chi* (NCL microfilm), 2/54a; Kuo Ju-lin, *Shih-ch'üan shan-fang wen-chi* 石泉山房文集 (NCL microfilm), 8/1a; Hsiao Yen蕭彦 (cs 1571), *I-yüan jen-chien* 掖垣人鑑 (NCL microfilm), 13/15b; Shunzo Sakamaki, *Ryukyu: a Bibliographical Guide to Okinawan Studies* (Honolulu, 1963), 76; W. Franke, *Sources*, 7.8.2; J. K. Fairbank, ed., *The Chinese World Order* (Cambridge, Mass., 1968), 141.

Hok-lam Chan

CH'EN Lin 陳璘 (T. 朝王[朝爵?], H. 龍崖), died 1607, was a native of Weng-yüan 翁源 in the prefecture of Shao-chou 韶州, Kwangtung. In 1562 he responded to the appeal of the supreme commander of Kwangtung for volunteers to assist in the campaign against the pirate, Chang Lien (*q.v.*), and was given the rank of deputy company commander. During the following two years he took an active part in the suppression of the bandits in the Shao-chou area. In 1564 he was awarded the hereditary rank of an assistant commander of the sub-guard station at Shao-chou. After five years of fighting successfully against banditry in the mountainous region of northern Kwangtung, he was promoted in 1570 to garrison commander of Che-lin 柘林, near the border of Fukien. There was a squadron of warships under his command and this first-hand experience in naval matters added substantially to his military knowledge. He also gained merits by taking part in suppressing coastal bandits and pirates. In 1573 he received a promotion to the rank of an assistant commissioner of the regional military commission of Kwangtung.

At this time the most formidable band of pirates on the coast of Kwangtung and Fukien was the one led by Chu Liang-pao 諸 (朱) 良寶 (d. 1578), an associate of the pirate chiefs Lin Tao-ch'ien and Lin Feng (*qq.v.*). Ch'en Lin proposed to the supreme commander of Kwangtung, Yin Cheng-mao 殷正茂 (T. 養實, H. 石汀 1513–92, cs 1547), a plan for the capture and destruction of the pirate base located on the seashore near Ch'ao-chou. The plan was approved. In order that he might have independent command over a force of three thousand men, the number he had requested, he was given the temporary rank of regional assistant commander. In his advance on the pirate stronghold Ch'en and his men carried bundles of faggots and rushes to pave their way over the marshland until they were within range of the enemy fort. Then, occupying the high ground and protecting themselves with shields, they opened up a barrage of rocket fire (shen-chi chien 神機箭), which killed many of the pirates including their chief, Chu Liang-pao. For this victory, as on similar occasions, the court rewarded Ch'en with a sum of silver.

In 1575, after his promotion to be mobile corps commander of Chao-ch'ing 肇慶, his rank as regional assistant commander was confirmed, and in that capacity he was assigned in March, 1576, to Kao-chou 高州. In the following year he took part in the campaign led by the supreme commander of Kwangtung, Ling Yün-i 凌雲翼 (T. 洋山, cs 1547), against the Yao 猺 tribal people in the Lo-p'ang 羅旁 mountainous area, a strategic region through which the West River flows to connect Kwangtung with Kwangsi. It is a fertile territory where Chinese farmers were then beginning to settle. After the Yao tribes were forced into submission, the region was formally occupied and divided into the subprefecture Lo-ting 羅定, and the districts Tung-an 東安 and Hsi-ning 西寧. Ch'en Lin became regional assistant commander for Tung-an with the rank of a regional vice commander, assigned to constructing offices, army barracks, highways, and bridges, a job which occupied his attention for several years.

In 1583, when he tried to tighten up the discipline of his troops, which had become lax during the years of peace, a hundred of them mutinied. They joined forces with the Yao tribesmen in pillaging the countryside until they were apprehended by Ch'en. The mutiny, itself a minor incident, was a turning point in Ch'en's career. A regional censor reported to the court that Ch'en had driven his soldiers to revolt by treating them with undue severity and that he had compelled them to furnish labor and supplies for the construction of temples. Although the charges were dropped and he was transferred, late in 1584,

to be regional vice commander of Lang-shan 狼山 (naval base guarding the Yangtze River at Nan T'ung-chou 南通州), his record had been marred. His biography in the *Ming-shih* states that he was dismissed, that he was "sullied by avarice," and that no one would recommend him for office. An earlier account of his life, written by Yü Cheng 喻政 in the Ming period, was more sympathetic. It records that the minister of War, Wang Ch'ung-ku (*q.v.*), had proposed further advancement for Ch'en, but the recommendation failed of approval because his detractors charged that he lacked probity and that, owing to his harsh treatment, his men mutinied. According to Yü, Ch'en was hurt by these slanders and resigned from the service.

Ch'en lived in retirement for eight years. When the Japanese invaded Korea in 1592 and the Ming court decided to intervene, many high officials in Peking remembered Ch'en and had him recalled to duty. He was given the rank of an assistant commander and assigned to training the seventh regiment of the firearms corps in the Imperial Guards, but the supreme commander of Kwangtung pointed out that the Japanese might also harass the coast of south China and suggested that Ch'en's service would be of greater value in his own province.

When the Japanese overran Korea and it was feared that they might push on to invade Liaotung, Ch'en was again ordered to proceed to Peking. He was given the rank of a vice commander in the Imperial Guards and the responsibility of training the sixth regiment of the firearms corps, but early in 1593 the orders were changed, and he was promoted to be regional vice commander of the coastal defense forces of Pei-Chihli. As soon as he arrived in north China, however, the Ming government at the instigation of the minister of War, Shih Hsing (*see* Li Ju-sung), agreed to an armistice with Japan, and Ch'en returned to Kwangtung. At this time he sent some expensive gifts to Shih Hsing, who, exposed the matter in a memorial to the throne, and, according to the *Ming-shih*, Ch'en was dismissed. (*See* below Editors' note.)

He lived in retirement until 1596 when the provincial military authorities again sought his help in the suppression of a rebellion of the Yao tribesmen in Ts'en-ch'i 岑溪, Kwangsi. Instead of taking command of the regular troops, he called in men from his former command and supported them with his own funds, almost bankrupting himself. Leading his men into the mountains of Kwangsi, he helped to quell the rebellion. The court commended him for his action and, with the resumption of hostilities in Korea in 1597, promoted him to be assistant central commissioner-in-chief, eligible to be a general officer as soon as a vacancy occurred. His action in impoverishing himself also temporarily silenced the critics who had accused him of avarice.

The truce with Japan ended in 1597 when Hideyoshi rejected the peace terms proposed by the Ming government. In the spring the Korean king reported that the Japanese were crossing the straits in force. The Ming court, which had been lulled into a sense of false security by Shih Hsing and his peace party, was surprised and shocked. Shih Hsing was dismissed and in May a new supreme commander for Liaotung, Hsing Chieh (*see* Yang Ying-lung) was dispatched to direct the Chinese forces in Korea.

The Korean king asked the Ming government to send a naval force immediately to reinforce the base at Hansan 閑山 Island, but the fear that the Japanese might strike at the seaboard provinces of south China hampered the plans for the relief of Korea. For land forces, the Ming government could summon the army in Liaotung under Li Ju-sung and the Szechwan army under Liu T'ing (*q.v.*), both of which had previously seen service in Korea. But it would be months before Liu's troops could reach Korea. As for naval forces, the proposals of the ministry of War and the approval of the emperor to send units from the south encountered opposition from the provincial authorities. Only after much urging did they agree to detach a thousand men from the Nan-Chihli fleet and another thousand from the Fukien.

Meanwhile the Japanese carried out their second invasion of Korea virtually unopposed. Their navy had been considerably strengthened and now included new and large warships, heavily armed with artillery. In contrast to the campaign of 1592-93, when their ships were sunk and their supply lines cut by the Korean fleet led by Yi Sun-sin 李舜臣 (1545-98), Japanese transports now freely ferried troops across the straits for the coming offensive. The Korean army had deteriorated during the years of truce and Yi, having been involved in party politics, had been disgraced and dismissed. His successor, Wŏn Kyon 元均 (killed in action August 28, 1597), further hastened the degeneration of the navy by making unconcerted piecemeal assaults on the Japanese. At the end of August they seized the base at Hansan Island, destroying the bulk of the Korean fleet and, in the following month, they occupied Namwŏn 南原 and Chinju 晉州. Frantically the king of Korea recalled Yi Sun-sin and sent messages to the Ming court asking for artillery and for the dispatch of Chinese naval forces. There was not much that Yi could do for, of the once powerful fleet, only a fraction was left. In response, the Ming government ordered a general mobilization and hastily dispatched to Korea whatever troops it could spare. Under the over-all supervision of Hsing Chieh and the field oversight of Yang Hao (ECCP), the general, Ma Kuei (*see* Li Ju-sung), was made commander-in-chief of the Chinese expeditionary forces.

The advance guards consisting of 17,000 men crossed the Yalu in the summer to buttress the Korean army. At the urgent plea of the Korean court for naval support, 150 vessels of the Chekiang fleet were sent to Lü-shun 旅順 on the southern tip of the Liaotung peninsula in September, and they were augmented in the ensuing months by 2,000 men from the Nanking fleet and 2,000 in 82 vessels from the Wu-sung 吳淞 fleet. These vessels were flat-bottomed ships (sha-ch'uan 沙船) and galleys (pa-la-hu ch'uan 叭喇唬船), for the provincial authorities, fearing Japanese raids on the China coast, were reluctant to release combat vessels from their fleets. The main naval force, consisting of warships from the Kwangtung fleet under the command of Ch'en Lin, was not expected to arrive until March of the following year.

By October the Japanese again approached the Korean capital city. With the situation in Korea rapidly deteriorating and the Korean army in disarray, Hsing Chieh decided to launch a counteroffensive without waiting for land and sea reinforcements to arrive. Ma Kuei blunted the Japanese drive at Chiksan 稷山 and pushed the Japanese back to the southeastern coast of Korea. Here the Japanese held on, in a fortified line from Sunch'ŏn 順天 in the south, through Pusan 釜山, to Ulsan 蔚山, farther north along the coast. In December, after driving the Japanese under Katō Kiyomasa (see Konishi Yukinaga) to their third and last line of defense at Ulsan, the Chinese received word that the Japanese fleet had left Pusan and was sailing up the Naktong River 洛東江. To avoid being outflanked, the Chinese pulled back and the withdrawal turned into a rout when wild rumors caused the troops to panic. In March and April, 1598, a 6,700-man contingent of Liu T'ing's Szechwan army reached Korea. Naval forces, under the over-all command of Ch'en Lin, arrived at Shanhaikuan in May. They consisted of 5,000 men of Ch'en's own Kwangtung squadron and a Chekiang squadron commanded by Teng Tzu-lung 鄧子龍, a native of Feng-ch'eng 豐城, Kiangsi. For his service in pacifying bandits and Miao tribesmen in Kwangtung Teng had risen

from deputy company commander (pa-tsung) to battalion commander (tu-ssu). In 1583 he collaborated with Liu T'ing in a campaign against the Burmese and was promoted to be deputy regional commander of Yunnan. After taking part in the war against Burma in 1590, he was censured and dismissed (1592). He remained in retirement until 1598 when his rank was restored and he was sent to Korea in command of a naval squadron. Ch'en's deputy, Wu Kuang 吳廣, came from his native district in Kwangtung and had been assistant commander of the southern area of Fukien. He was assigned to command a naval detachment to cooperate with Liu's land forces. From Shanhaikuan the Ming fleet sailed to Lü-shun to pick up Korean pilots for the voyage to its stations on the south Korean coast. In Korea Ch'en had the difficult task of uniting the Chinese and the Korean naval forces into an effective fighting unit. The Chinese had the men, but most of their ships were not combat vessels. Consequently, since the Koreans were building twenty-two large warships to augment the thirteen under Yi Sun-sin's command, Ch'en arranged for the joint use of these ships by the seamen of both countries. Each would have a crew of a hundred Korean oarsmen and thirty to forty Chinese fighting men, most of whom were to be selected from the Chekiang units.

Ch'en also had to play the role of a diplomat. At Shanhaikuan some of his men had mutinied and he was reprimanded for being lax, but in Korea when he tried to impose discipline the Koreans charged that he was too harsh. A biography of Yi Sun-sin by Yi Pun 李芬, written many years later, states that Ch'en was a vain and arrogant man, and, fearing friction, the king of Korea secretly instructed Yi to receive Ch'en with special courtesy. But contemporary documents, such as those selected from the *Yijo Sillok* 李朝實錄 and collected in the *Sadae Mungwe* 事大文軌, reveal that the Korean king distrusted Yi Sun-sin, while Ch'en vouched for his loyalty and commended him as the finest naval officer in Korea.

The Chinese offensive, scheduled for June, had to be postponed because of a revolt in Liaotung which not only drew off a portion of the Ming forces but also gave the Japanese more time to strengthen their line of forts along the coast from Ulsan to Sunch'on. It was defended, according to Arima Seiho 有馬成甫, by 64,700 men. The strong points were Ulsan, held by 10,000 under Katō Kiyomasa; Sach'ŏn 泗川, held by 10,000 under Shimazu Yoshihiro 島津義弘; and Sunch'ŏn, held by 13,700 under Konishi Yukinaga. In addition, according to Yi Hyŏn-sŏk (see Ch'en Chien), a Japanese fleet of 500 ships manned by 12,200 sailors, was based at Pusan.

The land forces of the Chinese and Korean allies numbered over 100,000, but when their offensive was launched in the middle of October there were still troops marching southward from Seoul, and the allied armies which engaged the enemy came to 50,600 Chinese and 17,800 Koreans, a total of 68,400 men. The largest army, consisting of 24,000 Chinese and 5,500 Koreans and under the command of Ma Kuei, laid siege to Ulsan. Tung I-yüan 董一元, with 13,000 Chinese and 2,300 Koreans, pressed against the enemy center at Sach'ŏn. Liu Ting's army, consisting of 13,600 Chinese and over 10,000 Koreans, attacked Sunch'ŏn, the southern anchor of the Japanese defense line. Ch'en Lin commanded the allied naval forces composed of 13,200 Chinese and 7,300 Koreans in about 500 ships, large and small, and operated in the waters off Sunch'ŏn. The offensive was thus mainly a Chinese effort, carried out under Chinese commanders and mainly by Chinese forces.

On October 19 the Chinese-Korean allies launched their general offensive by land and sea, driving the Japanese back to their third and last line of defense. In their assault on Sach'ŏn, October 30 to November 1, Tung I-yüan's troops breached the Japanese defenses but, just as they were about to exploit their advantage,

the enemy's magazine store exploded, either inadvertently ignited by the attackers' gunfire or touched off by the defenders. The Japanese sortied and inflicted heavy casualties on the fleeing Chinese. The setback, which exposed their flanks, compelled the allies to raise their siege of Ulsan.

In their assault on Sunch'ŏn the troops under Liu T'ing and the naval forces under Ch'en Lin also made no headway, although in one engagement Ch'en succeeded in destroying a Japanese convoy of a hundred boats, which was attemping to bring supplies to their beleaguered troops. On October 30 the allied attack was renewed. Two days later, when Ch'en's ships sailed up a narrow inlet, the tide ebbed. The Japanese then attacked the immobilized Chinese vessels, sinking 19 ships and 24 galleys. Ch'en escaped in a small boat. On land, after failing to penetrate Konishi's defenses, Liu's troops also withdrew.

The war now settled into a stalemate. Meanwhile, an outside development interposed. Hideyoshi died and on November 13 the regents, who took over the Japanese government, ordered the withdrawal of their forces in Korea by the end of the month. In a round-about way, via Liu-ch'iu, Fukien, and Peking, the Chinese commanders in Korea received the news of Hideyoshi's death in early December, and Hsing Chieh immediately launched another offensive. For Katō up at Ulsan in the north the evacuation posed no problem, but Konishi at Sunch'ŏn in the south, under pressure from Liu's forces on land, was blockaded by the allied fleet under Ch'en. Konishi, it is said (mainly in Japanese sources), reached an understanding with Ch'en and officials of the Korean court to permit withdrawal. There were even charges, unconfirmed from the Chinese side, that Ch'en had been bribed and that the naval battle of Noryang Straits 露梁津 took place when Ch'en broke his agreement. It is reported, on the other hand, that Konishi had sent emissaries to parley with Ch'en in order to gain time for the Japanese fleet at Pusan to arrive and cover his withdrawal.

On December 4 the allied fleet under Ch'en, totaling 15,000 men in about 500 ships (according to Yi Hyŏn-sŏk), congregated at the south end of the Noryang Straits, a narrow passage between the mainland and Namhae 南海 Island and the main route from Pusan to Sunch'ŏn, to block the junction of the two Japanese forces. Konishi began embarking his troops at Sunch'ŏn two days later, but it was not until December 14 that the Japanese fleet from Pusan, 12,200 men in 500 ships under the command of Shimazu Yoshihiro, was sighted coming down the Straits from the north. Ch'en had alerted his men to prepare for a night battle, but it was not until ten o'clock on the morning of December 15 that the two navies met. Teng Tzu-lung, commanding the left wing of the allied fleet, was the first to engage. With 200 of his men from Kiangsi and Chekiang he had transferred to a large Korean warship. Mistaking them for enemy boarders. an allied warship coming up from behind opened fire on them. After suffering heavy casualties, and with their ship disabled, Teng and his men were attacked by the Japanese and killed. Ch'en, in command of the central division of the fleet, had sailed ahead, leaving his other warships far behind. He was surrounded by attacking Japanese vessels. When Yi Sun-sin, commander of the right wing, saw Ch'en's plight, he at once turned around to go to the latter's succor and Yi too was encircled by the Japanese. His men opened fire with their mortars (hu-tsun p'ao 虎蹲礮), and one of the missiles hit and killed Yi. Meantime the heavy guns (fa-kung 發熕) from Ch'en's ship sank several Japanese vessels and, personally leading his men, Ch'en repelled repeated assaults by Japanese boarders. By this time the warships, led by his second in command, Ch'en Ts'an 陳蠶, arrived and drove back the Japanese. The latter lost 200 ships in the battle

of Noryang, but this diversion gave Konishi the opportunity to escape by another channel. Ch'en followed his victory by recapturing Namhae and other islands, using his guns to root out Japanese stragglers hiding in caves. In these mopping-up operations he also destroyed nearly a hundred Japanese ships.

In October, 1599, when Emperor Chu I-chün (q.v.) conferred honors for war service in Korea, the highest reward for the field commanders went to Ch'en Lin in recognition of the contribution made by the navy in bringing the war to a victorious conclusion. He received promotion to vice commissioner-in-chief of the central military commission, and one of his sons was given the hereditary rank of assistant commander of a guard. Liu T'ing received second honors, Ma Kuei third, and Hsing Chieh the honorary title of grand guardian of the heir apparent. Meanwhile several generals active in the Korean war were ordered transferred to southwest China to suppress the rebellion of Yang Ying-lung, chief of Miao tribesmen of Po-chou. Ch'en Lin was appointed regional commander of Hukuang, while Liu T'ing was returned to Szechwan. Under the supervision of Li Hua-lung (q.v.), the supreme commander of Szechwan, Hukuang, and Kweichow, Liu, Ch'en, and Wu Kuang also took part in the fight against Yang. After successfully concluding the war in 1600 Ch'en again received commendation for his part in the victory. The entire campaign lasted only three months. The pacification of these tribes in Po-chou permitted the government to attend to other Miao rebellions in Kweichow. In 1601 Ch'en and his army marched south to the area of Yung-ts'ung 永從 in southeastern Kweichow near the borders of Hunan and Kwangsi where the P'i-lin 皮林 Miao were in revolt. Assisted by troops from Hukuang, Ch'en had no difficulty in subduing the rebels. In one battle he brought his guns up a steep mountain to fire down on the tribesmen in their caves and fortified positions, forcing most of them to capitulate and the rest to escape to Kwangsi.

During this campaign Ch'en's integrity was again impugned by censors, when he was about to receive official commendation for the success of the Po-chou operations. They charged that he and Liu T'ing had attempted to bribe Li Hua-lung. Liu was reprimanded but the emperor dismissed the charges against Ch'en. The issue was also raised in 1602 when Ch'en was recommended for the post of regional commander of Kweichow. The emperor once more interceded so that his appointment was confirmed. In 1604 Ch'en was promoted to be a senior commissioner-in-chief of the central military commission, and one of his sons received the hereditary office of a guard commissioner.

The devastation of war in Kweichow and the misery and distress that came in its train drove the Miao peoples to rebel again in 1606. The uprising extended from the area of Hsin-t'ien 新添 (now Kuei-ting) and P'ing-yüeh, home of the Chung-chia 仲家 Miao, to the mountains west of T'ung-jen 銅仁 inhabited by the Highland 山 Miao. Ch'en, in command of 5,000 Chinese and non-Chinese troops and supported by two other armies totaling 15,000 men, encircled the region of T'ung-jen to blockade the Highland Miao. After killing 3,000 rebels in skirmishes and taking twelve chiefs as prisoners, he brought about the submission of 13,000 tribesmen in a campaign of ninety days. He then led his men against the Chung-chia Miao in the region of Hsin-t'ien, pacifying them in less than a month.

This was his last active campaign. Shortly after his subjugation of the tribes he was transferred to Kwangtung as regional commander while still holding the office of senior commissioner-in-chief of the central military commission. He died in June, 1607. Later in the year he was honored posthumously with the title of grand guardian of the heir apparent, and one of his sons was made a hereditary centurion.

Although not specifically stated, the accounts of Ch'en Lin's career bear out one fact: he was an artillery expert. In his military operations he relied largely on the employment of firearms, from rockets (shen-chi chien), which he used in his early campaign against the bandits and pirates in Kwangtung, to heavy cannons (fa-kung) and mortars (hu-tsun p'ao), which he employed in the naval engagements in Korea, and portable guns which he used in the wars against the Miao tribesmen.

Chinese firearms played a key role in the Korean war. The Koreans were supplied by the Ming government with 300 heavy guns in the beginning of the war in 1593 and an undisclosed number in 1597–98, and, according to Arima, many of these guns were placed on Korean warships. As for the armament of Chinese vessels, according to the *Chi-hsiao hsin-shu* by Ch'i Chi-kuang (*q. v.*), a large-sized Fukien war junk carried one heavy bombard (ta fa-kung), six large culverins (ta fo-lang-chi 佛郎機), three falconets (wan-k'ou ch'ung 碗口銃), and 60 p'en-t'ung 噴筒 (rudimentary flame-throwers?); a hai-ts'ang 海滄 ship had four culverins, three falconets, and 50 p'en-t'ung; and a Ts'ang-shan 蒼山 boat had two culverins, three falconets, and 40 p'en-t'ung. According to the *Wu-pei chih* (*see* Mao Yüan-i), the flat-bottomed sha-ch'uan were not very seaworthy and, having an exposed top deck, were unsuitable for combat. In the battle of Noryang Straits, according to the *Ming-ch'ao chi-shih pen-mo* by Ku Ying-t'ai (ECCP), the Chinese used Ts'ang-shan and pa-la-hu ships. The Ts'ang-shan were vessels propelled by sails and by six pairs of oars and the pa-la-hu were galleys 40 feet in length, propelled by 8 to 10 pairs of oars. The Kwangtung war junks, again according to the *Wu-pei chih*, were bigger than the Fukien war junks and were armed with as many, if not more, heavy bombards, culverins, and falconets. The bombards (fa-kung) were cast in bronze, each weighing about 500 catties (about 600 lbs.) and firing solid lead balls weighing four catties apiece, and the mortars were two feet long, 30 catties in weight, firing 105 *ch'ien* (0.43 oz.)pellets in one discharge. [Editors' note: Ch'en Lin was twice accused of sending expensive gifts to his superiors. In each case it was the superior who exposed him, namely, the minister of War Shih Hsing, in February, 1594, and the supreme commander Li Hua-lung, in 1600. According to the *Wan-li ti-ch'ao*邸鈔, his gifts to Shih Hsing included rolls of scarlet and green velvet and other European goods. As to the gift to Li, it was presented when Li's father died. Li had announced to all his subordinates that only nominal gifts would be accepted but was surprised when no gifts were presented to him personally by the generals, Ch'en and Liu T'ing. He was incensed, however, when he discovered that the two officers had each sent a large sum cf silver to his home.]

Bibliography

1/222/29b, 247/17a, 316/6b, 320/22a; 3/222/15b; MSL, 1940 (Shen-tsung), 242/11a, 306/6a, 307/3a, 308/3b, 311/3b, 313/5a, 314/2a, 316/3b, 318/3a, 321/3b, 329/4a; KC (1958), 4717, 4732, 4793; Ku Ying-t'ai, *Ming-ch'ao chi-shih pen-mo*, ch. 62, 64; Mao Jui-cheng, *Wan-li san ta-cheng k'ao*, 18; Yü Cheng (late Ming), *Ch'en T'ai-pao chuan* 太保傳 in *Shao-chou-fu chih* (1966 reprint of 1873 ed.), 34/12a; Chien Yu-wen 簡又文, "Ming-tai Kuang-tung ying-hsiung Ch'en Lin te shih-chi," in *Kuang-tung wen-wu t'e-chi* (1949), 93; *Wan-li ti-ch'ao* (Taipei, 1968), 816; Ch'i Chi-kuang, *Chi-hsiao hsin-shu*, ch. 18; Li Hua-lung, *P'ing Po ch'üan-shu*; Mao Yüan-i, *Wu-pei chih*, ch. 116; *Tongguk saryak* 東國史略: *Sadae mungwe* (ca. 1618), publ. in *Chosen shiryo shukan* 朝鮮史料叢刊 (1935), 19/43, 24/16, ch. 29, 30/39a, ch. 39, 63, 143; Yi Hyön-sök, *Imjin chollan sa* 壬辰戰亂史 (Seoul, 1967), 1066, 1117; Arima Seiho, *Chosen eki suigun shi* 朝鮮役水軍史, 1942; Aoyagi Tsunataro 青柳綱太郎, ed., *Ri Shun-shin zenshū* 李舜臣全集 (Seoul, 1916), Vol. 2, 76; Horace H. Underwood, "Korean Boats and Ships," *Trans. of the Korea Br. of the R.A.S.*, XXIII (1934), 1, 79; John L. Boots, "Korean Weapons and Armor," *ibid.*, XXIV: 2 (December, 1934), 20.

Jung-pang Lo

CH'EN Lung-cheng 陳龍正 (T. 惕龍, H. 幾亭, 龍致, 發蛟), 1585–1645, thinker and official, was a native of Chia-shan 嘉善, Chekiang. His father, Ch'en Yü-wang 于王, served as surveillance commissioner in Fukien. His elder brother, Ch'en Shan-yü 山毓 the (T. 賁聞), who came out first in the provincial examinations of Chekiang in 1618 and yet failed to obtain the *chin-shih*, was an accomplished poet and scholar, but died at the age of thirty-seven. The two brothers studied together under Wu Chih-yüan 吳志遠 (T. 子往), through whom Ch'en Lung-cheng came to know the famous scholar Kao P'an-lung (*q.v.*), becoming one of his disciples. Another disciple was Wei Ta-chung (*see* Kao P'an-lung). Ch'en Lung-cheng placed third on the list of candidates for the *chü-jen* in 1621. In 1625, when Wei Ta-chung was arrested and taken to the capital, Ch'en accompanied him as far as Wu-hsi, where he and Kao P'an-lung conversed for several days. Having earlier interested himself above all in letters and the art of government, Ch'en regretted his lack of spiritual comprehension, and began to concentrate on the understanding of his own mind and heart. This led him to realize the importance of being completely sincere and of extending one's love to all men. Acquiring the *chin-shih* in 1634, when he was already forty-nine years of age, he was appointed (1637) a drafter in the central drafting office of the Grand Secretariat. He remained in this rather humble post for several years, but did not hesitate to express opinions on the political situation of his time when occasion offered. In mid–1638 an astronomical event, thought to presage uncertain political fortune for the country, occurred. The planet Mars was observed to linger for over twenty days in the Antares (hsin 心) constellation—one of the twenty-four lunar mansions (hsiu 宿) in the eastern zone. This could be interpreted as an ominous sign (war or disaster), the result of bad government. Ch'en Lung-cheng submitted four memorials, pointing out especially the abuses of power by the

Eastern Depot in its irresponsible manner of imprisoning and punishing innocent persons. His protests yielded some effect, and the emperor (Chu Yu-chien, ECCP) commanded the Depot to exercise restraint in its activities. Ch'en's rebukes of the Grand Secretariat itself for recommending for office men known to it by personal connections rather than the really worthy, also won the approval of the emperor. But it angered his own superior officials. Late in 1639, when the appearance of a meteor again caused the emperor to seek advice, Ch'en urged him always to maintain a charitable disposition and a willingness to listen to advice, regardless of celestial phenomena. When a thunderstorm, accompanied by hail, struck the capital on the first day of winter that year, Ch'en attributed the occurrence to a ritual issue, suggesting that the date for the sacrifices to Heaven be changed. The emperor summoned the Secretariat to discuss this question. This resulted in a refutation of Ch'en's proposals. Undaunted, he submitted three more memorials on the subject, and requested retirement from office when these were not heeded. Permission refused, Ch'en wrote treatises on the same subject, entitled *Chiao-ch'i tzu-ying* 郊期咨應 and *Tung-t'ien min-chuan* 東天民傳.

In 1640 Ch'en Lung-cheng returned on leave to his native place, and then went back to the capital two years later. Responding to the emperor's renewed request for counsel, he submitted several memorials concerning the campaigns against roving bandits, the defense of the frontier, and the correct ways to increase national wealth. All received imperial approval. A memorial written on the subject of the opening of new land for agriculture, however, was detained by the grand supervisor of instruction, Huang Ching-fang 黃景昉 (T. 太穉, H. 東厓, 1596–1662, cs 1625), who appropriated Ch'en's ideas and submitted his own memorial first. Ch'en wrote another memorial on the subject which also did not reach the throne. He then prepared a treatise on government,

entitled *Chang-shang lu* 掌上錄, recommending to the sovereign the importance of rectifying his own mind and practicing discretion in the selection of men for public office. This was sent to the printer by Grand Secretary Chang Te-ching (*see* Aleni), and attracted much attention. At that time Ch'en Lung-cheng was, on one hand, being recommended for higher office by the scholar Liu Tsung-chou (ECCP), and, on the other, being accused, especially by Huang Yün-shih 黃雲師 (cs 1640) of the ministry of Personnel, and Huang Shu 黃澍, a censor, who criticized him for propagating false doctrines. Probably in order to defend himself, Ch'en submitted another memorial (1643) which purported to analyze false learning .The Ming government was then facing a grave crisis, as the rebel Li Tzu-ch'eng (ECCP) had penetrated T'ung-kuan 潼關, Shensi. The following year, Ch'en Lung-cheng was transferred to Nanking as proctor of the National University. In April he returned home, only to receive news in June of the fall of the capital to the marauding troops of Li Tzu-ch'eng and the suicide of the emperor. Ch'en was shocked. When Chu Yu-sung, then prince of Fu (ECCP), was proclaimed emperor in Nanking about a month later, Ch'en received an appointment as vice director of the bureau of sacrifices, but made excuses and did not assume the post. In mid–1645 Nanking itself fell to the invading Manchus. About the same time, when Ch'en Lung-cheng heard about the suicide, by starvation, of his friend Liu Tsung-chou, he was much moved. Already sick himself, he refused to take food and died soon afterwards.

As a thinker, Ch'en Lung-cheng manifests the same belief in the unity of all things as did his master Kao P'an-lung, for whose *Kao-tzu i-shu* (Surviving works) he wrote a general preface, as well as a special preface to each of its various sections. He is, however, better known for his social and political writings. Ch'en emphasized constantly the need for the scholar to take upon himself the responsibility of seeking peace for the world, maintaining that the cultivation of self would not be complete without active involvement in social and political affairs. While Kao P'an-lung had severely criticized Wang Shou-jen (*q.v.*), Ch'en on the other hand shows a sincere admiration for this philosopher, who had been at the same time a great statesman, and singled out for praise Wang's promulgations of the community compact (hsiang-yüeh 鄉約) for southern Kiangsi and of the ten-family joint registration system (pao-chia 保甲). Ch'en's name was not included in the list of the three hundred nine Tung-lin partisans which the eunuch Wei Chung-hsien (ECCP) made public in 1626. Owing to his connection with Kao P'an-lung, however, he is known as a Tung-lin scholar, and his biography may be found in the *Tung-lin lieh-chuan*東林列傳 (printed 1711) of Ch'en Ting (*see* Tao-chi). Huang Tsung-hsi's (ECCP) history of philosophy also cites him as a Tung-lin philosopher, but points out that Ch'en's absorption in social and political matters marks him out in a special way.

Ch'en Lung-cheng left many writings. A collection of works—*Chi-t'ing ch'üan-shu* 幾亭全書, 64 *ch.* —published by his son, Ch'en K'uei 揆, in 1665, a copy of which is in several libraries, includes his political writings: *Chi-t'ing cheng-shu* 政書, 20 *ch.*, his scholarly sayings, *Hsüeh-yen* 學言, 3 *ch.*, *Hsüeh-yen hsiang-chi* 詳記, 17 *ch.*, his essays, letters, and poems, *Chi-t'ing wen-lu* 文錄, 20 *ch.*, a shorter *Yin-shu* 因述, 2 *ch.*, and some biographies of the Ch'en family, *Chia-chuan*家傳, 2 *ch.* Two more collections of his works appeared later, namely, the *Chi-t'ing tsai-chi* 再集, which contains such supplementary material as *Hsü hsüeh-yen* 續學言, 3 *ch.*, and *Sui shih-chien* 隨時間, *tsai-chi*, *Chi-t'ing hsü wen-lu* 文錄, 8 *ch.*; and the second, *Chi-t'ing wai-shu* 外書, which includes *Chia-chü* 家距, 1 *ch.*, and *Chü-yeh su-yü* 舉業素語, 1 *ch.* Of these, it is known that *Chi-t'ing wen-lu* was first published in 1631. This work is in the National Central Li-

brary, Taiwan, and a microfilm copy is available. [Editors' note: The reason for the rarity of *Chi-t'ing ch'üan-shu*, *Chi-t'ing wen-lu*, and *Chi-t'ing wai-shu* is that they were all proscribed in the 1780s.] The *Ssu-k'u* catalogue also lists two other works by Ch'en. The first is the *Chiu-huang ts'e-hui* 救荒策會, 7 *ch.*, described as an amended edition of *Ku-chin chiu-huang huo-min shu* 古今救荒活民書, a 3 *chüan* work compiled by Tung Wei 董煒 (cs 1194), and continued and supplemented by others after him. Ch'en's presentation is essentially the same as Tung's but without its repetitious sections, and gives corrections of the more bizarre accounts added by others. It also provided information concerning vegetation available for the alleviation of hunger during a famine in Ch'en's native place, Chia-shan, in the years 1640–41. The second work purports to present an improved edition of *Er-Ch'eng i-su* 二程遺書 edited by Chu Hsi (1130-1200), without its repetitions but including also writings not contained in Chu's edition. According to the local gazetteers, Ch'en is said to have compiled two other works, *Chu-tzu ching-shuo* 朱子經說, and *Ming-ju t'ung* 明儒統, both of which are probably no longer extant.

Bibliography

1/258/37a; 3/218/15a; 39/110/19a; 59/16/4a; 77/1/18a; 83/61/7a; KC (1958), 5811, 5850, 5925, 5930, 5946; *Chia-shan-hsien chih* (1894 ed., 1919 reprint), 20/5a; *Chia-hsing-fu chih* (1879 ed.), 54/22b; *Chia-ho cheng-hsien lu* (*see* Wang Wen-lu), 29/7a; *Chekiang t'ung-chih*(1934), 3058; SK (1930), 82/9a, 84/5a, 95/4a; L. of C. *Catalogue of Rare Books*, 1030; *Chi-t'ing wen-lu* (1631); Sun Tien-ch'i(1957), 177; Joseph Needham, *Science and Civilisation in China*, Vol. III (1959), 232, 398; W. Franke, *Sources*, 5.9.3, 6.2.14.

Julia Ching

CH'EN Pang-chan 陳邦瞻 (T. 德遠, H. 匡左), died 1623, scholar-official, was born in Kao-an 高安, Kiangsi. His father, Ch'en Tan 旦 (T. 覺山), a tribute student of the Chia-ching era (1522–66), became prefectural instructor of Kan-chou 贛州,

Kiangsi. His uncle Ch'en Ju-i汝錡 (T.伯容) also a tribute student who served as assistant instructor of Chien-yang 建陽, Fukien, was the author of *Kan-lu-yüan ch'ang-shu* 甘露園長書, 6 *ch.*, and *tuan 短 shu*, 11 *ch.*, the second of which Ch'en Pang-chan was to publish after eliminating approximately one tenth of its contents. A fellow-townsman criticized Ch'en for his audacity, and restored and published the book in its original form.

After graduating as *chü-jen* (1582) and *chin-shih* (1598), Ch'en became successively assistant secretary of the Grand Court of Revision, director of a bureau in the ministry of personnel (both in Nanking), left administration vice commissioner of Chekiang, surveillance, then right, administration commissioner of Fukien until the death of one of his parents. After the period of mourning, Ch'en returned to office as right administration commissioner of Honan. At this post he initiated canal projects in Chang-te 彰德, and other prefectures which irrigated several hundred thousand *mou* of land. Subsequently he was elevated to the post of left administration commissioner.

In 1619 came his appointment as right vice censor-in-chief and governor of Kwangsi. In August the younger brother and son of Huang Te-hsün黄德勛, native headman of Shang-lin 上林, Kwangsi, rebelled against Huang and took refuge with Ts'en Mao-jen岑茂仁, native chief of T'ien-chou 田州. Ts'en then took Shang-lin by surprise, killed Huang, abducted his wives and daughters, and seized the seals of office. He asked the native authorities to have Huang's son installed in his father's office under the pretense that the headman had succumbed to illness. Ch'en Pang-chan disbelieved the account and called for a punitive expedition. On the succession to the throne of Chu Ch'ang-lo (ECCP) in 1620, Ch'en became concurrently right vice minister of war, right assistant censor-in-chief, supreme commander of military affairs in Kwangtung and Kwangsi, and governor of Kwangtung (September 12).

When Ts'en ignored the emperor's order to give up the seals and surrender his fellow rebels, Ch'en Pang-chan, with the use of both government and tribal soldiers, subdued him.

While in Kwangtung Ch'en protected the coast against Lin Hsin-lao 林莘老, and his pirate force, and ordered the burning of the Portuguese fortifications at Ch'ing-chou 青洲 (Ilha Verde) in present-day Macao. He next received an appointment as right vice minister of Works, but before this could be effected he was made a vice minister of War. On June 12, 1622, Ch'en counseled the throne on court economy and military training to meet the deteriorating situation. A reprimand was his reward. Subsequently he became also concurrent vice minister of Revenue and Works, charged with the specific task of supervising military provisions. He died in harness in 1623, and was posthumously named minister of War. In 1632 his tablet was installed in Kao-an's shrine for local men of note.

Ch'en is remembered as a man who delighted in study, and who was a person of undeviating principles. Though he served for over thirty years in various offices, no wrong-doing sullied his reputation throughout his career.

Ch'en wrote or edited several works. He completed a topical survey of Sung dynastic history started by Feng Ch'i(*q.v.*), the *Sung-shih chi-shih pen-mo*, 10 *ch.*, first engraved in 1605, and then proceeded to compile a similar history of the Yüan dynasty, the *Yüan 元-shih chi-shih pen-mo*, 4 *ch.*, which, with the editorial assistance of Tsang Mou-hsün 臧懋循 (cs 1580), was printed in the following year. There are 109 articles in the first (including also the history of Liao and Chin), 27 in the second. Both were copied into the *Ssu-k'u* Imperial Library, whose editors regarded the former as indispensable for the study of Sung dynastic history, and the latter as praiseworthy in its treatment of Yüan education and canalization.

Another of his writings, rare because

of its listing in the *Index Expurgatorius* of the 18th century, is the *Ho-hua-shan-fang shih-kao* 荷華山房詩稿, 26 *chüan*, printed probably about the same time. The National Library of Peking has a copy. Still another book by him, *Ho-hua-shan-fang chai* 摘 *kao*, 7 *ch.*, is reportedly extant. In his advanced years, Ch'en started a compilation of the history of the Sung dynasty which he left unfinished.

Bibliography

1/242/1a, 318/25b, 325/23a; 24/3/144b; 40/58/13a; 64/庚19/9a; 84/丁下/64b; MSL (1940), Hsi-tsung, 17/5b; KC (1958), 5168-5170; SK (1930), 49/2b, 125/2a; *Kao-an-hsien chih* (1871), 14/42b, 26/49b; *Kuang-hsi t'ung-chih* 廣西通志 (1891), 252/6a; L. of C. *Catalogue of Rare Books*, 124, 125; Sun Tien-ch'i (1957), 28, 45, 153.

*L. Carrington Goodrich
and C. N. Tay*

CH'EN Shih-yüan (陳士元 T. 心叔, 孟卿, H. 養吾, 環中迁叟), 16th century, official and scholar, was a native of Ying-ch'eng 應城, Hukuang. Information on his life and his family is limited, but he left over thirty works, some no longer extant. He became a *chü-jen* in 1537 and a *chin-shih* in 1544. In the following year he took up his official post in Luan-chou 灤州, Pei-chihli, as magistrate. His official career, however, was a short one. In less than three years (1547) he retired from his post and never resumed official life. He is described nevertheless as an able and conscientious administrator. Among his accomplishments was the compilation of the first local gazetteer of Luan-chou, the *Luan-chou chih* 志, 5 *ch.*, for which Chang Chü-cheng (*q. v.*), a fellow provincial, wrote a preface.

After retiring from official life, Ch'en first fulfilled one of his long cherished wishes, namely, to visit the five sacred mountains. He left separate accounts to commemorate these trips. Then he settled down at home and devoted his time mainly to writing. He wrote on many topics: the Classics, history, geography, language, and religion. He also edited the gazetteers of Hsiao-kan 孝感 district in 1555 and of Te-an 德安 prefecture in 1579. The *Ssu-k'u* catalogue notes eleven of Ch'en's works, five of which were copied into the Imperial Library. In 1746, Ch'eng Ta-chung 程大中 (cs 1757), also from Ying-ch'eng, compiled a list of Ch'en's writings including such interesting titles as *Hsin Sung-shih* 新宋史 and *Hsin Yüan-shih* 新元史 (new histories of the Sung and Yüan), neither of which is extant. In pointing out Ch'en's importance as an author, Ch'eng compared him with two other prolific Ming writers, Yang Shen and Chu Mou-wei (*qq. v.*); he also questioned the wisdom of the *Ming-shih* editors in listing a number of Ch'en's works in the bibliographical section but neglecting to provide a sketch of his life in the biographical.

Almost a century later (1833) another scholar from his native place, Wu Yü-mei 吳毓梅, reprinted his *Kuei-yün pieh-chi* 歸雲別集, a collection containing ten titles. According to the author's own introductory remarks, the *Kuei-yün pieh-chi*, 74 *ch.*, was first printed in 1583. Of the ten titles of this collection five deal with the Classics: the *Lun-yü lei-k'ao* 論語類考, 20 *ch.*, the *Meng-tzu tsa-chi* 孟子雜記, 4 *ch.*, the *I-hsiang kou-chieh* 易象鈎解, 4 *ch.*, the *I-hsiang hui* 彙 *-chieh*, 2 *ch.*, and the *Wu-ching i-wen* 五經異文, 11 *ch.*; three on names and surnames: the *Hsing-hui* 姓匯, 4 *ch.*, the *Hsing-hsi* 觿, 10 *ch.*, and the *Ming-i* 名疑, 4 *ch.*; one deals with the corrupted forms of the written characters, the *Ku su-tzu lüeh* 古俗字略, 5 *chüan* with 2 *chüan* of appendices, and one deals with the prognostication of dreams, the *Meng-chan i-chih* 夢占逸旨, 8 *ch.* In a short preface to the last mentioned work, Ch'en relates an anecdote to the effect that in 1562 he dreamed one night of meeting a distinguished looking old man, who presented him with an antique book. While offering thanks, Ch'en asked the old man if it were not a dream, and received the reply, "What encounter would not be a dream, and what dream would not be real?" This induced Ch'en to write his book on dreams.

Ch'en Shih-yüan was involved also in another dream. The story runs that just before his birth, his father dreamed of Mencius arriving at his home. After he was born, his father gave him the *tzu* meng-ch'ing 孟卿. Years later, when he was magistrate of Luan-chou, it happened that during a ceremony in the temple of Confucius, the tablet of Mencius suddenly fell on a sacrificial vessel, knocking it to the ground. Ch'en, unhappy over this seemingly inauspicious omen, decided to leave office. The *Meng-chan i-chih* not only recounts dreams, their meanings, and the results predicted, but also weaves in explanations of traditional Chinese beliefs. In 1850 it was reprinted in the *I-hai chu-ch'en* 藝海珠塵, and in 1939 was included in the *Ts'ung-shu chi-ch'eng*.

The *Ssu-k'u* catalogue lists Ch'en as the author of another work on dreams, the *Meng-lin hsüan-chieh* 夢林玄解, 34 *ch.*, for which Ho Tung-ju (*q. v.*) supplied additional material. Under the entry of Ho Tung-ju's *Ming-tsu ssu ta-fa* 明祖四大法, Ho's name is unfortunately written as Ch'en Tung-ju. This error in the Imperial Catalogue should be corrected.

A collection of notes on Ch'en's native province, the *Chiang Han ts'ung-t'an* 江漢叢談, 2 *ch.*, bearing his preface written in 1572, was reprinted in 1882, and later included in the *Hu-pei* 湖北 *ts'ung-shu* (1891) and in the *Ts'ung-shu chi-ch'eng* in the 1930s. Several titles of Ch'en's works may be found either in the above mentioned *Hu-pei ts'ung-shu*, or in the *Hu-pei hsien-cheng i-shu* 先正遺書 (1923), two collections by Hupei authors.

Bibliography

Ying-ch'eng-hsien chih (1882), 10/23b; *Hu-pei t'ung-chih* (1921), 2066; *Luan-chou chih* (1896), 3/18b, 14/4a; Chang Chü-cheng, *Chang T'ai-yüeh chi* 張太岳集 (1828), 7/17a; SK (1930), 5/2b, 34/1b, 36/4b, 43/5b, 50/10b, 54/1b, 70/10b, 111/14a, 136/1b, 137/10a; TSCC (1885-88), XIV:128/7a; Chu Shih-chia 朱士嘉, *Chung-kuo ti-fang chih tsung-lu* 中國地方志綜錄(Shanghai, 1958, enlarged ed.); Yeh Te-hui (BDRC), *Hsi-yüan tu-shu chih* 郋園讀書志 (1928), 9/56b.

Lienche Tu Fang

CH'EN Tao-fu 陳道復 (*ming* Ch'un 淳, T. 復甫, H. 白陽山人), 1483-1544, painter and calligrapher, was a native of Soochow. His grandfather, Ch'en Ch'iung 璘 (T. 玉汝, H. 成齋, 1440-1506, cs 1478), served as censor-in-chief in Nanking (1500-5). Ch'en Tao-fu studied in the National University in Peking. His family was well-to-do. After the death of his father, he left the management of his property to others. Following his return from Peking, he discovered that he had suffered heavy financial losses. He continued, however, to devote himself to art and literature. He studied under Wen Cheng-ming (*q. v.*), and later developed a style of his own.

In Soochow Ch'en had a well-planned country seat, distinguished for its beautiful old trees, flower beds, fishing ponds, rocks, and a small zoo. The garden was called Wu-hu t'ien-she 五湖田舍 (Five lake country house). Here he entertained his literary comrades, artists, and others, where they indulged in drinking and artistic pursuits. Usually, after imbibing much wine, he would devote himself to painting and writing. One of his sons managed the residence in the city. In his later years, his reputation as an artist was exceeded only by that of Shen Chou (*q. v.*) and Wen Cheng-ming. He had two sons, Ch'en Mei 枚 and Ch'en Kua 栝, both of whom achieved some note, the first as a calligrapher, the second as a painter.

Wang Shih-chen (*q. v.*) comments in his *I-yüan chih-yen*: "Ch'en Tao-fu originally imitated Yüan painters, sometimes adapting features initiated by Mi Fu (1051-1107) and his son Mi Yü-jen (1074-1153). The style is unusual and impressive. His creative talent is really best shown in his flowers and birds." In the opinion of Wang Shih-min (ECCP), "Ch'en Tao-fu's birds and flowers are at their best when he painted them at a time of complete relaxation and seemingly without paying much attention to detail." To sum up, Ch'en's paintings are generally unadorned and of genuine beauty.   His artistic skill was chiefly due to his intellectual objectivity. Connoisseurs of paintings admired his flowers and birds more than his landscapes. Indeed, his naturalness attained a high degree of refinement when he used light ink and simple brush strokes. As we learn from Wang Chih-teng (*q. v.*) in his *Tan-ch'ing chih*, Ch'en used bright colors sparingly; his drawings were entirely free from artificiality and looked like living flora and fauna. Wen P'eng, son of Wen Cheng-ming, relates the following anecdote: "One evening under candle light, Ch'en Tao-fu took a piece of paper to the inkstone; he crumpled it a bit and dipped it in the ink so as to paint clouds!" In calligraphy too Ch'en Tao-fu developed his own individual style, especially in the hsing-shu (running style).

To illustrate his popularity in his own day, it is worth noting that when the property of Yen Sung (*q. v.*) was confiscated after his death, the inventory listed 57 examples of Ch'en's paintings and calligraphy. His art is well represented in various collections in the world, especially in the Palace Museum, Taipei. His collected literary works bear the title *Pai-yang chi* 白陽集. He seldom took pains in writing verse. His poems resemble those of Shen Chou, being expressed with conversational directness. Ch'ien Ch'ien-i (ECCP) called the works full of platitudes, attributing this to the ineptitude of their compiler.

Bibliography

1/287/3a; 3/268/2b; 40/50/1a; 64/17/11a; 65/6/6b; 84/丁中/5a; 86/14/33b; Chang Huan 張寰 (1486-1561), "Pai-yang hsien-sheng mu-chih-ming," *Huang Ming wen-hai* (microfilm), 19/1/14; Wang K'o-yü, *Shan-hu ts'ung-shu* ed.), 30; Liu Feng劉鳳 (cs 1544), *Hsü Wu hsien-hsien tsan*, 續吳先賢贊, 13/15; *Shih-ch'ü pao-chi san-pien mu-lu* 石渠寶笈三編目錄, Vol. 4; *Su-chou-fu chih* (1883), 86 /31; Cheng Ch'ang 鄭昶, *Chung-kuo hua-hsüeh ch'üan-shih* 中國畫學全史 (1929), 390.

Liu Lin-sheng

CHE'N Ti 陳第 (T. 季立, H. 一齋, 子野子, 溫麻山農), March 29, 1541-April 26, 1617, scholar and military officer, was a native of Lien-chiang 連江, Fukien. His grandfather emerged from poverty through trading activities to become a landowner, and his father, a student in the local school, served for a time as a yamen clerk, Ch'en Ti and his elder brother, Ch'en Ku 穀 (T. 季實, H. 又山, d. 1606), devoted themselves in their youth to study. Ch'en Ti was especially interested in swordsmanship and the study of military strategy. This was the time of Mongol invasions in the north and piratical activities along the coast. It is said that in 1562, when General Ch'i Chi-kuang (*q.v.*) was fighting the pirates in Fukien, Ch'en advised the general on the use of some tactical weapons, such as a halberd with hooks called lang-hsien 狼筅 and sleds for the coastal swamps, both apparently well known to local fishermen and hunters.

From 1561 to 1573 Ch'en competed four times in the provincial examinations without success.   While in Foochow in 1566 he became acquainted with (or a disciple of?) the religious leader, Lin Chao-en (*q. v.*). In 1569 Ch'en gave some lectures at Chang-chou where many students came to hear him. During the following four years he lectured at an academy in Foochow. In 1574, apparently dissatisfied with this kind of sedentary life, he answered the call of Yü Ta-yu (*q. v.*), the recently discharged commander-in-chief of Fukien, to serve on the general's personal staff. Along the Great Wall at this time, under the direction of the minister of War, T'an Lun (*q. v.*), and Ch'i Chi-kuang, a training program for soldiers had been developing rapidly over a period of years. Yü, then seventy years of age, asked T'an for service in the north, in a letter in which he boasted of his virility and strength, saying that his concubines were still bearing children and that he was strong enough to ward off the attack of twenty men. This was the era of reform under Chang Chü-cheng (*q. v.*), when most appointments were based on talent. So Yü was granted his wish, summoned to Peking, and given charge of the training of troops in the use of military carts. Ch'en accompanied Yü and served with distinction in this program for two years, during which he became an expert on the military use of wheelbarrows. He requested and received military rank in 1576. That autumn he took part in the command of a contingent of three thousand troops from Peking on patrol duty along the Great Wall. By embarking on a military career instead of that of a prospective civil official with higher status, Ch'en won the admiration of his superiors, T'an Lun, Ch'i Chi-kuang, and others who presented him with poems of encouragement. Early in 1577, on the recommendation of T'an Lun, he was appointed commandant of Fort Ch'ao-ho-ch'uan 潮河川 controlling the pass Ku-pei-k'ou古北口, a post he held for four years. His command actually consisted of a series of forts built shortly after the Mongols had broken through to invade China in 1550 (*see* Ch'iu Luan). While keeping peace and order on the border he took charge of building a stone bridge across the Ch'ao-ho. It was three hundred feet in length and had seven arches; the engineer was from Fukien.

In 1580 Ch'en, when about to be recommended by his superior, Ch'i Chi-kuang, for promotion to an easy and highly remunerative position, indicated that at forty he was eligible, in his opinion, for a much more difficult appointment. In accordance with his own wish he was made the following year commander (with the rank of major) of the vanguard military cart battalion as acting lieutenant colonel, stationed at Han-er-chuang 漢兒莊. Later he was awarded the privileges of a colonel. He not only maintained order and kept up training but also established schools to educate all youths from six to twenty in the area under his jurisdiction, regard-

less of military or civil registry. He likewise encouraged his soldiers to marry and to drive away camp followers. His assignment at Han-er-chuang lasted for two years only, however, as the era of reform under Chang Chü-cheng was coming to an end.

Shortly after Chang's death in July, 1582, Ch'en was approached by a man (probably a quartermaster) with a gift and the offer of five thousand rolls of black cloth to be distributed among the soldiers at twice the market price and to be paid for by deducting the amount from each soldier's pay. Ch'en refused the gift, rejected the offer, and reported the matter to his superiors. This man was a cousin of Wu Tui 吳兌 (T. 君澤, H. 環州, 1525–96, cs 1558), then supreme commander of Chi-liao (1581–82), and so the direct supervisor of Ch'i Chi-kuang and Ch'i's subordinates, one of whom was Ch'en. As a result, although Ch'en received repeated commendations from inspectors sent from Peking, Wu judged him incompetent and cashiered him. Meanwhile Ch'i Chi-kuang was also removed and transferred to Kwangtung.

On the way home Ch'en climbed Mt. T'ai in Shantung and visited other scenic heights. He was then only forty-two years of age, but he decided to lead a life of retirement and study. From 1583 to 1597 he remained chiefly at his home in Lien-chiang, only occasionally taking a short trip, such as the one in 1585 to Chekiang to see his former superior, Ch'i Chi-kuang (then on his way from Kwangtung back to Shantung), and another one, in 1589–90, to Ch'ao-chou in Kwangtung. After his wife's death and burial early in 1596, he became driven by wanderlust. From 1597 to 1615, except for a few brief periods, he lived away from home, sometimes staying with friends and sometimes traveling to faraway places, much as Hsü Hsia-k'o did half a century later (see Hsü Hung-tsu, ECCP).

Although well acquainted with Buddhist literature, Ch'en did not believe in

Buddhism; but during his travels, at least in the first few years, he probably wore Buddhist or Taoist garb and called himself fang-wai 方外 or "non-secular." There is a strong possibility that he joined the sect founded by Lin Chao-en and that his travels, if not actively on behalf of Lin's movement, were at least facilitated by the widespread establishments of Lin's believers. He started in 1597 by visiting Chang-chou and Foochow and came to know two men important in his life, namely, Lin P'ei 林培 (T. 定宇, H. 培之, 1547–99) of Tung-kuan 東莞, Kwangtung, and General Shen Yu-jung (q.v.) of Hsüan-ch'eng, southwest of Nanking. Early in 1598 he accompanied Lin P'ei to Kwangtung. On their way they paid their respects at Lin Chao-en's temple in P'u-t'ien. Ch'en stayed in the south for two and a half years, visiting many places in Kwangtung and Kwangsi, returning home by way of Kiangsi. Early in 1603 he accompanied General Shen on the latter's voyage to Taiwan to fight the Japanese pirates then harassing the natives (called Tung-fan 東番, "barbarians on the east"). On January 19 twenty-one ships ran into a squall near the Pescadores. Seven ships were lost; fortunately the flagship survived. During the storm Ch'en composed a poem saying that to think of the sea as land and the boat as a house one did not care where one was to be buried, at the base of a hill or in the center of the ocean. Later the fleet encountered seven pirate ships, sank six of them, took fifteen heads as trophies, and rescued some three hundred seventy captives. While in Taiwan Ch'en made notes on the aborigines and later wrote an account of them, entitled *Tung-fan chi* 記; this is one of the first and fullest descriptions of the Taiwan aborigines. After returning to Amoy Ch'en remained as Shen's guest until late in 1603, when with Shen's help he printed the documents on his military service, entitled *Chi-men ping-shih* 薊門兵事, 2 *ch.*

In 1604 Ch'en traveled to Nanking where he made the acquaintance of Chiao Hung (ECCP) who encouraged him to concentrate on the phonological study of the Book of Poetry, in order to re-establish the ancient phonetic readings by a systematic arrangement of the rhyming words. After consulting Chiao's fine collection of books Ch'en verified his findings and completed the work in 1605, in which year he took the manuscripts to Te-hsing 德興 in northeastern Kiangsi to show to his brother Ch'en Ku, then serving as director of the district school. After visiting the Huang 黃 mountains he returned to Nanking in 1606 to supervise the printing of his book which he entitled *Mao-shih ku-yin k'ao* 毛詩古音考, 4 *ch.* Just then he learned of the sudden death of his brother and hurried back to Te-hsing where he burned a copy of the newly printed book in a ceremony at his brother's coffin.

After his brother's burial, Ch'en Ti lived for a while in Lu shan 盧山 in northern Kiangsi and a year later, in 1607, sailed up the Yangtze to Wuchang and then up the Han River to Wu-tang 武當 shan, the center of northern Taoism. Thereafter he based himself chiefly on Nanking, probably always in Chiao Hung's home, but made pilgrimages whenever possible to various scenic regions among which may be mentioned the coastal ranges of Chekiang (1609, 1612, and 1613). About this time (1609) he determined to see all the five sacred mountains, only one of which he had already climbed, namely, Mt. T'ai in 1583. Subsequently he visited Mt. Sung in Honan in 1611, Mt. Hua in Shensi in 1612, Mt. Heng in Shansi in 1614, and finally the last of the five, Mt. Heng in Hukuang in 1615. Before he started on the last pilgrimage he wrote two poems entitled "Ch'ing-ssu shih" 請死詩 (Welcoming death), remarking that at seventy-five *sui*, with hearing and sight still good, and teeth quite strong, to die then might be called kuei-ch'üan 歸全 (to return unimpaired); also that after studying and writing during his forties and fifties and visiting mountains and rivers for the past twenty years he welcomed an end to a life filled with activity. In a letter to a friend he wrote that he was planning to climb the sacred mountain of the south and that every time he looked forward to such a trip his grey beard turned black and his foot sores healed as if the mountains and rivers (collectively) could serve as the god of medicine. After climbing Mt. Heng he returned east by way of Kiangsi, arriving at Lien-chiang late in 1615. In 1616 he became restive and started on a trip to Szechwan; he fell ill on the way, however, and was brought home where he died soon afterwards. In his last will he specified a simple funeral, early burial, with no Buddhist or any other kind of religious ceremony.

The foremost contributions of Ch'en are his *Mao-shih ku-yin k'ao* and its accompanying volume, *Ch'ü Sung ku-yin-i* 屈宋古音義, 3 *ch.*, compiled in 1614, the latter being a study of the rhyming system in the writings of Ch'ü Yüan (*ca.* 340 B.C. -*ca.* 278 B. C.) and Sung Yü (290-223 B. C.). Both works were included in the *Ssu-k'u* library and recognized by the compilers of the *Ssu-k'u* catalogue as pioneer works on ancient phonology, a field of study that was continued by Ku Yen-wu (ECCP) and other scholars up to the present day. In methodology, too, Ch'en first demonstrated the effective application of inductive reasoning.

Here are some moot questions perhaps never raised before. Did Ch'en have any contact with the Jesuits, and if he did, could his study of phonology have been in any way influenced by a European? It is at least quite improbable for him not to have been aware of the foreigners for first, during his travels in Kwangtung and Kiangsi from 1598 to 1600 he passed through all the Jesuit centers; second, from 1604 to 1614 he lived chiefly in Nanking where in 1598 the Jesuits had established a church; and third, his friend and host in Nanking, Chiao Hung, was acquainted with Matteo Ricci (*q.v.*) when that missionary visited the city (1599-

1600). It was in 1605 that Ricci published his treatise on Latin alphabetic writing in Chinese *Hsi-tzu ch'i-chi* 西字奇跡, but long before that he had tried to explain it to Chinese scholars, among them perhaps Chiao Hung. That Ch'en began to work on the *Mao-shih ku-yin k'ao* in 1601 right after his return from Kwangtung and that he wrote the book in Chiao's home in 1604 to 1606 shortly after Chiao's acquaintance with Ricci seem to indicate a possible connection between western phonetic writing and Ch'en's approach to the study of ancient phonology.

Ch'en left two more works on the Classics, namely, the *Fu-hsi t'u-tsan* 伏羲圖讚, 2 *ch.*, and *Shang-shu shu-yen* 尙書疏, 衍, 4 *ch.*, both printed in 1612. The former is an attempt at cosmology which the compilers of the *Ssu-k'u* catalogue regarded as insignificant except for some incidental information on the correct pronunciation of certain words. The latter is a sound study of the Book of History except that Ch'en upheld the ancient text (*see* Mei Tsu). Among other serious works of his may be mentioned the three collections of essays, *Miu-yen* 謬言, printed in 1595, *I-yen* 意言, and *Sung-hsüan chiang-i* 松軒講義, and a collection of letters, *Shu-cha ou-ts'un* 書札偶存. As a book collector he left a catalogue, *Shih-shan-t'ang shu-mu* 世善堂書目, printed by Pao T'ing-po (ECCP) in 1795. In the postface Pao said that an earlier bibliophile of Hangchow discovered a copy of the catalogue about 1750 and went to Fukien to see the books but was disappointed to learn that the collection had been dispersed. It seems that Pao and this bibliophile did not know that Chu I-tsun (ECCP) had already obtained this intelligence as early as about 1705 when he sent a Fukienese friend to investigate. According to Cheng Chieh (*see* Hsü Po) Ch'en's books were destroyed by his wife.

As a poet Ch'en used a direct and forceful style. In 1601 he edited his poems written during his years of military service under the title *Chi-men sai-ch'ü* 薊門塞曲 and those during his travels in

Kwangtung, entitled *Liang-yüeh yu-ts'ao* 兩粵遊草, which were printed by his friend, General Shen Yu-jung, in that year. Sometime after that Ch'en published another collection of poems entitled *Chi-hsin-chi* 寄心集, 6 *ch*. In 1616 he assembled all his poems written during the travels to the five mountains, and printed them in a collection entitled *Wu-yüeh yu-ts'ao* 五嶽遊草, 7 *ch*.

Ch'en's writings were appreciated by only a few of his contemporaries, probably because he was neither a *chin-shih* nor a man of influence. By the 18th century, even after some of his works were highly praised in the *Ssu-k'u* catalogue, he was practically ignored by scholars as his collected work *I-chai chi* 集 was listed about the same time in the Index Expurgatorius for excision of a few words in one poem. In 1848 the *I-chai chi* was reprinted in Fukien but the event went unnoticed because of the civil war in the following two decades. In the last years of the 19th century even the great scholar, Yü Yüeh (ECCP), had difficulty in identifying him. Hu Shih (BDRC) referred to him in 1924 as "fl. 1600." Liang Ch'i-ch'ao (BDRC), in his works on the history of scholarship, does not seem to mention him at all. There are two chronological biographies of Ch'en Ti, one by Ch'en Yü-jui 陳毓瑞, printed in 1922, under the title *Ch'en I-chai nien-p'u* 陳一齋年譜, and the other by Chin Yün-ming 金雲銘 entitled *Ch'en Ti nien-p'u*, printed in 1945. Following the printing in 1959 of Ch'en's description of the Taiwan aborigines (*see* Shen Yu-jung) there has been a resurgence of interest in him in Taiwan.

Bibliography

3/267/7a; 40/49/9b; 64/已18/3a; Ch'ien Ch'ien-i (ECCP), *Lieh-ch'ao shih-chi*, 丁 11; Chin Yün-ming, *Ch'en Ti nien-p'u*; Chu Chiu-ying 朱玖瑩, "Ch'en Ti, the first scholar to visit Taiwan" (in Chinese), in *Wen-shih hui-k'an* 文史薈刊, no. 1; Mao I-po毛一波, ms. biography of Ch'en Ti in Chinese; Kuo Po-ts'ang郭柏蒼, *Ch'üan-Min Ming-shih-chuan* 全閩明詩傳 (1889), 31/1a; Shen Yu-jung, *Min-hai tseng-yen* 閩海贈言, 24, 28, 85, 96; Chu I-tsun, *Ching-i k'ao*, 88/6b, 90/2b, 114/3b; SK (1930), 8/7a, 12/5a, 42/8a; Yao Chin-yüan (1957), 32; T. Watters, *Essays on the Chinese Language* (Shanghai, 1889), 83-84; Laurence G. Thompson, "The Earliest Chinese Eyewitness Accounts of the Formosan Aborigines," MS, XXIII (1964), 170.

Chaoying Fang

CH'EN To 陳鐸 (T. 大聲, H. 秋碧), early 16th century poet and painter, was of the military registry in Nanking. According to Shen Te-fu (*q.v.*), they collaborated once in writing the famous ch'ü(曲) "Tung-feng chuan sui-hua" 東風轉歲華 (the east wind turns the season round). Ch'ien Ch'ien-i (ECCP), in writing the preface to the poems of the Hsi She 夕社 (the Evening Club), said in part: "During the Hung-chih and Cheng-te eras Ch'en To and Hsü Lin (*q.v.*) were well known in Nanking as writers of dramatic lyrics." In any event, Ch'en To was a marked man in this element in his day. His great-grandfather was Ch'en Wen 文 (1325–84, Pth. 孝勇), a general who supported the first Ming emperor, and was posthumously raised to the rank of a marquis. Ch'en To inherited the command of a guard in Nanking, but he distinguished himself more by writing lyrics than by military exploits. He named his studio Ch'iu-pi hsüan 秋碧軒 (Autumn verdure) and his hall Ch'i-i chü 七一居 (Seven-one dwelling).

Ch'en was one of the first writers of san ch'ü 散曲 (dramatic lyrics) of the Ming dynasty. Shen Te-fu considered them as beautiful as those of the Yüan masters. They were known as *Ch'iu-pi yüeh-fu* 樂府, 1 *ch.*, and *Li-yün chi-ao* 梨雲寄傲, 1 *ch.*, both reprinted in modern times. His other writings, known as *Ch'iu-pi-hsüan chi* 軒集 and *Hsiang-yüeh-t'ing chi* 香月亭集, seem to be no longer extant. He wrote two operas, *Na-chin-lang* 納錦郎, of which only four acts remain, and *Hao-yin-yüan* 好姻緣, which has been lost. The former is found in *Ch'en Ta-sheng tsa-chü*

大聲雜著, a Ming edition. Neither of these is mentioned in the *Ssu-k'u* catalogue.

Although Nanking was first established as the capital by Chu Yüan-chang, literary activities there were hardly known in the early years of the dynasty. It was in the Cheng-te era that Ch'en To, Hsü Lin, Chin Ts'ung 金琮 (T. 子玉, 1449–1501), and Hsieh Hsüan 謝璿 (name changed later to Hsieh Ch'eng-chü 承舉, T. 文卿, 子象, 1460–1524) joined in making it an artistic and literary center. The golden age came when Ku Lin (*see* Yüan Ch'iung) became the recognized leader of the day.

About the same time there was another Ch'en To (T. 木宣, H. 鹿崖), a native of Nanking, who left a collection of literary writings entitled *Tien-yu chi* 滇游集.

Bibliography

1/286/19b; 5/115/33a; 40/38/7b; 43/3/6b; 64/丁/1287; 65/4/1a; 84/丙/95b; 86/11/16b; Wang Shih-chen, *I-yüan chih-yen*, 152/21b; Shen Te-fu, *Yeh-hu pien* (1959 ed.), 25/640; Lu Ch'ien 盧前, *Yin-hung-i so-k'o ch'ü* 飲虹簃所刻曲(1932); *id., Chung-kuo hsi-ch'ü kai-lun* 中國散曲概論 (1936), 76; Jen No 任訥, *San ch'ü kai-lun* (Taipei, 1964), 77; *id., Ch'ü hsieh* 諧 (Taipei, 1964), 3/52; Fu Hsi-hua 傅惜華, *Ming-tai ch'uan-ch'i ch'üan-mu* 明代傳奇全目 (Peking, 1959), 18; *Kiang-nan t'ung-chih* (1736), 151/23, 166/44; Ch'en Tso-lin 陳作霖, *Chin ling t'ung-chuan*金陵通傳 (1904), 14/8b.

Liu Lin-sheng

CH'EN Yu-liang 陳友諒, 1320/21–October 3, 1363, a native of Yü-sha hsien 玉沙縣 which was incorporated into Mien-yang 沔陽, Hukuang, in 1376, was a leading rebel at the end of the Yüan dynasty. Ch'en assassinated Hsü Shou-hui (*q.v.*), the emperor of T'ien-wan, and founded the succession state of Han 漢 in June, 1360. Throughout his reign of three years he was the principal antagonist of Chu Yüan-chang, whose forces were to defeat and kill him in the battle of Poyang Lake. The state of Han survived until the surrender of the second emperor on March 22, 1364.

Ch'en Yu-liang owed his surname to the fact that his grandfather, surnamed Hsieh 謝, had joined his wife's household and taken her name. Ch'en's family for generations had been fishermen and he, too, learned the trade. He managed, however, to become sufficiently schooled to serve as a clerk in the government of his district. A physically powerful man with military ambitions, he found clerical work distasteful and the rebellion of Hsü Shou-hui in 1351 provided him with an opportunity to leave it for a career more to his liking. He entered the service of Ni Wen-chün, one of Hsü's most prominent military officers (*see* Hsü Shou-hui). Presumably because of his clerical experience, he began as a secretary but soon persuaded his patron to give him a military command. He prospered in this role, won a formidable reputation, and built up a following of his own. During the years from 1357 to 1360, he proceeded to enlarge his power within the state by assassinating Ni Wen-chün, a military rival, Chao P'u-sheng (*see* Hsü Shou-hui), and finally his emperor. In each instance he absorbed most of the victim's retainers. This now left him at the head of what was, in effect, a loose coalition, and he undertook to build his new state of Han with the vast material resources of the one that he had just overthrown. According to the available sources about Ch'en and his state, all written by authors supporting his opponent, Chu Yüan-chang, it was a brash and ill-omened beginning. After he had accomplished the murder of Hsü, Ch'en hurried to the stronghold of Ts'ai-shih采石, which had been the scene of the crime, selected a temple there to serve as his temporary palace, and had himself installed as emperor under the defiant reign-title Ta-i 大義 (Greatly righteous). Since there was no one in Ch'en's entourage capable of managing such matters properly, the inaugural ceremony was bungled and Heaven's displeasure manifested in a torrential downpour that drenched the hats and gowns of the participants. The task of absorbing the defunct state, moreover, was never successfully accomplished. Ch'en did succeed in forming a loyal central government, but local power remained in the hands of military men who often disputed his authority. In the central government, Ch'en's chief counselor (丞相), Chang Pi-hsien 張必先, and Grand Marshal (太尉) Chang Ting-pien 張定邊 had probably been his followers. Hsü's old associate, the messianic sectarian Tsou P'u-sheng (*see* Hsü Shou-hui), continued in the office of grand preceptor. He gave the title of prince to each of his brothers. Ch'en Yu-jen, called the fifth prince (五王), was conspicuous as a military leader and as a favorite of Ch'en Yu-liang. One of Ch'en's first acts as emperor was to attempt a diplomatic coup against his rival and eastern neighbor, Chu Yüan-chang. He sent a representative to Chang Shih-ch'eng (*q.v.*), Chu's opponent on his eastern flank, proposing a joint attack against the common enemy. Fortunately no doubt for Chu, Chang was not moved to action and Ch'en had to undertake his expedition down the Yangtze without cooperation. Chu was aware of his intentions, and led him into a well-prepared trap at Lung-wan 龍灣 (near the present Hsia-kuan 下關, northwest of Nanking). Ch'en fled the ensuing disaster in a single small vessel, but Chang Chih-hsiung 張志熊, leading the former subordinates of Chao P'u-sheng, who resented the assassination of their late chief, defected to Chu after the battle. Chu sent forces in pursuit of Ch'en, who escaped to Chiang-chou 江州 (modern Kiukiang), his capital.

After his disastrous first campaign as emperor, Ch'en remained generally on the defensive against Chu Yüan-chang. Although he put up a stiffer resistance as he fell back on the center of his state, he was undermined by the frequent defections that were to continue to occur throughout his reign. One of the most damaging of these came in October, when Ou P'u-hsiang 歐普祥 surrendered the city of Yüan-chou 袁州 (Kiangsi) to Chu. As an early associate of Hsü Shou-hui, Ou had taken part in the messianic disorders of 1351. The following year he was sent into Kiangsi, where he campaigned successfully against the Yüan and became notorious for the swath of destruction he left behind along his line of march. By the end of 1353 he had firm control over the burned and battered area of Yüan-chou, and Hsü subsequently rewarded him with the title of duke of Yüan 袁國公. After Ch'en assassinated Hsü, he attempted to conscript soldiers in Ou's territory. This precipitated an open breach, and, with the encouragement of an agent of Chu Yüan-chang who had been in Yüan-chou since the year before, Ou now secretly made his submission. When Ch'en belatedly learned of the defection, his brother, Ch'en Yu-jen, was sent to recapture the city. The attempt failed, however, and the latter was captured, given a whipping, and imprisoned. Tsou P'u-sheng, representing Ch'en Yu-liang, negotiated Ch'en Yu-jen's release by entering into an agreement that Ch'en and Ou should thenceforth respect each other's borders. In February of 1361 Ou, now apparently safe from reprisal, reaffirmed his earlier allegiance to Chu and, until his death in 1364, he was the ruler of Yüan-chou. Ch'en suffered more reverses in 1361. After recovering and then losing Anking in August and September, he abandoned in quick succession his capital at Chiang-chou with its large stores of grain, Nan-k'ang 南康, and, in the area of Hsü Shou-hui's uprising, Ch'i-chou 蘄州 and Huang-chou 黃州. The Han capital had now to be moved farther up the Yangtze to Wuchang and a number of Ch'en's Kiangsi officers made this the occasion to surrender more cities to Chu Yüan-chang. During 1362 the Han showed some signs of reviving militarily. Helped by furious dissension among some of the officers who had gone over to Chu and by some redefections, Ch'en was able to reclaim several Kiangsi cities. North of the Yangtze, Ch'i-chou at least was also recovered. Early in 1363, however, Ch'en found Chu Yüan-chang still firmly entrenched in what, at one time, had been the southern and eastern portions of Han.

Ch'en Yu-liang now gathered strength for a supreme effort to reverse the course of the war. With a force said to have numbered in the tens of thousands, he descended the Yangtze to Poyang Lake, and crossed it to the south shore, where, on June 5, 1363, he began a siege of Hung-tu 洪都 (modern Nanchang). The city, defended by some of Chu Yüan-chang's best officers, did not fall and on August 25 Chu himself appeared with a relief expedition off Hu-k'ou 湖口, where the arm of the lake meets the Yangtze. Ch'en abruptly broke off the siege, reembarked his army, and sailed north to meet the approaching force. The two fleets met August 29 off K'ang-lang 康郎 Island and commenced a four-day battle. Ch'en, who had lost two of his brothers, Ch'en Yu-jen and Ch'en Yu-kuei 友貴, in the fighting, then withdrew to an anchorage where he remained for several weeks. Here two of his officers, despairing of victory, defected with their following. Chu attempted to goad Ch'en to attack by sending him letters in a tone calculated to infuriate him, but it was not until October 3, when Ch'en's food was exhausted and a foraging expedition had failed, that he made a last attempt to escape through Chu's fleet to the Yangtze. On that day, Ch'en was struck by an arrow and killed. This loss demoralized his officers and most of them surrendered within a few days. Chang Ting-pien and Ch'en Li 陳理, Ch'en Yu-liang's son, escaped by night to the Yangtze and brought the emperor's body back to Wuchang.

The state of Han succumbed less than six months after its founder's death. Ch'en Li was installed as the second emperor under the reign title Te-shou 德壽 at Wuchang. There were other cities than the capital still garrisoned by Han officers, but few of these remained loyal. Wuchang was invested at once, with Chu coming from Nanking at the year's end and again in March to direct the assault. The failure of a relief expedition led by Chang Pi-hsien so disheartened the defenders that Ch'en Li was persuaded by an old Han officer, now employed by Chu, to surrender. On the 22d of March, 1364, Ch'en Li, stripped to the waist, his jade ring in his mouth, prostrated himself before Chu. Chu dealt magnanimously with the defeated House. Ch'en Li, his paternal grandfather, Ch'en P'u-ts'ai 普才, and two surviving uncles, Ch'en Yu-fu 富 and Ch'en Yu-chen 眞, were all granted titles of nobility and Ch'en Li was allowed to keep the contents of the treasury. Years later (1372) Ch'en Li and the similarly dispossessed heir of Ming Yü-chen (q.v.) quarreled with some of Chu's supporters, and, for their own safety, were placed under the protection of the king of Korea. After Ch'en Li's surrender, the destruction of surviving Han forces continued into 1365. Hsiung T'ien-jui 熊天瑞, a former musician of Ching-chou 荆州 (Hukuang), and one-time adherent of Hsü Shou-hui, still held the upper portions of the Kan River 贛江 valley. After ignoring orders to come to the aid of Ch'en Yu-liang at Poyang Lake, he went to the succor of Chang Shih-ch'eng, then fighting for his life against Chu Yüan-chang. Captured by Chu's forces at the collapse of Soochow, he suffered execution (October 1, 1367).

[Editors' note: According to *Annam tsūshi* 安南通史 by Iwamura Shigemitsu 岩村成允, Ch'en Yu-liang was the son of an Annamite prince. We owe this reference to a communication from Chan Hok-lam who, while reading Hsü Yün-ch'iao's 許雲樵 Chinese translation of Iwamura's work, found this surprising information, heretofore unknown to Chinese historians, and brought it to our attention. In Iwamura's account, Ch'en Yu-liang led an army to the border between Annam and China to ask for peace and marriage. In 1355 Chu Yüan-chang, then named Chu Te-yü 德裕, called himself emperor and became the founder of the Ming state; in 1359, at war with Ch'en Yu-liang, he sent an embassy to

Annam to ask for friendly relations, and Annam sent back a messenger to find out the results of his war with Ch'en; in 1360 Ch'en Yu-liang enthroned himself as emperor of Han; in 1361 Chu defeated Ch'en and asked for the help of Annam, which was denied. In 1366 the Han state came to an end. Also according to Iwamura, the name of Ch'en Yu-liang's father was Ch'en I-chi 益稷, who was a younger brother of the Annamite king, Trần Khoan 陳晃 (r. 1258–78), and held the Annamite title of prince of Chieu 昭國王; he surrendered to the Mongols in 1285, was given the title of king of Annam, but the Mongol forces were defeated that year and in 1288, and so failed in their plan to return him to his own country. A check of the *Yüan-shih* shows that Ch'en I-chi lived in Wu-chang the rest of his life, was given by the Mongol emperor various honorary titles and even appointed an associate governor of Hukuang (湖廣行省平章政事), with a grant of two hundred *ch'ing* of land or over three thousand acres; when he died in 1329 at seventy-six *sui* (born in 1254?), he was accorded the posthumous name, Prince Chung-i 忠懿王. Now, if Ch'en Yu-liang were indeed such a man's son, it seems rather incredible that he should have started his career as a yamen clerk, as the Ming records assert. The age of Ch'en I-chi seems, furthermore, to militate against such a relationship.]

Bibliography

1/123/1a; 3/113/7b; 5/119/2a; 61/89/17b; MSL (1962), T'ai-tsu, 0166, 0364; Ch'ien Ch'ien-i (ECCP), *Kuo-ch'u ch'ün-hsiung shih-lüeh* 國初羣雄事略, *ch.* 4; Sung Lien, *P'ing Han lu; id., P'ing chiang-han sung*; Ku Ying-t'ai (ECCP), *Ming-ch'ao chi-shih pen-mo, chüan 3; Iwamura Shige-mitsu, Annam tsūshi* (Tokyo, 1941), 98, 109, 118 (tr. into Chinese by Hsü Yün-ch'iao, *An-nan t'ung-shih* (Singapore, 1957), 67, 74; Nakayama Hachiro 中山八郎, "Chin Yū-ryō no daiikkai Nankin kōgeki" 陳友諒の第一回南京攻擊, *Suzuki Shun Kyōju Kanreki Kinen Tōyōshi Ronsō* 鈴木俊教授還暦記念東洋史論叢 (Tokyo, 1964), 447.

Romeyn Taylor

CH'EN Yü-chiao 陳與郊 (T. 廣野, H. 隅陽, 虞陽, 禹陽, 玉陽仙史), March 16, 1544 –January 17, 1611, scholar-official, came from the well-known Ch'en family of Hai-ning 海寧, Chekiang. He was the eldest son of Ch'en Chung-chien 中漸 (T. 風山) and the brother of Ch'en Yü-hsiang (ECCP, p. 96) whose branch of the family produced several high officials in the Ch'ing period. After achieving the *hsiu-ts'ai* at the age of fifteen, Ch'en Yü-chiao married the daughter of a family named Chu 朱 from Chin-t'an 金壇 in the prefecture of Chinkiang. They were of the same age. After graduating as *chü-jen* in 1567 and *chin-shih* in 1574, he received an appointment as prefectural judge of Ho-chien-fu 河間府, but was transferred to Shun-te 順德-fu in the same capacity the following year. In 1582 he was summoned to Peking as a supervising secretary of the office of scrutiny for Personnel, rising six years later to be head of that office. In the years 1586 and 1589 he took part as an assistant examiner in the metropolitan examinations. His last appointment (made Feb. 23, 1590) was as vice minister of the Court of the Imperial Sacrifices and overseer of the College of Translators. A few months later, however, he retired to attend a function honoring his mother on her eightieth birthday, but she died just before his arrival.

Ch'en's career as a bureaucrat seems to have been only moderately successful. Having passed the metropolitan examination under the supervision of Wang Hsi-chüeh (*q.v.*) and having later attached himself to the party of Shen Shih-hsing (*q.v.*), his progress up the official ladder was good only during the years in which they were in power, from 1584 to 1591. On February 29, 1592, during the mourning period following his mother's death, the censor Chang Ying-yang 張應揚 (T. 以言, 1550–1600, cs 1583) accused him of having received bribes when he was officiating in the metropolitan examinations. As a result he was cashiered.

The Ch'en clan in Hai-ning had become prosperous over several generations through its enterprise in the salt monopoly. After his years in government employ Ch'en Yü-chiao lived for a time in luxury. He renovated a country villa in Hai-ning which he named Yü-yüan 隅園, and started on his writing career. [Editors' note: This garden has an interesting history. First built in the 12th century for the descendants of General Wang Ping, who lost his life in 1126 defending Taiyuan against the invading Jurchen, it passed centuries later into the hands of the Ch'en family who maintained it through most of the Ch'ing dynasty. A current story had it that the Ch'ien-lung emperor was the son of a lady of this family. This is said to have accounted for his frequent visits to the Ch'en home and garden, the name of which he changed to An-lan yüan. (*See* ECCP, p. 97, and Meng Sen [BDRC], "Hai-ning Ch'en-chia" 家)]. Unfortunately, in 1605, his eldest son, Ch'en Tsu-kao 祖皐, became involved in a fight between salt merchants and government salt-control guards. The incident occurred when Ch'en Tsu-kao was staying at his father-in-law's place, his boat encountering the feuding parties on the river. One government officer lost his life in the affair. As a result, Ch'en Tsu-kao was sentenced to prison for about ten years, and his wife in shame hanged herself in 1606. Ch'en Yü-chiao spent most of his fortune in an effort to free his son, and then broke down and died in 1611; six months after his death his wife also died. His son was exonerated and released in 1615.

Though Ch'en Yü-chiao was not a marked man in his public career, he did achieve some fame in the field of literature, leaving quite a number of literary and dramatic works. The editors of the *Ssu-k'u* catalogue mention several of them, but copied none into the Imperial Library. Among the books Ch'en edited or compiled one may mention: *Tan-kung chi-chu* 檀弓集註, 2 *ch.*; *Fang-yen lei-chü* 方言類聚, 4 *ch.*; *Kuang hsiu-tz'u chih-nan* 廣修辭指南, 20 *ch.*, a supplement to

the *Hsiu-tz'u chih-nan* compiled by P'u Nan-chin 浦南金 (T. 伯兼, cj 1522) in 1557; *Tu-lü shih chu* 杜律詩註, 2 *ch.*, a punctuated edition with commentary on the *Tu-lü yen-i* 演義, the poems of Tu Fu (712-70) with annotations by Chang Hsing 張性 of the Yüan; and *Wen-hsüan chang-chü* 文選章句, 28 *ch.* All of these have survived. He himself wrote the *Ch'en feng-ch'ang chi* 陳奉常集, which includes, besides his dramatic works, three collections of his essays entitled *Yü-yüan chi* 集, 18 *ch.*, *Huang-men chi* 黃門集, 3 *ch.*, and *P'in-ch'uan chi* 蘋川集, 8 *ch.* His collection of dramas entitled *Ling-ch'ih-fu* 詅癡符 consists of four plays, or ch'uan-ch'i 傳奇 The first of these plays is the *Ying-t'ao meng* 櫻桃夢, based on the T'ang romance *Ying-t'ao ch'ing-i* 青衣 (*see T'ai-p'ing kuang-chi* 太平廣記, *ch.* 281). The second play is a revised version of the *Pao-chien chi* by Li K'ai-hsien (*q.v.*) entitled *Ling-pao tao* 靈寶刀, based on the story of Lin Ch'ung 林沖 in the *Shui-hu chuan* (*see* Lo Kuan-chung). The third is the *Ch'i-lin chui* 麒麟墜 (or *Ch'i-lin jih* 闚), based on the story of Han Shih-chung (1089-1151) and his wife Liang Hung-yü 梁紅玉, which seems to be a revised version of the *Shuang-lieh chi* 雙烈記 by an earlier dramatist Chang Ssu-wei 張四維 (T. 治卿, H. 年山, 屏山, 五山秀才). The fourth is a romantic play based on the T'ang story *Yü-hsiao chuan* 玉蕭傳, entitled *Ying-wu chou* 鸚鵡洲. It is interesting to note that in this drama collection Ch'en used pen names such as Kao Man-ch'ing 高漫卿 and Jen Tan-hsien 任誕軒. It is possible that he considered, as did many of his contemporaries, that playwriting was below the dignity of a one-time official. A recent edition of his four *ch'uan-ch'i* is included in the *Ku-pen hsi-ch'ü ts'ung-k'an* 古本戲曲叢刊, series 2. Ch'en wrote also five plays in the Northern style, or tsa-chü 雜劇, two of which are lost. The three extant ones included in the *Sheng Ming* 盛明 *tsa-chü* are: *Chao-chün ch'u sai* 昭君出塞, *Wen-chi ju sai* 文姬入塞, and *Yüan shih i-ch'üan* 袁氏義犬. The motive for writing the last, according to the editors of *Yeh-hu pien* 野獲編 and *Hang-chou-fu chih* 杭州府志, is that Ch'en intended to discountenance his students for their refusal to help him in his efforts to release his son from prison. But the author of the *Ch'ü-hai tsung-mu t'i-yao* 曲海總目提要 considered that his targets were certain disgruntled students of Chang Chü-cheng (*q.v.*) and Wang Hsi-chüeh.

His other writings have been lost, but they are listed in the *Hai-ning-chou chih-kao* 志稿 and the *Hang-chou-fu chih* (1685). From the little information available, one gathers that when the *Ku ming-chia tsa-chü* 古名家雜劇, a collection of dramas of the Yüan and Ming periods, was published by the bookseller Hsü 徐 of Hsin-an 新安, at the end of the Wan-li period, Ch'en was one of its editors, and aimed at collecting the plays then popular in Peking.

Bibliography

1/217/9a, 220/17a, 230/3b, 231/1b, 16b, 19a, 235/1a 236/5a, 305/6b; KC (1958), 4413, 4548, 4596, 4618, 4622; MSL (1966), Shen-tsung, 4018, 4112, 4115, 4116, 4551; SK (1930), 24/2b, 43/1b, 56/7a, 138/3a, 174/3a, 179/6a, 191/1a; *Hai-ning-chou chih-kao* (1922), 8/8a, 10a, 11b, 12/ 典籍 2/10, 3/ 2b, 4a, 29/文苑/2b; *Hang-chou-fu chih* (1888, reprinted 1922), 134/16a, 18a, 141/6b; Li Wei-chen 李維楨, *T'ai-ch'ang shao-ch'ing Ch'en-kung mu-chih-ming* 太常少卿陳公墓誌銘, *Huang Ming wen-hai* (microfilm), *ch.* 77; Shen Te-fu, *Wan-li yeh-hu-pien* (Peking, 1959), 423; Fu Hsi-hua傅惜華, *Ming-tai tsa-chü ch'üan-mu* 明代雜劇全目 (Peking, 1958), 152; *id.*, *Ming-tai ch'uan-ch'i ch'üan-mu* (Peking, 1959), 108; *Ku-pen hsi-ch'ü ts'ung-k'an*, ser. 2 (1955); Shen T'ai 沈泰 (late Ming), *Sheng Ming tsa-chü*, *ch.* 9,10, 11; Ch'en Yü-chiao, *Yü-yüan chi* (NCL microfilm); Ya-gisawa Hajime, *Mindai gekisakka kenkyū* (*see* K'ang Hai), 269; Meng Sen, "Hai-ning Ch'en-chia," *Kuo-li Pei-ching ta-hsüeh wu-shih chou-nien chi-nien lun-wen chi* 國立北京大學五十週年紀念論文集 (Peking, 1948), 12.

Ching-hwa Ho Jen

CH'EN Yü-pi 陳于陛 (T. 元忠, H. 玉壘), 1545 January 30, 1597, grand secretary from 1594 to 1597, was a native of Nan-ch'ung 南充, Szechwan. His ancestors for centuries lived in this western province, first in Lang-chung 閬中, then in Nan-ch'ung, both districts situated on the Chia-ling River嘉陵江, not far north of Chung-king. The Ch'en family originally was of peasant stock, but after the time of Ch'en Chi 紀, five generations before Ch'en Yü-pi's time, they moved into the scholar-gentry class. It seems that this social change developed through marriage. The record suggests that by marrying into the P'u 蒲 family over several generations, the Ch'en family was able to obtain schooling for its sons over a long period. Finally, Ch'en Ta-tao 大道, one of Ch'en Yü-pi's grand-uncles, passed the metropolitan examinations and became a *chin-shih* in 1517.

Ch'en Yü-pi's father, Ch'en I-ch'in 以勤 (T. 逸甫, H. 松谷, 青居山人, October 11, 1511-August 3, 1586, did even better; he not only became a *chin-shih*, but was also selected *shu-chi-shih* 庶吉士 to study in the Hanlin Academy in 1541. Rising steadily in officialdom, Ch'en I-ch'in was appointed grand secretary in 1567. Confronted with many difficulties as a high official in the central government, he very wisely retired at the age of sixty *sui* in 1570. Hence, he was able to enjoy a life of leisure for sixteen more years at his home in Szechwan. After his death, he was given, along with other honors, the name Wen-tuan 文端·

Ch'en Yü-pi was born in Peking at the time that his father was serving as a corrector in the Hanlin Academy. A precocious youth, he obtained the *chü-jen* degree in 1561 at the early age of seventeen *sui*. Seven years later, he became a *chin-shih* and was made a member of the Hanlin in 1568, when his father was grand secretary. In 1570, appointed a compiler, he took part in the compilation of the *shih-lu* of both the Chia-ching and Lung-ch'ing periods (1522–72). When his father retired, Ch'en Yü-pi accompanied him on the trip to Szechwan. Shortly after his return to Peking in 1572, his mother died, and he once more had to go to the ancestral home to observe the mourning period. On his father's seventieth birthday (actually sixty-ninth) in 1580, and then on his father's death in 1586, he also had to interrupt his official career to return to Szechwan.

After his recall to Peking in 1589, following the observance of mourning for his father, his promotions were rapid. By 1594 he was appointed grand secretary of Tung-ko 東閣. While performing some ceremonial duties during the winter solstice of 1596, he caught cold. From this illness he never recovered and died in January of the following year. All appropriate honors were accorded him, including the posthumous name of Wen-hsien 文獻.

During this last sojourn in the capital he submitted memorials on various topics. He advised on the importance of an early investiture of the heir apparent; he admonished the emperor for not holding court; he made suggestions on both civil and border affairs; and in the winter of 1594/95, he protested the wholesale demotion and castigation of censorial officials. Memorials at this time, however, were too often left unanswered and even unacknowledged; so most of his efforts were in vain.

Nevertheless, one of Ch'en Yü-pi's memorials proved to be an exception, namely, his suggestion to establish a project for the compilation of an official history of the Ming dynasty, to be called *Kuoch'ao cheng-shih* 國朝正史. Not only was it accepted, but it was also followed up and carried out. The emperor favored the idea, the ministry of Rites made certain deliberations, and other high officials supported it with further suggestions. On May 15, 1594, thirty-one officials were appointed to undertake the task with Ch'en Yü-pi at the head of the list, and all the grand secretaries as joint official editors-in-chief. Following another four months of preparation, the office for its compilation was duly opened on September 15, 1594. Plans were made to collect source materials and government documents, as well as private works and family records. From time to time more scholar-officials were added to the staff. Altogether about fifty were involved, including many well-known names, such as Chiao Hung, Tung Ch'i-ch'ang (both in ECCP), Yeh Hsiang-kao (*q. v.*), and Yüan Tsung-tao (*see* Yüan Hung-tao).

The project seems to have progressed smoothly under Ch'en Yü-pi's direction. His untimely death was certainly a blow. Then a catastrophic fire in the palace followed on August 1, 1597, and the project's quarters were destroyed. Five days later, Chang Wei 張位 (T. 明成 or 名誠, cs of 1568, and grand secretary, 1592–98), memorialized asking for a temporary halt to the compilation project because of the fire. It was stopped, not just temporarily, but for good. Indeed, about a decade later, one official did ask for its resumption, but his suggestion produced neither result nor enthusiasm. The project came into existence without fanfare, and died almost without any trace. When a recent scholar studied the compilation of the *Ming-shih*, he dealt strictly with its history in the Ch'ing period, and the Wan-li project received no mention. (Li Chin-hua 李晉華, *Ming-shih tsuan-hsiu k'ao* 明史纂修考, YCHP monograph 3, 1933). T'an Ch'ien (*q. v.*) asserts that he once saw some parts of the unfinished draft of the work and remarks that it was mediocre.

Notwithstanding the ill-fated adventure, the official Ming history project of 1594 to 1597 appears not to have been as fruitless as it seemed. First, the Chien-wen reign of four years (1399–1402) was officially restored to history. Prior to this time, the Hung-wu reign was recorded as four years longer to cover the Chien-wen period. In recording years the use of Chien-wen had been forbidden by Chu Ti (*q. v.*). The official Ming history project served to rectify this misrepresentation. Second, several of the compilers on the project left writings which seem to be without much doubt works done for the official history. The most memorable are the following titles: the *Huang Ming tien-li chih* by Kuo Cheng-yü (*q. v.*, appointed compiler 1594); the *Kuo-shih ho-ch'ü chih* 國史河渠志 by Wu Tao-nan 吳道南 (T. 會甫, H. 曙谷, 1550-October 11, 1623, cs 1589, appointed compiler in 1594, and grand secretary 1613-17); the *Huang Ming ping-chih k'ao* 皇明兵志考 by Shih Chi-hsieh 史繼偕 (T. 聯岳, 世程, cs of 1592, appointed compiler in 1594, and grand secretary 1620-21, d. *ae.* 75 *sui, ca.* 1629); and the *Yüeh-lü chih* 樂律志 by Huang Ju-liang 黃汝良 (T. 明起, cs of 1586, appointed compiler 1594). These titles suggest the intended sections on the rites, the river system, the military system, and music for the official history. It is not without interest that at this same juncture Chu Tsai-yü (*q. v.*), though not a compiler, was laboring on the calendar and on music; he submitted his *Li-shu* in 1595 and completed his *Lü-lü ching-i* in 1596. Last but not least, one must mention Chiao Hung's *Kuo-shih ching-chi chih*, which was definitely prepared as the bibliographical section for the official Ming history. Even Chiao's larger work, the *Kuo-ch'ao hsien-cheng lu* 國朝獻徵錄, a collection of Ming biographies with sources generally cited, was inspired by his participation in the history project. Furthermore, compilation of the *Kuo-ch'ao cheng-shih*, in spite of its brief existence, established a trend and influenced many late Ming scholars to make similar attempts.

Ch'en Yü-pi himself left only one slender volume of notes, entitled *I-chien* 意見, which, although listed in the Index of the 18th century, came to be printed in several collectanea, the most recent being the *Ts'ung-shu chi-ch'eng* 叢書集成. The notes, totaling eighty-one, are all short, mostly on Classics and the conduct of life. There are about a dozen notes on Ming topics. He criticized Wang Yang-ming's (Wang Shou-jen, *q. v.*) philosophy as superficial and Buddhistic. In one note on literature, he emphasized the importance of having one's own opinions (意見)

from which the title was perhaps derived. His collected works, known as *Wan-chüan-lou chi* 萬卷樓集, are probably not extant.

The *Ming-shih* points out that throughout the Ming dynasty the only instance of a father and son both rising to the high official position of grand secretary was that of Ch'en I-ch'in and Ch'en Yü-pi. About the same time there was another Ch'en Yü-pi who was a native of Ch'ü-chou 曲周, Pei-Chihli, and a *chin-shih* of 1559.

Bibliography

1/193/14a, 217/5a; 5/17/41a, 183a; MSL (1966), Shen-tsung, 5040, 5107, 5812; KC (1958), 4725, 4733, 4798; *Ming-shih i-wen chih, pu-pien, fu-pien* 明史藝文志補編, 附編 (Peking, 1959), 659; SK (1930), 125/3a; Sun Tien-ch'i (1957), 178.

Lienche Tu Fang

Ch'en Yung-pin 陳用賓 (T. 道亨, H. 毓台, Pth. 襄毅), fl. 1547-1617, a native of Chin-chiang 晉江, Fukien, *chü-jen* of 1567 and *chin-shih* of 1571, distinguished himself as governor of Yunnan, a post he held for fifteen years (1593-1608). His initial office was the magistracy of Ch'ang-chou 長洲 (Soochow), 1572-75. He then received an appointment as a censor, in which capacity he served as salt inspector in Shansi, in 1577, and at Huai-an 淮安 (1579). Early in 1582, he was appointed junior assistant administration commissioner in Szechwan, then promoted to surveillance vice commissioner in Chekiang (1584-87), and later made administration vice commissioner in the same province (1587-90). After serving a three-year term, as the administration commissioner of Hukuang, he was made governor of Yunnan early in 1593.

Beginning in 1253, when the Mongols overran Ta-li 大理, and down to Ch'en's time, there were intermittent hostilities between China and Burma. Realizing that the deeply rooted problem could not be solved easily, Ch'en Yung-pin paid much attention to border defense. Shortly after his arrival in Yunnan he made a series of inspection trips to the frontier. When he saw the strategic importance of Man-ha 蠻哈, he established a military outpost there. In addition, he weeded out the older soldiers and built up a new army directly under his own control. When the Burmese resumed their petty raids in 1593, he launched a diplomatic maneuver before taking any military action. Knowing that the Siamese and the Burmese were enemies, he sent a messenger to Siam asking the king to take action on behalf of the Chinese. The mission proved a fruitful one. The attack on Burma from both the Siamese and the Chinese sides brought Ch'en a decisive victory over the Burmese. For this he was promoted to the rank of a vice minister of War while concurrently holding the position of governor of Yunnan. His strategy was followed nearly two centuries later by the Ch'ienlung emperor (see Hung-li, ECCP), who sent a punitive expedition to Burma during the years 1765 to 1769.

Immediately after the war was over, Ch'en made another inspection trip to the border areas. He found that the distance between Teng-yüeh 騰越 and the pacification offices of Meng-yang 猛養, Mu-pang 木邦, and Nan-tien 南甸, was too great for the officer in charge of defense stationed at Teng-yüeh. In order to strengthen the ties among them, he added eight strategic military outposts known as T'ung-pi 銅壁, T'ieh-pi 鐵壁, T'ien-ma 天馬, Shen-hu 神護, Wan-jen 萬仞, Han-lung 漢龍, Chü-shih 巨石, and Hu-chü 虎踞. Since these border areas had been repeatedly used as a battleground, the inhabitants there were either frightened away or killed. He therefore encouraged the people of overpopulated regions to migrate into these borderlands, alloting land to them and equipping them as military colonists. His arrangements put the frontier more effectively under the control of the Yunnan government.

During the decade from 1593 to 1603 the borderlands were quiet; no major armed clash occurred between China and Burma. (It was also these eight outposts which provided the Chinese and British diplomats with some bases for negotiations in the 1890s, and the demarcation of the southern section of the Sino-Burmese borderline was, by and large, drawn according to the line of these outposts in 1897.)

During his term of office Ch'en turned to the promotion of local education, inviting learned men as teachers to Yunnan. New schools were also added while the old ones were enlarged and improved. He did so because he knew that Yunnan had only recently been annexed and its education was backward.

The state of equilibrium on the Sino-Burmese borderlands, however, was broken shortly after Emperor Chu I-chün (q.v.) accepted in 1600 the suggestion of Yang Jung 楊榮 (d. April 1606), a eunuch tax-collector, to reopen the ruby mine at Meng-mi 猛密. Yang Jung and his colleagues, like many of the eunuchs of the time, were arrogant and corrupt. After they came to Meng-mi, they began to mistreat and enslave the tribal people. Even the aboriginal officials were sometimes insulted. As the relations between local authorities and the eunuchs deteriorated, Ch'en became keenly aware of the gravity of the situation. He pled with the emperor to call back the eunuchs and stop the mining at Meng-mi. The emperor paid no heed to his suggestion.

In 1603 the eunuchs killed several innocent aboriginal officials; a rebellion then broke out in Meng-mi where the people sided with the Burmese. After he rebuffed the allied invaders, Ch'en submitted his important memorial of August 8, in which he stated that Meng-mi was a military outpost of strategic significance and vital to the security of Yunnan. To continue mining rubies there would not only lead to further outbreaks but also give the Burmese an excuse to raid the border areas. It would be advisable, he held, to call back the eunuchs and stop the mining. His plea was once more ignored.

Exactly as Ch'en predicted, rebellion broke out again in Meng-mi in 1605. He knew that the eunuchs were the main source of the unrest and also that it was useless to ask the emperor to order them home. Ch'en withheld his troops until the eunuchs, including Yang Jung, were killed by the rebels. He next charged several officials, who had a close tie with the eunuchs, with causing the revolt, and put them in jail. He then pled with the emperor again to stop the mining. This time the emperor could not but accept Ch'en's suggestion, for Meng-mi was no longer under China's control. What Ch'en did of course was good for the nation, but it cost him the favor of the emperor and made him a bitter enemy of the eunuch group.

In 1607 a rebellion led by Feng A-k'o (see Chou Chia-mu) occurred at Wu-ting 武定. The rebels quickly reached the provincial capital, Kunming, laid siege to it, and demanded the Wu-ting prefectural seal. Unprepared to give battle, Ch'en decided to comply with the rebels' demands. As soon as they left, however, he summoned enough troops to have them suppressed early in 1608. Instead of an award, he was accused of cowardice in yielding the prefectural seal. He was sentenced to death and imprisoned awaiting execution. Several high ranking officials, such as Li T'ing-chi 李廷機 (T. 爾張, H. 九我, cs 1583, Pth. 文節) and Chou Chia-mu, implored the emperor to grant Ch'en's release. Their efforts, however, were challenged by a number of censors, apparently friends of the eunuch group, who said that these officials had been bribed. The emperor knew quite well that Ch'en was unjustly sentenced, yet he shrank from lessening the penalty because Ch'en had not protected his favorite eunuch, Yang Jung. Consequently Ch'en suffered imprisonment in Peking for nine years. During this time he turned to the study of Taoism. Ts'an-t'ung-ch'i 參同契, Chin-tan chen-li 金丹眞理, and other Taoist works became his favorite reading. He died in 1617 shortly after

being released from the jail for medical treatment. According to his biography in Ch'üan-chou-fu chih 泉州府志, he wrote a number of books, but none seems to have survived.

Ch'en Yung-pin was regarded as a competent and honest administrator and strategist as well. The people of Yunnan were grateful to him not only for his military achievements but also for his promotion of education; as a result a number of gazetteers of the province record his memorials and provide a biography of him.

Bibliography

1/315/8b; 21/19/13a; MSL(1966), Shen-tsung, ch. 121-457; CSL (1937), Kao-tsung, 783/1a, 787/2b; Yunnan t'ung-chih (1736), 16/66b, 19/21b; Teng-yüeh-chou chih (1912), 2/2a, 3/30b, 8/7a; Ch'üan-chou-fu chih (1927), 43/74b; Tien-hsi 滇繫 (1887), 8/7a; Ming-chi 明紀 (1962), 473, 477; Wang Yen-wei (ECCP, p.383), Ch'ing-chi wai-chiao shih-liao, 1/16; Hsüeh Fu-ch'eng (ECCP), Yung-an ch'üan-chi, 2/15, 37, 6/2; Chang Ch'eng-sun 張誠蓀, Chung Ying tien-mien wen-t'i 中英滇緬問題 (1937), 144; Yüan Wen-k'uei 袁文揆, et al. ed.), Tien-nan wen lüeh 滇南文略 (1900), 4/1a; Henry Randolph Davies, Report on the Expedition Sent with the Chinese Official to Find the Hu-chi, Tien-ma, and Han-lung Gates, Rangoon, 1894.

Stanley Y. C. Huang

CHENG Ho 鄭和 (1371–1433), eunuch and commander-in-chief of the Ming expeditionary fleets in the early years of the 15th century, was born into a family named Ma 馬 at K'un-yang 昆陽 in central Yunnan. His great-grandfather was named Bayan 拜顏, and his grandfather and father were both named Ḥājjī 哈只, which suggests that the two probably visited Mecca and that the family had a long tradition of Islamic faith and may have been of Mongol-Arab origin. At the beginning of the Ming dynasty, a number of generals who fought on the frontier were in charge of recruiting eunuchs for the court. In 1381, when Yunnan was pacified by an army under Fu Yu-te (*q.v.*), Cheng Ho, at that time about ten years old, was one of the children selected to be castrated. As a trainee for eunuch service, he was assigned to the retinue of Chu Ti (*q.v.*). In his early twenties, he accompanied Chu Ti on a series of military campaigns and in the course of them took up a career in the army. As his family records relate, "when he entered adulthood, he reportedly became seven feet tall and had a waist about five feet in circumference. His cheeks and forehead were high but his nose was small. He had glaring eyes and a voice as loud as a huge bell. He knew a great deal about warfare and was well accustomed to battle."

Cheng Ho's performance during the campaigns against the Mongols outside the Great Wall from 1393 to 1397 first won him the recognition and confidence of his master. During the rebellion (1399–1402), by means of which Chu Ti usurped the throne, Cheng Ho played a significant role in several vital campaigns, including the blockade of Peking in August, 1399, and the southern expedition that ended with the capture of Nanking in July, 1402; hence when Chu Ti became emperor, Cheng Ho became one of his most trusted aides. In the midst of the conflagration, the dethroned emperor Chu Yün-wen (*q. v.*) reportedly fled the capital. His subsequent whereabouts became a mystery, and it seemed probable, at least to Chu Ti, that his rival might be wandering abroad (*see* Hu Ying). As a consequence (though he doubtless had other good reasons), Chu Ti sent out expeditions overseas under the command of Cheng Ho which resulted in the most extensive maritime enterprises in the nation's history. In a period of twenty-eight years (1405–33), Cheng Ho directed the fleets which seven times visited no fewer than thirty-seven countries, beginning with Champa in the east, to the Persian Gulf, the Red Sea, and the east African coast in the west.

Cheng Ho first achieved official prominence early in 1404 when he was pro-moted to the position of director of eunuch affairs and granted the surname of Cheng. Shortly afterward he received the appointment of commander-in-chief of the first expedition. Meanwhile local officials of the eastern coastal regions were ordered to build ocean-going vessels. By July, 1405, some 1,180 ships of various sizes and types had been constructed. The large or treasure ships 寶船 were, according to measures of that time, as much as 440 feet long and 186. 2 wide, and those of medium size, or horse ships 馬船, 370 feet long and 150 wide. There were supply ships 糧船 which measured 280 feet in length and 120 in breadth, and billet ships 坐船 measuring 240 feet by 94. The battleships 戰船 equipped with cannon were much smaller, measuring only 180 feet by 68. Most of the treasure ships were the product of the Lung-chiang shipyard near Nanking (*see* Li Chao-hsiang). None of these has survived, but near the site of the shipyard was recently discovered (1957) a large wooden rudder (length 11 meters) thought to have been fashioned for one of the bigger vessels. It is now preserved in the Kiangsu provincial museum.

The first voyage began in the summer of 1405 with a 27, 800 man crew and 62 (or 63) large and 255 smaller vessels carrying cargoes of silk, embroideries, and other valuable products. Accompanied by Wang Ching-hung (*q.v.*), the second in command, Cheng Ho set sail from Liu-chia-kang 劉家港, the present Liu-ho 瀏河 in the lower Yangtze estuary, and headed toward Wu-hu-men 五虎門 on the Fukien coast and then turned south. The fleet first anchored at Hsin-chou 新州 (Quinhon) in Champa, whence it proceeded along the coast of the peninsula.

As the expedition approached the coast of Sumatra, it encountered the fleet of a powerful pirate, Ch'en Tsu-i (*see* Shih Chin-ch'ing), who for some years had been a threat to voyagers passing through the Malacca Strait. A Cantonese, who in the early 1370s fled overseas with his family, he had gathered a group of men, had usurped the chieftainship of Chiu-kang 舊港 (Palembang), and was engaged in plundering ships in the vital sea lane. Cheng Ho demanded his surrender. Pretending to comply, Ch'en mnaeuvered to attack the expeditionary fleet. One of the local Chinese leaders, Shih Chin-ch'ing, disclosed the plot to Cheng in time for him to frustrate the scheme and defeat Ch'en in a sharp engagement. More than five thousand of his crew were killed, ten vessels burned, seven others damaged, and Ch'en and his two lieutenants were captured. Ch'en was taken to the capital and executed in October, 1407, while Shih received the designation of pacification commissioner of Palembang. The victory paved the way for safe passage through the Strait, and at the same time notably enhanced the prestige of the Ming court in tropical Asia.

The second voyage took off in the late autumn of 1407, and for the first time the fleet entered the waters of the Indian Ocean. Its objective was to reach Calicut, which then commanded a focal position in maritime trade in the Indian Ocean. On account of Calicut's frequent delivery of tribute to the Ming court, Cheng Ho was instructed to extend imperial gifts and greetings to its king and his subordinates. This set the pattern for the expedition's dealings with many other native states during the subsequent voyages. During the visit a tablet and a pavilion were erected to commemorate the occasion. On the way back the expedition visited Siam and then stopped at Java. Prior to its arrival, Java had been divided into a number of hostile principalities; the Chinese believed there were merely two which they called "the East King," and "the West King." They are probably to be identified as Wikramawarddhana, ruler of the empire of Madjapahit, in Central Java, and Werabhumi of Eastern Java. Unaware that the former had gained ascendancy over the island, Cheng Ho landed his crew on the shore once controlled by the ᴍast King.

One hundred seventy members of the expedition were slaughtered by the men commanded by the West King, who then offered sixty thousand taels of gold as indemnity. The commander rejected the offer and set up a descendant of the East King as ruler. In the summer of 1409 Cheng Ho returned to Nanking to report on his mission to the emperor. Here he built a temple in honor of T'ien-fei 天妃, the goddess of the sea, to whose virtue and power he attributed the safe voyages of his fleets. The inscription on the stele erected later (May 3, 1416) has been partly translated into French by Claudine Lombard-Salmon; the complete Chinese text may be found in the book by Louis Gaillard.

After a brief stay in the capital, Cheng Ho was again sent overseas, accompanied by Wang Ching-hung and Hou Hsien (q.v.). His third voyage was comparable to the first and second in the number of men but with only 48 vessels; it lasted from September, 1409, to June, 1411. This expedition reached the same destination on the Malabar coast of India, but along the way several excursions were made, including brief visits to Siam, Malacca, Sumatra, and Ceylon. It also undertook lumbering operations and gathered fragrant herbs in the Sembilan Islands.

Two major events are attributed to this voyage. An exhibition was held near Galle in Ceylon during which some of the best Chinese products were put on display, including gold and silver candlesticks, silk embroidery, valuable textiles, incense burners, and other articles used in Buddhist ceremonies. To commemorate this occasion, a tablet, which is still extant, was erected bearing the date equivalent to February 15, 1409, and carrying a trilingual inscription (Chinese, Persian, and Tamil). The native king, Alagakkonāra (Vijaya Bāhu VI?), with some fifty thousand troops, had designs on the ships and goods of the visiting fleet, but was outgeneraled by Cheng Ho in a midnight encounter. The king was captured and taken together with his family and ministers to Nanking in July, 1411. Ceylonese legends and the account of Huang Hsing-tseng (*q.v.*) suggest that the *de jure* claimant to the throne was also brought to Nanking. The captives were shortly afterward set free and sent home.

It was the fourth voyage, which began in 1413 and ended in August, 1415, that took the expedition far beyond its earlier destinations. Under the same command but with a crew of 27,670 men and some 63 large vessels, the expedition touched at a number of new places, including the Maldives, Hormuz, the Hadramaut coast, and Aden. In Sumatra the expedition became involved in a local power struggle at Ch'iao-shan 陷 山 (Samudra-Pasai). A usurper by the name of Su-wa-la 蘇幹 剌, after murdering the king, directed his forces against the expedition, but was subsequently defeated and pursued as far as Lambri, where he and his family were captured. The prisoners were taken to Nanking on the return of the fleet. As a result of this voyage, nineteen countries sent envoys and tribute to the Ming court. Chu Ti was so pleased with the results that he rewarded all participants in the expedition according to their ranks.

In December, 1416, Cheng Ho was commissioned to escort home the envoys of the nineteen states, and embarked, possibly in the autumn of 1417, on his fifth voyage, which lasted up to August, 1419. The returning envoys, who had witnessed the delight of the Ming emperor at his first sight of a giraffe, spread the news to other countries. Hence an impressive collection of strange animals, among them lions, leopards, single-humped camels, ostriches, zebras, rhinoceroses, antelopes, and giraffes offered by rulers of several states highlighted this journey. Malindi, a new addition to the itinerary, also offered one or more giraffes. Taiwan was possibly also visited by members of the expedition during this voyage (*see* Wang Ching-hung).

The spring of 1421 saw the launching

of the sixth voyage, but Cheng may not have joined the fleet until later. It returned on September 3, 1422, accompanied by a large number of envoys from such states as Hormuz, Aden, Djofar, La-sa (Al-shṣā?), Brawa, Mogadishu, Calicut, Cochin, Caīl, Ceylont, he Maldive Islands, Lambri, Sumatra, Aru, Malacca, Kan-pa-li (Coyampadi?), Sulu, Bengal, Borneo, Ku-ma-la 古麻剌 (-lang 朗, Cabarruyan Islands?), and Ts'eng-pa 層拔 (Zanzibar). The number of countries visited on this trip has not been listed, but the expedition reached at least as far as Aden, near the mouth of the Red Sea, and Mogadishu and Brawa on the coast of east Africa. On February 27, 1424, according to the *shih-lu* (February 16, according to the *Ming-shih*), the Chinese chief of Palembang, Shih Chi-sun (*see* Shih Chin-ch'ing), requested the court to install him as pacification commissioner of Palembang, to succeed his father, and to give him a new seal. The emperor, in approving, appointed Cheng Ho to carry out the mission. Apparently, however, he never set sail, for the *shih-lu* under date of September 17, 1425, records that a certain Chang-fo-na-ma (*see* Shih Chin-ch'ing) was sent back with a seal.

In the meanwhile Chu Ti had died (August 12, 1424), and almost at once the idea of another maritime expedition came under attack. The emperor designate, Chu Kao-chih (*q.v.*), promptly (August 28) released from prison Hsia Yüan-chi (*q. v.*), perhaps the most outspoken critic of the treasure fleets, and on September 7, the very day of Chu's accession to the throne as the fourth Ming emperor, other voices joined Hsia's in recommending their abolition. This protest seems to have settled the matter, for in the following February Cheng Ho received an appointment as garrison commander of the Nanking district, and was told to maintain order in his own expeditionary forces, and consult with Wang Ching-hung and two other eunuchs. We learn further that they were apparently dissatisfied with the palace buildings as they found them, the capital having been moved to Peking five years previously, and requested that the officials in Nanking be instructed to repair them and purchase gold leaf for their ornamentation.

Only a few months later the fourth emperor died and for several years the plan to launch another expedition lay dormant. Finally in June, 1430, his successor, the fifth emperor, Chu Chan-chi (*q.v.*), issued an order for the seventh (and what proved to be the last) voyage, but it was not to leave the Fukien coast until a year and a half later. It returned in July, 1433. The mission was intended to regenerate the tributary relationships once maintained under Chu Ti, which had significantly weakened since his death. A score of states were revisited, including those along the coasts of the Arabian peninsula and eastern Africa. In this instance too ambassadors returned with the fleet, bringing such gifts as giraffes, elephants, and horses. Cheng Ho, who was already in his sixties, did not perhaps visit all of them in person, and some of the side missions were conducted by his aides. A mission from Calicut to Mecca, for example, was carried out by a eunuch named Hung Pao 洪保. The visit to Sumatra was headed by Wang Ching-hung, who also commanded part of the fleet on a mission to Java in 1434 after Cheng Ho's return. What happened to Cheng Ho from this point is not clear. It has customarily been said that he died in 1435 or 1436 at the age of sixty-five, no specific date or site of burial being indicated in contemporary sources. A later source, the *T'ung-chih Shang Chiang liang-hsien chih* 同治上江兩縣志 (preface of 1874), 3/39a, however, maintains that Cheng Ho died at Calicut and was buried at Niu-shou-shan 牛首山 outside Nanking. If this be true, he must have passed away early in 1433. So far no stone tablet has been found to confirm the place of burial. What has been found in the vicinity is a tomb attributed to another Ming eunuch named Cheng Ch'iang 鄭強.

Cheng Ho's private life is very much overshadowed by his military career, official activities, and political prominence. He did have a home built in Nanking in his early thirties. He probably had an adopted son, for in 1489 a man by the name of Cheng Hao 灝 claimed inheritance as a descendant of the eunuch.

The career of Cheng Ho is unique. For a eunuch to be able to achieve such prominence, command such a powerful force, and exert so much influence on national policy is extraordinary. He sailed the longest distance and covered the widest expanse of water during his lifetime of anyone in the world up till then. Undoubtedly he was a man of outstanding ability. This was first revealed in his early military exploits, then in his role in the rebellion of Chu Ti, and later fully demonstrated by his skill in planning and organization, and by the respect he was able to command from his subordinates. At least six images of Cheng Ho are preserved in temples in the south seas.

In the retinue he assembled were such knowledgeable individuals as Ḥasan 哈三, Ma Huan (*q.v.*), and Kuo Ch'ung-li 郭崇禮, all Muslims and fluent in Arabic. A Buddhist monk, Sheng-hui 勝慧, is also known to have participated in some of the voyages. Literary men such as Fei Hsin (*q.v.*) and Kung Chen (*see* Fei Hsin) were attracted to the expeditions. Cheng Ho's own Muslim background facilitated his dealings with rulers of many Islamic states, although he also showed an interest in Buddhism and took the religious name Fu-shan 福善. It was he who erected the tablet at Ch'ang-lo 長樂 on the Fukien coast to give honor once more to the sea goddess T'ien-fei.

The effects of his activities, which lasted for nearly three decades, are manifold. The frequent official exchanges and the distribution of gifts to rulers of various lands expanded the market for Ming products and stimulated the handicraft industries at home, especially in silks and porcelains. It was at this time too (1407) that the Ssu-i kuan 四夷館 came into being; established as a school for interpreters, it was to endure throughout the dynasty, and result in several useful vocabularies which have survived (*see* Mao Jui-cheng). The broadening of Chinese geographical horizons was particularly significant. Much of the information gathered heretofore was either secondhand or fragmentary. It was throughrecords kept by the participants and other contemporary scholars that the locations of certain distant lands were ascertained and others added to the map.

During the first three voyages, the major sea route linking China and the Muslim countries in the far west and its subsidiary sea lanes were systematically explored. From that time on, the splitting up of the fleet (分粽) from which small flotillas were dispatched to places far off the main route became a common maneuver. This approach not only helped to reduce the cost and accomplish minor missions, but also enabled the expeditions to exercise greater mobility and flexibility in visiting more distant and less accessible places. Hsin-chou, the chief port of Champa frequented by the expeditions, became the point of departure for trips to Cambodia, Siam, and the Malay peninsula in the west and Brunei, Sulu, Mindoro, and other islands in the Philippines in the east. Palembang and Java, with their large Chinese settlements and long trading relations, served as the staging areas for voyages toward Karimata, Madura, Timor, and other islands in the Lesser Sunda. Malacca, with a specially built large warehouse, was undoubtedly a major supply base for missions to places in the Straits of Malacca and northwestern Sumatra. While Calicut was the key place in the promotion of trade and diplomatic relations with the Indian states, Hormuz was unquestionably the most strategic point in the missions along the coast of Arabia, as was Mogadishu in the African visits.

A contemporary navigational chart attributable to the expeditions and preserved in the *Wu-pei chih*, compiled by Mao Yüan-i (*q.v.*) in 1621, indicates that the fleet, or probably part of it, while sailing along the coast of Africa, passed a number of places such as Mogadishu, Brawa, Juba, Malindi, Mombasa, and several others farther south in the direction of Kilwa, which is the Ch'i-er-ma乞兒馬 (and Ch'i-li-ma-er 乞力麻兒) of the *Ming-shih*. There is good indication that the fleet had taken advantage of the prevailing winds, and in so doing had sailed through the Straits of Mozambique. Some of the ships reached as far as a place called Ha-pu-er 哈甫兒, which may be identified as Kerguelan Island in the Antarctic Ocean; if this is correct, it would be the southernmost point in the world of Chinese and Arabian geographical knowledge up to that time. Other features of the map are also worthy of note: in open water the navigators reached a speed of 6 1/4 miles an hour (though often less); the words chih 指 (finger) and chiao 角 (horn) used for certain latitudes reflect a method of Arabic notation; and the omission of navigation instructions in and out of harbors may indicate the employment of pilots at this time.

In conclusion it is well to remember that, though Ming and Ch'ing historians played down the exploits of Cheng Ho, Wang Ching-hung, Hou Hsien, Ch'en Ch'eng (*q.v.*), and others of their age, a writer of fiction celebrated the admiral's voyages over one and a half centuries after their conclusion. This was Lo Mou-teng 羅懋登, author of the *San-pao t'ai-chien hsia hsi-yang chi* 三寶太監下西洋記, 20 *ch.*, published in 1597. Mixed with much that is fantastic, including an episode telling of a visit to the Underworld, which has echoes of Buddhist, Islamic, Iranian, and Christian material, are data of genuine value on the travels of the great eunuch and on the vessels which sailed the southern seas. [Editors' note: According to Professor Lien-sheng Yang, the second voyage, said to be from "late autumn,

1407" to the "summer" of 1409, could not have taken place during these years. In the first place it seems inconceivable for Cheng Ho to have returned in October, 1407, and started on his second voyage in "late autumn" of that same year. Second, the hostilities between the Chinese and the West King of Java occurred during the first voyage. Third, the *shih-lu* has no reference to a voyage under Cheng Ho during these two years. Hence the third voyage should be considered as the second, etc., until the one lasting from 1421 to 1422, which should be changed from sixth to fifth. Perhaps the one authorized in 1424, but soon canceled after the death of Chu Ti in that year, counted as the sixth at first but was later left out.]

Bibliography

1/ch. 5-9, ch. 129, ch. 304/2b, 332; 3/283/2b; MSL (1963), T'ai-tsung, 0685, 0987, 0997, 1114, 1477, 1639, 1859,1940, 2149, 2256, 2267, 2344, 2427, Jen-tsung, 0016, 0232, Hsüan-tsung, 1576, 2341; KC (1958), 1216; Cha Chi-tso (ECCP), *Tsui-wei lu, chih* 志, 32A/14a, *chuan* 傳 29/5a, 36/15a: Fei Hsin, *Hsing-ch'a sheng-lan*; Ma Huan, *Ying-yai sheng-lan*; Kung Chen, *Hsi-yang fan-kuo chih* 西洋番國志 (ed. by Hsiang Ta 向達, Peking, 1961); Hsiang Ta, ed., *Cheng Ho hang-hai t'u* 航海圖, Peking, 1961; Huang Hsing-tseng, *Hsi-yang ch'ao-kung tien-lu*; Mao Yüan-i, *Wu-pei chih*, 240; Chu Yün-ming, *Ch'ien-wen chi*, 36; Li Chao-hsiang, *Lung-chiang ch'uan-ch'ang chih*, 117; Wu Han 吳晗, "Shih-liu shih-chi i-ch'ien chih Chung-kuo yü Nan-yang" 十六世紀以前之中國與南洋, CHHP, Vol. XI (January, 1936), 137; Cheng Ho-sheng 鄭鶴聲, *Cheng Ho*, Chungking, 1945; *id., Cheng Ho i-shih hui-pien* 遺事彙編, Shanghai, 1948; Pao Tsun-p'eng包遵彭, *Cheng Ho hsia hsi-yang chih pao-ch'uan k'ao* 下西洋之寶船考, Taipei, 1961; Li Shih-hou 李士厚, *Cheng Ho chia-p'u k'ao shih* 家譜考釋, Kunming, 1937; Chin Yün-ming金雲銘, "Cheng Ho ch'i-tz'u hsia hsi-yang nien-yüeh k'ao-cheng"七次下西洋年月考證, *Fu-chien wen-hua* 福建文化, 26 (December 15, 1937), 1; Fang Hao 方豪, *Tung-fang tsa-chih* 東方雜誌, 復刊, I: 2 (August 1, 1967), 45; Han Yü-hsüan 韓毓萱 in *Wen-wu ts'an-k'ao tzu-liao*文物參考資料 (1957), no. 12, 20; N. J. Krom, *Hindoe-Javaanische Geschiedenis* (The Hague, 2d ed., 1931), 427; Yamamoto Tatsuro, "Cheng Ho no saisei" の西征, TG, XXI (1934), 374, 506; J. J. L. Duyvendak, *Ma Huan Re-examined*, Amsterdam, 1933;

id., "The True Dates of the Chinese Maritime Expeditions in the Early Fifteenth Century," TP, Vol. 34 (1939), 341, "The Mi-li-kao Identified," Vol. 35 (1940), 215, "A Chinese *Divina commedia,*" Vol. 41 (1952), 255, "Desultory Notes on the *Hsi-yang chi,*" Vol. 42 (1954), 1; *id., China's Discovery of Africa,* London, 1949; P. Pelliot, "Les grands voyages maritimes chinois au début du XVe siècle," TP, Vol. 30 (1933), 237, "Notes additionelles sur Tcheng Houo," Vol. 31 (1935), 274, "Encore à propos des voyages de Tcheng Houo," Vol. 32 (1936), 210, "Les caractères de transcription *wo* ou *wa* et *pai,*" Vol. 37 (1944), 128; Chang Kuei-sheng, "A Re-examination of the Earliest Chinese Map of Africa," *Papers of the Michigan Academy of Science, Arts, and Letters,* XLII (1957), 151; W. Z. Mulder, "The 'Wu Pei Chih' Charts," TP, Vol. 37 (1944), 1; L. Carrington Goodrich, BSOAS, XIV, pt. 2 (1952), 386 ; William Willets, "The Maritime Adventures of Grand Eunuch Ho," *Journal of South-East Asian History,* V: 2 (1964), 31; Lo Jung-pang, "The Decline of the Early Ming navy," OE, 5 (1958), 149; Louis Gaillard, *Nankin d'alors et d'aujourd'hui* (Shanghai, 1903), 303; Claudine Lombard-Salmon, "La communauté chinoise de Makasar," TP, LV (1969), 272; Keith Stevens, "Three Chinese Deities," JRAS Hong Kong br., Vol. 12 (1972), 192.

Chang Kuei-sheng

CHENG Hsiao 鄭曉 (T. 窒甫, H. 淡泉, 海上大笠生), 1499-September 26, 1566, administrator and the first writer to attempt a comprehensive history of the Ming dynasty up to his time, was a native of Hai-yen 海鹽, Chekiang. In the mid-14th century his ancestor served as a leader of local militia on the side of the Yüan government against the rebel invaders; he barely escaped with his life in 1367 when the army of Chu Yüan-chang conquered that area. Cheng Hsiao's grandfather, Cheng Yen延 (T. 世昌, H. 東谷), and father Cheng Ju-t'ai 儒泰 (T. 道亨, H. 吾孩), were successful as tutors in their family's private school, but both failed to pass the provincial examination. Cheng Yen became a student in the National University at Nanking (1462), and later acted as deputy director of customs in Kwangtung (1475-

ca., 1481), where he became a friend of Ch'en Hsien-chang (*q. v.*). Cheng Ju-t'ai, also a student of the National University, served for a few months as assistant instructor in a district school. It is said that he became so discouraged by his and his father's repeated failures in the civil examinations, in spite of their scholarship, that he at first decided to prevent his son from having a classical education. When he discovered Cheng Hsiao's capabilities, however, he looked after him with devotion, molding his character as well as directing his studies.

Cheng Hsiao proved worthy of his father's expectations. In 1522 he passed first in the provincial examination. A year later he became a *chin-shih*. Appointed a secretary in the bureau of operations in the War ministry, he took the opportunity to study the documents and maps in the archives and became well informed on military history and strategy. In August, 1524, at the command of the minister, Chin Hsien-min 金獻民 (T. 舜舉, H. 蓉溪, cs 1484), he produced an atlas of the northern frontiers with explanations, which reportedly circulated widely in manuscript. That same year, at the time of the great debate over the honors to be accorded the parents of the emperor (*Ta-li i, see* Chu Hou-ts'ung), Cheng became involved. Urged by his colleagues, he drew up a memorial which went against the wishes of the young monarch. Cheng and the cosigners of the petition further annoyed the emperor when they joined other officials in kneeling at a palace gate to beg the emperor to change his mind. On his refusal, the two hundred twenty officials wailed and rattled the gate, whereupon the emperor ordered their arrest and detention. Those of the fourth grade or higher escaped with fines only, but those of lower grades, Cheng among them, were flogged twice, seventeen of them dying as a result. Eleven were sent into exile (*see* Yang Shen). The rest somehow survived the ordeal, and most of them returned to their posts. Cheng, after

being nursed back to life by his father, continued to serve in the War ministry. Then he retired on his mother's death (1525). Less than a year after he resumed service (1528) his father died, and he retired again This time he stayed home for ten years, on account, according to some reports, of his refusal to join the faction under Chang Fu-ching (*q. v.*). In 1539, on the recommendation of the minister of Personnel, Hsü Tsan (*q. v.*), Cheng Hsiao was recalled from retirement to serve as a secretary in Hsü's ministry. In a few years he worked his way up to the directorship of the bureau of evaluation in the same ministry. It happened to be a time when political rivalry among the grand secretaries became more and more acute, and Cheng very soon found himself at odds with another powerful grand secretary and incurred his displeasure. When Hsia Yen (*q. v.*) was dismissed from the office of the chief grand secretary in 1542, the emperor ordered an evaluation of all the court officials, because he thought that the censors and the supervising secretaries had been remiss in failing to impeach Hsia Yen. Thereupon Yen Sung (*q. v.*), who had just found favor with the emperor and coveted the grand secretaryship, determined to get rid of the officials he disliked. Cheng, however, recommended the dismissal of thirteen persons, most of whom, it is said, were close to Yen Sung. Naturally Yen was resentful. Later, when Cheng was transferred to the directorship of the bureau of appointments, Yen wanted to place one of his protégés, Chao Wen-hua (*q. v.*), in the ministry as director of the bureau of evaluation, the post Cheng had just vacated. It happened that not long before, when Huang Chen 黃禎 (T. 德兆, H. 北海野人, cs 1523) was appointed director and Li K'ai-hsien (*q. v.*), a native of Shantung like Huang, was recommended to be the evaluation director, the emperor preferred not to have two men from the same province head these sensitive offices simultaneously. Cheng, by reminding the minister,

Hsü Tsan. of this precedent, helped him to resist Yen's recommendation. Yen desired also to have his son, Yen Shih-fan (*see* Yen Sung), appointed as director of the seal office. On the ground that proper procedures called for the promotion of a vice prefect of the metropolitan area to the rank of prefect and that there was no precedent for a vice prefect to be promoted to the directorship of the seal office, Cheng refused to recommend Yen Shih-fan. Exasperated, Yen Sung had Cheng demoted to the position of vice prefect of Ho-chou 和州 (Anhwei) early in 1544, explaining that Cheng had recommended those officials who had been downgraded by imperial order less than a year before (in one case the official had had been deprived of his post for only four months)—an action which showed disrespect to the emperor, and at the same time one which sought to please other officials. Originally Yen had wanted to downgrade Cheng to the status of commoner. The emperor, however, modified Yen's proposal and decreed that Cheng should be dropped three grades in rank. With Cheng out of the way, Yen succeeded in getting his son the directorship he coveted.

Beginning late in 1544 Cheng served in different capacities in the southern capital, rising eventually to minister of the Court of Imperial Sacrifices (1553). His official career then was comparatively steady and smooth-sailing, yet no man of ambition was content to serve in Nanking. Throughout most of this period, however, Yen was at the height of his influence, and this was one of the reasons why Cheng was content to remain there. Then the political situation suddenly took a different turn, because of the depredations of the *wo-k'ou* in the southeastern provinces. Besides, at the capital, a new political force was emerging around the resourceful Hsü Chieh (*q. v.*), who had passed the metropolitan examination in the same year as Cheng and was a good friend of his. It was largely through Hsü's influence that Cheng was summoned back to Peking to serve as junior vice minister in the ministry of Justice (November 13, 1553).

Hardly had Cheng settled in Peking, however, than he was transferred (January 11, 1554) to be a junior vice minister of War with the concurrent title of junior assistant censor-in-chief in charge of grain transportation and also of the administration of the region north of the Yangtze. At that time the regions north and south of the great river were being ravaged by pirates, and transportation was seriously threatened. Cheng served until he was promoted to be senior vice minister of Personnel (May 13, 1555). Short as his tenure was, he did contribute to the stabilization of the region under his jurisdiction and to the efficient management of grain transportation. Upon his request a large sum of money was appropriated for the building of warships, the erection of defense forts, the training of troops, and the purchase of military provisions. Being a native of Chekiang and therefore well informed about the smuggling and piratical problems, Cheng succeeded in capturing and punishing some who had given aid to the pirates. He also recruited salt smugglers and other able-bodied men into the army, thus preventing them from joining the pirates. He likewise fortified most of the strategic areas in his region.

Compared with his contemporaries, Cheng was one of the few who concerned himself with the piracy problem and studied it from several angles. He was alarmed over the increasing number of poor and discontented Chinese who associated themselves with the pirates, and he kept voicing his alarm in both private letters and public writing. His concern over piracy was partly motivated by personal reasons, for his own family in Hai-yen suffered serious losses in 1553 and, 1554. He was not opposed to foreign trade, and yet he argued against granting permission to trade as requested by the smugglers when piracy was spreading. His arguments were widely quoted.

A year after his return to the capital he was promoted to be minister of Personnel in Nanking (May 2, 1556), but four days later was moved to the post of junior censor-in-chief with the concurrent title of junior vice minister of War to assist in the management of the Peking divisions. In April, 1558, he received the post of minister of Justice. Immediately after this, in the absence of Yang Po (*q. v.*), who had been sent to Tatung to cope with the serious situation caused by the younger brother of Altan-qaγan (*q. v.*), Cheng served concurrently for three months as acting minister of War. At that time, in spite of the emergency, about thirty-five thousand men from the Peking divisions were assigned to menial jobs. This brought a sharp protest from Cheng, and the throne approved their return to the barracks. It seems that Cheng also made a good reputation as minister of Justice, for he, Ma Shen 馬森 (T. 孔養, H. 鍾陽, cs 1535, d. 1580), the chief minister of the Court of Revision, and Chou Yen 周延 (T. 南喬, H. 崦山, 1499–1561, cs 1523), the censor-in-chief, were called the San p'ing 三平 (Three fair judges).

Cheng's presence in the capital, together with his high position in the government, naturally involved him in the political rivalry between the two grand secretaries Yen Sung and Hsü Chieh. Cheng and Hsü, as has been noted, were on friendly terms and shared almost similar political views. In one of Hsü's letters to a friend, he described Cheng as one of "our group." Accordingly, when in 1558 three of Hsü's supporters vehemently attacked Yen, Cheng resisted pressure from Yen and protected them from overly harsh punishment. It also happened that, during Cheng's tenure as minister of Justice, several celebrated trials came up. In the case of Supreme commander Wang Yü (*see* Wang Shih-chen), who had been charged with losing territory to the Mongol invaders, and in the case of Kuo Hsi-yen (*see* Chu Hou-ts'ung), who had been charged with

meddling in the question of imperial succession, Cheng advocated mild sentences while Yen demanded harsh ones. On the other hand, in the case of the mutiny of the soldiers in the Nanking area, resulting in the death of a vice minister, and in the case of some pirates, Cheng asked for severe punishments while Yen proposed lighter ones. Then in the cases of the governor of Fukien, Juan O 阮鶚 (T. 應薦, H. 函峰, 1509–67, cs 1544), the supreme commander of Hsüan-fu 宣府 and Tatung regions, Yang Shun 楊順 (cs 1541, d. 1568), and Censor Lu K'ai 路楷 (cs 1550), the first for misappropriation of money, the others for malfeasance in office, it was said that Yen used his influence to protect them. Since the compilers of the Ming history criticize Cheng for failing to mete out the severe punishment the three officials deserved, it may be assumed that in this case at least Cheng was on Yen's side. All this seems to show that Cheng was more independent and less partisan in politics than many of his contemporaries.

According to the *Ming-shih* and to the chronological biography of Cheng by his own son, Cheng antagonized Yen so much that Yen succeeded in engineering his dismissal from office in May, 1560. The issue arose as to whether the judicial offices in the central government should have jurisdiction over legal cases in the local districts bordering on the metropolitan area. In the past it had been customary for the ministry of Justice to exercise its jurisdiction over the neighboring districts. But the inspecting censor, Cheng Ts'un-jen 鄭存仁 (cs 1550), issued an order to the neighboring prefectures and districts concerned forbidding the sending of witnesses to the ministry of Justice on the ground that litigation should start at the lowest level. Disagreeing with this argument, Cheng and the two vice ministers appealed to the throne in support of the ministry's traditional privileges; to this the emperor agreed. The inspecting censor, however, submitted a second memorial questioning these privileges. The emperor referred the matter to the Censorate which was to discuss the issue with the ministry involved and offer a recommendation. Before the Censorate replied, however, Cheng again presented his arguments in a stronger tone. This annoyed the emperor, and he accused Cheng of arrogance and ordered his dismissal and permanent exclusion from government service, at the same time dictating a lighter punishment for the two vice ministers. While Yen has been represented as having been responsible for Cheng's retirement, the facts seem to indicate that Cheng brought it on himself.

Cheng died six years later. Not long afterwards, the title of minister of Justice was restored posthumously (January 3, 1567), and the title of junior guardian of the heir apparent conferred. He was canonized as Tuan-chien端簡 (March 16, 1567); for his military merits the privilege of sending a son to the Imperial Academy was also granted.

In the opinion of Chiao Hung (ECCP), Cheng Hsiao was unusually well versed in the history of the Ming dynasty. That Cheng came to be so highly esteemed by the scholars of later generations is because his writings show not only his interest in current developments, but also his keen insights and his historical perspective. Of all his writings the most important are the *Wu-hsüeh-pien*吾學編, 69 *ch.*, *Chin-yen* 今言, 4 *ch.*, *Ku-yen* 古言, 2 *ch.*, the collection of his essays, *Wen-chi* 文集, 12 *ch.*, and the collection of his memorials, 14 *ch.* The *Wu-hsüeh-pien*, published not long after his death (1567) and reprinted in 1599, contains a wealth of information on Ming history down to 1521, while the *Chin-yen*, his essays, and memorials provide discerning reflections on the events of his lifetime.

Cheng had three sons. The editors of the *Ming-shih* accorded a biography to the eldest, Cheng Lü-ch'un 履淳 (T. 叔初, 伯寅, b. 1536, cs 1562); he is chiefly remembered for his courageous act of remon-

strating (February 1, 1570) with the emperor, Chu Tsai-hou (*q. v.*). For this he received a hundred strokes and suffered imprisonment, and was not restored to the bureaucracy until August, 1572, when he was made vice director of the Court of Imperial Entertainments. The second son, Cheng Lü-chun 準 (b. 1538), served as secretary in the supervisorate of imperial instruction. Of Cheng Hsiao's five daughters, one married Hsiang Tu-shou, the brother of Hsiang Yüan-pien (*q. v.*), who, under the influence of the father-in-law, also became keenly interested in the history of his time.

Bibliography

1/199/18a, 215/10b; 3/178/23a; 5/45/43a; MSL (1965), Shih-tsung, 7079, 7303, 7729, Mu-tsung (1965), 1001; KC (1958), 3825, 3850, 3905, 4121; Cheng Hsiao, *Wu-hsüeh-pien*; *id.*, *Cheng Tuan-chien kung tsou-i*奏議; *id.*, *Cheng Tuan-chien kung wen-chi*; Cheng Lü-ch'un, *Cheng Tuan-chien kung nien-p'u* 年譜 (1568 ed.); Li Chih, *Hsü-ts'ang-shu* (1959 ed.), 384; *Hai-yen-hsien chih* (1876), 15/35a; Hsü Hsüeh-mo, *Shih-miao chih-yü lu*, 21/1a; Sheng Feng 盛楓 (cj 1681), *Chia-ho cheng-hsien lu* 嘉禾徵獻錄, 9/1a; SK (1930), 13/4b, 37/3b, 50/10b, 53/6a, 125/1a, 177/3b; Sun Tien-ch'i (1957), 76; Wang Kuang-wei 王光煒, *Pei-ta yen-chiu-so kuo-hsüeh-men chou-k'an* 北大研究所國學門周刊, II, 17 (Peking, February 3, 1926), 23; W. Franke, *Sources*, 2.1.1, 2.2.3, 4.1. 4, 4.2.2, 5.5.7; L. of C. *Catalogue of Rare Books*, 127, 130, 622, 1154.

Kwan-wai So

CHENG Jo-tseng 鄭若曾 (T. 開陽, H. 伯魯), fl. 1505–80, a native of K'un-shan 崑山 in the prefecture of Soochow, distinguished himself as a geographer. He was born into a family of literary background sustained through several generations, but his father interrupted the family tradition and became a merchant. In his teens Cheng Jo-tseng was sent to study under Wei Chiao 魏校 (T. 子才, H. 莊渠, 1483–1543, cs 1505), where he became acquainted with another student, Kuei Yu-kuang (q.v.). Wei Chiao had a wealthy cousin by the name of Wei Hsiang 庠 (T. 子秀, 1487-1554). Later Cheng and Kuei married daughters of Wei Hsiang. Cheng became a student of the district school(1520s) and later a student in the National University in Peking, but failed repeatedly in the provincial examination. He taught at home, therefore, and subsequently became known as a disciple of Chan Jo-shui (q.v.). Many leading scholars, among them Mao K'un, Lo Ch'in-shun, and T'ang Shun-chih (qq.v.), became his friends. This small group shared the view that, as a Confucian, one should contribute something to society. As a result each of them not only conducted serious research but also had his own field of specialization, such as military arts or history.

In the mid-16th century China's coastal provinces suffered from a series of raids by the Japanese pirates, known as wo-k'ou. Many cities from the Yangtze valley to Kwangtung were sacked and thousands of people lost their lives. Cheng decided to put aside what he was engaged in and to turn his attention to the strategy of coastal defense. His decision was highly applauded by his friend T'ang Shun-chih. With T'ang's encouragement and financial aid, he started in the late 1540s to collect source materials. After several years of strenuous effort, he completed the Yen-hai t'u-pen 沿海圖本, a strategic atlas of the Chinese coastal region ranging from the Liaotung Peninsula to southern Kwangtung (including the offshore islands), totaling twelve maps with a short text of explanation. This finished, he began to work on his magnum opus, the Ch'ou-hai t'u-pien 籌海圖編. He was such a serious scholar that, when his home city K'un-shan was besieged in 1554, he even ventured into the area, believing that only such field investigations would provide him with a better understanding of the tactics of the wo-k'ou and the weapons they used. Unfortunately T'ang Shun-chih passed away in 1560; so it fell to Wang Tao-hsing 王道行 (T. 明輔, H. 龍池, cs

1549), the newly appointed prefect of Soochow, to help Cheng continue his work without interruption. The Yen-hai t'u-pen was then published under Wang's patronage.

As the piratical raids on the coast of Chekiang increased, Hu Tsung-hsien (q.v.) was appointed governor of Chekiang and later supreme commander of Nan-Chihli. He recruited a number of competent officials including Hu Sung 胡松 (T. 汝茂, H. 柏泉, October 30, 1503-December 3, 1566, cs 1529, Pth. 莊肅) and T'ang Shun-chih. In addition, he invited a few scholars such as Mao K'un and T'ang Shu (see T'an Ch'ien) to become his advisers. On reading the Yen-hai t'u-pen, Hu Tsung-hsien was impressed. Learning that Cheng was then planning a new book of strategic value, Hu invited him to Hangchow as his adviser (spring of 1560), at the same time encouraging him to continue his work on the book. In order to gain more reliable information Cheng undertook a series of interviews with the captured Japanese pirates. By accident he learned that they had relatively little geographic knowledge of the Chinese littoral. Their raids on China were mainly dependent upon native pirates. Cheng therefore suggested to Hu that he sow discord between the Japanese and the Chinese to weaken their military strength. This tactic helped Hu win a decisive victory over the wo-k'ou. For this Cheng was offered a military rank (November 1560), but he declined.

By this time Cheng had just finished the first draft of the Ch'ou-hai t'u-pien. He handed it to an experienced editor, Shao Fang 邵芳 (a native of Yangchow), who was also working under Hu. With Shao's help, the draft became more systematic and readable. When the book was being printed, Cheng resigned his post under Hu and returned to K'un-shan, either at the end of 1560 or the beginning of 1561. In any event he could not have served under Hu for more than one year. Supervised by Hu Sung, then an administrative commissioner of Chekang (he was not promoted to be governor of Kiangsi until September, 1561) and a considerable publisher of the day, the first edition of *Ch'ou-hai t'u-pien* was handsomely printed and cased. It contained prefaces by Hu Sung, Mao K'un, and T'ang Shu, a postscript by Lu T'ang (*q.v.*), and an acknowledgement by Cheng himself. Since it is a voluminous work, and the process of printing a book at that time, drawing maps, and cutting blocks, was not an easy job, it appeared later than the dates shown in the prefaces. Unquestionably it was printed before Hu Tsung-hsien was put in jail (December 7, 1563) as quite a few passages relating to Hu, in the rare Princeton University copy, were stained with black ink, probably to delete the passages relating to Hu.

The scope of the *Ch'ou-hai t'u-pien* initially was fairly small. Cheng planned to compile only a handbook of *wo-k'ou* activities which he thought might help the coastal officials in dealing with the pirates. Later, with the sponsorship of Hu Tsung-hsien, it was greatly enlarged and became an encyclopedic reference book on coastal affairs. It totals 13 *chüan* and is divided into eight parts: part I has maps of the eastern world and of the offshore islands along the Chinese coast; part II includes a history of Sino-Japanese relations from the earliest times to late Ming, including a table of Japanese relations with China, and a short history and map of Japan; part III has maps of Chinese coastal areas from the Liaotung Peninsula to Kwangtung and the areas which suffered from the *wo-k'ou* raids, together with an account of the distribution of Chinese troops along the coastal areas during the Ming; part IV contains a chronological table of the *wo-k'ou* raids in this same region; part V has an account of the routes used by the *wo-k'ou*; part VI contains an account of the methods the Ming forces under the command of Hu Tsung-hsien used in defeating the pirates; part VII gives a list of those Chinese officers and civilians who lost their lives in the struggle against the *wo-k'ou*; part VIII contains a history of the way the Ming government dealt with the pirates, including an illustrated account of the vessels and weapons used by both sides.

The *Ch'ou-hai t'u-pien* has been called one of the most scholarly works in its field. A recent critic, Wang Yung 王庸, for instance, has characterized it as a solid contribution to Chinese historical geography in the Ming period. The section on Japan has also been shown to be fairly accurate, Japanese scholars such as Tanaka Takeo 田中健夫 and Fujita Motoharu 藤田元春 regarding it as one of the most important documents in its sphere. Although Cheng showed some originality, he owed much to one earlier work and to certain friends. The *Kuang-yü t'u* by Lo Hung-hsien (*q.v.*) was published in 1558. His maps and up-to-date data supplied Cheng with much information. According to Cheng's own acknowledgement, the maps in his *Ch'ou-hai t'u-pien* are largely based on Lo's work. Under the sponsorship of Hu Tsung-hsien, he enjoyed the privilege of interviewing the captured Japanese pirates directly. In addition, he was also in a position to gain access to government documents and archives, including the confidential reports by the men commissioned to go to Japan (*see* Chiang Chou) to ask the Japanese government to curb the pirates. Consequently he received first hand material not usually obtainable. When he served under Hu Tsung-hsien, many of his colleagues were themselves knowledgeable about geography and might have helped him; among them was a mathematician, Chou Shu-hsüeh 周述學 (T. 繼志, H. 雲淵子, fl. 1530-58).

The significance of the *Ch'ou-hai t'u-pien* is not alone because of its contents. It marks a turning point in geographic studies in China. Prior to the Ming period, China's major threats came from the north. Geographers had hitherto emphasized the northern frontier areas, and paid relatively little attention to other sections of the country. Only after the publication of the *Ch'ou-hai t'u-pien* did they begin to shift, or at least to include the coastal areas. It also stimulated other geographical studies. Important works, such as *Liang Che hai-fang lei-k'ao* 兩浙海防類考 (1575), compiled by Liu Tsung-tai 劉宗岱 (cs 1559), *Liang Che hai-fang lei-k'ao hsü-pien* 續編 (1602) by Fan Lai 范淶 (T. 原易, H. 希暘, cs 1574) and Shih Chi-ch'en 史繼辰 (T. 應之, H. 念橋, cs 1577), and *Wu-pei chih* (1621) by Mao Yüan-i (*q.v.*), were either inspired by or followed the pattern of Cheng's opus.

During the years from 1564 to the end of the Ming, the *Ch'ou-hai t'u-pien* was republished at least three times: in 1572 with a preface by Wu P'eng 吳鵬 (T. 萬里, H. 默泉, 1500-79, cs 1523); in 1592 (under a different title and in 12 *ch.*) with a postscript by Fei Yao-nien 費堯年 (T. 熙之, cs 1562); in 1624 edited by Hu Tsung-hsien's grandsons, Hu Teng (*see* Hu Tsung-hsien), Hu Ming-kang 鳴岡 (cj 1621), and Hu Chieh-ch'ing 階慶 (cj 1615). There is also a reprint of the last with the original preface of Mao K'un and a new one by Hu Ssu-shen 思伸 (cs 1595) of 1624. The editors of the last two editions simply dropped Cheng Jo-tseng's name as the author and supplanted it with the name of their grandfather. They also deleted the prefaces by Hu Sung and T'ang Shu, the postcript by Lu T'ang, and the acknowledgement by Cheng because all these indicated clearly that Cheng was the author. Cleverly enough, they preserved Mao K'un's preface, for it mainly applauds the military achievements of Hu Tsung-hsien and Hu's contribution, with only a few sentences relating to Cheng. Wherever Cheng Jo-tseng expressed his own opinions, he usually added his name "tseng" at the beginning of a passage. This they also dropped and substituted the character 予 (ego). Consequently if one did not have a chance to see the first edition, he would not question Hu's authorship. The compilers of the Imperial Catalogue, for instance, apparently saw only the 1624 edition. They therefore took Hu Tsung-hsien to be the author. The seals on the copy at Princeton University show it to have passed through the hands of several collectors, including the famous poet and bibliophile Chu I-tsun (ECCP).

[Editors' note: In the 19th century, when the study of coastal defense was revived, the book was usually referred to as Cheng's, as in *Fang-hai pei-lan* 防海備覽 (1811), in Alexander Wylie's *Notes on Chinese Literature* (1867), and in H. F. Holt's "Catalogue of the Chinese manuscripts in the Library of the Royal Asiatic Society" (JRAS, 1890, p. 75). In the early 1930s the library of Tsinghua University, Peiping, obtained a copy of the 1572 edition of the *Ch'ou-hai t'u-pien*. The librarian, Shih T'ing-yung 施廷鏞 (T. 鳳笙), wrote an account (in which he quoted from the original prefaces) describing the different editions of the book and establishing its correct authorship. (*See* Wang Yung, *Chung-kuo ti-li t'u-chi ts'ung-k'ao* 中國地理圖籍叢考, 1947, p. 83-86.)]

Cheng also compiled ten other texts, generally with maps: 1) *Hai-fang er-lan t'u* 二覽圖 (a strategic map of China's littoral from the Liaotung Peninsula to Kwangtung, including the offshore islands), 1 *ch.*, his co-author being T'ang Shun-chih (completed in 1561, published in 1604); 2) *Jih-pen t'u-tsuan* 日本圖纂 (a map of Japan with text describing the country and its inhabitants, together with a glossary of Japanese-Chinese which may be one of the earliest such vocabularies in China; *see* Ch'en K'an), 1 *ch.* (preface by the author 1561, published in 1662); 3) *Chiang-fang t'u-k'ao* 江防圖考 (a map of the Yangtze River from Kiukiang to the sea with text), 1 *ch.* (published in 1604-5); 4) *Ch'ao-hsien t'u-shuo* 朝鮮圖說 (a map of Korea with a description), 1 *ch.*; 5) *Liu-ch'iu* 琉球 *t'u-shuo* (a map of the Liu-ch'iu with a description), 1 *ch.* (published in 1662); 6) *An-nan* 安南 *t'u-shuo* (a map of Annam with descriptive comments), 1 *ch.* (published in 1662); 7)

Wan-li hai-fang t'u-lun 萬里海防圖論 (a map of the seacoast from the Liaotung Peninsula, including Korea and Japan, to the Yangtze valley), 2 *ch.*, the maps of Korea and Japan being very similar to those in *Jih-pen t'u-tsuan* and *Ch'ao-hsien t'u-shuo* (published in 1604; 8) *Hai-yün* 海運 *t'u-shuo* (a map indicating the route by sea from the Liaotung Peninsula to Foochow), 1 *ch.*; 9) *Huang-ho* 黃河 *t'u-shuo* (a map with text showing the course of the Yellow River), 1 *ch.*; 10) *Su-sung fou-fu* 蘇松浮賦 (treatise on the grain tax in the southern part of Nan-Chihli), 1 *ch.*

Most of Cheng's comments and maps in the above group are either overlapping or slightly different from those in his *Ch'ou-hai t'u-pien*. In addition they are all poorly organized. In some cases the repeated narrations and rambling discussions would certainly discourage one from reading them through. These shortcomings, combined with the fact that Hu Tsung-hsien used some summaries of these monographs in his memorials presented to the emperor, suggest that they might be Cheng's original drafts for his major work before he handed it to Shao Fang. During the K'ang-hsi reign (1662-1723) these monographs were edited and revised by Cheng's descendants in a single book entitled *Cheng K'ai-yang tsa-chu* 開陽雜著, reprinted in 1932 with a postscript by Liu I-cheng (BDRC). Also extant are five of Cheng's short essays, such as "Hu-fang t'u-shuo," preserved in the *Huang Ming ching-shih wen-pien* of Ch'en Tzu-lung (ECCP).

Since Cheng received no high degree, nor did he hold any significant position in the government, the sources about his life are few and not entirely accurate. The short notices in the *Ssu-k'u* catalogue, the *Soochow-fu chih*, and *K'un Hsin liang-hsien hsü-hsiu ho-chih* 崑新兩縣續修合志 virtually duplicate each other. The exact dates of his birth and death are nowhere cited, but we do know that he was a contemporary of Kuei Yu-kuang, that according to Kuei he enjoyed good health into his sixties, and that he was twice recommended in the

late 1570s to serve as a historian—an offer he declined. These points suggest that he may have lived until *ca.* 1580.

Bibliography

MSL (1965), Shih-tsung, 5665, 7612, 7649, 7653, 8265, 8459; *K'un Hsin liang-hsien hsü-hsiu ho-chih* (1880), 17/10a, 18/4a, 19/4a, 26/18a, 30/14b, 49/13b, 51/22b; *Hui-chou-fu chih* 徽州府志 (1827), 9/pt.3, 43a, 51b, 52b, 12/pt.2, 65b, 76a; *Soochow-fu chih* (1877), 24/47a, 93/10b, 11b; SK (1930), 69/8a; TSCC (1885-88), XXIII: 105/93/6a; Cheng Jo-tseng, *Ch'ou-hai t'u-pien* (1564 and 1624 eds.); id., *Cheng K'ai-yang tsa-chu*; Ch'en Tzu-lung, *Huang Ming ching-shih wen-pien* (Taipei, 1964), Vol. 16, 1, 607, Vol. 17, 157, 283; *Chekiang t'ung-chih* (1934), 2637; Kuei Yu-kuang, *Chen-ch'uan ch'üan-chi* (Hong Kong, 1959), 187, 234; Wang Yung, "Ming-tai yü-t'u hui-k'ao" 明代輿圖彙考, *T'u-shu chi-k'an* 圖書季刊, III (1936) 7; id., *Chung-kuo ti-li hsüeh-shih* 中國地理學史 (1937), 83, 92, 152; Tanaka Takeo, "Chūkai zuhen no seiritsu" in *Nippon rikishi* 日本歷史, 57 (February 1953), 18; Fujita Motoharu, "Min-jin Tei Jakuso no nihon chiri" in *Rikishi to chiri* 歷史と地理, 34: 4, 5 (1934), 154; Joseph zeedham, *Science and Civilisation in China*, III (Cambridge, 1959), 51, 105, 143, 516, IV (1965), 510; W. Franke, *Sources*, 7. 8. 10, 11, 14, 20; *Title Index to the Catalogue of the Gest Oriental Library* (Peking, 1941), 1057; L. of C. *Catalogue of Rare Books*, 388; Alexander Wylie, *Notes on Chinese Literature* (Shanghai, 1867), 49.

Stanley Y. C. Huang

CHENG Kuei-fei 鄭貴妃, *ca.* 1568-July 5, 1630, the favorite consort of Emperor Chu I-chün (*q.v.*), was the mother of his third son, Chu Ch'ang-hsün 朱常洵 (February 18, 1586–March. 6, 1641). The emperor's partiality toward her and her son was the main cause of the most serious controversy of his reign. A native of Peking, she was chosen for assignment to the palace by the eunuchs commissioned in September, 1581, to select young girls to serve as concubines to the emperor who, after three years of marriage to Empress Wang (*see* Chu I-chün) and having also had other mates, still had no son. In March, 1582, he selected nine from the new girls and raised them to the rank of pin 嬪, or second grade imperial concubine. Lady Cheng, one of the nine, was given the title, Shu 淑 pin. In September, 1583, she was raised to the first grade with the title Te-fei 德妃, and a year later to head of the first grade as kuei-fei. On New Year's Day by the lunar calendar, she gave birth to Chu Ch'ang-hsün. Two months later her title became huang 皇-kuei-fei, or senior consort, ranking next to the empress. The emperor showered favors on her and her family, and would have liked to name her son the heir apparent but for the fact that by the rule of primogeniture the prior right to inherit the throne belonged to his eldest son, Chu Ch'ang-lo (August 28, 1582, ECCP). The latter was the issue of a maid serving the emperor's mother. It is said that she was older than the emperor and that when he heard of her conception he tried to deny it until his mother showed him the daybook kept by the eunuchs in her palace. In July 1582, perhaps on his mother's orders and at the insistence of Chang Chü-cheng (q. v.), the young emperor reluctantly gave the maid the title of Kung-fei 恭妃; after that, however, he ignored her, keeping her in her own quarters until she died in October, 1611.

It was common knowledge that Lady Cheng held the emperor's attention, and a story circulated that he had promised to make her son his heir. As soon as he was born the officials, led by Grand Secretary Shen Shih-hsing (q.v.), submitted memorials, jointly and singly, asking the emperor to name his eldest son formally as the heir apparent. The emperor demurred, saying that his eldest was too young and too infirm to stand the ceremony and that the matter could wait a few years. Annoyed by their insistence, he showed his anger by punishing two lower grade officials with demotion (see Shen Ching). Thus began the controversy, later known as cheng kuo-pen 爭國本, or contention for the trunk line of the dynasty, with, on one side, the majority of the court pressing

the emperor to name the date on which he would make Chu Ch'ang-lo the heir apparent, and on the other side, the emperor using various excuses to postpone it. His main excuse, that the boy was infirm, proved to be untrue when the grand secretaries found the boy early in 1590 to be healthy and well favored. They reminded the emperor that it was already late for the youth at his age to start formal education, but the emperor again procrastinated. In 1593 the latter gave a new excuse, namely, that his empress was still not too old to bear a son and that, because the son of the empress had prior rights to inherit the throne, the matter of naming the heir apparent should wait a while longer. His obvious insincerity did not draw any comments, for it was known that he had been living with Lady Cheng and other consorts, not the empress. Then he gave an order to confer princedoms on his three sons (Chu Ch'ang-lo, Chu Ch'ang-hao 浩, Chu Ch'ang-hsün) at the same time, which was another way to postpone naming the heir apparent. Protests from the officials forced him to rescind the order (see Wang Hsi-chüeh). Late in 1593 even Lady Cheng's uncle, Cheng Ch'eng-en 承恩, came out to plead that he pronounce Chu Ch'ang-lo the heir apparent, but received a scolding from the emperor and was deprived of his ranks and titles.

Finally, in March, 1594, the emperor yielded to pressure and permitted Chu Ch'ang-lo to receive the necessary education, but denied him the ceremony and equipage to which he was entitled. It is reported that he made the boy study on hot summer days without relief and on severely cold mornings without proper heat. This revealed an attitude of malice bordering on sadism. Meanwhile Lady Cheng, perhaps with the emperor's encouragement, made an effort to present herself in a better light. One month later, in April, she contributed five thousand taels of silver to famine relief in Honan. The emperor made a special announcement of her contribution. Then the emperor gave her a copy of the book on exemplary women, *Kuei-fan t'u-shuo*, published by Lü K'un (*q. v.*) in 1590. She had the book reprinted in August, 1595, with a preface in her own name; in this she announced her concern for the people's education just as much as for their livelihood, as manifested in her using her own funds to print the book and in her contribution-to-famine relief. It was obviously a propaganda stunt, which gave rise to speculation that the publicity was aimed at showing her as the mother of an heir apparent-to-be. In June, 1598, there appeared in Peking a tract entitled Yu-wei hung-i 憂危竑議 by someone using the pseudonym, Chu Tung-chi 朱東吉, in which Lü K'un was attacked as being in collusion with Lady Cheng in a plot to harm the emperor's eldest son in favor of her own. It happened that shortly before this a supervising secretary, Tai Shih-heng 戴士衡 (T. 章尹, cs 1589) and a magistrate, Fan Yü-heng 樊玉衡 (T. 以齊, 欽之, H. 友軒, cs 1583), had each submitted a memorial along similiar lines. Lady Cheng's uncle, the above mentioned Cheng Ch'eng-en, alleged that Tai was the author of the tract. The emperor had both Tai and Fan sentenced to banishment and ordered the matter closed.

After three more years of wrangling, Chu Ch'ang-lo was formally declared heir apparent on November 9, 1601, and his marriage was permitted to take place in March, 1602. Then late in 1603 another anonymous tract appeared in Peking under the title, Hsü 續 yu-wei hung-i, attacking several officials for continuing to plot against the heir apparent in favor of Lady Cheng's son. Among those accused were the grand secretary Shen I-kuan (*q. v.*) and several members of the Cheng family. The investigation lasted half a year, during which innocent people were involved (*see* Chen-k'o, and Kuo Cheng-yü). The case was considered closed with the execution of a man without his confession (*see* Ch'en Chü). Then in June, 1615, a maniac with a stick entered the gate to the heir apparent's quarters, and was subdued after he had beaten several eunuchs. The case, known as t'ing-chi 梃擊, or striking with an acrobat's pole, again involved Lady Cheng's family. There were some who even alleged that her cohorts had hired the man to assassinate the heir apparent. Finally the emperor told Lady Cheng to plead her innocence directly with the heir apparent, and the case was closed with only the madman executed.

Meanwhile Lady Cheng's son, Chu Ch'ang-hsün, stayed with her after his designation as prince of Fu 福王 in 1601, his marriage in January, 1604, and even after the construction of his palace in Loyang, Honan, in 1612. His residence cost over four hundred thousand taels, twice as much as the most elaborate princely house of the past and twenty times costlier than regulation allowed. Furthermore, to his fief was at first assigned forty thousand *ch'ing*, or over six hundred thousand acres of land. After years of hunting for unclaimed properties and public land in several provinces, much less than half the desired number of *ch'ing* were found. The provincial authorities reported that the people had been squeezed dry and were in a rebellious mood, especially where famine conditions existed, Eventually, after hundreds of memorials urging the emperor to send the prince to his own fief, he did so in April, 1614. The prince's retinue and impedimenta required 1,172 boats for transport. To feed this army of laborers the prince was given, in addition to the income from land, the privilege of controlling part of the government salt monopoly. Yet the court sighed with relief, for every day this prince remained in Peking the security of the heir apparent was threatened. At least, that was the belief of those who held that they were supporters of the heir apparent and identified themselves as the "good elements" (*see* Kao P'an-lung). Even after the prince had left, the group's suspicion of the emperor and Lady Cheng continued unceasingly, as evidenced by the t'ing-chi case.

While the Ming court was paralyzed chiefly by this controversy, which polarized most of the able and conscientious officials against the emperor, Nurhaci (ECCP), the Jurchen chief, had been gathering his strength, and rose in rebellion in 1618, defeating the Ming army in 1619. During this period of confusion the emperor was failing in health. His empress died in May, 1620, and he followed her in death three months later. Even in his last will he ordered his successor, Chu Ch'ang-lo, to raise Lady Cheng to the rank of empress. This directive, however, was not followed, the ministry of Rites objecting. When she died ten years later the posthumous title of Kung-k'o hui-jung ho-ching 恭恪惠榮 和靖 huang-kuei-fei was granted her. Ironically she, the emperor's lifelong favorite consort, was not buried with him but in a separate grave west of Peking. In the emperor's tomb were interred two women to whom he had not shown any affection in life, namely, the empress and the mother of Chu Ch'ang-lo.

Lady Cheng gave birth to two sons and several daughters. Her second son, born October, 1587, died a year later. Possibly the emperor's favorite daughter, Princess Shou-ning 壽寧公主, was one of her offspring. In 1609 this princess married Jan Hsing-jang 冉興讓. One night in 1612 he came home late and found her nurse had locked the gate. Probably inebriated, he struck the woman. The following day she gathered together a number of eunuchs and waylaid Jan, giving him a beating. The emperor sided with his daughter's nurse. So Jan left his cap at the palace gate and went into hiding in the mountains. He was later captured and ordered to study for one year at the National University. He and his wife were killed in 1644 by the rebels entering Peking.

Because of Lady Cheng's position, her family received certain favors. In 1584 her father, Cheng Ch'eng-hsien 承憲 (d. 1589), was made a hereditary chiliarch in the Imperial Guard and appointed a regional commissioner. He was accused of various crimes, including even murder, but was never prosecuted. After he died with the rank of a central commissioner, Lady Cheng's brother, Cheng Kuo-t'ai 國泰 (d. March, 1617), was made a regional commissioner of the Imperial Guard. Later he was promoted to be a central military commissioner. When his son, Cheng Yang-hsing 養性, received the same rank, there was much objection, and the rank was reduced to assistant central commissioner. At the death of Emperor Chu Ch'ang-lo in September, 1620, after only one month on the throne, those with an irrational hatred of the Cheng family suspected that Lady Cheng and Cheng Yang-hsing were somehow responsible. One official even invented a story that she had presented several girls to the emperor just before he died. In 1622, on the suggestion of Kao P'an-lung (q. v.), Cheng Yang-hsing was retired from the court.

Bibliography

1/114/10a, 244/25a, 300/21b; KC (1958), ch. 72-91; MSL (1966), Kuang-tsung, 0001; Liu Jo-yü, *Cho-chung chih*, ch. 1-3; Shen Te-fu, *Wan-li yeh-hu-pien* (1959), 474, 873, 877; Huang Ching-fang 黃景昉, *Kuo-shih wei-i* 國史唯疑 (Taipei, 1969), 583, 620, 641, 716; Tung Ch'i-ch'ang (ECCP), *Shen-miao liu-chung tsou-shu hui-yao* (1937), 禮1/ 4a, 刑2/1b, 4b, 7b, 9b, 13a; Ku Ying-t'ai, *Ming ch'ao chi-shih pen-mo*, ch. 66-68; Li Tz'u-ming (ECCP), *Yüeh-man-t'ang tu-shu-chi* 越縵堂 讀書記 (1963), 361.

Chaoying Fang

CHENG Shan-fu 鄭善夫 (T. 繼之, H. 少谷 山人), December 26, 1485–January 31, 1524, official, poet, calligrapher, and painter, was a native of Min (Foochow). Shortly after he achieved the *chin-shih* in 1505, his parents successively passed away, and in consequence he spent the next six years in mourning. His first appointment came in 1511 when he was made secretary in charge of taxes and customs of the ministry of Revenue at Hu-shu-kuan 滸墅關

on the Grand Canal, eight miles west of Soochow; here he developed a reputation as a person of integrity. When he became conscious of the way that affairs of state were being mishandled by the favorites of the emperor (Chu Hou-chao, *q. v.*), he retired to his native place and devoted himself to study and reflection, living a life of simplicity. Hoping that the political atmosphere might have improved during his interval of retirement, he reentered the bureaucracy in 1518, and was appointed a secretary in the ministry of Rites, and the next year a vice-director of a bureau. In April, 1519, when he learned that the emperor proposed making an inspection in the south, he and one hundred six of his colleagues, including Hsia Liang-sheng 夏良勝 (T. 於中, 1480–1536) and Wang Wen-sheng (*see* Mao Po-wen), memorialized in groups criticizing the proposal sharply. They were flogged openly in court and ordered to kneel in the yard from morning to dusk for five days. Later the leaders were punished by more flogging, which resulted in the deaths of eleven of them. Certain others were demoted or banished. Cheng himself escaped any further punishment, but he felt, under the circumstances, that he could no longer remain in office. After repeated requests for retirement he was finally permitted to leave (1520?). In 1522 he was recalled and appointed a department director in a ministry in Nanking, but on his way to the new post he paid a visit to the scenic Wu-i Mountains; there he fell ill and died.

Cheng Shan-fu was regarded by some critics as an outstanding poet from Fukien and was compared to the great Tu Fu (712–70) in style. Ch'ien Ch'ien-i (EC CP) selected sixty-three of his poems for inclusion in the anthology *Lieh-ch'ao shih-chi*. His collected works, edited by the above-mentioned Wang Wen-sheng, then serving as prefect of Foochow (*ca.* 1524), were engraved under the title *Cheng Shao-ku chi* 鄭少谷集; they consist of poetry in 13 *chüan* and prose in 15 *chüan*. A copy of the 1824 edition in 24 *chüan* in the National Central Library is available on microfilm. There is a small collection of notes credited to Cheng, entitled *Ching-shih yao-t'an* 經世要談, which seems to be spurious, for it contains several mistakes including the date of his flogging, given as 1521 instead of 1519. He is also recorded as a painter of note; unfortunately none of his paintings seems to have survived.

Bibliography

1/16/1a, 11a, 189/13b, 289/20a; 5/27/69a, 68/29a, 70/73a; 84/丙/77b; MSL (1965), Wu-tsung, *chüan* 172; SK (1930), 124/5b, 171/10b; *Cheng Shao-ku chi*; Ch'ien Ch'ien-i, *Lieh-ch'ao shih-chi*, 丙13/7b.

W. Pachow

CH'ENG Ta-yüeh 程大約 (T. 幼博, 君房, 士芳, H. 篠野), 1541–1616?, ink-tablet designer and printer of colored woodblock illustrations, was a native of the village of Yen-chen 嚴鎮, She-hsien 歙縣 in the prefecture of Hui-chou, south of Nanking. Hui-chou is a locality long noted for its artistic attainments in the fields of painting, woodblock engraving, paper, and ink manufacture. Both the *Ssu-k'u* catalogue and the *She-hsien chih* (1936) are in error in regarding Ch'eng Ta-yüeh and Ch'eng Chün-fang as two persons. Actually Chün-fang is one of Ch'eng's alternate names.

The youngest of three sons of a well-to-do merchant, Ch'eng at fourteen *sui*, like his brothers before him, followed in the family tradition. In 1564 he purchased the privileges of a student in the National University in Peking and apparently took the provincial examination a number of times without success. In 1592 he secured a post as an usher in the Court of State Ceremonial, another rank open to purchase. When Weng Cheng-ch'un 翁正春 (T. 兆震, H. 青陽, 1553–1626, *chuang-yüan* 1592, Pth. 文簡), obtained the *chin-shih* degree in that year, he noted that Ch'eng in his capacity as usher led the procession. He left that minor official position in the following year and returned to his native place. Shortly thereafter he was charged with murder and imprisoned. Vehemently denying the allegation and insisting on his innocence, Ch'eng was finally exonerated and released in 1600.

After gaining his freedom, Ch'eng actively engaged in the manufacture of ink-sticks and ink-cakes on which he embossed elaborate artistic designs. Samples of his products were widely distributed among the élite and some even presented to the emperor. A few of them are preserved in the Metropolitan Museum of Art in New York City. This absorption in the making of ink-tablets, however, was not a new passion with Ch'eng, for ever since his youth he had taken great interest in them and had spared no expense in acquiring a large collection of ink-tablets of artistic merit as well as of utilitarian value, many made by master craftsmen of earlier times.

Ch'eng began his ink manufacturing enterprise also in his youth, his own establishment being known then as the Pao-mo chai 寶墨齋. In later years he asserted that he conceived his formula of mixing oil and lacquer in a dream and that he purchased his raw materials from distant places. His devotion to the art after 1600, however, was greatly stimulated by the success of the illustrated catalogue of ink-tablets by his former partner and later enemy, Fang Yü-lu (q.v.). It seems that he had befriended Fang and taught him the art. Some samples of 1576 bear the names of both men, and one at least as late as 1602. Later, however, not only did Fang become a professional competitor but, it is said, he also coveted and later succeeded in marrying the concubine whom Ch'eng was forced to relinquish on account of the jealousy of his wife. All these factors contributed to precipitating an acrimonious feud between two of the greatest ink makers in the Ming dynasty, provoking much gossip and developing into a *cause célèbre*.

Ch'eng's bitterness extended also to many other people, including his own brother, some clansmen, and business associates. His quarrel with Fang, however, resulted in the production in 1606, almost eighteen years after the appearance of Fang's work, of his own catalogue of ink-tablets, the *Ch'eng-shih mo-yüan* 程氏墨苑, an album of designs and illustrations of great beauty, together with essays, poems, eulogies, and testimonials from supposedly grateful and appreciative recipients. The book was subsequently edited and reissued several times, some illustrations being added after its initial appearance. The few surviving copies today vary not only in the number of *chüan*, but also in the arrangement of contents. A complete set should comprise 23 *chüan*, 9 *chüan* of text containing laudatory compositions, correspondence, pertinent articles, and anecdotes relating to ink and ink-making, together with 14 *chüan* containing some five hundred illustrations. In addition, there are at the end of the book three appendices. It is listed in the *Ssu-k'u* catalogue and elsewhere as in 12 *chüan* although not included in the Imperial Library itself. (The *She-hsien chih* makes it 24.)

Ch'eng's album surpassed its prototype in both artistic excellence and in the number of pictures it contained. No doubt he benefited from Fang's pioneer work. A comparison of the two albums reveals that many of the illustrations are identical, including even the captions. In issuing the album Ch'eng attempted to outdo his rival; he spared neither effort nor expense in engaging the best talents. He persuaded the eminent artist Ting Yün-p'eng (q.v.) to furnish the bulk of the illustrations; leading scholars and officials were prevailed upon to contribute literary pieces and calligraphy. Many of the latter were meticulously transferred to woodblocks by Huang Ying-t'ai 黃應泰, Huang Tao 道, and Huang Lin 鏻, all leading craftsmen of the Hui-chou area, who affixed their names to some of the blocks they engraved.

He arranged the illustrations under such categories as natural and unusual phenomena, geography, famous personalities, animal kingdom, and Confucian, Buddhist, and Taoist lore. They are usually accompanied by literary pieces written by a galaxy of luminaries, of whom nearly two hundred are listed at the beginning of the book. The roster of contributors reads like a "who's who" of the literary world and officialdom at that time, with the conspicuous absence of members of the Wang clan, headed by Wang Tao-k'un (*q. v.*), who were decided partisans of Ch'eng's rival, Fang Yü-lu; one list arranged according to the contributors' native places and the other according to their names together with their degrees and dates obtained, their official positions, and lists of titles of the pieces they contributed. Among the contributors may be mentioned Chiao Hung (ECCP), T'u Lung (*q. v.*), Tung Ch'i-ch'ang (ECCP), Ting Yün-p'eng, and Matteo Ricci (*q.v.*), the erudite Jesuit.

Ch'eng himself composed more than one hundred thirty pieces of varying length including some brief personal narratives in the text, venting his grievances and relating the unfair treatment he had received from ungrateful people whom he had befriended and helped. In one of the appendices, the "Hsü chung-shan lang chuan" 續中山狼傳, he included also the fable of the wolf bent on devouring the man who had saved his life from a hunter. Subsequenty a passerby killed the wolf. In reprinting this fable and supplying a sequel to it in 1606, Ch'eng included a number of fine illustrations depicting the scenes. Another appendix is the "Yüan-chung-ts'ao" 圜中草, a collection of poems written when he was in prison; the third one is entitled "Pu-er-chia wen" 不二價文.

The *Ch'eng-shih mo-yüan* is one of the best exemplars in the annals of Chinese printing; the woodcuts are impeccably executed. When the book was first struck off, about fifty of the five hundred illustrations appeared in several colors in a very limited number of copies—probably not more than a score. This Ch'eng did by simultaneously tinting each block with the desired colors, not as was developed a few years later, with a suite of blocks each in different color for the same picture, known as t'ao-pan.

Another special feature of the *Ch'eng-shih mo-yüan* is that it contains four Biblical pictures, skillfully copied by Chinese artisans from engravings made by Antoine Wierx, Jérôme Wierx, and Crispin de Passe in Antwerp. These Matteo Ricci gave to Ch'eng together with three essays of exhortation in Chinese. In addition, he included an essay dedicated to Ch'eng, dated January 9, 1606. In it Ricci relates that he met the ink-maker earlier at a party given by Chu Shih-lu 祝世祿 (T. 世功, H. 石林, cs 1589). He was much impressed with Ch'eng and commended him for his skill. The Chinese texts, presumably in Ricci's own handwriting, are accompanied by Portuguese phonetic spelling of the sound of characters with notation of accents. This was a memorable event because it marked one of the earliest attempts at romanization of Chinese characters, a scheme which Ricci had adopted in 1598 (*see* Lazzaro Cattaneo).

The late bibliophile Cheng Chen-to (BDRC) took great pride in describing a copy of the *Ch'eng-shih mo-yüan* which he acquired from a fellow collector, T'ao Hsiang 陶湘 (1871–1940). After Cheng's death in an airplane accident in 1958, his library was donated to the National Library of Peking. The Sonkeikaku Bunko in Japan has another copy of the book in color. An incomplete set of the album with some of the illustrations in color is in the library of the Percival David Foundation of Chinese Art in London. There are more sets of the monochrome edition in existence today.

Very little is known of the later years of Ch'eng Ta-yüeh. There are allusions to the fact that he became interested in Buddhism and was often in the company of a distant cousin, Ch'eng Chüan 程涓 (T. 巨源, H. 泰滄), who incidentally contributed, next to Ch'eng Ta-yüeh himself, the largest number of pieces to the album. He was still living in 1616, for one of the ink-tablets he manufactured bears that date. According to the *She-hsien chih* (1936), Ch'eng was accused of murder for the second time and subsequently languished and starved himself to death in prison.

Ch'eng was also author of the *Ch'eng Yu-po chi* 程幼博集 in 6 *chüan*, which likewise is listed in the *Ssu-k'u* catalogue but was not copied into the Imperial Library. Edited by Yü Shen-hsing (*q. v.*) with a preface by Chiao Hung, it consisted of 2 *chüan* of essays aud 4 *chüan* of poems. It is doubtful whether it is in existence today.

Ch'eng is reported as having been tall of stature, impressive in appearance, hospitable and generous to friends. He was very fond of traveling, his wanderlust taking him to many parts of the country.

[Editors' note: Concerning Matteo Ricci's inscription in the *Ch'eng-shih mo-yüan* as quoted in Ch'en Yüan (BDRC) *Ming-chi chih ou-hua mei-shu chi lo-ma-tzu chu-yin* 明季之歐化美術及羅馬字注音 (1927), and discussed by P. M. d'Elia, "Le origini del'arte cristiana cinese, 1583-1640," (Rome, 1939) and J. J. L. Duyvendak, TP 35 (1940), 386-87, the question of Ricci's transliteration of 遇寶像三座 as yu teú siám san çoo seems to have puzzled these and other scholars. Actually one may quite simply explain this by the fact that Ricci took teú to mean Deus. Hence the phrase may be translated as "Three pieces of molding depicting scenes of meeting with God." The character pao is a literal translation of Deus, following Buddhistic tradition. Had Ricci used tou 寶 to transliterate Deus, as suggested by Duyvendak, the character, to a Chinese reader, would have meant literally, "an opening" or "a hole," whereas by using the character pao he could at least convey the meaning of an object of worship, as in the phrase san-pao 三寶 (*triratna* or "The Three Holies"). By giving the reading of the character pao as teú he indicated precisely that he intended it to mean Deus.]

Bibliography

She-hsien chih (1936), 10/31b, 15/8a; Ch'eng Ta-yüeh, *Ch'eng-shih mo-yüan* (1606); SK (1930), 116/3b, 179/1b; Hu Yü-chin 胡玉縉, *Ssu-k'u ch'üan-shu tsung-mu t'i-yao pu-cheng* 四庫全書總目提要補正 (1964), 907; *Chung-kuo pan-k'e t'u-lu* 中國版刻圖錄, Vol. 1 (1961), 108; Cheng Chen-to, *Chieh-chung te-shu chi* (1956), 35; Chao Wan-li 趙萬里, *Ch'eng-shih mo-yüan tsa-k'ao*" 程氏墨苑雜考 in *Chung-Fa Han-hsüeh yen-chiu-so t'u-shu-kuan kuan-k'an* 中法漢學研究所圖書館館刊, no. 1 (March, 1945), 1; T'ao Hsiang, *She-yüan mo-tsui* 涉園墨萃 (1927); Kuo Wei-ch'ü 郭味蕖, *Chung-kuo pan-hua shih-lüeh* 中國版畫史略 (1962), 107; Wang Po-min 王伯敏, *Chung-kuo pan-hua shih* (1961), 108; Shen Te-fu, *Fei-fu yü lüeh* 飛鳧語略 in *Hsüeh-hai lei-pien* 學海類編 (1920), 103/8b; *T'ien-lu lin-lang hsü-pien* 天祿琳瑯續編 (1884), 17/21a; Lu I-tien 陸以湉, *Leng lu tsa-shih* 冷廬雜識 (1856) in *Ch'ing-tai pi-chi ts'ung-k'an* 清代筆記叢刊, 3/27b; Wang Chi-chen, "Notes on Chinese Ink," *Metropolitan Museum Studies*, Vol. 3, part 1 (1930), 114; P. M. d'Elia, *Fonti Ricciane*, I (Rome, 1942), 34, n. 4, II (Rome, 1949), 97, n. 4, 354, n. 2; Paul Pelliot, "La peinture et la gravure européennes en Chine au temps de Mathieu Ricci," TP, XX (1921), 1; Jos. Jennes, "L'art chrétien en Chine au début du XVIIe siècle," TP, XXXIII (1937), 129; *Arts of the Ming Dynasty* (London, 1958), 62 and pl. 25; W. Fuchs, *Chinesische und Mandjurische handschriften und seltene drucke* (Wiesbaden, 1966), 75.

K. T. Wu

CHI Ch'eng 計成 (T. 無否, H. 否道人), fl. early 17th century, painter and garden architect, was a native of Wu-chiang 吳江 in the prefecture of Soochow. In his early years he was a landscape painter, following the style of two masters of the latter half of the 10th century, Kuan T'ung 關仝 (同, or 童, or 幢) and Ching Hao 荊浩 (T. 浩然, H. 洪谷子). After sojourns in Peking and Hukuang, he settled in Chinkiang, northeast of Nanking. It was at this juncture that he first became fascinated with rock gardens, and began to direct his attention to garden architecture. As his knowledge developed and his fame spread, he was invited to draw plans for private gardens in estates on both sides of the Yangtze River. Following his success in these ventures, Chi made a compilation of his designs and patterns, and composed a text to which he gave the title *Yüan-mu* 園牧 (garden groom); later, at the suggestion of a friend, who noted that the work, including so many original ideas, should not be considered merely a collection of standard designs, he accepted a change of title to *Yüan-yeh* 冶 (garden smith).

The *Yüan-yeh* in three *chüan* was first printed in 1635, bearing one preface by Juan Ta-ch'eng (ECCP) dated 1634, another by Cheng Yüan-hsün 鄭元勳 (T. 超宗, cs 1643) of 1635, and Chi's own introduction of 1631. Three centuries later, this work was reprinted twice, in 1931, in the *Hsi-yung-hsüan ts'ung-shu* 喜詠軒叢書, and in 1933 by the Society for Research in Chinese Architecture. After a short essay on architecture in general and another on gardens, Chi divided his material as follows: 1) locale, 2) foundations, 3) structures, 4) lattices for screens and balustrades, 5) doors and windows, 6) walls and fences, 7) pavements, 8) artificial mounds (rockery), 9) selection of rock, and 10) consideration of the view (use of environment). It contains over two hundred thirty engravings illustrating the construction of buildings, patterns of lattice work for screens and balustrades, doors and windows, and ornamental styles of masonry for walls, fences, and pavements.

Chi Ch'eng laid special emphasis on the tenth of his categories. He differentiated between the distant views and the immediate setting, and took into consideration the contour and the size of the property, its natural environment, and the influence of the four seasons. In his essay on architecture he quote a Chinese proverb which notes that in construction work three-tenths

depends on the craftsman, but seven-tenths on the master (三分匠七分主人). He followed this up immediately by pointing out that the master here did not mean the owner, but the master builder—the architect. There is little recorded about Chi's life in the availablable sources, but it is fortunate that his unique work *Yüan-yeh* has been well preserved.

Bibliography

Chi Ch'eng, *Yüan-yeh*, *Hsi-yung-hsüan ts'ung-shu* ed.; Daniel Sheets Dye, *A Grammar of Chinese Lattice* (Cambridge, Mass., 1949), 12. (In this work Chi's *tzu* 無否 is romanized as Wu-fou, but it appears that the second character 否 here should be read as p'i.) Chu Hsiang 儲祥, *Chung-kuo hua-chia jen-ming ta-tz'u-tien* 中國畫家人名大辭典 (Taipei, 1962), 301, 721.

Lienche Tu Fang

CH'I Ch'eng-han 祁承爜 (T. 爾光, 越凡, H. 夷度, 曠翁), 1565–1628, official, bibliophile, and garden designer, was a native of Shan-yin 山陰, Chekiang. [Editors'note: His name is often mispronounced Ch'i Ch'eng-yeh, as in the biography of his son, Ch'i Piao-chia, ECCP, p. 126.] His ancestors, originally from Honan, moved south at the end of the Sung dynasty. His great-great-grandfather, Ch'i Ssu-yün 司員 (T. 宗規, H. 梅川), a *chin-shih* of 1478, rose in 1496 to be prefect of Ch'ih-chou 池州, a prefecture under the direct jurisdiction of Ying-t'ien 應天 (Nanking). His grandfather, Ch'i Ch'ing 清 (T. 子揚, H. 蒙泉, 1510–70), a *chin-shih* of 1547, died while serving as assistant administration commissioner of Shensi. Ch'i Ch'ing's wife, née Chin 金 (1508–94), came from a well-to-do family, and proved to be a capable manager of their properties. She lived to see five generations of the family prosper. Ch'i Ch'eng-han's father, Ch'i Ju-sen 汝森 (T. 蕭卿, 1539–72), died early, but under the supervision of his grandmother and mother, the youth studied industriously and succeeded in passing the examinations for *chü-jen* in 1590 and *chin-shih* in 1604. He received as his first appointment in the following year the magistracy of Ning-kuo

寧國(Anhwei), whence he was transferred two years later to that of Ch'ang-chou 長洲 (prefecture of Soochow); both of these were under the jurisdiction of the Nanking capital area. In the years from 1612 to 1615 he headed the bureau of equipment in the ministry of War in Nanking. It was in 1615, under his direction, that the administrative duties of this bureau were revised, and a new guidebook of instructions issued. Professor Meng Sen (BDRC) of Peking University in 1933 pointed out its importance for Ming history, and printed it under the title of *Ming Nan-ching ch'e-chia-ssu chih-chang* 明南京車駕司職掌. In 1615 Ch'i became perfect of Chi-an 吉安, Kiangsi, the highest provincial post he ever held. He went into retirement in 1617, but returned to officiate in I-chou 沂州, Shantung, in 1619, and then in Su-chou 宿州 (in the Nanking capital area) two years later. He retired finally in 1624.

In the intervals between his official terms, Ch'i remained at home, devoting his time and energy to building his garden and collecting books. About his garden—the Mi-yüan 密園—he left detailed accounts, the *Mi-yüan ch'ien-chi* 前紀 and the *Mi-yüan hou* 後-*chi*. He declared that he never liked to imitate; so he tried to achieve something unusual in laying out his garden. He placed emphasis on water, bamboos, and space, and on their blending with the environment. At one point he remarked: "No matter how small the body of water it should look boundless; no matter how many bamboos they should not conceal the view; inside the garden even one small mound or a single pool must not look detached; outside the garden, even numerous bodies of water and many rocky cliffs must present a harmonious view; if the area is small, it must borrow from space; if one's resources are limited, one must rely on natural grace; if ingenuity is desired, one must also insist on the simple and the unadorned."

His fondness for garden planning occupied his mind beyond his waking hours. Many landscape details, he reported, were formed in his dreams. His accounts of the Mi-yüan, besides general descriptions, mention thirty-two structures and scenic spots. While Tan-sheng-t'ang 澹生堂 seems to have been the main building, there was the K'uang-t'ing 曠亭, from which one of his sobriquets, K'uang-weng, must have derived. The names which he gave to certain buildings, Wo-tu-shu kuei 臥讀書庋, K'uai-tu chai 快讀齋, Mai-wang wo 脉望窩, and Hsiao lang-hsüan 小嫏嬛, all refer to books. The Wo-tu-shu kuei was a cottage with a single small room lined with book shelves on all sides and a bed in the middle. Ch'i Ch'eng-han explained that he enjoyed reading in bed; accordingly he designed it so that he could reach the books without getting up. In a note he also mentioned a Shu-liao lou 輸廖樓, where, he said, he housed other books, and on which he prepared a separate account but no such document is included in his collected literary works. The catalogue of his library is entitled the *Tan-sheng-t'ang ts'ang-shu mu* 藏書目.

Of his love for books he reminisced that, after his father's death, he began to develop a special fascination for the books in the family library. Occasionally he went to look at them. He could understand little, but the mere handling of the volumes gave him pleasure. His mother would call him to hurry to school. If he lingered he knew he would be scolded. After his marriage, he exchanged certain items from his wife's dowry for books. At that time a whole set of the dynastic histories was very difficult to obtain. When Kuo Tzu-chang (*q.v.*) printed about a hundred copies of these histories by movable type, Ch'i immediately bought a set, which made him feel like a poor boy suddenly become rich. He read the volumes day and night, and as a result suffered from insomnia for several months. By 1597 he had a library of over 10,000 *chüan*, housed in the Tsai-yü-t'ang 載羽堂; this became unfortunately a total loss by fire in the winter of the same year. Then in Peking and in Nanking he started to collect again. In 1613, in the midst of his official duties, he had the opportunity of staying at home for a period, and with the help of his sons he began to put his collection in order, and prepare a classified catalogue. He made a contract with his sons about the future of the library which came to be known as the "Tan-sheng-t'ang ts'ang-shu-yüeh" 約. The contract stipulates that 1) during his own lifetime there should be new additions every month; 2) in the lifetime of his sons there should be new additions every year; 3) whoever was able to read the books should be the sole keeper; if no appropriate person were available, all should share the responsibility; 4) books should not be taken from the library; 5) damage caused by mice or worms should be repaired immediately; 6) books after use should be returned to the shelves, and never taken to anyone's private quarters; 7) should relatives or friends wish to borrow any books, only those of which there were duplicate copies might be lent, and the better copy should never leave the Mi-yüan; 8) with ever increasing volumes, the catalogue should be brought up-to-date in every five to ten years; and 9) the collection should not be divided, or treated like waste paper, or sold to book dealers. In comparison with the principles of present day library management, the contract was not an inferior document.

Seven years later, in 1620, in accord with the contract he had designed himself, Ch'i Ch'eng-han reexamined and brought up-to-date the catalogue of his library. This time he established four guidelines for the classification: 1) to follow the general rules of the ssu-pu 四部 (four main classes); 2) to add more subdivisions to adjust to more recent trends and developments; 3) to employ analytic topics; and 4) to institute cross references.

The *Tan-sheng-t'ang ts'ang-shu mu*, 14 *ch.*, now may be found in the third series of the *Shao-hsing hsien-che i-shu* 紹興先哲遺書, printed in 1892. Although the Tan-

sheng-t'ang library contained literature of all periods, the catalogue gives one the impression that more emphasis was placed on Ming works, which naturally were easier to obtain. In the class of history, it provides a special category for Ming titles, and in the class of individual collected literary works, Ming authors are well represented. Furthermore, Ch'i also added a sub-division of *ts'ung-shu*, practically a new development in Ming times (*see* Hu Chen-heng). Furnished with the materials from his excellent collection, Ch'i compiled two large *ts'ung-shu* himself, the *Tan-sheng-t'ang yü-yüan* 餘苑 and the *Kuo-ch'ao cheng-hsin ts'ung-lu* 國朝徵信叢錄. The former, a collection of a general nature of 188 items in 604 *chüan*, the latter of 132 titles in 212 *chüan*, included only source materials for Ming history. It seems that neither of these has ever been printed.

Ch'i's own collected literary works, the *Tan-sheng-t'ang chi* 集, 21 *ch.*, 6 of poetry and 15 of prose, were printed in 1626. The accounts about his garden, Mi-yüan, appear in *chüan* 11, the library contract in *chüan* 14, biographies of his grandparents and parents in *chüan* 15, and some of his official papers in the last three *chüan*. This works suffered condemnation in the 1780s, and so is rare. But the copy preserved in the National Library of Peiping has been made available on microfilm. Another of his works, the *Mu-ching* 牧津, 44 *ch.*, citing exemplary local administrators known to history, receives a notice in the *Ssu-k'u* catalogue, but was not copied into the Imperial Library.

Ch'i Ch'eng-han had five sons, Ch'i Lin-chia 麟佳, Ch'i Feng 鳳-chia, Ch'i Chün 駿-chia, Ch'i Piao-chia, and Ch'i Hsiang 象-chia. Of the five, Ch'i Piao-chia, who died a martyr to the Ming cause, is the best known. He proved himself not only to be an able official and erudite scholar, but also inherited his father's fondness for both garden planning and book collecting. To satisfy his own whim he built himself a second garden, the Yü 寓-yüan, known besides as Yü-shan 山, in which he created a library, the Pa-ch'iu 八求-lou. One part of his garden, featuring the building Yüan 遠-shan-t'ang, is said to have been the handwork of the famous contemporary garden architect, Chang Lien (ECCP). It was because of this structure that Ch'i gave himself the sobriquet Yüan-shan chu-jen 主人.

In recent years, several of Ch'i Piao-chia's works have been either printed for the first time, or reprinted from not readily accessible sources. His diary, the *Ch'i Chung-min kung jih-chi* 忠敏公日記, covering the years 1631 to his death in 1645, with a *nien-p'u* preserved by Liang T'ing-nan (ECCP) in the 1830s, was printed in 6 *ts'e* in 1937. Sections of this work, dealing with the years 1644-45, and the *nien-p'u*, were later reprinted by the research department of the Bank of Taiwan in 1969 under the title *Chia-i jih-li* 甲乙日曆. His collected works, the *Ch'i Piao-chia chi*, 10 *ch.*, containing writings, largely poetry by members of his family (as appendices), originally compiled and printed in 1835 under the title *Ch'i Chung-hui* 忠惠 *kung chi* by two brothers, Tu Hsü 杜煦(1780–1850) and Tu Ch'un-sheng 春生 of Shan-yin, were rearranged, reedited, and reprinted in Shanghai in 1960. Of the 10 *chüan*, #5 and #6 deal with famine relief; #7, the "Yü-shan chu" 寓山注, is a long description of his garden; #8, the "Yüeh-chung yüan-t'ing chi" 越中園亭記, is an account of gardens in Chekiang; and #10 is a group of biographical materials about Ch'i Piao-chia. The appendices include works of his wife, Shang Ching-lan 商景蘭 (T. 媚(眉)生, 1605-1676+), a daughter of Shang Chou-tso 周祚 (cs 1601 and minister of Works in Nanking, 1627), his three daughters, Ch'i Te-yüan 德淵 (T. 弢英), Ch'i Te-ch'iung 瓊 (T. 修嫣, d. 1662), and Ch'i Te-ch'ih 茝 (or 莊, T. 湘君), his two sons, Ch'i Li-sun (b. 1627) and Ch'i Pan-sun (b. 1632, both in ECCP, p. 126), and his two daughters-in-law, Chang Te-hui 張德蕙 (T. 楚孃, wife of Ch'i Li-sun

and a granddaughter of Chang Yüan-pien, *q.v.*), and Chu Te-jung 朱德容 (T. 趙璧, wife of Ch'i Pan-sun, and a granddaughter of Chu Hsieh-yüan 燮元 [T. 懋和, H. 衡岳, Pth. 襄毅, 1566-1638, cs 1592, minister of War in 1624-25 and junior preceptor]). It was indeed a talented family.

Another work of Ch'i Piao-chia, the *Yüan-shan-t'ang Ming ch'ü-p'in chü-p'in chiao-lu* 明曲品劇品校錄, was a catalogue of dramatic works by Ming authors in his collection, each item being given some brief introductory or critical remarks. This unique contribution to the study of Ming drama was compiled and edited by Huang Shang 黃裳 and first printed in Shanghai in 1955. According to the publisher's notice, 376 items out of the 677 listed in this catalogue had never been mentioned in other works of a similar nature. The editor in this postscript reports that he discovered the battered manuscript in the early 1950s when many volumes of the Tan-sheng-t'ang collection appeared in the Shanghai book market. Only after he had patched it and compared it with other sources did this work in its present form emerge. The editor believes that probably the first two sections of part one are still missing. An abridged and slightly variant version of this catalogue was printed in T'ai-nan 台南, Taiwan, the title being shortened to *Ming ch'ü-p'in chü-p'in*, and the name of the editor given as Chu Shang-wen 朱尚文.

In 1645 the Ch'i family library was moved to the Lu-hua-ssu 鹿化寺, a monastery attached to the family cemetery. It was somehow kept together until 1666, when the bulk of the collection went to Huang Tsung-hsi and Lü Liu-liang (both in ECCP), between whom a dispute arose because Huang appropriated the choice items for himself. According to another early Ch'ing scholar, Chu I-tsun (ECCP), however, the collection of dramatic works was left intact. Apparently the Ch'i books were not entirely scattered until the early 1950s when the volumes still remaining finally found their way into the Shanghai book market.

Bibliography

40/59/22b; 86/20a; 87/1/3b; TSCC (1885–88), XIV: 42/4b; *Chekiang t'ung-chih* (1934), 2348, 2471; Ch'i Ch'eng-han, *Ming Nan-ching chü-chia-ssu chih-chang*, Research Inst. of Peking Univ. (Commercial Press, Shanghai, 1934); *id.*, *Tan-sheng-t'ang chi* (NLP microfilm), nos. 797, 798; SK (1930), 80/6a; Yeh Ch'ang-ch'ih (BDRC), *Ts'ang-shu chi-shih* (1958), 162; Jung Chao-tsu容肇祖, "Lü Liu-liang chi ch'i ssu-hsiang" 呂留良及其思想, *Fu-jen hsüeh-chih* 輔仁學誌, Vol. II, nos. 1–2 (December, 1936), 42; Sun Tien-ch'i (1957), 217; P. Pelliot, "Quelques remarques sur le Chouo Fou," TP, 23 (1924), 193.

Lienche Tu Fang

CH'I Chi-kuang 戚繼光 (T. 元敬, H. 南塘, 孟諸), January 10, 1528–January 17, 1588, military officer, was born of a hereditary military family at the Teng-chou 登州 guard in Shantung. His sixth generation ancestor, Ch'i Hsiang 詳, a native of Ting-yüan 定遠, adjacent to the birthplace of Chu Yüan-chang, joined the latter's army in the conquest of the empire, and died in action in Yunnan (*ca.*1382), receiving the award of hereditary rank of an assistant commander of the Teng-chou guard. In 1478 Ch'i Chi kuang's father, Ch'i Ching-t'ung景通 (T. 世顯, 1473–1544), succeeded to the family rank, later rising to be an assistant commander of a firearms unit in Peking (1535–38). For years Ch'i Ching-t'ung had longed for a son. When in his fifty-fifth year Ch'i Chi-kuang was born, the father saw to it that he receive a well-rounded education in the Classics and literature in addition to the military arts.

After assuming his father's rank in 1544, Ch'i Chi-kuang performed his duties well; one of his assignments was to lead a Shantung detachment annually to man the Great Wall north of Peking. He did this five times from 1548 to 1552. In between these responsibilities, he took the military examinations and in 1549 received the military *chü-jen* in Shantung. A year later, after he failed to pass the higher examination in Peking (held November 21), he remained in the capital for some duty, and was still there when the Mongols broke through the Great Wall and reached the suburbs. He took part in the defense of the city, and submitted a plan to fight the Mongols on the frontier to prevent any other invasion. In 1553 he received an appointment as an acting assistant commissioner of the Shantung regional military commission, in charge of coastal defenses. Thus at the age of twenty-six he had risen to be a field officer. It is said that he won the name of a disciplinarian after he punished, for failure to obey his orders, an officer much older than himself. From then on his orders were carried out with alacrity. Later he visited the man, actually his maternal uncle, and sympathized with him. Two years later he was transferred to the Chekiang commission in charge of the military farms.

At this time the *wo-k'ou* raids along the Chekiang coast intensified, and selected military officers were being brought into the province to strengthen the local military organization with tactical commands (*see* Yü Ta-yu). In 1556 Ch'i received the appointment of assistant commander in charge of defending the area east of the Ch'ien-t'ang 錢塘 River, and supporting the important cities of Ningpo, Shao-hsing, and T'ai-chou台州. He cooperated with the T'ai-chou prefect, T'an Lun (*q.v.*), in training local troops to fight the pirates. T'an recognized Ch'i's great potential, and during the remainder of his career, which included the post of minister of War (1572–77), managed to keep Ch'i with, or close by, him.

From the bitter experience of inroads by the Japanese pirates, Ch'i formed a plan to train volunteers to defeat the invaders. His plan met with the approval of the supreme commander, Hu Tsung-hsien (*q.v.*), in 1557, and he trained three thousand men from the Shao-hsing area. In 1558, when he took part in the unsuccessful campaigns against the pirates on Chusan Islands, he found the Shao-hsing natives disappointing. He decided that it was difficult to turn urbanites into good soldiers and suggested training farm boys only. In the following summer, because of his failure to dislodge some pirates from his territory, he was cashiered. Thus freed from command, he was assigned to train three thousand volunteers from I-wu 義烏, about 60 miles south of Hangchow. One of his innovations in the training program was the tactical formation known as the yüan-yang chen 鴛鴦陣 (mandarin duck formation) composed of basic units of twelve men each, consisting of one leader, two shield men, two with bamboo lances, and four with long lances, two fork men, and a cook. They were to advance in that order, or in two five man columns dividing the weapons equally, but with the strict ruling that all acted to protect the leader from being wounded. If the leader lost his life, during a battle that ended in defeat, any survivor in his unit was to be executed. Thus each man was drilled in the spirit of win or die. At the same time the weapons were designed especially to fight the Japanese whose long bows were deadly and whose sharp swords could sever any Chinese hand weapon. In Ch'i's tactics the shield was to take care of the arrows, and the bamboo lance, with its bushy branches intact, could slow down the onslaught and entangle the swordsman making it possible for the other lancers to dispatch him. In his experience the Japanese swordsmen were formidable combatants and he needed these five-to-one odds. He organized four basic units to a platoon, four platoons to a company, three companies to a battalion of about six hundred men. To each company was assigned a few muskets and to each battalion, a battery of cannon. But these firearms were not the decisive factor in the 1560s on the China coast. It was Ch'i's trained volunteers. In March, 1560, he was reinstated as assistant commander of the area of T'ai-chou, Yen 嚴-chou, and Chin-hua 金華, and continued the training. A year later, when the T'ai-chou

coast was invaded by a large fresh contingent of pirates, Ch'i led his newly trained volunteers to fight them, and of nine engagements within a single month he won every one. The enemy was annihilated, with only a few casualties among his own men. This complete victory won him promotion to regional commissioner. It also gained for him such prestige that the authorities in Kiangsi requested his help to fight a local uprising in that province. The expedition took place in November. 1561, and within a month it was crushed, The people of Kiangsi noticed a new phenomenon in China, the marching of a disciplined army, well fed, well led, and well trained in coordinated fighting.

In June, 1562, Ch'i led a relief expedition to Fukien against the pirates who had drifted south out of Chekiang. After several victories, Ch'i returned to Chekiang. Then in December the wo-k'ou, reinforced by newly arrived Japanese, captured a large area in Fukien, including the guard city of P'ing-hai 平海 and the prefectural city of Hsing-hua 興化. Early in 1563 Ch'i was appointed vice-commander on the north Fukien coast, while T'an Lun was made grand coordinator. They cooperated in dealing the pirates several heavy blows, recovering both cities by May. Ch'i received a raise in rank to central vice commissioner-in-chief.

Near the close of 1563 he was transferred to Fukien and became area commander for the coasts of Chekiang and Fukien. Ch'i's success against the pirates may be attributed not only to his selection and training of troops, but also to his defense plans and his close collaboration with civil authorities. He chose to recruit his men primarily from places near the area of conflict. He hired them with the help of the local magistrates, and paid them well. He trained and disciplined them so that they charged at the wo-k'ou rather than turning back. While in Chekiang in 1560 he wrote down his training methods in Chi-hsiao hsin-shu 紀效新書 (A new treatise on disciplined service), 18 ch. A major debate of the day among authorities involved in fighting the pirates was whether to meet them on water or on land. Because it was difficult to move men overland, and the troops were not numerous enough to distribute evenly in great numbers along the coast, some thought it wise to meet them on the sea. On the water, others argued, the pirates were in their element and at their best. Ch'i preferred to meet them on the land and set up a three-tiered defense system which entailed an early warning net on the islands off the coast of Fukien, a number of strong garrisons defending important cities, and a highly mobile group under his own personal command to rush to the area of invasion once given warning by this net. In this plan he had the close cooperation of the governor, T'an Lun, and the army inspector, Wang Tao-k'un (*q.v.*). By 1567 Ch'i and his forces had cleared the Fukien coast of the pirates. In honor of the general the local people erected a shrine in that year called Ch'i kung tz'u 公祠 in Fu-ch'ing 福清-hsien (near Foochow); it was restored in 1733, and again (when the Japanese were attacking north China) in 1937. A major reexamination of the defense of the northern frontier was under way at Peking, and Ch'i was recommended as a successful trainer of troops to take command of the forces north of the capital. When he took leave of the Chekiang and Fukien region, he left many of his former subordinates in important positions of military leadership. In the years after. 1574 three former members of the "Ch'i army" were simultaneously area commanders of Chekiang, Fukien, and Kwangtung. Ch'i arrived in the capital in November, 1567, and was appointed vice commander of the firearms division of the Capital Army in which his father had served before him. This was not close enough to the action for Ch'i; so he requested the command of Chi 薊-chou, Liaotung, Ch'ang-p'ing 昌平, and Paoting defense areas. T'an Lun had preceded Ch'i to the capital and was supreme commander of those four areas; he joined in recommending Ch'i's appointment. At the end of May, 1568, Ch'i was made superintendent of training for the three defense areas of Chi-chou, Ch'ang-p'ing, and Paoting, and the following year was given the title of concurrent area commander of Chi-chou.

Ch'i's fifteen years along the Great Wall in charge of the defense against the Mongols were quiet compared with the active days of fighting the pirates on the coast. This was chiefly due to the peace treaty concluded with the Mongols in 1571 (*see* Altan qaɣan), but Ch'i's training of an effective corps and the defenses set up by him under the direction of Chang Chü-cheng (*q.v.*) and T'an Lun certainly served as deterrents. First, Ch'i succeeded in making the shift from tactical commander to military administrator with ease and with enthusiasm. He reorganized the defense of the Chi-chou area in four tiers, much in the same way in which he had reorganized the Fukien coastal defense. He repaired the Wall, built more observation towers (to serve as his early warning net), organized training centers, and concentrated on drilling cavalry and wagon troops. He thought that the Mongols, like the pirates, were strongest in their element: in their case, on horseback on hard ground. Ch'i's defense strategy emphasized attacking the Mongols once they had either penetrated, or been allowed to penetrate, the Great Wall. In his training efforts, Ch'i requested the transfer of some of the military officers and personnel of his Chekiang days. This was refused on principle, although some of his junior officers did come north with him, and eventually nine thousand troops were sent to help him. While at the Chi defense area, Ch'i compiled the *Lien-ping shih-chi* 練兵實記 (A practical account of troop training), 9 *ch.* +*tsa* 雜-*chi*, 6 *ch.*, a manual and record of the drilling and defensive tactics which he implemented in that area.

T'an Lun left his post as supreme

commander in 1570, and became minister of War, but Ch'i remained at the Chi defense area under four more supreme commanders. During these years Ch'i received several promotions and various awards. In 1570 he was named junior commissioner-in-chief. A year later, on the partial completion of the construction of towers on the Great Wall (*see* T'an Lun) Ch'i received the hereditary rank of a chiliarch in the Teng-chou guard. In 1574 he became senior commissioner-in-chief, the highest military rank in the empire. Seven years later he was awarded an additional hereditary rank, that of centurion in the Embroidered-uniform Guard and, besides, the exalted title of junior guardian and concurrently senior guardian of the heir apparent. He was the only military officer not of the nobility in the entire dynasty to receive such a designation, although four others received the higher title of grand tutor. Also quite extraordinary was his long tenure of fourteen years as area commander at Chi-chou, where, in the previous fifteen years there had been eight holders of the post. This lengthy tenure was due not only to Ch'i's proven ability as a military officer, but perhaps also to his having friends in power in the capital: T'an Lun as War minister and Chang Chü-cheng as grand secretary until his death in 1582.

Less than six months after Chang's death, Ch'i was impeached and in the following year removed from his post (February, 1583). He returned to Teng-chou, was later recalled for duty in Kwangtung, but retired in 1585, and returned again to Teng-chou where he died. The great scholar, Wang Tao-k'un, then in retirement, penned his tomb inscription. Three decades later the court awarded him the posthumous name Wu-i 武毅. Shrines in his memory were erected at the places where he rendered service, at least three of them being recorded at Hsinghua. Ch'i had a younger brother named Ch'i Chi-mei 美, who rose to be regional commander of Kweichow (July, 1582).

It is interesting to note that, whereas the late president, Yüan Shih-k'ai (**BD RC**), placed him high on his list of China's military heroes, he is said to have been a hen-pecked man and afraid of his wife, a woman of strong character who in 1561 took charge of the defense of a fort surrounded by pirates. They were married in 1545 and she bore no children. After 1563 he took several concubines but hid them from her. By these women he had five sons; the eldest, Ch'i Tso-kuo 祚國, was born in 1567. In May, 1630, his third son, Ch'i Ch'ang 昌-kuo (b. 1573), who was serving as a commander in charge of the police court of the Embroidered-uniform Guard in Peking, memorialized on the distinguished exploits of his father, and requested an official designation for the shrine in Teng-chou. The emperor granted it the name Piao-chung 表忠 tz'u.

Ch'i Chi-kuang's two manuals on military training, reprinted many times, have come to be regarded as classics on military matters. The first, *Chi-hsiao hsin-shu*, was initially printed by Ch'i himself about 1562. It is known to have been reprinted in Szechwan *ca.* 1566. The Library of Congress has a 1569 edition, with a preface by the governor of Honan, Li Pang-chen 李邦珍 (cs 1550), who added some documents as preliminary *chüan* (卷首). There are some editions that contain numerous changes, such as the one published in 1588 by General Li Ch'eng-hsün 李承勛 (fl. 1550-1600, of the Ch'u-chou 處州 guard); this is a revised and completely rearranged edition in 14 *chüan*, incorporating parts of Ch'i's other works as well as some new information supplied by Li himself. Ch'i's second work, *Lien-ping shih-chi*, was first printed about 1571, and reprinted around 1580 as part of Ch'i's collected works, entitled *Chih-chih-t'ang chi* 止止堂集; this included, in addition to the first two works, his miscellaneous notes, *Yü-yü kao* 愚愚稿, 2 *ch.*, and his poems and prose, *Heng-shuo* 橫槊 *kao*, 3 *ch.* His writings on military matters have been frequently abridged or reedited and printed under spurious titles, such as *Li-jung yao-lüeh* 苙戎要略, or *Ch'ang-tzu hsin-ch'ien* 長子心鈐. Several of Ch'i's works, in full or in part, are included in various *ts'ung-shu*. Both Tseng Kuo-fan (ECCP) and Chiang Kai-shek have signaled their importance for men on the field, the latter writing in his preface to the Whampoo edition of Ch'i's works on military training: "These are the best books written on the practical use of troops since Sun-tzu [3d cent. B.C.]." Some of Ch'i's important memorials arecontained in *Huang Ming ching-shih wen-pien* by Ch'en Tzu-lung (ECCP), and additional memórials and poems are included in his chronological biography edited and compiled by his son, Ch'i Tso-kuo.

Bibliography

1/212/11a; 3/196/9b; 5/106/54a; MSL (1965), Mu-tsung, 0358, 0544 (1966), Shen-tsung, 2474; KC (1958), 5529; SK (1930), 99/5b, 6a, 100/5a, 178 /12a; *Shantung t'ung-chih* (1934), 1438, 4743; *Fu-chou-fu chih* 福州府志 (1754, Taipei repr.), 15/384; Sun Tien-ch'i (1957), 36; Ch'i Chi-kuang, *Chi-hsiao hsin-shu* (NLP microfilm, no. 564); *id., Lien-ping shih-chi* (NLP microfilm, no. 559); NCL *Catalogue*, 453, 454; L. of C. *Catalogue of Rare Books*, 471; Naikaku Bunko *Catalogue*, 183; Ch'en Tzu-lung, *Ming ching-shih wen-pien*, ch. 346-350; Hsieh Ch'eng-jen 謝承仁 and Ning K'o, 寧可, *Ch'i Chi-kuang* (Shanghai, 1961); Ch'i Tso-kuo, *Ch'i shao-pao* 少保 *nien-p'u, 12 ch.* (Hsien-yu仙遊, Fukien, 1878); Su T'ung-ping蘇同炳, *Ch'i Chi-kuang* (Hong Kong, 1959); James F. Milling-er, "Ch'i Chi-kuang, Chinese Military Official," (Ph. D. dissertation, Yale, 1968); J. Edkins, *A Catalogue of Chinese Works in the Bodleian Library*(Oxford, 1876), #54, #55; A. Wylie, *Notes on Chinese Literature* (repr. of 1922), 91; R. F. Johnston, "Chinese Cult of Military Heroes," *New China Review*, III (1921), 86; Howard S. Levy, *Warm Soft Village* (Tokyo, 1964), 14.

J. F. Millinger and Chaoying Fang

CH'I T'ai 齊泰 (T. 尚禮, H. 南塘), died July 25, 1402, statesman and martyr, was probably a native of Li-shui 溧水, one of the districts lying just south of Nanking and belonging to the capital prefecture. As is true of many of the officials who

were executed for resisting Chu Ti (*q.v.*) biographical data for Ch'i T'ai are missing, or reported inconsistently in the standard biographical sources. Under the name of Ch'i Te 德 he achieved first place in the provincial examination at the capital in 1384, passed the *chin-shih* examination in 1385, and was appointed a secretary in the ministry of Rites. It is said that as one of those who had no demerit after nine years of service, he was chosen to accompany the emperor in rites conducted at the Temple of Heaven. By imperial order his name was changed from Te to T'ai. About 1395, as a director of a bureau in the ministry of War, he showed his detailed knowledge, during a discussion at court on frontier defense, by giving the correct names of each commander on the northern border. When the emperor further questioned him about the maps, charts, and documents relevant to the subject, Ch'i drew from his sleeve a small manual he had prepared, reducing all the complex information to a clear and simple format, and presented it to Chu Yüan-chang. The emperor, impressed, promoted him (1395) to vice minister of War. Shortly before his death in 1398, the monarch is said to have charged Ch'i with special responsibility to guard his grandson and heir, Chu Yün-wen (*q. v.*).

Whether the old emperor's favor was a factor or not, the young emperor on coming to the throne in June of 1398 relied heavily on Ch'i T'ai and another civil offiicial, Huang Tzu-ch'eng (*see* Lien Tzu-ning) They became informal chief ministers in the outer court, and the emperor's closest advisers. Huang became chancellor of the Hanlin Academy and, on July 3, Ch'i was appointed minister of War. Almost from the moment of the new emperor's accession, these two officials were totally absorbed in the problem of how to reduce the power of the imperial princes (the emperor's uncles and cousins), some nine of whom held significant and growing power as heads of large military contingents subordinate to their princedoms (*see* Chu Yün-wen). This problem had several thorny aspects. First, the princedoms with their garrison forces and defense responsibilities, represented a key element in the structure of power devised by Chu Yüan-chang, hence not easily altered. The problem had to be met both in terms of specific legal rights of the princes established in the founder's binding *Huang Ming tsu-hsün* (Ancestral Instructions), and as part of more general considerations of state structure. That is, it was both an imperial clan matter and a state matter. Second, any imbalance in the delicate set of arrangements might open up the northern borders to incursions of powerful external enemies or might provoke rebellion, thereby becoming a domestic military problem. Third, and somewhat less certain, is the probability that the initiative lay in the hands of Chu Ti, eldest of the founder's surviving sons; Ch'i T'ai and the young emperor may have had good evidence that Chu Ti was planning insurrection whether or not the court took steps to reduce the princedoms, and therefore were forced to respond in haste rather than work out an ideal solution.

Ch'i T'ai's long-acknowledged expertise in border defense and military matters naturally made him a well-qualified minister of War. He and Huang Tzu-ch'eng, being the two officials most obviously identifiable with the policy of reducing the princedoms, Chu Ti made them symbols of evil in his war propaganda. His way of legitimizing his uprising was to appeal to an article in the Ancestral Instructions giving the princes responsibility to intervene with force in the affairs of the court should a youthful or disabled emperor come under the evil domination of treacherous ministers. Chu Yün-wen was past twenty, therefore a mature adult by Chinese reckoning when he came to the throne, but Chu Ti insisted that he was a perverse and unfilial youth, and that the plan to reduce the princedoms, illegal in the light of the Ancestral Instructions and

therefore unfilial, was conceived in the treacherous minds of Ch'i and Huang. Thus they were named in many of the usurper's proclamations as the real objects of his campaign; all the official accounts, constructed during the succeeding reign to replace the destroyed archives, excoriate them. At the same time, later accounts sympathetic to Chu Yün-wen also offer mostly unfounded reconstructions of the events, and in the spirit of shielding the young emperor from blame, often charge Ch'i and Huang with well-intentioned incompetence. Neither of these extreme views is credible.

From some of the information that can be pieced together about the Chienwen reign, it appears to be quite possible that Chu Yün-wen encouraged two or even three factions within his government, perhaps permitting them to serve as checks on each other. He quite obviously used them to provide a varying tone to his government, coordinated to the varying attitude he assumed toward prosecution of the civil war. That is, Ch'i and Huang were employed prominently when the war was going well, to symbolize uncompromising extirpation of the rebellion. Ju Ch'ang (*q. v.*), Li Ching-lung (*see* Li Wenchung), and others more acceptable to Chu Ti, were employed when he wished to approach Chu Ti to negotiate a compromise settlement. Ch'i's career illustrates this: he was promoted to minister of War in July, 1398; he was dismissed and replaced by Ju Ch'ang in December, 1399, after Li Ching-lung's serious defeats; he was reappointed minister of War in January, 1401, after the victories of Sheng Yung (*q. v.*) permitted an air of confidence to return to the Nanking government; he was again dismissed and replaced by Ju Ch'ang in July of that same year, after further defeats. At that time Chu Yün-wen sent a letter to his uncle announcing that inimical elements in the government had been dismissed and punished, and that through negotiation they could settle their differences. Chu Ti labeled this a hollow device intended to deter him, and replied that, although the "two traitors" had been dismissed, their policy had not been displaced, so negotiation was impossible. Chu Ti's observation was accurate enough, for indeed Ch'i T'ai's alternate appointments and dismissals seem to have been merely part of the public posturing that accompanied the struggle; whether in office or out, Ch'i T'ai seems to have kept the emperor's favor and to have remained an important adviser. Yet Ch'i and Huang did not always agree on important issues. Ch'i strongly opposed, though unsuccessfully, Huang's nomination of Li Ching-lung to be commander-in-chief of the forces sent north against Chu Ti in the fall of 1399, and there are other fragments of evidence to show that the civil officials at the imperial court constituted two factions, while the military officials represented still a third power group. Thus Ch'i T'ai and Huang Tzu-ch'eng, contrary to the propaganda emanating from Chu Ti's camp, must be regarded as loyal servants of the throne, and not as dictators who could control the emperor and determine the course of events.

Several events in Ch'i T'ai's career that are reported in most historical accounts probably are spurious, and must be credited either to the falsifications created as part of later official accounts, or to the mass of legend that arose following the usurpation, and grew throughout the dynasty. These include Ch'i's supposed visit to Peiping and Chu Ti's attempted bribery of him, and his advice to the young emperor at the time of Chu Yüan-chang's death, or again the following winter, or on both occasions, not to permit Chu Ti to visit the court at Nanking. In fact Chu Ti did not visit the court during the entire period from 1398 onward, nor would he have attempted to do so.

Throughout the last year of the Chien-wen reign Ch'i was not only out of office but away from the court, and it appears that he and Huang were assigned to important and semi-secret activities in the central and lower Yangtze provinces, recruiting and organizing the training of local militia that could be called upon if the civil war should extend to the region near the capital. Shortly after the capital was seriously threatened, in June of 1402, they were recalled, but Nanking was surrounded and entered before either could reach it. Both took steps to conceal their identity and flee to points where resistance could be organized. Ch'i was identified at Kuang-te 廣德 (Anhwei), captured, and delivered to Chu Ti at Nanking. While the latter had hopes that some prominent officials would come over to him, he had publicly proclaimed for two and one half years that Ch'i and Huang must die. They conducted themselves nobly, berating their captor and expressing loyalty to Chu Yün-wen to the end. On July 25 they and many others were publicly executed and their families ordered exterminated. More distant clan relatives and other associates were banished to the frontiers. Chu Kao-chih (*q. v.*), soon after coming to the throne in 1424, issued a proclamation of amnesty for survivors of families involved in the events of 1402. Ch'i T'ai is said to have had a five-year old son who was spared but sentenced to exile; at this time he reportedly came forth to claim the family property, under the amnesty. [Editors' note: According to one source, when Chu Ti ordered Ch'i T'ai's son, Ch'i Te-i 得義, to go into exile, a close associate of Ch'i T'ai by the name of Li Yu-lieh 李友烈, fearing that Ch'i's only heir might be harmed, secretly sent his own son to take his place. Ch'i's son thus lived under the name of the Li family. During the Ch'eng-hua period, Ch'i Te-i's descendants returned to settle in Li-shui, but did not resume their family name until the K'ang-hsi period. If this story be true, the man who reportedly came forward to reclaim the Ch'i family property was not of Ch'i T'ai's own blood, but the son of Li Yu-lieh whose descendants continued to assume the Ch'i family name.] In 1525 a shrine in honor of Ch'i, called Piao-chung tz'u 表忠祠, was erected at Li-shui. During the post-Ming period of resistance to the Manchu conquest, the short-lived southern Ming court of the prince of Fu, Chu Yu-sung (ECCP), at Nanking in 1645 bestowed posthumous honors on a number of Chien-wen loyalists. Ch'i T'ai was granted the honorific of Chieh-min 節愍, "the highly principled, unafraid to die." In 1776 the Ch'ien-lung emperor (see Hung-li, ECCP) bestowed upon Ch'i T'ai the posthumous name Chung-ching 忠敬. None of his writings has survived.

Bibliography

1/141/1a; 5/38/11a; 63/5/1a; MSL (1962), T'ai-tsu 3453, Jen-tsung (1963), 157; KC (1958), ch. 11–12, 6171; Li-shui-hsien chih (1882), 8/9a, 9/3b, 11/7a, 12/2b, 19/18a; Chu Ta-shao 朱大韶, Huang Ming ming-ch'en mu-ming 皇明名臣墓銘 (1969), Ch'ien chi 乾集, 55; T'u Shu-fang 屠叔方 (cs 1577), Chien-wen ch'ao yeh hui-pien 建文朝野彙編 (NCL microfilm), 8/17a; Wang Ch'ung-wu 王崇武, Ming ching-nan shih-shih k'ao-cheng kao 明靖難史事考證稿 Shanghai, 1948; id., Feng-t'ien ching-nan chi chu 奉天靖難記注, Shanghai, 1948.

F. W. Mote

CH'I Te, see CH'I T'ai

CHIANG Hsin 蔣信 (T. 卿實, H. 道林, 正學), September 28, 1483-December 31, 1559, thinker and official, had forebears who were natives of Feng-yang 鳳陽 (Anhwei). In the 14th century, at the beginning of the Ming dynasty, his ancestor Chiang Wen-chü 文舉 took office as magistrate at Ch'ang-te 常德, Hukuang, and settled there. His father, Chiang Ching 經 (H. 惠庵, d. 1496), although of modest means, was well regarded for his generosity. Chiang Hsin is described as a handsome and diligent child. His father's death came as a serious blow, affecting his health. At the age of eighteen, having qualified as a hsiu-ts'ai, he filled a vacancy as a salaried graduate. He became known for his careful observance of the rules of propriety. In spite of his needs, he declined all monetary aid offered by district officials. For about five years, from the age of twenty-four on, he used to discuss philosophy with his fellow townsman Chi Yüan-heng (see Wang Shou-jen). Both were interested in the Hsi-ming 西銘 (Western Inscription) of Chang Tsai (1020–77). In 1510 Wang Shou-jen passed Ch'ang-te on his way to Lu-ling 盧陵, Kiangsi, while returning from exile in Kweichow, and met both Chi Yüan-heng and Chiang Hsin. Together they spent time in meditation in a temple. Some time after that, Chiang fell seriously ill with tuberculosis. He eventually moved into the Tao-lin 道林 monastery, where, refraining from medical help, he spent his time day and night practicing meditation in a quest for purity of heart and detachment from life itself. After having done so for over six months, he found himself one day suddenly bathed in perspiration and surrounded by a bright light. He experienced then a certain enlightenment accompanied by a consciousness of himself being one with the universe. He also discovered that his disease had left him.

Chiang Hsin was then thirty-one years of age. He derived much profit from this experience, finding in the Confucian Classics the confirmation of his insights. His reputation for learning and wisdom gradually increased. After the death of his mother in 1518, Chiang built a house near Tao-lin, where he taught his disciples the art of quiet sitting and the meaning of the Confucian quest for jen 仁 (human-heartedness, given a universal connotation as consciousness of man's oneness with all things). In 1522, he attempted the provincial examinations, but failed to pass them, as he was prevented by ulcers on his elbows from writing properly; nevertheless, he returned home filled with joy and serenity. The following year he went as a tribute student to Peking, and met Chan Jo-shui (q.v.) for the first time. Enlisting formally as Chan's disciple, he stayed with him for several months, before returning to his home. In 1525 he visited Chan again when the latter was chancellor of the National University in Nanking, and entered this institution as a student, winning Chan Jo-shui's praise, especially for an essay written on the doctrine of Ch'eng Hao (1032–85) as to how a scholar might realize in himself the truth of jen. He entrusted him with the instruction of some of his own numerous disciples, while Chiang's friendly manner attracted many others to himself. In 1526 Chiang returned home where once more his former disciples assembled around him. He finally (1528) succeeded in passing the provincial examinations at Nanking, and four years later qualified for the *chin-shih* at the age of forty-nine. Appointed first as observer in the ministry of Revenue, he was later made secretary in the Fukien bureau of that ministry. Together with several others who had also acquired their degrees in the same year, such as Hsü Yüeh (*see* Ho Hsin-yin) and P'an Tzu-cheng 潘子正 (T. 汝中, H. 十泉), Chiang Hsin frequently discussed philosophical and scholarly subjects. He once received an order to take soldiers' rations to Shensi, and, unlike others who had been similarly commissioned, carried it out without making any profit for himself. In 1536 he was promoted to be vice director in the bureau of equipment in the ministry of War, his parents and wife all receiving honors. His wife, née Liu 柳, sought then to give him a maid as a concubine, but Chiang showed no interest. That same winter he was promoted to be assistant surveillance officer of the irrigation circuit in the Szechwan surveillance office. While there he corrected several administrative abuses, particularly in the horse and tea trade, giving peace to a region then beset by Miao tribesmen, settling difficult criminal cases, and inspecting schools. In 1539 he made a trip to Peking on the occasion of the emperor's birthday. The following year Chiang supervised the Szechwan provincial examinations. A few months later, he received a transfer to Kweichow as vice-commissioner of education. Proceeding there in 1541, he remained for three

years, gaining during this time the respect of the regional inspector, Chao Ta-yu 趙大佑 (T. 世胤, H. 方厓, 1510–69, cs 1535) for settling an aboriginal uprising; for this Chao recommended him to the court for higher office, but to no avail. While in Kweichow, Chiang built two academies, named Wen-ming 文明 and Cheng-hsüeh正學. In 1543 he requested sick leave, but his request was denied. When he was sent afterward as emissary from Kweichow to a conference in Ch'en-chou 辰州, Hukuang, on military problems affecting the three provinces of Szechwan, Hukuang, and Kweichow, Chiang completed his business within a month and also recovered his health, perhaps because the climate there was more congenial. Instead of returning immediately to his post, Chiang spent some time at home. For this, the censor, Wei Hung-mien 魏洪晃 (H. 古厓), charged him with having left his post without proper permission. It has been said that Wei's action was prompted by personal animosity. In any case, Chiang was deprived of his official rank. When he left Kweichow the people gave him a tearful farewell.

Chiang Hsin in1544 joined his elderly master, Chan Jo-shui, at Mount Heng 衡山 in Hukuang, where the latter had built a shrine in honor of Ch'en Hsien-chang (*q.v.*). Chiang went from there to Mount Shan-te 善德 where a number of his disciples, old and new, joined him. In 1548 a censor of Hukuang, Wang Ssu-chih 王思質, recommended him for service at the court, but without success. That same year, when Chiang revisited Mount Heng, he was invited by his friend and classmate, P'an Tzu-cheng, who then held a surveillance post in Heng-yang 衡陽, to give lectures in the academies established by Chan Jo-shui, the Kan-ch'üan ching-she 甘泉精舍 and Shih-ku shu-yüan 石鼓書院. Chiang then went to Kwangtung to see Chan and, after giving lectures in the Tu-kang 獨岡 shu-yüan, returned home in the following spring. It was after that journey that he built the T'ao-kang 桃岡

ching-she for his disciples. In 1551 he received a visit from Chao Chen-chi and the following year from Hu Tsung-hsien (*qq.v.*), then regional inspector in Hukuang, who aided him with donations for his academy. Three years later he sent his son, Chiang Ju-ch'uan 如川, to Kwangtung to congratulate Chan Jo-shui on the latter's ninetieth (*sui*) birthday. He had several exchanges of correspondence (1555) with Lo Hung-hsien (*q.v.*) on the subject of the "investigation of things." He saw Chan Jo-shui once more in 1557 on Mount Heng. By 1559 Chiang was seventy-six years of age, and seemed in good health. In November of that year, however, he fell sick and soon died. He demonstrated great serenity during his last days, which he spent writing poems in the presence of his two sons and his numerous disciples, as well as Hsieh Hsi-ming 謝錫命 (T. 東湖), a disciple of Chan Jo-shui sent there by the master to congratulate Chiang Hsin on his birthday. The latter is said to have been discussing the meaning of shen-tu 愼獨 (vigilance in solitude) in his final hours.

As a thinker, Chang Hsin has been classified by Huang Tsung-hsi (ECCP) as a follower of the school of Wang Shoujen. In reality, Chiang was influenced much more by Chan Jo-shui than by Wang Shoujen, as Huang Tsung-hsi himself admits. Besides, Chiang had met Wang before the latter had developed his central doctrine of liang-chih (knowledge of the good). For this reason, Chiang himself seldom spoke of this concept, preferring that of hsin (or the mind). Nevertheless, in so far as he had met and discussed learning with Wang Shou-jen, and also to the extent that Wang's philosophy resembles that of Chan Jo-shui, Chiang Hsin's teaching manifests various points of similarity with that of Wang Shou-jen. Chiang emphasized the doctrine of the unity of man with all things, but explained it in terms reminiscent of Chang Tsai, as the result of the underlying ch'i 氣 which permeated all things. He also favored the practice of quiet sitting as a method of cultivation, maintaining that it could lead to the knowledge of one's own mind and heart, which contains in itself the power of perfecting one's character. He did not, however, underestimate the importance of action, as his own busy official life amply demonstrates.

In his writings Chiang Hsin paid little attention to style, but aimed rather at being clear and simple, giving expression to the thoughts of his heart in a spontaneous and direct fashion. According to the *Ssu-k'u* Catalogue, Chiang left two important collections. The first is the *Chiang Tao-lin wen-ts'ui* 文粹, 9 *ch.*, compiled by his disciple Yao Hsüeh-min 姚學閔, and published in 1577. It includes the prefaces he wrote to some of Chan Jo-shui's writings, in particular to the *Hsin-hsing shu* 心性書 and the *Chia-hsün* 家訓, his own prose writings on philosophical subjects, taken from Confucian texts and from the Sung thinkers, his letters, and various epitaphs written in honor of relatives and friends, including Chi Yüan-heng. The National Central Library of Taipei has a copy of this work and a microfilm is available. The second work, *Tao-lin chu-chi* 諸集, compiled by another disciple, Chang P'ing 章評, is not divided into *chüan*. This work includes a treatise on the meaning of the Great Learning, lectures, dialogues, as well as academy rules at T'ao-kang, and certain notes taken during his illness. The editors of the *Ssu-k'u* Catalogue mention this work, but did not copy it into the Imperial Library. It seems to be no longer extant. Chiang's teaching and writings exerted a certain influence especially in the Hukuang region.

Chiang Hsin's son, Chiang Ju-ch'uan, was also known as a scholar. He served for a time as a district magistrate in Yunnan. His other son, Chiang Ju-chih 止, became a tribute student. His grandson, Chiang Meng-ch'i 孟奇, was instructor in the Confucian school in I-yang 益陽, Hukuang. His great-grandson, Chiang Hsing 釖, a poet, was killed, after the fall of Ch'ang-te, by troops of Chang

Hsien-chung (ECCP), in 1643.

Bibliography

3/185/16b; 5/103/62a; 83/28/1a; *Ming-shih* (Taiwan ed.), 162, 3183; Chiang Hsin, *Chiang Tao-lin hsien-sheng wen-ts'ui* (1577); Hsü Hsüeh-mo, *Hsü-shih hai-yü chi wai-p'ien* (1577), 40/14a; *Hunan t'ung-chih* (1934), 3379; SK (1930), 96/4b 177/9b; *Wu-ling-hsien chih* (1868), 21/41b; Wang Shou-jen, *Wang Wen-ch'eng kung ch'üan-shu* (SPTK, 1st series, double-page lithograph ed.), 32/911.

Julia Ching

CHIANG Pin 江彬 (T. 文宜), died July 11, 1521, a native of Hsüan-fu 宣府 (in modern Chahar), was a military official, known for his skill in archery and horsemanship. He was violent, crafty, and of commanding stature. At first he was made assistant commander of the Yü-chou Guard 蔚州衞 (also in Chahar). In 1511, as an officer in Tatung, he and his troops under orders from the regional commander, Chang Chün 張俊, hurried southward to attack the rebels, Liu Liu 劉六, Liu Ch'i 劉七, and Ch'i Yen-ming (*see* Yang T'ing-ho), all natives of Wen-an 文安, Pei-Chihli. Later in the same year, when he was fighting against them near the River Huai 淮河, he was hit by three arrows, one of which struck his face and lodged in his ear. In spite of his pain, he himself extracted the arrow and went on fighting. This manifestation of courage received the plaudits of Emperor Chu Hou-chao (*q.v.*).

In 1512, after the suppression of the rebellion, the frontier troops returned to their original stations; Chiang Pin, however, was ordered to remain in Peking. Some time later he offered a large bribe to the eunuch Ch'ien Ning (*see* Sayyid Ḥusain), one of the emperor's adopted sons and the head of the Embroidered-uniform Guard; this resulted in his being granted an audience with the emperor. As soon as the latter saw Chiang's scar, he said admiringly: "What a strong, brave man!" Seizing the opportunity thus given,

Chiang talked with the emperor about military matters to the latter's obvious satisfaction. Shortly afterward Chiang Pin received a promotion to be assistant commissioner of a regional military commission. From then on, he often frequented the Pao-fang (or Leopard House, *see* Sayyid Ḥusain), and remained there.

As Chiang Pin's position as favorite was being consolidated, Ch'ien Ning became jealous of him. He frequently spoke ill of Chiang to the emperor, but the latter paid no heed. Knowing that Ch'ien Ning envied him and that there were many of Ch'ien's adherents at court, Chiang determined to use the frontier troops to strengthen his position. Accordingly, he reported to the emperor that they were stronger than the metropolitan, and suggested that the emperor order these two commands to exchange stations, so as to make them familiar with each other's locale. The emperor complied. Consequently, at the end of 1512, selected troops of the four defense areas, viz. Liaotung, Hsüan-fu, Tatung, and Yen-sui 延綏, moved to the capital. This army, also known as Wai-ssu-chia 外四家 (the army of the four frontier commands), often went through its military exercises at the capital, and the emperor, accompanied by Chiang Pin, frequently went to see them drill. Since he, as well as Chiang, was in military dress on these occasions, they were hardly distinguishable from each other when riding side by side.

In 1513 Chiang Pin was made commander of the Shen-wei division 神威營. About this time he was granted the imperial surname Chu 朱 and became another of the emperor's adopted sons. Two years later he was appointed to be assistant commissioner-in-chief of a chief military commission. On his recommendation, the regional commissioner of the Wan-ch'üan 萬全 military commission, Li Tsung 李琮 (d. 1521), and the regional commissioner of the Shensi military commission, Shen Chou 神周 (d. 1521), were also given the imperial surname and became the emperor's adopted sons; furthermore, both of them were ordered to reside in the Pao-fang where the emperor usually lived.

Chiang Pin, knowing the emperor's interests, encouraged him to make tours of the frontier. Chiang is reported to have said: "Among the sing-song girls in Hsüan-fu there are many who are beautiful. If His Majesty goes there, he will see them. Besides, His Majesty will be able to have a good ride and be able to observe the engagements between our soldiers and the enemy along the frontier. I know that His Majesty is now often troubled by certain courtiers. If so, why does he not go to Hsüan-fu and other places near the border to enjoy himself?" Finally persuaded, the emperor left on August 17, 1517, traveling incognito to Ch'ang-p'ing 昌平, Pei-Chihli, accompanied by a small retinue of attendants including Chiang Pin. He returned to Peking a few days later, but on September 8 left a second time, passed through the Wall at Chü-yung kuan 居庸關 on the 16th of the month and reached Hsüan-fu. Under the direct supervision of Chiang, a palace called Chen-kuo fu 鎮國府 had been erected there for the emperor, and every piece of furniture, jewelry, and other treasures in the Pao-fang were transferred there; also a number of serving girls in Peking were ordered to go to Hsüan-fu to attend the emperor. The latter, accompanied by Chiang, sometimes entered people's residences at night to seek out women for his harem. His guards even wrecked their houses to get material for fuel when they were in need of firewood. It was a calamitous time for the simple folk of the region. The emperor, however, was elated. He liked Hsüan-fu so much that he came to call the new palace Chia-li 家裡 (his own home), and almost forgot the capital.

When the emperor was at Yang-ho 陽和, Shansi, in October, 1517, the Tatar chief Hsiao-wang-tzu 小王子 or Batü Möngke (q.v.), unexpectedly led fifty thousand horsemen in a raid against the Chinese frontier near the town. The emperor promptly gave directions to his troops to fight. He was nearly captured in this battle, but in the end the enemy was obliged to retreat. During these years the emperor called himself generalissimo Wei-wu, Chu Shou 威武大將軍朱壽, also duke of Chen-kuo 鎮國, and his station chün-men 軍門 (military post). No national business, important or trivial, could be presented to him except through Chiang Pin. Great delays thereby ensued in the transmission of government dispatches, the response to some memorials even being delayed for two or three years. Many officials remonstrated with the emperor against his irresponsibility but he paid no attention. On February 15, 1518, he returned to the capital from Hsüan-fu. Yet his thoughts often strayed in that direction; so on March 2 he went once more with Chiang in his train. A few days later, however, he returned to the capital as his legal grandmother, Empress-dowager Wang (see Wan Kuei-fei), had died on March 20. On August 7 of the same year the emperor appointed himself supreme commander of military affairs and concurrently regional commander to guard the northern frontier. About the same time Chiang was made vice generalissimo Wei-wu. On August 14 the emperor, guided by Chiang, once more started a tour of the northwest. They went to Hsüan-fu and Tatung, where on October 21 Chiang was given the title earl of P'ing-lu 平虜 (the earl who subjugates the caitiffs). They then crossed the Yellow River, and arrived at Sian via Yü-lin 榆林 and Sui-te 綏德 (both in Shensi). Subsequently they visited Taiyuan by a circuitous route through P'ien-t'ou kuan 偏頭關. During these months many girls and even married women all along the way were seized for the emperor's seraglio; one of them, Liu Niang-niang 劉娘娘, the daughter of Liu Liang 良, and the wife of Yang T'eng 楊騰 (a musician of Shansi), became a special favorite. As soon as the emperor reached Hsüan-fu from Taiyuan on February 16, 1519, he appointed Chiang Pin to be general commandant of the twelve integrated divisions of Peking. By this time the emperor, in full military attire, had ridden several thousand miles. Having faced the weather, braved the snow, and proceeded over difficult terrain on the march, most of his attendants were greatly fatigued, and some of them were ill. His own condition, however, remained good.

After returning to the capital from Hsüan-fu on March 8, he decided to go on a southern tour. Hearing that the prince of Ning, Chu Ch'en-hao (*see* Wang Shou-jen), had risen in rebellion on July 10 the same year, Chiang, falling in with the emperor's wishes, asked him to lead the army in person. The emperor agreed with alacrity, though many officials were opposed. Accordingly Chiang Pin was made superintendent and adviser on confidential military affairs and concurrently supervisor of the Eastern Depot and the Embroidered-uniform Guard. At this time, the eunuch Chang Jui 張銳 (T. 退之, exiled 1521, d. soon after), in charge of the Eastern Depot, and Ch'ien Ning of the Embroidered-uniform Guard, were both under Chiang Pin's supervision. Clearly his star was in the ascendant. On September 15, leading his punitive force, the emperor left Peking for the south; in the retinue, Chiang Pin was the most important figure. Although the emperor had received the report that Chu Ch'en-hao had been arrested and that Wang Shou-jen had already crushed the rebellion, he did not stop. He reached Nanking on January 15 of the following year. Later in that same year, because of a rumor amongst the troops that Chiang Pin was about to rebel, the emperor began to doubt his loyalty and insisted on returning. On September 23 he left Nanking and on the 22d of the next month he proceeded to Ch'ing-chiang-p'u 清江浦, north of Nanking, where he spent several days in sport and relaxation. Later, while diverting himself fishing in a pond near the town, his skiff was upset and he fell into the water. Though rescued, he was ill for a time. When he reached T'ung-chou 通州, near Peking, on his return (December 5), Chiang Pin requested him to make another tour of Hsüan-fu. Many officials being opposed, and the emperor himself being exhausted, Chiang's request was denied. On January 18, 1521, the emperor, a very sick man, reached the capital. Feigning an order from above, Chiang on April 14, gave an additional title, Wei-wu, to the training divisions 團練營, and made himself one of their commanders.

On April 20, 1521, the emperor breathed his last at the Leopard House. Immediately afterwards, Grand Secretary Yang T'ing-ho, announcing that it was the late emperor's will, ordered the disbandment of the so-called Wei-wu training divisions and the transfer of the frontier troops, then stationed in and around the capital, to their original positions. At this juncture, noting the rapid deterioration of his carefully laid plans, Chiang and his men considered rebellion; but under pretext of illness, he kept to his quarters. On the 24th of the same month, however, Yang T'ing-ho lured him into the palace on pretence of having him share in the imperial obsequies; being alone and unprotected, he was seized, and on the same day, on order of Empress Dowager Chang 張 (widow of Chu Yu-t'ang, d. 1541), his adherents Shen Chou and Li Tsung were also arrested and thrown into jail.

Chu Hou-ts'ung (*q.v.*) ascended the throne as emperor on May 27, 1521. A month and a half later Chiang was put to death; on the same day four of his sons were also executed. Meanwhile his wife, his youngest son, and three of his daughters were all ordered to become slaves in the homes of certain officials. In addition, his property was confiscated; it included 70 chests of gold, 2,200 chests of silver, and many other treasures.

Bibliography

1/307/12a; 3/285/10b; 6/46/16b; 61/154/11b; MSL (1965), Shih-tsung, 0121; KC (1958), 3230; *Chi-fu t'ung-chih* 畿輔通志 (1934), 980, 7917; *Huang Ming wen-hai* (microfilm), 112.

Chou Tao-chi

CHIANG T'ao, *see* HUNG-jen

CHIAO Fang 焦芳 (T. 孟陽, H. 守靜), 1436-April 12, 1517, who rose to be a grand secretary in the years 1506-10, was a native of Pi-yang 泌陽 in southern Honan. An ancestor served as a myriarch under the Mongols. His grandfather, Chiao Hsien 顯 (cj 1414), appears to have been the first to have had any scholarly interests; he became an instructor in the palace of the prince of Han韓, Chu Ch'ung-yü 朱沖烒 (grandson of the first emperor, enfoeffed in 1410, d. January 14, 1441). After graduating as *chü-jen* in 1459 and *chin-shih* in 1464, Chiao Fang served in the Hanlin Academy successively as bachelor, compiler, and senior expositor. It was at this point in his career (April 1480) that he made an enemy over an innocent mistake, which halted for a time his ascent in the bureaucratic hierarchy. As he was expounding the Classics to the heir apparent, Chu Yü-t'ang (*q. v.*), he encountered the expression chih yü 智愚 (intelligent and stupid) in a place where he was convinced that chih-ssu 知思) knowledge and experience) was intended. Nevertheless, as best he could, he explained the text as it was written, namely chih-yü wei-yu so chu智愚未有所主 (without intelligence and stupidity to guide one); then later checked it against other sources. Finding that they confirmed his doubts, he reported the matter to Grand Secretary Wan An 萬安 (T. 循吉, cs 1448, d. April 11, 1489, Pth. 文康), and accused the chief supervisor of instruction, P'eng Hua 彭華 (T. 彥實, H. 素菴, 1432-November 10, 1496, cs 1454, Pth. 文思), of being the one responsible for altering the characters. P'eng admitted to Wan that the mistake was his. In 1486 a case of bribery occurred during which the minister of Personnel and a number of officials were found guilty and punished. Chiao was involved and demoted. Most of the courtiers who lost out were, like Chiao, natives of northern provinces and they generally agreed that the southerners were responsible. Chiao thus had a strong aversion to men from Kiangsi like P'eng.

During the next few years Chiao served in a number of provincial posts; as subprefect of Kuei-yang-chou 桂陽州, Hukuang, as magistrate of Ho 霍-chou, Shansi, and as surveillance vice commissioner of education in Szechwan. As he was being transferred to Hukuang in March, 1490, Chiao dispatched a memorial to the emperor, his former student, to explain what had happened a decade earlier so that his record might be cleared. From Hukuang he was shifted to the office of transmission in Nanking, thence to become vice minister of the Court of Imperial Sacrifices in Peking and concurrently a senior expositor of the Hanlin. He was now back in the position from which he had been dismissed. From this point on Chiao progressed steadily up the ladder. He became assistant vice minister of Rites, associate vice minister, then minister of Personnel (May, 1506). Already under the baneful influence of the eunuch Liu Chin (*q. v.*), Chiao came to be considered a partisan of the "Eight Tigers" (*see* Chu Hou-chao) who did so much to bring the Cheng-te reign into disrepute. It was Chiao, reportedly, who, when the Grand Secretaries Liu Chien and Hsieh Ch'ien (*qq.v.*) urged the emperor to put these eunuchs out of the way, forewarned Liu Chin and his coterie. The "Eight" immediately leapt to their own defense, not only thwarting the demand of the two high officials, but also terminating their careers (October 28, 1506). Exactly four days later Chiao became a grand secretary.

Two years after this his son, Chiao Huang-chung 黃中, said to be a brilliant student, came up for the palace examination. Chiao Fang wanted him placed first, but when the list was posted he was actually named fourth (first in the second group). As only the three in the first group received immediate appointments, Chiao Fang changed the regular procedure and made his son a corrector. At the same time, to make it look less obvious, the first man in the third group, Hu Tsuan-tsung 胡纘宗 of Ch'in-an 秦安-hsien, Shensi (119th name in the list), was likewise named a corrector in the Hanlin. Liu Chin, however, did not like Chiao Huang-chung and induced him to quit.

In June, 1510, Chiao Fang was dismissed, and may well have devoted his last years to writing. A year or so after his dismissal, it is said that when bandits burned his house in 1511 or 1512, they robbed him of his hoard of gold and silver, and beheaded his effigy. This was in sharp contrast to the time when marauders entered Yü-chou 禹州 and left inviolate the house of Ma Wen-sheng (*q. v.*) whom they admired. The *Nan-yang-fu* 南陽府 *chih* credits Chiao with the authorship of four books, but not one of them seems to have survived. He is remembered still, however, for his editorship of the *Hsiao-tsung shih-lu* (completed 1509), a work often criticized, as Wolfgang Franke puts it, "for distortion of facts and for defamation [of character] of people he disliked." This may explain how it happens that his memorial, telling of his altercation with P'eng Hua, appears in its pages.

Bibliography

1/306/2a; 3/286/9a; 5/14/57a; 6/46/15b; 61/157/23b; MSL (1964), Hsiao-tsung, 0764, Wu-tsung (1965), 0379, 0547, 1392, 2873; KC (1958), 3124; *Nan-yang-fu chih* (1807), 5/129a; Tu Lien-che 杜聯喆, "Ming-ch'ao kuan-hsüan lu" 明朝館選錄, CHHP, 5: 2 (December, 1966), 36.

L. Carrington Goodrich

CHIEN I 蹇義 (T. 宜之, Pth. 忠定), 1363-February 12, 1435, served the first five Ming emperors for a total of fifty years, half of the time as minister of Personnel. A native of Pa-hsien 巴縣 (Chungking), Szechwan, he became a *chin-shih* in 1385 under the name Chien Jung 瑢. Appointed a drafter in the secretariat, he handled official papers with such scrupulous care that Emperor Chu Yüan-chang, pleased with his work, retained him on his personal staff after his regular three-year tenure. The monarch also changed his name to Chien I in recognition of his diligence and loyalty. Under Emperor Chu Yün-wen (*q. v.*) he became right vice minister of Personnel. In 1402 Chien was among those who shifted their allegiance to Chu Ti (*q. v.*). Before the year was over he was appointed minister. Two years later he became concurrently grand supervisor of instruction or official tutor to the heir apparent, the future emperor Chu Kao-chih (*q. v.*).

Chien was never recognized as a man of superior talent. His long-time friend and colleague, Yang Shih-ch'i (*q. v.*), described him as "full of doubts but little decision." His rise to prominence and occupation of a key position at court, according to his contemporaries, came about mainly because of his moderation and humility. The fact that he nevertheless survived the purge of 1402, profited by it, and earned the trust of emperors of widely differing personality, and that even in disagreement he maintained a cordial relationship, at least on the surface, with the critical Yang Jung and the outspoken Hsia Yüan-chi (*qq.v.*), suggests that he was very shrewd.

Chien's close association with the heir apparent was an important factor in his career. Although later Chu Kao-chih occupied the throne for eight months only, prior to his accession he frequently acted as prince regent during his father's long absences from the capital. Gentle by nature, in these intervals he succeeded in bringing the monarchy more in to harmony with the Confucian concept of benevolence. Chien, as tutor and senior adviser, undoubtedly wielded considerable influence, but in the last few years of Chu Ti's reign, the prince was somewhat alienated from the emperor. Rumors circulated alleging either that the monarch was ready to dispose of his heir or that the son was conspiring against the father. At one point, reportedly, Chu Ti actually contemplated his execution. The two finally became reconciled, however. Under circumstances such as the foregoing, Chien I was arrested by the emperor in the autumn of 1422. Yang Shih-ch'i, another counsellor of the prince, had been jailed several days earlier, also on trivial and freakish charges. While Yang was confined for ten days, Chien's imprisonment lasted six months. As soon as he was released, however, he was ordered to resume his ministerial duty. Contemporary sources do not elaborate on these arrests beyond recording the superficial charges lodged against the men. Only one account indicates that Chu Kao-chih, upon his accession, treated Chien and Yang with unusual courtesy because both had lived through so anxious and uncertain a period.

In the autumn of 1424 the new emperor revived the positions of the san-kung san-ku 三公三孤 (three dukes and three solitaries). Chien, continuing as minister of Personnel, was at first made junior guardian. A month later he was promoted to junior tutor and two months after this to be junior preceptor. In later years officials held such positions merely as an honor, but in the early 15h century the appointees were actually counsellors to the throne and expected to participate in decison making at court. Chien, in addition to his ministerial portfolio and by virtue of his concurrent appointment, outranked all other civil officials. This meant his inclusion in the inner circle which met the emperor informally to deliberate on state affairs. Along with Yang Shih-ch'i, Yang Jung, and Chin Yu-tzu (*see* Empress Hsü) he received a special seal from the throne which authorized him to submit confidential memorials criticizing the sovereign. By the time Chu Chan-chi (*q. v.*) suc-

ceeded his father in the summer of 1425, Chien's position as the senior elder statesman had been assured. Chu Chan-chi, also a ruler of Confucian stamp, retained Chien as a counsellor and confidant. In the campaign against Chu Kao-hsü (*q. v.*) in 1426, he accompanied the emperor to the field. Two years later he was relieved of routine ministerial duties. But even after another official took over the portfolio, Chien never relinquished his title as the senior head of the ministry. His free and informal access to the throne continued.

Chien's lack of accomplishment in office was deplored by his contemporaries. Even while acknowledging his virtues, his admirers emphasized that his very magnanimity made him too ready to forgive and to demand adherence to his own opinion.His reluctance to voice any criticism may be observed from the fact that the censorate under Liu Kuan (*see* Ku Tso) became notoriously corrupt but Chien, surely aware of the situation, remained silent. Only after Liu's case was brought up by Yang Jung and an investigating censor (1428) did Chien, following public opinion, advise that impeachment proceedings be carried through. In 1426, when Emperor Chu Chan-chi began to entertain the idea of abandoning Annam, Chien and Hsia Yüan-chi did try to dissuade him from taking so drastic an action; they did not press the issue, however. Under his long administration as minister of Personnel (1402–35) the Ming civil service was noticeably tightened. More degree holders from the triennial examinations were immediately appointed to administrative duty. After the first decades of the 15th century, these examinations became virtually the exclusive path to office. A hard line between officials and lesser functionaries was drawn. Regulations governing promotions, demotions, and personnel reviews became more elaborate and sophisticated. But while Chien I was partially responsible for those changes, the numerous entries in the *shih-lu* attest that most of the policies were dictated from above, largely by Emperors Chu Ti and Chu Chan-chi.

Two of Chien's memorials appear in the *Huang Ming Ching-shih wen-pien*. Students of Ming government may note the concise and incisive style of these documents, in contrast to the long and polemic discourses typical of the writings of court officials in later days.

[Editors' note: There were two prominent Chien families of Chungking in the Ming period. Chien I's was the older, having settled there for centuries. The other was founded late in the 14th century by a soldier of the Chungking guard; a descendant, Chien Ta 塞達 (T. 汝上, 汝循, H. 理庵, 1542-1608, cs 1562), served as governor-general of the northeastern frontiers (Chi-Liao薊遼, 1590-92, 1602-8), and was noted for his success in having the notorious eunuch and tax collector, Kao Huai 高淮, recalled from Liaotung in 1608.]

Bibliography

1/149/1a; 5/24/19a; MSL (1963), T'ai-tsung, 0170 0205, 0534, 2269, 2349, 2369, Jen-tsung, 0025, 0078, 0147, Hsüan-tsung, 0137, 0421, 0530, 0998, 1132, 1152, 1154, Ying-tsung, 0020; Cheng Hsiao, *Wu-hsüeh-pien* (1572), 28/1a; *Szechwan t'ung-chih* (1815), 146/11b; *Ching-shih wen-pien* (1964), 99; C. O. Hucker, *The Censorial System of Ming China* (Stanford, 1966), 261; Lo Jung-pang in Hucker (ed.), *Chinese Government in Ming Times: Seven Studies* (1969), 57.

Ray Huang

CHIEN Jung, *see* **CHIEN I**

CH'IEN Ku 錢穀 (T.叔寶, H. 罄室), 1508-*ca.* 1578, poet, editor, and painter, was a native of Ch'ang-chou 長洲, prefecture of Soochow. He owned a seal reading Wu-Yüeh-wang i 吳越王裔, "descendant of the king of Wu-Yüeh," *i.e.*, Ch'ien Liu (852-932). Orphaned while still a youth, he did not receive formal education until as an adult he became a pupil of Wen Cheng-ming (*q.v.*). Supposedly Ch'ien Ku

was introduced to Wen by the bibliophile Ch'ien T'ung-ai 同愛 (T. 孔周, H. 野亭, 1475-1549). Perhaps because he began his studies relatively late in life, Ch'ien Ku read omnivorously in the large library owned by the Wen family; eventually he became an avid book collector, devoting himself to copying and collating old texts. Several works are mentioned as ones he edited but the only one apparently preserved is the *Wu-tu wen-ts'ui hsü-chi* 吳都文粹續集 (56 +2 *ch.*), a continution of the study of literary remains and topographical records of Soochow, *Wu-tu wen-ts'ui,* 9 *ch.*, begun by Cheng Hu-ch'en 鄭虎臣 (fl. 1275). Subsequently copied into the Imperial Library, it has been photographically reproduced. Since the work as it now exists is considerably smaller than the version described by Chu I-tsun (ECCP), it may well have been revised by Ch'ien Ku's elder son, Ch'ien Fu 府 (T. 允治, H. 功文, 少室), who, in addition to being an artist, followed his father's example in copying and editing old texts. Even in his old age Ch'ien Fu is said to have continued to work from dawn to dusk. He died childless when over eighty *sui* and the family library was dispersed. A second son, Ch'ien Hsü 序 (T. 次甫), also an artist, excelled in landscapes.

In his leisure time Ch'ien Ku practiced painting, being influenced by the style of Wen Cheng-ming, which was dominant in Soochow during the 16th century. Ch'ien Ku's attitude toward painting is summed up in his statement: "Painting is a fusion whereby an artist takes a spiritual model to revive the breath of heaven. In daubing the void between fineness and coarseness, I guide the brush only. Afterwards, if that which I have painted grasps the original concept, how can it be said to be arranged or planned?" The innumerable fan paintings, as well as those albums illustrating scenic spots along the routes of Ch'ien's travels in the estuary of the Yangtze, are particularly noteworthy. Working within these relatively small formats, his experimentation with tiny, rather decorative textural areas and playfully executed architectural units, is more successful than in larger scrolls. In addition to his paintings in private collections, examples of Ch'ien's work are in the National Palace Museum, Taipei; Palace Museum, Peking; Museum für Ostasiatische Kunst, Cologne; and Musée Guimet, Paris. His earliest dated painting mentioned in the records was executed in 1529.

Ch'ien Ku became so engrossed in his studies and painting that he completely neglected household matters. On one occasion Wen Cheng-ming is said to have visited Ch'ien's ramshackle home and over the door he wrote the two characters Hsüan-ch'ing 懸磬 (empty jar). Whereupon Ch'ien replied with a smile, "My intention exactly." His collection of poetry is known as Hsüan-ch'ing-shih shih 室詩. Although the date of Ch'ien's death is usually given as 1572, paintings dated as late as 1578 are recorded.

Bibliography

1/287/3b; 2/396/20b; 3/268/2b; 5/115/96a; 24/3/76b; 32/24/39b; 40/50/2a; 65/4/1b; 84/丁中/14b 86/14/34b; Huang-fu Fang, *Huang-fu ssu-hsün chi* 51/6b; SK (1930), 189/7b; *Chung-kuo li-tai ming-hua chi* 中國歷代名畫集(Peking, 1965), 4/77; John C. Ferguson, *Index of Artists* (Nanking, 1934), 428a; Osvald Sirén, *Chinese Painting*, Vol. IV, 191, Vol. VII, 172; E. J. Laing, *Chinese Paintings in Chinese Publications, 1956-1968* (Ann Arbor, 1969), 160; V. Contag and C. C. Wang, *Seals of Chinese Painters and Collectors*, rev. ed. (Hong Kong, 1966), no. 390.

Thomas Lawton

CH'IEN Shih-sheng 錢士升 (T. 抑之, H. 御冷, 塞菴), 1575–1652, official and scholar, came from a wealthy clan of Chia-shan 嘉善, Chekiang. The clan traced its ancestry back to a high officer at the end of the T'ang dynasty, and boasted a number of officials of prominence who served under the Sung and Yüan. They were centered on the city of Chia-hsing 嘉興, but early in the Ming, a branch of the clan moved to the neighboring town of Chia-shan. Ch'ien Shih-sheng's great-grandfather, Ch'ien Chen 貞, was a vice prefect of Ju-ning 汝寧, Honan. Both his grandfather, Ch'ien Wu-jen 吾仁, and his father, Ch'ien Chi-k'o 繼科 were *hsiu-ts'ai*.

When Ch'ien Shih-sheng was fourteen *sui*, he placed first in the prefectural examination. In 1615 he was successful in the *chü-jen* competition and in the following year became *chuang-yüan* or optimus in the palace examinations. After serving as compiler in the Hanlin Academy, he requested permission (1621) to return home to care for his mother. Three years later he was offered, but declined to accept, the office of senior director of instruction.

Before Wan Ching 萬燝 (T. 闇夫, H. 元白, cs 1616) was publicly beaten to death and his property confiscated in 1624 by Wei Chung-hsien (ECCP), Ch'ien made every effort to secure his release. The following year Wei Ta-chung (ECCP, p. 893) also lost his life. In 1627 Chao Nan-hsing (*q.v.*), one of the leading members of the Tung-lin politico-literary group, was fined and exiled by the eunuch. Ch'ien attempted to help all these men, and after their deaths he gave their families financial assistance. During the early years of Wei Chung-hsien's dominance at court, Ch'ien was in retirement, and it is perhaps for this reason that he did not come into direct conflict with the eunuch and was never included in the official list of Tung-lin party members (*see* Feng Ch'üan, ECCP). Because of his efforts in the cases mentioned above, however, Ch'ien was greatly esteemed by the Tung-lin members. At the beginning of the Ch'ung-chen reign, Ch'ien received the appointment of junior supervisor of instruction and was put in charge of the Hanlin Academy in Nanking. In the following year he became grand supervisor of instruction. His former teacher, Ch'ien Lung-hsi 錢龍錫 (T. 稚文, H. 機山, 1575–1645, cs 1607), a native of Hua-t'ing 華亭, Nan-Chihli, and a Tung-lin partisan, however, was accused by his enemies

(1630) of being largely responsible for the defeat suffered by Yüan Ch'ung-huan (ECCP) whom he had recommended. When Ch'ien Lung-hsi received the death sentence, Ch'ien Shih-sheng and several other officials resigned in protest and the sentence was commuted to banishment.

Ch'ien rose the following year to the position of junior vice minister and acting minister of Rites in Nanking. Later, in 1633, when Chou Yen-ju (*q.v.*) was dismissed from the government, Ch'ien was summoned to serve as a grand secretary. His appointment, while clearly following the traditional line of promotion established in early Ming, was no doubt due in part to the emperor's desire to appoint men who had no specific political connections, and also to his peculiar reliance upon divination as an auxiliary method for selecting grand secretaries.

Upon entering the government in 1634, Ch'ien immediately memorialized against the sale of offices—a practice rife at the time—the debasement of currency, and the employment of eunuchs in the provinces. Although the emperor approved these suggestions, Wen T'i-jen (*q.v.*), the senior grand secretary from 1633 to 1637, ignored them, so that no changes were instituted. During this period Wen Chen-meng (*q.v.*), a grand secretary, and his nephew, Yao Hsi-meng 姚希孟 (T. 孟長, 現聞, 1579–1636, cs 1619), the grand supervisor of instruction, were the leading Tung-lin partisans at court. Wen T'i-jen, with evidence supplied by Ch'ien Shih-sheng, managed to expose their clique connections and succeeded in having Wen dismissed and Yao demoted. Ch'ien was also instrumental in securing the promotion of Wen T'i-jen's partisans such as Hsieh Sheng (ECCP). It so happened that Ch'ien Shih-sheng had a brother, Ch'ien Shih-chin 晉 (T. 康侯, H. 昭自, 1577–1635, cs 1613), a secretary in the ministry of Justice who was promoted (1629) from administration commissioner of Shantung to provincial governor of Yunnan, where he gained a considerable reputation for his

diligent and incorruptible administration. A little later (1635) Wen T'i-jen determined to get rid of Ch'ien Shih-sheng. When some false charges of corruption were brought against Ch'ien Shih-chin, Wen conspired with Lin Han 林釬 (T. 實甫, H. 鶴昭, cs 1616), another grand secretary, to implicate Ch'ien Shih-sheng in his younger brother's case. Before the charges could be formally presented, however, the brother died and consequently the matter was dropped. Wen T'i-jen, nevertheless, gained his ends the following year.

In the spring of 1636, a military licentiate, Li Chin 李璡, submitted a memorial in which he discussed the considerable land holdings of the gentry of the lower Yangtze valley and suggested that their names, along with a list of their holdings, be reported to the government for the purpose of taxation. He further recommended that those guilty of misrepresentation should have their property confiscated. Ch'ien naturally abominated such a plan and argued that members of the gentry were not only the source of the common people's livelihood, but also the first line of defense against famine, banditry, and rebellion. His outspoken persistence, however, greatly angered the emperor and by the end of the year he was forced to resign.

Ch'ien Shih-sheng had two sons. The elder, Ch'ien Shih 杸, died in 1642. In that same year Ch'ien's wife died. In 1645 the younger son, Ch'ien Ping 楝 (T. 仲馭, cs 1637), who before the fall of the Ming had risen to the office of director of the bureau of appointments in the ministry of Personnel, died while participating with other gentry in the defense of his home region against the Manchus. Ch'ien Shih-sheng's adopted son, Ch'ien Fen 棻 (T. 仲芳, H. 潁山, 八還道人, cj 1642), achieved some note as a landscape painter during the Ch'ing period.

Ch'ien's published works include his memorials *Lun-fei tsou ts'ao* 綸扉奏艸, 3 *ch.*;

notes on the *Chuang-tzu, Chuang ch'üan* 莊詮, 2 *ch.*; records of officials loyal to Chu Yün-wen (*q.v.*), *Piao chung chi* 表忠記, 10 *ch.*; the *Nan Sung shu* 南宋書, 60 *ch.*; the *Tz'u-yü-t'ang chi* 賜餘堂集, 20 *ch.* (published 1739); and the *Hsün-kuo i-shu* 遜國遺書, 7 *ch.* His unpublished works include random thoughts on the *I-ching, I k'uei* 易揆, 10 *ch.*; explanations of the Śūraṅgama sūtra, *Leng-yen chieh* 楞嚴解, 10 *ch.*; and a family genealogy. The *Tz'u-yü-t'ang chi* was listed on the *Index Expurgatorius* of the 18th century but copies have survived.

Bibliography

1/251/9a; MSL (1940), Ch'ung-chen 9/5b; *Ch'ung-chen wu-shih tsai-hsiang chuan* 崇禎五十宰相傳, x/9b; *Chia-shan-hsien chih* (1894), 19/9b, 31/19a; *Wu-shih fu-ch'en k'ao* 五十輔臣考, 3/1a; *Ming-ch'ao chi-shih pen-mo*, 66/18, 72/40; *Ming-chi nan-tu hsün-nan chi* 明季南都殉難記, x/68; *Ming-chi pei lüeh* 明季北略, 12/4a; Sun Tien-ch'i (1957), 213; SK (1930), 8/6b, 50/12b, 54/4a, 62/6a; *Chia-ho cheng-hsien-lu* 嘉禾徵獻錄, 1/11a (in *Tsui-li* 橋李 *ts'ung-shu*, 1932); W. Franke, *Sources*, 3. 2.4.

Donald L. Potter

CH'IEN Tai 錢岱 (T. 汝瞻, H. 秀峯), 1541–June 30, 1622, official, was a native of Ch'ang-shu 常熟, Nan-Chihli. The Ch'ien family considered itself descended from Ch'ien Liu (851–932), founder of Wü-Yüeh (895–978), one of the ten states during the period of the Five Dynasties. Ch'ien Tai's grandfather, owner of much land and apparently the target of jealous schemers, was accused of some wrongdoing, found guilty, and died in jail. The family thus lost a large part of its properties. Then, because a granduncle, Ch'ien Shu 庶 (H. 三溪), became a *chin-shih* in 1550, the family began to recover some of its losses, but about a year later, when Ch'ien Shu suddenly died, their fortunes again suffered. All through these ups and downs Ch'ien Tai's father, Ch'ien Heng 亨(T. 仲嘉, H. 龍橋, *ca.* 1520–87), managed to surmount the crises. He even won the praise of his

fellow citizens after serving a year as tax collector for the entire district.

It is said that just before Ch'ien Tai was born, his father had a dream about the arrival of a monk from the sacred mountain in Shantung, T'ai-shan 泰山, and so named him Tai, the alternative name of that eminence. When he passed the *chin-shih* examination in 1571, his chief examiner was Chang Chü-cheng (*q.v.*), whose sobriquet, T'ai-yüeh, happened to be another title for the same sacred mounain. The coincidence could not have escaped the notice of Ch'ien Tai. In any case, his official career was seriously affected by that of his mentor. After a full term of three years (1572–75) in Canton as prefectural judge, a very lucrative post, Ch'ien Tai served seven years as a censor. In the latter capacity his office was chiefly in Peking, but twice he was sent out as regional inspector, in 1580 to Shantung and in 1582 to Hukuang. During these ten years when Ch'ien was in official employ, Chang Chü-cheng, now senior grand secretary, essentially wielded the authority of a regent and maintained a strict policy of law and order, including regular checks on the qualifications and behavior of members of the bureaucracy. The official evidence on Ch'ien indicates that he observed the regulations faithfully; he seems to have limited his activity in the capital to remonstrating with fellow officials. When in Shantung, he managed to capture by a ruse a murderer who was hiding in the palace of a prince and had the man, a relative of the prince, brought to book. On another occasion (July, 1580) his report on several officials, who had made illegal demands on the postal service, eventuated in the dismissal of a subprefect and the demotion of two prefects and two provincial commissioners. Back in Peking in 1581, Ch'ien took part in conducting the triennial review of the records of high officials which resulted in the forced resignation of a minister (T'ao Ch'eng-hsüeh 陶承學, T. 子述, H. 泗橋, 1518–98, cs 1547), two vice ministers (including Wang Tsung-mu, *q.v.*), and two governors (one being Tseng T'ung-heng 曾同亨, T. 子野, H. 見臺, 1533–1607, cs 1559). While in Hukuang in 1582, Ch'ien's reports forced the retirement of several assistant commissioners. These actions, though not unusual for a regional inspector, must have gained him a considerable number of enemies who considered him one of Chang's henchmen. He was certainly regarded with fear and presumably treated with flattery. He probably had some forebodings, however, when, officiating in Hukuang, he learned of the death of Chang in July, 1582. Two months later he took part in supervising the provincial examination at Wuchang. Immediately after the conclusion of the examination, he received notice of the death of his mother and went home for the mourning period, perhaps with a sense of relief.

After Chang Chü-cheng was posthumously condemned early in 1581, his former associates were closely investigated for possible reproval. Apparently nothing incriminating Ch'ien came to light. In April, 1584, however, shortly before Ch'ien was to resume his office, two unsubstantiated accusations were lodged against him by a memorialist. Both charges concerned his participation in the Hukuang provincial examination of 1582. The first, that Ch'ien had orally suggested to Chang Chü-cheng that he send his youngest son to Wuchang for the *chü-jen* test (only Chang's untimely death preventing the son from following that course), was obviously a figment of the imagination. The second, that Ch'ien made it possible for Wang Chih-heng 王之衡, the son of a vice minister of Personnel, to pass the examination, seems equally farfetched, for Ch'ien was only a supervisor of the examination and had nothing to do with grading of the candidates. The charge could have been easily proved false by a review of Wang Chih-heng's papers or a test of his ability. The emperor, however, arbitrarily assumed Ch'ien to be guilty, unjustly deemed the review as unnecessary, and peremptorily ordered the demotion of Ch'ien by three grades.

Ch'ien had indeed been on friendly terms with Chang, who apparently saw in Ch'ien a keen, strong-minded official, able and willing to support his efforts to revitalize the ailing central power and curb the ever-growing privileges of the imperial family and the official class. The allegation, however, that Ch'ien had curried the grand secretary's favor is not borne out by a scrutiny of the data at hand. In the first place, no reasonable evidence was ever produced against him. Second, while Chang was in power, Ch'ien remained a censor for seven years without promotion. Third, a fellow townsman, Chao Yung-hsien (*q.v.*), who had been flogged at court for antagonizing Chang, remained a close friend of Ch'ien and even wrote the epitaph of his father in 1587. Ch'ien's conduct in government must have been above reproach or Chao would conceivably have deleted these writings from his collected works. Ch'ien had a younger relative, Ch'ien Ch'ien-i (ECCP), who wrote his epitaph, describing him as unusual in bearing and stature, eloquent, possessed of a resonant voice, and masterly as a writer. A rich man, he was generous towards the poor and destitute among his clansmen, but strangely rather imperious towards members of the gentry. Possibly this was because the latter had been the cause of his grandfather's death and his father's worries. In any case, during forty years of retirement Ch'ien Tai applied his talents to expanding the family holdings in farmland and other properties. He built a mansion in the western section of Ch'ang-shu city, and about 1585 constructed an enormous villa which he called the Hsiao-wang-ch'uan 小輞川 after the famous mountain retreat of the T'ang poet, Wang Wei (701–61), whom he admired. According to the account of T'u Lung (*q.v.*) about the villa, all the buildings, brooks, and hillocks sported designations after those in its eighth-century prototype. It is said that Ch'ien kept a troup of actresses trained to perform such classical song-dramas as the *Hsi-hsiang chi* (*see* Chin Jen-jui, ECCP) and *P'i-pa chi* (*see* Kao Ming) as well as those by contemporary writers such as T'ang Hsien-tsu (ECCP). He enjoyed a life of music and wine, playing chess and entertaining friends. About 1620, when the magistrate suggested that he be named as the honored elder of the district, a jealous fellow townsman, Ku Ta-shao 顧大韶 (T. 仲恭, younger brother of Ku Ta-chang (ECCP, p. 893), wrote a long denunciation publicly declaring him wicked and corrupt, and accusing him of embezzlement. It appears that Ku's father had on one occasion suffered indignities at Ch'ien's hands and so this seems to have been an act of revenge. It failed to deter the authorities from according Ch'ien the honors, however. After Ch'ien died, an anonymous acquaintance wrote a semi-fictitious account of his life entitled *Pi-meng* 筆夢 (a dream-like life). It has sometimes been erroneously listed in bibliographies as *Pi-meng hsü* 敘, mistaking a prefatory caption for the title of the whole work. The author may well have been envious of Ch'ien's good fortune and attributed it to destiny.

Ch'ien Tai is said to have compiled a work on the two Chin dynasties (265-419), entitled *Liang-Chin ho-tsuan* 兩晉合纂, but it is apparently no longer extant. He had five sons, two of whom became *chin-shih* and two *chü-jen*; of his fourteen grandsons and great-grandsons another eight were eventually registered as officials. His eldest son, Ch'ien Shih-chün 時俊 (T. 用章, H. 仍峯, cj 1600, cs 1604), first served as secretary in the ministry of Works, later rising to surveillance vice commissioner in Hukuang.

Bibliography

21/19/9a; MSL (1966), Shen-tsung, 0928, 1230, 1404, 1992, 2096, 2424, 2740; Ch'ien Ch'ien-i, *Mu-chai ch'u-hsüeh-chi* (SPTK ed.), 76/1a, 82/5b; *Pi-meng* (*Shuo-k'u* 說庫 ed.); Chao Yung-hsien, *Sung-shih-chai chi* (1635 ed., NLP microfilm no.

876), 文 10/16b, 14/8a, 16/39a, 18/18b, 詩 4/15a; *Hai-yü wen cheng* 海虞文徵 (1905), 2/31b, 11/41b, 23/10a; *Ch'ang Chao ho-chih kao* 常昭合志稿 (1904), 25/35b; *Su-chou-fu chih* (1824), 61/23b, 62/42b; *Chiang-nan t'ung-chih* (1737), 123/3a, 129/1b; *Kuang-tung t'ung-chih* (1934), 384; *Shan-tung t'ung-chih* (1915), 49/35b; *Hu-kuang t'ung-chih* (1733), 28/35b; *Hu-nan t'ung-chih* (1934), 2476; Wang Shih-chen, *Yen-chou shan-jen hsü-kao*, 107/1a.

Chaoying Fang and Bodo Wiethoff

CH'IEN Te-hung 錢德洪 (early ming 寬, T. 洪甫, H. 緒山), January 2, 1497-November 10, 1574, thinker, was, like Wang Shou-jen (*q.v.*), a native of Yü-yao 餘姚, Chekiang. His family claimed descent from Ch'ien Liu (d. 932), king of Wu-Yüeh. He became a disciple of Wang Shou-jen on the latter's return to Yü-yao following his success in 1521 in defeating the rebel prince, Chu Ch'en-hao (*see* Wang Shou-jen). One year later, Ch'ien received the *chü-jen* degree. By that time Wang Shou-jen had so many disciples that he asked Ch'ien and Wang Chi (*q.v.*) to help with the instruction of the newcomers. In 1526 Ch'ien and Wang Chi went together to Peking to take the *chin-shih* examinations. Angered by the veiled attacks made against Wang Shou-jen's teachings in some of the questions, they returned to Yü-yao without completing their papers. Three years later the two went again to Peking for the examinations, but on account of the master's death they returned south for a second time in order to attend the funeral. Building a hut near Wang's grave they mourned for him as for a deceased parent—in Ch'ien's case, with the permission of his own father. The time was spent collecting and editing Wang Shou-jen's recorded conversations and writings, talking with fellow disciples, as well as giving moral support to Wang's widow and infant son, who was betrothed, partly through their negotations, to the daughter of Huang Wan (*q.v.*). Thus it was not until 1532, on completion of their mourning, that Ch'ien and Wang Chi once more proceeded to Peking for the examinations. This time, both competed successfully.

After a short stay in Peking, Ch'ien received at his request an official appointment as instructor in the Soochow prefectural school, which enabled him to be near his aging parents. In 1534 he was sent to Kwangtung to supervise the provincial examination. He returned home the following year to mourn the death of his mother. On completing the prescribed period he was transferred to be proctor in the National University, moving later to the ministry of Justice, where he rose to become vice director of a bureau. His involvement in the case of Marquis Kuo Hsün (q.v.), however, resulted in his imprisonment and removal from office. A favorite of Emperor Chu Hou-ts'ung (q.v.), Kuo had been imprisoned in 1541 for disobedience to the emperor's summons. The case was submitted to the ministry of Justice. On account of Kuo's high connections, the officials hesitated to pass any sentence. Ch'ien took it upon himself to draw up a list of Kuo's offences, and recommended the death penalty. For this act he incurred the displeasure of the emperor, who had not desired to punish Kuo with any severity. Ch'ien was in turn accused of erroneous judgment and clapped into prison where he remained until 1543, the year after Kuo's death. Ch'ien passed his time in prison studying the Book of Changes in the company of other imprisoned scholar-officials. After his release, he spent nearly thirty years traveling about the country, teaching Wang Shou-jen's doctrine of liang chih (see Wang Shou-jen), until he reached the age of seventy, when he decided to settle down quietly at home. On the accession of Emperor Chu Tsai-hou (q.v.), he was restored to his former rank and permitted to retire. Emperor Chu I-chün (q. v.) raised his rank by one grade. In the autumn of 1574 Ch'ien went, as was his custom every year, to the T'ien-chen Academy (see Wang Chi) for a regular meeting with other disciples of Wang Shou-

jen. He died peacefully there in his seventy-eighth year. His wife, née Chu 朱, had died earlier, in 1558. He was survived by the younger of his two sons, Ch'ien Ying-lo 應樂 (cj 1573), who served several times as magistrate and whose first wife was the daughter of Wang Shou-jen's adopted son, Wang Cheng-hsien 正憲.

Ch'ien was a good judge of character. While living at home he advised Hu Tsung-hsien (q.v.), magistrate of Yü-yao from 1549 to 1551, to study Wang Shou-jen's military writings with a view to preparing himself for a military career. Later, when Hu was in charge of fighting against the pirates, Ch'ien counseled him on the organization of local militia, recommending the service of a disciple, Ch'i Chi-kuang (q.v.), who later became famous for his part in repelling these raids.

As a philosopher, Ch'ien developed his thought in close association with two men: his teacher Wang Shou-jen and his fellow disciple Wang Chi. His philosophy depended heavily on the teachings of his master, which he sought primarily to understand and to explain, thus differing from Wang Chi, who showed a much greater independence of mind. The principal differences between the two men's thought stemmed especially from the interpretations each gave to Wang Shou-jen's Ssu-chü-chiao 四句教 (Four Maxims): first, that the absence of good and evil characterizes the "mind-and-heart-in-itself" (hsin-chih-t'i 心之體); second, that the presence of good and evil characterizes the movement of its intentions; third, that the knowledge of good and evil characterizes its liang-chih; and fourth, that doing good and avoiding evil characterizes its investigation of things. Wang Chi regarded these maxims as the summing up of a tentative teaching on liang-chih, from which certain logical conclusions could be inferred. He held that, following from the first maxim, there comes the further recognition that the intentions themselves (i 意), knowledge (liang-chih), as well as "things," or better, "acts" (wu 物), are all beyond the categories of good and evil (wu-shan wu-o 無善無惡). On the other hand, Ch'ien's admiration for Wang Shou-jen caused him to consider the maxims to be part of the master's sacred teaching in its final form. He preferred to take the first maxim as descriptive of mind-and-heart-in-itself, in the state of "pre-stirred equilibrium" (wei fa chih chung未發之中), the recovery of which is the object all self-cultivation. The three following maxims would therefore appear as the embodiment of a practical teaching, aimed at the instruction of all whose hearts are no longer in possession of pristine innocence and purity. The distinction between good and evil must be maintained for the activities of the intentions, for the moral judgment of liang-chih, as well as for its application in acts through the "investigation of things."

In 1527, on the eve of Wang Shou-jen's departure for the military campaign in Kwangsi, the two disciples presented their difficulties to him. To their astonishment Wang judged that both interpretations were correct. He explained that the issue was one of pedagogy rather than doctrine. Thus, he said, while a man of superior spiritual intelligence might penetrate quickly into the nature of mind-and-heart-in-itself, as Wang Chi had described it, the less talented must learn how to do good and avoid evil in thought and intention, until his mind-and-heart-in-itself becomes clear and manifest. Nevertheless, Wang Shou-jen warned that few persons in the world would be so gifted as not to need to make efforts towards self-cultivation, they were more likely merely to meditate upon mind-and-heart-in-itself. In other words, he recognized with Wang Chi that a sudden and total experience of inner enlightenment could elevate a person to a higher state, transcending good and evil, but understood, with Ch'ien, that such experience was not at the beck and call of all, and therefore, that self-cultivation must not be neglected.

Wang Shou-jen said that Ch'ien had a firm and persevering nature, while Wang Chi was endowed with a quickness of perception. Each would develop in his own manner certain tenets of the master. After the latter's death, Ch'ien remained faithful to the teaching of gradual cultivation through careful development of liang-chih. To resolve the seeming contradiction between the first maxim and Confucian teachings on the goodness of human nature, he explained that the absence of good and evil refers also to the fullness of moral goodness in the mind-and-heart, the promptings of which one must always follow. His interpretation was called that of the Ssu-yu 四有 (Four positives), that is, of affirming the goodness in mind-and-heart (hsin), intention (i), knowledge (chih 知), and things, especially acts (wu). Together with Wang Ken (q.v.), another of Wang Shou-jen's disciples, Wang Chi exercised a great influence over the emergence of the so-called left-wing or T'ai-chou 泰州 branch of the school of Wang Shou-jen, which became a popular movement during the late Ming.

Comparing Ch'ien Te-hung with Wang Chi, Huang Tsung-hsi (ECCP) remarked that Ch'ien lacked Wang's penetrating perception, but surpassed him in diligent self-cultivation. In the end, Wang Chi became virtually a Ch'an Buddhist in Confucian disguise, while Ch'ien never strayed from orthodox teachings, although he contributed little to the further development of the incipient ideas contained in Wang Shou-jen's philosophy. He was, above all, the faithful disciple. He was not an original thinker.

Ch'ien Te-hung and Wang Chi remained good friends all their lives, seeing much of each other, and cooperating in various ways. After Ch'ien's death, Wang composed his hsing-chuang 行狀. Ch'ien's published works include the Hsü-shan hui-yü 緒山會語, 25 ch., and the P'ing-hao chi 平濠記, 1 ch. The first gives Ch'ien's recorded sayings and instructions, poems, and essays, as well as supplementary material.

It was compiled by his son, Ch'ien Ying-lo, but appears to have been lost, except for excerpts cited in such histories of philosophy as the *Ming-ju hsüeh-an* and the *Li-hsüeh tsung-chuan* of Sun Ch'i-feng (ECCP). The second supplies much information concerning Wang Shou-jen's campaign against Prince Chu Ch'en-hao, as related by Wang himself and by other eye-witnesses, much of which was not recorded in the memorials or in Wang's chronological record, and could not have been told until after Wang's death. It is available in the *Ts'ung-shu chi-ch'eng* edition, while a shorter version, given under the title *Cheng Ch'en-hao fan-chien i-shih* 征宸濠反間遺事 and dated 1535, is included in Wang's complete works.

Ch'ien's major work, however, was the editing of Wang Shou-jen's recorded conversations, letters, essays, and poems, which he had worked on since 1527, with the master's permission. He published the first installment in 1535 as *Yang-ming wen-lu* 文錄. It included certain material compiled earlier by Wang's other disciples, especially Hsü Ai, Hsüeh K'an, and Nan Ta-chi (*see* Wang Shou-jen). In 1566 he published additional sayings, recorded by himself and others, as *Wen-lu hsü-p'ien* 續篇. And lastly, in 1572, responding to the request of Hsieh T'ing-chieh (*see* Lei Li), who was preparing Wang's complete works, *Wang Wen-ch'eng kung ch'üan-shu*, for publication, he added to these other material, especially Wang's work, *Chu-tzu wan-nien ting-lun* 朱子晚年定論. Hsieh's collection has remained the standard version of Wang's complete works.

Ch'ien was also the chief compiler of Wang Shou-jen's *nien-p'u*. He had spent thirty years collecting facts and data on Wang's life. Finally, following the urging of Lo Hung-hsien (*q.v.*), he worked in isolation for four months on this work and published it in 1563. It gives an extensive treatment of Wang's philosophical teaching, and somewhat less attention to his military career. It is also included in Wang's complete works.

Bibliography

1/283/10b; 3/185/13a; 32/51/25b; 83/11/5b; MSL (1965),Shih-tsung, 263/la; SK(1930), 53/7b, 96/4a; Chou Ju-teng, *Wang-men tsung-chih* (Ming ed. in Naikaku Bunko), 10/la; Sun Ch'i-feng, *Li-hsüeh tsung-chuan* (1666 ed., Taipei reprint, 1969), 21/4a; Wang Chi, *Wang Lung-hsi ch'üan-chi* (1882 ed., Taipei reprint, 1970), 20/la; Wang Shou-jen, *Wang Wen-ch'eng kung ch'üan-shu* (SPTK, lst series); *Yü-yao-hsien chih* (1899), 18/22b, 19/58a, 23/10b; Lü Pen 呂本 (T. 汝立, H. 期齊, 1504–87), *Mu-chih ming* 墓誌銘, *Huang Ming wen-hai* (microfilm), ch. 158.

Julia Ching

CHIH-hsü 智旭 (T. 蕅益, H. 八不道人), June 24, 1599– February 26, 1655, Buddhist monk, was a native of Mu-tu 木瀆 near Soochow, a town on the banks of Lake T'ai. His father, Chung Chih-feng 鍾之鳳 (T. 岐仲), and mother, Chin Ta-lien 金大蓮, were pious Buddhists. They had been married for more than ten years without offspring and prayed to Kuan-yin for a son. Finally the wife dreamed that Kuan-yin in person brought her a son, and indeed she gave birth to Chih-hsü. As a boy he studied Confucian literature and developed an antipathy towards Buddhism and Taoism. He even wrote a long dissertation, *P'i-Fo lun* 闢佛論 (on exposing Buddha). The turning point in his life came when at the age of sixteen he read two works by the famous monk Chu-hung (*q. v.*), the *Tzu-chih lu* and the *Chu-ch'uang sui-pi*. He destroyed his dissertation but continued to study the *Lun-yü* and came to realize what Confucius meant by cultivation of the mind. In the winter of 1618 he lost his father and, while studying the *Kṣitigarbha Pūrvapraṇidhana-sūtra* (*Ti-tsang Pen-yüan ching* 地藏本願經), began to think of becoming a monk. He then proceeded to study the *Śūraṅgama-sūtra* but was in doubt as to whether he could attain enlightenment from contemplation of the void, as this text proclaims. Finally, in 1621 he decided to enter the clergy, pronounced his 48 vows in front of a statue of the Buddha, and adopted the name of upāsaka Ta-lang 大朗優婆塞.

We are told that during a single month in 1622 he dreamed three times of Te-ch'ing (q. v.) and wanted to become this famous teacher's pupil. At that time, however, Te-ch'ing was residing in Shao-chou韶州 (Kwangtung), so Chih-hsü resolved to go to one of his followers named Hsüeh-ling 雪嶺. Through him he was finally ordained and received the name of Chih-hsü (1622). His later monastic life shows no marked dramatic events; it is rather a story of unceasing spiritual effort. For a while after his ordination he studied at the center of the Nien-Fo 念佛 (Invocation of Buddha) school, the Yün-ch'i 雲棲 monastery near Hangchow. There he listened to the teachings of Ku-te 古德, who had been a pupil of Chu-hung. Ku-te's theories about the incompatibility of the existing schools of thought perplexed him, so he retired for some time to Ching-shan 徑 山 monastery near Hangchow in order to meditate. There he concluded that there were no basic contradictions among the various theories. In 1625 he turned to a study of vinaya (monastic discipline) texts. During the following year his mother died and he went into seclusion to pray and meditate. As a result of his studies of monastic discipline he wrote (1629) a treatise, Pi-ni chi-yao 毘尼集要 (Essentials of discipline)because he wished to remedy the supposed lack of discipline in the Dhyana (Ch'an) school. In the same year he visited Shantung and then stayed in Nanking for a while. In 1631 he went to the Ling-feng 靈峯 monastery near Hangchow, a place which later became so much associated with him that it is one of the names by which he is known. Among the many places where he took residence temporarily, we may mention Chiu-hua 九 華 Mountain (Anhwei), where Wang Shou-jen (q. v.) had studied (1636), Ch'üan-chou 泉州 (1639), Chang-chou 漳州, Fukien (1640), and Hu-chou 湖州, Chekiang (1642). In 1644 he went back to the Ling-feng monastery,

and in 1645 he stayed for a while at Nanking. In 1649 he again returned to Ling-feng. In 1652 he wrote his autobiography, the Pa-pu tao-jen chuan 八不道人傳. In the summer of 1653 he went to a retreat in the T'ien-ma yüan 天馬院 in Hui-chou. He used the quiet autumn days for extensive travel in nearby scenic mountains. In the second month of 1654 he returned to Ling-feng for the last time. He fell ill during the summer but recovered sufficiently to compose some additional works. His final illness occurred in the tenth month of 1654 and he eventually succumbed the following year. His pupils honored him with the posthumous name of Shih-jih ta-shih 始日大師.

Among his disciples Ch'eng-shih 成時 (1618–78, ordained 1645) should be mentioned. He assisted Chih-hsü in composing certain books and also edited his miscellaneous writings and prose under the title Ling-feng Ou-i ta-shih tsung-lun 藕(蕅)益大師宗論 (printed in 1801, reprinted 1875). Chih-hsü was a prolific author, being responsible for well over fifty different works, partly compilations made from earlier Buddhist writings, partly exegetical commentaries on the basic sūtras. Three of his works have been included in the Taishō edition of the Tripiṭaka (nos. 1762, 1850, and 1939); the Zoku Zōkyō contains 47 more by Chih-hsü. From the colophons which are appended to many of these one may assume that he worked very fast. He composed, for example, his A-mi-t'o ching yao-chieh 阿彌陀經要解 (Explanations of important points in the A-mida sūtra) within nine days in 1647. His most important contribution was the Yüeh-tsang chih-chin 閱藏知津 in 44 ＋ 4 chüan (printed in China 1664, 1709, 1892, in Japan 1709, 1782, and 1897/98), which contains a new bibliographical arrangement of the Tripiṭaka which was followed later by the Tokyo edition of the Buddhist Canon (1880–85). Chih-hsü also paid tribute to the fashion of his time by attempting a harmonization of Confucianism and Buddhism as is evidenced by his Chou-

i ch'an-chieh 周易禪解 (Ch'an explanation of the *Chou-i*), 10 *ch.*, and *Ssu-shu Ou-i chieh* 四書澫益解 (Ou-i's explanation of the Four Books), 1 *ch.*

Chih-hsü was in his lifetime much less an activist than, for example, Chen-k'o (*q. v.*), and must be regarded as a follower of the more contemplative Chu-hung who advocated a syncretism of the existing Buddhist schools of thought, the differences among which had long ceased to be meaningful. Chih-hsü's teaching, like that of Chu-hung, aimed at a synthesis of Ch'an and Pure Land meditation. He had also found that there was no basic difference in contemplation, the study of the scriptures, and monastic discipline. All this he achieved, however, very gradually, having suffered many doubts and scruples. He once even drew lots before the Buddha to choose among four ways to salvation: T'ien-t'ai, Hua-yen, Fa-hsiang, and founding a school of his own. T'ien-t'ai won out, although he found that particular school of the Ch'an sect too exclusive in practice. Chih-hsü is, in a way, the last great representative of syncretistic Buddhism in the mid-17th century. He continued to have some influence on later Buddhism through his pupils, and is regarded as the head of the so-called Lingfeng school which remained in vogue in China during the second half of the 17th and the first half of the 18th century. [Editors' note: According to Ch'eng-shih's notes on Chih-hsü's autobiography, the master lived "thirty-four years after ordination" 法臘三十四 (late in 1622 to 1655), but could count only nineteen summers of priesthood, for he declared himself independent one day in 1633(癸酉自恣日) and did not return to it until the spring of 1645. Chih-hsü hinted in his own writings that once he had pointed out certain incorrect practices in monasteries, and proposed a radical change in monastic regulations to conform to the laws recorded in Buddhist literature. After the rejection of his proposal, he either voluntarily left the monastery or was expelled.]

Bibliography

Pa pu-tao-jen chuan, in *Ling-feng Ou-i ta-shih tsung-lun*, ch. 1; *Ching t'u sheng-hsien lu* 淨土聖賢錄 (*Zoku Zōkyō* ed.), 2 B, 8, 2, p. 15la; *Chiang-ning-fu chih* 江寧府志, in TSCC (1885–88), XVIII: 194/70/6b; *Bukkyō Daijiten*, Vol. 3, 2730, Vol. 4, 3561, Vol. 10, 1183; Mochizuki Shinkō 望月信享, *Chūgoku Jōdo kyōri-shi* 中國淨土教理史 (1954), 501; Araki Kengo 荒木見語, "Minmatsu ni okeru Jubutsu chōwaron no seikaku" 明末における儒佛調和論の性格, *Nihon Chūgoku Gakkai Hō* 日本中國學會報, Vol. 15 (1966), 210; "Chigyoku no shisō to Yōmeigaku" 智旭の思想と陽明學, *Bukkyō Shigaku* 佛教史學, Vol. 13, no. 3 (1967), 1; Kenneth K. S. Ch'en, *Buddhism in China* (1964), 447; Leon Hurvitz, "Chu-hung's One Mind of Pure Land and Ch'an Buddhism," *Self and Society in Ming Thought*, ed. by W. T. de Bary (1970), 451.

Herbert Franke

CHIN Chung *see* ESEN Tügel

CHIN Ying 金英, fl. 1426–50, a eunuch of obscure origin, was, together with Hsing An (*q. v.*), one of the most favored imperial servants during the early years of the Ming dynasty. He first served under Emperor Chu Chan-chi (*q. v.*), gained his favor, and rose to become head of the directorate of ceremonial, the most powerful eunuch agency. In 1432 Chin and Fan Hung (*see* Wang Chin), a fellow eunuch of Annamite origin serving in the same directorate, received lavish awards from the emperor. They were given a silver seal with insignia, and a patent insuring their immunity from the death sentence in the event that they committed a crime. Through imperial favor they gradually exerted influence in high places.

Chin Ying continued his service under Emperor Chu Ch'i-chen (*q. v.*) as head of the directorate and was held in high esteem. But, when the emperor came under the domination of Wang Chen (*q. v.*) around 1442, Chin lost his influence, and Wang succeeded to his position. During this time it was revealed that Chin had abused his office by engaging in profitable pursuits. He was found in May, 1437, for example, to have operated several shops in the capital and attempted to monopolize certain businesses. In June, 1443 he and Fan Hung were indicted for illegally pasturing their herds in the imperial park and for stealing hay from the peasants. Chin was thrown into prison for these violations, but soon gained his release and was reinstated. In May, 1449, the emperor sent him to take charge, together with representatives from the three judicial offices, of the trial of convicts charged with serious offenses. The trial was conducted at the Grand Court of Revision, in which Chin Ying, representing the emperor, occupied the central seat, whereas the judicial officials, from the minister down, sat on either side of him. Such trials were convened once every five years. This procedure marked the formalization of the practice of putting a eunuch in charge, along with the three judicial office representatives; it was initiated by the appointment of Hsing An in 1441.

In the aftermath of the T'u-mu battle and the capture of Chu Ch'i-chen by the Oirat in September, 1449, Chin Ying, together with Hsing An, lent full support to Yü Ch'ien (*q. v.*) and the war faction, and rejected the proposal presented by Hsü Ch'eng (*see* Hsü Yu-chen) to abandon the capital and seek shelter in the south. As the reinstated head of the directorate of ceremonial, Chin probably also played a role, late in September, in the designation as heir apparent of Chu Chienshen (*q. v.*). It was due to his sustained support of the captured emperor that he incurred the displeasure of Chu Ch'i-yü (*q. v.*), who had taken over the throne from his brother.

Shortly after Chu Ch'i-yü's enthronement Chin Ying became the target of impeachment by his enemies who accused him of committing a number of misdeeds; in the absence of imperial backing, he suffered disgrace. In July, 1450, certain censors reported that Chin's servants, who

were probably working for their master, seized a sizable amount of the official salt, and appropriated private boats for shipment of their goods. As a consequence the offenders were apprehended and executed, and several censors who connived in the eunuch's activities for fear of reprisal were cashiered. Chin Ying, however, escaped reprimand. Then, in December, Chin was charged with a more serious offense, that of accepting a bribe from a commander in the Embroidered-uniform Guard in order to insure his position. When Chin was brought to trial, the censors revealed more instances of the same sort; this affected the career of a number of officials, including the minister of Works, Shih P'u 石璞 (T. 仲玉, cj 1411), who should have been punished as a member of Wang Chen's clique, but escaped impeachment through Chin's support. The authorities demanded capital punishment for Chin Ying and the confiscation of his properties, but the emperor, in a gesture of leniency, commuted the sentence to imprisonment. Nothing is heard of him after this, his position being taken over by Hsing An. Chin had an adopted son named Chou Ch'üan 周全. He served in the Embroidered-uniform Guard, holding the rank of regional assistant commander at the time of his death in August, 1487.

Bibliography

1/95/14a, 304/5b; 5/117/10a; 61/158/11b; MSL (1963), Ying-tsung, 580, 2196. 3438, 4048, 4119, 4150, 4201, Hsien-tsung (1964), 4937; Wang Shih-chen, "Chung-kuan k'ao" 中官考, in *Yen-shan-t'ang pieh-chi*, 90/14b, 91/13b; Teng Ch'iu 鄧球 (cs 1535), *Huang Ming yung-hua lei-pien* 皇明泳化類編, 123/9b; Hsia Hsieh夏燮, *Ming t'ung-chien* 明通鑑 (1959), 1026; Ting I 丁易, *Ming-tai t'e-wu cheng-chih* 明代特務政治 (1950), 102.

Hok-lam Chan

CHING Ch'ing 景清, died September 12, 1402, statesman and martyr of the usurpation, was a native of Chen-ning 眞寧,

Ch'ing-yang 慶陽-fu, Shensi. His actual surname was Keng耿, but it was recorded as Ching at some point in his youth through a scribal error. (Keng and Ching have similar pronunciations in some northern dialects.) He apparently used the surname Ching throughout his public life, but in certain historical works the error is corrected and he is referred to as Keng Ch'ing.

Except for one or two anecdotes about his student years, presenting him as a person of unusual intellectual capacity and moral force, little is known of Ching's early life. Having placed second in the palace examinations of 1394, he was assigned to the Hanlin Academy as a compiler, and after three years became a censor. In February, 1397, Emperor Chu Yüan-chang, pleased by his talent and intelligence, appointed him an acting (?) senior assistant censor-in-chief. Shortly thereafter, however, Ching and two other censors were impeached and imprisoned for some procedural errors in the conduct of their work. The emperor pardoned him (in May) and sent him on a mission to investigate tea-smuggling on the Szechwan-Shensi border, after which he received an appointment (December) as prefect of Chin-hua 金華, Chekiang. This demonstrated the emperor's continued confidence.

Shortly after Chu Yün-wen (*q. v.*) came to the throne in May, 1398, Ching Ch'ing was appointed censor-in-chief, and apparently held that post throughout the Chien-wen reign, with one interruption. That occurred early in the period when he was temporarily given the assignment of assistant administrative commissioner at Yen 燕 (Peiping), actually an investigative position of great trust and importance in view fo the relations at that time between Chu Yün-wen and his uncle, Chu Ti (*q. v.*). The latter used the occasion to associate cordially with Ching and to test him in conversation, as he did many officials sent from Nanking. He was favorably impressed by Ching, praising his intelligence and upright demeanor. Ching's

stay in Peiping was brief, and on his return to Nanking he became one of the circle of prominent civil officials at the court, associating with Fang Hsiao-ju (*q. v.*) and others.

Ching Ch'ing's place in history is based almost entirely on the special circumstances of his death. By early 1402 officials in Nanking were aware that they might have to compromise or die for their loyalty. Ching had been active in a group planning resistance to the usurpation, and with Fang Hsiao-ju and others had sworn to die if necessary. When Chu Ti entered Nanking in July, 1402, and proclaimed himself emperor, Ching, to the surprise of many, was among those courtiers who appeared to take the change in stride, perfunctorily assuming their places at court. The new emperor on seeing him referred to their previous encounter at Peiping, and with cordial comment reappointed Ching Ch'ing to his old post in the Censorate. On September 12 Ching was in attendance at the court when something suspicious in his manner, or secret information from spies, caused the emperor to have Ching seized and searched. He was found to be concealing a dagger in his robe, and, when questioned readily admitted that he had hoped to avenge Chu Yün-wen by murdering Chu Ti. He burst into a tirade of indignant abuse, and the emperor ordered the guards to pull out his teeth to silence him. The accounts say that the still-defiant Ching spat a mouthful of blood on the robes of the emperor who stood before him conducting the interrogation. He was immediately executed and, according to the same accounts, his corpse was skinned, the skin stuffed with straw and hung at the main palace entrance as a warning to others. Whether that detail is accurate or not, Chu Ti did make Ching the object of a terrifying vengeance, not only exterminating all his blood and marriage relations, and their kinfolk, but eventually ordering as well that every individual in his native village in Shensi be executed.

The most tenuous connection with Ching was enough to implicate a person in his crime; from his case emerged the term "melon-vine tendrils guilt" 瓜蔓抄. It described the limits to which guilt-by-association could be extended.

All of the accounts tell that Ching Ch'ing had a powerful spirit that could frighten away ghosts, and that, after his own death, his ghost visited the emperor and threatened him, until Chu Ti had his corpse ground to bits. These may be fanciful explanations of the emperor's often irrational vengeance; a sounder explanation may be that Chu Ti hoped to intimidate any one else who might be scheming to assassinate him. Despite the deep-seated resentment and willingness to die on the part of many loyalists, Ching and Lien Ying 連楹, a censor who seized the bridle of Chu Ti's horse and tried to stab him, were the only two persons known to have been ready to do violence to the usurper. They have provided neo-Confucian historians with a subject about which to moralize. A few loyalists openly regretted their failure. Most historians, however, while comparing them with the assassins discussed as heroes in the *Shih chi* of Ssu-ma Ch'ien (135-93? B.C.), have added serious reservations about the intended act of violence against the imperial personage. But it is a difficult subject for the biographer, for both Ching Ch'ing's righteous loyalty and Chu Ti's possession of the mandate had to be upheld.

Ching Ch'ing was one of the Chien-wen loyalists awarded the posthumous name Chung-lieh 忠烈 by the Southern Ming court at Nanking in January, 1645.

Bibliography

1/141/13a; 5/54/20a; 61/103/6b; 63/6/1a; MSL (1962), T'ai-tsu, 3610, 3646, 3686; KC (1958), 748, 770, 815, 874, 6171; T'u Shu-fang, *Chien-wen ch'ao yeh hui-pien,*建文朝野彙編 (NCL microfilm), 10/30a; Cha Chi-tso (ECCP), *Tsui-wei lu,* 傳 /9 上 /22a.

F. W. Mote

CH'IU Chün 邱 (or 丘) 濬 (T. 仲深, H. 瓊台, Pth. 文安), 1420–February 28, 1495, a native of Ch'iung-shan瓊山, Kwangtung, is one of the most prolific writers of Ming times; his treatises and essays on a variety of subjects, especially those dealing with governmental institutions, established him as a leading political thinker as well as a writer of stature. [Editors' note: Ch'iu's year of birth is problematical, being given variously as 1418, 1420, and 1421. The *Ming shih-lu*, Hsiao-tsung, 1088, records a memorial by Ch'iu, written in 1491, in which he remarks that he was then seventy-one *sui*. This would put the date in 1421. In the *Hsü-chou-fu chih* 叙州府志 (1895), however, there is a testimonial given by Ch'iu, dedicated to Chou Hung-mu (*q.v.*, 1419-91), in which Ch'iu says that he is Chou's junior by one year. This makes his year of birth 1420.]

Ch'iu ranked first in the provincial civil service examinations of 1444 and subsequently attended the National University. Upon his qualification for the *chin-shih* a decade later, he was selected to enter the Hanlin Academy and thenceforth, except for a period of mourning and leave of absence (1469–73), served the same institution continuously for almost a quarter of a century. He became an expositor-in-waiting (1465) and participated in the compilation of several important works under imperial auspices including the *Ying-tsung shih-lu* and *Huan-yü t'ung-chih* (*see* Shang Lu). In that same year he wrote a long letter to Grand Secretary Li Hsien (*q.v.*) proposing certain policies in dealing with the Yao 猺 tribesmen in Kwangtung and Kwangsi. Li brought this letter to the attention of Emperor Chu Chien-shen (*q.v.*) who approved it and ordered that Ch'iu's recommendations be carried out. This helped Ch'iu gain prominence. In 1477 he was appointed chancellor of the National University. Three years later, still as chancellor, his rank was elevated to right vice minister of Rites.

Two months after Chu Yu-t'ang's (*q.v.*)

accession (1487), Ch'iu dedicated to the throne his monumental work, *Ta-hsüeh yen-i-pu* 大學衍義補, 164 *ch.*, including appendices. The emperor was duly impressed and immediately ordered that the book be published and its author promoted to the rank of a minister of Rites. The new honor accorded to Ch'iu, however, was titular only; his function as a court erudite continued. In the next three years the compilation of the *Hsien-tsung shih-lu* occupied most of his time. His active participation in governmental affairs started only after he became grand secretary in 1491, when he was already over seventy.

This last appointment, as Ming wiriters have pointed out, established a precedent. Before Ch'iu's time it had not been uncommon for grand secretaries to be given ministerial titles to increase their prestige, but never before had an official who already held a ministerial rank entered the Grand Secretariat. Ch'iu's appointment, therefore, demonstrates the rise in importance of the grand secretaryship in the last part of the 15th century.

Ch'iu's performance in the cabinet, however, was lackluster. In 1491 he petitioned the emperor requesting that the suggestions outlined in his *Yen-i-pu* be put into effect. The emperor agreed. For reasons which historians have so far been unable to establish, few of his many constructive ideas were brought to realization. In his last years Ch'iu lost the sight of his right eye. Constantly troubled by illness, he became more and more impatient. Often he involved himself in quarrels with his fellow officials. One time in a fit of anger he tossed his hat to the ground while arguing with his colleague in the Nei-ko. His relationship with the minister of Personnel, Wang Shu (*q.v.*), worsened so that the two were not on speaking terms. The impeachment of Wang by an imperial physician which resulted in the former's retirement in 1493, was, according to consensus, instigated by Ch'iu, though he emphatically denied the charge.

Ch'iu is described by his contemporaries as "unimpressive in appearance." His simple style of living was widely known, his assiduity in scholarly pursuit universally acknowledged. But beyond this opinions about his character differ. His critics charge him with being selfish and treacherous. His admirers insist that he was straightforward and uncompromising. That Ch'en Hsien-chang (*q.v.*) was unable to obtain an official position at court, the critics assert, was entirely because Ch'iu, fearful of competition, elbowed him out of Peking. Ch'iu's supporters not only hold the accusation false, but also present correspondence and poems exchanged between the two learned men from Kwangtung to evidence their enduring friendship. The significance of such divergent opinion is that certain reviewers of Ch'iu's writings, among them the editors of the *Ssu-k'u* catalogue, use an *ad hominem* approach.

Possessed of a versatile talent, Ch'iu was responsible for numerous books, his list embracing geography, history, political economy, etiquette, education, philosophy, medicine, poetry, and drama. Among them the most celebrated work is undoubtedly the above mentioned *Yen-i-pu*. In his introduction Ch'iu indicates that his purpose is to supplement the *Ta-hsüeh yen-i* written by Chen Te-hsiu (1178–1235). Chen's work set a standard for righteous living, the scope of the book applying only to individuals and households, while Ch'iu's book, imitating Chen's plan, extends the coverage to public affairs. In reality, however, the two works bear no resemblance to each other except in form. Whereas Chen concentrates on philosophy and ethics, Ch'iu's compilation is by and large a comprehensive handbook on public administration, dealing with every aspect of governmental function including military defense, public finance, personnel management, transportation, water control, etc. Under each entry the historical background is presented, different approaches to every problem are discussed, the author's own opinion is enunciated, and, whenever possible, considerable numerical data are appended. Aside from its practical use, the work is noted for the painstaking research behind it and for its historical value. Being widely read, it exercised a genuine impact on Ming scholarship.

Following publication of the *Yen-i-pu* Ch'iu became recognized by many a Ming official as an early promoter of transportation by sea. Those who championed the sea traffic after his time seldom failed to quote him to support their argument. But unlike the later-day promoters who focused their attention on the route along the coast (*see* Liang Meng-lung), Ch'iu calls for construction of seaworthy ships sailing out into the open sea and for navigation by compass. In his opinion, not only should the current law forbidding sea traffic be rescinded, but also, to encourage maritime commerce, a moratorium of three years on the levy of custom duty should be declared. He emphasizes that promotion of sea trade is the best way to build a naval reserve. Writing of corvée labor, Ch'iu advocates the commutation of the service levy altogether. He urges that the commuted payments be made in lump sums on an annual basis. He thus anticipates the singlewhip-method (*see* P'ang Shang-p'eng and Wang Tsung-mu) almost a century before its implementation.

Nevertheless, not all of Ch'iu's ideas are far-sighted. The *Yen-i-pu*, for instance, reveals the author's preoccupation with the bullion theory. He insists that every coin minted by the government must contain enough metal to be worth its face value. Present-day scholars have not hesitated to seize on this passage in the book as evidence to support their thesis that Ming political thinkers failed to develop a modern concept of money, and in this respect their vision compares unfavorably with that of their Yüan counterparts. And again Ch'iu never separates himself from the traditional neo-Confucian bond. Holding that the harmony between the yin and the yang is essential to universal orderliness, he insists that ritual, following the principle of yang, and music, following the principle of yin, are two basic tools of sound government. In the *Yen-i-pu* he devotes large sections to a detailed discussion of state ceremonies.

As a historian, Ch'iu endorses the conventional view with certain reservations. He sees Empress Wu (624-705) as wantonly evil and has few kind words for Wang An-shih (1021-86). His admiration for Chu Hsi 朱熹 (1130-1200) is beyond question. On the other hand, he urges his readers to revise their traditional concept of dynastic history, which over-glorifies the rise of the Han and the T'ang and paints too dark a picture of the fall of the Ch'in and the Sui. During the compilation of the *Ying-tsung shih-lu*, he is said to have been instrumental in putting Yü Ch'ien's (*q.v.*) position in proper historical perspective. In spite of his moderation, however, critics have charged him with being different for difference's sake. Among many others, Li Chih (*q.v.*), a rebel himself, leans to the side of Ch'iu's detractors. The greatest controversy involving Ch'iu Chün as a historian concerns certain remarks which he is supposed to have made, which imply that Ch'in Kuei (1090-1155) was a sound statesman, Fan Chung-yen (989-1052) something of a fool, and Yüeh Fei (1104-42) only a single-minded warrior, thus reversing the recognized roles of heroes and villains in traditional Chinese historiography. A storm of criticism followed. But Ch'iu's defenders argue that the whole story is fabricated, that Ch'iu never made such statements, which, they further point out, would be incompatible with the sentiments expressed in his poetry. (Cf. Ch'iu, *Wu-lun ch'üan-pei chung-hsiao chi* 五倫全備忠孝記 [NLP microfilm, roll no. 1032]; see Shao Ts'an [*q.v.*], *Wu-lun chuan hsiang-nang chi*. In the latter Ch'in Kuei does appear as a villain and Yüeh Fei a hero in compliance with the conventions. There is some doubt, however, about the authorship of this play.)

The Gest Library at Princeton and the Hoover Library at Stanford each has a rare edition of the *Ta-hsüeh yen-i-pu*, and it has recently been reproduced in the *Ssu-k'u ch'üan-shu chen-pen* 珍本, series 2. Other important works by Ch'iu include *Shih-shih cheng-kang* 世史正綱, 32 *ch.* (reprinted 1936), *Chu-tzu hsüeh-ti* 朱子學 的, 2 *ch.*, *Ch'iung-t'ai yin-kao* 瓊台吟稿, 12 *ch.*, *Ch'iung-t'ai lei-kao* 類稿, 52 *ch.*, *Pents'ao ko-shih* 本草格式, 1 *ch.*, and *Chia-li i-chieh* 家禮儀節, 8 *ch.* He also wrote the *P'ingting Chiao-nan lu* 平定交南錄, 1 *ch.*, which recounts the military campaign in Annam of 1406-7; it has been included in a number of collections, such as the *Chi-lu hui-pien*, *chüan* 47, of Shen Chieh-fu (*q.v.*). In the 1620s a descendant extracted parts of the *Ch'iung-t'ai yin-kao* and *lei-kao* to form a work entitled *Ch'ung-pien* 重編 *Ch'iung-t'ai hui-kao*, 24 *ch.* *Chüan* 7-8 contain fourteen of Ch'iu's memorials. The combined works by Ch'iu and Hai Jui (*q. v.*), entitled *Ch'iu Hai er-kung ho-chi* 丘海 二公合集 have been recently reprinted.

Bibliography

1/181/4a; 5/14/29a; 63/11/33a; 64/ 乙 19/2a; MSL (1963), Hsien-tsung, 0294, 3068, 3591, Hsiaotsung, 0134, 1088, 1395, 1773, 1775; *Huang Ming wen-hai* (microfilm) 7/la; *Hsü-chou-fu chih* (1895), 35/12a; *Kwangtung t'ung-chih* (1934), 1152, 1212, 5159; *Ch'iung-shan-hsien chih* (1917), 19/3a, 20/5a, 24/6a, 28/31a; Wu Chi-hua 吳緝華, *Ming-tai hai-yün chi-yün ho-ti yen-chiu* 明代海運 及運河的研究 (Taipei 1961), 140; SK (1930), 48/ 2b, 93/3a, 170/10b; W. Franke, *Sources*. 5. 4. 3, 6. 6. 6, 7. 6. 2, 9. 2, 1.

Chi-hua Wu and Ray Huang

CH'IU Luan 仇鸞 (T. 伯翔, H. 杸齋), 1505-August 31, 1552), generalissimo charged with the defense of the frontier against the Mongols from 1550 to 1552, was a native of Chen-yüan 鎮遠, a strategic point on the Ninghsia 寧夏 border.

His family, engaged in military service for several generations, was originally (end of the 14th century)stationed at Yangchow, but later transferred to the northwest. Both his great-great-grandfather and his great-grandfather died in action in Ninghsia; so the family was given a hereditary military post there. His grandfather, Ch'iu Yüeh 鉞 (T. 延威, Pth. 武襄, 1465-1521), came into prominence because of the part he played in quelling the rebellion of the prince of An-hua, Chu Chihfan (*see* Yang T'ing-ho). He was first made earl of Hsien-ning 咸寧伯; then, because of additional military achievements, he was elevated to be marquis, a title which Ch'iu Luan inherited in 1522. It is said that he was an apt student, could write well, and that his residence at Suchou hu-t'ung 蘇州胡同 in Peking was modestly kept like the house of an ordinary civil official. In 1524 he was one of sixty-three civil and military officials joining Marquis Kuo Hsün (*q.v.*) to take the side of the emperor, Chu Hou-ts'ung (*q.v.*), in the *Ta-li i* controversy and so enjoyed imperial favor.

Late in 1524 Ch'iu was appointed commandant of one of the twelve guard divisions of Peking. Five years after this he received promotion to regional commander of Kwangtung and Kwangsi. He requested sick leave in the latter part of 1534, but because he left his post before imperial sanction arrived he was censored in 1535 and fined three months' stipend. As problems of succession were stirring in Annam (*see* Mac Dang-dung), the court decided in 1539 to make preparations for a punitive expedition. Ch'iu was made commander-in-chief with Mao Po-wen (*q.v.*) his chief of staff. While waiting for the troops to be assembled, Ch'iu was made one of the assistant commanders under Kuo Hsün to lead the imperial guard which accompanied the emperor on his visit to Hukuang in the months of February to May 1539. In September it was finally decided to send

Ch'iu and Mao to Kwangsi to assume their command. It seems that they did not arrive until the following year and finally submitted a plan of mobilization in July, 1540. Meanwhile Ch'iu and the Kwangtung regional commander, Liu Hsün 柳珣, the fifth marquis of An-yüan 安遠侯 (d. 1543), quarreled about certain points of etiquette, when Ch'iu arrogantly ordered Liu to kneel; the latter, however, proudly refused. Both appealed to the emperor who in October judged in favor of Liu, made him commander-in-chief, and had Ch'iu recalled. Just then a new turn of events made the use of force unnecessary, and the expedition ended in May, 1541, with Mao and Liu receiving high awards and Ch'iu a minor one.

In 1543 Ch'iu received an appointment as assistant commissioner of the left chief military commission in Peking. In the following year he became regional commander of Kansu, where he was later brought into close contact with Tseng Hsien (*q.v.*), who assumed the post of supreme commander of the three frontiers of Shensi in 1546. Tseng, who advocated the recovery of the Ordos region from the Mongols, found his subordinate (Ch'iu) uncooperative, ineffective, and corrupt. In a severely critical memorial, Tseng accused Ch'iu of ten crimes. Ch'iu was therefore relieved of his command and taken to Peking (winter of 1547) in the custody of the Embroidered-uniform Guard. Early in 1548, however, because of opposition to the Ordos region policy and a change of mind on the part of the emperor, Tseng himslf was indicted and taken to the capital. Seizing a rare opportunity, Ch'iu in a persuasive memorial voiced his own grievances, accused Tseng of disloyalty, and spoke of the latter's plan as ill-conceived. It was rumored that Yen Sung (*q.v.*) was really at the back of this memorial, as he objected to Tseng Hsien, was jealous of Hsia Yen (*q.v.*) and was critical of the Ordos proposal. Ch'iu was then released from prison and for some time he resided quietly in the cap-

ital.

The year 1550 was one of crisis, as the Mongols swept into the environs of Peking that summer. In imminent danger, the government revealed its impotence and the military its helplessness. Early in July Altan-qaγan (*q. v.*) led his forces to attack Tatung, and Chang Ta 張達, the regional commander, died in the fighting. This created a vacancy which demanded immediate replacement. On the recommendation of the ministry of War, Ch'iu was given the command with the additional designation by imperial edict of grand guardian of the heir apparent. Some sources suggest that a bribe to Yen Shih-fan (*see* Yen Sung) helped him secure this post. Ch'iu Luan may well have been tempted by the high office; actually he had neither the dedication nor the stomach to fight the Mongols. He avoided a head-on confrontation with the enemy. First taking up a stand east of Tatung, he then retreated to the Chü-yung Pass 居庸關, justiying his act by reporting that with the Mongols advancing toward Chi-chou 薊州, his forces would be in a better position to protect Peking by having them stationed inside the Great Wall rather than farther to the east. In the meantime, most sources agree, he sent confidants bearing expensive gifts to the Mongols, making a pact with them not to invade Tatung. The Mongols then proceeded eastward. By September 27 the enemy had reached the Pai River 白河 and camped some 20 *li* from Peking. The capital was shaken and called for outside troops to help in the defense. As Ch'iu's Tatung forces were stationed at Chü-yung Pass, close to Peking, he and his men arrived the following day. For this the emperor was grateful, rewarding him with special gifts, granting him the favor of confidential and direct reporting to the throne, and making him generalissimo in charge of the defense of the entire north 平北大將軍.

The crisis created sudden demands on the capital, which it was not prepared to meet. One of the most urgent was the feeding of the troops brought in from the outside. As this eventuality had not been anticipated, Ch'iu's men plundered the countryside, assaulted other troops, and harassed the officials. When the Mongols became surfeited with loot, they took off for the Great Wall at Ku-pei-k'ou 古北口. Thus far, having managed to keep at a safe distance from the invader, Ch'iu now began to follow them. North of Ch'ang-p'ing 昌平, however, he was unexpectedly brought face to face with the enemy. In a brief encounter, he lost more than a thousand men; wanting, however, to claim a victory, he produced as evidence eighty heads, allegedly secured by devious means.

During the crisis the Mongols reiterated their demand for tribute-trade arrangements, including the exchange of Mongol horses for Chinese silk. As it seemed to be one way to placate them, Ch'iu supported the reopening of horse fairs. Two actually did take place in 1551, one in Tatung and another in Yen-ning 延寧. Later the Mongols requested trade in cattle and sheep in exchange for grain. At the same time this arrangement neither stopped their raids, nor did it serve as any guarantee against future invasions. The emperor then ordered the trade suspended.

Although the capital was saved, it was a shocking experience and one which called for military reorganization. A reform plan was adopted and hurriedly carried out. The original twelve army corps and the two east and west special units 東西兩官廳 were all abolished, but three grand army corps were established under one over-all commander-in-chief, his office being known as the Jung-cheng-fu 戎政府, or Jung-cheng-t'ing 廳. The three grand army corps were the Wu-chün-ying 五軍營 with 66,660 men and 196 officers, the Shen-shu-ying 神樞營 with 40,000 men and 208 officers, and the Shen-chi-ying 神機營 with 40,000 men and 182 officers, making a total of 146,660 men and 586 officers. In nomenclature the reorganized Peking army was similar to that of the Yung-lo period, the only change being that of the name San-ch'ien-ying 三千營 to Shen-shu-ying; in actual fact, however, never before under the Ming was such military power entrusted to a single individual. The emperor gave Ch'iu this power, casting a special seal for him which bore the designation Tsung-tu ching-ying jung-cheng 總督京營戎政, commander of the military affairs of the Peking corps. Later, after Ch'iu's ill-fated end, the name Jung-cheng-fu continued, but the power of the command was reduced. By 1570, under Emperor Chu Tsai-hou (q.v.) the office was abolished and the corps were put under three separate commanders.

After the selection of aides, the assemblage of supplies, and the amassing of more troops, Ch'iu announced an expedition against the Mongols to take place in 1551. The expedition was put off after a great deal of commotion. In the spring of 1552, Altan-qaɤan again swept through the Great Wall, this time via Tatung. Ch'iu, told to stop the invaders, failed and was ordered back to Peking. By this time he had already incurred the displeasure of both Yen Sung and Lu Ping (q.v.), who had formerly been his supporters. Ch'iu felt uneasy and requested retirement, but was refused. Late in August he became very ill, having a carbuncle on his back. As alarming news came in daily, the minister of War, under the pretext that no one had the power to meet the emergency with Ch'iu still holding his appointment and his seal, secured an imperial order to deprive Ch'iu of both. This was immediately carried out on the night of August 28. Most probably this further aggravated Ch'iu's condition. He died three days later.

About the time of his death, his confidants, the same men who had served as liaison between him and the Mongols in former days, were caught on their way to the enemy near the frontier. Some sources suggest that this was all maneuvered by Lu Ping. Be that as it may, these renegades confessed at their trial. Ch'iu was posthumously adjudged a traitor and rebel. His corpse was decapitated; his parents, wife, and sons, and the renegades were all executed. His concubines and granddaughter were given to the families of deserving officials as slaves.

In his long reign of forty-five years, Emperor Chu Hou-ts'ung had a habit of favoring certain high officials. Very few escaped tragic ends, however, and Ch'iu was no exception.

Chao Shih-ch'un (see Wang Shenchung) who wrote an account of Ch'iu Luan (contained in the *Kuo-ch'ao hsiencheng lu*), was a contemporary, and knew him personally. And Kao Tai (*q.v.*), the author of the *Hung-yu lu* in which he devoted a chapter to Ch'iu, witnessed the critical situation in Peking in 1550.

Bibliography

1/89/5b, 175/5b; 5/10/64a; Cha Chi-tso (ECCP) *Tsui-wei lu*, 19/27a; MSL (1965), Shih-tsung, 1144, 3641, 3653, 4721, 4849, 4880, 4972; *KC* (1958), 3798; Fan Shou-chi, *Su-huang wai-shih*; Kao Tai, *Hung-yu lu* (TsSCC ed.), chüan 197–202; *Huang Ming wen-hai* (microfilm), 17/1/14; Henry Serruys, *The Tribute System and Diplomatic Missions 1400-1600* (Brussels, 1967), 15, 35, 50, 66, 526; Louis Hambis, *Documents sur l'histoire des Mongols à l'époque des Ming* (Paris, 1969), 55.

Lienche Tu Fang

CH'IU Ying 仇英 (T. 實父, H. 十洲) died 1552 (?), painter, was a native of T'aits'ang 太倉, near the mouth of the Yangtze. Early in his life he moved to Wu-hsien 吳縣 in the prefecture of Soochow. Some recent studies have suggested a very short career, ending after 1552, the date of his last known painting. All authorities agree that Ch'iu Ying came from a humble family. It is not certain when he was befriended by Chou Ch'en (*q.v.*) but he probably stayed with Chou for only a

brief period, until 1530–31 when his own talent came to be appreciated. The poet Wang Ch'ung (*q.v.*), who died in 1533, inscribed many of Ch'iu Ying's paintings of this time, and a close relationship between them is suggested for the last years of Wang's life. By the middle of the decade Ch'iu Ying had unquestionably established his reputation, and visits to the young painter's studio by collectors and other painters in the region are recorded for this period of his life. His independence was apparently short lived; we are informed by a number of writers that by the end of the decade Ch'iu Ying had begun residing with a series of collectors in the area. The first of these was a minor official, Ch'en Te-hsiang 陳德相, who had a mountain retreat where Ch'iu spent "several successive years," according to the painter P'eng Nien (*q.v.*), a close friend of both men. Ch'iu's reputation as an excellent copyist of old masters was well known by this time, and collectors began seeking him out for his special talents. Thus it is not surprising that he was invited to spend some time at the home of the greatest collector of antiquities in the region, Hsiang Yüanpien (*q.v.*). Precisely when he began with Hsiang and how long the association between the collector and painter continued is not clear, but a reasonable conjecture would place the two men together between the years 1545 and 1550, when Ch'iu had reached his maturity as a painter, and the youthful Hsiang was beginning to take a serious interest in the arts of painting and calligraphy. That at least part of Ch'iu's time with Hsiang was spent copying old masterpieces is evidenced by the existence of an album of landscapes preserved today in the National Palace Museum, Taiwan. An inscription accompanying the album indicates that Ch'iu executed the six leaves after different masters at the specific request of Hsiang in 1547. The relationship between the two was an intense one, according to Hsiang's grandson, and during the period

Ch'iu turned out hundreds of paintings. But it was not with Hsiang that Ch'iu stayed the final years of his short life, for, according to other commentators such as Chang Ch'iu (*q.v.*), writing a half century later, Ch'iu Ying's prime years were spent with another "lover of antiquities," a certain Chou Yü-shun 周于舜 of nearby K'un-shan 崑山, whose seals appear on many of Ch'iu's known paintings. Again it is the story of the celebrated copyist housed by a wealthy collector which is conveyed to us in this last association; yet a study of existing paintings by Ch'iu, which contain the seals of Chou Yü-shun or Hsiang Yüan-pien, reveals an artist of quite varied talents who certainly did much more than merely copy old masterpieces.

Ch'iu Ying's wide output of paintings is difficult to summarize. As might be expected of someone who gained such great distinction for his abilities as a copyist, a high degree of technical proficiency is evident in all his paintings. But it was the great diversity in his works that separated him from the merely accomplished craftsmen of his time, and it was his skill in so many different styles of painting which made him popular in his own lifetime among such a varied assemblage as the literate, fellow-professional painters, and collectors. In more modern times, however, Ch'iu Ying's name has been associated almost exclusively with the highly polychromed works featuring painstakingly detailed draftsmanship and bright mineral pigments, focusing often on the theme of pretty court ladies at their leisure. Although there is no question that Ch'iu did execute paintings of this type, a study of older collectors' catalogues indicates clearly that such paintings were relatively few and formed only a small part of the painter's total oeuvre. A few dated paintings in this coloristic style, such as the handscroll of 1530 in the Chicago Art Institute, which illustrates T'ao Ch'ien's famous poem "T'ao hua-yüan chi" 桃花源記 (The peach blos-

som spring), gives some evidence of Ch'iu's very early involvement with the kung-pi 工筆, or meticulous manner of painting. Other examples of the bright polychromatic style reveal an interesting interpretation of the "blue-and-green" mode of T'ang dynasty landscape painting. A particularly fine example of Ch'iu Ying's special archaistic manner is the handscroll in the Nelson Gallery, Kansas City, illustrating another ancient and famous poem, the "P'i-pa hsing" 琵琶行 (Lute song) of Po Chü-i (772–846). And in the traditional "court lady" category of painting may be cited the exquisite scroll in the National Palace Museum, "Han-kung ch'un-hsiao" 漢宮春曉, depicting a spring morning in the Han palace. The marvelous visual effects achieved in this one painting alone may explain why Ch'iu's name became so intimately connected with this kind of courtly-style painting, leading to the many later and less inspired imitations. At the same time, it is worth noting that the National Palace Museum contains other works of Ch'iu which are quite the opposite in style from the tightly controlled performance of the "Spring Morning." Among these looser and more freely rendered paintings may be included the pair of hanging scrolls depicting men in conversation under wu-t'ung 梧桐 trees(T'ung-yin ch'ing-hua 桐陰清話) and musicians in the shade of banana leaves (Chiao-yin chieh-hsia 蕉陰結夏). The brushwork in these paintings is bold and powerful, a distinct departure from the delicate refined touch evident in the coloristic works, and such a contrast in styles serves only to underline the range of Ch'iu's talents. The great majority of his paintings fall somewhere between the extremes represented by the bold and free on one hand and the meticulous and tight on the other. Paintings such as the masterful depiction of the "Chien-ko 劍閣 Pass" (a T'ang emperor's journey to Szechwan) in the Shanghai Museum, the pair of hanging scrolls, "T'ao-li-yüan" 桃李園 and "Chin-ku 金谷-yüan," portraying famous T'ang gardens, preserved in the Chion-in, Kyoto, the superb "Liu-t'ang yü-t'ing" 柳塘漁艇 (Fishing boat on the willow stream) and the powerful hanging scroll entitled "Ch'iu-chiang tai-tu" 秋江待渡 (Waiting for the ferry in autumn), both in the Palace Museum, and the exquisitely painted "Ts'ang-lang Yü-ti" 滄浪漁笛 (Fisherman playing a flute) in the Crawford Collection, New York, do not fall into any one category of style or subject matter. They are paintings free of any theorizing and they fit few preconceptions about schools or style. They have in common, however, a high quality of workmanship and a faultlessness of handling throughout. In the very disciplined way he practiced his craft, Ch'iu gained the respect of a highly critical audience in Soochow, and overcame the handicap of inferior status associated with the professional artist. By the end of the 16th century Ch'iu Ying was numbered among the "four masters of the Wu district" along with Shen Chou, Wen Cheng-ming, and T'ang Yin (*qq.v.*).

Ch'iu Ying left no real disciple, although his son-in-law, Yu Ch'iu 尤求 (T. 子求, H. 鳳丘, fl. 1572-83), occasionally echoed him in a limited way, especially in paintings of historical subjects. His daughter, painting under her *hao*, or literary name, Tu-ling nei-shih 杜陵內史, executed a few figure paintings which capture some of her father's grace of handling, but her subject matter was limited as was her reputation.

Bibliography

Wang Chih-teng, *Wu-chün tan-ch'ing chih* (1563) in *Mei-shu* 美術 *ts'ung-shu*; Chang Ch'ou, *Ch'ing-ho shu-hua fang* (preface 1616); Chiang Shao-shu 姜紹書, *Wu-sheng shih-shih* 無聲詩史 (*ca.* 1700); Wen Chao-t'ung 溫肇桐, "Ch'iu Shih-chou" 仇十洲 in *Ming-tai ssu-ta hua-chia* 明代四大畫家, Shanghai, 1946; Osvald Sirén, *Chinese Painting*, VII (New York, 1956–58), 174; E.J. Laing, *Chinese Paintings in Chinese Publications, 1956-1968* (Ann Arbor 1969), 161.

M. W. Young

CH'OE Pu 崔溥 (T. Yŏn-Yŏn 淵淵, H. Kŭmnam 錦南), 1454-1504, a Korean official and traveler in China, was a native of Naju 羅州, a prefectural town in Chŏlla province 全羅道. He passed the *chinsa* examinations in 1477, the civil service examinations (重試) in 1482, and the second examinations in 1486, and was selected to study in the Hodang 湖堂 library. In his varied offic career, he served successively in the printing office 校書館, military supplies commission 軍資監, national academy 成均館, office of the inspector-general 司憲府, office of special counselors 弘文館, Yongyang garrison 龍驤衛, and other posts, rising as high as director of the ceremonies office 禮賓寺正 before falling victim to political enemies. In 1498, as a member of the defeated faction in the first of the great "literati purges" of the Yi dynasty, he was banished to Tanch'ŏn 端川 and in 1504, the year of the second purge, was put to death.

In an official career of no more than eighteen years he held several responsible offices; contributed to an important scholarly work, the *Tongguk t'onggam* 東國通鑑 (1484), a history of Korea from ancient times; and established a reputation among his friends for learning, administrative competence, and adherence to moral principles. He was returned to honor posthumously in 1506.

An accident established his connection with China when he was still a comparatively young official. In 1487 he was sent to Cheju Island to check the registry for escaped slaves to be returned to the mainland. He had been at his new post less than three months when a family slave arrived (February 12, 1488) from Naju and told Ch'oe of his father's death. As the boat that was to carry Ch'oe back to the mainland put out from its harbor a storm swept it up and, after some fourteen days of heavy weather, carried the party of forty-three Koreans to the coast of Ningpo prefecture. From there Ch'oe and his men traveled under escort up the

Grand Canal to Peking and from Peking via Liaotung back to Korea, arriving at Uiju, the border town on the Yalu River, at the beginning of summer. Before reentering the capital, Ch'oe received a command from the king for an account of his journey. The diary he produced, *P'yohae-rok* 漂海錄 (A Record of Drifting Across the Sea) provides concrete information of conditions in China in the middle of the dynasty.

As a reporter, Ch'oe wrote from the viewpoint of a foreigner well educated in Chinese, and especially neo-Confucian, letters. At the same time he wrote as one active in Korean politics, a lively field at that time, so that his diary, in its expression of some emphases and attitudes, protrays a Korean Confucianist as well as it portrays China. It is the latter aspect, however, that counts here.

Among Ch'oe's general observations, the broadest is the discrepancy in apparent prosperity between north and south China. The south, with its rich scenery and expansive and splendid cities, strikes Ch'oe as having a liveliness and richness unmatched in the north, even in Peking. The south also displays more social order and cultivation than the north, the former seeming to be characterized by harmonious, industrious, and literate people, the latter by quarrelsome and even criminal wastrels.

The Ming Canal, an object of pride to Ch'oe's Chinese escorts, is adequately maintained and administered. The party moves up its course without administrative delay at a rate of approximately one hundred *li* a day. In addition to stations and posts all along the way, the Canal has locks, ramps, moles, paved towpaths, and other facilities. The postal route from Peking to the Yalu River is less elaborate but still maintained with distance markers and walled stations. The road is poor, however, and travel arduous as well as dangerous.

Among great issues of the time, the one Ch'oe encounters directly is concern over Japanese pirates, the famous *wo-k'ou*. The villagers who first arrest him and the officials who later take charge of him assume that the party consists of Japanese raiders and treat them with a truculence suggestive of bitter experiences in the past, a reception that is the more remarkable for the lack of any notice of *wo-k'ou* in the *Ming-shih* for at least the two preceding decades. In several interviews Ch'oe's primary task is to dispel the notion that he is Japanese. It is partly from this need as well as from a desire to impress others with the quality of Korean cultivation that he always displays his adherence to Confucian ethics, knowledge of Chinese letters, and competence in Chinese poetry.

At the same time, he makes clear his pride in Korea and his loyalty to the Korean king. He shows, for example, a ready knowledge of Korean history, geography, and famous men (stressing Confucianists, statesmen, and warriors); and praises his king as a respecter of learning and a wise ruler. He also chooses to say rather little about Korean military strength and relations with countries other than China. The thought of benefiting his countrymen leads him to learn the way of making a kind of water wheel that he introduces to the Korean court after his return and to describe carefully the construction of embankments and locks, and the floods along the Grand Canal.

Other incidents in the diary speak of bureaucratic practices, the public behavior of eunuchs, and the impact on officials of the accession of Chu Yu-t'ang (*q.v.*) adding political details to social and physical observations of life at mid-dynasty. Among his other impressions that are notable are the prevalence of Taoism, Buddhism, and animism, and the eagerness of everyone, even the powerful, to make money.

Ch'oe, as a castaway, was in no position to converse with the great men of the age, but coincidence or the normal workings of government brought him at least for a moment to the attention of such figures as Cheng Chi 鄭紀 (T. 延綱,

Chu Yüan-chang (1328–98); painted *ca.* 1368

Chu Yüan-chang (1328–98); painted *ca.*
1377

PLATE 1

Chu Yüan-chang (1328–98); painted *ca.* 1397

Empress Ma (1332–82)

PLATE 2

Chu Ti (1360–1424)

Empress Hsü (1362–1407)

PLATE 3

Chu Kao-chih (1378–1425) and Empress Chang (d. 1442)

Chu Ch'i-chen (1427–64) and Empress Ch'ien (1428–68)

Chu Chan-chi (1399–1435) and Empress Sun (d. 1462)

PLATE 4

Empress Chou (1430–1504), mother of Chu Chien-shen

Chu Chien-shen (1447–87) and Empress Wang (d. 1518)

PLATE 5

Chu Yu-t'ang (1470–1505) and Empress Chang (d. 1541)

Chu Hou-chao (1491–1521) and Empress Hsia (d. 1535)

PLATE 6

H. 東園, cs 1460), at the time surveillance vice-commissioner of schools in Chekiang; Ch'ang Heng 暢亨 (T. 文通, cs 1478), regional investigating censor of Chekiang; Yü Tzu-chün (*q.v.*), minister of War; Tai Hao 戴豪 (T. 師文, cs 1478), senior secretary of the bureau of Maps 職方清吏司, ministry of War; Chou Hung-mu (*q.v.*), minister of Rites; and Tung Yüeh董越 (T. 尙矩, cs 1469, who himself went on an embassy to Korea in 1488, leaving a diary *Shih tung jih-lu* 使東日錄 in 1 *chüan*, as well as a fu on Korea, *Ch'ao-hsien fu* 朝鮮賦, and some notes on the country, *Ch'ao-hsien tsa chih* 雜志, in 1 *chüan*), chancellor of the Hanlin Academy. The generous treatment of the Chinese court, which made gifts of clothing to the Koreans and arranged to return the party safely to the Yalu River, impelled the Korean court to send an embassy of thanksgiving within a month of Ch'oe's return. References in the diary to other castaways and official missions, incidentally suggest a lively intercourse between Peking and Seoul.

After Ch'oe presented *P'yohae-rok* to the king in 1488 the book was stored in the archives. Whether it was printed at first is not clear, but by 1569 Ch'oe's grandson, Yu Hŭi-ch'un 柳希春, had prepared the book for printing, and it was published in an edition that apparently made it available to many readers for the first time. A copy of this edition is in the Yōmei Bunko, Kyoto. Four years later another edition of the book was printed, indicating a continuing demand. A copy of the 1573 edition is in the Kanazawa Bunko, Yokohama. Another early copy, printed from movable type unlike the wood-block copies just mentioned, is in the Tōyō Bunko, Tokyo. Manuscript copies also exist in Japan.

That the diary interested Japanese as well as Koreans was evident in the publication in 1769 of an abbreviated translation by the Confucianist, Seida Tansō 清田儋叟 (1721–85), entitled *Tōdo kōtei-ki* 唐土行程記, which was, of course, also

commonly known by its original title.

Ch'oe's writings other than *P'yohae-rok* were collected and published under the title *Kŭmnam-chip* 錦南集, but no copy has been available for this article.

Bibliography

Yŏllyŏsil kisul 燃黎室記述(Keijo: Chōsen Kosho Kankō-kai, 1912, ch. 6: *Yŏnsan-jo kosa ponmal muo tangjok* 燕山朝故事本末戊午黨籍); Kim Chong-jik 金宗直, *Munin-rok*門人錄 (in *Chŏmp'ilje Sŏnsaeng munchip* 佔畢齋先生文集, 1892, 8 fascicules); Cho Sin 曹伸, *Yu-mun soe-rok* 諛聞瑣錄 (in *Taedong yasŭng* 大東野乘, Keijo: Chōsen Kosho Kanko-kai, Vol. I, 1909–1911); *Haedong chamnok* 海東雜錄 (in *Taedong yasŭng*, Vols. IV,V); *Yŏnsan-gun ilgi* 燕山君日記, ch. 56: 10/10 *wu-yin, hsin-ssu, jen-wu*; *P'yohae-rok* (in Makita Tairyō 牧田諦亮, *Sakugen nyūmin-ki mo kenkyū* 策彥入明記の研究 *Kyoto*: Hozō-kan, II, 1959); *Ch'oe Pu's Diary: A Record of Drifting Across the Sea*, tr. by John Meskill, Tucson, 1965.

John Meskill

CHŎNG To-jŏn 鄭道傳 (T. 宗之, H. 三峯, Pth. 文憲), 1342-October 6, 1398, statesman, scholar, and official under both Koryŏ and Chosŏn dynasties, was a native of Ponghwa 奉化 (north Kyŏngsang) and the son of Chŏng Un-gyŏng鄭云敬 (1305–66), minister of Justice (1359–63) under King Kongmin 恭愍王 (r. 1352–74). A disciple of the famous scholar Yi Saek 李穡 (1328-June 2, 1396), Chŏng To-jŏn took his *chinsa* 進士 degree in 1362. When in 1375, after the assassination of the anti-Mongol king, the pro-Mongol faction at court intended to receive the envoy from the Northern Yüan, Chŏng staunchly opposed their move and was banished to Hoejin 會津 (modern Naju 羅州 in south Chŏlla 全羅 province). Released in 1377, he withdrew to his studio at the foot of Mt. Samgak 三角山, near the capital city, Kaesŏng. His fame as a Confucianist and essayist in Chinese brought him many students. In the winter of 1383 he joined the staff of General Yi Sŏng-gye (*q. v.*), regional commander of the northeast with headquarters at Hamju 咸

州, thus beginning a close relationship with the man who later overthrew the Koryŏ dynasty and founded the Chosŏn dynasty. Chŏng, impressed by Yi's leadership, is said to have given the latter a hint that with such an army he might easily usurp the throne.

In the autumn of 1384 he served under Chŏng Mong-ju (*see* Yi Song-gye) on the mission to Nanking for the celebration of the Ming emperor's birthday. Known as sŏngjŏlsa 聖節使, it was one of the four annual tribute bearing missions of that period, the other three being sent for congratulations on New Year's Day (hajŏngsa 賀正使), at the time of the winter solstice (tongjisa 多至使), and on the occasion of the birthday of the heir apparent. The Chŏng Mong-ju mission of 1384, however, was a special one. It was the tenth year of the reign of Sin U (*see* Yi Sŏng-gye) and yet, after repeated requests, the king had not been granted confirmation of his title by the Ming emperor. Relations with China were in such a low state that the envoys of the preceding mission were flogged by the emperor and sent into exile. Chŏng Mong-ju, Chŏng To-jŏn, and others on the mission conducted themselves tactfully and intelligently, thus paving the way for the improvement of relations with China in the following year. In 1385, upon his return from Nanking, he became head of the National (Sŏnggyungwan) Academy. Later in that year he served as prefect of Namyang 南陽, then as headmaster of the National Academy. The return of General Yi Sŏng-gye's army from Wihwa Island on the Yalu in 1388 marked another step in the rise of the Yi party. In order to consolidate its power, Chŏng helped Cho Chun 趙浚 (d. July 23, 1405) to enforce land reform, a course of action which caused the ruin of most of Koryŏ's aristocracy.

Late in 1389 Chŏng To-jŏn took part in the successful coup to enthrone King Kongyang (Wang Yo, *see* Yi Sŏng-gye), and was rewarded with the hereditary rank of Ponghwahyŏn Ch'ungŭigun 奉化縣 忠義君, listed among the nine men of merit (Kongsin 功臣), and given land, slaves, silver, a horse, and the office of a director (grade 3A) of the Samsa 三司. In 1390 he was again sent on a mission to Nanking, returning to Kaesŏng late in that year. Early in 1391 he was appointed one of the three army commanders to assist the commander-in-chief, Yi Sŏng-gye, in carrying out a policy of reform in the military organization. Meanwhile he advised the king to promote Confucianism, discredit Buddhism, and punish those loyal to Sin U, such as Yi Saek. These pointed memorials and his land reform measures made him unpopular at court. At the same time his support of Yi Sŏng-gye marked him as an enemy to the so-called loyalists led by Chŏng Mong-ju. In October, 1391, he was accused of having harbored an evil mind and again banished.

After the assassination of Chŏng Mong-ju on April 26, 1392, and the subsequent exile of the other leaders of the loyalists, Yi Sŏng-gye came into undisputed control at court. On August 5 he dethroned the last Koryŏ king and launched the dynasty Yi. Chŏng To-jŏn now became the most influential scholar-statesman of his day, enjoying the complete trust of the new king. Late in 1392 he was sent to China on a mission and was well received in Nanking. It was he who gave names to palaces and halls, wards and gates of the new capital Seoul(1395), established the institutions, and formulated the national policy of the new kingdom. In 1393 he wrote eulogies in praise of the cultural accomplishments and military exploits of the founder. He compiled such handbooks as the *Chosŏn kyŏng-guk chŏn* 朝鮮經國典 (1394), *Kyŏngje mun'gam* 經濟文鑑 (1395; printed in 1397), and *Kyŏngje mun'gam pyŏlchip* 經濟文鑑別 集 (1397), which served as the basic references in the new government organization and administration. In 1395 he presented to the throne a chronological history of Koryŏ, consisting of 37 kwŏn which is no longer extant. An expert strategist, he drew up new battle formations and trained soldiers in accordance with his diagrams.

Chŏng To-jŏn had long been a professed pro-Ming Confucianist, and was noted for his lucid essays in Chinese. Hence it came as a shock to him and to the Korean court when suddenly in 1396 the Ming emperor named him as the one responsible for some disrespectful remarks in two memorials sent by the Korean king, and demanded that he be delivered to the Chinese capital. Several Korean envoys were detained in Nanking, including two sent by the Korean king who had actually drafted the documents in question. The king refused to deliver Chŏng To-jŏn on the pretext that he was seriously ill. Instead he elevated Chŏng to the rank of earl (伯). In the end the Ming emperor did not insist on compliance with his order but repeatedly reminded the Korean king of the lack of wisdom in retaining such an evil person as Chŏng as adviser.

The explanation of this episode probably lies in the emperor's pathological suspicion of writers for their alleged use of homophones and insinuations that he was once a monk and a rebel. Some such words might have been unwittingly included in the memorials. In any case Chŏng's reputation was damaged and the more so when late in 1397 it was ascertained that three of the envoys detained had been executed in Nanking. Still he retained the king's confidence and early the following year was even sent to the northeast border region as viceroy to supervise the repair of the royal ancestral tombs, the building of city walls, and the establishment of postal routes and post stations. On his return (April 7) he was banqueted and thanked.

On October 6, 1398, while at the height of his influence, in the full confidence of the king, and acting as a tutor to Yi Pang-sŏk (*see* Yi Pang-wŏn) the heir apparent who was the king's youngest son, Chŏng To-jŏn was caught unawares in the *coup d'état* engineered by the king's fifth son, Yi Pang-wŏn (*q. v.*). The latter succeeded in seizing power, assassinating the heir apparent, forcing the king to abdicate, and enthroning his own elder brother. Chŏng To-jŏn was captured while being entertained in the house of a friend and put to death. He was blamed for failing to nominate as heir apparent the eldest son of the king's first wife, as a Confucianist perhaps should have done. Other accusations against him included such fabrications as that of being loyal to the heir apparent, which was not a crime, or of plotting against the king's other sons, which was apparently untrue.

The contents of the *Sambong chip* 三峯集, the collected works of Chŏng To-jŏn, consisting of 14 kwŏn are: poems including *tzu*, *fu*, and eulogies, edited by Sŏng Sŏk-nin 成石璘 (1338-1423), kwŏn 1-2; prose works such as memorials, prefaces, and sketches (kwŏn 3-4); *kyŏngje mun'gam* (kwŏn 5-6); *Chosŏn Kyŏngguk chŏn* (kwŏn 7-8); *Pulssi chappyŏn* 佛氏雜辨 ("Essays against Buddhism") written during the summer of 1398 shortly before his death, with a preface of Kwŏn Kŭn (*q. v.*), kwŏn 9; essays on the neo-Confucian *li*, with a preface of Kwŏn Kŭn (kwŏn 10); *Kyŏngje mun'gam pyŏlchip* (kwŏn 11-12); essays on military science (kwŏn 13); appendices including his life and essays in his honor by various hands (kwŏn 14). His poems were first collected and printed by his eldest son, Chŏng Chin 津in two kwŏn (1397). In 1464 his great-grandson Chŏng Mun-hyŏng 文炯 (1426-1501) printed another edition, with prose works added, in Andong 安東; a revised edition with new materials appeared in 1486. In 1791 another woodblock edition, based on the manuscript copy in the Royal Library, appeared in Taegu 大邱. In 1961 the Korean History Compilation Committee issued a printed edition (as No. 13 in the series), based on a copy of the 1791 edition.

Bibliography

*T'aejo sillok*太祖實錄 (*Chosŏn wangjo sillok* ed., 1955), 14, 19b; *Chŭngbo munhŏn pigo* 增補文獻備考 (Kojŏn kanhaeng hoe ed., 1957), 244/ 5b, 247/9b; *Yŏllyŏsil kisul* 燃藜室記述 (1912-14 ed.), 2, 92–93; MSL (1963), Tai-tsu, 3353, 3583, 3605, 3711; *Ming shih tsung* 明詩綜, 95, 6a; Suematsu Yasukazu 末松保和, "*Sambong chip* henkan kō" 三峯集編刊考, *Chosŏn gakuhō*, 1 (1951), 55; Yi Sang-baek 李相栢, "Chŏng To-jŏn," *Chindan hakpo*, II (1935), 1–45, and III (1935), 41 (later reprinted in his *Hanguk munhwasa yŏn'gu non'go* 韓國文化史研究論考, 1954), 251; Ku Chieh-kang (BDRC), "A Study of Literary Persecution during the Ming," tr. by L. Carrington Goodrich, *HJAS*, III (1938), 264; id., "Sino-Korean Relations at the end of the XIVth Century," *Transactions of the Korea Branch of the Royal Asiatic Society*, XXX (1940), 35.

Peter H. Lee

CHOU Ch'en 周臣 (T. 舜卿, H. 東邨), *ca.* 1450-*ca.* 1535, a painter of landscapes and figures, was a native of Wu吳, prefecture of Soochow. For many years he studied with Ch'en Hsien 陳暹 (T. 季昭, H. 雲樵), a skilled artist from the same region, and learned the techniques of his predecessors in the Sung dynasty. Because of his fondness for kung-pi-hua 工筆畫 (fine, delicate drawings), and his interest in portraying the unglamorous life of the peasant or some folk heroes, he was never considered a member of the Wu school noted for its literati painting. On the contrary, he was regarded as a prominent representative of the academy style of previous dynasties.

Chou is best remembered for his refined and well executed drawings and his subtle use of rich ink and colors. His "Ch'ang-chiang wan-li" 長江萬里 (Ten thousand *li* of the Yangtze), dated October 11, 1535, about one and a half feet high and seventy feet long, was an ambitious undertaking. It consists of several sections, each dealing with a particular stretch of local scenery. To every one he applied the techniques of one or another of his predecessors. It is more an exhibition of Chou's consummate skill

and his well balanced academic eclecticism than of his originality. His "Sung-ch'üan shih-ssu" 松泉詩思 (Poetic thoughts inspired by pines and a spring), in color, dated September 22, 1534, in the National Palace Museum, Taipei, an imitation of a work by Tai Chin (*q.v.*), and his "Pei-ming" 北溟 (The North Sea), in color, undated, in the Kuwana collection, may be included in this category.

Chou took special delight in his portrayal of everyday life, especially the joys and sorrows of the peasnts and the sad state in which the oppressed lived. What was more—he expressed it with eloquence and force. A majority of his best works are in this genre. In "T'ien-chia" 田家 (A farming village), in light color, undated, in the Motoyama collection, Chou depicts a scene of two furious fighting cocks. The villagers, young and old, have all turned out to watch. The excitement and tension aroused are reflected vividly and unmistakably on the faces of the onlookers. In the words of Osvald Sirén, the painting "is all described in detail with unadulterated realism and a faculty for characterization not devoid of humor." In "Liu-chuang feng-yü" 柳莊風雨 (The willow village in wind and rain), in light color, undated, Chou portrays two men, clad in raincloaks, heading hurriedly home as a sudden squall sweeps over the rice fields. It is full of life and country flavor. His most original and expressive composition is, however, the "Liu-min" 流民 (The vagrants), dated August, 1516, in ink and color, an album of twenty-four figures— half of it in the Cleveland Museum of Art and half in the Honolulu Academy of Arts. It is a work of social protest in which the harshest, meanest aspects of life are depicted through the representation of a group of beggars, mendicant monks, conjurers, and tricksters—characters whom the artist often saw in the streets and market place. Because Chou was a keen and sympathetic observer of this gloomy side of humanity, and because he was a cultivated artist, he was able to portray his subjects with stark realism. Ever since Cheng Hsia (d. 1119) voiced his political criticism (in April, 1074) through a painting having the same title "Liu-min," few Chinese artists have ventured to paint meanness and hopelessness of the human condition. The reappearance of such a lowly, undignified theme in Chou's works against the dominant trend of his time is both refreshing and worthy of remark.

Another aspect of Chou's art is the representation of popular figures who appear in folk stories. One example is his "Nan-shan ch'ü-pa" 南山驅魃 (Subduing the demons at Southern Hill), in ink, undated, included in I-yüan i-chen 藝苑遺珍. It is not an original idea. The hero, Chung K'uei 鍾馗, a legendary being believed to be capable of exorcizing demons, had previously been portrayed by no less than Wu Tao-hsüan (d. 792) and Chou Wen-chü (d. 975). With his gift for characterization, however, Chou Ch'en managed to break new ground in a centuries-old theme. The painting depicts Chung K'uei passing by Nan-shan on an ox, with his sister following behind on a horse. A number of demons, all with different expressions on their faces, some pulling, some pushing, and others carrying banners, etc., escort the two. The effect of their gaiety and humor is hilarious.

Chou is also credited with several paintings on album leaves. Nearly all of them are landscapes done in the conventional manner. Like many professional painters of his time, Chou also lectured on his art. Two of his pupils, T'ang Yin and Ch'iu Ying (qq.v.), later achieved lasting fame. It is said that after T'ang Yin became famous, he sometimes was too lazy to paint the scrolls that were requested of him, and had Chou Ch'en execute them instead.

Bibliography

34/13/15a; 65/3/15a; Hsia Wen-yen 夏文彥 (fl. 1365) and Han Ang 韓昂 (fl. 1519), T'u-hui pao-chien 圖繪寶鑑, 6/167; Chiang Shao-shu 姜紹書 (fl. 1640), Wu-sheng shih-shih 無聲詩史, 2/9; Wang Chih-teng 王穉登 (1535-1612), Wu-chün tan-ch'ing chih 吳郡丹青志, 4; Pien Yung-yü 卞永譽, Shih-ku-t'ang shu-hua hui-k'ao, hua-chuan 式古堂書畫彙考, 畫卷 (Taipei, 1958), 26/449; Chu Hsiang 儲祥, Chung-kuo hua-chia jen-ming ta tz'u-tien 中國畫家人名大辭典, 246; Wu-hsien chih (1933), 75/17a; Soochow-fu chih (1883), 109/17a; Ku-kung shu-hua lu 故宮書畫錄 (Taipei, 1958), 中 /312; Wang Shih-chieh 王世杰 (1891-), I-yüan i-chen (Hong Kong, 1967), Vol. 3, pt. 13; Nihon genzai Shina meiga mokuroku 日本現在支那名畫目錄 (Tokyo, 1938), 152; O. Sirén, Chinese Painting, Leading Masters and Principles, VII (New York, 1956-58), 177; id., A History of Later Chinese Painting (London, 1938); E. J. Laing, Chinese Paintings in Chinese Publications, 1956–1968 (Ann Arbor, 1969), 163; The National Palace Museum Bulletin, I (November. 1966), no. 5. 8; Gustav Ecke, Chinese painting in Hawaii: in the Honolulu Academy of Arts and in Private Collections, I (Honolulu, 1965), 274; Bulletin of the Cleveland Museum of Art (January, 1966), 6.

Lee Hwa-chou

CHOU Chia-mu

CHOU Chia-mu 周家謨 (T. 明卿, H. 景松, 訒士), 1546-1629, a native of Han-ch'uan 漢川, Hukuang, was one of the elder statesmen involved in the palace controversies which disturbed the reign of Chu Yu-chiao (ECCP) in the 1620s. After his qualification for the chin-shih in 1571, Chou labored in bureaucratic posts for over half a century, the first forty years as a civil and military administrator of the southwestern provinces. He served successively as prefect of Shao-chou 韶州, Kwangtung (1577), vice surveillance commissioner (1582), surveillance commissioner (ca. 1587), and right administration commissioner (ca. 1606) of Szechwan. In the midst of these assignments, however, he observed a prescribed period of mourning and took a prolonged leave of absence.

In September, 1608, he was appointed governor of Yunnan, then a trouble spot. It is said that at that time only thirty per cent of the population of the province was Chinese, the rest being members of minority ethnic groups. Even though the local government was partially modeled on the Chinese system, in actuality many magistrates, including some prefects, were native chieftains. Nominally the provincial military administration was under a chief military commissioner, a post which, beginning with the late 14th century, had been inherited by the descendants of Mu Ying (*q. v.*) who were enfeoffed either as dukes or as marquises. By the early 17th century members of the Mu family had enlarged their estates out of all proportion. The then duke of Ch'ien, Mu Ch'ang-tso 黔國公沐昌祚 (fl. 1571-1625) and his son Mu Jui 叡 (d. 1609) who at times acted for his father, wielded unspecified authority, their duties being equally undefined. As their land holdings covered the territory of many prefectures and their estate managers dealt with the local population, this posed a serious problem for the civil administrators. Chou's predecessor as governor, Ch'en Yung-pin (*q.v.*), based his policy of governing local tribes on military suppression and intrigues in which he sometimes took advantage of the tribal conflicts among the natives. He was also preoccupied with the problem of Burma.

In the meantime Emperor Chu I-chün (*q. v.*) dispatched eunuch commissioners to the province to operate mines. Adventurers who associated themselves with the mining mission and the Mu family managers presented a double threat to the natives, the inarticulate aborigines suffering the most. Early in 1607 A K'o 阿克 (also known as Feng 鳳 A-k'o), a chieftain in Wu-ting 武定 (about thirty miles northwest of Kunming), decided to rebel. The tribesmen took the prefectural city and besieged the provincial capital, causing considerable anxiety to officials at court, and bringing about the dismissal and arrest of Ch'en Yung-pin. When Chou took over the governorship, the rebellion had already been put down, but an uneasy truce still obtained. In his report to the emperor, Chou listed the abuse and exploitation of the natives by civil and military

officials as causes leading to the uprising. In 1611 he sent another memorial to the throne criticizing the size of Mu Ch'ang-tso's land holdings. The duke's estates, he pointed out, consisted of 803,137 *mou* (about 120,500 acres) as of 1588 and after that the holdings had continued to increase. Ming law never allowed aristocrats to maintain fiefs as such, nor to collect feudal dues. Levies from their lands, even though set aside as aristocratic estates, were supposed to be collected by civil officials and handed to the noblemen as stipends. But the Mu family managed their properties as though they were autonomous, collecting funds far in excess of any prescribed rates. In conclusion Chou recommended the domains be taken over by the civil government, and the duke's managers evicted. The emperor concurred in these recommendations; nevertheless little has been recorded as to how they were carried out.

As governor Chou had also to deal with the tribesmen through the use of force. In the winter of 1610-11 the tribes under An To-min 安多民 rebelled near the present Sino-Burmese border. Only after his repeated offer of peaceful settlement was of no avail did Chou take up arms. His campaign of suppression involved twenty thousand troops and lasted ten days, climaxing with An's death. Upon quashing the revolt Chou forbade reprisal; he installed the rebel's younger brother as the new chieftain. In general Chou's administration seems to have been more enlightened than that of his predecessors. A local historian describes him as "reserved and stable." He is said also to have lived simply and to have been revered by the people.

In 1614 he was promoted to governor-general of Kwangtung, but did not assume the position until mid-1615. In his two years there he reorganized coastal defense and repaired many river dikes in his territory. In 1617 he became minister of Revenue in Nanking. Two years later he was called to Peking to assume the same position in the ministry of Works. Between July 4, 1620, and December 30, 1621, he served as minister of Personnel. In the latter capacity he strove to be a stabilizing force in the court, but in time fell victim to partisan politics.

Two emperors died in quick succession in the summer of 1620. As the senior minister Chou attended at the death bed of each departing emperor and saw to it that his successor promptly held audience at court. On the day Chu I-chün died, Chou conferred with him on filling key positions in the government. Chu I-chün's last testament, which directed the recall of all eunuchs operating in the provinces and the reappointment of banished courtiers, seems to have been composed under Chou's influence. The next service Chou performed was to carry out the deceased emperor's will by rehabilitating scores of dismissed officials, among them many Tung-lin partisans. At the same time the anti-Tung-lin courtiers were maneuvered into leaving their offices while Chou was in charge.

On the so-called Three Cases (*see* Kao P'an-lung) Chou definitely sided with the Tung-lin group. Huang K'o-tsuan 黃克纘 (T. 紹夫, cs 1580), minister of Works and concurrently minister of War in charge of ordnance, differed with Chou. In the winter of 1621 Huang became minister of Justice. He and Chou further clashed on minor issues which were under their joint jurisdiction. At this point both ministers requested leave to retire and absented themselves from their offices. In the end the emperor accepted Chou's resignation.

Sources differ as to the circumstances of Chou's retirement. The editors of the *Ming-shih* assert that the resignation was accepted by Wei Chung-hsien (ECCP) in the name of the young emperor. T'an Ch'ien (*q.v.*) suggests that both Chou and Grand Secretary Liu I-ching 劉一燝 (T. 季晦, 1567–1635, cs 1595) would have been banished by the emperor except for the intervention of Yeh Hsiang-

kao (*q.v.*) The *shih-lu* records, however, that in spite of impeachment by Chou's antagonists, the emperor on three occasions urged him to continue in service. It was only when Chou insisted, and abruptly returned his official seal, that the emperor finally acquiesced. On January 5, 1622, the *shih-lu* also discloses, the emperor received him at a farewell audience. Such divergencies are typical of histories written in the last years of the Ming wherein facts are distorted by partisan viewpoints.

Early in 1626 Wei Chung-hsien blacklisted Chou Chia-mu and removed his name from the civil service register. Reinstated by Emperor Chu Yu-chien (ECCP) on August 9, 1628, as minister of Personnel in Nanking, Chou died in office a few months later.

The *Han-ch'uan-hsien chih* lists nine publications by Chou, not one of which appears in current bibliographies. Some of the titles, such as *Shu-cheng chi-lüeh* 蜀政紀略 and *Tien-yüeh tsou-i* 滇粵奏議, seem to suggest works of genuine historical promise.

Bibliography

1/241/1a, 313/17a, 314/34b, 315/8b; 39/18/12a; 64/ 庚 10/3a; 77 (1936)/2/12b; MSL (1940), Shen-tsung, 443/6a, 449/5b, 8b, 473/11b, 475/8b, 485/3a, 497/4a, 525/5a, 529/10b, 13a, 536/11b, 543/14b, 553/4b, 555/4a, 584/25b, 595/6b, 10b, 11a, 596/14a, Kuang-tsung, IX/5a, X/15b, XI/4a, 15b, XII/23a, 34a, Hsi-tsung 4/10b, 5/25a, 11/11b, 26b, 12/5b, 62/4b; *Han-ch'uan-hsien chih* (1873), 20/64a; *Hupei t'ung-chih* (1934), 3336; *Yunnan t'ung-chih* (1876), 24/15b; Shih Fan 師範, *Tien-hsi* 滇繫 (1887), 2/35b, 7/8/10a, 8/2/13b; *T'ien-hsia Chün-kuo-li-ping-shu* (SPTK), 44/9a, 10b, 11a, 45/60a, 65a; KC (1958), 5196, 5449; Li Wei-chen 李維楨, *Ta-pi shan-fang chi* 大泌山房集 (NLP microfilm roll no. 888), 30/又23b; Li Yen 李棪, *Tung-lin tang-chi k'ao* 東林黨籍考 (Peking, 1957), 54; C. O. Hucker, *The Censorial System of Ming China* (Stanford, Cal., 1966), 186, 200, 359.

Ray Huang

CHOU Chih 周砥 (T. 履道, H. 東皋, 菊溜生), died *ca.* 1367, a native of Wu 吳-

hsien (Soochow), lived as a youth in nearby Wu-hsi 無錫. He is known as a poet, a scholar, a painter, and a calligrapher. He probably held a minor position in the Yüan government and later served in a literary capacity in the government of Chang Shih-ch'eng (*q.v.*) in Soochow.

The best recorded event of his life is his association with another poet, Ma Chih馬治 (T. 李常, H. 元素). In 1354 and 1355, when Soochow and Wu-hsi were being ravaged by the fighting among the armies of various rebellious groups that led to the capture of Soochow by Chang Shih-ch'eng in 1356, both Chou and Ma Chih took refuge in I-hsing 宜興 in the home of a Mr. Chou whose children they taught. During their stay these, they were able to visit some of the scenic spots of Mts. Yang-hsien 陽羨 and Ching-ch'i 荊谿. This association resulted in a set of poems known as "Ching-nan ch'ang ho chi 荊南唱和集 (Poetic exchanges from the south of Ching-ch'i), for which the poets Cheng Yüan-yu 鄭元祐 (T. 明德, 1292–1364) and Hsü Pen (*q.v.*) both wrote prefaces at a date; another poet, Kao Ch'i (*q.v.*), who helped to preserve the poems, added an epilogue. A well-recorded painting now in the Boston Museum of Fine Arts entitled "I-hsing hsiao-ching" 小景 (Scenery of I-hsing), dated 1356, is one of the artistic products of Chou's stay there.

It was after his return to Soochow that Chou became more involved in the events of that famous city. After Chang Shih-ch'eng had established his headquarters there, he made peace with the Yüan authorities (1358) and attracted many of the intellectuals to serve under him. It was probably during this period that Chou and others, especially the group of poets known as the Pei-kuo shih-yu 北郭十友 (Ten friends of the north wall), including Kao Ch'i, Yang Chi, Chang Yü (*qq.v.*), Wang Hsing 王行 (T. 止仲, H. 淡如居士, 1331–95), Sung K'o (*q.v.*), and Hsü Pen, all came to work under Chang Shih-ch'eng. Kao Ch'i mentions that his

friendship with Chou began in 1360 and that they held each other in high esteem. A number of other leading poets and painters of this period from Soochow and the surrounding areas were also his good friends. Later, probably due to the literati's disillusionment with Chang Shih-ch'eng because of his ambition and corruption, Chou left Soochow for K'uai-chi 會稽, Chekiang. He died when caught in the fighting between the forces of Chang and Chu Yüan-chang during their final struggle. His poems were collected and preserved by his friend, Lü Min (*see* Hsü Pen), another one of the "ten talents."

This meager amount of material on his life and the scarcity of his remaining artistic and poetical works seem to show that he was a typical literatus of the last years of the Yüan. Extremely individualistic and very shy, he was able only in the company of like-minded intellectuals, poets, and painters to find the fellowship that he truly enjoyed. It is in his painting, calligraphy, and poetry, however, that he achieved a measure of self fulfillment.

"The scenery of I-hsing" is a short handscroll depicting a retreat in the midst of mountains and rivers. His brushwork is quite personal and free, expressing a sense of purity and naturalness close to those of Ni Tsan (*q.v.*) and Huang Kung-wang (1269–1354). This is borne out by comments from his friends and later connoisseurs. Commenting on his poetry and painting, Ku Ying (*see* Ch'en Ju-yen) reports that they are comparable to those of his good friend Ni Tsan. Li Jih-hua (*q.v.*) holds that Chou's painting is superior to the art of Wang Meng (*q.v.*) and Huang Kung-wang in his ability to achieve a feeling of simplicity, purity, and remoteness—something very close to the work of Ni Tsan. These qualities are reflected in the "I-hsing hsiao-ching." It is interesting that this painting is now mounted together with a painting by Shen Chou (*q.v.*), dated 1499, entitled "T'ung-kuan shan-se" 銅官山色 (The landscape of T'ung-kuan). According to Shen's inscription, he was so inspired by Chou's painting that he executed a similar short handscroll as a gift to the owner of that time. Another well-recorded painting, "Yang-hsien t'u" (Scenery of Yang-hsien) seems to be no longer extant. A third landscape entitled "Ch'ang-lin yu-hsi" 長林幽溪 (Lonely stream in an extensive forest), dated 1365, now in the Osaka Museum, is very different in style and brushwork from the Boston painting and has never been recorded in standard Chinese catalogues.

In calligraphy he was skillful in various styles imitating the script of Su Shih (1037–1101). It is said that he always had a very firm and balanced control of his brush and his spacing. As to his poetry, it appears that only a few scattered pieces in various anthologies have survived. He wrote both shih 詩 and tz'u 詞, his contemporaries highly prizing his work.

Bibliography

1/285/19a; 3/266/14a; 24/1/52a; 34/11/12a; 40/11/12b; 65/2/3b; 84/甲前/19a; 88/10/17a; Shao Yüan-p'ing (see Wei Yüan, ECCP), Yüan-shih lei-pien, 36/28b; Tseng Lien 曾廉, Yüan shu 元書 (1911), 89/19a; Ku Ssu-li 顧嗣立(1669-1722), Yüan-shih hsüan 元詩選, 3/ 庚集; Ku-su chih 姑蘇志 (1965), 54/32a; Wu-chung jen-wu chih 吳中人物志, 9/16b; Shu shih hui-yao 書史會要, 7/13b; Tzu-t'ao-hsüan tsa cho 紫桃軒雜綴, 1/29b; Kao Ch'i, Kao t'ai-shih ta ch'üan chi (SPTK), 12/17a, 26a, 14/21a; id., Fu tsao chi, 2/10b; Chang Hsüan 張宣, Ch'ing-yang chi 青暘集, 1/9b, 2/2a, 3a; Hsü Pen, Pei-kuo chi, 1/3b; Lu Hsin-yüan (ECCP), Pi sung-lou ts'ang-shu chih, 117/12b; SK (1930), 188/7a; Soraikan kinsho 爽籟館欣賞, I (Osaka, 1930), 26; Chūkoku bi jutsu gosen-nen ten 中國美術 5,000 年展 (Osaka, 1966), pl. 54; Wen Cheng-ming; Fu-t'ien chi 甫田集, 23/4b; K. Tomita and H. C. Tseng, Portfolio of Chinese Paintings, Yüan to Ch'ing Dynasties (Museum of Fine Arts, Boston,1961), pls. 16-18.

Chu-tsing Li

CHOU Ching 周經 (T. 伯常, H. 松靈), 1440-May 7, 1510, was a native of Yang-ch'ü 陽曲, Shansi, who distinguished himself for his probity in high office. He was the son of Chou Hsüan 瑄 (T. 延玉, H. 蔡軒, 1447-May 24, 1484, cj 1435, Pth. 莊懿) who served as minister of Justice in Nanking from April, 1469, to January, 1478. After Chou Ching qualified for the *chü-jen* in 1459 and *chin-shih* in 1460, he was made a bachelor in the Hanlin. He then became a compiler but for eighteen years held no more responsibility than to participate in the compilation of the *Ying-tsung shih-lu* (completed 1467), and to serve as an assistant examiner of the metropolitan examination of 1469 and as a director of the provincial examination held at Nanking in 1477. According to his biographers, the reasons why Chou Ching was given no opportunity to demonstrate his worth in the early years of his career were partly because of his homeliness and partly because he refused to seek promotion, by becoming a sycophant to powerful eunuchs or officials.

His fortunes began to turn in 1478 when he was promoted to senior secretary in the directory of instruction and served as a tutor to the heir apparent (Chu Yu-t'ang, [q. v.]). Among other things he lectured on the *Wen-hua ta-hsün* (completed in 1482, see Chu Chien-shen). Chou refused a suggestion that he should kneel so the prince might remain sitting to listen to him, insisting that the prince had to observe the proper decorum. Perhaps this impressed the prince, for, as soon as he was enthroned, he promoted Chou Ching several grades to the post of vice minister of the Court of Imperial Sacrifices while he still retained the title of a reader in the Hanlin. In 1489 he was promoted to vice minister of Rites and two years later was transferred to the ministry of Personnel, where he served for five years. In these capacities he did his best to advise the emperor not to grant excessive requests from eunuchs or members of the imperial family.

When Chou was appointed minister of Revenue in 1496, certain people at court doubted his ability to handle the office, as he was mainly a Hanlin scholar and had

had little experience in dealing with financial matters. His achievements, nevertheless, were substantial. He based his policies on principles of economy, continued his firm stand against abuses of the eunuchs and imperial relatives, and constantly advised against extravagant undertakings. (Not all eunuchs did he condemn. In May, 1497, he and several others at court put in a plea on behalf of the eunuch Ho Ting [*q. v.*], but without avail. The senior eunuch, Li Kuang [*q. v.*], had Ho beaten so severely that he died of his wounds.)

He also considered it his duty to speak on behalf of the people. He was critical, for example, of a regulation which gave promotion to local officials according to the quantity of grain accumulated in their granaries, a practice which doubtless would lead some magistrates to making excessive demands. His suggestion that promotion should depend on other factors besides meeting the tax quota was well taken. Also, on his insistence, the emperor gave up the idea of summoning some seven thousand people from Shantung as corvée labor for the reconstruction of the Ch'ing-ning palace 清寧宮, which had been partially destroyed by fire. Instead, the emperor allowed him to use the surtax silver retained by the ministry of Revenue to hire people in Peking for the purpose.

But all was not work while he served in his high office. On the occasion of his sixtieth *sui* (June 12, 1499), he invited nine of his friends to his garden in Peking. The month also happened to mark the birth dates of a fellow minister, T'u Yung (*see* T'u Lung) and another official, Ssu Chung 倪鍾 (1440-December 14, 1511, cs 1466). This event might have passed unnoticed save for the fact that Wu K'uan (*q. v.*) recorded the celebration in a volume of woodcuts in 7 folio pages, entitled *Chu-yüan shou-chi t'u* 竹園壽集圖 (Scenes at a birthday party in the bamboo garden), a copy of which is in the possession of the Library of Congress. Lü Chi (*q. v.*) painted the birds and Lü

Wen-ying 呂文英 the human figures. The nine friends were the following: T'u Yung, then minister of Personnel; Ssu Chung, associate censor-in-chief; Wu K'uan, vice minister of Personnel and chancellor of the Hanlin; Wang Chi 王繼 (1433-May 24, 1503, cs 1466), surveillance commissioner of Shansi, Min Kuei (*see* Li Tung-yang), censor-in-chief; Ch'in Min-yüeh 秦民悅 (1434-March 23, 1512, cs 1457), vice minister of Personnel; Hsü Chin (*q. v.*), vice minister of Revenue; Li Meng-yang 李孟暘 (1432-August 8, 1509, cs 1472), associate vice minister of Revenue; and Ku Tso 顧佐 (1443-November 1, 1516, cs 1469), right vice censor-in-chief. These ten men were not all in the top rank of officialdom, but two were already ministers (Chou Ching and T'u Yung), and the rest were on their way up. Ssu Chung succeeded Chou as minister of Revenue the following year, Wu K'uan became minister of Rites in 1503, Wang Chi minister of War in Nanking in 1501, Min Kuei minister of Justice in August, 1499, Ch'in Min-yüeh minister of Personnel in Nanking in September, 1499, Hsü Chin minister of War in 1506, Li Meng-yang minister of Works in Nanking in 1502, and Ku Tso minister of Revenue late in 1506. (For similar garden parties *see* Yang Jung and Li Tung-yang.)

As a result of his efforts to curtail the abuses at court, Chou necessarily made numerous enemies. When, therefore, in 1500 he asked permission to resign, his request was granted. Yet for years after his retirement it is reported that more than eighty memorials were submitted to the throne suggesting his reappointment. When Chu Hou-chao (*q.v.*) succeeded his father in June, 1505, one of his first acts was to invite Chou to become minister of Revenue in Nanking. But Chou was able to decline, pleading the death of his step-mother. Three years later, however, he accepted the post of minister of Rites in the southern capital, only to retire in seven months due to illness. The fact that the new emperor showed him these favors, according to a contemporary, was because of the influence of Ts'ao Yüan 曹元 (T. 以貞, 1449–1521, cs 1475), his son-in-law, and soon to be minister of War and member of the Grand Secretariat. Two years after his death Chou was honored with the title of Grand Guardian (太保) and given the posthumous name Wen-tuan 文端.

Chou's family included several individuals who carried on the tradition of service in the government. His younger brother, Chou Hung 紘 (cs 1478), became an administration commissioner in Shantung; his eldest son, Chou Meng孟, officiated (1505) as prefect of Han-yang 漢陽, Hukuang; and his second son, Chou Tseng 曾 (cs 1496), acted for a time as assistant administration commissioner of Chekiang (ca. 1504).

Bibliography

1/183/8a; 3/166/7a; 5/24/78a, 33/43a;61/127/11b; 63/17/10a;MSL (1964), Hsien-tsung, 1317, 3132, 4260, Hsiao-tsung(1964), 0662, 2216, 2365, 2926, Wu-tsung (1965), 1348; KC (1958), 2269, 2394, 2490, 2591, 2690, 2704, 2715, 2751, 2845, 2912, 2931, 2967; *Yang-ch'ü-hsien chih* (1932), 5/3a, 10a, 13/14b; Wu K'uan, *P'ao-weng chia-ts'ang-chi*, 45/6b; A. W. Hummel, *Annual Report of the Library of Congress for the Fiscal Year Ended June 30, 1940* (Washington, 1941), 164.

Angela Hsi and L. Carrington Goodrich

CHOU Hung-mu 周洪謨 (T. 堯弼, 堯佐, H. 箐齋, 南皋子, Pth. 文安), 1419-April 1, 1491, official, writer, and educator, was a native of Ch'ang-ning 長寧, Szechwan. Upon his qualification for the *chin-shih* in 1445 (as second on the list), he received an appointment as Hanlin compiler. Later promoted to be reader-in-waiting (1456) he was given charge of the Academy and the National University in Nanking (1458). In 1465 he was back in Peking participating in the compilation of the *Ying-tsung shih-lu*, and after two years made the chancellor of the National University at the capital. In 1476 he became right vice minister of Rites. Advanced at first to left vice minister and then to minister (1481), he served continuously in the same office for over a decade.

Chou's official career was devoid of turbulent events; nor is there a long list of accomplishments to his credit. As a learned man, however, he had the opportunity to express his opinions on a variety of issues. His numerous proposals on administrative matters illustrate the role of a court adviser performed by an erudite in Ming times. In general Chou appears to have been pedantic and authoritarian. He proposed that Confucius should be given a posthumous title of emperor and that the dances and music performed at the sacrificial services in the Confucian temple be in accord with the standards set in ancient times. In advancing his arguments he elaborated on such minute details as the precise number of performers who should take certain positions in the ceremonial hall. Once he induced Emperor Chu Chien-shen(*q.v.*)to arrest a minor official and at another time to imprison a district Confucian instructor, merely because the former suggested changes in the established ritual and the latter recommended calendar reforms. Charging that the astronomical equipment then in use did not follow ancient specifications, Chou produced an observatory instrument of his own and it was accepted by the emperor. But his three memorials explaining the construction of the instrument (preserved in the *Hsü-chou* 叙州-*fu chih*) disclose that, with his dubious knowledge of astonomy, he chose to speculate, rather than conduct experiments on how it should be made, his purpose being to revive a very early device. (This misadventure occurred at the time when the court was troubled by inferior astronomical calculations; eclipses were incorrectly predicted.)

Chou's other recommendations dealt with education, state finance, military strategy, the selection of official personnel, the control of foreign tributary missions, etc. Most of his suggestions were either very broad and general or extremely minor and trivial. What historical justifications he cited to support his suggestions were as a rule no more than isolated occurrences. A number of his ideas were impractical. In 1483, for example, he championed the use of poisoned arrows by the army; this suggestion the emperor disapproved of on the ground that firearms were superior. Of genuine merit was his proposal for the rehabilitation of displaced persons. For more than a decade millions of people affected by famines in Hukuang and Honan had been wandering in the western sectors of these two provinces, often being driven back and forth by orders of provincial officials. In 1476, at Chou's suggestion, the emperor finally dispatched an imperial commissioner to the region to see that these persons be satisfactorily settled. Ch'iu Chün (*q.v.*), long-time colleague and friend of Chou, in an essay indicates that Chou Hung-mu also helped establish the permanent procedures governing civil service examinations and educational institutions, though he does not indicate what specific contributions were the latter's.

Chou is described as austere and inaccessible. His own writing reveals that he traveled quite extensively. He apparently was trusted by Chu Chien-shen, despite the fact that the emperor did not always follow his counsel and on occasion reprimanded him. The enthronement of Chu Yu-t'ang (*q.v.*), however, marked Chou's downfall. In 1488 two impeachment actions were brought against him, one charging him with allowing members of his household to make illegal profits, the other indicting Chou himself for graft and extortion. As a consequence he was forced to retire.

Chou left four works. *Ch'ün-ching pien-i-lu* 羣經辨疑錄, 3 *ch.*, is a notebook on the Confucian Classics in which he challenges Chu Hsi's annotations. In 1478 he presented the draft to Chu Chien-shen in the hope of imperial patronage of the book, only to be rebuffed by the latter on the ground that Chou was trying to revise the standard text which had already been adopted universally; and should not be altered because of one man's opinion. *Ch'ien-chai tu-shu lu* 簪齋讀書錄, 2 *ch.*, is a similar notebook in which Chou enunciates his personal understanding of Confucian Classics and history. Critics point out that he indulges in versicular speculation and is much too opinionated. His poetry and miscellaneous papers may be found in *Nan-kao-shan chi* 南臯山集, 20 *ch.*, and *Ch'ien-chai chi*, 50 *ch.*

Another man of the same name is Chou Hung-mu 周洪謨 (T. 宗稷), a native of Shan-yin 山陰, Chekiang. He graduated as *chin-shih* in 1616, and was among those blacklisted by Wei Chung-hsien (ECCP) early in 1627. He was a close friend of Chou Shun-ch'ang (*q.v.*). Serving as a supervising secretary of Revenue from 1624 to 1626, he impeached Hsiung T'ing-pi (ECCP) in 1625 and the same year was sent as an envoy to Korea. He is said also to have initiated impeachment action against Wei Chung-hsien and to have thwarted the latter's scheme for increasing the grain tribute quota of his native province. On April 21, 1626, he was dismissed by Emperor Chu Yu-chiao (ECCP). After Chu Yu-chien's (ECCP) enthronement he was recalled, serving successively as supervising secretary for Personnel, War, and Rites. In 1631 illness brought on his retirement. Seven of his memorials are included in the *Chien-yüan ch'i-shu* 諫垣七疏, 1 *ch.*

Bibliography

1/31/4b, 184/1a; 5/33/29a; 64/217/12b; MSL (1963), Hsien-tsung, 0082, 0185, 0336, 0928, 2491, 2795, 3554, 3568, 3694, 3873, 4117, Hsiao-tsung, 0143, 0191, 0452, 0970; *Szechwan t'ung-chih* (1815), 148/6a; *Hsü-chou-fu chih* (1895), 35/2b; SK (1930),34/1a, 126/2a; Cheng Hsiao, *Wu-hsüeh-pien* (1572), 40/2a; Ku Chieh-kang, "A Study of Literary Persecution during the Ming," tr. by L. Carrington Goodrich, HJAS, III (1938), 294. *Bibliography* for the second Chou Hung-mu, cs 1616. MSL (1940), Hsi-tsung, 57/26b, 59/31a, 64/27a; *Chekiang t'ung-

chih (1934), 2844; Li Yen 李楼, *Tung-lin tang-chi k'ao* 東林黨籍考(Peking, 1957), 86; *Shan-yin-hsien chih* (1803), 10/47a, 14/62b.

Ray Huang

CHOU Ju-teng 周汝登 (T. 繼元, H. 海門), 1547–1629 (?), official, teacher, and advocate of a fusion of Confucian and Buddhist thought, was a native of Ch'eng 嵊-hsien, Shao-hsing prefecture, Chekiang. His family belonged to the military category, but his branch developed a literary tradition. His father, Chou Mo 謨 (T. 居正, H. 雙溪, 1496–1560), after failing eight times at the provincial examinations, obtained by purchase in 1553 the qualification of a student of the National University, and beginning in 1554 held for four years the position of an assistant instructor in the district school of Ching-hai 靜海, near Tientsin. There Chou Ju-teng visited his father in 1559, and they returned home together later the same year. He had only one more year to study under his father before the latter died. He then came under the influence of his father's main wife, Ting-shih丁氏(1498–1580), and his own mother, née Huang黃 (1516–*ca*. 1605), a concubine. Intelligent and with a highly retentive memory, Chou made good progress, and in 1567 joined seven local young scholars at the Lu-shan shu-yüan 鹿山書院 to form a literary society. In 1570 he traveled to Shao-hsing with a cousin to listen to some lectures by Wang Chi, the outstanding disciple of Wang Shou-jen (*qq.v.*). Perhaps Chou went out of curiosity, for he was then preparing for the civil examinations, which he succeeded in passing: *chü-jen* in 1573 and *chih-shih* in 1577. He then served several months in the ministry of Works as a probationer.

A year later he received an appointment as secretary in the ministry of Works in Nanking where he gained the reputation of a champion player of wei-ch'i 圍棋 (a game like chess, called *go* in Japan). He was assigned to Wu-hu in 1579 as head of the ministry's tax office collecting transit duties on commodities, especially lumber. According to his biographers, an order went out to double the annual quota amount of collection from twenty to forty thousand taels, with which Chou, out of compassion for the traders, refused to comply, and so was demoted. On examining the *Ming shih-lu* and other sources, one discovers that the matter was not so simple. The assignment at Wu-hu was a lucrative post, especially during the expansion of trade in the mid-16th century; it was limited to a one-year term, and on completion would normally yield much more than the quota. A part of this surplus income was regularly distributed in the Nanking ministry as supplementary pay. By this time the powerful grand secretary, Chang Chü-cheng (*q.v.*), had introduced a system of accounting whereby some taxes, such as the revenue from farm land, were reduced, while others were raised realistically. In June, 1580, on the suggestion of a censor, the court ordered the tax collector at Wu-hu, on his return to his home office in Nanking, be examined as to his accounts and reputation. Three months later, the holder of that assignment was so examined, found guilty of accepting bribes, and removed from office to stand trial. It was then Chou's turn for that assignment, but in February, 1581, after only about half a year in office he had to return home to mourn the death of his father's main wife. It was under such a situation that he was adjudged incompetent for failure to meet the quota, which probably would not have happened had he completed his term of office in a normal way. In any case, he received the notice that he had been demoted one grade (6A central to 6B provincial). Obviously he resented the injustice, and found it difficult to demean himself by applying for a lower office. He remained at home for eight years (1581–89) during which he became an expert in locating auspicious sites as burial grounds, and for a time taught some students in Shao-hsing.

Also at this time he began to investigate the philosophical subjects of mind and nature and became a disciple of Lo Ju-fang (q.v.). In the preface to a poem, "San-fa Shan-hsi" 三發剡溪 (My third embarkation from Shan-hsi), he described how, on the urging of his mother, he started (1584) from Shan-hsi, the river in his home town, for Peking but turned back after reaching the Yangtze River, and how he repeated the performance in 1588 after reaching the Yellow River, and now finally, in the autumn of 1589, he was determined to complete the journey. Later in that year he accepted the appointment of assistant salt commissioner in charge of the ten salt fields of the T'ai-chou 泰州 area, northeast of Yangchow. With his own funds, he established at each field a free school. Every month he assembled the students for lectures and tests. T'ai-chou was the native place of Wang Ken (q.v.), the head of the so-called left wing of the Wang Yang-ming school. Chou paid his respects at the temple in honor of Wang Ken, and enthusiastically promoted the latter's teachings, especially as propagated by another native of that place, Wang Tung (see Wang Ken). Chou thus confirmed his association with the T'ai-chou school to which his master, Lo Ju-fang, also belonged.

In the summer of 1592 he was restored to his former rank in Nanking where he later served as secretary in the ministries of War (1593-94?) and of Personnel (to 1597). During these five years in the southern capital he engaged actively in meetings discussing philosophical subjects. At one such affair, attended by Hsü Fu-yüan (see Hsü Chieh), who was in Nanking as a vice minister of War from about May, 1595, to 1598, Chou discussed the debate of seventy years earlier between Wang Chi and Ch'ien Te-hung (q.v.) and the final conclusions of their master, Wang Shou-jen. The episode, known as T'ien-ch'üan cheng-tao 天泉證道, took place on October 2, 1527, on the T'ien-ch'üan bridge in Wang Shou-jen's academy

in Shao-hsing. It happened on the eve of Wang's departure for Kwangtung. The argument turned chiefly on the essence of Wang's teaching embodied in the poem, the first line of which reads "The absence of good and evil characterizes the mind in itself" 無善無惡心之體. After listening to Chou's exposition upholding this teaching, Hsü raised some questions in a paper entitled "chiu-ti" 九諦 (the nine inquiries) to which Chou replied in his paper, "chiu-chieh" 解 (the nine explanations). These and others of Chou's lectures were printed under the title, Nan-ching hui-yü 南京會語.

In February, 1597, Chou was promoted to be assistant surveillance commissioner of Kwangtung in charge of military farms, salt monopoly, and irrigation. There he again held meetings with the students. The record of their dialogues came to be known as the Tung-yüeh 東粵 hui-yü. He also became a friend of the Buddhist priest, Te-ch'ing (q.v.), and encouraged him to compile a history of the Nan-hua 南華 monastery in Shao-chou 韶州, entitled Ts'ao-hsi chih 曹溪志, 4 ch., to which Chou contributed a preface in 1604. Because he did not care for the climate of Kwangtung he requested retirement in 1598. Late that year, on receiving notice of his promotion to be vice administration commissioner of Yunnan, he repeated his request, and it was finally granted in 1599.

Back in Shao-hsing, one of the first things he did was to collect his disciples at the shrine of Wang Shou-jen to offer a prayer in which Chou compared Wang to Confucius and the Shao-hsing area to the sage's home state of Lu 魯. There are indications that for a time Chou attempted to organize a school of the Wang cult with himself as head of the fourth "philosophical generation" after Wang Chi and Lo Ju-fang. In this endeavor he was supported by his disciples, especially T'ao Wang-ling (see Yüan Chung-tao). On the fifteenth day of the eighth moon, 1601, they and about fifty students held a dinner party under the full moon at the T'ien-ch'üan bridge, where Wang Shou-jen and his two chief disciples had conversed seventy-four years previously. Chou also reminded his students how in 1524, Wang and over a hundred of his disciples had a similar celebration during the autumnal festival at the same spot. Chou then carried on the propagation of the cult for several more years. His activities, however, were limited to the eastern Chekiang area, as shown in the dialogues, *Yüeh-chung* 越中 *hui-yü*, *Shan* 剡-*chung hui-yü*, and *Wu-lin* 武林 *hui-yü*. The greatest distance he went at this time was to Hui-chou 徽州 (Anhwei) in 1602. In this period Chou published two important books summarizing his work of these years. One is the *Sheng-hsüeh tsung-chuan* 聖學宗傳 (Orthodox transmission of the sacred learning), 18 *ch.*, which traced the succession from the time of the earliest sage-kings to that of Wang Shou-jen's disciples, ending with Wang Tung and Lo Ju-fang. The book, printed about 1606, became very scarce in China (there is a copy preserved in the Library of Congress). In 1931, the bibliophile, Liu Ch'eng-kan 劉承幹, found a slightly damaged copy and had it reproduced by lithography. This book leaves the impression that Chou might have considered himself as the successor in the line of transmission. He gives some indications of this in his collected works, entitled *Tung-yüeh cheng-hsüeh lu* 證學錄 (Testimonials to learning in Shao-hsing), 16 *ch.* It has two prefaces, one by T'ao Wang-ling and the other, dated 1605, by Tsou Yüan-piao (*q.v.*). As the book contains writings of 1609, it was probably printed in that year. There is a copy preserved in the National Central Library, Taipei, which was reproduced in 1970. Other works by Chou in this period include *Yang-Shao shih-wei* 楊邵詩微 and *Wang-men tsung-chih* 王門宗旨, 14 *ch.*; the latter is rare, possibly because the title appeared in the 1780s on the list of books to be expurgated (but a copy is in the Naikaku Bunko).

There is the record of Chou's appointment in 1606 as an assistant administration commissioner of Hukuang, but it is not known whether he took up that office. In any case, in March, 1608, he was in Hang-chow attending some lectures by the governor of Chekiang, Kan Shih-chieh 甘士价 (H. 紫亭, 1553-1609, cs 1577), at the annual gathering in honor of Wang Shou-jen at his shrine in the T'ien-chen 天眞 academy. A year later he planned to present to the governor at the ceremony a painting, "T'ien-chen chiang-hsüeh t'u" 講學圖, but Kan died before it took place. Little is known about Chou's life in the following two decades. There are records showing that he was appointed the Nanking minister of the court of the Imperial Seal in 1612 and promoted to be Nanking minister of the Court of the Imperial Stud sometime later and to be commissioner of transmission in 1624. Possibly he did hold these offices in Nanking. It is said that he was later promoted to be junior vice minister of Revenue, and then retired; about the time he died (in 1629) he was named minister of Works. The *Ming shih-lu* does not corroborate these details. It is known only that he was buried in his home district. The year of his death is given in all available sources as 1629, but in *Kuo-ch'üeh* there is a passage which states that in April, 1630, a censor, Ch'i Piao-chia (ECCP), recommended Chou in a memorial. Ch'i was a native of Shao-hsing and his father, Ch'i Ch'eng-han (*q.v.*), had been a student of Chou Ju-teng. Ch'i Piao-chia himself had studied under Chou's son. According to the gazetteer of Ch'eng-hsien, Ch'i Piao-chia was also present at Chou's funeral. Thus, unless the date of the Ch'i memorial is misplaced in *Kuo-ch'üeh*, some further investigation seems to be necessary.

Chou Ju-teng had one son, Chou Yün-ch'un 孕淳 (T. 無遷) who became a *chü-jen* in 1618.

As a thinker, Chou is noted for his promotion of the T'ai-chou interpretation of Wang Shou-jen's doctrines (*see* Wang

Ken), particularly that concerning the mind being in itself "without good and evil" (wu-shan wu-o). In his rebuttal to Hsü Fu-yüan in the *Nan-ching hui-yü* and elsewhere, Chou sought to uphold the similarity between Wang Shou-jen's teachings and those of the sages, particularly Mencius, by maintaining Wang's acceptance of the goodness of human nature, and of that of liang-chih, or innate knowledge. Hsü explained liang-chih as expressive of the mind-and-heart in its pre-stirred equilibrium (wei-fa chih-chung 未發之中), attributed the doctrine of the Four Negatives (ssu-wu 四無) to Wang Chi rather than to Wang Shou-jen, and advocated the careful and systematic pursuit of self-cultivation as the means of acquiring sagehood. Chou Ju-teng responded by the explanation that, while doing good and avoiding evil was usually taught as a secure measure of cultivating human virtue, it could be best done through a thorough realization of the mind-and-heart and human nature as being "without good and evil." Besides, he regarded mind-and-heart as the residue of the Absolute, which is beyond differentiation and without opposite. It could be compared to the t'ai-hsü 太虛 (great void) precisely on account of its emptiness, represented also by the original innocence of the child's mind-and-heart, which is one with his intention, knowledge, and action, and which is given by Heaven to all. He insisted that true cultivation is without effort, since genuine good can be practiced only with disinterestedness. Finally, he concluded that the doctrine of the Four Negatives was the true although secret teaching of Wang Shou-jen, which Wang Chi had rightly described as that which was fit for persons of superior endowment.

Chou Ju-teng was criticized by Huang Tsung-hsi (ECCP) for contributing to the misunderstanding of Wang Shou-jen's teaching, especially by stretching the "absence of good and evil" to cover both human nature (hsing 性) as well as the mind-and-heart(hsin 心). In Chou's defense,

it must be pointed out that, in Wang Shou-jen's highly integrated and unitary thinking, it is rather difficult to discern any real difference between human nature and the mind-and-heart. Chou had rather developed further the discovery of the Absolute, the One behind the Many, which was already incipient in Wang Shou-jen's thought, and which Chou preferred to describe in negative terms. This brought him very near the Ch'an Buddhist teaching of reality being "empty" (śūn-yatā), as Huang correctly remarked. Chou, of course, never denied the reality of all things. Rather, he promoted the cultivation of a certain religious sense, of faith in ultimate reality, regarded as present in the mind-and-heart, which possesses in potentiality the fullness of sagehood.

Bibliography

1/283/15a; 3/185/20a; 40/53/16a; 83/36/1a; MSL (1966), Shen-tsung, 1983, 2025, 5727, 7985, 9301, Hsi-tsung, 2245; KC (1958), 5526; *Chekiang t'ung-chih* (1934), 3074, 3261; *Ch'eng-hsien chih* (1870), 8/6a, 13/22a, 21/7a; SK (1930), 62/3a, 96/7b, 179/7a; Chou Ju-teng, *Sheng-hsüeh tsung-chuan* (preface, 1609) in Naikaku Bunko; id., *Tung-Yüeh cheng-hsüeh lu* (1605 ed., Taipei reprint, 1970); id., *Wang-men tsung-chih* (preface, 1609) in Naikaku Bunko; Sun Ch'i-feng (ECCP), *Li-hsüeh tsung-chuan* (Taipei reprint, 1969), 26/54a; Yao Chin-yüan (1957), 25; Naikaku Bunko *Catalogue*, 97, 175; L. of C. *Catalogue of Rare Books*, 213, 1008; Okada Takehiko, 岡田武彦 *Ō Yōmei to Minmatsu no jugaku* 王陽明と明末の儒學 (Tokyo, 1970), 206.

Chaoying Fang and Julia Ching

CHOU Shun-ch'ang 周順昌 (T. 景文, H. 蓼洲, 冰條), September 20, 1584-July 10, 1626, a native of Wu 吳-hsien, Soochow prefecture, was one of the "seven Tung-lin Party heroes" who died by order of the eunuch dictator Wei Chung-hsien (ECCP, *see also* Kao P'an-lung), and whose arrest provoked a sensational riot among the people of Soochow.

Chou had only a decade-long official

career. After passing the metropolitan examination of 1613, he was appointed prefectural judge of Foochow, Fukien. Then in 1619 he was summoned to the capital for reassignment, and in 1621–22 served as secretary of all four bureaus of the ministry of Personnel in turn, finally being promoted to the vice director-ship of the bureau of appointments. Before the end of 1622 he went home to Soochow on leave of absence and never took office again. While in service Chou acquired a reputation for rigid integrity and uprightness, and while living at home he was a champion of popular local causes. He did not consider himself a Tung-lin partisan, and his name was omitted from the earliest Tung-lin lists drawn up for Wei Chung-hsien in 1624. But Chou made enemies among those who stood against the Tung-lin group.

Chou reportedly "hated wickedness as a personal enemy," and he found much to dislike in Wei's rise to power. In 1624 the popular governor of the Nanking-Soochow area, Chou Ch'i-yüan (see Chang Hsieh), was dismissed from office and his name deleted from the civil service roster for having denounced Li Shih 李實, eunuch supervisor of imperial textile manu-factories in Soochow and Hangchow. Chou Shun-ch'ang wrote an essay in Chou Ch'i-yüan's honor, making sharp criticisms of current trends at court. Both Li Shih and Wei Chung-hsien took note. Then in 1625, upon the arrests of six Tung-lin leaders who were ultimately put to death in a pal-ace prison, Chou openly befriended one of them, Wei Ta-chung (see Kao P'an-lung), when he was escorted through Soochow en route to Peking, and even betrothed a daughter to Wei's grandson. In the pres-ence of Wei's escort of imperial guards-men, Chou repeatedly shouted curses about Wei Chung-hsien. When this news reached the capital, one of the eunuch's henchmen, the investigating censor Ni Wen-huan 倪文煥 (cs 1619), impeached Chou for con-sorting with a criminal and Chou's name was removed from the civil service register.

By early 1626 Wei Chung-hsien and his sycophants wholly dominated the court and a purge of their old enemies was at its height. With the connivance or acqui-escence of Li Shih, Wei now prepared imperial orders for the arrest of seven eminent Tung-lin men of the populous, rich, and influential southeastern region: Chou Ch'i-yüan (see Chang Hsieh), Chou Shun-ch'ang, Miao Ch'ang-ch'i (q.v.),Huang Tsun-su (ECCP, p. 351), Chou Tsung-chien, Li Ying-sheng, and Kao P'an-lung (for the last three see Kao P'an-lung).

Imperial guardsmen arrived in Soo-chow on April 1 bearing an order for the arrest of Chou Tsung-chien. The guards-men lingered as long as they dared, col-lecting bribes to assure the prisoner's fair treatment. The arrest order was not for-mally promulgated until April 6, and the guardsmen did not depart until April 8. At about the same time other guardsmen arrested Miao Ch'ang-ch'i of nearby Chiang-yin 江陰 -hsien. Chou Shun-ch'ang contributed money in both cases. He had to pawn his formal official robes and hats to do so, for he was by no means wealthy. Meantime, rumors abounded as to who might be the next victim, and the city grew restless.

On April 11 another detachment of imperial guardsmen, apparently numbering sixty men, arrived with an order for the arrest of Chou Shun-ch'ang. On their in-structions the local magistrate, Ch'en Wen-jui 陳文瑞 (cs 1625), who had earlier studied under Chou and was a close friend, placed him in detention in his yamen pending formal promulgation of the order, when the prisoner would be delivered to the guardsmen. For three days the guardsmen postponed action, as-siduously collecting bribes on Chou's behalf from the townspeople. Crowds began milling about the yamen, muttering vague threats; and Chou was moved to other yamen in succession as the local authori-ties tried to keep tensions down.

It was finally announced that the

order for Chou's arrest would be promulgated publicly at noon on April 14 at a yamen backing on the city wall near one of its great gates. This was a dark, rainy day. Nevertheless, "several tens of thousands" of Soochow townspeople reportedly jammed the route by which Chou was taken to the ceremony in a caged cart, and most of the city's normal activities stopped for the day. Waving incense burners and chanting "Save our Chou! Save our Chou!" the crowd repeatedly blocked the procession despite Chou's own pleas for restraint and order.

At the yamen where imperial guardsmen awaited Chou, more than five hundred literati of the region also waited in formal garb; and townspeople were packed in the courtyard and atop the city wall overlooking it. The presiding officials —the incumbent governor of the Soochow region, Mao I-lu 毛一鷺 (cs 1604), and the Censorate's resident regional inspector, Hsü Chi 徐吉 (cs 1616), — arrived only to be surrounded by literati urging postponement, appealing for leniency, and charging that the arrest order had been falsified by Wei Chung-hsien. While such arguments went on both the massed townspeople and the imperial guardsmen, not understanding what was happening, became impatient and uneasy. Pushing and shoving started, and then a full riot broke out. The presiding officials escaped the melee with little dignity, and two guardsmen were killed. Many other persons were hurt and lay in the yamen courtyard until night, when rescue parties arrived. Crowds milled about the city all day.

In late afternoon of the same day it happened that another detachment of imperial guardsmen docked in the canal outside the Soochow city wall en route to Chekiang province to arrest Huang Tsun-su. The Soochow mob assumed they were reinforcements and set upon them also, burning their boats and dumping their gear. The guardsmen—mostly northerners who could not swim—floundered across the river only to be chased anew by

farmers brandishing rakes and hoes. Most of this group finally turned up in Nanking, bedraggled, dispirited, and without any official documents.

On the night of the 14th troops from a local garrison occupied Soochow, and Chou Shun-ch'ang was taken to a secret place of detention. The local authorities finally decided not to reschedule the public promulgation ceremony, and Chou was quietly taken out of town on the night of April 21 or 22. He reached Peking on May 19 and died in the palace prison after weeks of torture.

In consequence of the April 14 disorders, five Soochow commoners were executed as ringleaders of the mob: Yen P'ei-wei 顏佩韋, son of a wealthy merchant, Ma Chieh 馬傑, Shen Yang 沈揚, a salesman, Yang Nien-ju 楊念如, a haberdasher, and the sedan-chair bearer Chou Wen-yüan 周文元. Five others were banished to frontier military service; three more survived sixty blows of the heavy bamboo; and the butcher Tai Yung 戴鏞 was arrested but died before sentencing. Also, five Soochow literati were stripped of their honorable status. Eventually, after Wei Chung-hsien's fall from power, the citizens of Soochow reburied the five executed men in a memorial temple that had originally been built in the eunuch dictator's honor by the governor, Mao I-lu; and it is said that in 1629 Wei Chung-hsien's head was brought there and offered in sacrifice to the spirits of his victims. It is also said that the ghosts of the five Soochow martyrs subsequently called on Mao I-lu, and he died suddenly without apparent cause; and that the ghost of Chou Shun-ch'ang once appeared in broad daylight to his former impeacher, Ni Wen-huan.

After the Soochow riot, Wei Chung-hsien and his advisers came to the conclusion that stability in the rich Nanking-Soochow region, where taxes on grain supported the empire's northern military defenses, could not be further endangered. Imperial guardsmen were not again sent southward to make arrests, and punishments of Tung-lin partisans continued only in isolated instances and in less severe forms. It would seem reasonable to give the Soochow rioters major credit for thus diminishing the tempo and vigor of Wei Chung-hsien's purge of his enemies.

Under the last Ming emperor Chou Shun-ch'ang was posthumously named chief minister of the Court of Imperial Sacrifices and canonized Chung-chieh忠介. His collected writings were gathered and published by his descendants and friends under the title *Chou Chung-chieh-kung chin-yü chi* 公燼餘集, 3 *ch*. They were copied into the Imperial Library and are preserved in the collectaneus *Chieh-yüeh shan-fang hui-ch'ao* of Chang Hai-p'eng (ECCP) with an appendix in 1 *chüan*, containing a biography of Chou by Yin Hsien-ch'en 殷獻臣 (d. 1645), and *Ch'ien-k'un cheng-ch'i chi* of P'an Hsi-en (ECCP, p. 347). His memorial criticizing Wei Chunghsien, entitled *Chou Tuan-hsiao hsien-sheng hsüeh-shu t'ieh huang*周端孝先生血疏貼黃, 1 *ch*., was, as the title indicates, written in his own blood.

Bibliography

1/245/5a; 3/232/4b; 31/1/26a, 2/30b; 39/3/12a; 61/110/1a; 77/5/14b; MSL (1940), Hsi-tsung, 56/8b, 63/35a, 65/7b, 16a, 17a, 67/18b, 68/25a; KC (1958), 5328; SK (1930), 172/15a; Wen Ping (ECCP, p. 425), *Ku-su ming-hsien hsü-chi* 姑蘇名賢續記 (*Chia-hsü ts'ung-pien* 甲戌叢編 ed.); Chin Jih-sheng (*see* Kao P'an-lung), *Chou Shun-ch'ang chuan* 傳 (*Sung-t'ien lu-pi* ed.); *K'ai-tu ch'uan-hsin* 開讀傳信 (*Sung-t'ien lu-pi* ed.); Chu Tsu-wen朱祖文 (d. 1626), *Pei-hsing jih-p'u* 北行日譜 (*Chih-pu-tsu-chai ts'ung-shu* 知不足齋叢書 ed.); Yang T'ing-shu 楊廷樞(1595-1647), *Ch'üan Wu chi-lüeh* 全吳記略 (*Ching-t'o i-shih* 荊駝逸史 ed.); Chang Shih-wei 張世偉 (1568-1641), *Chou Li-pu chi-shih* 周吏部紀事 (*Sung-t'ien lu-pi* ed.); Yao Hsi-meng 姚希孟 (1579-1636), *K'ai-tu shih-mo* 始末 (*Yao Meng-chang ch'üan-chi* 姚孟長全集 ed.); *T'i-ch'i chi-lüeh* 緹騎紀略 (*Sung-t'ien lu-pi* ed.); *Hsü Hsün-an chieh-t'ieh* 徐巡按揭帖 (*Yu-man-lou ts'ung-shu*又滿樓叢書 ed.); C. O. Hucker, "Su-chou and the Agents of Wei Chung-hsien: a Translation of *K'ai-tu ch'uan-hsin*," *Silver Jubilee Volume of the Zinbun-Kagaku-kenkyusyo* (Kyoto, 1954), 224.

Charles O. Hucker

CHOU Ti, *see* **Chou Chih**

CHOU Yen-ju 周延儒 (T. 玉繩, H. 挹齋), 1588-January 15, 1644, high official, was a native of I-hsing 宜興, Nan-Chihli. In 1613 he took first place in both the metropolitan and the palace examinations and was appointed a Hanlin compiler, first class. After the usual promotions he was named in 1628 a vice minister in the ministry of Rites. At this time there was a revolt of soldiers in Chin-chou 錦州 (between Mukden and Shan-hai-kuan) as a consequence of which Yüan Ch'ung-huan (ECCP) sent in a petition for funds needed to meet their pay, pointing out that its withholding had provoked the uprising. At a meeting summoned by the emperor the court ministers were of the opinion that the necessary funds should be drawn from the privy purse as the government treasuries were apparently very low. Chou, however, quick to notice the reluctance of the emperor, opposed the views of his colleagues. This pleased the emperor immensely and from that day forward he showed great interest in Chou.

After the dismissal of the grand secretary, Liu Hung-hsün 劉鴻訓 (T. 默承, H. 青岳, 1561-1632, cs 1613), at the end of 1628, a council was summoned to propose a substitute. When the list of candidates was presented to the throne, the emperor was disappointed to find that Chou's name was missing. The Tung-lin party supported Ch'ien Ch'ien-i (ECCP), whose claims to the office were high. Wen T'i-jen (*q. v.*), however, intrigued unscrupulously to keep the name of Ch'ien off and Chou Yen-ju helped him in this. They succeeded in influencing the emperor, which resulted in Ch'ien's dismissal; but Chou was not named grand secretary until fifteen months later (February 9,

1630), when in addition he was also appointed minister of Rites. A half year after this (July 22, 1630) Wen T'i-jen also was appointed grand secretary. By skillful maneuver, however, Chou succeeded in becoming senior grand secretary, his adulation of the emperor securing for him favors from the throne. Wen pretended friendship towards Chou, though secretly he waited for a chance to wrest power from him. The revolt of K'ung Yu-te (ECCP) in 1632, together with scandals caused by members of Chou's family, made Chou Yen-ju a target of severe criticism. He was impeached by the censors on a set of charges which included the receipt of bribes from a rebel leader. This aroused the anger of the emperor, who ordered the case investigated thoroughly. In his embarrassment Chou sought help from Wen T'i-jen. Not unnaturally Wen regarded Chou's predicament as a golden opportunity. Far from doing anything to help him, he did all he could to heighten the emperor's anger. Ultimately Chou was forced to resign (July 25, 1633) and Wen stepped into his place.

In his retirement Chou cultivated the friendship of members of the Tung-lin party whom he had offended in the Ch'ien Ch'ien-i incident. Among these were Chang P'u (ECCP) and Ma Shih-ch'i (see Ku Hsien-ch'eng) whom Chou had selected for the chin-shih degree at the metropolitan examination of 1631. The unhappy choice of grand secretaries made after Chou's fall had seemingly worried the Tung-lin party so much that they thought Chou's collaboration worth seeking for the sake both of the government and of their own party. They therefore approached Chou and persuaded him to promise a change of policy if he were reappointed. When he agreed, the Tung-lin members began secretly to work for his recall. After spending sixty thousand taels of silver in bribing various government officials and eunuchs, they ultimately succeeded in restoring Chou to office (October, 1641). Chou kept his promise

and did his best to improve the administration, exempting poor farmers from taxes, pardoning prisoners condemned for minor crimes, promoting officials of merit, and summoning back innocent ministers from exile. People on all sides lauded him as the ideal grand secretary and he enjoyed the respect of the emperor as well.

Wu Ch'ang-shih 吳昌時 (a native of Chia-hsing 嘉興, Nan-Chihli), one of the men who had helped him reenter government service, gave him a good deal of trouble. In April, 1643, Wu was rewarded with the office of director of the bureau of appointments, the office he had long coveted, but his indiscreet behavior caused serious scandals, and this eventually led to Chou's fall. Despite his attempt to be a worthy grand secretary, Chou was unable to resist the temptation to accept bribes, and for this he was once again impeached by court ministers. In this time of difficulty he found few to support him, for he had become increasingly unpopular.

Meanwhile the Manchus invaded Shantung and on their return north threatened the capital. Wu Sheng (q. v.), one of the grand secretaries, had volunteered to direct the suppression of the rebels in Hukuang province. Chou therefore offered to fight the invaders. This the emperor accepted with great relief. The send-off was impressive, but Chou's army stayed in T'ung-chou 通州 and no action was taken against the enemy. Rumor had it that the officers bribed Chou to issue false reports of victory which the emperor, unaware of the facts, took to be true. When the Manchus withdrew in June, Chou laid claim to victory over the enemy, and was honored with the rank of grand preceptor which he declined. His son, however, received the rank of drafter in the central drafting office.

Shortly after this Chou Yen-ju was accused of having given the Manchus their chance to escape; but the emperor treated this as slander and dismissed the charge. The eunuchs, however, tried to make clear what had actually happened in T'ung-chou. This was in revenge for what Chou had done to them when, at the beginning of his period of office, the emperor had, on his advice, suppressed the imperial secret service headquarters organized and run by the eunuchs and the Embroidered-uniform Guard. The eunuchs' efforts succeeded; in a rage the suspicious emperor ordered an inquiry and Chou was dismissed (July 10, 1643) though the emperor still treated him with consideration.

Chou was not forgotten even after his dismissal. He was still the target of impeachment, the misdeeds of Wu Ch'ang-shih being imputed partly to him. Accusations of having received bribes and especially of having entered into secret communication with eunuchs caused imperial concern. The matter seemed so serious that the emperor himself conducted the trial of Wu Ch'ang-shih. The most cruel tortures could not break the will of Wu, who stubbornly refused to admit any of the accusations. He was, nevertheless, condemned to death. Meanwhile an imperial order had been issued for the arrest of Chou. He arrived in Peking in November, 1643, and two months later was sentenced to death by strangulation and his property confiscated. To display imperial leniency, however, the emperor allowed him to take his life by his own hands.

Chou's biography in the *Ming-shih* is listed among traitor ministers （奸臣傳）. It is perhaps too harsh to say that he was responsible for the fall of the empire, which by this time was beyond saving. There is no doubt that he obtained his high positions through cunning, for he was quick to read the mind of the emperor and was able to win his confidence. Greed which led him to conspire with certain eunuchs eventually caused his ruin. As an administrator he achieved scarcely anything worthy of his reputation. Hsia Yün-i 夏允彝 (T. 彝仲, cs 1637, 1596-1645) records that Chou, when chief minister, was once accused of having improperly supported officials at the border. In answer to this accusation he emphatically denied that he had ever had any correspondence with frontier officials, his response being equivalent to asserting that the affairs of the borders were no concern of the office of the grand secretary. Elsewhere we read that in 1643, when the Manchus were approaching the capital, one of the actions Chou took was to gather Buddhist and Taoist monks together to pray for protection. One thing, however, does stand to his credit: the temporary suppression of the imperial secret service headquarters, a cruel institution that destroyed many innocent lives during the Ming.

Bibliography

1/308/22b; 3/237/1a; 27/15a; *Ch'ung-chen ch'ang-pien* 崇禎長編 (Shanghai, 1940), 48; Chi Liu-ch'i 計六奇 (fl. 1671), *Ming-chi pei-lüeh* 明季北略 (Shanghai,1936), 260; Chiang P'ing-chieh 蔣平階, *Tung-lin shih-mo* 東林始末 (Shanghai, 1940), 47; Hsia Hsieh 夏燮, *Ming t'ung-chien* 明通鑑 (Shanghai, 1959), *Vol.* 4; Hsieh Kuo-chen 謝國楨, *Ming Ch'ing chih chi tang-she yün-tung k'ao* 明清之際黨社運動考 (Shanghai, 1934); *Fu-she chi lüeh* 復社紀略 (Shanghai, 1940), 205; *KC* (1958), 5423, 5461, 5606, 5612, 5971, 5977, 5999, 6005.

Albert Chan

CHU Chan-chi 朱瞻基, March 16, 1399–January 31, 1435, fifth emperor of the Ming, also came to be known by his reign title Hsüan-te 宣德 (1426–35), by his temple name Hsüan-tsung 宣宗, by his posthumous name the emperor Chang 章, and by the designation of his tomb Ching-ling 景陵. A strong and conscientious monarch, he was also a talented poet and painter and the sponsor of bronze and ceramic manufactures that have become world famous. His era was generally considered a time of peace, stability, prosperity, and cultural flowering—in short, of good governance unparalleled in other Ming reigns.

Chu Chan-chi was the eldest of the ten sons of Chu Kao-chih (*q.v.*). His mother, Empress Chang 張, a strong woman, eventually became regent for her grandson Chu Ch'i-chen (*q.v.*). Chu Chan-chi was formally established as imperial heir once removed (皇太孫) in 1411 by his grandfather, Chu Ti (*q.v.*), and thereafter generally accompanied him on inspection jaunts to the new capital, then being built at Peiping, and on military expeditions into Mongol territory to the north. Chu Ti was fond and proud of him, assigned distinguished scholar-officials to tutor him, and drilled him in the military arts and in hunting. The third emperor was repeatedly tempted to set Chu Kao-chih aside as heir apparent in favor of his more vigorous and flamboyant brother, the prince of Han, Chu Kao-hsü (*q.v.*), but young Chu Chan-chi was so promising in all regards that Chu Ti was always easily persuaded not to tamper with the normal succession.

Chu Kao-hsü, who was to rebel against his nephew in 1426, enjoyed being rude and arrogant toward the fat, sickly Chu Kao-chih; the latter could always be counted on not only to endure his contempt, but even to intercede for him when he provoked their father's anger. Once the latter sent the two brothers to visit the tomb of the dynastic founder outside Nanking; and when Chu Kao-chih, although supported by two eunuchs, was constantly losing his footing, his younger brother jibed, "When the man ahead stumbles, the man behind knows enough to take warning." Young Chu Chan-chi immediately retorted from the rear, "And the man behind *him* knows enough to take warning too!" Chu Kao-hsü is reported to have looked around in startled surprise, and no doubt with respect for his nephew's pride and mettle.

His father formally made Chu Chan-chi heir apparent on November 1, 1424, in Peking. Because Nanking had suffered several earthquakes, he was sent the following spring to reside in that now auxiliary southern capital as a symbolic gesture of appeasement to the forces of nature. But he had barely reached Nanking when he was summoned to Peking by news of his father's unexpected death after a short illness. On June 27, 1425, he was officially installed as emperor, at the age of twenty-six.

The new ruler inherited from his grandfather and his father a coterie of experienced, talented, and respected advisers, some of whom had already served him as tutors. Notable among them were Grand Secretaries Yang Shih-ch'i and Yang Jung, the minister of Revenue Hsia Yüan-chi, and the general Chang Fu (*qq. v.*). He was in the habit of listening and learning without standing in awe of them. He frequently called in one or more for private consultations, and at times he dropped in on them at work unannounced, bringing bottles of good wine and chatting at leisure about Confucian philosophy or Buddhism and Taoism, or historical events and persons, or perhaps one of his own new paintings or poems. Out of his intimate and trustful association with such ministers grew one of the Ming dynasty's distinctive governmental institutions, the Grand Secretariat, as an agency for screening memorials and drafting rescripts (*see* Yang Shih-ch'i).

After the turbulent, dynasty-building eras of the harsh emperors, Chu Yüan-chang and Chu Ti, Chu Chan-chi came to the throne at a time ripe for retrenchment and consolidation, and his personal inclination seems to have been well suited to the time. He had no ambitions for expansionist adventures or dramatic new enterprises. Rather, he was inclined toward tightening up of the governmental mechanism and perhaps above all alleviating distress among the people.

The gravest threat to stability and prosperity that he inherited from his predecessors was an expensive, losing war against rebels in Annam (Chiao-chih), which had been forcefully incorporated into the Chinese empire in 1407. From about 1418 the nationalistic Annamite, Lê Lọ'i (*q.v.*), had conducted guerrilla warfare against the Chinese authorities. In 1424 Lê had begun more aggressive, offensive campaigns against Chinese occupation forces, and Chinese power in Annam had begun to wither. Early in 1426 the Ming commander Fang Cheng (*see* Ssu Jen-fa) was routed in open battle, and the emperor sent one of his most prestigious military officers, the marquis of Ch'eng-shan, Wang T'ung (*see* Huang Fu), to take charge as grand defender of Annam. Wang in his turn was defeated by Lê Lọ'i late that year, and two great reinforcement columns from Yunnan and Kwangsi provinces soon thereafter were beaten off at the Annam border. Wang T'ung found himself fighting a wholly defensive war under constant siege, and in the autumn of 1427, having been defeated once more in the field, he made a peace treaty with Lê Lọ'i and withdrew Chinese military forces and civil officials. Upon returning to Peking, since he had abandoned Annam without imperial authorization, Wang was impeached, tried, and sentenced to death. But the problem of Annam remained, and court officials debated whether or not, in order to restore Chinese prestige, a great effort should be mounted to chastise Lê Lọ'i and recover Annam. The emperor himself wanted peace, but it was only by overriding strong opposition at court that he prevailed. Lê was officially pardoned and became *de facto* ruler of Annam, albeit under pretense that he was only temporarily in charge, pending identification of an heir of the traditional Annamite ruling family. The emperor in the end even remitted Wang T'ung's death sentence, stripping him, however, of all official and noble status.

The abandonment of Annam after a two-decade effort to control it is the major fault that later Chinese historians found with Chu Chan-chi and his principal peace-party supporters, Yang Shih-ch'i and Yang Jung. It has been felt that China's withdrawal dangerously eroded the whole tributary-system edifice and invited other neighboring peoples to show disrespect to the Chinese throne. From a twentieth-century perspective, however, it might appear that the emperor's decision was a realistic and, in its own way, a courageous act releasing China from an unjustifiable and heavy burden of expenditure and loss of life, and not having any consequences that were seriously disadvantageous to China. Whether wise or not, it was clearly his policy to keep China free of foreign wars. In a somewhat similar situation in 1428, when tribespeople of northern Burma provoked China in ways that could easily have led to war (*see* Ssu Jen-fa), he vetoed military action on grounds that it would prove too burdensome.

Chu Chan-chi could always justify his peace policies in the south by reference to the continuing need to be ready for potentially much more serious actions in the north, where the Mongols remained a threat under the leader Aruɣtai (*q.v.*). Fortunately for China, the Mongols had now divided into two mutually antagonistic groups, Eastern and Western Oirat and spent more effort maneuvering and fighting against each other than harassing China. In 1434 Aruɣtai was killed by Oirat enemies, and the way opened for an Oirat burgeoning that was to lead to a disaster for China in 1449. But in Chu Chan-chi's time, China was relatively free of Mongol pressures. The distinguished old general Hsüeh Lu 薛祿 (original ming 貴, 1358–1430), who under Chu Ti had risen from the ranks to be a military commissioner-in-chief and marquis of Yang-wu 陽武, and on whom Chu Kao-chih had conferred the eminent honorary title grand guardian, defeated Mongol raiders at K'ai-p'ing 開平 (modern To-lun 多倫) in 1427; and another raid in the same area had to be repulsed in 1429. The emperor himself, while on an inspection tour of the northern frontier in October, 1428, led three thousand picked troops outside the Great Wall in pursuit of raiders from the Uriyangqad tribes and won a victory at K'uan-ho 寬河, about twenty miles northeast of Hsi-feng-k'ou 喜峯口, reportedly killing three Mongols with his own bow. But the northern frontier, on the whole, was remarkably untroubled in his time.

In the interior there were incessant military troubles with the Man and Miao aboriginal peoples of Kwangsi, Kweichow, and Szechwan provinces, in some part related to China's activities in Annam. Such regional commanders as the marquis of Chen-yüan 鎮遠, Ku Hsing-tsu 顧興祖 (T. 世延, d. 1449?), the earl of Hui-ning 會寧, Li Ying (q.v.), Ch'en Huai (see Wang Ao, d. 1447), Shan Yün 山雲 (d. 1438), Hsiao Shou 蕭授 (d. 1445), and Fang Cheng were kept successively occupied in the southwest, and hardly a year passed without one aboriginal tribe or another being suppressed. But the campaigns mounted against these tribespeople were part of on-going policing activities that did not disrupt the empire generally.

By far the most dramatic political and military event of his reign was the rebellion in 1426 of the emperor's bellicose uncle Chu Kao-hsü. This prince of Han had always resented the fact that his brother had been chosen heir apparent rather than himself, and when his young nephew within a year succeeded to the throne, he decided, despite earnest efforts on Chu Chan-chi's part to show him deference, that he should and could overthrow him as Chu Ti had overthrown his nephew in 1402. He took on imperial airs and sent agents to organize a fifth column in Peking. In efforts to avert open hostilities, the emperor sent investigators and then personal letters to the prince's base at Lo-an 樂安 in Shantung province. But the prince became increasingly insulting, and Chu Chan-chi finally had no choice but to initiate military action against him. Officers suffering punishment were all pardoned and called to duty, imperial gifts were distributed to the troops, and a grand army was assembled at Peking. The emperor's first inclination was to send Hsüeh Lu to sup-

press the rebellion, but Yang Jung argued that it was important for the emperor personally to overawe the enemy, and in the end he led the campaign. He stubbornly resisted his advisers' pleas for overwhelming assaults on Lo-an, however, and instead plied the rebel prince with threats and warnings so that Chu Kao-hsü surrendered without a battle. The emperor refused to move then against his other uncle, the prince of Chao, Chu Kao-sui (see Chu Kao-hsü), whom court officials denounced as an accomplice. The emperor even ignored arguments that Chu Kao-hsü should be put to death on the spot; he was content to have the imperial army and its prisoners march triumphantly back to Peking. The prince and his relatives were reduced to the rank of commoners and incarcerated in detention quarters specially built for them within the imperial palace. Eventually—apparently not earlier than 1429—the emperor in a fit of anger had Chu Kao-hsü put to death in a peculiarly gruesome way and apparently wiped out all his sons. Eventually too, judicial proceedings growing out of the rebellion resulted in the death, disgrace, or exile of some three thousand persons. But the emperor ordered that all soldiers and civilians who had clearly been coerced into the rebel prince's service should not be implicated; and as soon as the campaign was over he sent out teams of officials to assess damages to crops where the army had passed through and to recommend appropriate tax remissions.

The domestic scene in Chu Chan-chi's time was on the whole placid and prosperous, but some evidence suggests that parts of China were then experiencing cyclical natural disorders such as droughts and locust infestations, which occasionally resulted in wide-spread distress. The emperor worked earnestly to cope with such problems within the inherited institutional pattern, and out of his efforts emerged some significant changes. Relief measures or tax remissions were repeatedly ordered for disaster areas:

for Pei-Chihli in 1427, 1428, 1432, 1433, and 1434; for Nan-Chihli in 1427, 1432, 1433, and 1434; for Shantung in 1426, 1433, and 1434; for Shansi in 1427 1428, 1430, 1432, and 1434; for Honan in 1427, 1433, and 1434; for Shensi in 1427 and 1433; for Hukuang in 1433 and 1434; for Chekiang in 1432 and 1434; and for Kiangsi in 1433 and 1434. A general 30 percent reduction in taxes on all lands classified as "government lands" (官田) was ordered in 1430. Permanent tax reductions were repeatedly ordered for specially troubled places, particularly in the rich but very heavily taxed southeastern prefectures around the mouth of the Yangtze River. To have more effective supervision over conditions of life among the people and over local administration, he assigned two high-ranking officials (in 1425) to "tour and soothe" (hsün-fu巡撫) Nan-Chihli and Chekiang, and in 1430 assigned such grand coordinators (hsün-fu) on a regular rotational basis to all provincial areas. Thus regularized, these representatives of the central government "on tour" in the provinces became in effect provincial governors, a new element in the Chinese administrative hierarchy.

In another innovative effort to regularize fiscal administration, he assigned two high-ranking capital officials in 1428 to manage (ching-lüeh 經略) the multi-province grain transport operation along the Grand Canal. He thus provided a precedent for the later spread of multi-province coordinators of various sorts (especially military) generally called supreme commanders (ching-lüeh or, most commonly, tsung-tu 總督). Then in 1430, on the advice of the Grand Canal Supreme Commander Ch'en Hsüan (q.v.), he ordered that the people should be relieved of the time-consuming burden of transporting their own grain taxes to the capital and that henceforth this activity should be carried out by special tax-transport army divisions established along the Grand Canal.

The emperor's concern for the people's welfare was no mere lip service. On one occasion, while traveling, he observed a plowman at work and paused to try his own hand at the plow. Then he said to his attendants, "After taking only three turns at the plow, we are already unequal to the labor. What if one does this constantly? Men always say there is no toil like farming, and they are right!" Subsequently he handed out money to all the farmers he met on the road. In 1426 he angrily rebuked the veteran censor-in-chief Wang Chang 王彰 (T. 文昭, 1366–1427, cj 1387) for reporting only insignificant matters on returning from an inspection trip to Nanking. The emperor then turned to the officials in audience and complained: "The two capitals, southern and northern, are several thousand li apart. We are constantly fearful that postal couriers going and coming might cause oppression and harassment, or that there might be calamitous damages from flood or drought or disease, so that people suffer and starve. All these things We want to hear about. Yet ministers go and return and censors make tours and not one reports about them. We sent Wang Chang on tour to inspect, hoping to learn the truth. Now he speaks only of petty trifles of no essential significance. If great ministers can do no better than this, what can We any longer hope for?" He made similar complaints about ministerial indifference repeatedly.

Conditions in the military establishment also attracted his concerned attention. The system of hereditary soldiers and officers that the first emperor had created was susceptible to abuse and corruption in the handling of personnel and to general deterioration in military effectiveness. Chu Chan-chi's awareness of such problems is clearly revealed in an edict of April 1434: "Military administration is one of the most urgent national concerns. From the time of Our ancestors, laws have been worked out for the understanding and lenient treatment of soldiers and for the setting in order of military defenses. We have repeatedly warned the metropolitan and provincial military officers to observe the law and to take appreciative care of the troops, but in recent times the officers of the provincial military commissions, the guards, and the battalions have given themselves over completely to graft. When there are campaigns, they dragoon the poor and sell exemptions to the rich; and when requisitions are levied they pass along tenfold demands. Some make soldiers their private attendants; some make them hand over their monthly wages; some wrongfully permit them to engage in trade; some usurp their monthly rations; some hold back the issuance of winter uniforms. Their exactions and harassments are of such myriad sorts that soldiers become desperate for clothing and food to the extent of even abandoning their wives and children and running away."

In efforts to tighten up military administration in 1426 and again in 1428, he dispatched teams of capital officials to inspect and improve military conditions in the provinces. Such ad hoc inspections were later to become regularized in the form of military roster clarification (清軍) commissions for investigating censors. Chu Chan-chi also promulgated a new set of rules in 1428 governing the conscription of troops and the capture of deserters, the new set increasing the articles from eight to nineteen. Then in 1429 he issued a whole new set with twenty-two articles. The emperor took military training units at the capital out on tours of the northern frontiers and on great hunting expeditions; and in 1429 he conducted one of the Ming dynasty's few great public military reviews outside Peking.

He was especially noted for leniency and mercy in judicial matters. During his reign almost all crimes could be redeemed by commutation payments of grain according to prescribed rules; and when it was pointed out that poor people, who could not afford such payments, suffered by being held in prison indefinitely, he approved a proposal that such convicted

criminals might substitute special labor tasks or return to their normal occupations at home, where they would have some hope of accumulating the prescribed payments. What is particularly evident is that he was extraordinarily reluctant to approve death penalties. In 1426, for example, the censor-in-chief Liu Kuan (see Ku Tso) memorialized for permission to execute seventy fierce bandits and murderers then held in prison. The emperor acknowledged that by law they might not be pardoned, but he ordered that another judicial review be conducted. Liu replied that such reviews had been conducted repeatedly without revealing any injustice and that the prisoners really deserved to be put to death. The emperor finally assented, but, when the audience had been terminated, he nevertheless sent a eunuch to tell Liu that the executions should be suspended, and that a full report of the cases should be sent in for his own perusal. Reviews of all cases of criminals detained in prison were repeatedly ordered. In 1426 more than three thousand prisoners were released after the review and in 1433 more than five thousand.

His conscientious concern for the people's welfare and for effective administration must be evaluated in conjunction with its corollary, his impatience with officialdom. Censorial officials in particular, comprising the "avenues of criticism" that were relied upon to maintain surveillance over the administration as a whole, he held to a high standard and repeatedly chastised for failing in their duty. He objected to their bureaucratic habit of quibbling about minutiae. He railed against their "venal and vile" ways and lamented that "they connive and consort with inferiors. Some presume upon the public law to get harsh and cruel revenge for private resentments, and assuage their feelings by a reckless disregard of it without care or dread." In 1428 he dismissed the censor-in-chief Liu Kuan and replaced him with the stern disciplinarian Ku Tso, and a consequent purge of the Censorate staff brought the mass dismissal of forty-three investigating censors. In the same year the emperor unprecedentedly displayed three investigating censors and five other capital officials in the portable pillories called cangues, because of their licentiousness, drunkenness, and flagrant neglect of their duties. The emperor's unhappiness with his censorial officials caused him in 1428 to order that henceforth new appointees to investigating censor posts must serve probationary terms before being confirmed for substantive appointments, a practice that was subsequently institutionalized.

Chu Chan-chi was only slightly less stern in dealing with non-censorial officials of the civil service, and when extremely provoked he could resort to very cruel treatment (*see* Li Shih-mien). The only official group that he treated consistently with lenience was the corps of military officers, and when these had to be punished, he was usually quick to pardon them and restore them to duty. Since military officers were not normally exposed to Confucian education, he felt that it was unfair to measure their conduct by strict Confucian standards. He was always ready, however, to lecture them and warn them to reform.

His sternness and occasional harshness in disciplining officials is one of two characteristics that later historians have lamented, as blemishes in the character of an otherwise admirable emperor. The other is his penchant for using palace eunuchs on governmental assignments outside the palace. He was by no means the first Ming emperor to rely on eunuchs, and in general he employed them with great care and restraint. One of his first acts, in 1425, was to recall eunuch purchasing agents who were then gathering supplies for the palace in the provinces; on being told that such eunuchs annoyed the citizenry, requisitioned far more than was required, and disrupted local trading conditions, he exclaimed: "How could we have foreseen that they would make trouble like this!" and put an immediate

stop to their activities. Also, in 1426 he insistently established the rule that no imperial edict delivered by a eunuch was to be considered authentic until supervising secretaries had memorialized and obtained confirmation, a device intended to prevent possible eunuch tampering with official documents. Furthermore, when eunuchs transgressed, the emperor normally showed them little mercy. Thus in 1427 the eunuch Chang Shan 張善 was put to death for corruption and abuses while on commission in the provinces; and in 1431, when it was discovered that the eunuch Yüan Ch'i 袁琦 had organized a large-scale network for graft, he was put to death by slow torture and ten of his eunuch associates were beheaded.

On the other hand, eunuch-commanded maritime expeditions, which had been halted in 1424, were renewed in his reign. The great eunuch admiral Cheng Ho (*q.v.*) led his seventh and last expedition into the Indian Ocean and down the east coast of Africa in 1431-33, and in 1434 his associate Wang Ching-hung (*q.v.*) led the fleet on a mission to Java. The emperor, moreover, perpetuated and probably expanded Chu Ti's practice of assigning eunuchs as military supervisors, called grand defenders (鎮守), in the provinces and frontier regions. That this was widely resented is suggested by the fact that one of the first edicts issued, after his death in 1435, called for the abolition of such eunuch grand defenders in the thirteen provinces. Most of all, later historians have lamented his creation in 1426 of a school for palace eunuchs, called the Nei-shu-t'ang 內書堂. This was a direct violation of the first emperor's announced policy of keeping eunuchs illiterate so that they could not possibly interfere in governmental administration, and historians have often pinpointed this one act as the seed from which eunuch dictatorships were later to grow. That Chu Chan-chi was aware of historic eunuch abuses and of potential future troubles with eunuchs is well established; he even complained that censors and other officials seemed unaccountably afraid of eunuchs. Whether he rationalized his policy with expectations of regulating and improving eunuch behavior by exposure to Confucian indoctrination is not clear.

The judgment of the historians is that he was one of the best intentioned, most conscientious, and most capable rulers of the Ming dynasty. His fame as a patron of the arts, however, has superseded this judgment. As late as the 20th century it was commonplace for Chinese craftsmen in bronze and especially in ceramic wares to dignify their most elegant and stylish products by stamping them with his era name, so that the term Hsüan-te (with the second character consistently written 德) is known to collectors and curators throughout the world.

Bronze works of his time are not as widely known as are the Hsüan-te porcelains, but they were produced in great quantities and furnished the Ming palaces and temples for generations. Incense burners, sacrificial vases, small utensils of many sorts—they are distinguished by a golden or gold-flecked color and have been praised for "their purity of shape and soft lustre" (see L. Sickman). An inventory of the great bronzes of the Hsüan-te era was compiled by the emperor's order and has been preserved under the title *Hsüan-te ting-i p'u* 鼎彝譜.

Hsüan-te porcelains are known and appreciated everywhere. Best known are blue-and-white wares, their brilliant blue color being derived from mineral cobalt possibly imported. Monochrome red wares were another notable Hsüan-te product, and there were also polychrome combinations of underglaze red with blue and white, or even with brown and green enamels. The colors were piled on in layers, achieving effects like those that painters obtain with oils; and the forms are clean, for the crudities and other imperfections, that give some Sung dynasty wares their charm, were now no longer tolerated. The best porcelains of this era were pro-

duced for imperial use in the kilns at Ching-te-chen 景德鎮, in northern Kiangsi province and elsewhere. Representative collections of Hsüan-te porcelains may be found in various museums including the Freer Gallery of Art in Washington, the Metropolitan Museum of Art in New York, the British Museum, the Victoria and Albert Museum, and the Percival David Foundation in London, and most abundantly in the National Palace Museum, Taipei, and the National Central Museum, Taichung.

He was the first Ming emperor who seriously patronized artists, and at his court he gathered together a coterie of painters who carried on the academy style inherited from the Sung dynasty emperor Hui-tsung (1082–1135). Later writers have referred to Chu Chan-chi's Painting Academy, but it existed only in an informal sense; most of the court painters had nominal appointments in the imperial bodyguard. Probably the most talented of the emperor's protégés was Pien Wen-chin (*q. v.*). The now more famous Tai Chin (*q. v.*) was summoned to court in the emperor's time but seems to have been neither happy nor appreciated there; he was permitted to depart and started a tradition of semi-professional landscapists in the unacademic Hsia Kuei (*ca.* 1170-*ca.* 1230), Ma Yüan (*ca.* 1176-*ca* 1240) style in his home province, Chekiang. This was also a time when much building was still going on in Peking (*see* Wu Chung and Juan An).

The emperor himself was a talented but not remarkable poet, and he painted with skill and distinction. Modern critics are not unanimous in their evaluations of his extant works. James Cahill observes: "Hsüan-tsung in particular produced charming pictures of birds, flowers and animals in a very orthodox style. In this and also as a patron of art, imposing his taste upon the painters under him, he no doubt fancied himself a latter-day Hui-tsung; but neither he nor the artists he patronized and encouraged were capable of matching the achievements of the great Sung emperor and his Academy." Osvald Sirén writes of his paintings: "They are executed in color with a very fine brush, the soft silky fur of the animals is rendered with consummate skill and every single flower and leaf is perfectly defined, the interest in detail being pushed to such a degree that it obscures the general impression of life and atmosphere." Laurence Sickman writes: "The emperor himself was a painter of marked ability. Indeed, of all the emperors after Sung Hui-tsung who painted or pretended to paint, it seems probable that Hsüan-te alone possessed any real talent. He specialized in animals, dogs, cats, monkeys, goats, frequently in combination with bamboo or the flowers and rocks of a garden, following in his compositions the traditions of Northern and Southern Sung academies. He was, if one may judge from his surviving pictures, a keen observer, a painter with a light and easy touch, and a certain rather dry, imperial humor. He frequently signed his pictures with, 'playfully painted by the imperial brush'.... Hsüan-te's animal paintings have none of the hard brilliance of the Northern Sung Academy, being more realistic, in a visual sense; as knowledgeable, sensitive studies the best of them will bear comparison with the work of earlier and more famous masters."

One often reproduced work of his, an ink-on-paper painting of two Afghan hounds dated 1427, is owned by the Fogg Museum of Art, Cambridge, Mass. Another 1427 painting, a small dog in front of bamboo, is preserved in the Nelson Gallery of Art, Kansas City. A 1427 watercolor on silk of a white parrot, inscribed as a gift for the grand secretary, Yang Shih-ch'i, now in the Seattle Art Museum, and a 1429 handscroll of five kittens in a garden, now in the Metropolitan Museum of Art in New York, may likewise be genuine. Four or five paintings unquestionably by the emperor are preserved in the National Palace Museum, Taipei; and Sirén reports having seen two others in the People's Museum, Peking.

Chu Chan-chi died at the end of January, 1435—as in his father's case, unexpectedly after a short illness. He was survived by two daughters and had two sons, the elder, Chu Ch'i-chen, succeeding to the throne. Because the elder was then only eight years old, Chu Chan-chi's mother (now Grand Empress-dowager Chang) at first reportedly thought to set him aside in favor of one of her other sons; but she served him in a regency council with several eminent ministers until her death in 1442. Chu Chan-chi was buried in a tomb north of Peking known as the Ching-ling. His original principal consort, who became empress in 1425, was Empress Hu 胡. Unable to bear Chu Chan-chi a son, she was asked to retire after a secondary consort, Madame Sun (see Chu Chien-shen) gave birth to Chu Ch'i-chen in 1427. Madame Hu survived until 1443. Madame Sun became empress in 1428 and enjoyed status as empress-dowager until her death in 1462. Some later historians have suggested that Chu Ch'i-chen was neither Chu Chan-chi's nor Madame Sun's natural child but was taken as an infant from another woman by Madame Sun, who presented him as her own in an effort to win the emperor's favor. Such gossip, of course, can be neither proved nor disproved. Ten of the emperor's concubines followed him in death.

[Editors' note: The *Ming Hsüan-tsung shih-lu* records in its concluding chapter that Chu Chan-chi died at the age of thirty-eight *sui*, which is an error, for it would make the year of his birth 1398. At the beginning of the same annals, however, his date of birth is given correctly as *chi-mao* 己卯 year, 2d month, 9th day, or March 16, 1399, making his true age at death thirty-seven *sui*. The mistake of the *Ming shih-lu* has been repeated by several works of the Ming dynasty, later even by the official *Ming-shih*. Among the books that give the correct age (thirty-seven *sui*) may be mentioned the *Tsui-wei lu* (see Cha Chi-tso, ECCP), *Huang Ming ts'ung-hsin lu* and *Myŏngsa Kangmok* (for both *see* Ch'en Chien), and also *The Rulers of China* by Moule and Yetts.

In general Chu Chan-chi fared better than most other Ming emperors at the hands of the historians, but it seems that he also indulged in many extravagant interests. As soon as he died an edict was issued by the empress dowager, in the name of his successor, recalling all the eunuchs and orderlies he had sent out throughout the empire to search for, or, in certain areas, to take charge of manufactures, silk goods, embroideries, paper, bronze, hardwood furniture, porcelain, precious minerals, nonmilitary supplies, falcons, exotic animals, insects, fish, plants, rocks, etc. Thus he demanded from the people much more than just fighting crickets (*see* K'uang Chung). There is, however, still another side of his life not recorded at all in Chinese sources, namely, the staffing of his harem. In this respect he was rather like his father who, right in the middle of the mourning period, violated Confucian decorum by sending eunuchs as far as Fukien in search of girls, for which he was openly chided by a Hanlin reader (*see* Li Shih-mien). Chu Chan-chi, however, more discreetly, like his grandfather, sent for virgins from Korea. Chu Ti's messengers were eunuchs of Korean origin, one of whom is known to have arrived in Nanking in 1402 in the company of several of them. Chu Chan-chi sent his eunuchs to transmit his orders verbally, so as to leave no record, but he had no idea that the Korean court was recording these orders and the subsequent events in its annals. According to the recently reproduced *Chosŏn wangjo sillok* 朝鮮王朝 實錄 in April, 1426, the eunuchs bearing the first order for virgins, eunuchs, and female cooks arrived at the Korean court Later other demands made on Korea included falcons, dogs, and leopards, obviously for the sport of hunting, and indicated the revival of the Korean tribute system of the Mongol period.

The Korean king set up a special office (known as jinhŏn-saek 進獻色) to meet these demands, at the same time ordering the postponement of all marriages of young women in his kingdom until the virgins had been selected; he also printed circulars with illustrations of various kinds of eagles and hawks to familiarize the populace with the genera desired. Finally the king personally selected seven virgins, who, with ten cooks, sixteen maids, and ten youthful eunuchs, left Seoul in August, 1427, arriving in Peking in October. In November, 1428, another girl, known for her beauty, was sent to Peking on demand. As the emperor acquired a taste for Korean food, he demanded in 1429 and received from Korea eleven more cooks as well as large amounts of fish and pickles. Even late in 1434, shortly before his death, Chu ordered the king to send another batch of cooks, as he delighted in the Korean culinary art, especially dishes with bean curd. In 1429 he had likewise asked for eight girl singers, eleven eunuchs, hunting dogs, falcons, etc.

In April, 1435, two months after his death, fifty-three Korean women, who wished to return to their own country, were sent back.]

Bibliography

1/9/1a; *MSL* (1963), Hsüan-tsung; Ku Ying-t'ai (ECCP), *Ming-ch'ao chi-shih pen-mo*, 28/1a; *Meng Sen* (BDRC), *Ming-tai shih* (Hong Kong, 1957), 119; *Chosŏn wangjo sillok*, Vol. 3 (1955), 13, 14, 83, 103, 179, 190, 605; *Blue-and-white Ware of the Ming Dynasty*, Vol. IV, bk. 2, parts 1 & 2 (1963) and *Enamelled Ware of the Ming Dynasty*, Vol. VII, bk. 1 (1966), comp. by the National Palace Museum and the National Central Musem, Taichung, and publ. in Hong Kong; C. O. Hucker, *The Censorial System of Ming China* (Stanford, 1966), 110; O. Sirén, *A History of Later Chinese Painting*, Vol. 1 (London, 1938), 28; J. Cahill, *Chinese Painting* (Geneva, Switzerland, 1960), 117; L. Sickman and A. Soper, *The Art and Architecture of China* (Harmondsworth, 1956), 163, 170; R. L. Hobson, *The Wares of the Ming Dynasty* (reprint, Rutland, Vt., 1962), 45; "Ming Blue-and-White,"

Philadelphia Museum Bulletin, Vol. XLIV, no. 223, 1949; *Great Chinese Painters of the Ming and Ch'ing Dynasties*, N. Y., 1949; Harrie Vanderstappen, "Painters at the Early Ming Court (1368–1435) and the Problem of a Ming Painting Academy," MS, XV (1956), 259, XVI (1957), 315; J. M. Addis, "More on the Problem of the 'Imperial Kilns,'" *Archives of Asian Art*, XXII (1968–69), 96.

Charles O. Hucker

CHU Ch'ang, *see* HSIA Ch'ang

CHU Ch'i-chen 朱祁鎮 (November 29, 1427–February 23, 1464), who had the distinction of reigning over two periods—Cheng-t'ung 正統 (1436–1449) and T'ien-shun 天順 (1457–1464)—was the elder son of Emperor Chu Chan-chi, the brother of Emperor Chu Ch'i-yü, and the father of Emperor Chu Chien-shen (*qq.v.*). His posthumous name was Jui 睿, his temple name Ying-tsung 英宗, and his remains were interred in the Yü-ling 裕陵. Between his two reigns for about a year he was a captive of the Mongols, and the other six and a half years he lived in confinement in Peking while his brother reigned as emperor under the title Ching-t'ai.

Chu Ch'i-chen's birth gave his father great delight. On February 20, 1428, at the age of three months he was declared heir apparent. In March his mother, Lady Sun (*see* Chu Chien-shen), was raised to empress to replace the dethroned empress with whom his father had been at odds for some time. In his childhood his father showered him with marks of favor and affection. Reports had it that he was precocious and striking in appearance; particularly noticeable was his large forehead which required hats of extra size. It was also said that his father would sometimes set him on his lap and ask him whether he would be able to keep peace in the empire when he became emperor. Always clearly and unhesitatingly he would answer, "Yes, I can." Again his father would ask him whether in an emergency he would have the courage to lead an army in person. He would answer, "Yes, I would." This pleased his father immensely. After putting down the rebellion of Chu Kao-hsü (*q.v.*) and leading expeditionary forces outside the Great Wall, Chu Chan-chi apparently regarded himself as a courageous figure and this must have impressed his son. In 1433 the emperor ordered the recruitment of ten thousand physically strong and presentable boys, aged eleven to twenty, to form a detachment of youth-guards (幼軍) for the heir apparent. In about six months a unit of 7,112 was formed and perhaps began to be trained with the son playing the role of commander. Meanwhile Chu Ch'i-chen started to learn to read and write, his first teacher being probably the eunuch and former pedagogue Wang Chen (*q.v.*). In March, 1434, the heir apparent held his first audience in the Wen-hua-tien 文華殿 (Hall of literary brilliance). Seven months later, when the emperor was about to set out on an inspection tour of the northern frontier, he put responsibility for the protection of the imperial city into the hands of five eunuchs of high rank, Wang Chen among them. Wang was obviously entrusted too with looking after the interests of the heir apparent.

When his father died in January, 1435, Chu Ch'i-chen was only eight years of age. Someone in the palace proposed placing a mature ruler on the throne, and suggested the name of his uncle, Chu Chan-shan 瞻墡 (the prince of Hsiang 襄王, 1406–78, Pth. 憲), whose mother was the dowager-empress Chang (*see* Chu Chan-chi). According to Mao Ch'i-ling (ECCP), she was the one who made the proposal, but the editors of the *Ming-shih* later represented her as upholding the rights of her grandson, Chu Ch'i-chen. It is said that she summoned the grand secretaries, Yang Shih-ch'i, Yang Jung, and Yang P'u (*qq.v.*) to the residence hall and, pointing to her grandson on the throne, said that this was the new emperor. Then and there the grand secretaries made their obeisances to the child emperor, later to be followed by the entire court. This was the first time in the Ming dynasty for this to happen when the emperor was not yet of age. By order of the founder of the dynasty, decisions in state affairs could come only from the ruling emperor; there was no provision for the contingency of a minor on the throne. Neither the empress-dowager nor anyone else could assume the functions of a regent. Yet the affairs of state had to be conducted as usual, as if the child emperor were in full control. On this occasion a *de facto* regency was set up with the grandmother, Dowager-empress Chang, as arbiter on vital issues, with the head eunuchs of the Directorate of Ceremonials, including Wang Chen, making the decisions for the emperor, but in consultation with the three grand secretaries who would draft the edicts in formal language. Soon it became obvious that Wang Chen, who enjoyed the emperor's complete trust, assumed greater powers than the rest, and the officials knelt in his presence. He was faithful to the emperor and conciliatory to the three grand secretaries. Hence harmony prevailed.

It happened that of the three men, all named Yang, two had served in the Grand Secretariat since 1402 and the third, Yang P'u, since 1426. Their experience, prestige, and personalities helped to make the Cheng-t'ung reign of Chu Ch'i-chen one of the best governed periods of the dynasty. In June, 1442, Chu Ch'i-chen married the lady Ch'ien (*see* Chu Chien-shen). A few months later his grandmother died. Evidently he assumed full powers then, but otherwise the government carried on as usual.

This was a period of significant transitions, especially in the provinces, where civilians were entrusted with more military power, probably as a result of the deterioration of the quality of military personnel which for years had been drawn only from hereditary ranks. During the two campaigns against Ssu Jen-fa (*q.v.*) in the

Yunnan-Burma border region (1441–49), it was the civilian, Wang Chi 驥 (*q.v.*), who was the actual commander and who was rewarded in 1442 with an earldom. To be sure, both the eunuch, Ts'ao Chi-hsiang (*q.v.*), who was in charge of firearms, and the marquis of Ting-hsi 定西侯, Chiang Kuei 蔣貴 (T. 大富, 1380–1449, Pth. 武勇), the commander-in-chief, contributed to the success of these campaigns, but it was Wang Chi who had the title of tsung-tu chün-wu 總督軍務 (supreme commander), the first civilian to be given such powers in the field.

The victory of the second Yunnan campaign was celebrated in Peking in March, 1449. About the same time the suppression of the rebellions in Fukien was reported (*see* T'eng Mao-ch'i, Yeh Tsung-liu). These victories probably encouraged the emperor to overestimate the effectiveness of his troops, and to try personally to lead an army in the field. He was then twenty-two years of age and had been on the throne fourteen years. With the faithful Wang Chen shouldering most of the responsibility, the young emperor probably became used to giving rash orders, and when any difficulty arose relying on Wang to straighten it out. On July 20 there was a report of border raids by the Oirat chieftain Esen (*q.v.*); the emperor at once ordered four generals and forty-five thousand Peking soldiers to proceed to Tatung and Hsüan-fu to guard the frontier. On August 3 he appointed his younger half-brother, Chu Ch'i-yü, to be regent while he himself was to lead an expedition to fight the invaders from the north. In his entourage were some twenty seasoned generals, most of them holders of ranks of nobility (*see* Chang Fu) and about an equal number of civilian officials of high rank. They were assisted by hundreds of officials of lower ranks. The total number on the expedition is usually given as half a million. Even under the best of conditions such a large army would have been difficult to manage. Hastily assembled, poorly prepared, and incompetently led, it became a disaster. The emperor left Peking on August 4 and, delayed by a storm, arrived at Hsüan-fu seven days later. Many appealed to the emperor to turn back, but Wang Chen, speaking for him, gave the order to advance. Finally Tatung was reached on August 18. On the way many men died from hunger rather than from any serious fighting. Two days later the emperor, realizing the dangerous situation, gave the order to retreat. At Hsüan-fu on the 30th it was learned that the rear guard had been crushed and a relief force of forty thousand was also annihilated. The following evening the expedition encamped at the post station called T'u-mu-i 土木驛 where there was no water. In the morning of September 1, the Mongols attacked. Hungry and thirsty, the emperor's men were nearly all massacred in the field without offering any resistance. Only a few escaped with their lives (see Han Yung, Yang Shan). Wang Chen met his end and so did two dukes (see Chang Fu), two marquises, five earls, several generals, and hundreds of officials. Tens of thousands of firearms, in addition to armor (including helmets) and other equipment, were later picked up by the Chinese troops when they re-occupied the area. The victory was such a surprise to the Oirat that, instead of pressing their advantage, they just took what they could carry and returned north with their biggest prize, Emperor Chu Ch'i-chen. As a consequence, the Ming had time to recover but not to the extent of resuming any serious offensive action (see Wang Yüeh, Yang Po).

In captivity for twelve and a half months, Chu Ch'i-chen was allowed to live and travel in his own yurt and have the service and companionship of Yüan Pin (see Esen), an officer captured at the same time, and Yang Ming (q.v.), an interpreter. On several occasions his captors took the ex-emperor with them on their raids inside the Great Wall, for he could demand gifts for them from the garrison commanders. Once Esen reminded him of this kindly treatment and asked him what torture he, Esen, would get from the Chinese had the situation been reversed. When Chu Ch'i-chen was returned to China, he and the Oirat parted like friends.

Meanwhile many changes had taken place in Peking. When the news of Chu's capture reached the capital, his mother, Empress-dowager Sun, gave the order that his son, Chu Chien-shen, then less than two years old, be named heir apparent, with Chu Ch'i-yü continuing as regent. At an audience the officials demanded the punishment of Wang Chen who was blamed for the disaster, but when the regent demurred, they rose in a rage and had a eunuch and two other followers of Wang beaten to death. On the insistence of Yü Ch'ien (q.v.), the regent agreed to have Wang's properties confiscated and his entire family executed. Made minister of War, Yü directed the defenses of the city, the assembling of a new army, and the stabilization of a situation potentially dangerous. On September 17 Chu Ch'i-yü ascended the throne and proclaimed his elder brother superior emperor 太上皇帝. Under the new regime the empire was saved, but there soon developed a subtle campaign to discredit Chu Ch'i-chen. He was regarded as a failure, and unwanted. The frontier commanders were warned not to receive him. Because of Esen's offer to return the ex-emperor, however, two missions were sent to negotiate his surrender (see Li Shih, Yang Shan). Finally he was released.

In September, 1450, an escort brought Chu Ch'i-chen back to China. The officials were forbidden to give him welcome. Only two or three of them (see Shang Lu) were sent to meet him with only one sedan chair and two horses. On his arrival on the 20th the reigning emperor, Chu Ch'i-yü, met him at a side palace gate and at once sent him to Nan-ch'eng 南城, an enclosure with a residence hall southeast of the imperial palace. There he lived for six and a half years, practically a prisoner, with the walls guarded by soldiers and the gate sealed. Ex-empress Ch'ien and his concubines were sent to live with him, and three of his sons (5th, 6th, and 7th) were born there, but their supplies were meager and the seclusion oppressive. Every year on his birthday the officials would request permission to go to his gate and congratulate him. Their request was invariably denied. In June, 1452, Chu Ch'i-yü's own son was declared heir apparent to replace Chu Chien-shen. It is said that in that same year, when the monastery, Lung-fu ssu 隆福寺, was built and lumber was needed, some pillars were taken from Nan-ch'eng for that purpose. It is also related that the tall trees in its yard were cut down as they obstructed surveillance.

Suddenly, on the night of February 11, 1457, the quiet of Nan-ch'eng was disturbed by shouting and clamor. Soldiers were ramming the gate and scaling the walls. After entering, their leaders came to Chu Ch'i-chen, told him that he was to be restored to the throne, and forthwith bore him by chair to the palace gate. Forcing their way in, they helped place him on the throne in the audience hall, and rang bells to summon the court. By daybreak the *coup d'état* was a *fait accompli*, and he started his second reign under the title T'ien-shun. The episode came to be known as to-men 奪門, signifying the forcing of the palace gate.

This neatly executed feat, taking but a few hours, was perpetrated by a small group of conspirators, the leaders being the eunuch military expert, Ts'ao Chihsiang, and the generals Shih Heng (*q.v.*), Chang Yüeh (*see* Chu Ch'i-yü), and the strategist, Hsü Yu-chen (*q.v.*). They forced the Nan-ch'eng gate with only about four hundred troops, mostly Mongols, and were later joined by two thousand eight hundred men, half of whom followed the emperor and the other half deployed to guard strategic points. Reportedly they had secretly communicated with Chu Ch'i-chen two days earlier, but another story indicates that

he was not aware of the plot beforehand. In any case he rewarded the leaders of the conspiracy with noble ranks and meted out promotions to all the participants. Soon, however, he became tired of their demands, and, when they fell out with each other, had them removed one by one. First to go was Hsü Yu-chen (August, 1457). Then Shih Heng died in prison (February, 1460), and Ts'ao Chi-hsiang and his entire family were executed for treason (August, 1461). Later even the designation to-men, was considered too crude and so changed to fu-p'i 復辟, or restoration of the throne. Furthermore, he punished a number of men who had offended him or who were now accused of having done, by word or deed, any harm to him or to the interests of his son, Chu Chien-shen. Some of the executed were falsely accused, especially Yü Ch'ien, who should have been rewarded for his responsibility in saving the empire. The same may be said of the Ching-t'ai emperor whose death was possibly by strangulation (*see* Chu Ch'i-yü). His aversion to Chu Ch'i-yü extended to books in the latter's name: the one containing exemplars of sovereigns in history, *Li-tai chün-chien* 歷代君鑒, 50 *ch.*, published in 1454; and the gazetteer of the empire, *Huan-yü t'ung-chih* (*see* Shang Lu), printed in 1456. The former was banned and the latter suppressed (fortunately original editions of both are still extant), but a new edition of the geographical work was issued under the title *Ta Ming i-t'ung-chih* (*see* Shang Lu) with little improvement. In sharp contrast to his treatment of Chu Ch'i-yü and his supporters, he gave Wang Chen an official burial (in effigy), had a statue made of him in the monastery Chih-hua ssu (*see* Wang Chen), and ordered a shrine honoring him with the name Ching-chung 旌忠 (reward for loyalty).

These acts of injustice made the first year of his second reign unpopular. It seems that he tried to improve his image. His choice of Hsüeh Hsüan and Li Hsien (*qq.v.*) as grand secretaries met with approval. After Hsüeh retired in the middle of 1457 the emperor sought another respected Confucianist and found him in the person of the country teacher, Wu Yü-pi (*q.v.*), who was reputed to consider it against the spirit of Confucianism to serve a court established through an unjustified rebellion and by a regicide. Wu was escorted to Peking and given an honorary position but allowed to retire. Meanwhile, however, the emperor relied heavily on his police and secret service for security and the suppression of unfavorable criticism.

Politically the second period of Chu Ch'i-chen's reign was marked by the secret strife between the northerners and southerners, a phenomenon existing as early as 1397 when the examiners who favored the southerners were punished (*see* Liu San-wu). In 1448, when no southerner was selected to enter the Hanlin Academy (*see* Wang Shu), it was attributed to the pro-north bias of Wang Chen. Then followed the Ching-t'ai reign of over seven years during which many southerners rose in power, such as Shang Lu, Yü Ch'ien, Yeh Sheng, and Han Yung (*qq.v.*). After the restoration Chu Ch'i-chen relied chiefly on Li Hsien, a Honanese, for advice. It would appear that in appointment and promotion the emperor gave the northerners some preference, and the southerners blamed Li, regarding him as leader of a northern party. The strife did not emerge in the open but is recorded in the notes and essays of that day.

According to Li Hsien and P'eng Shih (*q.v.*), Chu Ch'i-chen was an early riser and attended daily to the affairs of state with dispatch. Before he died he ordered a stop to the custom of having concubines commit suicide so as to accompany the master in death. This shows that he was essentially a man of compassion. Among his other acts similarly commendable may be mentioned the release of the descendants of Li Ching-lung (*see* Li Wen-chung) and the freeing of the younger

son of the Chien-wen emperor (*see* Chu Yün-wen) from the Nanking prison in 1457.

Chu Ch'i-chen was not particularly known for an interest in Taoism, but perhaps, persuaded by the eunuchs, he gave his name to the inscriptions commemorating the restoration of the Ch'eng-huang miao 城隍廟 and the Tung-yüeh 東嶽 miao, both dated in 1447. The inscription in his name on the monument in Hung-en ling-chi-kung 洪恩靈済宮 in 1436 was apparently authorized by someone else. During his reign the reprinting of the Buddhist and Taoist classics was completed. The former, *Ta-tsang-ching* 大藏經, 6,361 *chüan* in 636 cases, includes his preface dated 1440. The latter, *Tao-tsang*, commissioned in 1406 (*see* Chang Yü-ch'u), appeared in 1445 in 5,305 *chüan*, in 481 cases. A supplement in 32 cases was printed by imperial order in 1607 and the entire collection reproduced in 1926.

Under his reign also the work of exemplars of ethics, *Wu-lun shu* 五倫書, 62 *ch.*, was finished and printed in 1443. Incidentally, it was he who ordered that the images of Confucius dressed in Mongolian style (tso-jen 左衽) with buttons on the left be changed to the Chinese style of buttoning on the right. The emperor too gave orders to prohibit Mongolian dress and speech in Peking. He was perhaps not especially interested in the arts. His order forbidding the private sale of blue-and-white porcelain in 1439 was no doubt for the protection of the imperial monopoly. The order was repeated and extended on January 22, 1448, when the emperor forbade anyone in Jao-chou 饒州 (where Ching-te-chen is located) from the manufacture for private sale of porcelain of the yellow, purple, red, green, dark blue, and light blue, in addition to the blue-and-white; the penalty for breaking this law was to be as harsh as that for treason. These two prohibitions help to explain the scarcity of porcelains with the Cheng-t'ung, Ching-t'ai, and T'ien-shun nien-hao 年號 —a period known to western specialists as the "Ceramic Interregnum."

In 1443 the emperor wrote, or had written for him, the preface to the new edition of a Sung work on acupuncture, entitled *T'ung-jen shu-hsüeh chen-chiu t'u* 銅人腧穴針灸圖, 3 *ch.* The original work consisted of the text and illustrations engraved on stone, to accompany a bronze model of the human body showing 360 points where needles might be inserted. In the preface to the new edition the emperor described the bronze figure as tarnished and the stone inscription as eroded, and so ordered a new inscription of the text and the casting of a new and better model for the Imperial Academy of Medicine. One of the bronze figures has been installed in the Historical Museum in Peking, and another was taken (in 1900?) to Leningrad, where it is on exhibit in the Hermitage. It is said that the stone inscription was removed to Tokyo in 1900.

Bibliography

1/ch. 10 & 12, 83/3b, 103/14a, 119/4b; MSL (1963), Ying-tsung (supplement) *Pao-hsün* 寶訓; KC (1958), Cheng-t'ung and T'ien-shun periods; Ho Ch'iao-yüan, *Ming-shan ts'ang* (Taipei, 1971, photo reprint of 1640 ed.), ch. 11, 12, 14; Ku Ying-t'ai (ECCP), *Ming-ch'ao chi-shih pen-mo* (1658 ed.), ch. 29-36; Shen Chieh-fu, *Chi-lu hui-pien* (Changsha, 1938, photo-reprint of Wan-li ed.), ch. 16-23; Li Chin-hua 李晉華, *Ming-tai ch'ih-chuan shu-k'ao* 明代勅撰書考 (Harvard-Yenching Institute, Sinological Index Series, Supplement no. 3, 1932), 43; Sun Ch'eng-tse (ECCP), *Liang-ch'ao* 兩朝 *tien-ku pien-nien k'ao* (microfilm), ch. 43-55; W. Franke, *Sources*, 8.1.1; L. of C. *Catalogue of Rare Books*, 461; Naikaku Bunko *Catalogue*, 91, 191; John A. Pope, *Chinese Porcelains from the Ardebil Shrine* (Washington, D. C., 1956), 101; *Palace Museum Weekly*, nos. 143, 376, 377.

Lienche Tu Fang and Chaoying Fang

CHU Ch'i-yü 朱祁鈺, September, 11, 1428 -March, 14, 1457, who ruled under the reign-title Ching-t'ai 景泰 (1450-57), was the second son of Chu Chan-chi (*q.v.*) and became the seventh emperor of the Ming dynasty. His mother, the daughter of the commissioner-in-chief Wu Yen-ming 吳彥名 of Tan-t'u 丹徒, Nan-Chihli, had been raised to the rank of hsien-fei 賢妃 in 1428. After the death of his father in 1435, his elder half-brother, Chu Ch'i-chen (*q.v.*), ascended the throne and installed Chu Ch'i-yü as prince of Ch'eng 郕王.

In August, 1449, Emperor Chu Ch'i-chen left Peking in the company of a great number of leading officials for the ill-fated campaign against the Oirat chieftain, Esen (*q.v.*). He ordered the prince of Ch'eng to remain behind and take charge of the defense of the capital. After the catastrophe at T'u-mu which resulted in the capture of the emperor, Empress-dowager Sun (widow of Chu Chan-chi and alleged mother of the emperor), now the highest authority of the empire, appointed Chu Ch'i-yü as acting head of the administration and, four days later, on Septmber 4, 1449, as regent. On September 15, the leading civil and military officials asked the empress-dowager to install the prince of Ch'eng as emperor in order to stabilize the government which had been badly shaken by the T'u-mu disaster and by the imminent attack of the Oirat on the capital itself. The heir apparent, a small child, had just been installed and the emperor's only brother, Chu Ch'i-yü, was thus the only adult person eligible for the position. Being a rather timid, weak, and irresolute personality, and giving no indication at any time of imperial aspirations, Chu Ch'i-yü reportedly was frightened when asked to ascend his brother's throne. He eventually agreed after having refused three times according to the prescriptions of propriety. His refusal, however, seems not to have been just a matter of convention. His installation as emperor was primarily a political device of some leading officials —in particular of Yü Ch'ien (*q.v.*)—to reduce the importance of the imperial prisoner in the hands of the Oirat. The Chinese state, in having its emperor a captive of the barbarians, suffered an unbearable loss of prestige, whereas to have an ex-emperor in enemy hands meant a great deal less.

In the days immediately preceding Chu's enthronement, Yü Ch'ien persuaded the emperor to adopt various administrative measures to overcome the initial confusion prevailing in the capital. The administration was purged of the most notorious collaborators of Wang Chen (*q.v.*), the all-powerful eunuch mainly responsible for the debacle; important civil and military positions, which had become vacant with the death or capture of many high officials at T'u-mu, he filled with new men. Some high officials and eunuchs advocated the removal of the capital south to Nanking. During the heated debate, this proposal, in the light of the tragic precedent of the Sung dynasty, was rejected and its originators, in particular Hsü Yu-chen (*q.v.*), were rebuked by Yü Ch'ien, the new minister of War, who had emerged as the strong man during this crisis. On September 22, Chu Ch'i-yü formally ascended the throne, proclaiming Ching-t'ai as reign-title beginning in 1450 (January 14). His immediate problem was the defense of the capital. Yü took charge of organizing precautionary measures against the Oirat. An attack immediately after the Chinese defeat at T'u-mu would probably have made it easy for Esen to occupy Peking and to establish his rule over a large part of northern China. But he wavered for almost two months, thus providing time for the Chinese to reorganize and to become prepared. Not until October 27 did he advance on Peking. Seeing no chance to take the now heavily fortified city, he retreated after a siege of only four days. Thus did a period most critical for the destiny of the Ming dynasty end. The new emperor played an almost entirely passive role during this time. He relied upon a number of able officials (in particular Yü Ch'ien), being at least superior to his brother who had permitted himself to be manipulated by irresponsible and inefficient people like

the eunuch, Wang Chen.

The new authorities in Peking declined all offers by Esen to release the ex-emperor for ransom and demanded his return without any conditions. At the same time the Chinese government pursued a firm policy of resistance against the Oirat without openly showing much concern for the imperial captive. As a result Esen began to consider his prisoner more burdensome than useful. In the autumn of the following year (1450) he was prepared to release the ex-emperor without any further conditions. Chu Ch'i-yü had shown himself not only disinclined to consider the question of his brother's release, but also unwilling to send emissaries of high rank to welcome him upon his return. Nor would he offer him a reception in accord with the dignity of an ex-emperor, for fear that his brother might contest the throne. Chu Ch'i-yü is reported to have said: "Originally it was not my intention to ascend the throne; the idea was initiated and pressed by you, the officials." It was only after he was assured that the ruler was not to be changed, and after his brother had written a letter renouncing the throne, that Chu Ch'i-yü agreed to welcome him in a proper way. But apparently he did not have the necessary self-confidence to deal with Chu Ch'i-chen in a tolerant way. He always remained suspicious and he continued to be anxious lest his brother should claim the imperial dignity again for himself. He approved the strong policy of resistance against the Oirat at least partly out of fear that Esen might enforce the reenthronement of his former captive. Chu Ch'i-yü virtually interned the ex-emperor in the "Southern Palace" 南宮 (according to tradition the later P'u-tu-ssu 普度寺, southeast of the imperial palace), and tried to isolate him from all connections with the higher officials. The antagonism between Chu Ch'i-yü and his brother overshadowed the whole Ching-t'ai period. Even the reorganization of the army carried out under the supervision of Yü Ch'ien seems to have had some relation to this antagonism, since the new system was abolished at once after the restoration of Chu Ch'i-chen. Chu Ch'i-yü's lack of resolution did not help, and he took no step to eliminate his antagonists, as had usually been the practice of his predecessors in similar situations.

It is possible that prior to his enthronement, the empress-dowager privately advised Chu Ch'i-yü that he was expected to occupy the throne only temporarily and to resign after the return of his brother. We may infer this from the fact that, on the same day Chu Ch'i-yü became regent, she ordered the installation of Chu Chien-shen (*q.v.*), born 1447, eldest son of Chu Ch'i-chen, as heir apparent. After his enthronement, however, Chu Ch'i-yü was apparently determined to keep the throne not only for himself but also for his descendants. A memorial presented by an hereditary native official of Kwangsi, Huang Hung 黄竑 (d. 1454), who was charged with the murder of his brother and was eager to please the emperor in order to save himself and his family from prosecution, gave him the reason he wanted. Learning of the emperor's wishes, Huang memorialized proposing that Chu Ch'i-yü name a new heir apparent. The emperor accepted the memorial with alacrity and ordered the release of Huang Hung. The grand secretaries and other leading officials opposing this procedure were silenced by being given special favors and by being intimidated, thus deterring them from coming out in open resistance. On May 20, 1452, Chu Ch'i-yü ordered the demotion of the heir apparent Chu Chien-shen, installing him as prince of I, and put his own son Chu Chien-chi 見済 (Pth. 懷獻世子, 1440?-1453) in his place. Empress Wang 汪 was deposed on the same day in favor of Chu Chien-chi's mother, the imperial consort, née Hang 杭. The heir apparent, however, died only a year and a half later and Empress Hang in 1456. Chu

Ch'i-yü had no other sons and installed no successor. A few officials, such as a director in the ministry of Rites, Chang Lun 章綸 (T. 大經, Pth. 恭毅, cs 1439, d. 1484+), and the censor Chung T'ung 鍾同 (T. 世京, 1428-55, cs 1451), ventured to suggest the reinstatement of Chu Chien-shen. This provoked the emperor and they were imprisoned and ill-treated, Chung T'ung and certain others being flogged to death. His appointment of his son as heir apparent as well as his behavior towards his brother seriously impaired the prestige of the emperor. His unfitness for rule roused a number of ambitious people to plot for his eventual overthrow and the reinstatement of his brother.

The leading figures in the conspiracy were Shih Heng, Ts'ao Chi-hsiang, (*qq.v.*), Hsü Yu-chen, and Chang Yüeh 張軏 (Pth. 勇襄, 1393-1458), a former commissioner-in-chief of the central military commission. An opportunity offered itself when, at the beginning of the eighth year of his reign (1457), Chu Ch'i-yü fell seriously ill. For several days he was unable to hold audience and had to cancel the New Year ceremonies. The court was even prepared for his death. Requests to install an heir apparent had no result, and a general atmosphere of unrest and anxiety prevailed. Then during the early morning of February 11, 1457, the conspirators with armed protection brought ex-Emperor Chu Ch'i-chen from his residence into the audience hall of the imperial palace, put him on the throne, and to the surprise of the assembled officials, asked him to hold the morning audience. This *coup-d'état* is known as to-men 奪門 (the forcing into the palace gate). The reenthroned emperor at once made important changes among the highest officials. The men who had plotted the restoration received leading positions; former influential people were removed and put on trial; some were killed, such as Yü Ch'ien, Wang Wen (*see* Yü Ch'ien), and three high-ranking eunuchs. The reign-title of the year that had just begun was changed to T'ien-shun. Chu Ch'i-yü was downgraded to prince of Ch'eng. He never recovered from his illness, however, and died on March 14. Some contemporaries even state that he was murdered. [Editors' note: According to Lu I 陸釴 (T. 鼎儀, 1439–89, cs 1464), a eunuch, Chiang An 蔣安, strangled Chu Ch'i-yü. The same account appears in *Kuo-ch'üeh* by T'an Ch'ien (*q.v.*) and *Tsui-wei lu* by Cha Chi-tso (ECCP), the latter giving the additional information that the deposed emperor was murdered after he had recovered from the illness which was one of the causes of dethronement. Lu I's account can be found only in his collection of notes, *Ping-i man-chi* 病逸漫記. He was a Hanlin academician who had served as an editor of the *Ying-tsung shih-lu* (completed in 1467; *see* Chu Ch'i-chen). He had also taught in the palace school for selected eunuchs. With his qualifications and access to written and verbal sources of information, his assertion seems unimpeachable.]

Chu Ch'i-yü received the posthumous name Li 戾 (the rebellious one) and was buried far away from the area of imperial mausolea at a site near Yü-ch'üan shan 玉泉山 (the Jade Fountain). Some officials proposed the cancellation of his reign-title as Emperor Chu Ti (*q.v.*) had done with the reign-title Chien-wen (*see* Chu Yün-wen), but the emperor did not agree. Only under his successor, in 1475, was Chu Ch'i-yü canonized as Kung-ting k'ang-jen Ching huang-ti 恭定康仁景皇帝, a posthumous title not on a par with those of other Ming emperors. There are no separate Veritable Records for Chu Ch'i-yü, his reign being included in the *Ying-tsung shih-lu* with the subtitle *Fei-ti Ch'eng li-wang fu-lu* 廢帝郕戾王附錄 (Appendix concerning the deposed emperor, the rebellious prince of Ch'eng). During the Wan-li period (1573–1620), proposals were made to compile separate Veritable Records and bestow a temple-name on him; but it was only after the downfall of the dynasty that the Southern Ming court at Nanking granted him a posthumous title corresponding fully with that of the other Ming emperors and the temple-name Tai-tsung 代宗. Usually he is known by the name Ching-ti 景帝.

Besides his only son mentioned above, Chu Ch'i-yü had one daughter (two according to *Ming-shih*), the princess of Ku-an 固安公主. In 1469 she married Wang Hsien 王憲 (d. Dec. 28, 1514), a great-grandson of Wang Chi (*q.v.*).

After Chu Ch'i-yü died, his consorts were ordered to commit suicide (hsün殉), but the deposed Empress Wang was allowed to live in a house outside the palace. It is said that her nephew, the newly restored heir apparent, Chu Chien-shen, gave her his protection and permitted her to take all her possessions. Later Emperor Chu Ch'i-chen made a search of her house and removed some two hundred thousand ounces of silver as well as other treasures. She lived to the age of eighty and died in January, 1507. She received the posthumous name Chen-hui ching huang-hou 貞惠景皇后 and burial in the mausoleum of Chu Ch'i-yü.

While politically this was a tempestuous reign, culturally it could boast at least some advance. It is known particularly for the development of cloisonné enamel, an art probably introduced from Persia during the Yüan. In fact, a large proportion of the cloisonné enamel objects made during the Ming, which bear a reign mark, date from this period. As a consequence the common term for the ware is Ching-t'ai lan 藍.

Bibliography

1/11/1a, 113/11b, 16b, 121/12a; 5/2/50a, 61/20; *Ming-shih* (Taiwan ed.), 1475; MSL (1940), Ying-tsung, *chüan* 180; Ku Ying-t'ai (ECCP), *Ming-ch'ao* (*shih*) *chi-shih pen-mo*, *chüan* 33 and 35; KC (1958), 1772, 2033, 2581, 2877; Lu I, *Ping-i man-chi* (*Chi-lu hui-pien* 記錄彙編 ed.), 201/16b; Cha Chi-tso, *Tsui-wei lu* (1936), *Pen-chi* 8/3a; Wang Shih-chen, *Yen-shan-t'ang pieh-chi* (late Ch'ing ed.), 31/5b; Lang Ying, *Ch'i-hsiu lei-kao* (1959), 190, 204; W. Franke, "Yü Ch'ien, Staatsmann und Kriegsminister, 1398-

1457," MS, 11 (1946), 87; D. Pokotilov, *History of the Eastern Mongols during the Ming Dynasty from 1368 to 1634*, tr. by Rudolf Löwenthal, *Addenda and Corrigenda*, by W. Franke (Chengtu and Peiping 1947 and 1949); F. W. Cleaves, "The Sino-Mongolian Edict of 1453 in the Topkapi Sarayi Müzesi," HJAS, XIII (1958), 43, pls. I–VIII; Walter Fuchs, "Der perische Fürstenname in Pekinger Edikt von 1453," OE, I (July, 1954) 26; National Palace Museum *Newsletter*, Taipei I:9 (July, 1969).

[Editors' note: It is not without interest that a Sino-Mongol edict of this emperor, dated January 8, 1453, is preserved in the Topkapi Sarayi Museum, Istanbul. It appears to be the only one of its kind discovered so far. The decree orders that eleven bolts of silk of various colors be sent to Prince Yanglirgi (alternatively: Mieh-li-er-chi) of the city of Lar, capital of the district of Lāristān, to the southeast of Fars, in southern Iran. It is reproduced in full by Frances W. Cleaves. No mention of the edict or of a mission to Iran at this time appears in the *shih-lu*.]

Wolfgang Franke

CHU Chien-ju, *see* CHU Chien-shen

CHU Chien-shen 朱見深, December 9, 1447–September 9, 1487, whose name was changed in 1457 to Chu Chien-ju 濡, was the eighth emperor of the Ming dynasty. During his life of forty years he was known as the heir apparent (1449–52, 1457–64), as the prince of I 沂王 (1452–57), and by his reign title: the Ch'eng-hua 成化 emperor. After his death he was also referred to by his temple name Hsien-tsung 憲宗, by his posthumous name Ch'un huang-ti 純皇帝, or by the name of his mausoleum Mao-ling 茂陵.

He was the eldest son of the sixth emperor, Chu Ch'i-chen (*q.v.*); his mother was Madame Chou 周, recorded in history as Empress Hsiao-su 孝肅 (1430–1504, also known by the titles Kuei-fei 貴妃, 1457–64, Empress-dowager 皇太后, 1464–87, and Empress-dowager Sheng-tz'u jen-shou 聖慈仁壽, 1487–1504). It appears that from infancy he was brought up under the care of his foster grandmother, Madame Sun 孫, the Empress Hsiao-kung 孝恭 (d. Sept. 26, 1462), second empress of the fifth emperor, Chu Chan-chi (*q.v.*). In September, 1449, when the Oirat captured his father, Chu Chien-shen, then twenty months old, was named heir apparent, while his uncle, Chu Ch'i-yü (*q.v.*), served as regent. A few days later his uncle assumed the imperial title as the seventh emperor of the dynasty. Chu Chien-shen remained as heir apparent for three more years until displaced by his uncle's own son, Chu Chien-chi (*see* Chu Ch'i-yü). In 1453 Chu Chien-chi died, and for over three years the position of heir apparent was left open, a situation that gave rise to speculation and intrigues at court. Thus Chu Chien-shen's childhood during these years could hardly have been a happy one, for he must have been made aware of his precarious position as potential pretender. It is known that he acquired the habit of stuttering (especially when uttering sibilants), possibly the result of some traumatic experience during this period of insecurity.

His fortunes changed after the *coup d'état* of February 11, 1457, whereby his father regained the throne, and he was again declared the heir apparent (March 1). In the proclamation announcing his restoration his name was given not as Chien-shen but as Chien-ju, which caused a great deal of conjecture about his identity, and no explanation about the time and reason for the change has ever been offered. Perhaps the name Chien-shen, having been chosen for him by his uncle in 1449 when Chu Ch'i-chen was taken captive, was unacceptable to his father after the *coup*. The editors of the *Ming-shih*, however, write his name as Chien-shen and state (without any foundation) that his earlier name was Chienchün 濬, a mistake that has not been questioned since the publication of the *Ming-shih pen-chi* in 1739. Of Ming and Ch'ing writers on this subject so far consulted, only Fu Wei-lin (ECCP) correctly states the change from Chien-shen to Chien-ju, as did A. C. Moule among western authors. Most others mention only the name Chien-shen. The great Ming historians, Wang Shih-chen (*q.v.*) and Chiao Hung (ECCP), both erroneously state that his name was changed from Chien-shen to Chien-chi (the name of his cousin). No other emperor's personal name has caused so much confusion. To be sure, in Ming times the taboo in respect to an emperor's personal name was not taken seriously until perhaps towards the end of the dynasty. On the other hand, for an emperor to leave so much uncertainty about his own name seems to indicate the characteristics of an introvert accustomed to be passive and non-assertive, and of one easily influenced by stronger wills.

It is said that his father, who probably noticed these characteristics, had some doubts about his fitness for the imperial role; these doubts were finally allayed by the chief grand secretary, Li Hsien (*q.v.*). When his father died (February 23, 1464), therefore, Chu Chien-shen was confirmed as the successor. During the five days before he ascended the throne, twelve men were appointed to serve as a council of regents, namely, four senior eunuchs, Liu Yung-ch'eng (*q.v.*), Hsia Shih 夏時, Fu Kung 傅恭, and Niu Yü 牛玉; two military men, Sun Chi-tsung 孫繼宗(T. 光輔, 1395-January 9, 1480, marquis of Hui-ch'ang 會昌侯, Pth. 榮襄), and Sun T'ang 孫鏜 (T. 振遠, 1392-1471, marquis of Huai-ning 懷寧侯, Pth. 武敏); and six civil officials, Li Hsien, Wang Ao 王翱, Nien Fu, P'eng Shih (*qq.v.*), Ma Ang 馬昂 (T. 景高, H. 伯顒, 1399-1476, cj 1423, Pth. 恭襄), and Ch'en Wen 陳文 (T. 安簡, H. 裝齋, 1405-68, cs 1436, Pth. 莊靖). Sun Chi-tsung (a younger brother of the emperor's foster grandmother), had since 1457 occupied the highest ceremonial position at court. Later Sun and Liu Yung-ch'eng jointly commanded the Peking guards. (Of the two men the senior eunuch had more experience in military affairs, and when he died he was even accorded a shrine.) Through these twelve and many others at court, the first half of the Ch'eng-hua

reign was considered to be one of the few enlightened periods in Ming history. Among the acts and attitudes that met with general approval may be mentioned: the rehabilitation of those unjustly punished in the preceding reigns (*see* Chu Ch'i-yü, Yü Ch'ien), the generous measures of relief to famine stricken areas, the respect for scholarship (*see* Ch'en Hsien-chang), and his attention to public affairs. Especially notable was the revival of military training of units of the Peking guard. In May, 1464, he ordered the training corps reestablished and divided into twelve divisions, known as the Shih-er-t'uan-ying 十二團營. This corps, first introduced by Yü Ch'ien in 1449, had been disbanded in 1457 when the troops returned to their original units, namely, the Wu-chün ying 五軍營 (chiefly infantry), the San-ch'ien 三千 ying (Mongol cavalry), and the Shen-chi 神機 ying (firearms brigade). As reconstructed, each training division consisted of ten thousand men drawn from all three units to learn tactical cooperation. The over-all command of these divisions, as mentioned above, was entrusted to Sun Chi-tsung and Liu Yung-ch'eng, but each division was also headed by a eunuch official, known as Chien-ch'iang nei-ch'en 監槍內臣 (palace attendant in charge of firearms), for these weapons were to be jealously guarded by the emperor's trusted personnel alone. The newly trained Peking corps took part in several successful campaigns on the northern frontiers, such as the defeat of the Mongols in 1471, 1473, and 1480, and of the Jurchen in 1467 and 1479. In civil warfare it seems that the corps, with its reputation for excessive slaughter, was so dreaded that, during the campaign against the rebels in western Shensi in 1478 (*see* Hsiang Chung), the corps was put on the alert but, on the advice of P'eng Shih, held at the capital until there was no need for its dispatch. In doing so P'eng risked his own life in order to spare the people of Shensi the disaster that assuredly would have been inflicted on them. On the other hand, a small contingent of the corps took part in the suppression of Yao tribesmen in Kwangsi (*see* Han Yung). Although in later years it was often criticized as not being up to strength, because a part was utilized as a labor force in public or private works, the corps during the early Ch'eng-hua years proved to be a fairly effective fighting force in frontier warfare.

In both civil and military affairs Chu Chien-shen, by relying on such men as Li Hsien and P'eng Shih, did fairly well. By nature he was kind, compassionate, and permissive, allowing the officials free rein. There was some dissension among the officials, especially those with regional prejudice against each other, but the situation never reached a crisis. Inside his palace, however, he was troubled several times by the conflicts among the women, which eventually gave a bad name to the latter part of his reign.

The first incident occurred on the day he ascended the throne, when a dispute arose over conferring the title of empress-dowager on his father's widow, Empress Ch'ien 錢 (1426-68). According to regulations she was automatically entitled to it. But his own mother, Madame Chou, made the inordinate claim that she herself deserved the title, for Empress Ch'ien was not only barren but also had lost the use of a leg and an eye as a result of the deprivations she suffered during the seven years she stayed by her husband at his place of confinement; for this act of fidelity she was generally regarded as worthy of praise. Yet the emperor's mother could not be denied. At the suggestion of P'eng Shih and Li Hsien, both women were made huang-t'ai-hou皇太后, but Empress Ch'ien's title had two extra characters, Tz'u-i 慈懿, preceding it. Madame Chou apparently resented this discrimination. Four years later, when Empress Ch'ien died and was to be interred in her husband's tomb, Madame Chou again showed her perversity by raising objections, asserting

that honor should be reserved for her. After insisting on this demand for four days, she was forced to yield by several hundred officials who, led by Yao K'uei (*q.v.*), wailed at the palace gate for eight hours (July 19, 1468). Even so, when she died in 1504 and the tomb was opened, it was revealed that on her order Empress Ch'ien had been buried in a separate chamber entirely sealed off. In this conflict between mother and foster mother, Chu Chien-shen let the officials voice their opinions and then secretly gave them his encouragement; outwardly, however, he acted with apparent reluctance.

It was probably this Madame Chou who wanted to celebrate the lantern festival of 1468 with elaborate decorations, including poems to be indited by Hanlin members. When three of the Hanlin scholars refused, and advised the young emperor to express his filial piety towards the two dowager-empresses by refusing to allow such frivolous activities in the light of the sufferings of the people, all three were beaten at court and demoted (*see* Chang Mou). Although they mentioned both empresses they seem to have been referring only to Madame Chou. It was to placate his mother, therefore, that the emperor dealt with the three men so harshly. Except for this, his reign was unusually free from maltreatment of officials—a commonplace under most of the other Ming emperors.

In another conflict inside his palace, which also started in 1454, he was forced to make a positive decision. This time he took the side of his mistress, Wan Kuei-fei (*q.v.*), and dethroned his empress (Wu) one month after marrying her because she had asserted her rights by giving Lady Wan a severe beating. His second empress (Wang 王) kept her place and her title too by yielding to Wan the top place in the women's quarters (*see* Wan Kuei-fei). Chu Chien-shen permitted himself to be dominated by the Lady Wan, who, seventeen years his senior, began as his nursemaid and then became his mistress. In

1466 she gave birth to his first son who died when less than a year old. Four years later the emperor had a son by another consort, who was declared heir apparent in December, 1471, but soon died also. It was general conjecture that Lady Wan had a hand in his death. Meanwhile the young emperor had an affair with a Kwangsi girl, née Chi (see Chu Yu-t'ang), probably originally a Yao captive sent to the palace about 1467. As the story goes, when it became known that she was with child, those who disliked Lady Wan concealed the girl in the quarters of the dethroned Empress Wu, where, on July 30, 1470, she gave birth to a boy. The secret was well kept for it was not until June, 1475, while the emperor was lamenting the lack of an heir, that a eunuch revealed to him the child's existence. Whereupon the boy was brought forward, and officially given the name Chu Yu-t'ang (q.v.). A month later the child's mother died under suspicious circumstances. It was evidently at this time that Chu Chien-shen began to live apart from Lady Wan, for from 1476 to 1487 the records show that five different women gave him eleven sons and six daughters, all of whom with the exception of one boy lived to maturity.

It was thus for the safety of his son that Chu Chien-shen drew away from Lady Wan in 1475, but his devotion to her remained constant to the end. He acted almost as if he were trying to compensate for his lack of attention. During the second half of his reign he seldom, if ever, interfered in her activities (often illegal) in the pursuit of wealth, such as the sale of ranks and titles, and the appointment of eunuchs to sensitive posts in the empire to acquire silver, gold, and expensive baubles for her. Her agents are known to have been active in mining in Yunnan for copper, silver, gold, and precious stones, in foreign trade and pearl gathering in Kwangtung, tax collecting in the lower Yangtze valley, and the salt monopoly. Her chief eunuch, Liang

Fang (q. v.), managed the imperial store in Peking, where outwardly innocent transactions in jewelry could serve as cover for the sale of offices. By either selling a valuable piece cheaply or purchasing an ordinary object at an exorbitant price, an expectant official could secure the appointment to a government position without going through the qualifying examinations conducted by the ministry of Personnel and other agencies concerned. This was done by the simple procedure known as ch'uan-feng 傳奉, whereby a eunuch transmitted an imperial order to the Grand Secretariat to draw up a patent appointing a certain person to an office, or posting an official to a higher one. This practice used to be limited to service personnel such as physicians, artists, carpenters, jewelers, astrologers, Taoist priests, Buddhist monks, and the like, and even they were subject to review by the ministries. After 1475, however, ch'uan-feng cases became suddenly more frequent and the appointees increased in number; sometimes Lady Wan even dictated promotions to high offices.

The notorious eunuch Wang Chih 汪直 (q. v.), who controlled the secret service in Peking from 1476 to 1480, was at first an attendant in Lady Wan's service in her palace; possibly his mistreatment of some officials under arrest was in obedience to her order as a way to intimidate the outspoken ones. When some of them attacked Wang Chih in 1477, they themselves were bested and forced out of office (see Shang Lu, Hsiang Chung). It seems that by this time only those cooperating with her or keeping silent could stay in office. From the way Chu Chien-shen warded off the attacks on Lady Wan and her eunuch henchmen, it would appear that he was not entirely guiltless but an active participant in their activities, and shared their ill-gotten gains. One of his pet statements to parry criticism was that on any matter concerning palace affairs he himself made the decisions. It was chiefly in his reign that imperially

owned farmland grew from a small holding to over two hundred thousand acres,
and by the early 16th century expanded
to sixteen times that figure. Meanwhile
powerful families received generous grants
of land too—a loss both to the rightful owners and to the national treasury.
From various family records it may be
inferred that it was about this time that
the trend of land tenure in the Soochow
area underwent a change, whereby the
powerful and wealthy began to expand
their holdings, reversing a trend started
in the early years of the Ming when such
families began to establish branches in
the national capitals where the government milked them as it wished. A case in
point is Han Yung who came from such
a Soochow family living in Peking. After
he became a high official, however, his
son began to acquire land and properties
in Soochow. When Han retired in 1474,
it was not to his place in Peking but to
his ancestral home in Soochow, safe now
for a man of his status.

As to the sale of ranks and offices
which was blamed on the eunuchs under
the control of Lady Wan, Chu Chien-shen
as indicated above cannot be excused
from responsibility. Many ch'uan-feng officials were his own favorites, such as Taoist priests, Buddhist monks, Tibetan magicians, and even a grand secretary, all
known to be pornographic or aphrodisiac
experts. When one of the eunuchs he had
sent to purchase rare items in the Soochow
area in 1483 acted so outrageously that
the local gentry and officials almost rose
up in arms, the emperor ordered the eunuch executed, remarking: that he had no
way of anticipating the excesses of the
culprit. Obviously the historical records
are incorrect in asserting that the responsibility for the evil doings in Chu Chien-
shen's reign was chiefly that of the eunuchs and Lady Wan. These people could
not have acted as they did without the
emperor's approval. As a whole, however,
the reign of Chu Chien-shen must be
regarded as one of the better periods of
Ming history.

The excesses of the eunuchs and the
secret service personnel were far outbal-
anced by the positive features of his reign
which had lasting effects. The most important accomplishment was the penetration from 1465 to 1472 into the Yao
territory in Kwangtung and Kwangsi,
which secured the valley of the West River
and some of its tributaries for transportation and settlement. Likewise the expeditions in 1465 against the Shan-tu-chang
山都掌 aborigines south of Lu-chou 瀘州,
Szechwan, eliminated a threat to transportation on the Yangtze River in that area.
The advance into the Jurchen territory in
1465 and 1479 succeeded in keeping the
Chien-chou 建州 tribesmen weak and
divided for over a hundred years until
the rise of Nurhaci (ECCP). The building
of the Great Wall for six hundred miles
along the northern border of Shensi in
1474 lessened the threat of the Mongols
at the bend of the Yellow River. These
exploits and the training of the Peking
guards marked a period of revival in
Ming military power from its lowest days
after the defeat of 1449.

Politically and culturally the Ch'eng-
hua era was apparently a transitional
one; it marks the rise of civilian domination of the military, the increase
of the power of southerners, and the
shift of the center of culture from
Kiangsi to the lower Yangtze valley. The
practice of putting reign marks on porcelain manufactured at the imperial kilns at
Ching-te-chen (see Chu Chan-chi), discontinued for some thirty years, is a notable
event, for Ch'eng-hua ware ranks among
the best in design and decoration. Of
particular importance is the development
of polychromy, known as tou-ts'ai 鬥彩
(a competition of colors), an art that has
been imitated ever since. (We read that
a hundred years later, the emperor's great-
great-grandson, Chu I-chün [q. v.], became
fond of tou-ts'ai porcelain, which he collected and ordered to be copied; this affected the rise of its market value to that of

the finest jade.)

Chu Chien-shen is known too for his calligraphy. He left a scroll depicting in color the immortal Chung K'uei (*see* Chou Ch'en), entitled "Sui-chao chia-chao" 歲朝佳兆 (Good luck on New Year's Day) in the Palace Museum collection. The date of the painting is 1481. It shows the legendary master of ghosts Chung K'uei and a gnomish ghost bearing good omens for the year, viz. sprigs of pine 栢 (for pai 百100), persimmons 柿 (for shih 事 or affairs), and a ju-i 如意 (as you wish). He is said also to have enjoyed the theater and music, and had a troupe of eunuch actors. There are several stories about a clown who satirized court events. Once he declaimed about six thousand troops when everybody knew the line should be eight thousand. When asked about the missing two thousand, he replied that they were building a house for the Protecting State Duke (Chu Yung, head of the Peking training corps). Another time on stage he feigned sleep even when someone shouted that His Majesty was on his way, but stood at once at attention when told that the senior eunuch Wang Chih had arrived.

Chu I-chün's feeling for Ch'eng-hua porcelain seems to have been a manifestation of a certain likeness between his great-great grandfather and himself. Their personalities and careers, and in particular their relations with women and eunuchs, parallel each other so closely that one may assume that Chu I-chün consciously followed the other's example. Both also had mothers who sponsored Buddhist monks. Chu Chien-shen's mother had a younger brother who probably was a mental case; he ran away from home in his youth and lived a vagrant's life, spending his nights behind an idol in a temple. He was discovered about 1460 and, after his sister became empress-dowager in 1464, was made abbot of the temple, Pao-kuo ssu 報國寺. Rebuilt in 1465 and renamed Ta-tz'u-jen 大慈仁 ssu, it is located in the southwestern part of the south city

of Peking. Chu Chien-shen wrote a commemorative essay about the temple, which was inscribed on a monument possibly still standing. The essayist, Kuei Yu-kuang (*q. v.*), in 1570 left an account about the temple, the grounds of which at that time included large tracts of land supporting hundreds of monks. More Buddhist temples seem to have been built or rebuilt in Peking during the Ch'eng-hua and Wan-li reigns than in other periods of the Ming dynasty. The five Indian-style pagodas on a fifty foot high square foundation west of Peking were built in 1473 by order of Chu Chien-shen, and he composed an essay commemorating the event. This is perhaps the only distinctly Indian-style architecture to be found in the Peking area (*see* Pandita).

After Chu Chien-shen died, his annals and selected edicts were edited under the titles *Hsien-tsung shih-lu* 實錄 and *Hsien-tsung pao-hsün* 寶訓, respectively. He is known to have left a collection of poems in 4 *chüan*, compiled in 1478, which seems to have vanished. Early in 1483 he wrote the preface to the *Wen-hua ta-hsün* 文華大訓, a compilation of instructions to the heir apparent. In 1473 he sponsored the printing of *Tzu-chih t'ung-chien kang-mu* 資治通鑑綱目, 60 *ch.*, by Chu Hsi (1130–1200), and ordered the compilation of its continuation, *Hsü 續 Tzu-chih t'ung-chien kang-mu*, 27 *ch.*, both being printed in 1476. He also is credited with editing revisions of a Yüan dynasty anthology of essays, entitled *Ku-wen ching ts'ui* 古文精粹, 10 *ch.*, in 1475. It was published by the palace printing plant (Ching-ch'ang 經廠); a copy is preserved in the National Central Library, Taipei.

Chu Chien-shen had two grandsons who became emperors, Chu Hou-chao (*q. v.*), the only son of Chu Yu-t'ang, and Chu-Hou-ts'ung (*q.v.*). The latter was the son of Chu Yu-yüan (*see* Chu Hou-ts'ung), whose mother was Lady Shao 邵, a native of Hangchow. She was purchased by a eunuch who taught her to read and write and to recite hundreds of T'ang poems.

She became a favorite of Chu Chien-shen and gave birth to three of his sons: Chu Yu-yüan in July, 1476, Chu Yu-lun 倫 in November, 1478 (d. Dec. 3, 1501), and Chu Yu-yün 橒 in June, 1481 (d. 1507).

The portraits of Chu Chien-shen show him to be rather robustly built with a full face, bright eyes, big ear lobes, a well-clipped moustache, and a handsome beard. The same central Asian features may be remarked on portraits of his father and his predecessors, back to his great-great-grandfather. His successor, Chu Yu-t'ang, although bearded, looks quite delicate. All of his other descendants seem to be much less barbate and of the southern type.

Bibliography

1/13/1a, 14/7b, 104/16a, 108/5b, 113/13a, 119/16b, 121/12b, 300/8a, 304/12b, 307/8a; Fu Wei-lin, *Ming-shu*, ch. 10, 53; MSL (1964), Hsien-tsung; KC (1958), Hsien-tsung; Portraits in *Palace Museum Weekly*, nos. 144 (May 25, 1932), 379 (August 25, 1934), 380, and painting 426; Chiao Hung, *Huang Ming jen-wu k'ao* (1595), 1/7a, 14b; *Kwangsi t'ung-chih* (1599, reproduced 1965), 1/10b; Wang Shih-chen, *Yen-shan-t'ang pieh-chi* (1965), 1367; P'eng Shih, *Pi-chi(Chi-lu hui-pien*, 1968 ed.); Shen Te-fu, *Wan-li yeh-hu pien* (1959), 25, 73, 81, 652, 683, 856; *The Arts of the Ming Dynasty*, London, 1959; S. W. Bushell, *Chinese Art, I* (London, 1924), 55; Lady David, "The Ch'eng-hua Treasures," *National Palace Museum Quarterly*, II:2 (October, 1967).

Chaoying Fang

CHU Chih-fan 朱之蕃 (T. 元介 (价), 元升, H. 蘭嵎), 1564–?, official, poet, calligrapher, and a painter of minor note, was a native of Nanking. His ancestral home was in Shih-p'ing 茌平, Shantung, but the family had transferred their residence to Nanking in the early days of the Ming dynasty when Emperor Chu Yüan-chang carried out the policy of population resettlement. His father, Chu I 衣 (T. 正伯, H. 杜村, cj 1564), who served as magistrate of several districts in both northern and southern China, was also a poet and art collector. Chu Chih-fan became a *chin-*

shih in 1595, and subsequently topped the list in the palace examination, capturing the title of *chuang-yüan* 狀元. He was then appointed senior compiler in the Hanlin Academy. In 1605 he was sent to Korea as an envoy. Here his fame as a calligrapher spread far and wide. Many Koreans solicited his writings and gave him presents of ginseng and sable. Chu Chih-fan sold all these to buy paintings, pieces of old calligraphy, and other objets d'art. In 1609 he received a promotion in the Hanlin Academy. Two years later he held the concurrent post of junior supervisor of instruction and helped in the compilation of the imperial genealogy. He was transferred to Nanking to be vice minister of Rites in the auxiliary capital. After the death of his mother, he lived in retirement at home, where he kept a fine garden, and enjoyed his rich collection of antiques. As he is known to have written a postscript dated 1624 for *Chin-ling ku-chin t'u k'ao* 金陵古今圖考 by Ch'en I 陳沂 (T. 魯南, H. 石亭, 1469–1538), he must have lived beyond his sixtieth year. His calligraphy followed the style of Chao Meng-fu (1254–1322), with some adaptations which he took over from the writing of Yen Chen-ch'ing (709–85) and Wen Cheng-ming (*q.v.*). According to report he could write ten thousand characters a day, small ones of the size of flyspecks and large ones of 1 1/2 feet square. His calligraphy may easily be found in publications of Ming date where prefaces were printed in his handwriting. He never failed to respond in verse when his colleagues presented him with a poem. His paintings of landscapes imitated those of Mi Fu (1051–1107) and Wu Chen (1280–1354), and of bamboos those of Su Shih (1037–1101).

Chu Chih-fan's literary works are entitled *Feng-shih kao* 奉使稿, 4 *ch.*, *Nan-huan tsa-chu* 南還雜著, 1 *ch.*, *Chi-sheng shih* 紀勝詩, 1 *ch.*, and *Lo hua shih* 落花詩, 1 *ch.* Another, the *Lan-yü shih-wen chi* 蘭嵎詩文集 (Collected works of prose and poetry) may have included some or all of the above mentioned items. He also compiled a collection of lyric poems, entitled *Chiang-nan ch'un tz'u* 江南春詞, printed in 1891 in the *Su-hsiang shih* 粟香室 *ts'ung-shu*. His anthology of Ming poetry known as *Ming pai-chia shih-hsüan* 明百家 詩選, 34 *ch.*, a selection of the contributions of 318 Ming poets, is criticized by the editors of the Imperial Catalogue. A book of his verses on Nanking, the *Chin-ling t'u-yung* 金陵圖詠, 1 *ch.*, contains illustrations drawn by Lu Shou-pai 陸壽柏, depicting forty scenic spots in Nanking. All the poems were printed in the image of Lu's own handwriting. Chu wrote poems frequently, but Ch'ien Ch'ien-i and Chu I-tsun (both in ECCP) concurred in the criticism that his verses were overly long and a little trite.

The *Feng-shih kao*, originally entitled *Feng-shih Ch'ao-hsien kao* 奉使朝鮮稿 (Mission to Korea), tells among other things about his emotions in traveling through the pass at Shan-hai-kuan, about the repair of roads and canals in Liaotung, about a shrine built for a certain General Yu 尤, and includes as well the poems of a vice minister in Korea, Yu Hae 柳楷, and his essays composed at the palace examination of 1595. Some of his impressions about Liaotung were later considered seditious and were ordered extracted and burned a century and a half after his time.

One of his younger brothers, Chu Chih-shih 之士 (T. 蘭室), was also known as a painter. His son, Chu Ts'ung-i 從義 (T. 無外), entered the Imperial Academy through the yin privilege, and rose to be intendent of the Wen-chou 溫州 and T'ai-chou 台州 circuits in Chekiang.

Bibliography

40/58/1a; 64/庚 18/1a; 84/丁上 /87b; 86/16/20b; SK (1930), 179/13a, 193/4a; KC (1958), 5048; *Chiang-ning-fu chih* (1880), 40/4b, 54/12b; Ma Tsung-ho 馬宗霍, *Shu-lin tsao-chien* 書林藻鑑, 11/30b: Ch'en Tso-lin 陳作霖, *Chin-ling t'ung-chuan* 金陵通傳 (1904), 19/8b; T'ang Pin-yin 湯賓尹 (cs 1595), *Chuang-yüan t'u-k'ao* 明狀元圖考 (1875), 下 /64a; Yao Chin-yüan (1957), 21; L. of C. *Catalogue of Rare Books* (1957), 319, 592.

Liu Lin-sheng and Lienche Tu Fang

CHU Ch'üan 朱權 (H. 大明奇士, 臞仙, 涵虛子, 丹邱先生), May 27, 1378–October 12, 1448, prince and man of letters, was the seventeenth son of the first emperor and his consort, née Yang 楊. In 1391 he received the title prince of Ning 寧王 and in 1393 took up residence at his establishment at Ta-ning 大寧 (east of present Jehol city). Ta-ning was at that time an important border town with a garrison of reportedly eighty thousand soldiers, and the seat of the Ta-ning area branch military commission, strategically situated to guard against the Mongols of that region.

In 1399, during the critical months at the beginning of the rebellion of Chu Ti (*q.v.*), Chu Ch'üan was summoned by imperial edict to Nanking; he failed to comply, however, staying on at Ta-ning. By an adroit ruse Chu Ti captured the city, thereby greatly reinforcing his rebel army, especially with Mongol horsemen. Ta-ning and the area north of the Great Wall were then abandoned to the Mongols, and the military commission by that name was relocated at Paoting. Chu Ch'üan and his whole household were moved to Peiping where, on behalf of the prince of Yen, he occasionally drafted summons to war against the reigning emperor, their nephew Chu Yün-wen (*q.v.*). In 1402, after Chu Ti had won the final battle and had ascended the imperial throne, Chu Ch'üan requested investiture in another fief. After being refused Soochow and Hangchow, he finally received Nanchang in Kiangsi province. During the Yung-lo reign (1403–24) he generally kept aloof from political affairs and occupied himself with study and the writing of books. He also played the lute and cultivated flowers and bamboos. In the Hsüan-te period he several times incurred the displeasure of the emperor,

Chu Chan-chi (*q.v.*), by his unreasonable requests and extravagant behavior, and was repeatedly rebuked. In his old age he became increasingly interested in Taoism, alchemy, and the means of attaining immortality. He was canonized as Hsien 獻. Chu played a role of some importance in the accession of Chu Ti, though mainly in a passive way. He is, however, known to posterity principally as a man of letters. Well versed in Taoism and Buddhism, he was also at home in the Classics, in history, and in literature (especially drama), as well as in astronomy and medicine. In addition he was expert in making artistic censers and inkslabs. During his residence in Nanchang he contributed to the cultural elevation of the region and furthered the reprinting of rare books.

Chu was a voluminous and many-sided author. Altogether some fifty titles of works ascribed to him (including his lyrical dramas) are known. The subject matter ranges from the Classics and history to phonetics and literary criticism. To six of them the editors of the *Ssu-k'u* catalogue devoted descriptive notes without including them in the Imperial Library. Only ten works of his have received a wider circulation by their inclusion in *ts'ung-shu* or by being reprinted in modern editions. They are for the most part in the field of literature. In all probability his most important work and the best known is *T'ai-ho cheng-yin p'u* 太和正音譜, 2 *ch.*, which treats of the Northern lyrical drama (tsa-chü 雜劇), including short lyrical pieces (san-ch'ü 散曲). The first chapter contains, *inter alia*, a list of titles of 678 lyrical dramas by authors belonging to the Yüan period and the beginning of the Ming period. The last part of the first chapter and the whole of the second chapter are taken up by ch'ü-p'u 曲譜 (a tune book) of the Northern drama, the first one of its kind; 335 ch'ü-p'ai 牌 (lyrical melodies), arranged according to twelve basic tunes (kung-tiao 宮調), each exemplified by a fragment of an existing drama; the tone of each character is carefully indicated. This *ch'ü-p'u* is by far the most important section of the book. The work was completed in 1398 and printed soon after; two manuscript facsimiles (ying-hsieh pen 影寫本), each of a different edition of that time, have been preserved. The most recent critical edition (1959) is contained in Volume III of *Chung-kuo ku-tien hsi-ch'ü lun-chu chi-ch'eng* 中國古典戲曲論著集成.

Two other works of his on drama, *Wu-t'ou chi-yün* 務頭集韻 and *Ch'iung-lin ya-yün* 瓊林雅韻, may not be extant. Two of the twelve tsa-chü which he wrote have been preserved in the rich collection of plays of the famous Ch'ing bibliophile Ch'ien Tseng (ECCP). In 1941 they were included in the collection *Ku-pen Yüan Ming tsa-chü* 孤本元明雜劇 (reprinted in 1957), and are entitled *Ch'ung-mo tzu tu-pu ta-lo-t'ien* 冲漠子獨步大羅天 and *Cho Wen-chün ssu-pen Hsiang-ju* 卓文君私奔相如. The first is about the attainment of immortality by the recluse Ch'ung-mo tzu (probably Chu himself) and is indicative of the author's strong Taoistic leanings. The theme of the second drama is the popular story of the celebrated Han poet Ssu-ma Hsiang-ju (d. 118 B.C.) and his elopement with the rich widow Cho Wen-chün, a favorite subject of Chinese dramatic literature.

The well-known lengthy or Southern lyrical drama (ch'uan-ch'i 傳奇), *Ching-ch'ai chi* 荊釵記, has been ascribed to Chu Ch'üan instead of to the author to whom it is traditionally credited, K'o Chiu-ssu 柯九思 (T. 敬仲, H. 丹邱生, 1312–65) by the famous scholar and literary critic Wang Kuo-wei (BDRC); his view has been accepted by other prominent scholars such as Cheng Chen-to (BDRC). As long as there is no more conclusive evidence for this ascription than the *hao* both men have in common (丹邱 or 丹丘), it would seem safer to leave the question of the authorship of the *Ching-ch'ai chi* temporarily open.

A music book for the lute which

Chu wrote, entitled *Shen-ch'i mi-p'u* 神奇祕譜, 3*ch.*, has survived in Ming edition of which there exists a photolithographic reprint of 1956. The following works listed under his name have been included in various collections: *Ch'ü-hsien shen-yin* 瞿仙神隱, 4 *ch.*, on agriculture; *Fen-hsiang ch'i-yao* 焚香七要, 1 *ch.*, on burning incense; *Ti-li cheng-yen* 地理正言, 1 *ch.*, on geomancy; *T'ien-huang chih-tao t'ai-ch'ing yü-ts'e* 天皇至道太清玉册, 8*ch.*, on Taoism, in *Hsü Tao-tsang* 續道藏; and *Keng-ho chung-feng shih-yün* 賡和中峯詩韻, 1 *ch.*, a collection of his poems. A collection of his kung-tz'u 宮詞 (palace poems) has been incorporated in the *Chieh-yüeh-shan fang hui-ch'ao* 借月山房彙鈔. One work of his, entitled *Yüan shih mi-shu* 原始祕書, 10 *ch.*, sharply criticized by the *Ssu-k'u* editors, was put on the prohibited list in the 18th century. It seems not to have survived.

His interests reached also into the field of medicine and chemistry. About the year 1421 he published the *Keng-hsin yü-ts'e* 庚辛玉册, a description of natural products, such as metals and minerals, used in alchemy and in the pharmacopoeia. (Unfortunately this work seems to have disappeared.) He was responsible too, it appears, for an illustrated record of 168 foreign countries and places entitled *I-yü t'u-chih* 異域圖志, completed about 1430, but not printed until 1489; reprinted 1609. (A rare copy of the original edition is in the Cambridge University Library.) As some of the places named and some of the animals pictured (such as the zebra and giraffe) were unknown to the Chinese prior to the Yung-lo reign, it seems quite likely that the author was beholden to an informant from the staff of the eunuch Cheng Ho (*q.v.*).

Chu is not the only instance of a Ming prince who was interested in drama and even wrote plays himself. Another example is Chu Yu-tun (*q.v.*). Chu Ti is reported to have invited dramatists to his princely residence in Peking and to have treated them generously.

Because he survived his eldest son,

Chu P'an-shih 盤烒, Chu Ch'üan was succeeded by his eldest grandson, Chu Tien-p'ei 奠培 (1418-91), who achieved some distinction as a poet. The princedom of Ning was abolished in 1519 after the rebellion of Chu Ch'üan's great-great-grandson, Chu Ch'en-hao (*see* Wang Shou-jen).

Bibliography

1/102/5b, 117/14a; 3/109/6b; 5/1/70a; 61/87/5a; MSL (1963), Ying-tsung, 3280; KC(1958), 561, 610, 1747; TSCC (1885-88), XI: 99/12a; *Chung-kuo ku-tien hsi-ch'ü lun-chu chi-ch'eng*, III (1959), 3; Wang Chi-lieh 王季烈, *Ku-pen Yüan Ming tsa-chü t'i-yao* 提要 (1957), 18a; Fu Hsi-hua 傅惜華, *Ming-tai tsa-chü ch'üan-mu* 明代雜劇全目 (1958), 49; SK (1930), 52/9b, 89/3b, 111/11b, 137/7b, 147/10b, 200/8b; L. Carrington Goodrich, *Literary Inquisition of Ch'ien-lung* (Baltimore, 1935), 87; A. C. Moule, "An Introduction to the I Yü T'u Chih," TP 27 (1930), 179; J. Needham, *Science and Civilization in China*, III (Cambridge, England, 1959), 512, IV: 2 (1965), 570, 3 (1971) 493.

D. R. Jonker

CHU Hou-chao 朱厚照, November 14, 1491-April 20, 1521, was the tenth emperor of the Ming dynasty. During his lifetime he was first known as the heir apparent (1492-1505), and on his assumption of the throne (June 19, 1505) as the Cheng-te emperor. Following his death he came to be called by his temple name Wu-tsung 武宗, by his posthumous name I huang-ti 毅皇帝, or by the name of his tomb K'ang-ling 康陵. He was the eldest son of Emperor Chu Yu-t'ang (*q.v.*) and Empress Chang 張. It was rumored, however, that the empress had appropriated as her own the new-born baby from a certain consort, but this gossip has never been substantiated. Owing to the fact that for three reigns the empresses had not provided heirs to the throne and that the boy comported himself well, the emperor naturally took a liking to him. On occasions of imperial tours he always had the boy accompany him. Later, when he noticed his son's aptitude for riding and archery, he looked on with approval. In all likelihood the father probably spoiled the child (*see* Chu Yu-t'ang). The day before he died, he summoned the members of the Grand Secretariat, Liu Chien, Li Tung-yang, and Hsieh Ch'ien (*qq.v.*), and bade them serve his successor well. He remarked that the heir apparent was an intelligent youth (he was then not yet fourteen) but at the same time one who loved ease and pleasure; so he urged his ministers to guide him in the proper way.

In contrast to his father, who exercised imperial prerogatives in moderation, who saw to it that the power delegated to others was not abused, and who was always attentive to his duty, Chu Hou-chao refused to concern himself with state affairs. He had other interests, however. Besides riding, archery, and hunting, he enjoyed music; he loved to compose songs and to sing; this resulted in better music for the court. He liked playing the part of a merchant with his eunuchs; as a consequence a number of royal shops came to be established and managed by eunuchs. He doted on all kinds of entertainment: wrestling, acrobatics, magic, fireworks, and the like. His was a restless spirit, repelled by the dominant orthodox philosophy of the officials of the time. He would be the last man to be a stickler for rules, rituals, and ceremonies expected of a ruler. The didactic, high-sounding remonstrances of his ministers and officials he abhorred, but the obsequious coaxing and entreaty of the eunuchs, some of whom had served him from his childhood days, delighted him. One day, after an imperial lecture session, he complained about the verbosity of the lecturer. As a rule in these first years, he tried to shy away from court audiences and official discourses on Confucian themes.

Alarmed by the behavior of the young emperor, a group of high-ranking ministers, headed by Liu Chien and Hsieh Ch'ien, saw the need for action. They put the blame for his improper conduct on those eunuchs who waited on him, especially the so-called Eight Tigers or the Eight Group, viz. Liu Chin, Ku Ta-yung, Chang Yung (*qq.v.*), Kao Feng 高鳳, Ma Yung-ch'eng 馬永成, Wei Pin 魏彬, Ch'iu Chü 丘聚, and Lo Hsiang 羅祥. Allied with a few other eunuchs, Liu Chien and Hsieh Ch'ien insisted not only on the removal of the eight men but even on their execution, and refused to retreat from this demand. They were apparently unaware that Liu Chin had already assumed command of the guards and that the eight men also had allies among certain ministers and officials, one of whom, Chiao Fang (*q.v.*), had turned informer. The young emperor was at first shocked; then, when assured that, if placed in positions of trust, the eight eunuchs could meet with the threat, he sided with them and demoted and exiled the several rival eunuchs who had been allies of the Liu-Hsieh group. Now Liu Chin was promoted to be the chief eunuch in charge of the secretarial section of the directorate of ceremonial, while Ma Yung-ch'eng and Ku Ta-yung were given control of the Eastern and Western depots respectively. Liu Chien and Hsieh Ch'ien were then compelled to retire, and some other high ranking ministers also took their leave. Li Tung-yang remained in the Grand Secretariat to be joined by Chiao Fang and others amenable to the new powerful eunuch group in the palace.

From October, 1506, to September, 1510, the eunuch-official alliance under Liu Chin dominated the court. Not being being well educated, Liu had to rely on such able men as Chang Ts'ai 張綵 (cs 1490; d. Novmber 17, 1510) for the operation of the government. Conventional historians have often bitterly criticized Liu and his allies. But it is well to point out that Liu and his group did try to carry out reforms to arrest the deteriorating conditions of central authority, to improve administrative efficiency, and to put a stop to the growing self-serving attitude of the officials at large. The reforms, in fact, preceded, and may be compared favorably with, those launched under the leadership of Chang Chü-cheng (q.v.) about seventy years later. Unfortunately it was a eunuch who initiated them and this fact naturally disturbed the majority of tradition-minded government officials. The conduct of Liu and his allies and, indeed, of their policies, moreover, were subject to criticism.

While Liu Chin took care of state matters for him, the young monarch could spend his time as he pleased in the search for excitement. It is said that one day when Chu Hou-chao was amusing himself, Liu Chin presented state papers for his study and signature. Much put out, he scolded Liu and told him that it was the eunuch's duty to handle such matters for him. From then on, it is reported, Liu did not consult the emperor on state affairs. Now completely free, the emperor could enjoy his pleasures in a newly built section of living quarters called the Pao-fang (Leopard House, see Sayyid Ḥusain), where he was happily surrounded by sycophant eunuchs, military commanders, musicians, lama monks, and beautiful girls. In the early years of his reign, two men, Ch'ien Ning (see Sayyid Ḥusain) and Tsang Hsien 臧賢, were given special imperial favor. Ch'ien, a child of very humble origin, had been sold to Ch'ien Neng 錢能, a eunuch of the previous reign, and had become the latter's favorite, and hence adopted Ch'ien as his family name. Upon the death of his patron, he had been given the post of company commander of the Embroidered-uniform Guard. Through his service under Liu Chin, he had come to wait on the emperor. He was strong and skilled in archery, could pull the bow with either hand, and hence became an imperial favorite. The emperor adopted him and gave him the imperial surname, often hobnobbing with him, and, when drunk, using his body as a pillow. Tsang Hsien, an actor himself and also a deputy director of the office of music, won the imperial favor because of his musical talent. Since the two men had

ready access to the emperor, they became influential personages in the eyes of government officials and office seekers, a great number of whom flocked to their doors for favors.

Like his grandfather, Chu Chien-shen (q.v.), Chu Hou-chao became attracted to Lamaism. From the time of his accession, he showed an unflagging interest in that religion. He treated the Tibetan monks with partiality: he not only built new temples inside the Forbidden City but also continually conferred such high titles as imperial advisors on, and gave material rewards to, their leaders. He learned to chant the Lamaist scriptures and, sometimes donning Tibetan garb himself, presided at religious ceremonies. Once he initiated some palace women as nuns. For the burial service of his grandmother in 1518, he led the Lama monks in performing the rite before the start of the funeral procession.

The young monarch's interest in certain women began early. At the age of fifteen, one year after his accession, he officially took as empress the daughter of a vice commissioner-in-chief, née Hsia 夏, and also two girls as consorts. But his sexual desires were too strong to be confined to his official living quarters. In the Leopard House, under the influence of various self-seekers, he indulged in carnal pleasure. At the suggestion of Yü Yung 于永, a vice commissioner-in-chief of the Embroidered-uniform Guard, who was of central Asian descent, he summoned to his quarters Uighur dancers. One day, after some drinking, he ordered Yü to fetch his own daughter, reportedly beautiful. Yü instead brought in a neighbor's daughter and, for fear of discovery, retired from office in favor of his son. As time went on, wherever he went, the emperor's henchmen would search far and wide for beautiful girls. He sometimes demanded the concubines of his commanders, and even became enamored of a commander's younger sister who was not only married but also pregnant;

once he went on board a boat to snatch a concubine from an official; he had a troop of prostitutes paraded before him for his inspection. Shortly before his death he desired Liu Niang-niang (*see* Chiang Pin), the wife of a musician of a princely household. His depravity shocked the ordinary neo-Confucian believer, yet ironically enough, he has been immortalized in folkore for his interest in the opposite sex. The emperor also acquired the habit of heavy drinking. It was open knowledge that often he became intoxicated, sometimes for days at a time; his retinue always had his favorite potables ready. Some critics have conjectured that his attendants were partly responsible for his condition because, with him in a drunken state, they could do as they pleased to feather their own nests.

In 1510 he was roused from his life of debauchery, for in May Prince Chu Chih-fan (*see* Yang T'ing-ho), whose fief was in Ning-hsia, launched a rebellion. An ambitious man, the prince thought to avail himself of the opportunity afforded by the dissipations of the young emperor and also by the mounting opposition to Liu Chin, who was having trouble over his reforms. In only eighteen days, however, the commander of Ning-hsia, Ch'iu Yüeh (*see* Ch'iu Luan), succeeded in putting down the uprising and capturing the prince. Despite the quick suppression, the rebellion provided the chance for Liu Chin's foes to start a conspiracy against him. This time it was another member of the clique of eight, Chang Yung, who, allied with the officials headed by Yang I-ch'ing (*q.v.*), succeeded in outwitting Liu. The emperor appointed Chang to supervise the armed forces (under Yang) sent to pacify the Ning-hsia region. Immediately upon his return, following the strategy devised by Yang, Chang charged that because of the Ning-hsia incident, Liu Chin had been hatching a plot against the person of the emperor. Liu was thrown into prison, and finally executed in September, 1510.

Soon after the removal of Liu and his collaborators, the government had to deal with the spread of banditry in a few northern provinces. Beginning in November of the same year, outlaws under the ringleaders Liu Liu, Liu Ch'i, and Chao Sui (for all three *see* Yang T'ing-ho), and others, infested the regions of Pei-Chihli, Shantung, and Honan. They seldom remained in one place, and wherever they went they recruited the poor and malcontent to swell their numbers or forced the innocent to march in front of their regulars against the imperial troops. At first the government endeavored to stop them whenever they appeared, but city after city fell, and local officials and officers often fled or surrendered with the populace. The pacification campaign dragged on until the government found it necessary to send for frontier troops from such strategic northern regions as Hsüan-fu, Tatung, and Liaotung to help in suppressing the banditry. When the government at last tightened the ring around them, the rebels spilled over into the regions of Shansi, Hukuang, Kiangsi, and the lower Yangtze valley. The dispersal further weakened the rebel forces and they collapsed in September, 1512.

During the middle years of the reign there were also bandit troubles in other parts of the empire. In the region of Szechwan, brigandage first flared up in 1508. In 1509 some outlaw groups swelled to one hundred thousand strong, threatening not only the entire province but also Hukuang. The government forces succeeded in having them contained mainly in Szechwan and finally suppressed in 1514. Besides, the roving bandits in the hilly area of southern Kiangsi stubbornly resisted government efforts at pacification. Brigandage was first reported in 1511 and then different groups erupted one after another. With the appointment of Wang Shou-jen (*q.v.*) as governor of southern Kiangsi, the region was at last completely pacified in 1518.

Throughout his reign Chu Hou-chao conferred special favor and trust on the eunuch group. They gave intelligence and police reports directly to the emperor; they were sent as imperial deputies with supervisory status over the army in its task of frontier fighting and the suppression of internal rebellions; they were also dispatched to oversee not only such agencies as those which manufactured silk goods and porcelain wares for the court, but also regional governments. For their services, the emperor was more than generous in his rewards. A goodly number of the eunuchs' relatives were granted titles of nobility. For instance, for their part in the suppression of the bandits in Pei-Chihli, the younger brother of Ku Ta-yung and the nephew of Lu An 陸闇 were each given the title of earl. On the relatives of Ma Yung-ch'eng alone he bestowed over ninety offices.

The Liu Chin incident and troubles with bandits failed completely to jolt Chu Hou-chao to his senses. He continued his usual carefree ways. Ever since his accession, he had loved to watch the display of lanterns made in different shapes and sizes. Every year he spent a large sum of money on them. In 1514 Prince Chu Ch'en-hao (*see* Wang Shou-jen) presented several hundred different lanterns of novel design and even sent expert workmen to the palace to erect them. One night the Ch'ien-ch'ing Palace 乾清宮 burned to the ground. Even when the fire was raging at its fiercest, the emperor still wanted to go over to the Leopard House. On the way there, he looked back and laughingly exclaimed, "What a magnificent display of fireworks!"

The internal events above mentioned did affect him to a degree, for they directed his interests into a new channel. Once a bandit group ravaged the metropolitan province and even threatened the capital. Now he began to take a strong interest in military affairs and came to admire those fighting in the campaign against outlaws. He was particularly impressed by Chiang Pin (*q.v.*), a man of remarkable

physique and then (1511) a local commander of Tatung, who reportedly continued fighting even after being struck by three arrows. He generously bestowed favor on whatever able-bodied young officers attracted him. On one occasion he made one hundred twenty-seven men his adopted sons and conferred on them the imperial family name. After the suppression of the rebels in the northern provinces he retained the frontier detachments in the capital area. As the metropolitan soldiers were not well trained, he ordered the system of rotating frontier troops for garrison duty in the Peking region. He showed Commanders Chiang Pin, Hsü T'ai 許泰, Shen Chou (*see* Chiang Pin), and Liu Hui 劉暉 special favors and their men were called by others the Wai-ssu-chia 外四家 (army of the four frontier commands). He himself led a group of eunuchs trained in the art of fighting. Day in and day out he drilled them inside the palace; time and again he paraded them for inspection, and the noise of the drilling and of explosive devices could often be heard far and wide.

His interests in military matters grew. He came to enjoy martial pomp, and liked to dress in military costume, and see civilian officials don it too. At that time the military personnel all wore a yellow mesh-like armor which became the vogue of the day. Even civilians who dressed in silk or embroidered silk clothes would put on the armor to be in fashion. As headgear the officers wore sunshade hats adorned with one to three large blue goose plumes. When the minister of War, Wang Ch'iung (*q. v.*), was given a one-plumed hat, he considered it a signal honor. The emperor also ordered the construction of 162 luxurious yurts, as he enjoyed camping. One time, when he was on his way back to the capital from the frontier, the officials were given special silk material to make new court costumes, together with a special headgear to wear for his welcome. He kept them waiting until evening when, in the light thrown from the torches placed between the spears, he appeared in uniform, wearing a sword, and astride a chestnut mount. To the grand secretaries who were waiting on him, he even boasted that he had personally decapitated a barbarian.

Chiang Pin has usually been blamed for enticing the young ruler to tour the north and northwest frontier between August, 1517, and March, 1519. Since there was a keen rivalry between Chiang and Ch'ien Ning, Chiang tried to monopolize the emperor's attention and hence persuaded him to make the trip. Once the latter had reached the frontier he was fascinated by the novel experience. He began to establish his headquarters in Hsüan-fu and ordered the government to appropriate a large sum of money for the building of a mansion for that purpose and also moved to the new quarters the things he needed from the Leopard House. When he had to return to the capital, he began to miss his new home in Hsüan-fu. While he was still on the frontier in October, 1517, Batu Möngke (*q. v.*), leading 50,000 Mongol horsemen, unexpectedly raided the area, where they were met by the imperial forces. Though nearly defeated, the emperor personally led his army when the Mongols withdrew. Notwithstanding more losses on the imperial side than on the enemy's he and his generals claimed a victory. A large number of officers and troops were rewarded, and for their part Chiang Pin and Hsü T'ai received the titles of earl.

In 1518 Chu Hou-chao conferred on himself the title of supreme commander of military affairs charged with the task of touring the northern frontier and the suppression of barbarians and also with the pacification of rebels in Honan, Shansi, and the two metropolitan areas. Later in the same year he added to his titles that of duke of Chen-kuo 鎮國公 with an annual emolument of 5,000 *tan* of grain. Then in the last part of the year he started his journey to the northwestern part of Shensi before returning to the capital in March, 1519.

The northern tours whetted the emperor's appetite for more. When news of his desires to travel to the southeastern part of the empire came to light, people at court were disturbed; they worried not only for the safety of his person, but also about peace and order in the empire. When he became adamant about it, a large number of officials memorialized against the plan, to his annoyance. More than one hundred forty officials received punishments for antagonizing him: they were flogged, then were either thrown into prison, or pilloried, or made to kneel before the palace all day for five days; a considerable number were demoted to regional posts. At least fourteen people died soon after the flogging. All this seems to have dampened his enthusiasm for the tour which might not have materialized had it not been for the rebellion in July, 1519, of Prince Chu Ch'en-hao. The prince had long been ambitious, especially when he saw that the emperor was in ill repute throughout the land. With his wealth the prince had cultivated his own influence in the inner court, and in the central and local governments. Among those whom he had bought or bribed were several eunuchs including the deceased Liu Chin, as well as Minister of War Lu Wan 陸完 (T. 全卿, H. 水村, 1458-1526, cs 1487), and General Ch'ien Ning. In later years, as Chu Hou-chao had no issue of his own, the prince had been eager to have his eldest son named the heir apparent but without success. Because of his vainglorious and overbearing conduct, the court was about to reprimand him. Apprehending severe punishment he rebelled. He had completely miscalculated the situation. In about forty days (July 10-August 20, 1519) he ended up as the prisoner of Wang Shou-jen.

The rebellion revived the emperor's interest in the southern tour. He and his entourage, with Chiang Pin serving as his deputy, left the capital on September 15, 1519. Ch'ien Ning, Tsang Hsien, and others, having been exposed as the prince's allies, were either thrown into prison or punished in other ways. Chiang Pin became the most influential man, for he directed the officers of the Eastern depot and the Embroidered-uniform Guard. The eunuch, Chang Yung, was also dispatched southward in the capacity of chief military adviser and charged with investigating the rebel group's property. It has been reported that some of the military commanders and eunuchs strove to lay claim to achievements that rightly belonged to Wang Shou-jen and his colleagues, and that some of them even suggested to the emperor that the prince be set free so that the emperor himself might have the satisfaction of taking him captive. Wang Shou-jen apparently had a staunch sponsor in Wang Ch'iung who had gotten along well with the military commanders and also found Chang Yung reasonable to deal with. Consequently, Wang Shou-jen handed over to the latter all the prisoners from the prince on down, thus managing to avoid confrontation with the ambitious commanders and eunuchs.

In the meantime the emperor had enjoyed his trip southward, taking the route along the Grand Canal and arriving in Nanking in mid-January, 1520. On the way he issued an order forbidding people to raise hogs, as the word for hog had the same pronunciation as the imperial surname. One may also conjecture that certain eunuchs, or frontier military commanders of the Islamic faith, might have influenced him in the matter. In Nanking he sojourned until September 23 when he began his return trip northward. Before his departure he formally accepted the captive rebels—to complete the mission he had set out to accomplish. On the way back, while he was fishing in Ch'ing-chiang-p'u 清江浦 (in what is Huai-yin-hsien 淮陰縣 today), his boat capsized but he was pulled out of the water by his attendants. He became ill and was worse when he arrived in Peking in mid-January, 1521.

A few days later, when he was performing a ceremony to Heaven in the southern suburb, he spat blood and fainted. He lingered on for three months and passed away in the Leopard House.

Chu Hou-chao died without heir. Consequently the empress dowager and the Grand Secretariat headed by Yang T'ing-ho decided to select Chu Hou-ts'ung (q. v.) as his successor. At the same time the situation in the capital was tense, as Chiang Pin and other military commanders still controlled the troops there. The people worried especially about Chiang, who was suspected of having sinister designs. Allied with a eunuch group, Yang and his colleagues succeeded in quietly taking Chiang and his allies into custody. During the reign of the new emperor, almost all of Chu Hou-chao's favorite eunuchs and commanders were punished, either by being degraded or exiled, or both. First Ch'ien Ning, and then Chiang Pin, together with their sons (with the exception of Chiang's youngest), and several others were executed. Reportedly, Chiang Pin's property, confiscated at this time, included 70 chests of gold, 2,200 chests of silver, and other treasures. Naturally all were charged with having contributed to the disreputable conduct of the deceased emperor.

It was during the last years of Chu Hou-chao's reign that the Portuguese envoy Tomé Pires (q. v.) arrived with the intent of establishing relations with China. Pires came with Huo-che Ya-san (Hōja Asan, see Pires) from Malacca. Through Chiang Pin, Huo-che Ya-san came to wait on the emperor in Nanking and accompanied him on the trip north. Sometimes the emperor even mimicked the interpreter's native language. But after the death of the emperor Chiang was executed (1521). As a result, the Portuguese mission was rejected and Pires sent back to Kwangtung.

As the emperor apparently had no cultural interest, imperially sponsored arts were hardly encouraged in his day.

Nevertheless fine porcelain (blue-and-white, polychrome, monochrome, enameled ware, underglaze ware, etc.) continued to be produced in some quantity, and— for the foreign trade— a number of pieces, inscribed in Sanskrit, Persian, and Arabic, were fashioned. Ambassadors from Samarkand and Mecca continued to come with tribute and were undoubtedly presented such pieces in return. At the Ardebil Shrine in Iran several beautiful examples of Cheng-te date are still preserved—mute witness of this exchange of precious goods.

One type of pottery which may have had its start in these days, through private initiative, is known as I-hsing yao 宜興窰 after the name of a site on the western bank of Lake T'ai. The presumed originator of this ware was Kung Ch'un 龔(or 供)春. According to Dr. S. W. Bushell, it is a finely levigated ware which the Chinese prefer "to any other, even to porcelain, for infusing tea, and for jars to preserve the flavour of delicate sweetmeats." The pieces are often made in fantastic forms. A number of early date may be found in several western collections, such as the Percival David Foundation of Chinese Art (London) and the Freer Gallery of Art (Washington, D.C.). The Portuguese gave the ware the name boccaro and exported it to Europe where it exerted a strong influence on Johann Friederich Böttger of Meissen, beginning in 1708.

[Editors' note: In referring to the pregnant woman who became Chu Hou-chao's favorite for a time, the *Ming-shih* (307/14b) describes her as a singer (in Turkestan music, according to Mao Ch'i-ling, ECCP), horsewoman, archer, and one who could understand foreign languages. These qualities and the surname Ma 馬 indicate strongly that she was of Uighur origin. Her mastery of military arts may have served as a reminder to Chu of his grandfather's favorite consort, Wan Kuei-fei (*q. v.*). Ming records also reveal that Chu Hou-chao and Chiang Pin t'ung wo-ch'i 同臥起 (slept and rose together), making plain the emperor's homosexuality, which is apparently confirmed by his preference for the Leopard House as a residence (to which he brought military officers and other male favorites) instead of the palaces where the empress and other women lived. In fact, the records give the impression that he generally avoided normal relations with women.

The private life of Chu Hou-chao might be regarded simply as aberrant were it not that it affected so decisively the course of the dynasty and the trend of Chinese society. In the first place, because he did not leave an heir, a cousin succeeded to the throne, giving rise to the controversy concerning the status of the latter's parents, an episode known as the *Ta-li i* (*see* Chu Hou-ts'ung). Secondly, because of his eccentricities and his neglect in the performance of imperial duties as defined by his ancestor (*see* Chu Yüan-chang), the power to rule fell first to the eunuch, Liu Chin, who was familiar with the tradition of the court and the government; then, when the power was shared by his intimate favorites (as military men they often gave ridiculous advice), a chaotic situation resulted. To make the government function properly it behooved the grand secretaries and ministers to adopt remedial measures; this shifted the governing power from the emperor (assisted by eunuchs) to the grand secretariat, especially in the person of the chief grand secretary. In this way Yang T'ing-ho assumed almost imperial prerogatives in 1521, in sharp contrast to his predecessor, the meek Li Tung-yang (the last of the old type chief grand secretaries).

This relaxation of imperial control is also reflected in the rise of the social status of the scholar-officials in their own native communities. Taking advantage of their tax exemption privileges, they increased their land holdings insatiably, shifting the tax burden to the common people. This trend, sometimes partially arrested (*see* Hai Jui), continued until the end of the dynasty.

In the fourth place the summoning of frontier troops to serve in Peking, even for short periods, effectively altered the Ming military organization, resulting in the disruption of the training of the imperial capital army and the heightening of the unruliness of certain frontier units. This is especially true of the Tatung battalions which rose in rebellion several times (*see* Liang Chen.)]

Bibliography

1/ch.15–16, 181–190, 304, 307; MSL (1965), Wu-tsung, ch. 1–197; KC (1958), ch. 46–52; Chang Wei-hua 張維華, *Ming-shih fo-lang-chi lü-sung ho-lan i-ta-li-ya ssu-chuan chu-shih* 明史佛郎機呂宋荷蘭意大里亞四傳注釋 (Peiping, 1934; Ch'en Hao 陳鶴 (1757–1811), *Ming-chi* 明紀, ch. 24–27; Chu Kuo-chen (ECCP), *Huang Ming ta-cheng chi*, ch. 22–24; Ku Ying-t'ai (ECCP), *Ming-ch'ao chi-shih pen-mo*, ch. 42–49; Li Mo 李默 (d. 1556), *Ku-shu p'ou-tan* 孤樹裒談, ch. 10; Mao Ch'i-ling, *Ming Wu-tsung wai-chi* (*Kuang-wen* 廣文 *shu-chü* ed.); *id.*, *Hsi-ho wen-chi* (*Wan-yu wen-k'u* 萬有文庫 ed.), 1640; Wang Ao, *Chen-tse chi-wen*; *id.*, *Chen-tse chang-yü*; Wang Ch'iung, *Shuang-ch'i tsa-chi*; Paul Pelliot "Hōja et la Sayyid Husain de l'histoire des Ming," TP, 38 (1948), 81; J. A. Pope, *Chinese Porcelains from the Ardebil Shrine* (Washington, 1956), p. 34, 195, pls. 75–76, 115–17; S. W. Bushell, *Chinese Art*, Vol. II (London, 1924), fig. 3, p. 8; *Blue and White Ware of the Ming Dynasty*, Book 4 (Hong Kong, 1963), p. 44; *Underglaze Red Ware of the Ming Dynasty* (Hong Kong, 1963), 78; *Enamelled Ware of the Ming Dynasty* (Hong Kong, 1966), pls. 1–12; Geoffrey Hedley, "Yi-hsing Ware," T. O. C. S., 14 (1936–37), 70.

Kwan-wai So

CHU Hou-ts'ung 朱厚熜, September 16, 1507–January 23, 1567, the eleventh emperor of the Ming dynasty, was on the throne from 1521 to 1567, the second longest reign among the Ming emperors, known as the Chia-ching 嘉靖 period. After his death he was given the temple name Shih-tsung 世宗 and posthumous name of Su 肅; his mausoleum was known as Yung-ling 永陵. He was a grandson of Chu Chien-shen, a nephew of Chu Yu-t'ang, and a cousin of Chu Hou-chao (*qq.v.*). Because the last died having neither a son nor a brother, this cousin was brought in from a princedom to succeed to the throne. If Chu Hou-ts'ung had agreed to be the adopted son of Chu Yu-t'ang, the direct line of succession would nominally have continued, but as events unfolded, it was broken. The controversy that developed is known in history as the *Ta-li i* 大禮議. In the early years of his long reign the emperor's attention was focused domestically on this struggle, and in the later years he turned to the cult of religious Taoism in a search for a life without death. Both concerns ruined many able officials, and wasted the energy and wealth of the empire. In foreign relations these years saw Mongol bands sweeping across the Great Wall almost at will, raiding and killing from the northwestern frontier to the Liaotung peninsula. Along the southeast coast the *wo-k'ou* caused equal suffering and destruction, and erupted just as often. In spite of his concentration on selfish whims and the menace on his borders, Chu Hou-ts'ung never let anyone usurp his power and authority. In his time the rich grew richer and the poor became impoverished, particularly in the lower Yangtze area. Wealth bred leisure, which demanded luxuries and entertainment; it also encouraged the development of theatre, art, literature, and printing. The political vigor of the empire, however, began to decline, and the house of Ming showed signs of senescence.

Chu Hou-ts'ung's father, Chu Yu-yüan 朱祐杬 (July 21, 1476–July 13, 1519; the last character is sometimes erroneously written 杭), was the third son of Chu Chien-shen, and the eldest of three sons born to Lady Shao (*see* Chu Chien-shen). In 1487 Chu Yu-yüan was made prince of Hsing 興王. Early in 1491 he married a daughter of Chiang Hsiao 蔣斅, a native of Ta-hsing 大興, Pei-Chihli. Later in the same year he was given An-lu 安陸 in Hukuang, as his princedom, and this became his residence in 1494. It was there that Chu Hou-ts'ung was born and spent his childhood. After his father's death, in spite of his tender age, Chu Hou-ts'ung succeeded to the title of prince of Hsing. The conclusion of the *Ta-li i* controversy resulted in elevating Chu Yu-yüan posthumously to the status of emperor with the name Hsien huang-ti 獻皇帝 and the temple name Jui-tsung 睿宗; his widow, née Chiang (d. December 21, 1538), became Empress Hsien.

At his father's death, Chu Hou-ts'ung was only twelve years of age, but he acted as prince regent. After the observance of the prescribed mourning period early in 1521, succession by imperial order was made official. Twenty-four days later Chu Hou-chao died leaving the throne without an heir. Empress-dowager Chang (*see* Chu Yu-t'ang) and Grand Secretary Yang T'ing-ho (*q.v.*) between them selected Chu Hou-ts'ung to be the inheritor of the throne, in accordance with the wish of the deceased emperor, in an edict said to have been dictated on his death bed. Perhaps no one at the time anticipated any trouble from a boy of his age. In spite of Yang's extraordinary ability in governmental affairs, he must have overlooked the wording in this important document, assuming that the successor to the throne should certainly consider himself the heir of the imperial line, younger "brother" of Emperor Chu Hou-chao, and adopted son of Emperor Chu Yu-t'ang. This oversight, probably to Yang's regret, made for many turbulent years and involved a host of people.

On May 7, 1521, the prince left An-lu, reaching Peking on the 27th of the same month. Before entering the capital, he refused to be welcomed by the rites prepared for an heir apparent. Quoting the deceased emperor's edict, he argued that he came as successor to the throne, not as an heir apparent (嗣皇帝位, 非皇子也). He was firm, making no compromise whatsoever in response to the protestations of the court officials. They gave in finally, presenting a petition which urged him to ascend the throne immediately. Chu Hou-ts'ung then entered Peking with all the prerogatives and full regalia of an emperor. On the same day he was enthroned, proclaiming the following year (1522) to be the first year of the Chia-ching reign.

The primary concern of the new emperor was the honors to be accorded his own father. While the majority of the court officials argued that the emperor was indeed not only the successor to the throne, but also the heir who would propagate the direct imperial line, Chu Hou-ts'ung insisted on being considered the son of his natural parents, and that he must accord them their rightful due. On the question of the welcoming ceremony for his mother he again refused to follow the suggested rites for a princess. In the end he himself decided the details and on November 2, 1521, his mother was received into the palace like an empress-dowager. In the meantime a small group of officials led by Chang Ts'ung (who later changed his name to Chang Fu-ching, *q.v.*), sided with the emperor, and presented some cogent arguments. The emperor, delighted, finally had his way. His father was accorded the title of Hsing-hsien emperor and his mother put on an equal footing with Empress-dowager Chang, the widow of Emperor Chu Yu-t'ang. Not wholly satisfied, the emperor made further demands; at first he addressed his parents as pen-sheng 本生 (my own progenitors), then he dropped these qualifying characters. On August 14, 1524, a large group of officials protested by raising their voices in lamentation outside the palace gate. This action incensed the emperor. One hundred thirty-four officials were put in the prison of the Embroidered-uniform Guard, many were flogged, and sixteen died from their wounds (*see* Feng Hsi and Yang Shen). Chu Hou-ts'ung even suggested the removal of his father's remains from Hukuang to a mausoleum by the other imperial tombs near Peking. Though this was not carried out, a special shrine was built in the palace precincts

for his father's tablet. The emperor e-
merged completely victorious. Then he ordered the compilation of an official history
of the *Ta-li i* affair. It was published first
early in 1525, under the title *Ta-li chi-i*
(集議), but later this title was changed
to *Ming-lun ta-tien* 明倫大典, published in
1528 in 24 *chüan*, and is still extant.

On the heels of the *Ta-li* affair there
followed another known as the Ta-yü 大
獄 controversy. In 1526 a Shansi rebel,
Li Fu-ta (*see* Chang Fu-ching), escaped
from the consequences of his guilt, but
later worked for, and gained, the protection of the powerful Kuo Hsün (*q.v.*). Ma
Lu (*see* Chang Fu-ching), as regional inspector of Shansi, tried to reopen the case
and bring Li Fu-ta to justice. Kuo Hsün
wrote to Ma, asking that he drop the
matter, but Ma refused. As in the *Ta-li i*
officials lined up in two opposing camps.
One, following the lead of Chang Ts'ung,
took Kuo's side, arguing mistaken identity.
In the following year Li Fu-ta was released, and Ma Lu imprisoned, flogged, and
banished. Documents on this case were
collected and promulgated at its conclusion, and entitled *Ch'in-ming ta-yü lu* 欽明
大獄錄.

To his parents went ever more honors
and longer titles. Chu Hou-ts'ung also
rearranged the ancestral temples to suit.
All this led the emperor to be interested
in the revival of certain rites and ritual
music. It was for these services that Hsia
Yen (*q.v.*) came to imperial favor and
prominence. Toward the end of 1538,
when the emperor's mother died, the question arose as to whether he should bury
his parents together in the south or in
the north. For this reason he made a
trip of inspection and revisited his old
home in 1539 (*see* Lu Ping). After some
indecision, he finally decided to send his
mother's remains south to be interred
with his father's in the Hsien-ling 顯陵,
near An-lu. To let him achieve real imperial status, he had ordered previously
(1531) the compilation of a *shih-lu* for
his father (*see* Yang I-ch'ing), and re-

named An-lu as Ch'eng-t'ien-fu 承天府 so
that it might be on a par with Shun-t'ien-
fu (Peking) and Ying-t'ien-fu (Nanking).
A gazetteer, the *Ch'eng-t'ien ta-chih* 大誌,
40 *ch.*, was compiled under the supervision of Hsü Chieh (*q.v.*).

A short work of 12 chapters of instructions for women, entitled *Nü-hsün* 女訓,
allegedly written by his mother, was published (1530) together with a biography
of Empress Ma (*q.v.*), the *Kao huang-hou-
chüan* 高皇后傳, and the Household Instructions of Empress Hsü (*q.v.*). Empress
Ma was the wife of Chu Yüan-chang, the
founding emperor, and Empress Hsü the
wife of Chu Ti (*q.v.*), who was in a way
also a founding emperor as he installed a
different branch of the family on the imperial throne. Would it be reasonable to
suggest that, by publishing the *Nü-hsün*,
Chu Hou-ts'ung was not only honoring
his mother, but also indicating that his
father too was the founder of a new line
of the imperial family? Confirmation of
his idea about Chu Ti as founder is seen
from his decree of 1538 making his temple name Ch'eng-tsu.

It was common belief that people
from central China, the Hukuang area,
from the time of the ancient state of Ch'u
楚, tended to be superstitious. There is no
way to tell whether this milieu really
influenced Chu Hou-ts'ung's childhood,
but his persistent devotion to religious
Taoism, with its weird theories, and strange
practices in search for a life without
death seem to substantiate it. As early as
the second year of Chia-ching (1523),
Grand Secretary Yang T'ing-ho memorialized, advising the young emperor not
to indulge in Taoist services (齋醮). As
the emperor produced no heir in the first
ten years of his reign, certain high officials even suggested that the performance
of Taoist rites might be appropriate.
From then on Taoist activities were on
the increase in the palace grounds. An
unfortunate incident which happened in
1542 may have also intensified his interest in the Taoist cult.

An extraordinary event took place in the palace on the night of November 27 of that year. A group of palace serving girls attempted to assassinate the emperor. While he was sleeping in the quarters of his favorite consort, Tuan, née Ts'ao (端妃曹氏), the girls tied a rope around his neck to strangle him. The plot failed, however, as they had tied the wrong kind of knot. One of the girls panicked, and informed the empress, who hurried over and saved the emperor. Before he had regained the power of speech, the empress ordered the eunuchs to round up the whole group (18 girls) along with the consort Ts'ao and a secondary consort Wang (王), led them to the public execution place in Peking, and had all done away with, together with some members of their families. The emperor personally considered his favorite Ts'ao innocent, and regretted the empress' abrupt decree. From thta day on the emperor took up his residence in the Hsi-yüan 西苑, and never returned to the inner palace quarters. Hsi-yüan also was the center for Taoist rituals.

Events in the palace were usually regarded as taboo, although the emperor issued an edict in relation to this matter when he recovered. Yet this strange case was not recorded in detail. One source hints that it was probably due to the emperor's harsh treatment of the palace girls. Wang Shih-chen (q.v.) wrote twelve verses of palace poems (宮詞) on the Chia-ching period. In one verse, referring to the young girls selected for palace service, the poet relates that before they reached maturity, they had already made a contribution (as one ingredient) to the drug taken to promote longevity. Several times indeed during the Chia-ching reign the selection of young girls before the age of puberty was conducted. Could the Taoist pursuit of long life have had something to do with the palace girls' revolt?

Taoists and their adepts of various persuasions found their way to the palace to offer their services. For some the end was severe punishment or death, because their magic failed or because of their careless conduct. Members of the traditional Taoist establishment of Kiangsi (see Chang Cheng-ch'ang) achieved no special rapport with the emperor. His trusted counselors were first Shao Yüan-chieh and later T'ao Chung-wen (qq.v.). For Taoist worship special structures and buildings were erected, special incense, pearls, ambergris, gold, and other valuables were required. Huge quantities of timber from Szechwan were cut and transported. One high official reported that for the year 1537 expenditure for palace building projects reached six million taels. Shen Te-fu (q.v.) in his Yeh-hu-pien records that, whenever a Taoist prayer service was conducted in the palace, among other material needs, several thousand ounces of gold dust were required. Literary decorations, tablets, and couplets were all written in gold. The official scribes would purposefully change their writing brushes as they wrote. They then would take home the discarded brushes saturated with gold paste. By this means, some actually became well-to-do, Shen reports. The prayer services also occurred more and more often, lasted longer and longer, at first services of one day, then of three, but toward the end of the reign there were services of twelve and thirteen, lasting day and night.

At different times the emperor also took seriously the professed Taoist magic, such as the planchette board, the art of changing base metals into gold, and symbols of omens, etc. Rain or snow that fell when needed, multiple heads of grain, animals white in color, rabbits, deer, turtles, sparrows, and geese were all regarded as good omens. About 1556 chih 芝 (a fungus with purple stalk) was introduceds. Orders were issued to gather the plant of different sizes and colors from special localities, with the result that mounds of it were piled up in Hsi-yüan. One enterprising person named Wang Chin 王金 stole 181 stalks from such a mound, arranged them in a heap, called it Wan-sui chih shan萬歲芝山 (the ten-thousand-year chih hill), and presented it to the emperor as a birthday gift. He was handsomely rewarded.

In connection with Taoist worship, the revival and emphasis on the literary form known as ch'ing-tz'u 青詞 was another peculiar feature of the Chia-ching reign. They were supposed to be prayers and praises offered to the Taoist gods written on black paper. The style is poetic and full of Taoist allusions and references. Because of the emperor's fondness for ch'ing-tz'u, high officials were often favored for their ability in this form of writing rather than for their statecraft. As both Yen Sung (q. v.) and Hsia Yen were skilled in this, they were derogatorily known as ch'ing-tz'u tsai-hsiang 宰相 (ch'ing-tz'u premiers). Along the same line were the long Taoist titles coined for the emperor and his deceased parents. In 1556 the emperor gave his father a Taoist title of twenty-six characters, his mother one of twenty-two, himself one of thirty-seven, and another of thirty-five characters.

Throughout the reign, Mongol invasions along the northern frontier occurred almost yearly. Very often the Mongol horsemen dashed in, raided, and left as speedily as they came. Several times they reached the vicinity of Peking, and martial law had to be declared. The worst was in 1550, when Altan-qaγan (q. v.) led his forces to T'ung-chou 通州, endangered the imperial tombs, and came so close to the capital that they could be seen from the city wall. Under duress China gave in to their demand to establish horse-trading markets (馬市). The capital's military system was reformed as a result (see Ch'iu Luan). Yet when the danger subsided the emperor gave credit to T'ao Chung-wen for the latter's prayers to Taoist deities.

China fared no better along the southeast coastal provinces because of the constant depredations of the wo-k'ou (see Hu Tsung-hsien, Yü Ta-yu, and Ch'i Chi-kuang). Wealthy localities in the lower Yangtze area, such as Ningpo, Hangchow, and Shao-hsing, or Shanghai, Soochow, Yangchow, and Nanking—not one could escape repeated harassment. Farther south, in Fukien and Kwangtung, prominent coastal cities suffered equally. Even the provincial seats of Foochow and Canton were no exception. The most frequent and devastating raids took place in the 1550s and 1560s: on the lower Yangtze area in the late 1550s, Fukien and Kwangtung in the 1560s. The losses in life and property were incalculable.

Chu Hou-ts'ung had three empresses. The first née Ch'en 陳 (d. 1528), daughter of Ch'en Wan-yen 陳萬言, a native of Yüan-ch'eng 元城 (Pei-Chihli), became empress in 1522. Her death, it is said, was because of a miscarriage, due to fright over the emperor's sudden outburst against her. Even after her death, the emperor expressed displeasure by according her lesser funeral rites, and gave her the uncomplimentary posthumous name Tao-ling 悼靈. Not until 1536, following Hsia Yen's advice, was the name changed to Hsiao-chieh 孝潔. The second empress, née Chang 張 (d. 1536), was elevated from Consort Shun (順妃) after the death of the empress. Early in 1534 the emperor suddenly announced her deposition without apparent reason. Some sources suggest that it was because she attempted to put in a good word for Empress-dowager Chang (see Chang Ho-ling). As the emperor disliked the Chang family he was incensed. The third empress, née Fang 方 (d. 1547), was a native of Nanking, selected to be a secondary consort in 1531. After Empress Chang was deposed, the Ming-shan ts'ang relates, the emperor asked Hsia Yen if she would make a good choice for empress. Hsia congratulated him on the idea, and continued "Heaven is round and the earth is square [方 means square], it would be most suitable." The emperor was pleased, and the lady Fang was made empress nine days later. In 1542 she saved his life from the attempted assassination by the palace girls. He expressed his gratitude by giving her more favored funeral rites after her death. Her posthumous name Hsiao-lieh 孝烈 was the emperor's personal choice. Yet Ho Ch'iao-yüan (*q. v.*) links her death to the palace fire which took place about a fortnight before. When the palace burst into flames, Ho writes, one eunuch reported the conflagration to the emperor, asking permission to summon rescuers, but the emperor made no answer. Ho suggests that the reason was the execution of the emperor's favorite consort Ts'ao back in 1542. The author hints that even Hsia Yen's tragic end might also have had some connection with this event. A fourth consort née Tu 杜 (d. February 12, 1554), was the mother of the next emperor.

Chu Hou-ts'ung had eight sons and five daughters, but only two sons and two daughters grew to maturity. The second son, Chu Tsai-jui 朱載壑 (October 20, 1536-April 14, 1549), was designated heir apparent in 1539, and named regent during the emperor's trip to the south in the same year. He died two days after his capping ceremony (冠禮). The third son, Chu Tsai-hou (*q. v.*), succeeded to the throne. The fourth son, Chu Tsai-ch'uan 朱載圳 (enf. 1539 as Prince Ching 景王 d. Feb. 9, 1565), reached his estate in Te-an 德安, Hukuang (approximately the same territory as his grandfather's princedom, *see* Chu Tsai-hou), in 1561. Of the two daughters, one, Chu Lu-chen 祿媜, entitled Ning-an kung-chu 寧安公主, who married Li Ho 李和 in 1555, later was elevated to be ta-chang (大長) kung-chu in 1572. The other, Chu Su-chen 素媜 (d. 1564), became Chia-shan 嘉善 kung-chu, and married Hsü Ts'ung-ch'eng 許從誠 in 1557.

In the long reign of four decades and a half, a number of other events worthy of mention occurred; they include natural calamities. On the night of January 23, 1556, a disastrous earthquake shook the three provinces of Shensi, Shansi, and Honan, with Shensi suffering the most in the regions of Wei-nan 渭南, Hua-chou 華州, Ch'ao-i 朝邑, and San-yüan 三原. It started as rumbling thunder, which aroused the domestic animals; dogs barked, and cocks crowed. Houses and city walls collapsed. Both the Yellow and Wei 渭 Rivers overran their banks. Fissures opened in the earth, 20 to 30 feet in depth in some places, while in others level ground rose in hummocks. In certain areas tremors lasted for several days. It was estimated that over 830,000 people perished. Among the dead were some very prominent figures: Han Pang-ch'i (*q. v.*), the retired minister of War in Nanking; Ma Li 馬理 (1474-1556, T. 伯循, H. 谿田, cs 1514, native of San-yüan), the retired minister of the Court of Imperial Entertainment in Nanking; and Wang Wei-chen (*see* Ho Liang-chün), to name a few. Wang was on his way to his new post as chancellor of the Nanking National University, but had hurried home to see his sick mother, when he was caught in the disaster. Reports of earthquakes were frequent, and occurred in many areas. In a period of ten months, from July, 1523, to May 1524, as many as thirty-eight were recorded. Nanking, which has not been known in recent years to have earthquakes, reported fifteen in one month in 1425, and six in a single day.

The abolition of images in the Confucian temples also deserves special notice (*see* Chang Ts'ung and Hsü Chieh). When the founding emperor prohibited the worship of Confucius in Taoist and Buddhist sanctuaries, he also suggested the use of tablets in place of images. This decree, however, was not enforced, and the change not definitely made until 1530. Following his victory in the *Ta-li i*, Chu Hou-ts'ung became enthusiastic about revising other rites and rituals. Concerning the worship of Confucius, in addition to abolishing images for characters written on tablets, a separate chapel for the father of Confucius and the fathers of three Confucian disciples was added to the rear of the main temple. This, apparently, was also a reflection of the emperor's filial feeling toward his own father.

As the population of the princedoms grew by leaps and bounds, and its members were not allowed to participate in the "four professions" with ordinary people, their welfare became a financial problem for the government. In bringing up-to-date the Record of the Imperial House (玉牒 Yü-tieh) in 1549, the Imperial Clan Court presented the following statistics: 19,893 male members from princes to commoners; an estimate of another 1,000 not counted; and 9,782 titled daughters of various degree (郡主, 縣主, 郡君, 縣君). The total number of the three categories comes to 30,675, not including the female members (wives and concubines and service staff), and the husbands of the titled daughters. In 1529, while compiling the *hui-tien* 會典, Huo T'ao (*q. v.*) noted that, because of the population increase of the princedoms, their allowances constituted too heavy a drain on the economy. Citing the princedom of Chin (晉) in Shansi as an example, he wrote that, in the early years of Hung-wu, there had been only the prince of Chin, who received an allowance of 10,000 *shih* of grain annually, but now, in addition to the present prince, there were 2,851 members of the eight lesser degrees in that princedom, altogether receiving a total allowance of 870,000 *shih* of grain annually, an 87-fold increase. On the other hand, Huo continued, the taxable acres of land of Shansi were on the decrease. Under such circumstances, Huo T'ao asked how that province could meet its obligations. At the same time some clansmen families became very poor, and members of others resorted to violence and crime. Welfare and problems of the imperial clans reached an acute stage in Chu Hou-ts'ung's reign.

The *Ming-shih* considers Chu Hou-ts'ung a mediocre monarch, criticizes him for his *Ta-li* action and for his absorption in religious Taoism; it points out that during his reign the national wealth began to decline. Most Ming authors, probably on principle, called his obstinacy and harshness strength and firmness, praised the *Ta-li* episode as responsible for the revival of rites, rituals, and music, and approved his refraining from common vice, and never favoring the eunuchs. In reviewing the history of the Chia-ching reign, however, one can hardly fail to bear in mind the many officials who died or suffered unjust and excessive punishment (*see* Yang Chi-sheng, Chang Ching, Yang Chüeh, and Shen Lien). Even for his favorite officials, there were sad endings: Kuo Hsün died in prison, Ch'iu Luan was beheaded after death, Hsia Yen was executed, and Yen Sung ended his life in desolation. Only Lu Ping, who died rather early, and Hsü Chieh, who came into favor rather late, escaped tragic fates. Chu Hou-ts'ung was harsh, obdurate, and lacked compassion. He was also the only Ming emperor devoted to Taoism alone, and the only one to suppress Buddhism. In 1536 the Buddhist temple in the palace was dismantled, over 3,000 catties (斤) of so-called bones of the Buddha were destroyed, and 169 Buddhist images of gold and silver were melted down. Comments on Chu Hou-ts'ung are certainly many and varied. Perhaps the most sarcastic and derogatory is the statement that as emperor he committed only two good deeds, manifested in his enthroning edict and his dying one. The former was drawn up by Yang T'ing-ho and the latter drafted by Hsü Chieh.

Bibliography

1/ch. 17, 18, 114/4a, 115/5a, 120/2a, 121/14a; MSL (1965), Shih-tsung, *Pao-hsün* 寶訓 (MSL supplement); KC (1958), 1244, ch. 52-64; Ho Ch'iao-yüan, *Ming-shan ts'ang* (Taipei, 1971, photoprint of 1640 ed.), ch. 22–28, 30/24a, 26b, 32/4b, 34/1a; Fu Feng-hsiang 傅鳳翔 comp., *Huang Ming chao-ling* 皇明詔令 (Taipei, 1967, photoprint of Chia-ching ed.), ch. 19–21; Shen Te-fu, *Wan-li yeh-hu pien* (Peking, 1959), 42, 49, 59, 65, 87, 90, 361, 743, 799, 803, 892; *Ming-lun ta-tien* (NLP microfilm, #504); Fan

Shou-chi, *Su-huang wai-shih*, ch. 21-24 in Lei Li, *Huang Ming ta-ch'eng chi* (Wan-li ed.); Hsü Hsüeh-mo, *Shih-miao chih-yü lu* (Taipei, 1965, photoprint of Ming ed.); Ku Ying-t'ai (ECCP), *Ming-ch'ao chi-shih pen-mo* (1658 ed.), ch. 50-59; Wang Shih-chen, *Yen-chou shan-jen ssu-pu kao* (Wan-li ed.), 47/13a; Li Chin-hua 李晉華, *Ming-tai ch'ih-chuan shu k'ao* 明代勅撰書考, (Harvard-Yenching Inst. Sinological Index Ser., Supplement no. 3, 1932), 53, 58; Ch'en Mao-heng 陳懋恆, *Ming-tai wo-k'ou k'ao-lüeh* 明代倭寇考略, Peking, 1957; Liu Ts'un-yan, "The Penetration of Taoism into the Neo-Confucian Elite," TP, 37 (1971), 51.

Lienche Tu Fang

CHU-hung 袾宏 (T. 佛慧, H. 蓮池), February 23, 1535-July 29, 1615, was a Buddhist monk, later also called the master of Yün-ch'i 雲棲大師, after the monastery restored for him. He was born in Jen-ho仁和 (Hangchow), the eldest son of a family named Shen 沈. His father, said to have excelled in calligraphy as well as in the medicinal and divinational arts, never served in an official capacity and seems to have had a strong aversion to the bureaucracy. Chu-hung, however, became a student in the local school at the age of sixteen and achieved a certain reputation for his knowledge of Confucianism and Taoism. He sat for the higher examinations several times, but without success.

Chu-hung became interested in Pure Land Buddhism when he saw an old woman who lived next door to him call Amitābha's name every day. When he asked her why she did so, she replied that her husband had called Amitābha's name all his life, and such was the virtue of this practice that, when he died, he did so without suffering any illness. He was deeply moved by the old woman's story, and from that day on treasured the motto: Sheng ssu shih ta 生死事大 (The matter of life and death should be of primary concern).

When Chu-hung reached the age of twenty-six his father died. Shortly afterwards his wife and only son passed away. He was then remarried to a woman surnamed T'ang 湯. He vowed to himself that, if he failed the examinations in the following three years, he would become a monk. Three years passed. Not only did success evade him but his mother too passed away. Accordingly the next year, when he was thirty-one (1566), he bade farewell to his second wife (she later became a nun) and, entering the Buddhist priesthood, he embarked on a mendicant's tour in north China to seek further knowledge. On his way to Tung-ch'ang 東昌, Shantung, he experienced his first enlightenment, and wrote a gātha, the first lines of which may be rendered:

Things of twenty years ago may be held in doubt, It is no wonder that I encounter my enlightenment 3,000 *li* away.

It is known that he traveled all the way to Mount Wu-t'ai in Shansi. Later in Peking, he sought instruction from a Ch'an master, who told him that he should not concern himself with fame or profit but should concentrate on self-discipline and invocation of Buddha's name, a down-to-earth approach to Buddhism that remained with Chu-hung for the rest of his life. In 1571, after five years of travel, Chu-hung went to Mount Yün-ch'i in his native Hangchow. Finding the quiet surroundings much to his liking he decided to settle there, living in a hut some laymen erected for him. There he continued his efforts at meditation, eating but once a day and fasting at one time for as long as seven days. It is said that he hung an iron plaque around his neck on which appeared these words, "I will talk to people only when flowers bloom on the iron tree."

For about forty *li* around Mount Yün-ch'i tigers infested the area. Each year more than twenty people and many more domestic animals lost their lives. To put an end to these calamities Chu-hung asserted that by his recitation of Buddhist scripture and performance of tantric rituals (shih-shih 施食 [bestowing food on hungry ghosts]), the tigers of the neighborhood ceased their depredations. He also held that his prayers ended a great drought. In any case, in gratitude the local people volunteered to rebuild for him an abandoned monastery, originally constructed in 967 for the Ch'an master known as Fu-hu 伏虎 (tamer of tigers), which had been left in ruins for nearly one hundred years following the flood of 1492. After its completion in 1577 Chu-hung gave the monastery its original name, Yün-ch'i ssu 寺. Soon it attracted many monks and became a center of Buddhism. According to Chu-hung, the monks at the monastery were mainly followers of the Pure Land sect. In winter months they concentrated on Ch'an practices, while during the rest of the year they devoted themselves to Pure Land teachings which involved attendance at lectures and the recitation of scriptures.

In Chu-hung the parallel practice of Pure Land and Ch'an Buddhism, first instituted by Yen-shou (904-75), also a native of Hangchow, reached its culmination. He felt certain that only faith in Pure Land could satisfy people of varied capacities. He set his ideas down in the commentary to Kumārajīva's (344–413?) translation of the Lesser *Sakhāvatī-vyūha*, entitled *Fo-shuo A-mi-t'o ching shu-ch'ao* 佛說阿彌陀經疏鈔, 4 *ch.* In the commentary he made an effort to explain his assertion that, "One's nature is the Amitā-bha Buddha, and one's mind is set towards the Pure Land" 自性彌陀惟心淨土. Calling on Buddha's name will ultimately produce the state of single-mindedness, that is, the convergence of one's mind and the object of concentration. As a result all delusions arising from ordinary states of consciousness cease. Chu-hung explains this conception of the one mind as of two levels of comprehension, one for the dull and the other for the bright. The first is the shih i hsin 事一心 (one mind of particulars). To attain this level, one simultaneously utters the name of Amitābha, listens to the name, and dwells on it. If this be done for a long time one arrives at a state where one is pervaded by the single thought of Amitābha. The second is the li i hsin 理一心 (one mind of principle). This level is deeper than the first, for here not only does one achieve a continuous state of thinking and remembering Amitābha, but also one realizes that the mind which thinks and remembers (neng nien 能念) and the Amitābha which is thought and remembered (so nien 所念) are identical. In other words, although one calls or dwells on Amitābha's name (nien fo 佛), one is actually dwelling on one's own mind (nien hsin 心). The pursuit of this practice will lead to the realization that both Buddha and one's mind, being identical, are ultimately beyond ordinary reasoning. Not one of the four categories, being, non-being, both being and non-being, neither being nor non-being, describes the true state of the mind. Here Chu-hung succeeded in bridging the difference between Pure Land and Ch'an, for, starting from the concrete invocation of Buddha's name, nien fo, he ended up with the abstract Ch'an state of wu-nien 無念 (no thought). To supply followers of dull or sharp faculties with different means of cultivation, he followed Tsung-mi's (780-841) precedent in listing four types of nien fo. The first type is called ch'eng ming 稱名 nien fo, the invocation of Amitābha's name either aloud or silently or by moving one's lips soundlessly. The second type is called kuan hsiang 觀相 nien fo, which is to gaze attentively at the image of Amitābha. The third type, kuan hsiang 想 nien fo, was to contemplate the characteristics or signs of the Amitābha Buddha in the manner described in the *Shih-liu kuan ching* 十六觀經. This contemplation may be either of one particular sign or of the total person of Amitābha. The fourth type differs sharply from the other three; it is called shih hsiang 實相 nien fo, or invocation by being in accord with reality, which means to rid oneself of all artificial conceptions such as those of life and death, being and non-being, as well as speech and name. This is the intuitive knowledge of one's own pure nature which the "one mind of principle" achieves, whereas the first three types of nien fo lie in the realm of the "one mind of particulars."

The desire to combine Ch'an meditation with faith in Pure Land came from Chu-hung's deep disillusionment over the conduct of his fellow monks, many of whom, though they professed to be Ch'an practitioners, were in fact monks in name only. In order to revive strict adherence to monastic discipline, monks in his Yün-ch'i monastery were required to recite the Vinaya contained in the *Fan-wang ching* 梵網經 (Brahma-sūtra) once every fifteen days. In fact, his first scholastic effort after his enlightenment was the composition of *Fan - wang ching chieh shu fa yin* 戒疏發隱, a commentary on the T'ien-t'ai master Chih-i's (538-97) exposition of the same work. He also compiled primers on monastery life and discipline such as the *Chü chieh pien meng* 具戒便蒙, *Sha-mi yao-lüeh* 沙彌要略, *Ni chieh lu yao* 尼戒錄要, *Seng hsün jih-chi* 僧訓日記. It is interesting to note also that Chu-hung paid particular attention to the ritual aspect of receiving commandments. He was in favor of observing the strict rules of the chieh-t'an 戒壇 system as made known by the vinaya master, Tao-hsüan (596-667). Since, however, it had fallen into disuse, Chu-hung felt even more the necessity of stressing discipline.

Chu-hung's concern for morality also made him active among the laity. In this regard he created opportunities for lay Buddhists to achieve merit by setting captured animals free. In his writings he also protested the slaughter of animals and the infliction of harsh penalties on people. Being a man of his time, Chu-hung often employed stories of a supernatural character to substantiate his theory of rewards and retributions. It seems that he was quite successful in this endeavor and won a number of followers many of whom belonged to the gentry-official class.

Just as he held an anti-sectarian viewpoint towards Buddhism, so he maintained a conciliatory attitude towards Confucianism and Taoism. There is ample evidence of his admiration for Confucius and other early Confucianists in *Chu ch'uang sui-pi* 竹窗隨筆 and its sequels, *Er* 二 *-pi* and *San* 三*-pi*. He also revised the Taoist system of recording merits and demerits (*see* Yüan Huang) and wrote the *Tzu chih lu* 自知錄. He was not in favor, however, of the amalgamation of the Three Teachings which was very popular during his time (*see* Lin Chao-en). He was definitely hostile to Catholicism, as may be seen from the four rebuttals supposedly addressed to Matteo Ricci (*q.v.*) contained in the *San-pi*.

Chu-hung died at the age of eighty-one. His last words to his followers were, "Invoke the Buddha's name with honesty and sincerity." He was buried on the north side of the mountain opposite the stūpa of his second wife who had passed away a year earlier. He came to be known as one of the four illustrious monks of the last decades of the Ming and the eighth patriarch of the Pure Land sect. A portrait of him is included in his collected works, *Yün-ch'i fa-hui* 法彙, and reproduced in *Fonti Ricciane.*

Bibliography

Chu-hung, *Yün-ch'i fa-hui* (1897), 28/50b, 55a, 41b, 34/2a, 11a, 23a; Yü Ch'un-hsi 虞淳熙 (cs 1583), "Yün-ch'i lien-ch'ih ta-shih chuan 傳," *Huang Ming wen-hai*, 20/2/8; P'eng Shao-sheng (ECCP) and P'eng Hsi-su (ECCP, p. 620), *Ching-t'u sheng hsien lu* (1783), 5/13a; *Taishō daizō-kyō*, Vol. 49, no. 2038, p. 952; Ming-ho 明河, *Pu hsü Kao-seng chuan* 補續高僧傳 (1621), 5/55a; *Chekiang t'ung-chih* (1934), 3880; P. M. d'Elia, *Fonti Ricciane*, II (Rome 1949), pl. 19, p. 306.

Chun-fang Yü

CHU I-chün 朱翊鈞, September 4, 1563-August 18, 1620, thirteenth emperor in the Ming line, was also known by his reign title Wan-li 萬曆 (1573-1620), by his temple name Shen-tsung 神宗, by his posthumous name the emperor Hsien 顯, and by the designation of his tomb Ting-ling 定陵. In his youth he gave himself the studio title Yü-chai 禹齋, alluding to King Yü of ancient times. He ruled over a united China longer than anyone before him since Han Wu-ti (141-87 B.C.) —for forty-eight years beginning on July 19, 1572. The third-born but eldest surviving son of Chu Tsai-hou (*q.v.*), he was proclaimed heir apparent in the second year of his father's short reign, 1568, and was only nine years of age (ten *sui*) when he was enthroned. His reign is remembered chiefly for administrative reforms promoted by Chang Chü-cheng (*q.v.*) in the first ten years, rancorous factional controversies at court thereafter, unprecedented interference by eunuchs in provincial administration, elaborate construction projects and extravagant production of cloisonné and polychrome porcelain wares, re-introduction of Christianity in many places in China by European missionaries, the war against the Japanese invaders in Korea in the 1590s, some campaigns against Mongol raiders on the northern frontier, the suppression of aboriginal rebels in the southwest, and the rise to power in the northeast of Manchus who were to succeed the Ming dynasty in 1644.

The population had probably doubled since the early Ming years, to a total in excess of 100,000,000. Agriculture thrived, in part because of supplementary crops newly introduced from the Americas: maize, sweet potatoes, and peanuts. Manufacturing flourished under state and private auspices alike; and trade on regional, interregional, and national scales was esteemed and profitable to a degree not reached since the 13th century. The greatest cities, such as Peking, Nanking, Soochow, and Hangchow displayed the affluence of a society becoming increasingly urbanized and commercialized; and foreign traders (including Portuguese newly settled at Macao) sought business privileges at every frontier and coastal market. Tradi-

tional learning was stimulated by the spread of private academies (shu-yüan 書院), which, though many were closed by the order of 1579, assumed great political influence in the early 1600s. Expanding literacy encouraged the production of popular literature including how-to-do-it encyclopedias of many sorts and such fictional masterpieces as the novels *Hsi-yu chi* (*see* Wu Ch'eng-en) and *Chin P'ing Mei* (*see* Wang Shih-chen). Affluence combined with the liberating thought of Wang Shou-jen (*q.v.*) had created a ferment of innovative, iconoclastic self-expressionism among thinkers, writers, and artists (*see*, for example, Li Chih, Hsü Wei, and Yüan Hung-tao). It was a vigorous, creative, productive, and exploratory age.

It was also an ominously transitional age. When the emperor died in 1620, the far northeast frontier (modern Manchuria) had been overrun by the Manchus; ruinous tax increases or extortions had driven large numbers of people into banditry or rebellion in all parts of the empire, and state coffers were nevertheless drained; posts in both central and provincial government agencies were vacant as often as not, and officials on duty were locked in partisan antagonisms that almost paralyzed the government; and for a quarter century the emperor had done his best to neglect affairs of state. Extravagance, corruption, and ineptitude had become so normal that post-Ming historians have consistently attributed the collapse of the dynasty in the 1640s to trends that developed in Wan-li times, specifically blaming the emperor himself.

The first Wan-li decade was perhaps the most peaceful, prosperous, and stable of the Ming. The boy emperor was guided and dominated by a remarkably harmonious and effective triumvirate: his mother Li-shih (*q.v.*), the chief eunuch Feng Pao (*see* Chang Chü-cheng), and the senior grand secretary Chang Chü-cheng. The northern frontier was made secure by the vigorous and prestigious generals. Ch'i Chi-kuang (*q.v.*) northeast of Peking, and Li Ch'eng-liang (ECCP) in the Liao basin of Manchuria, under the capable direction of the ministers of War T'an Lun and Wang Ch'ung-ku (*qq.v.*). The great Tümed Mongol chief Altan-qaγan (*q.v.*), who had harassed the northern frontier since the 1520s, had finally made peace with China in 1570/71, and, until his death in 1583, he conducted tributary trade at frontier fairs and spent his energies converting his tribesmen to Lamaism. The nominal grand khan of all the Mongols, the Chahar chief Tümen-qaγan (*see* Chang Chü-cheng), based farther to the northeast on the border of the Liao basin, also devoutly Lamaist, made probing raids on Li Ch'eng-liang's outposts almost annually but was not a serious threat. In 1579 Li and Ch'i Chi-kuang mounted a combined pincers operation against his raiders and routed them decisively. In domestic affairs Chang Chü-cheng provided stern leadership in restoring bureaucratic discipline and efficiency. His authoritarian leadership was possible chiefly because he enjoyed the confidence and support of the Empress-dowager Li-shih. She insisted on making extravagant contributions for building temples and shrines (*see* Fu-teng), which Chang disapproved of; but in general she admonished the young emperor always to heed Chang, and she did not hesitate to chastize him angrily when he did not.

Ming emperors generally had been headstrong and temperamental. It could not have taken many years for Chu I-chün to weary of the tight discipline under which he grew to manhood. While the great grand secretary lived, the emperor treated him with the greatest deference, showered compliments and favors on him, and unhesitatingly punished and drove out of service officials who dared to criticize him. When Chang died in mid-1582, however, the emperor seems to have determined never again to subject himself to such domination. He still stood in awe of Feng Pao. But Feng now had no prestigious collaborator in the bureauc-

racy and was vulnerable to criticism because while Chang lived he had grown carelessly arrogant and corrupt. Before the year ended, the emperor, seizing opportunities afforded by censorial denunciations, sent Feng Pao into retirement at the auxiliary capital, Nanking. Empress-dowager Li protested but was mollified by false assurances that Feng would be recalled. Soon, however, Feng was ruined by the confiscation of his private household, which yielded more than one million taels of gold and silver, for the emperor's private vaults. Almost at the same time, Chang's favorite general, Ch'i Chi-kuang, after sixteen years of effective command on the northern frontier, was peremptorily transferred to a lackluster post in Kwangtung. Censorial critics of Chang who had previously been punished were simultaneously recalled to duty. The emperor's mood became ever more plainly apparent, and denunciations of Chang himself began to pour in from censorial and other officials Early in 1583 the emperor announced Chang's posthumous degradation, ruined Chang's family, and began purging officials whom Chang had patronized.

Through the remainder of the Wan-li era the emperor refused to have close relations with grand secretaries and increasingly closeted himself in the palace. At the beginning of his reign, because of his youthfulness, it had been arranged that he take personal part in daily court audiences only nine days each month (on "3-6-9 days"; that is, the 3d, 6th, 9th, 13th, 16th, 19th, 23rd, 26th, and 29th), other days being devoted to study under the tutorship of Hanlin Academy officials. By 1586, however, the emperor had become notoriously negligent in both these activities; and after the eighth month of 1589 he ceased appearing at general audiences entirely for more than twenty-five years—until the fifth month of 1615. In the second month of 1590 he permanently terminated his tutorial contacts with Hanlin scholars, and in 1591 he completely ceased taking personal part in the great public sacrificial ceremonies that were traditional annual highlights of Peking life. The emperor did not even participate in the elaborate funeral of the queen mother Li-shih in 1614. Imperial interviews with grand secretaries, already irregular in the late 1580s, became notoriously rare after 1590. There were two interviews in 1593 and one in 1594, one in 1602, another in 1615, and then no more until the emperor was dying in 1620. A whole generation of officials came into the government without ever having seen their emperor; some grand secretaries had no direct contact with him throughout their tenures. The early Jesuit missionary Álvarō Semedo (*q.v.*) wrote about the consequent widespread rumors that a Chinese emperor "never suffereth himself to be seen, and that he is always shut up in a glasse, and only sheweth one foot, and such like things."

Since the Ming governmental system concentrated all significant decision-making power in the emperor, Chu I-chün's seclusion put great strain on the grand secretaries, who bore responsibility for submitting recommendations to him and then transmitting his decisions to the appropriate administrative agencies for implementation. Eunuchs had to be relied on to shuttle papers back and forth between the grand secretaries and the emperor, and sometimes grand secretaries had to rely solely on eunuchs' oral reports of what the emperor intended. Matters were made more awkward when in 1587 the emperor began to ignore memorials that offended him, and retained them in the palace unanswered. From 1591 this became his normal reaction to almost all memorials: there was simply no response except in matters relating urgently to defense and taxation.

There were two particularly serious consequences of the emperor's inattentiveness—or, properly speaking, his refusal to be bothered. On one hand, personnel administration stagnated. Appointments, transfers, leaves, retirements, and disciplinary actions were blocked for years at a

stretch because of imperial inaction. Official vacancies went unfilled, so that even routine administration was imperiled. In 1596 the ministry of Personnel and censorial officials complained about understaffing throughout the government and its unfortunate effects—for example, the people's growing difficulties in getting important litigations resolved. Despite continuing complaints, the personnel situation deteriorated steadily. In 1602 nine of the Censorate's thirteen regional inspectorships were unstaffed; the central government's six ministries were short three ministers and ten vice ministers, the Censorate and the six offices of scrutiny were ninety-four men below normal staffing levels; three provinces had no governors; lesser provincial-level vacancies totaled sixty-six; and twenty-five prefectures lacked prefects. By 1612 administration was at a virtual standstill. There was only one grand secretary and he had been ill and secluded in his Peking residence for months; there was only one ministry head, charged with concurrent responsibility for the three ministries of Personnel, of War, and of Justice; the ministries of Revenue, of Rites, and of Works each had only one vice minister on duty; the Censorate had not had a regular censor-in-chief for eight years; in the Censorate circuits and in the offices of scrutiny officials commonly held several posts concurrently; a number of regional inspectors had not been relieved or replaced for more than a decade; provincial-level vacancies abounded; and it was estimated that some fifty per cent of all prefectural and district posts were vacant. Several thousand expectant appointees were reported idling in Peking simply because there was no one in the appointing agencies who could certify their appointments. Subsequently the six offices of scrutiny, normally staffed by more than fifty supervising secretaries, sank to a total staff of four men, at which point five of the six offices had no one in charge; and at one time only five men were assigned to the Censorate's thirteen circuits, which had a total normal staff of over one hundred investigating censors. The fact that prisoners languished and died in prison solely for want of trial judges was only one unfortunate effect of the failing personnel system: administration in all areas was beset by creeping paralysis.

A second consequence of the emperor's inaction was the rise of vicious, endemic partisan strife in officialdom. Partisan quarreling as much as anything else actually discouraged the emperor from making appointments and otherwise tending to governmental business, and his inaction naturally gave ever freer rein to partisan wranglers. The bureaucrats had resented Chang Chü-cheng's authoritarian discipline as much as the emperor had, and after Chang's death they shared the emperor's determination not to permit the emergence of another dictatorial grand secretary. Chang's successors as senior grand secretary therefore had embattled, frustrating tenures. They notably included Shen Shih-hsing (q.v.), who was dominant in the Grand Secretariat from 1583 to 1591; Wang Hsi-chüeh (q.v.), 1593-94; Chao Chih-kao (see Shen I-kuan), 1594-98; Shen I-kuan (q.v.), 1598-1606; Chu Keng (see Shen I-kuan), 1606-08; Yeh Hsiang-kao (q.v.) 1608-14; and Fang Ts'ung-che (see Wang Ying-chiao), 1614-20. The Ming system made the grand secretary's role a difficult one at the best of times, since emperors normally expected him to serve the imperial interest above all else but suspected him of being a tool of the bureaucracy, whereas the officials in general normally expected him to be their spokesman above all else but suspected him of being a tool of the emperor. It took an extraordinarily strong personality and an extraordinarily fortuitous combination of circumstances (a boy emperor, a strong and trusting empress-dowager, and a strong and cooperative chief eunuch) to produce a Chang Chü-cheng. In the post-Chang years grand secretaries were caught between a sullen uncooperative emper-

or and a clamorously quarrelsome officialdom increasingly split into feuding factions, and they got blamed by all sides no matter what happened.

In the earliest post-Chang years the emperor tried to impose some restraint on the people at court. In 1586, at Shen Shih-hsing's urging, he ordered officials to stop memorializing about matters outside their individual spheres of responsibility. In 1591 he threatened severe punishments to anyone who slandered a grand secretary. In the same year, because of unfavorable astrological portents, he imposed one-year salary suspensions on all officials of the Censorate and the offices of scrutiny. In 1595 a total of thirty-four censorial officials of these agencies were demoted, fined, or otherwise punished in one burst of the emperor's anger. In the 1580s, generally, the emperor did not hesitate to vent his spleen against those who offended him in cruel punishments such as floggings in open court and lifelong banishment to distant frontiers. In the 1590s he was mostly content to fine or demote, but he dealt cunningly with people who seemed to be taking advantage of his leniency. In the case of the thirty-four censorial officials who were fined or demoted in 1596, for example, when a grand secretary protested their mistreatment, the emperor took no action against the grand secretary but increased the severity of the original victims' punishments by sending them all into demeaning frontier posts; and when the minister of Personnel objected to that, he ordered all thirty-four to be dismissed from service entirely. This became commonplace: the more the emperor was opposed, the more truculent and punitive he became. At the same time, however, he was learning to ignore many complaints of sorts that had infuriated him in the 1580s. As early as 1591 he was taking no notice of many complaints whose authors, he felt, were merely seeking to attract attention to themselves; he refused to cooperate by making martyrs of them.

Whereas some officials consequently thought the emperor was mellowing in a promising way, the current minister of Personnel, Sung Hsün 宋纁 (T. 伯敬, cs 1559, d. July, 1591, Pth. 莊敏), observed ruefully that "censorial officials argue about the good and bad points of things so vigorously in order to influence the emperor. Even if they are punished, at least the emperor's thinking gets a shaking-up. His disregard of them is like a paralysis for which there is no cure." Sung's fears were premature: through the 1590s outspoken officials were often fined, demoted, or relieved of office, and occasionally offenders were dealt with more severely—by being flogged in court, tortured in prison, or dismissed from service. But after 1601–2, except for rare outbursts of anger, the emperor consistently ignored criticisms and protests, along with most other presentations from officialdom.

The more unresponsive the emperor became, the more crippling were the effects of partisan controversies among those in office. It had become a point of honor for any one of them when publicly denounced, to withdraw from duty pending exoneration. When the emperor took no action at all, accused officials customarily begged for retirement and accusers became more clamorous. In 1609 the supervising secretary, Wang Yüan-han 王元翰 (T. 伯舉, H. 聚洲, 1565–1622, cs 1601), under partisan attack, felt so humiliated by the emperor's refusal to exonerate him, or even to acknowledge the accusations against him, that he left his post and went to his provincial home without authorization. The ministry of Personnel then denounced him for disloyally abandoning his duty, but this too was ignored. Thereafter scores of officials followed his example, after repeatedly but in vain requesting retirement for whatever reasons; and it was in this fashion that official vacancies multiplied in the late Wan-li years. In 1613 the ministers of Personnel and of War both abandoned their offices without imperial permisson. The

most extreme case of this sort was that of Li T'ing-chi (see Ch'en Yung-pin). Appointed grand secretary in 1607, Li repeatedly asked permission not to serve because of censorial disapproval, but in vain. While on duty he offered his resignation again and again, and after less than a year he began remaining in his Peking residence to avoid provoking further attacks. Since attacks still did not cease, he then sought obscurity in a deserted temple. Finally, in 1613, after more than a full year of such total seclusion from public affairs, during which he continued to be subjected to censorial criticism, Li abandoned the Peking area entirely and on his own authority withdrew to his home in the far southeastern province of Fukien. His resignation had been submitted more than one hundred twenty times, always to be rejected or ignored. Having been nominally a member of the Grand Secretariat for more than five years, he had actually performed the duties of his office for only nine months.

In this way partisans not only harassed grand secretaries and other officials, but they also effectively prevented their victims from serving. It took no more than an accusation, however unfounded, to drive many an enemy from the court arena; and Peking soon abounded with sulking off-duty civil servants. Many officials simply could neither serve nor live in such an atmosphere. Qualified officials by the hundreds, therefore, discontentedly lived in their provincial homes in voluntary if not involuntary retirement, while state administration foundered because of understaffing. Whereas in some other Ming reigns officials may have lived in a state of constant terror, the prevailing mood of the Wan-li era—at least after the mid-1590s—was one of frustration, despair, and withdrawal.

Bureaucratic in-fighting of the Wan-li period developed out of resentment of Chang Chü-cheng's power into general anti-administration (that is, anti-Grand

Secretariat) sentiments. It was widely resented that Chang had wrested control over appointments and over other aspects of personnel administration from the ministry of Personnel, which had traditionally been the prestigious leader of the "outer court" (the line administration, so to speak) vis-à-vis the "inner court" (the Grand Secretariat and palace eunuchs). The prestige and influence of the ministry of Personnel were restored at Grand Secretariat expense in the 1580s, but by the late 1590s had ebbed away to perhaps their lowest point in Ming history because of the emperor's general lack of interest in personnel matters. Another institutional element in the anti-administration disputes was the traditionally privileged role of the censorial agencies, the Censorate and the offices of scrutiny. These had been intimidated and purged of independent minded critics and remonstrators by Chang Chücheng. Later censorial officials, therefore, were almost compulsively critical of the post-Chang grand secretaries, and also played provocative parts in almost all struggles among various outer court factions. By the late Wan-li years censorial officials intimidated and dominated the whole outer court and the Grand Secretariat as well. Meanwhile, however, anti-Grand Secretariat feelings in the outer court and factional wrangling among outer court officials also had all become confusingly intermingled with, and overshadowed by, suspicions and then anxieties and alarms on the part of outer court officials and grand secretaries alike, and even some members of the palace establishment, about the emperor's waywardness. His inattentiveness and his disdainful mistreatment of officials have already been noted. His greed, his drunkenness, his extravagance, his sensual indulgences, and most of all his irresponsibility regarding the naming of and caring for an heir apparent—anxieties about all these imperial aberrations, when not directly at issue, were always in the background of the long series of controversies that dominate the

chronicles of his reign.

The incessant controversies of the Wan-li era, which left a heritage of endemic factionalism for subsequent reigns, involved two groups that can be defined only vaguely and never achieved stable homogeneity. On one hand were self-proclaimed "good elements" (shan-lei 善類 or ch'ing-liu 清流) —men who conservatively advocated traditional morality and integrity in government, who were mostly anti-Grand Secretariat by inclination, and who insistently called the emperor to task for his shortcomings. Some "good elements" while in retirement founded a Tung-lin ("Eastern Grove") Academy at Wusih west of Soochow in 1604, and there engaged in philosophical discussions that attributed current political troubles to pervasive self-indulgence stemming from the individualistic thought of Wang Shoujen; they advocated a moral reinvigoration founded on the thought of Chu Hsi (1130-1200), the great systematizer of Sung dynasty neo-Confucianism (see Ku Hsien-ch'eng and Kao P'an-lung). Beginning in 1610, the "good elements" at court were collectively termed a Tung-lin Party (tang 黨), and to the end of the dynasty men were freely categorized as Tung-lin partisans even if they had no connection at all with the Tung-lin Academy. The opposition, in the eyes of the "good elements," consisted of weak grand secretaries who either did not try or failed to persuade the emperor to do his duty, together with their opportunistic, sycophantic outer court adherents. The opposition eventually became recognizable, and geographically identifiable: one faction from Chekiang, another from Shantung, and a third from Hukuang, all loosely coordinated under the leadership of a supervising secretary from Shantung, Ch'i Shih-chiao (see Kao P'an-lung). After the emperor's death in 1620, the so-called Tung-lin Party gained ascendancy in government only to run afoul of the dictatorial chief eunuch Wei Chung-hsien (ECCP). who purged it ruthlessly from 1625 to 1626.

The controversies that absorbed governmental attention in Wan-li times arose in the following succession:

1585: The argument over the imperial tomb. A site had been chosen for the new emperor's "eternity palace" (shou-kung 壽宮) in the hills northwest of Peking two years before. Now, when construction work had already begun, the censor Li Chih (see Shen Shih-hsing, not to be confused with his contemporary whose name is romanized similarly) began arguing that the site was too stony to be auspicious; he accused Grand Secretary Shen Shih-hsing of advising the emperor unwisely about it. Shen defended himself. Li and his principal supporters received six-month salary suspensions but persisted in their arguments; then other censorial officials began attacking them. The emperor finally made a personal inspection tour to the site and pronounced it eminently suitable. Li Chih was demoted to a provincial post. Some of his friends angrily demanded that they be dismissed but were ignored. Chao Yung-hsien (q. v.) memorialized in defense of Li, and denounced the villainy and the dangers of partisan favoritism.

1586-1601: the case of "the trunk of the state" (kuo-pen 國本). This had to do with the formal designation of an heir apparent, which was thought essential to the smooth continuance of the dynasty and thus to the stability of the empire (see Cheng Kuei-fei).

1593: The struggle over merit evaluations (see Chao Nan-hsing and Ku Hsien-ch'eng).

Meanwhile there arose the controversy over eunuch tax commissioners. The dispatch of palace eunuchs on special missions outside the capital had been a practice of Ming emperors at least since the early decades of the 15th century when missions to foreign lands were officered by eunuchs and when fleets led by eunuch admirals roamed the South China Sea and the Indian Ocean (see Cheng Ho). But never before had their activities been so much a matter of concern among civil service officials, apparently, as after 1594, when Chu I-chün approved a request that silver mines be opened throughout the empire to replenish state coffers that were being depleted by wars in Korea and on inland frontiers. Then in 1596 the emperor's residence halls were ruined by a fire, and a year later the main audience halls were also burned down. The emperor used the rebuilding of these structures as excuse for sending out eunuchs to supervise the mining projects and to impose a special mine tax. Their numbers increased as more and more special taxes were added to the regular tax structure—levies on shops, on boats, on market stalls, and others. Finally in 1599 eunuch commissioners were given supervisory control over all the taxes of the various provinces. Civil service officials were almost entirely united in opposition to this development and angrily reported scores of gross abuses that were being committed by the eunuch commissioners and their henchmen, ranging from extortion to murder. Local officials whom the eunuchs accused of obstructionism were arbitrarily punished. Court and provincial officials bombarded the emperor with protests. On March 9, 1602, the emperor (who thought he was dying) issued a proclamation correcting these abuses, but recalled it when he recovered (see Shen I-kuan). The clamor against eunuch tax commissioners continued until 1606, when the emperor authorized an order canceling the mine taxes and transferring control of all local taxes back to the regular civil service authorities. Since the special taxes had been imposed, the eunuch commissioners had submitted some three million taels of silver and countless precious stones and other rare commodities obtained largely by extortion.

Even though the special taxes had thus been terminated, the emperor refused to recall his eunuch tax commissioners from the provinces. They continued to harass local officials and well-to-do fami-

lies until the end of the Wan-li reign, and
both grand secretaries and outer court
officials continued endlessly to protest
their abusiveness. Popular uprisings in
Hukuang province were provoked repeatedly between 1596 and 1601 by the
eunuch tax commissioner Ch'en Feng (*q.
v.*) who was finally recalled to the palace
at his own request to escape being murdered. In 1599 an uprising in Shantung
resulted in the murders of thirty-seven
henchmen of the local tax eunuch. Six
retainers of a eunuch were murdered by
a mob in Soochow in 1601, and in 1602
notable popular uprisings against eunuchs
occurred in Kiangsi, Kwangtung, Kwangsi,
and Yunnan provinces. In 1606 the eunuch commissioner Yang Jung (*see* Ch'en
Yung-pin) and more than two hundred of
his retainers were killed by aroused aboriginal tribesmen of Yunnan; whereupon
the emperor became so agitated that he
was unable to eat for several days.

1603: The controversy over the Ch'u
princedom. Relations between Shen I-kuan
and his antagonists worsened dramatically
in 1603 in a dispute over the legitimacy
of the prince of Ch'u, Chu Hua-k'uei (*see*
Kuo Cheng-yü). When the emperor finally
decided that the prince was genuine and
degraded his accusers, Kuo submitted his
resignation amid charges that, because of
an old grudge against the prince, he had
himself instigated the original accusations

1603: The case of "the subversive
books" (*see* Cheng Kuei-fei, and also Chu
Ch'ang-lo in ECCP).

1604: A new controversy over merit
evaluations (*see* Shen I-kuan and Kuo
Cheng-yü). In the ensuing clamor of
accusations and denials Wen Ch'un (*see*
Shen I-kuan) was permitted to retire; some
of his defenders were sent into frontier
military service and then dismissed from
service entirely; and Ch'ien Meng-kao 錢
夢皐 (cs 1589), who was thought to be
Shen's principal outer court agent, was
dismissed.

1607: The abortive recall of Wang
Hsi-chüeh. Unwilling to leave an enemy

in control of the Grand Secretariat, Shen
I-kuan on his retirement in 1606 had connived to have Shen Li dismissed simultaneously. Chu Keng for several months
was the solitary grand secretary, but the
emperor announced additions to the Secretariat in the fifth month of the next
year. To everyone's astonishment, the
long-time controversialist, Wang Hsi-chüeh,
was recalled from retirement to serve a
third term, having more than sufficient
seniority to become the dominant grand
secretary. The "good elements" were exasperated beyond restraint (*see* Ku Hsien-
ch'eng). Immediately an almost universal
furor against Wang arose, and his recall
to service was not insisted upon.

1611: Yet another controversy over
merit evaluations. In preparation for the
merit evaluations that were due once
more in that year, the emperor had recalled from retirement a long-time anti-administration stalwart, Sun P'ei-yang (*q. v.*),
to be minister of Personnel. At this time
Yeh Hsiang-kao, a friend and defender
of Tung-lin men, was a solitary grand
secretary. The prospect of the new evaluations was therefore an ominous one for
enemies of the "good elements" (*see* Yeh
Hsiang-kao and Sun P'ei-yang). The emperor, however, approved the ministry of
Personnel's recommendations. What then
seemed to be a great triumph for the
"good elements" quickly turned into disaster. So savage were the attacks on all
concerned that "good elements" leaders,
including Sun P'ei-yang, began retiring
without imperial consent. When Yeh was
permitted to leave the Grand Secretariat
in 1614 after submitting his resignation
more than sixty times, enemies of the
Tung-lin Party dominated the central government. They manipulated the next merit
evaluations in 1617 to weed out remaining or newly emerging "good elements."

1612-14: The controversy over the
prince of Fu 福. In the winter of 1612 a
princely establishment was completed at
Loyang for Lady Cheng's son, Chu
Ch'ang-hsün (*see* Cheng Kuei-fei), who

had been named prince of Fu in 1601 and was now twenty-six years of age. His extraordinarily prolonged presence at Peking had been provocative indeed, and there was accumulated resentment that his wedding had cost the state 300,000 taels and that construction of his residence at Loyang had cost another 280,000, ten times the normal allowance. Late in the spring of 1613 the emperor yielded to increasingly urgent demands; he announced that the prince would be sent to Loyang in the following spring—but of course, he added, this could be assured only when an estate of 40,000 *ch'ing* of land had been designated for the prince's support.

1615: The case of "the attack with the club." In the summer of 1615 public attention was dramatically drawn once more to the situation of the heir apparent and the problem of the imperial succession when an uncouth commoner burst into the heir apparent's compound in the palace, clubbed the gatekeeper, and tried to force his way into the residence proper (*see* Kao P'an-lung).

The demoralization and deterioration of government resulting from all the personnel problems and factional feuds that flowed from the lack of firm leadership in the central government after Chang Chü-cheng's time coincided with a long series of natural disturbances. Beginning in the 1580s, strange astrological portents were commonplace. Earthquakes, typhoons, and other storms repeatedly devastated large areas in every part of the empire. Floods and droughts, with resultant famines, were reported almost annually from one area or another. The northwestern provinces, long relied on to support defenses against the Mongols on the frontier, were in process of becoming a permanently distressed area; and the empire's great grain-producing regions in the Yellow River plain, the Yangtze valley and delta, and the southeastern provinces were often troubled by climatic irregularities. No doubt in part be-

cause of abuses by eunuch tax supervisors, trade declined; harassed merchants went out of business, market places were closed down, and whole regions slipped into economic recession. In the last decade of the Wan-li reign, tax quotas seemed hopelessly beyond attainment and tax arrearages accumulated by the millions of taels.

Economic conditions in the empire constituted one realm in which the emperor recognized a vital interest. A major reason for his refusal ever to recall his eunuch tax commissioners from the provinces was his belief that they could look after his fiscal interests more efficiently than the bureaucracy and that the disadvantageous consequences—bureaucratic antagonisms and even occasional popular uprisings—were not sufficient to offset the presumed advantages. The emperor was easily persuaded, at least through the 1590s, to remit taxes and distribute emergency relief funds when these traditional ways of being merciful to distressed areas were called for. He also had huge waterworks projects undertaken to prevent or minimize water disasters. Between 1593 and 1604 a new canal was constructed, with great difficulty, from the confluence of the Yellow and Huai Rivers north into Shantung province, providing a reliable tributary of the Grand Canal that was necessary for adequate provisioning of the far northeast. In 1596 he authorized construction of new dikes and ramparts that guided excess waters of the Yellow and Huai Rivers into the sea and kept the Grand Canal navigable through the Huai basin to the Yangtze. More construction in the same region was completed in 1606, employing half a million laborers for six months. Additional repairs were necessitated a decade later between Kaifeng and Hsü-chou, where the Yellow River persistently breached its dikes. The Grand Canal waterways complex was thus kept operational at great cost, to meet the food-transport needs created by wars in Korea in the 1590s and in Liaotung in the later Wan-li years.

On the excuse of rebuilding the audience and residence halls destroyed by fire in 1596 and 1597 the emperor sent more eunuchs out to exact taxes and acquire lumber. By 1604 the main residence hall, Ch'ien-ch'ing-kung 乾清宮, was rebuilt but, although taxes arrived regularly and lumber accumulated, the audience halls remained in ruins until 1615. A half-hearted rebuilding program started then but was soon suspended. The halls were finally rebuilt in 1626 and 1627 under the direction of the eunuch Wei Chung-hsien

The emperor was also extravagant in more personal ways. His wedding clothes in 1578 cost 90,000 taels. Setting up his brother, the prince of Lu, in a residence in Hukuang province subsequently cost 200,000 taels. The weddings of two imperial princesses reportedly cost a total of 1,200,000 taels. The investiture ceremonies for the emperor's five sons in 1601 were originally budgeted for an astonishing 24,000,000 taels; in the end officials were able to dissuade the emperor from such heavy expenditures, but even so the investitures and weddings of the princes cost a cumulative total of more than 12,000,000 taels. Total annual revenue of the government at all levels has been estimated, for this era, at about 26,000,000 piculs of grain and about 14,000,000 taels of silver, of which only a small fraction found its way to the central government. Outlays on the scale mentioned were therefore lavish indeed; moreover, they had few beneficial effects on the general economy, for they were devoted primarily to jewelry, clothing, and similar personal items of adornment or curiosity. Investment of capital in such unproductive ways became widespread in the late Ming years, partly as a reflection of the Wan-li emperor's example.

The emperor was nevertheless notoriously tightfisted. The expenditures mentioned above were not made from his personal vaults; they were made possible by requisitions from regular governmental treasuries. Revenues that had traditionally been kept in reserve by the administrative agencies of the central government were transferred to the palace in unprecedented amounts throughout the reign; and for extraordinary needs, such as palace construction and princely investitures, funds were called in from provincial and local government reserves throughout the empire. The emperor's own income—the 1,200,000 taels paid him annually from state revenues, plus whatever income derived from the multiplying imperial estates and miscellaneous other sources—all went into palace vaults, inaccessible for general governmental purposes and unaccounted for. It was especially resented that for every tael delivered to the palace by the hated eunuch tax commissioners, as many as ten taels had to be spent by governmental agencies for support of huge entourages that accompanied the eunuchs. Officials always believed that an inexhaustible fortune was hoarded in the palace; and particularly in the late Wan-li years, when funds were desperately needed for defense against the Manchus in Liaotung and general governmental reserves were all but exhausted, there were clamorous demands that the emperor open his vaults. The emperor rarely acceded; he consistently complained that the palace treasury was as dangerously depleted as any other Outer court critics were delighted when the long-championed heir apparent, upon the emperor's death, found it possible immediately to release 2,000,000 taels of silver from the palace treasury for use in Liaotung.

Defense of the frontiers, of course, was another realm in which the emperor recognized a vital interest, and defense was costly. The peace achieved with Altan-qaγan in 1570–71 had a price; what resulted was an extension to the Tümed and Ordos Mongols north of Shansi, Shensi, and Kansu of the reverse tribute system that had long been enjoyed by the Uriyangqad Mongols settled immediately northeast of Peking. That is, the

Ming government tried to keep the whole northern frontier stable by admitting the Mongols to trading privileges at frontier markets (where the Chinese acquired horses for their military needs) and by granting various Mongol chiefs "rewards" that amounted to annual subsidies. The Chahar chief Tümen-qaɣan, on the western border of the Liao basin to the north, disdained such tributary relations; but his successors Sečen-quɣan (r. 1593—1603) and Ligdan-Qutuɣtu-qaɣan (r. 1604-34) had no such scruples. They demanded subsidies as regularly as did Altan's successors Cürüke (*see* Altan qaɣan) and Bušuɣtu (*see* Li Ju-sung). Payments of this sort increased steadily through the Wan-li years, but the policy did keep the northern frontier relatively stable, resulting in savings in military spending.

Fortunately for the Chinese, the Mongols were in a transitional status without strong or unified leadership after Altan-qaɣan. His successors were largely figureheads, often manipulated by Ordos Mongol strongmen.

The Ordos Mongols occasionally gave trouble, especially while migrating back and forth across Kansu to visit Lamaist shrines in Kokonor. Thus in 1590 they were pursued and routed in Kokonor by the frontier supreme commander Cheng Lo 鄭洛 (cs 1556). In 1592 an uprising in the Ning-hsia area was led by a Chahar Mongol formerly in the Ming military service, Pübei (*see* Li Ju-sung), and his son. They occupied Ning-hsia city most of that year, besieged by a grand army summoned from all nearby provinces and as far away as Chekiang, which finally forced the city to yield by diverting Yellow River waters to flood it. Chinese historians have considered the relief of Ning-hsia to be one of "the three great punitive campaigns" of the Wan-li era (others being the war with the Japanese in Korea from 1592 to 1598 and a campaign against southwestern aboriginal tribesmen in 1599-1600). In 1595 Yung-shih-pu 永什卜, a

nephew of Altan-qaɣan who had long been settled on the Kansu-Kokonor border and had recurringly raided Kansu, was chastened when caught in a pincers operation by Ming forces from Kansu and cooperating Tibetan or Uighur tribesmen from his rear. In 1598, again with the cooperation of Tibetans or Uighurs, Chinese forces in the Ordos region defeated the Mongols. The latter moved into Kokonor, where in 1603 and in 1607 the Chinese reported great victories. In the latter year the figurehead khan Cürüke died, and for an interval the Mongols were preoccupied with internal feuding (*see* Altan-qaɣan).

By 1613 the Tümed and Ordos tribes were so fragmented that Bušuɣtu had almost no control over them, and they were less threatening to China than ever before. They kept demanding market privileges and subsidies, however; and in 1613 and 1616 substantial campaigns had to be waged against them in the Yen-sui and Sui-yüan regions.

The southwestern frontiers were unstable through most of the Wan-li era. Burma in particular was experiencing both internal wars and wars with the Thai, and Burmese groups often violated nearby Chinese territories. A large Chinese campaign was mounted against them in 1584; Chinese forces invaded as far as the northern Burmese capital of Ava, and the Burma-Yunnan frontier was stabilized for a time. In 1594 Burmese groups were pushed out of Yunnan once more, but by 1606 the Burmese had by persistence won lasting control over some marginal zones (*see* Ch'en Yung-pin).

Aboriginal tribes of the southwest continued to be occasionally rebellious as had been true throughout the Ming, and government forces were repeatedly mobilized to suppress them. The most significant action was occasioned by the rebellion of the Po-chou chieftain Yang Ying-lung (*q. v.*). Po-chou had been a virtually autonomous state on the Szechwan-Kweichow border since the T'ang. When Yang's rebellion was put down in 1600 under the able direction of the supreme commander Li Hua-lung (*q. v.*), Po-chou was incorporated into the regular civil administration, divided into two prefectures attached to Szechwan and Kweichow provinces. In 1608, after the suppression of an aboriginal uprising in Yunnan, the rebels' territory was similarly incorporated into the regular provincial administrative structure. Sinification of the aborigines concerned was accelerated significantly in each instance.

Prior to the emergence of the Manchus, the most prominent challenge to Chinese dominance of the east Asian mainland perhaps in the whole Ming era—was Japan's invasion of Korea in the 1590s, which prompted extensive debates at the Ming court and extraordinary demands on the country's military and logistics systems. This war resulted from the ambition of Toyotomi Hideyoshi, newly emergent military dictator of Japan, to constitute a far-flung east Asian empire including China (*see* Ch'en Lin and Konishi).

Added to other things, the war in Korea made the 1590s a spectacularly troubled and expensive decade. The "three great punitive campaigns" reportedly drained a total of between 10,000,000 and 12,000,000 taels of silver from the central government's reserves, beyond normal continuing defense allocations. Special land tax increments had to be imposed to help pay war costs in Korea and the southwest; these were terminated in 1599 and 1600 respectively. There were also the great palace conflagrations in 1596 and 1597; and it was in 1599 that a proclamation called for 24,000,000 taels in special assessments to provide for the anticipated investitures of the imperial princes. These needs intensified the activities of eunuch tax supervisors in the provinces. The turn of the century was unquestionably a critical point in the fiscal and economic history of Ming China.

The threat that hung heaviest over China in the last Wan-li years emanated from the far northeast—the region between the Liao basin and Korea. Tungusic-speaking peoples had occupied the area since the beginning of the dynasty, under loose tributary arrangements. The young Manchu chief Nurhaci (ECCP) began building a coalition of tribes there in 1583, to some extent under the patronage of Li Ch'eng-liang of the Liaotung command. By 1616 Nurhaci had proclaimed himself emperor of a successor state of the Jurchen empire that had ruled north China in the 12th and 13th centuries. His open rebellion reached an early climax two years later, when his forces besieged and captured Fu-shun 撫順, a disaster which galvanized the court into emergency action. The emperor contributed 1,000,000 taels of silver from his palace vaults to help in massing a grand punitive expedition under the veteran generalissimo Yang Hao (ECCP). The Manchus met Yang's columns separately and routed them one by one in the most devastating Ming defeat since that at T'u-mu in 1449. Nurhaci then quickly reduced Ming garrisons at T'ieh-ling and K'ai-yüan in northernmost Liaotung, posing the gravest possible threat to the whole northeastern establishment. The victim of censorial clamor at court, as well as of Manchus in the field, Yang Hao was recalled, imprisoned, and sentenced to death. A more aggressive official, Hsiung T'ing-pi (ECCP), also experienced in Liaotung service, was recalled from retirement to replace Yang. When the emperor died that August, Hsiung had stabilized the situation in Liaotung temporarily, but the best he could hope for was to prevent new inroads by the Manchus, who were growing ever stronger and more confident.

People have long been fascinated by events in the Wan-li reign associated with the appearance and spread in China of Jesuit missions under the leadership and inspiration of Matteo Ricci (*q. v.*). When Ricci died in Peking in 1610, the emperor was persuaded to give the Jesuits a small suburban property once belonging to a eunuch, where he might be buried.

Historians have naturally been puzzled by the personality of this long-secluded emperor. He himself in 1589 told grand secretaries that his inactivity was due not to lack of interest, but only to the fact he was often dizzy and short-tempered and could not bear anxieties. In his later years he was reported to suffer backaches and sore legs or feet, and he became so obese that he had to be supported while erect. Modern students have suspected he might have suffered glandular disorders, and some modern Chinese historians, without citing any early textual evidence, have stated outright that the emperor was one of China's earliest opium addicts. His death followed more than two months of painful illness, apparently involving uncontrollable diarrhea and swelling of his extremities. On his deathbed he confessed to the heir apparent that he had been a neglectful ruler and insisted upon minimal mourning.

The three sons left by the emperor in addition to the heir apparent and the controversial prince of Fu were the prince of Jui 瑞, Chu Ch'ang-hao, the prince of Hui, Chu Ch'ang-jun, and the prince of Kuei, Chu Ch'ang-ying (for all, see ECCP, p. 176). The emperor sired three more sons who did not survive infancy. Of ten daughters, only two reached maturity: the Jung-ch'ang kung-chu 榮昌公主 (married 1596, d. 1616) and the Shou-ning kung-chu (see Cheng kuei-fei). The official empress, née Wang 王, died only a few months before the emperor in 1620. The heir's mother, also née Wang, died earlier, in 1611, having finally been granted the honored kuei-fei consort rank when the heir's first son was born in 1606. Another consort, née Liu 劉, who held the rank of chao-fei 昭妃, survived until 1642, when she died in the palace at the age of eighty-six. Cheng Kuei-fei, mother of the prince of Fu, apparently enjoyed the emperor's principal favor until his death; his will instructed that she

be promoted to the rank of empress, but she never received such honors. She survived until 1630.

The emperor's tomb, called Ting-ling, was constructed over a six-year span during the 1580s at a reported cost in excess of 8,000,000 taels of silver. The emperor was buried there together with his official empress. At the insistence of his grandson, the remains of the Lady Wang who mothered his heir were transferred there in 1621, and she was posthumously promoted to the rank of empress. Excavation of the tomb was carried out in 1956–58 by a team of Chinese archaeologists, who found it to be a lavish, large-scale underground palace. It quickly became a sightseeing attraction rivaling the Great Wall in popularity among Chinese and foreign visitors alike.

Bibliography

Ming-shih, ch. 20–21; Fu Wei-lin, *Ming-shu*, ch. 16; MSL, Shen-tsung, ch. 1–596; Ku Ying-t'ai, *Ming-ch'ao chi-shih pen-mo*, ch. 61–68; KC (1958), ch. 68–83; Shen Shih-hsing, *Chao-tui-lu* 召對錄 (TsSCC, 1936); Hsia Hsieh, *Ming T'ung-chien*, ch. 66–76; Ch'ü Chiu-ssu, *Wan-li wu-kung lu*, ch. 7–14; Mao Jui-cheng, *Wan-li san ta-cheng k'ao*; Wen Ping, *Hsien-po chih-shih*; Wu Ying-chi, *Tung-lin pen-mo*; Shen Shih-hsing, *Sheng-ch'u hui-lu* 升儲彙錄 (Wan-li ed.); Chu Keng, *K'an Ch'u shih-mo* 勘楚始末 and *Yao-shu chi-shih* 妖書記事, in *Chu Wen-i kung tsou-shu* 朱文懿公奏疏 (Wan-li ed.), 2/43b, 50b; Li Kuang-pi 李光璧, *Ming-ch'ao shih-lüeh* 明朝史略 (1957), 126; Meng Sen (BDRC), *Ming-tai shih* 明代史 (1957), 268; Li Tung-fang 黎東方, *Hsi-shuo Ming-ch'ao* 細說明朝 (2 vols., 1964–65), 21/373; Hsieh Kuo-chen 謝國楨, *Ming-Ch'ing chih chi tang-she yün-tung k'ao* 明清之際黨社運動考 (1934), 1; Ting I 丁易, *Ming-tai t'e-wu cheng-chih* 明代特物政治 (1950); Li Wen-chih 李文治, *Wan Ming min-pien* 晚明民變 (1948), 1; Li Kuang-t'ao 李光濤, *Wan-li er-shih-san-nien feng Jih-pen kuo-wang Toyotomi Hideyoshi k'ao* 萬曆二十三年封日本國王豐臣秀吉考 (1967); A. Semedo, *The History of that Great and Renowned Monarchy of China*, tr. from Italian (London, 1655), 110; C. O. Hucker, "The Tung-lin Movement of the Late Ming Period," in J. K. Fairbank, ed., *Chinese Thought and Institutions* (1957), 132; Henry Serruys, *Sino-Mongol Relations During the Ming, II: The Tribute System and Diplomatic*

Missions, 1400–1600, MCB, XIV, 1967, 91: P. M. d'Elia, ed., *Fonti Ricciane,* 3 vols., Rome, 1942–49; Hsia Nai, "Opening an Imperial Tomb," *China Reconstructs,* Vol. VIII, no. 3 (March, 1959), 16.

Charles O. Hucker

CHU Jo-chi, *see* TAO-chi

CHU Kao-chih 朱高熾, August 16, 1378–May 29, 1425, fourth emperor of the Ming dynasty, ruled China for less than a year from 1424 to 1425. He is known to history by his posthumous temple name, Jen-tsung 仁宗. He was the eldest son of Chu Ti and his consort, née Hsü (*qq.v.*), later (1402) emperor and empress of China.

As a young man Chu Kao-chih showed little inclination for the vigorously physical aspects of leadership that so notably characterized his father and his grandfather, Chu Yüan-chang. Once in the time of the first emperor, on being sent out with other princes to review troops at dawn, Chu Kao-chih returned unexpectedly with the explanation that the early morning was too cold; he would have breakfast and then review the troops. He grew up fat and sickly, often having trouble with his feet, perhaps gout. Chu Ti repeatedly thought to set him aside as heir in favor of his tall, powerful, arrogant brother, Chu Kao-hsü (*q.v.*). But the youth took readily to the civil aspects of governance and displayed such a sober sense of responsibility and such sound judgment that Chu Ti never openly threatened his status.

Chu Kao-chih was officially established as heir to his father's princedom of Yen in 1395. From 1399 to 1402, during his father's rebellion against his cousin Chu Yün-wen (*q. v.*), the heir administered affairs ably at the Yen base in Peking, while Chu Kao-hsü distinguished himself in battle. Only in 1404 was Chu Kao-chih finally summoned from Peking to the national capital, Nanking, to be invested as heir apparent to the throne. Thereafter, during the emperor's many absences from the capital—on military campaigns against the Mongols, or while residing in the new national seat being built at Peking—he acted as regent in Nanking. He won the respect and support of the officials and gained unusual experience in administration. He was constantly harassed by plots against him engineered by supporters of his two brothers (*see* Chu Kao-hsü), but he consistently persuaded the emperor not to punish them when the plots were exposed. After the latter's death, Chu Kao-chih formally took the throne on September 7, 1424. Less than nine months later (May 29, 1425), he too died following a brief illness. His era name, Hung-hsi 洪熙 (vast prosperity), includes only the lunar year 1425.

His primary concern as emperor was to alleviate distress among the people. Once, when a local famine was reported and the ministry of Revenue proposed that grain from state granaries be issued to the needy as loans, the emperor retorted, "Forthwith issue it in relief! What would loans accomplish?" On another occasion when popular distress was reported to him, he promptly told his chief adviser, Grand Secretary Yang Shih-ch'i (*q.v.*), to order tax remissions and the cessation of government requisitions in the area. Yang pointed out that it was proper for the ministries of Revenue and Works to be consulted before issuing any such orders. The emperor replied angrily, "Be patient? Relieving people's poverty ought to be handled as though one were rescuing them from fire or saving them from drowning. One cannot hesitate. But the authorities, worried about possible insufficiencies for the state's needs, are always stolid and indecisive. You just be still, sir!" He sent a eunuch after paper and ink, had Yang write out a proclamation on the spot, affixed the imperial seal, and sent it off with a runner. Only then did he turn back to Yang and say, no doubt with a smile, "Now sir, you may inform the ministries of Revenue and Works that We have ordered remissions and cessations."

His impulsiveness, however well intentioned, sometimes gave him cause for regret. He repeatedly urged his officials to speak up about current problems and if necessary to remonstrate with him vigorously about his own mistakes. He sometimes lost his temper, however, when they did so. Less than a month after making one urgent plea for fearless remonstrance, he flew into a rage at an official at the Grand Court of Revision named I Ch'ien 弋謙 (cs 1411) for speaking out "provocatively" and barred him from subsequent audiences. Soon thereafter he noticed that the officials in audience were not participating in discussion and complained that he could not rule effectively if his ministers were not outspoken with him. On Yang Shih-ch'i's advice, he then restored I Ch'ien's rights to come to audience and proclaimed that the officials should not take I's regrettable case to be a prohibition of remonstrance. Yet only two months later he was overcome by anger once more. His victim on this occasion was Li Shih-mien (q.v.), who submitted a memorial in which, among other things, he observed that during the mourning period the emperor should not be intimate with concubines. He was immediately summoned and beaten, and cast into the palace prison of the imperial bodyguard, where he remained for more than a year before the next emperor, Chu Chan-chi (q.v.), restored him to office.

Chu Kao-chih's irascibility put a great strain on the atmosphere of freedom that, on the whole, he tried to foster. His redeeming grace was that he recognized and repeatedly apologized for his aberrations; and they seem to have been greatly counterbalanced by his many benevolent acts and his sincere eagerness to serve the public interest. He released all officials who had been imprisond for offending his

father, Emperor Chu Ti, including the eminent ministers Hsia Yüan-chi (q.v.) and Yang P'u (see Yang Shih-ch'i). Reinstating other officials whom Chu Ti had sent away in disgrace, he restored to honorable status the supporters of the deposed Emperor Chu Yün-wen and their survivors. He lessened punishments generally, particularly ordering limitations on the death penalty and on castration, and forbade the implication of criminals' relatives in punishment except in cases of high treason. He ordered the cessation of requisitioning of local commodities for use in government agencies, and its replacement by a fair purchasing system. He also discontinued wasteful government enterprises such as the sending of trading ships into the "western ocean" (see Cheng Ho) and westward expeditions to acquire horses. Believing that the civil service examination system was unfairly discriminatory, favoring southerners, he instituted a quota system guaranteeing northerners 40 per cent of all metropolitan degrees; this policy endured with slight modification throughout the Ming and Ch'ing dynasties.

Chu was not happy about the transfer of the national capital to Peking and early in 1425 initiated plans to return it to Nanking. Thereupon all governmental agencies at Nanking nominally became the principal agencies without qualification, whereas those at Peking nominally became "auxiliary" (行在) ones. Although the capital was not moved, this unrealistic pattern of nomenclature persisted until 1441.

In 1424 Chu Kao-chih recalled from Annam the respected and popular official Huang Fu (q.v.). Huang had served in Annam for seventeen years as administration and surveillance commissioner. He and the general Chang Fu (q.v.) are said to have been the only Chinese whom the Annamites respected. Later critics suggested that the emperor's recall of Huang Fu opened the way for the Annamite rebel, Lê Lợi (q.v.), already successfully organizing against the Chinese, to win the great victories that were to bring about a Chinese withdrawal under the emperor's successor. He is also blamed for the rise to influence of eunuchs. When he ordered cessation of China's overseas expeditions, the emperor consoled the famous eunuch admiral Cheng Ho with the post of garrison commander at Nanking. Cheng was thus the first Ming eunuch to hold an important regional military command, and the fact that the next emperor subsequently appointed eunuch grand defenders in almost all provinces and frontier regions has made this appointment by Chu Kao-chih seem in retrospect to be an ominous precedent.

In all matters Chu relied heavily and respectfully on the counsel of a group of distinguished ministers who at this time formed an embryonic Grand Secretariat. These included Yang Shih-ch'i, Yang Jung, Hsia Yüan-chi, Chien I (*qq.v.*), and Chin Yu-tzu (*see* Empress Hsü). The emperor gave each of these men a silver seal inscribed "Rectify faults and shortcomings" 繩愆糾繆 with instructions that they use it to submit secret memorials of protest whenever he himself misbehaved.

The emperor's principal consort, Empress Chang 張 (Pth. 誠孝昭皇后) survived until 1442—as empress-dowager under Chu Chan-chi and then as grand empress-dowager under Emperor Chu Ch'i-chen (*q.v.*). Her father, Chang Ch'i 麒 (d. *ca.* 1411, Pth. 恭靖), a native of Yung-ch'eng 永城, Honan, was made an officer in 1393 on the occasion of her marriage. In 1424 he was posthumously given the hereditary rank of earl of P'eng-ch'eng 彭城伯, which was inherited by his elder son, Chang Ch'ang 昶 (1374–1438), a general in his own right. Chang Ch'i's younger son, Chang Sheng 昇 (T. 叔暉, 1379–1441), rose in the ranks to be a general officer, and in 1440, by order of his sister, the empress-dowager, was created earl of Hui-an 惠安 伯, also hereditary. In 1529, by imperial order, the ranks granted to imperial relatives were made non-hereditary. Only the two earldoms of the Chang family were especially exempted from that rule, because they were not merely inherited but earned by meritorious service. The empress seems always to have been an influence for stability on her husband and son, and after the latter's death she was a powerful and respected regent for her grandson (not yet eight when he came to the throne).

Chu Kao-chih had a total of ten sons and seven daughters, nine of the sons and four of the daughters reaching maturity. The eldest, Chu Chan-chi, inherited the throne. The other children were installed as hereditary princes and princesses. The practice of immolation of imperial concubines (殉), introduced by the Mongols and followed in the Hung-wu and Yung-lo reigns, was continued in the Hung-hsi era. Ten consorts of Chu Kao-chih followed him in death.

History has adjudged Chu Kao-chih a good emperor comparable to traditional Chinese paragons of simplicity, kindness, and earnestness, such as the Han dynasty's Emperors Wen and Ching. He was canonized as Chao Huang-ti 昭皇帝. His tomb outside Peking, called Hsien-ling 獻陵, where his empress was buried with him, was built in an austerely simple fashion that differentiates mid-Ming tombs from the splendid ones of the earlier and some later emperors. [Editors' note: According to Lu I in his *Ping-i man-chi* (*see* Chu Ch'i-yü), the suddenness of Chu Kao-chih's death gave rise to speculations that it was caused by lightning or poison, but a chief eunuch Lei 雷 told Lu that it was due to some yin-cheng 陰症, perhaps indicating heart failure.]

Bibliography

1/8/1a; 5/3/10a; MSL (1963), T'ai-tsung and Jen-tsung; C. O. Hucker, *The Censorial System of Ming China* (Stanford, 1966), especially pp. 112–113.

Charles O. Hucker

CHU Kao-hsü 朱高煦, *ca.* 1380–1429?, the prince of Han 漢, was the second son of

Emperor Chu Ti and Empress Hsü (*qq.v.*). Born when his father was the prince of Yen, Chu Kao-hsü in 1426 unsuccessfully attempted to overthrow his nephew Chu Chan-chi (*q.v.*), and was then referred to in history as "the commoner of Han" (庶 人). He grew into a tall, powerful, athletic man in much the same mold as his father, and with a life-long envy of his fat, sickly elder brother Chu Kao-chih (*q.v.*) who inherited the throne in 1424.

As a youth Chu Kao-hsü was impatient of scholastic pursuits and won a reputation for his quick temper and arrogance. During his father's rebellion of 1399–1402 against the second Ming emperor, Chu Yün-wen (*q.v.*), while his brother was left in charge of his father's princedom at Peiping, Chu Kao-hsü distinguished himself repeatedly as a battle leader, and on several occasions he rescued his father from personal danger and turned imminent defeats into victories. His father publicly gave him much credit for the eventual success of the rebellion, and the young prince became increasingly arrogant and ungovernable. He liked to compare himself to the great T'ang dynasty emperor T'ai-tsung, who won the empire for his father and in whose favor the father soon abdicated.

After his father won the throne in 1402, Chu Kao-hsü's influential friends tried to persuade the emperor to name him heir rather than the eldest son. The fact that Chu Ti postponed a decision on this matter until 1404 suggests that he perhaps wavered. But then he invested Chu Kao-chih as heir apparent and named Chu Kao-hsü prince of Han, to have control of Yunnan province. Chu Kao-hsü protested, "What crime have I committed, to be banished a myriad miles!" He refused to go to Yunnan, and the emperor ultimately indulged him and allowed him to remain at the capital, Nanking.

During his father's many campaigns northward into Mongol territory, while the heir apparent remained as regent in Nan-king, Chu Kao-hsü always accompanied him, ingratiating himself and trying to undermine his brother. Through his machinations two members of the embryonic Grand Secretariat, who strongly supported Chu Kao-chih, lost favor and were imprisoned. These were Hsieh Chin (*q.v.*), who died in prison, and Huang Huai (*q.v.*), who remained in prison ten years, until after Chu Ti's death.

In 1415 Chu Kao-hsü was given a new fief at Ch'ing-chou 青州 prefecture, Shantung. Again he protested. His father rebuked him angrily, and only then did he take up provincial residence. He quickly gathered together a private army of more than three thousand men, indulged in many abusive irregularities, and put to death an army officer who interfered. Learning of these things, the emperor recalled the prince to Nanking in 1416, imprisoned him, and would have disowned him entirely but for the intercession of his brother, the heir apparent. In 1417 Chu Kao-hsü was sent in disgrace to a lesser fief at Lo-an 樂安 sub-prefecture, Shantung. Chu Kao-chih repeatedly sent him friendly letters of warning, and when he succeeded to the throne in 1424 he increased the prince's income and installed his sons as princes of the second degree. But Chu Kao-hsü sulked angrily.

When Chu Kao-chih died and was succeeded (1425) by his son, Chu Chan-chi, Chu Kao-hsü seems immediately to have started planning to dethrone his nephew, as his father had dethroned his cousin two decades before. The emperor treated him with deference, but this only fed his ambition and envy. Early in September, 1426, he emerged in open rebellion, establishing imperial-style army designations and official titles. Chu Chan-chi reluctantly ordered an army into the field and then, on the advice of Grand Secretary Yang Jung (*q.v.*), took personal command of the campaign. When the imperial army appeared outside Lo-an, and when imperial cannon shook the city walls in warning, the prince lost all his bravado and gave himself up. The emperor, ignoring proposals that he be put to death on the spot, took him and all his family captive to Peking.

The rebellion having collapsed so ignominiously, Lo-an sub-prefecture was renamed Wu-ting 武定 (militarily pacified) All civil officials and military officers, who had collaborated with the rebel prince, were put to death. The number is reported to have exceeded six hundred forty. Another fifteen hundred persons were sent in disgrace to serve as soldiers at the frontier, and seven hundred twenty others were banished to live as vagrants there.

The *Hsüan-tsung shih-lu*, the contemporary official chronicle compiled under the supervision of Yang Shih-ch'i (*q.v.*) and other trusted ministers, reports that "the commoner of Han," his wife, and his sons were all incarcerated in a special compound built for them by the ministry of Works just inside the capital's Hsi-an西 安 gate—a compound apparently known popularly as "the carefree quarter" (逍遙 城)—and that their needs were provided for them in normal fashion. The chronicle notes also that in 1429 the emperor's granduncle, the prince of Ning, Chu Ch'üan (*q.v.*), asked in vain that Chu Kao-hsü be pardoned, but it does not report what eventually happened to the prince and his family. In its biography of the prince the later official history *Ming-shih* reports merely that Chu Kao-hsü and his sons died successively, as if of natural causes. Elsewhere, however, in its tabular presentation of the histories of all imperial princedoms, *Ming-shih* clearly indicates that the prince was burned to death after being incarcerated and that his wife and sons were all done away with.

Unofficial histories consistently and in gruesome detail tell a story that could only have been most embarrassing to the Ming ruling family. It appears that on one of the emperor's visits of inspection to "the carefree quarter," presumably not earlier than 1429, Chu Kao-hsü mischievously stuck out a foot and tripped him up; and the angry emperor then had the prince covered with a great 300–catty copper vat, built a coal fire on top, and watched the melting copper broil him to death. It is suggested that the rest of the prince's family was then disposed of, but no details are to be found.

Chu Kao-hsü had ten sons, the eldest of whom, Chu Chan-ch'i 瞻圻, spied on his father and repeatedly disclosed his wrongdoings. It is said that he hated his father for having killed his mother, but no further clarification of these matters is available. Chu Kao-chih in any event became so disgusted at Chu Chan-ch'i's lack of both loyalty and filial piety that he angrily sent him away "to attend the imperial tombs" at Feng-yang, the ancestral home of the first emperor, where he apparently died before his father's rebellion occurred. The other nine sons seem not to have survived their later imprisonment so that the Han princedom had no posterity.

Chu Kao-chih's youngest brother by the same mother, Chu Kao-sui 燧 (enfeoffed 1404 as the prince of Chao 趙, d. 1431, Pth. 簡), grew up to be similarly spoiled and envious, but was not such a threat to the throne as was Chu Kao-hsü. In 1409 his father rebuked him severely for his misbehavior, and assigned special officials to give him stern guidance. Thereafter he was relatively inoffensive until 1423, when, the emperor having fallen ill, some of his cronies forged and released an edict setting aside the heir apparent in the prince of Chao's favor. On recovering, the emperor became furious at the prince, but Chu Kao-chih persuaded him that Chu Kao-sui had not been responsible. In 1425, during Chu Kao-chih's brief reign, Chu Kao-sui took charge of a fief at Chang-te 彰德 prefecture, Honan. When the prince of Han's rebellion failed in 1426, many officials urged Chu Chan-chi to attack this other uncle as a major accomplice of the rebel, and the prince of Han himself admitted having plotted together with his brother. The emperor nevertheless took no action against Chu Kao-sui other than to send him copies of the complaints filed against him, as warnings. His princedom was inherited by his descendants to the end of the dynasty.

Bibliography

1/9/3a, 103/2b, 118/16b; 3/110/1b; 42/24/1a; 61/88/1a; MSL (1940), Hsüan-tsung, 20/1a, 21/1b; KC (1958), 1298, 1300, 1303; Ho Ch'iao-yüan, *Ming-shan ts'ang* (Ming ed.), 39/1a; Cheng Hsiao, *Wu-hsüeh pien* (1567 ed.), 16/3; Cha Chi-tso (ECCP), *Tsui-wei lu* (SPTK), 4/84b; Ku Ying-t'ai (ECCP), *Ming-ch'ao chi-shih pen-mo*, 27/1; TSCC (1885-88), XI: 99/43/1a; Wang Ch'ung-wu 王崇武, *Ming ching-nan shih-shih k'ao-cheng kao* 明靖難史事考證稿 (Shanghai, 1948), ch. 7.

Charles O. Hucker

CHU Lu 朱鷺 (original *ming*: 家棟, T. 白民, H. 西空老人), 1553-1632, scholar and painter, was a native of Wu 吳-hsien in the prefecture of Soochow. The son of an instructor in a local school, Chu Lu spent his early years studying under his father. He showed a talent in literary matters, particularly in poetry, and a keen interest in the history of the early years of the dynasty, especially the reign of Emperor Chu Yün-wen (*q. v.*). Little is known of his activities until about 1590 when he reportedly enrolled in the National University at Nanking and made an impression on the instructor, Feng Meng-chen 馮夢禎 (T. 開元, 1546-1605, cs 1577). He took the prefectural examination at Nanking in 1594 but failed. In subsequent years he taught in a local school to support his aging parents; after their death, he forsook his teaching career and made no further attempts to acquire a degree. He became interested in the *I-ching* and in metaphysics, but later embraced Buddhism, particularly the teachings of Te-ch'ing and Chu-hung (*qq. v.*). During his leisure, he took delight in traveling. He supported himself by selling his paintings on bamboo which he modeled with superb skill, after those of Wen Cheng-ming (*q.v.*), and by engraving seals for ready customers. Some of his works bear such names as I-nien ch'an 一念禪 and Ch'ing-fou-tzu 青浮子, indicating his obsession with Buddhism.

Chu Lu devoted a great part of his life to the preparation of a historical work, later known as *Chien-wen shu-fa ni* 建文書法擬, to justify the restoration of the reign-title and the award of posthumous honors to Emperor Chu Yün-wen. During the reign of Chu I-chün (*q. v.*), many officials memorialized the throne making similar requests in conjunction with the preparation of an official history of the dynasty (*see* Ch'en Yü-pi). Chu insisted that justification was due the deposed emperor, as he came to the throne legitimately, and argued that Chu Ti (*q. v.*), who overthrew his nephew, had never intended to blot out his name and place in history. It was official historians, he maintained, who had tried to put Chu Ti's usurpation in a more favorable light by distorting the records of Chu Yün-wen's reign and eliminating his title from the chronicles. Chu Lu maintained that such an action had done equal harm to Chu Ti, who could be charged with usurpation, and that the restoration of Chu Yün-wen's place in the official records would afford a more objective appraisal of his role in history. He reportedly spent twenty-eight years over his project, but before he was able to present his *magnum opus* to the throne after its completion late in 1594, Emperor Chu I-chün had already decreed the restoration of Chu Yün-wen's reign title; it was not until June, 1644, however, that Emperor Chu Yu-sung (ECCP) conferred the posthumous honorifics. Having missed the opportunity to make his point, Chu Lu dropped his plan; it was this work nevertheless that preserved his name in history.

The *Chien-wen shu-fa ni*, 5 ch.—*ch'ien-pien* 前編, 1 ch., *cheng* 正 -*pien*, 2 ch., *fu* 附-*pien*, 2 ch. — was revised in 1615 and engraved in 1621.   It includes Chu Lu's own preface of 1604 in which he calls himself Tung-wu huang-shih shih 東吳荒史氏, and another by Chiao Hung (ECCP) dated 1615. The prologue presents a collection of documents on the official views of the Chien-wen reign and a proposal for exonerating the dethroned emperor and members of his court; this is supplemented by an outline of principles (shu-fa 書法) for a new history of Chu Yün-wen and brief chronology of events, as well as a list of the Chien-wen martyrs. The main body of the text features the annals of the Chien-wen reign, interspersed with Chu's critical notes on controversial episodes, often in refutation of the official version, biographical data, as well as arguments for the restoration of the honors of the Chien-wen emperor and his officials. The epilogue presents a selection of eulogies, poems, and essays by later writers on the dethroned emperor and his slain supporters; this is supplemented by *Yung-hsü yü-t'an* 擁絮迂談, a collection of notes by Chu Lu devoted to the historiographical problem of Chu Yün-wen and Chu Ti growing out of a discussion with his younger brother in the winter of 1594 The *Chien-wen shu-fa ni* lists over sixty titles of official and private pieces of literature on the subject, some of which are no longer extant; as such, it supplements the *Chien-wen ch'ao-yeh hui-pien* by T'u Shu-fang (*q. v.*) as an important source for a study of the Chien-wen reign. It differs from the former, however in that it is not a mere compilation of historical records, but a critical appraisal of the period aimed at restoring the rightful place of Chu Yün-wen in history. The *Chien-wen shu-fa ni* was proscribed in the Ch'ing dynasty but copies survive in major libraries; an abridged edition of the *Yung-hsü yü-t'an* is included in the *Shuo-fu hsü* 說郛續, *chou* 弓, 7.

Shortly after the enthronement of Emperor Chu Yu-chien (ECCP) in 1628, when there was an auspicious omen, Chu Lu made a trip to Peking, and is said to have presented to the emperor a laudatory essay, together with a memorial on state affairs. During this time the capital was in danger of invasion by the Manchu forces, but Chu remained calm and reportedly whiled away his time by annotating the *Chin-kang ching* 金剛經 (Diamond sūtra). When the threat was over, Chu returned home; he then lived as a hermit on Mt. Hua 華 and adopted the title Hsi-k'ung西空. He died at the age of seventy-nine. Wen Chen-meng (*q. v.*), who composed his tomb-inscription, hailed Chu Lu and two of his friends, Chao Huan-kuang 趙宦光 (T. 凡夫, 1559-1625) and Wang Tsai-kung 王在公 (T. 孟夙, d. 1627, cj 1594), as the most talented and virtuous men of Wu-hsien of their time.

Chu Lu had a son who did not survive him. His grandson, Chu Tan 旦, took part in the restoration movement after the fall of the dynasty. Late in 1645 he organized a force trying to recapture Soochow from the Manchus, but was killed by government troops in the abortive attempt.

Bibliography:
40/67/11b; 59/46/10a; 64/ 庚 30 下 /9b; 65/7/7a; 86/19/4a; Chu Lu, *Chien-wen shu-fa ni* (NLP microfilm no. 170); Tsou I 鄒衍,*Ch'i-Chen yeh-ch'eng* 啓禎野乘 (1936), 14/4a; Ch'ien Ch'ien-i (ECCP), *Mu-chai ch'u-hsüeh chi* (SPTK), 71/1a; Wen Ping 文秉, *Ku-Su ming-hsien hsü-chi* 姑蘇名賢續記, in *Chia-hsü ts'ung-pien* 甲戌叢編, I (1934), 8a; Te-ch'ing, *Han-shan ta-shih nien-p'u su*, 108; Chiang Shao-yüan 姜紹原, *Wu-hsing shih-shih* 無聲詩史, in *Hua-shih* 畫史 *ts'ung-shu* (1962), 4/70b; Li Shu-ch'ang (ECCP), *Sung-ling wen-lu* 松陵文錄 (1874), 17/13a; Sun Tien-ch'i (1957), 115; Shang Ch'eng-tso 商承祚, *Chung-kuo li-tai shu-hua chuan-k'o chia tzu-hao so-yin* 中國歷代書畫篆刻家字號索引 (1960), 161; Wu Chi-hua 吳緝華, "Ming-tai Chien-wen ti tsai chuan-t'ung huang-wei shang ti wen-t'i" 明代建文帝在傳統皇位上的問題, *Ta-lu tsa-chih* 大陸雜誌, 19:1 (July 16, 1959), 14; W. Franke, *Sources*, 2. 4. 3; V. Contag and C. C. Wang, *Seals of Chinese Painters and Collectors*, rev. ed. (Hong Kong, 1966), 111, 649; O. Sirén, *Chinese Paintings*, V: 3, 74, VII: 182; E. J. Laing, *Chinese Paintings in Chinese Publications, 1956-1968*(Ann Arbor, 1969), 165.

Hok-lam Chan

CHU Mou-wei 朱謀㙔 (T. 明父, H. 鬱儀), died 1624, scholar and bibliophile, a 6th class noble of the blood (chen-kuo chung-wei 鎮國中尉), was a seventh generation descendant of Chu Ch'üan (*q.v.*), prince of Ning, enfeoffed in Nanchang, Kiangsi. Because of his learning and character he was repeatedly recommended to the emperor by local officials, first in 1591 to be director of his immediate branch of the imperial clan, then in 1593 to be manager of the affairs of the princely household of Shih-ch'eng 石城王府. The first prince of Shih-ch'eng was Chu Tien-t'u 朱奠堵 (d. 1486), a grandson of Chu Ch'üan. Chu Ch'en-fu 宸浮 (d. 1548), grandson and heir of Chu Tien-t'u, succeeded as prince in 1498, but in the following year was degraded for certain offenses, thus bringing officially to an end the line of the princes of Shih-ch'eng. Yet the members bearing lower designations continued and the population of the branch grew. At the time when Chu Mou-wei became manager of affairs (not counting the non-titled members, the female members, or the people in service) there were 293 titled males in the Shih-ch'eng branch of the imperial clan. In this position he remained for thirty years, looked after the welfare of the members, and exercised control over unruly elements. He commanded the respect not only of his own clan but also of the people of the locality

His great-grandfather, Chu Ch'en-han 宸浤, a 3d class noble of the blood (chen-kuo chiang-chün 將軍), was a younger brother of Chu Ch'en-fu, the deposed prince. By refusing to associate with the rebel prince of Ning, Chu Ch'en-hao (*see* Wang Shou-jen), Chu Ch'en-han and family escaped the unfortunate consequences which befell the former. His grandfather, Chu Kung-k'ai 拱概, was a 4th class noble (fu 輔-kuo chiang-chün), and his father, Chu To-liang 多煓, was a 5th class noble (feng 奉 -kuo chiang-chün). A man devoted to learning, the father had great influence on the son, teaching him the Classics himself. The date of birth of

Chu Mou-wei is not known, but through a poem he wrote we may ascertain that at the time of his death he was over sixty *sui*. After his death his followers honored him with the unofficial posthumous name of Chen-ching hsien-sheng 貞靜先生.

Chu Mou-wei is said to have written one hundred twelve works of various lengths which deal with a wide range of subject matter. In the bibliographical section of the *Nan-ch'ang-fu chih* 南昌府志, twenty-two titles are given, and the *Ming-shih* lists eight. The *Ssu-k'u* catalogue notes four of his works: *Chou-i hsiang-t'ung* 周易象通, 8 *ch.*, *Shih-ku* 詩故 (a work on the Book of Poetry), 10 *ch.*, *P'ien-ya* 駢雅 (a lexicon after the style of *Er-ya*), 7 *ch.* and *Sui-ku chi* 邃古記 (a history of antiquity), 8 *ch.* Both the second and third were copied into the Imperial Library, and both were reprinted in the *Yü-chang ts'ung-shu* 豫章叢書 (1915, 1920). The *P'ien-ya*, which was first printed by his eldest son Chu T'ung-wei 統鏸 (T. 伯壘, H. 羣玉山樵), in 1587, may also be found in three other *ts'ung-shu*. In a postscript, the son attributed his father's broad learning and profound understanding partly to the fact that he did not occupy himself in preparing for the examinations. In this the editors of the *Ssu-k'u* concurred. He left one important work on contemporary history, the *Fan-hsien chi* 藩獻記, a genealogical and biographical work on the Ming princedoms, which the Imperial Catalogue failed to list. This work in 4 *chüan* was first printed sometime before he died and later an abbreviated version in 1 *chüan* was included in the *Shuo-fu hsü* (*see* T'ao Tsung-i). Another work, which might interest students of Ming history, is the *Nan-ch'ang ch'i-chiu chuan* 耆舊傳, biographies of eminent people of Nanchang; unfortunately it is not clear whether it was ever printed, or if it is extant. He also annotated the Water Classic, the *Shui-ching chu chien* 水經注箋, 40 *ch.*, first printed in 1615 in Nanchang. A copy of the original edition, with a postscript of three pages by Hu Shih (BDRC), written in April, 1946, is now among the rare holdings of the East Asian Library of Columbia University.

The catalogue of Chu's library, the *I-chai shu-mu* 一齋書目, reportedly listed many rare titles. According to Ch'ien Ch'ien-i (ECCP), Chu Mou-wei offered his library resources to Ch'ien urging him to write a history of the Ming. After going to the trouble of having many items copied from the library, before they were to be transported to Ch'ien's home near Soochow, he suffered the loss of them all by fire. The name of Chu Mou-wei is often bracketed with that of Chu Mu-chieh (*see* Chu Su) as the two foremost bibliophiles among the members of the imperial descendants. As to their two collections of books, one perished by fire, and the other by water.

Chu Mou-wei had eight sons, both the eldest, Chu T'ung-wei, and the third, Chu T'ung-huang 鎤 (T. 孝穆), being known for their achievements in the arts of painting and calligraphy. His fourth son, Chu T'ung-chih 鉒 (T. 夢得), whose early name was Chu Pao-fu 寶符, was a *chü-jen* of 1633 and a *chin-shih* of 1634. A cousin, Chu Mou-yin (*see* T'ao Tsung-i), was interested in art history; this inspired him to compile a work on painting, the *Hua-shih hui-yao* 畫史會要, 5*ch.*, and also a 1 *chüan* supplement (*hsü-pien* 續編) to *Shu* 書*-shih hui-yao* of T'ao Tsung-i on calligraphy (completed 1631). Both titles are included in the Imperial Library; the former has been reproduced (1970–71) in the *Ssu-k'u ch'üan-shu chen-pen er-chi* 珍本二集.

In the early days of the dynasty members of the imperial clan were not allowed to take part in the examinations. As their numbers increased and the expense of supporting them became a burden to the government, this regulation was abrogated in 1602 (*see* Chu Tsai-yü). In 1606 it was decreed that examinations should be opened to all nobles of the blood of the six lower classes, the three grades of chiang-chün, and the three grades of

chung-wei. It was not until 1622 that the name of the first noble of the blood appeared on the list of successful *chin-shih*. To the end of the dynasty there were only ten or so who obtained the *chin-shih* degree, mostly members of the Kiangsi branch.

Bibliography

1/117/20a; 5/1/73a, 76b; 40/85/12a; 64/ 甲2下/ 11a, 15a; 84/ 閏 /98a; SK (1930), 8/1a, 16/3b, 40/5a, 50/12a, 113/1a, 3a; TSCC (1885–88),XIV: 74/10b, XXIV: 125/4b, 5b; Cheng Chung-k'uei鄭 仲夔, *Er-hsin* 耳新 (TsSCC ed.), 1/1a, 2/12b, 5/ 29a; *Chiang-hsi t'ung-chih* 江西通志 (1881), 138/ 15b; *Nan-ch'ang-fu chih* (1873), *chüan* 20, 62; T'an Ch'ien, *Tsao-lin tsa-tsu*, 聖集 /13a (*Chang-shih Shih-yüan ts'ung-shu* 張氏適園叢書 ed.); Yeh Ch'ang-ch'ih 葉昌熾, *Ts'ang-shu chi-shih shih* 藏書記事詩 (Shanghai, 1958), 70.

Lienche Tu Fang

CHU Piao 朱標, October 10, 1355–May 17, 1392, eldest son of Chu Yüan-chang (*q.v.*), was born at T'ai-p'ing (Anhwei), the stronghold on the south bank of the Yangtze River which had been captured that summer, and which served as Chu's base until he was able to seize Nanking in the spring of 1356. His mother (according to official sources) was the future Empress Ma (*q.v.*). In 1364, when his father assumed the title of prince of Wu, Chu Piao was designated his heir to the princedom 世子, and when the former was proclaimed emperor in 1368, Chu Piao was simultaneously designated the imperial heir apparent 皇太子.

From his early boyhood in the late 1360s Chu Piao was assigned important formal and ritual tasks as well as responsibilities intended to acquaint him with the problems of rulership. When he was only twelve or thirteen years of age, Sung Lien (*q.v*), eminent literatus, was designated his tutor in classical studies, and a succession of prominent statesmen and scholars guided his formal studies, evidently interesting him in literature. He seems to have had the gentle and humane characteristics of his mother. His father, who disdained such qualities in his courtiers and who himself possessed none of the same attitudes, is said nevertheless to have been proud of his heir. In 1377, when Chu Piao was twenty-two, he was ordered to participate under the scrutiny of his father in daily policy and administrative conferences, and in the review of punishments. His career during more than twenty years in the Eastern Palace, as the residence of the heir apparent traditionally was known, is difficult to evaluate in political terms. His father's personality totally overshadowed all aspects of government; moreover, the future conflict between Chu Piao's son, Chu Yün-wen, and the latter's uncle, Chu Ti (qq.v.), led to the suppression and distortion of much information bearing on the period, and especially on these personalities. Historical accounts have all been favorable to Chu Piao as heir apparent, partly perhaps because, by contrasting him with his tyrannical father and strong-willed brother, some psychological satisfaction was achieved. Even so, there is some evidence that Chu Piao was temperamentally quite the opposite of his father, and that his father both noted and in some degree took satisfaction in that. Yet what kind of ruler he might have been remains a matter of speculation.

In the early autumn of 1391 Chu Piao was given his most important political task; his father commanded him to make a tour of inspection of Shensi, with the responsibility of considering the transfer of the capital from Nanking to Ch'ang-an (Sian), the site of former capitals in Chinese history. Accompanied by a retinue including a number of important officials, Chu Piao carried out the mission between September and December, and on his return presented to his father his charts of Shensi and reports on Ch'ang-an, Loyang, and other cities. It is not known what recommendation Chu Piao may have made about moving the capital; but, before any action could result from his reports, he fell ill, and further considera-tions of the issue were set aside. The nature of his illness is not known; he lingered for several months, from January until his death in May, 1392. His father, the aging emperor, is said to have been so deeply grieved that he forsook all administrative responsibilities for a longer time than ritual formality demanded and finally had to be persuaded by his entire court, led by the officials responsible for rites, to put aside mourning. In September Chu Piao was buried in a mausoleum adjoining on the east the Hsiao-ling 孝陵, at that time being prepared for his father at the foot of Mt. Chung 鍾 in the northeast suburb of Nanking. He was given the posthumous honorific: heir apparent I-wen 懿文太子. In March, 1399, shortly after Emperor Chu Yün-wen's succession, he posthumously elevated his father to the dynastic title of the Hsiao-k'ang Emperor 孝康皇帝 with the temple name of Hsing-tsung 興宗. Chu Ti, however, Chu Piao's younger brother, upon usurping the throne, restored the original and less elevated posthumous title of heir apparent I-wen. From late Ming times onward, and especially after Chu Yün-wen's reign title was restored in 1595, the dynastic title Hsiao-k'ang Emperor returned to currency; it is the one adopted by the *Ming-shih*.

Chu Piao's principal consort was a daughter of General Ch'ang Yü-ch'un (q.v.). She was invested in May, 1371, and posthumously honored as empress in 1399. On November 21, 1374, she bore him his eldest son, Chu Hsiung-ying 雄英, who died on June 12, 1382. She also bore him his third son; she herself died on December 11, 1378. Chu Piao's secondary consort was the daughter of Lü Pen 呂本 (d. *ca.* 1381), a late Yüan official of Shou-cho 壽州 (Anhwei), who came into Chu Yüan-chang's service early in his rise to power. The consort Lü was alive when her eldest son, Chu Yün-wen, came to the throne, at which time she was elevated to the rank of empress-dowager. She bore him also two other sons who, with their half-brother by the consort Ch'ang, were given princely titles by Chu Yün-wen. They suffered demotion and personal hardship after Chu Ti's seizure of power in 1402 and did not long survive. One of them, the fifth and youngest, Chu Yün-hsi 允熙 (1391–1406, Pth. 哀簡), was given the title prince of Ou-ning 甌寧王 in 1404 and charged with conducting the sacrificial ceremony at his father's tomb, but died two years later in a fire. Thereafter the sacrifices were conducted by an official from the Court of Imperial Sacrifices until 1590 when it was decreed that to show proper respect an officer of general rank was to officiate instead. Incidentally, no one could explain why it was that, while at the tomb of Chu Yüan-chang, the sacrifices were offered only three times a year, at that of Chu Piao they were offered nine times annually. Shen Te-fu (*q.v.*), in recording this oddity, reasoned that the practice probably started by order of Chu Yün-wen as an emperor showing respect to his father; but no one bothered to change it after July, 1402. In any case, Chu Piao's line apparently came to an end when Chu Yün-wen's two sons died, the first in 1402 and the second without known heir in the T'ien-shun period.

Bibliography

1/115/1a, 118/16a; 5/1/1a; MSL (1962), T'ai-tsu, 0037-3194; KC (1958), 446, 511, 566, 619, 724, 729, 928, 2057; TSCC (1885-88), XIV: 406/14b; Cheng Hsiao, *Wu-hsüeh-pien* (1567), 14/8b; Wang Huan-piao 王煥鑣, *Ming Hsiao-ling chih* 明孝陵志 (1934), 25; Wu Han 吳晗, *Chu Yüan-chang chuan* 傳, 1948; Li Chin-hua 李晉華, "Ming I-wen-t'ai-tzu sheng-mu k'ao" 明懿文太子生母考, CYYY, VI: 1 (1936), 45; *id.*, "Ming Ch'eng-tsu sheng-mu wen-t'i hui-cheng" 明成祖生母問題彙證, *ibid.*, 55; Shen Te-fu, *Wan-li yeh-hu-pien* (1959), 8; Wang Shih-chen, *Yen-shan-t'ang pieh-chi*, 33/1b.

F. W. Mote

CHU Sheng 朱升 (T. 允升, H. 楓林), 1299–January, 1371, scholar, called himself a native of Hsiu-ning 休寧 of Hui-chou 徽州

prefecture, where the Chu family had settled since the middle of the 9th century; by the time of Chu Sheng, however, the family had moved to She 歙-hsien, some twenty miles to the east. A student of Ch'en Li (1252–1334), his fellow townsman, Chu Sheng went in 1343 to Kiukiang to study under Huang Tse (1260–1346), a renowned Confucian scholar. The following year he became a *chü-jen* and began lecturing in the local school. In 1348 he received an appointment as instructor of the prefectural school of Ch'ih-chou 池州, then plagued by financial difficulties due to official corruption. When he came to office in 1350, he reportedly improved the administration, rooted out fraudulent activities, and bolstered student morale by strict discipline; whereupon the school began to flourish. Its prosperity, however, was cut short by the outbreak of rebellions in 1351. When his term of office expired the following year, he returned home, devoting himself to study and writing, but had to seek shelter in the mountains to avoid harassment by rebel groups.

In August, 1357, after the forces of Chu Yüan-chang captured Hui-chou and through the recommendation of General Teng Yü (*q.v.*), Chu Sheng's name was brought to the attention of the rebel leader. He called upon Chu Sheng for advice on the future course of action when he came to Hui-chou late in 1358. There is the story that Chu Sheng offered three points, namely, to build high walls around Nanking, to accumulate ample provisions, and to delay the proclamation of kingship. This was very shrewd counsel, for by this time Chu Yüan-chang still needed to consolidate his strength before taking a further step in achieving his objectives. Chu Sheng's first recommendations were designed to give Chu Yüan-chang a solid base for future maneuvering, while the last served as a warning that any premature indication of his ambition might catch the attention of his rivals and jeopardize his chances. If this story is authentic, Chu Sheng's word must have had a considerable impact on the policy of Chu Yüan-chang. During the next ten years Chu Sheng was frequently called upon for advice on Confucian rites and music, for the drafting of decrees, for recommending talented people, and for consultation on strategy and policy matters. A letter addressed to him by Chu Yüan-chang dated December, 1367, indicates that he played a substantial role in the campaigns against rival contenders, Ch'en Yu-liang, Chang Shih-ch'eng (*qq.v.*), and others. On these occasions, he is said to have invoked his specialized craft, divination by means of the Book of Changes, to advise on the proper course of action, and to have accurately predicted the outcome of certain battles. These somewhat fictional accounts were further embroidered by Chu Sheng's descendants in an attempt to enhance the name of their distinguished ancestor.

Early in 1367 Chu Sheng received an appointment as a senior expositor and was put in charge of drafting decrees and the compilation of national chronicles. The next year, when Chu Yüan-chang assumed the imperial title, it was Chu Sheng who was mainly responsible for the ceremonial rites for the occasion. He was then appointed chancellor of the Hanlin Academy. On the emperor's instruction he compiled a code of conduct for women, called *Nü-chieh* 女誡, which he submitted together with a compendium of exemplary models of virtuous women of the past. In September, 1369, the emperor ordered his advisers to prepare a new code of rites, with Chu Sheng in charge of the section on seasonal sacrifices; this was completed in October of the following year, and became known as *Ta Ming chi-li* 大明集禮, 53 *ch.* In April, 1370, pleading old age, he was allowed to retire. The emperor favored him personally by writing the inscription on a plaque bearing the name of his residence, called "Mei-hua ch'u-yüeh lou" 梅花初月樓 (Studio of plum blossoms and the new moon). It is

said that he declined the imperial offer of title and gifts except for a "safe conduct" for his only son, Chu T'ung 同 (T. 大同, H. 朱陳遺民, 紫陽山樵, 1338-85). Though this was granted, it unfortunately did not give Chu T'ung immunity when he was charged with a breach of conduct.

Chu Sheng's main contribution to scholarship seems to have been "interlinear notes" (p'ang-chu 旁註) to many of the Classics, as well as his notes on the *Lao-tzu* and the *Sun-tzu*. These were designed to provide a guideline to students to distinguish between the commentary and the text, and help them to capture the original impression of the masters. Many of these notes are no longer extant, but copies of the *Shu-ching* 書經 *p'ang-chu*, 6 *ch.* (1526), and the *Chou I* 周易 *p'ang-chu hui-t'ung* 會通, 14 *ch.* (1618), are preserved in the National Central Library, Taipei. Chu also compiled a manual of instruction for students, called *Hsiao ssu-shu* 小四書 (Little "Four Books") in 5 *chüan*, after the model of Chu Hsi (1130-1200), incorporating four guides by Sung and Yüan writers. A copy of this work, which is rare, is in the Naikaku Bunko. Chu's collected works entitled *Chu Feng-lin chi* 楓林集, 10 *ch.*, were assembled and engraved by his fifth-generation descendant in 1616. This collection, however, represents only a fraction of Chu's original writings, which were scattered due to the lack of care by his descendants.

Chu T'ung, an instructor in the district school, was recruited for government service in 1380 and served as a vice director, then as a vice minister of Rites in 1382. A year later, however, being implicated in a scandal, he was put into prison and died shortly after. A man of many talents, he was a favorite of Chu Piao (*q.v.*). His collected works, entitled *Fu-p'ou* 覆瓿 *chi*, 24 *ch.*, with a sequel, *shih-i* 拾遺, 2 *ch.*, was engraved shortly after his death. Another version, 8 *ch.*, appeared in 1616. Copies of these editions are available in the Naikaku Bunko and the National Central Library. A photolithographic edition, also in 8 *chüan*, reproduced from the *Ssu-k'u* transcription, is included in the *Ssu-k'u ch'üan-shu chenpen*, 1st ser. (1935).

Bibliography

1/136/5a; 5/20/47a; MSL (1962), T'ai-tsu, 523, 526, 535, 769, 807; KC (1958), 282, 358, 382, 387, 436; SK (1930), 7/3a, 13/2b, 169/4b, 175/1b, 191/6a; TSCC (1885-88), XI: 275/ 10/2a; XXIII: 93/81/13b; *Hui-chou-fu chih* 府志 (1566), in *Ming-tai fang-chih hsüan* 明代方志選 (1965), 288, 325; Chu Sheng, *Chu Feng-lin chi* (1616); *id.*, *Fu-p'ou chi* (1935), 7/15a, 16b, 8/4b; Huang Yü (*see* Huang Tso), *Shuang-huai shui-ch'ao*, 1/9a; Naikaku Bunko *Catalogue*, 277, 345; NCL *Catalogue*, 102, 105.

Hok-lam Chan

CHU Su 朱橚, also known by his title and posthumous name as Chou-ting-wang 周定王, August 9, 1361-September 2, 1425, was the first prince of Chou. He was the fifth son of the founder of the Ming dynasty, Chu Yüan-chang, and, according to the official records, Empress Ma (*q. v.*). In 1370, when princedoms were created for the emperor's second to tenth sons, Chu Su was given the title Wu-wang 吳王, the prince of Wu of the Soochow-Hangchow area. In 1374, when it came time to build residences for the princes, a proposal to assign Hangchow to Chu Su was rejected by the emperor on the ground that the area was too valuable to the government as a source of revenue. It seems that during the following four years the matter was left unsettled.

Meanwhile Chu Su entered upon his education as a prince. His first duties were rather unusual. In October, 1374, on the death of the emperor's favorite consort, Sun Kuei-fei 孫貴妃 (1343-74, Pth. 成穆), who left two daughters but no son, Chu Su was charged with the filial duty of wearing mourning apparel for her for three years. Heretofore on the death of a concubine it was the custom for only her own son to wear mourning apparel at all and it was for one year rather than three

as in the case of mourning for a father. The sons by the wife or other concubines, moreover, were not required to wear mourning. These practices Chu Yüan-chang considered incorrect, reasoning that a son should undertake all the rites of mourning for his mother regardless of her status and that proper respect should be given to all the father's womenfolk. He ordered the compilation of a book embodying the regulations on the degree of mourning in a family; it was entitled *Hsiao-tz'u lu* 孝慈錄 and promulgated in December, 1374. For this book the emperor wrote a preface specifying that at the death of a concubine her own offspring should wear mourning attire for three years and the sons of other women in his household should observe similar mourning for a single year. Ostensibly his purpose was to elevate the status of concubines. Actually Chü Yüan-chang was motivated by his abhorrence of the Mongol practice of a son's inheriting the women of the deceased father. His ultimate purpose therefore was to solidify the patriarchal authority. Why Chu Su was chosen to play the part of the filial son is not recorded. Sun Kuei-fei might have nursed him during his childhood or by a remote possibility she may have been his real mother (*see* Chu Ti).

In 1376 Chu Su was sent with four other princes to take part in the training of troops at Feng-yang 鳳陽, a city set apart as the ancestral home of the imperial family. Two years later the designation of his princedom was changed to Chou-wang 周王 with residence at Kaifeng, Honan. About this time (early in 1378) he married one of the daughters of General Feng Sheng (*q. v.*), then stationed at Kaifeng, and entrusted with the construction of the fort and residence of the Chou princedom on the site of the palace of the Sung dynasty. In 1381 Chu Su began to live there and, together with his father-in-law, looked after the military affairs of the province of Honan. In December, 1389, he was charged with visiting

Feng-yang without authorization (*see* Feng Sheng) and his father considered the offense serious enough to warrant the sentence of transportation to Yunnan. His palace was then assigned to another prince. Twenty days later, early in 1390, these orders were rescinded. He was confined to Nanking but his palace was given back to his family and temporary charge given to his eldest son, Chu Yu-tun (*q.v.*). Late in 1391 the princedom was restored to him.

At this time a prince of the first class like Chu Su was allowed the annual stipend of fifty thousand *shih* of grain (reduced to ten thousand *shih* in 1395), assigned civil officials as managers and advisers, and given command of three bodyguard divisions called hu-wei 護衞. Chu Su's three divisions were designated as the Honan Left (the former Feng-yang Left Guard), Honan Right (the former Shen-wu 神武 Guard), and the Honan Central (the former Honan Guard comprised of soldiers from Hangchow and other places, including some local Kaifeng men). These soldiers numbered perhaps as many as fifteen thousand. Together with their families the population of military registry under Chu Su reached possibly a hundred thousand. His elder brother by one year, Chu Ti, was given command of even more troops because of his duties on the northern frontier. The two brothers were brought up together intimately and their combined military strength was regarded by some courtiers at Nanking as a potential threat to the imperial power. As soon as their nephew, the Chien-wen emperor, ascended the throne in June, 1398, a policy to reduce the power of the princes was set in motion. The elimination of the weaker ones began with Chu Su in August, 1398. On the accusation of treason by his own second son, Chu Yu-hsün 朱有勳 (Yu-tung 有燈, b. March 11, 1380, according to *Ming-shih*), Chu Su, and his eldest son, Chu Yu-tun, were arrested by the general, Li Ching-lung (*see* Li Wen-chung), escorted to Nanking, deprived of

their ranks, and sentenced to exile in Yunnan as commoners. Chu Su was confined at Meng-hua 蒙化 and Chu Yu-tun at Lin-an 臨安. It is said that Chu Yu-tun, in order to spare his father any further suffering and indignity, confessed that he himself had committed all the crimes of which they were accused and so secured his father's pardon and recall to Nanking early in 1402.

In 1399 the Nanking program of abolishing the princedoms was carried out in earnest against four more princes. Chu Kuei was reduced to the status of commoner and imprisoned in February; the prince of Hsiang, Chu Po, committed suicide in May; the prince of Ch'i, Chu Fu, was imprisoned in Nanking in June (for these princes *see* Chu Yüan-chang); and the prince of Min, Chu Pien (1379–1450, Pth. 莊, residence after 1425 at Wu-kang 武岡, Hukuang), was sentenced to confinement in Yunnan in July. In August, 1399, Chu Ti, the next to be dealt with, rose in rebellion. After a war of three years he entered Nanking victoriously on July 13, 1402. One of his first acts as emperor was to release Chu Su and Chu Fu from confinement. They and the other deposed princes were all restored to their former ranks. Chu Yu-tun was recalled from Yunnan and eight of Chu Su's younger sons were invested as princes of the second class. Even the notorious Chu Yu-hsün, who had inflicted so much suffering on the family, was given (or confirmed in) the rank of prince of Ju-nan 汝南, but, as a punishment for his unfilial act, was sent to live in Tali, Yunnan.

In the first few years of the Yung-lo reign Chu Su basked in imperial favor. When Chu Su found Kaifeng ruined by flood and his own palace in disrepair, the emperor granted his request to have a new palace built in Loyang, but the project was abandoned two years later when he reported his preference to remain in Kaifeng and to have his old palace renovated. While other princes received their stipend of ten thousand *shih* or less, he was allowed twice the amount, or twenty thousand *shih* a year. The taxes collected in Kaifeng city and other privileges were his as well as large presents made from time to time, which included, besides money, gold and silver, imported cloth, musical instruments, musicians, and eunuchs. Soon the emperor began his own policy of reducing the princely power. In 1405 Chu Su was repeatedly admonished when the men he sent on errands came into conflict with local officials. He was reminded that his authority was limited to his own establishment and that matters involving the officials in other cities should be referred to the imperial government. Late in 1405 he submitted a memorial admitting his excesses and asking forgiveness. Yet the extent of his realization of the new situation seems to have been limited, for in 1406, when he sent three thousand of his bodyguards to search for deserters in the mountains, he requested permission to assume personal command and had to be reminded that his place was in his own palace. In June, 1409, a secret report reached the emperor saying that Chu Su had expressed dissatisfaction and made disloyal remarks. The emperor considered the matter serious enough to send a secret message to his son, then the regent at Nanking, to be on the alert. No measure, however, was taken against him at this time. In 1409 Chu Su was one of five princes each of whom was told to provide several thousand troops to take part in the expedition into Mongolia in the following year. This expedition was successful and presumably the troops sent by Chu Su were properly rewarded. Late in 1410 Chu Su was again reprimanded for overstepping his bounds when it was reported he had built a temple honoring his father, the first emperor—an action which was considered an imperial prerogative. In 1415 he was ordered to send five thousand soldiers to take part in the projected maneuvers of 1416 but because of a famine the exercise was called off.

The next event in his life was an extraordinary one. He was accused in November, 1420, of treason by members of his own bodyguard. The leader of the accusers, who were all from the Honan Central Bodyguard Division, was a Jew of Kaifeng by the name of An San 俺三 (*see* Chao Ch'eng). After the accusation was confirmed by an investigation An San was rewarded on January 17, 1421, with the rank of an assistant commander in the Embroidered-uniform Guard and permitted to change to the Chinese name, Chao Ch'eng. In March Chu Su was summoned to Peking, and, confronted with the evidence, admitted his guilt; the emperor magnanimously permitted him to return to his princedom with a warning only. Then in June Chu Su returned the three bodyguard divisions to the capital. A small contingent was left to serve the prince and the rest of that division was reorganized and held at Kaifeng; another was transferred to Peking, and the third incorporated into other guards.

Apparently the accusation by Chao Ch'eng was just what the emperor needed as an excuse to relieve the prince of his military command. (According to the records of the Jewish community in Kaifeng concerning this event, "a physician, An Ch'eng, received in 1421 an order from the Prince of Chou to bestow incense and to rebuild the synagogue. In 1423, because of his merits in making report to the throne, the emperor gave An Ch'eng the family name Chao, the rank of commander in the Embroidered-uniform Guard, and promotion to assistant commissioner of the Chekiang Regional Military Commission." An Ch'eng, the physician, is undoubtedly An San the soldier. The year 1423 is in error as to the awards but is probably correct as to promotion. In reference to the prince's contributions to the rebuilding of the synagogue of Kaifeng, in honor of a former retainer who had brought humiliation and near calamity to his princedom, it was obviously an act of appeasement probably not voluntarily given. On the other hand there is a strong possibility that Chao Ch'eng took part in the prince's compilations on medicine and botany and that the two men had enjoyed a closer relationship than would be normal for a prince and a soldier in his bodyguard.)

Chu Su died in 1425 aged sixty-four. His wife bore him two sons, Chu Yu-tun and Chu Yu-hsün, and died in 1423. The rest of his fourteen sons were born to concubines. He also had at least ten daughters. He left the greatest number of progeny of any of Chu Yüan-chang's twenty-six sons. It is said that by 1600 his descendents numbered more than thirty-two thousand, altogether over one third of all the imperial clansmen. A few hundred were well off but many lived in poverty. The twelfth prince of Chou, Chu Kung-hsiao 朱恭枵 (who inherited the title in 1589), took part in the defense of Kaifeng against the bandits in 1641 and in 1644 escaped to south China, serving for a time in the court of Chu I-hai, prince of Lu (ECCP).

The most noteworthy of Chu Su's descendents was his great-great-great-grandson, Chu Mu-chieh 朱睦㮮 (T. 灌甫, H. 西亭先生, 東坡居士, 1517–86). His rank was Chen-kuo chung-wei 鎮國中尉, a noble of the blood of the sixth degree. He was fond of reading and accumulated a large library of over four thousand titles in almost fifty thousand *chüan*, for which he compiled a catalogue entitled *Wan-chüan-t'ang shu-mu* 萬卷堂書目, also known as *Chü-lo-t'ang i-wen mu-lu* 聚樂堂藝文目錄. He headed the school of the Chou princedom from 1577 until his death. Among his works still extant are, in addition to the catalogue of his collection, three works on the Confucian Classics, entitled *Chou-i chi-i* 周易稽疑, *Wu-ching* 五經 *chi-i*, and *Shou-ching t'u* 授經圖, together with a work on the history of the Chien-wen period, entitled *Ko-ch'u i-shih* 革除逸史. The last three were copied into the *Ssu-k'u ch'üan-shu* manuscript library. He was

chief editor of the gazetteers, *Honan t'ung-chih* of 1555, 45 *ch.*, and *K'ai-feng-fu chih* of 1585, 34 *ch.*, and also the author of the biographical sketches of 138 Honanese of the Ming dynasty, entitled *Huang-ch'ao chung-chou jen-wu chih* 皇朝中州人物志, 16 *ch.*, engraved in 1570. The East Asian Library of Columbia University has a manuscript copy of this work made about 1914.

Chu Su himself left two compilations, both copied into the *Ssu-k'u* library. One is a collection of prescriptions, *P'u-chi-fang* 普濟方 in 168 (426?) *chüan*. The other and more important work is the one on food plants entitled *Chiu-huang pen-ts'ao* 救荒本草, 4 *chüan* in 2 volumes, first printed in 1406. This book is significant in several respects. First, it is an original study of 414 plants found in the Kaifeng area, each described as to characteristics and edibility. Only 138 of these plants had been noticed in earlier works. Second, each plant is illustrated with an excellently executed woodcut sixty-nine years before the publication of the first book of this kind in Europe (the 1475 Augsburg edition of Cunrat von Megenberg's *Buch der Natur*). The 1406 edition of the *Chiu-huang pen-ts'ao* is probably not extant. It was reprinted in 1525 at Taiyuan, Shansi, by Governor Pi Chao 畢昭 (T. 蒙齋, cs 1499). Another edition was made in Kaifeng by Lu Chien 陸柬 (T. 道函, cs 1550) who, however, credited the work to Chu Yu-tun, an error that was repeated by almost all later Ming writers, including Hsü Kuang-ch'i (ECCP) and Li Shih-chen (*q.v.*), as well as in the Japanese editions of 1716 and 1799. The *Chiu-huang pen-ts'ao* has been greatly appreciated in recent years. In the 1880s the botanist Emil Vasilievitch Bretschneider (1833–1901) made a study and identified 176 of the 414 plants. The English pharmacologist Bernard E. Read (伊博恩, 1887–1949) identified 358 and published his study in 1946 in Shanghai under the title *Famine Foods listed in the Chiu huang pen ts'ao*. In 1959 the Chung-hua Bookstore published a facsimile edition reproduced from a copy said to be the 1525 edition. The *Naikaku bunko kansetsu bunrei mokuroku* (1956) lists a literary collection under the authorship of Chu Su, entitled *Ting-yüan jui-chih chi* 定園睿製集, 10 *ch.*, printed in 1469. It is perhaps the only copy extant.

Bibliography

1/116/9b, 100/17b; 3/108/12a; 5/1/17a; MSL (1963), T'ai-tsung, 2229, 2242, 2258, 2263, 2275; *Tsui-wei-lu* biography, 4/18a; *Hsin-ch'eng-hsien chih* 新城縣志 (1693), 7/8a; *Hsiang-fu-hsien chih* 祥符縣志 (1898), 16/27a; SK (1930), 102/2b, 104/5a; Amano Motonosuke 天野元之助, "Min-dai ni okeru kyukō sakumotsu chojutsukō" 明代にすける救荒作物著述考 in TG, 47:1 (1964.6); R. Hoeppli, *Parasites and Parasitic Infections in Early Medicine and Science* (Singapore, 1959), 252; *Yü Chia-hsi lun-hsüeh tsa-chu* 余嘉錫論學雜著 (1963), 560.

Chaoying Fang

CHU Ta, 朱耷 better known as Pa-ta shan-jen 八大山人 (H. 雪个, 個山, etc.), *ca.* 1626-*ca.* 1705, painter, calligrapher, and Buddhist monk, was a native of Nan-chang, Kiangsi. He may originally have been known as Chu T'ung-luan 朱統鑾, a member of the I-yang 弋陽 branch of the princedom of Ning 寧. It is known that as a boy he was a student in the local school, preparing to enter government service. But in 1645 the Ming regime in Nanking fell to the Manchu conquerors who soon came to Nanchang. When he found that they were searching for him, he hid in nearby mountains, took the tonsure, and became a Buddhist monk (1648) to avoid the Manchu command that every man wear a queue. At this time, apparently, his name was Ch'uan-ch'i 傳綮, and his sobriquet Hsüeh-ko 雪个. Later, about 1660, he discarded the Buddhist garb and adopted the Taoist style, letting his hair grow and wearing a headgear much like that of a Ming scholar. It is surmised by some authors that he did this in order to marry, for it is recorded that he had

a son.

In any case, in 1661, under the name Chu Tao-lang 道朗 (T. 良月, H. 破雲樵者), he founded a Taoist temple named Ch'ing-yün-p'u 青雲譜, about five miles southeast of Nanchang, where in over a decade he raised sufficient contributions to build three main halls and some residential quarters. As abbot he resided in a small chamber called Shu-shih 黍室 or millet room. Here he lived quietly, training young apprentices and working at his art, for his painting and calligraphy gradually became known nationally. About 1666 he began to use the sobriquet Pa-ta shan-jen.

There is a story that in his middle years he often feigned insanity and drunkenness, and yet appeared completely normal in congenial or trusted company. This must have been in the years 1674 to 1681 during the rebellion of the former Ming general Wu San-kuei (ECCP). For a time Wu and his allies occupied most of south China, including the southern part of Kiangsi. There were assuredly Manchu government agents watching the Taoist master who was known to be descended from the Ming imperial family. It is not surprising that when a magistrate invited him to be a guest he accepted and lived in the yamen for more than a year, until he was thought to be out of his mind. Perhaps he was approached by agents from Wu's side too, and his acting insane was understandably for self-protection. When Wu's rebellion was crushed in 1681 and the last Ming resistance on Taiwan ended in 1683, Chu Ta later that year celebrated his sixtieth birthday at his temple Ch'ing-yün-p'u.

By this time he was apparently no longer apprehensive over his safety. Two or three sketches of his life were written in these years. One was authored by Shao Ch'ang-heng (ECCP) in 1688 describing his meeting in a Buddhist monastery in Nanchang, where Chu Ta had painted a mural for their mutual friend the abbot. Ten years later Chu Ta received a request from his fellow Ming imperial clansman, Tao-chi (*q.v.*), to paint the latter's newly built country place called Ta-ti ts'ao-t'ang. Tao-chi, who had just returned from a stay in Peking, obviously had money received from Manchu noblemen and highly placed patrons, and apparently shared some of it with his more scrupulous clansman. At any rate, in 1699 the two masters and cousins met in Yangchow. This seems to be the longest trip Chu Ta made out of Nanchang.

Chu Ta reportedly lived in his temple until he died, although he is said to have retired in 1687. He left an account of the temple, the *Ch'ing-yün-p'u chih*, for which he wrote a postscript in 1681. A later edition of this work contains a list of the abbots, beginning with Chu Ta as the founder, but the obvious mistakes in his dates of birth and death show that the list was added by someone probably with intention to defraud. The *Nan-ch'ang-hsien chih* of 1919 includes several accounts of the temple. A writer in 1960 reported that it had become a memorial building in honor of the painter Pa-ta shan-jen. Also in 1960 the Palace Museum in Peking included nine examples of Chu Ta's paintings and calligraphy in its exhibition of ten great artists, and the Palace Museum, Taipei, recently reported an album dated 1659, signed by Ch'uan-ch'i.

Chu Ta is known especially for his paintings of flowers, fruit, vegetables, bamboo, rocks, trees, birds, and animals, all in a distinctive nonconforming style that sometimes suggests anger, dissatisfaction, or wariness. He was generally ignored in China during the Ch'ing period, but was appreciated by some Japanese collectors. Two centuries after his death his popularity took a sudden change because the mood he depicted suited that of a revolutionary age, and because he was considered an anti-Manchu patriot. His style, like that of Hsü Wei (*q.v.*), became recognized as creative, and led to a new school of painting. The demand for his work and his comparative-

ly easily imitated style have tempted some artists to forgery as pointed out by Wen Fong, in his discussion of the letter written in 1698 by Tao-chi to Pa-ta shan-jen.

Bibliography

Shao Ch'ang-heng, *Ch'ing-men lü-kao* 青門旅稿 and *Liu-hsi wai-chuan* 留溪外傳 (both in *Ch'ang-chou hsien-che i-shu* 常州先哲遺書); Ch'in Tsu-yung 秦祖永, *T'ung-yin lun-hua* 桐陰論畫, II (1846), 1/9b; *id.*, *T'ung-yin lun-hua hsü-pien* 續編, (1882) 1a; I-ting 一丁, "Pa-ta shan-jen sheng-nien chih-i" 生年質疑 in *I-lin ts'ung-lu* 藝林叢錄 (1962), 2, 280; Hsieh Chih-liu 謝稚柳, *Chu Ta*, Shanghai, 1961; Kuo Wei-ch'ü (ed.), *Sung-Yüan-Ming-Ch'ing shu-hua chia nien-piao* 宋元明清書畫家年表, Peking, 1958; *id.*, "Ming i-min hua-chia 明遺民畫家 Pa-ta shan-jen," *Wen-wu* 文物, no. 6 (Peking, 1961), 35; Li Tan 李旦, "Pa-ta-shan-jen ts'ung-k'ao chi Niu Shih-hui k'ao" 叢考及牛石慧考, *Wen-wu*, no. 7 (Peking, 1960), 35; H. Franke, "Zür Biographie des Pa-ta shan-jen," in *Asiatica, Festschrift für Friedrich Weller* (Leipzig, 1954), 125; O. Sirén, *Chinese Painting*, Vol. V (London, 1956-58), 149, VII, 322; R.H. van Gulik, *Chinese Pictorial Art* (Rome, 1958), 374, 376; Wen Fong, "A Letter from Shih-t'ao to Pa-ta-shan-jen and the Problem of Shih-t'ao's Chronology," *Archives of the Chinese Art Society of America*, XIII (1959), 22; V. Contag and C. C. Wang, *Seals of Chinese Painters and Collectors of the Ming and Ch'ing Periods* (Hong Kong, 1966), 106, 647; E. J. Laing, *Chinese Paintings in Chinese Publications, 1956–1968* (Ann Arbor, 1969), 229; James Cahill, *Fantastics and Eccentrics in Chinese Painting* (New York, 1967), 76; Tseng Yu-ho Ecke, *Chinese Calligraphy* (Philadelphia, 1971), 82.

Chiu Ling-yeong and Chaoying Fang

CHU Ti 朱棣, May 2, 1360-August 12, 1424, third emperor of the Ming dynasty, was also known by his princely designation Yen-wang 燕王, by his reign title Yung-lo 永樂 (1402-24), by his posthumous name Wen-huang-ti 文皇帝, by the designation of his mausoleum Ch'ang-ling 長陵, and by his two temple names, T'ai-tsung 太宗, and Ch'eng-tsu 成祖, the latter conferred on him in 1538 (*see* Chu Hou-ts'ung). He was the fourth son of the Ming founder, Chu Yüan-chang, but although he claimed to be the fourth of five sons born to the Empress Ma (*q.v.*), the founder's principal consort, modern scholars have in general agreed in a suspicion recorded at least as early as the late Ming that he was born to one of the lesser consorts, variously alleged to be a Mongol or a Korean. The facts remain uncertain. This matter, like so many historical details of his life and reign, is relevant to his usurpation of the throne from his nephew, Chu Yün-wen (*q.v.*), and to his subsequent attempts to bolster the legitimacy of his accession. Throughout his reign, elaborate efforts were made to expunge embarrassing facts and to replace them with carefully contrived counter statements; basic sources were destroyed, the *shih-lu* of the Hung-wu reign was twice rewritten, and various fictions were artfully woven into the fabric of the recent history. The specific issue with regard to Chu Ti's maternity is that the founder's *Tsu-hsün* (Ancestral Admonitions) clearly lays down a rule limiting the succession to sons of principal consorts. By asserting that he was the fourth son born to the founder's principal consort, Chu Ti did not supersede thereby the rights to the succession legitimately held by Chu Yün-wen and his heirs, but he put himself among the legitimate potential heirs; moreover, he became thereby the generational senior among such clan members, with responsibility to intercede in basic policy disagreements stemming from his interpretation of the Ancestral Admonitions. The civil war of 1399–1402 was, by this interpretation, an intra-clan affair, and not a matter in which the statesmen of the realm could rightfully intervene. Thus the issue of Chu Ti's maternity is of central importance to the history of his era.

Similarly subject to systematic exaggeration or falsification are most of the statements describing the character, learning, and personal qualities of himself as a young prince. The record makes him out to be a paragon of filial submission with humane and friendly qualities, a brilliant scholar of the classical tradition, a heroic young warrior, the object of all his less able brothers' envy and slander, yet the apple of his father's eye. The recent scholar Wang Ch'ung-wu (*see* Ch'ang Yü-ch'un) has demonstrated that the successively revised *shih-lu*, studied systematically in comparison with other contemporary documents, show enough inner inconsistencies to cast doubt on certain statements in it. It is unlikely that historians ever will be able to clear up all questions concerning the man and his period.

Nonetheless, Chu Ti clearly was a vigorous and crafty, perhaps even a brilliant, young man, possessing many of the personal traits of his able yet ruthless father. In 1370, when Chu Yüan-chang enfeoffed his nine elder sons, he gave to Chu Ti the title prince of Yen, with seat at Peiping, the former Yüan capital. He had decided that his sons should play an important role in garrisoning the northern and western borders, defending the state against Mongol incursions, and providing a military base for the family's dynastic interests. The Yen princedom, and that of Chin (northern Shansi) granted to his third son, Chu Kang (*see* Chu Yüan-chang), were the most important of the northern bastions. Chu Ti was ten years old when enfeoffed; he did not take up residence at Peiping until 1380. By that time he had received an excellent general education at the hands of eminent scholars at the court, and had begun to develop military leadership skills under the tutelage of the dynasty's leading generals, especially Hsü Ta (*q.v.*), whose eldest daughter was given to him in marriage (*ca.* 1376) at the founder's wish (*see* Empress Hsü).

On Chu Ti's arrival in Peiping he became aide-de-camp to General Fu Yu-te (*q.v.*). In the following year he joined in the successful campaign against Nair-buqa 乃兒不花 (d. 1393). During the next few years the Mongols held their peace, and Chu engaged in military exercises, until, in 1387, he was able to participate more actively in the campaign against Naɤaču (*q.v.*). He seems genuinely to have won his spurs in 1390, when, serving again with Fu, he was given his own command. He led his men, during a time of heavy snow, through the pass at Ku-pei-k'ou 古北口 to engage Nair-buqa at I-tu 迤都 (later known as Ch'in-hu-shan 擒胡山). His conduct in this affair elicited praise from his father. His last campaign into the northwest as prince came in 1396, when, as commanding officer, he defeated the Mongols east of the bend of the Yellow River, and pursued them to the territory known as Uriyangqad 兀良哈.

In spite of the emperor's pleasure over his fourth son's success, there were signs of strain between the two. Some evidence of this appeared on the occasion of the death of Empress Ma, and it showed again, more obviously, in 1392, when his eldest brother, the heir apparent Chu Piao (*q.v.*), died, and five months later his nephew Chu Yün-wen was chosen successor. It was precisely the potential for independent action on the part of Chu Ti and the princes which gave rise to the major problem facing Chu Yün-wen on his accession in 1398. The new emperor's principal advisers in Nanking, especially Ch'i T'ai (*q.v.*), were convinced that the "feudatories," i.e., the princedoms having military garrisons and regional powers granted to the principal sons of the founder, were an anomaly that must be eliminated. A policy, called in Chinese hsiao-fan 削藩 (reducing feudatories) was openly adopted by the emperor late in 1398. It brought to a head the real conflict of power interests between the central government and the princes, among whom Chu Ti was the eldest survivor, the most able, and the most ambitious (*see* Ch'i T'ai). If that was the principal element in the conflict between Nanking and Peiping, it was not the only one. Chu Ti also insisted that he was deeply disturbed about the treachery and villainy of his young nephew's advisers,

saying that not only were they leading him into dissolute personal ways, but also that they were inducing him to make changes in the structure and character of imperial government that would violate the founder's intentions (*see* Fang Hsiao-ju).

The young emperor in Nanking may have had no choice but to take military measures against Chu Ti in 1399, for one well-argued view is that revolt had long been urged upon Chu Ti by his advisers, and had in fact long been in secret preparation. The Nanking court appears to have sought earnestly to devise a thoughtful policy. One official, Kao Wei (*see* Chu Yün-wen), had argued for a policy of moderation and generous accommodation in a memorial submitted as late as the end of 1398, although that was a minority view at that time. He analyzed the crisis confronting the Ming state in terms of the dynasty's favorite source of analogies to itself, Han dynasty history, and urged the emperor to adopt a similarly gracious policy and to avoid direct conflict within the imperial clan. Chu Yün-wen is reported to have held back Kao Wei's memorial, unable to decide on the appropriate response to it, and from this it has been inferred that the decision to eliminate the princedoms by force had already been taken, however reluctantly, within a few months following the accession, and that there was to be no turning back.

Chu Ti's three sons were residing at the court at Nanking, potential hostages. Both sides had spies and agents observing and reporting from the other's seat of power. Chu Ti resorted to curious actions, feigning illness, then madness, during the winter of 1398–99, and through the period of early 1399 when the actions against other princes were under way. He requested the return of his sons, and early in June, 1399, it was decided to allow them to return, to allay their father's suspicions, and to lead him to believe that the actions against the other princes were in punishment for specific violations and not part of a general plan to abolish all the powers of all the princes. Returning the young princes to their father at Peiping has been judged by later historians one of Chu Yün-wen's serious errors.

Open hostilities did not break out until the summer of 1399. At that time, a military official loyal to the emperor seized two of Chu Ti's military subordinates, finding clear evidence of sedition, and took them to Nanking to be executed. But before the court could take further action, Chu Ti grasped the initiative, and proclaimed that he would "clear away the disasters, in response to Heaven's will," thus opening a military campaign which he called feng-t'ien ching-nan (see Chu Yün-wen).

The ensuing civil war was fought in Pei-Chihli and Shantung for two years, during which Chu Ti and his aggressive younger sons fought in the field, leading armies and fighting in every action; his wife, the future Empress Hsü, and his heir, the less martial Chu Kao-chih (q.v.), devoted themselves with great energy and initiative to defending the city and maintaining a center of civil government there. In contrast, the Nanking court failed to achieve a similarly intense sense of involvement, and the emperor scarcely participated in prosecuting the war. The larger numbers of troops that Nanking was able to put into the field, and their superiority in firearms, counted heavily in their favor, but they suffered in part from an occasional incompetent or irresolute commander. Chu Ti, on the other hand, was more experienced, had efficient Mongol horsemen, and was more determined to win.

The war started in central Pei-Chihli when the imperial army of about 130,000 moved into position around Ho-chien河間. In September, 1399, it was defeated with heavy losses. A month later Chu Ti, to protect his rear, and possibly to draw the enemy up to his own territory, left Peiping for the princedom of Ning 寧, and succeeded by a ruse in forcing his half-brother Chu Ch'üan (q.v.) to join him, and add his military units, especially his Mongol cavalry, to aid in the rebellion. Meanwhile the imperial army under Li Ching-lung (see Li Wen-chung) advanced to the walls of Peiping (November 12) and laid siege to it and other nearby points, such as T'ung-chou 通州. Chu returned just in time to save his citadel, defeating Li in a three-day battle, and reentering Peiping on December 4; while Li —abandoning many of his men and supplies—retreated to Te 德-chou, Shantung. Chu Ti next (January, 1400) proceeded to the northwest into Shansi, and in March succeeded in taking Tatung after a siege of several weeks. By so doing he protected another flank. Li Ching-lung, reluctant to take his southern troops northward in the dead of winter, had waited until March to proceed to the relief of the beleaguered Tatung. He was too late, never did engage the rebels, and had to return with an exhausted army to Te-chou, while Chu came back to Peiping in triumph.

The next main encounter was in central Pei-Chihli, near Paoting, by the banks of a stream known as Pai-kou 白溝河. Here the imperial forces, in two divisions (under the command of Li Ching-lung), planned to crush the rebel army in a pincers attack, but were frustrated (May 14) by cloudbursts and heavy flooding. The two sides, numbering some 600,000 men, engaged in a show of strength four days later. An interesting feature of the engagement was Li's use of explosive weapons and what appear to have been land mines (一窩蜂揣馬丹). In spite of this advantage, the imperial army gave way, Li retreating in disorder, first to Te-chou (May 30), then to Tsinan. But Chu was in danger too, for a cavalry column led by General P'ing An 平安 (an adopted son of Chu Yüan-chang, d. March 28, 1409), pursued him until forced to give way by a troop of several thousand horse, which emerged from Peiping, commanded by Chu Ti's son Chu Kao-hsü (q.v.). Chu

Ti then returned to the attack, advancing on Te-chou (June 1) and next on Tsinan (June 5), which he besieged throughout the summer. This was not a secure position for him, however, for during August both Sheng Yung (*q.v.*) and P'ing An stole out from the city to attack his rear, even recapturing Te-chou on August 19. With the news that a relief force was on the way from Nanking, Chu lifted the siege (September 4) and made his way home.

During the autumn, while Chu recouped his strength, occasionally making feints and diversionary attacks in southwest Pei-Chihli, Sheng Yung and T'ieh Hsüan (*q.v.*) moved to confront him at Tung-ch'ang 東昌, in western Shantung (January 10, 1401). At the mid-point in the battle P'ing An arrived with his cavalry, and overwhelmed Chu's army. Here too the imperial forces employed explosive weapons with devastating effect. Several commanding officers and thousands of his men were slain, and the prince himself nearly lost his life. This defeat was the low point in his rebellion. But Chu still had sufficient manpower to continue guerrilla tactics. On April 6 the armies met at the River Hu-t'o 滹沱河 (in southern Pei-Chihli). Again the elements gave Chu Ti the advantage. A typical dust storm blew in from the northeast, blinding the southern soldiers. Discomfitted, they left the field to the rebels. All of the southern part of the province was soon in Chu Ti's hands. In midsummer he followed up his success by sending General Li Yüan 李遠 (enfeoffed 1402 as marquis of An-p'ing 安平侯, d. 1409, aged fifty, Pth. 忠壯) with a troop of horsemen, all dressed in loyalist uniforms, to destroy points along the Grand Canal in southern Shantung and northern Nan-Chihli, as well as barges and supply depots. This action debilitated the government forces in northern Shantung, but Chu still had to ward off attacks both from the west and the east. The severest came on May 23, when Hsü Hui-tsu (*see* Hsü Ta) dealt him a heavy blow at Ch'i-mei shan 齊眉

山 (in northern Anhwei). Surprisingly enough, he was able to recover sufficiently three days later to turn the tables on the imperial force at Ling-pi 靈壁 nearby, capturing P'ing An and other officers.

This victory was just what Chu Ti needed. Avoiding the well-fortified posts along the Canal, he proceeded southeast to Yangchow, taking Ssu 泗-chou and Shou 壽-chou along the way (June 7, 8), crossing the Huai 淮 (June 9), and reaching his destination on June 17. The great river was now his major obstacle. After mopping up several government units along the north bank, he reached P'u-tzu-k'ou 浦子口, across the Yangtze from Nanking, on July 1. Here Sheng Yung stopped him in his tracks. Relief came, however, led by his son Chu Kao-hsü, who attacked with his Mongol horsemen, and cleared the way. Soon the naval forces too surrendered.

Li Ching-lung, who, following his replacement as generalissimo in September, 1400, had continued to serve as a prominent courtier and adviser, appears to have been the symbolic leader of a faction within Chu Yün-wen's court that opposed the war policies (*see* Ch'i T'ai). Together with Ju Ch'ang (*q.v.*) and others associated with that faction he was sent on July 8 to make offers of peace to Chu Ti at Lung-t'an 龍潭. They returned to report unsuccessful negotiations, and apparently to prepare secretly to end the civil war by other means. In any event, five days later, on July 13, Li conspired with Chu Hui (*see* Chu Yüan-chang), who was commanding the defense of the Chin-ch'uan 金川 Gate, to open it and welcome Chu Ti as conqueror.

In the disorders that followed, the palace enclosure was set afire and Chu Yün-wen is presumed to have died, along with his empress. Bodies identified as theirs were buried, and on July 18, after having symbolically and repeatedly refused, Chu Ti acceded to the pleas of his courtiers and ascended the throne. But many highly placed courtiers refused to acknowledge this usurpation. These defiant loyalists were made the objects of intimidating slaughter of all their relations to the ninth or the tenth degree, including neighbors, teachers, students, servants, and even friends. This act equaled in ferocity any of the bloody purges of Chu Yüan-chang. So, by force and with terror, commenced the reign for which the era name Yung-lo (lasting joy) was chosen. In fact, it was a very successful reign in many ways, especially in the domestic area, but hardly less in the foreign.

One of Chu Ti's first considerations on achieving empire was the location of his capital. He was not comfortable in Nanking with its many reminders of his father and nephew, and with a burned-out palace to boot. As early as 1403 he began to consider his old seat in the north, in 1409 making his decision definite. A final decree (1420) proclaimed a change of name to Pei-ching 北京 (northern capital), and the official transfer was effected in the following year. There are numerous references to the construction of walls, palaces, and other buildings before 1421 (see Juan An), but one of special interest, describing the city on December 14, 1420, comes from the pen of an envoy of Shāhrukh, son of Timur, named Hāfiz-i Abrū: "It was a very magnificent city, so that every one of its walls was a farsang long, total circumference being four farsangs. All around the city wall owing to the fact that it was still under construction there were set up one hundred thousand poles, each one of which being fifty cubits long, in the form of scaffoldings. Since it was still early dawn the gates had not yet been opened, the envoys were admitted to the city through the tower which was being constructed and made to alight at the gate of the Emperor's palaces. At the entrance to the citadel there had been constructed pavement of cut stones of the size of seven hundred paces in length." The city was greatly foreshortened at this time, the northern wall being

made to run far to the south of that of Ta-tu, possibly because the population was smaller, or possibly because it was thus made easier to defend.

Perhaps more aware of dangers from the north and west than any other man of his day, Chu Ti learned early in 1405 of the ambitions of Timur (Tamerlane) in faraway Samarkand, and began to make plans to frustrate his advance at the Chinese frontier. Fortunately for him Timur died at Otrar (February 17, 1405) while on his way with 200,000 men to recover China for the Mongols. There were later threats, altogether six during the Yung-lo reign: 1) in 1409, the Chinese led by Ch'iu Fu (see Qorγočin), marched out to the border, were drawn into a trap, and completely routed with a loss of almost all the commanding officers; 2) in 1410 the emperor himself took the field, pursuing the Mongols as far as the River Onon 斡難, where he defeated them (on his back he encountered and crushed roving bands led by Aruγtai, q.v.); 3) again in 1414 Chu took command of a combined army of Chinese and Eastern Mongols, and defeated the Oirat in a battle by the River Tola; 4, 5, 6) in the years 1422-24 three campaigns were mounted against the Eastern Mongols of Aruγtai in modern Jehol and Chahar, all successful, except that in the last, the emperor died on the way home at a place called Yü-mu-ch'uan 榆木川 (situation unknown). Three inscriptions telling of his victories were cut in stone, two at Dairiganga (1410) and one near Dolonor.

In addition to the emperor's efforts to quell all attempts of the Mongols to resume their control of China, Chu Ti embarked on what the French call "pénétration pacifique" of the northeast (modern Manchuria, the Amur region, and the Maritime Province of Siberia), establishing commanderies to control the restless tribes—descendants of the Jurchen conquerors of north China under the dynasty of Chin (1115-1234)—who might prove a threat to his country and his power. In so doing he was also countering the moves of the Yi dynasty of Korea which was trying almost simultaneously (from 1393 on) to make subjects of the same tribespeople. His father had initiated this policy, but it was left to the son to carry it through to completion. Henry Serruys, who has made the most thorough study of this question, believes that Chu Ti established altogether some 178 commanderies in this vast area. Their chieftains were induced to surrender by receiving ranks, titles, and economic advantages, as the exchange of presents from the Ming (silk, cotton, clothes, paper money, etc.) for tribute offerings (most commonly horses) was an ill-disguised form of barter, which inevitably benefited the chiefs more than it did their people. All this irked the Koreans, but they were obliged to give in to superior pressure, though they continued to complete with the Chinese wherever possible. A curious sidelight on Chu Ti's interest in the Jurchen is that, while still prince of Yen, he is said to have married the daughter of one of their chieftains, Aqaču (A-ha-ch'u 阿哈出) of the commandery of Chien-chou 建州.

Annam was another area of concern, although Chu Ti never fought there. In 1403, according to the *shih-lu*, the second son of Lê Quí-ly (*q.v.*), called Lê Han-thu'o'ng (Hồ-Dê 胡奎 in Chinese), asked the Ming court for investiture; with some hesitation, the court granted the request. But later, because of pleas from the king, Trân Thiên-bình (*see* Lê Quí-ly), who insisted that Lê Han-thu'o'ng had usurped the throne, Chu Ti decided to intervene (1406). This resulted in a short conflict, starting with an invasion (November, 1406) by Chang Fu (*q.v.*) and Mu Sheng (*see* Mu Ying), leading armies from Kwangsi and Yunnan respectively. By May, 1407, the Chinese had routed the Annamites and succeeded (in June) in capturing both Lê and his son who had fled to the south. Chu then formally incorporated Annam into the empire as the province of Chiao-chih, and saw to the

renaming of its divisions and its reorganization. All was not quiet in the new territory, however. For several years sporadic outbreaks occurred in which both Generals Chang and Mu had their ups and downs against the guerrilla attacks of the Annamites. Not until 1416 does their resistance to Chinese overlordship seem to have crumbled. But two years later, under the leadership of one of the ablest of the guerrilla leaders, Lê Lọ'i (*q.v.*), the rebels forced another protracted effort at pacification. Lê generally avoided frontal attacks, preferring to keep the Ming occupation army off balance, blocking their supply routes, making surprise attacks. By 1424 Chu Ti was dead. Though the Ming generals continued their efforts to ward off the inevitable, by the end of 1427 they were obliged to admit failure, and withdrew, leaving Lê Lọ'i king in fact.

Chu Ti used other means besides war and military penetration to keep his frontiers secure. One of his first acts as emperor was to extend an invitation to Japan to become a tributary state, and he followed up this approach by dispatching the transmission commissioner, Chao Chü-jen, and attendant envoys to Japan to enter into friendly relations with Yoshimitsu (for both, *see* Chang Hung 張洪), the third Ashikaga shōgun (d. 1408). The result was a commercial agreement, concluded 1404, which made for peace between the two countries for over a decade. A short period of uneasy truce followed. Then the *wo-k'ou* again began their raids on the China coast, once (1419) being soundly defeated by Liu Jung (*see* Maḥmud), then commanding the army in Liaotung. But Chu Ti refused to take punitive action against Japan. Instead he twice (1417, 1418) sent strongly worded rescripts to the next shōgun, Yoshimochi, by the hand of a vice director of the ministry of Justice, Lü Yüan 呂淵, in a vain attempt to restore relations to the *status quo ante*.

He also dispatched embassies from the capital to Tibet and Nepal (*see* Hou

Hsien), to Herat and Samarkand (*see* Ch'en Ch'eng), and other places—generally, but not always, with eunuchs in charge—in the interest of amicable relations and of personal aggrandizement, and to bring intelligence reports to the throne. Missions from all these states and kingdoms came in return, bearing gifts (and merchandise), and it is to one of these that we owe a description of His Majesty, then aged fifty-eight. It was written by the above mentioned Hāfiz-i Abrū, who saw the emperor shortly after daybreak (December 14, 1420): "The emperor was of middle height; his beard neither very large nor very small; nevertheless about two or three hundred hairs of his middle beard were long enough to form three or four curls on the chair he was seated."

The great voyages of Cheng Ho (*q.v.*) belong in the same category, though perhaps with them there was more interest in the import of precious goods. A reason explicitly mentioned both in the *Ming-shih* and in the official biography of the grand eunuch—the search for his imperial nephew—can only have been a minor one. After looking for him in all the provinces (*see* Hu Ying), Chu Ti may well have entertained the thought that he had disappeared abroad, and so ordered his envoys to raise the question wherever they went. As China's warships at this time were held in dread by all its island and peninsular neighbors, it seems more likely that the emperor's main concern was to overawe them into becoming proper tribute-bearing states. In any event, a fleet of over sixty treasure ships and many smaller vessels was built, equipped, and manned, and for the next seventeen years Cheng and his fellow-commanders (*see* Wang Ching-hung) visited the East Indies, coastal India, Ceylon, the Persian Gulf, the Red Sea, and the east coast of Africa. Ambassadors came to China in return, bearing gifts of "local products." Among the visitors, probably an unwilling one, was the king of Ceylon, Alagakkonāra, together with his queen

and their children (1411). Interesting developments resulting from these embassies were the establishment (April, 1407) of the Ssu-i-kuan (*see* Cheng Ho), a college for training interpreters, and the compilation of vocabularies for their instruction (*see* Wang Tsung-tsai and Mao Jui-cheng). It is worthy of note that the emperor had the Ssu-i-kuan attached to the highly respected Hanlin Academy, and authorized students of the bureau, under special conditions, to present themselves for the *chin-shih*, where their knowledge of foreign languages would be taken into consideration.

Vastly more important was the decision in the first year of his reign (July, 1403) to make an effort to preserve all known literature up to his day. The need was voiced by Hsieh Chin (*q.v.*), and for a year he served as general director with a staff of 147 assistants. But by December, 1404, when the manuscript was laid before the emperor, he called it insufficient, and ordered his long-time adviser Yao Kuang-hsiao (*q. v.*) and Liu Chi-ch'ih 劉季篪 (*ming*: 詔, 1363–1423, cs 1394) to serve as codirectors, aided by some 2,180 scholars. Was this huge enterprise undertaken just to keep alive the literary treasures of the past? Or may it have been partly to quiet the restless men of letters of the day, many of whom were doubtless unemployed and secretly held Chu Ti in contempt for his usurpation? The work, completed in 1408 in 22,877 *chüan*, received the approval of the emperor who, granting it the name of his own reign, gave it the title *Yung-lo ta-tien* 大典. Two other enterprises of major importance for their impact on all candidates for higher degrees, and as such on the Confucianism of the next few hundred years, were the compilation (1415) of the *Wu-ching ssu-shu ta-ch'üan* 五經四書大全 (for some reason the work copied into the Imperial Library of the 18th century includes the *Ssu-shu* in 36 *chüan* only) and the *Hsing-li* 性理 *ta-ch'üan*, 70 *ch.*, containing the opinions of one hundred twenty philosophers of the Sung dynasty. Whereas the first emperor had come to power as a near illiterate, and discovered the heinous doctrines about the rights of the people in the *Mencius* only after being on the throne for a number of years (*see* Liu San-wu), his son had had a good education, and apparently realized the importance of having the entire canon, including the unexpurgated *Mencius* (published about 1411) made available. For good measure he brought to the people the complete body of the commentaries on the canon by the thinkers of the 11th to 13th centuries. These works were to become required reading for every candidate for the highest degree. As for the *chin-shih* examinations, they were conducted during eight years in the twenty-two of the Yung-lo period, as against only six in the thirty-one of the Hung-wu reign; Chu Yüan-chang had suspended them between 1371 and 1385. Chu Ti also initiated the custom (February 14, 1405) of selecting twenty-eight *chin-shih* to study in the Hanlin Academy. From then on this practice became institutionalized.

Chu Ti's ascent to the throne was marked by domestic strains as well as the far larger problems of statecraft. One of the brothers of his wife (now empress), Hsü Tseng-shou (*see* Hsü Ta), was reportedly slain by Chu Yün-wen just prior to his own death. Another brother, Hsü Hui-tsu, a stanch loyalist, may have committed suicide at the same time. Chu's own son, and probably his favorite, Chu Kao-hsü, had a rebellious temper, often made no pains to hide it, and had frequently to be put in his place. To his brothers and half-brothers, who had suffered at the hands of Chu Yün-wen, Chu Ti was particularly magnamimous, restoring both their freedom and their ranks. One brother, Chu Su (*q.v.*), however, came close to rebellion, and had to be deprived of his military power and watched with care. His wife died in 1407, and soon afterwards Chu Ti started to repair the Pao-en monastery 報恩寺, situated outside

the Chü-pao gate 聚寶門 (Nanking), and undertook the construction in her honor (1413) of the justly acclaimed octagonal porcelain pagoda of nine stories, over 276 (English) feet high, known as Pao-en or Liu-li t'a 琉璃塔. There it remained until 1854, when the Taiping rebels razed it to the ground. S. Wells Williams once wrote: "It stood pre-eminent above all other similar buildings in China for its completeness and elegance, the material of which it was built, and the quantity of gilding with which its interior was embellished." In this connection it seems reasonable to assume that the porcelain tiles of this pagoda, completed in 1431, came from Ching te-chen 景德鎮, in Jao-chou 饒州, Kiangsi. Tradition has it that funds for its erection derived from the profits accruing from the expeditions of Cheng Ho.

Chu Ti seems to have had a genuine concern for the propagation of Buddhism. The National Central Library records two books for which he is held responsible: *Chu Fo shih tsun ju-lai p'u-sa shen-seng ming-ching* 諸佛世尊如來菩薩神僧名經, 10 *ts'e*, engraved in the palace in 1417, and *Kan-ying ko-ch'ü* 感應歌曲, 16 *ts'e*, engraved by the same printing office in 1419. He was responsible too for initiating (1420) the so-called northern edition of the *Tripiṭaka*, completed in 1440 in 6,771 *chüan*.

In civil matters Chu Ti followed in general the policies of his father in bringing the whole country to heel, especially in the southwest where Ming administrators (and possibly eager landowners as well) frequently aroused the hostility of local elements, including the tribespeople. In one respect, however, he failed to follow the strict injunction of the first emperor, who, in 1381, ordered that eunuchs should not involve themselves in affairs outside the imperial household; "those who do will be beheaded." The eunuchs Chu Ti employed were perhaps necessary in his case, as he distrusted the scholars who had served his nephew. He used them as envoys, as officers on military expeditions, and as spies on the bureaucrats and the common people, in 1420 establishing the tung-ch'ang 東廠 (Eastern depot) as a secret service. But those scholar officials who had not officiated in the Chienwen reign, such men as Yao Kuang-hsiao, Hsieh Chin, Hu Kuang (*q. v.*), and the three Yang (*see* Yang Jung and Yang Shih-ch'i) proved to be a bulwark of strength. It was to Chu Ti's credit that he consulted them on extraordinary issues and let them receive memorials addressed to the throne, one of them even assuming responsibility for drafting decrees for him to issue.

The northern provinces had suffered bitterly during the years of civil war—a book of doggerel entitled *Yen-wang sao pei* 掃北 (The prince of Yen sweeps the north), 4 *ch.*, was still circulating in the 1930s—and had to be rehabilitated, and people encouraged to settle or return. The local history of Ting 定 -chou, situated south of Paoting, for example, reports that in 1401, when the prince passed through, he so stripped the countryside that "the roof swallows nested in the trees," and the district had to be repopulated by bringing large numbers of families from Shensi. To the same end the Grand Canal required repair, and all ancillary structures, such as supply depots, had to be completely restored. A major figure in this work was Ch'en Hsüan 陳瑄 (*q. v.*), who initially built a large granary in Tientsin for the storage of grain (1411), and then erected more granaries along the route of the Canal. He also constructed new channels and new dikes, and directed the stationing of corvée laborers along the waterway to maintain it properly.

In supervising the rebuilding of Peking, Chu Ti had no desire to be buried near his father and his elder brother in the vicinity of Nanking. He selected instead a magnificent site, 26 miles north of Peking in the foothills of the mountain chain that runs to the west of the capital, and there (beginning 1409) he erected

his own mausoleum, where he was buried on January 8, 1425. His wife's remains were laid to rest in the same mausoleum. Chu Ti was followed in death by sixteen of his concubines (*see* Chu Kao-chih).

Bibliography

1/ ch. 1–3; MSL (1963), T'ai-tsung; KC (1958), ch. 11–18; SK (1930), 36/3b, 93/2b; Li Chin-hua 李晉華, "Ming Ch'eng-tsu sheng-mu wen-t'i k'ao-cheng kao," 生母問題考證稿, CYYY, VI: 1 (1936), 55; Chu Hsi-tsu 朱希祖, "Tsai po Ming Ch'eng-tsu sheng-mu wei kung-fei shuo" 再駁明成祖生母爲碩妃說 in *Tung-fang tsa-chih* 東方雜誌, 33:12 (1936), 5; Wang Ch'ung-wu 王崇武, *Ming ching-nan shih-shih k'ao-cheng kao* 明靖難史事考證稿 (Shanghai, 1948); id., *Feng-t'ien* 奉天 *ching-nan chi-chu* 記注 (Shanghai, 1948); Meng Sen (BDRC), *Ming-tai shih* (1957); Wu Han (BDRC), *Chu Yüan-chang chuan* (1948); anon., *Yen-wang sao-pei* (no date); Ko Yin-liang 葛寅亮, *Chin-ling fan-ch'a chih* 金陵梵刹志 (*ca.* 1607), 31/1a, 15a; Paul Pelliot, *Notes on Marco Polo* (Paris, 1963), II, 660; id., "Le Hōja et le Sayyid Husain de l'histoire des Ming," TP, 38 (1948), 228; S. J. Shaw, "Historical Significance of the Curious Theory of the Mongol Blood in the Veins of the Ming Emperors," CSPSR, 20 (1937), 492; Yi Sang-baek 李相佰, *Han'guk sa: künse chŏn'gi p'yŏn* 韓國史近世前期篇 (Seoul, 1962), 115; D. Pokotilov, "History of the Eastern Mongols During the Ming Dynasty from 1368–1634," tr. by R. Loewenthal, *Studia Serica*, ser. A., no. 1 (Chengtu, 1947), 15, 23; Wolfgang Franke, *Addenda and Corrigenda* (Chengtu and Peiping, 1949), 25; id., *Sources*, introduction; id., "Yung-lo's Mongolei-Feldzüge," *Sinologische Arbeiten*, III (Peiping, 1945); Wang Yi-t'ung, *Official Relations between China and Japan, 1368-1549* (Cambridge, Mass., 1953), 23; H. Serruys, *Sino-Mongol Relations During the Ming*, XIV, MCB (1967); id., "Sino-Jurčed Relations during the Yung-lo Period (1403-1424)*, (Wiesbaden, 1955); id., "The Mongols in China: 1400–1450," MS, 27 (1968), 233; Jung-pang Lo, "The Decline of the Early Ming Navy," OE, 5 (1958), 149; H. Friese, "Der Mönch Yao Kuang-hsiao (1335-1418) und seine Zeit," OE, 7 (1960), 158; V. M. Kasakevitch, "Sources to the History of the Chinese Military Expeditions into Mongolia," tr. by R. Loewenthal, MS, 8 (1943), 328; Hafiz Abru, *A Persian Embassy to China*, tr. by K. M. Maitra (Lahore, 1934), 56; L. Carrington Goodrich, "More on the Yung-lo ta-tien," JRAS,

Hong Kong branch, 10 (1970), 17; Sidney D. Gamble, *Ting Hsien, a North China Rural Community* (New York, 1954), 3; S. Wells Williams, *The Middle Kingdom*, I (New York, 1883), 102; Robert B. Crawford, "Eunuch Power in the Ming Dynasty," TP, 49 (1961), 119, 126, 131; Margaret Medley, "Ching-te-chen and the Problem of the 'Imperial Kilns,'" BSOAS, XXIX, pt. 2 (1966), 326; J. M. Addis, *Archives*, XXII (1968–69), 96; *id.*, "Yung-lo Blue and White," *Oriental Art*, V (1959), 157.

F. W. Mote and L. Carrington Goodrich

CHU Tsai-hou 朱載垕, March, 4, 1537–July 4, 1572, twelfth emperor of the Ming dynasty, was also known by his princely designation Yü-wang 裕王 (1539-66), by his reign title Lung-ch'ing 隆慶(1567–72), by his temple name Mu-tsung 穆宗, by his posthumous name Chuang-huang-ti 莊皇帝, and by the designation of his tomb Chao-ling 昭陵. He was the third son of Emperor Chu Hou-ts'ung (*q.v.*) and Consort K'ang 康妃 (d. February, 1554, a native of Peking and the daughter of Tu Lin 杜林, posthumously given an earldom in 1567).

The eldest son of Chu Hou-ts'ung died in infancy, and his second son, the heir apparent Chu Tsai-jui (*see* Chu Hou-ts'ung), was about six months old at the time of Chu Tsai-hou's birth. A little over a month later the fourth son Chu Tsai-ch'uan (*see* Chu Hou-ts'ung) was born. In February, 1539, on the same day that Chu Tsai-jui was proclaimed heir apparent, Chu Tsai-hou and Chu Tsai-ch'uan were respectively made prince of Yü and prince of Ching 景王. Ten years later the heir apparent died, leaving Chu Tsai-hou as the eldest living son and logically first in line of succession. Yet the emperor procrastinated in naming a new heir apparent despite repeated requests from his ministers. In March, 1552, the two sons, Chu Tsai-hou and Chu Tsai-ch'uan, were capped in a joint ceremony. They began their schooling together in September of that year, and two months later their future wives were selected at the same time. Their marriage ceremonies took place four days apart in February, 1553, and they were assigned separate residences with a wall in between. They were treated so much on the same footing that it naturally gave rise to speculations and aspirations. As a matter of fact, the emperor did favor the mother of Chu Tsai-ch'uan and kept her for a long time in his company (until 1565?). As to Chu Tsai-hou's mother, K'ang-fei, she was treated quite ungraciously. When she died, the officials in drawing up her funeral plan had to revise it downward twice because the emperor refused to sanction any part of the ceremony that would indicate her status to be higher than her rank as the mother of a potential heir apparent. In March, 1560, when an official memorialized on the urgency of designating Chu Tsai-hou the heir apparent, the emperor was so offended that he ordered his immediate execution. Later in that year, however, the emperor had a change of mind, and in October ordered Chu Tsai-ch'uan to leave Peking and proceed to his own princedom in Te-an, Hukuang (*see* Hsü Hsüeh-mo). Only then was Chu Tsai-hou more assured of his position, although he was still denied the designation of heir apparent and excluded from his father's presence. In the meantime he was treated rather shabbily and neglected. Reportedly his monthly allowance was once delayed, and he had to appeal to the son of Yen Sung (*q.v.*) to speed it up.

Unquestionably Chu Tsai-hou was not in his father's favor. There is a story that, when his elder half-brother, the heir apparent, died in 1549, the emperor was overwhelmed with sorrow and regret, and blamed himself for failing to take heed of the counsel of his Taoist adviser, T'ao Chung-wen (*q.v.*), who had allegedly warned that "two dragons should avoid seeing each other." Since the dragon was the symbol of an emperor, presumably for this reason he did not give Chu Tsai-hou the title of heir apparent and also refused to see him. On the other hand, there is the story that the emperor held Chu Tsai-hou in contempt, because he failed to observe the decorum of abstinence during the mourning period. Apparently this alluded to the fact that eighteen months after his mother's death a son was born to him in October, 1555. Whatever the reason, the fact is that Chu Tsai-hou as a prince lived practically in seclusion and grew up with little or no paternal guidance. Although twenty-nine years of age at his father's death, he was by no means well indoctrinated in statecraft or prepared properly to take up the reins of government. By nature, furthermore, he was neither strong nor ambitious, had no interest in national affairs, and sought pleasure only. It is said that his love of amusement and luxury was in compensation for his early years under the stern eye of his father. In court audiences he generally kept silent, and hardly ever initiated any policies, or assumed the power and responsibility of a sovereign. His dislike of governing naturally resulted in a tendency to keep his ministers at a distance, and to draw more closely to the eunuchs. In comparison to his father, however, he was a much more kindly and amiable man. Throughout his short reign, in contrast to the previous years, few high officials were abused or suffered the extreme penalty.

In the name of the deceased emperor's "dying commands," the new reign began with measures of redress and reform. Many officials who had been punished unjustly for their loyal advice were recalled to office if living or given posthumous honors if deceased. The Taoist adepts, who had exercised so much influence over the previous emperor, were thrown into prison and their rituals forbidden. The orders for the search and collection of various materials and substances demanded by the Taoists for their religious performances were rescinded. Hai Jui (q.v.), who had braved death in remonstrating against the Taoist influence, for

example, was immediately freed from prison and reinstated. These welcome "dying commands," were actually composed by Hsü Chieh (q.v.), now serving as senior grand secretary. The fact that Hsü failed to share the credit for them with his associates led to an irreparable breach between him and Kao Kung (see Chang Chü-cheng). As one commentator pointed out, it was lamentable that two such able men could not work together for the good of the nation, but instead should become deadly enemies. Kao Kung was discharged as grand secretary in the summer of 1567, and Hsü Chieh the following year. When Kao came back into office early in 1570, he and his followers revenged themselves on Hsü and his sons. The emperor's inability to assume authority was doubtless a contributing factor to the instability and confusion in the Grand Secretariat.

It was under such circumstances that Chang Chü-cheng, acclaimed by many as the most able senior minister of the Ming dynasty, rose to power. Though Chang received the *chin-shih* in 1547, his ascendancy in officialdom dated from 1567 when, as one of the emperor's former instructors, he was promoted to grand secretary. Notwithstanding his junior position, he had already formulated his scheme of governing, which he laid out in an important memorial; it was not theoretical or idealistic, but entirely practical and met the needs of the time. For a decade and a half thereafter, Chang Chü-cheng remained in the Grand Secretariat with ever increasing power, and came to be the most celebrated of Ming officials.

In external affairs the Lung-ch'ing period was in very real measure a peaceful one. Except for Kwangtung, the southeast coast was freed of Japanese (and Chinese) piratical raids, which had so disturbed the region in the Chia-ching period. In the north, thanks to the able handling by supreme commander Wang Ch'ung-ku (q.v.) and an intelligent decision on the part of Chang Chü-cheng and Kao Kung, a peaceful settlement with the Mongols was reached, and from then on their leader, Altan-qaɤan (*q.v.*), called himself a vassal.

Another event, of little significance perhaps, also merits mention. This was a grand review of troops held by the emperor in the autumn of 1569. Throughout the Ming dynasty it was the second of three times that this ceremony was held, the others being in 1429 and 1581. The colorful show with the emperor in the center also developed from a suggestion made by Chang Chü-cheng. Much occupied with the strengthening of border defense and the rejuvenating of the army, Chang must have believed that an imperial grand review would boost the morale of the forces. On the other hand, one cannot help suspecting that Chang's intention may partly have been to humor the emperor in the latter's rather monotonous and sheltered life.

Chu Tsai-hou had four sons. His first wife, whom he married in February, 1553, and who gave birth to his eldest son Chu I-shih 朱翊鈝 (October, 1555–May, 1559, Pth. 憲懷太子), died in April, 1558. Half a year later he married again, a lady née Ch'en 陳 (d. 1596), who became empress after his succession, but for some reason lost his favor and was made to live separately in her own quarters in 1569. She had no issue. His second son also died young. The third, Chu I-chün (*q.v.*), succeeded to the throne. The fourth, Chu I-liu 朱翊鏐 (1568–1614, Pth. 簡), was given a princedom in Wei-hui 衛輝, Honan, with the title of prince of Lu 潞王. Both Chu I-chün and Chu I-liu were born of the same mother Li-shih (*q.v.*). Of his seven daughters, four reached maturity.

Chu Tung-jun 朱東潤 in *Chang Chü-cheng ta-chuan* 大傳 asserts that Chu Tsai-hou died of a cardiac condition. According to Kao Kung's account, however, his death was possibly due to other causes for he was ill for several months before he died and also had a sore on his wrist that took a long time to heal.

Bibliography

1/ch. 19, 57/7b, 114/7b, 120/2b; MSL (1940), Shih-tsung and Mu-tsung; KC (1958), Shih-tsung and Mu-tsung; Kao Kung, *Ping t'a i-yen* 病榻遺言 in *Kao Wen-hsiang kung wen-chi* 高文襄公集; Chu Tung-jun, *Chang Chü-cheng ta-chuan* (Shanghai, 1947); Henry Serruys, "Four Documents Relating to the Sino-Mongol Peace of 1570–1571," MS, 19 (1960), 1.

Lienche Tu Fang and Chaoying Fang

CHU Tsai-yü 朱載堉 (T. 伯勤, H. 句曲山人), 1536–May 19, 1611, scholar, musician, mathematician, and first highly precise formulator in numerical terms of the equal temperament in music, was a descendant in the sixth generation of the fourth Ming emperor (Chu Kao-chih, *q.v.*). He was born in Ho-nei 河內 (Huai-ch'ing-fu 懷慶府), Honan, the heir apparent of the sixth prince of Cheng 鄭, Chu Hou-huan 厚烷 (1518–91). Although a prince, Chu Hou-huan was a strict Confucianist of austere temperament and modest habits and in 1548 incurred the displeasure of the emperor, Chu Hou-ts'ung (*q.v.*), for submitting a memorial criticizing the emperor's excessive observance of Taoist ceremonies, and urging personal reform. Two years later the emperor took revenge when a disgruntled cousin of the prince, who himself coveted the princedom, accused the prince of treason in a memorial enumerating forty crimes. A state investigation declared the accusations groundless except for some trivial offenses. Nevertheless the Prince was deposed and confined in the prison for convicted imperial clansmen at Feng-yang 鳳陽 (Anhwei).

Then fourteen years old, Chu Tsai-yü felt keenly the injustice endured by his father and signified his grief by living alone in a small cottage outside the ancestral palace gate until his father had been released and restored to the princedom, seventeen years later (1567). Only then did he marry, in 1570, at thirty-five *sui*. His wife was a great-great-granddaughter of a celebrated local scholar-official, Ho T'ang (*q.v.*). Late in life the latter helped Chu Tsai-yü's father in his studies, especially in the fields of mathematics, the calendar, and music.

During his years of solitary living Chu Tsai-yü devoted hlmself to study and, under the influence of his father, took a deep interest in the writings of Ho T'ang on the mathematical principles of music and the calendar. In 1593, two years after his father's death, Chu Tsai-yü, when he should have assumed the princely title, begged the throne to appoint the aforementioned disgruntled cousin to the princedom. This unprecedented, self-denying request was finally granted in 1606, after repeated urging on his part. Nevertheless, a special edict permitted him to retain his rank of shih-tzu 世子, the heir apparent of a prince of the first degree. Hence, after his death Chu Tsai-yü was known as Cheng Tuan-ch'ing Shih-tzu, Tuan-ch'ing 端清 being his posthumous name.

Like his father, Chu Tsai-yü was compassionate and considerate of the welfare of others. He suggested to the throne that imperial clansmen who wanted to study and serve the government be permitted, like commoners, to take the civil examinations and become eligible for appointment to office. This proposal was approved in 1602, thus affording talented imperial clansmen the opportunity of escaping the fate of drones. His own son, Chu Ch'ang-chieh 常潔, became a *hsiu-ts'ai* in the district school and later (1635) the seventh prince of Tung-yüan 東垣, a princedom created for their ancestor who was a nephew of the first prince of Cheng. Incidentally, the discontented cousin who became the seventh prince of Cheng died soon after he was confirmed in that rank in 1606; and his son, the eighth prince, was ignominiously condemned to take his own life in 1640.

Chu Tsai-yü left twenty-eight or twenty-nine works, mainly on music and the calendar, the rest being concerned with dancing, mathematics, and phonology. Twenty-one of these works are known to be extant. One of the first to be completed was the "Coordinated (mathematical) study of the pitchpipe and calendar," *Lü-li jung-t'ung* 律曆融通, 4 *ch.*, with an appendix, a glossary (*Yin-i* 音義) in 1 *chüan*, and a preface dated 1581. It describes the method by which the notes in the orthodox Chinese scale were calculated, their relation to the months, the trigrams, etc.—all more or less a recapitulation of the traditional Chinese musical and calendrical theory. Three years later he completed his "New account of the science of pitchpipes," *Lü-hsüeh hsin-shuo* 律學新說, 4 *ch.* Starting with measurements of the pitchpipes, it goes on to all standards of measurement recorded in Chinese history. In the ensuing ten years his works on music and mathematics were for the most part completed, some of them based on studies advanced by his father.

Both Chu Tsai-yü and his father were disturbed by inaccuracies that had developed in the Ming calendar since its initiation in 1384—inaccuracies revealed in mistaken calculations of eclipses and other phenomena repeatedly made by the imperial board of astronomy. Named the Ta-t'ung-li 大統曆 this calendar was calculated by the "quarter method," ssu-fen-shu 四分術, on the basis of three hundred sixty-five and a quarter days to a year (as against the actual 365.24219879 days), or about 0.0078 days longer than a year, resulting in an error of one day in 128 years. For more than a hundred years proposals to improve these calculations had been rejected by the professional and hereditary officials on the board. In 1591 Chu's father died and he alone carried on the work of modifying the calculations. In May, 1594, a bureau for writing the dynastic history was established, and books for reference were solicited (see Ch'en Yü-pi). Seizing this opportunity, Chu Tsai-yü submitted to the throne in 1595 his calendrical proposals in a set of three works in 10 chüan, which he called the Li-shu 曆書 (Books on the calendar). In addition to the aforementioned Lü-li jung-t'ung, it consists of the following works: Sheng-shou wan-nien li 聖壽萬年曆 (Imperial longevity permanent calendar), 2 ch., and Wan-nien-li pei-k'ao 備考 (Permanent calendar notes), 3 ch. In the latter work he included the calculations for several solar and lunar eclipses, and proposed that observations be made at the time he predicted to test the accuracy of his method as against that used by the board of astronomy. The members of the board were greatly annoyed, but hesitated to criticize a prince. Meanwhile in 1596 another official, Hsing Yün-lu 邢雲路 (T. 士登, cs 1580), submitted a memorial advising a revision of the calendrical method. To this the board replied threateningly, saying that rumors of astronomical miscalculations might lead to unrest or rebellion. Nonetheless, possibly in 1597, Chu ordered his Li-shu carved on blocks. It was appended to the documents in the case, including the board's memorial trying to silence the voices proposing reforms. Oddly enough, however, had Chu's own proposals been adopted the calendar probably could not have been much improved, for he too based his calculations on the inadequate "quarter method." The importance of his efforts lies in the fact that they prepared the way for the eventual employment of westerners to help revise the calendar three decades later (see Hsü Kuang-ch'i, ECCP).

Meanwhile Chu Tsai-yü considered submitting to the throne the work on music which he valued most. Hence early in 1596 he wrote a preface to the work giving it the title Lü-lü ching-i 律呂精義 (Essentials of music). It consists of a nei-pien 內編, main book, and a wai-pien 外編, futher notes, each in 10 chüan. Written apparently between 1584 and 1596, it contains at the very beginning his crown-

ing achievement in acoustics, which was to express in numerical terms that precise system of equal temperament based on the formula $12\sqrt{2}$ towards which musicians in the West as well as in the East had been feeling their way for over a thousand years. He was the first to appreciate that equal semitones do not require equal intervals as expressed in terms of measured lengths of strings or pipes, but an equal ratio between their lengths. He found that 12 semitones could be arrived at by dividing the length of each successive string or pipe in the twelve-semitone system by the 12th root of 2. Still more remarkable is the fact that in using open notched pipes for his experiments he appreciated that the end-effect of the pipes would be counteracted with almost perfect accuracy by reducing the diameters of the pipes, i. e., by dividing each successive diameter by the 24th root of 2, though in that age there was naturally no knowledge of the physics of end effect.

Chu Tsai-yü himelf was well aware of the importance of his great discovery: the calculation for equal temperament. In the preface to the Lü-lü ching-i he remarks that his book should in reality have at the beginning of the title the words, Ta Ming 大明 (The great Ming dynasty), "because this book did not exist in any of the earlier dynasties; it appears for the first time under our House." He planned to offer it to the throne about 1596 but refrained from doing so probably because of the discouraging answer he had previously received to his proposals for calendrical reform. Not until 1606 did he finally submit to the throne twelve works on music and dancing under the collective title, Lü-shu律書(Books on the pitchpipe), attributing the delay to the time required to execute the woodcuts for the very exacting illustrations. As a matter of fact, his illustrations rank among the best in a dynasty noted for its elegant woodcuts.

Fortunately the Lü-shu was well received by the emperor, and Chu was commended for his diligence and devotion. It consists of these titles: 1, 2) *Lü-lü ching-i nei-pien* and *wai-pien;* 3) *Lü-hsüeh hsin-shuo,* 4 *ch.;* 4) *Yüeh-hsüeh hsin-shuo* 樂學新說 (A history of music); 5) *Suan-hsüeh hsin-shuo* 算學 (On mathematics), engraved in 1603; 6) *Ts'ao-man ku-yüeh p'u* 操縵古樂譜 (Treatise on ancient melodies with accompaniments, including music for the lute in ancient notations); 7) *Hsüan kung ho-yüeh-p'u* 璇宮合樂譜 (Treatise on melodies and transposition, as illustrated by the music for the formal dance of the Kuan-chui 關雎 Ode); 8) *Hsiang-yin shih yüeh-p'u* 鄉飲詩樂譜, 6 *ch.* (Treatise on music for the odes sung at district banquets); and 9–12) four illustrated books of instructions on dancing for boys, namely, the *Ling-hsing hsiao-wu p'u* 靈星小舞譜 (Dances of the six ancient dynasties, featuring both civil and military themes), the *Hsiao-wu hsiang-yüeh p'u* 小舞鄉樂譜 (Music, instructions, and instruments for the above dances); and *Er-i chui-chao t'u* 二佾綴兆圖 (Coordinated steps for dancing teams of 2 × 2 persons, i. e., for the *shih* 士 or scholar-gentry grade). The steps in the illustrations in the last work are represented by shoes showing the direction of turns.

The collection of these works in 38 *chüan* on music and dancing, together with the four titles in the *Li-shu,* 10 *ch.,* printed about 1597, was given in 1606 the comprehensive title *Yüeh-lü ch'üan-shu* 樂律全書. It became a favorite among contemporary collectors, thus accounting for the large number of copies extant. (One of the four sets in the Library of Congress, according to Wang Chung-min 王重民, is from an "imperial edition," the other three being described as printed by the author. Wang's premise that the *Lü-shu* was submitted in 1595 and the *Li-shu* in 1606, however, is incorrect.)

Among Chu Tsai-yü's other works the following may be mentioned: *Chia-liang suan-ching* 嘉量算經, 3 *ch.,* a mathematical treatise on the measure of capacity (reproduced in 1935 from the *Wan-wei pieh-ts'ang* 宛委別藏 manuscript library); *Yüan-fang kou-ku t'u-chieh* 圓方勾股圖解, a work on geometry; the *Se-p'u* 瑟譜, 10 *ch.,* a work on the music for the ancient lute-like instrument, which was reproduced about 1930 in the *Pai-ch'uan shu-wu ts'ung-shu* 百川書屋叢書 from a Chi-ku-ko (*see* Mao Chin, ECCP) manuscript copy; and the *Lü-lü cheng-lun* 律呂正論, 4 *ch.,* written and printed in 1610 when Chu was seventy-four years old. About the same time he also wrote a work in defense of his theories on music, entitled *Lü-lü chih-i pien-huo* 質疑辨惑.

Although Chu Tsai-yü openly declared in his *Lü-lü ching-i* that his discovery in music was unique, and had never been made by anyone before him, few people in China understood what he meant. During the Ch'ing dynasty it seems that only the scholar Chiang Yung (1681–1762, *see* ECCP, p. 695) wrote understandingly about him, in the year 1757. Chiang had been a student of mathematics and music all his life and in that year, aged seventy-one, for the first time came across a copy of Chu's *Yüeh-lü ch'üan-shu.* It was Liu Fu (BDRC) who in 1933 published the first comprehensive treatise on Chu's contribution to musical theory.

In the world of music, Chu Tsai-yü should be given credit for being the first to formulate the system of equal temperament based on $12\sqrt{2}$, his crowning achievement in the field of acoustics, not only for the lucidity of thought which gave it birth, but also for the successful completion of the laborious calculations which were necessary in an age before the invention of logarithms. His work was written before the earliest known reference to such a formula in Europe, namely the unpublished paper of Simon Stevin.

Bibliography

1/119/3b 103/8b; KC (1958), 4725, 4759, 4785, 4798, 4948, 5040; *Huai-ch'ing-fu chih* (1794), 31/14b; Ku Ying-t'ai (ECCP), *Ming-ch'ao chi-shih pen-mo,* 73/8b; Liu Fu, *Shih-er teng-lü ti fa-ming-che* 十二等律的發明者 *Chu Tsai-yü* in *Studies presented to Ts'ai Yuan P'ei on His Sixty-fifth Birthday*, CYYY, I (Peiping, 1933), 279; Chuang Pen-li 莊本位, *Chung-kuo ku-tai chih p'ai-hsiao* 中國古代之排簫, Academia Sinica, Taiwan (1963), 59, 98; L. of C. *Catalogue of Rare Chinese Books*, 55; J. Amiot, "Mémoire sur la musique des Chinois," in *Mémoires concernant l'histoire, les sciences, les arts, les moeurs, les usages, etc., des Chinois*, VI (Paris, 1780), 1; Maurice Courant, "Essai historique sur la musique classique des Chinois," *Encyclopédie de la musique et Dictionnaire du conservatoire, première partie* (Paris, 1913), 79; Joseph Needham, *Science and Civilization in China*, IV, part I (Cambridge, Eng., 1962),128, 139, 220; L. E. R. Picken, "The Music of Far Eastern Asia," I, China, in *New Oxford History of Music*, I (Oxford, 1957), 100; John Hazedel Levis, *Foundations of Chinese Musical Art* (Shanghai, 1936), 67, 120, 123, 189, 206, 217.

Kenneth G. Robinson and Chaoying Fang

CHU Ts'un-li 朱存理 (T. 性甫，性父，性之， H. 野航), 1444-August 25, 1513, author, bibliophile, and calligrapher, was a native of Ch'ang-chou 長洲 (Soochow), and came from a well-to-do family. His father Chu Hao 朱灝(顥) (T. 景南) was posthumously awarded a memorial tablet in1475 for his fililial piety. In his youth Chu Ts'un-li found the traditional education, which was solely to prepare for the government competitve examinations, not to his taste; so he soon gave it up. He then became a pupil of Tu Ch'iung (*q.v.*) a noted scholar and painter, also a native of Soochow. As a result of Tu Ch'iung's coaching Chu Ts'un-li became fond of reading extensively, and continued this interest throughout his life. Whenever he heard of some rare books, he would make every effort to ferret them out and copy them himself. Indeed, his handwritten copies, covering all subjects, included works by more than a hundred authors.

His home was just outside Fu-men 葑門 (葑 is ordinarily pronounced Feng), a gate in the east wall of Soochow. Once he was engaged as a teacher by a Wang 王 family in a village not far from Soochow. One night his host entertained him with wine, and when he retired he left Chu alone. Watching the full moon riding in the sky Chu composed a verse which delighted even himself: "A cup in hand surpasses all; how many times does one see the moon?" 萬事不如杯在手，一生幾見月當頭. He then shouted to his host who immediately joined him for more drinking and praised his effusion. The next day the former asked some poets of Soochow to respond in verse, and later celebrated the occasion.

According to Wen Cheng-ming (*q.v.*), who wrote the tombstone inscription, Chu Ts'un-li befriended Wu K'uan, Shen Chou (*qq.v.*), and himself. Wen also said: "Chu Ts'un-li's poems, elegant in style, often show ideas." His poetical work, known as *Yeh-hang chi* 野航集, contained a preface by Yang Hsün-chi (*q.v.*), who remarked that Chu's verses tended to be simple in diction, but profound. In calligraphy Chu was an expert in the orthodox pattern, approching the style of the Tsin dynasty (265–420), although he was also noted for his seal script. As to his complete writings, Wen Cheng-ming enumerated a number of them, mostly lost. As the years went on he remained a man of robust vigor, but his financial condition worsened. His considerable collection of books and art objects as well as his manuscripts became scattered and lost.

Again according to Wen Cheng-ming, there lived in Soochow two scholars surnamed Chu, both highly respected for their learning and exemplary behavior, neither of whom entered political life. One was Chu Ts'un-li, the other Chu K'ai 朱凱 (T. 堯民, d. 1512). Both men were acquainted with the lore of their city and loved to tell of it. After their death, the people of Soochow wearied of any who tried to imitate them.

Chu Ts'un-li passed away at the age of sixty-nine and was survived by two sons, Chu Yen 延 and Chu Chien 建. One of them was adopted by the Lu family whose best known descendant, Lu Kung

陸恭 (T. 謹庭, 1741–1818), became an art critic.

The most controversial matter regarding authorship revolves around the book, *T'ieh-wang shan-hu* 鐵網珊瑚, in 16 *chüan*, attributed to Chu. The Ming edition of this book was later reprinted by Nien Hsi-yao 年希堯 (T. 允恭, d. 1738), younger brother of Nien Keng-yao (ECCP). It included a postscript written by Chao Ch'i-mei (*see* Chao Yung-hsien), a bibliophile, who the editors of the *Ssu-k'u* catalogue assert was the compiler. Weng Fang-kang (ECCP), an eminent art critic, disagreed, however, writing a long postscript to the *Shan-hu mu-nan* 木難 in four volumes in which he declared: "Chu Ts'un-li wrote two books: *T'ieh-wang shan-hu*, 16 *ch.*, in printed form, and *Shan-hu mu-nan*, 8 *ch.*, in manuscript. The present book in four volumes is the original draft of the aforementioned books. I have checked them against the former and found forty items identical." Ch'en T'ien (*see* T'ien Ju-ch'eng) in his *Ming-shih chi-shih* 明詩紀事 reached the conclusion that *T'ieh-wang shan-hu* was written by Chu Ts'un-li and supplemented by Chao Ch'i-mei. The book deals with famous paintings and calligraphy. In this connection it should be recalled that a book bearing the same title and written by Tu Mu (*q.v.*) is a publication of similar nature but quite different content.

In regard to the *Shan-hu mu-nan*, the editors of the *Ssu-k'u* catalogue maintain that it was in manuscript. It was later printed by a bibliophile, Chang Chün-heng (ECCP, p. 19), in a series called *Shih-yüan ts'ung-shu*. This book contains numerous pieces of prose, poetry, colophons on paintings, and calligraphy. These collections came mostly from the families of Wen Cheng-ming, Wang Chih-teng (*q.v.*), and Wang T'eng-ch'eng 王騰程 (T. 莊叟), Chu Ts'un-li's own collection being included therein.

In spite of heavy loss of manuscripts, Chu Ts'un-li's prose and poems were later printed under the following titles: *Ching-hsiao lu* 旌孝錄, 1 *ch.*, *Lou-chü tsa-chu* 樓居雜著, 1 *ch.*, *Yeh-hang wen-kao* 稿, 1 *ch.*, *Yeh-hang shih-kao* 詩稿, 1 *ch.*, and *fu-lu* 附錄, 1 *ch.* They are found in various series: *Fang-chi pa-k'o* 芳溪八刻, *T'ien ch'ih-lou ts'ung-ch'ao* 天尺樓叢抄 (in manuscript), and *Heng-shan ts'ao-t'ang-ts'ung shu* 橫山草堂叢書.

In addition to the above, Chu also compiled a supplement 補遺 to the *Ts'un-hui-chai kao* 存悔齋稿 by Kung Su (1266–1331); both of these works have been reprinted in the *Heng-shan ts'ao-t'ang ts'ung-shu*. As he had seen many valuable paintings and examples of calligraphy when he was compiling his *T'ieh-wang shan-hu* and *Shan-hu mu-nan*, it was natural for him to read and copy many of the colophons on those artistic treasures which captured his imagination.

Bibliography

5/115/38a; 32/22/21a; 34/11/11a; 40/23/15b; 64/丙 10/7a; 73/x/3a; 84/ 丙 /54a; 86/8/8a; SK (1930), 60/3b, 113/1a, 166/12b, 170/12b; Weng Fang-kang, *Fu-ch'u-chai wen-chi*, 31/8a; *id.*, *Fu-ch'u-chai chi wai-wen* 外文, 4/14a; *Su-chou-fu chih* (1881), 86/11a; Wen Cheng-ming, *Fu-t'ien chi* (late Ming printing), 29/5b; Yeh Ch'ang-ch'ih 葉昌熾, *Ts'ang-shu chi-shih shih* 藏書紀事詩 (Shanghai, 1958), 88.

Liu Lin-sheng

CHU Wan 朱紈 (T. 子純, H. 秋崖), September 29, 1494–January 3, 1550, official, was born into a family registered under the artisan category in Ch'ang-chou (Soochow). His father, Chu Ang 昂 (T. 圭庵, d. 1515), was an instructor at a district school in Chekiang but was dismissed from office two years before Chu Wan was born. Chu Wan's mother, a concubine, née Shih 施 (d. 1536), was persecuted by the wife and her grown-up sons. Three days after Wan was born they tried to starve him. Miraculously he survived this and other vicious attempts on his life by his half-brothers, the last one as late as 1546.

In 1521, after passing the *chin-shih* examination, Chu served an apprenticeship in the ministry of Works. The following year he was appointed subprefectural magistrate of Ching-chou 景州, Pei-Chihli, and in 1523 was transferred to K'ai-chou 開州 about one hundred miles to the southwest. His next commission brought him to Nanking (1527) where he served as vice-director in the ministry of Justice. Then he became director of a bureau in the ministry of War (1529) and in the ministry of Personnel (1530–32), both in Nanking. His next transfer took him away from the central bureaucracy into the provinces where he was to serve until his death. Chu Wan was appointed (1532) assistant administration commissioner in Kiangsi where he successfully coped with the inhabitants of the newly established district Tung-hsiang 東鄉, who by every possible means tried to escape labor service. After that he was sent to Szechwan, with the rank of surveillance vice commissioner serving as intendant of Wei-chou/Mou-chou 威州/茂州, where he put an end to the practice of paying off the native tribes in the area by launching a counterattack when they came out on one of their regular raids. He pacified the tribes and set up a new scheme of supply for the frontier guards.

Chu was appointed administration vice commissioner of Shantung in 1541. Since contingents from that province serving in places as far away as a thousand *li* had to look after their own supplies, he suggested to the throne that these troops be released from their duties and added to the defense of Shantung. His suggestion was followed immediately. Two years later Chu Wan had to travel again: this time to Yunnan where he served as surveillance commissioner. In 1544 he moved back into the provincial administration office of Shantung, a transfer which was accompanied by a promotion to the rank of an administration commissioner. One year later (1545) he was appointed to the same office in Kwangtung. The following year Chu was entrusted with yet a higher commission. He became vice censor-in-chief to the right and was delegated as governor of Nan-kan 南贛.

Due to the ever increasing number of raids by pirates along the southeastern coast, the central and provincial authorities had been looking for some time for a proper remedy. Following the receipt of a memorial from the regional inspector, Yang Chiu-tse 楊九澤 (T. 子德, cs 1538), suggesting the creation of a central command in Chang-chou, Fukien, with a high ranking official in control of the military and civil institutions of north Kwangtung, Fukien, and Chekiang, an edict was issued on July 10, 1547, to appoint a governor of Chekiang with jurisdiction also over the coastal regions of Fukien. Only a fortnight later (July 24) Chu Wan was named to this powerful position. North Kwangtung had not been added to the commission. According to the imperial decree Chu had to investigate and fight coastal piracy as well as the bandits in the mining area of southwestern Chekiang.

Although Chu Wan's headquarters were to be in Hangchow, he first (November, 1547) went to the center of the trouble, Chang-chou, where he soon discovered that the military readiness of the coast guard and the moral discipline of the coastal inhabitants had sunk to the lowest level. Only two warships out of ten remained serviceable and hardly a thousand soldiers were still on duty against a supposed twenty-five hundred. Chu Wan discovered, moreover, that a great many well-to-do families and members of the gentry privately traded with foreigners, or built big merchantmen under the name of ferryboats (tu-ch'uan 渡船 or yü-huang 艅艎) in order to trade in faraway countries such as Malacca and Japan. This was not only smuggling but also high treason as stipulated by the various laws and edicts promulgated first by the founding emperor, Chu Yüan-chang. Two centers of activity outranked all others in importance, and as Chu Wan put it, "in danger" were Chang-chou/Ch'üan-chou with its chief harbor Yüeh-kang 月港, the nucleus of the district later known as Hai-ch'eng 海澄, and Ningpo/Wenchou with its trading outpost Shuang-hsü-kang 雙嶼港 on Liu-heng Island 六橫島. Some of the pirate-merchants (hai-k'ou 海寇 or wo-k'ou) who worked with members of the gentry class on the mainland had earlier escaped from prison and set up family connections with their harboring hosts (wo-chu 窩主). Two of them were the unquestioned masters of Shuang-hsü-kang: Li Kuang-t'ou (see Lu T'ang) from Fukien and Hsü Tung 許棟 from She 歙 (Anhwei). In Fukien, Lin Hsi-yüan (q.v.), a former judge of the Grand Court of Revision, was one of the most important unauthorized shipowners and overseas merchants. The situation went from bad to worse when the credit granted by the lawless traders to their gentry-partners ran into tens of thousands of ounces of silver. Their former partners not only did not pay what was due but also cut off supplies and sent government troops after them. As a result the merchants turned to piracy, raided the mainland, and slaughtered their one-time associates.

Chu Wan immediately issued a proclamation strictly prohibiting anyone from venturing out to sea on pain of beheading. He made use of all ships for the defense of the coast. Concurrently he strengthened the traditional system of mutual protection and responsibility (pao-chia 保甲). Chu no doubt was lacking in tact in his dealings with the gentry of Fukien and Chekiang who profited from maritime trade. It so happened that the Japanese envoy, Sakugen Shūryō 策彥周良 (1501–79), had arrived with four ships and more than six hundred men before the date set for official delivery of tribute. The emperor ordered Chu to make a recommendation on whether to accept the mission. Chu asked Shūryō to wait offshore until the proper time had come. He treated the Japanese politely and diplomatically, inviting Shūryō and twenty-one sick sailors into the guest-house at Ningpo (April, 1548). Meanwhile his troops were ready to attack Shuang-hsü-kang. Under the command of Regional Military

Commissioner Lu T'ang (q. v.) and the surveillance vice commissioner, K'o Ch'iao (see Lu T'ang), a large fleet left Wenchou on the 15th. They took the settlement by surprise, caught a number of outlaws, but were unable to stop the flight of Li Kuang-t'ou, Wang Chih (see Lu T'ang), and the rest of the group. Lu T'ang, always under the orders of Chu Wan, had the entrance to the harbor barricaded and all installations destroyed. Shuang-hsü-kang disappeared from the list of outposts of illegal trade. Chu Wan and his military leaders were granted substantial rewards in silver. Shortly afterwards, they succeeded in pacifying the mine robbers of southwestern Chekiang. Illegal trade became more difficult and dangerous, since Chu, fearless as always, clearly stated the names of the influential persons engaged in this activity. As a result, the parties interested tried to curb his power. With the help of the censor Chou Liang 周亮 (cs 1532), a native of Foochow, and the supervising censor Yeh T'ang 葉鏜 (T. 汝聲, cs 1541), a pretext was found to reduce Chu to the position of inspector general (hsün-shih 巡視, a temporary assignment), the argument being that one man alone was unable to look after two provinces at the same time (August 4, 1548). Chu Wan was indignant and intensified his fight against what he termed treacherous people.

In the spring of the following year he again ordered Lu T'ang and K'o Ch'iao to set sail and attack the rest of the Shuang-hsü band who had congregated near Chao-an, Fukien, and set themselves up in business. Among the men and women caught alive there were some foreigners, but most of them were Chinese, headed by Li Kuang-t'ou. [Editors' note: In his memorial of April 15, 1549, recorded in the current edition of the *P'i-yü tsa-chi* (see below), Chu reported the number of people taken captive as two hundred six: three chiefs, sixteen white barbarians, forty-six black barbarians, one hundred twelve pirates (Li Kuang-t'ou et al), and twenty-nine barbarian women; thirty-three others were beheaded.] On orders from Chu many were beheaded forthwith (*see* Lu T'ang). This time he was accused of going beyond his authority, a moment long hoped for by his opponents. The censor, Ch'en Chiu-te 陳九德 (cs 1541), accused him of having killed, without imperial sanction, people who merely wanted to trade (April 27, 1549). Chu was promptly dismissed pending a thorough investigation by the supervising censor Tu Ju-chen 杜汝禎 (cs 1538). As for Chu Wan's end there are two versions. While the *Ming-shih* maintains that he was too proud to endure such indignity, the *Ming ming-ch'en yen-hsing lu* reports that he was awaiting the outcome of the inquiry when an official of his acquaintance was arrested and brought to Peking. In the first source Chu is said to have taken poison to evade further insults; in the second he reportedly committed suicide due to a false message saying that the bailiffs were on their way to make his arrest. In any case he died before the investigation was completed. Before his death he signed the preface (dated October 6, 1549) to his collected writings, which he had printed in order to keep the record straight, and he also wrote an autobiographical epitaph. Tu Ju-chen's verdict (submitted August 23, 1550) was that Chu had killed his prisoners without authorization, so a sentence of death was posthumously decreed. Lu T'ang and K'o Ch'iao shared the same sentence. Although the *Ming-shih* records that no governor was installed afterwards, Wang Yü (*see* Wang Shih-chen) was commissioned to Chekiang and Fukien only three years later (August 9, 1553).

Chu Wan's name was rehabilitated by imperial order on December 22, 1587, when a reprinting of his collected writings was accorded an imperial preface; no posthumous honors, however, were conferred on him. He was the victim of an influential clique from Fukien; his own personality no doubt contributed to his failure and tragic end. He was a loyal official, but remarkably narrow-minded and hot-tempered. Not stopping to realize that trade had become an economic necessity along the southern coast, he added to the instability prevalent in the Chia-ching period (cf. T'u Tse-min, *q. v.*).

The first edition of Chu's collection of writings called *P'i-yü tsa-chi* 甓餘雜集, in 12 *chüan*, has not been reported as extant. The edition now available containing Chu's picture is the one collated by his grandson Chu Huang-chung 篁仲 and printed by his great-grandson Chu Chih-yeh 質野 about 1587. *Chüan* 1 to 9 contain Chu Wan's memorials, proclamations, and communications written between 1547 and 1549; *chüan* 10 comprises poems and essays composed during this period; *chüan* 11, which exists separately under the title *Mou-pien chi-shih* 茂邊紀事, includes reports and poems on his actions in Szechwan. The last *chüan* is a collection of grave inscriptions and biographical sketches of his forefathers. There is a copy extant in the Naikaku Bunko and another in the Seikadō. The *Mou-pien chi-shih* was also included in the collection *Chin-sheng yü-chen chi* 金聲玉振集. The *Huang Ming ching-shih wen-pien* (*chüan* 205-6) of Ch'en Tzu-lung (ECCP) includes six memorials and three orders written by Chu Wan, all relating to the Chekiang and Fukien coastal affairs of 1547 to 1549.

Bibliography

1/205/1a; 3/188/14a; 5/62/44a; 8/59/11a; *Fu-chien t'ung-chih* (1868), 129/10a; SK (1930), 53/5b, 176/17b; KC (1958), 3703, 3717, 3732; MSL (1965), Shih-tsung, 6167, 6285; W. Franke, *Sources*, 5. 5. 12, 7. 5. 7; C. R. Boxer, ed., *South China in the Sixteenth Century* (London, 1953), xxvii, lii; P. Pelliot, TP, 38 (1947), 196, n. 230; T'ien-tse Chang, *Sino-Portuguese Trade from 1514 to 1644* (Leyden, 1934), 81.

Bodo Wiethoff

CHU Wen-chung, *see* LI Wen-chung

CHU Yu-t'ang 朱祐樘, July 30, 1470-June

8, 1505, the ninth Ming emperor and the most humane, was also known by his reign title as Hung-chih 弘治, by his temple name as Hsiao-tsung 孝宗, by his posthumous name Emperor Ching 敬, and by the name of his tomb as T'ai-ling 泰陵. He was the third but eldest surviving son of Emperor Chu Chien-shen (*q.v.*) and a maid in charge of a storeroom in the palace (*see* Wan Kuei-fei). His mother was probably an aborigine (a Yao 猺?) captured as a child during the suppression of a rebellion in Kwangsi and brought up in the palace by a eunuch. Even her family name has never been positively identified; generally accepted to be Chi 紀, it was also reported to be Li 李. As soon as pregnancy was indicated she was kept hidden from the emperor because his favorite, Wan Kuei-fei, had the reputation of being fanatically jealous, and had even forced him to displace his first empress, Lady Wu (*see* Wan Kuei-fei). This dethroned empress, in her secluded quarters, helped to conceal Chu Yu-t'ang and his mother until he was almost five years old. When his father, yearning for a son, was told about his existence, he greeted him with joy and gave him recognition. This happened in June, 1475. A month later his mother, the Lady Chi, died under suspicious circumstances. From then on, according to report, his security was entrusted to his grandmother, Empress-dowager Chou (*see* Chu Chien-shen).

On December 5, 1475, Chu Yu-t'ang was proclaimed heir apparent. An old and learned eunuch, T'an Chi 覃吉, his first teacher, taught him to read the Four Books, and in March, 1478, he began his formal education in the hall of literary excellence, Wen-hua tien 文華殿. A book on exemplary heirs apparent in history was compiled in 1482 especially for his edification. Apparently he took the teachings to heart, for in later life he followed the Confucian rules of conduct more closely than any other emperor in the Ming dynasty, always showing great self-restraint instead of lashing back at critics. By the time he married in February, 1487, he was already a mature youth. His consort came from a Chang 張 family of Hsing-chi 興濟, a town on the Grand Canal one hundred miles south of Peking. It is said that he was devoted to her, and was probably a monogamist, the only case in China's imperial history. His two sons were presumably hers, and so too his three daughters.

On September 4, 1487, he was named regent because of his father's illness. Five days later his father died. He ascended the throne on September 17. One of his first acts was to proclaim Lady Chang his empress. Another was to give his own mother the posthumous rank of empress-dowager with the title Hsiao-mu huang-t'ai-hou 孝穆皇太后. He then ordered a search for her family. Two men of Ho-hsien 賀縣, Kwangsi, asserting that they were her cousins, submitted a chart of the genealogy of the Chi family. They were brought to Peking and in October, 1478, made officers of the Imperial Guard. Actually they came from a Li family. It happened that another man related to the Li, in conspiracy with a eunuch, had already insisted that he was a cousin of the emperor's mother. Both parties in their accusations against each other were discovered to be impostors, and the Chi genealogical chart a forgery; they were punished by banishment. The case was closed in July, 1480. The emperor ordered the erection of a temple in Kwangsi in honor of his mother's ancestors, although none could be identified. Inside the palace he built (January, 1488) a special shrine, Feng-tz'u tien 奉慈殿, in memory of his mother. It was in a compound on the east side of the residence halls. Presumably after he failed to find any of her relations, he felt keenly the loneliness of being her only survivor. His yearning for a close relative may partly explain his devotion to Empress Chang. After she gave birth to the eldest son in October, 1491, he showered favors on her father and two brothers (*see* Chang Ho-ling) and all their relatives. The Chang brothers were given large tracts of land, the management of the imperial stores in Peking (*see* Liang Fang), and the privilege of selling salt from the government monopoly. One of the few complaints about his reign was over the protection he extended to the Chang family when the brothers were accused of excesses. Conceivably he did so because he regarded them as his son's nearest of kin.

Another aspect of his reign which aroused criticism was the trust and tolerance he showed towards certain eunuchs. After the abolition of the office of the prime minister by the founder of the dynasty, no succeding Ming emperor could escape entrusting them with part of his heavy responsibilities. A conscientious and rational ruler, Chu Yu-t'ang tried to employ only those eunuchs worthy of trust, and eliminate the unworthy. As soon as he ascended the throne he degraded or sent into exile the most notorious of his father's favorites, among them those generally blamed for his excesses and extravagance, such as Liang Fang. To head the eunuch organization, the directorate of ceremonial, the youthful monarch chose only the best, such as Huai En (*q.v.*) whom he recalled from retirement. During his reign there were two serious cases having to do with eunuchs. One involved Chiang Tsung 蔣琮, a native of Peking, who for many years held the important position of head of the triumvirate in control of the government in Nanking. In 1489 he started a feud with the censors when they accused him of appropriating the income from rent of some alluvial land near Nanking; he in turn accused them of failure to report the illegal activities of their own group. Possibly what Chiang received from the rent went to defray the expenses of the emperor's palace. Early in 1490 the emperor decided the case in Chiang's favor, but the officials continued to attack the eunuch until he was finally removed in 1494 on the ridiculous charge that

some construction excavations of his had disturbed the geomantic configuration of the southern capital.

The second eunuch case involved Li Kuang (*q.v.*) who was forced to commit suicide on October 28, 1498, because of a similar charge, that a pavilion he had built on the island in the imperial garden was a geomantic mistake which somehow brought about several disasters, including the death of the emperor's eldest daughter (October 1) and the burning down of the imperial residence halls (October 26). Li Kuang, maligned by the officials for several years, was the one whom the emperor entrusted to raise funds to meet the expenses in the palace by such means as the sale of licenses and official appointments and promotions.

It seems that neither Chiang Tsung nor Li Kuang had really committed any serious crimes. Actually the eunuchs of that period behaved better than those under most Ming emperors. Yet they were criticized as severely as in other reigns. It was almost as if the officials, professing to be Confucianists, had to denounce the eunuchs on principle, just as they felt it necessary to object repeatedly to the emperor's conferring titles and other favors on the Taoists and Buddhists. Even if the emperor himself did not believe in these religions, there were many in his palace who did, such as his mother and his wife. Also there were millions throughout the empire devoted to these popular beliefs. As to the lama priests, their service was demanded by many in the Peking area, chiefly among those of Tibetan and Mongol origin. There is also the financial side of the matter, for the sale of permits and titles added to the emperor's privy purse. He himself was not extravagant, but he wanted his empress to be amused and their son well provided for. Hence he even permitted the heir apparent to own a tract of land for a private estate.

On the whole Chu Yu-t'ang ruled wisely and his reign came to be characterized as harmonious and generally uneventful. Besides his initial act of ridding the court of undesirable elements he also demoted some three thousand people who had acquired their promotions and high titles not by merit but by purchase (*see* Chu Chien-shen), among them Taoists and Buddhists and hundreds of lama priests. Meanwhile he summoned competent and upright men from retirement. The most noted, besides Huai En, was Wang Shu (*q.v.*) whom he appointed minister of Personnel to help in the selection of the right men for the court. Among his other ministers were Ma Wen-sheng and Liu Ta-hsia (*qq. v.*). The former successively headed the Censorate and the ministries of War and Personnel, and gave sound advice in his memorials. The latter, as minister of War during the last five years of his reign, was frequently summoned to his presence for consultations, an unusual event in Ming history. Also consulted but usually as a group was his grand secretaries. Of the three from the preceding reign he dismissed two who had an unsavory reputation, retaining only Liu Chi 劉吉 (T. 祐之, H. 約庵, 1427-93, cs 1448, Pth. 文穆), who, however, was severely attacked by some censors. His other grand secretaries, Liu Chien, Hsü P'u, Ch'iu Chün, Li Tung-yang, and Hsieh Ch'ien (*qq.v.*) were all men of integrity. The harmony of his court was so remarkable that Ku Ying-t'ai (ECCP) used the heading "Hung-chih chün-ch'en" 君臣 for his chapter on the reign.

During the Hung-chih reign the acquisition of land by influential people, which began in the middle of the 15th century, became more pronounced, especially in the two national capital areas. Wealthy families of Soochow started to compete with the nobility in the purchase of objects of art. The so-called Wu school of artists began to flourish (*see* Shen Chou, Wen Cheng-ming, T'ang Yin, and Ch'iu Ying). Grand Secretary Li Tung-yang was the arbiter of the arts of painting, calligraphy, and poetry. The emperor himself was fond of Shen Tu (*q.v.*) and sponsored some court painters such as Lü Chi (*q.v.*). A valuable traveler's view of east China at this time, stressing the prosperity of the lower Yangtze valley may be found in the account of Ch'oe Pu (*q.v.*), a Korean official whose ship was wrecked on the Chekiang coast in 1488.

Chu Yu-t'ang conducted himself with restraint. As mentioned above, he was monogamous; he also abstained from meat on certain days of the month. He attended audiences regularly, and only infrequently was he late at the early morning assembly. He seldom showed his temper and, even when offended by an official, never humiliated him by a beating in the public courtyard, nor by any other inhumane and cruel punishment. He apparently accepted most of the Confucian ethical principles he was taught, and practiced them during his life. His reign, especially the first five years, has been compared by some historians to the golden age of a Confucian sage-king. Perhaps that was why among Ming emperors he was the only one who showed no martial spirit nor a desire to match the military achievements of the two ancestors (Chu Yüan-chang and Chu Ti). His great-grandfather led an army over the Great Wall into Mongolia in October, 1428, but apparently only as a demonstration. His grandfather followed that example in 1449 and suffered a disastrous defeat. His father, a peaceful man, loved a woman who sometimes dressed in military attire (*see* Wan Kuei-fei). He himself, however, aspired only to be a ruler of the Confucian ideal: to conquer with virtue rather than by force. About the only notable military campaigns of his reign were the minor expeditions to Hami in 1495 (*see* Hsü Chin, Ma Wen-sheng) and the suppression of some small-scale rebellions. Once he said something about leading an expedition on the northern frontier but was dissuaded from it. He probably tried to imbue in his son the same peaceful ideals. Of his two sons, the second, born in 1495, died a year later. To the survivor, Chu Hou-chao (*q. v.*), he conceivably gave as much affection as he could—something he himself had missed in childhood. The boy probably rebelled against his teachings at heart if not openly. In June, 1505, shortly before the emperor died, he summoned the grand secretaries and asked them to look after the affairs of his son whom he described as being too fond of ease and pleasure. Actually the boy had a mind of his own, and chose to ignore and perhaps ridicule the Confucianists as hypocrites, while he found his true friends among the eunuchs who played military games with him. To judge from his later behavior, he must have looked down on his father for his pacifism, for he regarded himself as a military commander.

As to the youth, the records tell of a soldier named Cheng Wang 鄭旺 who asserted that the prince was the son of his daughter, Cheng Chin-lien 金蓮, a maid in the palace. This suggests that a rumor must have spread that some of the emperor's children were born to women other than his empress. In any case Cheng Wang was tried and sentenced to death, but was later released during an amnesty. His eunuch accomplice, however, was executed by the slicing process. When Chu Hou-chao succeeded to the throne, Cheng Wang continued to make the same claim. In December, 1507, he was arrested and executed. The rumor, however, was later revived by the ambitious prince, Chu Ch'en-hao (*see* Wang Shou-jen), who used Chu Hou-chao's reported illegitimacy as one of the excuses for starting a rebellion.

During the reign of Chu Yu-t'ang two important works were compiled. One was the *Ta Ming hui-tien* (*see* Li Tung-yang), and the other the *Wen-hsing t'iao-li* 問刑條例, which contained 297 articles as supplement to the code of the dynasty (*Ta Ming lü*, *see* Chu Yüan-chang). The latter was completed (and printed?) in March, 1500. The documents used as sources for the *Wen-hsing t'iao-li* had been preserved in the Censorate where a censor, Tai Chin 戴金 (T. 純甫, cs 1514, minister of War 1544-45), made a copy (1527?) and started to classify the documents under the names of the six ministries. After he had edited the first two thirds in 50 *chüan*, the work, it seems, was interrupted, the rest being left unclassified. A copy of Tai's unfinished work, with several supplementary items at the end dated 1527, and given the title *Huang Ming t'iao-fa shih lei tsuan* 皇明條法事類纂, was acquired by the library of Tokyo University and reproduced in 1966 in 745 pages in two volumes. The fact that it contains a preface, supposed to have been written by a Ming emperor, which was actually a composite of excerpts taken from two different imperial prefaces to the *Ta Ming hui-tien*, casts some doubt on the editorship, on the authenticity of the title, and on all the colophons. But the documents (except those at the end dated in 1527) are genuine, and were collected at the time the *Wen-hsing t'iao-li* was being compiled.

The editors of the *Ta Ming hui-tien* have been criticized for failing to include the functions of the eunuch offices and the regulations governing them, thus making it impossible to check the illegal activities of some emperors and their eunuchs. The same criticism was made about Ch'iu Chün's *Ta-hsüeh yen-i pu*, the printing of which was also sponsored by the Hung-chih emperor.

The chronicles of his reign, the *Hsiao-tsung shih-lu*, 224 *ch.*, were edited by Li Tung-yang, *et al.* It is said that Chiao Fang (*q.v.*) had a hand in them and was responsible for some of the untruthful accounts about certain of Chiao's enemies. The praise accorded the emperor, however, should be regarded as truly representing the opinion of the day.

Chu Yu-t'ang, not yet thirty-five when he passed away, was buried in the hills north of the tomb of his great ancestor, Chu Ti. His consort, Empress-dowager Hsiao-k'ang 孝康, who died on August

28, 1541, was laid to rest beside him.

Bibliography

1/15/1a, 114/1a, 300/17a, 304/19b; MSL (1964), Hsiao-tsung; KC (1958), 2287, 2355, 2544; Meng Sen (BDRC), *Ming-tai shih* 明代史(1957), 186; Mao Ch'i-ling (ECCP), *Sheng-ch'ao T'ung-shih shih-i chi*; Huang Ching-fang 黃景昉, *Kuo-shih wei-i* 國史唯疑 (1969), 238; Shen Te-fu, *Wan-li yeh-hu pien* (1959), 23, 75, 149, 160, 192, 738; *Ch'oe Pu's Diary: A Record of Drifting across the Sea*, tr. John Meskill, Tucson, 1965; *Palace Museum Weekly*, nos. 143, 376, 377.

Chaoying Fang

CHU Yu-tun 朱有燉 (H. 全陽子, 老狂生, 錦窠道人, 誠齋), February 7, 1379–July 8, 1439, prince and dramatist, was the eldest son of Chu Su (*q.v.*), the first prince of Chou 周王, whose residence was in Kai-feng, Honan. During the period when his father was in disfavor late in 1389, Chu Yu-tun was put in charge of affairs at the establishment in Kaifeng for more than a year. In 1391 after his father's restoration to the princedom, Chu Yu-tun's formal installation as heir apparent took place. In 1398 he and his father were accused of treason by his younger brother, Chu Yu-hsün (*see* Chu Su), and banished to Yunnan. Wishing to spare his father any further hardship, he confessed to the crimes as charged, and took full responsibility on himself. In this way his father was given his freedom and permitted to live in Nanking. In 1402 they were both reinstated by Emperor Chu Ti (*q.v.*) who wrote a poem especially commending Chu Yu-tun for his filial conduct. After the death of his father in 1425, Chu Yu-tun inherited the title of prince of Chou. In 1428, at his request, he was permitted to construct an ancestral temple in his palace. In the same year, his younger brother, Chu Yu-hsün, who formerly had charged his own father with rebellion, now repeatedly made false accusations against Chu Yu-tun. Afterwards Chu Yu-hsün and a younger brother, Chu Yu-hsi 熺, were convicted of a plot

against Chu Yu-chüeh 爝 (d. 1452), another younger brother, and both were downgraded to the status of commoners; Chu Yu-hsi in addition was found guilty of robbery and cannibalism. Chu Yu-tun died without heir and was succeeded by Chu Yu-chüeh. He received the posthumous name of Hsien 憲, hence was often referred to as the Chou Hsien Wang.

Shortly before his death Chu Yu-tun submitted a memorial to the emperor (Chu Ch'i-chen, *q.v.*) saying that he would prefer a simple and inexpensive burial, did not want any of his women to hsün 殉 (i.e., to commit suicide so as to be buried at the same time), and would rather send home concubines still young and with parents living. The emperor thereupon sent an order to Chu Yu-chüeh to observe these wishes, but it was too late. The princess, née Kung 鞏氏 (married in 1429), and six of the concubines had already taken their lives. Each was given a posthumous name. It seems that this was one of the last observances of the custom of hsün in the Ming imperial house, for in 1464 the emperor specified in his will that the custom could not be tolerated and was to be discontinued.

Chu Yu-tun, who never played a political role, is known chiefly as a dramatist. He was also, however, a skillful calligrapher and painter. A collection of famous specimens of calligraphy, made when he was heir apparent, was copied by himself and engraved on stone; it was entitled Tung shu-t'ang chi-ku fa-t'ieh 東書堂集古法帖. Devoted to music and theatre, Chu Yu-tun left at least thirty-two Northern lyrical dramas, collectively known as the *Ch'eng-chai tsa-chü* 誠齋雜劇. They were written between the years 1404 and 1439 and printed chiefly in the last decade of his life, especially in 1433, his most productive year. Popularly performed, these dramas were reprinted in several Ming collections. Remarkably all thirty-two from the original edition are reported to be extant. Wu Mei 吳梅 (T. 瞿安, H. 霜厓, 1883–1939) asserted that twenty-two were in his possession. He published them, along with two more from another collection, in his *She-mo-t'a-shih ch'ü ts'ung er-chi* 奢摩他室曲叢二集 (1928). This type-set collection contains an appendix with Wu's comments on each of the twenty-four dramas. The National Peiping Library later acquired a set of twenty-five dramas also said to be from the original edition. In the *Ku-pen hsi-chü ts'ung-k'an ssu-chi* 古本戲劇叢刊四集 (Peking, 1958), there are eighteen of Chu's dramas reproduced from Ming manuscripts or printed editions, but none from the original edition.

In his lyrical dramas Chu Yu-tun introduced some innovations which exerted a certain influence on the further development of the tsa-chü during the Ming period. Deviating from the strict rules of the Yüan tsa-chü such as four acts to a drama and a single singing part in each act, he sometimes added a fifth act, often assigned lyrical parts to be sung by more than one actor in one act, and occasionally used melodies of the Southern drama. This may have been due to the influence of the Southern or lengthy lyrical drama (ch'uan-ch'i 傳奇), which about that time had started to reappear, *inter alia* with its most famous drama, the *P'i-pa chi* (*see* Kao Ming). The prose dialogues of Chu Yu-tun's dramas, which have been transmitted in their original state, are superior to those of most Yüan tsa-chü, partly due to the fact that the dialogues of the Yüan dramas were mainly reworded by their Ming editors.

He left a collection of short lyrical pieces (san-ch'ü 散曲), entitled *Ch'eng-chai yüeh-fu* 樂府, 2 ch., which was included in the *Yin-hung-i so k'o-ch'ü* 飲虹簃所刻曲 (Nanking, 1932). His collections of poetry and prose seem not to have survived. One hundred of his poems on the palace life of the Yüan dynasty entitled *Yüan kung-tz'u* 元宮詞, as well as forty-six other poems, appear in the anthology, *Lieh-ch'ao shih-chi* of Ch'ien Ch'ien-i (ECCP). Appended to the *Yüan kung-tz'u* are five poems on the palace life of the Chou princedom, entitled *Chou fan-wang kung-tz'u* 周藩王宮詞, attributed to Niu Heng 牛恆 (cs 1535, native of Wu-kung 武功, Shensi).

Bibliography

1 (Po-na ed.) 100/17b, 116/10b; 3/108/12b; 5/1/19b; 61/86/10b; 84/乾下/2b; KC (1958), 1571; MSL (1962), T'ai-tsu 1973, 2981, 3093, Ying-tsung (1963), 1062, 1068, 1071; Fu Hsi-hua 傅惜華, *Ming-tai tsa-chü ch'üan-mu* 明代雜劇全目 (1958), listing 31 dramas by Chu 朱, lacking the one entitled *Shan-chih-shih k'u-hai hui-t'ou* 善知識苦海回頭; Aoki Masaru 青木正兒, *Chung-kuo chin-shih hsi-ch'ü shih* 中國近世戲曲史 (transl. by Wang Ku-lu 王古魯, 1957), I, 142–156; Wang Chi-lieh 王季烈, *Ku-pen Yüan Ming tsa-chü t'i-yao* 古本元明雜劇提要 (1957), 19a; *Lieh-ch'ao shih-chi* 乾下, 7b.

D. R. Jonker

CHU Yüan-chang 朱元璋 (T. 國瑞), October 21, 1328–June 24, 1398, was born into a poor family in Chung-li 鍾離, Hao-chou 濠州 (modern Feng-yang, Anhwei) and eventually became the founder of the Ming dynasty. His early ancestors, according to his own account, were once settled in Chü-jung 句容 (near Nanking) and moved thence to Ssu-chou 泗州 (Anhwei). Some time in the 14th century his father, Chu Shih-chen 世珍, defaulting on his taxes and refusing to perform his corvée duties, moved to Chung-li. Chu Yüan-chang was the youngest of four boys and two girls. Difficulties in supporting such a family forced his parents to arrange for the adoption of his second and third older brothers and to marry off his sisters early. Information about Chu Yüan-chang's early life to his seventeenth year is meager. It is said that as a child he was frequently ailing and his father wished to have him reared in a Buddhist monastery, but his mother, née Ch'en 陳, objected. Later he developed into a robust youth, whose main physical characteristic was a protruding lower jaw. He probably assisted in work on the farm, and had no schooling.

An important turning point in his life

came in 1344 when a serious famine and pestilence took the lives of his father on the 18th of May, his eldest brother on the 21st, and his mother on the 3d of June. Only three other members of the family besides himself, a sister-in-law, a nephew Chu Wen-cheng 文正 (d. 1365), and his second older brother, Chu Hsing-sheng 興盛, survived. Their destitution was such that burial of the dead was impossible until a kind-hearted villager, Liu Chi-tsu 劉繼祖 (T. 大秀), donated a piece of land for the purpose. After the funeral the youth had no recourse but to put himself in the care of Buddhist monks as his father had wished. He was admitted to the Huang-chüeh 皇覺 monastery near Hao-chou as a novice, and did such menial work as burning incense, beating drums and bells, carrying water, and gathering fuel for the kitchen. After fifty-two days (October, 25–December, 16), the abbot had to let his disciples go for lack of food. During the next three years (1345–47) Chu became a mendicant, begging for food in both cities and rural communities west of the Huai River (western Anhwei and eastern Honan). Wherever he passed he observed the topography, listened to the talk of bystanders, and made himself familiar with conditions. Eventually he returned to the monastery, remaining there for four years (1348–52). It was probably during this time that he began to learn to read and write, and to be initiated into Buddhist doctrine. Judging from the amount of knowledge that he accumulated and was to reveal in his later writings, he must have been diligent and blessed with a retentive memory. But the times in which he lived were not conducive to quiet study, nor would he allow himself to live in isolation. [Editors' note: There are rumors that Chu may have served as a soldier under the Mongols. According to a manuscript biography of Cho Ban 趙胖 preserved in Korea, Cho and Chu, in their early days, campaigned together under the Mongol general Toγto (1313–55). The biography, however, contains fictional elements and may be disregarded. A report of a similar kind is B. Hulbert's rendering of a letter sent by Chu Yüan-chang to the Korean king and delivered by the Chinese envoy Hsieh Ssu (*q. v.*) in 1369; one sentence of this reads as follows: "At first we entered the Mongol army and there beheld the evils of the Mongol reign." Unfortunately this does not accord with the letter as recorded in the official Korean annals.]

A spirit of rebellion was in the air, induced by discrimination, unsound fiscal policy, political corruption, and the increase of famine conditions in certain areas. Secret societies, dormant in times of plenty and good government, sprang to life. Chu was drawn into the counsels of one or other of the leaders in rebellious movements. One who reportedly approached him, P'eng Ying-yü (*see* Hsü Shou-hui), also a mendicant Buddhist in the western Huai region, believed in the reincarnation of Maitreya Buddha and the reappearance of a Radiant Prince (Ming Wang 明王) who would save the people from their miseries. The doctrine he preached, which had spread from western Asia to China in the 7th century, included among its beliefs the idea that the dual principles of light and darkness were fundamental elements of the cosmos. Light generated intelligence and brightness; darkness produced ignorance and evil. This religion, known in Iran after the name of its founder Mani, the Chinese called either Mo-ni chiao 摩尼教, Manichaeism, or Ming-chiao 明教, Religion of Light. The Radiant Prince and Maitreya Buddha shared the same avowed purpose of saving people from suffering. The Ming-chiao and Pai-lien chiao 白蓮教 (White Lotus sect) were almost indistinguishable. Their members intermingled, burned incense, and covered their heads with red turbans. As a consequence, their military band came to be known as the Red Army 紅軍 or Red Turbans 紅巾. A branch of this band numbering some five thousand men started to riot in Kiangsi in 1338, only to be suppressed by the authorities. P'eng Ying-yü fled to the north where he continued to preach in the area where Chu was living.

Among the leaders of the White Lotus sect was Han Lin-er (*q.v.*) who was persuaded by a chief of the Red Army, Liu Fu-t'ung (*see* Han Lin-er), to claim descent from the imperial house of Sung. In 1351 Liu made Han king, calling him Hsiao-ming wang 小明王, or the Young Radiant Prince of the erstwhile Sung dynasty. In this same year breaks in the neglected dykes of the Yellow River resulted in an inundation of the Huai River region. Hundreds of thousands of people, many of whom were reportedly secret society members, were forced to repair the damage, Han's father, noticing the laborers at work, spread the rumor that it was "a oneeyed stone man which had disturbed the River, and the whole empire was about to revolt." Actually such a figure had been secretly buried in the mud. When it was discovered, the credulous people believed the prophecy and joined the rebel force.

In the autumn of the same year a cloth peddler, Hsü Shou-hui (*q.v.*), founded the state of T'ien-wan and called himself emperor with the reigning title Chih-p'ing, establishing his capital first at Ch'i-shui and then (1356) at Han-yang. About the same time Chih-ma Li 芝麻李 (Sesame Li) rebelled in Shantung, but Li was soon killed by the Mongols. P'eng Ta 彭大 (d. *ca*. 1354) and Chao Chün-yung 趙均用 (d. 1359) took insurgent action in Hsü-chou on the Shantung border. Earlier (1348) a salt smuggler and pirate on the Chekiang coast, Fang Kuo-chen (*q. v.*), had also rebelled. Nearer home, a well-to-do fortune teller, Kuo Tzu-hsing (*q.v.*), revolted and occupied the city of Hao-chou. Chu must have watched these developments with concern. Although he is said to have been familiar with the tenets of both Manichaeism and the White Lotus Society, he refused to join any of the rebels, as if awaiting a more favorable turn of events.

The Mongol generals who were dispatched to suppress these outbreaks fought among themselves instead of obeying orders. Chancellor Toyto was at odds with General Ha-ma 哈麻 (T. 士廉, d. 1356), and the two failed to cooperate in the suppression of Chang Shih-ch'eng (*q. v.*); both were eventually put to death. The emperor, Toyon-temur (*q.v.*), ordered others to put down the insurgents, but with no better success. As the Mongol officers and men lacked leadership, their military effectiveness decreased to such an extent that a number of rebel officers found it possible to establish themselves in various parts of the country, and anarchy prevailed. The Huang-chüeh monastery among many other structures was burned by the Mongols, and numerous young people were pressed into service. It became clear to Chu that he must cast his lot one way or the other. Repeated divinations along with common sense indicated that he should side with the rebels. He took the step in April, 1352, enrolling as a soldier under the local leader, Kuo Tzu-hsing.

Chu was quick to catch the attention and gain the confidence of his commander, marrying his foster daughter, née Ma (*q.v.*), who later became his empress. This brought a swift change in status. From now on he was addressed as Chu kung-tzu 朱公子, a term commonly applied to the son of a prince or of a family of the highest class. In due course he was to succeed to Kuo's command, following the latter's death (1355). His ability to read and write marked him out from many of his fellow officers and men. He was quick at making plans and arriving at decisions. His prowess as a soldier and unwearied attention to detail earned him rapid promotion. At the same time he succeeded in persuading men from his own district to join Kuo's army. By 1354 he had recruited several hundred; of these, twenty-four, including Hsü Ta and T'ang Ho (*qq.v.*), became members of his personal staff. He was unwilling at the start to serve under Han Lin-er, seeming to have made up his mind from the beginning to be second to none. As soon as his strength was sufficient he disposed of Han. On January 31, 1367, he established his own calender, initiating the kingdom of Wu 吳元年.

Chu differed from other rebels and Mongol officers in refusing to permit his men to kill and plunder. Another characteristic which set him apart was his continuing effort to seek out well-educated people to serve as his mentors. When he took Ting-yüan 定遠 (Anhwei), he persuaded Li Shan-ch'ang (q.v.) to join his staff; when he seized Ch'u-chou 處州, Chekiang, he succeeded in acquiring the services of Sung Lien and Liu Chi (qq.v.). These three and several others became his advisers, giving him not only political and military counsel but also informal lessons in Chinese history and literature. It was Feng Kuo-yung (see Feng Sheng), for example, who advised him to make Chin-ling 金陵 (later called Nanking) his capital, Li Shan-ch'ang who counseled him to pattern his career after that of the first emperor of the Han, pointing to that monarch's understanding of human nature and ability to employ men of diverse talents, and Yeh Tui 葉兌 (T. 良仲), who made suggestions as to the conquest of his rivals. Chu accepted their advice whenever it tallied with his imperial ambition. With a staff of this sort, well disciplined soldiers, an economic and communications center at Nanking, in addition to his own ability and drive, Chu succeeded in gaining popular support and overcame his rivals.

Once settled at Nanking, he took Chinkiang and several other cities in the lower Yangtze valley (1356). In the following year he conquered Ning-kuo 寧國 and Hui-chou 徽州 (Anhwei), and then the key city of Yangchow. Near the end of 1358, it is said that he heeded a scholar's advice to build high walls around his capital, accumulate ample provisions, but delay the proclamation of kingship, and begin to pay close attention to the problems of farming and irrigation. In 1361 he assumed the title of duke of Wu 吳國公, and three years later that of prince 吳王, in spite of the fact that his rival in Soochow, Chang Shih-ch'eng, was also so named. By 1366 the Huai valley was under his control.

In the meantime Chu had countered the challenge of Ch'en Yu-liang (q.v.). After meeting with one setback at T'ai-p'ing 太平, near Wu-hu, he threw his entire naval force against Ch'en in a decisive engagement at Lake Poyang (1363) destroying Ch'en's fleet with explosive fire and killing Ch'en in the action. Four years later, following a series of battles, Chang Shih-ch'eng succumbed as well to the superior power and strategy of Chu. Chang was arrested and taken to Nanking, where he died in 1376. Chu's last rival for supremacy was Fang Kuo-chen, who managed to maintain an independent regime along the coast of Chekiang from 1348 to 1367. At last Fang saw the futility of combat and surrendered without a struggle. Pockets of resistance remained in Kwangtung, Kwangsi, Fukien, Szechwan, and Yunnan, but were gradually eliminated—the first three in 1368, Szechwan in 1371, and Yunnan in 1381. Generals Hsü Ta and Ch'ang Yü-ch'un (q.v.) meanwhile were in command of a large army proceeding northward in the direction of Ta-tu 大都 (later called Peiping, Peking). Chu, now emperor, issued a public declaration condemning the Mongols and reassuring the people that China was about to be restored to the Chinese. This goal was reached on September 14, 1368, when the last Yüan emperor, Toγon-temur, fled in the direction of Shang-tu 上都 (in Chahar), and Mongol rule came to a halt. Hsü Ta and others continued their advance according to plan to Shansi, Shensi, and Shangtu, whence Toγon-temur continued his flight to the northeast, to Ying-ch'ang 應昌, dying in 1370. By 1372 the victorious forces had pushed across the Gobi into Outer Mongolia. When the Liaotung area in the northeast came under Chinese sway (1377), the conquest and unification of China came virtually to a close. The over-all director of this vast effort was Chu, "a general who never lost a major battle."

On January 23, 1368, Chu, then not quite forty years of age ascended the throne, proclaimed Ming 明 (bright or enlightened), as the dynastic name, and adopted as the reign title Hung-wu 洪武 (grand military achievement). He conferred the posthumous honorary title of emperor upon his ancestors to the fourth generation, and that of prince upon his maternal grandfather, his elder brothers, and his male cousins. Madame Ma he named Empress, and his eldest son, Chu Piao (q.v.), heir apparent. His seat of government remained at Nanking. He greatly enlarged the city, saw to the construction of many edifices, and surrounded it with the longest wall in China, some twenty-three miles, pierced by thirteen gates. Li Shan-ch'ang and Hsü Ta became his ministers of the left and right. In 1370, as a token of gratitude, Chu bestowed the posthumous title of prince on Kuo Tzu-hsing to whom he owed his initial rise to power.

Even as an emperor Chu suffered from self-consciousness and a pronounced inferiority complex. Hardly had he come to the throne when he issued a decree prohibiting unorthodox religious sects (June 30, 1370), especially mentioning the White Lotus sect and the Ming-chiao, as he apparently wished to erase his connection with secret societies and was apprehensive that their members might undermine his own position. The act of prohibition was later (1397) incorporated in his legal code. During his reign he put to death many scholar-officials whose writings contained comments apparently alluding to monk, tonsure, shining bald pate, beggar, or thief, all of which he took to satirize his own early life. He was, nevertheless, fond of calling himself a commoner (pu-i 布衣) from west of the Huai, who rose to power from humble beginnings. Repeatedly he used such expressions as Huai-yu 淮右 pu-i in his collected writings.

Chu had also a superiority complex. In a number of his actions he imitated not only the first emperor of the Han, whose birthplace was not far from his own, but also Ch'in Shih-huang (259–210 B.C.); it was clearly his intention to build an empire and fashion a government which would last for many generations. His desire for possession—possession of the empire for himself and his family—was obsessive. He may also have intended to be an enlightened ruler: to improve the lot of the common people and govern them justly. His concept of sovereignty was absolutism, tempered with benevolence and magnanimity. Appearing to be a Confucianist, he was actually a legalist. He exercised the strictest discipline, determined to dominate the empire and perpetuate his line. Trusting no one, he appointed officers to govern newly captured cities, but he required their wives and children to live in his capital as hostages. In addition he delegated more than twenty adopted sons to serve as overseers of these officers. He placed no reliance on his women folk or on eunuchs; all were forbidden to meddle in state affairs. Furthermore, he set up an espionage network to spy upon his subordinates throughout the empire, in both their public and private lives.

One of his schemes for control was to register the entire population; this was known as the li-chia 里甲 system. Every ten households formed a chia with one man as chief; ten chia made a li which, together with ten chia chiefs, made a total of one hundred ten households headed by a leader. Each household was required to put up a doorplate indicating the names, ages, and professions of its members. This registry served as a basis for labor service as well as a security check. All members of a single li were supposed to know each other and guarantee everyone's behavior. Anyone who traveled a distance of over a hundred li (thirty-three miles) was required to have a passport, the lack of which would subject him to a beating of eighty strokes or three years' imprisonment.

With peace and security finally established, Chu, following largely the military and political systems of the dynasties which preceded his—especially that of the Yüan under which many of his subordinates had served—began to make changes. The branch, or traveling Central Secretariat 行中書省, which exercised over-all power in a province under the Yüan, he changed in 1376 to a system of administrative commissioners 承宣布政使 with duties limited to civil and financial matters. In addition, for each of the provinces, he provided surveillance commissioners 按察使 for judicial affairs and a regional commissioner 都指揮使 for military matters. Thus the centralized authority of the Yüan provincial control was broken up into three divisions to make it easier for the emperor to oversee. In the central government Chu held to the administrative system of the Yüan until 1380, when he abolished the chancellorship of the Central Secretariat headed by Hu Wei-yung (q.v.). He allowed the six ministries, Personnel, Revenue, Rites, War, Justice, and Works, to handle routine administrative affairs and serve as his agents. As consultants he appointed four assistant officials, but this institution, known as the Ssu-fu kuan 四輔官, existed for only a short time (1380–82). As the state documents were too numerous for him to read, the emperor appointed four grand secretaries (ta hsüeh-shih 大學士) in 1382 to assist him in reviewing the less important ones, as well as to serve as clerks, attendants, and consultants.

For several years the central military commission (ta tu-tu fu 大都督府) was under the control of Chu Wen-cheng (now prince of Nanchang). It was taken out of his hands in 1380 for fear of his possible usurpation of power, and divided into five military commissions 五軍都督府 paralleling the six ministries. Each commission took charge of military activities in a certain geographical area. The power of mobilization and transfer of troops from one spot to another rested with the ministry of War. The emperor, through the ancient method of divide and rule and other checks, saw to it that the soldiers were controlled by the state, not by individual officers.

The name of the tribunal of censors was changed in 1380 from Yü-shih t'ai 御史台 to Tu-ch'a-yüan 都察院. The function of a censor—to remonstrate with an emperor if he found him in error—was reduced to a minimum. The investigating censors 監察御史 were increased in number to one hundred ten, and served as the eyes and ears of the monarch, reporting directly to him. The office of transmission 通政司, a message center set up in 1377, made all reports directly to the throne.

Although this highly centralized government was thus modified, its smooth functioning had still to be worked out. At the start many bureaucrats attempted to exercise independent judgment. To put a stop to this, the emperor resorted to legalist methods. His Embroidered-uniform Guard formally organized in 1382 (though it had been in existence from the 1360s) became his secret service. It exercised almost unlimited police and judicial authority over both officials and commoners, possessing its own jail, torturing instruments, and other means to extract information. Court flogging 廷杖 of outspoken and noncooperative high officials was one of the emperor's ways of intimidating them. Several men of high degree suffered death from the bastinado.

Three significant criminal cases or purges which took a heavy toll of lives helped Chu get rid of people he considered likely to thwart his plans or contend with him for power. The first was in connection with Chancellor Hu Wei-yung, executed along with a number of accomplices in 1380. Later on, more than thirty thousand people allegedly involved in Hu's case were ferreted out by the secret police over a period of fourteen years. The second, occurring in 1385, was the case of Kuo Huan 郭桓 (d. May 7, 1385), vice-minister of Revenue, who, on the charge of having embezzled more than seven million piculs of government grain, was put to death together with hundreds of others, including tax collectors, landlords, and granary owners who stored the grain. The third, which took place in 1393, was that of General Lan Yü (*q.v.*). This veteran officer, who had been granted the title of duke, was reported by a commander of the Embroidered-uniform Guard to be arrogant, self-willed, and, (most important) involved in a plot to overthrow the emperor. He, his family, clan members, and many friends, a total estimated at over fifteen thousand, suffered the extreme penalty. By this time most of Chu's old comrades-in-arms, like those of the first Han emperor fifteen centuries earlier, had either died a natural death or had been eliminated.

The slaughter of so many people, many of them innocent, stands out in sharp contrast to Chu's record of clemency before he became emperor. He cared nothing, however, for consistency. He would rather be unpredictable and paradoxical like Lao-tzu, whose book he liked so much he made a commentary of it. On the sentence (in *chüan* 74): "The people are not afraid of death, why then frighten them with death," he wrote in 1375: "The empire has recently been pacified, the people are treacherous, and officials are accustomed to malpractice; even though ten persons are executed in the morning, a hundred will still be engaged in evil-doing in the evening." Such being the conditions as he saw them, the emperor substituted imprisonment with labor for execution. In less than a year, he reported, the fear in his own mind decreased. Strangely enough, however, the executions in the above-mentioned criminal cases all took place after 1375. There

seem to be only two possible explanations for his shift in policy. Either he had become a paranoiac, especially after the death in 1382 of his wife who exercised some restraint over his temper, or conditions were getting out of hand, and he could think of no other recourse but extremist measures. His cruelty is vividly described, largely by himself, in the three compilations of the *Ta-kao* 大誥 (Great instructive warnings). The end result of these three cases was the elimination of many self-seeking bureaucrats and their collaborators. But who can say how many innocent people, men who might have counteracted the influence of evildoers, also lost their lives? In any event, he put his imperial authority beyond challenge, and became one of the most powerful and despotic emperors in the history of China.

His reign is characterized also by a great deal of reconstruction. He understood the Confucian theory that the prime requisites of good government are sufficient food and an adequate military force; then the confidence of the people in their ruler will be won. His comments on *chüan* 61 and 63 of the *Lao-tzu* make this very clear. On numerous occasions he exempted people from taxation in one region or another should any natural or man-made catastrophe occur. Local officials, including magistrates, prefects, and others, were often summoned to the palace; there he would instruct them to take care of the people and permit them to recover from the long years of strife. As early as 1358 he appointed a commissioner of irrigation and agriculture 都水營田使. He also established an office of agriculture 司農司, which was empowered to transport people from crowded areas to work where there was much unclaimed land, as in Honan and the area now known as Anhwei. Each family was given free seed, cattle, fifteen *mou* (over two acres) of land, plus two additional *mou* for vegetable plots. The rich he treated differently; he ordered many wealthy families, especially those from Soochow, to move to the capital, to be under his control. Some scholars have considered this action as a penalty for their earlier adherence to the cause of Chang Shih-ch'eng. Collectors of the land tax 糧長 were nevertheless chosen by the central government in 1371 from among the landlords, the emperor regarding this as a policy of "using good people to rule good people." Contrary to his expectations, however, the government within a few years faced mounting trouble with land-tax collectors; these paid but little on their own properties but extracted much more from the poor. The *Ta-kao* records many such collectors, and the punishments meted out to them.

For effective collection of taxes, Yellow Books 黄册, something like the English Domesday Book, and Fish-scaled Plots Books 魚鱗圖册, were painstakingly prepared. The former was a register of the civil population for labor tax; the latter a register of land with charts indicating the shapes of plots joined together, after the manner of scales of fish, as a basis for the tax on land. These registrations were vast enterprises which occupied many public servants for years. The result was gratifying, for near the end of the Hung-wu period more acres of arable land were accounted for than in any records until the latter part of the dynasty.

The emperor likewise provided for the issuance of paper currency, discontinued during the last years (1357-67) of the Yüan dynasty. Called Ta Ming pao-ch'ao 大明寶鈔, it first appeared in April, 1375, in five denominations. It proved unpopular, however, and the value of the notes declined rapidly. His successors, nevertheless, continued to print issues for over a century after his time using his reign name as a kind of guaranty. Another of the emperor's revivals was government control over salt and salt exchange, his regulatious eliciting praise by certain modern scholars.

The system of population classification which Chu inherited from the Yüan grouped the people under three heads: military men, civil officials, and craftsmen. Freedom to shift from one classification to another was forbidden. As early as 1358 he appointed a myriarch in control over ten thousand families of military personnel who had to do farm work in time of peace, and fight in time of war. Under this system, known as *t'un-t'ien* 屯田, half military, half agricultural, it was expected that soldiers would be self-supporting and would put no burden for their maintenance on the rest of the population. Garrison posts dotted the empire, especially along frontiers. Soldiers changed posts frequently so that long quartering at any one place might be avoided. The emperor inaugurated maritime defense to ward off piratical raids, mainly from Japan, ordering General T'ang Ho to establish fifty-nine garrison posts at strategic points on the littoral. In the 1380s more posts were set up, ships constructed, and guards trained for special duties. As a result of these measures, Chu made the country secure. In his twenty-sixth year as emperor the size of the army was put at one million, two hundred fifteen thousand men, and the supply of horses at nine thousand eighty head. Modern scholarship has calculated that his military establishment was substantially self-supporting.

In the field of education, the emperor aimed for practical results. He stood willing to make use of any scholar, whether Chinese, Mongol, or other, who would serve his administration. He reorganized the Hanlin Academy and the National University, and ordered the opening of other schools within and without the capital. To Confucius he gave lip service, spreading the ideas of neo-Confucianism to schools throughout the land. He restored the system of civil service examinations and promoted in them the use of the eight-legged essay, a feature which had a vague beginning during the time of Wang An-shih (1021-86) and was to become stereotyped a century after his day. By these means he tried to control the thought of students. They were not permitted to comment on current affairs nor to disobey their teachers. Punishments for violation of school regulations included whipping, life-long imprisonment, hard labor, banishment, and decapitation. Those who survived this discipline received good treatment from the emperor, and the bulk of them rendered loyal service to the state. He made use of the more advanced students as modern cadres are utilized today: they taught school, repaired temples and dykes, checked the Yellow Books, and audited fiscal reports. Certain among them rose to be provincial judges and governors, or filled other responsible posts. After the purge in the case of Lan Yü in 1393, more than a thousand students filled the vacancies created. In honor of the holders of the *chin-shih* degree, many of whom had been students in the National University, the emperor had their names inscribed on a stone tablet which he erected in the courtyard of the Kuo-tzu chien—a practice continued by successive emperors from 1388 to 1904. [Editors' note: The examinations for the *chin-shih* were held in 1371, but not again until 1385. In the meantime there was eliminated from the *Mencius* all anti-autocratic ideas; 85 sections were dropped and some 170 allowed to remain (*see* Liu San-wu). The emperor also had the tablet of Mencius removed from the temple of Confucius.] For his lettered subjects the emperor required that they learn by heart his *Ta-kao* in its three successive editions. Each family had to keep the work in its home, and punishment was reduced by one degree if a criminal could prove that he possessed it. He put out as well a *Ta-kao wu-ch'en* 武臣 (Instructive warnings to military officers). For the illiterate there were the "Sheng-yü t'u-chieh" 聖諭圖解 (Sacred instructions) of the emperor with hortatory comments and six illustrations; they contained the following admonitions: "Be filial to parents, show respect to elders, live in harmony with neighbors, instruct sons and grandsons,

be content with your calling, and do no evil." These "Instructions," proclaimed in 1388 and again in 1399, were posted on school walls and inscribed on stone tablets erected before Confucian temples and examination halls. Six times monthly village heads summoned their neighbors by a village clapper and then read them aloud. A translation of the Sacred Instructions into French by E. Chavannes is available.

We know little of the private life of Chu. The biography of Empress Ma describes her as kind-hearted, helpful, and beyond criticism. On many an occasion when her husband was in a mood to do away with high officials and close relatives she quietly counseled clemency and induced him to change his mind. It is impossible to tell how many consorts Chu had besides the empress; three concubines are given brief notices in the *Ming-shih*: Sun Kuei-fei (*see* Chu Su) who died in 1374 at the age of thirty-two *sui*, Li Shu-fei 李淑妃, who died young, and Kuo Ning-fei 郭寧妃, who bore his tenth son, Chu T'an 檀 (prince of Lu 魯, March 15, 1370-January 2, 1390). Their biographies are given in only 274 characters. Altogether Chu had thirty-six sons and sixteen daughters. We know nothing of the mothers of his daughters, but the concubines who bore him sons include the following: Hu Ch'ung-fei 胡充妃, mother of his sixth son Chu Chen 楨 (prince of Ch'u 楚, April 5, 1364-March 21, 1424); Ta Ting-fei 達定妃, mother of his seventh and eighth sons, Chu Fu 榑 (prince of Ch'i 齊, December 28, 1364-1428), and Chu Tzu 梓 (prince of T'an 潭, October 6, 1369-April 18, 1390); Kuo Hui-fei 郭惠妃, daughter of Kuo Tzu-hsing and mother of his eleventh, thirteenth, and nineteenth sons, Chu Ch'un 椿 (prince of Shu 蜀, April 4, 1371-March 22, 1423), Chu Kuei 桂 (prince of Tai 代, Pth. 簡, Aug. 25, 1374-December 29, 1446), and Chu Hui 穗 (prince of Ku 谷, April 30, 1379-February 22, 1417); Hu Shun-fei 胡順妃, mother of his twelfth son, Chu Po 栢 or 柏 (prince of Hsiang 湘, H. 紫虛子, Pth. 獻, September 12, 1371-June

1?, 1399); Li Hsien-fei 李賢妃, mother of his twenty-third son, Chu Ching 桱 (prince of T'ang唐, September 30, 1386-September 8, 1415); Liu Hui-fei 劉惠妃, mother of his twenty-fourth son, Chu Tung 棟 (prince of Ying 郢, June 21, 1388-December 12, 1444); and Ko Li-fei 葛麗妃, mother of his twenty-fifth son, Chu I 㰘 (prince of I 伊, July 9, 1388-October 8, 1444). Other women who bore him sons—the fourteenth, fifteenth, sixteenth, seventeenth, and twentieth—but who were not accorded the title of fei (imperial concubine), are known simply by their family names of Kao 郜, Han 韓, Yü 余, Yang 楊, and Chou 周. Not even the family names of the mothers of the ninth, eighteenth, twenty-first, twenty-second, and twenty-sixth sons are mentioned. Obviously he was well supplied with women, Mongol and Korean as well as Chinese, having taken them from different sources and by various means: by force from the Yüan palace and from Ch'en Yu-liang's harem, peaceably through traditional selections of desirable girls. In this respect his reputation is above that of many another occupant of the dragon throne.

Chu saw to his sons getting a sound education from such well-known scholars as Sung Lien. As he reached maturity, the heir apparent was given the opportunity of engaging in some state business. For the security and perpetuation of the empire, the emperor assigned each of his other sons to an area where the prince maintained a palace with an annual revenue of some ten thousand piculs of grain and a guard of from three thousand to nineteen thousand soldiers, and had other privileges and honors. All the sons, except the ninth and twenty-sixth, who died in infancy, were men of capability. To his second, third, and fourth sons, Chu Shuang 樉 (prince of Ch'in 秦, December 3, 1356-April 9, 1395), Chu Kang 朱棡 (prince of Chin 晋, December 18, 1358-March 30, 1398), and Chu Ti (q. v.), he entrusted the task of fighting against the Mongols on the northern and north-

western frontier. The last eventually became the third emperor. The fifth son, Chu Su (q. v.), excelled in botanical and pharmaceutical studies. The sixth, Chu Chen, fought against the aborigines on the Hukuang-Szechwan border along with Generals T'ang Ho and Chou Te-hsing 周德興 (executed August 28, 1392), both of whom had been comrades of his father. The seventh son, Chu Fu, followed his brother Chu Ti in defense of the northern frontier, but later suffered degradation to the status of a commoner because of his violent temper. The eighth, tenth, eleventh, and sixteenth sons, Chu Tzu, Chu T'an, Chu Ch'un, and Chu Chan 朱栴 (prince of Ch'ing 慶, February 6, 1378-August 23, 1438) had the reputation of being well bred and fond of literature. The twelfth son, Chu Po, showed an interest both in literature and in military affairs. The seventeenth, Chu Ch'üan (q. v.), dissatisfied with his lot, wrote nearly twenty books on Chinese history and other subjects. The thirteenth and twenty-fifth sons, Chu Kuei and Chu I, turned out badly; they mistreated, even killed, the people in their areas at their pleasure. Many later Ming princes followed their example; certain others were no better than parasites.

After establishing control of the empire the emperor passed away in 1398 at the age of seventy, and was given the temple name of T'ai-tsu 太祖. He had chosen his grandson, Chu Yün-wen (q.v.), as his successor. In his last will he ordered a simple funeral, and bade his sons stay away from the capital for fear they might cause trouble. Even as early as 1373 he decreed that princes might visit him once a year, but they should not come simultaneously. In the same will he acknowledged that he had enjoyed the mandate of Heaven for thirty-one years, but that anxieties and fears had constantly made him distraught. He had worked hard night and day, he continued, in the hope that what he did might be of benefit to the people. He and Empress Ma were buried in a tomb known as Hsiao-ling 孝陵, located at the foot of Chung-shan 鍾山, east of Nanking. (It is well described in Bouillard et Vaudescal, "Les sepultures imperiales des Ming," BEFEO 20, 1920, 117.) Following his death, in accord with Mongol custom, thirty-eight of his forty concubines gave up their lives 殉.

Chu Yüan-chang is a controversial character. Some scholars say that he paid more attention to the welfare of the people than other emperors; though he put to death many officials, he did not kill many commoners. This is not entirely true, for the clan executions (tsu-chu 族誅) necessarily included hundreds of innocent commoners, and he slew some sixty or seventy thousand Miao and Yao tribesmen during the pacification of Yunnan and Kweichow. His ruthlessness cannot be forgotten. Other scholars say that Chu betrayed the peasantry and favored the landlords. Chao I (ECCP) gives this estimate of the man: "The founder of the Ming combined in his person the nature of a sage, hero, and robber." There is plenty of material for any characterization. Whatever his shortcomings, Chu was an outstanding emperor, and may be compared with Ch'in Shih-huang, Sui Yang-ti, and other eminent rulers of China. A man without formal education, he could yet write swiftly and quote readily from histories and the Classics to support his position. That he made a commentary on the Lao-tzu in ten days in the midst of other duties is proof of his mental ability. His reorganization of the political, military, legal, economic, and social systems he inherited exercised a marked influence on both the Ming and Ch'ing dynasties.

Chu is credited with a number of writings issued to honor his ancestors, impress his contemporaries, and instruct his successors. Among these one may list: *Huang-ling pei* 皇陵碑 (Epitaph for the imperial tomb), *Hsi-cheng chi* 西征記 (The western expedition [against Ch'en Yu-liang]), *P'ing hsi Shu wen* 平西蜀文 (Pac-

ification of western Szechwan), *Chi-meng* 紀夢 (Account of a dream [about his experience before entering the army of Kuo Tzu-hsing]), *Chou tien hsien-jen chuan* 周顛仙人傳 (Biography of the crazy immortal Chou), and *Hsiao-tz'u lu* 孝慈錄 (Filial piety and cermonial [illustrated]). All these titles are preceded by the term *Yü-chih* 御製 (imperially written), and may be found in the *Chi-lu hui-pien* of Shen Chieh-fu (*q. v.*). A collection of the emperor's essays and poems is known under the title *Kao Huang-ti yü-chih wen-chi* 文集, 20 ch. Also under his name are such books as *Tz'u chu-fan chao-ch'ih* 賜諸蕃詔敕 (Proclamations and imperial commands to foreign nations), *Hsiao-ling chao-ch'ih* 孝陵詔敕 (Proclamations and imperial commands compiled posthumously), which deals with domestic issues such as the conquest of the Mongol capital and dismissal of Wang Kuang-yang (*q. v.*) and Hu Wei-yung, *Ch'en-chieh lu* 臣誡錄 (Instructions to ministers), and *Hsiang chien* 相鑒 (References to chief ministers). The last two are preserved in beautiful palace editions of the Hung-wu period.

Two important books compiled under imperial auspices are *Hung-wu cheng-yün* 正韻 (Correct rhymes of the Hung-wu period, reproduced in Taipei, 1963) and the code of law *Ta Ming lü* 大明律 which went through three major revisions before its final promulgation in 1398. Towards the end of his reign Chu tended to be more benevolent. As a consequence many cruel punishments listed in the *Ta-kao* are not incorporated in the code. The *Ta-kao* remains, nonetheless, an essential source for an understanding of the socio-economic and governmental conditions prevailing during the early years of the Hung-wu period. Of like importance is the *Huang Ming tsu-hsün* 皇明祖訓 (Ancestral Instructions of Imperial Ming), a work the tenets of which the emperor expected his descendants to obey for all time.

[Editors' note: On the excavation of the

tomb fo Chu T'an in 1970/71 in the region of Tsou-hsien 鄒縣, Shantung, there were discovered many artifacts including clothing, mortuary figurines, his seal, inkslab, ch'in (zither), two Sung and Yüan paintings, Yüan calligraphy, and a number of Yüan dynasty printed books. See *Wen-wu* 文物 (May, 1972), 25.]

Bibliography (highly selective)

1/ch. 1–4; MSL (1962), T'ai-tsu, ch. 1–257; KC (1958), ch. 1–11; *Yüan-shih*, ch. 42–47; Hsieh Chin, *T'ien-huang yü-tieh*; Wang Wen-lu, *Lung-hsing tz'u-chi*; anon., *Kuo-ch'u li-hsien lu* 國初禮賢錄; Lu Shen, *P'ing Hu lu*; T'ung Ch'eng-hsü 童承絃 (cs 1521), *P'ing Han lu* 平漢錄; Wu K'uan, *P'ing Wu lu*; Huang Piao 黃標 (fl.1544), *P'ing Hsia lu* 夏 *lu*; Kao Tai, *Hung-yu lu*; Ch'ien Ch'ien-i(ECCP), *Kuo-ch'u ch'un-hsiung shih-lüeh*; Fu Wei-lin (ECCP), *Ming shu*, ch. 1–4; Hsia Hsieh 夏燮 (1799–1875?), *Ming t'ung-chien* 通鑑, ch. 1–4; Ch'üan Heng 權衡 (14th cent.), *Keng-shen wai-shih* 庚申外史; Ku Ying-t'ai (ECCP), *Ming ch'ao chi-shih pen-mo*; Wu Han 吳晗, *Chu Yüan-chang chuan* (Shanghai, 1949); Fang Chüeh-hui 方覺慧, *Ming T'ai-tsu ko-ming wu-kung chi* 革命武功記 (Taipei, 1964); Teng Ssu-yü, "Ming *Ta-kao* yü Ming-ch'u chih cheng-chih she-hui," 大誥與明初之政治社會, YCHP, 20 (December, 1936), 455; Wan Kuo-ting 萬國鼎, "Ming-tai chuang-t'ien k'ao-lüeh," 莊田考略, *Chin-ling* 金陵 *hsüeh-pao* 3:2 (November, 1933), 295; Edouard Chavannes, "Les saintes instructions de l'empereur Hong-wou," BEFEO, III (October-December, 1903), 552; C. O. Hucker, "Government Organization of the Ming Dynasty," HJAS, 21 (1958), 1; Kao Yu-kung, "A Study of the Fan La Rebellion," HJAS, 24 (1962–63), 53; Ku Chieh-kang, "A Study of the Literary Persecution during the Ming Dynasty," tr. by L. Carrington Goodrich, HJAS, III (1938), 254; F. W. Mote, *The Poet Kao Ch'i* (Princeton, 1962), chap. 1; Henry Serruys, "Mongols in China during the Hung-wu Period," MCB, XI (1959); id., "Remains of Mongol Customs in China during the Early Ming Period," MS, 15 (1957), 137; B. Hulbert, *History of Korea* (Seoul, 1905, repr. 1962), 261; L. Carrington Goodrich, "Sino-Korean Relations at the End of the XIVth Century," *Transactions of the Korea Branch of the R.A.S.*, XXX(1940), 33.

                                        Teng Ssu-yü

CHU Yün-ming 祝允明 (T. 希哲, H. 枝山, 枝指生), January 17, 1461-January 28, 1527, scholar, calligrapher, was born into a literary family in Ch'ang-chou 長洲, prefecture of Soochow, a flourishing center of cultural and intellectual activities. His grandfather, Chu Hao 顥 (T. 惟清, cs 1439, 1405-January 23, 1483), a capable administrator and accomplished scholar, concluded his career as a vice administrative commissioner of Shansi, and left a collection of writings, *T'ung-hsüan chi* 侗軒集, 5 *ch.* His son, Chu Hsien 瓛 (H. 仁齋, d. 1483), married Hsü Shu-tuan 淑端 (1442-76), the daughter of Grand Secretary Hsü Yu-chen (*q.v.*). She was a talented woman who became the mother of Chu Yün-ming.

Chu Yün-ming reportedly looked rather unimpressive: he was near-sighted and had an extra finger on one of his hands; hence he came to be known as Chu Chih-shan 枝山, or Chih-chih sheng 枝指生 (extra finger). A precocious child, Chu Yün-ming is said to have been able to write simple characters when he was only four years of age and compose poems by the time he was eight. During his early years he studied the Classics and literature under the instruction of his elders, and made a mark for his ability. He struck his seniors, moreover, by his unorthodox thinking and behavior, such as his skepticism about orthodox neo-Confucianism and his contempt for conventional values and practices, on which he expounded in his first publication, a collection of notes on the Classics called *Tu-shu pi-chi* 讀書筆記, in 1488.

As he reached manhood, a fellow townsman, Li Ying-chen (*see* Wen Cheng-ming), a noted scholar-calligrapher who was then vice minister of the Court of the Imperial Stud, impressed by his promise, betrothed his daughter to him. In 1492 Chu belatedly graduated as *chü-jen*. He made an impression on the chief examiner Wang Ao 鏊 (*q.v.*), but abandoned his attempt for an official career after several failures in later examinations. He then went into retreat at home, absorbed himself in scholarly and literary pastimes, and took occasional trips to gain inspiration. He had the company frequently of three distinguished belle-lettrists of his locality, Hsü Chen-ch'ing, Wen Cheng-ming, and T'ang Yin (*qq.v.*), who became his life-long friends. They traveled together, exchanged poems and specimens of calligraphy, and collectively earned the epithet Wu-chung ssu chieh 吳中四傑 (four talents of the Wu district).

Eventually in 1515, through the recommendation of senior authorities, Chu received an appointment as magistrate of Hsing-ning 興寧, Kwangtung, where he officiated during the next five years. He won the appreciation of the natives by his devotion to justice, guidance in proper Confucian conduct, and promotion of public education. He was particularly remembered as editor of the local gazetteer, *Hsing-ning-hsien chih*, 4 *ch.*, with his own preface dated January, 1517. This edition, noted for its meticulous attention to financial and military institutions, was a model of its kind, and still survives in incomplete form. A transcription of the original draft in Chu Yün-ming's "running style" calligraphy was reproduced in 1962 by the Chung-hua 中華 Book Company under the title *Chu Chih-shan shou-hsieh* 手寫 *Hsing-ning-hsien chih kao-pen* 稿本. Around 1520, through the recommendation of Wu K'uan (*q.v.*), Chu gained promotion to be assistant prefect of Ying-t'ien (Nanking) in charge of fiscal matters. Before long, however, unhappy over official routines, and suffering from poor health, he pleaded for permission to retire. He spent the last few years at home, where he erected a pavilion called Huai-hsing-t'ang 懷星堂 (1525) and devoted himself to scholarly and literary pursuits. He was survived by two sons. The elder, Chu Hsü 續 (T. 遙緒, cs 1511), first served as a Hanlin bachelor, then as a superising secretary, and lastly as an administrative commissioner of Kwangsi.

Chu Yün-ming was an outstanding representative of an exceptional group of intellectual and literary people of the Soochow area in the latter half of the 15th century. There emerged not only accomplished scholars who distinguished themselves in official careers, but also certain "pure" literary figures who were unsuccessful in officialdom but who enjoyed prestige by virtue of their literary distinction. These individuals possessed two personality traits. First, they were individualistic nonconformists who prided themselves on their romantic self-indulgence, and sustained their reputation through the patronage of scholar-officials who valued their achievement. Second, they were social and political iconoclasts who questioned the values and standards of neo-Confucian orthoxy, and concerned themselves with the ills of society in their quest for justice and freedom. In so doing they became a group of social critics—the Japanese scholar Miyasaki Ichisada 宮崎市定 dubbing them "shih-yin" 市隱—who constantly spoke out on issues despite their nonofficial capacities. Besides Chu Yün-ming and his three talented friends, other outstanding members of this group of literati included Shen Chou, Wang Ch'ung and his brother, and later Huang Hsing-tseng and his brothers (*qq.v.*).

Chu Yün-ming made a mark both for his literary versatility and for his nonconformist thinking and behavior. He was above all a romantic, disdaining conventions, enjoying travel and female companionship, and indulging in drinking and gambling. One of the most popular anecdotes about him records that he abhorred those who requested examples of his writing and condescended only when he was intoxicated or at the bidding of a courtesan. On the other hand, he was an iconoclast typical of his group. His personality inspired numerous anecdotes and stories, these culminating in a modern novel called *Chu Chih-shan feng-liu shih* 風流史 (The romance of Chu Yün-ming), or *Chu Chih-shan ku-shih* 故事. In a mélange of imaginative and colorful anecdotes, the anonymous author dramatizes Chu as a romantic belle-lettrist, unorthodox thinker, and just administrator; this helped to popularize him.

Chu Yün-ming's revolt against the orthodox neo-Confucian tradition, his championing of rationalism, and his unconventional attitude toward individuals and society may be gleaned from his own writings. Chu produced voluminous and diverse collections of literary works and miscellanies. The bulk of his output on social and political issues was assembled and collated by his sons sometime after his death under the title *Chu-shih chi-lüeh* 氏集略, 30 *ch*. This collection, first engraved in 1558, was reprinted as *Huai-hsing-t'ang chi*, also 30 *ch*., in 1609. A later supplement, *Chu-shih wen* 文 -*chi*, 10 *ch*., assembled by his fellow townsman Hsieh Yung 謝雍 (T. 元和, 1464-1544 +) in manuscript transcription, was once preserved in the National Library of Peiping. These two were recently reproduced under the title *Chu-shih shih* 詩-*wen chi*, by the National Central Library, Taipei, in 3 vols. (1971)—by far the most comprehensive collection of Chu Yün-ming's writings.

In his numerous essays, particularly in a series of discourses on classical studies, Chu vented his criticism of the orthodox neo-Confucian tradition as well as the authoritarian political institutions of his age. He criticized the formalistic doctrine of Sung neo-Confucianism for its inhibiting effects on intellectual development, and advocated the study of pre-Sung commentaries for new concepts. He also chided his contemporaries for flirtation with vulgar religions and philosophies, such as superstitous Taoist beliefs and practices, and proposed the suppression of literature of this type. Similarly, he rebuked the hypocritical scholar officials for their disposition to enhance their prestige by falsifying their genealogical records, or by exaggerating the achievement of their ancestors in laudatory essays. In veiled but unmistakable language he also attacked the inept and overbearing administrators, particularly those officials and eunuchs presiding over the Soochow area, and exposed their unsavory conduct and misdeeds.

Chu Yün-ming culminated his attack on the neo-Confucian orthodoxy and its moral and ethical standards by publishing in 1522 a long treatise which he apologetically called *Chu-shih tsui-chih lu* 罪知錄, 10 *ch*. In separate essays he attacked the traditional evaluation of illustrious historical personalities from antiquity down to the Yüan dased on conventional moral and ethical criteria, and submitted his own versions through a critical appraisal of certain specific situations. He challenged the adulation of several ancient heroes such as Emperors T'ang of the Shang and Wu of the Chou, Minister I Yin of the Shang, and the Duke of Chou. He criticized both Hsün-tzu and Mencius for their one-sided views of human nature, characterizing the latter as no sage, and hailed Chuang-tzu as the greatest philosopher after Confucius. He also disputed the standard evaluation of a number of historical personalities—emperors, statesmen, military officials, philosophers, belle-lettrists—citing examples of their achievements or misdeeds which invalidated the stereotyped categories of conventional judgment. They include Yang Hsiung (53 B.C.-A.D. 18), Yen Kuang (37 B.C.-A.D. 43) of the Han, Hsieh An (320-85) and Hsieh Hsüan (343-88) of the Chin, Wei Cheng (580-643), Han Yü (768-824), and Li Te-yü (787-849) of the T'ang, Emperor Chao K'uang-yin (927-76), Fan Chung-yen (989-1052), Ssu-ma Kuang (1019-86), and Han T'o-chou (1151-1207) of the Sung. He also challenged the traditional views on such leading personalities of the last period as Wang An-shih (1021-86), Ou-yang Hsiu (1007-72), Su Shih (1037-1101), Ch'eng I (1033-1107), and Chu Hsi (1130-1200), decrying their achievements in philosophy and literature. He was particularly critical, however, of Chinese scholars who served under the Mongols, such as Hsü Heng (1209-81), Liu Ping-chung (1216-74), Wu Ch'eng (1249-1333), and

Chao Meng-fu (1254-1322), contending that their services betrayed the Chinese cause, and jeopardized their status as true Confucianists. This somewhat harsh attitude, while reflecting Chu Yün-ming's disdain of officialdom, perhaps exemplifies the increasing anti-Mongol sentiment sparked by the T'u-mu defeat of 1449 (see Wang Chen).

In a similar vein, Chu Yün-ming attacked Sung neo-Confucianism, particularly the school represented by Chu Hsi and the two Ch'eng brothers, charging that their interpretation distorted the meaning of the ancient sages, and that the adoption of their commentaries for examinations arrested the country's intellectual development. He also questioned the neo-Confucianists' refutation of Buddhism focusing on its doctrines of salvation and reincarnation, arguing that the Buddhist contribution to humanity and metaphysics supplements those of the Confucian and Taoist traditions. In this case his views reflect the san-chiao (three teachings) synthesis formulated by the Chin philosopher Li Ch'un-fu (better known as Li P'ing-shan, 1185-1231) and expounded a generation before his day by Ching-lung 景隆 (original name Ch'en Tsu-t'ing 陳祖庭, 1393-1444), a Ch'an monk from Soochow who exerted considerable influence on the intellectuals of the 15th century. In various ways, therefore, Chu Yün-ming's attack on the Ch'eng-Chu school, his unorthodox views on historical personalities, and his advocacy of the san-chiao syncretism provided a source of inspiration for later iconoclastic thinkers such as Li Chih and T'u Lung (qq.v.). As the Japanese scholar Manno Senryū 間野潛龍 points out, Li Chih's categorization of historical personalities and his criteria for praise and blame expounded in his Ts'ang-shu evidently were stimulated by Chu Yün-ming's writings.

Chu was also famous as author of several random jottings on historical and contemporary events and of semifictional miscellanies on prodigies and miraculous happenings. Three of his best known works from the first category are: Ch'eng-hua chien Su-ts'ai hsiao-tsuan 成化間蘇材小纂 (1499), 1 ch., Ch'ien-wen chi 前聞記 (ca. 1500), 1 ch., and Yeh-chi 野記 (also known as Chiu-ch'ao 九朝 yeh-chi, 1511), 4 ch., all of which are extant. These collections contain a medley of records on and valuable insights into historical and contemporary events, as well as a wide range of notes of a fictional nature, including fabulous tales and heresies. They underscore Chu Yün-ming's concern for the transmission of worthy records of history, as well as for the preservation of elements of China's heritage, not for blind acceptance but for future evaluation. Despite the charges of critics of their fictional nature, many of the accounts add to the existing sources on the personages and social and political conditions of the Ming dynasty. The first item, Ch'eng-hua chien Su-ts'ai hsiao-tsuan, presents a collection of biographies of the eminent people of Soochow by a contemporary author, and adds an important source for the reign chronicles of Chu Ch'i-chen and Chu Chien-shen (qq.v.). The other two titles, despite fictional trappings, also noted for valuable information on the early reigns of the dynasty, particularly on illustrious figures, institutions, and customs, social and political conditions of the Soochow area. The Ch'ien-wen chi, for instance, preserves a document on the uprising of Li T'an (d. 1262) during the early Yüan, and another on the launching of the maritime expeditions of Cheng Ho (q.v.) which supplement the standard sources. The Yeh-chi contains a rich collection of notes on the early Ming rulers, particularly those on Chu Yüan-chang and Chu Kao-chih (qq.v.), which not only supplement the official records, but also vividly illustrate the popular impression of the early rulers of the dynasty. Another work in this category that merits attention is the Chiang-hai chien-ch'ü chi 江海殲渠記, a narrative on the uprising (in 1510) of Liu Liu (see Yang T'ing-ho) in Honan and Shantung that has been highly rated for its historical value. In addition, Chu Yün-ming left at least three items of semifictional miscellanies: *Wei-t'an* 猥談, *Chih-kuai lu* 志怪錄, and *Yü* 語 *-kuai*. In these he records a number of miraculous and uncanny events and anecdotes that may seem highly improbable; he defended himself, however, by stating that he intended to warn people against indulging in superstition, and to preserve for the record affairs that seem to have been inexplicable in his own day.

Otherwise, Chu Yün-ming was highly reputed in the literary and artistic fields: he was a distinguished essayist, poet, and calligrapher. His essays are characterized by their rich content, creative and ornate style, and elaborate but expressive phraseology. In poetry he emulated the masters of the Six Dynasties and the late T'ang, and developed a refreshing, invigorating style replete with elegant, novel expressions that ranked him as one of the outstanding poets of his time. An example of his poetic creation was the "Ta-yu fu" 大游賦, a lengthy narrative prose-poem in which he expounded his views and criticism of Confucian orthodoxy and of ancient social and political institutions, interspersed with notes, from antiquity down to the early Ming. He often expressed his joy and sorrow in prosaic and poetic forms; many of these items he dated, thus providing material for his biography.

In calligraphy, Chu Yün-ming's achievement was very high. He devoted his lifetime to this art, and outshone his peers by his distinctive styles and prolific output. Early in life Chu Yün-ming received guidance from his elders and later gained inspiration from his maternal grandfather Hsü Yu-chen in the cursive style, and his father-in-law Li Ying-chen in the regular style. He then emulated the work of early masters from Chung Yu (151-230), Wang Hsi-chih (321-79), Chang Hsü (8th cent.), and the eccentric monk Huai-su (624-97), down to Chao Meng-fu, and developed a variety of styles characteristic of his personality and temperament. In his middle years he perfected his calligraphy by copying the stone inscriptions of the Han-Wei and Six Dynasties periods, and produced a distinctive running and cursive style in his later life. Among the best samples, we may cite his transcription (1506) of the "Huang-t'ing ching" 黃庭經 by Wang Hsi-chih and the "Ch'u-shih piao" 出師表 (1514) attributed to Chu-ko Liang (181-234). They are characterized by vigorous strokes in a well-assembled composition that exemplify the best in classical Chinese calligraphy. In both the running and cursive styles, in which he followed Chang Hsü and Huai-su, Chu's achievement was outstanding. He wrote with the dash and impulse of a child. His running style is best illustrated by his transcription of the *Hsing-ning-hsien chih*, and by the *Li-sao ching* 離騷經 (1525), and his cursive style by his reproduction (1521) of the illustrious "Chih-p'i 赤壁 fu" attributed to Su Shih, and by his "Ho T'ao Yüan-ming shih" 和陶淵明詩 (1525), all of which have been preserved and reproduced in several calligraphy albums. In addition to these items, a sizable number of examples of Chu's calligraphy have been reproduced in albums in Shanghai and in Japan during the early Republican period; many others are preserved in libraries and museums in mainland China, Taiwan, Japan, and the United States. Some of the best representations have been reproduced in such collections as *Ku-kung po-wu yüan ts'ang li-tai fa-shu hsüan-chi* 故宮博物院藏歷代法書選集; *Shanghai po-wu kuan* 館 *ts'ang li-tai fa-shu hsüan-chi*; *Shōdō zenshū* 書道全書, and *Chinese Calligraphy*.

Bibliography:

1/286/16a; 3/267/12a; 5/75/57a; 22/5/40a; 34/11/1a; 40/27 上/2b; 43/2/7a; 61/151/3b; 64/丁 12/1a; 84/丙/50b; KC (1958), 3344; SK (1930), 61/4b, 124/4b, 5a, 143/5b, 144/3a, 171/6a; Chu Hao, *T'ung-hsüan chi* (NCL microfilm), appendix; Chu Yünming, *Chu-shih shih-wen chi*; id., *Chu-shih tsui-chih lu* (NLP microfilm no. 235); Wang Ch'ung,

Ya-i shan-jen chi (Taipei, 1968 ed.), 10/1a; Ho Liang-chün, *Ssu-yu-chai ts'ung-shuo*, 23/16a; Hsü Hsüeh-mo, *Hsü-shih hai-yü chi wen-pien*, 23/16a; Chang Hsüan, *Hsi-yüan wen-chien lu*, 23/4a, 25/5a, 4/8a, 7/4a, 8/67a, 14/12a, 16/21a, 30/25a, 103/19a, 106/2a; Wang Shih-chen, *I-yüan chih-yen*, 6/4a; Wen Chen-meng, *Ku-su ming-hsien hsiao-chi* (1925), 上/35a; *Ying-t'ien-fu chih* (1577), 6/10a; *Ch'ang-chou-fu chih* (1598), 14/25a, 41a; *Su-chou-fu chih* (1748), 60/14b, 61/21b; Hsiao Yen 蕭彦 (cs 1571), *I-huan jen-chien* 掖垣人鑑 (NCL microfilm), 12/23b; Ma Tsung-huo 馬宗霍, *Shu-lin tsao-chien* 書林藻鑑 (Taipei, 1965 ed.), 310; Chang Lung-wen 張龍文, *Chung-hua shu-shih kai-shu* 中華書史概述 (Taipei, 1965),189; (*Tseng-ting pen*) *Ku-kung shu-hua lu* (增訂本) 故宮書畫錄 (Taipei, 1965), 1/101, 2/7, 3/75; *Ku-kung po-wu yüan ts'ang li-tai fa-shu hsüan-chi*, Vol.19 (Peking, 1963); *Shanghai po-wu kuan ts'ang li-tai fa-shu hsüan-chi*, Vol. 17 (1964); Lo Hsiang-lin 羅香林, "Ming Ch'ing Hsing-ning-hsien chih k'ao," CYYY, 36: 2(June, 1966), 435; *Ku-kung chi-k'an* 故宮季刊, 3:1 (July, 1968), 3:3 (January 1969); *Shōdō Zenshū*, Vol. 17, Tokyo, 1930-32; Fujiwara Kakurai 藤原鶴來, *Wakan Shodōshi* 和漢書道史 (1956), 170; Miyasaki Ichisada, "Mindai So-Shō chihō no shitai fu to minshu" 明代蘇松地方の士大夫と民衆, *Shirin* 史林, 37:3 (June, 1954), 1; Manno Sanryū, "Shu In-min no Bukkyō" 佛教, *Ōtani gakuhō* 大谷學報, 39:4 (March, 1960), 39; id., "Shu In-min no shigaku" 史學, *Shirin*, 61:1 (June,1968), 26; Ch'en Chih-mai, *Chinese Calligraphers and their Art* (Melbourne, 1966),136; Tseng Yu-ho Ecke, *Chinese Calligraphy* (Philadelphia, 1971), 45, 46.

Hok-lam Chan

CHU Yün-wen 朱允炆, December, 5, 1377 -probable death date July 13, 1402, second son of Chu Piao (*q.v.*), reigned as the second emperor of the Ming dynasty from the death of his grandfather, Chu Yüan-chang, on June 24, 1398, until he perished or disappeared in the burning of the imperial palace at Nanking. This was the day the armies of his uncle, Chu Ti (*q.v.*), entered Nanking and completed the military phase of the usurpation, leading to the proclamation of the Yung-lo reign period to commence the following year. Simultaneously the four years which had been numbered by Chu Yün-wen's Chien-wen 建文 reign title (1399–1402) were "expunged" from the record and by quite artificial *post facto* fiat renamed as the years Hung-wu 洪武 32 to 35. The ruler as well as those four years, therefore, are often referred to by the term koch'u 革除 (the expunged). The Chien-wen reign title was officially restored to the dynastic history by action of Emperor Chu I-chün (*q.v.*) in October, 1595; but Chu Yün-wen was denied a dynastic temple name and posthumous honorific for 242 years until July, 1644, when the southern Ming emperor, Chu Yu-sung (ECCP), in an attempt to rectify this miscarriage of justice, assigned the temple name Hui-tsung 惠宗 and the posthumous name Jang-huang-ti 讓皇帝. Chu Yu-sung's one year reign, however, was not recognized by the Ch'ing regime which in September, 1736, gave Chu Yün-wen the title of Kung-min Hui 恭愍惠 huang-ti. Hence in the official Ming history he is referred to as Kung-min-ti, but in Wang Hung-hsü (ECCP), *Ming-shih kao* as Chien-wen ti.

His elder brother having died as a young child ten years earlier, Chu Yün-wen was designated the heir apparent at the age of fourteen, on September 28, 1392, over five months after the death of his father. For six years after this he underwent careful training for rulership at the hands of his grandfather, as had his father before him. The youth displayed some of the temperament of his father—bookishness, gentleness, and extreme devotion to the Confucian proprieties. The grandfather may have had some doubts about such a youth's ability to head a government that he himself felt could be made to function reliably only when an emperor ruthlessly intimidated his civil and military officials. The purge of officialdom conducted in 1393 when the Lan Yü (*q.v.*) conspiracy was suppressed, and which led to the execution or banishment of thousands of individuals having some connection with the officials implicated, may have been the founder's last effort to ensure obedience to his heir. By overdoing it, however, Chu Yüan-chang eliminated the very military leaders who, had they survived him, might have been able to give his heir the protection and security he needed.

Most of the facts concerning the period are at best elusive. The entire decade from Chu Piao's death through the usurpation presents unusual difficulties, for the planned distortion of the record in the following reign was thorough, and largely effective. That distortion accuses Chu Yün-wen and his advisers of flagrant profligacy and personal immorality as well as treasonous official actions in displacing the dynastic institutions. The campaign leading to the usurpation was therefore announced as an effort to "clear away the disasters, in response to Heaven's will," or feng-t'ien ching-nan 奉天靖難. To justify his insurrection against the Chien-wen reign, Chu Ti had to prove that only by such drastic action within the imperial family could the founder's will be upheld, and since an objective reading of the record could scarcely be expected to uphold that view, another had to be created. Thus a succession of official works, including the twice-revised Veritable Records of the Hung-wu reign and an official white paper called the *Feng-t'ien ching-nan chi* 記, systematically if inconsistently suppressed facts about the decade 1392–1402 and substituted counter versions. Since mid-Ming times historians have speculated about the inconsistencies and the lacunae, but recent scholars have made considerable strides in overcoming some of these. Yet still today an account which limited itself to the incontrovertible facts would be able to say very little. The following attempts to summarize both the substantiated facts and the areas of controversy about which historians continue their investigations and continue to produce varying interpretations.

What Chu Yüan-chang did was to depart somewhat from the tendencies developed in previous Chinese dynasties in that he gave the princedoms granted to his many sons real powers and responsibilities. These important princedoms were located at places of strategic significance for defense, mostly along the northern and northwestern frontier. Although technically the princes did not possess civil government authority, they controlled large garrisons and were encouraged to acquire military skills. The emperor expected them to defend the dynasty against all its enemies within and without, but especially against the Mongols who had only recently been driven out of China. When Chu Yün-wen ascended the throne (June 30, 1398), the founder's second and third sons, Chu Shuang, prince of Ch'in, and Chu Kang, prince of Chin (for both *see* Chu Yüan-chang), had already died, This left Chu Ti, enfoeffed prince of Yen at the former Yüan capital (then called Peiping), as the senior son. He also held the most important base and controlled the largest armed force of any of the nine older sons. Chu Ti, a man of intellect and cunning, had enlarged his armed forces and taken other liberties with the powers and privileges originally granted to him, and had developed an independent mode of acting. He was in many ways a more impressive figure than his young nephew, and possibly ambitious men began to urge him along the path toward rebellion. Chu Ti proved to be the sole example of a successful usurper by military means within a dynastic line during the last thousand years of Chinese imperial history (if we except the Mongol Yüan dynasty whose imperial line scarcely attempted to adopt Chinese modes and values).

Meanwhile Chu Yün-wen and his close advisers from the time of his succession obviously embarked on a policy of reducing the semi-autonomous power of the princes, his uncles (especially Chu Ti) and his cousins. This policy, called in Chinese hsiao fan 削藩 (reducing the feudatories), was the result of long deliberations. Two courses of action were considered, whether to abolish the princedoms outright or to reduce them to political and military irrelevance. The Chienwen court chose the former and afforded Chu Ti the excuse of taking up arms in self-defense (*see* Ch'i T'ai and Lien Tzuning). Had Chu Yün-wen and his advisers devoted their full attention to the war, victory might have been theirs. But they diverted their energy to the far from urgent task of re-vamping the governmental structure, perhaps aiming at a moderation of the excesses of centralization to conform to his ideals. The full extent of the changes and whether they would have led to fundamental reformation may never be known, but from the few evidences on record it seems they involved the elevation or reduction of some ranks and the substitution of archaic titles. In any case, Chu Ti asserted that such institutional modifications were against the dynastic founder's explicit instructions. This seems to have given his insurrection additional justification. When the war was over, one of his first edicts was to eliminate all the changes and restore the entire governmental organization to that of 1398 (*see* Fang Hsiao-ju).

The decision to reduce the princedoms usually is said to have been urged upon Chu Yün-wen by the principal adviser, Huang Tzu-ch'eng (*see* Lien Tzu-ning), who had been his tutor since his years as heir apparent. The founding emperor had appointed Huang in 1392 to guide the imperial heir's studies and, according to reports, in those years Chu Yün-wen had already discussed with Huang what a ruler should do if powerful princes were to rebel against the central authority. Huang is supposed to have offered the comforting analogy of the rebellion of the Seven Feudatories in the Former Han, which the Emperor Ching had suppressed in 154 B.C. On other occasions too the analysis of Chu Yün-wen's relations with his uncles was made in terms of the Han emperor's relationship with the enfeoffed scions of the Han imperial house, implying that they inevitably would be the

source of trouble, so that the state could and should eliminate them. The analogy is misleading, but is typical of the kind of bookish unreality which, according even to many of the sympathetic accounts, pervaded the advice of Huang and of Ch'i T'ai. One of Chu Yün-wen's first acts as emperor was to promote Ch'i T'ai to minister of War and Huang Tzu-ch'eng to chancellor of the Hanlin Academy. Simultaneously both were charged with the responsibility of participating in policy formulation; in effect, they greatly influenced the new emperor's government. They devoted their full energies primarily to the problem of the princedoms; and later Chu Ti named them the principal villains in the struggle between himself and the government.

To prevent a coalition among the princes under the leadership of Chu Ti, the court decided first to remove some of the other princes against whom clear-cut charges of misconduct were pending. In February, 1399, the prince of Tai, Chu Kuei (*see* Chu Yüan-chang), who was the most flagrantly guilty of many infractions of the regulations was stripped of his powers, declared a commoner, and put under house arrest in Tatung, his seat. In June, 1399, the prince of Hsiang, Chu Po (*see* Chu Yüan-chang), one of the more able sons of the founder, was summoned to the court to answer charges of having committed illegal and seditious acts. In rage and no doubt in fear that he would be unable to prove his innocence, he set fire to his palace at Ching-chou 荊州 (Hukuang), burning his family to death, and then rode his charger into the flames committing suicide. Six days later (June 7) the prince of Ch'i, Chu Fu (*see* Chu Yüan-chang), was called to the capital and charged with numerous crimes; he was stripped of all power and rank and held at Nanking under house arrest. In the following month (July 4) the prince of Min, Chu Pien(*see* Chu Su), was similarly treated, and ordered held under house arrest in Yunnan. A year earlier,

in August, 1398, Chu Su, the prince of
Chou with seat at Kaifeng (and Chu Ti's
younger brother, hence considered his
closest potential collaborator) had been
involved in accusation of treason coming
from within his own family; he had been
reduced to commoner status and held
under guard first in Yunnan and then at
Nanking. Therefore, by the summer of
1399, one year after Chu Yün-wen's accession, five of the senior and more strategically located of the princedoms had
been eliminated. Of the others, the prince
of Ch'in at Sian and the prince of Chin
at Taiyuan had died and their junior
heirs, under effective surveillance, were
considered to be safe. Chu Ti at Yen was
becoming isolated, and the court confidently deliberated on steps against him.
While some advised drastic action, Kao
Wei 高巍 (T. 不危, Pth. 忠毅, d. 1402)
in a memorial in December, 1398, suggested a policy of leniency and consideration: stripping the prince of his powers
gradually and peacefully. Chu Yün-wen is
reported to have held back Kao's memorial, unable to decide on the appropriate
response to it, and from this it has been
inferred that the decision to eliminate the
princedoms by force had already been
taken and that there was to be no
turning back. It is also possible on the
other hand that Chu Yün-wen had no
time for gradual solutions, for there is
some evidence that Chu Ti's advisers,
especially the ex-monk Yao Kuang-hsiao
(q.v.), had long been encouraging him
to think dangerous thoughts and had assisted him in seditious preparations. Rather
than an importunate young emperor in
Nanking too hastily provoking his uncles
to rebellion, the truth may be that Chu
Yün-wen came to the throne faced with
a well-developed plan of insurrection.
What may have delayed Chu Ti in part
was that his three sons were residing at
the Chien-wen court, potential hostages.
On his request, his sons were returned to
him in June, 1399. It was an act supposedly that could allay their father's suspi-

cions and lead him to believe that the
actions against the other princes were in
punishment for specific violations and not
part of a general plan to abolish all the
powers of all the princes; the result was
to remove from Chu Ti's mind the last
cause for hesitation. This particular act
has been judged by later historians as
one of Chu Yün-wen's serious errors, indicative of his humane and indecisive
personality.

Late in July, 1399, Ni Liang 倪諒, a
battalion commander in Chu Ti's guard
unit, observing evidence of sedition, seized
two of Chu Ti's trusted military subordinates, and took them to Nanking to be
executed. He also reported fully on suspicious affairs within the prince's household. On the basis of his evidence, charges
were under preparation to which Chu
Ti would be required to reply, but his
intelligence sources had kept him informed. Before the court could make a
public issue of the case against him, he
seized the psychological initiative, and on
August 5 proclaimed his resounding slogan:
"feng-t'ien ching-nan."

At the beginning of the civil war,
Chu Ti controlled only his own palace
and household precincts in Peiping; the
city, the prefecture, and the province
were administered by personnel appointed
by the court at Nanking. His first act was
to seize and execute the principal agents
of the emperor in the city, bringing it
and its immediate environs under control.
He quickly extended that control to the
important prefectures on all sides, and
soon was able to neutralize or incorporate the garrison forces of the princedom
of Ning, lying to his east, and the princedom of Chin to his west. He also appears
to have built up a basis for cooperation
that would at least prevent the Korean
kingdom, nominally subordinate to Nanking, from providing support to the emperor. And it is likely that he had been
cultivating Mongol chieftains (the great
enemy against whose threats he was supposed to be guarding the northern bor-

ders) so that they would not seize the opportunity to attack his rear and flank while he was engaged in civil war in the south. There is evidence that he even obtained or arranged for military assistance from some of them. Thus Chu Ti had secured the rear and the important flanks.

Chu Yün-wen, responding to the civil war from his capital, had the resources of the entire empire to utilize against a local rebellion. It has been customary to regard Huang Tzu-ch'eng and Ch'i T'ai as primarily responsible for the decisions and the strategy, until their dismissal from office in early 1400. They were eliminated in an effort to placate Chu Ti after a series of defeats in the north, but returned to office a few months later after some victories by the government's forces, and were then again dismissed (*see* Ch'i T'ai). It is probable that their dismissals were merely part of the public posturing and that even when out of office they continued to advise the emperor. They frequently disagreed between themselves, and with other leading officials, however, on policy, and we cannot fix the blame for the errors of judgment that the government committed over and over again. Chu Yün-wen is seen as a serious young emperor, armed with his sense of righteousness and bound by his extraordinary sense of Confucian propriety; he emerges as the restrained and the humane as well as she inept and vacillating victim of a determined enemy. He apparently was served by assistants, moreover, whose talent for governing was limited and who, in some cases, also were capable of treachery. Even their errors and their treachery, however, could have been overcome had the emperor himself played a forthright role, made decisions, and for example, taken to the field at the head of his armed forces. Instead, he seemed preoccupied with other matters during the early phases of the civil war, and incapable of prosecuting it with the clarity and vigor which its seriousness demanded,

while Chu Ti and his able sons personally led their forces in every engagement, Chu Yün-wen never visited the front, and spent his days pondering antique principles of ritual and of rulership. In the last year of the civil war Fang Hsiao-ju, who was his adviser in these civil matters, seems to have become his principal consultant on military policy as well.

Fang Hsiao-ju during the Hung-wu years came to be most highly regarded for scholarly acumen and uprightness of character. Chu Yün-wen knew this, and summoned him in 1398 to service in Nanking. Fang had already begun to think in terms of reform, based on the ancient classic, the *Chou-li*, and commenced putting forward certain proposals which attracted the young emperor as they were in line with his own ideals. Many features of the reform have earned the praise of historians. They included humane corrections of the mistakes made during Chu Yüan-chang's long reign; prisoners long held in custody from the campaigns early in that reign were at last released; taxes were remitted in many areas; the idea of exacting punitive taxation from areas that the founder had resented for their support of his early enemies was renounced in principle and tax schedules were altered accordingly. The emperor apparently was deeply concerned over the burdens borne by the people, and attempted to improve their lot. In his personal life and in the conduct of his court, he accepted conscientious criticism, and encouraged discussion and advice in ways quite unheard of in the previous reign. His appointments show that he energetically sought out worthy persons and advanced them in office and that he was attempting to inculcate a spirit in the executive arm of government that would be free of the terror which Chu Yüan-chang had consciously nourished there. It seems that the strong centralizing tendencies and the authoritarian character of the government were coming under critical review and, had the usurpation not occurred, they might have been weakened or reversed. Although the reduction of the princedoms in itself affirmed the principle of centralization, that may not be as contradictory to Fang Hsiao-ju's and the young emperor's ideals as it would seem, for the princedoms did not represent the kind of decentralization and local autonomy that their ideal system would have called for.

The military action in the civil war was concentrated initially within the immediate perimeter of the prince of Yen's territory; from August, 1399, until midsummer of 1401 the fighting was more or less confined to the area around Peiping and nearby strongholds such as Tsinan in Shantung. The court sent large armies northward, one after another, and these attempted to hold major garrison points along the Grand Canal route by which they were supplied, intending also thereby to block any southward movement of Chu Ti's armies (*see* Sheng Yung). Chu Ti's strategy was to fight a war of attrition, to inflict losses rather than to seize and hold territories. In 1401 he began to take the initiative, launching guerrilla-like raids on the Grand Canal supply route and destroying warehouse and transport facilities, thereby threatening the governments armies in the north. Chu Yün-wen and his advisers became quite concerned; they commenced recruitment of militia throughout the central provinces closer at hand to the capital, and began to build a strong defense line along the lower Huai 淮 River, a hundred miles north of the Yangtze. Chu Ti's drive to the south began in the spring of 1402; throughout he avoided major battles, skirted heavily garrisoned points, and depended heavily on subversion and pre-arranged surrenders. After the one major pitched battle of the entire southward drive, his somewhat fortuitous victory at Ling-pi (Anhwei) at the end of May 1402 (*see* Sheng Yung), he began in early June a lightninglike drive to the Yangtze across northwest Nan-Chihli. Yangchow was taken on June 17 without a fight, its garrison

surrendering under suspicious circumstances. The Yangtze was crossed near Chinkiang on July 3, Chinkiang entered on July 6, and the push to surround Nanking was completed within the next two or three days. Ch'i T'ai and Huang Tzu-ch'eng had been dismissed and sent to recruit militia in the provinces. When the capital was threatened by the first penetration below the Huai River defense line, Fang Hsiao-ju noted that massive walls could withstand siege, that within it were 200,000 troops and adequate stores of provisions. He predicted that the Yangtze barrier. in any event, would stop the rebel armies. An unanticipated surrender of naval forces with barges allowed Chu Ti an easy crossing. Then followed discussion about fleeing up-river to the central provinces where sentiment in favor of the emperor was strong, and where reserve military units could be called upon. Fang again advised the emperor incorrectly, urging him to remain in the capital, defying the siege until armies from nearby points in the provinces arrived to lift it, after which a counterattack could be made. The logic was sound, but again Fang failed to consider the possibility of treason. Nanking fell when some of its defenders opened the Chin-ch'uan Gate 金川門 to the enemy (*see* Ju Ch'ang).

In the melee that followed the entrance of Chu Ti's armies, the imperial palace enclosure within the city walls was set afire. The badly burned bodies of Chu Yün-wen's empress (daughter of Ma Ch'üan 馬全, married in 1395) and her eldest son were found in the rubble, and finally it was announced that the emperor's body also had been recovered. All were buried on July 20 with minimal rites appropriate to an imperial family. The tomb, located near that of the founder, was not identified or maintained as that of an emperor. On July 17, after having refused on three successive days, Chu Ti accepted the pleas of his court and ascended the throne. Ch'i T'ai, Huang Tzu-ch'eng, and other loyal ministers were rounded up and executed on July 25, as was Fang Hsiao-ju whom the new emperor first attempted to enlist into his service. These defiant loyalists were slaughtered together with all their relations and also their neighbors, teachers, students, servants, and even friends. The slaying of these equaled in ferocity any of the bloody purges of Chu Yüan-chang.

Chu Yün-wen's eldest son and heir apparent, named Chu Wen-k'uei 文奎, was born to the empress on November 30, 1396, and thus was not quite six years old at the time of his death. The second son, Chu Wen-kuei 圭 (or 垚), also a child of the empress, was born in December, 1401; he was imprisoned but finally released in 1457. He died shortly thereafter and is not known to have had any heirs.

Unofficially, and increasingly as time passed, many Ming scholars and common people came to believe that Chu Yün-wen had survived the tragic events of 1402, and that his sons and grandsons flourished thereafter, in widely varying identities. Although Chu Ti reigned ably and advanced the fortunes of the dynasty, Chu Yün-wen in retrospect was readily turned into an unusually attractive ruler, and one who had suffered a vast injustice. His place in history grew far larger than his unsuccessful efforts during a brief reign would seem to justify; the legendary Chien-wen emperor became a far larger figure than the historical one. The development of the legend reveals much about the nature of Chinese civilization and the workings of its popular culture. The Yung-lo emperor had to acquire legitimacy in the eyes of his officialdom and in the eyes of his people at large, in order to make his reign secure. He could not do that by fiat. He could intimidate people who tried to resist but he also had to win cooperation through persuasion. He could suppress facts, but he also had to present an acceptable record of personal virtue in order to gain acceptance. He could encourage slanderous insinuation about his nephew, but he also

had to maintai a ncertain amount of credibility with a critical audience. In short, the more systematic the attempt to present a legitimizing account of the usurpation, the more the people, both elite and commoners, nurtured their counter legends. The greater the attempt to destroy historical records, the more the fragments of the original record, or items purporting to be part of that record, acquired value and drew interest. Apparently the Nanking court in 1645 followed the popular belief in this legend when it conferred on Chu Yün-wen the afore-mentioned title Jang huang-ti (the abdicated emperor). Chao Shih-che 趙士喆, a scholar writing in the middle of the 17th century, compiled a relatively sober *Chien-wen nien-p'u* 年譜 (Chronological biography of Chienwen), *2 ch.*, the second and longer of which argues for the historicity of the events it records for Chu Yün-wen's life between 1402 and 1440. Ch'ien Ch'ien-i (ECCP) in a preface dated 1658 praises it as a serious attempt to draw together and evaluate the more reliable traditions concerning these years in the former emperor's life. While Ch'ien Ch'ien-i does not necessarily accept all of the data included in the *nien-p'u*, he expresses the opinion that the true measure of Chu Yün-wen's character is seen in his acceptance of the usurpation, and his willingness to "abdicate" in the interests of dynastic stability; he implies that the Yung-lo emperor became aware of this intent near the end of his life, after long years of searching for the fugitive at home and abroad, and died accepting it. The modern historian Meng Sen (BDRC) applauds Ch'ien for his perceptive insight, and apparently accepts the same view. But many other historians repudiate the idea of Chu Yünwen's supposed existence after 1402, and prefer to believe that there is no single item of evidence for his survival, even though they recognize that Chu Ti apparently could find no unambiguous evidence for his death. [Editors' note: The author in his original biography wrote at some length on the course the legend about the Chien-wen emperor took in ensuing centuries; this we found necessary to curtail.]

One of the arguments that Chu Yün-wen's life actually did come to an end in 1402 is based on an entry in the *Ying-tsung shih-lu,* under date of December 12, 1440 (given also in *Kuo-ch'üeh* with commentary). It records the arrival in Kwangsi from Yunnan of a monk of ninety-some years, who asserted that he was the Chien-wen emperor. The local official dispatched him to Peking, where, upon interrogation, he confessed that his real name was Yang Hsing-hsiang 楊行祥 (or Yang Ying 應 -hsiang), a native of Chün-chou 鈞州, Honan, who became a monk in 1384. He was put in prison where he died four months later. It may well be that a garbled account of this unhappy imposter gave rise to the vast legend that developed not only about Chu Yün-wen, but also about his sons and officials loyal to him, from this time on. Wang Ch'ung-wu(*see* Ch'ang Yü-ch'un) has written in conclusion to his exhaustive study of all the elements of the Hui-ti legend:

"To summarize, the Hui-ti story intrinsically is one of such tragedy that it was diffused broadly everywhere and made a profound impact on men's hearts. The legend grew from simplicity to complexity, from vagueness to explicitness, from the account of his recurrent sufferings and humiliations to one of his repeated revenge. More than two hundred years later the chieftain of the roaming bandits, Li Tzu-ch'eng, could still make effective use of the legend to promote his own rebellion. Ming loyalists in the early Ch'ing period such as Li Ch'ing (ECCP) and Chang I 張怡 (1608-95) stoutly believed that the fall of the dynasty was the ultimate working out of Hui-ti's revenge. Still today in the remote border regions of the nation there are persons who claim to be Hui-ti's descendants. Moreover, all of those officials who remained steadfastly loyal and died with

their emperor had sons and grandsons who acquired fame and honor, while on the contrary the Emperor Ch'eng-tsu(Chu Ti) and his officials all suffered eventual humiliation and disgrace. Although the legend bears no relation to historical fact, the manner of its gradual growth and development displays sense of righteousness and the sympathies that existed among the people and which gave the legend its enduring qualities."

That provides an appropriate evaluation of the legend itself as an aspect of Ming history; no facts about Chu Yün-wen after July 13, 1402, exist at present, and modern historians must form their own opinions about the intriguing puzzle of whether he survived.

Bibliography

1/ch. 4, 116-118, 141-144; 63/ch.5-7; MSL(1962), T'ai-tsu, 1892, 3233, 3520, T'ai-tsung (1963), 0126, 0129, 0135, 0140, Ying-tsung (1964), 1419; KC (1958), ch. 11-12, 1597; Tu Shu-fang, *Chien-wen chao-yeh hui-pien* 建文朝野彙編 (NCL microfilm), ch. 1; Chu Lu, *Chien-wen shu-fa ni*; Li Chin-hua 李晉華, "Ming I-wen t'ai-tzu sheng-mu k'ao" 明懿文太子生母考 and "Ming Ch'eng-tsu sheng-mu wen-t'i hui-cheng" 明成祖生母問題彙證 in CYYY, VI/1 (1936), 45, 55; Meng Sen, *Ming-tai shih* (posthumous publ., 1957); Wu Han 吳晗, *Chu Yüan-chang chuan* 朱元璋傳, 1948; Wang Ch'ung-wu, *Ming ching-nan shih-shih k'ao-cheng kao* 明靖難史事考證稿, 1948; *id.*, *Feng-t'ien ching-nan chi chu* 記注, 1948; Huang Chang-chien 黃彰健, "Ta Ming lü kao k'ao" 大明律詁考 in CYYY, XIV (1953); Wu Ch'i-hua 吳緝華, "Ming-tai Chien-wen-ti tsai ch'uan-t'ung huang-wei shang ti wen-t'i" 在傳統皇位上的問題, *Ta-lu tsa-chih*, XIX: 1 (1959), 14; Ch'en Wan-nai 陳萬鼐, Ming Hui-ti ch'u-wang k'ao-cheng 出亡考證, Taipei, 1960; David Chan, "The Problem of the Princes as Faced by the Ming Emperor Hui (1398-1402)," *Oriens*, XI: 1-2 (1958), 183; Susuki Tadashi 鈴木正, "Ken-bun-tai shatsu-bō zei kōshō" 建文帝出亡說考證, *Shikan* 史觀, Vol. 65: 6-7 (October, 1962), 160, Vol. 68 (May, 1963), 50; L. S. Yang, "Ming Local Administration," in C. O. Hucker, ed., *Chinese Government in Ming Times* (1969), 1; Wolfgang Franke, *Sources*, 15.

F. W. Mote

CHÜ Chieh 居節 (T. 士貞, 貞士, H. 商谷), fl. 1531-85, was a native of Soochow, and one of the better-known followers of Wen Cheng-ming (*q.v.*), the acknowledged leader of the Wu school of painting during the first half cf the 16th century. Chü is said to have studied originally with one of Wen's sons; his handling of the brush so impressed Wen Cheng-ming that he agreed to accept the young man as his own student. While Ch'ien Ku (*q.v.*), another student of Wen, is reported to have achieved the master's massiveness, Chü Chieh is said to have acquired his elegance. Apparently Chü Chieh maintained a close relationship with several generations of the Wen family. Many of his paintings are inscribed byWen Cheng-ming and his sons, Wen Chia and Wen P'eng (*see* Wen Cheng-ming). The latter's son, Wen Chao-chih 文肇祉 (T. 基聖, H. 鴈峯, 1519-87), inscribed poems on some landscapes by Chü Chieh as late as 1583. Chü excelled in painting landscapes, his work being characterized by relatively simple compositions executed in ink on paper. Small areas of precisely delineated foliage or mountain rocks accentuate larger areas of light washes or blank paper. The one portrait recorded among his paintings is of the patriot Yang Chi-sheng (*q.v.*) executed in the spring of 1551; in the autumn of the following year, Yang himself added an inscription. In addition to his paintings in private collections, examples of Chü's work are in the National Palace Museum, Taiwan; the Museum for Far Eastern Antiquities, Stockholm; and the Metropolitan Museum of Art, New York. Chü is also mentioned occasionally as a poet. Examples of his verse are found in his inscriptions on his own paintings; they record the visits of friends or the passage of the seasons; they also make frequent reference to his being in poor health. Ch'ien Ch'ien-i (ECCP) includes sixty-seven of Chü's poems in his *Lieh-ch'ao shih-chi*. Apparently Chü Chieh's collection of poetry, entitled *Mu-shih chi* 牧豕集 (The swineherd's collection), has never been published.

According to Ch'ien Ch'ien-i, Chü Chieh's family was at one time connected with the imperial textile factory in Soochow, one of the three located in Nanking, Soochow, and Hangchow, which furnished silk for the government and the imperial household. When Sun Lung 孫隆 (d. July 2, 1601), reportedly the eunuch in charge of the Soochow factory, heard of Chü Chieh's reputation, he summoned the young artist to appear before him. On Chü's refusal to obey, Sun Lung was so furious that he tried to ruin the Chü family. Chü then went to live on scenic Hu-ch'iu 虎丘 Mountain, located northwest of Soochow. According to inscriptions on his paintings, Chü often entertained friends at his cottage there. The name of his studio, Hsing-yen chai 星硯齋, is mentioned in inscriptions dated as early as 1537.

The exact dates of Chü's birth and death are unknown. While he is said to have died at 59 or 60 *sui*, his recorded dated works span the relatively long period from 1531 to 1585. Chü Chieh's son Chü Mou-shih 懋時, also a painter, continued the Wen family tradition into the early years of the 17th century.

Bibliography

2/396/21b; 22/12/16a; 24/3/77a; 40/50/2b; 64/己17/13a; 65/4/2b; 84/丁中/11b; 86/14/35a; TSCC (1885–88), XVII: 786/20/9b; Ch'en Jen-t'ao 陳仁濤, *Ku-kung i-i shu-hua mu chiao-chu* 故宮已佚書畫目校注, 22b; John C. Ferguson, *Index of Artists* (Nanking, 1934), 173b; Osvald Sirén, *Chinese Painting*, Vol. VII (London, 1958), 184; Aschwin Lippe, "The Waterfall," *Metropolitan Museum of Art Bulletin*, Vol. XII, no. 3 (November, 1953), 60.

Thomas Lawton

CH'Ü Yu 瞿祐 (or 祐, T. 宗吉, H. 存齋), August 20, 1347-1433, poet, story-writer, and literary critic, was a native of Hangchow. He came from a scholarly family and had a great-uncle, Ch'ü Shih-heng 士

衡, who passed the provincial examination in 1359 and who was a close friend of the poet Yang Wei-chen (*q.v.*). Yang and other scholars praised Ch'ü for his ability to compose poems. In the civil war that ravaged the Hangchow area during the last years of the Yüan, he and his family sought refuge in other cities, one of which was Yin-hsien (Ningpo). Close to the end of the Hung-wu period, probably about 1390, Ch'ü, who had won a reputation as a poet and a student of the Classic, *Spring and Autumn Annals*, was appointed supervisor of a district school, in which capacity he served in Jen-ho 仁和 and Lin-an 臨安 in Chekiang and in I-yang 宜陽 in Honan. In 1400 the court recalled him to Nanking and appointed him to the rank of instructor in the National University. In 1403 he joined the staff of Chu Su (*q.v.*), prince of Chou, as administrator. This prince was himself a literary figure and a patron of writers. In 1408 Ch'ü for some unknown reason, perhaps because of an offensive poem as one source suggests, was incarcerated in the prison of the Embroidered -uniform Guard of the capital where several other literati were serving their sentences, among them the Buddhist monk Ju-lan 如蘭 (T. 古春). Finally Ch'ü was deprived of his official rank and banished to the frontier garrison of Pao-an 保安, about one hundred miles northwest of Peking. In 1425 he was pardoned through the initiative of the famous general Chang Fu (*q.v.*). After serving as teacher in Chang's family school for a while he was permitted to return to Hangchow where he died.

Ch'ü is chiefly remembered as the author of a collection of short stories in the literary language, the *Chien-teng hsin-hua* 剪燈新話 (New tales of wick-trimming hours). In the 1378 preface to the *Chien-teng hsin-hua* he writes that sometime before this he had completed a collection of notes and stories in 40 *chüan* under the tititle *Chien-teng lu* 錄 (Tales of wick-trimming hours). Seeing his interest in such

matters, his friends then supplied him with anecdotes of recent years which he wrote up and included in these "new tales." The *Chien-teng lu*, never printed, is presumably lost. The first printed edition of the *Chien-teng hsin-hua*, containing twenty stories in 4 *chüan*, was published towards the end of the Yung-lo period by a nephew of the writer, Ch'ü Hsien 暹. Another known Ming edition belongs to the Wan-li period. From the 17th century on, the *Chien-teng hsin-hua* gradually fell into oblivion although individual stories from the collection were reprinted here and there and some even incorporated in the encyclopedia *T'u-shu chi-ch'eng*. But the impression of the stories on Ch'ü's contemporaries must have been considerable because even during the author's lifetime and probably prior to the printed Yung-lo edition, an imitation was written, i. e., *Chien-teng yü-hua* (Additional tales of wick-trimming hours) by Li Ch'ang-ch'i (*q.v.*). It is easy to see why these stories were successful among the educated readers of the early Ming period. They are written in a fluent and graceful prose modeled on the language of the T'ang novelists and contain much subtle lyric poetry. Their subject matter is varied— they tell of ghosts, supernatural events, and romances. An additional attraction for the readers must have been that they are without exception set in an almost contemporary environment and frequently mention historical events and persons of the 14th century. Not a few contain social criticism directed against corrupt officials, usually in the form of retribution in the afterlife. Also their geographical and social background is briefly but concisely outlined with a high degree of realism. Several tales were later adapted for the stage, e. g., no. 15 (*Ts'ui-ts'ui chuan* 翠翠傳) by Yeh Hsien-tsu (*q.v.*) in his play *Han-i chi*, and by the seventeenth-century playwright Yüan Sheng 袁聲 in his *Ling-t'ou shu* 領頭書. Apart from Li Ch'ang-ch'i's collection of similar stories, another comparable cluster was published as late as *ca.* 1600, namely, Shao Ching-chan's 邵景詹 *Mi-teng yin-hua* 覓燈因話 (Imitation tales of light searching hours), containing eight tales in 2 *chüan*. A profusely annotated edition of all three collections, under the title *Chien-teng hsin-hua*, edited by Chou I 周夷, was published in 1957 in Shanghai.

The popularity of Ch'ü's short stories must indeed have been great because the work was prohibited in 1442 after a memorial had been presented by Li Shih-mien (*q.v.*). Li complained that scholars. instead of studying the Confucian Classics, preferred lighter reading such as the *Chien-teng hsin-hua* and were led astray by the unorthodox ideas of this and other similar works. Apart from adaptations for the stage some stories have also been used by later writers. Ling Meng-ch'u (*q.v.*) rewrote three from the *Chien-teng hsin-hua* in colloquial language in his *P'ai-an ching-ch'i* 拍案驚奇.

The influence of the *Chien-teng hsin-hua* in Korea and Japan was more pronounced than it was in China. Even during the 15*th* century the Korean poet, Kim Si-sŭp 金時習 (1435-93), wrote a series of short stories in imitation of the collection, entitled *Kum-o sin-hua* 金鰲新話, and several reprints of the original text of the Chien-teng corpus followed during the 16th century. Ch'ü's tales were also reprinted, translated, and imitated in Japan. The first partial translations appeared in the Tembun period (1532-55) when Nakamura 中村, prefect of the Bungo 豐後 province, translated several and incorporated them in his *Kiizatsudanshū* 奇異雜談集. Japanese writers of the early and middle Tokugawa period frequently adapted the plots of the *Chien-teng hsin-hua*, setting them in a Japanese environment. This was done, for example, by Asai Ryōi 淺井了意 (d. 1691) in his *Otogibōko* 伽婢子 (published 1666) and by Ueda Akinari 上田秋成 (1734-1809) in his famous *Ugetsu-monogatāri* 雨月物語. Western sinologists have only quite recently begun to pay attention to Ch'ü Yu and his fiction, and there is no complete translation available.

Apart from these stories on which his fame chiefly rests, Ch'ü Yu wrote a great number of works on a broad variety of subjects, ranging from the Confucian Classics to domino games, family handbooks, and divination. His own poetry was considered by some critics as somewhat feminine and too much under the influence of the romanticism of Yang Wei-chen. His collected poems, *Ts'un-chai shih-chi* 存齋詩集, seem to be lost but the specimens preserved in various Ming and Ch'ing anthologies allow us to form at least a general impression. Ch'ü was a friend of several minor poets of the late 14th century who, like himself, belonged to the Yang Wei-chen school, and amongst whom one at least should be mentioned, Ling Yün-han 淩雲翰 (T. 彥狲, cj 1359), who also wrote a preface to the *Chien-teng hsin-hua*. Much anecdotal material on contemporary poets is to be found in Ch'ü's *Kuei-t'ien shih-hua* 歸田詩話 in 3 *chüan* (preface dated 1425) which was first printed in 1466 and reprinted in the *Chih-pu-tsu chai ts'ung-shu* (*see* Pao T'ing-po, ECCP). Although the editors of the imperial *Ssu-k'u* catalogue (which does not mention Ch'ü's stories) have merely listed the *Kuei-t'ien shih-hua*, this work must be regarded as a valuable source for early Ming ideas on contemporary and ancient poetry.

Bibliography

Ting Ping (ECCP), "T'i-pa" 題跋, 28, quoted in *Kiangsu Kuo-hsüeh t'u-shu kuan* 江蘇國學圖書館, 4 (Nanking, 1931); 1/285/17a; 22/2/29a; 32/42/3a; 40/19 上 /la; 43/1/7a; 64/ 乙 13/1a; *Lieh-ch'ao shih-chi* (*see* Ch'ien Ch'ien-i, ECCP) 乙 5/1a; Lang Ying 郎英, *Chi-hsiu lei-kao* 七修類稿 (Shanghai, 1959), 503; T'ien Ju-ch'eng, *Hsi-hu yu-lan chih-yü* 西湖遊覽志餘 (*Wu-lin chang-ku ts'ung-pien ed.*), 12/18a; Lu Hsün 魯迅, *Hsiao-shuo chiu-wen ch'ao* 小說舊聞鈔 (Peking, 1953), 48-50; Sawada Yoshio 澤田瑞雄, "Sentō Shinwa no hakusai nendai" 剪燈新話の舶載年代, *Chūkoku Bungaku* 中國文學 35 (1938), 186-88; Kubo Tenzui 久保天隨 and Hayakawa Kōsaburō 早川光三郎, "Sentō Shinwa to Toyo Kindai Bungaku no oyoboseru

Eikyō" 剪燈新話ト東洋 近代文學ニ及ボセル影響, *Kangakkai Zasshi* 漢學會雜誌, 3/2, 168; *Bungakka Kenkyū Nenpō* 文學科研究年報 1, 1 (1935), 139; Herbert Franke, "Eine Novellensammlung der frühen Ming-Zeit: Das *Chien-teng hsin-hua* des Ch'ü Yu," ZDMG, 108 (1958), 338-82; W. Bauer and H. Franke, *The Golden Casket*, tr. by C. Levenson (New York, 1964), 219-63.

Herbert Franke

CHUNG Hsing 鍾惺 (T. 伯敬, H. 退谷, and 晚知居士), August 13, 1574-August 4, 1624, poet, and anthologist, was born in Ching-ling 景陵, Hukuang. After twelve years of unsuccessful attempts, following his graduation as *hsiu-ts'ai*, he obtained the *chü-jen* in 1603 and the *chin-shih* in 1610. He then became for eight years a member of the messenger office in the ministry of Rites, during which the court dispatched him to Szechwan and Shantung, and ordered him to preside over the provincial examination in Kweichow (1615). In the next four years he served successively as secretary of a bureau in the ministry of Works in Peking, secretary of the bureau of sacrifices, and then director of the bureau of ceremonies in the ministry of Rites in Nanking, and education intendant in Fukien. The death of his adoptive father (his father's elder brother) necessitated his return to his native place, where after observing the full period of mourning he also died. His remains were laid to rest three years later (November 25, 1627) in a tomb situated northeast of the *hsien* city. His biographers record that in appearance he was thin and ugly, in demeanor severe and austere, intolerant of ordinary people but eager to discover men of talent, recommending them to office without their knowledge. He also enjoyed traveling to famous mountains, lakes, and rivers, and went far to see and explore them, putting up in temples overnight. The achievement that brought him lasting fame was in literary criticism. During 1614 and 1615 he and T'an Yüan-ch'un (*q.v.*), a fellow townsman much his junior, jointly edited the anthologies, *Ku-shih kuei* 古詩歸 (Ancient poetry at culmination), 15 *ch.*, and *T'ang* 唐-*shih kuei*, 36 *ch.*, both printed in 1617. They were immediately acclaimed as the leaders of the Ching-ling 竟陵 (ancient name of their native place) school. In advocating the imitation of the true spirit in masterpieces of the past, they were not far removed from their earlier contemporaries, the Yüan brothers of Kung-an (*see* Yüan Hung-tao). Yet Chung and T'an considered the followers of the Kung-an school as ignoring refinement in style (li 俚) and using obscure expressions (p'i 僻), while they themselves were criticized also on these two points by a junior contemporary, Ch'ien Ch'ien-i (ECCP). They did succeed, however, in attracting a sizeable number of followers during the decades of the Ming dynasty. Some time after the fall of the dynasty there appeared an anthology of Ming poets, the *Ming-shih kuei*, 10 + 2 *chüan*, attributed to their editorship but obviously the work of someone else. This was pointed out by Ku Yen-wu (ECCP) as quoted in the *Ssu-k'u* catalogue. It was listed for suppression in the 18th century.

Some of Chung's own effusions are included in his volume of poetry and essays entitled *Yin-hsiu-hsüan chi* 隱秀軒集, 33 *ch.*, printed by means of woodblocks in 1622 and reprinted with movable type in 1936 as *Chung Po-ching ho* 合-*chi*. This too the Ch'ien-lung commissioners condemned, possibly because of an assertion in one poem that the Ming emperor was ambitious to "gobble up the barbarians." Chung made anthologies of literary pieces as well: essays dating from the Chou, the Han, the Sung, including the three Su (Su Hsün, Su Shih, and Su Ch'e), and some from his own time.

While stationed in Nanking, Chung rented a house on the bank of the Ch'in-huai 秦淮 River where he studied historical works far into the night, recording whatever critical thoughts came to his mind. This resulted in a book entitled *Shih-huai* 史懷, 17 or 20 *ch.*, published by a friend after his death, and reprinted 1891 and 1939. Other historical works attributed to Chung but of doubtful authorship include the *Ming-chi pien-nien* 明紀編年, an annalistic work in 10 *chüan*, printed in1660, the *Ming t'ung-chi tsuan* 明通紀纂, also in 10 *chüan*, printed probably in the Ch'ung-chen period, the *Chieh-lu ta-ch'üan* 捷錄大全, 4 *ch*., containing a number of items dating from the beginning of the Ming to the T'ien-ch'i period, and a more general work on Chinese history, entitled *T'ung-chien* 通鑑 *tsuan*, 20 *ch*. He is said likewise to have edited the *Tzu-chih* 資治 *t'ung-chien cheng-shih ta-ch'üan* 正史大全, 74 *ch*. These works, probably all produced by unscrupulous publishers, came to be listed on the *Index Expurgatorius* of the Ch'ien-lung era, but copies have survived. Of the same category may be listed several works on the Classics such as *Wu-ching tsuan-chu* 五經纂註, 5 *ch*., *Shih-ching t'u-shih ho-k'ao* 詩經圖史合考, 20 *ch*., *Mao-shih chieh* 毛詩解, and the *Chung p'ing Tso-chuan* 鍾評左傳, 30 *ch*. The *Shih-ching*, 4+1 *ch*., printed in 1620, a work on the Odes with commentary, is possibly the only one from Chung's own hand. Perhaps the most interesting of such spurious publications is the *Ju-mien-t'an* 如面譚, 16 *ch*., a book on letter writing, touching on a wide variety of subjects, which reflect Chinese life and society in the mid-seventeenth century. This book too fell under the ban, but the National Library of Peking and the Columbia University library both have copies published at the end of the Ming.

In his late forties, Chung turned to Buddhism, and studied the *Śūraṅgama sūtra* in earnest. From this came his commentary *Leng-yen ju-shuo* 楞嚴如說, 10 *ch*. There are even some landscape paintings accredited to him. The *Ssu-k'u* catalogue listed eleven of his works, three of which are adjudged spurious, namely, *Wu-ching tsuan-chu*, *Ming shih kuei*, and an anthology of poems by women, *Ming-yüan* 名媛 *shih-kuei*, 36 *ch*. Most of the remaining works, however, should be further exam-ined before they can be accepted as from Chung's personal editorship. It seems that from 1616 to 1621 Chung edited a few collections of "eight legged" essays for the examination hall trade and his popu-larity in that respect and in the field of poetry writing induced some unscrupulous publishers to capitalize on his name.

Bibliography

1/288/13b; 3/269/10a; 24/4/14a; 40/60/12a; 64/ 庚 5/10b; 84/丁中 /88a; 86/17/8a; TSCC (1885–88), XVII: 788/22/1a, XXIII: 108/96/12b; *Chung Po-ching ho-chi* (1936), 43; Chuang Ch'i-ch'uan's 莊啓傳 preface in Chang 編 (1933); *Ssu-k'u Hsiang* 張相, *Ming wen-tsai chien-pien* 明文在簡 (1930), 17/5a, 30/7b, 90/3b, 134/3b, 193/6a; Hsü Pang-ta 徐邦達, *Li-tai liu-ch'uan shu-hua tso-p'in pien-nien-piao* 歷代流傳書畫作品編年表 (Shanghai, 1963), 117; *Hupei t'ung-chih* (1934), 92, 664, 3089, 3096, 3756; *Ming-shih i-wen-chih* (1959), 89, 114, 120, 580, 589, 592, 625, 676, 771; L. of C. *Catalogue* (1957), 12, 13, 144, 868, 992, 1061, 1100, 1119; Sun Tien-ch'i (1957), 49, 103, 125, 133, 146, 149, 178, 234, 236; Kuo Shao-yü, *Chung-kuo wen-hsüeh p'i-p'ing chih* (1961), 363; Sun K'ai-ti 孫楷第, *Chung-kuo t'ung-su hsiao-shuo shu-mu* 中國通俗小說書目 (1957), 23.

L. Carrington Goodrich and C. N. Tay

COCCHI, Angelo (Kao 高), 1597–November 18, 1633, missionary to China, was born in Florence, Italy, became a Dominican at Fiesole on November 30, 1610, and professed his vows there on May 24, 1613. He studied theology at Salamanca where he became a deacon, and in 1620 left Cádiz with Juan Bautista de Morales (*q.v.*) for Mexico. Cocchi and Morales were ordained priests there, and on March 25, 1621, left Acapulco for Manila, arriving in the middle of 1622.

Cocchi was successively assigned to Abucay (1625), to Cavite (1627) where he was directed to learn the "Chincheo" lan-guage, and then to Tan-shui 淡水, Taiwan, where he became vicar in 1628. At the request of the governor of the Philippines, who wanted to establish good commercial relations with China, Cocchi was sent as envoy to the governor of Fukien, then Hsiung Wen-ts'an (*q.v.*). He left Tan-shui for the mainland at the end of December, 1631, on a boat carrying pirates in disguise. His companion, Tomás Sierra, was slain and the boat sunk, the intent being to drown all the passengers, but Cocchi managed to survive and on January 2, 1632, landed at Ch'üan-chou 泉州, Fukien. He was taken to the garrison commander of Fu-ning 福寧, who treated him kindly, and sent him to the governor at Foochow. As Cocchi had lost his credentials in the encounter with the pirates, the governor refused to recognize him as an envoy; he did, however, have the pirates apprehended and severely punished in spite of Cocchi's plea for mercy, and then ordered Cocchi to leave the country. He managed to remain until June, and then eluded the authorities by sending out a Christian Japanese dressed in his garb; he proceeded to Fu-an 福安, Fu-ning prefecture, in a sedan chair. There he was welcomed by ten scholars who had been converted by the Jesuits (*see* Giulio Aleni), and he used the studio of one of them as a meeting place.

It was soon evident to Cocchi that the scholars reflected the attitude of the Jesuits and did not sufficiently stress the doctrine favored by the Dominicans. He concentrated on this and with the help of these scholars obtained a number of conversions, and established the first Dominican mission and church in China, and later another church at Ting-t'ou 頂頭, in the same prefecture. He then appealed for help, and Morales, accompanied by a Franciscan, Antonio Caballero (*q. v.*), joined him at Fu-an in July, 1633, where they resumed the study of the Chinese language. In September Cocchi informed the Jesuit, Bento de Matos (1600–52) of their presence in China and asked for his cooperation toward a common goal. Matos replied that they should have come by way of Macao in order to obtain the permission of the bishop, or of the Jesuit vice-provincial, in compliance with Portu-

guese patronage. The vice-provincial, Manuel Dias (*q. v.*), was, however, displeased with their intrusion and, fearful of a clash of methods, was uncooperative.

In November Cocchi met an untimely death; among his effects were some interesting mission reports. Morales and Caballero carried on his work at Ting-t'ou.

Bibliography

José Maria González, *Historia de las Missiones Dominicanas de China 1632–1700*, Vol. I (Madrid, 1964), 71, 233, 634, 681, 686; K. S. Latourette, *A History of Christian Missions in China* (New York, 1929), 108; Antonio Sisto Rosso, *Apostolic Legations to China in the Eighteenth Century* (South Pasadena, 1948), 104.

Antonio Sisto Rosso

CRUZ, Gaspar da, *c a.* 1520, February 5, 1570, a native of Évora, east of Lisbon, arrived in China in 1556, and became the author of the first complete book on China of the Ming dynasty, published in Europe. Virtually nothing is known of his origins or his education. He entered the Order of St. Dominic at the convent of Azeitão (year unknown), and in 1548 sailed for Goa, along with eleven other Dominican friars, led by the Vicar General Diogo Bermudes. During the next four years his missionary labors carried him to the west coast of India (where he established convents in Goa, Chaul, and Cochin), Malacca (where he founded a convent), and Cambodia (where, in 1555, his hope of converting the king proved unsuccessful). Finding a Chinese vessel in the harbor, and the Chinese sailors amenable, he was permitted to take ship to Canton.

Within a month after his arrival, signs appeared in the streets of Canton prohibiting the inhabitants, on pain of heavy punishment, from having any dealings with the Portuguese. In spite of this warning, Cruz was so carried away by the sight in a temple of images that he tumbled them to the ground. Aroused by this act of vandalism, the onlookers protested, but, on hearing his reasons for the act (one wonders what the language of communication was), they let him go unharmed. Finding himself unwelcome everywhere, he left China after less than a year, and sailed to Ormuz. (It was this same year, according to Cruz's own report, that Leonel de Sousa (*q. v.*) was negotiating successfully with certain Chinese for permission for Portuguese merchants to land and trade at the island of Lang-po-kao, near Ao-men[Macao].)

At Ormuz Cruz continued his missionary endeavors, and founded a religious house. In 1569, after his return to Portugal, King Sebastian (r. 1557-78) offered him the bishopric of Malacca, but he declined the honor. At this particular juncture, a serious epidemic was raging. He and fellow friars labored day and night to help the afflicted. Cruz finally succumbed to the disease, and died in Setúbal (south of Lisbon) early the following year, aged about fifty. His remains were taken to the convent of Azeitão, where he became the object of veneration. Gaspar da Cruz was the author of *Tractado em que se cotam muito por esteso as cousas da China, co suas particularidades e assi dormuz cõposto pozel.... Dirigido ao muito poderoso Rey dom Sebastiam nosso señor. Impresso com licença, 1569.* (We are beholden to C. R. Boxer for a complete English translation, with introduction and explanatory footnotes, of this important work.) It was published in Évora just a few days after the author's death, February 20, 1570, according to a notice at the end of the book (and republished in 1829 and 1937). There are twenty-nine chapters in all. They deal with almost every aspect of the China of his day: its name, geographical setting, the number of provinces, the city of Canton, its architecture, the princes and the official class, shipping, occupations of the people, including farmers, craftsmen, and merchants, the clothing and customs of both men and women,

their feasts, music, burials, the education of the elite, their writing, provisions for the bureaucracy, their methods of dealing out justice, the emperor together with his harem and eunuchs, the experiences of Portuguese merchants, the religious practices of the people, Muslims in China, and the difficulty of propagating Christianity. The book concludes with an account of certain natural calamities that befell China in 1555 and 1556; the author regards them as a judgment from God. An appendix, which may not be from the hand of the author, deals with the kings of Ormuz.

The work is not without its mistakes, but it is astonishing how much useful data it does include, considering the length of time Cruz spent in the country. It is written with verve. He acknowledges his indebtedness to Galiote Pereira, whose account in Portuguese is dated 1561, and published in Italian in abridged form in Venice in 1565. He made contributions of his own, however. Boxer writes *inter alia*: Gaspar da Cruz "adds much information ···about Chinese social life which clearly fascinated him···He is the first recorded (and for a long time the only) European to appreciate Chinese music, and he found Chinese practices in husbandry and navigation superior to those in Europe··· It might, perhaps, be going too far to claim that Gaspar da Cruz made better use of his few weeks' stay in Canton than did Marco Polo of all the years he spent in Cathay; but there can be no doubt that the Portuguese friar gives us a better and clearer account of China as he saw it than did the more famous Italian traveller."

Bibliography

Luis Cacegas, *Historia de S. Domingos particular do Reino, e Conquitas de Portugal*, revised and enlarged by Luis de Sousa (4 vols., Lisbon, 1767), v. 3, bk. 4, chap. 8, bk. 6, chap. 9; Diogo Barbosa Machado, *Bibliotheca Lusitana Histórica, Critica e Cronológico* (Coimbra, 1966, reprint of Lisbon ed. of 1747), II, 347; *Dicionário de*

História de Portugal (Lisbon, 1971), I, 754; Artur Basilio de Sa, compiler and annotator, *Insulindia*, Vol. 2 (1550–62), 178; C. R. Boxer, *South China in the Sixteenth Century* (London, 1953), 1viii, 44.

Albert Chan and L. Carrington Goodrich

DAYAN-Qaɣan, *see* **BATU Möngke**

dGE-'DUN-GRUB, 1391–January 1475, posthumously reckoned as the first Dalai-lama of Tibet, was born on a small farm in the Srad valley not far from Sa-skya in southern Tibet. At an early age he became a pupil of the great reformer Tsong-kha-pa (*q. v.*), a distant relative. After the death of the latter, dGe-'dun-grub became the head of the new dGe-lugs-pa school (the Yellow Church of the Chinese texts), but only very gradually; and it was not until the 17th century that he was acknowledged as an incarnation of spyan-ras-gzigs (Avalokiteśvara). During the whole of his life he was not even elected as abbot of one of the three great monasteries of his sect in central Tibet: 'Bras-spungs, dGa'-ldan, Se-ra; the actual head of the sect was at first Tsong-kha-pa's chief pupil mKhas-grub-rje (1385–1438). Only after the death of the latter did dGe-'dun-grub come to the fore.

His work lay above all in the internal organization of his sect, whose solid and yet elastic disciplinary structure is mostly due to him. Like his immediate successors, he was a great traveler, and his missionary work untiring, above all in gTsang (southern central Tibet), where he founded in 1447 the great monastery of bKra-shis-lhun-po. And yet gTsang remained for two centuries the sore spot for the Yellow Church, soon to be organized into a strong state by the princes of Rin-spungs, who supported the Karma-pa sect. After the middle of the 15th century the influence of the dGe-lugs-pa centered on Se-ra, dGa'-ldan, and 'Bras-spungs in dBus(central Tibet), on bKra-shis-lhun-po in gTsang,

and on Chab-mdo (Chamdo), founded in 1437 in Khams (eastern Tibet). Under dGe-'dun-grub the Yellow Church did not as yet take a direct part in the political life of Tibet; it merely built up its spiritual and economic ascendancy based on a network of landed estates and on close connections with the aristocracy, chiefly of dBus.

It does not appear that dGe-'dun-grub ever had contacts with China, although his biographer mentions the arrival of two Chinese officials, who reached 'Bras-spungs on the day following his death. There is no hint of their dispatch in the *Ming-shih*, the *shih-lu*, or other works, and it may be taken as unhistorical; a Chinese embassy arriving during the last days or months in the lives of the first Dalai-lamas seems to be a standard cliché.

dGe-'dun-grub was a prolific, although neither original nor important, author in the fields of logic, dogmatics, and liturgy. His collected works (*gsung-'bum*) include twenty-one items, printed in five volumes.

Bibliography

Ye-shes-rtse-mo, *rJe thams-cad-mkhyen-pa dGe-'dun-grub-dpal-bzang-po'irnam-thar-ngo-mtshar-rmad-byung nor-bu'i'-phreng-ba,* 1494; G. Schulemann, *Die Geschichte der Dalai-Lamas,* 2d ed. (Leipzig, 1958), 183; L. Petech, "The Dalai-Lamas and Regents of Tibet: a Chronological Study," TP, 47 (1959), 370; Y. Kanakura, R. Yamada, T. Tada, and H. Hadano, *A Catalogue of the Tōhoku University Collection of Tibetan Buddhism* (Sendai, 1953), nn. 5522; G. Tucci, *Tibetan Painted Scrolls* (Rome, 1949), 122.

Luciano Petech

dGE-'DUN-RGYA-MTSHO, December, 1475–March 1542, posthumously reckoned as the second Dalai-lama of Tibet, belonged to the Sreg-mi family and was born near rTa-nag rDo-rje-gdan, to the northwest of Shigatse. His was the first instance of succession by incarnation in the series of the leading hierarchs of the Yellow Church. Although no regular search for a new incarnation was instituted as became the rule afterwards, the child soon attracted the attention of the leaders of the dGe-lugs-pa sect, and in 1483 he was brought to 'Bras-spungs and recognized as the rebirth of dGe-'dun-grub (*q.v.*). He received a sound education in that large monastery.

Soon after he reached his majority, he had to face a serious crisis in the secular fortunes of his church. The Karma-pa gained the upper hand and their protector, the prince of Rin-spungs, occupied Lhasa and its district in 1498. The dGe-lugs-pa were excluded from the celebration of the smon-lam (the New Year's prayers), the most important annual event of their sect, and the Karma-pa of the gSang-phu monastery took it under their control. dGe-'dun-rgya-mthso in the meantime undertook extended travels in central and southern Tibet; it was a kind of exile, but also a (not very successful) search for potential allies. Only in 1518 was Lhasa wrested from Rin-spungs by the Phag-mo-gru secular ruler, the Gong-ma chen-mo and the management of the smon-lam given back to the dGe-lugs-pa. dGe-'dun-rgya-mtsho returned to 'Bras-spungs, where he built the dGa'-ldan pho-brang palace. This palace was his seat and that of his immediate successors, and theoretically remained the seat of the Dalai-lama down to modern times, although the fifth Dalai-lama shifted the actual residence to the Potala in Lhasa. dGe-'dun-rgya-mtsho became abbot of 'Bras-spungs in 1521 and of Se-ra in 1524.

Although there was no question as yet of a temporal power, the influence of dGe-'dun-rgya-mtsho increased during the latter part of his life. Thus his intervention contributed decisively in saving the Phag-mo-gru rulers from military defeat at the hands of the princes of Rin-spungs. He was not so successful in 1537, when the abbot of the Red sect monastery of 'Bri-gung threatened Lhasa; he had to abandon 'Bras-spungs for some time. But soon the menace passed, and he came back to 'Bras-spungs, where he passed his last years peacefully. dGe-'dun-rgya-mtsho was an able administrator. He held under strict control the management of the temporal concerns of 'Bras-spungs and of the dGe-lugs-pa sect in general; for this purpose he created the post of sde-pa (at first: steward; later: regent). The estates of the greater monasteries were likewise administered by treasurers (p'yag-mdzod-pa).

Like most of the Dalai-lamas, dGe-'dun-rgya-mtsho wrote several works, mostly small tracts on liturgy, but also commentaries on the *Nāmasaṅgīti*, on the *Mūlamadhyamakāvatāra* of Nāgārjuna, and on a work of Tsong-kha-pa (*q. v.*); his collected works (*gsung 'bum*) include forty-four items in three volumes.

So far as we know, he never had any official contact with China. It has sometimes been asserted that the unlucky mission of the eunuch Liu Yün (*see* Halima), who started for Tibet in 1516 and met with armed resistance on his way, was addressed to dGe-'dun-rgya-mtsho. The actual letter sent by the emperor is preserved, however, and it shows that Liu Yün was dispatched to a Karma-pa leader, the eighth Zhva-nag-pa Mi-bskyod-rdo-rje (1506–54), who already in his childhood was widely known as a miracle-worker.

Bibliography

Ngag-dbaṅ-blo-bzang-rgya-mtsho (fifth Dalai-lama), *rJe-btsun thams-cad-mkhyen-pa'i gsung-'bum thor-bu-las rje-nyid-kyi rnam-thar* (actually a diary of his religious life with only slight information thereon which stops abruptly with 1528); G. Tucci, *Tibetan Painted Scrolls* (Rome, 1949), 39, 124, 162; G. Schulemann, *Die Geschichte der Dalai Lamas*, 2d ed. (Leipzig, 1958), 194, 202; L. Petech, "The Dalai Lamas and Regents of Tibet: a Chronological Study," TP, 47 (1959), 371; Y. Kanakura, R. Yamada, T. Tada, and H. Hadano, *A Catalogue of the Tōhoku University Collection of Tibetan Buddhism* (Sendai, 1953), nn. 5543; H. Richardson, "The Karma-pa Sect: a Historical Note, pt. 2," JRAS (1959), 6.

Luciano Petech

DE BŽIN gśegs pa, *see* HALIMA

DIAS, Manuel (Manoel Diaz 陽瑪諾, T.
演西, known as the Younger to distinguish
him from a missionary of the same name
李瑪諾, 1559-November 28, 1639), 1574-
March 1 or 4, 1659, Jesuit missionary,
was born at Castello-Branco, Portugal,
entered his novitiate in 1592, and left in
1601 for Goa, where he completed his
education as a member of the Society of
Jesus. About 1605 he was dispatched to
Macao and there taught theology for six
years. Accompanied by Gaspar Ferreira
(*q.v.*), also a native of Portugal, he was
next (1611) sent to Shao-chou 韶州, where
Matteo Ricci(*q.v.*) had already established
a church (1589). Here the animosity of
officials, scholars, Buddhist monks, and
others was too great for them; they were
forced out and their residence pillaged
(April 13, 1612). By a curious circumstance the river (Pei-chiang 北江) flooded
its banks at this point, causing widespread
destruction in the city. The two missionaries somehow managed to make their
way by boat upstream to Nan-hsiung 南雄,
situated close to the northern border of
Kwangtung, and to establish themselves
without opposition (July 31). In 1614
Dias was ordered to travel to all mission
locations to inform fellow Jesuits of the
decision (soon withdrawn) that they
must do no more teaching of mathematics
or any other science—only the Gospel. It
is at this very time that he completed
and published his treatise on Ptolemaic
astronomy, the *T'ien wen lüeh* 天問略, 1
ch. (Peking, 1615). In 1616 he was back
in Nan-hsiung, but a year later was
obliged to retreat to Macao, because of
the persecution of the church (*see* Shen
Ch'üeh). In 1621 it was possible for him
to return to Peking, where he lived successively in the country homes of Hsü
Kuang-ch'i (ECCP) and of another Chinese convert. From there he made frequent trips into the city in the interests
of the church.

One of the reasons given for permitting Catholic missionaries to reenter the
capital was the plea, made to the new
emperor (Chu Yu-chiao, ECCP) by officials favorable to the new religion, that
they might aid, in the face of the increasing Manchu menace, in reforming the
army and (above all) in improving the
artillery. Nicolo Longobardi (*q.v.*) and
Dias were chosen (1622) for this task,
although they themselves insisted that
their business was not war but peace and
service to the Lord of Heaven. In spite
of this declaration they were given freedom to pursue their calling. The ministry
of War even offered them a residence.
In the meantime both they and the officials awaited a detachment of Portuguese
soldiers and a shipment of western cannon from Macao. This moment of calm
was all too brief. When the cannons arrived one exploded with disastrous results.
Shen Ch'üeh, who had returned to power
(September, 1620) as minister of Rites,
seized the opportuntity to denounce the
missionaries and banish them from Peking.
Again, the home of Li Chih-tsao (ECCP)
in Hangchow became a welcome haven.
It was at this time (1623) that Dias and
Longobardi collaborated on the fashioning
of a terrestrial globe, more up-to-date
than the world map of Ricci (*see also*
Guilio Aleni). For an illustration see Nigel
Cameron, *Barbarians and Mandarins*
(Tokyo, 1970), 205.

In this same year (according to Pfister, but Cordier makes it 1626) Dias was
named vice-provincial of the order in
China. As China and Japan had now become
distinct entities in Jesuit administration,
he was able to give his full time to the
work of the China mission; from all accounts he fulfilled his responsibilites to
the general satisfaction, although the
Franciscan priest (a Spaniard) Antonio
Caballero (*q.v.*) accused him of being
uncharitable to a brother missionary. Dias
held the post twice, from 1626 to 1636
and 1645 to 1654, according to Cordier.

In 1626 we find him briefly in Nanking, but, banished from there, he went on to Sung-chiang 松江 nearby. The official who was responsible for his first ouster followed him and tried to arrest him. Dias then moved to Shanghai to the home of Hsü Kuang-ch'i. This, however, was hardly a place of refuge as Shanghai was under the jurisdiction of Sung-chiang. He considered returning to Sung-chiang as a test of faith, but Hsü counseled against this, and advised seeking refuge instead in Hangchow. Here (1627) he erected a church, at the expense of Yang T'ing-yün (ECCP) and founded a seminary. The ensuing years were spent in various centers: in Chia-ting (December, 1627), in Ningpo, in Nanchang (1634), in Foochow (1638) —his arrest had been ordered in Foochow in 1637—back in Ningpo (1639), in Yen-p'ing-fu 延平府, Fukien (1648), and again in Hangchow. Here he died in March, 1659, and was buried outside the city wall at the site known as Ta-fang ching 大方井, where Lazzaro Cattaneo (q.v.) and other Jesuits had already been laid to rest.

Dias was responsible for several works in the religious sphere, such as an incomplete translation of *De imitatione Christi*, attributed to Thomas à Kempis (1379?-1471), but now held to be the work of John Gerson, O.S.B. (fl. 1230), known as *Ch'ing-shih chin shu* 輕世金書, written in the classical style (2 vols., 1640). A second is the *Sheng-ching chih chieh* 聖經直解 (containing explanations of the Gospels of Sundays and Feast days) which he apparently adapted from a much larger work by Sebastian Barradas, S.J. (1542-1615). This bears his preface of 1636, and was published in Hangchow in 1642 in an original edition of 15 *chüan*; it was later reprinted at least four times (1790, 1800, 1866, and 1915). Fang Hao remarks in regard to this book: "A special characteristic of the work is that it has an index—the first time such a feature ever appeared in a Chinese book." In this too Dias was following Barradas. Besides these, as already

mentioned, he had a hand in making the terrestrial globe, the first of its kind in China, save for the famous model brought to Qubilai in 1267 from Maragha. Another work is the *Ching-chiao pei ch'üan* 景教碑詮 in 1 *chüan* (Hangchow, 1644; reprinted T'ou-se-we 土山灣 1878), the first European treatise on the Nestorian monument of 781. This book tells of the find ("in Kuan-chung 關中, while people were digging the ground under government orders in 1623") and its installation, gives the entire Chinese text of the inscription, adds a commentary on each phrase and each important word of the text, and concludes with wood-cut illustrations of three crosses found shortly before in Fukien (*see* Aleni). An appendix includes the account of the discovery written by Li Chih-tsao in 1625. The third is the above-mentioned work on astronomy, which, over one hundred fifty years later, was copied into the *Ssu-k'u ch'üan-shu*, and still later included in three other collections. In his conclusion Dias reports the most recent discoveries (1609) made: the observations of Saturn, the four moons of Jupiter, and the Milky Way, all being the work of Galileo and his telescope, though the name of the astronomer is nowhere mentioned. Ten Chinese scholars, including Hsü Kuang-ch'i, Yang T'ing-yün, and Li Chih-tsao, are listed by name in the book as "proofreaders."

Bibliography

Pfister (1932), 105; Sommervogel, III (1892), cols. 44-45; George H. Dunne, *Generation of Giants*, Notre Dame, 1962; Antonio Sisto Rosso, *Apostolic Legations to China of the Eighteenth Century* (So. Pasadena, 1948), 106; Pasquale M. d'Elia, *Galileo in China*, tr. by Rufus Suter and Matthew Sciascia (Cambridge, Mass., 1960), 7, 90, n. 61; id., *Fonti Ricciane*, II (Rome, 1949), 5, n. 4; Helen M. Wallis and E.D. Grunstead: "A Chinese Terrestrial Globe, A. D. 1623," *British Museum Quarterly*, XXV (1962), 83; P. Y. Saeki, *The Nestorian Documents and Relics of China* (2d ed., Tokyo, 1951), 27; A. C. Moule, *Christians in China Before the Year 1550*,

London, 1930; H. Cordier in *La Grande Ency-clopédie*, 14 (Paris, 1892), 457; SK (1930), 106/5a; C. R. Boxer, "Portuguese Military Expeditions in Aid of the Mings Against the Manchus, 1621–1647," THM, 7 (August, 1938), 24; Alvaro Semedo, *The History of That Great and Renowned Monarchy of China* (London, 1655), 99; Hou Wai-lu 侯外廬, *Chung-kuo ssu-hsiang t'ung-shih* 中國思想通史, 4B, 1195; Fang Hao 方豪, *Chung-kuo T'ien-chu-chiao shih jen-wu chuan* 中國天主教史人傳物 (Hong Kong, 1967), 173.

L. Carrington Goodrich

ESEN (Yeh-hsien 也先), died 1455, Oirat chieftain, ruler of a vast territory stretching from Hami in the west to the Jurchen dominions in the east, and self-proclaimed khan of the Mongols, captured Emperor Chu Ch'i-chen (*q.v.*) at the battle of T'u-mu 土木 and besieged Peking for several days in 1449. His father Toγon (T'o-huan 脫懽, d. 1439/40) laid the foundations for his power. In the 1430s Toγon killed two rival Oirat chieftains and subsequently united the various Oirat tribes. In 1434 he defeated the Eastern Mongol minister, Aruγtai (*q.v.*), the last important threat to his position as *de facto* ruler of the Mongols. Not being a descendant of the original Mongol royal family, however, he was unable to proclaim himself khan. Instead he married his daughter, Esen's elder sister, to the young khan, Toγto-buqa (T'o-t'o-pu-hua 脫脫不花). It was left to his son Esen to implement his designs on the Mongol khanate.

Esen had demonstrated his military prowess even before his father's death. In the 1420s he waged three campaigns against Eastern Moghulistan, twice capturing its ruler Vays Khan (*see* Ḥājjī 'Alī). He expanded Oirat influence as far west as Bishbalik. In the 1430s he assisted his father in destroying Aruγtai. After his father's death he adopted the titles t'ai-shih 太師 and Huai-wang 淮王 and pressed forward against the guards (wei) on China's northwestern border. Hami was the first of these to suffer at his hands. In 1443 a contingent of three thousand Oirat troops raided Hami and captured the mother and the wife of the prince. Esen sought to coax the prince to visit the Oirat camp, thereby accepting Esen's overlordship, but the prince refused. The Ming court complained bitterly about Esen's raid, and he, unwilling as yet to challenge the Chinese, finally released his royal prisoners. But in 1445, evidently feeling more confident about his strength, he again attacked Hami and recaptured the mother and the wife. He repeated his invitation to the prince, and in 1448 after some hesitation the latter consented to visit the Oirat lands. The prince, while assuring the Ming court that he would never acquiesce in Esen's demands, left Hami for an extended stay in Esen's entourage. Esen not only controlled Hami but also threatened the other northwestern guards. Initially he sought to annex them peacefully. In 1443 he had sent envoys demanding marital alliances with the chiefs of the Sha-chou 沙州 and the Ch'ih-chin 赤斤 Mongol guards. They procrastinated and requested assistance from the court, repeatedly warning of Esen's hostile intentions. The Chinese failed to act and thus inadvertently encouraged Esen. In 1445 he forced the rulers of the two guards to accept Mongol titles. He also created a "provincial government of Kansu," thus formally acknowledging his intention to conquer that area. By 1446 most of Sha-chou's people were so frightened that they decided to flee. A few joined Esen, but most requested and received sanctuary in China. The Mongols of Ch'ih-chin, however, resisted the Oirat, though Esen continued to threaten them. They often asked for permission to desert their land and move into Chinese territory, but the emperor rejected their appeals, asserting that (as Henry Serruys renders it) if they "kept a watchful eye on the situation in the west and in case of an impending invasion warned the Ming generals [they] would receive help in time and be quite safe." The emperor also gave them grain and other provisions to induce them to stay in their own land. Most of them remained even though as late as 1454 Esen attempted to coerce them into an alliance.

Esen also pursued an aggressive policy in the northeast. In the early 1440s he had formed an entente with the three guards of the Uriyangqad (Wu-liang-ha兀良哈) which he sealed by marrying the daughter of the chief of the T'ai-ning 泰寧 guard, In the following years they served as his spies in China. Yet he failed to help them when the court, angered by the Uriyangqad raids on Chinese settlements, dispatched a punitive expedition in 1444. Instead he took advantage of their weakness to plunder their territory. By 1447 he had conquered T'ai-ning and To-yen 朵顏, two of the Uriyangqad guards, and compelled the people of Fu-yü 福餘, the other guard, to migrate. With this last conquest, he now virtually controlled the land north of China from present-day Sinkiang to Korea.

The Ming court was apprehensive about Esen's territorial gains, but was perhaps even more concerned over tribute and trade relations. It complained about the excessive number of envoys on his tribute embassies, their rude and occasionally criminal behavior, and the poor quality of the tribute. Prior to Esen's accession, the majority of Oirat missions consisted of fewer than a hundred men, but he dispatched 2,302 in the mission of 1442, 1,867 in 1444, and over 2,000 in the winter of 1448/49. China's expenditure in feeding, transporting, and providing gifts for these people became burdensome. On the other hand, Chinese mistreatment of several of the envoys and the inadequate and occasionally paltry Chinese gifts and payments perturbed Esen. He repeatedly asserted that Chinese merchants and officials shortchanged his people in commercial trans-actions and that the court unfairly lowered its price for his horses.

The Ming made few efforts either to resolve these disputes or to prepare for an Oirat attack. In the early 1440s Grand Secretary Yang Shih-ch'i (q.v.) had warned of a possible Oirat incursion, and urged the emperor to acquire more mounts for frontier troops. Numerous border officials also submitted memorials requesting additional soldiers and supplies to withstand the Oirat. The government, however, failed to provide this support. Its basic policy was to drive a wedge between Esen and Toγto-buqa. It provided elaborate presents for the khan and treated his envoys courteously. Apparently he contemplated an alliance with China, but the government evidently did not realize that Esen (in the words of H. H. Howorth) "was clearly the autocrat of the desert, and the khan his protégé was probably of little more consequence than the later Merovingians in the hands of the two Pepins." The Chinese also either underestimated or were unaware of Esen's growing power. Even when deserters reported that Esen was massing his forces for an attack, the Ming court merely sent an envoy to ask Esen whether the report was accurate.

Two incidents transformed these arguments into armed conflict. One involved the Oirat tribute embassy of 1448 when its complement of over two thousand men reached Peking with an offering of horses. In order to obtain more gifts, they falsely asserted that their embassy numbered over three thousand men. The court, and particularly the eunuch Wang Chen (q.v.), infuriated upon learning of such deception, gave them only 20 per cent of the presents they requested. Esen was annoyed by this rebuff, but perhaps more friction was generated by an even more personal rejection. It is reported that a few Chinese interpreters, without any authorization, assured Esen that his son could marry into the imperial family. When Esen sent the proper ritual presents for the forthcoming marriage, however, the court, totally ignorant of Esen's discussion with the interpreters, curtly rejected the proposed betrothal. According to this unlikely story, the second rejection or insult provided Esen with another pretext for an invasion of China.

In late July of 1449 Esen launched his most grandiose campaign. He ordered Toɣto-buqa, who, according to Chinese sources, attempted to dissuade him from attacking China, to lead the Uriyangqad in a raid on Liaotung. He also instructed his subordinate, the chih-yüan 知院 A-la 阿剌, to lay siege to Hsüan-fu. He led his own troops toward Tatung. Upon hearing of Esen's scheme, Wang Chen apparently convinced Emperor Chu Ch'i-chen to witness, or even perhaps lead, the Chinese forces against the Oirat. [Editors' note: The scholar-officials who wrote the Ming histories despised eunuchs, and it may be that the account of Wang Chen's role in the ensuing catastrophe is unduly derogatory (see Chu Ch'i-chen).] Arriving at Tatung early in August, the emperor soon learned that Esen had routed the Chinese forces at Yang-ho 陽和 and was rapidly approaching Tatung. The Chinese sources attribute the defeat at Yang-ho to the lack of supplies and to the stupidity and corruption of the eunuchs who commanded the armies.

Wang Chen and the military commanders now decided upon a retreat. They moved east to Hsüan-fu, but Esen's troops met them there in late August. The Oirat won the ensuing battle, forcing the emperor to seek refuge in T'u-mu. His military and civilian advisers urged a speedy withdrawal to Huai-lai 懷來, a more secure sanctuary, but Wang Chen, fearing that such haste would lead to the loss of the emperor's baggage and the army's supplies, opposed and in effect vetoed the proposal. The Chinese, thus slowed down, camped at T'u-mu. Esen's forces arrived and surrounded the area. The Chinese found the water supply at T'u-mu inadequate and soon men and horses were parched. On September 1, Esen, after feigning a withdrawal, surprised and overwhelmed the weary and thirsty Chinese troops, killing Wang Chen and capturing Chu Ch'i-chen. According to a fanciful story in the *Altan*

Tobči, the Oirat twice considered executing the emperor but this action was not taken. Esen finally assigned Yüan Pin 袁 彬 (T. 文質), a captured prisoner and an officer in the Embroidered-uniform Guard, and several others to serve the emperor.

Esen inexplicably did not immediately press an attack on Peking, thus allowing the Chinese time to recuperate and to mass their forces for the defense of the capital. Instead he returned to Tatung, demanding gold and silk from the besieged garrison. The commander-in-chief, Kuo Teng (see Pai Kuei), gave Esen thirty thousand *liang* of silver and also made a vain effort to rescue the emperor. Shortly thereafter a report that the emperor's younger brother had taken the throne reached Esen. The latter, realizing that this considerably reduced the value of his captive, determined to place the ex-emperor on the throne. He quickly moved to Peking, fully expecting to take it with ease. But the new minister of War, Yü Ch'ien (q.v.), had calmed the panic-stricken inhabitants of the city and insisted on defending it. When Esen sent an envoy to demand one hundred million *liang* of silver as ransom, the Chinese reply was negative. Annoyed by this rejection, Esen laid siege to Peking from October 27 to October 30. Surprised by the stiff resistance he encountered, he finally lifted the siege and withdrew when he learned that a Chinese relief army was approaching Peking. On his return trip to Tatung he avenged his failure by plundering Lianghsiang 良鄉. At Tatung he again sought a ransom for the ex-emperor; instead the Chinese forces made a second unsuccessful attempt to free the prisoner.

Chinese policy towards Esen in late 1449 and early 1450 remained hostile. The officials tried to woo other Mongol leaders away from Esen. They entered into negotiations with Toɣto-buqa and A-la, and amply rewarded the Mongol envoys. They also offered to grant fifty thousand *liang* of silver, ten thousand of gold, and an official title to anyone who assassinated Esen. As late as May, 1450, they refused to meet with an Oirat delegation which wished to negotiate the release of the emperor. Yü Ch'ien asserted that the so-called peaceful embassy was merely a ruse and that Esen intended either to attack or to make great financial demands on China. The court also hesitated to negotiate with Esen because the newly-enthroned emperor, Chu Ch'i-yü (q.v.), feared that the ex-emperor would depose him—a factor that Yü Ch'ien necessarily kept secret. On the other hand, Esen was extremely conciliatory. The accounts of Esen's Chinese prisoners, as well as those of the Chinese envoys to the Oirat, all agree that Esen, perhaps for ulterior motives, was considerate towards Chu Ch'i-chen. He proffered elaborate banquets to the former Chinese ruler, provided attendants, and even sought to give him his sister in marriage. He also dispatched a stream of envoys to offer tribute and to arrange for his release.

Esen's gestures finally brought results in the latter half of 1450. A few Chinese ministers and eunuchs persuaded the reigning emperor that the return of his elder brother was essential. They also assured him that he need not relinquish his throne. In late June the emperor ordered the vice minister of Rites, Li Shih (q.v.), and several other officials to go to Oirat territory to demand the immediate release of Chu Ch'i-chen. Esen was pleased with Li's mission and immediately sent Pir Muhammad (P'i-er-ma-hei-ma 皮兒馬黑麻) to Peking to request that higher ranked Chinese officials be dispatched to escort the ex-emperor back to China. The Chinese instead sent a clever negotiator, a vice minister of Rites, Yang Shan (q.v.). In a delightful dialogue recorded in the *shih-lu* Yang obtained Esen's confidence, was granted a festive banquet, and secured the release of the ex-emperor. According to the undoubtedly exaggerated Chinese accounts, Esen was so saddened by the departure of his captive that he accompanied the Chinese convoy for a considerable distance and bowed down and wept at the final leave-taking.

After the release of Chu Ch'i-chen, Esen turned his attention to his relations with Toγto-buqa. In the winter of 1450 he and the Mongol khan cooperated in an invasion of Jurchen territory and overran the area of Hai-hsi 海西. But tension between the two arose concerning the succession to the khanate. Esen insisted on a particular candidate who was unacceptable to Toγto-buqa. He was also concerned lest Toγto-buqa form an alliance with the Chinese and with A-la to destroy the Oirat hegemony over the Eastern Mongols. Toγto-buqa was initially successful in his battles against Esen, but in the winter of 1451 his own brother betrayed him to the Oirat, and Esen defeated him in an area tentatively identified as the region of Turfan, called Qara (Ha-la 哈喇). The khan fled to the northeast, but early in 1452 a local chieftain, perhaps of the Uriyangqad peoples, killed him.

During and even after his struggles with Toγto-buqa, Esen and the Ming court generally maintained harmonious relations. Esen sent tribute embassies, most of which were permitted entry into Peking. One source reports that the Chinese needed and desired Oirat horses, and even when over two thousand eight hundred envoys arrived early in 1454 and received approximately ninety thousand bolts of coarse silk and ten thousand hats, the Chinese raised no objections. The Chinese complained, however, about the rudeness of the envoys on this and other missions. In addition, they did not always grant the goods that the Oirat sought. In 1453 they refused Esen's request for fine silk and gold wine vessels. But in general they maintained good relations with him. When Esen proclaimed himself khan in 1453, therefore, the emperor, though somewhat hesitantly, approved.

Esen's adoption of the title khan led to his downfall. He was not descended from the original Mongol ruling family and had no valid claim to the title. According to the Chinese sources, opposition also arose as a result of Esen's increasingly debauched ways, notably his fondness for liquor. His refusal to grant the title Tayisi, the second highest ranking position in the Oirat hierarchy, to A-la and another important chief, precipitated an intratribal war. Surprisingly enough, Esen was easily vanquished and met his death at the hands of Buqun (Pu-kun 布衮), son of a man whom he had executed.

Several significant Chinese accunts of Esen's relations with and treatment of the captured emperor are still extant. Yang Ming (*q.v.*), one of Esen's prisoners, wrote the most important of these works, the *Cheng-t'ung lin-jung lu*, a record in colloquial Chinese of the ex-emperor's experiences. Yüan Pin presented a sketch which formed the basis for the *Pei-cheng shih-chi* 北征事蹟, a valuable source for the study of Chu Ch'i-chen's life among the Oirat. The *P'i-t'ai lu* by Liu Ting-chih (*q.v.*), though not as valuable as the other records, deals both with the defense of Peking in 1449 and with Esen's campaigns in 1449 and 1450. Li Shih wrote the *Pei-shih lu*, an account of his negotiations with Esen. All of these sources are available in the *Chi-lu hui-pien*, a collection edited by Shen Chieh-fu (*q.v.*).

Esen's defeat of China underlined many problems that would plague China throughout the Ming. One was the shocking decline of the army since the victorious campaigns of Chu Yüan-chang and Chu Ti against the Mongols. Another was the growing influence of the eunuchs in the military and political spheres. Still another was the inability of the Chinese to enforce their own regulations on the size and frequency of tribute embassies.

Bibliography

1/148/8a, 155/3a, 170/4a, 173/8a, ch.328; MSL (1963), Ying-tsung; Fu wei-lin, *Ming shu* (Shanghai, 1937), 3332; Ku Ying-t'ai (ECCP), *Ming-ch'ao chi-shih pen-mo* (1658), ch. 32; Teng Ch'iu 鄧球, *Huang Ming yung-hua lei-pien* 泳化類編 (Taipei, 1965), 129/20a, 23a; Hsia Hsieh 夏燮, *Ming t'ung-chien* 通鑑 (Peking-Shanghai, 1959), 916, 933, 945, 961, 985, 989, 994, 1015, 1051, 1061, 1073; Jumpei Hagiwara 萩原淳平, "Doboku no henzengo—keizai mondai o chūshin to shite mita Min-mō kōshō" 土木の變前後一經濟問題を中心として見た明蒙交涉, *Tōyōshi kenkyū* 東洋史研究, 11 (1951), 193; L. Hambis, *Documents sur l'histoire des Mongols à l'époque des Ming* (Paris, 1969), 29, 97, 98, 104; David Farquhar, "Oirat-Chinese Tribute Relations, 1408-1446," *Studia Altaica: Festschrift für Nikolaus Poppe* (Wiesbaden, 1957), 60; Henry Serruys, "The Mongols of Kansu during the Ming," MCB, X (1955), 301; *id.*, "Notes on a Few Mongolian Rulers of the 15th Century," JAOS, 76 (1956), 83; *id.*, "Sino-Mongol Relations during the Ming: The Tribute System and Diplomatic Missions (1400–1600)," MCB., XIV (1967), 129, 166, 341; C. R. Bawden, *The Mongol Chronicle Altan Tobči* (Wiesbaden, 1955), 167, 172; D. Pokotilov, *History of the Eastern Mongols during the Ming Dynasty from 1368 to 1634*, tr. by R. Loewenthal, *Studia Serica*, ser. A, no. 1 (Chengtu, 1947), pt. 1, 43; W. Franke, "Addenda and Corrigenda," *Studia Serica*, ser. A, no. 3 (1949), pt. 2, 36; *id.*, "Yü Ch'ien, Staatsmann und Kriegsminister, 1398–1457," MS, 11 (1946), 87; *id.*, *Sources*, 2.5.1, 2, 3, 4, 5, 6; H. H. Howorth, *History of the Mongols* (London, 1876), pt. 1, 361; E. Bretschneider, *Mediaeval Researches from Eastern Asiatic Sources*, II (London, 1910), 165, 213, 218.

Morris Rossabi

ESEN Tügel 也先土干, died October 29, 1431, a Mongol chieftain who surrendered to the Chinese in 1423, was one of the better known Mongol princes in the service of the Ming in its first decades. Accounts about his ancestry and background are confusing; though he is often referred to as "king" in Chinese records, it is doubtful that he was ever an independent ruler. In his early years he served as a subordinate chieftain under Aruγtai (*q.v.*). When Aruγtai received (July, 1413) from the Ming the title of prince, Esen Tügel was granted the military title of tu-tu 都督 (commissioner-in-chief), the highest rank conferred by the Chinese on a Mongol. In March, 1416, Emperor Chu Ti (*q.v.*) rewarded him for his part in defeating the Oirat. Twice, in June, 1419, and February, 1420, Esen, along with

Aruγtai and other chieftains, sent tribute to the Ming court. He is referred to as a "Tatar king from the north" in the *shih-lu* under date of August 15, 1423, when the arrival of four envoys bearing tribute is reported. These were sent on Esen's own initiative and would indicate that by then he was trying to establish direct relations with the Ming.

In the same month Aruγtai broke with the Ming, and Emperor Chu Ti organized an expedition under his own command against him. On November 9, after reaching Shang-chuang-pao 上莊堡 near present-day Kalgan, the emperor received a dispatch from Ch'en Mou 陳懋 (T. 舜卿, 1384-1463, earl of Ning-yang 寧陽伯, Pth. 武靖), who commanded the vanguard. Ch'en reported that the Eastern Mongols had recently been routed by the Oirat north of the Kerülen River and that Esen Tügel, who was among the defeated, had offered to surrender with his followers. Ch'en's message was accompanied by a letter from Esen himself, who explained the reasons for his action; he said that he had been continuously on the move with his subjects under the pressure of the Oirat and that Aruγtai had become increasingly suspicious and was waiting for an opportunity to get rid of him. The *shih-lu* mentions that later he was urged to submit to the Ming by his sister's son Badai, who also surrendered. On receipt of these communications, the emperor sent orders to Ch'en Mou to accept Esen's surrender and escort him to his presence. On November 24 Esen and his retinue arrived and received a warm welcome. That same day the emperor honored him with the title of Chung-yung wang 忠勇王 (loyal and courageous prince) and gave him the Chinese name Chin Chung 金忠. He also granted the rank of tu-tu to Badai, and bestowed lavish gifts on Esen's staff. (Earlier Chu Ti had in his employ a physiognomist, also by the name of Chin Chung [T. 世忠, 1353-1415, Pth. 忠襄], who served as Chu's chief adviser when he was endeavoring to supplant his nephew. As a consequence Chin Chung enjoyed the imperial favor. He was minister of War from May, 1404, until his death in May, 1415. It is worth speculating that Chu Ti may have had this man in mind when he chose a Chinese name for Esen Tügel.)

Chu Ti immediately used Esen's surrender as a pretext to cut short his expedition, and returned to Peking with Esen, now known as Chin Chung, in his entourage. The unusual honor bestowed on Esen and the enthusiasm over his submission suggest that he was an important Mongol chieftain. This was in fact not quite the case. Evidently the emperor hoped that a good reception for him would make a favorable impression on the Mongols and induce them to follow his example. On the other hand, Chu Ti seems to have exaggerated Esen Tügel's importance deliberately in order to conceal the fruitlessness of his campaign against Aruγtai.

Meanwhile, Aruγtai was giving indications of hostility and on February 7, 1424, Chu Ti again decided upon a campaign against him and once more took the field. According to the *shih-lu*, if the information is accurate, the initiative came from Chin Chung himself, who volunteered to lead the vanguard against Aruγtai to avenge his subjects for their suffering. On April 1 the emperor ordered the formation of a Sino-Mongol expeditionary force with Ch'en Mou and Chin Chung commanding the forward units. Evidently Chin Chung led his own Mongol soldiers. The campaign, however, yielded no result, as the emperor died in Mongolia on August 12, 1424.

Shortly after the enthronement of Chu Kao-chih (*q.v.*), Chin Chung received a promotion (Oct. 21) to the rank of grand guardian of the heir apparent. In addition he was granted some one hundred acres of unoccupied land south of the capital, which he might turn into pasture for breeding horses. In October, 1428, when the succeeding emperor, Chu Chan-chi (*q.v.*), decided to launch a campaign against the Mongols northeast of Peking, Chin Chung and his nephew again volunteered to undertake a patrol. At that time some officials, who had misgivings about Mongols serving in China, objected to the offer on the ground that they would take the opportunity to defect. The emperor, however, overruled the objection. The two fully lived up to his confidence, and, when they returned with a number of prisoners, they received new honors from the emperor. Late in March, 1429, Chin Chung was promoted to the rank of grand guardian; in December of the following year, a number of his staff also received new military titles. Chin Chung died in October, 1431, without an heir. His nephew Badai then took over the management of his estate. Chin Chung was known to have a brother by the name of Möngkë Buqa 猛哥卜花, also a commander in the Chinese army.

Badai himself was a distinguished officer in the Ming service. In November, 1427, he received the Chinese name Chiang Hsin 蔣信 from Emperor Chu Chan-chi, but continued to be known as Badai. He served in October of the following year in the expedition against the Mongols in the Uriyangqad commanderies, and was rewarded for his outstanding performance. Later he became an earl (May, 1444) and inherited his uncle's title Chung-yang, with an annual stipend of 1,100 shih of rice. In July, 1448, together with several other nobles, he was indicted for failing to pay respect to the emperor; the latter forgave him but suspended his stipend for a year. He took part in the battle of T'u-mu against the Oirat in September, 1449, and was carried off to Mongolia as a captive with Emperor Chu Ch'i-chen (q.v.) and other high officials. He stayed with the emperor through the entire period of captivity and returned with the imperial entourage upon the latter's release almost a year later. During this time, because of his former affiliation, many people believed him to be a renegade rather than a prisoner of war, but it appears that the court finally realized that he had never intended to betray the Ming, and so restored his salary and rank. Upon his death on June 27, 1454, Badai received the canonized name Hsi-shun 僖順 (cautious and obedient) with his rank raised posthumously to that of marquis.

Badai was survived by a son, Chiang Ye-er-po-hu 也兒孛忽, who inherited his title in September, 1454, with half of the stipend. In March, 1457, the young Chiang adopted the Chinese name Chiang Shan 善, and then in April received the full share of his father's stipend. He died early in 1461 without an heir, and the earldom was abolished. In May of the same year the emperor granted his mother, née Wang 王, a stipend of ten shih of rice per month for subsistence.

Bibliography

1/156/5a, 106/37b; 3/144/4b; 61/99/1a; MSL(1963), T'ai-tsung, 1915, 2138, 2386, 2405, 2412, 2423, 2436, Jen-tsung, 23, 85, Hsüan-tsung, 397, 1141, 1143, 1231, 1412, 1909, Ying-tsung, 1299, 1352; Chang Hung-hsiang 張鴻翔, "Ming-shih chüan i-wu-liu chu-ch'en shih-hsi piao," 明史卷一五六諸臣世系表, Fu-jen hsüeh-chih 輔仁學誌, 5: 1–2 (1936), 19; Henry Serruys, "Mongols Ennobled During the Early Ming," HJAS, 22 (1959),228; L. Hambis, Documents sur l'histoire des Mongols à l'époque des Ming (Paris, 1969), 24.
For Badai: 1/156/6a, 107/11a; 3/144/3b; 61/99/4a; MSL (1963), Hsüan-tsung, 842, 1141, Ying-tsung, 2317, 3239, 3669, 4080, 5266, 5306, 5849, 5873, 6743; Yang Ming, Cheng-t'ung lin-jung lu, 6a, 8b, 10b, 24a; Yüan Pin (see Yang Ming), Pei-cheng shih-chi, 2b, 6a; Chang Hung-hsiang, op.cit., 20; Henry Serruys, op. cit., 233.

Hok-lam Chan

FAN-CH'I 梵琦 (T. 楚石, H. 西齋老人), July 21, 1296–August 17, 1370, monk and poet, was born into the Chu 朱 family of Hsiang-shan 象山, Chekiang, and was named T'an-yao 曇曜 (Dharma-light) after a monk had told his father that the infant was the "Buddha-sun" who would one day be a light unto darkness. In his fourth sui, both his parents died. His grandmother took him into her custody and taught him to recite the *Lun-yü* (Analects) by heart.

At nine *sui* the boy entered Yung-tso 永祚 monastery in Hai-yen 海鹽, Che-kiang, as a novice. He then moved to Ch'ung-en 崇恩 monastery on the bank of West Lake (西湖) where he met the scholar-calligrapher-painter Chao Meng-fu (1254-1322), who often came to visit his ancestors' graves. Chao was impressed by the boy, and paid the fee for his *tu-tieh* 度牒 (clerical certificate) to the government, thus enabling him at sixteen *sui* to shave his head at Ch'ung-en and take the monk's vow of the two hundred fifty commands 具足戒 at Chao-ch'ing 昭慶 monastery in Hangchow.

Four or five years later, while in charge of the library at Ch'ung-en monastery, Fan-ch'i was struck by certain passages in the *Śūraṅgama sūtra* 楞嚴, *chüan* 4, whereupon he composed the following lines:

The myriad veils of mystery were rent asunder,
The pearl [of self-nature] burst out full and clear.

Thenceforth he could read both Buddhist and Confucian texts with a measure of comprehension but was unable to feel their import in himself. This led him to seek instruction from the Ch'an master, Yüan-sou 元叟 (1255-1341), then presiding over the monastery at Ching-shan 徑山 (near Hangchow), a Ch'an center during the Sung and Yüan dynasties. Yüan-sou, however, tossed back the same question which Fan-ch'i himself had put to him, and when Fan-ch'i tried to answer, the Ch'an master shouted and sent him away in bewilderment.

Early in the 1320s the Yüan emperor Suddhipala (temple name: Ying-tsung, 1321-23), summoned Fan-ch'i, who was respected for his calligraphy, to the capital to take part in the transcription in gold of the *Tripiṭaka*. One night (February 6, 1324) during the Chinese New Year's festival, the drums sounded outside the city gate near his quarters. Fan-ch'i shuddered, suddenly realizing that Yüan-

sou meant to ask him to seek his own self-nature which no words could express. He returned to Ching-shan that year and the Ch'an master confidently made him his chief lieutenant and understudy in answering the questions of inquirers. Before long the branch headquarters of the Buddhist patriarch summoned Fan-ch'i to assume office as abbot of the Fu-chen 福臻 monastery in Hai-yen. There followed successive appointments as head of Yung-tso ssu (1328) where he had first served as a novice, Pao-kuo 報國 ssu in Hang-chow (1335), and Pen-chüeh 本覺 ssu in Chia-hsing (1344). In 1347 the Buddhist patriarch in Peking named him Fo-jih p'u-chao hui-pien ch'an-shih 佛日普照慧辨禪師 (Wisdom discerning Ch'an master, universal light of "Buddha-sun"). Fan-ch'i then retired to Yung-tso monastery (1357), where he later (1359) built the Hsi-chai (West studio) for his retreat and styled himself Hsi-chai lao-jen, signifying his following of both the Pure Land and the Ch'an practices. For a time (1363-68), after the demise of the abbot who had succeeded him, he resumed charge of Yung-tso at the magistrate's insistence, but in the final year he went again into seclusion, recommending his chief disciple as his replacement.

On October 22, 1368, Emperor Chu Yüan-chang, concerned over the spirits of soldiers and civilians slain during his take-over, summoned Fan-ch'i and others to Chiang-shan 蔣山 (later Ling-ku 靈谷) monastery outside Nanking, to preach sermons and perform services for their deliverance. Another ceremony took place the next year (April 19, 1369), and Fan-ch'i preached once more, after which he was feted, received in imperial audience, and, following ten days' sojourn as guest at the T'ien-chieh 天界 (Devagati) monastery, sent off with gifts of silver from the imperial treasury.

In the summer of 1370 the emperor demanded to know what the canon had to say about departed spirits. Fan ch'i and his party went again to T'ien-chieh ssu

(August 3) and proceeded to deliberate on relevant data to present to the imperial audience. On August 13 he felt indisposed. Four days later he asked his attendant to prepare his bath; after bathing he put on fresh attire and, sitting cross-legged in meditative posture, he composed a *gātha* and bade farewell to his fellow Ch'an master. Asked where he was about to go, he replied, sukhāvatī (West). His inquirer pressed him: "Can you find Buddha only in the West and not in the East?" At this Fan-ch'i shouted (dispelling the man's doubt and dissipating any wavering of his own at the last moment), and expired.

This same year the emperor forbade the practice of cremation; out of respect for Fan-ch'i, however, he made an exception of Buddhist monks. After the incineration Fan-ch'i's teeth, tongue, and rosary beads remained intact, while variegated *Śarīra* 舍利 (relics) were heaped high among the ashes. One disciple retrieved these and deposited them on September 18 in a *stūpa* built for the purpose at the Yung-tso monastery, where in his former quarters lay the bowl and cassock given him by the emperor. His friend, Sung Lien (*q.v.*), wrote his epitaph. Fan-ch'i's biographers included Yao Kuang-hsiao and Chu-hung (*qq.v.*), who regarded him as the greatest of Ming patriarchs, and criticized the *Tripiṭaka* councils for not having included his discourses in the 1420 *Pei-tsang* 北藏 and the 1589 *Ming-tsang*. Throughout the land, as well as in Japan and Korea, inquirers who had come to him and received his advice wrote out his words and treasured them.

Fan-ch'i's was an eclectic age when the first emperor could dub monk Tsung-lo (*q.v.*) "Lo *hsiu-ts'ai*," and call Hanlin reader-in-waiting Sung Lien "Sung *ho-shang*" 宋和尚. Fan-ch'i's works reflect Ch'an spontaneity and Pure Land simplicity as well as Confucian erudition. Among them are his Ch'an discourses, edited by his disciples, *Ch'u-shih* 楚石 *Fan-ch'i ch'an-shih yü-lu* 語錄, 20 *ch.*, which include his

own eulogy and epitaph and the two sermons to the dead, and a preface by Sung Lien who styled himself wu-hsiang chü-shih 無相居士 (Upāsaka Animitta); his Pure Land poems, *Hsi-chai ching-t'u shih* 淨土詩, 3 *ch.*, some 200 *shih*, and 32 *tz'u* 詞 to the melody *Yü-chia-ao* 漁家傲 with his own preface beginning with a reference to the Book of Odes, first published by Chu-hung's disciple at his master's command in 1615, and included in part by Chih-hsü (*q.v.*) in his *Ching-t'u shih-yao* 十要 as one of the ten basic books of the Pure Land sect; his 360 poems which used the same rhymes as those of the three T'ang dynasty masters of T'ien-t'ai, *Ho T'ien-t'ai san-sheng shih* 和天台三聖詩, printed in 1398 and re-engraved in 1625 and 1884; also other pieces using the rhymes of T'ao Ch'ien (365-427) and Ch'an master Yen-shou (904-75); 300 poems on his northern travels in *Pei-yu shih* 北遊詩; and other verses in a collection entitled *Feng-shan chi* 鳳山集. Selections of his poems were included in *Ming-shih tsung* by Chu I-tsun (ECCP), who commented that the *Pei-yu shih* gives full expression to life in the northern land and its style made even T'ang poet-monks seem inferior.

The following is the eighth of ten five-syllable "regulated poems" entitled *Mo-pei huai-ku* 漠北懷古 (Recalling the past north of the Gobi):

Oft beset by ice and frost,
   Forever in search of water and pasture,
They hunt with drawn bows wherever
   they go,
   And fish from hollowed logs in nearby
     streams.
Kumis [they drink] like tea,
   Their camel hide cloaks excel embroidered silk [in warmth].
These robust men are blue-eyed
   And read from left to right.

Bibliography

40/90/5a; 84/閏/1a; *Hsi-chai ching-t'u-shih* (TsSCC), 131, 151; Sung Lien, *Sung hsüeh-shih wen-chi* (SPTK), 5/15b; Chu-hung, *Huang Ming ming-seng chi-lüeh* 皇明名僧輯略, 12a, and *Chu-ch'uang san-pi* 竹窗三筆, 53a in *Yün-ch'i fa-hui* 雲棲法彙 (1897),

Vols. 17 and 26 respectively; *Taishō Daizōkyō* 大正大藏經, No. 945; *Zokuzōkyō* 續藏經, pt. 2, case 29, Vols. 1–2; Hsü Ch'ang-chih 徐昌治 (fl. 1654), *Kao-seng chai-yao* 高僧摘要 (*Zokuzōkyō*, pt. 2b, case 21, Vol. 4), 345a; Ch'en Yüan (BDRC), *Shih-shih i-nien-lu* (1939), 6/52, 9/16a, 10/1a; Lü Ch'eng 呂澂, *Fo-tien fan-lun* 佛典汎論 (1935), 30b; *Ming-shih i-wen-chih* 明史藝文志(1959), 87; *Chekiang t'ung-chih* (1934), 3889; *Chin-ling fan-ch'a chih* 金陵梵刹志 (1936), 3/1a.

C. N. Tay

FAN Shou-chi 范守己 (T. 介儒, H. 御龍子, 九二閒人), 1542–*ca.* 1611, scholar and official, was a native of Wei-ch'uan 洧川, Honan. The family prospered from farming and the ownership of land. His grandfather, Fan Pen 本 (T. 宗源, 1474–1515), purchased a clerical post in the district. His father, Fan Chiu-en 九恩 (T. 士寵, 1515–47), who was able to enter the district school, hoped to embark on an official career via the examination system but died before realizing his ambition. Perhaps partly because of this, his elder brother, Fan Shou-chieh 守節 (T. 希武, 1539–74), discontinued his own schooling while still young. As a consequence, Fan Shou-chi was the first member of the family able to continue his education; he succeeded in the examinations and eventually entered the official ranks.

After failing three times in the provincial examinations, he finally became a *chü-jen* in 1570. Four years later he qualified as *chin-shih*. In 1575 he received an appointment as prefectural judge of Sung-chiang 松江, Nan-Chihli. For six or seven years from 1581 on he held posts in the Nanking ministry of Justice, probably first as secretary then as bureau director. Perhaps because of his landed interests, he strongly opposed the land tax policy of Chang Chü-cheng (*q.v.*). Early in 1583 he drafted a scathing memorial denouncing Chang posthumously; it was never presented to the throne, however, and remains only in his literary work, the *Ch'ui-chien ts'ao* 吹劍草. By 1587 he became

assistant administration commissioner of Shensi, and three years later (1590) he rose to be educational commissioner of Shansi. Later he headed the military defense circuit of Chien-ch'ang 建昌, Szechwan, and then was demoted to prefect of Ch'a-ling 茶陵, Hukuang. In 1610–11 we find him in Peking as vice director of the bureau of operations in the ministry of War. It was at this time that he spoke out on the calendrical bureau's miscalculation of the eclipse of the sun (*see* Sabatino de Ursis). Our sources indicate that at this juncture he was being considered for more important posts in the central government, but before any action could be taken he died.

A collection of his writings entitled the *Yü-lung-tzu chi* 御龍子集, 77 *ch.*, was printed in Shansi in 1590. It includes the *Fu-yü*膚語 (study notes), 4 *ch.*, *T'ien-kuan chü-cheng* 天官舉正 (on astronomy), 6 *ch.*, *Ts'an liang t'ung-chi* 參兩通極 (on the neo-Confucian principles governing the world), 6 *ch.*, *So-t'an* 璅談 (on the places he had visited such as Soochow, Nanking, Peking, Ch'ang-an, Yangchow, and Shansi), 4 *ch.*, *Ch'ü-wei hsin-wen* 曲洧新聞 (reports on contemporary scenes), 4 *ch.*, and *Ch'ui-chien-ts'ao* (poetry and prose), 53 *ch.* In the prose section we find also a biography of Wang T'ao-chen (*q. v.*), the controversial daughter of Wang Hsi-chüeh (*q. v.*); a Fan family genealogy, 6 *ch.*; *Tsao Hsia lüeh* 造夏略 (an account of the first Ming emperor's founding of the dynasty), 3 *ch.*; biographical sketches of thirty-two officials under the Chia-ching and Lung-ch'ing (1522–72) reigns, 1 *ch.*; and a *nien-p'u* 年譜 (chronological biography) of the early Ming philosopher Ts'ao Tuan (*q.v.*).

Fan Shou-chi left as well an annalistic history of the Chia-ching period, the *Su-huang wai-shih* 肅皇外史, 46 *ch.*, for which he himself wrote a preface dated 1582. It seems that this book has never been printed as an individual work, but was included (1602) as part of the *Huang Ming ta-cheng chi* (*see* Lei Li) by a Nanking book dealer and publisher. This edition of

the *Huang Ming ta-cheng chi* in 25 *chüan*
consists of Lei Li's *Ta-cheng chi* (*chüan*
1–20), Fan Shou-chi's *Su-huang wai-shih*
(*chüan* 21–24), and the account of the
Lung-ch'ing period by T'an Hsi-ssu (*q.v.*)
extracted from his work, the *Ming ta-
cheng tsuan-yao* (*chüan* 25). According to
the notice in the *Ssu-k'u* catalogue this
printed edition is an abridgment of the
original work. This, however, is incorrect;
it is actually the same version, only combined and redivided, reducing to 4 *chüan*
what originally came to 46. The manuscript copy on microfilm has a different
preamble from the 1582 preface found in
his collected works, and the printed 4
chüan edition has neither. Because the
printed edition is hidden under another
title its existence must have escaped the
attention of many readers, among them
the contemporary bibliophile, P'an Ching-
cheng 潘景鄭. In taking note of a copy
belonging to the T'ien-i-ko (*see* Fan Mou-
chu, ECCP) which he had seen, or possessed, P'an remarked that the *Su-huang
wai-shih* was known only in manuscript.

The *Ssu-k'u* catalogue has a notice as
well on the *Yü-lung-tzu chi*. The editors
begin by indicating that the *Ch'ü-wei hsin-
wen* by the same author has already been
described. Actually their statement is
incorrect, undoubtedly an error caused by
lack of coordination among the cataloguers. Their comment that Fan's extremely
unfavorable treatment of Chang Chü-
cheng is personal and unfair is just. In
addition to these two works the editors
took note also of the *Ying-wu chi* 郢堊集,
12 *ch.*, another collection of Fan's literary
works. None of these three was copied
into the Imperial Library. From other catalogues we find that two more titles are
attributed to Fan's authorship: the *Ch'ou-
pien t'u-chi* 籌邊圖記 and the *Chien-ch'ang
chiang ch'ang k'ao* 建昌疆場考. Whether
these are extant is not known. Fan Shou-
chi owned a moderate library. In matters
of belief he was probably quite sympathetic to Taoism.

Bibliography

Ming-shih (Taiwan, 1963), 1603; Fan Shou-chi,
Yü lung-tzu chi (NLP microfilm no. 785, 786);
SK (1930), 54/1b, 179/6b; *K'ai-feng-fu chih*
開封府志 (1863), 26/35a; P'an Ching-cheng,
Chu-yen-lou shu-pa 著硯樓書跋 (1957), 62; *Ch'ui-
chien-ts'ao*, 42/1.

Lienche Tu Fang

FANG Hsiao-ju 方孝孺 (T. 希直, 希古, H.
遜志, 侯城生, 正學), 1357-July 25, 1402,
statesman and neo-Confucian thinker, was
from a family of Hou-ch'eng-li 侯城里,
Ninghai 寧海, Chekiang, prominent through
Sung and Yüan times for having produced
several scholars and officials. His grandfather had served the Yüan as director
of the district school at nearby Yin 鄞
-hsien (Ningpo). His father, Fang K'o-
ch'in 克勤 (T. 去矜, H. 愚菴, 1326-76),
was also a reputable scholar and administrator. Late in the Yüan period, Fang
K'o-chin took the provincial examination
of 1344 but failed to pass. Early in 1370
he joined the administration of Chu Yüan-
chang as a teacher in the local school. A
year later he passed a special examination
in Nanking and was appointed prefect of
Chi-ning 濟寧, Shantung, where he performed reasonably well for four years, but
was falsely accused of a minor misappropriation and lodged in prison in Nanking,
awaiting trial. He was then sentenced to
labor service in Chiang-p'u 江浦, forty *li*
northwest of Nanking. He was to have
been released from that and restored to
office, but became implicated (1376) in
the celebrated "Case of the pre-stamped
documents" (*see* Yeh Po-chü), and was
again put in prison where he died (most
likely was executed) December 5, 1376.

When his father was imprisoned, Fang
Hsiao-ju submitted a request to the prime
minister's office that he be allowed to
bear his father's punishment instead, but
without result. In the spring of 1377 he
took the corpse home for burial, and on
that occasion wrote a lengthy biography
extolling his father's character and learning. Though deeply influenced by the
latter's moral zeal, he was not alienated

from the emperor and dynasty that had caused his father's unjust imprisonment. He is said to have resolved at this time to prepare himself in learning and in moral discipline to become an aid to a sage emperor, thereby establishing a purpose in his life.

Like his father, Fang Hsiao-ju was something of a child prodigy whose literary capacities and ethical awareness astounded the Ning-hai community; he was called Hsiao Han-tzu 小韓子 (a little Han Yü) in reference to the late T'ang scholar who was regarded as the fountainhead of the neo-Confucian movement. At the age of fourteen (1371) he alone among his family members accompanied his father to Chi-ning, and he resided there while his father served as prefect; for the young Fang this was an opportunity to make pilgrimages to the tomb of Confucius, the shrine of the duke of Chou, and other sites associated with China's antiquity. He observed and, to some extent, participated in his father's strenuous but successful encounters with problems of governing amidst post-war devastation, the decline of learning in the north, and the concomitant loss of Confucian morale; but he acquired the conviction that the vigorous efforts to reconstitute local government could be successful.

At nineteen years of age, career decisions faced him. With the examination system not yet fully reestablished as the virtually exclusive route to higher officialdom that it had been and later again became, and with the government eagerly recruiting talent, it was not necessary for Fang Hsiao-ju to concentrate on the examination route. He later became an examiner, but he seems never to have intended to sit for the examinations. He needed to become known, to acquire sponsorship, and to further his studies. He later wrote that, up to that time, he had read virtually nothing by recent writers, but at the age of fifteen had seen some essays by Sung Lien (q.v.), and had come to regard him as the pivot of China's intellectual world.

In the late spring of 1376, shortly before his father's troubles commenced, Fang went to Nanking, sought an audience with Sung, showed him some of his writings, and so impressed the old man that they found a quiet place to talk for three hours. Fang asked to become Sung's pupil, and Sung, struck by the impressive qualities of his mind, consented. But shortly thereafter the elder Fang's difficulties and death intervened, and Fang Hsiao-ju went into mourning at Ning-hai. Sung Lien himself reached retirement age at the end of 1376 and withdrew from the court to live at his home in Chin-hua early the next year. In midsummer of that year, Fang traveled the one hundred or so miles westward from Ning-hai to Chin-hua and, to Sung's great delight, asked to take up the student relationship (contrary to what the Ming-shih biography states), before coming out of mourning for his father. Except for regular visits of filial obligation to his family, Fang lived at Chin-hua in close attendance upon Sung for the next three and a half years; in the autumn and winter of 1379/80 he accompanied the retired statesman on his annual attendance at court, frequently helping Sung respond to the innumerable demands on his writing brush by composing essays and other writings for him. Fang returned to Ning-hai on a family visit in October, 1380, and probably had planned to stay through the midwinter; in any event, he seems to have been there when Sung was arrested early that winter and sent into exile with all his family to distant Szechwan. Sung died the following year, like Fang's father five years earlier a victim of the Ming founder's suspicious nature and violent intimidation of officialdom. In 1382 Fang married the daughter of a fellow townsman by the name of Cheng 鄭.

Fang Hsiao-ju's polished literary style and his intellectual maturity gained much from Sung's tutelage; his spreading reputation derived principally from Sung's having acknowledged him as first among his many brilliant students. The remainder of his life was spent earnestly seeking opportunities to live up to the ideals exemplified for him by his father and his teacher, in service to the dynasty which had both claimed their loyalty and destroyed them. Eventually Fang emerged as a more seminal thinker than either of them, one of the more original Chinese minds of his century. He was the intellectual force behind an emperor's efforts to make perhaps fundamental modifications of the Ming dynastic style. Such changes might have been intended, among other things, to weaken the autocratic despotism and alter its increasing reliance on the very intimidation and force which destroyed so much human talent. Eventually, however, Fang failed utterly to bring about those changes, or even to have much impact on Ming intellectual life. In that failure, many historians have judged him impractical and unrealistic for the methods he chose. Yet one must counter that judgment with the question: what choices were open, in the first reign of the Ming dynasty, to a man imbued with the neo-Confucian ideal of the just society, equipped with the political knowledge of his civilization, alarmed about the disintegration of values that the Mongol conquest had induced, and endowed with his qualities of mind and spirit? The Ming dynasty was the legitimate instrument, the only one available, and Fang was committed to the activist's role in constructive use of that instrument. His life is a study in working out the available courses of action; at the same time, it may reveal more zeal and idealism than practical sense for the political realities.

The events of Fang's life during the 1380s and early 1390s are not readily reconstructed. The larger portion of his writings did not survive their suppression after 1402, and the number of precisely dated items among those that did survive is suspiciously small. Many of the references to him that one would expect to find in the *shih-lu* appear to have been deleted. From the extant writings, espe-

cially the occasional poems, one can learn that Fang lived mostly at his home in Ning-hai during those years, and both taught and continued his own studies and writing. In 1382/83, on the recommendation of an eminent scholar-official from Chin-hua, Wu Ch'en (*see* Chan T'ung), the court invited Fang for an interview with the emperor who, reportedly, was impressed, but said that this talent should be allowed to mature fully before being employed. In October, 1392, the emperor again interviewed him, and said on this occasion: "This is not yet the time to employ Fang Hsiao-ju." That apparently meant only that the moment had not come to use him prominently at the court, which was then troubled by the purge following the alleged conspiracy of Lan Yü (*q. v.*). Noting Fang's urgent concern for "transforming through teaching" the emperor appointed him director of Confucian studies for the prefecture of Hanchung 漢中, far off in southwest Shensi. Shortly after he took office in May, 1393, and again in 1396, Fang was twice summoned to Nanking to serve as one of the examiners at the provincial examinations for the metropolitan district. In the meantime he tried to make the best of what must have been a very trying assignment at Han-chung, which he held until after the emperor's death in the summer of 1398. In one surviving letter to a friend he describes the difficult travels, north through Honan, west along the Yellow and Wei Rivers to Sian and Pao-chi 寶雞, then south to Han-chung, almost 7,000 *li*, requiring one hundred twenty-four days. After arrival there he found it a poor, isolated, mountain-ringed outpost. The schools were poor, the few students were mostly below standard, and complete sets of the Classics were not even at hand to use for teaching. The decline of education and learning under the Mongol regime was even more serious in the poorer northwest than what he and his father had found in Shantung twenty years earlier.

One feature of life in these years that

must have made the experience worth-while was Fang's relationship with the eleventh son of the Ming founder, Chu Ch'un (*see* Chu Yüan-chang), designated Prince Hsien of Shu (in 1378), who took up his residence at Chengtu in 1391. Chu Ch'un was the most literary-minded of the imperial princes; at this time he was a mild-mannered young poet who recognized literary values and cultivated scholars. Han-chung lay on the main post route about twelve days' travel northeast from Chengtu; in the isolation of the west this made them neighbors. In 1393 he invited Fang to serve as director of the Szechwan provincial examination. Fang declined because the central government at Nanking had already summoned him to take charge of the provincial examination at the national capital. So he proceeded to Nanking. Returning to Han-chung in the spring of 1394, he traveled up the Yangtze River to Szechwan to pay his respects to the prince, and on the way stopped at K'uei-chou 夔州 to visit the tomb of his mentor, Sung Lien. There he saw Sung's grandchildren at their home, giving them aid and assistance and avuncular advice. Sung I (*see* Sung Lien), the eldest of the surviving grandchildren, was later brought to the attention of the prince who generously became his patron, and who later (after 1402) supplied funds for moving all the Sung family tombs and the family to Chengtu, where the latter was given a grant of land as endowment to maintain both the tombs and the family. These actions (perhaps also the prince's professed admiration for Sung Lien) must have been instigated by Fang. In any case, as titular tutor to the prince's infant heir, Fang made frequent visits to Chengtu. [Editors' note: This son, named Chu Yüeh-lien 悅燫, 1388-July 16, 1409, deserves special mention as his tomb was discovered in 1970. It had been robbed long ago, but tri-color glazed pottery figurines were found intact.] Sometimes he joined the prince in his travels to famous scenic spots such as Mount O-mei, and he participated in events such as the celebration to mark the prince's restoration of Tu Fu's famous "thatched cottage" near Chengtu. When Fang was away from Szechwan attending to his duties in Han-chung, the prince sent him poems and gifts in return for scholarly advice and literary guidance. From the surviving correspondence between the two, it is possible to reconstruct something of Fang's relationship to the latter. In his letters to Fang, the young prince displays extreme deference to the learned scholar and authority on Confucian learning, while Fang in return both lauds him as a sage-ruler and reminds him of his Confucian responsibilities. It was the prince who in these years bestowed on Fang the study-name "Cheng-hsüeh" 正學 (Correct Learning); that remained the name by which Fang was to be known in the context of Confucian studies.

In 1396 Fang made another trip to Nanking to take charge of the provincial examination at the national capital. The accession of Chu Yün-wen (*q.v.*) in June, 1398, abruptly and radically altered Fang Hsiao-ju's life. The young grandson of the Ming founder, who now came to the throne, was under the influence of scholar officials who advised him on staffing the court with men of character and intellectual distinction. Fang Hsiao-ju's reputation was that of a Confucian man of principle who had ideas on statecraft; so the emperor immediately summoned him to the court as erudite, then expositor-in-waiting, in the Hanlin Academy. For a third time he served as director of the Nanking provincial examination, a rare honor which shows how much he was appreciated for his scholarship and personality. This is even more evident when he was made director of the metropolitan examination in 1400. Politically he was drawn into the inner circle of trusted advisers. The young emperor was soon forced to defend his throne against the rebellion of his uncle, Chu Ti (*q.v.*), the prince of Yen. The Nanking court's conduct of current affairs and its military policies were influenced most strongly by the minister of War, Ch'i T'ai (*q.v.*), and the chancellor of the Hanlin Academy, Huang Tzu-ch'eng (*see* Lien Tzu-ning). Fang was not prominently identified with the policy of "reducing the feudatories," designed by them, which lay at the center of the conflict between the emperor and his uncle. His influence was significant in another area of policy; the young emperor undertook a study of political institutions and philosophy, with Fang his intellectual adviser. Fang Hsiao-ju's professed ambition to aid an enlightened ruler usher in a golden age seemed to be on the point of fulfillment. Together they examined the *Chou-li*, reputed to be the repository of Chou dynasty political wisdom, as a possible model for reforms in the structure of government. They talked endlessly about the means by which the Confucian virtues could be inculcated so as to "transform the people through teachings" and thereby reduce the necessity for harsh controls, about how the ancient "well-field system" of land-holding and tithing could restore the health of society at the base level and eliminate many social and political evils, and how government could be made simpler and more effective. It is difficult to know in concrete detail what Fang's intentions were, and how far the emperor and court might have been led along the reform path had the civil war not intervened. Scholars have seen in Fang's intellectual orientations strong elements of the Chin-hua school's neo-Confucian ethical fundamentalism, of which Sung Lien was representative, combined with traces of utilitarian reformism. The latter is best known through such a Sung dynasty figure as Wang An-shih (1021-86), who, like Fang, also had drawn heavily on the *Chou-li* for his political ideas. Subsequently, in the Southern Sung period, there were other thinkers whose political thought continued in that mold. This strain in Sung thought may have been transmitted to Fang through

Wu Lai (1297-1340), one of the formative influences on Sung Lien. Scholars have speculated whether such background influences on Fang may have been significant; with or without this element in the explanation, Fang must be seen as an original thinker in several aspects of political thought. He went somewhat beyond any previous thinker in imperial times in attempting to define the relationship between the Chinese, the bearers of mankind's civilization, and the alien peoples on China's borders whose more primitive ways, coupled with their military aggressiveness, made them potential threats to civilization. His models and his terms were ancient, but Fang's conceptualization clearly reflected his observation of China's recent historical experience under a succession of alien conquest dynasties. Fang also developed original views on the origins of the ruler institution, and the nature of the ruler's responsibilities and functions. These accepted the neo-Confucian dualistic (or rationalist, li-hsüeh) ontology and cosmogony, that by Fang's time were highly conventional; but on those grounds he developed nonetheless some fairly original political theories. Finally, and perhaps of greatest interest, Fang took the idealistic views of government stemming from the Mencian tradition and reaffirmed by neo-Confucianism, views stressing the importance of the people, the practical utility of some antique ideals of communal organization and cooperation, and the necessity for maintaining the ethical foundations of human relations, and attempted to formulate concrete measures for applying these. For example, he believed that antique social institutions such as the well-field system, as described in *Mencius* (Legge, *Chinese Classics*, II, 119) could be made to work in the rural society of his time. From the Ming dynasty onward, even scholars sympathetic to Fang's noble ideals, have criticized him for the impracticability of such suggestions, but perhaps not with total justice, for Fang was not blind to the great changes in society since ancient times. He seems to have advocated a practical modification of the antique ideal, carefully adapted to the varying regional conditions of Chinese rural society. Fang was not merely a bookish scholar; he had observed the practical problems of local government in his native Chekiang, in Shantung, and in distant Shensi and Szechwan, widely disparate regions, and he embraced the Ming founder's stress on rebuilding local government through greater reliance on responsible local interests. His efforts to combine that basic Ming policy with Confucian-inspired ideals, validated by reference to antique models, may not have been as foolishly literal-minded or as unreasonable as has often been assumed. Fang's opportunity to apply his ideas was very brief, and an effort was made by the usurper to obliterate all traces of the political acts of the Chien-wen reign. About the only actual modifications in the structure and form of government that were promulgated, before the usurpation cut all that short, were changes in the names of government buildings, in titles of office, and in other such superficial and probably merely preliminary steps to make Ming government accord with *Chou-li* models. We have thus no way of judging what the practical import of Fang's political thought might have been had his career and his emperor's reign not been terminated.

To the prince of Yen, the Chien-wen reign held both actual and plausible threats to the Ming dynastic system, made sacred by the founder's Ancestral Instructions. There is no doubt that the policies of Ch'i T'ai and Huang Tzu-ch'eng threatened his power and prerogatives, and the vaguer political ideals of Fang Hsiao-ju too may have seemed to undermine the system. Whether Chu Ti's motives were those he proclaimed—*i.e.*, to protect the dynasty from policies that would weaken or destroy it, and the young emperor from advisers who were using him insidiously—is problematical. In any event,

he could make a significant if not wholly convincing argument that duty forced him to intervene. During the civil war that commenced in the late summer of 1399 Fang was not prominently involved in the war policy, although later historians have argued that by distracting the emperor with his idealistic reform schemes he in fact prevented a more clear-minded attention to the rebellion's suppression. During the last months of the civil war, however, in the spring and summer of 1401, as the Yen armies crossed the Huai River in their southward offensive and began to threaten the capital at Nanking, and with Ch'i T'ai and Huang Tzu-ch'eng both on assignment away from the capital, the emperor appears to have leaned more heavily on Fang for day-to-day advice about the war. That advice was disastrously incorrect, first in assuming that the Yangtze River would stop the northern forces, and then in judging the city of Nanking to be impregnable. In both cases, it was treason rather than military conquest which proved Fang mistaken, and finally, on July 13, 1401, Nanking's gates were treacherously opened to the usurper. The palace area was set afire, the emperor was assumed to be dead, and Fang Hsiao-ju was made prisoner, along with most of the court and government. Fang, however, was not so prominently identified with the policy of "reducing the feudatories" that his death was a foregone conclusion, and the usurper seems to have desired sincerely to win so eminent a man of integrity over to his cause, thereby to gain much in popular validation of it. The stories of how Chu Ti commanded Fang, first in polite terms, to draft the rescript announcing his succession, how Fang berated him as a criminal and usurper, how the usurper then tortured him physically and psychologically, but to no avail, have become legend. In the ruthless purge of Chien-wen supporters, the execution of Fang Hsiao-ju and his brother, then all his kin, all his associates, his students, friends, neighbors, and all persons even loosely connected with him, the various accounts numbering them from almost nine hundred to more than one thousand, stands out for the ferocity and thoroughness with which this vindictive act of intimidation was accomplished. The *Ming-shih* follows most sources in indicating that Fang's wife and four children committed suicide just before he was put to death. Many rumors concerning the survival of an heir developed later, however, and, despite the exposure of some fraudulent claims, these rumors may have had some substance; a brief article by the modern scholar, Li Mi 李洣, has argued the case. During the Yung-lo period the penalty for possessing even a scrap of Fang's writings was death (*see* Yang Shan), and although the suppression relaxed somewhat after that, the ban on his works was not lifted for a century. Yet he became the popular hero of his age, a venerated martyr, and, among Confucian ethical philosophers thereafter, his uncompromising stand in defiance of the usurpation had profound impact as a moral example.

The official exoneration of Fang Hsiao-ju and his fellow Chien-wen martyrs, however, was slow in coming. Despite repeated imperial gestures towards pardoning their descendants during the next one hundred fifty years, no positive action was taken until the reign of Emperor Chu I-chün (*q. v.*). In the spring of 1584, on the urging of the censor, T'u Shu-fang (*q. v.*) and others, the emperor decreed the release and rehabilitation of the surviving descendants of Fang and other condemned individuals, totaling over fifty thousand men and women. About the same time, the emperor ordered the erection of a shrine in Nanking in honor of the Chien-wen martyrs, called Piao-chung tz'u 表忠祠, with Fang Hsiao-ju second on the list. Fang was not, however, accorded a posthumous honor until 1645 when the Southern Ming court bestowed on him the name Wen-cheng 文正 (cultured and upright); on the same

occasion, the court granted the name Chen-min 貞愍 (chaste and mournful) to his wife. In 1775 the Ch'ien-lung emperor (*see* Hung-li, ECCP) honored Fang Hsiao-ju with the canonized name Chung-wen 忠文 (loyal and cultured), and in 1863 his spirit tablet was placed in the Confucian temple.

Fang Hsiao-ju frequently expressed disdain for those writers who sought purely literary values for their own sake, but he nonetheless had a keen appreciation of his literary heritage, and was accounted one of the finest essayists of his time. He was also an accomplished poet. Most of his writings were scholarly and philosophical; among the works which he is known to have written, but which seem not to have survived, are: a critical study of the *Chou-li*, a work on the Book of Changes, works on Chou, Han, and Sung history, and several others. He was editor-in-chief of the *shih-lu* of the Hung-wu reign compiled in 1400 (but subsequently superseded), and of another official compilation of the Chien-wen era no longer extant (*see* Li Wen-chung). He is said to have drafted many of the proclamations and rescripts of the Chien-wen period. Besides his literary talent, Fang is credited with excelling in sketching bamboos.

Fang Hsiao-ju's collection of writings, known as *Hsün-chih-chai chi* 遜志齋集, banned during the Yung-lo period, came to be scattered. They were later collected by his disciple, Wang Yü 王稌 (T. 叔豐, 1384–1441), and were preserved under the guise of another title, *Hou-ch'eng* 侯城*chi*. This collection was engraved under the original title in 1463. An enlarged version of the *Hsün-chih-chai chi*, 40 *ch.*, plus *wai-chi* 外紀, I *ch.*, appeared in 1480. This was condensed into 24 + 1 *ch.* by Ku Lin (*see* Yüan Ch'iung), who contributed a preface dated 1520. Two other editions, based on the 1520 version, appeared in 1541 and 1561 respectively; the latter was reproduced in the *Ssu-pu ts'ung-k'an* series (1937). These were followed by yet another edition with *wai-chi*, 2 *ch.*, in 1612.

Several editions of this collection appeared during the Ch'ing dynasty. The earliest of these, based on the 1612 version, came out in 1698, including a *nien-p'u* 年譜 compiled by Lu Yen 盧演. This edition, in most cases minus the *nien-p'u*, was reprinted several times in the Republican period, in Korea, and in Japan. In Ch'ing times, a scholar by the name of Fang Hsüeh-hang 方學沆 (a clansman ?), produced a supplement to Fang's collected works, entitled *Hsü* 續 *Hsün-chih-chai chi*, 14 *ch.*, a copy of which is preserved in the Naikaku Bunko. There are several partial selections of Fang's writings in the anthologies of the Ming and Ch'ing. The earliest of these, in 1 *chüan*, edited by Li Chih (*q. v.*) with his commentary, was printed together with the writings of two other Ming martyrs, Yü Ch'ien and Yang Chi-sheng (*qq. v.*), under the title *San i-jen chi* 三異人集, 11 *ch.* A copy of this work is also preserved in the Naikaku Bunko. In addition, some of Fang's essays on family instruction and on etiquette for the young are available as individual items in various *ts'ung-shu*.

Bibliography

1/117/1a, 141/4b, 281/3a; 5/6/1a, 20/53a, 96/1a; 42/79/16; 61/102/6a; 63/5/7a; 83/43/2a; KC (1958), 733, 789, 854, 860; T'u Shu-fang, *Chien-wen ch'ao-yeh hui-pien* (NCL microfilm), 7/1a; Ho Ch'iao-yüan, *Ming-shan ts'ang* (Taiwan 1970 ed.), 5082; Cha Chi-tso (ECCP), *Tsui-wei lu*, *chuan* 傳, ch. 9, pt. 1, 1a; SK (1930), 95/9a, 170/2a, 192/9b; Hu Yü-chin 胡玉縉, *SKCS tsung-mu t'i-yao pu-cheng* 補正 (1962 ed.), 1482; *T'ai-chou-fu chih* (1936), 101/2a; Li Mi, "Shu *Ming-shih* Fang Cheng-hsüeh hsien-sheng chuan hou" 書明史方正學先生傳後, *Wen-lan hsüeh-pao* 文瀾學報, 3: 1 (1937), 1; Hsiao Kung-ch'üan 蕭公權, *Chung-kuo cheng-chih ssu-hsiang shih* 中國政治思想史 (Taipei, 1954), 526; Ch'ien Mu (BDRC), "Tu Ming-ch'u k'ai-kuo chu-ch'en shih-wen chi" 讀明初開國諸臣詩文集, *Hsin-ya hsüeh-pao* 新亞學報, 6: 2 (August, 1964), 320; Harrie Vanderstappen, "Painters at the Early Ming court (1368-1435)," MS, 15 (1956), 289; R. B. Crawford, H. M. Lamley, and A. B. Mann, "Fang Hsiao-ju in the Light of Early Ming Society," MS, 15 (1956), 303; *Ku-kung shu-hua lu* 故宮書畫錄 (rev. ed., 1965), 1/93.

F. W. Mote

FANG Kuo-chen 方國珍, also recorded as Fang Ku-chen 谷珍 or 谷貞, 1319/1320–May 8, 1374, was a native of Huang-yen chou 黃巖州 in T'ai-chou lu 台州路 (modern Huang-yen in Chekiang) who maintained a virtually independent regime in the east-coast Chiang-Che from 1348 to 1367. During most of this time, he was at least nominally an official under the Yüan or under Chu Yüan-chang or, for several years, under both at the same time. He supported himself in part by revenue from cities subject to his control and in part by raids on coastal towns and on public and private shipping.

Conditions of governmental inefficiency and corruption in Fang Kuo-chen's native place were favorable for piracy and his own experience fitted him for a life of maritime adventure. His forebears were salt traders who had moved from a salt-drying center in Fukien to Huang-yen, where they also engaged in fishing. Accused of collaborating with pirates, Fang was on the point of arrest late in 1348 when he escaped with his brothers to the sea. Rough characters now flocked to his side, so that in a month's time he had a following of several thousand. An official sent to apprehend him was captured instead, and forced to recommend him to the Yüan court for a government post. He was accordingly given a modest military rank but he continued his piratical attacks on government ships transporting grain. The Yüan court at Peking depended heavily on the annual delivery of tax —grain from east and south China shipped chiefly by sea. Thus Fang's attacks constituted an increasingly serious threat to the life line of the Mongol court, especially after the uprisings in central and eastern China from 1352 on forced the government to concentrate its naval forces along the Yangtze River. Fang took advantage of the situation and by alternately surrendering and rebelling three more times during the following eight years he obtained increasingly higher rank, expanded his fleet to more than a thousand ships, and came into control of the coastal area from Hangchow Bay to the Fukien border. His second surrender took place in the autumn of 1351 after he had defeated the navy and captured its commanders; he then was offered the post of a chiliarch commander of coastal defense at T'ai-chou. When the rebellions in central China began in the spring of 1352 (see Kuo Tzu-hsing), Fang returned to his piratical activities. In 1353, while the provincial government deliberated on an attractive offer to Fang to secure his surrender, a minor official, Liu Chi (q.v.), criticized the plan as one fostering lawlessness and argued that such offers should be given to loyalists, not to a rebel like Fang. For this sound advice Liu was placed in confinement as an obstructionist. On the other hand, when the government offered Fang an inland office he suspected a trap and once more returned to piracy. This time his successes were even greater as he crushed the navy and took Huang-yen and T'ai-chou in 1354 and then Ch'ing-yüan 慶元 (Ningpo) and Wen-chou 溫州 in 1355. These cities were to remain in his possession until they fell to the forces of Chu Yüan-chang in 1367.

In 1356 the Yüan government was further weakened by losing P'ing-chiang (Soochow) to Chang Shih-ch'eng (q.v.) and Chi-ch'ing (Nanking) to Chu Yüan-chang. It was finally forced to recognize Fang's position as ruler of the Chiang-Che coast by giving him the offices of myriad commander of the sea-route grain transportation service （海道運糧漕運萬戶府) and myriad commander of the sea route escort service （海道運糧防禦萬戶府). Thus induced to surrender for the fourth time, he changed his role from that of a marauder to that of guardian angel and presumably made some deliveries of grain to Peking during the following decade.

He even answered the call of the Yüan government to send an army against Chang Shih-ch'eng in 1357, and helped to force the latter to accept a nominal appointment. For his services Fang was rewarded with frequent promotions in the Chiang-Che provincial government. In this same year he was given the concurrent rank of an assistant to the governor, and a year later, that of associate governor. He was then promoted to chief administrator in November, 1359, and finally, to chief counselor for a time of Huai-nan 淮南 (October, 1365) with the hereditary rank of duke of Ch'ü 衢國公, and the honorary rank of t'ai-wei 太尉 (grand marshal).

Yet Fang tried to maintain his freedom of action, and in 1358 even annexed by force the government held city of Shao-hsing 紹興. Perhaps he hoped to preserve this independent position indefinitely by maintaining his ties with Peking but at the same time cultivating good relations with all his neighbors, such as the Yüan loyalist in Fukien, Ch'en Yu-ting 陳友定 (T. 安國, d. 1368), and the rebel, Chu Yüan-chang, to the northwest. In January of 1359 Chu's forces advanced south to Chin-hua 金華 and Chien-te 建德, directly threatening Fang's territory to the east. On Chu's call to surrender Fang sent an obsequious reply, asking for a feudatory position. Late in that year he received an order from Chu to head the administration of Fukien, a territory that was still held by Ch'en Yu-ting. Fang did not refuse the appointment nor did he take action. He continued to use the Yüan calendar much to the annoyance of Chu, and sought to placate the latter on various occasions with money and words. In May, 1367, he received a letter from Chu accusing him of twelve "crimes" and calling on him to surrender or be destroyed. In August, on the eve of the complete conquest of Chang Shih-ch'eng's state by Chu's forces, Fang was given a final warning by Chu to surrender, but still he procrastinated. In October Chu commenced military conquest of Fang's territory which he quickly accomplished (*see* T'ang Ho). At the last moment Fang boarded a ship to escape capture, and then sent a letter to Chu offering to surrender. The letter was so expertly composed that Chu was moved to give him assurance of leniency. Fang finally surrendered in mid-December, 1367.

An accounting of Fang's forces surrendered to the Ming state of Chu Yüan-chang indicated about nine thousand foot soldiers, fourteen thousand seamen, six hundred fifty officials, and four hundred twenty ships. The ships immediately served as part of the fleet that transported T'ang Ho and his men southward to the conquest of Fukien (*see* Liao Yung-chung).

Fang was taken with his family to Nanking. In November, 1368, Chu, now emperor, gave him the title and stipend of a vice administrator of Kwangsi but held him at Nanking where he died. He was buried with honors. His sons, Fang Li 禮 and Fang Kuan 觀 (also written 關 or Wan 完) were given military ranks. In 1376, at their request, permission was given for the erection of a memorial monument eulogizing Fang Kuo-chen. By imperial order, Sung Lien (*q.v.*) wrote the inscription representing the rude adventurer as a victim of many injustices whose sole purpose had been to preserve his own life in a time of trouble and to give protection to the people in his care.

Fang and his brothers were illiterate but they brought a few learned men into their service. Or rather, some men of letters came to serve under them for protection and for subsistence. At the time of surrender in 1367, a few were beaten to death by the conquerors, among whom was Liu Jen-pen 劉仁本 (T. 德元). Hundreds were sent to Hao-chou (Feng-yang) perhaps to work as laborers. Some were invited to serve in the new regime; for example, Ch'iu Nan 邱楠, who was made sub-prefect of Shao-chou 韶州, and Chan Ting 詹鼎 (T. 國器), who became an official in the ministry of Justice.

Chan Ting was the one who composed Fang's letter of surrender in 1367, the acceptance of which saved Fang. But Chan lost his life when he became involved in a bribery case sometime after 1375.

Bibliography

1/23/11b; 61/90/21b; MSL(1963), T'ai-tsu 1560; Sung Lien, *Sung hsüeh-shih wen-chi*, 40/12b; *Hsin Yüan shih* 新元史, 227/1a; Ku Ying-t'ai (ECCP), *Ming ch'ao chi-shih pen-mo*, ch. 5; Hsia Hsieh 夏燮, *Ming t'ung-chien* 明通鑑; *T'ai-chou-fu chih* 台州府志 (1936), 117/6b, 10a, 133/3a; Cha Chi-tso (ECCP), *Tsui-wei lu*, biography 6/4a.

Romeyn Taylor

FANG Ts'ung-i 方從義 (T. 無隅, H. 方壺, 上清羽士, 鬼谷山人, 不芒道人, 金門羽客), *ca.* 1301–93, a talented painter, was a native of Kuei-ch'i 貴溪, Kiangsi. Little is known of his early years, except that he seems to have become interested in Taoism when quite young, possibly because of the proximity of his home to Mt. Lung-hu, the religious center from the 11th century on of the descendants of the Taoist Chang 張 family (*see* Chang Cheng-ch'ang). He joined the Taoist order at the Hun-ch'eng yüan 混成院 on this eminence, studied the art of immortality under one of its adepts, and formed a society which included Chang Meng-hsün 張孟循 and Lu Po-liang 盧伯良.

Fang must have attracted attention when still relatively young. In 1338 he executed a painting entitled "yün-lin t'u" 雲林圖 (Cloudy forests), depicting the mountain retreat in Lin-ch'uan 臨川 where his "old friend" Wei Su (*q.v.*) used to study. This painting, no longer extant, drew the plaudits of several of his contemporaries: Ch'en Lü (1288–1343), Yü Chi (1272–1348), K'o Chiu-ssu (*see* Chu Ch'üan), and Chang Yü 張雨 (1277–1348), another Taoist, all of whom wrote colophons for it. In addition to these men, he also became acquainted with some other literati in Ta-tu 大都, the Yüan capital, for he was known to have spent some time there most likely during the 1340s and 1350s. They included Chang Yen-fu 張彥輔, another Taoist from Mt. Lung-hu, who painted a landscape of Mt. Sheng-ching 聖井山 (a mountain near Lung-hu shan) for Fang, with prefaces by Wei Su and Yü Ch'üeh (1303–58), testifying to Fang's nobility of character. In the capital Fang was known as a man who did not go there to seek a position in the court but to display his talents in art and literature. Also, during his stay in the north, he visited some mountains and passes to gain inspiration for his art.

Fang probably returned to Kuei-ch'i during the 1350s and became a priest in the Shang-ch'ing-kung 上清宮, the chief Taoist place of worship on Mt. Lung-hu, where he seems to have stayed until at least 1375. During these years he became a friend of a number of people, especially a group of well-known Taoists, such as Teng Yü and Chang Yü-ch'u (qq.v.). In addition, several literati of the late Yüan and early Ming were among his acquaintances, for all wrote poems for him. They include Li Ts'un 李存 (T. 明遠, d. 1377), Kao Ch'i, Chang Yü (qq.v.), Cheng Chen 鄭眞 (T. 千之, H. 滎陽外史, cj 1372), and Kao Ping (see Lin Hung). Fang is said to have been skilled in both poetry and prose, although at present—except for several poems incorporated in the *Yüan shih hsüan* 元詩選—there is no volume of any kind credited to him. In calligraphy he was reputedly adept in archaic, li 隸, and grass 草 styles. Examples of the last two may be found among the inscriptions he wrote on some of his paintings.

Fang is best known as a painter of landscapes following the examples of cloudy mountains by Mi Fu (1051–1107) and his son, Mi Yu-jen (1074–1153), and Kao K'o-kung (1248–1310). Their works were all known for their elusive and fleeting effect. Fang Ts'ung-i, however, instead of following their models closely seems to have made use of their approach in a peculiarly Taoist way. His main contribution lies in adapting this tradition to express the Taoist interest in the mountains of the immortals. Although he seems to have had a long and active life, at present only some thirty extant paintings are attributed to his name. Of these perhaps half are generally accepted. Most of them, if dated, are works of his last forty years. From these some notion of his development and his style can be reconstructed. One of the earliest dated paintings is the "Wu-i fang cho t'u" 武夷放棹圖 (Boating on a lake on Mt. Wu-i), now in the Chi-ch'ien Wang collection, New York. His inspiration, according to his own inscription, was derived from a landscape by the monk Chü-jan (d. 976+) and was painted in 1359 when he was residing on Wu-chün shan 烏君山. The composition and brushwork, however, are more indebted to one of his senior contemporaries, Wu Chen (1280–1354), who followed the same tenth-century painter, but the brushwork is quite personal and free. The "T'ai-po lung chiu 太白瀧湫 t'u" (Waterfall on Mt. T'ai-po), dated 1360, in the Abe collection of Osaka Municipal Museum, and the "Shen yüeh ch'iung lin 神嶽瓊林 t'u," dated 1365, in the Palace Museum, Taipei, seem to have taken up the late Yüan composition exemplified by Wang Meng, Hsü Pen (qq.v.), and some other artists. Another scroll, well recorded but hitherto unpublished, is the "Tung-chin feng liu t'u chüan" 東晉風流圖卷 (Literary expression of Eastern Chin), dated 1360, now in the Wang collection, which was painted as a companion piece for the copy by Chao Meng-fu (see T'ao Tsung-i) of the famous "Lan-t'ing hsü" 蘭亭序 (Introduction to the Lan-t'ing literary gathering) of Wang Hsi-chih (321–79). The "Yün-shan ch'iu-hsing 雲山秋興 t'u" (Autumn feeling for cloudy mountains), dated 1368 (published by K. Harada), and the "Shan-yin yün hsüeh 山陰雲雪 t'u" (Clouds and snow in Shan-yin), dated 1375 by a colophon, now in the Palace Museum, Taipei, seem to have been more original in composition and more personal in execution. Another hand-scroll, the "Yün 雲-shan t'u" (Cloudy mountains), in the Wang collection, is also a variation on the same theme. They represent his indebtedness to Mi Fu and Kao K'o-kung as well as to some of his contemporaries.

Several other paintings, some dated and some undated, appear to represent the last period of his life, when Fang was quite free in execution and bold in composition. They include the "Yün-shan t'u" of 1378 (published by Cheng Chen-to (BDRC), which, though a very small painting, shows his free strokes most prominently. Another painting of the same title, not dated (published in *T'ang Sung Yüan Ming Ch'ing hua hsüan* 唐宋元明清畫選, pl. 30), is even freer in the strokes. The "Wu-lao ch'iu-feng 五老秋風 t'u" (Autumn winds over Mt. Wu-lao), also undated (published by Harada), follows a theme of Kao K'o-kung, but shows the mountains as if in motion, a rather new departure from that tradition. The "Kao-kao-t'ing 高高亭 t'u" (Pavilion on a steep terrace), also undated, now in the Palace Museum, Taipei, is original in both composition and brushwork. The "Yün-shan shen-ch'u 雲山深處 t'u" (Retreat on cloudy mountains), 1392, his last dated work, now in the Shanghai Museum, is again a very free and powerful expression of his own. One of his last works is probably the "Mo-pi shan-shui hsiao fu" 墨筆山水小幅 (Small ink landscape), now in the Wang collection (formerly published in the Nansō Ihatsu 南宗衣鉢, IV). Unsigned and undated, it is identified only by a seal and some colophons. The painting, if accepted, is the freest among all of his works and freer than any Yüan paintings reflecting both his and early Ming developments. All these paintings represent his consistent evolution. Besides landscapes he painted some bamboos. One of these is now in the Masagi Museum in Izumi-Otsu near Osaka.

Fang Ts'ung-i is known to have had at least one pupil, Lin Chüan-a 林卷阿, who mentions this relationship in his only extant work, "Shan-yai tui-tso 山崖對坐 t'u" (Sitting face to face at the mountain cliffs), now in the Palace Museum, Taipei. Since Lin refers to both Fang Ts'ung-i and his associate Chang Meng-hsün as his teachers, he must also have been a Taoist. The painting is dated 1373. In addition, Kao Ping is said to have become known for is paintings after receiving high praise from Fang, although he was probably not his own pupil.

Fang Ts'ung-i was one of the most original and creative artists of his time. As a Taoist and an eccentric, he saw no need to conform to the accepted norms of his day and developed his own style by going beyond the limits set in the models of the Mi tradition and in those of the Yüan literati painters. For as a Taoist Fang seems to have tried to express, through a style which was among the most untraditional in his day, his desire to be free of worldly things as a means of attaining the realm of the immortals. That this ideal seems of have been very much in his heart may be seen in the names he adopted for his later years as well as in the names of the mountains he depicted in his paintings. Wu-lao, T'ai-po, Wu-i, and others, are all peaks frequently mentioned in the literature as a-bodes of famous immortals. This is why he is often mentioned in later art criticism as an artist in the i-p'in 逸品 group along with Ni Tsan (*q.v.*). One of his contemporaries, Li Ts'un, had this to say about him: "Fang-hu 方壺 reached the utmost limit in studying the art of the immortals. He gave shape to things which have no shape and returned things which have shape to the shapeless. As he was able to do this in his paintings, he must have reached the utmost limit. How could he have done it without being an immortal?" (Sirén translation).

Bibliography

Hsia Wen-yen 夏文彥, *T'u-hui pao-chien* 圖繪寶

鑑(1365), 5/108; T'ao Tsung-i, *Shu-shih hui-yao*, 7/21a; Chiang Shao-shu 姜紹書, *Wu-sheng shih shih* 無聲詩史, *Hua-shih* 畫史 ts'ung-shu ed., 1/8b, 13a; Ku Ssu-li 顧嗣立 (1669-1722), *Yüan shih hsüan*, 33/20b; *Yüan shih hsüan, kuei chi* 癸集, 壬上/7b; *Kuang-hsin-fu chih* 廣信府志 (1783), 24/20a; *Kuei-ch'i-hsien chih* (1871), 8/10/2b; *Lung-hu-shan chih* (1740), 7/22b; Ch'eng T'ing-kuei, *Chü-chu-hsüan chi* 居竹軒集, 1/15a, 2/17a; Li Ts'un, *Ssu-an chi* 俟庵集, 26/6b; Yü Chi, *Tao-yüan hsüeh ku lu* 道園學古錄 (new Taipei Commercial Press ed.), 28/251b, 29/26la; Yü Ch'üeh *Ch'ing-yang chi* 青陽集, 4/12b; Cheng Chen, *Jung-yang-wai-shih chi*, 滎陽外史集, 90/16, 22, 23; Wang Shih-chen, *Yen-chou-shan-jen ssu-pu kao*, 137/18a; *id.*, *I-yüan chih-yen* (Yü Chien-hua 俞劍華, *Chung-kuo hua-lun lei-pien* 中國畫論類編 [1957], 117); Chang Ch'ou, *Ch'ing-ho shu-hua fang* 清河書畫舫, 10/22a; Yü Feng-ch'ing 郁逢慶, *Yü-shih shu-hua t'i-pa chi* 郁氏書畫題跋記後篇 (1911), 3/33a; Pien Yung-yü (ECCP), *Shih-ku-t'ang shu-hua hui k'ao*, 23/1a; Yang En-shou 楊恩壽, *Yen fu p'ien* 眼福篇, 1/9/37a; Ch'en Pang-yen (ECCP, p.88) ed., *Li-tai t'i-hua shih lei* 歷代題畫詩類, 13/6b; Cheng Chen-to, *Wei-ta-ti i-shu ch'uan-t'ung t'u lu* (Shanghai, 1954), Section VIII, pl. 11; Osvald Sirén, *Chinese Painting*, Vol. IV (New York, 1958), 58; Sherman E. Lee and Wai-kam Ho, *Chinese Art Under the Mongols: The Yüan Dynasty (1279-1368)* (Cleveland, 1968), 268; Harada Kinjirō, *Shina meiga hokan* (Tokyo, 1936), pls. 381, 383.

Chu-tsing Li

FANG Yü-lu 方于魯 (T. 建元, original name 大滶), fl. 1570-1619, ink maker and minor poet, came from a family living in She 歙-hsien in the prefecture of Hui-chou 徽州 (Anhwei). He was born, however, in Chiang-ling 江陵, Hukuang, where his father was engaged in business. In his youth he reportedly squandered a large fortune of his friend; as a consequence he entered adult life in a state of destitution. It was as a pioneer printer of woodcut illustrations that he made his mark and won acclaim. He is also known for an acrimonious feud with his fellow townsman and business rival, Ch'eng Ta-yüeh (*q.v.*). Actually what we know of Fang's life is chiefly based on Ch'eng's account written after the break in their friendship, hence perhaps exaggerated.

According to Ch'eng, Fang, impoverished and desperate, begged Ch'eng to teach him the art of ink making. Ch'eng agreed, boarded, clothed, and taught him all he knew about the business. An apt student, Fang became proficient in the art. It is said that he mixed his ingredients with bear's gall and his ink was therefore bitter in taste. After parting, Fang became a keen competitor of his former benefactor. This started a quarrel that lasted a long time, each side with its own clique and partisans.

Ch'eng alleged that Fang was once arrested and flogged for selling ink tablets which the latter asserted were made by former masters but which were proved to be spurious, and that he was imprisoned for other fraudulent practices. There is also the story that Ch'eng had a concubine whom he was forced to give up because of the jealousy of his wife. It happened that Fang was infatuated with the concubine and eventually married her, further infuriating Ch'eng. With consummate skill and imagination Fang in 1588 produced after five years of preparation the first printing of an album of the designs and pictures on his ink tablets which were executed by two of the outstanding artists of his time, Ting Yün-p'eng (*q.v.*) and Wu T'ing-yü 吳廷羽 (T. 左千, from Hsiu-ning 休寧, Anhwei) under the title *Fang-shih mo-p'u* 方氏墨譜, 6 *ch.* The woodblocks were cut by Huang Shou-yen 黃守言, a member of the Huang clan in the Hui-chou area which furnished the most skilled craftsmen for woodblock engraving. The album contains upwards of three hundred eighty illustrations, arranged under six broad categories. They include designs for jade tablets or batons, imperial seals, ornaments for wearing apparel, also representations of antiques, Buddhist and Taoist legends, and a whole *chüan* (no. 5) devoted mainly to Tibetan (Lamaistic) symbols. He prevailed upon a great number of celebrities and friends to contribute relevant compositions for inclusion in the album. Some of the ink tablets bore dates, ranging from 1573 to 1616. It is said that he presented a copy of the album to the emperor, possibly about 1594 (*see* Ch'en Yü-pi).

Fang was a pupil and close friend of his fellow townsmen Wang Tao-k'un (*q. v.*), a one-time senior minister of War, and his brother, Wang Tao-kuan 貫 (T. 仲淹). Together with a cousin, Wang Tao-hui 會 (T. 仲嘉), they formed a famous trio which for a time dominated the social and literary world. All of them wrote laudatory essays for Fang's album. The older Wang was a scholar of great repute who gathered around him a coterie of literary and artistic celebrities. On the recommendation of the Wang brothers, Fang joined the exclusive Feng-kan she 豐干社, a prestigious literary and social club of his day over which Wang presided. On the occasion of a dragon boat festival, Fang with fellow members of the club took a boat ride on the Feng River during a downpour. As the water rose alarmingly their craft moved swiftly downstream in the rapids. This experience furnished the source of inspiration for literary compositions commemorating the occasion. The close relationship between Fang and Wang Tao-k'un was resented by the former's benefactor Ch'eng Ta-yüeh who denounced him as an ingrate, a fraud, and a sycophant. Fang was also a friend of the Wang brothers, Wang Shih-chen and Wang Shih-mou (*qq.v.*), both scholars of distinction. They too contributed essays for his album.

In addition to his fame as an ink maker, Fang was a poet of some note. His collection of poems was published in 1608 under the title *Chia-jih-lou chi* 佳日樓集, 13 *ch.*, which is listed by title only in the *Ssu-k'u* catalogue as *Fang Chien-yüan shih-chi* 建元詩集. Two of Fang's poems are incorporated in the *Ming shih tsung,* an anthology of Ming poets edited in 1705 by Chu I-tsun (ECCP). Fang's collection

of *tz'u* is included in the *Chia-jih-lou tz'u* in a single *chüan*. The anthology *Ming tz'u tsung,* edited by Wang Ch'ang (ECCP), also includes one of Fang's pieces.

The *Chia-jih-lou chi* is extremely rare today. A copy was acquired by the late Cheng Chen-to (BDRC), together with the *Ch'eng-shih mo-yüan* of Ch'eng Ta-yüeh. In his descriptive note Cheng Chen-to draws attention to an essay on slander which Fang wrote on his feud with Ch'eng Ta-yüeh. Fang stated that following his misfortune as a result of embroilment with his one-time benefactor, whom he had not seen for over ten years, he had repeatedly been abused. He quoted an old adage; to stop slander, there is nothing like discreet behavior. Although he made no mention of his so-called enemy by name, he was bitter in tone and vowed to perpetuate the vendetta.

Fang traveled widely and was interested in antiquities and famous retreats in various parts of the country; but in his later years he lived in She-hsien. In one of the poems included in the *Ming shih tsung* he stated that he had not left his home town for ten years and was delighted to entertain visitors from distant places. He had a son named Fang Chia-shu 方嘉樹 (T. 子封), who followed his father's trade and became a famous ink maker in his own right. Some examples of Fang Chia-shu's handicraft are also included in the *Fang-shih mo-p'u.*

Bibliography

40/64/24b; 43/5/4a; 86/18/6a; Ch'eng Ta-yüeh, *Ch'eng-shih mo-yüan* (1606); SK (1930), 116/4a, 178/13b; *She-hsien chih* (1937), 15/8a; Cheng Chen-to (BDRC), *Chieh-chung te-shu chi* (1956), 35; Kuo Wei-ch'ü 郭味蕖, *Chung-kuo pan-hua shih-lüeh* 中國版畫史略 (1962), 107; Wang Po-min 王伯敏, *Chung-kuo pan-hua shih* (1961), 108; Wang Chi-chen, "Notes on Chinese ink," *Metropolitan Museum Studies*, Vol. 3, pt. 1 (1930), 114; Paul Pelliot, "La peinture et la gravure européennes en Chine au temps de Mathieu Ricci," TP, XX (1921), 2; *Arts of the Ming Dynasty* (London, 1958), 20.

K. T. Wu

FEI Hsin費信 (T. 公曉), 1388-1436?, author of one of the records of expeditions of Cheng Ho (q.v.), was a native of K'un-shan 崑山, and belonged to a family of military register in the T'ai-ts'ang 太倉 guard, northeast of Soochow. We find him first serving in the garrison at T'ai-ts'ang, and it was in this same guard at Liu-chia-kang 劉家港 that Cheng Ho's fleets congregated before sailing out to sea. He was apparently pressed into service for the third expedition of 1409-11, and again for the fifth (1417-19), and the seventh (1431-33). With the clear exception of Bengal and Mecca, he probably visited the same places as Ma Huan (q.v.). Fei may not have started writing his book, known as Hsing-ch'a sheng-lan 星槎勝覽 (Captivating views from a star guided vessel), 2 ch., until after his return from the last voyage, that is, nearly twenty years after Ma began to compile his own. This may explain its lack of freshness and immediacy in comparison with Ma's. There is a possibility that Ma Huan's manuscript was available to him, as well as to Kung Chen 鞏珍 (T. 養素生), another soldier who went on the voyages and wrote a book, Hsi-yang fan-kuo chih 西洋番國志 (Record of foreign countries in the western ocean), 1 ch. (preface 1434). These two works by Fei and Kung, therefore, supplement Ma Huan's; but even Fei's, which is markedly more original than what survives of Kung's, might have been influenced by the work of Ma.

The Hsing-ch'a sheng-lan was probably first printed in 1436, some fifteen years earlier than the Ying-yai sheng-lan of Ma Huan. Again there is a marked difference between Fei Hsin's original version and the better-known edited and polished version which Feng Ch'eng-chün (BDRC) believes was the work of a fellow townsman named Chou Fu-chün 周復俊 (T. 子籲, H. 木涇子, 1496-1574, cs 1532). Fei Hsin's original version was preserved only in manuscript form until the 20th century. The earliest surviving manuscript is the one copied from the version printed in the Kuo-ch'ao tien-ku of Chu Tang-mien (see Ma Huan). This was preserved in the T'ien-i-ko library of the family of Fan Mou-chu (ECCP), and was the version collated by Lo Chen-yü (BDRC) early in this century, and printed in the Liu-ching-k'an 六經堪 ts'ung-shu. An even more authoritative version is the Ming manuscript collated by Lo I-chih 羅以智 (fl. 1840), which Feng Ch'eng-chün used as the basis of his anotated edition, the Hsing-ch'a sheng-lan chiao-chu 校注.

The slightly abbreviated Chou Fu-chün edition has survived in several collections, the earliest printed version in the Ku-chin shuo-hai of Lu Chi (see Lu Shen) and another somewhat better one in the Chi-lu hui-pien of of Shen Chieh-fu (q.v.). There are at least six other versions of this edition in various collectanea. Feng Ch'eng-chün, who has examined all of them, has pronounced the one in the Chi-lu hui-pien best; his authoritative edition is based on it.

The books by Ma Huan and Fei Hsin contribute a great deal of information about the world overseas as known to the Chinese after the great Cheng Ho expeditions. They tell us about Chinese relations with these southern and western regions, about Chinese attitudes towards alien cultures, about Chinese shipping, navigation, and commercial interests, most of all, about the conditions of most of the countries along the shores of the South China Sea, the Straits of Malacca, and key parts of the littoral of the Indian Ocean. They were the only major works of travel in Asia during the 15th century and fill the gap between Marco Polo and Ibn Batuta on one hand and the Portuguese writings of the early 16th century on the other. Furthermore, no other earlier work tells us more accurately and describes to us more vividly the conditions of the major countries in southeast Asia prior to the arrival of the Europeans after 1500. Significantly both for Chinese and for Asian history (and especially southeast Asian history), the two books were never known outside China and were never widely known even in China itself. They received the attention they deserved only in the 20th century.

Bibliography

1/97/29b; *T'ai-ts'ang-chou chih* (1500, repr. 1909), 8/12b; *Hsing-ch'a sheng-lan chiao-chu* (ed. by Feng Ch'eng-chün, 1935); SK (1930), 78/4b; Kung Chen, *Hsi-yang fan-kuo chih* (the edition annotated by Hsiang Ta 向達, 1961); Ma Huan, *Ying-yai sheng-lan: The Overall Survey of the Ocean's Shores (1433)*, tr. and edited by J. V. G. Mills (Cambridge, 1970); J. J. L. Duyvendak, *Ma Huan Reexamined* (Amsterdam, 1933); id., "The True Dates of the Chinese Maritime Expeditions in the Early Fifteenth Century," TP, 34 (1938), 341; P. Pelliot, "Les grands voyages maritimes chinois au début du XVe siècle, " TP, 30 (1933), 237; id., "Notes additionelles sur Tcheng Houo et sur ses voyages," TP, 31 (1935), 274; id., "Encore à propos des voyages de Tcheng Houo," TP, 32 (1936), 210; W. W. Rockhill, "Notes on the Relations and Trade of China with the Eastern Archipelago and the Coasts of the Indian Ocean during the Fourteenth Century," TP, 16 (1915), 61; Joseph Needham, *Science and Civilization in China*, IV: 3 (Cambridge, England, 1971), 492.

Wang Gungwu

FEI Hung 費宏 (T. 子充, H. 健齋, 湖東, 鵝湖, Pth. 文憲), March 20, 1468-November 15, 1535, official, a native of Ch'ienshan 鉛山, Kiangsi, served three times as grand secretary during the years 1511 to 1535. Becoming a *chü-jen* at the age of only sixteen *sui* in 1483, he entered the National University at Peking in the following year after failing to pass the metropolitan examination. Three years later, in 1487, he captured the highest honors and became the youngest *chuang-yüan* in the entire Ming period. He received appointment as first class Hanlin compiler, and assisted in the preparation of the *Hsien-tsung shih-lu* 憲宗實錄. Before its completion, however, Fei took sick leave and returned home, where he remained until 1495, and then he was appointed director of instruction of the heir apparent. When his parents died one after the other, he retired once more. Not until 1503 did he return to Peking to resume his official career. In 1506 he took part in the compilation of the *Hsiao-tsung* 孝宗 *shih-lu*, rising to be junior vice minister of Rites in 1507. Elevated to minister of Rites in 1510, Fei became a grand secretary in 1511. Honored as grand guardian of the heir apparent and grand secretary of the Wu-ying-tien 武英殿, he was given the title of minister of Revenue.

Because of the personality and the unrestrained conduct of the emperor, the Cheng-te years were difficult for responsible officials. At first there was the usurpation of power by the eunuch Liu Chin (*q.v.*), followed by other imperial favorites such as Ch'ien Ning (*see* Sayyid Ḥusain). In addition to periodic local disturbances in interior China, trouble also erupted on the frontier. Finally there came the rebellion (in 1519) of Chu Ch'en-hao (*see* Wang Shou-jen), a prince of the imperial family, who openly contended for the throne.

As early as 1507 Chu Ch'en-hao requested permission to restore to his princedom in Kiangsi the guards which had previously been withdrawn. Liu Chin saw to the granting of this request; after Liu's execution, however, it was denied. In 1514 Chu renewed his request, at the same time bribing important personages at court such as Ch'ien Ning. Sensing the prince's designs, Fei strongly opposed approval of the measure, antagonizing both Chu Ch'en-hao and Ch'ien Ning. On May 26, 1514, Fei was forced to retire. A younger cousin of his, Fei Ts'ai 費寀 (T. 子和, H. 鐘石, 1483-January 11, 1549, cs 1511), then a Hanlin compiler, also lost his post. As their native place was in the shadow of Chu's princedom, they were in extreme jeopardy. It was said that they were harassed on their trip home, their houses set on fire, and even their family graveyard pillaged. This dangerous situation lasted until Wang Shou-jen crushed Chu Ch'en-hao's rebellion. During Wang's campaign, Fei Ts'ai corresponded with him and made certain helpful suggestions.

With the advent of the new emperor, Chu Hou-ts'ung (*q. v.*), Fei Hung was promptly summoned back to court, and reinstated as grand secretary (November 26, 1521). For the following six and a half years, Fei enjoyed increasing honor and favor. During the *Ta-li-i* controversy (*see* Feng Hsi), he seems to have shown more understanding and greater sympathy than other courtiers toward the young emperor. Although he signed certain collective memorials in protest, he never submitted any individual memorial attacking the emperor's position. For this the emperor was grateful. Exactly for the same reason, he aroused the jealousy of the newly advanced officials who had taken the emperor's side, namely, Chang Fu-ching and Kuei O (*qq.v.*). Early in 1527 Fei begged to retire, and did so with no loss of honor. Had there been more high officials with his conciliatory attitude, the controversy might have caused less of an uproar.

After his departure, Chang Fu-ching became grand secretary. Eight years later, when Chang retired, the court recalled Fei Hung and made him grand secretary for the third time. About two months after his arrival at Peking, however, he died at his post. Accorded various posthumous honors, he was canonized as Wen-hsien 文憲. His eldest son Fei Mou-hsien 費懋賢 (T. 民猷), a *chin-shih* of 1526, officiated as a bureau director in the ministry of War.

Fei Hung left a collection of literary works in 12 *chüan* known as the *Wen-hsien chi* 文憲集 and his collected verse, the *Ming t'ai-pao Fei Wen-hsien-kung shih-chi* 明太保費文憲公詩集, 15 *ch.*, first printed by Huang Chung 黃中 (T. 文卿, H. 西野, cj 1531) during Huang's term as magistrate of Ch'ien-shan (1543-47). The National Central Library of Taipei has two works by Fei: *T'ai-pao Fei Wen-hsien-kung chai-kao* 摘稿, 20 *ch.*, printed in 1555, and *Fei Wen-hsien-kung wen-chi hsüan yao* 文集選要, 7 *ch*. The younger cousin, Fei Ts'ai,

who rose in office to be minister of Rites, was given the posthumous name Went'ung 文通. Fei Ts'ai's collection of literary works, entitled *Chung-shih hsien-sheng wen-chi* 鐘石先生文集, 24 *ch.*, was first printed in 1570.

The special concern with dreams looms significantly in Ming literature. Accounts of dreams are many and varied. As the primary attention of students and scholars was focused on the examinations, a large proportion of the recorded dreams are also centered on these competitions. Of the eighty-nine *chuang-yüan* who graduated between 1371 and 1643, over half were involved in premonitory dreams. Besides their own dreams, other people too dreamed of their success, several *chuang-yüan* were the subject of more than one dream. Fei Hung's is a case in point. In 1484, when he was en route to Peking to take part in the metropolitan examinations, he stopped at Hsü-chou 徐州 to visit his uncle, Fei Hsüan 費瑄 (T. 仲玉, H. 復庵, cs 1475), then a bureau secretary in the ministry of Works charged with river conservancy and relief works in this vicinity. Fei Hsüan advised his nephew that in the event of failure that year, it would be best for him to enter the National University in the capital, rather than return home. It is said that the uncle once dreamed of his nephew entering the university and receiving the bamboo slip (place card), which had belonged to P'eng Shih (*q.v.*). To the uncle this was an omen that Fei Hung eventually would capture the *chuang-yüan* honor just as P'eng Shih had done in 1448. One of Fei Hung's biographers wrote that this dream really foretold much more than the uncle conceived at the time, because similarities between P'eng Shih and Fei Hung went further than both becoming students of the university and achieving top honors—they both became grand secretaries, both died at their posts, and both were given the identical posthumous name of Wen-hsien.

Dreams of two of the *t'ung-nien* 同年

(competitors passing their examinations in the same year) of Fei Hung also involved him, making his success the key to their own. Chang Fu 張黼 of Shanghai once dreamed of passing the metropolitan examinations with a rank above that of the *chuang-yüan*. This depressed him, for it was neither logical nor possible. In 1487 he finally passed the hui-shih 會試 as number 15 on the list, and next to him, number 16, was Fei Hung. When the latter emerged as *chuang-yüan* after the palace examinations, Chang Fu realized how prophetic his dream had been. Liu Liang 劉良 (1437-1527) of Ning-yüan 寧遠, Hukuang, had passed his provincial examinations in 1453, but after that failed ten times in Peking. Once he dreamed of some deity, who told him that he would be successful only in the year when the *chuang-yüan*'s name was Fei Hung. Indeed he finally succeeded in 1487 when he was already fifty years old. Both dreams were said to have occurred before Fei Hung was born.

Bibliography

1/193/1a; 5/15/53a; 64/ 丙 9/1a; *Huang Ming wen-hai*, microfilm 1/7/3, 4, biographies by Hsia Yen and Li K'ai-hsien; TSCC(1885-88), XI: 245/11b, 798/21a, XIV: 458/6b, 7a; SK (1930), 73/4a, 175/18a, 176/10b; Wang Shih-chen, *Yen-shan-t'ang pieh-chi*, 5/11b (1965 Taiwan reprint); *Kuang-hsin-fu chih* 廣信府志 (1872), 9/I/49b, 52b, 53b, 9/II/42b, 43a; *Ming chuang-yüan t'u-k'ao* 明狀元圖考 (1875), 上 60; NCL *Catalogue of Rare Books* (1967), 1026.

                                              Lienche Tu Fang

FENG Ch'i 馮琦 (T. 用韞, H. 琢庵, Pth. 文敏), January 1, 1559-April 13, 1603, served the court of Chu I-chün (*q.v.*) for twenty-five years without involving himself in any significant controversy. He is not known to have impeached any of his fellow officials, nor to have been impeached himself. Except for a brief assignment as the provincial examiner in Hukuang, he never held an appointment outside the capital. His relatively uneventful life is worthy of the attention of modern scholars mainly because, being amply documented, it may serve as an additional focal point for students of Ming government who wish to form a better idea of bureaucracy in Peking during the middle years of the Wan-li period.

Feng was born in Lin-ch'ü 臨朐, Shantung, of a scholar-official family. His achievement of the *chin-shih* degree in 1577 made him the fourth consecutive generation of the family to be so honored: his grandfather, Feng Wei-no 惟訥 (T. 汝言, H. 少洲, cs 1538, d. 1572), and his great uncle, Feng Wei-min (*q.v.*), being particularly distinguished as scholar and dramatist respectively. Within the Hanlin Academy he worked his way up to the directorship of that institution in 1593. In the interim he participated in the compilation of the *Ta-Ming hui-tien* (1581-87) and, in collaboration with his close friend, Yü Chi-teng 余繼登 (T. 世用, H. 雲衢, Pth. 文恪, 1544-1600, cs 1577), lectured on history before the emperor (1589). In 1599 the court appointed him right vice minister of Rites. In July of that year he was transferred to the ministry of Personnel, rising to left vice minister in August, 1601. Two months later the emperor promoted him to minister of Rites. While holding these positions he retained his membership in the Hanlin Academy.

It would do him an injustice to call him compliant. A loyal official of the Confucian tradition, Feng tried to use his influence with the emperor. His memorials mention the evil of exorbitant taxation, the undesirability of dispatching eunuchs as mining commissioners, the need to fill vacant official positions, and the necessity of installing an heir apparent, citing comets, earthquakes, and palace fires as portents. To all these matters Chu I-chün turned a deaf ear. Feng carried on with tact and patience. While his advice was generally disregarded, his humility pleased the emperor. When the latter refused to recall the eunuchs in charge of mines, Feng offered a compromise solution which would limit each mining area to one of three *li* in diameter and replace the most notorious commissioners with ones of better repute. The installation of the heir apparent in 1601 took place a fortnight after he became minister of Rites. As funds on hand were insufficient to meet the ceremonial expenses, he went so far as to call back his brother Feng Yüan 馮瑗 (cs 1595), who, then a secretary in the ministry of Revenue, was on his way to Liaotung to deliver forty thousand taels of silver to the army. The intercepted military funds enabled Feng to carry on the celebration without reducing its expected grandeur.

His biographers assert that he never took part in any factional quarrel at court. On occasions when his fellow officials offended the throne he did his utmost to placate the emperor and to minimize their offenses. In 1601, along with Chu Kuo-tso 朱國祚 (T. 兆隆, H. 養淳, optimus of 1583), he was nominated for a grand secretaryship. Only a secret memorial by Shen I-kuan (*q.v.*), arguing that both men were too young for the office (i. e., not yet fifty) caused the emperor, who was on the point of making the appointment, to suspend action on it. Ironically, Feng's own policy on personnel management especially emphasized the observance of seniority. When junior officials were qualified for important jobs, he would make the appointments but withhold their promotion rank. His attitude toward education was even more conservative. He recommended that the numbers of students in state educational institutions be strictly limited, that students should not be permitted to write compositions containing unorthodox ideas, and that any of them who quoted a Buddhist sūtra once be punished by having his stipend suspended for a month. To blend the ideas of Motzu with those of Confucius he considered a serious offense; so also any unorthodox interpretation of history. Note too in this connection his attitude towards Li Chih

(*q.v.*). He asked for strict enforcement of the edict, issued in 1601, which made provincial officials in charge of education responsible for censoring all new books before they were put in print.

Feng's papers are preserved in *Feng tsung-po chi* 馮宗伯集 (81 *ch.*), probably published in 1607. Aside from poetry, personal letters, memorials, tombstone inscriptions, and biographies, the collection also contains questions and answers for the civil and military examinations over which he presided, and the notes for his lectures before the emperor. Occasionally these papers yield valuable information on current affairs. For instance, he mentions that the Chinese naval strength during the early days of Toyotomi Hideyoshi's invasion was fewer than three thousand men, that during the campaign against Yang Ying-lung (*q.v.*) the provincial governors constantly worked against each other, and that the mining ordered by Emperor Chu I-chün, as originally proposed, was not strictly a government enterprise, sixty per cent of the profit being passed along to the civilian population. There is, however, no systematic exposition of any of these topics. Most of the 282 letters found in the collection are casual personal notes, but the addressees included many prominent figures in the period. The work was listed for suppression in the 18th century, possibly because a few of his letters had to do with frontier affairs. Both the Library of Congress and Columbia University have copies of the original edition. The *Pei-hai chi* 北海集 (46 *ch.*), published about the same time, duplicates the *Tsung-po chi* in certain respects.

Feng started work on two books, but finished neither before his death. The *Ching-chi lei-pien* 經濟類編 (100 *ch.*), is a collection of quotations and anecdotes and was copied into the Imperial Library. Basically dealing with administrative matters, it also includes such divergent topics as witchcraft, liquor, lutes, and tripods. It is said that Feng arranged the chapters of his original draft in four groups. As published there are twenty-three parts. It is quite possible that his brother, Feng Yüan, who edited the work, added much new material. A copy is in the Harvard library. The *Sung-shih chi-shih pen-mo* 宋史紀事本末 (109 *ch.*), not only covers the rise and fall of the Sung, but also discusses the Liao and Chin at length. Several chapters describe the origins and governmental institutions of the Mongols. Most of the chapters are short, but the one on Wang An-shih (1021-86) takes fifty-four double pages. The author's disapproval of Wang is apparent (Feng himself was named after Han Ch'i, 1008-75, one of Wang's opponents); nevertheless he refrains from making a direct comment. The writer's position is reflected by his selection of material. The whole work is centered around each significant individual's personality; quotations appear often. The topics follow a chronological order. The 1874 edition names Feng as the originator and Ch'en Pang-chan (*q.v.*) as the one who brought the book to completion, with commentaries added by Chang P'u (ECCP). It is said that Feng contributed only about thirty per cent of the draft, but the book fails to specify which portion is done by which writer. Another edition appeared in 1935.

At his death Feng was buried in a tomb a little north of his place of birth. Over two decades later (1626) Wei Chung-hsien (ECCP) included Feng's name on his black list.

Bibliography

1/216/9b; 64/庚 12/2b; MSL (1940), Shen-tsung, 333/9b, 335/10a, 356/4a, 361/9b, 363/8a, 364/2a, 4a, 381/6b; *Shantung t'ung-chih* (1934), 1430, 4735; SK (1930), 49/2b, 136/2b, 189/4a; Wang Hsi-chüeh, *Wang-wen-su-kung wen-chi* (NLP microfilm no. 1964, roll nos. 885–887), 10/53b, 12/25b; *Feng tsung-po chi*; *Sung-shih chi-shih-pen-mo*; L. of C. *Catalogue of Rare Books*, 993; Ch'iu K'ai-ming 裘開明, in CHHP, n.s., II (1961), 98.

Ray Huang

FENG En 馮恩 (T. 子仁, H. 南江), 1491-1571, a censor of note, was a native of Hua-t'ing 華亭, Sung-chiang 松江 prefecture. At the beginning of the Ming dynasty Feng En's ancestor was sent to Yunnan as a soldier in one of the newly established guards. His great-grandfather, however, who was a local teacher at Hua-t'ing, changed to the Chin-wu 金吾 guard in Nanking. It is said that while performing his duties as a soldier Feng En impressed the inspecting censor, Fang Feng 方鳳 (T. 時鳴, H. 改亭, cs 1508), with his literacy and talents and was permitted to enter the prefectural school at Nanking. Later (about 1510) he changed to the Sung-chiang prefectural school, becoming a *chü-jen* in 1525 and a *chin-shih* the following year. He then received the appointment of messenger, in which capacity he was sent to Kwangsi in May, 1528, to present imperial awards to Earl Wang Shou-jen (*q. v.*) for his pacification of the rebellion of aborigines in the western part of that province. Feng arrived at Wang's headquarters at Nan-ning 南寧 on September 21. It is said that, after paying homage to the distinguished philosopher and military commander, Feng became one of the last of his disciples, for Wang died four months later.

In September, 1529, Feng was appointed a censor in the Nanking Censorate. Some months later he was given the assignment of inspecting the military posts along the Yangtze River west of Nanking. When he found that the regulation to reward the soldiers by the number of captured robbers encouraged them to arrest innocent people, he gave the order to reserve the best rewards for a unit reporting no robbery in its territory. In this way law-abiding residents were no longer molested. In 1531 he induced the censors and the supervising secretaries of the southern capital to submit a memorial on procedures in the sexennial central civil service review. This proposal pointed to the desirability of having all evaluation filed beforehand so that the ministry of

Personnel might base its decisions on them. The censor-in-chief in Peking, at that time Wang Hung (*see* Hsi Shu), objected on the ground that it was contrary to the usual practice of previous reigns. In a subsequent memorial Feng En indicated the incorrectness of Wang's arguments and attacked him for scheming to obstruct criticism. The emperor referred the matter to the ministry of Personnel, which reported that precedent upheld Feng's contentions, adding in the report the astute observation that criticism should be judged on the basis of merit, not on timing. The emperor consequently overrode Wang's objections and ordered that the evaluations be completed by the end of the year previous to the sexennial review.

On the appearance of a comet in September, 1532, just a year after one later known as Halley's, the phenomenon was interpreted as an omen signifying the presence of a disloyal minister at court; the grand secretary, Chang Fu-ching (*q.v.*), was accordingly ordered to retire. When the comet remained to dominate the night sky for several months (115 days all told), the emperor was impelled to solicit more criticisms; they came in abundance. The emperor and his favorites were subjected to so much admonition and reproof that he began to retaliate by finding fault with the faultfinders. At this juncture Feng submitted a memorial (November, 1532) which reviewed the conduct of twenty high officials, giving a favorable appraisal of ten, but speaking slightingly of the others, especially singling out Fang Hsien-fu (*see* Kuei O), Chang Fu-ching, and Wang Hung for denunciation. Their transgressions, he held, warranted punishment by death. The enraged emperor ordered Feng's arrest. After being escorted to Peking in chains, he was tried on the charge of conspiring to disturb the administration and was remanded to the prison of the Embroidered-uniform Guard. There he was tortured continuously in an effort to extract a confession and the

names of his alleged accomplices. Many officials courageously came to his defense, but to no avail, for the emperor maintained that Feng's real intention was to discredit him for the *Ta-li i* case (*see* Feng Hsi and Chu Hou-ts'ung). According to an account by his son, Feng suffered bruises all over his body and had to be resuscitated several times by an officer of the Guard, Lu Ping (*q.v.*), who took pity on him. In March, 1533, for want of a confession, the minister of Justice, Wang Shih-chung 王時中 (T. 道夫, H. 海山, 1466–1542, cs 1490), proposed the sentence of banishment, but the emperor, still angry, accused Wang of collusion, and sent him home as a commoner. Feng was then given the capital sentence of imprisonment awaiting execution.

At the autumn assizes that year, when the cases of prisoners sentenced to death were reviewed, Wang Hung, as minister of Personnel, served on the review board. When Feng En's case came up, according to one account Wang Hung sneered at him and ordered him to kneel. Feng knelt facing the north towards the throne. Wang ordered the gendarmes to force Feng to turn east facing him. Feng then raised himself erect, refusing to kneel. When Wang called him a hypocrite who received gifts while in prison, Feng replied that they were gifts made out of pure kindness, not like the ones which Wang had received, and which had led him to hand out favors in return. In a temper Wang leaped to his feet with fist raised but was calmed by the others. Wang then voted for Feng's execution but the others on the board disagreed. After Feng was returned to prison, he came to be known as the ssu-t'ieh yü-shih 四鐵御史 (censor of four steely parts, alluding to his tongue, knees, bones, and gall). When the emperor's first son was born in September, 1533, and a general amnesty proclaimed, Feng was specifically excluded. The emperor would not change his mind even when Feng's eldest son, Feng Hsing-k'o 行可 (T. 見卿, H. 勑齋, *ca.* 1521-*ca.* 1609, cj 1540), then twelve years old, offered his own life to save his father's.

Late in 1534 Feng Hsing-k'o again went to plead for his father, writing the memorial in blood from his own arm. Reportedly Feng En's mother, about eighty *sui*, also came to the palace gate asking for mercy. Wang T'ing-hsiang (*q. v.*), then censor-in-chief, was one of several officials who transmitted the son's pleas to the throne, with the recommendations of the group for a lessening of the sentence. In July, 1535, the sentence was converted to banishment to Lei-chou 雷州, Kwangtung, where Feng spent five years or so. He then received a pardon and permission to return home (probably as a result of the amnesty of 1539 on the installation of the heir apparent).

Feng En seems to have lived the rest of his life in Sung-chiang, amid surroundings of exceptional affluence. Perhaps he learned to do business while in exile in Kwangtung; his nation-wide fame as a dauntless censor undoubtedly helped in his dealings. In any case he became the owner of thirty thousand *mou* (about five thousand acres) of rich farm land as well as houses, gardens, and business properties. He built a tower a hundred feet high that overlooked the entire city of Sung-chiang, noted for its wealth and for being one of the centers of a budding textile industry. Conceivably Feng was one of the first to take part in the early stage of European trade. However that may be, for some thirty years from about 1540 he led a life of great luxury. As his son describes the situation, he had ten women ranked as concubines and many more maids. He traveled in style and, on a whim to move to Nanking to live, he purchased two houses there, which later served as lodgings for those of his sons taking the provincial examination. He arranged displays of fireworks to amuse his mother and is said to have discontinued them only after her death (about 1547) at the age of ninety-five. He was noted in local history for fulfilling his filial duties, as was

his grandfather whose mother also lived to an advanced age.

Early in 1567, after Chu Tsai-hou (*q.v.*) ascended the throne, he recalled to service many officials who had been discharged or exiled by his father. Feng was given the title of a vice minister of the Grand Court of Revision and, on account of his age, was granted the right to live in retirement. His eldest son, who had become a *chü-jen* but had failed in higher examinations, was given an imperial citation for filial piety. He was then made head of a bureau in the Court of Imperial Entertainment and a younger half-brother, Feng Shih-k'o (*q.v.*), became a *chin-shih* in 1571; Feng En thus had two sons at court at the time of his death. Probably because he did not have a will and his eldest son was absent, quarreling broke out in the household he left behind, some of his sons and their mothers appropriating all they could. When Feng Shih-k'o returned home, his second elder half-brother, Feng Ta-k'o 達可 (T. 善卿, H. 頤齋, b. 1524), secretly handed over to him the titles to some land and properties worth thousands of taels, but later Feng Shih-k'o had to yield these to other members of the family in order to avoid further disputes. He eventually made his home in Soochow to keep at a distance from them.

Feng Hsing-k'o returned to his office in 1574, was later promoted to be assistant prefect of Ying-t'ien (Nanking), and retired about 1581. After he died, a shrine was erected in memory of his father and himself. He had a son, Feng Ta-shou 大受 (T. 威甫), a *chü-jen* of 1579, who was a calligrapher of some note and left two collections, *Hsien-fu shih-chi* 咸甫詩集 and *Chu-su-yüan chi* 竹素園集. He served as magistrate of Yang-shan 陽山, Kwangtung (1613–16), and of Ch'ing-yüan 慶元, Chekiang (1620–23).

Bibliography

1/27/11a, 209/3b, 7b; 3/193/1a, 4b; 5/65/85a; 40/51/25b, 53//20b; 61/108/9a, 12a; 64/ 卢 10/4b,

12/19b; 86/15/8a; *Huang Ming wen-hai* (microfilm), 9/1/4, 7/11; 10/1/16; MSL (1965), Shihtsung, 3286, 3338, 3480, 3487, 3516 (1966), Mutsung, 0212; KC (1958), 3379, 3410, 3451, 3472, 3487; *Hua-t'ing-hsien chih* (1878), 6/10a, 14/24a, 32b, 20/4b, 5b, 16b, 18a, 31a; *Sung-chiang-fu chih* 松江府志 (1819), 53/6b, 54/6a, 64/8b, 72/2a, 36b; *Kwangtung t'ung-chih* (1934), 438; SK (1930), 28/8b, 30/4a, 105/7a, 122/6b; TSCC (1885–88), XI: 357/19/7b; Fan Shou-chi, *Su-huang wai-shih*, 22/8a, 86b, 89b; Lei Li, *T̩a-cheng-chi*, 22/110a; Feng Shih-k'o, *Feng Yüan-ch'eng hsüan-chi*, 52/8a, 53/52a, 60/1a; Ch'en Tzu-lung (ECCP), *Ming ching-shih wen-pien*, *chüan* 200; Cha Chi-tso (ECCP), *Tsui-wei lu*, biographies, 13 中/28a.

Chaoying Fang and L. Carrington Goodrich

FENG Fang 豐坊, later known as Feng Tao-sheng 道生 (T. 存理, or 禮, H. 人翁, 南禺道人, or 外史), cs 1523, official, author, and calligrapher, was a native of Yin 鄞-hsien (Ningpo), Chekiang. His father Feng Hsi (*q.v.*), for a time chancellor of the Hanlin Academy in Nanking, became so involved in the *Ta-li i* case that he was flogged and banished, a punishment which had its effect also on the son.

Feng Fang, like his father, was an able student, coming out first in the *chü-jen* examinations of 1519 in Hangchow; his performance in the *chin-shih* test, however, was less distinguished (32d in the second group). His first appointment was that of secretary of a bureau in the ministry of Rites, but, as a result of the political storm partly engineered by his father (August 1524), he was transferred to a similar post in the ministry of Personnel in Nanking and then demoted (1526) to the vice-magistracy of T'ung-chou 通州, near the mouth of the Yangtze River. He was dismissed in 1529. After several years in retirement and itching for greater activity in public affairs, he conceived a scheme which he hoped might lead to official employment. Returning to Peking, he sent to the throne (July, 1538) a memorial in which he proposed two actions, both of which were designed to exalt the memory of the deceased father of the emperor. One was to construct a Ming-t'ang 明堂 (or Hall of Light, as W. E. Soothill has called it), in which the father, Chu Yu-yüan (*see* Chu Hou-ts'ung), might be considered to associate in a banquet with Heaven; the second, to call the father, already accorded the posthumous rank of emperor, the name of Jui-tsung 睿宗. The emperor was delighted with the proposals and carried out the second (October 3), but running into opposition from his court, he dismissed the first. Not only was Feng not reappointed, but his memorial made him an object of such criticism for retreating from the brave stand taken by his father that he found himself an unwelcome guest in the homes of his acquaintances. The following year he presented a poem entitled "Ch'ing yün ya-shih" 卿雲雅詩 (The colorful cloud) to the emperor, who, instead of giving him some reward, simply filed it in the bureau of historiography. Completely disheartened, Feng returned home, and died a dejected man.

Feng was a considerable writer, in particular on the Confucian canon. The editors of the Imperial Catalogue list five of his studies, totaling 88 *chüan*, but only one of his books, the *Shu-chüeh* 書訣 (Secrets of calligraphy), 1 *ch.*, doubtfully ascribed to him, is included in the *Ssu-k'u ch'üan-shu*. According to the critics he ventured a number of novel theories in his exposition of the Classics—theories which, he asserted, were based upon rare books, or books of Korean or Japanese origin. But these, it appears, were his own invention and failed of acceptance. Another work, *Tzu-kung shih-chuan* 子貢詩傳 (A commentary on the Odes by Tzu-kung, a favorite disciple of Confucius), the *Ming-shih* editors held to be an outright fabrication. One book, not mentioned by the *Ssu-k'u* editors, entitled *Nan yü chi* 南禺集, has a preface by a fellow townsman and fellow *chin-shih*, Chang Shih-ch'e 張時徹 (T. 維靜, H. 九一, 東沙, 1500-77, cs 1523), who comments bluntly that it is a pity that the author, though of unusual talents, should have allowed himself to spoil them by his bragging and other eccentricities. Apparently Feng often contradicted himself and sometimes treated his friends as foes.

Feng's home included a library, known as the Wan-chüan lou 萬卷樓 (ten thousand *chüan* studio), some of its holdings being quite rare. Here he could revel in his family's collection of books, ancient rubbings, paintings, and specimens of calligraphy. [Editors' note: There is an essay in rhyme, Chen-shang-chai fu 眞賞齋賦, discovered by Miao Ch'üan-sun (BDRC) in 1908 and printed in his collection, *Ou-hsiang ling-shih*. The essay was signed Feng Tao-sheng and dated 1549. In it he boasts of the treasures in his family's possession, including some rare books, and gives the pronunciation and meaning of some unusual characters. The name of the studio, Chen-shang, means "authentic connoisseurship," another example of his boastfulness.] Besides his reputation as a classicist he was known for his ability as a calligrapher, but this view was not universal. Wang Shih-chen (*q.v.*), acknowledging that Feng's acquaintance with the subject was unexcelled, commented wryly that his execution was inferior. He could also paint landscapes and flowers.

Bibliography

1/17/12a, 191/20b; 3/76/19b; 22/7/15a; 40/39/26a; 84/丁上/1b; MSL (1965), Shih-tsung, 4373, 4409; KC (1958), 3558, 3560; Chang Hsüan, *Hsi-yüan wen-chien lu*, 105/56a; SK (1930), 7/7b, 13/4b, 17/3a, 30/3b, 113/2a; Wang Shih-chen, *Yen-chou shan-jen ssu-pu kao*, 136/20a; Chiang Hsüeh-yung 蔣學鏞 (cj 1773), *Yin-chih kao* 鄞志稿, 14/13a; Chu Chia 祝嘉, *Shu-hsüeh shih* 書學史 (Shanghai, 1947), 13/363; *T'ung-chou chih-li chou chih* 直隸州志 (1875), 8/18b; Huang Tsung-hsi (ECCP), *Huang Li-chou wen-chi* (Peking, 1959), 83; Yeh Ch'ang-ch'ih 葉昌熾, *Ts'ang-shu chi-shih shih* (Shanghai, 1958), 110; TSCC (1885–88), XXIII: 105/93/5b, XXIV: 123/29/1b; W. E. Soothill, *The Hall of Light* (London, 1951), 109.

Liu Lin-sheng

FENG Hsi 豐熙 (T. 原學), 1468-1537, official and scholar, was a native of Yin-hsien 鄞縣, Chekiang. He came from an old family which had lived in this eastern coastal province for centuries, tracing its genealogy back to Feng Chi (1033-1107, cs of 1059), a renowned official in the time of Northern Sung. In the early years of the Ming dynasty, Feng Yin-ch'u 寅初 (T. 復初, H. 復齋), was summoned to the court and given a post as director of studies in the Imperial Academy. It was said that Feng Yin-ch'u lived to the grand old age of one hundred five *sui*, and died at the beginning of the 15th century. His son, Feng Ch'ing 慶 (T. 文慶, cs of 1439) rose in his official career to be administration commissioner of Honan.

Feng Hsi was Feng Ch'ing's grandson. In 1499 Feng Hsi himself became a *chin-shih*, capturing the second highest honor in the palace examination, and was appointed a compiler in the Hanlin Academy. Early in the Cheng-te period (1506-21), he was promoted to director of instruction under the supervisorate of imperial instruction, but because of his opposition to the powerful eunuch Liu Chin (*q.v.*) he was removed from the capital to Nanking to head the Hanlin Academy there. It is not clear exactly when he was recalled to Peking, but we find him in the capital in the early years of the Chia-ching reign (1522-66), deeply involved in the case which concerned the conferring of honors on the father of the emperor (*see* Chu Hou-ts'ung), known as the *Ta-li i*. This involvement not only ended his own official career, but also affected the advancement of his son, Feng Fang (*q.v.*).

The story of the *Ta-li i* episode began with the accession of Chu Hou-ts'ung. When Emperor Chu Hou-chao (*q.v.*) died without an heir, a younger cousin of the same generation, Chu Hou-ts'ung, was brought in to ascend the throne. This was not the regular procedure of succession since the traditional way was from father to son, or from older generation to a younger generation, so that the succeeding emperor, if not the son or grandson of the deceased emperor, would be his adopted son. Hence Chu Hou-ts'ung's succession posed problems derived from certain Confucian teachings, and gave rise to a great political controversy. It was made particularly difficult as the young emperor tried to be a very filial son, who upheld the saying that filial piety was the most important of all the virtues. Indeed, if the fathers and ancestors of officials deserved to receive honors equal to those of their more illustrious sons and grandsons, why then, of all people, should not the father of an emperor? Thus Chu Hou-ts'ung wanted to give his father the posthumous title and honors of an emperor. Many officials in the court strongly opposed his line of reasoning, but many others not only sided with the emperor but also supported his contention with great vigor. The end result was that the former were punished and the latter gained favor and were elevated to high positions. On August 14, 1524, Feng Hsi, as one of the leaders of a large group of officials, staged a remonstrance with lamentations at one gate of the imperial palace. This made the emperor very angry. As a result over two hundred officials, high and low, were flogged and thrown into prison. Eighteen of them died as a result. On August 20, sentences were meted out to the surviving offenders. Feng Hsi was sentenced to banishment to Chen-hai wei 鎮海衛 in Fukien. Over a decade later, when many others who had been punished for the same reason received pardons, the emperor refused to extend similar amnesty to Feng Hsi, so he remained in banishment and died in his place of exile in 1537.

In looking back now at this famous case in Ming history, one finds it difficult to understand the heat and fury generated at the time. Perhaps one may regard it as a case of Confucianism in action. Undoubtedly too the politics and traditions and manners of officialdom of that day intensified the affair. In his essay, the *Ta-li i pien* 辨 (or *Pien-ting Chia-ching* 定嘉靖

Ta-li i), Mao Ch'i-ling (ECCP), the early Ch'ing scholar, blamed the high officials for their choice of a successor from the same generation as the deceased emperor. Mao probably assessed the matter correctly.

In scholarship, Feng Hsi was reported to be a specialist on the Book of Rites. He is credited with three works on the Classics and two collected literary works: *Lu-shih cheng-shuo* 魯詩正說, *Ku-i chuan-i* 古易傳義, *Li-chiao i-chieh* 禮教儀節, *Pai-an chi* 白庵集, and *I-chai chi* 一齋集. None of these titles is known to be extant.

Feng Hsi had two sons, Feng Fang, distinguished in his own right, and Feng Ch'ih 墀.

Bibliography

1/191/19b; 3/181/18b; 5/20/35a; MSL (1940), Shih-tsung, 41/5a, 32b; KC (1958), 3304; Chiang Hsüeh-yung 蔣學鏞, *Yin-chih kao* 鄞志稿, 1/5b, 4/8b, 6/6a, 7/6b (*Ssu-ming ts'ung-shu* 四明叢書, 3d series).

Lienche Tu Fang

FENG Meng-lung 馮夢龍 (T. 猶龍, 耳猶, 子猶, H. 龍子猶, 墨憨齋主人, 姑蘇詞奴, etc), 1574–1646, poet, dramatist, fiction writer, and editor, was a native of Ch'ang-chou 長洲, prefecture of Soochow. He and his two elder brothers were widely known as the "three Feng brothers in the Wu region." Feng Meng-lung, talented and learned as he was, had little success in the state examinations. It was only in 1631, at the age of fifty-seven, that he was sent to the National University by his local school, and then qualified for a minor appointment. He was interested in education and is said to have served as sub-director of schools in the district of Tan-t'u 丹徒 (prefecture of Chinkiang). The highest official position he obtained was that of magistrate of Shou-ning 壽寧, Fukien, from 1634 to 1638. His administration was distingnished for its fairness, honesty, and leniency, as well as for its encouragement of literary pursuits. Among other things he prepared the local gazetteer, *Shou-ning-hsien chih* 縣志 (1637), 2 *ch.*, a copy of which is preserved in the Ueno Park Library, Tokyo.

Some sources describe Feng Meng-lung as having died as a result of the collapse of the Ming, but this does not seem to have been the case, although he was loyal to the dynasty and resentful of both the Chinese rebels and the Manchu invaders. Two of his poems entitled "Li-luan ko" 離亂歌 bear out this contention. His enthusiastic support of the Ming princes in the south, particularly Chu Yü-chien (ECCP), may be seen from his book *Chung-hsing wei-lüeh* 中興偉略, 1 *ch.*, which he finished in 1645 and wherein he speaks of himself as an old official of seventy-two *sui*. So far as is known, he did live until the following year, 1646, when that book was published in Japan. It is doubtful, however, that he actually escaped to Japan, as Jung Chao-tsu 容肇祖 has proposed. The exact circumstances under which he met his end remain unknown.

Feng Meng-lung was undoubtedly a man of superior talent and erudition, his academic interests covering a wide spectrum of subjects ranging from Confucianism to gambling. His books, *Ch'un-ch'iu chih-yüeh* 春秋指月 and *Ch'un-ch'iu heng-k'u* 衡庫, 30 *ch.*, were just as popular with Confucian scholars as his books, *Ma-tiao chüeh-li* 馬吊脚例, 1 *ch.*, and *P'ai-ching* 牌經, 1 *ch.*, were with gambling experts. He was responsible too for editing a collection of reports and accounts of what happened in 1644, entitled *Chia-shen chi-shih* 甲申紀事 (printed 1645/46), 14 *ch.*, which has been reprinted in the *Hsüan-lan-t'ang ts'ung-shu*, compiled by Cheng Chen-to (BDRC). Feng's greatest contribution as a writer and scholar, however, does not lie in the study of either Confucian Classics or gambling rules, but in the preservation, promotion, and creation of popular literature.

From 1620 to 1627 Feng Meng-lung compiled and published three collections of hua-pen 話本 (colloquial short stories) entitled *Yü-shih ming-yen* 喻世名言 (initially called *Ku-chin hsiao-shuo* 古今小說), 40 *ch.*, *Ching-shih t'ung-yen* 警世通言, and *Hsing-shih heng-yen* 醒世恆言, which from the word yen common to each of the titles, later became known together as the *San-yen* 三言. These three collections, each containing forty stories, preserve practically all the Sung and Yüan hua-pen still extant in Feng's time. As we know, in the late Ming period Sung and Yüan hua-pen had become rare items for book collectors, and Feng must have taken pains to collect them from various sources. Without his effort and enthusiasm these stories might have been lost, considering what happened in China during and after late Ming times. In these collections are also preserved many Ming hua-pen, including Feng Meng-lung's own works. As an editor he often drastically revised and restyled the stories he collected, and on the whole his revision and restyling were for the better in view of their readability. A number of these have been rendered into English and other languages.

Not only colloquial short stories but also other forms of fiction attracted his attention. It was he who first recognized the true literary value of the *Chin P'ing Mei* (*see* Wang Shih-chen) in its manuscript form, and boldly advised his friend Shen Te-fu (*q.v.*) to publish the novel. It was he who revised the historical romance *Lieh-kuo chih* 列國志, 108 回, and the supernatural novel *San-sui p'ing-yao chuan* 三遂平妖傳, 48 *ch.* It was also he who wrote the biographical novelene *Wang Yang-ming hsien-sheng ch'u-shen ching-luan lu* 王陽明先生出身靖亂錄, 3 *ch.* Besides, he wrote and edited a great number of tales, anecdotes, and jokes, as may be seen in his books *Ku-chin t'an-kai* 古今譚概, 36 *ch.*, *Hsiao-fu* 笑府, 1 *ch.*, *Ch'ing shih lei-lüeh* 情史類略, 24 *ch.*, *Chih-nang* 智囊, 28 *ch.*, and *Chih-nang pu* 補, 28 *ch.*

It is quite conceivable that Feng Meng-lung owned or was closely connected with a printing concern. The rapidity of the publication of memoranda on current events in a manner not unlike journalistic literature of today, and the repetition and rearrangement of many short stories printed in different collections, both point to the validity of this conjecture. For example, the *Chih-nang pu*, although the title gives the impression that it is a supplement to the *Chih-nang*, actually is a reshuffled new edition. Perhaps it is also worth mentioning that the short stories dealing with Ming plots in Feng's collections are mostly based on contemporary events. Lienche Tu Fang in a recent article demonstrates this point.

As a dramatist Feng Meng-lung followed in the footsteps of Shen Ching (*q.v.*) a leader of the prosodic school of Ming drama. His book *Mo-han-chai hsin-ting tz'u-p'u* 墨憨齋新定詞譜 clearly shows his emphasis on metrical rules and music patterns in drama. In his lifetime, he wrote only two plays entitled *Shuang-hsiung chi* 雙雄記, 2 *ch.*, and *Wan-shih tsu* 萬事足, 2 *ch.*, both of which are noted for their metrical excellence. But he also edited and revised at least twelve plays—namely, *Hsin kuan-yüan* 新灌園, 2 *ch.*, *Chiu-chia yung* 酒家傭, 2 *ch.*, *Nü chang-fu* 女丈夫, 2 *ch.*, *Liang-chiang chi* 量江記, 2 *ch.*, *Ching-chung ch'i* 精忠旗, 2 *ch.*, *Meng-lei chi* 夢磊記, 2 *ch.*, *Sa-hsüeh t'ang* 灑雪堂, 2 *ch.*, *Ch'u-chiang ch'ing* 楚江清, 2 *ch.*, *Feng-liu meng* 風流夢, 2 *ch.*, *Jen-shou kuan* 人獸關, 2 *ch.*, *Yung t'uan-yüan* 永團圓, 2 *ch.*, and *Han-tan meng* 邯鄲夢, 2 *ch.*

In the field of poetry Feng Meng-lung was equally productive. Most of his poems written in the traditional style are in his book *Ch'i-lo-chai kao* 七樂齋稿. According to traditional critics, he was skillful only in making rhymes in the colloquial language and therefore could not compose good poetry. But from the point of view of modern critics, his ability to use the colloquial was precisely his great strength. Besides poems of the traditional type, he also wrote a large number of san-ch'ü 散曲 and folk songs, all filled with vivid colloquial expression of the common people. His best lyrical songs are perhaps those written after his separation from the singsong girl, Hou Hui-ch'ing 侯慧卿, with whom he had fallen in love. Practically all his colloquial songs are included in the three collections he edited: *T'ai-hsia hsin-tsou* 太霞新奏, 14 *ch.*, *Kua-chih-er* 掛枝兒, 9 *ch.*, and *Shan-ko* 山歌, 10 *ch.* It is particularly for his preservation of the popular songs of the Wu region that he is remembered by lovers of folk poetry.

Bibliography

38/4/24a; 40/71/23a; 88/20/10b; *Chiang-nan t'ung-chih* 江南通志 (1737), 165/43b; *Fu-ning-fu chih* 福寧府志 (1875), *ch.* 17; *Su-chou-fu chih* (1748), *ch.* 136; Huang Wen-yang黃文暘, *Ch'ü-hai tsung-mu t'i-yao* 曲海總目提要 (Peking, 1959), 9/7b, 10b; *Ming-shih i-wen chih, pu-pien, fu-pien* 明史藝文志, 補編, 附編 (Peking, 1959), 25, 589, 673, 675; SK (1930), 30/6a, 132/3b; Chih T'ang 知堂 (Chou Tso-jen 周作人), "T'an Feng Meng-lung yü Chin Sheng-t'an," 談馮夢龍與金聖歎, *Jen-chien-shih* 人間世, XIX (1935); Jung Chao-tsu, "Ming Feng Meng-lung te sheng-p'ing chi ch'i chu-shu"的生平及其著述, *Ling-nan hsüeh-pao* 嶺南學報, II, no. 2 (1931), 61; *id.*, "Ming Feng Meng-lung te sheng-p'ing chi ch'i chu-shu hsü-k'ao" 續考, *ibid.*, II, no. 3 (1932), 95; Shen Te-fu, *Yeh-hu pien* (Fu-li shan-fang 扶荔山房 ed., 1827), *ch.* 25; Sun K'ai-ti 孫楷第, "San-yen er-p'ai yüan-liu k'ao" 三言二拍源流考, *Kuo-li Pei-p'ing T'u-shu-kuan kuan-k'an* 國立北平圖書館館刊, V (1931), no. 2, 11; Yeh Ju 野孺, "Kuan-yü 關於 Feng Meng-lung te shen shih" 身世, *Ming Ch'ing hsiao-shuo yen-chiu lun-wen chi* 明清小說研究論文集 (Peking, 1959), 34; *id.*, "Kuan-yü 'San-yen' te tsuan-chi-che" 纂輯者, *Ming Ch'ing hsiao-shuo yen-chiu lun-wen chi* 論文集 (Peking, 1959), 29; Cheng Chen-to, *Hsi-ti shu-mu* 西諦書目 (1963); Hsieh Kuo-chen, *Wan-Ming shih chi k'ao* 晚明史籍考 (Peking, 1933), 3/1a; Lienche Tu Fang, "Ming-jen hsiao-shuo chi tang-tai pen-shih chü-li" 明人小說記當代奇聞本事舉例, CHHP, n. s., VII: 2 (August, 1969), 156; Sun Tien-ch'i (1957), 55; Nagasawa Kikuya 長澤規矩也, "'Sangen' 'Nihaku' ni tsuite" "三言" "二拍" について, *Shibun* 斯文, X (1928), no. 9, 592, XI (1929), no. 5, 377; Ono Shihei 小野四平, "Fu Mu-ryō no shōsetsu kan" 馮夢龍の小說觀, *Shūkan Tō-yōgaku* 集刊東洋學, no. 6 (September., 1961), 49;

Shinoya On 鹽谷溫, "Min no shōsetsu 'Sangen' ni tsuite" 明の小說 "三言" に就て, *ibid.*, VIII (1926), no. 5, 309, no. 6, 375, no. 7, 468; Cyril Birch, *Stories from a Ming Collection* (Bloomington, Indiana, 1959), intro.; John Lyman Bishop, *The Colloquial Short Story in China: A Study of the San-yen Collections* (Cambridge, Mass., 1956); Li Chi-t'ang, "The tragedy of Ts'ui Ning," THM, X:4 (April, 1940), 377; A. Waley, "Notes on the History of Chinese Popular Literature," TP, 28 (1931), 346; Harold Acton and Lee Yi-hsieh (tr.),*Glue and Lacquer*, London, 1941; W. Franke, *Sources*, 2. 9. 6, 4.4.2. [Editors' note: Cheng Chen-to, in the catalogue of his own library, lists among the titles under Feng's authorship an incomplete edition of a work on the Four Books, *Ssu-shu* (四書) *chih-yüeh*, and a novel, *Lieh-nü yen-i* 列女演義, 6 *ch.* Hsieh Kuo-chen (*see* T'ien Ju-ch'eng), in his bibliography of sources on the late Ming era, gives eight titles by Feng, most of which are items included in the *Chia-shen chi-shih*. The Tōyō Bunko kenkyujō 東洋文化研究所 (Tokyo University, 1965) has in its holdings a late Ming edition of *San-chiao ou-nien* 三教偶拈, compiled by Feng Meng-lung. As late as 1941 a collection of Feng's san-ch'ü(宛轉歌) brought together by Lu Ch'ien 盧前 (1905–51) was published by the Commercial Press in Changsha.]

Tien-yi Li

FENG Sheng 馮勝, original names Kuosheng 國勝 and Tsung-i 宗異, *ca.* 1330–February 22, 1395, was a native of Ting-yüan 定遠 (in present Anhwei). He and his elder brother, Feng Kuo-yung 國用 (1324–May 13, 1359), were reported as literate; as they apparently were not wealthy, their background may be designated as lower middle class. In 1351, when insurgents began to be active near their home, the two brothers joined a group of local people to establish a hiding place in the mountains. Feng Kuo-yung became leader of the group and Feng Sheng distinguished himself by his archery. In 1354 they joined Chu Yüan-chang when the latter went to Ting-yüan to enlist men for the rebel cause. It is said that Feng Kuo-yung gave the future founder of the Ming dynasty some pertinent advice and

was trusted as a close companion, ranking always below Li Shan-ch'ang (*q. v.*), however. As members of Chu's bodyguard, the two brothers took vigorous part in his campaigns from 1354 to 1359. Feng Kuo-yung became commander of the bodyguard division in 1356 but died during the battle of eastern Chekiang in 1359. He was posthumously given the title duke of Ying 郢國公, conferred about 1369 when his plastic statue was placed in the Temple of Worthy Subjects 功臣廟. His command was transferred to Feng Sheng, then known as Feng Kuo-sheng.

In 1360 Feng Sheng distinguished himself in the battles against Ch'en Yu-liang (*q.v.*). During the following seven years he shared in most of the major campaigns, serving usually as second in command under Hsü Ta (*q. v.*). In 1367, as commissioner of the central military commission and as commander of the bodyguard, he took part in the arrest and trial of a former Yüan official, Chang Ch'ang 張昶, who was accused of treason and executed. Later in that year, after the conquest of the Wu kingdom of Chang Shih-ch'eng (*q.v.*), Feng, then under the name of Feng Tsung-i, ranked fourth among the thirteen generals receiving rewards. He served next under Hsü Ta and Ch'ang Yü-ch'un (*q. v.*) in the expedition to the north, taking Shantung (late 1367 to early 1368), Pien-liang 汴梁 (or Ta-liang 大梁, April, 1368), and T'ung-kuan 潼關, Honan (May, 1368).

By this time Chu Yüan-chang had enthroned himself as emperor of the Ta Ming state, with the reign title Hung-wu. He went to Pien-liang in person, changed its name back to K'ai-feng-fu, and designated it as the northern capital of his new empire. Situated at the junction of the canal transportation systems of that day, Kaifeng was made a base for military operations to the north and northwest. Feng Sheng was appointed commander of that base, and here he made his headquarters for almost twenty years. Meanwhile he took part in the conquest of Shansi

(1368) and Shensi (1369), and in the
northern expeditions into Kansu and Mongolia (1370, 1372). Early in 1370 he was
named third among twenty-nine generals
rewarded for their exploits, and late in
November of that year he was fifth among
the thirty-five awarded hereditary ranks,
his appointment being duke of Sung 宋國
公 with the stipend of three thousand
shih. The emperor also gave him a cast
iron testimonial embodying an oath which
guaranteed to posterity inheritance of the
dukedom in perpetuity. In 1379 his daughter was married to the emperor's fifth
son, Chu Su (q. v.), the prince of Chou,
whose residence at Kaifeng was built
under Feng's supervision. All this seems
to indicate that Honan, particularly the
Kaifeng region, constituted Feng's special
area of interest, perhaps even his fief as
mentioned in an imperial edict in 1381
(Ta-liang nai er so-feng-chih-ti 乃爾所封
之地).

In 1385 Feng Sheng was appointed
commander-in-chief of the campaign
against the last Mongol military force,
that of Naɤač;u (q. v.), in the area of the
Liao and Sungari River valleys. Feng's
title was Cheng-lu ta-chiang-chün 征虜大
將軍 (Generalissimo to conquer the northern barbarians) for by this time those
who outranked him had all died, and he
naturally succeeded to the supreme command. Extensive preparations were made to
support the expeditionary force of about
two hundred thousand men. A like number
of civilians were conscripted to transport
one and a quarter million shih of rice to
be stored at four advance bases near the
Great Wall. By April, 1387, the army was
ready to advance and three months later,
after crossing the Liao River, it made
contact with Naɤaču, forcing the latter to
surrender together with some two hundred
thousand followers. The victory was gained
without much fighting and with one million shih of rice still left in storage.

Feng Sheng, however, emerged from
the successful expedition discredited, and
was sent into retirement. He was charged

with mistreating the surrendered Mongols,
appropriating good horses to himself and
assigning his son-in-law, Ch'ang Mao (see
Ch'ang Yü-ch'un), to escort Naɤaču, with
the result that through some misunderstanding Ch'ang wounded the Mongol general. These and other charges, even if
true, were apparently magnified by the
emperor to provide an excuse for depriving Feng of his fief in Honan and his
military command, and packing him off
to Feng-yang 鳳陽, perhaps under surveillance. (When Chu Su secretly visited
Feng-yang late in 1389 and was punished,
it was conceivably for a matter involving
Feng.)

The last years of Feng Sheng's life
are scantily recorded. It is said that in
1388 he was ordered to escort some Mongol troops from Shantung to Yunnan and
from 1391 to 1392 he served as inspector
of several Guards in Shensi. In 1393 the
court summoned him and Fu Yu-te (q.v.)
to Nanking, probably to witness the execution of the twenty thousand persons involved in the case of Lan Yü (q. v.).
They were then dispatched to Peiping to
serve under the prince of Yen (see Chu
Ti). It is unknown at what time Feng
and Fu returned to Nanking. Fu died in
December, 1394, and three months later
Feng also died. His nine sons had all
predeceased him; so the title of duke of
Sung lapsed.

Different versions about the deaths of
Fu and Feng range from their committing
suicide (Kuo-ch'üeh) to their execution
(Kuo-shih k'ao-i). One source (Huang
Ming k'ai-kuo kung-ch'en lu) asserts that
Feng died peacefully on "Hung-wu 32d
year, 10th month, 10th day," i. e., November 7, 1399, or seventeen months after
the Hung-wu emperor himself had passed
away. The existence of these discrepancies
may mean that all these versions are speculations. As the T'ai-tsu shih-lu was revised twice during the Yung-lo period to
meet the approval of Chu Ti, it may not
be too far-fetched to presume that the
death and defamation of these two men

had something to do with the Yung-lo emperor, for the last assignment of both was to serve under him when he was a prince in Peiping.

A contemporary officer of the same name, Feng Sheng (native of Shou-chou 壽州, Anhwei), retired because of old age in 1381 with the hereditary rank of a centurion, has often been confused with the duke as in the *Combined Indices to Eighty-nine Collections of Ming Dynasty Biographies.*

Bibliography

1/129/1a; *Ming-shih* (Taiwan, 1962), 1635; 5/6/1a; 20/1/62a, 31/34a (the other Feng Sheng); KC (1958), 752; MSL (1962), T'ai-tsu, 3447.

Chaoying Fang

FENG Shih-k'o 馮時可 (T. 敏卿, H. 元成), born *ca.* 1547, was a native of Hua-t'ing 華亭, prefectural seat of Sung-chiang 松江, near Shanghai, who achieved a reputation as an official, a scholar, and a prolific writer. He was the eighth son of Feng En (*q.v.*), the famous censor who was exiled in 1535 to Kwangtung, where he began to amass a fortune. He returned about 1540 and lived in luxury, accumulating a household of over a hundred persons, among whom were ten concubines, two being girls he brought back from Kwangtung. They could not speak the Wu dialect and, ostracized by the other women, lived in separate quarters. Feng Shih-k'o's mother, née Ma 馬 (1520–87), who possibly had been a maid-servant to the Cantonese women, taught them the Wu speech and acted in their interest; after she was raised to the status of concubine, the three lived together, each looking after the other's children as her own. She was the youngest of the ten, and had two children, Feng Shih-k'o and a daughter. After Feng En died in 1571 and a scramble for the movable properties ensued, she kept inside her quarters; when what was left of the silver was divided, she was handed five hundred taels, a very small portion of the share that was properly hers and her son's. She did not complain, quoting the old proverb that a good son does not depend on inheritance for a living, for Feng Shih-k'o had earlier that year succeeded in passing the *chin-shih* examination, the only one of Feng En's nine sons to achieve that honor.

After the mourning period Feng Shih-k'o went to Peking in 1574 and received an appointment as secretary in the ministry of Justice. From then on he served eight years in the central government, after which he held seven provincial posts. On each he left a lucid account describing his experiences in a somewhat complacent way. These stories provide invaluable information on the inner workings of the government on both central and provincial levels. It was his prose style which first won him recognition by his superiors, the ministers of Justice, Wang Chih-kao 王之誥 (T. 告若, cs 1544) and Wang Ch'ung-ku (*q.v.*). Then the minister of War, T'an Lun (*q.v.*), had him transferred (1577?) to his ministry to take charge of the drafting of state papers. He held that trust for four years during which he rose to be a bureau director. For a time he also served jointly with Hsiang Tu-shou (*see* Hsiang Yüan-pien) in compiling the ministerial documents to be incorporated in the collected institutes, *Ta Ming hui-tien* (*see* Shen Shih-hsing). He was very proud to have been the one to draft the memorial in 1580 which paved the way for discontinuing the policy of farming out war horses among the people of the Peking and Nanking areas; for more than a hundred years these people had suffered greatly over the requirement to provide the government annually with a specified number of colts. By paying in silver in lieu of colts the people of these regions, and of Honan and Shantung, were henceforth spared the risks involved in the health and grade of the animals and the exactions made by officials in charge of reception and inspection. It was the powerful grand secretary Chang Chü-cheng (*q.v.*) who made this reform possible.

In 1581 Feng Shih-k'o received the appointment of surveillance vice commissioner of Kweichow in charge of education. He served two years in that province, promoting scholarship and self-cultivation, printing books, and rebuilding academies. While traveling throughout the area, he had certain roads repaired and several bridges constructed. Early in 1583 he used his influence to help Tsou Yüan-piao (*q. v.*) leave his place of exile even before the order of pardon had arrived. Among the books Feng printed in Kweichow are two collections of excerpts of his lectures, *Ch'ien-chung yü-lu* 黔中語錄, and some examples of pa-ku essays, *Ch'ien-chung ch'eng-shih* 程式.

In 1583 Feng was granted sick leave and returned home. On the excuse that the Sung-chiang way of life was too luxurious for his taste he made his home in Soochow. The real reason seems to be that he wished to keep a distance from some of his clansmen who tried to use his name and influence in lawsuits to embarrass him. In 1591 he was named director of education of Szechwan, but unfavorable comments, such as reference to his passion for visiting scenic places, forced the minister of Personnel to change the appointment to the inferior office of surveillance vice commissioner of Kwangsi in charge of military inspection. After demurring he agreed to accept. Arriving at Kweilin the following summer, he found much of the military land, originally assigned to the guards through a long period of fraudulent practices, now yielding nothing to the government. After examining the records and titles he cleared sixty thousand *mou* (10,000 acres) for additional military revenue, enough to support five thousand soldiers. While serving as acting intendant of Kweilin he rebuilt the road along the Kuei 桂 River to Wu-chou 梧州 with funds which in general practice were used

by that office to meet the demands of his superiors. After two years in Kwangsi he was given the promotion to administration vice commissioner of Hukuang in charge of the intendancy at Yün-yang 鄖陽. On his arrival in the summer of 1594 he found the area famine stricken yet the people still burdened with taxes and labor service. He did what he could to reduce the unnecessary expenses, to supervise a fair distribution of relief, and to help the peasants with the planting of the next crop. In deposing several magistrates for cruelty or corruption, he incurred the displeasure of their sponsors and two years later was transferred to be intendant of southern Chekiang with residence at Wen-chou 溫州. Again he encouraged frugal practices and tried to introduce reforms for the benefit of the people. One of the burdens of the taxpayers was the excessive surcharge. It happened that the collection of taxes, which used to be assigned to wealthy persons whose turns rotated seasonally, had at some juncture been changed to the conscription of heads of chia 甲 (100 families) or pao 保 (10 families) with a more rapid turnover. Hence, the demands by the magistrate from the tax collectors, previously a quarterly affair, had now to be met much more frequently. For self-protection each collector increased his fee for handling by manipulating the weights and measures to the disadvantage of the taxpayers. Feng Shih-k'o changed the procedure to permit taxpayers to go directly to the magistrate's office, and have only delinquents assigned to tax collectors. On inspection tours he specified for himself the simplest accommodations and food; this was such a contrast to the demands by other officials that they showed their resentment by making fun of him. It was the time when eunuchs began to be sent to the provinces to open silver and gold mines, but they were prevented from coming to his territory by his plea that there were no such mines, and by his warnings on the possibility of riots. Indeed an attempt to start a riot was discovered in a town bordering on Fukien, but by swift and decisive dispatch of troops he nipped it in the bud. Yet he was not rewarded but downgraded and removed from office on a minor charge (probably in connection with a former subordinate in Hukuang accused of misconduct late in 1597). The news of his demotion delighted the eunuchs and many officials but saddened the people. He tells in an account of this episode that the people tried to stop him from leaving and then escorted him for a long distance on his departure. His name was later inscribed on the list of benevolent officials in the provincial shrine in Hangchow.

This time Feng's retirement lasted another eight years. When he returned to Soochow in 1598, he sold his inherited properties in Sung-chiang, including a house and some three hundred acres of land, in order to build his home and garden north of Soochow city. In 1600 he added a library and gave it the name Yen-ch'ing ko 延清閣. He lived comfortably on the remuneration which came from his writings, epitaphs, biographies, birthday and other congratulatory essays, prefaces, etc., which were in high demand. By 1605 he became restless and traveled to Peking to apply for an appointment, accepting in 1606 even the office of an assistant surveillance commissioner of Kwangtung, a demotion from 3B to 5A. On arrival early in 1607, he was assigned the intendancy of western Kwangtung with residence at Chao-ch'ing 肇慶, where he served for five years. While there he headed a list of subscribers to a fund for the restoration of the main hall of the temple, Nan-hua-ssu (*see* Te-ch'ing). In 1611 he was promoted to assistant administration commissioner of Yunnan and some time later served a term as surveillance vice commissioner of Hukuang in charge of the western circuit at Ch'ang-te 常德. He is mentioned in the *shih-lu* as having received a promotion in July, 1615, to administrative vice commissioner of Hukuang, but some time thereafter he must have been

demoted, for the *shih-lu* has a reference to him as an assistant administration commissioner of Kweichow who was criticized in November, 1617, by a supervising secretary as being unfit for that appointment. This seems to have been the last office of his long career of over forty years following his attainment of the *chin-shih*.

A prolific writer, Feng published small collections of his works from time to time, each under a different title such as *Yen-ch'i kao* 巖棲稿, 10 *ch.* (1585), *Yü-hang yin-kao* 雨杭吟稿, and *Feng Wen-so shih-kao* 文所詩稿, each in 3 *chüan*, *Shih-hu* 石湖 *kao* and *Chin-ch'ang* 金閶 *kao*, each in 2 *chüan*, *Nu-ju* 蒘茹 *kao*, 6 *ch.*, *Hsi-cheng chi* 西征集, 10 *ch.*, *Ch'ao-jan lou* 超然樓 *chi*, 12 *ch.* (Chekiang, 1597), and at least six more. Under the editorship of Tsou Yüan-piao, a selection of Feng's writings appeared with the title *Feng Yüan-ch'eng hsüan-chi* 選集, 24 *ch.* This title was placed on the prohibited list in the 18th century. About 1611 a much larger collection in 83 *chüan* came out bearing the same title, which is available in microfilm from a copy once belonging to the National Library of Peiping. It contains a wealth of information about Feng himself, his family, acquaintances, and career, and is an invaluable source on the social and political conditions of his day. His was a time of maladministration in government and a widening cleavage between the wealthy and the poor, as described vividly by Feng in his accounts. He shows a tendency to be overly self-assertive, but this may be explained as a compensation for his feeling of frustration when his public spirited acts won for him only resentment and disgrace.

Anthologists seem to be prejudiced against Feng's poetry, and most of them ignored his prose writings too. Only Ch'en Tzu-lung (ECCP) in the *Ming ching-shih wen-pien* and the anonymous compiler of the collection of biographies, *Huang Ming wen-hai* 皇明文海, seem to have tapped to a certain extent the enormous amount of Feng's prose. In the latter anthology Feng is represented by 116 articles, exceeded only by two others, Wang Shih-chen (*q.v.*) by 191, and Li Wei-chen (*see* Hsieh Chao-che) by 192. Feng also has a work of exempla, *Pao-shan-pien* 寶善編.

Among other works by Feng included in the *hsüan-chi* are his study notes on the Confucian Classics, historical works, the ancient philosophers, neo-Confucian tenets, and the Taoist and Buddhist religions. The last eleven *chüan* (73–83) constitute a series of literary criticisms of the Han through T'ang periods, under the subtitle *I-hai chiung-cho* 藝海洄酌. He is represented in the Imperial Library by his notes on the Spring and Autumn Annals, *Tso-shih shih* 左氏釋, 2 *ch.*, and his miscellaneous notes, *Yü-hang tsa-lu* 雜錄, 2 *ch.* The latter work, first published by Ch'en Chi-ju (ECCP) in *Pao-yen-t'ang pi-chi*, is the best known of his writings. A work on medicine, *Shang-ch'ih tsa-shuo* 上池雜說, is given notice in the *Ssu-k'u* catalogue only, but has been recently reprinted in China, together with his small collection of verified prescriptions, *Ching-mu lü-yen liang-fang* 經目屢驗良方. The collection, *Shuo-fu hsü* (*see* T'ao Tsung-i), includes excerpts of three of Feng's works, *P'eng-ch'uang hsü-lu* 蓬窗續錄 (miscellaneous notes), *Tien-hsing chi-lüeh* 滇行紀略 (travel to Yunnan), in which he makes passing reference to Matteo Ricci (*q. v.*), and *Lin-chien she-yüeh* 林間社約 (rules of his poetry club). The second title undoubtedly came from his collection of writings in Yunnan, *Tien-nan* 滇南 *chi*; this and his writings in Ch'ang-te, entitled *Wu-ling* 武陵 *chi*, are probably the last of his works. Neither seems to have survived, except the few leaves contained in the *Shuo-fu hsü*.

Bibliography

Feng Yüan-ch'eng hsüan-chi, *chüan* 20–24; MSL (1966), Shen-tsung, 10092, 10610; *Yunnan t'ung-chih* (1894), 121/15b; *Chao-ch'ing-fu chih*(1876), 12/8a; *Hunan t'ung-chih* (1934), 2216; *Sung-feng yü-yün* 松風餘韻, 5/6a; P. M. d'Elia, *Fonti Ric-ciane*, I (Rome, 1942), 35, n. 1; Sun T'ien-ch'i (1957), 165; Te-ch'ing, *Han-shan lao-jen meng-yu-chi*, 54/23a; *Huang Ming wen-hai*, microfilm, 9/1/4, 7/11; *Hua-t'ing-hsien chih* (1878), 6/10a, 14/24a, 32b, 20/4b, 5b, 16b, 18a, 31a; Ch'en Tzu-lung (ECCP), *Ming ching-shih wen-pien*.

Chaoying Fang

FENG Tao-sheng, *see* **FENG Fang**

FENG Ts'ung-wu 馮從吾 (T. 仲好, H. 少墟), 1556–1627(?), official and philosopher, was a northwesterner from Ch'ang-an 長安, Shensi, the son of Feng Yu 友 (T. 益卿, 1507–65), a provincial graduate of 1534 who eventually became vice prefect of Paoting. Feng Ts'ung-wu is considered a member of the Kan-ch'üan 甘泉 school of neo-Confucianism, which opposed the ideas of Wang Shou-jen (*q.v.*) about the self-sufficiency of the individual mind. Like the Tung-lin academicians, he disliked the Buddhist influences in Wang's thought and advocated stern moral training. He was an early admirer of the Tung-lin leader, Ku Hsien-ch'eng (*q. v.*), whom he first met in Peking in 1582.

Feng placed high in the metropolitan examination of 1589 and was made a Hanlin Academy bachelor. In September, 1591, he was appointed an investigating censor. Six months later he submitted a memorial criticizing the emperor, Chu I-chün (*q.v.*), for his inattention to duty and for his alcoholic and sexual indulgences. This so infuriated the emperor that he threatened to have Feng beaten publicly at court. Through a grand secretary's intervention Feng was saved from the punishment. Soon thereafter, in May, 1592, he took sick leave and went home. Early in 1596, probably soon after he resumed office in Peking, he was one of fourteen censors who were cashiered on the charge of dereliction of duty. This charge, made by the emperor himself, was entirely unjustified. It happened that the emperor's favorite eunuch had suddenly fallen into disgrace and the censors and many other officials were blamed for having failed to report on the offender. Apparently the emperor was using the occasion to rid the court of offiicials he disliked, among whom Feng may have been the foremost. In any case Feng's name was erased from the civil service register.

For the next twenty-five years Feng lived a calm life of study, writing, and teaching in the Kuan-chung 關中 Academy in Ch'ang-an. When recalled to duty in Peking in 1621, with status as vice minister of the Grand Court of Revision, he was successively promoted (1622) to be assistant censor-in-chief and vice censor-in-chief. After retiring from office at the end of 1622 because of the Shou-shan Academy controversy(see Tsou Yüan-piao) he was repeatedly offered new appointments in 1623 and 1624, but he preferred retirement. In 1625, when Wei Chung-hsien (ECCP) was in power, he was for the second time stripped of his civil service status. He is said to have died in 1627 (perhaps earlier) of a long illness induced by his vexation and distress over the anti-Tung-lin outrages of 1625 and 1626. He was eventually given posthumous rank as grand guardian of the heir apparent and canonized as Kung-ting 恭定.

Feng's collected writings, Feng Shao-hsü chi 少墟集, 22 ch., were originally printed in 1612, reprinted in the 1620s, and again in the K'ang-hsi era (1662–1722), and copied into the Imperial Library. Early copies are owned by the Academia Sinica and the National Central Library in Taiwan. Some uncommon collectanea include other Feng works. T'ung-ko ch'üan-shu 桐閣全書 and Kuan-chung tao-mai ssu-chung shu 道脈四種書 both have the Feng Shao-hsü kuan-hsüeh pien 關學編, 5 ch., plus 1 introductory chüan and Feng Shao-hsü Kuan-chung ssu hsien-sheng yao-hsüeh lu 四先生要學錄, 4 ch. Hsi-ching ch'ing-lu ts'ung-shu 西京清麓叢書 includes Kuan-hsüeh yüan-pien 原編, 4 ch., plus 1 introductory chüan. A separate 1756 edition of Kuan-

hsüeh pien, in 4 ch., is owned by Columbia University; and the second series of Chih-fu-chai 知服齋 ts'ung-shu preserves Feng's intellectual history of the Yüan dynasty, Yüan-ju k'ao-lüeh 元儒考略, 4 ch., which was disparaged as a rather mechanical compilaion by the eighteenth century Ssu-k'u chüan-shu editors but nevertheless copied into the Imperial Library. Works called Feng-tzu chieh-yao 馮子節要, 14 ch., and Ku-wen chi-hsüan 古文輯選, 6 ch., were known to the Ssu-k'u editors but seem no longer extant. Also lost, it appears, is an enlarged collection, Feng Kung-ting ch'üan-chi 全集, 24 ch., plus a hsü-chi, 4 ch. Feng is said to have compiled as well a genealogy of his clan, Feng-shih tsu-p'u 馮氏族譜, 1 ch., and to have collaborated in compiling a gazetteer of his native province, Shensi t'ung-chih 通志, 35 ch; the first seems no longer extant, but copies of the second, printed in 1611, are among the holdings of the National Library of Peking and the Naikaku Bunko, Tokyo.

Bibliography

1/243/19b; 3/227/17a; 39/13/13a; 83/41/6b; KC (1958), 4766, 5212; SK (1930), 58/3b, 96/9a, 172/13b, 193/3a; Tsou I 鄒漪, Ch'i-Chen yeh-sheng 啓禎野乘 (preface of 1679, reprint 1936), 1/13b; TSCC (1885–88), XI: 359/21/11b.

Charles O. Hucker

FENG Wei-min 馮惟敏 (T. 汝行, H. 海浮山人), October 1511-78 (?), a native of Lin-ch'ü 臨朐 in Shantung, was a prominent writer of san-ch'ü 散曲 (song poems or dramatic verse) in the Ming era. He was the third of four sons of Feng Yü 裕 (T. 伯順, H. 閭山, cs 1508), who had risen to become surveillance vice commissioner in Kweichow from a family of military registry in Kuang-ning 廣寧, Liaotung, but who later moved a part of the family back to the ancestral home in Lin-ch'ü. Of Feng Wei-min's three brothers, Feng Wei-no (see Feng Ch'i) achieved prominence as a finance commissioner in Kiangsi; his grandson, Feng Ch'i, was to become minister of Rites. Feng Wei-min's father became a follower of Ch'en Hsien-chang (q.v.) and, as a lover of poetry, contributed to a poetry club, Hai-tai-hui 海岱會, from which a collection entitled *Hai-tai-hui chi* 集 in 12 *chüan* was edited by Feng Ch'i and, in the 18th century, copied into the *Ssu-k'u* library. As a boy Feng Wei-min accompanied his father to various appointments in Nanking, Kansu, and Kweichow. Through his father's intellectual interests and his own early experiences in areas so far apart the youth received an education broader than that of boys who remained at home.

The Shantung education intendant, Wang Shen-chung (q.v.), lauded the young man's talent, calling it superior to his own. Feng passed the provincial examination in 1537 but failed several times in the metropolitan, whereas two of his brothers were successful in 1538. This gave Feng Wei-min the theme for one of his two dramas. He lived for over two decades about 25 *li* from Lin-ch'ü at the foot of Hai-fou 海浮 Mountain, whence his *hao* is derived. He is described as leading the leisurely life of a rural gentleman, roaming the countryside and writing poems in a region said to be nearly southern in climate. In 1557/58 an exceptionally greedy and unlawful regional inspector in Shantung named Tuan Ku-yen 段顧言 (cs 1550) got him into trouble and even into jail for reasons not wholly clear, but probably due to Feng's sharp criticism of the censor's abuse of power. Another high official in the province saw to his release because of his outstanding contributions to literature. This anticipates later divided judgments of his literary talent and oeuvre. About four years after this incident (1562) Feng went to the capital to apply for a post. He was entrusted with the magistracy of the district Lai-shui 淶水 in Pei-Chihli, serving in this capacity for more than a year, until he was removed on some unjustified charges by a eunuch whom he had forced

to pay delinquent taxes on land and other properties. He was demoted to instructor of the prefectural school of Chinkiang, where he served from 1565 to 1569, keeping close contact with poets, playwrights, and painters in the Nanking area, then a cultural center of importance. In 1567 he was invited to Yunnan to be a provincial examiner. After a stay at home because of illness he went to officiate (1569) as vice prefect in Paoting-fu for another two years. Orders then came for him to go to the court of Chu I-t'an 朱頤坦, prince of Lu 魯王 (enfoeffed 1551, d. 1594), in Yen-chou 兗州, Shantung, but he pleaded ill health and returned home. He was sixty-one then and lived the last years of his life in his Hai-fou villa. It is not fully clear when he died; internal evidence leads to the year 1578 when he had reached the age of sixty-seven.

During the Ming some poets made use of the popular song forms of the Yüan period to write operas, as well as compound and single song poems, for which the common term ch'ü 曲 was employed. A compound poem, t'ao-shu 套數, was formed with one rhyme and a common set of melodies, thus corresponding to one act in the drama as did a single poem, hsiao-ling 小令, to one aria. The term "dramatic verse" to translate the Chinese san-ch'ü fits the genesis of this type of poetry. Feng Wei-min wrote two dramas himself, the *Liang chuang-yüan pu-fu-lao yü-tien ch'uan-lu chi* 梁狀元不伏老玉殿傳臚記 and the *Seng-ni kung-fan ch'uan-ch'i* 僧尼共犯傳奇 (both reproduced from a Ming edition in 1958 in the *Ku-pen hsi ch'ü ts'ung-k'an* 古本戲曲叢刊, 4th series). These plays show freshness in style and freedom in narrating the plot; the ancient story of the ironic success of an eighty-year-old examination candidate is used to criticize the system as it existed during the Chia-ching period; and the call to return to society from monastic life is educed in rapid and simple language full of humor and goodwill. But Feng Wei-min's main contribution was in the field of dramatic verse. Almost fifty compound poems and more than five hundred single poems are known, having been collected in the *Hai-fou shan-t'ang tz'u-kao* 詞稿, 4 *ch.*, of which the *San-ch'ü ts'ung-k'an* edition of 1931 was a rearrangement with deletions by Jen Chung-min 任中敏 from a late sixteenth-century edition. Feng's poems in classical style were assembled in the *Shih-men chi* 石門集 (1596 ed.); another collection, *Feng Hai-fou chi*, edited by Yü Hsien 俞憲 (T. 汝成, H. 岳率, cs 1538) during the author's lifetime, has been incorporated in the *Sheng Ming pai-chia shih* 盛明百家詩. Of his prose not much is left; there is, *inter alia*, the introduction to his poetical collection and his editorial work on the two local gazetteers, the *Lin-ch'ü-hsien chih* (1552 ed.) and the *Pao-ting-fu chih* 府志 (1570 ed.).

Feng Wei-min's dramatic verse has been both praised and censured by contemporaries and later critics. Wang Shih-chen (*q.v.*) among the more prominent called them superior but not flawless because they had too much local color and were all northern in tone. The dominating musical style in dramas at that time was the southern k'un-ch'ü崑曲 style. Only in the 20th century has Feng become recognized as one of the outstanding poets of san-ch'ü dramatic verse. He covered a wide range of themes and moods —from individual melancholy and gloom about unrequited love to social criticism of a cutting sharpness, together with much descriptive detail. Original talent and family background combined to produce, it seems, Ming China's greatest san-ch'ü poet, as Jen Chung-min suggests in his *San-ch'ü kai-lun* 概論.

Bibliography

40/45/19b; 64/戊8/6b; 84/丁上/21b; 86/13/22b; *Lin-ch'ü-hsien chih* (1884), 9上/2b, 12上/7b, 14上/24a; *Pao-ting-fu chih* (1881), 4/5a; Li Wei-chen 李維楨, "Feng-shih chia-chuan" 馮氏家傳 in *Ta-mi shan-fang chi* 大泌山房集, 65/12b; Cheng Ch'ien 鄭騫, "Feng Wei-min chi ch'i chu-shu" 及其著述, YCHP, no. 28 (December, 1940), 133; id., "Feng Wei-min yü san-ch'ü ti chiang-lai"與散曲

的將來, in *Ts'ung shih tao ch'ü* 從詩到曲 (Taipei, 1961), 209.

Tilemann Grimm

FERREIRA, Gaspar (Gaspard, Gaspare, 費奇觀, T. 揆一), 1571-December 27, 1649, missionary, was born in Fornos, Portugal. Following his novitiate (1588) and four years devoted to the study of rhetoric and philosophy, he left before ordination for Goa (1593). For four years he taught humanities, then concluded his study of theology at Macao. In 1604 Alessandro Valignano (*q. v.*) sent him to Peking. On the way he received harsh treatment from the eunuch assigned to escort him to the capital, suffered shipwreck in the river at T'ung-chou 通州 (near Peking), and lost much of his luggage and many valuables which he had expected to present to the emperor and others at the court. Some of the boxes were deliberately pilfered or thrown overboard by the sailors, but later partly recovered. Feng Ying-ching (*see* Matteo Ricci), despite the fact that he was himself in prison, succeeded through his connections in bringing the culprits to book and in restoring certain things to Ferreira; but the latter refused to press charges against the offenders.

For the next two years Ferreira and Diego de Pantoja (*q.v.*) worked in the region of Pacting-fu (some eighty miles south of Peking) and developed a Christian community of both men and women, as well as children. At the end of 1607 he was sent to Nanchang and then posted to Shao-chou 韶州 (Kwangtung) but not for long. On April 27, 1612, he and Manuel Dias the Younger (*q.v.*) and two Chinese brothers were forced to leave, transferring their mission to Nan-hsiung 南雄 in the northern part of the province. On November 21, 1612, Ferreira became a priest. During the persecution of Christian missionaries and their adherents in 1616 and 1617, Ferreira and his colleagues decided to sell their residence, and joined others seeking shelter at the hospitable home of Yang T'ing-yün (ECCP) in Hangchow.

His experiences and places of labor following the persecution are only vaguely reported. We know that in 1620 Ferreira was appointed instructor in Chinese for the newcomers to the mission in Chia-ting 嘉定 (*see* Lazzaro Cattaneo), one of them being Johann Terenz (*q.v.*). In the 1630s he was in Chien-ch'ang 建昌, Kiangsi. It was there that the Franciscan, Antonio de Santa Maria Caballero (*q.v.*), encountered him on December 16, 1633, Ferreira inviting him to celebrate mass in his chapel. In this year he boldly took issue with Nicolo Longobardi (*q.v.*), who had previously been superior of the China mission, on the question of the term for God. This for at least two decades had been a matter of warm debate. Matteo Ricci (*q.v.*) had approved of both Shang-ti 上帝 and Tien-chu 天主 for God. Longobardi questioned these and other terms and raised the issue again and again; he rebutted Ferreira's arguments and went so far as to reject both Shang-ti and T'ien-chu and come out for a sinicized rendering of Deus. Eventually T'ien-chu won the day.

At the time of the Manchu conquest Ferreira was forced to retreat to Canton, probably in 1646, and remained there (with Francesco Sambiasi, *q. v.*)—bowed down with years — until his death three years later. He left a number of works, mostly in Chinese, on religious matters, except for several tracts, refutation of the arguments of Longobardi, and a Chinese-Portuguese dictionary in manuscript, entitled *Diccionario da lingua Chinese e Portugueza.*

Bibliography

Pfister (1932), 21; L. J. Gallagher, *China in the Sixteenth Century, The Journals of Matthew Ricci, 1583–1610* (New York, 1953), 444; G. H. Dunne, *Generation of Giants* (Notre Dame, 1962), 105; A.S. Rosso, *Apostolic Legations to China of the 18th Century* (South Pasadena, 1948), chap. 4; Sommervogel, Cols. 682–683; P. M. d'Elia, *Fonti Ricciane*, II (Rome, 1949), 279, n. 1, 281, 356, 465; Robert Streit, *Bibliotheca Missionum*, V (Münster-Aachen, 1929), 695.

L. Carrington Goodrich

FU-TENG 福登 (family name Hsü 續, H. Miao-feng 妙峰), 1540–February 8, 1613, an architect and a Ch'an Buddhist monk, was born at P'ing-yang 平陽, Shansi. His parents died when he was six years of age and since the family was poor the boy became a shepherd. He entered a monastery at the age of eleven but was dissatisfied and left after a few years. When he was seventeen he went begging at nearby market places. He slept at night under the porch of the Wen-ch'ang ko 文昌閣 in the temple Wan-ku ssu 萬固寺, in P'u-chou 蒲州, Shansi. The Wen-ch'ang ko had been built for the temple by a prince of the imperial family, Chu Chün-cha 朱俊柵 (Shan-yin wang 山陰王, d. 1603), who lived there. The prince, impressed by the promising appearance of the young beggar, decided to develop the latent abilities he saw in him, and from then on became Fu-teng's protector and adviser.

He chose a monastery, the Hsi-yen 棲巖 ssu, on the other side of the mountain, Chung-t'iao shan 中條山, and here, it is said, Fu-teng meditated and attained enlightenment. On a return visit to the prince, the latter seemed not as impressed as expected but sent him to a temple in the Chieh-hsiu 介休 hills where Fu-teng applied himself to study of the sūtras and finally at the age of twenty-six received ordination.

The prince next advised him to see more of the Buddhist world so, as a mendicant monk, he traveled to P'u-t'o 普陀 shan, an island dedicated to Kuan-yin on the Chekiang coast. Back in Ningpo he contracted a disease during an epidemic there and while still ill he went to Nanking in 1567, lodging at the monastery T'ien-chieh 天界 ssu. There he made the acquaintance of a learned monk, Te-ch'ing (*q.v.*), later to become his close friend and biographer.

From Nanking Fu-teng retraced his steps to his benefactor the prince, who built for him, or had him build, a refuge deep in the wilderness on the southern side of the Chung-t'iao shan. There he lived in seclusion for several years until in 1572, at the request of the prince, he went to Peking to secure a copy of the *Pei-tsang* 北藏, a collection of Buddhist works initiated by Emperor Chu Ti (*q. v.*). At the capital he met Te-ch'ing again and the following year the two friends traveled together to deliver the sūtras to his patron. In 1574 they decided to settle on Wu-t'ai shan. On their way they passed Fu-teng's native place where many years previously his parents, because of their poverty, had been buried without ceremony. Concerned that this neglect might cause them difficulties in their future lives, he arranged for a reburial with all due regard to the proprieties.

After the burial the monks finally arrived at Wu-t'ai shan, where they stayed in the coldest places, "enduring much hardship." Both were anxious about the future lives of their respective parents so each decided to make a copy of the *Hua-yen ching* 華嚴經 (*Avataṁsaka-sūtra*). Te-ch'ing wrote a golden text, the golden ink made by blood and water, and Fu-teng a red text with blood from his tongue. Having finished the transcription, Fu-teng wanted to hold a great meeting on Wu-t'ai shan in commemoration of their work. The two monks were already well known for their pious lives and strange deeds; so, when Fu-teng in 1581 walked out of the mountains to invite everybody to their meeting, several thousand people, monks and laymen, came. The meeting lasted a hundred twenty days from the end of 1581 to the spring of 1582, taking place in the monastery T'a-yüan 塔院 ssu, which two years previously had been restored at the request of Empress Dowager Li-shih (*q.v.*). The subject of the meeting was the *Hua-yen ching*, but coincidentally the empress dowager sent messengers to the temple beseeching the monks to pray for the birth of an heir apparent. This petition was included in the daily prayers at the meeting.

Immediately afterward the two friends parted and left Wu-t'ai shan. Fu-teng went to Lu-ya 蘆芽 in Wu-chai hsien 五

寨縣, Shansi. In the eighth month of the same year (August 28, 1582), the emperor's eldest son, Chu Ch'ang-lo (ECCP), was born; in gratitude the empress dowager asked Fu-teng to build a big Hua-yen temple on Lu-ya shan. From that moment the imperial treasury was open to any temple building that Fu-teng might propose. He was forty-two years of age when he built the Hua-yen ssu and an iron pagoda of seven stories on the top of the mountain. The temple and its pagoda are mentioned but no details given in his biography or in the provincial gazetteer. In the latter it is recorded that both were completely destroyed during the wars that brought the Ming dynasty to an end.

His next work was the rebuilding of the temple Wan-ku ssu, where as a young man he had met the prince. The temple had been founded during the T'ang dynasty, but by the 1580s had fallen into disrepair. At the request of Wang Ch'ung-ku (*q.v.*) he rebuilt and enlarged the temple, staying there for three years to supervise the construction. What remains today is entirely his work and proclaims him to have been a skillful and experienced architect with a very personal style, though nothing is told about where and how he acquired his professional knowledge.

He erected a pagoda of thirteen stories and a main hall flanked by two smaller buildings, all three of two stories made entirely in brick. The traditional Chinese timberwork of eaves and cantilevers was imitated in brick. In the main hall the traditional cone-shaped ceiling ending in a circular "heaven well" 天井 was also in brickwork. The doors and windows had vaulted lintels. These so-called wu-liang tien 無梁殿 (beamless) buildings are characteristic of all Fu-teng's temple constructions. An inscription on the pagoda dates it in 1586.

His skill and experience with vaulted brick constructions led the minister of Justice, Li Shih-ta (*see* Ku Hsien-ch'eng), a native of Shensi, to ask him to repair a bridge of thirteen arches over the Wei River 渭水, a work which he completed in two years. On his way back to Lu-ya, Fu-teng passed a vertical cliff near Ning-wu 寧武 (Shansi). This inspired him to construct a cave temple, measuring approximately forty feet each in height, width, and depth. The walls he decorated with delicately carved figures of the ten thousand Bodhisattvas.

His next work was a challenge to his skill as an engineer. A bridge over the Yang-ho 洋河 was needed in Hsüan-hua hsien 宣化縣, just south of the Great Wall at a strategic place on the road to Mongolia, strong enough to resist the inevitable floods and broad enough to carry soldiers and horses. Several architects had tried in vain. Because of Fu-teng's success with the bridge over the Wei, the governor of Pei-Chihli, Wang Hsiang-ch'ien 王象乾 (cs 1571), asked him to construct one. In a record of 1599 there is praise for his achievement and a description of it, called Kuang-hui ch'iao 廣惠橋, which is said to have been about 1380 feet long and to have had twenty-three arches. It tells too, without further explanation, that the bridge was double or reinforced. As nothing is left of the bridge today, it is impossible to discover exactly what is meant. The record shows that an unusually large amount of metal was used for this bridge, and Fu-teng's later buildings indicate that through the bridge construction his skill increased and he learned how not only to put up large vaults but also to cast metal as well and to combine brick and metal in his structures.

At about this time Fu-teng conceived what he hoped might be his major achievements, namely, to build on each of three holy mountains a bronze hall around a gilded sculpture of the Bodhisattva to which each mountain was dedicated: Kuan-yin (Avalokiteśvara) on P'u-t'o shan, Wen-shu 文殊 (Mañjuśri) on Wu-t'ai shan, and P'u-hsien 普賢 (Samantabhadra)

on O-mei shan, in Szechwan. His idea was probably inspired by a visit to Chu Hsiao-yung 效鏞, then Prince of Shen 藩 (enf. 1580) at Lu-an 潞安, Shansi. The prince had cast a gold alloy statue of P'u-hsien to be delivered to Mt. O-mei. Apparently Fu-teng was requested for this mission. When the monk revealed his dream of building a temple on that mountain at a cost of some ten thousand taels, the prince promised to finance it. Thus assured, Fu-teng went to Ching-chou 荆州, Hukuang, to supervise the casting of the metal parts, which were then shipped upstream. The fact that his friend Wang Hsiang-ch'ien was then serving as governor of Szechwan greatly facilitated Fu-teng's work.

On the highest peak of O-mei shan, Chin-ting 金頂, in the monastery Yung-ming Hua-tsang 永明華藏 ssu, Fu-teng constructed his hall for the Bodhisattva in brick. In the mountain chronicle it is recorded that "the beams and pillars, the posts and rafters, the window latticework and roof tiles as well as the walls above and below were all covered with a layer of bronze." On the walls were carvings of the ten thousand Bodhisattvas. Outside, by each of the four sides of the hall, he put up four bronze pagodas and south of the hall a library, Ts'ang ching lou 藏經樓. The emperor bestowed the name Yung-yen 永延 ssu on the monastery. Today only two of the bronze pagodas remain, and a bronze plate with an inscription dated 1609, placed there apparently some years after the buildings were completed.

About 1603 Fu-teng was in Ching-chou supervising the bronze work for the P'u-t'o project, which was partly financed by Wang Hsiang-ch'ien. Later Fu-teng learned at Nanking that the monks of P'u-t'o objected to his project. Hence late in 1603 he chose a place southeast of Nanking, the Pao-hua 寶華 shan in Chü-yung 句容, and asked the empress dowager for funds to erect a bronze hall for Kuan-yin there. He immediately received the sum he requested. The empress dowager personally donated the gilt figure of Kuan-yin and gave the name Lung-ch'ang 隆昌 ssu to the monastery in 1605. The bronze hall which he built around the figure on the top of the mountain is of almost the same size as the hall on O-mei shan: some 32 feet in height, 21 feet in length, and 18 1/2 feet in width. By it he erected two smaller two-story buildings, a P'u-hsien tien on the right and a Wen-shu tien on the left; both are "beamless" brick structures. The ceilings are barrel vaulted. These two buildings dated 1605 still remain and so do the brick walls of the bronze hall. The roof was destroyed together with the rest of the temple compound during the T'ai-p'ing rebellion.

Fu-teng's main works occupied his last years. In the years following the birth of the heir apparent the empress dowager continued to hold both Fu-teng and Wu-t'ai shan in veneration; in 1605 she invited him to build what is now the main temple on Wu-t'ai shan, the Hsien-t'ung 顯通 ssu. It had been part of the oldest temple, the Ta-fou ling-ch'iu 大孚靈鷲 ssu, around the great white pagoda, but was separated from it when the T'a-yüan ssu was restored in 1579 as the temple of the pagoda. To compensate for the loss of its main reliquary Fu-teng built a vast temple compound with hall behind hall surrounded by living quarters and store houses, all in brick. The innermost building on top of the mountain was a two-story bronze hall for the gilt figure of Wen-shu. It is flanked by two "beamless" libraries and in front of it stood four bronze pagodas. The bronze hall remains in its original shape and corresponds exactly to the description of the bronze hall on O-mei shan. Of the bronze pagodas, today only two are left.

The monk-architect did not restrict his endeavors to the enlargement of the Hsien-t'uang ssu, on which the emperor bestowed the name Sheng-kuang yung-ming 聖光永明 ssu. He built rest houses for pilgrims where tea and medicine were distributed at the expense of the emperor.

Nothing is left of these buildings now; we know them only through inscriptions. For the benefit of the pilgrims he constructed a new road through the mountains with bridges over gorges and rivers.

It must have been at this time too that he built the monastery Tz'u-yu yüan-ming 慈佑圓明 ssu in Fu-p'ing 阜平, Pei-Chihli. His latest works are surely the two thirteen-story brick pagodas at Yung-tsu 永祚 ssu in Taiyuan, Shansi, imposing structures that in style are closely related to the pagoda at Wan-ku ssu. An inscription dates them in 1611.

In 1612 he was asked to build a bridge over the Fen River 汾水 south of Taiyuan, but during his labors he fell ill and in the autumn he returned to Wu-t'ai shan, where he died in February, 1613. The imperial family contributed rich gifts for his funeral. The emperor had a tomb pagoda raised for him near Hsien-t'ung ssu and in an inscription called him Chen-cheng fo-tzu 真正佛子.

Since all his great building activities were accomplished within the short span of thirty years, he must have had a numerous and well-trained staff of craftsmen acquainted with his intentions and methods. That may account for the several "beamless" brick temples built during the last years of the Ming dynasty. Many buildings within the compound of the Yung-tsu ssu are similar to the works of Fu-teng, but only the two pagodas are ascribed to him. His tomb pagoda follows the style of his own buildings so closely that it could well have been designed by himself.

Bibliography

Te-ch'ing, *Han-shan ta-shih Meng yu ch'üan-chi* 憨山大師夢遊全集, 39/317 (in *Hsü-tsang-ching* 續藏經, pt. 2, case 32); *Pao-hua shan chih* (*ca.* 1860), 5/3a, 6/1a, 12/1a; Li Wei-chen 李維楨, *Sheng-kuang yung-ming ssu chi* 記 (in his *Ta-pi shan-fang chi* 大泌山房集), 54/28b; Tsang Chin-shu 臧晉叔, *Fu-pao t'ang-chi* 負苞堂集, ch. 4; Po Huan 白煥, *Wu-t'ai shan wen-wu* (1958); *O-mei shan t'u chih* 峨嵋山圖志 (1889), 2/88b;

Hibino Takeo 日比野丈夫, *Myōhō Fukuto no jiseki ni tsuite* 妙峰福登の事蹟について in *Tsukamoto Hakushi Shoju-kinen Bukkyō-shigaku ronshū*塚本博士頌壽記念佛教史學論集(1961), 583-95; Sekino Tadashi 關野貞, *Shina Bunka shiseki* 支那文化史蹟 (1940), *ch.* 18; Hibino Takeo & Ono Katsutoshi 小野勝年, *Godaisan* 五台山 (1942), 235; Mizuno Seiichi水野清一and Hibino Takeo, *Sansei koseki shi* 山西古蹟志(1956), 207; Yü-ch'ien 喻謙, *Hsin hsü kao-seng-chuan* 新續高僧傳 (1923), *ch.* 33; *Ch'ing-liang shan chih* 清涼山志 (1933), 3/29a, 5/8b, 5/14a; J. Prip-Møller, *Chinese Buddhist Monasteries* (Copenhagen, 1937), 275.

Else Glahn

FU Yu-te 傅友德, d. December 20, 1394, eminent general, was a native of Su-chou 宿州 (northern Anhwei). His family, like many peasant families in the region, fled the Yellow River floods and attendant social disorders that had become general throughout the northern Huai River plain, and went to live at Tang-shan 碭山, some 120 miles east of Kaifeng, and then at Ying-chou 潁州 (Anhwei). Although an unlettered man of poor rural background, Fu possessed personal qualities and acquired military skills that in those unsettled times made him a village leader as a young man. As the Yüan government gave increasing evidence of its incompetence, it began to be challenged by numerous rebellions. The Red Turban uprising in this region, dominated by Liu Fu-t'ung (*see* Han Lin-er), produced widespread and general disorder from 1351 onward. Fu Yu-te joined a local band of rebels at Hsü-chou 徐州 (*ca.* 1351), but after Liu proclaimed in 1355 the establishment of a "Sung" rebel dynasty, Fu decided to serve under his banner. He was made a junior commander in the army of one of Liu Fu-t'ung's generals, known as Li Hsi-hsi (*see* Han Lin-er), who was active in plundering Yüan cities in Shantung and the metropolitan area from about 1355. Li suffered a series of defeats, however, which drove him into the far northwest in

1357, and forced further retreats into Szechwan in 1358. Fu Yu-te became discouraged with Li's leadership and left him that year to join another rebel leader, Ming Yü-chen (*q.v.*), who had recently (1355-56) conquered Szechwan for Hsü Shou-hui (*q.v.*), leader of another branch of the sprawling Red Turban movement based in the central Yangtze valley. Again Fu Yu-te failed to find satisfying recognition for his talents, and sometime after Ch'en Yu-liang (*q.v.*) murdered Hsü in 1360, Fu left Ming Yü-chen and joined Ch'en Yu-liang's newly proclaimed "Han" dynasty in Hukuang. But again he felt that his talents were not recognized. About a year later, on September 19, 1361, when Chu Yüan-chang, in personal command of his armies in the field, had just driven Ch'en's forces westward from the environs of Chin-ling (Nanking), and had succeeded in wresting Anking from "Han" control, Fu with the force under his immediate command surrendered to Chu. The future Ming founder gladly accepted him.

Fu Yu-te had traveled a long route from the Huai region, under a succession of overlords into the northwest, into Szechwan, and downriver into central China. In Chu he found at last the leader who recognized his qualities; moreover, he had come back to the command of a fellow peasant from the Huai, and a fellow Red Turban leader. In social background, in regional associations, in dialect, he fitted very well into the military leadership group around Chu. In the years that followed, he was to assume one of the leading positions within that group, and to contribute importantly to the military tasks associated with the establishment of the new dynasty.

During the next nine years, Fu served in many campaigns, sometimes directly under Chu, at other times under the command of Hsü Ta or Ch'ang Yü-ch'un (*qq.v.*). He rose rapidly in rank and honors, and participated with great valor in the campaigns which overcame Ch'en Yu-liang's Han state in 1363–64, and the Wu state of Chang Shih-ch'eng (*q.v.*) in 1366–67. Then he was assigned to the northern expeditionary force which drove north to the Mongol capital in 1367–68, and to subsequent campaigns through 1370, which drove the Mongol court into the steppe and pursued remnants of their power along the Great Wall frontier (*see* Hsü Ta, Ch'ang Yü-ch'un, and Li Wen-chung). On November 25, 1370, Hsü Ta and his entourage returned to Nanking, and on the 26th Hsü submitted his reports detailing the events of the successfully concluded campaigns against the Mongols. On November 29 the emperor held an audience at which rewards were announced, explaining that he was personally responsible for all decisions and illustrating by example how he had avoided favoritism and had maintained objectivity. Six officers, including Hsü Ta, were given honorary titles of duke; Fu Yu-te was among twenty-eight awarded the next highest level of honors his title being marquis of Ying-ch'uan 潁川侯, in recognition of his place of residence. His rank among the twenty-eight, however, as indicated by the amount of annual income and supplementary gifts, was near the bottom of the list.

Fu Yu-te was overshadowed by the figure of Ch'ang Yü-ch'un until Ch'ang's death in 1369. They were commanders of the same caliber, shrewd field tacticians with immense personal courage, always fighting at the head of their forces. Fu was famous for accepting any challenge, fighting on after receiving many wounds, leading his group of daredevils to the top of any hill, dueling the opponent's leading general in hand-to-hand combat. But he came into Chu Yüan-chang's service five years later than Ch'ang and was often referred to as "second only to Ch'ang"; he was not given as prominent a role as long as Ch'ang was alive, and by the time of Ch'ang's death, the major military tasks in founding the dynasty had been accomplished. Fu received important independent commands, however, in two remaining military undertakings, and in both he proved himself highly competent in the role of generalissimo, conducting independent operations of large scope. These were the conquest of Szechwan (1371), still held by Ming Yü-chen's heir, and the campaign against the Liang 梁 princedom in Yunnan, ten years later.

The Szechwan campaign, to eliminate the rival state of Hsia established there in 1362, was launched in January, 1371. Two expeditionary commands were organized, one under T'ang Ho (*q.v.*), including naval forces under Liao Yung-chung(*q.v.*) was to move westward along the route paralleling the Yangtze. The other under Fu Yu-te, including both infantry and cavalry, was to enter Szechwan from Shensi. The emperor had worked out a plan which he expected his commanders to follow in detail; it included secret instructions to Fu to strike with lightning speed against the central basin and the city of Chengtu while the enemy, anticipating that the other army coming from the east along the Yangtze was the main invasion force, were concentrated there to repel that thrust, Fu Yu-te was assigned the same route by which he had entered Szechwan fifteen years earlier.

While T'ang Ho's forces got bogged down and lagged behind the prearranged schedule, Fu sent a succession of victory notices to the court, having accomplished his part of the conquest ahead of schedule. He took Chengtu in August, and forced the surrender of other main cities. Resistance collapsed and T'ang was able to join forces with Fu in September. Ming Yü-chen's heir, a boy of nine, was sent to Nanking and pardoned, given a title, and relocated in Korea. Provincial government for Szechwan was established, the city of Chengtu enlarged and its walls rebuilt, and the followers of Ming's state of Hsia intimidated or won over. The generals returned to Nanking where the emperor praised Fu for having achieved the major share of the Conquest and reproved T'ang for having failed to do

better. Rewards of money in modest a-
mounts were announced on January 19,
1372. Historians have criticized the emperor's niggardly attitude in this instance;
Fu and Liao Yung-chung, they say, should
have received dukedoms in reward for
military exploits of the first magnitude.

During the next eight years Fu served
prominently along the northern frontier
and was frequently cited and rewarded
for victories. In addition to leading campaigns in Kansu and Inner Mongolia, he
supervised construction of defenses along
the Great Wall, which in these years was
being largely rebuilt in the form which it
has retained into the present century. Fu
also instructed the heir and other imperial
princes in the military arts.

After the conquest of Szechwan, Chu
Yüan-chang determined to bring Yunnan
into the empire. Previously a loose con-
federation of tribal states known as Nan-
chao, the region had been conquered by
Qubilai Khan in 1254, and had existed as
a princedom ruled by a branch of the
Mongol imperial line thereafter; the Chinese referred to it as the princedom of
Liang. In the late 14th century it was a
region populated mostly by non-Han
(principally Tibeto-Burman) tribal peoples,
ruled by hereditary chieftains. The cities
had a veneer of Chinese culture, although
on the fringes of the tribal world. It
probably assumed importance in Chu's
mind because it was an outpost of a remnant of Mongol power. In 1372 he sent
an envoy, the eminent literatus Wang Wei
(*q.v.*), to persuade the reigning Liang
prince Basalawarmi to recognize the disappearance of Mongol hegemony and
submit to the Ming dynasty. Wang was
murdered there in February, 1374, but
diplomatic efforts continued. In the same
year a Mongol prince, who had surrendered to the Ming court on the northern
frontier, was sent to convey the same
message. There was no response. In 1375
Liang envoys to the Mongols in Mongolia
who were captured by Hsü Ta, were
forced to accompany a Chinese sent from

Nanking bearing further messages to the
Liang prince; when they reached Yunnan,
but before presenting themselves to the
prince, they murdered the Chinese court's
representative.

Diplomacy having failed, the court
decided on military measures. In the autumn of 1381 the emperor named Fu Yu-te
commander-in-chief of a vast military
force, numbering three hundred thousand
troops, with Lan Yü and Mu Ying (*qq.v.*)
as vice commanders, and with many other
eminent officers on his staff. The troops
were mostly from the Nanking region;
since most of them remained as permanent garrison forces, they exerted considerable cultural influence on the population
of the region. The emperor had studied
the maps and accounts of Kweichow and
Yunnan and had devised a detailed plan
which Fu was compelled to follow. The
conquest was by no means as rapid or as
decisive as the conquest of Szechwan ten
years earlier, but Kunming, the Liang
prince's capital, was taken in January,
1382, and many tribal leaders surrendered.
Ta-li 大理, the second city of the region,
fell to Mu Ying's army in April. The
Liang prince and his staff had committed
suicide when Kunming was threatened;
others of their regime, however, fled into
mountain strongholds, and were prepared
to resist. Tribal leaders who had surrendered often reversed themselves and resumed warfare against the Chinese. Following a plan sent from Nanking, Fu divided
the region into prefectures and districts,
established the provincial government at
Kunming, and installed military guards in
certain important cities. But warfare
dragged on well into 1383 and the
outcome semed uncertain. Early that
year the emperor sent a message to
Fu Yu-te acknowledging the protracted
hardship of his troops and encouraging
them; he added that even when Fu and
the main army returned, Mu Ying should
plan to remain with the army indefinitely to garrison the region. Late in the
summer Chu Yüan-chang sent another

message to Fu, saying: "For a long time I have hoped to be able to recall you to the capital, but I fear that it still is not possible to do so." He was obviously deeply concerned about the fate of his field forces. He sent dozens of long messages, warning about various dangers, and particularly about the food supply problem. His attitude was never that of impatience or anger; often he closed his long letters reviewing problems and suggesting solutions with a sentence such as: "I sit back here calculating and planning, but whether my suggestions can be carried out is something that must be judged in the light of the military realities." Clearly the conquest of this area offered both psychological and military-administrative problems quite unlike those encountered in reuniting the empire, and also quite different from the familiar ones of defense along the Great Wall frontier.

Early in 1384 the task of bringing Yunnan under control was declared accomplished. About April 1 Fu Yu-te and Lan Yü left with portions of the army to return to Nanking, and on May 5 the rewards for the campaign were announced. Fu was elevated to the dukedom of Ying-kuo 穎國公, with right of inheritance and an annual stipend of 3,000 *shih*; Lan and other generals, who already had marquisates, were given additional income and nominal honors, and the inheritance privilege was added to their titles.

After returning from Yunnan, Fu alternated between routine military assignments, mostly on the northern frontier, and returns to Yunnan. In 1385 he was assigned to the military command at Peiping, but early the next year tribal leaders, who had previously submitted, rebelled in Yunnan, and Fu was returned to Yüeh 越-chou (modern Ch'ü-ching 曲靖), east of Kunming, to help quell the revolt of a Lolo chieftain; then in the summer he joined Mu Ying in putting down a large uprising of tribes to the north, in the Tung-ch'uan 東川 (modern Hui-tse 會澤) region. He was recalled to the court in October. That winter (January 21, 1387) he was named vice commander to Feng Sheng (*q.v.*), who had been given a special commission to go to Liao-yang (modern Manchuria) to attack Naγaču (*q. v.*), a leader of the Eastern Mongols, who had rebelled. Fu served with conspicuous personal merit in a campaign that was otherwise discredited by the performance of Feng and other officers attached to his staff. Summoned back after the campaign had successfully terminated late in the summer, Feng was relieved of his command and severely rebuked, and Fu was at first left to take charge of the military defenses northeast of Peiping, but shortly thereafter was recalled to Yunnan. Throughout 1388 Yunnan was seriously threatened by the revolt of the Shan chieftain Ssu Lun-fa (*see* Ssu Jen-fa). Although Mu Ying achieved a brilliant victory over the Shan tribes, that emergency permitted other groups to rebel. Fu again led campaigns against the tribes at Tung-ch'uan, and throughout the second half of the year and most of 1389 was kept busy trying to suppress the repeated uprisings of the Lolo east of Kunming. After being ordered to establish a military garrison at Yüan 沅-chou (modern Chih-chiang 芷江 in western Hukuang), he apparently returned to Nanking before the end of the year, for in January of 1390 he was named on the merit list of 57 men, and then assigned to accompany the princes of Chin 晉 and of Yen 燕 in military excursions into Mongolia. He did not return to Yunnan and through the remaining three or four years of his life held somewhat routine assignments in north China, inspecting garrisons, reviewing and training troops, and participating in minor campaigns in the steppe.

The only imperial criticism made of Fu in his entire active career was in response to his request for a grant of almost a thousand *mou* of land in his home region on which to establish a private estate. He submitted the request in March of 1392, and received an angry rebuke from the emperor who reminded him that he had been generously rewarded. Many historians in Ming and later times have felt that Fu had received shabby treatment from the emperor, considering the scale of his achievements. But the matter passed, and it seems to have had no influence on Fu's career, nor was it related to his death by suicide two years later. At the beginning of March (1393), Lan Yü was denounced as a traitor and executed, and there followed a purge of thousands of persons associated with him. In September, however, the aging emperor apparently decided that the killing had gone far enough, and ordered that no new charges be made against anyone in connection with either the Hu Wei-yung (q.v.) conspiracy case of 1381 or the Lan Yü case. Yet senior officials, especially military leaders, saw the two cases as excuses for the emperor to get rid of all persons of status and power who might become threats to dynastic stability. Those who had survived the latter are said to have felt that their days were numbered, and that the emperor would find some reason for doing away with them. Between December 20, 1394, and February 23, 1395, three of the senior survivors were forced to commit suicide or executed on false charges; they were, first, Fu Yu-te, then Wang Pi (see Lan Yü), and finally Feng Sheng. Historians have linked their deaths, generally accepting the view that the emperor simply wanted to eliminate them. Fu Yu-te's death has been the most lamented, for his entire career was not only spectacularly successful in ways that brought immense benefits to the dynasty, but also was unmarked by any evidence of personal shortcomings or failings.

The circumstances surrounding Fu's end are obscured by widely varying accounts. The *Ming-shih* simply has it that he was "ordered to commit suicide." Other records state that he was in attendance at an imperial banquet when the emperor accused him, or his son, of some impropriety constituting *lèse majesté*. Various explanations exist of what that act may have been: 1) that Fu was ordered to leave and return with his two sons, and that the emperor sent guards to apprehend him as soon as he had left the room; 2) that he then committed suicide at the palace gate; 3) that a guard erroneously told him that the emperor expected him to return after having commanded his sons to commit suicide; 4) that he returned to the banquet to confront the emperor, bearing the heads of his two sons; when the emperor expressed shock, Fu is said to have replied: "You wanted the heads of my sons and myself, so here they are," after which he removed a dagger from his sleeve and slit his own throat. Many well-regarded traditional historians have offered some version of this account as the true story, but there are many reasons to discount most of it. We know only that some infraction of regulations or of propriety was the basis for his having been forced to end his life.

As to his two sons, the elder, Fu Chung 忠, married Chu Yüan-chang's ninth daughter, the imperial princess Shou-ch'un kung-chu (see Ning-kuo kung-chu), in 1386. His second son, Fu Jang 讓 who held a minor military rank, became the adopted son of Fu Yu-te's elder brother, Fu Yu-jen 仁, also a military officer. A daughter became consort of Chu Chi-hsi 濟熺, heir of the prince of Chin 晉, in 1391. Accounts of another son, supposedly his eldest, who is said to have been separated from his father in the early 1350s and never reunited with him, are not granted much credibility by most historians. Fu Chung and Fu Jang apparently did not survive their father, and may have died as he did for the same reason. Fu Chung's son was specially spared on acount of his mother, and some descendants are known to have been alive in Shansi in the 16th century, but none achieved any prominence. Later attempts to rehabilitate the line and restore their titles and properties were refused, but in 1522 the governor of Yunnan, Ho Meng-ch'un (*see* Li Tung-yang), requested and was granted permission to erect a memorial shrine to Fu Yu-te in Yunnan. In 1645 the Southern Ming court granted him the honorific title Wu-ching 武靖.

Bibliography

1/129/5b; 5/6/8a; 20/5/1a; 61/93/1a; 63/4/23a; MSL (1962), T'ai-tsu, *ch.* 9–234; KC (1958), 293, 458, 605, 641, 752; Ho Ch'iao-yüan, *Ming-shan-ts'ang*, "Ch'en-lin chi," 3; Cha Chi-tso (ECCP), *Tsui-wei lu*, "Chuan" 傳八上 8-a, 54a; P'an Ch'eng-chang 潘檉章, *Kuo-shih k'ao-i* 國史考異, *ch.* 3, no. 16; Ku Ying-t'ai (ECCP), *Ming-ch'ao chi-shih pen-mo*, ch. 11, 12.

F. W. Mote

FURTADO, Francisco 傅汎際 (T. 體齋, François Huertado), 1587-November 21 (or April 12), 1653, Catholic missionary, later vice provincial, then Visitor, of the China mission, was born on Fayal, one of the Azores. He entered the Society of Jesus in 1608. After his ordination as priest, he embarked in 1618 in the company of Niklaas Trigault (*q. v.*) who was returning to China. A few months after his arrival in Macao (1620) he was posted to Chia-ting 嘉定 in the Yangtze estuary to study Chinese (arriving January 15, 1621). During the ensuing decade he became a companion of Li Chih-tsao (ECCP) and remained with him in Hangchow until the latter's death in 1630. Two works in translation are the product of their association.

In 1631 Furtado was sent to Sian in Shensi where he established a church (1634). Two years later he received the appointment of vice provincial of the China mission, and during the next six years visited each of its centers, and performed a variety of tasks. One of the more important was to attempt to persuade the Holy See, in the light of the growing controversy between the Jesuits and other missionaries, Dominicans and Franciscans, to parcel out the mission field among the various orders, so that evangelization might proceed without friction. The Propaganda Fide, however, took no action, and the church suffered as a result.

The China mission was divided in 1641, due to mounting political unrest, Giulio Aleni (*q.v.*) keeping the southern branch, with the northern assigned to Furtado. Shortly after the Manchus took Peking, Dorgon (ECCP) as regent named Johann Adam von Bell Schall (*q.v.*) director of the bureau of astronomy. But Schall did not wish to serve. It fell to Furtado repeatedly to order him to accept the appointment. Later (1649), strangely enough, because of trouble stirred up by the Portuguese Jesuit Gabriel de Magalhães 安文思 (T. 景明, 1609-May 6, 1677), Furtado and others petitioned, unsuccessfully as it happened, that Schall be dismissed. In 1651 Furtado was named Visitor and returned to Kwangtung and to Macao, where he served until his death and where he was buried.

Furtado is especially remembered for the translation, with Li Chih-tsao, of Aristotle's *De coelo et mundo*, rendered as *Huan yu ch'üan* 寰有詮, 6 *ch.*, published in 1628, and the *Logica* of the University of Coïmbra, entitled *Ming li t'an* 名理探, 10 *ch.*, published by the son of Li Chih-tsao, Li Tz'u-pin 李次彬, whose preface is dated in the spring of 1639. The former is listed, incorrectly, in the *Ming-shih*, as the work of Fu Chao 兆 -chi, but this mistake was not carried over into the *Ssu-k'u* catalogue; the latter has been reissued three times in recent years in an edition of 5 *chüan*.

Bibliography

1/98/19b; SK (1930), 125/9b; Fang Hao 方豪, *Chung-kuo T'ien-chu-chiao shih jen-wu chuan* 中國天主教史人物傳 (Hong Kong, 1967), 208; P. M. d'Elia, *Fonti Ricciane*, II (Rome, 1949), 170 n.; Pfister (1932), ♯45; George H. Dunne, *Generation of Giants* (Notre Dame, 1962), 264, 269, 292, 325.

L. Carrington Goodrich

GOES, Bento de (Armenian name: Abdullah Isâi; Chinese name: O-pen-tu 鄂本篤), 1562 (or 1561)-April 11, 1607, was a native of Villa Franca do Campo, in the Azores, and the first Jesuit to cross Asia to the frontier of China. At the age of twenty he made his way to India as a soldier. One day, when with the Portuguese fleet on the coast of Travancore, he happened to enter a chapel of the Virgin, and then and there decided to give up his profession and enter the Society of Jesus. In February, 1584, the society accepted him as a lay brother. After residing in Goa for six years he became a companion of Jerome Xavier (1549-1617), a Jesuit priest and grandnephew of the famous Francisco Xavier. For several years both were associated with the great Mogul ruler Akbar (r. 1556-1606). While in Lahore (1598), Xavier learned from a Muslim merchant that he had sojourned for thirteen years in Cathay, that its ruler lived in Khanbaliq, and that one might reach the capital by traveling overland. This unexpected intelligence led Xavier to recommend to the Jesuit superior in Goa that someone be charged with trying out the route. (One of the chief reasons why the Jesuits should be interested in this exploration was to determine whether the way might be more feasible than the long and dangerous journey by sea.) The superior, aware that Matteo Ricci (*q.v.*) had written of the probable identity of Cathay and China, decided to propose that Goes, whom he had come to admire for his character, native wit, and physique, should undertake the journey. Philip II (r. 1580-98) in Portugal gave his consent and asked his viceroy to collaborate in any way possible. Akbar too helped, furnishing letters of commendation addressed to some of the princes on the way and contributing funds for the expedition.

Goes, assuming an Armenian name and Persian dress, left Agra on October 29, 1602, with a party consisting of two Greeks (one a priest, the other a merchant, named Demetrius) and four servants.

Reaching Lahore in December, he dismissed the servants as unnecessary and found another traveling companion, an Armenian named Isaac (or Is'ai) who was to be faithful to the end. Two months later (February 24, 1603) they set out with a caravan of some five hundred people and a long string of animals and wagons. In spite of stormy weather, mountainous terrain, and bandits, they arrived in Kabul after six months. To defend themselves they had been forced to engage four hundred soldiers on the way. At this point the two Greeks took their leave. Another eight months went by before a new caravan was formed. By November, 1603, or thereabouts, they were in Yarkand after surmounting the Pamirs and crossing the Pamech Desert. Goes reports from here that he had lost several of his horses on the way because of the intense cold. Now word soon spread that a non-Muslim had arrived in the city. His life in danger, Goes diplomatically called on the prince, gave him a few presents, and so impressed the ruler that he ordered him to explain the religion he professed. Again there was a delay, possibly of twelve months' duration. The old caravan having disbanded, a new one, to take shape as an embassy to Peking, had to be assembled. It consisted finally of seventy-two travelers, headed by one leader and four others having the title of envoys. While these negotiations were under way, Goes made a side excursion to Khotan to acquire jade in exchange for a loan he had earlier made to the mother of its prince. By the time of his return, he was again joined by the Greek merchant Demetrius, who had remained behind in Afghanistan.

On November 14, 1604, they set out once more, traveling along the road north of the Takla Makan, via Aksu, Kucha, Turfan, and Hami. At Aksu he received a kind reception from the young ruler, with whom he exchanged presents; also from the prince's mother. At a place he calls Cialis (Chalish, according to Paul Pelliot) Goes had a dispute with the

mullahs, in the presence of the prince; in
the end he so satisfied the latter that he
was entertained sumptuously and detained
for the night, to the consternation of
Isaac, who feared the worst. It was here
that a party of merchants returning from
Peking made their appearance. As they
had been housed in the same hostelry for
foreign envoys as Matteo Ricci, they
were able to give Goes exact information
about him and his colleagues. So for the
first time was he assured that China and
Cathay were indeed one.

From Cialis, bearing letters from the
prince, he and his two companions and a
few others took leave of the main caravan.
Both at Turfan and at Hami they lingered
for a month, then moved on to Chia-yü-
kuan 嘉峪關, where they were obliged to
await the pleasure of the Chinese governor. On this portion of the trip across
the desert Goes nearly met his end. With
his companions traveling on ahead, he
chanced to be thrown from his horse,
and lay for a long time half dead. Eventually the faithful Isaac missed him, went
out in search, and succeeded in bringing
him to the place of encampment. After
twenty-five days' wait permission came to
proceed. (In Ricci's account, the permit
had to come from a viceroy. Could this
have been Hsü San-wei 徐三畏, T. 子敬,
H. 理齋, cs 1577, d. October 28, 1608,
who, on December 12, 1605, was named
governor of Kansu and, on January 14,
1606, became t'i-tu 提督, or commander-
in-chief, of the northwestern frontier 三
邊?) The party then moved through the
Great Wall to Su-chou 肅州, reaching the
city approximately on Christmas Day,
1605. Here once more they met a caravan
of Muslim merchants, just arrived from
Peking, who were able to assure them of
the presence of European priests at the
capital. Goes immediately dispatched a
letter to Ricci, but, unaware of his Chinese name, had to address him in European
writing. This apparently went astray. Finally, in November, 1606, a Muslim trader
placed in Ricci's hand a missive dispatch-

ed on March 26. A few days later (December 11), he sent off a youth named
Chung Ming-li 鍾明(or 鳴)禮 (a native of
Kwangtung, 1581-1620, baptized as Gio-
vanni Ferdinando [Fernandes, Fernandez])
who had learned Portuguese in Macao.
Chung reached Goes, but just in time.
He had fallen gravely ill, and was to die
eleven days later in the knowledge that
he had at last succeeded in his quest.

During his journey Goes had kept a
careful journal. Most unfortunately, immediately following his death, some of his
fellow travelers pounced on this and his
other possessions, eager to take what they
could and to destroy any record of loans
made to them en route. What remained
Chung and Isaac were able to turn over
to Ricci months afterward in Peking.
With this battered and incomplete manuscript and their own narratives to guide
him Ricci edited an account of Goes'
journey. (It may be consulted either in
English or Italian translation by Sir Henry
Yule and P. M. d'Elia respectively.) The
route followed has been reconstructed,
inter alia, in an excellent map included
in d'Elia's work. In 1907, on the occasion
of the tercentenary of the doughty traveler's death, the Sociedade de Geographia
de Lisboa commemorated his achievement
with appropriate ceremony, and the people
at his place of birth erected a statue of
him, dressed like a Persian merchant. An
illustration of this appears in Wessels'
book.

Bibliography

Kansu t'ung-chih (1736), 27/23a; KC (1958),
4947, 4949, 4994; Fang Hao 方豪, "Chung-kuo
T'ien-chu-chiao shih jen-wu chuan" 中國天主教
史人物傳, I (Hong Kong, 1967), 163; Pfister,
#27, 34; C. Wessels, *Early Jesuit Travellers in
Central Asia, 1603-1721* (La Haye, 1924), chap.
1; Paul Pelliot, review in TP, 24 (1926), 387; P.
M. d'Elia, *Fonti Ricciane*, II (Rome, 1949), 396;
Sir Henry Yule, *Cathay and the Way Thither*, rev.
by H. Cordier, IV (London, 1916), 169; Henri
Bernard, *Le Frère Bento de Goes chez les*

Musulmans de la Haute Asie (1603-1607), (Tientsin, 1934), 38, 152.

L. Carrington Goodrich

HA-MING, *see* YANG Ming

HAI Jui 海瑞 (T. 汝賢, H. 剛峯), January 23, 1513-November 13, 1587, an official celebrated for his integrity, was a native of Ch'iung-shan 瓊山, the capital of Hainan Island. It is said that his great-great-grandfather, a native of Canton by the name of Hai-ta-er 答兒 (Haidar, a non-Chinese ?), was sent in 1383 to the Hainan guard as a soldier, but his descendants prospered by becoming bureaucrats following success in the civil examinations. Hai Jui's grandfather, Hai K'uan 海寬 (cj 1456), served as a magistrate in Fukien and an uncle, Hai Ch'eng 海澄 (cs 1475), became a censor.

At the age of three Hai Jui lost his father. His mother, née Hsieh 謝 (d. 1575) taught him to recite the Classics and looked after his education. At the prefectural school where he remained for some twenty years, he was noted for his exemplary conduct and earned the respect of his fellow students. About 1546, perhaps by order of his mother, he divorced his first wife, who then sued him for the return of her dowry. To avoid a court trial and publicity he borrowed money and reimbursed her.

In 1549 he became a *chü-jen*. A year later, when he went to Peking for the higher examination, he submitted a memorial to the throne on the pacification of the Loi 黎 tribesmen in the central highlands of Hainan. The plan, referred to the ministry of War and Kwangtung officials, was rejected as impractical. Actually the main points of his plan involved the building of military highways intersecting at the center of the island and the establishment of a magisterial administration for the sinification of the aborigines. These measures were essentially carried out in the late 19th century when Chang Chih-tung (ECCP) initiated the modern development of the island.

In 1553, after failing the metropolitan examination for the second time, Hai applied for an appoinment. Named instructor of the district school of Nan-p'ing 南平, Fukien, he arrived at his post early in 1554, and at once declared to his students that Confucian teaching laid stress on self-cultivation for the achievement of unyielding integrity and strict observation of regulations. At this time obsequiousness towards one's superiors was the general attitude among provincial officials, even to the extent of kneeling, while the regulation on etiquette required standing only. Hai often found himself the sole one erect at an audience. He also preached public mindedness and frugality as prerequisites to incorruptibility. He found a chance to prove that he practiced what he preached when, in 1558, he was promoted to be magistrate of Ch'un-an 淳安, Chekiang. On assuming office the made a declaration to his subordnates, clerks, students, and elders that he would strictly observe the law and would try to promote the general welfare. He summarized the rules and orders he proclaimed in Ch'un-an in a work entitled *Hsing-ko t'iao-li* 興革條例. (For a discussion and translation of extracts of this work, see the thesis of Michel Cartier.)

Ch'un-an is a mountainous district producing chiefly tea, bamboo, and some lumber. What little tillable land existed was concentrated in the hands of the people of consequence. It is on the waterway between Hui-chou 徽州 and Hangchow, hence plagued by demands for porters by travelers on government business. When, in the 15th century, the influential people of the locality increasingly evaded their share of the taxes and of labor service, the burden fell more and more on the poor, many of whom, forced to abandon their properties, became migrants. By reassessment, after a survey of the land, Hai made a more equitable distribution of the tax burden based on land holding, known as the "single-whip" system. He also attacked corrupt practices, built the city wall, resisted illegal demands by superiors, and brought the clerks under control. He himself led a simple life, even raising his own garden vegetables. There is a story that, when he celebrated his mother's birthday, he gave the most extravagant feast, purchasing two catties of pork. It is said that the clerks in his office, who used to enrich themselves by manipulating judical cases, became impoverished through Hai's honest way of dispensing justice; so he permitted some of them to return to their farms.

The people worshiped Hai but some of his superiors abhorred him. One such was Yen Mao-ch'ing 鄢懋卿 (T. 景修, cs 1541). In 1560 Yen went to Chekiang to inspect the salt gabelle, dispatching to officials on his route an announcement that he desired only simple service from their districts. In reality his demands were more exacting than usual. Hai sent Yen a memorandum quoting his own pronouncement which was to be followed to the letter if he came through Ch'un-an. Yen took the hint and proceeded by another route, but, reportedly because of his influence, the censor Yüan Ch'un 袁淳 (T. 育眞, cs 1556) criticized Hai for a minor irregularity and prevented his promotion. Hai was then adjudged qualified only for a secondary district. Another Chekiang magistrate, whose career was affected by having refused to yield to Yen Mao-ch'ing's demands, was Huo Yü-hsia, the son of Huo T'ao (q.v.), who also happened to be a Cantonese. In 1562, soon after Hai Jui published a collection of public papers, Ch'un-an kao 稿, he was sent as magistrate to Hsing-kuo 興國, Kiangsi, where he remained for two years. He was called then to Peking and, on the recommendation of the vice minister of Personnel, Chu Heng (see P'an Chi-hsün), was appointed a secretary in the ministry of Revenue. To reduce expenses, Hai Jui sent his family south to Hainan and went north to his new post, ac-

companied by only two personal servants. His life in the capital was obviously a lonely one. For almost a year he brooded over the erratic conduct of the emperor, Chu Hou-ts'ung (q.v.), with disapproval and despair. Finally (November, 1565) he submitted a memorial criticizing him for his failure as sovereign, father, and husband, and for his inattention to the public business in the previous twenty years. This he said resulted in the prevalence of injustice, corruption, military weakness, heavy taxation, and destitution among the common people, as shown in the popular pun on his reign title, Chia-ching 嘉靖, rendered as 家淨 (every family cleaned out). He found fault with the emperor for his vanity as shown by his search for longevity, for his senseless involvement of the court in Taoist prayer ceremonies, and for his eccentric ways of constructing buildings on the palace grounds. It was the first severe attack on His Majesty's personal conduct since the imprisonment of Yang Chüeh (q.v.) in 1541. The emperor is said to have been deeply disturbed by the memorial, throwing it to the floor and then picking it up to read again. There is also the story that he called Hai a beast and ordered guards dispatched to Hai's home to prevent him from slipping away, but was calmed by a eunuch who said that a man like Hai would never go into hiding, for he had already purchased a coffin and made funeral arrangements before submitting the memorial. The emperor pondered Hai's accusations for three months, wondering if the reason behind them was to force him to abdicate in favor of the heir apparent. In February, 1566, he ordered Hai to prison, there to be interrogated on his motives and to divulge the names of possible conspirators. Hai almost died of the tortures used to extract a confession. Finally the minister of Justice suggested the sentence of death by strangulation on the ground that Hai had committed the crime of disrespect and malediction, but the emperor died before acting on this proposal. During

Hai's confinement only one minor official submitted a memorial on his behalf. This man was promptly sent to prison and beaten almost to death. Throughout the empire, however, Hai's courage in speaking the truth aroused admiration and sympathy.

Early in 1567, a few days after Chu Hou-ts'ung died, Hai Jui was released from prison and restored to his former rank. After several promotions he became transmission commissioner of Nanking. In the middle of 1569 he received the appointment of governor of Ying-t'ien (Nan-Chihli), with headquarters at Soochow, and concurrently chief inspector of grain and storage. Once more, when he assumed office, he made a declaration of his policies, which included the elimination of all corrupt practices. Awed by his reputation as a strict disciplinarian, some officials tendered their resignations and a few apprehensive people of substance even moved away. One who had sported a red lacquered gate blackened it overnight, and a eunuch quietly reduced the number of carriers of his sedan from eight to four.

The region was then suffering from a disastrous flood which resulted in large arrears in taxes and an urgent demand for relief. Hai Jui saw that the only solution to the problem of water control was to dredge the rivers, a task shunned for decades by his predecessors. According to the practices of that day an undertaking of such magnitude meant the enrichment of the officials and gentry at heavy cost to the people. Hai, however, was confident of popular trust and cooperation. He first obtained imperial sanction to use part of the relief fund as payment for materials and labor. Then he made a detailed plan. In March, 1570, he started to dredge the Woosung River, and completed the operation in about a month with little cost to the government. The success encouraged him to dredge and dike several other streams and canals. He also started surveying the land to determine the amount of tax and labor service to be exacted

from each household on the basis of the land it owned.

At the same time Hai made it known that he would investigate a complaint against any landlord illegally assuming the title of other people's land. Thousands of plaintiffs appeared, especially in the Sung-chiang 松 江 area where since about 1550 the acquisition of land had become an obsession among families of influence. One of the landlords of consequence in that area was Hsü Chieh (*q.v.*), the former grand secretary, whose sons and relatives were notorious for their harsh dealings. At the trial of Hsü's sons, Hai insisted on justice and ignored the entreaties of many officials on Hsü's behalf. During the conflict between Hsü Chieh and Kao Kung (*see* Chang Chü-cheng) in 1567 Hai sided with Hsü. Hai declared that his former support had been a mistake for he now realized that Hsü had used his influence for personal gain and had failed to uphold the law. It happened that early in 1570 Kao Kung was restored as chief grand secretary and his supporters in Soochow tried to please him by harassing his former opponent, Hsü Chieh. Hai, however, seems to have acted on his own in this case. When Hai forced Hsü and other landlords to return some land to their original owners, these powerful families jointly plotted his removal. In March, 1570, just after Hai reported on the dredging of the Woosung River, a censor attacked him for sheltering the evildoers and harming the gentry. At once some people of rank in Peking advised the emperor that Hai, though highminded, lacked the ability to be governor and should be replaced. Then in April Hai, about to go to Nanking to his office of chief inspector of grain and storage, learned that that post had been abolished. He was thus forced to retire, but not before submitting a memorial in which he vented his ire on the courtiers who had failed to stand up for him, calling them womenfolk. One story has it that Hsü's sons boasted that the removal of Hai had cost them only a thousand taels; other accounts, however, give higher figures. Some local gentry, such as Wang Shih-chen and Ho Liang-chün (*qq. v.*), praised Hai for his honesty and public spirit, but also criticized his methods. Wang wrote a poem, "Chih chung-ch'eng" 直中丞 (The honest governor).

During the fifteen years of retirement Hai accumulated a large library, but lived simply in a modest house on his small plot of land. There is a painting of him reproduced in the *Kuo-ts'ui hsüeh-pao* 國粹學報 in 1910, complete with Hai's own colophon, dated summer of 1575; it shows him relaxing in a chair beside a brook in a garden of rocks and trees. It is said that on the instruction of Chang Chü-cheng (*q.v.*) an official paid a visit to Hai to inquire into his circumstances and to see if he had indeed engaged in anti-Chang activities as reported. The official left with only admiration for Hai's integrity. In 1580 he printed his second collection of public papers and essays, *Pei-wang chi* 備忘集, 10 ch. (reprinted Taiwan, 1969). He may also have indulged at this time in the painting of landscapes and orchids of which only one example of each is recorded. Several times recommended for recall to service he was barred, it is said, by Chang Chü-cheng who did not approve of Hai's treatment of Hsü Chieh. Early in 1585, several years after Chang died, Hai was appointed assistant head of the Censorate in Nanking. Apprised of his recall to service the septuagenarian at once started on his way north. He traveled so modestly that he appeared to be voyaging incognito. Soon after arrival at Nanking he was transferred to the ministry of Personnel as vice minister and for about a month as acting minister. Again he offended the bureaucrats by forbidding any official to charge the local people for expenses not specified by law; his action naturally pleased the people and enhanced his popularity. In a memorial denouncing illegal practices he mentioned the harsh treatment meted out to corrupt officials two hundred years previously by the founder of the dynasty; this further antagonized other officials, even arousing some censors to accuse him of proposing to reinstitute such cruel punishments as flaying an offender alive.

In March, 1586, Hai was promoted to be censor-in-chief in Nanking. Once more his insistence on the letter of the law drove certain officials to scheme for his removal. One who was apprehensive of being exposed as a bribe-taker assumed the offensive and in June submitted a memorial attacking Hai for pomposity and hypocrisy. There were mutual accusations but general opinion was on Hai's side. He died in office a year later. A subordinate, Wang Yung-chi 王用汲 (T. 明受, Pth. 恭質, 1528-93, cs 1568), finding that Hai had no relative in attendance and had left very little money, solicited contributions from his colleagues to purchase a coffin. When his body was being transported from Nanking to the River, the funeral procession, like that of K'uang Chung (*q.v.*), is said to have been participated in by people from miles around. The court recognized Hai's strength of character and gave him the posthmous name Chung-chieh 忠介 (loyal and incorruptible). Admirers bought prints of his portrait to worship at home. Shrines were erected at the places where he had held office. The one in his home town honored also the Sung poet and one-time exile on Hainan, Su Shih (1037–1101), and Hai's fellow townsman, Ch'iu Chün (*q.v.*). Hai was likewise celebrated in legend and folk literature, one piece being the fictionalized account of his life and the proceedings in his court and his pronouncement of judgment, *Hai Kang-feng chü-kuan kung-an chuan* 海剛峯居官公案傳, 4 *ch.*, printed in 1606, a copy of which is preserved in the National Central Library in Taipei. In the Ch'ing period several novels were written about him, such as *Hai-kung ta hung-p'ao ch'üan-chuan* 海公大紅袍全傳 and *Hai-kung hsiao* 小 *hung-p'ao ch'üan-chuan*, and also the drama

San-nü ch'iang-pan 三女搶板 (or *Sheng-ssu p'ai* 生死牌).

There are several editions of Hai's collected works. The *Hai Chung-chieh kung wen-chi* 文集 was printed in 1594 and reprinted in 1618. Another edition appeared in 1624, and was enlarged in 1631. A third, entitled *Pei-wang chi*, 10 *ch.*, was printed in 1602, in 1688, copied into the Imperial Library of the 18th century, and reprinted in 1905. In 1962, the authority on Ming history, Wu Han (BDRC), published a new and most nearly complete edition, entitled *Hai Jui chi*, which also includes bibliographical and biographical information painstakingly collected from various sources. In addition it has reproductions of a portrait, a calling card, impression of a seal, and some examples of his calligraphy. The introduction is an essay, "Lun 論 Hai Jui, " written by Wu in September, 1959.

Wu Han, deputy mayor of Peking from 1949 to 1966, a cataloguer of Chinese rare books in the library of Yenching University in 1931, was graduated from Tsinghua University in 1934, and served on its faculty until 1948. He specialized in the history of the Ming dynasty. His study of the life of its founder, entitled *Chu Yüan-chang chuan* 朱元璋傳 (1949, first published in 1943 as *Ming T'ai-tsu chuan* 明太祖傳 and then as *Ts'ung seng-po tao huang-ch'üan* 從僧鉢到皇權) has come to be regarded as a classic in Chinese biographical writing. He became a leader of the Democratic League, a political party at first advocating an Anglo-American form of government, but in 1948 he sided with the Communist regime and some years later even became a member of the party. In 1959 he interested himself in Hai Jui, publishing several articles about his life and personality, his fearless criticisms of the emperor, and his consistent efforts to help the people against their oppressors, the bureaucrats in and out of office. In June, 1959, he published the "Hai Jui ma huang-ti" 罵皇帝 and three months later, the "Lun Hai Jui" (both in the People's Daily, *Jen-min jih-pao*). The following year he wrote another essay, "Hai Jui," in which he compared Hai with K'uang Chung, showing how K'uang's reduction of the rate of taxation favored the landowners but Hai, by trying to reduce large landholdings and equalize tax burdens, himself came under attack by wealthy landlords. Meanwhile Wu wrote a drama, *Hai Jui pa-kuan* 罷官, for the Peking opera which was revised seven or eight times before its final version of 1961. The opera enjoyed great success but in May, 1964, it began to be adversely criticized. Then in November, 1965, it was severely attacked by a critic as full of misrepresentations and as having a covertly anti-party and anti-socialist stance. During the discussions which ensued Hai Jui was adjudged completely loyal to his own class and to the emperor, for in order to produce more taxes he adopted policies which favored not the common people but the smaller landowners. Wu was forced to submit a confession of self-criticism in January, 1966. It became the target of further attacks, especially after the publication of his correspondence with Hu Shih (BDRC) written in the early 1930s in the People's Daily of June 3, 1966. By this time it was obvious that the criticism of Wu was just the prelude to a serious systematic and large scale purge which continued for over two years and became known as the "great cultural revolution" (文化大革命). The purge led to the mobilization of the youth as "red guards" whose excesses caused disturbances in cities, the loss of many lives, destruction of numerous national treasures, slowing-up of production, and the ruin of several writers and scholars, including Wu Han himself who reportedly committed suicide sometime in 1967. It remains a mystery as to whether, in writing about Hai Jui, Wu had indeed alluded to General P'eng Te-huai (BDRC, purged in 1964), or whether his description of Hai criticizing the emperor was a covert attack on Mao Tse-tung (BDRC).

During his sixteen years in office Wu had himself taken part in the political struggles and purges, sometimes denouncing his own colleagues of the Democratic League as the party line demanded. On the other hand it is said that he never attacked his mentor, Hu Shih. Probably because of his lack of proficiency in speaking or writing English, he strove to distinguish himself in the composition of Chinese essays and in the study of Ming history; for his success in these fields he will long be remembered.

In 1968, under the editorship of Chester Leo Smith, there appeared a mimeographed edition of an English version of the drama *Hai Jui pa-kuan* under the title *The Dismissal of Hai Jui.*

Bibliography

1/226/1a; 5/64/28a; Chang Chü-cheng, *Chang T'ai-yüeh wen-chi*, 22/1a; Ho Liang-chün, *Ssu-yu-chai ts'ung-shuo* (1959), 108; Wang Shih-chen, *Yen-chou shan-jen hsü-kao* (ca. 1590), 2/17a; *Hai Jui chi*, 2 vols., Peking, 1962; Wu Han, *Ch'un-t'ien chi* 春天集 (1961), 228; id., *Teng-hsia chi* 燈下集 (1962), 146; *Wu Han wen-chi* 文集, Hong Kong, 1967; *Ch'ang-tuan lu* 長短錄, Hong Kong, 1966; *Li-shih yen-chiu* 歷史研究, no. 6 (1965), no. 2 (1966); Yeh Kung-ch'o (BDRC), *Hsia-an t'an-i-lu*遐庵談藝錄(1965?),4; *Ling-nan hua-cheng-lüeh* 嶺南畫徵略 (1961), 23; Ch'en Feng 陳風, "Wu Han p'i-p'an ching-wei" 批判經緯, *Tsu-kuo* 祖國(Hong Kong, 1966), no. 8, 26; *Ch'iung-shan-hsien chih*, 191/726/17a; American Consulate General, Hong Kong, *Current Background* (March 21, 1966), 783 (June 29, 1966), 792; Picture of Hai's tomb in *Wen-shih hui-k'an* 文史薈刊, no. 1 (Tainan, 1959), 75; L. Carrington Goodrich (tr.): "A Study of Literary Persecution During the Ming Dynasty," by Ku Chieh-kang, HJAS, III (1938), 27; Moscow, TASS, International Service in English, September 25, 1967; Michel Cartier, *Le Xing-ge tiao-li de Hai-rui, 1562* (summary of thesis presented to the Faculté des Lettres et Sciences Humaines de Paris—Sorbonne. Série "Recherches," t. 53, 1969; Ernest Wolff, "A Preliminary Study of Hai Jui, His Biography in the *Ming-shih*," *Jo. of the Oriental Soc. of Australia*, 7 (December, 1970), 147; Tseng Yu-ho Ecke, *Chinese Calligraphy* (Philadelphia, 1971), 55.

Chaoying Fang

ḤĀJJĪ ’Alī (Ha-chih A-li 哈只阿力), fl. 1469–78, was the chief of Turfan when conflict between that state and China first erupted in 1473. Several scholars have identified him with Yunus Khan, the ruler of Moghulistan. Though the Persian sources on Yunus and the Chinese sources on ’Alī are occasionally contradictory, this identification seems to be accurate. The *Ming shih-lu* and the *Tarikh-i-Rashidi* of Mirza Muhammad Haidar agree that ’Alī, or Yunus, resided in the area of Turfan in the 1470s, that he campaigned against the Oirat during that time, and that he had a son named Aḥmad or A-hei-ma (*q. v.*) who succeeded him. But Muhammad Haidar fails to mention Yunus' relations with China. The Persian historian also states that Yunus (’Alī) died in 1487, while the *shih-lu* gives 1478 as the date. Around 1478 Yunus moved to the west, leaving his son Aḥmad in charge of Turfan and eastern Moghulistan; and the Chinese historians mistook his departure for his death.

According to the Persian account Yunus was the son of Vays Khan (d. 1428), the ruler of Moghulistan. After Vays Khan's death, the followers of Yunus and those of his brother Esen-buqa engaged in a struggle for power, and the loser, Yunus, who was scarcely in his teens, was exiled to Persia. He must have received a good education, for a later visitor described him as "a person of elegant deportment with a full beard and a Tajik face and such refined speech and manners, as is seldom found even in a Tajik." He seems also to have acquired a taste for the niceties of urban life and was reluctant to revert to the nomadic existence of Moghulistan. But, after his brother's death in 1462, he, with the aid of the Sultan of Herat, returned and by 1472 had unified Moghulistan under his rule.

Almost immediately after this his relations with China became strained. The Ming court was upset by the frequency and size of the tribute embassies from Turfan, because of the expense it incurred in feeding, sheltering, and entertaining the increasing number of envoys. On the other hand, Turfan's rulers and merchants, who obtained Chinese silks, porcelains, and other goods in trade or as gifts, sought to send even more tribute embassies to Peking. The court was also concerned about Turfan's territorial expansion. It feared that its conquest of Karakhoja (Huo-chou 火州) and Lukchak (Liu-ch'eng 柳城) presaged further incursions even closer to China.

In 1465 the controversy was made public when the court approved the proposal of Yao K'uei (*q. v.*), the minister of Rites, that only one mission from Turfan be allowed to enter China every three to five years and that it consist of no more than ten envoys. ʼAlī, involved in consolidating and unifying his territory, initially failed to react to these regulations. But in 1469 he sent an envoy who informed the emperor that his ruler had adopted the title "Sultan" and wished to buy or receive as gifts gerfalcons, a four-clawed dragon robe, colored silk, and other goods. Yao replied that Chinese regulations forbade the export of most of these goods and that some, such as the dragon robe, were granted infrequently and only by imperial authority. Instead of the goods ʼAlī had requested, the emperor gave him textiles. In the same year ʼAlī's envoys again asked for specific Chinese goods, but received a second refusal. These incidents embittered relations between ʼAlī and the court and caused him to adopt a more aggressive posture. He had an excellent opportunity both to avenge himself on China and incidentally to enrich himself through neighboring Hami. Noticing that the succession to the throne was creating a crisis and weakening Hami, he plotted to conquer it. In 1473 he mobilized his troops for the attack and within a short time occupied Hami, captured Nu-wen-ta-shih-li 弩溫答失里, the mother of the former prince of Hami, and confiscated the city's seal, which had been granted by the Ming emperor. He plun-

dered the area and then withdrew, leaving his brother-in-law, Ya-lan 牙蘭, with a small force to guard this vital gateway to central Asia and the Middle East.

The emperor responded immediately to the loss of Hami. He urged the Mongols of Ch'ih-chin 赤金 Guard to oust them and attempted to "use barbarians to regulate barbarians" (i-i-chih-i 以夷制夷), a tactic that was employed as early as the Han dynasty. Apparently the leaders of Ch'ih-chin hesitated to act on their own, because several months later the Chinese organized their own punitive expedition. On July 26, 1473, the emperor ordered the vice commissioner-in-chief, Li Wen (*see* Li Ying) to lead a military force to Ch'ih-chin and Han-tung 罕東, and to gain the support of these two guards in the campaign against Turfan. Within a few months Li succeeded in raising the necessary troops.

By early 1474 Li's forces reached the outskirts of Hami. Li sent a mission led by Ma Chün 馬俊 urging ʼAlī to retreat and to return the city's seal and the mother of the prince. ʼAlī refused and detained Ma for over a month. A report that 30,000 Chinese-led troops were poised for an attack on Hami and Turfan, however, caused him to release Ma and to prepare several banquets for the Chinese mission. During one of them, Nu-wen-ta-shih-li appeared. Noticing that soldiers from Turfan surrounded the area, she told the Chinese envoy that Hami was already destroyed and that she did not wish to return. Later that night she was able to send a secret message to Ma pleading that he oust ʻAlī from Hami. On returning to the Chinese camp Ma conveyed this message to Li. The latter was about to march on ʻAli's base when rumors that Turfan's ruler planned to attack Ch'ih-chin and Han-tung reached his troops. The Ch'ih-chin and Han-tung contingents hastily departed to protect their own homelands. Left with a much smaller force, Li was also obliged to retreat. Having achieved a notable success in inducing the withdrawal of the Chinese expedition, 'Alī became ever more demanding in his relations with the court. Late in 1474 he sent tribute, and his envoy requested an elephant as a gift. The request was rejected. Undaunted, 'Alī demanded, a few months later, that more embassies be exchanged between China and Turfan. His envoy pointed out that Turfan controlled Hami and had routed the Oirat and the Ch'ü-hsien 曲先 Guard, implying that China would suffer the same fate if it failed to accede to 'Alī's request. The emperor answered that if 'Alī sincerely offered tribute as a vassal the court would forgive him his past crimes. Some officials wished to take drastic action against 'Alī for his continued insolence in occupying Hami, but the minister of War, Hsiang Chung (*q.v.*), argued that he was a petty barbarian and not worthy of concern.

From 1475 to 1478 'Alī and the court remained hostile. In 1478 the Chinese sources record his death. Actually he migrated to the west to lead the urban life that he preferred. His departure provided China with a brief respite from frontier problems in the northwest, but other cities and states in central Asia were not as fortunate. 'Alī continued his marauding, capturing Sairam in 1482 and Tashkent in 1485, until his death in 1487 from a stroke. His capture of Hami posed a serious threat to China's trade and tribute relations with central Asia and the Middle East; and China's inability to recapture and restore Hami exposed its military weakness on the northwestern frontier.

Bibliography

1/329/6a, 20b; MSL (1964), Hsien-tsung, 1406, 2224, 2238, 2270, 2342, 2380, 2393, 2407, 2465, 2541, 2575, 2580, 2856; Hsü Chin, *P'ing-fan shih-mo* 平番始末, 1/2a; Ma Wen-sheng, *Hsing-fu Ha-mi chi*, 1b; *Ming-shih* (Taipei, 1964), 97; Fu Wei-lin, *Ming shu* (Shanghai, 1937), 3294; E. Bretschneider, *Mediaeval Researches from Eastern Asiatic Sources* (London, 1910), II, 181, 195; R. Grousset, *L'empire des Steppes* (Paris, 1939), 569; N. Elias (ed.), *The Tarikh-i-Rashidi of Mirza Muhammad Haidar, Dughlat*:

A History of the Moghuls of Central Asia, tr. by E. D. Ross (London, 1895), "Introduction," 103; D. Pokotilov, *History of the Eastern Mongols during the Ming Dynasty from 1368 to 1634*, tr. by R. Loewenthal, *Studia Serica*, ser. A, no. 1 (Chengtu, 1947), pt. 1, 87; W. Franke, "Addenda and Corrigenda," *Studia Serica*, ser. A, no. 3 (1949), pt. 2, 50; V. V. Barthold, *Four Studies on the History of Central Asia*, tr. by V. and T. Minorsky, I (Leiden, 1956), 147; M. C. Imbault-Huart, *Le Pays de Hami ou Khamil* (Paris, 1892), 37; P. Pelliot, *Notes Critiques d'histoire Kalmouke* (Paris, 1960), 17, 77; M. Rossabi, "Ming China's Relations with Hami and Central Asia, 1404–1513," Columbia University Ph. D. Dissertation (1970), 184.

Morris Rossabi

HALIMA 哈立麻 (also written Ko-li-ma 葛哩麻), 1384-1415, the fifth Tibetan hierarch, is the designation by which, in the early years of the Ming era, the Chinese knew the Zhwa Nag (Black Hat) hierarch of the Karma-pa sect of Tibet, whose principal seat is Mtshur-phu, some fifty miles west of Lhasa.

Known to the Tibetans as De bžin gśegs pa, he was born at Nyaṅ 'Dam in the rKoṅ-po region of Tibet on the eighteenth day of the sixth month of the Wood Male Rat year in the Tibetan cycle —July/August, 1384. His parents were Gu-ru-rin-chin, a Tantric adept, and Lha-mo-skyid. The family was of the lineage of Sna Nam, one of the great noble clans at the time of the Tibetan kingdom cf the seventh to ninth centuries. Because of the miraculous occurrences which preceded and accompanied his birth, he was speedily recognized as the reincarnation of the fourth hierarch, Rol-pa'i rdo-rje (1340-83), and thus the third reincarnation of the founder lama, Dus-gsum mkhyen-pa (1110-93). He was ordained a monk at the age of seven. From his eighteenth year he traveled and preached extensively in the eastern part of Tibet. In 1402 he returned to rKoṅ-po to take his final monastic vows, after which he went to Mtshur-phu in central Tibet.

Although some time before the fall of the Yüan dynasty the exercise of authority in Tibet had passed from religious dignitaries nominated by the Mongol emperors into the hands of an independent monk-prince of the P'ag-mo-gru family, the early Ming emperors prudently tried to cultivate friendly relations with leaders of the principal Tibetan sects. Accordingly, on March 10, 1403, Emperor Chu Ti (q.v.) invited Halima to come to his court. A Tibetan translation of the letter, which is polite and complimentary, is preserved in a sixteenth century Tibetan history. The fourth Karma-pa hierarch had declined a similar invitation from Emperor Chu Yüan-chang; there was, therefore, no precedent for a visit to the Ming court, but in 1405 Halima set out on a round of travels which took him, by the end of 1406, close to the borders of China. In response to further exhortations from the imperial court he proceeded slowly to Nanking. There on April 10, 1407, after a ceremonious welcome, he presided at religious services for the benefit of the emperor's deceased parents. The twenty-two days of his stay were marked by miraculous occurrences. These were recorded in five languages on a great scroll some fifty feet long by two and one-half feet high which also contained paintings illustrating the various miracles. The scroll, bearing the emperor's seal, was preserved, at least until the Communist occupation of Tibet in 1951, at the monastery of Mtshur-phu.

Tibetan histories record that Halima dissuaded Chu Ti from any thought of attempting to impose his authority on Tibet by military means, as the Mongols had done. The emperor conferred on the lama a long title which may be abbreviated to Ju-lai ta-pao-fa-wang 如來大寶法王. Thereafter the Karma-pa hierarchs were usually referred to as Ta-pao fa-wang—one other great Fa-wang, Ta-ch'eng 大乘 fa-wang, being the Sa-skya hierarch.

After receiving lavish presents the lama left Nanking on May 17, 1408, for Mt. Wu-t'ai in Shansi where he conducted further services in memory of the emperor's parents. He returned to Tibet where he continued to enhance his reputation for learning and prescience and also undertook extensive travels from monastery to monastery, a characeristic activity of Karma-pa lamas. On three occasions he exchanged presents with the Ming emperor. In 1415, after giving indications of his hoped-for reincarnation, he died at Lhasa at the age of thirty-one.

Ming recorders, as quoted by Professor G. Tucci in *Tibetan Painted Scrolls*, appear unaware that he had died and that it was another Karma-pa, De bžin gśegs pa's reincarnation Mthong-ba-ldon-ldan (1416-53), with whom communications were exchanged down to the end of the Cheng-t'ung period.

In other respects too Ming records are vague on the subject of the Karma-pa lamas. It seems that the Zhwa Nag hierarch and the other Fa-wang (that of Sa-skya), were not on the list of those from whom "tribute" was received every three years. The reason given for this, that they were itinerant monks with no fixed seat, is only partially true. Lamas of the Karma-pa sect in partic ar were expected to spend much of their time in travel but they were masters of many great monasteries throughout Tibet, including their chief seat at Mtshur-phu. The Sa-skya lamas too had a great monastery at Sa-skya and others elsewhere. Again Ming records fail to note—and in this western scholars have been equally negligent—that it was to invite another Karma-pa lama, the eighth hierarch, Mi-bskyed-rdo-rje (1507-54), that the dilatory, abortive, and scandalous mission of the eunuch Liu Yün 劉允 (T. 子允) was dispatched in 1516. The story is well documented in records of the Karma-pa sect.

Bibliography

1/6/1b, 6a, 331/2b;3/283/31a; MSL (1963), T'ai-tsung, 0310, 0890, 0896, 0910, 0915, 1057;*Ch'ing-liang-shan chih* 清涼山志 (1596, repr. of 1755),

4/9b, 8/21a; 'Gos-lo-tsa-ba, *Deb-ther-sngon-po*, 1476; Dpa'-bo-gtsug-lag-'phreng'ba, *Chosbyung*, 1565; Collected *rnam thar* of the Karma-pa hierarchs, XIX century; G. Tucci, *Tibetan Painted Scrolls* (Rome, 1949), 628, 686; H. E. Richardson, "The Karma-pa Sect, a Historical Note, Part 1," JRAS (1958), 139, "Part 2," (1959), 1; H. Sato, "Mondai Chibetto no hachidaikyo-o ni tsuite," *Tōyōshi-kenkyū*, 21 (1963), 295, and 22 (1963), 203, 488.

Hugh Richardson

HAN K'uang 韓爌 (T. 象雲, *ca.* 1558–*ca.* 1637), a leading statesman for most of the last four decades of Ming rule, was a native of P'u-chou 蒲州, Shansi, the son of Han Chi 楫 (T. 伯通, H. 天川, cs 1565) who had served as a supervising secretary in the ministry of Justice. His paternal uncle, Han Chan 柟, for a time was magistrate of Hsin-ts'ai 新蔡, Honan. Numerous other members of the Han clan held offices in both the national and provincial administrations. Having placed high in the *chin-shih* examination of 1592, Han K'uang was appointed to the Hanlin Academy as a compiler. He rapidly advanced to the office of supervisor of imperial instruction and served as a lecturer to the heir apparent. In 1617 he became vice minister of Rites, and assisted in administering the grand supervisorate of imperial instruction. Later he was charged with overseeing the education of the Hanlin bachelors.

A few days after Chu Ch'ang-lo (ECCP) succeeded to the throne (August, 1620), Han K'uang was made grand secretary and concurrently nominal minister of Rites. During his early tenure as a grand secretary, Han was known for his concern with the northeast defenses. His interest in this area, however, is a moot point. In 1619 Li Ju-po (ECCP, p. 451), a scion of a well-known military family of Liaotung, had been defeated in battle and retreated before the invading Manchu forces. He and his brother, Li Ju-chen (ECCP, p. 451), who had failed to defend his ancestral home, were arrested

to await trial. The throne, however, pardoned both. Han K'uang, acting in conjunction with another grand secretary, Liu I-ching (*see* Chou Chia-mu) ordered Li Ju-po's re-arrest. In 1621 the latter committed suicide in prison. This case, not unlike those of Yüan Ch'ung-huan, Hsiung T'ing-pi (both in ECCP), and Wen T'i-jen (*q. v.*) merits further investigation.

In October, 1620, as a special favor on the occasion of his enthronement, the succeeding emperor, Chu Yu-chiao(ECCP), made Han grand guardian of the heir apparent and nominal minister of Revenue. He worked closely with Liu I-ching, then the chief grand secretary following the forced retirement from office of Fang Ts'ung-che (ECCP, p. 176). Following the emperor's marriage (July 23, 1621), Han was promoted to junior guardian and nominal minister of Personnel, while one of his sons received appointment to the Seal Office through the yin privilege. Shortly thereafter, on receipt of word of the successful suppression of a Miao rebellion in Kweichow, Han and other grand secretaries received additional honors.

In May, 1622, the minister of Rites, Sun Shen-hsing (ECCP), accused the former grand secretary, Fang Ts'ung-che, of conspiring with Li K'o-shao (ECCP, p. 176) to poison the late emperor, Chu Ch'ang-lo. Since the court was sharply divided over this accusation, Han K'uang presented a clarifying memorial. He pointed out that originally, when Li suggested that he possessed an effective elixir, Fang was disturbed and urged the emperor to take no drugs. In this advice Han and other court ministers had concurred. But on September 25, his condition worsening, the emperor himself had ordered the elixir prepared. After taking the preparation he improved slightly and ordered another. The next day, September 26, he expired. Han argued accordingly that the death of the emperor was natural, and that his successor should make an announcement to that effect. Although later commentators have held Fang culpable because he was chief grand secretary, Han's version is entirely plausible. Despite Fang's probable innocence, Han failed to mention the very likely complicity of eunuchs in the demise of the emperor. His memorial seems to have been more an attempt to smooth over court conflicts and to get on with the serious business of administering the country than to discover the true villains—an almost impossible task in any case.

Early in 1623, on the suppression of bandits in Shantung, additional honors came to Han K'uang, and by the following year he ranked second only to the chief grand secretary, Yeh Hsiang-kao (*q. v.*). It was at this time that Yang Lien (ECCP), a senior vice-president of the Censorate, denounced the eunuch Wei Chung-hsien(ECCP) in a memorial listing twenty-four crimes. When Wei turned to Han for assistance, Han rebuffed him, and thus incurred his undying enmity. After Wei managed to remove Yeh from office (August, 1624) Han became head of the Grand Secretariat, but not for long. He had led Chu Kuo-chen (ECCP) and other high court officials in defending Yang Lien, Chao Nan-hsing, and Kao P'an-lung (*qq.v.*). Chu, however, who had little inclination for political intrigue, was eventually dismissed (January 30, 1625). Finding himself completely ineffective in his role as chief grand secretary, Han retired (December 28, 1624).

In August, 1625, a supervising secretary in the ministry of War, Li Lu-sheng 李魯生 (cs 1613), a supporter of Wei Chung-hsien, falsely accused Han of having accepted a bribe. Han's name was erased from the rolls (August 29), and members of his family suffered imprisonment and death. According to one biography, in order to help those still alive in prison, he sold the family lands and borrowed from both friends and relatives.

After the death of the emperor in September, 1627, Han's colleagues tried to have the former chief grand secretary reinstated, but they were blocked by one of the remnants of the eunuch party, a censor named Yang Wei-yüan 楊維垣 (cs 1616). On December 30, 1628, however. Han, responding to a special summons from the new emperor, returned to the capital and resumed his post as chief grand secretary. Together with Li Piao 李標 (T. 汝立, cs 1607). and Ch'ien Lung-hsi (*see* Ch'ien Shih-sheng), he participated in the compilation of the *Yen-tang ni-an* 閹黨逆案, a list of the partisans of Wei Chung-hsien and their degrees of complicity.

In 1629, in the interest of economy, Han advised the emperor to discontinue the courier-post system in the more remote areas. In Shensi the system was the principal mode of transport, dependent on conscription and heavy government subsidy. Its discontinuance caused considerable economic dislocation in the area.

In the autumn of 1629, the chief ministers at court recommended Ch'ien Ch'ien-i (ECCP) to serve in the Grand Secretariat. When Wen T'i-jen, who coveted this position, attacked Ch'ien, a censor, Jen Tsan-hua 任贊化 (cs 1622, d. 1629), immediately impeached Wen. Thereupon, Wen accused Jen and Ch'ien of partisan conspiracy. Han K'uang, who was favorably disposed towards the Tung-lin politico-literary group, did his utmost to defend both of them. He was rebuffed by the emperor, however, and they were dismissed from the government. During his tenure of office Han tried to mitigate the conflict between opposing groups. He protected Wang Yung-kuang (*see* Wen T'i-jen) from the censorious attacks of partisans. For this defense of Wang, Han has been criticized by later pro-Tung-lin writers.

In the spring of 1637 Li Tzu-ch'eng (ECCP) captured P'u-chou where Han had retired after having resigned in February, 1630, from a court of increasing partisan strife. The bandit demanded to see the former chief grand secretary. Upon being rebuffed, Li seized Han's only grandson; thus forcing an audience. Shortly thereafter Han died at the age of seventy-nine, a bitter and disappointed man.

Bibliography

1/240/13b; 3/224/5b; 4/15/21b; 8/78/5a; 27/×/8a; 30/1/19a; 39/17/16a; 77/1/5a; MSL (1966), Hsi-tsung, 0547; KC (1958), 5168, 5172, 5204, 5213, 5309, 5431, 5435, 5463, 5468, 5472, 5482, 5514; *P'u-chou-fu chih* (1755), 12/39a; *Wu-shih fu-ch'en k'ao* 五十輔臣考 (NCL microfilm), 1/31.

Donald L. Potter

HAN Lin-er 韓林兒 (known also as Han Lin in contemporary accounts), died January, 1367, was the first and only emperor of the Red Turban Sung 宋 reign (1355 -66), which for a few years overran most of north China and prepared the way for the fall of the Yüan dynasty. He and his father Han Shan-t'ung 山童 (executed January 26, 1355) were scions of a hereditary house of White Lotus sect leaders, originally from Luan-ch'eng 欒城 (Pei-Chihli) but later exiled to Yung-nien 永年 of the same province in punishment for their secret organizing activities.

In 1350, when preparations were being made by the Yüan chancellor of the right, Toɤto (1313-55), to rechannel the course of the Yellow River, which had burst its dikes in 1344 and inundated the area west of the Shantung uplands, a children's conundrum or jinglet began to be circulated: "A stone man with one eye; when they channel the Yellow River, the empire will rebel." A few days after one hundred seventy thousand corvée laborers were assembled for work in the spring of 1351, some of the men happened to dig up a one-eyed stone figurine from an embankment. The inscription on its back read: "Do not say the stone man has only one eye; when you excavate this, the empire will rebel." The figurine, and perhaps the jinglet too, had been deliberately planted by Han Shan-t'ung as an answer to the children's prophecy and in hopes of gathering recruits for rebellion among the corvée workers. Not many of the latter

actually joined the rebellion for the river project continued without stop until its completion late in 1351; enough adherents, however, were gathered from among such other groups as dismissed clerks and officials, local bandits, market place idlers, and male and female religious fanatics, to produce a small rising at Ying-chou 潁州 (Anhwei), after local officials forced the rebels' hand by moving in and arresting Han Shan-t'ung.

The propaganda message prepared by Han and his White Lotus followers included features which were shared by earlier Yüan-time religious uprisings plus some novel elements. Chief among the former were a belief in the imminent rebirth of the Buddha Maitreya, a messianic figure with a long tradition in Chinese history, whose advent is supposed to bring on an era of universal felicity and joy; and, fused with the Maitreya doctrine, a belief in the appearance of a Radiant Prince and the conquest of light over darkness—a Manichean tenet with a tradition almost as long. But Han Shan-t'ung also made political capital of an old popular legend, which had it that the heirs of the Sung Dynasty (960-1279) had never really perished but were only in hiding in Korea and Japan waiting for a chance to come back; Han himself posed as a descendant in the eighth generation of the Northern Sung emperor Hui-tsung (r. 1082-1135). To this religious and legitimist propaganda was added an appeal to the disinherited: "While poverty is extreme south of the Yangtze, wealth is boasted beyond the Great Wall."

The loosely organized mobs, known as Red Turbans 紅巾 after the cloths they wound around their heads as insignia, and as the Incense Army 香軍 for their practice of burning incense in honor of the Maitreya, overran a dozen cities in the upper Huai by the early autumn of 1351, scoring some spectacular successes in the field against ill-trained and ill-led Yüan forces. Although the mobs' banners proclaimed their intent to march upon the Yüan capital of Ta-tu (Peking) and restore the Sung empire, the rebels were content at this stage with burning, pillaging, murdering local officials, and chanting sūtras *en masse*.

Word of the Red Turbans' successes touched off other outbreaks: Chih-ma Li (*see* Chu Yüan-chang) took Hsü-chou 徐州 in August, 1351; the Ma-ch'eng 麻城 Red Turbans under Hsü Shou-hui (*q.v.*) rebelled a month later, and Kuo Tzu-hsing (*q.v.*) took Hao 濠-chou in February of the following year.

While the Yüan court devoted its main efforts to the extermination of other rebel movements near the Grand Canal, a landowner named Čaɣan Temür (*see* Kökö Temür), whose domains lay in an area the rebels of Han Shan-t'ung had overrun, recruited an army and during 1352 was partly instrumental in turning back the Red Turbans' advance. The rebels were forced gradually to shift their base eastward upon the cities of An-feng 安豐, Po-chou 亳州, and Ying-chou (all in An-hwei). Probably because it was too greatly ravaged, the rebels never attempted to regain the western Huai area that they abandoned at this time.

During 1353 and 1354, the rebels seem to have taken no action. The Yüan forces were successfully quelling revolts in other parts of China, and probably the followers of Han Shan-t'ung would have been dispersed eventually had the Yüan been able to press its campaigns to a successful conclusion. The disaster at Kao-yu (*see* Chang Shih-ch'eng) changed all this, and the Sung revolt, together with a number of other moribund rebel movements, revived. In January, 1355, the Yüan finally executed Han Shan-t'ung. In March Han Lin-er, who had been taken into hiding by his mother after his father's arrest, was brought to Po-chou and enthroned there as emperor of the Great Sung 大宋 dynasty under the reign title of Lung-feng 龍鳳 (Dragon and Phoenix). Han was also known by the Manichean title of Radiant Prince, Hsiao-ming wang 小明王. The

choice of Po-chou for the capital may have been suggested by the fact that it had been the capital of the Sung 宋 state during antiquity. Chosen as prime minister and *de facto* ruler of the dynasty was Tu Tsun-tao 杜遵道, who had once served briefly as a minor secretary in the military affairs bureau of the Yüan. Sometime during 1355, Tu was murdered and replaced as prime minister by Liu Fu-t'ung 劉福通, a White Lotus organizer from Ying-chou who posed as the descendant of a famous Sung general, Liu Kuang-shih (1089-1142). The revived Sung movement replaced the earlier mob action with a degree of planning and direction under a central government and with more-or-less regularlarly constituted military forces.

In 1356 the Sung rebels under Liu Fu-t'ung initiated a series of long-range running attacks which reached as far west as Ning-hsia, as far north as Shang-tu 上都 (the Mongol "Upper Capital"), as far east as Sŏgyŏng 西京 (Pyongyang), and as far south as the parts of Nan-Chihli that were occupied by Chu Yüan-chang. These raids were for the most part led by outside rebel groups with which Tu and Liu contracted alliances. Already in 1355, a group of rebels at Ho-chou 和州 (Anhwei), which had split off from the original forces of Kuo Tzu-hsing at Hao-chou, made contact with Tu Tsun-tao and arranged to submit to the Sung in order to prevent another man from taking control. The Sung appointed Chu Yüan-chang third in command at Ho-chou at this time. In the following year, two rebel commanders named Li Wu 李武 and Ts'ui Te 崔德 were brought up with their men from Hsiang-yang, and launched an attack at the eastern end of the Wei 渭 River valley of Shensi, while the Ho-chou rebels, after having crossed the Yangtze, reduced the city of Chi-ch'ing 集慶 (Nanking). After his two superiors were killed in action, Chu Yüan-chang was given a provincial title by the Sung and put in full control in the south.

During 1357, the rebel leader Mao

Kuei 毛貴, sought out in his native area of Liaotung, launched a seaborne invasion of the Shantung peninsula and occupied it as far west as the Grand Canal. Just west of him, a militia commander in Yüan service named T'ien Feng 田豐 rebelled and went over to the Sung side. Troops under Liu Fu-t'ung's own command reduced a number of cities in the south end of the T'ai-hang Mountains 太行山 and east along the Wei 衛 River. Finally, a group of Green Turban 青巾 rebels led by Li Hsi-hsi 李喜喜, Pai Pu-hsin 白不信, and Ta-tao Ao 大刀敖 (Big Knife Ao) were brought up from Szechwan for an attack on western Shensi.

The year 1358 represents the watershed of the rebel Sung movement. Liu Fu-t'ung conquered Pien-liang 汴梁, the old capital of the Northern Sung dynasty, and reestablished the rebel capital in this symbolically more suitable location. A grand assault, led by Kuan To 關鐸 (also known as "Master" Kuan 關先生), P'an Ch'eng 潘誠 (cracked head P'an 破頭潘), and Sha Liu Er 沙劉二 (Sandy Liu the second) was thrust against the Fen 汾 River valley, Shansi, while Mao Kuei made a direct attempt upon the Yüan capital. But the Yüan managed to thwart Mao, who retreated to Shantung; the invasion into Shansi failed to establish a permanent foothold; and the remnants of the Green Turbans were scattered, some to Ning-hsia and some back to Szechwan where they were eventually subdued by Ming Yü-chen (q.v.). Li Wu and Ts'ui Te were driven into the mountains, finally surrendering to Li Ssu-ch'i 李思齊 (T. 世賢, 1323-74) in 1361. The rebel forces in Shansi split into three parts at the north end of the Fen valley late in 1358, with Kuan, P'an, and Liu taking the main part and heading toward Shang-tu.

A further blow was dealt the Sung in 1359, when the rebel leader Chao Chün-yung (see Chu Yüan-chang) went north to Shantung from Huai-an and murdered Mao Kuei. After Chao was murdered in his turn, the men elevated Mao's young son to his father's position; but this action did not succeed in quelling disputes among the older rebel chieftains, and thus the possibility of another attack on Ta-tu was eliminated. In September of the same year, the Sung were driven from their capital of Pien-liang by Čaγan Temür. Liu Fu-t'ung transferred Han and the central government to An-feng in the southeast.

Delayed by a struggle with his rival Bolod Temür (see Kökö Temür), Čaγan Temür waited until 1361 before attacking the divided Sung remnants that still remained in Shantung. The rebels' last stand was made at I-tu 益都. After a year's siege, in the course of which Čaγan was assassinated by T'ien Feng, the city fell; Liu Fu-t'ung could make only a token attempt to aid the defenders.

The power of the Sung, now confined to An-feng, eroded even further when Chang Shih-ch'eng besieged the city early in 1363. Han was rescued by his adherent Chu Yüan-chang and was brought to Nanking where preparations were made for his enthronement—a step favored by most of Chu's generals and men, for they seem to have been believers in the idea of a Sung restoration and in the religious propaganda of the White Lotus. Han Lin-er in turn awarded posthumous titles to Chu's ancestors. Chu's mentor Liu Chi (q.v.), who had objected to Han's rescue in the first place, now convinced Chu that it would be a mistake to enthrone Han and continue the White Lotus heresies, thus losing gentry support for the incipient dynasty. When Ch'en Yu-liang (q.v.) launched a counterattack against Chu in June, 1363, the plan to elevate Han was quietly dropped, and he and Liu Fu-t'ung (some accounts, however, have it that Liu was killed at An-feng) were sent back across the Yangtze to Ch'u-chou 滁州 (near Nanking). There they remained until January, 1367, when the boat bringing them to Nanking a second time was capsized in a prearranged accident (see Liao Yung-an), and both the Sung emperor and his prime minister lost their lives. Chu himself donated a site for Liu Fu-t'ung's burial in the latter's native village near Ying-chou.

After Han Lin-er's death, Chu Yüan-chang made strenuous efforts to eradicate all traces of his connection with the Red Turban Sung regime. The Sung reign-title of Lung-feng was erased from all official documents and replaced by the Yüan Chih-cheng 至正 designation. Even a stone stele set up at Chiang-yin 江陰 some years previously in commemoration of a victory there was obliterated because it had the Lung-feng reign-title. Officially the rebel Sung dynasty never even existed: only the words "Liu Fu-t'ung of An-feng" appear in a list of twenty defeated rebels which Chu submitted to the gods in a sacrificial prayer upon assuming the throne as emperor of the Ming in January, 1368.

Liu Fu-t'ung undoubtedly was the mastermind behind the Sung advances during the years from 1355 to 1358, and his obvious purpose was to conquer all of north China. But when Kuan To burned Shang-tu and proceeded east across the Liao-tung plains in the winter of 1359, he was no longer under orders from Liu Fu-t'ung. Kuan joined another group of Red Turbans under Mao Chü-ching 毛居敬 at Liao-yang, and both men led invasions of Korea: Mao late in 1360, and Kuan in 1361. The Koreans repulsed both attacks, and remnants of the defeated armies straggled back to north China through 1363; those who remained in Liao-tung were eventually subdued by Naɤaču (q.v.).

Of all the Sung rebels in the north, the best administration seems to have been that of Mao Kuei, who set up three hundred sixty military-agricultural colonies in Shantung, instituted a regular tax-collection system, and tried to bring able men, including former Yüan officials, into his regime. The central administration under Liu Fu-t'ung, in spite of its large size, is not credited with any such constructive measures. Liu's greatest strategic mistakes were probably two: he sent his

allies out to attack without ever trying to bring them under centralized control; and second, dispatched them in all directions at once, rather than having them concentrate upon building a solid core area from which attacks could be launched gradually later on. Thus, as soon as one of his columns moved through an area, loyalist forces would follow behind and recover it; or they would keep hitting the overextended rebels and prevent them from establishing themselves permanently.

Bibliography

1/122/3b, 129/12b; 5/119/7b; 61/89/8b; *Yüan-shih* (Po-na ed.), *ch.* 42–45, 139, 141, 142, 144-5, 183, 194, 207; *Hsin Yüan-shih, ch.* 225; MSL (1962), T'ai-tsu, 478; *Koryŏ-sa* (1908), I, 584; Lu Shen, *P'ing Hu lu* (TsSCC ed.); T'ao Tsung-i, *Cho keng lu* (TsSCC), 439; Ch'üan Heng, *Keng-shen wai-shih* 庚申外史 (TsSCC); Liu Ch'en 劉辰, *Kuo-ch'u shih-chi* 國初事蹟; Wang Yüan (ECCP), *Chü-yeh-t'ang chi*, 6; Wang Ch'ung-wu 王崇武, *Ming pen chi chiao-chu* 明本紀校注 (Hong Kong, 1967), 40; Ch'ien Ch'ien-i (ECCP), *Kuo-ch'u ch'ün-hsiung shih-lüeh* 國初羣雄事略, *ch.* 1; *Wo-yang feng-t'u-chi* 渦陽風土記 (1924), 15/6a; *Lu-ch'eng-hsien chih* 潞城縣志 (1885), 3 下/55b; *Feng-t'ien t'ung-chih* 奉天通志 (1934), 10/21b; *Hsin-yang-chou chih* 信陽州志 (1925), 11/15b; Yen Han-sheng 閻瀚生, "Liu Fu-t'ung fen-mu tiao-ch'a hsiao-chi" 墳墓調查小記, *Li-shih chiao-hsüeh* 歷史教學, 8 (1955); Shigematsu Toshiaki 重松俊章, "Sō-Gen jidai no kōkingun to Gen-matsu no Miroku-Hakuren kyōhi ni tsuite (naka)," 宋元時代の紅巾軍と元末の彌勒白蓮教匪に就いて中, *Shien* 史淵, 27 (November, 1941); Wada Sei 和田清, "Min no Taiso to kōkin no zoku" 明太祖と紅巾の賊, *Tōyō Gakuhō* 東洋學報. Vol. XIII, 2 (July, 1922).

John Dardess

HAN Pang-ch'i 韓邦奇 (T. 汝節, H. 苑洛), 1479-January 23, 1556, official, scholar, and thinker, was the highest ranking official to die during the disastrous earthquake of 1556. Born in Chao-i 朝邑, prefecture of Sian, he was the second son of Han Shao-tsung 紹宗 (T. 裕後, H. 蓬峯, 1452-May 19, 1519, cs 1478), who served nine years in the ministry of Justice and was later a surveillance vice commissioner of Fukien (1492-98). Both Han Pang-ch'i and his younger brother, Han Pang-ching 靖 (T. 汝慶, H. 五泉, 1488-1523), graduated as *chin-shih* in 1508. Han Pang-ch'i was appointed a secretary in the bureau of evaluations of the ministry of Personnel, and three years later promoted to be vice director of the bureau of appointments. Following an earthquake in Peking (December 1, 1511), he submitted a memorial pointing out the inadequacies of the administration, but it came to nothing. Soon afterwards, when the censors and supervising secretaries jointly impeached more than thirty officials, including Han, for various offenses, he was demoted to assistant prefect of P'ing-yang 平陽, Shansi. In March, 1514, he received promotion to surveillance vice commissioner in charge of the prefectures, Hangchow and Yenchou 嚴州, Chekiang. While there he observed that the imperial prince, Chu Ch'enhao (*see* Wang Shou-jen), was engaged in various illegal activities, such as gathering several thousand people in a monastery in Hangchow, ostensibly for the purpose of feeding Buddhist monks, but perhaps soliciting supporters for a plot. One of the prince's relatives sent some emissaries, under pretence of offering tribute, to Peking, via Ch'ü-chou 衢州, Chekiang, which was on the direct route to the north. Han did not hesitate to disperse the men gathered at the temple and to intercept the emissaries. He also discovered how tribute-collecting eunuchs oppressed the people of the Hangchow area, famous for its tea and samli fish (much enjoyed by the emperor), and did what he could to control them, composing a dirge to express the people's complaints. The eunuchs, resenting his interference, brought various charges against him. He was arrested, taken to Peking in chains, and tortured in the prison of the Embroidered-uniform Guard. Finally, in November, 1516, he was sentenced to dismissal from office and reduction in status to a commoner. Numerous protests against this flagrant injustice

Emperor Chu Hou-chao (*q.v.*) ignored.

A month after Chu Hou-ts'ung (*q.v.*) ascended the throne (June, 1521), Han was recalled to service and appointed an assistant administration commissioner of Shantung. About the time he assumed office, the emperor's mother was traveling through Shantung toward Peking on the Grand Canal. A vice magistrate offended some eunuchs in her entourage and was reported to the throne. The emperor at once ordered his arrest and trial by the court of the Embroidered-uniform Guard. Han submitted a memorial reminding the emperor of the correct legal procedure in such a case, namely that the provincial authorities should first investigate and then recommend a person for trial if he were considered guilty. In Han's opinion an official, however lowly in rank, should not be convicted just on the word of a eunuch. He soon discovered, however, that he was quite alone in his struggle against the excessive use of imperial power, and that all his superiors in the provincial government had already obsequiously acquiesced, as if their subordinate had indeed committed a crime. Finding himself ostracized, Han tended his resignation (October, 1521?), and went home.

In February, 1523, he was joined there by his brother, Han Pang-ching, who had resigned from his post as intendant of Tatung. In May the latter died. Three months later a mutiny broke out at Tatung, the soldiers of the garrison murdering both a commanding officer and the governor. Late in August, while a new governor and several generals were dispatched there, Han Pang-ch'i was hurriedly called back to service, raised in rank to an assistant administration commissioner, and made intendant of Tatung, the office his brother had recently held. He found that his brother had built up such a good reputation among the people and soldiers that his own prestige was enhanced. He courageously faced the mutineers and helped the governor in calming the situation, with the result that without much fighting the culprits were brought to book and the uprising quelled. He then resigned on the plea of illness. This time he stayed home for nearly four years. In November, 1527, he was named surveillance vice commissioner of Szechwan, but within a few days the appointment was changed to that of instructor in the supervisorate of Imperial Instruction, with the concurrent title of a senior Hanlin compiler. This was an unusual honor, for in practice this office was reserved for one who had been a junior member of the Academy. Han served in that capacity, however, for only ten months. It happened that, after he directed the provincial examination held in Peking in September, 1528, a censor pointed out that he had made several mistakes in the printed questions. There being no way to argue his way out of this, Han was demoted to assistant minister of the Court of the Imperial Stud in Nanking. Meanwhile the censor who had accused him had also made several mistakes in his memorial; so his rank too was lowered.

It is said that Han then decided to retire from public life, but apparently he stayed home for only one year. In September, 1529, he was appointed a surveillance vice commissioner of Shantung. Sometime later, it seems, he was transferred to Honan, for in May, 1532, it was from that province that he was promoted to vice minister of the Grand Court of Revision. In March of the following year he was made governor of the Hsüan-fu area north of Peking. Over a year later (August,1534) the court summoned him to Peking to serve as deputy head of the Censorate with the rank of vice censor-in-chief. When in May the court received the report of a mutiny in Liaotung, Han was posted there as its governor, but within a few days a new assignment took him to Shansi. It is said that he had the reputation of a disciplinarian, but this did not suit the emperor as he had decided to pursue a lenient policy towards the mutineers. In

any event, during his service of three years in Shansi, Han took part in repulsing several Mongol invasions and in directing the repair of a section of the Great Wall. He lived frugally, always paying for his own needs. In July, 1538, at the age of fiftynine, the throne accepted his request to retire. This time he remained at home for six years.

When recalled to service (August, 1544), Han was appointed director-general of the conservancy of waterways with the rank of vice censor-in-chief. Within six months he became vice minister of Justice and a year later he was transferred to the ministry of Personnel. Then in October, 1546, he was made censor-in-chief of the Nanking Censorate, and a year later, minister of War, also in Nanking. After more than two years in that responsible position he pleaded illness, and was finally (January, 1550) permitted to retire. He lived in peace at home for six years until the great earthquake that brought havoc to the Honan, Shansi, and Shensi area, perhaps the most destructive in history as indicated by the enormous number of casualties (more than four-fifths of a million identified, with many unknown and unreported). The emperor, on receiving the report of his death, awarded him posthumously the name Kung-su 恭 肅 and the title of grand guardian of the heir apparent.

Han Pang-ch'i was a follower of the San-yüan 三原 school of Wang Shu (q.v.), which got its inspiration from the early Sung thinkers, especially Chou Tun-i (1017 –73) and Chang Tsai (1020–77). Han was particularly attached to Chang's teaching, but he was less an original thinker than a versatile scholar. The Ssu-k'u catalogue mentions nine of his works, three of which were copied into the Imperial Library. These are the I-hsüeh ch'i-meng i-chien易學啓蒙意見, 5 ch., on the Book of Changes, the Yüan-lo chih-yüeh 苑洛志樂, 20 ch., on the theory of music, and the Yüan-lo chi 集, 22 ch., his collected essays and poems. His approach to the study of the Changes stressed the astrological aspects, and in this field he also wrote two more works, entitled *I-chan ching-wei* 易占經緯, 4 *ch.*, and *Hung-fan t'u-chieh* 洪範圖解, 2 *ch.* The latter was printed in 1521; a copy of this original edition is now preserved in the National Central Library, Taipei. In the same library may be found the original editions of the *Yüan-lo chih-yüeh* (printed in 1548) and a collection, *Hsing-li san-chieh* 性理三解, consisting of the *I-hsüeh ch'i-meng i-chien*, the *Hung-fan t'u-chieh*, and a shorter primer on music, *Lü-lü chih-chieh* 律呂直解, 1 *ch.* A copy of the *Yüan-lo chi*, printed in 1552, is in the National Peiping Library collection, now in Taipei, and is available on microfilm.

His brother, Han Pang-ching, was a brilliant youth who acquired the *chü-jen* at the age of thirteen and became a *chin-shih* at twenty. In 1514, while serving as a secretary in the ministry of Works, he was cashiered for outspokenness. Restored to office in 1521, he was appointed an assistant administration commissioner of Shansi (1522). A year later at a time of famine in Tatung, Han Pang-ching requested the government to distribute alms. When this was refused, he addressed a memorial in protest, tended his resignation, and left for home without waiting for a reply. He died soon afterwards, leaving a collection of poems, available in the National Library of Peking, entitled *Wu-ch'üan Han Ju-ch'ing shih chi* 五泉韓汝慶詩集, 4 + 2 *ch.*, printed *ca.* 1558. He also took part in the compilation of the local gazetteer, *Chao-i-hsien chih* 縣志, 2 *ch.*, published in 1519, and frequently reprinted.

Bibliography

1/201/12b; 3/264/10b; 5/42/72a, 90/62a, 97/59a; 16/94/26b, 102/27b, 119/17b, 124/20a; 32/104/7a; 40/33/7a; 83/9/6b; MSL (1965), Shih-tsung, 2122, 2437, 2485, 3229, 3426, 5899, 6394; SK (1930), 5/1b, 13/3b, 38/4a, 39/2b, 68/9a, 96/2a, 110/2b, 111/7a, 143/6b, 171/11a, 176/11a; KC (1958), 3116, 3464, 3502, 3514, 3559, 3659, 3694, 3866; NLP microfilm, no. 907, 965; NCL *Catalogue*, 55, 445, 512, 520; Honda Shigeyuki 本田成之, "Min-gaku gairon" 明學概論 in *Takase hakushi kanreki kinen shinagaku ronsō* 高瀨博士還曆紀念支那學論叢 (1931), 285; manuscript biography by Huang P'ei.

Chaoying Fang and Julia Ching

HAN-SHIH 函昰 (T. 麗中, 天然), November 21, 1608-September 25, 1685, Buddhist patriarch who, during the Ming-Ch'ing transitional period, gave refuge to many Ming loyalists by tonsuring them as his disciples, was born into a Tseng 曾 family in a village of the P'an-yü 番禺 district, Kwangtung. The village, situated about twenty-five miles north of Canton city, became in 1685 a part of the newly created district of Hua-hsien 花縣; hence both districts claim him as a native son. In his youth he prepared for government service. Under the name of Tseng Ch'i-hsin 起莘 (T. 宅師) he was selected to be a student of the district school in 1624, passed the *chü-jen* examination in 1633, and went twice (1634, 1637) to Peking to take the metropolitan examination. During these years he joined the T'ien-kuan 天關 and other local literary societies, associating especially with a number of young scholars who, while preparing for civil examinations, sought solace in Buddhism, a noticeable trend among Confucianists of that day, especially in south China. In later years Han-shih recalled how one day in 1625 he picked up from a friend's desk a copy of the *Shou-leng-yen ching* 首楞嚴經 (Śūraṅgama sūtra) which struck a sympathetic chord and started his study of other sūtras. Meanwhile he continued his other pursuits. He married and by 1629 had a son. Five years later, on his way home from Peking, he fell seriously ill with fever at a river port in Kiangsi. One night, after the physicians had given up hope for his recovery, he prayed to the Buddhist deities and made a pledge to devote the rest of his life to religious studies. He then fell asleep, had a dream, broke into perspiration, and when he awoke, the fever was gone. He lived up to his word and even persuaded his entire family to follow the Buddhist practice of abstinence and celibacy.

Early in 1640, while traveling north for the third time to take the examination in Peking, he changed his mind and decided to become a monk. At Nan-k'ang 南康, Kiangsi, he went to the Kuei-tsung-ssu 歸宗寺 to visit its abbot, Tao-tu 道獨 (T. 宗寶, H. 空隱, 1600–61, born into a Lu 陸 family of Canton), and begged for acceptance as a disciple. The abbot agreed and he thus became the first of the gentry class with as high a degree as *chü-jen* to do so. He was tonsured and given the name of Han-shih, for all of Tao-tu's disciples had the character han in their names, just as in later years Han-shih's own disciples had names which included the character chin 今. A year previously, in 1639, another member of the Cantonese gentry, Han Tsung-lai 韓宗騋 (T. 猶龍, January 6, 1612–January 9, 1660), the eldest son of the minister of Rites, Han Jih-tsuan 日纘 (T. 緒仲, H. 若海, 1578–1635, cs 1607, Pth. 文恪), had been tonsured by Tao-tu and received the name Han-k'o 可 (T. 祖心, H. 剩人).

In 1641 Han-shih accompanied his master, Tao-tu, back to Kwangtung, serving for a time as the latter's coadjutor (首座) at the Hua-shou-t'ai 華首臺 monastery on Mt. Lo-fu 羅浮, about fifty miles northeast of Canton. A year later he returned to Canton at the invitation of local scholars, led by Ch'en Tzu-chuang (ECCP) to give a series of lectures at the Ho-lin 訶林 hall in the chief Buddhist temple of that city, Kuang-hsiao 光孝 ssu. These won him high regard. It is said that he laid stress on the Confucian teachings, loyalty and filial piety, in expounding Buddhist doctrines. A year later the lectures were published under the title *Ho-lin yü-lu* 語錄.

During the Manchu conqest of China, Canton suffered heavily from destruction and famine. The city first fell to the in-

vaders in January, 1647. One of the Ch'ing generals, Li Ch'eng-tung (ECCP), rebelled in May, 1648, and returned the Canton area to Ming rule. Finally, after a siege of several months, the city was retaken in November, 1650, by Ch'ing forces under Shang K'o-hsi (ECCP). It is said that some seven hundred thousand inhabitants lost their lives, some because they took up arms against the invaders, as Ch'en Tzu-chuang did in 1647, and others when Shang entered the city. Any male who had disobeyed the Manchu order to shave the top of his head and braid a queue at the back was regarded as a rebel and killed on sight. The only way to avoid wearing a queue and escape death was to be tonsured as a Buddhist monk. Many Ming loyalists of the gentry class, acquaintances of Han-shih, begged him to accept them as disciples. They found him an understanding master who tonsured them whether they took up monastic life as did Chin-shih 今釋 (*see* Chin Pao, ECCP), or lived as laymen as did Ch'ü Ta-chün (ECCP). It is said that Han-shih had thousands of such disciples. Conceivably they contributed heavily to the institutions under his control or headed by his disciples. Perhaps this accounts at least partly for the prosperity of the Buddhist monasteries in this period. An examination of their records shows that at this time many of them expanded their properties, decorated their buildings, and increased their publication activities.

Han-shih could not have foreseen such prosperity when he took his oath in 1640. From all accounts he led a life of devotion and self-discipline. In 1647 he had quietly buried the bodies of many of the loyalists, including several Ming imperial clansmen. Early in 1648 he himself had to take refuge in the Lung-hsing 隆興 monastery on Lei-feng 雷峯, some fifteen miles southeast of Canton, where his disciple, Chin-chan 今湛 (T. 旋庵, 1613–77), officiated as abbot. From then on Han-shih had a lifelong association with this monastery where, as its patriarch, he took up residence off and on for more than eighteen years (1648-53, 1658-67, 1674-78, 1685). It was here that his father was tonsured in 1650, and a year later his son, Tseng Tsung 琮, who changed his name to Chin-mo 今摩 (T. 訶衍, 1629-98). Han-shih's mother and wife had become nuns in 1642, his two sisters about 1647, and his son's wife some time after 1651. Thus his entire family entered monastic life. Later a cousin and some other members of his family also became monks. The recruitment of these close relatives seems to imply a motive not purely religious, but indicates rather the demands of an expanding business as the name of the monastery so clearly suggests. In any case, during an extensive program of rebuilding in 1658, its name was changed to the poetic sounding Hai-yün 海雲 ssu (Monastery of the sea cloud).

Having a large number of former officials and gentry under his guidance, Han-shih felt the necessity of imposing strict rules to ensure the safety of the community. About 1652 he published the *T'ien-jan ho-shang t'ung chu hsün-lüeh* 天然和尚同住訓略, a set of regulations on communal life in a monastery with exhortations to good behavior. He warned its members to be frank with each other but to be discreet and polite with outsiders. It was the time when the local survivors of the massacre were cowering before the conquerors under General Shang; the latter, however, tried to be friendly towards Han-shih and contributed to the casting of a huge copper Buddha, beautifully gilded. Probably for the sake of the safety of his flock, Han-shih responded to the general courteously.

In 1653 he traveled to the Kuei-tsung monastery in Kiangsi, where his master, Tao-tu, had once served as abbot. It is said that he went there because a famine had stricken Canton in that year. In any event he took with him his mother and several disciples. In the autumn of 1654 he accepted the position as superior of Ch'i-hsien 棲賢 ssu, a monastery on Mt.

Lu blessed with striking scenery. Here he built for his mother and sisters a nunnery. Late in that year he went to Yung-feng 永豐 (Kuang 廣-feng) in eastern Kiangsi, ostensibly to attend a memorial meeting on the seventy-ninth birthday of Tao-tu's own master, Yüan-lai 元來 (T. 無異, 1575-1630). The meeting was held at Yüan-lai's tomb in the Po-shan 博山 monastery, attended by many of his disciples and their disciples. The real purpose of the meeting was to discuss the recently published genealogy of Ch'an Buddhism, *Wu-teng yen-t'ung* 五燈嚴統, 25 *ch.* (printed in 1654), by T'ung-jung 通容 (T. 費隱, 1593-1661), who excluded Yüan-lai and his school from the legitimate lines of transmisson. At this time there were two main sects of Ch'an, namely Lin-chi-tsung 臨濟宗 and Ts'ao-tung 曹洞-tsung. T'ung-jung belonged to the former and Yüan-lai to the latter. Any doubt on the ancestry of Yüan-lai, or attack on his position in the 32d generation of the Ts'ao-tung sect, would render the legality of his line of transmission insecure. This in turn could jeopardize the property rights of his disciples, including Han-shih. Because of the protests at the meeting late in 1654, the printing blocks of the *Wu-teng yen-t'ung* were destroyed.

In 1658 Han-shih returned to Canton and resumed his residence at Hai-yün ssu. Late in the same year some admirers presented him with a building in Tung-kuan 東莞 which he named Chieh-an 芥菴 (Mustard chapel), a retreat to which he frequently repaired during the ensuing years. For a time in 1662 he served as abbot of the famous Hai-chuang 海幢 ssu, south of Canton, and then handed it over to his favorite disciple Chin-wu 今無 (T. 阿字, 1633-81, of the Wan 萬 family of Canton). At this time a certain family gave to Chin-shih their estate on Mt. Tan-hsia 丹霞 in Jen-hua 仁化 district, about 130 miles north of Canton. Chin-shih converted it into a monastery named Pieh-ch'uan 別傳 ssu. There Han-shih resided as patriarch for five years beginning in 1666. Late in 1671, on the invitation of his friend, the prefect of Nan-k'ang, Liao Wen-ying (*see* Mei Ying-tso), and the entire monastic population of Kuei-tsung ssu, Han-shih went there once more as its abbot. This time he remained three years. At the beginning of the Wu San-kuei (ECCP) rebellion in 1674, Han-shih returned to Canton and stayed in Hai-yün monastery until 1678. Then he again returned to Kiangsi, this time as head of the Ch'i-hsien 棲賢 monastery. Here he built himself a chapel named Ching-ch'eng ching-she 淨成精舍 where from 1681 on he lived in retirement. Early in 1685, when he heard that the local authorities had issued an order to organize the monks on Mt. Lu into mutual watching units (保甲), he left Kiangsi and returned to Hai-yün ssu, and there he died.

As a Ch'an monk, Han-shih left several important works. At each monastery where he gave lectures, notes were taken and printed. They were collected as the *T'ien-jah Shih ch'an-shih yü-lu* 禪師語錄, 12 *ch.*, printed 1670, with two appended collections of poems, *Mei-hua shih* 梅花詩, 1 *ch.*, and *Hsüeh* 雪 *shih*, 1 *ch.*, in the Chia-hsing 嘉興 edition of *Hsü-tsaug-ching* 續藏經. His works, *Leng-chia hsin-yin* 楞伽心印, 4 *ch.*, printed 1670 (on the Laṅkāvatāra sūtra) and *Shou-leng-yen chih-chih* 直指, 10 *ch.*, printed 1678 (on the Śuraṅgama sūtra) were also included in the *Hsü-tsang-ching*. His collection of poems, *Hsia-t'ang shih-chi* 瞎堂詩集, 20 *ch.*, was printed shortly after he died and reprinted probably in the Tao-kuang reign (1821-50). Both the lecture notes and the collected poems contain writings by Chin-shih, and, when the latter's works were ordered destroyed in 1776, Han-shih's books were also banned. The poems and most other works of his, however, were later reprinted.

While Han-shih propagated the Ts'ao-tung sect of Ch'an Buddhism in south China, the other disciple of Tao-tu, Han-k'o, did the same in Liaotung in north-eastern China. It happened that Han-k'o was in Nanking in 1645 when the city fell to the Manchus. In 1647, when he was leaving the city, the soldiers at the gate searched his luggage and found records of the Ming loyalists fighting against the Manchus. The Ch'ing commander, Hung Ch'eng-ch'ou (ECCP), who issued him a passport, thus became involved in the case. Han-k'o was tried in Peking and sentenced to exile in Liaotung. In 1648 he arrived at Shen-yang where he was lodged in the Tz'u-en ssu 慈恩寺. There he learned that his brothers and their families in Kwangtung had lost their lives during the war against the invaders. Later he became abbot of the monastery Lung-ch'üan 龍泉寺 on Mt. Ch'ien 千山, Liao-yang 遼陽. He soon bcame such a popular lecturer that many believers, including the scholar Hao Yü (ECCP) who was a fellow exile, came to listen to him. In a few years he developed the monastery into a great Buddhist center. His collected sayings, *Ch'ien-shan sheng-jen ch'an-shih yü-lu* 剩人禪師語錄, 6 *ch.*, was printed in 1654 and reprinted in 1690. It was later banned, but a copy was reproduced in Hong Kong in 1970, with 54 pages of additional biographical matter.

Bibliography

Wang Tsung-yen 汪宗衍, *T'ien-jan ho-shang nien-p'u* 年譜, 1966; *P'an-yü-hsien chih* (1871), 49/6b; Ch'en Yüan (BDRC), *Ch'ing-ch'u seng-cheng chi*; Sun Tien-ch'i (1957), 21, 30, 212; Han-k'o, *Ch'ien-shan sheng-jen ch'an-shih yü-lu*, Hong Kong, 1970.

Chaoying Fang

HAN Wen 韓文 (T. 貫道, H. 質菴), October 10, 1441-March 27, 1526, an official of outstanding probity known for his impeachment of the eunuch Liu Chin (*q.v.*), was a native of Hung-tung 洪洞, Shansi. The Han family, who claimed descent from the minister of state, Han Ch'i (1008-75), one of the chief opponents of the reforms of Wang An-shih (1021-86), originated in Hsiang-chou 相州 (modern An-yang, Honan). They moved to Shansi during the Jürchen invasion at the end of the 11th century, and took up farming. Han Wen was the first in the family, following his distinguished ancestor, to pursue an official career. There is a story that shortly before Han Wen's birth, his mother had a dream: a Taoist arrived, announcing that he was delivering the reincarnation of Wen Yen-po (1006–97), a famous statesman of the Northern Sung, to be her son; so his father named the boy Wen.

Having qualified for the *chü-jen* in 1465, Han Wen achieved the *chin-shih* the following year. He then took advantage of the special leave granted to successful degree holders to spend two years with his family. In April, 1469, he became a supervising secretary in the ministry of Works. Three years later Han Wen joined with several of his colleagues in memorializing Emperor Chu Chien-shen (*q. v.*), charging Wang Yüeh (*q.v.*), the censor-in-chief and concurrently governor of Ta-tung, with the responsibility of provoking the Mongols in the Ordos region. He then recommended the recall of the senior officials, Wang Hung (*see* Han Yung) and Li Ping 李秉 (T. 執中, cs 1436, d. 1489, Pth. 襄敏), who had been disgraced because of their criticism of the throne, to assume duty on the northern frontier. His latter recommendation, however, offended the emperor, and he suffered punishment by the bastinado, and reduction of a grade in rank. In January, 1474, acting on the accusation of a censor against the demeanor of the commanders responsible for the campaign in Wei-chou 韋州, Ning-hsia prefecture, the court dispatched Han Wen to look into the situation. Three months later Han submitted a report charging Liu Chü (*see* Liu Yung-ch'eng), then commander-in-chief in the area, Ma Wen-sheng (*q. v.*), governor of Shansi, Wang Yüeh, and others, with exaggerating the record of their military exploits. His candid exposition led to the

punishment of those responsible, but he antagonized certain powerful officials, and they took revenge by thwarting recommendations for his promotion.

In December, 1479, after having served over ten years in the same post, Han Wen received promotion to be an assistant administration commissioner of Hu-kuang and supervisor of the administration of the Taoist temples and shrines on Mt. T'ai-ho 太和. He stayed in this post for the next seven years, during which he had some success in curbing the expenses in sacrifices incurred by the eunuch in charge (*see* Wei Kuei), but withdrew to mourn the death of his father in 1486. Following the accession of Chu Yu-t'ang (*q. v.*) in 1488, he was reinstated but soon received a transfer (June, 1489) to be administration vice commissioner of Shantung, and then administration commissioner of Yunnan (September, 1490). He officiated in Yunnan for the next three years, during which he distinguished himself in the provisioning of the army charged with the suppression of a tribal uprising in Kweichow, and by introducing effective measures to relieve the local population stricken by poor harvest. In January, 1495, he was transferred to a similar post in Honan, being promoted to be an assistant vice minister of Revenue at the end of this year. Two years later (June, 1497) his mother died and he retired to observe the mourning requirement. He returned to office late in 1499 but was soon transferred to the ministry of Personnel as an associate vice minister.

In June, 1503, Han Wen received a summons to Nanking to serve as grand adjutant and minister of War. During the time in this office he was credited with resolving a rice shortage crisis by releasing government reserves to the public and by suppressing hoarding and speculation. In recognition of his service the court appointed him (December, 1504) minister of Revenue in Peking—his highest post. Four months later he submitted a lengthy memorial proposing measures to remedy the breakdown in the salt monopoly system, which was caused by inefficient management, official corruption, and the administration's failure to deal with the problem of supply and demand in an expanding market. He recommended the following: (1) strictly enforcing the k'ai-chung 開中 barter system to ensure that the merchants, who acquired the salt vouchers, make prompt delivery of grain to the northern frontier; (2) suppressing illegal transaction in salt produced by private individuals; (3) forbidding lower prices for official licenses in order to induce merchants to transport salt from the outlying regions; (4) revoking the practice of allowing imperial favorites to purchase licenses for surplus salt for private disposal; (5) forbidding merchants to make transactions in salt in excess of the amount stipulated in the official quota; (6) prohibiting disposal of salt outside the designated areas; (7) revamping the salt distribution superintendency to promote efficiency and forestall corruption and abuses. The emperor accepted his recommendations, but before these could be implemented, the monarch passed away.

Following the accession of Chu Hou-chao (q. v.), Han Wen remained as minister of Revenue and continued his effort to strengthen the fiscal health of the state by improving the administration, doing away with abuses, and curbing unnecessary expenses involving both the state and the imperial family. He memorialized the throne denouncing the extraordinary expenditure for the emperor's wedding, for financing the inner court, and for granting excessive rewards to religious dignitaries; he also proposed suspending such expensive imperial undertakings as the purchase of precious metals and increased manufacture of textiles. He also pleaded with the young monarch to forbid his relatives the privilege of acquiring licenses for the disposal of the surplus salt in violation of the monopoly system, and, to eliminate abuses, recommended the removal of a number of eunuchs

from positions in charge of the granaries. He paid attention to the military preparations at the northern frontier, and proposed strengthening the army by increasing the grain reserves against possible need. He recommended as well three major procedures to increase the income of the state: reimposing taxes on the produce derived from the imperial domains, improving the military farms to make them self-sufficient, and reassesing the land held by privileged individuals to ensure against tax evasion. Han's recommendations, however, fell on deaf ears, as the erratic emperor abhorred the duties expected of him, indulged in sensual pursuits, and ignored the remonstrances of his ministers. In due course the administration of the state fell under the domination of a group of junior eunuchs headed by Liu Chin, who kept the emperor amused with diversions and obstructed the counsel of the ministers.

Despairing of the situation, Han Wen and his senior colleagues at court, such as Hsieh Ch'ien, Liu Chien (qq. v.), and others, persisted in their efforts to persuade the emperor to ignore his favorites, but to little effect. After several futile attempts, Han Wen, supported by Hsieh and Liu, decided to take a drastic step. On October 28, 1506, Han, who had drafted a memorial with the assistance of Li Tung-yang (q. v.), made a dramatic plea before the emperor in an audience which included several of his colleagues. He proposed a sentence of death for the eunuchs. Unfortunately, before the emperor acted on this plea, Han's plan was prematurely exposed; the eunuchs, forewarned, succeeded in convincing the monarch of their fidelity. This accomplished, Liu Chin and his cronies emerged all-powerful. Thereupon Hsieh Ch'ien and Liu Chien submitted their resignations, and Han Wen was cashiered in December, an action which involved also his two sons who held junior posts. In May of the following year, Han's name was placed, after those of Hsieh and Liu, at

the head of a black list of officials branded as conspirators against the throne. A
year later (September, 1508), still smart-
ing from Han's action, Liu Chin clapped
Han into prison on the charge of dereliction of duty, and fined him one thousand
bushels of rice, half of which he was
required to ship in person to the granaries in Tatung. Following this, Han was
fined three times, the total amounting to
over two thousand bushels of rice; this
bankrupted him. In January, 1510, Liu
Chin further disgraced Han Wen and his
colleagues by obtaining an imperial order
revoking the honors and gifts granted
them by the emperors of previous reigns.

In November, a month after Liu
Chin's execution, Han Wen, like many
another official banished by the eunuch,
was exonerated; he was allowed to retire,
retaining his official rank. In subsequent
years, despite several recommendations for
his recall, Han Wen received no further
official appointments, but his reputation
was such that a flood of laudatory essays
reached him when he was observing his
eightieth (*sui*) birthday in October, 1520.
His son, Han Shih-ch'i 士奇 (cj 1489, cs
1502), later compiled these essays, together
with the imperial decrees of the previous
reigns, in a booklet entitled *Wan-ming
jung-shou lu* 完名榮壽錄; this is no longer
extant but many of the essays and imperial decrees have been preserved in Han
Wen's collected works. Han Wen's honors
were fully restored during the next reign.
In August, 1521, the imperial successor,
Chu Hou-ts'ung (*q. v.*), sent a special
messenger to inquire after him, and rewarded him with a monthly stipend of four
bushels of rice and six servants. In June
of the following year the emperor further
honored him with the rank of grand guardian of the heir apparent, and appointed
his grandson, Han T'ing-jui 廷瑞, acting
assistant minister of the Court of Imperial
Entertainments. Han Wen died at home
early in 1526, at the age of eighty-five.
(The *shih-lu*, followed by the *Kuo-ch'üeh*,
however, records his death on August 6,

probably the date when the news reached
the court.) On August 25 the emperor
awarded Han the canonized name Chung-
ting 忠定 (loyal and determined), and the
honorary rank of grand tutor.

Han Wen's collection of writings was
first engraved by his sons early in the
1520s under the title *Chih-an ts'un-kao* 質
菴存稿, 6 *ch.*, which had a limited circulation. In 1580 the magistrate of Hung-
tung brought out a revised version entitled
Han Chung-ting kung chi 公集, 4 *ch.*; a
copy of this edition is preserved in the
National Central Library, Taipei, and is
available on microfilm. This collection
includes his memorials, poems, as well as
his autobiography which he composed in
1518, at the age of seventy-seven, and a
number of imperial decrees, laudatory
essays, and biographies by his contemporaries. It therefore supplies the basic sources for his biography. The *Ming ching-
shih wen-pien* by Ch'en Tzu-lung (ECCP)
contains a selection of his memorials entitled *Han Chung-ting kung tsou-shu* 奏疏,
1 *ch.* Two of his essays not included in
his collected works are preserved in the
gazetteer of Hung-tung (1917 ed.).

Han had three sons and several grandsons who achieved some reputation in
their official careers. The eldest son, Han
Shih-ts'ung 聰 (cj 1492), served first as
magistrate of the subprefecture Kao-t'ang
高唐, Shantung, then as secretary of a
bureau in the ministry of Justice, but was
cashiered on his father's dismissal. His
second son, Han Shih-ch'i, held posts
successively in the ministries of Justice
and War, as magistrate of Ch'i-chou 祁州
(Pei-Chihli), vice prefect of Feng-hsiang
鳳翔 (Shensi), prefect of Huai-ch'ing 懷
慶 (Honan), and surveillance vice commissioner of Shensi. He rose to his highest
office, shortly after his father's death, as
administrative vice commissioner of Hukuang. Han Wen's youngest son, Han
Shih-hsien 賢 (cj 1495), served successively
as assistant prefect of Chia-hsing 嘉興
(Chekiang), vice prefect of Kaifeng, and
held his highest post as vice commissioner

of the salt distribution superintendency in the Huai region. At least two of Han Wen's grandsons became *chin-shih*, but their official careers were modest.

Han Wen is often confused (as in the case of the *Harvard-Yenching Index no. 24*, 111, p. 135) with a contemporary of the same name and surprisingly enough of the same *tzu*, who was a native of Hsin-ch'eng 新城, Pei-Chihli. A *chin-shih* of 1457, this Han Wen was appointed a messenger, and was sent, in April, 1471, as special vice envoy to the Liu-ch'iu (Ryūkyū) for the investiture of the new king. Upon his return in the following year, he served successively as director of a bureau in the ministry of Revenue, in the administration office of Shensi (December, 1478), rising to the rank of administration commissioner (February, 1488), and as vice censor-in-chief in charge of the prefecture of Ning-hsia (June, 1490), retiring four years later. His date of death is reported as August 25, 1499.

Bibliography

1/186/1b; 5/29/1a; 16/33/6b; 61/107/14a; 84/丙 5/19b; MSL (1964), Hsien-tsung, 1820, 2362, 2403, 3451, Hsiao-tsung, 589, 863, 1755, 1949, 2762, 3697, Wu-tsung, *ch.* 1–70, Shih-tsung (1965),160, 485, 1505; KC (1958), 2823, 3338; TSCC (1885–88), XI: 311/2/14a; Han Wen, *Han Chung-ting kung chi* (NCL microfilm); Li Meng-yang, *K'ung-t'ung-tzu chi*, 39/14a, 52/8a; Ho T'ang, *Ho Wen-ting kung wen-chi*, 5/8a, 12b; Ho Ch'iao-yüan, *Ming-shan ts'ang* (Taipei, 1970 ed.), 4159; *Hung-tung-hsien chih* (1917), 4/8b, 12/10a, 15a, 17b, 17/54b; Han Wen II: 5/61/1a; 16/129/11a; 32/14/26a; MSL (1964), Hsien-tsung, 1490, 1730, Hsiao-tsung, 195, 801, 1654, 2691; TSCC (1885–88), XIV: 162/4/11b; *Hsin-ch'eng-hsien chih* (1890), 9/5a.

Hok-lam Chan and L. Carrington Goodrich

HAN Yung 韓雍 (T. 永熙), November 22, 1422-November 9, 1478, the celebrated military commander who was credited with the pacification of tribal uprisings in Kwangsi in the 1460s, came from a well-to-do peasant family originating in Ch'ang-chou 長州 in the prefecture of Soochow. Late in 1403, under an imperial order requiring thousands of wealthy families from Soochow and Chekiang to resettle in the Peking region, his father, Han Kuei 貴 (T. 公顯, 1385–1468), moved there and became a registered taxpayer of Wan-p'ing 宛平, a district that included the western half of Peking city. It was here that Han Yung was born and brought up. Turning out to be an able student, he entered the prefectural school in 1436 and wa graduated as *chü-jen* in 1441 and as *chin-shih* in 1442. A year later he received an appointment as censor. Thereafter he served as regional inspecting censor in Nanking and in the Grand Canal area to watch over the transportation of grain. In 1448 he was transferred to Kiangsi where he established a reputation as an upright and competent official. He exposed the chicanery of certain powerful officials and promptly settled a number of judicial cases. Late in the same year, he was charged with suppressing remnants of the bandits led by Yeh Tsung-liu (*q.v.*) who had recently been killed by government troops. It was during this time that he paid his first visit to his ancestral home in Ch'ang-chou, Because of his performance he was recommended to remain in Kiangsi for an additional term (until 1450). In May, 1451, he and his friend, Hsiang Chung (*q.v.*), were both promoted to be surveillance vice commissioners of Kwangtung.

Han's record soon brought him back to Kiangsi. In February, 1452, upon the recommendation of Ch'en Hsün (*see* Ch'en Ch'eng), a native of Kiangsi and then grand secretary, the court appointed Han assistant censor-in-chief to serve as governor of the province. At that time the people of Kiangsi were overburdened by a corrupt corvée system which favored the rich. Han examined the discrepancies and initiated procedures to insure an equal share of duties among people on all social levels. In addition he made an effort to accumulate a surplus in the provincial granaries to meet any situation that might arise. To this end Han submitted a memorial (October, 1452) asking permission to invite wealthy families to contribute grain to the government, holding out an official cap and sash as a possible reward. Acting on this recommendation, the ministry of Revenue reviewed its regulation for such contributions. Within the next two years (1455–56), Han requested these families to donate approximately two million *shih* of grain and two thousand rolls of cotton cloth. It was due to his foresight and competent management that, when Kiangsi was struck by a serious drought in 1456, the people were spared the usual attendant panic and suffering. It is said, moreover, that the regulation and procedure of government that he set up during his administration had become the guideline for his successors.

Late in 1456 Han became involved in the dispute between Chu Tien-p'ei, the successor to the princedom of Ning (*see* Chu Ch'üan), and his younger brother, Chu Tien-chien 奠壏, the prince of I-yang 弋陽 (d. June 1461). Chu Tien-chien, who presented his case before Han, accused his brother of taking the life of his consort, née Chang 張, of pocketing the stipend of the imperial guards assigned to the princedom, and of more than ten other unlawful acts; whereupon Chu Tien-p'ei submitted a counter-charge. In December Emperor Chu Ch'i-yü (*q.v.*) ordered Han and other officials to investigate the case; they found Chu Tien-p'ei guilty of the charge, but the emperor forgave his imperial kinsman. For this reason Chu Tien-p'ei bore a grudge against Han. The occasion for revenge came shortly after Chu Ch'i-chen (*q.v.*) regained the throne, when Han was appointed the surveillance vice commissioner of Shansi (March, 1457). In August Chu Tien-p'ei criticized Han for his arrogant manner of traveling by sedan chair, and charged him with violating protocol by having an elaborate ceremony when he was recalled from duty in

Kiangsi. Han was subsequently imprisoned, but the emperor soon pardoned him, ordering him to retire. Han returned to his ancestral home in Soochow where, by this time, he had acquired some property.

In March, 1458, Han was recalled to become vice minister of the Court of Imperial Sacrifices; a few days later he was reinstated as an assistant censor-in-chief in Peking. He interrupted his duties when his mother died in November 1459, but by imperial order returned to the same office four months later (March, 1460). In December of the same year he was appointed governor of the Tatung and Hsüan-fu 宣府 regions. During this period Han overhauled the administration, improved the methods for military provisioning, constructed fortifications, and strengthened the defense along the border. Under his leadership the Ming forces successfully repulsed several incursions by Oirat tribesmen. His achievements brought him promotion (May, 1463) to be vice minister of War. In February, 1464, shortly after the enthronement of Chu Chien-shen (*q.v.*), Han became involved in the case of Ch'ien P'u 錢溥 (T. 原溥, H. 九峯, 1408–88, cs 1439), a reader-in-waiting in the Hanlin Academy who was accused of communicating with a palace eunuch of the late emperor in the hope of an appointment to the Grand Secretariat. Ch'ien was put into prison, whereas Han, being close to Ch'ien who is said to have thought of proposing him as minister of War, was demoted to be the vice administration commissioner of Chekiang, where he served until the following year.

At this time the rebellious Yao 猺 tribesmen of Kwangsi, under the leadership of their able chieftain Hou Ta-kou 侯大狗 who exploited the vacillating policy of the government, not only ravaged Kwangtung but expanded their depredations into Kiangsi and Hukuang. In February, 1465, shortly after Chu Chien-shen ascended the throne, the court adopted a hard-line policy and proposed to dispatch an expeditionary army to Kwangsi to suppress the rebels. Immediately upon the recommendation of the minister of War, Wang Hung 王竑 (T. 公度, H. 休菴, 1413-88, cs 1439), the emperor appointed Chao Fu 趙輔 (T. 良佐, made earl of Wu-ching 武靖 in November, 1466, d. July 13, 1486, Pth. 恭肅), the commander of the expeditionary army, with Han as censor-in-chief and concurrent associate in military affairs, and the senior eunuchs, Lu Yung 盧永 and Ch'en Hsüan 陳瑄 (T. 德新, H. 靜菴, d. 1475), as supervisors. In July the leaders convened at Nanking to deliberate on strategy. Earlier, in February, Ch'iu Chün (q.v.), an expositor-in-waiting of the Hanlin Academy and a native of Kwangtung, had submitted to Grand Secretary Li Hsien (q.v.) his two-point recommendation: namely, to quell the bandits in Kwangtung and besiege those in Kwangsi. By this time some officials, invoking Ch'iu's recommendation, proposed to send two separate units, one to Kwangtung to crush the insurgents, and another to Kwangsi to lay siege to the rebel stronghold in Ta-t'eng hsia 大藤峽 (grand rattan gorge). Han, however, disagreed. He argued that, to suppress the rebellious tribesmen, it would be necessary to strike at the source of trouble in Ta-t'eng gorge; once the rebels' headquarters in Kwangsi was destroyed, it would not be difficult to deal with the enemy in Kwangtung. His plan, which included a thousand Mongol cavalry commanded by Toɤto Bolod (see Aruɤtai), was adopted.

Leading a contingent of thirty thousand men, Han and others marched into Kwangsi, defeated the Miao 苗 rebels in Ch'üan-chou 全州 in August, and arrived at Kweilin in October. In the following month, joined by the local troops with a numerical strength of one hundred sixty thousand men, the punitive forces routed the rebel hideouts in Hsiu-jen 修仁 and Li-p'u 荔浦, killing, it is said, over seven thousand tribesmen. As a result several thousand of them flocked to the side of the government. Riding the tide of victory, the government troops arrived in Hsün-

chou 潯州 at the entrance to the gorge. At that time some local elders pointed out that the gorge, covering a vast area, was mountainous, abounding in dense forests, swamps, and waterways; and since it was difficult of access, it could be a dangerous trap; hence, they implored Han to assemble the troops on the outskirts and surround the region, awaiting the chance to attack. Han, who pointed out the impracticability of laying siege to an area with a perimeter of six hundred li, rejected their advice. Realigning his troops in fifteen units, Han directed the army into the gorge and assaulted the enemy from the front and rear.

The Mongol cavalry, with their skill in archery, proved highly successful. In the following January, after a series of bloody clashes, the government troops reached the heart of the gorge, captured Hou Ta-kou and over seven hundred of his men, and killed three thousand. Following this, Han smashed the sprawling huge rattans linking the two sides of the gorge, changed its name to Tuan 斷-t'eng hsia (broken rattan gorge), and erected a memorial tablet to commemorate the occasion. (The gorge was renamed Yung-t'ung 永通 hsia [ever-accessible gorge] in 1516 by the then governor, Ch'en Chin 陳金 [T. 汝礪, R. 西軒, 1446-1528, cs 1472] after his successful campaign against another tribal uprising in this region.) At this point, Han submitted a memorial proposing several administrative changes in the government of the region. He advocated making the gorge the seat of a new subprefecture called Wu-ching chou 武靖州 within the jurisdiction of Hsün-chou-fu, the setting up of several police offices, and the founding of a chiliad in T'eng-hsien in the center of the gorge. He also recommended competent natives to fill these posts. Han's proposals approved, they were carried out immediately to consolidate the Chinese administration over this region.

Han remained in Kwangsi in charge of the suppression of the undefeated rebels, while the contingent of the victorious army under the command of Lu Yung and Chao Fu returned to the capital (July, 1466). In December, in addition to a monetary reward, he received a promotion to be the vice censor-in-chief with the concurrent title of superintendent of military affairs and governor of Kwangsi and Kwangtung. In February, 1468, stricken by illness, Han begged for relief from duty, but the ministry of Personnel turned a deaf ear. In the following month Han memorialized the court proposing a division of authority between the civil and military in Kwangsi and Kwangtung. He pointed out that, as the two provinces encompassed a vast territory ravaged by sporadic uprisings, it was difficult for one official of his status to oversee both civil and military matters; he requested the court, therefore, to name two governors, and appoint two superintendents of military affairs (one civil and one military) to be stationed in Wu-chou 梧州 on the border of the two provinces to coordinate military operations. In April, having approved Han's proposal, the court appointed him the civil superintendent of military affairs and designated two governors, one for each province. The court also appointed a general officer as military commander of the region and a eunuch as supervisor with the title of chen-shou 鎮守, or grand defender. Wu-chou thus became the command center for all the officers: the civil supreme commander, the military commander, and the grand defender. Before matters took shape, however, Han's father died (November), and he had to leave office. After his departure, the problem of coordination of military operations between the two provinces became acute; so the local censors urged the court to appoint an official with full authority over the civil and military affairs of the entire region. In January, 1470, the court approved the recommendation, appointed Han as supreme commander and concurrently governor of Kwangsi and Kwangtung, with headquarters in Wu-chou as he had

earlier recommended. By this time Han had not completed his mourning period; so he begged to decline the appointment (February, 1470) but, the emperor overruling his petition, Han assumed the duty and held this post until his retirement in April, 1474. From this time on the post of supreme commander of the two was regularized.

In this capacity Han played the combined role of a military commander and civil administrator. His task was twofold. On one hand he overhauled the military system, disciplining his troops by regular training and keeping them alert to possible uprisings. He also constructed forts, improved the communication facilities, and registered the population to prevent intrusion of potential spies. On the other hand, Han offered the people assistance in agriculture so that they could help support the troops, and provided them with relief in times of hardship. In addition he improved the school system, tried to raise the ethical standards of the people, and administered the region with justice. Under him the two provinces enjoyed relative stability amid sporadic uprisings, while official corruption was kept in check under his vigilant eyes. His pacification of the tribesmen and subsequent governorship in Kwangsi were so memorable that they soon became a source of legend.

Han's rigorous policy, however, annoyed unscrupulous officials who viewed his presence as injurious to their interests, and they began to intrigue against him. Being aware of his precarious situation and dogged by ill health, Han begged for permission to retire (November, 1473), but the emperor ignored his plea. Han's apprehension was not unfounded. Late in the year the junior eunuch, Huang Ch'in 黃沁, then grand defender of Kwangsi, submitted a memorial calling for the impeachment of Han for concealing his failure to suppress the rebels and for indulging in luxury and high living, an accusation which involved several of his subordinates also. The emperor subsequently ordered an investigation, which turned up only partial evidence in support of the allegation; he pardoned Han but ordered him to retire (April, 1474). For the next four years Han lived in seclusion at his residence, called Fu-ch'i ts'ao-t'ang 莩溪草堂, in Ch'ang-chou, until his death at the age of fifty-six. (The *shih-lu*, however, records Han's death on May 8, 1479, which is probably the date the court conferred posthumous honors on him.) The emperor then ordered an elaborate burial for him, and granted a son the privilege of becoming a student at the National University. In August, 1515, Emperor Chu Hou-chao (*q.v.*) awarded Han the posthumous name Hsiang-i 襄毅, and a year later granted his son Han Hsün 勛 the yin privilege of enrolling in the National University.

In the decade following his death, shrines in his honor sprang up in many localities. In 1497, through the memorial of the supreme commander and governor of the two Kwang provinces (1495-1500), Teng T'ing-tsan 鄧廷瓚(T. 宗器, 1430-1500, cs 1454), a shrine known as Han-kung tz'u 公祠 was built in Wu-chou. In 1518, upon the recommendation of the censor from Soochow, Lü Kuang-hsün 呂光洵 (T. 信卿, H. 沃州, 1518-80, cs 1532), who had served in Wu-chou, the magistrate of Ch'ang-chou set up another. In 1723 the commissioner of education of Kwangsi, Hsü Shu-p'ing (ECCP, p. 311), removed Han's spirit tablet from the shrine and placed it beside that of Yüan Chieh (723-72), a celebrated T'ang official, in the Ch'uan-ching shu-yüan 傳經書院, known as Yüan-Han er-kung 元韓二公 tz'u. Similar shrines were erected in Ts'ang-wu 蒼梧, Kuei-p'ing 桂平, T'eng 藤-hsien, and several other districts in Kwangsi.

In spite of his civilian background Han was a gifted commander and a brilliant strategist. His quality of leadership lay in his sound judgment and ability to make decisions, his capacity to recruit dedicated officials to his staff, and maintenance of discipline over the rank-and-file. One of

the officials, T'ao Lu 陶魯 (T. 自强, H. 節菴, 1434-98), whose ability Han Yung recognized, later became his trusted lieutenant and rose in rank. Han owed his success to some extent, however, to his cordial relations with the eunuch Ch'en Hsüan who seldom interfered with his decisions. This is particularly significant in view of the fact that his downfall was caused by the allegation of a junior eunuch. In addition to his military ability Han was a man of letters. His essays were written in a plain and lucid style. One of the best examples is his "Tz'u yu hsi-yüan chi" 賜遊西苑記, composed on the occasion of a visit to the Imperial Park in June, 1459 (*see also* Li Hsien, who used the same title for a short book). His poetry too received high acclaim. One of the outstanding pieces is his "P'ing 平 tuan-t'eng hsia," which described his campaign against the tribesmen of the Ta-t'eng gorge. Han is reported to have left several other literary pieces as well as memorials, but none of these seems to have survived. His extant collection, the *Han Hsiang-i kung chia tsang wen-chi* 家藏 文集, 15 ch., with samples of his poems and essays, but few memorials, was printed by his descendants some time after his death, and is available in microfilm and recently reprinted (1970) — a chief source for some of the information in this biography.

Bibliography

1/178/6a; 5/58/1a; 9后/17/8a; 34/3/1a; 40/20/ 13a; 63/16/15a; 64/乙17/8b; MSL (1963), Ying-tsung, *ch.* 105–351, Hsien-tsung(1964), *ch.* 13–126, Wu-tsung (1965), 2551, 3197; KC (1958), 1940, 1994, 2010, 2164, 2183, 2197, 2201, 2414, 2715; SK (1930), 170/9a; *Ch'ang-chou-hsien chih* (1635), 6/9b, 23a, 11/10a, 13/12b, *i-wen chih* 藝文志, 3/24a; Wang Ao 王鏊, *Chen-tse chi-wen* in *Chi-lu hui-pien*, 124/19b; *Kwangsi t'ung-chih* (1965 reprint of 1599 ed., Taipei), 7/18a, 25/19a (also Taipei 1968 ed.), 91/9a, 137/2a, 144/19b, 145/2b, 247/15a; *T'eng-hsien chih* (Taipei 1968 reprint of 1908 ed.), 406, 779; *Huang Ming wen-hai* (microfilm), 8/1/8, 10/2/14; Liu Yao-hui 劉堯誨 ed., *Ts'ang-wu tsung-tu chün-men*

chih 總督軍門志 (NCL microfilm), 18/1a, 29/1a;
Yang Hsün-chi, *Wu-chung ku-yü*, in *Wu-ch'ao hsiao-shuo* 五朝小說 (Ming ed.), Vol. 100, 3a;
Wang Shih-chen, "Chung-kuan k'ao" 中官考, 3, in *Yen-shan-t'ang pieh-chi* (Taipei, 1965), 92/1a;
Han Yung, *Han Hsiang-i kung chia-tsang wen-chi*, Taipei, 1970; Huang Tso, *Nan-yung chih*, 4/83b.

Hok-lam Chan

HAO Ching 郝敬 (T. 仲輿, H. 楚望), 1558
-1639, a native of Ching-shan 京山, Hu-kuang, was a courageous official whose de-nunciations of corruption in the bureauc-racy led to his retirement and his concen-tration on classical studies. His father Hao Ch'eng-chien 承健 (H. 玉吾, cj 1561), who served for a time as an instructor in a school at Ting-chou 定州, and then as magistrate of Su-ning 肅寧, Pei-Chihli, was himself a poet and essayist, author of *Tsai-shan-ts'ao-t'ang chi* 載山草堂集.

Following Hao Ching's graduation as *chü-jen* in 1588 and *chin-shih* in the next year, he became magistrate (1591–95) of two hsien: Chin-yün 縉雲 and Yung-chia 永嘉, both in Chekiang. When word of his ability came to public attention, he was made supervising secretary, first of the office of scrutiny for Rites and sec-ond of a comparable office in the ministry of Revenue. He served at a time when, to obtain money for various imperial objects, the emperor was imposing heavy taxes on mines. The chief tax agent—appointed to this activity in the autumn of 1596—the eunuch Ch'en Tseng 陳增 (fl. 1584 –99), he denounced (in February, 1599) for exceeding the revenue schedule. (His memorial is preserved in the *Ching-shan-hsien chih.*) Hao saw fit also to accuse of disloyalty to the throne the grand secretary Chao Chih-kao (*see* Shen I-kuan), whose special prerogative it was to pass on ap-pointments and accept tribute. Hao's charges cost him a demotion and transfer first to I-hsing 宜興, west of Lake T'ai, as assistant magistrate, and next (1600–03) as magistrate of Chiang-yin 江陰, a port on the south bank of the Yangtze River, a few miles to the northeast of I-hsing. Fur-ther demotions so discouraged him that he resigned and gave himself up to schol-arship.

Hao wrote numerous books on the Five Classics, the *I-li, Chou-li, Lun-yü, Meng-tzu, Shih-chi*, etc., thirteen of his writings being listed in the Imperial Cata-logue; not one, however, was copied into the *Ssu-k'u ch'üan-shu*. One of the titles so listed, the *Hsiao-shan ts'ao* 小山草, 10 *ch.*, was in the same decade ordered par-tially expunged; in it he reviles the Bud-dhist doctrine, discusses the probable meaning of the Confucian canon, includes a few letters and a register of his clan in 3 *chüan*. The censorial board found fault with passages in the 4th and 9th *chüan*. A copy of this, printed in the Wan-li period, has survived, as has also his *Hsiao-ts'ao-t'ang chi* 堂集, printed at the same time. His *Chien ts'ao* 諫草, 2 *ch.*, is included in the *Shan-ts'ao-t'ang chi, nei pien* 內編.

Hao Ching died at the age of eighty-one, and was buried twenty *li* west of Ching-shan. One son, Hao Hung-fan 宏範 (cj 1642), survived him.

Another man of the same name, a native of Yüan-chiang 沅江, Hukuang (cj 1408), became a magistrate of Yung-ning 永寧, Honan. His principal achieve-ment was to open up several irrigation ditches, including one named Wan-hsiang 萬箱, which provided for the cultivation of over a hundred thousand *mou* of land (say, 15,000 acres), and by so doing he won the gratitude of the population.

Bibliography

1/288/2a; 3/269/10b; 21/5/4b, 40/55/31b; 64/庚 16/14a; 83/55/1a; 86/16/9b; KC (1958), 4826; SK (1930), 8/2b, 14/1a, 17/4a, 23/2b, 8b, 24/3a, 30/ 5a, 34/2b, 37/5a, 46/8a, 125/5a, 179/11a; *Hupeh t'ung-chih* (1934), 658, 3071, 3082, 3087, 3755; *Ching-shan-hsien chih* (1882), 10/3a, 8a, 13/1a, 23/10a, 16a, 23a/1a; *Chiang-yin-hsien chih* (1878) 11/76a; *Chin-yün-hsien chih* (1880), 6/5a, 32b; *Yung-chia-hsien chih* (1882), 9/18b; Sun Tien-ch'i (1957), 20, 21; Naikaku Bunko *Catalogue*, 588. For the 2d Hao Ching: *Hunan t'ung-chih* (1934), 3376; *Ch'ang-te-fu chih* 常德府志 (1813),

27/14a, 37/2a; *Lo-ning* 洛寧*-hsien chih* (1917),
3/16b, 30a; TSCC (1885–88), XIV: 525/7b.

L. Carrington Goodrich

HO Chen 何眞 (T. 邦佐), 1322–April 11,
1388, military leader, official, was a native
of Tung-kuan 東莞, Kwangtung, but made
his home in the neghboring city of Hui-
chou 惠州. Intelligent and robust, he studied both calligraphy and swordsmanship
and in his youth served under the Mongol
regime as a transport tax collector in Ho-
yüan 河源 and later as a salt tax collector in Kuei-shan 歸善, both in Hui-chou
prefecture. For some reason he lost this
position and was at home when local
banditry developed about 1354. Ho Chen
organized a defense unit to fight the
bandits and probably operated for a time
like one himself, for it is said that he
was named for arrest on a false accusation
and became a fugitive. With the support
of his younger brother, Ho Ti 廸 (d.
1393), and other followers, Ho Chen recaptured for the Mongol regime the city
of Hui-chou and its neighboring area
from a group of rebels. For this service
he was appointed the subprefect of that
prefecture by the Yüan court and concurrently a commander of the provincial
troops. In 1363, for his recovery of Canton from another rebel, he was promoted
to be assistant administrator of his native
province. Meanwhile Ho Ti was made a
commander of the provincial troops.

Although frequently harassed by
rebels and invaders Ho Chen set up a
creditable administration with the help of
several well-known scholars of his day,
such as Liu San-wu and Sun Fen (*qq.v.*). In
1368 he surrendered his province to the
commander of the Ming troops marching
south to conquer Fukien and Kwangtung
(*see* Liao Yung-chung), and was himself
sent to Nanking for an audience with the
first Ming emperor. He must have impressed
the latter; he was appointed an assistant
administrator first in Kiangsi, and then in
Shantung. His next move, 1371, was to

Canton to collect the officers and men
formerly under his command and to transport them with their families to Honan
where they were assigned to Chang-te
彰德 and other guards. It seems that
later he returned to Shantung and officiated there until 1376, and that for some
reason he was cashiered and lived in
retirement for several years. In 1380 he
offered his third son, Ho Kuei 貴 (T. 奉
先), to the court to serve as a bodyguard
of the heir apparent. A year after that he
and Ho Kuei, who had been made chief
of police of northern Nanking, were
named quartermasters in the expeditionary
forces during the conquest of Kweichow
and Yunnan (*see* Fu Yu-te and Mu
Ying).

By 1382(?) Ho Chen had redeemed
himself and was made a commissioner of
administration of Shansi but in 1383 he
was again returned to Canton to select
men for military service. It is said that
he collected over twenty thousand men formerly under his command and sent them
and their families to Nanking. There is
evidence that he also enlisted others whom
he assigned to the Nan-hai Guard 南海衞
which had been established in 1381 in his
native city, Tung-kuan. He was then reinstated in the government, being appointed
commissioner of administration successively in Chekiang (1385–86) and in Hukuang
(1386–87). When he finally retired in 1387
he was awarded the hereditary rank of earl
(伯) of Tung-kuan at an annual stipend
of 1500 *shih*, and an iron plaque bearing
an embossed patent dated 11th day of 8th
month, Hung-wu 20th year; it recorded
that, although he had made some mistakes
while serving as an official, his action in
surrendering the Kwangtung province
without resistance was in his favor; hence
the award of the earldom with rights of
perpetual inheritance and the pledge of
two future pardons from any crime warranting a death sentence except for that
of treason.

Ho Chen died in 1388, apparently in
Nanking, for he was buried several miles

south of that capital city. Only five years later his sons were involved in the case of Lan Yü (*q.v.*) and were executed. Had Ho Chen been alive he himself would assuredly have been put to death just like hundreds of the other men who had received patents and pledges from the emperor. All his sons were probably executed at this time, including the eldest, Ho Jung 榮 (T. 耀先 inheritor of the earldom), the third, Ho Kuei, and the sixth, Ho Hung 宏 (T. 彥先). Ho Chen's younger brother, the afore-mentioned Ho Ti, was in Tung-kuan when he learned about the execution of his nephews. Apprehensive for his own life, he rose in rebellion, killed some three hundred guardsmen, and escaped to an island. He was later captured and executed too.

Ho Chen's earldom was abolished and his properties confiscated, including the hundreds of acres of land in Hui-chou which he had given to the Ho clan as communal property and about which Sung Lien (*q.v.*) wrote a eulogistic essay. Two centuries later, in 1586, there was a re-evaluation of Ho Chen's contribution to the dynasty and permission was granted for a shrine in his memory to be erected in Tung-kuan. In 1645 Chu Yu-sung, the prince of Fu (ECCP), conferred on Ho Chen the rank of marquis and the posthumous name Kung-ching 恭靖.

Bibliography

1/130/21a; 5/10/1a; *Tung-kuan-hsien chih* 55/1a; *Tung-kuan shih-lu* 詩錄 (1924), 4/1a; MSL (1962), T'ai-tsu, 2418; P'an Ch'eng-chang (ECCP), *Kuo-shih k'ao-i*, 2/8b, 3/34b.

Chaoying Fang

HO Ch'iao-hsin 何喬新 (T. 廷秀, 天苗, H. 椒丘), 1427-January 19, 1503, official, scholar, and bibliophile, was a native of Kuang-ch'ang 廣昌, Kiangsi. His father, Ho Wen-yüan 文淵 (T. 巨川, H. 東園, 鈍菴, cs 1418, d. May 7, 1457), served as minister of Personnel from 1451 to 1453. After the restoration in 1457 (*see* Chu

Ch'i-chen), Ho Wen-yüan fell into disgrace because of his association with the former emperor (especially in connection with the displacement of Chu Chien-shen [*q.v.*] as heir apparent). Overcome by the prospect of arrest, he committed suicide. Ho Ch'iao-hsin (cj 1450, cs 1453) first entered government service in the ministry of Works. In 1456 he became a secretary in the Nanking ministry of Rites. When his father died, he went home; soon afterwards his mother also passed away.

Following the mourning period which ended in the early 1460s, he was appointed a secretary in the ministry of Justice, rising to the directorship of the bureau which had charge of cases relating to the Embroidered-uniform Guard. By adhering strictly to the law, Ho kept its unruly officers, who had long enjoyed special privileges, under control and won a reputation for probity. His next promotion (1468) was as surveillance vice commissioner in Fukien. Here he suppressed a group of a thousand miners who had resorted to banditry on the Chekiang border. From 1473 to 1480 he served successively as surveillance commissioner in Honan and administration commissioner in Hukuang. During these years he helped to relieve famine in Honan and modify compulsory service in Ching-chou 荊州, Hukuang, by setting up grades of service on the basis of wealth. At the close of 1480 he became governor of Shansi. One of his duties was the defense of the northern frontier, where he won some minor engagements against the Mongol invaders. In 1482 he was brought to the capital to become minister of Justice, and three years later returned to Shansi to supervise the relief work during a severe famine which affected all the northern provinces. Through his organizational efforts many thousand lives were saved during a six months' period. He went back to the capital in August, 1485. In October, 1486, he was sent to the borderland of Kweichow and Szechwan to investigate a charge made by Yang Yu 楊友

against his half brother Yang Ai 愛, the aboriginal chief of Po-chou 播州. The Yang clan had governed Po-chou and its adjoining areas for hundreds of years (see Yang Ying-lung); actions taken by its members, therefore, weighed heavily in local politics. For that reason any misjudgment on Ho's part might have led to grave consequences. After careful investigation Ho declared Yang Ai innocent. By his decision Ho was able to restore peace. His long memorial dealing with the situation, entitled *K'an-ch'u Po-chou shih-ch'ing shu* 勘處播州事情疏, 1 *ch.*, is one of the important sources for information on the aboriginal tribes in the Ming period.

One month after the enthronement of Chu Yu-t'ang (*q.v.*) in September, 1487, Ho Ch'iao-hsin was promoted to minister of Justice in Nanking, and four months later (February 7, 1488) to the same office in Peking. Within the next two years his health failed and he was twice compelled to take leave to recuperate. As minister he memorialized the throne, recommending that the Embroidered-uniform Guard be forbidden to make arrests without court orders, and that people in the capital should be prohibited from speaking Mongol and from wearing Mongol attire. These measures received imperial approval. His strict adherence to the letter of the law, however, provoked a number of officials, notably the powerful grand secretary Liu Chi (*q.v.*), who made life difficult for him. On various minor charges he was assessed fines, which were deducted from his pay with the result that he was without salary for two years. Early in 1491 a censor named Tsou Lu 鄒魯 (T. 公輔, cs 1475) accused him of receiving bribes and giving unlawful help to his relatives. After proving his innocence he asked for retirement in September, 1491. It was in 1517, fourteen years after he died, that he was given the posthumous name Wen-su 文肅.

Ho spent the last years of his life writing and editing. The following are attributed to him: *Chiao-ch'iu wen-chi* 椒丘

文集. 34 *ch.*, *wai-chi* 外集, 1 *ch.* (a copy of which is in the Library of Congress); *Ts'e-fu ch'ün-yü* 策府群玉, 3 *ch.*; *Chou-li-chi-chu* 周禮集注, 7 *ch.* (also in the Library of Congress); *Pai-chiang chuan, hsü pien*百將傳, 續編 (in *Wu-hsüeh ching-chuan* 武學經傳 of 1553); and the above mentioned memorial which may be found in the *ts'ung-shu*, *Chi-lu hui-pien*, made by Shen Chieh-fu (*q.v.*) and printed in 1617. Several other works credited to him seem not to have survived. The collection of his writings, *Chiao-ch'iu wen-chi*, was republished in 1694 under the title *Ho Wen-su chi*. This work, banned in the 1780s, survived and was reprinted in the mid-nineteenth century. Ho's reputation derives largely from his knowledge of the law, and the vigor with which he attempted to protect the weak, the wronged, and the distressed. He is also known as a bibliophile, having made a collection of thirty thousand *chüan*, almost all of which he carefully collated. He had a taste too for rare items; if a book were scarce and not for sale he would borrow it and have it transcribed.

Two of his great great-grandsons achieved some note: Ho T'ao 濤(T. 仲平), who took first place in the Kiangsi provincial examination of 1549 and compiled a work entitled *P'ing-shan wen-chi* 平山文集, 8 *ch.*, and *shih-chi* 詩集, 8 *ch.*, both listed in the *Ssu-k'u* catalogue; and Ho Yüan 源 (T. 仲深, Pth. 靖惠, 1519–89), who rose to be senior vice minister of Justice, and who wrote the *Hsin ch'üan-chi* 心泉集, 25 *ch.*, also listed in the same catalogue.

Bibliography

1/183/1a; 3/166/a; 5/44/48a; 8/32/10a; 40/21/9a; MSL (1963), Ying-tsung, 5913, Hsiao-tsung (1964), 3577; *Shansi t'ung-chih* (1892), 103/12a; *Honan t'ung-chih* (1914), 54/37a; *Chien-ch'ang-fu chih* 建昌府志 (1872), 8/21b; SK (1930), 23/1a, 137/8a, 170/11a, 178/1a, 6a; Sun Tien-ch'i (1957), 25, 41, 85; *Huang Ming-wen-hai* (microfilm), 6/5/16; Ch'ien Ch'ien-i (ECCP), *Lieh-ch'ao shih-chi*, 丙/5b; *Huang Ming tsou-shu lei-ch'ao* 奏疏類鈔, 56/4a; Ch'en Tzu-lung (ECCP), *Huang Ming ching-shih wen-pien*, 67/1a; L. of C.

Catalogue of Rare Books (1957), 18, 904; W. Franke, *Sources*, 7.5.1.

                                        Lee Hwa-chou

HO Ch'iao-yüan 何喬遠 (T. 穉孝, H. 匪莪), September 12, 1558-February 10, 1632, official and historian, was a native of Chinchiang 晉江, prefectural seat of Ch'üanchou 泉州 in Fukien. His father, Ho Ch'iung 炯 (T. 思默, H. 作菴, d. 1582), a student of the National University in the 1550s, served as assistant instructor in An-fu 安福, Kiangsi, and from 1560 to 1565 as instructor in Ching-chiang 靖江, Nan-Chihli. He spent the remaining years of his life at home lecturing and writing. Among his works is the *Ch'ing-yüan wen-hsien* 清源文獻, 18 ch., which records the writings, beginning with the T'ang dynasty, of men of his own prefecture. It was edited by Feng Meng-lung (*q.v.*) *et al.*, and printed in the Wan-li period. Two copies of this work are preserved in the Naikaku Bunko.

Ho Ch'iao-yüan, born in An-fu, studied with his father in his youth. A *chü-jen* of 1576, he became a *chin-shih* in 1586. Early in that year his mother died, so he hurried home from the capital for the mourning period and in 1588 returned to Peking. In May he received his first assignment—the post of secretary of the Yunnan bureau in the ministry of Justice. As it was a relatively unimportant position, he had time and leisure to compose poems and to undertake the task of compiling a history of the Ming dynasty, *Ming-shan ts'ang* 名山藏, and a treatise on litigation, *Yü chih* 獄志. He next served in the ministry of Rites, first as vice director of the bureau of provisions, then as director of the bureau of ceremonies. In 1594 he helped formulate the regulations on how members of the imperial clan might enter government service (*see* Chu Tsai-yü). In May of that year he memorialized against the negotiations for peace with the Japanese in Korea. Two months later he strongly protested the demotion of Ku Hsien-ch'eng (*q.v.*) and for this he was demoted to registrar of the provincial administration office of Kwangsi. His stay there was cut short by the untimely death of his wife. He returned to his native place and spent the next twenty-five years at home lecturing on Confucian Classics and writing books. He taught successively at three different academies in Ching-chiang. His reputation traveled far and wide. Chao Nan-hsing, Tsou Yüan-piao, Feng Ts'ung-wu (*qq. v.*) and he were called the Four Gentlemen 四君子. It was also during this period that he took part in compiling the gazetteer of his prefecture, *Ch'üan-chou-fu chih* (1612).

On September 6, 1620, soon after Chu Ch'ang-lo (ECCP) came to the throne, Ho was appointed vice minister in the Court of Imperial Entertainment. During the following years he occupied a series of posts: vice director of the Court of the Imperial Stud (1621), left transmission commissioner (1622), director of the Court of the Imperial Stud (1623), and transmission commissioner (January, 1624). In the middle of 1624 he requested retirement, pleading ill health. His petition granted, he received an honorary title as right vice minister of Revenue. For the next five years he lived in retirement at Ching shan 鏡山 (Mirror Hill) in Ching-chiang. During this period he helped local officials secure the services of Cheng Chih-lung (ECCP) for the defense of the coast against both the pirates and the Dutch.

Brought back to government service in October, 1629, he served as right vice minister of Works in Nanking. His measures for reducing the number of superfluous officials and in developing high morale within the bureaucracy apparently angered a number of people at court. In 1631, after presenting a memorial in which he asked the government to lift the ban on traveling by sea, he sent in his resignation and retired for the last time. For a while he lectured at Ch'üan-shan shu-yüan 泉山書院. He also wrote two expository essays: *Ch'eng-fen chieh* 懲忿解 (How to restrain one's anger) and *Chih-yü* 窒慾 *chieh* (How to restrain one's lusts). He died a year later at the age of seventy-three. His associates and disciples gave him the posthumous name Ching-shan hsien-sheng (Master of Mirror Hill). A shrine (何鏡山祠) was erected in his honor in 1632 shortly after his death.

Ho Ch'iao-yüan's fame rests chiefly on the following: 1) *Min shu* 閩書, a gazetteer of Fukien, 154 *ch.*, preface 1619, printed 1630; 2) *Ming-shan ts'ang*, 106 *ch.*, published 1640; and 3) *Huang Ming wen cheng* 皇明文徵, 74 + 1 *ch.*, an anthology, printed in 1631. These have to do with three of his major interests: his native province and the history and literature of the dynasty in which he served. For long these books have not been widely known, partly, one may presume, because the editors of the *Ssu-k'u* did not think highly enough of the first two to include them in the Imperial Library, and partly because the second was placed on the prohibited list in the 1780s. It had a preface by Ch'ien Ch'ien-i (ECCP) — always sufficient to make it suspect by Ch'ing officials—and in discussing the Mongols, Ho made unflattering comments, which drew the ire of the Manchus. Fortunately all three are available; there are copies of the *Min shu* in mainland China and in Japan, *Huang Ming wen cheng* in the Library of Congress and Naikaku Bunko, and *Ming-shan ts'ang* has recently (1971) been reprinted in Taipei.

Wolfgang Franke has this to say about the *Min shu*: "Comprehensive monograph on the province of Fukien from ancient times to 1620, but with particular consideration to the Ming period. Divided into twenty-two subjects such as geography, buildings, customs, population and taxation, civil and military officials officiating in Fukien, examinations and eminent men and women of Fukien, description of Liuch'iu Islands, plants, animals and other products, etc." To this description one should add that Ch'en Yüan (BDRC), fol-lowed by Paul Pelliot, has found in *chüan* 7 important material about the history of the Manichean religion in China and especially in Fukien, data which have recently been confirmed by discoveries made in the area of Ch'üan-chou. The *Ming-shan ts'ang*, also known as *Shih-san ch'ao i-shih* 十三朝遺史, contains historical data on the first thirteen reigns of the dynasty, i. e., from *ca.* 1368 to 1572. He drew materials not only from the *shih-lu* of each reign covered, but also from informal histories, and romances. Again, to quote Professor Franke, it includes "the imperial annals, chronicles of empresses, imperial princes, and hereditary nobles, biographies, and monographs on administrative subjects like geography, law, river-regulation, grain-transport, coining, military, horses and horse-markets, salt, etc." To this historical work should be added (*Ho-shih*) *Wan-li chi* (何氏)萬曆集, 30 (or 33) *ch.*, and *Hou chi*, 8 *ch.*, *T'ai-ch'ang* 泰昌 *chi*, 4 *ch.*, *T'ien-ch'i* 天啓 *chi*, 18 *ch.*, and *Ch'ung-chen* 崇禎 *chi*, not divided into *chüan*. The last must have been compiled by other hands, and (according to Sun Tien-ch'i, who supplies this information) was probably printed after 1644. The *Huang Ming wen cheng* is an anthology of prose and poems of literary figures (including priests and women), one hundred eighteen in all from the beginning of the dynasty to the reign of Ch'ung-chen. It is arranged by genre and within each genre subdivided by subject. Its scope and arrangement are modeled to a certain extent after the *Sung-wen chien* 宋文鑑, 150 *ch.*, by Lü Tsu-ch'ien (1137–81).

Several other books are credited to Ho. These include the *Ssu-ch'ao hsing yen chi* 四朝幸闈記 (Favorite eunuchs of four reigns), in which he dilates on Wang Chen 王振, Wang Chih 汪直, Liu Chin (*qq.v.*), and Wei Chung-hsien (ECCP), a collection of his prose and verse entitled *Ho Ch'iao-yüan chi* 集, 80 *ch.* (according to the essay on literature of the *Ming shih*), and *Ching-shan ch'üan chi* 全集, ? *ch.* (according to Huang Yü-chi, ECCP).

Ho had an elder brother, Ho Ch'iao-ch'ien 遷 (T. 齊孝, H. 屏臺), who became a *chü-jen* in 1576, and eventually served as judge in the Grand Court of Revision. Among Ho Ch'iao-yüan's three sons, the second, Ho Chiu-yün 九雲 (T. 舅悌, H. 培所), became a Hanlin bachelor shortly after he received the *chin-shih* in 1643. Then in 1644 he was promoted to be a compiler in the Hanlin Academy; but within a few days the army led by Li Tzu-ch'eng (ECCP) pressed northward toward the capital. As a result, Ho Chiu-yün was compelled to journey home. There he lived in quiet retirement until his death occurred not long after. A grand-nephew of Ho Ch'iao-yüan, Ho Yün-liang 運亮 (T. 中寅, H. 紫屏), also a *chin-shih* of 1643, held a series of posts: magistrate of Hai-k'ang 海康, Kwangtung (1643), prefect of Canton (1644), and vice minister in the Court of the Imperial Stud. Later he entered the Buddhist order and adopted the clerical name Chin-hsüan 金宣, though he also called himself Hsüeh-feng hsing-che 雪峯行者.

Bibliography

1/99/19b, 242/9b; 3/29/16a; 24/3/123a; 40/55/4b; SK(1930), 74/5b, 193/3a, 4b; MSL(1966), Kuang-tsung, 0166, Hsi-tsung, 2238; KC (1958), 5249, 5579; *Chin-chiang-hsien chih* (1765, repr. 1967), 173, 181, 231, 237; *Kwangtung t'ung-chih* (1934), 389, 632; *Kwangsi t'ung-chih* (1966), 12228; TSCC (1885–88), XIV: 215/3/15b, XXIII: 115/103/10a; Sun Tien-ch'i (1957), 71, 85, 186; Huang Yü-chi, *Ch'ien-ch'ing-t'ang shu-mu*, 25/17a; Hsieh Kuo-chen 謝國楨, *Wan Ming shih-chi k'ao* 晚明史籍考(Peiping, 1932), 5/17b; Chou Ch'üeh 周彀, "Kuan-ts'ang Ch'ing-tai chin-shu shu-lüeh" 館藏清代禁書述略, *Kuo-hsüeh t'u-shu-kuan* 國學圖書館 (Nanking, 1930), 23; Tsou I 鄒漪, fl. 1657, *Ch'i Chen yeh ch'eng* 啟禎野乘(1936), 7/33; *Ch'üan-chou-fu chih* (1870), 50/35b; Naikaku Bunko *Catalogue*, 425; L. of C. *Catalogue of Rare Books*, 1107; Ch'en Yüan, "Manicheism in China," Catholic University of Peking *Bull.*, no. 4 (May, 1928), 59; P. Pelliot, "Les tradi-tions manichéens au Fou-kien," TP, 22 (1923) 195, 198; L. Carrington Goodrich, "Recent Discoveries at Zayton," JAOS, Vol. 77 (1957),

164, Vol. 78 (1958), 48; W. Franke, *Sources*, 2.1.5, 8.13.4.

Lee Hwa-chou and L. Carrington Goodrich

HO Ch'in 賀欽 (T. 克恭, H. 醫閭山人, 醫閭先生, 閭山先生), April 16, 1437–January 3, 1511, official and thinker, was the only son of a merchant named Ho Meng-yüan 孟員 (April. 19, 1379–March 26, 1462). He held that his family originated in Ting-hai 定海, Chekiang. As his grand-uncle, Ho Chih-ch'u 志初, was ordered to serve in the garrison station of Kuang-ning 廣寧, Liao-ning, in the early years of the Yung-lo period, his father accom-panied him, settling at I-chou義州 nearby. So Ho Ch'in was born and brought up in a garrison area, bordering Jurchen ter-ritory, and started life as a student of military affairs. In 1456 he qualified for the *chü-jen*, and ten years later the *chin-shih*, a feat which was acclaimed by the people of I-chou, a place which had pro-duced few successful graduates. His offi-cial life commenced in 1467 with ap-pointment as supervising secretary of the office of scrutiny for Revenue. In 1468, during a drought, he suggested that the emperor improve his personal life and reform the administration. That same year, he became a disciple of Ch'en Hsien-chang (*q. v.*), then at the National University, and, under Ch'en's influence, decided to resign from the bureaucracy and return to private life in I-chou. When recalled to government service in 1488 as assistant administration commissioner of Shensi, he submitted a four-point memor-ial, urging the new emperor, Chu Yu-t'ang (*q. v.*), to promote true Confucian teach-ings, recruit the talented, control the eunuchs, and give due attention to pro-priety. But his advice went unheeded. The death of his mother made him go into mourning and retirement. He recommend-ed to the emperor's attention the merits of his teacher, Ch'en Hsien-chang, but also to no effect. In 1509 the local people of I-chou rose up in protest against the corrupt officials there, who assisted the eunuch Liu Chin (*q.v.*) in his misgovernment. Thanks to Ho Ch'in's efforts, they were calmed down, and bloodshed avoided. After his death, he is said to have been canonized as Kung-ting 恭定, but this was changed (1621) to Kung-ching 靖.

Although a disciple of Ch'en Hsienchang, whose portrait he kept on his wall for some thirty years, Ho Ch'in did not depart far from the teachings of Chu Hsi to whose book, *Chin-ssu lu*, he had been attracted from his early years. He was also a diligent reader of Lu Chiu-yüan (1139–92). Besides, unlike Chu Hsi, he did not pursue extensive study, but dwelt constantly upon the Four Books, the Five Classics (the *I-ching*, particularly), the *Chin-ssu lu*, and the *Hsiao-hsüeh* 小學. Under the influence of Ch'en Hsien-chang, he practiced quiet-sitting for the sake of gaining inner tranquility, and increasingly gave emphasis to the maintentance of reverence (ching 敬) and the recovery of the "dissipated" mind or heart (see *Mencius* 6A: 11, Legge, *Chinese Classics* II, 414). In his old age, he developed an even deeper interest in the Book of Changes. Although he founded no philosophical school, his influence in Liao-ning, where philosophy was little known, was important.

Ho Ch'in had five sons. The eldest, Ho Shih-tzu 士諮 (T. 士閻), acquired the *chü-jen* in 1492, and is said to have submitted a twelve-point memorial which met with no response. Ho Ch'in's grandson, Ho Ling-t'ai 凌臺, was a scholar who taught students on Mount I-wu-lü 醫無閭 山, the place where Ho Ch'in himself lived in retirement and studied philosophy. Ho's writings were published as *I-lü chi* 醫閭集, 9 *ch.* (or 10 *ch.*, according to one edition); this was later copied into the Imperial Library. A part of *chüan* 7 of this work appears as the *I-lü man-chi* 漫記 included in volume 10 of the *Chin-hsien hui-yen* 今 獻彙言, Shanghai, 1937. It had been listed for destruction during the latter part of

the Ch'ien-lung period as was also another book of his, dealing with various schools of thought, the *Pai-chia tsa-shuo* 百家雜說. This last work seems to have been lost. A third work, *I-lü yen-hsing lu* 言行錄, 8 *ch.*, is credited to him by Huang Yü-chi (ECCP) in his *Ch'ien-ch'ing-t'ang shu-mu*.

Bibliography

1/283/4a; 3/265/3b; 5/94/38a; 32/98/44a; 40/24/11a; 61/113/1a; 63/21/10a; 83/6/3a; MSL (1940), Hsitsung, 1/13b; KC (1958), 5184; Ho Ch'in, *I-lü chi* (1936); SK (1930), 171/2a; Lo Hsüeh-p'eng 羅學鵬, *Kuang-tung wen-hsien* 廣東文獻 (1863), 1st ser., introd. 3a, 4/6a; *Chen-hai-hsien chih* 鎮海縣 志 (1879), 17/20a; 21/18b, 21a; Yao Chin-yüan (1957), 168; Sun Tien-ch'i (1957), 237; Huang Yü-chi, *Ch'ien Ch'ing-t'ang shu-mu*, 10/17b.

Huang P'ei and Julia Ching

HO Ching-ming 何景明 (T. 仲默, H. 白坡, 大復山人), September 7, 1483-August 31, 1521, poet and man of letters, was a native of Hsin-yang 信陽, Ju-ning 汝寧 prefecture, Honan. His grandfather was a police officer of a local district; his father, Ho Hsin 信 (T. 文實, H. 梅溪, d. 1509), had charge of a post station in Shensi. In addition to Ho Ching-ming, who was the youngest child, Ho Hsin had two other sons by his first marriage, Ho Ching-shao 韶 (T. 仲律, cj 1483), and Ho Ching-yang 暘 (T. 仲升, cj 1498).

Ho Ching-ming spent his early years (1493–96) in Shensi accompanying his father. He returned home in 1497 and, a year later, at only fifteen years of age, was graduated as a *chü-jen*. He spent the following year in Pa-ling 巴陵, Szechwan, where his elder brother had lately been appointed vice magistrate. In 1502 he achieved the *chin-shih* but did not receive an appointment immediately. He spent the next two years in the capital, where his talents in literature soon brought him into the circle of the leading men of letters, such as Li Meng-yang, Pien Kung, Hsü Chen-ch'ing (*qq. v.*), and others.

In 1504, Ho became a drafter in the

central drafting office. When Emperor Chu Yu-t'ang (*q. v.*) died in June, 1505, Ho was ordered to make a trip to Yünnan to announce His Majesty's death to the tribespeople. Shortly after returning in June, 1507, because of his opposition to the eunuch Liu Chin (*q. v.*), he begged relief from duty under the pretext of ill health; but before the request could be approved in the following year, the eunuch had already succeeded in having him cashiered. Like most other officials who were so banished, however, Ho was exonerated immediately after Liu's downfall, but was prevented from assuming office owing to the death of his parents in May, 1509. In 1511, through the recommendation of Li Tung-yang (*q. v.*), Ho was reinstalled as drafter and served as an exegesist in the Grand Secretariat. It was in the following year that he came to the rescue of Li Meng-yang, then surveillance vice commissioner in charge of education in Kiangsi. The censor Chiang Wanshih (*see* Li Meng-yang) charged Li with intruding on the authority of the prince of Ning, Chu Ch'en-hao (*see* Wang Shou-jen), by inflicting punishment without prior consultation on his servants over disputes with students. Because of his friendship with Li, Ho solicited the assistance of Yang I-ch'ing (*q.v.*), the minister of Personnel, through whose intervention Li was spared punishment.

In February, 1514, the Ch'ien-ch'ing 乾清 palace was destroyed by fire. Emperor Chu Hou-chao (*q. v.*), interpreting the incident as an indication of Heaven's disapproval of his rule, invited his ministers to submit remonstrances. Ho then presented a bold and outspoken memorial pleading with the emperor to devote more attention to his administration, listen to the counsel of the ministers, and dissociate himself from the eunuchs and other imperial favorites who were meddling in state affairs. In 1517, after marking time in the central drafting office for a decade, Ho received a promotion as vice director of the bureau of honors in the ministry of Personnel, concurrently serving in the Grand Secretariat. In August of the following year he received a promotion to surveillance vice commissioner in charge of education in Shensi. There he improved the administration, promoted ethical principles, and initiated the students into Ch'in-Han models of composition. Being dissatisfied with the current curriculum, Ho drew up a new syllabus and compiled several selections from the Classics for instruction. A copy of this syllabus, entitled (*Ho Ta-fu* 大復) *hsüeh-yüeh ts'un-mu* 學約存目, 3 *ch.* (original preface 1531), has been reprinted in *Lung-t'an ching-she ts'ung-k'o* 龍潭精舍叢刻 by Liu Hai-han 劉海涵 (1922), who was also the author of Ho's chronological biography (年譜), included in the same collection. During this time Ho also initiated his students into the compilation of a comprehensive gazetteer of Shensi, called *Yung-ta chi* 雍大記, 36 *ch.*, which was not completed until after his death. Copies of this work are available in various collections including that at the Library of Congress.

Shortly after his appointment to Shensi, Ho was afflicted with ill health. In March, 1521, his condition deteriorated and in July he obtained permission to retire. He died a month later before reaching thirty-eight years of age. His immediate descendants were successful scholar-officials. His second son, Ho Li 立 (T. 豫甫, b. 1515), became a *chü-jen* in 1543. Ho Li's two sons, Ho Lo-wen 洛文 (T. 啟圖, cs 1565) and Ho Lo-shu 書 (cs 1577), were selected to be Hanlin bachelors. In 1562, on the initiative of Hsü Chunghsing (*q. v.*), the vice-prefect of Ju-ning, the local authorities erected a shrine in honor of Ho Ching-ming.

Ho owed his fame to his achievement as a poet and essayist. He has been paired with Li Meng-yang as the pioneer of a literary movement attempting to discard the ornamental style promoted by Li Tung-yang and emulate the model of the Ch'in-Han essayists and T'ang poets. After Li Meng-yang, Ho occupied the leading position among the writers of this movement, first in a group called ch'ien ch'i-tzu (seven early masters), and later in another, called ssu ta-chia (four great masters; *see* Li Meng-yang). In spite of his close association with Li, Ho himself was a critic of originality and a creative writer. He followed the principles espoused by Li in emulating the Ch'in-Han essayists and the T'ang poets, but was more concerned with substance than format, and was opposed to Li's emphasis on conformity in' both content and style. Noting this deviation and considering it injurious to his cause, Li sent Ho a letter in 1509, admonishing him to modify his stand and reasserting the correctness of his own guidelines. To Li's surprise, Ho refused to concede and instead expounded his own views about literature and poetry in his rejoinder of 1510. He denied that he was departing from Li's principles, arguing that he was only trying to point out the importance of capturing the spirit of the early masters when emulating their work rather than simply imitating their style. In this sense Ho stressed creation rather than imitation, while Li adhered to format and discouraged nonconformity. This exchange of polemics was followed by further debates between the followers of the two masters, and further strained their friendship.

This seems to have been the cause of cleavage between the two. But, as later writers see it, their difference has little to do with their principles; rather it has to do with the style and temperament of the two individuals. In style, Li was eloquent and invigorating, while Ho appeared more elegant and refined. In temperament, Li was more learned, tended to be bookish, and therefore more reserved, while Ho, being sentimental and unrestrained, was predisposed to inventiveness and change. This latter difference was visible not only in Ho and Li, but also became apparent among other members of the group. The reconciliation between the two, however, was made difficult because of Li's doctrinaire and haughty disposition, and the schism widened as their followers began to take sides, although Li and Ho still had much in common. It is interesting to note that when Ho was dying, he expressed the wish that Li compose his tomb-inscription, but his disciples refused to comply. They feared that Li might turn down the request, or else that he might insert unfavorable comments about their master because of their earlier differences. It was finally resolved, therefore, to let Ho's disciple Fan P'eng 樊鵬 (T. 少南, cs 1526) compose the record of conduct (行狀), and Meng Yang 孟洋 (T. 望之, 有涯, 1483–1534), his sister's son-in-law, compose the tomb-inscription. As a result, we are denied the post-mortem judgment of Ho by his senior and rival.

Ho Ching-ming left a prodigious collection of writings. His prose and poetry, collected by his friend K'ang Hai (*q. v.*) shortly after his death, were first engraved in 1524, and again in 1531, under the title of *Ho-shih chi* 何氏集, also known as *Ho Chung-mo* 仲默 *chi* or *Ta-fu chi*, 26 *ch.* An enlarged edition in 36 plus 1 *chüan* was printed in 1558 and reprinted in 1577 with slight amendments. This is the basis for the revised edition of 1749, 38 *ch.*, which was successively reprinted in 1858, 1889, and 1909. A selection of his poetry, entitled *Ho Chung-mo hsien-sheng shih-chi*, 15 *ch.*, was printed in 1603, together with that of Li Meng-yang, collectively known as *Ho-Li er* 何李二 *hsien-sheng shih-chi.*

In addition to the above writings, Ho compiled at least three other collections of poetry and prose-essays, presumably as textbooks for students, when he was in charge of the prefectural school in Shensi. Except for the selection on poetry of the Han and Wei periods, which is reported lost, those on the pre-Han yüeh-fu and on the classical essays are still extant. A copy of the former, entitled *Chi ku yüeh-fu* 輯古樂府, 3 *ch.*, is in the Columbia University Library and a copy of the latter, known as (*Ho Ta-fu hsien-sheng*) *hsüeh-yüeh ku-wen* 古文, 10 *ch.*, is in the National Central Library, Taipei.

Several of Ho's essays, originally presented in the enlarged version of his collected works, appear under separate titles in a number of *ts'ung-shu*. These include, among others, *Ta-fu lun* 論, essays on philosophical topics, in Yüan Chiung (*q. v.*), *Chin-sheng yü-chen chi* (Peking, 1959), vol. 2; *Ssu-chen tsa-yen* 四箴雜言, combining his "Four Admonitions" with a miscellany of sayings, in Wang Wen-lu (*q. v.*), *Po-ling hsüeh-shan* (Changsha, 1940), vol. 14; and *Ho-tzu* 何子 *tsa-yen* and *Hsiang-she chih-chih* 鄉射直指 in *Shuo-fu hsü* (*see* T'ao Tsung-i).

Bibliography

1/286/13b; 5/94/64a; 40/30/1a; 61/146/18a; 63/26/17a; 64/丁1/10a; 84/丙/71a; 86/10/2b; MSL (1965), Wu-tsung, 1486, 2217; Shih-tsung, 183; *Ho Ta-fu chih* (NLP microfilm nos. 912, 926); Chang Hsüan, *Hsi-yüan wen-chien lu* 6/23a, 8/63a, 11/10a; *Ju-ning-fu chih* (1796), 19/18a; *Hsin-yang-chou chih* (1925), 8/4a; SK (1930), 73/3a, 171/9b, 174/5b; Liu Hai-han, *Ho Ta-fu hsien-sheng nien-p'u* (*Lung-tan ching-she ts'ung-k'o*); Kuo Shao-yü 郭紹虞, *Chung-kuo wen-hsüeh p'i-p'ing shih* 中國文學批評史 (Shanghai, 1961), 304; Yoshikawa Kojirō 吉川幸次郎, *Gen-min shi kaisetsu* 元明詩概說 (Tokyo, 1962), 184; Yokota Terutoshi 橫田輝俊, "Ho Ching-ming no bungaku" 何景明の文學, *The Hiroshima University Studies (Literature Department)* 廣島大學文學部紀要, Vol. 25, no. 1 (December, 1965), 246; James J. Y. Liu, *The Art of Chinese Poetry* (Chicago, 1962), 79.

Hok-lam Chan

HO Hsin-yin 何心隱 (original name Liang Ju-yüan 梁汝元, T. 夫山, H. 桂乾), 1517–79, writer and thinker, was a native of Yung-feng 永豐, Kiangsi. Although he passed the civil examination with highest honors at the district level in 1546, he did not serve in the government. It was probably at this time that he met his teacher, Yen Chün 顏鈞, a member of the T'ai-chou branch of the Wang Yang-ming school (*see* Wang Ken), who led him to become a member of it. Liang organized his clan into what was called Ts'ui-ho-t'ang 萃和堂, which handled all matters concerning education, ceremonies such as weddings, funerals, and libations, payment of taxes, labor service for the government, and relief for the old and poor. All the young members of the clan lived and ate together with complete equality until their marriage. The practice of having the clan organization collect taxes from each member and then deliver them to the government in one payment prevented government officials from exacting bribes; this annoyed the local bureaucracy (1559). Thanks to the intervention of Hu Tsung-hsien (*q.v.*), famous for his exploits against the wo-k'ou, Liang escaped severe punishment, and changed his name to Ho Hsin-yin. Shortly after this, Ho went to Peking with a friend of his who held a high office in the government. There he befriended Keng Ting-hsiang and Keng Ting-li (*see* Keng Ting-hsiang), and through them (in 1560) met the future Grand Secretary Chang Chü-cheng (*q.v.*), but the two did not see eye to eye. Ho opened a hui-kuan 會館, a kind of club, to befriend people in all walks of life who boasted of any specialty. The wording fang-chi tsa-liu 方技雜流 in *Ming-ju-hsüeh-an* of Huang Tsung-hsi (ECCP) suggests that many of the club members were of plebeian origin and in questionable professions. Reportedly it was a magician friend of Ho who planted seeds of doubt in the mind of the superstitious emperor with respect to the loyalty of Yen Sung (*q.v.*). This eventually led to the downfall of Yen and his son (1562), heretofore the most powerful and most hated men in the capital. But before that could happen Ho had to flee the capital for fear of retaliation.

From 1562 to 1564 he traveled over much of Fukien giving lectures in the traditional neo-Confucian fashion. He appears to have stayed for a while with Lin Chao-en (*q.v.*). During the following three years he wandered in the Yangtze valley, continuing to give lectures on Confucian themes, visiting his increasing circle of friends, which included Lo Ju-fang (*q.v.*), then prefect of Ning-kuo. In 1567 he traveled to Chungking with the prefect designate of that city, and there they ran into a serious uprising of members of the White Lotus sect. The pacification campaign was concluded within a month, and Ho was given some responsibility for its swift success. He set up another organization in that city, but the nature of it is obscure. In 1569 he resumed his travels up and down the Yangtze valley. There is even less information about his activities during the next decade. It is known that he was frequently in the company of the brothers Keng Ting-hsiang and Keng Ting-li, who were probably the most gregarious among the prominent neo-Confucians of the time. In 1576 the governor of Hukuang issued an order for Ho's arrest on the charge of banditry, but Ho went into hiding just in time. He returned to his native place (1577) to build his parents' graves, and continued to evade the authorities until 1579 when he was apprehended at Ch'i-men 祁門 (Anhwei). There was much public agitation over his arrest, his friends and disciples in and out of the government trying in every way to rescue him from prison. Chang Chü-cheng, who had since become senior grand secretary, is said to have harbored a personal grudge against Ho, allegedly for the latter's criticisms of himself, and hence was in no mood to show mercy. Ho was moved first to Nanchang and then to Wuchang where he died in prison as a result of injuries suffered from flogging, about six months after his arrest.

What remains of Ho's complete works amounts to only slightly over one hundred pages. In his writings he tends to uphold the brand of Confucianism which was acceptable to the more orthodox of the Confucian school. He recognized that all human desires arise from nature and he advocated moderation in everything. In his lecturing he traced the transmission of truth all the way back to such mythical figures as Fu Hsi and Shen Nung. This is interpreted by the modern scholar, Hou Wai-lu 侯外廬, as an attempt on Ho's part to appeal to the superstitions of the "proletariat." It is worth noting that the topics Ho dealt with—quietude, reverence, doctrine of the mean, and reinterpretation of the Book of Changes—are those which interested the Sung Confucians most. Such contemporary problems as good and evil, liang-chih (良知), unity of action and knowledge, choice between sudden enlightenment and general cultivation, ultimate truth (pen-t'i 本體) are nowhere touched upon in Ho's extant writings. In fact there is no mention of any of the names of the school of Wang Shou-jen (*q.v.*). Ho's thinking can hardly be regarded as original or provocative, and his historical importance must be attributed to his personality and activities. His martyrdom certainly attracted much sympathy, even from Ku Hsien-ch'eng (*q.v.*), who was no admirer of the T'ai-chou movement.

Ho Hsin-yin was a fourth-generation spiritual descendant of Wang Shou-jen, whose teaching he supposedly received through Yen Chün, disciple of Hsü Yüeh 徐樾 (T. 子直, H. 波石, cs 1532), the best-known disciple of Wang Ken. According to Huang Tsung-hsi, the departure from orthodox neo-Confucianism, already visible in Wang himself, reached its apogee in Yen Chün and Ho Hsin-yin. Huang's judgment may have been directed more at the actions of these thinkers than at their philosophy. Yen did believe in the purity of the original nature of man and hence in the spontaneity of action unbridled by conventional morality. But he advocated nothing more radical than that. Lo Ju-fang, another of Yen's disciples, who befriended both Ho Hsin-yin and Li Chih (*q.v.*), thus serving as a link between the two, since they never met, also taught nothing more extreme.

The actions of these men are worth comparing. Yen's teacher, Hsü Yüeh, died in battle. Yen went personally to the battleground to search for his remains which he took home for burial. When a friend of his was banished to an inhospitable region, he went along to share the hardships. He often traveled from place to place offering assistance to those in distress. On the other hand, he is portrayed by his enemies as barely literate, greedy, and unscrupulous. According to Wang Shih-chen (*q.v.*), Ho Hsin-yin eventually disassociated himself from Yen Chün and did not continue to acknowledge him as master.

In the case of Ho Hsin-yin, we have reports of transgressions even more serious. He is said to have sent Lü Kuang-wu 呂光午, a disciple of his who also happened to be a well-known knight-errant, to travel all over the country to seek people of talent and ambition. Lü, taking along several followers and a great deal of money, met and enlisted people who were monks, merchants, servants, and even thieves and hoodlums. It is hinted that Ho was plotting the seizure of power. When Ho died, Lü and another follower, braving the fury of the chief grand secretary, wept in public over Ho's corpse and took it home for burial.

When one looks for a common pattern in the lives of these men, one discovers a readiness to take action against injustice, a willingness to place loyalty to friends above one's obligations to the state and family, and even above one's own life, a disregard of such matters as money, an unscrupulousness in selecting means if the end were worthy, a freedom in choosing associates, and a personal courage that belittled death, which distinguish them from all Confucianists since the beginning of the Sung dynasty (960). As for Ho Hsin-yin, in whom these qualities found their fullest expression, there is added the use of aliases, his perpetual peregrinations, and the strange circumstances of his death. We are then tempted to accept the opinion shared by one of his critics and one of his eulogists, and consider him a knight-errant in the guise of a Confucian.

Ho Hsin-yin left one work, the *Ts'uan-t'ung chi* 爨桐集, which Chang Su 張宿 published in 1625. A copy of this edition is preserved in the Peking National Library. Another collection, even shorter and probably never published, is entitled *Liang Fu-shan i chi* 夫山遺集. Jung Chao-tsu (*see* Feng Meng-lung) consulted both in publishing in 1960 *Ho Hsin-yin chi*, a complete collection of Ho's extant writings, together with all relevant historical and biographical accounts related to Ho's life and death. This includes Ho's longest philosophical essay, *Yüan-hsüeh yüan-chiang* 原學原講, 1 *ch.*, originally written as a defense of public philosophical discussion shortly after the downfall of Chang Chü-cheng in 1579, various shorter essays and letters, 3 *ch.*, as well as those accounts and documents which were culled from the works of Ku Hsien-ch'eng, Li Chih, Huang Tsung-hsi, Keng Ting-hsiang, and Wang Shih-chen, and from local gazetteers. A selection of Ho Hsin-yin's own writings has been translated into English by Ronald G. Dimberg.

Bibliography

83/32/1a; *Ming-shih* (Taiwan ed.), 18/130; *KC* (1958), 3977; Ku Ying-t'ai (ECCP), *Ming ch'ao chi-shih pen-mo* (1658), 54/25a; Jung Chao-tsu (comp.), *Ho Hsin-yin chi* (Peking, 1960); *id.*, *Ming-tai ssu-hsiang shih* 明代思想史 (Taipei, 1962), 218; Hsi Wen-fu 嵇文甫, *Wan-Ming ssu-hsiang shih-lun* 晚明思想史論 (Chungking, 1944), 35; Hou Wai-lu, *Chung-kuo ssu-hsiang t'ung-shih* 中國思想通史 (Peking, 1960), 1003; Okada Takehiko 岡田武彥, *Ō Yōmei to Minmatsu no jugaku* 王陽明と明末の儒學 (Tokyo, 1970), 231; W. T. de Bary (ed.), *Self and Society in Ming Thought* (New York, 1970), 178; Ronald G. Dimberg, *The Life and Thought of Ho Hsin-yin 1517–1579, The Sage and Society — A Sixteenth Century View* (doctoral dissertation, Columbia University, 1970).

Wu Pei-yi and Julia Ching

HO Liang-chün 何良俊 (T. 元朗, H. 柘湖居士, 青溪漫士), 1506-73, scholar, was a native of Hua-t'ing 華亭, Sung-chiang 松

江 prefecture. His family had lived since the early years of the Ming in a town called Che-lin 柘林 situated on the coast, some twenty-five miles southeast of Shanghai. His grandfather, a frugal farmer, left about one hundred acres of rich farmland, inherited by his two sons, Ho Ssu 嗣 (1457-1535) and Ho Hsiao 孝 (January, 1460-1538), who with their families lived together. Ho Ssu, tall and dignified and a man who commanded respect, served from about 1490 to about 1515 as one of the liang-chang 糧長 (grain tax collectors) for his section of the district. He invited the best teachers for his younger brother and later for the latter's three sons, Ho Liang-tso 佐 (T. 參之, H. 五山, 1496-1563), Ho Liang-chün, and Ho Liang-fu 傅 (T. 叔皮, H. 大壑, 1509-63, cs 1541). Ho Ssu did not have a son. According to the rules of inheritance, whereby the eldest branch of a family, if without male issue, must be continued by adoption from the nearest branch, he made Ho Liang-chün his heir.

In 1513 Ho Liang-tso was selected to be a student in the district school. Nine years later Ho Liang-chün and Ho Liang-fu also received that honor. The magistrate who conducted the examination and passed the two younger brothers was the philosopher Nieh Pao (q.v.). Ho Liang-chün graduated from the district school in 1532 and moved on to the National University at Nanking, but failed to pass the higher examinations. The younger brother, Ho Liang-fu, however, became a chü-jen in 1540 and a chin-shih in the following year. The latter's success was probably a serious blow to Ho Liang-chün's ego, for he considered himself the better scholar. He ranked his own learning and character so high that he named his studio Ssu-yu-chai 四友齋 (Four friends hall). In this he alluded to Chuang-tzu, Wei-mo-chieh (Vimalakīrti, a legendary disciple of Buddha), Po Chü-i (772-846), and himself. He failed once more (1546) in the provincial examination. This and the death of his wife must have affected him. He began to complain of what apparently were stomach ulcers and probably suffered from mental depression too, for he later described himself as having been frequently irritated by an argument, bursting out with abusive language or unorthodox ideas. After two years of suffering he began to recover by taking a different attitude towards life, changing to a relaxed enjoyment of sensuous pleasures. He kept a troupe of young actresses trained in song-plays, and he himself studied music and choreography. This change may be illustrated by a story he told in later years about a party in Soochow around the year 1562, at which he produced a tiny shoe belonging to the famous prostitute of Nanking, Wang Sai-yü 王賽玉, to serve as a wine cup; this inspired the scholar, Wang Shih-chen (q.v.), to write an impromptu poem celebrating the occasion.

In 1550 Ho Liang-chün completed a book of exempla culled from the Classics and the Histories, entitled Ho-shih yü-lin 何氏語林, 30 ch. (recently reproduced in the Ssu-k'u chen-pen 珍本, ser. 3). It followed the style of the Shih-shuo hsin-yü 世說新語 by Liu I-ch'ing (403-44) and in fact was designed as a supplement to that classical work. The famous scholar-artist, Wen Cheng-ming (q.v.), contributed a preface highly praising Ho's thought and style. By this time Ho had abandoned all hope of succeeding in the civil examinations and planned a different way of entering officialdom. By publishing the Ho-shih yü-lin he probably wanted to prove to the world his attainment in scholarship and literary proficiency, that his failure in the examinations was not due to any lack in these qualities. Wen Cheng-ming happened also to have failed in the examinations and obtained a minor government position by recommendation.

Ho went to Peking (1552) to apply for an appointment, hoping that his status as a scholar in the National University would help him. It happened that the grand secretaries of that time, Yen Sung, Hsü Chieh (qq.v.), and Lü Pen (see Cheng

Ching) were all old acquaintances of his. In addition, the minister of War, Nieh Pao, was his former patron. On the recommendation of these men, Ho was appointed k'ung-mu 孔目 (chief clerk) in the Nanking Hanlin Academy—a post low in rank but usually filled by a man of letters. During the five years in that office (1553-58) he was treated courteously by such superiors as Chao Chen-chi (*q.v.*) and with deference by such other high officials as Sun Sheng 孫陞 (T. 志高, H. 季泉, 1501-70) and Wang Wei-chen 王維楨 (T. 允寧, H. 槐野, 1507-January 24, 1556). His younger brother, Ho Liang-fu, was in Nanking too, having served in the ministry of Rites there since 1549. Ho Liang-fu retired because of illness in 1555 and Ho Liang-chün himself terminated his service three years later. Both had to stay on in Nanking, however, because their house in Che-lin, including the library known as Ch'ing-sen-ko 清森閣, had been destroyed in 1555 during the disturbances caused by pirates. Two years later Ho Liang-fu returned to Che-lin to oversee rebuilding. At this time the Ho family also contributed substantially to the construction of walls around the town.

Ho Liang-chün remained in Nanking until he moved to Soochow in 1561. Two years later, following the death of his younger brother, he returned to Che-lin to look after family affairs. There he rebuilt his home, which he called Hsiang-yen ching-she 香嚴精舍, and continued to use the name "Four friends hall" for his study. There he edited the collected works of Ho Liang-fu, entitled *Ho Li-pu chi* 禮部集, 10 *ch.*, engraved about 1563. Later he edited a collection of his own poems and essays, entitled *Ho Han-lin chi*, 28 *ch.*, engraved in 1565. Both works were reproduced in 1932 under the collective title *Yün-chien liang Ho-chün chi* 雲間兩何君集. In his last years he edited his collection of miscellaneous notes, entitled *Ssu-yu-chai ts'ung-shuo* 叢說, which he printed with movable type in 1569 in 30 *chüan*. Later he continued to add to the collection and had completed several more *chüan* in manuscript before his death. In 1579 a new edition of the *Ssu-yu-chai ts'ung-shuo*, 38 *ch.*, was engraved. This work represented his important contribution to scholarship, for it contains not only his writings of literary criticism, classical studies, opinions on music, painting, ethics, and so forth, but also important records of contemporary affairs and anecdotes about his acquaintances; this constitutes a valuable source for the student of his time. The book, distinguished by a lucid and interesting style, was reengraved in 1621. Parts of it appeared in various collectanea and a complete edition was printed in 1959.

Born to a landlord family and having a foster father who had been a tax collector, Ho was conversant with the problems of taxation and tenancy. According to him the system of liang-chang began to be abused in the Cheng-te period, which was the reason why his foster father gave up the service. From that time on the tax collectors, working in collusion with the magistrates' offices, enriched themselves by taking bribes to exempt the wealthy. They tried to make up the quota by exacting more from the rest of the population. The result was that in his native place the annual tax quota could seldom be met in time after 1510, and the tax collectors were no longer respected members of the local society. Other abuses by government officials also increased in severity as time went on. Contemporary records confirm his observations.

Ho Liang-chün also lamented the decline of the study of Confucian Classics, blaming that trend on the regulation of the Yung-lo period which required every candidate in the civil examinations to base his replies chiefly on the commentaries of Sung men, especially those by Chu Hsi. He also pointed out some of Chu's mistakes and advocated the printing of pre-Sung commentaries. In these respects he anticipated the scholars of the following centuries.

Bibliography

1/287/4a; 5/23/28a; 64/戊 8/13a; 84/丁上 /73b; Wen Cheng-ming, *Fu-t'ien-chi*, 17/19a; Yeh Ch'ang-ch'ih 葉昌熾, *Ts'ang-shu chi-shih-shih* 藏書紀事詩 (1958), 123; Li Tz'u-ming (ECCP), *Yüeh-man-t'ang tu-shu-chi* (1963), 966; *Sung-chiang-fu chih* 松江府志 (1817), 53/19a; Naikaku Bunko *Catalogue* (1962), 268, 283; L. of C. *Catalogue of Rare Books*, 754.

Chaoying Fang

HO T'ang 何瑭 (or 塘, T. 粹夫, H. 虛舟, 栢齋), December 8, 1474-October 27, 1543, scholar and thinker, was born in Wu-chih 武陟, Huai-ch'ing 懷慶 prefecture, Honan. The Ho family, originally from Yangchow, settled in Honan in the early Ming when Ho's great-grandfather, a platoon commander, was assigned to the Huai-ch'ing Guard during the reign of the first emperor.

Quiet and serious, and the first in his family to distinguish himself in scholarship, Ho topped the list in the provincial examination of 1501 and achieved the *chin-shih* a year later. He was appointed a Hanlin bachelor, then became a compiler (1504), and after the death of Emperor Chu Yu-t'ang (*q.v.*) took part in the composition of the Veritable Records, *Hsiao-tsung shih-lu*. In 1507, shortly after Chu Hou-chao (*q.v.*) became emperor, Ho submitted a memorial urging the restoration of the post of diarist for recording history, but received no response. Following the completion of the *Hsiao-tsung shih-lu* (May, 1509), he was promoted to be a senior compiler (June) and served as tutor to the eunuchs in the palace. In the following year, however, he offended the notorious eunuch Liu Chin (*q.v.*) by not kneeling before him, while criticizing a certain member of the Hanlin for doing so. It is said that Liu Chin sent his agents to spy on Ho, but when they found only good to report, Liu became Ho's admirer and was about to promote him when Ho pleaded ill health and obtained permission to retire (April, 1510). He was reinstated in his former position (March, 1511) after Liu's downfall.

In the next two years Ho submitted a number of recommendations, aimed at better management of state affairs and the general welfare of the people. In three-point memorandum he suggested ways to eliminate corruption as the first step to improve the administration, strict discipline to boost the morale of the military, and careful use of resources to strengthen the state. In addition, he presented five papers on defense matters to the Grand Secretariat, but none of these received serious attention. In May, 1513, he was assigned to lecture on the Classics before the emperor at a formal audience; he appeared in shabby attire and ungroomed, and spoke incoherently. This was Ho's natural habit, but the emperor took it as a show of disrespect and ordered him flogged. After the Grand Secretaries pleaded for him, he was saved from the beating but demoted to be the vice magistrate of K'ai-chou 開州, Pei-Chihli. While at this post, he initiated a reallocation of taxes in three grades according to land productivity, and expedited the repair of embankments in Huang-ling kang 黃陵岡 to prevent the flooding of the Yellow River. As a reward for his performance he was promoted to be the vice prefect of Tung-ch'ang 東昌, Shantung (June, 1515), but left office five months later due to illness. He then spent the following eight years in his native place, during which period his father died (1521).

In September, 1522, shortly after Chu Hou-ts'ung (*q.v.*) ascended the throne, Ho received a summons to be the surveillance vice commissioner of Shansi, but was unable to accept because of mourning requirements. In 1523 he was appointed surveillance vice commissioner in charge of education in Chekiang. In this capacity he exhorted the students to place a higher value on serious study, and discouraged them from taking short cuts to achieve a bureaucratic career. Early in 1526 Ho became the vice minister, then (May, 1527) the minister of the Court of Imperial Sacrifices. In July of this year he was promoted to be vice minister of Works in Nanking. While in this office he scrutinized the records and proposed a number of measures to reduce governmental expenses. In the next two years he served as vice minister of three different ministries in Peking: Works (September, 1528), Revenue (January 1529), and Rites (April). In June, 1529, he became censor-in-chief in Nanking, but after serving for only a short time he asked permission to retire on the ground of ill health. His initial request was disregarded, but after a second plea the emperor finally allowed him to take leave.

During his retirement Ho led a simple, unspectacular life, and spent his time in study and teaching. He was devoted to his mother, and when she died early in 1543, it is said that he was so emotionally disturbed that he became seriously ill. He passed away shortly afterwords, at the age of sixty-eight. In January, 1568, he received the posthumous honorific of minister of Rites and the canonized name Wen-ting 文定 (cultured and resolute).

Ho distinguished himself as a scrupulous official and capable administrator, but perhaps was better known as a thinker. He was close to the Chu Hsi orthodoxy in his emphasis on the doctrine calling for the investigation of things and applying oneself to practical problems. What was of prime importance, according to him, was the rectification of one's own conduct and, by extension, matters that concerned the state. Perhaps as one of the northern school he disliked pretentiousness and ornateness of expression for he contended that the words of the sages were all contained in the Classics; hence, he held it pertinent to examine the ancient works rather than rely on pedantic commentaries by later scholars.

Like most of his contemporaries, Ho expressed a deep interest in the theories of yin and yang, two key concepts in the neo-Confucian philosophy of cosmology. He believed that the two, representing "form" and "spirit" as the primal forces of creation, in fact complement each other and are inseparable. On this basis Ho developed his theory on mathematics, the calendar, music, and medicine. He further elaborated his view in reply to the challenge of Hsü Kao (q.v.) and Wang T'ing-hsiang (q.v.), who disagreed with Ho's findings. The pros and cons of their argument have been summarized in *Ming-ju hsüeh-an* (*chüan* 9) by Huang Tsung-hsi (ECCP). Ho's attitude towards Buddhism and Taoism is also worthy of note. He is said to have detested Buddhism so much that he could not bear the sight of the statue of Maitreya. But, like many Confucianists of his time, he was moderately tolerant of religious Taoism. In one instance he compared Taoist priests and female shamans to the junior staff in a prefectural or magisterial office, commenting that they appropriate the power of the heavenly deities in the same fashion as the junior functionaries appropriate the authority of their superiors. Ho was, moreover, a devoted teacher. During his retirement he recruited scores of students, the most outstanding being Chu Hou-huan, father of the celebrated musician and mathematician Chu Tsai-yü (q.v.). The latter, under the influence of his father, took a deep interest in Ho's writings on the mathematical principles of music and the calendar. Probably for this reason, Ho was mentioned in the biography of Chu Tsai-yü in the *Ch'ou jen chuan* (Biographies of mathematicians and scientists) compiled by Juan Yüan (ECCP). The connection between the two families was further strengthended by Chu Tsai-yü's marriage to Ho's great-great-granddaughter in 1570.

Ho's collection of writings entitled *Ho Po-chai wen-chi* 栢齋文集, including his memorials, essays on neo-Confucianism, prose and poetic works, were printed by Chu Hou-huan in 1549, six years after Ho's death. A later edition, 10 *ch.*, slightly condensed, appeared in 1554. The revised version, called *Ho Wen-*

ting kung wen-chi, 11 *ch.*, was printed in 1576 and again in 1580. A collection of his essays on neo-Confucianism, including the *Ju-hsüeh kuan-chien* 儒學管見, and *Yin-yang kuan-chien*, is presented in *Ming-ju hsüeh-an* and in *Kuang li-hsüeh pei-k'ao* 廣理學備考, edited by Fan Kao-ting 范鄗鼎 (1825), volume 5. (The *Yin-yang kuan-chien* is also available in *Pai-ling hsüeh-shan* 百陵學山 [1940], Vol. 13.) A sample of his tz'u poetry, called *Po-chai hsien-sheng yüeh-fu* 先生樂府, is included in *Yin-hung-i so-k'o ch'ü* 飲虹簃所刻曲 by Lu Ch'ien 盧前 (1905-51).

Bibliography

1/282/34a; 5/64/18a; 8/49/11a; 40/28/5b; 64/丁 13/6a; 83/49/1a; MSL (1964) Hsiao-tsung, 3416, 4082; Wu-tsung (1965), 1123, 1152, 1346, 1598, 2067, Shih-tsung, 220, 1677, 1715, 2079, 2258, 2359, 2394, Mu-tsung, 409; KC (1958), 3383, 3392, 3401, 3648; *Huai-ch'ing-fu chih* (1786), 17/10a, 25b; 29/8b, 31/21a; (*Ho*) *Po-chai chi* (NLP microfilm no. 1002); Cheng Hsiao, *Chin-yen*, in *Chi-lu hui-pien*, 146/49a; SK (1930), 105/5a, 134/1b, 171/9a; Juan Yüan, *Ch'ou-jen chuan* (Taipei, 1965), 31/371; Liu Ts'un-yan, "The Penetration of Taoism into the Ming neo-Confucian Elite," TP, LVII, 1–4 (1971), 86.

Hok-lam Chan

HO Ting 何鼎 (T. 文鼎), died 1497/8, a eunuch in the service of Emperor Chu Yu-t'ang (*q.v.*), known for his persistent remonstrances with the monarch and criticism of imperial sycophants, was a native of Yü-hang 餘杭, Chekiang. Described as frugal, upright, and bookish, Ho Ting expressed a deep concern for the well-being of the state. His constructive proposals for reform in government affairs, however, came to annoy the emperor who charged him with presuming on his prerogatives, and his confrontation with the brothers of the empress, Chang Yen-ling and Chang Ho-ling (*q.v.*), brought his life to a tragic end.

In July, 1489, Ho Ting, then a junior palace attendant, submitted the first of a series of memorials to the emperor in which he complained that the court had been filled with an extraordinary number of officials, civil and military, who had acquired their positions through improper channels. He pointed out that there had been too many promotions in the ranks of the Embroidered-uniform Guard which were not only unnecessary, but which also placed an extra burden on the treasury. He also charged that the excessive use of the ch'uan-feng procedure, whereby a eunuch transmitted an imperial order directly to the Grand Secretariat to appoint a certain person to an office or to make a promotion, had produced an inordinate number of unqualified functionaries (*see* Chu Chien-shen). Ho then urged the court to look into the records of civil and military personnel dating back to 1457, and cashier those who did not possess proper credentials, or had obtained their positions on other grounds than their own merits. The matter was referred to the ministry of Personnel for deliberation and resulted in a considerable diminution of abuses.

Three years later (September, 1492), Ho Ting, then a vice director of the firewood office, memorialized again. In this communication he pointed out that the granaries in T'ung-chou 通州 (Pei-Chihli) being located southwest of the city wall, were at a spot not conveniently accessible to the soldiers in the capital and not easy to defend in times of trouble. He then proposed the construction of new granaries within the walls of Peking and the dredging of the section of the Hui-t'ung 會通 River (also known as Ta-t'ung 大通 River) at its northern end, which connected ultimately with the Grand Canal (*see* Juan An). This was to enable the grain boats to unload their cargoes by the Ta-t'ung bridge (close to Peking) to expedite delivery. The officials in the ministry of Revenue seconded his proposal on the new granaries in the capital, but delayed action on account of the cost; however, they implemented his suggestion to dredge the Hui-t'ung River.

In the next few years Ho Ting submitted several additional memorials, with a few anonymous ones, expressing his frank opinion on state affairs, and on various occasions pleaded with the emperor to appoint him to a more responsible position. His persistent memorializing and carping criticism finally exhausted the patience of the monarch, and his attack on the empress's brothers cut short his career. It is said that Ho Ting, who had long detested Chang Ho-ling and Chang Yen-ling for their unbecoming behavior, struck them with a guard's weapon on one occasion when they tried to spy on the emperor in his private quarters. Learning of this, the empress was outraged and had Ho consigned to the custody of the Embroidered-uniform Guard.

When the news of Ho's arrest leaked out in April, 1497, several court officials, including the supervising secretary of Justice, P'ang P'an (*see* Liu Lin), and the minister of Revenue Chou Ching (*q.v.*), hurried to his defense and besought the emperor to pardon him. They held that, if Ho Ting were to be penalized for having submitted frank opinions on state affairs his punishment would have a bad effect on the court officials, who might be afraid of speaking their minds. Their appeal, however, disturbed the emperor, who charged his critics with meddling in the private affairs of the monarch, and punished them accordingly. In the meantime, while Ho languished in prison, the eunuch Li Kuang (*q.v.*), a sycophant of the empress, had him so severely beaten that Ho soon died of his wounds. In November of the following year, accepting the protest of a secretary of the ministry of Justice, Ch'en Feng-wu 陳鳳梧 (T. 文鳴, H. 靜齋, cs 1496, 1475–1541), the emperor granted Ho a posthumous patent of merit with a proper burial, and approved the erection of a stele in his memory.

Bibliography

1/304/19a; 5/117/24a; MSL (1964), Hsiao-tsung, 602, 607, 1272, 2205, 2216, 2492; KC (1958), 2588, 2703; T'ang Shu 唐樞, *Kou-shen chi* 國琛集 in Shen Chieh-fu, ed., *Chi-lu hui-pien*, 103/43a; Ho Ch'iao-yüan, *Ming-shan ts'ang* (1970), 5417; *Yü-hang-hsien chih* (1919), 26/9a.

Hok-lam Chan

HO Tung-ju 何棟如 (T. 子極), cs 1598, the son of Ho Chan-chih 湛之 (T. 公露, H. 矩所, 疎園, 1551–1612, cs 1589), a onetime assistant administration commissioner of Chekiang, was a native of Chiang-ning 江寧 (Nanking), who, in his official career, suffered because of his outspokenness. After graduating as *chin-shih*, Ho Tung-ju became prefectural judge of Hsiang-yang 襄陽, Hukuang. Highly correct in his actions, he incurred the displeasure of Ch'en Feng (*q.v.*), a eunuch serving as tax collector, for resisting his attempts to make improper demands on the miners in Ho's area. Ho was cast into prison, his name being stricken from the register. His fellow prisoner was Feng Ying-ching (*see* Matteo Ricci), who, as assistant surveillance commissioner of Hukuang (appointed 1600), had suffered an identical fate at the hands of Ch'en Feng (March, 1601). Together they discussed the worsening conditions in the body politic, and how to counteract them. Both agreed that the type of rule that should obtain was that advocated by Chu Yüan-chang. Ho thereupon set about compiling a work based on the *T'ai-tsu shih-lu* which eventually (1614/15) appeared under the title *Huang-tsu ssu ta-fa* 皇祖四大法 (The august emperor's four major methods [of governance]), 12 *ch*. He divided it into four sections, with the sub-titles: Hsin 心 -fa (Appealing to the emotions of the people), *ch.* 1–2, Chih 治-fa (Public policy), *ch.* 3–8, Ssu 祀-fa (Uses of sacrifices), *ch.* 9–10, and Ping 兵-fa (Military methods), *ch.* 11–12. After Ho's release he was allowed to return home, where he remained for seventeen years.

Following the death of the Wan-li emperor and the accession of Chu Yu-chiao (ECCP), Ho was called back into service as secretary of a bureau in the ministry of War in Nanking. Hardly had he reached his post when word came of the military successes of Nurhaci (ECCP) in Liaotung. The important cities of Shen-yang and Liao-yang had fallen in May, 1621. Ho promptly volunteered to help in the defense of the northeastern frontier and succeeded in raising sufficient funds to enlist 6,700 recruits from Chekiang. But many of these had no stomach for fighting north of the Great Wall, and withdrew. As a consequence, the supervising secretary of the ministry of Revenue, Chu Ch'in-hsiang 朱欽相 (T. 如容), accused him of embezzlement, of enlisting soldiers just to plunder army supplies. At this time, however, Ho was already leading men up to the Great Wall.

His next post (ca. 1623) was as vice minister of the Court of Imperial Stud in Peking. As such he became involved in military strategy. Reportedly Ho was quick witted, but not overly tactful. He took to task both Hsiung T'ing-pi and Wang Hua-chen (both in ECCP), rival generals in the northeastern theater, defending China against the Manchus. For this, certain censors castigated him. In reply he invited the emperor at his own convenience to investigate the bureaucracy in the capital, and purge it of the quarreling officials of both parties—the Tung-lin and the followers of Wei Chung-hsien (ECCP). His words irritated powerful figures at court, and once more he found himself in prison, but not for long. In 1625 he was dispatched to Ch'u-yang 滁陽 (Anhwei) to aid in putting down a rebellion in the area. In the following reign (1628-44), his official status restored, he retired.

Besides the *Huang-tsu ssu-ta-fa*, copies of which are available at Harvard, in Japan, and on microfilm, Ho wrote the *Ho T'ai-p'u chi* 太僕集, 10 *ch.*, which is included in the *Chin-ling ts'ung-shu* (*see* ECCP, p. 146). The first *chüan* of the latter includes ten of his memorials and certain of his official writings. Probably because of its comments on the enemy in Liaotung the title was put on the prohibited list in the following century. Another book, the *Nan-yin she yüan* 南音攝園, 2 *ch.*, seems no longer extant.

Bibliography

1/237/8a; 3/218/4b; 40/58/20b; 64/ 庚 19/18a; MSL(1966), Shen-tsung, 6657, Hsi-tsung, 2169; KC (1958), 4866, 5212, 5240, 5246; *Chiang-ning-fu chih* (1880), 31/10a; Yao Chin-yüan (1957), 151; *Huang-tsu ssu ta-fa* (NLP microfilm, 171); W. Franke, *Sources*, 2.3.16, 5.7.12.

Yang Chin-yi and
L. Carrington Goodrich

HOU Hsien 侯顯, a eunuch of outstanding ability, served on seven successive embassies for the imperial court during the years 1403 to 1427. Twice he accompanied the eunuch admiral Cheng Ho (*q.v.*) on his voyages into the Indian Ocean, and on five other occasions he went out either as a subordinate or as chief of mission to such places as Bengal, Tibet, and Nepal.

Bearing the title deputy grand eunuch of the directorate of ceremonial, Hou had as his first assignment (1403) the duty of accompanying the Buddhist monk Chih-kuang (*see* Pandita) to the Karma-pa abbots in Tibet. The purpose of the emperor was to invite the hierarch Halima (*q.v.*) to Nanking. In this he was successful, as Halima first dispatched envoys of his own with tribute, and then accompanied Hou and Chih-kuang on their way back to Nanking. On his return in 1407 Hou received a promotion to t'ai-chien (grand eunuch) and almost immediately had orders to associate himself with Cheng Ho and Wang Ching-hung (*q.v.*) on the admiral's second expedition (1407-9) and again on his third (1409-11). Hou's fourth assignment (Spring, 1413) took him into the Himalayas to make gifts of brocade and silk to two of its rulers, Saktisiṃha 沙的新葛 of Nepal and K'o-pan 可般 of Ti-yung-t'a 地湧塔 (Khopva, the Newari name for Bhatgaon—the "prince" being Jayasthiti Mala, according to Petech). Here the Nepalese ruler, whom the emperor appointed as king and to whom he awarded a seal of gilded silver and a patent, delegated a high official to accompany Hou back to China (1414). The following year he went by sea to Bengal and other states, again with a load of rich gifts. The ruler of Bengal, Saïfu-'d-Dīn 賽佛丁, had previously sent a giraffe and other presents to the Ming emperor, and Chu Ti (*q.v.*) dispatched Hou to reply in kind. In 1420 the emperor ordered Hou to proceed to the kingdom of Jaunpūr 沼納樸兒. It appears that the king, Ibrahim 亦不刺金, had invaded Bengal, and Saïfu-'d-Dīn had besought Chu Ti to come to his aid. Hou sailed with gifts of gold and silk and succeeded in persuading Ibrahim to cease his depredations. Hou Hsien's last mission (1427) was to Tibet and Nepal. At important stops along the way he presented brocaded velvet, hemp cloth, and silk to Lamaist abbots and princes. On his return brigands assaulted him and his party, but he finally succeeded in overcoming them.

The authors of the *Ming-shih* conclude his biographical sketch by remarking that, because of the intelligence and courage which he demonsrated on his various missions, Hou should be ranked on a par with Cheng Ho.

Bibliography

1/304/4b, 331/10b, 13a; MSL (1963), T'ai-tsung, 0311, 1665, 1777, 1859, 2226, Hsüan-tsung, 1321; Hsü Yü-hu 徐玉虎 in *Ta-lu tsa-chih* 大陸雜誌, 16 (April, 1958), 242; Yamamoto Tatsurō 山本達郎, TG, 21 (1934), 528; Paul Pelliot, TP, 30 (1933), 267, 283, 314; J. J. L. Duyvendak, TP, 34 (1938), 362, 383; G. Tucci, *Tibetan Painted Scrolls* (Rome, 1949), 682, 689, 693; L. Petech, *Mediaeval History of Nepal* (Rome, 1958), 205.

L. Carrington Goodrich

HSI Shu 席書 (T. 文同, H. 元山), May 14, 1461-April 11, 1527, who rose to be minister of Rites, was a native of Sui-ning 遂寧, Szechwan. After qualifying for the *chü-jen* in 1489 and the *chin-shih* a year later, he received an appointment first as magistrate of Yü-ch'eng 禹城 and then of T'an-ch'eng 郯城, both in Shantung. In recognition of his services he was made secretary (1498) of a bureau in the ministry of Works and in 1500 vice director of a bureau in the ministry of Revenue.

In 1503, because of a violent earthquake in Yunnan which caused the city of Ching-tung 景東 in that province to be shrouded in darkness for several days, the senior vice minister of Justice in Nanking, Fan Ying 樊瑩 (T. 廷璧, 1422-1508, cs 1464), was ordered to make an inspection. Acting on the assumption that these calamities were signs of maladministration in Yunnan, Fan Ying suggested to the emperor, Chu Yu-t'ang (*q.v.*), that he either demote or cashier three hundred officials in the province. Hearing of this, Hsi Shu addressed a memorial to the throne which read: "In my humble opinion, it is the court rather than the officials in Yunnan province which should be held responsible for these calamities. The current expenses of the palace are several times greater than they were a few years ago; there are thousands of supernumeraries in the government; temples are under construction everywhere; imperial sacrifices are performed too often; eunuchs are constantly assigned to various places throughout the country. These evil practices should be immediately stopped. I wonder why Fan Ying, as a minister, has not mentioned these things but has suggested instead the punishment of a large number of officials in Yunnan." The emperor, however, paid no attention.

At the beginning of the Cheng-te reign Hsi was appointed assistant surveillance commissioner of Honan. In 1509 he received a transfer to Kweichow as vice commissioner in charge of education. It was just at this time that Wang Shou-jen (*q.v.*) had been punished and sent to serve in the government dispatch station of Lung-ch'ang, also in Kweichow; many officials there dared not associate with him for fear of offending the powerful eunuch Liu Chin (*q.v.*), who was responsible for Wang's disgrace. Hsi, however, often invited Wang to come to the provincial capital, Kweiyang, to teach a number of students selected from all parts of Kweichow; this action on his part contributed measurably to the educational development of that province.

In 1510, through the recommendation of the minister of Personnel, Yang I-ch'ing (*q.v.*), Hsi was made administration vice commissioner of Honan. Shortly after this his father died and he went home. After completing the mourning period, he was appointed surveillance commissioner of Chekiang; in the following year he was sent to Shantung as junior administration commissioner. Subsequently he returned home because of the death of his mother. In 1517 he received orders to be successively junior right administration commissioner of Yunnan and senior administration commissioner of Fukien. Hearing that the prince of Ning, Chu Ch'en-hao (*see* Wang Shou-jen), had risen against the government (in July, 1519), he assembled twenty thousand soldiers and led them northward. By the time his troops had entered northern Kiangsi, Wang Shou-jen had already suppressed the rebellion; so he led his men back to Fukien.

On June 11, 1521, a few days after Chu Hou-ts'ung (*q.v.*) had succeeded to the throne, Hsi was promoted to be junior vice censor-in-chief and concurrently governor of Hukuang. Later, in May, 1522, he was made junior right vice minister of War in Nanking. At this time the people to the south of the Yangtze River were suffering from a serious famine occasioned by drought, while to the north the people were plagued by an equally serious famine occasioned by flood. Hsi was ordered to bring relief to the latter.

He set up many sheds in the area where gruel was prepared for the needy, and in this way saved many lives.

During his service in Hukuang as governor, the problem of appropriate titles to be granted to the parents of the new emperor came under discussion. Hsi found himself in agreement with the opinions expressed by Chang Ts'ung (*i.e.* Chang Fu-ching, *q.v.*) and Huo T'ao (*q.v.*) both of whom opposed the stand of Grand Secretary Yang T'ing-ho (*q.v.*); so he actively promoted their side of the argument. This eventually (1524) won the day. In the meantime Hsi was transferred to Nanking as vice minister of War (1522) and in 1524 the emperor summoned him to Peking to take charge of the ministry of Rites. Now precedent demanded that a minister or vice minister of Rites be selected from those officials who had served in the Hanlin Academy. Hsi therefore was ineligible. Many critics and censors, as a consequence, opposed the appointment, even falsely accusing him of having appropriated relief funds for his own use. Faced with this situation, Hsi decided to refuse the offer and remained in Nanking. The emperor persisted, however, and in September Hsi finally accepted and became minister of Rites.

Late in 1524 the frontier troops stationed in Tatung mutinied, killing Governor Chang Wen-chin (*see* Liang Chen) because of the severity of his discipline. To settle the mutiny, Grand Secretary Fei Hung (*q.v.*) wished to adopt a policy of appeasement and appoint as commander a man chosen by the mutineers themselves. Hsi, however, held that the soldiers should be punished severely. As a consequence, a distinct coolness developed between them. In the spring of 1525, in a memorial recommending the appointment of Wang Shou-jen to the Grand Secretariat, Hsi characterized all ministers then in office as men of little ability; only Wang was a man of stature. The emperor was not pleased, and Wang was passed over.

Hsi Shu's rank was raised to grand guardian of the heir apparent in January, 1526. In the autumn of the same year, under the supervision of Hsi and others, the *Jui-tsung Hsien-huang-ti* 睿宗獻皇帝 *shih-lu* (the Veritable records of Chu Yu-yüan, now lost), 50 *ch.*, was completed; in recognition of that achievement, his rank was elevated to junior guardian. Unfortunately, by this time he had become almost blind and fell ill. He begged repeatedly to be retired, meanwhile suggesting to the emperor the appointment of Lo Ch'in-shun (*q.v.*) as minister of Rites in his place. Early in 1527 the emperor acted on his proposal but Lo did not accept. By this time Hsi's condition had worsened; he passed away in April. Directly before his death, his rank was raised to grand secretary. He was posthumously given the title of grand tutor and canonized as Wen-hsiang 文襄.

Hsi Shu's younger brother, Hsi Ch'un 春 (cs 1517), served as an investigating censor in Yunnan. After several promotions, he became Hanlin chancellor. In 1533 he was transferred to be a vice minister of Personnel from the same office in the ministry of Rites. Subsequently, as hostility developed between him and the minister of Personnel, Wang Hung 汪鋐 (T. 宣之, Pth. 榮和, cs 1502, d. August 15, 1536), he was removed from office. A still younger brother, Hsi Chuan 篆 (cs 1514), rose to be a supervising secretary; he died about 1522.

Hsi Shu was the author of a book called *Yüan-shan wen-chi* 元山文集, a collection of essays, but whether it is extant is unknown. Another work, entitled *Ts'ao ch'uan chih* 漕船志 (monograph on shipping and transport on the imperial canal), 8 *ch.*, edited by him and later enlarged by Chu Chia-hsiang 朱家相, and published in 1544, was photolithographically reprinted in 1940 in the *Hsüan-lan-t'ang ts'ung-shu* 玄覽堂叢書, first series. The book deals with the shipyards, the number and types of boats constructed in each, and other matter involving regulations, personnel, and organization of the transport service.

Bibliography

1/197/1a; 3/183/1a; 5/15/105a; 6/2/22a, 10/25b, 12/34b, 14/47a, 30/6b, 11b, 35/11b, 38/10b, 12a; 7/41/11a; 10/14/30b; 42/70/5b; 61/155/20b; 63/12/55a; MSL (1965), Shih-tsung, 1111, 1158, 1227, 1397, 1487, 1506, 1660; KC (1958), 2799, 3309, 3349; *T'ung-ch'uan-fu chih* 潼川府志 (1897), 21/94a, 99a, 108a; *Shantung t'ung-chih* (1934), 2334; *Ch'ang-te-fu chih* (1813), 22/22a; Chao Shih-wei 趙士煒, "*Shih-lu k'ao*" 實錄考, *Fu-jen hsüeh-chih* 輔仁學誌, V (1936), 48; W. Franke, *Sources*, 6.5.4.

Chou Tao-chi

HSIA Ch'ang 夏昹 (T. 仲昭, H. 自在居士, 玉峯, 居易), September, 1388-September 9/10, 1470 (or June 14, 1470, according to Wang Shih-chen, *q.v.*), calligrapher, painter, and official, was a native of K'un-shan 崑山 in the prefecture of Soochow. Demonstrating his precocity at the age of six (he could already write k'ai-shu 楷書), he went on to pass the examinations for *chü-jen* in 1414 and for *chin-shih* the following year, and was selected a bachelor in the Hanlin Academy. At this time his name was Chu Ch'ang 朱昶. There is some speculation as to why he later changed his surname from Chu to Hsia. One account has it that, during the 1358 attack on K'un-shan by Fang Kuo-chen (*q.v.*), most members of the Hsia family lost their lives, and Hsia's father, then a child, was brought up by his maternal relatives whose name became his too. Another suggests that his mother remarried and that he took the name of his step-father. As Chu Ti (*q.v.*) favored Chu Ch'ang's calligraphy —he had achieved first place in a palace competition in k'ai-shu—he ordered him to write the inscriptions for the tablets mounted on the new buildings then being erected in Peking. The emperor, noticing Chu Ch'ang's name, objected to the way the character for Ch'ang was written, holding that it was inappropriate for the sun 日 to be put on the side of 永

(viz. 昶), and ordered it placed on top (晏), an arrangement which he followed the rest of his life. About the same time Chu Ch'ang requested permission to change his *hsing* to Hsia. (Presumably this request covered his entire family, including his elder brother Hsia Ping 昺 [T. 孟暘].) It is said that Hsia Ping, formerly named Chu Ping, also known as a painter and calligrapher, once (in 1407?) took part in the production of the *Yung-lo ta-tien* (*see* Chu Ti). While serving as assistant magistrate of Yung-ning 永寧, Honan, he was dispatched to escort a number of laborers to work on the imperial burial grounds north of Peking. On the way many laborers under his care defected; Hsia Ping was held accountable, and was exiled to the southern part of Yunnan. Hsia Ch'ang entered a plea for his brother's release, and eventually it was granted through the aid of Grand Secretary Yang Jung (*q.v.*). Meanwhile (March, 1421), he had been made a drafter in the central drafting office and his brother was then assigned to the same office, where they came to be known familiarly as the senior and junior drafters (大小中書).

A contemporary fellow townsman, Chang I 張益 (T. 士濂, H. 彥庵, Pth. 文僖, 1395–1449), who had graduated in the same year as Hsia Ch'ang and served in the Hanlin, also had a reputation as a calligrapher and a painter of bamboos. When Hsia came to realize that Chang's *fu* 賦 were superior to his own, he ceased writing poetry; and when Chang found he could not compete with Hsia in painting bamboos, he in turn gave up the art.

In 1422 Hsia Ch'ang received a transfer to the new capital. Three years later Yang Jung invited him to serve in the Wen-yüan hall 文淵閣. During this period he had to return home because of the death of his father. In the following reign (1426–35), he was shifted to the bureau of evaluations of the ministry of Personnel, again as secretary. In the Cheng-t'ung era his main assignment was to assist in the compilation of several imperial works, including the two *shih-lu* of Jen-tsung and Hsüan-tsung. (According to the *Hsüan-tsung shih-lu*, however, the former had already been completed in 1430. Was it subjected to some modification?) On the completion of the last, he received as reward a grant of money and a roll of silk (白金文綺). In 1439, because of his mother's age, he received leave to retire to serve her. During the years 1448 to 1452, he served as prefect of Jui-chou-fu 瑞州府, Kiangsi. His term there was marked by good administration. Then he found himself back in the capital as vice minister of the Court of Imperial Sacrifices, and five years later, when Chu Ch'i-chen (*q.v.*) resumed power, he made Hsia chief minister (March 2). Hsia had now reached the age of seventy *sui* and was permitted to retire in September, 1457.

During Hsia's lifetime he achieved an enviable reputation as a painter of bamboos and writer of k'ai-shu. The critics all remark on the influence of his calligraphic strokes on his paintings. His fame as calligrapher and painter spread even to Korea, Japan, and Siam. At present a number of examples are available. The Staatliche Museen (Berlin) has his "Spring Rain by the River Hsiang," dated 1455, and a handscroll featuring a bamboo-bordered stream is in the possession of the Art Institute of Chicago; other paintings, likewise dominated by bamboos, are in the National Palace Museum, Taiwan, and elsewhere.

Hsia Ch'ang had three sons. The second, Hsia To 鐸 (T. 文振), also achieved some note as a calligrapher, in 1466 receiving an appointment as drafter in the cental drafting office.

Bibliography

1/286/4a; 5/70/10a; 38/2/10b; 65/2/7b, 7/3a; MSL (1963), T'ai-tsung, 2257, Ying-tsung (1963), 5840, 6049, Hsien-tsung (1964), 1606; KC (1958), 2289; *Soochow-fu chih* (1874), 60/2b, 61/6a, 91/34a; *Jui-chou-fu chih* (1873), 2/3a, 7/24b, 8/8a; TSCC (1885–88), XIV: 15/15/11a, 438/8a, XVII: 783/17/13b, XXIII: 95/83/5a, XXIV:

118/24/7b; *Huang Ming wen-hai* (microfilm), 9/
2/1, 2; Ho Ch'iao-yüan, *Ming-shan ts'ang*, 99/3
下; Chiang Shao-shu 姜紹書 (fl. 1640), *Wu-
sheng shih-shih* 無聲詩史, 1/10; Hsia Wen-yen 夏
文彥 (fl. 1365) and Han Ang 韓昂 (fl. 1519),
T'u-hui pao-chien 圖繪寶鑑, 6/159; *K'un-shan
jen-wu chuan* 人物傳 (1724), 2/10b, 16a; *K'un
Hsin liang-hsien hsü-hsiu ho-chih* 新兩縣續修合志
(1880), 17/9a, 18/3a, 30/7b; Wang Chih-teng
王穉登 (1535–1612), *Wu-chün tan-ch'ing chih*
吳郡丹青志, 4; *Ku-su chih* 姑蘇志 (rep. of 1965),
113, 763; O. Sirén, *Chinese Painting*, VII (New
York, 1956–58), 186; E. J. Laing, *Chinese Paintings in Chinese Publications, 1956–1958* (Ann
Arbor, 1969) 166; Harrie Vanderstappen, "Painters at the Early Ming Court (1368–1435) and
the Problem of a Ming Painting Academy,"
MS (1956), 290; V. Contag and C. C. Wang,
Seals of Chinese Painters and Collectors, rev.
ed. (Hong Kong, 1966), 671.

L. Carrington Goodrich and Lee Hwa-chou

HSIA Yen 夏言 (T. 公謹, H. 桂洲), 1482–
October 31, 1548, poet and grand secretary
of the Chia-ching period, was descended
from a family registered in the military
class of Kuei-ch'i 貴溪, prefecture of
Kuang-hsin 廣信, Kiangsi. He had an uncle on military duty in Peking; so his immediate family had the privilege of living
there too. Hsia Yen's father, Hsia Ting 鼎
(T. 雨梅, H. 象峰, d. 1506), thus spent
all his student years in the capital city,
taking the *chü-jen* there in 1480 and becoming a *chin-shih* in 1496; later he served
as a prefectural judge of Yen-chou 嚴州,
Chekiang (1497–1500?), and as magistrate
of Lin-ch'ing chou 臨清州, Shantung, where
he died in office. Hsia Yen was born in
Peking and lived there with his father
until the age of fourteen; he was thus a
native speaker of the court language. In
his youth, he was known for his ability
to write and for his retentive memory.
After becoming a *chü-jen* (1510), he
failed twice in his attempt to achieve the
higher degree, and so in 1514 enrolled in
the Imperial Academy. He succeeded in
the metropolitan examination in 1517, but
as a *chin-shih* he was graded in the third
group and was appointed a messenger. In

1520 he received a promotion to supervising secretary of matters concerning the
ministry of War.

Early in his official career Hsia Yen
became known as an articulate figure at
court. When Chu Hou-ts'ung (*q.v.*) came
to the throne and declared his willingness
to correct the mistakes of the previous
reign, Hsia, as a supervising secretary,
was in a position to react accordingly.
Of reforms in which he took an active
part, the most famous was his settling of
the dispute of the Ch'ing-yang 青羊 Mountain incident in southeast Shansi. In 1528
a notorious outlaw, Ch'en Ch'ing 陳卿,
had collected a band on the mountain
and they were raiding the surrounding
areas. The court had dispatched detachments from many defense areas and succeeded in putting down the rebellion. The
matter was far from settled, however,
because the generals and officials who
had been in charge were quarreling over
who should be honored. Hsia was sent to
investigate.   He succeeded in correcting
the blunders of the officers and rehabilitated the disturbed residents by the establishment of a new district named P'ing-
shun 平順. The emperor showed his appreciation by transferring Hsia from the
post of supervising secretary of War to
that of chief supervising secretary of the
ministry of Personnel.

After his outspokenness and ability in
administrative work had earned him a certain prestige at court, Hsia's fortunes began another upward turn in 1530 when the
emperor adopted two of his suggestions.
First, he proposed that the empress should
personally direct the rite of cultivating
silkworms—a ritual through which women
might learn feminine virtues. A month
or so later, when he learned that the
emperor disliked the idea of using the
same altar and on the same date to make
sacrifices to both Heaven and Earth, he
suggested in an erudite memorial that His
Majesty should sacrifice to the former at
Yüan ch'iu 圜丘 in the southern suburb
on the winter solstice, and to Earth at

Fang-tse 方澤 in the northern suburb on the summer solstice. The emperor was so pleased that he bestowed on Hsia a special imperial gift and other favors, and also temporarily sent Huo T'ao (*q.v.*) to prison for his vehement attack on Hsia's suggestions. This marks the time of the construction of separate altars, T'ien t'an 天壇 and Ti 地 t'an, at their present sites. Altars to the sun and moon (Ch'ao jih 朝日 t'an and Hsi yüeh 夕月 t'an) were ordered at the same time for the eastern and western suburbs, respectively, and erected a year or so later. For his expertise on ceremonial matters Hsia was made minister of Rites (October, 1531). From that time until he became a grand secretary in June, 1537, his ambitious nature revealed itself. Power-driven and self-confident, he became constantly involved in factional struggles with other influential officials competing for the emperor's good graces. The first in his way was Chang Fu-ching (*q.v.*), together with his clique. The struggle between them began immediately after Hsia made the proposals about the silkworm ritual and the separate sacrifices to Heaven and Earth. According to Wang Shih-chen (*q.v.*), the biographer of the men involved, the ideas about both the ritual and the separate sacrifices originated with Chang Fu-ching, but Hsia pirated them at the right moment. When Chang discovered that he had lost both opportunities, and when he sensed that the attention of the emperor was shifting to Hsia, he naturally tried hard to get rid of the latter.

For a while the emperor seems to have been pleased to see such a struggle going on at court, for in this way he could always insure his own authority. But then, after a scheme to have Hsia falsely accused came to light, Chang was removed from office (1531). Although Chang was twice summoned back, his influence had diminished. Hsia, on the other hand, continued to rise partly because the emperor, who took for himself the responsibility of creating and revising rites and

music, found Hsia indispensable in such matters. In fact, it was under Hsia's editorship that the *Chiao-li t'ung-tien* 郊禮通典, 27 *ch.*, was compiled (1533). In addition, his bearing and his pronunciation without a provincial accent also pleased the emperor. The latter's liking for Hsia was revealed in frequent gifts, such as a special silver seal which Hsia could use in sending him secret memorials, and the donation of many specimens of his own writing; also in the fact that he removed the military status from Hsia's clan upon request. Early in 1537 Hsia finally became a grand secretary, and two years later earned the unprecedented honorary title of Shang chu kuo 上柱國 (Superior Pillar of State), the only civilian (Li Shan-ch'ang [*q.v.*] excepted) so honored in the Ming dynasty while living.

Secure in the belief that the emperor had confidence in him, Hsia Yen as grand secretary, and later (February, 1539) as chief grand secretary, held much of the decision making power in his hands and no doubt encroached upon the prerogatives of the six ministries. For this his biographers call him "overbearing," and "one who regards even the high officials below him beneath consideration." He underestimated, however, the emperor's trust in anyone who did not constantly comply with his wishes. He was blind in failing to see that the emperor, despotic and suspicious, distrusted anyone who overstepped his authority. The emperor's favor gradually began to cool. In 1538, when Hsia followed the emperor on a trip to the imperial tombs north of Peking, a fire broke out in Hsia's tent which spread and burned some special memorials marked with the emperor's comments. The emperor was angry at Hsia because, instead of sending a personal memorial to beg forgiveness, he joined in one with others. When the emperor expressed the desire to confer on his father a posthumous imperial reign title, Hsia, though not openly declaring himself against the idea, did nothing to encourage the emperor. According to a contemporary, this was the underlying reason for his downfall. In the following year, when the emperor made the tour to his father's tomb in Hukuang (see Lu Ping), Yen Sung (q.v.), praising the emperor's act as filial and humane, requested that other officials join in lauding the act. Hsia Yen, however, suggested that they wait until the emperor had returned to the capital. The emperor took offense at this too. After these incidents Hsia began to find himself in an uneasy position and was twice dismissed from office, for a few days in May, 1539, and September-November in 1541, both times over minor offenses.

Hsia nevertheless continued to make trouble for his enemies, such as Kuo Hsün (q.v.) and Yen Sung. Kuo, a descendant of an honored general at the beginning of the Ming, had gained his power and the emperor's favor by his support in the Ta-li i controversy, and his help to the emperor in his pursuit of Taoistic arts and practices. For almost two decades Kuo was one of the most influential men in Peking, and did not hesitate to indulge in various illegal activities to gain wealth, land, and houses, and to operate private businesses. In 1541, when a group of censors and officials began attacking Kuo and eventually brought about his collapse, Hsia was said to have been behind the whole scheme. Hsia did not really gain by this, however, for, when Kuo died in prison, the emperor's resentment against Hsia came to the surface as he considered that he himself had also been victimized by Hsia's maneuvers. The outcome of Hsia's political struggle with his fellow provincial, Yen Sung, was even worse, leading as it did to his eventual downfall and execution. Astute, tactful, and ambitious, Yen knew how to please Hsia in order to rise in the hierarchy. Totally unaware of Yen's real motives and needing a political ally at court, Hsia supported Yen in the jockeying for the post of minister of Rites (early 1537), and succeeded in bringing him into the inner circle of power. Once in personal contact with the emperor, Yen had no difficulty in winning the latter's favor. When Hsia realized that he had created for himself a formidable new political rival, he discovered that it was too late to remove Yen.

While Yen Sung was consolidating his position, the relationship between Hsia and the emperor continued to worsen. For one thing, the emperor was very jealous of his prerogatives. He declared in 1537, for instance, that no one except with his express permission might wear or make use of anything not appropriate to his rank. While he allowed his favorites to ride on horseback to see him at his Taoist Hall, he was greatly annoyed when Hsia came in a kind of sedan chair. Again, as the emperor preferred wearing a Taoist cap instead of the imperial headgear, he ordered five other Taoist caps made for his favorites. Hsia alone refused to wear one, arguing that it was not the proper official costume. Yen, however, donned one to please the emperor. Worse still, when two palaces were vacated upon the deaths of both empresses dowager, Hsia suggested that one palace be turned over to the heir apparent to save the cost of any new construction. The emperor was enraged, considering that Hsia's suggestion would clearly violate the principle of filial piety. In August, 1542, he dismissed Hsia, and Yen Sung gained admission to the Grand Secretariat.

In October, 1545, however, seeing that Yen was falling into the same errors as his rival, the emperor summoned Hsia back to maintain a balance of power. Once again in office as senior grand secretary, Hsia began to act overbearingly towards Yen who was now practically his co-equal. Not only did Hsia fail to consult Yen on important questions but even dismissed from office certain of Yen's clique. Since Yen and his son Yen Shih-fan were clearly disliked by many at court and by the general populace, Hsia's curbing of the Yen family's power was applauded. Hsia, however, neglected to cultivate closer relations with the emperor, who alone controlled the delegation of authority. He had never been a diligent man and now that he was older he became even more lax. He no longer composed Taoist prayers himself, but had his guests compose them for him or had old ones sent in. This of course greatly annoyed the emperor. Hsia had no way of getting information on the likes and dislikes of the emperor from the inner court, since he refused to ally himself with the eunuchs. Yen, on the other hand, did quite the opposite, not only complying in every way with the whims and fancies of the emperor, but also bribing eunuchs to speak on his behalf and to apprise him of the emperor's wishes so that he might be prepared. Sensing that Hsia was falling into disfavor, Yen succeeded in bringing about Hsia's downfall on the issue of recovering the Ordos region (see Tseng Hsien). Hsia was executed and his second wife, née Su 蘇, was exiled to Kwangsi. His nephew, Hsia K'o-ch'eng 克承, secretary of a bureau in the ministry of Rites, and grandnephew Hsia Ch'ao-ch'ing 朝慶, vice minister in the seal office, were dismissed from the court. Hsia's punishment was clearly the irrational act of a despotic monarch who disregarded the procedures of law and the special consideration granted to high officials. Hsia's offense (nominally the Ordos issue) was in reality his unwillingness to comply in every respect with an emperor who was now deeply engrossed in Taoistic practices. Although Hsia, like many other high officials during the Chia-ching period, was opportunistic, he nevertheless was frank and incorruptible. Early in the Lung-ch'ing reign all his honors and titles were restored, and he was granted the posthumous name Wen-min 文愍.

Hsia's death caused widespread grief. His support of Tseng Hsien's plan for the defense of the Ordos region, in the face of the strong opposition of Yen Sung and others, became part of a highly popular play known as *Ming feng chi* 鳴鳳記, allegedly written by Wang Shih-chen around the year 1565, the central theme of which turned on the viciousness of the Yen family. Hsia's calligraphy was sought after particularly when he was in the Grand Secretariat. He and his wife enjoyed greater note, however, for their poetry; Hsia's specialty, tz'u, was published in his *Kuei-chou hsien-sheng tz'u* 桂州先生詞, 9 *ch.*, to which his *Ou-yüan hsin-ch'ü* 鷗園新曲, 1 *ch.*, was appended. His regular poems were published separately in the *Kuei-chou shih-chi* 詩集, 24 *ch.* (Chia-ching period). His memorials were published first in 5 *chüan* under the title *Nan-kung tsou kao* 南宮奏稿 (*ca.* 1535) and later in an expanded edition, *Kuei-chou tsou-i* 議 (1539), 21 *ch.* Hsia is also known to have printed a collection of memorials of gratitude for imperial favors, *Tsou-hsieh lu* 奏謝錄, 3 *ch.* He wrote as well the *Tz'u-hsien-t'ang kao* 賜閒堂稿, 8 *ch.*, appendix 1 *ch.* (1546). He was responsible too for the editing of the *T'ai miao ch'ih-i* 太廟敕議, 1 *ch.* (1534) and for co-editing of the *Chia-ching shih-ssu nien chin-shih teng-k'o-lu* 嘉靖十四年進士登科錄, 1 *ch.* His collected work, *Kuei-chou hsien-sheng wen-chi* 文集, 50 *ch.*, first published in the Chia-ching years, has been reissued several times since then. A condensed copy under the same title, published in 1638, also contains his *nien-p'u*, though only down to the year 1531.

Bibliography

1/196/20b; 3/182/18a; 5/16/24a; 17/3/1a; 32/60/37b; 40/36/2a; 42/70/10a; 43/3/5a; 61/132/3b; 64/戊 13/4b; 84/丁中 /56a; 86/10/36a; MSL (1965), Shih-tsung, ch. 74-84; SK (1930), 55/8a, 56/4a, 83/3b, 176/15b; *Kuang-hsin-fu chih* (1873), 9/1/65b; Hsü Fu-tso 徐復祚, *Hua-tang-ko ts'ung-t'an* 花當閣叢談 (*Chieh-yüeh-shan-fang hui-ch'ao* 借月山房彙鈔 ed.), 2/6b; Shen Te-fu, *Wan-li yeh-hu-pien*, 8/206, 245; Huang Wan 黃綰(1480-1554), *Shih-lung chi* 石龍集 (Chia-ching ed.), 13/16a; TSCC (1885-88), VI: 335/12a, XIV: 438/11b, XXIV: 122/28/12b; Hsia Yen, *Kuei-chou wen-chi*, ch. 1; Ku Lin 顧璘 (1476-1545), *Ku Hua-yü chi* 華玉集(*Chin-ling ts'ung-shu* 金陵叢書 ed.), chia-chi 甲集, han 函 7, 13/5b,

17a, 15/11b, 20/3a; Liu Ts'un-yan, "The Penetration of Taoism into the Ming neo-Confucianist Elite," TP, 57 (1971), 35, 62; *Chung-kuo chin-shih hsi-ch'ü-shih* 中國近世戲曲史, tr. and annotated by Wang Ku-lu 王古魯 from a Japanese work by Aoki Masaru 青木正兒 (Peking, 1958), 192.

Angela Hsi

HSIA Yüan-chi 夏原吉 (T. 維喆), 1366–February 19, 1430, minister of Revenue during the years from 1402 to 1421 and from 1424 to 1430, was descended from a family of Te-hsing 德興, Kiangsi. His grandfather and father both served away from home; his father becoming an instructor at Hsiang-yin 湘陰, Hukuang, the family decided to settle there. [Editors' note: The accounts of Hsia Yüan-chi's grandfather seem as confusing as those of the parents of Yang Shih-chi (*q.v.*). In any event, Hsia's grandfather is said to have lost his life during the rebellious years of the Yüan dynasty, while serving as a chief clerk in the Hukuang provincial government. The Hsia family then lived in a place north of Yo-chou 岳州 until 1373 when Yüan-chi's father Hsia Shih-min 時敏 (d. 1378) received the above mentioned appointment. The family then registered in Hsiang-yin.] Hsia Yüan-chi passed his *chü-jen* examination in 1390 and was admitted to the National University. He was then selected to draft edicts in the inner court and came to the attention of Emperor Chu Yüan-chang (*q. v.*). Within two years he was appointed one of the secretaries in the ministry of Revenue and, except for short intervals, was to remain in this ministry until his death. The minister Yü Hsin (*see* Ch'en Hsüan) regarded him highly, and, after Hsia returned from over a year's leave to attend to his aging mother, he was promoted (July, 1398) to be junior vice minister. Under Emperor Chu Yün-wen (*q. v.*), he was sent in March, 1399, to Fukien as regional inspector (採訪使, something like a governor in later years) and then transferred to Ch'i-chou 蘄州 in Hukuang. He was still

there in 1402 when Chu Ti (*q. v.*) ascended the throne. There was some doubt as to whether he could be trusted, but the new emperor promoted him to be senior vice-minister and then junior minister of Revenue, all within about two months. He thus joined a team of young and promising men, all in their thirties and all picked by Chu Ti, who were to dominate the imperial administration during the next twenty to thirty years. In fact, he and four others went on to serve at least three rulers and provided the dynasty with great stability and continuity during a crucial and dynamic period. The other four were Chien I, Yang Shih-ch'i, Yang Jung (*qq. v.*), and Chin Yu-tzu (*see* Empress Hsü).

For the first three years, Hsia proved his administrative ability outside the capital at Nanking. He was asked to deal with the persistent problem of floods in the lower Yangtze valley which the local authorities had failed to solve and which needed large-scale help from the central government. After surveying the area with a team of officials and consulting with local irrigation experts, Hsia recommended channeling the flood waters into the main river courses leading from Lake T'ai to the Yangtze River and thence to the sea. The silting of previous years had become very serious and some of the courses were completely blocked. The main feature of his work was to deepen the rivers leading out at Pai-mao kang 白茆港 in Ch'ang-shu 常熟, at Liu-chia kang 劉家港 in T'ai-ts'ang 太倉, and at Wu-sung k'ou 吳淞口, north of Shanghai, and to build sluices and dikes where necessary. The task occupied over ten thousand men for more than a year. Hsia personally supervised the work for most of the year 1404. Although he did not permanently solve the flood problems, the area was free from severe inundation for several decades. It is worth noting that Hsia benefited greatly from the writings of Shan E 單鍔 (1031–1110) of the Northern Sung, whose classic study of the river systems of the lower Yangtze, the *Wu-chung shui-li shu* 吳中水利書, continued to be valuable to later Ming administrators in the region.

After Yü Hsin's death, Hsia took over the Revenue ministry (August, 1405) and directed it for more than sixteen years, until November, 1421. For over fifteen of these years he was in fact the sole minister; only during eleven months in 1421 did he have a junior minister, Kuo Tzu 郭資 (T. 存性, 1360-January 15, 1434). Kuo, an older official, had looked after the administration of Peking since the 1390s and was particularly successful as public works administrator at Peking during its period as a transition capital (1408-20), and served as minister from 1421 to 1424 and again from 1429 to 1434. During this period Hsia played a key part in dealing with all the financial problems of these eventful years. He was close to the emperor and accompanied him to Peking in 1409, 1413, and 1417, after which he stayed with him in Peking until the capital was officially moved there in 1420. It seems clear that he was usually present when major policies were being considered and his advice was sought on their financial feasibility. His main achievements, however, lay in his ability to organize the necessary supplies to support the emperor's ambitious plans. In particular, credit must go to him for his success in enabling the empire to sustain the very expensive Annam campaigns, the emperor's own northern expeditions against the Mongols, the first five voyages of Cheng Ho (*q. v.*) to the Indian Ocean, as well as the construction of the new capital at Peking and the transportation of at least a hundred thousand families from Nanking to Peking. Hsia Yüan-chi was noted for his ability to know exactly what funds and what grain supplies were available throughout the empire whenever the emperor wanted the information. He achieved this by constantly carrying with him figures of population, households, tax surpluses, and shortages.

Hsia was in no way an innovative administrator. He used basically orthodox methods of raising money; for example, cutting down on unnecessary expenses, regulating equitable taxes, tightly controlling permits to sell salt in exchange for food supplied to the frontiers, and checking currency and other profiteering abuses. He also encouraged the cultivation of new lands and the growth of legitimate trade. His methods were adequate for his purpose and there were no serious financial crises during the first period of his ministry.

Hsia's particular distinction in the eyes of his fellow officials and the traditional historians was in his rare combination of financial expertise and Confucian virtues. Unlike most finance specialists, he was not obsessed with expanding wealth either for himself or for the empire. He was far more concerned with prudence and stability, with responsible expenditure, and with the need for humanity and magnanimity in government rather than with brilliant schemes to swell the imperial coffers. In an era of military adventures, overseas expeditions, and large-scale construction works, this attitude was hardly to the court's liking and it was a measure of Hsia's integrity that he survived nearly twenty years under Emperor Chu Ti before he was sentenced to imprisonment in December, 1421.

In some ways, his brief disgrace may be considered a high point in his career. He had, on the grounds mainly of unnecessary expense, advised the emperor against personally leading a northern campaign against the Mongols. Despite the emperor's anger at this advice, Hsia remained firm and was himself jailed. This was a considerable risk, as the prisons of the Embroidered-uniform Guards, controlled by the eunuchs of the inner palace, were notoriously dangerous for officials who had offended the monarch. The danger was greatly increased because one of his colleagues, who had expressed the same views, had committed suicide and further angered the emperor. This was

Fang Pin 方賓 (minister of War 1409–21), whose death (December 11, 1421) led the emperor to confiscate Hsia's property. Although the latter was fortunate enough to survive his arrest until Chu Ti's demise in August, 1424, and resume his successful career under the next two emperors until his own passing in 1430, the disgrace of 1421 confirmed his image as a true Confucian official worthy of the highest respect by his colleagues and biographers. It was indeed rare that an emperor on his deathbed should remember a "disgraced" official and admit that he was mistaken and the official right. In Hsia's case Chu Ti's words shortly before he died on his way back to Peking were reported to have been, "Yüan-chi loved me."

Hsia's second period of five and a half years as minister of Revenue was a difficult one in a different way. The two emperors Chu Kao-chih and Chu Chan-chi (qq. v.) placed great trust in him. Chu Kao-chih was much indebted to Hsia for many subtle ways of protecting him while heir apparent from being harmed by intriguers. As to Chu Chan-chi, he came to know Hsia well when he was learning from him how to administer the Peking area as early as 1410. This was when his grandfather, Emperor Chu Ti, was campaigning north of the Great Wall and his father was looking after affairs in Nanking. For five months Hsia worked beside his young master, then only eleven years old, and impressed the boy with his ability and wisdom. Hsia later accompanied the youth on at least four trips between Nanking and Peking and also his father Chu Kao-chih, when the capital was officially moved to Peking. So, when it was known that Chu Ti remembered Hsia so warmly before his death, the way was clear for the latter to resume his place close to the next emperor's side and wield greater influence than before.

Hsia's last years as minister of Revenue were difficult not because he lacked security or power, but because the previous years of extravagance and ambitious enterprises had depleted the imperial coffers, and because he was unable to solve the main financial problems. The most serious one he had to deal with was that of the imperial paper currency which had been losing value for a number of years. He had to find a way of curbing drastic inflation and restoring the paper notes to normal use within a month of his reinstatement; this remained an unsolved problem until his death over five years later. His two main efforts at solution were based on the well established view that "when the notes are too plentiful, they are valued less; when they are scarce, they will be valued more." In September, 1424, he tried to withdraw notes from circulation by inducing the rich to buy the very profitable salt vouchers with paper notes instead of delivering grain to the frontiers. This was obviously inadequate, and in February, 1425, he introduced a few additional commercial taxes which had to be paid in paper notes, arranged to have old notes destroyed, reduced the issuing of new notes, and also prohibited the use of gold and silver in any transaction. In addition, he had persuaded Emperor Chu Kao-chih to reduce unnecessary expenses, to stop the unprofitable mining of gold and silver and the purchase of rare gems, incense, and spices, and also to put an end to the naval expeditions in "treasure ships" to southeast Asia and the Indian Ocean. He advised likewise against further commitments in Annam, and this advice later proved to be quite sound. Unfortunately Emperor Chu Kao-chih died after only ten months on the throne, and the young Chu Chan-chi was more ambitious and expected quick results. When it was obvious that Hsia's measures to curb inflation had failed, the emperor virtually retired him on the grounds of his age by making him a senior adviser at the end of 1428. Hsia was highly respected and was still paid his emoluments until his death, but his career as a financial administrator really came to an end then, when he was in fact if not in name

succeeded by two men who were bolder
and less scrupulous about increasing the
range of taxes in a desperate effort to
halt inflation and save the paper currency
system. It is interesting that one of them
was Kuo Tzu who had taken over from
him in 1421 but had been edged out at
the end of 1424. The fact that Kuo Tzu
was six years older than Hsia suggests
that Emperor Chu Chan-chi was not really
concerned about age but preferred Kuo
Tzu's aggressive methods to Hsia's conser-
vatism and excessive caution.

Hsia had one other claim to fame.
He was one of the directors in the revision of the Veritable Records (*shih-lu*) of
Chu Yüan-chang, during the years from
1411 to 1418, and then of the compilation of the Veritable Records of both Chu
Ti and Chu Kao-chih. He was, therefore,
one of the four men who had an important say in writing the history of the first
fifty-seven years of the Ming dynasty, The
other three men were Yang Jung, Yang
Shih-ch'i, and Chin Yu-tzu. Perhaps concurrent with this was his compilation on
the founding of the Ming entitled *I-t'ung
chao-chi lu* 一統肇基錄.

Hsia's very slight body of prose and
poetry was collected by his son, Hsia Hsüan
瑄 (T. 韞輝, 韞華, 1418–78), and known
as *Hsia Chung-ching kung chi* 忠靖公集, 6
ch. A new edition was brought out by his
grandson, Hsia Ch'ung-wen 崇文 (T. 廷章,
1456–1507), which includes much biographical material.

Bibliography

1/149/3b; 3/139/4a; 5/28/6a, 14b, 67/52, 77/62a;
16/32/7a, 83/6b, 100/8a, 105/7a, 106/6a, 154/10a;
63/8/4a; MSL (1962), T'ai-tsung, Jen-tsung,
Hsüan-tsung (to p. 1471); KC (1958), 788, 796,
900, 1016, 1035, 1176, 1186, 1216, 1356, 1383;
Huang Ming wen-hai (microfilm roll no.5), 4/5/6;
Hsia Chung-ching kung chi i-shih 遺事, 6/54a;
Yang Shih-ch'i, *Tung-li wen-chi*, 12/11b; Li Tung-
yang, *Huai-lu-t'ang chi*, 15/1a; Ch'en Tzu-lung
(ECCP), ed., *Ming ching-shih wen-pien* 明經世文
編, 14/4b; *I-t'ung chao-chi lu*, incl. in Huang
Ch'ang-ling 黃昌齡, *Pai-ch'eng* 稗乘, Wan-li ed.
(NLP microfilm), no. 536.

Wang Gungwu

HSIANG Chung 項忠 (T. 藎臣, H. 喬松),
March 13, 1421–September 11, 1502, a
celebrated military commander, was born
into a family which settled in the early
12th century at Chia-hsing 嘉興, Chekiang.
A *chin-shih* of 1442, he received the appointment of secretary in the ministry of
Justice. In 1449 he served on the expedition led by the emperor, Chu Ch'i-chen
(*q.v.*), which suffered the disastrous defeat at T'u-mu. Captured by the Mongols,
Hsiang was taken to the north and assigned to tending horses. He succeeded in
making his escape, taking two mounts;
after both were exhausted, he continued
seven days on foot before reaching a
border fort. He was later reinstated in his
ministry and rose to become an acting
bureau director.

In May, 1451, he and the censor, Han
Yung (*q.v.*), were promoted to surveillance vice commissioners, dispatched to
Kwangtung, and both charged with military duties. While Han received rapid
promotion, Hsiang remained at the same
post for three years. In 1454 he received
an increase in pay for his part in the
suppression of an aboriginal band, but
soon thereafter went home on learning
of the death of his father. After the
mourning period he was sent (1457 ?) to
Shantung without change in rank. In July,
1459, he was made surveillance commissioner of Shensi. As this was his first
promotion in eight years, Hsiang's friend
Han Yung sent him a poem of congratulation.

It seems that Hsiang continued to
display rather than to conceal his talents.
His administration of justice so pleased
the people of Shensi that on two occasions, when he had to leave his post, they
sent delegations to Peking to plead for
his retention in their province. This happened in 1462 on the death of his step-
mother, and a year later when he was
promoted to an office in Peking. Late in
1463 the emperor by a special decree
made him governor of Shensi, a post he
held for four years. One of his accomplish-

ments greatly appreciated by the people was the reopening of the irrigation canals north of Sian, which enriched over eleven thousand acres of land. Apparently by imposing strict measures of inspection on the lucrative tea trade he incurred the displeasure of certain powerful interests (including perhaps some eunuchs and princely establishments), which profited from it. In September, 1467, when the rules of inspection were promulgated, he was removed from Shensi and recalled to Peking as deputy head of the Censorate, subordinate to Lin Ts'ung (*see* Yeh Sheng).

After less than a year in Peking Hsiang went back to Shensi to help quell a rebellion which broke out in June, 1468, near Ku-yüan 固原 in the P'ing-liang 平凉 prefecture of western Shensi (later Kansu). The leader was Man Ssu 滿四 (or Man Chün 俊), grandson of Badan 把丹, the Mongol officer at P'ing-liang who had surrendered to the Ming army about 1369 and became a hereditary chiliarch of the P'ing-liang Guard, in command of the Mongols who submitted with him. The later generations of these Mongols, known as T'u-ta 土達, or native born Tatars, enjoyed the use of a vast pastureland exempt from taxation. Their increasing wealth invited harassment by covetous officials against whom they sometimes reacted with violence. On this occasion (1468) Man Ssu and his followers killed some police sent to arrest them and then occupied a stronghold in the mountains, called Shih-ch'eng石城, located about thirty-five miles northwest of Ku-yüan. They attracted thousands of followers after defeating a detachment sent from Ku-yüan. In July they routed an army of thirty thousand led by the Shensi provincial authorities: the Grand Defender Huang Pi 黃泌 (a senior eunuch), the governor Ch'en Chieh 陳价 (cs 1439), and the regional commander, Jen Shou 任壽 (second earl of Ning-yüan 寧遠伯). The three escaped death but were arrested and later banished as common soldiers. Several senior

officers and over five hundred men lost their lives. Meanwhile Man Ssu had assumed the title of king.

Due to the fear that the rebels might establish contact with the Mongols north of the Yellow River, the central government now roused itself to action. Early in August an expeditionary force was sent from Peking to join the provincial army against Man Ssu, with Hsiang Chung named supreme commander of Shensi. Sharing his authority were the senior eunuch, Liu Hsiang 劉祥, as supervisor, and the general, Liu Yü 劉玉 (T. 仲璧, Pth. 毅敏, earl of Ku-yüan, nephew of another eunuch), as regional commander. At the same time Ma Wen-sheng (*q.v.*) was appointed governor of Shensi. Some thirty thousand men all told assembled at Ku-yüan in the middle of October, and proceeded to assail the rebel stronghold. After several days of skirmishing they suffered a defeat during which a general, Mao Chung (*q.v.*), was killed by an arrow. It so happened that a comet was visible in the night sky when the report of the defeat reached Peking (November, 20) and the court, apprehensive of a panic among the people, published only stories of victory. The military insisted on sending imperial guards from Peking, but the civilians led by P'eng Shih and Shang Lu (*qq.v.*) advised the emperor to trust Hsiang Chung with the conduct of his mission without interference. The civilians prevailed, much to the chagrin of the military, who were thus denied the chance of gaining power, fame, and wealth. In this context Hsiang's strategy of encirclement and starvation worked. By December the rebels began to surrender. One of them, a Muslim, agreed to a plot to have Man Ssu enticed out of the fort. Man appeared expecting an easy victory but was surprised and captured. About three hundred prisoners, including Man Ssu, were sent to Peking where they were executed in February, 1469. The remaining rebels held out a few more days. When they tried to escape from the fort, they were either slaughtered or captured.

For this victory Hsiang Chung received an advancement of one grade as a reward and made right censor-in-chief and one of his sons was given a minor hereditary military rank in the Chin-i Guard. After returning to his post as deputy to Lin Ts'ung in the Censorate (February, 1469), he served on several missions. In August, 1470, after a serious flood, he supervised the relief of several hundred thousand famine stricken people in a vast area south and east of Peking. Before the relief work was completed, however, he was sent to Honan to assemble an army for the suppression of a rebellion in Hukuang. This took place in the western parts of the Ching-chou 荊州 and Hsiang-yang 襄陽 prefectures, known as the Ching-Hsiang area in the northwestern corner of Hukuang bordering on Honan, Shensi, and Szechwan, a region of some ten thousand square miles of mountains, forests, gorges, and valleys that had been officially closed to immigrants since 1368 when it was conquered by the Ming army under Teng Yü (q.v.). In time, however, it became the refuge of outlaws, tax evaders, and famine refugees, who, from 1437 on, had arrived in waves time and again. By 1465 nearly two million non-registered persons had illegally settled there, not under any particular governmental jurisdiction and not paying taxes. Here and there local strong men emerged as leaders. A schemer, Shih Lung 石龍, nicknamed Shih Ho-shang 和尙 or Shih the monk, began to unite them against the government. Their rebellion took place that year with Liu T'ung 劉通, nicknamed Liu Ch'ien-chin 千斤, or Liu the lifter of a thousand catties, as leader. Late in 1466 government troops commanded by General Chu Yung 朱永 (T. 景昌, 1429-96, earl of Fu-ning 撫寧伯, duke of Pao-kuo 保國公, Pth. 武毅) and the minister of Works, Pai Kuei (q.v.), assisted by the Hukuang regional commander, Li Chen 李震 (T. 懋學, d. August, 1486),

and other generals suppressed the uprising. They succeeded in killing most of the rebels, but left unresolved the problem of the one and a half million illegal residents. Four years later in 1470 another rebellion occurred, led by an outlaw, Li Yüan 李原 (also called Li Hu-tzu 鬍子, Li the Bearded), again assisted by Shih, the monk. In December Hsiang received the appointment of supreme commander of Honan and Hukuang in charge of the armies to put down the uprising. Han Yung again sent him a poem of congratulation, which included these words of caution, "great talents have always evoked much resentment, and so it would be advisable to keep one's brilliance under cover" (古來才大人多忌, 且閟精芒在劍函).

Early in 1471 Hsiang established his headquarters at Nan-yang in southwestern Honan. Together with Li Chen then still the regional commander of Hukuang, he set up blockades at entrances to the rebel held mountainous area. By promising immunity to those who would surrender themselves, Hsiang drew most of the people out of the mountains and had them escorted back to their native places for resettlement. Meanwhile his army fought its way into the rebel land, finally capturing Li the Bearded in August, 1471. In their joint report Hsiang and Li Chen said they resettled nine hundred thirty-eight thousand individuals, killed over a thousand rebels in combat, and captured twenty-eight thousand rebels and their families. Concerning the last category, Hsiang suggested banishment, saying that by taking one man from each family five thousand could be added to the military service. Late in 1471 Hsiang and Li submitted their report on the conclusion of the military action, stating that they had resettled over five hundred thousand more persons, captured two hundred eighty-six ringleaders, executed six hundred forty, and sentenced over thirty thousand to exile. Compared to reports on other campaigns in the Ming dynasty, these contained nothing unusual and would normally have been accepted without question.

It happened that on January 16, 1472, fifteen days after Hsiang's report was recorded in Peking, a comet appeared in the sky, and was visible during the next thirty-one nights. According to common belief, a comet conveyed heavenly displeasure at some wrongdoings by the emperor or his officials. As usual on such an occasion, a wave of memorials turned up, some bearing admonitions, some with confessions, but most naming someone's misdeeds as the possible cause of the omen. When one official suggested the possibility that among those killed and banished by Hsiang some might have been innocent or subject to pardon, those who disliked Hsiang took the rumor as fact and seized the opportunity to attack him, some even saying that such wanton killing would assuredly deserve heavenly retribution after death if not in this life. The emperor, however, was on Hsiang's side and called his accusers prejudiced. Then in June, 1472, Pai Kuei memorialized on some discrepancies in figures given in Hsiang's reports and suggested a formal investigation; but the emperor rejected Pai's suggestion and ordered immediate acceptance of Hsiang's final report as the basis for naming those to be given rewards. Hsiang and Li each received an advancement by one grade.

Incensed by the criticisms, Hsiang submitted a long memorial in his own defense, declaring that he had followed strictly the imperial order based on a century-old policy of forbidding immigration to the Ching-Hsiang area, and that the rebellion was the direct result of the failure of Pai Kuei and the generals who had directed the earlier campaign and had received rewards. He said that the figures in the final reports had been correctly checked and should supersede the preliminary figures in earlier dispatches. He also reported on the establishment of forts and police stations to guard the points of entrance to the forbidden area. The emperor approved Hsiang's conten-

tions and ordered him back to Peking. As to the Ching-Hsiang area which he tried to insulate against immigrants, on the recommendation of the associate censor-in-chief, Yüan Chieh 原傑 (T. 子英, 1417-77, cs 1445), a new policy was adopted in Peking in 1476 whereby the remaining settlers were legalized by registration and put under the jurisdiction of the new prefecture, Yün-yang-fu 鄖陽府, to be supervised by a governor and a branch regional commander.

Hsiang served two more years in the Censorate after his return to Peking. Late in 1474 he was appointed minister of Justice, but within a month was transferred to the ministry of War which he headed for over two years. Early in 1477 the emperor, Chu Chien-shen (q.v.), began to place his trust in the eunuch Wang Chih (q.v.) to coordinate the intelligence network, and in March permitted him to establish a new court of investigation, called the West Depot, which soon became a center of blackmail and torture. It is said that Wang became so powerful that even high officials meeting him in the street would yield him the right of way. One day Hsiang passed him without showing this courtesy and the following day a gang of imperial guards sent by Wang harassed and insulted him.

In June, after Grand Secretary Shang Lu requested the abolition of this Depot, Hsiang collected the signatures of high ministerial officers in a strong memorial supporting Shang. The emperor yielded to their demand and closed it. A few days later, however, Wang Chih returned to imperial favor, and Hsiang, finding his position untenable, requested sick leave. Before he could depart from Peking, however, the eunuchs had him brought to trial on the charge of accepting bribes from his military subordinates including the general, Li Chen. It is said that under torture Hsiang confessed as charged and was then deprived of all ranks and reduced to the status of a commoner. Li Chen, who had just received, in October,

1476, the hereditary rank of earl of Hsing-ning 興寧伯 for the pacification of the tribesmen in southwestern Hukuang, was deprived of the earldom. After the downfall of Wang Chih in 1483, both Hsiang and Li were restored to their former ranks. Hsiang then lived in retirement nineteen more years. When he died, he was accorded several posthumous honors including the name Hsiang-i 襄毅 and the hereditary rank of a deputy chiliarch of Chia-hsing. Thus he left his descendants two military ranks, one in his native place and the other in Peking.

Hsiang had ten descendants, who won the *chü-jen* degree during the Ming dynasty. Among them five advanced to *chin-shih*: a son, Hsiang Ching 經 (T. 誠之, cs 1487); two grandsons, Hsiang Hsi 錫 (T. 秉仁, H. 瓶山, cs 1523), and Hsiang K'o 銅 (T. 秉容, H. 南沙, cs 1562); a great-grandson, Hsiang Yüan-chih 元治 (T. 子聲, H. 星渚, cs 1556); and a great-great-grandson, Hsiang Ch'eng-fang 承芳 (T. 彥國, H. 見呂, cs 1593). He also had a famous great-grandnephew, Hsiang Yüan-pien (*q.v.*), the artist and collector. A great-great-grandnephew, Hsiang Te-chen 德楨, compiled a biography of Hsiang Chung, entitled *Hsiang Hsiang-i kung nien-p'u* 公年譜, 5 *ch.*, printed in 1598. It has two appendices, biographical data in 4 *chüan* and Hsiang Chung's own writings in 1 *chüan*.

The accusation leveled against Hsiang as a wanton killer is obviously a fabrication, for by the Ming code rebels were supposed to be dealt with harshly as a warning, and a combat soldier was rewarded according to the number of enemy heads or ears he could display. He was evidently also the victim of the inopportune appearance of the comet. In this respect one cannot help but remember the poem his friend Han Yung sent him in 1459 with the advice that a talented man should try to be discreet to avoid being hated.

Bibliography

1/178/1a, 156/11b, 164/22a, 166/12b, 176/13b; 5/38/62a; 7/29/1a; 8/31/1a; 61/100/4a; 63/16/5a; MSL (1964), Hsien-tsung, 1874, 1876, 1882, 1888, 1900, 2019, 2023, Hsiao-tsung, 3508; KC (1958), 2317; Sheng Feng 盛楓 (cj 1681), *Chia-ho cheng-hsien lu* 嘉禾徵獻錄, ch. 6; Ku Ming-t'ai (ECCP), *Ming-ch'ao chi-shih pen-mo*, ch. 38; Chu Kuo-chen(ECCP), *Ta-shih chi*, ch. 20; Chu Ta-shao 朱大韶, *Huang Ming ming-ch'en mu-ming* 名臣墓銘 (NCL microfilm) 震集; Wang Shih-chen, *Chung-kuan k'ao* in *Yen-shan-t'ang pieh-chi*, 92/11a.

Chaoying Fang

HSIANG Sheng-mo 項聖謨 (T. 孔彰, H. 易庵, 大酉, 胥山樵, etc.), 1597–1658, painter, calligrapher, and poet, was a native of Hsiu-shui 秀水, Chekiang. He was a grandson of Hsiang Yüan-pien (*q.v.*), the great art connoisseur and collector, and a son of Hsiang Te-hsin 德新 (T. 復初, 又新). He became celebrated for his smaller paintings, which are generally considered better than his large ones. Critics regard his work as showing the excellence of a scholar-painter and the skill of a professional artist. Because of his specialty in sketching pine trees, he came to be known as Hsiang Sung 松 (Hsiang the Pine). He was also skilled in depicting bamboos, rocks, trees, flowers, human figures, buildings, and, particularly, landscapes. The great artist Tung Ch'i-ch'ang (ECCP) remarked admiringly that Hsiang approached the excellence of Yüan artists, and that Hsiang Yüan-pien should be proud to have so outstanding a painter as his grandson. He himself reports that even as a child he was fond of painting. Exhorted by his father to concentrate on the study of the Classics for the official examinations, he could practice painting only at night. He learned by copying well-known ancient pictures in his family's collection and also by painting natural objects. "One night," he wrote, "I dreamed that my brush stood up like a pillar stretching upwards. There were steps along the pillar which was more than ten feet tall. I climbed up and occupied the top of it, clapping my hands, laughing and talking. Since then, I have felt as if I were inspired and have often achieved fine results while imitating the works of ancient artists."

In July, 1626, he painted his well-known "Chao-yin t'u" 招隱圖 (Summoning to the life of a recluse). In 1628 he traveled to north China, as far as the Great Wall. During a nine months' stay in Peking, he started to paint another of his masterpieces, "Sung-t'ao san-hsien t'u" 松濤散仙圖 (A lesser immortal amid wind-blown pines). One day, returning from an excursion, he fell from his horse and hurt his right arm. He was unable to move for some time, and the picture remained incomplete. Early in 1629 he returned home and finished the picture soon afterwards.

In his last years Hsiang lived in comparative poverty (after the pillage of the family property by the Ch'ing army in 1645), but maintained his integrity. He supported himself by selling his pictures, but he would not let them go to rich buyers whom he disliked, even if they offered high prices. Other works include a long scroll depicting himself from his youth to old age, entitled "Chiu-shih-chiu pien-hsiang t'u" 九十九變相圖 (99 metamorphoses), and "Ch'ang-chiang wan-li t'u" 長江萬里圖 (A myriad *li* of the Yangtze), the latter eliciting the approbation of Chu I-tsun (ECCP). Osvald Sirén lists sixty paintings credited to Hsiang, the latest one dated 1657, while J. C. Ferguson credits him with over a hundred. They may be found in museums and private collections all over the world.

Particularly admired among Hsiang Sheng-mo's poems was his series *Yen-tzu shih-chüan* 雁字詩卷. Lu Shih-hua 陸時化 (1714–79), art critic and author of *Wu Yüeh so-chien shu-hua lu* 吳越所見書畫錄, remarked on these: "Wang Wei (701–61?) was praised for the painting in his poetry and the poetry in his painting. Hsiang need not defer to him." There is an anecdote that a friend once presented him

with a jar of wine. The next day the friend came back asking for the empty jar, which a soldier unfortunately had broken. In compensation Hsiang painted a jar filled with peach blossoms and willow branches, some stretching out horizontally and some hanging downwards. It was an elegant tour de force. He also wrote on the picture a long explanatory poem.

Hsiang Sheng-mo is reported to have left a literary collection entitled *Lang-yün-t'ang chi* 朗雲堂集; he was also the compiler of *Mo-chün t'i-yü* 墨君題語, 2 *ch.*, which the editors of the *Ssu-k'u* catalogue mention by title only. His nephew, Hsiang K'uei 奎 (T. 子聚, H. 東井, 牆東居士, fl. 1681–92), was also an artist who specialized in painting chrysanthemums, orchids, and bamboos. His landscape in the Yüan style shows his fondness for using the "dry brush with black ink" technique.

Bibliography

64/辛27/19b; An Ch'i 安岐 (b. 1683?), *Mo-yüan hui-kuan lu* 墨緣彙觀錄, 3/180; Ch'en Lang 陳烺, *Tu-hua chi-lüeh* 讀畫輯畧, 7; *Chia-hsing-fu* 嘉興府 *chih* (1877), 53/36a; Ch'in Tsu-yung 秦祖永, *T'ung-yin lun-hua* 桐陰論畫, 上/4; CSK, Vol. *I-shu chuan* 藝術傳, 3, *Lieh-chuan*列傳 289, 5461; J. C. Ferguson and Shang Ch'eng-tsu 商承祚, *Li-tai chu-lu hua-mu* 歷代著錄畫目, 329b; Hsü Ch'in 徐沁 (fl. 1694), *Ming-hua lu* 明畫錄, 4/43; *Ku-kung shu-hua lu* 故宮書畫錄 (1956), 4/235, 5/409, 6/75, 8/95; *Ku-kung ming-hua* 名畫 (1968), VIII, 36; Lu Shih-hua, *Wu Yüeh so-chien shu-hua lu*, 2/100a; Tung Ch'i-ch'ang, *Jung-t'ai pieh-chi*, 6/50b; SK (1930), 114/5a; Tseng Yu-ho Ecke, *Chinese Calligraphy* (Philadelphia, 1971) no. 72; O. Sirén, *Chinese Painting*, VII (New York, 1958), 188; E. J. Laing, *Chinese Paintings in Chinese Publications, 1956–1958* (Ann Arbor, 1969), 167; V. Contag and C. C. Wang, *Seals of Chinese Painters and Collectors* (Hong Kong, 1966), 386, 701; James Cahill, *Fantastics and Eccentrics in Chinese Painting* (The Asia Society Inc., 1967), 20.

Liu Wei-p'ing

HSIANG Yüan-pien 項元汴 (T. 子京, H. 墨林山人), 1525–90, art collector and painter, was a native of Hsiu-shui 秀水

(Chia-hsing), Chekiang. He came from a family of wealth and had a great-grand-uncle Hsiang Chung (*q.v.*) who served in the years 1475-77 as minister of War. His father had three sons by two wives, nées Ch'en 陳 and Yen 顏. The one born to the lady Ch'en was the eldest, Hsiang Yüan-ch'i 淇 (T. 子瞻, H. 少嶽), who collected art and practiced calligraphy. The second son, Hsiang Tu-shou 篤壽 (T. 子長, H. 少谿, 1521-86), who married the daughter of the historian Cheng Hsiao, *q.v.*), a-chieved the *chin-shih* in 1562, served in the government until about 1575, and was the author of several works, including a collection of memorials under the title *Hsiao-ssu-ma tsou-i* 小司馬奏議, 6 *ch.*, and a collection of biographical sketches of persons in the Ming period under the title *Chin-hsien pei-i* 今獻備遺, 42 *ch.*, in which he lavished praise and ignored issues.

Hsiang Yüan-pien, the youngest son (hence his seal reading Hsiang Shu-tzu 叔子), attended the local school and took part in the provincial examinations until 1558 when his brother passed and he failed to qualify. Pleading ill health, he gave up hope of an official career, purchased the rank of a scholar in the National University, and resigned himself to a supposedly humdrum life as supervisor of the family estate. Meanwhile, his brother achieved the *chin-shih* and rose steadily in the civil service hierarchy. Probably driven by an ambition not to be overshadowed by his brother, Hsiang Yüan-pien devoted himself to the connoisseurship of art and with a passionate and urgent zeal built up an art collection of extraordinary proportions. He named the building housing his collection the T'ien-lai-ko 天籟閣, after an old iron lute inscribed with the characters *t'ien-lai*. Wen P'eng (*see* Wen Cheng-ming), who visited the place frequently, described it as surrounded by palm trees whose green leaves gave restful shade on summer days. Working before a window thus shaded, Hsiang entitled the booklet he composed *Chiao-*

ch'uang chiu lu 蕉窗九錄, or "nine chapters written before a palm shaded window," in which he described nine items in his collection—paper, ink stick, writing brush, ink palette, printed books, rubbings of inscriptions on stone, paintings, lutes, and incense. [The authorship of this work has been questioned.] His art collection, especially the paintings and calligraphic pieces in it, became widely known. At last he found a place for himself in the world and outshone his brother, the official, whose name became so unfamiliar by the eighteenth century that the editors of the *Che-chiang t'ung-chih* 通志 (1736) entered it incorrectly in the *chin-shih* list as Hsiang Tu-ch'un 春.

Hsiang Yüan-pien was a man of considerable business acumen. It was his practice to identify the contents of his collection by assigning a specific character to each group and a number to each item, characters such as 聚 and 讖 which were followed by a number. He usually added a note on each handscroll, indicating price, when and how acquired. This was a common way of keeping an inventory, and being a businessman himself, including the ownership of a pawnshop, it was only natural that he should adopt the practice for his art collection. Oddly enough, however, unlike so many other collectors, Hsiang Yüan-pien somehow failed to compile a complete catalogue of his collection, with the result that it is impossible to determine its exact size. His contemporaries generally believed that his collection surpassed that of Wang Shih-chen (*q.v.*) both in quantity and quality. In the year 1645, when the Ch'ing army sacked and took Chia-hsing, the collection was dispersed. Fortunately, its reputation was such that items known to have belonged to it were quickly acquired by other collectors. Many items bearing his seals were presented or added by purchase to the Ch'ing imperial collection. One of Hsiang Yüan-pien's admirers was the Ch'ien-lung emperor (*see* Hung-li, ECCP) who acquired the largest number of items from the Hsiang collection and mentioned him frequently in his inscriptions and colophons on works of art. The emperor even named a studio in the summer palace in Jehol the T'ien-lai shu-wu 天籟書屋 after the T'ien-lai-ko and selected four scrolls formerly owned by Hsiang to be stored in it. Items of the Hsiang collection which did not find their way into the Ch'ing imperial collection are now scattered in museums all over the world. Judging by the large number of Hsiang items extant, it is safe to say that, although the pillage of 1645 destroyed his collection as such, most of the items it contained have been preserved.

Besides labeling each item in his collection with loving care, Hsiang Yüan-pien also demonstrated his pride of possession by spattering his collector's seals on the mounting if not on the works of art themselves. According to a recent tabulation made from items in the Chinese National Palace Museum Collection (the former imperial collection) which once belonged to Hsiang, the Ming collector had at least ninety-three different seals. Victoria Contag and Wang Chi-ch'ien have reproduced seventy-four of them. Hsiang Yüan-pien has enjoyed the reputation of possessing a prodigious knowledge and a discriminating taste in matters pertaining to painting and calligraphy. A possible explanation of his lavish use of the collector's seals may have been his desire to make doubly sure that no unscrupulous art dealer could forge so many seals without being caught. That a work of art bears his many seals means generally that it had passed his close and expert scrutiny and is therefore the more treasured on that basis. Nevertheless, his habit of stamping too many seals on works of art does have the effect of harming their aesthetic appeal, and many connoisseurs are in agreement with Ch'en Chi-ju (ECCP) that such practice is "devilish."

In building up his collection, Hsiang Yüan-pien bought and sold. Like a true collector, the price paid for a work of art was a matter of paramount importance to him and must be duly recorded. According to Chu I-tsun (ECCP), who was related to the Hsiang family, when Hsiang thought he had paid too high a price for a particular item, he used to feel so remorseful that he would lose appetite. On such occasions, his elder brother Hsiang Tu-shou, the official, would come to his rescue by buying the item from him at the original price. Hsiang Yüan-pien's preoccupation with prices has led his detractors, among them Chu I-tsun, to call him a miser. Hsiang's emphasis on prices, however, was precisely the reason why he was able to assemble a princely collection without bringing his family fortune to bankruptcy. Imbued with the taste of a wealthy scholar for *objets d'art* and aided by the acumen of a pawnbroker in evaluation and authentication, Hsiang occupied a position almost without parallel among the art collectors of China. One wonders how his detractors would feel if they were ushered into an art auction in London or New York today.

Hsiang's fabulous collection was truly an extraordinary phenomenon in the art world of China. It included a large number of the greatest masterpieces, such as three manuscripts of the fourth-century calligrapher Wang Hsi-chih, and the Nü-shih-chen t'u-chüan 女史箴圖卷 (Admonitions of the palace instructress, now in the British Museum) by another fourth-century artist, the painter Ku K'ai-chih. Hsiang Yüan-pien seals may also be found on many of the more renowned works of the T'ang, Sung, Yüan, and Ming dynasties now in public and private collections. Before the invention of photographic reproductions, an aspiring artist considered it extremely fortunate if he were able to see and copy a few originals of the old masters. The vastness and variety of the Hsiang collection did, therefore, exert a tremendous influence on his contemporaries. For instance, in 1584, Tung

Ch'i-ch'ang (ECCP) was a needy student whom Hsiang employed as the tutor of his eldest son. This enabled Tung to gain an intimate acquaintance with the superb works of art in the Hsiang collection, an opportunity open only to the most fortunate few. In later years Tung was to acknowledge over and over again in his writings his great indebtedness to the Hsiang collection for his own achievements as the most outstanding calligrapher, painter, and critic of his age.

An art collector is to be judged by the merits of his collection. There is no doubt that Hsiang, a true lover of art, was possessed of an intense acquisitive instinct which enabled him to compete successfully with the other collectors of the day. Being an artist himself, his collection was in a way his own creative act, an extension of his personality, and an expression of his ideal image of himself. By and large, it may be said that Hsiang's collection, considering its enormous size, was one of very high quality, although inferior works, even a few late copies, had found their way into it. Laurence Sickman, an American student of Chinese art, has said of Hsiang Yüan-pien: "His enthusiasm outdistanced his discrimination, and his collection was distinctly uneven, though many famous paintings and calligraphies did enter his possession." This assessment appears to be too harsh.

Hsiang expectedly dabbled in calligraphy and painting himself. But he was an artist of decidedly limited attainment. In landscape painting he was an ardent admirer and imitator of the Yüan masters, especially Ni Tsan (*q.v.*). An example of his landscape painting is included in the album *Hsü-ching-tsai so-ts'ang ming-hua chi* 虛靜齋所藏名畫集 (reproduced by The Commercial Press, Shanghai, 1934). It presents a scene of a valley deep in the mountains with trees, rocks, and waterfalls, but no trace of human habitation. In his inscription on the top of the painting he wrote: "The mountains are so deep that no path exists; the pines so thick they enclose darkness by themselves. I sit here alone unconcernedly in the garden of art but dispatch my thoughts to the obscure far-away. The painting probably expresses my wish to escape from this world and live among woods and rocks." The painting was dated eighth day of the eleventh moon, chi-ch'ou year (December 15, 1589), one year before his death. The concept and the sentiments are very much in the Ni Tsan tradition. Tung Ch'i-ch'ang, in a landscape done in 1623, recalled in the inscription that Hsiang Yüan-pien once told him that among the masters of landscape Ni Tsan was the hardest to imitate because any minor deviation might prove fatal, impossible of concealment by alteration. In this painting, Hsiang tried his hand at imitating Ni Tsan, unfortunately with only limited success. Another example of his landscape painting is a handscroll in the John M. Crawford collection. The work is dated "Wan-li era, wu-yin year," namely, 1578. Although not distinctly in the Ni Tsan style, it is a work which properly belongs to the wen-jen-hua (literary man's painting) school. The Chinese National Palace Museum Collection contains a number of Hsiang paintings, all in the genre of flowers and birds, bamboos and orchids. One of them was included in the exhibition of Chinese art in Burlington House, London, 1935. Richard Edwards of the University of Michigan, commenting on Hsiang's works, said: "As an artist he must be viewed as the gifted amateur, not a famous artist-amateur like Wen Cheng-ming or Shen Chou (*q.v.*), but one who followed similar ideals without attaining a great name." This judgment appears to be judicious. Hsiang's calligraphic style belonged to the school of the Yüan master Chao Meng-fu (1254–1322). His contemporaries, according to Wu Hsiu (ECCP, p. 154), liked his calligraphy but not the way he inscribed his paintings and sometimes bribed his attendants to smuggle out his paintings before he had a chance to put inscriptions on them.

Appended to the chapter on the collection of paintings in his booklet *Chiao-ch'uang chiu lu* is a short discussion on the art of painting in which he expressed his preference for techniques employed by the Yüan masters, particularly the use of the k'o-jan 渴染, "dry brush staining." Hsiang Yüan-pien has erroneously been given credit for two books. One is a short treatise on the bronzes cast in the Hsüan-te period, entitled *Hsüan-lu po-lun* 宣鑪博論. The book bears Hsiang's name as the author but the date of composition is given as 1626—an obvious clue to its lack of authenticity. The other book is a work on porcelains with eighty-three colored illustrations, published first in Oxford, 1908, under the title *Chinese Porcelain, Sixteenth Century Colored Illustrations with Chinese Ms. text by Hsiang Yüan-p'ien*, translated and annotated by Stephen W. Bushell, and reissued in a lavish way in 1931 under the title *Noted Porcelains of Successive Dynasties with Comments and Illustrations by Hsiang Yüan-pien*, revised and annotated by Kuo Pao-ch'ang 郭葆昌 and John C. Ferguson. Included in the 1931 edition is an alleged portrait of Hsiang Yüan-pien and a picture of a pottery ink palette in the shape of a swan with Hsiang's name inscribed thereon. In the text attributed to Hsiang, references to other collectors are mostly vague and unidentifiable, but in one instance Shen Shih-hsing (*q.v.*), who died in 1614, is referred to by his posthumous title. This discrepancy was noticed by the annotators who offered the explanation that the text was altered by someone in the Hsiang family, which seems implausible. Another mistake unnoticed by the annotators is the erroneous reference to Wang Shih-mou (*q.v.*) as a member of the Hanlin Academy. This book was the subject of a long and critical review by Paul Pelliot in the pages of the *T'oung Pao* (1936), a rejoinder by John C. Ferguson in the *Journal of the North China Branch of the Royal Asiatic Society* for

the same year, and a riposte by Paul Pelliot in the *T'oung Pao* for 1937. Sir Percival David also wrote an article entitled "Hsiang and His Album" in the *Transactions of the Oriental Ceramic Society*, 1933–34, London, 1934. On the other hand, several of Hsiang Yüan-pien's own works in the *Chiao-ch'uang chiu lu* have been incorrectly attributed to T'u Lung (*q.v.*), another collector and connoisseur of note.

Forty-five years after his death, Hsiang Yüan-pien's tombstone eulogy was composed by his former protégé Tung Ch'i-ch'ang in which Hsiang Yüan-pien's art collection was compared with those of the Sung dynasty painters Mi Fu (1051–1107) and Li Kung-lin (1049–1106). Tung also said that in landscape painting Hsiang was able to capture the mood and atmosphere of the Yüan masters Huang Kung-wang (1269–1304) and Ni Tsan, while his calligraphy was as tasteful as that of the sixth-century monk Chih-yung 智永 (Wang Hsi-chih's descendant) and the Yüan master Chao Meng-fu. Tung Ch'i-ch'ang himself transcribed the eulogy and the original copy is now in the possession of Takashima Kaian 高島槐安. It was reproduced in 1962 in the series *Shōseki meihin sōkan* 書跡名品叢刊.

Hsiang Yüan-pien had six sons. Although none of them achieved high scholastic and official honors, they were all worthy inheritors of his talents in the arts. The eldest, Hsiang Te-ch'un 德純 (later changed to Hsiang Mu 穆, H. 貞元, 無稱子), was tutored by Tung Ch'i-ch'ang and authored a book on the theory and practice of calligraphy entitled *Shu-fa ya-yen* 書法雅言, included in the *Ssu-k'u ch'üan-shu*. Hsiang Yüan-pien's grandson, Hsiang Sheng-mo (*q.v.*), was an outstanding landscape and flowers-and-birds painter.

Bibliography

5/99/60a; 40/48/25b; 64/19/3a; 65/4/7b; Tung Ch'i-ch'ang, *Jung-t'ai chi* 文 8/30e; *Chia-hsing-fu chih* 嘉興府志 (1877), 首, 15/22b, 17/17a, 53/2b,

3b, 35a; Pien Yung-yü (ECCP), *Shih-ku-t'ang shu-hua lu, shu* ch. 27, *hua* ch. 29; Chu I-tsun, *P'u-shu-t'ing chi*, 53/1b, 54/8b; Wu Hsiu, *Lun-hua chüeh-chü* 論畫絕句; *Chinese Calligraphy and Painting in the Collection of John M. Crawford, Jr.* (1962), 25, 144, no. 66, pl. (detail) 42; Victoria Contag and C. C. Wang, *Seals of Chinese Painters and Collectors of the Ming and Ch'ing Periods* (Hong Kong, 1966), 610, 700; E. J. Laing, *Chinese Paintings in Chinese Publications, 1956–1968* (Ann Arbor, 1969), 168.

Ch'en Chih-mai

HSIAO Ta-heng 蕭大亨 (T. 夏卿, H. 嶽峯), April 6, 1532-February 23, 1612, an expert on Mongol affairs, was born in T'ai-an 泰安, Shantung. His father, a native of Chi-shui 吉水, Kiangsi, for some reason had previously taken up residence in Chi-ning 濟寧 on the Grand Canal. A legend has it that he dreamed, just prior to Ta-heng's birth, of the god of Mount T'ai, and so decided to establish his home at the foot of that sacred mountain. In 1549 Hsiao Ta-heng was accepted as a student in the T'ai-an subprefectural school, probably as a result of the sponsorship of his father-in-law, a landowner of the area, for as a rule it was difficult to change one's registration. After passing the civil examinations (cj 1561, cs 1562), Hsiao's first assignment was to the magistracy of Yü-tz'u 榆次, Shansi. In 1565 he became secretary in the ministry of Revenue. After being promoted some time later to director of a bureau in the same ministry, he was dispatched to the northern border of Shensi to oversee the provisioning and military equipment of the frontier forces. Except for a period at home to mourn the passing of his mother, he served in these regions for nearly two decades, seeing among other things to the repair of the irrigation canals at Ning-hsia. His capabilities were recognized by a series of appointments: governor of Ning-hsia (1580–81), and of Hsüan-fu (1581–87), assistant commander of the capital defense corps (1587), and vice minister of War (1587–

89). On March 27, 1589, the court directed him to escort the prince of Lu 潞, Chu I-liu (fourth son of Chu Tsai-hou and younger brother of the reigning emperor, Chu I-chün [qq.v.], March 3, 1568-July 4, 1614), to his domain in Wei-hui 衞輝, Honan. A drought was then afflicting the land in north China, and the court was apprehensive about the prince's safety enroute. After completion of the mission Hsiao was appointed governor-general of Hsüan-fu and Tatung where he served for six years (1589–95). One of the important events during his term of office was the rebellion of two Mongol chieftains, Shih-er-kuan 史二官 and Ch'e-ta-chi 車達雞, who had received permission to tend their flocks and herds in Chinese territory for over thirty years. In July, 1591, Hsiao ordered a subordinate officer to attack a raiding party sent by Shih-er-kuan and to retrieve whatever booty they had seized. The action was initially successful but it did not deter the Mongols in the Tatung region from continuing to make trouble. It happened that the chief of the Mongols in that area, Čürüke, a grandson of Altanqaγan (q.v.), for an unauthorized migration to the west in 1590, was punished by the Chinese court which ordered the suspension of trading in horses at Tatung. The loss of that lucrative trade forced the Mongol chief to ask for forgiveness and to be permitted to continue sending tribute. Hsiao and other commanders on the northern border took the opportunity to stipulate that one condition for the resumption of trade was the arrest and delivery of Shih-er-kuan. In May, 1592, Shih-er-kuan and other rebel leaders were duly delivered and the Mongol chief was richly rewarded. Hsiao, in order not to upset relations with the Mongols, treated the captives well and even permitted Shih-er-kuan's son, along with two hundred seventy horsemen, to move back inside the Great Wall. When a censor protested, Hsiao, while defending his policy, offered to resign (January 27, 1593), but the emperor would not hear of it. By the following spring (April 18, 1593) he explained his policy of forbearance towards the tribesmen, and the ministry of War, burdened as it was with responsibility for the defense of Korea, gave its approval, with the emperor concurring. In the following year he was given the honorary rank of minister of War.

It was at this point in his career that he undertook to put down on paper his impressions of the Mongols of the frontier. He completed the work at the end of 1594 (November 12). Half a year later (June 12, 1595) he was on his way back to the capital to become minister of Justice with the higher rank of grand guardian of the heir apparent. While serving in this capacity Hsiao made the acquaintance (1601) of Matteo Ricci (*q.v.*) and —along with several other scholar-officials —helped the latter in his composition of the catechism (*T'ien-chu shih-i* 天主實義, 1603). In 1602 Ricci baptized Hsiao's nephew as Michael. Hsiao Ta-heng served as minister of Justice through 1604 (November 28), but beginning in 1603 (July 30) was given the added responsibility of the ministry of War. The following year and until 1608 the latter became his sole charge. He retired with honor on December 23, and was named Pillar of State. Announcement of his death, aged eighty-one *sui*, reached the throne on March 18, 1612. Even before his retirement (October, 1608) his fellow townsmen erected a shrine and stele to him on Mt. T'ai; the shrine still exists, or did at the beginning of the century, when Edouard Chavannes saw it, but the stele is no more. One may add that following his death his funerary inscriptions were written by two grand secretaries, Wu Tao-nan (*see* Ch'en Yü-pi) and Shen Shih-hsing (*q.v.*).

In spite of the respect in which he was held throughout his long and arduous career Hsiao received not a single notice in any one of the eighty-nine compilations included in the Harvard-Yenching Sinological Series Index, number 24. The reason for this neglect was probably political.

His book on the Mongols, known originally as *Pei-lu feng-su* 北虜風俗 (Customs of the northern slaves) and latterly as *I su chi* 夷俗記 (Customs of the barbarians), was distasteful to the ruling group and was suppressed by the imperial commissioners in the 1780s. It receives, nonetheless, a brief notice in the *Ssu-k'u* catalogue, and has survived both in its original edition and as reprints in several *ts'ung-shu*. (Henry Serruys has examined both Wan-li and later editions and reports that the latter have neither Hsiao's preface nor the genealogical tables; otherwise they are almost completely identical.) The work contains, besides the foreword and the appendix giving the tables of the descendants of Batü Mongke (*q.v.*)— apparently added by another hand—, the author's comments on a wide range of topics: marriage, birth, inheritance, punishment for adultery, the judicial process, burial, Buddhism, hospitality, respect for teachers, farming and hunting, food and drink, headgear and dress, respect for superiors, prohibitions and tabus, animal husbandry, practices and preferences, training for war, the army on campaign, tribute and markets. These observations by one who knew the Mongols, at least those in his area, from many close contacts, who respected but did not fear them, are important for his time. We are fortunate in having an annotated translation into French by Serruys, who has also lived in the northwest. Besides this he has made two renderings of the tables, which must have been drawn up at the same time, as the latest date in them is equivalent to 1592.

Hsiao left other works (collections of essays, memorials, etc.) but these seem not to have survived. Both of his sons entered officialdom through the yin privilege. The elder, Hsiao Ho-chung 和中, became a vice minister of the Court of Imperial Stud, and the younger, Hsiao Hsieh-chung 協中 (T. 公融), received an appointment as assistant director of Imperial Parks. The latter committed suicide at the end of the dynasty. A piece of prose written for a stele and several of his poems are included in the local history. In 1726 his tablet was entered in the shrine devoted to men of loyalty.

Bibliography

1/112/21b, 23a, 218/11b, 225/10a; MSL (1940), Shen-tsung 226/4a, 227/5a, 236/4b, 247/11b, 255/10b, 258/5a, 285/3a, 385/7a, 402/4a, 452/4b, 492/8b; T'ai-an-hsien chih (1782), 10/4a, 16b, 11/47a, 12 序記/20b, 12 詩/6a; Yü-tz'u-hsien chih (1748), 3, 11; Huang Ming wen-hai 皇明文海 (microfilm), 5/9/2, 3; TSCC (1885–88), XIV: 191/7/11b; SK (1930), 78/5b; Pei-lu feng-su (Kuo-hsüeh wen-k'u 國學文庫 ed., Peking, 1936, and Pao-yen-t'ang pi-chi ed.; see Ch'en Chi-ju, ECCP); H. Serruys, "Pei-lu fong-su. Les coutumes des esclaves septentrionaux," MS, 10 (1945), 117; id., Genealogical Tables of the Descendants of Dayan-qan ('s Gravenhage, 1958); id., "A Mongol Settlement in North China at the End of the 16th Century," Central Asian Journal, IV (1959), 237; E. Chavannes, Le T'ai Chan (Paris, 1910), carte (#234), 150; W. Franke, Sources, 7. 3. 20; P. M. d'Elia, Fonti Ricciane, II (Rome, 1949), 155, 260, 300.

L. Carrington Goodrich

HSIEH Chao-che 謝肇淛 (T. 在杭), 1567–1624, official, poet, scholar, traveler, and collector of books, paintings, calligraphy, and ceramics, is best remembered as the author of the encyclopedic compilation *Wu tsa tsu* 五雜俎 (Five assorted offerings), 16 *ch.* He came from a family listed in the military category which, at the beginning of the Ming dynasty, had moved from the region of Chekiang to the small coastal town of Chiang-t'ien 江田, in Ch'ang-lo 長樂, Fukien, immediately south of the estuary of the Min 閩 River. By the 16th century the Hsieh family was one of the more prominent in this settlement facing the Straits of Taiwan.

Hsieh's immediate paternal ancestors, in spite of their earlier background, gained some note as scholars, administrators, and collectors of books. The great-great-grandfather, Hsieh Shih-yüan 士元 (T. 仲仁, H. 約菴, 1425–94, cs 1454), rose to be assistant censor-in-chief and concurrently governor of Szechwan (1488–89). Two of his sons acquired the *chin-shih* and left creditable records both in the bureaucracy and in the field of literature. The first, Hsieh Chao-che's grandfather, Hsieh T'ing-chu 廷柱 (T. 邦用, H. 雙湖, cs 1499), concluded his official career as assistant surveillance commissioner in Hukuang; the second, Hsieh T'ing-jui 廷瑞 (T. 邦應, cs 1502), became prefect of Ch'iung-chou 瓊州, Kwangtung. One of Hsieh Shih-yüan's grandsons, Hsieh Chieh 杰 (T. 漢甫, H. 天靈山人, cs 1574, d. 1604), served in 1576 on a mission to the Liu-ch'iu (Ryūkyū) Islands and later published a report on the embassy, *Shih Liu-ch'iu lu* 使琉球錄 (variously given as 2 and 6 *chüan*). Another of Hsieh Chieh's books is an illustrated sketch of coastal defense against Japanese pirates, entitled *Ch'ien-t'ai Wo tsuan* 虔台倭纂, 2 *ch.*, printed in 1595. It contains a long map of the Chinese coast and some remarkable illustrations of ships and firearms. The "Ch'ien-t'ai" in the title refers to the Nan-Kan 南贛 governorship Hsieh Chieh held from 1593 to 1595. Hsieh Chao-che's father, Hsieh Ju-shao 汝韶 (T. 其盛, cj 1558), left a collection of writings, *T'ien-ch'ih hsien-sheng ts'un kao* 天池先生存稿, 16 *ch.* (preface of 1608), a copy of which is preserved in the Naikaku Bunko, Tokyo. Hsieh Chao-che's maternal grandfather was Hsü Ang, a native of Foochow, who was likewise a writer, but is even better known as the father of the poets, Hsü T'ung and Hsü Po, the latter also a calligrapher and book collector (for Hsü Ang and Hsü T'ung, *see* Hsü Po). It was Hsü Po who later wrote a biography of his nephew (cited by Fou Yun-tseu 傅芸子) which is still extant. Hsieh Chao-che was born at Hangchow, Chekiang, where his father was serving as teacher in the Ch'ien-t'ang 錢塘 district school; hence his name, Chao-che and *tzu*, Tsai-hang.

After Hsieh Chao-che acquired the *chü-jen* in 1588 and the higher degree four years later, he became a prefectural judge in Hu-chou 湖州, Chekiang. While there he established a practice which he was to follow frequently thereafter: he investigated the customs of the area, and wrote his impressions, entitling the book *Hsi-Wu chih-sheng* 西吳枝乘, *2 ch.* He was then transferred to Tung-ch'ang 東昌, Shantung (1602-6?). After mourning his father he went to Peking in 1608 for a new assignment. In 1609 he received appointment to Nanking as a secretary in the ministry of Justice and then in the ministry of War. Later he was promoted to the directorship of a bureau in the ministry of Works in Peking (1610?-14?). In this capacity he had to make an inspection of the Ta-ch'ing ho 大清河 and the Grand Canal south of Tung-ch'ang, at the place where the river and Canal intersect. The result was a book-length study of the problems of the northern section of the Canal, entitled *Pei-ho chi* 北河紀, *8 ch.*, and a supplement, *chi-yü* 紀餘, *4 ch.* (Another version called *Pei-ho chi-lüeh* 略, *14 ch.*, is also credited to him.) This, however, was not the only fruit of his stay in Tung-ch'ang; he also brought together interesting data on the region in his *Chü Tung chi* 居東集, *6 ch.* (2 *chüan* each of poetry, essays, and anecdotes), an original edition of which is in the National Central Library (available on microfilm). One of the poems gives a moving description of the hardships of the men conscripted to labor on dike construction. The last part includes his recollection of curious events, strange people, precious products of the region, and gossip—all based on information gleaned during his stay in Shantung.

From this time on Hsieh's official career was in the provinces. Sent to Yunnan as administration vice commissioner, he immediately set to work to investigate the history and mores of that distant outpost and eventually published his findings as *Tien lüeh* 滇略, *10 ch.* Each *chüan* formed a separate section touching on 1) the region, 2) mountains and rivers, 3) produce, 4) customs, 5) leaders of note,

6) contributions to national life, 7) historical events, 8) literature, 9) aborigines, and 10) miscellaneous information. The organization of material foreshadows that of the *Wu tsa tsu*, and indeed a number of items in the latter are in all probability derived from the *Tien lüeh*: the information about the Lao 獠 tribespeople and their belief in sorcery, for example.

He was posted to Kwangsi from Yunnan as assistant surveillance commissioner, then as right administration commissioner, and finally (in 1621-22) as left administration commissioner, his highest rank (2), after which he retired. Hsieh was then in his middle fifties, and, except for the years *ca.* 1606 to 1608, he had been in official employ for thirty years. He was to live in retirement only two more; so he must have combined study and writing with official activity throughout his service with the government, for he was a prolific author.

Among the thirty or so titles ascribed to him are several which show the range of his interests and the extent of his wanderings. (In one of his prefaces he wrote: "I have traveled widely. There are few celebrated spots in the Empire where I have not left the imprint of my feet.") While in Kwangsi he became interested in both the region's folklore and its government, writing *Po-Yüeh feng-t'u chi* 百粵風土記, *1 ch.*, and *Yüeh-fan mo-i* 瀋末議, *2 ch.* Actually, in spite of its title, the former is primarily concerned with geography, having much to say about the land, its products, the historic sites, and the tribespeople. While passing through Honan he wrote on the Mu mountain, *Mu-shan chih* 姥山志, *2 ch.* In his own province he collected miscellaneous information about Ch'ang-ch'i 長溪, *Ch'ang-ch'i so-yü* 瑣語, *2 ch.*, edited the gazetteer of the famous mountain, *Ku-shan chih* 鼓山志, *8 ch.* (the Ming edition in Japan is in 12 *chüan*), and had a hand in the history of a neighboring district, *Yung-fu-hsien chih* 永福縣志, *6 ch.* (a manuscript copy of which, dated 1612, is in the Peking library). Another work concerned with his native province which has survived is the *Fu-chien yün-ssu chih* 運司志, 16 *ch.* (printed 1613), which he edited, writing in collaboration with Chiang Ta-k'un 江大鯤, a native of Ch'u-hsiung 楚雄, Yunnan, then director of the salt transport office in Fukien. It deals, under sixteen headings, with salt production and conveyance in the province, its organization and control, and is abundantly provided with maps. This has recently been reprinted in the *Hsüan-lan-t'ang ts'ung-shu* 玄覽堂叢書. A collection of his prose appears as *Hsiao-ts'ao-chai wen-chi* 文集, 28 *ch.*, with a supplement in 3 *ch.*; it was published in the T'ien-ch'i era (1621–28); at least two copies are recorded in Japanese libraries. Several others of his publications include selections of his poetry. In chronological order they are the *Yu Yen chi* 遊燕集, 2 *ch.*, telling of his experiences in poetic form of two trips to Peking in 1588 and 1591; the *Hsiao-ts'ao-chai kao* 稿, 1 *ch.*, written in 1589 when he was living in impoverished solitude in a cottage at the foot of Chiu-hsien shan 九仙山 (in Fukien); the *Hsia-ku chi* 下菰集, 6 *ch.* (preface of 1597), a collection of his poems selected by T'u Lung (*q.v.*) and five other contemporaries; and the *Chü Tung chi*, mentioned above. His poetry received high praise, T'u Lung going so far as to write: "His extraordinary talent rises above that of all of his fellow writers.... The delicacy of his verse puts him among the greatest masters." A supplementary collection, *Hsiao-ts'ao-chai hsü-chi* 續集, 3 *ch.*, is also preserved in Japan. Several of Hsieh's works receive notices in the *Ssu-k'u* catalogue, but only two, the *Tien lüeh* and the *Pei-ho chi*, were copied into the Imperial Library. both being recently reproduced in the *Chen-pen* 珍本, series 2 and 3, respectively. One of those noticed, the *Shih hsi* 史籯 (a guide to little-used and obscure phrases in the seventeen dynastic histories), 17 *ch.*, is dismissed with the comment: "Deficient in textual criticism, therefore insufficient for scholarly purposes." Some

of Hsieh's poetry is preserved in the *Ch'üan-Min Ming-shih chuan* (*see* Hsü Po) and other selections.

Another of Hsieh's compilations of interest is the *Hung-yün hsü-yüeh* 紅雲續約, a collection of regulations, records, and poems of a litchi (lichee) club be organized in 1608 in Foochow to satisfy his hunger for that peerless fruit of his native province. He had missed it during his official service away from home beginning in 1592. He was late for the litchi season of 1606, and the following year the crop failed. So in 1608, just before he left home for Peking, he and his friends indulged themselves in eating the fruit and writing poems, several of which are included in the *Hsü shuo-fu* (*see* T'ao Tsung-i) and in the *T'u-shu chi-ch'eng*.

Of all his writings the *Wu tsa tsu* remains his crowning achievement. Because of certain passages containing words offensive to the Manchus, this work was banned in the 18th century, and as a consequence is unmentioned by the editors of the Imperial Catalogue. Hence its rarity. Fortunately some copies of the original edition may be found both in China and in Japan; moreover, two woodblock reeditions appeared in Japan in 1661 and 1795. (The second diverges from the original text briefly but significantly at several points.) There is also a reprint in two volumes published in China in 1959. It is of interest to note that the writer of the preface to the Ming edition, Li Wei-chen 李維楨 (T. 本寧, 1547-1626, cs 1568), also contributed prefaces to books by such well-known contemporaries as Wang Shih-chen and Li Chih (*qq. v.*). The *Wu* 五 in the title denotes the number of categories in the 16 *chüan* text: Heaven, 2; earth, 2; man, 4; things, 4; and events, 4. Under such headings he was able to subsume a view of nature and the universe in all its diversity, making many observations drawn from his own experience as well as from his reading. Skepticism tempered with curiosity makes up the pervading tone.

Living as he did on the south China

littoral, Hsieh has much to say about overseas contacts, from the era of T'ang to his own day. Whereas other contemporaries tended to dwell only on the horror of Japanese depredations, he could note that some among the *wo-k'ou* were different. "The Japanese highly regard Confucian books and believe in Buddhism. They always purchase for good prices various books and works on the Classics, except for the book of Mencius; of this they say that any vessel carrying it will overturn and sink." Obviously the Japanese authorities, just like the first Ming emperor, Chu Yüan-chang, found that the *Mencius* taught the justification of rebellion, and so they tried to discourage its importation by circulating such a story.

Hsieh's observant eye also took in the sights around him: the itinerant drug peddlers who played magic tricks with mirrors, the sing-song girls in the entertainment districts, the variety of fruits, grains, wines, condiments, and meats available in different parts of China, the variant tastes and eating habits of people north and south, the ceramic ware known as ju yao 汝窰, rare even in his own day. "Those specimens used in palaces in Sung times generally had their rims bound with copper; consequently, they were of less value." Like any true collector he took delight in objects of art for their quality even though they might come from Korea or Japan. Such things he praised for "their beauty, unlike that of the Chinese," and sought out examples imported on "barbarian ships." He was one of the very few to record the painting of a giraffe brought as tribute from Bengal to Emperor Chu Ti (*q. v.*) in 1414. He noticed how rich merchants "squander gold like dust" on "concubines, prostitutes, and lawsuits." Footbinding he deplored, supersition also. Unorthodox or eccentric behavior were not for him. Of Li Chih, a near neighbor, he wrote, "Rash extremism may suffice to kill a man, and Li's case is a perfect example." He questioned

too the claims and motives of Lin Chao-en (*q. v.*), another Fukienese, and characterized the work of Yang Shen (*q. v.*) as "careless and full of errors." Of a man's attitude towards woman he gives a picture (in *chüan* 8) worthy of the best writers of his time; this is the tu fu 妬婦, recently rendered into English as "The Jealous wife" by Howard Levy. The story about the general, Ch'i Yüan-ching, and his jealous wife is a true story about Ch'i Chi-kuang (*q. v.*), Yüan-ching being his *tzu*. Another of his anecdotes about a jealous wife involves the consort of General Ch'ang Yü-ch'un (*q. v.*), one of the favorite officers serving under the first emperor. This may be found in another of Hsieh's books, the *Wen-hai p'i-sha* 文海披沙, a work of 8 *chüan* (preface of 1609).

Because of its breadth and scope and the personal touches that lighten almost every *chüan*, the *Wu tsa tsu* found a special niche in the hearts of the Japanese. Travel was severely restricted in Tokugawa Japan; so books offered the main source of knowledge about the outside world. The *Wu tsa tsu*, written by one who was richly informed both through experience and through books, many of which were generally unavailable in Japan, held more attraction for the ordinary reader than the matter-of-fact encyclopedias such as the *San-ts'ai t'u-hui* of Wang Ch'i (*q. v.*) or its Japanese derivative, *Wakan sansai zue*. For two centuries Japanese scholars treasured the *Wu tsa tsu* and consulted it frequently; only recently have western scholars begun to turn to it for its almost unrivaled picture of Ming society and culture of the author's day.

Like his fellow townsmen, Ts'ao Hsüeh-ch'üan (*q. v.*) and Hsü Po, Hsieh was a celebrated bibliophile. Some of the noted items in his library are manuscript (facsimile?) copies from Sung editions and other rare books. In 1609, when he was awaiting appointment in Peking, he had permission from the grand secretary,

Yeh Hsiang-kao (*q. v.*), to borrow books from the library of the Grand Secretariat. Hsieh records how, unable to employ high priced scribes, he himself made the copies at night with fingers stiff from cold. Collectors have since valued these treasures from his library, which came to be known as *Hsiao-ts'ao-chai ch'ao-pen* 鈔本 or as *Hsieh-ch'ao*.

Hsieh had several sons. One, his youngest named Hsieh Kao 昊 (H. 青門老人) lived on into the Ch'ing dynasty but refused to submit to the Manchus. He sold the family library and retired to a hermitage in the mountains by the coast. Chou Liang-kung (ECCP) purchased (*ca.* 1654) some of the Hsieh collection. A portion of the Hsieh family archives remained in the hands of a wealthy Hang-chow family until recent times, when it passed into the possession of the Shanghai library.

Bibliography

1/286/21a; 40/57/7b; 64/庚 1/9a; 84/ 丁下 /68a; 86/16/12b; SK (1930), 65/4b, 68/9b, 69/4a, 77/1b, 5b, 128/4b, 179/12b; KC (1958), 4925; *Ch'ang-lo-hsien chih* (1918), 14/33a, 54b, 19/5a, 7b, 11b, 20 上 /31a, 20 下/9a, 86a, 23/19b, 33a, 37b, 24/9a, 30/4b; Yeh Ch'ang-chih 葉昌熾, *Ts'ang-shu chi-shih shih* 藏書紀事詩 (Shanghai, 1958), 158; *Kwangsi t'ung-chih* (facsimile reprod. of 1800 ed.), III, 1569; *Yunnan t'ung-chih* (1835), 135/29a, 208/30b; *Tung-ch'ang-fu chih* (1808), 15/24b; Shen Tsu-mou 沈祖牟, "Hsieh Ch'ao k'ao" 鈔考, *Fu-chien wen-hua chi-k'an* 福建文化季刊, Vol. 1, no. 1 (March, 1941), 17; *Hsü Shuo-fu*, 29; TSCC (1885-88), Vol. XX, *chüan* 273-77; Yuasa Jōzan 湯淺常山(1708-81), comp., *Bunkai zakki* 文會雜記 in *Nihon zuihitsu zenshū* 日本隨筆全書 (1927-28), II, 622; *Gosō mampitsu* 梧窗漫筆 (1822-40) in *Nihon zuihitsu zenshū*, XVII, 246, 291; Fou Yun-tseu, "Etude biblio-graphique des oeuvres littéraires de Sie Tsai-hang (1567-1624)," *Han-hiue*, II: 4(Pekin, 1949), 373; L. of C. *Catalogue of Rare Books*, 289, 361; H. S. Levy, *Warm-Soft Village* (Tokyo, 1964), 10; W. Franke, *Sources*, 4. 3. 11; J. J. L. Duyvendak, TP, 34 (1938), 401; Percival David, bart., "A Commentary on Ju Ware," *Trans. of the Oriental Ceramic Soc.* (1936-37), 41; L. Carrington Goodrich, *The Literary Inquisition of Ch'ien-lung* (Baltimore, 1935), 62, 153, 246; Ping-ti Ho, *The Ladder of Success in Imperial China* (New York, 1962), 158, 263; *id.*, *Studies on the Population of China* (Cambridge, Mass., 1959), 139, 197, 262; Kuwabara Jitsuzo, MTB, II (1928), 13; Robert des Rotours, "L' Anthro-pophagie en Chine," TP, 54 (1968), 16.

Leon Zolbrod and L. Carrington Goodrich

HSIEH Ch'ien 謝遷 (T. 于喬, H. 木齋), January 11, 1450-March 6, 1531, scholar-official who served twice as grand secretary (1495-1506, 1527-28), was a native of Yü-yao 餘姚, Chekiang. The Hsieh family, originally from Honan, settled in K'uai-chi 會稽, Chekiang, when its distinguished ancestor, Hsieh An (320-85) became the minister of state of the Eastern Chin dynasty. Hsieh Ch'ien's branch, which claimed descent from Hsieh Shen-fu (cs 1166), a renowned minister of the Southern Sung, moved to Yü-yao during the 12th century. Hsieh Ch'ien's grandfather, Hsieh Ying 瑩 (T. 懷玉, H. 直菴, 1407-73), a minor official, ended his career as a secretary in the administration office of Fukien. Hsieh's father never held any post, but spent his time attending to the family estate and providing his children with a classical education. At the time of Hsieh Ch'ien's birth, it happened that the family had just moved to a new house; so Hsieh Ying gave his eldest grandson the name Ch'ien (moved).

Hsieh Ch'ien emerged as first in *chü-jen* list in 1474, and became optimus in the *chin-shih* examination the following year. He then received an appointment in the Hanlin Academy as senior compiler. Early in 1484 he was promoted to be an in-structor in the supervisorate of instruction for the heir apparent. During the next two years he served concurrently as at-tendant of the imperial heir, Chu Yu-t'ang (*q.v.*), and as lecturer on classical studies to Chu Chien-shen (*q.v.*). Late in 1487, shortly after Chu Yu-t'ang's enthronement, Hsieh rose to senior instructor, concurrently reader in the Hanlin Academy, and took part in the preparation of the Veritable Records of the preceding emperor, *Hsien-tsung shih-lu*. During this time a certain eunuch, attempting to ingratiate himself with the new emperor, proposed that a few girls be selected to fill the imperial harem. Hsieh then submitted, jointly with his colleague Liu Chien (*q.v.*), a strongly worded remonstrance against the proposal as it was not only premature for an eighteen-year-old monarch to receive concubines, but also a violation of the rites during the period of imperial mourning. The emperor accepted his advice. In September, 1491, upon the completion of the *shih-lu*, Hsien became an assisstant supervisor of imperial instruction and concurrently senior expositor of the Hanlin Academy. He left office two years later upon learning of the death of his mother; during this period his father also died, so he was further prevented from returning to government service. In March, 1495, after the death of Ch'iu Chün (*q.v.*), Hsieh and Li Tung-yang (*q.v.*) were both appointed to the Grand Secretariat. After completing the mourning period, Hsieh arrived in Peking in October, and was appointed concurrently grand supervisor of instruction. As part of his duties he also had the responsibility for several compilation projects including the preparation of the *Ta Ming hui-tien* (*see* Hsü P'u). In March, 1496, he directed the metropolitan examination, and two years later received title of junior guardian of the heir apparent, titular minister of War, and concurrently grand secretary of the Tung-ko 東閣 (East hall). Late in the same year, a fire destroyed the Ch'ien-ch'ing 乾清 and K'un-ning 坤寧 palaces. Responding to the emperor's request for remonstrance on this ominous disaster, Hsieh pleaded with the monarch to pay closer attention to state affairs and devote himself to providing for the welfare of his subjects. On the completion of the *Ta Ming hui-tien* (March, 1503), he was awarded the rank of grand guardian of the heir apparent, titular mi-

nister of Rites, and concurrently grand secretary of the Wu-ying 武英 Hall. Three months later he supervised the compilation of a compendium of works on the *Tzu-chih t'ung-chien* 資治通鑑, later known as *Tzu-chih t'ung-chien tsuan-yao* 纂要, 92 *ch.*, an incomplete set of which is available in the Peking National Library.

Among his services as grand secretary may be cited his remonstrance early in 1500 against the recommendation of his colleague, the minister of War, Ma Wen-sheng (*q.v.*), that a two-thirds surcharge be imposed on the southern provinces for every *shih* of revenue presented, to meet the military expenses involved in defense against the Mongol tribesmen (*see* Wang Ao 王鏊). Instead he proposed a restraint on government spending to meet the additional financial burden. On several other occasions Hsieh exposed the profiteering activities of the eunuchs in charge of government storage depots and granaries, as well as of the military personnel in the imperial guards, and urged the authorities to take steps to curb their illegal activities. He and his colleagues, Liu Chien and Li Tung-yang, came to be known as the three most distinguished statesmen of the Hung-chih period. The compilers of the *Ming-shih*, citing the opinion of their contemporaries, assert that Li excelled in planning, Liu in judgment, and Hsieh in outspokenness. Emperor Chu Yu-t'ang, expressing his confidence in all three, asked them (when he was dying in June, 1505) to serve as mentors to his heir, Chu Hou-chao (*q.v.*). In August the new emperor honored Hsieh with the rank of junior tutor and grand tutor to the heir apparent. He was put in charge, early in the following year, of the compilation of the *Hsiao-tsung shih-lu*; the actual work, however, was completed by his successor and political rival Chiao Fang (*q.v.*) and others, as Hsieh had retired late in 1506, three years before its completion.

It is interesting to note that the *Hsiao-tsung shih-lu*, compiled in an adverse political climate, includes several partisan comments sharply critical of Hsieh Ch'ien and his colleagues. One of these blames Hsieh for his advice to the emperor to decline a eunuch's proposal to recruit girls for his harem, asserting that this accounted for the paucity of imperial progeny. Another charge was that he had enlisted the assistance of the influential eunuch Li Kuang (*q.v.*) to gain admission to the Grand Secretariat, and that, when Hanlin scholar Ch'eng Min-cheng 程敏政 (T. 克勤, 1445-99 十, cs 1466) brought this to light, he had sought personal vengeance by pressing charges against Ch'eng.

In their service with the new emperor, Hsieh and his colleagues soon found to their dismay that the erratic young monarch preferred the company of eight eunuchs who kept him amused with diversions instead of attending to the advice of the elderly advisers. Gradually these favorites, known as pa-tang 八黨 (clique of eight), under their leader Liu Chien (*q.v.*), interfered with state functions and obstructed counsel. In March, 1506, out of frustration, Hsieh and Liu Chin submitted requests for retirement, but these were not approved. Seven months later they lent support to Han Wen (*q.v.*), the minister of Revenue, who made a dramatic plea before the emperor for a sentence of death for the eunuchs. Unfortunately Han's plan was prematurely exposed; so Hsieh and Liu submitted their resignations and went into retirement. Liu Chin and his cronies thus emerged all-powerful and dominated the court. Several junior officials who petitioned for the return of Hsieh were either cashiered or imprisoned. The vacancy left by Hsieh in the Grand Secretariat was now filled by Chiao Fang, Liu Chin's protégé. Chiao, earlier denied an appointment to this office because of Hsieh's support of Wang Ao and Wu K'uan (*q.v.*), saw an opportunity to get his revenge. Liu and Chiao falsely charged (in March, 1509) that Hsieh had attempted to bolster his power by overriding normal procedures, and filling the vacant official positions with his own townsmen;

they proposed punishing Hsieh by stripping him of his official title and status. They also introduced a ruling that in the future no candidates from Yü-yao be allowed to hold an appointment in the capital. In January, 1510, they further discredited Hsieh and his colleagues by revoking the imperial honors and gifts granted to them by the emperors of previous reigns, Their vengeance also involved Hsieh's brother, Hsieh Ti 廸 (T. 于吉, H. 石厓, 1467-1529), and Hsieh's second son, Hsieh P'i 丕 (T. 以中, H. 汝湖, May 5, 1482-December 25, 1556), whom they succeeded in ousting from office and reducing to the status of commoners. Following Liu Chin's execution in September, Hsieh was exonerated, but he did not return to office and lived for a number of years in retirement.

In August, 1521, shortly after his enthronement Emperor Chu Hou-ts'ung sent a messenger to enquire after Hsieh, granted him a monthly stipend of eight bushels of rice and ten servants, and rehabilitated his brother and son whom Liu Chin had banished. Hsieh then sent his eldest son Hsieh Cheng 正 to the court to express his gratitude, and, pleased with his response, the emperor appointed Hsieh Cheng a drafter in the central drafting office. Late in the same year, on the death of Hsieh Ch'ien's wife, née Hsü 徐, he stayed at home to observe the mourning rites. The emperor again in 1523 sent a messenger to visit him. At this same time several senior officials supported the emperor's desire for Hsieh's recall to the Grand Secretariat, each with a different motive. It is said that Chang Ts'ung (later known as Chang Fu-ching, *q.v.*), who had an eye on the Grand Secretariat, wished to use Hsieh to oust Fei Hung (*q.v.*) to make way for his own admission, and that, somewhat ironically (which coincided with Chang's plan), Fei also favored Hsieh as his successor out of personal friendship, as he was planning to retire. Yang I-ch'ing (*q.v.*), who was appointed grand secretary in 1525, on the other hand, wanted Hsieh Ch'ien to block the appointment of his rivals, Chang Ts'ung and Kuei O (*q.v.*). Late in the year Chang and Kuei simultaneously submitted their recommendations for his recall. Hsieh first declined the invitation on the excuse of ill health and old age, but, after several urgings from the court, finally gave in, and reported for duty late in 1527. He had expected that he would be given the post of senior grand secretary, and that Yang I-ch'ing, now holding this position, would step down in his favor. Yang, however, declined to do so, and Hsieh became the second man in the Grand Secretariat. It does not seem that he played much of a role in state affairs; instead, he was asked to serve as chief supervisor for the compilation of the *Ming-lun ta-tien* (*see* Yang I-ch'ing). Three months before its completion in July, 1528, however, Hsieh had already obtained permission to retire. Hsieh's second term in the Grand Secretariat was thus brief and devoid of achievement, a fact which was deplored by his contemporaries who considered that he should not have reentered official service at his age and in an unfavorable political climate. Retiring to his native place, Hsieh died three years later, at the age of eighty-one. (Hsieh's epitaph by Fei Hung records his death on March 6; the *Kuo-ch'üeh*, however, places it five days earlier, but the *Shih-tsung shih-lu* does not mention it until five months later, on August 11.) He received the canonized name Wen-cheng 文正 (cultured and upright), and the posthumous honorific of grand protector. His portrait appears in the *Ming chuang-yüan t'u-k'ao* of Ku Ting-ch'en (*see* Shen I-kuan).

Hsieh Ch'ien left a literary collection entitled *Kuei-t'ien kao* 歸田稿, 8 *ch.*, which contains writings he produced during his later years and represents only a fraction of his original work. The bulk of his output, including his earlier memorials and literary essays, was destroyed during the raid on his house by the *wo-k'ou* in the summer of 1547. The *Kuei-t'ien kao*, edited from surviving manuscripts by his descendant of seven generations later and engraved during the K'ang-hsi period, was copied into the Imperial Catalogue of the 18th century. It includes a *nien-p'u* by Hsieh's townsman, Ni Tsung-cheng 倪宗正 (T. 本端, H. 小野, cs 1505), and other biographical matter. This edition, however, is also rare; a manuscript transcription in 3 *ts'e* is preserved in the Seikadō Bunko, Tokyo.

The *Ming ching-shih wen-pien* by Ch'en Tzu-lung (ECCP) lists a memorial by Hsieh Ch'ien submitted shortly after Chu Yu-t'ang's enthronement against the proposal of the eunuch to recruit girls for the imperial harem during the emperor's mourning period. This, being the only piece represented in that collection, is not derived from Hsieh's own works, which Ch'en designates as *Hsieh Wen-cheng chi*, but was extracted from the original memorial Hsieh submitted jointly with Liu Chien; it had been preserved in Liu's collected works.

Hsieh Ch'ien also left a collection which contains poems he composed in response to his townsman, Feng Lan 馮蘭 (T. 佩之, H. 雪湖, cs 1469), a retired assistant superintendent of the education intendant circuit of Kiangsi, and those of Feng during Hsieh's retirement in Yü-yao (1506–15). This anthology, entitled *Hu-shan ch'ang-ho* 湖山唱和, 2 *ch.*, with an appendix, *Hu-shan lien-chü* 聯句, and Hsieh's own preface, was engraved around 1515. A copy of the 1524 reprint is preserved in the Peking National Library and is available on microfilm (no. 770).

Hsieh was survived by five sons and several brothers, some of whom also achieved distinction in official service. Among his sons, the second, Hsieh P'i who was later adopted by his uncle, had the most distinguished career. Entering the National University through the yin privilege in 1501, Hsieh P'i achieved the *chin-shih* in 1505, and served as Hanlin compiler for the next four years until his banishment in 1509. He returned to office in 1524 and served under Emperor Chu Hou-ts'ung, taking part in the preparation of the *Wu-tsung shih-lu*, and becoming an instructor in the supervisorate of instruction of the heir apparent a year later. In 1527 he advanced to be an assistant minister of the Court of Imperial Sacrifices, oversaw the College of Translators (August-December), and then returned to the Hanlin Academy as senior reader. He assumed charge of the Hanlin Academy eight years later, became assistant minister of Rites in June, and was transferred to the ministry of Personnel in October, 1536. He left office in May, 1537, upon the death of his step-mother; failing to obtain an official recommendation, however, he was not reinstated after he had observed the mourning period. He spent his remaining years in retirement, and died at the age of seventy-four.

Of Hsieh Ch'ien's brothers, Hsieh Ti, the second in the line, deserves mention. A *chin-shih* of 1499, he first served as a bureau secretary in the ministry of War, then as assistant minister, but was banished in 1509 due to Liu Chin's opposition. Recalled to office during the early years of the next reign, he became successively assistant administration commissioner of Kiangsi, surveillance commissioner of Honan, and administration commissioner of Kwangtung in 1527. He died on the return trip to Peking to present a routine report in 1529, at the age of sixty-two. As he had no sons, his line was continued by an adopted heir, his brother Hsieh Ch'ien's fourth son.

Bibliography

1/181/14a; 5/14/47a, 26/35a, 99/1b; 40/25/1a; MSL (1964), Hsien-tsung, 2598, 4180, Hsiao-tsung(1964), *ch.* 1-24, Wu-tsung(1965), 277, 324, 543, 553, 588, 1073, 1294, Shih-tsung (1965), 1380, 1811, 1942, 3042, 6326; KC (1958), 2944, 3437; SK (1930), 171/2b; *Yü-yao-hsien chih* (1899), 33/ 列傳 7, 8, 10; Wang Ao, *Shou-ch'i pi-chi*, in Shen Chieh-fu, *Chi-lu hui-pien*, 124/ 30a; Wang Shih-chen, "Shih-ch'eng k'ao-wu" 史乘考誤, in *Yen-shan-t'ang pieh-chi*, 25/19b, 26/6b; Shen Te-fu, *Wan-li yeh-hu pien, pu-i*(1959), 800; Hsü Hsüeh-mo, *Shih-miao shih-yü lu* (1965), 5/2a, 21/15b; Hsü Hsiang-mei 徐象梅, *Liang-Che ming-hsien lu* 兩浙名賢錄 (preface 1621, undated Ch'ing ed.), 14/17a; Li Chin-hua 李晉華, *Ming-tai ch'ih-chuan shu k'ao* 明代勅撰書考 (1932), 51, 55; *Ming chuang-yüan t'u-k'ao*, 2/23b.

Hok-lam Chan

HSIEH Chin 解縉 (T. 大紳, 縉紳, H. 春雨), December 6, 1369-February 22, 1415, scholar official, was born into a family that had settled in Chi-shui 吉水, Kiangsi, beginning with the 7th century, acquiring a reputation in civil service and scholarship in later periods. Hsieh Chin's father, Hsieh K'ai 開 (T. 開先, H. 筠澗, March 15, 1312-December 31, 1398), a learned scholar, who held no previous official position, declined an invitation from Chu Yüan-chang to help him in founding the dynasty. Two of his brothers subsequently joined the new government, and two of his three sons later distinguished themselves in official service and scholarship.

A child prodigy, Hsieh Chin topped the district examination of 1387, and achieved his *chin-shih* a year later, as did also his eldest brother, Hsieh Ching 經 (T. 大經, H. 滄江, 1343-November 10, 1411), who retired in 1391 after serving a term as instructor in the prefectural school of Ying-t'ien 應天 (*ca.* 1388-91). Immediately thereafter, Hsieh Chin received (April) an appointment as bachelor in the central drafting office, and attracted the attention of Chu Yüan-chang for his broad learning and literary excellence. A month later, at the emperor's command, he submitted a memorandum presenting his views on state affairs. He criticized with some eloquence the harshness of the law, the excessiveness of taxation, and the failure of the government to appoint people of caliber to public service, to maintain military effectiveness, and to elevate moral and ethical standards. In like fashion, he deplored the emperor's indulgence in unrefined literature and in the use of superstitous dogma for political persuasion, and he offered to compile a selection of essential readings of the Classics for the emperor. Following this, Hsieh submitted a ten-point formula known as t'ai-p'ing shih-ts'e 太平十策, which, if adopted, would, he predicted, inaugurate an era of peace and prosperity. His recommendations included such archaic measures as the introduction of a combined well-field 井田 and equal-field system of land tenure 均田 (which he thought to be a viable means to limit the landholdings of privileged individuals), a mixed system of feudal and prefectural divisions in local administration, clarification of the functions of the bureaucrats, promotion of Confucian rites and music, appointment of officials based on merit, renovation of the school system, elimination of supernumerary offices, reduction of taxes, encouragement of agriculture, and promotion of military studies. The emperor commended him for his insight but shrugged off his suggestions. Hsieh's unreserved outspokenness and arrogance, however, alarmed his seniors, and the emperor, wary of the consequences, transferred him to the Censorate. Nevertheless, he persistently criticized the court and antagonized his colleagues, and so disturbed the throne, when he submitted a memorial on the injustice done to the prime minister, Li Shan-ch'ang (q.v.), shortly after the latter's suicide (July, 1390), that the emperor decided to send him away. In June of the following year, having summoned Hsieh K'ai to his presence, Chu Yüan-chang ordered Hsieh Chin to escort his aging father back home to look after him, and to remain there to devote himself to study and reflection, stipulating that he was not to return to the capital for official appointment within a ten-year period.

When news of the death of Chu Yüan-chang (June, 1398) reached him, Hsieh proceeded to Nanking to pay homage, regardless of the ruling forbidding his return, and his violation of the cus-

tom against leaving home during the period of mourning for his mother, who had died in December of the previous year. For this he was demoted to be a lesser functionary in the Ho-chou 河州 guard in Shensi. He then pleaded with Tung Lun 董倫 (T. 安常, H. 貝川, 1323-August, 1402), a vice minister of Rites and Hanlin chancellor who enjoyed the confidence of the imperial successor Chu Yün-wen (q.v.), and gained his sympathy. Seven months later (July, 1399), through Tung's recommendation, Hsieh received an appointment as a Hanlin scholar (tai-chao 待詔, 9b). Following his usurpation in August, 1402, Chu Ti, impressed by Hsieh's promise, appointed him a reader in the Hanlin Academy. The new emperor then commanded Hsieh and his colleagues to screen the memorials and state papers that had been submitted to Emperor Chu Yün-wen, separating those on military and financial matters from the rest. These were to be prepared for the emperor's scrutiny; all others concerning the Chien-wen reign were to be destroyed. Late in the year Chu Ti elevated Hsieh to be a senior reader, and made him one of seven Hanlin members who were to advise him on important government issues and state affairs. The other members were Huang Huai, Hu Kuang, Yang Jung, Yang Shih-ch'i, Hu Yen (qq. v.), and Chin Yu-tzu (see Empress Hsü); this led to the establishment of the Grand Secretariat. The emperor held Hsieh in high esteem, entrusted him with the drafting of imperial edicts and orders, and often consulted him on matters of rites and music for the new reign. This responsibility gave Hsieh Chin a chance to exercise his penchant for scholarly contributions, and an opportunity to channel ideas and recommend capable people for government service.

In subsequent years, among other duties, Hsieh Chin occupied himself with work on several official compilations. He was appointed chief editor (November, 1402) in the first revision of the chronicles of Chu Yüan-chang, the *T'ai-tsu shih-lu*, in order to eradicate references that might challenge the legitimacy of Chu Ti's overthrow of his nephew. This revised version, 183 *ch.*, submitted to the throne in July, 1403, however, failed to satisfy the emperor, who subsequently ordered another revision (completed in 1418; *see* Li Wen-chung). In this connection, Hsieh was ordered to compile a genealogical record of the first emperor, known as *T'ien huang yü-tieh* 天潢玉牒, 1 *ch.*, which contains several statements exaggerating the accomplishments of Chu Yüan-chang, and asserting that Chu Ti was the son of Empress Ma (*q.v.*); this aimed at legitimatizing his succession. About the same time, Hsieh also supervised the compilation of biographies of past and present virtuous women, entitled *Ku-chin lieh-nü chuan* 古今列女傳, 3 *ch.* (*see* Empress Hsü), completed January, 1404, which is still extant. Then in mid-July, acting on Hsieh's recommendation of 1388, Chu Ti charged him and his colleagues with the compilation of a complete thesaurus of existing literature. This, temporarily known as *Wen-hsien ta-ch'eng*, they submitted to the throne in December; subsequently expanded, it received the title *Yung-lo ta-tien* when completed four years later (*see* Yao Kuang-hsiao).

In May, 1404, Hsieh received promotion to be Hanlin chancellor and concurrently grand secretary. Early in the following year (February 1405), the emperor entrusted him with a major assignment, that of selecting promising young scholars from among the holders of the *chin-shih* for further training. (Twenty-nine of them were selected; thirteen later worked on the *Yung-lo ta-tien* project.) About the same time, Hsieh became involved in the selection of the heir apparent. Some of the military officials headed by Ch'iu Fu (*see* Qorγočin) favored Chu Kao-hsü (*q.v.*), the emperor's second son, but Chu Ti preferred his eldest, Chu Kao-chih (*q. v.*). When consulted, Hsieh Chin also supported the candidacy of Chu Kao-chih,

thus presumably strengthening the emperor's decision to designate his eldest son over the opposition of the military. The matter was deliberated in great secrecy, but it was eventually revealed; as a result, Chu Kao-hsü bore a grudge against Hsieh Chin, who later became the victim of a plot instigated by the prince.

Shortly afterward, Hsieh twice offended the emperor. The first offense occurred in May, 1406, when Chu Ti ordered a punitive expedition to Annam to chastise the rebellious Lê Quí-ly (*q.v.*), and reduce Annam to provincial status. Hsieh vehemently criticized the undertaking as dangerous and adventurous, but his plea went unheeded. The second took place at a time when Chu Ti, disappointed with the heir apparent, began to favor Chu Kao-hsü. Hsieh again remonstrated, saying that this would widen the rift between the two princes. With imperial support declining, Hsieh came under increasing attack by his enemies. Some charged him with exercising arbitrary judgment as an examiner during the palace test of March, 1404. Chu Kao-hsü also accused him of revealing the controversy over the imperial decision on the choice of the heir apparent. Acting on these charges, Chu Ti demoted Hsieh (March, 1407) to the post of assistant administration commissioner of Kwangsi. Before long Hsieh suffered another slanderous attack from one of his rivals, and the court banished him (March, 1408) to the Chiao-chih 交阯 administration office to oversee the collection of revenue in Hua-chou 化州, Kwangtung.

Early in 1410 Hsieh Chin arrived in Nanking to present a memorial, but did not see the emperor, who had left for Mongolia with an expeditionary army. Hsieh instead had an audience with Chu Kao-chih. When Chu Ti returned to Nanking (August), Chu Kao-hsü accused Hsieh before his father, reporting that he had violated protocol by deliberately coming to see the heir apparent while the emperor was away. Chu Ti was annoyed.

Unaware that he had antagonized the emperor, Hsieh took a leisurely tour in Kwangtung with a Hanlin colleague on his way to Annam, and proposed the dredging of the Kan 贛 River in Kiangsi to facilitate communications between north and south. Irritated by Hsieh's conduct, Chu Ti ordered his arrest, charging him with squandering his time in travel and with presenting an unrealistic scheme that might incur unnecessary sacrifice on the part of the common people. Found guilty, in July, 1411, Hsieh was sentenced to imprisonment. His wife, children, and close relations were exiled to Liaotung. Several of Hsieh's colleagues, implicated in his case, also received prison terms. Four years later Hsieh died in prison at the age of forty-five reportedly because of the enmity of Chu Kao-hsü. When Chu Kao-chih, who had been friendly to Hsieh Chin, ascended the throne, he granted amnesty to the Hsieh family and appointed (February, 1425) Hsieh's second son, Hsieh Chen-liang 禎亮 (who married a daughter of Hu Kuang), to be a drafter in the central secretariat. Eleven years later (October, 1436) Emperor Chu Ch'i-chen (*q.v.*) returned the confiscated property to the family, and in 1465, through the petition of Hsieh Chen-liang, Emperor Chu Chien-shen (*q.v.*) restored Hsieh's official rank posthumously; then in January, 1591, the court conferred on him the canonized name Wen-i 文毅 (cultured and resolute).

Hsieh Chin's career illustrates the tragedy of an intellectual prodigy, serving under strong-willed monarchs, who became involved in palace intrigues. At the beginning his youth and candid expressions of opinion, together with his carefree and unconventional style, alarmed his colleagues, and he later fell prey to their slanders when imperial favor waned. Contemporary scholars describe him as kind-hearted, friendly, and eager to recommend people of caliber to office, citing his support of Yang Shih-ch'i who later became his colleague in the Grand Secretariat. In

scholarship, Hsieh expressed a genuine interest in genealogical studies, and in literature he made a mark with his fresh, invigorating narrative style, and became known for his skill in calligraphy; Chu Yün-ming (*q.v.*) later was to extol his skill in the last.

Apart from official compilations, Hsieh Chin left a collection of literary writings entitled *Hsieh hsüeh-shih* 學士 (*Wen-i kung* 公) *chi* 集 or *Hsieh Ch'un-yü hsien-sheng* 春雨先生 *chi*. The first edition, 30 *ch.*, engraved in 1457, contained many pieces which were adjudged spurious and so deleted by later editors. Several later editions reveal minor differences. One edition in 10 *chüan*, compiled by a descendant, Hsieh T'ung 桐 (cj 1540), appeared in 1562, and he subsequently reprinted it with an appendix, a *nien-p'u* 年譜, 2 *ch.* A slightly enlarged edition, 16 *ch.*, came out in 1719. The most comprehensive seems to be the 1766 edition, a reprint of the earlier one of 1719 to which was added a supplementary collection, known as *Hsieh Wen-i kung hou-chi* 後集, 6 *ch.* In the original 16 *chüan* version, there are six essays on calligraphy tracing the development of this literary art from antiquity down to his own time. These were later made into a separate volume, entitled *Ch'un-yü tsa shu* 雜述, 1 *ch.*, by Ch'en Chi-ju (ECCP) in his *Pao-yen-t'ang pi-chi*. The supplementary collection features forty prefaces to genealogical records of many families, mostly from Kiangsi. There are also six such prefaces in the original collection.

Bibliography

1/147/1a; 3/137/1a; 5/12/12a; 40/17/1a; 42/41/1a; 63/10/1a; 85/2/6; MSL (1963), T'ai-tsung, 166, 186, 256, 386, 475, 499, 535, 627, 1016, 1483; Hsi-tsung, 226, Ying-tsung, 417, Shen-tsung(1965), 4264; KC (1958), 684, 1064, 1112; TSCC (1885-88), XI: 243/63/4a, XXIV: 118/24a; SK (1930), 58/2a, 127/3b, 137/7a, 170/4a; Hsieh Chin, *Hsieh Wen-i kung-chi* (1766 ed., NCL microfilm); Yeh Sheng, *Shui-tung jih-chi*, 13/6b, 38/1a; Chu Yün-ming, *Chu-shih chi-lüeh* (NLP microfilm, no. 910), 26/10a; Liao Tao-nan, *Tien-ko tz'u-lin chi*,

3/9a; Chang Hsüan, *Hsi-yüan wen-chien lu*, 4/29a; Ho Ch'iao-yüan, *Ming-shan ts'ang* (Taipei, 1970 ed.), 3365; *Chi-shui-hsien chih* (1875), 12/39a, 30/1b, 32/21a, 37/11a; Li Chin-hua 李晉華, *Ming-tai ch'ih-tsuan shu k'ao* 明代勅撰書考 (Peiping, 1933), 26, 28, 37; Kuo Po-kung 郭伯恭, *Yung-lo ta-tien k'ao* (1938), 5; Chu Chia 祝嘉, *Shu-hsüch shih* 書學史 (Shanghai, 1947), 340; Wu Han (BDRC), "Chi *Ming-shih lu*" 記明實錄 in *Tu-shih cha-chi* 讀史劄記 (Peking, 1957), 186; *Ming-shih* (Taiwan, 1963), 1819; W. Franke, *Sources*, 2. 3.7; L, Carrington Goodrich, "More on the *Yung-lo ta-tien*," JRASHKB, 10 (1970), 19.

Hok-lam Chan

HSIEH Shih-ch'en 謝時臣 (T. 思忠, H. 樗仙), 1487–1567+, painter and poet, was a native of Wu 吳-hsien, prefecture of Soochow. We know almost nothing about him except for the precious information we may draw from the inscriptions on his paintings. It seems that he never took part in any civil service examination or followed a government career. As he came from a fairly well-to-do family, he had the leisure and means to devote his life to his art. For decades he lived mainly in a villa situated on a mountain overlooking scenic Lake T'ai. He probably took several short excursions to nearby regions during his lifetime. In 1547 he set out on a long journey. First he visited Mt. T'ai-ho 太和 in northwestern Hukuang and Mt. Ta-pieh 大別 on its northeastern border. From there he went south to Wuchang where he visited the Huang-ho lou 黃鶴樓 (Yellow crane tower) on a prominence overlooking the Yangtze River. He then went to the scenic Mt. Lu 盧 in Kiangsi before he took a boat down the River to return home. "Chiang-shan" 江山 (Rivers and mountains), a long scroll of three sections, dated 1547, was painted as a result of this trip. Although influenced by Shen Chou (*q.v.*), the foremost artist of the Wu school, Hsieh was able to develop his own style. He was not only more descriptive in his manner, but also painted large-sized landscapes in a bold fashion—both being out of step with the tradition of this school.

As a landscape painter Hsieh was noted for his river and lake scenes. Nevertheless, pines remained throughout his life his favorite motif. They appear in nearly all of his paintings. His fascination with them may be substantiated by reference to two of his inscriptions. In the undated "Ch'ing-sung pai-yün" 青松白雲 (Green pines and white clouds), in ink, he compares the pine to a dragon. In "Sung-shih" 松石 (Pines and rocks), in light color, undated, he professes that pines have human virtues, such as steadfastness and perseverance. Hsieh is remembered for the vitality of his art. In "Ssu-hao" 四皓 (Four old men), in light color, undated, a large-sized scroll eight feet high and three feet wide, in the collection of the Palace Museum, Taipei, Hsieh gives a dramatic representation of four serene elderly scholars enjoying a chess game outdoors in the midst of a heavy blow. In the background are layered mountains enveloped by misty clouds. Old pine trees stand out conspicuously, whereas the branches of some plum trees are only barely visible. The wind is strong, and the trees on high peaks are shaken and torn by violent gusts. The onrush of the storm is reflected in nearly every detail except the chess board and the human figures. It is not a realistic painting; nevertheless, it illustrates Hsieh's fondness for dramatic effect. "Feng-yü kuei-ts'un" 風雨歸邨 (Returning home through wind and rain), dated 1530, in the collection of H. Mueller, and "Ch'u-hsia" 出峽 (Passing through the gorge), in color, undated, included in *T'ang Sung Yüan Ming Ch'ing hua-hsüan* 唐宋元明清畫選, were executed in a more or less similar fashion. His "Shan-shui" 山水 (Mountains and streams), in light color, dated November, 1557, in Baron Dan's collection, however, demonstrates another aspect of Hsieh's brushwork. Here the audacity and virility exhibited prominently in "Ssu-hao" are absent. Instead, a certain poetic mood pervades it. The setting is early spring. On the left side of a winding stream is a low promontory with two huge willow trees standing on its bank, their leaves not yet in full bloom. A man, possibly a servant, is paddling a skiff toward the villa situated on the other side of the stream. A tutor looks out from the studio at the river view, while one of his pupils close by is absorbed in his books, and another is sitting in an adjacent room. A bridge on high supports may be seen upstream. In the background are a few lofty mountains with a covering of trees. The whole composition is done with mellow, consummate skill. Some of his works, such as "Chiang-shan wu-chin" 江山無盡 (The limitless view of rivers and streams), undated, in the Kuwana collection, and "Hsi-shan feng-yü" 溪山風雨 (Mountain and river in wind and rain), in light color, undated, in the Ōmoto collection, are distinguished for the same reason.

Besides the above, Hsieh provided pictures for several literary masterpieces. Two examples are his "Tsui-weng t'ing chi shu-hua ho-pi"醉翁亭記書畫合璧 (Pavilion of the intoxicated old man). in ink, dated 1559, which illustrates a passage by Ou-yang Hsiu (1007-72), and his "Yüeh-yang lou" 岳陽樓 (Tower of Yüeh-yang), in color, undated, which does the same for a piece of prose by Fan Chung-yen (989 -1052). Both are in the collection of the Palace Museum. Hsieh is also credited with three sketches on album leaves which are reproduced in *Ku-kung ming-shan chi* 名扇集.

Hsieh concentrated almost all of his energy on painting. Although skilled in the art, he seldom composed poetry. A score of his productions, however, are preserved through his paintings.

Bibliography

65/3/15b; Han Ang 韓昂 (fl. 1519), *T'u-hui pao-chien hsü-tsuan* 圖繪寶鑑續纂, 1/3; Chiang Shao-shu 姜紹書 (fl. 1640), *Wu-sheng shih-shih* 無聲詩史, 3/44; *Wu-hsien chih* (1933), 75/18a; *Soo-chow-fu chih* (1883), 109/17b; *T"ang Sung Yüan Ming Ch'ing hua-hsüan* (Shanghai, 1959), pl. 53; *Chung-kuo li-tai ming-hua chi* 中國歷代名畫集, IV (Peking, 1965), pl. 64; *Ku-kung shu-hua lu* 故宮書畫錄 (Taipei, 1956), 中/372; Pien Yung-yü, 卞永譽 (1645-1712), *Shih-ku-t'ang shu-hua hui-k'ao* 式古堂書畫彙考, *hua-chüan* 畫卷, 27/474; Sun Yüeh-pan 孫岳頒 (1639-?), *P'ei-wen-chai shu-hua p'u* 佩文齋書畫譜, 57/1b; *Ku-kung yüeh-k'an* 故宮月刊, 34(June, 1932), pl. 11; *Ku-kung shu-hua chi yüeh-k'an* 書畫集月刊, 10 (July, 1931), pl. 7; *Ku-kung po-wu yüan* 博物院, *Ku-kung ming-shan chi* 名扇集 (Peking, 1932-35), no. 8, pl. 17; *Sō Gen Min Chin meiga taikan* 宋元明清名畫大觀 (Tokyo, 1931), 130; *Nihon genzai Shina meiga mokuroku* 日本現在支那名畫目錄 (Tokyo, 1938), 171; *Kokka* 國華, 522/140 (May, 1934); E. J. Laing, *Chinese Paintings in Chinese Publications, 1956-1968* (Ann Arbor 1969), 169; O. Sirén, *Chinese Painting*, (New York, 1956-58), VII, 199; id., *A History of Later Chinese Painting*, I (London, 1938), 192.

Lee Hwa-chou

HSIEH Ssu 傈斯 (d. 1380+), envoy and administrator, was officially registered as a native of Li-yang溧陽, which was under the direct jurisdiction of Ying-t'ien-fu 應天府 (later Nanking). Actually, however, he was a descendant of an influential Uighur Manichean family which originated in Kao-ch'ang 高昌, situated on the Hsieh-nien River 傈輦河, from which the family derived its name. Hsieh Ssu's grandfather served the Yüan, and four of his uncles, all of whom became *chin-shih*, were known for their literary attainments. His father, also a *chin-shih* (1315), officiated for a time in Kwangtung. He appears to have had two sons; one was Hsieh Hsün 遜 (or Hsieh Po-liao 百僚 -hsün), cs 1345, who in 1358, to escape the upset conditions in north China, moved to Korea where he enjoyed highly favorable treatment. He was the author of *Chin-ssu-chai i-kao* 近思齋逸稿 and a minor poet. The other was Hsieh Ssu. According to *Koryŏ sa* 高麗史, he was Hsieh Hsün's younger brother.

At the end of the Yüan dynasty Hsieh Ssu was magistrate of Chia-ting-chou 嘉定州, in the prefecture of Soochow. In 1366 he surrendered to Chu Yüan-chang.

When Chu became emperor two years later, Hsieh Ssu first received a post as a vice director in the ministry of War, then an appointment as minister of the seal office. Late in the same year he was selected for the first mission to Korea, to proclaim the inauguration of the new dynasty. The trip by sea was long and hazardous. He reached his destination in the fourth lunar month of 1369. His mission remained about a month in Korea. As he refused to accept any gift, the Korean king ordered his scholar-officials to compose poems to present to Hsieh as a memento. A few months after the successful completion of his mission he was entrusted with another, this time to bear a golden seal, an imperial patent, an imperial edict formally endorsing the Korean king as sovereign, a copy of the Ming calendar, and gifts, not only to the king, but also to the queen, the king's mother, and several high officials. This time he arrived in Korea in the fifth lunar month of 1370.

During the early years of the Hung-wu period, although Korea carried on friendly communications with remnant Mongol groups, the first Ming emperor generally regarded Korea kindly for its early submission as a tributary state. At the same time Ming power had not yet been consolidated to the north and northeast. Under the Yüan dynasty kings of Korea were related by marriage to the Mongol imperial family. They even had Mongol names. As the Mongol power disintegrated, Korea managed also to have close connections with Mongol splinter groups, the Jurchen, and whatever local authorities happened to be in Liaotung, mainly because they were on their frontier. Under such circumstances, suspicions, rumors, and spying were common. Misunderstanding followed. Thus relations between China and Korea immediately after 1374 became strained.

Respected as an able administrator, Hsieh Ssu, from 1371 to 1376, officiated away from the capital, first as magistrate of T'ai-an 泰安, Shan-tung, then (1373) as prefect of Ho-chien 河間 in the Peiping adminstrative area. Recalled to Nanking in 1376 for a short period of time only, he became a bureau director, then minister of Revenue. In June, 1377, he was sent out to be vice commissioner of Shansi. Back in the capital in 1380, he was appointed minister of Personnel, then of Rites. In this last capacity he established the three categories of title designations, the k'ai-kuo 開國, the shih-hsi 世襲, and the chui-feng 追封; in this way distinctions were made clear among those who earned their titles by merit in the founding of the empire, their descendants who inherited the titles, and their ancestors who were given the titles posthumously. On July 27 of this same year Hsieh Ssu retired because of advanced age.

In supplementing the Chinese records, the Korean sources are invaluable: they reveal the other side of any given story, they fill up certain gaps, especially for the early Ming period, as the *shih-lu* was written and rewritten. For example, the *Koryŏ sa* reports that Chu Yüan-chang several times suggested a marriage alliance with Korea. Except on important official occasions, eunuchs were usually sent on missions to Korea. During the Hung-wu era these eunuchs were almost always Korean. When they returned to their homeland, as recorded in Korean sources, most of them were overbearing and demanding. More likely than not, some of them made unfavorable remarks in the presence of the emperor and planted ideas which led to his distrust and displeasure with Korea.

Hsieh Ssu's nephew, a son of Hsieh Hsün, Sŏl Chang-su 偰長壽, who rose to high office in Korea, headed a number of embassies to Nanking. Presumably well versed in Chinese, he was granted several audiences by the first Ming emperor. The conversations and spoken imperial orders are often found in the *Koryŏ sa* and the *Chosŏn wangjo sillok* 朝鮮王朝實錄. From such documents we realize that the Chinese spoken words of the 14th century were not too different from those of to-day, yet occasionally enough for us to take notice of them. In 1394, as superintendent of the bureau of translation, Sŏl Chang-su initiated a two-level government program for language teaching, and an examination system for the selection of language officials. In this program Chinese was undoubtedly the principal foreign tongue, but he also included Mongol and Uighur.

Bibliography

MSL(1962), T'ai-tsu, 0749, 0866, 2098; 5/24/12a; 40/95/1a; Ch'en Tso-lin 陳作霖, *Chin-ling t'ung-chuan* 金陵通傳 (photo-repr. of 1904 ed., Taipei, 1970), 9/3b; *Koryŏ sa* (1908), I/628 下, 633 下, 691 下, III/739 上, 757 下; *Chosŏn wangjo sillok* (1955), I/71 下, 93 上, 97 下, 103 下; Fang Chaoying, *The Asami Library* (Berkeley, 1969), 50; Ch'en Yüan 陳垣, *Yüan hsi-yü jen hua-hua k'ao* 元西域人華化考 (Peiping, 1935), 32 (tr. and annot. by Ch'ien Hsing-hai and L. Carrington Goodrich as *Western and Central Asians in China under the Mongols*, Los Angeles, 1966, 77); L. Carrington Goodrich, "Sino-Korean Relations at the End of the XIVth Century," *Trans. of the Korea Br. of the R.A.S.*, XXX (1940), 35.

Lienche Tu Fang

HSIEH Wu-lu, *see* SEMEDO, Álvarō

HSING An 興安, fl. 1441–57, a eunuch of obscure origin, was one of the most favored imperial subordinates during the early years of the Ming dynasty. Unlike his colleague Chin Ying (*q.v.*), Hsing An did not become generally known until the reign of Cheng-t'ung. In June, 1441, he was sent to Nanking as the imperial representative to take part in the trial of convicts, conducted by Ho Wen-yüan (*see* Ho Ch'iao-hsin) and others; this was an early instance in which a eunuch participated in such trials (*see* Chin Ying). During this time, however, Hsing An remained a minor figure under the dominating shadow of Wang Chen (*q.v.*). In the aftermath of the captivity of Emperor Chu Ch'i-chen (*q.v.*), Hsing An, together with Chin Ying, vigorously spoke out against the proposal that the court abandon the capital and seek shelter in the south. He gave support to Yü Ch'ien (*q.v.*) and his pro-war party, who demanded the defeat of the invaders. In November the new emperor, Chu Ch'i-yü (*q.v.*), sent him to assist Yü and his deputies in the defense of the capital.

Under the new emperor, Hsing An headed the directorate of ceremonial and rose in political influence. Early in 1450 he participated in the selection of the envoy Li Shih (*q.v.*) for a mission to the Oirat court to negotiate the release of the captive emperor, and played a considerable role in the deliberation of the strategy to be followed in these negotiations. In May, 1452, when Chu Ch'i-yü decided to depose the legal heir apparent appointed by his brother in favor of his own son, Hsing An, as his mouthpiece, transmitted the message to the court officials, and cowed them into accepting the decision.

As the most powerful eunuch at this time, Hsing An shared the predilection and vices of his predecessors and committed numerous unbecoming acts; his warped obsession with Buddhism was such that it led to excessive drafts on the imperial treasury. During the first three years of Chu Ch'i-yü's reign, through Hsing An's influence more than thirty thousand people entered the Buddhist order, drawing stipends and enjoying tax exemptions. In the summer of 1453 Hsing An, attempting to rival Wang Chen in his patronage, persuaded the emperor to spend large sums on the construction of a new monastery in the capital, known as Ta-lung-fu ssu 大隆福寺. It is said that he employed more than ten thousand workmen, and that one of the palace halls in Nanking occupied by the first emperor was stripped of its wood and marble to supply necessary materials. Upon its completion a year later, he invited the emperor to pay a visit, but the latter, swayed by the remonstrance of the censors, canceled the excursion. In December, 1454, two eunuchs were charged with illegally using government materials for the construction of several Buddhist monasteries in the palace area in the name of Hsing An. When the irregularity was revealed, Hsing pleaded ignorance and shifted the blame to his two subordinates. The judicial authorities recommended the death sentence for the offenders, but the emperor, presumably acting at the suggestion of Hsing An, exonerated them. He ordered only the destruction of the monasteries and the return of the building materials to the government depot.

Early in February, 1467, when Chu Ch'i-yü was gravely ill, Hsing and his associates tried to suppress the news from the court officials, but it was finally revealed to the opposition group led by Ts'ao Chi-hsiang and Shih Heng (*qq.v.*) who subsequently succeeded in restoring the ex-emperor Chu Ch'i-chen. Following this, Hsing An lost his influence and found himself in a precarious situation. Before long, the secretaries from the six supervisory offices and the censors from the thirteen branch offices of the Censorate submitted a joint memorial charging that Hsing An, in his service under the former emperor, had superseded the imperial authority, participated in the decision to put Chu Ch'i-chen in confinement after his return from captivity, and been responsible for the deposition of the rightful heir apparent, Chu Chien-shen (*q.v.*). They recommended capital punishment, but the reinstalled emperor, in a gesture of leniency, instead sent Hsing An into retirement. As a Buddhist, Hsing made a wish when he was dying that his body be cremated and the ashes given as an offering to the Buddha.

Bibliography

1/95/14a, 304/14b; 5/117/11a; MSL (1963), Ying-tsung, 3630, 4632, 5025, 5058, 5369, 5815; Li Shih, *Pei-shih lu*; Yang Hsüan 楊瑄, *Fu-p'i lu*; Yeh Sheng, *Shui-tung jih-chi*, in *Chi-lu hui-pien* ed. by Shen Chieh-fu, 17/1b, 21/1a, 142/20b; Wang Shih-chen, *Yen-shan-t'ang pieh-chi*, 90/17a, 91/16b; Teng Ch'iu 鄧球 (cs 1535), *Huang Ming yung-hua lei-pien* 皇明泳化類編 (Taipei, 1965), 123/9b, Lu T'ung, *Ti-ching ching-wu lüeh* (1957), 13; Hsia Hsieh 夏燮, *Ming t'ung-chien* 明通鑑 (Shanghai, 1959), 1055; L. C. Arlington and William Lewisohn, *In Search of Old Peking* (1935), 183.

Hok-lam Chan

HSIUNG Wen-ts'an 熊文燦 (T. 心開), d. November 16, 1640, one of the highest military commanders executed by order of the last Ming emperor, Chu Yu-chiao (ECCP), was of obscure origin but is recorded as having been a native of Lu-chou 瀘州, Szechwan, whence his family of military registry had moved from the Yung-ning 永寧 guard (about ninety miles southwest of Kwei-yang 貴陽, Kweichow). The gazetteers of both provinces list his name among the *chin-shih* of 1607. Where or when he passed his *chü-jen* examination, however, is not mentioned; presumably it was in Szechwan a few years earlier. In any case his first official post was as prefectural judge of Huang-chou 黃州, Hukuang. Here he became a friend of a member of the local gentry, Yao Ming-kung 姚明恭 (H. 崑斗, cj 1603, cs 1619, grand secretary, 1639–40). Later (1610?) Hsiung received a promotion to be a secretary in the ministry of Rites, eventually rising to a bureau director. According to his biography in the *Ming-shih* (practically the main source about him until recently), he was then sent on a mission to the Liu-ch'iu Islands (Ryūkyū), which is obviously an error for, after the Japanese invasion of those islands in 1612, the only mission from the Ming court was the one sent in 1634.

In January, 1621, Hsiung became intendant of the Grand Canal at Chi-ning 濟寧, Shantung, with the rank of an assistant administration commissioner. Fourteen months later a minister recommended him as one of the middle grade officials able to take up military duties. Soon thereafter he was promoted to surveillance commissioner of Shansi (May, 1622), assigned to the military intendancy at Chinghsing 井陘. In 1623 he returned to Shantung as an administration commissioner, but a year later, having learned of the death of a parent, he retired to observe the mourning rites. At this time he made his home in Ch'i-shui 蘄水, Hukuang, the native district of his friend, Yao Mingkung. (Reportedly Yao had a daughter who married one of Hsiung's sons.) Apparently Hsiung had invested in properties there and changed his registry to that district. This seems to indicate that his relationships with the authorities in both Kweichow and Szechwan had not been happy. The fact that the gazetteers of the two provinces have no record of him before he became a *chin-shih* indicates a possible blemish in his family's past.

When Hsiung returned to Peking early in 1628, the eunuch party had fallen. In this way he had escaped involvement in the violent political strife of the preceding three years. In March he was reinstated as administration commissioner and sent to Fukien where, due to failure in the suppression of piracy, the governor and the regional commander were both being removed. Just then a minister recommended Hsiung as capable of dealing with pirates. This resulted in his appointment as governor of Fukien (April). Meanwhile the leader of the pirates, Cheng Chih-lung (ECCP), who had had dealings with the Europeans in Macao, Manila, and the Japanese port, Hirado, and had been in command of a large fleet with western style ships and firearms since 1624, expressed willingness to surrender to the Fukien provincial government. When Hsiung arrived, he assumed the responsibility of accepting Cheng's offer, and made him a probationary officer to fight the other pirates. The move proved to be an immediate success. From 1628 to 1631 one after another pirate leader was killed or put out of action, and in September, 1631, Hsiung even reported that the end of piracy called for a return to normal and

the reopening of the coast to sea trade. He then sent Cheng to lead his command to southern Kiangsi to fight a group of roving bandits which operated in the vast mountainous area where Kwangtung, Fukien, and Kiangsi meet. Cheng gained several victories over the bandits and forced their leader to surrender. For these and other successes Hsiung received a promotion in March, 1632, to supreme commander of Kwangtung and Kwangsi, and Cheng was confirmed as yu-chi 游擊 (mobile force commander, 4th ranking military or naval officer; at this time in coastal provinces equivalent to a brigadier general or a commodore). In May, while Cheng pursued the remaining bandits to a point as far as T'ai-ho 泰和 in central Kiangsi, the new governor, Tsou Wei-lien 鄒維璉 (T. 德輝, H. 匪石, cs 1607, d. 1633), recalled him to Fukien because of the threat of an invasion by the Dutch and the emergence of another pirate, Liu Hsiang (*q.v.*).

It took Cheng another three years of bitter fighting before he could subdue Liu. During these years, because Liu several times operated on the Kwangtung coast, Hsiung Wen-ts'an frequently joined the Fukien authorities in directing the naval forces of both provinces. After Liu suffered a defeat in Fukien waters in May, 1634, and Cheng chased him back to Kwangtung, the pirate tried to negotiate his own surrender. Delighted over the prospect, Hsiung sent two intendants and two high officers to Liu's flagship to discuss the matter. The pirate, however, detained all of them as hostages. When Hsiung dejectedly reported this to the throne early in 1635, he shifted the blame to these officials themselves, accusing them of acting without his permission, which was obviously improbable. The emperor questioned him about this and ordered him to redeem himself by subduing the pirate. In May, 1635, Hsiung took pleasure in dispatching a memorial on Cheng's final victory over Liu. Thus did Hsiung regain his reputation as a master of the art of turning former rebel leaders to good use. In March, 1636, he received the higher concurrent rank of a vice minister of War.

Hsiung's post in Kwangtung was one of the most lucrative in the empire and at this time one of the most desirable, because a rebellion was then engulfing most of north China, and the Manchus were conducting raids from the northeast. There is a story that, after he had sent gifts to influential persons in Peking, he became confident of retaining his office. One day in 1637, while entertaining at his headquarters in Ch'üan-chou 全州, Kwangsi, a eunuch on an imperial mission to collect some medicinal herbs, Hsiung became inebriated and boastfully declared that if he were the commander-in-chief, he could suppress the banditti with ease. The eunuch stood up, confessed that his errand was really to evaluate Hsiung's ability, and promised to recommend him to the emperor. Realizing at once that he had gone too far, Hsiung made various demands as condition to his acceptance of any such appointment, viz., direct access to the throne, full authority over personnel, the appointment of a high official to take charge of financial matters, and so on. The eunuch, however, thought the demands evidenced the fact that Hsiung had a well-planned strategy, and so reported to the throne. In May, 1637, Hsiung received the appointment of supreme director (tsung-li 總理) of the military affairs of six provinces (Nan-Chihli, Hukuang, Shensi, Shansi, Honan, and Szechwan) in charge of the suppression of the rebels, with the rank of a minister of War and vice censor-in-chief.

When Hsiung left Canton, his three sons and their teacher, Liang Ch'ao-chung 梁朝鍾 (T. 未央, H. 車匿, cs 1643, d. January, 1647), accompanied him, along with a bodyguard of a thousand Cantonese equipped with firearms. When their boats reached northern Kiangsi, there came to meet them from Mt. Lu 盧山 several acquaintances, including Tseng Ch'i-hsin, known later as the monk Han-shih (q.v.).

Together they went to visit their mentor, Tao-tu (see Han-shih), who warned Hsiung not to overplay his luck by placing too much trust in converted rebels as he had with the pirates.

In November, when Hsiung arrived at his headquarters in Anking, he requested horses for the Cantonese, but Peking assigned to him the six thousand horsemen under General Tso Liang-yü (ECCP). As a result of Tso's objection, Hsiung had to remove his Cantonese bodyguard from his headquarters. Apparently he quartered them in his home town, Ch'i-shui, where they took part in defending the city from rebel attacks for two or three years before they returned to Canton. In any case, early in 1638, the emperor, following the suggestion of Yang Ssu-ch'ang (q.v.), made Hsiung responsible for a hundred twenty thousand troops commanded by ten governors. A contingent of several thousand imperial guards from Peking under the eunuch, Liu Yüan-pin 劉元斌 (executed November, 1642), was also ordered to take part in the encirclement of the rebels. The over-all plan was to check the guerrilla bands on all sides, force them into the area in northwest Hukuang and southwest Honan, and make it possible for the troops under Liu Yüan-pin, Tso Liang-yü, and the Yunnan general, Lung Tsai-t'ien 龍在田 (d. ca. 1647), to annihilate them there. The campaign was to last one hundred days and be financed by a surtax of 2.8 million taels.

Hsiung, as field director of the campaign, undoubtedly had the means and the power to carry out this strategy, but he lacked the wisdom and the will. From the beginning he tried pacification. It is said that from Anking he issued widely posted notices promising pardon to any rebel who would surrender. In February, 1638, one of the rebel leaders, Liu Kuo-neng 劉國能 (d. 1641), submitted; some others followed. In May, after the time limit had passed and Hsiung was about to be reprimanded, the strongest of the three rebels, Chang Hsien-chung (ECCP), began to negotiate terms of surrender. Hsiung thought his policy was approaching success and was pleased; so were his sponsors in Peking, Yang Ssu-ch'ang and the emperor.

Had Hsiung dealt with the surrendered rebels correctly, by dispersing them at once, he might have accomplished his plan. Instead he permitted Chang to retain command of his men, numbering over ten thousand, and settled them as military farmers at Ku-ch'eng 穀城 on the Han 漢 River in northwestern Hukuang. He then armed three thousand of them as government soldiers, but allowed them to camp at Ku-ch'eng without taking any effective measures to watch them. At this time Hsiung himself maintained his headquarters some thirty miles downstream at Hsiang-yang 襄陽. In October Lung Tsai-t'ien and his Yunnanese won a spectacular victory over the remaining rebels at Shuang-kou 雙溝, about twenty miles north of Hsiang-yang on the Honan border, forcing the bandits to winter in the mountains in southwest Honan. Soon thereafter another able outlaw, Lo Ju-ts'ai 羅汝才, also negotiated for surrender, and the end of the rebellion seemed in sight. Just at this time, however, the Manchu invaders were approaching Peking, and many veteran troops, including those under Tso Liang-yü, were transferred from Shensi, Honan, and other places to the national capital. This lifting of pressure gave the small bands of hard-pressed rebels several months to regain their strength. Although Tso Liang-yü later won several engagements over them in April, 1639, Chang Hsien-chung decided it was time to resume his profitable pursuit of banditry. In June he suddenly attacked Ku-ch'eng, killing its magistrate and other officials, and pillaging the city. He then took up positions in the mountains to the west. Soon Lo Ju-ts'ai and others joined him. Only Liu Kuo-neng remained loyal to the government. Late in August Chang inflicted a severe defeat on the pursuing army under Tso Liang-yü. For his failures Hsiung was stripped of his ranks and ordered to await

the arrival of his successor, Yang Ssu-ch'ang. In November Hsiung was placed under arrest and sent to Peking to be tried. At this time his friend, Yao Ming-kung, was serving as a grand secretry, but could do nothing to help. Hsiung was sentenced to death and executed. According to the gazetteer of Ch'i-shui, he was buried there, west of the city near a pagoda.

Hsiung's failure to suppress the rebels contributed to the eventual fall of the dynasty. He is described in some accounts as corrupt, mediocre, lacking in patience, and cowardly (貪庸躁怯), and was accused of boastfulness and untruthfulness. It is said that, when Chang Hsien-chung captured Ku-ch'eng in 1639, he inscribed on the wall of the magistrate's office a list of officials who had accepted bribes from him, with dates and amounts, and accused Hsiung of forcing him to rebel by insatiable demands. Chang named Wang Jui-nan 王瑞枏 (T. 聖木, cs 1625, d. 1647), the former intendant of Hsiang-yang, as the only official who had refused to accept anything from him.

As to Hsiung's persistence in his policy of appeasement, there is the possibility that he was influenced by his belief in Buddhist teachings of preservation, not destruction, of life. Liang Ch'ao-chung addressed him in a letter as chü-shih 居士, or lay Buddhist. In fact, while in Canton, Hsiung had private consultations with the priest Tao-tu, and it was this monk who introduced Liang to him to teach his sons. In Liang's collected works there are four letters to Hsiung and two to his eldest son, Hsiung Kuei 檜 (T. 遜木). According to Liang, Hsiung led a very frugal life while in Hsiang-yang, allowing only thirty cash a day for the family table. This seems to contradict the impression given in the *Ming-shih* and elsewhere. In any case, when Chang Hsien-chung occupied Ch'i-shui early in 1643 and massacred the townspeople, he is said to have paid particular attention to Hsiung's household there. The new magistrate found the city utterly devastated and strewn with corpses. Hsiung's two younger sons were never heard from again and presumably had lost their lives; but, according to Liang Ch'ao-chung, the eldest, Hsiung Kuei, escaped with his life and for a time lived as a guest of Cheng Chih-lung.

Bibliography

1/260/9b, 235/21b, 252/2a; MSL *fu-lu, Ch'ung-chen ch'ang-pien*, 0199, 0955, 1040, 1788; Ku Ying-t'ai (ECCP), *Ming-ch'ao chi-shih pen-mo*, ch. 76, 77; KC (1958), 5683, 5701, 5715, 5728, 5780, 5793, 5806, 5814, 5818, 5840, 5879; Wu Wei-yeh (ECCP), *Sui-k'ou chi-lüeh* (TsSCC ed.), ch. 6; Tai Li 戴笠, *K'ou-shih pien-nien* 寇事編年 (in *Hsüan-lan-t'ang* 玄覽堂 *ts'ung-shu*, 2d ser., 1947), 10/13b; *Ch'i-shui-hsien chih*(1880), 2/37b, 10/18b, 13/46a, 18/21b; *Hsiang-yang-fu chih* (1886), 16/32b, 21/29a; Li Ch'ing (ECCP), *San-yüan pi-chi*, 1/11a, 18b; *Ming Ch'ing nei-ko ta-k'u shih-liao* (1949), 505, 516, 522, 750; Li Wen-chih 李文治, *Wan-Ming min-pien* 晚明民變 (1948), 72; Liang Ch'ao-chung, *Yü-yüan chi* 嚛園集 (in *Kuang-tung ts'ung-shu*, 1941); James B. Parsons, *Peasant Rebellions of the Late Ming Dynasty* (Tucson, 1970), 54, 57, 64, 69.

Chaoying Fang

HSÜ 徐, **Empress** (Pth. 仁孝), 1362-August 6, 1407, wife of Emperor Chu Ti (*q.v.*), was the eldest daughter of Hsü Ta (*q.v.*). Although she seems to have been a woman of intellect and energy, the many virtues credited to her by Ming writers are obviously exaggerated. Practically all extant biographies are based on a single entry in the *shih-lu* under the date of her death, when she received the traditional adulation. Her marriage to Chu Ti, then prince of Yen, probably took place in 1376. On February 17 of that year she received the title of princess of Yen. Contemporary sources assert that the dynastic founder, Chu Yüan-chang, having heard of her good poise and disposition, selected her to be the consort of his son. It is more likely that the nuptials were arranged to strengthen the family alliance between the emperor and his former comrade-at-arms, as the princess' two younger sisters were also wed (much later) into the imperial family—one to Chu Kuei (*see* Chu Yüan-chang), the emperor's thirteenth son, the other to Chu Ying 楹, the twenty-second. It may be noted that in the early years of the dynasty consorts of imperial princes were usually chosen from the households of the new nobility; only later was this practice discontinued. Except for Empress Hsü, no other first lady of the Empire in the history of the dynasty had an aristocratic background. [Editors' note: Thereafter the wives and concubines of the princes were deliberately selected from families of humble origin. They were the daughters of lesser officials and commoners. The policy was apparently aimed at preventing the domination of the court by powerful imperial relatives, a situation which had cropped up all too often in earlier dynasties. Two extreme but interesting cases under the Ming are: the mother of Emperor Chu Yu-t'ang (*q.v.*) was the daughter of a native chieftain captured by the imperial army, and the grandmother of Emperor Chu Hou-ts'ung (*q.v.*) was a slave girl sold to a eunuch; the former was posthumously honored as empress, and the latter assumed the title of empress-dowager during her lifetime.] The princess reportedly served her mother-in-law, Empress Ma (*q.v.*), with becoming filial piety and on the latter's death in 1382 she is said to have followed a strict vegetable diet for three years, a practice consistent with her Buddhist background. In 1380 she accompanied her husband to his new princely domain at Peiping. Their devotion to each other, reported by contemporaries with delight, seems to be true, as she bore three of his four sons and four of his seven daughters, although Chu Ti is known to have had at least twenty-three concubines who received imperial titles. Two of them he particularly favored, both apparently entering his life after the death of the empress.

When the prince rebelled in 1399 against his nephew, Emperor Chu Yün-wen (*q.v.*), he set as his first goal the broadening of his base of operations and the strengthening of his army. In the autumn of that year he proceeded to attack Ta-ning 大寧 (in modern Jehol), a fief held by a half-brother, leaving Pei-ping in the hands of his son, Chu Kao-chih (*q.v.*). Upon hearing that the latter city was guarded by a skeleton garrison only, the imperial army under Li Ching-lung (son of Li Wen-chung, *q.v.*) dashed forward to besiege it. The princess, it is said, mobilized the army wives to assist her son's defense. Some women apparently even saw action on the city wall. Accounts of the battle indicate that some of them flung stones at Li's troops then attacking the Li-cheng 麗正 (now the Cheng-yang 正陽) gate.

In the summer of 1402 Chu Ti took Nanking and proclaimed himself emperor. The princess was installed as empress four months later. The triumph, however, cost dearly. The three years' fighting split not only his family, but hers as well. Before things settled she had lost two younger brothers (*see* Hsü Ta). At the outset of Chu Ti's rebellion both brothers were serving Chu Yün-wen's court at Nanking. The elder, Hsü Hui-tsu, who inherited the father's title of duke of Wei-kuo, was a stanch loyalist. The younger, Hsü Tseng-shou, a chief military commissioner, favored the prince of Yen. Each brother tried to serve his own master in a way detrimental to the other. On the eve of the rebellion Hsü Hui-tsu advised the monarch to detain all three sons of the prince then attending the funeral of Emperor Chu Yüan-chang in Nanking. Hsü Tseng-shou, on the other hand, urged him to let them return. Three years later, in defeat, Chu Yün-wen reportedly slew Hsü Tseng-shou with his own hands before disappearing in the palace fire. Hsü Hui-tsu not only fought with the imperial army, but also, the day Nanking fell to the prince, still carried on

the loyalist cause by directing street fighting inside the capital. When taken captive he refused the prince's offer to write a letter of apology, remaining defiant to the end. The outcome is not clear. Official sources state that he was under house arrest for life and died in 1407, the same year that Empress Hsü passed away. Another account indicates that he committed suicide while the prince of Yen, now emperor, was debating whether he should be executed and the empress, although grieving over his plight, did not dare to intercede inasmuch as her husband still regarded him with rage. Hsü Tseng-shou, on the other hand, was posthumously enfeoffed as duke of Ting-kuo 定國公, and a son inherited the position. The empress, according to her biographers, considering the award overgenerous, tried to stop the enfeoffment but without success.

While maintaining a keen interest in the state's well-being, Empress Hsü is not known to have intervened in governmental affairs. Only once, according to the records, did she advise the emperor, counseling that promotions of officials not be restricted by seniority. Well-schooled herself, she emphasized the importance of education and became concerned with the employment of erudite advisers in the court. In the autumn of 1404 the emperor gave audience to Hsieh Chin, Huang Huai, Hu Kuang, Hu Yen, Yang Jung, Yang Shih-ch'i (*qq.v.*), and Chin Yu-tzu 金幼孜 (ming 善, H. 退闇, 1368-1431, cs 1400, Pth. 文靖), all members of the Hanlin Academy, and indicated that the empress wished to meet their wives. When the ladies were ushered into the inner palace, Empress Hsü addressed them on womanhood and the role of an official's helpmeet. The session concluded with the women carrying away gifts from the hostess. There is little doubt that the event was faithfully recorded, as the most important state papers and chronicles of the early 15th century, including the *shih-lu* and the notes about the empress in it, are largely the works of the aforementioned scholar-officials. More significantly, several of them eventually rose to become outstanding statesmen in the dynasty's history. It suffices to say that the empress exerted some contributing influence on the increasing prominence of the Hanlin under her husband's reign, and perhaps, indirectly, under her son's as well.

The empress patronized literature and is credited with the authorship of two works of her own. The *Ku-chin lieh-nü chuan* 古今列女傳, 3 *ch.*, a collection of biographies of women noted for their humility, devotion, chastity, and varied accomplishments, compiled by Hsieh Chin *et al.*, with prefaces by the emperor, is said to have been prepared by order of Empress Ma but completed under Empress Hsü's auspices. The *Ssu-k'u* catalogue indicates that certain sections of the work were either dictated or edited by Empress Hsü. One of the books written by the empress herself is entitled *Nei-hsün* 內訓, 1 *ch.*, (Household instructions). Originally intended as a textbook for her own children, it was nevertheless promulgated by the emperor four months after her death. The other work carrying the empress' name is the *Ch'üan-shan shu* 勸善書, 20 *ch.* (Exhortations). The Peiping Library has an incomplete manuscript copy and two printed editions of this, the earlier one in large size characters, probably engraved shortly after its completion in 1407, and the other in smaller size characters, which seems to be the basis for the one published by the National University of Nanking. Each chapter of the work begins with a group of proverbs and quotations, followed by historical events and anecdotes illustrating them. In addition to its infusion of the traditional Confucian sense of morality, the work reveals certain Buddhist and Taoist influences. In some sections, for example, Buddhist terminology is used and sūtras are quoted. Unlike the *Nei-hsün*, this compilation was produced for popular reading and circulated as such. After his wife's death, Emperor Chu Ti ordered the performance of

Buddhist sacrificial ceremonies on her behalf. r He remains were buried eventually beside her husband's in Ch'ang-ling 長陵. near Peking.

Undoubtedly Empress Hsü strove to live up to the Confucian dictum that empresses should serve as models of motherhood for commoners. Her intention and decorum, both laudable, provided sufficient basis for elaboration by the court officials who tried hard to insist on the moral superiority of the imperial family. But in the end such effort had little result. The empress' moral precepts, if they affected the imperial subjects at all, did not move the members of her own household. Indeed, her eldest son, Chu Kao-chih, appears in history as a benevolent monarch. But as heir apparent he was so estranged from his father that the latter contemplated his execution (*see* Chien I). Her second son, Chu Kao-hsü (*q.v.*), was notoriously unruly; he did not hesitate to kill when he was angered. After his unsuccessful rebellion of 1426 and a later conspiracy, he was burned to death and his family terminated by his nephew, Emperor Chu Chan-chi (*q.v.*). Her youngest son, Chu Kao-sui (*see* Chu Kao-hsü), was involved in the attempted rebellion of 1426, but escaped the consequences. All the daughters of the empress married generals or sons of generals. The eldest daughter, Princess Yung-an 永安, married Yüan Jung 袁容, who achieved military merit in his father-in-law's rebellion. In 1406 he lashed a general nearly to death merely because the latter did not show appropriate courtesy by dismounting from his horse when passing Yüan's residence. The second daughter, Princess Yung-p'ing 永平, married Li Jang 李讓 in 1425. Her brother Chu Kao-chih, then emperor, stripped her of her aristocratic title, charging her ,with an unspecified conspiracy committed earlier. The two youngest princesses, An-ch'eng 安成 and Hsien-ning 咸寧, married brothers, Sung Hu 宋琥 and Sung Ying 瑛, the latter dying in 1449 fighting against Esen (*q.v.*).

Bibliography

1/113/7b, 18b, 21a, 118/16b, 121/9a, 125/9b; 61/
TsSCC/246, 1846; MSL (1963), T'ai-tsung, 0040,
0257, 0603, 0850, 0966; SK (1930), 58/2a, 93/
1b, 131/3a; KC (1958), 798, 836, 853; Cheng
Hsiao, *Wu-hsüeh-pien*, 52/3b; Ho Ch'iao-yüan,
Ming-shan-ts'ang (NLP microfilm no. 93–96),
K'un-tse chi 坤則記, 6a; *Ch'üan-shan shu* (NLP
microfilm no. 91); *Ku-chin lieh-nü chuan* (NLP
microfilm no. 134); Mao Ch'i-ling (ECCP),
Lieh-ch'ao t'ung-shih shih-i chi.

Chou Tao-chi and Ray Huang

HSÜ Chen-ch'ing 徐禎卿 (T. 昌穀, 昌國),
1479-April 2 (3), 1511, man of letters,
was born into a family registered in the
military category in T'ai-ts'ang 太倉 in the
prefecture of Soochow. Hsü's ancestors,
originally from Loyang, Honan, settled in
Soochow at the beginning of the Ming,
but in the time of his father they moved
to T'ai-ts'ang.

A talented boy, Hsü began to make
a name for himself in poetry while still
young. He entered the district school in
Ch'ang-chou 長洲, graduated as *chü-jen* in
1501, and achieved the *chin-shih* in 1505.
According to report, Hsü was under consideration for appointment as a Hanlin
bachelor by Emperor Chu Yu-t'ang (*q.v.*),
but when he found that Hsü looked rather unimpressive — short and slim —, the
emperor dropped his name from the list
of candidates. Instead, Hsü received an
appointment as a judge (7a) in the Grand
Court of Revision. Being unfamiliar with
legal procedures, however, he was found
unequal to his responsibilities; so he requested a transfer to a place nearer home
on the ground that he had to support his
aging parents. But the authorities frowned
upon his request, and made him an erudite in the National University (1509).
This, being an 8b post, implies demotion.
Two years later, however, he died at the
early age of thirty-two. His son, Hsü Po-
ch'iu 伯虯 (T. 子久, cj 1525), who survived him, was also a poet.

Hsü Chen-ch'ing owed his fame to
his achievement in literature, particularly
in the field of poetry. In his early years
he was grouped with T'ang Yin, Wen
Cheng-ming, and Chu Yün-ming (*qq.v.*), as
one of "The Four Talents from the District of Wu" (吳中四才子). Sometime after
1505 he fell under the influence of Li
Meng-yang (*q.v.*), the pioneer in the literary renaissance of the middle Ming period, and came to be known as a member
of the "Seven early masters" of Ming
literature, which included Li, Ho Ching-
ming, Pien Kung (*qq.v.*), and others. All
were northerners except Hsü, the only
one from south of the Yangtze River. It
is said that at this time Hsü began to
concentrate on the classical styles of the
T'ang masters and to adopt their criteria in
poetry. This changing attitude is evident
in the exchange of correspondence between
Hsü and his mentor during this period.
He was not just an imitator, however, but
proved himself a poet in his own right.
Certain critics have held that in some
ways his achievement in the last six years
of his life may well rival that of his seniors, Li Meng-yang and Ho Ching-ming.

Toward the end Hsü showed great
interest in religious Taoism, and became
quite obsessed with its concern for the
cultivation of longevity. Wang Shou-jen
(*q.v.*) reports on Hsü's tomb inscription a
conversation with him on this subject
when they met in the capital in the winter of 1510. In the presence of Chan Jo-
shui (*q.v.*), Wang's close friend, Hsü
raised the question as to whether a human
being could "bodily ascend to heaven"
(fei-sheng 飛昇) and become an immortal
with the assistance of a Taoist elixir. On
this occasion, while Chan dismissed the
possibility outright, Wang chose not to
dispute it, but tactfully contended that, if
a person is able to cultivate his mind,
nourish his physical self, and follow what
is natural in life, he may be said to have
done his best. Hsü appears to have been
convinced. His concern over popular Taoism made him distinct from the other disciples of Li Meng-yang, and this probably accounts for his changing attitude

toward life, and his indulgence in writing fictional accounts with a Taoistic flavor.

A prolific writer, Hsü left several collections of prose and poetry, but only the *Ti-kung chi* 廸功集, which he personally edited, seems to have survived. This collection, 6 *ch.*, with a preface by Li Meng-yang, and an appendix *T'an-i lu* 譚藝錄, 1 *ch.*, a treatise on poetic theory regarded as an important contribution to the field, was printed in 1520, and reprinted in 1528. A complete edition of Hsü's writings, entitled *Hsü Ch'ang-ku ch'üan-chi* 昌穀全集, 16 *ch.*, was printed during the Wan-li period. A copy of this work, listed as rare, is preserved in the Shanghai city library. A later edition of his poetry, 4 *ch.*, with appendices of *wai-chi* 外集, 3 *ch.*, and the *T'an-i lu*, were incorporated in the *Hung-chih ssu-chieh-shih-chi* 弘治四傑詩集, together with the works of Li, Ho, and Pien Kung, by Sun Tsu-t'ung 孫祖同 in 1895. His poems also appeared in many collections in the Ch'ing dynasty.

In addition, Hsü left several items of fiction, such as *Chien-sheng yeh wen* 剪勝野聞, 1 *ch.*, a collection of anecdotes and fictionalized accounts of outstanding events and personalities in the reign of the first emperor; *Hsin-ch'ien chi* 新倩籍, 1 *ch.*, an assemblage of five biographies of his contemporaies such as T'ang Yin and Wen Cheng-ming; *I-lin* 異林, 1 *ch.*, a miscellany of prodigious events and strange happenings. With Wen Cheng-ming, Hsü was also the author of *T'ai-hu hsin-lu* 太湖新錄, a collection of miscellaneous notes about T'ai Lake, which is included in *Kuang ssu shih chia hsiao-shuo* 廣四十家小說 by Ku Yüan-ch'ing 顧元慶 (T. 大有, H. 大石, 1487-1565), reprinted in 1915. Except for the last item, these writings are available in a number of Ming and Ch'ing collections of fictional writings. Hsü's tomb inscription by Wang Shou-jen has been rendered into Japanese in *Yōmei gaku* 陽明學; it also includes a reproduction of Hsü's calligraphy on the front page. One of Hsü's essays in his own calligraphy, entitled "Wei Chu-chün mu mai lü shu hou" 爲朱君募買驢疏後, is preserved in the art museum of Princeton University.

Bibliography

1/286/15a; 34/11/1b; 40/31/1a; 42/94/18a; 64/丁/2/1a; 84/丙/51b; KC (1958), 2996; Wang Shou-jen, *Wang Wen-ch'eng kung ch'üan-shu*, 25/709; Li Meng-yang, *K'ung-t'ung tzu chi*, 52/2b, 62/3a; Wen Cheng-ming, *P'u-t'ien chi*, 24/2a; Kuo P'an 郭槃, *Huang Ming t'ai-hsüeh chih* 皇明太學志 (NLP microfilm, no. 454), 11/4a; *T'ai-ts'ang-chou chih* (1548), 7/37b; *ibid.* (1859), 10/10a, 13b, 18/36b; *Wu-hsien chih* (1934), 66 上/19a; SK (1930), 171/10a, 190/5b; TSCC (1885-88), XXIII: 99/87/9a; Weng Fang-kang (ECCP), *Fu-ch'u-chai wen-chi* (1877), 8/12b; Wang Shih-chen (ECCP), "Er-chia shih-hsüan hsü" (fu-lu) 二家詩選序 (附錄), in *Yü-yang san-shih-liu chung*, vol. 68; Chu Tung-jün 朱東潤, *Chung-kuo wen-hsüeh p'i-p'ing shih ta-kang* 中國文學批評史大綱 (1960 reprint), 229; *Shanghai t'u-shu-kuan shan-pen shu-mu* 上海圖書館善本書目 (1957), 4/16a; *Ku-kung chi-k'an* 故宮季刊, 3: 3 (January, 1969), 39; *Yōmei gaku* (March 1, 1918), no. 111, front page, 22; Liu Ts'un-yan, "Taoist Cultivativtion in Ming Thought," in W. T. de Bary ed., *Self and Society in Ming Thought* (New York, 1970), 310; NCL *Catalogue of Rare Books* (1966), 1041, 1299.

Hok-lam Chan

HSÜ Chieh 徐階 (T. 子升, H. 少湖, 存齋), October 9, 1503-April 18, 1583, one of the more prominent grand secretaries, was officially registered as a native of Hua-t'ing 華亭 in the prefecture of Sung-chiang 松江. He was actually born in Hsüan-p'ing 宣平, Chekiang, where his father, Hsü Fu 黻 (T. 恩復, d. 1524), was then serving as assistant magistrate. Surviving the hurly-burly of court politics for three decades, Hsü Chieh gradually gained the confidence of Emperor Chu Hou-ts'ung (*q. v.*), and played an important role in the years 1562 to 1568. All his biographers like to indicate, as premonitions of his future greatness, the stories of his narrow escapes from death in childhood. Once he fell into a well, was rescued, and remained in a coma for three days. Another time he fell off a high cliff, but fortunately his clothing caught in the branches of a tree.

Hsü Chieh's father was a successful yamen clerk in the Sung-chiang prefectural office who, after being awarded the rank of a lower grade official, qualified as an assistant magistrate. In that capacity he served at Hsüan-p'ing and later at Ning-tu 寧都, Kiangsi. At this time any official who entered the bureaucracy as a *chin-shih* was likely to be arrogant towards those who came in as university students or yamen clerks. Having probably long suffered the humiliation and frustration as one of the latter category, Hsü Fu apparently saw to it that his son would be provided with the proper training to enable him to succeed in the civil examinations. In this respect Hsü Chieh satisfied his father's dreams beyond expectation for he not only became a *chin-shih* in 1523 but also attained the coveted title of t'an-hua 探花 reserved for the third highest on the list; he at once became a compiler in the Hanlin Academy. He was then granted a special leave to marry his betrothed, née Shen 沈. On his way back to the capital in September, 1524, however, the news of his father's death reached him; so he turned homeward again to observe the mourning period.

After resuming his former post in Peking (1527?), Hsü was assigned to the palace school for young eunuchs as a tutor. Unlike the other tutors he took the assignment seriously, never arriving late or leaving early. He also treated his students politely, saying that some of them in time would hold responsible positions affecting the destiny of the empire. In return they came to respect him.

In November, 1530, Hsü had an encounter with the powerful grand secretary, Chang Ts'ung (name changed later to Chang Fu-ching, *q. v.*), and suffered the only serious setback in his political career. Chang was then trying to revise the ritual regulations to conform to the emperor's insistence that his father be elevated to imperial rank, an episode known as the

Ta-li i. In the cult of Confucius, according to Chang, the image of the sage, flanked by those of his four associates (四配), was shown seated in the main hall, while his own father and three of their fathers were given inferior places in the side halls, thus presenting an appearance contrary to Confucian principles of filial piety. It was a situation closely paralleling the one which the emperor faced and was trying to rectify. Chang attributed the cause of this ethically improper way of seating to the time when the princely title Wen-hsüan wang 文宣王 was conferred on Confucius in A. D. 739, and when at various times lesser ranks of nobility were assigned to his relatives, disciples, and followers. As a remedy Chang suggested the erection of a separate shrine for the seating of the father of the sage as well as the fathers of some of his disciples. Chang asked the emperor, furthermore, to follow the sage's teaching of the rectification of names, to abolish all these posthumous noble titles, and to destroy all the images. In any case, he argued, the images were developed after the Buddhist example and were decidedly un-Chinese. In their place he suggested the use of tablets with such designations as, in the case of Confucius, Chih-sheng hsien-shih K'ung-tzu chih shen-wei 至聖先師孔子之神位 (the spiritual seat of the ultimate sage and first teacher, Master K'ung). He also suggested the designations hsien-hsien 先賢 for the disciples and hsien-ju 先儒 for the latter day Confucianists. The emperor who, during certain state ceremonies at the Confucian temple, had to pay homage to the sage as the universal teacher, had long been bothered by the impropriety of an emperor having to kowtow to a prince. Hence he enthusiastically wrote an essay to endorse Chang's memorial and ordered that both documents be circulated among Hanlin academicians for comment. While the others were awed into silence, Hsü Chieh alone submitted a memorial in opposition, listing eight reasons why the sage's princely title should not be withdrawn, nor the images destroyed. The emperor considered Hsü's arguments a covert attack on himself, taking particular offense at the statement that, since His Majesty had often insisted that he was a faithful follower of the rules set by his ancestor, the founder of the dynasty, it would be contradictory to order a change in this case. The emperor obviously resented such an affront and, when a group of censors also voiced their opposition to any change, he angrily ordered an investigation to establish Hsü as the ringleader of a group of dissenters. After being tortured in prison Hsü was told that he could not escape execution. Yet he kept his composure, refused to change his opinion, and admitted to no more than that His Majesty's "sagacious counsels overwhelmingly exceeded the discernment of this servent" (聖謨洋洋非臣所能窺測). Somehow the emperor interpreted this sarcastic remark as flattery and, accusing Hsü of obsequiousness, ordered the erection of a "Monument to the Sycophant" (ning-jen pei 佞人碑) to ridicule him (in the court of the Temple of Confucius?). Hsü was demoted to prefectural judge of Yen-p'ing 延平 in Fukien. The arrangement in the Confucian temples was changed as ordered, and has remained essentially the same to modern times.

An examination of the documents shows that Chang Fu-ching's arguments are rational while Hsü's memorial seems forced, appealing rather to emotion. It reads like a sophomoric tract in comparison with his other writing. Whatever his real motive, whether he sincerely believed that in so acting he was loyal to the memory of Confucius, or whether he shrewdly took the opportunity to try to express his objection to the *Ta-li i* innovations, he emerged in the contest from the obscurity of a Hanlin compiler to national prominence and philosophical if not active leadership of the opposition to Chang Fu-ching.

While in Fukien Hsü made the most of the situation by exerting himself in the discharge of his duties. Several times he officiated as acting prefect, once quelling a local rebellion easily. In 1534 he was promoted to assistant surveillance commissioner and director of education of Chekiang, and in October, 1536, rose to be vice surveillance commissioner in charge of education in Kiangsi. During these years he gained the respect of the scholars as a conscientious official of exemplary conduct and as an advocate of the school of thought of Wang Shoujen (*q. v.*). Meanwhile Chang Fu-ching retired in 1535 and died in February, 1539. Three months after Chang's death Hsü was recalled as a reader in the Hanlin Academy to serve in the retinue of the heir apparent. Apparently he had learned his lesson; when he felt compelled to differ with the emperor, he managed to yield at the critical moment. He then rose steadily in rank. After serving as chancellor of the National University (1543–44) and as a vice minister of Rites (1544–45), he was appointed a vice minister of Personnel, a post he held for four years (1545–49). Others in that office used to close their doors to visitors to avoid any suspicion of taking bribes. Hsü ridiculed the practice as stemming from a guilty conscience and said that only by interviewing the visitors, especially officials from the provinces, could he evaluate them and make the proper selections. So he kept his door open, saying that one must have faith in oneself. In March, 1549, he became minister of Rites. Four months later he was ordered to serve in the Wu-i palace 無逸殿 as a writer of Taoist prayers, because his composition of that kind of incantation pleased the emperor.

During the crisis of 1550, when the Mongols swept over the Great Wall and camped in the vicinity of Peking, Hsü Chieh assumed leadership at court because, when the invaders requested trade, it was technically a tributary matter under the control of his ministry. He rose to the occasion and acted with courage and decision, and at the same time shrewdly and sagaciously, for he knew he was walking a tight rope amidst various powerful personages in the emperor's circle. In a statesmanlike manner he often succeeded in calming the emperor, helped several upright officials, and smoothed over some rather difficult situations. After the capture of a few Mongol interpreters late in 1551, the emperor unbelievably called it a military success and, attributing it to his Taoist prayers, rewarded those who helped in the ceremonies. Hsü, as a result, received the hereditary rank of a centurion in the Embroidered-uniform Guard. After the emergency had ended, he placated the emperor's favorites, particularly Grand Secretary Yen Sung (*q. v.*), and the head of the secret service, General Lu Ping (*q. v.*). Meanwhile the youngest of his three sons married Lu's daughter and a similar relationship was contracted with Yen's family. In April, 1552, Hsü was promoted to be a grand secretary. Ho Liang-chün (*q. v.*), who was in Peking in the autumn of that year, has left a vivid account of the private lives of the three grand secretaries, describing Yen's home as full of activity, with people coming and going like a market place, Hsü's quiet and reserved, and the home of Lü Nan (*q. v.*) somewhere in between. In public affairs Hsü seems to have had some freedom in the first few years. With regard to the pirates in the Soochow area Hsü at first took part actively in directing the campaign, but after the execution of Chang Ching and Yang Chi-sheng (*qq. v.*) in 1555 Hsü suddenly became silent and left the matter in Yen's hands. At the same time Hsü's mastery of timing served him well when he struck out to remove an enemy or a political rival, such as the moment when in September, 1552, he joined with Lu Ping to denounce another of the emperor's favorites, General Ch'iu Luan (*q. v.*).

In 1562 Hsü seized the opportunity to weaken the emperor's confidence in Yen Sung. It happened that on December 31, 1561, the Yung-shou-kung 永壽宮, the emperor's residence hall for almost twenty years, burned down and the emperor expressed his wish to have it rebuilt. At a conference on the matter, Yen Sung said that the project should be postponed until after completion of reconstruction of the three main audience halls which had been destroyed by fire in 1557. Reportedly Yen balked at the cost and advised a delay, suggesting as the emperor's temporary lodgings the palace called Nan-ch'eng, where his great-grandfather, Emperor Chu Ch'i-chen (*q. v.*), had once been held prisoner. The emperor regarded this association with abhorrence. Hsü, however, declared that the rebuilding of the Yung-shou-kung could be immediately undertaken by making use of the accumulated lumber and other materials that had been rejected as unfit for use on the three main halls. The emperor gladly entrusted the project to the minister of Works, Lei Li (*q. v.*), assisted by Hsü Chieh and his eldest son, Hsü Fan 璠 (b. 1532). The work was accomplished with such dispatch that in four months the reconstructed palace was ready for occupancy. Delighted, the emperor renamed it Wan 萬 shou-kung and bestowed awards on all concerned. Hsü headed the list of those favored and received the exalted title of junior preceptor, the twentieth civilian in the dynasty to be so honored while alive. Hsü Fan was made a vice minister of the Court of Imperial Sacrifices. In this way Hsü replaced Yen in the emperor's highest esteem. Only two months later Yen, accused of corruption by a censor, was cashiered and his son, Yen Shih-fan (*see* Yen Sung), sentenced to exile. Two years after this, when Yen Shih-fan was rearrested on the more serious charges of having escaped from his place of exile and having lived at home like an independent baron, the ministry of Justice, according to the code, recommendeded the sentence of imprisonment which the emperor rejected. By imperial order a new trial was conducted on the charge that he had been plotting treason; this time the sentence was immediate beheading, which took place in April, 1565. There is a story, probably apocryphal, that the new and unsubstantiated charge of treason was brought up by a censor following a hint from Hsü Chieh, who knew how to put an end to any chance of a resurgence of the influence of the two Yen.

In any event from 1562 on the emperor listened to Hsü's advice, which was sound and sensible, sometimes affording the only restraint to the aging sovereign who often acted irrationally, for he was experimenting with drugs supposed to have aphrodisiac effect. In 1566, when the emperor became incensed by the criticisms of Hai Jui (*q.v.*), it may very well have been Hsü Chieh's advice that saved that official from execution. When finally the emperor succumbed early in 1567, Hsü seized the opportunity to repeat what his famous predecessor, Yang T'ing-ho (*q.v.*), had done in 1521 at the death of Emperor Chu Hou-chao (*q.v.*), i.e., to issue an imperial final will (i-chao 遺詔) in the deceased emperor's name, which enumerated the misdeeds, unjust decisions, and harmful undertakings during his reign, and instructed his successor to endeavor to redress and rectify. As the matter was fraught with extreme danger should anything go wrong, Hsü could collaborate only with someone he trusted completely. For that reason he excluded his fellow grand secretaries and selected his former student, the Hanlin chancellor, Chang Chü-cheng (*q.v.*). After drafting the will Hsü showed it for approval to the heir apparent, Chu Tsai-hou (*q.v.*), and had it proclaimed to a surprised court. By the authority of the document, Hsü was enabled in the new emperor's name, to correct most of what he regarded as past mistakes. In this way he put a stop to the Taoist ceremonies inside the palace, halted unnecessary construction, cleared

the palace grounds of unsavory persons, withdrew the honors conferred on them, freed those unjustly imprisoned, reinstated tens of officials who had been cashiered, and reversed the verdicts on almost all those involved in the *Ta-li i* and other cases. Thus at one stroke he redressed what had been generally considered as miscarriages of justice during some forty years.

These first acts of the new reign, amounting to a peaceful *coup d'état*, were hailed by a grateful empire, and Hsü, as the one who planned it and carried it through, rose to the zenith of prestige and power. His achievement, however, proved to be the cause of his downfall, for he became the target of jealous grand secretaries who resented his failure to take them into his confidence. The slight was keenly felt especially by Kao Kung (*see* Chang Chü-cheng), who, as a long time tutor of the new emperor, had the qualifications to take Hsü's place. When in six months Kao was attacked twenty-eight times, he suspected Hsü as the instigator. In June, 1567, a censor on Kao's side openly accused Hsü of having slandered the deceased emperor in the will. The censor was demoted and Kao forced to retire. By this time the emperor's favorite eunuchs began to work for Hsü's removal. Finally, after being severely attacked by a censor, Hsü at the age of sixty-five was permitted to retire.

It is said that more than any other high official of his day Hsü had acquired an enormous holding of farmland (the amount varying from forty to more than sixty-six thousand acres). The fact that his father had once been a clerk in the prefectural office, and so perhaps had access to the land registers, may serve as an explanation as to how Hsü surpassed his fellow landlords. In general Hsü Fan was blamed as the one who, taking advantage of the privilege of exemption from taxes accorded his father, obtained title to property at nominal prices. Hsü Chieh, however, was not allowed to enjoy his wealth in comfort, because in 1569 the governor, Hai Jui, whose life he had saved in 1566, was now determined to force him to release at least half of his holdings to their original owners. It happened that in January, 1570, Kao Kung returned to power as an associate grand secretary and resumed his vendetta against Hsü in earnest. This, however, had nothing to do with what Hai Jui had in mind. In a letter to another grand secretary, Hai said that his reason for trying to force Hsü to relinquish a part of his land was to insure that for a hundred years his descendants could live in safety among their neighbors, adding that Hsü had only himself to blame for acquiring such an excessive amount of property. There is a story that Hsü's son boasted that he effected the removal of Hai from the governorship by spending a thousand taels of silver in Peking. It seems that Hsü in this way managed to retain most of his land, as revealed in one of Hai's letters to Hsü complaining that the land the latter had given up totalled far less than what he should have relinquished. Shortly after Hai was transferred (March, 1570), the local authorities, acting on Kao Kung's order, pursued the matter with more zeal. In 1571 the case was concluded when Hsü Fan was sentenced to exile and his two younger brothers were reduced to commoner status. Some ten thousand acres of their land was confiscated. This harsh treatment lasted only about a year, for the pressure was taken off when Kao Kung was ousted in July, 1572, and Chang Chü-cheng became grand secretary. About 1580 a magistrate reported that his attempt at rendering some relief to the dispossessed drew a subtle hint from Hsü to desist (*see* T'u Lung). When Hsü reached his eightieth birthday in 1582, the court even sent special messengers to his home, bearing presents and greetings. After his death the following year, high honors were accorded him, including the title of grand preceptor and the posthumous name of Wen-chen 文貞.

Hsü Chieh is described as short, light complexioned, and delicate in appearance, always careful in manners and attire. In philosophy and learning he was influenced by Wang Shou-jen. Some of Wang's students were his close friends, such as Nieh Pao and Ou-yang Te (*qq.v.*). During Hsü's official years in Peking, academies flourished and lecture gatherings were held in the capital. They were prohibited later under Chang Chü-cheng. Hsü left two collections of literary works, *Shao-hu hsiensheng wen-chi* 少湖先生文集, 7 *ch.*, and the *Shih-ching-t'ang chi* 世經堂集, 26 *ch.* The former was printed in Fukien by local scholars in honor of Hsü on his departure from Yen-p'ing in 1534. The latter, a much larger work, was printed by his sons after his death. He is known to have left a collection of philosophical sayings entitled *Ts'un-chai yü-lu* 存齋語錄 and some examples of his handwriting entitled *Pao-lun-t'ang t'ieh* 寶綸堂帖.

Hsü Fan's eldest son, Hsü Yüan-ch'un 元春, a *chin-shih* of 1574, rose to the rank of minister in the Court of State Ceremonial. Hsü Chieh's hereditary rank of a centurion in the Embroidered-uniform Guard was inherited successively by Hsü Yüan-ch'un's son, Hsü Yu-ch'ing 有慶, and the latter's son, Hsü Pen-kao 本高 (T. 維嶽, d. *ca.* 1645). As an opponent of Wei Chung-hsien (ECCP), Hsü Pen-kao was cashiered about 1626 but was reinstated in December, 1627, later rising to commander of the Guard. In June, 1637, he was promoted in rank to vice commissioner in the central military commission (lieutenant-general) and sometime thereafter was given the title of grand tutor to the heir apparent.

In 1645, when the invading Manchu troops entered Sung-chiang, Hsü Chieh's great-grandson, Hsü Nien-tsu 念祖 (T. 無念) committed suicide in the mansion built by the government for Hsü Chieh. The house was then confiscated by the new regime and converted to serve as headquarters of the provincial generalissimo. In 1776, when the Ch'ien-lung emperor bestowed posthumous honors on Ming loyalists, Hsü Nien-tsu was given the name Chieh-min 節愍. Hsü Chieh's younger brother, Hsü Chih 陟 (T. 子明, H. 望湖, 達齋覺庵, 1513-70), a *chin-shih* of 1537, rose to be vice minister of Justice in Nanking. He had a great-grandson who was an active Ming loyalist. This was Hsü Fu-yüan 孚遠 (T. 闇公, H. 復齋, 1599-1665, cj 1642) who took part in the editing of the collection of state papers of the Ming dynasty, the *Huang Ming ching-shih wen-pien* (*see* Ch'en Tzu-lung, ECCP), and wrote one of the prefaces. In 1646 he served the Ming prince, Chu Yü-chien (ECCP), in Foochow, and, after the latter's fall, joined Prince Chu I-hai (ECCP). About 1649 Hsü was given the rank of an assistant censor-in-chief. In 1651 he followed the prince to the Chin-men 金門 Islands off the Fukien coast. Seven years later, while trying to proceed to Yunnan by way of Annam, he was detained at the Annamite court and had to turn back to Chin-men. It is said that, after the fall of that island in.1663, Hsü escaped to the mainland and lived the last two years of his life in the mountains near Jao-p'ing 饒平 in Kwangtung on the Fukien border. His collected works, *Tiao-huang-t'ang ts'un-kao* 釣璜堂存稿, 20 *ch.*, existed only in manuscript until it was printed in 1926, together with two smaller collections, *Chiao-hsing chai-kao* 交行摘稿 and *Hsü An-kung hsien-sheng i-wen* 闇公先生遺文. The *Chiao-hsing chai-kao* was first printed in the collection *I-hai chu ch'en* 藝海珠塵. The portraits of Hsü Chieh, Hsü Chih, Hsü Nien-tsu, and Hsü Fu-yüan may be found in an album of rubbings entitled *Pang-yen hua-hsiang* 邦彥畫像. The rubbings were made about 1909 by the acting director of the Sung-chiang school, Hsü Fen 芬 (T. 漱芳), from engravings that lined the walls in a hall of that school.

Bibliography

1/213/1a; 5/16/86a; *Ming Wen-hai* (microfilm), 1/10/1, 2 (biographies by Shen Shih-hsing and Feng Shih-k'o); Wang Shih-chen, *Yen-chou shan-jen hsü-kao*, ch. 136; MSL (1965), Shih-tsung, Mu-tsung (1965), and early Shen-tsung (1966) reigns; KC (1958), 4127, 5780; Wu Yüan-ts'ui 伍袁萃, *Lin-chü man-lu* 林居漫錄, ch. 2 (microfilm of Wan-li ed.); *Hua-t'ing-hsien chih* (1879), 13/29b, 35b, 14/30a, 42b, 15/34b, 21/4b; *Sung-feng yü-yün* 松風餘韻 (1743), ch. 6; Ho Liang-chün, *Ssu-yu-chai ts'ung-shuo* (1959), 71; Lo Chi-tsu 羅繼祖, *Ming tsai-hsiang shih-ch'en chuan* 明宰相世臣傳 (1936), 7a; TSCC (1885-88), XVIII: 201/8a; Hsia Hsieh 夏燮 (1799-1875?), *Ming t'ung-chien* 明通鑑 (1959), 2422; Chang Fu-ching, *Chang Wen-chung kung chi* (1935), ch. 7; Shen Te-fu, *Wan-li yeh-hu-pien* (1959), 214, 548, 556, 834; *Hai Jui chi* (1962), 431, 592; Henry Serruys, *Sino-Mongol Relations during the Ming* (Brussels, 1967), 55, 62.

Chaoying and Lienche Tu Fang

HSÜ Chin 許進 (T. 季升, H. 東崖), June 6, 1437-September 20, 1510, minister of War, and father of three sons who rose to ministerial ranks, was a native of Ling-pao 靈寶, Honan. It is said that he came from a long line of officials, his ancestor in the eighth generation, a military officer serving the Mongols, being the first to settle in Ling-pao, probably in the mid-13th century. His father, Hsü Chü 聚 (1402-66), after studying in the National University, served (1446) as an instructor in An-ting 安定, Shensi. Hsü Chin, who graduated as the highest *chü-jen* in his province in 1462, became a *chin-shih* in 1466; then he was obliged to retire to mourn the death of his father. He returned to Peking in 1469 and was appointed a censor, but a year later his mother died and he withdrew again. In 1473 he resumed his office in the Censorate where he served for nine years, during which he was sent out twice as regional censor inspector, to Kansu in 1475-76 and to Shantung in 1478-79. This was the time when the eunuch, Wang Chih 汪直 (*q.v.*), was in the emperor's confidence, a situation bitterly resented by many officials. In 1480 Hsü joined some other censors in supporting a colleague, Ch'iang Chen 强珍 (T. 廷貴, cs 1466), who tried to conduct an investigation of the wrong-doings of the eunuch's protégés. Because of some false claims made by Ch'iang himself, the case backfired. Hsü and those who had taken the same stand as Ch'iang were fined three months' stipends. This episode probably gave rise to the erroneous story cited in the *Ming-shih* that the eunuch pointed out a wrong word in a memorial by Hsü, and had him flogged at the main gate of the imperial palace, a punishment that almost cost him his life. The *Ming shih-lu* reports a case occuring in March, 1482, concerning the beating of two censors for quoting the Book of History incorrectly; but that took place in Nanking. Hsü had no part in it. As a matter of fact, he received commendation for completing nine years of meritorious service, and in September, 1482, was promoted to be surveillance vice commissioner of Shantung in charge of educational affairs. It is related that he was transferred to Liaotung early in 1487, where half a year later, for some reason, he was placed under arrest, tried in Peking, and not released until a year later; again the story seems apocryphal.

According to the *shih-lu*, Hsü was promoted early in 1488 from his post in Shantung to surveillance commissioner of Kwangsi. Barely a month passed before he received another promotion, to be governor of Tatung in charge of defense of the northern frontier. For having failed to get along with the eunuch Shih Yen 石巖, Hsü was demoted (1491) to serve as prefect of Yen-chou 兗州, Shantung; but in December, 1494, he was back as surveillance commissioner in Shensi. A month later, at the suggestion of Minister of War Ma Wen-sheng (*q.v.*), he became left assistant censor-in-chief and governor of Kansu. In the hope that he might retake Hami from Aḥmad (*q. v.*), Hsü received orders to assemble an army which could force its way to that central Asian city. The enemy, learning of his plans, vanished; so Hsü was able to march to the city unimpeded in Decem-

ber, 1495. Not wishing to remain, however, he withdrew his men, and Aḥmad promptly repossessed the area. Hsü's account of this expedition, the *P'ing-fan shih-mo* 平番始末, 1 (or 2) *ch.*, published in 1503, is a valuable record of the event, along with *Hsing-fu Ha-mi chi* of Ma Wen-sheng.

A year later (September, 1496) Hsü received a transfer to the governorship of Shensi; but he did not remain long. By August, 1497, he was summoned to the capital to be right, then (October, 1498) left, vice minister of Revenue, It was at this point in his career that he joined with nine other respected officials in a function at the Bamboo Garden belonging to Chou Ching (*q.v.*), illustrations of which were to be published by his seventh son. With war flaring up on the frontier north of Peking, he was sent there in May, 1500, to direct the defense. The Mongols crossed over into the region of Tatung and Ning-hsia, subduing every commander in their path, including Hsü. Three of the leading offiers were condemned to death; Hsü, however, was simply relieved of his office (July), and retired. At his home he took this period of enforced idleness to write his well known book. He left at least two other works, but these seem not to have survived. He also built a villa, known as Tung-yai ching-she 東崖精舍, where he could relax. He is known to have been a competent figure painter.

Hsü's knowledge of frontier affairs was not forgotten. In 1505 he became vice minister and then minister of War, serving throughout the latter half of 1506 before being called in November to preside over the ministry of Personnel. He held this office for two years. Because he clashed with the formidable eunuch Liu Chin (*q.v.*), who had the ear of the new emperor, Chu Hou-chao (*q.v.*), he again retired and for the last time. (According to one historian, he was driven to suicide but the *shih-lu* does not corroborate this.) He died two years later, aged seventy-three. In the following reign (1526) the court honored him posthumously with the title of grand guardian of the heir apparent and the name Hsiang-i 襄毅. He had two wives and one concubine. The first wife died early; the second, Madame Kao 高, who lived to be over eighty, bore six of his eight sons. The three who became prominent were Hsü Kao, Hsü Tsan, and Hsü Lun (qq.v.). Three others may also be mentioned: Hsü Chao 詔 (cj 1483) who died early, Hsü Shih 詩 (cj 1528), and Hsü Tz'u 詞 (T. 廷章), who through the yin privilege served as prefect of Yun-yang 郎陽, Hukuang, in 1536-40, and then of Pao-ning 保寧 -fu, Szechwan.

Bibliography

1/186/11a; 5/24/99a; 6/2/26a; 16/25/49b, 125/11b, 130/21b; 65/1/14b; SK (1930), 53/4b; Shan-chou chih-li-chou chih 陝州直隸州志 (1892), 7/17a, 8/16a, 17b, 12/34a, 36b, 14/53b; KC (1958), 2683, 2979; MSL (1964), Hsiao-tsung, 2088, 2267, 2452, 2895, 2952, Wu-tsung (1965), 0557, 0954, 1450; Ch'en Tzu-lung (ECCP), Ming ching-shih wen-pien, ch. 68; Yen-chou-fu chih (1769), 12/10a, 22/19a; Yün-yang-fu chih (1870), 5 上/17b; Pao-ning-fu chih (1821), 32/22a; W. Franke, Sources, 7. 4. 2; L. Hambis, Documents sur l'histoire des Mongols à l'époque des Ming (1969), 43, 142.

L. Carrington Goodrich and *Lee Hwa-chou*

HSÜ Chung-hsing 徐中行 (T. 子與, H. 龍灣), August 20, 1517-October 13, 1578, a noted poet, writer, and provincial administrator, was also known as T'ien-mu shan-jen 天目山人 (recluse of T'ien-mu) because he had lived and studied on the southern slope of T'ien-mu Mountain in Chekiang. He was a native of Ch'ang-hsing 長興 -hsien, Hu-chou 湖州 prefecture, Chekiang, born into a poor but respected family of scholars. At sixteen years of age, Hsü became a *hsiu-ts'ai* and later (*ca.* 1540) entered the National University in Nanking as a second-degree graduate. The date of his marriage is unknown, but it is reported that Hsü so impressed an official by the name of Ku Ying-hsiang (*q.v.*)

that he arranged for the young scholar to marry his niece. Ku later rose to be minister of Justice (August, 1550-March, 1551).

A *chin-shih* of 1550, Hsü received an appointment as a secretary of a bureau in the ministry of Justice. During this time he gained a reputation for his scholarly abilities and met the circle of acquaintances and colleagues who formed the literary group known as the Hou ch'i-tzu (Seven later masters; *see* Li P'an-lung). This group, led by Li P'an-lung and Wang Shih-chen (*q.v.*), originally consisted of five members, namely, Li, Wang, Hsü, Tsung Ch'en (*q.v.*), and Hsieh Chen 謝榛 (T. 茂秦, H. 四溟山人, 脫屣山人, 1495-1575). Some historians omit the name of the last, the original leader, and substitute either Wu Kuo-lun (*q.v.*) or Liang Yu-yü (*see* Huang Tso). This omission, however, is undoubtedly due to the lengthy quarrel between Hsieh Chen and Li P'an-lung, as a result of which Li eventually displaced Hsieh and took over as leader. The "Five" group was later expanded to include all of those mentioned. Hsü and his associates, along with the literary school of the previous generation called the Ch'ien-ch'i-tzu (Seven early masters; *see* Li Meng-yang), wielded considerable influence over Chinese letters. Dedicated to the renewal of Chinese culture, the two groups were bold imitators of earlier literary artists. The "Seven later masters" were especially careful to study only the best literature of antiquity, concentrating on prose writing of the Han dynasty, particularly the Western Han (206 B.C.-A.D. 9) and earlier, and poetry of the T'ang, particularly its middle years, and before.

Hsü was a natural addition to the group, not only because of his influential connections, but also because he had always maintained an intense interest in classical studies and archaic models of writing. He was a loyal friend and ardent supporter of these writers, being closest to Wang Shih-chen, Tsung Ch'en, and Wu Kuo-lun. But, due to the imitative approach, Hsü fell victim, along with many other talented writers who might have advanced Chinese letters to a new level, to the stifling restrictions placed on original and creative literature. Consequently, while Hsü was an able poet, he never attained the literary stature of the group leaders, especially Wang Shih-chen. Hsü was perhaps better known as an efficient and capable administrator while serving as a public official during his twenty-eight year career.

Soon after his appointment, Hsü openly supported Yang Chi-sheng (*q.v.*), a young official who was imprisoned for his denunciation of Yen Sung (*q.v.*). Yen, who kept a close eye on his political opposition, resented the fact that Hsü, along with Wang Shih-chen and others, would visit Yang in prison taking supplies and medicine while he was under sentence of death. When Yang was finally executed, Hsü accompanied twenty-three colleagues to claim the corpse for burial. This enmity was aggravated when Hsü rendered a legal decision in favor of Yen's opponent in the ministry of Justice. In retaliation, Yen schemed to cause trouble for this group and blocked several attempts to promote Hsü to the provincial surveillance office. In the meantime, Hsü had risen to the post of vice-director, and later, director of his bureau.

In 1557 Hsü was sent to T'ing-chou 汀州, Fukien, as prefect. He had just arrived when the outlaw, Hsiao Wu 蕭五, and his band invaded the area. After some panic-stricken people were trampled do death in the stampede toward the city from the surrounding districts, Hsü quickly ordered the gates opened and restored order among the refugees by allowing them to file into the city in a peaceful manner. He then made preparations for defense, and defeated the bandits by ambushing them. Hsü quickly won the respect of the people for his accomplishments and administrative policies. His recommendations for the protection of the area against bandits and pirates were

adopted after he had moved on. The people of T'ing-chou built a shrine in his honor at Mt. Wu-i 武夷山 later.

Hsü learned of his father's death while at T'ing-chou (1558) and quickly returned home. When the period of mourning was over, he was appointed to Ju-ning 汝寧, Honan, as prefect. His administration was fair and efficient, and he kept busy with administrative duties, repairing ruined buildings and constructing dikes, erecting shrines, and supporting a school. Several incidents occurred, however, which were to affect his future career. Some minor officials, under the influence of an imperial prince, assumed the authority to levy taxes on the people in order to build walls and fortifications as protection against marauders and outlaws. Hsü was able to persuade the prince, after some difficulty, to halt this practice and other illegal activities. A scandal soon followed in which an assistant magistrate committed suicide while being falsely accused of corruption, and Hsü had to arrest his antagonist for prosecution. Finally, due to Hsü's unusual fondness for entertaining numerous guests who continually took advantage of his generosity and came near to exhausting his wealth, he was forced out of office (1563) by the slander and gossip of his colleagues, and possibly too through the influence of Yen Sung. Hsü was demoted to the position of judge in the salt commission at Ch'ang-lu 長蘆, Pei-Chihli. He served in this capacity for three months, and then moved to Jui-chou 瑞州, Kiangsi, as vice prefect.

During his stay there (1564-65), he received the news both of his mother's death and of his promotion to assistant surveillance commissioner of Shantung. In order to observe the customary mourning period, Hsü did not take up his new post. He returned to public office, however, in 1568 as assistant surveillance commissioner with headquarters at Wuchang. While in this position, he gained a reputation for a keen sense of justice and respect for human dignity in his legal decisions. He brought about the capture of a notorious outlaw whose recovered store of contraband was sufficient to help feed over ten thousand people who had been affected by natural disasters. He also restored the national shrine, Huang-ho-lou 黃鶴樓 (Yellow crane hall), partly from his own funds.

In 1570 he was transferred as senior assistant administrative commissioner to Yunnan, where his tenure was marked by uneventful duties and literary pursuits. He also donated several thousand volumes from his personal collection of books to create a library in honor of the new emperor's ascent to the throne (1573). He moved then to Fukien as surveillance vice commissioner, and in the following year was made junior administrative vice commissioner. In 1575 he was promoted to surveillance commissioner (Fukien), and in 1576 served also as a provincial examiner. Elevated to the position of junior administrative commissioner of Kiangsi in 1577, he was finally shifted in the following year to senior administrative commissioner in the same province, with control over ten prefectures.

By this time Hsü was well known for his ability to eliminate corruption and to pacify the territory under his jurisdiction. He was equally effective in his last position, but while he had always been industrious in professional life, his duties here were more hectic than before. In his attempt to carry out these responsibilities and settle a serious quarrel between two imperial clansmen, he collapsed at his desk and died shortly afterwards, aged sixty-one. The news of his death brought a quick response from the people, his friends, and colleagues, for he had been a popular figure. Hsü was finally interred on December 25, 1579, at a scenic and peaceful spot near Mt. T'ien-mu and Lake T'ai. His literary works include the Ch'ing-lo-kuan chi hsü-chi 青蘿館集續集, 10 ch., and T'ien-mu-shan-t'ang (ch'ien)-chi 堂(前)集, 20 + 1 ch. The editors of the

Ssu-k'u list both titles in the Catalogue, but did not copy either work into the Imperial Library. The National Central Library, Taipei, has four copies of his T'ien-mu hsien-sheng chi 集, 21 ch.

Bibliography

1/287/16b; 3/268/13a; 5/86/21a; Hsü Chung-hsing, Ch'ing-lo-kuan shih ch'ien-chi 詩前集; id., T'ien-mu hsien-sheng chi; TSCC (1885–88), XIV: 60/6 /3a, XXIII: 106/94/7b; Kuo Shao-yü 郭紹虞, Chung-kuo wen-hsüeh p'i-p'ing shih中國文學批評史 (Shanghai, 1961), 315; Li P'an-lung, Ts'ang ming hsien-sheng chi, 16/14; Tsung Ch'en, Tsung Tzu-hsiang chi, 13/22, 62; Wang Shih-chen, Yen-chou shan-jen hsü kao, 45/10, 134/12, 152/9; Wang Shih-mou, Wang Feng-ch'ang chi, 5/12, 14/17, 25/11; Wang Tao-k'un, T'ai han chi, 63/6; Liu Ta-chieh 劉大杰, Chung-kuo wen-hsüeh fa-ta shih 發達史 (Taipei, 1966), 294; SK (1930), 178/1b, 2a; NCL Catalogue of Rare Books, II (Hong Kong, 1958), 149.

Dell R. Hales

HSÜ Fu-tso 徐復祚 (original *ming* 篤儒, T. 陽初, H. 暮竹, 陽（暘）初子, 三家村老, 慳吝道人, etc.), 1560-after 1630, dramatist and man of letters, was born into a family which had lived for generations in Ch'ang-shu 常熟, Soochow prefecture. His grandfather, Hsü Shih 徐栻 (T. 世寅, H. 鳳竹, 1519–81), became a *chin-shih* in 1547, served as governor of Kiangsi (1571 –72) and Chekiang (1576–78), was named minister of Works at Nanking (1579), and then retired, apparently with sufficient wealth to enable his son and grandsons to live in luxury for several decades.

In his younger days Hsü Fu-tso was twice involved in lawsuits, once in 1585, when he was accused of offering a bribe while participating in the metropolitan examinations. Another lawsuit, the details of which are obscure, is one which he noted with feeling as having lasted ten years or so. These experiences were probably sufficient to cause him to abandon the pursuit of a career through the examinations. With the chance to follow a life of leisure at home, he devoted himself to drama, paying special attention to music and the performing arts.

In 1610 he completed his first dramatic work, *Hung-li chi* 紅梨記, which received praise and became widely known. It seems that, because of some criticism, perhaps the result of jealousy, he gave up writing plays for a time. Later he produced five more dramas: *I-wen-ch'ien* 一文錢, *T'ou-so chi* 投梭記 (*so* 梭 in some places is mistaken for *shu* 梳), *Hsiao-kuang chi* (*chien*) 宵光記(劍), *T'i-ch'iao chi* 題橋記, and *Wu-t'ung-yü* 梧桐雨. The last two are no longer extant. The first was reproduced in the *Sheng Ming tsa-chü* 盛明雜劇 in 1918 and again in 1925. The second and third may be found in the recently printed *Ku-chin hsi-ch'ü ts'ung-k'an* 古今戲曲叢刊, series I, 1954, and series III, 1957.

A short work on drama under the title *Ming Ho Yüan-lang, Hsü Yang-ch'u ch'ü-lun* 明何元朗徐陽初曲論 appears, together with a number of notes extracted from the *Ssu yu-chai ts'ung-shuo* on the same subject by Ho Liang-chün (*q.v.*) in the second series of the *Ku-hsüeh hui-k'an* 古學彙刊 (Shanghai, 1912). The same material, with seven more notes in a different arrangement with Ho's work omitted, was later included in the *Hsin ch'ü-yüan* 新曲苑 (Shanghai, 1940) under the title *San-chia-ts'un wei-t'an* 三家村委談. Hsü Fu-tso was critical of his contemporary dramatists, mostly for their fondness for displaying their literary knowledge, and for their ignorance of instrumental music and voice accompaniment. As for Hsü himself, he was not only a master of poetic expression, but was also proficient in music and deeply aware of the difficulties involved in vocal performance. It is reported that he spent days and nights in directing his own plays. It was for this ability that Ch'ien Ch'ien-i (ECCP) compared him with Kao Ming (*q.v.*), the celebrated author of the *P'i-pa chi*.

More appreciated by students of history, however, are his miscellaneous notes, the *Hua-tang-ko ts'ung-t'an* 花當閣叢談, also known as the *Ts'un-lao wei-t'an* 村老

委談, 8 *ch.*, printed in the 15th series of the *Chieh-yüeh shan-fang hui-ch'ao* early in the 19th century (*see* Chang Hai-p'eng, ECCP), and later reproduced in 1920. The notes deal with Ming institutions, personalities, superstitions, and social mores, dialects, and local festivals of the Soochow area, etc. *Chüan* 8 is concerned solely with accounts of the *wo-k'ou* invasions written by people who had suffered from them. He had a keen sense of history and questioned why the written records often differed from what he heard from certain eye witnesses.

Credited to him also is the *Chia-er ssu-yü* 家兒私語, preserved for three centuries in manuscript and first printed in 1936 in the *Ping-tzu ts'ung-pien* 丙子叢編. In spite of some questionable dates assigned to his brothers, the work seems to be authentic. It is short, consisting of seven essays and notes relating a shocking story about the Hsü family. It happened that Hsü had an elder brother, Hsü Ch'ang-tso 昌祚 (T. 伯昌, 1558–1609), and a younger brother, Hsü Ting-tso 鼎祚 (T. 聞叔, 1562-*ca.* 1615). In 1578, as a reward to their grandfather (Hsü Shih), Hsü Ch'ang-tso was admitted into the bureaucracy as a student of the National University. He later rose to be the director of a bureau in the ministry of Justice (*ca.* 1604–05). According to Hsü Fu-tso's account, both Hsü Ch'ang-tso and his wife were niggardly and greedy. In 1591 they managed an unscrupulous ruse in which the victim was an aunt, a wealthy divorcée then living with the family. Using a foppish young artist as bait, they convinced her that the man wanted her to elope with him and, after swindling her of her wealth, they sent her to the rendezvous on a rainy night and had her drowned by the servants acting as guides. The scandal was whispered about in the family, then spread in the neighborhood, and later became the theme of several short stories. For lack of a plaintiff no official investigation was initiated until eighteen years later when the younger brother, Hsü Ting-tso, while disputing with Hsü Ch'ang-tso over the ownership of some family properties, perhaps in an attempt at blackmail, lodged a formal charge of murder against him. Hsü Ch'ang-tso was arrested and tried at the magistrate's court and committed suicide while confined in prison awaiting sentence.

This and similar tales as told by Hsü Fu-tso reflect a dramatic side of Ming society, especially concerning the self-indulgence and licentious transgressions of the well-to-do. Perhaps this accounts at least partly for the realism in literature achieved in the late Ming period.

It may also be pointed out that in Hsü's account of his elder brother, he referred to the magistrate of Ch'ang-shu, Yang Lien (1571–1625, ECCP), as bigoted and tyrannical. Hsü also described a neighbor and relative, Ku Ta-chang (ECCP, p. 893), as a scheming busybody who supplied Yang with information against Hsü Ch'ang-tso. Both Yang and Ku later became celebrated personages when they sacrificed their lives in the fight against the eunuch party, and the stories about the cruelties and indignities they suffered were naturally regarded with sympathy by the general public, especially after the fall of the eunuch party late in 1627. Hsü Fu-tso, however, pointedly declared that the sufferings of Yang and Ku were their just desserts because of their harsh treatment of others. Hsü wrote his story in October, 1627, two months before the condemnation of the eunuch party, and three months before the restitution of Yang Lien's name and reputation. One wonders if the author would have laid bare so much of his feelings towards Yang and Ku had he written only a few months later.

Bibliography

1/220/7a; 5/52/89a (here Hsü Shih's name is given incorrectly as 拭); Fu Hsi-hua 傅惜華, *Ming-tai tsa-chü ch'üan-mu* 明代雜劇全目 (1958), 135; *id.*, *Ming-tai ch'uan-ch'i傳奇 ch'üan-mu*(1959), 125; Wang Shih-chen, *Yen-chou-shan-jen hsü-kao* (1970), 77/1a; TSCC (1885–88 ed.), XI: 800/2b, XIV: 60/2b; *Ch'ang Chao ho-chih* 常昭合志(1898),

8/123b; Ch'ien Ch'ien-i, *Mu-chai ch'u-hsüeh chi* (1900), 85/2b.

Lienche Tu Fang

HSÜ Hsüeh-chü 徐學聚 (T. 敬輿, H. 石樓), cs 1583, an official and historian, was born into a scholarly family. His grandfather, Hsü P'ao 袍 (T. 仲章, cj 1534), reportedly taught several hundred students; his father, Hsü Yung-kuang 用光 (T. 成孚, H. 谷菴, 1526–60, cs 1553), became director of a bureau in the ministry of Works; while his uncle, Hsü Yung-chien 檢 (H. 魯源, cs 1562), who had studied under Hsü P'ao and Ch'ien Te-hung (*q. v.*), rose to be director of the Court of Imperial Sacrifices. All of these three favored the teachings of the neo-Confucian school, and quite naturally the young Hsü Hsüeh-chü imbibed much from them, especially from his uncle Hsü Yung-chien, the most prominent in their native Lan-ch'i 蘭谿, Chekiang.

After achieving the advanced degree, Hsü's first appointment was to the magistracy of Fu-liang 浮梁, Kiangsi, and then (1586) to that of Chi-shui 吉水 in the same province, where he served for about three years. Here his most noteworthy feat was the construction of a dam on the river Feng 豐, which successfully prevented serious flooding of the district.

The *shih-lu* reports that in December, 1589, Hsü, now supervising secretary of the office of scrutiny for Rites, memorialized the throne berating Mu Ch'ang-tso (*see* Chou Chia-mu), duke of Ch'ien (who inherited the title in 1571), for adding twenty eunuchs to his staff. A year later, according to the same authority, he showed his concern for the descendants of the rebel prince of Ning, Chu Ch'en-hao (*see* Wang Shou-jen), who had suffered the death penalty early in 1521, by suggesting to the emperor that a school be set up for these descendants. These two memorials of his appear to be the only ones recorded in the imperial records, although the Lan-ch'i local history refers to many more.

Three months after the second memorial (March, 1591), Hsü received the appointment of assistant surveillance commissioner in Hukuang, and subsequently administration commissioner in Fukien. While serving the latter capacity (June, 1604) he discomfited a crafty bandit named Wu Chien 吳建, who had several thousand followers, all members of the White Lotus Sect (*see* Chu Yüan-chang). Reporting to Peking on the success of his action, he reminded the throne that the province was without a governor. His appointment to that office followed (August 21), together with the concurrent title of assistant censor-in-chief.

Prior to this (in 1603), a eunuch, Kao Ts'ai (*see* Shen Yu-jung), had informed the emperor that a certain Chang I 張嶷 and a centurion (pai-hu 百戶) named Yen Ying-lung 閻應隆, (called in Spanish The Pacu, Liang Yameng). hearing that in Chi-i Mountain 機易山 in Cavite, Luzon, there were deposits of gold and silver, had gone to the island (May, 1603) to open up mines. They even reported that an annual production could amount to over a hundred thousand ounces of gold and two hundred thousand ounces of silver. On receiving this intelligence the emperor ordered the Fukien governor to appoint officials to accompany Chang to Luzon. Their coming outraged the Spanish governor of the Philippines, Bravo de Acuña, who took it to mark the first step in a possible invasion of the island. Though planning at first to execute the two and their retinue, he was dissuaded when informed that the Chinese had no intention of mounting an attack. Instead the governor sent the official party back to the mainland. Disquiet still prevailed in Manila, however, the governor deciding to make preparations for defense. In this general state of alarm there were outbreaks of violence on both sides, which led to the complete rout of the Chinese. They suffered great loss of life, over twenty thousand according to Chinese accounts, fifteen thousand according to Spanish. The wives and children were sent back to China. Hsü reported all this to the emperor and gave succor to those repatriated, Chang I excepted; he was executed for having falsely reported the existence of gold and silver in Luzon.

At about the same time the Dutch made a landing on the Pescadores. Again Hsü dispatched a memorial requesting the emperor to order them off, and lodged an accusation against the Chinese who had invited them (some of whom paid with their lives). The leader of the expedition was Admiral Wijbrand van Waerwijck (*see* Shen Yu-jung). Reportedly in the hope of gaining permission to trade, he gave three hundred thousand *liang* of silver to the eunuch, Kao Ts'ai (*see* Shen Yu-jung), who then wrote to the emperor suggesting that the Dutch be allowed to stay in the Pescadores. But in the face of Hsü's hostility and possibly Portuguese opposition as well, the admiral asked for the return of his money and took off with his expeditionary force (December 15, 1604).

Hsü by this time had had enough of Kao. He memorialized the emperor suggesting that the eunuch not only be recalled but also that he be ordered to turn over to the provincial government the tax money he had collected. As the local people were complaining that they had suffered from an excess of taxation, Hsü arranged for a lessening of their load. In this way the annual tax was reduced by a sum amounting to approximately 40,000 taels of silver. This was among his last official acts; Hsü left his post in mid-July, 1607.

Hsü's main claim to fame is his authorship of the *Kuo-ch'ao tien-hui* 國朝典彙, 200 *ch.*; although under the title *Ming-ch'ao tien-hui* it was criticized by the editors of the Imperial Catalogue and not included in the *Ssu-k'u ch'üan-shu*, it has become so highly valued in recent years as to be reprinted twice, in 1932 and 1965. The book may be considered as a chronicle of the years from the beginning of the Ming to 1572, being (in the words of Arthur Hummel) "a compendium on almost every aspect of Chinese governmental and social organization in the Ming period;" it treats the central imperial power structure (*chüan* 1-33) and also the activities of the six ministries (*chüan* 34-200). Hsü's experience with Kao is reflected in *chüan* 33. This chapter is devoted to the use made of eunuchs by the emperor. It is divided into three parts, and clearly reveals his concern over this branch of the government, which in his time was overreaching itself. Hsü had a separate work on eunuchs in history, *Li ch'ao tang-chien* 歷朝璫鑒, 4 *ch.*, also recorded in the *Ssu-k'u* catalogue; in his preface Hsü declares that ninety percent of these eunuchs were evil-doers and that none had ever received such power as in his day.

The earliest preface to the *Kuo-ch'ao tien-hui* was written in 1601 by Feng Ch'i (*q. v.*), while Hsü was serving as education intendant in Shantung; according to his grandson, Hsü Chieh-shou 介壽 (T. 孟齡), however, the work was not finished at the time of his death (shortly after 1617). His sons, Hsü Yü-chi 與稽 and Hsü Yü-ts'an 參 (T. 嵩少, d. 1633), undertook to complete it. It was then printed by the latter some time after 1626, for that is the year that he went to Peking to seek posthumous honors for his father; and the book too cites Hsü Hsüeh-chü by his highest title, vice censor-in-chief. In 1632 some of the printing blocks were destroyed by fire. Hsü Chieh-shou then, with the help of the magistrate of Lan-ch'i, Wu Kuo-ch'i 吳國琦 (T. 公良, H. 雪厓, cs 1631), reproduced the lost blocks and brought out the edition of 1634. Evidently Hsü Chieh-shou tampered with all the blocks, for most of them bore Wu's name as collator, which could have happened only in the 1634 edition and not in the earlier one. As to the other collators, Feng Ch'i's name is given in the first *chüan*, and those of about a hundred others appear throughout the book. The last four were all the author's grandsons.

Hsü Chieh-shou, who at one time served as magistrate of Ch'i-hsien 祁縣 in Shansi, wrote an account of the collection of books in the family. Hsü Hsüeh-chü's earlier collection was lost in the rapids of a river in Fukien and of his second collection almost all were stolen or worm-eaten. Hsü Yü-ts'an, Hsü Chieh-shou's father, then formed his own collection, which amounted by 1626 to some fifty thousand *chüan*; he turned it over to Hsü Chieh-shou together with the library building, Po-ch'eng lou 百城樓. Both Hsü Yü-ts'an and Hsü Chieh-shou added to the collection after 1626, but in 1632 it was completely destroyed in a fire. A catalogue of the books collected between 1626 and 1632 was the only thing saved.

Bibliography

40/54/19a; 64/庚14/11b; 86/15/34b; MS (Taiwan ed.), 3701, 3732, 3737; MSL (1966), Shen-tsung, 4063, 4250, 7338, 7458, 7486, 7536, 7547, 8189, 8202, 8116; KC (1958), 4917; *Lan-ch'i-hsien chih* (1887), 5/79a, 89b, 98a, 103a; *Chin-hua-fu chih* 金華府志 (1965 reprint of 1578 ed.), 17/21a, 18/39b; *Chi-shui-hsien chih* (1875), 11/2b, 26/9a; *Fukien t'ung-chih* (1938), 10/2a, 11/4b; *Chekiang t'ung-chih* (1934), 2336, 2436, 2857, 2979, 3309; *Hunan t'ung-chih* (1934), 2471; SK (1930), 83/1b; Hsü Hsiang-mei 徐象梅, *Liang Che ming-hsien lu* 兩浙名賢錄 (reprint of 1621 ed.), 4/40b; Ch'en Ho 陳鶴 (1757-1811), *Ming chi* (SPTK ed.), 45/16a, 23a; Tung Ch'i-ch'ang (ECCP), *Shen-miao liu-chung tsou-shu hui-yao* (1937), 10/1a; Wang Ch'ung-ping 王崇炳, *Chin-hua cheng-hsien lüeh* 金華徵獻略 (1732), 6/21b, 12/13b; Ho Ch'iao-yüan, *Min shu* (Ch'ung-chen ed.), 45/18a; Ch'en Tzu-lung (ECCP), *Ming ching-shih wen-pien* (1964), 3913, 4116, 4726; Wang Ch'ung-ping 王崇炳 (ed.), *Chin-hua wen-lüeh* 文略 (1742), 4/50a, 60a; Sun Tien-ch'i (1957), 157; L. of C. *Catalogue of Rare Books*, 1159; A. W. Hummel, *L. of C. Qu. Jo. of Current Acquisitions*, 6 (February, 1949), 26; W. Franke, *Sources*, 6. 6. 3; T'ien-tse Chang, *Sino-Portuguese Trade from 1514 to 1644* (Leyden, 1934), 113; Alfonso Felix, Jr. (ed.), *The Chinese in the*

Philippines, 1570–1770 (Manila, 1966), 99; Emma H. Blair and James A. Robinson, tr. and ed., *The Philippine Islands, 1493–1803*, XII (Cleveland, 1904), 83, 87, 103.

Mou Jun-sun and L. Carrington Goodrich

HSÜ Hsüeh-mo 徐學謨 (T. 叔明, H. 太室, 二白居士, original *ming* Hsüeh-shih 學詩, T. 子言, 思重), 1522–January 22, 1594, official, scholar, and minor poet, was a native of Chia-ting 嘉定, Soochow. His ancestor in the fifth generation engaged in the distilling business and made the family fortune. Hsü Hsüeh-mo was the first descendant to enter officialdom. Praised as precocious in his youth, he became a *chü-jen* in 1543, and obtained the *chin-shih* degree in 1550. After passing the metropolitan examinations he changed his name. Allegedly he did this because one bureau director of the same name in the ministry of Justice, Hsü Hsüeh-shih (T. 以言, cs 1544, a native of Shang-yü 上虞, Chekiang), was in trouble at this time for his impeachment of Yen Sung (*q. v.*); Hsü Hsüeh-mo was afraid of complications through confused identity.

In 1551 he was appointed a secretary of the bureau of operations in the ministry of War. In that capacity he supervised the erection of lookouts in the suburbs of Peking for the army of Ch'iu Luan (*q. v.*). Before long, however, he was transferred to the bureau of records in the ministry of Personnel. Later his mother died and he retired to observe the mourning period. When he reported to Peking again he was given a post in the ministry of Rites and by 1555 rose to be a vice director of the bureau of sacrifices. At this time the emperor (Chu Hou-ts'ung, *q. v.*) was infatuated with religious Taoism. Special forms of literary compositions being required for the oft-held Taoist rituals, the work on them sometimes kept certain officials on duty day and night. As Hsü was proficient and well versed in these forms, his superiors came to rely on him.

Appointed prefect of Ching-chou 荊州 in 1559, Hsü Hsüeh-mo began his long service as a local official in Hukuang. He proved himself an able and conscientious administrator, dealing energetically with flood and pestilence, alleviating the burden on the people of an unfair land tax, and suppressing by military force and shrewd tactics a large band of three thousand brigands. Then he risked his own future by protecting the wealthy and strategic district of Sha-shih 沙市 from the attempted encroachment of Chu Tsai-ch'uan, the prince of Ching (*see* Chu Hou-ts'ung and Chu Tsai-hou). The prince left Peking to take up residence in Te-an 德安, Hukuang, in 1560. In the following year he asked for more land to enlarge his domain. Although Sha-shih was not mentioned in the original petition, the prince wanted it assigned to his estate. Not only did Sha-shih constitute an important part of Ching-chou prefecture, but the people of the district opposed its inclusion under the jurisdiction of the prince. Through his exercise of courage, diplomacy, and argument, Hsü succeeded in bringing about an agreement whereby an annual monetary settlement kept Sha-shih free of the prince's control. This earned him the gratitude of the local inhabitants, who later referred to the district as "Hsü-shih" in his honor. The prince, irritated by the rebuff, lodged complaints against Hsü with the result that he lost his post in 1563.

In the new Lung-ch'ing reign Hsü was reinstated. After a short term as prefect of Nan-yang 南陽, Honan, he returned to Hukuang as surveillance vice commissioner assigned as intendant of Hsiang-yang 襄陽. Late in 1568, he became involved in the affairs of another prince, Chu Hsien-chieh (*see* Chang Chü-cheng), prince of Liao 遼王, a seventh generation descendant of Chu Chih 朱植 (March 24, 1377–June 4, 1424, Pth. 簡), the fifteenth son of the founding emperor. Chu Chih first received a princedom in Liaotung, hence the designation Liao. During the Chien-wen period, however, Chu Chih was assigned a domain in Ching-chou, Hukuang. Chu Hsien-chieh, enfeoffed as prince of Liao in 1540, was at first regarded with favor by Emperor Chu Hou-ts'ung, as he professed to revere the Taoist cult as much as the emperor did. Greedy, licentious, and depraved in many ways, Chu Hsien-chieh incurred the hatred of the people, as well as of the local officials and numerous members of the imperial family besides. Repeatedly accused, he eventually was charged with seditious intent. Finally in 1568, degraded to commoner status and his princedom abolished, he was imprisoned inside the "high walls" (高牆), the place of custody designed for members of the imperial family in their place of origin, Feng-yang 鳳陽. In this case, Hsü Hsüeh-mo was not directly implicated, but as a local official he spoke out for justice against the apparently trumped-up charge of sedition. Later he wrote a biographical account of the last prince of Liao, which was printed in his second collection of literary works. Chu Hsien-chieh used to fancy himself as something of a poet, so he had poets as retainers. One was the eccentric northerner Sung Ch'un-teng 宋春登 (T. 應元, H. 海習, 鷲池生, fl. 16th century), who also happened to be a friend of Hsü and about whom Hsü also wrote a biography. Hsü might, therefore, have received certain information from Sung about the prince.

Hsü's promotions came rapidly thereafter; he served successively as surveillance vice commissioner, administration vice commissioner, and vice censor-in-chief and grand-coordinator with headquarters in Yün-yang 鄖陽. In 1578 the court summoned him to Peking to be vice minister of Justice. Two years later he became minister of Rites. For over a century the minister of Rites by tradition had been chosen from among Hanlin academicians. Exceptions were few and rare, and Hsü was one of three such cases. His unusual rise to this position is generally believed to have been due to the powerful influence of Chang Chü-cheng (q. v.), who is said to have appreciated Hsü's fight for Sha-shih against the prince of Ching, and for certain favors performed on behalf of Chang's family. Hsü's ability, however, must have been taken into account in this appointment for, in carrying out his duties in the ministry of Rites, he proved to be competent and energetic, and did not fail Chang's trust. After the death of Chang Chü-cheng, as Hsü was looked upon as a member of Chang's clique, it was natural that his days in Peking should be numbered. He was forced to retire in the winter of 1583, but without loss of honors. He lived at home for another ten years and died in his seventy-second year.

Of Hsü's writings, the *Ssu-k'u* Imperial Library includes his *Ch'un-ch'iu i* 春秋億, a work on the Spring and Autumn Annals in 6 *chüan*, originally a part of his collected literary works, which is reproduced in the *Ssu-k'u chen pen* 珍本 and the *Hsü-shih hai-yü chi* 徐氏海隅集, 43 ch., printed in 1577. Three other works receive notices in the *Ssu-k'u* catalogue: the *Shih-miao chih-yü lu* 世廟識餘錄, 26 ch., a history of the Chia-ching reign, written after his retirement, first printed in the 1580s and reproduced in Taiwan in 1965; the *Wan-li Hu-kuang tsung-chih* 萬曆湖廣總志, a history of Hukuang in 98 *chüan*, printed in 1591; and a second collection of literary writings, *Kuei-yu-yüan kao* 歸有園稿, 29 ch., printed in 1593 just before his death. *Chüan* 11 of the last mentioned work, which bears the chapter heading Chu-hsieh 麈諧, was later reprinted in the *Pao-yen-t'ang pi-chi* 寶顏堂祕笈 with the title *Kuei-yu-yüan chu-t'an* 麈談. Hsü also annotated the *Lao-tzu*, which, entitled *Lao-tzu chieh* 老子解, was printed in 1965 in Taiwan as no. 81 of the collection of 140 works on *Lao-tzu*, the *Wu-ch'iu-pei-chai Lao-tzu chi-ch'eng' ch'u-pien* 無求備齋老子集成初編 compiled by Yen Ling-feng 嚴靈峯. As helpful as the *Ssu-k'u* notices often are, if one has no opportunity of examining the items described, one may be misled. In Hsü's case, the *Shih-miao chih-yü lu* and his two collections of literary writings are actually more valuable as sources on Ming history than the notices infer.

In dealing with this period of history one cannot avoid the feeling that many Ming officials were petty and biased, their political fights often unsavory. In the Chu Hsien-chieh affair, the consensus was that Chang Chü-cheng's vendetta caused the prince's downfall. If this be true, and Hsü Hsüeh-mo once spoke in defense of the degenerate prince, this would put Hsü and Chang on opposite sides, which is contrary to fact.

Hsü's biography is not included in the *Hsien-cheng lu*, the outstanding collection compiled by Chiao Hung (ECCP); nor did the *Ming-shih* accord him a biography. His contemporaries, however, honored him with epitaphs and eulogies. These include Kuo Cheng-yü, Shen Shih-hsing (the father-in-law of Hsü's daughter), Wang Hsi-chüeh, and Feng Shih-k'o (*qq. v.*). Even the *Ming wai-shih* 明外史, as quoted in the *T'u-shu chi-ch'eng*, allotted considerable space to him.

Bibliography

62/ 下 /7a; 64/ 己 10/3b; 84/ 丁上 /32a; TSCC (1885–88), XI: 318/4b; *Huang Ming wen-hai* (microfilm), 5/2/12; SK (1930), 28/7b, 32/8b, 74/3b, 178/3a; Sung Ch'un-teng, *Sung pu-i chi* 宋布衣集, 1/22b, appendix in *Chi-fu ts'ung-shu* 畿輔叢書.

Lienche Tu Fang

HSÜ Hung-ju 徐鴻儒, also named Hsü Sung 誦, died December, 1622, a leader of the White Lotus sect (*see* Chu Yüan-chang), was a native of Chü-yeh 鉅野, Shantung. From June to December, 1622, he led a rebellion against the Ming government and even declared himself emperor with the reign title Ta-ch'eng hsing-sheng 大乘興勝 (and reportedly assumed the title of Chung-hsing fu-lieh ti 中興福

烈帝, which seems unlikely for it reads like a posthumous name). What qualified Hsü as a leader was chiefly his reputation as one who possessed certain magic skills. One account says that he could enable people to see gold, silver, and wheat hills, oil fountains, and liquor wells, and to have other visions; it also relates that those converted to his faith would never be poor in their lifetime. Another version has it that he was able to simulate combat among paper men and paper horses, a skill allegedly used centuries later by the Boxers at the end of the 19th century. A third version records that he could make people see themselves in the reflection of a basin of water with the costumes and hats of emperors, princes, generals, and ministers. All accounts stress the fact that Hsü attracted many followers who believed in his supernatural powers.

Hsü's mentor, a Mr. Kao 高, was said to be the founder of the Wen-hsiang chiao 聞香教 (the incense-smelling sect), a branch of the White Lotus sect, in the early years of the Wan-li period. Kao brought many people into the sect, including Hsü, in western Shantung. Contradictory evidence indicates that the Wen-hsiang chiao was founded by Wang Sen 王森 of Chi-chou 薊州, northeast of Peking. It is recorded that Wang learned from a fairy a magical skill for creating various odors. Wang thus came to call himself Wen-hsiang chiao-chu 主 (master of the Wen-hsiang sect). While there is no way to prove whether Wang or Kao was the original founder of the sect, the two groups evidently merged in the middle of the Wan-li period with Wang Sen as the leader and Hsü Hung-ju as co-leader (possibly after Kao's death).

Under Wang's leadership, headquarters were set up in Luan-chou 灤州, Pei-Chihli, and a definite organizion was established; leaders known as ch'uan-t'ou 傳頭 (head evangelist) and hui-chu 會主 (assembly chief) were appointed, but their functions are obscure. A regulation of the sect required that anyone who joined must contribute a sum of money, known as the ch'ao-kung-ch'ien 朝貢錢 (tribute). A kind of centralized system of communication among the groups of different regions was also effectively put into operation. These areas reportedly included Shantung, Pei-Chihli, Honan, Shansi, Shensi, and Szechwan, traditionally known for their White Lotus activities. This alarmed many officials, so much so that by 1595 Wang Sen was arrested by his local magistrate. But Wang was able to bribe his way to freedom, and resume his propagandizing in Peking. During the last years of the Wan-li reign, there is indication that the White Lotus members were active even among eunuchs and court ladies.

In 1614 Wang was arrested again; thereafter Hsü Hung-ju assumed the leadership of the sect. Hsü's personal charm and magical feats must have won more followers. Records show that many people went into bankruptcy without regret in order to contribute to Hsü, and others even brought their wives and children to join his sect. According to one account, the White Lotus members existed all over the country and came together in crowds wherever their leaders went. Many high officials again became concerned about this situation. Finally in 1619 a vice minister of Rites, Ho Tsung-yen 何宗彥 (T. 君美, cs 1595, d. March 4, 1621, Pth. 文毅), proposed that the White Lotus sect be severely suppressed; this received imperial approval in the following year. It is likely that the revolt was due in large measure to government suppression.

The immediate cause for Hsü's uprising was the Manchu advance in Liaotung. The drastic change in this area after March, 1621, resulted in numbers of refugees spilling over into northeast China. The social restlessness enabled Hsü and his cohorts to intensify their activities. Consequently, in the spring of 1622, the White Lotus leaders decided to start the insurrection on the 15th of the 8th month (September 19). Due to some unexpected occurence, however, Hsü three months earlier than the original plan declared himself emperor, established his military headquarters at Liang-chia-lou 梁家樓, appointed ministers with such titles as ch'eng-hsiang 丞相 (prime minister) and chün-shih 軍師 (military adviser), and made his brother, Hsü Ho-yü 和宇, and a son of Wang Sen, Wang Hao-hsien 好賢, princes. He then offered sacrifice to the banners and started the revolt.

During its initial stage Hsü was quite successful. The rebels occupied Tsou 鄒-hsien and T'eng 滕-hsien districts and even blocked the Grand Canal for some time. Their activities directly affected Shantung and parts of Pei-Chihli and Honan provinces. According to the official records the effects of this revolt were felt in Nan-Chihli, Shansi, Shensi, and Szechwan provinces, and involved many people. Hsü himself confessed that he had two million followers. This was the first large organized rebellion near the close of the Ming, and marked the beginning of the downfall of the dynasty. On the other hand, during the period of military revolt Hsü and his followers found it difficult to occupy even a small town if there were any militia forces. Such was true of Ch'ü-fou 曲阜 and Chü-yeh (Hsü's native place). As a whole, the rebels could not claim any decisive military victory on the basis of which a new government structure might be developed.

The government response at the beginning of the revolt was restricted by the number of available forces in the Shantung region. Troops previously stationed in the province had been sent to Liaotung early in 1621. As soon as the revolt broke out, the governor of Shantung, Chao Yen 趙彥 (T. 名字, cs 1583), appointed Yang Chao-chi 楊肇基 (d. 1630), the former commander in Tatung, as the commander-in-chief. Local militia in various districts were immediately organized and trained. Supplementary troops from outside of Shantung were requested. As a result the coast guard under the command of Lai

Ssu-hsing 來斯行 (T. 道之, H. 槎菴, cs 1607) came to their aid from Tientsin and proved effective. The joint effort of these soon won crucial victories which led to the defeat of Hsü and his men. The rebellion lasted six months. At the end of 1622, the main force was surrounded by government troops in T'eng-hsien. As a consequence Hsü surrendered, was taken to Peking, and executed in the market place.

Bibliography

1/240/22b, 257/5a, 300/22a; MSL (1940), Hsi-tsung, 17/19a, 23/4a; KC (1958), 5205, 5212; Chang T'ing-yü (ECCP), *Ming-chien kang-mu* (Shanghai, 1936), 8/478; Cha Chi-tso (ECCP), *Tsui-wei lu*, 31/57a; *Shantung t'ung-chih* (1934), 2307, 3318, 4744; *Chü-yeh-hsien chih* (1840), 17/45a; *Ts'ao-chou-fu chih* 曹州府志 (1756), 22/23b; *Tsou-hsien hsiang-t'u chih* 鄉土志 (1907), 9a; *Ch'eng-wu-hsien chih* 城武縣志 (1830), 13/2b; Ku Ying-t'ai (ECCP), *Ming-ch'ao chi-shih pen-mo* (1658), 70/1a; Noguchi Tetsurō 野口鐵郎, "Tenkei Jo-kō-ju no ran" 天啓徐鴻儒の亂, *Tōhō Shukyō* 東方宗教, Vol. 20 (1963), 35, Vol. 21 (1963), 41.

Yung-deh Richard Chu

HSÜ I-k'uei 徐一夔 (T. 大章), 1318-*ca.* 1400, scholar, was a native of T'ien-t'ai 天臺 in the then Chiang-nan Chekiang province. Hsü's early life is not recorded, but during it he acquired a broad knowledge of the Classics and became skillful in belles-lettres. At one time he made his home in Chia-hsing 嘉興 and then moved to Hangchow, where in 1350 he acquired a position as an assistant instructor in a local school. A few years later, through the recommendation of Wei Su (*q.v.*), he became an instructor in the prefectural school of Chien-ning 建寧, Fukien, but left office shortly afterward because of the uprisings of Fang Kuo-chen (*q.v.*), and led a secluded life in Chia-hsing until he received a summons from Chu Yüanchang.

In 1357, when Chu, then duke of Wu, instructed his officials to recruit men of scholarly attainment to his service, Hsü was called to the capital and put in charge of the drafting of decrees, but he relinquished that post six months later. In September, 1369, Chu, now emperor, ordered his advisers to compile a new code of rites, and appointed Hsü as the chief editor. When this work, known as *Ta Ming chi-li* 大明集禮, 53 *ch.*, was completed in October, 1370, Hsü was given a lavish reward, but he declined an official post on the grounds of illness. In March of the same year, the emperor also ordered the compilation of the history of the late Yüan period from 1333 to 1368, appointing Wang Wei, Li Shan-ch'ang, and Sung Lien (*qq.v.*) as joint editors. Wang then recommended Hsü to be compiler. At that time Hsü sent a memorandum to Wang in which he wrote about the importance of the *Jih-li* 日曆, or daily court records, which had been the basic source for the writing of dynastic history ever since T'ang times. He lamented the fact that in the Yüan dynasty the historiographers neglected to keep such a record; that only in the central secretariat was there an office for the compilation of historical documents, and this became the principal source of the *Yüan shih-lu* for the first thirteen reigns (to 1333); the only other official source was the *Ching-shih ta-tien* 經世大典, compiled in 1329-32. He concluded by stating that, for the history of the thirty-six years of the last reign, not even such works were available and all materials had to be collected first hand; it was a task for really experienced editors, certainly not for a sick man like himself. So he declined the honor, pleading lameness due to rheumatism. Nonetheless, his opinion about the *Jih-li* may have prevailed, for in the following year the emperor ordered the compilation of the daily court records of his own reign.

Early in 1373 Hsü received an appointment as instructor in the prefectural school of Hangchow. In October he was summoned to Nanking to take part in the compilation of the daily court records which, when completed in June, 1374, became known as *Ta Ming jih-li*, 100 *ch.* (*see* Chan T'ung). He declined an appointment to the Hanlin Academy and returned to his post in Hangchow, one which he held for the next twenty odd years and in which he acquired a reputation as an eminent teacher. The emperor, however, did not forget him entirely for, in 1383, shortly after the reconstruction of the Ling-ku monastery 靈谷寺 in Nanking, Chu Yüan-chang summoned him to compose a commemorative essay. Hsü complied and submitted it from Hangchow. Greatly delighted, the emperor again rewarded him. It is not certain at what age he died, but it seems that he may have lived to the end of the century, for the local gazetteer indicates that he remained as instructor of the prefectural school in Hangchow until about 1400. One source says that he retired to Chia-hsing and died there.

One of Hsü's dated writings is an epitaph written in 1399, one year after the death of the first Ming emperor. This seems enough to prove the spuriousness of the story that in a memorial he used certain words suspected by that emperor as being puns which ridiculed him, and that on that account Hsü was executed. It is known that the emperor did punish someone under such a circumstance, but it was not Hsü.

Apart from official compilations, Hsü also compiled a gazetteer of Hangchow, which is no longer extant. Hsü's collected works entitled *Shih-feng kao* 始豐稿, 15 *ch.*, first printed in the late years of the Hung-wu period, was salvaged and reedited by Ting Ping (ECCP) in his *Wu-lin wang-che i-chu* 武林往哲遺著 (1894), 14 *ch.*, with 1 *chüan* of biographical and bibliographical material in the appendix. Hsü divided his work into four sections in chronological order, the first three *chüan* for the period before 1367, *chüan* four to six for the period until 1377, *chüan* seven to nine for the period between 1377 and 1382, and the rest for the period after 1383. This order is followed in the present edition. Many of Hsü's writings give good descriptions of Hangchow in the 14th century, particularly of local schools and religious establishments; one exceptionally interesting piece is the "Chih-kung tui" 織工對 (A dialogue with weavers), which vividly describes the silk weaving industry in Hangchow at the end of the Yüan dynasty. Hsü is also credited with the authorship of the *I-p'u sou-ch'i* 藝圃蒐奇, 18 *ch.*, with a sequel *Pu-chüeh* 補闕, 2 *ch.*, a collection of jottings on odd items in literature and history, which the *Ssu-k'u* editors considered later writers to have fabricated.

Bibliography

1/285/14b; MSL (1962), T'ai-tsu, 875, 1113, 1507, 1573; TSCC (1885–88), XXIII: 92/80/7b; *Hangchow-fu chih* (1579), in *Ming-tai fang-chih hsüan* 明代方志選 (1965), 260, 1019; *Chekiang t'ung-chih* (1934), 3150; Chu I-tsun (ECCP), *P'u-shu-t'ing chi*, 64/4a; SK (1930), 82/3a, 134/1a, 169/6a; *Shih-feng kao* (1894); Sung Lien, *Sung hsüeh-shih chi* (SPTK ed.), 34/5a; T'ien Ju-ch'eng, *Hsi-hu yu-lan chih* 西湖遊覽志 (1896), 7/11b, 21/18a; Hsü Chen-ch'ing, *Chien-sheng yeh-wen* 翦勝野聞 in *Li-tai hsiao-shih* 歷代小史, 78/10a; Sheng Feng 盛楓, *Chia-ho cheng-hsien lu* 嘉禾徵獻錄, in *Tsui-li* 槜李 *ts'ung-shu* (1936), 42/2b; Cheng T'ien-t'ing 鄭天挺, "Kuan-yü 關於 Hsü I-k'uei 'Chih-kung tui'," LSYC (1958), no. 1, 65; Ku Chieh-kang, "A Study of Literary Persecution during the Ming Dynasty," tr. by L. Carrington Goodrich, HJAS 3 (1938), 263; W. Franke, *Sources*, 6. 4. 3; J. Prip-Møller, "The Hall of Lin ku ssu, Nanking," *Artes*, III (Copenhagen, 1935), 191; id., "Oldest Known Church Building in China," *Chinese Recorder* 66: 12 (December, 1935), 762.

Hok-lam Chan

HSÜ Kao 許誥 (T. 廷綸, H. 函谷), January 15, 1472-January 31, 1534 (according to the tomb inscription written by Wang T'ing-hsiang, *q.v.*), the second son of Hsü Chin (*q.v.*), and the lady Kao, rose to be minister of Revenue in Nanking. (Other sources give date of birth as November 17, 1471, and date of death June 28, 1534.) Following his graduation as *chü-jen* in 1495 and *chin-shih* in 1499, he became (1500) a supervising secretary, and, in June, 1506 (as his father was a vice minister of War), he was obliged by the regulations to leave his supervisory post, and was made a corrector in the Hanlin Academy. Two years later, after the eunuch Liu Chin (*q.v.*) had engineered his father's dismissal, Hsü Kao was demoted to the assistant magistracy of Ch'üan-chou 全州, Kwangsi. In 1510 he retired to mourn his father's passing. During this period he gave himself up to further study of neo-Confucianism and to teaching a number of students. In 1515 he received an appointment as director of the Seal Office, but, excusing himself on account of poor health, he continued to live at home.

Returning to government employ (1525), he served as assistant administration commissioner in the office of transmission in Nanking. Because of his fame as a student of neo-Confucian thought, many people came to call on him to seek his counsel. He was popularly regarded as the chief exponent of the school in the north, while in the south Wang Shou-jen (*q.v.*) held first place. Next he became expositor-in-waiting in the Hanlin Academy (1527) and as such gave lectures to the emperor on neo-Confucianism. Two years later the emperor asked him to take charge of the military examinations, and in 1529 he received a promotion to be director of the Court of Imperial Sacrifices and concurrently of the National University. In the last office he joined with Grand Secretary Chang Fu-ching (*q.v.*) in petitioning the substitution of tablets for images in the cult of Confucius (*see* Hsü Chieh). For this purpose the emperor consulted Hsü's work on the cult, *Tao-t'ung yüan-liu* 道統源流. In 1532 he served as right vice minister of Personnel and at the end of the year (December 23) as minister of Revenue in Nanking. (It is not without interest that at this same time his younger brother, Hsü Tsan (*q.v.*) held the same but more prestigious post

in Peking [October, 1531-October, 1534].) This was his final office; he died two years later. The court honored him with the name Chuang-min 莊敏.

Hsü produced a number of works, the bibliographical section of the *Ming-shih* recording several titles, including a collection of his memorials in 2 *chüan*. He is best remembered for his *T'ung-chien kang-mu ch'ien-pien* 通鑑綱目前編, 3 *ch.*, in which he attempted to give a record of the events which preceded the centuries included in the history devised by Ssu-ma Kuang (1019–86), later condensed by Chu Hsi (1130–1200) and his disciples, covering the years 403 B.C.-A.D. 959). The editors of the Imperial Catalogue took note of the book, but refused it a place in the *Ssu-k'u ch'üan-shu*. Hsü also wrote a book of poems entitled *Hsia-ch'eng chi* 霞城集, 20 *ch.*, which displeased the censors of two and a half centuries later for some of the author's comments on frontier affairs, particularly one alluding (according to the censors) to Altan-qaɣan (*q.v.*). This seems hardly likely, however, as Altan's star was yet to rise on the horizon. This book is very rare, but Sun Tien-ch'i reports having seen a copy of the Chia-ching edition during his long years in the book trade in Peking.

Bibliography

1/186/14a; 5/31/75a; 16/34/51a, 89/5a, 159/46b; 22/4/35a; 32/90/44b; 42/57/8a; KC(1958), 3500; MSL (1965), Shih-tsung, 3354, 3609; *Shan-chou chih-li-chou chih* (1892), 12/36b; SK (1930), 48/2b; Sun Tien-ch'i (1957), 231; Chu Ta-chao 朱大韶 (1517–77), *Huang Ming ming-ch'en mu-ming* 名臣墓銘 (Taipei, 1969), 1152.

L. Carrington Goodrich and Lee Hwa-chou

HSÜ Lin 徐霖 (T. 子仁, H. 九峰), 1462-July 27, 1538, calligrapher, painter, poet, and songwriter, was a native of Shang-yüan 上元, Nanking. He came from a Soochow family that had moved probably in the early years of the 15th century to nearby Sung-chiang 松江. His grandfather, sentenced for some offense to military service in Nanking, established a branch of the family there. A precocious child, Hsü Lin is said to have been able to compose poems at six years of age and write large-size characters at eight. In 1475 he passed the examinations to enter the district school as a stipendiary student. He reportedly had a full face, long ear lobes, and an impressive physique. Evidently outstanding in both appearance and intelligence he became recognized as a promising candidate for the higher degree. He failed, however, to pass the provincial examination after several tries, while in the meantime he gained a reputation for unconventionality. In 1490 he joined Tu Mu (*q.v.*) and six other young scholars in paying a visit to the great artist Shen Chou (*q.v.*). The occasion was depicted by another painter, Wu Lin 吳麟 (T. 瑞卿, fl. 1440–90), in a scroll known as "Pa-shih t'u" 八士圖 (The eight scholars), for which Shen wrote a colophon. Not long thereafter Hsü Lin was expelled from the district school, thus ending his hope for an official career. His biographers give the usual excuse, that someone brought a false accusation against him. Perhaps his popularity among certain circles so went to his head that he became even more effusive and unconventional, thus making him a target of jealousy and dislike; a minor indiscretion, ordinarily overlooked, may have been magnified in his case. Considering his love of music and acquaintance with singsong girls, it is not difficult to surmise the reason for his exclusion from the government school.

Proclaiming that a true scholar did not need any official garment to win respect, Hsü concentrated on achieving excellence in calligraphy, painting, and poetry. Soon his handwriting, especially in the seal style, won the praise of such eminent contemporary calligraphers as Li Tung-yang (*q.v.*) and Ch'iao Yü (*see* Huang Hsing-tseng), and his fame as an artist

reached Japan and Annam. It was the time when, stimulated by the rise in wealth of landed gentry, art studios began to flourish, and artists could become affluent. Hsü accumulated enough wealth to become the owner of a house in the entertainment area of Nanking on the Ch'in-huai River 秦淮河, near the Wu-ting Bridge 武定橋, inside the southwest gate, Chü-pao-men (*see* Shen Fu). His estate, known as K'uai-yüan 快園 (Satisfaction Garden), occupied several acres and was noted for its terraces, ponds, buildings, and flora. He had among his guests notables in various fields, and famous actors and actresses came to perform in his garden the song dramas of the day, for some of which he himself wrote the lyrics. It seems that he even had a troupe of his own. In his garden he was fittingly known as the Jan-hsien 髯仙 (bearded immortal).

In 1520, when Emperor Chu Hou-chao (*q.v.*) made his nine months' stay in Nanking, he summoned Hsü to an audience on the recommendation of the actor and musician, Tsang Hsien (*see* Chu Hou-chao). Reportedly Hsü pleased the emperor by the songs he had written and by his "Poem on New Year's Eve" (January 19, 1520); the monarch showered him with gifts, including a robe worn by first grade officials. Twice the emperor visited Satisfaction Garden, once arriving unannounced on a pleasure boat after midnight. Hsü could set a table of only ordinary fare, but the emperor enjoyed it. During the second visit, it is said, the emperor fished from a boat and auctioned off some goldfish to the eunuchs in attendance. There is the legend that the emperor fell off the boat, soaking his clothes; and so a pond in Hsü's garden became known as the Yü-lung-ch'ih 浴龍池 (dragon bathing pool). By imperial order, Hsü accompanied the emperor on the latter's return voyage to Peking. One source has it that he received an appointment to a minor military office. In any case, the emperor died shortly after his return and many imperial favorites were punished or sent way in disgrace. Apparently Hsü left earlier and so escaped the fate that befell the others. He lived the rest of his life in peace. On his seventieth birthday more than a hundred famous singsong girls came to take part in the celebration.

Hsü is the author of several works, none of which seems to be extant. Among them may be mentioned a history of Nanking, several anthologies, an annotated edition of the rhyme book, *Chung-yüan yin-yün* 中原音韻, and a work on calligraphers. He also left several small collections of poems. His collected poems and essays are entitled *Hsü Tzu-jen shih-chi* 子仁詩集, 4 *ch.*, and *Li-tsao-t'ang wen-chi* 麗藻堂文集. He also is credited with eight song dramas, none of which, unfortunately, is extant. Only parts of one, the *Liu-hsien chi* 柳仙記, are preserved in an anthology. Another one, *Hsiu-ju chi* 繡襦記 (Embroidered jacket), formerly published several times under his name as author, has of late been attributed to another dramatist.

Osvald Sirén cites a few of his paintings (landscapes and flowers) and Ellen Laing another (hare, chrysanthemum, bamboo, and rock, with a poem), now in the Palace Museum, Peking.

Bibliography

1/286/19b; 5/115/33a, 35a; 22/11/11a; 32/13/33b; 40/38/7b; 64/ 丁 12/10b; Ch'ien Ch'ien-i (EC CP), *Lieh-ch'ao shih-chi*, 丙 14/31b; KC (1958), 3206; Ho Liang-chun, *Ssu-yu-chai ts'ung-shuo* (1959), 132, 237, 268, 341; Huang Yü-chi (EC CP), *Ch'ien-ch'ing-t'ang shu-mu*, 22/22b; Fu Hsi-hua 傅惜華, *Ming-tai ch'uan-ch'i ch'üan-mu* 明代傳奇全目 (1959), 23; Chou Hui 周暉, *Chin-ling so-chih* 金陵瑣志 (1955 reprint of 1610 ed.), 187, 222, 234, 256, 429, 940, 979, 1112; O. Sirén, *Chinese Painting*, Vol. VII (New York, 1958), 193; E. J. Laing, *Chinese Paintings in Chinese Publications, 1956–1958* (Ann Arbor, 1969), 169.

Chaoying Fang

HSÜ Lun 許論 (T. 廷議, H. 嘿齋), 1495-November 19, 1566, the eighth son of Hsü Chin (*q.v.*) and the lady Kao, rose to be minister of War. It is recounted that as a youth (probably around the years 1505-6), when Hsü Chin was vice minister, then minister, of War, he became interested in frontier defenses. Hence the significance (after many years of later acquaintance) of his work, the *Chiu-pien-t'u-lun*, 九邊圖論 published in 1538. This includes, as Wolfgang Franke remarks, maps and description of the northern border regions, and is one of the first books of its kind. The maps, presented to the emperor in September, 1537, came to be especially appreciated by Lo Hung-hsien (*q.v.*) who used them in his own geographical compendium, the *Kuang-yü-t'u*, published some years later. Not surprisingly, the Manchu authorities banned Hsü's book in the 18th century, but a few copies are known to survive in the Bibliothéque Nationale, Library of Congress, and Naikaku Bunko.

On acquiring the *chü-jen* degree in 1519 and the *chin-shih* in 1526, he was made prefectural judge of Shun-te 順德, Pei-Chihli (1527). In 1531 he became secretary in the ministry of Revenue but retired for a time for reasons of health. On his return to the capital (1533) he became secretary in the ministry of War. A year later his mother's death obliged him to leave once more. In 1537 he was appointed a secretary in the ministry of Rites, after which he received a promotion to vice director, then director of the bureau of receptions in that ministry. From 1540 to 1544 we find him acting successively as vice minister of the Court of Imperial Entertainments in Nanking, assistant minister of the Grand Court of Revision, also in Nanking (1542), then governor of Peking (July, 1543). A year later illness again forced his resignation. Brought back to government service in 1550, he served as a vice minister of War, and became involved in matters of defense on the frontier, because of the attacks by the Mongols under Altan-qaγan (*q.v.*). In 1554 Hsü was made supreme commander north of Peking and tried to keep the enemy at bay. He succeeded Yang Po (*q.v.*) as minister of War in February, 1556. The year following he joined with Yen Sung in falsely accusing Shen Lien (*q.v.*) of connections with the Mongols. At the same time the concubine of Hsin-ai (son of Altan-qaɤan) is said to have had illicit relations with the chief of one of the tribes. Hsin-ai in pursuit failed to catch the chief as the local commander, Yang Shun (*see* Cheng Hsiao), to whom he had come for security, had packed him off to Peking and sent the concubine away, telling Hsin-ai of her whereabouts. In his anger Hsin-ai found and killed her, pillaged the whole area around Tatung, made an encirclement of the Yu-wei 右衞 Guard, and menaced the garrisons of Hsüan-fu and of Chi 薊 -chou (west of the capital). The court was alarmed. Yen Sung, after consulting with Hsü, considered the abandonment of the Yu-wei; but the emperor would not hear of it and sent reinforcements which in time forced the enemy's retreat.

During these critical years Yen Sung and his son were close to the seats of power, and made Hsü Lun's tenure difficult, though he generally concurred with their decisions. Besides the threats in the north and northwest there were the continuing incursions of the *wo-k'ou* on the southeast littoral. So Hsü was made a scapegoat and forced to retire (March 27, 1558) from the ministry. Nevertheless, the dangerous situation continued in the north, and for a while in 1559 he took charge of the defense of Chi, Liaotung, and Paoting, with his old title restored. He sent in so many memorials, however, that a censor accused him of trying to usurp the prerogatives of the emperor. So once again he was dismissed and deprived of title and honors. At his death his body was laid to rest in a tomb about three miles southeast of his native place. Early in the following reign of Lung-ch'ing, his third son, Hsü T'an 俊, announcing his father's demise, petitioned the court that it restore his rank. It obliged, and honored him with the posthumous name Kung-hsiang 恭襄.

In addition to his best-known book he produced a collection of writings, entitled *Mo-chai chi* 嘿齋集, 4 *ch.*; he was also responsible for the engraving (*ca.* 1560) of the *Er yüan chi*, the picturesque representation of two polite gatherings of notables in 1437 and 1499 (*see* Yang Jung and Chou Ching). Hsü Lun's father had been one of those present at the Bamboo Garden.

Hsü had three sons, the two elder, through the yin privilege, receiving military ranks; one became a chiliarch in the Embroidered-uniform Guard, then a supreme commander, the other a battalion commander. The third, Hsü T'an, was made prefect of Heng-chou 衡州, Hukuang, in 1584. A grandson, Hsü Mao-shun 茂橓, became an officer in the Embroidered-uniform Guard; another, Hsü Mao-ch'i 杞, was appointed a myriarch of the Hung-nung Guard 弘農衞 stationed at Ch'ang-p'ing 昌平, near Peking. A great-grandson, Hsü Hao-jan 浩然, through the same privilege, received the title of grand guardian of the heir apparent and vice commissioner-in-chief of a chief military commission. The son of Hsü Hao-jan, Hsü Ta-yin 達陰, who became a commander in the Embroidered-uniform Guard, lost his life in defending Peking against the forces of Li Tzu-ch'eng (ECCP). His cousin, Hsü Chia 佳 -yin, a commander of the Hung-nung guard, situated near his home, died when the rebels under Li destroyed Ling-pao in 1641.

At the end of the dynasty, during the years from 1633 to 1643, when guerrillas were operating almost continuously in the Honan region, the great Hsü family seems to have been wiped out. In the Shan-chou gazetteer of 1892 where almost six hundred names, most of them from other towns, are listed as having contributed to the printing of various editions of the work, only one man named Hsü appears and he was a merchant.

Bibliography

1/186/16b; 3/172/20a; 5/39/105a, 57/38a; 16/116/
11a, 117/25a; 32/90/56b; MSL (1965), Shih-tsung,
4253, 5386, 7375, 9039; KC (1958), 4034;
Huang Ming wen-hai (microfilm), 5/8/7; Ch'en
Tzu-lung, *Ming ching-shih wen-pien*, ch. 80;
Shan-chou chih-li-chou chih (1892), 12/37a; *Hunan
t'ung-chih* (1934), 2472; Sun Tien-ch'i (1957),
16; L. Hambis, *Documents sur l'histoire des
Mongols à l'époque des Ming* (Paris, 1969), 59;
H. Serruys, *Sino-Mongol relations during the
Ming* (Brussels, 1967), 295, 298; L. of C. *Cata-
logue of Rare Books*, 384, 1065; W. Franke,
Sources, 7. 3. 7.

L. Carrington Goodrich and Lee Hwa-chou

HSÜ Pen 徐賁 (T. 幼（以）文, H. 北郭生,
蜀山人), 1335-80, poet, painter, and official, was born into a family of Szechwanese origin settled at Ch'ang-chou 常州
in the Yangtze estuary. Afterwards he
moved to Soochow, the then P'ing-chiang
平江, which in 1356 became the capital
of the rebellious leader Chang Shih-
ch'eng (*q.v.*). Dwelling in the quarter outside the north wall of the city, he and
nine other young men of letters were
later called "Pei-kuo shih-yu" 北郭十友
(Ten friends of the north wall) by Kao
Ch'i (*q.v.*). All these men were poets, but
Hsü, Kao, Chang Yü, and Yang Chi (*qq.
v.*) distinguished themselves as "Wu-chung
ssu-chieh" 吳中四傑 (Four outstanding
figures of Soochow). With the exception
of the leading poet Kao, they were all
painters as well as poets.

After 1358, Kao Ch'i and Yang Chi
successively became the "guests" of Jao
Chieh 饒介 (T. 介之, H. 醉樵, d. 1367),
already in the service of Chang Shih-
ch'eng. Perhaps in order to escape possible involvement in official life, Hsü and
Chang Yü went to stay on two adjoining
hills of Wu-hsing 吳興 in Chekiang. On
the eve of Hsü's departure, Kao Ch'i
wrote the "Sung Hsü I-wen hsü" 送徐以
文序 as a farewell address. In 1364 he
composed the "Shu-shan shu-she chi" 蜀山
書舍記, an account of Hsü's newly built
house on Mt. Shu. According to this

essay, Hsü was already qualified for civil
service (in the Yüan government), yet he
was in no hurry to seek honor and preferred to pursue his studies. Kao praised
him as a far-sighted man who was preparing for greater achievement. Hsü stayed
in his mountain retreat almost ten years
with varying intervals of absence. His
life there and his excursions in the neighboring regions are known from his poems
and the poems of Chang Yü and others.
Some of these poems are on the subject
of his paintings of landscapes there.

In October, 1366, the armies of Chu
Yüan-chang seized Wu-hsing. One year
later P'ing-chiang was also captured after
ten months of resistance by Chang Shih-
ch'eng. Many of its wealthy residents who
collaborated with Chang were banished to
Hao-liang 濠梁 (Feng-yang 鳳陽). Since
Hsü suffered the same fate, he must have
been for some time in P'ing-chiang in
Chang's service. According to a poem of
Yang Chi composed in Hao-liang, he and
Hsü shared a house which he named
Meng-lu-hsüan 夢綠軒 because once Hsü
dreamed of the verdure south of the
Yangtze.

Released from his place of exile in
1369, Hsü returned to Mt. Shu. His artistic
activity in this period is especially marked
by two of his paintings, "Shu-shan t'u" 圖
(Shu Mountain) and "Tsui-chung 醉中
t'u" (On a drunken spree), both offered
to Lü Min 呂敏 (T. 志學, H. 無碍居士),
one of the "ten friends" who visited him
twice. In his poem inscribed on the first,
he expressed his enjoyment of life on Mt.
Shu and asked Lü to come to stay with
him. According to Lü's inscription on the
second, it was made in Hsü's studio Wu-
tan 悟澹 on the mount after he and Hsü
had been drinking together in the spring
of 1373.

It does not seem that Hsü received
an official appointment (as a censor ?)
from Chu Yüan-chang until 1374, about
the time of Kao Ch'i's death. Early in
1376 he was sent to Shansi on a tour of
inspection. At the end of the tour in

March, he gave a description of the journey in a series of fourteen poems entitled *Chin Chi chi-hsing* 晉冀紀行. Following this, he received an appointment as senior administration vice commissioner of Honan and in September was promoted to be the administration commissioner. In June, 1377, he was demoted to prefect of Huai-ch'ing 懷慶, Honan, the reason being that it was a punishment for his failure to provide adequate supplies for the expeditionary forces proceeding to the northwestern frontier under the command of Teng Yü (*q.v.*). In February, 1378, Hsü was promoted to be the administration vice commissioner of Kwangtung, a position which he held until his death in 1380. This date is supported by two poems of his contemporaries who lamented his passing, one by Lü Min dated August, 1380, and another by Sung Lien (*q.v.*), who himself died in 1381. The two poems were each inscribed on one of Hsü's paintings, namely "Hui-shan 惠山 t'u" (Hui Mountain) and "Chu-ch'uang feng-yü 竹窗風雨 t'u," (Wind and rain on the bamboo lattice) which are recorded in the *Shih-ku-t'ang shu-hua hui-k'ao*, compiled by Pien Yung-yü (ECCP).

According to Lü Min's inscription which follows his poem on the first painting, Hsü's poetic work was originally entitled *Wu-tan chi* 集, 10 *ch.*, by Hsü himself, after the name of his studio, but was also known as *Pei-kuo chi*. The latter title was adopted in 1487 when Chang Hsi 張習 (T. 企翔, cs 1469) published it for the first time. In a note appended to it, Chang relates that he had made an effort to collect Hsü's poems, which had already been dispersed, and some information about Hsü's life. This account of Hsü's life was partly based on hearsay and is full of errors, such as giving the year of death as 1393. Ch'ien Ch'ien-i (ECCP) pointed out this mistake in the *Lieh-ch'ao shih-chi*, citing as evidence the above mentioned poems by Lü Min and Sung Lien. Ch'ien's sketch of Hsü's life, however, also contains several mistakes.

Hsü is especially famous for his landscape painting. Seventeen paintings ascribed to him with eight reproductions are listed in Osvald Sirén's *Chinese Painting*. But five among them are doubtful. The one dated 1345 is too early in time. The other four bear dates after his death: one in 1393, two in 1395, and one in 1397. One of the two dated 1395 is the "Ch'un-yün tieh-ts'ui 春雲疊翠 t'u" (Spring clouds in alternate banks of white and blue) reproduced in *Kokka*. Similarly, two more, one dated 1381 and the other also dated 1395, are listed in the *Li-tai liu-ch'uan shu-hua tso-p'in pien-nien-piao*, compiled by Hsü Pang-ta (*see* Lu Chih). In addition to the eight reproductions of his paintings indicated by Sirén, another may be found in *Chinese Landscape Painting* by Sherman E. Lee. An important example of his art is the "Wu-hsing ch'ing-yüan 清遠 t'u" (Wu-hsing in the clear distance), distinguished for its brush strokes, reproduced in the *Chin-kuei ts'ang-hua* 金匱藏畫. With its extraordinarily fluent lines, it serves as one of the best example of wen-jen-hua 文人畫, the paintings of literati.

Bibliography

1/285/21b; 3/266/17b; 65/2/3a; 84/甲 8/1a; MSL (1962), T'ai-tsu, 1800, 1856, 1908; SK (1930), 169/9b; Hsü Pen, *Pei-kuo chi* (SPTK 3d series); Kao Ch'i, *Kao t'ai-shih ta-ch'uan chi, ibid.*, 1st ser., 3/19b, 4/8b; *id., Kao t'ai-shih fu-tsao chi*, 1/7b, 2/4b, 3/10b; Chang Yü, *Ching-chü chi, ibid.*, 1st ser., 1/34a, 4/4b; Yang Chi, *Mei-an chi, ibid.*, 3/10b; Pien Yung-yü, *Shih-ku-t'ang shu-hua hui-k'ao hua-pu* 畫部 (1922), 24; *Honan t'ung-chih* (1914), 31/14a; *Kwangtung t'ung-chih* (1934, 351; Ch'en Jen-t'ao 陳仁濤, *Chin-kuei ts'ang-hua* (Hong Kong, 1960), Vol. II, pl. 21; Osvald Sirén, *Chinese Painting* (London, 1959), Vol. VI, pl. 113, Vol. VII, 193; *Kokka* (April, 1946), 649/337; *Ku-kung ming-hua san-po-chung* 故宮名畫三百種 (Taipei, 1959), Vol. V, no. 206; Sherman E. Lee, *Chinese Landscape Painting* (Cleveland, 1954), pl. 36, p. 60; F. W. Mote, *The Poet Kao Ch'i* (Princeton, 1962), 97, 194.

T. W. Weng

HSÜ Po 徐燉 (T. 惟起, H. 興公), August 2, 1570–1642, bibliophile, calligrapher, and poet, was a native of Min-hsien 閩縣, Fukien. His father Hsü Ang 徐榻 (T. 子瞻, H. 相坡居士, 1513–91), who was a *kung-sheng* of 1565, officiated first as an assistant instructor in the local school of Nan-an 南安, Fukien, then as instructor in the district school of Mao-ming 茂名, Kwangtung, and finally as magistrate of Yungning 永寧, Chekiang. Hsü Po's elder brother, Hsü T'ung 徐熥 (T. 惟和, 1561–99), a *chü-jen* of 1588, was a celebrated poet. The two brothers and five of their fellow provincials (among whom was Hsieh Chao-che [*q.v.*], son of an elder sister of the Hsü brothers) were known as the Seven Poets of Fukien. Hsü T'ung left a collection of poems entitled *Man-t'ing shih-chi* 幔亭詩集, 15 *ch.*, which was included in the *Ssu-k'u* imperial library. He also compiled an anthology, *Chin-an feng-ya* 晉安風雅, 12 *ch.*, of the poetry of two hundred sixty-four Foochow authors who lived from 1368 to *ca.* 1600; this received a notice in the *Ssu-k'u* catalogue.

In his younger days Hsü Po in all probability lived in different provinces as his father moved from post to post. Even in later life, he seems to have traveled frequently and extensively, particularly in Chekiang, in the Soochow-Nanking area, in Kiangsi, and in his native province. He did not choose to follow the prevailing pattern of an educated man of his time. Reports have it that, after participating as a young man in one of the examinations, he refused to repeat the process because the confusion and undignified atmosphere repelled him; he remained a commoner to the end of his days. Because of his literary and artistic accomplishments, however, he earned the respect of his contemporaries. Perhaps it is reasonable to assume that his frequent trips and sojourns in various places in the lower Yangtze region were largely in response to calls for literary assistance, and that he supported himself in part by offering his talents to his official friends and wealthy acquaintances. One of his life-long friends, Ts'ao Hsüeh-ch'üan (*q.v.*), financed the construction of a building called Wan-yü-lou 宛羽樓 in 1634, to house Hsü's books, and late in 1642 composed a poem lamenting his death.

Hsü Po left a number of writings. The *Hsü-shih pi-ching* 徐氏筆精, a collection of notes in 8 *ch.*, was copied into the *Ssu-k'u* imperial library and later printed in the *Pi-lin-lang-kuan ts'ung-shu* 碧琳琅館叢書 (1908) and again in 1935 in the *Yü-yüan* 芋園 *ts'ung-shu*. Two others of his works, the *Jung-yin hsin-chien* 榕陰新檢, 8 *ch.*, classified biographical sketches of Fukien people, and the *Min-nan T'ang-ya* 閩南唐雅, 12 *ch.*, an anthology of Fukien poets of the T'ang period, received notices in the *Ssu-k'u* catalogue. His own collected literary works in 20 *chüan* bear the title *Ao-feng chi* 鼇峯集. As he was a connoisseur of the fruit, lichee or li-chih 荔枝 (his native province producing a high quality of this fruit), he wrote a supplement to the famous Sung work *Li-chih p'u* 譜 by Ts'ai Hsiang (1012–67), also from Fukien. In 1608, to celebrate the lichee season, Hsü Po initiated a series of gatherings in which everyone partook of the fruit and composed poetry in its appreciation. He named the events Red Cloud gatherings. The "Hung-yün she yüeh" 紅雲社約, which he sent out as a circular invitation, and his supplementary *Li-chih p'u* may be found in the *Hsü Shuo-fu* 續說郛 (1646). Hsü wrote a biography of the above-mentioned Ts'ai Hsiang, entitled *Ts'ai Tuan-ming pieh-chi* 端明別紀 (also known as *Ts'ai Chung-hsiang nien-p'u* 忠襄年譜), 10 *ch.*, printed *ca.* 1617. He likewise added a few notes to the *Min-chung hai-ts'o shu* 閩中海錯疏, a work on the sea food produced along the Fukien coast, written by T'u Pen-chün 屠本畯 (T. 田叔, H. 漢陂, d. 1622, *ae.* over 80 *sui*), an official in the salt administration in Fukien in the 1590s.

As a bibliophile, Hsü Po was well known in the last years of the Ming. In 1602, when he wrote the preface to the catalogue of his own library, he had a collection of some 53,000 *chüan*. He held that the happiest way of life is to read books at home, completely shutting out the world. "To acquire a rare book," he once wrote, "to learn an unusual character, to find a unique account, to read an exquisite line, each can make one leap with joy, give incomparably more pleasure than music to the ear or colorful silks to the eye." The original catalogue has been lost. Two of his admirers each made a collection of his bibliographical writings: Lin Chi (ECCP) in 1719 and Cheng Chieh 鄭杰 (T. 昌英) in 1798. In 1907 Miao Ch'üan-sun (BDRC) combined the two collections and re-edited them as *Ch'ung-pien hung-yü-lou t'i-pa* 重編紅雨樓題跋, 2 *ch.*, which was printed in 1910 and reprinted in 1925 in the *Ch'iao-fan-lou* 峭帆樓 *ts'ung-shu.*

Hsü Po's collection of books seems to have remained intact up to 1656, when his son, Hsü Yen-shou延壽 (T. 存永), left Fukien, but he did not take it with him. Many of the books were treasured by successive generations of collectors. Both Hsü Yen-shou and his son, Hsü Chung-chen 鍾震 (T. 器之), also attained some note as men of letters.

Bibliography

1/286/21a; 40/65/18b; 64/庚3/5a; 84/丁下/95a; 86/18/23b; TSCC (1885-88), XXIII: 105/93/9a, 108/96/14b, XXIV: 125/31/15b; SK(1930), 62/6b, 70/11a, 119/3a, 172/15b, 193/7a; Ch'ien Ch'ien-i (ECCP), *Lieh-ch'ao shih-chi* 丁 10/60a, 丁14/36a; *Fu-chien t'ung-chih* 通志 (1922), 文苑 6/33b, 34a; Kuo Po-ts'ang 郭柏蒼, *Ch'üan-Min Ming-shih chuan* 全閩明詩傳 (1889), 26/33b, 32/18b, 33/20b, 36/1a, 17a, 40/1a, 41/11a, 45/13b, 50/19a; Yeh Ch'ang-ch'ih (BDRC), *Ts'ang-shu chi-shih shih* (1958), 171; Ku Ching-hsing 顧景星, *Pai-mao-t'ang chi* 白茅堂集 (1887), 9/25b; *Yin-hsien chih* 鄞縣志 (1874), 37/21b.

Lienche Tu Fang

HSÜ P'u 徐溥 (T. 時用, H. 謙齋), September 1, 1428-October 15, 1499, who officiated for twelve years in the Grand Secretariat, was a native of I -hsing 宜興, situated a few miles west of Lake T'ai. Hsü was apparently from a well-to-do family, for it was known for its numerous charitable works. His grandfather, Hsü Chien 鑑 (T. 子明, 1371-1434), served as prefect of Ch'iung-chou 瓊州 -fu, Hainan Island, in the years 1430-34. Hsü P'u placed second in the *chin-shih* examination of 1454 and received an appointment as a compiler in the Hanlin Academy in the following year. In March, 1457, shortly after the *coup d'état* of Emperor Chu Ch'i-chen (*q. v.*), Hsü was assigned to the staff of the reinstated heir apparent, Chu Chien-shen (*q. v.*), and to the library of the supervisorate of imperial instruction. He took part in the final editing of the *Ta Ming i-t'ung-chih* (*see* Li Hsien), completed in May, 1461. In July, 1464, five months after Chu Chien-shen succeeded to the throne, Hsü was made an expositor. Next he was asked to clarify and summarize personnel dossiers of the military (貼黃). He left office in 1471 upon his father's death, but (after the mourning period) was assigned to be junior supervisor of instruction and concurrently a senior expositor. In the following spring (April, 1474), he and Ch'iu Chün (*q. v.*) were given the responsibility of conducting the metropolitan examination. Later, because of the death of his mother in 1477, he returned home. When he went back to Peking (1480), he was promoted to the directorship of the Court of Imperial Sacrifices and became concurrently chancellor of the Hanlin Academy. After conducting the metropolitan examinations a second time (1481), he received an appointment as senior vice minister of Rites. In 1484 he and Keng Yü (*see* Keng Chiu-ch'ou), then senior vice minister of Personnel, were sent to Shansi and Shensi to make sacrifices to the gods of mountains and rivers, and to pray for rains because of severe drought in the region. It is said that it was his sincerity which induced the rain to fall. In October, 1486, he was transferred to the ministry of Personnel as senior vice minister, and here he began to discharge his duties according to his own lights. He seldom demoted an official and often overlooked or even concealed small mistakes of certain individuals, as he believed it difficult to produce men of talent, and such people should not be shelved for minor faults. Until this time a great part of his official career had passed without significant achievements possibly because he had fallen ill or taken more leaves than usual, and possibly also, as one of his biographers has suggested, because he did not get along with the men in power.

When Emperor Chu Yu-t'ang (*q. v.*) ascended the throne (near the close of 1487), Hsü was immediately promoted to be titular minister of Rites and a grand secretary, along with Liu Chien (*q. v.*). In 1490, for the third time, he conducted the metropolitan examinations. In 1492, on the retirement of Liu Chi (*see* Chu Yu-t'ang), he became senior grand secretary, and two years later titular minister of Personnel. During the twelve years he spent in high office, he had a hand in a number of responsible tasks. One was his participation in the compilation of both the *Hsien-tsung shih-lu* and the first edition of the collected institutes of the empire, *Ta Ming hui-tien* 大明會典. The *shih-lu*, commissioned in 1488, was completed in the autumn of 1491. As a reward Hsü P'u was granted the titles of grand guardian of the heir apparent and minister of Revenue. The *shih-lu* itself, however, did not receive an altogether favorable reception. Wang Ao 王鏊 (*q. v.*) criticized it for its lack of objectivity as compared with the historical writing of the past. What it amounted to, Wang asserted, was nothing more than a conglomeration of memorials and official documents presented by various departments. Only officials above the third rank were accorded short biographies containing information mostly on birthplaces, promotions, ranks, and time of death. If criticism or praise were given,

the editors failed to be impartial. Hsü's assignment to compile the *Ta Ming hui-tien* came in April, 1497, with himself as editor, and Liu Chien, Li Tung-yang (*q. v.*), *et al*, as his associates; it was not completed until January 8, 1503 (after his death). This work (as T'an Ch'ien [*q.v.*] remarks in his *Kuo-ch'üeh*) has no entry dealing with the institution of eunuchs, possibly even the most eminent of the bureaucracy holding them in dread. The *hui-tien* was revised and supplemented subsequently, and finally printed in 1511. A palace edition in 180 *chüan* still exists. It was also included in the *Ssu-k'u ch'üan-shu*. The Korean royal house protested (1518) the section on Korea because of its failure to treat the Yi 李 genealogy properly, and asked that it be modified, but the court did not comply with this request until the next up-dated edition of 1587.

Fellow officials and contemporaries remembered Hsü, however, not for his literary achievements, but for a number of decisions he made while in high office and for certain deeds he performed for his clan. In conducting government affairs he adhered to a laissez-faire policy, for he believed that rules and regulations established by the early emperors were the results of their consideration for the masses. The problem was how to follow their instructions, not to create new ones. He was not totally inflexible, however. Because of his help, for example, the minister of Revenue, Yeh Ch'i 葉淇 (T. 本清, 1426-September 15, 1501, cs 1454), was able to establish a new salt regulation which changed the nature and organization of the trade, and which the salt merchants found to be of benefit to them. Previously they had been obliged to transport their "contributed" grain to frontier posts along the Great Wall where they exchanged it for certificates allowing them to obtain salt in the main salt-producing areas. With the passage of the new rule, the merchants could now purchase salt directly with silver, though paying a higher price. As a result of this new regulation, the government income was measurably increased, but the ruling also caused some controversy.

Although Hsü was responsible for no other far-reaching regulations, he did his best to guide the emperor. Upon his advice early in 1496, for example, the emperor gave up the idea of requiring the grand secretaries to compose san-ch'ing yüeh-chang 三清樂章, Taoist prayers used in sacrifices. After 1495 the emperor began to lose interest in government affairs, and became more and more involved in Taoist practices because of the influence of the eunuch Li Kuang (q. v.). Hsü (1497) took the lead in condemning them. The united voice of the grand secretaries impressed the emperor to such a degree that he granted them a special audience, the only one held during Hsü's service in the Grand Secretariat. The occasion was one at which the emperor drew up edicts with their aid, but did not touch on either Taoist practices or Li Kuang. Finally, because of the insistence of Hsü P'u and other grand secretaries, he consented to the release of the censors imprisoned because they had offended the emperor by speaking up on behalf of the eunuch Ho Ting (q. v.).

If Hsü appeared kindhearted to his colleagues, he was appreciated even more by his friends and the people of I-hsing. He lived a simple life, and was generous in helping old acquaintances in financial straits. At his request, Wu Yu-yün 吳友雲, from his neighborhood, a forgotten official of the Hung-wu period, was enshrined. He also collected and put into print poems of well-known officials of his region in a book entitled Chung-chieh lu 忠節錄. From the beginning of his career he frequently assisted the poor among his clansmen. In 1495 he purchased about 800 mou of fertile land to be established as an i-chuang (benevolent estate) to support the clan, the income from which would pay for sacrifices in the ancestral shrine, expenses of the clan school, and the cost of marriages and funerals. For this act of charity, the emperor granted exemption from corvée service to those working on the estate.

After he reached the age of seventy sui (1497), he requested permission to retire, but the emperor refused. In September of the following year he fell ill; this time the emperor relented and sent him off with presents of sheep, wine, rice, and vegetables, as well as gifts of robes, gold, and notes. One grandson received a post as drafter in the central drafting office. Following his death, aged seventy-one, Hsü P'u was honored with the posthumous title Wen-ching 文靖. He left his collected writings entitled Ch'ien-chai wen-lu 謙齋文錄, 4 ch.; included in chüan 1 are nineteen memorials which he submitted to the throne during his career. An original edition survives, as do the editions of 1876 and 1907.

Bibliography

1/181/1a; 5/14/20a; 40/21/9a; MSL (1964), Hsiao-tsung, ch. 5–154; KC (1958), 2119, 2347, 2741, 2793; TSCC (1885–88), XI: 24/64/15b, XIV: 59/5/9b; SK (1930), 81/4b, 170/11a; I-hsing-hsien chiu chih 舊志 (1882), 7/10a, 21b, 8/45a, 9/76b, 10/7a, 15a, 72b, 129b; Kwangtung t'ung-chih (1934), 4404; Hsü Chao 徐照, Ming-tai ta-cheng-chih chia: Hsü P'u nien-p'u 明代大政治家徐溥年譜, Taiwan, 1963; Hsü wen-hsien t'ung-k'ao, 20/2963; Wang Ao, Wang-wen-k'o-kung chi, 15/9b; Wang Ch'ung-wu 王崇武, "Ming-tai te shang-t'un chih-tu," 明代的商屯制度, Yü-kung pan-yüeh k'an 禹貢半月刊, 5: 12 (1936), 1; Naikaku Bunko Catalogue, 347; Wolfgang Franke, Sources, 1. 1. 6, 5. 4. 8, 6. 1. 2; L. Carrington Goodrich, "Korean interference with Chinese Historical Records," JNCBRAS, 68 (1936), 28.

Angela Hsi

HSÜ Shih-hsing, *see* **SHEN Shih-hsing**

HSÜ Shou-hui 徐壽輝 (original name Chen-i 眞一), died June 17, 1360, was a native of Lo-t'ien 羅田, Hukuang. Originally an itinerant peddler of cloth, he became founding emperor of the state of T'ien-wan 天完, reigning from October/ November, 1351, under the title Chih-p'ing 治平, until he was assassinated by Ch'en Yu-liang (*q. v.*).

In September, 1351, Maitreya-worship-ing disciples of the monk P'eng Ying-yü 彭瑩玉 (a native of Yüan-chou 袁州, Kiangsi) chose Hsü Shou-hui to lead them in revolt at Ch'i-shui 蘄水, Hukuang. Under another leader, Chou Tzu-wang 周子旺, the same sect had risen in 1338 in Kiangsi and had suffered defeat by local govern-ment troops. P'eng fled to the upper Huai region and his disciples, apparently un-discouraged by this failure of the prophe-sied arrival of their messiah and universal ruler, were now ready once again to pre-pare for his coming by attempting the overthrow of the imperial government. A Ma-ch'eng 麻城 (Hukuang) blacksmith, Tsou P'u-sheng 鄒普勝, had become a local leader of the sect. Tsou made the acquaintance of Hsü Shou-hui when he came to him to have some tools made. They then joined with others of the sect in preparing a rebellion. Hsü was made their chief, at least nominally, because his great size and powerful physique seemed auspicious, and because, it is said, he seemed to be aglow while bathing in a salt water pond. Wearing red headbands, like the doctrinally similar White Lotus sect of Han Shan-t'ung (*see* Han Lin-er), Hsü's forces took Ch'i-shui and the nearby Huang-chou in October, and in the following month Hsü was installed as emperor at Ch'i-shui, which served him as his capital until February, 1356, when he moved to Han-yang 漢陽.

The new state did not absorb P'eng Ying-yü's entire sect, nor, in any signifi-cant way, did he control it. Despite the fact that the messianic doctrine continued, for a time, to be a factor in Hsü's strategy of conquest, the name of P'eng Ying-yü does not appear in relation to the state after its founding. It is not sur-prising, therefore, that other self-styled followers of P'eng Ying-yü should have

initiated rebellions quite independently. Chao P'u-sheng 趙普勝 or "Two-Sword Chao" 雙刀趙, for example, rebelled as a member of the sect in 1352 at Han-shan 含山, near Nanking. Late in 1354 or in early 1355, this group was defeated by Yüan forces and retired westward to their ships on Lake Ch'ao 巢湖. They sub-sequently joined with Chu Yüan-chang, who was about to cross to the south bank of the Yangtze. Chao and some of his followers promptly defected to Hsü Shou-hui, but enough of the Ch'ao Lake fleet remained with Chu to effect the crossing (*see* Liao Yung-an).

T'ien-wan grew to be an immense but weakly organized state. It followed the teachings of the Maitreya sect and maintained a policy of avoiding wanton killing and raping, which contrasted sharp-ly with the ways of soldiers under the government commanders and in most of the other rebel camps. But it annexed towns and cities faster than effective local governments could be established in them. A little more than a year after the state's founding, the area defined by its conquered cities reached from west of Tung-t'ing Lake to Hangchow, which was briefly occupied in August, 1352. By the end of 1355 Szechwan as far west as Chengtu had been incorporated. Until 1357 the principal opposition came from Yüan forces. After a year of almost uninter-rupted reverses, the Yüan succeeded during 1353 in recovering about as many cities as its armies lost but their resistance weakened again thereafter and, by 1360, they appear to have been virtually elimi-nated from T'ien-wan territory. The Yüan officials, whether Mongol or Chinese, and some Chinese loyalist commoners, de-fended their cities with great courage, but were largely dependent on local Chinese militia and, city by city, they were overwhelmed. Several sieges ended only when the inhabitants had been reduced to starvation. A brief but spectacular reversal occurred at the end of 1353, when Yüan forces raided the T'ien-wan capital at Ch'i-shui, put Hsü Shou-hui to flight, and captured more than four hundred of his officials. The obduracy of the Yüan officials in the face of the rebellion made it impossible for T'ien-wan to meet its need for local governments merely by compelling the officials to change sides. Most of them are alleged to have died fighting, or in the course of physical torture (rather than submit to their captors), or to have fled to safety. Attempts by T'ien-wan to register conquered populations, as at Hangchow in 1352, contributed nothing to the economic viability of the state when local administration was inadequate and the cities often could not be held against counterattacks. Chu Yüan-chang's new state of Wu replaced the Yüan as Hsü's chief enemy, blocking its expansion northeastward down the Yangtze. Beginning in 1357, fighting between these rivals became increasingly heavy along their common boundary southeast of Nanking.

Hsü Shou-hui was little more than a figurehead during his imperial reign. For the first six years, the dominant figure was that of the naval commander, Ni Wen-chün 倪文俊, a former fisherman of Mien-yang 沔陽 (Hukuang). Ni distinguished himself in the first months of the rebellion and became premier councilor in the new state. His younger brother, Ni Wen-yü 郁, served with him and was granted the title prince of Changsha 長沙王. Ni Wen-chün and his water-borne forces played the major role in the capture of cities along the Yangtze and its tributaries. In February, 1356, Ni made Han-yang the new capital of T'ien-wan and brought Hsü to that city. It is said that in August, 1357, Ni in his thrust for power made an unsuccessful attempt on Hsü Shou-hui's life. Ch'en Yu-liang, who was Ni's subordinate, then pursued his fugitive chief to Huang-chou 黃州 and executed him. Ni's death resulted in the virtual secession of Szechwan (see Ming Yü-chen). Ch'en now emerged as the most powerful figure in the government, though contenting himself

for a time with the title of councilor. A rival appeared, however, in the person of his lieutenant, Chao P'u-sheng. While Ch'en extended his military conquests southwards in Kiangsi, Chao was heavily engaged with the forces of Chu Yüan-chang along the Yangtze. Chu perceived that the round of assassinations within T'ien-wan had engendered an atmosphere of mutual distrust among its officers. He succeeded in communicating with a brilliant adviser of Chao P'u-sheng, bringing him under suspicion, and making it necessary for him to desert. Chu then enlisted him as an agent serving in Ch'en's entourage, where he played on Ch'en's envy and mistrust of Chao. On April 27, 1359, Ch'en paid a visit to Chao's headquarters at Anking. Chao prepared a banquet and unsuspectingly went on board Ch'en's ship to pay his respects. Ch'en then murdered him and incorporated his victim's forces into his own command. Encouraged by this successful coup, Ch'en established his capital at Chiang-chou 江州 (modern Kiukiang) and assumed the title prince of Han. Contrary to Ch'en's expressed wishes, Hsü now insisted upon leaving Han-yang to make Chiang-chou his imperial seat. Late in 1359 Ch'en prepared for Hsü's arrival by setting an ambush outside the city gates; he slaughtered Hsü's retainers and made him prisoner. On June 17, 1360, following closely upon a major victory over Chu Yüan-chang at T'ai-p'ing, Ch'en arranged for Hsü to be bludgeoned to death by hired assassins.

Bibliography

1/123/1a; 61/89/15a; MSL (1962), T'ai-tsu, 8/5a, ch. 99-102; Ch'ien Ch'ien-i (ECCP), Kuo-ch'u ch'ün-hsiung shih-lüeh 國初群雄事略, ch. 3; Yüan-shih, ch. 42-45, 195; Wu Han 吳晗, Chu Yüan-chang chuan 朱元璋傳.

Romeyn Taylor

HSÜ Ta 徐達 (T. 天德), 1332-April 7, 1385, a native of Hao-chou 濠州 (Anhwei), ranked first among the military command-

ers in the founding of the dynasty, was
awarded the dukedom of Wei 魏國公, and
is often referred to by his posthumous
title as the prince of Chung-shan 中山王.
He was only twenty-one years of age
when he joined Chu Yüan-chang in 1353,
as sub-commander under Kuo Tzu-hsing
(*q.v.*). Hsü solidified his relationship
with Chu by personally taking his place
when he was captured by hostile forces.
When Chu led his followers south across
the Yangtze in July, 1355, Hsü was in
the vanguard. After the conquest of
Nanking (April, 1356), he was charged
with securing the northeastern flank by
taking the city of Chinkiang. This accomplished, he received the title of Huai-
hsing 淮興翼統軍元帥 (wing commander).
Success at Chinkiang brought Hsü into
conflict with Chang Shih-ch'eng (*q.v.*),
who controlled the lower Yangtze region.
It required a year of fighting to take
Ch'ang-chou 常州, the next city to the
east. Hsü was reprimanded and his subordinates demoted at one point for harshness
to those who had recently surrendered.
Ch'ang-chou fell in the spring of 1357
and Hsü moved up to the position of
assistant military commissioner. In the
following year he was entrusted with the
defense of Nanking while Chu Yüan-
chang was in the field.

In 1359 a series of campaigns were undertaken up the Yangtze to the southwest
against Ch'en Yu-liang (*q.v.*). After recapturing Ch'ih池-chou, Hsü Ta was promoted
to full general and vice commissioner-
in-chief of the Chiang-nan military commission. Hsü pursued Ch'en past Wuchang.
In January, 1361, Hsü was named to the
Secretariat. Two years later (March, 1363),
he joined the personal command of Chu
Yüan-chang in the recovery of An-feng 安
豐 from Chang Shih-ch'eng. Some months
afterwards came the showdown with
Ch'en Yu-liang in a great naval battle on
Poyang Lake. Having scored an initial victory, Hsü was sent back to guard Nanking
against possible attack by Chang Shih-
ch'eng, while Chu himself administered

the final coup to Ch'en Yu-liang.

By 1364, when Chu Yüan-chang took
the title prince of Wu, Hsü Ta had risen
to the second highest office in his entourage—that of left chief councillor just
below Li Shan-ch'ang (*q.v.*). The next
two and one half years were largely
taken up with the pacification of areas
north of the Yangtze. Lu 廬-chou was
occupied early in the first year. By the
second half of 1365 Hsü and his subordinate, Ch'ang Yü-ch'un (*q.v.*), moved into
the Huai River region, taking key points
like T'ai 泰-chou and Kao-yu 高郵.
In mid-1366 the generals assembled in
Nanking for the final campaign against
Chang Shih-ch'eng. Hsü Ta was made
commander and, assisted by Ch'ang Yü-
ch'un, he led a naval force rated at two
hundred thousand men against Hu 湖
-chou. Within just over a year he besieged
Chang Shih-ch'eng at P'ing-chiang 平江,
captured him, and sent him to Nanking.
When the army returned, Hsü Ta received
as his reward (in October) the title of
duke of Hsin-kuo 信國公. A month earlier
(September, 1367), Chu had selected Hsü
to lead the expedition to the north and
designated him commanding general of the
Mongol suppression campaign. The army
of some two hundred fifty thousand foot
and horse was to clear the northern plain
of Yüan resistance. As was usually the
case in these early years, the deputy commander was Ch'ang Yü-ch'un. The *Ming-
shih* gives considerable attention to contrasting these two generals. Typically, in
the discussion of strategy for the northern
expedition, it is Ch'ang Yü-ch'un who is
portrayed as advocating a direct attack
on the Yüan capital. Chu Yüan-chang
preferred a more cautious policy of first
securing Shantung, Honan, and the old
heartland beyond T'ung-kuan 潼關 so that
the capital would be isolated and fall
without fighting. Hsü Ta led the great
army north in the last months of 1367.
Other forces were sent to the south. This
was the culmination of Chu Yüan-chang's
conquest of China. A few months later,

on January 20, 1368, Chu took the throne as the first emperor of the new Ming dynasty. Hsü was named right chief councillor and junior tutor to the heir apparent. In the meantime the army pushed north to Tsinan in Shantung and, when resistance was encountered there, turned west and pushed across the plain to T'ung-kuan and on into the Wei valley. In the process of this sweep he liberated the old Sung capital at Kaifeng. In the late spring of 1368 the emperor traveled north to Kaifeng. He tentatively designated the city his northern capital 北京, and declared his intention to divide his time every year between his residence in Kaifeng and another in Nanking. This plan was never realized, but it reveals the importance of Sung precedents in the early stages of the Ming founding. When he reached Kaifeng, the emperor called Hsü Ta in from the field to plan the final campaign against Ta-tu (Peking). It was decided to drive north through Shantung, allowing the Mongol remnants to withdraw north of the Great Wall. Hsü Ta predicted that Kökö Temür (*q.v.*) would be forced to flee to the west. The emperor, conscious of his need to win support in an area which had not known Chinese rule for more than two hundred years, stressed the importance of not oppressing the populace.

In the summer of 1368 the Ming army under Hsü Ta's command crossed the Yellow River and pushed northeastward to Lin-ch'ing 臨清 (in Shantung) on the Grand Canal, and then north to T'ung 通-chou. The last stiff opposition was surmounted just south of T'ung-chou at Ho-hsi-wu 河西務. As the Ming armies approached Ta-tu, the Yüan ruler fled north with his court. The city surrendered without a fight. It was then in highly straitened circumstances. Because of the constant fighting in north China and the operations of pirates on the coast, the shipment of grain from the Yangtze valley had begun to fall off seriously after 1341. By 1359 rice deliveries dropped to almost nothing. Yeh Tzu-ch'i 葉子奇 (T. 世傑, H. 靜齋, (d. 1385?) reports in his *Ts'ao-mu-tzu* 草木子 that famine in the city was so severe in the last years that there were cases of cannibalism and that the Yüan could not control its soldiers. The people may even have welcomed the take-over. Hsü Ta's occupation of the Mongol capital is said to have been a peaceful and orderly process. He executed a number of Yüan commanders who refused to submit, but no one else was killed. The libraries and treasuries were sealed and the eunuchs were left to care for the palace women. One thousand men guarded the imperial precincts. He strictly prohibited soldiers from violence and looting, and allowed market activities to resume. Once Ta-tu was secure the emperor renamed the city Peiping. Hsü Ta undertook the reconstruction of the northern wall, moving it five *li* to the south, thus destroying the original symmetry of the Yüan city. The two gates in the north were named An-ting 安定 and Te-sheng 德勝 perhaps to signify that the Ming had pacified the area and gained a virtuous victory.

In the autumn of this year Hsü and Ch'ang Yü-ch'un pushed west into Shansi where they encountered the principal Yüan remnants under Kökö Temür. Hsü's plan was to lure the enemy commander toward Peiping and then strike at his base at Taiyuan, forcing him to turn back and fight in the open. A night attack on the Yüan camp led by Hsü was successful. Kökö escaped with a handful of followers, but his army suffered defeat. The Ming forces took Taiyuan and Tatung, and soon completed pacification of Shansi. In the spring of 1369 Hsü assembled his commanders at Feng-hsiang 鳳翔 to plan the campaign in Shensi and Kansu. Armies pushing out to the northwest and north cleared much of the area of Yüan resistance.

Hsü's preeminent position among the Ming generals was formally confirmed in the summer of 1369 with the erection of a temple of meritorious ministers (*see* Teng Yü). The first position was accorded Hsü, the second Ch'ang Yü-ch'un, and the third Li Wen-chung (*q.v.*). In October the emperor ordered Hsü Ta to return to Nanking. Three months later (January, 1370), Hsü received as reward for the conquest of the north five hundred ounces of silver and fifty rolls of silk. A few weeks later Hsü was again designated commander for the suppression of the Mongol forces, this time with Li Wen-chung as his second in command.

The campaign of 1370 was once again aimed at Kökö Temür, who still threatened the northwest. Hsü Ta led an army north through Shensi and engaged Kökö in battle. Although the Ming forces prevailed, he escaped. Great numbers of prisoners and animals were taken. One of the Ming commanders, Hu Te-chi, the adopted son of Hu Ta-hai (*q.v.*), was cowardly in battle and had to be sent back to Nanking in custody. A second series of battles took place west of Sian at Hsing-yüan 興元. Late in the year the emperor ordered Hsü Ta and Li Wen-chung back to the capital, and came out to greet them on their arrival. This time, when awards were given out, Li Wen-chung was named first in merit and Hsü Ta fourth behind Li Wen-chung, Teng Yü, and Li Shan-ch'ang (*q.v.*). Six titles of dukedom 國公 were conferred, and again Hsü Ta was in second position behind Li Shan-ch'ang. Hsü received the hereditary title duke of Wei-kuo with a stipend of five thousand piculs. In the following weeks and months the emperor took a number of steps to secure the positions of his closest supporters. He gave tracts of land at Lin-hao 臨濠 to the dukes, marquises, and high officials. This land was probably for the purpose of establishing family tombs near there. The next month he granted Hsü and other nobles a hundred or a hundred fifty grave-keeping households.

The year 1371 marked a new stage in Hsü Ta's career. In January he was ordered back to Peiping to repair walls and train troops. This was to become a regular pattern for the remainder of his life. He was stationed at Peiping, where he managed the defense of the northern border. Every winter the emperor ordered him to return to Nanking for a brief period. In 1371 Hsü concentrated on settling the population around Peiping and strengthening defenses. Early in the following year, with a force of one hundred fifty thousand men, Hsü was sent to deal with Kökö. He led the central column, while Li Wen-chung commanded the eastern, and Feng Sheng (*q.v.*) the western. In May Hsü's force suffered a defeat at the hands of Kökö, and tens of thousands of soldiers lost their lives. Li Wen-chung also did poorly. Only Feng Sheng was victorious on the battlefield. but he was charged with misappropriation of livestock and so went unrewarded. This was the only major defeat in Hsü Ta's career, and the emperor overlooked it in consideration of his remarkable record. The army was pulled back to Peiping and the commanders returned to Nanking. In the spring of 1373 Hsü was again sent north as Mongol suppression commander against Kökö Temür. Hsü's army marched to Peiping and then moved into Shansi. Kökö was beyond the Wall north of Tatung, but the emperor now urged caution in dealing with him. Hsü Ta returned to Nanking again in 1375.

In February, 1376, Hsü's eldest daughter married the emperor's fourth son, Chu Ti (*q.v.*), the prince of Yen whose fief was at Peiping, normally the base of Hsü's operations. Chu Yüan-chang was devoting a great deal of attention to his sons at this point. He drew up regulations to govern the management of their fiefs and revenues, and he sent them to Feng-yang 鳳陽 for training. He also ordered Li Wen-chung in this year to restore the old Yüan palaces at Peiping for the prince's use. After the prince took up residence there in 1380, he came under Hsü Ta's influence for a number of years. Then twenty years of age, Chu Ti got his first military experience patrolling the border under the general's direction. This doubtless had an affect on him, for in later years, when he became emperor, he marshaled all the resources of his state to lead campaigns personally into the northern deserts.

Hsü Ta led a large force north in 1381 to deal with the threat of Nair-buqa (*see* Chu Ti). His deputy commanders were T'ang Ho and Fu Yu-te (*qq. v.*). It was customary in these years for the emperor to send long instructions to his commanders advising them on how to proceed. He urged caution and above all the collection of intelligence on the enemy's capability prior to engaging him in combat. Increasingly the Ming policy became one of garrisoning strong defensive points. By 1385 Hsü Ta was able to report to the emperor that Peiping had seventeen guard units with more than a hundred five thousand men.

Although a clever and resourceful strategist, Hsü was not a man of polish. He was a field general who shared the lot of his men and instilled respect and loyalty in his subordinates. Uneducated and inarticulate, he played little role in court affairs. He held the title of right chief councillor from 1368 to 1371. The function of this office was probably to clarify his standing with the emperor. He stood before all the other generals, but second to Li Shan-ch'ang who held the principal administrative post. There is little evidence to indicate that Hsü ever served as an administrator or even that he was literate. His accomplishments were all military, although he was a close confidant of the founder. By virtue of shared origins and long association Hsü developed a unique relationship with Chu Yüan-chang. The founding emperor frequently referred to the fact that they had both been commoners from the same community. Even after the founding they continued to eat and drink together as friends. This relationship put Hsü Ta at a disadvantage since he was

in constant danger of overstepping his position, but the emperor continued to shower him with favors. He ordered built for Hsü, in front of the old palace, a new home with an archway bearing the name Ta-kung fang 大功坊 (Great merit residence), and publicly praised him for his diligence, honesty, and freedom from vices and personal ambition. The fact that he was repeatedly entrusted with the command of military forces in the north is testimony to his political reliability. He was one of a very small number of generals who participated in the founding of the empire and still escaped the purges and executions of the Hung-wu period.

In 1384, while still residing in Peiping, Hsü Ta became ill. Chu Yüan-chang sent Hsü's eldest son Hsü Hui-tsu 輝 祖 (1368–1407), north to comfort him, and later ordered the general to return to Nanking. Even with the best medical attention available in the capital, Hsü's condition continued to worsen and in the following spring he died at the age of fifty-three. Despite the existence of popular stories to the effect that the emperor poisoned him, it appears that the former was grieved at the loss of his closest comrade. Court business was suspended. A tomb site was granted on the north side of Mt. Chung 鍾山. The emperor himself composed the text of the memorial spirit path inscription, and granted him the posthumous title of prince of Chung-shan and the name Wu-ning 武寧. His ancestors in the preceding three generations were also raised to the level of prince.

Hsü Ta's family was intimately connected with the Ming imperial house. Three of the general's daughters were married to sons of the founder. His eldest daughter, consort of the prince of Yen and later Empress Hsü (*q. v.*), was a strong-willed and colorful person with some of her father's spirit. Two other daughters were consorts of the prince of Tai, Chu Kuei (*see* Chu Yüan-chang), and the prince of An, Chu Ying (*see* Empress Hsü).

Hsü Ta had four sons: Hsü Hui-tsu, Hsü T'ien-fu 添福, Hsü Ying-hsü 膺緒, Hsü Tseng-shou 增壽. [Editors' note: There is some confusion in the records as to their order of birth. This is the one followed by the editors of the *Ming-shih* in the biography of Hsü Ta. But the tables 表 show Hsü Tseng-shou as the second son 次子, while Wang Shih-chen (*q. v.*) makes him the third.] Hsü T'ien-fu died young and Hsü Ying-hsü served as a minor military officer. The eldest and the youngest sons became involved in the prince of Yen's usurpation of the throne.

Late in 1389 Hsü Hui-tsu succeeded to his father's title as duke of Wei. His original name, Yün-kung 允恭, was changed (after 1392) to avoid conflict with Chu Yün-wen (*q. v.*) when the latter was named imperial grandson. An able and vigorous man, Hsü Hui-tsu distinguished himself during his father's lifetime by managing the left chief military commission. Continuing an active military career for the remainder of the Hung-wu period, he was granted the title of grand tutor to the heir apparent early in the Chien-wen reign (September, 1398). At the time of the prince of Yen's revolt he remained loyal to Chu Yün-wen. When the prince's son, Chu Kao-hsü (*q. v.*), fled Nanking just prior to the outbreak of hostilities, Hsü Hui-tsu is said to have tried to stop him despite the fact that the prince was his nephew. Hsü Hui-tsu later led troops in Shantung against the Yen forces and scored a victory at Mt. Ch'i-mei 齊眉山 (in Anhwei) after which he was ordered back to Nanking. When the prince of Yen took the capital, Hsü refused to submit. In consideration of Hsü Ta's part in the founding, the new emperor spared the son's life but removed his title and put him under house arrest. He died a few years later. His fidelity to Chu Yün-wen was not recognized until the Wan-li period when a temple was erected at Nanking to honor loyal officials of the Chien-wen period (*see* T'u Shu-fang). Hsü Hui-tsu was ranked at the head of the list and later received a promotion to grand tutor and the canonized name of Chung-chen 忠貞. Immediately after Hsü Hui-tsu's death, his eldest son, Hsü Ch'in 欽, succeeded to the title of duke of Wei. He also offended the Yung-lo emperor and was reduced to commoner status in 1421. He was reinstated in 1424, but he died late that year. From the middle of the 15th century to the end of the dynasty successive holders of the title of duke of Wei were appointed grand commandant at Nanking with concurrent command of the middle chief military commission.

The career of Hsü Ta's youngest son, Hsü Tseng-shou, was in marked contrast to that of the eldest. This one betrayed the Chien-wen emperor and abetted the cause of the prince of Yen by relaying information about conditions in Nanking. When his disloyalty became known the emperor put him to the sword in the palace. Following Chu Ti's enthronement, Hsü Tseng-shou was granted a posthumous title, marquis of Wu-yang 武陽侯, and given the name Chung-min 忠愍. His posthumous rank was soon raised to a hereditary status as duke of Ting-kuo 定國公 with an annual stipend of twenty-five hundred piculs and a residence in Peiping. His son, Hsü Ching-ch'ang 景昌, was named to succeed him (July, 1404). His descendants successively inherited this title and pursued military careers to the end of the dynasty. Thus of all the meritorious officials who participated in the Ming founding, only Hsü Ta produced two ducal lines—the dukedom of Wei and the dukedom of Ting. This double honor was made possible by divided loyalties at the time of Chu Ti's revolt against his nephew.

Bibliography

1/105/2a, 106/20b, 125/1a; 5/5/1a, 16b; 63/3/1a; KC (1958), 651; MSL (1962), T'ai-tsu, ch. 3–171; Wang Shih-chen, *Yen-chou shan-jen hsü kao*, 69/1a, 80/1a; Hsü Tao-lin 徐道鄰, "Sung Lien yü Hsü Ta chih ssu" 宋濂與徐達之死 in

Tung-fang tsa-chih 東方雜誌 I: 4 (October, 1967), 56; T'an Hui-sheng 譚慧生, *Yüan Ming wei-jen chuan-chi* 元明偉人傳記, Vol. II (Taipei, 1965), 98.

Edward L. Farmer

HSÜ Tsan 許讚 (T. 廷美, H. 板皐), July 28, 1473–August 28, 1548, the third son of Hsü Chin (*q.v.*) and the lady Kao, served from 1529 to 1544 in high ministerial posts, concluding his career as Grand Secretary at the end of 1545. He qualified for the *chü-jen* in the same year (1495) as his elder brother Hsü Kao (*q. v.*), but succeeded in graduating as *chin-shih* in 1496, three years ahead of him. His initial appointment was as prefectural judge of Ta-ming 大名, Pei-Chihli, in which office he received high praise. After a year's leave due to illness (1506), he became an investigating censor, but was obliged to transfer, because of his father's appointment as minister of Personnel (November), to be a compiler in the Hanlin Academy. This must have been a proud moment for the father—to have reached the rank of minister and have two sons in the Academy. But it was quickly soured by the eunuch Liu Chin (*q.v.*), who crossed him at every turn and forced the dismissal of all three. Hsü Tsan's next appointment (1509) was the magistracy of Lin-tzu 臨淄, Shantung. In 1510, on the death of his father, he had to retire; about 1513 he was transferred to Chekiang as assistant surveillance commissioner, and in 1518 he became vice-commissioner in control of the sea coast. During the following years he occupied a series of provincial posts: educational administrator in Shansi (1519), administration vice-commissioner and surveillance commissioner in Szechwan (1521), right (1524), then left (1525) administration commissioner in Chekiang. At this point (1527) the emperor summoned him to be (in turn) director of the Court of Imperial Entertainments, vice minister of Justice, and from October, 1529, to October, 1531, minister of Justice. There followed his appointment as minister of Revenue about the same time that his brother was holding a similar post in Nanking. In October, 1534, he was obliged to leave to mourn his mother's loss.

Ordered back in April, 1536, to become minister of Personnel, Hsü did not appear at court until the end of January, 1537, probably to observe the full period of mourning. For twelve years he held this high office. Yen Sung (*q. v.*), who wielded great power at this time, trusted Hsü, who probably was willing to compromise to hold his post. The director of a bureau in the Personnel ministry, Wang Yü-ling 王與齡 (T. 受甫, H. 泿泉, 1508-64, cs 1529), protested (July, 1543) that Hsü should try to effect Yen's ousting, and he actually joined with Wang in a memorial to this effect. The emperor, however, would make no move, as he leaned heavily on Yen; Wang, as a consequence, lost his post, and Hsü was berated for his part in the proposal. After this Hsü was more cautious than before, and may even have been tempted with bribes. Hsü's final assignment to the Grand Secretariat came on September 27, 1544. He requested retirement after fourteen months in office, pleading ill health. The emperor accused him of dissembling, and dismissed him summarily, depriving him of his rank and titles. He died three years later. Four years after his death, his second son, Hsü Yü 儫, reported his passing to the emperor. Whereupon the latter, regretting his former action, restored all of Hsü Tsan's honors, gave him the name Wen-chien 文簡, and provided for an appropriate funeral.

It is said that at his native place Hsü repaired the temple of Confucius, and built several altars to the hills and streams. He was something of a poet and left a number of writings, best known of which is a collection entitled *Sung-kao chi* 松皐集, 26 *ch*. The Naikaku Bunko has a copy of the original edition (1543) in 24 *chüan*. His wife, née Li 李 (1474-

1545), bore him two sons: one died early; the second Hsü Yü, through the yin privilege, became eventually a vice director of a bureau in the ministry of Rites, then a drafter in the central drafting office.

Bibliography

1/186/15a; 5/16/16a; 16/13/25a, 56/58a; 40/27 下/1a; 84/ 丙 /1a; MSL (1965), Shih-tsung, ch. 105-67, 195-305, p. 6175; KC (1958), 3526, 3721; *Shan-chou chih-li-chou chih* (1892), 7/17a, 12/37a, 14/21a; *Ta-ming-fu chih* (1853), 13/119b; *Honan t'ung-chih* (1735), 60/71a; *Chi-fu t'ung-chih* (1934), 6859; *Shantung t'ung-chih* (1934), 2377; *Chekiang t'ung-chih* (1934), 2091, 2093, 2635; TSCC (1885-88), XIV: 409/3/5a; Naikaku Bunko *Catalogue*, 351; Ch'en Tzu-lung (ECCP), *Ming ching-shih wen-pien*, ch. 71.

L. Carrington Goodrich and Lee Hwa-chou

HSÜ Wei 徐渭 (T. 文長, H. 天池, 田水月, 青藤, 山陰布衣, etc.), March, 12, 1521–1593, essayist, poet, dramatist, painter, and calligrapher, was a native of Shan-yin 山陰 in the prefecture of Shao-hsing, Chekiang. His father, Hsü Ts'ung 鎗 (cj. 1488, d. 1521), listed in the military registry of Kweichow, who had served as magistrate of various places in Yunnan and as vice-prefect of K'uei-chou 夔州, Szechwan, during the Cheng-te period, was forced to retire because of illness, and returned home. By his first wife, née T'ung 童, Hsü Ts'ung had two sons, Hsü Huai 淮 (T. 文東, H. 鶴石山人, 1492–1545) and Hsü Lu 潞 (T. 元邦, 1501–40). She died while Hsü Ts'ung was in Yunnan; so he married the daughter of a member of the literati of the Miao 苗 clan, and also took a concubine. It was the latter who gave birth to Hsü Wei. When the father died (June 19, 1521), it fell to the lady Miao, who was childless, to bring him up. As her stepson, Hsü Huai, was a Taoist devotee and liked to spend his time in travel to famous mountains and lakes, he had run through much of the family property by the time Hsü Wei was nine. So the lady Miao, forced to

cut down expenses, did away with the serving staff, including Hsü Wei's mother. Not until later did Hsü Wei bring her back into his household, probably by purchase. She lived on until 1568.

The boy's intelligence was noticed at an early age, and he was soon launched on a classical education. He also learned how to play the lute, and at the age of fourteen took up swordsmanship for a while. Hsü Wei achieved the *hsiu-ts'ai* in 1540, but, in spite of numerous tries (eight in all), he failed in the higher examinations. In the following year he married into the family of P'an K'o-ching 潘克敬, a deputy magistrate and student of law. and went to live with them in Kwangchow. After four years of marriage, his wife bore a son, named Hsü Mei 枚, but she died soon afterwards, aged only eighteen. Hsü remained in the P'an household for a time, then (1546) left to start one of his own, inviting his mother to live with him. He visited T'ai-ts'ang 太倉 briefly, but in 1547 settled in Shaohsing and started teaching. His studio there he named I-chih-t'ang 一枝堂 (Twig Hall). For a time he studied with Chi Pen 季本 (T. 明德, H. 彭山, 1485–1563, cs 1517), a disciple of Wang Shou-jen (*q.v.*). Confucian thought seems, however, to have taken no special grip on him, for he was later to confess that he had found a special interest in the *Śūraṅgama sūtra* (首楞嚴), the *Chuang-tzu*, the *Lieh-tzu*, and ancient medical lore. In 1550 a lawsuit nearly pauperized him, obliging him to retreat to a monastery, supported by a friend. At this juncture, fortunately, a stipend from the district saved him, enabling him to continue trying to pass the *chü-jen* examination. Eventually he became a professional writer, and began to take an interest in the theatre. At the same time he advised the authorities of Shao-hsing on schemes to resist the invasions of the Japanese pirates. In spite of his involvement in the defense against them, Hsü continued his literary activity, turning out poems, essays, and plays, which to a degree reveal the political and social conditions of the day. About 1557 his name came to the attention of Hu Tsung-hsien (*q. v.*), then commander-in-chief of the armies defending the southeastern provinces, who asked him to join his staff. Hsü accepted with some hesitation, and in the end became his secretary. His reports to the court, written in the name of Hu, are said to have delighted the emperor. One of them, the "Chin Pai-lu piao" 進白鹿表 (memorial of the white deer), is especially remembered, It was while serving in this capacity that he came into increasing contact with T'ang Shun-chih (*q.v.*), with whom he shared some of the same independent theories in respect to literature. But his main task was to advise Hu on strategy. The general valued him so highly that, despite his frequent lapses and indulgence in wine, he rewarded Hsü with a large house on spacious grounds, to which Hsü gave the name Ch'ou-tzu-t'ang 酬字堂 (Reward for words hall). Hsü remained with Hu until 1562.

Having cast aside his wife of two years, née Wang 王 (1559), Hsü married for the third time a woman née Chang 張, who a year later bore him his second son, Hsü Chih 枳. This marriage again proved unsatisfactory. When, in 1565, Hu Tsung-hsien lost his high post and was thrown into prison, Hsü became terrified, fearing that he too might be implicated. He attempted suicide and confesses, in an unusually frank "obituary," that he was pretending madness. In this mood anything could upset him. His wife aroused his suspicions. Perhaps it was his own fault, for he had destroyed his testicles. In any event, he beat her to death, and consequently was imprisoned (1566). The sentence was death; but his friends pleaded for him, and after seven years he gained his release, thanks to Chang Yüan-pien (*q.v.*), then a member of the Hanlin Academy. His time in jail was not wholly wasted. He continued to read and write, and was able to see his friends occasionally.

On emerging from his long confinement (1573). Hsü returned to his profession of writing and painting. At the invitation of numerous people he composed a stream of prefaces, epitaphs, and poems. For four months in 1575 he assisted Chang Yüan-pien in compiling the *K'uai-chi chih* 會稽志, 16 *ch.*, published the same year. His part included the introduction and commentary on various sections in which he criticized certain social and economic conditions to which the local people were subjected. His comments on population and taxation show particular insight. In the following summer, at the invitation of a fellow townsman and schoolmate, Wu Tui (*see* Ch'en Ti), he went north to Hsüan-fu. Wu, then governor, is reported to have valued Hsü's counsel in his problem of defending the area against Mongol infiltration.

On his return to Shao-hsing (September, 1577), Hsü's one-time pupils came again to study poetry, prose, drama, and calligraphy with him. At the same time he continued his own writing and painting. It must have been a restless life, for he seems not to have lived under his own roof, shifting instead to the homes of one or another of his friends, asserting that it was the fault of his sons who made him move. He passed away finally, aged seventy-two, at the house of the wife of his son Hsü Chih.

Hsü Wei was the author of numerous books, most of which seem to have been preserved, although several were criticized in the 1780s for careless writing and errors of fact. The first edition of his collected works entitled *Hsü Wen- ch'ang ch'u-chi* 文長初集, 10 *ch.* (1590), was followed immediately by *Ch'üeh-pien* 闕編, 5 *ch.* (1590), and later (1600) by *Hsü Wen-ch'ang san-chi* 三集, recently reprinted in Taipei in four volumes, with his portrait. The complete collection of his literary remains, *Hsü Wen-ch'ang ch'üan* 全 -*chi*, 29 +1 *ch.*, appeared in 1614; it contains the commentary of Yüan Hung-tao (*q.v.*), who was the first to accord him the highest praise. A supplementary collection, *Hsü Wen-ch'ang i-kao* 逸稿, 24 *ch.*, appeared in 1623. Though scorned by the editors of the Imperial Catalogue as trifling—they cite such essay themes as "the obscene chatter of strolling players" and "eating a sour pear"—it was printed again in 1936. Besides these he was responsible for numerous short pieces on divination, medicine, physiognomy, the horoscope, and the three religions 三教, many of which may now be found in various collectanea. Hsü also compiled several anthologies of literature and anecdotes, such as the *Ku-chin ch'ih-tu chen-ya yün chien* 古今尺牘振雅雲箋, 10 *ch.*, probably printed before 1620, and the *Ch'ing-t'eng shan-jen lu-shih* 青藤山人路史, 2 *ch.* (Copies of original editions of both survive in the Naikaku Bunko and elsewhere.) In addition he edited, with commentary, a number of collections of T'ang and Sung literature, and of writers of his own day.

Hsü's plays came out under the collective title *Ssu sheng yüan* 四聲猿 (Four ape cries), and are known by the titles "K'uang ku-li yü yang san nung" 狂鼓吏漁陽三弄, "Yü ch'an-shih ts'ui hsiang i meng" 玉禪師翠鄉一夢, "Tz'u Mu-lan t'i fu ts'ung chün" 雌木蘭替父從軍, and "Nü chuang-yüan tz'u huang te feng" 女狀元辭凰得鳳. Josephine Huang Hung sketches the plots of all but the second. Two of these plays, frequently performed ever since, strike a very modern note; they show that Hsü believed in "women's rights": a girl could become a great general or the top scholar of the empire. Hsü also wrote two books on the drama of his day: the *Nan tz'u hsü lu* 南詞敘錄 (Story of the southern drama), a descriptive catalogue of the four chief divisions of stagecraft (it lists, *inter alia*, the titles of sixty-five plays of the "southern opera" of Sung and Yüan times, many of which are not to be found in the *Yung-lo ta-tien* [*see* Yao Kuang-hsiao] or elsewhere). His name is associated with those of T'ang Hsien-tsu (ECCP) and Li Chih (*q.v.*), in an edition of certain plays of the Yüan

period, known as *San hsien-sheng ho-p'ing Yüan pen pei hsi hsiang* 三先生合評元本北西廂, 5 *ch.* This rare work, printed at the end of the Ming, is available on microfilm from the collection of the National Library of Peiping.

Ascribed to Hsü, but according to modern critics by an anonymous author, is a revised version of the *Huang Ming k'ai-yün ying-wu chuan* 皇明開運英武傳 (a popular historical account of the Ming founding attributed to Kuo Hsün, *q.v.*), popularly entitled *Yün-ho ch'i-tsung* or *Ying-lieh chuan*, printed 1616. Then too, in the introduction to Bernard Miall and Franz Kuhn's condensed translation of the *Chin P'ing Mei* (*see* Wang Shih-chen) Arthur Waley offered the suggestion that Hsü Wei was the author of the famous romance, on the ground that Hsü was "not only an important political figure, but also…the author of several popular plays;" furthermore, he added, "the only discoverable complete manuscript of the *Chin P'ing Mei* was procured from the Hsü family." Waley's proposal has not, however, gained general acceptance.

Hsü appears to have been as prolific in painting as he was in prose and poetry. His subjects included landscapes, figures, flowers, bamboos, and rocks. Examples are known in many museums in China, Japan, and abroad. He also did the illustrations for the *K'un-lun nu* 崑崙奴 (The African slave). For examples both of his paintings and of his calligraphy see, *inter alia*, Tseng Yu-ho Ecke's "A study on Hsü Wei." She writes of his craft: "He bursts out; his words are replete with feverish impetus. Even rational aesthetic theories are handled by him in a totally irrational way. His paintings are turbulence itself." And she quotes with approval one remark of Hu T'ing 胡廷, the writer of a preface, dated 1617, to Hsü's *I-chih-t'ang i-kao*, "Out of ten units in Hsü Wei, nine are uninhibited personality, only one part luck; yet he moved between the two, a sage perhaps, a saint, a demon, or a devil."

To the eye of a non-artist, it would seem that he was really the founder of a school of modern Chinese painting, later carried on by Wu Ch'ang-shih (ECCP, p. 716) and Ch'i Pai-shih (BDRC) whose works have become extremely popular.

Bibliography

1/288/3a; 5/115/112a; 40/49/17b; 65/6/8b; 84/丁中 /78b; Ho Lo-chih何樂之, *Hsü Wei*, in *Chung-kuo hua-chia* 中國畫家 *ts'ung-shu*, no. 15 (Shanghai, 1958); Hsü Lun徐崙, *Hsü Wen-ch'ang* (Shanghai, 1962); SK (1930), 114/4a, 128/1a, 178/11b; *Shan-yin-hsien chih* (1936), 14/20b; *Shao-hsing-fu chih* (1789), 54/33b; *K'uei-chou-fu chih* (1827), 23 上/17a; Sun Tien-ch'i (1957), 135, 139; Hsü Wei, *Ch'ing-t'eng shu-wu wen-chi*書屋文集;*id., Hsü Wen-ch'ang i-kao*; *Hsü Wen-ch'ang i-ts'ao* 佚草; *Hsü Wen-ch'ang san-chi; I-chih-t'ang kao*稿;*Ko-tai hsiao* 歌代嘯; *Nan-tz'u hsü lu*; *Ssu-sheng yüan*; Yüan Hung-tao, *Hsü Wen-ch'ang chuan* 傳; Ch'ien Nan-yang 錢南揚, YCHP mon. no. 7, 1381; Aoki Masaru 青木正兒, "Jo Sei-tō no geijutsu" 徐青藤の藝術, *Shinagaku* 支那學, II: 3 (November, 1921), 4 (December, 1921); Sugimura Yūzō 杉村勇造, *Jo Bun-chō, Sekitō, Chō Shi-ken* 徐文長, 石濤, 趙之謙 (Tokyo, 1964); NLP microfilm nos. 45, 861, 970, 1035; L. of C. *Catalogue of Rare Books*, 979; Naikaku Bunko, *Catalogue* 269, 358, 426; Yao Hsin-nung, "The Rise and Fall of K'un Ch'ü", THM, 2 (January, 1936), 66; Arthur Waley, Introduction of *Chin P'ing Mei*, tr. by Miall and Kuhn (N.Y., 1940), xviii; Josephine Huang Hung, *Ming Drama* (Taipei, 1966), 74; Tseng Yu-ho (Ecke), "A Study on Hsü Wei", *Ars Orientalis*, V (1963), 243; *id., Chinese Calligraphy* (Philadelphia, 1971), #57; Osvald Sirén, *Chinese Painting*, VII, 194; E. J. Laing, *Chinese Paintings in Chinese Publications, 1956–1968* (Ann Arbor, 1969), 170.

I-cheng Liang and L. Carrington Goodrich

HSÜ Yu-chen 徐有貞 (orig. *ming*理, T. 元玉, H. 天全), 1407-August 23, 1472, scholar-official and artist, was from Chi-hsiang-li 集祥里, Wu 吳-hsien, in Soochow prefecture. The family is said to have lived in the Chiang-nan area for many centuries, and was registered as artisan （匠籍） at Wan-p'ing 宛平 -hsien in Peking. Hsü Yu-chen was the second of three brothers, and reportedly very small in stature. Being extremely gifted, he became a *hsiu-ts'ai* at an early age. After he studied in Peking under Wu No and Hu Yen (*qq.v.*), he passed the provincial examination in 1432 and graduated as *chin-shih* the following year. His first appointment was as Hanlin bachelor. Two years later, after the death of Emperor Chu Chan-chi (*q.v.*), he was named compiler and ordered to take part in the compilation of the *Hsüan-tsung shih-lu*. He not only knew the Confucian Classics, but was at the same time well versed in such subjects as astronomy, geography, military tactics, water conservancy, magic, and geomancy. His decisions seem to have been often influenced by astrological considerations. In connection with his interest in military affairs he became aware of the quickly deteriorating military position of the Chinese in the face of the growing strength of the Mongols, and memorialized early in 1443 on the situation. He proposed measures to strengthen the military efficiency of the army defending the northern border. The emperor, Chu Ch'i-chen (*q.v.*), appreciated his proposals, but did not implement them. In 1447 Hsü Yu-chen was promoted to the rank of expositor-in-waiting.

When in August, 1449, the emperor set out on his ill-fated campaign against the Oirat chieftain Esen (*q.v.*), Hsü was most pessimistic about its outcome. Foreseeing a catastrophe, he ordered his wife and children to leave the capital for the south. On September 2, the day after the T'u-mu debacle (*see* Chu Ch'i-chen), Chu Ch'i-yü (*q.v.*), prince of Ch'eng and younger brother of the emperor, who acted as head of the government, summoned the remaining high officials to deliberate on how to cope with the critical situation. Hsü proposed removal of the capital to the south in order to avoid a still greater calamity. But several leading officials, such as the minister of Rites Hu Yen, the vice minister of Revenue Ch'en Hsün (*see* Lü Yüan), and the vice minister of War Yü Ch'ien (*q.v.*) opposed the move. Yü even went so far as to ask capital punishment for those advocating the transfer, thus greatly humiliating Hsü.

On October 13 he was sent as acting investigating censor to Chang-te 彰德 in northern Honan to recruit and train solders for defense against the Mongols. In the following year, when the enemy had retreated and military conditions had improved, he was recalled to the capital and reinstalled in his previous position of Hanlin expositor-in-waiting. Being eager for promotion, however, Hsü asked someone close to Yü Ch'ien to approach Yü on his behalf. Yü, now minister of War, was at that time most influential, and he actually did propose Hsü's promotion to the emperor. But the latter, remembering Hsü's former inopportune suggestion to remove the capital to Nanking, was unwilling to agree to it. When Hsü learned of this decision, he was gravely disappointed and became resentful of Yü whom he incorrectly suspected of obstructing his advancement. On May 11, 1452, he was concurrently appointed to the position of an instructor to the heir apparent. In view of Hsü's failure to receive promotion, Ch'en Hsün advised him to alter his personal name in order to avoid the permanent association with the proposal of 1449. Hsü followed this suggestion and changed it from Ch'eng to Yu-chen.

Eventually, on November 11, 1453, Hsü achieved the long awaited preferment, being appointed assistant censor-in-chief, and sent to take charge of the maintenance of the northern branch of the Yellow River at Sha-wan 沙灣, southeast of Shou-chang 壽張, in western Shantung, where it joins the Grand Canal. The main course of the Yellow River at that time was south of Shantung. From 1448 on, the northern branch of the river repeatedly burst its banks. The effect was not only that the region of Chang-ch'iu 張秋 was inundated, but also that the Grand Canal farther to the north, near Lin-ch'ing 臨清, got insufficient water. As a result the traffic on the Canal was often

obstructed. Up till then all efforts to control the stream at this critical junction had had but temporary success, and the Sha-wan dikes broke again and again. Hsü eventually succeeded in controlling the water by rebuilding the Sha-wan dikes and by constructing a canal connecting the northern course of the Yellow River with the Ta-ch'ing ho 大清河 which flows into the sea at Li-chin-hsien 利津縣 south of what was later to be the main course of the Yellow River. Thus the water could flow off; at the same time several locks provided for a sufficient quantity of water for the Grand Canal. On May 22, and again on August 14, 1455, Hsü Yu-chen reported to the throne that the diking and other works had been completed; he had employed fifty-eight thousand laborers over a period of 555 working days. The new canal received the name Kuang-chi ch'ü 廣濟渠. During this and the following year Hsü went twice on an inspection tour to supervise the water conservancy at this strategic point of the Grand Canal. The emperor expressed great satisfaction, rewarding Hsü and promoting him on Jauuary 3, 1457, to the rank of vice censor-in-chief. Hsü's conservancy work was so substantial that it lasted thirty-four years.

Hsü Yu-chen was now fully rehabilitated, but apparently his ambitions were still not satisfied. He gladly gave his consent when General Shih Heng (q.v.), upon the suggestion of the chief minister of the Court of Imperial Sacrifices, Hsü Pin 許彬 (T. 道中, cs 1415), approached Hsü asking him to collaborate in the conspiracy to restore the ex-emperor, Chu Ch'i-chen, to the throne. When, after the coup d'état, the victorious conspirators opened the trial against Yü Ch'ien and others, Hsü was able to prevent the reenthroned emperor from commuting the death penalty for Yü Ch'ien. The day after the restoration Hsü was promoted to the rank of a chancellor and attached to the Grand Secretariat. He was, however, not yet satisfied, and through the good offices of

Shih Heng, he was (on April 3) made minister of War, the position formerly held by Yü Ch'ien; he was also made earl of Wu-kung 武功伯 with an annual stipend of 1,100 *tan* of rice. Three days later he was in addition named grand secretary of Hua-kai tien 華蓋殿. Together with Shih Heng and Ts'ao Chi-hsiang (*q.v.*), Hsü now became one of the three most influential men at court. The close collaboration of the former conspirators was, however, not a lasting one. Often they differed, and as early as the summer of 1457 they began to intrigue against each other. On June 28 Hsü was arrested for undue assumption of authority, and subsequently demoted and transferred as administrative vice commissioner of Kwangtung. Shih and Ts'ao, however, still felt uneasy about him and sought his life. They managed to have Hsü arrested on his way to the south and sentenced to a new trial, making use of a faked memorial. The death sentence for Hsü was proposed, but the emperor commuted it to banishment to Chin-ch'ih wei 金齒衛 in present day Pao-shan-hsien 保山縣 in western Yunnan, between the rivers Mekong and Salween. He was deprived of all his ranks and titles, and made a commoner.

In January, 1461, almost a year after Shih Heng had been arrested and died in prison, Hsü Yu-chen was recalled from exile and permitted to return to his home district, but he received no further appointment. Although it became evident that the charges made against him by Shih and Ts'ao were unfounded, his responsibility for the death of Yü Ch'ien prevented influential people at court from speaking on his behalf. All his biographers praise his knowledge and ability, but many condemn his personal character. Hsü also made a name as a painter of landscapes and as a calligrapher. He had a son Hsü Shih-liang 世良 (original *ming* 鑄, T. 嗣勳, 1446-1502), who was appointed (April, 1457) to the rank of commander of the Embroidered-uniform Guard. Hsü Yu-chen spent his last years in peace at home. One of his daughters became the mother of the great calligrapher, Chu Yün-ming (*q.v.*).

Hsü's collected writings, *Wu-kung chi* 武功集, 5 *ch.*, are included in the *Ssu-k'u ch'üan shu*, but apparently have never been reprinted. Two memorials and an inscription written on the occasion of the completion of the water conservancy work of 1455 are contained in the *Huang Ming ching shih wen-pien* 經世文編, *chüan* 37.

[Editors' note: Legends about Hsü Yu-chen abound, especially on his power of divination and ability to predict by means of astrology. According to a certain story, one night (about 1465) he looked at the stars and predicted that a man from Soochow was going to be victorious as a military commander. He thought it meant himself. So he began to prepare for reinstatement. Soon, however, he was told of the appointment of Han Yung (*q.v.*) as supreme commander of Kwangtung and gave up hope. Ch'ien Ch'ien-i (ECCP) considered Hsü's tz'u 詞 (poems of irregular meter), written in his last years, as expressive as those of Hsin Ch'i-chi (1140–1207). When inspired by scenery and warmed by spirits, Hsü would compose these songs and write them in the grass calligraphic style, wielding the brush with speed. As Ch'ien stated, in Soochow's cultural life Hsü was invariably regarded as the leading light.]

Bibliography

1/171/7a; 5/10/31a; 16/10/50a; 34/2/6b; 63/13/28a; Ch'ien Ch'ien-i, *Lieh-ch'ao shih-chi* (1652), II, 6/14b; MSL (1963), Ying-tsung, 2001, 3594, 5108, 5463, 5515, 5764, 5873, 5879, 5968, 5972, 6018, 6689; KC (1958), 1926; SK(1930), 170/8b; Shen Te-fu, *Yeh-hu pien* (1959), 186; Lu Ts'an 陸粲 (1494–1551), *Keng-chi pien* 庚巳編 (in *Chi-lu hui-pien. ch.* 169), 6/1a; Chu Yün-ming, *Chu-shih chi-lüeh* (NLP microfilm, no. 910), 15/4a; Hsü Tzu-yang 徐子陽, *Huang Ming T'ien-ch'üan hsien-sheng i-shih* 天全先生遺事 (*Shuo-k'u* 說庫 ed., 1963), 12/954; P'eng Yün-ts'an 彭蘊燦, *Hua-shih hui-chuan* 畫史彙傳 (1825), 5/13a; Wu Chi-hua 吳緝華, "Ming-tai Liu Ta-hsia te chih ho yü Huang-ho kai tao" 明代劉大夏的治河與黃河改道, in *Yu shih hsüeh-pao* 幼獅學報, Vol. 1: 2

(Taipei, 1959), 2; *id.*, *Ming-tai hai-yün chi yün-ho te yen-chiu* 海運及運河的研究 (Taipei, 1961), 104; Liu Ts'un-yan, "The Penetration of Taoism into the Ming neo-Confucianist Elite", TP, 57 (1971), 78.

Wolfgang Franke

HSÜAN Ni 軒輗 (T. 惟行 [衡], H. 靜齋), died June 8, 1464, a capable administrator noted for his uprightness and frugality, came from a family of obscure origin that had settled in Lu-i 鹿邑, Honan. Graduating as *chü-jen* in 1420, Hsüan Ni achieved the *chin-shih* in 1424, the same year as his distinguished contemporary Keng Chiu-ch'ou (*q.v.*). He immediately received an appointment as vice director of the messenger office. Seven years later he was promoted (March, 1431) to be a censor, assigned to Fukien and Chekiang. In October, 1436, he was one of seventeen censors ordered to check the military registry throughout the nation. During their tour of duty, they uncovered numerous cases of desertion and other abuses. Upon their return in the following year, the group, headed by Hsüan Ni, submitted a five-point memorandum with these recommendations: 1) any captured deserter found to be overage or disabled should be replaced by an able-bodied man selected from the same household; 2) the substitute of the above, who has been taken from his household and assigned to a military post, should be immediately released; 3) to each guard or chiliarch an official from the nearby highest civil administration should be assigned exclusively to checking its military registry; 4) when a military unit (guard or chiliarch) has been notified three times by the civil authorities that a household is truly without any able-bodied male, that unit should strike out the said household from its registry and not include it again on the list for replacement; 5) a substitute should not be permitted to evade transportation by involving himself in a lawsuit; except in such a serious case as murder or worse, the substitute should be transported to his destination and a younger member of the family be designated to represent him in the lawsuit. Early in 1440 he submitted another memorial, pointing out that imperial sanction must be secured first before a censor is assigned any additional task.

A few months later (May) Hsüan Ni was promoted to be surveillance commissioner of Chekiang. He stayed there for the next nine years, during which he showed himself to be a competent, scrupulous official noted for his austerity and discipline. He improved the administration, rooted out official corruption and the profiteering activities of certain well-to-do families, and insured peace and order within the province. At the beginning of 1444, when the court deliberated on reopening the silver mines in Chekiang to provide additional income for the treasury, Hsüan Ni spoke out against the proposal as an added burden to the people and likely to cause popular unrest. The court at first acceded to his remonstrance, but after further prodding by eunuchs and their profit-minded colleagues it reversed its stand. The consequence of this action, as Hsüan Ni had predicted, seems to have led to the subsequent uprisings of the miners in Chekiang and Fukien (*see* Yeh Tsung-liu). In July, 1448, expressing concern for the welfare of the nation based on his experience in Chekiang Hsüan submitted a four-point memorandum. He urged the court to ensure the recruitment of men of high caliber by warning the provincial authorities that anyone who recommended a person who later turned out to be an offender was to be punished accordingly; to enforce full daytime office hours; to admonish the officials to study the code, so that they might avoid making misjudgments; and to forbid usury.

The following year witnessed the invasion of the Oirat tribesmen, the captivity of Emperor Chu Ch'i-chen (*q.v.*), and the succession of Chu Ch'i-yü (*q.v.*). Hsüan was promoted to deputy censor-in-chief and governor of Chekiang. In February, 1450, he was given the additional duty of the salt administration of the province. During the next two years he distinguished himself in his office by suppressing several insurrections by local bandits, including one band in Ch'u-chou 處州 (May, 1450) and was later rewarded with a raise in salary.

In May, 1451, Hsüan received a transfer to Nanking as director general of grain storage for military supplies. In due course, the court extended his authority to the Soochow region after the local inhabitants complained that their land had been misappropriated by the garrison soldiers seeking to expand their military farms. His duties were regarded as so indispensible that, when his father died in October, 1453, the court granted him leave only to attend the burial. In March, 1454, he became head of the Censorate in Nanking. Falling ill the following year, he submitted a request for retirement, but the emperor rejected it. Three years later, shortly after the reinstallation of Chu Ch'i-chen, Hsüan Ni received a promotion to be minister of Justice. Soon after he went to Peking to assume his new duties, he ran into difficulties due to domination of the court by the eunuch Ts'ao Chi-hsiang and his associate Shih Heng (qq.v.). Following the banishment of Keng Chiu-ch'ou in June, Hsüan, aware of his precarious situation, submitted a request for retirement on the ground of illness and advanced age. The emperor summoned him for an audience, found him indeed not well, and let him go home. A year later he was recalled to serve again as director general of grain storage in Nanking with the rank of censor-in-chief. Early in 1464, again a sick man, Hsüan begged for permission to retire, and left before his request was approved. He died six months later, but received no posthumous honor until April, 1593, when the canonized name Tuan-su 端肅 (upright and majestic) was awarded. Following this, acting on the recommenda-

tion of his townsman, Shen Li 沈鯉 (T. 仲化, H. 龍江, Pth. 文端, cs 1565, 1531-1615), then minister of Rites, the court approved the request of the local authorities for the erection of a shrine in his memory. Upon its completion, another fellow townsman, Lü K'un (q.v.), then assistant censor-in-chief, composed a laudatory essay in praise of his character and achievements.

Distinguished as an administrator, Hsüan Ni also became known as one of the few scholar-officials during this period extolled for their integrity and discipline. His contemporaries describe him as a man of reserve who rarely showed his emotion and seldom acceded to the views of others. His aloofness often annoyed his colleagues but they nonetheless admired his character and individuality. Among his associates, only Keng Chiu-ch'ou is said to have possessed qualities equal to his.

Hsüan Ni had a son, Hsüan Wei-ming 惟明 (T. 克清), known also for being upright and economical. He was appointed, through the yin privilege, to be the magistrate of Kuang-tsung 廣宗, Pei-Chihli, in 1469, where he gave a good account of himself, but died three years later. Hsüan Wei-ming had a daughter, Hsüan Ch'un-chieh 春節, who committed suicide after the death of her fiancé; she is listed in the local gazetteer as a woman of virtue.

Bibliography

1/158/13b; 5/59/1a; 8/28/3a; 9/ 后 3/15a; 61/119 /17a; MSL (1963), Hsüan-tsung, 1752, Ying-tsung, ch. 22–326, Hsien-tsung(1964), 145, Shen-tsung (1965), 4796; KC (1958), 2172; Ho Ch'iao-yüan, Ming-shan ts'ang (1971 ed.), 3735; Lu-i-hsien chih (1896), 3/15a, 12 上 /2b, 14 上/ 14a, 16b, 15 上 /3a.

Hok-lam Chan

HSÜEH Hsüan 薛瑄 (T. 德溫, H. 敬軒), August 31, 1389-July 15, 1464, was a native of Ho-chin 河津, Shansi, the son of Hsüeh Chen 貞 (1355-1425, cj 1384), an education official. Hsüeh Hsüan passed first in the provincial examination in 1420, and achieved the *chin-shih* a year later. He remained at home a few years after his father's death, but in 1428 received an appointment as censor, in which capacity he served a year in Hukuang (1430) as inspector of silver mines.

In 1438 he was made assistant education surveillance commissioner of Shantung. There he instructed the students especially in the rules which Chu Hsi (1130–1200) had laid down for the Po-lu-tung 白鹿洞 Academy. He was next promoted to vice minister of the Grand Court of Revision through the recommendation of the eunuch Wang Chen (*q.v.*), his fellow townsman. It is said that he later incurred the wrath of this powerful eunuch, however, and after being falsely impeached, received a sentence of death in July, 1443, but won a reprieve. After the catastrophe at T'u-mu in 1449 (*see* Chu Ch'i-chen) and the collapse of the Wang Chen clique, Hsüeh received an appointment in October of the same year as assistant minister of the Court of Revision. When the Oirat, led by Esen (*q.v.*), attacked Peking, he defended the north gates. In 1451 he became the chief minister of the same Court in Nanking. During a famine in the lower Yangtze area, when the poor people of a village asked a wealthy family for rice and were refused, the irate villagers burned the house to the ground. The government condemned them to death for rebelliousness, but Hsüeh strongly defended their cause, pointing out the injustice of this verdict.

When the eunuch Chin Ying (*q.v.*) visited Nanking, Hsüeh alone among the higher officials did not attend the dinner party given to flatter him. Upon returning to the capital, Chin Ying reported that the only man of integrity in Nanking was Hsüeh Hsüan. When Chu Ch'i-chen resumed power, Hsüeh was appointed (February 13, 1457) grand secretary with the rank of a vice minister of Rites and chancellor of the Hanlin Academy. Hsüeh interceded on behalf of Wang Wen (*see*

Yü Ch'ien) and Yü Ch'ien when they were condemned to death, but was unable to save their lives. He has sometimes been criticized for not having done more for them. In any case, he is said to have become disillusioned afterwards over intrigues at court, and resigned from office on July 1, 1457. He returned to his native place and devoted the remaining years of his life to teaching his numerous disciples. After his death, he was honored with the name Wen-ch'ing 文清. His portrait may be found in the *Sheng-hsien hsiang tsan* of Lü Wei-ch'i (*q.v.*).

Hsüeh Hsüan was an assiduous follower of Ch'eng I (1033–1107) and Chu Hsi, and an admirer of the Yüan philosopher, Hsü Heng (1209–81). Unlike Sung Lien and Fang Hsiao-ju (*qq.v.*), who were scholars in the broader sense, and experts in letters, history, and politics, as well as in philosophy, and who thus exemplified Chu's doctrine of the "extension of knowledge," Hsüeh concentrated on that which had a direct bearing on personal conduct and the quest for Tao: the study of the Four Books and of the Sung philosophers. He was especially fond of the *Hsing-li ta-ch'üan*, compiled by Hu Kuang (*q.v.*) and others, which he eagerly devoured, frequently to the point of neglecting his sleep. Hsüeh manifested in his life the Ch'eng-Chu doctrine of "reverence" (ching 敬), in the practice of which he sought to acquire perfection and recover the original goodness of his human nature (fu-hsing 復性). As he once said, "Ever since Chu Hsi made the Tao clear, there is no more need to write about it. All that is necessary is to put it into practice." For this, it has sometimes been held that Hsüeh Hsüan himself made little original contribution to learning and thought. Huang Tsung-hsi (ECCP), however, carefully repeated the comment of his own teacher, Liu Tsung-chou (ECCP), who alluded to Hsüeh's poem, written toward the end of his life, regarding the way his mind sensed the oneness of nature (hsing) and Heaven (T'ien 天), and declared it probable that Hsüeh actually acquired wisdom, in the Tao, in his old age.

Hsüeh's chief philosophical works are the *Tu-shu lu* 讀書錄, 11 *ch.*, and the *Tu-shu hsü-lu* 續錄, 12 *ch.* Huang Tsung-hsi has described them as "basically commentaries on the Diagram of the Supreme Ultimate, the Western Inscription, and the Correction of Youthful Folly," and has likewise pointed out Hsüeh's many repetitions. Huang went on to note that Hsüeh had merely recorded the insights which derived from his practice of the recommendations of Ch'eng I and Chu Hsi, for his own reference, and with no intention of presenting them systematically. Even in so doing, Huang remarked, Hsüeh had added to the Ch'eng-Chu legacy by his teaching the interpenetration of li 理 and of ch'i 氣, and by denying that the former is prior to the latter. He also gave more emphasis to the development of the mind (hsin), which is the special characteristic of Ming thinkers. It may be pointed out in addition that, with all his reputation for orthodoxy, Hsüeh was free from the antagonism against Buddhism and Taoism which many others manifested. He did not, indeed, show much interest in, or knowledge of, Ch'an Buddhism. But he once defended the Buddhists as sincere seekers after personal perfection. He also devoted one chapter of the *Tu-shu lu* (ch. 6) to the *Yin-fu* 陰符 Canon, a book of Taoist origin, which, of course, was also a favorite of Chu Hsi.

Hsüeh Hsüan is said to have been fond of writing poetry in his youth, but to have burned his poems later on, when he decided to devote his time to the study of philosophy. Those poems he wrote which have come down to us, however, have been praised for their literary excellence; they call to mind the poetry of earlier times, and do not always have philosophical content. Certain of his poems manifest a conscious effort to imitate the *Chi-jang chi* 擊壤集 of Shao Yung (1011-77).

In his history of philosophy, Huang Tsung-hsi has listed Hsüeh Hsüan at the head of the Ho-tung hsüeh-an 河東學案, including, with him, that group of thinkers, mostly natives of the northern provinces, who sought, above all, to observe the teachings of the Sung thinkers. Huang pointed out how these men had been faithful to Sung learning, whereas the disciples of Wang Shou-jen had not even been able to keep to Wang's own teaching. The best known of Hsüeh's immediate followers were Yen Yü-hsi 閻禹錫 (T. 子與, cj 1444), a native of Loyang, who rose to be censor, and Chang Chieh 張傑 (T. 立夫, H. 默齋, 1421-72), a native of Shensi. Yen Yü-hsi's disciple, Tuan Chien 段堅 (T. 可久, H. 容思, 1419-84, cs 1454), a native of Kansu, is also noteworthy for the transmission of the teaching of reverence. Through him, Hsüeh's teaching passed to Wang Hung-ju 王鴻儒 (T. 懋學, H. 凝齋, cs 1487), a native of Honan, and later minister of Revenue in Nanking, and Chou Hui 周蕙 (T. 廷芳, H. 小泉), native of Shansi, a famous teacher. Chou's best-known disciple was Hsüeh Ching-chih 薛敬之 (T. 顯思, H. 思庵, 1435-1508), native of Shensi, a friend and fellow student of Ch'en Hsien-chang (*q.v.*).

In 1571 Emperor Chu Tsai-hou (*q.v.*), responding to the requests of many officials, in particular the supervising secretary Han Chi (*see* Han K'uang), allowed Hsüeh's tablet to be placed in the Confucian temple. He thus became the first Ming scholar of the four to be so honored.

Besides the *Tu-shu lu* and *Hsü-lu*, Hsüeh Hsüan left other writings. These include the *Tao-lun* 道論, 1 *ch.*, and *Ts'ung-cheng lu* 從政錄, 1 *ch.*—also called *Ts'ung-cheng ming-yen* 名言—, both of which are extant, and available in the *Ts'ung shu chi-ch'eng* edition. The former gives philosophical comments which do not add much new insight to what is already included in the *Tu-shu lu*, while the latter contains his reflections on political life and its ethics. The Naikaku Bunko catalogue reports the existence also of *Hsüeh tzu ts'ui-yen* 子粹言, 3 *ch.*, compiled by Wu T'ing-chü (*see* Ch'en Hsien-chang) with preface dated 1501, and *Hsüeh Wen-ch'ing kung yao-yü* 要語, 2 *ch.*, compiled by Ku Chung-hsü 谷中虛 (T. 聲甫, cs 1544), published in 1604. There are two collections of his poetry, separately published, the *Ho-fen shih-chi* 河汾詩集, 8 *ch.*, and the *Wu-yu* 五友 *shih*, 1 *ch.*, the latter being in the Naikaku Bunko, while the former, according to the *Ssu-k'u* editors, has been mostly incorporated in Hsüeh's collected works.

There are several versions of the last. The *Wen ch'ing Hsüeh hsien-sheng wen-chi* 文集, 24 *ch.*, gives his poems, letters, essays, and a few memorials. It was compiled by his disciple Chang Ting 張鼎, and published in 1614 by his descendant, Hsüeh Shih-hung 薛士弘. There is also the *Hsüeh Wen-ch'ing kung ch'üan-chi* 全集 in 40 plus 1 *ch.*, which includes the same contents as the 24 *chüan* version, with the *Tu-shu lu*, and a few biographical accounts. It was published in 1615. The Naikaku Bunko has the longest extant version, *Hsüeh Wen-ch'ing hsien-sheng ch'üan-chi*, 53 *ch.* It is to this collection (1713 ed.) that Hsüeh's *nien-p'u* 年譜, by Yang Ho 楊鶴, is attached. Another *nien-p'u*, originally compiled by Yang Hsi-min 楊希閔 (1877) but never finished, and published without corrections by the Yenching University Library in 1934, contains errors.

Both the *Tu-shu lu* and Hsüeh's collected works have been edited and included in several collections. Chang Po-hsing (ECCP) selected what he considered to be Hsüeh's important sayings and writings, and published *Tu-shu lu* in 8 *chüan*, and *Hsüeh Ching-hsüan* 敬軒 *chi* in 10 *chüan*.

Bibliography

1/109/18a, 282/7a; 3/159/5a; 4/6/23a; 5/13/41a; 16/10/59a; 32/100/13a; 40/18 下/13a; 42/72/4a; 61/111/17b; 63/10/55a; MSL (1963), Ying-tsung, 2141, 3623, 5792, 5976, Mu-tsung, (1966), 1484; SK (1930), 93/2b, 95/9b, 170/7b, 175/7b; Hsüeh Hsüan, *Hsüeh Wen-ch'ing kung ch'üan-chi* (NLP microfilm nos. 959–960); *id.*, *Hsüeh Ching-hsüan chi* (*Cheng-i-t'ang ch'üan-shu* ed.); *id.*, *Tao-lun* (TsSCC ed.); *id.*, *Ts'ung-cheng lu* (TsSCC ed.); *id.*, *Tu-shu lu* (*Cheng-i-t'ang ch'üan-shu* ed.) *id.*, *Tu-shu lu* and *Tu-shu hsü-lu* (1827 ed.); *id.*, *Wen-ch'ing Hsüeh hsien-sheng wen-chi* (1614); Chou Ju-teng, *Sheng-hsüeh tsung-chuan*, 12/1a; Keng Ting-hsiang, *Keng T'ien-t'ai hsien-sheng wen-chi* (1598 ed., Taipei reprint 1970), 13/6a; Yang Hsi-min, *Ming Hsüeh Wen-ch'ing kung nien-p'u* (1934); L. of C. *Catalogue of Rare Books*, 901; Naikaku Bunko *Catalogue*, 173, 174, 346, 529, 530, 559; Jung Chao-tsu 容肇祖, *Ming-tai ssu-hsiang shih* 明代思想史 (Taipei reprint, 1962), 13; Wing-tsit Chan, "The Ch'eng-Chu School of Early Ming" in W. T. de Bary(ed.), *Self and Society in Ming Thought* (New York, 1970), 31.

Cze-tong Song and Julia Ching

HSÜEH Ying-ch'i 薛應旂 (T. 仲常, H. 方山), 1500-after February 1, 1573, official, teacher, and historian, was a native of Wu-chin 武進, a city on the Grand Canal north of Lake T'ai. As a youth he received instruction first from Shao Pao 邵寶 (T. 國賢, H. 二泉, Pth. 文莊, 1460-August 1, 1527, cs 1484), an adherent of the neo-Confucian school of the Ch'eng brothers (11th cent.) and Chu Hsi (1130-1200); second from Ou-yang Te (*q.v.*), a distinguished follower of Wang Shou-jen (*q. v.*); and third from Lü Nan (*q.v.*) who persuaded him to return to the Ch'eng-Chu fold. Along the line Hsüeh acquired the degrees of *chü-jen* (1534) and *chin-shih* (1535), receiving as his first assignment (1536-38) the magistracy of Tz'u-ch'i 慈谿, near Ningpo. While in this office he acted in the autumn of 1537 as one of two officials responsible for the provincial examinations in the neighboring province of Fukien. At Tz'u-ch'i he found that people were taxed excessively, almost beyond endurance, and suggested to the provincial government the reduction of all levies except the land tax. The latter approved his suggestions and circulated his petition among all officials in the province, instructing them to follow his example. His measures also met with widespread approval of the common people; the rich and the influential, including some officials, however, opposed them. Furthermore, he found himself at odds with the prefect; so on the plea of poor health he asked for transferral and became instructor of the prefectural school at Kiukiang, where for some time he also lectured at the famous Pai-lu shu-yüan 白鹿書院 (White Deer Academy).

His next office (1545) was that of secretary, later director, of a bureau of the ministry of Personnel in Nanking. At this time Yen Sung (q.v.), who had formed a dislike for the supervising secretary of the office of scrutiny for Rites, Wang Yeh 王燁 (cs 1535), instructed a protégé named Chu Chieh 諸傑 to write Hsüeh, telling him to get rid of Wang. Hsüeh, however, proved stubborn and wrote the all-powerful grand secretary that Chu was not to be trusted. According to Hsüeh's own account, Yen, incensed, told the censor Kuei Jung 桂榮 (T. 君用, cj 1522) to accuse Hsüeh of some misdemeanor. Whereupon the latter found himself appointed assistant prefect of Chien-ch'ang 建昌, Kiangsi, where he served for two years (1545-47). At this point someone at court maintained that Hsüeh's shift from Nanking had been an improper one; so he was brought to Peking (1547) as vice director of a bureau in the ministry of Justice and later made director of a bureau in the ministry of Rites. By this time Hsüeh, again according to his own account, was in the good graces of Yen Sung, who praised him for some of his writings. Because, allegedly, of Yen's support, Hsüeh received a promotion (1551) to the post of surveillance vice commissioner in charge of education in Chekiang, where he took part in the civil and military provincial examinations of 1552. His concern for this institution led him to stamp out the irregularities he found, such as the falsification of papers by some of the candidates. His reforms irritated certain people, who accused him of beating students found guilty, and reported that he had no ability for the post. These charges led to another change of scene, Yen reportedly arranging for his transfer (1553) to Shensi as surveillance vice commissioner and intendant of the military defense circuit of the northeastern borders of that province. He soon discovered that some of the officials in the region were so mistreating the people, who were very poor, that a number were being driven into banditry. Those responsible he had dismissed. At the same time he did what he could to relieve the poverty of the population, partly by lessening the tax burden. Inevitably his actions encountered opposition, the censor T'u Chung-lü 屠仲律 (cs 1550) voicing it in a memorial to the throne. In his own defense Hsüeh intimated that Yen Sung may have sent him to the frontier region in the hope that the Mongols might conveniently put him out of the way. Apprised of this report, Yen promptly arranged for his dismissal (1555). Meanwhile, Hsüeh took part in the Shensi provincial examinations of 1555, reading some of the papers submitted. He seems to have been responsible for the selection of Tsou Ying-lung (see Lin Jun), who was to become a chin-shih (1556) and later (1562) gain fame, as a censor, for impeaching Yen and his son and bringing about their downfall. Another anecdote is told of Hsüeh as he was about to leave for home. It seems that he had accused the magistrate of Lo-ch'uan 洛川 (in Fuchou prefecture), Yang Hsü 楊勗 (cj 1540), of peculation. Whereupon Yang fled, leaving behind 1,027 ounces of silver. The assistant prefect of Yen-an 延安 handed the entire sum to Hsüeh for his travel expenses; Hsüeh turned the money over to the provincial government, saying that all through his career he had never accepted payment of this kind.

While in retirement Hsüeh devoted himself to teaching and writing. Among his students were Ku Hsien-ch'eng (q.v.)

and his younger brother. As indicated above, Hsüeh had become a follower of the Ch'eng-Chu school, but he had also come under the influence of the Lu-Wang school. He spent much of his time at this stage trying to harmonize the two, among other things undertaking a revision of the *K'ao-t'ing yüan yüan lu* 考亭淵源錄 of Sung Tuan-i 宋端儀 (T. 孔時, H. 立齋, 1447–1501, cs 1481), and reprinting the *Chu-tzu wan-nien ting lun* 朱子晚年定論 (Master Chu's final conclusions arrived at late in life) by Wang Shou-jen. Through his promotion these two books made a substantial impact on the thought of his time. But more important perhaps was his effect on the two Ku brothers, the elder of whom came to dominate the Tung-lin group in its earliest days.

Hsüeh's writings cover a wide field. While in Shensi, as he became involved in problems of defense, he printed a copy of *Sun-tzu shuo* 孫子說, a discussion of the ancient military classic. On his return to Wu-chin and discovery that the Japanese were raiding the coast nearby, he wrote the *Yü k'ou lun* 禦寇論 (How to resist the pirates). This is included in his collected work, *Fang-shan* 方山 *Hsüeh hsien-sheng ch'üan-chi* 全集, 68 *ch.* His experiences in public life led him to write the *Hsien chang lu* 憲章錄, 46 *ch.*, a year by year record of governmental development from 1368 to 1521. Though based in large measure on the *shih-lu*, it was found wanting by the editors of the *Ssu-k'u* catalogue who criticized the author for failing to consult all existing sources; one may assume too that its title appeared on the list of banned books for including comments unfavorable to the ancestors of the Manchus. The Library of Congress and Princeton University both possess copies printed in 1573. His own reflections on the bureaucracy may only be assumed, but he does make the revealing comment in a preface to another book, the *Chih sheng lu* 治生錄, also quoted in his complete works, that no official could depend solely on his salary; each one had to find other means of support.

In the area of classical studies he left a discussion of the Odes, entitled *Shih shuo* 詩說, which in the main follows the lead of Chu Hsi. Another contribution is his study of individuals mentioned in the Four Books, *Ssu-shu jen-wu k'ao* 四書人物考, 40 *ch.*, published in 1558. The book was so popular that several annotated or enlarged editions soon appeared. A 1637 edition is in the library of Columbia University. Like other writings by Hsüeh, it has been criticized for his failure to indicate the source of his data. One may mention here also his addition to and revision of the famous *Kao-shih chuan* 高士傳 by Huang-fu Mi (215–82), which originally contained the biographies of ancient scholars.

History likewise claimed his attention, the longest contribution being the *Sung Yüan* 宋元 *tzu-chih t'ung-chien*, 157 *chüan*, a continuation of the great Mirror of History of Ssu-ma Kuang (1019–86). With this too the *Ssu-k'u* editors found fault, and it was prohibited, probably because it came to be edited by Ch'en Jen-hsi (*q.v.*) and because of necessity it discussed Liao 遼 and Chin 金 history and the relations between the Chinese and their northern and northwestern neighbors during the years 960 to 1367. Hsüeh himself said that he granted the Mongol rulers imperial status only from the year the last Sung emperor died (1279) to the year the Ming founder joined the rebels (1353). Another criticism of Hsüeh is that he emphasizes in his treatment the individual and how well or ill he observes i-li 義理, or the right way of life, while the standard historical method was to stress the chih-tao 治道, or proper governance of the state. In other words, Hsüeh wrote history as though he were writing on the canon. An interesting feature of this work is his indication of the importance of Taoist principles in ruling the land. Points in his favor are his discussions of the neo-Confucianism of the centuries in question, and his comments on the invasions by border peoples. This book has, up till now, been displaced by the work of Pi Yüan (ECCP), published in 1801, covering the same period, which reflects the Manchu viewpoint. Hsüeh's history has nevertheless been preserved (in the Library of Congress and the libraries of Columbia and Princeton Universities, among other collections) in two editions, one printed in 1566 and another, edited by Ch'en Jen-hsi, printed in 1625.

Another history which has received higher praise is his gazetteer of Chekiang province, the *Chekiang t'ung-chih*, 72 *ch.*, published 1561. Alexander Wylie a century ago called it "one of the best of the class as to its plan of arrangement and general treatment of subjects." Fortunately a few copies of this have been preserved in mainland China, Japan, and Taiwan. In the chronological category there is his *Chia-tzu hui-chi* 甲子會記, 5 *ch.*, which starts with the legendary period and concludes with the year 1563.

Hsüeh left also a short book of jottings, entitled *Fang-shan chi-shu* 紀述, which has been reprinted in several collectanea, besides his collected works, mentioned above, a copy of which (in the National Library of Peiping) is available in microfilm. The latter includes discussions of the books he wrote. One may conclude by remarking that, though much of his output has suffered from criticism and prohibition and neglect, his pa-ku essays were much admired.

Two of Hsüeh's grandsons, Hsüeh Fu-chiao (*see* Ku Hsien-ch'eng) and Hsüeh Fu-cheng 政 (T. 以心, H. 純臺, cs 1607), entered government service and were authors in their own right. The former joined Ku Hsien-ch'eng in helping to found the Tung-lin; the latter rose to be regional inspector of Szechuan.

Bibliography

1/231/18a; 3/216/17a; 40/42/12a; 64/戌 19/21a; 83/25/23a; 86/12/27b; *Fang-shan Hsüeh hsien-sheng ch'üan-chi* (NLP, microfilm nos. 935–936); Huang Tsung-hsi (ECCP), *Ming-ju hsüeh-an* (1693 ed.), 2/1a, 17/1a, 25/1a, 12a, 58/1a; TSCC (1885–88), XIV: 523/4/8b, XXIII: 105/93/15b; *Wu-chin Yang-hu* 陽湖 -*hsien chih* (1879), 19/12a, 28/8b, 13a, 15a; *Tz'u-ch'i-hsien chih* (1899), 16/23a, 23/19a; *Chien-ch'ang-fu chih* (1910), 6/16a, 37a; *Lo-ch'uan-hsien chih* (1806), 8/5a, 16/3b; *Shang-jao* 上饒 -*hsien chih* (1873), 19A/31a; *Wen-hsi* 聞喜 -*hsien chih* (1919), 14/6b, 16B/3a; *Chekiang t'ung-chih* (1934), 2639; *Shensi t'ung-chih* (1735) 22/42a; SK (1930), 37/4a, 48/3b, 61/4a, 96/5a, 177/12b; *Kung-chü k'ao-lüeh* 貢舉考略 (compl. ca. 1839), 2/5b, 9b; Sun Tien-ch'i (1957), 75, 218; L. of C. *Catalogue of Rare Books*, 99, 108, 117; I. V. Gillis, *An Index to the Catalogue of the Gest Oriental Collection* (Princeton, 1941), 427, 574; A. Wylie, *Notes on Chinese Literature* (Shanghai 1867, repr. of 1922), 45; W. Franke, *Sources*, 1.3.1, 8.10.1.

Mou Jun-sun and L. Carrington Goodrich

HU Chen-heng 胡震亨 (T. 孝轅, H. 遯叟), 1569–1644/45, bibliophile, scholar, and official, was a native of Hai-yen 海鹽, Chekiang. His grandfather, Hu Hsien-chung 憲仲 (T. 文澄, 文徵, H. 仰崖, 1514–53), was a *chin-shih* of 1550, who served as a secretary in the ministry of Works, and his father, Hu P'eng-shu 彭述 (T. 信甫), was a book collector, owning a library named Hao-ku lou 好古樓. Hu Chen-heng himself qualified as a *chü-jen* in 1597, but, after failing several times to pass the metropolitan examinations, took a post as instructor in the district school of Ku-ch'eng 故城, Pei-Chihli. Promoted to be magistrate of Ho-fei 合肥 (Anhwei) he served for five years, receiving plaudits for the efficiency and justice of his administration. Because of his mother's advanced age, however, he chose to return home, and lived in retirement for some twenty years. Not until 1637 did he resume his official career as magistrate of Ting-chou 定州, Pei-Chihli. Later, for a brief period, probably about 1640 or 1641, he became a vice director of the bureau of operations in the ministry of War in Peking. Realizing the helpless situation of the Ming government and the ineffectiveness of the high officials in the ministry of War, Hu retired once more. It is said that under the administration of Ch'en Hsin-chia 陳新甲 (cj 1612, vice minister of War, 1638-40, and minister of War, 1640-42, executed 1642), Hu had high hopes of effecting certain changes to combat the deteriorating conditions in the state, resulting from both outside encroachment and internal disorder. When he found how unpopular Ch'en was, however, he begged leave to resign.

During the earlier period of retirement, Hu together with a friend and fellow provincial, **Shen Shih-lung** 沈士龍 (T. 海 (汝) 納, cj 1597), collected and printed in 1603 the *Pi-ts'e hui-han* 秘册彙函, a *ts'ung-shu* of twenty or twenty-two titles. Unfortunately, the blocks of this compilation as well as Hu's library were partially destroyed by fire in 1621. Later the remaining blocks passed into the possession of Mao Chin (ECCP), and became the nucleus of Mao's much larger collection, the well-known *Chin-tai pi-shu*. Included in the *Pi-ts'e hui-han*, as well as in the *Chin-tai pi-shu*, is an item entitled *Sui-hua chi-li* 歲華紀麗, 4 *ch.*, a reference work classified by calendrical order, attributed to Han O 韓鄂 (*ca.* 9th cent.). Its authenticity has been debated, the Ch'ing scholar Wang Shih-chen (ECCP) declaring that it was written by Hu Chen-heng. (Ming scholars such as Yang Shen, Feng Fang, and Yao Shih-lin [*qq.v.*] have all been accused of writing under names of earlier authors. Possibly this practice was not regarded then as a serious misdemeanor.)

In the first years of the 1620s the Hai-yen local government under Magistrate Fan Wei-ch'eng 樊維城 (T. 紫蓋, cs 1619, d. May 10, 1643) undertook several learned projects, for which it relied principally on the aid of local scholars. One of them was the production of a new edition of the Hai-yen local history, which in 1622 Fan entrusted to Hu Chen-heng. Almost single-handedly, Hu completed the work entitled *Hai-yen-hsien t'u-ching* 圖經, 16 *ch.*, in 1624; a copy of the original edition is in the Library of Congress. Simultaneously another project, collecting

works by Hai-yen authors, got under way; for this work, the *Yen-i chih-lin* (*see* Yao Shih-lin), he solicited the assistance of another local bibliophile and friend. The notice in the *Ssu-k'u* catalogue has little to say for this ts'ung-shu, criticizing it in particular for its treatment of the dictionary of Ku Yeh-wang (519-81), entitled *Yü-pien (Kuang-yün) chih-yin* 玉篇 (廣韻) 直音.

Perhaps the most ambitious work that Hu undertook was the *T'ang-yin t'ung-ch'ien* 唐音統籤, a comprehensive collection of T'ang poetry in over one thousand *chüan* in ten parts. As the work was so vast, it was never printed in its entirety. In 1703, when the *Ch'üan T'ang-shih* was compiled on imperial order, Hu's manuscript copy of the *T'ang-yin t'ung-ch'ien* served as the basic source (*see* Ts'ao Yin, ECCP). By 1685 Hu's grandson, Hu Ch'eng-chih 成之 and great-grandson, Hu Ch'i 頎, printed part 9 of the gigantic work in 265 *chüan* under the title *T'ang-yin wu* (戊)-*ch'ien*, containing poems of late T'ang authors and some authors of the Five Dynasties. A printed edition of part 10, entitled *T'ang-yin kuei* (癸)-*ch'ien*, 33 *ch.*, appeared in the Nanking book market in 1718. This, the last part of Hu Chen-heng's original work, containing comments on interesting episodes and other relevant materials concerning T'ang poetry, was reprinted in 1959 in mainland China and has been reproduced in *Ssu-k'u...chen-pen* 珍本, series 3. An abridged version of the *T'ang-yin kuei-ch'ien* was also included in the *Hsüeh-hai lei-pien* (*see* Ts'ao Jung, ECCP) under the title *T'ang-shih t'an-ts'ung* 談叢. In the years from 1635 to 1642 Hu completed a study of the two greatest T'ang poets, Li Po and Tu Fu, the *Li Tu shih-t'ung* 李杜詩通. Hu also left a work supplementing the famous *Wen-hsüan* 文選 of Hsiao T'ung (501-31), the *Hsü* (續) *wen-hsüan*, and a historical work on the Sung dynasty, the *Ching-k'ang tzu-chien lu* 靖康咨鑒錄, probably with the intention that it might serve as a warning for the people of his time. After the accumulation of writings of several centuries, perhaps it was time by the 16th century for Chinese scholars to do some collecting and sorting out of this material for safekeeping. Although the *Po-ch'uan hsüeh-hai* (*see* Wang Wen-lu) appeared in the Sung period, and the *Shuo-fu* (*see* T'ao Tsung-i) was compiled at the end of the Yüan, the development of the printing of *ts'ung-shu* really began in the middle of the Ming dynasty. It is true that there were bad selections, incorrect assignment of authorship unsound judgments, abridgments, and other imperfections, as later scholars pointed out; yet through these *ts'ung-shu* many works have been saved. Similarly praiseworthy was the endeavor to preserve in anthologies and collections literature of past dynasties and of their own time. The labors of Mei Ying-tso and Chang Hsieh (*qq. v.*), for example, must have opened the way for Yen K'o-chün (ECCP) to succeed in producing the "Complete Collection of Prose Literature from Remote Antiquity through the Ch'in and Han Dynasties, the Three Kingdoms, and the Six Dynasties."

As a bibliophile, Hu is said never to have wearied in the search for rare items in collating, correcting the errors in old texts, patching up fragments, and making incomplete books as nearly complete as possible. One of his sons, Hu Hsia-k'o 夏客 (T. 宜子), who also engaged in scholarly pursuits, was a student in the National University in the early Ch'ing period. Another son, Hu Chi-ying 季瀠 (T. 子甫, H. 念齋), became a *kung-sheng* in 1648 and rose to be prefect of Soochow and then of Kiukiang.

Bibliography

40/58/10a; 64/庚 18/8a; *Hai-yen-hsien chih* (1876), 15/59b, 16/2b, 17/18b 末 /32a, 58b, 67a; SK (1930), 74/6a, 134/3b, 137/1b, 190/1a, 193/4b, 196/3a, 197/10a; Chang Hsin-ch'eng 張心澂, *Wei-shu t'ung-k'ao* 偽書通考 (1954), 945, 975; Yü Ta-kang 俞大綱, "Chi 記 T'ang-yin t'ung-ch'ien" in CYYY, Vol. VII, part 3 (1937), 355.

Lienche Tu Fang

HU Chih 胡直 (T. 正甫, H. 宜舉, 廬山), 1517-June, 1585, thinker and official, was a native of T'ai-ho 泰和, Kiangsi. In his youth he seems to have been barely restrained by the influence of his father, Hu T'ien-feng 天鳳, a trusted disciple of Wang Shou-jen (*q.v.*). When the father died, Hu Chih, then seventeen years of age, led a carefree life, scoffed at and belittled the teachings of the master. He fell in with the vogue of the times in praising the merits of ancient prose 古文, emulating in his own writings especially Li Meng-yang and Ho Ching-ming (*qq.v.*). It was not until 1542 that Hu Chih began to follow any particular school of thought. He listened to Ou-yang Te (*q.v.*), another disciple of Wang Shou-jen, discoursing on the *Lun-yü*, and decided to become a follower of the Wang school. The next year he passed the *chü-jen* examination, but it was not until thirteen years later that he attained the *chin-shih*. In 1547 he went to visit Lo Hung-hsien (*q.v.*) at Chi-shui 吉水, Kiangsi, where the latter had just a year before built the Shih-lien tung 石蓮洞 for purposes of contemplation. After staying a month meditating and studying, he became Lo's disciple. In 1548 he went to Shao-chou 韶州, Kwangtung, where the prefect Ch'en Ta-lun 陳大倫 (cs 1529) employed him to teach at the Ming-ching Academy 明經書院. There he studied Taoism and dhyana Buddhism. He sat for days in quiet meditation, hoping to drive out distracting thoughts and discover his own true nature. In the autumn of that year he met Ch'ien Te-hung (*q.v.*) and tried to learn from him but to no avail. It is reported that one day while standing on a height he received sudden enlightenment, declaring that the unity of all things lay in his heart's mind.

Five years later, Hu became instructor in the Confucian school of Chü-jung 句容 near Nanking, and in 1556 after getting the higher degree he was appointed a secretary in the ministry of Justice. From 1560 on he served in various administra-

tive commissioner posts in Hukuang, Szechwan, and Kwangsi, often taking charge
of local education. In 1573 he received
an appointment as surveillance commissioner of Kwangtung, but asked to be relieved in the winter of that year to look
after his aged mother. Between 1573 and
1581, when his mother died, Hu led a life
of retirement and labored on his *Hu-tzu
heng-ch'i* 胡子衡齊, 8 *ch*. In 1584 he was
recalled to serve as surveillance commissioner of Fukien where he died.

Hu's thought, chiefly expressed in his
Heng-ch'i, a collection of his conversations
with his disciples, among whom was Kuo
Tzu-chang (*q.v.*), is an extension of the
Wang Yang-ming system. Hu, more than
his intellectual progenitor, openly advocated the Ch'an Buddhist notion of the
mind as the sole source and repository
of truth and reality, and criticized the
contention of the neo-Confucian masters
of the Sung that the principle (理) of
things was an external standard. Hu did
try to differentiate between Buddhism
and Confucianism, as he considered
himself a Confucianist. He said that even
though the Buddhists were right in saying
that all reality is in the heart-mind of
man and strove to understand this inner
nature, they nevertheless denied the
world. In the end even the heart-mind is
unimportant. The Confucianists, on the
other hand, were world affirming; moreover, because they too entertained reality
in the heart of man, they were all the
wiser to deal with worldly affairs since
they already comprehended everything
before action was taken.

From the Taoist and Ch'an Buddhist schools, Hu also took the idea that
feeling is human nature, that there is no
point in separating mind, feeling, in-
tuition, and nature. Cultivating-to-know
for him meant cultivating inner capacities
for feeling the entirety of existence. Like
Wang Shou-jen, he also maintained the
essential unity of knowledge and action,
implying the test by experience of
inner knowledge. This experience was to

be subjective and personal. Hu Chih thus
can be thought of as a latter-day articu-
lator of Wang's thought, bold in his attempt to infuse Confucianism with Buddhist and Taoist ideas, but remaining
loyal to the subjective, moral idealism of
the master.

Hu Chih's writings include the *Heng-
ch'i* (reprinted in the *Yü-chang* 豫章 *ts'ung-
shu*, 1916); the *Heng-lu ching-she ts'ang-kao*
衡盧精舍藏稿, 30 *ch*., and *hsü-kao* 續稿, 11
ch., originally collected for printing by his
disciple Kuo Tzu-chang. The *K'un hsüeh
chi* 困學記 is appended to the *hsü-kao* in
the 1902 edition.

This Hu Chih is not to be confused
with another Hu Chih (T. 敬方), a native
of Chi-shui, Kiangsi, who flourished in
the 14th century.

Bibliography

22/10/47a; 40/44/13b; 83/22/1a; Biography by
Keng Ting-hsiang, in *Keng T'ien-t'ai ch'üan-shu*,
ch. 12; Jung Chao-tsu, *Ming-tai ssu-hsiang shih*
明代思想史, 206; SK (1930), 96/6a, 172/9b.

D. W. Y. Kwok

HU Ching, *see* **HU Kuang**

HU Chü-jen 胡居仁 (T. 叔心, H. 敬齋,
1434-April 7, 1484), thinker and educator
was a native of Yü-kan餘干, Kiangsi. His
ancestors originally lived in T'ai-chou 泰州
(prefecture of Yangchow), whence they
moved south about 1126 with the first
emperor of the Southern Sung dynasty.
For generations the Hu family had been
poor farmers. By the time of Hu Chü-
jen, their poverty had become rather
acute. About 1445 his family moved to a
neighboring district, An-jen 安仁, where
in 1452 he received special instruction in
the Spring and Autumn Annals from Yü
Chun 于準 (T. 世衡, sub prefect of Sung-
chiang 松江 in 1474), a disciple of Wu
Yü-pi (*q.v.*). On Yü's recommendation, Hu
went (in 1454) to study under the direction of Wu Yü-pi at the latter's home in

Ch'ung-jen 崇仁, some sixty miles to the south. Hu Chü-jen manifested a deep attachment to Wu and appreciation of his teaching, hoping to attain sagehood by living according to the Confucian code of conduct. He accompanied Wu on a trip to Fukien (1456), and followed his example by refraining from taking the civil examinations (see Wu Yü-pi). To attain his goal, Hu stayed in his native place, living as a farmer to support his parents, while studying by himself and instructing disciples. He moved in 1465 to the Mei-hsi 梅溪 hill near Yü-kan, where he had built some mud houses with thatched roofs. After the death of his father (1466), Hu observed strict mourning. In 1468 he was invited to give lectures at the famous White Deer Academy in Kiangsi, but had barely the time to lay down certain academic rules, as a supplement to the ones originally given by Chu Hsi, before he was called back to his native place, this time to mourn the death of his mother. Soon afterwards he also lost his wife. Perhaps the bereavements and protracted mourning affected his health, for Hu reported in a letter to a friend (1479) that he had not been well for about eight years. In 1480 he was invited once more to the White Deer Academy, to take over its direction. He remained there for four years until his death, which occurred in 1484.

Hu Chü-jen had one son, Hu Ch'ung-hsiu 崇修. His best known disciple, Yü Yu (q.v.), was also his son-in-law. In 1578, by imperial order, a shrine in Hu's memory was erected in his native Yü-kan, with the designation Cheng-hsüeh tz'u 正學祠. His tablet was placed in the Confucian temple in 1584, together with those of Ch'en Hsien-chang and Wang Shou-jen (qq.v.). He was also canonized Wen-ching 文敬.

Hu Chü-jen was an ardent admirer of the teachings of Chu Hsi. He followed the basic doctrines of the Ch'eng-Chu school, which gave equal emphasis to the inner cultivation of the mind and the outer investigation of things. But, like his mentor, Wu Yü-pi, Hu showed no interest in such metaphysical subjects as T'ai-chi 太極 (Ultimate), yin-yang, li 理, and ch'i 氣. For him moral principles are embodied in the mind and should therefore be sought in oneself. As the Ming-shih says, "He considered loyalty (chung 忠) and faithfulness (hsin 信) to be of first importance, and the discovery of the lost mind to be essential." He regarded the practice of reverence (ching 敬) to one's inner self as so important that he named his study Ching-chai 敬齋. Huang Tsung-hsi (ECCP) has observed that Hu's "whole life was built on the strength of reverence, and consequently his practice of virtue showed excellent results." Nor did Hu neglect the investigation of things, which meant for him actual practice, not empty speculation. He manifested this concern by his personal study, not only of government, society, and education, but also of the calendar and of methods of irrigation. He desired as well the restoration of the well-field 井田 system.

Hu Chü-jen was a fellow-pupil of Lou Liang (q.v.) and Ch'en Hsien-chang, both of whom studied also under Wu Yü-pi. But Hu put more emphasis on the cultivation of the mind than Wu himself. A serious and upright man, he was of the same character as Hsüeh Hsüan and Ts'ao Tuan (qq.v.). He criticized Ch'en Hsien-chang for the latter's Ch'an Buddhist sympathies, drawing the comment from Huang Tsung-hsi that Hu was closer to the "cautious" (chüan 狷) type of Confucian disciple, whereas Ch'en was closer to the "eccentric" (k'uang 狂; see Legge, Chinese Classics, I, 136). The editors of the Ssu-k'u Catalogue add, "Ch'en Hsien-chang learned [from Wu Yü-pi] quiet observation and self-cultivation, while Hu Chü-jen learned from him earnest resolution and vigorous practice."

Hu Chü-jen left several written works. The I-hsiang ch'ao 易象鈔, 4 ch., gives his insights into the Book of Changes, which he studied for twenty years, and on which he once (1483) gave a lecture in the presence of Prince Chu Ch'i-ch'üan 朱祁銓 of Huai 淮 (d. 1502). It has been published in the *Ssu-k'u ch'üan-shu chen-pen* 珍本, first series. His main philosophical work is the *Chü-yeh lu* 居業錄, 8 *ch.*, which gives his recorded dialogues, as compiled by Yü Yu and published in 1504. It resembles Hsüeh Hsüan's *Tu-shu lu* in both form and content. The book exists also as the *Chü-yeh lu lei-pien* 類編, 31 *ch.*, compiled and edited by Ch'en Feng-wu (*see* Ho Ting), who put the original recorded sayings into thirty-one categories. Hu's letters, essays, and poems have been collected and published in the *Hu Wen-ching kung chi* 公集, sometimes entitled *Hu Ching-chai chi*, 3 *ch.* This collection shows too Hu's simplicity of style and purpose. He spoke against Chu Hsi for having written commentaries on the Taoist classics, *Ts'an-t'ung ch'i* and *Yin-fu ching*. He himself was so careful to remain orthodox that he commented only on the Spring and Autumn Annals and the Book of Changes.

Bibliography

1/282/11a; 5/114/26a; 42/72/11a; 63/21/6b; 38/2/1a; MSL (1940), Shen-tsung, 155/5a; KC(1958), 2489; SK (1930), 5/2a, 93/3a, 95/10a, 171/5b; Hu Chü-jen, *Chü-yeh lu* (TsSCC ed., lst ser., 1936); *id., Chü-yeh lu* (*Cheng-i-t'ang ch'üan-shu* 正誼堂全書 ed.), Vol. 17; *id., Hu Ching-chai chi* (TsSCC ed., lst ser., 1936); *id., Hu Ching-chai chi* (*Cheng-i-t'ang ch'üan shu* ed.), vol. 9; Yang Hsi-min 楊希閔, comp., *Hu Wen-ching kung nien-p'u* 年譜, in *Shih-wu-chia* 十五家 *nien-p'u* (1878), Vol. 9; manuscript biography by Huang P'ei.

Julia Ching

HU Kuang 胡廣 (T. 光大，晃菴), 1370-June 21, 1418, scholar-official, was a native of Chi-shui 吉水, Kiangsi. His father, Hu Tzu-ch'i 子祺 (*ming* 壽昌, 1333-77), is reported to have persuaded Chu Yüan-chang to spare the lives of his fellow townsmen who had been forced to join Ch'en Yu-liang (*q.v.*); eventually (1387) he was made censor, then prefect of Yen-p'ing 延平, Fukien. Hu Kuang was his second son and became a marked man by graduating as *optimus* in the palace examination of 1400. Emperor Chu Yün-wen (*q.v.*), finding his name to be the same as that of the Han minister Hu Kuang (A.D. 91-172), ordered him to change it to Hu Ching 靖, and appointed him compiler in the Hanlin Academy. Following the enthronement of Chu Ti (*q.v.*) he reverted to his former name. In due course he and several other Hanlin members came to be much favored by the new emperor. Hu received a promotion to expositor-in-waiting in the Hanlin and later was ordered, together with Hsieh Chin, Huang Huai, Hu Yen, Yang Jung, Yang Shih-ch'i (*qq.v.*), and Chin Yu-tzu (*see* Empress Hsü) to participate in deciding important governmental issues at court. This led to the establishment of the Grand Secretariat.

In 1404 Hu and three others were asked by the emperor for their judgment of a book which Chu Chi-yu 朱季友, a commoner, had written and presented to the emperor. Because the author denounced the opinions of the neo-Confucian school, all four officials condemned the work. Three of them suggested either to burn the book or to flog the author. Hu alone remarked, "I hear that the author is already seventy *sui*; to burn his writings would be sufficient warning." The emperor adopted the majority opinion, and ordered not only that the book and other writings of Chu be burned, but also that the unhappy author be publicly flogged before the provincial officials and scholars of his native province, Kiangsi.

Hu was made chancellor of the Hanlin Academy and Grand Secretary of the left directory of instruction in 1407, and was ordered along with others to tutor the eldest grandson of the emperor, Chu Chan-chi (*q.v.*). In 1410 and again in 1414 he, Chin Yu-tzu, and Yang Jung accompanied the emperor on his northern expeditions. The emperor's regard for these three learned advisers is vividly described in Chin Yu-tzu's account of these events in his *Pei-cheng lu* 北征錄. On the first campaign the emperor took them along not for their advice on military arts, of which they knew little, but for their discussion of literature and governmental affairs. On the second campaign they continued their service as tutors of Chu Chan-chi, who was in the emperor's entourage to observe how actual battles were fought. In 1416 Hu rose to be Grand Secretary of the Wen-yüan hall 文淵閣, the highest post in the court, and maintained this position until his death. His other significant administrative work was to serve twice (1403, 1411) as director of the provincial examinations held in Nanking.

As an official Hu was known for his care and restraint. His advice to the emperor, always well taken, was based on reason and understanding, and he never attacked other officials for making an error. He particularly refused to betray the emperor's confidence in personal or important governmental affairs, not even to his closest relatives or friends. It was he who urged the emperor to cancel the order to exterminate the partisans of his deposed nephew Chu Yün-wen. Because of his consideration for others and lack of forcefulness Hu was not given the kind of power his colleague Yang Shih-ch'i enjoyed. The emperor's deep trust in Hu, however, may be seen in the fact that the emperor either ignored those who accused or slandered him, or dismissed others who presented criticisms. On his death Hu was granted the posthumous name Wen-mu 文穆, one of the two civil officials to be given such an honor during Chu Ti's reign, the other being Yao Kuang-hsiao (*q.v.*).

Hu was also a well-known classical scholar, and is said to have been as well a student of medicine, astrology, Taoism, and Buddhism. A collection of his writings, *Hu Wen-mu chi* 集, unfortunately does not appear to be extant, but a small collection of miscellaneous notes entitled *Hu Wen-mu tsa-chu* 雜著 was copied into the eighteenth century Imperial Library, and has recently been reproduced in the *Ssu-k'u ch'üan-shu chen-pen*, series 2 珍本二集. His literary talent led to his drafting of many edicts and participation in the compilation of the *Ku-chin lieh-nü-chuan* (*see* Empress Hsü) and to his being put in charge of the compilation of the second revision of the *T'ai-tsu shih-lu* (1418) and the compilation of the *Wu-ching Ssu-shu* and *Hsing-li ta-ch'üan* (*see* Chu Ti), completed on October 17, 1415. In his private life he enjoyed the beauty of nature and the tranquillity he found in his garden. According to Yang Shih-ch'i, his calligraphy in running hand style was the best of his time. It was to Hu that the emperor turned for writing the inscription on the memorial tablet for his deceased empress and for the monuments along the routes of his campaigns. Many people from all over China came to request examples of his penmanship. The critic Wu K'uan (*q.v.*), however, considered Hsieh Chin's hand better. His eldest son Hu T'ung 穜, by imperial favor, was made a Hanlin graduate of the third degree. Another son, Hu Chung 種, fared less well; he is reported to have been found guilty of manslaughter.

Bibliography

1/147/10b; 3/137/14b; 5/12/18a; 61/119/11a; 64/乙 4/1a; 84/ 乙 /9a; 86/6/17b; MSL (1963), T'ai-tsung, ch. 33-217; KC (1958), 870, 883, 887, 909, 920, 928, 947, 997, 1012, 1036, 1152; Teng Yüan-hsi, *Huang Ming-shu* (1606), 15/21a; TSCC (1885-88), XI: 243/63/8b, XXIV: 118/24/2b; Chin Yu-tzu, *Chin-wen ching-kung-chi* 金文靖公集, 7/2b, 10/59b, 62b; *id.*, *Pei-cheng lu*; Yang Shih-ch'i, *Tung-li wen-chi*, 4/2b, 9, 9/9a, 21b, 12/9b; Hsü Hung 徐紘 (cs 1490), *Huang Ming ming-ch'en wan-yen lu* 皇明名臣琬琰錄(NCL microfilm), 19/1; Ho Ch'iao-yüan, *Ming-shan ts'ang*, Ch'en-lin chi 臣林記 (NLP microfilm, rolls 93-96), 5/32a; Cheng Hsiao, *Wu-hsüeh pien* (1567), Ming-ch'en chi 名臣集, 8/10a; Yeh Sheng, *Shui-tung jih-chi* (1965 reprint), 28/1a; Wu K'uan, *P'ao-weng-chia ts'ang-chi*, SPTK ed. (Chi-pu 集部), 55/1b; Li Mo 李默 (d. 1556), *Ku-shu-p'ou-t'an* (NLP microfilm, roll 247), 1/23a, 3/4a, 11a, 14a, 16b, 4/1a, 4a; SK (1930), 36/3b, 93/2b, 122/5a; *Yen-p'ing-fu chih* (1873), 34/30a; Shen Te-fu, *Wan-li yeh-hu-pien*; Ku Chieh-kang, "A Study of the Literary Persecution during the Ming," tr. by L. Carrington Goodrich, HJAS, III (1938), 293; W. Franke, *Sources*, 1.1.1.

Angela Hsi and L. Carrington Goodrich

HU Ta-hai 胡大海 (T. 通甫), died March 3, 1362, native of Hung 虹 -hsien (modern Ssu-chou 泗州, Anhwei), was an early military supporter of Chu Yüan-chang and helped conquer and administer Che-kiang. When he was assassinated by a treacherous subordinate, Hu's personal retainers and the people of Chin-hua 金華 (Chekiang), where he had his head-quarters, thought of him as a great soldier and made him the object of a local cult.

Hu Ta-hai and his adopted son, Hu Te-chi 德濟 (T. 世美, 1337-February, 1379), began their service under Chu Yüan-chang at Ch'u 滁 -chou (Anhwei) early in 1354. It is likely that Hu Ta-hai was already a veteran of the rebellion because he was appointed right away to Chu's vanguard and he must have been about Chu's age or older, because Hu Te-chi was able to begin his active military career at the same time. The two Hu, father and son, crossed the Yangtze with Chu Yüan-chang in July, 1355, and campaigned with him for about two years, participating in the capture of Ch'ang 常 -chou from Chang Shih-ch'eng (*q. v.*) in November, 1356, and Ning-kuo 寧國 from the Yüan in May, 1357. Under the command of Teng Yü (*q. v.*), his fellow townsman, Hu continued towards the south and invaded the Yüan-held prefecture of Hui 徽 -chou in July. After he took the prefectural seat, the name was changed to Hsing-an 興安- fu, and Teng became its administrator. In a few months of campaigning in the field Hu conquered most of the prefecture and later (November ?) helped Teng beat off an attack by the Yüan commander Yang Wan-che (Öljei) and his Miao army (*see* Chang Shih-ch'eng).

In the spring of 1358 Hu joined with Teng Yü and Li Wen-chung (*q. v.*) in a campaign into Chekiang. After several sharp engagements they occupied the Chien-te 建德 prefectural seat in April. In the course of the reorganization of the administration, which was undertaken at once, ill-feeling appeared in the relationship between Hu and his younger colleague, Li Wen-chung. Chu found it necessary to intervene with instructions for both men; Hu received a promotion to the rank of assistant military commissioner, which satisfied him, while Li was made responsible for the defense of the prefectural seat. Hu then (May) assisted in the defense of Hui-chou against new attacks by Yang Wan-che, and resumed his eastward march in November, capturing Lan-ch'i 蘭溪 in Chin-hua prefecture. He was ordered to take the prefectural seat in December. As he was unsuccessful in his first attempt, Chu Yüan-chang arrived with heavy reinforcements to take charge. When the Yüan general Shih-mo I-sun (*see* Chang I) foolishly sent a relief force in armored "lion wagons" northward from Ch'u 處 -chou through difficult terrain, Hu Ta-hai was sent to trap them in the mountains, where he defeated them easily. The defenders of Chin-hua were disheartened by the failure of the relief expedition to get through. One of the gates was soon breached and, after many of the Yüan officials had been killed or captured, the city was won. Hu now was rewarded for his services by promotion to the rank of vice military commissioner.

Following the victory at Chin-hua in January, 1359, Hu invaded Chang Shih-ch'eng's territory, turning northeast to take Chu-chi 諸暨 (named Chu-ch'üan 全 in 1359-66) in Shao-hsing-fu in February and entering Hsiao-shan 蕭山-hsien on the coast (May). His attacks on Shao-hsing, however, were turned back by General Lü Chen (*see* Chang Shih-ch'eng), and in June Hu was recalled to Chin-hua by Chu

Yüan-chang. Chu was on the point of returning to his capital at Nanking, and was persuaded that Hu could be relied upon to take charge of the defense of Chin-hua and win the active cooperation of its people. Chu appointed the scholars Wang K'ai 王愷 (T. 用和, 1317-62) and Luan Feng 欒鳳 to assist Hu in civil and military administration. Before he accepted this new assignment a tragic circumstance occurred. At some time during the half year that Chu maintained his headquarters at Chin-hua, he discovered that one of Hu's own two sons had violated his stern order against the manufacture of liquor (a measure adopted to conserve grain). Hu Ta-hai was then campaigning in Shao-hsing and Wang K'ai urged clemency in order "to set Hu Ta-hai's mind at rest" (by which he meant not to upset him and drive him into the arms of Chang Shih-ch'eng). Chu replied that he would rather see Hu in revolt against him than "allow his law to be disregarded." He then executed the offender with his own hand. It does not appear that the faithful Hu Ta-hai wavered in his loyalty then or afterwards.

At the end of June Hu had to return to Chu-chi in order to help defend it against an attack by Lü Chen. Lü dammed the river below the city so that the backed-up water would flood it, but Hu turned the tables on him when he demolished the dam and flooded Lü's camp instead. Lü then presented a broken arrow as a token of truce. Hu accepted it and allowed him to withdraw. Wang K'ai urged Hu to violate the truce and attack Lü because he was a "treacherous bandit," but Hu refused to break his word. Late in November Shih-mo I-sun's carefully planned defenses in Ch'u-chou were breached when his follower, Hu Ch'en (*see* Chang I) deserted to one of Hu Ta-hai's subordinates, Keng Tsai-ch'eng 耿再成 (T. 德甫, Pth. 武莊). Hu Ta-hai and Keng then occupied the entire prefecture. In June and July, 1360, when Ch'en Yu-liang (*q. v.*) mounted his great offensive against

Chu Yüan-chang, Hu was ordered to create a diversion by capturing Kuang-hsin 廣信 in Kiangsi. He succeeded in doing so and established a garrison there. At about this time Hu submitted a memorial pointing out the resentment caused by the "stockade grain" (寨糧), an arbitrary tax levied by Chu's garrison troops on the local inhabitants. The tax was promptly abolished. Hu was promoted in June, 1361, to the rank of assistant administrator of the Che-tung sub-branch secretariat and stationed at Chin-hua. In the same month he had to return to Kuang-hsin to help its outnumbered defenders under his son Hu Te-chi against an attack by Ch'en Yu-liang's general, Li Ming-tao 李明道. The two Hu defeated Li, captured him and sent him to Chu, but Chu ordered him released in order to encourage more defections among Ch'en's officers in Kiangsi. Hu then turned his attention again to Shao-hsing, but failed once more to take it, and in September had to return to Chin-hua.

The Miao army commanders at Chin-hua, Chiang Ying 蔣英 and Li Fu 李福, submitted to Li Wen-chung in September 1358, with their leader Yüan Ch'eng 員成. Hu Ta-hai liked their combative spirit and accepted them under his command. Chiang and Li rebelled in March, 1362, and with the aid of their followers assassinated Hu Ta-hai, his son, Hu Kuan-chu 關住, and Wang K'ai. Hu's only surviving heir, Hu Te-chi, and Li Wen-chung hurried to the scene, but the two conspirators had fled to Chang Shih-ch'eng's territory. Li Wen-chung was welcomed as a deliverer, however, and the elders told him of the reign of terror under which they had lived during the revolt. Four years later, the assassination was spectacularly avenged. When Li Wen-chung captured Hangchow from Chang Shih-ch'eng in December, 1366, one of the captured officers was Chiang Ying. He was sent to Nanking where Chu Yüan-chang executed him and reportedly offered his blood as a sacrifice before Hu Ta-hai's portrait. Hu was posthumously invested as the duke of Yüeh-kuo 越國公 and later accorded the canonized name Wu-chuang 武壯.

Hu Ta-hai's death moved many of his followers and the people of Chin-hua to join together to build a temple to his spirit. Sung Lien (*q. v.*) wrote an account of the building and the ceremonies that marked its completion late in 1363. A formal composition was recited in two parts—one by his retainers and one by the citizens—praising Hu for having conferred the blessings of peace, justice, and wealth on the community. Sung also related that when people observed Hu when he went out at night, his eyes shone like lamps, and that after his death he came to people in their dreams, filling the void with his light and with the sounds of his protecting army on the march. The image of the beneficent army is also seen in the catechism he required each of his soldiers to commit to memory: "I am a military man. I am uneducated. I know only three things: I do not slaughter people; I do not commit rape; I do not burn or destroy people's houses." In 1368 Hu Ta-hai was given first place among the deceased officers to whom sacrifices were offered at the capital, and the following year his portrait was hung in the place of highest honor in the temple of meritorious officials.

Hu Te-chi, whose original surname was Lin 林, was a native of Ch'u滁-chou. His skill in riding and shooting caught the attention of Hu Ta-hai, who adopted him. He remained under his command until Hu Ta-hai's death, and continued in military service in Chekiang for another five years, rising to the rank of vice administrator of that province. In 1368 and 1369 he campaigned in Szechwan and Shantung, and in 1370 he served in the northwest with Hsü Ta (*q. v.*). This time he proved ineffective and was relieved, demoted to ordinary cavalryman, and sent back in shackles. Chu Yüan-chang pardoned him, however, in 1371; he restored his surname to Lin and granted him the

ming Chi-feng 濟峯. In this year he was given a new command to assist T'ang Ho (*q. v.*) who was campaigning against Ming Yü-chen (*q. v.*), the overlord of Szechwan. Four years later he was appointed a regional commander of Shensi. Late in 1378 he was allowed to return home on grounds of illness and died the next year at the age of forty-two.

Bibliography

1/133/6a; 5/6/20a; 61/9 4/1b; MSL (1961), T'ai-tsu, ch. 10; Lin Pi 林弼, *Teng-chou Lin hsien-sheng hsü-chi* 登州林先生續集 (NLP microfilm, no. 993), 3/5b; Hsü Mier 1-chih 徐勉之, *Pao yüeh lu* 保越錄, TsSCC ed.; Huang Chang-chien, "*Ming-shih* tsuan-wu" 纂誤, CYYY, Vol. 31 (1960), 326.

Romeyn Taylor

HU Tsung-hsien 胡宗憲 (T. 汝貞, H. 梅林), 1511-December?, 1565, supreme commander of Chekiang, Nan-Chihli, Fukien, and Kiangsi in the struggle against the Japanese pirates and other insurgents, was a native of Chi-hsi 績溪, Hui-chou 徽州 prefecture, about 150 miles south of Nanking and approximately the same distance west of Hangchow. Hui-chou is a mountainous, forested area, where the inhabitants, because of their location, probably suffered less from the effects of civil wars than those living in lowland urban areas; for this reason they were able to preserve their old customs and speech, and especially their clan traditions. There were several large Hu clans in Chi-hsi. Hu Tsung-hsien's is known by the name of the ancestral village as the Hu clan of Lung-ch'uan 龍川. He had a great-great uncle, Hu Fu 富 (T. 永年, 1445-1522, cs 1498, Pth. 康惠), who served as minister of Revenue in Nanking from January, 1512, to January, 1516. Hu Tsung-hsien's own branch of the family, although well-to-do, did not produce anyone of distinction until he himself became a *chü-jen* in 1534 and a *chin-shih* four years later. His first appointment was as magistrate of

I-tu 益都, Shantung, where his administration of justice won the acclamation of the people. They liked to relate stories about him, such as the one that he arrived during a drought and rains came after he prayed to the city god; and an even stranger one that, just when locusts were destroying the crops, magpies flew in from the north and ate them all. When several thousand miners threatened brigandage, he selected a thousand of them to be trained as volunteers, and easily disbanded the rest. Just then, in 1541, the governor (Tseng Hsien, *q.v.*) received an imperial order to send Shantung soldiers against a possible large scale invasion by the Mongols. He called on Hu's corps of volunteers to take the assignment. They saved the province both time and money. Hu was recommended for promotion, but in May, 1542, he retired on account of the death of his mother. Then, two years later, his father passed away, and he remained home three more years.

In July, 1547, Hu received an appointment as magistrate of Yü-yao 餘姚, Chekiang. The gazetteer of that district describes him as tall and stout, being concerned only with matters of consequence, disdaining the routines of office. It happened that he publicly owned a cliff of an eminence about a mile north of Yü-yao city, known as Mt. Sheng-kuei 勝歸, which was being defaced by men who in some way had secured title to part of the cliff. Their sale of the rocks cut from it was a profitable enterprise. Hu summoned the owner of the largest section, and at the assessed price of ninety taels purchased it for the district with his own funds. This shamed the other owners into donating their holdings without compensation. Early in 1548 the gentry erected a monument on the cliff to mark Hu's generosity and public spirit. Several months later he was summoned to Peking for promotion and in December, 1548, appointed a probationary censor. Half a year later he became a regular member of the Censorate.

During his six years in this office Hu distinguished himself as an able memorialist. Late in 1549 he was given the assignment of serving as censor inspector of Pei-Chihli and sent to Hsüan-fu where a group of soldiers, unwilling to be transferred to another frontier fort, showed signs of restiveness. Hu settled the matter with alacrity and tact. His tour of duty at Hsüan-fu was an extremely demanding one, for it was the year that the Mongols penetrated the Chinese defense line in September, advancing as far as Peking and pillaging the suburbs (*see* Ch'iu Luan). The raiders broke through at Ku-pei-k'ou 古北口, about one hundred fifty miles east of Hu's area of responsibility. When the Hsüan-fu front held and its troops were even sent to aid in the defense of Peking, Hu was cited and given fifteen taels of silver as reward. This marks the beginning of the emperor's recognition of his ability.

In the summer of 1551 Hu was transferred to Wuchang in Hukuang where a year later he took part in the final phase of the suppression of a Miao rebellion on the border of that province and Kweichow. There he gained firsthand knowledge of the loyal Miao chieftains whose troops later took part under him in fighting the pirates. Hu next served two years in the Censorate in Peking (1552–54). Late in 1553 he participated in a conference of inspecting secretaries and censors to evaluate the performance of high officials for promotion or punishment. Among those recommended by the conferees for promotion were Yang Po, Chang Ching 經, and Hsü Lun (*qq. v.*). Hu probably drafted the document, for it is included in his collected memorials.

This was the time when the country was threatened by the Mongols on the northern frontier and by the pirates, known as the *wo-k'ou*, who raided the south China coast. By mid-1554 the pirates had defeated the Chekiang troops under Yü Ta-yu (*q.v.*) and other generals, and pillaged at will in the Hangchow-Soochow area, establishing their head-quarters at Che-lin, a coastal town near Sung-chiang (*see* Ho Liang-chün). They even extended their operations north of the Yangtze River, threatening the Grand Canal. At this time (May, 1554) Hu and several other censors in Peking submitted a joint memorial recommending a number of measures to meet the emergency, such as to employ Miao and other abo-rigine troops, to solicit contributions from the wealthy inhabitants whose properties were threatened, to enforce military dis-cipline, and to permit the field commander to make critical decisions in order to seize the initiative. As a result of these suggestions Chang Ching was appointed (June, 1554) supreme commander of Nan-Chihli, Chekiang, Shantung, Kwangtung, Kwangsi, and Fukien, with full authority to control supplies and rations, and to deal with his subordinates of or below the fifth rank civil, or the second rank military (regional). In the Ming dynasty this was the first and only time one man was given such immense military and civil authority. It was granted to Chang Ching, probably because he was expected to ac-complish the task in short order. It seems that the emperor soon became apprehen-sive about him and dispatched at least two officials to scrutinize his actions, namely, the vice minister of Works, Chao Wen-hua (*q.v.*), and the censor, Hu Tsung-hsien. Chao was to offer sacrifices to the sea-god, and Hu to be inspector of Che-kiang.

Hu arrived in his office in Hang-chow late in 1554. One of his first acts was to ask permission to send represent-atives to Japan in an effort to persuade its authorities to stop piracy; it was granted. As to the fighting against the pirates, for half a year he could report nothing but defeats and serious loss of life and prop-erty. He blamed the ineffectiveness of the government troops on lack of discipline and poor leadership. In May, 1555, about eight thousand Miao troops from the Hu-

kuang-Kweichow border arrived in Soo-chow, and some Thai troops from Kwangsi also reached Sung-chiang. Chao called a war council in Hangchow, attended by Chang Ching, Hu Tsung-hsien, and the governor of Chekiang, Li T'ien-ch'ung 李天寵 (T. 子承, d. 1555). According to Hu's account, Chang promised at the conference to send the Miao troops to Chekiang, but a day later changed his mind and kept them at Soochow, because of the intelligence that pirates were ap-proaching the city. Meanwhile Chao memo-rialized the emperor, accusing Chang of ignoring the needs of Chekiang and of other acts showing incompetence as su-preme commander. Chao also accused Li of failures as governor. Just after Chao wrote the memorial, Chang assigned the Miao troops to the command of Yü Ta-yu and sent them into battle. After a vic-tory, east of Soochow, they pursued the pirates south to Wang-chiang-ching 王江涇, a town on the Grand Canal at the northern border of Chekiang, dealing them a crushing defeat (May 19–20; *see* Chang Ching). When Chao learned of the victory, it was too late for him to recall his memorial against Chang, and so, it is said, he immediately submitted another memorial slighting Chang's vic-tory and asserting that the pirates were easily defeated, as Hu Tsung-hsien had weakened them by getting them intox-icated or poisoned. Acting on Chao's ear-lier memorial accusing Chang, the emper-or ordered (June 4) his arrest for trial in Peking. Three days later Chang's report of the Wang-chiang-ching victory arrived. The emperor angrily commented that Chang had heard of Chao's memo-rial and only then started to fight. Accord-ing to the *shih-lu*, Grand Secretary Yen Sung (*q.v.*) told the emperor that it was Chao and Hu Tsung-hsien who had made the victory possible, and that Hu person-ally had gone to the field in a suit of armor. Thus misinformed, the emperor gave 60 taels of silver to Chao and 30 to Hu as prize money for the victory; Chang received the death sentence. Actually Hu was in Hangchow and learned about the battle after it was over, but he went along with Chao Wen-hua and began to attack Chang too, saying that the latter became arrogant after the victory and neglected to strengthen the defenses of Hangchow. Shortly thereafter Li T'ien ch'ung was also cashiered and placed under arrest. Both were executed in November (see Yang Chi-sheng).

The tragic story of Chang Ching has always been attributed to the evil conspiracy of Yen Sung and Chao Wen-hua with Hu Tsung-hsien as a third villain. A close examination of the facts seems to indicate that Chang brought on his own demise. Having been invested with excessive authority over six wealthy provinces, he was too conceited to realize that the power was begrudgingly granted to him for a short time only, and that if he failed to end the piracy quickly he would assuredly be suspected of being overly ambitious. Perhaps the emperor at first wanted only to remove Chang from that office so as to substitute someone else with reduced power. The fact that without any explanation Chang's successor, Chou Ch'ung 周 琉 (cs 1532), was given jurisdiction over three provinces only—Nan-Chihli, Chekiang, and Fukien—indicates such a possibility. It was still a post with too much responsibility, controlling an area producing the major part of the national revenue; but the detachment of the other three provinces did make it less formidable. Chang's life would probably have been spared if he had not argued stubbornly in his own defense; he may possibly have said something offensive to the emperor.

More realistic in court politics and perhaps somewhat intimidated by the influence of Chao and Yen, Hu Tsung-hsien followed their tactics and won rapid promotion. In June, 1555, even as a censor, he was first assigned the duty of checking the military reports and then given the authority to direct the coastal defense of Chekiang. A month later he received the unusual promotion from censor (7A) to assistant censor-in-chief (4A) to replace Li as governor of Chekiang. There is no denying his ability as a military commander, for he did succeed in winning many engagements. In April, 1556, he was awarded another spectacular promotion, this time to supreme commander of Nan-Chihli, Chekiang, and Fukien. He was the last of three in that post, but he held it longer than the other two—for over six and a half years. He established his headquarters in Hangchow, and made it much like a royal court. By wisely using the large funds at his disposal, he collected some able men on his staff, such as Mao K'un, Hsü Wei, and Cheng Jo-tseng (qq.v.), who helped to advise him in diplomacy and strategy. Hence, although he had at this time an army composed chiefly of hastily assembled, multi-racial, undisciplined troops, he could still achieve some victories and make signal gains. In August, 1556, for example, he succeeded in persuading one of the pirate leaders, Hsü Hai (see Chao Wen-hua) to surrender and then forced him into a trap where he was killed. Hsü's Japanese followers, who tried to escape, were waylaid at sea. Some of them were captured and executed in Peking. Their heads and that of Hsü Hai were displayed at the imperial ancestral temple, as the emperor considered it a major victory. It was to Chao Wen-hua, however, that the chief credit was accorded, and he received as reward the title of junior guardian and the hereditary rank of a chiliarch in the Imperial Guard. Hu Tsung-hsien was raised only one grade to censor-in-chief.

In February, 1557, Hu was given the additional concurrent post of governor of Chekiang. He now continued his efforts to prevent the Japanese in authority from helping the pirates by promising them trade, and to persuade the Chinese pirate leader in Japan, Wang Chih 直 (see Lu T'ang), to surrender. Wang came from the same prefecture as Hu, and it is said they were old acquaintances. In August some Japanese trading ships came to Chusan Island, but the court in Peking refused to sanction the reopening of trade. Late in that year Wang Chih swallowed Hu's bait, came to his headquarters, and was immediately detained. This betrayal was resented by Wang's Japanese friends and his Chinese followers alike, who, from their base on Chusan Island, intensified their raids on the Chekiang and Fukien coast (see T'an Lun). In March, 1558, Hu directed a large scale naval and land attack on Chusan, his vessels converging from six points, but failed to dislodge the pirates. Actually, the government troops were forced to retreat. It seems that the original documents on the Chusan affair, like almost all of Hu's memorials from mid-1555 to the time of his death, were lost or destroyed, and only summaries, frequently by biased parties, survived. In any case, evidently Hu blamed the failure on the military leaders, including Yü Ta-yu, the naval commander, and Ch'i Chi-kuang (q.v.) in charge of one of the six contingents. Meanwhile (April, 1558), Hu cleverly sent to the emperor, Chu Hou-ts'ung (q.v.), as an auspicious omen, a white deer captured on Chusan, which the superstitious ruler accepted as a gift from heaven, and celebrated the event in a report to his ancestral temple. Later Hu presented another white deer and two white turtles (August, 1560)—all accepted with elation and gratitude, for the emperor was pleased to find Hu a fellow believer in these Taoist symbols of longevity and felicity.

Early in 1559, when the pirates left Chusan and moved to the Fukien coast, Hu again blamed the failure to contain them on Generals Yü and Ch'i. In April Yü was arrested and escorted to prison in Peking. Although Ch'i was cashiered too he was commissioned by Hu to train three thousand I-wu volunteers (see Ch'i Chi-kuang). Late in that year the emperor ordered Hu to have Wang Chih

executed in Hangchow. Although Hu had taken an oath to guarantee Wang's life, he had to obey the imperial order. The event was again celebrated in Peking as a signal victory, and Hu was rewarded with the title of a grand guardian of the heir apparent and given the hereditary rank of a vice chiliarch in the Imperial Guard. In June, 1560, he was raised in rank to be a titular minister of War and granted full authority to supervise the governors under his jurisdiction. At this time, Hu, Chao Wen-hua, and others connected with the suppression of the pirates were accused of misappropriation of funds (see P'ang Shang-p'eng), but while Chao and the others were subjected to investigation Hu alone was exempted by the emperor from having his accounts examined.

It happened that the three thousand I-wu volunteers trained by Ch'i Chi-kuang in 1559 proved to be effective as a fighting force, winning several spectacular victories, for which Hu received in October, 1561, the higher title of a junior guardian. When Kiangsi was invaded by bandits in that year, Hu was temporarily given the additional jurisdiction over that province too, and he sent Ch'i to help in suppressing them. In July, 1562, he ordered Ch'i to lead his men on an expedition to Fukien to dislodge the Japanese pirates on an island near Ning-te 寧德, fifty miles north of Foochow. Ch'i accomplished the mission with dispatch. At this time the Kwangtung bandit leader Chang Lien (q.v.) had been captured, and it was generally believed that the emergency in the southern provinces was over. The people, especially those in Chekiang, credited Hu with rescuing them from the pirates, and in gratitude to him built a shrine in Hangchow called the Pao-kung tz'u 報功祠 with a plastic image of him and wall paintings depicting his battles. A similar shrine was erected in his home district.

Hu had now reached the zenith of his career. When in June, 1562, Yen Sung lost his position to Hsü Chieh (q.v.), and even after some officials regarded as Yen's clique began to be replaced, Hu misjudged the political situation and made no move to retire. He failed to take a hint when late in November he was ordered to relinquish his supervision over Kiangsi, because the bandits there had been suppressed. The end came swiftly. A group of Nanking secretaries and censors attacked him in a rambling memorial accusing him of various wrongdoings summarized as ten major crimes. He was accused of having been overfriendly with the pirate Wang Chih; of enjoying the luxurious life in Hangchow instead of fighting in the field; of wastefulness in expending the war funds supplied by several provinces; of mishandling other funds; of imposing surtaxes at will; of selling government ranks and titles; of permitting an ex-official, Mao K'un, to purchase some public land technically belonging to the Hangchow Guard; of assigning troops as personal guards to his own son; and lastly of marrying the daughter of a native of Hangchow and allowing the wives of subordinates to visit his chambers. On close examination these accusations all seem to be explainable, such as being friendly to Wang in order to entice him to surrender, granting titles to contributors to the war fund as permitted by imperial order, or assigning an escort to his son to protect him from kidnaping by pirates for blackmail. Corruption and misappropriation could be chargeable to any commander of that day because of the unhealthy court politics and the inadequate accounting system. Living eight years in Hangchow, Hu's marriage (second ?) to a local woman is understandable, and so is some social visiting. Hu's father-in-law happened to be Hung Pien 洪楩 (T. 子美, fl. 1500-60), the grandson of Hung Chung 鍾 (T. 宣之, H. 兩峯, 1443-1523, cs 1475) and publisher of the famous collection of short stories, *Ch'ing-p'ing-shan-t'ang hua-pen* 清平山堂話本. (This last marks the beginning of the recognition of this form of popular literature by the

scholar-official class.) Perhaps Hu took part in its publication as he did in sponsoring the 1556 edition of the *Yang-ming wen-lu* (*see* Wang Shou-jen) and the 1561 edition of the *Chekiang t'ung-chih* (*see* Hsüeh Ying-ch'i). Hu himself wrote an intelligent preface to the former work, and Grand Secretary Hsü Chieh composed the preface to the latter. Apparently Hu also had something to do with printing the *Huang Ming ching-chi wen-lu* (*see* Wan Piao), for in the *Hang-chou fu-chih* of 1579 this work is listed as one of his compilations, with the printing blocks stored in the administration commissioner's office.

In any event, on rather flimsy grounds, an order was issued to arrest Hu for trial in Peking. When Hu arrived on January 19, 1563, the emperor commented that Hu owed all his promotions not to Yen Sung but to himself; that during the eight or nine years of service Hu had three times presented symbols of favor from heaven; that he had written memorials with his own hand; that the sudden attacks on him recently were partisan; that he had been inadequately rewarded because the ministry of War retracted its promise of an earldom to the one who captured Wang Chih; and that if he were punished it would prevent others from rendering faithful service. So the emperor released Hu and let him live in retirement with his rank and titles intact.

The emperor's comments indicate that he knew someone wanted to incriminate Hu as one of Yen Sung's clique, but none of the accusations was serious enough to warrant punishment. There is the possibility that the attack on Hu was ordered from above just for the purpose of removing him from his powerful office, now that the threat of piracy had subsided. As in the case of Chang Ching, once the incumbent was removed from office the authority of that post was reduced. This time the position of supreme commander of the three provinces was abolished. A governorship of Chekiang with specified military powers succeeded it. Had Hu foreseen the inevitable he could have saved himself the hardship and indignity of being apprehended as a culprit by voluntarily requesting the abolition of his post. In any case, as soon as he was arrested, several of his former subordinates and staff members cooperated in writing accounts of his victories over the pirates, perhaps intending to influence a favorable decision in the event of a trial (*see* Mao K'un). Some of them are included in *chüan* 9 of the work on the Japanese pirates, *Ch'ou-hai t'u-pien* (*see* Cheng Jo-tseng), compiled originally and financed by Hu's order. The accounts are intended to present Hu in a favorable light, and so sometimes show bias in the choice of words, in omissions, and in the sequence of presentation.

Back home in Chi-hsi, Hu reportedly acquired some properties and lived quietly for two years. When a former protégé, Lo Lung-wen (*see* Yen Sung), was executed in April, 1565, and his estate confiscated, there was found a letter from Hu to Lo asking the latter to present a bribe to Yen Shih-fan (*see* Yen Sung). A censor there used this undelivered letter as evidence to accuse Hu of corruption. At the same time he was charged with employing ruffians to intimidate his neighbors and of giving shelter to Lo's son, thus enabling the latter to escape punishment. In November, 1565, the emperor again ordered Hu arrested and brought to Peking for trial. While in prison Hu submitted a memorial asking for mercy on account of his past services. It was then discovered that he had died. Some said he committed suicide by taking poison. At the time of his arrest the prefect of Hui-chou had his residence surrounded by troops in anticipation of the order of confiscation. As usually happened in such cases the family was to be put in an enclosure and the properties held under seal. Soon, after Hu's death, the emperor ordered the case closed. According to Keng Ting-hsiang (*q.v.*), Hu's second son, Hu Sung-ch'i 松奇, the inheritor of the vice chiliarch who had

now been deprived of that rank, transported his coffin from Peking to about sixty miles north of Chi-hsi; he abandoned it on the roadside on hearing that the local people (perhaps instigated by the prefect?) had risen and had been threatening the family. Keng, then the censor in charge of education of Nan-Chihli, happened to be passing by and had the coffin removed to a temple for shelter. Apparently it was later taken to Chi-hsi for interment. According to report, the magistrate of Chi-hsi, named Yü Lan 郁蘭 (T. 文芳, cj 1534), an admirer of Hu, took the personal risk of guaranteeing the accountability of Hu's family and estate, and prevented the prefect from mistreating them. Then followed the long process of Hu's rehabilitation. In 1569 the people of Hangchow built a new shrine in his memory. In 1572 by imperial order his titles and ranks were restored and sacrifices were offered at his tomb in Chi-hsi. In 1589, on the appeal of his grandson, Hu Teng 燈 (T. 元亮, cj 1582), a recounting of his exploits took place, and Hu was accorded state burial and offered sacrifices nine times. In 1595, during the war against Japan in Korea, he was further remembered by being canonized as Hsiang-mao 襄懋. His hereditary rank was then raised to that of an assistant commissioner of the Imperial Guard; this went to his grandson, Hu Tun 焞, and was inherited twice more before the fall of the dynasty.

Hu Tsung-hsien reportedly had two sons, the elder being Hu Kuei-ch'i 桂奇, who succeeded through the yin privilege in becoming a student in the National University and an official. In either 1589 or 1595 it was ordered that a descendant of Hu be admitted as stipend student in the government school of Jen-ho 仁和, one of the two districts of Hangchow, so as to officiate at his shrine, the Pao-kung tz'u. A branch of the Hu family thus became natives of Hangchow.

It seems that there was also an economic factor in the connections of Hu

Tsung-hsien with Hangchow. During and immediately after the war with the Japanese pirates, many wealthy families in need of cash had to frequent the pawnshops. There is the possibility that Hu, with his control of the military funds, helped his fellow townsmen engage in banking in the Hangchow area. In any case, the Hui-chou pawnshops became prominent from that time on. Even when the proprietors were natives, especially men of influence, such as Hsiang Yüan-pien (q.v.), who came from a family with a hereditary rank in the local guard, the staff of the shop were usually professionally trained men of Hui-chou. Whatever Hu's part in this enterprise, it was immediately after him that Hui-chou merchants became active in Hangchow and other coastal cities in various kinds of business, including the salt monopoly, publishing, engraving, sale of writing brushes, ink, tea, lumber, etc.

A large part of Hu's life is still obscure because so few of his own writings are extant. Most of his important memorials were collected in the *Tu-fu tsou-i* 督撫奏議 and *Hsü 續 tu-fu tsou-i*, each in 6 *chüan*, printed by himself about 1560 or 1562 but both were lost and are practically unknown today. His memorials written as a censor (1549-54), entitled *San-hsün* 三巡 *tsou-i*, 3 *ch.*, were printed in 1556 by Yeh K'o-ch'eng 葉可成 (cs 1553), the magistrate of Shan-yin 山陰, Chekiang, hence a subordinate. There are thirty-eight memorials in this collection, which are evidently all that could be found in the late Ming period; they constitute the only source for Hu's memorials in the *Ming ching-shih wen-pien* (*see* Ch'en Tzu-lung, ECCP). The *San-hsün tsou-i* became extremely rare until a copy preserved in the Mori 毛利 family of Tokuyama 德山, Japan, was reproduced in 1964, thus throwing some light on Hu's early activities. There is also a *P'ing-wo* 平倭 *tsou-i* listed under his name. Among his other writings only a few essays and poems may be found in some gazetteers.

Bibliography

1/205/8a; 5/57/43a; 8/59/19a; 32/37/14a; MSL (1965), Shih-tsung, 7845; KC(1958), 3851, 3854, 3880, 3900, 3984, 4018; Chu Kuo-chen (ECCP) *P'ing-wo lu* 平倭錄 in *Ch'ou-hai t'u-pien*, 9/44a; Hsü Hsüeh-chü, *Kuo-ch'ao tien-hui*, ch. 169 (a part of this chapter has been published by book dealers as the *Chia-ching tung-nan* 嘉靖東南 *P'ing-wo t'ung-lu*); Ts'ai Chiu-te 采九德, *Wo-pien shih-lüeh* 變事略; *Chia Lung shu-ch'ao* 嘉隆疏鈔 19/63a; Chao Wen-hua, *Chao t'i-tu tsou-shu* 提督奏疏 (manuscript in NCL on microfilm); *Chi-hsi-hsien chih* (1963 Taipei reprint of 1756 and 1810 editions with supplement); *Hang-chou-fu chih* (1965, Taipei reproduction of 1579 ed.); Wu Chung-han 吳重翰, *Ming-tai Wo-k'ou fan-hua shih-lüeh* 犯華史略 (Changsha, 1938), 86; Yüan Wei 袁煒, *Yüan Wen-jung chi* 文榮集 (NCL microfilm), 8/25b; Keng Ting-hsiang, *Keng T'ien-t'ai chi*, 12/37b; *Chung-ching-t'ang hui-lu* 忠敬堂彙錄 (not consulted).

Chaoying Fang

HU Wei-yung 胡惟庸, died February 12, 1380, the prime minister from 1377 to 1380, was executed by order of the first emperor, Chu Yüan-chang, on charges, many of them trumped up, such as plotting to overthrow the throne. Because of the contradictions and anachronisms in the official records about him, many historians during the last six hundred years have studied his case to sift the evidence with varying degrees of success. All this has impeded our effort to present a true portrait of this important figure.

Little is known of Hu's early years. A native of Ting-yüan 定遠 (Anhwei), he went to Ho-chou 和州 in 1355 to join the rebel army under Chu Yüan-chang and was made a messenger. Two years later, through the recommendation of his fellow townsman, Li Shan-ch'ang (q.v.), he was appointed assistant magistrate, then magistrate of Ning-kuo 寧國 (Anhwei). Clever and capable, Hu soon won the favor of Chu Yüan-chang. In 1364 he became an assistant prefect of Chi-an 吉安, Kiangsi, being promoted to assitant surveillance commissioner of Hukuang two years later. The following year Hu received the post of vice minister, then minister of the Court of Imperial Sacrifices. After Chu assumed the imperial title, Hu became an assistant administrator of the Central Secretariat and was promoted to vice administrator in January, 1371. In August, 1373, Chu Yüan-chang named him to fill the post of junior chief administrator of state that had been left vacant by the banishment of Wang Kuang-yang (*q.v.*) in February. Eventually Chu elevated him to prime minister in October, 1377.

Hu Wei-yung's colleagues, however, viewed his rise with misgiving. Liu Chi (*q.v.*), for example, is said to have pointed out Hu's reckless character, and warned the emperor not to place too much trust in him. Before long, the emperor, alarmed by Hu's growing arrogance and worried about his possible treachery, took steps to curb his power. The official records later charged that Hu abused his position to expand his influence, organized a faction, conspired against his rivals, and usurped the imperial prerogatives. He reportedly manipulated communications to the throne by ordering that all memorials be directed first to the Central Secretariat for inspection, and, moreover, took the law into his own hands, passing out rewards or punishments at will. Again, according to the official accounts, Chu Yüan-chang took action when reports reached him (October, 1379) that the officials in the Central Secretariat had failed to inform the court of the arrival of the envoys from Champa. Outraged, the emperor ordered the arrest of those responsible; this involved both Hu Wei-yung and Wang Kuang-yang, who had been recalled. Both were subsequently put in prison. In January of the following year, the vice censor-in-chief T'u Chieh 涂節, who was reportedly in contact with Hu and feared that he might be implicated, revealed to the emperor that Hu was engineering the overthrow of

the throne. Another official followed with a similar allegation. These charges may have been spurious, but they provided a good excuse for the emperor to eliminate the accused. He sentenced to death not only Hu Wei-yung, but also T'u Chieh, and the censor-in-chief Ch'en Ning 陳寧 (original *ming* Liang 亮), who were indicted as the chief co-conspirators. Other officials implicated included Sung Shen, a grandson of Sung Lien (*q.v.*), who was sent into exile at the same time. The purge was extended to the friends and associates of the culprits and their descendants, and involved reportedly over fifteen thousand individuals. Following this, to safeguard future abuse of his authority, Chu Yüan-chang ordered the abolition of the office of the Central Secretariat, as well as that of the chief military commission, replacing them with the six ministries and the five chief military commissions. In addition, he commanded the court scholars to compile two compendia of biographies of the "treacherous officials" of the past as a reminder of the "crime" of his former chief minister. This resulted in the *Ch'en-chieh lu* 臣誡錄 (Instruction for officials), 10 *ch.*, completed in July, 1380, and the *Chien-ch'en chuan* 姦臣傳 (Biographies of the treacherous chief ministers), 4 *ch.* (forming part of the *Hsiang-chien* 相鑒 [References to chief ministers], 20 *ch.*), completed in January, 1381. When promulgating his instructions for posterity (*i.e. Huang Ming tsu-hsün*) in July, 1395, Chu Yüan-chang again warned his descendants not to reinstate the office of the Central Secretariat, and advised that those who dared put forth such proposals should be severely punished.

The nature of Hu Wei-yung's crime, however, remains obscure. The official version, leaning heavily on the verdict promulgated by the emperor as late as 1390 in an attempt to emphasize Hu's guilt, presents only one side of the story. The absence of alternative sources, because of the silence of Hu's contemporaries for fear of persecution, has prevented historians from making a more objective appraisal of the case. The difficulty confronting them may be seen in the study made by Wu Han (BDRC), an authority on Ming history, who has given by far the clearest exposition of this episode. In the light of his evidence, the most serious of the charges seems to have been that of organizing factions to plot the overthrow of the throne, while that of Hu's responsibility for the death of Liu Chi appears to be peripheral. The latter accusation, it seems, was intended to add to the enormity of Hu's guilt, for it appears that Liu died of natural causes, and not of Hu's poison. We do not know, however, exactly how Hu and his associates conspired against the throne, nor are we certain of the connections between Hu and those executed in later years as his accomplices.

The story of Hu Wei-yung's crimes became magnified, and he acquired a notorious character as time went by, Chu Yüan-chang invoking the case to prosecute people he wished to eliminate. He then saw to it that more of Hu's "crimes" were revealed to the public, especially details of the plot against the throne. The first of these charges, publicized in the *Ta-kao* late in 1386, implicated a certain Lin Hsien 林賢, a commander of the Ming-chou 明州 guard, Chekiang. This held that Lin had received instructions from Hu Wei-yung to go to Japan to solicit help in his plot from a certain daimyō. The latter, it is said, agreed to send a contingent of armed men to China disguised as a tribute mission. The scheme, however, fell through; whereupon Lin and his family, friends, and associates were executed. This episode, reported only in official dispatches, is not substantiated by contemporary records. It may have been a trumped-up charge against people associated with Hu Wei-yung, as well as a pretext for breaking off relations with Japan in the midst of a diplomatic impasse.

The story that Hu Wei-yung sought alliance with China's neighbors to realize his ambition became a *cause célèbre* in later years when reports circulated that he had sounded out Korea, the Mongols, and even Śrivijaya, these actions coming to light in 1384, 1390, and 1397 respectively. The allegation that Hu had sought assistance from the Mongols was the basis of the accusation against Li Shan-ch'ang and several of his old comrades in arms. According to this, Hu had sent a certain former official by the name of Feng Chi 封績 (whose existence is doubtful), in secret to the Mongol chieftain seeking an alliance. The former, reportedly captured by General Lan Yü (*q.v.*) in 1388, was found carrying a document in Li Shan-ch'ang's handwriting. When the trial was held, Li's family servants further revealed that Li was close to Hu Wei-yung and had helped him to advance his plot. Whatever the truth of these allegations, they provided the pretext the emperor wanted to eliminate Li Shan-ch'ang, who subsequently committed suicide, and many others.

According to the *Chao-shih chien-tang lu* 昭示姦黨錄, a black list of officials prosecuted by the emperor published in 1388, which Ch'ien Ch'ien-i (ECCP) examined and reported on in his study of this episode, twenty-two high-ranking officials, including several who had passed away, were among those charged as Hu Wei-yung's accomplices and were executed accordingly. Those who shared the fate with Li Shan-ch'ang included: Chao Yung 趙庸, the marquis of Nan-hsiung 南雄, Cheng Yü-ch'un 鄭遇春, the marquis of Ying-yang 熒陽, Fei Chü (*see* Keng Ping-wen), the marquis of P'ing-liang 平涼, Hua Chung (*see* Li Wen-chung), Huang Pin 黃彬, the marquis of I-ch'un 宜春, Lu Chü 陸聚, the marquis of Honan, Lu Chung-heng (*see* Ning-kuo Kung-chu), T'ang Sheng-tsung (*see* Lan Yü), and army officers Ch'en Fang-liang 陳方亮, Keng Chung (*see* Keng Ping-wen), Mao Hsiang 毛驤, Yü Hsien 於顯, and his son Yü Hu 琥. Those who had passed away, but were branded as members of Hu's clique and whose families suffered, included: Ch'en Te (*see* Keng Ping-wen), Chin Ch'ao-hsing 金朝興 (Pth. 武毅, d. 1382), the marquis of Hsüan-te 宣德, Chu Liang-tsu 朱亮祖 (d. 1380), the marquis of Yung-chia 永嘉, Hu Mei (*see* Teng Yü), Ku Shih (*see* T'ang Ho), Wang Chih 王志 (Pth. 襄簡, 1335–86), the marquis of Lu-an 六安, and Yang Ching 楊璟 (Pth. 武信, d. 1382), the marquis of Ying-yang 熒陽.

The purge, however, was far from over. In September, 1392, Yeh Sheng (*see* Lan Yü) was executed for having had communications with Hu Wei-yung. This was later extended to implicate Lan Yü, who was accused of plotting a rebellion, and was executed in March, 1393, along with his accomplices. In October of this year Chu Yüan-chang proclaimed that he would spare those accused of having connections with the two culprits, with the exception of those who had already been indicted for their part in the alleged conspiracy. According to an official estimate, over forty thousand individuals were involved in these cases. The significance of this case in the history of the early Ming was far-reaching. In political terms, it climaxed the hostility of the first emperor towards his one-time comrades in arms. He was determined to be supreme. The dissolution of the Central Secretariat and the chief military commission brought the country under the absolute control of the emperor himself. The purges, moreover, had economic implications. Through these executions the government confiscated the property of the offenders and was enabled to take over much of their wealth. This action enriched the imperial treasury, and at the same time weakened the economic base of the bureaucracy, significantly doing away with potential threats to the throne. Lastly, these purges heightened the terror throughout the land during the latter half of the reign of the first emperor. Hu Wei-yung's case inaugurated periods of mass slaughter lasting over fourteen years; it bears witness to another aspect of absolutism in Chinese history. The fact that historians have stigmatized Chu Yüan-chang as one of China's most tyrannical emperors is to a large extent due to his brutal persecutions, which began with his prime minister.

Bibliography

1/308/2a; 5/11/17a; 16/1/26a, 131/4a; 42/31/9b; 61/157/1b; MSL (1962), T'ai-tsu, 436, 488, 958, 1487, 1884, 2037, 2100, 3023, 3228, 3478; KC (1958), 581, 707, 710, 716, 744, 757, 775; Chu Yüan-chang, *Ming T'ai-tsu yü-chih wen-chi* (1965), 83; *id.*, *Ta-kao san-pien*; *id.*, *Ch'en-chien lu*; *id.*, *Chien-ch'en chuan*; *id.*, *Huang Ming tsu-hsün*; *id.*, *Hsiao-ling ch'ao-chih*, in *Ming-ch'ao k'ai-kuo wen-hsien* 明朝開國文獻 (1966), 327, 1459, 1586, 1589, 1880, 1891, 1905, 1929; Wang Shih-chen, *Yen-shan-t'ang pieh-chi* (1965), 20/6b; Ch'ien Ch'ien-i, *Mu-chai ch'u-hsüeh chi* (SPTK), 103/11b, 104/1b, 105/8b; Ku Ying-t'ai (ECCP), *Ming-ch'ao chi-shih pen-mo* (1658), 13/1a; P'an Ch'eng-chang (ECCP), *Kuo-shih k'ao-i* (TsSCC), 2/42; Chao I (ECCP), *Nien-er-shih cha-chi* (1963), 32/678; Li Chin-hua 李晉華, *Ming-tai ch'ih-chuan shu k'ao* 明代敕撰書考 (1932), 12; Wu Han, "Hu Wei-yung tang-an k'ao" *Yen-ching hsüeh-pao*, 15 (1934), 163; Wang Yi-t'ung, *Official Relations between China and Japan* (Cambridge, 1953), 20; Teng Ssu-yü, "Ming T'ai-tsu's Destructive and Constructive Work," *Chinese Culture*, Vol. VIII, no. 3 (September, 1967), 14.

Hok-lam Chan

HU Yen 胡儼 (T. 若思, H. 頤菴), 1361– September 20, 1443, scholar-official, was a native of Nanchang, Kiangsi. He graduated as *chü-jen* in 1387, and, after passing the metropolitan examination in the following year, received an appointment as instructor in a district school. In that capacity he served at Hua-t'ing 華亭, Nan-Chihli (1388), Ch'ang-yüan 長垣, Pei-Chihli (1396), and Yü-kan 餘干, Kiangsi. In 1399 he was promoted to be the magistrate of T'ung-ch'eng 桐城, north of Anking, where he served for the next three years and won acclaim for his capable and enlightened administration. Early in 1402, through the recommendation of the censor-in-chief Lien Tzu-ning (*q.v.*), Hu received a summons from Emperor Chu Yün-wen (*q.v.*). Before he was offered an appointment, however, the rebel army under Chu Ti (*q.v.*) had invested the capital.

When Chu Ti entered Nanking in July as victor, Hu was among the scores of officials who came to the city gate to offer their submission. Before long the ministry of Personnel forwarded his name to the new emperor for prospective appointment. Impressed by his scholarship, especially in astrology, Chu Ti offered him a position in the newly reorganized Hanlin Academy, first as corrector (August), and then as reader (December). In this capacity he took part in the compilation of the *Ku-chin lieh-nü chuan*, a collection of biographies of virtuous women (*see* Empress Hsü), and in the first revision of the veritable records of Chu Yüan-chang, the *T'ai-tsu shih-lu* (*see* Ju Ch'ang). In the same year he was admitted to the Wen-yüan Hall 文淵閣, where, together with Hsieh Chin, Huang Huai, Hu Kuang, Yang Shih-ch'i (*qq.v.*), and two others, he became one of the first group of scholars selected to perform Secretarial and advisory duties for the emperor. His initial appointment to the secretariat was brief; in May, 1404, he concurrently served as tutor to the heir apparent, Chu Kao-chih (*q.v.*), then in October he became chancellor of the National University. It is said that his colleagues, nettled by his candor and parade of learning, recommended his promotion in order to remove him from the Secretariat. If so, they had done Hu a favor, for he held the chancellorship for over twenty years.

At this post Hu devoted himself to assisting in reorganizing the administration, upgrading the standards of the institution, strengthening the lecture program, and modifying the harsh sentence of exile imposed on pupils taking leave on various pretexts. Meanwhile he continued to hold the title of reader in the Hanlin Academy, frequently taking part in certain compilation and other projects, and making occasional trips to Peking at the call of the emperor. In December, 1404, for example, he was appointed one of the directors in the compilation of the *Yung-lo ta-tien* (*see* Chu Ti). When Chu Ti led his army into Mongolia early in 1410, Hu took leave of several months to go to Peking to assist Chu Chan-chi (*q.v.*) who had been charged with the custody of the auxiliary capital. In November of the following year Hu served as chief director in the second revision of the *T'ai-tsu shih-lu* (*see* Li Wen-chung). After it was decreed that Peking was to become the capital in 1420, Hu moved his office to the north while another chancellor was appointed for the National University in Nanking. He retired in 1425, receiving from Emperor Chu Kao-chih the privilege of exempting his immediate descendants from corvée service. When Chu Chan-chi ascended the throne in 1426, he offered Hu the post of assistant minister of Rites, but Hu declined. He lived to the advanced age of eighty-two. In February, 1490, his tablet was included in the shrine honoring meritorious officials in his native district.

Hu earned his name not as a statesman but as a scholar and teacher. He held the longest term in the dynasty as head of the National University, and was responsible for the preparation of a generation of scholars for government service. As a man of letters Hu left a considerable body of writing, including a number of edicts and commemorative essays composed in the name of the emperor. His collected work, *Hu Chi-chiu (I-an) chi* 祭酒（頤菴）集, 30 *ch.*, was printed sometime after his death. The original edition is presumably lost, but a fragment in 8 *chüan* (*ch.* 16–23 of the original) survives and is available on microfilm. A manuscript copy of a selection of his writings, known as *I-an wen-hsüan* 文選, 2 *ch.* (prose and poetry, 1 *ch.* each), is preserved in the Seikado Bunko. A collection of his comments on literature and history, entitled *Hu-shih tsa-shuo* 氏雜說 is included in *Shuo-fu hsü, chou* 弓 15. According to the *Ming-hua lu* 明畫錄, Hu was also skilled in painting, specializing in birds and flowers. A specimen of his calligraphy is preserved in the Palace Museum, Taipei.

Bibliography

1/147/13b; 5/12/45a; 9/24/6a; 16/10/1a, 19/51b, 159/8a; 61/118/20b; 64/乙 3/2b; 65/6/1b; 84/2/9b; MSL (1963), T'ai-tsung, 158, 256, 477, 535, 603, 627, 1314, 1517, 2081, Jen-tsung (1963), 237, Ying-tsung (1963), 2178; KC (1958), 845, 883, 1653, 2598; SK (1930), 170/5a; Hu Yen, *Hu Chi-chiu (I-an) chi* (NLP microfilm), no. 993; Huang Tso, *Nan-yung chih*, 2/7a, 19/6b; Wu Han 吳晗, "Chi *Ming shih-lu*" 記明實錄, in *Tu-shih cha-chi* 讀史劄記(Peking, 1957), 194; Wang Chung-min 王重民, "*Yung-lo ta-tien* tsuan-hsiu jen k'ao" 永樂大典纂修人考, *Wen-shih* 文史, no. 4 (Peking, 1965), 176, *Ku kung shu-hua lu* 故宮書畫錄 (Taipei, 1965), 413.

Hok-lam Chan

HU Ying 胡濙 (T. 源潔, H. 潔菴,) 1375–1463, who served six emperors in seven reign periods covering a span of almost sixty years, may well have had the longest official career of anyone in the Ming dynasty. His family originated in the lower Huai 淮 River valley, moved to Kiangsi, and then settled in the district of Wu-chin 武進 in the present province of Kiangsu. Beginning with the 5th century A.D. and on through the T'ang, Sung, and Yüan periods, his ancestors are recorded as officials.

A *chü-jen* of 1399, Hu Ying became a *chin-shih* in 1400 and received the post of supervising secretary first in the office of scrutiny for War, and later in the office of scrutiny for Revenue, The political upheaval which brought the downfall of Chu Yün-wen (*q.v.*) and the succession to the imperial throne of his uncle Chu Ti (*q.v.*) does not seem to have affected Hu, for within a few years he gained the confidence of the new emperor. In 1407 he was sent on a strange mission which involved traveling all over the empire in search of the Taoist immortal Chang San-feng (*see* Chang Chung). It has always been believed, however, that the real purpose of the mission was to ascertain whether Chu Yün-wen had escaped the burning of the palace area in Nanking and was still alive somewhere. For what had happened to the latter on that summer day of 1402 remains a mystery even to our own time. Did he die in the conflagration, or did he succeed in slipping away in disguise to live at first as a Buddhist monk and then as a Taoist priest?

To carry out his mission Hu traveled for some thirteen or fourteen years. He returned to court in 1416 after the news of his mother's death reached him. It was probably about this time that he was promoted to the vice-presidency of the ministry of Rites. Although the sources differ, he may have been sent on the road again in the following year, as the emperor refused to grant him the usual period of mourning for his parent. Finally in 1423 he completed his mission and reported to the emperor in Hsüan-fu, where the latter had just established his headquarters for the northern expedition against the Mongols. As the report was not vouchsafed to anyone but the emperor, it has aroused much speculation. One story, which may well be fictitious, has it that Hu actually saw the erstwhile emperor somewhere in Hunan, but pretended not to recognize him, so the latter's life was spared. Two years before the initiating of Hu Ying's mission, Cheng Ho (*q.v.*) had been sent on an ocean voyage to foreign lands (1405). Many have surmised that Cheng's mission was for the same purpose, but the emperor probably had much weightier reasons for launching the overseas expeditions.

Included in the official order to Hu, according to some sources, was also the task of distributing the government printed *Hsing-li ta-ch'üan* 性理大全, the *Wei-shan yin-chih* 為善陰隲, and the *Hsiao-shun shih-shih* 孝順事實. These were all works compiled by imperial order partly for students preparing for civil service examinations and partly for the purpose of exhorting people to live virtuous lives. Since these works were completed respectively in 1414, 1419, and 1420, their distribution could not have been possible previous to these dates; such an order must have been issued in the later years of Hu's mission.

Retribution in the emperor's case worked all too swiftly, for he faced problems in his own succession. Although he proclaimed his eldest son the heir apparent, he showed favor to his younger sons, who in turn schemed against their brother. Because of certain rumors in 1418, the emperor ordered Hu to check on the prince then acting as regent in Nanking. As a result Hu submitted a confidential memorial emphasizing many of the prince's virtues; this allayed the emperor's suspicions.

During the Hsüan-te reign, Hu was called to Peking from Nanking and shortly afterwards (May 10, 1426) promoted to be minister of Rites. After accompanying the young emperor on the campaign to crush the rebellion of the emperor's uncle Chu Kao-hsü (*q.v.*), Hu was repeatedly rewarded with slaves, houses, land, and seals. The emperor named him one of the four ministers who had rendered important services in the early years of his reign. The other three were Chien I, Yang Shih-ch'i, and Yang Jung (*qq.v.*). It was during this reign that the seventh and last of the expeditions of Cheng Ho took place (1431–33). With him came ambassadors from a number of lands with a wide variety of gifts. On the 14th of September, 1433, Hu felicitated the emperor on the arrival of the giraffes in particular, considering them to be animals of good omen.

Hu continued to be a trusted minister in the following reign (1436–49). In 1444, on reaching the age of seventy *sui*, he begged to be retired, but his request was refused. When the emperor, Chu Ch'i-chen (*q.v.*), embarked on his ill-fated expedition against the Mongols in 1449, Hu was made grand tutor to the heir apparent and remained in Peking to assist in government affairs. Under Chu Ch'i-yü (*q.v.*) in 1451, he again asked to retire, but once more was refused; he was named junior tutor and later promoted to grand preceptor to the heir apparent. After 1453 he annually repeated his request to retire, but to no avail. In 1456 he suddenly became ill and was unable to walk. He was then eighty-two *sui*. In the following year, after the imperial restoration, he was deprived of the higher titles previously conferred by the dethroned emperor but permitted to retire with honor. At home he enjoyed seven more years of leisurely life. He had three younger brothers, all over seventy *sui* at the time, so he named his family hall Shou-k'ai-t'ang 壽愷堂 (the Hall of the venerable brothers). He had four sons; the eldest Hu Hung 胡祆 (T. 長寧) held a hereditary judgeship in the Embroidered-uniform Guard.

Hu is credited with several books, none of which seems to be extant. His collection of literary works is known as *Chih-hsüan chi* 芝軒集 or *Tan-an chi* 澹菴 集. While traveling in the empire, he made a collection of prescriptions and medical formulae from many localities, entitled *Wei sheng i-chien fang* 衞生易簡 方. Another work, the *Lü-shen kuei-chien* 律身規鑑, probably dealt with personal conduct. His memory is (or was?) still kept green in the metropolitan area, for his signature appears on a tablet (dated 1443) standing in the main court of the Fa-hai monastery 法海寺 located in the hills west of Peking, which had just been rebuilt. Hu was then minister of Rites.

In his official life of nearly six decades, Hu participated as an examiner no fewer than ten times in the metropolitan examinations. As a consequence a large number of the officials of the time were considered to be his "pupils."

Comments on him are divided. Some

have praised him for his caution and strict self-discipline, while others have criticized him for obsequiousness. Perhaps these are more or less the two sides of a single coin. Could anyone, at any time, especially in the Ming period, achieve such a long and successful official career without being extremely cautious, or tolerant, under many trying circumstances?

Bibliography

1/169/2a; 5/33/17a; 42/42/12b; 61/119/12a; 63/8/18a; TSCC (1885-88), XI: 316/10a, XIV: 85/9b; MSL (1963), Hsüan-tsung, 2341, Ying-tsung, 5782, 5825; Yao K'uei, Mu-chih-ming 墓誌銘 in *Huang Ming wen-hai* (microfilm), 5.1.5; Li Chin-hua 李晉華, *Ming-tai ch'ih-chuan shu-k'ao* 明代勅撰書考 (1932), 37; *Huang Ming ching-shih wen-pien* (*see* Ch'en Tzu-lung, ECCP), *ch.* 19; Paul Pelliot, TP, 31 (1935), 297, 303.

Lienche Tu Fang

HU Ying-lin 胡應麟 (T. 元瑞 and 明瑞, H. 石羊生, 少室山人), June 25, 1551–1602, scholar and bibliophile, was born in Lanch'i 蘭溪, Chekiang. His father, Hu Hsi 胡僖 (T. 伯安, H. 公泉, b. 1524, cs1559), rose to be director of grain transport in the Hukuang area (1565) and later an assistant surveillance commissioner of Yunnan. Hu Ying-lin himself became a *chü-jen* in 1576 at the age of 26 *sui*. From 1577 to 1598 he competed at least eight times for the *chin-shih* degree without success. From youth on he had professed a distaste for the examination system as well as for the prevailing Yao-chiang 姚江 school of philosophy signalized by Wang Shou-jen (*q.v.*). Thereupon he led a retired life devoted to wide reading in history and philosophy and also in fiction, a field in which he had made a collection when he was fifteeen.

In his youth, the family was described as poor but, as his father rose in official position and seeming affluence, Hu Ying-lin was enabled to satisfy a passion for book-collecting. The items he acquired came mostly from the bookstalls of Peking, Nanking, Soochow, and Hangchow. He likewise borrowed and copied and sometimes commissioned friends to obtain publications for him in out-of-the-way places, such as northwest China and Yunnan. While perusing these books he made countless notes, many of which were later printed in his massive collected works.

We learn from a preface which his mentor and sponsor, Wang Shih-chen (*q.v.*), wrote for one of these collections, that by the time Hu was barely thirty years of age (1580) he had accumulated a library of 42,384 *chüan* which reportedly included titles on the Classics to the number of 370, on history 820, on philosophy 1,450, and in the field of *belles lettres* 1,346. Conceivably the collection was expanded in later years but unfortunately the catalogue is no longer extant. An examination of Hu's writings shows that he stressed the practical and was not enamored of rare books. To house his collection, he built a retreat in the hills north of his native city, which he first called Shao-shih shan-fang 少室山房, a name which figures in the the titles of several collected works. Later he named the library Er-yu 二酉 shan-fang after a legendary book depository.

The *Ssu-k'u* editors, in some of the notices in which they deal with Hu's works, minimize the significance of his literary achievements, asserting that he rose to note by currying the favor of the aforementioned Wang Shih-chen who was the literary light of the day and was Hu's senior by twenty-five years. In particular, they charge that Wang indulged in extravagant praise of Hu's verse which, in their estimation, could be classed only as conventional. The same judgment, or bias, apparently influenced the editors of the official *Ming-shih*. At any rate, they did not accord to Hu an independent biographical sketch, but featured him under his patron, Wang Shih-chen.

Notwithstanding these strictures, Hu's reputation was revived after 1917, by the critical-minded historians of the Literary

Renaissance. It both surprised and pleased them to find embedded in one of Hu's collected works on miscellaneous subjects, *Shao-shih shan-fang pi-ts'ung* 筆叢, a small treatise entitled *Ssu-pu cheng-o* 四部正譌 (Forgeries in four branches of literature), 3 *ch.*, which he completed in 1586 when he was 36 *sui*. For them it furnished evidence, if more were needed, that from early times China had scholars who approached the study of history in a critical spirit. Accordingly, it was edited by Ku Chieh-kang (BDRC) and for the first time circulated independently in 1929. Some critics declared it to be the first Chinese monograph to concentrate specifically on the identification, the history, and the transmission of known or reputed forgeries. To be sure, long before this scholars had singled out individual titles as spurious. One of the first to do so on a modest scale was Kao Ssu-sun 高似孫 (cs 1184), who questioned the authenticity of about forty philosophical items in an essay named *Tzu-lüeh* 子略, 4 *ch.* It was similarly edited by Ku Chieh-kang and printed separately in 1928. A still more rigorous inquiry into some forty works was produced in 1357 by Sung Lien (*q.v.*) under the title *Chu-tzu pien* 諸子辨 (Philosophical works discriminated). Submerged in the author's collected works, it too received little attention until published independently in 1926 with modern punctuation by Ku Chieh-kang.

While compiling this *Ssu-pu cheng-o* in 1586, Hu had the advantage of a rich library, ample leisure, and a resolute interest in the subject. He singled out some one hundred works which he regarded as forgeries—laying down principles leading to their detection, and speculating on the motives that prompted their producers. He separated them into twenty categories of which the following are typical: those pieced together from older known writings; those suggested by genuine works the texts of which are lost; those composed for self-aggrandizement; those written to disparage others; those

forged only in part; those falsely attributed to a known writer of former times; those long stamped as spurious, but later found to be genuine.

The above-mentioned collection, *Shao-shih shan-fang pi-ts'ung*, as reprinted in the *Kuang-ya ts'ung-shu* (ECCP, p. 28), consists of twelve works of miscellaneous notes probably all originally printed by Hu in the late 16th century. Besides the *Ssu-pu cheng-o*, there are three titles on books in general and book collecting, *Ching-chi hui-t'ung* 經籍會通, 4 *ch. Er-yu chui-i* 二酉綴遺, 3 *ch.*, and *Chiu-liu hsü-lun* 九流緒論, 3 *ch.* Of books on history, there are the *San-fen pu-i* 三墳補逸, 3 *ch.*, and *Shih-shu chan-pi* 史書佔畢, 6 *ch.* Also worth mention are notes on Taoism, *Yü-hu hsia-lan* 玉壺遐覽, 4 *ch.*, on Buddhism, *Shuang-shu huan-ch'ao* 雙樹幻鈔, 3 *ch.*, and on various subjects including drama and fiction, *Chuang-yüeh wei-t'an* 莊嶽委談, 2 *ch.* An admirer of Yang Shen (*q.v.*), Hu read Yang's works carefully and jotted down the mistakes with corrections, which were assembled in three works, *I-lin hsüeh-shan* 藝林學山, 8 *ch.*, *Tan-ch'ien hsin-lu* 丹鉛新錄, 8 *ch.*, and *Hua-yang po-i* 華陽博議, 2 *ch.* Hu likewise published a collection of jottings written during his stay in Peking in 1594 and 1595, entitled *Chia-i sheng-yen* 甲乙剩言, 2 *ch.*, which contains a few items about the war against the Japanese invaders in Korea. It was printed separately and included in several later collections such as *Pao-yen-t'ang pi chi* (ECCP, p. 84).

Hu Ying-lin also wrote a work entitled *Shih-sou* 詩藪, 18 *ch.*, and *Hsü shih-sou*, 2 *ch.*, printed in 1589 in which he discusses the various forms of poetry that prevailed from the Chou dynasty to the Yüan, a span of over two millennia. The copy in the Library of Congress, six volumes on Korean paper, is described in that Library's catalogue of Chinese rare books as having been printed from Korean brass movable type, although there are some critics who believe it was struck off from wood-blocks. However that may be, it has a preface by Wang Tao-k'un (*q.v.*) reproducing by wood-block print the handwriting of an assistant in Hu Ying-lin's studio who had the name Ch'eng Pai-er 程百二. Tseng Yu-ho has translated into English a few examples of his prose and poetry.

Bibliography

1/287/20a; 3/268/17a; Ch'ien Ch'ien-i (ECCP), *Lieh-ch'ao shih-chi* 丁, 6/36a; SK (1930), 123/7a, 172/11b, 179/7a, 197/8b; Wu Han 吳晗, "Hu Ying-lin nien-p'u," *Tsing Hua Journal*, 9 (1934), 183; *Lan-ch'i-hsien chih* (1887), *ch.* 8; Ts'ao Yang-wu 曹養吾, "Pien-wei hsüeh shih" 辨偽學史 (The history of forgery detection), in *Ku-shih pien* 古史辨, II (1930), 388; Chang Hsin-cheng 張心澂, *Wei-shu t'ung-k'ao* 偽書通考 (The investigation of forgeries, 1954); L. of C. *Catalogue of Rare Books*, 1124; Tseng Yu-ho, "Hsüeh Wu and Her Orchids in the Collection of the Honolulu Academy of Arts," *Arts Asiatiques*, II: 3 (1955), 201, 203.

Arthur W. Hummel

HUA Ch'eng, *see* HUA Sui

HUA Ch'ien, *see* HUA Sui

HUA Sui 華燧 (T. 文輝, H. 會通, 梧竹), 1439–1513, scholar and printer, was a native of Wu-hsi, west of Soochow. He was a fourteenth-generation descendant of the O-hu 鵝湖 branch of the Hua clan, which had first moved to the area at the end of the Northern Sung dynasty (960–1126). He inherited several thousand *mou* of good land, but his neglect of the property caused a decrease in family fortune during his time. He applied himself to the study of the Classics and histories in his youth but soon, occupied with business matters, he had no opportunity for scholarly pursuits until the age of fifty. Then his strong will and perseverance enabled him to read persistently and diligently and to practice what the Classics taught. Thus his contributions to scholarship in collating

books, printing with bronze movable type, and writing on the canon and the histories, were all made during or after his middle years.

His later devotion to study was complete. He used to get up early in the morning and immediately start to read and practice calligraphy, continuing until late every evening. He had all the books in his library arranged along the walls with several boys in attendance, each charged with the care of a section so that materials might be available whenever needed. His bookish knowledge was frequently applied to his way of living. It is said that he often read books out loud by the main road of the town, paying no attention to others around him. He tried to apply the theory of the so-called well-field system mentioned in the Classics to the management of his own land but without success.

Hua also demonstrated filial piety in the care of his father, Hua Fang 方 (T. 守方, H. 時茸, 1407–87), who was confined to bed with foot trouble. Whenever his brothers retired after the routine duty of attending their ailing father, Hua Sui would stay and read in a room next to the old man to keep him company. When his father died, he lived in a cottage beside the latter's tomb and remained there for years writing a book on the mourning ceremony, entitled *Chih-sang ch'ieh-wen* 治喪切問. Every time he offered sacrifice to his ancestors, he and his three sons, Hua Yün 塤 (T. 允和), Hua K'uei 奎 (T. 允昭), and Hua Pi 壁 (T. 允章), would prepare themselves by abstinence before the occasion, so as to perform the rites with respect and sincerity. He also engaged in the compilation of the genealogical record of the Hua clan, known as the *Hui-t'ung p'u* 會通譜 in which he carefully traced both the chronological sequence and collateral relationships of the family. He wrote several works on the Classics and histories, including the *Chiu-ching yün-lan* 九經韻覽, a rhymed work on the nine Classics, and the *Shih-ch'i-shih chieh-yao* 十七史節要, excerpts from the seventeen standard histories. He was likewise responsible for his own epitaph before he died at the age of seventy-four.

Hua Sui is noted for his interest in collating books and in printing, especially with bronze movable type. All books printed by him and his cousin, Hua Yu 煜 (fl. 1495), contain the signature Hüi t'ung kuan 館 (Studio of mastery and comprehension), by which he meant that he had mastered the process of using movable type in printing. Several dozens of titles are said to have been printed by Hua Sui, but only a few are known to have survived. These include a movable type edition of *Sung chu-ch'en tsou-i* 宋諸臣奏議, a collection of memorials by Sung officials in 150 *chüan*, printed in 1490; the *Chin-hsiu wan hua ku* 錦繡萬花谷, a Sung encyclopedia in three series, 80 *ch*, printed with blocks in 1494; *Jung-chai sui-pi* 容齋隨筆, miscellaneous notes in five series, 74 *ch.*, by Hung Mai (1123-1202), printed with bronze movable type in 1495 (reprinted in the *Ssu-pu ts'ung-k'an* , second series); *Chiao-cheng yin-shih ch'un-ch'iu* 校正音釋 春秋, commentaries on the Spring and Autumn Annals in 12 *chüan*, printed with bronze movable type in 1497; *Ku-chin ho-pi shih-lei ch'ien-pien* 古今合璧事類前編, another Sung encyclopedia, first series in 63 *chüan*, printed in 1498; and the *Wen-yüan ying-hua tsuan-yao* 文苑英華纂要, a summary of the complete collection of literature in 84 *chüan* with *pien-cheng* 辨 正 in 10 *chüan*, printed with bronze movable type in 1506.

Several other members of the Hua family also engaged in printing with either conventional blocks or bronze movable type. One was Hua Ch'eng 珵 (T. 汝德, H. 夢萱, 尚古生, 1438-1514), second son of Hua Chi 濟 (fl. 1400-50), a descendant of the Lung-t'ing 隆亭 branch of the Hua clan and a secretary in the ministry of Revenue by purchase. Hua Ch'eng studied at a local Confucian school together with his younger brother, Hua Chüeh 珏 (T. 汝和, cs 1484), who became a director of the bureau of records in the ministry of Personnel. After failing seven times in the examinations, Hua Ch'eng entered the National University and later obtained an appointment as a deputy in charge of food supply at the Court of Imperial Entertainment. It was known that this office was usually liable to corruption, the supply of provisions being under eunuch control. But Hua was dutiful and honest and liked by his superiors. He resigned, however, after serving for a short period and returned home in 1499 on the plea of poor health.

Hua Ch'eng was an easy-going person and enjoyed a leisurely life. He frequently entertained friends in his garden, traveled to scenic places in neighboring provinces, and engaged in collecting art objects and books and in printing and other hobbies. He built a house called Shang ku chai 尚古齋 (Studio for esteeming antiquities), where many precious vessels, specimens of calligraphy, paintings, books, and rubbings were treasured. All the furniture and utensils he used in the house were in imitation of the antique style. He was especially noted for his ability to evaluate art objects; it is said that his knowledge and judgment were second only to those of the artist Shen Chou (*q. v.*). The two friends frequently exchanged visits to show each other their prize possessions.

Hua Ch'eng was also fond of collecting books. Whenever he obtained a rare work, or his friends supplied him with a manuscript, a copy of the book was soon put out. Among those printed by him known or extant today are the *Wei-nan wen-chi* 渭南文集, the literary collection of Lu Yu (1125-1210) in 50 *chüan*, printed with movable type in 1502 (reprinted in the *Ssu-pu ts'ung-k'an*); and the *Pai-ch'uan hsüeh-hai* 百川學海, one of the earliest *ts'ung-shu* in 160 *chüan* compiled by Tso Kuei (d. after 1274), printed in 1501 with conventional blocks. All the books published by Hua Ch'eng bear the signature Shang ku chai.

Another printer of the Hua family was Hua Chien 堅 (T. 允剛, fl. 1513-16), youngest son of Hua Chiung 絅 (T. 文熙, H. 南湖, 1428-1504), the elder brother of Hua Sui. All books printed by Hua Chien bear the notation Lan-hsüeh-t'ang 蘭雪堂 (Hall of orchids and snow) and a preface written by him. Among those printed with bronze movable type known to be extant are the *Po shih ch'ang-ch'ing chi* 白氏長慶集, a collection of poems in 71 *chüan* by Po Chü-i (772-846) printed in 1513; the *Ts'ai Chung-lang chi* 蔡中郎集, a literary collection in 10 *chüan* by Ts'ai Yung (132-92) printed in 1515 (reprinted in the *Ssu-pu ts'ung-k'an*); the *I-wen lei-chü* 藝文類聚, a T'ang encyclopedia in 100 *chüan* with a preface by Hua Ching 鏡, elder son of Hua Chien, printed in 1515; and the *Ch'un-ch'iu fan-lu* 春秋繁露, a philosophical work in 17 *chüan* by Tung Chung-shu (*ca*. 175-105 B. C.), printed in 1516.

Some scholars have inferred that Hua Chien may have learned the technique of using bronze movable type in printing from An Kuo (*q. v.*), also of Wu-hsi. From the dates of various editions extant, however, it appears that Hua Sui was the earliest to use this process; his publications appeared in 1490-1506, Hua Ch'eng's in 1502, Hua Chien's in 1513-16, and An Kuo's around 1520-30. The type may have been from the same font, transmitted from one to another in the Hua family and later to the An family. All the books printed by the Hua family, however, have been criticized by a number of scholars for faults in printing technique and carelessness in collation and proofreading, as numerous mistakes and omissions have been detected in the text. Their productions cannot be compared in quality or technique with those printed by the An family of the same locality.

Bibliography

5/71/27a; 32/28/51b; *Ch'ang-chou-fu chih* 常州府志 (1695), 25/10a; *Wu-hsi Chin-kuei-hsien chih* 無錫金匱縣志 (1881), 25/7a; *Hua-shih tsung-p'u* 華氏宗譜 (1872), *chüan shou* /6a, 24a; *Hua-shih pen-shu* 華氏本書 (1905), 30A/2b, 7a; Shao Pao 邵寶 (1460-1527), *Jung-ch'un-t'ang hou-chi* 容春堂後集 (1518), 4/9b, 7/34b; *T'ien-lu lin-lang shu-mu* 天祿琳瑯書目 (1775), 10/11b; Yeh Ch'ang-ch'ih (BDRC), *Ts'ang-shu chi-shih-shih* (1918), 7/20a; Yeh Te-hui (BDRC), *Shu-lin ch'ing-hua* (1920), 8/8b; K. T. Wu, "Ming Printing and Printers," *HJAS*, 7 (1943), 214.

Tsuen-hsuin Tsien

HUA Yün 花雲, 1322-June 17, 1360, military officer, was a native of Huai-yüan 懷遠, Feng-yang 鳳陽 prefecture, Nan-Chihli. Hua lost his father when he was a child and his mother, who later married again, raised him to manhood. He grew to be tall and robust, brave and daring, and, with a dark complexion, looked rather impressive. In 1353, at the start of the rebellion in Hao-chou 濠州 (Feng-yang, *see* Kuo Tzu-hsing), Hua Yün joined the rebels and was selected by the young and ambitious leader, Chu Yüan-chang to be one of the twenty-four men who served as the core of his personal command. During the next three years Hua followed him in campaigns against the government forces as well as against other rebels in the lower Yangtze valley, overrunning a number of cities. In 1356 he received a promotion to the command of a thousand men on account of his able performance. In combat Hua often rode courageously ahead of his forces and galloped into the enemy vanguard, earning the sobriquet of Hei chiang chün 黑將軍 (black general).

In July, 1356, when Chu Yüan-chang founded a branch chief military commission in T'ai-p'ing 太平, near Wu-hu, Hua became an assistant commissioner with the concurrent title Generalissimo of An-yüan 安遠大將軍. In the following year he gained a victory north of Soochow and was given the command of the ten thousand men captured. After some more fighting he was ordered to return to T'ai-p'ing to defend the city against the rival contender, Ch'en Yu-liang (*q.v.*). On June 14, 1360, Ch'en brought his naval squadron down the Yangtze and launched an offensive against T'ai-p'ing. Being out-numbered, Hua Yün's forces could hold out against the enemy for only three days before the city wall was breached. Hua was captured in the ensuing melee, but he reportedly managed to break loose and killed several enemy soldiers before he was tied to a pole and shot to death by archers. In 1364, after inaugurating the reign of Wu, Chu Yüan-chang bestowed upon him the posthumous title Marquis of Tung-ch'iu chün 東丘郡侯, and ordered a shrine of loyal ministers (忠臣祠) built in T'ai-p'ing in honor of Hua and two other officials who shared a similar fate, Hsü Yüan 許瑗 (T. 栗夫, 1317-60, Pth. 忠節) and Wang Ting 王鼎.

During the siege, Hua Yün's wife, née Kao 郜 (1326-60), aware that she might follow her husband in death, entrusted to her maid née Sun 孫 the care of her three-year-old son. After the city's fall Lady Hua committed suicide, and the maid tried to carry the child away, but was intercepted by the enemy soldiers and taken to Kiukiang. She managed to shelter the boy, however, and, taking advantage of the chaotic situation follow-ing Ch'en's defeat months later, freed herself and the child, though not without difficulties on the way, and brought him into the presence of Chu Yüan-chang in Nanking early in 1361. Delighted over the safety of Hua Yün's heir, Chu bestowed upon him the name Wei 煒, and ordered that he be reared in the palace. Following in the footsteps of his father, Hua Wei became a deputy commander of a battal-ion at thirteen *sui* and was promoted in 1377, then only twenty *sui*, to be an assist-ant guard commander of the navy. Ear-lier that same year he brought an effigy of his father and his mother's remains from T'ai-p'ing and buried them in Shang-yüan 上元 -hsien, near Nanking.

Early in 1522, acting on the request of Hua Yün's fifth-generation descendant, an assistant commander of the Fu-chou 復州 guard in Liaotung, whose name is not available, Emperor Chu Hou-ts'ung (*q.v.*)

bestowed upon Lady Hua the posthumous honorific of Chen-lieh fu-jen 貞烈夫人, and upon the maid the title of An-jen 安人. The emperor also ordered a shrine erected in Liaotung in honor of Hua Yün and gave his descendant the hereditary title of assistant commander of the Fu-chou guard. In 1523 the magistrate of T'ai-p'ing memorialized the court propos-ing the erection of a statue of Hua Yün in the shrine of loyal ministers; the request was granted and its name then changed to San-chung tz'u 三忠祠 (shrine of the three loyal ministers). In December, 1583, acting on the petition of the super-vising secretary of the office of scrutiny for War, Wang Liang 王亮 (T. 茂大, H. 樓峰, cs 1577), Emperor Chu I-chün (*q. v.*) ordered the authorities to look for the descendants of Hua Yün and register their names for prospective appointments. In October, 1644, Emperor Chu Yu-sung (ECCP) of the Southern Ming court con-ferred on Hua the posthumous name Chung-i 忠毅 (loyal and resolute).

The dramatic end of Hua Yün later became a subject of heroics in literature. Li Tung-yang (*q.v.*), for example, com-posed a ballad entitled "Hua Chiang-chün, ko" 歌, in praise of his gallantry in battle. His story is likewise dramatized in the late Ming historical romance, *Ying-lieh chuan* (*see* Kuo Hsün). The title probably alludes, in the word *Ying*, to the bravery of Hua, and in the word *Lieh*, to the chastity of his wife. It was later adapted and became a popular play called *Chan* 戰 *T'ai-p'ing* or *Hua Yün tai-chien* 帶箭, and was per-formed in many provinces with local var-iations. Hua Yün's story also received yet another dramatic twist in a play entitled *Hu-fu chi* 虎符記 (The tale of the war tally), attributed to Chang Feng-i (*q.v.*), 2 *ch.* In this the author has Hua Yün escape death and survive as a captive while his wife fails in her attempt at sui-cide; he also makes Hua hand his war tally to his son as a means of identifica-tion, and the son later becomes a gallant general, defeating the enemy and freeing his father; the play thus ends in a joyful reunion. His reworking of the story followed a common practice of Ming dramatists who liked to transform a tragedy into a play with a happy conclusion.

Bibliography

1/289/2b; 5/8/37a; 8/2/7a; KC (1958), 264, 289; MSL (1962), T'ai-tsu, 92, 95, Shih-tsung (1965) 347, Shen-tsung (1965), 2662; KC (1958), 289; Teng Ch'iu 鄧球, cs 1535, *Huang Ming yung-hua lei-pien* 泳化類編 (1965), 110/16a; Chi Liu-ch'i 計六奇, *Ming-chi nan-lüeh* 明季南略 (1936), 5/108; Ch'ien Ching-fang 錢靜方, *Hsiao-shuo ts'ung-k'ao* 小說叢考 (Shanghai, 1957), 136; *Huai-yüan-hsien chih* 縣志 (1819), 18/21a; *Anhui t'ung-chih* 安徽通志 (1877), 55/6b; Li Tung-yang, *Huai-lu-t'ang chi* (1803), 2/33a; *Ku-pen hsi-ch'ü ts'ung-k'an ch'u-chi* 古本戲曲叢刊初集 (Shanghai, 1954, Hoover microfilm 1968, reel 8); *Ying-lieh chuan* (Shanghai, 1956), ch. 29; Huang Wen-yang 黃文暘, *Ch'ü-hai tsung-mu t'i-yao* 曲海總目提要 (Peking, 1959), 17/3b; Fu Hsi-hua 傅惜華, *Ming-tai ch'uan-ch'i ch'üan-mu* 明代傳奇全目 (Peking, 1959), 48; Kung Te-po 龔德柏, *Hsi-chü yü li-shih* 戲劇與歷史 (Taipei, 1962), 354.

Hok-lam Chan

HUAI En 懷恩, died January, 1488, was a chief eunuch during the Ch'eng-hua period. His original surname was Ma 馬, and his native place Soochow. There is no information as to when and why his family changed its name, but by his father's time it had become Tai 戴, and their place of residence Kao-mi 高密, Shantung. (One may speculate, however, that the family was originally Muslim, descended from central or western Asian forebears, who came to China under the Yüan.) Huai En's father (Tai) Hsi-wen 希文, who had attained the position of minister of the Court of the Imperial Stud, was cashiered (*ca.* 1424, during the Hsüan-te period because of a crime committed by his nephew, Tai Lun 綸 (then vice minister of War). The latter's transgression was considered so serious that punishment was extended to the entire clan. [Editors' note: No official record of this crime exists. Only some vague stories can de found, which seem to indicate that Tai, having been entrusted by Emperor Chu Ti (*q.v.*), to serve the heir apparent, Chu Kao-chih (*q.v.*), reported on some misconduct of the prince. When the latter ascended the throne, Tai, then vice minister of War, was sent to the distant post of Annam. During the reign of the next emperor, Chu Chan-chi (*q.v.*), Tai reportedly was recalled and put to death on the charge of having plotted against the emperor's father, one of the most serious crimes in the code. There are several variations of the story, however, affecting its credibility. In one version it is said that, while Tai definitely came from Shantung, Huai En was a native of Soochow and so possibly from a different family.] As a boy Huai En (original name unknown) suffered castration and was sent to the palace. At that time he received the name Huai En, meaning grateful (for his life).

During his first thirty-some years we know little of Huai's activities. His advancement in the court, however, must have been steady for, at the beginning of the Ch'eng-hua period he was in line for the post of director of Ceremonial. It was in 1467, when Ch'en Wen (*see* Chu Chien-shen), then minister of Rites, was looking for an ally in the inner court, that he supported Huai for that office. Huai held the position through almost the entire reign.

Huai En is recorded as a man of principle. He was loyal to the emperor, and more, he was loyal to the law and to tradition. Throughout these years, many events witness to his struggle for justice. He never withdrew from a contest even when he found himself in opposition to the highest authority. The first such case came in his effort to save Liu Ta-hsia (*q.v.*), a director in the ministry of War, who was put in prison on the false charges of a eunuch, and was released when Huai intervened.

A case in 1485 was much more serious, and Huai En had to risk his own life to try to save Lin Chün (see Li Meng-yang), then a vice director in the ministry of Justice. Lin had accused a favored eunuch of the emperor, Liang Fang (*q.v.*), of bringing a Buddhist priest into the palace to teach the emperor sexual techniques. This led Lin to lodge a complaint against Liang Fang. Unfortunately Lin's action directly impinged upon the personal concerns of Emperor Chu Chien-shen; as a result he had Lin clapped into the Guard's prison, with the intention of having him put to death. At this time no one in the court dared to speak up for Lin for fear of the emperor's wrath. This fear was not without foundation, for, when Huai En tried to defend Lin Chün, the emperor exploded, seized an inkstand from his desk, and flung it at Huai. At the same time he asked how Lin could learn of things which took place within the palace unless Huai had served as his informer. At no point did the emperor deny the basis for Lin's charge. Huai En was put out of the palace, and not until the emperor had calmed down was he allowed to return, and Lin Chün to regain his freedom.

This experience did not stop Huai from speaking up when occasion called. Sometime after 1485 (no precise date given) the emperor one day asked Huai to inform the court of the appointment of a certain Chang Chin 章瑾 as judge of the Embroidered-uniform Guard. This appointment had been made after Chang had presented the emperor with precious stones. Knowing this, Huai refused to announce the appointment. His reason was that the judge of the Guard controlled all the prisons, and such a position should not be filled by some person who might be subject to bribery. The emperor asked him whether he intended to disobey his order. Huai replied that he did not mean to disobey the emperor, but he was afraid of breaking the law.

Huai En's strict observance of the Code finally brought his relation with the emperor to an end. The last encounter between Huai and Chu Chien-shen happened toward the end of the latter's reign; it concerned the heir apparent. The background of this incident has to do with the problem of gold in the palace treasury. There was a practice in the earlier years of the dynasty of reserving a special fund in the treasury, said to be ten vaults of gold (another source makes it seven), for border emergencies. But during the middle of the Ch'eng-hua period, under the influence of the eunuch Liang Fang and others, all the reserved gold was used for building temples, refining cinnabar, entertaining monks and priests, and other activities of a superstitious sort. One day the emperor in essence said to Liang Fang, "You people were responsible for exhausting all the gold." Liang responded, "All of it was used in Your Majesty's own interests." After a short pause, the emperor replied that the time would come when someone else would deal with Liang and others on this matter. This "someone else," as interpreted by Liang Fang, was the prince. From this time on Liang determined to plot behind the scenes for the change of the heir apparent. His scheming was so successful that one day the emperor called Huai in and asked his opinion on the matter. Without any hesitation Huai held that a change could never be made, saying that he would rather be executed by the emperor for not endorsing the proposal than be cursed by the whole world. The emperor did not execute him, but demoted him to serve the imperial tombs in Feng-yang 鳳陽 (Anhwei). The status of the heir apparent remained unchanged.

Shortly after Chu Yu-t'ang (*q.v.*) ascended the throne (1487), Huai was recalled to Peking to serve again as the director of Ceremonial. His appointment, however, lasted only a few months. He died early in 1488. His last contribution to the new reign was his suggestion to dismiss Wan An (*see* Chiao Fang) and to appoint Wang Shu (*q.v.*) as minister of Personnel. With this shift many good officials were brought into the bureaucracy.

The above record explains why the editors of the *Ming-shih* classified Huai En as one of the few good eunuchs during the Ming. After his death, he was honored with a shrine, Hsien-chung tz'u 顯忠祠 (illustrious and loyal).

Bibliography

Ming-shih (Taiwan ed.), 162/1945a, 168/1995a, 180/2115a, 182/2138a, 194/2263a, 304/3409b; 5/117/15a, 17a; MSL (1964), Hsiao-tsung, 10/17b; Teng Yüan-hsi, *Huang Ming shu* (1606), 13/18a; *Shantung t'ung-chih* (1729), 28/2a; *Kao-mi-hsien chih* (1754), 8 甲/4b; Shen Te-fu, *Wan-li yeh-hu pien*, 6/159; T'ang Shu 唐樞 (1497–1574), *Kuo-ch'en chi* 國琛集, 103/43a; Wang Ao 鏊, *Shou-ch'i pi-chi*, 124/22a; Wang Shih-chen, *Yen-shan-t'ang pieh-chi*, 92/11a.

Yung-deh Richard Chu

HUANG Chung, *see* **K'UANG Chung**

HUANG Fu 黃福 (T. 如錫, H. 後樂翁), 1363-February 7, 1440), administrator of Chiao-chih 交阯 between 1407 and 1424, was born in Ch'ang-i 昌邑, Shantung. In 1384 he passed the examination for *chü-jen* and, after failing the metropolitan examination, was admitted to study in the National University. Two years later he received an appointment as an assistant magistrate at Hsiang-ch'eng 項城, Honan, and still later was transferred to Ch'ing-yüan 清源, Shansi. He then rose to become a chief clerk of a Guard regiment and, sometime after that, became registrar of another Guard. While still in this lowly position, he memorialized on affairs of state and gained the notice of Emperor Chu Yüan-chang himself. On the strength of this memorial, he received the exceptional promotion from a registrar (7th grade) to vice minister of Works (3d grade). This was on April 29, 1398, about two months before the emperor's death.

During the brief reign of Chu Yün-wen (*q.v.*), Huang Fu continued to be highly trusted and was once sent to Szechwan as inspector (ts'ai-fang shih 探訪使). In 1402 he was named one of the twenty-nine men on the black list of Chu Ti (*q.v.*). When Chu Ti captured Nanking and usurped the throne in July, 1402, however, Huang Fu, insisting that disloyal officials had misled them, was among those welcoming the victors; Huang was pardoned and allowed to remain as vice minister of Works. Three months later he became minister. He was in a vulnerable position and soon found himself the target of attack from the vigorous censor-in-chief, Ch'en Ying (*see* Ju Ch'ang). This led to his transfer to be a minister in the secondary capital at Peking in May, 1405. Even there he was criticized, in February, 1406, for the errors of his previous subordinates at the Works ministry and received a sentence of imprisonment followed by a demotion. Fortunately for him, however, he was given an opportunity, in July, 1406, to redeem himself under the senior general Chu Neng (*see* Chang Fu) and, when Chu was sent as expeditionary commander to Annam, Huang Fu joined him to take charge of military supplies. Later, when Chang Fu conquered Annam, Huang had the chance to make his mark as an able and respected administrator. On July 5, 1407, by imperial edict, the name Annam was changed to Chiao-chih, and Huang Fu received appointment as administration and surveillance commissioner.

In this capacity Huang faced many grave difficulties. His authority was seriously limited by the presence of the expeditionary army needed throughout his seventeen years in Chiao-chih for the pacification of rebellious elements. In 1408/9 there was the revolt of Emperor Gian-dinh which was continued in 1410 to 1414 by Trăn Quí-khoáng (for both see Chang Fu). To deal with these two major revolts, Chang Fu received general authority over the provinces for most of the time from 1409 to 1416. Afterwards, Li Pin (*see* Lê Lọ'i) served as expeditionary commander from 1417 to 1422, almost continuously fighting a series of Annamite uprisings against Chinese rule. During the entire period of Huang Fu's administration, problems of feeding and coping with a large mobile army were immense. He also had to deal with problems of security in the countryside, revival of peasant agriculture under conditions of disorder, collection of taxes, and keeping land and census records.

Huang Fu's second difficulty was that of his mixed Sino-Annamite administration. While only a few Annamites were given responsible positions at the provincial capital, the greater number of local prefectural district level officials were Annamites whose loyalty to the emperor was at best uncertain. As for the Chinese administrators available to Huang Fu, only a few of them were able and qualified. It was noted that many were men from Kwangtung, Kwangsi, and Yunnan who had failed in higher civil examinations and were dispatched to Chiao-chih because they were willing to take up unpopular appointments at the frontier regions near their own provinces. These men had not been formally trained as local administrators and lacked both skill and a sense of responsibility. Huang Fu was so short of able assistants that he often sought the help of court and provincial officials who had been exiled to Chiao-chih, even recruiting some of them into his administration. But the shortage of good, trained staff remained a serious handicap to his provincial government throughout his stay.

His third difficulty was the presence of eunuch commissioners who had been sent either as army inspectors or as special duty officials in charge of gold and silver mines, pearl fisheries, and the bureau of foreign trade. These were in a position to communicate directly with the court and were effectively outside of Huang's jurisdiction. Their misconduct in office was resented deeply by the Annamites, however, and marred his administration.

Despite these difficulties, Huang consistently carried out his many-sided duties and did not hesitate to advise on military and defense affairs as well. During the campaigns against Gian-dinh and Trần Quí-khoáng, he advised on new ways to supply the large army and arranged for additional thousands of piculs of grain to be transported by sea from Kwangtung. In 1410 he also introduced the k'ai-chung (開 中) method of salt vouchers to induce merchants from Yunnan and other provinces to transport grain to supply the large forces in Chiao-chih. To save grain for military supplies, he also parceled out public waste lands to provincial and local officials for their own cultivation in lieu of emoluments paid out in grain. And for reasons of health, convenience, and security, he advocated the development of an alternate route into Kwangsi by following the coast to Ch'in-chou 欽州 and upstream on the Ch'in River to Ling-shan 靈山, Kwangtung, and thence by portage to the Yü 鬱 River in Kwangsi; besides, he proposed the building of garrison forts and post stations along the way.

Huang was particularly concerned with financial administration. One of his first recommendations in 1408 was to ask that the tax structure be standardized and the burden lightened as one of the measures to win over the Annamite population. This remained a crucial problem as the Annamite revolts of 1408-14 spread through a greater part of the province. And what became especially acute was the difficulty in finding officials to carry out the new tax policies. In 1410, and again in 1411, Huang proposed measures to ensure a steady supply of both Annamite and Chinese administrators at all levels with the requisite skills and experience. His provincial vice commissioner also commented on this in 1411 and pointed out how serious the consequences of this shortage were on the efforts to maintain the goodwill and cooperation of the Annamite subjects. He also proposed methods to improve educational facilities for Annamite scholars and potential officials.

The continuous campaigns against rebels until 1414 delayed the implementation of many of Huang's constructive proposals. His educational plans were not effected until June, 1416, when offices were set up for Confucian education in 12 prefectures, 19 subprefectures, and 62 districts; offices for astrologers in 6 prefectures, 14 subprefectures, and 26 districts; offices for medical knowledge in 5 prefectures, 13 subprefectures, and 31 districts; offices for Buddhist affairs in 3 prefectures, 16 subprefectures, and 56 districts; and, not least, offices for Taoist affairs in 6 prefectures, 15 subprefectures, and 37 districts. This was the most important step in the policy of sinicization Huang embarked upon. Unfortunately for him, the policy was soon undermined by new revolts which Lê Lợi (*q.v.*) and others started in 1418. Continuous unrest kept the regional commander Li Pin and his successors busy until Chiao-chih had to be abandoned in 1427. After Huang was recalled on September 26, 1424, a full-scale rebellion by Lê Lợi made all administration impossible. Only a few fortified towns and garrisons survived under conditions of siege until the final withdrawal.

Huang was himself fortunate to have been recalled. He was spared the experience of seeing his lifework disintegrate and the fate of his successor, Ch'en Ch'ia (*q.v.*), who lost his life in a battle against Lê Lợi. When the situation became desperate in 1426, Ch'en Ch'ia did ask that Huang Fu be sent back to Chiao-chih, but he arrived too late in 1427. On the defeat and death of the expeditionary commander Liu Sheng (*see* Lê Lợi), Huang Fu was captured; but his life was spared because the Annamites remembered him as a benevolent administrator, and they escorted him back to Kwangsi.

In every Chinese account of the Annam debacle, it is noted that, after Huang Fu left Chiao-chih, the Chinese could not keep their new province, that the Annamites had really admired Huang, and that even Lê Lợi himself commented that if every Chinese official were like Huang he would not have rebelled. Also, the Chinese accounts blame the worst administrative abuses on eunuchs like Ma Ch'i 馬騏 (T. 文祥, army inspector in Chiao-chih from about 1410 to 1427) whose activities demoralized the Chinese officials and turned the Annamites against the Ming empire. Other accounts emphasize the incompetence of the generals after Chang Fu, especially the cowardice of Wang T'ung 王通 (T. 彦亨, d. 1452) and the rash stupidity of Liu Sheng. Huang Fu himself, in one of his letters to Chang Fu, dated about 1415, analyzing the situation in Chiao-chih after the decisive Chinese victories over Trần Quí-khoáng, expressed the opinion that what was needed to control the province was a substantial number of reliable Chinese troops stationed at strategic points. This would have been an admission that the Annamites could not be easily won over and that their fierce pride and resistance could be met only with force. It also implied that the thousands of Annamites in the provincial and local administration and the garrisons were merely awaiting the opportunity to rid their country of the Chinese.

The Chinese failure in Annam was never fully investigated at the time. Those who died for the empire were posthumously rewarded and those who came back were punished or reassigned. The emperor, Chu Chan-chi (*q.v.*), was happy to abandon the expensive campaign. Only Huang Fu was highly respected for his work there. He was promoted to grand supervisor of instruction of the heir apparent while retaining his office as minister of Works. He continued to make himself useful in the work of grain transportation, of organization of military supplies, of ways and means to increase agricultural productivity, and even of the establishment of military colonies along and close to the northern sections of the

Grand Canal (1429-30). For his contributions he was made minister of Revenue in 1430.

In 1432, in reward for his long service, he was sent to Nanking to a less strenuous post, still as minister of Revenue and then as minister of War. In the latter position, Huang Fu, during the last years of his life (1435-40), acted as adjutant to Li Lung 李隆 (T. 彥平, d. 1447), the second earl of Hsiang-ch'eng 襄城伯, who for fifteen years served on the military directorate at Nanking (1425-40, *see below* editors' note).

Huang left a work collected by one of his sons, Huang Tsung 琮, entitled *Chung-hsüan chi* 忠宣集, 13 *ch.* (also listed as 8 or 30 *ch.*), which is still extant. (Chung-hsüan is the posthumous name awarded him [1467?]) . His best known work, however, is the *Feng-shih An-nan shui-ch'eng jih-chi* 奉使安南水程日記, 1 *ch.*, of which several editions are known.

Bibliography

1/154/7a, 321/1a; 3/136/6b; 5/31/5a; 16/15/4b; 63/8/10a; KC (1958), 1581, 2231; MSL (1963), Ying-tsung, 1195, Hsien-tsung, 0839; *Huang Chung-hsüan kung wen-chi* 公文集, *pieh-chi* 別集, *chüan* 1-6.

[Editors' note: After the national capital was moved to Peking in 1420, a subordinate central government was left in Nanking. As to the highest military authority, there does not seem to have been anyone so empowered. Perhaps for a time all matters had to be referred to Peking. In 1424, as soon as Chu Kao-chih (*q. v.*) ascended the throne, he appointed the senior eunuch, Wang Kuei-t'ung (another name [?] for Wang Ching-hung, *q. v.*), to bring his troops, just returned from their south sea voyage, to serve as the guards at Nanking. Wang was instructed to consult with two other senior eunuchs, Chu Pu-hua 朱不花 (a Mongol ?) and T'ang Kuan-pao 唐觀保, on all matters concerning the Palaces in Nanking, and also with two members of the nobility. Earl Li Lung was probably appointed early in 1425 to serve on the directorate, about the same time as Cheng Ho (*q. v.*), who had apparently just returned from his sixth expedition. It seems that Cheng replaced Wang at this juncture, or perhaps Wang's role was to act for Cheng until his arrival. Huang Fu's appointment to the directorate in 1440, with the concurrent office of minister of Revenue, was definitely made because of his logistical experiences in Annam. From then on the directorate of military affairs (chi-wu 機務) at Nanking consisted of a grand eunuch as imperial representative, one or two members of the nobility as head of the military forces (the chief one holding the directorship of the military central commission), and a civilian who from 1487 on was the southern minister of War.]

Wang Gungwu

HUANG-FU Fang 皇甫汸 (T. 子循, H. 百泉子), 1503-82, poet and official, the third of four famous brothers, was a native of Soochow. This area was for centuries a center of affluence, and many of its sons became leaders in arts and letters. During the 16th century it seems to have reached a high plateau, producing, besides the Huang-fu, such families as those represented by Wen Cheng-ming (*q. v.*). the brothers Huang Hsing-tseng (*q. v.*), and Huang Lu-tseng (*see* Huang Hsing-tseng) and their sons, and Chang Feng-i (*q. v.*) and his two brothers. The two Huang brothers were cousins of the Huang-fu. The three Chang brothers and the Huang-fu brothers were fondly referred to by their fellow townsmen in the expression: "First the four Huang-fu, and then the three Chang" (前有四皇, 後有三張). The four brothers were also known collectively as the "Four outstanding Huang-fu" (皇甫四傑). In the *I yuan chih-yen*, Wang Shih-chen (*q.v.*) praised their achievement in poetry.

Wealth or official position, and often both together, constituted the background of these families. Usually too, rich families were allied by marriage to other well-to-do families. Huang-fu Fang is a case in point. He married twice, both wives being from families even wealthier than his own. His first wife, née Shen 沈 (1502-27), came from a fabulously rich household nicknamed Shen Pan-chiang 沈半江, probably implying that it owned half of the Chiang-tung 江東 area of Soochow.

Her father, Shen Chao 沈照, was a *chin-shih* of 1502 and rose in official position to assistant surveillance commissioner of Kwangtung in 1520–21. His second wife, née T'an 談 (1514–52), also from Soochow, whom he married in 1531, was from a family which owed its wealth to the textile trade. Her father, T'an Hsiang 祥 (T. 惟善), was said to have been a man trusted by all merchants, and the factories of his family reportedly produced materials of the newest design and the most resplendent colors.

Huang-fu Fang described himself as a precocious child, one who could compose poetry at the age of seven *sui*. Among the four brothers, he was indeed the first to obtain the *chü-jen* degree (1525), and the first to become a *chin-shih* (1529). Initially he refused the appointment to a district magistracy, taking a minor post in the National University in Peking instead. Later he became magistrate of Ch'ü-chou 曲周, Shansi, for three years, and returned to the capital as vice director of the bureau of irrigation and transportation in the ministry of Works in 1534. In 1538, when he incurred the displeasure of Kuo Hsün (*q. v.*), he was thrown into the prison of the Embroidered-uniform Guard and downgraded to the post of prefectural judge of Huang-chou 黃州, Hukuang. Two years later he received an appointment as bureau director in Nanking, but as his father died he retired that same year to his home. When the mourning period expired, he became director of the bureau of records in the Nanking ministry of Personnel. Again, after getting into trouble with a superior, he was dispatched (1545) to the provinces to be a minor official. His mother died the following year. Even at home in the observance of mourning he antagonized a censor and was impeached. He ended his official career as subprefect of K'ai-chou 開州, Szechwan, then of Ch'u-chou 處州, Chekiang, and finally as assistant surveillance commissioner of Yunnan (1554-55).

His literary friends included Ho Liang-chün (*q. v.*), who not only exchanged poems with him but also expressed high regard for his poetic attainment. Huang-fu Fang's poems were first grouped by periods and printed at different times under such individual titles as *Ch'an-ch'i chi* 禪棲集, *San-chou chi* 三州集, and *Nan-chung chi* 南中集. In 1574 he collected and reedited his own literary pieces into a work of 60 *chüan*, 33 of poetry, and 27 of prose, and printed it under the unified title *Huang-fu ssu-hsün chi* 司勳集. The *Ssu-k'u* editors included this work in the Imperial Library and agreed with other critics in calling Huang-fu Fang an accomplished poet of the mid-Ming era. (It has recently been reproduced in the *Ssu-k'u chen-pen* 珍本, ser. 3.) Two other items by him also received notices in the *Ssu-k'u* catalogue, the *Po-ch'üan-tzu hsü-lun* 百泉子緒論, a short book attacking the irresponsible pronouncements of the censors and the injustices flowing therefrom, and the *Chieh-i hsin-yü* 解頤新語, a collection of notes on poetry. Huang-fu Fang loved music, entertainments, and other sensual pleasures. Even in old age he hardly changed his pattern of life. Ch'ien Ch'ien-i (ECCP) characterized him as a braggart of sorts, and pointed to this failing as the root of many of his troubles.

Huang-fu Ch'ung 沖 (T. 子浚, H. 華陽山人, 不菴叟, 1490-1558), the eldest brother of the four, was a *chü-jen* of 1528. He was the only one to fail in the metropolitan examinations, and never held any official post. In his younger days while living in Peking with his father, he led a rather intemperate life, indulged in sensual pleasures, such as games of chance, and enjoyed hunting and polo. He took delight in discussing strategy and tactics of warfare. Later he traveled to Szechwan when his father was an official there. His collected literary works, 40 *chüan* of poetry and 20 of prose, known as the *Hua-yang chi* 華陽集, may never have been printed. He is said to be the author of a dozen other works on many subjects, including a family genealogy, but none seems to be extant except some scattered poems and essays to be found in anthologies and in his brothers' works.

Huang-fu Hsiao 涍 (T. 子安, H. 少玄子, 1497–1546), the second of the four brothers, died the earliest. He qualified for the *chü-jen* in 1528, and became a *chin-shih* in 1532. After serving in the ministry of Works, he received a transfer to the ministry of Rites, where he became vice director of the bureau of ceremonies. Grand Secretary Hsia Yen (*q. v.*) is said to have regarded him favorably, and had him draft several important memorials. His rise probably antagonized others in officialdom in Peking, for he was demoted in 1539 and sent out to be assistant prefect of Kuang-p'ing 廣平, Pei-Chihli. After he received an appointment as a bureau director in the ministry of Justice in Nanking the following year, his father died. Reinstated in Nanking after the observance of the mourning period, he later became assistant surveillance commissioner of Chekiang. Rated inadequate in 1545, he was retired from office. Soon after his mother's death in 1546, he too passed away. His elder brother edited his literary works and wrote his biography. The *Huang-fu shao-hsüan chi* 少玄集 in 26 *chüan* was printed in 1551. An addition of 10 *chüan*, the *wai-chi* 外集, was printed in 1566. (These have both been reproduced in the *Ssu-k'u chen-pen*, ser. 3.) He is also the author of one hundred biographical sketches of people, living from Chin 晉 to Sung 宋 (roughly 4th to 13th centuries), who led idealistic lives as nonparticipants in worldly affairs. This work entitled *I-min chuan* 逸民傳, 2 ch., was printed in the *ts'ung-shu*, *I-men kuang-tu* by Chou Lü-ching (*see* Ts'ao Chao) in 1596.

The *Ssu-k'u* editors wrote appreciatively of Huang-fu Hsiao's poetry and included *Huang-fu shao-hsüan chi* in the Imperial Library. Their notice of the *I-min chuan*, however, is open to criticism. Basing themselves on the *Ming-shih* and the *Chiang-nan t'ung-chih* 江南通志, they assert that the real author of the *I-min chuan* was not Huang-fu Hsiao, but Huang-fu Lien (see below), the youngest of the four brothers. It seems that both the *Ming-shih* and the *Chiang-nan t'ung-chih* are at fault, and the *Ssu-k'u* editors were misled. According to Huang-fu Hsiao's biography, written by Huang-fu Fang, he left a work entitled *Hsü Kao-shih chuan* 續高士傳, supposedly a continuation of the famous work *Kao-shih chuan* by Huang-fu Mi (215–282), but he makes no mention of any work with the title of *I-min chuan*. His description, however, fits the *I-min chuan* which is available now in the *I-men kuang-tu*; furthermore, Huang-fu Fang also wrote a biography of Huang-fu Lien, the possible author suggested in the *Ssu-k'u* notice, in which no such work is mentioned either.

What happened, if one may attempt a conjecture, is that the altering of the original title *Hsü Kao-shih chuan* to *I-min chuan* was the act of Chou Lü-ching. If one makes a careful examination of the *I-min chuan* in the *I-men kuang-tu*, one finds at the end a sketch of Chou Lü-ching himself, which he has surreptitiously added. Perhaps he assumed that to call himself a *kao-shih* would have been presumptuous, so he deleted this expression and changed the title to *I-min chuan*. The notice in the *Ssu-k'u* catalogue also gives Ping Yü 邴郁 for Teng Yü 鄧郁. As to the remark that the names of Yü I 庾易 and Seng Shao 僧紹 appear only in the table of contents and that their biographies were omitted in the edition examined, this too is not true for the *I-men kuang-tu* edition.

Huang-fu Lien 濂 (T. 子約, 道隆, 理山, 1508–64), the fourth and youngest of the brothers, was a *chü-jen* of 1534, and a *chin-shih* of 1544. After a short term as a secretary in the bureau of construction in the ministry of Works, he retired to observe the mourning period for his mother in 1546. In 1548 he again received an appointment in the same ministry, this time as secretary in the bureau of irrigation and transportation. Incurring the displeasure of a superior, he was demoted to a minor post in the Honan provincial surveillance office. In due course he earned a promotion and became assistant prefect of Hsing-hua 興化, Fukien. After 1556 he gave up his official career, and turned to religious Taoism in the search for immortality. Following his death his brother, Huang-fu Fang, edited his literary works and printed them in 20 *chüan* under the title *Huang-fu shui-pu chi* 水部集. It is said that he also annotated the *Tao-te ching*, and was a calligrapher, and a painter of flowers, birds, trees, and rocks.

The father of these four brothers, Huang-fu Lu 錄 (T. 世庸, H. 近峯, 1470–1540), became a *chin-shih* in 1496. In the capital he served the ministries of Works and Rites. Later he became prefect of Shun-ch'ing 順慶, Szechwan (1511–14). Both the *Ming-shih* and the *Ming wai-shih* 明外史, as quoted by the *T'u-shu chi-ch'eng*, mistook Shun-ch'ing for Ch'ung-ch'ing (Chungking). The editors of the *Ssu-k'u* catalogue notice three of his works, the (*Huang*) *Ming chi-lueh* 紀略, the *Chin-feng wen* 近峯聞 (*chi*) -*lüeh*, and the *Hsia-p'i chi-t'an* 下陴紀談, all of which are in the category of random notes. Under the first item the editors point out the error of mistaking Shun-ch'ing for Chungking in the *Ming-shih*. This *Huang Ming chi-lüeh*, a miscellany of anecdotes, deals with various subjects of Ming history, the more important ones being on population, official salaries, the transport of grain, and Emperor Chu Chan-chi's (*q. v.*) hobby of cricket fighting. It was first printed in the late Ming years by Wu Shih 吳栻 in the *Li-tai hsiao-shih* 歷代小史. Recently the Commercial Press reprinted it twice, first in 1936 in the *Ts'ung-shu chi-ch'eng*, then in 1940 separately as one of the ten rare editions of the Yüan and Ming. The *Chin-feng chi-wen* 紀聞, a short work of eighteen notes, may be found in the *Po-ling hsüeh-shan*, edited and printed by Wang Wen-lu (*q. v.*). Unfortunately the author's name is printed incorrectly; instead of Huang-fu Lu (T. Shih-yung), it reads Huang-fu Yung (T. Shih-lu). Small wonder that the meticulous Ch'ing scholars often remarked with despair on the poor editing of Ming times. This is another glaring example. Another *ts'ung-shu* compiled about the same time, the *Chi-lu hui-pien* (*see* Shen Chieh-fu), includes a *Chin-feng chi-lüeh chai-ch'ao* 摘抄 of seventeen notes, identical except for the omission of the first note. The *Hsia-p'i chi-t'an* is supposedly a group of jottings on the observations Huang-fu Lu made on the defense against bandits of Shun-ch'ing while he was prefect. It is not clear whether it is still extant. In addition to the above mentioned three titles, he left a collection of official documents on the regulation of the princes and their domains, the *Huang Ming fan-fu cheng-ling* 藩府政令, compiled when he was director of the bureau of ceremonies in the ministry of Rites under Pai Yüeh 白鉞 (T. 秉德, 1454–1510, cs 1484, minister of Rites, 1508–10). A manuscript copy in 6 *chüan* of this work is in the National Peiping Library collection of rare books and available on microfilm.

Bibliography

1/287/11a; 5/51/119a; 64/戊5/1a, 4b, 14a, 20a; 84/丁上 /37b, 40a, 41b; TSCC (1885–88), XIV: 584/10b, XVII: 786/16a, XXIII: 103/1b; *Su-chou-fu chih* (1862), 86/19b, 30a; SK (1930), 61/9b, 124/8a, 143/5b, 172/4b, 197/7b; Wang Shih-chen, *I-yüan chih-yen*, 7/15b (*Yen-chou shan-jen ssu-pu kao* ed.), 7/15b; Ho Liang-chün, *Ssu-yu-chai ts'ung-shuo* (1959 ed.), 240.

Lienche Tu Fang

HUANG Hsiao-yang 黃蕭養, died May, 1450, rebel leader, was a native of the village of Ch'ung-ho-pao 沖鶴堡 in Nan-hai 南海 (later Shun-te 順德) -hsien, southwest of Kuang-chou-fu 廣州府 (Canton). In the autumn of 1448, while imprisoned in Nan-hai for robbery, he managed to break jail with nineteen fellow prisoners. Boarding a boat secreted at a prearranged meeting place, they escaped to the sea. In a short while he was joined by thousands of local ruffians and malcontents, especially among the riverboat people. The latter constituted a small minority, and, like the Hakka, were discriminated against. All these formed a rebellious force of some magnitude. It happened that selected Kwangtung troops had been sent to Lung-shui 瀧水 (name changed to Lo-ting-chou 羅定州 in 1577) to fight the Yao 猺 tribesmen, and to the eastern border to fight the bandits of Fukien. The provincial authorities were thus unable to nip Huang's uprising in the bud. Meanwhile he collected hundreds of vessels operating in the Pearl River estuary. Then, in mid-September, 1449, news arrived from Peking that the imperial army had been annihilated by the Mongols and that Emperor Chu Ch'i-chen (*q.v.*) had suffered capture. Seizing the opportunity thus offered him, Huang declared himself Shun-t'ien wang 順天王 (King obeying heaven) with the reign title Tung-yang 東陽, and led a fleet of three hundred ships to attack Kuang-chou. He found the city well defended and the walls too strong to breach. On the river outside the city, however, he was in his element, and on October 4 overwhelmed a fleet of two hundred warships led by Chang An (*see* Wang Tso), then provincial commander-in-chief. In the battle Chang lost his life (reportedly by drowning while drunk), and his deputy was taken prisoner along with a full complement of firearms and other military equipment. Even with these additional weapons Huang could not take Kuang-chou and could only blockade it, the siege lasting over eight months. During this time the rebels occupied the surrounding area and pillaged many households.

In the meantime the Peking government had begun to mobilize troops from Kwangsi and Kiangsi to come to the rescue. In mid-October, on the recommendation of the minister of War, Yü Ch'ien

(*q.v.*), Yang Hsin-min 楊信民 (cj 1420, d. 1450, Pth. 恭惠), a former assistant commissioner of Kwangtung, then on military duty north of Peking, was made governor of Kwangtung and sent to Kuang-chou to deal with the rebellion. It is said that the people of that province believed in Yang's integrity and compassion, and even Huang, the rebel leader, considered surrendering to him. Yang, however, died suddenly in April, 1450. Meanwhile the government troops from several provinces, under command of Tung Hsing 董興 (created earl of Haining 海寧, February, 1457, d. December, 1475), arrived at the scene. In a battle on May 21 Huang was killed by an arrow. His followers carried on the fighting for a while longer, but were crushed early in June. The rebel leaders who were captured, including Huang's father and the rest of his family, were escorted to Peking to be executed. By Tung's order Huang's native village and other towns, where fighting took place, were destroyed. Thousands of people, mostly innocent villagers, were either massacred or rendered homeless. It is said that the people of Kuang-chou went to the shrine erected in memory of Yang Hsin-min and wailed that were he alive he would have prevented their suffering in such a way. After intensive campaigning, involving tens of thousands of troops from three different provinces, the government had finally succeeded in crushing the rebellion which had lasted more than a year, and had done extensive damage to Kuang-chou and adjacent territories.

Two years after the conclusion of the campaign, the court approved the recommendation of the local authorities for the creation of a new hsien which included these depopulated villages, to be called Shun-te (submitting to the imperial virtue). It was made up of four southern villages of Nan-hai and the northern section of Hsin-hui 新會 -hsien. To forestall trouble, as a result of possible cooperation between the pirates and remnants of the rebels, the court reissued its edict against people of Fukien and Kwangtung engaging in seafaring activities. The death of Huang Hsiao-yang, however, did not put an end to the rebellions. In subsequent years remnants of his band, in alliance with pirates and Yao tribesmen, broke out in sporadic uprisings around the prefectural city and in the border regions of Kwangsi, and did not desist until the end of the 15th century (*see* Yeh Sheng and Han Yung).

Bibliography

1/11/1b, 172/10b, 175/3a; 5/63/1a; 61/161/16b; MSL (1963), Ying-tsung, ch. 183–193, 207; KC (1958), 1739, 1764, 1795, 1844, 1854; Huang Yü (*see* Huang Tso), *Shuang-huai sui-ch'ao*, 7/2a; Lu I (*see* Chu Ch'i-yü), *Ping-i man-chi*, 201/11b; (Wan-li) *Nan-hai-hsien chih* (NLP microfilm, no. 496), 2/11a; *Kuang-chou-fu chih* (1879), 78/8b; Mao Ch'i-ling (ECCP), *Hou-chien lu*, in *Mao Hsi-ho hsien-sheng ch'üan-chi*, no.78), 1/7b; Ch'ü Ta-chün (ECCP), *Kuang-tung hsin-yü*, 1/16b, 4/18b; *Fo-shan chung-i-hsiang chih* 忠義鄉志 (1923), 11/2a, 14/1a; P'eng I-lo 彭伊洛, "Ming chung-yeh Huang Hsiao-yang tsai Kuang-chou ch'i-i te she-hui pei-ching chi ch'i ching-kuo" 明中葉黃蕭養在廣州起義的社會背景及其經過, *Shih-hsüeh yüeh-k'an* 史學月刊, no. 10 (1957), 5; Hsü Hsü 徐續, "Kuan-yü 關於 Huang Hsiao-yang ch'i-i te chi-ko wen-t'i" 幾個問題, *ibid.*, no. 11 (1958), 32.

Hok-lam Chan

HUANG Hsing-tseng 黃省曾 (T. 勉之, H. 五嶽山人), 1490-August 25 (?), 1540, scholar, author, poet, publisher, and bibliophile, the best known of the Huang family of belle-lettrists, was a native of Wu 吳-hsien (Soochow). This area, because of the productivity of its land and its flourishing commerce, was for centuries a center of affluence and literary activity. During the 16th century it produced, besides the Huang brothers, such well-known families as those of Wen Cheng-ming, Huang-fu Fang, and Chang Feng-i (*qq.v.*). Huang Hsing-tseng and his elder brother Huang Lu 魯 -tseng were cousins of the Huang-fu brothers.

The Huang family, originally from Honan, settled in Yüan-chou 袁州, Kiangsi, at the beginning of the 12th century. Huang's sixth-generation ancestor Huang Pin 斌 (d. 1375), a muscular man skillful in the military arts, joined the rebel leader Hsü Shou-hui (*q.v.*) after Hsü's forces seized Yüan-chou from government hands in April, 1352, and was appointed a miliarch commander.

He stayed on in Hsü's camp even after Hsu's the assassination by Ch'en Yu-liang (*q.v.*) in June, 1360, but surrendered to Chu Yüan-chang after Chu captured Chiang-chou 江州 (Kiukiang) from Ch'en in September of the following year. Early in 1370, Chu Yüan-chang, now emperor, rewarded Huang Pin with the rank of battalion commander, and assigned him to Soochow, where he raised his family. During the last two years of his life (1373–75), Huang Pin officiated in the transportation of grain along the coast from the Yangtze valley to Liaotung. After his death his two sons successively inherited the military rank, and continued in the same service intermittently for over thirty years from 1378 to 1410. Huang Pin's second son had an heir who remained in the military service; he raised three sons, the youngest, Huang Wei 暐 (T. 日昇, H. 東樓, b. 1438), Huang Hsing-tseng's grandfather, was the first in the family to pursue a civil career.

Having qualified for the *chü-jen* in 1477, Huang Wei achieved the *chin-shih* belatedly in 1490, at the age of fifty-two. He then successively served as secretary in the ministry of Justice, and as director of a bureau in the ministry of Works. He became known as the author of a collection of notes on the history and folklore of the Soochow area. The original edition of this work, with a preface by Wang Ao 王鏊 (*q.v.*), dated 1526?, is extremely rare; the publisher of at least two later editions erroneously attributed the authorship to Yang Hsün-chi (*q.v.*), also a native of Soochow. A manuscript copy entitled *P'eng-hsüan Wu-chi* 蓬軒吳記, 2

ch., with a supplement *P'eng-hsüan pieh* 別 *-chi,* 1 *ch.*, is preserved in the former National Library of Peiping and is available in microfilm (no. 249). A collated edition entitled *P'eng-ch'uang lei-kao* 窗 類稿, 5 *ch.*, with slight variations, was printed in 1915 in the collection *Han-fen-lou pi-chi* 涵芬樓祕笈 (second series). Huang Wei's son, Huang I 異 (H. 葵菴), though not a scholar, made handsome provision for his two sons, Huang Lu-tseng and Huang Hsing-tseng, for their acquisition of books.

Huang Lu-tseng (T. 得之, H. 中南. March 25, 1487-August 10, 1561), was the second son of Huang I (his eldest having died early). Tall and impressive looking, Huang Lu-tseng graduated as *chü-jen* in 1516, but failed in the metropolitan examinations. He lived the rest of his life in Soochow and became the center of a small group of men of letters, including the Huang-fu cousins, Wang Ch'ung (*q.v.*) and his elder brother, and Chang Feng-i and his brothers. They were fondly referred to by their fellow townsmen as "two dragons of the Huang, two jades of the Wang, and four gems of the Huang-fu" (黃家二龍, 王氏雙璧, 皇甫四傑). Huang Lu-tseng was known for his generosity and readiness to help those in need. He is reported to have written several works. Among those that are extant may be mentioned the tsan 贊 (eulogies) to the *Ku Lieh-nü chuan* 古列女傳 attributed to Liu Hsiang (77-6 B.C.), and to the *Hsü* 續 *Lieh-nü chuan*, a continuation of the previous work by the same author, and the *Chung-Lü er-hsien* 鍾呂二仙 *chuan*, biographies of Chung K'uei (*see* Chou Ch'en) and Lü Tung-pin 洞賓, two famous legendary Taoist figures. He had a collection of poetry published under the title *Nan-hua ho-pi chi* 南華合璧集, 5 *ch.*, including a selection of the poems of Wang Ch'ung; it receives a notice in the Imperial Catalogue but it is not known to have survived.

Huang Lu-tseng had a son named Huang Ho-shui 河水 (original *ming* Te-shui

德水, T. 清父), who distinguished himself as a poet. He was the author of several collections of travelogues and poetry, and the co-editor of an anthology of T'ang poems entitled *T'ang-shih chi* 唐詩紀, 170 *ch.*, with a table of contents in 34 *chüan* printed by his collaborator Wu Kuan 吳琯 (cs 1571) in 1585, which is still extant.

Huang Hsing-tseng, the youngest son of Huang Wei, was generally acknowledged as superior to his brother in learning and literary achievement. Even as a young man without an official title, Huang attracted the attention of such distinguished individuals as Wang Ao, Li Meng-yang, Wang Shou-jen, and Huo T'ao (*qq.v.*). After repeated failure in the examinations, he became obsessed with an urge to travel, and adopted the sobriquet Wu-yüeh-shan-jen 五嶽山人 (recluse of the five sacred mountains). Late in 1517 he received an invitation from the minister of War at Nanking, Ch'iao Yü 喬宇 (T. 希 大 H. 白巖, 1457-1524, cs 1484, minister from 1515 to August, 1521, Pth. 莊簡), to come to the southern capital. Ch'iao entrusted him with the compilation of accounts of travelogues of that area, which he successfully completed in due course. Unfortunately, these accounts are not noticed in any catalogue. It was also during this time that he produced his famous work of historical geography, the *Hsi-yang ch'ao-kung tien-lu* 西洋朝貢典錄 (preface July, 1520).

Already in 1521, Huang, impressed by the teaching of Wang Shou-jen, had begun corresponding with this famous philosopher. Two years later, upon learning that Wang had returned to Chekiang, Huang proceeded to Shao-hsing to become one of his students. He compiled an account of Wang's conversation with his disciples, excerpts of which are preserved in the final section of the *Ch'uan-hsi lu* edited by Ch'ien Te-hung (*q.v.*). Huang's record, however, was later criticized by Huang Tsung-hsi (ECCP) as distorting the meaning of the master. When Wang Shou-jen was recalled from retirement to suppress the rebellion in Kwangsi in 1527, Huang continued his study under Wang's senior disciple Chan Jo-shui (*q.v.*), then chancellor of the National University at Nanking (1526–28). He took note of the differences between Wang and Chan, but contended that they differed only in emphasis and not in principle. By this time Huang's fame was such that, when Li Meng-yang, who had earlier discussed the art of poetry with him, was recuperating from illness at Ching-k'ou 京口 in the summer of 1529, he entrusted Huang with publishing his collected works; Huang complied and contributed a preface. After a brief sojourn in Nanking until 1530, Huang returned to Soochow; a year later, at the age of forty-one, he finally became a *chü-jen*, at the top of the list.

Huang did not, however, pursue an official career. In subsequent years, except for occasional travel, which included visits to Ch'ang-an and Peking, he spent most of his time in Soochow, devoting himself to writing, collecting, and publishing. In 1537 he enrolled in the National University at Nanking, but stayed there very briefly. During this year, he took a trip to West Lake in Hangchow, where he encountered another distinguished man of letters, T'ien Ju-ch'eng (*q.v.*). They traveled together and exchanged poems, producing a corpus of poetry known as *Hsi-hu yu-yung* 湖西遊詠. This collection, with prefaces by both Huang and T'ien dated 1538, is available in several collectanea. In November, 1539, his mother née Wang 王 died; overcome with grief he contracted an illness which became very serious. By July of the following year, worrying that he might not recuperate, he started writing his autobiography. Huang succumbed a month later, aged fifty, apparently of lung disease; before the end, he composed his own eulogy, which, together with his autobiography, is preserved in his collected works. He married twice but both wives died before him; the first bore him a son, Huang Chi-shui 姬水, who was also accomplished in letters and

scholarship.

Huang Hsing-tseng is reported to have been as impressive looking as his brother and quite conversant with the official speech, but he lived a rather carefree and unconventional life. Supported by the family estate and unhindered by official duties, he took delight in composing poetry and in pursuing antiquarian interests—a typical example of the "pure" literary man of his time (*see* Chu Yün-ming). He enjoyed the association and friendship of many leading scholar-officials and intellectuals, and benefited from their patronage and guidance; these associations he recounts vividly in his autobiography; yet, both in life and writing style, he remained individualistic. In philosophy, though he was a member of the Wang Yang-ming school, he did not distinguish himself; except for casual remarks indicating his skepticism about certain popular beliefs, such as fate and the efficacy of geomancy, he seldom discussed philosophy in abstract terms. In literature, particularly in poetry, despite his affiliation with Li Meng-yang, he did not follow his style. The breadth of his scholarship, marked by the copiousness and diversity of his writings, exceeded that of many of his contemporaries.

Huang Hsing-tseng wrote on subjects ranging from emendations of, and annotations, to, classical literature and miscellanies on history and geography, to treatises on plants and animals. His collected works of prose and poetry, entitled *Wu-yüeh-shan-jen chi* 集, 38 *ch.*, were printed by his family shortly before his death. A selection of his poems, brought out with those of his son, collectively known as *Er-Huang* 二黃 *chi*, is included in *Sheng Ming pai-chia shih (ch'ien-chi)* 盛明百家詩 (前集), edited by Yü Hsien (*see* Feng Wei-min). Most of his other writings survive either as independent works or as chapters in various collectanea. His supplements to classical literature include the "eulogies" to the *Lieh-hsien chuan* 列仙傳 ascribed to Liu Hsiang, the *Kao-shih* 高士 *chuan* by Huang-fu Mi (215–82), and the

Hsü hsien chuan by Shen Pan (of the Nan-T'ang, 923-36); and annotation of the *Shen-chien* 申鑒 by Hsün Yüeh (148-209) with preface of 1519, considered the most detailed and authoritative of its kind. His notes on the Odes and on the principles of poetry are available in several *ts'ung-shu*. His miscellanies on history and geography include: *Wu-feng lu* 吳風錄, a collection of jottings on the Soochow area, and the above-mentioned *Hsi-yang ch'ao-kung tien-lu*, which is probably his best known work. It is a record of the vassal states in central and southeast Asia that dispatched tributary missions to the Ming court from the beginning of the dynasty down to his time, based on the works of Ma Huan, Fei Hsin (*qq. v.*) and others, but with important emendations and corrections. This work is a valuable supplement to the earlier accounts of the Chinese maritime expeditions to the South Seas, and has been critically examined by J. J. L. Duyvendak, Paul Pelliot, and others. First circulated in manuscript, it was initially printed by Chang Hai-p'eng (ECCP), who collated the surviving fragments in his *Chieh-yüeh shan-fang hui-ch'ao* in 1808. His writings on plants, animals, and related topics encompass the following: *Tao-p'in* 稻品, on rice growing; *Ts'an-ching* 蠶經, on the silkworm; *Yü* 魚 *-ching*, on fish; *I-chü* 藝菊, on chrysanthemums; *Yü* 芋*-ching*, on taros; *Shou* 獸 *-ching*, on animals; and others. The first four were printed together under the title (*Hsin-k'o*) *Nung-p'u ssu-chung* (新刻) 農圃四種 in 1603. These are all available in a number of Ming collectanea, such as *I-men kuang-tu* 夷門廣牘, *Pai-ling hsüeh-shan* 百陵學山, *Kuang Pai-ch'uan hsüeh-hai* 廣百川學海, and *Ko-chih* 格致 *ts'ung-shu*.

Huang Hsing-tseng was also noted as a publisher. He supervised the engraving of a score of important works, ranging from classical literature and Buddhist and Taoist treatises, to miscellanies on philosophy, history, and geography; some of these also contained his own commentaries. In 1525 he printed the *Hsi Chung-san*

chi 嵇中散集, 10 *ch.*, being the collected works of the famous poet-musician Hsi K'ang (223-62). It bears the name of Huang's studio, Nan-hsing ching-she 南星精舍, and was later reproduced in the *Ssu-pu ts'ung-k'an* series. In 1534 he engraved another important book, the *Shui-ching chu* 水經注 of Li Tao-yuan (d. 527) which, though criticized by later commentators for its faults, was one of the important Ming editions. The *Wu-yüeh shan-jen chi* contains a number of prefaces and colophons to works of different kinds, indicating the books which Huang had printed. Some of these works bear the studio names of Fou-yü shan-fang 浮玉山房 and Wen-shih-t'ang 文始堂.

Huang Hsing-tseng's son Huang Chi-shui (T. 淳父, H. 質山, 1509-June, 1574) also distinguished himself in literature and scholarship. In his early years, at the instance of his father, whose handwriting was poor, he received instruction from the famous calligrapher Chu Yün-ming, and became superior in this art. He entered the prefectural school at the age of thirteen, but, like his father, Huang Chi-shui, suffered setbacks in the civil examinations. He delighted in literary pursuits, and spent large sums for the acquisition of books, paintings, and antique objects. His indulgence in these activities eventually sapped the family wealth, and he ceased to be a man of means toward his later years. By virtue of his literary achievement and secure in his family name, he became a well-known figure among his contemporaries. Early in 1555, when Soochow was threatened by the raids of the *wo-k'ou*, he accepted the invitation of Nieh Pao (*q. v.*), lately retired as minister of War to live with him in his native village, Yung-chi 永吉, Kiangsi. While he and his family were stopping over at Nanking on the way, his friend Ho Liang-chün (*q.v.*), who also sought shelter from the pirates, persuaded him to stay in the southern capital instead. Huang then made his temporary home in Nanking for the next six years. During this period he composed numerous poems, many of them his prized pieces. He returned to Soochow in 1561, where he died thirteen years later. Huang Chi-shui was the author of several collections of writings, most of which were printed by his son Huang Chia-fang 嘉芳, after his death. One of the earliest, known as *Pai-hsia* 白下 *chi* (Pai-hsia being an ancient name of Nanking), 11 *ch.*, contains many poems composed during his sojourn there. Another one entitled *Kao-su-chai* 高素齋 *chi*, 29 *ch.*, includes some of his later writings. Finally there is the *Huang Ch'un-fu hsien-sheng ch'üan-chi* 淳父先生全集, 24 *ch.*, which supplements the aforesaid collections. Copies of these works, though still extant, are quite rare. A selection of Huang Chi-shui's poems, entitled *Huang Chih-shan* 質山 *chi*, is printed together with those of his father in *Sheng Ming pai-chia shih*. Huang Chi-shui was also the author of *P'in-shih chuan* 貧士傳, 2 *ch.*, being a compendium of biographical sketches of scholars of the past who became poverty stricken. This appears to have been a work of his late years, an edition of which was included in 1922 in the *Pao-yen-t'ang pi-chi (cheng-chi)* (正集) by Ch'en Chi-ju (ECCP). Like his father, Huang Chi-shui also published books. One of his best-known works is a facsimile reproduction of a Sung edition of the *Ch'ien-Han chi* 前漢紀, 30 *ch.*, by Hsün Yüeh. This work was later reproduced in the *Ssu-pu ts'ung k'an* series. A specimen of his calligraphy is preserved in the Palace Museum, Taipei.

Bibliography

1/287/3a; 34/11/3a; 40/48/6a; 64 戊 17/19a; 83/25/4a; 84/丙/69b; *Su-chou-fu chih* (1862), 80/14a; *Wu-hsien chih* (1933), 66 上/23b; Huang Hsing-tseng, *Wu-yüeh-shan-jen chi* (NCL microfilm); Huang Chi-shui, *Pai-hsia chi* (NLP microfilm, no. 868); Wang Ao, *Chen-tse hsien-sheng chi*, 7/6a, 12a; Li Tung-yang, *Li K'ung-t'ung chi*, ch. 27, 67, 68; Wang Shou-jen, *Wang Yang-ming ch'üan-chi* (1936), ch. 3, 5; Huang-fu Fang, *Huang-fu ssu-hsüan chi* (NLP microfilm, no.

928), 36/9a; Ts'ai Yü 蔡羽 (d. 1541), *Lin-wu chi* 林屋集 (NCL microfilm), 11/11b, 13/7b; Ts'ui Hsien 崔銑 (1478–1541), *Yüan-tz'u* 洹詞 (Wan-li ed.), 12/23a; Ho Liang-chün, *Ssu-yu-chai ts'ung-shuo*, 24/16b, 26/12b; Ho Ch'iao-yüan, *Ming-shan ts'ang* (*Kao-tao chi* 高道記), 95/16b; Wen Chen-meng, *Ku-su ming-hsien hsiao-chi* (1925), B/12a; SK (1930), 78/5a, 91/5a, 124/8b, 137/9b, 177/8b; Yeh Ch'ang-ch'ih 葉昌熾, *Ts'ang-shu chi-shih shih* 藏書紀事詩 (1897), 2/57b; Cheng Te-k'un 鄭德坤, "Shui-ching chu pan-pen k'ao" 版本考, YCHP, 15 (1934), 214; Paul Pelliot, "Les grands voyages maritimes chinois au début du XVe siècle," TP, XXX (1933), 344; K. T. Wu, "Ming Printing and Printers," HJAS, 7 (1942), 241; Ping-ti Ho, "The Introduction of American Food Plants into China," *American Anthropologist*, 57: 2 (April, 1955), 191; *id.*, *Ladder of Success in Imperial China* (1962), 81; Hu Shih, "Note" in ECCP, 970; L. of C. *Catalogue of Rare Books*, 490. For Huang Wei: *Wu-hsien chih*, 66 上/16b; SK (1930), 144/9b. For Huang Lu-tseng: 84/丁上 /43b; Huang-fu Fang, *Huang-fu ssu-hsüan chi*, 34/5a; *Wu-hsien chih*, 66 上/23b; SK (1930), 61/4a, 192/4b. For Huang Chi-shui: 1/287/3a; 5/115/98a; 64/ 巳 20/9a; 84/ 丁上 /74b; Wang Shih-chen, *Yen-chou shan-jen hsü-kao*, 150/11a; SK (1930), 61/11a, 180/2b; *Ku-kung shu-hua lu* 故宮書畫錄 (rev. ed. 1965), 3/414.

Hok-lam Chan

HUANG Huai 黄淮 (T. 宗豫, H. 介庵), 1367–June 22, 1449, scholar and official, came from a wealthy family of Yung-chia 永嘉, Chekiang. A *chin-shih* of 1397, he was appointed a drafter in the central drafting office. In August, 1400, by order of Emperor Chu Yün-wen (*q.v.*), the drafters were transferred to the Hanlin Academy and their titles changed to shih-shu 侍書 (attending scribe); two years later, however, under the new Emperor Chu Ti (*q.v.*), all of Chu Yün-wen's innovations were abolished. Thus Huang Huai and eight others had their original titles restored. A month later he was returned to the Hanlin Academy as a compiler. Late in the same year he was promoted to reader. At the same time Hsieh Chin, Yang Jung, Yang Shih-ch'i,

Hu Kuang, Hu Yen (*qq.v.*), and Chin Yu-tzu (*see* Empress Hsü), also received promotions and became known as the seven Hanlin who served as the emperor's confidants and composed his edicts.

In 1404, after Huang and Hsieh had supervised the metropolitan examination, they were ordered to serve in the supervisorate of instruction to the heir apparent. Three years later Huang received a promotion to be a grand secretary in the supervisorate and in 1408 he became a tutor to the emperor's eldest grandson Chu Chan-chi(*q.v.*). In 1409, when the emperor left for the northern frontier to lead an expedition into Mongolia, Huang and Yang Shih-ch'i were ordered to remain in Nanking to assist the heir apparent, Chu Kao-chih (*q.v.*), in looking after the affairs of state. This command was repeated in 1413; but when the emperor returned to the capital he found fault with the heir apparent and his advisers, and sent Huang Huai, Yang P'u (*q.v.*), Chin Wen 金問 (T. 公素, 1370–1448), and others to jail. Huang languished there for ten years. His collection of poems entitled *Hsing-ch'ien chi* 省愆集, 2 *ch.*, was written at this time.

As soon as Chu Kao-chih ascended the throne in September, 1424, Huang Huai was set free, reinstated in office, then promoted to the transmission office, and became a grand secretary. About this same time he asked permission to retire to mourn his mother, but he was granted only a short leave of absence. In 1425 he received the title of junior guardian, and was appointed concurrently minister of Revenue. The following year, when Emperor Chu Chan-chi led an expedition to suppress the insurrection of his uncle, Chu Kao-hsü (*q.v.*), Huang was one of a commission of nine members appointed to look after the affairs of state in Peking during his absence. In September, 1427, he finally received permission to retire and was given many honors and awards. He was then sixty years of age and his father eighty-nine. When his father died

in 1431, more imperial honors were bestowed on him. For these favors he went to Peking early in 1433 to thank the emperor in person, and was entertained handsomely; this mark of attention included a tour of the imperial garden, accompanied by members of the nobility and high officials. When he took his leave, the emperor presented him with a long poem composed for the occasion and bade him attend the celebrations on the emperor's next birthday. During Huang's visit he was given the unusual honor for a retired official of serving as one of the directors of the metropolitan examination. He went again to Peking early in 1435 to attend the emperor's funeral. He died at home at the age of eighty-two, and was given the posthumous name Wen-chien 文簡.

He left two collections of prose and poetry, *Hsing-ch'ien chi*, printed in 1433, and *Chieh-an chi* 介庵集, 12 *ch.*, printed about the time he died. The first was copied into the Imperial Library of the 18th century, but the second the editors of the Imperial Catalogue mention by title only. There seems to be another edition of the *Chieh-an chi* but in 15 *chüan*, of which an incomplete copy, lacking *chüan* 4–7, forms the basis of the 11 *chüan* edition, printed in 1931 in the *Ching-hsiang-lou* 敬鄉樓 *ts'ung-shu*, 3d series. The *Hsing-ch'ien chi* was also reprinted in the same series.

Huang Huai was also partly responsible for the editing of the *T'ai-tsung* 太宗 *shih-lu* and the *Jen-tsung* 仁宗 *shih-lu*, both completed in 1430; also the *Li-tai ming-ch'en tsou-i* 歷代名臣奏議, an enormous work in 350 *chüan* which included memorials presented to the throne from ancient times (Shang and Chou) to the end of the Yüan dynasty. The last was also copied into the Imperial Library; a facsimile reproduction appeared in Taipei in 1964.

Bibliography

1/147/9a; 5/12/14a; 64/23/7a; 61/118/1a; MSL

(1963), T'ai-tsung, ch. 11–156; *Yung-chia-hsien chih* (1882), 14/28a, 27/9a, 28/28b, 32/50b, 59b, 71a, 77b, 84b, 34/27a; *Wen-chou-fu chih* 溫州府志 (1865), 20/27; Yang Shih-ch'i, *Tung-li wen-chi*, 10/14; *Wei-an chi* 畏庵集, 29/23; Wang Chia-ping 王家屏 (1537-1604), *Wang-wen-tuan-kung wen-chi* 王文端公文集, 29/16b; Liao Tao-nan, *Tien-ko-tz'u-lin chi*, 1/21; SK (1930), 55/10b, 170/6a, 175/4a; W. Franke, *Sources*, 1.1.2, 3; Ping-ti Ho, *The Ladder of Success in Imperial China* (New York, 1962), 146.

Liu Chia-chü

HUANG Lu-tseng, *see* **HUANG Hsing-tseng**

HUANG O 黃娥 (T. 秀眉), 1498–1569, poetess, was the wife of the celebrated belle-lettrist and scholar-official Yang Shen (*q.v.*). A native of Sui-ning 遂寧, situated about three hundred *li* east of Chengtu, Szechwan, Huang O was the second daughter of Huang K'o 珂 (T. 鳴玉, 1449-1522, cs 1466, Pth. 簡肅), a noted scholar-official who had served successively in the Censorate, the ministries of Revenue, Justice, and War (1511-14), and who retired as the minister of Works in Nanking (1515-19). Well known for her knowledge of the Classics and literature, Huang O spent her childhood in various places where her father was on official business, including both Peking and Nanking, and returned to Sui-ning upon her father's retirement. It was in that year, when she was twenty-one, that she was betrothed to Yang Shen, ten years her senior and less than a year after his first wife's death. Yang, who was on leave at his native Hsin-tu, north of Chengtu, made a special trip to Sui-ning to meet his future bride and make preparations for the wedding. The marriage had obviously been arranged by the family as Huang K'o was a good friend of Yang T'ing-ho (*q.v.*), Yang Shen's father. Huang K'o must have been pleased not only because Yang Shen was an optimus, and so a man of promise, but also because the Yang family, headed by Yang T'ing-ho, was at the peak of its political influence.

Shortly after their marriage, they took up residence in Peking, where Yang Shen served as a Hanlin compiler and exegetist to Emperor Chu Hou-chao (*q.v.*). Huang O accompanied her husband when he was sent in March, 1522, to perform sacrificial ceremonies to the spirit of the Yangtze River. Later in that year they went to Chengtu, and she paid a short visit home before returning to Peking. Late in that year she learned of her father's death. Huang O and her husband did not stay long at the capital for in August, 1524, Yang Shen was sent into exile at Yung-ch'ang guard, Yunnan, for his stand in the *Ta-li i* controversy. The two traveled together as far as the Yangtze; there they parted, Yang Shen proceeding on his journey, and Huang O going to Hsin-tu to look after her husband's property. She remained there until October, 1526, when Yang Shen took a short leave to return home on the pretext of visiting his father. He then took his wife to Yunnan, where they lived in several places during the next three years. In July, 1529, Yang returned home again, this time to mourn the death of his father, but when he departed in December, after fulfilling the minimum mourning requirements, he left his wife behind to attend to family matters. This marks the beginning of an almost permanent separation between the two. Huang O was then thirty-one years of age.

In spite of the fact that he was an exile, Yang generally received courteous treatment from local officials, who offered him various assignments which enabled him to stay away from Yung-ch'ang guard and even to live in more cultured and hospitable places in Szechwan. He founded a residence in Lu-chou, about seven hundred *li* southeast of Hsin-tu, where he reportedly led an easy life, surrounded by female companions, and where he indulged in his favorite occupation of reading and writing. Meanwhile Huang O remained in Hsin-tu and continued to supply Yang with funds. In 1534, while in Szechwan, Yang took a concubine, née Chou 周, who later bore him a son. This no doubt upset Huang O, as may be seen in the poems she exchanged with her husband; in them she upbraided him for his inconstancy, whereas he gave various excuses for his conduct.

The couple were temporarily reunited in June, 1540, on the occasion of the pending seventieth (*sui*) birthday of Huang O's mother, née Nieh 聶 (b. 1472); Yang took a short leave to escort his wife to her home. Later they returned to Hsin-tu, where they remained for a short time before Yang went back to Lu-chou. Two years later, while he was in Yunnan, Yang took a second concubine, née Ts'ao 曹, who also bore him a son. The husband and wife, however, were again reunited, perhaps for the last time, on the occasion of mourning the death of her mother in June, 1543. Huang O was not with her husband when he died in August, 1559. Following his death, she went to Lu-chou where she closed Yang's residence, and took the two sons by his concubines to Hsin-tu. In the remaining years of her life, she devoted herself to tending the family estate and to the education of the two boys, and eased her solitude and despondency by composing poems.

Huang O has been hailed for her literary talent and feminine virtue. A close friend of the Yang family, Chao Chen-chi (*q.v.*), author of the tomb-inscription for Yang T'ing-ho, praised her judgment and intelligence in connection with an incident over that statesman's burial. According to Chao, some members of Yang's family at that time proposed burying him in his grade 1A costume. Huang O, however, objected, saying that since Yang had been stripped of his official title and honor before his death, he should be buried in a commoner's dress. She pointed out that if the emperor came to know about this violation of rites, he might impose punishment on the whole family. Her advice was followed. Before

long, so it is said, Emperor Chu Hou-ts'ung did send a special messenger to inspect the corpse of Yang T'ing-ho and was satisfied to learn that his former opponent was buried as a commoner.

Huang O's literary ability developed independently of her husband. She has been acclaimed as one of the most talented poetesses in the history of the dynasty. She composed poems in a variety of genres, but excelled in the san-ch'ü 散曲 style. It was through poetry that she gave vent to the sadness of separation, her husband's inconstancy, and her irritation over his unbecoming conduct. She has been praised for her genuine, spontaneous outburst of feeling, natural, direct expressions in refined language, and skillful adaptation of the colloquial speech. In a conventional analogy many critics have compared her with Li Ch'ing-chao (1084–1147), the famous Sung poetess who also led a lonely life in her later years after her husband's death. Wang Yü-ying 王玉映 (*ming:* 端淑), a scholar of the Ch'ung-chen period, placed Huang O's work at the top of the list in his *Ming-yüan shih-wei ya-chi* 名媛詩緯雅集, 38 *ch.*, an anthology of poetry by women of the dynasty.

Of Huang O's poems, many of which she wrote in response to her husband's, only a small number have survived. The earliest extant edition of her poetic works, entitled *Yang fu-jen yüeh-fu tz'u-yü* 楊夫人樂府詞餘, 5 *ch.*, has a preface dated 1608. This collection also includes a number of Yang Shen's poems. On the basis of this the contemporary scholar, Jen Na 任訥 (T. 二北), produced a revised edition entitled *Yang fu-jen ch'ü* 曲, 3 *ch.*, which was printed in 1934 together with the *T'ao-ch'ing yüeh-fu* by Yang Shen, collectively known as *Yang Sheng-an fu-fu* 楊升庵夫婦 *san-ch'ü*. This was later reprinted by Lu Ch'ien 盧前 in his *Yin-hung-i so-k'o-ch'ü* 飲虹簃所刻曲 (1936), entitled *Yang fu-jen yüeh-fu*, 3 *ch.*, including a short but useful biography of Huang O which Lu composed.

Bibliography

40/86/7a; 43/11/1b; 86/23/5a; Ch'ien Ch'ien-i (ECCP), *Lieh-ch'ao shih-chi* 列朝詩集, 閏 /4/9a; Yang Shen, *Sheng-an ch'üan-chi*, 8/2b, 9/2a, 14a; Chu Meng-chen 朱孟震 (cs 1568), *Hsü Yü-ssu shih-t'an* 續玉笥詩談 (TsSCC ed.), 57; Lu Chin, "Hsin-tu Yang-shih ch'ü-lun," 新都楊氏曲論, *Wen-shih tsa-chih* 文史雜誌, 3: 5 (March, 1944), 80; Liang Jung-jo 梁容若, "Huang Hsiu-mei ho t'a te san-ch'ü" 黃秀眉和她的散曲, *Ch'un wen-hsüeh* 純文學, 7: 1 (July, 1970), 26.

Hok-lam Chan

HUANG Pin, *see* **HUANG Hsing-tseng**

HUANG Tso 黃佐 (T. 才伯, H. 希齋, 泰泉居士, 大霞子), 1490–1566, scholar and prolific writer, was a native of Hsiang-shan 香山, Kwangtung. He came from a family of military registry. One of his ancestors served as an officer under Ho Chen (*q.v.*), and another as an officer in the Kuang-chou 廣州 right guard stationed at Hsiang-shan; the latter made his home there, but several branches of the family have kept until recently their properties in Canton city and nearby regions. His grandfather, Huang Yü 瑜 (T. 廷美, 1426–97), became a *chü-jen* in 1456 and a student in the National University in Peking. After serving as a supernumerary official in the ministry of Revenue for some time, Huang Yü qualified in 1469 for a magistracy. As it was a time of war against the Yao 傜 and Chuang 僮 tribesmen of Kwangsi (*see* Han Yung), when a native of the southern area was permitted to serve in his own province, Huang Yü received the unusual appointment of magistrate of Ch'ang-lo 長樂, Kwangtung. Praised by the common people, but disliked by the powerful, he was later forced out of office. Subsequently, for a number of years, he kept school in Canton. He is chiefly remembered for his study notes on the history and institutions of the Ming dynasty, especially of Canton, entitled *Shuang-huai sui-ch'ao* 雙槐歲鈔,

10 *ch.*, printed in 1543 and again in 1684. Though banned in the 18th century for its comments on the Jurchen, it was reprinted in 1831 in the *Ling-nan i-shu* (*see* Wu Ch'ung-yüeh, ECCP). His interest in history apparently had some influence on his grandson.

An apt student of the Classics, Huang Tso came out on top in the provincial examination of 1510. Ten years later he achieved the *chin-shih*. Because of Emperor Chu Hou-chao's (*q.v.*) southern expedition in 1520 and his death in Peking early in the following year, the palace examination did not take place until June 30, 1521, after the succeeding emperor, Chu Hou-ts'ung (*q.v.*) had been on the throne little more than a month. The burning issue of the day was the controversy over the emperor's wish to grant imperial titles to his own parents by which he meant the continuance of his natural family relationship. The majority of the courtiers insisted that the emperor, as successor to the throne, should automatically become the adopted son of the deceased emperor, Chu Yu-t'ang (*q.v.*), and so should designate his own father "the prince uncle." At the palace examination the subject of the essay was on this question, and Huang Tso gave his honest opinion, which happened to concur with that of the majority. From then on, as Huang himself asserted in a letter to Yang I-ch'ing (*q.v.*), he was always regarded as an outsider by the faction that had agreed with the emperor during this controversy called the *Ta-li i*. In the official records about it, however, Huang's name is not mentioned at all.

In October, 1523, for the installation of some princes and princesses residing in Hukuang, he was sent as an associate of the imperial messenger, Duke Chang Lun 張崙 (d. 1535), to Ch'en-chou 辰州, Wu-kang 武岡, and other places. While Huang was away the *Ta-li i* controversy came to a head (1524), which may account for his escaping a possibly disastrous involvement. He continued to feel, however the hostility of the emperor's faction under Chang Fu-ching (*q.v.*) and so requested leave to look after his mother. This was finally granted late in 1526, but on account of the freezing of the Grand Canal he was detained for months near T'ung-chou 通州. Here he enjoyed the company of another Hanlin official, the artist Wen Cheng-ming (*q.v.*); they were finally able to leave the following spring. Huang continued his journey by a detour through Chekiang in order to pay a visit to Wang Shou-jen (*q.v.*), then living in retirement and giving lectures at Shaohsing. With Wang he debated spiritedly the conception of the integration of innate knowledge and action. He maintained that a Confucianist should pursue the acquisition of knowledge in order to control himself intelligently according to the moral code. Thus, in the world of thought dominated by Wang's school, Huang was regarded as an independent.

After he arrived home in 1527 he pleaded illness and was given a sick leave. About this time he served as chief editor of the gazetteer of his home prefecture, the *Kuang-chou-fu chih* 府志, which he completed in 70 *chüan*. It happens that he had long been interested in the significant figures of his native area, having written about them in a work entitled *Kuang-chou jen-wu chuan* 人物傳, 24 *ch.* (printed in 1831 in the *Ling-nan i-shu*). The work was evidently completed in 1526 just in time to be used as a draft of the biographical section in the gazetteer. Hence, although his edition of the *fu-chih* is lost, most of its biographical section is still available.

Meanwhile in Peking many Hanlin scholars, for their hostility to Chang Fuching in 1521, were now assigned to provincial posts. When Huang returned to the capital in 1529, he was appointed assistant surveillance commissioner in charge of education in Kiangsi but was soon transferred to Kwangsi where he remained for about a year. At the request of Lin Fu (*see* Lin Chao-en), then su-

preme commander of Kwangtung and governor of Kwangsi, Huang served concurrently as chief compiler of the first gazetteer of the latter province, the *Kwangsi t'ung-chih* 通志, 60 *ch.* (printed in 1532), a copy of which is available in the Naikaku Bunko, Tokyo. He also drafted for Lin Fu the memorial of 1529 requesting the reopening of Kwangtung to foreign trade, which had been forbidden since 1521, and which had resulted in the move by foreign traders to Fukien and Chekiang ports to the economic disadvantage of Kwangtung. Lin's request was granted.

Late in 1530, upon hearing of his mother's illness, Huang requested leave and without waiting for the imperial approval took off directly for home. In April, 1531, the emperor ordered Lin Fu to arrest Huang on the charge of showing disrespect to the throne. On Lin's recommendation for leniency Huang was cashiered without further punishment. In retirement Huang restored his grandfather's schoolhouse at Canton and taught there for eight years. It is said that students came to him from near and far. He also acted as a consultant to provincial and local authorities, and gave help in 1532 in the defense of Canton during the threat of attack by the pirate Hsü Chekuei 許折桂. In 1537 he advised against the military expedition to Annam (*see* Mac Dang-dung and Mao Po-wen). In 1539, after Hsia Yen (*q.v.*) became chief grand secretary, Huang was recalled as Hanlin compiler and a remonstrator in the office of instruction to the heir apparent. Early in 1541 he received promotion as reader-in-waiting and acting head of the Hanlin Academy in Nanking. About this time he compiled a book about that institution, entitled *Han-lin chi* 翰林記, 20 *ch.* (reprinted in 1831 in *Ling-nan i-shu*). Liao Tao-nan (*q.v.*) partly incorporated it later in his *Huang Ming tien-ko tz'u lin chi* 皇明殿閣詞林記, 22 *ch.* listing Huang as co-author. In September, 1543, Huang became chancellor of the National University in Nanking. While there he wrote an account of the university entitled *Nan-yung chih* 南雍志, *24 ch.*, printed in 1544. In 1626 there appeared a supplement, *Nan-yung hsü-chih* 續志, *24 ch.* edited by Huang Ju-ping 黄儒炳 (T. 士明, cs 1604). The Nanking Kuo-hsüeh library in 1931 published a lithographic reproduction of the *Nan-yung chih* from a copy of an early seventeenth-century edition; this has been referred to as an important new source on the history of education in China. Of interest as well is its bibliographical section compiled by Mei Tsu (*q.v.*), as also its section on music embodying Huang's own theories.

In 1544 Huang retired on account of his mother's death. Two years later, in November, 1546, on the recommendation of Hsia Yen, then chief grand secretary, Huang was recalled and appointed a junior supervisor in the office of instruction to the heir apparent. He was now qualified for the more powerful post of a vice minister of Personnel and probably made some political moves to enhance his chances when the opportunity arose. It happened that he had several competitors who made similar moves. At last in August, 1547, the office of the junior vice minister of Personnel became open through the death of the incumbent, Wang Tao 王道 (T. 純甫, H. 順渠, 1487-1547, cs 1511, Pth. 文定). To fill the vacancy the ministry of Personnel submitted the names of two candidates, Huang Tso and Ts'ui T'ung 崔桐 (T. 來鳳, H. 東洲, cs 1517), from which the emperor was to make a choice. Several supervising secretaries and censors presented strongly worded memorials against these two men on the flimsy ground that they and two others before them had engaged in factional politics and had openly fought against each other, thus showing a covetousness detrimental to an office requiring complete impartiality. The emperor took these charges into account and in September all four accused were ordered to leave government service. There is a story

that Huang was forced out of office in 1547 because he was opposed to Hsia Yen on the Ho-t'ao 河套 project (*see* Tseng Hsien). Be that as it may, Huang's official career came to an end, and he resumed his teaching at Canton.

In scholarship he was closer to the Ch'eng-Chu school of neo-Confucianism than the Lu-Wang school. In teaching he adopted as his principle the statement in the Analects, referred to by the characters po 博 and yüeh 約 signifying that one should study widely and restrain oneself by the rules of propriety. His disciples collected his philosophical sayings in a work entitled *Yung-yen* 庸言, *12 ch.* He wrote a treatise on proper conduct in family and communal life, the *T'ai-ch'üan hsiang-li* 泰泉鄉 禮, *7 ch*, which has been reprinted several times. He also left two works of instructions for teachers, *Hsiao hsüeh ku-hsün* 小學古訓 for the men and *Mu-hsün* 姆訓 for the women. Although respected as a Confucian he did not seem to be a straight-laced one. He left a poem with two liens about recollections of his youthful days when he held a beauty in his arm and sang the ballad Lien-hua-lao 蓮花落. It is said that his students were recognizable for their politeness in manners and care in attire. A few became noted scholars or writers. Five of them, Ou Ta-jen 歐大任 (T. 楨伯, H. 崙山, 1516-95), Li Min-piao 黎民表 (T. 維敬, H. 瑤石, cj 1534), Liang Yu-yü 梁有譽 (T. 公實, H. 蘭汀, cs 1550), Li Shih-hsing 李時行 (T. 少偕, H. 青霞, cs 1541), and Wu Tan 吳旦 (T. 而待, H. 蘭皋, cj 1537), came to be known as Nan-yüan hou wu-tzu 南園後五子 (the Later Five Poets of the Southern Garden), indicating a revival of excellence in literature since the days of the earlier five poets of the 14th century (*see* Sun Fen). This revival, as it is attributed to Huang's influence, seems to reveal the success of his stress on scholarship and self-control, not on meditation. It is interesting to note that another Cantonese of the same period, the historian Ch'en Chien (*q.v.*), held similar views.

During his later years Huang edited several local histories of his native area. About 1549 he edited the *Hsiang-shan-hsien chih*, 8 *ch.* In 1557 he supervised the compilation of the *Kwangtung t'ung-chih*, 70 *ch.*, published a year later and still extant. There is also an account of the scenic mountain of northeastern Kwangtung, *Lo-fu-shan chih* 羅浮山志, 12 *ch.*, which he edited in 1550 in collaboration with the above mentioned Li Min-piao. Among the rest of his prolific output are his earlier compilations, such as the one on the Book of Odes, *Shih-ching t'ung chieh* 詩經通解, 25 *ch.*, *ca.* 1517, and an account of the Chien-wen reign (*see* Chu Yün-wen), entitled *Ko-ch'u i shih* 革除遺事, 6 *ch.* The latter, compiled in 1521, was one of the earliest to recount the facts about which for a hundred years few men had dared to write for fear of being accused of contradicting the official version. It is said that Huang's work is an abridgment of his original manuscript in 16 *chüan*. He reportedly left also two works on music, *Yüeh-tien* 樂典, 36 *ch.*, and *Yüeh-chi chieh* 記解, 11 *ch.*

On his poetry the critics, such as Ch'ien Ch'ien-i, Ch'en Tzu-lung, and Chu I-tsun (for all three *see* ECCP), seem to agree that he ranked high among the Cantonese. Wang Shih-chen(*q.v.*), however, considered him mediocre, declaring that he only occasionally came up with a good line or two. The *Ssu-k'u* editors rated Huang's collection of poems, *T'ai-ch'üan chi* 集, 10 *ch.*, printed in 1542, as sufficiently important to include in the Imperial Library. (This has recently been reproduced in the *Ssu-k'u ch'üan-shu chen-pen* 珍本, ser. 2.) A larger collection of Huang's works, in 60 *chüan*, but with the same title, was printed after he died and presumably contains his later writings too. These appear as well in several anthologies. As Ch'ien Ch'ien-i says, Huang and Ch'iu Chün (*q.v.*) raised the literary standard of Cantonese writers to the highest level in the country.

Huang is to be chiefly remembered as a historian, however. In his preface to his grandfather's *Shuang-huai sui-ch'ao* he stated that at an old building of the Nanking branch of the Hanlin Academy, which he headed in 1541, he discovered a case full of documents, some reaching back to the beginning of the Ming dynasty. He said that even those dated in 吳 first year (1367) looked and felt like newly written ones. This probably means that these documents had never been touched until he used them in editing his grandfather's work and for the writing of his own history of the Hanlin Academy.

Huang accumulated a large collection of books in his library, Pao-shu-lou 寶書樓, in his home in Canton. The buildings became a shrine to him, known as Huang Wen-yü kung t'zu 黃文裕公祠, Wen-yü being the name conferred on him in 1571 when he was posthumously raised to vice minister of Rites. The buildings were destroyed by fire during the Japanese attack in 1939. Only a stone arch remains on the site, which in 1953 became a part of the Ch'ing-nien wen-hua kung 青年文化宮 (Cultural palace for youth).

Bibliography

1/287/4b; 3/268/3b; 83/51/1a; MSL (1965), Shih-tsung, 6022, 6030; KC (1958), 3237, 3440, 3542, 3570, 3694, 4167; *Chang-chou-fu chih* (1877), 10/11b; *Hsiang-shan-hsien chih* (1879), 13/13b, 17a, 18b, 21/17b, 23a; *Kwangtung t'ung-chih* (1934), 1162, 3974, 4768; *Kwangsi t'ung-chih*(1965 reprod. of 1602 ed.), 7/49b, 25/37a; SK (1930), 22/5b, 39/2b, 53/5b, 61/7b, 73/5a, 79/3b, 80/1b, 96/3b, 143/4b, 172/2b, 192/4b; Sun Tien-ch'i (1957), 240; Ch'ien Ch'ien-i, *Lieh-ch'ao shih-chi*, 丁 2/4b; Wen Cheng-ming, *P'u-t'ien chi*, 11/5b; *T'ai-ch'üan chi* (NLP microfilm roll no. 944); *T'ai-ch'üan chi wen-hsüan* 文選(in Lo Hsüeh-p'eng 羅學鵬, ed., *Kwangtung wen-hsien* 文獻, 1863, 3d ser.), 3/13a, 25b; *Nan-yung hsü-chih*(NLP microfilm roll no. 436), 19/19a; Wang Shih-chen, *Yen-chou shan-jen ssu-pu-kao*, 150/5b; Wen Ch'ien-shan 溫謙山, comp., *Yüeh-tung shih-hai* 粵東詩海, *chüan* 20, 22, 24, 25, 27, 31; L. of C. *Catalogue of Rare Books,* 1075; Hsü Shao-ch'i 徐紹棨, *Kwangtung ts'ang-shu chi-shih shih* 藏書紀事詩 (1963), 3; Paul Pelliot, TP, 38 (1947), 156.

Kwan-wai So and Chaoying Fang

HUANG Wan 黃綰 (T. 宗賢, H. 久庵, 石龍, 公綬), 1480-1554, philosopher, official, and scholar, was a native of Huang-yen 黃巖, Chekiang, where his family settled in the 10th century. His great-grandfather, Huang Yen-chün 彥俊 (cs1436), was a secretary in the ministry of War; his grandfather, Huang K'ung-chao 孔昭 (T. 世顯, H. 定軒, January 1429-July 23, 1491, cs 1460, Pth. 文毅), reached the post of a vice minister of works in Nanking (1487-91); and his father, Huang Fu 俌 (T. 汝修, H. 艾齋, 1450-1506, cs 1481), was director of the bureau of appointments in the ministry of Personnel (*ca.* 1495-*ca.* 1505). Huang Wan himself had no degree except that of a *yin-sheng* or honorary student of the National University, awarded through the meritorious service of his grandfather. In his youth an early love for scholarship, coupled with a disdain for the futility of youthful exertions, drove him for days to find some meaning in his books. The neo-Confucian notion of self-cultivation impressed him so much that he often punished his own body to achieve spiritual enlightenment. He decided to lead the life of a sage, thus breaking the pattern of a family of scholar-officials. The notable formative influence on Huang was the tutelage of Hsieh To 謝鐸 (T. 鳴治, H. 方石, 1435-1510, cs 1464, Pth. 文肅), who, together with his grandfather, Huang K'ung-chao, edited the collected works of their fellow-townsman, Fang Hsiao-ju (*q.v.*), the scholar-official who preferred death to serving in the court of Chu Ti (*q.v.*). His diligence and natural gifts earned him the attention of the Chekiang inspecting censor Ch'en Ch'üan 陳銓 (T. 秉衡, cs 1481), who asked him to take the provincial examination. Huang declined and went to the mountains to study and meditate.

In December, 1510, after he had become an assistant manager in a central military commission in Peking, Huang went to see Wang Shou-jen (*q.v.*), who had just been appointed a secretary in the ministry of Justice. The two, now joined by Chan Jo-shui (*q.v.*), became friends and formed a pact to study for sagehood. They even planned for their retirement together in the T'ien-t'ai mountains near Huang's native place. Huang left for home in 1512 but the other two were unable to join him. Ten years later, when Wang, newly awarded an earldom, was at his residence in Yü-yao, Huang visited him and heard him discourse on intuitive and innate knowledge. Huang acknowledged that he was deeply impressed and assumed the status of a disciple of Wang instead of a friend. The latter regarded him with esteem, little dreaming that Huang was later to revise his teachings.

By 1523 Huang Wan had been at home for eleven years. Now he returned to officialdom on the recommendation of a censor and was appointed registrar in the Nanking Censorate. There he became involved in the *Ta-li i* controversy (*see* Chu Hou-ts'ung) over the emperor's wish to honor his own parents. Yang T'ing-ho (*q.v.*), representing the Sung school, wanted the emperor to change his parents' titles to imperial uncle and aunt to comply with the normal requirements of an adopted son. Some members of the Wang Yang-ming school, represented by Huang Wan, Huo T'ao, Hsi Shu (*qq.v.*), Huang Tsung-ming 宗明 (T. 誠甫, cs 1514), and Fang Hsien-fu (*see* Kuei O), all of whom were either the friends or disciples of Wang, sided with the emperor, saying that ethical ties between father and son came first. They followed the leadership of Chang Fu-ching (*q.v.*) and Kuei O, and through them Huang Wan gained imperial favor; early in 1526 he became a vice bureau director in the ministry of Works in Nanking.

In 1527 Huang was summoned to Peking as vice minister of the Court of Imperial Entertainments to help in compiling the *Ming-lun ta-tien* (*see* Yang I-ch'ing). When the work was completed in 1528, Huang was promoted to be grand supervisor of instruction, the only *yin-sheng* in the Ming period to rise to such an office reserved for the members of the Hanlin Academy. While serving in the capital, Huang had numerous opportunities to memorialize the emperor in defense of Wang Shou-jen, who was now being attacked by Yang I-ch'ing and Kuei O. After Wang's death in 1529, Huang helped to settle the disputes over Wang's estate and betrothed his daughter to Wang's son, Wang Cheng-i (see Wang Shou-jen). Friends such as Ch'ien Te-hung, Wang Chi, and Wang Ken (qq.v.) took part in the betrothal ceremonies. By this time Huang had become vice minister of Rites in Nanking. In August, 1533, he was recalled to Peking to serve as left vice minister of Rites. There he came into close contact with Hsia Yen (q.v.), then a rising figure at court. Chang Fu-ching regarded this development with jealousy. Late in that year, when the soldiers at Tatung mutinied for the second time (the first mutiny taking place in 1524, see Liang Chen and Han Pang-ch'i), the supreme commander, Liu Yüan-ch'ing 劉源清 (T. 汝澄, H. 東圃, cs 1514), and the general, Hsi 郤 (or Chüeh 郤) Yung 永 (T. 世延, H. 龍泉, 1471–1548, 隱懷 Pth.), took harsh measures against not only the culprits but also the people of that area. This caused the mutineers to hold out and even to communicate with the Mongols for joint action. Huang Wan proposed a peaceful and more humane policy which further antagonized Chang Fu-ching. In March, 1534, the soldiers assassinated their leaders and surrendered to the besieging government troops. A month later Huang Wan was sent there ostensibly to distribute relief but actually to single out each culprit for punishment. He had the case settled within a few months. It was his conviction, however, that Liu and Hsi were responsible for the rebellion; as a consequence, they were punished by imperial order, much to the chagrin of Chang Fu-ching who had sponsored them.

In 1535 Huang returned home due to his mother's death. Four years later he was promoted to honorary minister of Rites and appointed chief envoy to Annam to convey some imperial messages but primarily to see what he could do to avert war which the general, Mac Dang-dung (q.v.), was threatening. Huang, sensing the danger of such a mission, delayed commencing the journey, then sent messages and memorials telling of difficulties and requesting honorable titles for his parents. The emperor finally became impatient and dismissed him. Much of Huang's retirement was spent in a mountain retreat near his home, where he studied and taught. In 1547 his son, Huang Ch'eng-te 承德, planned the printing of his lectures and daily records, Ming-tao pien 明道編, which has a colophon dated 1550. Huang Wan died shortly afterwards.

Huang is usually considered a thinker of the Wang Yang-ming school, although in his final years he criticized the teachings of the master, veering away from the inner and meditative aspects of Wang's thought, and placing more emphasis on the practical and practicable. His criticism of Wang was never frontal; instead he referred to his former master as "a recent friend" 近日朋友, blaming him nevertheless for adulterating the thought of Lu Hsiang-shan (1139–93), with whom Wang shared the idea of the identity of mind and principle but not the idea of the unity of knowledge and action. Huang Wan seemed particularly displeased with the anti-intellectualism and emptiness to which Wang's teachings had given rise. He also was displeased with the li-hsüeh 理學 of the Sung thinkers, saying that they were merely inspired by Ch'an Buddhism. The discovery of an incomplete copy of the Ming-tao pien in the National Peiping Library by Jung Chao-tsu (see Feng Meng-lung) in the 1930s brought this to light. What is extant is just the diary entitled Chiu-an jih-lu 久庵日錄, 6 ch., now preserved in the National Central Library in Taipei. It was reprinted in China in 1959 and is available on microfilm. It is probably the only copy extant and even the seventeenth-century historian of Ming thought, Huang Tsung-hsi (ECCP), does not seem to have had access to it. Huang Wan's collection of writings, *Shih-lung chi* 石龍集, 28 *ch.*, was printed about 1539. The copy in the National Central Library is available on microfilm. Other works by him do not seem to be extant, but the *Huang Ming ching-shih wen-pien* (comp. by Ch'en Tzu-lung, ECCP) contains four of his memorials.

The editors of the *Ming-shih* wrote disparagingly of Huang Wan calling him ch'ing chiao 傾狡 (unsteadfast and cunning), probably referring to his turning against his one-time benefactors, Chang Fu-ching and Yang I-ch'ing. Perhaps the editors also had in mind Huang's latter-day belittling of the teachings of Wang Shou-jen. It is interesting to note that although in the biography of his grandfather, Huang K'ung-chao, they call him clean and incorruptible, the account in the *Ming shih-lu* reporting his death in 1491 gives an entirely different impression, its author evidently having a personal grudge. In the *shih-lu* sketch he is sarcastically attacked on two main points. First he was ridiculed for declaring in his youth that he planned to pursue sagehood for life, but in 1456 he quietly changed his mind and took the *chü-jen* examination. Apparently Huang, in editing the works of Fang Hsiao-ju, followed the example of Wu Yü-pi (*q.v.*), in disdaining service in a court established by a rebel, but unlike Wu failed to persist. The second point against him was his long term of office in the bureau of appointments in the ministry of Personnel (1469-82); there he is said to have started poor but ended a wealthy landlord. Even his son, Huang Fu, was described as a well-to-do man obtaining the same office through bribery, but finally he had to resign due to a scandal. Huang Wan in his accounts of his two forebears gave them high praise, which was accepted by the editors of the *Ming-shih*. Huang admitted the rise in family fortune but explained that it was his mother, Pao-shih 鮑氏 (1451-1535),

who was responsible. When she married his father, she found the Huang household in straitened circumstances and, by selling her own jewelry, raised fifty taels of silver to purchase fifty *mou* of land. She managed the property so well that in twenty years the family acquired over a thousand *mou* (160 acres). It seems hard to believe that a woman of that day could expand landholdings twenty fold on her own initiative. What is remarkable is that the period of her activities corresponds closely with the rise in influence of Huang K'ung-chao, *i.e.*, *ca.* 1470 to 1490. So even if he were completely incorruptible as director of the bureau of appointments, the fact of his being head of that office would have unavoidably influenced local officials in family lawsuits or other transactions. On the other hand, the holder of that office had to reject and so antagonize someone in every appointment made. Whoever wrote the account about him in the *Ming shih-lu* must have been a bitterly disappointed man.

Bibliography

1/179/7a, 197/19b; 3/183/17a, 190/17b; 5/34/11a; 83/13/15b; MSL (1964), Hsiao-tsung, 1030; *Shih-lung chi*, 23/6b, 26/1a; Hou Wai-lu 侯外廬, preface to new ed. of *Ming-tao pien* (Shanghai, 1959), 1; Jung Chao-tsu, *Ming-tai ssu-hsiang shih* 明代思想史 (Taipei, 1969), 159; *id.*, "Wang Shou-jen te men-jen 門人 Huang Wan," YCHP, 27 (1940), 53; Wang Fen 王棻 (1828-99), *T'ai-hsüeh t'ung* 台學統, *ch.* 45; *Huang-yen-hsien chih* (1877), 18/20a.

Chaoying Fang and D. W.Y. Kwok

HUANG Wei, *see* **HUANG Hsing-tseng**

HUNG-JEN 弘仁 (T. 无智, H. 漸江), 1610-January 19, 1664, a native of She-hsien 歙縣 (Anhwei), was a Ch'an Buddhist monk and painter, whose secular name was Chiang T'ao 江韜 (T. 六奇). One source, the *She-hsien chih* of 1690, gives his secular name as Chiang Fang 舫 (T. 鷗盟). He may in fact have used both names; a painting dated 1639 is signed "Chiang T'ao," but he is later referred to as "Chiang Ou-meng" 鷗盟 by a friend in a dedication to a poem. Best known as a painter of landscapes, he came to be regarded as the foremost artist of the Anhwei school of the early years of the Ch'ing dynasty and one of the "Four Masters of Hsin-an" 新安四家, the others being Sun I 孫逸 (T. 疎林, 無逸), Wang Chih-jui 汪之瑞 (T. 無 (无) 瑞), and Cha Shih-piao (*q.v.*).

Chiang T'ao's family had been prominent for some years in the She-hsien region and fairly affluent, but the death of his father while he was still a boy left him and his mother impoverished. The boy did manual labor to support both of them, drawing water and selling firewood, and by so doing achieved a reputation for filial piety; on one occasion he carried rice for his mother over thirty *li*. Arriving too late for her customary mealtime, in his chagrin he wanted to hurl himself into the river and perish. Eventually, after diligent study, he was able to make some income by writing—just what kind is unspecified; reportedly, too, he graduated as a *chu-sheng* at the end of the Ming. When his mother died, he went into deep mourning and abandoned all thought of marrying or seeking an official career.

Chiang is said to have studied the Classics with one Wang Wu-yai 汪無涯 (or, in another account, Chang 張 Wu-yai), unknown, but possibly to be identified with, or related to, Wang Mu-jih 汪沐日 (1605–79), who is known to have traveled to Fukien in 1645 as Chiang T'ao did, and who was ordained with the name Hung-chi 弘濟 as a Ch'an Buddhist monk by the same Ku-hang (*see below*). Chiang and his teacher made their way south, presumably to escape from the turmoil and danger of the Manchu invasion, which had engulfed their home by the autumn of that year. The two may also have

been involved in some loyalist political movement, as several of Chiang's friends evidently were. Perhaps it was at this time that Chiang changed his name to Chiang Fang; other loyalists fleeing to Fukien and elsewhere are known to have assumed new names.

In Fukien, Chiang T'ao (or Fang) visited Mt. Wu-i 武夷山 in Ch'ung-an-hsien 崇安縣, and, at a temple on the Man-t'ing 幔亭 Peak there, met the Ch'an Buddhist master Ku-hang Tao-chou 古航道舟 (1585–1655), who in 1646 ordained him. Here he took the name Hung-jen and the *hao* Chien-chiang 漸江 after a river near his birthplace. He remained in Fukien for several years, returning to his home in She-hsien around 1651 or 1652. Except for a number of excursions, he lived in monasteries of the She-hsien and Huang-shan 黃山 region, such as the Yün-ku ssu 雲谷寺 and Tz'u-kuang 慈光 ssu, during his remaining years. His trips included a visit to Nanking in 1658, to Yangchow in 1661, and one to Lu-shan 盧山 in 1663, another mountain beloved of Chinese landscapists; he had attempted the last trip in the previous year but had been turned back by snow. He returned that summer to the Wu-ming 五明 monastery, located below the P'i-yün Peak 披雲峯 in the southwest of She-hsien. He died there after taking off his broken straw sandals and had to indicate an end to his wanderings, and crying out, "My Buddha, the Tathagata Kuan-shih-yin." He was buried at the monastery and his friends planted several dozen plum trees around his grave as he had requested; from this he acquired the posthumous name Mei-hua Ku-na 梅花古衲 (The old monk of the plum blossoms).

Hung-jen was devoted to painting from his early years, and throughout his life missed no opportunity to see and study works by great masters of the past. He himself owned a few paintings, including a scroll ascribed to the T'ang dynasty master, Wu Tao-tzu (d. 792); and landscapes supposed to be by two of the Four Great Masters of the Yüan dynasty,

Ni Tsan and Wang Meng (*qq. v.*); these were among the "Ten Gifts" which a group of his friends presented to him during or after his trip to Lu-shan in 1663. One contemporary states that Hung-jen painted for around thirty years, which would mean that he began about 1634; the earliest work now extant is dated 1639. Early accounts say that he imitated Sung dynasty painters in his youth, but after entering the Buddhist order turned to the Yüan masters as models, especially Huang Kung-wang (1269–1354) and Ni Tsan. He likened himself in a poem to the latter, who had given away all his possessions and left his family seat to escape from political disorders under the Mongol regime. He is credited by Chang Keng (ECCP, p. 99), writing in 1739, with having established the popularity of the Ni Tsan style in the Anhwei school of painting. Hung-jen also, however, affirmed the necessity of observing and studying the landscape, saying that just as Tung Yüan (d. 962), Huang Kung-wang, and Kuo Hsi (fl. 1020–90) had depicted the mountains and rivers of their native regions, so must he. For him the local scenery, to which many of his paintings are devoted, was of course the scenery of Huang-shan.

Concerning his teacher in painting accounts vary. Chou Liang-kung (ECCP), the noted Nanking collector and connoisseur, credits a certain Sun Wu-hsiu 孫無修, a Nanking artist, none of whose work is now known, with being the source of "every stream, every stone" in Hung-jen's paintings. Some have interpreted this statement to mean that Sun was Hung-jen's teacher. Another source names his older contemporary, Hsiao Yün-ts'ung (ECCP, p. 87); an inscription by Hsiao on a Hung-jen album, in which he writes of himself as "the old painting teacher," along with anticipations of some features of Hung-jen's style in Hsiao's works, bears this out. In any case, the sparse, angular style and bizarre scenery of his early work was common property among a number of artists of the time. It is rather in his later works, when basically the same mode of painting in dry-brush with a minimum of wash or surface texturing is used to construct landscapes of a monumental character, that Hung-jen achieves greatness. He worked typically in ink only, but occasionally used light washes of color. Besides landscapes, he painted pictures of branches of flowering plum, and pines and rocks. His major paintings all date from a period of five or six years, from 1657 until his death. Hung-jen had several direct followers, including his nephew Chiang Chu 注 and a wide circle of friends who were also painters.

Hung-jen was an accomplished calligrapher in various styles; on one occasion he inscribed, at the invitation of the monks of the Yün-ku monastery, a memorial text for the tomb of the Ch'an master Yü-an 寓安大師. In his late years he followed the style of Ni Tsan in calligraphy as well as in painting. His poetry has been collected under the title *Hua-ch'i* 畫偈, comprising some seventy-five poems, to which sixty or so more may be added from inscriptions on paintings and other sources. For important dated and other paintings by Hung-jen, see the landscape section of a collective handscroll done with four other Anhwei artists, signed "Chiang T'ao" and dated 1639, Shanghai Museum, unpublished; leaf in the album *Hsin-an ming-hua chi-chin ts'e* 新安名畫集錦冊 (publ. by Shen-chou Kuo-kuang she, 1920), so Hung-jen's leaf may be dated around that time; other leaves dated 1648 and 1649; section of collective handscroll painted with seven other artists, dated 1651 (same publisher, 1935); album of eight landscapes, dated 1657, painted in Nanking (*Shina Nanga Taisei*, XVI, pls. 124–131); landscape in the style of Lu Kuang (*q.v.*), dated 1658 (James Cahill, *Fantastics and Eccentrics in Chinese Painting*); landscape handscroll, dated 1661 (Sumitomo Collection, Sumiyoshi, Japan); "The Coming of Autumn," undated, (Honolulu Academy of Arts, *see* Gustav

Ecke, *Chinese Paintings in Hawaii*, pl. XLVI); landscape of Mt. Wu-i, undated (*Tō Sō Gen Min Meiga Taikan*, Tokyo, 1929, pl. 418). For a list of extant works *see* Osvald Sirén.

Bibliography

Wang T'ai-cheng 王泰徵 (1600–75), *Chien-chiang ho-shang chuan* 和尚傳; Ch'eng Shou 程守, *Ku ta-shih Chien-kung pei* 故大師漸公碑 (publ. after 1664); Hsü Ch'u 許楚, *Huang-shan Chien-chiang shih wai-chuan* 外傳(all in *Anhwei ts'ung-shu*, ed. 1932); *Huang-shan chih ting-pen* 定本 (1682), 2/97a; Yin Shu 殷曙, *Chien-chiang shih chuan* (see *Huang-shan chih*, 1666); *Huang-shan chih* (1673); *She-hsien chih* (1690), 10/5a rev. ed. (1937), 10/10a 16/63a; *Hui-chou-fu chih* 徽州府志 (1698); Chou Liang-kung (ECCP), *Tu-hua lu* in *Tu hua chai* 讀畫齋 *ts'ung-shu*, 2/9b; Chang Keng (ECCP, p. 99), *Kuo-ch'ao hua-cheng lu*(1887), 3/17b; Huang Pin-hung 黃賓虹 (1864–1955), comp., "Chien-chiang ta-shih shih-chi i-wen"事蹟佚聞, *Chung-ho yüeh-k'an* 中和月刊 (1940); Cheng Hsi-chen 鄭錫珍, *Hung-jen k'un-ts'an* 髡殘, Shanghai, 1963; Wang Shih-ch'ing 汪世清 and Wang Ts'ung 汪聰, *Chien-chiang tzu-liao chi* 資料集, Ho-fei 1964 (this contains the best compilation of biographical matter, literary works, lists of paintings, etc.); Osvald Sirén, *Chinese Painting* (New York, 1956-58), V: 116, 147, VI: pls. 351, 352; E. J. Laing, *Chinese Paintings in Chinese Publications, 1956–1968* (Ann Arbor, 1969), 248; Hsü Pang-ta, *Li-tai... shu-hua... nien-piao* (1963), 143, 345, 359, 364.

James Cahill

[Editors' note: Mr. Cahill wishes to acknowledge the aid of M. Jonathan Chaves in preparing this biography.]

HUNG Ying-ming 洪應明 (T. 自誠, H. 還初道人), who flourished in the Wan-li era, was an author of religious works. Nothing is known about his life and career, except that he was a contemporary of Yü K'ung-chien (*see* Ku Hsien-ch'eng). According to the editors of the *Ssu-k'u* Catalogue, Hung's *Hsien-fo ch'i-tsung* 仙佛奇蹤 (Wonderful deeds of immortals and Buddhas),

4 *ch.*, was completed in 1602. This book, preserved in the Palace collection (Taipei), deals with: 1) the *faits et gestes* of sixty-three Taoists, from Lao-tzu to Chang San-feng (*see* Chang Chung); 2) comments on immortality; 3) nineteen patriarchs of Indian Buddhism, from Śākyamuni to Prajñātāra (fl. A. D. 457), and forty-two patriarchs of Ch'an Buddhism, from Bodhidharma (fl. 502) to Ch'uan-tzu 船子 (9th c.), and 4) the mysteries of eternity. The immortals and Buddhist patriarchs are all portrayed.

Sheng-yin 聖印, a Buddhist priest in Taiwan, asserts that Hung Ying-ming was also the author of the following (lost) works: *Lien-chin* 聯瑾 (A string of gems), *Ch'iao-t'an* 樵談 (Simple sayings of the woodcutter), *Pi-ch'ou* 筆疇 (Fields reclaimed by the brush), and *Ch'uan-chia pao* 傳家寶 (Treasures transmitted in our family). He is, however, best known for his *Ts'ai-ken t'an* 菜根譚 (Vegetable root discourses), for which Yü K'ung-chien wrote a preface. A free translation of the title would be "Discourses on a simple life." It is divided into two parts of 222 and 134 paragraphs respectively. Each paragraph is actually an aphorism or maxim written in the so-called parallel style. For example, "People understand how to read a book with characters, but they do not understand how to read a book without characters. They know how to play a dulcimer with strings, but they do not know how to play a dulcimer without strings. They use the material, but do not avail themselves of the spirit. How can they grasp the essence of a dulcimer or a book?"

The author was an eclectic, drawing from Confucianism, Taoism, and the Ch'an sect. Generally speaking we may say that the first part of his work counsels integrity in office, whereas the second part describes the joys of living in retirement. Its general spirit is that of the "Golden Mean." One is tempted to compare the book with the *Meditations* of Marcus Aurelius or the *Maximes* of La Rochefoucauld.

The original edition of the *Ts'ai-ken t'an* seems to be no longer available in China. According to Ogaeri Yoshio 魚返善雄, the copy preserved in the Sonkeikaku Bunko is a Ming print. Its cover and Yü's preface have been lost. Another copy, preserved in the Naikaku Bunko, the editing of which was revised by Wang Ch'ien-ch'u 汪乾初, might, according to Imai Usaburō 今井宇三郎, be dated 1591. In China there exist two other editions: one printed in 1748 has a preface by San-shan Ping-fu T'ung-li 三山病夫通理, and a second has a colophon by Huan-ch'u-t'ang chu-jen 還初堂主人, dated 1794. The latter is a new arrangement with supplements taken from the *Hsü* 續 *Ts'ai-ken t'an* by Shih Ch'ing-chai 石清齋, 1736. The best modern Chinese edition, based on the Wan-li text, is the one by Sheng-yin, printed for the first time in 1958.

The *Ts'ai-ken t'an* was probably introduced into Japan around the middle of the Tokugawa period (1603–1867). Hayashi Yu 林楡 (1781–1836) revised the text, wrote a preface to it, and had it engraved on printing blocks made by his disciples. This first Japanese edition appeared in 1822. Under its Sino-Japanese title *Saikontan* Hung Ying-ming's work has enjoyed a tremendous popularity until the present day. More than two score annotated editions have been published in Japan since the beginning of this century.

Because of the antagonistic attitude of the Yi 李 government in Korea towards Buddhism, the *Ts'ai-ken t'an* (Sino-Korean: Ch'aegŭndam) was considered to be "undesirable reading." Four or five annotated editions, however, have been published in Seoul since 1920.

[Editors' note: A Manchu translation of the *Ts'ai-ken t'an* by Hesu (ECCP) is one of the items included in his *Ch'i pen t'ou* 七本頭 (ca. 1700).]

Bibliography

SK (1930), 144/5a; Sheng-yin, *Ts'ai-ken t'an chiang-hua* 講話, Taiwan, 1958; Yamada Takamichi 山田孝道, *Saikontan kōgi* 講義, Tokyo, 1908; Tomoda Yoshikata 友田宜剛, *Kaisetsu* 解說 *Saikontan*, Tokyo, 1938; Ogaeri Yoshio, *Saikontan*, Tokyo, 1955; Nobuhara Daisen 延原大川, *Shiyaku* 詩譯 *Saikontan*, Tokyo, 1966; Imai Usaburō, *Saikontan*, Tokyo, 1968; Han Yong'un 韓龍雲, *Chŏngsŏn kang'ŭi* 精選講義, Keijo, 1921; Cho Chihun 趙芝薰, *Sin* 新 *Ch'aegŭndam*, Seoul, 1959.

Frits Vos

HUO T'ao 霍韜 (T. 渭先, H. 兀厓, 渭厓, 石頭子), May 13, 1487-November 5, 1540, an official noted for his integrity but criticized for being too intolerant and contentious, was a native of Nan-hai 南海, Kwangtung. He came from a non-official family. His great-great-grandfather made a profitable business out of selling roast duck. His grandparents, suffering the loss of the ancestral house destroyed during a local rebellion, restored the family fortune by starting a small business with two cows and two pigs. In his youth, as he confessed in later years, Huo T'ao led a pampered and dissipated life, which indicates an affluent background. He turned over a new leaf at the age of eighteen, resolving to study seriously. After mastering the Classics and histories in a few years, he succeeded in rapidly passing the civil examinations, becoming a student of the prefectural school in 1512, placing second as a provincial graduate in 1513 and first in the metropolitan examination of 1514. At the palace examination he ranked fourth among the *chin-shih*. It is said that his paper might have earned him first honors had it not been stamped by a careless clerk with the official seal inverted.

After being assigned to the ministry of Personnel as an observer, Huo T'ao was probably reluctant to serve in the disorderly court of Emperor Chu Hou-chao (*q.v.*). He returned home on leave to marry, remaining there for seven years. On his way back to Peking, Huo learned of the death of the unmourned emperor (April, 1521) and the enthronement of his imperial cousin, Chu Hou-ts'ung (*q.v.*), who, though only fourteen, made the unexpected declaration that he was to ascend the throne not as an adopted son but by right of succession. Huo admired the young emperor for taking such an audacious stand in defiance of the recommendation submitted by the ministry of Rites; this was that the emperor should designate his own father as uncle, while acknowledging Emperor Chu Yu-t'ang (*q.v.*) as father by adoption. In July, after his arrival, Huo sent to the same ministry a document opposing its proposal as a distortion of the emperor's natural family relationship, attacking its basic canonical sources, namely, the quasi-classic *Chou-li* (Rites of Chou), and calling the historical precedents cited unsound. While he exchanged heated communications with the minister, Mao Ch'eng 毛澄 (T. 憲清, Pth. 文簡, optimus 1493, 1460-May 24, 1523), on the controversy, a new *chin-shih*, Chang Fu-ching (*q.v.*), submitted in August a memorial with views similar to those of Huo. Three months later Huo handed in his own memorial. By that time Chang had already become the recognized leader of the small group of junior officials including besides Huo, Kuei O, Hsi Shu (*qq.v.*), and Fang Hsien-fu (*see* Kuei O). For a time (1521-24) they were shifted to other posts but later they were recalled to court for about a decade and wielded power as imperial favorites because of their support of the emperor in the *Ta-li i* controversy, as it came to be known (*see* Chu Hou-ts'ung). They were vilified by the majority of contemporary officials; some historians considered them opportunists and sycophants.

For about a year, beginning in September, 1521, Huo served as a secretary in the ministry of War. He came to the attention of the emperor for his above mentioned memorial justifying the emperor's refusal to degrade his own parents. The following February he presented three long statesmanlike memorials advising the emperor on various matters. One of his suggestions, probably resulting from his

experience in business, had to do with the keeping and checking of accounts. Half a year later he offended the grand secretary, Yang T'ing-ho (*q.v.*), whom he described as unqualified for noble rank, and then antagonized the supervising censors by denouncing them for receiving imperial edicts while not properly dressed. Soberly he applied for sick leave but in his memorial he made an uncustomary statement to the effect that his impaired health was due to sexual excesses in his youth. His later explanation that it was intended as a warning to the young emperor did not keep it from being ridiculed. It seems, however, that he did suffer from hemorrhages and other symptoms suggestive of tuberculosis.

In 1524 the emperor finally decided to reject the advice of the majority of his court and proceeded arbitrarily to confer on his own father the imperial title and to designate the late Chu Yu-t'ang his uncle. Chang Fu-ching and others who had strongly supported the emperor in this controversy were brought to the capital and given rapid promotions. An urgent call was sent to Huo but he could not attend and remained at home for three more years. Meanwhile (1526) he was given the extraordinary promotion to the coveted post of a junior supervisor of instruction (from 6A to 3A). He finally assumed office in 1527 in time to take part in the editing of the *Ming-lun ta-tien* (*see* Chang Fu-ching). He then became supervisor of instruction, an office which he held for three years, and in which he begged to remain even when named minister of Rites (1528), for the supervisorate was an exalted position from which he could advise or criticize while unencumbered with administrative burdens. During this period he submitted more than thirty memorials. He also served as joint examiner with Chang Fu-ching at the metropolitan examination of 1529 and again took an unusual step by refusing to acknowledge as "disciples" those who passed the examination. He explained this decision by saying that these men should be known as disciples of the emperor, not of the examiners; others, however, averred that it was because the optimus, T'ang Shun-chih (*q.v.*), disagreed with him on the question of the *Ta-li i*. At this time the *Ta-li i* clique under Chang Fu-ching was at the height of its power and Huo actively helped to strengthen its influence. In other policy matters he took pains to rely on his own judgment and maintain his integrity though often criticized even by his own group for being loquacious and argumentative. Thus in 1530, when Chang sided with the supervising censor, Hsia Yen (*q.v.*), in advocating the separation of worship of the god of earth from the worship of heaven, quoting *Chou-li* as their authority, Huo offered his objection, denouncing the *Chou-li* as a work compiled under the direction of a traitor to the Han dynasty, Wang Mang (45 B.C.-A.D. 23). Unfortunately for Huo, the emperor had already set his mind on building four altars for the worship of heaven, earth, sun, and moon in the southern, northern, eastern, and western suburbs respectively. Hence when his memorial was attacked by Hsia Yen as covertly slandering the emperor, Huo was remanded in April, 1530, to the prison of the Censorate for investigation. Although a month later he was permitted to redeem himself by paying a fine and immediately restored to his former rank, he felt discouraged. Just then his mother died and he retired for the mourning period.

In 1533 Huo returned to Peking to serve as a vice minister of Personnel, a position he held for three years. During this time he seems to have succeeded in controlling his temper and even while reporting on irregularities and noting the rise of corruption he managed to avoid any dispute with the men in power. In 1536, however, he became involved in the case of Liu Shu-hsiang 劉淑相 (T. 養忠, d. 1537) and again came into open conflict with Hsia Yen. Liu, like Huo, was a *chin-shih* of 1514. Then serving as prefectural

governor of Peking, Liu tried to stop the fraudulent practices of certain wealthy families. They were receiving payment for services they never intended to fulfill. By bribery and judicious alliances with influential men in government, these families had enjoyed freedom from accusation for decades until Liu exposed them. But when Liu identified Hsia Yen as one of the men accepting bribes, the latter accused Huo of being the instigator. In this episode Hsia emerged as the victor. Liu was sent home as a commoner and Huo "promoted" to the innocuous post of minister of Rites at Nanking.

Some of the duties of this office had to do with religious orders and popular customs. In 1537 Huo obtained imperial sanction to close down all the Buddhist nunneries in the Nanking area on the ground that some were found to be houses of ill repute. Most of the seventy-eight buildings were converted to schools or shrines and the confiscated farmland reverted to public ownership. Older nuns (238 of them) were either returned to their families or sent to homes for the aged, while 210 younger ones were allowed three months to marry, those still single at the end of the period to be assigned to unmarried soldiers. Huo also paid attention to the fashion of women's clothing. He forbade the wearing of long sleeves that reached to the knee or blouses that hung down like robes, and specified that a woman's head-dress, currently five inches high and tipping backward, be changed to the older style of three inches in height and bending towards the front. Some of his orders were praised and well remembered by the people of Nanking, such as the one forbidding feasts and music at funerals.

In May, 1539, just after the emperor returned to Peking from his eventful visit to his father's tomb at An-lu 安陸, north of Wuchang, he decreed the reorganization of the office of instruction of the then heir apparent, Chu Tsai-jui (*see* Chu Hou-ts'ung). Huo was named a joint supervisor and given the title of junior guardian of the heir apparent and the titular rank of minister of Rites. In August, while he was still in Nanking, he and a subordinate, Tosu Shou-i (q.v.), jointly compiled an illustrated textbook on exemplary conduct for the three-year-old heir apparent. The emperor, after reading the book, suspected that some passages implied criticism of his own conduct. He ordered its destruction but let the authors off with a reprimand only. When Huo traveled to Peking in September, he noticed many evil practices by officials using the government post service and learned that, when the emperor passed through Honan earlier that year, the entourage made more excessive demands than customary. According to Huo, only Kuo Hsün (q.v.) and one other official were known to have refused gifts. Hence, when it was reported that another imperial tour was under consideration, Huo memorialized on its inadvisability, especially because the provinces in north China had been suffering from almost continuous famine for decades. Huo's memorial displeased the emperor but the projected tour never materialized. It is said that the people of Shantung and Pei-Chihli, who had been apprehensive about the the tour, regarded Huo as their savior. He died in Peking in his fifty-fourth year and was awarded the posthumous rank of grand guardian of the heir apparent and the name Wen-min 文敏.

The collected works of Huo T'ao, edited by his second son, Huo Yü-hsia 霍與瑕 (H. 勉齋, 1522-ca. 1592, cs 1559), were first printed in 1552 and reprinted in 1576 and 1709. Known as Wei-yai wen-chi 渭厓文集 or Huo Wen-min kung wen-chi, 10 ch., the book includes chiefly his memorials, official papers, and letters, some of which contain important information on the economic conditions and the political situation of his day. He was concerned about the welfare of his home province and wrote on sixty topics for the reference of the officials; this contribution known as Liang Kuang shih-i 兩廣事宜 forms part of chüan 10 of his collected works. In the

same chüan is an abridged version of his instructions to the junior members of his family, entitled Chia-hsün 家訓, which he wrote in 1529 and printed in 1530. The complete text of this work may be found in the second series of Han-fen-lou Pi-chi (see P'eng Sun-i, ECCP). Of special interest is the plan of a house which might enable a clan to live together. Here each apartment was to have a front door marked in red which opened on the lane, for use exclusively by men, and a door marked in black which led from the backyard to the lane, to be used exclusively by women. Some halls of this house were designated as public meeting places for cousins or for brothers and sisters.

In one of the letters to his sons Huo exhorted them to study hard, to be polite to their neighbors, to make full payment of taxes, and to meet all obligations. Especially were they warned not to accept gifts that might compromise their father for he wanted to be free at all times to denounce any kind of misdeed. Apparently his bluntness in criticising other officials was one reason why he was often described as biased, inconsiderate, contentious, and difficult in his personal relations.

One record has it that Huo wrote an autobiography entitled Shih-t'ou lu 石頭錄, 8 ch., Shih-t'ou being the name of the village where his ancestral home was situated. He owned several houses, one of which was in the scenic hills Hsi-ch'iao shan 西樵山, where he built an academy called the Ssu-feng shu-yüan 四峯書院. He built another academy near Canton city, known as the Shen-tu 慎獨 shu-yüan where a shrine was erected in his memory and where the printing blocks of his writings were stored. According to Li K'ai-hsien (q.v.), who wrote a eulogy of his mentor, Huo also wrote on the Classics and the Sung philosophers. None of these works seems to be extant. In the eulogy Li included some interesting episodes which reveal the fact that the careers of several officials of the third decade of the 16th century were affected by the feud between Huo

T'ao and Hsia Yen. Li's own removal from office in 1541 was conceivably due to his friendship with Huo, a relationship which Hsia resented.

In his early days Huo seems to have dabbled in painting, which he apparently gave up in later years. There is only one landscape under his name recorded in Wang Chao-yung 汪兆鏞, *Ling-nan hua cheng lüeh* 嶺南畫徵略. It was executed in 1510.

Huo had nine sons and six daughters. The second son, the above mentioned Huo Yü-hsia, served as magistrate of Tz'u-ch'i 慈谿, Chekiang (1559-61), but was removed from office about the same time as Hai Jui (*q.v.*) and for the same reason, namely, that he had the courage to refuse the illegal demands of one of the henchmen of Yen Sung (*q.v.*). Later Huo Yü-hsia served (1567) as magistrate of Yin (Ningpo) and as an intendant in Kwangsi. The collection, *Huang Ming ching-shih wen-pien* (*see* Ch'en Tzu-lung, ECCP), includes selections of Huo Yü-hsia's writings in *chüan* 368 and 369, under the title *Huo Mien-chai chi* 霍勉齋集. Selections from Huo T'ao's works form *chüan* 185–88 of the same collection.

Bibliography

1/197/7a, 283/8a; 5/18/12a; 22/6/15a; 32/111/14a; 40/35/1b; 42/60/1a; 83/53/8b; *Li K'ai-hsien chi* (1959), 402; SK (1930), 53/5a, 56/1b, 176/12b; *Kwangtung t'ung-chih* (1934), 3864, 3969, 4807, 4846; TSCC (1885–88), VI: 1306/4a, 1309/5b, 1313/7b; MSL (1965), Shih-tsung, 4888; *Ling-nan hua cheng-lüeh* (1961), 1/20.

Chaoying Fang

HUO Yüan-chieh, *see* **QONINČI**

IBRAHIM (I-pu-la 亦不剌, I-pu-la-yin 因, or Ibarai Tayishi of the Mongol chronicles), died 1533, was a Mongol leader whose dispute in 1510 with Batu Möngke (*q.v.*) resulted in his leading several raids on China's northwestern regions. The evidence concerning his ancestry is unclear. One source suggests that he was the grandson of the Oirat chief, Esen (*q.v.*). The *shih-lu* twice refers to him as a leader of the Wild Mekrid (Yeh Mieh-k'o-li 野乜克力), a Turkic tribe intimately involved in the struggles between Turfan and Hami in the late 15th and early 16th centuries. The chiefs of the Wild Mekrid frequently intermarried with the ruling family of Turfan, and Ibrahim's border compaigns indicate that, even if he were not related to Turfan's rulers, he communicated with them.

Prior to the schism with Batu, he sought Chinese permission to settle near the Chinese border. On January 24, 1495, while being pursued by a hostile Mongol chieftain, he appealed to the Chinese for sanctuary and permission to trade and pay tribute. Ma Wen-sheng (*q.v.*), the minister of War, allowed him to trade on the border, but, perhaps fearing that his tribute envoys might prove troublesome while traveling to the capital, refused to permit him to enter China. Ibrahim probably remained on the border for a few years but then returned to the region north of Shansi, in present day Chahar, after his opponents had abandoned the area. He continued to raid Chinese territory with varying degrees of success. In 1509 a Chinese force led by the Muslim general Ma Ang 馬昂 repulsed his troops at Mu-kua shan 木瓜山. This defeat may have precipitated splits among the Mongol leadership, principally between Batu and Ibrahim.

Batu's attempts to expand and consolidate his dominions exacerbated these tensions. Around 1510 Batu bestowed the title Chi-nung 濟農 (Jinong) on his son Ulus Bolod and appointed him regent of the Mongols in the west. Ibrahim, infuriated by Batu's action, killed the newly appointed Chi-nung. War erupted, and Ibrahim, accompanied by his ally, Mandulai Aɣolqo (known to the Chinese as A-er-t'u-ssu 阿爾禿斯), fled to the southwest. Ibrahim sought to regain power and prestige by capturing the border guards (wei) in

Hsi-hai 西海 (Kokonor, a region later called Ch'ing-hai) and the oases and towns on China's route to central Asia. In 1511 he repeatedly raided Chuang-lang 莊浪 and Liang-chou 凉州. In the following year he moved west and totally overwhelmed the Uighur tribes of An-ting 安定 and Ch'ü-hsien 曲先, causing their dispersal. The destruction of these two border guards dealt a severe blow to China, because they had served as a source of information on hostile foreign peoples, occasionally escorted tribute envoys to the Chinese border, and assisted in safeguarding the route to central Asia in the north and Tibet in the south. Ibrahim's invasion also disrupted the highly profitable and important trade, Chinese exporting tea and receiving horses in return from these guards.

Ibrahim's successes inspired an effort to control Hami, "the funnel for central Asian trade and tribute." In the winter of 1512 he dispatched an envoy to Su-chou 肅州 to seek permission for a marital alliance with Hami. The Chinese entertained and rewarded the envoy but rejected his request. Within a few months, Turfan, whose chief, Manṣūr (q.v.), was perhaps a relative of Ibrahim, occupied Hami, meeting little resistance from the inhabitants or the Chinese. Ibrahim also did not oppose Turfan. It seems likely that Manṣūr and Ibrahim agreed, either formally or informally, to divide the Chinese border areas into spheres of influence. Manṣūr would expand in the north around Hami and Ibrahim in the south from Kansu to Szechwan.

In 1513 Ibrahim, after several triumphant raids, requested permission to initiate trade and tribute relations with China and demanded a gift of a four-clawed dragon robe, a highly prized garment rarely bestowed on foreigners. The Kansu governor, Chang I 張翼 (cs 1484), fearful of antagonizing him yet unwilling or incapable (i. e. only the emperor could award dragon robes) to grant this prestigious costume, finally presented him with silk fabrics and succeeded in temporarily diverting him. Ibrahim briefly shifted his attention to raids on Tibet, but shortly thereafter returned to attack such border areas as Min-chou 岷州, T'ao-chou 洮州, and Sung-p'an 松潘, all centers for the tea-horse trade. According to the Ming-shih, the hai-k'ou 海寇 (lake bandits, the Chinese designation for Ibrahim's forces) allowed these regions no further peace or stability in the early 16th century. In addition they reached as far east as Ho-lan shan 賀蘭山, north of Ninghsia, by 1526.

While pursuing an aggressive policy against China, Ibrahim himself was threatened by the Eastern Mongols. In the first two decades of the 16th century Batu led several abortive campaigns against him. Batu's grandson, Gün-bilig-mergen (see Qutuγtai-sečen), was more successful, for in 1533, feigning an invasion of Yen-sui 延綏, he marched westward, and surprised and routed Ibrahim's forces. One source states that Ibrahim reached Hami where a local chieftain killed him. The Altan Tobči notes that one of his own allies assassinated him. Ibrahim's conquests of An-ting, Ch'ü-hsien, and other northwestern border areas, along with Manṣūr's seizure of Hami, limited China's contacts with central Asia in the 16th century. Tribute and trade missions from the Western Regions (hsi-yü 西域) were endangered; trade through which the Chinese acquired horses for their military was restricted; and hostile tribes replaced the previously friendly ones on the northwestern fringes of China.

Bibliography

1/182/11a, 187/22a, 198/5b, 327/15b; MSL(1964), Hsiao-tsung, 1847, Wu-tsung (1965), 1677, 1740, 1756, 2065, 2072, Shih-tsung (1965), 3407; Ch'en Jen-hsi, Huang Ming shih-fa-lu (Taipei, 1965), 70/30b, 71/32b, 36b, 40b, 47a, 49b, 52a, 57b, 72/1a, 16a, 27a, 29a, 32a; Hsü Hsüeh-chü, Kuo-ch'ao tien-hui (Taipei, 1965), 170/37a, 40a; Kansu t'ung-chih (1736), 46/24b, 27a, 30a; E. Bretschneider, Mediaeval Researches from

Eastern Asiatic Sources, II (London, 1910), 207, 211; L. Hambis, *Documents sur l'histoire des Mongols à l'époque des Ming* (Paris, 1969), 42, 45, 47; C. R. Bawden, *The Mongol Chronicle Altan Tobči* (Wiesbaden, 1955), 187; H. H. Howorth, *History of the Mongols, from the 9th to the 19th Century* (London, 1876), pt. 1, 373; D. Pokotilov, *History of the Eastern Mongols during the Ming Dynasty from 1368 to 1634*, tr. by R. Loewenthal, *Studia Serica*, ser. A., no. 1 (Chengtu, 1947), pt. 1, 98; W. Franke, "Addenda and Corrigenda," *Studia Serica*, ser. A., no. 3 (1949), pt. 2, 52; H. Serruys, "A Note on the Wild Mekrid," *MS* 22 (1963), 439; *id.*, *Genealogical Tables of the Descendants of Dayan Khan* ('s-Gravenhage, 1958), 40; Wada Sei, "A Study of Dayan Khan," *MTB* 19 (1960), 27.

Morris Rossabi

ISIHA (I-shih-ha 亦失哈), fl. 1409-51, a eunuch of Jurchen origin, was the leading figure in early Ming relations with the Jurchen tribes. Like so many other eunuchs in Chinese history, however, he receives scant attention from Chinese historians, and our view of him is limited to his public life. It appears, nonetheless, that he was from Hai-hsi 海西 and that Chinese forces captured him late in the 14th century. It also seems clear that he was related to the ruling family of the Wu-che 兀者 Guard which occupied an important area in the Hu-lan 呼蘭 River basin. As a eunuch he probably learned Chinese and undoubtedly proved himself sufficiently loyal to the throne to be entrusted with an important foreign mission. In 1409 the emperor, Chu Ti (*q. v.*), who had already exchanged envoys and established relations with the Hai-hsi and Chien-chou 建州 Jurchen in southern Manchuria, ordered him to make preparations for an expedition to the Nurkal 奴兒干 Jurchen in the remote northern section of present Manchuria. The court did not conceive of this expedition as a punitive force, but merely as a military demonstration to induce the Nurkal Jurchen to initiate cordial relations. The emperor was assembling an army for a campaign against the hostile Eastern Mongols and was not eager to fight on two fronts. [The *Shih-lu* gives 1409 as the date of the first expedition, but every other source consulted, including the inscription at the Yung-ning ssu, gives it as 1411.]

After two years of preparations, Isiha, leading an expedition of 25 ships and over 1,000 men, took off from Chi-lin 吉林 (Kirin), where his boats were constructed, towards the north. He met with little opposition and thus generously rewarded the local chieftains and established a regional military commission (tu-ssu 都司) in Nurkal. He also succeeded in stimulating the chieftains to send a tribute mission composed of 178 men to accompany him on his return. The emperor showed his appreciation of this mission by again dispatching Isiha to reward the Nurkal Jurchen. In 1413, during this second expedition, Isiha built a Buddhist monastery, the Yung-ning 永寧寺, in Jurchen territory and erected a stele to commemorate his success in "pacifying" Nurkal. The inscriptions, in Chinese, Mongol, and Jurchen, briefly recount the origin of the expedition and list the names of the leading Chinese and Jurchen who accompanied him. The Vladivostok Museum possesses the stele, and several photographic reproductions are available.

Isiha's missions promoted good relations with the Nurkal Jurchen. His knowledge of Jurchen customs and language evidently impressed the chiefs and they responded with tribute and trade embassies. The Chinese court, in turn, sent him as an envoy on three occasions to the Nurkal during the remaining years of Chu Ti's reign. The latter's successors temporarily pursued the same policy, and in 1425 the court ordered Liu Ch'ing 劉清, the regional commissioner of Liaotung, to build ships for Isiha's next expedition; this sailed in the following year. The retirement of the Nurkal chief and the enfeoffment of his successor prompted the last and most elaborate of Isiha's missions. In 1432 he reached Nurkal, conferred a seal on the new ruler, and presented gifts to the other chieftains. He also took this opportunity to repair and add to the Yung-ning ssu and erected a second stele which included a list of the Jurchen who acted as escorts on his journey. The court, which had at the same time ended the Cheng Ho (*q.v.*) expeditions, then terminated these missions to the Jurchen. It still employed Isiha to deal with them, however. In 1435 it appointed him grand defender of Liaotung, a position he occupied for over fifteen years. He received and probably deserves credit for China's cordial relations within and on the borders of Liaotung. The raids of Esen (*q.v.*) in 1449 ended his career as an official and sullied his reputation. Several Chinese sources accuse him of refusing to assist the Kuang-ning 廣寧 Guard in repelling the attacks of the Oirat-led troops. They also imply that he, along with many other Jurchen, sympathized with and perhaps abetted the Oirat. In addition, the court feared that the large force under his command might pose a threat. As a result, sometime between 1449 and 1451, it apparently relieved him of his duties, but, probably taking into account his years of service to China, did not punish him. The editors of the *Ming-shih* fail to accord him an independent notice but mention him in the biography of another eunuch, Ts'ao Chi-hsiang (*q.v.*).

Bibliography

1/304/11b; MSL(1963), T'ai-tsung, 1618, Hsüan-tsung, 0877, 1435, 2057, Ying-tsung, 3718; Meng Sen 孟森, *Ming yüan-Ch'ing hsi t'ung-chi* 明元清系通紀 (Peiping, 1934), 25b; Ejima Hisao 江島壽雄, "Ishiha no Nurukan shōbu ni tsuite," 亦失哈の奴兒干招撫に就いて *Nishi Nihon shigaku* 西日本史學, 13 (1953), 43; *id.*, "Taikan Ishiha ni tsuite, " 太監亦失哈に就いて, *Shien* 史淵, 50 (1951), 19; Pi Kung 畢恭, *Liao-tung chih* 遼東志 (1931–34), 9, 10b; Wada Sei 和由清, *Tōa shi kenkyū: Manshū-hen* 東亞史研究: 滿洲篇 (Tokyo, 1955), 353; Henry Serruys, *Sino-Jürčed Relations during the Yung-lo Period* (1403-1424), (Wiesbaden, 1955), 42; *id.*, *Sino-Mongol Relations during the Ming: The Tribute System and Diplomatic Missions* (1400–1600), MCB, XIV (1967), 102, 541; Li Chi, "Manchuria in History," *Chinese Social and Political Science Review*, XVI, No. 2 (July, 1932), 251; Lo Fu-i 羅福頤, "Nu-er-kan Yung-ning ssu pei pu k'ao" 奴兒干永寧寺碑補考 in *Manshū gakuhō* 滿洲學報, Vol. 5, 97.

Morris Rossabi

I-Shih-ha, *see* ISIHA

JU Ch'ang 茹瑺, died 1409, an official during the first three reigns of the Ming dynasty, was a native of Heng-shan 衡山, Hukuang. When he was sixteen *sui*, he was selected by the local school to study in the National University. (This was probably in 1371 when 2,728 students were enrolled; if so, then it places his date of birth in 1356). In 1381 he was appointed ch'eng-ch'ih lang 承敕郎. Subsequently, he became commissioner in the office of transmission. In 1390 he rose to be junior vice censor-in-chief, then minister of War. Two years later he was granted the additional honor of junior guardian of the heir apparent.

When Chu Yün-wen (*q.v.*) ascended the throne, Ju was shifted to the ministry of Personnel, retaining the same rank. Because Ju was not in accord with the policies of Huang Tzu-ch'eng (*see* Lien Tzu-ning), Pao Chao 暴昭 (native of Fou-shan 浮山, Shansi, d. July 25, 1402), minister of Justice and a member of Huang's party, succeeded in forcing him out of his position by accusing him of corruption. Ju then became administration commissioner of Honan. When the imperial army suffered a series of defeats at the hands of Chu Ti (*q.v.*), then prince of Yen, Huang Tzu-ch'eng was himself dismissed. Ju's recall followed, and once more he was minister of War.

On July 8, 1402, Chu Ti captured Lung-t'an 龍潭 on the south bank of the Yangtze, threatening the capital. In order to stave off his attack on Nanking, the emperor ordered Li Ching-lung (*see* Li Wen-chung), Wang Tso 王佐 (both military officers), and Ju Ch'ang to go to Lung-t'an where they were to propose a partition of the country. Part of north China was to be given Chu Ti in exchange for a cessation of hostilities and his promise to retire to Peiping. The latter not only refused to discuss the proposal, but mockingly told the imperial emissaries that he wanted only to visit the tomb of his father, after which he would return north. Possibly at that meeting Ju Ch'ang secretly aligned himself with the prince of Yen. It is not known whether he also took part in the plot which enabled the latter to penetrate the Chin-ch'uan Gate 金川門 at Nanking, later opened by Chu Hui, prince of Ku (19th son of Chu Yüan-chang).

When the prince of Yen captured the capital (July 13, 1402), Ju came at his bidding and was among the first to advise him to ascend the throne. Shortly afterwards (September 30), Ju was granted the title Chung-ch'eng po 忠誠伯 (loyal, sincere earl) with an annual stipend of 1,000 shih of rice for life. He continued to serve as minister of War and junior guardian of the heir apparent. The new emperor considered him one of his trusted advisers, and made his son, Ju Chien 鑑, consort of the princess of Ch'ang-an 長安郡主, a daughter of Chu Shuang (second son of Chu Yüan-chang).

It was during the year 1409 that Ju Ch'ang's troubles began. Returning to the capital on one occasion, he failed to escort Chu Kao-sui (see Chu Kao-hsü). For this negligence he was ordered to return to his native place. The sources are not clear, but apparently he was accused by his household retinue of committing an unnamed crime, arrested, and sent to the capital. Upon his release, he returned home, but, while passing Changsha, did not appear in audience before Chu Hui, who therefore insisted upon his arrest. The emperor esteemed his brother, for the latter was one of several who had opened Nanking to him and his army; but he also valued Ju Ch'ang. Apparently the emperor

tried to counter Chu Hui's insistence that Ju should be punished, but soon concluded that he had to accede to his brother's wish. Whereupon the censor-in-chief, Ch'en Ying 陳瑛 (executed 1411), impeached Ju Ch'ang for having violated ancestral regulations. He was seized and interned in the prison of the Embroidered-uniform Guard. Fearing that he would be executed, he ordered his second son, Ju Ch'üan 銓, to bring him poison and then on February 28, as recorded in the Ming shih-lu, he committed suicide. Cha Chi-tso (ECCP) lists Ju Ch'ang among the chien-jen 姦壬 (treacherous and obsequious).

The legal officials accused Ju Ch'üan of patricide but, upon further investigation, they decided that he had followed his father's command. His death sentence was commuted to military service, and he joined his elder and younger brothers and their families, totaling twenty-seven persons, in the guard of Ho-ch'ih 河池, Kwangsi. When Chu Kao-chih (q.v.) succeeded Chu Ti (1425), they were pardoned and allowed to return home. During the following reign their confiscated property was also restored.

Ju Ch'ang seems not to have engaged in any independent literary work but he did assist in the first revision of the T'ai-tsu shih-lu (1403).

Bibliography

1/151/1a; 3/141/1a; 5/10/7a; 16/23/34a; MSL (1962), T'ai-tsu, 3018, 3266, T'ai-tsung (1963), 1171; Huang Tso, Nan-yung chih, 1/12a, 23a; Cha Chi-tso, Tsui-wei lu, 30/4a; Wolfgang Franke, Sources, 1. 1. 1.

David Chan

JUAN An 阮安 (also known as A Liu 阿留), died 1453, was a eunuch of Annamite origin who acted as the chief engineer in the construction of the Ming capital at Peking in the 1430s and 1440s. He was one of a number of Annamite boys (see Wang Chin) selected for their looks and ability, castrated, and sent to Nanking in 1407 for service by Chang Fu (*q. v.*), the Ming commander who suppressed Lê Quí-ly (*q. v.*).

Juan An had a talent for the design and management of large-scale architectural and engineering projects. The *Ming-shih* credits him with the conception and planning of the new capital. This is difficult to substantiate since he is not mentioned in the principal sources for the Yung-lo period. Juan was probably a very young man when Emperor Chu Ti undertook to rebuild the capital city, which he decided to call Peking. Work was begun as early as 1406, but significant construction did not get underway until 1417 when canal transport was opened to the north, making it possible to supply a large work force. In that year building activity was placed under a unified command headed by Ch'en Kuei 陳珪, the marquis of T'ai-ning 泰寧侯 (1335–May 24, 1419, Pth. 忠襄, and ennobled as duke of Ching-kuo靖國公), who was concurrently in charge of the Peking branch rear military commission. The ministers of Works and Justice were Sung Li and Wu Chung (*qq. v.*) respectively, and Ts'ai Hsin 蔡信 headed the construction bureau. The initial phase of erection of the palaces, altars, and residences of the princes was completed in early 1421. In that year Peking was designated as the primary capital, Ching-shih 京師.

It is not clear what role if any Juan An played in this early work, but he was the dominant personality in the reconstruction which took place twenty years later. He is credited with having planned the walls, moats, temples, palaces, government offices, and other buildings. The ministry of Works and its artisans merely followed his specifications. In the Cheng-t'ung period Juan An was ordered to undertake large-scale repairs and improvements. Late in 1436 he supervised the repair of the nine gates of the main wall and construction of wall towers, as well as the repair of an embankment of the Lu-kou 盧溝 River, 40 *li* west of Peking. For the first, more than ten thousand

military personnel, temporarily in the capital on rotation for training purposes, were designated a labor force (work concluded May, 1439). To mark the occasion, a number of dignitaries, headed by Yang Jung (*q. v.*), composed laudatory poems in praise of Juan An. Unfortunately, according to a report, Wang Chen (*q. v.*) objected to their publication; so the collection was never printed. Sun Ch'eng-tse (ECCP) declares that it was printed as *Ying-chien chi* 營建紀. The poem by Yang Shih-ch'i (*q. v.*), however, survives in his collected works. The repair of the embankment was completed in the summer of 1437; the emperor then gave it the name Ku-an ti 固安堤. In March, 1440, Juan was charged with rebuilding the major palaces, the Feng-t'ien 奉天, Hua-kai 華蓋, and Chin-shen 謹身 pavilions. This project required a work force of sixty-six thousand soldiers and artisans. When it was completed late in 1441, the emperor rewarded Juan with 50 ounces of gold, 100 ounces of silver, brocade, and paper currency worth 100 strings of cash. In the autumn of 1443 Juan assumed charge of the construction of new buildings for the government schools in the capital. During the next two years he supervised three more public works: the repair of the Lu-kou (known to westerners as Marco Polo) bridge (April, 1444), the facing of the earthen wall of Peking with brick (July, 1445), and the building of the Yung-t'ung永通 bridge outside the eastern gate of the capital. Early in 1449 he was ordered to inspect the Grand Canal, especially the repairs in southern Shantung after a flood ruined many of the locks. This work was not completed until the autumn of 1453. While inspecting the reconstructed dikes in Shantung he died. He was devoted in his service to the emperor, for despite rewards he reportedly had no personal wealth on his death.

The *shih-lu* of the Ch'eng-hua period cites another Juan An, also an Annamite sent to China not as a eunuch but as a prisoner of war, who later served as an artisan. In July, 1467, this Juan An and over six hundred follow Annamite artisans were reported to have deserted. Juan was later captured, but received the emperor's pardon. He continued to serve as an artisan and became (late in 1484) an assistant chief (fu-shih 副使, 9B), of the artisan bureau (wen-ssu yüan 文思院) attached to the ministry of Works.

Bibliography

1/85/6b, 283/7a, 304/6b; 5/117/4a; MSL (1963), Ying-tsung, 0471, 1047, 1219, 1679, 2596, 3362, 4974, 5021; Hsü Hsüeh-chü, *Kuo-ch'ao tien-hui* (Taipei, 1965), 2248; TSCC (1885–88), VI: 3/2/5b; Yang Jung, *Yang Wen-min kung chi* (NCL microfilm), 9/6b; Li Shih-mien, *Ssu Chung-wen ku lien chi* (NCL microfilm), 2/1a, 5b, 6b; Yang Shih-ch'i, *Tung-li wen-chi hsü-pien* (NLP microfilm, no. 977), 23/16a; Yeh Sheng, *Shui-tung jih-chi*, in *Chi-lu hui-pien*, 139/28a; Teng Ch'iu 鄧球 (cs 1535), *Huang Ming yung-hua lei-pien* 皇明泳化類編 (1568, repr. 1965, Taipei), 123/7b; Chang Hsiu-min 張秀民, "Ming-tai Chiao-chih jen tsai Chung-kuo chih kung-hsien," 明代交阯人在中國之貢獻, in *Ming-shih lun-ts'ung* 明史論叢, Vol. 7 (Taipei, 1968), 63. For Juan An II: MSL (1964), Hsien-tsung, 876, 4344; Sun Ch'eng-tse, *Ch'un-ming meng-yü lu*, 3/3a.

Edward L. Farmer and Hok-lam Chan

JUAN Ch'in 阮勤 (T. 必成), 1423–May 9, 1499, an official of Annamite descent who won acclaim as a capable administrator, was born into a family originally from Phụ-dực 多翼, Tân-hung 新興 prefecture (renamed Hsin-an 新安 fu in 1407), in the northeastern interior of Annam. His father, Juan Ho 河 (Nguyen Hà, T. 大河, 1377–1445), a talented man with some knowledge presumably of the Chinese language and literature, rendered service to the commander of the Chinese expeditionary army, Chang Fu (*q. v.*), when the latter concluded his first campaign against Annam in 1407. Impressed by his promise, Chang Fu later appointed Juan Ho to be the police warden (典史) of Van-n'ai 雲屯, an island off the coast of Tinh-yên 靖安 prefecture. In 1416 Juan Ho was one of the hundreds of local officials who went to China to pay tribute to the Ming court. He remained at his post until about 1426 when the Annamite prince, Lê Lợi (*q. v.*) was completing his campaign against the Chinese; siding with the Ming, he then set sail with his family to seek shelter in Ch'in-chou 欽州, Kwangtung. Later he obtained permission to proceed to Peking, and was accorded a warm welcome by Emperor Chu Chan-chi (*q. v.*). Before long he received an appointment as police warden of Ch'ang-tzu 長子 district, Shansi, and served in this capacity to the end of his life.

Raised in Ch'ang-tzu, Juan Ch'in was by imperial order admitted to one of the district schools in Peking upon the death of his father, becoming *chü-jen* in 1453 and *chin-shih* a year later. He received an appointment as judge in the Grand Court of Revision and in September, 1463, was promoted to be the prefect of T'ai-chou 台州, Chekiang. He remained at this post for the following nine years, during which he achieved a reputation as an upright and competent official. He was credited with the improvement of the administration, with the repair of a number of schools, including the famous Shang-ts'ai shu-yüan 上蔡書院 which dated back to the 1260s, and with the construction of several shrines in the prefecture. His notable achievement, however, was the recommendation which led to the establishment of a new administrative unit within Huang-yen 黃巖 -hsien on the coast of Chekiang. This proposal was addressed to the government's problems in maintaining effective control over a territory of about 150 *li* from north to south where the population was unevenly distributed, and where the inhabitants were known to have exploited their proximity to the sea to engage in illicit activities. It suggested the formation of a separate administration of the three wards, Fang-yen 方巖, T'ai-p'ing 太平, and Fan-ch'ang 繁昌, in the southeastern part of Huang-yen-hsien. In January, 1470, the ministry of Revenue approved the changes, and T'ai-p'ing-hsien thus came into existence. It was then reported to have 4,564 *ch'ing* of land, and a population of 7,249 households. (The authorities in 1476 assigned a portion of the island Yü-huan 玉環 to the new hsien, which by 1497 had a population of 11,651 households as compared to Huang-yen-hsien's 11,129 households.) In May, 1471, Juan received an imperial patent in recognition of his service. By September of the following year, he had left office to become the left administration vice commissioner of Shantung, from which he advanced to be administration commissioner of the same province (April, 1477). As a tribute to him, the people of T'ai-chou erected a memorial epitaph and, after his death, included his tablet in the shrine honoring reputable officials.

In April, 1480, Juan Ch'in became vice censor-in-chief and was assigned to be the governor of Shensi, then a worrisome frontier region due to inroads by Mongol and Tibetan tribesmen and occasional natural calamities. During his three-year term of service, Juan paid attention to border defense by promoting military alertness and improving the provisioning of the guards, and devoted himself as well to the general welfare. In January, 1481, for example, he proposed to the court the construction of fourteen additional beacon-fire towers in the northeastern part of present Kansu. When drought followed by flood struck Shensi in the following year, Juan promptly introduced a number of measures to relieve the suffering of the population, such as a reduction in the amount of tribute of herb medicine and other local products, and requested the local officials to donate grain in proportion to their rank and stipend. He also submitted a plea to lift the ban forbidding private individuals from engaging in the lucrative tea trade, and to rescind eighty per cent of the revenue imposed on seven disaster-stricken prefectures which had failed to fulfill the assigned quota. Under his leadership the government forces repelled several incursions of Tibetan tribesmen, the people thus being spared the usual chaos resulting from the threat of war.

Juan became a vice minister of War in September, 1483. When late in 1485 the eunuch Wei Ching (*see* Yü Tzu-chün) accused the minister of War, Yü Tzu-chün, of improperly effecting the transfer of certain officials in charge of the defense of the frontier, Juan presented facts in defense of his senior, but withdrew his objection when the emperor insisted on an investigation. In March, 1485, Juan became involved in another case when several junior officials in the ministry of War were executed on the charge of illegally trading with the Jurchen delegates from the Chien-chou 建州 Guard in the hostelry for foreign envoys. Juan and several of his colleagues were clapped into prison for neglect of duty, but the emperor, released Juan and transferred him with the same rank as before to the ministry of Justice in Nanking.

In May, 1490, Juan completed his nine-year term of service; the new emperor, Chu Yu-t'ang (*q. v.*), then recommended a raise in stipend of two grades, and asked him to stay in office. By this time, however, Juan was already getting on in years; he pleaded for permission to retire, finally obtaining the emperor's approval in October. A censor proposed that Juan be recalled to service in November, 1493, but the emperor ignored the recommendation. Juan spent his remaining years in Ch'ang-tzu, where he died at the age of seventy-six.

Besides being known as a capable administrator, Juan was also a man of letters. He composed a number of memorial essays for the monuments erected in T'ai-chou and in Ch'ang-tzu, but few of these have been preserved. He left a collection of poetry on the scenery of Ch'ang-tzu entitled *Chang-yüan pa-ching shih* 漳源八景詩 (Eight views of Chang-yüan), Chang-yüan being the name of the western region of Ch'ang-tzu, so called because it is the source of the Chang River. This collection is reported lost, but a preface by Tu Ning 杜寧 (cs 1427) is preserved in the bibliograpical section of the *Ch'ang-tzu-hsien chih*.

Juan Ch'in was known to have two sons; the elder, Juan Shou 壽, achieved his *chin-shih* in 1474; the younger, Juan Fu 富, received the yin privilege to enter the National University in 1490. A grandson, Juan Chung 忠, who benefited also from the yin privilege (in August, 1501), later became an assistant director of the imperial parks.

Bibliography

1/178/14a; 5/49/4a; MSL (1963), Ying-tsung, 711, Hsien-tsung (1964), 1429, 1754, 2091, 2975, 3234, 3532, 3598, 3660, 3752, 3861, 3913, 3949, 3963, 4018, 4024, 4097, 4116, 4322, 4604, 4638, 4803, Hsiao-tsung, 789, 868, 1540, 2615, 3245; *Hung-chih* 弘治 *Ch'ih-ch'eng hsin chih* (NLP microfilm, no. 416), 5/7b; *Huang-yen hsien chih* (1877), 4/3a, 12b; *Wan-li Hsien-chü* 萬曆仙居-*hsien chih* (1935), 12/25b; *Ch'ang-tzu-hsien chih* (1888), 2/4b, 6/藝文志/4a, 8/集傳/2/6a, 11/7b; *T'ai-chou-fu chih* (1936), 63/15a, 65/15a; Yang Hsüan 楊璿(1416–74), *Yang I-hsien wen-chi* 宜閒 文集 (NCL mirofilm), 2/28a; Yang Shou-ch'en 守陳 (1425–89), *Yang Wen-i kung* 文懿公 *wen-chi* (NLP microfilm, no. 992), 8/9b, 18/1a; Ho Ch'iao-hsin, *Chiao-ch'iu wen-chi*(NCL microfilm), 12/18b; Chang Hsiu-min 張秀民, "Ming-tai Chiao-chih jen tsai Chung-kuo chih kung-hsien" 明代交阯人在中國之貢獻 in *Ming-tai kuo-chih kuan-hsi* 國際關係 (Taipei, 1968), 79.

Hok-lam Chan

JUAN Lang 阮浪, died July 28, 1452, was a favored eunuch of Annamite origin during the early years of the Ming dynasty. Upon the conclusion of his military campaigns in Annam, Chang Fu (*q.v.*) selected a number of native boys for their looks and ability, and had them castrated, and sent to Nanking in 1407 for service (*see* Wang Chin). All of them rose to eminence in the palace. Impressed by Juan's promise, Emperor Chu Ti (*q.v.*) had him placed under the care of tutors for instruction in the Classics; later he put him

in charge of the directorate of tailoring. Juan Lang continued this service into the next reign and was equally favored by the new emperor, Chu Kao-chih (*q.v.*).

Following his enthronement, Emperor Chu Chan-chi (*q.v.*) appointed Juan Lang to take charge of the superintendency of paper currency, during which he gained the emperor's confidence by his managerial competence. In 1426 Juan was sent to Kuang-chou 廣州 (Canton), to inspect the cargoes of the tribute-bearing missions from the South Seas and to insure their safe delivery to the capital, a task usually reserved for the most favored eunuchs. Late in November, 1428, Juan accompanied the emperor on a tour outside Peking to inspect the military defenses erected to prevent the intrusion of the Mongols. Upon their return the emperor made him an assistant supervisor of the directorate of furniture supplies.

Juan Lang stayed on to serve the next emperor, Chu Ch'i-chen (*q.v.*), who, in appreciation of his long service, made him a senior eunuch and rewarded him richly. Juan did not join the imperial retinue when Chu Ch'i-chen led an expedition in person against the Oirat (*see* Wang Chen), but, when the latter returned from captivity and lived in confinement in the "Southern Palace," Chu Ch'i-yü (*q. v.*), now emperor, assigned Juan to serve the former monarch. During this changeover Juan remained a loyal servant of the ex-emperor. It is said that he secured a painting of the deities patronizing longevity and secretly prayed for the prolongation of his former master's life. In 1452, however, Juan became involved in a scandal. It occurred in a tense political climate following Chu Ch'i-yü's displacement of the heir apparent in favor of his own son, an act which further strained the relations between him and his elder brother. Unfortunately for Juan Lang, it so happened that just then the former emperor gave him a delicate golden blade with an embroidered purse and that Juan then presented it to his friend, a messenger in the palace. This man later showed the gift to a commander in the Embroidered-uniform Guard named Lu Chung 盧忠. Being a vicious individual, who coveted an opportunity for advancement, Lu stole the blade and purse after making the messenger intoxicated; these he showed to the emperor as evidence that Juan Lang was plotting to overthrow him and reinstall the former emperor. Subsequently Chu Ch'i-yü ordered the arrest of Juan and several others. It was never made clear whether Juan indeed had plotted a rebellion, or whether it was a trumped-up accusation brought against him and the former emperor by their political enemy. Juan was thrown into prison and tortured, but he reportedly declined to give testimony implicating the former emperor. He died shortly afterward, at the age of approximately sixty. When Chu Ch'i-chen regained the throne, he elevated Juan Lang posthumously to the rank of grand eunuch and ordered an elaborate burial for him. At the emperor's command the Hanlin chancellor, Li Hsien (q.v.), composed an epitaph, which supplies the basic data about Juan Lang.

In June, 1457, Juan Lang's enemies were brought to justice. Lu Chung, then a chiliarch in the Liu-chou 柳州 guard, Kwangsi, and his accomplice, the eunuch Kao P'ing 高平, were arrested and sent to the capital for trial. The emperor ordered their execution and that their bodies be exposed for three days as punishment for their false accusation against Juan and the throne. Three months later he made a grant of forty-eight *mou* of land outside the southern gate to the east of the Peking city wall for Juan Lang's burial place, which he decreed should be exempted from rent tax.

Bibliography

1/304/7b; 5/117/5a; 42/25/10a; 61/158/9a; MSL (1963),Ying-tsung, 5933, 5972, 6046; Wang Shih-chen, "Chung-kuan k'ao" 中官考 in *Yen-shan-t'ang pieh-chi*, 91/18b; Hsia Hsieh 夏燮, *Ming t'ung-chien* 明通鑑 (1959), 1045.

Hok-lam Chan

K'ANG Hai 康海 (T. 德涵, H. 對山, 沜東漁夫, 湖西山人), July 22, 1475-January 10, 1541, poet, dramatist, and prose writer, was a native of Wu-kung武功, Shensi. His ancestor of the eighth generation, reportedly from Honan, had come here as a settler in the middle of the 13th century, and had become a man of property by employing hundreds of persons to cultivate land that had been laid waste probably during the Mongol conquest of that area in the 1230s. K'ang Hai's great-great-grandfather, K'ang Ju-chi 汝楫 (T. 濟川, H. 東里, January, 1350-January, 1412), served Chu Ti (q.v.) as an official in his princely household, and in 1403 was appointed a vice minister of the newly established auxiliary central government in Peiping. In 1425 K'ang Ju-chi was awarded posthumously the rank of minister of Works. K'ang Hai's father served in 1488 as assistant registrar (chih-shih 知事, 9A) of the P'ing-liang 平涼 prefecture. K'ang Hai was thus brought up in a gentry family of considerable affluence.

Together with Wang Chiu-ssu (q.v.), he was regarded as belonging to the group of Ch'ien-ch'i-tzu 前七子 (Seven early masters) of classical prose style (Ku-wen-tz'u; *see* Li Meng-yang). Four years after achieving the *chü-jen*, K'ang Hai became (in 1502) the empire's optimus, or *chuang-yüan*. His essay seems to have made a signal impression on the emperor, who reportedly remarked that there had been no such examination essay during the previous century and a half of Ming rule. K'ang was duly posted to the Hanlin Academy and appointed a first-class compiler. His fame as an outstanding master of san-ch'ü 散曲 (song poetry) developed only later. His position in the Hanlin brought him into contact with personalities in positions of influence. At least two of the grand secretaries became his foes because of his outspoken opposition to abuse of power and high-handed literary orthodoxy. He had once criticized Wang Ao 王鏊 (*q.v.*) for incorrectly placing an examination candidate, and Li Tung-yang (*q.v.*) for upholding the grand secretariat style (t'ai ko t'i), in prose writing. K'ang remained equally candid vis-à-vis his fellow provincial Liu Chin (*q.v.*), the powerful eunuch, who aimed at a dictatorial role and would have liked to have had the famous *chuang-yüan* in his entourage. K'ang, however, would not submit. In 1508 Li Meng-yang, another fellow provincial, fell into disgrace with the eunuch and was thrown into prison apparently to await execution. A friend persuaded him to call on his literary rival K'ang Hai for help. K'ang went to Liu to plead Li's case, much to the delight of the eunuch, who gave his consent for Li's release. This seems to indicate that K'ang had collaborated, however loosely, with the eunuch party while it was in power. K'ang retired later in 1508 owing to the death of his mother. After the eunuch's downfall in 1510, K'ang fell from favor and was cashiered. There is a commonly accepted story that when he asked Li for help Li refused. This lack of gratitude on Li's part is said to be depicted in K'ang's play, *Chung-shan-lang* 中山狼 (Wolf of Central Mountain; *see* Ch'eng Ta-yüeh). However this may be, there certainly are passages in K'ang's play criticizing the selfishness of high political leaders of the time without naming specific persons. Perhaps K'ang's expulsion from the Hanlin should be taken to be the result also of his personal attitude in office, in addition to any connections he had with the eunuch's faction. Some of his poems contain elements of "Zeitkritik" adding to his fame as a courageous critic.

He lived in his home district for thirty years. During this time he acted the part of a non-conformist hermit, together with his friend Wang Chiu-ssu, ignoring official visitors for fear of a renewed call to office. He used to sit drinking wine and plucking the p'i-pa lute until the official guest left in disgust. Both friends were noted for their noisy carousing, acting like fools in order to give expression to their grievances. In a letter to a friend, who would have liked to see him back in office, K'ang explained his position: officials do not act openly but criticize secretly and without mercy; Hanlin officials are mere tools of the Grand Secretariat; upright evaluation of able men has become dangerous; frank statements only enrage people who are accustomed to formal and false politeness; there is above all the wrong tendency of acquiring a literary name by spiritless poems; criticism is useless; friendly relations under such circumstances can only be strained and frustrating. So K'ang declared that return to office was out of the question. He died aged sixty-six *sui* (another source incorrectly says sixty-four) at the beginning of 1541.

K'ang left a collection of his writings, *Tui-shan chi* 對山集, 19 *ch.*, first printed in 1545 by Wu Meng-ch'i 吳孟祺 (T. 元壽, cs 1529); the edition copied into the *Ssu-k'u ch'üan shu* is in 10 *chüan* and edited by Sun Ching-lieh 孫景烈 (cs 1739). The Naikaku Bunko has an edition (preface dated 1582) in 46 *chüan*. There is a collection of song poems by K'ang, *P'an-tung yüeh-fu* 泮東樂府, 2 *ch.* (*San-ch'ü ts'ung-k'an* 叢刊 edition). An earlier edition of 1524 is said to exist with amendments (*pu-i* 補遺, 1 *ch.*). He served as editor of the local history of his district, *Wu-kung-hsien chih*, 3 *ch.* (1519), which has been frequently reprinted; and a genealogy of his mother's family, entitled *Chang-shih-tsu-p'u* 張氏族譜. His two dramas are the *Chung-shang-lang* and the *Wang Lan-ch'ing chen-lieh ch'uan-ch'i* 王蘭卿貞烈傳奇. Reportedly he taught several girls to sing his own songs; he was devoted to music, could play stringed instruments, and had a large collection of drums.

Bibliography

1/286/13a; 5/21/43a, 48b; 61/146/1901; *Chuang-yüan t'u-k'ao* 狀元圖考, 下/8; SK (1930), 68/9a,

171/8b, 178/4a; *Wu-kung-hsien chih* (TsSCC ed., no. 3202), NCL *Ming Index*, 500; Yagisawa Hajime 八木澤元, "Kōkai," in his *Mindai geki-sakka kenkyū* 明代劇作家研究 (1959), 109; Cheng Chen-to (BDRC), *Chung-kuo wen-hsüeh yen-chiu* (1957), 1123.

[Editors' note: There seems to be no doubt that in 1508 K'ang Hai persuaded Liu Chin to release Li Meng-yang from prison. The story that in 1510 Li repaid K'ang by refusing to answer the latter's request for help, thus provoking K'ang to write a drama on the ungrateful wolf of the central mountain is, however, entirely fallacious and probably a concoction of the 17th century.

It was the Japanese scholar, Yagisawa Hajime, who, after exhaustively assembling materials relating to the life of K'ang Hai, reported in 1959 that he could find no evidence of a break in the friendship between K'ang and Li, nor any record of Li's ever having persecuted K'ang; moreover, in all K'ang's writings no word exists of an accusation of ingratitude against Li. The first writer to record such a story was Wang Shih-chen (1634-1711, ECCP) who, in his collection of anecdotes, *Ch'ih-pei ou-t'an*, said that the *Chung-shan-lang chuan* 傳 by Ma Chung-hsi (*see* Yang T'ing-ho) was a covert attack on Li for his ingratitude to K'ang. According to Yagisawa, Ma's story, which was a refinement of an earlier one of the same title by a Sung dynasty writer, Hsieh Liang 謝良, served as the inspiration for two song dramas, one by K'ang Hai in four acts and another by Wang Chiu-ssu in one act. There is nothing in any of these writings that can be interpreted as indicating an attack on Li Meng-yang. The ungrateful wolf (or some other wild animal), furthermore, has been the theme of popular folktales among Hindus, Kirghiz, Koreans, and other peoples of Asia and Europe. Cheng Chen-to pointed this out in 1926. Apparently the theme caught the fancy of Ma Chung-hsi and the two dramatists.

In his study Dr. Yagisawa has certainly made a valuable contribution to the history of Ming literature. On further investigation we find another possible reason for Ma Chung-hsi to write on the wolf of central mountain. It happens that Ma's ancestor who first settled early in the Ming dynasty in Ku-ch'eng 故城, south of Peking, originally came from Ta-tu 大都, the Yüan capital city. This fact and his surname, a common one for central Asians to adopt, seem to indicate that he came from a non-Chinese family. Hence he might have heard the fable as a child, and, when he found Hsieh Liang's version, revised it in the light of his own background. As to K'ang Hai, his ancestor might have been in charge of a reclamation project under the Mongols in the mid-13th century, and so there is the possibility that he also came of alien ancestry. The fact that he describes his father as having an extremely light complexion and his grandfather as having a very prominent nose makes our speculation plausible. Perhaps K'ang's musical interests may also have derived from his ancestral origin. Report has it that, although Wang Chiu-ssu had to learn music before he started to write dramatic works, his version of the *Chung-shan-lang* contains chiefly dialogue and very few lyrics in sharp contrast to K'ang's drama. If our theory is not too farfetched, then we may add to the roster of Ming writers two more of possible central Asian origin].

Tilemann Grimm

K'ANG Mao-ts'ai 康茂才 (T. 壽卿), 1314/ 1315-August 24, 1370, official under both Yüan and Ming dynasties, was a native of Ch'i-chou 蘄州, Hukuang. He received a classical education in his youth. When Hsü Shou-hui (*q.v.*) and other White Lotus Society leaders rebelled in Ch'i-chou and Huang-chou 黃州 in the autumn of 1351, K'ang organized a militia to oppose them. He was appointed captain of the unit by the Yüan government and, soon afterwards, given the rank of military pacification officer. During the next few years he participated in successful attacks on rebel strongholds in Ch'i and, farther east, in Kiukiang. Later he encamped with his troops near Ho-yang 和陽 (in eastern Anhwei). Here he became a military official in the western Huai pacification office. Ho-yang fell to the forces of Kuo Tzu-hsing (q.v.) at the beginning of 1355 and was placed under the authority of Chu Yüan-chang. When Chu crossed the Yangtze on July 11 of the same year, his first objective was the strategically important city of Ts'ai-shih 采石. K'ang's forces, now on the south bank, were among the defenders. The city fell, but K'ang continued his resistance until, early in 1356, the fort to which he had withdrawn was destroyed by bomb-throwing catapults. He escaped and was rewarded for his loyal service with the office of assistant administrator (參知政事) of the Huai-nan branch secretariat at Nanking. He had been in office barely a month, when, in April, Nanking fell to Chu Yüan-chang. He fled eastward to Chinkiang. When this city also collapsed in the same month, K'ang surrendered with his three thousand men. In all he served the Yüan as a military officer for four and a half years.

As Chu Yüan-chang wished to make use of K'ang, he allowed him to retain his command. K'ang then served Chu during the rest of his life. In 1357 he was appointed commander of naval forces in the Ch'in-huai 秦淮 wing command which had been established at Chinkiang in April of the previous year. In August/September he defended Lung-wan 龍灣 on the southeastern outskirts of Nanking against the forces of Chang Shih-ch'eng (q. v.), and pursued and defeated the attackers, capturing some of their warships. He served next (1358) under Liao Yung-an (q. v.) in a successful campaign against the state of Hsü Shou-hui. In the same year K'ang was appointed superintendent of hydraulic works and agricultural projects (都水營田使). In his instructions to K'ang, Chu Yüan-chang explained that he was to be

responsible for the restoration of irrigation and flood-control, visiting each community to see that the work was going forward.

In 1360 one of Hsü Shou-hui's generals, Ch'en Yu-liang (q.v.), assassinated his chief and founded the state of Han. Ch'en was Chu's most formidable enemy at this time. A strategem adopted to conquer him was to induce him to attack and then ambush his army. In the autumn K'ang, who had known Ch'en some time before, was given the delicate task of guiding him into the trap. He "defected" to Ch'en and won his confidence. Ch'en attacked on K'ang's advice and suffered a serious defeat. K'ang subsequently played an active military role in Chu Yüan-chang's elimination of major rivals in the Yangtze valley. From 1360 to 1364, he served in the campaigns that destroyed the state of Han. Among his rewards was promotion to the office of associate commissioner in the newly established chief military commission. K'ang shared also in the successful campaigns of 1365 that ended Chang Shih-ch'eng's state in the east, and was further promoted to the office of vice-commissioner, a position he still held at the time of his death. In 1368 K'ang served under Hüs Ta (q. v.) in the capture of the Yüan cities in the Yellow River valley, Pien-liang 汴梁 (Kaifeng), Loyang, and Shan-chou 陝州. At Shan-chou he constructed a floating bridge that was used to effect a crossing of the Yellow River. He was then made responsible for the defense of the Ho-chung 河中 area (between the Fen 汾 and Yellow Rivers, north from Shan-chou). A year later he again took the field under Hsü Ta in a campaign westward to Han-chung 漢中 (Shensi). The following year he was recalled to Shan-chou, and died of illness on the way. Chu Yüan-chang poured a libation at his burial near Nanking (October 21), and composed an essay in his honor. K'ang was posthumously granted the title duke of Ch'i 蘄國公 and the name Wu-k'ang 武康.

Bibliography

1/130/3b; 5/6/43a; MSL (1962), T'ai-tsu, 1073; KC(1958), 274, 278, 279, 290, 295, 300, 318, 340, 354, 365, 392, 424; Sung Lien, *Sung hsüeh-shih wen-chi* (SPTK ed.), 2/17a; Chu Yüan-chang, *Ta Ming T'ai-tsu huang-ti yü-chih chi* (NCL microfilm); Ch'ien Ch'ien-i (ECCP), *Kuo-ch'u chün-hsiung shih-lüeh*; Ku Ying-t'ai (ECCP), *Ming-ch'ao chi-shih pen-mo* (1658 ed.); Fu Wei-lin (ECCP), *Ming-shu*, 95/1b.

Romeyn Taylor

KAO Ch'i 高啓 (T. 季迪, H. 青丘子, 槎軒), 1336–74, poet and official, was a native of Ch'ang-chou 長洲 in the prefecture then known as P'ing-chiang-lu 平江路 (Soochow 蘇州府 since 1367). He traced his ancestry, though by what evidence is uncertain, to Kao Huan, actual founder (d. 547) and father of the first emperor of the Northern Ch'i dynasty (550–77). Little is known about his early youth except that the family was of scholarly background, possessed property, and still had both a home within the city and a farm of over a hundred *mou* (about 17 acres) on the Woo-sung 吳淞 River, northeast of Ch'ang-chou. The young lad received a good education of the type intended to prepare one for the civil service, but it was an age of unrest and he probably never sat for any examinations. The prosperous and relatively stable area lying just south of the lower Yangtze River drew to it many uprooted officials, families of wealth, and men of literary talent at the end of the Yüan period. From his youth, early marked by unusual gifts, he kept the company of a circle of outstanding persons, many of whom became famous literary figures of his generation. The most prominent members of this circle, after Kao himself, were Hsü Pen (*q.v.*), poet, painter, and official; Chang Yü and Yang Chi (*qq. v.*), both poets and officials; these four together were classed as the "four outstanding figures of Soochow." Othe rintimates of this unusual circle of talents were the calligrapher Sung K'o (*q. v.*) and the monk Tao-yen, better known to history as Yao Kuang-hsiao (*q. v.*), and a dozen or more other figures of similar caliber.

In 1353 Kao married a daughter of the wealthy Chou 周 family of Ch'ing-ch'iu 青丘 (Green Hill), a village some ten miles east of P'ing-chiang city. They had three daughters and one son; a daughter and the son died while very young.

P'ing-chiang city fell (1356) into the hands of Chang Shih-ch'eng (*q.v.*), military leader of a rebellion who made that city his base, and for a short time called it by a new name, Lung-p'ing-fu 隆平府. During more than ten years Chang alternately displayed imperial ambitions, and accepted enfeoffment from the rapidly disintegrating Yüan state. For a resident of an area held by a rebel leader in these decades—whether or not to accept a position with the rebellion, to fight it in the name of loyalty to the legitimate but declining Yüan court, or to remain in some way uncommitted was the pressing question, although complete freedom to select among these alternatives did not always exist. The discredited Yüan dynasty clearly had no future, but the demands of loyalty to it still existed, reinforced by Confucian morality. Service to one of the rising leaders of rebellions was much more attractive, if one could be sure which rebel leader would gain the Mandate of Heaven. It was able and ambitious young men of Kao's generation who felt the dilemma most keenly, and who most actively sought solutions that would utilize their talents. Some of Kao's friends accepted service under Chang Shih-ch'eng, and Kao was under great pressure to do the same, but he hesitated. For a time he was engaged as a tutor to the sons of one of Chang's officials. In 1358 he withdrew completely from the scene of politics to take up residence at his wife's home village, Ch'ing-ch'iu, and wrote a long poem called "Ch'ing-ch'iu-tzu ko" 歌 (The song of the man of the Green hill), describing himself as one who scorned the world and wanted only to be a recluse. Despite the conscious incongruity of this self-identification, or perhaps because of it, he was known from that time onward by the sobriquet, Ch'ing-ch'iu-tzu. Pressures to join Chang Shih-ch'eng's government were still strong, and perhaps to escape them more effectively, or perhaps to find another cause with still greater promise to serve, he spent the years from late in 1358 to 1360 traveling in the area around Hangchow and farther south, which had fallen to Chang's control since the autumn of 1358. While there is little information on his activities in this period other than that provided by a series of travel poems, it may be assumed that the purpose of his journey was to seek involvement in the great enterprise of the time, and not merely to avoid direct connection with Chang's inadequate part in the enterprise of creating a new dynastic order. Although a literary man, Kao also cultivated the values and the skills of the yu-hsia 遊俠 (knight errant); among his associates were swordsmen, military strategists, and others of heroic mold. But he apparently found no outlet for these abilities, and he returned home. Chang at that time had abandoned his open rebellion to accept appointment as regional overlord from the Mongol court. This temporary "legitimacy" of Chang's movement made it even harder to escape involvement. Kao again managed to refuse office, but he had close personal connections with many who had accepted. In 1362 he took up residence on the bank of the Lou River 婁江, just east of the city and devoted himself assiduously to poetry and to the company of his friends, in a mood of increasing pessimism about the course of events. In 1363 Chang Shih-ch'eng again broke with the Yüan court, proclaimed himself prince of Wu, and announced dynastic pretensions, now in open rivalry with Chu Yüan-chang, founder of the Ming dynasty. Seeking detachment from the political and military currents, Kao continued to live in the country until 1365, at which time the

armies of Chu began to menace the area about P'ing-chiang. Kao moved back into the city for safety, and after the middle of 1366 was unable to leave even briefly because of the military situation. In that winter the city came under direct siege which continued for the better part of a year, with attendant suffering for the trapped population. Kao's second daughter died, perhaps as a consequence of the hardships. On October 1, 1367, the city collapsed; Chang Shih-ch'eng and his principal associates were captured and later most of them were executed. His former subjects then settled down to uneasy acceptance of the overlordship of Chu who changed the name of P'ing-chiang to Su-chou (Soochow) and who, a few months after this, was enthroned as the first emperor of the new Ming dynasty.

Kao's joy on having survived the siege of Soochow, like that of most of the city's residents, was tempered by apprehension over reprisals the Ming court might take against the population of the region, supposedly still sympathetic to the memory of Chang Shih-ch'eng. Kao's elder brother, his only close relative, most of his wife's relatives, and many of his former literary friends were banished, or had fled and were in hiding. Kao again took up the life of a poet-recluse on the bank of the Lou River, working on editing and revising his poems, presumably to remove incriminating references that might be used against him, as well as to improve their literary quality. Although only thirty-two years of age, his reputation as a poet and scholar was quite widespread, and probably was the reason for his being invited to go to Chu's capital around February, 1369, to accept appointment as one of the sixteen historian-officials assigned to write the official history of the Yüan dynasty, the *Yüan-shih*. Kao's early ambition to serve in high office was apparently thwarted by Chang Shih-ch'eng's emergence as the dominant political figure in the area in which he lived; now unexpectedly he found another opportunity. He served with the Historical Commission in Nanking throughout the period of its work, from February to mid-September, 1369, an extraordinarily short time in which to accomplish so large a task. [Editors' note: Kao's contribution to the *Yüan-shih* seems to include the treatise on the calendar and the biographies of women, for there are prefaces to these sections in his collected prose writings.] The inordinate haste is evident in the quality of the work; it was submitted in incomplete form, and the commission disbanded. A second commission was formed the following year; it spent several months adding the history of the last Mongol reign and otherwise filling out the work. As historical scholarship the product must have been unsatisfactory to men like Kao, but the activity brought other rewards. The commission was headed by the eminent literatus Sung Lien (*q. v.*), and included other leading figures with whom Kao formed close friendships. It gave the poet an opportunity to become immersed in the vigorous intellectual life of the capital at the time of the dynasty's rapid and complete success in achieving reunification of the Chinese world. The members of the Historical Commission were released from their assignments with rewards and high honors, and offered important posts in the civil service. Kao was retained in a Hanlin assignment without specific office for another year, until mid-summer of 1370, when he was summoned into imperial audience and offered a vice presidency of the ministry of Revenue, a very high post considering his youth and lack of civil service background. He declined, excusing himself on the grounds of youth and inexperience, and begged to be allowed to retire from government service. It is apparent from the poems of that time that he had come to find the life of a courtier onerous, and perhaps he was apprehensive about serving under an emperor who was already showing signs of the violent and cruel temper that increasingly marked his long reign. Kao's request

to resign granted, he returned to Soochow in the early autumn of 1370, again to live quietly as a poet and semi-recluse.

Four years later (1374) at the age of only thirty-eight, Kao was put to death on a charge of treason. Along with a fellow Soochow poet-scholar and former member of the Yüan Historical Commission, Wang Wei (*q.v.*), he was named an accomplice of Wei Kuan 魏觀 (T. 杞山, or 起山), the prefect of Soochow, in a plot to reestablish there an independent power base utilizing remnants of Chang Shih-ch'eng's rebellious movement. The three were sent to the capital and summarily executed. The charge against Wei was that in rebuilding the offices of local government he had inappropriately selected the site of Chang's former palace; Kao and Wang had commemorated the act in literary pieces having seditious import. Although the charge sounds farfetched, it could well have been designed to intimidate resentful anti-Ming elements in Soochow. Wei, however, was a scholar of irreproachable integrity who had served the rising Ming cause with considerable distinction, and within a month after his execution the emperor exonerated him and had him publicly rehabilitated. By implication, Kao and Wang were also exonerated, but this was never made explicit, and their names remained under a shadow. The whole case defies precise explanation. The informal writings of subsequent generations are filled with fanciful attempts to link Kao's poetry with *lèse majesté*, making his execution appear as the emperor's devious revenge. The principal objection to such theories is that the Ming emperor was under no necessity to be devious, and his usual manner was crudely direct. But it is not unreasonable to imagine that he could have been suspicious of a man like Kao, a self-proclaimed "knight errant" in his youth, an associate of plotters and strategists and experts on military affairs, a man having many links with the hated Chang Shih-ch'eng, and a man too proud to serve the new Ming dynasty. The true political significance of Kao's execution may have been simply that the emperor wished to intimidate potential dissidents.

Regardless of its political significance, Kao's death was a distinct loss to Ming literature. He is often ranked as the great poetic talent of his age, and had already achieved such recognition within his brief lifetime, although later critics have also felt that his powers had not reached their full development, and a mature style had not yet emerged. Most of his poetry is in the genres that reached the peak of their development in the T'ang, *i.e.* the lü-shih 律詩 (regulated poetry) and the (ku-shih 古詩 (ancient poetry), although he also wrote some lyrics (tz'u 詞 and ch'ü 曲) on Sung and Yüan models. He was famous for his ability to recreate the personal styles of the great T'ang poets, but at its best his work is highly individual in manner and marked by the force of his own thought and personality. In 1362 Kao prepared a collection of his own poems, calling it *Lou-chiang yin-kao* 婁江吟稿. A second collection called *Fou-ming chi* 缶鳴集, containing 732 poems dating from the period 1358 to 1367, was prepared in the latter year. After returning home in 1370 he enlarged the *Fou-ming chi* to 12 *chüan*, and included 937 poems. At the same time he developed an interest in local antiquities, and early in 1372 he completed the editing of a collection of 123 of his own antiquarian poems about the Soochow region, called *Ku-su tsa-yung* 姑蘇雜詠, which was printed in 1398. At least three copies from the printing blocks for this edition are known to be extant. In 1403 his nephew, Chou Li 周立, compiled and edited a more comprehensive collection of his poetical works, entitled *Ch'ing-ch'iu Kao Chi-ti hsien-sheng shih chi* 先生詩集, often referred to as *Ch'ing-ch'iu shih chi*. There also exists a brief collection of tz'u lyrics called *K'ou-hsüan chi* 叩舷集, 1 *ch.*, and a collection of prose writings under the title *Fu-tsao chi* 鳧藻集, 5 *ch.*, both printed in 1445 with a preface by Chou Ch'en 忱 (*see* Chang Hung 洪).

In 1450 there appeared another edition of Kao's collected poems, entitled *Kao t'ai-shih ta-ch'üan chi* 高太史大全集, 18 *ch.*, a copy of which, together with an original edition of the *Fu-tsao chi*, is reproduced in the *Ssu-pu ts'ung-k'an*. The eighteenth-century scholar, Chin T'an 金檀 (T. 星軺) of T'ung-hsiang, Chekiang, prepared an excellent critical and annotated edition of the poetical works in 20 *chüan*, and included a *nien-p'u* 年譜 and other supplementary material under the title *Ch'ing-ch'iu shih-chi chu* 注; this is included in the *Ssu-pu pei-yao*. There are several other Ming and Ch'ing editions of the poet's writings; several printings of his works were also made in Tokugawa and Meiji Japan, where he was quite popular. [Editors' note: It is an interesting coincidence that in 1962 there appeared two works on Kao Ch'i, both containing numerous translations of his poems; one in English by F. W. Mote entitled *The Poet Kao Ch'i* and the other in Japanese by Iritani Sensuke 入谷仙介, under the title Kōkei 高啓 which is No. 10 of the second series of *Chūgoku shijin senshū* 中國詩人選集.]

Bibliography

1/285/20b; Wang Ch'ung-wu 王崇武, "Tu Kao Ch'ing-ch'iu, Wei-ai-lun'" 讀高青丘威愛論, CYYY, 12 (1947), 273; Fu Tseng-hsiang (BDRC), *Ts'ang-yüan ch'ün-shu T'i-chi ch'u-chi*, 7/15b; Ting Ping (ECCP), *Shan-pen shu-shih ts'ang-shu chih*, 35/19b; reviews of Mote, *The Poet Kao Ch'i* by L. S. Yang, HJAS, 24 (1962-63), 291; D. Holzman, TP, 51 (1964), 278, and James J. Y. Liu, JAOS, 82 (1962), 599.

F. W. Mote

KAO Ming 高明 (T. 則誠), *ca.* 1305-1368+, scholar and official, and a native of Jui-an 瑞安, Wen-chou prefecture 溫州府, Chekiang, is best known as the author of the drama *P'i-pa chi* 琵琶記 (variously rendered as *The Story of the Guitar*, or *The Lute Song*), 2 *ch.* Kao came from a highly literate family. His paternal grandfather, Kao T'ien-hsi 天錫 (H. 南軒), and his uncle, Kao Yen 彥 (T. 俊甫, H. 梅庄), both wrote poetry which has survived. His grandmother, née Ch'en 陳, had three brothers all of whom composed both prose and verse. It is no wonder then that there are anecdotes about Kao Ming's precocity. In 1344 he became a *chü-jen* and the following year a *chin-shih*. His first appointment was that of recorder in Ch'u-chou 處州, Chekiang. When, near the end of 1348, Fang Kuo-chen (*q. v.*) started his rebellion in eastern Chekiang, many officials scattered to other parts of the country, but Fang succeeded in detaining Kao. In 1352, however, Kao gained his freedom and went to Hangchow. There he encountered an old friend, Chao Fang (*q. v.*), who was instrumental in persuading him to serve the Yüan once more. So for the next four years Kao acted as a censor in Kiangnan and in the provincial headquarters in Fukien. In 1356 he retired permanently to Yin 鄞 (Ningpo), living in the home of a family named Shen 沈. The writing of the *P'i-pa chi* may well have been a product of the next few years.

Shortly after his enthronement (1368) Chu Yüan-chang started to assemble a commission to compile the official history of the Yüan (*see* Kao Ch'i). Who proposed Kao Ming's name is unknown, but it may well have been Chao Fang, Sung Lien, Liu Chi, or Wang Wei (*qq. v.*), all of whom had made the acquaintance of Kao in their student days. (Liu Chi and Kao had both specialized in the *Ch'un ch'iu*, or Spring and Autumn Classic.) Kao was duly summoned to court, but he excused himself on account of his age and ill health, and returned to die in Ning-hai 寧海, Chekiang, date unknown.

The *P'i-pa chi*, also known as *Ts'ai Po-chieh* 蔡伯喈 (the name of the hero), is thought to have appeared originally in 1367. It could not have been published much later, for the title is among the pre-Ming "southern drama" listed in the *Yung-lo ta-tien*, prepared in the years 1403-8 (*see* Yao Kuang-hsiao), ch. 13,991. Two copies of this *chüan*, or volume, have

survived, according to the index of the table of contents of Dr. Iwai Hirosato 岩井大慧: one in the private collection of Mr. Hsü 徐 of Tientsin, and one in the National Central Library, Taipei. Ming printings are well known, such as those edited by Li Chih (*q.v.*) and Ch'en Chi-ju (ECCP). Not long ago Professor James J. Y. Liu discovered an edition of 1553 in the Royal Library of San Lorenzo, Escorial, Spain, which, in his opinion "may safely be regarded as a pre-Ming version," as the text has numerous divergencies from other known versions. The drama continued to be popular throughout the Ch'ing, and became one of the first to be rendered into a European tongue. The translator was Antoine Pierre Louis Bazin who gave it the title: *Le Pi-Pa-Ki, ou l'histoire du luth, Drame chinois de Kao-tong-kia représenté à Péking, en 1404 avec les changements de Mao-tse traduit sur le texte original* (Paris, 1841). Since then there have been a number of other translations, mostly incomplete, except for one in German by Vincenz Hundhausen, entitled *Die Laute, von Gau Ming* (Peking and Leipzig, 1930). The play appeared on Broadway in 1946, with Yul Brynner as Ts'ai Po-chieh and Mary Martin as his wife in the lead; they used a version adapted by Will Irwin and Sidney Howard in 1925, later published in Chicago.

Kao was the author too of *Jou-k'o-chai chi* 柔克齋集, 1 *ch.*, and *Jou-k'o-chai shih chi* 詩輯, 1 *ch.*, which are preserved in certain collectanea.

Bibliography

1/285/19a; 3/266/14a; 40/11/13b; 43/1/5b; 86/4/7b; Ch'ien Ch'ien-i (ECCP), *Lieh-ch'ao shih chi* 甲前, 11/21b; *Chekiang t'ung-chih* (1934), 2291, 3167; Wang Kuo-wei (BDRC), *Sung Yüan hsi-ch'ü k'ao* (1912, repr. 1957), 146; Aoki Masaru 青木正兒, tr. into Chinese by Wang Ku-lu 王古魯, *Chung-kuo chin-shih hsi lu* 中國近代戲錄 (1936, rev. ed. 1958), 94; Ch'ien Nan-yang 錢南揚, *Sung Yüan nan-hsi pai-i lu* 南戲百一錄, *Yenching Jo. of Chinese Studies*, mon. ser. no. 8 (Peiping, 1934), 60; Chang Li-hua 張隸華, *P'i-pa chi k'ao shu* 考述, Taipei, 1966; Tai Pu-fan 戴不凡, "Kao

Tse-ch'eng shih-lüeh 事略," *P'i-pa chi t'ao-lun chuan k'an* 討論專刊 (Peking, 1956), 325; Lo Chin-t'ang 羅錦堂, *Chung-kuo hsi-ch'ü tsung-mu hui-pien* 戲曲總目彙編 (Hong Kong, 1966), 283; Tung K'ang (BDRC, *Ch'ü-hai tsung-mu t'i-yao* (Shanghai, 1930), 5/2b; Chiao Hsün (ECCP), *Chü shuo*, Vol. 8, 2/106 [not seen]; Ch'ien Chi 錢 箕, *P'i-pa chi*, Peking, 1960; Iwai Hirosato, "Eiraku taiten genson kan mokuroku (shintei)" 現存卷目錄(新訂), *Iwai hakushi koki kinen tenseki ronshū* 岩井博士古稀紀念典籍論集 (Tokyo, 1963), 49; Martha Davidson (ed.), *A List of Published Translations from Chinese into English, French, and German,* Part I (Ann Arbor, 1952), 167; James J. Y. Liu, "The Feng-Yüeh Chin-Nang," 風月錦囊, JOS, 4 (1957), 93; *Kao-Tong-Kia's Lute Song*, adapted by W. Irwin and S. Howard, Chicago, 1952; Josephine Huang Hung, *Ming Drama* (Taipei, 1966), 87.

L. Carrington Goodrich

KAO P'an-lung 高攀龍 (T. 雲從, 存之, H. 景逸), August 13, 1562-April 14, 1626, scholar, official, and a principal leader of both the intellectual and the political movements associated with the Tung-lin Academy (*see* Ku Hsien-ch'eng), was one of seven sons born to a prosperous land-owner of the flourishing Grand Canal city of Wu-hsi 無錫, northwest of Soochow. His grandfather, Kao Ts'ai 材 (H. 靜成), had succeeded in the provincial examina-tion and had been a popular magistrate of Huang-yen 黃巖, Chekiang. Since his own father Kao Te-cheng 德徵 (H. 繼成, d. 1596) had many sons, Kao P'an-lung as a child was given in adoption to a childless paternal granduncle, Kao Chiao 校 (H. 靜逸, d. 1589). He was encouraged to study, succeeded in the provincial ex-amination of 1582, and was accepted as an official student in the National Uni-versity at Nanking in 1588, winning the *chin-shih* the following year.

Kao's progress toward a civil service career had been delayed by mourning for his foster mother (d. 1584), which prevented his attempting the metro-politan examination of 1586, and then again by mourning for his foster father, which delayed his presenting himself at Peking for an appointment until 1592. Meantime, he had become committed to a life of serious study. One early in-fluence in this direction came from his boyhood tutor, a local scholar, Hsü Shih-ch'ing 許世卿 (T. 伯勳, H. 靜餘, cj 1585); another was his master in the National University, Chao Yung-hsien (*q.v.*). But Kao always traced his real intellectual awakening back to hearing a lecture in 1586 by his fellow-townsman Ku Hsien-ch'eng with whom he was eventually to collaborate in reviving the Tung-lin Academy.

The metropolitan examination that Kao passed was presided over by Chao Nan-hsing (*q.v.*), who was thereafter an influential patron, colleague, and friend. Among Kao's fellow *chin-shih* of the same year were three of philosophical bent with whom he became lifelong friends and who, like himself and Chao, were eventually labeled Tung-lin partisans: Wang Shu-ku 王述古 (T. 信甫, H. 鍾嵩, 1564-1617); Ou-yang Tung-feng 歐陽東鳳 (T. 千仞, H. 宜諸), who as prefect of Kao's native Ch'ang-chou 常州 prefecture in 1604 gave official patronage to reestab-lishment of the Tung-lin Academy; Hsüeh Fu-chiao (*see* Ku Hsien-ch'eng), whose historian-classicist grandfather Hsüeh Ying-ch'i (*q.v.*) had in his old age tutored Ku Hsien-ch'eng and his younger brother Ku Yün-ch'eng (*see* Ku Hsien-ch'eng). Kao outlived all three of these friends and wrote their biographical memoirs or ep-itaphs.

Kao's first civil service designation in 1592 was as an appointee in the messenger office at Peking, where minimal demands on his time and the availability of a good library enabled him to broaden his studies. He became particularly enamored of the great Sung neo-Confucians, Ch'eng Hao (1032-85), Ch'eng I (1033-1107), and Chu Hsi (1130-1200), from whose writings he selected passages for his *Jih-hsing pien* 日省編 (Compendium for daily self-examina-tion), and *Ch'ung-cheng pien* 崇正編 (Com-pendium for venerating orthodoxy). It was no doubt portions of these compendia that later got published as a Ch'eng brothers' sampler entitled *Er-Ch'eng chieh-yao* 二程節要, 6 *ch.* Kao now developed a regimen of half-day meditation and half-day reading, which he tried to maintain the rest of his life. When an assistant surveillance commissioner in Szechwan, Chang Shih-tse 張世則 (T. 惟範, H. 準齋, cs 1574), submitted his own annotations of the Great Learning, *Ta-hsüeh ch'u-i* 大學初義, and urged that it be officially sanctioned in lieu of the standard Sung interpretations, Kao protested in a memorial that won a commendatory response from the throne. (Another work submitted by Chang at the same time, however, was accepted by the emperor. This was the *Tiao-tang shih-chien* 貂璫史鑑 a history of powerful eunuchs in past dynasties.) Kao's other memorials of this period, urging him to study philosophy and rectify irregularities, drew no response.

Kao was greatly stimulated by some young fellow officials in Peking with whom he discussed philosophy and who also later became known as Tung-lin partisans. When late in 1592 he was sent on a journey to deliver an imperial proclamation to Nanking, he took the opportunity to visit his family in Wu-hsi and meanwhile became acquainted with a number of scholars who were then widely known or becoming known: Tsou Yüan-piao (*q.v.*), Chu T'ing-i 朱廷益 (T. 汝虞, H. 虞岊, 1546–1600, cs 1577), Ch'ü Ju-chi 瞿汝稷 (T. 元立, H. 洞觀, 1548–1610), Ch'ien I-pen 錢一本 (T. 國瑞. H. 啓新, 1539–1610, cs 1583), and Wang Ching-ch'en 王敬臣 (T. 以道, H. 少湖, 1513–95).

During Kao's absence from Peking long-festering resentments between loose factions of officials—allies of the Grand Secretariat and the imperial palace eunuch corps on one side, and on the other self-styled "good elements" or "upright men" or "honest critics, " especially of the Censorate and the ministry of Personnel —culminated in a grand partisan debacle when the "good elements" tried to use the triennial personnel evaluations of 1593 to punish their enemies and were themselves punished in retribution (*see* Ku Hsien-ch'eng). Kao's patrons, Chao Nan-hsing and Chao Yung-hsien, were both dismissed from the civil service, and his friends Hsüeh Fu-chiao and Ku Yün-ch'eng were demoted to demeaning provincial posts. Ku Hsien-ch'eng was also discharged from the service the following year. Kao, returning to Peking late in 1593, vigorously denounced leaders of the recent purges. He was subjected to a formal inquiry before a court of Ministry and Censorate officials and was himself ordered demoted to minor employment "in a remote frontier region." His new assignment was soon specified as a supernumerary tien-shih 典史 (jail warden) in Chieh-yang 揭陽, Kwangtung.

Kao returned home from Peking early in 1594 and in the late summer traveled southward to take up his new and lowly post. En route, and while in residence at Chieh-yang, he assiduously visited academies and temples, and made many new scholarly friends. Undaunted by his demotion he attended seriously to his new duties and spent much of his time tutoring local scholars. After only three months on duty he was granted a leave of absence, and reached his Wu-hsi home at the beginning of 1595. The deaths of both his natural father and mother in quick succession the following year caused him to remain on leave indefinitely.

Until 1621 Kao remained out of service, devoting himself to study and writing. In the early years of his retirement he associated intimately with Kuei Tzu-mu, youngest son of the great Ming litterateur Kuei Yu-kuang (*q.v.*) and with Kuan Chih-tao (*see* Ku Hsien-ch'eng), an exponent of the doctrines of Wang Shou-jen (*q.v.*). In 1601 Kao began meeting in formal lecture sessions with other scholars of the region, and it was he who later suggested to the Ku brothers that the old Tung-lin Academy, if reconstructed, would provide a good setting for regular meetings of this sort. In 1604 the rebuilt academy was opened under Ku Hsien-ch'eng's leadership, and for the next two decades it remained one of the focal points of Ming politics and intellectual life. Kao was considered Ku's principal aide at the academy until Ku died in 1612, and then Kao was chosen master. From 1604 to 1621 Kao participated actively in the tutoring of students, which was a regular function of the academy, and in the monthly and annual assemblies of scholars that were scheduled there. Kao also, like Ku Hsien-ch'eng, traveled to lecture repeatedly at nearby satellite academies: the Yü-shan 虞山 in Ch'ang-shu 常熟 to the east, presided over by Keng Chü 耿橘 (T. 庭懷, cs 1601); the Ching-cheng 經正 in Wu-chin 武進 to the north, sponsored by Ch'ien I-pen, Hsüeh Fu-chiao, Ou-yang Tung-feng, and Sun Shen-hsing (ECCP); the Chih-chü 志矩 at Chin-t'an 金壇 to the northwest, sponsored by Yü K'ung-chien; the Ming-tao 明道 at I-hsing 宜興 to the west, sponsored by Shih Meng-lin (for Yü and Shih, see Ku Hsien-ch'eng); and the T'ien-hsin 天心 in Chia-hsing 嘉興 to the south, the home of Kao's now deceased friend Chu T'ing-i. Almost all of the scholars associated with these academies were, like Kao and Ku, anti-administration "good elements" now out of office.

During this period of his life Kao wrote with regularity. He carried on a widespread correspondence, and his academy lectures were often written out and quickly printed for wider circulation. He prepared annotated editions of several ancient Classics: *Ch'un-ch'iu chi-chu* 集註 (so mentioned in the *nien-p'u*, but known to the *Ssu-k'u ch'üan-shu* bibliographers as *Ch'un-ch'iu K'ung-i* 孔義, 12 *ch.*; *Mao-shih chi-chu* 集註; *Chou-i K'ung-i* (so mentioned in the *nien-p'u*, but known to the *Ssu-k'u* editors as *Chou-i I-chien shuo* 易簡說, 3 *ch.* [This is reproduced in the Ssu-ku chen-pen, ser. 3.] He completed a Chu Hsi sampler, *Chu-tzu chieh-yao* 要, 14 *ch.*, in 1602, a commentary on Chang Tsai (1020-77),

Cheng-meng chi-chu 正蒙集註 in 1603, an anti-Buddhist tract, *I-tuan pien* 異端辨 in 1605, a new edition of the old text of the Great Learning, *Ku-pen* 古本 *Ta-hsüeh*, in 1611, a treatise on quiescent meditation, *Ching-tso shuo* 靜坐説, in 1613, and a short intellectual autobiography, *K'un-hsüeh chi* 困學記, in 1614.

Kao was perhaps the most creative and influential of the original Tung-lin thinkers, who generally shared an admiration for the Chu Hsi school of neo-Confucianism and were alarmed by what they considered to be undisciplined ethical subjectivism and Buddhism-Taoism-Confucianism eclecticism deriving from the thought of Wang Yang-ming. Kao did not engage extensively in political polemics as did his teacher and friend Ku Hsien-ch'eng. He concentrated on the practice and teaching of self-cultivation through a balanced mixture of earnest study and intense meditation, the goal being a Confucian enlightenment that brought awareness of the monistic unity of the cosmos and acceptance of a stoic fatalism. He believed that he had himself attained such enlightenment in 1594 while en route to Chieh-yang, whereupon "with a start of comprehension I exclaimed, 'So this is how it is! In actuality there is nothing at all!' As soon as I realized this, my bindings were cut away, and it was suddenly as if a hundred-catty burden had all at once fallen to the ground, or as if a flash of lightning had flooded my being with illumination. Thereupon I became wholly fused and blended, indivisibly, with the great cosmic processes (ta-hua 大化), and there was no longer any separation betweeen heaven and earth, or between inner and outer." Because he denied the self-sufficiency of the individual mind, he believed that his forms of meditation and enlightenment differed fundamentally from Ch'an Buddhism and even more from the "mad Ch'an" (k'uang-ch'an 狂禪) eccentricities of latter day exponents of Wang Yang-ming's subjectivism. Yet he advocated a Ch'an-like stoicism. One of his mottoes was, "If you must die, then die." In a last letter to friends he wrote. "One's mind, like the Great Void, knows no such things as life and death. Why cherish illusions and long unduly (for life) ?"

As his philosophy dictates, Kao seems to have had a stolid, earnest temperament. In admonitions to his sons he warned against sexual lust, and he is reported to have known no woman but the one he married in 1581. He was careless of his own material comforts but freely supported needy students, friends, and relatives. Having come into a sufficient inheritance from his foster father in 1589, he used his share of his natural father's estate in 1596 to endow rent-free lands for the poor. In 1608 he endowed other lands to subsidize the hsien corvée payments, and in 1614 he organized a local good works society (t'ung-shan hui 同善會) to aid widows and orphans. Despite his protests that in growing old "there is no pleasure like the pleasure of being unoccupied," he was honored with an officially-sponsored community celebration (hsiang-yin 鄉飲) upon reaching the age of sixty *sui* in 1621. He liked to go into meditative retreats for weeks or even months at a time, and to this end in 1598 he had built for himself a rustic riverside resort that he called K'o-lou 可樓 in the hope that no intellectual achievements would be found impossible there. His meditative habits bred qualities that enabled him to end his own life stoically "as if he were going home" after he had become involved anew in political entanglements.

Despite the ousters of himself, Ku Hsien-ch'eng, and many others in the 1590s, the "good elements" had weathered controversial storm after storm at the Ming court until about 1614, by which time their enemies were openly calling their group Tung-lin tang (party). They struggled mainly to get the indolent, eunuch-dominated, long-lived emperor Chu I-chün (*q. v.*) to do his duty, but he ignored them to the point of not attend-

ing court audiences, not responding to memorials, and, in the end, not filling civil service vacancies. By 1614 the "good elements" had almost no spokesmen left at court, and the government drifted under a do-nothing grand secretary, Fang Ts'ung-che 方從哲 (T. 中涵, cs 1583, d. 1628). The ever fewer court officials were mainly of three anti-Tung-lin factions identified with Shantung, Hukuang, and Chekiang provinces, coordinated by Fang's vigorous young crony, the supervising secretary Ch'i Shih-chiao 亓詩教 (H. 靜初 cs 1598).

The Manchu attack on the Ming empire's northeastern frontier in 1618 (*see* Nurhaci, ECCP) persuaded the aging emperor that his administration must at least be restaffed if not reinvigorated. Appointments were authorized again, and a new generation of idealistic "good elements" with Tung-lin sympathies began to infiltrate the court. Among the new appointees were the supervising secretary, Yang Lien (ECCP), a devoted disciple of both Ku Hsien-ch'eng and Kao, and the investigating censor Tso Kuang-tou (*q.v.*). Shrewd political maneuvering by Yang and Tso soon brought about a schism in the Shantung-Hukuang-Chekiang group and opened the way for recalling some of the senior "good elements" to duty in Peking.

The Tung-lin tide swelled greatly when the emperor died on August 18, 1620, and was succeeded by a middle-aged son long championed by the "good elements," Chu Ch'ang-lo (ECCP). But the latter fell ill almost immediately and died on September 26 after a reign of barely one month. His death brought to the throne his not quite fifteen-year-old son, Emperor Chu Yu-chiao (ECCP), who was totally unprepared for his responsibilities and proved to be completely incompetent. The turbulent last years of Chu I-chün and the transition to his grandson had given rise to a succession of partisan controversies known as the "three great cases," which reverberated throughout the last three decades of the dynasty.

(1) "The case of the attack with the club" (t'ing-chi an 梃擊案 or ch'ih-t'ing an 持梃案), 1615—Chu Ch'ang-lo had been installed as heir apparent in 1601 only after bitter court controversies in the 1590s, and it was publicly accepted that Chu I-chün's favorite consort, Cheng Kuei-fei (q.v.), had by no means abandoned attempts to supplant him with her own son, the prince of Fu (see Cheng Kuei-fei). One May day in 1615 Peking was thrown into consternation when a Shantung man named Chang Ch'a 張差 (or Chang Wu-er 五兒) was captured rushing into the heir apparent's palace residence wielding a club against eunuch attendants, apparently intending to do away with the prince. Speculation about an intended palace coup spread so wildly that the emperor convened a general audience for the first time in some twenty-five years, at which he and the heir apparent together tried to assure the assembled officials of their mutual affection, and to persuade them that Chang Ch'a was clearly a madman who should be tried and executed forthwith without any innocents being implicated. Subsequent investigation by a junior official of the ministry of Justice, Wang Chih-ts'ai (ECCP), however, did wring from Chang Ch'a evidence of a plot involving some palace eunuchs, presumably under Madame Cheng's influence. A succession of trials resulted in the execution of Chang Ch'a and the death under interrogation of two eunuchs, but to "good elements" it always seemed that the sordid truth of the case had been suppressed by the palace. Because of their complaints about it, Wang Chih-ts'ai and some other "good element" sympathizers were dismissed from the civil service in the personnel evaluations of 1617, which were dominated by the anti-Tung-lin factions.

(2) "The case of the red pills" (hung-wan 紅丸 an), 1620—When the new emperor Chu Ch'ang-lo fell ill within a week of his accession, rumors of assassination again abounded. The emperor was slow to recover, and Madame Cheng hovered constantly at his side, conniving with his own favorite consort, née Li 李, to prevent the court officials from having access to him. They had a eunuch physician, Ts'ui Wen-sheng 崔文昇, give the emperor a laxative, which seemed to worsen his condition. There were frantic court assemblies. Led principally by Yang Lien and Tso Kuang-tou rather than by the ineffective grand secretary Fang Ts'ung-che, the officials insisted that Madame Cheng remove herself and that Ts'ui Wen-sheng be punished. Finally, after two weeks, a delegation of officials was able to visit the emperor's bedside. For another two weeks the emperor's condition fluctuated. Then on September 25, at the emperor's insistent order, a minor official of the Court of State Ceremonial, Li K'o-shao (ECCP, p. 176), was allowed to give him some red pills of Li's own making; and early the next morning the emperor died. For years following, there were factional disputes about who was responsible for the emperor's death.

(3) "The case of the removal from the palace" (i-kung 移宮 an), 1620—On learning of Chu Ch'ang-lo's death, a host of officials marched into the palace to do obeisance to the boy successor, Chu Yu-chiao (ECCP). But Madame Li had taken him into her custody in the imperial residence hall, and her eunuch attendants barred the way. While Yang Lien roared curses at the eunuch guards, the friendly eunuch Wang An 王安 (d. 1621) by a ruse whisked the boy emperor out of Madame Li's presence and into the custody of the officials. Though the latter promptly began to quarrel among themselves about when the emperor should be formally enthroned, they reunited quickly when Madame Li refused to move out of the imperial residence hall and announced that she would screen all government documents for Chu Yu-chiao. Yang Lien, Tso Kuang-tou, and others protested so vigorously against the possibility of a

female usurpation of power that her friends finally persuaded her to yield and move out so that the emperor could move in unchaperoned. The crisis ended, but for years court factions argued about the propriety of what had been done.

These controversies intensified the factional strife and contributed to the polarization of the Tung-lin group and their opponents. The recall to duty of banished Tung-lin partisans, begun under Chu Ch'ang-lo in 1620, continued under his son. It included many men who had been in enforced retirement for more than twenty years, among them Tsou Yüan-piao and Chao Nan-hsing. Kao P'an-lung was summoned in 1621 to be assistant minister of the Court of Imperial Enter-tainments. At the beginning of the next year he was promoted to vice minister and senior official on duty in the same court; and then, in quick succession, he was transferred to be vice minister of the Grand Court of Revision and promoted to chief minister of the Court of the Imperial Stud. In his memorials of this period he insistently urged emergency measures to fill civil service vacancies and as strongly argued about the "three great cases" of 1615 and 1620; it was of vital concern to all factions that the historical record be set right. Kao vigorously de-manded punishment of Fang Ts'ung-che as the one who, by transmitting to Chu Ch'ang-lo the medicine or red pill made by a minor official, should be held respon-sible for that emperor's death. For being overly insistent Kao was punished by having his salary suspended for one year. At the beginning of 1623, at the age of sixty-one, Kao begged for and was granted retirement and returned to Wu-hsi to take charge once more of the Tung-lin Academy which he had entrusted to disciples in 1621. But before the year ended he was recalled again. He asked permission to decline reappointment, but it was not granted. So in the spring of 1624 he set out for Peking to take up the office of vice minister of Justice.

The new ascendancy of the "good elements" had been signaled late in 1621 by the reappearance as senior grand sec-retary of Yeh Hsiang-kao (*q. v.*), who had been the principal Grand Secretariat defender of Tung-lin interests from 1607 to 1614. Fang Ts'ung-che had been re-moved from the Grand Secretariat at the end of 1620 under Tung-lin attack; and in the personnel evaluations of 1623, under the vengeful leadership of Chao Nan-hsing, the Tung-lin men succeeded in removing from the capital many of their remaining enemies of former days, begin-ning with the Shantung faction leader Ch'i Shih-chiao. By the latter part of 1624 the key posts at court were all held by Tung-lin partisans. Yeh Hsiang-kao was a highly prestigious senior grand secretary, Chao Nan-hsing was minister of Personnel, and Kao P'an-lung was named censor-in-chief.

The Tung-lin partisans, however, did not at any time have complete control of the government, and they suffered several reverses. One resulted from a controversy over the establishment in Peking in 1622 of the Shou-shan Academy (*see* Tsou Yüan-piao and Feng Ts'ung-wu). Much more ominous for the Tung-lin partisans was the rise in influence of the eunuch Wei Chung-hsien (ECCP), who became the young emperor's most trusted adviser in 1621 and 1622. After his first few months on the throne, Chu Yu-chiao rapidly wearied of the demands that government made on him and let Wei be his intermediary with the Grand Secre-tariat, with less and less supervision. During 1622 and 1623, despite their grasp of key positions, the Tung-lin partisans were steadily being undermined by a multitude of complicated intrigues that linked Wei to dissatisfied elements in the outer court. The crisis finally came in the summer of 1624, when Yang Lien (by then having risen to the rank of vice censor-in-chief) submitted a long denun-ciation of Wei in which he itemized "twenty-four great crimes." When Yang was severely rebuked for his audacity, the "good elements" presented an almost united front in defending him and re-iterating his accusations. The conflict between the Tung-lin men and Wei Chung-hsien had become open battle.

It was just at this tense juncture that Kao arrived again in Peking to accept his post. In the furor that followed Yang Lien's attack on Wei, one official of the ministry of Works, Wan Ching (*see* Ch'ien Shih-sheng) was publicly beaten in court in an effort by Wei to cow his at-tackers, and four days later Wan died. Soon Yeh Hsiang-kao, whose prestige had previously kept Wei from interfering in administration too openly, was shamed into resigning when a eunuch force besieged his residence accusing him of giving sanctuary to a protégé wanted for trial. With Yeh out of the way, govern-mental power steadily shifted into Wei's hands.

Early in October, 1624, when this drift was not yet wholly apparent, Kao P'an-lung was persuaded despite his pro-tests of inadequacy to assume the impor-tant post of censor-in-chief, and he plunged zealously into a reform program that caused contemporaries to liken him to famous censorate-purgers of the early 15th century (*see* Ku Tso). He posted strict prohibitions against bribery through-out the capital and proposed more than fifty new regulatory articles for governing the conduct of local and provincial affairs, under enforcement by the Censorate's regional inspectors. His proposals were based on the legalist-like premise that "in governing, one should select those who are worthy and talented, get rid of those who prey on the people, and restrain mediocre men. Such men are the most numerous in the empire. They should be curbed by laws, which do no harm to the worthy." His proposals were not accepted.

Kao also sternly inquired into the conduct of a regional inspector then re-turning to the Censorate from salt-control duty in the Huai River region, Ts'ui

Ch'eng-hsiu 崔呈秀 (cs 1613). Kao re-ported Ts'ui to the ministry of Personnel as being guilty of venality, and the min-ister, Chao Nan-hsing, proposed that Ts'ui be disgraced and sent to serve as a com-mon soldier at the frontier. This episode sealed the doom of the Tung-lin partisans; for Ts'ui, terrified, fled to Wei Chung-hsien for help, impressed him with the urgent threat to the eunuch posed by Tung-lin activities, and pledged himself to be Wei's adopted son. Ts'ui not only was reinsta-ted, but he got both Kao P'an-lung and Chao Nan-hsing removed from office (November, 1624), and began preparing black lists to guide Wei in an open, vicious purge that now moved to its full tide. (During the remainder of Wei's dominance—i. e., until the death of the emperor in September 1627—Ts'ui was Wei's most ruthless and feared outer-court agent, and quickly rose to be censor-in-chief in 1626. When the sequence of events at last turned against the eunuch and his partisans, Ts'ui, like Wei, strangled himself to avoid arrest, in late 1627).

Thus Kao P'an-lung found himself re-lieved of office in the autumn of 1624, and he reached his Wu-hsi home by the end of the year. Technically, he had been per-mitted to resign at his own request when his integrity was publicly questioned in a court debate about the appointment of a new governor for Shansi province; but his removal had clearly been arranged by the eunuch partisans, along with the almost simultaneous dismissals of Yang Lien, Tso Kuang-tou, and many other Tung-lin stal-warts in addition to Chao Nan-hsing.

It was characteristic of Wei Chung-hsien's purge that merely removing enemies from office was not satisfying enough; once discharged, many victims were pursued with further accusations and stripped of their civil service status en-tirely; then some of these, Chao Nan-hsing among them, were sent to serve as com-mon soldiers at the frontier, and others achieved martyrdom by being arrested and tortured to death in the palace prison maintained in Peking by the imperial bodyguard. Kao P'an-lung was not spared vengeful pursuit. In early summer of 1625 he was "erased from the register and made a commoner." Official histories indicate that the pretext for this action was that Kao had selfishly punished an official who had been responsible for his younger brother, Kao Ju-lin 如驎, being sent to the frontier as a common soldier on the charge of fraudulently passing the provincial examination.

In the summer of 1625 the purge of Tung-lin men brought the arrests and deaths by torture of Yang Lien, Tso Kuang-tou, Ku Ta-chang (see Ch'ien Tai), Wei Ta-chung 魏大中 (original name 廷鯾, T. 孔時, H. 廓園, Pth. 忠節, 1575-1625, cs 1616), Yüan Hua-chung 袁化中 (T. 民諧, H. 熙宇, 民協, cs 1607), and Chou Ch'ao-jui 周朝瑞 (T. 思永, H. 衡臺, Pth. 忠毅, cs 1607). Like Yang Lien, Wei Ta-chung had studied under Kao in the Tung-lin Academy; and when Wei passed by Wu-hsi under arrest en route to Peking, Kao made a point of welcoming and honoring him. Early in 1626 Kao conducted a memorial service at Wu-hsi for the six Tung-lin martyrs of 1625.

Meantime, in the late summer of 1625, the imperial court denounced Tung-lin type academies as subversive organizations and ordered their destruction throughout the country. Kao P'an-lung prevailed upon the local authorities to interpret this order loosely, so that only the principal meeting hall of the Tung-lin Academy was affected at this time. Thereafter Kao went into almost total isolation in his private retreat.

A second major wave of anti-Tung-lin terrorism loomed in the spring of 1626, when orders were given for the arrests of a recent governor of the Soochow region, Chou Ch'i-yüan (see Chang Hsieh), and six "good elements" of the area, including Kao. Six of these seven, like their 1625 predecessors, died under torture in the palace prison: Chou Ch'i-yüan, Chou Tsung-chien 周宗建 (T. 季侯, H. 來玉, Pth. 忠毅, 1582-1626, cs 1613), Chou Shun-ch'ang, Miao Ch'ang-ch'i (qq. v.), Li Ying-sheng 李應昇 (T. 仲建, H. 次見, Pth. 忠毅, 1593-1626, cs 1616), and Huang Tsun-su (ECCP, p. 351). Miao and Chou Tsung-chien had already been taken into custody and the metropolis of Soochow thrown into a turmoil of popular uprisings by the arrest of Chou Shun-ch'ang, when Kao learned on April 12 that mounted guardsmen of the dreaded imperial bodyguard had indeed arrived in Wu-hsi to arrest him as well. He spent a calm evening with his family, ostensibly making plans to go into town in the morning to give himself up, and then, alone after midnight, drowned himself in a pond on the family estate. In his study he left a farewell letter to friends and a memorial to be forwarded to Peking which explained that "although my name has been erased from the register, I formerly was a great minister, and when a great minister accepts disgrace the state is also disgraced. Therefore I have done obeisance toward the throne and have followed the example of Ch'ü P'ing (the ancient poet-official Ch'ü Yüan). I may not have requited the ruler's mercy, but I shall hope to do so in the hereafter."

In 1629, after the deaths of the emperor and Wei Chung-hsien, the reputations of the martyred Tung-lin partisans were officially rehabilitated. Kao was posthumously promoted to be junior guardian of the heir apparent and concurrently minister of War and was canonized as Chung-hsien 忠憲 (loyal and judicial). A chronological biography was prepared by his favorite disciple and fellow townsman Hua Yün-ch'eng 華允誠 (T. 汝立, H. 鳳超, 1588-1648, cs 1622), who was eventually put to death by the Manchus for refusing to adopt the queue. Kao's writings were collected and edited by another disciple, Ch'en Lung-cheng (q. v.), and were printed in 1632 under the title Kao-tzu i-shu 高子遺書, 12 ch. The work was reprinted in 1689 and again in 1876.

A more complete collection of Kao's

works was published in 1742 by Hua Hsi-min 華希閔 (T. 豫原, fl. 1682-1742), another member of the Hua family of Wu-hsi. It consists of ten titles: *Chou-i K'ung-i, Ch'un-ch'iu K'ung-i, Chu-tzu chieh-yao* (*see* above), *Ssu-shu chiang-i* 四書講義, 1 *ch.*, *Tung-lin shu-yüan hui-chiang* 會講, 1 *ch.*, *Ch'eng-tzu chieh-lu* 程子節錄, 4 *ch.*, *Ch'eng-tzu wen-chi-ch'ao* 文集抄, 1 *ch.*, *Chiu-cheng-lu* 就正錄, 1 *ch.*, *Kao-tzu wen-chi* 文集, 6 *ch.*, and *Kao-tzu shih-chi* 詩集, 8 *ch.* Unaccountably the *Kao-tzu ch'üan-shu* is very scarce, with only four copies recorded as extant. The only possible reason seems to be that it was affected by the banning of the *Kao-tzu i-shu* in the 1780s.

After Kao died in 1626, his elder son Kao Shih-ju 世儒, was charged with failure to guard his father from committing suicide and sent in disgrace to serve as a common soldier at the frontier but eventually was given a minor office. Another son, Kao Shih-ning 世寧, devoted himself to a life of quiet study. The Kao family remained prominent in Wu-hsi life, and especially in the region's intellectual life, for several generations. Kao P'an-lung's nephew Kao Shih-t'ai 世泰 (T. 彙旃, H. 石屋遺氓, 1604-76?, cs 1637) and his grandnephew Kao Yü 愈 (T. 紫超) were both known as scholars. From 1641 to 1643 Kao Shih-t'ai served as assistant surveillance commissioner of Hukuang in charge of education of the province's northern territory. He then retired and led the life of a member of the local gentry under the Manchu regime.

The Tung-lin Academy, partially destroyed in 1625, was totally demolished by government order soon after Kao's suicide in 1626. After the death of Emperor Chu Yu-chiao the official suppression of private academies terminated. Portions of the academy were restored in 1628-29, and scholarly activities resumed there under the leadership of Kao's disciple Wu Kuei-sen 吳桂森 (H. 覲華, d. 1632) of Wu-hsi. From Wu's death until 1643 the academy became inactive; then Kao's nephew Kao Shih-t'ai, having given up his official career, devoted the remaining thirty years of his life to being master of the academy. He rebuilt it almost entirely and maintained its lively intellectual activities. Then in the 1680s it became a government-supported institution and flourished on a new scale thereafter. Although destroyed by fire during the nineteenth-century Tai-p'ing rebellion, it was again rebuilt; and it survived into the twentieth century, transformed into a public elementary school.

The Tung-lin partisans have fared well in the judgment of history; almost all histories in the late Ming era are pro-Tung-lin. During the years 1625 to 1627, however, anyone accused of Tung-lin affiliation was liable to persecution and prosecution, suffering fates ranging from demotion and dismissal to death and confiscation of properties. An anti-Tung-lin viewpoint suffuses a special "white paper" published by Wei Chung-hsien's adherents compiled from February to June, 1626, entitled *San-ch'ao yao-tien* 三朝要典, 24 *chüan*. It concentrates on the documents of the "three great cases," citing the memorials by Tung-lin partisans chiefly for condemnation. By imperial order in June, 1628, the book was ordered destroyed but a few copies are extant. At least eight lists of Tung-lin partisans compiled by their enemies in Wei Chung-hsien's time, and ranging from thirty-five to three hundred ninety-three names, remain extant: *Tung-lin tang-jen pang* 黨人榜 (four complete texts, including that in *Tung-lin lieh-chuan* 列傳), *Tung-lin tien-chiang lu* 點將錄 (five complete texts, including that in *Hsien-po chih-shih* 先撥志始), *Tung-lin p'eng-tang lu* 朋黨錄, *Tung-lin hsieh-ts'ung* 脅從, *Tung-lin t'ung chih-lu* 同志錄, *Tung-lin chi-kuan* 籍貫, *Tao-che Tung-lin huo* 盜柘東林夥, and *Huo-huai feng-ch'iang lu* 夥壞封疆錄 (the latter six lists all in *Cho-chung chih-yü* 酌中志餘). Versions of seven of these lists were printed from an old manuscript in 1958 by the Kwangtung provincial Chung-shan Library, under the title *Tung-lin pieh-sheng* 別乘. Manuscript versions of six of the lists are owned by the Seikadō Library, Tokyo.

A Tung-lin party roster, compiled by a friendly hand, is one entitled *Chung-cheng piao-t'i* 衆正標題, which lists all those persecuted by the eunuch party, including chiefly Tung-lin members but also many who did not belong to the party. It seems to exist in only two versions:

(a) In Vol. IV of the old manuscript collection *Pi-ts'e ts'-ung-shuo* 祕册叢說, now in the possession of the Academia Sinica Library, Taiwan: 378 names, without attribution of authorship.

(b) In Vol. I of the Naikaku Bunko (Tokyo) copy of Chin Jih-sheng 金日昇 (T. 茂生, H. 東吳野臣), *Sung-t'ien lu-pi* 頌天臚筆: 379 names, with preface and postface both by Chin, dated 1633. This roster is also included in the Columbia University copy but not in several other copies consulted. The Columbia University copy, however, is printed from blocks that had eleven names deleted, possibly because they were later adjudged as not qualified.

Bibliography

1/243/15b; 3/227/13b; 39/2/14a; 52/x/7a; 61/115/23b; 77/5/6b (1936); 82/2/4a; 83/58/16a; SK (1930), 5/4b, 28/9a, 95/4a, 172/13a; Hua Yün-ch'eng, "Kao Chung-hsien-kung nien-p'u" 年譜 (*Kao-tzu i-shu* ed.); *Tung-lin shu-yüan chih* 書院志 (1881 rev. ed.), 7/45a, 47b; MSL, Shen-tsung, Kuang-tsung, and Hsi-tsung; Ku Ying-t'ai (ECCP), *Ming-ch'ao chi-shih pen-mo*, chüan 61, 65–68, 71; Li Yen 李棪, *Tung-lin tang-chi k'ao* 籍考, Peking, 1957; Wen Ping 文秉 (1609–69), *Hsien-po chih-shih* 先撥志始; Wu Ying-chi 吳應箕 (1594-1645), *Tung-lin pen-mo* 本末; Liu Hsin-hsüeh 劉心學 (1599–1674), *Ssu-ch'ao tacheng lu* 四朝大政錄; Ku Ling 顧苓 (fl. in 1940s), *San-ch'ao ta-i lu* 三朝大議錄; Liu Jo-yü, *Cho-chung chih*; Li Ch'ing 李清, *San-ch'ao yeh-chi* 三朝野記; Wu Ying-chi, *Ch'i-Chen liang-ch'ao po-fu lu* 啓禎兩朝剝復錄; Hsieh Kuo-chen 謝國楨, *Ming Ch'ing chih chi tang-she yün-tung k'ao* 明清之際黨社運動考 (Shanghai, 1934); id., *Wan-Ming shih-chi k'ao* 晚明史籍考 (1933); Chu Tan 朱倓, "Tung-lin tang-jen pang k'ao-cheng" 考證, YCHP, XIX(1936, 157–71; id., "Tung-lin chu-shu k'ao" 著述考, *Kuang-chou hsüeh-pao*, I (1937), 1; Takehiko Okada 岡

田武彦, "Toringaku no seishin" 東林學の精神, *Tōhōgaku* 東方學, no. 6 (June, 1953), 77.

Charles O. Hucker

KAO Tai 高岱 (T. 伯宗, 鹿坡居士), scholar-official, a native of Ching-shan 京山, Hukuang, came from a family of military registry. After graduating as *chin-shih* in 1550, he was assigned to the ministry of Justice. On becoming director of one of its bureaus, he became concerned over the harsh penalties meted out to three fellow officials in his ministry: two secretaries of a bureau, Tung Ch'uan-ts'e 董傳策 (T. 原漢, H. 幼海, cs 1550) and Chang Ch'ung 張翀 (T. 子儀, cs 1553, d. 1579), and a supervising secretary named Wu Shih-lai 吳時來 (T. 惟修, H. 悟齋, cs 1553, d. 1590, Pth. 忠恪). They had joined (April 16, 1558) in a memorial denouncing Grand Secretary Yen Sung (*q.v.*) and his son. Earnestly pleading their cause before the minister of Justice, Cheng Hsiao (*q.v.*), temporarily serving as minister of War, Kao Tai succeeded in obtaining a lessening of their sentences—from death to exile. Yen was incensed; so, when the prince of Ching, Chu Tsai-ch'uan (*see* Chu Hou-ts'ung), was on the point of leaving (1561) for his estate in Te-an 德安, Hukuang, Yen ordered Kao to accompany him as an administrator; this prevented future promotion.

Kao enjoyed writing and began, while in Peking, to collect material for a book on military actions beginning with the early successes of Chu Yüan-chang and concluding with the unhappy failures of Ch'iu Luan (*q. v.*) in 1550/51, of which Kao himself was a witness. This work, completed in 1557, entitled *Hung-yu lu* 鴻猷錄, 16 *ch.*, is divided into sixty topics. It was considered for suppression in the eighteenth century, but allowed to survive, — only a few sentences were ordered expunged from the text. It is rare, nonetheless. It was first printed in 1573 in Chengtu and again in Soochow in 1580. The Library of Congress has a copy of the latter edition. It is now available in the *Ts'ung-shu chi-ch'eng* and other collectanea. Kao also wrote other books, but these seem not to be extant. A collection of his poems, *Hsi-ts'ao shih-chi* 西 曹詩集, 9 *ch.*, printed in the Chia-ching period, has survived.

On his death Kao was buried west of Ching-yüan shan 京源山, in his native district, not far from the grave of one of the men he saved from execution, Chang Ch'ung.

Kao Tai had two younger brothers, also noted for their scholarship, Kao Ch'i 啟 (T. 叔宗, cs 1556) and Kao Yü 礐 (T. 季宗, H. 雲萍) who died aged eighteen *sui*, just after qualifying for the *chü-jen*.

Another Kao Tai (T. 魯瞻), a native of K'uai-chi, Chekiang, who received a military degree in the Ch'ung-chen period in Peking, and who served briefly under the prince of Lu, Chu I-hai (ECCP), is sometimes confused with the historian as in the *Harvard-Yenching Institute Sinological Index*, series no. 24.

Bibliography

40/45/25a; 64/乙7/4b; 84/丁上/59b; MSL (1965), Shih-tsung, 7738, 8188, 8221; *Ching-shan-hsien chih* (1882), 10/7b, 21/22b, 22/3b; *Hupeh t'ung-chih* 1934), 3060, 3755; SK (1930), 49/8a; Sun Tien-ch'i (1957), 127; *Hu-peh shih-cheng* 詩徵 comp. by Chang Hsing-hai 章星海 (1881), 26/9a; Kao Tai, *Hung-yu lu*, TsSCC, 3915; *Harvard Yenching Inst. Sin. Index*, no. 24, 165; *Hsi-ts'ao shih-chi* (NLP microfilm, no. 1048); *L. of C. Catalogue of Rare Books*, 126; W. Franke, *Sources*, 2.2.2.

L. Carrington Goodrich

KENG Ch'ing, *see* **CHING Ch'ing**

KENG Chiu-ch'ou 耿九疇 (T. 禹範, H. 恒 菴), May 20, 1396-September 13, 1460, scholar-official, was a native of Lu-shih 盧氏, Honan. Keng's ancestors, who had settled in P'ing-ting-chou 平定州, Shansi, for several generations, abandoned their military career after the fall of the Jurchen-Chin dynasty and became civil servants under the Mongols in the early years of the 13th century. His father, Keng Ch'iung 絅 (T. 汝明, November 10, 1347-June 28, 1411), a Confucian scholar, was appointed an instructor in the district school of Lu-shih in 1398, where he served until his death; his family remained to make it their home. Graduating as *chü-jen* in 1417, Keng Chiu-ch'ou achieved the *chin-shih* in 1424. For some unknown reason, he received no appointment until April, 1431, when he became a supervising secretary. In 1437 he rose to be a vice superintendent of the salt administration of the Huai River region with headquarters at Yang-chow. Keng toured the salt depots extensively and made several suggestions designed to insure justice and promote efficiency. One of the two measures, which the authorities subsequently adopted, was the maintenance of a fair distribution of shares of production among the salt households; the other was the reduction of samples of salt for examination, so that officials might be less likely to take any for their own use. When his mother died in April, 1443, he relinquished office to meet the mourning requirement. Before the period was over, however, he was recalled (February, 1445), through the recommendation of the eunuch Wang Chen (*q. v.*), who was impressed by his credentials, to fill the vacancy of superintendent of the salt administration.

In June, 1449, Keng became involved in a scandal which almost ruined his career. Upon investigation by officials from the ministry of Revenue into the misappropriation of government resources, they discovered that certain salt merchants who should have received payment in either salt or cash for shipping rice to the guards on the northern frontiers had made claims under both categories. Thereupon the secretary of the ministry, Ch'en Ju-yen 陳汝言 (T. 納之, cs 1442, d. January 22, 1462), accused Keng of accepting bribes to make this wrongdoing possible. Keng then submitted evidence and succeeded in convincing the emperor of his innocence; as a result he received promotion to be vice minister of Justice. In December the emperor sent him to Feng-yang 鳳陽 (Anhwei) to take charge of the rehabilitation of the refugees dislocated by the invasion of Esen(*q.v.*), with the order that they be alloted provisions and assistance in farming, and exemption from tax levies for three years. Keng was given (February, 1450) the additional duty of superintendent of the salt administration of the Huai River region, where he served for two years. During this time he introduced a rule forbidding merchants, charged with supplying grain to the north, to exchange their commodities for salt en route, instead of shipping the produce to its destination. Nine months later he became as well governor of Feng-yang and adjacent prefectures and sub-prefectures in the same area. In this capacity he overhauled the administration and settled numerous judicial cases. In November, 1451, the court recalled Keng to Peking, after which it transferred him to Shensi (April, 1452) as governor, later raising his rank to that of vice censor-in-chief (October, 1453), which gave him greater authority.

During his administration in Shensi, Keng devoted himself to strengthening the defense of the frontier against the intrusion of the Mongol tribesmen, and improving the welfare of the inhabitants. He discovered corruption among several military commanders, punishing one of them for subjecting the rank and file to hard labor in his own interest, and spurned a proposal by the military authorities to increase the number of frontier guards. He argued that efficiency could be achieved by strict discipline, whereas more guards would inevitably demand more grain and other supplies. He also stopped the local people from leaving the area in autumn and winter to avoid the Mongol intruders; it was the duty of the guards to protect them, he insisted, and under no circumstances should their daily occupations be interrupted for fear of invasion.

On an occasion when the emperor requested a frank opinion after the appearance of an ominous cosmological sign, Keng responded with a memorial pleading with the emperor to recruit learned scholars to give their advice, be judicious in exercising rewards and punishments, and appoint men of caliber for service in the local administration and border defense. The emperor is said to have accepted this with becoming grace.

Shortly after his reinstallation, Emperor Chu Ch'i-chen (*q. v.*) summoned Keng from Shensi and made him censor-in-chief (April, 1457). In June Keng submitted a five-point formula in which he proposed:1) arousing the moral awareness of the officials; 2) expediting the trial of convicted offenders; 3) paying further attention to agriculture; 4) reducing the grain allowance to soldiers to lighten the burden of the farming population; 5) bolstering the authority of the Censorate. Except for the fourth, the emperor ordered the adoption of his recommendations.

Before long, however, he became involved in the case of Yang Hsüan 瑄 (*q. v.*), a courageous censor, whom the eunuch Ts'ao Chi-hsiang and his associate Shih Heng (*qq. v.*) charged with spreading scandal about them. Probably because they supported Yang in discrediting these two imperial favorites, Keng and several of his colleagues were indicted as conspirators. They were subsequently cashiered and put in jail. A few days later, however, the court changed its decision; instead it demoted Keng to be a junior administration commissioner of Kiangsi and then a month later transferred him to Szechwan. In December, 1458, through the recommendation of Grand Secretary Li Hsien (*q. v.*), the court pardoned him and made him a minister of Justice in Nanking. Keng died at his post two years later at the age of sixty-four. The next emperor, Chu Chien-shen (*q.v.*), in May, 1465, gave, to Keng's grandson the privilege of enrolling in the National University. After two years (July, 1467), through the petition of his second son, Keng Yü 裕 (T. 好問, H. 青厓, 1430-February 3, 1496), he honored Keng Chiu-ch'ou with the posthumous name Ch'ing-hui 清惠 (honest and benevolent).

Keng Yü, a *chin-shih* of 1454 and a Hanlin bachelor, was assigned to be a supervising secretary in June, 1456. After twenty years in minor offices he became chancellor of the National University (January, 1477), vice minister of Personnel (August), and then as minister (September, 1486). Two months later the court transferred him to Nanking, where he served successively as minister of Rites and of War with the title of military adjunct (December, 1487). Following the enthronement of Chu Yu-t'ang (*q. v.*) he was recalled to Peking, and served both as minister of Rites (November, 1488) and for the second time—of Personnel (July, 1493). In October, 1494, he received the honorific of grand protector of the heir apparent and after his death the posthumous name Wen-k'o 文恪 (cultured and faithful). He is described by his colleagues as learned, broad-minded, and articulate, and had an impressive figure. Like his father he earned a reputation for uprightness and frugality. He is credited with two memorials which he submitted during the reign of Chu Yu-t'ang, remonstrating with the monarch for failure to pay attention to state affairs and unwillingness to undertake reforms in government administration. These are included in the *Ming ching-shih wen-pien*, edited by Ch'en Tzu-lung (ECCP), under the title *Keng Wen-k'o kung chi* 公集. The gazetteer of Lu-shih also contains a sample of his essay writing.

Bibliography

1/158/12a, 183/12a; 5/24/56a, 48/1a; 8/28/1a; 9/后 2/13b; 61/125/11a; 63/15/15a; MSL (1963), Hsüan-tsung, 1773, Ying-tsung, ch. 125–318, Hsien-tsung (1964), 146, Hsiao-tsung, 1980; KC (1958), 2109, 2685; Ho Ch'iao-yüan, *Ming-shan ts'ang* (1971 ed.), 3739, 3745; Ch'en Tzu-lung, *Ming ching-shih wen-pien* (1964 ed.), 339; *Lu-shih-hsien chih* (1892), 7/4b, 8/3a, 14/17b, 15/1a, 16/1a, 29b.

Hok-lam Chan

KENG Ping-wen 耿炳文, *ca*. 1335–December 18, 1404, a native of Hao-chou 濠州 (Anhwei), served as a military and civil official chiefly in Chekiang and Shensi in the Hung-wu era, and commanded the imperial army in 1399 against Chu Ti (*q.v.*). His family was of peasant stock and had long resided in the Hao-chou township, T'ai-p'ing hsiang 太平鄉, in which the family of Chu Yüan-chang had settled before the great famine of 1344. Keng, his father, Keng Chün-yung 君用 (d. 1356), his father's elder brother, Keng Chün-mei 美, and the latter's grandson, Keng Jui 瑞 (d. 1364), joined forces with Kuo Tzu-hsing (*q.v.*) at Hao-chou as had Chu Yüan-chang a few months earlier. According to some sources, another military leader, the chief military commissioner, Keng Chung 耿忠 (d. 1392), who joined at the same time, was Keng Ping-wen's younger brother, although his given name would seem to make this doubtful. The Keng family served with Chu in his early campaigns in Ch'u 滁-chou and Ho 和 -chou, and in 1355 Keng Ping-wen was one of the two officers whom Chu called to his side in his attempt to stop the battle between two allied forces at Ho-chou (*see* Kuo Tzu-hsing).

After crossing the Yangtze with Chu in 1355, they invaded the territory of Chang Shih-ch'eng (*q.v.*) to the southeast. Keng Chün-yung was promoted to the rank of regional military commander, but he was killed during the successful assaults on I-hsing 宜興, west of Lake T'ai in early 1356. Keng Ping-wen then inherited command of his father's army and took part in the seizure by Teng Yü (*q.v.*) of Kuang-te 廣德 (Anhwei) that summer. In February, 1357, Keng was sent back to Lake T'ai to take the city of Ch'ang-hsing 長興 (Chekiang). This city at the southwest end of the lake was described as the gateway to Chekiang and became a defensive strong-point blocking the westward expansion of Chang Shih-ch'eng, who still held Hu-chou 湖州 on the south shore. Keng was to spend ten years here in command of the garrison, successfully defending the city against repeated attacks by Chang Shih-ch'eng.

In March, 1357, the Yung-hsing wing commandery 永興翼元帥府 was established for local military administration and Keng appointed commander. His principal official subordinates were Liu Ch'eng 劉成 and Li Ching-yüan 李景元. He was also ably assisted by a mathematician and engineer, Wen Hsiang-ch'ing 溫祥卿, who later served in the Ming central administration, rising to the office of minister of War in February, 1385; he was soon demoted and sent to Szechwan where he died. In October the wing commandery was reorganized as the Ch'ang-hsing Guard with Keng as commander. Chang Shih-ch'eng's first great counterattack came in October, 1360, when he sent his general Lü Chen (see Chang Shih-ch'eng) across the lake with a large fleet. After the enemy had landed, Keng engaged them in a long and costly battle and finally drove them off. In June of the following year, in anticipation of new attacks, Keng asked Chu Yüan-chang to let him use some of the troops of T'ang Ho (q.v.) at Kuang-te. Chu denied his request and told him to train local recruits instead. This left Keng with a mere seven thousand men in December, 1361, when Chang Shih-ch'eng sent Li Po-sheng (see Li Wen-chung) at the head of an army, said to number one hundred thousand men, to attack him. Chu then dispatched relief forces from Nanking, Kuang-te, I-hsing, and Ning-kuo 寧國 under such eminent commanders as Ch'en Te 陳德, the marquis of Lin-chiang 臨江侯 (d. 1377), Fei Chü 費聚, the marquis of P'ing-liang 平涼侯 (executed 1390), and Hua Kao 華高, the marquis of Kuang-te 廣德 (d. 1371). These impressive forces suffered a disastrous defeat soon after their arrival, when Li destroyed their camp in a night attack and drove them off. Keng then retreated within the city walls and locked the gates. Liu Ch'eng was killed in a last futile sortie and Li began his siege. He built nine forts and a number of movable siege

towers, dammed the moat with earth and rocks, launched fire-boats against the city's water gates, and tried repeatedly to storm the walls. When the struggle had gone on for a month, Chu sent Ch'ang Yü-ch'un (q.v.) with another army and this time he was able to lift the siege.

In October, 1364, when the military organization underwent a series of changes, the wing commandery was abolished and the guard and chiliarch system were substituted. There were national capital guards and local garrison guards. Of the latter category, the first one established seems to have been the Ch'ang-hsing guards, of which Keng Ping-wen was appointed the hereditary commander. He thus defended the place of his own fief. In November Chang Shih-ch'eng sent his brother, Chang Shih-hsin (see Chang Shih-ch'eng) in a last attempt to take Ch'ang-hsing. Defeated in his first attack, Chang Shih-hsin returned with reinforcements, and in December Chu ordered T'ang Ho to help Keng. After an indecisive battle had been joined by Chang Shih-hsin and T'ang Ho, Keng led his troops out of the city and defeated the attacking force, lifting the siege. During the winter of 1366–67, from his base at Ch'ang-hsing, Keng supported the final campaign against Chang Shih-ch'eng by helping Hsü Ta (q.v.) capture Hu-chou.

After the fall of this city, Keng was rewarded for his services by appointment to the office of assistant military commissioner-in-chief. With the temporary field rank of general, he was assigned to Hsü Ta's command for the invasion of north China. While the main armies continued their campaigns towards the north and west, Keng's talents were turned primarily to administration. From the spring of 1369 until 1390, he was permanently stationed in Sian. Here, as the supreme military officer of the central government's chief military command in Shensi, he ranked above the provincial military command at Sian and its Kansu branch headquarters at Kan 甘-chou. In 1370 he was also appointed to the civil office of vice administrator of Shensi. In the same year, when an estate was created at Sian for the emperor's second son, Chu Shuang (*see* Chu Yüan-chang), Keng was made the prince's military councillor, and on November 29 invested as marquis of Ch'ang-hsing. Other officials came and went during these two decades, and more famous generals, such as Hsü Ta, T'ang Ho, Li Wen-chung, Mu Ying, Lan Yü, and Kuo Ying (*qq.v.*) led the great frontier campaigns in Shensi, while Keng wrestled with the day-to-day problems of agriculture, military recruitment, training and supply, external trade, and the suppression of local disorders. After his "retirement" in 1390, he repeatedly was sent back to Shensi on administrative missions and campaigns which extended his involvement in the affairs of the province to the very end of the first reign.

During the Hung-wu period, Shensi province appears to have been practically ungovernable. That Keng was able to bear a major share of the administrative burden there for twenty years testifies to his patience and good judgment. Very large numbers of troops were required in Shensi for the northern frontier, which reached out from the Kansu panhandle to eastern modern Sinkiang (Kansu under the Ming was administered as a part of Shensi), for the western frontier with its large Tibetan population, and for the southern frontier, including the Ch'in-ling mountains and the headwaters of the Han River, just north of the Szechwan border. All these troops (in 1391, Keng reported more than two hundred thirty thousand of them, including about one hundred twenty-five thousand men of the Shensi guards) had to be maintained in a province that was economically poor and thinly populated (294,526 families registered in 1392). When Shensi officials tried to find the revenue required to meet military and civil costs of government, they were caught between the overburdened and recalcitrant taxpayers and a central government in Nanking that was committed to the greatest possible economy during the period of recon-

struction, and was therefore inclined to resist frontier demands for subsidies. The resulting pressure of tax and compulsory service on the local population intensified local resistance to authority which, in turn, led to greater reliance on military measures of control and greater military costs.

The province's agricultural economy was in a depressed state. A censor, reporting in 1375 on his inspection of Shensi, offered a vivid description. Away from the irrigated plains of the Wei 渭 valley, he saw a pattern of shifting slash-and-burn cultivation, of temporary plots closely bound by thickets of wild growth from which leopards and tigers emerged at night to prey on the villagers. From the censor's point of view, this kind of cultivation was undesirable because it made assessment and collection of taxes practically impossible. He also observed that, when agents were sent to round up the taxpayers for their corvée service, they fled "like rats and snakes into their places of hiding." The solution he proposed was to restore ancient irrigation systems in areas where they had once flourished and had been allowed to break down. This would increase production and tie the Shensi farmers to permanent farming in the plains and therefore make them taxable. His optimism was tempered, however, by his judgment that the highland people would rather continue their hard but free existence than submit to taxation and administrative control. He proposed that farmers be lured out of the mountains on the promise of tax-exemption and limited corvée service. (But he failed to specify the period of exemption.) The emperor, impressed by the censor's arguments, ordered the provincial government to carry out his proposal.

Keng probably achieved a modest success in his efforts to increase agricultural production and public revenue. In 1375, the year of the censor's report, he carried out an order to dredge the Ching-yang Great Canal 涇陽洪渠, which watered a stretch of

200 *li* of land near the confluence of the Ching 涇 and Wei Rivers. Four years later Li Wen-chung's suggestion, that the Lung-shou 龍首 fresh-water canal serving Sian be restored and lined with stone, was approved, and the project completed by the prefectural authorities. For the first time in years, the inhabitants had water fit to drink. At the very end of the Hung-wu period, the Ching-yang system had silted up again and Keng was ordered to clear it; he dredged one hundred three thousand *chang* (or close to two hundred miles) of channel. When the irrigation system was functioning properly, the plain around Sian produced a large surplus of grain for use by military units in less favored areas, and in 1386 officials in Sian asked permission to commute that year's grain levies to money because the granaries were already filled. But the problem of the evasive mountain farmers remained, and in 1397 the emperor could still complain that ever since the pacification in 1368 poor Chinese and minority peoples in Shensi had been hiding and withholding their share of taxes and labor. Another approach to the problem of the grain deficit was the establishment of military agricultural colonies. A general order of 1380 called for two thirds of the Shensi guardsmen to engage in farming as their main occupation, a proportion that was modified from time to time thereafter. Also, thousands of guardsmen were moved from eastern Shensi to the Kansu region to establish colonies for the support of guards stationed there. The military agricultural colony system proved difficult to maintain, however, and in 1392 the emperor complained that most soldiers assigned to agricultural labor in the northwest were running away. The erosion of the tax base by emigration from the province had become so general by 1397 that the emperor felt compelled to order the troops guarding the eastern passes to turn back civilians and soldiers attempting to move into Shansi and Honan.

For all the efforts in agriculture, short-ages persisted and other means to lessen these had to be adopted. Officials traded cloth to aborigines, who did not grow textile fibers, in exchange for their grain and beans. The system of reimbursing merchants with salt certificates for transporting grain to the frontiers was used in Shensi. Military horses were obtained from the Tibetans in exchange for tea, most of which was grown in Szechwan. These measures were undermined by illegal private commercial competition in salt and tea, however, and consequently led to greater conflict between the authorities and the local population. Aside from these peaceful methods, large numbers of horses, cattle, and sheep were obtained as war-booty from the Tibetans and Mongols.

The provincial government, whether on its own initiative or on orders from Nanking, tried to improve its relations with the local population. Confucian academies were established, such as the three authorized in remote Yenan 延安 in 1382, to provide easier access to official careers. Another was established in Kan-chou, where the branch military command had complained in 1395 that the young men were growing up illiterate for lack of instruction, and that there were not enough clerks in the region even to draft official documents. Public grain storage quotas were established to provide for famine relief and, as elsewhere in the empire, tax remissions were ordered in times of poor harvests. Nanking sometimes supported the local population against the provincial authorities. The tendency of Keng and others to supplement military labor by conscripting civilians to work on fortifications was restrained by imperial orders, especially at times when this would interfere with agricultural production. Similarly, when tax payments were commuted to money for the year 1386, the emperor ordered a rate of commutation more favorable to the taxpayers than that proposed by the province. A minor point with the same implications for Shensi was that Keng's request in 1371 that his whole marquisate stipend of 1,500 *tan* per year be paid out of Shensi taxes was denied and instead was to be divided, 500 to come from Shensi and 1,000 from western Chekiang, the region in which his marquisate was situated. Efforts were also made to bring the Shensi Tibetans into the body politic. In 1374 Keng obtained official appointments for thirty-nine "chiefs" who had served him well. Three years later, however, the emperor, in going over military records, discovered that Tibetan guardsmen in Shensi were being discriminated against by their officers, who were issuing them rations below the quota, and ordered that they be paid as well as Chinese guardsmen since they were performing the same service. Special awards were sometimes given the Tibetan soldiers and, in 1393, officially approved chiefs were issued gold and copper tallies.

On the negative side, the provincial military authorities had to repel the attacks by Mongols on the northern frontier between 1376 and 1378, and suppress a great rebellion by the "Eighteen Tribes" of Tibetans near T'ao 洮-chou in 1379. Another campaign was made necessary by a rising of a coalition of non-Chinese peoples in Kansu under a certain Yüeh-lu t'ieh-mu-er 月魯帖米兒 in 1392. South of Sian, in the Ch'in-ling mountains and the upper Han River valley, banditry was a chronic problem. A great uprising occurred in 1397 under the leadership of Kao Fu-hsing 高福興 and the monk Li P'u-chih 李普治. In the later stages of the campaign, Keng, commissioned as the western campaign general, led one hundred fifty thousand troops from Shensi and Szechwan against the rebels. In this case, as after the rising of Yüeh-lu t'ieh-mu-er five years before, one measure taken to make the pacification permanent was to inscribe the names of the surrendered rebels and their families on the military registers. Beyond the borders of Shensi, Keng also served in two northern campaigns under Hsü Ta and Lan Yü in 1383 and 1388 and in a campaign against the Szechwan

Man rebels in 1386 under Fu Yu-te (*q.v.*).

Keng received only modest rewards for his long service in Shensi. He was not promoted in official rank after 1370. When allowed to return to his Ch'anghsing estate in 1390, he received two hundred ounces of yellow gold, two thousand ounces of silver, thirty bolts of brocade, and a large sum in paper notes. He had little time to enjoy this treasure, however, because in April of the following year he returned to Shensi on a tour of inspection. He became a relative of the imperial family by marriage in 1395, when his eldest son, Keng Hsüan 璿, married a daughter of the late heir apparent, Chu Piao (*q.v.*).

When Chu Ti rebelled in 1399 against the Chien-wen emperor, Keng remained loyal to the latter as a lifelong supporter of his grandfather. Called out of retirement to command the imperial armies, he led the army to the north, despite his years (he was then about sixty-four). He tried to confine the rebel forces by deploying his troops at various points around Peiping. The Yen army unexpectedly attacked and destroyed the imperial vanguard of nine thousand men at Hsiung-hsien 雄縣 west of Peiping. Forces in relief were ambushed and also destroyed. These reverses led to the defection of General Chang Pao 張保 at Mo-chou 鄚州. As the Yen army advanced, Keng withdrew his diminished forces southward into the city of Chen-ting 眞定. After several days of heavy fighting, the prince of Yen, recognizing that Keng, renowned for his skill in siege warfare, could not be easily defeated withdrew northwards. Meanwhile, however, word of the earlier imperial reverses had reached the emperor, who was persuaded by partisans of Li Ching-lung (*see* Li Wen-chung) to place command of the army in his incompetent hands. Keng was accordingly recalled and again retired to his home. In 1404 Keng was the subject of the improbable accusation of having furnished his house and wardrobe with utensils and clothes bearing insignia designed only for the emperor. When he had been informed of the charges, Keng hanged himself, and his sons suffered execution. The marquisate then terminated, although some survivors of the family lived on in Ch'ang-hsing.

Bibliography

1/88/1b, 130/6a; 5/8/3a; 20/4/1a; 42/8/3a, 26/9b; 61/95/19b; MSL (1962), T'ai-tsu, ch. 2–255, T'ai-tsung (1963), 0027, 0033, 0202; *KC* (1958), 943; Morris Rossabi, "Tea and Horse Trade with Inner Asia," *Journal of Asian History*, 4 (1970), 136.

Romeyn Taylor

KENG Ting-hsiang 耿定向(T. 在倫, H. 楚侗, 天臺), November 5, 1524-July 16, 1596, thinker and official, was a native of Ma-ch'eng 麻城-hsien, Huang-chou 黃州-fu, Hukuang. His grandfather and father, were gentlemen farmers who spent their lives in retirement in their native place. Keng Ting-hsiang was the eldest of four sons. His younger brothers were Keng Ting-li 理 (T. 子庸, H. 楚倥), Keng Ting-li 力 (T. 子健), and Keng Ting-yü 裕. Keng Ting-hsiang showed unusual ambition as a child, announcing to his grandfather, to whom he was much attached, that he wanted to become not just a government official, but a sage. At the age of thirteen he was sent away from home to study with a master, but returned for his grandfather's funeral. After an initial failure in the provincial examination of 1549, Keng Ting-hsiang studied assiduously, acquiring the *chü-jen* in 1552, and the *chin-shih* in 1556, with an excellent paper on the Spring and Autumn Annals. Late in the year, he was appointed a messenger, an employment which required constant travel between the capital and the provinces. He made good use of these occasions keeping contact with his brother, Keng Ting-li 理, with whom he was fond of discussing philosophy. Their circle of friends grew to include Wang Chi 畿, Lo Ju-fang, Ho Hsin-yin, Li Chih (*qq.v.*), and other important thinkers and scholars. In October, 1559, Keng Ting-hsiang was appointed a censor, assigned to the Yunnan branch office. At this time the government was under the control of Yen Sung (*q.v.*) and his son. Keng had the audacity to impeach (May, 1560) a protégé of Yen, Wu P'eng (*see* Cheng Jo-tseng) then minister of Personnel, and his son-in-law, Tung Fen (*see* Tung Ssu-chang), then Hanlin chancellor, for showing partiality in the exercise of their official duties and for accepting bribes. The emperor, Chu Hou-ts'ung (*q.v.*), took notice of the affair and rebuked Wu P'eng, but the protection of Yen Sung prevented the two men from receiving punishment. In May, 1561, Keng was transferred to Kansu, and, a year later, appointed education intendant in Nanking, where he and other thinkers participated in a meeting under Wang Chi's sponsorship (1565). In subsequent years, bothered by poor health, he submitted several memorials requesting sick leave, but without success. He is said to have recommended two persons to Yen Sung for official positions: Chang Chü-cheng (*q.v.*) and Lo Ju-fang. In September, 1567, after the accession of Emperor Chu Tsai-hou (*q.v.*), he was transferred to be assistant minister of the Grand Court of Revision, but the displeasure of Kao Kung (*see* Chang Chü-cheng), then in power, occasioned an unfavorable review of his exercise of duties, causing him to be demoted in 1570 to assistant magistrate of Heng-chou 横州, Kwangsi. After Kao's dismissal (July, 1572), Keng was promoted to prefectural judge in Heng 衡-chou, Hukuang, and then transferred to be secretary in the ministry of Works (1573), vice minister of the Seal Office (1574) and next of the Court of the Imperial Stud, then junior assistant censor-in-chief(1575). The death of his mother brought him back to his home for several years. In August, 1578, he was recalled to be governor of Fukien where he had some success in his effort to suppress the piratical activities of Lin Tao-ch'ien (*q.v.*). After mourning his father (d. 1580), he was appointed (April, 1584) a senior censor-in-chief, and rose to be vice censor-in-chief, then vice minister of Justice (May, 1585), censor-in-chief in Nanking (December, 1587), and finally minister of Revenue (October, 1589). But his official life was not without its small difficulties. On two occasions Keng had felt obliged to offer his resignation. The first occurred when the supervising secretary, Li I-ch'ien 李以謙 (T. 德光, H. 春臺, 1534–86, cs 1574), criticized him (late in 1584) for siding with Lu Kuang-tsu (*see* Lu Nan), vice minister of Personnel, after the latter had been impeached by the censor, Chao Chih-han 趙之翰 (cs 1592). But his request was ignored by the emperor. The second occasion (September, 1589) arose when Keng, as censor-in-chief, manifested his displeasure with a subordinate, Censor Wang Fan-ch'en 王藩臣, for having impeached Chou Chi 周繼 (cs 1565), governor of the southern metropolitan area, without giving him notice. Wang Fan-ch'en was punished by the loss of two months' salary, while Keng himself was in turn impeached by the supervising secretary, Hsü Hung-kang 許弘綱 (cs 1580), and others who defended Wang's action. Their appeal received an unfavorable hearing, and these men themselves were censured. At the time, Keng Ting-hsiang had already been named minister of Revenue; because of these events and his poor health, he insisted on resigning from office. After he had submitted nine memorials, his request was granted and he retired to his native place, where he made frequent visits to the scenic Mt. T'ien-t'ai 天臺, and earned the sobriquet Master T'ien-t'ai. He died seven years later, aged seventy-two. (The *shih-lu*, however, records his death belatedly on September 2, probably the date when the news reached the court.) He was awarded the posthumous name Kung-chien 恭簡 and the title of junior guardian of the heir apparent.

In spite of the incidents described above, Keng Ting-hsiang had a long and relatively smooth official career, serving successively under five grand secretaries: Yen Sung, Hsü Chieh, Chang Chü-cheng, Shen Shih-hsing, and Wang Hsi-chüeh (*qq.v.*). This was pointed out by Huang Tsung-hsi (ECCP), who criticised Keng for having compared Chang Chü-cheng to I-yin, the sage minister of King T'ang of early Shang at the time when Chang Chü-cheng had scandalized the country by choosing to remain in office as grand secretary instead of returning home to mourn his father's death (1578). Keng's praise of Chang amounted to flattery, which had earlier been criticized by Ku Yün-ch'eng (*see* Ku Hsien-ch'eng). Li Chih also found fault with him for not having intervened with Chang Chü-cheng in favor of Ho Hsin-yin, when the latter was imprisoned and sentenced to death. But Keng's disciple Chiao Hung (*q.v.*), who wrote a rather long biographical account of his master, pointed out that Keng had several times intervened on behalf of various persons, including Hai Jui (*q.v.*), when the latter was put in prison in 1566, and Hsü Chieh, who had disagreements with Kao Kung and was once (1571) severely criticized by a censor, Ch'i K'ang 齊康 (cs 1562). Keng contributed to Hsü's reinstatement and Kao's dismissal.

As a thinker, Keng Ting-hsiang, like Li Chih, belonged to the T'ai-chou branch of the school of Wang Shou-jen (*q.v.*). He criticized those scholars who considered intellectual knowledge itself to be wisdom, while attending only externally to the cultivation of character. He taught rather that ultimate truth, the Tao, was to be discovered in the mind (hsin 心) which in turn could be cultivated through a life of affairs (shih 事). He held that liang-chih 良知 was present and "already realised" (hsien-ch'eng 現成) in all, and need only be exercised in activity without requiring special effort toward inner development. All this shows the extent of Ch'an Buddhist influence on his thought. Keng Ting-hsiang objected to Li Chih nevertheless for openly admitting his Buddhist beliefs although he proved to be unequal to Li in debate. Huang Tsung-hsi later commented that Keng himself lacked a penetrating understanding of liang-chih, and had no real insight into ultimate truth.

Keng Ting-hsiang's two younger brothers each exemplified one side of his own interests. Keng Ting-li 理, the elder of the two, was a thinker and even more deeply influenced by Ch'an Buddhist teachings than Keng Ting-hsiang himself. It is said that as a young man, frequently reproved by his father for lack of success in his studies, he used to take solitary walks in the valleys, thus developing a fondness for silence and contemplation. He never served in any official capacity. As a teacher of philosophy he gave few lectures, preferring to enlighten his students as occasion arose. He was a good friend of Li Chih, to whose long speeches he gave quiet attention. He did not wholly approve of Keng Ting-hsiang's absorption in his political career, and remonstrated with him from time to time on his rationalization of such activity. The younger, Keng Ting-li 力, had an interesting official career. He acquired the *chin-shih* in 1571, was appointed secretary in the ministry of Works and, like Keng Ting-hsiang, rose to be censor-in-chief (1587) and afterwards vice minister of War in Nanking, and was awarded posthumously the title of minister of War.

Keng Ting-hsiang was a prolific writer. He was the author of two historical works; the first, *Hsien-chin i-feng* 先進遺風, 2 *ch.*, a compilation of the lives of selected Ming officials which he undertook during the time of power of Yen Sung, probably to admonish Yen and to promote the philosophy of Wang Shou-jen, was included in the *Pao-yen-t'ang Pi-chi hui-chi* 彙集 by Ch'en Chi-ju (ECCP); the second, *Shih-fu pao-chien* 碩輔寶鑑, 4 *ch.*, was first written during his term of office as education intendant in Nanking, and treats seventy-nine ministers of state including certain legendary personages of remote antiquity, as well as those of T'ang and Sung times. It was later expanded into 20 *chüan* to include people of the Ming period, supplemented by chronological tables, selected memorials, and other writings and poems. A copy of the original edition was recently reprinted in Taipei (1970). In 1585, when he was serving as vice minister of Justice, Keng collaborated with the minister Shu Hua 舒化 (T. 汝德, cs 1559) in compiling the *Ta Ming lü fu-li* 律附例 (Amplification of the official code), 30 *ch.* First ordered in 1373, the code was subjected to various additions and alterations in the next two centuries, but still needed revision. Arthur W. Hummel writes that Shu and Keng left 460 articles of the fundamental code untouched, but made corrections and alterations in 191 of the 382 supplementary statutes. It is said that the authors eliminated a number of cruel regulations of the Chia-ching period. The Library of Congress has a copy of the original edition, and it is available also in the *Hsüanlan-t'ang ts'ung-shu* of Cheng Chen-to (BDRC). Keng also left a selection of the savings of the Sung neo-Confucian philosopher Lu Chiu-yüan (1139–93), entitled *Hsiang-shan hsien-sheng yao-yü* 象山先生要語, 3 *ch.*, and a collection of philosophical and anecdotal notes called *Ch'üan-tzu* 權子, 1 *ch.* The former is a part of the *Lu Wang er hsien-sheng yao-yü lei-ch'ao* 陸王二先生要語類抄, edited and engraved (1574) by Hsiao Lin 蕭廩 (T. 可發, H. 兌嵎, cs 1565, d. 1587). The latter is included in the *Shuo-fu hsü* 說郛續, *chou* 弓 45. Keng's collection of writings, *Keng T'ien-t'ai hsien-sheng wen-chi* 文集, 20 *ch.*, which is devoted to his poetry, essays, memorials, correspondence, short biographies, and other works, as well as his recorded dialogues, was compiled in 1598 by his disciple Liu Yüan-ch'ing (*see* Chang Huang), and recently reprinted (1970) in Taipei.

Bibliography
1/221/5b, 7a; 3/207/5a; 5/29/63a; 16/38/6a, 59/9a, 74/5a, 76/7a, 97/7a, 106/5a, 153/9a; 32/79/37a; 42/77/3a; 83/35/1a, 7a; MSL (1965), Shen-tsung, 5626; KC (1958), 4022, 4607, 4775; *SK* (1933), 61/60, 95/109, 141/67, 178/92; Chiao Hung,

T'an-yüan chi (preface 1606), NLP microfilm no. 834, 33/1a, 35/15a; Keng Ting-hsiang, *Keng T'ien-t'ai hsien-sheng wen-chi* (1598 ed., Taipei repr.); *So-fu pao-chien* (Taipei repr., 1970); Li Wei-chen 李維楨, "Keng Kung-chien chia-chuan" 家傳, *Huang Ming wen-hai* microfilm, 4, 7, 1; *Ma-ch'eng-hsien chih* (1882), 18/13b; Wang Chi, Wang Lung-hsi ch'üan-chi (1822 ed., Taipei reprint, 1970), 4/13b, 27a, 10/7b; Okada Take-hiko 岡田武彦, *Ō Yōmei to Minmatsu no Jugaku* 王陽明と明末の儒學(Tokyo, 1970), 219; W. Franke, *Sources*, 5.6.14, 6.3.3. (5); A. W. Hummel, *The Library of Congress, Div. of Orientalia* (1938), 216; L. of C. *Catalogue of Rare Books*, 427.

Julia Ching

K'O Wei-ch'i 柯維騏 (T. 奇純, H. 希齋), 1497–1574, historian, came from a schol-ar-official family in P'u-t'ien 莆田, the prefectural city of Hsing-hua 興化, Fukien. One of the distinguished members of his family was his great-granduncle, K'o Ch'ien 潛 (T. 孟時, H. 竹巖, 1423–73), who headed the *chin-shih* list of 1451 and served successively as compiler (1451–64) and as chancellor of the Hanlin Academy (1464–74). In addition to participation in several official compilations, he left a col-lection of writings known as *Chu-yen wen-chi* 竹巖文集, 12 *ch.*, edited and printed by K'o Wei-ch'i; a manuscript copy of this is preserved in the Peiping National Library and is available on microfilm (no. 993). An enlarged version in 18 *chüan*, together with supplement and appendix, was printed in 1733. K'o Wei-ch'i's father, K'o Ying 英 (T. 汝傑, H. 西波, cs 1499), served as prefect of Hui-chou 徽州 (An-hwei) from 1508 to 1510. He had four sons, K'o Wei-ch'i being the youngest.

K'o Wei-ch'i graduated as *chü-jen* in 1516, and achieved the *chin-shih* in 1523. Following this K'o received an appointment as secretary of a bureau in the ministry of Revenue at Nanking, but was unable to assume office because of illness. When he finally recovered, a new regulation intro-duced by the ministry of Personnel (January, 1530), stipulating that officials who had failed to take office for more than three years, after the initial offer, be denied appointment. As a consequence, K'o Wei-ch'i remained at home, and devoted the rest of his years to teaching and scholarship. His reputation attracted a large number of students. He exhorted them to serious study and discouraged them from taking short cuts in the effort to enter officialdom. He also emphasized the principles of rever-ence and dedication, holding that the nour-ishment of these virtues would lead to a harmonious union with the cosmological order. In the following decades, two offi-cials, the censor Li Yüan-yang 李元陽 (T. 仁甫, H. 中谿, 1497–1580, cs 1526), and the governor of Fukien, T'an Lun (*q. v.*), reportedly submitted memorials recom-mending him for an appointment, but met with a negative response from the court. According to report, when P'u-t'ien was occupied by the pirates in December, 1562, K'o suffered serious losses and lived his remaining years in considerable poverty. About 1567 the secretary of Revenue at Nanking, Ts'en Yung-pin 岑用賓 (T. 允穆, cs 1559), is said to have recommended him again. This time, because of his age, K'o received only the honorary rank of ch'eng-te-lang 承德郎 (6b), a title usually reserved for scholars distinguised in his branch of scholarship. He died shortly afterwards at the age of seventy-seven.

K'o Wei-ch'i owes his reputation to his labors as a historian. His monumental work is the *Sung-shih hsin-pien* 宋史新編, 200 *ch.*, being a revision of the official history of the Sung dynasty published in 1345, in which the Yüan-appointed editors denied the Sung a place as the only legit-imate dynasty by putting its history on the same level as those of the Liao and Chin. During the Ming dynasty several attempts to rewrite the Sung history fail-ed to materialize; this included an official one in 1536 (*see* Yen Sung). It was Wang Chu 王洙 (T. 崇教, H. 一江, cs 1521), a contemporary of K'o Wei-ch'i, who after sixteen years, labor produced the first new Sung history called *Sung-shih chih* 質, 100

ch. (preface 1546), which is still extant. Wang's work, however, is considered inferior to that of K'o.

K'o apparently started his project about 1530 and brought it to completion before 1555. He placed the chronicles of the Liao and Chin in the "accounts of foreign nations" along with those of the Hsi-hsia, thereby legitimizing the Sung as the ruling house according to Ch'un-ch'iu principles. He also restored the imperial title of the last Sung emperors and accorded each of them a biography in the "imperial annals" which had been denied hitherto. In addition K'o rearranged the order of the biographies, assigning the first place to the neo-Confucian philosophers (tao-hsüeh 道學) instead of to the upright officials as in the official history. There is a story that K'o, wanting to concentrate on his work, castrated himself to keep from being disturbed by sensual and sexual thoughts. This anecdote, fanciful as it seems, may indicate K'o's deep devotion to his project. The *Sung-shih hsin-pien* was printed sometime around 1557;the original edition includes a preface by Huang Tso (*q. v.*), dated 1555, and a postscript by K'o's townsman, K'ang T'ai-ho 康太和 (T. 原中, H. 礪峯, cs 1535; 1499–1578), dated 1557. Though criticized by the compilers of the *Ssu-k'u* catalogue for its bias in favor of the Chinese, K'o's new Sung history is noted for its correction of errors, for elimination of duplicate sources, and for the addition of new biographies and chronological tables. It received praise from the eminent Ch'ing historian Ch'ien Ta-hsin (ECCP), though he also criticized it for its lack of new source materials. K'o's work was later modified and expanded by Wang Wei-chien 王惟儉 (T. 損仲, cs 1595), who renamed it *Sung-shih chi* 記, 250 *ch.*; this work, however, survives in manuscript only. A modern edition of the *Sung-shih hsin-pien* was reprinted in a single volume in 1936.

In addition K'o wrote an emendation of the *Shih-chi*, entitled *Shih-chi k'ao-yao* 史記考要, 10 *ch*. The original edition of this work may have been lost, but excerpts have been incorporated in the *Shih-chi p'ing-lin* 評林 by Ling Chih-lung 凌稚隆 (T. 以棟, H. 磊泉), completed in 1576. K'o's other works, including a collection of writings, the *I-yü chi* 藝餘集, 14 *ch.*, appears to have been lost. A selection of his poetry has been preserved in the *Ch'üan Min Ming shih chuan* 全閩明詩傳 (1889), edited by Kuo Po-ts'ang 郭柏蒼.

Bibliography

1/152/11b, 287/5b; 5/18/61a, 32/45a; 8/54/23a;40/39/25a; 64/戊 15/10a; MSL (1965), Shih-tsung, 2556; Shen Te-fu, *Wan-li yeh-hu pien, pu-i*, 4/922; Chu I-tsun (ECCP), *P'u-shu-t'ing chi*, 45/7b; SK (1930), 50/10a; *P'u-t'ien-hsien chih* (1879), 13/27a, 16/27a, 17/33a; T'u Ch'ing-lan 涂慶瀾, *P'u-yang wen-chi* 莆陽文輯 (1899), 3/42a; Kuo Po-ts'ang, ed., *Ch'üan Min Ming shih chuan*, 19/10b; *Nei-k'u ts'ang-shu mu-lu* 內庫藏書目錄 (1913 ed.), 3/48a; Huang Yün-mei 黃雲眉, "Yü Hsia ch'ü-ch'an lun kai-hsiu *Sung-shih* chu-chia shu," 與夏瞿禪論改修宋史諸家書, *Wen-lan hsüeh-pao* 文瀾學報, 2: 1 (1936), 1; Chin Yü-fu 金毓黻, *Chung-kuo shih-hsüeh shih* 中國史學史 (1957 ed.), 139;L. of C. *Catalogue of Rare Books*, 128.

Hok-lam Chan

KOFFLER, Andreas Wolfgang (known after 1643 as Andreas Xavier Koffler; Chinese name Ch'ü Sha-wei 瞿紗微, and sometimes Ch'ü An-te 安德, T. 體泰), 1603-December (?), 1651, missionary, was born in Krems, Austria, into a well-to-do Protestant family. When his father died, his mother moved to Ratisbon, Bavaria, where she raised her children in the Catholic faith. Joining the Society of Jesus in 1627. Koffler studied theology and mathematics and other subjects for several years before leaving for the East either in 1639 or 1640. He arrived in Goa in January, 1642. The end of the year found him in Batavia, and by 1643 he was in Macao. Here he spent the next two years acquainting himself with the language and the people, being specially valued, it is said, for his talent in mathematics. Here too he changed his name from Wolfgang to Xavier, doubtless under Portuguese influence. In 1645 Koffler proceeded to the court of Prince Chu Yu-lang (ECCP), who was to become the last claimant to the Ming throne in December, 1646. The latter was then at Chao-ch'ing 肇慶, Kwangtung, along with members of his immediate family and the eunuch P'ang T'ien-shou (ECCP, p. 195). A little later the court moved to Kweilin, Koffler fell in easily with this group and was taken into their confidence. P'an ghad become a Christian years earlier (see Nicolas Longobardi); so also had Ch'ü Shih-ssu (ECCP), governor of Kwangsi, and Chiao Lien (ECCP, p. 200), a military commander serving under Ch'ü. In this friendly atmosphere Koffler was able to make marked progress in evangelization. In the course of a few months he, together with P'ang, Ch'ü, and Chiao, succeeded in persuading several members of the imperial family to become Christians (1648). The widow of Chu Yu-lang's father, née Wang 王, was baptized as Helena; his own mother, née Ma 馬, as Maria, his wife the empress, also née Wang 王, as Anna; his infant son, the heir apparent Chu Tz'u-hsüan (ECCP, p. 195), as Constantine; the mother of Helena as Julia; and another princess as Agatha. These baptisms gave rise to protests from certain officials, but the ladies stood firm. It is barely possible that the emperor himself considered following their example but refrained; instead, he dispatched (October, 1648) two or three Christian officials to Macao with presents for the church, and the women of his household followed suit. In return, the Portuguese sent him gifts, including arms.

A little later, at the emperor's request, Koffler left Chao-ch'ing for Macao by way of Canton to seek military aid. The Portuguese responded (January, 1649) by sending a detachment of three hundred men (officered by two captains), two cannon, and other equipment, This was a time of considerable confusion both for the embattled Ming court and for the Jesuits. The Manchus in their sweep to the south were menacing the Ming remnants in Kwangtung and elsewhere. A defeat which they suffered (Spring, 1648) gave the Ming some respite and a chance to recover lost territory. By March of the following year, however, the Ming armies were again in retreat, and in February, 1650, Chu Yu-lang was obliged to leave Chao-ch'ing and move to his "water palace" in Wu-chou 梧州, and thence (after the fall of Canton in November) to Nanning 南寧, both in Kwangsi. As to the Jesuits, Francesco Sambiasi (q. v.) had died early in 1649 in Canton. Álvarō Semedo (q. v.), who had been serving as vice-provincial of the China mission, came to take his place. Instead of remaining in Canton, however, he pressed on to Chao-ch'ing, and returned to Macao about April. While there he asked Michal Piotr Boym (q. v.) to join Koffler at Chao-ch'ing. In 1650 Boym followed the court in its peregrinations. When in November the eunuch P'ang and empress-dowager Helena indited letters addressed to Pope Innocent X and to the Jesuit General Goswin Nickel, it fell to Boym to undertake the commission of delivering them to Rome. Meanwhile, following the collapse of Canton, Koffler set about joining the court, but traveling by an alternate route. Somewhere on the border between Kwangsi and Kweichow (probably T'ien-chou 田州), his boat was stopped by a Manchu outpost, and he was slain. The date usually given for his death is December 12, but this rests on dubious grounds.

Koffler left a number of letters and reports which remain largely unpublished. One short item in 12 folios, entitled *Summa del Estado del Imperio de la Chine*, published in Mexico in 1650, includes Koffler's letter, written in Canton in the latter part of 1648, telling of the relations between Emperor Chu Yü-chien (ECCP) and Sambiasi, the accession of Chu Yu-lang, and the baptism of members of the imperial family. This letter, together with one from Semedo, had been sent to the Jesuits in the Philippines, and thence to Mexico. A copy of it has been located in the archives of the Propaganda Fide in Rome. Another edition of the same work, published in Madrid, 1651, is known in two copies. An expanded translation of the *Summa del Estado*, published in Antwerp, 1651, which includes two additional letters of Koffler, written from Canton in November and December, 1648, seems to have disappeared.

Bibliography

Fang Hao 方豪, , *Chung-kuo T'ien-chu-chiao shih jen-wu chuan* 中國天主教史人物傳 (Hong Kong, 1967), 302; Pfister (1932), 265; Sommervogel (Paris, 1890, 1960), IV, col. 1156; Robert Chabrié, *Michel Boym jésuite polonais à la fin des Ming en Chine* (1646–1662), Paris, 1933; Paul Pelliot, "Michel Boym," TP, 31 (1935), 99.

L. Carrington Goodrich

KÖKÖ Temür 擴廓帖木兒, died September 17, 1375, originally named Wang Pao-pao 王保保, was a military leader who fought for the Yüan cause. He belonged to the family of the wife of Čaɤan Temür 察罕帖木兒 (also known as Li Ch'a-han 李察罕, T. 廷瑞, d. July 6, 1362), but was raised by Čaɤan as his own son. Čaɤan came from a family of Naiman origin, which followed the Mongol army in its invasion of north China and settled as landowners in Shen-ch'iu 沈丘, Honan. When the Red Turban rebels rose in 1351, Čaɤan and Li Ssu-ch'i (*see* Han Lin-er), a police chief from the nearby city of Lo-shan 羅山, gathered forces and helped to push the rebels out of the upper Huai area. Čaɤan and Li stationed themselves there until 1355, when they moved north to the vicinity of the Yellow River. In 1357 Čaɤan and Li took their troops west to Shensi. A year later, leaving Li there, Čaɤan led his men east to fight the rebels in southern Shansi, and in September, 1358, succeeded in dislodging the Sung rebels from their capital city of Pien-liang (Kaifeng, *see* Han Lin-er). He thus gained control, in the name of the Yüan court, of parts of each of the three provinces,

Shensi, Shansi, and Honan. In the following two years, however, he had to defend his territory in southern Shansi against an encroachment of the commander of the Yüan troops at Tatung, Bolod 孛羅 Temür (d. August 16, 1365). The Mongol emperor Toɤon Temür (*q.v.*), who needed outside support at this time in his struggle against rivals, sided with Bolod on this issue. By the spring of 1361, when Bolod moved his troops to Shensi against Li Ssu-ch'i, Čaɤan was left free to direct his campaign against the Red Turbans in Shantung.

The fall of the Red Turban capital in 1358 and the rapid success of Čaɤan's Shantung campaign in 1361 alarmed Chu Yüan-chang and the other warlords south of the Yangtze. In the summer of 1361, Chu was hemmed in by Ch'en Yu-liang (*q.v.*) on the west and Chang Shih-ch'eng (*q. v.*) on the east, and thus was eager to establish friendly relations with Čaɤan Temür and at the same time to spy on the northern situation. Čaɤan, however, favored Chang and Fang Kuo-chen (*q.v.*), who were nominal Yüan officials at this time, rather than Chu; this may be one reason why he prevented the envoy, whom Chu had sent to him, from returning south again. Yet Čaɤan seems to have had a hand in the complex arrangements which led to the sending of the Yüan envoy Chang Ch'ang (*see* Feng Sheng) to Chu for the purpose of getting the latter to surrender to the Yüan in return for an official position—an offer which Chu may have been about to accept until Čaɤan's assassination made it unnecessary.

Čaɤan's Chinese nephew Wang Pao-pao participated in this campaign in Shantung, and then Čaɤan sent him to the Yüan capital for the purpose of forming an alliance with the heir apparent Ayuširidara (*q.v.*) and his mother the Empress née Ki, who were leading a court faction in opposition to the emperor. It may have been at this time that the court honored Wang Pao-pao with the name Kökö Temür (the name meaning "blue iron"). In July,

1362, Čaɣan was assassinated by a Red Turban turncoat whom he had trusted; his former lieutenants then made Kökö Temür their commander by acclamation, a move which the Yüan court soon afterward confirmed. Kökö sent missions to the southern warlords announcing his succession, brought the Shantung campaign to a successful conclusion, and plunged with enthusiasm into the continuation of the struggle against Bolod Temür. Stationing himself at Taiyuan during the summer of 1364, Kökö attacked Bolod at four points along their common frontier. Outmaneuvered and steadily losing ground in the field, Bolod marched into the Yüan capital and ruled there as virtual dictator until his assassination on secret orders from the emperor in August, 1365.

The elimination of Bolod left Kökö supreme in north China. He escorted Ayuširidara back to Ta-tu, but refused to go along with the plot of the heir apparent and his mother to force the emperor to abdicate. Nor did he desire to dominate affairs in the capital as his rival had done; being a military man, Kökö was disliked by the court ministers and preferred in any case to be with his troops in the field. In November, 1365, the emperor made him prince of Honan 河南王. The grant of the princedom enabled Kökö to set up a branch provincial government (fen-sheng 分省) in the field, first at Huai-ch'ing 懷慶 and later at Chang-te 彰德. Kökö staffed the branch provincial government with some 2,600 officials of his own choosing, making an establishment that was said to rival the central government itself in size; further, he was allowed full authority over all plans, supplies, and promotions. The aim of this grant was to give Kökö all the latitude he needed in order to reconquer south China; the heir apparent had earlier volunteered for this duty, but the emperor preferred to let Kökö handle it.

Yet Kökö Temür seems never to have been particularly interested in invading south China. He made some moves south and east of Honan in 1363, but his main problem apparently was his inability to elicit unquestioning loyalty from Čaɣan's old comrades in arms; it was to the rectification of this rather than to the conquest of the south that he devoted his attention. At this time the warlords in Shensi, Chang Liang-pi 張良弼 and Li Ssu-ch'i, joined in refusing to obey the order of the court which put them under Kökö's command. In February, 1367, they made an alliance consisting of themselves and two lesser Shensi warlords over whom Li Ssu-ch'i was elected presiding officer (meng-chu 盟主). The pact was aimed at Kökö, who had begun attacking Shensi. The court tried ineffectually to arrange a truce between the two sides. Kökö also had trouble in Shantung with some of the local warlords there, and by August, 1367, he had a mutiny in his own ranks when Mo Kao 貊高, a former lieutenant of Čaɣan Temür, refused to attack Li Ssu-ch'i and rebelled. Mo Kao's mutiny coincided with a court-directed plan to strip Kökö of the newly granted military powers which it felt he had not been putting to legitimate use. On the same day as the mutiny, Kökö was openly denounced at court by civil officials for his refusal to obey orders, and a few days later a special supreme military bureau, called the Ta-fu-chün-yüan 大撫軍院, was set up by the heir apparent to handle the generals not under Kökö's command, as well as to assuage those of Kökö's generals who should choose to betray him. The heir apparent also won over most of the Shensi and Shantung warlords. In November, 1367, Kökö was relieved of command completely, and although ordered to Lo-yang, he actually stationed himself (with troops loyal to him) at Tse-chou 澤州 in Shansi.

The Yüan court may have been acting on poor intelligence when it relieved Kökö; it might better have tried to support him in his difficulties with the former followers of Čaɣan, for it was in November, 1367. that the Ming forces under Hsü Ta and

Ch'ang Yü-ch'un (*qq. v.*) began their northern expedition to drive the Yüan out of China. In the spring of 1367 Kökö had taken some action to shore up his southeastern flank, posting some of his generals and his younger brother Toyin Temür 脫因帖木兒 (d. 1388) in Shantung to keep the unruly local worlords in line; he also began strenghening his relations with the warlords of south China, Chang Shih-ch'eng and Fang Kuo-chen, in order to try to check Chu Yüan-chang. In March he deliberately provoked a skirmish near Hsü-chou 徐州 in order to entice Chu into entering his territory without adequate preparations.

Chu had first come into contact with Kökö Temür around January, 1363, when he received from the northern strong man a gift of horses and the return of the envoy he had earlier sent Čaɤan Temür. In his letter of reply, Chu gave immediate recognition to Kökö's succession, heaped praise on the deceased Čaɤan, and expressed a desire for close diplomatic and commercial relations. In March Chu had an envoy accompany a mission Fang Kuo-chen was sending to the Yüan capital, in order to get information on the struggle going on at that time between Kökö and Bolod, and to find out about Li Ssu-ch'i in Shensi. In January, 1365, Chu offered Kökö his support against Bolod, but by September of the same year he turned about and tried to get Ming Yü-chen (*q. v.*) to join him in opposing Kökö. In August, 1366, Chu wrote Kökö demanding the return of an envoy who had gone north three years before. He told Kökö that there was no need to detain the envoy if it were feared that he would give valuable intelligence on the northern situation, and enumerated the key facts that he already knew: the conflict with Li Ssu-ch'i, the untrustworthiness of the Shantung warlords, and the rift with the Yüan court. Chu ended by asking that the *status quo* be maintained, threatening a massive invasion of the north if these terms were not agreed to.

In February, 1367, while in the process of defeating Chang Shih-ch'eng, Chu fired off another minatory letter to Kökö and demanded again the return of the envoy. Later in the spring Chu began probing Kökö's southern flank at two key points—Ch'en-chou 陳州 (Huai-yang, Honan) and Shantung—by sending ambassadors with letters and gifts for the officers stationed there. By the autumn of 1367, when Chu had finished with Chang Shih-ch'eng and was ready to undertake the conquest of the north, he sent yet another letter to Kökö boasting of his victories, obliquely accusing Kökö of treason vis-à-vis the Yüan dynasty, hinting that he knew of the dissension within Kökö's ranks, and demanding for the third time the return of the envoys he had sent. In addition, Chu tried to steal a psychological march upon Li Ssu-ch'i and Chang Liang-pi by warning them in another letter that they had best not act as a duumvirate, but choose one of themselves as superior and present a unified front: he was apparently unaware that Li Ssu-ch'i had already been made "presiding officer."

Chu Yüan-chang thus began his northern campaign with many advantages in his favor. He was fresh from his victory over Chang Shih-ch'eng; he had definite plans in mind concerning the conquest of north China; and he was in full control of his military forces. Kökö Temür's position was by contrast ambiguous: he harbored within his over-all domains a congeries of unreliable local satraps, and within his own ranks a number of disloyal generals; there was a real question about his own loyalty to the Yüan dynasty; and, just as Chu's campaign began, he was relieved of supreme military control. The Yüan court tried through its newly formed military agency to unify command and coordinate defenses against Chu's approaching forces, but found itself too busy trying to achieve the former to have time to attend to the latter. Li Ssu-ch'i, for one, turned out to be no more eager to take orders from the heir apparent than he had been to heed Kökö Temür.

The Yüan court tried to occupy forcefully the grain-producing regions of Shansi upon which the strength of both Čaɣan and Kökö had heavily depended, mollifying Kökö by promising to restore his powers if he would move into Shantung and fight the forces of Chu. But Kökö moved instantly into his threatened supply base and killed all of the officials the Yüan court had posted there. For this act, the Yüan court in February, 1368, stripped him of all of his offices and honors and declared open warfare on him. Kökö, however, soon defeated Mo Kao and another general who had earlier rebelled against him, and reestablished himself in southwestern Shansi.

The Ming forces in the meantime marched practically unopposed into Shantung, taking time out on the way to carry out a sacrifice at Čaɣan Temür's tomb, and to address to his ghost a highly laudatory elegy. By September, 1368, the Yüan dynasty was obliged to make peace with Kökö Temür on the latter's own terms. When the Ming forces were in possession of the whole north China plain and were about to close in on Ta-tu, the supreme military bureau was abolished, its chief official executed, and all of Kökö's former offices and powers were restored. This done, the imperial entourage and most of the central government abandoned the capital and moved north to Shang-tu 上都.

The Yüan court was able to maintain only a tenuous contact with Kökö after its flight north. It sent numerous requests to him for help, but either he did not heed the requests, or the envoys never reached him. In December, 1368, Kökö was enfeoffed *in absentia* as Prince of Ch'i 齊王, and in February, 1369, was elevated to the post of chancellor of the Right, the highest civil position. A month earlier, however, the Ming forces took advantage of Kökö's attempt to retake Ta-tu (now renamed Peiping) to move into and occupy Taiyuan: Kökö was betrayed by one

of his own generals when he doubled back to save his supply base and was badly defeated. He fled north to Tatung and thence to Ninghsia.

With Peiping and Shansi in their possession, the Ming armies under Hsü Ta moved southwest into Shensi in the spring of 1369. Chang Liang-pi retreated about 140 miles to Ch'ing-yang 慶陽, and Li Ssu-ch'i fled some 200 miles west to Lin-t'ao 臨洮. Neither man offered any resistance. Chu had earlier written to Li, telling him that he had already missed his opportunity to set himself up as an independent ruler; he advised Li not to follow the Mongols into the steppes, for they were "not our kind" (fei wo tsu-lei 非我族類) and would probably distrust him, while his troops who were Chinese would desert and return to their homelands. Chu offered to treat Li as the founder of the Later Han had treated the warlord Tou Jung (16 B.C.-A.D. 60) if he should decide to "leave the barbarians and come over to China" (ch'ü-i chiu-hua 去夷就華).   Hsü Ta decided to attack Li at Lin-t'ao first and leave the less capable Chang Liang-pi until later, aiming to make use of the men and supplies which Li controlled. Li surrendered on May 19, 1369, when Ming forces under Feng Sheng (*q.v.*) approached; they had already captured Li's wife and children. Li aided the Ming in a number of expeditions in the northwest until his death in 1376. Chu himself wrote a eulogy for him, and allowed his son, Li Shih-ch'ang 世昌, to inherit the position of an assistant guard commander.

In June, 1369, the Ming forces attacked Ch'ing-yang; Chang Liang-pi fled west to Kökö Temür at Ninghsia, leaving his younger brother Chang Liang-ch'en 良臣 in charge. Ch'ing-yang finally fell in September after a three months' siege; Kökö Temür, having failed in his attempts to save the city, retreated to Yung-ch'ang 永昌, about 200 miles west of Ninghsia. Shortly after the fall of Ch'ing-yang, Chu Yüan-chang directed a letter to Kökö urging him to surrender, promising posts for his lieutenants and offering to allow his men to return to their homes in China. But Kökö had clearly cast his lot with the Yüan government-in-exile: after finally receiving one or more of its requests for aid, he sent an envoy late in 1369 to advise the court, which had by this time fled farther north to Ying-ch'ang 應昌 (on the west shore of Tari Nūr, about eighty miles north of Shang-tu), that rather than try to hold out there against the Ming it would be best to withdraw all the way to Karakorum.

After taking Ch'ing-yang the Ming commanders were called back to Nanking for rewards and consultations, and Kökö took advantage of their absence to force a reentry across the Yellow River. Toward the end of January 1370, Chu ordered a two-pronged attack against the Yüan: one group led by Hsü Ta against Kökö Temür in Kansu, and the other by Li Wen-chung (*q.v.*) against the Yüan court at Ying-ch'ang. On May 2, 1370, Hsü inflicted a heavy defeat upon Kökö at a place called Shen-er-yü 沈兒峪, about twenty miles north of Ting-hsi 定西, Kansu, capturing some 84,000 men, 15,000 horses, and 1,800 officers, some of whom were original followers of Čaγan Temür. Kökö, together with his wife and a few others, are said barely to have escaped by floating west across the Yellow River on tree trunks. From there he went north to Karakorum and joined the heir apparent Ayuširidara, who became emperor of the Yüan on May 23, Toγon Temür having died at Ying-ch'ang.

In 1372 the Ming sent out three columns consisting altogether of about four hundred thousand troops to attack the Yüan, who were still vaguely trying to reconquer China. Lan Yü (*q.v.*) defeated Kökö on the Tula 土剌 River in Mongolia on April 23, but on June 7 Kökö decimated Hsü Ta's forces and saved Karakorum. Kökö made intermittent raids on the Tatung area in 1373 and 1374, and later

followed the Yüan court from Karakorum west to Qara Noqai 哈剌那海 (probably near modern Jirgalanta, Mongolia). There he died in 1375. His wife, née Mao 毛, followed him in death.

Kökö Temür had at least two younger brothers, Toyin Temür and Chin-kang-nu 金剛奴, who served under him. A younger sister was married to Chu Shuang, second son of Chu Yüan-chang (*see* Chu Yüan-chang), on October 15, 1371. Čaγan Temür's father, Arγun 阿魯溫, prince of Liang 梁王, surrendered to the Ming in April, 1368; it was probably at this time that Kökö's sister fell into Ming hands. Chu Yüan-chang was never able to achieve his aim of capturing Kökö Temür or make him surrender. Calling him an "extraordinary fellow" (ch'i nan-tzu 奇男子), he rated him even above Ch'ang Yü-ch'un, his own favorite general. The Yüan court in 1376 forged a letter in Kökö's name and sent it to Korea, hoping thereby to use the dead hero's prestige to influence the selection of a successor to the Korean throne.

Biliography

5/11/20a; *Yüan-shih*, ch. 42–47, 141, 207; *Ming-shih* (Taiwan ed.), 1579, 3757; MSL (1962), Tai-tsu, 117–1703; Liu Chi 劉佶, *Pei-hsün ssu-chi* 北巡私記; Ch'üan Heng 權衡, *Keng-shen wai-shih* 庚申外史 (1369); Yeh Tzu-ch'i 葉子奇, *Ts'ao-mu tzu* 草木子; Liu Ch'en 劉辰, *Kuo-ch'u shih-chi* 國初史蹟; T'u Chi 屠寄 (1856–1921), *Meng-wu-er shih-chi* 蒙兀兒史記, 154/5b; *Ning-wu-fu chih* 寧武府志 (1857), 12/7a; *Mindai mammō shirryō* 明代滿蒙史料, I, 3–123; Wada Sei 和田清, "Kökö Temür no shi ni tsuite," 擴廓帖木兒の死に就いて, SZ, XLIV: 12 (December, 1933); id., "Min-sho no Mōko keiryaku," 明初の蒙古經略, *Toāshi kenkyū* (*Mōko hen*) 東亞史研究(蒙古編): *Tōyō Bunko Ronsō* 東洋文庫論叢 XLII (Tokyo, 1959).
                                John Dardess

KONISHI Yukinaga 小西行長 (early name 彌九郎, baptized Augustine), *ca.* 1558-November 6, 1600, also known as the Christian daimyo, was a military officer serving Toyotomi Hideyoshi (1536-98) in many campaigns, especially during the invasion of Korea. Konishi came from a merchant family of Sakai 堺, a seaport of greater importance in the 16th century than its northern neighbor, Osaka. His father, Konishi Ryūsa 隆（立）佐 (also named 壽德, *ca.* 1533-94), is said to have been a dealer in medicinal herbs in Kyoto and, perhaps because of business contacts in the Portuguese trade, became one of the earliest Christian converts, being baptized Joachin (1560?) by a Jesuit missionary. Later he served Hideyoshi as commissioner of military supplies (1586-87) and as an assistant administrator of Sakai (1586-94?); in 1590 he received the rank of Izumi no kami 和泉守.

Records about the family are scarce and some facts about Konishi Yukinaga's early life have been unearthed only after decades of research in missionary sources in several European languages. He was probably born in Kyoto. It is known that as son of a convert he received some instruction in religion and western affairs, possibly including naval science and the use of firearms. Reportedly he began his military service under Ukita Naoie 宇喜多直家 (1530-82), daimyo of Bizen 備前. In 1577 he came to the notice of Hideyoshi and some time later joined his staff as a retainer. Soon he rose in rank and in 1580 he is known to have been in charge of Murozu, a seaport west of Kobe. In May, 1582, as a naval commander in the suppression of piracy in the Inland Sea, he was given as his fief the Shōdoshima 小豆島 and Shiaku 鹽飽 Islands off the northeastern Shikoku coast. Two years later he took part in the campaigns to gain control of the Shikoku Island, and was awarded first the title of takumi no suke 內匠頭 and then the feudal rank of Settsu no kami 攝津守 (100,000 *koku* [bushels]).

About this time (1584?) Konishi was baptized by a Jesuit missionary. Following the feudal tradition the soldiers under his command were also converted to Christianity, and this may have enhanced their

unity. Besides Konishi there were several other officers under Hideyoshi who were Christians, the two prominent ones being Takayama Nagafusa 高山長房 (1553-1615) and Kuroda Yoshitaka 黑田孝高 (1546-1604). This fact, however, does not indicate that Hideyoshi exclusively favored the Christians. Another of his trusted lieutenants commanding troops using firearms was Katō Kiyomasa 加藤清正 (1562-1611), a devout Buddhist. These men brought Hideyoshi victories and honors until he became virtual head of the government; for on January 27, 1587, the imperial court gave him, a man of low birth, the title of Kanbaku 關白 (prime minister), a rank hitherto reserved for a Fujiwara only. He was also given the elegant surname Toyotomi 豐臣, to take the place of the one he gave himself in 1571, namely Hashiba 羽柴. He immediately permitted several of his lieutenants, including Konishi, to use it as their surname too. As to the Christian church, he relied on the missionaries to be his interpreters in diplomatic matters, and intermediaries in the Portuguese trade that brought him goods and revenue with which to wage the costly wars.

Early in the same year Hideyoshi started the campaign against the Satsuma daimyo, Shimazu Yoshihisa 島津義久 (1533-1611), to gain control of Kyushu in the final phases of the unification of Japan. For several years the Shimazu army had been advancing on northern Kyushu where the majority of the daimyo, such as Ōtomo Yoshimune 大友義統 (1558-1605), Arima Harunobu 有馬晴信 (1567-1612), Ōmura Yoshiaki 大村喜明 (1568-1615), and Matsuura Shigenobu 松浦鎮信, had embraced Christianity. It was on Ōtomo's plea for assistance that Hideyoshi made war on Shimazu. From May to July Hideyoshi personally directed the attack on Satsuma, finally forcing Shimazu to surrender, but permitting him to retain his fief of southern Kyushu. Immediately to the north of Satsuma, however, he, in July, 1588, gave Konishi Yukinaga the fief of half of Higo 肥後, and made him daimyo of Udo 宇土 (200,000 *koku*). The northern half of Higo he assigned to Katō Kiyomasa as daimyo of Kumamoto 隈本 (250,000 *koku*). Then he awarded to Kuroda Yoshitaka Buzen 豊前 province on the northern coast of Kyushu (180,000 *koku*). It was as if by design he posted these kinglets to watch each other. Then he made two moves which greatly affected Konishi's life.

The first was the Kanbaku's surprise decree, issued on July 25, ordering the expulsion of all missionaries on the ground that they had preached against Japanese national beliefs, and destroyed Shinto shrines and Buddhist monasteries. He evidently acted on the spur of the moment, for he never seriously enforced the law but knowingly let almost all the Jesuit missionaries stay on, particularly in Nagasaki, which had come under his direct control. He also made no objection when Konishi became the chief protector of the missionaries and their converts, and, after quelling a local uprising on Amakusa 天草 Island, allowed it to become another center of Jesuit activity. The mass conversion of the subjects in Konishi's fief is said to have reached tens of thousands in a year.

One of the reasons why Hideyoshi did not enforce his law banning missionaries was because of the second move he made at that time, namely, his ambitious plan to conquer China by way of Korea. To carry it out he needed the missionaries' help in the Portuguese sea trade. He also needed Konishi and other Christian daimyo and their warriors and sailors, mostly if not all converts. It was likewise in July, 1587, that Hideyoshi sent a message inviting Korea to join him in invading China or to give passage to his troops. Korean refusal brought on further negotiations in the following four years and finally, after completing the unification by conquering northeastern Japan in 1590, Hideyoshi ordered preparations for the invasion of the peninsula. In 1591 Konishi and other

daimyo of Kyushu built for him the Nagoya castle to serve as his headquarters.

Almost 300,000 men were mobilized for the Korean War. The invasion force in 1592 involved over 150,000. Konishi commanded the vanguard division of 18,700, all from the fiefs of Christian daimyo, including Ōmura, Arima, Matsuura, and Sō Yoshitoshi 宗義智 (1568-1615), adopted son of the daimyo of the Tsushima Islands and son-in-law of Konishi. The second vanguard division was commanded by Katō. Other commanders followed. On May 25, 1592, Konishi landed at Pusan. Twenty days later he took Seoul, the capital city. King Yi Yŏn (*see* Yi Hon) and his court fled north to Pyongyang (June 16), and, when that city was threatened two weeks later, went farther north, finally arriving at Ŭiju 義州 on the Yalu River on July 30. Meanwhile Katō advanced on northeastern Korea until in mid-September he reached the Tumen River.

After occupying Pyongyang (July 4), Konishi held up further advance for several reasons. One was the reverses suffered by the Japanese navy from the attacks of the Korean admiral, Yi Sun-sin (*see* Ch'en Lin), rendering the supply line insecure. Another was the rise of local Korean gentry-led volunteers who harassed the invaders. A third reason was the report that China had sent troops to the rescue of Korea. Although the Chinese vanguards were defeated at the first engagement at Pyongyang (September 4), the main army was known to be on the way. In the meantime China had also sent an agent to negotiate for peace in the person of an unofficial representative, Shen Wei-ching 沈惟敬 (T. 宇愚, fl. 1540?-1597?), a native of P'inghu 平湖, Chekiang. Shen is said to have been tall and bearded. In October he met with Konishi to discuss terms of peace, the latter agreeing in the end to a truce of fifty days to permit the former to return to Peking in an effort to obtain an answer from the throne. Shen finally returned to Pyongyang in mid-December but with a reply unsatisfactory to the Japanese; he then threatened them with an army of a million men. And indeed the general, Li Ju-sung (*q.v.*), had gathered together a force of 35,000 in Liaotung, and late in January, 1593, started crossing the Yalu. The Chinese army swept down on Konishi's headquarters, invested Pyongyang, and on February 8 forced him to retreat with heavy losses. The Chinese supreme commander, Sung Ying-ch'ang (*see* Li Ju-sung), reported 796 Chinese dead and 1,620 Japanese killed in action. After a punishing march, Konishi reached Seoul ten days later, collected his men, and with reinforcements defeated Li in a sharp engagement on February 27, about fifteen miles north of Seoul near the post station Pyŏkjegwan 碧蹄館. A stalemate ensued. Both Chinese and Japanese commanders were ready for a truce. In April and early May Konishi, now joined by Katō, held three conferences with Shen to discuss possible terms of peace. Neither side could dictate from a position of strength. On May 7 Konishi received from Hideyoshi the order to withdraw to a more defensible position, and eleven days later he began the evacuation of Seoul. He and Katō then returned to Pusan to await the conclusion of a peace treaty, but held on to southeastern Korea, establishing a cordon of fortified points over two hundred miles in length. While they had difficulty in obtaining supplies, and resorted to foraging for food, the Koreans were gaining in strength and making hit-and-run attacks.

In the meantime Sung Ying-ch'ang sent two officers to conduct negotiations in Japan, Shen Wei-ching acting as their adviser. From Pusan Konishi sailed with the three Chinese to Japan where they had an audience with Hideyoshi (June 21). The conference lasted over a month. While the peace negotiations went on, the Japanese army under Katō, on Hideyoshi's order, attacked and sacked Chinju 晉州 to retaliate for a defeat suffered in November of the preceding year. It is said that when the Japanese took the city on July 27 they massacred the defenders and inhabitants, totaling over 60,000. The Chinese mission learned of this atrocity after returning from Japan late in July, and questioned Konishi about it. The latter blamed Hideyoshi and Katō. Bv that time the three Chinese probably considered the conclusion of peace a more important task, for they had with them a memorial to the Ming emperor from Hideyoshi asking to be confirmed as a tributary prince (封爲藩王) and requesting permission to renew trade-tribute relations (貢). It is said that Hideyoshi demanded from China as price for peace an imperial princess and half of Korea, but that at Pusan Konishi and others moderated the demands in the final version of the memorial. The bearer of it was Hideyoshi's envoy to China, a retainer of Konishi by the name of Konishi Joan 小西如安 (original name Naitō Tokuan 内藤德安, baptized in 1564 as John; he is mentioned in the memorial by his rank as Konishi Hida-no-kami 飛驒守, but the Chinese, ignorant of Japanese etiquette, misnamed him in Ming records as Hsiao Hsi Fei 小西飛. For being a Christian he was exiled in 1614 to Manila where he died in 1626). The Ming court at first doubted the sincerity of the Japanese because of their massacre of Koreans at Chinju and their continuing hold on Pusan, and kept Konishi Joan waiting more than a year in Korea and Liaotung. Finally, late in 1594, he was brought to Peking, and, after a month of questioning and investigation, the Ming court decided to accept the Japanese request for investiture in return for their promise to withdraw from Korea and not to invade it again. As for renewal of the tribute-trade relations it was postponed for later consideration.

On February 8, 1595, Emperor Chu I-chün (*q.v.*), at the suggestion of the War minister, Shih Hsing (*see* Li Ju-sung), appointed assistant central military commissioner Li Tsung-ch'eng 李宗城 (T. 汝藩,

descendant of Li Wen-chung) as envoy and
regional commissioner Yang Fang-heng 楊
方亨 as his deputy to proceed to Japan to
invest Hideyoshi as king. On their arrival
in Korea (May, 1595) they found that
the Japanese were still entrenched on the
southern coast of Korea and showed no
signs of moving. They refused to proceed
unless the Japanese left. In May, 1596,
Li gave up his mission and Yang was
appointed in his place, Shen Wei-ching
succeeding him as second in command.
The impasse was broken when Konishi
had most of his troops withdrawn, leaving only a small force at Pusan. In July
he set sail with the Chinese mission, arriving at Sakai. Later a Korean mission
also arrived. At first the conference was
to take place at Fushimi 伏見, but due to
a severe earthquake the place was changed to Osaka. There, after all the prelimi-
naries had been disposed of, Hideyoshi, on
October 21, formally received the Chinese
envoys for the acceptance of the investiture. It is said that when the reader of
the imperial edict came to the passage
on investing Hideyoshi as king of Japan,
the latter lost his temper and broke up
the session. A more likely reason for his
angry outburst seems to have been the
Chinese insistence that he evacuate all
troops from Korea. In any event the
Chinese and Korean envoys were sent
packing, and by the following spring
Hideyoshi mobilized another expeditionary
force of over 140,000 men to re-invade
Korea. Konishi was again put in joint
command along with Katō, Kuroda, and
others. They met on the peninsula another Chinese expeditionary army (see Liu
T'ing), this time with a strong navy under
Ch'en Lin who cooperated with the
Korean navy under Yi Sun-sin. After
more than a year of fighting the war was
brought to an end because of Hideyoshi's
death on September 16, 1598. In November, just when Konishi received orders to
withdraw, the Chinese stormed his strongly built fortress of Wigyo 倭橋. This is
portrayed on a scroll, which also includes

the later naval battle of Noryang 露梁
Straits, where Yi Sun-sin died in action.
From the photograph of the scroll, one may
conclude that it was probably Ch'en Lin
who commissioned it, for it presents vividly
the naval actions that took place, viz., the
storming of the Japanese fortress, including its watch tower Tenshukaku 天守閣,
and the troops with their firearms. It is
quite a realistic portrayal of the warfare
of the late 16th century in East Asia.
(Two colophons on the scroll erroneously
describe it as a commemoration of the sea
battle of General Liu Chiang 劉江 against
Japanese pirates near Chin-chou 金州,
Liaotung, in 1419.)

Soon after their return to Japan, Konishi and Katō found themselves in the
midst of a factional dispute among the
officers who had served under Hideyoshi.
One group, following the lead of Ishida
Mitsunari 石田三成 (1560-1600), faithfully
supported the boy, Hideyori 秀賴 (1593-
1615), son of Hideyoshi. The other group
of daimyo aligned themselves under the
ambitious Tokugawa Ieyasu 德川家康(1543-
1616), who, with Edo 江戶 as his base
of power, controlled much of eastern
Japan and plotted to assume the role of
Hideyoshi. In this conflict Konishi joined
Ishida in support of Hideyori while Katō
took the side of Tokugawa. In the famous
battle of Sekigahara 關ケ原 (August, 1600)
Tokugawa emerged victorious, and eventually eliminated all opposition and became
founder of the bakufu government of
Edo, which ruled Japan for 264 years
(1603-1867).

Konishi escaped to a mountain retreat but was soon captured. Told to
commit suicide or face execution, he is
said to have chosen the latter because he
was a Christian. He was beheaded, along
with Ishida, on the bank of Rokujō River
六條河 in Kyoto. His eleven-year-old son
whom he entrusted to a fellow partisan,
Mōri Terumoto 毛利輝元 (1553-1625),
was put to death by the latter who sought
thus to placate Tokugawa. Konishi also
had two daughters, Maria, who married

Sō Yoshitoshi, was sent into exile for being a Christian; she died in 1605 in Nagasaki. The family properties were confiscated.

Though daimyo of Udo for twelve years, Konishi had spent only a short while there; still the place became a center of missionary activities. He was experienced in city planning, having taken part in laying out the city of Hakata in 1587 and of Sakai a little earlier. The castle of Udo was strongly constructed, with the yagura (watch tower or tenshu kaku) built plainly but solidly. After the battle of Sekigahara, Katō Kiyomasa was awarded the additional fief of Udo, and led his men to take the city by force. The defenders stoutly resisted, the siege lasting over a month until the news of Konishi's execution was verified. Late in November they surrendered the city. Konishi's tower was torn down in 1610 and its materials were used to build Katō's own castle in Kumamoto.

Konishi is said to have been kindly and considerate. After his baptism he supported numerous charities, including a leper asylum in Osaka. His name is mentioned frequently in the Jesuit letters, and after his death the church indited a funeral oration in his honor, now known as Argomento della Tragedia Intitolata Agostino Tzunicamindano re Giapponese, of which a handwritten copy, dated 1607, is preserved in Geneva. In Japan, however, his memory has been consistently ignored for two and a half centuries, partly because he was executed for fighting against Ieyasu, but chiefly because of the anti-Christianity policy maintained by the Tokugawa government.

It is interesting to note that, when Konishi Joan was being questioned in Peking on December 29, 1594, as to the sincerity of the Japanese in suing for peace, he gave an oath declaring that, after the investiture, the Japanese would not seek to revive tribute-trade, and would withdraw all their troops; if one word of this were false, Hideyoshi as well

as Konishi Yukinaga and Konishi Joan, would suffer unnatural death, and the descendants of the three would not prosper. As a matter of coincidence, this seems to be what did happen to Konishi and also what at least in part happened in the case of the two others.

Bibliography

1/320/14b, 322/18b; MSL (1966), Shen-tsung, 4775, 4835, 4917, 5172, 5191, 5208, 5434, 5511, 5526, 5559, 5721, 5732, 5764, 6085; KC (1958), 4744; Shen Te-fu, *Wan-li yeh-hu pien* (1959), 440; Sung Ying-ch'ang, *Ching-lüeh fu-kuo yao-pien* (1929), 附錄 35b; Mao Jui-cheng, *Wan-li san-ta-cheng k'ao* (1934), 33; Yi Hyŏngsŏk 李炯錫, *Injin Chŏllan-sa* 壬辰戰亂史 (1967), Vol. I, 240, 452, 719, 903, 926, Vol. II, 1102, 1433; *Chōsen-shi* 朝鮮史 (1932–40), pt. IV, Vol. 10; Ikeuchi Hiroshi 池內宏, *Bunroku keichō no eki* 文祿慶長の役 (1914); *id.*, *Toyo Bunko Ronsō*, ser. A 25 (1936); *Udo-shi shi* 市史 (1960); Matsuda Kiichi 松田毅, *Kinsei shoki Nihon kankei Namban shiryō no kenkyū* 近世初期日本關係南蠻史料の研究 (1967), 295, 756; Anesaki Masaharu 姊崎正治, *Kirishitan dendō no kōhai* 切支丹傳道の興廢; *id.*, *A Concordance to the History of Kirishitan Missions* (1930); C. R. Boxer, *The Christian Century in Japan* (1951), 139, 163, 180; James Murdock, *A History of Japan* (1903), II, 302; J. Laures, *Kirishitan Bunko* (1957), 204; Hugh Dyson Walker, *The Yi-Ming Rapprochement, Sino-Korean Relations, 1392–1592* (doctoral dissertation, 1971), 262.

Chaoying Fang and Toyoko Y. Chen

KU Cheng-i 顧正誼 (T. 仲方, H. 亭林), fl. 1575–96, painter and poet, was a native of Hua-t'ing 華亭, in Sung-chiang 松江, southwest of Shanghai. Son of a minor official, Ku became a student in the National University and was appointed a drafter of the central drafting office (*ca.* 1575). Mo Shih-lung (*q.v.*), a fellow native of Hua-t'ing, referred in his writings frequently to him and his art. The two author-painters were considered by followers and later writers as founders of the Hua-t'ing (Sung-chiang) school of landscape painting, spearheading the famous Southern School 南宗 movement in the history of Chinese painting.

While most sources repeat each other in describing Ku's style of painting as derived from Huang Kung-wang (1269-1354), Wu Chen (1280-1354), Ni Tsan, and Wang Meng (*qq.v.*), it has been pointed out that Ku began his career by studying the style of Ma Wan 馬琬 (T. 文璧, active 1328-66), another later Yüan painter. Tung Ch'i-ch'ang (ECCP), on the other hand, who as a young man had studied painting under Ku, once commented in a colophon that a certain work by Ku Cheng-i demonstrated the fact that Ku had gained profound understanding of landscape by studying Li Ch'eng (919-67). His admirers seem to have preferred his works in Huang Kung-wang's style.

Among the important painters of the Hua-t'ing school, Ku Cheng-i should be regarded as the first significant one, followed closely by Mo Shih-lung. Tung Ch'i-ch'ang came on the scene later and led this artistic revolution to a triumphant conclusion. Through their efforts, the elaborate and almost ornate landscape style, with an overwhelming amount of painstakingly executed details, developed around the middle of the 16th century; it became clarified and reorganized into three or four prominently stated passages, executed with confident virtuosity, using brush strokes akin to those employed in calligraphy. In the hands of their followers, however, the original intellectual directions became unclear, although the new landscape style meanwhile had established itself in a superficial way. A popular taste for it developed by the middle of the 17th century.

A fellow countryman from Hua-t'ing, Sun K'o-hung (*see* Lan Ying), and Sung Hsü (*q.v.*) from Chia-hsing 嘉興, Chekiang, were among Ku Cheng-i's painter friends. He benefited from discussing the art of painting with them.

Ku traveled widely and assembled a collection of important paintings. During his sojourn in Peking, it is said that a host of admirers "tripped over each other" to acquire his works. At home he enjoyed his gardens and the many buildings in them. His friends often gathered at his place to enjoy and create paintings, examples of calligraphy, and poetry. Mo Shih-lung in his poems mentions as belonging to Ku the gardens Tung-yüan 東園, Shu-fang 漱芳, and Chao-yin. 招隱, and the building P'i-yün-ko 披芸閣, where he had joined Ku and his company in literary and artistic gatherings. Ku Cheng-i left a work entitled *Shih-shih* 詩史, consisting of fifteen poems on events from Chinese history. It is mentioned in the *Ssu-k'u* catalogue, but with the unsupported suggestion that it was really the work of a fellow townsman, T'ang Ju-hsün 唐汝詢 (T. 仲言). In any case this work seems to have been lost. Not many paintings by Ku are extant. Of the half a dozen or so attributed to him, four are in the Palace Museum, Taipei. A hanging scroll known as "Hsi-shan ch'iu-shuang chou" 溪山秋爽 軸, dated 1575, is a good example of his landscape style.

Bibliography

1/99/20b; 65/4/9b; *Sung-chiang-fu chih* (1819), 61/14a; Hsü Ch'in 徐沁, *Ming-hua lu* 明畫錄, in *Hua-shih* 畫史 *ts'ung-shu* (Shanghai, 1962), 4/53; Chiang Shao-shu 姜紹書, *Wu-sheng-shih shih* 無聲詩史 (same ed.), 4/61; *T'u-hui pao-chien hsü-tsuan* 圖繪寶鑑續纂 (same ed.), 1/9; Mo Shih-lung, *Mo T'ing-han i-kao*, 4/57b, 7/28b, 42a, 14/11a, 14b, 15a; Chu Mou-yin 朱謀垔, *Hua-shih hui-yao*畫史會要 (1631 ed.), 4/大明, 56a; Tung Ch'i-ch'ang, *Hua-ch'an-shih sui-pi* (1720 ed.), 2/33b; *Ku-kung shu-hua-lu* 故宮書畫錄 (增訂本, 1965 ed.), 5/433; SK (1930), 90/3b; P'an T'ien-shou 潘天壽, *Chung-kuo hui-hua shih* 繪畫史, 174; Osvald Sirén, *Chinese Painting*, VI, pl. 270A; E. J. Laing, *Chinese Painting in Chinese Publications, 1956–1968* (Ann Arbor, 1969), 172.

Nelson Wu

KU Ch'i-yüan 顧起元 (T. 太初, 鄰初, H. 遯園居士), 1565-1628, scholar, belonged to a family which had served in the Chin-wu Guard 金吾衛 at Nanking. His great-grandfather, brought up by a family named Chang 張, took Chang as his surname. Ku Ch'i-yüan's father, who received the *chin-shih* degree in 1574 under the name Chang Kuo-fu 張國輔 (T. 惟德, H. 毅庵), held official posts in the provinces of Hukuang and Chekiang. I twas not until later in his career that the father petitioned the government to restore the family name of Ku, and change his own name to Ku Kuo-fu.

After passing the provincial examination in 1597, Ku Ch'i-yüan became a *chin-shih* in 1598. Ranked the third highest in the palace tests, he was appointed a compiler in the Hanlin Academy. From 1610 to 1613 he served as director of studies in the National University at Nanking, and in 1615 was reappointed there as chancellor. In April, 1616, he rose in rank to be an assistant supervisor of instruction to the heir apparent and later served as a vice minister of Personnel. He then retired to his home in Nanking where he devoted himself to study and writing, took time to enjoy the simple pleasures of nature, and built the Tun-yüan 遯園 (Garden of escape). Among the structures in that garden was a pavilion which named Ch'i-chao t'ing 七召亭 to commemorate the seven times that he declined to return to officialdom when summoned by the court. The posthumous name of Wen-chuang 文莊 was bestowed on him in 1645 by Chu Yu-sung (ECCP), then reigning in Nanking.

It is in his writings that Ku Ch'i-yüan is best remembered by posterity. A brief examination of various bibliographies reveals over twenty titles listed as his work, with most still extant, although not all easily accessible. They indicate a breadth of learning, from the Classics and history to philosophy and literature. The three largest productions are the following: 1) *Lan-chen ts'ao-t'ang chi* 嬾眞草堂集, collected literary works consisting of 20 chüan of poetry and 30 *chüan* of prose, first printed in 1618, which appears to have survived only in fragmentary condition, for the reprinted edition in the third series of the *Chin-ling ts'ung-shu* 金陵叢書 of 1914 consists only of the 20 *chüan* of poetry with *chüan* 11 to 17 missing, and *chüan* 8 possibly incom-

plete; 2) *Shuo-lüeh* 說略, 30 *ch.*, classified notes on various subjects, mainly drawn from historical sources, first printed in 1613, and the only one of his books to be copied into the Imperial Library (later included in the fourth series of the *Chin-ling ts'ung-shu*); 3) *K'o-tso chui-yü* 客座贅語, 10 *chüan* of notes on his native place, Nanking, as well as on the country as a whole, primarily dealing with the contemporary scene, first printed in 1618, and later included in the *Chin-ling ts'ung-k'o* 刻, printed in 1906. To students of Ming history the most interesting and noteworthy is undoubtedly the last work, for it provides not only descriptions of Ming political institutions, but also insights into Ming society and mores. There are items of information on taxation and labor service, grain transportation and communicatons, population, registration, and examination quotas, the monetary system, monuments and bronze inscriptions, fashions from men's boots to women's headdresses, and even something on fish and plants.

Of special interest in the *K'o-tso chui-yü* is a note cited by J. J. L. Duyvendak on the Pao-ch'uan ch'ang 寶船廠 in Nanking where the ships for the celebrated ocean voyages of Cheng Ho (*q.v.*) were built. By using the characters t'iao-pien 條編 rather than the homophonous 條鞭, Ku gives us a better understanding of the origin of the widely used term i-t'iao-pien, or "single whip" system of tax collecting (*see* Wang Tsung-mu). He also provides us with a good sketch of Matteo Ricci (*q.v.*) whom he must have known personally in Nanking. He was impressed by the picture of the Holy Mother and Child, which he describes as having a dimensional appearance with the facial features standing out; he furthermore reported on Ricci's explanation of the use of light and shade to achieve perspective in Western painting. Among other things in this sketch he mentions a tzu-ming chung 自鳴鐘 (self-striking clock), and remarked on the European's superior knowledge of astronomy and mathematics.

During the years 1616 to 1624, Ku printed eight of his shorter works under the collective title *Kuei-hung kuan tsa-chu* 歸鴻館雜著. One title in this small *ts'ung-shu* is *Ku-shih hsiao-shih* 顧氏小史, which is perhaps a history or genealogy of his own family. His three long works, cited above, as well as several shorter pieces, were put on the list of prohibited books in the 18th century. In the T'ien-ch'i period, when a compilation of the works of ancient philosophers, with annotations and comments, was printed under the title *Ho chu-ming-chia p'i-tien chu-tzu ch'üan-shu* 合諸名家批點諸子全書, Ku annotated the book of *Shang-tzu* 商子, or *Lord Shang*, which included the comments of another Ming scholar, Yang Shen (*q.v.*). A preface Ku wrote to a book on a collection of ink slabs, *P'an Fang-k'ai mo-hsü* 潘方凱墨序, was printed in the *Shih-liu-chia mo-shuo* 十六家墨說 in 1922.

Ku Ch'i-yüan was instrumental in printing the *Hsien-cheng lu* by Chiao Hung (ECCP) for which he also wrote a preface dated 1616. Even today this biographical compilation remains one of the most important sources on Ming history.

Ku had three younger brothers, Ku Ch'i-feng 鳳 (T. 羽王, 醒石), a *chü-jen* of 1609 and *chin-shih* of 1610, Ku Ch'i-nan 柟 (T. 周南), who died young, and Ku Ch'i-chen 貞 (T. 邃初, 太復), a *chü-jen* of 1621, who held minor official positions both in the provinces and in the central government, and who died at the advanced age of eighty-three *sui*.

Bibliography

40/58/11a; 64/庚19/1b; 84/甲/64a; KC (1958), 5046, 5067, 5072, 5086, 5101; Ch'en Tso-lin 陳作霖, *Chin-ling t'ung-chuan* 通傳 (1904), 19/13a; Ch'en Chi-sheng 陳濟生, *T'ien-ch'i Ch'ung-chen liang-ch'ao i-shih* 天啓崇禎兩朝遺詩 (Shanghai, 1958), biographical section (小傳), 1875; Sun Tien-ch'i (1957), 109, 145, 194, 214, 231, 243; SK (1930), 87/4b, 136/3a, 143/9b, 179/14a, 193/5b; J. J. L. Duyvendak, "Chinese Maritime Expeditions in the Early Fifteenth Century," TP, 34 (1938), 357, n. 5; Henri Bernard, *Le père Matthieu Ricci et la société chinoise de son temps* (Tientsin, 1937), Vol.1, 254; P. M. d'Elia, *Fonti Ricciane*, I (Rome, 1942), 32, n. 2.

Lienche Tu Fang

KU Hsien-ch'eng 顧憲成 (T. 叔時, H. 涇陽), September 17, 1550-June 21, 1612, scholar, official, and founder of the academy, Tung-lin shu-yüan 東林書院, was a native of Wu-hsi, northwest of Soochow. His clan had lived in a village north of Wu-hsi since Sung times. Some of his ancestors were known for their wealth, but by his grandfather's time the family had fallen into straitened circumstances. His father, Ku Hsüeh 學 (H. 南野, 1516-76), had to leave the clan establishment to make his own living in Ching-li 涇里, a village east of the district city, where, gaining a reputation for integrity, he succeeded in becoming a wealthy merchant in a few decades. Of his four sons, the eldest engaged in business, and the second in land reclamation through irrigation, thus enabling the two younger ones to pursue their studies. The third, Ku Hsien-ch'eng, passed first in the examination for *chü-jen* in 1576, achieving the title of a chieh-yüan 解元. He became a *chin-shih* in 1580, as did his younger brother, Ku Yün-ch'eng 允成 (T. 季時, H. 涇凡, 1554-1607), six years later.

Ku Hsien-ch'eng, after serving two years as a secretary in the ministry of Revenue (1580-82) and one year in the ministry of Personnel, took a leave of absence in the autumn of 1583 and went home for a period of three years.

From the beginning Ku sided with a group of officials, known as the ch'ing-i 清議 (pure critics), who applied Confucian standards most stringently to the government and public figures, especially the higher ranking ones in power, such as the grand secretary, Chang Chü-cheng (*q. v.*). Even before receiving an appointment Ku and two other chieh-yüan, Wei Yün-chung 魏允中 (T. 懋權, cs 1580, d. 1585, a native of Nan-lo 南樂, Pei-Chihli) and Liu T'ing-lan 劉廷蘭 (T. 國徵, H. 紉華, cs 1580, d.

1584, a native of Chang-p'u 漳浦, Fukien), came to the attention of Chang Chü-cheng through their uninhibited criticism of his administration. In the ministry of Revenue Ku found like-minded friends in Li San-ts'ai (q. v.) and Chiang Shih-ch'ang 姜士昌 (T. 仲文, cs 1580), who had both passed the *chin-shih* examination at the same time as himself. Soon they were joined by Chao Nan-hsing (q.v.) who was to become one of the leading figures of the "pure critics." One of their main grievances was that the officials who had protested against Chang Chü-cheng's staying in office during the period of mourning for his father and had been punished, such as Shen Ssu-hsiao 沈思孝 (T. 純父, H. 繼山, 1542–1611, cs 1568), Chao Yung-hsien, and Tsou Yüan-piao (qq.v.), remained ineligible for office. When Chang Chü-cheng was critically ill in 1582, and the court officials almost in a body went to Buddhist services held for his recovery, Chao Nan-hsing, Chiang Shih-ch'ang, and Ku refused to attend. Somebody had entered Ku's name on a list soliciting contributions for these services, but he hastened to remove it. The death of Chang saved him from reprisals.

The "pure critics" were gratified by the change of policy that took place after Chang Chü-cheng's death. Ku remarked that the abuses of Chang's administration had been corrected. He excepted, however, the favoritism shown to relatives of the grand secretaries at the public examinations. Here things had become so bad that Ku saw no other way to restore public confidence than to exclude the relatives of grand secretaries from the examinations altogether. This advice, given in a letter to Grand Secretary Hsü Kuo 許國 (T. 維貞, 1527–96, cs 1565) before the *chin-shih* examination of 1583, was not followed. After that examination Wei Yün-chen 魏允貞 (T. 懋忠, H. 見泉, 1542–1606, cs 1577, Pth. 介肅), the older brother of Wei Yün-chung, protested that irregularities had been committed in the graduation of sons of Grand Secretaries Chang Ssu-wei and Shen Shih-hsing (qq. v.). Wei

was demoted to a provincial post; and when Li San-ts'ai spoke up for him he was meted out the same punishment. Through Ku's efforts both Wei and Li were assigned to central government positions in Nanking. About this time Ku also warned the grand secretaries that the public seemed dissatisfied with various actions taken by the government.

During his first years in Peking Ku had already become known for his keen analysis of issues and acute appraisal of people. He and Chao Yung-hsien, then vice minister of Personnel, were regarded spokesmen of the "pure critics"; their pronouncements on the character and the actions of public figures carried great weight. After his return to Peking in the autumn of 1586, Ku was reassigned to the ministry of Personnel but barely half a year passed before he fell victim to a quarrel which developed between the Grand Secretariat and the "pure critics" as an aftermath of the scrutiny (beginning of 1587) of the metropolitan officials. It happened that the censor-in-chief, Hsin Tzu-hsiu 辛自修 (T. 子吉, 子言, H. 慎軒, cs 1556), who decided to apply the regulations with utmost rigor to the unworthy elements among the officials, was himself attacked by those censored by him, especially Ho Ch'i-ming 何起鳴 (T. 應岐, H. 來山, cs 1559), the minister of Works who had been marked for dismissal. Hsin saw himself finally compelled by the grand secretaries to resign, together with Ho. Several censors who protested against the discharge of Hsin were variously punished, one of them even being thrown into prison. Ku submitted a memorial in which he defended Hsin, attacked Ho as hsiao-jen 小人 (villain), and questioned the emperor's wisdom in punishing the censors. The memorial drew the imperial response that Ku was impetuous and self-seeking and was to be demoted three ranks and transferred to a provincial post. When an official said to the grand secretary, Wang Hsi-chüeh (q.v.), that the memorial of Ku had been moderate in tone and had not warranted punishment, Wang answered that Ku was a pedant who fell in with the talk heard on the street and knew nothing of the worries of the grand secretaries. Ku was given the position of assistant magistrate of Kuei-yang-chou 桂陽州, Hukuang. In the following year he became prefectural judge of Ch'u-chou-fu 處州府, Chekiang. He spent only two or three months in each of these positions, then asked for leave of absence and returned home. Soon he went into mourning for his mother, after which he received another provincial appointment, but before he left for it he was singled out as the most exemplary provincial official (first on a list of twenty or more) on the occasion of the scrutiny of provincial officials conducted by Lu Kuang-tsu (see Lu Nan), minister of Personnel, and Tsou Kuan-kuang 鄒觀光 (T. 孚如, cs 1580), director of the bureau of evaluations. In 1592 he was reinstalled in the ministry of Personnel in Peking—something, it is noted, that had never happened before during the Ming dynasty. Later he was promoted to vice director in the bureau of honors. At the beginning of 1593 he received a transfer to the bureau of evaluations, headed by his friend Chao Nan-hsing. Half a year later he was promoted to the rank of bureau director. As such he headed successively the bureaus of honors, evaluations, and appointments.

At the beginning of 1593 Ku took part in the fight for the selection as heir apparent of Chu Ch'ang-lo (ECCP), the first-born son of Chu I-chün (q.v.), whom the latter wanted to pass over in favor of Chu Ch'ang-hsün, the son of his favorite consort, Cheng Kuei-fei (q. v.). In this struggle, which was to embroil the court for the rest of the emperor's reign and to culminate in the famous "three cases," the "pure critics" held the emperor to the strict observance of the dynastic conventions while their opponents tried to accommodate the emperor and accused the "pure critics" of being fanatical and overly suspicious, and of lacking in respect and

consideration for the emperor and his consort. At this time the emperor issued an order that for the time being his eldest son, as well as the two younger sons, should be nominated simply to the rank of imperial prince, the nomination of an heir apparent to wait until the empress gave birth to a son. Wang Hsi-chüeh, who had just returned (February 15, 1593) to become chief grand secretary, approved the edict, but many opposed it. Ku led the officials of the four bureaus of his ministry in a memorial in which he gave nine reasons for opposing the imperial order. In a letter to Wang, Ku upbraided him for upholding the emperor. The request of Ku and other speakers that Chu Ch'ang-lo be forthwith made heir apparent was not granted, but the "simultaneous nomination of the three princes" was called off.

At the same time Ku, who had just become vice director in the bureau of evaluations, took an active part in the scrutiny of the metropolitan officials at the beginning of 1593, an event which was a landmark in the struggle between the "pure critics" and the Grand Secretariat. With Sun Lung 孫鑨 (T. 文中, H. 立峰, 1525-94, cs 1556) as minister of Personnel, Chao Nan-hsing as director of the bureau of evaluations, the neo-Confucianist Meng Hua-li 孟化鯉 (T. 叔龍, H. 雲浦, 1545-97, cs 1580) as director of the bureau of appointments, and Li Shih-ta 李世達 (T. 子成, H. 漸菴, cs 1556, Pth. 敏肅, 1531-99) as senior censor-in-chief, the reformers were for the first time in many years in almost complete control of the scrutiny and they decided to do a thorough house cleaning. To show their impartiality they cashiered at the outset a nephew of Sun and a relative by marriage of Chao, and then proceeded to remove all unworthy officials, among them many friends and relatives of grand secretaries. Wang Hsi-chüeh, who had just been recalled (see above), hurried to Peking, but found when he arrived that the recommendations of the scrutiny had been submitted the day before. The grand secretaries, however,

soon had their revenge. Censors friendly
to them accused Sun Lung of wanting to
keep in office Yü Ch'un-hsi 虞淳熙 (T. 長
孺, H. 德園, cs 1583) and Yang Yü-t'ing
楊于廷 (T. 道行, cs 1580) who had both
been impeached; and the emperor rebuked
the ministry of Personnel for "monopo-
lizing power and fomenting cliques." Ku,
answering in the name of Sun, politely
denied the charge; the emperor, declaring
that the culprits refused to confess, fined
Sun and demoted Chao to a post in the
provinces. Now Ku, together with his
colleague, Li Fu-yang 李復陽 (T. 宗誠, H.
元冲, 1551–1608, cs 1583), reported that
both of them had closely cooperated with
Chao in the scrutiny as a whole and in
the decision to keep Yü and Yang in
office. Chao, they said, had acted out of
loyalty for the country and ought to be
restored to his office, but if the charges
for which he was dismissed were allowed
to stand then both of them begged to be
punished with him. No answer was made
to this memorial, but now many other
officials spoke up for Chao, among them
Li Shih-ta, Wang Ju-hsün 王汝訓 (T. 師吉,
H. 泓陽, 1551–1610, cs 1571), Wei Yün-
chen, Yü K'ung-chien 于孔兼 (T. 元時, H.
景素, cs 1580), Ch'en T'ai-lai 陳泰來 (T.
伯符, 上交, cs 1577), Ku's brother Ku Yün-
ch'eng, Shih Meng-lin 史夢麟 (T. 際明, H.
玉池, cs 1583), and an instructor in the
National University, Hsüeh Fu-chiao 薛敷
教 (T. 以身, H. 玄臺, cs 1589). The emperor
became incensed and punished Yü and
Ch'en. When Li Shih-ta continued to protest, Chao Nan-hsing, Yü Ch'un-hsi, and
two others were cashiered. Ku Yün-ch'eng
and Shih Meng-lin had openly laid the
responsibility for the harsh measures at the
door of the grand secretaries. Shih was
in danger of being flogged but was let
off with the loss of his office; Ku Yün-
ch'eng, having been demoted to a provincial post, bade farewell to an official
career; Sun Lung was allowed to resign.

After Sun Lung's resignation, Wang Hsi-
chüeh proposed a Hanlin official, his friend
Lo Wan-hua 羅萬化 (T. 一甫, H. 康州,

1536–94, *optimus* of 1568), for minister of
Personnel. To this Ku strenuously objected
arguing that, since all grand secretaries
had been Hanlin members, the minister
of Personnel should not be a Hanlin too,
thus preventing the two powerful offices
from being manned by officials from the
same group. When the objections of Ku
were presented to Wang by Chao Yung-
hsien, the acting minister of Personnel,
Wang was furious but had to give up his
idea. Ch'en Yu-nien 陳有年 (T. 登之, H.
心穀, cs 1562, d. 1598) was appointed
instead.

In the summer of 1594, Wang Hsi-
chüeh, yielding to mounting public criticism, urgently requested that he be relieved
of his duties, and the emperor reluctantly
agreed. Before Wang left, the whole body
of court officials was ordered to submit
the names of six or seven candidates for
the office of grand secretary. Even collective nominations such as these were
presided over by the ministry of Personnel
and its bureau of appointments in particular. The minister Ch'en Yu-nien and
Ku saw eye to eye on this, so much so
that independently they came up with two
identical lists of candidates. Wang Hsi-
chüeh, still at court, asked that his friend
Lo Wan-hua be added to the list. Ku
again refused, this time giving Lo's character as his reason. Finally the emperor
rejected their selections and chose Shen
I-kuan and Ch'en Yü-pi (*qq. v.*). The emperor severely rebuked the ministry of
Personnel for arrogating to itself the nomination (going so far as to present unqualified applicants), and he had all officials
of the bureau of appointments demoted
to minor posts. Ch'en Yu-nien assumed
responsibility for the nomination and asked
that the officials of the bureau be reinstated. When this was refused, Ch'en
defended the nominations, saying that the
imperial order had asked for candidates
"irrespective of position or rank." All was
in vain; but upon the entreaty of the
grand secretaries punishment was limited
to the director of the bureau, Ku, who

was reduced to the status of a commoner. When Ku left the capital, he was seen off by a large crowd of friends. Although restored to his former rank on the occasion of the nomination of the heir apparent in 1601, he was never again to enter public life.

Some time after his return home late in 1594, Ku, who had suffered from frequent fainting spells during his last years in Peking, became critically ill, and not before the autumn of 1596 did his health begin to improve. As soon as he was able, he devoted himself to teaching, and many pupils flocked to him. When the neighboring temples could not accommodate all of them, Ku and his brothers built special apartments for them and a large hall called T'ung-jen-t'ang 同人堂. Among his pupils who later achieved fame were Ch'ien Shih-sheng (q. v.), who served as grand secretary under the last Ming emperor, Miao Ch'ang-ch'i (q. v.), one of the famous victims of Wei Chung-hsien (ECCP), Ma Shih-ch'i 馬世奇 (T. 君常, 1584-1644, cs 1631), who rose to be senior deputy supervisor of instruction of the heir apparent and committed suicide on the fall of Peking, and Chang K'o-ta 張可大 (T. 觀甫, cs 1601), who became junior military governor and was killed resisting the rebellion of K'ung Yu-te (ECCP).

Ku's deepest personal interest during his retirement was in neo-Confucian moral practice and theory. Soon after his return he began to keep a kind of philosophical diary, entitled *Hsiao-hsin-chai cha-chi* 小心齋劄記 (named after his studio), which he continued to the end of his life. He also played a leading role in the then popular neo-Confucian study meetings (講會) in the neighborhood. At conferences held in the Er-ch'üan shu-yüan 二泉書院, he had among other things amicable controversies with Kuan Chih-tao 管志道 (T. 登之, H. 東溟, 1536-1608, cs 1571), a former official at Nanking who had been ousted by Chang Chü-cheng. In 1603 Ku and his friends, following a suggestion of Kao P'an-lung (q.v.), decided to rebuild

the Tung-lin shu-yüan in Wu-hsi, the site where at the beginning of the 12th century Yang Shih (1053-1135), the foremost disciple of the Ch'eng brothers, had taught. During the following year they constructed the academy, and a shrine in honor of Yang Shih called Tao-nan tz'u 道南祠. In 1610 a small temple of Confucius, called Yen-chü miao 燕居廟, was added on the grounds of the shu-yüan. Local officials contributed public funds to the building project. The money was accepted; but to allay misgivings it was used for the expenses of the temple of Yang Shih while the academy proper was built with the contributions made by Ku and his friends. For the opening exercises of the academy, which took place from November 29 to December 1, 1604, Ku wrote the statutes (東林會約) in which he explained the meaning and objectives of the meetings and the frame of mind required to take part in them profitably, and the rules of procedure (會約儀式). The latter envisaged a major meeting every year and minor meetings eight months of the year; all meetings were to last three days. A feature distinguishing the Tung-lin meetings from other contemporary ones was the lectures (as a rule on chapters of the Four Books); they caused occasional comment by visitors accustomed to silent meditation typical of most other academies. The statutes also provided for community singing as a recreation after the sessions. Sometimes specially invited scholars gave series of lectures. Ku himself transferred his teaching activities from the T'ung-jen-t'ang in his home to the academy. Pupils of both Ku and Kao P'an-lung held study meetings of their own in the academy; from among them a choir was recruited which performed during the official meetings. For years Ku traveled back and forth between the Tung-lin and his home at Ching-li, a distance of about thirteen miles. It was not until 1608 that he moved to the district city.

From the beginning the Tung-lin enjoyed great prestige. Large gatherings of scholars appeared at the meetings. Most of them came from districts close to Wu-hsi, but some from as far away as Hang-chow in Chekiang and from Hukuang and Honan. Local officials were frequent guests. Even the provincial governor, Chou K'ung-chiao 周孔敎 (T. 明行, H. 懷魯, cs 1580), a close friend of Ku and Kao P'an-lung, was often seen at the conferences. Late in 1608 an agreement was made that, be-sides an autumn meeting in the Tung-lin, a great spring meeting should be held every year at which the Ching-cheng-t'ang 經正堂 in Wu-chin, the Ming-tao shu-yüan 明道書院 in I-hsing, and the Chih-chü-t'ang 志矩堂 in Chin-t'an 金壇 (Chinkiang) should by turn play hosts. Ku as a rule presided at these meetings and delivered lectures. With the help of notes which were usually taken during the lectures and the attendant discussions, Ku later pub-lished the transactions of these and other conferences under the title *Shang-yü* 商語.

Even in his retirement Ku kept up an active interest in public affairs, both local and national. In 1605 he spoke up against the minions of the eunuch com-missioners who were then the scourge of the country. A certain Chao Huan 趙煥 from Ku's native village had exposed abuses of the customs office in Hu-shu kuan 滸墅關 and had been killed by the underlings of the eunuchs. Ku's protests were later distorted and led to the accusa-tion in 1610 that the Tung-lin had inter-fered with the customs of Hu-shu. What Ku did was probably not unusual, but his continuing interest and participation in national politics was indeed highly uncon-ventional for one in retirement. He re-mained in contact with his political friends in Peking and throughout the empire; his pronoucements, to which friend and foe had paid attention while he was in the capital, remained as influential as before.

After the foundation of the Tung-lin Academy, Ku used the meetings quite deliberately for political discussion. For example, in a note written in the autumn of 1606 he invited Shih Meng-lin to come to the next conference and discuss the situation created by the impending resigna-tion of the grand secretary, Shen I-kuan. In time the movement for political criti-cism, centered in the Tung-lin Academy, developed into something like organized political agitation. Some members of the Tung-lin circle made it their task to act as intermediaries between the academy and the "pure critics" at the court and elsewhere. The most important of these self-appointed or semi-official agents were Yü Yü-li 于玉立 (T. 中甫, cs 1583), Huang Cheng-pin 黃正賓, and Wang Wen-yen 汪文言 (both natives of She 歙-hsien, An-hwei), all well versed in political intrigue. It was Ku himself, however, who drew nation-wide attention to the Tung-lin circle in the first place and gave its op-ponents occasion to coin the name Tung-lin tang 黨 (party) which was to remain the object of intense hatred by its enemies, and of intense pride by its followers, for the remaining years of the Ming dynasty.

After the resignation of Shen I-kuan in 1606, the emperor entreated his favorite, Wang Hsi-chüeh, to return as chief grand secretary. Ku felt moved to publish two pieces entitled *Wu-yen* 寤言 (Words of one awake) and *Mei-yen* 寐言 (Words of one asleep). They were narrative in form but actually described the situation at court as the "pure critics" saw it, with the challenge that Wang either accept the summons of the emperor and exert him-self to effect the necessary reforms, or stay home. Although Wang rejected the criticism of himself and his fellow grand secretaries, he stayed home. In 1608 the chief grand secretaryship fell to Yeh Hsiang-kao (*q.v.*) and hopes were high that the alarming deterioration of the governing process, due to a large extent to the indolence and avarice of the em-peror, might be reversed. The first step was to be the recall of ex-officials of proven ability and character. Great efforts in particular were made to have Ku re-stored to office. Late in 1608 the emperor gave his approval for Ku's appointment to the post of sub-director in the Court of Imperial Entertainments in Nanking. Ku discussed the question with his friends at a meeting in the Ching-cheng-t'ang in Wu-chin at the beginning of 1609, and then declined the appointment for reasons of health. Yeh Hsiang-kao and Ku's friends were beside themselves with frustration and urged Ku to reconsider. Finally Ku started for Nanking but en route he received word from his friend, Chao Nan-hsing, warning him against taking office; so, using a fit of illness as excuse, he returned home. In the following year he was recommended for two other posts, but the emperor no longer took any notice.

In the face of the growing influence of the "pure critics," their adversaries drew closer together. There were, in particular, the so-called Ch'i 齊, Ch'u 楚, and Che 浙, and the Hsüan 宣 and K'un 崑 factions. The first three were grouped around a core of censors from Shantung, Hukuang, and Chekiang; the last two were named after the native places of their leaders, the chancellor of the Nanking National University, T'ang Pin-yin 湯賓尹 (T. 嘉寬, H. 霍林, cs 1595) from Hsüan-ch'eng 宣城, and the instructor of the heir apparent, Ku T'ien-chün 顧天埈 (T. 升伯, H. 開雍, cs 1592) from K'un-shan 崑山. T'ang and Ku Hsien-ch'eng were the strategists of the factions. In 1610 the anti-Tung-lin censors concentrated their attack on the governor and director of grain transport, Li San-ts'ai, a stanch member of the Tung-lin faction, so as to prevent him from being appointed a chief censor. In defense of Li, Ku indiscreetly wrote some letters to high officials in Peking. Two of his letters, one to the grand secretary, Yeh Hsiang-kao, and the other to the minister of Personnel, Sun P'ei-yang (q.v.), were circulated in Peking and evidenced as proof of Ku's interference in national affairs. Early in 1611 Li was forced to retire. This was a serious loss to the party. During the scrutiny of 1611

the Tung-lin group succeeded in getting rid of many of their opponents, including T'ang Pin-yin, but this resulted in compelling the non-Tung-lin officials to join forces in their hatred and fear and in their urge for self-preservation. From then on the Ming court was split between Tung-lin and anti-Tung-lin factions, and their struggle, sometimes resulting in bloody strife, marked the remaining three decades of the dynasty.

Ku had no foreboding about the significant role his academy was to play. He seems to have been content with the conviction that he and those on his side were the upright (cheng-jen 正人 and chün-tzu 君子). Late in 1611 he supervised the printing of his collected works, the Ching-kao ts'ang-kao 涇皋藏稿, 22 ch., and the construction of an ancestral hall; this also became the headquarters for management of land which had an annual yield of a thousand shih of grain, contributed by himself and his father, brothers, and nephews. Part of the rent was used for payment of taxes and the remainder for the relief of indigent clansmen. After he died the direction of the Tung-lin Academy was taken over by Kao P'an-lung. At the height of persecution of the Tung-lin faction by the eunuch party, the buildings were destroyed (1625 and 1626), but a few years later they were partly restored, and the meetings there were resumed. Meanwhile posthumous honors to Ku were granted in 1622, revoked three years later, and restored in 1629. He was then given the name Tuan-wen 端文.

Ku's endeavors as a neo-Confucian thinker were first of all aimed at the cultivation of the Confucian way of life for oneself and its spread among one's fellow scholars. During the typical study meetings he and his friends sought moral enlightenment and mutual encouragement by delivering homilies based on the Classics and by subsequent discussion. For his ideas Ku was indebted to the neo-Confucians of both the Sung and Ming periods. His teacher, Hsieh Ying-ch'i (q.

v.), came from the school of Wang Yang-ming (Wang Shou-jen, *q.v.*), but in later years he had also come to appreciate the doctrine of Chu Hsi (1130–1200). In Ku and other Tung-lin scholars a definite movement away from Wang Yang-ming and back to Chu Hsi may be discerned. The turning away from Wang was due to reaction against the radical ethical subjectivism advocated by the extreme wing of the Wang school which led some of his followers to eccentricities and even licentiousness, and to tendencies of syncretism with Buddhism and Taoism on the other hand (*see* Lin Chao-en). Ku held certain utterances of Wang Yang-ming himself responsible for this development, especially his dictum that human nature in itself is neither good nor bad and the other that mind is principle (心即理). Ku did his best to refute the theme of the moral indifference of human nature in his controversy with Kuan Chih-tao. Another formula, which postulated that moral acts ought to be impromptu, or spontaneous (當下), not planned or reflected, Ku also fought. On the important question of the method of cultivation, on the other hand, Ku sided with Wang Yang-ming rather than with Chu Hsi. His chosen ethical motto, to strive for quiescence (主靜), was taken from Chou Tun-i (1017–73) whom Ku esteemed even more highly than he did Chu Hsi. Quiescence for him was freedom from selfish desires, objectivity, rule of the mind and not of the emotions. Ku tried to cultivate this quiescence, among other things, by sitting quietly (靜坐). To sum up, Ku was not a creative or original thinker but rather an eclectic who tried to select the best of the various thinkers. In his critical appraisal of the neo-Confucianists before him, Ku was so straightforward that some later scholars found fault with him, as Sun Ch'i-feng (ECCP) hints. On his contempories Ku's commanding personality seems to have made a deep impression; this can be seen from the exaggerated praise accorded to him by Kao P'an-lung and by Sun Ch'i-feng.

Ku wrote a number of works besides those already mentioned. The exposition of the goodness of human nature, which Ku considered as the central theme of his philosophy and the defense of this tenet against Buddhists, Taoists, and contemporary followers of Wang Yang-ming, is the subject of *Huan-ching lu* 還經錄 written in 1597 and its fuller version, *Cheng-hsing pien* 證性編 in 8 *chüan* (1600). In *Tang-hsia i* 當下釋 (1608) Ku discusses the impromptu morality of the extreme Wang school. Altogether Ku wrote five works on the Four Books, three of them treatises on the *Ta-hsüeh*. He also wrote several works of exempla which do not seem to be extant.

According to the *nien-p'u* of Ku, a collection of eight of his works was printed in 1610. It included the statutes of Tung-lin, the series of *Shang-yü*, the *Ta-hsüeh t'ung-k'ao* 大學通考, *Ta-hsüeh chih-yen* 質言, and the *Tang-hsia i*. To these, works called *Ching-kao pa-shu* 八書, the *I-ssu lu* 以俟錄 (documents concerning the controversy about Li San-ts'ai), and the *Ching-kao ts'ang-kao* were added during the lifetime of Ku, bringing the number up to ten so that the collection was now called *Ching-kao shih-shu* 十書.

The National Central Library of Taipei records a collection of his works, *Ku Tuan-wen kung chi*, which includes the *Ching-kao ts'ang-kao*, the *Tang-hsia i*, and eight of the *Shang-yü* series, printed about 1630. The woodblocks of all these editions were lost during the upheaval which accompanied the fall of the Ming dynasty. Towards the end of the 17th century a great-great-grandson, Ku Chen-kuan (ECCP, p. 662), undertook to publish a complete edition of the works of Ku under the title *Ku Tuan-wen kung i-shu* 公遺書 (printed *ca.* 1698, reprinted 1877), but in the end as many as eleven titles remained unprinted. The *I-shu* contained the diary, the statutes, six *Shang-yü*, the *Tang-hsia i*, the *Cheng-hsing pien* (6 of the 8 *chüan*), the *Huan-ching lu*, the *Tzu-fan lu* 自反錄 (about the political controversies in 1609 and 1610), the *Ching-kao ts'ang-kao*, and a life chronology, *Ku Tuan-wen kung nien-p'u* 年譜, *4 ch.* The last was edited in 1694 by Ku Chen-kuan, who based himself on family records.

Ku had two sons, Ku Yü-t'ing 與淳 born in 1574 and Ku Yü-mu 與沐 born in 1580. Ku Yü-mu graduated a *chü-jen* and rose to the positon of prefect of K'uei-chou-fu 夔州府 in Szechwan. The two eldest grandsons of Ku were both born in 1602, one being Ku Shu 樞, a *chü-jen* of the T'ien-ch'i period who played a role in the Fu-she (*see* Chang P'u, ECCP). After the downfall of the Ming dynasty, he lived in retirement, devoting himself to neo-Confucian philosophy and writing. Ku Chen-kuan was a great-grandson of Ku Yü-mu. He was born in 1637, graduated as a *chü-jen* (1666) during the K'ang-hsi period, and served as sub-archivist in the Mi-shu yüan (*see* Tu Li-te, ECCP, p. 778) in Peking. He was well known as a writer of tz'u 詞.

Bibliography

1/231/1a; 39/2/5a, 14a, *chüan* 21–22; 83/58/3a; MSL (1940), Shen-tsung, 273/7b, 275/8b, Hsi-tsung, 57/7a; KC (1958), 4552, 4693, 4696, 4729, 5021, 5309; SK (1930), 96/8b, 172/12b; Ku Ying-t'ai(ECCP), *Ming-ch'ao chi-shih pen-mo*, 66/1a; Wu Ying-chi (ECCP, p. 52), *Tung-lin pen-mo*, Shanghai, 1936; Hsü Hsien 許獻, *Tung-lin shu-yüan chih* 志 (1736); Li Yen 李棪, *Tung-lin tang chi k'ao* 黨籍考 (1957); H. Busch, "The Tung-lin Shu-yüan and Its Political and Philosophical Significance," MS, XIV (1949–55), 1; C. O. Hucker, "The Tung-lin Movement of the Late Ming Period," in J. K. Fairbank (ed.), *Chinese Thought and Institutions* (Chicago, 1957), 132, 367.

Heinrich Busch

KU Ta-yung 谷大用, died January, 1532, was a member of the pa-hu 八虎 or Eight Tigers (*see* Chu Hou-chao), imperially favored eunuchs during the Cheng-te reign. There is no knowledge of his birth-place, nor information about his family beyond the names of his father, Ku Feng 奉, his elder brother, Ku Ta-k'uan 大寬,

and his younger brothers, Ku Ta-ch'i 玘, Ku Ta-liang 亮, and Ku Ta-chung 中. All are recorded as receiving special favors through Ku Ta-yung's influence. His educational background and early career are also unknown. The first definite information about him is that he served Chu Hou-chao while the latter was still heir apparent. As soon as Chu ascended the throne (June, 1505), Ku was assigned the post of assistant commander of garrison forces in the capital, and before the year was over was made director of the Yü-ma chien 御馬監 (Imperial Stables), the routine work of which was partly a concern of the ministry of War. It was in this period that Ku first became known as one of the Eight Tigers. These eight eunuchs were responsible for providing various games and amusements for the young emperor to divert him from matters of state. Consequently, soon after the succession, the bureaucracy in the outer court and the old eunuch faction in the inner court launched an all-out attack against them. This struggle for power lasted about a year. By the autumn of 1506 the tension in the court was so great that it could be ended only by imperial intervention. The Eight Tigers emerged as winners (*see* Liu Chin). On October 27, both the inner and outer courts were reorganized. Ku Ta-yung was given an additional assignment as the head of the Western Depot, a newly restored secret agency (*see* Wang Chih 汪直); he held this position until the execution of Liu Chin in September, 1510.

The period from October, 1506, to September, 1510, may be regarded as the time when the Eight Tigers were at the height of their influence, and the first period of Ku Ta-yung's official career. One incident worth mentioning is that, on the date of the dragon-boat festival in 1508 (the fifth day of the fifth moon, June 3), a team of his agents viewed the boat race in Nan-k'ang 南康, Kiangsi. During that visit, the agents accused three local families of building dragon-boats (with imperial insignia) without authorization. As a result, their properties were confiscated. After this incident, people in that region would immediately spread the news whenever a stranger riding on a fast horse and speaking with a northern accent appeared. Such activities of imperial agents were rather usual throughout the dynasty. Another act which caused hostility among the people was his annexation of private properties to convert into pastures for imperial horses. His fencing-in of the area was done without proper compensation, an unlawful act which finally caught up with Ku after the death of the emperor. In spite of his lack-luster performance during these years, he must have pleased the emperor, for he received a number of imperial favors. In February, 1507, his brother, Ku Ta-chi, was made a centurion of the Guard, and in June was promoted to be an assistant commander. In October of the same year, his father, Ku Feng, was appointed a commander of the Guard. In May, 1508, Ku Ta-yung himself was made the commander of the Yung-shih and Ch'i-chün 勇士旗軍, two corps under the Yü-ma chien. Favor of this sort to the Eight Tigers came to an end due to their internal wrangling. In early 1510 a direct confrontation took place between the two most influential members, Liu Chin, director of ceremonial, and Chang Yung (q.v.), director of furniture supplies. Ku was instructed by the emperor to act as arbitrator. His success evidently did not last long, for Chang Yung finally was instrumental in the execution of Liu Chin in the autumn, upon Chang's return from the expedition to suppress the rebellion of the prince of An-hua, Chu Chih-fan (q.v.). The downfall of Liu Chin led to a reorganization of the intelligence networks. One of the consequences was the abolition of the Western Depot.

From October, 1510, to the death of the emperor in April, 1521, is the second period of Ku Ta-yung's career. During this decade he enjoyed the emperor's trust and favor. Even though he had lost his post as head of the Western Depot he was compensated (October 12) by having his elder brother, Ku Ta-k'uan, granted the title of earl of Kao-p'ing 高平伯; furthermore, the emperor made an attempt to restore the Western Depot, but was frustrated by the opposition of Grand Secretary Li Tung-yang (q.v.). Ku Ta-yung's fortunes rose again toward the end of 1511, when the rebellion of the Liu brothers, Liu Liu and Liu Ch'i (see Yang T'ing-ho), broke out in north China. The Liu brothers were natives of Wen-an 文安 in Pei-Chihli, and both were skilled in military arts. The local officials in the district often asked them to help keep the peace. Before Liu Chin's execution, however, one of his henchmen, Liang Hung 梁洪, tried to harass the two Liu, labeling them rebels. Whereupon their properties were confiscated, and the brothers fled to join the rebel group led by Chang Mao 張茂. Late in 1511 the Liu brothers initiated an uprising near the capital. Ku, appointed commander of the army of suppression, was assisted by Mao Jui (see Mao Chung) and Lu Wan (see Chu Hou-chao). Their forces, however, all lacked battlefield experience. Several months passed without any issue; but early in 1512 Mao's men had a brief encounter with the rebels at Ch'ang-yüan 長垣 (modern Ta ming-fu), and were badly mauled. At this point, Ku's own contingent was stationed in Lin-ch'ing 臨清, not far from Mao, but he dared not try to effect Mao's rescue. During the autumn of 1512, for some unknown reason, the rebels moved southward. When their main forces were crossing the Yangtze near Chinkiang, a severe storm struck, overturning several of their ferry boats. Lu Wan's pursuing forces seized the opportunity to make their attack, and crushed the main body of the rebels. Ku Ta-yung claimed a victory, and received generous rewards. On October 3, he was granted the hereditary position of commander of the Guard (to be inherited by a nephew) with forty-eight additional *shih* of rice annually, and the Western Depot was temporarily restored. It was soon closed again, however. Several of his adopted sons were also promoted, and in March, 1513, his brother, Ku Ta-liang, was made earl of Yung-ch'ing 永清 伯. Another brother, Ku Ta-chung, received a promotion to be a commissioner-in-chief of a chief military commission. Ku Ta-yung himself was appointed (December, 1513) one of the three joint chief commanders for the army in the capital region.

He enjoyed the imperial confidence throughout the rest of the Cheng-te period. In November, 1514, he and Chang Yung were given the responsibility of rebuilding the Ch'ien-ch'ing 乾清 and K'un-ning 坤 寧 palaces. Eight months later, when the command of the capital troops was reorganized, Ku remained in command. His close relationship with the emperor may be further illustrated by the fact that in August, 1517, when the emperor paid a visit to Hsüan-fu, Ku was sent ahead to assume the command of the Chü-yung Pass 居庸關, responsible for the security of the imperial party. During this assignment, Ku managed to arrest three travelers, accusing them of spying on the imperial activities. For this he received a reward of an additional twelve *shih* of rice annually. In the meantime, he was given a hereditary chiliarchy in the Guard (which later went to another nephew), and his brother, Ku Ta-chung, was promoted to be a commissioner-in-chief. In September, 1519, when the Ch'ien-ch'ing and K'un-ning palaces were completed, Ku was given another chiliarchy of the Guard (which was to go to another nephew). A few months later (January, 1520) the throne appointed him to a newly created position, viz. chang-shih t'ai-chien 掌事太監, or eunuch-in-charge to coordinate all the major offices in the court, while the emperor was on tour in south China.

The death of the emperor in April, 1521, initiated the beginning of the third period of Ku Ta-yung's career. As Chu Hou-chao died without an heir, the ruling coterie ordered Ku to serve as a temporary liaison between the empress-dowager and the Grand Secretariat to decide on a sucessor. They selected Chu Hou-ts'ung (*q.v.*), and dispatched an official party to his estate in Hukuang to welcome him. As a member of this party, Ku went on ahead and on his arrival immediately requested a private audience. The request was flatly turned down, which forecast his future under the new emperor. Less then six weeks after the death of Chu Hou-chao, Yen Hung 閻洪 (T. 尚友, cs 1517), a supervising secretary in the office of scrutiny for Personnel, led the way in an attack on Ku and his fellow eunuchs, and a few days after this they were sent to prison. Though the death penalty was recommended, they were banished from Peking instead. Ku Ta-yung was sent to Nanking as an attendant at the imperial tomb. Two years later he was charged with failing to compensate the owners of the land he had enclosed for horses when he headed the Court of the Imperial Stud. As a result he received a further demotion in his post in Nanking.

The following year his health declined rapidly. He requested special permission to return to Peking for treatment and recuperation on the ground that, after all, he had played a role in the welcome of the emperor. Early in 1525 he was called back to Peking to serve at K'ang-ling 康 陵, the tomb of his previous master, Chu Hou-chao. After this he led a quiet life until he died seven years later, though not without furtherattacks and impeachments. Following his death, Grand Secretary Chai Luan (*see* Yen Sung) recommended that his property be confiscated, a decision approved by the throne.

Bibliography

Ming-shih(Taiwan ed.), 16/112, 17/118, 156/1898, 181/2184, 190/2217, 206/2395, 304/3413, 3415, 5416, 332/3833; MSL (1965), Wu-tsung, ch. 4–197, Shih-tsung, ch. 1–133; *Ming t'ung-chien*

(1900 ed.), 40/1533, 1555, 1590, 1612; KC(1958), ch. 4552; Shen Te-fu, *Wan-li yeh-hu pien*, ch. 6; Chang Hsüan, *Hsi-yüan wen-chien lu*, ch. 101; Wang Shih-chen, *Yen-shan-t'ang pieh-chi*, ch. 95; Yeh Ting-i 葉丁易, *Ming-tai t'e-wu cheng-chih* 明代特務政治 (Peking, 1951), 33; Robert Crawford, "Eunuch Power in the Ming Dynasty," TP, 49 (1961), 120.

Yung-deh Richard Chu

KU Tso 顧佐 (T. 禮卿, H, 端臨), died 1446, an early Ming official particularly noted as a reformist censor-in-chief, was a native of T'ai-k'ang 太康 in the Kaifeng region of Honan. After winning the *chin-shih* in 1400, he was appointed magistrate of Chuang-lang 莊浪 in western Shensi (later Kansu province). In 1402 he was called to the capital, Nanking, to serve as an investigating censor and thus began a long career in censorial offices. In 1409 he was transferred to the new branch (行在) Censorate at Peking, which was then being readied for the transfer of the whole central government from Nanking. Promoted to be surveillance vice commissioner of Kiangsi (some texts say Shensi, but seem in error), he was further promoted to be governor of Ying-t'ien 應天, the metropolitan prefecture of Nanking; and when Peking was officially made the capital in 1421 he was transferred to the governorship of the metropolitan prefecture there, Shun-t'ien 順天.

Early in his career Ku established a reputation for integrity; in this regard people likened him to the famous Judge Pao (999–1062) of Sung times. But his resolute honesty discomfited many of his superiors at court, where moral laxity and bureaucratic apathy were becoming the norm in the last years of Emperor Chu Ti (*q.v.*). So in 1422 Ku was transferred away from court to be surveillance commissioner of the under-developed southwestern frontier province, Kweichow. Under Chu Ti's successor, Chu Kao-chih (*q.v.*), Ku was recalled to court as transmission commissioner, and in 1428 promoted to be right censor-in-chief by the new emperor, Chu Chan-chi (*q.v.*), on the recommendation of the grand secretaries, Yang Shih-ch'i and Yang Jung (*qq.v.*).

Chu Chan-chi was an earnest, moralistic ruler. He was gravely troubled by the licentious life of the capital and the venality of the bureaucracy, and he laid most of the blame for prevailing conditions on the long-time head of the Censorate, Liu Kuan 劉觀 (cs 1385, vice censor-in-chief 1404–8, censor-in-chief 1415–28), who was accused of intimidating his subordinate censors and allowing his son, Liu Fu 輻, without any official status, to rule the Censorate in his name. An investigation found Liu Fu guilty of keeping a wine shop, associating with prostitutes, and stealing government property. He was sentenced in 1429 to serve as a convict with the military service in Liaotung, and his father made to accompany him.

The emperor gave Ku Tso control of the Censorate for the specified purpose of preparing that agency to maintain more effective disciplinary surveillance over officialdom, and Ku was well disposed to this task. Before the end of 1428 he had swept thirty investigating censors and two of the Censorate's minor administrative officers out of their posts and recommended forty-five junior officials of good repute to become investigating censors. Late that year another disciplinarian, Shao Ch'i 邵玘 (T. 以先, 1375-1430, cs 1406), was given control of the Nanking Censorate as left vice censor-in-chief, with orders to purge it in like fashion; and in 1429, on Shao's recommendation, thirteen investigating censors were removed from the relatively small Nanking staff. Moreover, Shao is said to have brought about the dismissal of some eighty other officials. The disciplining of censors continued until by the end of Chu Chan-chi's reign at the beginning of 1435 a cumulative total of 118 disciplinary actions had been taken against investigating censors. The purge was long remembered; two centuries later court officials still talked about it when another head of the Censorate, Kao P'an-lung (*q.v.*), conducted a minor shakeup in it. Kao was praised for being like "Ku in the north and Shao in the south."

Ku was a sober man who took his censorial duties seriously, influencing both that institution and the mores of the capital. It was under his aegis that new, inexperienced *chin-shih* were banned from censorial office and that all new appointments as investigating censors came to be probationary, subject to confirmation only after three months (later, six months) of good conduct. It was also at his insistence that officials on duty in the capital were forbidden to entertain in houses of pleasure, which had become their custom. Ku's whole image in history is that of humorless severity. It is said that he deliberately did not fraternize with fellow officials and that he felt it not worthwhile to speak unless he had something to champion or something to denounce. In court audiences he sat to one side frowningly scrutinizing everyone. It is clear that he was held in awe by most of his peers; he came to be known as Ku tu-tso 獨坐 (Sit-alone Ku). He was no doubt over-zealous in purging the Censorate of undesirables, and occasionally was gently rebuked by the emperor for his hasty decisions about guilt. But Ku's integrity was never seriously questioned. Soon after he took office in the Censorate a lesser functionary impeached him, saying that Ku accepted money from some clerks in that office and secretly released them to go home. The emperor asked Yang Shih-ch'i about this, and the grand secretary said it was true of all offices in Peking because capital officials commonly followed this practice to supplement their meager salaries, as he did himself. The emperor regretted that high ministers were so poorly paid and turned the accuser over to Ku for punishment. When Ku merely urged that he change his ways, the emperor is reported to have become more pleased than ever with him.

Ku was held in such esteem by the throne that he was repeatedly made a member of regency councils set up to control the central government when the emperor was traveling, and when Ku fell seriously ill for more than a year in 1433-34 the emperor relieved him of most of his duties but would not permit him to go home on sick leave. Ku retired in 1436 under Chu Ch'i-chen (*q.v.*), thereafter lived quietly in Kaifeng, and died at home a decade later. A great-grandson, Ku Ta-sheng 大膾, in 1522 compiled a memorial volume of documents relating to Ku Tso's career, called *Tu yü-shih Kukung en-jung lu* 都御史顧公恩榮錄, which was printed in the Chia-ching reign. A National Library of Peiping copy is available in the Library of Congress microfilm series (roll #137).

At least one other Ku Tso and three other men named Liu Kuan attained some eminence in Ming times. The other Ku Tso (*see* Chou Ching), a native of Lin-huai 臨淮, Nan-Chihli, eventually became governor of Shansi province (1495-96) and, later, minister of Revenue (1506-8). Liu Kuan [II] of T'ai-ku 太谷, Shansi, was appointed a supervising secretary in 1394 and subsequently assistant transmission commissioner. Liu Kuan [III] (T. 崇觀, H. 臥廬先生, cs 1439, of Chi-shui 吉水, Kiangsi) did not take office but devoted himself to scholarship and teaching, attracting many disciples. Liu Kuan [IV] (cs 1451, of Wu-chin 武進, northwest of Soochow) served as supervising secretary, administration vice commissioner in Fukien, and finally as administration commissioner in Hukuang.

Bibliography

1/151/11a, 158/2b, 185/4b; 3/148/1a, 2b; 5/54/ 23a, 31a, 64/44a; 21/4/6a; 61/119/14b; 63/19/1a; TSCC (1885-88) XI: 353/15/8a; Wang Shih-chen, *Yen-shan-t'ang pieh-chi*, 23/2b; Yeh Sheng, *Shui-tung jih-chi*, 2/12a, 6/4b; MSL (1940), Hsüan-tsung,44/10a, 45/3a, 46/5a, 6a, 47/8a, 14b, 56/8a, 10b, 61/3a, 105/4b, 113/9b; C. O. Hucker, *The Censorial System of Ming China* (Standford, 1966), 63, 259.

Charles O. Hucker

KU Ying-hsiang 顧應祥 (early *ming* 夢麟,
T. 惟賢, H. 箬溪), 1483-September 29'30,
1565, official and mathematician, was a
native of Ch'ang-hsing 長興, Chekiang.
Following his graduation as *chin-shih*
(1505), he received an appointment (1508)
as prefectural judge of Jao-chou-fu 饒州
府, Kiangsi. Rebels were then disturbing
the peace at T'ao-yüan-tung 桃源洞 in
the T'ien-t'ai mountains, T'ien-t'ai 天臺
-hsien, and seized the magistrate, Wang
Ho 汪和 (cs 1505) of Lo-p'ing 樂平, Jao-
chou prefecture. Ku succeeded in effecting his rescue. He was next posted
(1516) to Kwangtung as assistant surveillance commissioner, and was also made
acting director of the bureau of maritime
commerce. As such, near the end of September, 1517, he became an eyewitness of
the arrival of the Portuguese fleet under
the command of Fernão Peres de Andrade.
Although the Portuguese had touched
the southern coast in 1514 and 1516, this
was the first contact between them and
the Chinese in which there are first hand
reports both in Portuguese and in Chinese. In this instance too the Portuguese
brought an ambassador, Tomé Pires (*q.v.*),
who, accompanied by a Portuguese retinue, was sent to Peking to be lodged in
the official residence for foreigners (the
Hui-t'ung-kuan 會同館), according to Ku
Ying-hsiang. They also stored the presents
destined for the emperor in the same
place. In his account Ku relates that Pires
and his escort remained there for about a
year. Meanwhile (the end of September,
1518) de Andrade took off for Malacca.

In these same years Ku became involved in the campaign to suppress the rebels entrenched in Fukien (T'ing-chou 汀州
and Chang 漳 -chou) who were overrunning three provinces. Wang Shou-jen (*q.v.*),
then governor of southern Kiangsi and
adjacent areas, requested him to come to
his aid. With the troops he collected and
with his supply of explosive weapons, Ku
was able to put to death fourteen hundred of the enemy. Later Ku had a hand
in suppressing uprisings in Hukuang and

elsewhere. From Kwangtung he was transferred to Kiangsi as surveillance vice
commissioner, and rose by a succession of
provincial appointments in Shensi (1526)
and Shantung (1527) until in 1538 (?) he
became a right vice censor-in-chief and
concurrently governor of Yunnan. After
several years in the southwest he was
shifted to Nanking as right vice minister
of War (August, 1549). A year later (August 29, 1550) he reached his highest rank,
that of minister of Justice in Peking; but
he held the office hardly more than half
a year because he displeased the grand
secretary, Yen Sung (*q.v.*), being downgraded (April 3, 1551) to minister of Justice, Nanking. Dismissed in March, 1554,
because of an accusation by an investigating censor in Nanking, named Li Shang-
chih 李尚智 (cs 1544), Ku went home.
He lived on for eleven more years, dying
at the age of eighty-two. He was laid to
rest at Ling-shan 靈山 in his native district, and was posthumously accorded the
title of junior guardian of the heir apparent.

Ku was responsible for a number of
books, the most noteworthy perhaps being
in the field of mathematics. His *Ts'e-yüan
hai-ching fen-lei shih shu* 測圓海鏡分類釋術,
10*ch.*, published 1550, according to Joseph
Needham and Wang Ling, "distinguishes
equations of the various degrees according to the signs of their coefficients,"
and gives fuller explanations for their solution than did his contemporary T'ang
Shun-chih (*q.v.*). A second work, *Hu shih
suan-shu* 弧矢算術, 1 *ch.* (1552), "system-
atized the formulae developed up to
that time for dealing with arcs and
circle segments." These were his only
works copied into the *Ssu-k'u ch'üan-shu*.
Three others are listed by title: the *Jen
tai chi-yao* 人代紀要, 30 *ch.*, a chronicle
of important events in Chinese history;
the *Nan-chao shih-lüeh* 南詔事略, 1 *ch.*, an
historical work on the Nan-chao written
while he was serving in Yunnan; and the
Hsi yin lu 惜陰錄, 12 *ch.*, a discursus on
thought, including the ideas of Wang

Shou-jen, written when he was eighty-one. Although acknowledgedly a pupil of Wang, he did not completely agree with the master, according to Huang Tsung-hsi (EC CP).

Bibliography

5/48/80a; 40/28/13a; 64/10/1b;83/13/3b;86/9/28b; MSL (1964), Wu-tsung, 3630, Shih-tsung (1965) 6469, 6618, 7110; KC (1958), 3209, 3668, 3736, 3752, 3775, 3828; *Ch'ang-hsing-hsien chih* (1874), 20/16a, 23/53b; *Chekiang t'ung-chih* (1934), 2820, 4043; *Shantung t'ung-chih* (1934), 1704, 1709; *Yunnan t'ung-chih* (1894), 120/15b, 135/24a; *Kwang-tung t'ung-chih* (1934), 367, 4285; Mao Yüan-i, *Wu-pei chih*, 122/7b; TSCC (1885-88), XXIV: 122/28/15a; SK (1930), 48/3a, 66/9a, 107/4b, 5b, 124/5b; L. of C. *Catalogue of Rare Books*, 428; NCL *Catalogue*, 2/116; Joseph Needham with the collaboration of Wang Ling, *Science and Civilization in China*, III (Cambridge, England, 1959), 51; Chang T'ien-tse, *Sino-Portuguese Trade from 1514 to 1644* (Leyden, 1934), 42; Paul Pelliot, "Le H̱ōja et le Sayyid H̱usein de l'Histoire des Ming," TP, 38(1947), 81, 88, 272; W. F. Mayers, *Notes and Queries on China and Japan*, 2 (1868), 129.

L. Carrington Goodrich

K'UAI Hsiang 蒯祥, 1398-1481, carpenter and construction worker, was a native of Soochow. His father K'uai Fu 福 served as an artisan in the ministry of Works in the early years of the Yung-lo period (1403-24). When the senior K'uai retired, his son succeeded him. In 1417, when Emperor Chu Ti (*q.v.*) went from Nanking to Peking, K'uai accompanied the imperial entourage. For more than six decades thereafter he participated as chief architect in nearly all the construction works involved in the restoration of Peking as the capital of the empire. The most outstanding achievement was perhaps his connection with the building of the audience and residence halls completed in 1441 (*see* Juan An). Other works included the erection of various government offices. For his industry and talent, K'uai was successively promoted in the ministry of Works first as assistant then chief of the bureau of construction, and later assistant director in the Court of the Imperial Stud. Finally in 1456 he was made a vice minister of Works. Lu Hsiang 陸祥 (d. 1470, a native of Wu-hsi), stone mason, concurrently received the same rank. When Emperor Chu Ch'i-chen (*q.v.*) died in 1464, his mausoleum was constructed under K'uai's direction. It was said that the last emperor he served, Chu Chien-shen (*q.v.*), used to address him as K'uai Lu Pan 魯班, Lu Pan being the patron god of carpenters. K'uai's grandparents and parents were honored posthumously, and one of his two sons was made a chiliarch in the Embroidered-uniform Guard, and the other appointed a student in the National University. Throughout the long history of China few construction men received comparable distinction. In the Ming dynasty, however, K'uai Hsiang was not alone; nearly a century later another carpenter and construction worker, Hsü Kao 徐杲, rose to an even higher position, but his career ended less fortunately than K'uai Hsiang's.

A native of Yangchow, Hsü Kao made his contributions largely during the reign of Emperor Chu Hou-ts'ung (*q.v.*) who, at first, was obsessed with a desire to honor his deceased father, and latterly became deeply concerned with Taoist rituals. Both pursuits required the erection of temples, altars, palaces, and special structures. Frequent fires, moreover, resulted in destruction in the palaces, requiring repairs and replacements. This second longest reign in the Ming dynasty saw perhaps more construction than any other. It is said that prior to any building project, Hsü Kao would first make a careful survey and then as work progressed it was observed that his calculations in every respect were entirely correct. Early in 1562, when the Wan-shou kung 萬壽宮 was completed, it pleased the emperor so much that promotions went to all concerned and Hsü Kao was elevated from vice minister to minister of Works, and his son, Hsü Wen-ts'an 文燦, was given the rank of a hereditary centurion in the Embroidered-uniform Guard, later rising to commander. After the death of the emperor, many of his favorites suffered reverses. In 1567 Hsü Kao was dismissed as minister of Works and his son cashiered. But misfortune did not stop there; before long a eunuch accused Hsü of earlier embezzlement while directing repairs to the Lu-kou ch'iao 蘆溝橋 (Marco Polo Bridge). Hsü was sentenced not only to pay the money reportedly misappropriated, but also to be banished.

In the case of both K'uai Hsiang as vice-minister and Hsü Kao as minister, they were accorded the title, rank, and salary of their posts, but not the ministerial duties. For this reason, in the various lists of high officials, their names are wanting.

It may be of interest to recall here that the imperial house of Ming also produced an ingenious carpenter. Chu Yu-chiao (ECCP), emperor of the T'ien-ch'i period, is recorded as never tiring of wood carving, lacquer work, and building miniature palaces and gardens. He even designed and constructed a fountain.

Bibliography

5/51/16a, 61/84; TSCC (1885–88), XXXII: 5/24a; MSL (1964), Hsien-tsung, 3710, Shih-tsung (1965), 8367; Teng Ch'iu 鄧球, *Huang Ming yung-hua lei-pien* 皇明泳化類編 (1568 Taiwan reprint), 679; Ch'en Chien and Shen Kuo-yüan 沈國元, *Huang Ming ts'ung-hsin lu* 皇明從信錄 (Wan-li ed.), 23/24a; Shen Te-fu, *Wan-li yeh-hu pien* 萬曆野獲編 (Peking, 1959), 2/5b; Shan Shih-yüan 單士元 and Wang Wen-pi 王文璧, *Ming-tai Chien-chu ta shih nien-piao* 明代建築大事年表 (Peiping, 1937); Chu Ch'i-ch'ien 朱啓鈐 and Liang Ch'i-hsiung 梁啓雄, "Che-chiang lu" 哲匠錄, in *Chung-kuo ying-tsao hsüeh she hui-k'an* 中國營造學社會刊 (Bulletin of the Society for Research in Chinese Architecture), Vol. III, no. 3 (September, 1932), 101.

Lienche Tu Fang

K'UANG Chung 況鐘 (T. 伯律, H. 龍岡, 如愚), September 3, 1383-January, 1443, celebrated prefect of Soochow, was a native of Ching-an 靖安, northwest of Nan-chang in Kiangsi. It is said that his father, K'uang I-shih 以實 (T. 仲謙, H. 遜齋, 1346-1418), was orphaned by the red-turbaned rebels under Hsü Shou-hui (*q.v.*) during the conquest of northern Kiangsi in 1351 or 1352; adopted as son and heir by a neighbor named Huang 黃, he was brought up under the name of Huang I-shih. That is why K'uang Chung's name in the first forty-six years of his life was Huang Chung; in 1429 he obtained imperial permission to restore his surname to K'uang in order to venerate his own ancestors. Out of gratitude to the foster family, he arranged to have his younger brother remain as a Huang to continue the worship of the ancestors of that family too.

While he was still in his infancy, K'uang Chung's mother died. Later his father and stepmother permitted him to study in preparation for the civil examinations. In 1406 the magistrate of Ching-an, Yü I 俞益 (cs 1404, d. 1435), enlisted him in a program of training as a clerk in the district office and later, noticing his talents, recommended him for service in a higher office. In 1414 he passed the examination for clerical staff at the ministry of Personnel in Peking and received an assignment to serve in the ministry of Rites. There a year later the minister, Lü Chen 呂震 (T. 克聲, 1365-1426, cj 1386), recommended K'uang Chung to the throne for a special promotion. After an audience with the emperor (Chu Ti, *q.v.*), he was adjudged qualified for an official appointment and made a secretary in the ministry of Rites. (At that time a promising yamen clerk had the same rights to promotion as a *chin-shih* or a student in the National University, a procedure for qualification in government service known as the three concurrent routes [三途幷用]. Later only the *chin-shih* received preferential treatment, the clerks being gradually discriminated against until they were practically barred from high ranks in the bureaucracy.) In 1416 he was selected to serve in the entourage accompanying the emperor from Peking to Nanking. A year later he retired to observe the period of mourning for his stepmother but was soon summoned by imperial order to forgo the mourning and return to his ministry. Then in 1418 his father died and again he was refused permission to complete the mourning period and was ordered to resume his service. So indispensable did his superiors in the ministry of Rites find him that, in 1424, after completing nine years of service as a secretary, he received the unusual promotion by special imperial decree to bureau director in his ministry.

When Emperor Chu Kao-chih (q.v.) died suddenly on May 29, 1425, the heir apparent Chu Chan-chi (q.v.) was serving as head of the government at Nanking. News of the death was kept secret while a commission went posthaste to the southern capital to summon the prince. K'uang Chung volunteered to represent his ministry on the commission. He is said to have traveled continuously for seven days on horseback to reach Nanking and then accompanied the prince to Peking for the enthronement.

At that time the emperor was concerned about local administration, especially in the larger and more populous prefectures where the collection of taxes, maintenance of order, and supervision of the local clerical staff demanded experienced men with superior ability as prefects. In the summer of 1430, nine such prefectural vacancies were filled with central government officials through special recommendation by their superiors. K'uang Chung, whose name headed the list of nine, was sent to the most difficult office of all, that of the prefect of Soochow. The commission given to these prefects included the right of directly memorializing the throne, full authority to deal with subordinates, and instructions to look after the welfare of the people, to equalize their burdens in tax and labor service, to ignore the intimidation of the powerful, and to detect the offenses of unprincipled clerks. So armed, K'uang Chung first demonstrated his ability by bringing the yamen clerks under control and removing twelve subordinates on various charges. It is said that his accusation of incompetence against one of these men was later found to be incorrect and he was reprimanded. The emperor, however, had confidence in him and he also had the backing of the governor, Chou Ch'en (see Chang Hung), and the grand secretary, Yang Shih-ch'i (q.v.). In 1431 when his second stepmother died and he again retired for mourning, more than thirty thousand people of Soochow submitted requests to have him resume his office as prefect. Thus once more he was recalled before completing the mourning period. In March, 1432, a superior, Ch'eng Chün 成均 (cj 1405, d. ca. 1439), tried to remove him by accusing him of improper conduct and corruption, a charge which K'uang refuted in a memorial. He did receive a reprimand for having misjudged a subordinate but was permitted to remain at his post, for the emperor was convinced of his honesty. He served ten more years as prefect of Soochow, receiving many honors in the meantime. In 1439 he was promoted to the third grade and a year later given the rank of a surveillance commissioner. In 1441, when by regulation he was in line for promotion, twenty thousand (some accounts say eighty thousand) local people succeeded in requesting the emperor to send him back to them.

The people of Soochow were grateful to K'uang Chung chiefly for his achievement in the reduction of the tax quota on grain. Since about 1368, the seven districts of Soochow, partly as a punishment for their support of the anti-Ming leader, Chang Shih-ch'eng (q.v.), had been assessed annually, in addition to heavy labor duties, large amounts of cloth, silk, weapons, and articles of luxury, a total of 2,779,109 piculs of rice. This was four percent more than the rice tax of the entire province of Chekiang. The people themselves, moreover, were charged with the transportation of rice to the imperial granaries—a tremendous task when the capital was at Nanking, but after 1403, with the building and later shifting of the capital to Peking, this burden became intolerable. The government-appointed liang-chang 糧長 (tax collectors), who were responsible for the delivery of the rice, had to increase the surcharge to meet the cost until it amounted to twice the tax, making a total of over eight million piculs collected from the people of Soochow every year. By 1430, when K'uang arrived at his post, some families had been ruined financially and many had left their lands and become migrants; the arrears in tax had accumulated to seven million piculs. K'uang followed an imperial order issued in March of that year promising a 20 to 30 percent reduction of all excessive rates of taxation, by requesting for the Soochow prefecture a decrease of 721,600 piculs (22%) in annual grain tax. The ministry of Revenue, however, refused to sanction the full reduction requested, on the excuse that the rate of taxation on much of the land in Soochow was fixed long before the Ming dynasty. After being rebuffed several times, K'uang advised the emperor not to retreat from his initial authorization to the prefects. The emperor reviewed the situation, overruled the ministry's decision (1433), and granted Soochow full reduction. K'uang further lessened the people's burden by halving the surcharges.

Meanwhile, by enforcing the regulations and disciplining the unruly, K'uang maintained order so that the law-abiding might live in peace. In 1432 almost forty thousand family groups, which had left the area, returned to the prefecture's tax register. K'uang is credited with reducing some taxes imposed in time of emergency, for the support of such items as remote post stations and the transportation of grain by the Grand Canal. He also won some altercations over illegal demands made by powerful persons such as eunuchs on imperial mission or hereditary guard officers. In matters of legal judgment, he was noted for his just decisions but no spectacular case is associated with his name. There is a story in the *Ching-shih t'ung-yen* (*see* Feng Meng-lung) about a murder case in Yangchow which, according to the teller, he settled while traveling by that city in a boat. It seems unlikely, however, that he would permit himself to meddle in affairs outside his own jurisdiction.

After K'uang died in office early in 1443 thousands mourned him. As a prominent native son, he came to be officially commemorated in a special shrine in Ching-an. Later in the Ming dynasty, because of his achievements, his name was officially celebrated in a shrine (rebuilt in 1709) in the Soochow prefectural school. In the compound of that school there also remain a monument bearing an inscription of his essay on an office building and another monument erected in 1436 by the local people, with his portrait and a sketch of his life. There are four Ming collections of his writings or materials about him, entitled *Chung-chen chi* 忠貞集, *Ch'uan-fang* 傳芳 *chi*, *Wen-hsien* 文獻 *chi*, and *Kao-yü* 膏雨 *chi*. In 1763 these were brought together under the title *K'uang Lung-kang kung chih-su cheng-chi ch'üan-chi* 況龍岡公治蘇政績全集. In 1826, when Ch'en Wen-shu (ECCP) and others in Soochow erected a special shrine to K'uang, a new edition of this collection was engraved under the title *K'uang t'ai-shou* 太守 *chi*, 16 *ch*. The shrine was destroyed by the T'aip'ing army in 1860 and rebuilt in 1872.

There is an edict in the collection which reflects on the imperial demands on the people of Soochow. It was issued in 1434, instructing K'uang that, because the earlier shipment of crickets was deficient in both quality and quantity he was to assist the two eunuchs on that mission in carefully selecting a thousand large and strong ones for the next shipment. Apparently the game of cricket fighting was then a fad in the palaces in Peking (*see* Chu Chan-chi), but it did not always result in pleasure for the people as may be noted in the story entitled "Ch'u-chih" 促織 in *Liao-chai chih-i* (*see* P'u Sung-ling, ECCP).

In two places in the 1826 adition of *K'uang t'ai-shou chi* (凡例 /2a, 3/2b) the editors in trying to praise K'uang stated that he did not employ any mu-pin 幕賓 (private secretary), writing documents himself. This anachronistic comment became the basis for some modern writers to infer that local officials in the Ming dynasty employed private secretaries. Actually all Ming local civil officials composed their own papers, perhaps letting a clerk make the first draft. Understandably, only military commanders employed help in legal, financial, or literary matters, and some high military leaders were assigned civil officials as staff. The system of employing private secretaries by civil officials developed in the early Ch'ing period. When the Manchus conquered China in the mid-seventeenth century, the military commanders continued the Ming tradition of employing experts to help. The Manchus appointed to civil posts, however, likewise needed such aid; thus the employment of mu-pin gradually took on the status of an institution, at first surreptitiously but later with imperial sanction. In time the Chinese civil officials did the same. By the 19th century it had become such an accepted procedure that the editors of the *K'uang t'ai-shou chi* considered a prefect who did not have the help of private secretaries as quite unusual, being of almost a remarkable virtue. Unfortunately this innocent mistake has led some modern scholars to cite it as a basis for the notion that the mu-pin as an institution existed in the 15th century.

The legend of K'uang Chung as an official of wisdom and integrity grew to such an extent that a story of the Sung dynasty, *Ts'o-chan Ts'ui Ning* 錯斬 崔寧, about a mistrial was recast substituting K'uang for the original hero in a mid-seventeenth century music-drama entitled *Shih-wu kuan ch'uan-ch'i* 十五貫傳奇, 2 *ch.*, by Chu Ho 朱𧮲 (T. 素臣, fl. 1650?). It became so popular that it was retold in perhaps every form of Chinese folk literature and adapted to several styles of opera. In 1956 there appeared several version in Communist China, including one for the Peking opera by Shu Ch'ing-ch'un ("Lao She," BDRC). Wu Han (BDRC) explained the popularity of the tales about K'uang Chung as due to the common people's detestation of all corrupt and arbitrary officials who oppressed them, and their gratitude towards such officials as K'uang who took their side. Ten years later the communists in power accused Wu of covertly inciting the people to oppose them and purged both Shu and Wu.

Bibliography

1/161/6a; 5/83/13a; 14/6/17a; 15/9/5a; 61/118/ 22a; 63/27/11a; *K'uang tai-shou chi* (1849 printing of 1826 ed.); KC (1958), 1392, 1404, 1429, 1433, 1435, 1445, 1526, 1574, 1604, 1637; MSL (1963), Ying-tsung, 2006; Shen Te-fu, *Wan-li yeh-hu-pien* (1958), 574; Ch'ü T'ung-tsu, *Local Government in China under the Ch'ing* (Cambridge, Mass., 1962), 258; *Chiang-nan t'ung-chih* 江南通 志 (1684), 113/36b; *Wu-hsien chih* 吳縣志(1933), 33/17b, 42/17a, 59/26a, Wang Ch'ang-shih 王昌 時, *Huang Ming chün-mu lien-p'ing chuan* 皇明郡牧 廉平傳 (Yangchow mimeograph, Ming ms., *ca.* 1955, *chüan* 2.

Chaoying Fang

K'UANG Yeh 鄺埜 (T. 孟質, H. 朴齋), 1385–September 1, 1449, minister of War from 1445 to 1449, was born into a family registered in the military category in I-chang 宜章, Hukuang, on the Kwangtung border. His father, K'uang Tzu-fu 子輔 (T. 雄德), served as magistrate of An-fu 安福, Kiangsi, during the reign of the first emperor. Following his acquisition of the *chü-jen* in 1405 and the *chin-shih* in 1411,

K'uang Yeh was assigned to the Censorate in charge of trying criminal cases. In January, 1414, he received promotion to be a censor in Peking. He had hardly assumed office when he was sent to Nanking to investigate an alleged attempt by the local merchants to discredit the monetary notes in favor of gold and silver currency. K'uang punished the ringleaders and restored the value of the paper money. Next he went to Liaotung to conduct the trial of soldiers indicted for deserting their posts in the face of *wo-k'ou* raids and exercised his authority responsibly. Then in June, 1417, after the court decreed the providing of medical care to the artisans engaged in construction work in Peking, K'uang was sent there as supervisor. In August of the following year, he received promotion to be the surveillance vice commissioner of Shensi and distinguished himself for his relief work during a period of natural calamities; he held this post until the death of his father in 1430.

In October, 1433, K'uang Yeh was promoted to be the prefectural governor of Ying-t'ien 應天-fu, an important post with jurisdiction over the metropolitan area of Nanking; this gave him direct access to the emperor. When the censors for Nan-Chihli behaved superciliously towards him and bullied his subordinates, K'uang memorialized (March, 1434) proposing the establishment of a special code of etiquette to be observed by the censors in their communications with the officials of his prefecture. His recommendation was accepted. K'uang stayed in this post until the end of the reign of Chu Chanchi (*q.v.*); during these years he improved the welfare of the inhabitants by adjusting the revenue quota in times of bad harvests, and by curtailing unnecessary government expenses, such as elaborate preparations for the prefectural examinations.

Late in 1436, shortly after the succession of Chu Ch'i-chen (*q.v.*), K'uang advanced to the rank of vice minister of War under Wang Chi (*q.v.*), taking charge of military planning against the intrusion of the Mongols along the northwestern frontier. Only after a few months in office (January, 1437), however, the young emperor put both K'uang and Wang into prison for failing to report promptly the military situation, but released them shortly afterwards. Late in the same year, as Wang Chi assumed command of an expedition against the Mongols in Kansu, K'uang was given charge of the ministry. His performance made an impression on the emperor who favored him (December, 1438) by removing his name from the military register, thereby exempting his descendants from conscription. During his tenure as Wang Chi's deputy, K'uang was noted for several recommendations. In November, 1437, he proposed that an order be issued to all commanders to recruit men of exceptional martial prowess for service on the northern frontier. When drought struck Pei-Chihli and Shantung in May, 1441, with the consequent loss of many cavalry horses, he suggested that those responsible for rearing animals for the army be spared from making good the losses. Three months later he joined with several high officials in submitting a memorial urging new regulations and reorganization of the curriculum of the military schools in the capital. K'uang completed his nine-year term of service in November, 1442, but the emperor asked him to remain in office; he then served under Hsü Hsi (*see* Wang Chen), minister of War from June, 1442, to November, 1445.

K'uang succeeded Hsü as minister and assumed full responsibility for the military operation against the Oirat who had increased their hostilities on the northwestern frontier. In a conference in November, 1447, he proposed several exigent measures: increase of grain storage for the border guards, strengthening defense preparations in Tatung and Hsüan-fu, and dispatch of high officials to inspect the frontier. The emperor approved his recommendations; the situation quickly deteri-

orated, however, as a result of corruption
in the army and the indecision of the
court. In August, 1449, urged on by the
eunuch Wang Chen, the emperor decided
to take personal command of a campaign
against the Oirat chieftain Esen (*q.v.*).
K'uang was among those summoned to join
the expedition. Together with many of his
colleagues, K'uang remonstrated with
Wang against this hazardous undertaking,
but the eunuch turned a deaf ear. On his
way to the frontier, probably due to inexperience, K'uang accidentally fell from
his horse and injured himself. He continued
on with the rest, however. After the
debacle at Hsüan-fu of Chu Yung (*see*
Hsiang Chung) on August 30, K'uang
again pleaded with Wang Chen to withdraw, but the eunuch once more shrugged
off his appeal. In the disastrous defeat at
T'u-mu on September 1, during which the
emperor and his retinue were taken prisoner, K'uang was killed in action, together
with many other high officials. He was
then sixty-four years of age.

Early in 1450, when the new emper-
or, Chu Ch'i-yü (*q.v.*), bestowed lavish
posthumous awards on the officials who
perished in the campaign, he honored
K'uang with the title of junior guardian,
and appointed his son, K'uang I 儀, to be
a secretary in the ministry of Revenue in
Nanking. Then in October, 1466, acting
on the recommendation of the minister
of Rites, Yao K'uei (*q.v.*), Emperor Chu
Chien-shen (*q.v.*) granted K'uang Yeh the
canonized name Chung-su 忠肅 (loyal and
majestic).

Bibliography

1/167/2b; 5/38/31a; 9/5/21a; 61/122/1a; MSL
(1962), T'ai-tsung, 1722, 2100, Hsüan-tsung,
(1963), 355, 2367, 2416, Ying-tsung (1964), ch.
3–181, p. 7033, Hsien-tsung, 673; KC (1958),
1776; Ch'en Hsün, *Fang-chou wen-chi* 芳洲文集
(NLP microfilm, no. 978), 7/33b; K'uang
Kuang-ning 鄺光寧, *Ku K'uang-kuo ts'ung-t'an*
古鄺國叢談 (Hong Kong, 1967), 209.

Hok-lam Chan

KUEI O 桂蕚 (T. 子實, H. 見山), died
October 3, 1531, grand secretary, was a
native of An-jen 安仁, Kiangsi. After
qualifying for the *chü-jen* in 1507 and the
chin-shih in 1511, he became magistrate of
Tan-t'u 丹徒, Chinkiang; later he suffered
flogging for opposing his superiors and
was cashiered. Restored to office as magistrate of Wu-k'ang 武康, Chekiang, in
1517, he was demoted in 1520 for contradicting a superior. Subsequently he
received a transfer to the magistracy of
Ch'eng-an 成安, Pei-Chihli, and in 1521,
when Chu Hou-ts'ung (*q.v.*) had ascended
the throne, he was promoted to be secretary of a bureau in the ministry of Justice in Nanking.

Shortly after the new emperor's assumption of power, one of the principal
proposals which he made concerned the
titles to be granted his parents (*see Ta-li
i* case in Feng Hsi, Chu Hou-ts'ung). Early
in 1524 Kuei O submitted a memorial
supporting the views of Chang Fu-ching
and Huo T'ao (*qq. v.*) as expressed in
their memorial of 1521, and recommended
the memorials written by Hsi Shu (*q. v.*)
and Fang Hsien-fu 方獻夫 (T. 叔賢, H. 西
樵, cs 1505, Pth. 文襄, d. June 26, 1544),
who were of like mind. From that time
on, Kuei repeatedly memorialized the
throne attacking the then grand secretaries,
especially the senior Yang T'ing-ho (*q.v.*).
The emperor, pleased with his expressions
of opinion, made him Hanlin chancellor
in July, 1524. In October of the same
year, following the suggestions of Chang
Fu-ching. Kuei O, and certain others, the
emperor's late father was awarded the
title the emperor demanded, and his mother, who was still alive, also received the
title he wished. A year later Kuei was
made grand supervisor of instruction and
continued as Hanlin chancellor.

In April, 1527, Kuei was elevated to
be right vice minister of Rites, while still
carrying the responsibility of the Hanlin
chancellorship. Five months later he was
promoted to be left vice minister of Personnel and in October made minister of

Rites. According to precedent, no minister could at the same time assume the post of Hanlin chancellor; Kuei was the first man to hold these two positions simultaneously. About one month later he was transferred to be minister of Personnel. He was in such favor with the emperor that he received the privilege of submitting sealed reports directly to the throne. As a matter of fact, he now had privileges equivalent to those of a grand secretary. His rank was raised on January 31, 1528, to that of grand guardian of the heir apparent, and later in June of the same year, when the *Ming-lun ta-tien*, 24 *ch.*, in which he had a hand (*see* Chang Fu-ching) was completed, to that of junior guardian and concurrently grand tutor.

Meanwhile (late in 1527) he sent in one report which is still recalled by older residents of Peking and its environs. A few miles west of the capital stands a well-known nunnery called variously the Huang ku ssu 皇姑寺 and the Pao Ming 保明 ssu. Kuei informed the emperor that the occupants were all harlots who sponsored debauchery of all sorts on the premises. Sent to investigate this charge, Huo T'ao confirmed it. The emperor was furious and ordered all nunneries destroyed and the nuns expelled. When news of this edict reached the Pao Ming ssu, its alarmed inmates sought aid through the eunuchs of the two dowager empresses. These succeeded in persuading the emperor to spare the temple. Others, however, were demolished and their nuns sent to the Pao Ming ssu to live. A mutilated stone, inscribed Hui ni pei 毀尼碑 (Destroy the nunnery tablet), used to stand in the temple court as mute evidence of this near catastrophe.

As soon as Kuei had the emperor's confidence, he began to seek revenge on certain officials for former injuries and insults. Individuals, especially those who had criticized him, became afraid of him. In 1527, having been rejected for some time, Wang Shou-jen (*q. v.*) was once more appointed left censor-in-chief and concurrently superintendent of military affairs of Kwangtung, Kwangsi, Kiangsi, and Hukuang. As one of those recommending him, Kuei had supported this appointment. In due course, however, he came to dislike Wang as the latter refused to be one of his partisans. Again and again he made trouble for Wang; even after Wang's death early in 1529, he attacked him violently. For this reason, the government did not honor Wang immediately.

On March 16, 1529, Kuei O was made titular minister of Personnel and concurrently grand secretary. At this level he came to take part in the highest decisions. Some years earlier (July, 1524), when Chang Fu-ching and Kuei O, responding to imperial summons, arrived at Peking from Nanking, a number of officials wanted to make life difficult for them because of their flattery of the emperor in the *Ta-li i* controversy. Once, fearing an attack, Chang and Kuei fled to the house of the marquis of Wu-ting, Kuo Hsün (*q. v.*). and escaped bodily harm. Later, Kuo was put in charge of the imperial bodyguard. Early in 1529, when disclosure of his receiving bribes came to light, Chang made every effort on his behalf. Kuei O, however, ascertaining that Kuo had fallen into the emperor's bad graces, accused him of other misdeeds, and as a consequence Kuo Hsün was cashiered. At first, Kuei's relations with Chang were quite friendly. As years went on, however, they became estranged. By 1529, when Kuei also entered the Grand Secretariat, their relations were even more strained.

In August of the same year, the supervising secretary of the office of scrutiny for War, Sun Ying-k'uei 孫應奎 (T. 文宿, H. 東穀, cs 1521), submitted a memorial, sharply criticizing Grand Secretaries Yang I-ch'ing (*q. v.*), Chang, and especially Kuei O. By this time, the emperor came to have doubts about Kuei, and bade him amend his ways if he wished to escape punishment. From then on Kuei became apprehensive. Later in the same month the supervising secretary of the office of scrutiny for Rites, Wang Chun 王準 (T. 子推, H. 石谷, cs 1523), memorialized the throne, accusing Chang and Kuei of putting some improper persons in office. This time Kuei would have been put out of the way if Chang had not enjoyed the emperor's confidence. A few days later, however, the supervising secretary of the office of scrutiny for Works, Lu Ts'an 陸粲 (T. 子餘, 浚明, H, 貞山, 1494-1551, cs 1526) presented another memorial violently accusing Chang and Kuei of still other wrongdoings. On September 15 both Chang and Kuei were removed from office; in the meantime, the imperial physician, Li Meng-ho 李夢鶴, who obtained the appointment entirely through Kuei's recommendation, was also dismissed. Shortly afterwards, in an effort to exonerate Chang and Kuei, the grand supervisor of instruction, Huo T'ao, lodged two memorials successively with the throne, in which he attacked Yang I-ch'ing severely, asserting even that the accusations of the supervising secretaries against Chang and Kuei were instigated by Yang. At the same time he remarked: "Chang Fu-ching, Kuei O, and I are all officials who received promotion for having advanced favorable opinions in the *Ta-li i* controversy. Now Chang and Kuei have been removed from office; how can I remain in the government?" As a result, in October Yang I-ch'ing was cashiered; Chang was recalled to the capital and became senior grand secretary; and on December 8, a decree was issued summoning Kuei to court too. On May 16 of the following year (1530), he returned to Peking and was reappointed titular minister of Personnel and concurrently grand secretary, with his former titles restored.

At first, Kuei was eager for honor and rank, and dared to bear responsibilities regardless of criticism. After the accusations and dismissal late in 1529, however, he became greatly depressed. When he returned as grand secretary, he worked very discreetly. At the end of that year, he repeatedly applied for retirement; his application was finally granted on February 6, 1531. He died at his native place a few months later, and was posthumously canonized as Wen-hsiang 文襄.

Kuei O was a considerable writer, most significantly perhaps in the field of geography. His part in the *Ming-lun ta-tien* has already been noted. but the *shih-lu* also draws attention to his submission, during the summer of 1529, of a map of the empire, *Yü-ti t'u* 輿地圖 (elsewhere called *Yü-ti chih-chang* 指掌 *t'u*), in 17 sections, with descriptive notes in 2 *chüan*. He was responsible as well for the *Li-tai ti-li* 歷史地理 *chih-chang*, 4 *ch.*, a historical treatment of China's geography, which doubtless accompanied the map. The last seems not to have survived but his prefatory remarks on the different sections have been gathered together in the *Ming ching-shih wen-pien* of Ch'en Tzu-lung (ECCP), along with certain other comments on related subjects and a few of his memorials. Collections of his essays, poetry, and other memorials seem to have disappeared. The editors of the Imperial Catalogue mention them but thought them unworthy of inclusion in the *Ssu-k'u ch'üan-shu*. [Editors' note: Wang Yung (*see* Cheng Jo-tseng) in his bibliography of maps, *Chung-kuo ti-li t'u-chi ts'ung-k'ao* 中國地理圖籍叢考 (1957), 8-9, asserts that Kuei's atlas, which he submitted to the throne in 1529, was based on the *T'ien-hsia yü-ti t'u* 天下輿地圖 by Li Mo (*see* Chao Wen-hua). In any case the atlas is considered rather inferior in cartography and information to the *Kuang-yü t'u* of Lo Hung-hsien (*q. v.*)]

Bibliography

1/97/2a, 196/10a; 3/182/8b; 5/16/9a; 6/2/22b, 41/27a, 6/16b, 7/7a, 11/26b, 20/12a, 35/9b, 38/11a; 42/70/7b; 61/155/20a; MSL (1965), Shih-tsung, 1012, 1673, 1723, 1767, 1894, 2295, 2400, 2420, 2526, 2663, 2902; KC (1958), 3450; Ku Ying-t'ai (ECCP), *Ming-ch'ao chi-shih pen-mo*, 50; *Kiangsi t'ung-chih* (1881), 102/16b, 109/1b, 162/31b; *Jao-chou-fu chih* (1872), 21/15b, 26/28b; *Hu-chou-fu chih* (1872), 6/22b; SK (1930), 56/3b, 72/1b, 102/4a; Ch'en Tzu-lung, *Ming ching-shih wen-pien* (Hong Kong ed.), *ch.* 178–182; Arlington and Lewisohn, *In Search of Old Peking* (Peking, 1935), 310.

Chou Tao-chi

KUEI Yu-kuang 歸有光 （T. 熙甫，開甫， H. 震川）, January 6, 1507-February 7, 1571, essayist, was a native of K'un-shan, east of Soochow. He came from an old landed family that had settled there for ten generations. One of his granduncles was an officer of the Soochow Guard, and his grandfather, Kuei Feng 鳳 (T. 應韶, cj 1474), served as magistrate of Ch'eng-wu 城武, Shantung. From childhood Kuei Yu-kuang studied for the career of a scholar-official, devoting himself to mastering the Confucian Classics and composing the kind of essays required in examination halls. He specialized in the study of *I Ching* (the Book of Change), winning acclaim in 1519 when he qualified as a student of the district school. Six years later he became a stipend student in the Soochow prefectural school and in 1536 was selected to be a scholar at the Nanking National University. Meanwhile he took the provincial examination six times, finally passing it in 1540 to become a *chü-jen*. By then his essays were known and his style imitated nationally. It was another twenty-five years, however, before he succeeded in becoming a *chin-shih*. He was then sixty *sui*.

For a talented man like Kuei Yu-kuang, it must have required patience, perseverance, and extraordinary self-discipline to survive the rejections time and again for some forty years, during which he had to see his friends, then students, and later even their children graduate to officialdom. His lot, however, was greatly eased by the prestige of his gentry family, by a modest inheritance of a house and some land, by fortunate marriages, and by his fame as a teacher, for many young men came to study with him. He also received some income from the writing of eulogies and epitaphs for wealthy families, especially for those in his neighborhood. He occasionally took an active interest in local affairs. In 1546 he published a book, the *San Wu shui li shu* 三吳水利書, 4 *ch.*, on the necessity of dredging the Woosung River in order to reduce the damage from annual floods in the Soochow area. He lamented the lack of wisdom in the government for its neglect of an area on which it depended for the main part of its revenue. His proposals surprisingly enough were not followed until twenty-three years later (*see* Hai Jui). Another project Kuei advocated was the strengthening of the local garrisons to fight the Japanese pirates, a subject on which he wrote several essays during the years 1553 to 1555.

After he graduated as *chin-shih* in 1565 Kuei was assigned for a period of training to the ministry of Works. Later he received an appointment as magistrate of Ch'ang-hsing 長興, Chekiang, where he assumed office early in 1566. Ch'ang-hsing is situated only some two hundred miles from his home on the other side of T'ai Lake and in the same dialect area. Through direct communication with the common people he learned of improper practices in the administration, which he tried to rectify. He discovered that the land register had not been revised for many years, resulting in serious inaccuracies in the records of land ownership and taxation. Some wealthy families which profited from such irregularities resented his meddling in their affairs and worked for his removal.

As magistrate Kuei was happy that after decades of preparation he finally was able, as a conscientious official, to translate his ideals into practice. His personal wealth made it possible for him to spend his magistrate's income on public works, such as the repair and extension of the living quarters of the resident official. During a drought he climbed to the top of a mountain to pray for rain and had the satisfaction of watching it fall heavily immediately thereafter. His duties included the supervision of the students. One night while in Hangchow he dreamed of repairing an ancient tripod. When three students of his district passed the provincial examination of that year (1567) and certain people interpreted the dream as an omen foretelling their success, he named the residence hall, newly rebuilt with his own funds, the Meng-ting-t'ang 夢鼎堂 (hall of the tripod dream). The monument which bears the inscription relating this episode, the "Meng-ting-t'ang chi" 記, has reccently been recovered in Ch'ang-hsing. The original inscription was written in the hand of Wu Ch'eng-en (q. v.), then serving as vice magistrate of Ch'ang-hsing. Incidentally, except for this and another inscription proving the association of the two scholars in that year, the writings of both so far available in print have betrayed not even a hint of their having ever met.

Kuei Yu-kuang's occasional visits to Hangchow on official duties, such as serving on the examination commission of 1567, probably provided his enemies with the opportunity to plot against him. Thus in 1568, even before his term of magistracy ended, he was promoted to assistant prefect of Shun-te 順德-fu, Pei-Chihli, in charge of the office concerned with farming out government horses among the people. He left his magistracy with bitterness for he resented the injustice of promotion (7A to 6A) to a post usually reserved for the senile, the invalided, or those with lower degrees. At first he complained, pleaded for another assignment, and even considered retirement. Later he changed his mind and assumed the office in Shun-te in 1569. His duties being light, he had time to study the file of documents and to write a long history of the administrative control of government horses (*Ma-cheng-chih* 馬政志). He also made proposals for extensive reforms (Ma-cheng-i 議) in order to alleviate the suffering of the common people involved. In 1570 he was given the title of assistant to the director of the Court of the Imperial Stud at Nanking, but was sum-

moned to Peking where he helped in the editing of the history of that court. Meanwhile the grand secretaries—Kao Kung (*see* Chang Chü-cheng), Chao Chen-chi, and Li Ch'un-fang (*qq. v.*) who admired him as a writer—assigned him to the Grand Secretariat to serve as a drafter and as a compiler of the Veritable Records, *Shih-tsung shih-lu.* Unfortunately he died a few months later. He was buried in 1575 in K'un-shan, the inscription on his tombstone being written by another grand secretary, Wang Hsi-chüeh (*q.v.*). The tomb has been repaired many times by magistrates of K'un-shan and by local admirers. Kuei Yu-kuang married three times. His first wife (married 1528, d. 1533) was the second daughter of Wei Hsiang (*see* Cheng Jo-tseng), the owner of several thousand acres of rich farm land, and his second wife (married *ca.* 1534, d. 1551) came from a Wang 王 family which had declined in wealth but still owned a country villa of a hundred rooms, known as the Shih-mei-t'ang 世美堂. One of his sons, Kuei Tzu-ning 子寧 (T. 仲粄, H. 徹園), was a military *chü-jen* of 1576 and another, Kuei Tzu-mu 子慕 (T. 季思, H. 陶庵), became a *chü-jen* in 1591.

It is said that there used to be a Fukien edition of samples of Kuei's writings in 2 *chüan*, but it probably no longer exists. After his death, a second collection was edited in 1574 and printed in Ch'ang-shu 常熟 under the title *Chen-ch'uan hsien-sheng wen-chi* 震川先生文集, 20 ch. His sons at once considered it inadequate and produced a third edition in 1575, *Kuei hsien-sheng wen-chi,* 30 ch., with one additional *chüan* of poems and another of biographical matter. In 1660 an admirer, Ch'ien Ch'ien-i (ECCP), helped one of Kuei's grandsons, Kuei Chuang (ECCP), to edit a fourth and larger edition, *Chen-ch'uan hsien-sheng wen-chi,* 30 ch., with an appendix, *pieh-chi* 別集, 10 ch.; these were printed in the years 1667 and 1675 respectively. The two together became the copy on which later editions were based. There is a manuscript collection compiled about 1580, entitled *Kuei Chen-ch'uan hsien-sheng wei k'o kao* 未刻稿, 25 *ch.*, in 6 fascicles, preserved in the National Central Library, Taipei. In 1799 there appeared the most nearly complete edition of his collected works entitled *Chen-ch'uan ta-ch'üan chi* 大全集 which added two supplements, *pu-chi* 補集 and *yü-chi* 餘集, each in 8 *chüan*. There are also some minor works attributed to Kuei as the writer or compiler. One collection *Chu-tzu hui-han* 諸子彙函, 20 *ch.*, was possibly assembled by a bookdealer who used his name for effect. During the 18th century certain of Kuei's books were listed for suppression, largely, it seems, because of their association with the names of Ch'ien Ch'ien-i and Lü Liu-liang (ECCP) who had edited some of them. These include the *Chen-ch'uan chi*, *Chen-ch'uan pieh-chi*, and *Kuei Chen-ch'uan shih wen kao* 詩文稿. In spite of this the *Chen-ch'uan wen chi* and *pieh-chi* form part of the Imperial Library.

The main writings of Kuei Yu-kuang are all assembled in the fourth edition of his collected works. The essays, written in a plain and lucid style, reveal the honesty and strength of the character of the author. The accounts relating to his mother ("Hsiang-chi hsüan chi" 項脊軒記) and to his deceased second wife ("Shih-mei-t'ang hou-chi" 世美堂後記) are masterpieces of tenderness. Through his letters and public documents he displayed the sensitivity of a scholar molded by Confucian ethics—unyielding in upholding justice, and compassionate. As an essayist Kuei belonged to the T'ang-Sung school (唐宋派, *see* Mao K'un and T'ang Shun-chih), which was opposed to the "archaic" school represented by the "seven later masters" (*see* Li P'an-lung). One of the seven, Wang Shih-chen (*q.v.*), apparently made some derogatory remarks about Kuei's prose. Kuei retorted by criticizing Wang as wang 妄 (overconfident) and yung 庸 (mediocre) to which Wang replied that he might be overconfident but never mediocre. Kuei's comment was that overconfidence is the result of mediocrity. In later years, however, Wang regretted his earlier opinions and acknowledged Kuei as a master essayist, comparing him with Han Yü and Ou-yang Hsiu. This appraisal was concurred in by late Ming and Ch'ing critics, especially those of the T'ung-ch'eng school (*see* Fang Pao in ECCP).

Bibliography

1/287/20b; 3/268/17b; *K'un-Hsin liang-hsien hsü-hsiu ho-chih* 崑新兩縣續修合志 (1880), 26/5a; Chang Ch'uan-yüan 張傳元, *et al.*, *Kuei Chen-ch'uan nien-p'u* 年譜, 1936; Ch'ien Ch'ien-i, *Lieh-ch'ao shih-chi*, 丁/12/1a; Kuo Shao-yü 郭紹虞, *Chung-kuo wen-hsüeh p'i-p'ing shih* 中國文學批評史 (1961), 314; *Kuei Chuang chi* 莊集 (1962), 289, 342, 347; Sun Tien-ch'i (1957), 209, 239; SK (1930), 172/11a; Yao Chin-yüan (1957), 74, 122, 170; Sun Tz'u-chou 孫次舟, "Chen-ch'uan hsien-sheng wen-chi pa-wei" 跋尾, in *Wen-shih tsa-chih* 文史雜誌, II: 1 (January, 1942), 63.

Chaoying Fang

K'UN-TS'AN 髡殘 (surname: Liu 劉; T. 介邱, H. 白秃, 石溪, etc.), fl. 1657-74, native of Wu-ling 武陵, Ch'ang-te prefecture 常德府, Hukuang, was a Buddhist monk also known as a painter and poet. Born possibly around 1610, he moved early to Nanking. His parents died when he was young; so he was brought up by others in the family circle. When they endeavored to arrange a marriage for him, he refused. The story goes that one day, on the approach of winter, his brother brought him a felt cap. He tried it on, repeatedly gazing at his reflection in the mirror. Suddenly he seized a pair of shears, cut off his hair, and applied for ordination as a monk. Eventually he reached the status of abbot in the Niu-shou monastery 牛首寺, some ten miles south of Nanking. There he became known for his abstemiousness and his asceticism, spending long periods of time alone in his cell, furnished only with one small stool and a metal recital knocker. He rarely communicated with his fellow inmates, going for days in complete silence. Though a sufferer from rheumatism from his boyhood and never free from pain, he did not complain. Once he visited Huang-shan 黄山 (in An-hwei), but his health did not permit him to indulge in other pilgrimages. He once wrote: "I regret that my feet are unable to travel to the famous mountains. My eyes cannot read the myriad books to exploit the experience of the great wide world. My ears have never heard a wise man's teachings. I do have a tongue, but am speechless the moment my mouth opens. Now I am old like a tired horse in the stable. I am unable to manage any-thing bodily."

K'un-ts'an's small circle of friends in-cluded Ch'eng Cheng-k'uei 程正揆 (early name: 葵, T. 正葵, H. 青溪老人, cs 1631), Kung Hsien 龔賢 (d. 1689), and Chou Liang-kung (ECCP). Although often linked with Tao-chi (*q. v.*) as one of the 二石 (Two Stones)—*cf.* Victoria Contag's *Die Beiden Steine*--, actually their art is quite different and they were acquaintances only. Technically he was not as versatile as Tao-chi, for he painted landscapes only. His mountains were heavily wooded. His style and brushwork may be compared with that of Huang Kung-wang (1269–1354) and Wu Chen (1280–1354). He never attempted to paint anything strange, yet his compositions are individualistic. One critic describes the art of K'un-ts'an with these words: [his] "dry, crumbling brush-work is the expression of a temperament as passionately single-minded as that of Cézanne." Not being a professional artist, he painted only on occasion; as a result comparatively little of his work survives. Nevertheless, as the lists of his paintings compiled by O. Sirén and E. J. Laing in-dicate, there is enough to show his talent.

Two volumes containing reproductions of K'un-ts'an's paintings and calligraphy were reproduced in 1934 and 1936, and since then several others.

Bibliography

Yin-te 9: 1/509/3a; *Wu-ling-hsien chih* (1868), 24/3a; K'un-ts'an, *Shih-ch'i ch'i-shan wu-chin t'u-chüan* 石溪谿山無盡圖卷, Shanghai, 1934; *id.*, *Shih-ch'i mao-lin ch'iu-shu* 茂林秋樹 *t'u-chüan*, Peiping, 1936; Chang Keng 張庚 (1685–1760), *Kuo-ch'ao hua cheng-lu* 國朝畫徵錄 (*Hua-shih* 畫史 *ts'ung-shu* ed.), 69; *Shih-ch'i hua chi* 畫集 (The Selected paintings of Shih-ch'i), Hong Kong, 1969; O. Sirén, *Chinese Painting* (New York, 1956–58), VII, 365; E. J. Laing, *Chinese Paintings in Chinese Publications, 1956–1968* (Ann Arbor, 1969), 263; V. Contag and C. C. Wang, *Seals of Chinese Painters and Collectors of the Ming and Ch'ing Periods*, rev. ed. (Hong Kong, 1966), 392, 702; J. Cahill, *Fantasics and Eccentrics in Chinese Painting* (NewYork, 1967), 56, 59; Michael Sullivan, "The Ch'ing scholar-painters and Their World," in *The Arts of the Ch'ing Dynasty* (The Oriental Ceramic Society, London, 1964), 9, pl. 4, 5.

Yu-ho Tseng Ecke

KUNG Yung-ch'ing 龔用卿 (T. 鳴治, H. 雲岡), 1500–63, scholar-official who headed a special embassy to Korea in 1536 to 1537, was a native of Huai-an 懷安, northwest of Foochow in Fukien. Kung's ancestors, originally from Kuang-chou 光州, Honan, moved to Fukien during the 11th century; they served as bureaucratic officials under the Sung rulers but refused to serve un-der the Mongols. Having qualified for the *chü-jen* degree in 1522, Kung passed first in the *chin-shih* examination of 1526. He then received an appointment as senior compiler in the Hanlin Academy and offi-ciated there for the next fourteen years, with only two periods of absence due to his father's death in 1532 and his special assignment later to Korea. As an academ-ician he participated in two major offi-cial compilations, the *Ming-lun ta-tien* (*see* Yang I-ch'ing) and the *Ta Ming hui-tien* (unpublished version, *see* Hsü P'u and Shen Shih-hsing), and presided over the metropolitan examinations of 1529 and 1532.

On November 13, 1536, to celebrate the birth of Chu Tsai-jui second son of Emperor Chu Hou-ts'ung (*q. v.*), the court appointed two special embassies, each led by a Hanlin official, to proceed to Annam and Korea to make the announcement. Five days later, Kung Yung-ch'ing was chosen to head the one to Korea, with a junior colleague Wu Hsi-meng 吳希孟 (T. 子醇, H. 龍津, cs 1532), a supervising secretary of Revenue, as his deputy. After spending some time drafting a code of rites and ceremonies, Kung and Wu departed late in the year. Journeying through Liaotung and crossing the Yalu River, they arrived in the Korean capital (modern Seoul) in April, 1537. The Korean king (Chungjong 中宗, r. 1507-44), after greeting the Chinese envoys and offering congratulations to their emperor, submitted two requests to Kung and asked that they be forwarded to the Ming court. First, he asked for a rectification of the genealogy of the Yi rulers as recorded in the *Ta Ming hui-tien*. Second, he presented a list of herb medicines suggesting that they be brought as gifts during the next visit of Chinese envoys. (It is not without interest that Kung's colleague came from a family known for its connection with the Imperial Academy of Medicine.) Kung accepted both requests for transmission to the throne. (The correction of the Yi genealogy, however, was not to appear until the updated edition of the *hui-tien*, published in 1587.) Upon the completion of their mission, Kung and his party made an extended tour of Korea, including a prolonged visit in modern Pyongyang in the north. They returned to Liaotung early in May but their arrival in the capital is not recorded in the *shih-lu* until October, a lapse of five months. Kung then presented a report to the court, together with a journal on the embassy, entitled *Shih Chao-hsien lu* 使朝鮮錄, 3 *ch.*, which he compiled in consultation with his deputy. This narrative, dealing mainly with the rites and ceremonies used during the diplomatic exchanges, but also including a geography of Korea, provides scant information on Kung's reception as compared to the Korean historical account.

The Korean *sillok* which records Kung's presence in detail, describes him and Wu as haughty and arrogant. Kung Yung-ch'ing, in particular, is pictured as quick-tempered, carping at trivia, and imprudent in manner and speech. He insisted that the Koreans conform to the Chinese protocol in their receptions, taking exception to their use of native music which featured female singers and dancers. Nevertheless, he enjoyed the girl performers and acrobats. He liked such Korean dishes as shellfoods, but, as a gourmet, found fault with their cooking. There is an anecdote about the embarrassment he caused his hosts. In the midst of a royal feast, as they apologized for the food, Kung asked for a brush and ink to write down his favorite recipe; carried away by the charm of the dancers, Kung got over-excited and spilled ink over them, causing a commotion. The Koreans considered this a display of very bad manners and a gross insult. They were also disturbed when they discovered that Kung had violated regulations by secretly giving exotic goods to his interpreters to dispose of for profit. Enchanted by the local scenery and the hospitality extended to them, Kung and his deputy twice delayed their departure, which the Koreans considered rather exceptional for Chinese envoys. During his visit, Kung composed numerous poems, said to have been over three hundred, depicting the local scenes, and wrote characters for tablets at many historic spots and antiquarian sites. Some of his verses are collected in the *Hwang-hwa chip* 皇華集, an anthology of poetry by Chinese envoys and Korean officials distributed at the Korean court and among the senior officials. As a belle-lettrist, Kung showed keen interest in the literary attainment of the Koreans. He asked the king for copies of the local gazetteers and for samples of the Korean examination registers. These he used as sources for his poetic and literary writings about Korea, and for his report on the geography of Korea.

Upon the designation of Chu Tsai-jui as imperial successor in January, 1538,

Kung was appointed instructor in the supervisorate of instruction of the heir apparent and reader in the Hanlin Academy. In April, 1540, he was one of twenty-three officials seconding the proposal to enshrine the late Confucian scholar-philosopher Hsüeh Hsüan (*q. v.*) in the Confucian temple. Following this Kung was promoted (July, 1541) to be chancellor of the National University in Nanking, and was credited, among other things, with the repair and construction of a number of classroom buildings and student quarters. Two years later, however, a supervising secretary of Justice, Chang Yung-ming 張永明 (T. 鍾誠, H. 臨溪, 1499–1566, cs 1535, Pth. 莊僖), charged him with corruption and dereliction of duty. In a lengthy memorial Chang reported Kung guilty of misappropriating government funds, accepting bribes from students to ignore their improper conduct and negligence in studies, behaving outrageously in public, flouting his subordinates, and committing other misdeeds. Whatever may have been the truth of these allegations, the court felt obliged to make an example of Kung to preserve the reputation of a national university. Kung was removed from office but asked to stay in Nanking to await another appointment, which never materialized. He then returned to his native place and lived sumptuously, spending his hours planting flowers, composing poems and essays. When the *wo-k'ou* pirates raided Foochow in April, 1559, Kung sought shelter with his family in Chien-an 建安, not far from the Kiangsi border. He died there four years later at the age of sixty-three. A portrait of him, somewhat stereotyped, is included in the *Ming chuang-yüan t'u k'ao* by Shen I-kuan (*q. v.*).

While he served in a number of capacities Kung Yung-ch'ing is remembered principally as author of the *Shih Chao-hsien lu*, which record his experience in Korea in two parts. The first part presents an account of the rites and ceremonies employed in conducting exchanges during his visit, a notice of his meeting with the Korean king, and a succinct geographical description based on local gazetteers. The second part contains a collection of poems and essays, some of which were written for, or in exchange with, his hosts, and an appendix giving transcripts of his conversations with Korean officials. Judging from Kung's preface, dated May, 1537, one may conclude that the first part of the journal was compiled during his sojourn in Korea, while the collection of poems may have been added to the text some time later. In content and style, Kung's work differs from its antecedent, the *Chao-hsien chi-shih* by Ni Ch'ien (*q. v.*), and supplies an important addition to the literature on China's relations with Korea during the Ming period. The original edition, engraved some time after 1537 and including Kung's preface and a second preface by Wu Hsi-meng, is extemely rare; it was reproduced in photolithographic form in 1937 by Liu I-cheng (BDRC), who contributed a colophon. There is a Japanese manuscript transcription, 2 *ch.*, in the Naikaku Bunko.

Kung's collected work, *Yün-kang hsüan-kao* 雲岡選稿, 20 *ch.*, compiled by his son and engraved during the Wan-li period, receives a notice in the Imperial Catalogue of the late 18th century. A copy of this edition, listed as rare, is preserved in the library of the former Research Institute of Humanistic Studies, Peking. There is an abridged version, entitled *Yün kang kung wen-chi* 公文集, 17*ch.*, in manuscript transcription in the National Central Library, Taipei.

Bibliography

5/74/14a; 16/160/32a; MSL (1965), Shih-tsung, 1448, 1452, 2364, 4066, 4071, 4266, 4522, 4806, 5025, 5410; SK (1930), 177/4b; *Fu-chou-fu chih* (1754, 1967 ed.), 40/51a, 60/30a; Yüan Chih, *Yüan Yung-chih chi* (NCL microfilm), 14/37b; Lin Wen-chün 林文俊 (1487–1536), *Fang-chai ts'un-kao* 方齋存稿 (NCL microfilm), 6/26b; Chang yung-ming, *Chang Chuang-hsi kung wen-chi: Nan-huan chien-ts'ao* 莊僖公文集: 南垣諫草 (NCL microfilm), 16a; Lin T'ing-chi 林庭機 (1506–81), *Shih-han-t'ang kao* 世翰堂稿 (NLP microfilm, no. 864), 8/25b; Shen I-kuan, *Ming chuang-yüan t'u k'ao*, 3/3a; Huang Tso, *Nan-yung chih*, 5/7a, 8/30a, 16/24a; Jen-wen ... *Catalogue* (Peking, 1938), Vol. 5, 10b; NCL *Catalogue*, 1059; Naikaku Bunko *Catalogue*, 133; *Chosŏn wangjo sillok* 朝鮮王朝實錄 (1953–56), Vol. 18 (Chungjong), ch. 84, 85; W. Franke, Sources, 7. 9. 4.; Chaoying Fang, *The Asami Library* (1970), 366.

Hok-lam Chan

KUNJILAI 困即來 was a chieftain from 1405, until his death in January, 1444, of the Sha-chou 沙州 guard, situated in modern Tunhuang, Kansu, China's strategic gateway to central Asia. His origin is obscure. Some sources assert that he was a Turk, others that he was a Mongol; perhaps he was of Turkish-Mongol extraction. Sha-chou had been a settlement of Turkish and Mongol people since the Yüan dynasty; a Chinese garrison was stationed there early in the Hung-wu period, but was withdrawn after 1390 as the Ming court felt it had overextended its line of defense. The settlers, however, remained friendly to the Chinese. Shortly after his enthronement Chu Ti (*q.v.*) set about consolidating control over the alien peoples on the northern and northwestern frontiers and established a commandery at Sha-chou. On November 11, 1405, Kunjilai and one other native chieftain were appointed commanders. In the following decades Sha-chou played an important role in the diplomatic and tributary exchanges between the western kingdoms and China, as it served as the meeting place for envoys going to and fro. Kunjilai was either well liked or hated by both the Chinese and the central Asians, depending on whether he helped, protected, and escorted embassies and merchants, or intercepted them and robbed them of their goods. At the same time, he relied on Chinese good will to protect his domain from the attack of hostile neighbors, first the people of the Han-tung 罕東 and Ch'ih-chin 赤斤 guards, then the Tibetans from Hami, and finally the Oirat Mongols.

During the reign of Chu Ti, Kunjilai demonstrated his loyalty to the Ming court by dispatching regular tribute-bearing embassies and by undertaking various assignments as was his due as chieftain of a Chinese protectorate. In May, 1410, he sent help to the Chinese commander of Su-chou 肅州 to suppress a Muslim uprising, and was rewarded with a promotion to assistant commissioner. Sha-chou enjoyed harmonious relations with its neighbors until the rise of the Han-tung tribe as trouble maker on the northwestern frontier two decades later. In May, 1434, Kunjilai memorialized the court that his commandery had been the target of attacks from the Han-tung and the Tibetans, and requested permission to move his people to an abandoned town named Ch'a-han 察罕. Emperor Chu Chan-chi (*q.v.*), however, denied his request and advised him instead to maintain friendly relations with his neighbors. In January, 1436, Kunjilai, under attack by Hami forces, brought his followers to the Chinese border appealing for food supplies and other assistance. It appears, however, that, though the Ming court understood Kunjilai's troubles and was ready to help, it did not contemplate moving his people inside Chinese territory as it wanted to keep Sha-chou as an advanced post in front of its own defense line.

Following the rise of both Hami and the Oirat as potential enemies on the Chinese western frontier, Kunjilai was given the additional assignment of collecting information on their activities. This was a task he eagerly accepted, as he was clearly aware of their threat, and of the need of Chinese assistance in times of trouble. In August, 1440, as reward for information supplied about Hami, Kunjilai received promotion to commissioner, and his son Nan-ko 喃哥, who is mentioned in the official records for the first time, became a vice commander.

Meanwhile, the powerful Esen (*q.v.*) began exerting pressure on Sha-chou and the neighboring Ch'ih-chin guard to make them conclude an alliance with him against the Ming. In September, 1442, Kunjilai reported that Hami had reached an agreement with the Oirat, and he requested permission to build the walls of an abandoned town about twenty *li* south of Ch'ih-chin against possible Oirat invasion. As this town once belonged to Ch'ih-chin, the emperor feared that such a proposal, if approved, would lead to a clash between the two commanderies; hence he ordered Kunjilai to fortify instead a ruined town called K'u-yü 苦峪 in the Sha-chou territory. Esen, during this time, delayed military action against Sha-chou as he feared Chinese reprisal. Instead, he tried to consolidate his position by compelling the two ruling families to form marriage alliances with his family, requesting Kunjilai, early in 1443, to send his daughter as bride for his younger brother, and pressing the chieftain of Ch'ih-chin to send his daughter to his son. These negotiations dragged on for almost two years without result; apparently Kunjilai was reluctant to commit himself to Esen and deliberately delayed making a final decision. The attitude of the Ming court on this matter was one of noninterference, although it clearly was to the advantage of the Chinese to keep the Mongol tribes divided among themselves. On several occasions the emperor wrote to Kunjilai that he was free to do as he saw fit, but that he should be aware of the danger of falling under Esen's domination. Before he had made up his mind, however, Kunjilai died, leaving his sons to tackle his unresolved problems. The most famous of his sons were Nan-ko, So-nan-pen 鎮南奔, and K'o-lo-o-ling-chan 克羅俄領占.

Nan-ko, said by the *shih-lu* to be Kunjilai's eldest son, served under his father as guard commander in various capacities, such as escorting the tribute-bearing embassies from Sha-chou and from the western kingdoms to the Ming court, and

Chinese envoys en route to Hami and central Asia. In September, 1444, eight months after Kunjilai's death, Emperor Chu Ch'i-chen (*q.v.*) appointed Nan-ko to succeed to his father's command, with the rank of assistant commissioner. It appears, however, that Nan-ko, like his father, did not always commit himself to the Chinese; rather, dictated by political and economic expediency, he paid lip service to the Oirat chieftains by accepting their official titles. In January of the following year, the emperor issued a stern warning to Nan-ko not to favor the Oirat, but as this had little effect, the Ming court began to watch the people of Sha-chou vigilantly. In the meantime, Esen stepped up his pressure on Sha-chou by demanding that Nan-ko, among other things, send his daughter to be the bride of his son; though the result is not known, it appears that Nan-ko was slowly being drawn into the Oirat camp. As it became evident that Nan-ko's resistance to Esen's advances was collapsing, the emperor decided to take strong action. He gave orders in August, 1446, to Jen Li (*see* Mao Chung), commander of the Su-chou guard, to strike at Sha-chou and bring the people back across the border into Chinese territory. In the face of this pressure, and as Sha-chou was striken by famine, a rift developed between Nan-ko and his brother, So-nan-pen. The former favored seeking shelter within the Chinese frontier; the latter, who had received the title of Ch'i-wang 祁王 from the Oirat, preferred joining the Mongols. Taking independent action, Nan-ko proceeded to Su-chou in person; while Jen Li dispatched his deputy, Mao Qara (later known as Mao Chung, *q.v.*), to Sha-chou to arrange for the settlement of the Sha-chou people. When the Chinese delegates arrived, however, some of Nan-ko's followers, under the influence of the pro-Oirat faction, attempted to flee; thereupon Mao Qara used force to bring them back to Kan-chou 甘州. The rest of the settlers, led by So-nan-pen, succeeded in escaping to Han-tung and gained the protection of its Mongol chieftain. This brought to an end the existence of the Sha-chou commandery; henceforth the region was occupied by the Han-tung people.

Nan-ko, leading a contingent of over twelve hundred strong, proceeded to their new settlement in Shantung (April, 1447). He and his deputies received a rich stipend and other monetary rewards, and were accommodated in the P'ing-shan 平山 and Tung-ch'ang 東昌 guards; the rest of his followers, however, were resettled in Ch'ing-p'ing 青平 and Po-p'ing 博平-hsien. They lived there in relative confinement, being forbidden to travel outside their territories, or to communicate with the local authorities. Meanwhile, Nan-ko died in Tung-ch'ang on January 5, 1448.

Following Nan-ko's surrender, the court continued its pursuit of So-nan-pen. Having failed to secure his extradition from Han-tung, the Chinese commander of Su-chou launched a campaign against him and succeeded in capturing him in August, 1448. The ministry of War demanded capital punishment, but the emperor, in a gesture of leniency, spared his life and sent him to Shantung to live under house arrest with his mother and brother. His people were established in P'ing-shan and Tung-ch'ang. Following the T'u-mu disaster (see Wang Chen), however, when the court became aware that overconcentration of alien peoples in north China might endanger internal security, there were plans to send So-nan-pen's followers farther south, below the Yangtze River.

K'o-lo-o-ling-chan, whom the shih-lu calls Kunjilai's third son, spent his early years serving under his father in various capacities. In 1444 he was appointed a commander and became the deputy of his brother Nan-ko, following him into China. He joined the expedition in October, 1449, of Mao Fu-shou (see Mao Sheng) against the rebellious tribesmen in Yunnan and Kweichow, receiving promotion to assistant central commissioner. In the following years he saw further action in south-

west China and was twice rewarded for distinguished service, rising to the rank of a central commissioner. Late in 1457, shortly after the reenthronement of Chu Ch'i-chen, K'o-lo-o-ling-chan adopted the Chinese name of Lo Ping-chung 羅秉忠, and was so known thereafter. In July of the next year he memorialized the court for permission to move his family and that of his brother So-nan-pen to the capital. His request was approved, but his followers in the Tung-ch'ang guard were reassigned to Nanking. The emperor favored him in December, 1459, with a grant of 80 ch'ing of land in the Ho-chien 河間 prefecture south of Peking. The official records are silent on his subsequent activities until early in 1463 when they report an accusation against him of implication in the rebellion of Ts'ao Ch'in (see Ts'ao Chi-hsiang) to overthrow the throne. He was subsequently put in jail and his properties confiscated, but the emperor, after reviewing the case, released him and sent him to Nanking in charge of drilling troops.

Shortly after the ascension of Chu Chien-shen (q.v.), Lo Ping-chung was recalled to active duty. Early in 1468 he received an appointment as mobile corps commander to assist Ch'eng Hsin 程信 (T. 彥實, 1417-79, cs 1442, Pth. 襄毅) in a campaign against the rebellious tribesmen in Szechwan. In September he was awarded the honorary rank of earl of Shun-i 順義伯. (Earlier, Arγaširi [d. November 5, 1433], who surrendered in 1409 and was later known by his Chinese name Chin Shun 金順, had been appointed to this earldom in August, 1429.) Lo died on January 24, 1481, and received the posthumous canonized name Jung-chuang 榮壯. His son Lo Chen- (te) 珍 (德) was not granted the privilege of inheritance, but received an appointment as commander in the Embroidered-uniform Guard. Lo Chen- (te) left no heirs, but the family was continued through the descendants of So-nan-pen, who also adopted the surname Lo. Lo Sheng 昇, one of So-nan-pen's grandsons, was appointed (August, 1523) a commander of the Embroidered-uniform Guard and his descendants subsequently inherited this rank until the end of the dynasty.

Bibliography

1/155/16b, 156/13b, 330/22b; MSL (1962), T'ai-tsung, 720, 1353, 1391, 1472, Hsüan-tsung (1963), ch. 13–110, Ying-tsung (1964), ch. 1–361, Hsien-tsung (1964), 1168, 3669; Chang Hung-hsiang 張鴻翔, "*Ming-shih* chuan i-wu-liu chu-ch'en shih-hsi piao" 明史卷一五六諸臣系表, *Fu-jen hsüeh-chih* 輔仁學誌, 5: 1–2 (1936), 37; Henry Serruys, "The Mongols of Kansu during the Ming," MCB, Vol. 10 (1955), 301; L. Hambis, *Documents sur l'histoire des Mongols à l'époque des Ming* (Paris, 1969), 138, 144.

Hok-lam Chan

KUO Cheng-yü 郭正域 (T. 美命, H. 明龍), 1554–July 21, 1612, an outspoken scholar-official, was a native of Chiang-hsia 江夏 (Wuchang), Hukuang. He came from a family of military registry which apparently held a hereditary officer's rank in the escort guard of the princedom of Ch'u 楚. His father, Kuo Mou 懋 (T. 子德, cj 1549), in 1562 became magistrate of Chao-chou 趙州, Pei-Chihli. Following his own success in the civil examinations (cj 1582, cs 1583), Kuo Cheng-yü was made a bachelor, then compiler in the Hanlin Academy. In March, 1594, he was named one of the tutors of Prince Chu Ch'ang-lo (b. 1582, ECCP), the eldest son of Emperor Chu I-chün (*q.v.*) and eventually successor to the throne in 1620. But at this juncture the prince was still denied formal installation as heir apparent because the emperor had not as yet made up his mind for, according to court gossip, he favored a younger son, Chu Ch'ang-hsün whose mother was his favorite consort, Cheng Kuei-fei (*q.v.*). Only after repeated requests and remonstrances by certain high officials, especially Wang Hsi-chüeh and Shen I-kuan (*qq.v.*), did the emperor reluctantly consent to the formal education of the elder, and assign-

ed Kuo, Chiao Hung (ECCP), and six other Hanlin members as tutors supervised by Wang. Four months later Shen I-kuan became a grand secretary and a supervisor of the tutors.

For some reason Kuo could not get along with Shen, and in September, 1598, was sent to Nanking as chancellor of the National University in the southern capital, a promotion in rank that was interpreted rather as a step backward. During his tenure of three years, however, his reputation as a scrupulous official became enhanced by his astuteness in handling some delicate situations. There is the anecdote about a student with very influential background, known to have been an informer and blackmailer, who was arrested on insufficient evidence. Kuo, posting a notice in the market place, called on those whom the student had wronged to bear witness before the judges. Fifteen hundred plaintiffs turned out. It is also recorded that a young nobleman, flogged by an instructor of the university for failing to dismount from his horse in front of the temple of Confucius, returned with a platoon of soldiers who began to damage the precincts. Kuo persuaded the high military authorities of Nanking to order the nobleman to desist, explaining that the instructor had the right to punish a student for any infraction, and that the nobleman, even though granted by imperial favor the status of a student in the university, was subject to this regulation. While in Nanking Kuo made the acquaintance of Matteo Ricci (*q.v.*) in February, 1599, and visited him again on his arrival in Peking over two years later, treating him, Ricci writes, with much familiarity (con molta familiarità). He showed especial interest in Ricci's terrestrial globe and clocks, and in certain mathematical instruments.

When Chu Ch'ang-lo was formally installed as heir apparent in 1601, Kuo was recalled to Peking to resume his tutorial activities with the title of supervisor of instruction. It is said that one morning that winter in a freezing cold, Kuo found the hall of instruction without any heat, and the prince and tutors shivering. He complained so vigorously that the eunuchs quietly brought out charcoal burners from their own quarters. The story indicates how indifferently the court treated Chu Ch'ang-lo and the way Kuo looked out for his interests. On February 15, 1602, Kuo was placed in charge of the tutors. In January, 1603, he received the concurrent posts of junior vice minister of Rites and acting chancellor of the Hanlin Academy. Three months later, on the death of Feng Ch'i (*q.v.*), Kuo became for a time acting minister of Rites and was generally considered a leading contender for the post of a grand secretary. The rise of Kuo was not at all to the liking of Shen I-kuan who had, since October, 1601, held the powerful position of senior grand secretary, and had been manipulating decisions and appointments to his own advantage. Kuo did not help matters by openly siding with Shen's rival, Grand Secretary Shen Li (*see* Hsüan Ni), well known for his sponsorship of the more public-spirited individuals, particularly the group later lumped together as the Tunglin partisans (*see* Ku Hsien-ch'eng and Kao P'an-lung). The latter began to designate Shen I-kuan and his protégés first as the southerners and later as the Chekiang faction, thus contributing to the unfortunate split of the court into groups identified by the native place of their leaders. Party strife brought on by differences on moral or legal issues alone now degenerated into contests for power and material gain. Meanwhile Kuo displeased the emperor and the eunuchs by his memorial in March, 1603, urging the emperor to recall all the eunuchs serving on mining and tax collecting missions. They preferred Shen I-kuan as more pliable.

The dispute between Kuo and Shen came to a head in May when the case of the legitimacy of the 9th prince of Ch'u 楚 was referred to Kuo's ministry.

The prince, Chu Hua-k'uei 朱華奎 (1572-1643), was officially registered as the elder of twin boys born half a year after the death of the presumed father, the preceding prince; from the beginning it was whispered that the babies were not the prince's sons but were adopted in secrecy. Before Chu Hua-k'uei was installed as prince in 1580, there had already been an official investigation into his legitimacy. In March, 1603, twenty-nine cousins of the prince brought up the matter again in a memorial. Shen I-kuan did not want the case reopened, but on Kuo's insistence an imperial order was issued in July, over Shen's protest, to have the governor and the inspecting censor of Hukuang conduct another investigation at Wuchang. During the trial some seventy witnesses refused even under torture to change their testimony supporting the legitimacy of the prince. When this report reached Peking in October, the emperor ordered the case closed and those accusing the prince punished. Now Shen I-kuan and his protégés gained the upper hand and charged Kuo with being in collusion with these accusers. In retaliation Kuo sent in a memorial insinuating that Shen had received a bribe from the prince. What Kuo offered as evidence the emperor rejected. Consequently Kuo resigned on November 17, 1603.

In mid-December, while Kuo was on his way home and had reached a point about seventy miles southeast of Peking, the case of the anonymous broadside, Hsü yu-wei hung-i, broke (*see* Cheng Kuei-fei). It intimated that a conspiracy was afoot to harm the heir apparent's rights in favor of Chu Ch'ang-hsün. The emperor ordered a thorough investigation and had hundreds of persons arrested for questioning. Shen I-kuan's protégés plotted to involve Kuo Cheng-yü. During the trial that lasted half a year, Kuo's eldest brother, Kuo Cheng-wei 位 (cj 1588), then serving as an instructor in the National University, was placed under surveillance; so also was Kuo's boat on the Grand Canal. Someone even hinted to Kuo Cheng-yü that he should commit suicide in order to escape the kind of death awaiting him, but Kuo declared his confidence in eventual vindication. Reportedly the heir apparent even sent a eunuch to Shen to plead for Kuo. At last clearance came and Kuo continued his voyage. Kuo spent the rest of his days mostly at home, and at death was buried nearby.

Four years later the throne honored him with the rank of minister of Rites, and in 1620 his one-time imperial student conferred on him the honorary title of junior guardian of the heir apparent, and the posthumous name Wen-i 文毅. During his years of retirement Kuo is said to have visited the Tung-lin Academy, and came to be much in sympathy with its position in state affairs. This relationship became strained, however, when in 1610 he learned that Tung-lin supporters at court had succeeded in bringing about the dismissal of two of his fellow provincials.

Both in and out of office Kuo gave much of his leisure time to writing. Three of his books are listed by the editors of the *Ssu-k'u* catalogue but not copied into the Imperial Library. They are the *P'i-tien K'ao-kung chi* 批點考工記 (1 *ch.*, according to the imperial cataloguers, 2 *ch.*, according to the Library of Congress catalogue), an attempt to correct and punctuate the chapter on technology of the *Chou-li* (*cf.* Tai Chen, ECCP); the *Ming tien-li chih* 明典禮志, 20 *ch.*, printed in 1613, describing the workings of the ministry of Rites; the *Han wen Tu lü* 韓文杜律, 2 *ch.*, dealing with the prose of Han Yü (786–824) and the poetry of Tu Fu (712–70). A collection of his prose and poetry, entitled *Huang-li ts'ao* 黃離草, 10 *ch.*, was printed in 1600. About 1612 there appeared an enlarged collection, *Ho-ping* 合併 *Huang-li ts'ao*, 30 *ch.*, which includes his later writings. One of them, later printed separately, is his account of the events of 1603 and 1604, concerning the case of the prince of Ch'u and the anonymous broadside, entitled *Ch'u shih yao-shu shih-*

mo 楚事妖書始末. The *Huang-li ts'ao* is rare, as it was proscribed in the 1780s, but copies still exist. He is credited as well with the compilation of two local histories, the *Wu-ch'ang-fu* 武昌府 *chih* and *Chiang-hsia-hsien chih*, but neither appears to have come down to modern times.

Bibliography

1/226/17b; 3/203/8a; 8/74/8a; 39/15/1a; 40/54/14b; 61/135/8a; 64/庚14/7b; 86/15/32b; MSL (1966), Shen-tsung, 6034, 6868, 6878, 7139, 7162, 7238, 7343, 7363, 9350; *Huang Ming wen-hai* (microfilm), 5/4/10, 11; Ch'ien Ch'ien-i (ECCP), *Ch'u-hsüeh chi*, 51/1a; SK (1930), 23/2b, 83/5a, 193/2b; TSCC (1885–88), XI: 276/11/4a; Sun Tien-ch'i (1957), 170; L. of C. *Catalogue of Rare Books*, 19, 421, 998; Hsieh Kuo-chen 謝國楨, *Wan Ming shih-chi k'ao* 晚明史籍考 (Peiping, 1933), 6/22a; *Chiang-hsia-hsien chih* (1882), 4/8a, 26a, 6/48b, 8/6b, 8a; *Hupei t'ung-chih* (1934), 595, 3080, 3083, 3086, 3319; *Chao-chou chih* (1897)5/14a; H. Busch, "The Tung-lin Shu-yüan and Its Political and Philosophical Significance," MS, XIV (1949–55), 145; P. M. d'Elia, *Fonti Ricciane*, II (Rome, 1949)43, 158.

Chaoying Fang and L. Carrington Goodrich

KUO Hsün 郭勛, 1475-November 15, 1542, marquis of Wu-ting 武定侯 and later Duke I-kuo 翊國公, was a favorite of Emperor Chu Hou-ts'ung (*q.v.*) and one of the most powerful men in Peking during the first two decades of the Chia-ching period. His ancestor, Kuo Ying, together with an older brother, Kuo Hsing (*see* Kuo Ying), became an early follower of Chu Yüan-chang, the founder of the Ming dynasty. Both brothers proved to be able military men in assisting the first emperor in the conquest of the empire. For their exploits each was given the hereditary noble rank of marquis. So close was the Kuo family to the imperial house that a younger sister of Kuo Ying became Imperial Consort Ning 寧妃 to Chu Yüan-chang; one of Kuo Ying's sons married a princess; two of his daughters became consorts to a prince; and later one of his granddaughters became a consort to Emperor Chu Kao-chih (*q.v.*). Because of family disputes, however, Kuo Hsün's grandfather, Kuo Ch'ang 昌 (d. 1461), was not able to succeed to the marquisate. Not until 1502 was the hereditary rank given back to Kuo Hsün's father, Kuo Liang 良 (T. 存忠, H. 實竹, 1454-1507). At his father's death Kuo inherited the marquisate Wu-ting.

About Kuo's early life information is scant, but by 1512, when his grandmother died, he was holding the military post of grand defender of Kwangtung and Kwangsi. At the time of the death of Emperor Chu Hou-chao (*q.v.*) in 1521, we find him in Peking as one of the two high ranking officers entrusted with the protection and security of the capital.

His rise to extraordinary power and prominence, nevertheless, began with the Chia-ching era, for he was one of the earliest supporters of the young emperor in the stormy controversy of the *Ta-li i* (*see* Chu Hou-ts'ung and Feng Hsi). As the emperor insisted tenaciously on the honorification of his own father, despite the opposition of most of the influential high court officials, he indeed needed their help; and he was grateful for this support throughout his life. It was said that when Chang Ts'ung (later called Chang Fu-ching) and Kuei O (*qq.v.*) came to Peking to support the emperor's stand on the *Ta-li i* against the majority of officials, they were boycotted, and even threatened with bodily harm. It was through the help of Kuo alone that they were able to see the emperor secretly in the night. The emperor stood firm, and the opposing officials were punished and disgraced, many dying as a result. For some twenty years thereafter, Kuo withstood criticism, weathered impeachments, and remained in favor until 1541. In the weird case of Li Fu-ta of 1527, generally known as Ta-yü 大獄 (*see* Chang Fu-ching), for example, it was due to Kuo's influence that the case was never really solved, and many high officials suffered injustice and indignity therefrom.

Early in 1522 Kuo was made commander of the Integrated Divisions, the important training center of troops in Peking. As he was impeached for bribery and the illegal treatment of an officer, this post, together with some other honors, was taken away from him in 1529, but a year later he was charged with the training of the Five Divisions, and by 1531 he was back as commander of the Integrated Divisions. Kuo also supervised many construction works in and around Peking. As both the training of troops and erection of buildings were expensive, Kuo had clashes with ministers of Revenue, especially Liang Ts'ai (*q.v.*). Kuo likewise assisted in various religious ceremonies and Taoist rituals. From 1533 on, he often represented the emperor at sacrificial functions.

It seems that Kuo was versed in literature as well, for he was one of the few selected to attend the emperor in his too frequently performed day and night Taoist rites, and participated in the composing of the peculiar type of sacrificial poetry known as ch'ing-tz'u 青詞 (*see* Chu Hou-ts'ung and Yen Sung). In gratitude for his services, the emperor bestowed on him the dignity of Left Pillar of State in 1536, grand tutor in 1538, and the dukedom of I-kuo in 1539.

When the emperor wen tsouth to visit his old princedom in An-lu (Hukuang) early in 1539, Kuo was a member of the imperial entourage. After the emperor decided to remove his mother's remains to An-lu to be interred beside his father's, he appointed Kuo one of the high officials in charge. In rapid succession Kuo received the rank of a hereditary centurion for one of his descendants, and then (1540) an additional annual stipend of one hundred *shih* of grain. The latter favor was for his introduction of the Taoist adept Tuan Ch'ao-yung 段朝用 (d. March 29, 1543) to the throne. Tuan professed to know not only how to prepare the elixir of life, but also how to turn base metals into gold and silver. As proof he presented to the emperor many pieces of silverware and utensils, which he said, if used in dining, could lengthen the user's life; he also gave ten thousand taels of silver to help in the construction of the altar of thunder 雷壇. This greatly pleased the emperor, who thereupon granted Tuan the official Taoist title Tzu-fu hsüan-chung kao-shih 紫府宣忠高士. Actually he had obtained the silver and silverware directly or indirectly from Kuo, most likely without the latter's knowledge. Tuan lost his life when his magic failed to work; his deception of the emperor contributed to the downfall of Kuo Hsün.

By 1540 and the early part of 1541, Kuo reached the peak of his power and political favor. His end followed hard after. First, a supervising secretary impeached him for many illegal acts, then others followed, accusing him of appropriating government labor for his own use, unlawfully acquiring land and houses, operating businesses without proper procedures, using government transportation for his own profit, and oppressing thc common people. The emperor, reluctant as he was to pursue the matter, nevertheless ordered an investigation by the Censorate. The result revealed that in the Peking area there were about a thousand shops owned by men in high positions, Kuo controlling the largest number of them. It was found too that he resorted to torture and imprisonment to serve his own interests. In rebuttal Kuo argued that, as to real property, he rented it, never exacting illegal payments; as for the business operations, they were all managed by his men and he had little knowledge of their transactions. Up to this point the emperor still hesitated to hold him responsible. The straw that broke the camel's back finally came when Kuo refused to receive an imperial written command commissioning him to investigate ill practices in the Peking Military Corps, because he resented the fact that two civil officials were appointed as his associates. As the matter turned personal, the emperor became angry and finally had Kuo arrested and put into the prison of the Embroidered-uniform Guard on October 1, 1541. Then more and more impeachments followed. After much deliberation, the officials sentenced Kuo to be executed, his family members enslaved, and his property confiscated. This document when presented to the emperor, however, was held over and never received imperial sanction; instead, more than once, the emperor told the prison officials to spare Kuo any physical punishment. After a little over a year, Kuo died in prison.

Eight years after his death, Kuo's son, Kuo Shou-ch'ien 守乾, petitioned to succeed to the title and perquisites of the marquisate Wu-ting; the emperor graciously gave his consent. In 1565 Kuo Shou-ch'ien's son, Kuo Ta-ch'eng 大誠, in his turn inherited the title. Kuo P'ei-min 培民 (d. 1643), a son of Kuo Ta-ch'eng, who met his end at the hands of the rebel forces of Li Tzu-ch'eng (ECCP) in 1643, was the last Marquis Wu-ting. So did the Kuo family hold this noble rank throughout the Ming dynasty.

Early in 1537 Kuo Hsün begged the emperor to have the name of his ancestor, Kuo Ying, inscribed in the Imperial Ancestral Temple, and the request was granted. Also in honor of his ancestor, he compiled the *San-chia shih-tien* 三家世典. a work recounting the history of the three notable families of Hsü Ta, Mu Ying (*qq.v.*), and Kuo Ying. Perhaps it was for this reason that some sources credited Kuo Hsün with the authorship of the *Ying-lieh chuan* 英烈傳, a popular novel about the founding of the Ming dynasty. Some even suggested that he wrote it to glorify his ancestor and to impress the emperor with this fact. The evidence to prove this theory is not adequate, however. According to the catalogue of Chinese popular novels compiled by Sun K'ai-ti 孫楷第, Kuo printed both famous novels, the *Shui-hu chuan* (*see* Shih Nai-an) and the *San-kuo t'ung-su yen-i* 三國通俗演義, and they have come to be known as the Wu-ting editions. Kuo Hsün is also cited as the compiler of a collection of lyrics selected from musical dramas, the *Yung-hsi yüeh-fu* 雍熙樂府, 20 *ch.*, first printed in the Chia-ching era and recently included in the second series of the *Ssu-pu ts'ung-k'an* 四部叢刊續編. In protecting him from physical punishment, the emperor defended himself by recalling the part played by Kuo Hsün in the *Ta-li i* and in the printing of the *T'ai-ho chuan* 太和傳. It is not clear what the *T'ai-ho chuan* was, but it reaffirms Kuo's association with the printing and publication of books. The account about the T'ai-ho Mountain, given in the provincial gazetteer of Hupei, states that the first book, or *chih* 志, on this mountain was compiled by Wang Tso 王佐, the eunuch overseer of the T'ai-ho Taoist establishments in the Chia-ching period, but apparently it is no longer extant. Could there be some connection between the two? The *T'u-shu chi-ch'eng* lists Kuo Hsün's name in its section on calligraphers. Kuo must indeed have been a man of many parts.

勛 and 勳 are interchangeable characters, so Kuo Hsün's name is also occasionally written as 勳, although as a rule the form 勛 is employed both in the *Ming shih-lu* and the *Ming-shih*. There was another Kuo Hsün 郭勳 (T. 希暘), native of Chiang-yin 江陰 in present day Kiangsu, who was a geomancer, and who lived much later. Perhaps the confusion in the two forms of this character was the reason for the omission of the citation in Kuo Ying's biography in the *Ming-shih* in the *Combined Indices to Eighty-Nine Collections of Ming Dynasty Biographies.*

Bibliography

1/130/8b, 10b, 131/5b; 3/119/9b; 87/2/12b (for the other Kuo Hsün); *Huang Ming wen-hai* (microfilm), biography by Ho Ch'iao-yüan; MSL (1965), Wu-tsung, 3645, Shih-tsung, ch. 1-267; KC (1958), 3211-3635; Li Tung-yang, *Huai-lu-t'ang chi* (*wen-hou-kao*), 29/5b; Liang Ch'u, *Yü-chou i-kao* (1912 ed.), 3/4a; SK (1930), 61/5a; Shen Te-fu, *Wan-li yeh-hu pien* (1959 ed.), 139, 140, 142, 643, 818; Sun K'ai-ti, *Chung-kuo t'ung-su hsiao-shuo shu-mu* 中國通俗小說書目 (1957 ed.), 182; Chao Ching-shen 趙景深, *Hsiao-shuo hsien-hua* 小說閒話 (1937 ed.), 208; *Hu-pei t'ung-chih* 湖北通志 (1934 ed.), 688; TSCC (1885-88), XXIV: 121/27/13a, Wang Kuo-wei (BDRC), *Kuan-t'ang pieh-chi* (i-shu 遺書 ed.), 8.

Lienche Tu Fang

KUO T'ing-hsün 過庭訓 (T. 爾韜, H. 成山), fl. 1570-1625, official and author of an important collection of biographies of Ming people, was a native of P'ing-hu 平湖, Chekiang. He probably hailed from a well-to-do family involved in the production of salt, as his name is put in the tsao 竈 category in the *chin-shih* lists. In any event, his forebears early began to make a collection of books, especially rare ones, which his grandfather Kuo Ch'iao 橋 (T. 龍濱) greatly expanded. Unhappily this library suffered a total loss in 1554, when the Japanese pirates burned and plundered his area. As a consequence, it is said that his father Kuo Hou 厚 (T. 九山), in teaching him, stressed moral behavior rather than book learning. When Kuo T'ing-hsün was seventeen years of age, his father died, leaving the family in financial straits. So to help his mother, he engaged himself as a teacher, for he had been selected a student in the district school in 1582. Reportedly he had as students the sons of a number of distinguished people. One day, in 1585, while visiting in the home of an eminent fellow townsman, Sun Chih 孫植 (T. 斯立, H. 晷川, Pth. 簡肅, cs 1535, minister of Justice in Nanking, 1567-70, and minister of Works there in 1584, d. 1586), Kuo happened upon a copy of the recently published *Wu-hsüeh-pien* by Cheng Hsiao (*q. v.*). A reading of this important compilation led him to an understanding of the characteristics of famous figures in earlier reigns of the dynasty. He decided to compile a compendium of eminent Ming individuals under two categories, people of upright behavior and those accomplished in government service, and began to collect biographical material. In 1592 Kuo became an instructor in the home of a neighboring Feng 馮 family, which had a library founded by Feng Ju-pi 汝弼 (T. 惟良, H. 佑山, cs 1532, 1499-1577). Spending part of his time tutoring Feng's grandson and part conducting his research in the Feng collection, he labored for over ten years on this task, collaborating with several friends, including Lu Chien 陸鍵 (T. 實甫, H. 開仲, cs 1607) and Chao Wei-huan 趙維寰 (T. 無聲, cj 1600).

The work was interrupted in 1603 when Kuo passed the provincial examination at Hangchow. He then went to Peking where, in 1604, he became a *chin-shih* and an official on probation. A year later he was appointed magistrate of Chiang-ling 江陵, Hukuang, where he served with distinction. In 1606 he took part in the provincial examination at Wuchang. One of the *chü-jen* he passed was Hsiung Kao 熊膏 (T. 雨亭, cs 1613, d. *ca.* 1628) whom he engaged for a time to teach his third and youngest son, Kuo Ming-fu 銘簠. In 1610 the court summoned Kuo to Peking to take office as censor. In his spare time he resumed research on the biographies. Meanwhile he published two of his minor works, one on philosophy, entitled *Hsing-li i-ming* 性理翼明, and one on Confucianists, *Sheng-hsüeh ti-p'ai* 聖學嫡派, 4 *ch.* During these years (1610-17) he served as inspecting censor in Pei-Chihli, Shantung, and Honan provinces, in 1616 being charged with the distribution of 160,000 taels of silver to the famine-stricken people in Shantung. After a period of mourning for the death of his mother, he was recalled to service and appointed in 1621 director of education of the Nanking area. It was here that he finally decided to limit the biographies to those of exemplary conduct and to arrange them by native provinces and prefectures. Hence he named the book *Pen-ch'ao ching-sheng fen-chün jen-wu k'ao* 本朝京省分郡人物考. This was printed in 1623 in 115 *chüan*, with the help of his disciple, Hsiung Kao, then serving as intendant of Soochow. At the head of the table of contents, the first part of the title is given as *Kuo* 國-*ch'ao* instead of *Pen-ch'ao*. This book was partially banned in the 18th century because of certain passages considered seditious in Manchu eyes. As a result it is rare, but has recently (1970) been reprinted in Taiwan (in 29 volumes with index), and has also been made available on microfilm.

About 1623, Kuo seems to have been appointed for a time as an administration vice commissioner of Kiangsi. In 1625 he served as intendant of Yüeh-chou 岳州, Hukuang. Later he became surveillance commissioner of Fukien, and finally received an appointment as vice governor of the Nanking metropolitan area but died before assuming office.

It seems that in 1629 a monument bearing an imperial eulogy was erected at Kuo's tomb, but it was removed three years later due to court politics. It happened that while serving as a censor from 1610 to 1617 Kuo had been unusually outspoken about the party wrangles of that day, criticizing Yeh Hsiang-kao (*q.v.*) and other Tung-lin members (*see* Kao P'an-lung) as severely as he did their opponents. For this reason he came to be labeled a Chekiang party man (浙黨). Consequently, while the Tung-lin men were being persecuted from 1625 to 1627 by the eunuch Wei Chung-hsien (ECCP), Kuo was receiving promotions. As a result some contemporaries considered him one of the eunuch's clique. Actually Kuo was a public minded official who reported candidly what he believed. For example, he submitted a memorial in 1614 on the dangers threatening the Liaotung border by the rising military power of Nurhaci (ECCP), and predicted a war which actually broke out three years later. The emperor, however, ignored his warning. Luckily the document was preserved, as Tung Ch'i-ch'ang (ECCP) included it in his collection of important memorials of that day.

Kuo left a collection of his poetry, entitled *P'ing-p'ing ts'ao* 平平草, 4 *ts'e*. Chu I-tsun (ECCP) includes a single example in his *Ming-shih tsung*, the title of which may be rendered "Traveling on an autumn day in 1621 to Mao-shan 茅山" (an eminence in the lower Yangtze valley).

Bibliography

32/preface; 40/5a/20b; 87/1/4a; KC (1958), 4531; *P'ing-hu-hsien chih* (1886), 13/7a, 15/51b, 23/16a, 25/2a; Tung Ch'i-ch'ang, *Shen-miao liu-chung tsou-shu hui-yao* (1937), 兵 2/11a; Sheng Feng 盛楓, *Chia-ho cheng-hsien lu* 嘉禾徵獻錄 (1932), 20/1a; SK (1930), 62/5a, Sun Tien-ch'i (1957), 41, 157; *Hunan t'ung-chih* (1934), 2493; *Chiang-ling-hsien chih* (1876), 17/53a; *Nai-kaku Bunko*, 97; Ping-ti Ho, *The Ladder of Success in Imperial China* (New York, 1962), 95; W. Franke, *Sources*, 3. 1. 5.

L. Carrington Goodrich and Chaoying Fang

KUO Tzu-chang 郭子章 (T. 相奎 H. 青螺, 蠙衣生), January 29, 1543–September 12, 1618, prolific author and official, was a native of T'ai-ho 泰和, Kiangsi. After graduating as *chin-shih* in 1571, he became successively prefectural judge in Chien-ning 建寧-fu, Fukien (1572–75), where he conducted the provincial examinations in 1573, secretary in and later director of a bureau in the ministry of Works in Nanking (1575–82), prefect of Ch'ao-chou 潮州, Kwangtung (1582–85), provincial director of education in Szechwan (1586–89), administration vice commissioner of Chekiang (1589–92), surveillance commissioner of Shansi (1592–93), and administration commissioner first of Hukuang (1593–95) and then of Fukien (1595–98). He returned home in 1598, but was not there for long. On April 2, 1599, he received an appointment as vice censor-in-chief and was dispatched to Kweichow as governor. This area, including the southern border region of Szechwan, for several years had been plagued by acts of rebellion and destruction by the Miao tribesmen, led by Yang Ying-lung (*q. v.*), the native chieftain of Po-chou. The local officials having apparently failed to quell the rebels, Kuo, Li Hua-lung, and several military commanders such as Ch'en Lin (*qq.v.*) were brought

in to crush them. This they did (July, 1600), though it was costly in human life.

After Kuo was granted his wish to retire in 1608, and finally left Kweichow in 1609, the residents of that province erected a shrine in his honor. This was not the first time that the people under his administration had expressed their gratitude towards him in this way, for similar shrines had been dedicated to him in Chien-ning, where he held his first office, and in Ch'ao-chou. The usual practice was to let a number of years elapse after the death of an official before dedicating a shrine to him; to do so while he was still alive meant either extreme flattery, as in the case of the eunuch Wei Chung-hsien (ECCP), or sincere gratitude. Later Kuo's admirers collected the documents and inscriptions commemorating him at each of these shrines, which they presented under the title *San-sheng sheng-tz'u lu* 三省生祠錄 (Records from three provinces of enshrinement [of Kuo] while he was still living). It is said that Kuo was one of the noted high officials who happened to be a dwarf.

The central government took particular note of his military successes. In November, 1604, for his part in the conquest of Yang Ying-lung and the establishment of two new prefectures in the area of the former native chieftainship, Kuo received the minor hereditary rank of an assistant commander of the Embroidered-uniform Guard; this went evetually to his eldest grandson, Kuo Ch'eng-hao 承昊 (b. 1593, military cj 1609). For the former's sucessful campaign against aborigines who rebelled in 1606 Kuo received in June, 1612, the title of minister of War and an upgrading in hereditary rank to vice commander. During the nine years of retirement certain censors recommended him as worthy of a high appointment. At the same time, however, he was also denounced by other censors whenever he was considered for a post. One censor even attacked him as warranting capital punishment because he had written that an emperor could be safe only in the company of women and eunuchs. Kuo did write such an essay in 1588, but he meant it to be a criticism of the monarchical system by which a sovereign guarded his power and wealth. Perhaps this essay is one reason why, after his death, he was given in 1620 only the routine honors such as an official burial and the title of junior guardian of the heir apparent, but no posthumous name.

Kuo's biographers all record that Kuo had remarkable gifts which distinguished him from his contemporaries; yet strangely he receives no biographical notice either in the *Ming-shih* or in the *Ming-shih kao*; not even in the far more copious *T'u-shu chi-ch'eng*. The *Ming-shih* does, however, list twenty-five titles under his authorship. The editors of the *Ssu-k'u* were also well aware of his writings. Although they excluded every one from the Imperial Library, they listed altogether seventeen of his books in the Catalogue, some with *chüan* numbers, unlike those in other lists or in printed editions. The first is a contribution to the study of the *I* (Book of Changes); the second, *Ch'ien-chung p'ing Po shih-mo* 黔中平播始末, 3 *ch.*, is an account of his part in the campaign against Yang Ying-lung; a third, *Sheng-men jen-wu chih* 聖門人物志, 12 *ch.*, is about the early disciples of Confucius; a fourth, *Yü-chang* 豫章 *chih*, 122 (or 124) *ch.*, is a history of his native province which gives some data on porcelain manufactured there; a fifth, *Chün-hsien shih-ming* 郡縣釋名, 26 *ch.*, printed in 1615, discusses the place names in the empire; a sixth is a gazetteer of a mountain near Ningpo entitled *A-yü-wang shan chih* 阿育王山志 (The record of King Asoka's mountain), with material on its monastery and śarīra stūpa; a seventh is a compilation of references on the double-edged sword, *Pin-i-sheng chien-chi* 蠙衣生劍記; the eighth is a similar compilation of quotations about the horse, *Pin-i-sheng ma* 馬 *chi*; a ninth is *Ch'ien-lei* 黔類, a compilation of quotations on various subjects, 18 *ch.*, a tenth is a

series of six anthologies of ballads, folk songs, riddles, augural sayings, jokes, and satire, 30 *ch.*; the eleventh is a collection of notes on Kiangsi poets, 6 *ch.*; and the twelfth through the seventeenth are six of his collections of prose and poetry. In the last category he is known to have left at least fifteen collections, each at the end of residence in a place or occupation of an office, or at the completion of an event. Among these may be mentioned *Yüeh-ts'ao* 粵草, 10 *ch.*, written in Kwangtung, *Shu* 蜀*-ts'ao*, 10 *ch.*, in Szechwan, and *Ch'ien ts'ao* 16 *ch.*, in Kweichow, all preserved in the National Central Library, Taipei. (The *Shu-ts'ao* is one of two works by Kuo listed for partial proscription in the 18th century.) The same library has three more of Kuo's collections in manuscript. The Library of Congress has copies of *Ch'ien-ts'ao*, *A-yü-wang shan chih*, *Sheng-men jen-wu chih*, and in addition has listed under Kuo's authorship a *T'ai-yang-chou Hsiao-hou miao chih* 太洋洲蕭侯廟志, 7 *ch.*, printed 1622, which is a treatise on the temple in T'ai-ho erected in honor of a local man of Sung times; an imperial decree of 1419 had singled him out for having saved the fleet commanded by some eunuchs returning from a voyage. This work is not mentioned in the gazetteers or in the list of ninety-two titles compiled by one of Kuo's clansmen in 1876.

Certain of Kuo's manuscripts and some printing blocks for his books were lost during the wars of the mid-seventeenth century, and most of the rest failed to survive the Taiping Rebellion two hundred years later. In 1876 the descendant of one of his cousins assembled what was available in a collection entitled *Ming ta-ssu-ma Kuo kung i-shu* 明大司馬郭公遺書, 35 *ch.*, also known as *Ch'ing-lo kung i-shu* 青螺 kung i-shu. Preceding this work is a chronology (*Kuo kung Ch'ing-lo nien-p'u* 年譜) originally compiled by Kuo Tzu-chang's second son, Kuo K'ung-yen 孔延 (b. 1574). Appended are writings by the other two sons: the *Ch'ui-yang kuan chi* 垂楊館集, 11

ch., by Kuo K'ung-chien 孔建 (T. 建公, 1573-98), and the *Ching-chuan cheng-wu* 經傳正誤; discussing a number of commonly mispronounced words in the Classics, by Kuo K'ung-t'ai 孔太 (b. 1576). The printing of these appendices was completed in 1879. The Columbia University copy of this work has a preface written about 1903 by the then minister of foreign affairs, Ch'ü Hung-chi (ECCP, p. 674), who praised Kuo as a true follower of the school of thought of Wang Shou-jen (*q.v.*), and pointed out the fallacy of the theory that the teachings of Wang were responsible for the decline and fall of the Ming dynasty. During the Manchu conquest in the late 1640s in the Ch'ao-chou area Kuo's shrine was destroyed. In 1661 a new one was erected celebrating ten former prefects, among whom were Kuo Tzu-chang and his clansman, Kuo Ch'un-chen 春震 (T. 以亨, H. 菊壇, cs 1529, prefect, 1545-47). The latter was editor of the gazetteer *Ch'ao-chou-fu chih*, 8 *ch.*, printed in 1547, a copy of which is in Japan. To this work Kuo Tzu-chang himself wrote a supplement, *Ch'ao-chung tsa-chih* 中雜志, 12 *ch.*

That Kuo was an observant and keen-witted man is clear. He happens also to have been among the first to appreciate the geographical contributions of Matteo Ricci (*q.v.*), whom he came to know while serving in Kwangtung. Years later, while governor of Kweichow, Kuo received a copy of the second edition (1600) of Ricci's *mappa mundi* and reproduced it in his *Ch'ien-ts'ao*. P. M. d'Elia has translated the preface, which is an interesting disquisition on the importance of Ricci's contribution to Chinese geographical knowledge.

Finally there is a collection of tales of judicial cases based partly on investigations and reports made by Kuo Tzu-chang during his service in six provinces, entitled *Hsin-k'o Kuo Ch'ing-lo liu-sheng t'ing-sung-lu hsin-min kung-an* 新刻郭青螺六省聽訟錄新民公案, 4 *ch.*, printed in 1605. The only known copy of this collec-

tion seems to be a manuscript written by a Japanese in 1744, now in the Taiwan University Library. According to the review by Mou Jun-sun 牟潤孫, the book contains forty-five cases listed under seven headings: embezzlement; manslaughter, murder, robbery, fraudulence, injustice, and usurpation. The style is that of someone with no claims to literary skill, who put into fiction judiciary reports, quite inferior to the contemporary collections of short stories such as those edited by Feng Meng-lung (*q.v.*). It signifies that Kuo enjoyed writing in a popular vein anecdotes which would meet the fancy of the common people.

Bibliography

40/51/7a; 64/庚10/5b; 86/15/8a; MSL (1966), Shen-tsung, 6144, 6478, 8258, 9314; KC (1958), 4838, 4855, 4933, 4978, 5123; Ch'en Tzu-lung (ECCP), *Ming ching-shih wen-pien*, ch. 419-20; SK(1930), 7/11a, 54/1a, 62/2a, 72/2a, 76/3a, 116/1a, 11a, 138/3a, 144/10b, 179/3b, 197/7b; *T'ai-ho-hsien chih* (1879), 12/23a, 17/35a, 22/15a, 17a, 25b, 32a, 33b, 56b; *Ch'ao-chou-fu chih* (repr. of 1775 ed.), 31/32b; *Kuei-chou t'ung-chih* (1911?), 19/12a, 41/44b; *Kwangtung t'ung-chih*(1934), 570, 4366; *Chekiang t'ung-chih* (1934), 2642; *Fukien t'ung-chih* (1922), 32/8b; Sun Tien-ch'i (1957), 246; Ch'iu K'ai-ming 裘開明, CHHP, n.s. II: 2 (1961), 105; Hung Wei-lien 洪煨蓮, "K'ao Li Ma-tou te shih-chieh ti-t'u" 考利瑪竇的世界地圖, *Yü-kung* 禹貢, 5 (April 11, 1936), 22; Jao Tsung-i 饒宗頤, *Ch'ao-chou chih hui-pien* 滙編 (1965), 51, 236, 249; Shen Te-fu, *Wan-li yeh-hu pien* (1959), 315; Mou Jun-sun, *Chu-shih chai ts'ung-kao* 注史齋叢稿 (1959), 235; P. M. d'Elia, *Fonti Ricciane*, I (Rome, 1942), 260, II(Rome, 1949), 60; L. of C. *Catalogue of Rare Books*, 213, 275, 375, 980; S. W. Bushell, *Description of Chinese Pottery and Porcelain* (Oxford, 1910), 173.

Chaoying Fang and
L. Carrington Goodrich

KUO Tzu-hsing 郭子興, posthumous title Ch'u-yang Wang 滁陽王 died April-May 1355, a native of Ting-yüan 定遠 (Anhwei), participated in the White Lotus Sect rebellion from 1351 or 1352 until his death. It was in his service that

Chu Yüan-chang first became involved in rebellion against the Yüan. Kuo grew up on the margins of respectable society in Ting-yüan, where his father prospered as a fortuneteller and practiced his art in the homes of the wealthy. His forebears were natives of Ts'ao-chou 曹州, Shantung. His father found a good market for his services in Ting-yüan where he settled after marrying a blind woman who had been living in the household of a client. They had a daughter and three sons, the second of whom was Kuo Tzuhsing. The sons inherited a considerable fortune from their father and set up separate households. Kuo Tzu-hsing had a wife and a concubine, both surnamed Chang 張. By the former he had three sons, and by the latter, a daughter. Another member was added to the household, probably in 1351, when a certain Mr. Ma left his daughter (the future Empress Ma, q.v.) in their care; according to the official accounts the Kuo family looked after her "as though she were their own." (Editors' note: For another version of this episode, see Empress Ma.)

In February or March, 1352, Kuo Tzuhsing took part in the capture of the city of Hao-chou 濠州 (Anhwei) on the Huai River. The year before, the White Lotus Society's armed bands had initiated successful rebellions farther west. Toward the end of that year, Kuo spent liberally to organize Ting-yüan farmers as sworn brothers. He and four other local leaders, Sun Te-yai 孫德崖, and Yü 俞, Lu 魯, and P'an 潘, who are known only by their surnames, joined forces and declared themselves yüan-shuai 元帥 (commanders) by authority of the Sect. They made Hao -chou their headquarters. In the autumn of 1352 Hsü-chou 徐州, another rebel-held stronghold, fell to the Yüan troops and two of the defeated leaders, P'eng Ta and Chao Chün-yung (for both see Chu Yüan-chang) escaped with some of their supporters to take refuge in Hao-chou. Both now outranked the local leaders but were themselves equal in rank. It was

impossible, therefore, to fix final responsibility locally and the higher authorities in the sect do not seem to have intervened to resolve the disputes at Hao-chou. The result was that, by the autumn of 1354, the redel camp of two years before at Hao-chou had split into two or three mutually hostile groups. One, under Kuo and Chu Yüan-chang, was the nucleus of the Ming dynastic regime. The second, originally under P'eng Ta and Chao Chün-yung, survived in what is now known as northern Anhwei for several years until Chao was assassinated in 1359, and P'eng Ta's son and heir, P'eng Tsao-chu 早住, was captured in 1366 by Chu Yüan-chang. A third group under Sun Te-yai may have operated independently for a time in the Huai River area.

Kuo was given too much to relentless personal feuds to take advantage of the fluid political situation within the rebellion. This was in marked contrast to Chu Yüan-chang, who rose from the lowest rank under him and became the founder of an empire. Chu arrived at Hao-chou as a refugee in April-May, 1352. He was at first held as a suspect, but was released by Kuo and taken into his service. Kuo's concubine, who had no son, presently suggested to her husband that this promising young officer might be permanently tied to their service by arranging his marriage to the Ma girl. This was done, and thenceforth Chu, his wife, and Kuo's concubine seem to have worked well together in the face of growing resentment on the part of the rest of the family.

When P'eng and Chao arrived at Hao-chou about October, 1352, Kuo was impressed by P'eng who was, like his father and probably like himself, a fortuneteller. At the same time that he cultivated P'eng's friendship, he made an enemy of Chao by treating him with contempt. Chao then joined Kuo's four old rivals in a plot against him. They captured Kuo on some excuse and imprisoned him in the house of Sun Te-yai. It was Chu

Yüan-chang who secured P'eng's help in breaking into Sun's house and had Kuo released. Soon after this the city was laid under siege by Yüan forces and the necessities of defense imposed a measure of unity on the leaders. Late in 1353, some months after the siege had been lifted, P'eng and Chao assumed the grandiloquent titles prince of Lu-huai 魯淮王 and prince of 永義王 Yung-i respectively.

Meanwhile Chu had been busy in Kuo's and his own behalf. He had recruited a large number of men in his native village and, in July and August of 1354, he negotiated or compelled the defection of several government militia units, some of them very large. At the same time, he recovered control of Ting-yüan, which had apparently been abandoned the year before to government forces. Then moving southeastward towards the Yangtze, he took the city of Ch'u-chou 滁州. While Chu was busy in the south, Kuo advanced northeastward along the Huai in the company of P'eng and Chao who captured Hsü-i 盱眙 and Ssu-chou 泗州. In September-October, 1354, P'eng and Chao vainly ordered Chu to come with his swollen army and take charge of the defense of the cities they had just occupied. Chu chose, instead, to remain at Ch'u-chou and build his strength there. Shortly after this, P'eng and Chao fell to fighting each other. There was heavy loss of life, and one of those killed was P'eng Ta, whose titles passed to his son P'eng Tsao-chu. This left Kuo's enemy Chao Chün-yung in full command. Kuo, who had been fortunate to survive P'eng Ta, was still in danger. Chu used persuasion and bribes to enable Kuo to escape with his followers to Ch'u-chou. This proved to be a permanent split in the old Hao-chou forces.

Kuo made his headquarters in Ch'u-chou and only Chu's strong arguments on grounds of prudence dissuaded Kuo from assuming a royal title. Now that he had been liberated from his rivals, his relations with Chu deteriorated. The latter had under his personal command a force much larger than Kuo's and his prestige and popularity had grown with his successes, all of which caused Kuo to regard him with apprehension and mistrust. All efforts to reduce Chu's prestige were unavailing, however, because Kuo repeatedly had to call on him for help, first to manage the defense of Ch'u-chou, which came under attack by Yüan forces in October-November of 1354, and then to take charge of the forces at Ho-chou 和州, which had been captured on Chu's advice in January-February of 1355. But the issues dividing the two men were evidently beyond solution. In April-May, 1355, when Sun Te-yai and others of the original Hao-chou group, now running short of food, came to Ho-chou for help, Chu, apparently seeing a chance to reunite the divided forces, generously invited them into the city. When Kuo learned of Chu's hospitality to his old enemies, he rushed to Ho-chou, where he called Chu to account. Sun was frightened and intended to leave at once but was detained by Kuo. Sun's men outside the city then seized Chu as hostage. To Kuo's credit, he exchanged Sun for Chu, thus saving the latter's life. Kuo died shortly after these events.

The question of the succession to Kuo's nominal command at Ch'u-chou was taken up by the White Lotus Sect authorities at Po-chou 亳州. Since Kuo's eldest son had died some time before this, his second son, Kuo T'ien-hsü 天敘, was appointed commander. Chang T'ien-yu 張天祐, a younger brother of Kuo's widow, was made first vice commander, while Chu Yüan-chang was relegated to the place of second vice commander. Chu, who had led the successful crossing to the south bank of the Yangtze and the capture of T'ai-p'ing 太平 in July-August, 1355, became, in effect, the chief commander by general agreement of the forces there. In any case, two or three months later Kuo and Chang were killed in an attack on Chi-ch'ing 集慶 (later Nanking) leaving Chu as the ranking officer. After Chu's capture of Chi-ch'ing in 1356 he assumed the title Duke of Wu 吳國公 and was appointed by the government at Po-chou as chief administrator while Kuo's only surviving son, Kuo T'ien-chüeh 爵, was appointed first assistant administrator, and some time after this plotted against Chu and was executed.

Kuo's last surviving child, excluding the adopted future Empress Ma, was the daughter by his concubine. According to the official records, Chu married her also and as the Hui-fei, she bore three sons: the 11th, Chu Ch'un, the 13th, Chu Kuei, and the 19th, Chu Hui (see Chu Yüan-chang).

In the third year of his imperial reign, Chu Yüan-chang granted his father-in-law the posthumous title Ch'u-yang Wang and had a temple built for him near his grave at Ch'u-chou. In 1383 Chu drafted a discreet biography of Kuo and ordered Chang Yü (q.v.) to rewrite it and have it engraved on a stone tablet to be installed in the Kuo temple.

In the late Ming historical romance, *Ying-lieh chuan* 英烈傳, Kuo Tzu-hsing is referred to as Kuo Kuang-ch'ing 郭光卿.

Bibliography

1/122/1a; 2/156/4b; 3/113/4a; 5/3/6a; Ch'ien Ch'ien-i (ECCP), *Kuo-ch'ün-hsiung shih-lüeh* 國初群雄事略; Chu Yüan-chang, *Yü-chih chi-meng*; Li Chih, *Hsü ts'ang-shu* ed. (1959), 6; Cha Chi-tso (ECCP), *Tsui-wei-lu*, 5/2a; *Ying-lieh chuan*, Shanghai, 1955.

Romeyn Taylor

KUO Ying 郭英, 1335-March 9, 1403, a native of Hao-chou 濠州 (Anhwei), was a leading military officer and favorite of Chu Yüan-chang from the time he entered his service in 1353 at the age of eighteen. He was large and physically powerful and, as his many wounds would testify, a man of great courage. Chu valued him for these qualities and for his personal loyalty. Probably until 1356 he acted as Chu's bodyguard on night watch. For another five or six years, he served in campaigns in the east against the Yüan forces and Chang Shih-ch'eng (q.v.). In 1362, when he was gravely weakened by his wounds, Chu called him to his side again in order to spare him. Still not fully recovered he fought at the battle of Poyang Lake and was credited with having shot the arrow that killed the enemy commander, Ch'en Yu-liang (q.v.). A few months later he saved the future emperor's life at Wuchang when Chu was caught relaxing in his campchair during a sudden counterattack by Ch'en Li's forces (see Ch'en Yu-liang). On this occasion, Chu took off his red battle coat and gave it to Kuo as an expression of his gratitude.

During the six years from 1365 to 1371 Kuo took part in the conquest of the north and northwest under the command of Hsü Ta, Ch'ang Yü-ch'un, and Li Wen-chung (qq.v.). In 1366 he was appointed a battalion commander in a select unit, the special cavalry guard 驍騎衞, later called the commandery rear guard 府軍後衞. Successive promotions led in 1370 to his appointment as commander of this unit. One of his more celebrated victories was under Hsü Ta's command at T'ung-chou 通州, east of the Yüan capital, in 1368. Here he lured the Yüan defenders out of their well-fortified city by pretending to retreat and then caught them in an ambush. In 1370, still in Hsü's army, he and a dozen or so other cavalrymen made a daring night attack on the camp of Kökö Temür (q.v.). Setting fires while other troops nearby fired cannon, they threw the enemy into confusion and scattered them.

In January, 1372, Kuo was rewarded for his twenty years of effort by appointment as Honan provincial military commander. He shared this office with Miao Tao 繆道, son of Chu's early follower, Miao Ta-heng 大亨 (d. 1363). Kuo was one of the first provincial commanders appointed under a new rule, viz., removal of this office from the category of hereditary military posts, and setting a limit of six years' tenure. He remained in office the full term, until 1376, when he was transferred to Peiping. It was probably during his years in Honan that his mother died. His conduct on this occasion is said to have been a model of filial piety. Although Honan had been disrupted by the war, the province recovered rapidly. The banditry that was widespread in 1371 soon subsided with no large-scale outbreaks occurring. In April, 1373, Kuo carried out the emperor's orders to round up Yüan army veterans, and registered seven hundred of them to fill vacancies in the ranks of his Honan guards. The registered population of Honan rose rapidly during these years, and in 1375 Kaifeng qualified for promotion to the status of a superior prefecture by meeting the census and tax return criteria. Although there is little evidence of Kuo's direct contribution to the peace and prosperity of the province, his final departure from Kaifeng is said to have been marked by a mass demonstration of dismay over his transfer, and the local citizens built a shrine in his honor.

From November, 1376, until some time in 1380, Kuo served as the Peiping provincial military commander. He was no doubt honored by this appointment because the city had recently been the Yüan capital and also because of its strategic situation near the northern frontier. His years here appear to have been as uneventful as those in Honan, however. Peiping at this time was headquarters for Hsü Ta as commander-in-chief of the northern army, and he and his own officers did most of such fighting and patrolling as were required. The emperor did not ignore Kuo, however. In December, 1379, he received an appointment as assistant military commissioner-in-chief. A few months later, the year in which the prince of Yen, Chu Ti (*q.v.*), was established in his palace in Peiping (1380), Kuo was recalled to the capital. In the reorganization of that year he was appointed assistant military commissioner-in-

chief of the forward army, and then sent to the northeast on a short expedition against bandits in Liaotung.

In September, 1381, an army under the command of Fu Yu-te, Lan Yü, and Mu Ying (*qq.v.*) proceeded to Yünnan to subjugate the Yüan prince of Liang, Basalawarmi (*see* Wang I). Kuo was assigned to serve with them. Mongol aristocrats and Man chieftains had created an immense, if thinly populated state, extending from the western frontier of Yünnan across the province into southern Szechwan and western Kweichow. The campaign lasted until April, 1383, by which time the main opposition had been broken, the prince of Liang driven to suicide, and many of the Man leaders reduced to at least outward submission to Ming authority and formally incorporated into the provincial administration. During these years, Kuo was almost continuously engaged in attacking and destroying the enemy forts and palisades that had sprung up on the slopes of the steep mountainsides of the region, and while doing so was wounded again. In May, 1384, after his return to the capital, Kuo was invested with the title marquis of Wu-ting 武定 and given an annual stipend of 2,500 *tan* and his iron certificate of legal immunity. In March of the following year he was also given a special grant of 500 *tan*.

Late in 1385 Kuo received the field rank of Ching-hai 靖海 General, and was sent to Liaotung to command defense forces there. At least since 1372 the Mongol general Naɣaču (*q.v.*) had conducted raids into this region, and in January, 1387, the emperor launched a great campaign against him. Kuo served in the third level of command under Feng Sheng (*q.v.*), Fu Yu-te, and Lan Yü. The main objective was attained with Naɣaču's surrender, but the army was ambushed on the way back and suffered heavy losses. Feng, moreover, had become embroiled in a bitter quarrel with his son-in-law, Ch'ang Mao (*see* Ch'ang Yü-ch'un), which ended in his sending the latter back to the capital in shackles. Ch'ang's report to the emperor persuaded him that Feng was at least partly to blame, and he relieved him of his command, appointing Lan Yü to take his place. Kuo, who had fought bravely as usual and suffered a spear wound in the abdomen, returned to Liao-tung. In November of the same year he was ordered out on another campaign to the north, this one against the Mongol khan, Tögüs Temür (*q.v.*), near Lake Büyür (modern Pei-er ch'ih 貝爾池 on the western border of Hei-lung-chiang). Lan Yü was in command with T'ang Sheng tsung (*see* Lan Yü) and Kuo Ying as his assistants. A surprise attack on the enemy camp resulted in a rich haul of captives and loot. The khan escaped, however, but his second son, Ti-pao-nu 地保奴, was among the captives. Kuo Ying received as reward for his part gifts of silver, paper money, and silk.

Kuo was permitted to return home after the campaign, probably in the autumn of 1388. In 1390 the emperor called him to the capital, gave him the privilege of remaining seated during a private audience, and put him in charge of the palace guards. On several occasions that year the emperor presented him more gold, silver, and paper money. In July he gave to him, as to other veteran officers, an escort guard of one hundred for his home, and authority to secure land enough to support the men. Kuo's duties at this time were probably light. He oversaw construction of the tomb of the prince of Lu, Chu T'an (*see* Chu Yüan-chang), in Shantung. The project did not go forward as rapidly as expected, and in April, 1390, the emperor refused to let him hire civilian labor in order to complete it. He suggested, perhaps with conscious irony, that, since Kuo was a military man and lacking in education, he didn't know that civilians should not be disturbed when they were busy with farming. The emperor may have considered the work unimportant because he had been angry with the prince for having

ruined his health by experimenting with elixirs, and had bestowed on him the posthumous epithet Huang 荒 (the besotted). In January, 1391, Kuo was assigned again to Fu Yu-te's command. The northern army, drawn on this occasion from the Shantung and Peiping guards, was to engage in training exercises and in protecting the northern frontier. In May, with Chu Fu (*see* Chu Yüan-chang) in nominal command, they were ordered beyond the Wall where they conducted a successful raid against the Mongol general Ajaširi 阿劄失理. This done, they returned to their defensive positions until their recall in October.

The years from 1392 to 1395 were a time of military activity, prosperity, and continued imperial favor for Kuo. The author of his spirit-path inscription asserts that the emperor considered him unique among the new nobility in that he did not seem to be bent upon enriching himself and his family. He was one of several nevertheless singled out by Li Hsin 李新 (marquis of Ch'ung-shan 崇山, enfeoffed January, 1383, d. November 21, 1395) in a memorial charging the meritorious officials with having acquired land and dependents beyond the standards proper to their station. The main result of the memorial was one of far-reaching significance. Originally the dukes and marquises had been given enough public land (together with farmers to work on it) to enable them to collect their own annual stipends directly. Now, however, the emperor determined that they should return these lands and tenants to the public domain and receive their stipends from the state tax granaries. Kuo had to give up some of his own tenants but, in 1393, the emperor relented and let him have them back again.

In 1394 Kuo's daughter was married to Chu Chih (*see* Hsü Hsüeh-mo). Kuo at about this time was in charge of building the prince's palace in the remote Liao valley outpost of Kuang-ning 廣寧. Insufficient supplies for the troops, bad morale, and the threat of attack by Jurchen and Koreans compelled the emperor to order the project stopped before it was finished. Kuo attacked the problem of supply by establishing agricultural camps and reserve granaries. The ranks of the Liaotung guards had been filled in part by some thirty thousand Jurchen and Korean soldiers. In August, 1395, their habit of pillaging under the pretext of hunting made it necessary for Kuo to order them back to their regular quarters. His services in Liaotung ended in May, 1397, when he was sent to assist Keng Ping-wen (*q.v.*) in the suppression of the rebellion of Kao Fu-hsing (*see* Keng Ping-wen) in southern Shensi. On his return to the capital in November a censor charged him with having acquired an excessive number of slaves (a hundred fifty) and with having killed fifty of them, including both men and women. The emperor stood by him and refused to make an inquiry. Other censors submitted memorials reiterating the charge, and the emperor then ordered a council of imperial relatives-by-marriage to discuss the case. Kuo, as the brother of an imperial consort, would thereby be judged by a friendly family court. They decided that he should be let off with a warning.

In August, 1398, the emperor, now close to death, commanded Kuo to assemble a great army drawn from guards all across the northern frontier in anticipation of a Mongol attack. The princes of Liao, Tai, Ku (Chu Chih, Chu Kuei, and Chu Hui, *see* Chu Yüan-chang), and Ning (Chu Ch'üan, *q.v.*) were also to take part. The name of the prince of Yen was added to the list when (years later) Chu Ti had the *T'ai-tsu shih-lu* revised; the eiditors also made it appear that the imperial order of 1398 had been addressed to him rather than to Kuo. It may be that Chu Yüan-chang had misgivings about his ambitious son and had deliberately sought to undermine him by leaving him out of the expedition. In fact, when the prince of Yen rebelled in 1399, the princes of Liao, Ning, and Ku all obeyed their recall to the capital rather than

remain in the north with him. Kuo fought for the loyalist side under Keng Ping-wen and Li Ching-lung (*see* Li Wen-chung) and then returned home where he died at the age of sixty-eight. He was posthumously elevated to the rank of imperial duke of Ying 營國公, and given the name Wei-hsiang 威襄 (majestic supporter).

Kuo had three brothers, the eldest dying in childhood. The second, Kuo Hsing 興 (also called Tzu-hsing 子興, 1330-December 22, 1384), advanced more rapidly than he, achieving the rank of assistant military commissioner-in-chief in 1368. In November, 1370, he was invested as marquis of Kung-ch'ang 鞏昌, and ranked fifteenth among the nobles at this time. He would have stood higher had his record not been marred by some infraction of the law. Also in 1370 he was appointed military instructor 武傅 to Chu Shuang, prince of Ch'in (*see* Chu Yüan-chang) in Sian, and concurrently an assistant commander in the Shensi military command. In both offices he was the subordinate of Keng Ping-wen. In 1371 he was allotted land to furnish his annual stipend as marquis in the amount of 1,000 *tan*. From 1371 to 1383 he served in campaigns in Szechwan and on the northern frontier. He was recalled to the capital in the latter year and died aged fifty-four. In 1389 his son, Kuo Chen 振, succeeded to the marquisate and in 1390 was given a large sum of money to defray the cost of building a residence for his family. Soon after this, however, he was accused of complicity in the Hu Wei-yung (*q.v.*) affair and his investiture voided.

The youngest, Kuo Te-ch'eng 德成. offered a striking contrast to his brothers. He remained at court as a military attendant and provided a kind of comic relief. The emperor once urged an important office on him that would be more in keeping with his place in a distinguished family of soldiers and as the emperor's brother-in-law. He refused the appointment, explaining that his addiction to wine would make him incapable of performing his duties. The emperor, pleased by his candor, subsequently kept him well supplied with good wine. Once after an imperial banquet Kuo Te-ch'eng was crawling about on his knees in a drunken stupor when his hat came off and revealed that his hair was falling out. The emperor thought this was amusing and suggested that it might be a consequence of his heavy drinking. Kuo thereupon confessed to the emperor that the only thing that could make him really happy would be to shave his head completely and become a monk. Here he was treading on dangerous ground because the emperor himself had left the monastic community to engage in a rebellion against the Yüan. When Kuo's avowal was followed by an ominous silence, he understood what he had done, and in his terror, feigned madness to turn away the emperor's wrath. Later, Kuo did indeed become a monk, and, according to one source, rejoiced in his success in remaining alive and happy while the noted men of the time were dying in battle or being executed in the great conspiracy trials. A younger sister became a secondary wife of Chu Yüan-chang and in 1384, following the deaths of the Empress Ma (*q.v.*) and the lady Li Shu-fei 李淑妃, she became the ranking consort. The circumstances under which the sister became an imperial consort may have been inspired by an apochryphal tale concerning the first Han emperor (r. 202-195 B.C.). As in that story, Kuo's father, Kuo Shan-fu 山甫, was a physiognomist. When Chu was still a monk, Kuo Shan-fu discerned his imperial destiny and sent his sons and daughter to serve him. The less romantic but more plausible account is that Kuo's two older sons entered the rebel stronghold at Haochou in the winter of 1352/53 as followers of Kuo Tzu-hsing (*q.v.*). There they soon became attached to Chu's forces and stayed with him when he broke with Kuo Tzu-hsing and his heirs in 1355.

Kuo Ying had eleven sons. The eldest, Kuo Chen 鎮, married the emperor's daughter, the princess of Yung-chia (*see* Ning-

kuo kung-chu). The second, Kuo Ming 銘, served Chu Chih, and was posthumously invested as marquis of Wu-ting when his son Kuo Hsien 玹 (d. 1447) was finally allowed to inherit the title in 1424. Two of Kuo Ying's nine daughters were married to Chu Chih and Chu Tung (*see* Chu Yüan-chang). Kuo Hsien, who became head of the clan, eventually got into difficulty over his seizure of land from the common people of Ho-chien 河間 (Pei-Chihli), and from the Tientsin agricultural colonies. He was pardoned for this, however, and his servants were punished in his stead. When Kuo Hsien died, there began an interminable succession dispute between two branches of the clan and at times the title had to be withheld pending a decision by the court. One holder of the title, Kuo Hsün (*q.v.*), was a ruthless and ambitious man who secured the favor of Emperor Chu Hou-ts'ung (*q.v.*), and persuaded him in 1537 to permit the placement of Kuo Ying's name tablet among the meritorious supporters of the dynasty celebrated in the imperial ancestral temple, the last of the seventeen so honored.

Bibliography

1/113/7a, 117/8b, 130/8b, 131/5b, 132/12a; 3/119/8a, 120/6b; 5/7/1a, 8/5a, 73/1a; MSL (1962), T'ai-tsu, *ch.* 4-257; *Ming hui-yao* 明會要 (typeset ed.), 789; Louis Hambis, *Documents sur l'histoire des Mongols à l'époque des Ming* (Paris, 1969), 14.

Romeyn Taylor

KWŎN Kŭn 權近 (earlier name Chin 晉, T. 可遠, 思叔, H. 陽村), January 4, 1353-February 28, 1409, the fourth son of Kwŏn Hŭi 僖 (1319-1405, the Great Lord of Yŏngga 永嘉府院君), was a poet, writer of eminence, and a Korean official who served first the Koryŏ kings and later the first three kings of the Yi dynasty. He passed the palace examination in the Koryŏ capital, Kaesŏng 開城 at the age of seventeen, and was appointed to literary duties at the court. When the Mongol envoy arrived (1375) after the assassination of King Kongmin 恭愍王, (1330–74, r. 1352–74), Kwŏn and Chŏng Mong-ju (see Yi Song-gye) advocated the severance of diplomatic relations with the Northern Yüan 北元. In 1383 Kwŏn is said to have memorialized the young and reckless King Sin U (see Yi Sŏng-gye) at least four times, admonishing him about his debauchery, harshness, irregular allotment of land, and misuses of authority.

In the sixth month of 1389, Kwŏn, together with Yun Sŭng-sun 尹承順 (d. February, 4, 1393), went to China to request an audience for Sin U. The mission was not successful, however, as the first Ming emperor (Chu Yüan-chang) disapproved of the idea, so they returned with a written reprimand from the ministry of Rites. It is said that on his way back Kwŏn secretly broke the seal of the ministry's memorandum and read the contents; then, on his arrival at court, instead of presenting himself to the all-powerful chief minister, Yi Sŏng-gye he reported to an official of the faction opposed to Yi. Apparently at this time Kwŏn was loyal to the Koryŏ house and probably sided with Chŏng Mong-ju in opposing Yi Sŏng-gye's attempt to usurp power. When Kwŏn tried to clear a friend of a false accusation, he was himself condemned to banishment. The following year, when the charge of opening a sealed official document without authority was brought against him, the death penalty was demanded by the judges. On the intercession of Yi Sŏng-gye, however, the punishment was reduced to one hundred strokes of the bamboo and transportation to Ch'ŏngju 清州. Later in 1390 he was released. While making his home temporarily in Ikchu 益州 (modern Iksan 益山 in North Chŏlla), he wrote the famous *Iphak tosŏl* 入學圖說 (Illustrated discussion on commencement of study), 1 *kwŏn*, a work widely read by neo-Confucianists of the Yi dynasty.

Yi Sŏng-gye overthrew the Koryŏ regime in 1392 and proclaimed himself king. Early in the following year, when he was at Hanyang 漢陽 supervising the establishment of his new capital there, he summoned Kwŏn to his court to assist Chŏng Ch'ong 鄭摠 in composing the inscription for his father's tomb, known as the Chŏng-nŭng 定陵, located east of Hamhŭng 咸興. In this way Kwŏn entered the service of the new dynasty. His talents as a writer of literary Chinese court style soon secured his position at court. In 1396, when the Ming emperor, offended by some phrases in a memorial from the Korean king, demanded the extradition of the presumed writer of the document, Chŏng To-jon (*q.v.*), Kwŏn volunteered to go to Nanking in his stead with a mission to present an apology to the emperor. During the interview with the emperor, Kwŏn explained that the rude expressions in the missive were due to the ignorance of the writers, that they were unfamiliar with proper procedure, and were thus unable adequately to manifest the loyalty and sincerity of the king. The emperor relented so far as Kwŏn was concerned and allowed him to tour the capital. When he learned of his erudition, the emperor ordered Kwŏn to compose some poems. Thereupon Kwŏn submitted eight on October 17, ten on October 24, and six on November 27, 1396. Chu praised him and his work, instructed him to attend an audience in Wen-yüan hall 文淵閣, and bestowed three poems on him, entitled "T'i Ya-lu chiang" 題鴨綠江 (The Yalu River), "Kao-li ku ching" 高麗古京 (The ancient Koryŏ capital), and "Shih ching Liao-tso" 使經遼左 (Serving on an embassy on the other side of the Liao), respectively. [Editors' note: The poems and the story seem apocryphal.] When Kwŏn returned to Korea on April 6, 1397, the king enrolled him as an associate in the roster of the Wŏnjong kongsin 原從功臣 which had been established on October 25, 1392, to honor the supporters of Yi Sŏng-gye before his enthronement. Several times after this

Kwǒn requested permission for a leave but was refused. In the third month of 1400 he was appointed inspector general (大司憲), and in the first month of the following year was enrolled in the roster of Chwamyǒng 佐命 kongsin. He became (1402) the director of the office of royal decrees （藝文館大提學: senior 2d rank) and in 1405 he *was ennobled receiving the title Kilch'ang kun 吉昌君 . A year later he was made second deputy director (貳師) in the heir apparent's tutorial office （世子侍講院）, By a royal order (1408), Kwǒn composed the inscription for the tombstone of Yi Sǒng-gye, who died in June and was buried in late September of that year. The tombstone, known as the Kǒnwǒllǔng sindobi 健元陵神道碑, was erected in Yangju 楊州 in May, 1409, three months after Kwǒn himself had died. Kwǒn was given the posthumous name Munch'ung 文忠. The second character meaning "loyalty" seems to be a misnomer from the strict Confucianist point of view for he served two dynasties. The first character, however, is most appropriate, for his achievement as a writer of the classical Chinese style is quite impressive, as testified to by his collected works in the *Yangch'on chip* 陽村集, 40 *kwǒn*, first published *ca.* 1426 and reprinted in1674, 1718, and 1937. Another book in which he had a hand is the *Tong-guk saryak* 東國史略, 6 *kwǒn*, a short history of Korea down to 1392, which has had both Chinese and Japanese editions.

Kwǒn had four sons, all of whom held high rank at court. His third son, Kwǒn Kyu跬 (Kilch'ǒn kun 吉川君), married Princess Kyǒngan 慶安公主, the third daughter of King Yi Pang-wǒn (*q.v.*).

Bibliography

40/95/1a; *Koryǒ sa* 高麗史 (Seoul, 1955), 107/19a; *Yangch'on sǒnsaeng yǒnbo* 陽村先生年譜, in the *Yangch'on chip* (1937), 1/1a;Kim Yuk 金堉, *Haedong myǒngsin nok* 海東名臣錄 (1914), 3/118; *Chǔngbo munhǒn pigo* 增補文獻備考 (1957), 242/6b, 245/13a, 246/2b, 6b, 247/10a; Yi Kǔn-ik 李肯翊, *Yǒllyǒsil kisul* 燃藜室記述 (1912-14), 2-95; Yi Pyǒng-do 李炳燾, "Gon Yōsun no Nyugaku tosetsu ni tsuite," TG, 17 (1929), 566; Pak Ch'ǒn-kyu 朴天珪, "Yangch'on Kwǒn Kǔn yǒngu," *Sach'ong* 史叢 9, December, 1964; Yun Hoe 尹淮 *et al.*, *T'aejong sillok* 太宗實錄 (*Chosǒn wangjo sillok* ed., 1955), 17/8b; *Chosen Kinseki sōran* 朝鮮金石總覽 (1919), II, 727, 732, 820; L. C. Goodrich, "Sino-Korean Relations at the End of the XIVth Century,"*Transactions of the Korea Branch of the Royal Asiatic Society*, 30 (1940), 35, Chaoying Fang (comp.)., Elizabeth Huff (ed.), *The Asami Library* (Berkeley, 1969), 82, 215, 291, 386.

Peter H. Lee

LAN Ying 藍瑛 (T. 田叔, H. 西湖外史, 石頭陀, etc.), 1585-*ca.* 1664, painter, was a native of Hangchow. Little is recorded about his life, which is the usual fate in the Ming and Ch'ing periods of professional painters who did not belong to the literati class. What anecdotes survive are vague and subject to challenge. He is said to have traveled to Kwangtung and Fukien and in the northern provinces, gaining experiences which were later reflected in his paintings. In his youth he may also have gone to Peking at the time that the paintings in the collection of Emperor Chu Chan-chi (*q.v.*) were being catalogued; but the story that court circles prized his paintings seems doubtful as few of them are recorded in the catalogues of the palace collection of paintings and specimens of calligraphy. Just as apocryphal is the sketch of Lan in the Hangchow local history of 1686, where it is recorded that early in his life he gained the esteem of Tung Ch'i-ch'ang (ECCP), Ch'en Chi-ju (ECCP), and Sun K'o-hung 孫克宏 (T. 允執, H. 雪居, 1533-1611). That he imitated their "ideals" is evident from his own painting; some of Lan's album leaves, especially those done in the "Mi" style (that of Mi Fu, 1051-1107), would seem to have been drawn from similar pantings attributed to Tung. In an album entitled *Fang ku shan-shui hua-ts'e* 仿古山水畫册, dated 1642 (published in 1959 by the Shanghai Museum), Lan records that he depicted one of the leaves after a painting which he saw in the collection of Ch'en Chi-ju. This may help to substantiate some connection with Ch'en, but Ch'en had already died three years before. As to Sun K'o-hung, he passed away when Lan was still quite young and some nine years before his first recorded painting.

It seems that Lan spent most of his days in the city of his birth. The *hao* which is found most frequently on his paintings—Hsi-hu wai-shih 西湖外史 (West Lake unofficial historian)—suggests this. Besides his associations with fellow professional painters, he had acquaintances among the literati, for he belonged to poetry circles in Hangchow. More than one source also praises the strength of his calligraphy, and he frequently adopted the literati manner of adding long inscriptions to his paintings.

Lan was the last leader of the Chekiang school (Che-p'ai 浙派), whose line began with Tai Chin (*q.v.*); on the other hand he was undoubtedly also influenced by Shen Chou (*q.v.*) and other masters of the Soochow school. One fellow artist, who figured largely in Lan's life, was Ch'en Hung-shou (ECCP). Ch'en's senior by over a decade, Lan is said to have been his teacher. A stylistic affinity does exist between the paintings of these two, particularly in the handling of mountain and rock forms. This is a little recorded fact, but Mao Ch'i-ling (ECCP), a later contemporary, does make note of it. Mao reports that Lan Ying and a fellow townsman, Sun Ti 孫杕 (T. 子周, H. 竹癡), together discovered the talents of Ch'en; Mao records further that Lan taught Ch'en how to paint orchids, in which area the student apparently came to surpass his master. Another writer, Hsieh Ch'eng-chün 謝誠鈞, has it that Ch'en Hung-shou so excelled his teacher in the depiction of figures that Lan changed to painting landscapes, rocks, orchids, birds and flowers—there is no extant painting

by Lan Ying himself where figures are the primary subject matter. In joint ventures with a well-known portrait painter, Hsieh Pin 謝彬 (T. 波臣, 1568–1650), Lan provided the landscape settings for Hsieh's figures.

Attributed to Lan Ying and Hsieh Pin as joint editors is a revised and enlarged edition of the work on painting and painters by Hsia Wen-yen夏文彥(fl. middle 14th century), entitled *T'u-hui pao-chien* 圖繪寳鑑, 5 *ch.*, first printed in 1365. In 1519 there appeared an edition with an added *chüan* of Ming artists compiled by Han Ang 韓昂 (T. 孟顯). Some one hundred twenty years later Mao Chin (ECCP) brought out an edition, also in 6 *chüan*, but with a different supplementary list compiled by Mao Ta-lun 毛大倫. The version attributed to Lan and Hsieh, known also as the *Chieh-lu ts'ao-t'ang* 借祿草堂 edition, contains Hsia's work, Mao's supplement, and a new supplement as *chüan* 7 and 8, bringing the list of artists to the late 17th century. On closer examination one finds that Hsia's text is not reprinted faithfully, deing presented with some deletions and revisions, and incorporating ideas of Lan's contemporaries, such as those of Tung Ch'i-chang. When Yü An-lan 于安瀾 edited the *Hua-shih ts'ung-shu* 畫史叢書 (Shanghai, 1962), he rejected these revisions as anachronistic, preferring the text from the Mao Chin edition, and chose the Han Ang supplement as the 6th *chüan*; he then made the supplementary part in the Lan-Hsieh edition a separate work under the title *T'u-hui pao-chien hsü-tsuan* 續纂, 3 *ch.*, but, after including a critical review by Yü Shao-sung 余紹宋, added a more caustic one himself in a long colophon.

The *T'u-hui pao-chien hsü-tsuan* deserves all these criticisms, especially in that it contains anachronisms and that it not only makes third person sketches of those mentioned as its editors, but also gives them preferential treatment in length as well as in the choice of words. Thus Lan

Ying is presented in flattering terms that suggest the work of an admirer or one intending to promote the Lan Ying "school." The book nevertheless preserves evidences of the existence of such a school in Hangchow, apparently flourishing in the late 17th century. It seems to have been in competition with the more scholarly Soochow school represented by the Four Wang (*see* ECCP, p. 834) which finally received imperial patronage. After failing to gain the upper hand in China, the Lan Ying "school" later found a favorable response in Japan and exercised considerable influence on Japanese artists of the Southern Style, or Nanga 南畫 school, through the importation of Lan's paintings. This happened in the second half of the 18th century at a time when original Chinese paintings were reaching Japan in great numbers. While artists like Tani Bunchō 谷文晁 and Nakamura Chikudō 中村竹堂 copied Lan Ying's compositions directly, others like Noro Kaiseki 野呂介石 and Kuwayama Gyokushū 桑山玉洲 would incorporate aspects of Lan's technique and imagery. Largely due to their interest, Japan today has more of Lan Ying's paintings than any other country in the world.

Because of the existence of so many of his works in Japan and elsewhere, and because he dated them with fair regularity over a period of some forty-five years (1620 to 1664), we are in a position to know their nature. He continually paid respects to significant historical figures. Besides he was somewhat of an innovator, experimenting with the long, narrow, vertical format, and contributing to the development of the so-called fantastic landscape. Working primarily in ink and pale local color, he occasionally used pure ink; and sometimes he painted in almost pure color, for which he demonstrated a keen sensitivity.

Bibliography

Hang-chou-fu chih (1686), 32/29; Mao Ch'i-ling, *Hsi-ho wen-hsüan*, 4/4; Hsieh Ch'eng-chün, *K'uei-chai shu-hua chi* 瞶瞶齋書畫記, 1/6; P'an T'ien-shou 潘天授, *Chung-kuo hui-hua shih* 中國繪畫史 (Shanghai, 1925), II/69; Chang Keng 張庚, *Kuo-ch'ao hua cheng lu* 國朝畫徵錄 (*Hua-shih ts'ung-shu* ed., Shanghai, 1963), 5/12; Hsü Ch'in 徐沁, *Ming-hua lu* 明畫錄 (same ed. as above), 5/63; Lan Ying and Hsieh Pin, *T'u-hui pao-chien hsü-tsuan* (same ed. as above), 4/14; Chiang Shao-shu 姜紹書, *Wu sheng shih-shih* 無聲詩史 (same ed. as above), 4/75; *Tung yin lun hua* 桐陰論畫, Yü Ying-yüan 魚英園 Collection, 4/6; V. Contag and C. C. Wang, *Seals of Chinese Painters and Collectors* (rev. ed., Hong Kong, 1966), 490; E. J. Laing, *Chinese Paintings in Chinese Publications, 1956–1968* (Ann Arbor, 1969), 173, *Illustrations*; *Ku-kung ming-hua san-pai chung* 故宮名畫三百種 (Taipei, 1959), VI, pl. 252; *Min-chin no kaiga* 明清の繪畫 (Tokyo, 1965), pls. 12, 13; *So-gen* 宋元 *min-chin meiga taikan* 名畫大觀 (Tokyo, 1932), pls. 177–181; *To-so gen-min* 唐宋元明 *meiga taikan* (Tokyo, 1929), pls. 381–384; *The Pageant of Chinese Painting* (Tokyo, 1936), pls. 698–705; *Portfolio of Chinese Paintings in the Museum* (*Ming to Ch'ing Periods*), Museum of Fine Arts (Boston, 1961), pls. 85; O. Sirén, *A History of Later Chinese Painting* (London, 1938), pls. 131–133; *id., Chinese Painting* (New York, 1958), Vol. VII, 286b–289.

Hugh Wass and Chaoying Fang

LAN Yü 藍玉 (executed March 22, 1393), a native of Ting-yüan 定遠, Nan-Chihli, was an outstanding general in the latter half of the Hung-wu reign. He was the younger brother of the wife of General Ch'ang Yü-ch'un (*q.v.*), and entered military service on the latter's personal staff, rising to the rank of an assistant commissioner-in-chief. As such he served under Fu Yu-te (*q.v.*) in Szechwan in 1371. Early in the following year he joined Hsü Ta (*q.v.*) in the great campaign against Kökö Temür (*q.v.*), and in April defeated part of the Mongol army on the Tula River.

During the next two years Mongol pressure on the northern border increased, and Lan Yü continued to command troops in that region. In 1374 he was sent in command of an expedition to destroy the Mongol concentration at Hsing-ho 興和 (30 miles north of Kalgan).

He defeated it in May, capturing its leader and occupying the city of Hsing-ho. In the following years he remained on the northern border, and was one of the generals in charge of the defense of Yen-an 延安. Lan was appointed in November 1378, deputy commander-in-chief under General Mu Ying (*q.v.*) in fighting against the Tibetans in Kansu. They crushed a tribal uprising in T'ao-chou 洮州, established a guard there, and after defeating the Tibetans in October, they returned home. In December Lan was one of twelve generals ennobled (his title being marquis of Yung-ch'ang 永昌) and he was granted an annual stipend of 2,000 *shih*; most of these men were later executed or otherwise punished for complicity in Lan's alleged conspiracy. Lan served under Fu Yu-te in September, 1381, on an expedition aimed at the conquest of Yunnan, then still in the hands of the Mongols. They defeated the Yüan army and captured its commander in January of the following year. Then Lan, leading a detachment, marched west to Ta-li 大理, captured the city from the Tuan 段 family, and gained control of northwestern Yunnan. As a reward for his part in these conquests Lan received a raise in stipend to 2,500 *shih* and was accorded the honor of having his daughter selected as the consort of the emperor's eleventh son, Chu Ch'un, prince of Shu (*see* Chu Yüan-chang).

Lan Yü, Fu Yu-te, and Feng Sheng (*q.v.*) were given charge of the army in Peiping in September, 1385. In January, 1387, they received orders to suppress the Mongols under Naγaču (*q.v.*), who had maintained himself in southeastern Mongolia and made repeated campaigns against Liaotung. Leading the vanguard Lan succeeded in destroying part of the Mongol army north of the Great Wall. Meanwhile the main force under Feng Sheng penetrated the Mongol headquarters. Lan received Naγaču's surrender in July at Chin-shan 金山, about 70 miles north of Shen-yang(?). The actual leadership of the Mongols now reverted to Toγus Temür (*q.v.*).

Two months later the emperor dismissed Feng Sheng from his command, leaving Lan Yü in temporary control of the Ming army in the northeast; he moved his headquarters east of Peiping. In November Lan, T'ang Sheng-tsung 唐勝宗 (marquis of Yen-an), and Kuo Ying (*q.v.*) received orders to wage war on Toγus Temür. By mid-May, 1388, the Ming army, said to be 150,000 strong, had marched to the northeast extremity of the Gobi. They located the Mongol camp northeast of Lake Bayur Naγur about 500 miles north of Peiping, and took the enemy by surprise. Though they failed to confront Toγus Temür, who had escaped, Lan's forces captured a number of his chief subordinates, along with several tens of thousands of Mongols and also domestic animals. On their return march the Ming forces destroyed the camp of another Mongol general, Qarajang, 哈喇章 capturing him and his followers, as well as thousands of horses (before June 5). Returning to Nanking late in September, Lan and his principal subordinates received lavish rewards from the emperor. On January 19, 1389, Lan was at last made duke of Liang 涼國, and his annual stipend was raised to 3,000 *shih*. It is said that the emperor had originally intended to confer on him the more elegant title of duke of Liang 梁, but abandoned this idea and almost refrained from promoting Lan at all when word came that he had taken one of the concubines of a certain Mongol ruler (who later hanged herself). The title as finally granted, though something of a let down, was the third new dukedom awarded to a living person after 1370 (the others being T'ang Ho [*q.v.*], 1378, and Fu Yu-te, 1384); Lan thus emerged as the foremost representative of the group of generals who had come to prominence after the civil wars of the 1360s.

In March Lan was sent to Szechwan in charge of drilling troops to keep them in readiness for the suppression of possible revolts of non-Chinese tribesmen. A year later Lan dispatched a division of his men to quell an uprising in the mountainous region of southwest Hukuang, and in July another division put down a second rebellion in the same province. On his recall to the capital in September, Lan received an increase in stipend to 3,500 *shih*. Together with two other dukes and several generals, Lan was sent in April, 1391, to Shensi to command the army on the frontier; these appointments coincided with other decrees which placed the provincial armies under the emperor's sons. By February, 1392, the emperor felt strong enough to recall the nobles holding field commands; in addition to Lan himself, Li Ching-lung (*see* Li Wen-chung), Ch'ang Sheng (*see* Ch'ang Yü-ch'un), and many others later connected with Lan Yü were recalled at this time. By now Chu Yüan-chang was deeply suspicious of the nobles as a class, but Lan, despite his often tactless behavior, still enjoyed imperial favor. In March he was placed in command at Lan-chou 蘭州 to defend the area against renewed Mongol incursions. While his army was on its way the commander of the Chien-ch'ang 建昌 guard, Yelü Temür 月魯帖木兒 staged a rebellion among the non-Chiinese tribesmen of Szechwan. After the local government troops failed to deal with the rebels, the emperor ordered Lan to transfer his forces to Szechwan. In compliance with the imperial order, Lan grudgingly abandoned his scheme to subjugate the Mongols, and hurried to Szechwan from Shensi. Before Lan arrived, however, the local commander Nieh Wei 聶緯 had scored (in July) a decisive victory over the insurgents. In December Yelü Temür was captured and sent to the capital for execution. Lan subsequently submitted a memorial in which he pointed out the vulnerability of Szechwan to tribal insurrections, and proposed the establishment of more military colonies and the transfer of the peasantry to the military registers. These recommendations, coming in the midst of an extended series of unsuccessful imperial attempts to curb the illegal use of troops and military lands by the hereditary officers, infuriated the emperor, who used them as a pretext to recall Lan Yü to Nanking and dismiss him from his commands.

The fall of Lan was the latest in a number of steps directed against the military nobility. Lan was dismissed late in December, 1391, but in August, 1392, Chou Te-hsing, marquis of Chiang-hsia 江夏 (*see* Chu Yüan-chang), had been accused of involvement with Hu Wei-yung (*q.v.*) and executed, and in September Yeh Sheng 葉昇, (the marquis of Ching-ning 靖寧, a relative of Lan Yü), had suffered an identical fate. In the same month several of the dukes and marquises, who had already lost their field commands, were forced to return to the state the lands which had previously been granted as rewards. Lan Yü resented his dismissal bitterly. Reportedly, when the emperor decided to grant him the honorific title t'ai-fu (grand tutor) in partial compensation for the loss of his other offices, Lan made no secret of his feeling that he deserved the still higher title t'ai-shih (grand preceptor) for his great victory of 1388. This display of bad manners so outraged the emperor that he abandoned the idea. Distrust between the two men developed during the first months of 1393. In the midst of this tense situation, the Embroidered-uniform Guard arrested some of Lan's subordinates, and under torture they confessed to the existence of a wide-ranging conspiracy to murder the emperor and seize control of the state. True or not, the report of this by the commander of the Guard, Chiang Hsien 蔣瓛, gave the emperor a pretext for dealing ruthlessly with a class of men whom he had come to regard as a threat. Lan was arrested and executed in March along with a number of his former associates. Many seem to have been involved, however, on thin excuses and trumped-up charges (*see* Chan Hui, Ho Chen, Sun Fen).

This was merely the beginning of a

wave of executions, as the families of the victims were also killed. and the provincial officials were ordered to investigate and denounce those who might be connected with Lan Yü or his followers. Late in April another noble, Chang Wen 張溫 (marquis of Hui-ning 會寧), and the commander Hsiao Yung 蕭用 were executed. Eventually, on October 15, the emperor issued a decree stating that so far fifteen thousand people had been executed in connection with the Lan Yü affair, and ordered that no one should ever propose posthumous pardons for any of them. This marked the end of the actual terror, but the emperor continued his policy of concentrating all field commands in the hands of his sons, and over the next two years Wang Pi 王弼 (marquis of Ting-yüan), Feng Sheng, and Fu Yu-te, the most celebrated of the surviving nobles, were forced to commit suicide. Lan Yü's biography in the *Ming-shih* lists fifteen commanders as victims; of the titled nobles themselves, an official account entitled *Ni-ch'en lu* 逆臣錄 (Record of the rebellious ministers) was published by the emperor in June, 1393, in defense of his action. Of the sixteen men denounced in this tract, some were only marginally connected with Lan Yü, but nine of the marquises had careers which paralleled his closely.

In Chu Yüan-chang's view Lan Yü and Hu Wei-yung were equally the leaders of factions plotting treason, and accounts of this period often refer to *Hu-Lan er-tang* 胡藍二黨 (The two factions [led by] Hu and Lan). The compilers of the *Ming-shih*, however, differentiated between the two: Hu Wei-yung's biography was consigned to a special chapter (*Ming-shih* 308) entitled *Chien-ch'en* 奸臣 (Villainous ministers), while the biographies of Lan Yü and his associates, (*Ming-shih* 132), take their places among those of the other great commanders of the first reign. Whatever justice there may have been in the charges against Lan, it appears likely that the emperor used his case as a pretext to destroy the last vestiges of the corporate independence of the military in order to bring the latter under his direct control.

Bibliography

1/2/9a, 11a, 132/5b; 3/118/10b; 5/6/15a; 61/96/13b; 63/4/32a; MSL (1962), T'ai-tsu, ch. 64–230; KC (1958), 739, 744; Cheng Hsiao, *Wu-hsüeh-pien*, 18/9b; Ho Ch'iao-yüan, *Ming-shan ts'ang* (*Ch'en-lin chi* 臣林記),3/15b; Chu Yüan-chang, *Hsiao-ling chao-ch'ih* 孝陵詔勅 in *Ming-ch'ao k'ai-kuo wen-hsien* 明朝開國文獻, 4 (1966), 1931; Ku Ying-t'ai (ECCP), *Ming-ch'ao chi-shih pen-mo* (1658), 12/1a; P'an Ch'eng-chang 潘檉章, *Kuoshih k'ao-i* 國史考異 (TsSCC), 2/72; *Ming-shih* (Taipei, 1962), 1682; Chao I (ECCP), *Nien-er-shih cha-chi* (1963), 32/678; Wu Han 吳晗, "Hu Wei-yung tang-an k'ao" 胡維庸黨案考, YCHP, 15 (1934), 163; D. Pokotilov, *History of the Eastern Mongols during the Ming Dynasty from 1368 to 1634*, tr.by Rundolf Loewenthal, *Studia Serica Mon.*, ser. A, no. 1), Chengtu, 1947), pt. 1, 9.

Edward L. Dreyer and Hok-lam Chan

LANG Ying 郎瑛 (T. 仁寶, H. 草橋), 1487-ca. 1566, author, bibliophile, and connoisseur of antiques, was a native of Jen-ho 仁和 (Hangchow), Chekiang, the youngest son of a family of antique dealers. His father was the first in Hangchow in this line of business to acquire bronze objects in Kaifeng and sell them on his return, thereby accumulating a sizable fortune. His mother was a devout Buddhist lay disciple. On reaching middle life they still had no son; in great anxiety, they began bestowing considerable charities in the hope that their offerings might invoke the blessing of Heaven. Their prayer was eventually answered, for at least two sons were later born to them. When Lang Ying was only five *sui*, his father passed away. His mother, oblivious of the worth of the antiques, had several valuable pieces recast into sacrificial vessels and Buddhist images and in the end few of the antiques were left. The husbands of his two elder sisters, tempted by the Lang family property, made several attempts on Lang Ying's life, but were not successful, and the two boys were left with the remnant of the estate to support their mother and themselves.

Lang Ying was a precocious child and entered the local school at an early age. He showed no desire to follow an official career, however, while his sporadic ailments eventually forced him to leave school altogether. It is said that he was such a lover of literature that, except for a small sum laid aside for his mother, he spent all his share purchasing books and art objects. Steadily the family's inheritance dwindled until they became impoverished, but this did not seem to deter Lang Ying from his studies. He is also reported to have been quite filial. Once, when his mother was taken ill, and he was probably too poor to afford pieces of meat, he cut off parts of his thigh for her to eat. At the same time, he bore no hard feelings against his relatives mentioned above; when they died, he took care of their burial.

Lang Ying lived a long life of over eighty years, but apart from his scholarly preoccupations we know little of his other activities due to the paucity of sources. Apparently he devoted his whole career to study, reading books on a wide range of subjects, taking notes on what seemed worthy of attention, and acquiring a broad circle of acquaintances who were attracted by his disposition and scholarship. Similarly he delighted in entertaining friends, meeting visitors, and conversing with them, at which times he would make perceptive remarks on current events and state affairs, some of these attracting the attention of the authorities. He is also reported to have been a man of justice and forthrightness, one who would not suppress his views in order to ingratiate himself with people of influence. Over long years of note-taking he accumulated a mass of information on various topics, out of which came several volumes. The most famous of these were the *Ch'i-hsiu lei-kao* 七修類稿, 51 *ch.*, with a sequel called *Hsü-kao* 續稿, 7 *ch.*, and the *Hsü*

ssu 巳 -*k'ao*, 1 *ch.*, included in *Shuo-fu hsü* 說郛續. Other works of his, now lost, included his collection of prose and poetry and two items of miscellaneous writings, the *Ts'ui-chung lu* 萃忠錄, 2 *ch.*, and the *Ch'ing-shih kun-yüeh* 靑史袞鉞, 60 *ch.*, probably collections of biographical accounts of upright officials and men of virtue of the earlier Ming period. It is not certain when he passed away, but we hear of no activities after he had produced the sequel to the *Ch'i-hsiu lei-kao* in 1566, when he was reported to be just eighty *sui*.

Lang Ying owes his fame to his authorship of the last, a collection of notes on various aspects of historical and political matters of the Ming period and on miscellaneous topics relating to philosophy, literature, and art. It is divided into seven categories: T'ien-ti 天地 (Heaven and earth), Kuo-shih 國事 (National events), I-li 義理 (Priniples of righteousness), Pien-cheng 辨證 (Verificaton of facts), Shih-wen 詩文 (Poetry and prose), Shih-wu 事物 (Things in general), Ch'i-nüeh 奇謔 (Strange and amusing items). Some of these notes grew out of the author's direct observation or memory, or out of conversation with his friends and visitors. Others were copied directly from literature at his disposal, some items of which are no longer extant today. Of these notes, what is of exceptional interest to historians of the Ming period is perhaps his candid account of the events of the founding of the Ming. While relatively little space is given to these events in works published in the earlier period, probably due to official censorship, the *Ch'i-hsiu lei-kao* contains vivid and detailed records of the vicissitudes of the arch-rivals of the Ming emperor, such as Ch'en Yu-liang, Chang Shih-ch'eng, and Fang Kuo-chen (*qq.v.*). Additional notes on contemporary political events, or anecdotes and remarks about literature and antiques, are also useful in supplementing other sources. The *Ch'i-hsiu lei-kao*, however, has also had its critics.

Some have charged that it is badly organized and insubstantial, and gives no indication of sources; others that too many mistakes occur in the transcription of earlier works. They have also criticized Lang Ying for being uncritical in his observations, for, instead of making his own evaluations, he sometimes tended to copy the remarks of others; if indeed he made a judgment, this proved often to be hasty and careless. For this reason scholars must exercise great care in using the *Ch'i-hsiu lei-kao* as a source in spite of its obvious merits.

It was first printed in the middle of the Chia-ching period and its sequel, the *Hsü-kao*, sometime after 1566. They were reprinted in 1775, with several passages deleted from the original text. This is because the *Ssu-k'u* editors discovered that they contained remarks which the Manchus found offensive. A new edition of the work, together with its sequel, was printed by the Chung-hua 中華 Bookstore in two volumes in 1958. The text is collated from two earlier editions, and includes the original prefaces and additional bibliographical material.

Bibliography

5/115/82a; TSCC (1885–88), XIV: 304/5a, XXII: 272/16/2b, XXIII: 103/91/6a; Chang Hsüan, *Hsi-yüan wen-chien lu*, 14/61b, 22/34b; *Ch'i-hsiu lei-kao* (1958), 41/592, 45/663, 46/674; *Hsü-kao*, 5/819; *Shuo-fu hsü chou* 易, 14; SK (1930), 127/6a; *Chekiang t'ung-chih* 通志 (1934), 3104; W. Franke, *Sources*, 4.3. 3.

Hok-lam Chan

LÊ Lọ'i 黎利 (the pronunciation of the name was changed from Lê Lê out of respect), ca. 1385–October 4, 1433, was the founder of the Annamite Lê dynasty, known as the Later Lê 後黎. He was the youngest of the three sons of a seigneur of the village of Lam-sơn 藍山, Thanh-hoá 清化 (northern Annam), situated between plain and mountain in the Annamite-müöng area. Founded by his great-grandfather Lê Hối 誨, a native of the region and married to a native, Lam-sơn by the following generation counted a thousand souls; it developed into an independent unit during the disturbed years at the end of the Trần 陳 dynasty. On the premature death of his eldest brother, Lê Lọ'i came into his inheritance. Of his early life we have but a recast tradition.

Lê Lọ'i appears in history, retrospectively around the year 1410—immediately after the first pacification of Annam by the Ming (*see* Lê Quí-ly)—as a partisan of the last pretender Trần Quí-khoáng (*see* Chang Fu). Chinese authorities (the *T'ai-tsung shih-lu* and *Ming-shih*) agree that Lê Lọ'i was his pseudo-general of the guard; he was not one of the intractables, however, and became, under the Ming, a local chief of Nga-lạc 俄樂 district with his fief in the same Thanh-hoá confirmed. A deadly rivalry, generated by interests of landholders and due to political ambition involving people who were both his neighbors and his equals, developed, precipitating his revolt. Denounced to the Chinese who attacked him he escaped into the jungle. At the beginning of 1418, after other forerunners had been successively wiped out by the Chinese, he adopted the title of pacifying king 平定王. Victorious in a frontal war, the Chinese discovered that they were now engaged in one that was diffuse. Wearied of distant campaigns, weakened in effectives and in command, their organization of the country compromised by insecurity and their occupation by misrule, the Chinese longed for peace which they hoped to achieve. Lê Lọ'i to them was at first only a marginal rebel, too weak to engage in regular confrontation and hence more likely to elude them. His way of fighting was to them what Plutarch calls a war of brigands, and what the *San lüeh* 三略 calls the art of giving serious battle with the slimmest of means 以寡勝衆者—ambushes, surprise attacks, always on the wing, constantly menacing. When Lê Lọ'i plundered they seized his possessions. According to the Chinese he disappeared for a year; according to the Annamites he drove them back once during the winter. The following summer (1419) he resumed his tactics and was beaten at Khá-lam 可藍柵 according to the Chinese; but according to the Annamites, he attacked Nga-lạc and pillaged Lôĩ-giang 磊江縣 (Thanh-hoá). He took shelter at Lao-chua 老撾 according to the Chinese, but according to the Annamites at Chí-linh 至靈山 (a spot difficult to determine) and at Lô-so'n 蘆山 (Ai-lao 哀牢). Insurrections broke out again from south to northeast; new pretenders, captured with their families, proceeded in cages to Peking. In the imperial reproof sent to Li Pin 李彬 (T. 質文, made marquis of Feng Ch'eng 豐城侯 in 1403, d. February 5, 1422, Pth. 剛毅), commander of the Chinese army in the area, Lê Lọ'i is still named (mid-1420) as only the second among the pretenders. According to the Chinese, Lê Lọ'i hid himself in Laos; but the Annamites credit him with success in Thanh-hoá and initial rallyings (Müöng Thôi 忙催, Ba-lẫm 波凜柵). By the winter of 1421 he became the sole rebel and China by various threats obliged Laos to hunt him down. Again, according to the Annamites, he disconcerts the Chinese in their pursuit into the defiles of Úng 甕隘 and of Kinh-lọng 勁弄隘, and he repulses the Laotians come to attack him. During the winter following (1422-23), a fresh reproof made to the new Chinese commander, Ch'en Chih陳智, stirs him to give chase. Lê was beaten at Xa-lai 車來縣 (Ninh-hoá 寧化州) and driven to Khôi 塊柵. He retrieves Chí-linh, where, blockaded for over two months, scarcity of supplies and the exhaustion of his band forces him to offer to submit. A truce saves him. The details are unclear, the sources poorly assembled. Lê, returning to Lam-so'n or Nga-lạc (in May, 1423?), seems to have handed over a dispensable numbcr of his followers, both men and women, and to have profited from a lull in the Chinese operations to rest and rearm his force. As a consequence he

is successful at Trà-long 茶隆州 (Nghệ-an). Ch'en Chih, in order to take action, asked for reinforcements; but Chu Ti (q.v.) was dead, and Chu Kao-chih (q.v.) busy with granting amnesties on the occasion of his accession to the throne. On October 5, 1424, to rally him to the Chinese side, the eunuch Shan Shou 山壽 brought to Lê from the court his nomination as prefect of Thanh-hoá. Lê put him off to the following autumn (the Chinese avoiding operations in the summer). He attacked Trà-long, defended by a native prefect, and beat it into submission after a long siege (January, 1425?). By this time the war had changed its character. Lê assembled his forces, raised recruits, and, continuing his surprise actions, turned to the offensive, driving the Chinese back throughout the south into their citadels. Nghệ-an 乂安 (February, 1425) and Tây-dô 西都 (Thanh-hoá, June) were invested, help from the north was intercepted at Khâ-lu'u可留 (upper Lam River 藍江), and a convoy of junks bound for Diên-châu 演州 (Nghệ-an) was stopped at Dá-gia 杜家縣 (Hà-tĩnh). Remote Tân-bình 新平 and Thuận-hoá 順化 capitulated. The hesitations of the imperial court, as well as the discord among, and incapacity of, its generals, discouraged its native partisans and created other disorders in the north, which connected with rebelliousness in Yunnan (the Red Coats 紅衣of Ning-yüan 寧遠州). The year 1426, the first year of Hsüan-te, opened with the suspension in Annam of the examinations established by the Ming, continued with the dismissal of the senior Chinese commander and his mediocre replacement by Wang T'ung (see Huang Fu), the amnesty offered to Lê and his invasion of Thanh-hoá, and the invasion of Tongking by his lieutenants who overran the capital in the north (the Chiao-chou 交州 or Chiao-chih ch'eng 交阯城 of the Chinese, Dông-quan 東關 or Dông-dô 東都, of the Annamites). Save for two towns, the Chinese evacuated Nghệ-an and Thanh-hoá by water, and concentrated at Dông-dô. Lê pursued them without lingering at Nghệ-an or at Taŷ-dô, camping nevertheless at Lỗi-giang and leaving to his lieutenants the task of engaging in decisive battles. There ensued another exchange of surprise attacks, the battlefield being by a secondary branch of the Red River, at Ninh-giang 寧江 to the west of Dáy, from So'n-tây to Hàdông 河東; but the Ming History (*chüan* 321) abridges the account of the action which the Lê Annals give in detail. Dông-dô, manned by the flower of the army of occupation, its walls and moats reinforced, attemped a disengagement which miscarried at Ninh-kiêù 寧橋 (south Hà-dông). The expeditionary force of Wang T'ung was mired there, defeated at Tốt-dông 崒洞 and nearby places; the Yunnan army, which had been joined to it, beat a retreat (September-November, 1426). The Ming History is cognizant of but one bridge of Ninh, while the Lê Annals name several and place the episode of the miring in a different ambush; but both agree on the issue. Wang T'ung cooped himself up in Dông-dô, leaving other citadels without aid. Lê, informed of this success, arrived with drums beating, records the Ming History (*chüan* 321), which compares him that year in *chüan* 127 to a conflagration 勢熾 (*cf. Sun-tzu* 孫子, *chüan* 7). The fortune of war depended in the following year (1427) on help from China. With Dông-dô invested, the majority of places besieged, more and more people submitting to him, Lê, according to the Annals, was reshaping Tong-king. He encamped at Bồ-dề 菩提 (by two ficus, or banyan, trees on the east bank of the river) with an office and an observation tower overlooking the town, and engaged in parleys by messenger which were broken off by lack of trust. Two new sorties made a turn for the better for the Chinese; Wang T'ung hesitating lost his advantage; Lê, protecting his camp with a palisade, attacked at five strategic points: Tam-giang 三江城 on the way to Yunnan (*i.e.*, Việt-trì, at the confluence of the rivers Thao 洮江, the upper

Red River, Lô 瀘江 and Dà 沱江, the rivers Clear and Black), Diêu-diêu 刁鷂, Thị-kiều 市橋, Xuo'ng-giang 昌江, and Khu'u-ôn 邱溫 on the route to Kwangsi. Diêu-diêu gave up in the first month (February, 1427), as well as Nghệ-an and Diên-châu; Tam-giang and Thị-kiều in the third (April). Khu'u-ôn was abandoned during the night; Xu'o'ng-giang resisted for nine months (according to the Ming History) or six months (according to the Annals) and was carried only by an extraordinary effort, after a heroic defense, ten days before help arrived from the north. The tardiness in sending reinforcements was fatal to the Chinese. Mu Sheng (*see* Mu Ying) in Yunnan and Liu Sheng 柳升 (Pth. 融國公, 襄愍) in Kwangsi had since the winter received an imperial order to proceed with a large army. Their prolonged preparations and their fear of the summer season gave Lê time to evacuate the population and to remove or isolate those supporting the Chinese along the two routes of invasion. The recklessness of Liu Sheng got him into ambushes; he perished in Lạng-so'n 諒山 at Chi-lăng 支陵隘 (according to the Annals) or at Da'o-mã pho 倒馬坡 (according to *Ming-shih*) in the ninth month (September-October), or the fourth (May) according to one version of the Annals (*cf.* Xu'o'ng-giang). The prudence which Mu Sheng exercised was also unfortunate. Making use of a ruse which had succeeded at Tam-giang, Lê sent him as prisoners the two subordinates of Liu Sheng with his seals of office. Frightened, Mu Sheng drew back, and his demoralized army was defeated at Li-hua 梨花 (Lào-kay, Shui-wei 水尾 in Chinese, Linh-thúy 冷水溝 in Annamite). Both columns were thus destroyed at the border. Wang T'ung, in expectation of their arrival, had renewed and prolonged his negotiations. Lê, close to making an assault upon him, sent him the same prisoners. This is the version of the Annals; the *Ming-shih* version reverses the order, placing the episode before the retreat of Mu Sheng, in this instance all too late in respect to Liu Sheng. Wang T'ung, in despair over the situation, made a decision. Hostages were exchanged, and an oath of peace with Lê was sworn to on the bank of the river on the 12th of October, 1427 (according to the *Ming-shih*) or on the 10th of December (according to the long version of the Annals, Toàn thư' 全書 10). The Chinese had numerous outposts and at least three other fortresses: Cổ lóng 古弄 (Nam-dịnh) and Tây-dô (Thanh-hoá) towards the south, Chí-linh 至靈 in Bắc-giang 北江, in the northeast were still in Chinese hands. Lê, according to the Annals, assembled junks and horses and put bridges and roads in working order. Wang T'ung did not wait for the imperial command to take off, and many men were lost.

One proposal, made to the Chinese generals, offered to the Ming emperor a pretended descendant of the house of Trăn—an honorable pretext for all, but fatal to the unhappy individual; the emperor (Chu Chan-chi, *q.v.*) granted his investiture, while in the spring following, Lê forced him to commit suicide. Successive embassies clashed over two insistent demands: the Ming calling for a Trăn and Lê asking for the regency. Lê obtained it only in 1431.

Actually, on the departure of the Chinese army, Lê became king in fact, and comported himself as a sovereign, imitating the empire. He maintained two capitals: Tây-dô-Lam-so'n, honorary and religious, and Dông-dô, the name of which he changed in 1430 to Tây-kinh 西京 and Dông-kinh 東京 (origin of the European term Tongking). He established five major circuits 五道 (according to the Annals; whereas the Ming History enumerates thirteen as of 1433, and the Geography of Nguyễn Trãi 阮廌 of 1435 describes fifteen), four in Tongking and one only in the south up to the Cham border, known as Nam-giói 南界; each had three courts 三司, derived from the Ming: administration, justice, and defense. Notably he imitated the Ming in respect to educa-tion, creating in its image schools, a royal college, Quốc-tú giám 國子監 (1429), and extending the examination system to include both the military and the clerical, which was given back to the commoners in the event of their failure. Confucianism, obscured by Buddhism under the Trăn, flourished once more. With a new hierarchy, a censorate, and (memorials of) remonstrance—"Ming customs substantially prevailed," wrote the Ming historians under the date 1433. Lê summoned or had promoted hidden talent. His code took as model that of the T'ang, its procedure revised. The army was reduced in size; a scheme of rotation maintained one fifth under arms, the balance on the farm (the Annals). Restoration of rice fields and distribution of vacant lands made up for the ruination caused by war and recompensed people for their sacrifices or settled a floating population grown large during the long years of hardship. Prohibition of gambling and of drinking forestalled other troubles (1428); for gamblers the penalty: mutilation of the fingers; for drinkers, the bastinado. A general reorganization of the villages accompanied the concessions. Census lists, civil and land registers served to fix imposts and charges. Provincial products for royal tribute, the resources of streams and mines, exacted harshly by the Ming, became the objects of fiscal inventories. A *Thuận-thiên* 順天 currency was created. Without waiting for imperial recognition, Lê assumed this reign title (Thuận-thiên) and gave to the country the name Dại-Việt 大越. He had achieved independence.

Traditionally he is said to have been extraordinary, with a lively eye, strong mouth, sonorous voice, an air of grandeur, and the histories record that he was a man of inhuman energy and inflexible will; essentially a warrior, shaped by Chinese tacticians, and a founder inspired by the first Han emperor. He knew how to surround himself with aids, whom he either rewarded or sacrificed. His strategy throughout the south was suggested to him by one who came from there, Lê Ch'ieh黎隻; his memorials, cited in the *Ming-shih*, his manifestos quoted in the Annals, are the product of the most famous scholar of his time, Nguyễn Trãi, and his chief victories are due to his lieutenants. Two among them, Trần Nguyêh-hãn 陳元扦 and Phạm Văn-Xáo 范文巧, illustrate through their tragic end Lê's temperament. The first had crowned his campaign at Xu'o'ng-giang, the second at Li-hua. Distinguished for the highest services in combat, both acceded to the loftiest posts in time of peace. But one was a scholar-soldier of a branch of the Trần family, and the other a man who had made himself popular with the people and was a native of the capital. Lê, encouraged by two denunciations, had both put to death one after the other (1429 and 1430). Old and sick, he ended his career with three expeditions against the Thai in high Tongking and Laos: at Thái-nguyên 太原 from the eleventh month of the third year to the third month of the fourth year of his reign 1430-31); at Ningyüan, from the first to the eleventh month of the fifth year (1432); at Ai-lao. Having returned from there during the first month following (January-February, 1433), he degraded and replaced his eldest son as heir apparent. In the sixth year of his reign, he died. On January 3, 1434, his body was laid to rest at Lam-so'n, where a stele in his honor still stands.

Bibliography

Annamite sources: The stele of Lam-so'n; the Lê Annals; the *Lam-so'n thật-lục* 藍山實錄; Nguyễn Trãi, *Quân trung tù'-minh tập*軍中詞命集; Lê Quí-Dôn 黎貴惇, *Dại-Việt thông-sú'* 大越通史; Chinese Sources: 1/7-9, 126, 154, 321; MSL (1963), T'ai-tsung, Jen-tsung, Hsüan-tsung; *An-nan ch'i-shou pen-mo* 安南棄守本末; Yamamoto Tatsurō 山本達郎, *Annan shi no kenkyū* 安南史の研究, I (Tokyo, 1950), 8; E. Gaspardone, JA, 1939, 405; *id.*, *Silver Jubilee Volume* (Kyoto University, 1954), 158; *id.*, *Annuaire du Collège de France* (1947, 1953-56, 1962-63); *id.*,

Stèles royales de Lam-so'n I, plates, Hanoi 1935.

Emile Gaspardone, tr. by L.C.G.

LÊ Quí-ly 黎季犛, *ca.* 1335-*ca.* 1407, Annamite usurper, was the founder of the ephemeral Hồ 胡 dynasty (1400-7). One of his ancestors is said to have been a native of Chekiang province named Hu 胡, who, in the period of the Five Dynasties (907-60), emigrated to Diễn-chou 演州. A descendant who went on to Thanh-hoá 清化 received there from an adoptive father the clan name of Lê 黎, which after four generations remained that of Lê Quí-ly up the time of his final *coup d'état* (1400). At that moment he assumed, or resumed, the name of Hồ and pretended descent from Yü Shun.

The histories give details of his life only at the height and termination of his career. The *Ming shih-lu* and the *Ming-shih* both maintain that he came from a family hereditarily in the royal service. The Annamite Annals in the year 1371 report the elevation of his family with entry into the harem of two of his aunts who bore two of the Trần陳 kings, Nghệ-tông 藝宗 (r. 1370-72) and Duệ-tông 睿宗 (r. 1373-February, 1377). He himself remarried the younger widowed sister of the first king and her cousin married the other. The Trần, shaken by a palace revolution (1369), declined in power. Troubles and natural calamities gave rise to pretenders (1379, 1389). The Cham in the south ravaged the provinces and came north to pillage the capital (1371, 1377, 1378, 1383). Duệ-tông in the course of an expedition against them imprudently entered their capital and perished there (1377). The feeble retired Nghệ-tông, already an old man, submitting to the ascendancy of Lê Quí-ly, supported by his relatives, deposed Dề Hiện 帝睍, son and successor of Duệ-tông (1389). The elder daughter of Lê Quí-ly became queen of the new king, aged thirteen, last son of Nghệ-tông, who soon passed sway (1396); his son was deposed (1398). His grandson, grandson too of Lê Quí-ly, was enthroned at the age of three, and was put aside shortly afterwards (1400). The Trần, progressively younger and less kingly, now disappeared.

Lê Quí-ly gradually took over the throne. A mediocre general but an audacious politician, he abandoned the army on campaign for intrigue at court (1389) to protect his own interests, eliminating all rivals by degrees (1389, 1391, etc.), suppressing plots (1388, 1392, *cf.* 1395, 1397), and interpreting his oath to his own advantage (1394, 1398). Finally, of the dynasty itself, he spared only the progeny of a prince, who, sensing his scheme, soon enough retired, was allied to him through marriage, and protected his blood by mingling it with his own (1385). Treasons and favors aiding his fortune, Lê Quí-ly succeeded for a time in the attempt to found his own order. He created an entirely new capital, Tây-dô 西都 (Thanh-hoá, 1397), with such haste that it was necessary very soon to repair the walls; he compelled the king to come there, and at the old capital, Thăng-long 昇龍 (Hanoi), which became Dông-dô 東都, he dismantled two palaces half of which were sunk en route to Tây-dô. Lệ Quí-ly made himself regent (1398), assumed the attributes of a sovereign (1399), proclaimed himself king (1400), with the era name of Thánh-nguyên 聖元 and changed his name from Lê to Hồ (Hồ Nhất-nguyên 胡一元 in the Chinese histories) and that of Annam to Dại-ngu 大虞. In 1400-1 he made himself father-royal 太上皇 and, without ceasing to reign, enthroned his second son Lê Hán-thu'o'ng 漢蒼 (Hồ Dễ 胡查 in the Chinese histories; Annamite er anames Thiêu-thành 紹成 and Khai-dại 開大).

The Annamite Annals report the accomplishments of the two Hồ rulers: the state put sternly to rights and the country launched on a risky political venture. Lê Quí-ly exchanged copper money for paper (1396); he reshaped the provinces (1397, 1403) and limited the extent or number of private lands (1397); registered or confiscated them (1398). He arranged, along with statute labor, for three sorts of taxes (1402) and for three taxes on merchant vessels (1400). Reduction of the number of private slaves increased those of the crown (1401), the inspection of markets compelled the use of paper money (1403). He paid great attention to the police and the army. The latter, deprived by him of its leadership, received the officers he appointed (1375, 1379, 1389, 1391). Secret investigations and denunciation filled the bureaucracy with his partisans. At the mouths of rivers and at passes, surveillance forces, which Lê Quí-ly had created in 1392, curbed Cham incursions and local brigandage. The crisis in Champa 占城, following the death of its warrior king, Chê' Bồng-nga 制蓬峩, gave the Hồ, in two attempts at conquest, the chance to annex new districts (1402, in Quãng-nam 廣南). Lê Hán-thu'o'ng transported to this area, evacuated by the Cham, those people without rice fields, registered them there, and branded them on their arms (1403); in the following year, when their families were sent for to rejoin them, a storm at sea cost many of them their lives.

The chief concern, however, was China. The empire and the two kingdoms, Annam and Champa (plus Korea, 1392), were then going through palace revolutions. The enfeeblement of Trần, according to Annamite sources, had tempted the Ming (1378); according to the Chinese, it made them wait patiently (1396). Annam multiplied its tribute offerings and extracted titles; China exacted rice for its armies in the south, also seed, and asked as well for Buddhist monks (*T'ai-tsu shih-lu* and *Ming-shih*, 1381, 1395; the Annals under the years 1384, 1385, 1395). The Ssu-ming 思明 frontier (Kwangsi), neither Annamite nor Chinese, came under dispute. The Yüan had shifted the border a hundred *li* to the south, and the Trần two hundred to the north. The Thai chief, Huang Kuang-p'ing 黃廣平, received as an equal with Annam at the Ming court, denounced the encroachment (*T'ai-tsu shih-lu* and *Ming-shih*, 1397, *cf.* 1381). Lê Quí-ly, summoned to give up the five districts, not only paid no attention to the order, but, his son having just been enthroned, he even seized others (1403); obliged in the end to yield, he saw to the poisoning of the local chiefs delegated by the Ming (Annals, 1405).

He made preparations for the inevitable confrontation. The registers of vital statistics aided recruitment (1401, 1406). The army was reorganized, and the navy increased its vessels (1404). Da-bang 多邦城, a key position, upstream from Dông-dô on the Red River, was fortified; the Bạch-hạc 白鶴江 opposite bristled with stakes, as did all mouths of rivers (1405). Junks were taken away, the population of the northeast withdrawn for these works and for defense (1406). A belt of embankments and palisades ran along the southwest bank of the great river and stretched from Tam-giang 三江 to the Ninh-giang 寧江 (over 700 *li*, according to the Annals; over 900 *li*, according to the *shih-lu* and *Ming-shih*); it aimed at the rivers from Bắc-ninh to Hai'-du'o'ng (1406). Supported at both capitals and shielded by these streams, Lê Quí-ly, now a septuagenarian, happy in all his misdeeds, bent on defending his dynasty, defied Chu Ti (*q.v.*) only recently enthroned.

Beginning in 1401, according to the Annals, in 1403 only according to the Chinese, Lê Hán-thu'o'ng asked for investiture. He invoked the extinct Trần, his own kin, and the election obtained by his clientele. The Ming hesitated, then accorded it (start of 1404). A little later Biù Bá-ki 裴伯耆, a Trần subject, arrived to denounce the usurpation (September), and some time afterwards, Trần Thiên-bình 陳天平 (Thiêm-bình 添平 of the Annals), like Buí, one who had escaped the cruelty of the Hồ, came from Lao-chua 老撾, Yunnan (October). An imposter in the eyes of the Annalists, an authentic prince in the minds of the Chinese, he was confronted by them with the An-

namite embassy which had arrived on New Year's Day; the latter fell at his feet (February, 2, 1405). Lê Hán-thu'o'ng, summoned by the emperor, pretended to offer him the throne (July, 1405 and January, 1406), and laid an ambush for Thiêm-bình and his Chinese escort (April 13). Chu Ti, who following Chu Yüan-chang, was deferring intervention, made his decision to do so.

The Ming with three ways of invasion made use only of the two by land. The Kwangsi army, commanded by Chang Fu (*q.v.*), was by the 24th of November at Cântram 芹站. Carrying several positions, setting up one half-way to Thị-cầu 市橋 (Dặp-cầu), helping itself by means of floating bridges, it pushed right on to Gia-lâm 嘉林, in front of the capital, for purposes of making a reconnaissance, and by means of the Xu'o'ng-giang 昌江 (Bắc-giang), advanced obliquely on the River Bạch-hạc and joined Mu Sheng (*see* Mu Ying) with the army from Yunnan. Mu Sheng camped opposite Da-bang, Chang Fu mopped up the river area, while Chu Jung 朱榮 (T. 仲華, Pth. 忠靖, d. 1425+) made a diversion at Gia-lâm. The Chinese attacked one night, passed over the ditches, scaled the walls, and seized Da-bang (January 19, 1407); Dâng-dô on the following day fell without a struggle, and six days later Tây-dô also (January 26). The Chinese went down the Phú-lu'o'ng 富良江 (the Red River) and swept the delta, accusing the Hồ, welcoming defections, and trying to rally the people. Lê Trù'ng 澄 (b. 1374), son of Lê Quí-ly, with three hundred junks (five hundred according to the *shih-lu*) was beaten at Mộc-hoán 木凡江, an affluent on the right downstream from Dông-dô (February 21), and defeated again with "ten *li* of junks," at nearby Phú-lu'o'ng on the north bank (May 4). Seeking refuge at the ports of Nam-dịnh, Muộn 悶海口 (in land today), then Dại-an 大安海口, the hounded Hồ gained Thanh-hoá by sea, where at Lỗi-giang 磊江, a branch of the Mã 馬江, the remainder of their force disbanded. They fled farther to the south, to the port of Kỳ-la 奇羅 and to Mt. Cao-vọng 高望山 (Hà-tĩnh), where they were captured (June 16 and 17). Sent in cages to Nanking, together with their house-holds and their seals of office, they met the emperor seated at the Feng-t'ien gate 奉天門 (October 5). Chang Fu's report is read. At the passage: "He killed his king, they usurped," the emperor asked, "Is that the way of a subject?" Lê Quí-ly and Lê Hán-thu'o'ng were silent. The reading concluded, they were all thrown into pris-on, except two: Lê Trù'ng and the heir to the throne, Lê Nhuề 芮, to whom the emperor extended clemency, and for whom he provided. People have embroid-ered this act of clemency and the end of the Hồ.

As a result of an Annamite petition presented on April 17, the name Annam, by an imperial edict issued July 5, was changed for the time being to Chiao-chih 交阯. Lê Quí-ly had believed that he would be able to wear out the Ming on the other bank, and Chu Ti that his armies would be able to avoid diseases endemic in the summer. Both presumed too much, for the war continued and the Hồ disap-peared. They had wounded half the peo-ple of importance and maltreated those of low degree, and had pressed into serv-ice a mass of individuals and provoked a warlike China. The Hồ showed no talent for fighting, only temerity and haste in fiight. Absent at Da-bang, they abandoned Dông-dô and burned Tây-dô. Alone Lê Tr'ùng was defeated at Mộc-hoàn. Lê Quí-ly, in spite of his age, governed un-der Hán-thu'o'ng. Two acts put the finishing touches to his portrayal: in a fit of temper he saw to the slaying of two ill-advised counselors, one at Lỗi-giang, and the other a month later at Kỳ-la.

The lives of the three principal Hồ are hardly separable, neither they them-selves nor the events in which they were involved. Lê Trù'ng, also known as Nguyên 元 Trù'ng, was the eldest of the sons of Lê Quí-ly. But in 1400, like Lê Quí-ly, he yielded to his younger brother Lê Hán-thu'o'ng. They were the children of two mothers; Hán-thu'o'ng was the son of Princess Huy-ninh 徽寧公主 who, being a daughter of Minh-tông 明宗, was related remotely to a Trần king — one of the three claims (*supra*) by which the Hồ legitimized their dynasty.

They were of the scholar class, reformed education and regulated Buddhism; the year of their accession saw a doctoral promotion (1400). Lê Quí-ly prided him-self on his writing and made it serve his ends. The Annals cite an Annamite poem of his (1387), a version in prose of the *Wu-i* 無逸 of the *Shu ching* (1395), some occasional Chinese verses (1405), and a *Minh dạo* 明道 in 14 chap-ters, a kind of Confucian philosophy of history, ill received by two orthodox scholars both of whom suffered punish-ment (1392); and those who criticized the Chinese verses fared even worse. Le Trù'ng is the author of an agreeable collection of historical and literary anec-dotes, the *Nan weng meng lu* 南翁夢錄 (in Annamite: *Nam êng mộng lue* in one *chüan* (1438), which still exists, handed down in Chinese collections. The *shih-lu* reports that Le Trù'ng, several years after his capture by the Chinese, was ordered to manufacture firearms in Peking. He worked inside the palace, and in 1436 was given the title of senior vice minister of Works. After a few decades of service he died on August 2, 1446, by which time he had been holding the honorary title of minister of Works for over a year. He received honors on his interment at a site in the hills west of the capital. It became customary for soldiers to pay their respects both to him and to their weapons at his tomb. Some of Le Trù'ng's descendants continued to manufacture firearms for the Chinese.

Bibliography

Chinese sources: 1/ch. 2–6 and 321; MSL (1962), T'ai-tsu (1963), T'ai-tsung, Hsüan-tsung, 0409,

Ying-tsung, 0428, 2082, 2586, 2827; Chang Hsiu-min 張秀民, "Ming-tai Chiao-chih-jen tsai chung-kuo chih kung-hsien" 明代交阯人在中國之貢獻 in *Ming-tai kuo-chi kuan-hsi* 國際關係 (Taipei, 1968), 74; Annamite sources: Annals (3 redactions); E. Gaspardone in *Annuaire du Collège de France*, Vol. 56 (1956), 292, Vol. 57 (1957), 358.

Emile Gaspardone, tr. by L. C. G.

LEI Li 雷禮 (T. 必進, H. 古和), 1505–August 28, 1581, a native of Hsün-she 鐔舍 in Feng-ch'eng 豐城, Kiangsi, was an official, builder, and author of works on the administrative system of the Ming dynasty in its formative and middle years. A descendant of Lei Ch'eng 誠 (T. 誠智, cs 1415) who had been prefect of Yen-p'ing 延平府, Fukien, he not unnaturally sought a career in public office. After achieving the *chin-shih* in 1532, he served as prefectural judge in Hsing-hua 興化, Fukien (1533–36), and Ning-kuo 寧國, south of Nanking (1539). In 1542 he was appointed a secretary of the ministry of Personnel in Peking, rising to the directorship of the bureau of evaluations (1547). His strict adherence to the rules of his office did not sit well with some of his superiors, especially Hsia Yen (*q. v.*); so later in 1547 he found himself posted, at a lower rank, to Ta-ming 大名府, Pei-Chihli, as assistant prefect. Here he probably found the time to write, or at least have a hand in, one of his first books, a local history of Chen-ting prefecture 眞定府, 33 *ch.*, printed in 1549. Next he was in Chekiang as surveillance vice commissioner in charge of education (1548–50), and then served in the years from 1550 to 1552 as vice-president of the Court of Imperial Stud in Nanking. His experience here in charge of horses, pasture lands, and grain supply led to a second of his books, the *Nan-ching t'ai-p'u-ssu chih* 南京太僕寺志, 16 *ch.*, on the work of the court. He must have given general satisfaction in this post for he was ordered back to Peking in the same office and was promoted to the presidency of the Court of Imperial Sacrifices. In 1553 he became prefectural governor of Peking and a year later was promoted to be vice-minister of Works, while another vice-minister of Works (Lu Chieh 陸杰, cs 1514, d. April 13, 1554) was dispatched to supervise the construction of tombs and palaces at the emperor's birthplace in Te-an 德安, Hukuang. Lei Li was placed in charge of the projects in Peking and of the imperial tombs north of the capital. When, in May, 1557, the three audience halls were destroyed by fire, Lei suddenly found himself engaged in the rebuilding of these huge edifices, as well as of the Wu-men 午門 (Meridian Gate), the towering entrance to the palace area.

On October 28, 1558, when appointed minister of Works, Lei reached his highest rank; he held the office for almost exactly ten years. This was a time of great activity in the construction and repair of government buildings inside and outside the capital, and the financial condition of the country was such that it seems to have been capable of bearing the expense. Which of the two, Lei Li or Hsü Kao (*q. v.*), the unofficial minister of Works, was the more responsible for the supervision of building one can only guess. Lei's was a lucrative post. It is reported that the cost of the projects for which he was responsible had been estimated at millions of taels, but he completed them at a tenth or less of the original estimates, much to the annoyance of those officials and eunuchs who usually profited from public works. Lei was the object of attacks, both open and covert, but maintained his position because the emperor recognized and valued his honesty. On April 17, 1562, in a general bestowal of awards, Lei received the title T'ai-tzu t'ai-pao (grand guardian of the heir apparent) and a few months later, after palace construction came to an end (October 8), the title was elevated (November 6) to that of T'ai-tzu t'ai-fu (Grand Tutor). During the last four years of the Chia-ching era quiet seems to have reigned in the ministry. With the coming of the new emperor, Chu Tsai-hou (*q.v.*) troubles began. On March 25, 1567, the eunuch Li Fang (*see* Chang Chü-cheng) accused Hsü Kao of misappropriating funds meant for the repair of Lu-kou ch'iao (Marco Polo Bridge), an accusation which cost that able engineer his post as titular minister. A year and a half later (October 5, 1568) Lei protested against the activities of a eunuch named T'eng Hsiang 滕祥 who, in his opinion, was going too far in his demands for funds and requisition of materials from the stocks of the ministry for use in temple worship. He concluded his protest by acknowledging that he had insufficient strength to do battle with the eunuchs and implored the emperor to intervene; else he must resign. Now T'eng had entered the palace, probably as a youth, in 1509, nearly sixty years before; so he had been acquainted with the pleasure-loving emperor from his childhood and knew how to pamper him. T'eng accordingly won the argument and Lei was forced to retire. He lived on at home for another thirteen years. It is probably at this time that he had the leisure to compile his other books.

In addition to the two works already mentioned, several other titles are credited to him. They include the *Huang Ming ta-cheng chi* 皇明大政記, 25 *ch.*, the first 20 *chüan* of which are due to Lei. (Another work with the same title is by Chu Kuo-chen; *see* ECCP.) It is a political history of the dynasty from its beginnings (1368) to 1521. Although rare, the Library of Congress and Columbia University each has a set of the edition of 1602. Another significant compilation is the (*Kuo-ch'ao*) *lieh-ch'ing chi* 列卿記, 165 *ch.*, a collection of notices of men in official employ from 1368 to 1566, tables supplying dates of appointment, and essays on government offices. This was reprinted (1970) in Taiwan in 24 volumes, together with a final volume constituting an index. An expanded work on the tables and essays, 129 of the former, 51 of the latter, in 139 *chüan*, was supplemented by Hsieh T'ing-chieh

謝廷傑 (cs 1559, a native of Hsin-chien 新建, Kiangsi) who brought the lists down to the 1570s. These works concern government on the national level, but Lei continued his interest on the local level as well, being responsible for a study of the operations of his own native place, entitled *Feng-ch'eng-hsien chih chi* 治記, a work which seems to have disappeared. His contemporaries expressed their admiration of the erudition of Lei with the saying: Lei Li is learned about the past, while Cheng Hsiao (*q. v.*) knows all about the present.

It is not without interest that certain of Lei Li's descendants tn the 18th and 19th centuries continued his work as builders of palaces in Peking and its environs, particularly at Wan-shou shan 萬壽山.

Bibliography
1/305/1b; 5/50/67a; 16/153/24a, 154/7b; 42/64/20b; KC (1958), 200, 3829, 4047, 4398, 4785; *Feng-ch'eng-hsien chih* (1873), 13/15b, 25, 32a, 35b; MSL (1965), Shih-tsung, 7382, 8363, 8417, 8441, Mu-tsung (1940), 24/6b, Shen-tsung, 118/3a; Yü Yin 余寅 (cs 1580), "Hsing-chuang" 行狀, in *Huang Ming wen-hai* (microfilm roll #9), ch. 61; O. B. van der Sprenkel, "The Chronological Tables of Lei Li," BSOAS (1952), 325; W. Franke, *Sources*, 1.3.3, 3.3.12; Joseph Needham, *Science and Civilization in China*, IV: 3 (Cambridge, England, 1971), 61.
L. Carrington Goodrich and Chaoying Fang

LENG Ch'ien 冷謙 (T. 起 (啓) 敬, H. 龍陽子), *ca.* 1310–*ca.* 1371, musician, painter, Taoist, was a native of Chia-hsing 嘉興 (or nearby Hangchow) although some records give his place of birth as Wu-ling 武陵, Hukuang. His life is shrouded in mystery. An examination of a number of the biographies written by Ming authors shows that they are scarcely more than a repetition of a doubtful colophon penned by a less identifiable Taoist named Chang San-feng (*see* Chang Chung) on the painting "P'eng-lai hsien-i t'u" 蓬萊仙奕圖 ascribed to Leng. Lang Ying (*q.v.*) demonstrated the spuriousness of this colo-

Empress Shao (d. 1522), mother of Chu Hou-ts'ung

Chu Hou-ts'ung (1507–67) and Empress Ch'en (d. 1528)

PLATE 7

Empress Tu (d. 1554), mother of Chu Tsai-hou

Chu Tsai-hou (1537–72) and Empress Li (d. 1558)

PLATE 8

Empresses Li (d. 1614) and Ch'en (d. 1596), mother of Chu I-chün

Chu I-chün (1563–1620) and Empress Wang (d. 1620)

PLATE 9

Empress Wang (d. 1612), mother of Chu Ch'ang-lo

Chu Ch'ang-lo (1582–1620) and Empress Kuo (d. 1613/14)

PLATE 10

phon in his *Ch'i-hsiu hsü-kao.* In Lang's opinion the author of the colophon knew neither the native place nor the post held by Leng at the beginning of the Ming dynasty. Instead he filled it with legends, such as the one which puts Leng's birth before the end of the Sung dynasty (960–1279). Lang's arguments are strong enough to show the unreliability of these biographies.

According to two inscriptions mentioned below, which are devoid of legendary elements, Leng was a friend of Sa-tu-la 薩都剌 and Liu Chi (*q.v.*), the former born in 1308 and the latter in 1311. His date of birth therefore may be placed at about the same time. One inscription, made in 1339 by Sa-tu-la on one of his own paintings, entitled "Yen-ling tiao-t'ai t'u" 嚴陵釣台圖, records that he and Leng paid a visit to Yen-ling (in T'ung-lu 桐廬, Chekiang), and that he painted this landscape at Leng's request. Another inscription, dated 1343 by Leng himself, may be found between his own poem and one by Liu Chi on a painting attributed to Leng, entitled "Po-yüeh t'u" 白岳圖, of which two copies are extant. This inscription states that he and Liu visited Po-yüeh Mountain (in Anhwei) together. Even if the authenticity of these two paintings may be questioned, the fact remains that the visit of Sa-tu-la to T'ung-lu is verified by a poem in his collected works.

Leng around this time became a Taoist hermit on a mountain known variously as Wu-shan 吳山 or Hsü 胥 -shan, situated near Hangchow. According to the preamble to a poem written by Chang Hsüan 張宣 (T. 藻重, a native of Chiang-yin on the Yangtze, d. 1373) in the summer of 1364, he and several friends visited Leng at the pavilion Ju-tz'u chiang-shan t'ing 如此江山亭 in his mountain retreat. To amuse them, the poem records, Leng played the lute, and to such effect that they called him Ch'in-hsien 琴仙 (immortal of the lute). Liu Chi's two poems were written after the year 1366, and both

describe Leng's playing on the instrument. Perhaps it was due to Liu's recommendation that, on September 4, 1367, Leng was appointed hsieh-lü-lang 協律郎, or court musician, at the time that Chu Yüan-chang proclaimed himself King of Wu. Leng was charged with the task of instituting the system of music and dancing for the court and of supervising the fashioning of numerous musical instruments after ancient models. As he was a Taoist, the pupils of music and dancing under his direction were all enrolled among the Taoists. This became the tradition during the early years of the dynasty. In 1371 he, together with T'ao K'ai 陶凱 (T. 中立, cj 1347) and Chan T'ung (*q.v.*), composed music to be used on the occasion of sacrifices and feasts. Leng's compositions are quoted or mentioned several times in the *Lü-lü ching-i wai-p'ien* of Chu Tsai-yü (*q. v.*). In Chu's opinion Leng understood the theory of composition very well, following the rules laid down by musicians of the Sung much better than Liu Lien 劉濂 (T. 濬伯, cs 1521), author of the *Yüeh-ching yüan-i* 樂經元義·

Three booklets have been ascribed to Leng. Two concern music and bear the titles: *Ch'in-sheng shih-lu fa* 琴聲十六法 and *T'ai-ku cheng-yin* 太古正音; both are listed in the bibliographies of Yu T'ung and Huang Yü-chi (both in ECCP). The third, entitled *Hsiu-ling yao-chih* 修齡要旨, deals with certain exercises generally performed by Taoists. Its authenticity is questioned by the editors of the *Ssu-k'u* catalogue. The second of these three works seems to have disappeared, but the other two are included in the *Hsüeh-hai lei-pien* (*see* Ts'ao Jung, ECCP), and the first in the *T'an-chi ts'ung-shu* 檀几叢書 of 1695. The *Ch'in-sheng shih-lu fa* is incorrectly ascribed in both. Though its authorship is disputed, R. H. van Gulik assumes it to be a genuine work of Leng Ch'ien, and has rendered the entire text into English in his *Lore of the Chinese Lute.*

Just as there is uncertainty as to his writings, so there is doubt as to various

paintings ascribed to him in later times.
Documentary evidence about them from
his own day is wanting. That is why Lang
Ying denied that Leng was a painter.
Nevertheless Hsü Ch'in 徐沁 (early
Ch'ing, a native of K'uai-chi, Chekiang),
author of the *Ming hua lu* 明畫錄, considered him one, and modern critics hesitate to regard all paintings assigned to
him as spurious. For example, as noticed
above, there are two copies of the "Po-
yüeh t'u" extant, and they differ from
each other in certain details. One is probably unauthentic; but are both? One of
them, "Yellow Mountain Chu Sha An,"
is reproduced in the *Ta-feng-t'ang ming-
chi* 大風堂名蹟.

As uncertainty clouds our knowledge
of Leng's early days, so does it affect our
knowledge about his end. The last firm
date is 1371; after that silence. Possibly
he offended the emperor, and was put out
of the way. This is suggested by the colophon of Chang San-feng, but one can
only surmise.

Bibliography

5/118/119a; 40/12/16a; 61/151/15a; 65/2/2a; 86/
4/19b; MSL (1962) T'ai-tsu, 0357; TSCC (1885-
88), XIV: 444/3b, XVII: 788/13a, XVIII: 256/
11a, XXIX: 30/30/4a; *Hunan t'ung-chih* (1934),
3088, 5073, 6004; Ch'en Chien and Shen Kuo-
yüan 沈國元, *Huang Ming ts'ung-hsin lu* 從信錄
(Wan-li ed.), 5/25a; Liu Chi, *Liu Ch'eng-i-po
wen-chi* (SPTK ed.), 11/25b, 13/49b; Lang Ying,
Ch'i-hsiu lei-kao (Peking, 1959), hsü kao 4/801;
Chang Hsüan, *Ch'ing-yang chi* 青暘集 (Chiang-yin
江陰 ts'ung-shu), 2/7b; Sa-tu-la, *Sa t'ien-hsi shih-
chi* 薩天錫詩集 (SPTK ed.), hou 85b; Chu Tsai-
yü, *Lü-lü ching-i wai-p'ien*, 1/17, 23, 3/15, 17,
18; Hsü Ch'in, *Ming hua lu* (TsSCC ed.), 2/13;
SK (1930), 39/2b, 147/10b; *Ku-kung shu-hua lu*
故宮書畫錄 (Taipei, 1959), 5/175, 251; Chang
Ta-ch'ien 張大千, *Ta-feng-t'ang ming-chi*, 4 vols.
(Kyoto, 1955–56), pl. 19; O. Sirén, *Chinese
Painting*, VII (New York, 1958), 120; R. H.van
Gulik, *The Lore of the Chinese Lute* (Tokyo,
1940), 104; E. J. Laing, *Chinese Painting in
Chinese Publications, 1956–1968* (Ann Arbor,
1969), 126.

                                    T. W. Weng

LI Ch'ang-ch'i, *see* **LI Chen**

LI Chao-hsiang 李昭祥(T. 元韜), fl. 1537–
53, official, best known as shipbuilding
director, was a native of Shanghai. He
took first place in the provincial examinations at Ying-t'ien (Nanking) in 1537,
and became a *chin-shih* in 1547. Li began
his official life by acquitting himself well
as magistrate of Lan-ch'i 蘭谿, Chekiang;
then in 1551, while serving as a secretary
of the ministry of Works in Nanking, he
was appointed executive director of the
Lung-chiang shipyard 龍江船廠, where he
was to make the major contribution of
his public career.

Established in the early years of the
Hung-wu reign near Nanking, the Lung
chiang shipyard was administered by the
ministry of Works and charged with the
construction of various types of ships for
government use, including warships, imperial barges, patrol boats, and fishing craft
(but not including grain transport boats
which were built elsewhere). The ministry
maintained a superintendent's office within
the shipyard premises, yet through the
years there was never a fixed procedure
for either the staffing or the administration of the yard. Government shipbuilding, it appears, remained in a state of
confusion throughout the Ming dynasty
with regard to the procurement and allotment of materials, the channels of accountability and responsibility among the
officials in charge, and administrative
efficiency in general. Meanwhile, demands
for watercraft increased for a time after
the capital was moved to Peking, but
decreased after the middle of the 15th
century. It was in this context that Li
Chao-hsiang assumed the directorship of
the shipyard.

Li's first acts were to restore and
renovate the physical plant of the yard,
most of which was lying in ruins through
years of neglect, the process of decay being aided two years previously by a fire
that razed the office compound of the

executive director. Li began by rebuilding this office in 1552, enlarging it in the process. Other buildings repaired or rebuilt at this time included the storehouse for tung oil and hemp and the paint shop. He also had wells dug and trees planted, and soon the shipyard was an entirely different place from the tumbledown establishment that Li took over. [Editors' note: Considerable interest was stirred when, in 1962, there was discovered, at what may have been the site of the shipyard, a sternpost rudder, said to be 36.2 ft. long and 1.25 ft. thick, constructed to swing a rudder blade of 19.7 ft. in length. Whether this dates from Li's time or a century and a half earlier is unknown. The assumption is that it was made for a junk between 480 ft. and 536 ft. in length. Cf. Joseph Needham, *Chinese Science and Civilization*, IV:3 (Cambridge, 1971), 404, 481, fig. 980.]

Li's second act was to write an account of this shipyard. Entitled *Lung-chiang ch'uan-ch'ang chih* 志 (with a preface of 1553 by Ou-yang Ch'ü 歐陽儞, cs 1526, native of T'ai-ho 泰和, Kiangsi), it is a work in eight *chüan* offering a general view of the history of the shipyard, the past laws and precedents governing this institution, the names and years of service of past superintendents and directors, the physical plant, the requirements in raw materials for building the different types of ships, and the needed reforms in administration. The book contains many sketches of the types of boats built at Lung-chiang, and the dimensions and brief history of each craft are given. For several centuries the work was unknown, but fortunately a copy was found and reproduced in 1947 in the *Hsüan-lan-t'ang ts'ung-shu*, 2d series (comp. by Cheng Chen-to, BDRC), volumes 117–19. Li was responsible for a number of other books, but this apparently is the only one known to have survived.

Li was evidently unable to carry out all of his intended reforms in the operation of the yard, however, for in his book he laments that, owing to the state of extreme decay of the shipyard and the lack of funds, he could do little but resign himself to the situation.

It is not known how many years Li served at Lung-chiang. Of his later life it is known only that he became a bureau director in the ministry of Works in Nanking and then retired. After his death he was accorded the shrine designation of his native place. The local history of Shanghai does not elaborate on Li's own career, but lists many of his descendants as successful degree holders and officials.

Bibliography

Ho Ch'iao-yüan, "Ts'ao-yün chi" 漕運記 (On grain transportation), in *Ming-shan ts'ang* 名山藏, ed. of 1628–44, 15b; *Shang-hai-hsien chih* 上海縣志 (1814), 10/21, 12/36b; *Sung-chiang-fu chih* 松江府志 (1817), 53/24b.

E-tu Zen Sun

LI Chen 李禎 (T. 昌祺, H. 運甓居士, 僑菴, 白衣山人), July 13, 1376–March 17, 1452, was an official, poet, and story-writer. He came to use his *tzu* (Ch'ang-ch'i) instead of his *ming*, presumably in order to avoid an infringement of the tabooed name of the Ming imperial prince, Chu Chen, sixth son of Chu Yüan-chang. A native of Lu-ling 廬陵, Kiangsi, he was a brillint student and obtained the *chin-shih* in 1404. Selected one of the twenty-eight graduates who were taken over as Hanlin bachelors, he was assigned to the compilation of the great thesaurus, which became known as *Yung-lo ta-tien* (*see* Yao Kuang-hsiao); after its completion he was promoted to the rank of director of the bureau of receptions in the ministry of Rites. His next office was that of left administration commissioner for the province of Kwangsi. This promotion took place on June 1, 1418, and was due to the influence of the heir apparent, Chu Kao-chih (*q.v.*). In less than a year, he was in what the sources call "an affair" and removed from office. Furthermore, he had to redeem himself by serving as a supervisor of forced labor at Fang-shan 房山 near Peking for two or three years. Then his father died and he went home. After the mourning period he was reinstated (May 23, 1425) as administration commissioner for the province of Honan. About 1429 he retired due to the death of his mother but when a famine was reported in Honan the court summoned him to return to his office before the completion of the mourning period. In 1436 he presented a memorial to Emperor Chu Ch'i-chen (q.v.) stressing the need for centralized supervision of local schools and urging measures against the practice of medicine by Taoists. He also suggested the erection of a memorial shrine for the celebrated Sung loyalist Wen T'ien-hsiang (1236–83) in Lu-ling, clearly from motives of local pride. Three years later Li applied for retirement on grounds of ill-health and old age, an application granted May 18, 1439. He spent the remainder of his life in frail health but in constant literary activity in his home town. He was buried in the family mausoleum near the Chao-i temple 招義院 on the Tzu-yün mountain 紫雲山 near Lu-ling. He was married twice. By his first wife née Ai 艾 he had one daughter, and by his second née Liu 劉 two sons, Li Hsüan 宣 and Li Ting 定, and two more daughters.

His collected poetry appeared in print during his lifetime (1436) and was reprinted after his death in 1459 under the title *Yün-p'i man-kao* 運甓漫稿 in 7 *chüan*. This work was incorporated in the manuscript library, the *Ssu-k'u ch'üan-shu*, in the 18th century but no later printed edition seems to have been made. Contemporary critics praised Li's poetry as refined and spontaneous. But Li's importance as a writer is chiefly due to his collection of short stories in the literary language, the *Chien-teng yü-hua* 剪燈餘話, written in 1419 at Fang-shan after he had read *Chien-teng hsin-hua* by Ch'ü Yu (q.v.). As the titles indicate Li intended his work in form and content to be a continuation of that of his elder contemporary. In so doing Li undoubtedly increased the popularity of Ch'ü's work because of Li's prestige and high official status. The social stratum in which Li moved is indicated by the position of those contemporaries who in 1420 wrote prefaces for his *Chien-teng yü-hua*. They were all *chin-shih* of 1404 like himself: Tseng Ch'i 曾棨 (T. 子啓, H. 西墅, Pth. 襄敏, 1372–February 22, 1432), *chuang-yüan* of that year who was a Hanlin academician; Wang Ying 王英 (T. 時彦, Pth. 文安, later changed to 文忠, 1376–June 26, 1450), one-time minister of Rites in Nanking; Lo Chien 羅簡 (or 肅, T. 沙敬, 1372–1439), a successful official who, after some time spent in the Hanlin Academy, served twice as ambassador to Annam and distinguished himself in the campaign against the Mongols in 1430; Liu Ching 劉敬 (T. 子欽, 1368–1454) who, like Li Chen and Tseng Ch'i, also took part in the compilation of the *Yung-lo ta-tien*.

The first printed edition of the *Chien-teng yü-hua* was published in 1433 through the efforts of Liu Ching. This edition was illustrated. Another edition followed in 1487. In later centuries only partial reprints were published in China until, in the 20th century, when the interest in early Ming fiction revived, a complete edition appeared. The collection consists of twenty-two stories; almost all of them seem to be modeled on certain ones in the collection of Ch'ü Yu. The subject matter also is similar: ghost and love stories, some of them mildly erotic. Like Ch'ü Yu, Li invariably chose the 14th century as historical background and like him took great care in providing realistic detail for even the most fantastic plots. It is evident how keen Li was to do better than Ch'ü Yu. This applies not only to the contents as such but also to the literary skill displayed throughout his work. Li was a master of difficult poetic forms such as the palindrome (hui-wen 廻文) and the cento (chi-chü 集句), of which many examples may be found in his stories. A literary tour de force is number 21: "Chih-cheng chi-jen hsing" 至正妓人行 (The life of a courtesan of the Chih-cheng period). This is a poem with a short introduction describing the splendor and decay of metropolitan life under the last Yüan emperor where, in addition to many historical allusions to his reign, much use is made of foreign, mostly Mongol, words which give a distinctly outlandish flavor to the poem. Number 22, *"Chia Yün-hua huan-hun chi"* 買雲華還魂記 (The return of the soul of Chia Yün-hua), is much longer than the other tales and more like a novel than a short story. It is a romantic and even sentimental love story set against the social background of two well-to-do families.

The *Chien-teng yü-hua* rapidly won great popularity. But like the work on which it is modeled it met the disapproval of stern Confucianists. When the censor, Han Yung (*q.v.*), made an application to erect a tablet to Li's memory, the plan failed because Li was the author of the *Chien-teng yü-hua*. Nevertheless the influence of this book lasted into the early years of the 17th century when several pieces of fiction were rewritten in colloquial language by Ling Meng-ch'u (*q. v.*) and other writers or adapted for the stage. Whereas in China the *Chien-teng yü-hua* was more or less forgotten in the 18th and 19th centuries, although some stories were incorporated in the encyclopedic *T'u-shu chi-ch'eng*, the collection became popular in Japan where a movable type copy was published during the Genwa period (1615-24) and reprinted in 1692. The Japanese editors continued to regard the work as an integral part of the literary heritage of China, and included it in such representative collections as *Shina Bungaku Taikan* 支那文學大觀 and *Kokuyaku Kambun Taisei* 國譯漢文大成.

Bibliography

1/161/3b; 3/151/1b; 5/92/1a (also in *Huang Ming wen-heng* 文衡, 82/9a); 40/18 上 /14a; 43/2/1b; 64/ 乙 9/5a; 86/6/22b; *Lieh-ch'ao shih-chi* (see Ch'ien Ch'ien-i, ECCP), 乙 5/8b; *Huang Ming hsi-chiang shih-hsüan* 西江詩選 (*Yü-chang ts'ung-shu* 豫章叢書 ed.), 8/1a; Herbert Franke, "Zur Novellistik der frühen Ming-Zeit: Das Chien-teng yü-hua des Li Ch'ang-ch'i," ZDMG, 109 (1959) 340; W. Bauer and H. Franke, *The Golden Casket*, tr. by C. Levenson (New, York, 1964), 264.

Herbert Franke

LI Chih 李贄 (original name, Tsai-chih 載贄, T. 宏父, 思齋, H. 卓吾, 溫陵居士, 百泉居士), November 23, 1527-May 6, 1602, the most independent and courageous thinker of his day, was a native of Chin-chiang 晉江, Fukien. His mother died shortly after he was born. "Left motherless," he wrote later, "I know not who was responsible for rearing me." His father, a man "seven feet tall, who never set his eye upon improper things," taught him to read when he was six. Making rapid progress in his studies, he took up in succession the Books of Changes, Rites and History. He confessed, however, that he found Chu Hsi's exegeses difficult to assimilate.

He gained the *chü-jen* in 1552, but financial circumstances prevented his trying for a higher degree. Entering officialdom in 1555, he assumed the post of district director of studies of Kung-ch'eng 共城 (modern Hui-hsien 輝縣) in Honan province. Four years later he rose to erudite in the National University, Nanking. After only a few months in Nanking his father died and Li had to return home to observe the traditional mourning rites.

In 1561 he took his wife and children to Peking where he waited for almost two years before he received an assignment in the northern National University. The news of his grandfather's death reached him two years later, on the same day that his second son died. He relinquished his new post, presumably with little regret, as he did not get along well with the libationer and the tutors, and went home again to observe the mourning rites. On the way south he stopped at Kung-ch'eng, bought a small farm and left his wife and children there to support themselves, for he planned to use the major part of the capital on hand to give a proper burial to his parents, grandparents, and great-grandparents.

Rejoining his family in 1566, he found that his second and third daughters had died of privation as a result of a local famine. He took the remaining members to Peking for the second time, where he received appointment as an office manager in the ministry of Rites. It was at this time that he became acquainted with Buddhism as well as with the teachings of Wang Shou-jen and Wang Chi (qq.v.). This proved to be a turning point in his intellectual life. He declared, "In my youth I honored Confucius, but I knew not why he deserved honoring . . . Thus before I was fifty I was like a dog barking as other dogs barked." (A preamble to the Sage's teaching 聖教小引.) The next year he changed his name to Chih, as Tsai was a part of the personal name of the newly enthroned emperor Chu Tsai-hou (q.v.).

From 1571 to 1576 he spent most of his time in Nanking, serving as vice director of a bureau in the ministry of Justice. While he was in the southern capital he met, among others, the two brothers, Keng Ting-hsiang and Keng Ting-li (qq.v.), and also Chiao Hung (ECCP) and Wang Chi, men who were to exert much influence on his thinking. By this time he had already begun holding discussions with friends and achieved a measure of intellectual independence.

He took up the post of prefect of Yao-an 姚安 in Yunnan province in 1578. At the end of the three-year term he was allowed to resign, thus ending an uneventful and largely unrewarding official career of twenty-five years. While he was an incumbent of the four or five government posts to which he was assigned, he incurred without exception the displeasure of his superiors and senior colleagues. Here in Yunnan the friction began to develop between himself and the governor as well as the circuit intendant. To remain longer in office would prove neither useful nor pleasant, even though many of the local inhabitants begged him to stay because he had served them well.

Now in his fifties, he began to devote himself completely to intellectual pursuits—discoursing with friends, expounding his views to all who came to listen, and putting his thoughts in writing—activities which were interrupted only by his death twenty years later. It was during these years that he gave his intellectual position its final definition and became the most outspoken critic of neo-Confucianism.

Instead of returning home he went (1581) from Yao-an to Huang-an 黃安 (in northeastern Hukuang) to enjoy the companionship of the Keng brothers, who were natives of the district, and to teach their sons. He was particularly close to Keng Ting-li and so, when the latter died (August 28, 1584), he was profoundly saddened. Meanwhile doctrinal disagreement between Keng Ting-hsiang and himself brought them into sharp disputes. Hopelessly estranged, he took leave of his host (1585), sent his wife back to Fukien, and moved to Ma-ch'eng 麻城 (a neighboring district southeast of Huang-an), where he found shelter in a Buddhist temple on the shores of a small lake, Lung-t'an 龍潭 (or Lung-hu 湖), outside the walled city. In 1588 he shaved his head. That action, he explained, was a way of letting his family know that he would never return home to rejoin them, and "to protect the reputation of the many undiscerning people of this locality," who considered him a heretic; so he assumed the outward form of one. The four short poems which he wrote at the time may be taken, however, as a truer indication of his feelings. The first three of these may be rendered as follows:

I

An ugly old man by the deep lake,
A Buddhist monk now I am:
Countless men shall I by the way save—

With the sun and moon long shines the
    Lamp.

II

To have a family truly is a hindrance,
And to get along with the world brings
    scorn.
Into the hills away I go, I go—
To a bowl of gruel when I arise each
    morn.

III

A Confucian half my life,
Many years have I lived on official pay.
But wishing to attain a Birthless patience
All family bonds I now cast away.

Although he was not an unfeeling
man and was indeed capable of strong
attachment to good friends, he did not entertain deep affection for his wife. He
confessed as much in the six short poems
written upon learning of her death in
1595, four of which merit quoting:

I

Marriage made us man and wife
But bonds of love neither of us had.
Today I hear of your death,
I cannot help but feel a trifle sad.

II

I mourn you—not because of affection;
I feel sad because you were great:
Not a single angry word came from you
In the forty years you were my mate.

IV

Kindly in heart, you denied yourself the
    things you gave away;
With self-discipline you managed the
    household well.
To seek the Buddha in earnest I have
    roamed far,
So I bid you farewell.

VI

Who could match you in your loyal feat,
Except those noble women of old?
Sorry that you could not follow me.

All within the four seas is a man's free-
    hold.

Li expressed identical sentiments in his
letter to Chuang Ch'un-fu 莊純夫, his son-
in-law. While Li extolled his wife's virtue
and ability, he regretted that she was unable to reach intellectual rapport with him.

This leads to Li's notion of the ideal
relationship between man and woman. In
his view it was indeed commendable for
a woman to act as befitted "a good wife
and worthy mother," but in order to be
loved (and not merely esteemed) she
must also be an understanding companion of her spouse, sharing his interests
and aspirations. Li assumed that intellec-
tually speaking man and woman are
equals. "It is incorrect to say that there
are male and female human beings. But is
it correct to say that there is a male or
female intelligence?" (Letter in reply to
"women being shortsighted are unfit to
seek truth" 答以女人學道為短見書.)

In 1590 the first edition of Li's collected works, *Fen-shu* 焚書, was published
in Ma-ch'eng. It contains some letters he
wrote to Keng Ting-hsiang attacking the
latter's pharisaical conduct. Probably as a
result of Keng's retaliation, Li left Ma-
ch'eng about this time. He went up the
Yangtze, visiting Wuchang and other
places. At Kung-an 公安 he met the Yüan
brothers and so impressed them that one
of them, Yüan Chung-tao (*q.v.*), kept a
record of the conversation (Cha-lin chi-
t'an 柞林記譚). After his return to Lung-
t'an in 1593, the three brothers visited
him. The admiration was mutual, as the
poems exchanged between host and guests
show. Yüan Chung-tao, who became one
of his biographers, describes Li's life
at this time in these words: "Each day
he locked his door and became absorbed
in reading. He loved to sweep the floor;
several men could not make enough
brooms to meet his needs. His clothes were
meticulously laundered and exceedingly
clean. Washing his face and bathing his
body were nothing short of a passion.

He detested visitors whom he considered vulgar. If by chance he failed to keep one of these out...he would keep the intruder at a distance, loathing the stench. But he chatted happily all day long with those people whose company he enjoyed." Li was actually no solitary recluse. He often "discoursed on learning" with each and all who appreciated his ideas, women not excluded.

In an essay, "Aloofness and purity" (高潔說), he justified his selective association with people by saying that because he sought friends that were truly worthwhile he could not avoid appearing haughty and unapproachable to those who courted the powerful and fawned upon the wealthy. One might surmise that, because he had had to conform to the conventional decorum of scholar-officialdom half of his adult life, he now determined to break with it. Shaving his head was intended possibly as much to dramatize his self-imposed exile from polite society as to symbolize his conversion to Buddhism.

Conversion is perhaps not a fully accurate word to define his relationship to that faith. He was after all a man who refused to restrict his intellectual horizon to any single persuasion, a man who believed that truth abides in the teachings of all sages and that one should, by his own personal insight and in his own individual way, find it in Confucianism, Taoism, Buddhism, or elsewhere. Such a free-thinking, non-conformist approach to truth stemmed from his conviction that each man possessed in himself the capacity to attain enlightenment. Taking Wang Yang-ming's doctrine of innate knowledge as a starting point, Li arrived at an uncompromising creed of intellectual freedom and independence. "Not a single man is born without knowledge," he said.

This creed, when applied to political life, led to startling conclusions for those accustomed to paternalism. While he was prefect at Yao-an, he wrote "Essay on Governance" (論政篇) in which he argued that, as there was more than one way for men to follow and as men's dispositions were not of one mold, it was altogether wrong to try to "enlighten" people so that they all would become alike. A meddlesome government, even with the most benevolent intentions, was detrimental to self-determination and therefore undesirable. Worse still was enforcement of conformity by means of law and punishment after persuasion had failed. Too often people suffered as much from "the benevolent" who sought to "benefit" them as from the tyrannical who frankly maltreated them, he said in a letter in reply to Keng Ting-hsiang. Indeed, "the superior man allows people to rule themselves; he dares not rule them because each man is capable of ruling himself." This being so, "all precepts, regulations, and proscriptions are unnecessary." Government existed to serve the people's interests, not to dictate to their minds.

Obviously, Li was indebted also to Buddhism for his idea of the intrinsic equality of men. "As heaven, earth, and I have the same roots, who [among men] is superior to me? And as myriad things are one with me, who is inferior to me?" (Answer to question concerning repeating the Buddha's name 念佛答問). Again, in a letter to Ma Li-shan 馬歷山 in which he discussed a passage in the Great Learning on "the enlightening virtue," he expressed the same sentiment: "Each man possesses the mirror of great perfect wisdom (大圓智鏡 [*i.e.*, the perfect all-perfecting Buddha wisdom]), which is none other than the so-called enlightening virtue. This virtue . . . is identical in countless sages and worthies. No man has more of it, as I do not have less of it."

From the concept of equality Li arrived at the notion of independence. He attached great importance to man's intellectual self-sufficiency. No person should take another, not even Confucius or any other sage, as his infallible preceptor. On the contrary, one must find his own place in the world. To suppose that one had to depend upon Confucius to attain fulfillment was tantamout to admitting that "all who were born before Confucius could not become fullfledged human beings." In fact, Confucius himself never required men to imitate him. Did he not say: "What the superior man seeks is within himself?" (Letter in reply to Keng Ting-hsiang.) Nor of course should one slavishly follow the Buddha. One should retain his freedom to choose, "sometimes to sit down and chat with the Buddha of the Western Region, and at other times to converse with the Buddhas of all the Ten Directions" without tying oneself down to any one of them (Letter to Li Wei-ch'ing 李惟清). By the same token, one should not accept any book, however time-honored, as indubitable authority. The Six Classics and the Confucian Analects contain much that does not come from the mouth of the Sage; and even those portions that are veritable records of his dicta may not be accepted without question, as they do not necessarily embody absolute or eternal truths. (On the Infant's Heart 童心説).

Li pursued this line of thought further in his work on historical judgments, the *Ts'ang-shu* 藏書, which Chiao Hung and others printed in Nanking early in the autumn of 1599. What Li undertook in this book was to pass judgment on historical figures and events by standards entirely of his own choosing, effecting a sort of transvaluation of neo-Confucian ideals. For instance, he rated the first emperor of the Ch'in as "the greatest emperor of all ages," in direct opposition to the view of traditional historians who condemned virtually everything he did. Feng Tao (882-954), widely disdained as a shameless fellow who transferred his allegiance in rapid sequence to no less than four different ruling houses and ten sovereigns, received Li's approval for having rendered good service to the people by averting wars of dynastic succession in total disregard of the neo-Confucian precept of unilateral loyalty. Confucian

ministers, glorified by traditionalists as paragons of virtue, were in Li's view perfectly useless prigs in possession of neither true wisdom nor practical ability. As for the neo-Confucian scholars, members of the Ch'eng-Chu school in particular, they were not merely incompetent but outright dishonest. Hypocrites all, they pursued selfish ends while they pontificated on "virtue, benevolence, and righteousness."

The opening remarks of the book set the keynote: "Human judgments are not fixed quantities; in passing judgments men do not hold settled views." Opinions varied among different men and with changing times and circumstances. Indeed, if Confucius had been living now, he would have thought differently from what he did two thousand years ago. This being so, each man should have the right to his own opinion irrespective of what others said, and at the same time allow the same right to other people. To force one's own judgment of what was right and wrong upon another was as culpable as to parrot the words of another without honest conviction. That, Li concluded, was his justification for evaluating history anew, even though he, like anyone else, could make no claim to finality.

On other occasions he formulated this cardinal tenet of his in slightly different terms. The individual's right to his own opinion, he pointed out, carried no warrant for dogmatism or bigotry. Firmness of conviction should not rule out intellectual receptiveness. In a conversation with his good friend Keng Ting-li in 1572 (Li was then forty-five), he came to the realization that "to regard oneself as always right" was as harmful as "to consider oneself never right." Similarly, in an undated "Essay on receptiveness and commitment" (虛實説), he observed that "when seeking truth, receptiveness is valuable; when bearing the burden of truth, commitment is precious. Through receptiveness one acquires excellence; through commitment one holds it with steadfastness."

The individual himself, then, held the key to truth and goodness. Be true to oneself or, more accurately, be oneself was thus a fundamental principle of intellectual life. Somewhat reminiscent of Mencius, Li attached great importance to obeying the dictates of "the infant's heart," a mind unburdened with arbitrary conventions and untrammeled by rigid codes. When a man was able to do what his heart desired, what his ability allowed, and what circumstances permitted, he would then be in a position to achieve his complete fulfillment. To do so was "to act in accordance with propriety" 禮. Notwithstanding what the neo-Confucians had said, propriety imposed no man-made rules upon the individual. Emanating from one's own nature, it operated "without calculation, endeavor, or study" on the part of the individual. To do otherwise—"to act on the basis of what one had seen or heard, or in imitation of what others had done in the past" —would be to act contrary to true propriety. (Essay on four avoidances 四勿說.)

This principle held good for men in every walk of life. A thinker, for instance, who encumbered his "infant's heart" with moralistic precepts foisted upon him from without, or a poet who submitted himself to stiff rules of conventional prosody, could not be expected to produce anything with a true ring. In spontaneity 自然 alone lay genuine philosophical or poetic inspiration. By the very nature of the case, spontaneity could not be consciously sought; it would be inhibited by the very act of seeking. Only when one permitted his sensibilities to flow freely of themselves would his writings be spontaneous. Incidentally, Li himself followed his own doctrine. As one of his biographers noted: "He gave his own nature free play, never forcing himself to do anything his heart did not desire."

The notion of the "infant's heart" (fraught with overtones of Ch'an Buddhism) had ethical implications. It led Li to insist that true ethicality stemmed from man's inborn nature and therefore had no contact with any external standard or authority. Ku Hsien-ch'eng (*q.v.*), who had no sympathy with the Wang Yang-ming school or with Li Chih, alleged not without reason that in Li's thinking each man was a "sage" and that socially upheld values, such as political loyalty, filial piety, chastity, and righteousness, were not spontaneous manifestations of human nature. The fact was that Li rejected the neo-Confucian view which saw man's salvation in the elimination of human desires in order to make way for "heavenly reason" and affirmed, on the contrary, the legitimacy of human desires. "Morality," he said in a letter to Teng Shih-yang 鄧石陽, "is nothing other than wearing clothing and eating food [as every man does]." So too it was not immoral to desire to accumulate wealth, to achieve social status, or to gratify the sexual impulse; these desires should not be decried and suppressed. Confucius himself had admitted that "riches and honors are what men desire," although the Sage rightly cautioned against acquiring them by improper means.

Even selfishness 私 had its place in life. "Only when a man is selfish does he reveal his mind." A peasant worked hard in his field because he wished to have the autumn harvests; a scholar studied diligently because he wished thereby to gain social advancement. Neo-Confucians who preached unselfishness really did not know what they were talking about. In propagating their forbiddingly lofty maxims they unwittingly promoted hypocrisy and in fact made hypocrites of themselves. True ethicality was a simple and unpretentious thing; goodness inhered in what was ordinary and common. "Cloth and silk, beans and rice are commonplace," Li wrote to Keng Ting-hsiang, "but how marvelously do they warm the cold and satisfy the hungry!" Those who elevated morality to superhuman sublimity (Li said in another place) actually stifled it.

As a consequence, "the teachings of ancient kings can now prevail only in remote hamlets and backwoods districts ... among illiterate men and women, but not among gentlemen who read many books and stand above ordinary people," (Biography of T'ang Kuei-mei 唐貴梅傳).

To say that man was intrinsically moral was not to suppose that all men were necessarily equal. Li recognized the fact of human inequality and traced it to unequal individual capacities. Many desired wealth, he remarked, but only people with sufficient aptitude for money-making became rich. Some were strong and others weak; the latter naturally submitted themselves to the former. Li voiced the pessimistic view that "men of the least worthy kind are the most numerous in the world" (letter to Teng Shih-yang) and that, except for a very small number of men qualified to be masters, the overwhelming majority were fit to be slaves. (Small talk under a wintry lamp 寒燈小話.) Moral inequality came from another source. When a man refused to obey the dictates of his inner nature, his "infant's heart," he forfeited his claim to goodness and thus became inferior to the common man. A moral renegade deserved to be looked upon with contempt and shunned.

This thought underlay Li's sharply discriminatory treatment of his contemporaries, warm acceptance of some and cold rejection of others. He explained his attitudes in his essay on aloofness and purity. "I am inclined to be aloof. Being aloof I am proud and find it difficult to tolerate people. But I refuse to accept those who themselves are overbearing merely on account of their wealth or power. I am ever ready to show respect to any man who has one modicum of ability or goodness, even if he is only a lackey or a slave. I like purity. Wishing to be pure I become narrow-minded and intolerant. But I cannot get along with those people who curry the favor of the mighty or flatter the rich. I am always willing to honor as my guest any man who possesses talent or moral worth, even if he is a high official or a nobleman."

Neo-Confucians of the Ch'eng-Chu school, though neither wealthy or powerful nor necessarily given to sycophancy, were despicable because of their moral and intellectual faults. Li disposed of them through ridicule or criticism. Two instances from his *Ts'ang-shu* may be cited. Ch'eng I (1033–1107) was said to have kept completely calm when his boat almost capsized, and to have accounted for his extraordinary composure by declaring, "I do maintain reverence in my mind." Li commented tartly, "Extreme nonsense." Chu Hsi (1130–1200) as is well known, took a view opposed to that of Ch'en Liang (1143–94), maintaining that no ruler since Han times had behaved worthy of the principles laid down by the ancient sage-kings. Li's comment again was "Nonsense." Neo-Confucian scholars were wont to blame "unprincipled persons" for the political disasters that so often punctuated Chinese history. Li countered this view by observing that the well-intentioned but ill-advised "superior man" could be even more damaging to a state than the proverbial "wicked minister." Confident that he was superior, the self-righteous man was likely to pursue a dangerous course with daring, stubborness, and a clear conscience. "Master Chu was like that," Li added. Lesser neo-Confucians who were simply inept did harm to the state by occupying most official posts and thereby depriving the capable and courageous of the opportunity to exercise their talents. (Reminiscences 因記往事.)

Inevitably Li antagonized and infuriated many of the scholar-officials. The situation deteriorated as his iconoclastic utterances became widely known. From about 1590 on he met with persecution almost everywhere he went. A particularly violent episode occurred in 1600 in Ma-ch'eng where some of the local neo-Confucians gathered a mob and demolished the temple in which he had lived for several years. Finally, in 1602, when he was a house guest of Ma Ching-lun 馬經綸 (T. 主一, cs 1589), a censor in T'ung-chou 通州 (near Peking), Chang Wen-ta 張問達 (T. 德允, 誠宇, d. 1625, cs 1583), a supervising censor, impeached Li in these terms: "Li Chih, who was an official in his early years, has shaved his head [and become a Buddhist monk] in his old age. Recently he has printed a number of books, including *Ts'ang-shu*, *Fen-shu*, and *Cho-wu ta-te* 大德, which, circulating throughout the country. work to mislead and confound the minds of men.... He considers the judgments of Confucius unreliable.... When he lived temporarily in Ma-ch'eng, he indulged freely in shameful conduct: disporting with worthless fellows in Buddhist temples, sharing baths with prostitutes in broad daylight, and inviting wives and daughters of respectable people to come to a temple to listen to his discourses—some of whom went so far as to bring bedding and pillows to spend the night there....A current report indicates that he has now moved to T'ung-chou, just forty *li* from the capital. If he chooses to come to the capital... what transpired in Ma-ch'eng may repeat itself here." Chang concluded his memorial by requesting the emperor to send Li back to his home district as a prisoner pending punishment and to have all his writings destroyed.

Yüan Chung-tao gave a vivid account of Li's arrest and trial. To the question why he wrote "perverse books," he replied, "The prisoner has indeed written many books which serve only to benefit the Sage's teaching and not to injure it." Without further hearing or formal charge he was kept in prison. One day he called for a barber to shave him. After having sent the latter away on some pretext, he slashed his throat with a razor. When an attendant asked him why he attempted suicide, he answered by tracing with a finger in the man's palm these words, "What does an old man of [over] sev-enty seek?" Two days later he died, and was buried north of the city of T'ung-chou.

Li apparently had anticipated his death. In a will dated March 16, 1602, he wrote, "Since spring I have often been ill. Luckily I shall die here in the hands of my good friend [Ma Ching-lun]." Then he went on to give precise instruc-tions regarding the manner of his burial which conformed neither to the Confucian nor to the Buddhist custom. In a way, he also had chosen the manner of his death. In an essay, "Five ways to die" 五死, written presumably about the same time he drew up his will, he considered heroic death for a worthy cause the most desirable; next in descending preference: to die in battle, to die as a martyr, to die as a loyal minister who had become a victim of calumny, and to die prematurely after one had accomplished his work or achieved renown. "An intelligent per-son should elect to die in any one of these five ways. One may be better than another, but each is a good way to end one's life. As for those who die in a sick bed, surrounded by wives and children—one finds them everywhere in the world .... That is hardly a way for a man to die.... As man is born for some good reason, how can he die but for some good cause? But I am already old. I am denied the opportunity to die in any one of the five preferable ways.... How then shall I die? For those who fail to under-stand me will I die—just to give vent to my resentment."

Actually, so it seems, Li died not merely out of resentment, but as a will-ing martyr for the cause of intellectual independence. He had said some time before that "scholars and officials in gen-eral hold uniform views. One look at my ideas makes them think either that I am crazy or that I should be put to death." (The dragon-fly song 蜻蛉謠.) These scholars and officials were of course none other than the people who upheld as sacred tradition the intellectual and moral values as defined by the neo-Confucianists. By following the lead of the T'ai-chou school (*see* Wang Ken), a left-wing development of Wang Yang-ming, and by going beyond it in radicalism, Li challenged that very tradition and thus committed himself to almost certain persecution.

The case did not rest with his death. Feng Ch'i (*q. v.*), a minister of Rites, for one decided to pursue it further. In a memorial he praised the emperor for having complied with Chang Wen-ta's request to punish Li Chih for his "crime of deluding the world and leading the people astray;" Feng then proceeded to affirm the importance of maintaining the indisputable authority of neo-Confucianism against men "who turn their backs on Confucius and Mencius, and flout Ch'eng I and Chu Hsi." These men, "looking upon morality as insufferable bondage and social convention as obnoxious superfluity," had been indulging freely in "indecorous words and deeds" and therefore should not go unpunished. And, convinced that Buddhism was a source of their inspiration, Feng suggested that any scholar who quoted words or phrases from Buddhist texts be duly penalized. The emperor agreed with him, pointing out that if the heretical tendencies were permitted to persist, the world would soon be devoid of "upright, loyal, and filial scholars" to render services to the state.

In addition to being a casualty in the traditionalists' "holy war" against heterodoxy, Li was possibly also an unsuspecting victim of political strife. Ma Ching-lun, his erstwhile host, put the matter thus: "As he [Li Chih] had chosen to remain apart from the men of today, he appeared to all of them as queer and aberrant .... Those who abhorred him [found it easy to] slander him, charging him with seduction and lasciviousness .... But to accuse a dying man of over seventy of such conduct is simply ridiculous. Actually, when they spoke of 'wives and daughters [of respectable people]' in Ma-ch'eng, they had in mind the widowed daughter of Mei Kuo-chen 梅國楨 (T. 克生, cs 1583, who wrote a preface to Li's *Ts'ang-shu*)... Scholar-officials of Ma-ch'eng who bore grudges against Mei used 'sexual laxity of monks and nuns' as a means to defame him and his family, intending thereby to ruin his official career. This, in sum, is the truth of the matter." (Letter to a high official 與當道書.) During the long career of Mei, who rose to the position of vice minister of War, he presumably had made enemies who would like to see his downfall. Seizing upon Li Chih's unconventional behavior, exaggerating and distorting it, they used it as their weapon against their foe. The net effect of their attack, however, turned out to be more detrimental to Li than to their object of hate. It might be noted that the widowed daughter of Mei Kuo-chen mentioned by Ma was one of Li's worshipful disciples who assumed the pseudonym Tan-jan ta-shih 澹然大士 (tranquil hearer, ta-shih being the Chinese equivalent for śrāvaka hearer or disciple of the Buddha). Li's letter to her, written probably in the autumn of 1599 before he returned to Ma-ch'eng, is preserved in the *Fen-shu*.

It is easy to exaggerate Li's iconoclasm. Despite the fact that he has been stigmatized by the defenders of tradition as a renegade from Confucianism, a destroyer of hallowed social and ethical values, he had actually done no more than call for a revolt against bigotry and deceit. He was a nonconformist without being a nihilist. A man of robust sentiments and lively intellect, he recoiled almost instinctively from the beginning from the rationalistic outlook of Chu Hsi. But it should be recalled that in his childhood and youth he had been steeped in Confucianism through uncritical study of the Classics. Contact with Taoism and Buddhism in later years enabled him to survey the Confucian teaching in a new light and in a broader perspective. These intellectual experiences did not result in his disowning the Master but gave him instead new understanding and perhaps deeper appreciation of him. Li emerged eventually as a sort of universalizing syncretist, paying homage to all the sages. "The teachings of Confucius, the Buddha, and Lao-tzu are one," he once declared. [Editors' note: One may remark that the san-chiao movement was fairly strong in his day. Li was a contemporary and fellow provincial of Lin Chao-en (*q.v.*), and may have been aware of Lin's ideas and activities even though he was independent of the movement.] Unfortunately, from Han times on the Master's doctrines had repeatedly suffered falsification. They ceased to be a guide for seekers of truth and became a passport to privilege. Many were those who "wore the garb of a Confucian scholar but acted like dogs and swine." (The three teachings converge in Confucianism 三教歸儒說.) Li, in other words, disdained neo-Confucianism but cherished the basic Confucian values. He rejected Confucian pharisaism in order to resurrect what he regarded as unadulterated Confucianism. And, in denouncing the neo-Confucians whose state-sanctioned precepts had been for centuries helping the emperors to rule the minds of men, he in effect was endeavoring to rescue Confucianism from political servitude and to reconstitute it into a personal credo. His concern with the intellectual and moral integrity of man prevented him from relegating himself to isolationist individualism, despite his uncompromising attitude toward people who violated his convictions. Thus he stood stanchly against conformity but he was not anti-social.

That he held Confucius in high esteem may be seen, for instance, from his frequent quoting of the Master's sayings to lend weight to his own and from the fact that he expressly referred to Confucianism as the Sage's teaching. Once he even put himself in the position of a defender of the faith. When he met Matteo Ricci (*q. v.*) in Nanking in 1599, he was favorably impressed by the stranger's brilliance but highly dubious of his intentions. It would be "very foolish," Li wrote, if he wished "to replace the teachings of Chou and K'ung with his own doctrine." (Letter to a friend 與友人書.) [Editors' note: An interesting by-product of the encounter between Li and Ricci is a poem the former struck off on the occasion, entitled Tseng hsi-jen Li Hsi-t'ai 贈西人利西泰 (presented to the occidental Ricci), translated into Italian by d'Elia, and preserved also in Ch'ien Ch'ien-i (ECCP), *Lieh-ch'ao shih-chi*.]

It is clear that Li did not place himself outside the pale of the Confucian "human relationships." In his letter in reply to Teng Shih-yang he expressed regret that though he had been an official for over thirty years, he had failed "to render even a tiny bit of service to the state." He found comfort in the thought that his parents had been properly interred and that his seven brothers and sisters had all married and begotten children. Having lost all of his four sons (and three of his four daughters), he alone was without male offspring. Already sixty and in uncertain health, he felt disconsolate because he would be unable to fulfill "this one great duty in a man's life." It was altogether natural, he added toward the end of the letter, for a man to desire a son upon whom he could depend for support and comfort in his declining years. There were people who, parading themselves as Confucian superior men, left their aged and dying parents to shift for themselves, while they sought the glories of officialdom. Such conduct outraged human nature as much as Confucian morality. Filial piety, Li said in another connection, was not an exclusively Confucian virtue; it also had a place in Buddhism. The Buddha himself must have been a filial son, like all other good human beings. (Postcript to Jo-wu's letter to his mother 讀若無寄母書.) Finally, commenting on a passage in the Analects, in which the Master taught that one should repay kindness with kindness, Li said that reciprocity was the foundation of human society, the very thing that sustained "the unalterable human bonds" 綱常. (Eight matters 八物.)

In the last analysis, then, in spite of Li's denunciation of outward conformity, he did not intend to destroy all Confucian values. What he demanded was that all values, intellectual as well as moral, be authenticated by each person's inward commitment.

Li's fearless crusade wrought no appreciable or lasting changes in the general intellectual atmosphere of sixteenth-seventeenth century China. By and large, scholar-officialdom remained dogmatically neo-Confucian, even after an alien dynasty displaced the native Ming. But his influence did not disappear completely after his death. His writings continued to circulate among presumably a small number of people, despite the government's proscription; twenty-three years after Li died the court still found it necessary to repeat the ban. When Ku Yen-wu (ECCP) wrote his *Jih-chih lu* decades later, he had to note, not without chagrin, that Li's writings were still circulating freely. In fact a few of his manuscripts were published posthumously by devoted friends, notably a collection of Ming biographies entitled *Hsü ts'ang-shu* 續藏書 in 1609 (a copy of which is in the Columbia University Library), and several others subsequently. What may have kept Li's name alive as much as anything else was the association of his name with certain popular pieces of fiction and drama such as the *Shui-hu chuan* (*see* Shih Nai-an) and *Hsi-hsiang chi* 西廂記.

[Editors' notes: (1) Recent reprinting of Li's works in China, including the *Ts'ang-shu*, *Hsü ts'ang-shu*, and *Hsü fen-shu* in 1959, and the *Fen-shu* in 1961, indicates a revival of interest in Li's life and philosophy that started in the 1930s. A carefully compiled bibliography of Li's works may be found in *Chung-kuo ssu-hsiang t'ung-shih* 中國思想通史 edited by Hou Wai-lu 侯外廬. Hou suggests, *inter alia*, that some of Li's ancestors may have been exposed to Islamic culture. There is no evidence, however, that Li ever remarked on that faith. (2) Joseph Needham is more categorical than Hou Wai-lu about the ancestry of Li Chih. He writes: "Li Nu 駑 who was at Ormuz in 1337, married an Arab or Persian girl and adopted Islam. Li Nu was an ancestor of the great Ming reformer Li Chih." (3) Among the books read by the Japanese patriot, Yoshida Shōin 吉田松陰 (1830–59), in the Noyama prison in June, 1859, were Li Chih's *Fen-shu* and *Hsü ts'ang-shu*. After copying the essays to his liking, the Japanese scholar often put his own comments in excellent Chinese on the margin. This was in June, shortly before he was transferred to the Edo prison where he was executed on November 21. One of the comments may be translated as follows "The way Li Cho-wu concluded his life is the full expression of greatness. Now if he, a septuagenarian, could do it in that way, why should I, just turning thirty, face it as an old weakling?" Apparently Yoshida took courage from Li's suicide to meet his own tragic end.]

Bibliography

1/221/7a; Yüan Chung-tao, *K'o-hsüeh-chai chin chi* 珂雪齋近集, 8; *T'ung-chou chih* (1879), 2 79b; P'an Tseng-hung 潘曾紘, *Li Wen-ling wai chi* 外紀, appendix to *Hsü fen-shu* (1609) P'eng Chi-ch'ing 彭際清, *Chü-shih chi* 居士集 43; Wu Yü (BDRC), *Wu Yü wen-lu*, 2; Huan Yün-mei黃雲眉,"Li Cho-wu shih-shih pien-cheng 事實辨正, *Chin-ling hsüeh-pao*, II, May, 1932 Jung Chao-tsu 容肇祖, *Li Cho-wu p'ing-chuan* 評傳, Shanghai, 1937; *id.*, *Li Chih nien-p'u* 年譜 Peking, 1957; Yeh Kuo-ch'ing 葉國慶, "Li Chi hsien-shih k'ao" 先世考, *Li shih yen-chiu* 歷史研究, 2, 1958; Wu I-feng 烏以鋒, "Li Cho-wu chu shu k'ao" 著述考, *Wen-shih yen-chiu-so chi-k'an* 文史研究所輯刊 I, June, 1932; Chu Ch'ien-chi 朱謙之: *Li Chih—shih-liu shih-chi Chung-kuo fan feng-chien ssu-hsiang ti hsien-ch'ü-che* 李贄——十六世紀中國反封建思想的先驅者 (Wu-han, 1956 2d printing 1957); Hou Wai-lu (ed.), *Chung-ku ssu-hsiang t'ung-shih*, IV: 2 (Peking, 1960 1048; Suzuki Torao鈴木虎雄, "Ri Taku-go nen pu," *Shina-gaku* 支那學, VIII(February and July

1934); (Chinese translation by Chu Wei-chih 朱維之 appears in *Fu-chien wen-hua*, III, April, 1935; this issue about Li Chih includes also articles on Li's personality, thought, and influence on Chinese literature of the 20th century); *Yoshida Shōin zen-shu* 全書, IX (Tokyo, 1935), 1; O. Franke, "Li Tschi" and "Li Tschi und Matteo Ricci," *Abhandlungen der Preussischen Akademie der Wissenschaften* nos. 10 & 11, 1937, and 1938); P. M. d'Elia, *Fonti Ricciane*, II (Rome, 1949), 66; Joseph Needham, *Science and Civilization in China*, IV:3, 495, ftn. g.

K. C. Hsiao

LI Ch'un-fang 李春芳 (T. 子實, H. 石麓), January 14, 1511–April 18, 1585, scholar-official, was a native of Hsing-hua 興化, Yangchow prefecture, who rose to be chief grand secretary during the years from 1568 to 1571. His ancestors had originally lived in Chü-jung 句容, near Nanking; so he is sometimes recorded as hailing from that district. During the year that he qualified for the *chü-jen* (1531), he fell under the influence of such important members of the school of Wang Shou-jen (*q.v.*) as Wang Ken, Chan Jo-shui, and Ou-yang Te (*qq.v.*) —an influence which was to persist throughout his life. Coming out first in the palace examination of 1547 Li was promptly made compiler in the Hanlin Academy. His rise from this point on was rapid: —vice minister of the Court of Imperial Sacrifices, vice minister successively of both Rites and Personnel until, in 1563 (April 8), he became minister of Rites, and in the following year (September 11), at the celebration of the emperor's birthday, he received the designation grand guardian of the heir apparent. On May 5, 1565, he entered the Grand Secretariat and three years later (February 12) became its head.

Li was known for his unruffled demeanour and incorruptibiliy. He had always lived frugally, and when he achieved high office in Peking he continued to live without ostentation. In his first associations with Emperor Chu Tsai-hou (*q.v.*), Li

advised him to conserve imperial finances by not rebuilding the Hsiang-feng lou 翔鳳樓 (a high building in the palace area), but the emperor paid no heed; so gradually Li stopped advising him about economies. In other respects, however, he continued to give counsel. He urged the emperor to favor, rather than punish, those courtiers who dared to speak out on matters of policy. When military men encountered official opposition in Peking to their proposal to construct watch towers along the line of defense in the northeast, Li gave them his whole hearted support at court; and they were eventually built. He also tactfully resolved the differences which cropped up between northern and southern officers guarding the frontier. Actually it appears that relations with the Mongols were one of his major concerns. He approved heartily of the policy of keeping them at bay, but opposed any invasion of Mongol territory. When the grandson of Altan-qaɣan, Dai-čing Taiji (*see* Altan-qaɣan), sought asylum in China, Li joined with Chang Chü-cheng (*q.v.*) and others in recommending that he be returned to Mongolia and a treaty of peace concluded with Altan-qaɣan.

In spite of his agreement with Chang Chü-cheng on certain issues, Li found cooperation with him difficult. Finally, after several times requesting permission to retire, the emperor gave his consent (June 9, 1571). On his death, aged seventy-four, he was honored with the title t'ai-shih 太師 (Grand Preceptor) and the posthumus name Wen-ting 文定. His townsfolk too erected a shrine in his memory, the local magistrate inscribing a stele.

Li was the author or co-author of several books. The only one of his listed in the *Ssu-k'u* catalogue is the *I-an-t'ang chi* 貽安堂集, 10 *ch.*, his memorials compiled by his second son, Li Mao-ts'un 茂村 (cj 1570), but the editors left it out of the Imperial Library; fortunately three copies are still available in Taiwan; it was published in 1589, with *fu-lu* 附錄, 1

ch. A second work, the *Ching-chung chuan* 精忠傳, 8 *ch.*, was condemned in the 1780s, the reasons given being that the author frequently failed to raise certain characters to the top of the line (out of respect for the throne?), and that he wrote critically of the Chin 金 people (ancestors of the Manchus). A copy of this work is in the Library of Congress. The local history reports also that he compiled the *Ming-chün* 明雋, 10 *ch.*, which too seems to have disappeared. He had a hand as well in the *Ch'eng-t'ien ta-chih* 承天大誌, 40 *ch.*, an official work, published 1566, dealing with the subject of the *Ta-li i* controversy: the father of Emperor Chu Hou-ts'ung (*q.v.*), his place of residence, and the honors posthumously accorded him. A rare copy exists in the Naikaku Library. Like other high officials of his day he was involved in the compilation of two other official publications: the *Shih-tsung* 世宗 *shih-lu* and a revision of the *Ta Ming hui-tien* (see Hsü P'u). He was likewise concerned with the decision (of September, 1562) to make a duplicate copy of the great *Yung-lo ta-tien* (see Hsieh Chin), and with its completion in June, 1567.

Li and his wife née Hsü 徐 had several descendants who achieved success. The above mentioned son, who became vice minister of the Court of Imperial Sacrifices, had a son named Li Ssu-ch'eng 思誠 (T. 次卿, 碧海, cs 1598) who, in 1626, served for ten months as minister of Rites. Two great-grandsons (brothers), Li Ssu-ching嗣京 (T. 嘉錫) and Li Ch'iao 喬 (T. 世臣), both achieved the *chin-shih*, the first in 1628, the second in 1619. Li Ssu-ching rose to be regional inspector of Fukien, and Li Ch'iao to be governor of Shensi. Two others (great-great-grandsons), were Li Ch'ing (ECCP) and Li Ch'ang-ch'ien 長倩 (cs 1634), who became assistant surveillance commissioner and education intendant of Kiangsi. After the Manchu army reached the Yangtze, he was transferred to Fukien. When this province too was overrun, he comitted suicide, and was posthumously made minister of Revenue.

Four other people named Li Ch'un-fang were near contemporaries. They acquired the *chin-shih* in 1502, 1521, 1550, and 1553, respectively. The best known of these is the last, Li Ch'un-fang (T. 元實, H. 鳳岡), a native of Ch'in-shui 沁水, Shansi. He became successively magistrate of Chou-chih 盩屋, Shensi, supervising secretary in the ministry of War and then in the ministry of Justice. Falling ill in 1567 he left office.

Bibliography

1/193/12b; 3/177/17b; 5/16/113a; 17/5/18b; 18/9/6a; MSL (1965), Shih-tsung, 8511, 8709, Mu-tsung, 0109, 0435, 1152, 1307, 1404; KC (1958), 4011, 4501; SK (1930), 177/18a; *Hsing-hua-hsien chih* (1852), 1/古迹 15b, 7/12a, 13a, 8/列傳 7a, 11b, 21b, 24a, 9/碑目 3a, 書目2a, 古文 10a; *Ch'in-shui-hsien chih* (1881), 6/5b, 11b, 8/24a; *Chou-chih-hsien chih* (1925), 5/7a; "Li-kung chi p'ei Hsü-shih mu-chih-ming" 李公暨配徐氏墓誌銘, in *Hsü Wen-mu kung chi* 許文穆公集, 11/14b (NCL microfilm); Ch'en Nai-ch'ien陳乃乾, *So-yin shih-ti chin-shu tsung-lu* 索引式的禁書總錄 (Shanghai, 1932), 1/49b; *Kuo-li chung-yang t'u-shu-kuan shan-pen shu-mu (tseng-ting-pen)* 國立中央圖書館善本書目 (增定本), (Taipei, 1967), III, 1078; *Title Index to Independent Chinese Works in the Library of Congress* (3d ed., Washington, D.C., 1932), II, 358; W. Franke, *Sources*, 2.7.3.

L. Carrington Goodrich and Yang Chin-yi

LI Hsien 李賢 (T. 原德, Pth. 文達), 1408–January 22, 1467, grand secretary from 1464 to 1467, was a native of Teng-chou 鄧州, Honan. One source indicates that the Li family in Teng-chou was known there during the Sung period. According to others, however, Li seems to have made a fresh start in the province, no father or grandfather being mentioned; Chu Mu-chieh (*see* Chu Su), in his collection of biographies of eminent people from Honan, proudly lists him at the top of one of its chapters. When twenty-four years of age (1432), Li passed the provincial examination and in the following year achieved the *chin-shih*. His first assignment took him to Shansi where he had to investigate a locust-stricken district. Here he made the acquaintance of Censor Hsüeh Hsüan (*q. v.*), later known as the head of the orthodox Ho-tung 河東 school, whom he followed for a while almost as a pupil. In 1436 he entered the capital bureaucracy as a secretary in the bureau of honors of the ministry of Personnel. In this post he found a niche in which he was to earn a good reputation, as many of the able men who served during his time and later were his selections.

Li Hsien started his career in a conventional way by memorializing the throne. He once argued that the Mongols in Peking, numbering about ten thousand, constituted a real danger; those receiving stipends were better paid than Chinese officials and made up a third of the city population (which in the 1430s must have numbered about thirty thousand individuals as heads of households), and that they would surely cause mischief and should be removed to the countryside. He held too that a decaying National University in the capital of China was a shame, when at the same time Buddhist monasteries flourished. Further, he opposed as impractical the handling of the promotion system. Through his memorials he tried to show his ability as a bureaucrat who was both nationalist and orthodox. In 1445 he rose to be a director, first in the bureau of evaluations, and then in the bureau of appointments of his ministry. In August, 1449, in place of his superior who pleaded illness, Li was obliged to march with the army to the north. He records then in a revealing note the feeling of hopelessness that swept over himself and a few intimates: "As the imperial expedition is to pass through Mt. Chi-ming 鷄鳴山 (near Hsüan-fu) on the morrow (August 13), everyone is becoming frightened and in despair. Overwhelmed by my emotions I approached several censors, expressing the opinion that the emperor is now in deep trouble, the army is losing its morale, and everyone is blaming Wang Chen (*q.v.*). If we might hire a brave warrior (武士) to seize Wang

and smash his skull right in front of the imperial entourage, his crime of usurping power and injuring the country would be exposed. Then the generals could go to Ta-tung, and heaven's will might be recovered. We tried to consult the duke of Ying-kuo, Chang Fu (*q.v.*), but failed to reach him, and the plot collapsed." Following the battle of T'u-mu, "on the fringe of death" he returned home.

His career took a favorable turn after that: in 1451, as junior vice minister first in the ministry of War, thus serving directly under the redoubtable Yü Ch'ien (*q.v.*); next in 1452, in the ministry of Revenue; and then in 1454 again in the ministry of Personnel. In the meantime he had been commissioned to investigate the officials' sincerity in the provincial administration of Szechwan. In 1457 the resumption of power of Chu Ch'i-chen (*q.v.*) did him no harm; on the contrary, he entered the Grand Secretariat as a Hanlin chancellor, being second only to Hsü Yu-chen (*q.v.*), a leader in the restoration clique. Li Hsien was now forty-nine years of age.

It is at this point that his life was to become of interest to historians. They noted his political adroitness during one of the most troubled periods of Ming rule. Though he had profited from both the T'u-mu and the restoration incidents, he never became a partisan of one of the related power groups. While his elder colleague, Hsü Yu-chen, had to leave the political scene in 1457, and the dominating figures, General Shih Heng and the eunuch Ts'ao Chi-hsiang (*qq. v.*), fell one after the other in 1460 and 1461, he survived and became the senior official in the later years of the T'ien-shun period (1457–64) because he knew how to combine caution with principle. He made himself a name because of the strong stand he took twice in favor of relief measures at the expense of the imperial treasury when the provinces suffered, 1457 in Shantung and 1462 in the Yangtze area. And he became famous for his daring move to have more than four thousand officials and officers who had won rank or promotion in assisting the restoration of Chu Ch'i-chen, downgraded, or at least their titles of special merit withdrawn. He convinced the emperor that legitimacy had been on his side, and that it had not been necessary to "seize the gate," and make this a meritorious act; such would only be a disservice to a legitimate cause in the future. He again took this stand after the enthronement of Chu Chien-shen (*q. v.*) when those demoted asked for their rehabilitation. Li Hsien is said to have suggested clearing Yü Ch'ien's name instead.

Li had been thrown into prison once in 1458 and had been wounded during the mutiny in 1461 of Ts'ao Ch'in (nephew of Ts'ao Chi-hsiang). This mutiny is of somewhat obscure origin. Some say that the arbitrary actions of the Embroidered-uniform Guard provoked it; others maintain that Ts'ao Chi-hsiang once more tried to win power and influence. When this last move of the dissolving faction of the eunuch miscarried, Li Hsien was instrumental in devising a novel plan for free discussion in the policy-making sphere at the capital and of moderation in the provinces. He developed a new selection system: the responsible ministries (Personnel and War) should propose two candidates for each vacancy so that the emperor might make a choice, and the Grand Secretariat should act on mutual agreement with the two ministries. This system was regarded as an advance over the mere sponsorship that Yang Shih-ch'i (*q.v.*) had practiced thirty-five years earlier. It worked well under the amicable cooperation between Li Hsien in the Grand Secretariat on one hand and Minister of Personnel Wang Ao 鏊 (*q.v.*) and Ma Ang (*see* Chu Chien-shen) on the other. In 1464, after the accession of Chu Chien-shen, Li Hsien at last became grand secretary in name though he had been this in fact for several years. He died early in 1467 in his residence and received all the honors due his rank and stature.

Apart from many memorials, he left a few prose writings: a concise and meticulous account of a visit to the Imperial Gardens, *Tz'u yu hsi-yüan chi* 賜遊西苑記, 1 *ch.*, some unrevealing notes of his personal views on various events in the T'ien-shun period, *T'ien-shun jih-lu* 日錄, 1 *ch.*, and some thoughts and recollections with a slight tinge of Zeitkritik, *Ku-jang tsa-lu* 古穰雜錄, 1 *ch.* [Editors' note: According to the editors of the *Ssu-k'u* catalogue, this work is in 3 *chüan*; the *Ming-shih i-wen-chih, pu-pien, fu-pien* list it variously as 2 and 3 *chüan;* but only the one *chüan* edition has survived. In addition Li wrote the *Ku-jang chi* 集, 30 *ch.*, which was copied into the Imperial Library. The *Ssu-k'u chen-pen*, series 2, has recently reproduced it.] A collection of model biographies apparently in the orthodox manner, *Chien-ku lu* 鑑古錄, 22 *ch.*, seems not to be extant. Because of his exalted position his name heads the list of the editors of the *Ying-tsung shih-lu*, 361 *ch.*, completed 1467, and the *Ta Ming i-t'ung-chih*, 90 *ch.* (Geography of the empire), completed 1461.

Most sources agree in calling Li Hsien a true man of state because he helped to restore power to the throne. But this was a dubious achievement. In the very last years of his life new troubles arose when the imperial agents of the Embroidered-uniform Guard started to usurp the emperor's power, and rebels in the Honan-Hukuang border region defied it. He was particularly criticized for failing to observe the full mourning period of twenty-seven months on the death of a parent. It happened that when his father died in April, 1466, the emperor permitted him leave to return home only for the burial, and sent eunuchs to see to it that he came back immediately. On his resumption of office in June, the optimus of that year, Lo Lun (*q.v.*), memorialized on this transgression of propriety. Lo was punished by demotion but earned fame for being a dauntless memorialist and defender of moral conduct, while Li was cited as the one who set an evil example (especially during a similar case one hundred twelve years later; *see* Chang Chü-cheng). In view of the fact that Li resumed his office only half a year before his death, it seems hardly worth mentioning this blemish on his reputation.

[Editors' note: The *Ming-shih* records, besides the above-mentioned, four other individuals of the same name; only one of them, however, lived at the same time, viz.,

Li Hsien II (1346–1425), earl of Chung-ch'in 忠勤伯, was a Tatar originally named Ch'ou-lü 丑驢. In the Mongol court he held the rank of minister of Works: he defected to the Ming at Nanking in 1388, was given the Chinese name, and sent to serve in the princely establishment of Chu Ti (*q.v.*). In the latter's reign he was charged with the translation of documents from or into Mongol, and rose in military rank to that of earl (non-hereditary).

Li Hsien III (d. 1451, Pth. 忠憲), second marquis of Feng-ch'eng 豐城侯, inherited that fief in 1423, and served as grand defender of Nanking in the years 1441–51.

Li Hsien IV, *fl.* 1524, was the adopted son of a eunuch, and

Li Hsien V, *fl.* 1622, was a native chieftain in Kweichow, who took part in a rebellion.]

Bibliography

1/106/23a, 154/17a, 156/3b, 176/1a, 192/11b, 249/24a; 3/159/1a; 5/13/45a; 8/24/1a; 33/8/1a; 61/125/2493; 63/11/1a; MSL (1963), Ying-tsung, 4514, 5840, 5873, 5972, 5997, 6808, Hsien-tsung (1964), 0509, 0515, 0590, 0736; KC (1958), 2165; SK (1930), 53/1a, 68/3b, 127/3b, 170/8b; Cheng Hsiao, *Wu-hsüeh pien*, 36/1a; Li Hsien, *Ku-jang tsa-lu* (in Shen Chieh-fu, *Chi-lu hui-pien*, 1937 ed.), 23/8a; Ch'en Tzu-lung (ECCP), *Ming ching-shih wen-pien* (Hong Kong ed.), 277; Henry Serruys, "Were the Ming Against the Mongols Settling in North China?" OE, 6 (1959), 148; W. Franke, *Sources*, 1.1.5, 2.5.6, 4.5.3, 8.1.2.

Tilemann Grimm

LI Hua-lung 李化龍 (T. 于田, H. 霖寰), April 11, 1554–January 17, 1612, military strategist and conqueror of the Po-chou 播州 native chieftainship, was born into a landed family of Ch'ang-yüan 長垣 at the southern tip of Pei-Chihli. His grandfather died in 1536, leaving a young widow, née Chang 張 (*ca.* 1510- *ca.* 1585), a son Li Tung 棟 (T. 良材, 1532–1600), and a daughter. It happened to be a year of failing crops and the family was harassed by tax collectors, causing a neighbor to remark that the Li family seemed to be on the downgrade. The widow rose to the occasion, tided over the disaster, and restored the family fortune. Having suffered at the hands of some minor bureaucrats, she saw that the way to revenge, or at least to be freed from the abuse of the tax collectors, was to have a male member of the Li family become an official. Her son did not seem to be of such caliber, but her two grandsons were promising. She was determined to have them properly educated to compete in civil examinations. She also married her daughter to a student in the government school who later became a *chü-jen*. Undoubtedly Li Hua-lung owed his early start in officialdom to this ambitious and determined grandmother.

Precocious and studious, he proved to be even more than all she could have hoped for. He first came under the notice of the prefect of Ta-ming 大名, Wang Shu-kao 王叔杲 (T. 陽德, H. 暘谷, 1517–1600, cs 1562), who enrolled him as a student in the local academy where he met other youths of promise, including Wei Yün-chen (*see* Ku Hsien-ch'eng). Li Hua-lung was the first among his fellow students to pass the *chin-shih* examination (1574), and at only twenty years of age was appointed magistrate of the Sung 嵩 district in Honan, where he served with merit for six years. It is said that when he arrived at his office, the local yamen clerks at first slighted him as one too young and inexperienced for such a responsible post, but he quickly managed to establish discipline. His grandmother accompanied him to Sung-hsien, thus having the satisfaction of seeing her dreams realized.

In 1580 Li Hua-lung was promoted to be a secretary in the Nanking ministry of Works. He held this rank for two years, during which time he served one term as supervisor of customs at Wu-hu, chiefly in charge of the collection of lumber as tax from merchants transporting it from Szechwan and Hukuang. Then he served four years (1582–86) in Nanking as a bureau director in the ministry of Personnel, a position with light duties. He made use of the leisure to store up knowledge about the workings of the government and occasionally to join some friends on excursions to scenic places. He then acted as director of education in Honan (1586–90) and Shantung (1590–92), administration vice commissioner of Honan (1592), vice minister of the Court of the Imperial Stud (1593–94), and commissioner of the Office of Transmission (1594).

In July of the same year he was promoted to the important post of governor of Liaotung where he served for three years. It was the time of the war against the Japanese in Korea when Liaotung became the base for supplies and reinforcements. Li arrived at his headquarters at Kuang-ning 廣寧 just after the region had suffered a raid by the Mongols. To secure the route of supply for the front in Korea, the Mongols had to be subdued. Anticipating another raid, Li and the regional commander Tung I-yüan (*see* Ch'en Lin), appointed 1593, prepared the battleground, drew the enemy in, and dealt them a crushing defeat at the fort, Chen-wu-pao 鎮武堡. For his part in this victory Li was rewarded (1595?) with the title of a vice minister of War and the hereditary rank of a chiliarch in the Embroidered-uniform Guard. Meanwhile the peace negotiations with the Japanese in Korea were in progress. Li reported in 1596 on their failure at Pusan and made

prepartions for the eventual resumption of warfare. Something then happened, forcing him to put in a request for leave pleading illness. He was finally permitted to quit his post in May, 1597. It seems that at this time the emperor, Chu I-chün (*q.v.*), had begun to send to the provinces eunuchs chosen by himself to exact silver and precious objects from the people. When the provincial authorities protested the unreasonable interference by these eunuchs and were ignored by the emperor, several governors and supreme commanders tried to force the emperor's hand by tendering their resignations. Their concerted action failed to impress the stubborn emperor and resulted in their being censored.

In April, 1599, Li was recalled from retirement to serve as supreme commander of the three provinces: Szechwan, Hukuang, and Kweichow, and concurrently governor of Szechwan. This post was created to meet the emergency of the open rebellion of Yang Ying-lung (*q.v.*), chief of the Miao tribesmen of Po-chou. The Po-chou hereditary chieftainship, commanding an area about the size of Switzerland, had been practically an independent kingdom ruled by the Yang family since the last years of the ninth century. In the middle of the 13th century the Mongol court conferred on its chief the rank of first class hereditary chieftain (Hsüan-wei shih 宣慰使). The Ming government, which continued the Yüan system of native chieftainship, confirmed the status of the Yang house of Po-chou in 1372. Two centuries later, in 1571, Yang Ying-lung succeeded to the chieftainship as the eleventh holder of that rank in the Ming dynasty. He proved to be a military leader, but was unpopular among the subordinate chiefs because he tried to assert his traditional tribal authority. In 1590 they accused him of treasonous acts for which he was convicted two years later at his trial in Chungking. Just then the war in Korea broke out and, on his promise to send five thousand troops and contribute twenty thousand taels of silver, he was released from prison by imperial order. Once he had returned to Po-chou, however, he broke his promise and made some impossible demands as excuses for not sending the men or money. Early in 1594 (mistaken as 1593 in *Ming-shih*, 312/8b) he dealt the Szechwan army a crushing defeat which gained for him almost six years of practically independent rule, during which he raided many border towns and villages. In 1599 his challenge of the imperial authority was finally accepted.

It was under such circumstances that Li Hua-lung became supreme commander and began to mobilize the resources of the three provinces: Kweichow under its governor, Kuo Tzu-chang (*q.v.*), Hukuang under Chih K'o-ta (*see* Ch'en Feng), and Szechwan under his own control. Li went to Chungking late in 1599, armed with the shang-fang-chien 上方劍 (imperial sword symbolizing supreme military authority), to direct the campaign and to supervise the logistical preparations. Early in 1600 he reported the arrival of reinforcements from Yunnan, Kwangsi, Shensi, Honan, Chekiang, Shantung, and Tientsin, mostly in small contingents under the assumption that, as he later commented, just the appearance of these troops from so many areas would dampen the spirit of the enemy and cause some of them to surrender. He divided his army into eight routes, four from Szechwan, all advancing southward, and four from points in Kweichow, two of which were to advance northward and two westward. They were to converge on Yang's headquarters. Each route consisted of around thirty thousand men, two thirds of whom were from native chieftainships in the five southern provinces. Many troops were veterans of the war in Korea; there were even some Japanese who had surrendered or been captured and assigned to the garrison in Tientsin.

The government troops began their advance in the middle of March, 1600. After three months of bitter fighting, they had encircled Yang's capital area. It took almost another month to capture his mountain stronghold Hai-lung-t'un 海龍囤, which fell on July 15. Yang Ying-lung committed suicide. His entire family were delivered to Peking where they were executed in January, 1601. Thus ended a kingdom which had endured for eight hundred years. Li Hua-lung commemorated the victory by melting the captured weapons in order to cast a memorial column, which he erected on the grounds of Yang's former palace, and some fifty tripods which he gave to the native chiefs of that area. The inscription on each tripod cited Yang's fate as a warning.

The success of this campaign was chiefly due to Li's leadership. His ability to inspire the generals until they gave their utmost in battle, his tactfulness in soliciting help from provincial authorities all over the empire, and his devotion to detail may be deduced from reading the collected documents of the campaign, entitled *P'ing Po ch'üan-shu* 平播全書, 15 *ch.*, printed about 1887 in the *Chi-fu ts'ung-shu* 畿輔叢書. The book was not copied into the *Ssu-k'u* library but the editors of the catalogue described Li's defeat of Yang Ying-lung as one of the few really successful wars of the Ming period. Yet it took almost four years before the announcemnt of the evaluation of merits and rewards. In November, 1604, Li was grudgingly given the titles of a minister of War and a junior guardian and the hereditary rank of a commander of the Embroidered-uniform Guard. Even the emperor questioned the rewards as not commensurate with his accomplishments, but Grand Secretary Shen I-kuan (*q.v.*) replied with the argument that the suppression of an internal rebellion was less meritorious than frontier warfare, and so ranks of nobility were denied Li and his generals. Apparently Shen was influenced by his partisan outlook on Li Hua-lung, who was a friend of Tsou Yüan-piao, Li San-ts'ai, and Chao Nan-hsing (*qq.v.*), and whom Shen obviously considered as belonging to the opposition (*see* Kuo Cheng-yü). Li, moreover, was known to have refused gifts of value from any of his subordinates and had even reported two generals who had secretly sent such gifts to his home in Ch'ang-yüan; hence it may be assumed that he did not have any dealings with men in power at the capital where just at this time corrupt practices were rampant. There must have been some attempts to discredit him by a close examination of his accounts, but apparently nothing censorable came to light. In fact his completely successful campaign cost only one and a half million taels, and from all the funds appropriated for this purpose he reported a surplus of about a million taels, part of which he requested should be used for the establishment of the new prefectures and other offices, including the building of city walls and the resettlement of the people. His undeniable integrity thus forced those who disliked him to resort to belittling his success, terming it an internal rebellion only.

Li Hua-lung seems to have been quite satisfied with just finishing a job entrusted to him. In 1601, shortly before the capture of Yang's headquarters, Li received the notice of his father's death. By imperial order he remained at his post to attend to the aftermath of the conquest. The Po-chou chieftainship was abolished. Out of its territory were created two prefectures, Tsun-i 遵義 as part of Szechwan (until 1726) and P'ing-yüeh 平越 in Kweichow. Also established was the guard Wei-yüan-wei 威遠衛. These tasks occupied him for almost a year before he was permitted to return home to observe the period of mourning.

In June, 1603, Li was recalled to service as vice minister of Works in charge of the conservancy of the Yellow River and Grand Canal. His notable contribution in this office was the opening of the Chia-ho 泇河 section of the Grand Canal. It happened that the Yellow River between Huai-an 淮安 and Hsü-chou 徐州 had served as part of the Ming canal

system since the early years of the 15th century (*see* Ch'en Hsüan, 1365–1433), but its rapids near Hsü-chou caused frequent shipwrecks resulting in the loss of life and grain; and the upstream pulling of the fully laden transports by human labor added to the burdens of the people. Li made a careful survey which convinced him of the advantages of the Chia-ho project advocated by several of his predecessors but never realized. Early in 1604 he obtained imperial permission to construct this new canal from Hsia-chen 夏鎮 on the Shantung border to reach the Yellow River at Tung-kou 董溝 near Su-ch'ien 宿遷. This new channel enabled the grain transports to by-pass the Hsü-chou rapids, and shortened the distance for the men conscripted to haul the boats upstream. It was apparently the first real improvement of the Grand Canal in two centuries. It took another quarter of a century, until the 1680s, before the Chia-ho channel was extended all the way south to Ch'ing-chiang 清江, making it possible to avoid traveling on the Yellow River completely except at the point of crossing.

Late in 1604 Li again retired, this time to observe the mourning period for his mother. While he was awaiting the arrival of his successor, the above mentioned belated rewards for the conquest of Po-chou were pronounced in Peking. The timing may be important, for it seems to indicate that Li, now in mourning, was not supposed to have any thought as to the appropriateness of a reward. It is not known whether Li ever voiced an opinion on the matter. In any case he was recalled in the middle of 1607 and, late in 1608 he succeeded Hsiao Ta-heng (*q. v.*) as minister of War. He died in office early in 1612 and was given posthumously the title of junior preceptor (later grand preceptor), the name Hsiang-i 襄毅, and, in addition to the two hereditary ranks in the Embroidered-uniform Guard, a third son was granted the rank of drafter in the central drafting office.

Li is known to have left several collections of poems, a work on military regulations and another on river conservancy, but all except the *P'ing Po ch'üan-shu* seem to have been lost.

According to Shen Te-fu (*q. v.*), Li was tall and stout ("eight feet tall and fifty inches at the waist"). Shen praised him as serene and attentive, quick-witted and meticulous, and above all a true scholar. In 1609, when Li was minister of War and worried about the rising power of the Jurchen, Shen suggested to him a plan to convert the military region of Liaotung to civilian provincial administration, which Li at once accepted as feasible but had to abandon on account of opposing views. Apparently the objection came from the eunuchs who profited from their control of the military on the frontier. As early as June, 1608, Li had memorialized on the dangers in Liaotung as a result of the exactions by the senior eunuch, Kao Huai (*see* Ch'ien I) who had impoverished the entire region, military and civilian, and had forced many to escape to live under the Jurchen tribesmen. Unforunately the emperor was the one who directed Kao Huai to collect silver regardless of the consequences. Li's memorial was ignored.

Bibliography

1/87/4a, 228/8b, 312/1a; 3/212/15a; 8/75/1a; 40/52/16a; 61/135/10b; MSL (1966), Shen-tsung, 4910, 5426, 5431, 5438, 5520, 5648, 7509, 7518, 7527, 9222; KC (1958), 4933, 5040; Chao Nan-hsing, *Chao Chung-i kung wen-chi*, 11/6b, 12b; NCL *Ming Index*, 193; *Huang Ming wen-hai* (microfilm), 5/8/14, 9/1; TSCC (1885–88), XI: 586/6b; *Ta-ming-fu chih* (1854), 19/101a, 21/78a, hsü 2/40b; Shen Te-fu, *Wan-li yeh-hu-pien*, 450, 561; Tung Ch'i-ch'ang (ECCP), *Shen-miao liu-chung tsou-shu hui-yao*, 兵 1/4b; Ku Ying-t'ai (ECCP), *Ming-ch'ao chi-shih pen-mo*, ch. 64; Chu Kuo-chen (ECCP), *Huang Ming ta-shih-chi*, ch. 42; Ch'en Tzu-lung (ECCP), *Ming ching-shih wen-pien*, 4547, 4584, 4592, 4720, 4729, 5275.

Chaoying Fang

LI Jih-hua 李日華 (T. 君實, H. 九疑, 竹懶居士), April 13, 1565-1635, official, artist,

and art critic, was a native of Chia-hsing 嘉興, Chekiang. He came from a peasant background, his great-grandfather being the first one in the family to rise from a yamen clerk to a lower rank official; he held a minor post, probably late in the fifteenth century, on distant Hainan Island. According to Li Jih-hua, his grandfather may have suffered from dipsomania and lost most of his property, forcing—after his death about 1539—his only son, then eight years old, to live with an aunt who had married into a Chou 周 family. Thus Li Jih-hua's father was brought up as a ward of the Chou, but after years of hard work he succeeded in developing half an acre of inherited land into a modest estate and besides became owner of farmland and of rentable properties in the business section of Chia-hsing. His prime ambition was to have his son educated for the competitive civil examinations, and in this he was not disappointed. Li Jih-hua became a *chü-jen* in 1591 and *chin-shih* a year later. Thus the family was accepted into the local gentry by men like Hsiang Yüan-pien (*q.v.*), and by a Li clan that claimed descent from the T'ang imperial house.

Li Jih-hua's first appointment was as prefectural judge at Kiukiang, Kiangsi, a post he held for six years (1592-98), during which he served once as acting prefect and at another time as acting magistrate of the nearby district, Jui-ch'ang 瑞昌. He felt happy and useful, for the people seemed to like him. His literary talents pleased those of his superiors who asked him to draft ceremonial essays in elegant styles. Once he composed the formal letter from the provincial administration to the ministry of Works on a shipment of porcelain from the imperial factory at Ching-te-chen 景德鎮, eighty miles to the southeast of Kiukuang. In 1597, when he was in the provincial capital, Nanchang, apparently on official business, he met the Jesuit missionary, Matteo Ricci (*q.v.*); he expressed his admiration in a poem which Pasquale M. d'Elia has rendered into Italian, and in prose which Lin Yutang has abridged and put into English. Li never saw the missionary again but mentions him twice in his diary (1609, 1614) and later(about 1623) opined that someone should utilize Ricci's maps to write a geography of the world.

Early in 1598 Li went to Ching-te-chen to supervise the selection and packaging of porcelain to be shipped to Peking. While there he learned that he had been denounced by a superior. Among the charges was one which he cited as a compliment, that he had paid more attention to Ch'an Buddhist thinking than to his official duties. According to his own account, the people of Kiukiang thought well of him and protested these charges, but he calmed them and returned home to await the results of the investigation. He was cleared of most of the charges, but was demoted one grade. In 1600 he went to Peking to apply at the ministry of Personnel for his new appointment, which was that of assistant sub-prefect of Ju-chou 汝州 in central Honan. A year later he received promotion to magistrate of Hsi-hua 西華, some seventy miles south of Kaifeng. Here he served a full term of three years and, being in line for promotion, he was given (1604) the temporary assignment in flood control work on a section of the Yellow River, a task he executed with credit. At this point his mother died and he went home.

When the mourning period was over late in 1606, he requested additional leave so as to take care of his aging father. The leave granted, he stayed home for almost two decades, during which he made the most of the leisurely life of a wealthy member of the gentry who happened also to be an artist and a collector. The court notified him (1616) of his appointment as a secretary in the Nanking ministry of Rites, but he requested an extension of his leave, pleading that his father, then eighy-five years of age, needed his attention more than ever. His father died in 1617. After the mourning period he suf-

fered from poor health for several years. In 1623, on a general order to select from local archives all pertinent documents to be submitted to the commission compiling the *Shen-tsung shih-lu*, the prefect of Chia-hsing made Li the chief edijor for that prefecture. Partly for this contribution Li was recalled to service in July, 1624, as a secretary in the ministry of Rites in Peking. Late in that year, while still at home, he was transferred to the Seal Office as an assistant to the director, a position he assumed in Peking in May, 1625. He left an account of his travels of this year under the title *Hsi-chao lu* 璽召錄. This was the time when the eunuch Wei Chung-hsien (ECCP) was dominating the scene. Later Li held that, in seeking a way to absent himself from the capital, he managed to obtain an order to represent the court at the funeral of the tenth duke of Ch'ien-kuo (for the first duke, Mu Sheng, *see* Mu Ying) by the name of Mu Ch'ang-tso (*see* Chou Chia-mu). The duke died in Yunnan, but his burial was to be near Nanking where the state was erecting his tomb. Li was thus permitted to stay at his home for over a year to await the funeral, which finally took place in May, 1627. After that Li returned to Peking, arriving in June. Three months later the new emperor, Chu Yu-chien (ECCP) ascended the throne and Wei Chung-hsien lost his power. Li hoped that he might serve under the new regime, and to that end submitted early in 1628 a memorial containing such sound advice as 1) the annual compilation, by each office, of the new regulations concerning it, and 2) the submission of local gazetteers to the central government. The memorial received some comments and then was ignored.

In August, 1628, Li was stricken by an illness which partially paralyzed him. Again he asked for retirement in a memorial relating that he had once stayed home for over a decade in order to be with his father. He received a warm reply from the emperor, refusing his request but granting him leave for recovery. In the rescript the emperor praised him for his filial piety, using the words, hsiao-ssu t'ien-chih 孝思恬致 (preferring retirement for filial reasons). Li considered it such an honor that he chose "t'ien-chih" for the name of the main hall at his Chia-hsing home. Meanwhile he was promoted to vice minister of the Court of the Imperial Stud, but he knew that at seventy-four he could not expect a speedy recovery. In October he managed to be assigned the mission of delivering some silver to the frontier guards north of Peking, after which he went south to his home by the government postal service. (To be sent on a non-essential mission was a common practice of the day for many officials in order to obtain a passport that could be used after the mission for a homeward journey.)

Back at home Li enjoyed the company of his son and three grandsons, who helped him in editing his works for publication. In 1635, on the first day of the seventh moon (August 13), he composed a prayer for his health to the Taoist deity, Mao-chün 茅君. This seems to be his last known writing before his death. Although he several times denounced the alchemists and sexualists in Taoist garb and pitied those of his acquaintances who had lost their money or even their lives by listening to these people, he was obviously a believer in the magic power of the Taoist deities. In 1610 he had paid a visit to the Pai-yüeh T'ai-su-kung 白嶽太素宮, the Taoist center in Hsiu-ning 休寧 (Anhwei), built by imperial decree in 1557. He left an account of this trip, entitled Li 禮 Pai-yüeh chi. Sometimes he would lead his whole family to pray at a Taoist shrine. On the other hand he also enjoyed the refreshing repartee in the company of Ch'an monks and attended frequently the Confucian lecture meetings at the local academy, Jen-wen shu-yüan 仁文書院. This seems to have been the pattern of spiritual life of late Ming gentry, enjoying fully the mundane pleasures of the wealthy and influential while feeling assured of immortality through their belief in Taoist preachings.

Primarily an artist, Li considered highly his own achievement in calligraphy and painting, especially bamboos done in ink, but critics agree with Ch'ien Ch'ien-i (ECCP) in ranking him in these respects lower than Tung Ch'i-ch'ang (ECCP). Li also was confident in his judgment as a connoisseur of objets d'art. In this respect Ch'ien considered him inferior to Wang Wei-chien (see K'o Wei-ch'i). This seems rather petty, for Li had not only seen the vast accumulations of the Hsiang family, but also had a collection of his own. In his diary he regularly records the arrival of some dealers bringing him scrolls, ink slabs, or porcelain to evaluate or to sell. He probably kept a diary all his life but only entries for the years 1609 to 1616 have survived. These were printed in 1919 in the Chia-yeh-t'ang 嘉業堂 ts'ung-shu under the title, Wei-shui-hsüan jih-chi 味水軒日記, 8 ch. Proud of his taste for tea, he was also particular about the water in which to steep it; hence the name Wei-shui-hsüan or Water-tasting pavilion. He ranked highest the quality of the water drawn from the spring on Hui-shan 惠山, Wu-hsi, west of Soochow, and had it regularly shipped to him, a distance of over sixty miles, in sealed jars. Once he issued a prospectus "Sung-yü-chai yün-ch'üan yüeh" 松雨齋運泉約 soliciting subscriptions to a monthly shipment of this water at tael 0.06 of silver per jar.

His Wei-shui-hsüan jih-chi is an important document on the everyday life of a Ming official in retirement. In one entry in 1610 he records that in 1598, before he left Ching-te-chen, he paid a craftsman, Hao Shih-chiu 昊十九, three taels of silver for a set of cups with colors of Li's own choosing and then forgot about it, and that twelve years later he received a letter from Hao saying that the set of fifty cups had been entrusted to assistant sub-prefect Shen of Hangchow (see Shen Pang) to be delivered. Li records that obviously Shen, in character, had kept them for himself.

About 1614 he published a collection of inscriptions on his own paintings, entitled *Chu-lan hua-sheng* 竹嬾畫賸, which, with its sequel, *Hsü* 續 *hua-sheng* (*ca.* 1625), has become a minor classic of its kind. It has been supplemented by Chou Liang-kung (ECCP) and others. Some three years later he brought out his first collection of miscellaneous notes, *Tzu-t'ao-hsüan tsa-ch'o* 紫桃軒雜綴, 3 *ch.* Its continuation *Yu* 又 -*ch'o*, 3 *ch.*, was published about 1623. In 1626 he issued a third collection, *Liu-yen-chai pi-chi* 六研齋筆記, 4 *ch.*, and later two sequels, *Liu-yen-chai er-pi* 二筆 and *san* 三 *pi*, in 1630 and 1635 respectively. These notes were apparently edited chiefly from his diary. His criticism of others' paintings of bamboos and other subjects, entitled *Chu-lan mo-chün t'i-yü* 墨君題語, was probably edited after he died by a disciple, Chiang Yüan-tso 江元祚 (T. 邦玉). A similar collection written by his son, Li Chao-heng 李肇亨 (T. 會嘉, H. 珂雪, fl. 1600-62), entitled *Tsui-ou* 醉鷗 *mo-chün t'i-yü*, was edited by Hsiang Sheng-mo (*q.v.*). Two years after Li Jih-hua's death his collected poems and prose were printed under the title *T'ien-chih-t'ang chi*, 堂集, 40 *ch.* There seems to be only one printed copy, formerly in the National Library of Peiping, now in Taipei, which is available on microfilm. It is obviously the same one sold by Sun Tien-ch'i. There is also a manuscript copy in the Naikaku Bunko, Tokyo. The rarity of this work is entirely due to its being listed among the prohibited books of the eighteenth century. Excerpts from it have been printed under individual titles, such as the *Wo-pien chih* 倭變志, 1 *ch.*, mentioned in the *Ming-shih*, which is part of *chüan* 39 of this work.

In 1768 a Chia-hsing scholar published Li's notes, travels, and art criticism in a collection, *Li Chu-lan shuo-pu ch'üan-shu* 說部全書, a copy of which is in the Library of Congress. About two decades later, the editors of the *Ssu-k'u* catalogue critically reviewed eleven of Li's works, only one of which was copied into the Imperial Library, namely, the *Liu-yen-chai pi-chi*.

There is a lithographic edition of this work reproduced about 1910 from a copy of the 1634 edition. The reproduction includes the marginal notes of a late nineteenth-century scholar, who, like the *Ssu-k'u* editors, considered Li passable as an artist and writer but not completely reliable in his factual data. Yet he enjoyed in his lifetime a reputation of being widely informed and referred to as erudite (*po-wu chün-tzu* 博物君子). In 1630 there appeared in Hangchow a collection of popular reference works attributed to him as editor. The collection, *Ssu-liu ch'üan-shu* 四六全書, contains five items naming him as the compiler, viz: *Hsing-shih p'u-tsuan* 姓氏譜纂, 7 *ch.*, a sort of biographical dictionary; *Kuan-chih pei-k'ao* 官制備考, 2 *ch.*, a government handbook stressing the proper way to address people; *shih-wu tien-hui* 時物典彙, 2 *ch.*, on miscellaneous matters; *Yü-t'u chai-yao* 輿圖摘要, 15 *ch.*, a geography of the empire; and *Ssu-liu lei-pien* 類編, 16 *ch.*, a classified anthology of samples of writings in the parallel style used chiefly in letter writing. The collection is evidently the work of a book dealer. In *Hsüeh-hai lei-pien*, the eighteenth-century collection attributed to Ts'ao Jung (ECCP), there is a work of remarks on poetry, *T'ien-chih-t'ang shih-hua* 詩話, 4 *ch.*, culled from Li's various publications. Also included in the *Hsüeh-hai lei-pien* is a short work by Li's son, Li Chao-heng, entitled *Fu-nü shuang-ming chi* 婦女雙名記. The latter is known to have left several collections of poems, one being the *Hsieh-shan-lou chin-kao* 寫山樓近稿, after the name of his studio. It is said that he eventually became a monk, taking the name Ch'ang-ying 常螢 and residing at the Ch'ao-kuo monastery 超果寺 in Sung-chiang 松江, southwest of Shanghai. V. Contag and C. C. Wang cite several of his paintings. One of his three sons, Li Hsin-chih 新枝 (T. 森玉), became a *chü-jen* in 1642. Three years later invading troops looted Chia-hsing and left much of it in ruins. The Hsieh-shan-lou, however, still remained standing in the early

18th century, according to Chu I-tsun (ECCP),

Bibliography

1/288/14b; 40/57/6a; 43/5/1b; 64/ 庚 7/3a; 65/4/8b; 84/ 丁下 /59a; 86/16/16a; KC (1958), 5442; Chou Liang-kung, *Tu-hua lu*, 1/1a; *Chia-hsing-fu chih* (1878), 45/67a, 50/45a; *Ch'en-chou-fu chih* 陳州府志 (1747), 13/25a; *Chiu-chiang-fu chih* (1874), 25/24b, 27/37a; *Chekiang t'ung-chih* (1934), 3116; SK(1930), 60/6a, 64/5a, 80/4a, 114/4b, 122/7a, 128/4b, 138/4a, 197/8b; Sun Tien-ch'i (1957), 58; *Li Jih-hua shan-shui* 山水, *Shang-wu ming-jen shu-hua* 商務名人書畫, no. 5 (Shanghai, 1921); Huang Yü-chi, *Ch'ien-ch'ing-t'ang shu-mu* (1916), 15/2a; Sheng Feng 盛楓, *Chia-ho hsien-cheng-lu* 嘉禾獻徵錄, 18/10a; P. M. d'Elia, *Fonti Ricciane*, II(Rome, 1949), 69, n. 1; Lin Yutang, *Translations from the Chinese* (1963), 287; L. of C., *Catalogue of Rare books*, 293, 403, 737, 1138; V. Contag and C. C. Wang, *Seals of Chinese Painters and Collectors* (Hong Kong, 1966), 545, 552; P. Pelliot, "Bibliographie," TP, 21 (1922), 348; Percival David, *Transactions of the Oriental Ceramic Soc.* (1936–37), 49; A. W. Hummel, *Annual Report of the Librarian of Congress*, for the fiscal year ended June 30, 1940 (Washington, 1941), 173; R. H. Van Gulik, MN, III (1940), 344; O. Sirén, *Chinese Painting, Leading Masters and Principles*, V (New York, 1958), 40, 65, VII, 206; E. J. Laing, *Chinese Paintings in Chinese Publications, 1956–68* (Ann Arbor, 1969), 175.

Chaoying Fang

LI Ju-sung 李如松 (T. 子茂, H. 仰城), December 29, 1549-May 17, 1598, military officer, a native of T'ieh-ling 鐵嶺, Liaotung, was the eldest son of Li Ch'eng-liang (ECCP), a regional commander of Liaotung for years, who in 1579 was made an earl with the designation Ning-yüan-po 寧遠伯. It is said that his ancestor in the sixth generation, Li Ying-ni 膺尼, was a Korean who moved to T'ieh-ling in the early years of the Ming from a town on the south bank of the Yalu River. After his son, Li Ying 英 (early 15th cent.), the recognized founder of the clan, had been made a hereditary secretary of the garrison at T'ieh-ling, his descendant in the direct line succeeded him. Li Ch'eng-liang,

the first prominent general of the family, distinguished himself by blocking repeated invasions of the Mongols and the Manchus in Liaotung. As a consequence several members of his family benefited, rising to high rank in the Ming army.

Li Ju-sung started his military career by inheriting the post of his father, and was ordered to serve in the honorary office of an earl, with the designation of Ning-yüan. After several promotions, due partly to his father's exploits but also to his own, he was appointed regional commander of Shansi in 1583. (According to a Ming source, he participated with his father [1582] in an encounter in which a number of Chien-chou 建州 chiefs, including the father and grandfather of Nurhaci [ECCP], were killed. Information on his role in the encounter is unclear, however.) As his father then held the post of a regional commander, a supervising secretary of the office of scrutiny attacked the appointment on the ground that both father and son should not concurrently be charged with important military posts in the frontier zone. Li Ju-sung was then transferred to the capital and for a time served as general commissioner of the metropolitan police. In 1587 he was appointed a regional commander of Hsüan-fu. In spite of repeated accusations lodged by supervising secretaries of the office of scrutiny against him and his brother, Li Ju-po (ECCP, p. 451), then a regional commander, for their licentiousness, the emperor, Chu I-chün (*q.v.*), cleared them. A regional censor also criticized Li Ju-sung for his arrogance; this resulted in the loss of his salary, possibly also in his transfer from Hsüan-fu to Shansi. Here too the censors charged him repeatedly with mismanagement of military affairs, and he was forced to resign from the frontier post.

In 1592, however, Li was again appointed regional commander to suppress the rebellion of Pübei (Po-pai哱拜), commander of the prefecture of Ning-hsia who had deserted to the Mongols. His success in this engagement firmly established his reputation. The course of the rebellion ran as follows: in March Liu Tung-yang 劉東暘 and Hsü Chao 許朝, a Chinese officer under Chang Wei-chung 張維忠, regional commander of Ning-hsia, rose in revolt, killing the governor, Tang Hsin 黨馨 (cs 1568), and a surveillance vice commissioner, Shih Chi-fang 石繼芳 (T. 克宵, cj 1555), because of their maladministration of military affairs. The rebellion became a formidable one when Pübei, who had been opposed to Tang Hsin, participated with Liu and Hsü together with his son, Hsü Ch'eng-en 許承恩, a regional vice commander, and T'u Wen-hsiu 土文秀, a guard commander. Pübei was a Mongol who had served under the Ming and later rose to high military rank as a reward for his frequent military exploits. T'u Wen-hsiu, too, was a son of a Mongol who held Ming rank. The rebels put their army in order, establishing Pübei as leader, Liu as regional commander, Hsü and his son as senior and junior regional commanders, T'u and Po-yün 哱雲, an adopted son of Pübei, as senior and junior local commanders. The rebels, taking Ning-hsia as their base, attacked its adjacent areas. After aligning themselves with a Mongol chief, J̌oriɤtu tayiji 着力兔 (probably Auba-joriɤtu-nayan 鄂巴卓哩克圖諾延), the rebels became so powerful that all of Shensi was in an uproar. J̌oriɤtu and his son(?) Dayičing tayiji 打正台吉 engaged in diversionary attacks, preventing the government troops under the supreme commander Wei Hsüeh-tseng 魏學曾 (T. 惟貫, cs 1553) from making any headway. In May Li Ju-sung, recommended strongly by Mei Kuo-chen (see Li Chih), a circuit censor of Chekiang, was appointed in spite of strong opposition a regional commander and concurrent superintendent of armies in Shensi to take charge of reinforcements recruited from Liaotung, Hsüan-fu, Tatung, and Shensi. He was the first general to become a superintendent. Learning in July that the rebels were awaiting reinforcements from the Ordos Mongols, the Chinese army, consisting of five divisions commanded by Yeh Meng-hsiung 葉夢熊 (cs 1561), a censor in Kansu, besieged Ning-hsia to frustrate any attempts on the part of the Mongols to join the rebels. But this proved fruitless as the rebels stood the siege even after the arrival at the end of the month of reinforcements brought up by Li. The government troops. now strengthened, made several assaults against Ning-hsia but failed to dislodge the defenders. Finally they decided to flood the city, constructing a long (ca. 11 1/2 miles) bank around its walls for this purpose. Pübei in dismay once more asked the Ordos Mongols for reinforcements. Consequently, Bušuɤtu 卜失兔 (or Bušuɤtu tayiji 博碩克圖, 1565–1624, became jinong in 1576), a chief of the Ordos Mongols, and Dayičing tayiji approached Ning-hsia with forty thousand cavalry to distract the Ming forces from the besieged fortress, but the Ming troops put them to rout. In September they suffered serious food shortages, and the city walls collapsed little by little. Around the end of the month J̌oriɤtu, with an army of ten thousand, crossed a river to rescue the besieged, and proceeded to Fort Chang-liang 張亮堡 where a battle took place. Li Ju-sung in the vanguard with a thousand men, aided by a large number of reinforcements under the command of Li Ju-chang 樟, one of his younger brothers, and Ma Kuei 麻貴 (a native of Tatung), was victorious. On October 7, when a contingent of the Chekiang army arrived to help Li, the Chinese forces set out to the attack using boats and rafts. Five days later they feinted against a northern barrier of the walls which had been flooded, while Li and Hsiao Ju-hsün 蕭如薰 (T. 季馨, a native of Yen-an 延安) successfully stormed the southern barrier. In the meantime dissension broke out among the besieged, the causes of which may be attributed partly to the supporters of the Chinese and partly to the prolonged siege. The rebel leaders, Hsü, Liu, and T'u all met their end because of the dissension. Learning that it had seriously weakened the morale of the rebels, Li and a Colonel Yang Wen 楊文 were the first to swarm over the northern barrier. The whole city now fell to the imperial army and the surviving rebel leaders, Hsü Ch'eng-en and Pübei, were either captured and executed or committed suicide. After the suppression of the rebellion which had lasted six months, Li was elevated to be a chief military commissioner and awarded the hereditary rank of a vice commander in the Embroidered-uniform Guard. Li was accused of arrogance, however, in declining to submit to the control of the supreme commander. In order to ease the impact of the accusation submitted by a supervising secretary and the minister of War, the emperor himself ordered him to obey the commands of his superior.

In May, 1592, while the fighting was still under way, the Japanese invaded Korea with the intention of conquering China. A division of their army led by Konishi Yukinaga (q.v.) took Seoul, the capital city of Korea, on June 13, and Pyongyang on June 24, meeting no serious resistance. Another division led by Katō Kiyomasa (see Konishi) reached Hoi-nyŏng 會寧 of Hamkyongdo 咸鏡道, and captured two Korean princes (September 2). Escaping from Seoul, the Korean king, Yi Yŏn (see Yi Hon), took refuge in Oiju 義州, the northernmost city of the Korean peninsula on the south bank of the Yalu River, and asked for Chinese reinforcements in order to recover his lost territory. The court at Peking was then made aware of the imminent crisis that might endanger the empire, and sent Tsu Ch'eng-hsün 祖承訓, a lieutenant colonel, in command of three thousand men. They attacked Pyongyang only to suffer disastrous defeat (August 23). Shocked by this reversal, the Peking court decided to send larger forces to repel the Japanese invaders. On September 23, Sung Ying-ch'ang 宋應昌 (T. 思文, H. 桐岡, October 17, 1530-March 18, 1606, cs 1565),

was given over-all command, with the rank of vice minister of War and supreme administrator of military affairs to guard the seacoast and to resist the Japanese in the areas of Chi 薊, Liaotung, Shantung, and Paoting. The commander of the expeditionary forces was assigned to Li with the title of regional commander of the armies to defend the seacoast and repel the Japanese. Thus Li was to play an important role in the second conflict of the three major wars in the Wan-li era. His army had three divisions, the right, the center, and the left, led by two regional vice commanders, Chang Shih-chüeh 張世爵 and Yang Yüan 楊元, and one regional commander, Li Ju-po. Another of Li Ju-sung's younger brothers, Li Ju-mei 梅, and a cousin Li Ju-wu 梧, were among his subordinates. The Chinese troops were said to total one hundred thousand men, but in reality they numbered perhaps thirty-six thousand, including mounted men from the north (Liaotung), artillerymen from Chekiang and foot soldiers. Several months later Liu T'ing (q.v.) participated in the expedition with his five thousand soldiers from Fukien, western Szechwan, and the southwest.

On January 27, 1593, Li's force, which the Koreans called the celestial army, arrived at Oiju where King Yi Yŏn awaited them. Five days later they encamped at Soonan 順安 to prepare for the attack. Before the expedition crossed over to Korea, and after Tsu Ch'eng-hsün had been repulsed at Pyongyang, Shen Wei-ching (see Konishi), who apparently could speak Japanese, had conducted conversations with Konishi about a possible truce. Shen demanded complete withdrawal of the invaders, while Konishi asked that China become a vassal and agree to tributary status; he also demanded session of Korea south of the Daetong 大同 River. Denouncing Shen's peace-making efforts, Sung and Li succeeded shortly in throwing the Japanese off their guard by reporting that Shen was ready to reopen conversations. On February 6 the Chinese,

aided by Korean soldiers led by Yi Il 李
鎰, a Korean general, besieged Pyongyang from all sides, encircling it with foreign cannon of various kinds. On the
following morning the general attack
began, The firearms and fire-arrows of
the Chinese, which surpassed the Japanese
muskets and cannon, proved effective in
destroying the stone walls and huge
wooden gates of Pyongyang. Li personally
urged on his soldiers, disregarding his
own safety though his horse was shot.
Lo Shang-chih 駱尚志, Wu Wei-chung 吳惟
忠, and other southern officers were the
first to penetrate the walled city of Pyongyang, while northern soldiers followed
hard after. It took only a few hours to
win the battle and liberate the city. Retreating to the earthen fortifications which
they had built around Yŏnkwang pavilion
練光亭, the Japanese continued to resist
fiercely. Consequently, Li, apprehensive
that a desperate resistance might bring
about much heavier losses, urged Konishi
to retreat with his security assured.
Thereupon the Japanese marched south to
Seoul, crossing the frozen Daetong River.

The loss of life on the Japanese side
during the fighting is given in Sung
Ying-ch'ang's report as sixteen thousand
forty-seven men. He also reported that
ten thousand men were burned to death
in addition to numerous men taken captive, estimating that hardly a tenth of the
Japanese soldiers who had been stationed
in Pyongyang (the *Ming-shih* asserts that
one hundred thousand men were in the
city) made their escape, exclusive of
one thousand men who were killed on
the way south by a detachment of the
Korean army. It is pointless, however, to
evaluate the Pyongyang victory by counting the number of enemy dead. The
victory meant a check on further Japanese
advances. There are good reasons also to
question the losses reported. Both Chinese
and Korean sources reveal outrageous
actions on the part of the Ming soldiery
who killed Korean civilians as well as
Japanese to exaggerate their exploits.

Actually Yang T'ing-lan 楊廷蘭 (cs 1586),
a supervising secretary in the office of
scrutiny in charge of personnel, accused
Li of exaggeration. A special investigator
was sent to Korea but no action was
taken as it was not pressed by the Korean
government, which, in spite of its out-
rage, had no wish to come into conflict
with Li.

The Pyongyang victory resulted in
the liberation of five provinces. Disturbed
by the defeat, Katō in Hamkyongdo retreated to Seoul, where Konishi's men had
already arrived. Kaesŏng 開城 was recovered by Li Ju-po soon afterwards on February 19. Even the detachments stationed
in Kyŏngsangdo 慶尙道, not to mention the
one in Seoul, prepared to withdraw after
reports of the Pyongyang defeat.

The key factor in the fighting in the
Pyongyang campaign has been attributed
to the firearms of the Ming troops,
namely, several kinds of "foreign cannon."
These cannon shot explosive shells,
it is reported, to a distance of five or
six *li*; the Japanese had nothing to compare with them. On February 27, after the
fall of Kaesŏng, Li Ju-sung, intoxicated
by his success, and accompanied by only
three hundred men, marched forward in
defiance of Sung's repeated warnings, to
Byŏkjegwan 碧蹄館 thirty *li* north of Seoul.
Belittling the enemy and misled by his
intelligence, Li ordered a vanguard of
three thousand men led by Cha Ta-shou
查大受 and a Korean general, Ko Ŏnbaek
高彦伯, to proceed in advance. Thus the
main body of the Chinese army was left
far behind. The vanguard met a Japanese
detachmeut of six or seven thousand men
at Byŏkjegwan and defeated it easily.
But shortly after this encounter, the vanguard was set upon by a large number
of Japanese led by Kobayakawa Takagage
小早川隆景 who vigorously opposed the
plan to evacuate Seoul. Apprised of the
situation in which the vanguard found
itself, Li dashed to its rescue and fought
at close quarters. If it had not been for
Li Yu-sheng's 李有昇 sacrifice of his own

life to protect the general, Li Ju-sung
would surely have been killed by Inoue
Gorobee 井上五郎兵衞, one of Kobayakawa's officers, who closed in on him.
Soon the main force commanded by
Yang Yüan arrived at the battlefield in
time to save the detachment from anni-
hilation. According to a Ming source, the
Chinese troops suffered a loss of only
three hundred lives in the hand-to-hand
fighting. But another Ming source and
some Japanese authorities tell of far
larger casualties on the Chinese side.
Upset by his defeat, Li returned to Pyongyang with Yang Yüan, letting Li Ju-po
encamp at Bosan 寶山, Cha Ta-shou on
the banks of the Imjin River 臨津江, and
Tsu Ch'eng-hsün at Kaesŏng. As Li and
his northern soldiers had no more will to
fight, the front became stagnant. The
Japanese army too was in no mood to
continue. The peace negotiations resumed
as a consequence. The Japanese first asked
the Ming troops to reopen the talks.
The serious deterioration of their strength
forced them to do so. A small unit of
chosen combatants led by Cha Ta-shou
stole into Yongsan 龍山, adjacent to Seoul,
and successfully destroyed the food accumulated there. The Japanese therefore
had hardly sufficient to feed their soldiers for a month; moreover, an epidemic
threatened. It was reported that the Japanese army then stationed in Seoul was
smaller by one third than when it first
set foot in Korea. The Korean army,
weak at the beginning but now stronger,
attacked at every place the Japanese
were encamped. They cooperated closely
with the militia in keeping the Japanese
from raising any crops locally. The
Korean navy commanded by Admiral Yi
Sun-sin (*see* Ch'en Lin) was so successful
in attacks against the Japanese fleets that
they had great difficulty in crossing the
Strait.

At the same time, the Chinese expeditionary forces also had difficulties which
made them accede to the Japanese proposals to resume negotiations. Li in despair,

following his defeat at Byŏckjegwan,
requested retirement for himself and withdrawal of his armies. In this Shih Hsing
石星 (T. 拱辰, H. 東泉, 1538-99, cs 1565),
minister of War from 1591 to 1597, supported him. The reasons for Li's desire
to withdraw included insufficient food for
his men, difficulty of his horsemen in
proceeding over Korea's wet lands in
the summer season, an epidemic which
proved fatal to many, and dissension
among the officers which weakened morale.
The top leaders, Li and Sung, who differed with each other from the beginning
because of Li's arrogance, became more
and more at odds; Sung, who opposed
withdrawal of the armies, wished to prepare both for negotiation and for fighting,
while Li advocated complete withdrawal
looking only towards negotiation. Among
the subordinate officers, too, there was
discord especially between the northerners
and southerners.

On July 28, in obedience to orders
from the Ming court, both Li and Sung
returned to Peking, together with the
bulk of the Chinese army. Several months
elapsed, however, before Li received any
reward for his service. Many at the capital denounced him for his appeasement
policy; but in October he was awarded
the title of senior guardian of the heir
apparent and the grant of an increase
in stipend. In Korea, the royal government
placed his portrait in a shrine erected at
Pyongyang in his honor. Until 1597 Li
lived in relative obscurity; then, in the
face of considerable opposition, he received the appointment of regional commander of Liaotung (his father's old post).
In May of the following year the Tumed
Mongols under Chao-hua 炤花 (probably
Suqaγ-joriγtu qung-bâtor 早禮克圖洪巴圖
魯, great-grandson of Dayan-qaγan), invaded the northern part of Liaotung.
Succeeding in destroying a detachment
of the enemy, Li led his soldiers in a
night attack, fell into an ambush, and
was slain together with a large number
of his men. On imperial command he was

canonized as Chung-lieh忠烈, and given
the honorary title of junior guardian of
the heir apparent and the honorary rank
of earl, with the designation Ning-yüan. A
shrine too was erected in his memory. He
was buried at Ch'ang-hsing-tien 常興店
(?) north of Liaoning.

To his brother, Li Ju-mei, went the
post at Liaotung; to his eldest son, Li
Shih-chung 世忠, the office of commander
in the Embroidered-uniform Guard, in
addition to the title of earl of Ning-yüan;
and to his second son, Li Hsien-chung 顯
忠, the hereditary title of commander of
the guard. His wife, née Yang楊, receives
a notice in the biographies of women of
the local history of Shu-lu 束鹿, her native
district in the prefecture of Paoting, as
she lived to the advanced age of ninety
sui.

Bibliography

1/238/10b; 3/220/8b; Shen Kuo-yüan沈國元(end
of Ming), *Huang Ming ts'ung-hsin lu* 皇明從信錄,
ch. 36, 37; Sung Ying-ch'ang, *Ching-lüeh fu-kuo
yao-pien* 經略復國要編; Ku Ying-t'ai (ECCP),
Ming-ch'ao chi-shih pen-mo (San-min shu-chü
ed.), 671; Wang Tsai-chin (ECCP), *San-ch'ao
Liao-shih shih-lu*; *Hui-chou-fu chih* 惠州府志
(1881), 32/24b; Li Kuang-t'ao 李光濤, "Ch'ao-
hsien jen-ch'en Wo-huo yü Li Ju-sung chih
tung-cheng"朝鮮壬辰倭禍與李如松之東征,CYYY,
22 (1950), 267; *Chosŏn wangjo sillok*, *Sŏnjo*朝鮮
王朝實錄, 宣祖, *kwŏn* 26-46; *Chōsen shi*, 4 hen/
9/kan/617; Yu Sŏngyong 柳成龍, *Chungpi lok*
懲毖錄, *kwŏn* 16 (in *Soaechip* 西厓集);Shin Ryŏng
申靈, *Chaijopŏnchi* 再造藩邦志, *kwŏn* 6 (in *Taitong
yasŏng*大東野乘, Vols. 7, 8; Sonoda Ikki 園田一龜,
"Li Sei-ryō to sono ichizoku" 李成梁と其の一族
に就て,TG, 26 (1937), 89; Ikeuchi Hiroshi 池內
宏, *Bunroku keicho no eki, shōhen* 文祿慶長の役
(1935); Suzuki Ryōichi 鈴木良一, *Toyotomi
Hideyoshi* (in *Iwanami shinsho* 岩波新書, 1950),
157.

Min Dugi

LI K'ai-hsien 李開先 (T. 伯華,H. 中麓, 中
麓山人, 中麓放客), September 28, 1502-
March 13, 1568, scholar, dramatist, poet,
and bibliophile, was a native of Chang-
ch'iu 章丘, Shantung. His father, Li Shun

李淳 (T. 景淸, H. 綠原, 1471-1520), passed
the provincial examination in 1510. Li
K'ai-hsien himself became successively a
chü-jen in 1528, a *chin-shih* in 1529, and a
secretary in the ministry of Revenue. In
1531 he was sent to the Ning-hsia 寧夏
garrison to deliver rations to soldiers and
to check their morale. On his way he met
by accident a famous man of letters,
K'ang Hai (*q.v.*), in Shensi. On his return
trip he visited K'ang and another man of
letters, Wang Chiu-ssu (*q. v.*), both living
in retirement in Shensi. Subsequently Li
spent more than twenty days with K'ang
and other scholars in Sian. Shortly after
he reached Honan, he fell ill and returned
home where he convalesced for over a
year.

In 1532 he resumed government service as secretary in the ministry of Revenue and in 1533 was sent to Hsü-chou
徐州 on the Grand Canal as inspector of
the granaries. Later he was transferred to
the ministry of Personnel. While serving
there he was called upon to evaluate
government officials. After several promotions, he became (1540) vice minister in
the Court of Imperial Sacrifices in Peking
in charge of the College of Translators.
This must have been an irksome responsibility, for he complained (on October 11
1540) that "many officials and students
are absent for months at a time, fail to
prepare their work, miss examinations,
and skip daily classes. Discipline should be
restored." Because of the fire in the Imperial Ancestral Temple on April 25, 1541,
all officials of higher rank were required
to submit memorials blaming themselves,
and to offer their resignations. Only twelve
were retired, Li among them. He spent
the remainder of his days in Chang-ch'iu
where, as owner of about one hundred
fifty acres of land, he led the life of a
country gentleman. He built a private
library named Ts'ang-shu wan-chüan lou
藏書萬卷樓, a school called the Chung-lu
Academy 中麓書院, and a group of buildings. He owned an extensive collection of
books, especially in the field of drama, for

which he came to be known as shih-shan ch'ü-hai 詩山曲海.

Throughout his retirement, Li devoted himself to writing, especially in the field of drama and folk songs. He probably printed most of what he wrote. The collection, *Li K'ai-hsien chi* 集, three volumes, published in Peking in 1959, seems to contain all that are extant.

Both in literature and in art Li advocates originality, individuality, and truthfulness. He denounces blind imitation of famous masters of arts. His work, whether in prose or in verse, is natural and straightforward. The *Hsien-chü chi* 閑居集, 12 *ch.*, is a collection of his miscellaneous writings which he wrote during his retirement years. Hsien-chü means leisurely living, suggesting indifference to gain and loss, and freedom from the burdens and pressures of official life. *Hua p'in* 畫品, 1 *ch.*, is a criticism of contemporary artists. In evaluating these artists, Li characteristically esteems those who show spontaneity and individuality in their paintings, and rebukes those who exhibit only ostentation and artificiality. Among the dramas he wrote or rewrote, *Pao-chien chi* 寶劍記, *Ta-ya-ch'an* 打啞禪, *Yüan-lin wu-meng* 園林午夢, and *P'i-chiang ts'an-ch'an* 皮匠參禪 are the best known. *Pao-chien chi* is an adaptation of an episode in the *Shui-hu chuan* (*see* Lo Kuan-chung). The hero Lin Ch'ung (*see* Ch'en Yü-chiao) is wrongfully accused of murder by a powerful commander called Kao Ch'iu 高俅, and of entering a forbidden hall without authority. Kao Ch'iu, who is infuriated by Lin's repeated charges against him, endeavors to put Lin to death. After appalling sufferings and hair-raising vicissitudes, Lin escapes and joins the brigands on Liang-shan-p'o 梁山泊, in Shantung. In the end, Lin is able to take revenge against Kao. Harold Acton has translated a portion of this into English. *Ta-ya-ch'an* and *Yüan-lin wu-meng* are two of the six short plays grouped under the collective title *I-hsiao san* 一笑散 printed in 1560. *Ta-ya-ch'an* is a religious satire. By unmasking the follies

and absurdities of two Buddhist monks and a butcher, the author skillfully attacks the corruption and degradation of certain Buddhist monks. In his opinion they are the ones who have done most harm to Buddhism. All except *P'i-chiang ts'an-chan*, which does not seem to be extant, are included in the *Li K'ai-hsien chi*. A play entitled *Tuan-fa chi* 斷髮記, of which only one act has survived, is attributed to him. Li also edited a collection of Yüan dramas entitled *Kai-ting yüan-hsien ch'uan-ch'i* 改定元賢傳奇 of which no copy is preserved. His own ballads entitled *Shih-ching yen-tz'u* 市井艷詞, *Yen-hsia hsiao-kao* 煙霞小稿, and *Pang-chuang-t'ai hsiao-ling* 傍粧臺小令, which do not seem to be preserved either, are believed to have made considerable contribution to the development of folk songs of his day. In addition, he wrote jointly with his friend Wang Chiu-ssu a book on southern ch'ü (lyrics) entitled *Nan-ch'ü tz'u-yün* 南曲次韻 which may be found in *Yin-hung-i so-k'o -ch'ü* 飲虹簃所刻曲 printed in 1936.

Besides the above mentioned works, Li also compiled *Ching-i tai-chih* 經義待質 and *Shuang-hsiu chieh-yao chi* 雙修揭要集. The former in 4 *chüan* is a study of the Classics, and the latter in 6 *chüan* is a selection of writings from religious Taoism. Both seem to have disappeared.

Li was a good player of hsiang-ch'i 象棋, or Chinese chess. He boasted of having won from such experts as Ts'ao Ch'i 曹起 and Chang I 張翼. As an amateur physiognomist, he was gifted in foretelling a man's fate from his general appearance. It is said that he made hardly any mistake in this art.

There are at least two other men named Li K'ai-hsien in the Ming period. Both lived in the early 17th century. One was from Feng-yang 鳳陽 and was a descendant of Li Pin (*see* Le Lo'i) and inherited his title, marquis of Feng-ch'eng. He was killed when Feng-yang was seized by the rebels at the end of the Ch'ung-chen reign. The other Li (T. 石麓, cj 1624), a native of Chiang-ling 江陵, Hukuang, committed suicide in 1643 when summoned by the rebel leader, Li Tzu-ch'eng (ECCP).

Bibliography

1/287/10a; 3/268/7b; 5/70/33a; 22/8/6a; 40/41/4b; 84/丁上/10b; 86/12/11b; *Shantung Chang-ch'iu-hsien chih* (1833), 9/38; "Lin Ch'ung Yeh Pên," tr. by Harold Acton in THM, IX, no. 2 (September, 1939), 180; Li K'ai-hsien, *Li K'ai-hsien chi* (Peking, 1959); Norman Wild, "Materials for the Study of the Ssŭ I Kuan," BSOAS, XI (1943–46), 640.

Lee Hwa-chou

LI Kuang 李廣, died October 28, 1498, date and place of birth unknown, was a eunuch who promoted Taoist arts at the court of Emperor Chu Yu-t'ang (*q.v.*) and, by so doing, won the empror's favor. When Li was at the peak of his power, imperial relatives and prince consorts had to treat him as their father, governors and regional commanders had to honor him as duke of the court. In September, 1495, Yüan Hsiang 袁相, a young man from a well-to-do family, bribed Li handsomely in the hope of being selected senior consort of an imperial princess. The bribe was soon discovered, and Li severely castigated by supervising secretaries and investigating censors. The emperor, however, decreed that Li be not punished as there was no concrete evidence to prove any wrong-doing. In the later part of his reign, the emperor began to indulge in Taoist practices. Li was always the one who saw to the emperor obtaining whatever he desired. In his maneuverings Li had the support of Empress Hsiao-k'ang (*see* Chu Yu-t'ang). Li, together with his supporters and fellow eunuchs, was able to monopolize the salt trade, to confiscate private lands, and to build a grand mansion for his own use. In 1497 the supervising secretary Yeh Shen 葉紳, (T. 廷縉, cs 1487) and simultaneously the censor, Chang Chin 張縉, (T. 廷肅, H. 良

菴, 1444-1512, cs 1481) accused Li of eight major crimes. The emperor, however, turned a deaf ear. Many a time the emperor would condescendingly pay Li a visit, which led Li to have more opportunities to intervene in imperial affairs. In 1498 Li induced the emperor to erect the Yü-hsiu pavilion 毓秀亭 on Mount Wan-sui 萬歲山 (present-day Ching shan 景山, Prospect Hill, in the Forbidden City, Peking). When the building was completed, an infant princess breathed her last (October 1). Soon afterwards (October 26), a fire occurred in Ch'ing-ning kung 清寧宮 (Pure and tranquil palace). Officials at the court then interpreted these calamities as due to the untimely erection of the pavilion. The empress-mother, after experiencing one misfortune after another, indicated that they were because of Li Kuang. He became so frightened that he committed suicide.

His death did not end the crisis in the court. The chief supervising secretary in the office of scrutiny for Justice, Chang Ch'ao-yung 張朝用 (cs 1484), and the investigating censor, Ch'iu T'ien-yu, 丘天祐, (T. 恆吉, cs 1481), reported in their memorials that Li Kuang had left thousands of taels of gold and a list of names of senior ministers who had collaborated with him; both suggested that all those linked with Li should either be punished or reprimanded. The emperor again refused to take action, for there were too many senior ministers involved and he maintained that their accusations were based only on hearsay. Memorials from other censors disclosed that Li Kuang had accepted bribes up to thousands of piculs of yellow and white rice from senior ministers. The emperor gave this too no credence until he was told that yellow rice meant gold, and white rice meant silver. He then became angry and decided to take action against the ministers involved. After the emperor had had a private audience with the marquis of Shou-ning, Chang Ho-ling (*q.v.*), he decided to take no further notice of Li Kuang's case.

Bibliography

1/304/19b; 3/283/19a; 20/31/29b; 42/25/16b; 61/158/27a; MSL (1964), Hsiao-tsung, 1891, 2218, 2320, 2449, 2456, 2462, 2476, 2486, 2491, 2527; Ting I 丁易, *Ming-tai t'e-wu cheng-chih* 明代特務政治, Peking, 1950; P'eng Sun-i (ECCP), *Ming-ch'ao chi-shih pen-mo pu-pien*, in *Han-fen lou pi-chi*, 5/12b; Chiu Ling-yeong 趙令揚, "Lun Ming-tai chih huan-huo" 論明代之宦禍, *United Journal* (Hong Kong, 1964), 3: 1; Chien Po-tsan 翦伯贊, "Lun Ming-tai yen-huan chi yen-tang cheng-chih" 閹宦及閹黨政治, in *Chung-kuo shih lun-chi*, 中國史論集 (Shanghai, May, 1947), Vol. 1.

Chiu Ling-yeong

LI Liu-fang 李流芳 (T. 茂宰, 長蘅, H. 香海, 泡庵, 慎娛居士, etc.), 1575-1629, painter, calligrapher, and poet, came from a family located in She 歙 -hsien (Anhwei), but is generally considered a native of Chia-ting 嘉定, northwest of Shanghai. After qualifying for the *chü-jen* in 1606 (along with Ch'ien Ch'ien-i, ECCP), he went to Peking to try for the higher degree, but was passed over. On a second attempt he failed to reach the capital on time because of travel conditions; so in 1622, at a time when Wei Chung-hsien (ECCP) was making life difficult for all officials not subservient to his will, he abandoned the effort to become a bureaucrat, and devoted himself to artistic and literary activity. He made a home for himself and his mother at Nan-hsiang 南翔, near Chia-ting, and laid out a garden known as T'an-yüan 檀園 (Sandalwood Gardens). Here he wrote and painted and entertained his friends. He loved to travel to scenic places, especially to the West Lake in Hangchow, where he often conversed with Buddhist monks in the temples and boatmen on the lake. His collected work is entitled *T'an-yüan chi* 集, 12 *ch.*; it includes poems (said to number 360), written after ancient and modern styles, 6 *ch.*; miscellaneous essays, 4 *ch.*, and colophons copied from scrolls of paintings, 2 *ch.* It was printed in 1629, and reprinted 1689. Though partially condemned in the 18th century for its inclusion of his biography and tomb inscription, both by Ch'ien Ch'ien-i, it still survives. "These passages extracted," wrote the critic, "the balance of the book may be saved." So it came to be copied into the Imperial Library, and received favorable treatment by the editors of the *Ssu-k'u* Catalogue. Both the National Library of Peiping and the Naikaku Bunko possess original editions. Another short contribution of his, which may be found in his *T'an-yüan chi* as well as in several collectanea, such as the *Mei-shu* 美術 *ts'ung-shu*, is the *Hsi-hu wo-yu t'u t'i-pa* 西湖臥遊圖題跋 (colophons on the paintings of one who delights in touring the West Lake through the medium of paintings), 1 *ch.* When Hsieh San-pin 謝三賓 (T. 象三, H. 賓山, cs 1625) was serving as magistrate of Chia-ting (1625), he printed a collection of the poetry of T'ang Shih-sheng 唐時升 (T. 叔達, 1551-1636), Lou Chien 婁堅 (T. 子柔, 1567-1631), Ch'eng Chia-sui (ECCP), and Li Liu-fang, entitling it *Chia-ting ssu hsien-sheng chi* 四先生集 (Anthology of the four masters of Chia-ting).

Li was a popular artist and the subjects of his brush are widely known. John C. Ferguson lists 78 entries under his name and Osvald Sirén over 50, the earliest being dated 1589 and the latest 1628. [Editors' note: Sirén's first date would make the painter fourteen. Hsü Pang-ta (*see* Lu Chih) writes that the first acceptable painting by Li is dated 1610; he agrees with Sirén on 1628 for the last.] An album of six of his landscapes, now in the Museum of Fine Arts, Boston, may serve as an example of his work. "The subjects treated," write K. Tomita and A. K. Chiu, "are based on short verses by poets of the T'ang dynasty. To accompany the pictures, which illustrated such themes as are expressed in the verses, the artist himself copied on the paintings the complete poems." The album includes, *inter alia*, an encomium by his old friend Ch'ien Ch'ien-i (written in 1641), together with the inscription for Li's tomb. "He was fond of fine natural scenery. Wherever he went, poetry and wine, brush and ink, followed him. He always satisfied the wishes of his friends and admirers by executing pictures. In paintings he drew his inspiration from Yüan masters, especially from Wu Chung-kuei [Wu Chen, 1280-1354]."(Trans. of Tomita and Chiu.) [Editors' note: It is ironic that the words of Ch'ien, ordered expunged in the 1780s, were copied into the imperial encylopedia of the 1720s, the *Ku-chin t'u-shu chi-ch'eng*, and not tampered with there.]

Li had two brothers and a son who were also gifted. His eldest brother was Li Yüan-fang 元芳 (T. 茂初), skilled in writing prose and poetry. A collection of his poems was graced by a preface written by Ch'eng Chia-sui, who praised his gifts. The next, Li Ming-fang 名芳 (T. 茂材), a good prose writer at an early age, became a *chin-shih* in 1592, was appointed a Hanlin bachelor, but died prematurely at the age of twenty-eight. Li Liu-fang's son, named Li Hang-chih 杭之 (T. 僧筏), whose techniques in painting and calligraphy resembled his father's, perished at the hands of the Manchu soldiery in 1645.

Bibliography

1/288/7b; 3/269/4b; 24/4/9a; 46/60/1a; 84/ 丁下 / 9b; SK (1930), 172/14b; Sun Tien-ch'i (1957), 233; *Chia-ting-hsien chih* (1880), 11/22a, 14/26a, 19/12b; TSCC (1885–88), XXIII: 114/102/11a; J. C. Ferguson, *Index of Artists* (Nanking, 1934), 139; Yü I 魚翼, *Hai yü hua-yüan lüeh* 海虞畫苑略 (*Hua shih* 畫史 *ts'ung-shu* ed.), 22; Sheng Ta-shih 盛大士, cj 1800), *Hsi-shan wo-yu lu* 谿山臥游錄, *ibid.*, 4/55; Chou Liang-kung (ECCP), *Tu-hua lu, ibid.*, 1/5; Chiang Shao-shu 姜紹書 (fl. 1644), *Wu-sheng shih shih* 無聲詩史, *ibid.*, 4/65; Hsü Pang-ta, *Li-tai liu-ch'uan shu-hua tso-p'in pien-nien piao* 歷代流傳書畫作品編年表 (Shanghai, 1963), 109, 111; V. Contag and C. C. Wang, *Seals of Chinese Painters and Collectors* (Hong Kong, 1966), 151, 656; O. Sirén, *Chinese Painting* (London, 1956–58), V: 45, VII: 207; Kojiro Tomita and A. Kaiming Chiu, "Album of Six Chinese Paintings Dated 1618, by Li Liu-fang (1575–1629)," *Bull. of the Museum of Fine Arts*, XLVIII (Boston, 1950), 26; E. J. Laing, *Chinese Paintings in Chinese Publications, 1956–1968* (Ann Arbor, 1969), 175.

L. Carrington Goodrich and Nelson Wu

LI Ma-tou, *see* **RICCI, Matteo**

LI Man-chu 李滿住, died October 27, 1476, Jurchen chieftain of the Huo-er-a 火兒阿 tribe, one of the three tribes which originated in the area of I-lan 依蘭 in the lower Sungari valley in what later became known as northeast Manchuria. In the late 14th century the tribe moved southwestward and settled in the area of Feng-chou 鳳州 in the upper valley of the Hui-fa 輝發 River, an affluent of the Sungari. As a result of the Ming pacification policy of the Jurchen in this area the Chien-chou guard (建州衞) was established in 1403 and Li Man-chu's grandfather Aqaču 阿哈出 (alias Li Ch'eng-shan 李誠善, or Yü-hsü-ch'u 於虛出) was nominated to be guard commander. Li Man-chu's father, Li Hsien-chung 李顯忠 (d. *ca.* 1420), visited Nanking several times and in 1410 was made assistant commissioner.

In May, 1424, because of the Mongol reprisals caused by Ming expeditions against them, Li Man-chu and his fellow tribesmen of about one thousand households moved south to the middle valley of the T'ung-chia 佟佳 River, an affluent of the Yalu. They frequently asked Korea for food supplies and sometimes ravaged Korean villages beyond the Yalu. Having no definite policy toward them, the Korean court vacillated between pacification and severance of relations. In the meantime Li Man-chu visited Peking and presented tribute to the emperor (March, 1426), being promoted to assistant commissioner, although his main purpose was to get food from Korea through the help of the Ming emperor.

In January, 1433, Jurchen mounted men looted Korean villages, and the Korean government ascribed the banditry to Li Man-chu, although he denied it. The Ming court tried to conciliate the two parties without success, and eventually in May, 1434, Korea sent an expeditionary force of fifteen thousand men, who took a number of captives and much loot. Li Man-chu fled to the upper valley of the Fu-er 富爾 River, an affluent of the T'ung-chia. For almost two years after that there was no warfare between Korea and the Chien-chou tribe. But starting in February, 1435, the Jurchen again success-fully invaded Korea and looted the countryside. In October, 1437, Korea sent against them for the second time a force of about seventy-eight hundred men, forc-ing Li Man-chu to move northward to the area of Chiu-lao-ch'eng 舊老城 in the Su-tzu 蘇子 River valley. This time Fanca (see Menggetimur) of the Left Chien-chou guard tried to mediate the dispute between the two parties but with no suc-cess. The Ming policy toward Korea and Li Man-chu at this time was inconsistent, sometimes favoring Korea, sometimes Li Man-chu.

After the Left Chien-chou tribe moved to the Su-tzu River valley, all the tribesmen belonging to the three guards of Chien-chou (i.e., the Chien-chou, the Left Chien-chou, and the Right Chien-chou), lived close to each other until around 1450. Meanwhile, starting in 1442, the Uriyangqad invaded Liaotung inces-santly for about ten years, and some Jur-chen even joned them. Ming officials in the region, believing that the Jurchen had been instigated by Li Man-chu, started to take positive measures for the defense of this area. To avoid Mongol invasions and Ming misunderstandings the Jurchen of the three guards returned to the middle valley of the T'ung-chia River in 1451.

Li Man-chu, having been promoted to vice commissioner-in-chief, retired in 1455 and his eldest son Ku-na-ha 古納哈 (d. October 27, 1467) took his place. For sev-eral years the Jurchen chieftains frequent-ed the Korean court, presenting tribute and receiving supplies in turn until the Ming prohibited further relations in 1459. In the meantime an assistant commission-er-in-chief of the Mao-lien guard 毛憐衛 was killed by a Korean local official, and

two years later a group of the Mao-lien tribe attacked the Korean border in re-venge. Soon the tribesmen of the Right Chien-chou joined them, and finally in 1465 it was rumored that the Jurchen of the three Chien-chou would concurrently invade Korea. At the same time sporadic Jurchen revolts irritated Ming officials; in the summer of 1467 the Ming emperor suddenly decided to attack them, suspend-ing, though temporarily, the traditional pacification policy, despite the fact that Jurchen chieftains, including Ku-na-ha and Tung-shan (see Menggetimur), were in Peking on a tributary visit at that time. In October of that year the Ming mobil-ized a force of fifty thousand and Korea ten thousand men; the latter force at-tacked the main body of the enemy and killed Li Man-chu, Ku-na-ha, and others; Tung-shan had been assassinated earlier by some Ming local officials on his way home from Peking. Thus all the three guards of the Chien-chou were subdued for the time being only to be revived a few years later.

Bibliography

MSL (1963), T'ai-tsung, Hsüan-tsung, and Ying-tsung; Wu Han 吳晗, "Kuan-yü tung-pei-shih shang i-wei kuai-chieh ti hsin-shih-liao" 關於東北史上一位怪傑的新史料, YCHP, 17 (Peiping, 1935); Hsü Chung-shu 徐中舒, "Ming-ch'u Chien-chou Juchen chü-ti ch'ien-hsi k'ao 明初建州女眞居地遷徙考, CYYY, 6:2 (1936); Sonoda Kazu-kame 園田一龜, Mindai Kenshū Jochokushi kenkyū 明代建州女直史研究 (Studies on the History of the Chienchou tribe of the Jurchen people under the Ming), 2 vols. (Tokyo, 1948 and 1953); id., "Kenshū san-i no ichini tsuite" 建州三衛の位置について (On the localities of the three Chien-chou tribes in the Ming period), Shigaku zasshi 史學雜誌, 60:4 (Tokyo, 1951); Wada Kiyoshi 和田清, "Minshono Manshū keiryaku" 明初の滿洲經畧, Man-Sen chiri rekishi kenkyū hōkoku 滿鮮地理歷史研究報告, 15 (Tokyo, 1937); Oshibuchi Hajimu 鴛淵一, "Kenshū saino senjūchinī tsuite" 建州左衛の遷住地について, Kuwabara ha-kushi kanreki kinen toyoshi ronsō 桑原博士還曆紀念東洋史論叢 (Tokyo, 1930); id., "Kenshū saino setsuritsu nendaini tsuite" 建州左衛の設立年代について, Rekishito chiri 歷史と地理, 26 (Tokyo, 1930); Ikeuchi Hiroshi 池內宏, "Senshono Tōho-

kukyōto Joshintono kankei" 鮮初の東北境と女眞
との關係, *ibid.*, 2, 4, 5, and 7 (1916, 1917, 1918,
and 1920); Inaba Iwakichi 稻葉岩吉, "Kenshū
Jochokuno genjūchi oyobi senjūchi" 建州女直の
原住地及び遷住地, *Manshu rekishi-chiri* 滿州歷史
地理, 2 (Tokyo, 1913); Henry Serruys, *Sino-
Jürčed Relations during the Yung-lo Period (1403-
1424)* (Wiesbaden, 1955), 39, 51.

Chun Hae-jong

LI Meng-yang 李夢陽 (T. 獻吉, H. 空同子)
January 16, 1473-October 30, 1529, poet
and man of letters, was born into a military
family of the Ch'ing-yang Guard 慶陽衛,
located some one hundred forty miles north
of Sian, Shensi. His great-grandfather,
probably a laborer, married (*ca.* 1390) the
daughter of Wang Chü 王聚 of Fu-kou
扶溝 (50 miles south of Kaifeng, Honan),
a soldier in the Ch'ing-yang garrison, who,
having no son of his own, adopted him
as heir and gave him the name Wang En
恩. He too became a soldier. It is said
that in 1399 he went with his unit to
fight against the rebel army of Chu Ti
(*q.v.*), and was killed in May, 1400,
during the battle of Pai-kou-ho, about
sixty miles south of Peking. His wife
then remarried, leaving two sons to shift
for themselves. The elder, Wang Chung忠
(1395-1447), after being apprenticed to
a trader, succeeded in acquiring some
means, but was murdered by an antagonist
in a lawsuit, and the family sank again
into poverty. He left three sons. The
youngest, Wang Cheng正 (1439-95), became
a student of the National University in
1473; he served for five years (1475-79)
as an instructor in the district school of
Fu-p'ing 阜平 (about sixty-five miles west
of Paoting) and for thirteen years in Kaifeng (1482-95) as tutor to a grandson of
Prince Chu Su (*q.v.*). It was probably at
this time that he restored the family name
to Li.

At the time of Li Meng-yang's birth
in 1473 his family suffered a disaster. His
granduncle (*ca.* 1396-*ca.* 1476), who was
an inebriate and a gambler, and was the
family member shouldering military serv-

ice, lost the family properties in a wager.
The family as a result became very poor.
When the boy was born, there was no
bedding and even the herb needed for
burning off the umbilical cord had to be
begged from a neighbor. Fortunately his
father became an official and the family
moved to Kaifeng, where Li Meng-yang
began to be recognized as a talented
young man. Using his ancestral connection with Fu-kou, he took part in the
Honan provincial examination of 1489 but
failed to pass. In 1490 he married Tso-
shih 左氏 (1475-1516), a great-great-
granddaughter of Prince Chu Su, and
had a son by her a year later. He then
brought his family back to his native
Ch'ing-yang, became at once recognized by
the director of education, Yang I-ch'ing
(*q.v.*), and in 1492 passed first in the
Shensi provincial examination at Sian. A
year later he graduated as *chin-shih* but,
owing to the death of his parents, lived
in Ch'ing-yang for the next five years,
teaching and studying.

Li Meng-yang returned to Peking in
1498 at the time when Grand Secretary
Li Tung-yang (*q.v.*) was the leader of a
group of young poets and writers who
met for literary discussions. Li Meng-yang
became an enthusiastic participant in the
circle. It happened that the senior grand
secretary, Liu Chien (*q.v.*), attached little
importance to lyrical achievement, commenting that even at its highest level
it was represented by inebriates like
Li Po (701-62) and Tu Fu (712-70).
When Li Meng-yang came up for
assignment he received an appointment as a secretary in the ministry of
Revenue. In 1499 he was sent to T'ung-
chou, east of Peking, to supervise the
reception of tribute grain on the Grand
Canal. A year later he was posted to
Yü-lin 榆林, Shensi, to distribute rewards to the border garrisons. In 1501,
when he was delegated to inspect the
customs stations, he found many cases of
tax evasion by merchants under the protection of powerful eunuchs and imperial

relatives. Trying to stop such abuses, he incurred the hatred of the profiteers who accused him of corruption and had him removed. He was exonerated at his trial and returned to the ministry. In 1503 he went to Ninghsia to take charge of the delivery of grain to border troops. Except for these missions he attended to his duties in Peking. Meanwhile he became a leading member of the young poets at the capital of whom may be mentioned the following: Ho Ching-ming, Hsü Chen-ch'ing, K'ang Hai, Pien Kung, Wang Chiu-ssu, and Wang T'ing-hsiang (qq.v.). Some time later they collectively became known as the "seven early masters" (前七子) of poetry. At this time Li was also a close friend of Wang Shou-jen (q.v.).

Those were the last years of an era. Peace and order reigned on the surface, but corruption, injustice, indulgence, apathy, and other corroding vices were already discernible. In March, 1505, Li Meng-yang submitted a long memorial, expostulating on eleven abuses that required attention. One of the abuses concerned the command of the imperial guards of Peking, officered by men whose chief qualifications happened to be their relations with eunuchs or powerful families. Another was the recent practice of granting farmland near Peking to privileged families, including those of some eunuchs. He concluded the memorial with a warning to the emperor that his leniency towards Empress Hsiao-k'ang's younger brothers contributed to their lawlessness, and might lead to their ruin (see Chang Ho-ling). The Chang brothers and their sister pressed the emperor to punish Li, and he was lodged in prison on the charge of involving the empress in a memorial. When it was explained that Li referred to the Chang family, not to the empress herself, he was fined and released. This was a few months before the emperor's untimely death (see Chu Yu-t'ang).

Under the new emperor, Chu Hou-chao (q.v.), Li was promoted in 1505 to deputy director of a bureau and early in

1506 to an acting director. In October, when Han Wen (q.v.) and most high officials, in a concerted move, attacked Liu Chin (q.v.) and other eunuchs of like mind for leading the young emperor astray, Li Meng-yang drafted the memorial. After the failure of their attempt, Liu Chin took revenge by having them dismissed and their supporters punished. A blacklist of forty-eight names was published. In February, 1507, Li was demoted to registrar and cashiered. On leaving Peking he was accompanied by another newly disgraced official, Wang Shou-jen. When they arrived at Pai-kou-ho, where Li's great-grandfather lost his life, he wrote a long poem on the battle that had taken place there one hundred five years previously. It happened that Wang also had a relative killed in the same engagement.

Li then made his home in Kaifeng where his elder brother owned a farm north of the city, near the Yellow River. Here he spent a quiet year teaching and writing. Among other things he composed some poems criticizing the court, now dominated by Liu Chin. When this was reported to Liu in February, 1508, he had Li arrested, brought to Peking in chains, and lodged in prison awaiting investigation. Li begged his friend, K'ang Hai, to appeal to Liu on his behalf, for it was widely known that Liu held K'ang in high esteem, although the latter had resisted the advances of the eunuch. For the sake of rescuing a friend, however, K'ang threw his scruples aside, paid a visit to Liu, and obtained Li's release. For this K'ang became identified as belonging to the eunuch's clique. In September, 1510, after Liu fell from imperial favor and was executed, K'ang was cashiered and never returned to office. In sharp contrast, Li Meng-yang received commendation for having opposed the eunuch, and in February, 1511, was first reinstated as deputy bureau director, and then appointed surveillance vice commissioner of Kiangsi in charge of education. It is said that Li failed to return the favors of his benefactor and did nothing towards the rehabilitation of K'ang Hai. Reportedly the latter wrote a drama on this theme, using the fable about an ungrateful wolf. On close examination we find no record of any break in friendship between K'ang and Li, and it is doubtful that K'ang was the author of the drama.

In any case, Li's return to official favor was short-lived. He arrived at Nanchang in 1511 in an expansive mood, for on his commission paper there was the imperial instruction to report not just on educational matters, but also on the provincial and local administration. He began by encouraging the students in the study of classical literature and exhorting them to maintain their self-respect in their dealings with local officials. He restored the White Deer Academy, founded by Chu Hsi (1130-1200), and compiled a new history of the institution, *Po-lu-tung shu-yüan hsin-chih* 白鹿洞書院新志, 8 *ch.*, a copy of which is preserved in the Library of Congress. He also ordered the building of local schools throughout the province. When his students refused to kneel in the presence of local officials and began to dispute their judgment, these pompous functionaries blamed him for inciting them to civil disobedience. In 1514 some of his students had a fight with the guards of a prince. Li took the side of his students and had the guards flogged. The prince reported him as showing disrespect to a member of the imperial clan. By imperial order an investigation followed. The officials of Kiangsi, one after another, accused Li of exceeding his authority and interfering with their jurisdiction. One official submitted his resignation, saying that he could no longer function on account of Li's interference. On his part Li memorialized on the incompetence and other faults of these officials. He also received help from his admirer, Chu Ch'en-hao (*see* Wang Shou-jen), the ranking prince at Nanchang. Finally, the minister of the Grand

Court of Revision, Yen Chung 燕忠 (T. 良臣, H. 西溪, cs 1484, 1459-1515), was sent from Peking to conduct the trial. Yen was afraid to go to Nanchang, for he knew that thousands of students were ready to fight for Li. So the trial took place at Kuang-hsin 廣信, about 130 miles east of Nanchang. When Li arrived late in February, 1514, Yen berated him and put him in prison. Even though the accusations against him proved to be groundless and his accusers were found guilty and their names stricken from the official register, Li was retired. In his account of the case he said that this failure to judge between right and wrong made him apprehensive for the future of the dynasty.

After his release in June, he went with his family by way of the Yangtze River, and thence up the Han to Hsiangyang 襄陽. Here they remained a short while before returning to Kaifeng. Now aged forty-two, as a man of moderate means, he began the life of a retired official. At the same time he was recognized as a poet nationally. When his wife died in 1516, he wrote three poems, "Chieh-ch'ang pien" 結腸篇, eulogizing her. The poems were put to music for the lute by a local master, and published under the title *Chieh-ch'ang ts'ao p'u* 操譜 (not extant). Meanwhile poets of distinction asked him to edit their works for publication. Among these was his mentor, Yang I-ch'ing who, living in Chinkiang on the Yangtze River after his retirement in September, 1516, frequently corresponded with Li.

In June, 1521, a censor accused Li of having had close connections with Prince Chu Ch'en-hao who staged an unsuccessful rebellion in August, 1519 (*see* Wang Shou-jen). Li was once more imprisoned and tried in Peking. The only evidence against him seems to have been some writings about one of the prince's studios, which he composed for the prince in 1513. He was exonerated and set free in September, 1522, but deprived of his official status. It is said that his release was granted on the recommendation of the minister of Justice, Lin Chün 林俊 (T. 待用, H. 見素, cs 1478, 1452-1527), who maintained that Li, who had stood up to imperial relatives and the powerful Liu Chin, might have been friendly to the prince but could never have been persuaded to be a partisan in the rebellion.

Reduced to a commoner, Li was resigned to his fate. His family was now in better financial shape. His eldest son, Li Chih 枝 (b. 1491), became a *chü-jen* in 1522 and a *chin-shih* a year later, and was appointed in 1525 a secretary in the ministry of Works in Nanking. Li Meng-yang himself received several strong recommendations, all ignored by the court: one by Wang T'ing-hsiang in 1524, naming him worthy of high office and another by Huo T'ao (*q.v.*) in 1528, comparing him to Han Yü (768-824). In May, 1529, he went to Chinkiang to consult a physican about his health. There he stayed in the house of Yang I-ch'ing who was then in Peking. Later Li had a visit from an admirer, Huang Hsing-tseng (*q. v.*), who came up from Soochow to meet him. Shortly after his return to Kaifeng he died. He was buried in the tomb of his wife at the site chosen by himself, some seventy miles southwest of Kaifeng and about ten miles north of Chün-chou 鈞州 (changed to Yü禹-chou in 1575 to avoid the personal name of Emperor Chu I-chün).

Towards the end of his life Li Meng-yang carefully edited his own works for publication. In 1524 he published his poems composed before 1522 under the title *Hung te chi* 弘德集, 33 *ch.*, written during the reigns of Hung-chih and Cheng-te. About this time there appeared in Soochow the *Chia-ching* 嘉靖 *chi*, 1 *ch.*, consisting of his poems of the years 1522 to 1524. In 1527 he edited the notes on philosophical and ethical matters, entitled *K'ung-t'ung-tzu* 空同子 in 8 chapters in 2 *chüan*. A year later he edited his writings in verse and prose and entrusted them to Huang Hsing-tseng to be engraved at Soo-chow, famous for fine printing. In 1529 Li, anxious over the delay in the printing, went to Chinkiang and met Huang, who apparently reported on the lack of funds as the reason for the delay. Later in a letter to Huang, Li mentioned sending thirty taels of silver to help in the printing. The collection, *Li K'ung-t'ung chi*, 66 *ch.*, finally appeared in 1531, two years after his death. His son, Li Chih, on receiving the first copy, presented it at his tablet in the ancestral shrine.

Meanwhile another edition, also entitled *Li K'ung-t'ung chi*, was printed in Feng-yang 鳳陽 by the prefect, Ts'ao Chia 曹嘉 (T. 守禮, cs 1517, Hanlin bachelor 1517-21, censor 1521-25), who was Li's nephew (a son of his eldest sister). Both editions were consulted in 1602 by the magistrate, Teng Yün-hsiao 鄧雲霄 (T. 玄度, cs 1598), and a writer, P'an Chih-heng 潘之恒 (T. 景升, b. 1559), in the printing of the second Soochow edition of *Li K'ung-t'ung chi*, 66 *ch.*, with 2 *chüan* of appendices. A number of copies of this edition are extant (preserved in the Library of Congress, Columbia University, and elsewhere). The editors added some notes and collected some biographical data, but they failed to point out the discrepancy concerning Li's date of death, for in a chronology and in the preface written by Huang Hsing-tseng it was given as the last day of the Chinese year, or January 28, 1530, which was evidently based on hearsay.

A collection of Li's poems, *Li K'ung-t'ung shih-chi* 詩集, 33 *ch.*, edited by Chu Mu-chieh (*see* Chu Su) in mid-16th century, was reprinted in 1578 in Shansi, and frequently in the following centuries. His poems also appeared in various anthologies and selected editions, for they were very popular in Ming and Ch'ing times in spite of the derogatory criticisms by Ch'ien Ch'ien-i (ECCP), Yüan Tsung-tao (*q.v.*), and editors of the *Ssu-k'u* catalogue. He is said to have advocated writing prose in the style of the Han or earlier and imitating Han and T'ang poets in their respective specialized styles; his critics, however, attacked him for this. Actually he said that each era had its own predominant style which was a worthy one; only that of Sung poets should be avoided as they tended to express philosophical thoughts in poetic form. He was well aware that the essence of poetry was spontaneity and sincerity, and even pointed out as examples some folk songs and popular lyrics of love and sorrow sung by illiterates. Some of his own poems in the ku 古 (ancient) style are indeed of high quality. Perhaps one reason for the severe criticisms of his poetry was the fame he gained as leader among the masters of lyrical craft of his day; hence more was expected of him. This is partly because of his vanity as evidenced in his editing his own poems, first by number of characters to a line and then by subject matter such as seasons, sorrow, death, happiness, etc. He was presenting primarily, not records of feeling and thought in poetical form, but his craft in composition to serve as a model for imitation. In poetic achievement and in literary criticism Li Meng-yang was a follower of Li Tung-yang, who was the real leader in the movement to study the Classics and to avoid the pitfalls of examination-hall style in writing. Li Meng-yang admitted in a poem of 1504 that his own rise in fame was chiefly due to the patronage of this master. In another poem, in which he deals with the poets of the Ming dynasty up to his time, he said that his models Yang I-ch'ing and Li Tung-yang rose majestically and turned the tide at the critical moment (我師崛起楊與李，力挽一髮回千鈞). It was the political disturbance of 1506, through which Li Tung-yang remained in office, that finally dislodged him in the popular mind, and unfairly discredited his leadership in the literary movement too. As to Li Meng-yang, as a fighter against evil political influences, he emerged in the role of a popular hero, but in literary achievement and

leadership he could not quite take the place of his mentor. In January, 1621, he was granted the posthumous name Ching-wen 景文.

Bibliography

1/286/10b; 5/86/68a; 40/29/1a; 64/丁/1/1a; Ch'ien Ch'ien-i, *Lieh-ch'ao shih-chi* 丙 11, 12; MSL (1964), Wu-tsung, 0543, 0605, 2200, 2280, Shih-tsung (1965), 0541; KC (1958), 2827, 2879, 3053, 3265; *Li K'ung-t'ung chi* (1602), 19/6b, 20/19b, 28/12a, 38/1a, 49/9a, 50/1b; NCL *Ming index*, 219; SK (1930), 124/5a, 171/6b; Kuo Shao-yü 郭紹虞, *Chung-kuo wen-hsüeh p'i-p'ing shih* 中國文學批評史 (Peking, 1961), 297; K. Yoshikawa, *Gem-min-shi kaisetsu* 元明詩概說 (1963), 169; L. of C. *Catalogue of Rare Books*, 392, 925; TSCC (1885-88), XXIII: 99/87/1a.

Chaoying Fang

LI P'an-lung 李攀龍 (T. 于鱗, 子鱗, H. 滄溟), 1514-70, an influential man of letters, was a native of Li-ch'eng 歷城, Shantung. He was the son of Li Pao 寶, a man of some wealth (d. *ca.* 1522), who took service under the prince of Te 德王, Chu Chien-lin 朱見潾 (second son of Emperor Chu Ch'i-chen [*q.v.*], enfeoffed in 1467, d. 1517). As he reportedly wasted his substance on strong drink, his wife, née Chang 張, was forced to take up needlework to provide their son with schooling. Thus enabled to continue his studies, Li P'an-lung, though deprived of his father at the age of eight, achieved the *chü-jen* degree in 1540 and the *chin-shih* in 1544. His initial appointment was as a secretary in the ministry of Justice. From this post he went on to the office of vice director of a bureau before his assignment to be prefect of Shun-te 順德, Pei-Chihli. His honesty and willingness to serve the populace won the trust of his superiors, who later promoted him to be assistant superintendent of education in Shensi. When Li's fellow provincial, Yin Hsüeh 殷學 (T. 時敏, H. 虛川, cs 1532) then governor of Shensi (1557-60) and his superior, ordered Li to write an essay for him, he retorted, "How can the writing of an essay be done by official order," and refused to comply. Just at that juncture, Shensi was shaken by a series of severe earthquakes; his fright as a result and his sudden concern for his mother prompted him to resign and retire on the pretext of illness.

At home he constructed for himself a building, Pai-hsüeh-lou 白雪樓 (white snow pavilion), where he discussed learning and philosopy with friends. His literary reputation grew day by day, but he refused to see all other visitors and made no exception of people of prominence. By so doing he antagonized many who came to regard him as haughty and insolent. He maintained close relationships only with Hsü Chung-hsing, Tsung Ch'en, Wu Kuo-lun (qq.v.), the Huang-fu brothers (see Huang-fu Fang), and a handful of others regardless of criticism.

One worthy of mention was Wang Shih-chen (q.v.), whom Li entertained when Wang arrived in Shantung on official service. But Li almost spoiled the relationship before it started by likening Wang to Tso Ch'iu-ming (and himself, as a consequence, to Confucius). When he noticed Wang's reaction and realized his blunder, he hastily corrected Tso to Lao-tzu.

In 1567, following ten years in retirement, he received an appointment to the office of provincial judge of Honan. His mother died shortly after he took up this assignment so he hastened home to bury her and, before the period of mourning ended, he too passed away. His body was laid to rest, according to one source, in a tomb south of Tsinan; according to another, east of Ma-an shan 馬鞍山; and according to a third, it was buried back of Niu-shan 牛山, then moved to Ma-an shan. His incorruptibility during his periods in office impoverished him, and left little for his wife and sons. It is reported that his favorite concubine, Lady Ts'ai, during her seventies had to hawk cake in the western outskirts of the city of Tsinan. Wang Chi-mu 王季木, the granduncle of Wang Shih-chen (ECCP), witnessed this episode and wrote a melancholy poem, two lines of which run

Pai-hsüeh buries a great literary man;
Lady Ts'ai has pawned all her patched clothing of gauze.

Prior to Li P'an-lung, Ming literature was under the influence of the so-called Sung-wen yün-tung 宋文運動 (a harking back to the essay style of the Sung) led by such writers as Wang Shen-chung and T'ang Shun-chih (qq.v). These literati tried to supersede the Ch'ien-ch'i-tzu (seven early masters) represented by such eminent stylists as Li Meng-yang and Ho Ching-ming (qq.v.), whose slogan was Wen-ch'ung-Ch'in-Han shih-pi-sheng-T'ang 文崇秦漢, 詩必盛唐 (Honor the essays of Ch'in and Han; venerate the poems of effulgent T'ang). Their effort appered to be on the way to success when it unexpectedly encountered an opposing group of scholars represented by Li P'an-lung, Wang Shih-chen, Tsung Ch'en, Hsü Chung-hsing, and Wu Kuo-lun (qq.v.), Hsieh Chen (see Hsü Chung-hsing), and Liang Yu-yü (see Huang Tso), who came to be known by the sobriquet of Hou-ch'i-tzu (Seven later masters). Their effort tipped the balance in favor of the literary style of Li Meng-yang and Ho Ching-ming.

The leader of the "Seven later masters" was first Hsieh Chen, but Li P'an-lung, supported by Wang Shih-chen, eventually displaced him. Thereafter, Li Meng-yang, Ho Ching-ming, Li P'an-lung, and Wang Shih-chen became the four idols of students of that day. Their shortcomings, however, were numerous and these led to their final downfall. Their readers came to complain of their tendency towards imitation and lack of creativity. In their poetry also, they were often guilty of plagiarism. These faults gave rise to another school—the Kung-an p'ai 公安派—led by three brothers, Yüan Tsung-tao, Yüan Hung-tao, and Yüan Chung-tao (qq.

v.). This school succeeded in ending the domination in the literary realm of Li P'an-lung, his colleagues, and his predecessors.

Li was the author of *Ts'ang-ming chi* 30+1 *ch.*, the *Pai-hsüeh-lou shih chi* 詩集, 10 *ch.*, the *Ku-chin shih shan*古今詩刪, 34 *ch.*, and several other works, some of which are doubtfully his. The first is the sole work of his copied in to the Imperial Library. Two or three of his anthologies were later condemned to expurgation because his co-compilers included the writings of men whose names were anathema to the Ch'ien-lung regime. The *Ming-shih hsüan* 明詩選, 12+1 *ch.*, printed in 1631, is one of these. His anthology of 465 poems of the T'ang period, *T'ang shih hsüan*, 7+1 *ch.*, is represented by three late Ming editions in the Library of Congress. A well-known Japanese scholar-collector of the 17th century, Ogyū Sorai 荻生徂徠 (1666-1728), who once owned one of these, wrote, as translated by Shio Sakanishi: "Wang Shih-chen, criticizing the poems of Li P'an-lung, says that they are like snow on the top of the Omei mountains—clear and brilliant. Li selected T'ang poems which, like his own, are excellent and individualistic.... Li says the thing that is always cloudless is the heart of man." His poetry has attracted little attention among western translators, but one example, rendered into English, appears in *The Penguin Book of Chinese Verse*.

One son, Li Chü 駒 (T. 千里, H. 松盤), who became a student in the National University, had some of his father's gifts as an essayist and won the praise of Wang Shih-chen.

Bibliography

1/104/1a, 287/15a; 3/268/12a; 40/46/1a; 61/147/11a; 64/丁1/1a; 84/丙/53a; Wang Chieh-hsi 王介錫, *Ming-ts'ai-tzu-chuan* 明才子傳, *Jih-pen nei-ko-wen-k'u ts'ang-shou ch'ao-pen* 日本內閣文庫藏手鈔本; TSCC (1885-88), XIV: 397/17/9a, XXII: 217/39/2b; XXIII: 106/94/4b; Teng Yüan-hsi, *Huang Ming shu*, 396/a; *Shensi t'ung-chih* (1735), 22/23a; *Chi-nan-fu chih* 濟南府志 (1924), 49/26b, 63/6b; SK (1930), 137/10a, 172/7a, 177/17a, 189/5b, 192/9a, 197/7a; Sun Tien-ch'i (1957), 102, 132; L. of C. *Catalogue of Rare Books*, 947, 1047, 1058; *Report of the Librarian of Congress* (1930-31), 286; A. R. Davis (ed.), *The Penguin Book of Chinese Verse* (Baltimore, 1962), 60.

Chin-tang Lo

LI San-ts'ai 李三才 (T. 道甫, H. 修吾), died 1623, official, was a native of Lin-t'ung 臨潼, Shensi. His father, a member of the Wu-kung 武功 right guard, made his home at Chang-chia-wan 張家灣, the canal port of T'ung-chou 通州, east of Peking, where Li San-ts'ai was brought up; hence he is also recorded as from T'ung-chou. A *chin-shih* of 1574, he was appointed to the ministry of Revenue as a bureau secretary, and subsequently promoted to bureau director. During this period he formed life-long friendships with such of his colleagues as Wei Yün-chen (*see* Ku Hsien-ch'eng) and Li Hua-lung (*q. v.*). These were young officials who took their public careers seriously and encouraged each other by discussions of the need for proper economic and administrative reforms. When Wei Yün-chen incurred great displeasure at court for criticizing several high officials with nepotism and was penalized, Li San-ts'ai, then vice director of a bureau in the ministry of Revenue, defended his friend in a memorial, with the result that Li himself was punished by demotion in May, 1583, to prefectural judge of Tung-ch'ang 東昌, Shantung. Later he was transferred to Nanking as a bureau director in the southern ministry of Rites. His act, however, earned Li San-ts'ai a high reputation among the reform-minded scholarly elite. Among his colleagues in Nanking also were Wei, Li Hua-lung, and another man of similar mind, Tsou Yüan-piao (*q. v.*), and the discussions on current affairs were carried on with greater fervor than ever before. In the following years Li was appointed to a number of provincial posts: assistant surveillance commissioner of Shantung; assistant administration commissioner and vice-surveillance commissioner of Honan; director of education of Shantung and then Shansi; assistant commissioner of the transmission commission at Nanking, and vice minister of the Grand Court of Revision.

In 1599 Li San-ts'ai became junior assistant censor-in-chief and was charged with the general supervision of grain transport, concurrently to serve as governor of Feng-yang. These were the years when the emperor, Chu I-chün (*q. v.*), in an effort to obtain additional funds, dispatched eunuchs to the provinces as tax collectors. These agents inflicted dire hardship on the population through their unprincipled conduct and earned the intense hatred of the people. The special tax collectors sent to Li San-ts'ai's territory included several very rapacious individuals, in particular Ch'en Tseng (*see* Hao Ching), collector of sales taxes, who felt himself powerful enough to treat provincial officials highhandedly. Li refused to yield to him, however, and proceeded to suppress Ch'en's henchmen, thus reducing the harm that Ch'en might have wrought in this region. Realizing at the same time the disastrous effects brought about by the new mining levies, which in many cases drove the people to open rebellion, Li presented two memorials in 1600 calling the throne's attention to the situation, but the emperor gave no response to the appeal. In 1602 during an illness the emperor ordered the cessation of mining levies, but this decision was soon reversed. Li again memorialized on the dangers of the situation, but his plea was in vain.

Annoyed by Li's memorials the emperor used occasion of the controversy over financing water conservancy works to try to get rid of him. Certain sections of the Grand Canal under his charge needed to be dredged and new locks built, and Li proposed the retention of the tribute rice as a way to finance the costs. When this met with strong opposition in

Peking, he sent in his resignation, which the emperor promptly accepted. A group of censors both in the capital and in the Huai region, however, interpreting this event in terms of the power struggle at court, raised strong objections to Li's removal, because the government "must not dismiss San-ts'ai on account of Ch'en Tseng." The emperor then ordered Li to remain at his post until a successor had been named. His replacement, however, was never appointed.

Li San-ts'ai had now made the abolition of the mining levies his cause. He continued to memorialize on the great misery of the common people brought about by these exactions, but his memorials were not forwarded to the throne. At the same time he determinedly carried on his war against Ch'en Tseng's clique, executing a number of individuals. This ended only with Ch'en's death in 1604. The vacillating measures of the throne regarding the mining levies brought forth fresh remonstrances from Li, who once so incensed the emperor that in 1606 he had to forfeit his official salary for five months as punishment. Nevertheless, Li persisted in offering his views to the throne on reforms and on the precarious situation in Liaotung. All fell on deaf ears. Friendly with such leaders of the Tung-lin group as Ku Hsien-ch'eng and Kao P'an-lung (*q. v.*), Li San-ts'ai was regarded as belonging to the anti-court faction. Enmities incurred as a result brought forth an impeachment from metropolitan officials, but his case dragged on for months. He was neither tried nor suspended; his friends petitioned the throne for some decision one way or another, so as not to impede the administration of the grain transport system; Li himself was reported to have memorialized fifteen times. When the throne still took no action he left his post of his own accord in 1611, yet this act brought no reprimand from the emperor. In fact, such occurrences were quite common during the latter part of the Wan-li period, when the bureaucracy appeared to be nearing the breaking point through financial and administrative maladjustments, one of the most obvious signs of which was the widespread neglect of matters concerning official appointments; numerous posts went vacant as the edicts naming the replacements were not forthcoming, while in some posts the incumbents who wished to be relieved of their responsibilities had no effective way of having their resignations properly processed.

Li San-ts'ai's voluntary retirement, however, brought no peace from his adversaries in Peking. New troubles broke out for him in November, 1614, when he was accused of embezzling some 220,000 taels worth of government timber for the building of his own mansion; the blow was made the worse by the fact that among the accusers were some officials whom he in the past had helped to advance. In deep chagrin he offered to have his home inspected by the government, and the entire case grew into a noisy scandal. His continued criticism of government policies and defense of the Tung-lin group deepened his disfavor at court, Although the evidence did not actually support the accusation. the censor who was sent to investigate the case repeated the original charges in his report, which resulted in Li's dismissal from office in 1616. In 1621, when the Manchu threat became critical, a metropolitan censor memorialized the new emperor for the re-employment of Li San-ts'ai, but without success. Finally, in February, 1623, Li was named minister of the southern ministry of Revenue at Nanking, but he died before he could assume office.

In 1625, when Wei Chung-hsien (EC CP) was wielding unlimited power, Li San-ts'ai was posthumously stripped of all titles and honors. These were restored in May, 1629.

Li was an able administrator whose thirteen-year governorship of the Huai region won him loyal support from the local population, especially as a result of his successful fight against the eunuch tax collectors. Conscious of his own high reputation and influence, he was fond of gathering round himself a coterie of friends and supporters, accepted freely the gifts presented by all and sundry, and tended to be rather extravagant in his personal tastes, particularly in regard to building his good collection of paintings, calligraphy, and antiques. For a number of years he remained a controversial figure in the government: there were those who fiercely attacked him, but there were others who supported him with equal stanchness. His views on public affairs as well as personal associations clearly placed him close to the Tung-lin group; it even appears that he himself might actually have been the leader of a lesser clique allied to the Tung-lin scholars. On many occasions he felt frustrated in his public career, and often his supporters thought that he really should be allowed to serve in the capital, to be placed directly in the center of power where important decisions were made. Some of Li's bitterness and sadness is reflected in a number of his poems, particularly those written after his initial removal from Peking to Nanking.

He is reported as the author of several collections of poems. Five of his poems may be found in the *Lieh-ch'ao shih-chi* (*see* Ch'ien Ch'ien-i ECCP). The *Ts'ao-fu hsiao-ts'ao* 漕撫小草. 15 *ch.*, which contains his memorials and documents, was printed in the early years of the 17th century, and is reported to be still extant. The *Huang Ming ching-shih wen-pien* of Ch'en Tzu-lung (ECCP) includes six of his memorials.

[Editors' note: According to the *T'ung-chou chih*, Li San-ts'ai had a concubine, née Ma 馬, who, after he died, committed suicide by starving herself twelve days. The event is recorded as of the 2d month, T'ien-ch'i 4th year (March/April, 1624), which would make Li's death as possibly occurring in 1624 instead of 1623. The year and month of a virtuous woman's

death as given in a gazetteer, however, frequently denotes not the actual
date of her death but the time the event
was officially recorded.   The time of Li's
death is generally given as shortly after
he received his last appointment, which
was issued on March 18, 1623.]

Bibliography

1/232/7b; 3/226/18a; 40/52/15a; 64庚11/2318; 84/
丁11/47a; Meng Sen 孟森, *Ming-tai shih* 明代史
(Taipei, 1957), 285; *T'ung-chou chih* (1879), 8/28a,
8/烈女 5a; KC (1958), 4440, 4854, 5040, 5215,
5485; biography by Sun Ch'eng-tse (ECCP) in
Huang Ming wen-hai (microfilm) 10/2/7; Chu
Tan 朱倓, "A bibliographical study of the literary works of Tung-lin scholars" (in Chinese)
in *Kuang-chou hsüeh-pao* 廣州學報 (1937); Li Yen
李楼, *Tung-lin-tang chi k'ao* 東林黨籍考 (Peking,
1957), 1; H. Busch, "The Tung-lin Academy,"
MS 14 (1949–54), 54; C. O. Hucker, "The Tung-lin
Movement," in *Chinese Thought and Institutions*
(Chicago, 1957), 147.

E-tu Zen Sun

LI Shan-ch'ang 李善長 (T. 百室), 1314–
July 6, 1390, a native of Ting-yüan 定遠
(Anhwei), was the first official holding
the title tso ch'eng-hsiang 左丞相 (prime
minister), in the Ming dynasty. Throughout the early years of the struggle for
power of Chu Yüan-chang, from 1354 to
1371, he was the ranking civil official in
Chu's service and principal leader of his
followers, both civil and military. Thus,
although he seems never to have won
recognition as a scholar, he officially outranked all the learned men in the new
regime, including Liu Chi, Sung Lien, and
T'ao An (*qq.v.*), and organized their labors
in major projects that were undertaken
in founding the state. It was Li, moreover, who presided over the ideologically
significant ceremonials that legitimized
Chu's assumption of the titles of prince
and emperor. His services were generously
acknowledged by his investiture as duke
of Hsüan-kuo 宣國公 in October, 1367,
and as duke of Han 韓國 in December,
1370. In 1368 he was given the title Shang

chu-kuo 上柱國 (High pillar of state), and
in 1370 made Tso chu-kuo (Pillar of state
of the left). In August, 1376, moreover,
he was linked to the imperial family when
Chu Yüan-chang gave his eldest daughter
to Li's son, Li Ch'i 祺 (T. 承先), in marriage. His tragic fall from imperial grace,
that culminated in his suicide in 1390,
resulted from his implication in the treason case of Hu Wei-yung (*q.v.*) and the
long-term factional struggles in which that
case was a major episode.

Li Shan-ch'ang's official biography
suggests that his credentials as a scholar
were a little shady. He is said to have
studied in his youth and to have become
versed in the writings of the "Legalist
School." There is no indication given of
important family connections and he
appears never to have held office under
the Yüan. One may assume, therefore,
that his social position when he met Chu
was, at best, barely within the category
of the literati. This occurred in the
summer of 1353 when Chu marched his
still small band of followers from Ting-
yüan towards Ch'u-chou 滁州. After conversing with Li, who was fourteen years
his senior, the rebel leader invited him to
take charge of his paper work and records, and to serve him as his adviser. Li
accepted the invitation and remained in
Chu's service for the next twenty years.

Li's loyalty and effectiveness were to
be tested almost at once. Chu Yüan-chang
at this time was in the service of Kuo
Tzu-hsing (*q.v.*), who in turn was in the
service of the State of Sung of Han Lin-er
(*q.v.*). Both the Sung State and Kuo's own
command were torn by internal dissension.
During 1354 Chu's following had grown
to such proportions that Kuo became
envious and fearful of his subordinate
and transferred many of Chu's officers to
his own command. He was particularly
determined to have Li in his own camp.
Li, however, refused, and implored Chu to
allow him to stay, which he eventually
did. The following year Chu was given
command of the newly captured city of

Ho-chou 和州 (Anhwei). Here Li assisted him in bringing to terms a number of insubordinate officers who had insisted on taking orders only from Kuo, and on one occasion helped to defend the city from Mongol assaults in Chu's absence. Soon after this, Kuo died, and Chu, now in independent command of a large following, made his fateful crossing of the Yangtze in July, 1355.

After the crossing, Chu began rapidly to build a permanent state. Li's role in this process is not clearly documented, but, as the administrative system expanded and higher offices were created, he was repeatedly promoted. Chu established his first regular governmental office, (太平興國翼元帥府) at T'ai-p'ing (Anhwei), and made Li the chief administrator directly under him. In August, 1356, after Chu Yüan-chang proclaimed himself the Duke of Wu, Li was appointed assistant administration commissioner of the Kiangnan branch secretariat. Early in 1364, following the establishment of the principality of Wu, he was appointed minister in the secretariat, and four years later, upon the founding of the dynasty, became prime minister with the concurrent title of junior guardian of the heir apparent. During these years Li was in close communication with Chu but with the emperor dominating the Secretariat. In subsequent years, Li played a major role in devising regulations for Chu's army, and in planning strategems to circumvent Chu's rival contenders, particularly Ch'en Yu-liang and Chang Shih-ch'eng (qq. v.). Li appears to have served more as a manager than as the major author of policy or strategy, except, perhaps, in the field of law.

One of Li's more specific contributions to the new state was in the preparation of a new code of law upon which Chu Yüan-chang relied heavily to replace the arbitrary precedents for the maintenance of order. In December, 1367, Chu appointed a commission with Li at its head to draft a new code. In his instructions to the commission, obviously under Li's influence, Chu advised his subordinates to consult the T'ang and Sung codes instead of the Yüan, which he thought confusing and badly drafted. He was most insistent upon the need for simplicity in the document so that all might understand it; otherwise corruption and chaos would result. The new code *Ta Ming ling* 令, 1 ch., was drafted quickly, with Chu himself informally joining in the discussions; Li presented it for Chu's final review about three weeks after the work had been begun. An additional work, the *Lü-ling chih-chieh* 律令直解, which served further to explain the laws, was completed soon afterwards (January 21, 1368) by the same commission.

As the head of the civil administration, Li bore a heavy responsibility for the financing of the growing state and its relatively enormous army (possibly around two hundred thousand in 1363). His biography in the *Ming-shih*, perhaps with some exaggeration, credits him with having filled the treasury without injury to public morale by instituting taxes on salt, tea, and fisheries, by introducing a new coinage, and by setting up iron foundries. These, however, were not innovations, but modified or continued traditional practice, and it seems that Li was more responsible in this matter of revenues for the setting-up and staffing of the necessary offices. In 1361 salt was taxed at 5 percent (soon increased to 10), and offices were established in tea-producing areas for the sale of certficates to tea merchants at a rate of 200 cash per 100 catties. At the same time a coin foundry at Nanking began production of the new coins.

Li Shan-ch'ang was also responsible for arranging the ceremonial to be used in the imperial enthronement, which took place on the twenty-third of January, 1368. Thereafter Li labored on the establishment of court ritual, such as the sacrifices to be made to Heaven and Earth, to the spirits of the rivers, and to Shang Ti. During the first few years of the dynasty, the Secretariat produced a flood of literature on law, ceremonial, history, and moral instruction for which Li, as prime minister, was officially responsible. It would seem, however, that his contribution was mainly administrative rather than scholarly, as in the case of the compilation of the *Yüan-shih*, which should be attributed to its chief compiler, Sung Lien, although it was Li who made the formal announcement of its completion (in September, 1369).

It was in the management of the civil and military administration on Chu's behalf that Li had both his greatest success and his final disaster. It is reported that he regularly interviewed and evaluated prospective official appointees who had been recruited or captured by the generals and then reported on them to the emperor. He is also said to have determined the policies regarding promotion and demotion, reward and punishment of officials, both civil and military, but the final judgment always rested with the emperor. On several occasions he intervened on behalf of officials threatened with punishment, as when he persuaded Chu to spare several generals, including Hsü Ta (*q.v.*), for having let their soldiers get out of hand on entering the city of Nanking in 1356. The fact that Chu's state appears to have been somewhat less troubled than its rivals by conflicts among its military leaders may also be to Li's credit.

During the first three years of the Ming, Li Shan-ch'ang as (senior) prime minister presided over the Secretariat and enjoyed the greatest official preeminence of his career. At the same time, however, social and political forces were already at work that were to undo him at the last. Even after the enthronement Chu kept around him a closely knit oligarchy of old comrades in arms, men who for the most part were soldiers by trade and poorly educated. At the same time he was energetically recruiting great numbers of new and more learned men, some of whom had served his rival contenders, in

subordinate ranks. Thus the stage was set for a struggle between a privileged and intimate inner group of relatively rustic and unlettered men, and the more normally qualified officials who were filling up the lower ranks. As the friction between the two groups gradually came to an open break, Li could not but be involved. As early as 1368 he became embroiled in a quarrel with Liu Chi over the latter's strong disapproval of one of Li's repeated attempts to secure special consideration for a friend in trouble with the law. Far more serious was his quarrel with Yang Hsien (*see* Empress Ma) who complained to Chu Yüan-chang that Li lacked the ability to serve effectively as prime minister, but the emperor supported Li. Nonetheless, the trouble with Yang came to a head at the end of 1370 when Li, during a temporarily incapacitating illness, was given permission to resign from the Secretariat. His choice for the succession to the vacated office was his long-time associate, Wang Kuang-yang (*q.v.*). Yang now charged that Wang, too, was not equal to the demands of the office. Li's protégé, Hu Wei-yung, then persuaded him to protect the position of the Huai valley men by bringing serious countercharges against Yang. As a result, Yang was tried and executed, and Wang was given the appointment. These events led to the beginning of a series of factional convulsions within the government.

If Li's involvement in bureaucratic politics could have ended with his retirement from the Secretariat, he might have been allowed to die a natural death. During his last year in office as prime minister he was appointed grand preceptor, an honorary title he retained until his death; this made him one of the Three Dukes. It was a distinction he then shared with Hsü Ta and the son of the late Ch'ang Yü-ch'un (*q.v.*). He was also reinvested as the hereditary duke of Han with an annual stipend of four thousand *shih* of grain. As additional marks of favor on the occasion of his retirement, he was given land in Hao-chou 濠州 (=Feng-yang, Anhwei), a hundred fifty families of tomb-guardians, fifteen hundred households of farm workers, and twenty families of honor guards. Yet his official services were not quite at an end. A year later, after he had regained his health, he was ordered to oversee the construction of the new palaces at Hao-chou (in accordance with an abortive plan to make that city an imperial capital) and the transportation there of one hundred forty thousand well-to-do families from south of the Yangtze to farm the surrounding fields. In 1375 he was commanded to share with Chu Liang-tsu (*see* Hu Wei-yung) responsibility for the program of military affairs, and in 1380, just before that office was abolished, he was appointed to fill a vacancy as senior vice censor-in-chief. Whether he wished it so or not, therefore, Li remained in official service and at a much lower level than before.

Beginning in 1377, if there is any truth to the charges later made against them, Hu Wei-yung tried to involve Li in what became a full-fledged plot against the throne. Hu had first been appointed to an office in the capital on the recommendation of Li Shan-ch'ang. Subsequently, they were involved together in the Yang Hsien case, and they were allied by the marriage of Li Yu 佑, the son of Li Ts'un'-i 存義, younger brother of Li Shan-ch'ang, to the daughter of Hu's elder brother. In a widely ramified secret fashion, Hu allegedly drew together under his control a number of civil and military officials who had reason to fear the emperor's wrath. In January, 1380, Hu's plot was discovered, and thousands of real or alleged conspirators and their families were savagely punished by execution. At this time, there were widespread demands among the officials that Li Shan-ch'ang and his family also be executed because of their undeniable proximity to the chief conspirator. The emperor, however, once again cited Li's long and effective service and let him off without an investigation.

This was far from being the end of the matter, however. Charges were brought again in 1385, and again Li was spared an investigation. On this occasion the emperor was angered by Li's failure to express his gratitude for the consideration shown him, which suggests that Li's position at court was becoming insecure. Finally, early in 1390, a sudden barrage of disclosures or allegations descended upon Li's head. First the Censorate asserted that in 1385 Lan Yü (*q. v.*) had captured in the Mongol camp a former Yüan official whom Hu Wei-yung had employed as a secret messenger in 1380. A document carried by the man was now said to have been in the handwriting of Li. It was further charged that in 1385 Li had known of the messenger's capture, and that he had concealed this from the emperor. The latter at first rejected the charge, but was soon persuaded to allow the arrest and interrogation of a number of individuals connected with the case, including the sons of Li Ts'un-i, Li Yu and Li Shen 伸. A relative of Li's by marriage, Ting Pin 丁斌, who had served in Hu's household, and some of Li's own domestic slaves were now induced to report that Li had been in close and secret communication with Hu before the latter's arrest in 1380. Ting testified that Li had received three hundred ounces of gold from him as the price of his recommendation of Hu for appointment in the capital, and that, in furtherance of Hu's designs, he had furnished him with forty servants, for which he received more gifts in return. This testimony was then supported by that of a slave in the household of Lu Chung-heng, the Chi-an marquis (*see* Ning-kuo kung-chu), who said his master, Fei Chü (*see* Keng Ping-wen), the P'ing-liang marquis, and Chao Yung, the Nan-hsiung marquis (*see* Hu Wei-yung), and Li Shan-ch'ang all had been in league with Hu. The emperor, shaken by these statements, asked that formal charges be prepared and the truth revealed. When the officials then demanded Li's execution,

Chu once again asked that the case be given a full hearing and a formal decision rendered. He also consented to the arrest of the marquises. He now learned, moreover, that Li had just received bribes from some of his associates who had caused disorders in the capital and were to be transported to the frontier, and had intervened on their behalf. Finally, T'ang Ho complained to the emperor that Li had illegally commandeered three hundred of his guardsmen to assist in the construction of a new residence. Chu now seemed on the point of abandoning him to his enemies and, when for the last time he offered excuses for the seventy-six year-old former prime minister on the ground that he was too elderly to be dangerous, Chu allowed himself to be persuaded by officials, who insisted that Li's guilt had been clearly proven, and that the law allowed no exemptions in such cases. Li then humbly made full confession in the emperor's presence, and returned home to hang himself. Some seventy members of his family including his nephews were granted the choice of suicide or being executed. Only his son, Li Ch'i, presumably because he was married to the Lin-an princess, was spared, but he too was exiled to Chiang-p'u 江浦, where he died shortly afterwards. The following year an official of the ministry of Works, Wang Kuo-yung 王國用, with the censor Hsieh Chin (q.v.) drafting the memorial for him, protested this disposition of the case on the ground that the charges against Li had been implausible in the absence of any possible motive he may have had for engaging in conspiracy, and that the elimination of such a reputable official would inspire general disrespect for the regime. Chu, according to Li's biography in the *Ming-shih*, read the memorial and was unable to make any reply. In October, 1644, the Southern Ming court of Nanking conferred on Li the canonized name Hsiang-min 襄愍.

Bibliography

1/127/1a; 3/122/1a; 5/11/1a; 8/3/1a; 20/1/20a; 61/93/15b; 63/2/47a; 88/2/25a; MSL (1962), T'ai-tsu, *ch.* 1-202; Chu Yüan-chang, *Kao-huang-ti yü-chih wen-chi*, 3/1a, 6/1a, 7/1a, 20a; Ho Ch'iao-yüan, *Ming-shan ts'ang* (*Ch'en-lin chi* 臣林記), 2/10a; *Ming-shih* (Taiwan, 1963), 1615; W. Franke, *Sources*, 6.3.1.

Romeyn Taylor

LI Shih 李實 (T. 孟誠, H. 虛菴), June 18, 1413-October 5, 1485, official, whose mission to Esen (q.v.) led to the safe return from Mongol captivity of ex-Emperor Chu Ch'i-chen (q.v.), was a native of Ho-chou 合州, Szechwan. In his youth he was an apprentice in trade. Once coming back from a business trip in the lower Yangtze valley, he almost lost his life when his boat was wrecked. After this experience he decided to try to enter the bureaucracy by preparing to take the civil examinations. Devoting his whole energy to study —a change in direction which proved successful—he became a *chü-jen* in 1441, and a *chin-shih* in the following year. Three years later he was appointed a supervising secretary in the ministry of Rites. Accused by an official of his native place of illegal and unbecoming acts, while staying at home after the metropolitan examinations, he was thrown into prison for a time in 1446.

The unfortunate T'u-mu defeat of 1449 (*see* Chu Ch'i-chen) left Peking with no emperor, no proper defense, and the central government in turmoil. Li Shih at this juncture memorialized on certain measures for the protection of the city and helped in the recruiting of men for the armed forces. Before long, for a memorial in connection with grain transport judged to be trivial and incorrect, he was again imprisoned, but was quickly released and reinstated. Refusing to be discouraged, he presented two more memorials early in 1450, one on permitting provincial officials to take their immediate families with them to places of assignment; another on dispatching additional military personnel to his home province to help control the Man 蠻, a minority people. His opportunity for promotion came in the middle of that year. He was first made chief supervisory secretary of the ministry of Rites, and then on August 4 elevated to right vice minister of Rites to head a mission to the Oirat. Some sources say that he volunteered, but the *shih-lu* is silent on this point. According to his own account, a list of names of officials from the third grade up was presented to Emperor Chu Ch'i-yü (*q.v.*). After an interview with the eunuch Hsing An (*q.v.*), Li Shih agreed to go on the mission. He had as his deputy envoys Lo Ch'i 羅綺 (cs 1430, right vice minister of the Grand Court of Revision) and an interpreter, Ma Hsien 馬顯 (grand commander, probably a Mongol). Separate imperial edicts addressed to three Mongol chieftains were entrusted to him. On examination, Li found no mention of the matter of the return of the imperial captive. Astonished over this omission, he enquired about it. Hsing An's reply was a sharp retort meaning "ask no questions."

The Li mission had sixteen members who traveled in the company of five Mongols going back to the Oirat. It was the practice of his day that a Chinese embassy would be dispatched with a returning mission of the Mongols and vice-versa. Since there was no peace and a language barrier existed, probably this was the best way to ensure a safe journey. The two groups started on August 8, 1450, and arrived at the Mongol camp on the 18th. At a conference Li Shih and Esen seem to have achieved mutual respect and understanding. The next day Li was escorted to the Chinese emperor, whose tent was some 30 *li* from Esen's camp. The emperor expressed himself as extremely anxious to gain his release. He vowed that he would be willing to become a commoner, or a keeper of his ancestral tombs, if only he might go back to China. Probably moved by the plea, yet remembering the reluctance of Chu Ch'i-yü who

was on the throne in Peking for the return of his brother, Li Shih offered some frank advice. He made it clear that, since His Majesty had relied on the wrong people (who had persuaded him to lead the army against the Mongols), perhaps he should now repent humbly and avoid any involvement in the imperial succession. At the time Li Shih thought his advice was well taken, but he did not foresee the possibility that this might end his official career. He observed that the imperial tent, made of felt cloth, had no tables, chairs, or beds inside, only the floor. Outside there was a horse and an ox cart for use in moving. As for food there was hardly any grain or vegetables, but every five days Esen did send over one head of cattle and a sheep.

After the audience Li again made his way to Esen's camp, where the Mongol chief expressed his willingness to let his captive return as soon as possible. One remark of interest he made was that holding the Chinese T'ai-shang-huang 太上皇 was meaningless. In such an atmosphere Li Shih's misson ended; he started back on August 21 and arrived at Peking on the 27th. On the following day he reported to the emperor, offering the opinion that the sooner the court welcomed the ex-emperor, the sooner peace might be made with the Mongols. Several grand secretaries also questioned him in detail in order to arrive at a government policy. In the meantime another mission headed by Yang Shan (*q.v.*) had started out on August 25; this finally escorted the ex-emperor to Peking, reaching the capital on September 20, 1450. For his efforts Yang Shan was later, after the restoration, made an earl and received a posthumous title.

Later in 1450 Li was promoted to right censor-in-chief and concurrently governor of Hukuang, at which post he remained until 1454. In 1451 Li Shih exposed, and assisted in putting down, an attempted rebellion by a member of the imperial family. Chu Hui-yeh 朱徽煠, prince of Kuang-t'ung 廣通王 (a son of Chu

Pien, *see* Chu Su), enfeoffed in Wu-kang-chou 武岡州, Hukuang, schemed to incite the Miao tribes to help him gain the throne. He failed and was degraded to the status of a commoner. About this time Li Shih was himself accused of being an overbearing administrator, but he suffered no ill as a consequence.

Soon after the return from his mission to Esen, Li Shih wrote a day-by-day account entitled *Pei-shih lu* 北使錄, also known either as Ch'u 出-*shih lu*, or *Shih-pei-lu*, an interesting and revealing document. It must have been his official report or a variation of it, which came to be published. When he once more became the target of an accusation by a local official in his native place, the *Pei-shih lu* was presented in evidence. Huang P'u 黃溥 (T. 澄濟, cs 1448), then governor of Szechwan, maintained that Li Shih's account demeaned the court and bragged about his own achievement. Although Li escaped personal punishment or official demotion, the book was ordered banned. After more unfavorable accusations in 1453 and 1454, he was recalled from Hukuang and ordered to take charge of the Censorate in Peking. Soon after the restoration of 1457, accusations were again lodged against him, and the *Pei-shih lu* was held to be a boastful and fictitious account. This time he was stripped of his official status and given the sentence that no descendants of his would ever be allowed to enter official life. As if this were not enough, in 1463 people of his native place sued him on the ground of violence and oppression; so he was taken to Peking, thrown temporarily into the Embroidered-uniform Guard's prison, and his home confiscated. Under the reign of a new emperor in 1465, Li Shih memorialized when he was released, protesting his innocence and begging to be of further service. By 1472 Li was actually recalled to Peking, but before he reached the capital new accusations reached the emperor; so he was again ordered to retire, but this time with his original official titles, and the throne allowed him the privilege of wearing his official garb. In spite of the repeated misfortunes of the *Pei-shih lu*, it seems to have circulated widely, and even in the preparation of the *Ying-tsung shih-lu*, it served as an important source.

In addition to the *Pei-shih lu* there are two other first-hand documents about Emperor Chu Ch'i-Chen's captivity, namely, the *Cheng-t'ung lin-jung lu* by Yang Ming (*q.v.*) and the *Pei-cheng shih-chi* by Yüan Pin (*see* Esen and Yang Ming). A partially first-hand account on the same topic is the *P'i-t'ai lu* by Liu Ting-chih (*q.v.*).

Bibliography

1/171/14a; 5/60/15a; MSL (1963), Ying-tsung, *ch.* 181–357, Hsien-tsung (1964), 0303, 2054; KC (1958), *ch.* 28–31; SK (1930), 53/1a; *Ho-ch'uan-hsien chih* 合川縣志 (1920), 35/3b; Li Shih, *Pei-shih lu*; W. Franke, *Sources*, 2.5.1–4.

Lienche Tu Fang

LI-shih 李氏, Imperial Consort, December 7 (15th day of the 11th moon), 1546-March 18, 1614, concubine of Emperor Chu Tsai-hou, mother of Emperor Chu I-chün (*qq.v.*), and known after August 24, 1572, as Empress-dowager Tz'u-sheng 慈聖皇太后, was a native of Kuo-hsien 漷縣 (T'ung-chou 通州), near Peking. Her father, Li Wei 李偉 (T. 世奇, H. 毅齋, Pth. 恭定, 1510-February 4, 1584), was descended from a native of Shansi, who settled in T'ung-chou after taking part in the rebellion of Chu Ti (*q. v.*). In 1550, during the Mongol invasion, he moved to Peking where his young daughter was selected as a maid servant for the palace of Chu Tsai-hou, then holding the title of the prince of Yü. She bore him two sons, Chu I-chün in 1563 and Chu I-liu (*see* Chu Tsai-hou) in 1568, and a daughter, Princess Jui-an 瑞安公主, who married Wan Wei 萬煒 (*ca.* 1570-1644) in 1585. In 1567, the year after the prince of Yü ascended the throne, she was given the title Kuei-fei 貴妃, or first grade imperial consort. In 1568, when her elder son was made heir apparent, her father was appointed vice commissioner-in-chief of a central military commission and given the title of earl of Wu-ch'ing 武清伯, later raised to marquis 侯 following his grandson's enthronement in 1572.

Heretofore, whenever a new emperor succeeded to the throne, the unqualified title of Huang-t'ai-hou (Empress-dowager) had been accorded the empress of the deceased emperor. If the new emperor were not her son but the son of a concubine of the former emperor, the concubine—as, in this case, Li Kuei-fei—would, according to precedent, also be recognized as an empress-dowager, but with a qualifying term implying lesser rank. With regard to Li Kuei-fei, however, the eunuch Feng Pao (*see* Chang Chü-cheng) proposed to Grand Secretary Chang Chü-cheng that she receive the identical title, Huang-t'ai-hou, implying equal rank with the empress of the deceased emperor. Debate was resolved by conferring the title of empress dowager on both ladies, the title in each case having a distinguishing and qualifying term—the title Jen-sheng 仁聖 Huang-t'ai-hou to Chu Tsai-hou's empress (née Ch'en 陳) and the title Tz'u-sheng Huang-t'ai-hou to Li Kuei-fei. The decision seems not to have caused any ill feeling between the two ladies, whose courtesies to each other were noted as late as 1584 when they visited together the imperial tombs north of Peking. Emperor Chu I-chün showed equal respect to both.

Though officially on a par with Empress-dowager Jen-sheng, Empress-dowager Tz'u-sheng exercised paramount authority. Until Chu I-chün came of age Grand Secretary Chang Chü-cheng directed state affairs, and his astuteness largely accounts for China's increase in wealth and military power during these early years of the reign. But the grand secretary's effectiveness depended upon Tz'u-sheng's support, and her trust in him evidences her generally sound judgment. When they disagreed, however, her will

prevailed, as in the matter of patronage of Buddhism and the increase in the number of Buddhist temples (*see* Fu-teng) with consequent mounting costs to both the court and the general population, an expense against which Chang Chü-cheng protested in vain. Tz'u-sheng did not hesitate, furthermore, to discipline members of her own family, including her father, who for some slight offense was promptly summoned to the palace, upbraided, and remanded to the Grand Secretariat to abide by penalties according to law. Over Emperor Chu I-chün himself Tz'u-sheng also exercised close supervision.

While Emperor Chu Tsai-hou was still alive, she had compelled the future emperor to attend court, personally rousing him from sleep early in the morning and supervising his attire and behavior, so much so that the eunuchs regarded her demands upon the boy as excessively severe. Throughout his minority she heard his lessons, followed his recitations to his tutors, and compelled him to remain on his knees before her as punishment for any lapse of attention. In February, 1578, when he was about to be married, she withdrew from the main residence hall, the Ch'ien-ch'ing palace 乾清宮, where she had resided since 1572 to be in charge of the young emperor, and returned to her assigned residence the Tz'u-ning palace 慈寧宮 (Empress-dowager Jen-sheng residing at the Tz'u-ch'ing 慈慶 palace). But though Tz'u-sheng signalized her withdrawal with a special order entrusting sole responsibility to Chang Chü-cheng—"the deceased emperor on his sickbed entrusted you with the care of my son. I hope that you will instruct him every day and never forget the emperor's wishes"—she continued to try to superintend the young emperor's decisions and behavior.

On at least one occasion she openly threatened to dethrone him. It happened that in a drunken rage in 1580, when annoyed that two attendants had apologetically declined his request to sing a new song, he threatened them with a sword and, though agreeing with the eunuchs' plea that the girls' lives be spared, struck off tufts of hair from their heads. Hearing of this episode, Tz'u-sheng had Chang Chü-cheng file a remonstrance with the emperor and draft a decree expressing self-reproach which the emperor was compelled to attest to and publish. She also forced him to remain on his knees in her presence, pardoning him only after long sustained coolness to his pleas.

She also took a hand in the emperor's decision respecting his heir apparent. Chu I-chün's eldest son was Chu Ch'ang-lo (ECCP), born in 1582 to a lady-in-waiting at the residence of Tz'u-sheng. A month prior to Chu Ch'ang-lo's birth, Tz'u-sheng had the young mother-to-be recognized by the title Kung-fei 恭妃, who, however, was thereafter ignored by the emperor. His second son died in infancy. The third son, Chu Ch'ang-hsün (ECCP, p. 195), was born in 1586, his mother being the emperor's favorite consort, Cheng Kuei-fei (q.v.). The emperor's delay in naming the heir apparent indicated his intention to appoint Chu Ch'ang-hsün. Shortly after the child was born, the supervising secretary Chiang Ying-lin 姜應麟 (T. 泰符, 1546-1630, cs 1583), and several other officials were sent into exile for presuming to urge that the elder son and first-born, Chu Ch'ang-lo, be at once appointed heir apparent. The emperor's partiality toward Chu Ch'ang-hsün brought immediate remonstrance from Empress-dowager Tz'u-sheng. When the emperor, summoned to dine with her, argued that Chu Ch'ang-lo was only the son of a lady-in-waiting, she rebuked him sharply and reminded him that at the time of his own birth she too was of lowly rank. Tz'u-sheng's insistence helped to bring about the naming of Chu Ch'ang-lo as heir apparent in 1601 (see Shen I-kuan). When (1606) Chu Ch'ang-lo's first son, Chu Yu-chiao (ECCP), was born, Chu Ch'ang-lo's mother, the long neglected Kung-fei, was allowed the title Huang-kuei-fei; she died in 1612.

Empress-dowager Tz'u-sheng continued unchallenged both in general affairs and in those of the imperial family. When (1596) the censor, Ts'ao Hsüeh-ch'eng (see Ch'en Chü) was condemned to death for having opposed the emperor's policy toward Japan, Tz'u-sheng—using the argument that such a sentence wonld hasten the death of his ninety-year-old mother—persuaded the emperor to commute the penalty to a ten-year prison term. In 1614 when Chu Ch'ang-hsün, who in 1601 had been awarded the title of prince of Fu, was finally ready to leave Peking for Loyang to take up residence on the estate assigned him there, Tz'u-sheng maneuvered to forestall efforts by both Chu I-chün and Chu Ch'ang-hsün's mother to postpone the prince's departure. The already thirteen years' delay was regarded by many courtiers as a threat to the status of Chu Ch'ang-lo as heir apparent. Chu Ch'ang-hsün's mother now argued for further delay on the pretext that her son should remain in Peking, at least into 1615, to attend the ceremonies in honor of Tz'u-sheng's attainment of the age of seventy sui. Tz'u-sheng promptly fended this proposal by announcing that, on this premise she would summon her own younger son, Chu I-liu, prince of Lu, who in 1589 had moved from Peking to his domain in Wei-hui, Honan (see Hsiao Ta-heng), to return to Peking for the ceremonies. The implications of this proposal had their anticipated effect; Chu Ch'ang-hsün withdrew to Loyang on May 2, 1614. Shortly thereafter Tz'u-sheng died. Álvaró Semedo (q.v.) gives a description of rites connected with her funeral in his history of China. She was canonized as Hsiao-ting ... Chuang 孝定莊 Huang-hou and was buried in the tomb of Emperor Chu Tsai-hou, her tablet being placed in a special shrine called Ch'ung-hsien-tien 崇先殿.

The Li family, especially the father Li Wei, is still held in remembrance by officianados of old Peking. At the site of his one-time garden, the Ch'ing-hua yüan 清華園, located to the north of the capital, the K'ang-hsi emperor (*see* Hsüan-yeh, ECCP) constructed his own pleasance (1687), the Ch'ang-ch'un-yüan. [Editors' note: Li Wei had three sons and eight daughters. His second daughter married a descendant of Ch'en Hsüan (1365–1433, *q.v.*) and became Countess P'ing-chiang. The two elder sons held the highest of military ranks. The third son, Li Chin 進, however, became a eunuch in the palace, holding in 1583 the rank of a grand eunuch and the office of director of the palace stud. Did this son enter the palace at the same time as his sister? In any case this is one of the manifestations of the close relationship between the emperor's relatives and superior military officers, who constituted the nobility, and the eunuchs of high rank.]

Bibliography

1/*chüan* 18–21, 114/8b; 3/107/8b; 5/3/47a; 81/x/82b; Fu Wei-lin (ECCP), *Ming-shu*, 21/15a; Cheng Ju-pi 鄭汝璧 (cs 1568), *Huang Ming ti-hou chi-lüeh* 皇明帝后紀略, 16b; MSL (1965), Shih-tsung, 8557, Mu-tsung, 0180, 9743; KC (1958), 4050, 4083, 4419, 4523; *Huang Ming wen-hai* (microfilm), 1/3/24; TSCC (1885–88), X: 96/14/12a, XXXII: 118/2/6b; C. B. Malone, *History of the Summer Pal aces under the Ch'ing Dynasty* (Urbana, Ill., 1934), 23; Á. Semedo, *The History of that Great and Renowned Monarchy of China* (tr. into English, London, 1965), chap. 17.

Chou Tao-chi

LI Shih-chen 李時珍 (T. 東璧, H. 瀕湖), 1518–93, naturalist and pharmacologist, was the compiler of China's most important pharmacopoeia, the *Pen-ts'ao kang-mu* 本草綱目, 52 *ch.* Not only does work constitute one of the chief sources of knowledge of proto-scientific developments in China up to his day, but it also records the author's attitude toward his subject, which distinguishes him from preceding and contemporary writers of comparable works. Li was born in Ch'i-chou 蘄州, Hukuang, into a family known for several generations for the practice of medicine and the sale of drugs. His grandfather had peddled them, and his father Li Yen-wen 言聞 (T. 子郁, H. 月池), reported to have been selected to be a scholar in the National University in 1549, was noted both for his skill as a physician and for his ability as an author. Samples of his writings are embedded as quotations in the *Pen-ts'ao kang-mu*, and six of his productions are known by title: one on the four techniques of diagnosis (*see* below), two on smallpox, one on the pulse, one on ginseng, and the last on mugwort (artemisia) of the Ch'i-chou area. As his three children (two sons and a daughter) were growing up, he came to look with special favor on Li Shih-chen, and persuaded the boy to study for and compete in the civil service examinations. At his first test, taken at the age of fourteen *sui*, Li Shih-chen passed and became a student in the district school, but in three tries at the provincial examination he failed. Thereafter his father allowed him to desist and give all his attention to the family profession.

In the diagnosis of disease Li followed the lead of his father and of earlier traditionalists; their methods, four in number, ssu chen 四診, were known as wang 望, consideration of the general condition, including skin color and tongue of the patient; wen 聞, the use of both ear and nose in diagnosis; wen 問, an inquiry into the patient's background and physical history; and ch'ieh 切, the use of fingers to determine symptoms by feeling the pulse at the wrists. Widely recognized as an authority on the pulse—Li published two useful contributions on the subject (sphygmology)—he conceded, as had his father before him, that no diagnosis on the basis of a study of the pulse alone was sufficient; all four diagnostic methods must be brought into play. Parenthetically it may be noted here that the work of Li Yen-wen on the four diagnostic techniques, *Ssu-chen fa-ming* 發明, is erroneously listed in the local history of Ch'i-chou as *Ssu-mo* 脈 *fa-ming* (the four sphygmological techniques).

As Li's fame as a practitioner spread abroad, Ch'i-chou became a focal point for people from far and near, who suffered from various ills, some of whom he treated free of charge. His reputation in due course came to the attention of the family of the prince of Ch'u 楚 (probably Chu Ying-hsien 朱英㷿, enf. 1551, d. 1571), resident in Wuchang, and he accepted appointment in the prince's court as superintendent of sacrifices (奉祠, 8th grade) with the additional responsibility of caring for the sick. Later, on the recommendation of a prince, he officiated in the Imperial Academy of Medicine (T'ai-i yüan 太醫院) in Peking, probably as an ordinary medical officer. Service in such establishments connotes prestige and may well have given him access to books and materia medica nowhere else to be found.

While practicing medicine Li soon came to feel the need for a better understanding of the principles involved both in diagnosis and in methods of treating disease. Even more he realized that the materia medica at hand must be more precisely identified and their medicinal values better defined than had been done by any earlier writer. So from 1552 to 1578, according to his own account, he devoted himself to the ambitious task of compiling a new edition of the pharmacopoeia known under the generic name of *Pen-ts'ao*. The earliest text of an herbal by this name possibly survived the burning of the books in the last quarter of the third century B. C., and subsequently went through many transcriptions, annotations, and especially amplifications. One of the first printed editions was the *Cheng-lei* 證類 *pen-ts'ao* compiled by T'ang Shen-wei (fl. 1094). It was printed in 1108 and reprinted eight years later. In 1249 Chang Ts'un-hui of P'ing-yang, Shansi, published an illustrated, revised, and enlarged version of T'ang's work entitled *Ch'ung-hsiu Cheng-ho ching-shih cheng-lei pei yung pen-ts'ao* 重修政和經史證類備用本草, 30 *ch.*, which remained an authoritative text for three hundred years. When

Li Shih-chen began to study it critically he found it contained errors or was impracticable in classification, identification, and explanation. Furthermore, a number of new drugs, some from other lands, had been introduced since its compilation. Hence he decided to undertake himself the colossal task of producing a revised and truly up-to-date encyclopedia of pharmaceutical natural history. This was an audacity, since in former times works of this magnitude and depth had generally been compiled by imperial commissions or financed by men of wealth.

With only modest means Li proceeded on his own, reviewing a vast quantity of literature and, wherever he happened to be, collecting necessary pharmacognostic specimens and medical formulae. In his published version he listed references to almost a thousand titles in three groups. The first consists of 43 pharmacological works on each of which he made some comments; the second consists of 361 medical books; and the third, 592 general works from the Confucian Classics to fiction; of these titles about three fourths in each category had been mentioned in no earlier pharmacopaeia. To cull the information from this impressive number of works he must also have consulted many books not on the list. Yet wherever possible he augmented the information from written sources with personal observation and study of specimens. The result was the *Pen-ts'ao kang-mu*, 52 *chüan*, with 2 *ch.*, of illustrations. It contains 1,892 entries, 275 belonging to the mineral kingdom, and 444 to the zoological, 1,094 having to do with botanical species, and 79 being miscellaneous substances. Of these, Li himself added 374, of which 39 were drugs utilized by his predecessors of the Chin, Yüan, and early Ming, though unrecorded in the materia medica of those periods (12th through 16th centuries). The prescriptions number over eleven thousand, more than two thirds of which Li himself collected or formulated. The third draft of the work was completed in 1578 but further revisions were probably made in the following decade.

In 1590 Li took his manuscripts to Nanking to the famous scholar Wang Shih-chen (*q.v.*), who was then serving as minister of Justice in the southern capital. Wang was impressed by what he read and wrote a preface in which he described the author as a unique scholar, tall and slender, with a devoted look and flowing speech, and the book as a comprehensive treatise on the investigation of natural phenomena.

Probably on the strength of Wang's preface a printer at Nanking, Hu Ch'eng-lung 胡承龍, agreed to publish the *Pen-ts'ao kang-mu*. In 1593, when the printing was barely completed, Li died. In the imprint he was given as the compiler with the title of "magistrate" of P'eng-hsi 蓬溪, Szechwan, which is actually an honorary title conferred on him about 1578 at the request of his eldest son, Li Chien-chung 建中 (T. 龍源, d. *ca.* 1596, cj 1564), who held that post from 1575 to *ca.* 1578. It was the custom of the day for an author to name his sons in the imprint. Thus Li Chien-chung and the second son Li Chien-yüan 建元 (student of Huang-chou prefectural school) were recorded as proofreaders, and the other two, Li Chien-fang 建方 (a physician in the Imperial Academy of Medicine) and Li Chien-mu 建木 (T. 泰階, student of the Ch'i-chou school), as subordinate proofreaders. A grandson, Li Shu-pen 樹本, was named as calligrapher. The imprint at the beginning of the illustrations lists Li Chien-chung as compiler, Li Chien-yüan as artist, and another grandson, Li Shu-chung 樹忠, as proofreader.

When the project to compile the national history was initiated in 1594 in Peking (*see* Ch'en Yü-pi), an imperial proclamation called for the presentation of worthwhile books for reference. The Li family presented a copy of the *Pen-ts'ao kang-mu* to the throne in 1596. An edict acknowledged the receipt of the book and referred it to the ministry of Rites. After a fire in 1597 the project was abandoned and the government took no further action with respect to Li's book. There does not seem to be any basis for the story in the *Ming-shih* that the book received imperial approval to be printed and nationally distributed. In any case the printing was already complete and, as a work of high quality answering a practical need, it did not depend on imperial sanction for promotion. After the first edition of 1593 at least eight reprintings appeared during the 17th century; namely: the first Nanchang edition of 1603 issued by the Kiangsi provincial government, the Wuchang edition of 1606 issued by the Hukuang provincial government, the Shih-ch'ü-ko 石渠閣 edition (*ca.* 1620, at Nanchang?), the Chiu-shou-t'ang 久壽堂 edition (*ca.* 1630), the Hangchow Ch'ien 錢 family edition of 1640, the Hangchow Wu 吳 family edition of 1655, the second Nanchang edition issued by the Kiangsi governor's office in 1657, and a 1684 edition. The Imperial Library edition is based on the edition of 1655. While seven copies of the 1593 edition have been accounted for (one in Washington, one in Berlin, two in China, and three in Japan), only one copy of the 1606 Wuchang edition, with a hitherto unknown preface by Tung Ch'i-ch'ang (*ECCP*), has come to light and that recently. There have been many editions since 1700. In 1885 the retired general of Ho-fei (Anhwei), Chang Shao-t'ang 張紹棠 (fl. 1835-85), published an elegant edition with newly engraved illustrations. Among its appendices (as in many earlier editions since 1603) are three works by Li Shih-chen on sphygmology, *P'in-hu mo-hsüeh* 瀕湖脈學 (completed 1564), *Mo-chüeh k'ao-cheng* 脈訣考證, and *Ch'i-ching pa-mo k'ao* 奇經八脈考 (completed 1572). The first explains the 27 pulse types and is still used in China today. The last is a treatise on the eight auxiliary tracts of pneuma circulation. It is recorded that Li also authored several other works on medicine and physiology and also a collection of poems. None of these seems to be extant, except for some excerpts found in the *Pen-ts'ao kang-mu.* (For example, his work on the Ch'i-chou snake, *Pai-hua-she chuan* 白花蛇傳, is partially preserved in *chüan* 43.) There is a manuscript entitled *T'ien-k'uei lun* 天傀論 in the library of the Chinese Medical Association in Shanghai which bears his name as author. A manuscript collection of medical books, copied in the 18th century, *Li P'in-hu ch'ao i-shu* 李瀕湖抄醫書 in four volumes, is preserved in the National Central Library, Taipei. Two poems under his name have been found in anthologies. Judging from these samples he should be considered among the better poets of his time. His prose is lucid and precise.

All of Li's other works pale into insignificance when compared to his *Pen-ts'ao kang-mu.* This is not just a pharmacopoeia. It is far more, as the author's introduction clearly indicates. Li purposely spread his net wide, including matter of interest in the whole world of nature that he found in ancient literature or that he discovered himself, whether of use to a physician or not. As a result his work is concerned in chapters 5 to 11 with inanimate substances (water, fire, earth, metals, and stones), in chapters 12 to 36 with plants (herbs, grains, vegetables, fruits, and trees), in chapter 37 with garments and utensils useful to the practitioner, and in chapters 38 to 52 with animal life (insects, animals with scales and shells, birds, quadrupeds, and humans). In addition there are at the beginning two chapters of illustrations or woodcuts of minerals, plants, and animals, more than eleven hundred in number, and a bibliography. In each department of his work he gives attention to historical developments, and mentions his sources with care, correcting or supplementing them when necessary. Names of all substances are treated historically, the earliest one being taken as standard, later ones as synonyms. His observations here are frequently acute, such as the one on the

name for the solitary wasp: i-weng 蠮螉. This, he writes, is like the sound the wasp makes. Occasionally the author indicates a mistake in one or other of the synonyms. While often accepting without comment dicta from the past he also sometimes expresses his skepticism. Take, for instance, this entry about sa-pa-er 撒八兒 (turtle semen): "Liu Yü 劉郁, in his *Hsi-yü chi* 西域記 (correct title: *Hsi shih* 使 *chi*, published 1263), reports that this derives from the western sea. It is the semen of the tortoise. The crocodile eats it and then vomits. In a year or so the vomit hardens. As its price is equal to that of gold, there are false subsitutes such as the feces of the rhinoceros. I consider that a substance of such value must be efficacious, though I do not know whether there is such a thing as tortoise semen and have no means of ascertaining the facts. So I leave the problem here for other scholars to find out." Li also indicates wherever known the source of each substance, both within China and without, and in the case of interior China, where certain varieties may be had. He was keen in his appreciation not only of drugs known to earlier practitioners, but also of substances introduced nearer to his own time. Maise and sweet potato, for example, probably brought from the New World around 1550, are well described and their medicinal uses noted. Li remarks also on the entry of a new disease, syphilis. "In ancient times this was unknown; only with the reigns of Hung-chih (1488-1505) and Cheng-te (1506-21) did it become prevalent, the people taking mercury as a cure. The sickness first appeared in Kwangtung, spread northwards, and then to all parts of the empire." Although the people of China and India had been in contact for well over fifteen hundred years up to Li's time, only 26 percent of the plants listed are, according to Dr. Bernard Read, identical with those in Indian materia medica. Basically, it would appear, the Chinese developed their own cures for disease.

The world-wide influence of the *Pen-ts'ao kang-mu* began as early as 1607 when a copy of the 1593 Nanking edition that had been brought to Nagasaki, Japan, was obtained by the Confucian scholar, Hayashi Razan 林羅山 (1583-1657), and presented to the shôgun, Tokugawa Ieyasu. (This copy was deposited in the Kōbazan Bunko in Yedo in 1614 and is now preserved in the Naikaku Bunko, Tokyo.) Since then there have been ten or more reprints in Japan and the study of it in its various aspects—pharmaceutical, botanical, minerological, and zoological—has come to be known as honzō-gaku 本草學. One of the proponents, Ono Ranzan 小野蘭山 (1729-1810), made an annotated translation in 1802 under the title *Honzō kōmoku keimō* 本草綱目啓蒙, 48 *ch.* Another translation appeared in 1931.

How early the *Pen-ts'ao kang-mu* began on make any dent on the European mind is difficult to determine. For several decades before its publication certain travelers were interested in ascertaining Chinese achievements in medicine. We learn from Juan González de Mendoza's *Historia* (published in Rome in 1585, and translated into English in 1588 as *Historie of the great and mightie kingdom of China...* Part I, Book III, Chap. xvii) that among the books which the Augustinian friar Martín de Rada (*q.v.*) brought to Manila from Fukien in 1575 were "manie herbals, or books of herbes, for phisitions, shewing how they should be applied to heal infirmities;" also "many other books of physicke and medicine, compiled by authors of that kingdome, of antiquitie and of late daies, containing in them the manner how to use the sicke, and to heale them of their sickness, and to make preservatives against all sicknesses and infirmities." At least one such book, the *Hsü-shih chen-chiu* 徐氏鍼灸 (Methods of acupuncture and moxibustion of the Hsü family) by Hsü Feng-t'ing 徐鳳廷, which bears his preface of 1502 and was published in 1531, found its way to the Escorial in Spain at an early date. Although both Johann Terrenz and Michaĺ Boym (*qq.v.*) were trained in medicine they seem to have made no reference to the *Pen-ts'ao kang-mu* in their writings. The first certain use of Li Shih-chen's work by a European is that of Julien Placide Hervieu (赫蒼璧, T. 儒良, 子梫, January 14, 1671-August 26, 1746); his contribution is incorporated in Jean-Baptiste du Halde, *Description géographique, historique, chronologique, politique de l'empire* (4 vols., Paris, 1735), III, 435-525, and bears the title: "Extrait du Pen tsao cang mou, c'est-a-dire de l'Herbier chinois, ou Histoire naturelle de la Chine pour l'usage de la médecine." Hervieu points out with fair correctness that the work was by Li che tchin, revised and enlarged by his son, presented to the Wan-li emperor in the 24th year of his reign [1596], and that it was reprinted in the 22d year of K'ang-hsi [1683]— probably the edition he himself utilized. As the work of du Halde appeared successively in English (two volumes, 1738-41), in German, and in Russian translation, one may take it for granted that the *Pen-ts'ao kang-mu* had some influence on the scientific thought of Europe in the 18th and early 19th centuries. Carl von Linné (1707-78) reflects it; so also do Charles Darwin (1809-82) and the Russian physician, A. Tatarinov, writing in 1853. Certainly by the last decades of the 19th century the writings of Dr. E. V. Bretschneider, to name only one scholar, brought it to the attention of the scholarly world through his *Botanicon Sinicum*, which first appeared (imperfectly) in *The Chinese Recorder* of 1870 and 1871, and again, with revisions, in the *Journal of the Royal Asiatic Society*, China branch, in 1881, 1890-91, and 1894-95; see especially his introductory remarks in Volume 16. His contributions were reprinted in London (1882) and Shanghai (1892 and 1895). In the 20th century the name of Dr. Bernard E. Read (see bibliography) stands out especially for his more particularized researches and

translations made with the able assistance
of one Korean and three Chinese scientists.

Extensive research by Japanese, Chinese, and western scholars has revealed
to science Chinese knowledge of inocula-
tion against smallpox, the use of kaolin
as medicine, chaulmoogra oil for sufferers
from leprosy, a certain marine algae (containing iodine) for alleviation of goiter,
and ma-huang (ephedrine) as an antidote
for colds; also strychnos nux vomica,
stramonium, rhubarb root, opium, iron fil-
ings, asafetida, aconite, and the secretion
of the toad's poison gland (now known
to contain a digitalis-like substance).
Scholars have likewise found Li's opus of
high utility in the study of plant and
other transmissions, iron and steel processing, meterorite and fire, wild and domestic animal life in China and on its borders, a long list of trees (such as cam-
phor, cinnamon, pine, willow, bamboo,
tamarisk, mulberry), and the social and
religious ideas and practices of the common people. In his time Li Shih-chen was
regarded highly as a learned man and as
a physician especially by his fellow townsmen, among whom may be mentioned
a prince of the imperial clan (the prince
of Fu-shun 富順王, Chu Hou-k'un 朱厚焜,
fl. 1514-76) and the two Ku brothers, Ku
Wen 顧問 (T. 子承, H. 日巖, cs 1538)
and Ku Ch'üeh闕 (T. 子良, H. 桂巖, 1528-
1613, cs 1553). After Li's eldest son (Li
Chien-chung) became a *chü-jen* in 1564
and then a magistrate, his social position
rose locally. It was Ku Ch'üeh's grandson
Ku Ching-hsing 景星 (T. 黃公, 1621-87)
who wrote the biographies of several generations of the Li family, including the
most famous grandson of Li Shih-chen,
Li Shu-ch'u 樹初 (T. 客天, 1587-1643, cs
1619, intendant of Ch'ih-ch'eng 赤城 in
present Hopei). About 1627 Li Shu-ch'u
erected a memorial arch in Ch'i-chou in
honor of his grandfather (Li Shih-chen)
as well as his father (Li Chien-chung)
and foster father (Li Chien-mu). The arch
had an inscription Liu-ch'ao wen-hsien

liang-chen kan-ch'eng 六朝文獻. 兩鎮干城
notables of six reigns [Cheng-te to T'ien-
ch'i]; defender of two military posts [prob-
ably referring to Li Shu-ch'u himself]).
Killed by bandits in 1643 when Ch'i-chou
fell into their hands, Li Shu-ch'u was
celebrated as a martyr and given a posthumous title in the 18th century. In
time, however, his name became so
unfamiliar that even the compilers of
the *Chi-fu t'ung-chih* 畿輔通志 of 1884
failed to identify him (1934 ed.. D. 962).

As a pharmacologist Li's fame has
been sustained by his *Pen-ts'ao kang-mu*.
Some adventurous publishers even used
his name to promote sales. But facts
about his life did not begin to interest
Chinese scholars until the early 1950s.
Before that even his birth and death
dates were not determined and were given
variously as flourished 1596 or 1522-96,
etc. Then in 1954 an article appeared in
the *Chung-hua i-shih tsa-chih* 中華醫史雜
誌, no. 1, asserting that the correct dates,
based on sources found at Li's tomb, were
1518-93; these have been currently accepted. In 1955 a memorial stamp was issued in Peking in his honor. An imaginative portrait of him appears on the
stamp, which has since been reproduced
as his likeness. Another likeness of Li,
equally imaginative, may be found in K.
C. Wong and Wu Lien-teh, *History of
Chinese Medicine* (2d ed., Shanghai, 1936),
opposite page 78. In 1957 a film was
made about his life. The legend of Li
Shih-chen is accumulatively in the making.

The stature of Li Shih-chen has
grown from that of a pharmacologist to
one versed in several fields of science in
which his attainments need to be more
carefully evaluated. Such a study should
begin with the separation of what had
already been known before his time from
his own contributions. It is in the latter
respect that the personage of Li Shih-
chen may be fully revealed and better
appreciated. Dr. Bernard E. Read and

his colleagues have led the way in this investigation.

Bibliography

1/101/1a, 299/19a; *Pen-ts'ao kang-mu* (1603; NLP microfilm nos. 589–92); TSCC(1885–88), XIV: 73/8/18a; Ku Ching-hsing, *Pai-mao-t'ang chi* 白茅堂集, 38/1a, 45/13b; *Ch'i-chou chih* 蘄州志 (1882), 9/13a, 14b, 10/9a, 11/3b, 12/11a; SK (1930), 104/8a; L. ofC., *Catalogue of Rare Books*, 549; Watanabe Kōzō 渡邊幸三, "Various editions of Li Shih-chen's herbal" (in Japanese) in *Tōyōshi-kenkyu*, XII, 4 (June, 1953); Yen-yü 燕羽, "Shih-liu-shih-chi ti wei-ta k'o-hsüeh-chia Li Shih-chen" 十六世紀的偉大科學家李時珍 in *Chung-kuo k'e-hsüeh chi-shu fa-ming ho k'e-hsüeh chi-shu jen-wu lun-chi* 中國科學技術發明和科學技術人物論集 (Peking, 1955)314; Chang Hui-chien 張慧劍 (author) and Chiang Chao-ho 蔣兆和 (illustrator), *Li Shih-chen* 李時珍 (Shanghai, 1954); Fang Hao 方豪, "Liu-le yü Hsi P'u ti Chung-kuo wen-hsien" 流落於西葡的中國文獻の科學技術史 part 1, *Hsüeh-shu chi-k'an* 學術季刊 I:2 (December 1952), 154; Yabuuchi Kiyoshi 藪內清 Yoshida Mitsukuni 吉田光邦 (eds.), *Min-shin jidai no kagaku gijutsu* 明清時代の科學技術, Kyoto, 1970; Kotari Shirai, Tomitaro Makino, *et al*, *Kokuyaku honzō kōmoku*, 15 vols., 1931; Joseph Needham and Wang Ling, *Science and Civilization in China*, IV, part I (1962), 64; Bernard E. Read with Liu Ju-ch'iang, Li Yü-t'ien, Ya Ching-mei, and Pak Kyebyǒng—see bibliography in Needham and Wang, IV, part 1, 388; Lung Po-chien, Li Tao, and Chang Hui-chien: "Li Shih-chen—Ancient China's Great Pharmacologist," *People's China* (January 1, 1955), 31; Cheng Chih-fan: "Li Shih-chen and his *Materia Medica*," *China Reconstructs*, XII: 3 (March, 1963), 29; Donald F. Lach, *Asia in the Making of Europe*, I, bk. 2 (Chicago, 1965), 778 and n. 276; S. Elisseeff, Bibliography, HJAS, I (1936), 261; Lu Gwei-djen, "China's Greatest Naturalist; a Brief Biography of Li Shih-chen," *Physis*, 8 (1966),383.

*L. Carrington Goodrich and
Chaoying Fang*

LI Shih-mien 李時勉 (*ming* 懋, but preferred his *tzu*, H. 古廉), 1374–1450, a member of an old Nanking family which had recently moved to An-fu 安福, Kiangsi, was one of a small group of officials who suffered grievously for giving personal offense to the otherwise notably just emperors, Chu Kao-chih and Chu Chan-chi

(*qq.v.*). Li's case, in particular, was a palace scandal that was kept well obscured throughout the Ming dynasty.

After winning his metropolitan degree in 1404, Li was successively a Hanlin bachelor, a bureau secretary in the ministry of Justice, and a reader in the Hanlin Academy. In the last capacity he worked on the editorial boards of both the *Yung-lo ta-tien* (*see* Yao Kuang-hsiao) and the *T'ai-tsu shih-lu* (*see* Hu Kuang). Late in 1421 he offended Emperor Chu Ti (*q.v.*) by arguing that the newly built capital in the north, Peking, was not yet a suitable place for the reception of foreign envoys. Parenthetically it may be noted that, just a year before (December 14, 1420), the famous embassy of Shāhrūkh had arrived in Peking and was received in audience by Chu Ti. Following the audience (acording to the Persian chronicler) "they were conducted to the Yamkhana or hostelry where they found everything handsomely provided for them." The embassy remained until about May 18, 1421. No mention of this appears in the *shih-lu*. Li was imprisoned for more than a year before being released in 1423 at the urging of the influential grand secretary, Yang Jung (*q.v.*). Then in 1425 he was imprisoned again by the new emperor Chu Kao-chih, and again more than a year passed before he was released by Chu Chan-chi.

Compilers of the contemporary official chronologies, *Jen-tsung shih-lu* and *Hsüan-tsung shih-lu* —in both instances dominated by Grand Secretaries Yang Shih-ch'i (*q.v.*) and Yang Jung—reported that in 1425 Li was transferred to be an investigating censor "because he spoke out about things," that "those in authority" immediately after the death of Chu Kao-chih imprisoned him, and that in 1426 Chu Chan-chi "learned of his literary scholarship" and released him to resume his former duties. The *Ying-tsung shih-lu*, in noting Li's death in 1450, makes clear that it was Chu Kao-chih himself who, in a characteristic fit of temper, had Li severely beaten and then cast into prison; and that Chu Chan-chi later ordered Li put to death for having insulted the former monarch, only to pardon him after learning from Li the content of his memorial to Chu Kao-chih. The chroniclers give no inkling of what Li had in fact said.

No Ming historian seems to have reported more fully, except that Hsü Hsien 徐咸 (cs 1511) in his *Hsi-yüan tsa-chi* 西園雜記 and Ch'en Chien (*q.v.*) in his *Huang Ming t'ung-chi* indicate that Li had memorialized about "current policies and violations of morality" 時政違節. Cheng Hsiao, Li Chih, Yin Shou-heng (*qq.v.*), and Fu Wei-lin (ECCP) all report that they did not know what was in the memorial; and Ku Ying-t'ai (ECCP) writes merely that it had been something "very provocative." Ch'en Chien and Cha Chi-tso (ECCP) both wondered why the famous "three Yang" (*see* Yang Shih-ch'i and Yang Jung) or other eminent ministers of the time had not protested against imperial mistreatment of Li. But the substance of Li's memorial seems to have remained secret until preparation of the imperially sponsored *Ming-shih kao* 明史稿 (1723) and *Ming-shih* (completed 1739, finally published *ca.* 1782). Then it was at last revealed that, when angrily interrogated by Chu Chan-chi, Li confessed that he had urged Chu Kao-chih, among other things, not to keep the heir apparent in Nanking far from the court (perhaps sufficient to mollify the emperor), and to cease recruiting a harem of imperial concubines while he was still in formal mourning for his father, Chu Ti (certainly sufficient to anger Chu Kao-chih). What purports to be the verbatim substance of Li's memorial was finally published in 1781 in the imperially sponsored *Ming-ch'en tsou-i* 明臣奏議, and an abbreviated version appeared in 1817 in the similarly sponsored *Ch'in-ting Ming-chien* 欽定明鑑 with editorial comment: "Jen-tsung [Chu Kao-chih] was a worthy ruler, and Shih-mien was an upright minister. When an upright minister and a worthy ruler

are in confrontation, why should they be mutually antagonistic to such an extreme? ... Thus the study of cherishing virtue cannot but be earnest, and the striving for self-restraint cannot but be determined." The Manchu emperor (Yung-yen, ECCP), himself posthumously called Jen-tsung, appended an ode in honor of Li Shih-mien, concluding, "We sincerely commend Shih-mien's loyalty, and we are sorely grieved with Jen-tsung." Perhaps this criticism by a Ch'ing emperor may be considered quite rational, for indeed none of the Manchu emperors before the mid-nineteenth century seems to have committed such excesses as Li mentioned in his memorial. He dwelt on these four points: that the emperor should consider the unbearable burden on the people and stop his extensive construction work in the palace area, that he should set an example for the observance of mourning on the death of a parent by refraining from such acts as sending eunuchs to far away places like Fukien to search for virgins, that he should rise early to attend the morning court before sunrise, and that he should every day spend more time with scholarly officials and less with eunuchs and women.

It appears that Chu Kao-chih, on first receiving Li's memorial, summoned him to private audience on May 22, and, infuriated by his candid explanations, ordered him beaten seventeen times with a mace-like weapon called a Chin-kua 金瓜 (golden gourd). Three ribs were broken, and Li was dragged away in a faint. The emperor announced that Li was to be transferred from the Hanlin Academy to the Censorate—perhaps as an ironic gesture suggesting that Li belonged in one of the "speaking offices" if he insisted on being so outspoken. As a censor he was ordered to conduct a trial every day in addition to submitting a memorial; in either case any mistake could be used against him. After three days of this kind of mental torture he was sent to prison where, it is said, an officer took pity on him and brought him back to normal with some unusual medicine. There is the story that a few days after these events, and shortly before his sudden death, the emperor still spoke in anger about Li's personally insulting him.

When released by Chu Chan-chi in 1426, Li resumed his former duties as Hanlin reader. In 1430 he became Hanlin reader-in-waiting, and under Chu Ch'i-chen (*q. v.*) he was promoted (1438) to be chancellor of the Hanlin Academy, and three years later chancellor of the National University. He won special fame in the latter post, both as a lecturer on the Classics (even court officials came to listen) and as a conscientious and liberal patron of students.

For repeatedly snubbing the increasingly powerful eunuch Wang Chen (*q. v.*), Li got into trouble again in 1443. On the pretext that Li had trimmed a tree on the National University grounds without proper authority, Wang Chen forced him to sit in disgrace at the university gate pilloried in a hundred-catty cangue. More than a thousand students demonstrated angrily in front of the imperial palace on Li's behalf, and influential friends persuaded the emperor to release him after three days of humiliation. (The *Ying-tsung shih-lu* avoids mentioning this incident in its biographical notice about Li.)

Li had already passed his seventieth birthday and had begun requesting retirement. His repeated requests were not heeded until 1447. Then more than three thousand officials and students escorted him out of the capital in a farewell ceremony demonstrating rare affection and esteem. On his death three years later he was canonized Wen-i 文毅. Subsequently, at the request of his family, the canonical name was changed to Chung-wen 忠文. Li was also posthumously promoted to vice minister of Rites.

A grandson, Li Yung 顒, published Li's collected writings in the Ch'eng-hua period under the title *Ku-lien chi* 古廉集, 11 *ch.*, with a 1 *chüan* supplement of bio-graphical material. The work was copied into the Imperial Library in the 18th century and has been reproduced in the *Ssu-k'u chen-pen* 珍本, series 3. An original copy of 1474 in 10 *chüan* is in the National Central Library, Taipei, and is available on microfilm. At the time (May, 1425), when Li Shih-mien was sent to prison for criticizing Emperor Chu Kao-chih, another Hanlin member, Lo Ju-ching 羅汝敬 (*ming* 簡, H. 寅庵, 1372–1439, cs 1404), was also jailed and made a censor for the same reason. Later Lo held the rank of vice minister of Works and served on missions to Annam (November, 1427, June, 1428) and Chekiang (August, 1429), and several times as director of military farming (later grand coordinator) in Shensi from 1431 to 1438. Several officials were also known to have suffered scandalously for offending the next emperor, Chu Chan-chi, by their indiscreet advice. Among them may be mentioned Ch'en Tso 陳祚 (T. 永錫, H. 退庵, 1382–1456, cs 1411), Kuo Hsün 郭循 (T. 循初, 1395?–1450, cs 1421), convicted in 1431, Tai Lun (*see* Huai En), and Lin Ch'ang-mao 林長懋 (T. 景時, cj 1405), jailed in 1425.

Ch'en and Kuo were accused of disrespect—Ch'en for suggesting a primer for the imperial study and Kuo for accusing the emperor of extravagance. As to Tai and Lin, they had both been tutors to the emperor while he was a prince and reproved him for his love of riding, hunting, and military exercises. On his enthronement he sent both to prison, where Tai died, and Lin was not released until 1435.

Bibliography

1/162/3b, 4b, 163/1a; 3/143/5b, 147/4a; 5/19/34a, 73/7a, 90/75a, 99/27a; 34/1/11a; 42/61/4a; 61/121/3b; 63/19/6b, 9a; 64/乙9/x, /乙10/x; MSL (1940), Jen-tsung, 10/3b, Hsüan-tsung, 22/9b, Ying-tsung, 151/7b, 190/19b, 191/13b, 193/26a; SK (1930), 170/7a; Li Hsien, *Ku-jang tsa-lu* (*Chi-lu hui-pien* ed.), x/14b; Yeh Sheng, *Shui-tung jih-chi*, 2/9a; Chu Yün-ming, *Yeh-chi*, x/32a; Hsü

Hsien, *Hsi-yüan tsa-chi* (*Yüan Ming shan-pen ts'ung-shu* 元明善本叢書 ed.), 2/4a; Cheng Hsiao, *Wu-hsüeh pien*, 34/1a; T'ang Shu唐樞(1497–1574), *Kuo-shen chi* 國琛集 (*Chi-lu hui-pien* ed.), 1/24b; Wang Shih-chen, *Yen-shan-t'ang pieh-chi*, 8/6b, 28/13a; T'an Hsi-ssu, *Ming ta-cheng tsuan-yao*, 17/21a, 18/22a; Chu Kuo-chen (ECCP), *Huang Ming shih-kai*, 9/24a, 10/11a, 11/4a, 13b, 12/12a, 13/3a; Ch'en Chien, *Huang Ming t'ung-chi ts'ung-hsien-lu*, 15/6a, 37a, 17/11b, 29a; Cha Chi-tso, *Tsui-wei lu* (SPTK ed.),13A/33a; Huang Yü 黃瑜, *Shuang-huai sui-ch'ao* 雙槐歲鈔, 4/5a; Chu Lin 朱璘 (fl. 1685), *Ming-chi chi-lüeh*明紀輯略, 4/41b, 46b; Ku Ying-t'ai, *Ming-shih* (orig. title *Ming-ch'ao*) *chi-shih pen-mo*, 28/14a, 27b, 29/7b; *Ming-ch'en tsou-i* (TsSCC ed.), 2/21; *Ch'in-ting Ming-chien* (1817 ed.), 7/10b; Hsia Hsieh 夏燮 (1799–1875?), *Ming t'ung-chien*明通鑑 (late Ch'ing ed.), 17/12b, 17a, 19/11b; Kuo Po-kung郭伯恭, *Yung-lo ta-tien k'ao* 永樂大典考(1938), 43; Ku Chieh-kang (BDRC), "A Study of Literary Persecution during the Ming," tr. L. Carrington Goodrich, HJAS, III (1938), 270; "The Embassy Sent by Shah Rukh to the Court of China, A.D. 1419–1422,"in Yule and Cordier, *Cathay and the Way Thither*, I (London, 1915), 280; *A Persian Embassy to China*, tr. by K. M. Maitra (Lahore, 1934, repr. N.Y., 1970), 64.

Charles O. Hucker

LI Shih-ta 李士達(H. 仰槐, 仰懷, 邵甫, 通甫), fl. 1580–1620, an artist noted for landscapes and figure compositions, was a native of Wu 吳-hsien (Soochow). Little is known of Li. The assertion is sometimes made that he attained the *chin-shih*, but this confuses him with a man of the same name, a native of Sian (cs 1574). He is described as being a proud man, full of self-esteem. He once narrowly escaped difficulties when he refused to kneel in the presence of Sun Lung (*see* Chü Chieh), merely making a deep bow and then departing. He went into hiding and constables sent to arrest him could not find him. It is said that the wealthy and powerful who sought Li's paintings were unable to obtain them at any price. He was active as an artist when he was seventy-three years of age, but he may not have begun painting until somewhat late in life since the earliest date on any of his paintings corresponds to 1601.

Li's artistic abilities were quite varied. Among his works are paintings in which the landscape and the figures are stylistically akin to the styles current in the late 16th and early 17th centuries, such as a fan showing a bustling ferryboat landing, dated 1612, or another fan painting, "Ch'i-lü hsün-mei t'u" 騎驢尋梅圖 (On donkeyback seeking plum-blossoms), dated 1619, depicting a traveler in a wintry landscape. He was equally attracted to the art of the past and selected models from all eras. Through exaggeration and emphasis of salient features, he adeptly exploited and reworked antique styles and compositions. The bright blue and green mineral pigments seen in the landscape background of a fan painting depicting the pastimes of scholars, now in the Hashimoto collection, is based on a technique which, according to tradition, originated in the T'ang dynasty. A painting in the Seikado collection in Tokyo, entitled "Shan-t'ing t'iao-wang 山亭眺望 t'u" (Gazing from a mountain pavilion), dated 1618, is a daring and striking revision of the Southern Sung "one-cornered" composition. The open vistas and the large, gnarled pine trees in the immediate foreground of "Tso-t'ing sung feng 坐聽松風 t'u" (Listening to the wind in the pines), dated 1616, in the National Palace Museum, derive from the horizontal tripartite compositional divisions familiar in Yüan dynasty landscape paintings. Yet another, "Chu-li ch'üan-sheng 竹裡泉聲 t'u" (Listening to the sounds of a spring in a bamboo grove), shows the influence of the artist Hsieh Shih-ch'en (*q. v.*).

As themes for his figure compositions, Li Shih-ta portrayed not only the diversions of the literati, but also specific famous ones among them, as in the hanging scroll now in the University of Michigan Museum of Art, "T'ao Ch'ien shang-chü 陶潛賞菊 t'u" (T'ao Ch'ien [365–427] admiring chrysanthemums), dated 1619, or the handscroll "Hsi-yüan ya-chi 西園雅集

t'u" (The elegant gathering in the western garden). The latter is a delightfully inventive depiction of the sixteen Northern Sung luminaries, including Su Shih (1037-1101), Huang T'ing-chien (1045-1105), Mi Fu (1051-1107), and Li Kung-lin (1049-1106), with their attendants, in a setting of arching pines, curved-leafed palms, and mammoth rounded boulders. The figures of the gentlemen are exaggeratedly rotund and paunchy, repeating the massive shapes of the boulders behind them, while the extraordinarily slim servants and ladies echo the slender verticals of the tree trunks and bamboo stalks.

With one exception all the known and recorded paintings by Li are either landscapes or figure paintings; thus, a hanging scroll "Jui-lien 瑞蓮 t'u" (Auspicious lotus), dated 1606, in the National Palace Museum, is his only flower painting and is the only one by him executed in a free fashion, employing flowing strokes and pools of ink and green color. Li lived in retirement at Hsin-kuo 新郭 (probably a peninsula in the northern part of Shih-hu 石湖 near Soochow), and at the age of eighty years still enjoyed night-long carousing; at that advanced age "the pupils of his eyes were bright, his wrists supple, and his body like an immortal's." He wrote a treatise on painting of which only a summary (?), as noted by Chiang Shao-shu 姜紹書, has survived: "Landscape has five excellences—vigor 蒼, spontaneity 逸, creativity 奇, completeness 圓, and harmony 韻; landscape has five faults—timidity 嫩, stiffness 板, laboriousness 刻, incompleteness 生, and confusion 癡."

Li Shih-ta had at least one pupil, a certain Shen Chen 沈軫 (T. 文林). In addition, some of the paintings executed by Sheng Mao-yeh (*q. v.*) reveal the influence of Li Shih-ta.

Bibliography

Chiang Shao-shu, *Wu-sheng shih-shih* 無聲詩史 (*Hua-shih* 畫史 *ts'ung-shu* ed.), 4/70; Hsü Ch'in 徐沁, *Ming hua lu* 明畫錄(*ibid.*), 1/12, 5/66; Hsü Pang-ta, *Li-tai…shu-hua … nien-piao* (Shanghai, 1963), 91; Kuo Wei-ch'ü 郭味蕖, *Sung Yüan Ming Ch'ing shu-hua-chia nien-piao* 宋元明清書畫家年表 (Peking, 1962); *Wu-hsien chih* 吳縣志 (1642), 53/16b; Ch'en Jen-t'ao 陳仁濤, *Chin-k'uei ts'ang hua chi*, Vol. 1 (Hong Kong), pl. 38; *Su-chou po-wu-kuan ts'ang hua chi* 蘇州博物館藏畫集 (1963), pls. 23–25; *Ku-kung chou-k'an* 故宮週刊, no. 11, 302, 432; *Kokka, no.* 309; O. Sirén, *Chinese Painting* (New York, 1956–58), Vol. V: 27, VI: 276, 277, VII: 208; *Masterpieces of Chinese Painting in the National Palace Museum* (Taipei, 1970), pl. 38; *Kyūka Inshitsu Kanzo Garoku* 九華印室鑑藏畫錄, Vol. 1, Kyoto, 1920; KKSHC, no. 28.

E. J. Laing

LI Tai 李戴 (T. 仁夫, H. 對泉), *ca.* 1531-March 1, 1607, an official who served as minister of Personnel for five and a half years, was a native of Yen-chin 延津, Honan. Following his graduation as *chin-shih* in 1568, he became magistrate for three years (1568-71) of Hsing-hua 興化, in the prefecture of Yangchow, and then supervising secretary of the ministry of Finance. Early in the Wan-li period, he was made successively chief supervising secretary of Revenue (April, 1576), right administration vice commissioner in Shensi, then surveillance commissiner. From all accounts Li left a favorable impression everywhere he officiated. During his days in Hsing-hua three floods inundated the region. On one hand, he besought the government to exempt the people from taxation and grant them financial aid; on the other, he urged the people not to leave, and personally aided them out of his own resources. Four letters from him, two of them written from Shansi to his friends in Hsing-hua, are preserved in the Hsing-hua local history. Not surprisingly the people erected a shrine in his honor. Under the vigorous leadership of Chang Chü-cheng (*q.v.*), he was shifted first to the office of left administration commissioner of Shansi, and second to that of right assistant censor-in-chief and concurrently governor of Shantung. Unlike others in provincial posts, during the days when Chang was in power, Li Tai continued his benevolent administration. After this he served as vice minister of Justice, minister of Finance in Nanking (appointed October 13, 1594), and minister of Works in Nanking (appointed June 19, 1595). A few months later he retired to mourn the loss of his stepmother. At the conclusion of the mourning period the court ordered him to Peking to become minister of Personnel (July 25, 1598).

At this time many parts of the country were upset by the emperor's insistence on ever higher taxes on mines. Li Tai objected sharply to the exorbitance of these demands, especially those made by such eunuchs as Ch'en Feng (*q.v.*), who was in charge in Hukuang, but to no avail. Ch'en urged his arrest, but the emperor took no action even when Li Tai accused Ch'en and Kao Huai (*see* Chien I), another eunuch stationed in Liaotung, of recruiting soldiers simply to make further extortions from the people. An unexpected denouement came in March, 1602: the emperor fell ill and in alarm agreed to the abrogation of the mining tax and the release of those in prison who had opposed it. The very next day, however, he recovered and immediately withdrew his previous commands. Li Tai and others urged him to change his mind, but the emperor brushed them angrily aside. While the Grand Secretariat was still pondering the question of procedure, Li continued his protests to the throne. Whereupon the minister of Justice, Hsiao Ta-heng (*q.v.*), chided him for improper procedure, and the chief minister of the Court of the Imperial Stud, Nan Ch'i-chung 南企仲 (T. 伯墀, 1561–1643, cs 1580) also took him to task for delaying his request for the release of those imprisoned. Li Tai requested permission to resign, but without successs.

Another matter that disturbed his period as minister was the case of Chao Pang-ch'ing 趙邦清 (cs 1592), a director of a bureau in the ministry, and an upright official, who was unfairly charged by the censors Tso Tsung-ying 左宗郢 (cs 1589) and Li P'ei 李培 (cs 1589). When Li came to Chao's support, they criticized him for incompetence as minister. Again he asked to be allowed to resign, but the emperor refused.

Li Tai, like many another knowledgeable official of his day, had an inquiring mind and developed an interest in both Buddhism and Taoism, and—after making the acquaintance of Matteo Ricci (*q.v.*)—in Christianity. He wrote a preface, dated 1601, to the *Leng-yen-ching shu chih* (on the *Śuraṅgama sūtra*) by his old friend of Hsing-hua days, Lu Hsi-hsing (*q.v.*), and at his urging sought help from others to finance its printing. In the same preface he also praised two others of Lu's compilations: the *Fang-hu wai-shih*, a work on Taoist physical education, and the *Nan-hua chen-ching fu-mo*, his Taoist exposition. About the same time he made the acquaintance in Peking of the newly arrived Jesuit missionary. Matteo Ricci recounts that he was frequently a guest in Li's house where the two devoted many hours to discussing religion and the after life. But Ricci could not dislodge Li's convictions. "If your God is the lord of heaven," Ricci has him say, "the Buddha is supreme on earth." Later (1608) Ricci was to write a small book, the *Chi-jen shih p'ien*, which devotes some space to his talks with Li and the minister of Rites, Feng Ch'i (*q.v.*).

During the winter of 1603–4 the capital was thrown into an uproar over the appearance of the anonymous broadside, *Hsü yu-wei hung-i* (*see* Cheng Kuei-fei), which cast aspersions on the imperial house. Among those involved happened to be a nephew of Li Tai, named Chou Chia-ch'ing 周嘉慶, an officer of the Embroidered-uniform Guard. Inevitably Li was implicated and suffered the loss of all his insignia and his office (January 16, 1604). While in retirement he donated

money to build a free school (義學) for
the local boys and also purchased sufficient
land, the income from which would support it indefinitely. Three years later,
probably at the age of seventy-six or
seven, he died peacefully at home. (Ricci
records that he was seventy when they
met in 1601.) The throne subsequently
honored him with the posthumous title
shao-pao 少保 (junior guardian of the
heir apparent). He had earlier, July 2,
1601, earned the lower title t'ai-tzu t'ai-
pao 太子少保.

Bibliography

1/225/8a; 3/209/8a; MSL (1966), Shen-tsung,
1113, 5117, 5281, 6009, 6719, 6881, 7357, 7382,
8111; TSCC (1885–88), XI: 304/6/9a; *Hsing-hua-
hsien chih* (1852), 6/ 秩官1/10a, 仕蹟 11a; *K'ai-
feng-fu chih* 開封府志 (1863 repr. of 1695 ed.),
26/34b; *Shansi t'ung-chih* (1892), 12/18a; *Shantung
t'ung-chih* (1934), 2307; Liu Ts'un-yan, *Buddhist
and Taoist Influences on Chinese Novels*, Vol. I:
The authorship of the *Feng shen yen i* (Weisbaden, 1962), 259; P. M. d'Elia, *Fonti Ricciane*,
II (Rome, 1949), 157, 182, 190, 300.
Yang Chin-yi and L. Carrington Goodrich

LI Tan 李旦, died August 12, 1625, an
important merchant in the China Sea
trade, but referred to in some Chinese
official accounts as a pirate, was a native
of Ch'üan-chou 泉州, Fukien. He is described as a smuggler who thrived on the
prohibited trade with foreign countries
and who, escaping from the local authorities, lived in Japan as a man of influence. He is mentioned in dispatches and
memorials of 1623–24 during the Dutch
occupation of the Pescadores. At first he
was condemned as a pirate who, by keeping the Japanese from giving military
assistance to the Dutch, helped in forcing
the latter to leave the Pescadores. Probably for this reason he was not molested
when in 1624 he returned to Amoy to
visit his ancestral tombs and collect from
his debtors; he was even permitted at this
time to leave with a cargo of silk and
other goods (*see* Nan Chü-i). According

to another Chinese source, Li Tan was
the pirate captain whom Cheng Chih-
lung (ECCP) first served as a lieutenant
and later succeeded as chief.

This has been practically all that was
known about Li Tan until in 1958 Iwao
Seiichi 岩生成一 published his article entitled "Li Tan 李旦, Chief of the Chinese
Residents at Hirado, Japan, in the Last
Days of the Ming Dynasty." In this he
identified Li Tan as the "China Captain,"
"Andrea Dittis." and Tojin Capitan 唐人
カビタン or China Captain 支那甲必丹 in
English, Dutch, and Japanese accounts. C.
R. Boxer had earlier mentioned the "Fukienese trader, Li Han Kok, alias Andrea
Dittis, alias 'Captain-China'" but had not
dealt with Li's career. Based on the Iwao
article and other sources, one may reconstruct the early life of Li Tan as follows.

Soon after the Spaniards in 1571
established a settlement in Manila on the
island of Luzon, Chinese traders flocked
there in increasing numbers. These Chinese, who came chiefly from Amoy, the
port of Chüan-chou, and the south China
coast, had probably been denied by the
Cantonese the opportunity of taking
part in the profitable foreign trade at
Macao just as the Portuguese had denied
it to the English, Dutch, and Spanish,
These Fukiense first came and went in
junks to barter with the Spanish, but soon
began to settle in numbers in the Parián
or Chinese quarter. Li Tan was one of
them. It is unknown whether he started
his career as a sailor or as a merchant.
Also unknown is the time he first arrived
in Manila. In any event he rose to be a
leader in the quarter and was even described by Cocks in 1616 as having been
"governor of the Chinas at Manila... and
in the end the Spaniards picked a
quarrel on purpose to seize all he
had, to the value of above 40,000 taels
and put him into the galleys, from
whence he escaped some nine years since
and came to Firnando, where he hath
lived ever since" (letter of Richard Cocks
dated February 25, 1616). The seizure of

his property probably took place between the massacre of October, 1603, and either 1607 or 1608 when he landed in Japan.

It was at about this time that the Chinese population in Japan suddenly increased many fold. Chu Kuo-chen (1557–1632; ECCP) quotes a report that "beginning with 1608 the Chinese traders who arrived at Nagasaki Island numbered about twenty, and within less than a decade more than two or three thousand have come." Was this a coincidence? Or did Li Tan, mistreated by the Spanish, lead some of his countrymen to a new haven? Whatever happened, he became the leader of the growing community in Hirado, and in 1620 (writes Cocks in his *Diary*, II, 309) "this Andrea Dittis is now chosen captain cheefe commander of all the Chinas in Japon, both at Hangasaque, Firando and elsewhere."

In these days the Tokugawa government at Yedo was encouraging foreign trade, and the local Japanese were treating the Chinese with respect. The rise of Li Tan to affluence and influence may be attested by the reports that between 1613 and 1617 a number of Japanese of high rank, including the governor of Nagasaki, called on him or were entertained by him, and on one occasion he made a loan of sixty thousand taels to the feudal lord, Shimazu 島津. A Dutch account reads: "He is a sly man; he has magnificent houses at Nagasaki and here at Hirado and several pretty wives and children." At the end of 1617 a fire in Nagasaki consumed three of his houses and warehouses, but he seems to have survived this loss without difficulty.

The wealth of Li Tan and other members of his family was built on trade with south China and southeastern Asia. Because of Ming China's prohibition of overseas commerce except at Macao, business had to be transacted at such neutral points as Taiwan and the Pescadores (P'eng-hu 澎湖) or secretly at such foreign ports as Manila and Nagasaki. A Japanese source records, under date of February 19, 1614, that the Shogunate granted the younger brother of Li Tan named Li Hua-yü 華宇 (known also as Whowe, Whow, or Whaow, d. 1620) a license for voyaging to Cochin China 交趾, repeated the following year, and in 1616 one for travel to Tongking 東京. Cocks reports in a letter of February 15, 1618: "Andrea Dittis and Capt. Whow, his brother, are the greatest adventurers for [Taiwan]. They sent 2 small junckes the last yeare, and bought silks for the one halfe they pay ether at Cochinchina or Bantam." Such voyages continued for several years, not always, however, with complete success. During the years from 1614 to 1635 there are records of twenty-three expeditions conducted by Hua-yü and himself, their destinations being Cochin China, Tongking, Luzon, and Taiwan, especially the last, which accounted for eleven of them. At least one other excursion may have been made to Java in the first part of 1625. Throughout these years they were closely in touch with the English and Dutch. The former were eager to trade directly with the Chinese on the mainland, as they found the Japanese disinclined to buy their commodities; furthermore, they wished, if possible, to effect this without show of force. To this end Cocks approached Li Tan, who proved a willing agent. Under date of July 11, 1615, Cocks tells in his diary of receiving a call from Li, who said that his brother in China was acting as agent; that three thousand pesos, presented to certain high officials, was paving the way, but they advised waiting until the aging emperor, Chu I-chün (*q.v.*), was out of the way and his son had succeeded him. On January 20, 1621, Cocks wrote a letter to the East India Company which said in part: "... the new Emperor hath granted our nation trade into China for two shipps a yeare, and the place appointed near Fuckchew, and that there wanted but the fermes of ij vizroys of ij provinces to conferme it; and that the goshon or passport will be sent us the next moonson, and had been heare before now, had it not byn letted per the wars of Tartaria. Thus much our China frendes tell me, and I hope it will prove true." But it did not prove true, in spite of the advances made by Cocks to Li Tan for the purpose. Between 1615 and 1621 these totaled 6,250 taels in silver, in addition to presents made to him and his brother personally. When the East India Company decided in April, 1623, to withdraw its factory from Hirado none of this money had been repaid, and the officers accused Cocks of simplemindedness for allowing himself to be deluded by the promises of Li Tan.

The Dutch had likewise for several decades been concerned to gain a foothold on the mainland, either by force or by guile. Apparently unaware of the failure of Cocks in working through Li Tan, they entered into negotiations with him in April, 1623, on the occasion of his stop-over in Taiwan en route to Hirado. Adam Verhult was subsequently authorized to present him with a scarlet woolen cloth, and remarked: "This is for asking for [Li Tan's] every assistance and turning his kind intentions towared us." A little later he asked the Dutch for a loan of four thousand taels in silver, and they obliged. In January of the following year he left Hirado again for Taiwan, but this time the Dutch were forewarned by their representative in Hirado:"I have no doubt that Your Honour [Cornelis Reijersen, commander of the Dutch fleet in the China sea] will be satisfied with his payment and everything else will be serviceable. But you must take utmost care not to hand him a large sum of money, for he is a sly man, with fine mansions and several lovely wives and children at Nagasaki and here at Hirado. Still he owes the Englishmen 7,000 taels in silver money." Based on this warning, the officials at Batavia ordered Reijersen to recover the four thousand taels previously lent to him.

The Chinese authorities in Fukien were in no mood to accommodate the Dutch any more than they had the English, and prepared to drive them out of any mainland outpost and the Pescadores as well. A fleet of four ships under Christian Francs was attacked in Amoy harbor in October, 1623, the fiagship sunk, and its commander and others taken captive. The following year a succession of Chinese fleets crossed over to the Pescadores and by the end of August succeeded in overcoming all resistance, and in driving out the Dutch. The only hope of the latter was in Li Tan. When he arrived in Taiwan on August 17, he agreed to help, and forthwith proceeded to the mainland in the company of the commander of the Chinese forces. First he wrote from Amoy (on October 19) that he was ill and could not proceed to Foochow; two days later that he was still sick, and besides was being detained by the authorities, but that in their opinion no difficulties would he encountered in the matter of an agreement to trade. On November 14, 1624, he returned to Taiwan with a letter from an official in Amoy who promised that he would proceed to Foochow to confer with the provincial authorities "and try to strike up a friendship between you and us." This was no license to trade, however, and none such was ever vouchsafed. The ugly suspicion has arisen that Li Tan was playing both sides. Chinese accounts of the time make him a member of a small group of Chinese in foreign pay, who were trying to buy Chinese silk and other goods for their masters. Another was Hsü Hsin-su 許心素 (d. 1627), an agent of the Dutch who had been imprisoned. A passage in the *Hsi-tsung shih-lu* under date of May 6, 1625, gives this intelligence, reported by the governor of Fukien: "Li Tan, a native of Ch'üan-chou, has lived a long time in Japan, and is in charge of affairs there. Hsü Hsin-su, with whom Li was on intimate terms, is now in prison. We might, therefore, capture Hsü's son as a hostage, and dispatch Hsü to Li to try to persuade him to return to allegiance..."

Li Tan lived on in Taiwan for some months before he finally (July 1, 1625) received permission from the Dutch to return to Japan. He set sail two days later. The Dutch were not sorry. Immediately after his departure they discovered that he had not only misappropriated funds but had also plundered junks plying between Taiwan and the mainland. Li Tan had little chance to enjoy these ill-gotten gains. He was even then a sick man. and he died in Hirado on August 12, 1625. His burial place is not certainly known but it may have been in the temple grounds of Hōon-ji 法音寺, in Hirado.

Among his children the best known was Li I-kuan 一官, called by the English and Dutch Augustin (or Augustjin) Iquan, who entered into business with his father at least as early as 1618 and continued to operate between Japan and Taiwan up to 1633 if not later. Following the death of Li Tan, several of his followers, including Yen Ssu-ch'i 顏思齊 and Cheng Chih-lung, may well have contended for leadership. The latter in 1628 finally surrendered to the governor-general of Fukien and Chekiang. Apparently Li I-kuan still had control of part of the fleet for in 1633 there was a rumor in China that the followers of the pirate Liu Hsiang (q.v.) were planning to enlist his aid and that of the Satsuma Japanese in assembling a combined fleet to plunder the Fukien coast. This rumor is mentioned in a memorial dating from the middle of 1633.

One of the sons of Li I-kuan, a convert to Christianity, was executed for his faith on October 18, 1635, along with eight Japanese and foreigners.

Bibliography

1/264/3a; MSL (1966), Hsi-tsung, 2662; *Ming Ch'ing shih-liao*, 2/7/605, 657; Ch'in Chiung 秦烔, *Chao-an-hsien chih* 詔安縣志 (1691), 12/8b; Liao Han-ch'en 廖漢臣, "Cheng Chih-lung k'ao," *T'ai-wan-wen hsien*, X, 4 (1959), XI, 3 (1960); Mao I-po 毛一波, "Cheng Chih-lung shih-liao chung ti Li Tan ho Yen Ssu-ch'i,"*ibid.*, XIV: 1 (1963), 88; Iwao Seiichi, "Li Tan 李旦, Chief of the Chinese at Hirado, Japan, in the Last Days of the Ming Dynasty," MTB, 17 (1958), 27; C. R. Boxer, *Fidalgos in the Far East, 1550–1770, Fact and Fancy in the History of Macao* (The Hague, 1948), 73; id., *The Great Ship from Amacon*; *Annals of Macao and the Old Japan Trade, 1555–1640* (Lisbon, 1959), 72; Wm. Foster, Letters received by the East India Company from Its Servants in the East, Vol. IV (London, 1900), 51; William Lytle Schurz, *The Manila Galleon* (New York, 1939), 71.

*Chaoying Fang and
L. Carrington Goodrich*

LI Ts'ai 李材 (T. 孟誠, H. 見羅), *ca.* 1520-*ca.* 1606, thinker and official, was a native of Feng-ch'eng 豐城, Kiangsi. He came from a distinguished family that produced several scholar-officials. His father, Li Sui 遂 (T. 邦良, H. 克齋, 羅山, 1504-66, cs 1526), a disciple of Ou-yang Te (*q. v.*), served as governor of Feng-yang 鳳陽 and Huai-an 淮安 (1557-59) and later as minister of War in Nanking (1561-66). Li Ts'ai himself studied under Tsou Shou-i, the disciple of Wang Shou-jen (*qq. v.*). After Li became a *chin-shih* in 1562, and was appointed a secretary in the ministry of Justice, he requested home leave to further his philosophical studies. On the way south he visited several followers of the school of Wang Shou-jen, in particular T'ang Shu (*see* T'an Ch'ien), Wang Chi, and Ch'ien Te-hung (*qq. v.*). After completing the mourning for his father, he returned to the capital to serve as director of a bureau in the ministry of War. In February, 1571, he was promoted to assistant surveillance commissioner in Kwangtung. There he defeated the bandits of Hsin-hui 新會 and other native tribesmen west of Canton (1572). He also repelled the raiding pirates and rescued thousands of women captives. For such meritorious service, he was promoted in 1574 to be surveillance vice commissioner, but soon resigned from office, possibly because he had incurred the displeasure of Grand Secretary Chang Chücheng (*q. v.*). In August, 1583, Li Ts'ai returned to official service as administrative vice commissioner in Shantung. Three months later he was transferred to Liaotung, but early in 1584 he was sent to Tali, Yunnan, as administrative vice commissioner in charge of military affairs in the western border region. In dealing with the aboriginal chiefs of Meng-yang 孟陽 and Man-mu 蠻目, Li directed their warlike instincts against the Burmese tribes, defeating them after a seemingly spectacular victory on the battlefield (1585). Later that year he was rewarded with a promotion to surveillance commissioner. Before any official assessment was made of the battle, he received a second promotion (August, 1586) to be assistant censor-in-chief and governor of Yün-yang 隕陽, Hukuang. It was there that he allowed his disciples to persuade him to make the local commander's headquarters a Confucian school. This decision provoked a mutiny instigated by the local commander, Mi Wan-ch'un 米萬春, who had the students' houses burned, and coerced Li Ts'ai into writing a memorial attributing guilt for the mutiny to the vice commissioner, Ting Wei-ning 丁惟寧 (T. 少濱, cs 1565) and the vice-prefect, Shen Fu 沈鈇 (cs 1574). The two were consequently imprisoned, while Li was ordered to return to his native place to await the results of a thorough investigation of the incident. Even after a report following the investigation, however, Mi Wan-ch'un received only a slight punishment. In the meantime, Li Ts'ai got into further trouble when the Yunnan regional censor, Su Tsan 蘇酇 (cs 1577), who was instructed to assess Li's handling of the battle against the Burmese in Yunnan, turned in an unfavorable report (1588), saying that Li had confused the dates and locations of the battles and exaggerated the results of his victory. One of the dates mentioned is Li's own birthday (17th day of the 7th moon), on which occasion his subordinates came to Yung-ch'ang 永昌 to see him; hence he could not have been a hundred miles away directing the campaign. As has been pointed out, the accuracy of such a report, furnished three years after the battle had taken place, and allegedly based on investigation made on the spot, is difficult to determine. In any case, Li Ts'ai was put into prison together with two of his former subordinate officers. While the others were given lesser punishments, Li was sentenced to death, and granted a reprieve only after the intercession of Shen Shih-hsing (q.v.) and T'ang Yao-ch'in 唐堯欽 (T. 寅可, H. 韋軒, cs 1571), then supervising secretary. His friend, Hsü Fu-yüan (see Hsü Chieh), then governor of the Peking metropolitan area, submitted a memorial in protest and was demoted two grades. Li stayed in prison for five years, until a second investigation of the Yunnan affair was completed; this yielded the conclusion that Li's merits were still not sufficient to make up for his official failures. This time, the intervention of Grand Secretary Wang Hsi-chüeh (q. v.) obtained for him a reduction of the sentence, and Li Ts'ai was exiled in July, 1593, to the Fukien coast as a soldier in the Chen-hai 鎮海 guard, near Chang-chou 漳州. He remained there for about thirteen years, continuing his work of teaching philosophy. The local people built for him the Ming-tsung 明宗 Academy in P'u-t'ien 莆田. When Hsü Fu-yüan was governor in Fukien (ca. 1595), he paid frequent visits to Li Ts'ai, and was astonished to find that Li was still using his former insignia of administrative vice commissioner. Li listened to Hsü's counsels, and gave up this illicit practice.

Li Ts'ai's son, Li Chiung 熲 (T. 宏明, cj 1606), had just married when his father was imprisoned in 1588. He rushed to the latter's side, waiting on him in prison for five years, and following him to exile in Fukien. The local gazetteers report that Li Chiung asked for pardon for his father in 1621, on the accession to the throne of Emperor Chu Yu-chiao (ECCP). According to a eulogy by Kao P'an-lung (q. v.), however, written in 1613, Li had been dead seven years. Thus he probably died in 1606. It seems that his memory was rehabilitated in 1620 or 1621, as a result of the amnesties (*see* Chu Ch'ang-lo [ECCP] and Chu Yu-chiao). At any rate, one source quoted in his biography in the Feng-ch'eng gazetteer of 1874 states that he was pardoned in 1621, returned home and then died, which seems to be a mistake in the light of Kao's evidence.

Li Ts'ai's disciple, Hsü Chi-teng 徐繼登 (T. 德俊, H. 匡嶽, cs 1583), was serving in the ministry of Rites when Li was imprisoned. He too sought to save Li Ts'ai during his trial and captivity, waiting on the master in prison and listening to his instructions. He rose later to be education surveillance vice commissioner in Fukien.

It has been said that Li Ts'ai consciously took Wang Shou-jen as his model, and sought, like Wang, to achieve distinction both as a soldier and as a thinker. Although a student of Tsou Shou-i, he gradually evolved his own distinctive ethics. This called for a return to human nature (hsing) and its original goodness, with the immanent "four beginnings" of virtue described by Mencius (cf. Legge, *Chinese Classics*, II, 278). Li pointed out the importance especially of these words of the Great Learning: "knowing the roots" (chih-pen 知本) and "knowing where to rest" (chih-chih 知止), and explained these in terms of the cultivation of self (hsiu-shen 修身). For this reason, he summed up his own learning in the two words: chih-hsiu 止修 , saying that "rest" (chih) refers to the theory (chu-i 主意), and "cultivation" (hsiu) refers to the practice (kung-fu 工夫) of his spiritual doctrine. His thought thus represented also a conscious return to the insights of the Sung thinkers, of Chu Hsi (1130–1200) and the Ch'eng brothers. Like Lü Nan (*q. v.*), Hsü Fu-yüan, and others, Li made an attempt to stem the tide of rising individualistic eccentricity and moral indifference which resulted partly from the successes of the T'ai-chou

movement, and for this, he should be given due credit. He cannot, however, be called an original thinker.

The *Ssu-k'u* catalogue reports three works of Li Ts'ai. The first, *Chiang-chiang chi* 將將記, 24 *ch.*, treats of military matters, giving the exploits of seven emperors during the Han, T'ang, and Sung dynasties (9 *ch.*), as well as the military successes and failures during the whole of Chinese history until Sung times (11 *ch.*). Li Ts'ai also quotes profusely (3 *ch.*) from classical texts, literature, history, and philosophy to support his assertions and judgments. While giving Li due credit for his own achievements as a soldier, the *Ssu-k'u* editors consider this book to have been written from too subjective a viewpoint, including too many irrelevant and pedantic references. The second work, *Kuan-wo-t'ang chai-kao* 觀我堂摘稿, 12 *ch.*, includes Li's treatise on the meaning of the old text of the Great Learning, 1 *ch.*, his letters, 10 *ch.*, and other miscellaneous writings 1 *ch.* The third work, *Li Chien-lo shu* 見羅書, 20 *ch.*, compiled by his disciple, Li Fu-yang (*see* Ku Hsien-ch'eng), presents the same treatise on the old text of the Great Learning, 1 *ch.*, Li's letters, 9 *ch.*, a treatise on the goodness of human nature, 1 *ch.*, another on the meaning of the Analects, 4 *ch.*, accounts by Li's disciples, 4 *ch.*, and the prefaces, included at the end, 1 *ch.*

The Japanese library catalogues also report the existence of other works by Li. These include *Chien-lo hsien-sheng Cheng-hsüeh t'ang kao* 正學-*t'ang kao* 稿 (Wan-li ed.), 24 *ch.*, *Chien-lo Li hsien-sheng Fu* 福-*t'ang kao* (Wan-li ed.), 2 *ch.*, and the *Chien-lo Li hsien-sheng Kuan-wo-t'ang kao* (Ming ed.), 22 *ch.*, as well as a copy in 12 *chüan* (Wan-li ed.), both to be found in the Naikaku Bunko. The last named collection may be identical with the *Kuan-wo-t'ang chai-kao* described earlier.

Bibliography

1/227/5b; 3/265/11a; 5/41/30a, 42/82a; 32/57/47b; 83/31/2a, *Shih-shuo* 師說/22a; *KC* (1958), 4536,

4564, 4567, 4577, 4579, 4586, 4749; SK (1930), 96/6b, 100/4b, 178/7a; TSCC (1885-88), XIV: 397/11a; Kao P'an-lung, *Kao-tzu i-shu*, 1632 Preface (NLP microfilm no. 792), 8A/1a, 9A/24b; *id.*, "Kao (告) Li Chien-lo hsien-sheng wen," in *Kao-tzu wei-k'o k'ao* 未刻稿 (Manuscript, NLP microfilm); Ku Hsien-ch'eng, *Ku Tuan-wen kung chi*, Ming ed. (NLP microfilm no. 811), 6/21a; *Chia-ch'ing ch'ung-hsiu i-t'ung chih* 嘉慶重修一統志 (SPTK ed.), 310/13b; *Chao-ch'ing-fu chih* 肇慶府志 (1876), 16/39a; *Feng-ch'eng-hsien chih* 豐城縣志 (1873), 15/15b; *Fu-chien t'ung-chih* 福建通志 (1938), 11/4b; *Hsing-hua-fu P'u-t'ien-hsien chih* 興化府莆田縣志 (1879), 9/32a; *Yün-yang-fu chih* 鄖陽府志 (1870), 5C/21a; *Nan-ch'ang-fu chih* 南昌府志 (1873), 39/52b, 43/22a; *T'ai-chou chih* 泰州志 (1908), 17/29b; *Yunnan t'ung-chih* 雲南通志 (1736), 13/69a, 19/23b; Okada Takehiko, *Ō Yōmei to Minmatsu no Jugaku* (Tokyo, 1970), 275.

Julia Ching

LI Tung-yang 李東陽 (T. 賓之, H. 西涯), July 21, 1447-August 20, 1516, poet, calligrapher, and grand secretary, was born in Peking into a family of military registry, belonging to the Chin-wu 金吾 Left Guard. His great-grandfather, a native of Ch'a-ling 茶陵 in the Changsha prefecture of Hukuang, served in the bodyguard of the prince of Yen, Chu Ti (*q.v.*); his grandfather, who fought for that prince during the latter's rebellion (1398-1402), attained merely the rank of a corporal assigned to a bureau in the imperial household and became a foreman in charge of laborers. Li Tung-yang's father, Li Ch'un 淳 (T. 憩庵, d. 1486), was probably the first one in the family to study for the civil examination, and, when in 1441 he was in line to inherit the military service, his younger brother took his place. Decades later Li Tung-yang wrote a moving account about this uncle who shouldered without complaint his military duties as well as the support of an elder brother and the latter's family for many years.

Li's father achieved little of note except perhaps the rearing of a precocious child, for when Li Tung-yang was three years old in 1450 his fame was such that he was presented to the emperor, Chu Ch'i-yü (*q.v.*). At the audience he demonstrated his precocity by writing a few complicated characters. In 1454, after a third audience, he was permitted by imperial grace to register as a student in the district school. In 1463, aged sixteen, he became a *chin-shih*, one of the youngest to achieve that distinction. A year later, having been selected a bachelor of the Hanlin Academy, he embarked on a career of literary service which lasted forty-nine years under the three reigns, Ch'eng-hua, Hung-chih, and Cheng-te. His rise during the first two reigns was unhurried and regular. First he held the following offices in the Hanlin Academy: compiler (1465-74), expositor (1474-83), and senior expositor (1483-94). During these years he made a special journey to Ch'a-ling to visit the home of his ancestors (1472) and traveled to Nanking in 1480 as director of the provincial examination. Later he also served as director of the provincial examination at Peking (1486) and of the metropolitan examinations of 1493 and 1499. As a lecturer in to the emperor in the Classics he won commendation for his wise and daring exhortations, especially in 1492 when he explained certain passages from Mencius.

In September, 1494, when the grand secretaries, Hsü P'u, Ch'iu Chün, and Liu Chien (*qq.v.*), were pressed with urgent matters—probably planning for the dispatch of an expeditionary force to Hami (*see* Hsü Chin)—they were permitted to have a supernumerary member to assist in drafting imperial orders of a routine nature, chiefly the honorary patents (kao-ch'ih 誥勅). Li received appointment to that office with a promotion in rank to vice minister of Rites and senior reader of the Hanlin Academy. In 1495, after Ch'iu Chün died, Li and Hsieh Ch'ien (*q. v.*) were selecfed to serve in the Grand Secretariat as probationary counselors. In March, 1499, the court formally gave Li the title of grand secretary of the Wen-yüan-ko with the concurrent rank of a minister of Rites and junior guardian of the heir apparent. It also had such faith in his integrity that, during the metropolitan examination of 1499, he was placed in charge of an investigation of one of his colleagues accused of receiving bribery (*see* T'ang Yin). Five years later, on the completion of the first edition of the *Ta Ming hui-tien* 大明會典, 180 *ch.*, printed in 1509, he received the higher rank of a grand guardian of the heir apparent. In 1504 the court sent him to Shantung to represent the emperor in the dedication of the reconstructed Temple of Confucius, which had been destroyed by fire in 1499. In June, 1505, the dying emperor, Chu Yu-t'ang (*q.v.*), entrusted him and the two other grand secretaries, Liu Chien and Hsieh Ch'ien, to serve as mentors to the heir apparent, Chu Hou-chao (*q.v.*).

The grand secretaries soon found to their distress that the erratic youth, now emperor, preferred the company of eight junior eunuchs who kept him amused with diversions. Gradually the favorites, known as pa-tang 八黨 (the clique of eight), interfered with matters of state, the emperor parrying or ignoring the admonitions and remonstrances of his highest officials. At last, by threatening to resign unless the eight were put to death, the grand secretaries forced the emperor to propose sending the eight into exile. Liu and Hsieh adamantly insisted on the death sentence while Li wavered. During the night of October 27, 1506, the leader of the eight eunuchs, Liu Chin (*q.v.*), succeeded in persuading the emperor to appoint him chief of the directorate of ceremonial. In this way he became the spokesman for the emperor and emerged all powerful. Of the three grand secretaries, Liu and Hsieh were immediately sent into retirement while Li was requested to stay on as head of the Grand Secretariat with the exalted rank of junior preceptor. Soon the eunuch arrogated more powers to himself and behaved outrageously. In 1507 when Li, as head of the

editorial board of the general history, *Li-tai t'ung-chien tsuan-yao* 歷代通鑑纂要, 92 *ch.*, presented the book to the throne on its completion, Liu Chin pointed out a few mistakes and, after forcing Li to admit carelessness, had about twenty compilers cashiered. Two years later on the completion of the Veritable Records of the preceding reign (*Hsiao-tsung shih-lu*), when all compilers were in line for awards, Liu Chin, in the emperor's name, had them first reduced in rank or salary on the trumped-up charge of being too extravagant during the compilation of an earlier work (*Ta Ming hui-tien*). When the awards were made, it was merely a restoration to their previous status.

Under such trying circumstances Li Tung-yang kept on, managing somehow to hold the trust of the emperor and even to command the eunuchs' respect for his incorruptibility. He used his influence to restrain them occasionally from excessive misdeeds and to rescue some of their victims. He bided his time until in 1510 with one stroke he had Liu Chin removed. This crucial task was accomplished without any revelation of his part in the planning and direction of the coup. As a reward for his share in the Ning-hsia campaign (*see* Yang I-ch'ing) Li was given the exceptional rank of T'e-chin tso chu-kuo 特進左柱國 (Left Pillar of State), marking the first time a grand secretary was so rewarded for military victory. Late in 1511, on the completion of nine years as a grand secretary, he was given extra stipends and a testimonial dinner in the main hall of the ministry of Rites. Shortly thereafter the emperor found a new group of favorites, the foremost being the notorious general Chiang Pin (*q.v.*). A year later, when the emperor instructed the Grand Secretariat to draft an order assigning Tatung troops under Chiang Pin to the imperial bodyguard, Li first tried to dissuade the emperor, and then obstructed the issuance of the order by refusing to submit a draft. In the end the emperor issued the order without a draft from the Grand Secretariat. This was too much. Li quit and received permission to retire on February 2, 1513.

After having held the premier civil office in the empire for over a decade, Li left office with honors but apparently not well off. Fortunately people sought him out for his writings and calligraphy, and this helped take care of household expenses. Although usually referred to as a man from Changsha, he did not own any property there. His only home was the one in Peking to the west of the palace, in a lane known to this day by his name Li ko-lao hu-t'ung 李閣老胡同. After he died in 1516 he was accorded many high honors including the rank of grand preceptor and the name Wen-cheng 文正.

He married three times. His first wife, née Liu 劉, the daughter of an officer, died about 1471. The second, a daughter of Yüeh Cheng 岳正 (T. 季方, H. 蒙泉, 1418-72, cs 1448), died in 1475, a few months after giving birth to a son, Li Chao-hsien 兆先 (1475-1501). His third wife, a daughter of Chu I 朱儀 (T. 炎恒, Pth. 莊簡, 1427-96, third duke of Ch'eng-kuo 成國), bore a son who also died young, and a daughter (1483-1510) who married a descendant of Confucius in the 62d generation, Duke K'ung Wen-shao 孔聞韶 (T. 知德, d. 1546). There was an adopted son, but the family seems to have died out in a few decades. In 1565 Keng Ting-hsiang (q.v.) headed a group of admirers who purchased a part of the house and converted it to a shrine, called the Li Wen-cheng kung tz'u 公祠. Liu T'ung (q.v.) visited the place some sixty years later and recorded, in his guide book on Peking, that among the relics were two small shoes and a coat of coarse cloth said to be what Li had worn as a child in 1450 at his first imperial audience. Li was buried about three miles west of the northwestern gate of Peking. Late in the 18th century a tomb was identified as his by the scholar of

Mongol descent, Fa-shih-shan (ECCP), who had it restored (1801) and built a shrine in front of it. For some time an annual gathering took place there on his birthday, the 9th day of the 6th moon. Fa-shih-shan also owned a portrait of Li, originally painted in 1503. It happened that Fa-shih-shan lived in a house on the lake, Shih-ch'a-hai 十剎海, north of the imperial palace in Peking, and discovered that it was where Li Tung-yang's family once resided. In 1798 he asked a friend to paint twelve scenes of the area and many scholars wrote colophons on the album. This album, "Hsü Hsi-yai shih-hua ts'e" 續西厓詩畫册, was reproduced by the Chung-hua Bookstore in 1921.

In Ming literature Li Tung-yang occupies a significant position during the transitional period of the late 15th and early 16th centuries. The last of the grand secretaries to dominate the literary world, especially in the style known as t'ai-ko-t'i 臺閣體 (censorate-grand secretariat style, usually connoting scorn), he was also the forerunner of the renaissance movement, fu-ku yün-tung 復古運動, of which the recognized leaders (see Li Meng-yang) had either been his disciples or entered officialdom under his tutelage. As a critic of poetry Li stressed the choice of the right word for musical effect and held that poets should acquire extensive knowledge; in the matter of following the styles of the great masters Li warned against slavish imitation of any one school or period. As Ch'ien Ch'ien-i (ECCP) has pointed out, Li's own poems may be considered to be in the style of one or other of the masters of the past, but the ideas are his alone.

Before he died Li edited his own collected works entitled *Huai-lu-t'ang kao* 懷麓堂稿, 100 *ch.* The book is divided into shih ch'ien-kao 詩前稿, 20 *ch.*, wen 文 ch'ien-kao, 30 *ch.*, shih hou 後-kao, 10 *ch.*, wen hou-kao, 30 *ch.*, and tsa-chi 雜記, 10 *ch.* First published in 1518, it was reprinted at least twice, in 1682 and 1803, and was copied into the Imperial Library.

After Fa-shih-shan published in 1804 a chronological biography, *Ming Li Wen-cheng kung nien-p'u* 年譜, 7 *ch.*, it was reprinted in 1809 and issued as a part of the 1803 edition. A work not included in the collection is his account of an audience, *Yen-tui lu* 燕對錄, 1 *ch.* Some parts of the collection appeared as separate works, such as his criticisms of poetry, *Huai-lu-t'ang shih-hua* 詩話 (also called *Lu-t'ang shih-hua*), 1 *ch.*, also copied into the Imperial Library. The most celebrated of Li's works is a collection of 101 poems in the ballad style of Han times, entitled *Ni-ku yüeh-fu* 擬古樂府, 2 *ch.*, first published about 1504. One of the Ming editions, entitled *Hsi-yai ni-ku yüeh-fu*, contains extensive annotations by a disciple, Ho Meng-ch'un 何孟春 (T. 子元, H. 燕泉, Pth. 文簡, 1474-1536, cs 1493), author of the collection of miscellaneous notes, *Yü-tung hsü-lu* 餘冬序錄. Reprinted both in Korea and in Japan, the *Ni-ku yüeh-fu* influenced the writing of Chinese poetry in these lands too. One of the imitators of Li's style was the Japanese scholar, Rai San-yō 賴山陽 (1780-1830), in his *Nihon gakufu* 日本樂府, published in 1830.

The two characters in Li Tung-yang's posthumous name signify excellence in literature and correctness in behavior. In both aspects, conduct and literature, Li underwent some severe criticisms by his contemporaries. His relations with Liu Chin appeared too smooth to be explained away entirely on the ground that he held the eunuch's respect. Many, including some of his protégés, such as Lo Ch'i 羅玘 (T. 景鳴, H. 圭峯, 1447-1519, cs 1487), never forgave him for staying on in 1506 when his colleagues had to leave the Grand Secretariat. He offered no explanation himself. Some admirers in later years made these observations: that in 1506 he did not resign because, as one of the triumvirate entrusted to be mentors to the young emperor, he may have felt the moral obligation to remain in office when Liu Chin forced the other two to resign; that outside of Peking he

obviously had no place to retire to, nor any land holdings; and that he probably thought that by remaining he might be able to render some constructive service. As it happened he did accomplish the dangerous task of ridding the court of the evil eunuch without any unnecessary ado, which indicated diplomacy of a high order. This seems to be the opinion of all his admirers, such as Li Chih (*q.v.*), Li Fu, Shen Te-ch'ien (both in ECCP), *et al.* Li Chih even went so far as to use harsh words in commenting on one of Li Tung-yang's detractors.

On the other hand many of Li's contemporaries could not tolerate him for overlooking the activities of the eunuch. Huo T'ao (*q.v.*) considered him a hsiang-yüan 鄉愿 (something like a pharisee, *see* Mencius VII/2/37/8,12). Wang Shih-chen (*q.v.*) in his *I-yüan chih-yen* relegated Li's position in the renaissance movement of Ming poetry to a place subordinate to such men as Ho Ching-ming and Li Meng-yang. In his later years, however, Wang changed his opinion, declaring Li's *Ni-ku yüeh-fu* an exceptional achievement in that style of poetry, and in this judgment most later critics seem to concur. In any case Li was undoubtedly the leading arbiter in the literary circle of his day. It is said that often after leaving office in the afternoon men of letters would gather at his house and discuss cultural matters. An anecdote relates that one winter morning before daybreak, when Li was on his way to office, he was seen joining a young scholar in a cup of hot wine. He was then a grand secretary and in his sixties. The Ming short story, "Shih-san-lang wu sui ch'ao-t'ien" 十三郎五歲朝天 in *Chin-ku ch'i-kuan* (*see* Feng Meng-lung), may be partially based on the legends concerning Li Tung-yang's childhood.

There is a scroll entitled "Chia-shen shih t'ung-nien t'u" 甲申十同年圖, painted in 1503 by the famous artist Lü Chi (*q.v.*), depicting ten men who became *chin-shih* in 1464, and who held an anniversary reunion in Peking. All were of ministeral rank or higher. Li Tung-yang, as the one occupying the top post, wrote an introduction in which he identified each one, recording that the artist drew the portraits at individual sittings. The ten men in order of age on that occasion are: Min Kuei 閔珪 (T. 朝英, 1430-1511, Pth. 莊懿), age 73; Chang Ta 張達 (T. 時達, H. 柏庵, 1432-?), age 71; Tseng Chien 曾鑑 (T. 克明, 1434-1507), age 69; Hsieh To (*see* Huang Wan), age 67; Chiao Fang, age 67; Liu Ta-hsia, age 66; Tai Shan, age 65 (*qq.v.* for the last 3); Ch'en Ch'ing 陳清 (T. 廉夫, 1439-1521), age 64; Wang Shih 王軾 (T. 用敬, 1439-1506, Pth. 襄簡), age 64; and the youngest, Li Tung-yang, age 56. Only Chiao Fang failed to be present at the reunion; his portrait was made from a previous one. Each one wrote one or more poems to celebrate the occasion, and inscribed them on the scroll in his own hand. Then nine duplicate copies were made, so that each might keep one as a memento. The one in Min Kuei's family, which has several later colophons including one by Wang Shih-chen, written in 1569, was reproduced by lithography in 1935. Of special interest are the reliable likenesses of these men and samples of their handwriting. Li Tung-yang's beautiful running style serves as an outsanding example of his calligraphy.

Bibliography

1/181/16b; 5/14/37a; 19/8/1a; 42/68/25b; KC (1958), 2989, 3110; SK (1930), 53/2b, 64/2a, 89/4b, 170/12a, 191/9b, 196/2a; Ch'ien Ch'ien-i, *Lieh-ch'ao shih-chi*, 丙 nos. 1-2; Wang Shih-chen, *Yen-shan-t'ang pieh-chi*, 12/10b; Li Tung-yang, *Huai-lu-t'ang chi*, 1803; Li Chih, *Hsü ts'ang-shu* (1959), 208; Cha Chi-tso (ECCP), *Tsui-wei lu*, 11B/21a; Ho Liang-chün, *Ssu-yu-chai ts'ung-shuo* (1959), 60, 67; Yoshikawa Kojiro, *Gemmin-shi kaisetsu* 元明詩概說 (1963), 161; a copy of Li's 1503 portrait, made in 1801, is reproduced in *Kuo-ts'ui hsüeh-pao* 國粹學報, 1911.

Chaoying Fang

LI Wen-chung 李文忠 (T. 思本, childhood name Pao-er 保兒) , 1339-March 22, 1384, was the nephew and adopted son of Chu Yüan-chang. He served the dynastic founder from the age of thirteen until his death at the age of forty-five. During most of his career, he was a military officer, but held several civil posts as well. Li was the son of Li Chen 貞 (1303-November 1, 1378) and the second sister of Chu Yüan-chang. Her name was Chu Fo-nü 朱佛女 (1317-52), and she was posthumously granted the title of grand imperial princess of Ts'ao 曹國長公主. Li Chen's father was the eldest of five sons in a peasant family of Hsü-i 盱眙 (Anhwei) and a fisherman by trade. After his father's death, Li Chen took charge of his family. In the midst of the disorders of 1351 he took his family, including his wife and son, to Chu Yüan-chang's home district of Chung-li. A year later they were practically exterminated, whether by disease or as casualties of the fighting is not clear. As the only survivors, Li Chen and Li Wen-chung lived a fugitive existence for two years, avoiding the armed bands of rebels and government soldiers. In 1354, hearing that Chu Yüan-chang had established his headquarters at Ch'u-chou 滁州, they went there to seek protection, and stayed until 1358, when Li Chen accompanied his son on his first campaign in Chekiang. In that same year he brought a group of mutinous captives to Nanking where he was detained, Chu providing him with a mansion in the city. There he lived until around 1368. During his years in the future capital, he was a favorite of his nephews, the imperial princes, who were frequent visitors in his home. As their only uncle to survive the early years of the rebellion, he helped the Empress Ma (*q. v.*) look after them when Chu was away. Some years before his death, he was maintained in another home in T'ung-lu 桐廬, Chekiang. When his deceased wife was posthumously given the title of princess, he was invested as En-ch'in hou 恩親侯 (kindly and affectionate marquis). His posthumous title was prince of Lung-hsi 隴西王, and he was awarded the name Kung-hsien 恭獻.

When Li Chen and Li Wen-chung joined Chu Yüan-chang, the latter had not been married long and still had no sons of his own. Like some other military leaders of that time, he made it his practice to adopt orphaned and destitute youths who he thought might prove useful. There were at least six of these and probably more: Chu Wen-kang 文剛 (d. 1362), Chu Wen-hsün 遜 (d. 1360), Chu (originally Ho 何) Wen-hui 輝 (d. 1376), Chu Wen-ying (better known as Mu Ying, q. v.), and a fraternal nephew, Chu Wen-cheng (see Chu Yüan-chang). Thus it was that in 1354 Li Pao-er became Chu Wen-chung. (In 1367 he became known as Li Wen-chung; see below.) He and his adoptive brothers, as soon as they were old enough, were added to the dynastic founder's group of politically reliable military and civil officers. In Ch'u-chou, Li Wen-chung was placed directly under the authority of Chu Wen-cheng, his first cousin. They probably stayed together at least until 1356, when they were sent on a joint mission to Nanking, after which their careers diverged. Chu Yüan-chang took pains to have Li Wen-chung well trained for a career in his service, in both the military and literary fields. Between 1357 and 1368, Li gained much practical experience in military art and politics during the chaotic struggle for control of Chekiang. This region was contested by Chu Yüan-chang, Chang Shih-ch'eng, Fang Kuo-chen (qq. v.), an army of Miao aborigines, and a number of loyal Yüan officials and local bandits, with all the actors alternately involved in conflicts or alliances with one another. He began this decade as an assistant guard commander and ended it as the chief administrator of the province.

In the spring of 1358 Li Wen-chung served under Teng Yü and Hsü Ta (qq. v.) in an invasion of western Chekiang and the capture of Chien-te 建德. His uncle left him there and directed him to hold the city, while the other leaders continued their campaign. For the next five months, the principal threat to Chien-te was posed by the Miao army, recruited by the Yüan authorities and commanded by Yang Wan-che (see Chang Shih-ch'eng). Li defeated several detachments of their forces before the fall of Chien-te. Trouble with the Miao ended temporarily in September, 1358, when Yang Wan-che committed suicide in his encampment near Hangchow, and most of his army scattered. A local Miao commander, Yün Ch'eng 員成 in T'ung-lu, consequently offered his submission along with his following of thirty thousand. Chu Yüan-chang directed Li Wen-chung to conclude the agreement.

From the autumn of 1358 to the beginning of 1362, Li's service at Chien-te was marked by repeated victories over Chang Shih-ch'eng's forces. During this time he received the office of vice commissioner in the bureau of military affairs (October, 1360) and second vice administrator of the Che-tung sub-branch secretariat with full command of all military forces stationed in, roughly, the western half of Chekiang (March, 1362). But later his task was greatly complicated by political problems within his command. On March 3, 1362, three of the Miao army commanders who had submitted in 1358 carried out a bloody coup at Chinhua 金華, killing Hu Ta-hai (q. v.) and several other officers, and seizing control of the city. Li dispatched a punitive expedition against the rebels, who immediately departed, taking many kidnaped women and children with them. In the meantime an officer at Ch'u-chou was inspired by news of the revolt to kill his commander, Keng Tsai-ch'eng (see Hu Ta-hai), one of Chu Yüan-chang's earliest followers. Chang Shih-ch'eng, taking advantage of Li's preoccupation with the revolts, undertook another invasion, this time sending his younger brother, Chang Shih-hsin (see Chang Shih-ch'eng), to lay siege to Chu-ch'üan (see Hu Ta-hai). Li had few troops to send in relief of the garrison commander, Hsieh Tsai-hsing 謝再興. Chu Yüan-chang, then pressing his campaign against Ch'en Yu-liang (q. v.) in Kiangsi, had to dispatch reinforcements. In June, 1363, Hsieh Tsai-hsing rebelled and assassinated the prefect of Chu-ch'üan, marching off with his troops to Shao-hsing, where he submitted to Chang Shih-ch'eng. Chang sent his general, Li Po-sheng 李伯昇, with a great army of two hundred thousand (March 1365) in a last effort to conquer western Chekiang. This time Li Wen-chung was not thwarted by defections, and, drawing troops from throughout the province, was able to win a major victory.

During his years at Chien-te, Li managed to spend some time in the company of literati and to continue his studies. Among his teachers were two classical scholars of Chin-hua, Hu Han (see Wang I) and Fan Tsu-kan 范祖幹 (T. 景先). When Li was promoted to the office of second vice administrator, Chu Yüan-chang sent Yang Hsien (see Empress Ma) from the metropolitan adminstration to assist him. Liu Ch'en 劉辰 (T. 伯靜, 1335-August 29, 1412), author of the *Kuo-ch'u shih-chi* 國初事蹟, 1 *ch.*, and compiler of an early draft of the *T'ai-tsu shih-lu*, served as his secretary. The scholar's role as adviser or secretary to a general was an awkward one. Liu Ch'en asserted that the generals usually blamed their own mistakes on their scholar-secretaries. According to Liu Ch'en's account, there was at least one early crisis in the relationship between Li Wen-chung and his uncle. Yang Hsien informed Chu that Li was keeping a prostitute in his quarters. Chu summoned him to the capital, demanded an explanation, sent an emissary to Chien-te to execute the woman, and was on the point of transferring him to another post when the future Empress Ma interceded for him on the ground that Chien-te was strategically important and the people there would have no confidence in anyone sent

to replace him. Li was then allowed to go back to Chien-te. On his arrival, two of his scholar-advisers pointed out to him that a second such summons to Nanking would probably be his last and that he would be well advised to start making his own plans. Accordingly he entered into negotiations with Chang Shih-ch'eng, thinking that he might defect. Before the negotiations could bear fruit, Chu, perhaps in a spirit of contrition, invited Li back to Nanking for a banquet. He bravely accepted, was lavishly entertained and, assured of his uncle's affection, returned once again to Chien-te. He then killed several of his advisers, who, he feared, might divulge his near treason. In 1365, moreover, when Chu punished his other nephew, Chu Wen-cheng, for what he held to have been gross insubordination, he was troubled about the effect this might have on the attitude of Li Wen-chung. He therefore sent him a long letter of explanation in which he enumerated "the donkey's" provocations and advised Li not to emulate Chu Wen-cheng while reminding him once again of their ties of mutual affection.

The final campaigns against the state of Chang Shih-ch'eng in the autumn and winter of 1366 and his subsequent activities at Hangchow, provided the setting for the climax of Li's early career. While Hsü Ta and Ch'ang Yü-ch'un (q. v.) stormed Chang's capital city of Soochow, Li was ordered to complete the conquest of the northern part of Chekiang, including the provincial metropolis of Hangchow. In December, 1366, the commander at Yü-hang 餘杭 (the rebel Hsieh Tsai-hsing) guarding Hangchow on the west was persuaded to submit on the promise that his life would be spared. Li provided him with an excuse for thus deserting his post by suggesting to him that he had only entered Chang's service out of respect for his brother who had done so before him. The ranking officer at Hangchow, P'an Yüan-ming (see Ch'en Ju-yen), was also persuaded to submit without a fight. P'an was allowed to retain the title but not the substance of his office as provincial chief administrator. In January, 1367, Chu founded the Chekiang branch secretariat at Hangchow and appointed Li Wen-chung to be the chief administrator. Also, at this time, he commanded his nephew to resume his original surname in recognition of his having become a man of considerable stature in his own right.

Li served in his provincial office less than two years. His uncle expected him while there to demonstrate in his own conduct both frugality and self-discipline, and so cause the people of Hangchow to forswear their "habitual extravagance"and "their evil practices." One may doubt whether he was successful in remolding the population, but he did provide for the defense of the region against piracy by establishing garrisons in the coastal districts, and he won Chu's permission to abolish a much resented agricultural surtax that had been levied on Chin-hua as an emergency measure in 1359. He also led an expedition into Fukien from February to September, 1368, to stabilize the situation there following the conquest of the province (see T'ang Ho).

Li retained the title of chief administrator of Chekiang until January, 1371, when he was replaced by P'an Yüan-ming, who now actively resumed his former office. Li's work in Chekiang ended, however, in the spring of 1369. At that time he was assigned to a campaign against the Mongols north of the Great Wall. This marked the beginning of the second phase of his career. For the next seven years he served on the northern frontier, leaving it only for an expedition to Szechwan and three trips back to Nanking. Li was ordered to assist Ch'ang Yü-ch'un in an expedition against the Yüan emperor, Toɣon Temür (q. v.), in his Shang-tu refuge north of the Wall. The campaign began well enough when in July they compelled the Mongol emperor to retreat and captured many of

his men and horses. The next month, however, Ch'ang suddenly became ill and died. Although Li was newly arrived on the frontier, Chu immediately ordered him to take charge of the leaderless army. In a letter to Li he confessed his misgivings about the change in command. He said that he had been increasingly out of touch with the army in recent years and would have to rely upon Li to get to know his subordinates intimately and evaluate them as both Hsü Ta and Ch'ang Yü-ch'un had been able to do. In September Li acquitted himself well in his new command when he broke the Mongol siege of Tatung; he then returned to Peking.

When a new campaign was ordered against the Mongols in January, 1370, Li was to pursue the Yüan ruler far into Mongolia and capture him there. while Hsü Ta, the supreme commander, was to attack Wang Pao-pao (Kökö Temür, q. v.) and the main Mongol army on the northwest frontier. Li accordingly passed through the Wall again north of Peking, then turned westward, dispersing Mongol detachments as he went. Presently he heard that Toɣon Temür was in Ch'ing-yang 慶陽 in northern Shensi. He hastened there by forced marches, traveling day and night, but learned on his arrival that the Yüan emperor had died and his newly-enthroned heir, Ayušíridara (q.v.) had escaped northward. Despite this, however, he did capture the new emperor's son and heir, Maidiribala (see Ayušíridara) and several imperial consorts and high officials. He also obtained the Yüan and Sung imperial seals and certain regalia which the Mongols had taken in their flight from the court in 1368. Although he continued his pursuit, Li was unable to overtake the fugitive emperor and, late in October, Hsü Ta and he were ordered to return. Maidiribala, meanwhile, had been sent under escort to the capital along with Li's victory memorial. Chu found the language of the memorial excessively boastful and ordered it revised. Further, to guard against the hubris he detected in his nephew and other officials, he treated his distinguished captive with great courtesy, granted him a marquisate, and ordered ex-officials of the Yüan to refrain from sending congratulatory gifts.

The northern expeditionary army returned in November, 1370, in time for a mass investiture of meritorious officials. Li stood third (in the honors list) after Li Shan-ch'ang (*q.v.*) and Hsü Ta, and was invested as duke of Ts'ao 曹國公 with an annual stipend of 3,000 *tan*. Included in the document of investiture were a threat and a promise. Along with the usual words of fulsome praise and sentimental reference to family ties, Chu Yüan-chang assured Li that if he should ever be involved in a plot against the throne, he would be punished without mercy, but that if he should commit any other capital offense, his life would be spared twice. His sons, moreover, would enjoy the same immunity on one occasion. A few days after his investiture Li was appointed to head the chief military commission, in Nanking. His service in this office was soon interrupted, however, by new orders that sent him to Szechwan in August, 1371. This province had just been pacified (*see* Ming Yü-chen), and Li's services were required to help establish the Ming authority there and provide for its defense. Before he left for Szechwan, however, his uncle compelled him to carry out a purge in his own command. The emperor informed him by letter that a eunuch would visit him bearing a list of names of men who had "broken the law," and warning him against showing any partiality towards those who were to be beaten or executed. Nothing less would suffice to maintain Li's authority over his army. The letter ended by informing him that his family had just been moved from Hangchow and installed in new quarters in the capital, and that the emperor's mind was at rest. In the context, this would seem to suggest that they were to be kept as hostages

against full compliance with the order.

Li was once again sent to the northern frontier under Hsü Ta in February, 1372. This time he remained for three years, returning to the capital in March, 1375, although Hsü and the other generals were recalled earlier. He was mainly engaged in patrolling the Wall from Peking to Kansu and harassing the Mongols. During the summer of 1372, however, Hsü, Feng Sheng (*q.v.*), and Li were ordered to make one last—and as it proved—fruitless attempt to capture the Yüan imperial entourage, which had retreated beyond the Gobi to Karakorum. Li's column soon ran into difficulty. They had left most of their supplies behind in order to be able to travel faster, keeping only twenty days' rations. The Mongol troops steadily retreated, drawing them ever farther into Mongolia, across the Tula River to the Orkhon. By this time enemy cavalry began to gather around them in great numbers, and Li was forced to retreat, leaving many dead in his wake. On their return across the Gobi, they nearly died of thirst. Remnants of the army were saved, according to a story, when, in answer to Li's prayer, one of the horses galloped off a certain distance, dug up the ground with his hoof, and uncovered a spring. When the soldiers returned to Peking, they circulated tales of the terrors of the desert to account for the failure of their mission. In one of these they reported that they had been warned to turn back by the apparition of a chüeh-tuan 角端, a unicorn like the one that, according to another legend, caused Jenghis Khan and his adviser, Yeh-lü Ch'u-ts'ai (1189-1243) to retreat from India. For whatever reason, Chu was finally dissuaded from further attempts to send armies across the Gobi.

In the spring of 1376 Li received orders from a new source; his young cousin, Chu Ti (*q.v.*), imperiously instructed him to construct or repair buildings for his princely establishment in Peiping. The job done, Li returned to Nanking in July, this time in the role of a senior statesman. He made just one last campaign, against the eighteen Tibetan tribes who had revolted in Kansu in the spring and summer of 1379, but he did so with obvious reluctance. He tried in vain to persuade his uncle that the maintenance of troops there would result in an unjustifiable burden on the people, but this objection was dismissed with the assertion that enough sheep and cattle could be captured from the tribesmen to feed the army for two years. Except for this operation, Li stayed at home, resumed his classical studies with the help of local scholars, and attended to his official business. As chief military commissioner, he was frequently consulted at court, and in 1383 he was appointed concurrently head of the National University with responsibility for restoring discipline and respect among the sons and younger brothers of "meritorious officials" who studied there. Also on occasion he was sent on tours of inspection to military installations and princely estates, and performed state sacrifices on the emperor's behalf.

The circumstances of Li's death were the subject of rumor and conjecture at that time. The widely accepted account is instructive as evidence of the sense of fear and insecurity that prevailed in Nanking especially after the Hu Wei-yung (*q.v.*) purge trials. Li gathered into his household in Nanking a large number of clients including both scholars and soldiers, a circumstance that caused his uncle some misgivings. Moreover, in 1383, he began to criticize the emperor directly on a number of sensitive issues. He opposed a plan to send an expedition against Korea, and pointed out that he had unsuccessfully opposed a campaign in Yunnan the year before that had turned out badly. No less daringly, he criticized the emperor's violent treatment of followers suspected of disloyalty, and suggested that his uncle should reduce his household expenses by having fewer eunuchs. He added that it was improper for an emperor to be too intimate with mutilated persons. The reference to eunuchs was particularly infuriating because the emperor often spoke in praise of frugality and against the eunuchs. He allegedly replied that his nephew's comment about the eunuchs could have been inspired only by the classical scholars with whom he associated. The deaths a few years before of Li Chen and the Empress Ma had removed two people who might have deflected the emperor's wrath. Angered by the criticism, Chu sent soldiers to kill several members of Li's household, and the latter returned to find his house strewn with corpses. Soon afterwards, he became ill and died, allegedly as the result of poison administered by Hua Chung 華中, the second marquis of Huai-an 淮安 (enf. 1376), who had been sent to him with "medicine" from the emperor. Chu Yüan-chang then downgraded the marquis and executed a large number of doctors, and also women and eunuchs of Li's own household as responsible for his death.

Whether or not Chu Yüan-chang had really intended the death of Li Wen-chung, he honored him posthumously with the title of prince of Ch'i-yang 岐陽王, the canonized name Wu-ching 武靖, and, in 1386, allowed his eldest son to inherit the ducal title. His other two sons held offices in the imperial guards. Li Ching-lung 景隆, the eldest, even became something of a favorite. After a few minor assignments, he was appointed military commissioner of the left, and to the court rank of grand tutor of the heir apparent. In the Chien-wen period, when Chu Ti defeated the loyalist general, Keng Ping-wen (*q.v.*), Li Ching-lung replaced him. Li marched north at the head of an immense army of five hundred thousand men after a gala farewell banquet provided by Emperor Chu Yün-wen (*q.v.*). His own officers regarded him as an incompetent fop who proved quite unable to lead them. After Li had suffered several defeats, the emperor tried to bolster his crumbling authority by sending him a splendid set of weapons: a yellow battle-ax, bow, and arrows. He promptly lost these tokens of imperial favor when his boats were swamped during a battle. The emperor, trusting him still, sent him another set. Li, at the head of a reinforced army of six hundred thousand, suffered another defeat, left his new weapons behind on the battlefield, and returned to Nanking. The Hanlin compiler, Huang Tzu-ch'eng (*see* Lien Tzu-ning), who had recommended his promotion to command the army, now recommended his execution, but the emperor instead sent Li to the prince of Yen to try to make peace. Li, instead of doing so, simply surrendered, and when the prince became emperor, he gave Li a court rank and a large annual stipend. One of the major assignments the new emperor gave him was to supervise the revision of the *T'ai-tsu shih-lu* (November, 1402), with the purpose of eradicating references that might challenge the legitimacy of his replacement of his nephew as the imperial successor. This was completed in July of the following year, but the emperor, still displeased with the contents, rejected it and later (1411, *see* Yao Kuang-hsiao) ordered a second revision. In August, 1404, Li was accused of keeping a band of armed personal retainers, making false prophecies, and plotting against the throne. His younger brother, Li Tseng-chih 增枝, was also implicated by having failed to inform on Li Ching-lung, and by having acquired a great establishment of his own, including several country estates, each with a thousand or more dependent households. Li Ching-lung was then imprisoned and his title revoked. Li Tseng-chih's lands were expropriated for the public domain, and he and his family placed under house arrest. Other relatives were banished to Liaotung. A subsequent attempt by his partisans to rescue Li Ching-lung from prison failed and resulted in a number of executions. Li reportedly died toward the end of the Yung-lo period. Years later, early in 1448, some thirty-eight members of the Li family still in detention were released. In 1532 a descendant was created mar quis of Lin-huai 臨淮侯, and this title passed on early in 1537 to Li T'ing-chu 庭竹 (d. 1575), whose grandson was Li Tsung-ch'eng (*see* Konishi Yukinaga).

Bibliography

Yüan-shih, *ch.* 47; 1/105/5a, 126/1a; 3/117/1a; 5/5/87a; 61/92/1a; MSL (1962), T'ai-tsu, 2469, T'ai-tsung (1963), 199, 233, 577, 588, Ying-tsung (1964), 3142, Hsiao-tsung (1965), 1184; KC (1958), 640; Chu Yüan-chang, *Ming T'ai-tsu yü-chih-wen-chi* 御製文集 (1965), 5/7a, 9/1a, 20/3a; Liu Ch'en, *Kuo-ch'u shih-chi*, in *Chin-sheng yü chen-chi*, ed. by Yüan Chiung; Sung Lien, *Sung hsüeh-shih wen-chi*, 5/53a; Wang Shih-chen, *Yen-shan-t'ang hsü-kao*, 81/9a; Yu K'un 郁衮, *K'o-ch'ao i-chung lu* 革朝遺忠錄 (1969), *fu-lu* 附錄, 4a; *Ch'i-yang shih-chia wen-wu t'u hsiang ts'e* 岐陽世家文物圖像册, ed. by Ch'ü Tui-chih 瞿兌之 (Peiping, 1937); Wang Ch'ung-wu 王崇武, *Feng-t'ien ching-nan chi chu* 奉天靖難記注, Shanghai, 1948.

Romeyn Taylor

LI Ying 李英, died 1442/3, a military officer ennobled during the reign of Emperor Chu Chan-chi (*q.v*) for distinguished service, was descended from a family of Mongol-Turkish extraction that had settled in Hsi-ning 西寧, Kansu, for several generations. The Li clan, which was subdivided into six important branches during the early 14th century, traditionally claimed descent from the Sha-t'o tribe of Li K'o-yung, founder of the non-Chinese dynasty of T'ang (923–36). Li Ying's father, Li Nan-ko 南哥 (1338-February 6, 1430), who headed one of the major branches of the Li clan, served under the Yüan as a vice-magistrate of Hsining. Following his surrender (*ca.* 1371) to Emperor Chu Yüan-chang with his clansmen, he became a pacification officer (鎮撫) of his settlement. He served under the Mongol chieftain Dorji-šige 朵兒只失結 when the latter was appointed (February, 1373) head of the newly created Hsi-ning guard. In the following years, besides dispatching tribute-bearing missions to Peking, Li Nan-ko performed various military assignments for the Ming court, as was his due as a native chieftain of a Chinese protectorate. He is credited, among other activities, with assistance in the establishment of the An-ting 安定 and Ch'ü-hsien 曲先 guards in Kansu in the 1370s, inducing the tribesmen from central Asia to pay tribute to the Chinese court, and in suppressing the rebellious settlers in his own territory. One of his notable achievements, which contributed to the spread of Tibetan Buddhism, was the construction of a monastery in Hsi-ning, to which the Ming emperor gave (February, 1394) the name Ning-fan ssu 寧番寺 (monastery of the appeased barbarians). Some time later Li Nan-ko was promoted to the rank of commander and continued to discharge his various duties under Emperor Chu Ti (*q.v.*) until retirement (*ca.* 1407). Li Nan-ko died in 1430 at the advanced age of ninety-two. At Li Ying's request the Hanlin scholar Chin Yu-tzu (*see* Empress Hsü) composed an epitaph in his memory; it was engraved on a stele subsequently erected in Hsi-ning.

Li Ying, who began his career under his father, assumed command over his clansmen in Hsi-ning upon the retirement of Li Nan-ko. The *shih-lu* first mentions him in December, 1407, in a report that he, then an assistant commander, dispatched a mission to Peking to present tribute horses. In the following years, like his father before him, Li Ying undertook various military assignments for the Ming court. Late in August, 1412, when the Mongol settlers in Kansu led by Lao-ti-han 老的罕 rebelled, and the court appointed Li Pin (*see* Lê Lọ'i) in charge of their suppression, Li Ying was ordered to lead a contingent of his clansmen to join the Chinese command. They distinguished themselves by successfully crushing the uprising; whereupon Li Ying received promotion (December) to regional assistant commander. He then returned to Hsi-

ning to oversee his clansmen, and periodically dispatched tribute embassies to Peking. During this time, a Tibetan monk in Hsi-ning by the name of Chang Ta-li-ma 張答里麻, who had been appointed an assistant secretary of the central Buddhist registry by Emperor Chu Ti because of his knowledge of Chinese, had been accused of plundering and seizing the tribute embassies from the Western regions passing through his territory. Li exposed him, presumably because the presence of such an undesirable figure might jeopardize his own interests, and brought the monk to justice.

Li Ying was recalled to active military duties nine years after his first campaign when, late in 1421, the Mongol chieftain Aruɣtai (*q.v.*) began amassing forces for an assault on the Chinese northern frontiers. In April of the following year Li arrived in Peking with several other native chieftains from Kansu, and a large contingent of their tribesmen to strengthen the Chinese forces. A month later Li and his clansmen joined the expedition led in person by Chu Ti in a major offensive against Aruɣtai, returning to Hsi-ning upon the conclusion of the campaign late in this year. Li then asked the emperor for permission to erect a Taoist shrine in Hsi-ning for the deity Chen-wu 眞武, ostensibly in gratitude for its blessings but actually for his own glorification. Upon the completion of the shrine (January, 1427), Emperor Chu Chan-chi granted the name Kuang-fu kuan 廣福觀 (phalanstery of extensive felicity), and the Hanlin scholar Tseng Ch'i (*see* Li Ch'ang-ch'i) composed an epitaph in Li Ying's honor. In April, 1424, Li returned to Peking with a contingent of his men in response to a summons by Chu Ti, who was preparing another campaign against Aruɣtai. The expedition, however, was cut short by the sudden death of the emperor; whereupon Li Ying returned to the capital with the Chinese forces in September. A month later Emperor Chu Kao-chih (*q.v.*)

awarded him a promotion to deputy regional commander of Shensi.

In the summer of 1425 Li Ying saw military action again when he was ordered to lead an expeditionary force, made up of the native soldiers of Kansu, to chastise the rebellious tribesmen of the An-ting and Ch'ü-hsien guards. This was in reprisal for the attack and slaying by the local chieftains of the Chinese embassy to central Asia, led by the eunuchs Ch'iao Lai-hsi 喬來喜 and Teng Ch'eng 鄧成, towards the end of Chu Ti's reign. The expeditionary force pursued the enemy beyond their homeland in northern Kansu several hundred *li* past Mt. K'un-lun 崑崙山, slaughtering about five hundred and capturing over seven hundred of the rebels, seizing a stock of animals totaling 140,000 head, and dispersing the Uighur-Mongol settlers in this area. Subsequently the chieftain of An-ting proceeded to the Ming court and apologized for their action. In September Li Ying was promoted to the hereditary rank of commissioner in the right military commission, drawing a stipend from this office but not attending to its duties. On October 13, 1427, Li Ying reached the peak of his career when Emperor Chu Chan-chi ennobled him as earl of Hui-ning 會寧伯, with an annual stipend of 1,100 bushels of grain. His ancestors of three generations, including his father Li Nan-ko, also received honorary titles. This appointment led Li Ying to reside in Peking, leaving his sons and family servants to tend to his properties in Hsi-ning.

Li Ying's rise in prestige, coupled with his arrogant personality, lust for power, and impatience with routine, before long antagonized the court and his colleagues, and precipitated his downfall. Late in 1428 the court heard of the conflict between Shih Chao (*see* Wang Chin), the regional commander of Hsi-ning, and Li Ying's father when the latter memorialized reporting that Shih Chao had slandered him. The emperor intervened and the matter was dropped. In the meantime, Li Ying aroused the emperor's apprehension when he made the unprecedented request in May, 1429, to retain fifty-one of the guards, who had followed him in campaigns, to serve him in the capital. The authorities charged him with flouting the rules, but the emperor did not punish him. Following this, in August, 1431, the minister of War, Hsü K'uo 許廓 (T. 文超, cs 1399, 1377–July 7, 1432), accused Li Ying of giving shelter to over seven hundred households of deserted soldiers in his domain, and of making them till his land. The emperor, convinced by Li's plea that he was implicated by his family servants, again pardoned him, and ordered Shih Chao to turn the fugitives over to the civil authorities. A year later, however, Li Ying was charged with a more serious offense for which he was eventually brought to justice. It happened that in this year Ch'i Chen 祁震, a native chieftain, representing a branch of the settlers in Hsi-ning, who held the rank of deputy commander, died, and, according to custom, his heir, Ch'i Ch'eng 成, should succeed him. Ch'i Ch'eng's candidacy, however, was challenged by his half-brother, Ch'i Chien-tsang 監藏, who was the son of Li Ying's sister, and who gained Li's support. Ch'i Ch'eng then sent his uncle to represent him in Peking to plead his case. Li Ying, however, sent men to intercept the party on its way. They captured Ch'i Ch'eng's uncle and his adopted son, had the latter flogged to death, and made off with the tribute they were bringing. In August the censors brought the case before the court; Li Ying and his accomplices were subsequently arrested and condemned to capital punishment, but were not immediately executed.

A year after his enthronement, Emperor Chu Ch'i-chen (*q.v.*) reviewed Li's case (May, 1437) and decided to spare his life but revoked his title. Sometime later, Li was released from prison with the order to retire. In September, 1442, in response to Li's plea, the emperor granted him a monthly stipend of five bushels of grain for subsistence, but he died shortly afterwards. As a result of Li Ying's dishonorable behavior, the Li clan was discredited for the next twenty years until the second reign of Chu Ch'i-chen. It was rehabilitated largely through the effort of the earl of Kao-yang 高陽, Li Wen 文 (T. 孟華, d. January 17, 1490), Li Ying's nephew, who found favor with the emperor through having supported his reinstallation. Li Ying's memory was redeemed in 1475 when his son, Li Ch'ang 昶 (or 昶, T. 明遠, 1430-May 29, 1493), erected his stele in Hsi-ning.

Li Ch'ang, the eldest and best known of Li Ying's sons, was only a little over ten years of age when his father died. When he became an adult, he followed in the footsteps of his ancestors by joining the army. In August, 1450, he was one of sixteen members of a mission, headed by Li Shih (*q. v.*), to the Oirat court of Esen (*q. v.*) to negotiate the release of the captured Emperor Chu Ch'i-chen. Upon his return the court rewarded him richly and made him a corporal in a guard in Peking, but he declined the appointment in order to return to Hsi-ning. In April, 1459, shortly after the reinstallation of Chu Ch'i-chen, he was appointed, presumably through the recommendation of his cousin Li Wen, to the hereditary rank of deputy commander of the Embroidered-uniform Guard. Seven years later (September, 1466) he became an acting assistant commissioner first of the left, and then of the right, military commission in Peking. During the next three years he was assigned to the training of the military corps organized by Yü Ch'ien (*q.v.*), known as shih-er t'uan-ying (*see* Chu Chien-shen). In August, 1470, he was ordered to accompany the censor-in-chief Hsiang Chung (*q. v.*) to supervise the relief of several hundred thousand famine-stricken people in a vast area south and east of Peking; he return-ed to his post six months later. During

the next several years, he supervised a number of public work projects including the repair of the walls of Peking (1473), and that of the Lu-kou 蘆溝 bridge (1479) in the vicinity of the capital (*see* Juan An). Early in 1480, when the eunuch Wang Chih 汪直 (*q. v.*) assumed charge of the military corps, Li Ch'ang was relieved of his training duties, but was recalled, through the recommendation of the minister of War, Yü Tzu-chün (*q. v.*), to supervise the drilling of the shen-chi ying (firearm brigade) following Wang's execution a year later. Before long he submitted a request to retire, but it was denied. In 1485 he obtained permission to return to Hsi-ning to visit his ancestors' tombs; there he erected a villa, adopted the sobriquet Sung-yen cho-sou 松嚴拙叟 and prolonged his stay for over a year until his recall. Early in 1488, Li Ch'ang made another plea for permission to retire, but it was ignored. In March, 1492, on the occasion of the designation of Chu Hou-chao (*q. v.*) as heir-apparent, Emperor Chu Yu-t'ang (*q. v.*) elevated Li to the full rank of assistant commissioner. By this time, however, he was gravely ill and was unable to assume office. He died a year later at the age of sixty-two, sur-vived by twelve sons. The Hanlin scholar Ch'eng Min-cheng (*q. v.*) later composed his tomb-inscription, giving a favorable account of his career.

Li Kung 玑 (cs 1489), Li Ch'ang's second son, was the first member of the Li clan to acquire a literary degree. He served as an assistant minister of the Seal Office at the time of his father's death, later rising to the rank of minis-ter. As Li Kung pursued a civil career, Emperor Chu Yu-t'ang appointed (August, 1493) his son Li Ning 寧 to the heredi-tary rank of commander of the Embroi-dered-uniform Guard. In 1568, some time after Li Kung's death, the officials of Hsi-ning erected an arch in his honor; upon its completion, Emperor Chu Tsai-hou (*q. v.*) gave it the name Ch'ing-yün fang 青雲坊, Li Ning's descendants subsequently inherited the military rank through the end of the Ming into the Ch'ing dynasty.

Li Wen, whom the *shih-lu* calls Li Ying's nephew and a registered taxpayer of Hua-yin 華陰-hsien, Shensi, but who may have come from a different branch of the Li clan, also distinguished himself in military service. An assistant commander of the Hsi-ning guard, Li Wen took part in the campaign under Li Ying's command in 1425 against the rebellious tribesmen from the An-ting and Ch'ü-hsien guards. Four years later (April, 1429), as a reward for his suppression of a local rebellion, he was promoted to be an assistant commissioner of the Shensi regional commission in command of his clansmen in Hsi-ning. Little is known of his activities in the next twenty odd years. In February, 1457, Chu Ch'i-chen, now emperor again, because of Li's support of his reinstallation, awarded him the rank of an assistant commissioner of the right military commission. As a result of his standing with the monarch, members of the disgraced Li family, such as his cousin Li Ch'ang, also received official appointments. In the following month Li Wen was sent to Tatung as area commander in charge of defense against possible intrusion by Mongol tribesmen. In July the Chinese forces under his command annihilated a contingent of invaders led by their leader Po-lai (*see* Mao Chung); and on August 16 he received the honorary rank of earl of Kao-yang 高陽伯, drawing an annual stipend of 1,000 bushels of grain. Early in 1460, while serving in Tatung, Li submitted a request for promotion to full commissioner for his part in the re-enthronement of the emperor, citing the example of other officials so rewarded. His request, however, was denied; naturally he bore a grudge against the throne. This probably explains why late in this year, when Po-lai launched a counter offensive against Tatung, Li Wen refused to mobilize his troops, a failure which resulted in a major defeat for the Chinese forces. He and other senior officials, including the eunuch Ch'en Hsüan (*see* Han Yung), were subsequently arrested and indicted for dereliction of duty. The Censorate demanded capital punishment, but the emperor treated them leniently. He took away Li Wen's title, demoted him one rank, but gave him the opportunity to redeem his honor by fighting against the Mongols in Yen-sui 延綏. Finally, in June, 1470, he proved his merit by subduing a band of invaders, and so regained the rank of deputy commander.

In August, 1473, Li Wen was ordered to accompany the junior transmission commissioner, Liu Wen 劉文 (T. 宗華, cs 1436, d. September 24, 1477), to lead an expeditionary force against the Turfan chieftain who had lately seized the capital of Hami and forced its leader to seek shelter in Kansu in the midst of a succession crisis. The Chinese forces, short of manpower and supplies, were unable to recover Hami; instead they held their defense line on the Kansu border, and gave support to the exiled leader who retrieved his lost territory five years later. Li Wen was recalled less than two years after his appointment. In August, 1478, pleading advanced age, he submitted a request to retire. The emperor granted his wish, and appointed his son Li Yung 鏞 to the hereditary rank of centurion, who became commander of the Hsi-ning guard when Li Wen died twelve years later. In July, 1508, Emperor Chu Hou-chao restored to him the title of earl of Kao-yang as a posthumous honor. Li Yung's descendants subsequently inherited the military rank through the end of the Ming into the Ch'ing dynasty in the same manner as did the offspring of Li Ning.

[Editors' note: The history of the Li clan, aside from official records, is also adumbrated in a family genealogy compiled by a descendant of Li Ying during the early Ch'ing, and a report by a modern visitor to Hsi-ning in the late 1940s. These documents, as evaluated by L. M. J. Schram, are not highly reliable as they contain excessive adulation and have a number of chronological errors.]

Bibliography

1/107/4a, 25a, 116/25a, 156/6a; 3/144/5b; MSL (1962), T'ai-tsu, 3372, T'ai-tsung (1963), *ch*. 15-269, Jen-tsung, Hsüan-tsung, *ch*. 31-90, Ying-tsung (1964), *ch*. 28-323, Hsien-tsung, *ch*. 33-180, Hsiao-tsung, 731, 1428, Wu-tsung (1965), 916; Chin Yu-tzu, *Chin Wen-ching kung chi* 金文靖公集 (1969), 9/27a; Ch'eng Min-cheng, *Huang-tun Ch'eng hsien-sheng wen-chi* 篁墩程先生文集 (NLP microfilm, no. 918), 25/1a, 46/13b; *Hsi-ning-fu hsin chih* (1762; 1969 ed.), 7/17a, 10/4a, 24/8a, 27/9b, 35/6a; *Kansu hsin t'ung-chih* (1909-11), ch. 30, 42; Chang Hung-hsiang 張鴻翔, "*Ming-shih* chüan i-wu-liu chu-ch'en shih-hsi-piao" 明史卷一五六諸臣世系表, *Fu-jen hsüeh-chih* 輔仁學誌, 5: 1-2(1936), 21; Wei Chü-hsien 衞聚賢, "Li K'o-yung hou-i ti tsu-p'u" 李克用後裔的族譜, *Shuo-wen yüeh-k'an* 說文月刊, 3: 10(1943), 127; Ma Hao-t'ien 馬鶴天, *Kan-Ch'ing-Tsang pien-ch'ü k'ao-ch'a chi* 甘青藏邊區考察記 (1947), 180; Ts'en Chung-mien 岑仲勉, "Ch'ao Ming Li Ying cheng Ch'ü-hsien (chin K'u-chü) ku-shih ping lüeh-shih" 抄明李英征曲先（今庫車）故事幷略釋, CYYY, 15(1948), 375; D. Pokotilov, *History of the Eastern Mongols during the Ming Dynasty from 1368 to 1634*, pt.1, tr. Rudolf Loewenthal, *Studia Serica* (Chengtu, 1947), series A, no. 1, 87; L. M. J. Schram, *The Monguors of the Kansu Tibetan Frontier: their origin, history and social organization*, Tr. of the American Philosophical Society, n. s., Vol.44, pt.1, 3(1954, 1958); Henry Serruys, "The Mongols of Kansu during the Ming," MCB, X(1955), 243, 287; Louis Hambis, *Documents sur l'histoire des Mongols à l'époque des Ming* (Paris, 1969), 128, 141.

Hok-lam Chan

LIANG Chen 梁震, flourished 1528-39, was a native of Hsin-yeh 新野, Honan. He began his career as hereditary commander of the Yü-lin guard 楡林衞. In 1528 he was appointed commander of Fort Hsing-wu 興武, in the Ning-hsia area, and in the year following he became commander of a mobile battalion of Yen-sui 延綏 in northern Shensi. Late in 1533, as regional vice commander of Yen-sui, he assisted the regional commander Wang Hsiao 王斅 (Pth. 武襄, d. 1537) in turning back a barbarian attack at Chen-yüan-kuan 鎮遠關,

the fortified position 60 *li* north of P'ing-lu 平虜 (the present P'ing-lo 羅) in Ning-hsia. After being promoted to assistant commissioner-in-chief he led his forces in a great victory over the Tatar chieftains Gün-bilig-mergen (*see* Qutuγtai-sečen) and Altan-qaγan (*q.v.*) at Huang-fu ch'uan 黃甫川, 70 *li* northeast of Fu-ku 府谷 in extreme northeast Shensi. He turned back a third Mongol attack at Hua-ma-ch'ih 花馬池 in August, 1534, and gained yet another victory over Gün-bilig-mergen at Kan-kou 乾溝, some 80 *li* north of Hui-ning 會寧 in Kansu. At the latter engagement the enemy is said to have numbered a hundred thousand cavalry. Liang directed the construction of a wall and trench system at Kan-kou to impede future raiding.

Liang moved to the rank of vice commissioner-in-chief and in 1535 became regional commander of Shensi, a region relatively untroubled by Mongol raiding. On October 15, 1536, however, he was transferred to Tatung in northern Shansi where both mutiny and repeated raiding had been endemic. Previously in August, 1524, a mutiny broke out in Tatung when the garrison refused to obey orders to construct five forts. The governor, Chang Wen-chin 張文錦 (T. 閭夫, cs 1499, Pth. 忠愍, native of An-ch'iu 安邱), and a few other senior officers were assassinated, and succeeding administrators failed to restore order. Finally the court sent Liang to the scene. He took with him five hundred robust and loyal followers and together they assumed command of the situation. With promises of fair and equable administration they restored discipline to the garrison.

Over the next few years Liang led his forces on a series of expeditions which brought the border under some measure of control. On the battlefield Liang displayed great personal courage and dash; he was, moreover, a serious student of the military art and he instilled in his troops both discipline and loyalty. In July, 1539, Liang assisted Mao Po-wen (*q.v.*), the minister of War, who was responsible for the defense of Shansi, in the reconstruction of five frontier outposts, a task which was completed after only three months of intensive labor. His efforts came to naught, however, for the outposts were abandoned soon after his death, not long after completion of the project.

In the years 1540 to 1542 the enemy took advantage of Liang's death and the abandonment of his outposts by making three successful invasions, reaching Tai-yüan and threatening P'ing-yang. It was in the midst of these difficulties that the court commemorated Liang's work by bestowing on him the posthumous name Wu-chuang 武壯.

Bibliography

1/211/3a; 3/195/3a; 63/14/284; KC (1958) 3493–3585; *Huang Ming wen-hai* (microfilm roll 20) 17/1/11; Ku Ying-t'ai (ECCP), *Ming-ch'ao chi-shih pen-mo*, 57.

Benjamin E. Wallacker

LIANG Ch'en-yü 梁辰魚 (T. 伯龍, H. 少伯, 仇池外史), *ca.* 1510-*ca.* 1582), dramatist, poet, and musician, was a native of K'un-shan 崑山, near Soochow. He was reportedly tall of stature and bearded, a handsome, talented man. After repeated failures in the examinations he purchased the title of scholar in the National University and pursued the life of a romantic writer. It happened that in the same locality there was a well-known musician and composer, Wei Liang-fu (*q. v.*), who is believed to have devoted ten years to the classical opera and the popular music of the lower Yangtze valley. It was he who combined the two, which resulted in a highly sophisticated form later called K'un-ch'ü 崑曲. Wei's new technique, which unconditionally excluded ranting and shouting, necessitated a total reorganization of the dramatic orchestra, involving the replacement of noisy instruments with subtler, quieter accompaniment. Liang, who had a full and pleasing voice himself, learned the dramatic arts from Wei and wrote a special play entitled *Huan-sha chi* 浣紗記, making use of the newly developed technique. It incidentally made the K'un-ch'ü a stage success. Thus it may be said that through Liang's efforts the prestige that this school of theatrical art enjoyed was established. From now on Wei and Liang were men of repute, so much so that a number of scholars and musicians came to work under them; at the same time other schools of drama began to be influenced by the new developments in the theater. Eventually K'un-ch'ü of the southern style drama prevailed for more than two centuries over all other forms, at least among sophisticated theater-goers. Some of the tunes from the *Huan-sha chi* may be found in *Na-shu-ying ch'ü-p'u* 納書楹曲譜.

In the years from 1553 to 1575, Liang traveled extensively at the invitation of wealthy officials, probably in the capacity of adviser in theatrical matters. He also wrote in the lyrical San-ch'ü style a book entitled *Chiang-tung pai-chu* 江東白苧, 2 *ch.*, with a supplement *Hsü* 續 *Chiang-tung pai-chu*, 2 *ch.* Other works of his include a collection of poems, *Yüan-yu kao* 遠遊稿 and two shorter dramatic works of the tsa-chü style, namely, *Hung-hsien nü yeh-ch'ieh huang-chin ho* 紅線女夜竊黃金盒 and the *Hung-hsiao-chi shou-yü ch'üan-ch'ing* 紅綃妓手語傳情. The former, commonly known as the *Hung-hsien nü*, may be found in the collection *Sheng-Ming tsa-chü* 盛明雜劇, printed in 1919.

A friend once wrote a poem addressed to Liang, which contains the following lines:

The man of penetration prefers the epicurean way
Disdaining all strictures····
Charming songs from his colorful pen
Bloom resplendent like spring flowers.
With a pint of wine, a song at night,
A Soochow girl in an old man's embrace,
And no savings at all, he is followed by a flock of youths····

This picture of a man about town reflects one phase of metropolitan life in the Yangtze delta of the 16th century; Liang Ch'en-yü's life may be considered a typical one.

Bibliography

22/11/39a; 38/8/36b; 84/丁中/16a; 86/14/42b; *K'un Hsin liang-hsien hsü-hsiu ho-chih*崐新兩縣續修合志 (1880), 30/明36; Li T'iao-yüan (ECCP), *Yü-ts'un ch'ü-hua* 下/20; Shen Te-fu, *Ku-ch'ü tsa-yen* 顧曲雜言, 10; *Su-chou-fu chih* (1877), 93/32; *Na-shu-ying ch'ü-p'u* (1792), 正集 3; A. C. Scott, *The Classical Theatre of China*, 32; Yao Hsin-nung 姚莘農, "The Rise and Fall of the K'un Ch'ü" in THM, II, no. 1 (1936), 63.

Lee Hwa-chou

LIANG Ch'u 梁儲 (T. 叔厚, H. 厚齋, 鬱洲), August 8, 1451-April 25, 1527, grand secretary, was a native of Shun-te 順德, a district created in 1450 out of the southern part of Nan-hai 南海, the provincial capital area in Kwangtung. His family was well-to-do, his father even contributing his own funds to organize a militia for the protection of the neighborhood during the Huang Hsiao-yang (*q.v.*) rebellion of 1449-50. It was due partly to this rebellion that the Shun-te district was formed to facilitate supervision. Liang Ch'u became a *chü-jen* in 1474. Four years later he headed the list at the metropolitan examination, passed fourth among the *chin-shih*, and was selected a bachelor of the Hanlin Academy where he became a compiler in 1480. During the following three decades he performed chiefly the duties of a Hanlin member, serving as a tutor to the heir apparent (1486-87, 1496-1505) and to Hanlin bachelors (1502-4), as an assistant examiner of the metropolitan examination in 1487, and three times as the director of provincial examinations, in Peking in 1492 and 1501, and in Nanking in 1498. Late in 1498 he was sent to Annam as head of the embassy to confirm the succession of a new king. His biographers put special emphasis on his refusal to accept gifts from the Annamite court and report that he returned with little luggage.

From 1500 to 1509 Liang Ch'u held the concurrent post of chancellor of the Hanlin Academy while he served as supervisor of instruction, vice minister of Personnel (1503-6), minister of Personnel in charge of writing eulogies (1507-9), and director of the metropolitan examination (1508). He then spent a year as the minister of Personnel in Nanking. In 1510, after the fall of the powerful eunuch, Liu Chin (*q. v.*), Liang was recalled from the south and appointed a grand secretary with the honorary ranks of minister of Personnel and junior tutor. In 1514 he served for the second time as director of the metropolitan examination. The candidate he selected to pass with first honors was his fellow townsman, Huo T'ao (*q. v.*). Later Huo passed fourth at the palace examination. It happened that Liang had also passed first at the metropolitan and fourth at the palace examination. Perhaps it was not a pure coincidence, for it was not uncommon in those days for the ranking of *chü-jen* and *chin-shih* to be manipulated (*see* T'ang Yin).

During his eleven years in the Grand Secretariat, Liang Ch'u first served under the chief grand secretary, Li Tung-yang (*q. v.*), and from 1513 under Yang T'ing-ho (*q. v.*) except for the period from April, 1515, to November, 1517, when Yang was absent to mourn the death of his father. Liang's biographers praise him for his modesty and prudence in yielding to Yang in 1517 the position of head of the grand secretariat. Actually Liang had no choice in the matter. Yang was far superior in talent and dominating in personality, and besides he enjoyed an overwhelming popularity. It is said that when he arrived at T'ung-chou at the northern terminus of the Grand Canal, the twelve-mile stretch of the highway to Peking was lined by nobles and high officials as well as by thousands of commoners who came to welcome him. This report contrasts sharply with the frequent accusations of incompetence, nepotism, and other irregularities lodged against Liang. An example is what happened to him in the case involving a member of his own family. In 1514 his eldest son, Liang Tz'u-shu 次攄, a centurion of the Embroidered-uniform Guard, not only murdered his rival in a feud for the acquisition of a large tract of land near Canton, but also killed more than two hundred persons, wiping out some thirty families. For such a crime Liang Tz'u-shu received merely a sentence of service at a frontier post to redeem himself, which amounted to no more than a fine. This flagrant miscarriage of justice was excused in official records as an imperial favor granted to Liang Ch'u. It seems more likely, however, that the grand secretaries, including Liang himself, were responsible for the sentence.

In 1518 the emperor decided to appoint himself field marshal, ignoring the protests made by Liang and the other grand secretaries. A year later the emperor, overruling all objections, proceeded south to fight the rebel prince, Chu Ch'en-hao 朱宸濠, even after receiving Wang Shou-jen's (q. v.) reports of the crushing of the rebellion and the capture of the prince. Liang Ch'u and another grand secretary, Chiang Mien 蔣冕 (T. 敬之, 敬所, 1463-1533, Pth. 文定, cs 1487), were members of the imperial entourage but were helpless in their efforts to restrain the headstrong emperor or his favorites. It is said that in September, 1520, the two grand secretaries wept as they knelt for hours in front of the palace gate in Nanking before the emperor finally promised to return to Peking instead of traveling farther in south China. That seems to be one of the few positive actions of Liang during his long term of office.

After the emperor died in 1521 without issue, and Yang T'ing-ho and others decided to designate as successor to the throne the emperor's cousin, Chu Houts'ung (q.v.), Liang Ch'u, then seventy years of age, went on the mission to Hukuang to welcome the emperor-elect. A few days after their return to Peking, several censors attacked Liang Ch'u for incompetence and for consorting with evil men. Someone even made the assertion that Liang's properties, if confiscated, might be used to supply half the annual revenue. Without offering any defense, Liang requested retirement, and this was granted. For six years he stayed quietly at home; during this time he was the recipient of some special imperial favors. After the notice of his death reached Peking, the controversy concerning him revived. Kuei O (q. v.), as vice minister of Personnel in charge of the granting of posthumous honors, submitted a collection of memorials by censors who had denounced Liang at various times in the past, and pointed out that both his private life and his conduct in office had given cause for severe criticism. Ordinarily Kuei's report would have been sufficient for disqualification. In this case, however, the emperor, on the doubtful excuse of giving consideration to Liang's services under the deceased emperor, granted him the posthumous title of grand preceptor and the name Wen-k'ang 文康. The emperor's real motive in this unusual act of indulgence may perhaps be explained by what chiefly concerned him at the time, the punishment of those who had objected to the conferment of imperial title on his own father. Yang T'ing-ho, in particular, was then the object of his animosity. Honors to the deceased Liang were probably intended as a slap at Yang, then living apprehensively in retirement.

At this time a concerted move seems to have been afoot to give Liang Ch'u a favorable name in history. His protégé, Huo T'ao, served as the standard bearer. Huo wrote a sketch of Liang which came to be quoted by later writers without question. A close examination of the facts will show that Huo's sketch is full of discrepancies and stories obviously fabricated to cover up Liang's weaknesses and to refute the accusations lodged against him. In one case Liang was praised as modest and prudent when he was simply being realistic. He was also pictured as a man unconcerned with money, for it is related that he did not add a foot to his land during forty years in government. He did not need to, looking on tolerantly, as he did in 1514, when his son did away with two hundred persons in order to acquire possession of a tract of land, and manipulating the courts so that the son went almost scot-free. Incidentally Huo, perhaps as a way to repay his mentor, even recommended Liang Tz'u-shu, the culprit, for a military appointment, which shows how rampantly nepotism flourished at that time.

One of the events Huo described to illustrate Liang's virtues was the following: Liang in 1517 succeeded in dissuading the emperor from issuing an edict granting a prince's request for a large tract of land to serve as pasturage; he worded the draft of the edict in such a way as to make the emperor realize the potential dangers of granting land to a prince for such a purpose. All biographers of Liang seem to have accepted the story without question, except Mao Ch'i-ling (ECCP) who, as a compiler of the official draft of the *Ming-shih* about 1679, was given the assignment of editing the section on the Cheng-te period covering the entire reign of Chu Hou-chao. Mao discovered that the case of the prince's request for pasture land was recorded in the *Ming shih-lu* in 1524, and that the vivid story of Liang's drafting of an edict in 1517 was evidently a fabrication. So Mao wrote a public letter about this discovery to the directors of the commission charged with the compilation of the *Ming-shih*. Yet in all versions of the official Ming history the story has been retained as told by Huo, as if Mao never uttered any dissent. This may serve as an interesting case study of Ming historiography.

The collected works of Liang Ch'u, entitled *Yü-chou i-kao* 鬱洲遺稿, were first printed in 1553 in 6 *chüan;* subsequently it was enlarged to 10 *chüan* and printed in 1566. The reprint of 1913 contains three additional poems attributed to Liang Ch'u. One of the poems, on the subject of retirement in 1518, is obviously written by another and mistaken as Liang's. The other two poems also seem spurious, as are ten poems attributed to the great Cantonese scholar, Ch'en Hsien-chang (*q. v.*), and dedicated to Ts'ang-yung 藏用 and several other disciples; in this the assertion is made that Ts'ang-yung was a courtesy name once taken by Liang Ch'u. On further study this seems to be a fiction due to someone who tried to include Liang's name among Ch'en's disciples, and may well have been inserted after 1584 when Ch'en's tablet was placed in the Confucian temple.

Bibliography

1/190/10b; 5/15/46a; 84/丙/14a; MSL (1965), Wu-tsung, 1681, 2176, Shih-tsung, 1777; *Ming-shih* (1962), 2225; 42/69/5a; 61/129/1a; Cha Chi-tso (ECCP), *Tsui-wei-lu*; biographies and other sources in *Yü-chou i-kao*; Mao Ch'i-ling, *Hsi-ho ho-chi* 西河合集 *cha-tzu* 劄子, 1/3b; *Pai-sha men-jen-k'ao* (*see* Ch'en Hsien-chang), 14.

Chaoying Fang

LIANG Fang 梁芳, a notorious eunuch in power from about 1476 to 1487, was a native of Hsin-hui 新會, Kwangtung. Little is known about his early life. It may be assumed that he was one of the attendants in the entourage of the heir apparent, Chu Chien-shen (*q.v.*); after the latter ascended the throne in 1464, he rose in the eunuch ranks until he became head of the directorate of wood craft and bookcraft (Yü-yung-chien 御用監). As the one in charge of furnishing the imperial living quarters, Liang supplied and perhaps also anticipated the needs of the young emperor and his favorite lady, the first class consort, Wan Kuei-fei (*q.v.*). Among his duties was the production of books. It is said that he gathered together a number of experts on elixirs and aphrodisiacs to cull from Taoist, Buddhist, and fictional writings such passages as might interest or amuse the emperor; these he presented in beautifully copied volumes with invented titles. On his recommendation some of these experts became advisers to the emperor and received official appointment or promotion as rewards. Among such men of unsavory repute were Li Tzu-hsing 李孜省 (d. January, 1488), a Taoist magician, and Chi-hsiao 繼曉 (d. 1488), a Buddhist monk.

Many ingredients in the aphrodisiac or alchemical formulae prescribed by these charlatans were exotic and expensive; for example, pearls. At one of the sources of supply, the oyster bed at Ho-p'u 合浦 in Kwangtung, a eunuch was stationed as tax collector. Liang Fang received an appointment as manager of the emperor's own stores in Peking, apparently to engage in the trade of pearls, precious stones, and ornaments, the prices of which he was able to manipulate. Large tracts of farmland were registered in his name perhaps to subsidize his activities. In 1480 and again in 1482 he also received subsidies in the form of salt-sale certificates. This certainly would result in an expanded market bringing the price of salt down and in the long run reducing the government revenue. He remained in Peking, the exception occurring in 1485 when he was dispatched to Shantung to search for mercury. While in the capital he directed the business of collecting money to meet palace expenses.

Liang had a brother, Liang Te 德, who, on the pretext of making an annual visit to their mother and bringing Kwangtung products back to Peking as tribute to the emperor, obtained a permit to travel by government postal service. Conceivably the interest of the Liang family in these business transactions exceeded, or at least mingled with, that of the imperial household. When Liang Te asked the administration commissioner, P'eng Shao (q.v.), to endorse the permit as renewable

every year, P'eng submitted a memorial recommending that the permit not be renewed. For this and his other efforts to curb the activities of the eunuchs, P'eng was removed from Kwangtung.

Much to the displeasure of the regular officials at court, Liang and several other eunuchs were put in charge of the sale of patents for the Taoist and Buddhist priesthood, swelling the number of those exempted from taxation. But what irked the officials most was the sale of official ranks by direct imperial order instead of through the proper channels in the minstries of War and Personnel, thus admitting many men of ill repute. Some of them even purchased promotions, the price ranging from a hundred to a thousand taels. Such was the need for money to meet the expenses of the palace.

The eunuchs, as usual, were blamed for excesses and exactions while in truth they merely followed instructions as agents of the emperor. Some of them indeed acted outrageously and arrogated power and wealth to themselves, but many just performed their duties as required. Even the notorious Wang Chih 汪直 (q.v.) conducted certain investigations, not on his own but on orders from above, and the money he collected by extortion or intimidation went apparently into the emperor's privy purse. In spite of frequent denunciations against him for avarice, depravity, and currying of imperial favor, Liang was not known to have much wealth in his own name. The ranks in the Embroidered-uniform Guard conferred on his relatives in 1482 were not out of the ordinary and probably were paid for by himself. It is said that when Ch'en Hsien-chang (q.v.) was summoned to Peking in 1483 and placed in the dilemma of determining whether to degrade himself by taking an examination in the ministry of Personnel or to incriminate himself by rejecting an imperial order, he appealed to Liang, his fellow townsman, who prevailed upon the emperor to permit Ch'en to retire with the title of a Hanlin academician. In gratitude, as one story has it, Ch'en presented the eunuch with ten poems expressing his appreciation. If this be true, then Liang saved the situation for Ch'en and at the same time earned for the emperor the image of one who sponsors scholarship. Later Ch'en was criticized as presumptuous for parading the paraphernalia of a Hanlin corrector when he left Peking. It seems somewhat out of character for Ch'en to have been so crudely ostentatious but rather befitting a eunuch's idea of pageantry. Perhaps the banners and tablets in Ch'en's procession were supplied by Liang following a desire to serve the emperor in a way that he deemed most fitting. In any case, as soon as Emperor Chu Chien-shen died in September, 1487, his successor, Chu Yu-t'ang (q. v.), made some radical changes in court and palace personnel, as usually happened on such an occasion. Li Tzu-hsing, who had been promoted (1486) to the office of transmission commissioner with the honorary rank of a vice minister of Rites, now received the blame for many of the evils of the preceding reign and was sentenced to banishment along with nine other Taoists and magicians holding high office. Hundreds of the supernumerary personnel were cashiered and many more downgraded. Liang Fang and two other eunuchs, Wei Hsing 韋興 and Ch'en Hsi 陳喜, were held responsible for the sale of government offices and forced to retire to Nanking, after being demoted. Two months later, in November, the three eunuchs, as well as Li Tzu-hsing and five other magicians, were re-arrested and interrogated in the prison of the Embroidered-uniform Guard. This time they were charged with squandering government money on the erection of temples and shrines. Li died of torture and the others were exiled to the frontiers.

Liang Fang was sent back to Nanking probably with a further reduction in rank. Late in 1488, following the execution of Chi-hsiao, Liang was flogged eighty strokes for having been the one who recom-

mended that Buddist monk some nine years previously. In time, however, both Liang Fang and Wang Chih received pardons. In 1498 two censors criticized the emperor for having forgiven them and for recalling them from Nanking. This is the last word on them to be found in the Veritable Records.

Bibliography

1/304/17a, 183/6a, 307/7b; 5/67/5a, 118/136a; 42/25/14a; MSL (1963), Hsien-tsung, 3897, Hsiao-tsung, 0138, 0152, 0204, 2462, 2471; KC (1958), 2480; Wang Shih-chen, *Yen-shan-t'ang pieh-chi*, 93/5a, 14b; Ting I 丁易, *Ming-tai t'e-wu cheng-chih* 明代特務政治 (1950); Ch'en Tzu-lung (EC CP), *et al.*, *Huang Ming ching-shih wen-pien*, 711.

Chaoying Fang

LIANG Ju-yüan, *see* **HO Hsin-yin**

LIANG Meng-lung 梁夢龍 (T. 乾吉, H. 鳴泉, Pth. 忠敏), 1527-1602, one of the trusted lieutenants of Chang Chü-cheng (*q.v.*), was a native of Chen-ting 眞定, Pei-Chih-li. After receiving the *chin-shih* degree in 1553 and being appointed Hanlin bachelor, Liang worked in the academy at the time that Chang Chü-cheng was in charge of the institution. Later he was referred to by his contemporaries as Chang's favorite disciple. In November, 1555, he was made a supervising secretary. A month later he initiated impeachment of the minister of Personnel, Li Mo (*see* Chao Wen-hua). Although Li died in jail later (1556), he stood at this time high in the favor of Emperor Chu Hou-ts'ung (*q.v.*), and Liang's impeachment action was dismissed. After a tour of duty in Shensi province, Liang was promoted to be chief supervising secretary. In 1561 he brought charges against both the minister of Rites, Wu Shan 吳山 (T. 日靜, H. 筠泉, d. 1577, cs 1535), and the minister of Personnel Wu P'eng (*see* Cheng Jo-tseng). The two officials were cashiered as a result. This built up Liang's fame as "the one who impeached two ministers." Yüan Wei 袁煒 (T. 懋中, H. 元峰, 1508-65, cs 1538), who succeeded Wu Shan, had written Taoist prayers for the emperor and was well regarded by the monarch. Hearing that Yüan was about to be appointed grand secretary, Liang proposed to the throne that grand secretaries be limited to those whose learning was "pure and orthodox" and that the appointment be not restricted by seniority. This angered the emperor. Liang apologized and was fined six months' salary.

In 1562 he was promoted to be prefect of Shun-t'ien 順天 (Peking). [Editors' note: The general rule forbidding natives of a particular province from serving in any office in its government was not always strictly observed, particularly in Pei-Chihli. *Cf.* James B. Parsons, "The Ming Dynasty Bureaucracy," in *Chinese Government in Ming Times: Seven Studies*, ed. by C. O. Hucker, New York, 1969, p. 196.] The break in the Yellow River dike near P'ei-hsien 沛縣 in 1565 gave him an opportunity to distinguish himself. Since at that time this section of the Yellow River constituted a part of the water system conventionally known as the Grand Canal, its maintenance was vital for the transport of grain supplies to Peking. Liang was nominated for the repair project on account of his unusual capability and talent. Appointed deputy commissioner in charge of waterways in Honan, he assisted Chu Heng (*see* P'an Chi-hsün), minister of Works, in constructing a new channel for the Yellow River from P'ei-hsien to Hsü-chou 徐州, about sixty miles long. The construction was completed in 1566. During the next four years Liang received a series of transfers, accompanied almost every time by a promotion: left administration vice commissioner, Shensi province, provincial surveillance commissioner, Shansi (1568), and right administration commissioner, Honan (1569). This was climaxed by his elevation to the governorship of Shantung province with the rank of a right assistant censor-in-chief (1570).

In 1571 he received instructions to find a sea route for the shipment of tributary grain from Huai-an 淮安 to Tientsin. The previous year the Yellow River dike had broken again north of Huai-an near Su-ch'ien 宿遷 with the loss of eight hundred boats from the tributary grain fleet; the court was eager to find an alternate route for grain transportation. Once involved, Liang became an ardent promotor of the sea route. He posted notice of awards for information on the sea route and recruited volunteers for test runs. He personally surveyed the coast and ordered the military colonies in Shantung to provide guides and assistance to the forthcoming traffic. During the summer two test runs were conducted under his direction. One flotilla of five ships loaded with two thousand piculs of husked rice sailed from Huai-an. Another with three ships and twelve hundred piculs of wheat left from Chiao-chou 膠州. Both hugged the coast of the Shantung peninsula and arrived in Tientsin without loss. The first took forty-five days to complete the voyage, the latter thirty-five. Information about islands, shoals, harbors, and storm shelters en route was gathered, charts were prepared, and the distance of each leg of the journey recorded. With this initial success Liang memorialized the throne proposing the implementation of the coastwise traffic on a larger scale. The governor of Huai-an in charge of the grain tribute, Wang Tsung-mu (*q.v.*), who had only recently served as the left administration commissioner of Shantung, was also in favor of the sea route. At their suggestion the court ordered that one hundred twenty thousand piculs of grain be shipped from Huai-an by sea and construction of new ships started. Army units operating the grain ships on the Grand Canal were reorganized to participate in the undertaking. Liang ordered signal stations set up in his territory and army units re-deployed to provide security along the coast.

In the spring of 1572 the consignment of grain was loaded on three hundred ships, which were organized into six squadrons to take to the sea. The whole fleet was reported to have arrived in Tientsin without mishap. For their services Liang and Wang were commended by the emperor, and each received a raise (by one grade) in their salaries, together with a reward of thirty taels of silver and two bolts of silk. It was further decided that an annual consignment of 201,150 piculs of grain be shipped by the sea route regularly to supplement the canal operation. After all this, however, a supervising secretary charged that during the spring operation eight ships had capsized and that Wang Tsung-mu, knowing that he himself was responsible, had purchased sufficient grain to cover up the loss. Wang defended himself and requested the court to conduct an inquiry. It seems that none ever took place and the coastwise operation continued until the following year when seven ships were definitely lost in a storm off the Shantung coast near Chimo 即墨. Now the new governor of Shantung, Fu Hsi-chih (see P'an Chi-hsün), who had succeeded Liang, along with a censor and a supervising secretary, argued against the whole operation. The sea route was then abandoned. Meanwhile Liang had been appointed right vice censor-in-chief and sent to Honan as governor.

The accession of Chu I-chün (q.v.) as emperor in mid-1572 marked Chang Chü-cheng's coming to power. Liang was recalled to Peking for ministerial assignments. He became successively right vice minister of Revenue, right, then left, vice minister of War. Early in 1578 the court sent him to the northern frontier as governor-general of Chi-chou 薊州, Paoting, and Liaotung. About a year later he was made right censor-in-chief and concurrently minister of War, but maintained his post as governor-general. (The Ming governmental system permitted the appointing of more than one minister

to each ministry. Only one, however, actually managed the business of the office. The rest, all having other functional assignments, received the title only. While Liang assumed the title approximately from 1579 to 1581, the "actual" minister of War was Fang Feng-shih 方逢時 (T. 行之, H. 金湖, cs 1541). As governor-general Liang had the cooperation of the generals, Li Ch'eng-liang (ECCP) and Ch'i Chi-kuang (q.v.). The latter was especially instrumental in the reconstruction of the section of the Great Wall near Ku-pei-k'ou 古北口, which remains an imposing sight to this day. After the completion of the work on the Wall, Ch'i received a minor hereditary rank and Liang the title of junior guardian of the heir apparent. A month later, on May 16, 1581, Liang was recalled to Peking to take over the ministry of War. In November, 1582, he became minister of Personnel.

Before Chang Chü-cheng died in 1582, he submitted to the emperor a list containing the names of several officials capable of administering state affairs, Liang's name among them. When Chang's party was purged, however, Liang's position became untenable. Several censors brought impeachment action against him, charging him with handing out bribes and conspiring with Chang Chü-cheng's eunuch associate, Feng Pao (see Chang Chü-cheng). Liang submitted his resignation, which was accepted early in 1583; he had served only two months. Returning to his native Chen-ting, he lived in retirement for the next nineteen years.

Some contemporaries criticized Liang for his aggressiveness in courting personal favor and his shameless advancement of his own career. But his reputation as an efficient administrator was never challenged. Vigorous in action, he planned deliberately and supervised lower echelon work in person. In constructing the Yellow River channel, he camped with the workers in the field. As governor of Shantung, he inspected the coastal area by boat. In the 1579 campaign against marauding tribes in Liaotung, he personally commanded three thousand mounts and saw action east of Shan-hai-kuan 山海關. As a reward for his exploits, all four of his sons received official titles. Two of his grandsons became *chü-jen*, Liang Wei-shu 維樞 (T. 慎可) in 1615 and Liang Wei-pen 本 in 1621. Both later served as officials under the Manchus. Three great-grandsons held important positions in the Ch'ing court. Liang Ch'ing-k'uan 清寬 (cs 1646) and Liang Ch'ing-yüan 遠 (T. 遹之, H. 葵石, 1608-84, cs 1646) served as vice ministers of Personnel; Liang Ch'ing-piao 標 (T. 玉立, H. 蕉林, 1620-91) was minister of War and a grand secretary.

Six books by Liang have been cited in various sources. They are: *Hai-yün hsin-k'ao* 海運新考, 3 *ch.*, *Tz'u-lin-t'ang chi* 賜麟堂集, *Tu-shu jih-lu* 讀書日錄, *Li-kuan piao-tsou ch'ao* 歷官表奏抄, *Hsiao-chung lu* 效忠錄, and *Shih-yao-pien* 史要編. These titles suggest that, besides being a capable administrator, he was also a diligent scholar.

The *Hai-yün hsin-k'ao* is included in the *Hsüan-lan-t'ang ts'ung-shu* (comp. by Cheng Chen-to, BDRC). It is a collection of forty documents, all dated in the years 1571 and 1572. The present edition is a reproduction of the original work of 1579 with two maps attached. The discourse is formal and repetitious, the short-lived sea route remaining the main topic. Nevertheless this book also yields much interesting information about late 16th-century China. It mentions, for instance, that the sea route from Huai-an to Tientsin had been used by the civilian population some twenty years before the grain fleet followed the course. Commodities such as sea food, salt pork, fruit, beans, yeast cakes, porcelain, paper, cotton cloth, and herbs had long been transported here by sea. Merchants engaged in the trade came from Shantung, Nan-Chihli, Chekiang, Fukien, and Liaotung. The route from Huai-an to Tientsin was calculated at 3,310 *li* or about 1,000 miles. When the wind was favorable, the voyage took only twenty days; if not, it might take two months or longer.

The vessels in the coastwise operation ordered by the Ming court never attemped to venture out into the open sea, but followed the coast closely, slipping from one harbor to another, or to an off-shore island, making many stopovers. The maps appearing in the work are crude, not even employing the grid system of earlier maps, nor indicating any use of a compass for navigation; several documents, however, list all the islands and harbors en route. The avoidance of the open sea was deliberate. Both Liang and Wang regarded the direct route from the south of the Yangtze to the Pohai Gulf as unfeasible, for in their opinion it would expose to possible loss not only the grain, but also the lives of those operating the fleet. Another consideration was the increased insecurity from piratical raids. The emperor concurred in their opinions and also forbade his subjects to construct ships of more than one mast or to sail into the open sea. Tribute missions bound for the capital were prohibited from following the same route as the vessels carrying grain, and special regulations were issued for Chinese merchants engaged in coastwise traffic.

New ships planned for the coastwise operation numbered 436, of which at least one prototype was constructed in 1572. Each vessel was to have a capacity of 600 piculs of grain plus a 200 picul allowance for drinking water, provisions, and other necessities. A twelve-man crew was employed, of which nine were army personnel, three recruited seamen. The dimensions of the craft were not specified; based on the details above, however, it is estimated that each vessel may have had a capacity of between fifty and seventy tons. The construction cost of each craft was about three hundred taels of silver. The ships were expected to last from fifteen to thirty years. Those used before the construction was completed came either from the regular grain fleet operating on the Grand Canal or from a private source. Every one that Liang utilized in his test runs was leased and of the type regularly engaged in the coastwise commerce; they seem to have had curved hulls.

The documents in the *Hai-yün hsin-k'ao* indicate that signal posts were installed along the entire littoral: flags to be flown by day, lanterns, protected by iron frames and weatherproof, to be lit by night. Men in two small fishing smacks attended each signal post. Ceremonies were not forgotten. When each squadron took out from shore or entered a harbor trumpets were ordered blown, drums beaten, and flags broken out. At temples en route prayers were said. A proposal made to the court concerned the construction of a special shrine to the goddess of the sea near the mouth of the Huai River. The statue of the goddess was to be made of iron, to counteract the influences of dragons and winds—both thought to belong to the category of wood. Each vessel too had to maintain on board a small replica of the deity, housed in a cabin.

Financing the operation proved to be difficult. No special funds were available. Eventually part of the money was obtained by diverting the local funds that previously had been committed to maintaining the grain fleet on the Grand Canal. When that was insufficient, it was supplemented by funds derived from fines and confiscations collected by several coastal prefectures. Small expenses incurred in local communities on the coast were met by additional impositions on the corvée labor.

As indicated above, the project to transport annually one hundred twenty thousand piculs of grain by the sea route was unwisely abandoned in 1573, because some ships were lost in a storm. Opponents of the project seized upon this to emphasize the risk of the sea route. Late in 1572 Wang Tsung-mu requested an investigation but the powerful minister, Chang Chü-cheng, let the matter pass without action. He had no desire for an investigation which might result in an impeachment of Liang or Wang. Nor did he have any strong argument for the sea route because just then reports had come in saying that the Grand Canal had already been restored to its former capacity and the crisis of any shortage of food in Peking no longer existed.

Bibliography

1/86/14a, 193/2a, 212/15a, 216/2a, 223/13b, 225/4b, 238/1a; MSL (1965), Shih-tsung, 8199, 8251, 8367; MSL (1940), Shen-tsung, 4/3a, 6/5a, 14/4a, 110/6a, 116/3a; *Chi-fu t'ung-chih* 畿輔通志 (1934), 7833; Ch'ien Ch'ien-i(ECCP), *Yu-hsüeh-chi* (SPTK ed.), 28/10; *Hai-yün hsin-k'ao* (*Hsüan-lan-t'ang ts'ung-shu* ed.); Ni Yüan-lu (ECCP), *Ni Wen-cheng-kung ch'üan-chi* (1772), wen-chi, 14/5; Chang Chü-cheng, *Chang T'ai-yüeh wen-chi* (1612), 24/8b, 24a, 25/12a, 16b; A. W. Hummel, *Report of the Librarian of Congress* (1938), *Div. of Orientalia*, 235.

Ray Huang

LIANG Ts'ai 梁材 (T. 大用, H. 儉菴), 1470-November 2, 1540, minister of Revenue during the years from 1529 to 1531, 1534 to 1538, and 1539 to 1540, was descended from a family registered in the military category in the Chin-wu 金吾 right guard, Nanking. Liang's ancestors originally hailed from Ta-ch'eng 大城, Shun-t'ien 順天 prefecture, Pei-Chihli. Graduating as *chü-jen* in 1495 and as *chin-shih* four years later, Liang Ts'ai received his first assignment as magistrate of Te-ch'ing 德清, Chekiang. He served an eight-year term, and made a mark for his competence and industry. In 1507 he was promoted, first as a secretary in the ministry of Justice, next as vice director (1509), and then as a censor in April, 1510. In this last capacity, Liang was entrusted with drafting a public statement denouncing Liu Chin (*q.v.*), when the court decided to make known the crimes of the formidable eunuch following his execution in September. It is said that Grand Secretaries Li Tung-yang and Yang T'ing-ho (*qq.v.*), who were to prepare a document on this case for the bureau of history. withdrew their draft after they had reviewed Liang's and found it superior.

Early in 1511, in recgnition of Liang's caliber and performance, the court appointed him prefect of Chia-hsing 嘉興, Chekiang, but soon transferred him to the more important and populous seat of Hangchow, where he served for the next five years. Besides being known for his discipline and uprightness, Liang demonstrated his talent in fiscal administration by standardizing the land tax quota according to acreage and productivity, and by introducing effective measures to relieve the population stricken by bad harvests. In 1516 he received an appointment to be an administrative vice commissioner of Chekiang, from which he rose to be surveillance commissioner of the same province two years later (March, 1518). When the prince of Ning, Chu Tsai-hou (see Wang Shou-jen), rebelled in July, 1519, the eunuch Pi Chen 畢眞 (d. 1520), then overseeing the administration of Chekiang, attempted a coup in Hangchow. Liang is credited with devising a plan to expose the eunuch's intent, thereby preventing the rebellion from spreading into Chekiang. Before there was time for his services to be rewarded, however, Liang had to withdraw to mourn the death of his parent, and stayed at home until the end of the Cheng-te reign.

In 1523, shortly after the accession of Chu Hou-ts'ung (q.v.), Liang Ts'ai returned to office as surveillance commissioner of Yunnan, where he mediated several disputes between native chieftains by acceding to local customs. A year later (September, 1524) he was appointed an administration commissioner of Kweichow, and then of Kwangtung (1525), where he officiated with distinction during the next two years. He received promotion in July, 1527, to be vice censor-in-chief and governor of Kiangsi, but three months later was named a vice minister of Justice. In April, 1528, when the court ordered an expedition against the rebellious tribes-

men in Yunnan, Liang Ts'ai was appointed vice minister of Revenue, and given charge of the supply of military rations. He followed the commander, minister of War Wu Wen-ting (see Wang Shou-jen), to Yunnan, assisted him in the suppression, and returned to his post upon the conclusion of the campaign in August. Five months later (January, 1529), Liang Ts'ai was appointed minister of Revenue, succeeding Tsou Wen-sheng 鄒文盛 (T. 時鳴, 1459–1536, cs 1493, Pth. 莊簡), a rapid promotion for Liang in view of his record.

When Liang assumed office, he was confronted with a state deficit of 1,100,000 taels of silver, resulting from the unrestrained spending of the previous monarch and the new emperor during his first years. To redress the imbalance, Liang resorted to the conservative method of tightening expenses, eliminating abuses and corruption, without attempting to exploit new resources at the expense of the population. In March, 1529, his ministry was ordered to examine the feasibility of several suggestions presented by Huo T'ao (q.v.). Two months later, after a court conference, Liang presented a long list of proposals which may be summarized as follows: a) concerning imperial princedoms, to limit the recipients of stipend grain, to levy taxes on lands under princely control, and to reduce the number of employees in princely households; b) concerning the military, to eliminate corruption in the management of military farms, to check strictly the qualifications for promotion, and to give half pay to inactive army officers; c) concerning the junior bureaucracy, to reduce the pay of those appointed by favoritism or purchase, and to eliminate supernumerary employees; d) concerning the inner court, to reduce funds for extravagant items, such as gold and precious stones, and to limit the expenses on entertainment. Finally, he urged a stern enforcement of regulations governing the delivery of tax cash and grain contributions from the prov-

inces to the central government at designated periods, to ensure a regular flow of
revenue to the imperial treasury. The emperor approved of most of his recommendations but withheld those on the reduction
of stipends for the inactive army officers,
probably out of concern that this might
hurt the morale of the military.

During this period, another problem
facing Liang Ts'ai was the financing of
the defense of the northern frontier of
Pei-Chihli, Shensi, and Shansi, which constituted the bulwark against the intrusion
of the Mongols. Those in positions of
responsibility continually complained of
fiscal difficulties due to bad harvests and
the unstable environment for farming
under the threat of invasion. Liang's solution was again one of restraint in spending by reallocating existing resources and
by eliminating abuses, instead of acceding
to the demands of the provincial governors for increases in budgetary appropriation. In addition, he endeavored to eliminate the vested interests of the imperial
favorites by proposing to remove the eunuchs from supervision of a number of
granaries, and to reassess the landholdings
of the imperial relatives to prevent illegal
appropriation. Although these measures
hurt the privileged individuals whom the
emperor was reluctant to offend, they
curtailed government spending, improved
the fiscal health of the state, and lessened
the burden of the people. Notwithstanding its good intent, Liang's policy antagonized a number of imperial sycophants
and powerful officials, but because of his
integrity and competence, which temporarily arrested the unfavorable fiscal situation, the emperor stood behind him. In
November, 1531, however, he had to leave
office to mourn the passing of his mother, thus concluding his first term as financial minister.

Three years later, on the conclusion
of his mourning, Liang Ts'ai was recalled
to succeed Hsü Tsan (q.v.), and became
minister of Revenue for the second time.
In these years he renewed his effort to
strengthen the finances of the state by
curtailing spending and eliminating abuses,
at the same time devoting his attention to
improving the general welfare. Liang's
tight rein on fiscal matters, coupled with
his strong personality, however, soon
brought him into conflict with his colleagues at court and in the provinces. The
first instance occurred in March, 1536,
when Fan Chi-tsu 樊繼祖 (T. 孝甫, H. 双
岩, cs 1511), governor of Tatung, complaining of financial difficulties, requested
an increase in appropriation for strengthening military preparation against the
Mongols. Liang pointed out that the annual appropriation had exceeded over
770,000 taels of silver, and argued that
he could live within his resources by a more
effective use of them. He recommended
instead an allocation of 40,000 taels as
emergency funds, and declined further
petitions for increases by the governor.
In the second instance, Liang clashed
with Kuo Hsün (q.v.), the powerful duke
of I-kuo, over his requests for increase
of funds for construction under his
supervision of new palaces and imperial
mausolea. In July, 1537, for example, he
sternly rejected Kuo's plea for an additional supply of grain, winter garments,
and summer clothes for his work force—
reportedly 70,000 strong—to supplement
the regular provisions. Kuo then proposed
reopening the mines in Shun-t'ien, Shantung, and Honan to yield additional income for his projects, but Liang again
dissented, arguing that such undertakings
would not be profitable in view of the
costs, and that they would only increase the
burdens of the people. As a result, Kuo
bore a grudge against him, and Liang's
continual disagreement with the powerful
commander eventually caused his downfall.

Between these events, nettled by the
criticism of his colleagues, Liang submitted
in the autumn of 1536 a request for transfer to be minister of Revenue in Nanking on the pretext of ill health, hoping
that a shift to this less prestigious position
would placate his critics. A supervising

secretary of Revenue, however, subsequently took the lead in criticizing him for evading responsibilities, and recommended punishment. The emperor pardoned Liang, retaining him in office, but began to lose confidence in him. In July of the following year, when bad harvests affected a number of provinces, both north and south, Liang implored the court to implement an earlier injunction approving a thirty percent reduction of land tax and grain contribution countrywide. To this the emperor agreed, but became increasingly annoyed by Liang's policy of restraint; so he retired Liang in April, 1538, upon the completion of less than a four-year term, allowing him to retain his title. Two months later Liang was demoted to be vice minister when the court, after reexamining a previous dispute between him and an imperial prince over land usage, charged him with dereliction of duty. In June of the following year, however, when Li T'ing-hsiang 李廷相 (T. 夢弼, H. 蒲汀, 1481-1544, cs 1502, Pth. 文敏) retired as financial minister, the emperor reinstated Liang and further honored him with the title of junior guardian of the heir apparent. The recall of Liang, it seems, suggests that the emperor felt the need for a steady hand to guide the state during a period of fiscal difficulties, and was willing to overlook his former attitude. It is said that the emperor, impressed by Liang's judgment, entrusted him with the annual review of the performance of the officials in the capital and the trial of important cases of offenses, a function normally reserved for the ministries of Personnel and Justice. In the meantime Liang continued to find fault with certain powerful officials; this was particularly true of Kuo Hsün, whose continued spending for construction of imperial buildings he was attempting to curtail.

It happened that during the previous year Kuo, who had reportedly 46,000 men under him for his projects, complained of numerous desertions from his force, and requested the court to grant a sum at the rate of 1.2 taels of silver per absentee to hire a total of 4,000 civilian substitutes in the autumn session, and 5,000 in the spring session. In addition, he requested an appropriation of grain for substitutes at the rate of 4 tou 斗 per person; this the outgoing minister, Li T'ing-hsiang, agreed to supply for two months, but Liang Ts'ai, suspecting that Kuo had misappropriated much of the funds, refused to comply. Kuo then brought a complaint against Liang. When the matter was deliberated at court, the minister of War, Chang Tsan (see Yang Po), supported Liang, but Kuo succeeded in convincing the monarch and won his case. Before this was over, Kuo, who had already hired thousands of substitutes for his work force without prior authorization, again asked for new recruits to fill the vacancies; this would increase the burden on the treasury. Both Chang Tsan and Liang rejected his plea. Outraged by their stand, Kuo launched a counter attack, charging them with intrigue against the court, and violating the established regulations. The emperor again supported Kuo Hsün, and punished both Chang and Liang. Chang Tsan was later pardoned, but Liang Ts'ai was ordered to retire, though allowed to retain his title. This was in July, 1540. According to the *Ming-shih*, however, the reason the emperor cashiered Liang was not because of his liking of Kuo Hsün, but rather because Liang failed to supply the ambergris (龍涎香) needed for making an elixir and for conducting Taoist sacrifices. This seems plausible in view of Liang's earlier remonstrances with the monarch against indulgence in Taoist festivities, and of the fact that certain sycophants ingratiated themselves with the emperor by submitting such exotic items. Four months after his dismissal, Liang died at his home aged seventy. Despite his outstanding record and dedication, he did not receive a posthumous honor until July, 1567, when Emperor Chu Tsai-hou (q.v.) awarded him the canonized name Tuan-su 端肅 (upright and majestic), and subsequently the honorific of grand protector. One of his sons, Liang Shan 山, received the yin privilege (June, 1535) to be enrolled in the National University, but did not distinguish himself in government service.

Liang Ts'ai was not a vigorous, innovative financial minister who would propose bold solutions to complicated problems, but rather a cautious, managerial-type administrator who tried to arrest the fiscal deterioration of the state by modest, conservative means. Described as honest, frugal, competent, and disciplined, Liang served well in his terms as minister of Revenue. It is said that the emperor, impressed by Liang's ability, once exclaimed metaphorically that if he could recruit twelve ministers like Liang, he could set his house in order. Unfortunately, Liang was unable to convince the emperor of the virtue and necessity of thrift, and, in attempting to discharge his duties honestly, ran into the concerted opposition of privileged individuals, twice antagonizing the emperor.

Liang Ts'ai left a collection of memorials entitled *Liang Tuan-su kung tsou-i* 公奏議, 14 *ch.*, containing those he submitted to the court during his first two terms as minister of Revenue; they were engraved by his descendants during the Wan-li period. A copy of the original edition, listed as rare, with a preface by Chiao Hung (ECCP), dated 1607, is preserved in the Naikaku Bunko. A partial selection of his memorials, 5 *ch.*, is included in the *Ming ching-shih wen-pien*, edited by Ch'en Tzu-lung (ECCP).

Bibliography

1/194/19a; 5/29/32a; 8/52/1a; 10/14/42b; 11/4/53a; 12/25/4a; 16/33/23b; 61/129/23b; MSL (1964), Wu-tsung, 2780, 3056, Shih-tsung(1965), *ch.* 100–30, 161–242, Mu-tsung (1965), 263, 276; KC (1958), 3599; *Hang-chou-fu chih* 杭州府志 (1579, reprint 1965), 63/51a; Hsü Hsüeh-mo, *Shih-miao shih-yü lu* (1965 ed.), 259; Chang Hsüan, *Hsi-yüan wen-chien lu*, 12/24b, 14/42b, 15/6b, 35/3b, 40/1b, 76/24b; Ku Ch'i-yüan, *Lan-chen ts'ao-t'ang*

chi (1970 ed.), 18/23b; Ch'en Jen-hsi, *Huang Ming shih-fa lu* (1965 ed.), 89/23a; Ho Ch'iao-yüan, *Ming-shan ts'ang* (1970 ed.), 4598; Chiao Hung, *Ching-hsüeh chih* 京學志 (1965 ed.), 5/77b, 8下/66a; TSCC (1885–88), XI: 597/7a; *Ta-ch'eng-hsien chih* (1896), 9上/13b; Ch'en Tso-lin 陳作霖, *Chin-ling t'ung-chuan* 金陵通傳 (1904), 15/9a; W. Franke, *Sources*, 5.5.19.

Hok-lam Chan

LIAO Tao-nan 廖道南 (T. 鳴吾, H. 玄素子), died 1547, official and author, came from a family registered in the military category in P'u-ch'i 蒲圻, Hukuang. His grandfather at one time served as an instructor in a prefectural school; his father, Liao Han 漢 (T. 天章, cs 1493, d. 1537), director of a bureau in the ministry of Revenue, raised a large family. Liao Tao-nan was the second of twelve sons. A *chü-jen* of 1513, he achieved his *chin-shih* in 1521, topping the list of second class honors, but was unable immediately to obtain an appointment due to the death of Emperor Chu Hou-chao (*q.v.*). In December, 1522, the new emperor, Chu Hou-ts'ung (*q.v.*), named him a Hanlin bachelor. Subsequently Liao served as compiler of official records, as expositor of the Classics, and occasionally as supervisor of civil examinations. In February, 1527, he was appointed to the commission charged with the compilation of documents which sought to justify the emperor's bestowal of posthumous honors on his father in the aftermath of the *Ta-li i* episode (*see* Feng Hsi and Chu Hou-ts'ung). This, when completed in July, 1528, came to be known as the *Ming-lun ta-tien* (*see* Yang I-ch'ing). Following this Liao took part in the preparation of a supplement to the *Ta Ming hui-tien* (completed in 1550 but never published; *see* Shen Shih-hsing). On the occasion of the appearance of an ominous cosmological phenomenon (February, 1529), Liao submitted a memorial exhorting court officials to perform their duties and promote the study of Confucianism; he also advised the throne to be cautious in the appointment of military officers.

In the following year Liao presented a memorial requesting the removal from the imperial ancestral temple of the tablet of Yao Kuang-hsiao (*q.v.*), the one-time Buddhist priest who became adviser to Chu Ti (*q.v.*). The emperor, acting on his recommendation, ordered the transfer (in September) of Yao's tablet to the Buddhist monastery, Ta-hsing-lung ssu 大興隆寺. Later Liao occupied himself with the rectification of rites and music arising out of the *Ta-li i* episode, and delighted the emperor by submitting pieces of laudatory rhymed prose on auspicious occasions. From November, 1530, to March, 1536, he served on a commission headed by Grand Secretary Chang Fu-ching (*q.v.*) to prepare a collection of documents on sacrificial rites in the imperial ancestral temple in consequence of another episode concerning the *Ta-li i* (*see* Huo T'ao). Liao became a senior expositor in February, 1532. Seven months later he submitted a memorial urging the restoration of the post of diarist for recording history (*see* Ho T'ang), and the training of talented scholars in the Hanlin Academy for the compilation of historical chronicles. Though pleased with Liao's memorial, the emperor does not seem to have acted on his recommendations.

In subsequent years Liao was involved in several incidents which brought an end to his career. The first occurred in August, 1533, when the daily expositor of the Classics, Ku Ting-ch'en (*see* Shen I-kuan), happened to be absent due to illness. Chang Fu-ching then recommended Liao to take his place, but Liao hesitated to comply because it was against the regulations. Displeased, the emperor demoted Liao to assistant prefect of Hui-chou 徽州 (Anhwei), but reinstalled him in April, 1534. Four months later, however, he was charged with negligence during his supervision of the provincial examination in Peking and fined a year's stipend. He was involved next (August, 1536) in the case of the vice minister of Person-

nel, Huo T'ao, who lost out in a confrontation with his rival, Grand Secretary Hsia Yen (*q.v.*). Liao was indicted as an instigator along with Huo and was deprived of two months' stipend as punishment. In September Liao left office to mourn the death of his mother; fifteen months later his father also died, so he was unable to return to duty. During the mourning period he was involved in yet another episode which resulted in his retirement. It happened in September, 1539, when the secretary of Personnel, Hsüeh T'ing-ch'ung 薛廷寵 (T, 汝承, H. 萃軒, cs 1533), and some censors submitted a memorial accusing Yen Sung (*q. v.*) and a number of his favorites of dereliction of duty. The emperor, in defending Yen, sought to placate the critics by making a number of officials, including Liao, scapegoats. He was thus ordered to retire. His death eight years later is not mentioned in the dynastic records.

Liao left a collection of writings, *Hsüan-su-tzu chi* 玄素子集, 17 *ts'e*. A copy of an undated original edition is preserved in the Naikaku Bunko. His better known works, however, are the *Tien-ko tz'u-lin chi* 殿閣詞林記, 22 *ch.*, and *Ch'u-chi* 楚紀, 60 *ch.*, both completed in 1545. The *Tien-ko tz'u-lin chi*, a collection of notes on the Grand Secretariat and biographies of the grand secretaries from the beginning of the dynasty to the early Chia-ching period, is an invaluable compendium for the study of this important institution. According to Liao's preface (1545), he collaborated with Huang Tso (*q.v.*) on parts of this work; the sections from *chüan* 9 to 22, for example, are derived from Huang's *Han-lin chi*. A copy of the undated original edition is preserved in the collection of the former National Library of Peiping and is available on microfilm (no. 286). This was reprinted in the *Hu-pei hsien-cheng i-shu* 湖北先正遺書, shih-pu 史部, by Lu Ching 盧靖 in 1923. The *Ch'u-chi* is a gazetteer of Hukuang on which Liao is said to have spent over ten years and to have attempted to show the importance of his native area, which had served as the base of the founder of the dynasty as well as the fief of Chu Hou-ts'ung when he was a prince. This was written apparently in an effort to please the emperor. In the concluding section Liao gave an account of his ancestry and a résumé of his career, modeling it after the pattern of the grand historian Ssu-ma Ch'ien in his postscript to the *Shih-chi*. A copy of the original edition, with a preface by Ying Chia (*see* Mao K'un), is preserved in the Naikaku Bunko. A specimen of his calligraphy is preserved in the Palace Museum, Taipei.

Bibliography

5/19/38a; 40/37/7a; 64/戊14/13a; MSL (1965), Shih-tsung, 593, 2278, 2364, 2759, 2802, 3172, 3293, 3455, 3582, 3657, 3986, 4734; *P'u-ch'i-hsien chih* (1866), *ch.* 5, 7, 8; SK (1930), 53/6a, 58/2a; Chou Fu-chün 周復浚 (1496–1574), *Ching-lin chi* 涇林集 (NCL microfilm), 7/35a; Li Chin-hua 李晉華, *Ming-tai ch'ih-chuan shu k'ao* 明代勅撰書考 (1932), 52, 61, 63; Shen Te-fu, *Wan-li yeh-hu pien*, 800; *Ku-kung shu-hua lu* 故宮書畫錄 (rev. ed., 1965), 3/14; W.Franke, *Sources*, 6.2.6, 8.12.1.

Hok-lam Chan

LIAO Yung-an 廖永安 (T. 彥敬), 1320–September 2, 1366, naval officer, was a native of Ch'ao 巢-hsien (Anhwei). His family probably engaged in some activities on Lake Ch'ao, such as fishing or transportation. During the decline of the Yüan authority about 1352, local uprisings of religious sects were frequent in the northern part of the province. He joined one group led by P'eng Tsao-chu (*see* Kuo Tzu-hsing), and after P'eng died became one of the leaders who jointly operated a piratical fleet of hundreds of boats on that lake. It seems that Liao himself did not belong to the Maitreya sect at this time as did some of colleagues, especially Chao P'u-sheng (*see* Hsü Shou-hui). In June, 1355, pressed by another rebel leader, the pirates proposed to join Chu Yüan-chang, whose power was then in the ascendant at Ho-chou, about thirty-five miles

to the northeast. Chu was then planning to cross the Yangtze River with his command of about thirty thousand men and was in desperate need of means of transportation. Hence he went in person to take command of Liao's fleet. Just then a summer storm flooded the canal between Lake Ch'ao and the Yangtze River, enabling the fleet to float down easily. About this time Chao P'u-sheng defected but Liao stayed on with Chu. At the confluence Yü-hsi-k'ou 裕溪口, Liao directed his highly maneuverable small boats on June 27, 1355, to attack the large government ships guarding that port. After winning the battle they moved northeast downstream to Ho-chou where Chu's soldiers boarded the boats. On July 11 they crossed the river, routed the surprised Yüan troops, and went on to take the city of T'ai-p'ing 太平, thus launching Chu's career of conquest.

During the following five years Liao Yung-an took part in most of the battles that resulted in the conquest for Chu of the cities of Chi-ch'ing (Nanking) and Chinkiang in 1356, and Ch'ang-chou 常州 and Ch'ih-chou 池州 in 1357. He commanded the naval forces which defeated the enemy fleet under Chang Shih-ch'eng (*q.v.*) on the Yangtze River at Fu-shan 福山 on the south bank and Lang-shan 狼山 on the north (August, 1358). Later in that year, in a battle against Chang's men on the lake, T'ai-hu 太湖, near I-hsing 宜興, Liao was captured by the enemy and brought to Chang in P'ing-chiang (Soochow). He refused to surrender and died a prisoner eight years later. In October, 1364, two years before he died, he was remembered by Chu Yüan-chang and given the hereditary rank of Duke of Ch'u 楚國公.

After the subjugation of P'ing-chiang in 1367, Liao's body was brought to Nanking for burial. Chu Yüan-chang came out the city gate to meet the procession and to offer sacrifice. In 1369 Liao was honored in the Imperial Ancestral Temple as first among the seven generals who had died in service. Among the remaining six men, three were Liao's associates in the pirate days and joined Chu's service together in 1355, namely, Yü T'ung-hai (*q.v.*) of Ch'ao-hsien, Chang Te-sheng 張德勝 (T. 仁甫, d. 1360) of Ho-fei 合肥, and Sang Shih-chieh 桑世傑 (d. 1358) of Wu-wei 無爲.

In 1373 Liao Yung-an was given the posthumous name, Wu-min 武閔. Seven years later his rank was changed to duke of Yün 鄆國公; the change from Ch'u, a large state, to Yün, a small district, indicates a kind of downgrading. In any case, because he did not have a son, his rank did not survive him. His adopted son, a nephew, Liao Sheng 昇, received a minor hereditary rank.

Bibliography

1/133/1a; 5/6/32a; *see also* Liao Yung-chung.

Chaoying Fang

LIAO Yung-chung 廖永忠, 1323-75, naval officer, was a native of Ch'ao-hsien 巢縣 (Anhwei) and a younger brother of Liao Yung-an (*q.v.*) under whom he served from 1355 to 1358 in the naval campaigns in support of Chu Yüan-chang. After his brother was captured by the enemy in 1358, Liao Yung-chung succeeded to the command of the naval forces. During the following eight years he took part in most of the fighting against Ch'en Yu-liang and Chang Shih-ch'eng (*qq.v.*) that involved the use of naval units. In the battle on Lake Poyang 鄱陽 it was Liao who in 1363 helped to set fire to the large ships in Ch'en's fleet, gaining a victory at perilous odds, and a name for bravery.

Late in 1366, after both Ch'en and Chang had been overcome and Chu Yüan-chang had extended his control over the entire lower Yangtze valley, there arose the delicate question involving the titular head of the Sung state, Han Lin-er (*q.v.*), under whose reign title, Lung-feng 龍鳳,

Chu had been doing all the fighting. Han wanted to remove his capital from Ch'u-chou 滁州 to Nanking and Liao was entrusted with the transportation of Han's party across the Yangtze River. Han's boat sank and he was drowned. Irrespective of whether the murder—for that is what it must have been—was perpetrated by higher order or on Liao's own initiative, it gave Chu a free hand in assuming a royal title shortly thereafter (1367) and in ascending the imperial throne a year later (January 23, 1368). During this time Liao was given a plaque to hang in front of the gate to his house inscribed with eight characters: Kung ch'ao ch'ün chiang, chih mai hsiung shih 功超羣將, 智邁雄師 (Merit outstrips other generals; intelligence transcends a strong army). The *Ming-shih* dates this plaque in 1364.

In 1367 Liao was made a deputy central administrator and late in that year was appointed deputy commander of the expedition to conquer the south. The commander, T'ang Ho (*q.v.*), together with another deputy commander, had already advanced by land to occupy Ch'ing-yüan (Ningpo) on the Chekiang coast. Liao's mission was to command the naval vessels collected at that port to transport the troops by the sea route. They set sail on January 6, 1368, and twelve days later, after some fighting, took the city of Foochow. After the conquest of Fukien T'ang Ho was recalled. Liao, succeeding as commander, sent a message calling on Ho Chen (*q.v.*), then in control at Canton, to surrender. When Liao's fleet arrived at Swatow in April, he received Ho's reply of submission. Later in the month when Liao disembarked at Canton he took over the city from Ho Chen, and, although he met some resistance here and there, occupied both Kwangtung and Kwangsi provinces by July. After organizing the civil and military governments in these provinces, he returned by boat to Nanking late in October, 1369, and was honored by being met at Lung-wan 龍灣, the river port of Nanking, by the entire court with the heir apparent at its head. It is said that he tried in 1370 to find out from someone close to the emperor the hereditary rank to be awarded to him. This displeased the emperor and, in November of that year when he created six dukedoms and twenty-six marquisates, Liao was openly accused of trying to influence the emperor in the matter and so, although he merited a dukedom, was given a lower rank. He was made marquis of Te-ch'ing 德慶侯 with a stipend of 1,500 *shih* of rice.

In 1371 two armies were sent to conquer Szechwan, one on land by way of Shensi under the command of Fu Yu-te (*q.v.*), the other by water up the Yangtze under T'ang Ho. Liao was again made a deputy commander under T'ang and, leading the advance naval units, forced his way through the gorges in a series of heavy battles in July. On approaching Chungking early in August he received the enemy's offer to surrender (*see* Ming Sheng) but ordered the commanding officer to wait until T'ang Ho arrived so as to let the superior general have the honor of acceptance. Later in the same month Chengtu surrendered to Fu's army. Early in 1372, when awards were distributed among the generals for the conquest of Szechwan, Liao ranked with Fu in receiving the highest honors.

In April, 1373, Liao was ordered to supervise the transportation of grain by the sea route to Liaotung. According to his biography in the *Ming-shih* he also took part in the Mongolian expedition of 1372 and in some naval action against Japanese pirates in 1373.

The *Ming shih-lu* records that when Liao died the emperor sent gifts to his family and let his son, Liao Ch'üan 權 (d. 1384), succeed to his rank. Obviously this was not entirely correct for, according to contemporary documents, Liao Yung-chung was executed. His biography in the *Ming-shih* summarized his crimes as follows: for being the one responsible in the eyes of the emperor,

for the drowning of Han Lin-er, for being a partisan of Yang Hsien (*see* Empress Ma), the assistant central administrator, executed in 1370; and for other minor offenses, such as wearing decorations designated for imperial use exclusively. The responsibility for the drowning of Han Lin-er, however, seems to be the main reason for Liao's downfall. He perhaps acted on orders and later became indiscreet.

Liao Ch'üan married a daughter of T'ang Ho. He did not inherit his father's rank until 1380. Shortly thereafter he took part in Fu Yu-te's campaign in Yunnan (1381-83). Liao Yung 鏞, Liao Ch'üan's son, a disciple of Fang Hsiao-ju (*q.v.*), was executed in 1403 for that relationship, and his mother, and other female members of the family were enslaved as washwomen in the laundry attached to the imperial household. The male members were exiled to frontier military posts. It was not until 1645 that the sentence imposed on Liao Yung-chung was revised in Nanking, at which time he was posthumously given the title duke of Ch'ing 慶國公 and his grandson, Liao Yung, was designated a successor to the title marquis of Te-ch'ing. By that time the dynasty was in its last days.

The *Ming-shih* holds that when Chu Yüan-chang met Liao Yung-chung in 1355 he found Liao the youngest of the pirate leaders and asked him a question as if talking to a boy or a young man. Actually in that year Liao Yung-chung was thirty-two years of age and five years Chu's senior. Hence the account must be a fabrication.

Bibliography

1/129/10a; *Ming-shih* (1963), 1646; MSL (1962), T'ai-tsu, 1674; Cha Chi-tso (ECCP), *Tsui-wei lu* 傳, 8下/4a; KC (1958), 520; Wang Shih-chen, *Yen-shan-t'ang pieh-chi*, 20/18b; *Huang Ming wen-heng* 文衡, 97/2b; P'an Ch'eng-chang (ECCP), *Kuo-shih k'ao-i*, 1/36b, 2/10a; Ch'ien Ch'ien-i (ECCP), *Ch'u-hsüeh chi*, 103/6b.

Chaoying Fang

LIEN Tzu-ning 練子寧 (*ming* An 安, H. 松月居士), died July 25, 1402, statesman, literatus, and martyr of the usurpation, was a native of Hsin-kan 新淦 district in Lin-chiang-fu 臨江府, Kiangsi. His father, Lien Po-shang 伯尚 (*ming* Kao 高), minor poet and official, held various posts during the early years of the Hung-wu period. As diarist 起居注 at the imperial court, Lien Po-shang antagonized Emperor Chu Yüan-chang by his frankness, and in punishment was demoted to serve in a succession of local government posts in Nan-Chihli, in Lin-chiang, and in remote Kwangsi. Lien Tzu-ning accompanied his father to these posts in his youth and studied with local teachers. He apparently received some of his education at his native place, for it is recorded that he and a fellow townsman, Chin Yu-tzu (b. 1368, *see* Empress Hsü), studied the Spring and Autumn Annals together at Hsin-kan and were noted as "friends whose talent earned them great reputations at that time."

Lien Tzu-ning passed the metropolitan examinations in 1385. At the following palace examination, at which the new *chin-shih* were again tested so as to be ranked by the emperor, Lien displayed some of the same temperament that had caused his father's demotion. When asked to respond orally to the emperor on the subject of employing talent, he replied with daring criticism of the court and, by implication, of the tyrannical Ming founder himself. The emperor then placed Lien second among the top three candidates, thereby indicating his approval of the courageous remarks. In April Lien was appointed Hanlin compiler, but almost immediately was forced into temporary retirement to observe mourning for his mother. He somewhat exceeded the norms by rigorously observing antique rites. Coming out of mourning, he was reinstated in his former position, and became vice minister of Works in 1395.

When Chu Yün-wen (*q. v.*) came to the throne in 1398, Lien was at hand, a young but experienced official just below the highest rank, a man of scholarly background and literary achievement, and one already famous for his courageous and upright conduct. He was precisely the type of official that the new emperor drew to his court and with whom he probably intended to create a new era in government. He served as vice minister of Personnel beginning in October, and is said to have "taken it as his personal responsibility to ensure that merit alone be the standard for promotion" throughout the entire civil service. But he soon was transferred to the Censorate as vice censor-in-chief, for, on April 9, 1400, when that title was changed from fu tu-yü-shih 副都御史 to yü-shih chung-ch'eng 中丞, Lien is recorded as holder of that office.

It is difficult to judge how important a role Lien played in determining policy during the civil war of 1399-1402. Too little information about the Chien-wen reign has survived the destruction of archives and the ban on private reporting that followed the usurpation. In one or two significant incidents, however, Lien's part is known. He is famous for having joined with Huang Tzu-ch'eng 黃子澄 (*ming* 湜, T. 伯淵, cs no. 3 in 1385, d. 1402, aged fifty), Ch'i T'ai, and Fang Hsiao-ju (*qq. v.*) in September of 1400 in support of their demand that Li Ching-lung (*see* Li Wen-chung) be executed for his unsatisfactory conduct of the punitive campaign against Chu Ti (*q. v.*), but it is unlikely that he charged Li with treason, as most of the accounts say. The emperor on this occasion ignored his chief civil advisers and sheltered Li. Lien is often grouped with Ch'i, Huang, and Fang as "the four outstanding martyrs" of the usurpation episode. He is also often named with Fang Hsiao-ju as the two scholar-officials enjoying the emperor's highest esteem and confidence. Lien and Fang probably were the two civil officials that Chu Ti would most have wanted to acknowledge his succession in July, 1402. The perhaps apocryphal account, but one imbedded deeply in the historical consciousness of Ming China, describes his encounter with Chu Ti at that time. Lien was in chains, facing the usurper, violently berating him for his crime. Chu Ti ordered that Lien's tongue be cut out to silence him, realizing that there was no hope of winning him over, but explaining: "I desired only to emulate the Duke of Chou coming to support young King Ch'eng." This use of the analogy to the heroic Duke of Chou, son of King Wen and brother of King Wu, who in the 12th century B. C. had nobly assisted King Wu's infant son and heir, was most inappropriate to the early Ming situation. Lien Tzu-ning displayed his contempt for Chu Ti by dipping his finger in the blood streaming from his mouth and using it to write on the floor at the usurper's feet: "But where is King Ch'eng?" King Ch'eng, *i. e.* the Chien-wen emperor, of course was dead or had vanished, and stubborn loyalists like Lien would have to join him.

Lien was executed and his family eradicated; some accounts say that one hundred fifty-one immediate family members were done to death and several hundred more distant clan relatives and associates banished to the frontiers. But some accounts relate that a concubine who was pregnant was among those banished, and that in exile she bore a son, named Lien Shan-ch'ing 善慶, who was able to return from exile, claim the family property, and continue the line after the amnesty of 1424. It must be remembered, however, that the legends which developed (*see* Chu Yün-wen) provided all of the martyrs with descendants; lacking better verification, this account should be regarded with suspicion.

Lien Tzu-ning was looked upon in his time as an essayist and poet of considerable distinction. Only fragments of his writing have survived. During the Hung-chih period, those that could be found were collected and published under the title *Chin-ch'uan yü-hsieh chi* 金川玉屑集, 2 *ch.*, edited by Wang Tso 王佐 (T.

廷輔, 1440–1512, cs 1478). This was republished in 1611 with biographical and commemorative addenda under the title *Lien-kung wen* 文-chi, 2 *ch.*, with appendices of *Ch'ung-ssu shih-chi* 崇祀實紀, 1 *ch.*, *shou-chi* 手蹟, 1 *ch.*, and *i-shih* 遺事, 1 *ch.* A copy of an early Ch'ing reproduction of this edition is held by the National Central Library. The Naikaku Bunko has a copy of his *shou-chi* printed 1610. There have been later reprintings under slightly different titles. Some of his fugitive pieces may also be found in the *Hsin-kan-hsien chih.* The famous literary figure Li Meng-yang (*q. v.*) became interested in Lien while serving from 1511 to 1512 in Kiangsi as surveillance vice commissioner; he founded at Hsin-kan a Chin-ch'uan academy as a memorial to him. Finally, Lien received the canonized name Chung-chen 忠貞 when the Southern Ming court awarded posthumous honorifics to the loyalists of the Chien-wen era in February, 1645.

Bibliography

1/141/9a; 5/54/18; 63/5/5a; 84/甲/118, 150; KC (1958), 652, 791, 815, 820, 856, 6171; *Hsin-kan-hsien chih* (1873), 7/進士/12a, 鄉舉 1b; 8/文苑/6b, 忠義3a, 9/書目/3a, 文徵/42a, 86a, 106a (古體詩), 4a, 8b, 25a, 29b, 44b; T'u Shu-fang 屠叔方, *Chien-wen ch'ao yeh hui-pien* 建文朝野彙編 (NCL microfilm), 10/15a; NCL *Catalogue of Rare Books* (Taipei, 1967), 1006; Naikaku Bunko *Catalogue* (Tokyo, 1956), 252.

F. W. Mote

LIN Chao-en 林兆恩 (T. 懋勛, H. 龍江, 子谷子), 1517-98, a native of P'u-t'ien 莆田, Fukien, was a religious leader who propagated the essential oneness of the three religions: Confucianism, Taoism, and Buddhism; hence, he was also known as San-i-chiao-chu 三一教主. He came from a prominent clan, which produced several degree holders and officials in the Ming dynasty. His grandfather, Lin Fu 富 (T. 守仁, H. 省吾, *ca.* 1472-*ca.* 1538), was a *chin-shih* of 1502 who rose in official career to be vice minister of War and acting supreme commander in Kwangtung and Kwangsi. His father, Lin Wan-jen 萬仭 (T. 樅谷, 養浩, d. 1544), had two other sons: Lin Chao-chin 金 (T. 懋南), a *chin-shih* of 1550, and Lin Chao-chü 居 (T. 懋協).

At the age of four *sui*, Lin Chao-en was taken by his father to meet the great philosopher, Wang Shou-jen (*q.v.*), who is reported to have predicted that the boy was destined to be unsuccessful in the examinations, but would achieve even greater distinction. The meeting had not been difficult to arrange, as his grandfather was a close associate of Wang in official and military affairs in Kwangsi. Although not precocious, Lin succeeded in becoming a *hsiu-ts'ai* at the age of eighteen *sui*, his writings gaining praise chiefly for their thoughtful approach. After his father's death, he returned some one thousand taels' worth of notes to the family's debtors, refusing repayment. It was probably at this juncture that he made the decision to refrain from taking any more examinations as he had already failed three times in those at the provincial level. In the meantime, he began a serious inquiry into the teachings of Confucianism, Taoism, and Buddhism. For a few years he visited many exponents of greater and lesser fame, who advocated one or another of the three doctrines. Prehaps it was his devotion and single-mindedness which led him to dream of Confucius passing on to him the essence of the *Lun-yü*, and confiding in him that therein lay the tao 道 (way) that had never previously been revealed. In like manner, Lao-tzu led him to a comprehension of hsüan 玄 (mystery), and Buddha gave him an understanding of k'ung 空 (emptiness). He stressed the significance of the character ni 尼 in all three names: Chung-ni 仲尼 (Confucius), Ch'ing-ni 清尼 (Lao-tzu), and Shih-chia-mou-ni 釋迦牟尼 (Sakyamuni Buddha), which in his opinion hinted at a oneness in the masters of the three religions. A pun like this may be regarded today as preposterous, but in the 16th century it may have proved an attractive element in the popularization of Lin's San-chiao religion.

About this time Lin came to know another individualist of his native place and the two became fast friends. This man, Cho Wan-ch'un 卓晚春 (H. 無山子, 上陽子, d. probably in the late 1560s), a Taoist adept, who is said to have been a wizard at numbers as a boy, and later, without any formal education, wrote poetry and achieved a good hand in calligraphy in the running style. Cho paid no attention to personal appearance or comfort—he was always barefoot and his hair disheveled; sometimes he bathed in the streams even in freezing weather. His ability to deal with numbers helped him in prognosticating the fortunes of individuals as well as approaching events. Before leaving P'u-t'ien in 1554, he predicted the area would undergo twelve years of adversity. It so happened that just at this time coastal Fukien was preyed upon by pirates, and the city of P'u-t'ien ransacked (1562). Cho is reported to have died in a Buddhist monastery in Hangchow. For his alleged magical powers, he was also known as Cho Hsiao-hsien 卓小仙 Cho the minor immortal). Other sources say that Cho was a native of Szechwan, an accomplished painter, and one who could change a pebble into silver by holding it in his mouth for a moment. Accounts of Cho are similar to those of many others in the Ming period categorized as Taoist immortals and generally described as men of odd behavior and supernatural gifts. The bond of friendship between Cho Wan-ch'un and Lin Chao-en certainly had marked influence on the latter.

In 1553 Lin began seriously to promote, by preaching and writing, the doctrine calling for the amalgamation of the three religions. His first group of disciples formed at this time included his younger brother Lin Chao-chü. When the rebel Ming thinker, Ho Hsin-yin (*q.v.*), was in

Fukien (1562-64), he paid his respects to Lin and is reported to have praised Lin's writings as the greatest ever produced in the Ming era, even surpassing those of Wang Shou-jen.

When pirates attacked P'u-t'ien, Lin Chao-en took the lead in raising volunteers to defend the city, and in burying those who died as a result of both raids and an epidemic which broke out simultaneously. Reports have it that in 1561 and 1562 nearly ten thousand corpses were interred under his supervision. Finally, due to Ch'i Chi-kuang's (*q.v.*) military successes, the pirates' activities subsided. It was again under Lin's leadership that a shrine was built for Ch'i in P'u-t'ien to express the people's gratitude. He was acquainted with Ch'i personally, and later corresponded with the great general. A note in Ch'i's own collected writings records that Lin once advised him to take up the Taoist practice of striving for longevity, but in reply Ch'i declared that the duty of a general is to die for the preservation of peace in the empire, so how could he embrace the Taoist practice of seeking long life.

In 1565, when Lin was puzzling over a title for a newly written tract, he had a dream about someone holding a manuscript, the cover of which bore the characters Hsia-yü 夏語. Thereupon he adopted these characters as the title of his new work, although he could not explain their meaning when asked. From this title one more of his names, Hsia Wu-ni 夏午尼, is derived, in which he used the character *ni* to match the names of the masters of the three religions. In the following year (1566) he designed a special garb, the san-kang wu-ch'ang i 三綱五常衣, which may be rendered as "the gown of the three bonds and five principles"; this was made by sewing together three pieces of cloth in front and five pieces in back. He called the cap san-kang chin 三綱巾 and the shoes wu-ch'ang lü 五常履.

In the ensuing years he traveled and preached in Fukien as well as in Kiangsi, Chekiang, and Nanking, making thousands of converts, and many acquaintances among scholar-officials. San-chiao shrines sprang up in all these places. In this repid spread of Lin's doctrine, his declared power of healing the sick was surely an important factor. He called his method the Ken-pei fa 艮背法 and referred to it also as Hsin-fa 心法. Several stories about his healing powers have come down. One high official had eye trouble, but after a conversation of a few minutes with Lin, the condition cleared up. Another high official's father was sick, but after Lin talked to him the patient became well. A third official suffering from a nervous disorder quieted down the day after Lin treated him. This mysterious religious healing quality may have been psychic, presumably a kind of hypnosis.

Other magic gifts, such as the ability to still a storm, or to keep ghosts away in the night, etc., were also credited to him. His followers included all kinds of people, high and low, rich and poor. One of his close disciples was a Buddhist monk. While some branded his teachings as heretical, others spoke up for him vigorously. His contemporary, Yüan Huang (*q. v.*), also a religious scholar, asserted that in his younger days, whenever he encountered difficult passages in reading, he could always find satisfactory explanations in Lin's writings. Lin's family background and social status must have helped him in his religious activities, but his escape from serious persecution, the kind that befell Li Chih (*q.v.*) and Ho Hsin-yin, is probably because he limited his activities to south China. If Li and Ho had also remained in the south and had abstained from politics, they too might have avoided tragic ends. Ye tLin was not entirely free from minor difficulties with the local authorities, who were concerned over his ability to attract large congregations of people and over some of his publications. Even after his death, a writer in collaboration with an enterprising bookdealer produced a piece of fiction about him entitled *San-chiao k'ai-shu yen-i* 三教開述演義which, apparently derogatory in tone, was destroyed by his disciples. Hsieh Chao-che (*q.v.*), another Fukien scholar, records that Lin suffered from loss of his faculties in his last years and therefore questioned how anyone who laid claim to having attained the real tao could have come to such an unhappy end. Hsieh expressed regret that Lin who came of an official family should have been led astray, and reported that the evil activities carried on in Foochow by some of Lin's disciples after his death proved to be harmful and might also be a source of danger to the state.

Most of Lin's writings were printed during his lifetime; some went through several editions. About 1631 they were collected and printed under the general title *Lin-tzu ch'üan-chi* 林子全集, to which a biography, the *Lin-tzu hsing-shih* 行實, is appended. The Gest Oriental Library at Princeton has a copy of this collection including forty individual titles. The work includes discourses on the three religions, discussion of his own doctrine, information on his psycho-religious healing, his prose and poetry and letters, and one *chüan* of poetry by Cho Wan-ch'un. Lin's writings lack clarity in thought and lucidity in presentation. It is not surprising, therefore, that *Lin-tzu ch'üan-chi* receives an unfavorable notice in the *Ssu-k'u* catalogue.

The seventeenth-century scholar and thinker, Huang Tsung-hsi (ECCP), wrote a biography of Lin Chao-en in which he most appropriately summed up Lin's doctrine as an attempt to bring Taoists and Buddhists into the Confucian framework by abolishing their observance of monasticism, and to lead Confucianists to practice certain Taoist and Buddhist ways, while respecting Confucius as the chief master. His doctrine, Huang continued, was quite insubstantial and had no logical basis. Huang also attributed the religious sectarian disturbances of his own time to the influence of Lin's teachings.

Another early Ch'ing scholar, Chu I-tsun (ECCP), included Lin Chao-en both in his anthology of Ming poetry, the *Ming shih-tsung*, and in his notes on Ming poetry, the *Ching-chih-chü shih-hua*. But Chu erroneously recorded Lin's *tzu* as 谷子, a mistake derived from Lin's religious name 子谷子. Chu's one-sentence evaluation of Lin, however, in which he classified Lin and Li Chih together as the two heretics of Fukien, is direct and succinct.

Although Lin never in his writings mentions the Ch'üan-chen sect of Taoism (*see* Chang Yü-ch'u), there is no doubt that he was somewhat influenced by the teachings of that sect which stressed the amalgamation of the three religions under Taoist dominance. Like Yüan Huang, Lin taught the supremacy of Confucianism in the san-chiao. Yet in the development of religious Taoism, the two, Lin and Yüan, certainly may be described as Ch'üan-chen Taoists in Confucian garb. Lin apparently had a desire to visit the center of that sect on the mountain, Wutang shan (*see* Chu Ti), for he started twice on such a journey, but both times he failed to reach his goal. It may well be that he was attempting to find the source of his religious inspiration there.

Bibliography

40/50/27b; 86/14/43a; *Lin-tzu ch'üan-chi* (in microfilm); Huang Tsung-hsi, *Huang Li-chou wen-chi* (1959), 46; biography by Yang Shu-liang 楊樹樑 in *Fu-chien wen-hua* 福建文化, III, no. 17 (January, 1935), 41; article tr. from Japanese by Hsiu-hsiu-sheng 休休生, *ibid.* n. s., II, no. 1 (January, 1944), 23; TSCC (1885–88), XIV: 3/10b, 4/1a, XVIII: 6/9b; SK(1930), 125/7a; *Hsing-hua P'u-t'ien-hsien chih* 興化莆田縣志 (1963), 32/4b; Hsieh Chao-che, *Wu tsa-tsu* (Japanese ed., 1795), 8/36b, 44a; Ch'i Chi-kuang, *Yü-yü-kao* (in *Chih-chih-t'ang chi* 止止堂集), 上/11a; Ch'en Yüan (BDRC), *Nan-Sung ch'u Ho-pei hsin Tao-chiao k'ao* (1958).

Lienche Tu Fang

LIN Ch'un-tse 林春澤 (T. 德敷, H. 旗峯), November 15, 1480-June 4, 1583, scholar, official, a native of Hou-kuan 侯官, Fukien, was to be a marked man because of his long life. From a family of some prominence since the 10th century, he became known as a precocious youth, talented in composing poetry. A *chü-jen* of 1510, he became a *chin-shih* in 1514. In the following year, however, he retired to observe the mourning period for his father. He resumed his official career as a bureau secretary in 1518 in the ministry of Revenue. Appointed a supervisor of the Lin-ch'ing levy station (臨清關), he did his best to protect the merchants from the exactions of the subordinates of Chiang Pin (*q.v.*) in 1519 during the emperor's tour of the south. Later he supervised the granaries of Peking, T'ung-chou 通州, and Ch'ang-p'ing 昌平 with fairness and efficiency. After three years he was promoted to bureau vice director in the same ministry. For some reason he was demoted to Kiangsi province, first to Ning 寧-chou, then to Chi-an 吉安 as assistant prefect. From there he received a transfer to Kwangtung, first as vice prefect of Chao-ch'ing 肇慶, then as acting prefect of Kao 高-chou in the years from 1531 to 1533. It was a time when the *wok'ou* were raiding the southeast coastal regions. Aware of the fact that the people might suffer equally from the government forces, Lin Ch'un-tse laid emphasis on the use of native volunteers for defense. Then he was appointed a bureau director in the Nanking ministry of Justice. From Nanking he advanced to his last official post, that of prefect of Ch'eng-fan-fu 程蕃府 (later Kuei-yang 貴陽) in the southwest province of Kweichow. Many non-Chinese tribespeople in Ch'eng-fan were living according to their own customs and social mores. Lin promoted Confucian teachings among them and elevated the level of education; this laid the foundation for their active participation in the examination system. From this post he retired probably abut 1540, and led a long and quiet life at home.

At his 100 *sui* anniversary in 1579,

the local authorities erected an arch in his honor, calling it Jen-jui fang 人瑞坊 (Arch of the auspicious man). Four years later, shortly before his death, the authorities put up another arch which bore the inscription Liu-ch'ao ta-lao fang 六朝大老坊 (Arch of the grand old man of six reigns). On both occasions it is said that he was hale and hearty, capable of performing all the genuflections the ceremonies required. Also in the last year of his life he wrote a poem celebrating the birth of a great-great-grandson. In recording the names of people who enjoyed longevity in Ming times, Wang Shih-chen (*q.v.*) in his *Huang Ming sheng-shih* could enumerate only seven centenarians since the founding of the dynasty, but none could compare with Lin Ch'un-tse in achievement. Besides his collection of prose and poetry, entitled the *Jen-jui-weng chi* 翁集, 12 *ch.* (a copy of which, in the original edition of 1580, is in the Naikaku Bunko), he produced a work on the Rites, the *Li-chi ch'üan-t'i* 禮記荃蹄, 16 *ch.*, and *Chia hsün shih-liu p'ien* 家訓十六篇 (Family teachings in 16 sections). He was a good friend of another Fukien poet, Cheng Shan-fu(*q.v.*), whose daughter married his eldest son. This son, Lin Ying-liang 應亮 (T. 熙載, H. 少峯, 1507–92), a *chin-shih* of 1532, rose in official position to be vice minister of Revenue; his collected works appeared under the title *Shao-feng ts'ao-t'ang shih-chi* 少峯草堂詩集, 1 *ch.* (apparently no longer extant). Lin Ying-liang's son, Lin Ju-ch'u 如楚 (T. 道茂[翹], H. 碧麓), (1543–1623), who became vice minister of Works, graduated as *chin-shih* in 1565; a collection of his writings, known as *Pi-li-t'ang chi* 碧麓堂集, seems not to have survived. It was indeed a family of longevity and prominence.

Bibliography

Huang Ming wen-hai (microfilm), 14/7/17; 40/35 /23b; 64/戊12/12a; 84/丙13/21a; Wang Shih-chen, *Huang Ming sheng-shih*, in *Yen-shan-t'ang pieh-chi*

(Taipei, 1965), 221; Kuo Po-ts'ang 郭柏蒼, *Ch'üan-Min Ming-shih chuan* 全閩明詩傳 (1889), 16/1a; *Fu-chien t'ung-chih* 福建通志 (1938), *lieh-chuan* 列傳, 23/6b; Naikaku Bunko *Catalogue*, 357; SK (1930), 176/13b, 177/10b.

Lienche Tu Fang

LIN Feng 林鳳 (variants: Limahong, Dim Mhon), fl. 1572–76, was a native of Jao-p'ing 饒平, Ch'ao-chou 潮州, Kwangtung. His great-uncle was a famous freebooter who, associated with such pirate chiefs as Wu P'ing and Tseng I-pen (for both *see* Lin Tao-ch'ien), had ravaged the coasts of Chekiang, Fukien, and Kwangtung. The first mention of Lin Feng appears in the *Ming shih-lu* in an item for the year 1572 which, summarizing the dispatches from the provincial authorities of Kwangtung and Fukien, states that he, in command of five to six hundred men, had asked to submit. At the time, the military officials of Kwangtung and Fukien were preparing a campaign to eradicate piracy and, on their recommendation, the ministry of War issued an order that no quarter should be given to the pirates. Lin Feng's request was therefore denied.

In July, 1574, after he had been defeated by the Fukien naval forces led by the regional commander Hu Shou-jen 胡守仁, Lin again asked for amnesty, and once more his request was refused. Thereupon, he and his band continued to harass the coast of Fukien and Kwangtung (*see* Lin Tao-ch'ien). At this time the provincial authorities reported that Lin Feng had ten thousand men under his command and that his activities extended as far as Hainan Island. Late in October Lin Feng decided to transfer his base from Makung 媽宮 Island in the P'eng-hu group to the west coast of Taiwan. The new base was the haven Wang-kang 魍港, now known as Yen 鹽-kang, in Tung-shih chen 東石鎮, west of Chia-i 嘉義. While his fleet was sailing across the Straits it was surprised and intercepted by a Fukien naval squadron, which scattered and sank a large number of Lin's ships.

After this engagement the name Limahong began to appear in Spanish records in the Philippines.

The first contact between the Chinese and the Spaniards took place in May, 1570, when Martín de Goyti, in command of two ships and fifteen praus, sailed north from Cebu to Luzon. Near Mindoro they encountered and, after a brisk fight, captured two Chinese merchant junks. Two weeks later the Spaniards arrived at Manila where they found a colony of forty Chinese. When the town of Manila was established in the following year the number of Chinese residents had increased to one hundred fifty, and more and more Chinese ships came to trade. Spanish control over the region was, however, far from assured.

After his defeat Lin returned to his old base, Makung Island, to rebuild his fleet. While he was there his war junks captured a Chinese merchantman homeward bound from Manila, and he learned from its captain that Luzon was weakly garrisoned because the Spanish troops were away on expeditions to other islands. Immediately gathering his forces at hand Lin set sail for the Philippines. His fleet consisted of sixty-two vessels carrying about two thousand men and over a thousand women. Besides arms the pirates also brought along farming implements, indicating the colonizing aim of the venture.

On November 23, 1574, the pirate fleet sailed by Ilocos Sur, captured a Spanish galliot, and seized its armaments. Spanish soldiers ashore who witnessd the action immediately sent word to warn Manila of the coming of the pirates. Six days later, after plundering several coastal villages, the pirate fleet entered the bay of Manila and anchored off the island of Corregidor. On the following day, November 30, Lin ordered a Japanese lieutenant of his named Sioco 莊公and two hundred men to land at Paranaque and to attack Manila. The corsairs spent their time looting and burning; then, taken by surprise, they were driven back despite their killing of Martín de Goyti and others among the Spanish defenders. Lin decided to give his men a day's rest before undertaking the assault on Manila. The delay enabled the governor, Guido de Lavezares, to strengthen his defenses, and permitted reinforcements under Captain Juan de Salcedo (*see* Martín de Rada) to arrive. On December 2 a thousand pirates landed and, under the personal command of Lin Feng, advanced on Manila. Again the attack failed and, after suffering two hundred casualties, the pirates withdrew to the beach. That night Lin decided to give up his plan to occupy Manila and, on the following day, his men embarked and set sail. Instead of returning to their base at Wang-kang Lin headed for Lingayen Bay in northern Luzon, and at Pangasinan near the mouth of the Agno River built a fortified stockade.

Although Lin's attempted assault on Manila did not receive widespread response from the Filipinos, it did touch off sporadic revolts in the vicinity of the city, north and south of the Pasig River, and on the islands of Mindoro and Cebu. These disturbances occupied the attention of the Spaniards so that they were unable to mobilize troops for an expedition against the Chinese pirates until March, 1575. This force, consisting of 256 Spanish soldiers and a large contingent of native auxiliaries (500 men according to Mendoza and 2,500 according to Francisco de Sande) under the command of Salcedo, set out in two ships and fifty-seven small boats. It arrived at the entrance of the Agno River on March 30 and, while a landing party struck at the pirate stronghold, the flotilla headed for the pirate fleet anchored nearby. The assault took the Chinese by surprise. With most of the crew ashore, the Chinese ships were virtually unmanned and, as a result, the attackers were able to sink and burn all thirty-five ships of the pirate fleet.

On land the attempt to take the Chinese fort was unsuccessful. The Spaniards and their Filipino allies then brought artillery ashore and on April 1 bombarded the Chinese defenses. At one point they almost broke through, but Lin rallied his men and drove them off, seizing some of their guns. After this setback Salcedo and his men made no further attempt to storm the fort. Instead, they cordoned it with their troops and waited. But the initiative was not theirs. Time and again Lin and his followers sallied out and fired into the Spanish-Filipino camp. Friendly natives in the neighborhood supplied the pirates with food and firewood. In small boats the Chinese sailed out to adjacent areas to bring back timber with which they built thirty-seven ships. Then on August 4, after four months of siege, their ships sailed out from a canal which they had secretly dug, and it was after they were at sea that the Spaniards found that they had escaped.

In December, 1575, reports came to the Chinese government of Lin's raids on the coastal towns of eastern Kwangtung. Defeated in his attempts to enter Fukien waters, he withdrew to his base at Wang-kang. On January 15, 1576, when he again ventured near the coast of Kwangtung and Fukien, he was met by the naval forces of Hu Shou-jen, which pursued him across the Taiwan Straits. Off Tan-shui 淡水 at the northern tip of Taiwan the government fleet caught up with the pirates, and in the engagement sank twenty of their ships. Lin Feng fled to the country of the Hsi-fan 西番 (western barbarians), which Li Kuang-ming 黎光明 identifies as Indochina. His followers, numbering 1,712 men, laid down their arms and were pardoned, and 688 men and women who had been taken prisoners by the pirates were freed.

One of the reasons which prompted Lin to evacuate his fort at Pangasinan was the appearance in early April of two ships which he recognized to be Chinese government naval vessels. Led by Garrison Commander Wang Wang-kao (*see*

Rada), known in Spanish records as Omocon, they had been sent by the governor-general of Kwangtung and Kwangsi, Ling Yün-i (*see* Ch'en Lin), to search for Lin and his pirates. When the Chinese officers came ashore, they explained their mission to Salcedo and told him that the Chinese government would reward the Spaniards for the capture of the pirates. Salcedo replied that this was assured and he invited them to go to Manila. At Manila Wang Wang-kao was well received by Governor Lavezares who asked him to take a Spanish mission with him back to China. The embassy, consisting of two Augustinian friars, Martín de Rada and Jerónimo Marín, and two army officers, left Manila on a Chinese warship in the middle of June. They landed at Amoy and then at Chang-chou 漳州, whence they traveled overland to Foochow. There they were graciously received by the governor of Fukien, Liu Yao-hui (*see* Rada), who agreed to forward to Peking their letters requesting the opening of trade and permission to propagate Christianity.

Relations between the Chinese and their visitors were soon strained. The Spaniards behaved with the arrogance of the hidalgos, as represented in the person of Martín de Rada, who in 1569 had urged the conquest of China by Spanish arms. They were annoyed because the Chinese officials did not immediately accede to their requests nor permit them to travel freely in the interior. The Chinese regarded the Spanish party as no better than a mission from Patani or Brunei, deserving therefore no special consideration, and they were suspicious of the Spaniards' good faith, especially when they heard that pirates, believed to be Lin Feng and his band, were committing depredations on the coast. Wang Wang-kao was sent to the Philippines to find out. If the pirates were caught, he was to bring them back to China and to hand over the gifts to the Spaniards as reward. Wang left Foochow late in August with the members of the Spanish mission on board his fleet of ten warships. Delayed by storms, they did not reach Manila until the end of October. Wang Wang-kao was furious when he learned that Lin Feng and his pirates had escaped and he refused to hand over the gifts. The new governor, Francisco de Sande, accused the Chinese of a breach of faith and charged that Wang had sold the gifts for his own profit. In his anger, he wrote to King Philip II of Spain suggesting the dispatch of troops to invade and conquer China. The misunderstanding and ill-feeling ended early attempts to establish amicable relations between China and Spain.

Bibliography

MSL (1965), Shen-tsung, 179, 421, 584, 607, 623, 628, 646, 673, 731, 997, 999, 1014, 1050, 1107, 1267, 1313, 1725; *Ch'ao-chou-fu chih* (1893), 38/36b, 4o/3b; *Kwangtung t'ung-chih* (1804), 188/22a; Chang Chü-cheng, *Chang T'ai-yüeh wen-chi*, 26/18b, 27/16a, 28/6b, 25a; Chang Hsing-lang 張星烺, "The Real 'Limahong' in Philippine History," 斐律賓史上'李馬奔'之眞人考, YCHP, VII (1930), 1469; Li Kuang-ming, "Further Notes on the Identity of Limahong in the History of the Philippine Islands" 補正, *ibid.*, X (1931), 2061; Ch'en Ching-ho 陳荊和, *Shih-liu shih-chi chih Fei-li-pin hua-ch'iao* 十六世紀之菲律賓華僑 (Hong Kong, 1963), 31; Wu Ching-hung 吳景宏, "Supplements to a Study of References to the Philippines in Chinese Sources from Earliest Times (?–1644)," *Journal of East Asiatic Studies* (Manila), VII: 4 (October, 1958), 334; Wang Te-ming, "Lim Ah-hong's Affair," *ibid.*, VIII: 1(January-April, 1959), 21; Francisco de Sande, "Relation of the Philippine Islands, June 7, 1576," in Emma H. Blair and James A. Robertson, *The Philippine Islands, 1493–1803*, IV (1898), 24; Juan Gonzales de Mendoza, *History of the Great Kingdom of China* (1586), *ibid.*, VI, 91; Martín de Rada, "Narrative of the Mission to Fukien, June-October, 1575," in C. R. Boxer, ed., *South China in the Sixteenth Century* (London, 1953), 243; Isabele de los Reyes, *Expedecion de Li-Ma-Hong contra Filipina en 1574*, Manila, 1888.

Jung-pang Lo

LIN Hsi-yüan 林希元 (T. 思虙, 懋貞, 茂貞, H. 次崖), *ca.* 1480-*ca.* 1560, official, scholar, overseas merchant, was a native

of T'ung-an 同安, Fukien. Born into a
family of the military category, he passed
his *chin-shih* examination in 1517. His
first assignment took him to Nanking,
where he became junior judge in the
Grand Court of Revision. After Chu Hou-
ts'ung (*q.v.*) ascended the throne in 1521,
Lin Hsi-yüan submitted a detailed memorial strongly recommending the recall of
all eunuchs to the palace, particularly
those with supervision over the military
in the provinces. His arguments found
approval at court, whereupon he was
promoted to the rank of senior judge. In
this capacity he openly opposed a decision
of his superior, Ch'en Lin 陳琳 (T. 玉
疇, cs 1496), with the result that he was
downgraded and transferred to Ssu-chou
泗州 (Anhwei) to serve .as assistant magistrate. When a famine struck the region,
he worked without ceasing to bring relief
to the people. Once he single-handedly
dispersed a crowd of several hundred men
and women who had gathered to plunder
the granaries, insisting that he was in
this way looking out for their best interests. His action and his words succeeded
in pacifying the population. Before long,
however, he resigned because he felt that
he had been treated improperly by a certain censor Liu 劉. He returned home,
where he stayed for more than three
years.

In 1527, on the recommendation of
Huo T'ao (*q.v.*), Lin was restored to his
former office in Nanking. A short time
later the court ordered him transferred to
Peking to serve as director of the northern Grand Court of Revision; but before
leaving Nanking he was made assistant
surveillannce commissioner of Kwangtung
and put in charge of the salt monopoly and
the military farmland. Later he was given
control of the Kwangtung education intendant circuit. During this period he wrote
a little pamphlet called *Huang-cheng ts'ung-
yen* 荒政叢言 about his experiences in Ssu-
chou and the measures he had taken. The
emperor ordered it printed and had it
circulated throughout the empire. Although

it was not part of his normal duty, Lin
successfully defeated a band of robbers
near Hui-chou 惠州 with a small military contingent. As a reward, he was
moved back to the Grand Court of Revision in Nanking, this time (1530) as
chief judge. When the garrison of Liaotung mutinied in April, 1535, Lin openly
voiced his opinion in a memorial to the
throne, saying that such rebellious behavior was the result of leniency. "Troops
should be employed against troops," he
said. This was a formula clearly critical
of the central policy. He was charged
with false reporting and downgraded in
July to subprefectural magistrate of Ch'in
欽-chou, Kwangtung, the southwestern
region of the empire bordering Annam. For some time this area had
been neglected, and Lin found the need
for a wide range of public works into
which he could throw all his energies.
When a punitive expedition was planned
against Mac Dang-dung (*q.v.*), who a few
years before had usurped the throne of
Annam, Lin collected all the information
about the military and social situation of
that country he could obtain, and composed several memorials strongly advising
the throne to capture Mac Dang-dung
(1540). Again going beyond the duty
assigned to him, he now considered as
his principal task the reclamation of the
area of Ssu-t'ung 四峒, which the An-
namese had been cccupying for some
time.

Instead of eliciting the enthusiastic
approval of the central government, he
was ordered to assemble soldiers and
ships in the vicinity of Chang-chou and
Ch'üan-chou, Fukien. The contingents
were disbanded before their arrival in
Kwangtung because Mac Dang-dung had
given in, dispatched a tributary mission,
and restored Ssu-t'ung to China. Lin had
to leave Ch'in-chou and was made · assistant surveillance commissioner and intendant of the circuit of Hai-pei 海北, Kwangtung, where within a year's time he pacified a band of local outlaws. Meanwhile

his activity in the Annam affair was still being considered at court. An investigation followed, and Lin was found guilty of usurpation of authority and neglect of his proper duty. He was dismissed and returned home, this time for good.

Between 1530 and 1533, when he was a chief judge in Nanking, Lin made the acquaintance of Wang Tao (*see* Huang Tso) and Ou-yang Te (*q.v.*) with whom he had many discussions on doctrine and interpretation of the Classics, without, however, always concurring in their opinion. Although he had studied the canon intensively for some time, particularly during his three-year stay at home after his return from Ssu-chou, the acquaintance with Wang Tao and Ou-yang Te first prompted him to amend the commentary of Chu Hsi (1130-1200) on the Four Books and the Book of Changes, not, as he pointed out, in order to criticize Chu Hsi or the Ch'eng brothers (11th c.), but in order to support their interpretation and to discredit the ancient Han tradition. The latter he considered unsuitable and impracticable for the times. The amended versions he entitled *Ssu-shu ts'un-i* 四書存疑, 12 *ch.* (there is a copy in the Naikaku Bunko), and *I-ching ts'un-i* 易經存疑, 20 *ch.* Another product of this period was the *Ku-wen lei-ch'ao* 古文類抄, 20 *ch.*, which is also preserved in the Naikaku Bunko. He submitted the two *Ts'un-i* for imperial inspection in 1551, together with a revised edition of the textbook for schools *Ta Hsüeh ching-chuan ting-pen* 大學經傳定本. The books were found to deviate from the orthodox tradition and ordered burned. At the same time Lin was cashiered and made a commoner. Somehow the *Ts'un-i* manuscripts were preserved and published in 1742 by his descendant Lin T'ing-p'ien 廷玝, and thence apparently copied into the *Ssu-k'u* over thirty years later. Likewise his collected writings, which his son, Lin Yu-wu 有梧, collected under the title *Lin Tz'u-yai wen-chi* 林次崖文集, 18 *ch.*, were published in 1753, a copy of which is also in the Naikaku Bunko. This collection makes it quite clear that Lin strongly opposed Wang Shou-jen (*q.v.*), whose idealistic concept he rejected as useless for practical purposes. Intellectual activity for him had to be applicable in the concrete world of affairs. This resulted in a style as uncompromising and individual as he was himself, characterized by a mixture of coarse and refined diction. Lin Hsi-yüan specialized in textbook literture. Apart from his collected writings, the work on famine relief, and the *Chu-tzu ta-t'ung chi* 朱子大同集, 13 *ch.*, by the Southern Sung scholar Ch'en Li-yung (containing poems and essays by Chu Hsi written when he was assistant magistrate of T'ung-an) which he re-edited, practically all other works he wrote or compiled were meant in the first place to be a guide and a source of study for pupils and examination candidates. This applies also to at least ten other works credited to him.

After his return from Kwangtung, Lin does not seem to have confined himself to his studies. Being a highly active individual eager for enterprise, and not without useful connections in the judicial hierarchy, he found a new field of endeavor outside the normal career of a scholar-official. He engaged in the lucrative, but illegal, private overseas trade. Living by the sea, close to the highly frequented bay of Amoy, he apparently made his first acquaintance with pirate-merchants (hai-k'ou 海寇) when he was still young. During the Hung-chih period his father Lin Ying 應 had to move with his family into the interior for some time, because he had reason to fear the revenge of the pirates whom he had reported to the authorities. In contrast to his father, Lin secured the cooperation of the pirate-merchants, acting as their "harboring host" (wo-chu 窩主); that is to say, he took their merchandise on commission and sold it in the inland market. But he had ships built for himself too. When Chu Wan (*q.v.*) became governor of Chekiang and military superintendent of Fukien in 1547, Lin Hsi-yüan owned a large fleet of oceangoing junks which he had declared as ferry-boats (yü-huang 餘艎), in order to evade prosecution. Independent supercargoes, or as the case might be, dependent ones, regularly transacted business for him overseas, particularly in southeast Asia. Upon their arrival in China (usually half a year later), the supercargoes first returned the capital Lin Hsi-yüan had given them. Furthermore, they had to pay interest on this capital and divide the remaining gross income with him. Such a huge income, together with his official associations, made Lin Hsi-yüan nearly impervious to attack; he had become the overlord (t'u-hao 土豪) of his district. Although this activity was subject to the most severe punishment, neither military nor civil authorities dared to intervene once the traders had been identified as having connections with Lin Hsi-yüan. Disregarding the prevailing policy of maritime prohibition he openly supported the local population in their attempt to profit by selling everyday supplies out at sea to the Portuguese and to mariners from other countries who were not allowed to enter a Chinese harbor officially. All this ran counter to Chu Wan's concept of coastal defense and was an offense against the imperial statutes. Chu Wan accused him of conspiring with pirates and oppressing the local authorities; but no investigation followed. Instead, Chu Wan was downgraded and for fear of persecution committed suicide. Whether Lin Hsi-yüan himself exerted his influence is not known. As Chu Wan said, however, people from Min (Fukien) in the central government, and on the provincial and local level, all connived to cover up their business with foreigners and pirates.

After having had his insignia as an official stripped from him, due to his unorthodox commentaries on the Classics, Lin lived on for another decade. About 1584, some twenty years after his death, an official sacrifice to his spirit was conducted in T'ung-an, as a result of the efforts of Wang Shih-mou (*q.v.*). His fellow townsmen celebrated Lin's name in the local temple to Chu Hsi, and erected a shrine in his honor about 1614 inside the compound of the temple of Confucius. This shrine was restored several times, the last time in 1926.

Bibliography

1/282/14b; 3/263/15b; 5/102/69a; 40/36/13b; 64/戊13/20a; SK (1930), 5/2a, 174/12a, 176/15b; *Fu-chien t'ung-chih* (1868), 212/37b; *T'ung-an-hsien chih* (1798), 28/1a; *ibid.* (1928), 7/12a, 14/10b, 15/4b; Lin Hsi-yüan, *Lin Tz'u-yai wen-chi* (1753); Chu Wan, *P'i-yü tsa-chi* (Wan-li ed.), 2/19a; Katayama Seijirō 片山詩二郎, "Mindai kaijo-mitsu bōeki to enkai chihō kyōshinsō," in *Re-kishigaku kenkyū* 歷史學研究 (1953), 164.

Bodo Wiethoff

LIN Hung 林鴻 (T. 子羽), a native of Fu-ch'ing 福清, Fukien, was a poet of the latter half of the 14th century. He proved to be an important man of letters in Fukien, and influenced to some extent the development of literature in the Ming period. In his early life he was described as an idealist, a nonconformist, and an undisciplined scholar. He had an excellent memory, however, and because of his talent was recommended by one of the local officials to take the palace examination at the capital. Early in the Hung-wu period, he wrote two poems, "Lung-ch'ih ch'un-hsiao" 龍池春曉 (Spring dawn at the Dragon Lagoon) and "Ku yen" 孤雁 (The lonely wild goose), which pleased His Majesty when he made a personal appearance at the examination hall. Lin became famous in the capital overnight.

Unsuccessful in the examination, Lin was appointed assistant instructor of the Confucian school at Chiang-lo 將樂 (Fukien). He served at this post for seven years before being promoted to be vice director of the bureau of provisions of the ministry of Rites. Because of his independent and romantic nature, Lin was evidently not suited to administrative work. Under the efficient but stringent regime of the first emperor he became dissatisfied with the lack of opportunity to demonstrate his talents, and so resigned while still in his thirties and returned to private life.

[Editors' note: One of Lin's poems refers to his living in exile. In another he mentions an invitation to a party given by the minister of Rites, Chang Ch'ou 張籌 (T. 惟中), whose second term of office lasted four months (October, 1379-January, 1380), apparently ending at the time of the execution of the premier, Hu Wei-yung. Lin's possible involvement might explain his banishment. Since he was then not yet forty years of age, he perhaps was born about 1340.]

Lin now devoted his time entirely to traveling, studying, and writing poetry. He isolated himself, and refused to see any visitors except a few of his literary colleagues. His two closest disciples were Chou Hsüan 周玄 (T. 微之) of Min-hsien 閩縣 and Huang Hsüan 黄玄 (T. 玄之) of Hou-kuan 侯官, popularly known as the two Hsüan. A third, and perhaps more important, associate was the poet and artist Kao Ping 高棅 (T. 彦恢, H. 漫士, later ming 廷禮, 1350-1423), who together with Chou Hsüan and six others formed the literary group popularly called the "Min-chung shih ts'ai-tzu" 閩中十才子 (The ten masters of Fukien). Lin was the best and most famous poet of this association and its acknowledged leader; but some of the others also led active lives, three of them being called to help prepare the Yung-lo ta-tien (see Yao Kuang-hsiao), and one labored on the T'ai-tsu shih-lu.

Lin became part of the literary restoration movement in the Ming era by copying the prosody of the T'ang dynasty. He particularly venerated the poets of the literary period called the "flourishing T'ang" (713-56), and took Li Po and Tu Fu as standards of excellence. The call to imitate the old masters was adopted by Lin's associates, with Kao Ping articulating very clearly the poetic theories of the group in his massive study, T'ang-shih p'in hui 唐詩品彙, a work of 90+10 chüan. This is important in Ming literary history for several reasons: 1) it divided T'ang poetry into four distinct periods—early T'ang, flourishing T'ang, mid-T'ang, and late T'ang; 2) it strongly urged the emulation of the T'ang poets, especially those of the middle years; and 3) the work influenced later poets and scholars of the orthodox school, including the group known as the Hou ch'i-tzu (Seven later masters; see Wang Shih-chen).

The practice of simulating ancient literature became prevalent in the Ming period and had an unfortunate effect on the progress of Chinese letters, including the poetic genre. Critics have accepted the fact that Lin was obviously a gifted poet, but censured him for dissipating his creative energies in copying the works of others. The most penetrating criticism of Lin's style centers around one basic weakness: that although he could almost reproduce exactly the T'ang form in tonal and metrical requirements, his excessive imitation failed to integrate a high quality of poetic content within this formal structure. Though he fell short of the T'ang achievements, his verse had merit and some artistic individuality. His influence on others, however, seems to have been a type of literary corruption, because the creations of these Fukienese poets have the appearance of being written by one person. This situation is clearly illustrated by the following anecdote about Lin Hung:

A man by the name of P'u Yüan 浦源 (fl. 1398, T. 長源, H. 梅生, of Wu-hsi 無錫, near Soochow), who once served in the government about the same time as Lin, traveled some distance to visit the poet. Lin would not receive him, however, and sent his two disciples Chou and Huang to meet the guest. In spite of Lin's strange behavior, P'u Yüan disregarded this rebuff and explained that he had

come for Lin's opinion of his own poems
which he had brought with him. He offered his work to the disciples, and, as
Chou and Huang read the following lines:
"The road on Mt. Pa spirals up to the
clouds. The waters of the Han resound
through the forest" 雲邊路遠巴山色，樹裏
河流漢水聲, they exclaimed in surprise:
"This is just like our style of poetry."
This was true enough because, in addition
to being a very good couplet in terms of
tonal and parallel structure, it followed
very closely Tu Fu's style. The two disciples persuaded Lin to receive P'u Yüan,
and the new arrival got along so well
with the group that Lin moved out of his
own quarters to make way for him. Writing poetry every day with his companions,
P'u was welcomed into the club, and
gradually became well known.

In spite of Lin's imperfections, the
state of Ming poetry cannot be attributed
entirely to him, for it was simply a reflection of the mood of the times. Lin's
work was of sufficient quality that the
poets and scholars of Fukien considered
him as the model to follow (he had a
number of disciples), and many of his
poems are still enjoyed today. Some of
his writings were brought together in the
Ming sheng chi 鳴盛集, 4 *ch.*, printed in
1467, which was later copied into the Imperial Library. Two other works preserved
in various *ts'ung-shu* are *Lin shan pu shih*
膳部詩 5 *ch.*, and *Lin yüan wai chi* 員外
集, 1 *ch.*

Bibliography

1/286/1b; 3/267/1b; 5/35/77a; 40/10/18b; *Fukien
t'ung-chih* (1871?, reprint of 1968), 3913; Ho
Ch'iao-yüan, *Ming-shan ts'ang*, 85/3; *Yen-p'ing-fu*
延平府 *chih* (1873), 34/31b; *Foochow-fu chih*
(1754, repr. of 1967, Taipei), 1138; TSCC
(1885-88), XIV: 359/3/1b, XXIII: 95/83/1b,
XXIV: 117/23a; SK (1930), 169/9b, 189/1b; KC
(1958), 538, 576; Lin Hung, *Ming sheng chi*
(NLP microfilm, no. 978); Shen Te-ch'ien (EC
CP), *Ming shih pieh ts'ai*, in *Wan-yu-wen-k'u
hui-yao* 萬有文庫薈要, nos. 667 and 668; Kuo
Shao-yü 郭紹虞, *Chung-kuo wen-hsüeh p'i-p'ing shih*
中國文學批評史 (Shanghai, 1961), 286; Kuo Po-
ts'ang 郭柏蒼, *Ch'üan Min Ming-shih chuan* 全閩
明詩傳 (1889), 3/9a, Ch'ien Ch'ien-i (ECCP),
Lieh-ch'ao shih-chi 甲, 20/1a, 乙3/16b.

Dell R. Hales

LIN Jun 林潤 (T. 若雨, 九霖, H. 敬輿),
ca. 1530-70, a censor of renown, was a
native of P'u-t'ien 莆田, Fukien. A *chü-jen*
of 1552 and *chin-shih* of 1556, he became
magistrate of Lin-ch'uan 臨川, Kiangsi,
where he served for three years, from
1556 to 1559. Early in 1558, three thousand bandits from Fukien attacked Nan-
feng 南豐, a city about sixty miles to the
south, while Lin was on official duty
there. The local people asked him to
direct its defense. After seven days of
fighting the bandits withdrew. In gratitude to Lin, the people of Nan-feng
erected a shrine in his honor.

In October, 1559, Lin received a
promotion to censor in Nanking. Half a
year later he accused the chancellor of
the National University, Shen K'un 沈坤
(T. 伯載, optimus of 1541, d. 1560 or
1561), of acts of extreme cruelty. Shen,
during the piratical invasion of the region
north of the Yangtze River in 1559, had
raised a corps of volunteers under his
own command. The charges against him
included cutting off a man's hands and
killing some peasants thought to be escaped
soldiers. Shen was arrested and lodged in
jail where he died. According to T'an
Ch'ien (*q. v.*), one of Shen's enemies
had manufactured the accusation, and
after he died no one bothered to clear
his name because he had been arrogant
and generally detested.

In 1561 Lin Jun accused the powerful
Yen Mao-ch'ing (*see* Hai Jui) of corruption in his direction of the distribution
of salt, thus establishing himself as a
courageous censor daring to speak out
against influential officials, for Yen Mao-
ch'ing was sponsored by no less than
Grand Secretary Yen Sung (*q. v.*). The
following year he memorialized the
throne about the unruly behavior of the

Prince of I, Chu Tien-ying 伊王朱典楧, a fifth generation descendant of Chu I, the twenty-fifth son of Chu Yüan-chang, accusing the prince of overstepping his prerogatives in the construction of palaces, and of oppressing the people in various ways. The prince was warned and some of his aides were reprimanded. As the prince showed no remorse and continued his willful behavior, he was eventually imprisoned and the princedom of I abolished. On another occasion Lin submitted a memorial calling the attention of the emperor to the plight of members of families in the various princedoms.

Meanwhile another young censor, Tsou Ying-lung 鄒應龍 (T. 雲卿, H. 蘭谷, cs 1556), by astute timing and courage, had brought about in 1562 the dismissal of Yen Sung and the exile of his son, Yen Shih-fan (see Yen Sung). As Yen Shih-fan and his cohort, Lo Lung-wen (see Yen Sung), did not remain in their places of exile, but returned and lived luxuriously at home, Lin Jun found another opportunity to exercise his censor's duty. While on an inspection tour in the Kiangsi area in 1564, he learned of this situation and quickly dispatched a memorial. Before the culprits could return to their rightful stations Lin had already received orders from Peking to arrest them. Both were sent to the capital and subsequently executed.

In 1567, under the new reign of Chu Tsai-hou (q. v.), Lin Jun was first promoted to minister of the Court of Imperial Sacrifices, and then to right assistant censor-in-chief and concurrently governor of Nanking. As the chief administrator of this rich area, he ordered a survey of the agricultural land of the prefecture of Sung-chiang 松江, and promoted a simple and fair scheme of taxation, which greatly benefited the people. Three years later he died at his post at the age of forty sui. Just before his death he had assembled his memorials and sent them to Wang Shih-chen (q. v.), requesting a preface. Wang obliged, stating that the collection numbered fifty-six memorials, As Lin Jun is known to have left a collection of memorials entitled the Yüan-chih shu-kao 願治疏稿, it is not clear whether it is the same as the one for which Wang had written.

Concerning Tsou Ying-lung, who came from Shensi, there is some uncertainty as to his native place; some say Ch'ang-an 長安 others Lan-chou 蘭州. The official chin-shih list gives the former. In 1561 he was selected to be a censor. Hardly a year passed before he seized the opportunity to bring about the downfall of Yen Sung, a feat that many had tried before but which brought them only harsh punishment or death. It is said that at this time the Taoist adept and planchette expert Lan Tao-hang (see Yen Sung) was a favorite of the emperor. Once His Majesty asked who were the good and who the bad among high officials at court. The planchette placed Yen Sung and his son in the latter category. While taking refuge from rain in a eunuch's quarters, Tsou Ying-lung overheard this; and so he submitted his memorial. Another story relates that when Tsou was composing this document which might seal his own end, he was unable to formulate a good line of presentation. As the candle light flickered and the wax streamed down like tears, he dozed off at his desk. In those few moments he had a dream. He fancied that he was on a hunting trip, equipped with bow and arrows, and mounted on horseback. Confronting him was a high mountain with a two-story structure on the east side. He shot an arrow toward the mountain; nothing stirred. Then he shot another toward the building; it instantly collapsed. He awoke and pondered the strange dream. Suddenly it dawned on him that "high mountain" must mean Yen Sung, since the character 嵩 was formed with "mountain" and "high," and the "east two-story structure" must mean Yen's son, because Yen Shih-fan had 東樓 as his hao. Tsou realized it would be of no use to attack the elder Yen, but if he concentrated on the younger his strategy might work. Thereupon he wrote a memorial attacking only Yen Shih-fan. Whatever the truth of this anecdote, Tsou must have been a keen observer, who sensed that the emperor's favor of the Yen father and son was on the wane.

For his courageous act Tsou was promoted first to assistant administrator in the office of transmission and later to vice minister of the Grand Court of Revision. It is said that Tsou was always apprehensive that before Yen Shih-fan's execution, Yen might take vengeance on him, but this never happened. Rapid promotions came to him during the Lung-ch'ing reign: minister of the Courts of the Imperial Stud and Imperial Sacrifices, and then vice censor-in-chief to supervise the salt administration in the provinces of Hukuang, Chekiang, Fukien, Kwangtung, Kwangsi, Yunnan, and Kweichow. By 1570 he had risen to vice minister of Works, and a year later was appointed vice minister of War, concurrently assistant censor-in-chief to govern Yunnan.

Tsou Ying-lung remained there nearly four years. In dealing with the disturbances of some of the aboriginal tribes, he seems to have been successful at first, but as trouble continued Tsou was blamed and he was retired early in 1575. As he left office without waiting for the imperial order, he was stripped of his official status. He died sometime before 1585. In 1588, in response to the plea of the governor of his native province, the official titles of governor of Yunnan and left vice minister of War were restored to him posthumously.

The exceptional scarcity of biographical data leaves us with neither information about Tsou Ying-lung's forebears, nor any about his immediate family. The interesting Ming drama, *Ming-feng chi*, on the downfall of Yen Sung, the authorship of which has been attributed to Wang Shih-chen by some, presents Tsou Ying-lung and Lin Jun as the two leading characters; it weaves together all the events relating to this famous episode. This drama records that Tsou's father was a minor official in Hangchow. After the father's death, the family was too poor to return to their native place. There Tsou Ying-lung married into a Shen 沈 family and lived in his wife's home. It was also in Hangchow that he first met Lin Jun and they became fast friends.

Bibliography

1/210/21b, 24a, 314/2a; 5/62/102a; TSCC (1885–88), XI: 358/1b, 2b; MSL (1965), Shih-tsung, 8048, 8247, 8267, 8386, 8433, 8448, 8737, 8789, Mu-tsung, 0224, 0486, Shen-tsung (1966), 0964, 1452, 2966, 2974, 3697; KC (1958), 3929, 3936, 3962, 3964, 3977, 3981, 3983, 3986, 4006, 4015, 4019, 4045, 4050, 4055, 4062, 4074, 4081, 4095, 4100, 4147, 4172, 4236, 4238, 4264, 4270, 4277, 4318, 4508, 4576; Ch'en Tzu-lung (ECCP), *Ming ching-shih wen-pien, chüan* 329; *P'u-t'ien-hsien chih* (1879), 17/76b; Kuo Po-tsang 郭柏蒼, *Ch'üan-Min Ming-shih-chuan* 全閩明詩傳 (1889), 26/3a; *Lan-chou-fu chih* 蘭州府志 (1882), 9/3b; Li Yüan-ch'un 李元春, comp., *Kuan-chung liang-ch'ao wen-ch'ao* 關中兩朝文鈔 (1832), 人物考略, 7a, 8/103a; Chu Tung-jün 朱東潤, *Chang Chü-cheng ta-chuan* 張居正大傳 (1947), 53; Wang Shih-chen, *Yen-chou shan-jen ssu-pu-kao* (1577), 66/9a; *id.*, *Ming-feng chi*, 1959.

Lienche Tu Fang

LIN Liang 林良 (T. 以善), fl. 1455–1500, a painter of birds and flowers, was a native of Nan-hai 南海, Kwangtung. Around 1455, while he served in the provincial administration office in Kwangtung, his talents caught the attention of his superior Ch'en Chin 陳金 (T. 汝礪, cs 1433), the left administration commissioner. Later he became an assistant to the head of the construction office under the ministry of Works. His fame as an artist reached Emperor Chu Yu-t'ang (*q.v.*), who finally installed him in the Jen-chih palace 仁智殿, and granted him the title of a commander in the Embroidered-uniform Guard. Both he and Lü Chi (*q.v.*), another painter of birds, came to be held in high esteem. O. Sirén praises Lin Liang as "the greatest master of bird painting in the monochrome hsieh-i 寫意 [expressionist] manner." He quotes the *Ming hua lu* as remarking: "He painted birds, flowers, and fruits in colour very skilfully in a refined manner using ink only for mist and waves with flying and feeding wild geese, which he painted very smoothly and clearly." Although Lin studied the works of Huang Ch'üan (*ca.* 905-65) and Pien Wen-chin (*q.v.*) — both painters of the orthodox school,—Lin was innovative enough to develop his own style. Instead of giving an almost photographic portrayal of birds in color, in the fashion of his predecessors, he tried to breathe life into his subject. With his skillful use of different tones of black ink, he gave spirited representations of feng 鳳 (often incorrectly called the Chinese phoenix), wild geese, eagles, cranes, and the like. In "Feng-huang" 鳳凰, undated, in ink, in the possession of the Sōkoku monastery, Japan, Lin depicts with dynamic force the haughty airs of such a bird. The wet and free application of washes for clouds and mists in the background—a characteristic feature of Lin's art—is more evident here than in his other paintings. His "Geese," in ink, in the collection of the British Museum, is executed more in line with the orthodox school; only the contrasts of black and white—the result of subtle gradations in the use of ink, and the cursive calligraphic strokes applied in his drawing of the reeds by the stream—are uniquely his.

Judging from several of his preserved paintings in light color, Lin was also a master in this medium. In "Ch'iu ying" 秋鷹 (An eagle in the autumn), in ink and light color, in the collection of the National Palace Museum, Taiwan, Lin portrays an eagle circling above and preparing to swoop down and pounce upon its prey, a mynah. The coloring is both refined and appropriate. Lin also excelled in his portrayal of lotus flowers, camellias, reeds, and willow branches. The swift, cursive strokes applied in paintings of this genre show the influence of his ts'ao-shu 草書 (cursive) style. One outstanding example is his "Hua niao" 花鳥 (Flowers and birds), in color, included in *Shina meiga shū* 支那名畫集.

Lin's son, Lin Chiao 郊 (T. 子達), also a painter of birds in ink, achieved first place in a palace competition for painters in 1494. Consequently, the emperor, Chu Yu-t'ang, installed him in the Wu-ying palace 武英殿, and made him a judge in the Embroidered-uniform Guard. Later he retired to Lung-tzu ling 龍子嶺, near Nan-hai, where he gave himself up to the study of alchemy.

Bibliography

65/6/3a; *Kwangtung t'ung-chih* (1934), 5445 下; *Chung-kuo li-tai ming-hua chi* 中國歷代名畫集, IV (Peking, 1965), pl. 26; *Shanghai jen-min mei-shu ch'u-pan-she*上海人民美術出版社, *T'ang Sung Yüan Ming Ch'ing hua-hsüan* 唐宋元明清畫選 (Shanghai, 1960), 37; Wang Chao-yung 汪兆鏞 (1860-1939), *Ling-nan hua-cheng lüeh* 嶺南畫徵略 (Hong Kong, 1961), 1/9; P'eng Yün-ts'an 彭蘊燦, *Li-tai hua-shih hui-chuan* 歷代畫史彙傳 (Shanghai, 1922), 39/2b; *Ku-kung shu-hua lu* 故宮書畫錄 (Taipei, 1956), 中/288; Chiang Shao-shu 姜紹書 (fl. 1640), *Wu-sheng shih-shih* 無聲詩史, 2/19; Hsia Wen-yen 夏文彥 (fl. 1365) and Han Ang 韓昂 (fl.1519), *T'u-hui pao-chien*圖繪寶鑑, 6/162; *Nihon genzai Shina meiga mokuroku*日本現在支那名畫目錄 (Tokyo, 1938), 138; *Shina nanga taisei* 南畫大成, 6 (Tokyo, 1935-36), pl. 62; *Shina meiga-shū*, 2 (Tokyo, 1907), pl. 34; *Sō Gen Min Chin meiga taikan* 宋元明清名畫大觀 (Tokyo, 1938), pl. 92; O. Sirén, *A History of Later Chinese Painting*, I (London, 1938), 61; E. J. Laing, *Chinese Paintings in Chinese Publications, 1956-1968* (Ann Arbor, 1969), 176; H. A. Giles, *An Introduction to the History of Chinese Pictorial Art* (Shanghai, 1918), 178.

Lee Hwa-chou

LIN Tao-ch'ien 林道乾 (variants: Lintoquian, Lim Dao Kiam), fl. 1566-80, pirate chief, was a native of Hui-lai 惠來, in the prefecture of Ch'ao-chou 潮州, Kwangtung. Lin began his career as a clerk in the district yamen but soon forsook it to join the bandits Wu P'ing 吳平 and Tseng

I-pen 曾一本 (d. 1569) who, in collusion
with the Japanese pirates, had ravaged the
coasts of Chekiang, Fukien, and Kwangtung. In the early years Lin was inseparable
from his mentors, but after Wu's defeat
in April, 1566, Lin began to assume independent command and challenged his
senior, Tseng I-pen, for leadership. In this
year Lin and his band raided several
coastal districts, Chao-an 詔安 in June
and Nan-ao 南澳 in October, but were
repeatedly repulsed by government units
led by Ch'i Chi-kuang, Yü Ta-yu (*qq.v.*),
and others. After several setbacks, according to the gazetteer of Ch'ao-chou, Lin
fled to Pei-kang 北港 (on the Taiwan
coast), where he regrouped his followers
and built ships in preparation for new
ventures. From then on Lin's name occurred more frequently in official records.

Lin and his band resumed their piratical activities on the mainland late in
1567 and twice, in January and in March
of the following year, raided Ch'eng-hai 澄
海 in Ch'ao-chou. Thereafter Lin extended his piracy to Lei-chou 雷州 and Hainan Island, where dispatches indicate the
repeated failure of the local officials to
curb his activities. Some officials at this
time proposed extending conciliatory gestures to Lin to secure his surrender, but
the governor of Kwangtung insisted on
stern measures against the outlaws. Hence
a price was placed on the heads of both
Lin and Tseng: 1,000 taels of silver if
dead and thrice that figure if captured
alive. Meanwhile the court dispatched
Yü Ta-yu, supreme commander of
Kwangsi, to Kwangtung to help in the
suppression of the rebels. Yü presented a
two-point formula: the strengthening of
the Kwangtung guards by equipping them
with superior vessels and better trained
naval units from Fukien; and the turning
of one bandit against the other by exploiting the differences between Lin and
Tseng. The first step would be to pacify
Lin and turn him against his rival; after
this, to take appropriate measures against
Lin to assure the end of the pirates. The

first part of the strategy worked as planned, for, with Lin's assistance, government naval units killed Tseng in action in
June, 1569, while Lin annihilated remnants of his followers in another encounter
in August.

Lin's position, however, remained
ambiguous. His submission to the government and offer of assistance to suppress his rival were probably a tactical
move to preserve his own strength and
recuperate from losses inflicted by government forces. The provincial officials,
due to tardiness and indecision, failed to
follow up Yü Ta-yu's plan for dealing
with Lin, although they had been suspicious of his latest movements. Meanwhile,
pretending submission in his shelter in
Ch'ao-yang 潮陽, Lin began to attract
new recruits and repair his fleet, and in
time accumulated a far stronger force
than before. According to a dispatch of
July, 1569, Lin already possessed a following of over five thousand men, with
about a hundred small ships and six larger
ones. A contemporary report avers that
Lin once sent his ships, equipped with
Portuguese firearms, to aid the government in recovering Jao-p'ing 饒平 from
the *wo-k'ou*. During the next three years
reports about Lin alternated between his
submission and rebellion; much effort,
however, was wasted in the futile competition between the Fukien and Kwangtung
officials for the credit of suppressing
Lin. The corruption of the military officials, who often exaggerated the account
of the piracy to cover up their own
failures, also helped to perpetuate the
fortune of the outlaws.

It is not certain when Lin next rebelled and took to the seas to resume his
piratical activities. According to the
report of June, 1573, he fled overseas
with his fleet shortly before Yin Cheng-
mao (*see* Ch'en Lin), the new governor
of Kwangtung who was opposed to the
pacification policy, was put in charge of
the suppression of piracy. Lin's subsequent movements were hard to trace, for,

as pirates on the high seas they probably maintained a highly mobile operation. The *Ming-shih* account of Lin at this time confuses him with the contemporary pirate, Lin Feng (*q.v.*), who had fled to the Philippines after having been defeated by government forces. The Portuguese account by Juan Gonzalez de Mendoza (*see* Li Shih-chen) states that the two had fought a battle near the Pescadores (P'eng-hu澎湖 Islands) around 1574, during which Lin Tao-ch'ien suffered a disastrous defeat, and that his men and ships were incorporated into those of his rival. This incident, however, does not seem to have occurred at this time, for later events show no indication of any setback and Lin appeared far stronger than before. The encounter, if it happened at all, must have taken place earlier, probably during Lin Tao-ch'ien's flight to Taiwan.

Some acconts, however, hold that Lin fled to K'un-lun Island 崑崙山 (Pulo Condor) in the South China Sea, which from 1574 on he made his base for raids on the coasts of Siam, Fukien, and Kwangtung. Around 1578 Lin was found to have moved to the Indochina peninsula and to be operating from bases in Cambodia, Pattani, and Siam. (Pattani, Po-ni 淳泥 , or Ta-ni 大泥 in Chinese, was a Malay kingdom in southern Siam, whose ruler was a traditional vassal of the Thai. Some historians have erroneously identified Pattani with Brunei, another Po-ni kingdom in north Borneo.) While Lin was in Cambodia, Liu Yao-hui (*see* Martín de Rada), then governor of Fukien (1573–77), had attempted to capture him with the help of a renegade bandit headman, but the plan was reportedly revealed by the Kwangtung officials who were jealous of Liu's possible success.

Keng Ting-hsiang (*q.v.*), the new governor of Fukien (1578–80), then enlisted the assistance of the kings of Cambodia and Siam for the capture of Lin, but the plan did not materialize. In an effort to settle the quarrel between the Fukien and Kwangtung officials over the suppression of Lin Tao-ch'ien, Grand Secretary Chang Chü-cheng (*q.v.*) proposed a compromise by designating the responsibility to the Fukien officials if Lin fled to Cambodia, and the same task to the Kwangtung officials if he appeared in Siam. Following his setback in Cambodia, Lin transferred his base to Pattani from which he made sporadic raids on Siam. He was reportedly the man behind Pattani's invasion of Siam in 1580, for in May of this year a Siamese envoy informed the court of the incident and volunteered to capture Lin. Several months later (September) a Cambodian chieftain presented to the court the captured subordinates of Lin and reported that he was still at large in Siam. A later account, however, holds that Lin changed his name to Wu-liang 浯梁, and that, acting on the information of the envoy, the governor of Kwangtung recruited a Portuguese officer and a sea captain for his punitive force and succeeded in driving Lin to Malacca.

These official reports about Lin's whereabouts in Indochina, therefore, lend factual support to the prevailing legends about Lin in Pattani and Siam. According to these, Lin had conquered Pattani with his forces, founded a settlement called Tao-ch'ien kang 港 (Port of Tao-ch'ien), married the king's daughter, and died in an explosion while supervising the manufacture of firearms, said to be in imitation of the Portuguese model, after which the natives of Pattani later claimed him as their progenitor. In Siam the legend about Lin fused with the historical facts that Lin offered assistance to the Thai king in campaigns against the neighboring Tung-man Niu 東蠻牛 (Tong U), a Burmese kingdom, and Champa, and that the king rewarded him by offering him his daughter in marriage. It is not certain when and where Lin died, presumably somewhere in Indochina, as local legends insist.

Bibliography

1/222/28b, 323/17b; MSL (1965), Shih-tsung, 9003, Mu-tsung, 299, 451, 676, 855, 906, 964, 986, Shen-tsung (1966), 421, 836, 1693, 1725, 1977, 2025; KC (1958), 4225, 4230, 4276, 4364; *Ch'ao-chou-fu chih* (1893), 38/37a, 40/53a; *Chang-chou* 漳州-*fu chih* (1888), 47/26a; *T'ai-wan* 臺灣-*fu chih* (1763), 19/42b; *P'eng-hu-t'ing* 廳 *chih* (1963), 351; *Hai-feng* 海豐-*hsien chih* (1931), 35b; Ch'en Tzu-lung (ECCP), *Ming ching-shih wen-pien*, 3248, 3251, 3484; Yü Ta-yu, *Cheng-ch'i-t'ang hsü-chi* (1934), 1/20b; *id., Hsi-hai chin-shih*, in *Cheng-ch'i-t'ang hsü-chi*; Chang Chü-cheng, *Chang T'ai-yüeh wen-chi*, ch. 26, 28, 31, 32; Keng Ting-hsiang 耿定向 (1524-96), *Keng T'ien-t'ai hsien-sheng wen-chi* 耿天台先生文集 (NCL microfilm), 2/27b; Chung Ping-wen 鍾秉文, *Wu-cha mu-fu chi* 烏槎幕府記, ed. by Fan Wei-ch'eng 樊維城 (cs 1620) in *Yen-i chih-lin* 鹽邑志林 (Shanghai, 1937), 44/3b; Liu Yao-hui, *Ts'ang-wu tsung-tu chün-men chih* 蒼梧總督軍門志 (NCL microfilm), 21/31a; Mao Ch'i-ling (ECCP), *Hou-chien lu*, 4/7b; Hsü Yün-t'iao 許雲樵, "Lin Tao-ch'ien lüeh-chü Po-ni k'ao" 略居浡泥考, *Tung-fang tsa-chih* 東方雜誌 32: 1 (1935), 81; *id., Pei-ta-nien shih* 北大年史 (Singapore, 1946), 111; Wu I-lin 吳翊麟, *Sung-ch'ia chih* 宋卡志 (A history of Songkhia, Tai-pei, 1968), 149; Chiao Hung (ECCP), *T'an-yüan chi* (NLP microfilm, no. 834), 33/10a.

Hok-lam Chan

LING Meng-ch'u 淩濛初 (alternate *ming* 波, T. 玄房, 波斤, H. 初成, 即空觀主人), 1580-February, 1644, scholar, poet, drama-tist, and, above all, short story writer, was a native of Wu-ch'eng 烏程, prefec-ture of Hu-chou 湖州, Chekiang. He was born into a scholar-official family. His father, Ling Ti-chih 迪知 (T. 稚哲, H. 繹泉, cs 1556), was a celebrated publisher besides being an accomplished scholar. As a youth, Ling Meng-ch'u took part in his father's wood engraving and publishing activities. Many of the woodblock editions of scholarly and literary works published under the auspices of the Ling family were so remarkable for their excellence in collating, printing, and related crafts-manship that they were highly valued by book dealers and collectors.

Although he obtained the *hsiu-ts'ai* at an early age, Ling Meng-ch'u did not advance much beyond that initial achieve-ment. He spent most of the prime years of his life in reading, writing, and edi-ting books. Not until his middle fifties did he shift his interest from literary pursuits to governmental administration. It was in 1634 that, as a senior licentiate, he secured an appointment as assistant mag-istrate of Shanghai. For eight months after his appointment, he actually served as the magistrate of that city. Later he was assigned the additional duty of supervising coastal defense, and he received credit for eliminating corrupt practices in the administration of the salt yards in the area under his jurisdiction. In 1642, after eight years of unin-terrupted administrative work, he was transferred to the post of second-class assistant prefect of Hsü-chou 徐州 (northwest of Nanking), and in his new official capacity he took charge of river control work at Fang-ts'un 房村, nearby. A highly sensitive man and patriot, he was concerned about the rising tide of rebellion and banditry in the Huai River and Hsü-chou region. He is said to have offered to the official and military leader Ho T'eng-chiao (ECCP), then also serving there, a ten-point plan to fight the ban-dits. He was brave enough, moreover, to ride alone to a bandits' camp, and through persuasion bring about their surrender to Ho. In recognition of his unusual merit, the court appointed him to a high-er post in Hukuang; instead of accept-ing the appointment, however, he remain-ed at his post at Fang-ts'un. In mid-Feb-ruary, 1644, when the rebels led by Li Tzu-ch'eng (ECCP) invaded the prefec-ture of Hsü-chou, Ling Meng-ch'u swore to fight to the death in defense of his territory. Together with more than ten others he died when Fang-ts'un fell. Af-terwards the people there erected a shrine in his memory.

Ling was one of the few late Ming writers genuinely and passionately inter-ested in writing and promoting the hua-pen 話本 or colloquial short story. In that special field of literature he made a greater contribution than any other contemporary author excepting, perhaps, Feng Meng-lung (*q.v.*). His two collections of colloquial short stories, *P'ai-an ching-ch'i* 拍案驚奇, 40 *ch.*, completed in 1628, and *Er-k'o* 二刻 *p'ai-an ching-ch'i*, 40 *ch.*, printed in 1632, which have become collectively known as the *Er-p'ai*, won him as great a fame as the *San-yen* did for Feng Meng-lung. (A microfilm copy of the original in manuscript of the *Er-k'o* in 39 *chüan*, kept in the Naikaku Bunko, is now available.) The *Er-p'ai* were significant in the eyes of the literary critics of his time, as they represented the first two collections of colloquial short stories written by one author on the basis of earlier versions. All previous collections of such stories were merely aggregations of writings produced by different authors at different times. The fact that he finished eighty hua-pen stories of considerable length in only a few years was itself a prodigious feat rarely seen in the history of classical Chinese fiction.

Although vigorously engaged in the promotion and writing of the colloquial short story, Ling never lost sight of his broad academic and literary interests, which went far beyond the scope of fiction. In terms of productivity his performance was equally remarkable in the fields of poetry, drama, literary theory, and textual criticism. In drama he was responsible for the *Nan-yin san-lai* 南音三籟, a selection of southern style theatrical pieces and lyrics. In 1963 a publisher in Shanghai brought out a reproduction of this work in four elegant volumes, together with 16 pages of illustrations. (The catalogue of the library of the late Cheng Chen-to [BDRC], *Hsi-t'i shu-mu* 西諦書目, lists a copy of this as printed in 1668.) In addition he published fresh editions of the Yüan drama *Hsi-hsiang chi* 西廂記 and the *P'i-pa chi* of Kao Ming (*q.v.*). (Copies of these are noted also in the above mentioned catalogue.) Other than works of fiction and drama, he produced altogether twenty or more books, notably *Sheng-men ch'uan-shih*

ti-chung 聖門傳詩嫡冢, 16 *ch.*, *Yen-shih i yen* 言詩翼, 6 *ch.*, *Shih-ni* 詩逆, 4 *ch.*, *Ni Ssu Shih Han i-t'ung pu-p'ing* 倪思史漢異同補評, 32 *ch.*, *Kuo-men chi* 國門集, 1 *ch.*, *Kuo-men i* 乙-*chi*, 1 *ch.*, *Tung-p'o ch'an-hsi chi* 東坡禪喜集, 14 *ch.*, *Ho-p'ing hsüan-shih* 合評選詩, 7 *ch.*, *T'ao Wei ho-chi* 陶韋合集, 18 *ch.*, *Hsi-hsiang chi wu-chü wu-pen chieh-cheng* 五劇五本解證, 1 *ch.*, *Ch'iu-jan Weng* 虬髯翁, 1 *ch.*, *Tien-tao yin-yüan* 顛倒因緣, 1 *ch.*, and *Sung Kung-ming nao yüan-hsiao tsa-chü* 宋公明鬧元宵雜劇, 1 *ch.* Several of these are mentioned in the *Ssu-k'u* catalogue, but none was copied into the Imperial Library.

Bibliography

Hu-chou-fu chih (1874), ch. 59; *Wu-ch'eng-hsien chih*(1746), 6/28b, (1881), 10/18b, 16/8a, 31/17a; Fu Hsi-hua 傅惜華, *Ming-tai ch'uan-ch'i ch'üan-mu* 明代傳奇全目 (Peking, 1959), 343; SK (1930), 17/6a, 174/8a, 180/7a, 193/6b, 7a; *Ming-shih i-wen chih, pu-pien, fu-pien* 藝文志補編附編(Peking, 1959), 17, 581, 746, 771; Cheng Chen-to, "Ming Ch'ing er-tai te p'ing-hua chi" 明清二代的平話集, *Chung-kuo wen-hsüeh lun-chi* (Shanghai, 1949, 3d ed.), II, 530; *id.*, *Hsi-t'i shu-mu* (1963), 5/34b, 40a, 60b; Tien-yi Li 李田意, "The Original Edition of the *P'ai-an ching-ch'i*," CHHP, n.s. 1, no. 3, 120; *id.*, "Ch'ung-yin 重印 *Er-k'o p'ai-an ching-ch'i hsü*," *Er-k'o p'ai-an ching-ch'i* (Taipei, 1960), 1; Wang Ku-lu 王古魯, "Pen-shu te chieh-shao" 本書的介紹, *ibid* (Shanghai, 1957), 1; Wang Kuo-wei (BDRC), *Sung-Yüan hsi-ch'ü shih* (Shanghai, 1930), 102; Yeh Te-chün 葉德均, *Ling Meng-ch'u shih-chi hsi-nien* 事跡繫年, unpublished; Sun K'ai-ti 孫楷第, "San-yen er-p'ai yüan-liu k'ao" 三言二拍源流考, *Kuo-li Pei-p'ing t'u-shu-kuan kuan-k'an* 國立北平圖書館館刊, V (1931), no. 2, 11; Shinoya On鹽谷溫, "Mindai no tsuzoku tampen shosetsu" 明代の通俗短篇小說, *Kaizo* 改造, VIII (1926), no. 8, 130; Toyoda Minoru 豐田穰, "Minkan yonukambon Hakuan kyōki oyobi Suiko shiden hyōrin kambon no shutsugen" 明刊四十卷本拍案驚奇及ひ水滸志傳評林完本の出現, *Shibun*斯文, XXIII (1941), no. 6, 34: A. Waley, "Notes on the History of Chinese Popular Literature," TP, 28 (1931), 346; Naikaku Bunko *Catalogue*, 438; Arthur W. Hummel, *Library of Congress Quarterly Journal*(February, 1951), 35; K. T. Wu, "Colour Printing in the Ming Dynasty," THM, 11 (August-September, 1940), 39.

Tien-yi Li

LIU Chi 劉基 (T. 伯溫), July 1, 1311–
May 16, 1375, statesman, thinker, literatus, mathematician, a native of Ch'ing-
t'ien 青田, Ch'u-chou 處州-fu, Chekiang,
was descended from a family originally
from Shensi, distinguished in military
service. One ancestor, Liu Kuang-shih
(1089-1142), who moved to Chekiang,
had a brilliant military career under the
Southern Sung emperor, Kao-tsung (r.
1127-62), advancing to the title of
duke and grand preceptor. Liu Chi's
great-grandfather Liu Hao 濠 was well
known for his chivalrous deeds during
the last years of the Sung. From this
time on scholarship became a tradition in
the family. Liu Chi's grandfather, Liu
T'ing-huai 庭槐, was a prolific writer on
astronomy, geography, and medicine. His
father, Liu Yüeh 爚 (T. 如晦), was an
instructor in an academy at Sui-ch'ang 遂
昌, Chekiang.

A precocious child, Liu Chi became well
versed in the Classics and works of ancient thinkers. He was unwilling, however,
to confine himself to this rather circum-
scribed literature, and instead, like his
grandfather, took up the study of astronomy, mathematics, geography, and the
art of war. After graduating as *chü-jen*
in 1326, Liu studied under Cheng Yüan-
shan 鄭元善 (H. 復初, cs 1318), developing
an interest in "hsin-hsüeh" 心學 (studies
of the mind), a branch of neo-Confucianism, and achieved the *chin-shih* in 1333.
Three years later (1336) he was appointed
assistant magistrate of Kao-an 高安, Kiangsi, but was cashiered for disregarding
the wishes of his seniors after only two
years in office. Next he served as chief
clerk in the Kiangsi branch secretariat
(1339-40) and assistant inspector of public
academies in Hangchow (1343), but resigned
thereafter on the pretense of ill health
but actually because of a dispute with his
superiors in the tribunal of censors. During the following years, he assisted the
authorities of Chekiang in fortifying several local sub-prefectures against bands of
rebels, notably those from the west under

Hsü Shou-hui (*q.v.*), and the pirates of
the Chekiang coast under Fang Kuo-chen
(*q.v.*). In 1352 he was appointed an
assistant secretary by the provincial authorities to take part in the defense of the
coastal region, and a year later became
an assistant secretary in the Che-tung 浙
東 branch secretariat with headquarters
at Hangchow. Liu's career was again
arrested when he criticized the provincial
government's deliberation on an attractive
offer to Fang to secure his surrender. At
the instigation of his enemies, Liu Chi
was placed in confinement in Shao-hsing
as an obstructionist. Three years later
(March, 1356) he was reappointed as secretary and sent to the aid of Shih-mo I-
sun (*see* Chang I), assistant prefect of
Ch'u-chou, in the defense of the city. In
the following year he raised a band of
volunteers and conducted a successful
campaign against the outlaws. His successes, however, did not win him any recognition from the Yüan authorities; in despair he abandoned his official career and
retired. This concludes the first phase of
Liu's career under the Mongols.

Liu Chi's withdrawal to Ch'ing-t'ien
was understandable. This was a period of
social and political crises, an era of lawlessness and disorder and the breakdown
of civil authority. Liu was loyal to the
Mongol regime but blamed its misrule on
those officials who were self-seeking and
unscrupulous. He showed no sympathy for
the leaders of rebellion either, for in his
eyes they were no more than agents of
destruction and disorder. Disillusioned by
the political climate and powerless as an
individual, he felt that the time was inopportune for government service, and
remained at home devoting himself to
study and writing. One product was a
series of essays entitled *Yü-li tzu* 郁離子,
2 *ch.*, divided into 18 sections, in the style
of ancient philosophers, and expounding his social and political views. Here
he developed his vision of an ideal government administered by men of caliber
and virtue; he criticized the government

for mismanagement and ineptness which had brought on misery and political collapse.

In December, 1359, the rebel leader Chu Yüan-chang extended his conquest to Ch'u-chou. Immediately he sent for Liu and three other scholars: Sung Lien, Chang I (*qq. v.*), and Yeh Ch'en (*see* Chang I); they responded and arrived in Nanking (then known as Chin-ling 金陵) in April of the following year. A pious tradition asserts that Liu's powers as astrologer enabled him to forecast Chu's fortunes; in reality, however, it seems that Liu took note of Chu's leadership, and saw an opportunity to advance his own career. In any case, when Liu Chi presented himself, he reportedly submitted an eighteen-point memorandum on government policies which Chu accepted. For two years Liu Chi remained at the latter's headquarters. Because of his knowledge of the art of war, he was frequently consulted on military strategy and operation, but his greatest service to Chu Yüan-chang lay in his political advice. He was instrumental in persuading him to take immediate military action against Ch'en Yu-liang (*q.v.*), Chu's rival and western neighbor. He also advised Chu to be his own master and sever allegiance to Han Lin-er (*q.v.*), nominal overlord of the Sung kingdom. Chu launched his campaign against Ch'en in September, 1361, and successfully occupied cities up the Yangtze as far as Kiangsi. Liu was a central figure in military planning in these campaigns, his success lying, according to legend, in his astute observation of heavenly phenomena. In March, 1362, Liu temporarily left Nanking to mourn his mother's passing. During his stopover at Ch'u-chou he assisted the defender of the city in suppressing several mutinies headed by commanders of Miao 苗 origin (*see* Hu Ta-hai). While in Ch'ing-t'ien, he devoted himself to rallying his clansmen to the support of Chu Yüan-chang. During Liu's absence, Chu frequently dispatched messages to Ch'ing-t'ien, seeking Liu's counsel on current affairs, especially on military operations.

Returning to Nanking early in 1363, Liu persistently implored Chu Yüan-chang to attack Ch'en Yu-liang and, after subduing him, to deal successively with Chang Shih-ch'eng (*q.v.*) in the east and the Mongols in the north. At this point Chu almost invited disaster when he disregarded Liu's admonition against sending a reinforcement to lift the siege of An-feng 安豐 (Anhwei), capital of Han Lin-er's kingdom, by the army of Chang Shih-ch'eng. Learning his lesson, Chu acted on Liu's plan against Ch'en Yu-liang, and annihilated Ch'en in May to October, 1363, at the battle of Lake Poyang, Kiangsi. During this engagement, Liu stayed with Chu Yüan-chang and, as tradition has it, he saved his chief's life from catapult missiles. According to this, he moved Chu to another boat when a correct reading of a celestial portent indicated imminent danger.

During the following years Liu Chi continued to serve Chu Yüan-chang as adviser on political and military affairs, and, as reported, he often correctly forecast the outcome of military engagements. In August, 1365, Chu, now prince of Wu, appointed Liu director of the newly instituted bureau of astronomy, and asked him to prepare a calender for his new reign. A year later (September, 1366) he entrusted Liu with designing a plan for enlarging the city of Nanking, and for constructing new palaces and quarters. Accordingly Liu placed the new palace to the north of Mt. Chung 鍾, two *li* to the east of the old city; the new wall was extended northeast to the foot of Mt. Chung, with a perimeter of fifty odd *li*. The construction, begun in January, 1367, and completed two months later, thus laid the foundation of Chu's future capital. In November Liu assumed charge as vice censor-in-chief in the reorganized Censorate, concurrent with his duties in the bureau of astronomy; a month later, he submitted a calendar for the following year, known as *Wu-shen ta t'ung*-li 戊申 大統曆, 4 *ch*. Late this year he was commissioned, together with Li Shan-ch'ang (*q.v.*) and others, to draft a new code of law, hurriedly completed in less than a month, known as *Ta Ming ling*, 1 *ch*.

Following Chu Yüan-chang's enthronement in February, 1368, Liu remained in the Censorate, with the additional title of counselor to the heir apparent, and continued to advise his chief on state and military affairs. He urged the new emperor to be magnanimous and affectionate to his people, and remonstrated against the proposal of designating Feng-yang 鳳陽 (Anhwei), the emperor's birthplace, as the capital, proposing Nanking instead. At the same time he drafted the regulations for the new military system, known as wei-so 衛所 (or guard system), based on the Mongol model, and reportedly drew up the syllabus for the civil service examination, using the Four Books and Five Classics with the orthodox Ch'eng-Chu commentaries as the prescribed texts. In this same year he participated in the compilation of a new treatise on rituals, known as *Ta Ming chi-li*, 53 *ch*., completed two years later (October, 1370; *see* Hsü I-k'uei). During this time the government decided to raise the land tax to meet financial requirements; consequently, that of Ch'u-chou was increased ten times. As a tribute to Liu's service, the emperor reduced the land tax in Ch'ing-t'ien and six other adjacent subprefectures to one half of the original Sung rate, *i.e.*, five ho 合 (0.5 pint) per *mou*.

Liu Chi's rising prestige, coupled with his strong personality and sense of justice, soon brought him into conflict with his colleagues, particularly Li Shanch'ang. In April of this year the emperor visited Pien-liang 汴梁 (Kaifeng), presumably to investigate its suitability for his capital, and entrusted Liu and Li Shanch'ang with the administration of Nanking. Liu, deploring the laxity of certain officials, insisted on enforcement of dis-

cipline, and more than once clashed with Li, who indulged in nepotism. Upon the emperor's return, Li slandered Liu, without success, and, finding it increasingly difficult to work with his colleague, Liu took the pretext of his wife's death (September), and begged leave to return home. Before he departed, he left two memoranda for the emperor: first, not to move his capital to Feng-yang; second, not to underestimate the strength of the Mongol general Kökö Temür (*q.v.*). In late December, the Ming forces suffered a sharp setback in Shansi at the hands of the Mongols, and so the emperor, recalling Liu's early admonition, summoned him to Nanking for consultation. Delighted over his presence, the emperor lavished gifts on him and awarded posthumous honors to his ancestors.

Until his retirement in 1371 Liu Chi continued to channel advice to Chu Yüan-chang. On various occasions he tried to inculcate in the emperor the Confucian ethics of benevolence and propriety, and pleaded for a more lenient and dignified treatment of court officials. He also performed such tasks as preparing the designs of costumes to be worn by civil servants during court ceremonials. His remonstrances and criticism, however, incurred the displeasure of the emperor, who had become uneasy over his relations with the scholar-officials. Earlier, Chu Yüan-chang, unhappy with Li Shan-ch'ang as prime minister, contemplated replacing him with a more cooperative official. When the emperor raised the question with him, Liu declined the offer, and, despite his previous accusation, spoke in Li's favor, citing his competence. In November, 1369, Chu again brought up the subject of prime minister, and asked Liu to present his views. The emperor had three candidates in mind: Yang Hsien (*see* Empress Ma), Wang Kuang-yang, and Hu Wei-yung (*qq.v.*). In his reply, Liu recommended none. Yang, he said, had the ability but lacked magnanimity, Wang was too narrow-minded, and Hu too reckless. When the emperor proffered Liu the post, he again declined with the excuse that he was too sensitive to sit in judgment on others, and too impatient to carry the burden of high office. His candor, however, upset the emperor, and his reservation about Hu Wei-yung antagonized his rival. Nevertheless, Chu Yüan-chang remained courteous to him. In May, 1370, he appointed Liu a bachelor in the newly instituted College of literature (Hung-wen kuan 弘文館), an organization the members of which were charged with offering counsel, and lecturing on Classics to the emperor. Seven months later (December) he invested Liu as earl with the appellation Ch'eng-i 誠意 (sincerity), an honor carrying with it a stipend of 240 bushels of rice but no rights of inheritance. In reality, however, the emperor was beginning to shy away from his counsel and remonstrances. So, in January, 1371, he appointed Hu Wei-yung a vice administrator of the central Secretariat, and Wang Kuang-yang junior prime minister. Greatly disheartened at his rivals' ascent to positions of power, Liu begged leave to retire and returned home the same month.

During his retirement, Liu lived a quiet life and stayed clear of political affairs. The emperor, however, occasionally dispatched messages asking him about cosmological phenomena, and after Liu sent him his explanations, he used to burn his correspondence. Liu seldom went to Nanking himself, and sent any communication addressed to the throne through his eldest son Liu Lien 璉 (T. 孟藻, 1348-79). Early in 1374, however, he became involved in a scandal provoked by his chief antagonist, Hu Wei-yung, lately appointed junior prime minister. The case was as follows: earlier, while in Nanking, Liu submitted a recommendation directly to the throne proposing the establishment of a police office in Tan-yang 淡洋, 170 *li* south of Ch'ing-t'ien, for the suppression of illicit salt traffic. In 1372 the police office was set up as recommended.

Hu Wei-yung, however, regarded his failure to transmit the message through the central Secretariat as a personal affront. He felt further humiliated when Liu, having discovered that certain local officials failed to report a disorder, sent his son to reveal the facts, without first informing Hu's office. Hu then instructed a junior official to slander Liu, reporting that Liu's recommendation was due to his discovery that his knowledge of geomancy revealed that Tan-yang would produce a prince of royal stature, and that he intended to use the police office to force the local inhabitants to vacate a certain piece of land for his grave site. Though the emperor was influenced by the charges, he did not punish Liu severely, suspending his stipend only. Nevertheless, Liu was worried and proceeded to Nanking (August) to beg forgiveness. Wary of further provoking the wrath of the emperor, Liu stayed in the capital and attended the court, although his health was failing. In April of the following year his condition deteriorated, and he asked for permission to return home. He died a month later, at the age of almost sixty-four. During his last hours, Liu handed over his astrological books to his eldest son, instructing him to submit them to no one else but the emperor, and asked his second son, Liu Ching 璟 (T. 孟光, Pth. 忠節, 1340-1402), to convey his last thoughts to the emperor on current political problems.

The circumstance of Liu Chi's death, however, has puzzled historians, since most of the surviving records about it have been distorted to substantiate the charges against Hu Wei-yung who was executed for alleged treason early in 1380. The official records and the privately written biographies contend that, while Liu was sick in bed, Hu Wei-yung sent a physician to attend him. Medicine was prescribed, and a month later Liu died. This gave rise to the speculation that Hu in fact had ordered the physician to poison him, presumably on the emperor's initiative, since Hu is said to have visited

Liu on his sick bed on Chu Yüan-chang's orders. A modern scholar, Wang Chih-p'ing 王之屏, after scrutinizing the evidence in Liu's own writings, has questioned these contentions, arguing that Liu died of natural causes after a long illness, though Hu Wei-yung's prescribed medicine may have hastened his end. The allegation that Hu Wei-yung poisoned Liu Chi, it seems, originated with Chu Yüan-chang's trumped-up charges against his ambitious prime minister; the emperor, presumably eager to substantiate Hu's guilt, added this particular item to his numerous "crimes," which came to be publicized and accepted as historical truth.

Informed of his late confidant's death, Chu Yüan-chang suspended his court audience and dispatched a special messenger to Ch'ing-t'ien to offer sacrifices. In the summer of 1377 Liu Lien arrived in Nanking to submit his father's astrological books; delighted at his presence, the emperor appointed him a censor. Liu Lien died in July, 1379, presumably a victim of the intrigue of Hu Wei-yung. Following Hu's execution early in 1380, Liu Chi's stipend was restored, and his descendants became his beneficiaries. In January, 1391, Chu Yüan-chang summoned Liu Chi's second son to the capital, and appointed him an attendant in a princely fief. In accordance with regulation, the emperor granted Liu Lien's son, Liu Chien 薦 (T. 士端), the privilege of inheriting the earldom Ch'eng-i. Because of Liu Ching's opposition to Chu Ti (q. v.) and his death in the occupation of Nanking (1402), the fortunes of the family declined, and the hereditary earldom was probably canceled at this time. The improvement in the family's situation was slow in coming. In 1439 the local authorities in Ch'ing-t'ien erected a memorial hall in honor of Liu Chi as well as Liu Ching. Thirteen years later (December, 1452) Emperor Chu Ch'i-yü (q. v.) commanded that members of the Liu family be registered for future favors and official

appointments; he then appointed a descendant, Liu Lu 祿, to the hereditary rank of erudite of the Five Classics. In 1457 a shrine was erected in Ch'ing-t'ien in Liu Chi's honor, and another two years later. In 1500 Emperor Chu Yu-t'ang (q. v.) appointed a descendant, Liu Yü 瑜 (T. 公謹), to the hereditary rank of commander of the Ch'u-chou guard. Liu Chi's honors reached their peak when, in January, 1514, Emperor Chu Hou-chao (q. v.) bestowed upon him the posthumous name Wen-ch'eng 文成 (cultural attainment) and the honorary title t'ai-shih 太師 (grand preceptor). In 1531 Emperor Chu Hou-ts'ung (q.v.) recommended that Liu's name be enshrined in the imperial temple, and a year later restored the earldom as a hereditary investiture with Liu Yü as the third earl. The last inheritor, the sixth earl, Liu K'ung-chao 孔昭 (T. 復陽), served as a military commander in charge of the defense of Nanking in the last years of the Ming; but he disgraced his ancestors by deserting the capital on the entry of the Manchu invaders in June, 1645.

Although his political career was marred by the uncertainties of his age, Liu Chi has been accorded a high place in history as an exemplary imperial adviser. He was also an outstanding figure in Ming intellectual and literary history, and a thinker of note in 14th-century China. In the political sphere he championed the Mencian concept of Heaven as the ultimate source of authority, with the sovereign as its agent, and that the highest goal of government, whether Chinese or non-Chinese, is concern for the peoples' welfare. Similarly he espoused the equalitarian concept of "great harmony" (ta-t'ung 大同), a theme closer to the Taoist school of Chuang-tzu than Confucianism and which, ironically, played down the superiority of the Han race over alien tribes. In the social sphere, he deplored the rigidity of the system which held women in low esteem and which did not improve the lot of the peasants, and he expressed much nostalgic admiration for the ancient well-field (井田) program as a possible solution to the manifold problems created by the over-concentration of property in the hands of a few landowners. Liu Chi is, moreover, rated by modern historians as a man with a distinctly scientific mind and a mathematician of some significance in his time. His status as an astronomer and geomancer has also gained recognition. In the literary sphere, Liu Chi is considered one of the fine writers of the day; his prose is praised for its expressive yet refined style, and his poetry appreciated for its freshness and elegance. He is also said to have been skillful in painting and calligraphy. Despite all his achievements, however, Liu Chi received in his day somewhat stereotyped biographical treatment which emphasized conventional Confucian morality and certain popular legends. In Confucian literature he has been credited with a more important role in the founding of the Ming dynasty than he deserves. Like many other outstanding personalities in China's past, his life has been mythologized in popular fiction; for example, in the late Ming historical romance *Ying-lieh chuan* (*see* Kuo Hsün and Hsü Wei) and its various adaptations. His exceptional qualities as politician and scholar have been attributed to his possession of occult powers, while the stories thus created have transformed him into a legendary Taoist mystic and efficacious prognosticator.

Liu Chi left many writings such as *Yü-li tzu*, a treatise on political and social philosophy which has been discussed; *Fu-p'ou chi* 覆瓿集, a collection of prose and poetry written during the Yüan; *Li-mei kung* 犁眉公 *chi*, a similar assemblage of literary specimens composed during the Ming and compiled by his grandson Liu Chien; *Hsieh-ch'ing* 寫情 *chi*, an anthology of tz'u 詞 poetry; *Ch'un-ch'iu ming-ching* 春秋明經, a discourse on the Spring and Autumn Annals, and others. These five items were first printed independ-

dently and not brought together into one collection until 1470. This edition, containing 20 *chüan*, incorporated a compendium of biographical material, imperial edicts, and correspondence known as *I-yün lu* 翊運錄, which was also compiled by his grandson and first printed as an independent work. Following a preliminary revision in 1536, the collection was thoroughly revised in 1572 and became known as *T'ai-shih Ch'eng-i po Liu Wen-ch'eng kung chi* which includes a portrait of Liu Chi as a man with "curly whiskers and torch-like eyes" (虬髯電目). This edition was reprinted several times, including a reproduction in the *Ssu-pu ts'ung-k'an*, under the title of *Ch'eng-i po Liu Wen-ch'eng kung wen-chi*.

As legend has it, Liu Chi wrote extensively on astronomy, cosmology, geomancy, physiognomy, and even divination. The *Ming-shih i-wen chih* and the *Ssu-k'u* catalogue list more than ten titles attributed to his authorship. One of these works, the *T'ien-yüan yü-li* 天元玉歷, a treatise on heavenly phenomena, is listed as a banned book in the Index Expurgatorius drawn up in the 18th century. A concise discussion of most of these writings attributed to Liu Chi is included in an appendix to the *Liu Po-wen nien-p'u* 年譜 by Wang Hsin-i 王馨一 (Shanghai, 1936), a highly scholarly work on Liu's life. The authorship of some of these works, however, is highly questionable. Inasmuch as the historical truth about Liu Chi has been subject to popular legend-making, it is only at one's peril that one attributes the authorship of these works to any single person.

Some of these books, nevertheless, have gained wide popularity. These include the *Ch'ing-lei t'ien-wen chih-sheng fen-yeh chih shu* 清類天文直省分野之書, 24 *ch.* (completed 1384), a treatise on the origin of the Ming prefectural divisions which are said to have been arranged according to the positions of the twelve heavenly stars; the *Pai-yüan (ching) feng-yü (chan-hou) t'u* 白猿(經)風雨(占候)圖,

1 *ch.*, a study of cosmological phenomena with a preface attributed to Liu Chi dated 1372; the *San-ming ch'i-t'an ti-t'ien sui* 三命奇談滴天髓, 1 *ch.*, a treatise on physiognomy; the *Ti-li* (*k'an-yü*) *man*-hsing 地理 (堪輿)漫興, 3 *ch.*, and the *Tso-yüan chih-chih* (*t'u-chieh*) 佐元直指 (圖解), 10 *ch.*, being two important treatises on geomancy (the former regarded as a work of some significance by Joseph Needham); and the *Shao-ping ko* 燒餅歌 (the Hot roll ballad), a widely circulated book of prophecies that has gained popularity as one of the most important of the so-called *Chung-kuo wu-ch'ien nien chih yü-yen* 中國五千年之預言 (Prophetical books on China's five thousand years) in which Liu is said to have forecast the fortunes of China in the five hundred years to follow (*see* Chang Chung). These works, in fact, are more broadly circulated and widely read than his treatises on political philosophy or his prose and poetry.

Bibliography

1/105/21b, 128/1a; 3/123/1a; 5/9/1a; 63/2/4a; 84/甲前/5a, 甲/6a; MSL (1962), T'ai-tsu, ch. 8–99, Ying-tsung (1963), 4849, Wu-tsung (1964), 2192, Shih-tsung (1965), 2972, 3254, Shen-tsung (1966), 2662; KC (1958), 287, 522; Liu Chi, *Ch'eng-i po Liu Wen-ch'eng kung chi*, SPTK; Yao T'ung-shou 姚桐壽, *Yüeh-chiao ssu-yü* 樂郊私語 (pref. 1363), in Fan Wei-ch'eng 樊維成 (cs 1619) ed., *Yen-i chih-lin* 鹽邑志林 (1937 ed.), 17/2a; anon., *Kuo-ch'u li-hsien lu* 國初禮賢錄 in Shen Chieh-fu, ed., *Chi-lu hui-pien*, ch. 14; Sung Lien, *Hung-wu sheng-cheng chi*; Liu Ch'en 劉辰 (1335–1412), *Kuo-ch'u shih-chi* 事蹟 in Yüan Chiung, ed., *Chin-sheng yü-chen chi*; Wang Shih-chen, *Yen-chou shan-jen hsü-kao*, 85/1a; Li Hsü 李詡 (1476–1563), *Chieh-an man-pi* 戒庵漫筆 (*Ch'ang-chou hsien-che i-shu* 常州先哲遺書, 1897 ed.), 2/1b; Ho Ch'iao-yüan, *Ming-shan ts'ang* (Taipei 1970 ed.), 3065; SK (1930), 109/2b, 110/7b, 124/3b, 130/1b, 169/1b; Mao Chi-ling (ECCP), *Mao Hsi-ho hsien-sheng ch'üan-chi*, Vol. 62, *Shu-hou* 書後, 2b; *Ch'ing-t'ien-hsien chih* (1875), 10/4b, 12/40a; *Ying-lieh chuan* (1955), ed. and collated by Chao Ching-shen 趙景深 and Tu Hao-ming 杜浩銘; Yüan Fu 袁阜, *Chung-kuo li-tai pu-jen chuan* 中國歷代卜人傳 (Canton, 1948), 11/14; Ch'ien Chi-po 錢基博, *Ming-tai wen-hsüeh* 明代文學 (1933), 7; Hsiao Kung-ch'üan 蕭公權, *Chung-kuo cheng-chih ssu-hsiang shih* 中國政治思想史, IV (Taipei, 1961), 521; Wang Chih-p'ing, "Liu Chi chih ssu k'ao-i"之死異考, *Ching-shih chi-k'an*經世季刊, 2: 3 (April, 1942), 59; Jung Chao-tsu 容肇祖, "Liu Chi ti che-hsüeh chi ch'i she-hui cheng-chih kuan-tien" 的哲學及其社會政治觀點, *Che-hsüeh yen-chiu* 研究(1961), 3, 25; Kao Hai-fu 高海夫, "T'an Liu Chi ti Yü-li tzu," *Wen hsüeh i-ch'an tseng-k'an* 遺產增刊 (Peking, 1962), 73; Ch'ien Mu (BDRC), "Tu Ming-ch'u k'ai-kuo chu-ch'en shih-wen chi" 讀明初開國諸臣詩文集, *Hsin-ya hsüeh-pao*新亞學報, 6: 2 (August, 1964), 267; Fukumoto Masaichi 福本雅一, "Ryū Ki shi josetsu"詩序説, *Chūgokū Bun-gakūho*中國文學報, 18 (Kyoto, 1963), 91; Nakayama Hachiro 中山八郎, "Chin-yū-ryō no dai-ichiji kai Nankin kōgeki" 陳友諒の第一次回南京攻撃, in *Suzuki Shun kyōju kanreki kinen Tōyōshi ronsō* 鈴木俊教授還暦紀念東洋史論叢 (Tokyo, 1964), 447; Joseph Needham, *Science and Civilization in China*, II (Cambridge, 1956), 388; Hok-lam Chan, "Liu Chi (1311–75) in the *Ying-lieh chuan*: the Fictionalization of a Chinese Scholar-hero," *Journal of the Oriental Society of Australia*, 5: 1–2 (December, 1967), 26; *id.*, "Liu Chi (1311–75) and His Models: the Image-building of a Chinese Imperial Adviser," OE, 15: 1 (June, 1968), 34; *id.*, "Tu Liu Po-wen *Shao-ping ko*," in *Essays on Chinese Studies Presented to Professor Lo Hsiang-lin* (Hong Kong, 1970), 163.

Hok-lam Chan

LIU Chien 劉健 (T. 希賢, H. 晦菴), February 27, 1433-December 9, 1526, scholar-official, who served as a grand secretary during the years from 1487 to 1506 under Emperors Chu Yu-t'ang and Chu Hou-chao (*qq. v.*), was a native of Loyang, Honan. The Liu family originally hailed from T'ai-k'ang 太康, Kaifeng prefecture, Honan. Liu Chien's great-grandfather served as a provincial administrator under the Mongols until he died in the early 1360s. Liu Chien's grandfather, then an eight-year-old boy, went with his mother to live with a maternal uncle in Loyang, where he grew up and raised a family. Liu Chien's father, Liu Liang 亮 (T. 彥明, 1387-December 21, 1463, cj 1420), the first in the family to acquire a literary degree, spent his entire career, from 1430 on, as an instructor in the local schools in Shensi, Shantung, and Honan. His last post until retirement in 1456 was in San-yüan 三原, Shensi. During his service in Hua-chou 華州, Shensi, in 1433, his concubine gave birth to Liu Chien, the third among his four sons.

A precocious and quiet youth, Liu Chien entered the local school in Loyang in 1452, and qualified for the *chü-jen* a year later. He then devoted himself to the study of neo-Confucian thought. Following his acquisition of the *chin-shih* in 1460, Liu Chien was appointed a Hanlin bachelor. Two years later (October, 1462) he became a compiler, then withdrew on the passing of his father late in the same year, but was recalled by special imperial order in December, 1464, to take part in the compilation of the *shih-lu* of Emperor Chu Ch'i-chen (*q.v.*). Three years later (September, 1467) Liu rose to be a senior compiler, and participated (March, 1473) in the compilation of the *Hsü Tzu-chih t'ung-chien kang-mu* (*see* Chu Chien-shen). In July, 1476, he was appointed a junior instructor in the supervisorate of instruction for the heir apparent, where he officiated for over a decade until his advancement to be assistant minister in the same office in February, 1486. In his capacity as tutor to the heir apparent, Chu Yu-t'ang, he cultivated a cordial relationship with the future emperor, and gained political importance during the next reign.

Late in 1487, following Chu Yu-t'ang's enthronement, Liu Chien received an appointment as Hanlin chancellor and junior grand secretary, with the titular rank of vice minister of Rites. Early in the following year (February, 1488) he was appointed chief editor in the compilation of the *shih-lu* of the late emperor Chu Chien-shen, and then lecturer on classical studies to the new emperor. During this time Liu, together with his colleague Hsieh Ch'ien (*q.v.*), submitted a strongly worded remonstrance, charging as premature and a violation of the rites of imperial mourning the proposal of a certain

eunuch that a few girls be selected to fill the harem of the eighteen-year-old monarch. The emperor accepted their counsel. Following the completion of the chronicles of Chu Chien-shen in September, 1491, Liu Chien was appointed grand secretary of the Wen-yüan 文淵 hall, with the titular rank of minister of Rites. Three years later (September, 1494) Liu Chien was promoted to be grand secretary of the Wu-ying 武英 hall with the rank of grand guardian of the heir apparent, and served (April, 1497) as chief editor in the compilation of the *Ta Ming hui-tien* (*see* Hsü P'u). A year later (March, 1498), Liu was advanced to be grand secretary of the Chin-shen 謹身 hall, with the title of grand tutor of the heir apparent and the titular rank of minister of Revenue. In this capacity he replaced Hsü P'u as senior grand secretary when the latter retired in August.

During the next few years, together with his colleagues Hsieh Ch'ien and Li Tung-yang (*q.v.*), Liu Chien devoted himself wholeheartedly to his duties, offering counsel to the emperor on state affairs, and protesting his favoritism for certain eunuchs and sycophants, and obsession with Buddhist and Taoist festivities under the influence of his mother and grandmother (*see* Chu Yu-t'ang). They jointly submitted a persuasive memorial, following a fire destroying the Ch'ien-ch'ing 乾清 and K'un-ning 坤寧 palaces in November, 1496 (which the emperor interpreted as an ominous sign), remonstrating against his conduct of Taoist prayers, and proposing that he release convicted prisoners as a means of forestalling future calamities. They urged him to stay away from court parasites, listen to the counsel of his worthy ministers, and maintain impartiality in matters of reward and punishment; they spoke out furthermore against the proposal of an imperial servant to erect a shrine in honor of the eunuch Li Kuang (*q.v.*), who had just committed suicide for fear of punishment for his misdeeds. To their chagrin, the emperor paid them no heed; this occurred before the full disclosure of Li's crimes. In March, 1503, upon the completion of the *Ta Ming hui-tien,* the emperor awarded Liu the title of junior tutor and made him concurrently grand secretary of the Hua-kai 華蓋 hall, with the titular rank of minister of Personnel. During these same years, particularly from 1501 to 1504, Liu Chien and his two colleagues persisted in their effort to persuade the emperor against expensive undertakings, such as textile weaving and elaborate religious festivities, to prevent a drain on the treasury. They exhorted him, for example, not to conduct Taoist ceremonies on Mt. T'ai and Mt. Wu-tang 武當, not to erect Buddhist images and pagodas in the capital or to print Buddhist and Taoist scriptures; they sternly rejected several invitations to compose laudatory essays in honor of religious celebrities, and opposed the granting of an honorific title to the Taoist patriarch, Tu Yung-ch'i 杜永祺 (March, 1504). In most cases they succeeded in their efforts; the monarch, out of high regard for his senior tutors, often accepted their counsel. With imperial support, Liu Chien Hsieh Ch'ien, and Li Tung-yang became the three outstanding statesmen during the Hung-chih period. The compilers of the *Ming-shih,* citing the opinion of their contemporaries, assert that Liu excelled in judgment, Hsieh in outspokenness, and Li in planning. Emperor Chu Yu-t'ang, expressing his confidence in all three, asked them, when he was dying in June, 1505, to serve as mentors to his heir, Chu Hou-chao. The emperor remarked that his son, then not fourteen years of age, was intelligent but undisciplined, and urged his counselors to give him proper guidance.

Following Chu Hou-chao's accession in August, Liu Chien received the exalted rank of tso chu-kuo 左柱國 (left pillar of state), drawing the stipend of a 1A official, and remained as senior grand secretary. A few months later (January, 1506)

he assumed charge of the compilation of the *shih-lu* of Chu Yu-t'ang, but was unable to see the project through as he retired later that year, three years before its completion. In their service with the new monarch, Liu and his colleagues, Hsieh Ch'ien and Li Tung-yang, soon found to their dismay that the erratic young emperor showed little concern for state affairs. He spent his time in martial exercises—riding, archery, hunting,—and in sensual entertainments (singing, wrestling, magic, fireworks, and the like). Instead of attending to the normal duties of a monarch, he preferred the company of eunuchs who amused him with diversions and kept him from seeing court officials. With the emperor shirking his duty, the operation of government fell into the hands of his favorites. Headed by Liu Chin (*q.v.*), a group of eight junior eunuchs, known as pa-tang 八黨 (the clique of eight), dominated the court and obstructed the counsel of the senior statesmen. Greatly disturbed, Liu Chien and his associates submitted a series of remonstrances to the emperor. They exhorted him to pay more attention to state affairs, abstain from excesses, and curb the power of his servants, and forewarned him of the advent of disaster if these errors were not immediately corrected. The young monarch, however, turned a deaf ear. In great distress, Liu and Hsieh pleaded (March, 1506) for permission to retire, but the emperor refused.

Having failed in their request, they decided to take steps against the eunuchs to remove the source of trouble. Thus late in October they lent support to Han Wen (*q.v.*), the minister of Revenue, who made a dramatic plea before the emperor for a sentence of death for the eunuchs. Unfortunately Han's plan was prematurely exposed; so Liu and Hsieh tendered their resignations, and went into retirement to avoid possible humiliation. Liu Chin and his cronies thuse merged all powerful, and dominated the court. Several junior officials who petitioned for the reinstatement of the two were either cash-iered or imprisoned. Six months later (May, 1507), the names of Liu and Hsieh were placed at the head of a black list of thirty-three officials branded as conspir-ators against the throne. In March, 1509, being implicated in a trumped-up charge against Hsieh Ch'ien, Liu Chien was re-duced to the status of a commoner. Ten months later (January, 1510), Liu Chin further disgraced Liu and Hsieh by obtain-ing an imperial order to revoke the honors and gifts granted to them by the emperor of the previous reign. Following Liu Chin's execution in September, Liu Chien and Hsieh Ch'ien were exonerated, but Liu did not return to office and spent the rest of his years in retirement.

Late in 1521 the imperial successor Chu Hou-ts'ung (*q.v.*), expressing concern for the senior statesmen of the previous reign, sent a special messenger to inquire after Liu Chien, and awarded him a monthly stipend of eight bushels of rice and ten servants. In June of the following year the emperor granted his grandson, Liu Ch'eng-hsüeh 成學, the *yin* privilege to be a drafter in the central secretariat. A month later, having heard that Liu Chien had reached his ninetieth year, the emperor again sent a messenger with lavish gifts to visit him. Late in 1526 Liu died at home, at the advanced age of over ninety-three. (The *shih-lu*, followed by *Kuo-ch'üeh*, however, records his pass-ing almost four months later on April 5, 1527, probably the date on which the em-peror granted him posthumous honors.) It is said that Liu left a memorial to the emperor exhorting him to devote himself to studies, stay away from sycophants, and listen to the senior statesmen. He was awarded the posthumous honorific of grand tutor and the canonized name Wen-ching 文靖 (cultured and tranquil). Liu Chien's wife bore him two sons who both died before him. He was survived by a son born to his second wife, and two grandsons, but none of them accomp-lished anything in the bureaucracy. In

addition to official compilations, Liu Chien left a collection of memorials entitled *Liu Wen-ching kung tsou-shu* 公奏疏. The ori-ginal edition of this collection does not seem to be extant, but a partial selection, in 2 *chüan*, is included in the *Ming ching-shih wen-pien* by Ch'en Tzu-lung (ECCP).

Later historians hailed Liu Chien as an upright, dedicated official, distinguished for his unreserved and frank counsel of the monarch. Contemporaneous literature gave a favorable account of him except in the case of *Hsiao-tsung shih-lu*, which, completed under the direction of his rival Chiao Fang (*q.v.*), who had close connec-tions with the eunuchs, contains several slanderous statements about him. One of these falsely accused him of siding with Hsieh Ch'ien against the Hanlin scholar, Ch'eng Min-cheng (*see* Hsieh Ch'ien), and held him partially responsible for Ch'eng's death (July, 1499).

Bibliography

1/181/6a; 3/164/3b; 5/14/24a; 8/30/7a; 16/11/50a; 32/90/20a; 61/126/21b; 63/11/26a; MSL (1964), Ying-tsung, 6561, 6959, Hsien-tsung, 186, 940, 2813, 4616, Hsiao-tsung, *ch.* 7–124, Wu-tsung (1965), *ch.* 1–67, Shih-tsung, 320, 484, 496, 1657; KC (1958), 2871, 3349; Liu Lung 劉龍 (1477–1553), *Tzu-yen wen-chi* 紫巖文集 (NCL micro-film), 41/8a; Li Tung-yang, *Huai-lu-t'ang chi* (wen hou-kao), 18/6b; Liao Tao-nan, *Tien-ko tz'u-lin chi*, 2/14a; Ho Liang-chün, *Ssu-yu-chai ts'ung-shuo*, 8/3a, 15/5b; Chang Hsüan, *Hsi-yüan wen-chien lu*, 78/17a, 89/19a; Wang Shih-chen, "Shih-ch'eng k'ao-wu" 史乘考誤, *Yen-shan-t'ang pieh-chi*, 26/6b; Ho Ch'iao-yüan, *Ming-shan ts'ang* (Taipei, 1970 ed.), 4145; Ch'en Tzu-lung, *Ming ching-shih wen-pien* (Hong Kong, 1964 ed.), *ch.* 52, 53; *Lo-yang-hsien chih* (1813), 30/8a, 45/28a; *Huang Ming wen-hai* (microfilm), 1/5/17; Li Chin-hua 李晉華, *Ming-tai ch'ih-chuan shu k'ao* 明代勅撰書考 (Peiping, 1932), 49, 52; W. Franke, *Sources*, 1.1.6.

Hok-lam Chan

LIU Chin 劉瑾, died September 27, 1510, a native of Hsing-p'ing 興平, Shensi, was the most powerful as well as the most hated eunuch during the early years of the Cheng-te period. His tenure in power lasted less than five years, and was concluded by the severest of punishments. Little is known about his family background and childhood except that his original surname was T'an 談. Like many eunuchs of his time Liu as a youth had submitted himself to castration. In the 1450s he began to serve in the palace through the recommendation of another eunuch, named Liu 劉, and as a consequence changed his surname to his benefactor's. The first event which brought him out of obscurity took place during the Ch'eng-hua period, when reportedly he once put on a play in the palace theater. Next we read that early in the Hung-chih years he committed a crime deserving of capital punishment, but further details are lacking. Certain court officials possibly betrayed him; if so, this may explain why he was so antagonistic toward officials opposing him when he came to power. How he escaped the death penalty is not vouchsafed. Instead he was sent to serve at Mao-ling, the tomb of Chu Chien-shen (q.v.) north of Peking. In 1492, when Chu Hou-chao (q.v.) was made heir apparent, Liu was recalled through the recommendation of Li Kuang (q.v.).

When Chu Hou-chao ascended the throne in June, 1505, Liu was promoted to be the head of the Chung-ku ssu 鐘鼓司 (eunuch bureau of music and theatricals). In the meantime, along with seven other eunuchs who served the emperor before his accession, Liu became known as one of the "Eight Tigers" (see Chu Hou-chao). In this position he won further imperial favor by providing the emperor (then scarcely fourteen) with a variety of amusements. He also saw to it that the youth took a number of tours outside the palace. Within a short period of time, Liu came to be the director of the Nei-kuan chien 內官監 (directorate of palace builders), and on February 7, 1506, was also put in charge of the San-ch'ien garrison 三千營, one of the three major

military units in the capital. Only four months or so later, Liu's power increased when he was put in command of the entire imperial military training corps. In this capacity he assigned eunuchs to control all the gates of the imperial city, an action directly counter to the will of the former emperor, Chu Yu-t'ang (q.v.). Besides, Liu also enclosed over three hundred imperial estates (huang-chuang 皇莊) in the name of the throne. These actions not only alarmed the court officials, but also made Liu supreme among all the eunuchs in the inner palace. It is not surprising therefore to find Liu's faction soon in open conflict with many of the officials at court, supported by certain senior eunuchs in the palace.

Signs of opposition to the "Eight Tigers" started almost from the beginning of the reign. Open challenge, however, came a little later. On April 26, 1506, the duke of Ying-kuo, Chang Mou (see Chang Fu), together with several other officials, memorialized the throne expressing their concern over various activities of the young emperor. There was no response. Two months afterward (June 27), Censor Wang Huan 王渙 (T. 時霖, H. 毅齋, cs 1496), formally impeached the "Eight Tigers" for their bad influence on the emperor. Simultaneously, Grand Secretaries Liu Chien and Hsieh Ch'ien (qq. v.), and other high officials at court flooded the throne with memorials against the "Eight Tigers." These efforts were all in vain.

The situation changed drastically when on October 13 a junior official in the directorate of astronomy, Yang Yüan (see Yang Hsüan 瑄), drew attention to a series of omens which suggested Heaven's discontent with the emperor's personal behavior and his neglect of the people's welfare. Yang's memorial infuriated Liu Chin who had him bastinadoed (30 blows). When, on his release, Yang pointed to still other signs, Liu doubled the punishment, as a result of which Yang died (1507). These omens spoke louder than any of the previous memorials, and as a consequence the emperor began to show some concern. A second wave of attacks on Liu Chin and his clique came on October 28, when the minister of Revenue, Han Wen (*q.v.*), led other officials, including Grand Secretaries Liu Chien and Hsieh Ch'ien, to ask for the execution of Liu Chin and the other "Tigers." This recommendation was also supported by the old eunuch group in the palace, headed by the director of Rites, Wang Yüeh (*q.v.*). At this critical moment, Liu's political ally, Chiao Fang (*q. v.*), the minister of Personnel, forewarned Liu. As a result Liu Chien and Hsieh Ch'ien were dismissed, a third grand secretary, Li Tung-yang (*q.v.*), requested permission to resign, but his request was refused, and Wang Yüeh and other leading eunuchs were ordered to Nanking. They were murdered on the way.

Liu Chin now became the director of Rites. Two of his close associates, Ma Yung-ch'eng (*see* Chu Hou-chao) and Ku Ta-yung (*q.v.*), were made heads of the Eastern and Western Depots respectively. Chiao Fang was made a grand secretary, and worked closely with Liu Chin for the next four years. Other major personnel involved in the opposition, within a short period of time, were quietly demoted, jailed, exiled, or executed on various trumped-up charges.

As a person Liu has been described as cruel and cunning in nature. He took Wang Chen (*q.v.*), the powerful and evil eunuch under Emperor Chu Ch'i-chen (*q. v.*), as his hero and model. While he had little education, Liu was known as a persuasive person and a sharp talker. In dealing with the emperor he was very adroit. It is said that he sometimes asked for instructions on official matters when the former was absorbed in some amusement. This nettled the emperor who instructed Liu to handle the business himself. Consequently reports and memorials had first to be channeled through Liu. He was assisted in his labors by two

persons, Sun Ts'ung 孫聰, his brother-in-law, and Chiao Fang, the grand secretary.

Beginning with 1507 Liu's power was further extended. He became responsible for promoting and dismissing all military and civilian officials. He assigned trusted fellow eunuchs to head military posts along the border garrison stations. He required all officials, except those with distinguished honors, to kneel when they appeared before him. The following events may illustrate his exercise of authority. On April 19, 1507, through an imperial edict, he assembled all the court officials and had them kneel in the yard outside the audience hall where he read off a list of rebellious officials. This list included the names of grand secretaries and other top officials at court, all of whom had been involved in the movement against his clique the year before. On July 26, 1508, there appeared an unsigned leaflet pointing out his various crimes. Again he gathered all the courtiers together and had them kneel in front of the Feng-t'ien gate 奉天門 (sometimes called Ch'eng-t'ien 承天 gate) as a kind of group punishment. It was a hot summer day. By late afternoon three elderly officials had passed away. On the same night over three hundred officials were detained in prison. The following day the market of the capital went on strike protesting his cruelty. In the meantime, word leaked out that the leaflet was probably written by a eunuch in the palace. Officials in prison were then freed.

In 1509 Liu's power reached its height. On September 10, 1508, a new agency had been created, called the Nei-hsing ch'ang 內行廠 (palace depot), and also put under Liu's control. Its function was to supervise the other two depots. In that same year, Liu Chin's father, Liu Jung 榮 and his brother, Liu Ching-hsiang 景祥 (d. July, 1510), were both made vice commissioners-in-chief of the chief military commission. Other family members were also given high posts in the military.

Liu Chin's punishment included the

following. Penalties of one adjudged guilty extended to his family, neighbors, and friends. Liu often had officials beaten in public; many were physically disabled as a result. He also devised special methods of punishment. Two popular ones were cutting the rations 罰米法 and torturing by means of the cangue 枷法. The latter caused the death of many. Another special punishment during Liu's time was to decrease the quota of degree holders in different provinces. Kiangsi and Chekiang suffered as a result. At the same time, he practiced favoritism. He increased the quota of degree holders in his native province by thirty-five, Chiao Fang's province (Honan) by fifteen, Shansi by twenty-five, Shantung by fifteen, and Szechwan by ten. He rewarded his own men lavishly. His acceptance of bribes is recorded on almost every other page of the *Kuo-ch'üeh* (*see* T'an Ch'ien) during his period in power. It became the practice for any official returning from an inspection tour to present him with an expensive gift. It is recorded that the supervising secretary of the ministry of War, Chou Yüeh 周鑰 (cs 1502), unable to gather enough money together after a tour of duty, committed suicide on his way home. From 1508 on, another informal regulation required that any provincial administrative commissioner visiting the court on official business was supposed to give Chin twenty thousand taels of silver. The commissioners in turn collected the money from the people in their own regions, and this became a disturbing factor in many localities. From all these sources Liu collected a very large fortune. By the time of his arrest investigators found in his house, among other valuable things, three hundred thousand ounces of gold (one version says 2,500,000), over fifty million ounces of silver, and twenty bushels of precious stones.

Liu Chin respected no traditions. He made changes in almost every field, some of them good, which may even be described as reforms. In 1507 he altered the laws concerning the salt monopoly. In 1510 he modified items in the criminal section of the military code. By the time of his downfall it has been calculated that, during his years of control, twenty-four items having to do with the ministry of Personnel were changed, thirty some with the ministry of Revenue, eighteen with the ministry of War, and thirty with the ministry of Works. Before his day all edicts were sent from the palace to the ministries through their chiefs. In his time edicts were issued in Liu's residence, and sent directly to the ministries. Memorials and reports were all dispatched directly to him. One of Liu Chin's characteristics which finally contributed to his downfall was his superstitious nature. In his lifetime Liu built several temples. The best known are the Hsüan-ming kung 玄明宮, put up outside the Ch'ao-yang men 朝陽門, and the I-yung wu-an wang phalanstery 義勇武安王廟 in his native place. He also erected a shrine for himself. But what harmed him most was his belief in fortunetelling. A certain practitioner in the art, named Yü Yüeh-ming 俞曰明, told him that his adopted son (actually his nephew—one version incorrectly calls him his great-great-grandson 從孫) Er-han 二漢, would become a super noble. This Liu took to mean that Er-han would become emperor. This may have been the reason why he had people fashion armor and weapons to be hidden in his own house. These later were produced as evidence of his intention to rebel.

Liu's downfall was due to numerous factors. The decisive one was perhaps his innumerable personal enemies. He antagonized many in the bureaucracy, a number among the old eunuch group, and above all several among his close associates, the "Eight Tigers." The one most responsible for his end was one of the "Tigers," Chang Yung (*q.v.*). It all started in May, 1510, when the prince of An-hua, Chu Chih-fan (*see* Yang T'ing-ho) rose in rebellion. In his declaration, the prince related the crimes that Liu had committed. This report was not shown to the emperor. After the suppression of the rebellion, a special mission was appointed, headed by the eunuch Chang Yung and General Yang I-ch'ing (*q.v.*). On the date of their return to Peking (September 13, 1510), Chang Yung proceeded directly to the emperor and showed him the declaration of the rebellious prince, convincing him that Liu Chin might have evil designs. That same night Liu was arrested. On September 16, the emperor went in person to Liu's residence to confiscate his property. In the great accumulation of treasures the emperor saw many weapons, a ready-made seal, and two sharp knives hidden in a fan which Liu often used in his presence. On September 20 all of Liu's close associates were demoted and all the changes he had made in the regulations were rescinded. A week later, Liu was executed by the slicing process.

Bibliography

1/304/21b; 5/117/76a; *Ming-shih* (Taiwan ed.), 107/23a, 162/1951b, 181/2124a, 202/2357a; MSL (1965), Wu-tsung, *ch.* 1–66; Ch'en Hao 陳鶴 (1757–1811), *Ming-chi* 明紀 (SPPY ed.), *ch.* 24, 25; Ku Ying-t'ai (ECCP), *Ming-ch'ao chi-shih pen-mo, ch.* 43; Hsia Hsieh 夏燮 (1799–1875?), *Ming t'ung-chien* 明通鑑 (1900 ed.), *ch.* 41, 42/ 29; KC (1958), *ch.* 46–48; Wang Shih-chen, *Yen-shan-t'ang pieh-chi*, 90/2b, 21b, 94/7b; *id.*, *Feng-chou tsa-pien*, 4/106a; Ch'en Hung-mou 陳洪 謨 (1474–1555), *Chi-shih chi-wen* 繼世紀聞 (TsS CC), Vol. 2823, 1/1a; Ho Liang-chün, *Ssu-yu-chai ts'ung-shuo*, 8/66, 15/124; Kao Tai, *Hung-yu lu, ch.* 12; Shen Te-fu, *Wan-li yeh-hu-pien*, 18/33a; Sun Chih-lu 孫之騄, *Er-shen yeh-lu* 二申野錄 (1901), 1/54, *ch.* 3; Wang Ao 王鏊, *Chen-tse ch'ang-yü, hsia* 下/24; *id.*, *Chen-tse chi-wen, hsia* 下/11; Yeh Ting-i 葉丁易 (d. 1954), *Ming-tai t'e-wu cheng-chih* 明代特務政治 (Peking, 1950), 96, 116, 130, 359, 464, 487, 502.

Yung-deh Richard Chu

LIU Ching-t'ing 柳敬亭 (original *ming* Yü-ch'un 遇春), a storyteller, who lived to be over eighty *sui* and died sometime after 1669, was a native of T'ai-chou 泰州 in the prefecture of Yangchow. His family name was originally Ts'ao 曹. At fifteen he was involved in a serious crime and took refuge in a neighboring town. It is said that at this time he decided to adopt the name of Liu, a character meaning willow, because he had saved himself from the police by hiding among the willow trees.

Apparently possessing a gift for storytelling, he began to make a living in this way. Even in those early days he was popular. Unfortunately, being fond of gambling, he was unable to save money. An old man came to his rescue by collecting cash from his audience, saving it for him, and providing him with food and lodging. After some time he drifted south across the Yangtze River. In Hua-t'ing 華 亭 he met a scholar by the name of Mo Hou-kuang 莫後光 under whom he learned Confucian principles, and since he was so well instructed in his own art, he was to become the storyteller of the era. Mo told him that, although storytelling was regarded as of little consequence, if one intended to excel, one had to analyze human nature and observe human behavior. In presenting a story, he said, the introduction must be brief and to the point, and the conclusion must be neat yet create a lasting effect. The listener would thus be absorbed in the story and forget himself. Liu was struck with the force of Mo's counsel and assiduously put it into practice. After a month's time he went back to see his teacher and gave a fresh demonstration of his art. Mo told him that indeed he had improved; that now he was capable of making his audience elated, astonished, or roar with laughter. When he returned after a second month's interval, Mo said that he had again achieved further effectiveness; that now he could make the faces of his auditors change color, force them to sit up in their seats, cause their hair to stand up straight and their mouths to gape. With another month's concentration, he went back a third time to his scholar friend. This time Mo showed genuine surprise.

He told Liu that he had now really mastered the fine points of the art. With the expression of his eyes and gestures with his hands and feet, he was able to prepare the atmosphere for either a comedy or a tragedy. He could hold his audience spellbound during his act and make it regret the ending of his performance. Mo predicted that as a storyteller Liu could henceforth be successful anywhere in the empire. After taking leave of his teacher, Liu traveled to all the major southern cities: Yangchow, Hangchow, Soochow, and finally Nanking.

In the last years of the Ming dynasty, due to the turbulent conditions in the north, many official families left Peking and congregated in Nanking. As a top performer of his day, Liu Ching-t'ing became acquainted with several rich and powerful people. He was favorably regarded by Grand Secretaries Fan Ching-wen (q.v.) and Ho Ju-ch'ung 何如寵 (d. 1641, T. 康侯, 芝岳, cs 1598, and grand secretary, 1628-31, Pth. 文瑞). Later in 1643 or 1644, through General Tu Hung-yü 杜弘域, Liu was introduced to Tso Liang-yü (ECCP), who not only appreciated his storytelling, but also valued him as an adviser. Tso was a military man with little education. The scholars in his secretariat with their elaborate literary styles often irked him. He found Liu's colloquialisms understandable, his stories pleasing, and he delighted in his fictionalized historical episodes with their appeal to a soldier's creed. Thus Liu's activities were no longer limited to entertaining; he was even entrusted with some important missions. Soon after the establishment of the Nanking regime under Chu Yu-sung (ECCP), Tso Liang-yü found himself at variance with the clique in power in the new capital. With the excuse of "clarifying the surroundings of the throne," Tso led his army down the Yangtze from Wuchang to pose a threat to Nanking. On the way Tso died suddenly. Before long Nanking fell into the hands of the Manchus. From a position of wealth and influence, Liu

found himself once more impoverished and a mere entertainer. When, in his old age, he lost his son, Liu could not even afford a proper burial. To help him out, Ch'ien Ch'ien-i (ECCP) circularized a plea on his behalf, asking for aid not only for the funeral expenses of his son, but also for the provision of land for a burial place for Liu on his own demise.

Several other scholars and poets of the Ming-Ch'ing transitional period left accounts or poems about Liu. Wu Wei-yeh (ECCP), for example, wrote, besides several poems, a sketch of Liu's life eulogizing the storyteller in ecstatic terms. This proved too much for Huang Tsung-hsi(ECCP), who rewrote the sketch to put Liu in his place, so to speak, and pointed out that he was far from being literate and that it was a reflection on the upbringing of Tso Liang-yü that he trusted such a man.

Liu Ching-t'ing is described by Chang Tai (ECCP) as tall, dark, and pock-marked; hence, the nickname Liu the pock-face (柳麻子). He had a fine voice, expressive eyes, and dressed in good taste. Chang reported that once he listened to him telling the story of "Wu Sung killing the tiger" (武松打虎), an episode from the Shui-hu-chuan (see Lo Kuan-chung). He found Liu's wording quite different from that of the romance, and his delivery and presentation effective and moving. In describing the scene of Wu Sung entering the wine shop, the storyteller related that when Wu saw no attendants he gave forth such a roar that the empty earthen jars all echoed in unison. Chang Tai also remarked that it was such dramatic details which held his audiences spellbound. At this time Liu's price was one silver tael a day, and as he was extremely popular, the reservation for his service had to be made ten days in advance.

In 1653 when Liu was in Ch'ang-shu 常熟, Chou Jung 周容 (T. 茂三, 1619-79), listened to him for days on end. Chou notes in his account that Liu told stories

of Kuan Yü (d. 219), of Kuo Tzu-i (697–
781), and of Yüeh Fei (1104–42). One
could visualize the fighting, the battle-
grounds, the corpses, and feel the chilly
wind, see only those famous heroes, and
forget the presence of the performer. On
the other hand, said Chou Yung, when
Liu told a love story, or described some
ordinary daily occurrence, he was gentle
or comic as the situation demanded. In
the drama *T'ao-hua shan* 桃花扇 (Peach
blossom fan) by K'ung Shang-jen(ECCP)
Liu Ching-t'ing and his contemporary Su
K'un-sheng 蘇崑生, a famous singer, are
made the instruments which bring together the various incidents in the plot.

Bibliography

Chang Tai, *T'ao-an meng-i* (*Shuo-k'u* ed. 說庫,
1915), 5/3; Ch'ien Ch'ien-i, *Mu-chai yu-hsüeh chi*
(SPTK ed.), 6/7b, 41/12a; Chou Jung, *Ch'un-
ch'iu-t'ang wen-ts'un* 春酒堂文存 (*Ssu-ming ts'ung-
shu* 四明叢書, 1st ser), 2/29b; Huang Tsung-
hsi, *Li-chou wen-chi* (1959), 86; Mao Hsiang
(ECCP), *Ch'ao-min shih-chi* 巢民詩集 (*Ju-kao
Mao-shih ts'ung-shu* 如皋冒氏叢書), 6/10a; K'ung
Shang-jen, *T'ao-hua shan*, annotated by Liang
Ch'i-ch'ao (BDRC), (*Ying-ping-shih chuan-chi* 飲
冰室專集, also 1954 ed.); Wu Wei-yeh (ECCP),
Mei-ts'un chia-ts'ang kao (SPTK), 10/1a, 26/2b,
52/3b, 53/2b; Yen Er-mei 閻爾梅, *Yen Ku-ku
ch'üan-chi* 閻古古全集 (1919), 5/11a; Ch'en Ju-
heng 陳汝衡, *Shuo-shu shih-hua* 說書史話 (Peking,
1958). (The suggestion in the last work that
Liu Ching-t'ing visited Peking in 1662 is not
convincing.)

Lienche Tu Fang

LIU Hsiang 劉香, referred to also as Liu
Hsiang-lao 老, or, in contemporary Dutch
records as Jan Glaew (Jang Laew?), was
a pirate leader active on the south China
coast from 1632 to May 23, 1635, when
he died during a sea battle. Probably
from a seafaring family of Hai-ch'eng 海
澄, Fukien, he turned to piracy under
Cheng Chih-lung (ECCP). When in 1628
Cheng surrendered to Hsiung Wen-ts'an
(*q.v.*), then governor of Fukien, his fleet
became a naval unit in government service assigned to suppress the remaining

privateers. Later in that year, however,
one of his lieutenants, Li Chih-ch'i 李芝
奇 (or Li K'uei 魁-ch'i), succeeded in
leading a group to mutiny and turned a
large part of the fleet back to piracy. Liu
Hsiang was one of the mutineers.

After restoring his strength in ships
and men, Cheng pursued the pirates and
fought them bitterly for three years. In a
series of engagements he captured Li
Chih-ch'i early in 1630, and a year later
annihilated a large number of the remaining corsairs. By March, 1631, Governor
Hsiung was so sure of the end of piracy
on the Fukien coast that he sent Cheng
to fight some roving bandits in southern
Kiangsi. A year later Hsiung himself was
promoted to supreme commander of Kwangtung and Kwangsi. It was at about this
time, early in 1632, that Liu Hsiang gathered together the remnants of the pirates
and sixty or seventy ships, and in a few
months brought his strength up to two
hundred ships and ten thousand men.

It seems that, about the middle of
the same year, Liu began to have communications with the Dutch who, after being
forced out of P'eng-hu 澎湖 Islands (Pescadores) in 1624 (*see* Nan Chü-i), had been
operating from Fort Zeelandia on Taiwan
(Formosa), guarding their own trade route
between Japan and Batavia while preying
on ships of other nations. The exact relationship between Liu and the Dutch is
not clear. By May, 1632, the Dutch had
returned to the Pescadores. This threat
and the renewed piratical activities made
it necessary for Hsiung's successor, as
governor of Fukien, to recall Cheng from
Kiangsi. While Cheng was trying to
rebuild his navy, the Dutch in September
raided T'ung-shan 銅山, one of the
southermost islands on the Fukien coast.
Early in November Liu Hsiang was reported to be conducting raids on the Chekiang coast, extending his operations as far
north as Ch'ang-kuo 昌國 peninsula. He
met some resistance there and is next
reported as again pillaging in Fukien, inflicting considerable damage on the coast-

al communities east of Foochow; he was defeated, however, by the government navy under Cheng Chih-lung at Hsiao-ch'eng 小埕 and Ting-hai 定海, both in Lien-chiang 連江 district. Liu then turned south to plunder the Kwangtung coast. After Hsiung authorized an attack on the pirates in Kwangtung, Cheng led his Fukien fleet in pursuit, defeating Liu on April 4, 1633, at the battle of Ch'ih-kang-t'ou 赤岡頭 (on the east side of the Pearl River estuary). After losing fifteen ships, Liu sailed west, but Cheng defeated him again in Lei-chou 雷州 bay on May 19. In this engagement one of Cheng's brothers lost his life when his ship was wrecked. Liu then returned to Fukien with Cheng following him. Meanwhile the Dutch at Batavia, who had been well informed of Liu Hsiang's activities, had adopted the policy of using force to open some places on the Chinese coast to trade; this apparently meant cooperation with Liu Hsiang when necessary.

On July 11, while Cheng was removing barnacles from his ships on the beach at Fort Chung-tso-so 中左所 on Amoy Island, a Dutch fleet suddenly appeared and attacked, causing great havoc. Officially fifteen ships were reported lost, ten of them belonging to Cheng's squadron. From the wording of the reports it is evident that the Fukien authorities tried to lessen Cheng's responsibility in the defeat, for he was deemed indispensible—the only one who could meet the pirates and the Dutch on equal terms. Even so, upon investigation, Cheng was found negligent; he received a reprimand and a demotion by one grade.

Meanwhile (July 26) Liu Hsiang took advantage of the situation to return to the coast of Ch'ang-lo 長樂, east of Foochow. Reportedly he led a fleet of three hundred vessels and sailed into the mouth of the Min 閩 River. Cheng, however, soon had his revenge, for on October 22 he caught the joint fleet of about sixty ships of the Dutch and the pirates at Liao-lo 料羅 Bay on the south side of

Quemoy Island. With about one hundred fifty units Cheng attacked savagely. Of six Dutch warships one was sunk, one captured, and one seriously damaged. The rest escaped with Liu Hsiang on board one of them; he left behind a hundred captured and thousands dead. The battle is described as a great victory and credited chiefly to Cheng Chih-lung.

For about five months, apparently, Liu rested his men on the Pescadores. In November, 1633, two Dutch ships, dispatched on a mission to purchase his loot for four thousand florins, and also to join him in an attack on Fukien, were separated in a storm, only one being accounted for later off the Cambodian coast. Four months after this a Dutch agent was sent to Liu with only a thousand florins. At this time (late in 1633) the Chinese authorities decided on a new policy of negotiating with the Dutch for peace and promised them trade on Taiwan. During the discussions with the Chinese, the Dutch told Liu to leave the Pescadores and avoid making trouble. For this reason the pirate fell out with the Dutch, and on April 10, 1634, in command of fifty ships, attacked Fort Zeelandia, but was defeated. Later, however, he captured Dutch vessel with thirty men whom he commandeered to serve in pairs as gunners on his ships. That same month he sailed again to Kwangtung. On April 27 he conducted a raid on the coast of Hai-feng 海豐. While cruising off the coast of Quemoy, he was overtaken (May 20) by Cheng Chih-lung and suffered a defeat in the ensuing encounter. He then returned to Kwangtung where he gained some victories, and enlarged his fleet with captured ships. From this improved position he asked Hsiung Wen-ts'an for permission to surrender. Hsiung was delighted and late in the year dispatched a mission headed by two intendants and two high officers to negotiate terms. Liu, however, detained them as hostages, thus forcing Hsiung to abandon his policy of appeasement. A joint Kwangtung and Fukien fleet under Cheng was soon made ready. The battle took place on May 23, 1635, at sea off T'ien-wei 田尾 Point, on the coast of Chieh-shih 碣石 guard, about seventy miles southwest of Swatow. Cheng, with the title of Wu-hu fu-tsung-ping 五虎副總兵 (Five-tiger-decorated vice admiral), personally directed the encirclement of the pirates, concentrating on Liu's flagship. At the end of the engagement, Liu set fire to his own ship and perished with it. Many of his men lost their lives. Among the 147 captives, some were found to be Japanese and Dutch. Five months later in October, the remnants of Liu Hsiang's followers numbering over a thousand, including about sixty members of his own family, sailed to the Chekiang coast and surrendered at the Huang-hua 黃華 naval base to the commander of the Wen-chou 溫州 area. Piracy lessened for a while but official reports soon mention it again. There was even a story that Liu did not die but continued to lead additional raids. In any case sporadic fighting on the Fukien coast persisted for five more decades.

Bibliography

MSL *fu-lu* 附錄 (1967), *Ch'ung-chen ch'ang-pien* 崇禎長編, 3603, 3624, 3664, 3758, 3770, 3781; KC (1958), 5591, 5604, 5611, 5634, 5683, 5701, 5715; *Ming Ch'ing shih-liao* 明清史料乙編, 7/657, 688, 8/701, 戊編, 1/9; *Ming-chi Ho-lan-jen ch'in-chü P'eng-hu ts'an-kao* 明季荷蘭人侵據澎湖殘稿 (1962), no. 154 in *Taiwan wen-hsien ts'ung-k'an* 臺灣文獻叢刊; *Cheng-shih shih-liao ch'u-pien* 鄭氏史料初編 (1962), no. 157, same series; Cheng Hsi-fu 鄭喜夫, "Cheng Chih-lung mieh hai-k'ou Liu Hsiang shih-mo k'ao" 滅海寇劉香始末考, in *Taiwan wen-hsien*, 18: 3 (September, 1967), 19; C. R. Boxer, *The Dutch Seaborne Empire* (1965), 304; *Pa-ta-wei-ya ch'eng jih-chi* 巴達維亞城日記, 2 vols. (Taipei, 1970), 79, 94, 107, 131 (Chinese trans. by Kuo Huei 郭輝 from the Japanese tr. by Murakami Naojirō 村上直次郎, of the first part (1624–45) of *Dagh-Register gehouden int Casteel Batavia van passerende daer ter plaetse als over geheel Nederlandts India, 1624–1682* (Batavia, 1896–1931).

Chaoying Fang

LIU Hsiao-tsu 劉效祖 (T. 仲修, H. 念菴), August, 1522–March, 1589, poet and official, was a native of Pin-chou 濱州, Shantung. Although this is the place where his name was registered, actually his great-great-grandfather, who belonged to the Wu-hsiang left guard 武驤左衞, had moved from there to Peking in the reign of Chu Ti (*q.v.*). It was at the capital then that Liu qualified for the *chü-jen* (1540) and the *chin-shih* (1550). His initial appointment (1551) was as director of judicial proceedings in Wei-hui 衞輝 prefecture, Honan. Here he reversed a number of decisions, saving, in one case at least, the life of a wrongly accused individual. Other anecdotes too are told of his aid to people in need and of his incorruptibility. At the end of three years he was appointed secretary of a bureau in the ministry of Finance. In 1556 he assumed charge of transport in Tientsin. Two years later he was promoted to director of the Yunnan bureau, and it became his duty to purchase gold and pearls for the palace. Here too he proved his honesty and his competence in handling financial matters. Yen Sung (*q.v.*) and others tried to recruit him for their staffs but he declined. He was then sent to Shensi as surveillance vice commissioner in charge of the Ku-yüan 固原 circuit where his reputation for courage in opposing vested interests continued. For example, he supported the supreme commander, Kuo Tsung-kao 郭宗皋 (T. 君弼, 1499-1588, cs 1529), in his request to return home to bury his mother, even though this move was being blocked by certain officials at court. He likewise stood up for the surveillance commissioner, P'ei Shen 裴紳 (T. 子書, H. 右山, 1513-67, cs 1538), when a local prince was making trouble for him. Liu's special moment came when, at the time of a Mongol assault on the Hua-ma-ch'ih 花馬池 fortress, he led the populace in mounting the wall. Seeing this posture of defense, goes the story, the enemy withdrew. In 1563, on the occasion of the bureaucratic scrutiny, Liu was cashiered. He spent the remainder of his life in retirement, dying twenty-six years later.

During this period he lived the life of a scholar and poet, and was highly productive, although not much of his writing has been preserved. Report has it that he was proud of his skill in versification, and that some of his poems even penetrated the palace—the emperor, Chu Tsai-hou (*q.v.*), going so far as to send some of his eunuchs out to the market for them. An anthology of his poetry, *Tz'u-lüan* 詞欒, 1 *ch.*, is contained in the *Yin-hung i so k'o-ch'ü* 飲虹簃所刻曲 (1932) of Lu Ch'ien 盧前. Perhaps the work by which he is best remembered today is his *Ssu chen san kuan chih* 四鎮三關志, 10 *ch.*, which concerns the four frontier centers: Chi-chou 薊州, Ch'ang-p'ing 昌平, Paoting, and Liaotung, and the three passes: Chü-yung kuan 居庸關, Tzu-ching 紫荊 kuan, and Shan-hai 山海 kuan. He worked three years on this (1574-76), visiting the passes in question, and included maps of the areas. The book was prohibited two centuries later, particularly because of certain statements in the 10th *chüan* considered objectionable in Manchu eyes. Fortunately a few rare copies of the 1576 edition have been preserved.

Bibliography

5/94/81a; 22/10/18b;40/44/2a; 64/已10/7b; 84/丁上/24a; 86/13/5b; *Pin-chou chih* (1860), 9/4a, 8a, 11/記14b; *Shantung t'ung-chih*(1934), 2742, 2823; *Chi-fu* 畿輔 *t'ung-chih* (1934), 7688; *Shun-t'ien-fu chih* (1884 ed., repr. 1965), 7294, 8823, 9838; *Honan t'ung-chih* (1867), 32/53a; *Huang Ming wen-hai* (microfilm) 11.2.21; TSCC (1885-88), XXIII: 106/94/1a; Sun Tien-ch'i (1957), 60; L. of C. *Catalogue of Rare Books*, 299; *Kuo-li chung-yang t'u-shu-kuan shan-pen shu-mu, tseng-ting pen* 國立中央圖善本書目, 增訂本 (Taipei, 1967), I: 299.

Yang Chin-yi and L. Carrington Goodrich

LIU Jo-yü 劉若愚, March/April, 1584-*ca.* 1642, a grand eunuch, was the author of *Cho-chung chih-lüeh* 酌中志畧, 24 *ch.*, popularly known as the *Cho-chung chih*, an enlightening account of life in the imperial palace. Known by the name of Liu Shih-t'ai 時泰 until 1620, he came from a military family of the Yen-ch'ing 延慶 Left Guard stationed at the Chü-yung 居庸 Pass, northwest of Peking. According to his autobiography, his ancestor, Liu Ta-hai 大海, was one of the twenty thousand men of Ting-yüan 定遠 who joined the rebellion under Chu Yüan-chang early in 1354. Liu Ta-hai was awarded the hereditary rank of chiliarch of the Yen-ch'ing Left Guard, and after his son was killed in action, the family rank was raised (about 1402) to that of assistant guard commander. The sixth inheritor of the rank was Jo-yü's father, Liu Ying-ch'i 應祺 (1560-1605), who served (1603-5) as regional vice commander of Liao-yang 遼陽. Liu Jo-yü's elder brother inherited the rank, served for a time as a local commander, and lost his life in 1634 defending the imperial tombs at Ch'ang-p'ing 昌平 against the Manchu invaders.

As a younger son Liu studied for a civil career but in the autumn of 1598, influenced by a dream, he voluntarily subjected himself to castration and began to study medicine and dietetics in search of an elixir. He then applied for service in the palace, giving his native place as Hsiang-yang to spare his family any embarrassment. The reason for his choice of Hsiang-yang was probably because he recalled that his mother had dreamed before his birth of a Buddhist priest telling her that he came from there. In 1601 his wish was granted, and the grand eunuch, Ch'en Chü (*q.v.*), chose him to study in the school for young eunuchs. Soon marked for his ability as a writer, Liu was about to embark on a career suited to his talents when, in 1611, for some offense he was sentenced to being chained to a stone and not released until after the enthronement of Chu Ch'ang-lo (ECCP) in 1620. On the announcement of the new emperor's reign title, T'ai-ch'ang, Liu changed his name from Shih-t'ai to Jo-yü.

Sponsored by the grand eunuch, Kao Shih-ming 高時明, Liu was first appointed a calligrapher, and soon rose to the rank of an assistant grand eunuch in the directorate of ceremonial, which at that time was practically the nerve center of the empire. Late in 1621, having incurred the displeasure of the powerful eunuch, Wei Chung-hsien (ECCP), Liu was sent to serve in the directorate of stables. For two years he had nothing more important to do than to edit for Kao Shih-ming a work on Taoism. In 1623, recalled to the directorate of ceremonial, he became a subordinate of Wei's chief lieutenant, Li Yung-chen 李永貞 (1583–1628, entered the palace in 1601), and for four years witnessed from close quarters the assumption and wielding of supreme power by Wei, who was in charge of the imperial secret service from 1620 to 1627, and who dominated the directorate of ceremonial beginning in 1621.

This directorate had the responsibility of processing all memorials and edicts, copying the latter as drafted for the emperor by the grand secretaries. The drafts were supposed to be read, edited, and approved by the emperor in person before copying, but sometimes an emperor would delegate the power of approval to a trusted eunuch in the directorate. Hence the regular requirement for appointment to that sensitive office was someone with a well rounded education, usually chosen from among those who had studied in the eunuch school. Wei Chung-hsien, however, was an illiterate, and his appointment to that office was entirely due to the trust placed in him by the youthful emperor, Chu Yu-chiao (ECCP), who preferred woodcraft to statecraft. In 1624 Wei survived a concerted attack by Tung-lin officials (see Kao P'an-lung) and emerged with undisputed power; he depended, however, on a number of educated eunuchs such as Li Yung-chen, to read and explain the memorials to him and to draft

imperial replies. Another of this inner group was the seal-holding director of ceremonial, Wang T'i-ch'ien 王體乾 (entered the palace in 1578, died in prison 1640), who served as the nominal head of that office. Later at his trial Liu Jo-yü asserted that he was merely an adviser and secretary to Li Yung-chen. During the four years when Wei and his cohorts received various awards, Liu was not cited even once, showing that his assertion seems credible. In any case, late in 1627, after the new emperor, Chu Yu-chien (ECCP), had disposed of Wei, a censor accused Li and Liu of being Wei's accomplices in criminal activities. Early in 1628 both eunuchs were sentenced to exile, but in April, when another censor brought more charges, they were returned to Peking and held for trial. The charge against Liu was that, with his superior knowledge of law, he could twist the wordings to suit the wish of Wei and Li. Li was charged with manufacturing false accusations against Chou Shun-ch'ang (q.v.) and six others of the Tung-lin faction, and with ordering the eunuch at Soochow to submit against these men a memorial in which certain parts were to be written in red, or to be left blank to be filled in or blackened in Peking. An examination of the original document revealed these passages in red ink, later covered by writings in black, thus establishing Li's guilt. He received the death sentence and on August 17, 1628, was executed; his confiscated properties were valued at two hundred ninety thousand taels. At the same time Liu received the sentence of imprisonment awaiting decapitation. His first appeal in October was rejected, but in 1633 this sentence was reduced to death by strangulation. Eight years later, during a general amnesty, his case came up for review but somehow he was not released. He died in prison probably late in 1641 or 1642.

While in confinement Liu wrote the *Cho-chung chih-lüeh*, partly to record what he knew about the events of his day and the life in the palace, but chiefly to rationalize his own part in the activities of Wei Chung-hsien. The latest date mentioned in the book is the summer of 1641. Li Ch'ing (ECCP), who took part in one of the reviews of Liu's case in 1639 or 1640, once read the manuscript of Liu's book and predicted that it would certainly become an important source of information for future historians, but lamented that one so talented as Liu had allowed himself to be involved with Li Yung-chen and to die in prison. Li Ching's prediction proved to be correct but his lament seems rather off the mark. After years of frustration by being denied service in the directorate of ceremonial, a position for which he had been especially trained, Liu was ready to take any offer to be in that office. He expressed his gratitude to Li Yung-chen for giving him that opportunity (in 1623) in a long biography of Li, including a eulogy written in 1633. (Both Liu and Li were noted for their long beards, a feature unusual among eunuchs.)

In the first 2 *chüan* of *Cho-chung chih-lüeh* Liu included the texts of some rare documents, such as the Yu-wei hung-i and Hsü yu-wei hung-i, and the prefaces to the *Kuei-fan t'u shuo* (*see* Cheng Kuei-fei). In *chüan* 3 and 4 he describes the early lives of Chu Yu-chiao and Chu Yu-chien. In *chüan* 5 and 7 he records the lives of important eunuchs of the Wan-li period. *Chüan* 8 to 15 he devotes to the period of Wei Chung-hsien's ascendancy, describing his rise in power and naming the eunuchs and officials who supported him. *Chüan* 16, with the heading Nei-fu ya-men chih-chang 內府衙門職掌, is a detailed account of the eunuch organization, and *chüan* 17, Ta-nei kuei-chih chi-lüeh 大內規制紀略, tells of a tour of the imperial palaces. In *chüan* 18 he describes bookmaking and the imperial printing establishments, listing the books by title, each with the number of stitches and leaves. *Chüan* 19 has a description of the habiliments of the eunuchs and *chüan* 20 is a gastronomical calendar. *Chüan* 21 contains criticisms of the general, Li Ch'eng-

liang (ECCP). *Chüan* 22 records various matters and events, and *chüan* 23 is an autobiographical account. The appendix, an attack on Feng Ch'üan (ECCP), is later given in printed versions as *chüan* 24.

At first the *Cho-chung chih-lüeh* circulated only in manuscript, one copy of which is preserved in the Columbia University Library. Liu's original manuscript copy with corrections and deletions in his own hand was once in the possession of the historian, Ch'üan Tsu-wang (ECCP). The official *Ming-shih* in several passages includes quotations which are taken from Liu's work or are based chiefly on it. Yet his book was named among those banned in the 18th century. It seems that someone using the name Lü Pi 呂毖 (H. 蘆城赤隱) made an abridged version in 5 *chüan* which later passed the censorship under such titles as *Wu-shih hsiao-ts'ao* 蕪史小草 and *Ming kung-shih* 明宮史. This second version was even included in the Imperial Library with a lengthy comment by the editors, who obviously feigned ignorance of the fact that it derived from a banned book. Thereafter the *Ming kung-shih* appeared in print (1802–4 in the *Hsüeh-ching t'ao-yüan* (ECCP, p. 36), and other collectanea. By the middle of the 19th century a printed edition of the complete work under the title *Cho-chung chih*, 23 *chüan*, with a one *chüan* appendix, appeared in the collection *Hai-shan hsien-kuan ts'ung-shu* (ECCP, p. 606).

The *Cho-chung chih-yü* 餘, 2 *ch.*, is a collection of twelve titles on the struggle of the Tung-lin group against the eunuchs under Wei Chung-hsien. Its anonymous editor probably meant it to be a supplement to Liu's work. It consists of eight lists of Tung-lin members (*see* Kao P'an-lung), two lists of Wei's faction, and two works of anecdotal poetry about the court and palace in the T'ien-ch'i period.

Bibliography

1/305/29a; *Cho-chung chih* (1849), 9/5a, 21/1a,

23/1a; KC (1958), 5423, 5473; MSL *Ch'ung-chen ch'ang-pien* (1967), 0185, 0307, 0339, 0346, 0761; Hsieh Kuo-chen 謝國楨, *Wan-Ming shih-chi k'ao* 晚明史籍考 (1933), 4/15a; Li Ch'ing, *San-yüan pi-chi* (1927), 1/37b; SK (1930), 82/4b; *Sung-t'ien lu-pi* (see Kao P'an-lung), 3/12b, 16b; Yao Chin-yüan (1957), 53, 103, 135; Sun Tien-ch'i (1957), 134; W. Franke, *Sources*, 4.2.7.

Chaoying Fang

LIU Lin 劉麟 (T. 元瑞, 子振, H. 南坦, 坦上翁), November 7, 1474-April 15, 1561, scholar-official, a native of Nanking, was descended from a military family registered in the Kuang-yang 廣洋 Guard. His ancestors, who hailed from Honan and served as provincial administrators under the Sung, moved to An-jen 安仁, Kiangsi, in the last quarter of the 10th century. Liu's great-great-grandfather, a junior officer in the Mongol army, who surrendered with his followers to Chu Yüan-chang shortly after the founding of the Ming, was appointed chiliarch commander of the Shuo-chou 朔州 Guard, Shansi. His descendants pursued similar military careers. Liu Lin's father, Liu Ts'ang 蒼 (T. 伯春, 1444-1511), who inherited his father's rank in 1452 as deputy chiliarch commander of the Ying-yang 鷹揚 Guard, Nanking, was later assigned to the Kuang-yang Guard, where he established his home. Unlike his ancestors, Liu Ts'ang was versed in letters and prepared his sons for official careers. Born and schooled in Nanking, Liu Lin was the first in the family to distinguish himself in the civil service.

A *chin-shih* of 1496 Liu Lin received his first assignment as an apprentice in the ministry of Works. In April of the following year he drew attention by submitting a joint memorial with a fellow graduate, Lu K'un 陸崑 (T. 如岡 [or 如玉], H. 玉崖, 1465-1530), in defense of the supervising secretary P'ang P'an 龐泮 (T. 元化, H. 芹齋, 1450-1516, cs1484) and his colleagues, who had been indicted for supporting the eunuch Ho Ting (*q.v.*) for impeaching the imperial relative Chang Ho-ling (*q.v.*). Shortly afterwards, Liu left office to observe the mourning requirement for his mother, and stayed home for several years. In 1550 he was appointed a secretary in the ministry of Justice, and rose to be a bureau director a few years later. In this capacity Liu served capably but antagonized several powerful officials, including the eunuch Liu Chin (*q.v.*), who later dominated the court. In December, 1507, Liu Lin was appointed prefect of Shao-hsing 紹興, Chekiang, but, after only a few weeks in office, he was ordered to retire on Liu Chin's recommendation, charged with a minor offense. Despite the brevity of his stay in Shao-hsing, Liu earned the appreciation of the local people by correcting the abuses of the previous administrator who, incidentally, was also called Liu Lin (cs 1487, a native of Hsin-kan 新淦, Kiangsi, appointed in 1505). Shortly after his departure, the people of the prefecture erected a shrine in his honor, called Liu T'ai-shou tz'u 太守祠. They generally referred to him as the "new" Liu (新劉), to distinguish him from Liu Ch'ung 寵, governor of Shao-hsing in the Later Han period, who also enjoyed considerable popularity there.

Following his dismissal, Liu Lin proceeded to Ch'ang-hsing 長興, Chekiang, at the invitation of his friend Wu Ch'ung 吳琮 (T. 汝琇, H. 甘泉), a noted scholar-mathematician and wealthy local landowner with whom he later became allied in marriage. He then built a lodge in a locality south of Lake T'ai called Nan-t'an 南坦, made it his permanent residence, and adopted the name for his sobriquet; hence he was also known as T'an-shang weng (elder from Nan-t'an). There he enjoyed the company of three other belle-lettrists and former scholar-officials, including the famed poet Sun I-yüan (*see* Sun Lou); this group came to be known as Hu-nan wu-yin 湖南五隱 (Five hermits from south of Lake T'ai). They founded a social club devoted to mutual aid and intellectual discourse called Hu-nan Ch'ung-ya she 崇雅社, for which Liu Lin drafted the regulations for membership and meetings. Shortly after Liu Chin's execution in September, 1510, Liu Lin was recalled to be prefect of Sian, but interrupted his service when his father died in Nanking a year later. Being unable to escort the coffin back to An-jen for burial because of a local rebellion, he interred his father's body in Ch'ang-hsing.

In February, 1514, having fulfilled the mourning requirement, Liu Lin received an appointment as assistant administration commissioner of Shensi in charge of the supply of military rations. During this time he had a clash with the deputy censor-in-chief, Teng Chang 鄧璋 (T. 禮方, H. 煙村, cs 1487, d. November 29, 1531), then supervisor of defense to repel the invading Mongol tribesmen, over Teng's proposal for an increase in revenue to meet the rising military expenses. Liu pointed out that the local population, having recently suffered from natural calamities, could not afford the additional burden; instead, he increased the resources of the province by thwarting official corruption and preventing tax evasion by the powerful families. In June of the following year Liu Lin received a promotion to be surveillance commissioner of Yunnan, but left office in August, 1516, because he was suffering from hemorrhoids, and spent the next five years in Ch'ang-hsing recuperating.

In June, 1521, following the accession of Chu Hou-ts'ung (q.v.), Liu Lin was recalled to be minister of the Court of the Imperial Stud, from which office he rose to become deputy censor-in-chief and concurrently governor of Paoting and adjacent prefectures (May, 1523). Liu then devoted the next two years to strengthening the military against possible Mongol intrusion, rooting out unscrupulous officials, including a eunuch, and improving the welfare of the population. In a memorial dated October, 1524, Liu submitted recommendations on frontier defense and on measures to redress the inequities in local production, such as

ceasing to grant farmland to the imperial relatives and nobles at the expense of legal landowners, and distributing fairly labor and expense to local inhabitants in the maintenance of postal stations.

Liu Lin, however, discharged his duties under considerable physical strain, as he suffered from chronic internal disorders shortly after taking office. Within two years he submitted several requests for permission to retire, but not until May, 1525, after he had made the fifth plea, was his request granted. Liu then stayed home to regain his health until his recall in October, 1527, to serve as minister of the Grand Court of Revision. He received two promotions in the following year, first to be assistant minister of Justice (April, 1528), and then minister of Works four months later. The latter appointment, which lasted for only one year, marked the crowning point in his career.

As minister, Liu Lin was concerned with the financing of his administration, hurt by overspending and misappropriation of government resources by unscrupulous officials and eunuchs. He introduced a number of measures to correct abuses, reduce expenditure, and make more efficient use of existing resources through reorganization in administration and reorientation of priorities. First, he ordered an inventory of all materials on hand and an accounting of the funds allotted for public works and manufacturing to be undertaken in the capital or in the provinces during the preceding several years. He then introduced two hsün-huan pu 循環簿 (rotating registers), one kept by the ministry and the other by the officials in charge of projects. They were required to record on a yearly basis all materials or cash to be sent or requisitioned for specific projects or for general purposes and the date of collection or disposal of such articles. The officials were to submit their registers for examination and for cross-checking at specified periods, ranging from a month to a year, depending on the distance between locality of assignment and the capital.

Next Liu proceeded to overhaul the service system of artisans which had nearly collapsed, as a large number had deserted their duties or sought replacement by paying for a substitute, and as many of the conscripts converging on the capital had not been accorded proper job assignments. He then proposed that the compulsory service be discontinued and that the ministry should provide for a system whereby an able-bodied individual from a registered household of artisans might pay a fixed sum in cash to hire a replacement. Liu's suggestion, which stemmed from a precedent set in 1485, inaugurated a new arrangement which came to be adopted nationwide in 1562.

To further his effort to conserve government resources and to avoid corruption, Liu proposed a consolidation of the storage plants of the four major bureaus in his ministry into a single storehouse under centralized accounting and supervision. This created, in April, 1529, the chieh-shen ta-k'u 節慎大庫 (frugally and carefully managed grand storehouse) which came under the direction of a special keeper (ta-shih 大使, grade 9a), who handled the transaction under the supervision of a representative from the Censorate. Two years later (April, 1531), a fire broke out in buildings of the ministry of Works, destroying the storage plants of all the bureaus, but, as the bulk of government properties had already been transported to the grand storehouse, the losses were not considered serious.

Finally, Liu Lin turned his attention to the various agencies of public works and manufacturing under the management of the eunuchs, who had hitherto not been subject to ministerial supervision. He charged that a considerable quantity of materials had been squandered because of the eunuchs' profiteering and mismanagement, and undue burdens had been placed on the population for contracting assignments not in immediate demand. He then (July) submitted a memorial listing items of work to be proportionately curtailed or temporarily suspended until the treasury could take care of demands, and there were genuine needs for them. These affected several public works bureaus and shops—silk-weaving, sewing, hat and shoemaking, the armory, a number of eunuch agencies, and even the Court of Imperial Entertainments. The throne responded favorably to Liu's proposals and adopted some of his recommendations, but the new policies displeased the eunuchs as they deprived them of much authority and vested interests. It was the eunuchs' annoyance that brought an abrupt termination to Liu Lin's career.

Earlier Liu had proposed the suspension of certain items of silk-weaving in the factories in Soochow, then under the charge of the eunuchs, as part of his stringent economic policies. It so happened that, due to some confusion, the stoppage mistakenly held up the weaving contract for the emperor's regalia. The eunuch Wu Hsün 吳勳 then charged Liu with dereliction of duty. Liu shouldered the blame and was under orders to retire. This was in August. Two years later (May, 1531), Liu received another reprimand when a leak was discovered, during a heavy downpour, in a building of the imperial mausoleum, the construction of which he supervised. This ended his tour in office.

Going back to Ch'ang-hsing, Liu Lin spent the next thirty years in retirement, taking occasional trips to neighboring districts, and gathering around him a host of belle-lettrists for exchange of poems and essays. Though he had suffered from illness during his years in office, he later enjoyed good health, said to have been due to his practice of Taoist methods of achieving longevity. He aroused considerable excitement among his literary friends when, approaching the age of eighty, he told of yearning for the comfort of a storied house which he could not afford building. It is said that Liu Lin had a rattan settee suspended from a beam and used it as his bed. According to a contemporary account, at Liu's birthday celebration in 1553, Wen Cheng-ming (*q.v.*), the renowned artist, presented him with a scroll, entitled "Shen-lou t'u" 神樓圖, depicting an imaginary dwelling. This was followed by an outpouring of literary writings from his friends, lauding his noble conduct and honesty in government. He lived to the ripe age of nearly eighty-seven, and was survived by two sons, one daughter, and a number of grandchildren. The court awarded the name Ch'ing-hui 清惠 (honest and benevolent) some time after his death.

Liu Lin was accomplished in letters, particularly in poetry and calligraphy. With Hsü Chen-ch'ing (*q.v.*) and Ku Lin (*see* Yüan Chiung), he was known as one of the three talented belle-lettrists from the Soochow and Chekiang area during his time. His collection of writings, known as *Liu Ch'ing-hui kung chi* 公集, 12 *ch.*, was edited by his great-grandson and engraved in Ch'ang-hsing in 1606 with the financial assistance of the local prefect. A copy of the original edition, listed as rare, used to be preserved in the National Library of Peiping, and is available on microfilm. It contains several of his memorials on fiscal and administrative reforms and includes an appendix of biographical materials, which constitutes the principal source for this biography. Two specimens of his calligraphy are preserved in the Palace Museum, Taipei.

Bibliography

1/194/21b; 5/50/43a; 40/27下/1b; 61/129/27a; 84/丙/76b; MSL (1965), Wu-tsung, 0824, 1486, 2228, 2504, 2739, Shih-tsung, ch. 1–103, 8205; KC (1958), 3405, 3957; *Shao-hsing-fu chih* (1792), 26/21a, 37/10b, 43/3b; *Ch'ang-hsing-hsien chih* (1874), 12/20a, 13/11b, 23上/57b, 26/8b, 29/37b, 31下/30b; (*T'ung-chih*) *Shang-Chiang liang-hsien chih* (同治) 上江兩縣志 (1874), 22/12a; *Hu-chou-fu chih* 湖州府志 (1874), 59/40b, 90/28b; SK (1930), 171/7b; Liu Lin, *Liu Ch'ing-hui kung chi* (NLP microfilm, #920); Wen Cheng-ming, *P'u-t'ien chi*, 16/6a; Lü Nan, *Ching-yeh hsien-sheng wen-chi* (1832), 13/7a, 36/8a; Ting Yüan-chien 丁元薦 (cs 1586), *Hsi-shan jih-chi* 西山日記, 上/古道/5b, in *Han-fen-lou mi-chi* 涵芬樓祕笈, Vol.7 (1925); Ch'en Tso-lin 陳作霖, *Chin-ling t'ung-chuan* 金陵通傳 (1904), 12/8b; *Ku-kung shu-hua lu* 故宮書畫錄 (Taipei, 1965), 94, 365.

Hok-lam Chan

LIU San-wu 劉三吾 (original *ming* Ju-sun 如孫, 崑孫, H. 坦翁, 坦齋), 1312-July, 1399 (?), scholar, was a native of Ch'a-ling-chou 茶陵州, Hukuang, where his family had lived for several generations beginning with the Sung Dynasty. His grandfather, father, and two elder brothers all served as minor officials. He himself, after studying for an official career, also held minor offices in the Yüan government, serving in Kwangsi as an assistant director of a prefectural school. When the forces of Chu Yüan-chang took over in Kwangsi in 1367, Liu returned to his native place and lived for some time in seclusion.

In 1384, through the recommendation of the transmission commissioner, Ju Ch'ang (*q.v.*), Liu received an appointment in the Hanlin Academy, later rising to its chancellorship. An erudite scholar, Liu soon found favor in the eyes of Chu Yüan-chang, who often consulted him on literary matters, Confucian rites, and principles of government. In the following years he was put in charge of the compilation of a number of official works and contributed prefaces to several writings composed in the name of the emperor. For example, he contributed in 1384 a preface to the *Ta-kao*, the first of a series of the emperor's instructive warnings to posterity. He then compiled the *Hsing-kung lu* 省躬錄, 10 *ch.*, a record of the portents relating to the ministers (1385), and wrote a postscript to the new annotation of the "Hung-fan" 洪範 chapter of the Book of Documents (1387). In February, 1390, a censor criticized him for neglect of duty in the instruction of the sons of Prince Chu Kang (*see* Chu Yüan-chang). Acting on these charges,

Chu Yüan-chang demoted him to be an erudite in the National University, but restored his position a few months later.

Shortly after this incident, Liu suffered another disgrace on account of the misdeeds of some members of his family. In January, 1393, according to the *shih-lu*, his son-in-law Chao Mien 趙勉 (cs 1385), the minister of Revenue, was charged with accepting stolen goods from racketeers and was sentenced to death, together with his wife (January 28). To save himself from possible punishment, Liu acknowledged his failure to give Chao proper guidance and asked to be relieved of his duties. The emperor accepted his resignation but recalled him to office in October. There is another version of this episode: that the one executed was not his son-in-law but the husband of his granddaughter, Shan Ch'ing 單慶, a battalion commander who was charged with membership in the clique of Lan Yü (*q.v.*).

In the next few years, under Liu's supervision, several important official works were produced. Early in 1394 Chu Yüan-chang instructed him to undertake a revision of the Mencius, which resulted in the expunction of eighty-five sections which the emperor found distasteful to his authority. This abridged version, entitled *Meng-tzu chieh-wen* 孟子節文, 7 *ch.*, with some one hundred seventy sections, then became the prescribed text for civil examinations. (The National Library of Peiping has an original copy. This text, however, was abandoned in 1414/15 when Chu Ti [*q.v.*] restored the original classic.) In the same year two more major works attributed to his authorship were produced: in October the *Shu-chuan hui-hsüan* 書傳會選, 6 *ch.*, a revision of the elucidation of the Book of Documents by Ts'ai Ch'en (1167–1230) on the basis of the commentary by Chu Hsi (1130–1200); in December, the *Huan-yü t'ung-ch'ü shu* 寰宇通衢書, a treatise on national geography, based on the incomplete version of 1380. In January, 1396, he produced a handbook on current rites, known as *Li-chih chi-yao*

禮制集要, 1 *ch*. In the same year, at Chu Yüan-chang's direction, he drew up a series of models of the format and style of memorials for congratulating the emperor on auspicious occasions, collectively known as piao-chien 表箋. These completed, the emperor promulgated them, ordering all officials to follow these examples in presenting their congratulations.

Meanwhile, in July, 1397, Liu committed a blunder in his supervision of the metropolitan examinations. On that occasion it so happened that all the successful candidates came from south of the Yangtze. This created a commotion among the northerners. They brought the case to the throne and charged Liu with undue prejudice in supervising the test. The emperor then personally conducted a reexamination in which he passed sixty of the candidates, all from the north. Whereupon Liu and his associates were also accused of being members of the Lan Yü clique, for, by passing the wrong candidates, they harmed the state. Two of his fellow examiners were put to death, but out of consideration for Liu's advanced age, the emperor sentenced him to exile only. This incident is known as the Nan-pei pang 南北榜 (the episode of the southern and northern examination results' scandal).

There are various dates given for the year of Liu's death. Cheng Hsiao (*q.v.*) reports that he died in exile in July, 1399, following the scandal; this seems to be the most plausible.

Apart from the official compilations Liu left a collection of prose and poetry entitled (*Liu*) *T'an-chai hsien-sheng wen-chi* 坦齋先生文集. First printed in 1488 in 2 *chüan*, a collated edition with considerable variations in content appeared in 1578. An enlarged edition, 15 *ch.*, with *pu-i* 補遺, 1 *ch.*, was compiled in 1873. The latter contains the prefaces and colophons to several imperial writings, various specimens of piao-chien, a number of epitaphs of leading officials of the early Ming composed under imperial command,

and an appendix of biographical material.

Bibliography

1/127/1a; 5/20/20a; 8/4/15a;61/143/6a;64/甲/18a; MSL (1962), T'ai-tsu, 2583, 2684, 2727, 3073, 3268, 3354, 3422, 3529; KC (1958), 478, 774; *Liu T'an-chai hsien-sheng wen-chi*; Huang Yü (*see* Huang Tso), *Shuang-huai sui-ch'ao*, 2/2b; SK (1930), 12/3a, 175/2a; P'an Ch'eng-chang (EC CP), *Kuo-shih k'ao-i* 國史考異 (TsSCC ed.), 3/ 8b; NLP, *Catalogue of Rare Books*, series A (1933), 1/9b; Li Chin-hua 李晉華, *Ming-tai ch'ih-tsuan shu k'ao* 明代勅撰書考 (Peiping, 1932), 15, 19, 20; Huang Chang-chien 黃彰健, "Ming-shih tsuan-wu hsü" 明史纂誤續, CYYY, 36, pt. 2 (1966), 505; L. Carrington Goodrich (tr.), Ku Chieh-k'ang, "A Study of Literary Persecution during the Ming Dynasty," HJAS, 3 (1938), 259.

Hok-lam Chan

LIU Shih-t'ai, *see* **LIU Jo-yü**

LIU Ta-hsia 劉大夏 (T. 時雍, H. 東山, Pth. 忠宣), January 31, 1437-June 29, 1516, who directed the project of channeling the Yellow River into its southern course in 1495, and who suffered persecution at the hands of the eunuch Liu Chin (*q.v.*) in 1506, was regarded by certain Ming historians as an outstanding statesman. According to his tombstone inscription composed by Lin Chün (*see* Li Meng-yang), his ancestor was a Sung general who followed the army of Yüeh Fei (1104–42) to Hukuang and subsequently settled there. Liu Ta-hsia was the thirteenth-generation descendant of that general. Liu was born in Jui-ch'ang 瑞昌, Kiangsi, at the time when his father was serving as district magistrate, but his native place is listed as Hua-jung 華容, Hukuang, where the family took permanent residence. In 1441 a friend of his father, Yang P'u (*see* Yang Shih-ch'i), saw him in Peking and liked him so much that he named him Ta-hsia and affianced him, then only four years old, to a distant relative of the Yang family. In 1463,

while Liu was participating in the metropolitan examinations, a fire broke out in the examination buildings, resulting in the deaths of more than ninety candidates. The emperor conferred posthumous degrees on those who perished in the fire and directed that the palace competition be held the following year. Having narrowly escaped the disaster, Liu subsequently (1464) passed the test and was chosen to enter the Hanlin. A year later, accompanied by a fellow *chin-shih*, Chang Fu-hua (*q.v.*), he besought Grand Secretary Li Hsien (*q.v.*) to reassign them to ministerial offices to gain administrative experience. Li offered him the appointment of supervising secretary, but Liu declined in spite of its honor and prestige, on the ground that the post necessarily involved its occupant in controversial matters which might lead to serious consequences, and it was therefore unsuitable for a man with obligations to his parents. Li agreed, recommending him instead for the post of a secretary in the ministry of War, where he subsequently served almost consecutively for two decades, interrupted only by the prescribed period of mourning (1476–79) upon the death of his father and a short period in prison (1483). Beginning in 1473 he became director of a bureau. Later he won renown for his service in the ministry, not because of his sound strategic planning but, ironically, for outwitting both a powerful eunuch and an emperor. According to a chronological biography written by a relative and edited by a grandson of Liu, a eunuch Wang Chih 汪直 (*q.v.*), while pressing Emperor Chu Chien-shen (*q.v.*) to retake Annam (1465), demanded that the ministry deliver the files relating to the campaign of 1407 in that country (*see* Lê Quí-ly). Upon hearing the news, Liu went to the file depository a step ahead of the clerk and removed the required documents. As the clerk failed to locate them, he was bastinadoed, but in the meantime talk about the southern expedition subsided. Afterward Liu confessed his action to Minister of War Yü Tzu-chün (*q.v.*), and won his approval. In connection with this incident, he is supposed to have said that he would sacrifice the life of one clerk rather than jeopardize the lives of thousands. In 1473 he repeated his manipulation of the files, carrying away the records of earlier maritime expeditions to the South Seas, as the emperor was contemplating the dispatch of a similar mission. This time the clerk was beaten three days in a row. In the interim a sufficient number of offiicials opposed to the proposal prevailed upon the emperor to put off the suggested expedition. As he had before, Liu made a confession after the dust settled to the minister of War, Hsiang Chung (*q.v.*), who applauded his deed. Stories such as these are hard to verify. The aforementioned version is, to say the least, a gross distortion of the facts, as it puts the two ministers of War in the wrong order and antedates Yü's appointment and Wang's rise to power by more than a decade. Neverthless both the *shih-lu* and the *Ming-shih* include the incident concerning Annam in Liu's biography. In both cases the exact date is omitted, although the *Ming-shih* does indicate that the suggested invasion of Annam was conceived to take advantage of a recent defeat of that tributary state at the hands of the Laotians, which, according to verifiable sources, took place in 1479. Liu's brief imprisonment in 1483 marks his first victimization by a eunuch. It came about after he had flogged a junior officer. The officer's brother, who happened to be a palace attendant close to the throne, reported to the emperor that while His Majesty was praying for rain, during which time all penalties were supposed to be suspended, a ministerial official dared to disregard the regulations. An imperial order went out for Liu's arrest. After he had suffered twenty strokes of the bamboo, he returned to duty.

Liu's appointment as right vice administration commissioner of Fukien was anounced either late that year or early the next. His tour of duty was terminated in the autumn of 1486 on the death of his mother. After mourning he returned to the capital (1488). Six months later he was promoted to right administration commissioner of Kwangtung. Four years after that he became left administration commissioner of Chekiang. While his biographers elaborate on the benevolence of his administration in the three provinces, the numerous episodes that they cite to illustrate it can be summed up as no more than routine. Li Tung-yang (*q.v.*), a friend, describes Liu as "magnanimous and gentle, always ready to give credit to others rather than assume it himself." He had now had thirty years in the civil service and commanded the respect of his fellow officials. His integrity and thrift were widely acknowledged. In 1493, when Emperor Chu Yu-t'ang (*q.v.*) was searching for a commissioner to direct the restitution of the Yellow River system, Liu received the most favorable recommendation. He was called from Chekiang, and promoted to right vice censor-in-chief to assume the office.

Before Liu came to the scene havoc caused by the Yellow River had troubled the court for many years. Beginning with 1489, the river's lower course had divided into numerous branches, those running southward spilling into the Huai 淮 and those going to the north running into the Grand Canal. But the dike which broke near Ching-lung-k'ou 荊隆口 (or Chin-lung 金龍 -k'ou) in the summer of 1492 worsened the situation, as the major volume of water turned north, inundating the northern section of the Grand Canal and preventing the transportation of grain to Peking. Liu embarked on his task of reconstruction in three stages. The first was to construct a new channel near the break which enabled the northbound grain ships to pass. The second was to repair the dikes, seal the breaks, and dredge the silted channels running to the southeast, giving special emphasis to directing the major current of the river into the Huai and its tributaries. The principal dike break at Chang-ch'iu 張秋 near the confluence of the Grand Canal and the Yellow River he succeeded in closing by the winter of 1494–95. The rest of the repair work was completed in early 1495. This accomplished, Liu received the emperor's approval to launch the third stage of construction work which aimed at blocking all branches of the Yellow River flowing north and northeast from Chinglung-k'ou. Since the main stream had already been diverted to the south, sealing those channels in the dry season was made easier. In fifteen days he blocked the watercourses at seven places, nine hundred (Chinese) feet and more in width. Thereafter the full volume of the Yellow River took its southeast course from Honan to Nan-Chihli, and flowed via Hsü-chou 徐州 and Huai-an 淮安; here the Yellow and the Huai Rivers converged to empty into the Yellow Sea. Although relocations of its lower stretch continued to be effected during the dynasty (see P'an Chih-hsün), not until 1855 did the Yellow River find another outlet to the sea.

A fundamental consideration behind the project was to safeguard the northern section of the Grand Canal; this is what dictated Liu's scheme. In executing the work Liu is not known to have introduced any new technological devices. To plug the gap in the stream he generally followed the method employed by Chia Lu 賈魯 in 1351, which called for assembling a flotilla of ships filled with stones and lined up ready for scuttling between the river banks. As the ships sank, they were covered by huge blocks of compacted earth, packed in fascine bundles of twigs one inch thick, laced with ropes no less than three inches in diameter, and covered by a thick layer of vegetation. Inside the blocks were wooden frames so built as to hold the earth in place. (In Chia Lu's project such blocks were as large as

one hundred fifty feet long and twenty feet high; they required several thousand men to haul each into place.) The effort was a continuing operation; often the stream washed the blockading material away and this required correction. The final sealing of the break at Chang-ch'iu took about seventy hours. After the gap was closed, Liu reinforced the earthwork with shaped rocks.

Not being a hydraulic engineer himself, Liu employed the talents of specialists. That he completed so stupendous a project within a little over two years demonstrated his organizing ability. The laborers he employed numbered one hundred twenty thousand, a body of men obviously requiring leadership of a high order. While his work was in progress there was considerable criticism at court. In the summer of 1494 the emperor dispatched a eunuch named Li Hsing 李興 and the earl of P'ing-chiang, Ch'en Jui 平江伯陳銳 (1439–1502), to assist him. Even though neither of them made any substantial contribution to the project, in Liu's reports he always scrupulously allowed their names to precede his own. When the mission was accomplished in the autumn of 1495, the administration and surveillance commissioners of Honan, it is said, each presented Liu with two thousand taels of silver, calling the gifts funds unexpended on the construction project. Liu declined both gifts.

After his return to Peking he retained his censorial rank for a short time and was then made right, and next, left vice minister of Revenue. In the latter capacity he was dispatched (1497) to Shansi to take charge of military supplies. After service on the frontier for about a year he requested retirement on account of illness. The emperor granted him a leave of absence instead. In the autumn of 1500, on the recommendation of several officials, Liu was appointed supreme commander and concurrently governor of Kwangtung and Kwangsi, with the rank of right censor-in-chief. A year later he became minister of War.

At this point Liu was about as close to Emperor Chu Yu-t'ang as any courtier could be. Often called to the emperor's living quarters for consultation, he and the monarch discussed a variety of issues without being disturbed by attendants, the sessions sometimes lasting a whole morning. As was his wont, the emperor lay on the couch, while Liu knelt before him. Their dialogue was never recorded except in Liu's memoir of some twenty double pages, written years later when he was in exile. Liu also accompanied the emperor to the Cabinet whenever the latter gave informal audiences. Another official who was so privileged was Tai Shan (q. v.), left censor-in-chief.

Despite his nearness to the throne in the four and a half years he served as minister of War, Liu accomplished little. He had hopes of elevating the periodic military service examinations to the same plane as those of the civil service, but they failed to show any appreciable results even when he was in office. Beginning with the autumn of 1502 he was put concurrently in charge of the garrison forces around the capital. In 1504, however, when the Tatars were making incursions on the northern frontier, Grand Secretary Li Tung-yang reported that the garrison, after dispatching ten thousand troops to the north, was unable to fulfil a second demand which called for another ten thousand men. The garrison had the paper strength of one hundred fifty thousand. Desertion had thinned its ranks and large numbers of the remaining soldiers were employed as construction laborers in the capital. Liu, fully aware of the situation. in both his memorials and conversations with the emperor described the suffering of the soldiers in detail, yet he offered no remedy. He was approaching seventy with his health failing. Although the emperor's confidant, he evidently had difficulty with other officials, as the monarch one time authorized him to submit sealed reports; but he declined to exercise this privilege on the ground that such a practice would disturb the proper functioning of the government and create a bad precedent. Most Ming writers, impressed by Liu's moral character, hesitated to comment on his lack of accomplishment as minister. But Wang Shih-chen (q. v.) remarked that Liu was "weak" and his work "insubstantial." That Liu upheld the Confucian ethical standard is beyond question. As minister of War, he several times induced the emperor to remit land taxes, order famine relief, and reduce the number of attendants and artisans employed in the palace. He dissuaded the emperor from launching a punitive expedition on the northern frontier in which Chu Yu-t'ang had desired to exercise personal command. His main concern was to create good will through economic retrenchment. In no instance did he conceive an institutional reform.

The reason for his persecution by Liu Chin remains to this date a puzzle. He is not known to have given the eunuch any personal affront. About a year after Emperor Chu Hou-chao (q. v.) ascended the throne (June, 1505), Liu Ta-hsia requested retirement, which was promptly granted. Liu therefore was not involved in the move to eliminate the eunuch late in 1506 (see Han Wen). Nor was his name included in the blacklist proclaimed by the eunuch in the spring of 1507. In the autumn of 1508, when Liu Chin launched a vigorous campaign to punish and harass his antagonists, however, Liu was arrested. Some historians suggest that Liu, while serving as Chu Yu-t'ang's confidant, had blocked the promotion of Liu Yü 劉宇 (T. 至大, cs 1472) and alienated Chiao Fang (q. v.), and that, when these two officials collaborated with the powerful eunuch, they persuaded him to include Liu Ta-hsia in the purge. Another theory is that Liu's suggestion to reduce the number of palace attendants annoyed numerous eunuchs who now incited their leader to eliminate him. Reportedly when the captain of the imperial guard heard of it, he purposely brought in a smaller number of attendants during the morning audience. The emperor, suspecting Liu, was not pleased.

Liu Chin, it is said, had every intention of putting the retired minister of War to death. For some time no appropriate charge could be found to justify the extreme penalty. At last someone discovered that six years before, as supreme commander in Kwangtung, Liu Ta-hsia had suggested the transfer to a neighboring province of a native tribal leader, who had inherited the position of prefect of T'ien-chou 田州, but who continued to defy the imperial order. A rescript to this effect was issued but never carried out. This chieftain, continuing to hold T'ien-chou, became only more defiant. Under this accusation Liu was indicted for "mismanagement which agitated subordinates to open rebellion," a charge punishable by death. Following the intervention of several officials, however, he was sentenced to life exile as a foot soldier in Su-chou 肅州 on the northwest frontier.

Liu reported to the army post accompanied by two servants. The military commanders apparently treated him with consideration. But a story persists that he carried a lance and answered the roll call of his troop, though the officers wanted him to stay behind. His exile lasted one and a half years. A general amnesty proclaimed in the spring of 1510 enabled him to return to his native Hua-jung. Four months later, after the downfall of Liu Chin, he was reinstated and all his titles and honors restored.

Liu left three works. A collection of his poems, known as the *Tung-shan shih-chi* 東山詩集, 2 *ch.*, includes *inter alia* certain verses concerning his journeys to and from his place of exile. Some of his memorials appear in *Liu Chung-hsüan* 忠宣 *kung chi* 公集, 1 *ch.*, and fifteen others in the *Ching-shih wen-pien* of Ch'en Tzu-lung (ECCP). The *Hsüan-chao lu* 宣召錄, 1 *ch.*, dated July 17, 1509, by the author, was written at Su-chou. This work con-

tains a report of twenty discussions that Liu had with Emperor Chu Yu-t'ang. As one might expect, Liu wrote with extreme care, refraining from any trace of criticism. This description nonetheless depicts the monarch as well-intentioned, yet somewhat naive. In the concluding paragraph Liu indicates that the compilers of the *Hsiao-tsung shih-lu* asked him to submit such a manuscript, but he declined for fear of causing trouble. This memoir may still have been submitted on demand as in the same paragraph he asks twice because of failing memory to have his omissions excused. The work is included in the chronological biography listed below. Liu was also something of an artist. His painting "Bamboos in the snow" is in the National Museum, Stockholm.

Bibliography

1/83/11a, 182/14a; 5/38/77a; 84/丙/12b; MSL (1963), Hsiao-tsung, 1355, 1628, 1786, 1826, 1870, 1887, 1899, 1916, 2031, 2242, 2439, 2447, 2980, 3166, 3315, 3323, 3327, 3481, 3499, 3576, 3869, 3994, 4006, 4022, 4054, Wu-tsung, 0064, 0087, 0213, 0263, 0396, 0404, 0475, 0972, 0983, 1461, 2713; Ku Yen-wu (ECCP), *T'ien-hsia chün-kuo li-ping shu* (SPTK), 18/23b, 31b; *Hunan t'ung-chih* (1885), 170/4b; *Ching-shih wen-pien* (1964), 697; Li Tung-yang, *Huai-lu-t'ang wen-kao* (NLP microfilm no. 950), 6/17b; Liu Shih-chieh 劉世節, *Liu Chung-hsüan kung nien-p'u*, 1786; Chang Hsüan, *Hsi-yüan wen-chien lu*, 33/25b; Chu Ta-Shao 朱大韶 (1517-77), *Huang Ming ming-ch'eng mu-ming* 名臣墓銘 (1969 repr.), V. 3, 857; Lo Jung-pang in C. O. Hucker (ed.), *Chinese Government in Ming Times, Seven Studies* (New York, 1969), 62; J. J. L. Duyendak, TP, 34 (1939), 395; Ping-ti Ho, *The Ladder of Success in Imperial China* (New York, 1962), 75; O.Sirén, *Chinese Painting*, VII (New York, 1958), 212.

Ray Huang

LIU Ting-chih 劉定之 (T. 主靜, H. 呆齋), 1409-September 15, 1469, scholar-official, was a native of Yung-hsin 永新, Kiangsi. He came from a literary family, being the eldest son of Liu Mao 劉髦 (T. 孟恂, 1373-1445, cj 1408), a teacher of some note with a number of devoted disciples, and the author *inter alia* of a study of the Book of Changes—an interest which the son was to continue. Liu Ting-chih's younger brother, Liu Yin-chih 寅之, became a *chin-shih* (in 1454) and rose to be assistant administration commissioner of Hukuang.

Liu Ting-chih took first place in both the provincial examination of 1435 and the metropolitan of 1436, but emerged as third in the palace examination a few weeks later. He became immediately a compiler in the Hanlin Academy and then an expositor-in-waiting. In 1452 he began service in the library of the supervisorate of imperial instruction and in 1456 was made a member of the directorate of instruction. The following year he received an appointment as left assistant administation commissioner in the office of transmission and concurrently expositor-in-waiting, rising to chancellor of the Hanlin Academy in January, 1458. In 1464 he was appointed vice minister of the Court of Imperial Sacrifices and on January 24, 1467, he entered the Grand Secretariat. For his service on the commission that compiled the *Ying-tsung shih-lu* (*see* Chu Ch'i-chen), Liu was appointed vice minister of Works in 1467 rising in the following year to left vice minister of Rites. He fell ill in 1469, and, in spite of the ministration of the court physician sent by the emperor, breathed his last in September. He was duly honored with the title minister of Rites and the posthumous name Wen-an 文安.

Besides being known as a man of high ethical standards and incorruptibility in official life, Liu gave a good account of himself as a writer both of poetry and of prose. While serving at the capital he was one of those responsible for the compilation and editing of the *Ta Ming i-t'ung-chih* (*see* Li Hsien) completed in 1461, and the *Ying-tsung shih-lu*. In these same years he submitted a considerable number of memorials to the throne. For example, in 1439, as Hanlin compiler, when the metropolitan area around Peking suffered from a flood, he made a

series of proposals; among them, the dispersal of prisoners of war to the south, the appointment of men with long service in the capital to posts in the interior in order to improve administration throughout the country, the instruction of sons of military officers in the science of war, and the prohibition of political activity on the part of Buddhist monks and nuns. Again, following the disaster at T'u-mu in 1449 (*see* Chu Ch'i-chen), he sent in another series of suggestions, most of them relating to the improvement of the empire's military posture, but proposing too the selection of experienced officials for the handling of foreign affairs and an increase in the emperor's authority over the central administration. Early in 1467 and once more in 1468 he memorialized when a disastrous famine struck Kiangsi and Hukuang, to be followed by a serious drought in Kiangsi. In the first instance he urged the cessation of taxation in the area, and this was done; in the second he held, among other things, that the drought might be alleviated if the emperor would pay some attention to his empress and other palace ladies, not just to the concubine Wan Kuei-fei (*q. v.*) a woman seventeen years his senior! (There is no record as to the emperor's reaction to this invasion of his privacy.) Liu also averred that it was high time that the daughter of Chu Ch'i-yü, the princess of Ku-an (*see* the emperor's biography), be given in marriage. This indeed took place in the following year (December 22, 1469) when she married Wang Hsien, the fourth earl of Ching-yüan (*see* Chu Ch'i-yü).

Liu wrote a number of books. The editors of the *Ssu-k'u* catalogue list five, but pass them over for inclusion in the Imperial Library. His *I-ching t'u-shih* 易經圖釋, 12 *ch.*, is an illustrated exposition of the Book of Changes. The *P'i-t'ai lu* 否泰錄, 1 *ch.*, gives an account of the defeat and capture of Emperor Chu Ch'i-chen in 1449 and his subsequent release in 1450; this must be based on first-hand reports, for Liu was in Peking at the time. The *Sung (shih) lun* 宋 (史) 論, 3 *ch.*, discusses certain points in the early history of the Northern Sung dynasty (960-1126). *Ts'e-lüeh* 策略, 10 *ch.*, written when he was twenty-five years of age, was initially published in 1513, and came to be known as *Wen-an ts'e-lüeh* or *Shih-k'o* 十科 *ts'e-lüeh*. It is a reference work for the style of essays submitted in the examination hall. It was included in his collected work, *Tai-chai chi*呆齋集, 45 *ch.*, printed in 1729, but was listed for suppression a half century later. (The *Tai-chai ts'ang-kao* 藏稿, 6 *ch.*, in manuscript, and *Tai-chai ts'un-kao* 存稿, 24 *ch.*, an early sixteenth-century print, are among the rare books of the National Library of Peiping, and are available on microfilm.) All of these, together with a small collection of his miscellaneous writings, entitled *Liu-shih tsa-chih* (or *shuo*) 劉氏雜志 (說), 1 *ch.*, and his prose and poetry, *Liu Wen-an kung wen-chi* 公文集, 16 *ch.*, and *shih* 詩-*chi*, 6 *ch.*, have been made widely available in various collectanea.

Bibliography

1/176/19b; 3/159/18a; 5/13/68a; 40/20/7a; 64/乙 16/10b; 84/乙/26b; SK(1930), 7/4a, 53/1a, 89/4a, 137/8b, 175/10a; Sun Tien-ch'i (1957), 12; Liu Ting-chih, *P'i-t'ai lu* (TsSCC ed.); NLP microfilm, no. 990; MSL (1963), Ying-tsung, 6106, Hsien-tsung (1964), 0738, 1094, 1378; *Yung-hsin-hsien chih* (1874), 11/14a, 36b, 38a, 16/18a, 21經 /4b, 史/22b, 28b, 集/4b, 25/2a; *Chi-an-fu chih* 吉安府志 (1876), 26/55b; *Kung-chü k'ao-lüeh*貢舉考略 (1825), 1/11a; Cheng Hsiao, *Wu-hsüeh pien*, 23/1a; T'ao T'ing (*see* T'ao Tsung-i), *Shuo-fu hsü*, 易 15; TSCC (1885–88), XI: 244/64/13b; W. Franke, *Sources* 2. 5. 1; Wada Sei 和田淸, *Toachi kenkyū, Mōkō* hen 東亞史研究, 蒙古篇, (Tokyo, 1959), 867.

Ching-hwa Ho Jen and
L. Carrington Goodrich

LIU T'ing 劉綎 (T. 省吾), *ca.* 1552-April 17, 1619, army commander, also known by his sobriquet Liu Ta-tao 大刀 (Big Sword Liu) because of his ability to brandish a 120-catty sword on horseback, was born when his father, General

Liu Hsien (*see* Chang Lien), was serving in the northern part of Nan-Chihli. Liu Hsien was a native of Nanchang, Kiangsi province. He had had some education, but was so poor that at one time he even contemplated suicide. Going to Szechwan he found employment as a village school teacher, then, passing himself off as a native Szechwanese, he graduated as a military *chü-jen*, and joined the army. By 1555, in the campaign to pacify the Miao tribesmen in the region of I-pin 宜賓, he distinguished himself and was promoted be a chiliarch commander and a guard assistant commander. Transferred to Nanking, he served as an instructor to train recruits in the Chen-wu encampment 振武營. For his success in repulsing Japanese pirates east of Yangchow in 1557, he was promoted, and in 1559 became a deputy area commander of Chekiang. Despite difficulties with some of his civilian superiors he was promoted to be area commander for Kwangtung in 1562, and in the following year led his troops into Fukien to collaborate with Ch'i Chi-kuang and Yü Ta-yu(*qq.v.*); this resulted in the victory at P'ing-hai平海 in 1563 against the *wo-k'ou*. After serving as area commander for Lang-shan 狼山 at the mouth of the Yangtze River and as area commander of Chekiang, he rose to be the grand defender of Kweichow. In 1573 he led an army of one hundred forty thousand men in a successful campaign against a rebellion of tribal people in I-pin in Szechwan, for which he was promoted to be vice commander of the central military commission.

His son, Liu T'ing, through his yin status, had been appointed a commander and had taken part in the campaign in the region of I-pin. After a brief term of service in Yunnan he served for a while as a military instructor at Nanking. In 1582 he was transferred to Yunnan, which was then invaded by the Burmese. The Burmese, Shans, and other tribal peoples of southwest China had long been chafing under Chinese rule, and their defiance of Chinese authority became stronger at the beginning of the Wan-li period. When the sawbwa of Mien-tien (Upper Burma) at Ava revolted, many of the tribes in Upper Burma, Laos, and Yunnan joined in, the insurrection being furthered by a Chinese merchant from Kiangsi named Yüeh Feng 岳鳳, who poisoned the sawbwa of Lung-ch'uan 瀧川, seized control, and sought the support of the Burmese. The border principalities, which resisted, were handicapped by insufficient supplies and delay in Chinese help. By 1582 the rebellion threatened such Chinese cities in Yunnan as T'eng-ch'ung 騰衝, Yung-ch'ang 永昌, and Ta-li 大理.

The Ming high command launched a counteroffensive in November, 1582, with Liu T'ing, mobile corps commander of T'eng-ch'ung, and Teng Tzu-lung (see Ch'en Lin) the area assistant commander of Yung-ch'ang, each leading five thousand men, plus native auxiliaries. After a major battle at Yao-kuan 姚關, in which the Chinese defeated an elephant charge, the Chinese recovered the lost principalities and pushed on to Ava. The Burmese submitted and Yüeh Feng, who had fled there, was captured and executed. The whole region was pacified. Liu T'ing was recommended for promotion to be deputy area commander, but he was accused of accepting bribes from a native chieftain and of failure to prevent his troops from looting T'eng-ch'ung. Promotion was denied, and he was ordered to await transfer. A stele set up there after his invasion of Burma was discovered in 1929.

While awaiting a new appointment, Liu T'ing was asked by the governor of Kwangsi to assist in putting down a rebellion fomented by two sorcerers in the region of Ch'ü-ching 曲靖 (now Nanning). Some ten thousand rebels laid down their arms, and only fifty of their leaders were executed. Liu T'ing was commended for his humaneness. But again he was accused of failure to report his appropriation of the private possessions of the chief, so instead of promotion, he was made only an area assistant commander for Kwangsi, and later for Szechwan.

In 1592 he was appointed area assistant commander of the third brigade of the Central Five Armies, but , before he started out for Peking, war had broken out in Korea betweeen China and Japan. When he asked to be sent to the front with five thousand Szechwan troops, the request was approved and he was promoted to be area vice commander. By the time Liu T'ing arrived, the Japanese had evacuated Seoul. Under the over-all command of Li Ju-sung (q.v.) the Chinese pressed on southward. The Japanese had set up a road block in the Choryŏng 鳥嶺 pass in Sangju 尙州, but Liu T'ing and forces under two other officers bypassed and outflanked the Japanese, forcing them to withdraw to Pusan. Liu and other Chinese forces then occupied Taegu and Chungju while Korean forces blockaded Pusan.

When Japanese reinforcements arrived and Konishi Yukinaga (q.v.) launched a counter offensive, Liu T'ing and his men were able to check one of the Japanese columns in line from Hyŏpch'ŏn 陜川 to Hamyang 咸陽 and Namwŏn 南原. When peace talks began, the Ming government withdrew their main forces under Li Ju-sung, leaving an occupation force of seventy-six hundred men under Liu and another officer.

Liu T'ing proved to be a good diplomat during his stay in Korea. Reports by Korean officials included in the *Yijo Sillok* commend him for his modesty and courtesy, his refusal to accept gifts, and the discipline of his men. They report that Liu wanted to fight but was restrained by orders from Peking, where peace-seeking ministers expected to arrange a truce with Japan. The Korean sources also describe the troops and equipment of Liu's contingent of five thousand. They revealed that the bulk of his troops were non-Chinese tribesmen from the southwestern frontier regions, including some Siamese.

Liu remained in Korea for two years until he was promoted to be regional commander for Szechwan to assist in putting down the rebellion of the Po-chou chieftain Yang Ying-lung (*q.v.*). According to the *Ming-shih*, Liu thought that he deserved greater recognition from the government. He bribed a censor to speak for him, but instead, the censor exposed him, and the ministry of War deprived him of the honors he had previously re-ceived, and demoted him to area vice commander for Szechwan. When Yang Ying-lung came to terms, Liu was transferred to Kansu with the temporary rank of area commander to take charge of the newly established headquarters at Lin-t'ao 臨洮 for the suppression of Ch'ing-hai banditry. His rank and honors were restored to him in 1596 when one of his officers defeated the outlaws and captured twenty thousand head of cattle.

In 1597 when hostilities resumed in Korea, Liu T'ing was ordered to proceed there with Chinese and tribal forces under his command. He reached Korea just when the Japanese drive had been blunted and the invaders had withdrawn to a fortified line from Ulsan 蔚山 through Sach'ŏn 泗川 to Sunch'ŏn 順天. According to one source, Liu T'ing had under his command an army of thirty-six thousand Chinese and Koreans, but since the bulk was held in reserve at Seoul, he had at the front thirteen thousand, six hundred Chinese and ten thousand Koreans, with whom he laid siege to Sunch'ŏn, the southern anchor of the Japanese line, defended by Konishi. On his left was the army under Tung I-yüan (*see* Ch'en Lin) besieging Sach'ŏn, and operating offshore was the combined Chinese-Korean naval force under Ch'en Lin. Attached to Liu's headquarters was a small naval unit under his former comrade in arms in Burma, Teng Tzu-lung. During the spring and summer of 1598 there was a stalemate along the entire front. On October 19 the Chinese and their Korean allies launched a general offen-sive by land and sea. The Japanese were pushed back to their third and last line of defense which they firmly held. The Chinese then began their siege. From October 30 to November 1, the forces under Tung I-yüan assaulted Sach'ŏn and succeeded in piercing the Japanese line until one of the enemy magazines blew up, throwing the Chinese attackers into disorder. This reverse compelled the Chinese to withdraw. At Sunch'ŏn, the joint assault by the land forces under Liu T'ing and the naval under Ch'en Lin also failed. During the offensive, the Chinese vessels suffered heavy losses when they were stranded in a narrow estuary and attacked by the Japanese. Liu was censured for pulling his men back instead of going to the aid of the navy units.

After these reverses the fighting slackened. While the Chinese retreated to recover their strength, the Japanese received word of the death of Hideyoshi (*see* Konishi) and began to make plans for evacuation. The Koreans, who wanted to seize the Japanese supplies before the Japanese destroyed them, complained that the Chinese commanders, including Liu T'ing, were not aggressive enough. Relations between the allies became strained. At length the order for the allies to take the offensive came. Liu moved up to take Waegyo 倭橋 on December 6 when Konishi began his evacuation. After the naval battle of Noryang 露梁 started on December 15, in which the Chinese and Korean allied fleet defeated the Japanese who were attempting to evacuate Konishi, he and his men escaped by another channel, and Liu T'ing was able to take Sunch'ŏn unopposed.

For his services, Liu T'ing was promoted to be vice commissioner in the central military commission, with the hereditary rank of a chiliarch for one of his sons. He returned to his old post as regional commander of Szechwan with orders to resume the campaign for the suppression of the rebellion of Yang Ying-lung in Po-chou. Of the eight government columns which converged on the rebel stronghold under the over-all command of Li Hua-lung (*q.v.*), four were from Szechwan, and the main force under the command of Liu T'ing had the responsibility of driving down via Chi-chiang 綦江, the route which was the most strongly defended by the rebels. The offensive was launched in February, 1600. In the battle of San-tung 三洞 he routed the enemy but killed only forty men, and in subsequent battles he checked the enemy assault and killed several hundred of them. The military censors reproved him for failing to advance and to exterminate the rebels by more aggressive action. At the height of the campaign, he was relieved of his command, and ordered transferred to Nanking with the rank of assistant commander. Liu refused to accept the appointment and, when the commander-in-chief, Li Hua-lung, memorialized that Liu T'ing was needed in the campaign against Yang Ying-lung, he was restored to his command.

Liu led his troops into the mountain fastness of Kweichow, through terrain the rebels had heavily fortified with blockhouses and ditches. He advanced cautiously, carefully building camps as he moved forward. Although one of his officers had rashly led his men into an ambush with heavy losses, Liu steadily demolished the enemy outposts and threw a cordon around their headquarters at Hai-lung tun (*see* Li Hua-lung).

For the suppression of the rebellion of Yang Ying-lung, Liu T'ing was cited as the military officer chiefly responsible for the victory, but again recognition was denied. Censors accused him of having accepted bribes from the rebel, and of giving valuable presents to his commander-in-chief Li Hua-lung, including a jade belt, one hundred ounces of gold, and one thousand ounces of silver. The victory over Yang Ying-lung was stricken from official records, although Liu was promoted to be a commissioner in the central military commission and one of his sons was given a hereditary appointment as commander.

After serving as regional commander in Yunnan (in 1608) he was given the same office in Szechwan in 1612 where he put down a rebellion of the Kuo 猓 tribesmen. He directed the movements of eight columns and in fifty-six engagements destroyed the rebel bases, killing three thousand three hundred of the enemy. Instead of honors, however, Liu T'ing was reprimanded for striking a magistrate, and was deprived of his salary for half a year.

Liu then resigned and returned home. In 1618, after the Manchus under Nurhaci (ECCP) had proclaimed their independence from Ming rule and had invaded and seized two cities near the border, he was recalled, and promoted to be an assistant commissioner in the central military commission. In the following year he was sent north to take command of one of the four armies which the Ming government was sending against Nurhaci. Yang Hao (ECCP), who had served with Liu in Korea twenty years before, was the commander-in-chief, with headquarters at Liao-yang. The four Ming columns totaled fewer than ninety thousand men, but for propaganda purposes was proclaimed to be two hundred forty thousand (and exaggerated to four hundred seventy thousand in Ch'ing sources). The Manchu forces numbered sixty thousand. The Ming army was to converge on Hsing-ching 興京 on April 14, but, because of the difficulty of the terrain, they did not all arrive on time. The main forces of thirty thousand men under Tu Sung (ECCP, p. 886) advanced from Fu-shun 撫順 and reached Sarhu 薩爾滸 about forty miles from Hsing-ching, when it was attacked by the Manchus at night. The Ming troops were well equipped with firearms, but their gunflashes revealed them to the Manchus. Tu Sung's forces were scattered. The Manchus then turned on the army of fifteen thousand men under Ma Lin (ECCP, p. 886) ten or twelve miles away, defeating them the following day. Manchu soldiers, wearing uniforms of Tu Sung's men who had fallen, rode to report to Liu T'ing that Tu Sung was attacking Hsing-ching and needed his help immediately. At the time, Liu's own Szechwan troops had not arrived and he had command of ten thousand other Chinese troops and ten thousand Korean allies. The Koreans were ill equipped; they wore paper armor with wicker breastplates and were reluctant to advance. Delayed by the Koreans, Liu pushed ahead with his own troops, marching in good order. When he received the false information that he was needed by Tu Sung to assault Hsing-ching, he left his artillery train behind while he went ahead with a small force. At a mountain pass he was ambushed and killed on April 7. The Manchus then attacked during a windstorm when the Chinese gunners could not see, and captured their artillery. The Koreans laid down their arms without a fight. Liu T'ing was granted the title of junior preceptor in 1621 and canonized Chung-lieh 忠烈 and also as Chung-chuang 壯.

In evaluating his career, the *Ming-shih* relates: "(Liu) T'ing was the most courageous of the commanders. In the campaigns against the Burmese, the Miao, the Japanese in Korea, the rebels in Pochou, and the Lolos, he distinguished himself by his valor. After his death, the dangers on the frontiers were intensified." As his biography shows, Liu T'ing, for one living in an age of brutality and violence, has the distinction of being a humane person for an army officer. One Korean officer reported a conversation which he had with Liu in which, while discussing the setback suffered by the Chinese troops under Yang Hao at Sach'ŏn, Liu remarked, "Yang Hao does not understand war, so his men suffer many casualties. I desire to have not a single soldier killed in order to pacify the enemy." The Korean officer went on to say that perhaps Liu T'ing felt that the

war was already won; hence further bloodshed was unnecessary. [Editors' note: A recently discovered long scroll depicting the scenes of the attack and capture of the Japanese fort at Waegyo and the naval battle of Noryang Straits gives a credible representation of the weapons and uniforms of the Chinese, Japanese, and Korean armed forces of the late 16th century. The picture of the Japanese fort is remarkably realistic. The scroll is in a private collection, but a series of twelve photographs of it is available at the Department of Fine Arts, University of California at Berkeley.]

Bibliography

1/247/1a; KC (1958), 3893, 3895, 3921; Ho Ju-chao 何如召, *Liao-tso liu chung shu* 遼左六忠述 (NCL microfilm); Wang Tsai-chin (ECCP), *Tu-tu Liu chiang-chün chuan* 都督劉將軍傳 (in *Hsüan-lan-t'ang ts'ung-shu*, ser. 1, ed. by Cheng Chen-to [BDRC], *ts'e* 95); Wang Ch'ung-wu 王崇武, "Liu T'ing cheng tung k'ao" 征東考, CYYY, XIV (Taipei, 1959), 137; Yi Hyong-sok 李炳錫, *Imjin Chŏllan-sa* 壬辰戰亂史 (Seoul, 1967), II, 1102.

Lo Jung.pang

LIU T'ung 劉侗 (T. 同人), died 1637, native of Ma-ch'eng 麻城 northeast of Wuchang in Hukuang, was a literary figure of the last years of the Ming dynasty, principally remembered for his guide book on Peking, the *Ti-ching ching-wu lüeh* 帝京景物略. In the history of literature of the late 16th and early 17th centuries, two schools, the Kung-an (*see* Yüan Hung-tao) and Ching-ling (*see* Chung Hsing), played a prominent part. The leaders of both were from present-day Hupeh province. Liu T'ung, generally regarded as a member of the Ching-ling school, was a friend of T'an Yüan-ch'un (*q.v.*), one of the best-known leaders of that school. It is said that he and T'an were once reprimanded at one of the provincial examinations for their unconventional style of writing. About 1630 Liu

T'ung went to Peking and entered the National University. With his Embroidered-uniform Guard's registration, he was permitted to compete in the *chü-jen* examinations in Peking, which he passed in 1633, and became a *chin-shih* the following year. In 1637 he received an appointment to be magistrate of Wu-hsien 吳縣 (Soochow). En route to assume this office, he died on the boat moored in Yangchow. There is a poem written by him in this same year lamenting the death of T'an Yüan-ch'un.

In the compilation of the *Ti-ching ching-wu lüeh* Liu T'ung had as associate Yü I-cheng 于奕正 (original name 繼魯, T. 司直, d. *ca.* 1635 in Nanking), who was a *hsiu-ts'ai* of Wan-p'ing 宛平. Being a native of the capital area and a collector of bronze and stone inscriptions, Yü shouldered the task of collecting data, while Liu was responsible for the writing. Actually there was a third man who also took an active part: Chou Sun 周損 (T. 遠害, cj 1639), likewise a native of Ma-ch'eng. Chou's task was to assemble poems pertaining to each site, which were then appended to the descriptions. Although he included some poems by earlier writers, the large majority were by Ming authors. Among them we find ten poems each by Liu and Yü. Liu also left a few other poems later published in anthologies.

The *Ti-ching ching-wu lüeh*, a book of 8 *chüan*, deals with some 130 topics grouped under five geographical headings. The original edition includes a preface by Liu dated the winter of 1635, and an explanatory introduction by Yü. Both acknowledge the contribution of their friend Chou. This work was apparently printed immediately after its completion in 1635 or 1636, and seemingly enjoyed great popularity from the start. It was quoted at length by Chu I-tsun (ECCP) in his compendium on Peking, *Jih-hsia chiu-wen*, but was not included in the *Ssu-k'u* Imperial Library. The editors of the *Ssu-k'u* catalogue did give it a notice, with some reserva-tions as to its value. Some of the criticisms appearing in the notice we may disagree with today, such as those concerning the stone drums in the Kuo-tzu chien, or the tomb of Li Chih (*q.v.*). In spite of this, however, Chi Yün (ECCP) must personally have been fond of it, for some seven years prior to his appointment as chief editor of the *Ssu-k'u*, while at home observing the mourning period for his father, he had edited and made an abridged edition of the work, even adding some notes of his own. The most important abridgment was the elimination of all the poems. Chi printed his edition in 1766; in 1957 this was reprinted in Shang-hai. In the mid-seventeenth century, when the *Shuo-fu hsü* (*see* T'ao Tsung-i) appeared, it included the calendar of festivals from *chüan* 2 bearing erroneously the title "Ti-ching ching-wu lüeh," and the section on the raising and fighting of crickets from *chüan* 3 under the title "Ts'u-chih chih" 促織志.

The work covers the most famous sights in Peking and its environs including the South Cathedral, the tomb of Matteo Ricci (*q.v.*), shrines and temples, gardens and natural scenery, as well as markets and mores. Besides all the information offered, the book is spiced with gossip, legend, and some fictitious anecdotes which contribute to its quality, and make it a materpiece of literature. A passage on the shrine of Yü Ch'ien (*q.v.*), in *chüan* 2, serves as an example—a moving story involving dreams. It relates that after the execution of Yü Ch'ien, his wife was banished to Shan-hai kuan 山海關. One night she dreamed that her husband asked her to lend him the luster of her eyes, so that he might appear to the emperor and present his grievance. She became blind the next morning. Meanwhile the emperor, Chu Ch'i-chen (*q.v.*), saw Yü Ch'ien's image in the flames of a palace fire. Then Yü's wife received a pardon. When Yü Ch'ien appeared again in her dream, he returned the borrowed luster, and so she regained her eyesight.

As a matter of fact, Yü Ch'ien's wife, née Tung 董, had died eleven years before. Out of respect for his deceased spouse, Yü had neither remarried nor had he ever taken a concubine. It is an interesting story, but without foundation.

Bibliography

24/4/79a, 138a; 40/68/24a, 76/10b; 64/辛20/3a, 25/1a; *Huang-chou-fu chih* 黃州府志 (1884), 19/23a; *Wu-hsien chih* 吳縣志 (1933), 2/18b; *Hu-pei t'ung-chih* 湖北通志 (1934), 3112, 3115, 3355, 3752; Ting Su-chang 丁宿章, *Hu-pei shih-cheng chuan-lüeh* 湖北詩徵傳略 (1883), 19/12b; Liao Yüan-tu 廖元度 (1640–1707), *Ch'u-feng pu* 楚風補 (1753), 31/17b; Wang Ch'ung-chien (ECCP), *Ch'ing-hsiang t'ang wen-chi*, 8/52a; L. T. Fang, "Ming Dreams," CHHP n. s. X:1 (June, 1973),55.

Lienche Tu Fang

LIU Yen 劉儼 (T. 宣化, H. 時雨), 1394-September 30, 1457, scholar-official, came from Chi-shui 吉水, Kiangsi. He is said to have been an unusual child, a diligent student, and to have had an upright character. Graduated as *chü-jen* in 1417, he placed first in the *chin-shih* examinations of 1442. His assignments throughout his official career were chiefly literary. In 1443, as a compiler in the Hanlin Academy, he helped to edit the *Wu-lun shu* 五倫書, 62 *ch.*, printed in 1448. An imperial undertaking concerning the five relationships of the Confucian tradition, it was initiated in the Hsüan-te period, possibly as a result of the Korean publication in 1434 of the elegantly illustrated book of exempla, *Samgang haengsil* 三綱行實. Liu was promoted to expositor-in-waiting in 1451, and in the following year he was concurrently made associate director of instruction; Emperor Chu Ch'i-yü (*q.v.*) had then succeeded in having his own son established as the heir apparent in place of Chu Chien-shen (*q.v.*). Liu next took part (1453) in editing the *Li-tai chün-chien* 歷代君鑑 (Mirror for rulers), 50 *ch.* (a copy of which is in the Princeton University Library), for which he was awarded silver and embroidered silk. In March of the next year he and P'eng Shih (*q.v.*) were ordered to tutor the new bachelors in the Hanlin Academy. Meanwhile he was one of those working under the editorship of Grand Secretary Ch'en Hsün (see Lü Yüan) on the *Huan-yü t'ung-chih* (Geography of the empire, which also gives in *chüan* 114–118 information on twenty-four states in Asia with which China had relations), 119 *ch.*, completed in June, 1456. That done he was promoted to vice minister of the Court of Imperial Sacrifices and concurrently expositor-in-waiting, and made associate editor for a continuation of the *T'ung-chien kang-mu* 通鑑綱目 of Chu Hsi (1130-1200). This was completed in 1457 in 27 *ch.*, under the title *Sung-Yüan* 宋元 *t'ung-chien kang-mu*. It was reedited in 1473 as the *Hsü Tzu-chih t'ung-chien kang-mu* by order of Chu Chien-shen.

Liu's last assignment got him into trouble. In September, 1456, he and Huang Chien 黃諫 (T. 廷臣, third in the *chin-shih* list of 1442) were ordered to conduct the *chü-jen* examinations in the capital. The grand secretaries, Ch'en Hsün and Wang Wen 王文 (see Yü Ch'ien), later accused them of setting questions which broke various taboos, of requiring answers to material which could be found only in the as yet unpublished *Huan-yü t'ung-chih* and the *Sung Yüan t'ung-chien kang-mu*, and of failing to pass properly qualified candidates—particularly, it would seem, their own sons, Ch'en Ying 瑛 and Wang Lun 綸. The emperor promptly appointed Grand Secretary Kao Ku 高穀 (T. 世用, 1391-February 2, 1460, Pth. 文義) to re-examine the essays and report back. His considered judgment was that Liu Yen and Huang Chien may have been careless, but that they were guilty of no corruption; also that Ch'en Hsün and Wang Wen, in making their accusation, were thinking only of their own selfish interests and should be punished. The emperor followed Kao's initial recommendation with respect to Liu and Huang, but refused to punish their accusers. Liu Yen, now restored to office, died a few months later, and received the posthumous name Wen-chieh 文介.

Bibliography

1/152/11b; 5/20/37; MSL (1963), Ying-tsung, 5208, 5646, 5652, 5699, 5708, 5710, 5714, 6057; KC (1958), 1624, 1715, 1892, 1926, 1973, 2007, 2011, 2055; SK (1930), 175/10b; *Chi-shui-hsien chih* (1873), 28/17a, 33/3a, 53/24b; *Ming-shih i-wen-chih, pu pien, fu pien* 藝文志補編附編 (Peking, 1959), 53, 66, 451, 549, 671; L. of C. *Catalogue of Rare Books*, 461; *Title Index to the Catalogue of the Gest Oriental Library* (Peking, 1941), 255; Ku Chieh-kang, "A Study of Literary Persecution during the Ming," tr. by L. Carrington Goodrich, HJAS, III (1938), 277; L. Carrington Goodrich, "Geographical Additions of the XIV and XV Centuries," MS, 15 (1956), 203; Chao-ying Fang, *The Asami Library* (1970), 188.

L. Carrington Goodrich and Angela Hsi

LIU Yung-ch'eng 劉永誠, 1391–1472, a eunuch who participated in several of the Ming military campaigns on the northern frontiers, was a native of Peking. The sources note that "he looked fierce and imposing," and was an excellent horseman and a highly proficient archer. These talents served him well during his half century of military action. He took part in three of the campaigns of Chu Ti (*q. v.*) against the Mongols and emerged as "supervisor of war chariots." During the reign of Chu Chan-chi (*q.v.*), he continued to serve in expeditions against rebellious northern peoples and provided valuable intelligence reports to the court. He achieved greatest renown during one of the campaigns against the Uriyangqad. The latter appeared to be in league with the Oirat chief Esen (*q.v.*), and the court, under strong pressure from the eunuchs, decided on a punitive expedition to reassert its authority over them. In 1444 four separate detachments, under the over-all leadership of Chu Yung (*see* Hsiang Chung), set forth. Each contingent, composed of ten thousand men, had not only a military commander but also a eunuch supervisor. Liu Yung-ch'eng ac-

companied the forces of Ma Liang 馬諒. Though the expedition was on the whole unsuccessful, Liu distinguished himself, and, according to one account, captured an unnumbered horde of Uriyangqad tribesmen. His fine performance led to an appointment as a general in Kansu in the late 1440s. He led at least two impressive expeditions against troublesome "barbarians" in the northwest before being recalled in the aftermath of the Oirat capture of the emperor in 1449. This decisive defeat caused a reduction in Chinese offensive campaigns, and Liu no longer led forays into alien territory. Instead he became the commander of the t'uan-ying 團營 (integrated divisions), which trained military forces. Perhaps because he missed combat action, he appeared unhappy in his new position and repeatedly sought to retire. Early in the reign of Chu Chien-shen (*q.v.*), the court granted his request and gave him a home, salary, and various goods. He rejected these gifts and lived in a hut simply and frugally "like an old Buddhist monk." He died in 1472, after having had the satisfaction of seeing his nephew, Liu Chü 聚 (d. April 24. 1474), whom he had adopted, become earl of Ning-chin 寧晉 in 1471.

In May, 1472, Liu Chü requested the throne to confer a title of nobility and a posthumous name on his deceased uncle, and to give a name to his temple. The ministry of Rites advised the emperor to reject the title and name for lack of a precedent, but to grant an appellation to the temple, citing as example the Ching-chung 旌忠 temple in honor of the eunuch, Wang Chen (*q.v.*). The emperor, after assigning the characters Pao-kung 褒功 (in appreciation of military merits) to Liu's temple, insisted that the grand secretaries suggest a posthumous name and a noble title. This time P'eng Shih (*q.v.*) and other grand secretaries refused to comply and the matter was dropped.

The court granted Liu Chü the rank of nobility for his military exploits on the northwestern frontier, and in 1473 this was made hereditary. When he died he was given the higher title of marquis of Ning-chin and the posthumous name Wei-yung 威勇 (martial and brave).

Bibliography

1/107/29a, 304/12b; 3/283/4b; 61/158/4a; MSL (1964), Hsien-tsung, 1725, 2005, 2262; W. Franke, "Addenda and Corrigenda to Pokotilov's *History of the Eastern Mongols During the Ming Dynasty from 1368 to 1634*," *Studia Serica*, ser. A, no. 3 (1949), pt. 2, 37.

Morris Rossabi

LO Ch'in-shun 羅欽順 (T. 允升, H. 整菴), December 8, 1465-May 13, 1547, scholar and official, was a native of T'ai-ho 泰和, Kiangsi. In 1492 he won first place in the provincial examination. One year later, he placed third in the metropolitan examination, and was appointed compiler in the Hanlin Academy. So enwrapped in study did he become that he shunned all society. In 1502 he was made director of studies of the National University in Nanking. From 1503 to late in 1504 he and the chancellor Chang Mou (*q.v*) improved the standards in the university. At this time he began to concern himself exclusively with the Four Books, the Five Classics, and the writings of the Sung philosophers. After a lengthy and total immersion in this literature he said that the two Ch'eng brothers (Ch'eng Hao, 1032–85, and Ch'eng I, 1033–1107), Chang Tsai (1020–77), and Chu Hsi (1130–1200) had all studied Buddhism and investigated its essence, but when they came to understand Confucianism thoroughly, the errors of Buddhism in general (and particularly those of the influential Ch'an 禪 sect) became so apparent that they not only veered away from Buddhism but also made every effort to refute it. In another place he remarked that Chu Hsi's criticism of Lu Chiu-yüan (1139–92) was well grounded.

During the first five years of the reign of Emperor Chu Hou-chao (*q.v.*), the eunuch Liu Chin (*q.v.*) tried to enforce the regulations. When Lo accompanied his aged father home later in 1504, he requested extension of his leave. This was denied as against the rules, but he remained home. For this he was deprived of both office and rank in 1508. Two years later, after the eunuch was executed, Lo was restored to his previous post. In 1511 he was promoted to be vice minister of the Court of Imperial Sacrifices in Nanking. In 1515 he received another promotion, being made junior vice minister of Personnel in Nanking, in which capacity he served four years before rising to the position of senior vice minister. Later (1521) he was transferred to the same post in Peking and distinguished himself by his scrupulous honesty and discrimination; for example, if any person were to come asking for promotion on the strength of a letter from a eunuch he would be handed over to the ministry of Justice for punishment. In this same year (November 29), following the death of the emperor, Lo became one of the editors of the *Wu-tsung shih-lu*, the Veritable Records of the years 1505–21. Shortly after his elevation to be minister of Personnel in Nanking (May 14, 1522), he requested permission to retire to be with his aged father. At the latter's death in May, 1523, he went into mourning and although called back in 1527, first to the post of minister of Rites and later to his former post of minister of Personnel, he declined so persistently that his request for retirement was finally granted (1527). During his last twenty years he lived quietly at home and died at the age of eighty-two. He was posthumously given the title of grand guardian of the heir apparent and the name Wen-chuang 文莊. It is interesting to note that his spirit-way inscription was written by Yen Sung (*q.v.*). In 1724 his tablet was placed in the Temple of Confucius.

Lo was a man of admirable discipline.

Every morning he arose early and went to his library in an old hall where, after receiving the greetings of his family and disciples, he began to study. He was also abstemious. The complete lack of frivolity in his character is demonstrated by the fact that he built no garden houses or pavilions in his residence and that he provided no such entertainment as music and dancing when he gave a dinner party. All his family members were modest and thoughtful in their treatment of each other. In praising Lo's personality Lin Hsi-yüan (*q.v.*) wrote, "From his first service in the Hanlin Academy to the post of minister, Lo presents himself, both publicly and privately, as pure as gold and as fine as jade; indeed there is nothing in his conduct which may be criticized."

Lo's works include the *K'un-chih chi* 困知記, 6 *ch.*, and miscellaneous writings under the title *Cheng-an ts'un-kao* 整菴存稿, 20 *ch.* These were first printed about 1552 (National Peiping Library copy on microfilm). The *K'un-chih chi* was later expanded to 8 *chüan*, and together with the *ts'un-kao* was reprinted 1620–23 (copy in Library of Congress). There is also a *Cheng-i-t'ang ch'üan-shu* 正誼堂全書 edition of 1710. Both were copied into the Imperial Library seventy years later. The *K'un-chih chi*, as Lo himself repeatedly stated, is the crystalization of his ideas after thorough immersion in Confucianism for more than twenty years. It contains his philosophical thoughts and, more significantly, reflects his spirited defense of the Confucian orthodoxy then under the threat of the Lu-Wang school and Buddhism (*see* Wang Shou-jen). Nine days before his death he wrote his own epitaph in which he summarized his whole life as having been dedicated to the investigation of the principle of endowed nature, and this had led to the writing of his important work. He often expressed regrets that in his early life he had studied merely for the civil examinations and promotion. Not until the age of forty did he begin to appreciate the profundity and comprehensiveness of Confucian teaching. After more than a score of years of laborious study and thinking did he become convinced in the belief that "mind" and "nature" were distinct. Since "mind" is distinct from "nature," it follows that the statements "The mind is principle" of the Lu-Wang school and "The nature is principle" of the Ch'eng-Chu school likewise differ.

As a scholar Lo was noted for his theory of the inseparability of "li" (理) and "ch'i" (氣) which offers the solution of Chu Hsi's dualism. He is remembered too for his debate with Wang Shou-jen and his remarkable rebuttal of Buddhist claims. The debate between Lo and Wang began with the latter's publication in 1515 of the *Chu-tzu wan-nien ting-lun*. To bolster his position, Wang had written this treatise in which he maintained that Chu Hsi, though in early life differing from Lu Chiu-yüan, had in his later years regretted his error and modified his views to accord with those of Lu. When this appeared, it aroused much discussion among the followers of the Ch'eng-Chu school, some of whom wrote rebuttals to prove that Chu and Lu's teachings were really not the same. In his first letter to Wang dated 1520 Lo concerned himself with the interpretation of the "investigation of things" and "extension of knowledge." He went back to the *Ta-hsüeh* where the expressions "investigation of things" and "extension of knowledge" first appeared and showed that Wang's understanding of the *Ta-hsüeh* was incorrect. His second letter written in 1528 contained discussions of some fundamental philosophical problems. He disagreed with Wang in his definition of the "investigation of things." Unfortunately, Wang died before Lo sent the second letter.

Lo Ch'in-shun wrote at length about Buddhism. He quoted from the sūtras and attempted to refute them. Kao P'an-lung (*q.v.*) said that there had been no one since the T'ang (618–906) so brilliant and comprehensive as Lo in this field.

Bibliography

1/282/15b; 3/264/4a; 5/25/17a; 83/47/1a; MSL (1965), Shih-tsung, 0285, 0462, 5980; KC (19 58), 2984; SK (1930), 93/4a, 171/6b; Lo Ch'in-shun, *K'un-chih chi*; id., *Lo Cheng-an hsien-sheng* 先生 *ts'un-kao*, in *Cheng-i-t'ang ch'üan-shu*; Wang Shou-jen, *Chu-tzu wan-nien ting-lun* in *Yang-ming ch'üan-shu*, Vol. 3; Jung Chao-tsu 容肇祖, *Ming-tai ssu-hsiang shih* 明代思想史 (Shanghai, 1941), 183; Sung P'ei-wei 宋佩韋, *Wang Shou-jen yü Ming li-hsüeh* 王守仁與明理學 (Shanghai, 1933), 86; Ch'ien Mu (BDRC), *Sung-Ming li-hsüeh kai-shu* 宋明理學概述 (Taipei, 1953), 216; Fung Yu-lan, tr. by Derk Bodde, *A History of Chinese Philosophy*, Vol. 2 (Princeton, 1953), 620; Carsun Chang, *The Development of Neo-Confucianism*, Vol. 2, New York, 1963; Wang Yang-ming, *Instructions for Practical Living and Other Neo-Confucian Writings*, tr. by Wing-tsit Chan (New York, 1963), 157; O. Franke, "Li Tschi—Ein Beitrag zur Geschichte der chinesichen Geisteskämpfe im 16 jahrhundert," Abhandlungen der Preussischen Akademie der Wissenschaften, No. 10, 1937.

Tu Ching-i

LO Fu-jen 羅復仁 (d. 1371), official, was born in Chi-shui 吉水, Kiangsi. Noted for his knowledge of astronomy and astrology, he was called to service by the rebel leader, Ch'en Yu-liang (*q.v.*), and appointed a Hanlin compiler. He was soon disillusioned with Ch'en and, when in 1362, the army of another rebel leader, Chu Yüan-chang, reached Kiukiang, he defected to Chu, who kept him as a personal adviser. The following year he accompanied Chu to Poyang Lake and was present at the naval battle at which Ch'en went down to defeat. It fell to Lo to exhort the people of Kiangsi to surrender to Chu.

In 1364 Chu proclaimed himself prince of Wu and led an army to Wuchang, then held by Ch'en Yu-liang's son, Ch'en Li (*see* Ch'en Yu-liang). Lo went along as consultant in the Secretariat. Because of his former service under Ch'en Yu-liang, he was ordered to use his arts of persuasion to bring about Ch'en Li's surrender. After obtaining Chu's promise that he would not harm Ch'en Li, Lo went to the latter's headquarters and succeeded in securing his capitulation.

Lo was then appointed instructor in the National University. Well on in years, he was granted the use of a wheeled vehicle. Even when appearing before the prince, he was allowed to keep his seat. In the spring of 1366, he was sent to Shansi, carrying a message to the Yüan general Kökö Temür (*q.v.*), presumably to prevail upon him to surrender also. The sources are not clear about the purpose, but mention that previous emissaries had been detained by the general. Lo, however, managed to return to Chu's headquarters.

In the first year of Hung-wu (1368), he was promoted to the position of compiler of the Hanlin Academy. He was dispatched as envoy to Annam in 1369, with instructions to order the king to stop encroaching upon the frontier of Champa. The king acquiesced, at the same time recognizing the suzerainty of China. When Lo was about to return home, he was offered gold, cotton goods, and other local products, but he declined them all.

In 1370, when the Secretariat, Hung-wen kuan 弘文館, was established, Lo and Liu Chi (*q.v.*) were both appointed chancellors. As such they were permitted to speak critically to the emperor about governmental matters. Lo was something of a rustic, and when he spoke in his native dialect it delighted Chu as being natural and unaffected. The latter particularly enjoyed Lo's outspokenness, calling him "honest Lo." Once the emperor visited his home, which was situated in a rather forlorn and unpopulated area. As the emperor approached without warning, he caught Lo at work painting the walls. Lo called excitedly to his wife to fetch a bench for the emperor. Taking note of his situation, the emperor, a short time later, provided him with a residence inside the capital.

At Lo's retirement, the emperor gave him a long gown made of plain cloth. On the lapel of the gown was a poem in which the emperor praised him for his contributions. His retirement was shortly interrupted when he was asked to return to serve the court. After three months' service, he retired again. His death was reported to the throne on May 29, 1371.

One of his grandsons, Lo Ju-ching (*see* Li Shih-mien), while serving as an expositor in 1425, was imprisoned for offensively criticizing the emperor, Chu Kaochih (*q.v.*). Two days later the emperor died and Lo was then released and appointed a censor. Later he rose to be a vice minister of Works, served twice as envoy to Annam (1428), and wrote a book entitled *Yin-an chi* 寅菴集 (in 8 *chüan*) which receives a notice in the *Ssu-k'u* catalogue.

Bibliography

1/137/17a; 3/128/3a; 5/20/68a; 16/5/13b; 32/63/4b; 61/116/12b; MSL (1963), T'ai-tsu, 1217; *Chi-shui-hsien chih* (1875), 32/19a; SK (1930), 175/6a.

David B. Chan

LO Ju-fang 羅汝芳 (T. 惟德, H. 近谿), June 13, 1515-October 21, 1588, thinker and official, was a native of Nan-ch'eng 南城, Kiangsi. He received his elementary education from his mother. At an early age he began to show an interest in the quest for sagehood. The words of Hsüeh Hsüan (*q. v.*) in the *Tu-shu lu*, regarding the recovery of one's original purity of mind and heart, fired him with enthusiasm. In 1532 he shut himself up in a Buddhist monastery in order the better to pursue this goal. There he meditated daily, facing a mirror in front of which he had also put a basin of clear water. The aim of the exercise was to render his heart as pure and undefiled as the mirror and the water, capable of reflecting all things. Instead of bringing him near this goal, however, the practice induced in him a strange sickness of heart. Disturbed by this development, Lo's father taught

him to read the *Ch'uan-hsi lu* of Wang Shou-jen (*q. v.*). The malady gradually subsided, but did not completely disappear. In 1536 Lo was admitted to the local school to prepare for the civil examinations. Four years later, at the age of twenty-five, on a visit to Nanchang, a sign promising cures for "sicknesses of the heart" led him into the monastery where Yen Chün (*see* Ho Hsin-yin), a disciple of Wang Ken (*q. v.*), was giving lectures. Much impressed, Lo stayed behind to ask advice of Yen. After hearing about Lo's efforts to attain an unperturbed state of mind and heart with regard to questions of life and death, success and failure, Yen explained that Lo had been aiming, not at the personal realization of jen 仁 (human-heartedness), but at the control of the passions. He then instructed the younger man to cultivate a more positive attitude, based on Mencius' teaching of the presence of the four beginnings of virtue in man—of human-heartedness, justice, propriety, and wisdom (cf. Legge, *Chinese Classics*, II, 278). He said that one ought to develop these virtues to the fullest rather than work against one's natural tendencies. Lo became formally Yen's disciple, spending some time with him, and learning as much as possible. Yen predicted then that Lo would soon be cured of his sickness, make progress in learning, and succeed in the examinations.

In 1543 Lo Ju-fang acquired the *chü-jen*, and the following year proceeded to the capital for the *chin-shih* examinations, but decided to return home without taking the final palace tests, because (so say some sources) his father was ill, or (as other sources put it) Lo himself was ill or did not consider himself sufficiently mature to undertake any official responsibility. He then built (1545) a small house, the Ts'ung-ku shan-fang 從姑山房, where he pursued his studies, and in the same years traveled about from time to time in search of teachers and friends. It was during this period of continued quest for wisdom that he also requested instruction in the *I Ching* (Book of Changes) of his former student, Hu Tsung-cheng 胡宗正 (H. 清虛). After three months of intense study, Lo mastered Hu's interpretations, but he remained preoccupied with the exact meaning of the "investigation of things" of the *Ta-hsüeh* (Great Learning), and searched through many commentaries for an answer to this problem. After about three years it suddenly dawned on him one night that the message lay in an integrated view of the entire text, taken as a presentation of the method of cultivation which should be followed in one's search for sagehood. Rushing to his father's bed in the middle of the night, he quickly communicated this discovery, and obtained approval for this interpretation, after answering his father's question regarding the diverse roles of the classical text itself and of the commentaries.

Early in 1553, on his way to the capital for the palace examinations, Lo passed through Lin-ch'ing 臨清, Shantung, and fell suddenly ill. While resting on a couch, he dreamed of an old man telling him that the energy he had put into his study and into self-cultivation had brought upon him a chronic sickness of the heart, which might have disastrous effects on his health in general. Lo awoke astonished and perspiring, and from then on slowed down his mental activity. Passing the palace examinations in the spring, he received an appointment the same year as district magistrate of T'ai-hu 太湖 (Anhwei), from which post he was promoted to secretary of a bureau in the ministry of Justice.

After a period of mourning for his father, Lo was named (1562) prefect of Ning-kuo 寧國 (Anhwei), where he concentrated his efforts (until 1565) on the improvement of education, giving instructions also to the prison inmates. On a visit to the capital to render account of his official duties, he had occasion to visit Grand Secretary Hsü Chieh (*q. v.*),

who was impressed with his character and talents. At a meeting organized in a Taoist temple in Peking, the Ling-chi kung 靈濟宮, Lo gave a moving speech in the presence of a large audience of scholars and officials. Shortly after his return south, however, news reached him of Yen Chün's imprisonment at the capital. Lo sold his land, borrowed money from friends, and went north with his two sons and a disciple, and was able to obtain a commutation of the death penalty to one of exile. Later on, he was to take Yen into his own home and wait on him as a son would his own father, even though Yen's idiosyncrasies, including the habit of giving away Lo's money, frequently caused embarrassment in the family circle. In 1573, on completion of the mourning for his mother, who died in 1569, Lo went back to the capital where he saw Chang Chü-cheng (*q. v.*), then in power. It was a much less happy meeting than that with Hsü Chieh. He then served as prefect of Tung-ch'ang 東昌, Shantung, where he took as much pains to fulfill his duties as he had earlier in Ning-kuo. The following year he was transferred to Yunnan as vice commissioner in charge of the military farms. He improved the irrigation facilities of the region, and continued his instruction of disciples. On the occasion of a Burmese invasion, Lo arranged to cut off the supply routes of the invaders, and could have annihilated them had it not been for the hesitation of the governor, Wang Ning 王凝 (T. 道南, cs 1556), who refused to send reinforcements. Lo later became surveillance vice commissioner of Yunnan, and was sent to the capital on a gift-bearing mission. There again he gave lectures in a Buddhist monastery, the Kuang-hui ssu 廣慧寺. The displeasure of Chang Chü-cheng, however, led to his impeachment and resignation. Lo retired to his native place, but often traveled about in the Yangtze valley and in Fukien and Kwangtung. In September, 1588, he fell suddenly ill, but refused to cease teaching. On October 19 he dressed himself in ceremonial hat and robes, paid reverence to Heaven, Earth, and his ancestors, and sat up in the hall, surrounded by his disciples. In their presence he wrote what might be termed a spiritual testament, explaining how the Tao pervades the universe, uniting each person to all and the present to the past, and how the Tao is to be found, not by examining words and propositions, but by freeing the heart of all its preoccupations. The following day, the first of the ninth moon (October 20), he washed himself, and sat up again. Then he asked his grandchildren to offer wine to all present. After this act of courtesy, he bade farewell to his family and disciples. With much anguish, they begged him to remain with them one more day. He agreed. The next day, helped by his grandchildren, Lo sat up straight again and died serenely in that position. He was then seventy-three years of age.

Lo had two sons, Lo Hsüan 軒 and Lo Lu 輅, eight grandchildren, and ten great-grandchildren. Two of his grandsons, Lo Huai-tsu 懷祖 and Lo Huai-chih 懷智, showed exceptional talent. Lo was well acquainted with the thinkers and scholars of his time. Wang Chi (*q. v.*) thought highly of him. Of his numerous disciples, several were celebrated for their contributions to scholarship and thought. These include Tsou Yüan-piao, Chou Ju-teng (*qq.v.*) and T'ang Hsien-tsu (ECCP). They gave him the private canonization of Ming-te 明德.

Lo Ju-fang had an unusual spiritual evolution, moving from his earlier practice of earnest contemplation and assiduous study, as recommended by the followers of the school of Ch'eng I (1033–1107) and Chu Hsi (1130–1200), especially by Hsüeh Hsüan, to the freer, more spontaneous cultivation of the mind and heart, as encouraged by the T'ai-chou followers of Wang Shou-jen (*see* Wang Ken). He can therefore be said to have known by personal experience the value of each of these ways to sagehood. Lo

had been accused of being a Taoist and Ch'an Buddhist. But Huang Tsung-hsi (ECCP) pointed out Lo's repudiation, in later life, of Buddhist and Taoist doctrines and practices, to the point of forbidding his grandson to read Buddhist literature. The same historian of thought also compared Lo to Wang Chi, saying that while Wang was better as writer than as lecturer, Lo was superior as lecturer, able to impart understanding and enthusiasm to those least acquainted with learning. While Yen Chün and his disciple, Ho Hsin-yin, had attracted much attention to the T'ai-chou branch of the school of Wang Yang-ming by their unconventional behavior and relative lack of learning, Lo Ju-fang stood out as a serious and disciplined scholar, whose main eccentricity was his dogged determination to seek and attain sagehood.

Lo Ju-fang laid much emphasis on the understanding of the Four Books, and he considered that the Doctrine of the Mean should be studied before the Great Learning. As a thinker of the Wang Yang-ming school, Lo was much imbued with the importance of liang-chih, the capacity for moral discernment and development, and he emphasized in particular its innate character. For this reason, he frequently discoursed on the "heart of the infant" (Ch'ih-tzu chih hsin 赤子之心; cf. Legge, *Chinese Classics*, II, 198) which he described as being full of "the principle of Heaven" (T'ien-li 天理). The sage, therefore, is the man who has allowed this child's heart in himself to develop to the fullest his love for others (jen) which enables him to become one with all things. Lo had a high regard for the Sacred Instructions of Emperor Chu Yüan-chang, and made use of these especially in his efforts to extend moral education among the masses, through lectures given during community meetings.

Lo Ju-fang's writings have been published in many forms. The editors of the *Ssu-k'u* catalogue list the *Chin-hsi-tzu wen-chi* 近溪子文集, *5 ch.*, which his great-grandson, Lo Wan-hsien 萬先, published. There are also the *Chin-hsi-tzu chi*, 6 *ch.*, compiled by his disciple Yang Ch'i-yüan (*q. v.*) and published in 1582, the *Hui-yü hsü-lu* 會語續錄, 2 *ch.*, also compiled by Yang, the *Chin-hsi-tzu Ming-tao lu* 明道錄, 8 *ch.*, compiled by his disciple Tu Ying-k'uei 杜應奎, and the *Hsü-chiang* 盱江 *Lo Chin-hsi hsien-sheng ch'üan-chi* 全集, 10 *ch.*, comprising his recorded dialogues, poetry, and biographical accounts written by friends and disciples, published in 1618. Many of these are to be found in various Japanese libraries, especially the Naikaku Bunko. A microfilm copy of the first, the *Chin-hsi-tzu chi*, is also available. A copy of the last on the list, the *ch'üan-chi*, is in the National Central Library, Taipei. The Naikaku Bunko has another edition in 13 *chüan*, the last three being Lo's instructions on filial piety, human-heartedness, the community compact (hsiang-yüeh 鄉約), and other essential sayings (yü-yao 語要). Lo's other philosophical works include the *Hsiao-ching tsung-chih* 孝經宗旨, which gives the general meaning of the Classic in a question-answer style, the *I-kuan pien* 一貫編, 5 *ch.*, which purports to interpret the central message of the Five Classics and the Four Books. Lo also edited the essay entitled *Shih-jen p'ien* 識仁編 by Ch'eng Hao (1032–85), although this edition may not be extant. His non-philosophical works include the *Ming t'ung-pao i* 明通寶義, 1 *ch.*, and the *Kuang* 廣 *t'ung-pao*, 1 *ch.*, which treat the history of monetary exchange. These works too may no longer be extant. The *Ch'ien-ch'ing-t'ang shu-mu* (*see* Huang Yü-chi, ECCP) also lists the titles of *Chin-hsi chi-yü* 集語, 12 *ch.*, *Wen-ch'iu cheng-tu* 問求正牘, 2 *ch.*, and the *Pa-chiu ping-t'a hsin-tsung* 八九病榻心宗, 2 *ch.*

Bibliography

1/283/14a; 3/185/19b; 4/10/4b; 32/61/23a; 42/77/1a; 61/114/22b; 63/22/41a; 83/34/1a; *KC* (1958), 4824; *Ch'ien-ch'ing-t'ang shu-mu*, 2/13a; Hsüeh Hsüan, *Tu-shu lu* with *Hsü-lu* 續錄 (1827 ed.), 1/23a; *id.*, *Wen-ch'ing kung Hsüeh hsien-sheng wen-chi* 文清公薛先生文集 (1614); *Yunnan t'ung-chih* (1894), 121/8b, 29b, 135/29b; *Nan-ch'eng-hsien chih* (1872), 8A/9a; *T'ai-hu-hsien chih* (1922), 15/8a, 16/2a; *Ning-kuo-fu chih* (1919), 3/15a, 5/26b, 30b; *Tung-ch'ang-fu chih* (1808), 15/17a, 20/40b; *Chia-ch'ing ch'ung-hsin i-t'ung chih* 嘉慶重修一統志 (SPTK ed.), 321/9b; SK (1930), 32/5a, 84/3a, 124/10b, 125/1a, 10b, 178/4b; Lo Ju-fang, *Chin-hsi-tzu chi* (NLP microfilm) no. 869; *id.*, *Hsiao-ching t'ung chih*, TsSCCed.; *id.*, *Hsü-chiang Lo Chin-hsi hsien-sheng ch'üan-chi* (1618), 10 *ch.*; Wang Chi, *Wang Lung-hsi ch'üan-chi* (1822 ed., 1970, Taipei reprint), 11/26a, 14/26b, 30a; Chou Ju-teng, *Sheng-hsüeh tsung-chuan* (Ming ed.), 18/9; Tsou Yüan-piao, "Chin-hsi Lo hsien-sheng mu-pei 墓碑," *Huang Ming wen-hai* (microfilm), 14/1/6, 18/6/5; Okada Takehiko, *Ōyōmeito Minamatsu no jugaku* (Tokyo, 1970), 192.

Julia Ching

LO Kuan-chung 羅貫中, known also as Lo Pen 本 (T. Kuan-chung), Lo Kuan (T. Kuan-chung), or Lo Tao 道-pen (T. Kuan-chung, H. 名卿), was an author of popular fiction, a playwright, and also (according to some later sources) a publisher. He lived during the late Yüan and early Ming period; in all events he was alive during the second half of the 14th century and probably died after 1370. He was either a native of Taiyuan, or (according to some later sources) of Ch'ien-t'ang 錢塘 (Hangchow). It is likely that he was born in the first city but spent his later years in the latter. Little is known of him. Later scholars and writers have provided confusing and contradictory information. He is even described as a man of the Southern Sung by at least one source, the reliability of which has been questioned. His authorship of part or all of the several historical romances and "variety plays" (tsa-chü 雜劇) that have been attributed to him by different accounts is open to doubt. Modern scholars, especially Yen Tun-i 嚴敦易, have cast considerable doubt on Lo's identity as established by later records and on the information about him revealed in these sources and on the title pages of the works attributed to him. According to the only surviving contemporary notice of him found in the *Lu kuei pu hsü-pien* 錄鬼簿續編, the preface of which is dated 1422, Lo was an older contemporary of Chia Chung-ming (*see* Meng Ch'eng-shun), probably the author of the book. According to Chia, Lo, whom he treats as a poet and playwright rather than as a writer of historical romances, was styled Hu-hai san-jen 湖海散人 (Wanderer on lakes and seas). Chia recounts that he had not seen Lo since 1364, over sixty years earlier. As implied in Chia's account, Lo had and cared for few friends. He was probably a very lonely and peculiar man. He seems to have led a wandering life in his last few years. As suggested by Roy Andrew Miller, he was probably a disappointed and rejected scholar-official who turned to assembling works of historical romance due to his complete disillusionment with the current situation. According to Wang Ch'i (*q.v.*) in his *Pai-shih hui-pien*, written a century and a half later, Lo was involved in a movement against Mongol rule toward the end of the Yüan dynasty; after his leader was finally defeated, Lo had to be content with writing historical romances to express his revolutionary sentiments. The reliability of this information is questionable, and the rest has no solid evidence to support it. Lo received little attention both during his lifetime and after his death; he is barely mentioned in Ming literature. Modern scholars have attempted to speculate on his life primarily on the basis of Chia Chung-ming's account.

Following are the works attributed in whole or in part to Lo: the *San-kuo-chih yen-i* 三國志演義 (The Romance of the Three Kingdoms), the *Shui-hu chuan* 水滸傳 (The Water Margin), the *Ta T'ang Ch'in-wang tz'u-hua* 大唐秦王詞話 (The tz'u-hua on the prince of Ch'in of the Great T'ang), the *Sung T'ai-tsu lung-hu feng-yün hui* 宋太祖龍虎風雲會 (The Romance of heroic encounters in the time of Sung T'ai-tsu), the *Sui-T'ang liang-ch'ao chih-chuan* 隋唐兩朝志傳 (The Romance of the two dynasties, Sui and T'ang), the

Ts'an T'ang Wu-tai-shih yen-i chuan 殘唐五代史演義傳 (The Romance of the Declining T'ang and the Five Dynasties), and the *San Sui p'ing-yao chuan* 三遂平妖傳 (The Three Sui quell the demons' revolt).

Since some of the works attributed to Lo are now lost and the several that have survived have been greatly revised by later writers, it is impossible to extract anything significant about him from these works. The sheer bulk and mutual divergencies of style, moreover, are difficult to reconcile with a single author. All that can be said is that they reflect a life-long concern with and interest in history, since they are all more or less historical plays and romances.

Of all the tales traceable to the authorship of Lo Kuan-chung, scholars, such as C. T. Hsia, are generally agreed that the *San-kuo-chih yen-i* bears the closest resemblance to what must have been his original version. In addition, of all the works attributed to him in whole or in part, only this can be reasonably accepted as his original compilation, for the name of Lo Kuan-chung appears not only in the earliest surviving edition but also in practically all subsequent ones. Later bibliographical sources too almost unanimously attribute the text of the work to him with no verifiable evidence existing to the contrary.

Of the other books that have been traced wholly or partially to Lo, only the *San Sui p'ing-yao chuan* and the *Ts'an T'ang Wu-tai-shih yen-i chuan* have been more widely accepted as his original compilations. In recent years, however, scholars, notably Patrick Hanan and Liu Ts'un-yan, have cast serious doubt on both attributions, that of the *Shui-hu chuan* to Lo being even more questionable.

The role which Lo has played in the creation and composition of the *San-kuo-chih yen-i* is open to debate. Most scholars are agreed that Lo should be regarded as the original author. It should be pointed out, however, that it probably reached its present form through many hands and a slow process of evolution, despite the fact that it reflects much less popular, folk, oral taste and quality than other works of the yen-i type. Also, it reveals in many respects a conscious departure from the tradition of the storytellers. It is rather unfair to attribute the entire work to a single author. It is most likely that Lo compiled the work from a variety of sources, oral as well as literary. Capitalizing on the old San-kuo story cycle, he succeeded in injecting new personality into the old cycle by refining the narration and by reducing the falsification of authentic history. He did add new elements to the cycle by creating some fictional episodes and historical characters in accordance with historical reality without contradicting history to any serious extent and by, to a lesser extent, fictionalizing and dramatizing historical events. Though the work should be regarded as mostly his own compilation, his primary role in its creation and composition was more likely that of editor, redactor, compiler, or recreator rather than original author.

Certain San-kuo figures and events had been romanticized by poets, story tellers, and playwrights long before the earliest edition of the *San-kuo-chih yen-i* appeared. Since the publication of its earliest surviving version in 1522, numerous editions have been printed. It has become the most popular historical romance in China, Korea, and Japan, and established for the succeeding generations the yen-i type of historical fiction, which has become something unique in world literature. In the late 19th century European language translations of selected chapters from the work began to appear. The first full English translation was completed by C. H. Brewitt-Taylor in 1925, and this was followed by Franz Kuhn's German translation in 1953, V. A. Panasiuk's Russian version in 1954, and Nghiêm Toan's and Louis Ricaud's 30-chapter French translation in 1960–63. As for the *Shui-hu chuan*, see the biography of Shih Nai-an.

Bibliography

Hsieh Wu-liang 謝无量, *Lo Kuan-chung yü Ma chih-yüan* 與馬致遠 (Shanghai, 1930); Li Ch'entung 李辰冬, *San-kuo Shui-hu yü Hsi-yu* 與西遊 (Chungking, 1945); *San-kuo yen-i ts'an-k'ao tzuliao* 參考資料 (Peking, 1954); Yen Tun-i, *Shui-hu chuan te yen-chiu* 的研究 (Peking, 1957), 225; C. H. Brewitt-Taylor (tr.), *Romance of the Three Kingdoms* (with an introduction [in 2d ed.] by Roy Andrew Miller), 2 vols. (Shanghai, 1925; Rutland, Vt., 1959); Patrick Hanan, "The Composition of the *P'ing yao chuan,*" HJAS (1971), 201; C. T. Hsia, *The Classic Chinese Novel* (New York, 1968), 34; id., "The Military Romance: A Genre of Chinese Fiction" (ms., 1971); Franz Kuhn (tr.), *Die Schwurbrüder vom Pfirsichgarten. Roman aus dem alten China*, 2 vols. (Berlin, 1953); Tien-yi Li, *Chinese Fiction* (New Haven, 1968), 133; Liu Ts'un-yan, "On the authenticity of Lo Kuan-chung's historical romances" (ms., 1970); Lu Hsün, *A Brief History of Chinese Fiction*, tr. by Yang Hsien-yi and Gladys Yang (Peking, 1959), 166, 183; Nghiêm Toan and Louis Ricaud (tr.), *Les Trois Royaumes*, 2 vols. (Saigon, 1960); V.A. Panasiuk (tr.), *Troetsarstvie* (Moscow, 1954); B. L. Riftin, *Istoricheskaia epopeia i folklornaia traditsiia Kitae* (Moscow, 1970).

Winston L. Y. Yang

LO Hung-hsien 羅洪先 (T. 達夫, H. 念菴, 青蓮居士, Pth. 文恭), 1504-64, has long been known as a thinker of the Wang Yangming school. His achievements in geography, however, have received less attention. Lo was born into a scholar-official family in Chi-shui 吉水, Kiangsi. His father, Lo Hsün 循 (T. 遵道, H. 霍泉, cs 1499, 1464-1533), was regarded as a competent official of his day. Lo Hsün paid much attention to his son's education and shared in his instruction. At the age of thirteen, Lo Hung-hsien told his father that he would like to further his studies under Wang Shou-jen (*q.v.*). His request, however, was not approved; instead Li Chung 李中 (T. 子庸, Pth. 莊介, cs 1514, 1479-1542), a local scholar, became his tutor. While with the latter, Lo used his leisure time to study Wang's *Ch'uan-hsi lu*, and was deeply affected by it.

Lo's career started promisingly. After achieving the *chü-jen* in 1525 he was selected as optimus in the *chin-shih* examination of 1529, and received the appointment of compiler in the Hanlin Academy. Soon afterwards, however, he left for home because of his father's illness, and there he remained sharing in the latter's care. Later he returned to Peking, but had to go home again in 1533 because of his father's death. Then his mother died (1535). He did not resume official life until 1539 when he received an appointment as assistant secretary in the supervisorate of instruction.

At that time the emperor, Chu Houts'ung (*q.v.*), had long absented himself from daily audiences. Lo Hung-hsien, T'ang Shun-chih (*q.v.*), and Chao Shih-ch'un (*see* Wang Shen-chung), as a consequence, submitted separate memorials in which they suggested that, since the emperor was unable to attend because of illness, it would be appropriate for the heir apparent to be present at the New Year's day audience. The emperor, however, took affront at their proposals, for they seemed to hint that his recovery was out of the question. Consequently all three were dismissed and their names removed from the civil service register in 1541.

As noted, Lo had early become an admirer of Wang Shou-jen. His intensive study of neo-Confucianism during the years of mourning further confirmed him in his desire to devote himself to scholarship. After his dismissal he studied and taught at home. He moved to the countryside in 1546 and lived at Shih-lien grotto 石蓮洞 where he established a school.

Early in its life the neo-Confucian movement appeared threatened by the popularity of Buddhism and Taoism. While working strenuously to establish a new philosophy, the Confucians also tried to distinguish themselves from the Buddhists and the Taoists. By the end of the 15th and 16th centuries, however, the threat no longer seemed a problem. But Lo saw things differently; he thought it still an important issue and made it his duty to promote the neo-Confucian move-

ment with all his mind and strength. He determined to distinguish himself as a thinker of the Wang Yang-ming school and to help the state by making contributions to the geographical knowledge of his time. As early as the Northern Sung (960-1126), the Confucians had already pointed out that the main difference among the Buddhists, Taoists, and themselves lay in their varying attitudes toward society. The Buddhists and Taoists assumed a more or less negative attitude. Though they positively affirmed the individual's freedom and their own transcendant value, they had no effect on the status of other individuals. Their ultimate goal was to become hermits and withdraw from society. The Confucians, on the other hand, took a positive stand. They enjoyed participating in society and felt it their duty to guide it. Fan Chung-yen (989-1052) thus proclaimed that "a (Confucian) scholar should be the first to become concerned with the world's troubles and the last to rejoice in any success he achieved." Lo went one step further than Fan's maxim by saying that "within one's capacity, everything related to society or public affairs should be deemed one's responsibility and it should be accepted without hesitation."

Lo was a thinker who put what he believed into practice. When he noticed that the assessment of taxes in Chi-shui required of the rich and the poor was unfair, he suggested that the local authorities should make some adjustments. They hesitated to accept his suggestion, for it was not an easy task. Lo then volunteered his services. Wang Chi (*q.v.*) was deeply impressed when he saw Lo working vigorously in the hot weather resurveying the lands at the time he visited him in the summer of 1548. After six laborious years Lo completed a new tax register for the local government. Again, in the late 1550s, when Chi-shui was besieged by a large number of bandits and the local defenders were frightened away, Lo took charge of defenses and saved the city from being sacked.

It was his belief in social responsibility that led Lo to study geography. Japanese piratical raids on the maritime provinces were a crucial issue during the Chia-ching reign. The government urgently needed maps for defense. As few accurate ones existed, Lo decided to provide some and spent three years collecting source material. Among other items he discovered a manuscript or epigraphic copy of the *Yü-ti t'u* 輿地圖 by Chu Ssu-pen (*ca.* 1273-1337). As Chu had used the method of indicating distances by a network of squares, the *Yü-ti t'u* was more accurate. Lo therefore revised and enlarged it under the title *Kuang-yü t'u* 廣輿圖. Chu's map was originally seven (Chinese) feet both in length and width, and therefore inconvenient to unroll. Lo rearranged it in book form. Chu Ssu-pen, moreover, had been preoccupied with the topographical aspects; Lo supplied additional details from other sources of Yüan and Ming times. The original *Kuang-yü t'u*, according to Hu Sung (*see* Cheng Jo-tseng), contained forty main maps (16 leaves of the various provinces, 16 of the border regions, 3 of the Yellow River, 3 of the Grand Canal, 2 of sea routes) and sixty-eight supplementary maps. Since the *Kuang-yü t'u* came to be revised several times by different hands during the late Ming period, however, and each time it was supplemented or changed in some way, there are no two editions alike. Probably the earliest edition of the *Kuang-yü t'u* is the one now located at the Library of Congress. It is a revision dated 1558. When Cheng Jo-tseng (*q.v.*) compiled his *Ch'ou-hai t'u pien* (1562), he referred to it. The *Kuang-yü t'u* must therefore have been first printed earlier than 1558. According to Hu Sung, Lo compiled the *Kuang-yü t'u* some two decades before he handed it to Hu for printing. He probably started his compilation shortly after his dismissal from the government in 1541. One of the widely circulated editions was that of Ch'ien Tai

(*q.v.*), published in 1579.

Lo's achievements in geography are significant. The *Kuang-yü t'u* provides us with some clues as to how Chu Ssu-pen compiled his *Yü-ti t'u*. It also informs us as to other valuable sources of his time, in particular the map of the northern expedition of Emperor Chu Yüan-chang. When Matteo Ricci (*q.v.*) brought out his *Yü-ti shan-hai ch'üan-t'u* in 1584, he introduced the idea of latitude and longitude to China. Despite this fact, the method of indicating distances by a grid system, first used by P'ei Hsiu (224-71) and refined by Chu and Lo, still exercised a dominant influence on Chinese cartography throughout the late Ming and early Ch'ing periods. Most of the maps and atlases published in this period were mainly based on Lo's *Kuang-yü t'u*. It is also highly likely that Ricci, who undoubtedly used the Mercator map of 1569 and the Ortelius map of 1570 for his information on most of the world in his first mappa mundi, depended on the 1579 edition of the *Kuang-yü t'u* as a source for eastern Asia.

From the Northern Sung onward the question of how an ordinary man might become a sage was a frequent topic of discussion among the neo-Confucians. Their studies reached a new stage when Wang Shou-jen expounded his theory of liang-chih 良知 (innate knowledge) in the early years of the 16th century. As his arguments, however, were subjective, they opened up almost unlimited possibilities for individual self-expression. Lo conceived it his mission to explore these possibilities to the limit. He compared Wang's theory with the ideas of other neo-Confucians. In addition he consulted several leading thinkers of the time, including Nieh Pao, Wang Chi, and Ch'ien Te-hung (*qq.v.*) either through correspondence or through personal confrontation. Wang Chi and Ch'ien Te-hung first visited Lo in the spring of 1540 before Lo's dismissal from the government, then in the summer of 1548, and again in the winter of 1554. Each time they met, they visited various places in Hukuang and Kiangsi together while sharing each other's ideas. They concluded that they should give further study to the problems which remained in Wang Shou-jen's philosophy.

Lo and Nieh Pao seem to have been much closer in their points of view than Lo and Wang Chi. Nevertheless, their differences did not affect the friendship between Lo and Wang. The latter regarded Lo as one who helped him clarify his thought.

Lo's philosophy is actually a synthesis of the thought of Ch'en Hsien-chang (*q.v.*) and Wang Shou-jen while absorbing some of Chou Tun-i (1017-73). He distinguished the function of liang-chih from its substance. Lo disagreed with Wang Chi, who believed that "liang-chih is inborn, and everyone's liang-chih is equally good." According to Wang, liang-chih can be easily realized naturally; and if one trusts his own liang-chih and uses it to regulate behavior, he will sooner or later become a sage. Lest Wang Chi's arguments might mislead one towards belief in Ch'an 禪 Buddhism, Lo emphasized the importance of chih 致 (to realize or to obtain). "Liang-chih might be inborn," he argued, "but the coming and going of good and evil ideas in our minds always prevent us from realizing it. If liang-chih can be easily obtained, why should Wang Shou-jen say 'Chih liang-chih,' instead of saying 'liang-chih.' Since the coming and going of good and evil ideas in our minds always disturb our moral self and prevent us from realizing liang-chih, one needs to make some effort to obtain or realize liang-chih," he continued. He thought the best way to do so was by way of kuei-chi 歸寂 (return to tranquillity). To practice kuei-chi one must separate oneself temporarily from all affections, stop all volitional ideas, and then abide in a state of inner tranquillity to mediate between the substance and the function of liang-chih. Lo always took Wang Shou-jen as an example, reminding others that, after Wang was demoted and sent to Lung-ch'ang 龍場 and prac-

ticed kuei-chi there, only then could he expound the theory of the realization of liang-chih. Both Lo and Nieh Pao were natives of Kiangsi; they were thus later classified as belonging in that section of the Wang Yang-ming school in order to distinguish them from others.

Lo Hung-hsien was a broad-minded scholar. He studied Buddhism and Taoism and struck up an acquaintance with a number of Buddhist monks and Taoist priests. Yet he never gave up his Confucian beliefs, and criticized those who tried to make compromises. His interest in Buddhism and Taoism and his relationship with their adherents, however, may have misled his own disciples. Some of them, such as Lin Chao-en (*q.v.*), made similar studies and became leaders of the attempt to unify the three faiths.

In the late 1550s China suffered a number of setbacks at the hands of the Jurchen and of the *wo-k'ou*. The Ming court thought that it should recruit more competent officers to deal with the invaders. In 1558, when both Lo and T'ang Shun-chih were recommended by Grand Secretary Yen Sung (*q.v.*) for their knowledge of strategy and military affairs, they once more received appointments, this time in the ministry of War. Lo, however, declined the offer; instead he worked with Ch'ien Te-hung to revise the chronological record of Wang Shou-jen, *Wang Wen-ch'eng kung nien-p'u* 王文成公年譜. They printed their revision in 1562. This work done, Lo was urged by Wang Chi and Ch'ien Te-hung to acknowledge himself as a disciple of Wang Shou-jen, a concession he did not make during the latter's lifetime. Lo died shortly afterwards and was granted the posthumous title of Wen-kung 文恭 in 1567.

Lo Hung-hsien was one of the earliest thinkers to point out that Wang Chi's philosophy would lead scholars to neglect their studies and research and become superficial. The decline of intellectual activity was certainly disastrous for the country. It is not important whether

Lo's arguments are correct or not. The significance is that his view was later shared by many Chinese scholars including Ku Yen-wu and Huang Tsung-hsi (both in ECCP). They and a number of others held that the Ch'an-like studies of the last decades of the Ming were one of the main reasons for the collapse of the dynasty. They therefore praised Lo and hailed him as a true disciple of Wang Shou-jen. Lo's philosophical writings are contained in the *Nien-an Lo hsien-sheng ch'üan-chi* 念菴羅先生全集 and the *Nien-an Lo hsien-sheng chi.*

Bibliography

1/383/16b; 5/19/65a; 8/54/7a; 42/76/1a; 63/22/36b; 83/18/1a; MSL (1965), Shih-tsung, 4593; Lo Hung-hsien, *Nien-an Lo hsien-sheng ch'üan-chi* (1565 ed.), 1/18a, 22b, 35a, 42a, 51b, 2/1a, 20b, 31b, 3/1a, 26a, 34a, 41b, 5/1a; Wang Chi, *Lung-ch'i Wang hsien-sheng ch'üan-chi* (1615 ed.), 2/19b, 24a, 25a, 3/18b, 22a, 4/4b, 6/1a, 10/2a, 14/23b, 18/3a, 19/10a, 21/27b; *id., Wang Lung-ch'i yü-lu* (1960 ed.), 1a; Cheng Jo-tseng, *Ch'ou-hai t'u-pien,* fan-lieh 凡例, 3a, 5a; *Chi-shui-hsien chih* (1873), 5/19b, 8/7a, 23a, 32b, 39a, 12/43a, 18/2a, 36/10a, 51/30b, 53/34a, 54/10b, 55/14a, 56/27b, 66/31a; Jung Chao-tsu容肇祖, *Ming-tai ssu-hsiang shih* 明代思想史 (Taipei, 1962), 119, 138; Wang Yung王庸, *Chung-kuo ti-li hsüeh-shih* 中國地理學史 (Changsha, 1938), 85; Ch'ien Mu (BDRC), *Sung Ming li-hsüeh kai-shu* 宋明理學概述 Vol. 2 (Taipei, 1952), 241; Naitō Torajirō 內藤虎次郎, tr. by Hu Han 吳晗, "Ti-li hsüeh-chia地理學家 Chu Ssu-pen," in *Kuo-li Pei-p'ing t'u-shu-kuan kuan k'an* 國立北平圖書館館刊 (March-April, 1923), 11; Mishima Akira 三島復, *Oyōmei no tetsugaku*王陽明の哲學(Tokyo, 1934), 588; Walter Fuchs, "Die Ausgaben des Ming-Atlasses Kuang-yü-t'u" in *Man-sen shi ronsō* 滿鮮史論叢 (Keijo, 1938), 537; Joseph Needham, *Science and Civilization in China,* III (Cambridge, England, 1960), 517, 552; L. of C. *Catalogue of Rare Books,* I, 307; Pasquale M. d'Elia, *Fonti Ricciane,* I(Rome, 1942), 14; Arthur W. Hummel, *Report of the Librarian of Congress, Division of Orientalia,* 1937 (Washington, D. C., 1938), 174.

Stanley Y. C. Huang

LO Lun 羅倫 (T. 應魁, later changed to 彝正, H. 一峯), February 22, 1431-October 19, 1478, scholar, official, and thinker,

was the son of an obscure scholar named Lo Hsiu-ta 修大 (H. 火山), a native of Yung-feng 永豐, Kiangsi. Lo Lun began his studies at the age of six, in poor circumstances. He tried to study even when tending animals or gathering fuel. At the age of thirteen, he was able to earn money to help the family by teaching other boys. A year later he became a licentiate student at the prefectural school. In 1456 he graduated as *chü-jen.* In 1463 he sat for the metropolitan examination. But the hall caught fire, and about ninety candidates lost their lives. Although Lo Lun escaped, he had to hurry home to attend his father's funeral. In 1466 he took the examination again, and passed as *optimus.* He wrote a long examination essay, in part of which he cautioned the emperor to avoid undue association with eunuchs and concubines. Although some of the examiners advised him to delete a few lines, in order to avoid annoying the young monarch, Chu Chien-shen (*q.v.*), Lo Lun refused to modify his position. Appointed a Hanlin compiler, Lo continued to manifest this same steadfastness with regard to moral principles. He counseled Li Hsien (*q.v.*), the grand secretary who continued in office during the months following the death of his father, to observe the prescribed ritual. When Li disregarded this piece of advice, Lo submitted a long memorial, urging the throne to instruct Li to comply with the rites. Instead of listening to the young scholar, the emperor ordered his demotion to assistant inspector of the maritime trade superintendency in Ch'üan-chou 泉州, Fukien. Fortunately for him, however, the death of Li Hsien (January, 1467) and the restoration of Shang Lu (*q.v.*) to the Grand Secretariat in the spring of the same year marked the end of his short exile. Lo was restored to his former position, but stationed in Nanking rather than at Peking. He remained there nearly two years, and then resigned from office, pleading ill health, to spend the rest of his life teaching and studying. He established two studios, Ching-kuan 靜觀 and Chih-mi 止密, on Mount Chin-niu 金牛, south of Yung-feng.

Lo was a follower of the school of Ch'eng I (1033-1107) and Chu Hsi (1130-1200) and a friend of Ch'en Hsien-chang (*q.v.*). Like many Ming scholars, he emphasized the role of tranquillity (ching 靜) in the quest for perfection. He was partial to the *Hsiao-hsüeh* 小學 and *Chin-ssu lu* 近思錄, both compiled by Chu Hsi, and passed his time annotating the ancient Classics during the ten years after his retirement. He described himself as having a quick temper. It is said that he once paid a visit to Wu Yü-pi (*q.v.*) in Ch'ung-jen 崇仁 and was visibly angered at the latter's reluctance to receive him. The courage he showed as Hanlin compiler linked his name with three others, who had also memorialized the throne on a different issue, but about the same time. They were Chang Mou (*q.v.*), Chuang Ch'ang, and Huang Chung-chao (for both *see* Chang Mou). They were jointly acclaimed as the "Four Hanlin remonstrators" (Han-lin ssu-chien 翰林四諫). Even as a retired scholar, he attracted much attention by his scholarship and virtue. It is reported that, after his death in 1478, the emperor himself composed a eulogy. In 1521 he was honored posthumously as an assistant supervisor in the supervisorate of imperial instruction, and canonized as Wen-i 文毅.

Lo Lun had four sons, the eldest of whom became a senior licentiate, and served as instructor in a district school. The second qualified for the *chü-jen* in 1495. Lo's writings were published in a collection entitled *I-feng chi* 集, 10 *ch.*, copied later into the *Ssu-k'u ch'üan-shu*. One edition of this work in 14 *ch.*, known as *I-feng hsien-sheng wen* 文-*chi*, dated 1550, is preserved in several Japanese libraries. His poems were published separately in the *I-feng Lo hsien-sheng shih* 詩-*chi*, 4 *ch.*

Bibliography

1/179/1a; 3/162/1b; 5/21/29a, 23/15a, 86/112a; 32/66/22a; 40/24/3b; 42/73/1a; 63/21/15a; 83/45/5a; MSL (1940), Shih-tsung, 8/6b, 30/2a, 10b, 37/7b; KC (1958), 2210; SK (1930), 171/1a; Ch'en Hsien-chang, "I-feng hsien-sheng chuan" 傳, *I-feng hsien-sheng wen-chi* (Ming ed.), NLP microfilm, no. 957, 1a; Lo Lun, *ibid.*; Ts'ao Jung 曹溶, "Lo Wen-i chuan," *Huang Ming wen-hai* (microfilm), 3/3/18, 18/6/14.

Huang P'ei and Julia Ching

LONGOBARDI, Nicolo (Longobardo, Nicolas 龍華民, T. 精華), 1565–December 11, 1655, a Jesuit missionary, was born into a patrician family at Caltagirone, Sicily. (Some sources, such as Sommervogel, Pfister, and his tombstone, give variant dates of birth and death, such as 1559-1654; we prefer to follow P. M. d'Elia.) He entered into his novitiate at Messina in 1582, and for the next few years continued his education in the humanities, philosophy, and theology. After another five years of teaching and performance of other duties he sailed from Lisbon in 1596 with a number of missionaries, arriving in China 1597. While pursuing language study he mailed reports, extreme in their optimism, back to the homeland. His first charge was at Shao-chou 韶州, Kwangtung, whither he was sent (December 28, 1597) along with a Chinese brother, to join Lazzaro Cattaneo (*q.v.*). Here he became so active in evangelistic work among both common folk and the scholar class that he stirred the Buddhist monks and others into active persecution. They resented his effort to evangelize the women through their men folk, and his opening and blessing of a church. In 1603 a scheme to kill him went astray. In 1606 he came to the defense of a Jesuit lay-brother Huang Ming-sha 黃明沙 (d. March 31, 1606) accused of being a spy from Macao, who had been thrown into prison in Canton and subjected to the bastinado. His memorial to the governor-general resulted in a finding of innocence for Huang, but it was too late to save the latter, who had already succumbed to the wounds inflicted.

This did not please his enemies, who secretly lodged an accusation of adultery against him. He succeeded, however, in confounding his persecutors.

In 1609 Longobardi was shifted to Peking, and there (on May 11, 1610) Matteo Ricci (*q.v.*) proclaimed him his successor—superior of the Jesuit mission in China. This was irregular as at that time Longobardi was not fully qualified, having the status of spiritual coadjutor. Not until December 24, 1617, was his status regularized. His appointment came at a time when a number of his co-workers were becoming exercised over the problem both of nomenclature and of accommodation to Chinese customs. What, for example, should be the name for God? What should the church do about ancestor worship? Ricci had opted for "provisional and partial accommodation." Longobardi kept his peace on these questions as long as Ricci was alive, but after becoming superior he voiced his concern, pressed to take a position in part because of his own convictions, in part because of agitation from Japan where the problem was acute and where the church was suffering from apostasies. For the next few years debate and conflicting orders were frequent, Longobardi never conceding his stand. In 1621, after the then Visitor of the order called a convention in Macao at which Ricci's position prevailed, Longobardi refused to accept its conclusions and drew up a long treatise (in 1623), pointing out, *inter alia*, the difficulties in which such scholars as Hsü Kuang-ch'i and Li Chih-tsao (both in ECCP) found themselves when equating Shang-ti 上帝 and the God of the Bible. Incidentally, the latter advised the missionaries not to concern themselves with the question, but Longobardi refused to be guided by their advice. The controversy continued, growing ever more acute, and becoming a source of embarrassment to successive Visitors of the church. One of them, André Palmeiro (1569–April 4, 1635), following a meeting called at Chia-ting 嘉定 in 1628, took the side of Longobardi,

only to be opposed by the Jesuits at the court. Longobardi replied in 1631 with "Annotationis contra usum nominis Xamti," to which Gaspar Ferreira (*q.v.*) issued a rejoinder entitled "Refutatio argumentorum P. Longobardi." This debate was not to end for over a century; enough has been said, however, to indicate Longobardi's attitude and persistence.

Meanwhile he was busy with other matters. In 1613, apparently on his own authority, he sent Niklaas Trigault (*q.v.*) to Europe to obtain certain concessions from the Pope and the general of the Society, to enlist recruits and funds, and to obtain books for the mission; he wanted every residence to have a library. His own words, as translated by H. Verhaeren, best express his last desire: "It is from the Sovereign Pontiff that we must hope for the principal library destined for Peking. To obtain this more easily, we will dedicate to him the translation of the Commentaries of Fr. Ricci. The portrait of the Pope will perpetuate in the eyes of the Chinese the souvenir of the donation. Besides this principal library, which must vie with the best we have in Europe, we need others, more modest for the other houses in China." The books acquired by Trigault from Paul V and other donors for Peking still remain, in Verhaeren's words, "the richest part of the Nant'ang library." From the Pontifical Library he counts 534 works in 457 volumes, and from other sources 223 works in 172 volumes. Among the recruits who came—Longobardi had repeatedly begged for mathematicians and astronomers—were such eminent figures as the Bohemian Wenceslas Pantaleon Kirwitzer (1586–May 22, 1626), the Italian Giacomo Rho, the Swiss Johann Terrenz, and the German Johann Adam Schall von Bell (*qq.v.*).

In 1616, when Shen Ch'üeh (*q.v.*) started his persecution, Longobardi, then in Nanking, hastened to Peking with funds contributed by Li Chih-tsao whom he stopped to visit at Kao-yu 高郵 (in Yangchow-fu). His efforts to bring it to a halt through the influence of friendly officials were of no avail, but he remained in Peking along with Francesco Sambiasi (*q.v.*), neither of whom was named in the edict of February 14, 1617, which ordered all missionaries out of China. They stayed unmolested in the residence of Hsü Kuang-ch'i. The church and residence of the missionaries in the capital too were protected by Chinese associates.

In 1622 he ceased being superior of the mission, this charge passing on eventually to Manuel Dias the Younger (*q.v.*). At the time of the next persecution (1622) he again returned to Peking, reoccupying the house acquired by Ricci in 1605. It was then that officials of the ministry of War asked Longobardi and Dias to obtain Portuguese cannon and cannoneers (*see* Dias). Years later (1631) the Korean envoy Chŏng Tu-wŏn 鄭斗源 was to express his astonishment over Longobardi's knowledge of these weapons. When forced out of the city, he returned with several others to the hospitable residence of Yang T'ing-yün (ECCP) in Hangchow, and collaborated with Dias in the fashioning of a terrestrial globe (*see* Giulio Aleni). Later he was back in Peking, for we find him producing a book (1624) on earthquakes, one of which had just shaken the city and its environs. In 1629, following a mistaken calculation by the imperial mathematicians of an eclipse which occurred on June 21, Hsü Kuang-ch'i and Li Chih-tsao asked him to serve as their assistant in the correction of the calendar, but he begged off on account of age.

It must have been between these years, 1624 to 1629, that he and others in the church became increasingly concerned over the power of the eunuchs, and determined to bring some of them into the fold. Ten at least were fully persuaded, one being P'ang T'ien-shou (*see* Chu Yu-lang, ECCP), whom he baptized as Achilles. P'ang himself was in due course to make Christians of a number of members of the family of Prince Chu Yu-lang, who in 1646 assumed the title "administrator of the realm" as the Ming dynasty was approaching its end. This led eventually (1650) to the well-known appeal for aid by the mother of the prince, the Empress-dowager Helena, née Wang 王, to Pope Innocent X and the Jesuit general (*see* Michał Piotr Boym).

During the last quarter of his life, in spite of increasing years, he was continuously active in evangelistic work in Shantung, often going long distances on foot until 1638, when he allowed himself the luxury of travel on horseback. On occasion he fell into trouble. In Tsinan-fu Buddhist monks lodged a complaint with the magistrate against him, but the latter was deterred by his appearance: "If it were not for the respect in which I hold your long white beard," he is reported to have said, "you would not leave here without being subjected to sixty lashings with a bamboo." His companion, however, did not elicit the same respect, and was forced to suffer imprisonment. On another occasion he was waylaid by robbers who stripped him of all he possessed. Fortunately a local prince (see note) saved him and gave him lodging. The stories of his success in the province strain one's credulity: here an impoverished man of eighty, there an official with all his family, at another place a Buddhist monk, and at still another over a period of two months the baptism of eight hundred individuals. At the time of the Manchu conquest he was seized and thrown into prison; only the high authority and influence of Schall brought about his release in 1645. At his death, aged ninety-five he was mourned not only by his associates, but also by the Shun-chih emperor (Fu-lin, *see* ECCP), who previously had had his portrait painted, and who now provided 300 taels for the expense of his tomb. His body was laid to rest at the cemetery set aside for Catholics at Cha-lan 柵欄 , outside the P'ing-tse men 平則

門, Peking. Though the cemetery, together with all its monuments and remains, was violated in 1900, the monument of Longobardi, inscribed in Latin and Chinese, was later restored to its original location.

Longobardi wrote a number of books and tracts largely in the religious field. Of the latter, one of the more interesting is his rendering into Chinese of the lives of Barlaam and Josaphat, principal characters of a legend of Christian antiquity which (though he was unaware of the fact) derives ultimately from one of the legends of the Buddha. The title as given by L. Pfister is *Sheng Jo-se-fa hsing shih* 聖若瑟法行實 (1 *ch.*, published in Shao-chou, 1602). Paul Pelliot renders it as *Sheng Jo-se-fa shih-mo* 始末 (1 *ch.*, published before 1610 in Peking). M. Courant cites another edition published in Foochow in 1645. A second work is a controversial discussion of certain phases of the religion of the Chinese, which appeared in *Tratados historicos, politicos, ethicos y religiosos de la monarchia de Chine* by Dominique Navarrete (Madrid, 1676) and in French and Portuguese translations. G. W. von Leibniz also gave it a new rendering in his *Epistolae ad diversos* II. His writings in the secular field, besides his work on the terrestrial globe mentioned above, include *Breve relatione del regno della Cina* (sent from Shao-chou October 18, 1598), published in Mantua in 1601, in 32 pages, and a treatise on earthquakes, *Ti-chen chieh* 地震解, 1 *ch.*, Peking, 1624 (1679).

[Note: Dunyn-Szpot and Colombel, followed by Pfister, record that in 1641, when Longobardi was robbed on his way from Peking to Ch'ing-chou 青州 he was rescued by a prince of the imperial line resident there, and was invited to stay in his house. It seems that the prince was a man of letters and much attracted by the teachings of Islam. His conversations with Longobardi almost persuaded him of the prior claims of the Christian church; to remove all doubts, however, he invited several "doctors of the Koran" to discuss points of difference. Fully convinced by Longobardi's arguments he accepted baptism, to be followed by his entire family, several other officials of Ch'ing-chou, Tsinan, and other towns in Shantung, and "the most illustrious scholar in the province." The latter was given the name of Nazaire or Nazarius, and the prince the name of Paul. Who was this prince? Pfister has tried without success to identify him. The tables in the *Ming-shih* include one for the princes of Heng 衡王 (in 104/24a) who were established in 1500 in Ch'ing-chou. In the fifth and last generation one finds the name of Chu Ch'ang-shu 朱常㵒 who was enfeoffed in 1580 and inherited the title in 1596. (His father had died in 1592.) As he receives no biography in the *Ch'ing-chou-fu chih* of 1859 and only passing mention elsewhere it cannot be determined if he is the man involved. It is barely possible, however, that this is the prince who in his seventies or eighties succumbed to the persuasive pleadings of another octogenarian. (Joseph Dehergne, however, identifies the prince as Chu Yu-tsou 朱由枞, whom we cannot place.) As to Nazaire, one meets the same name in 1621 in Peking in Pfister's biography of Manuel Dias, the younger. But this must he another individual.]

Bibliography

Fang Hao 方豪, *Chung-kuo T'ien-chuchiao shih jen-wu chuan* 中國天主教史人物傳, I (Hong Kong, 1965), 96; Pfister (1932), 58; P. Pelliot, TP, 31 (1935), 98, n. 2; *id.*, *Notes on Marco Polo*, II (Paris, 1963), 752; M. Courant, *Catalogue des livres Chinois* (Paris, 1900-1912), 6758; Sommervogel, cols. 1931-1933; J.M. Planchet, *Le cimitière et les oeuvres Catholiques de Chala, 1610-1927* (Peking, 1928), opp. pp. 24 & 56, 230; *Enciclopedia Italiana*, VII (Rome, 1957), 116; H. Havret, *La stèle chrétienne de Si-nganfou*, II (Shanghai, 1897), 22 n.; H. Verhaeren, *Catalogue of the Pei-t'ang library*, Peking, 1949, introd.; P. M. d'Elia, *Galileo in China*, tr. by R. Suter and M. Sciascia (Cambridge, Mass., 1960), 21; *id.*, *Fonti Ricciane*, I (1942), 385, II (1949), 232, 382; A. M. Colombel, *Histoire de la mission du Kiang-nan* 江南 (ms., 1895-1905), 410; Thoma-Ignatio Dunyn-Szpot (1633-1700?), *Archivum Societatis Iesu, Jap. Sin*, 103, Historiae

Sinarum, Partis II, Liber V, 22; "Annua della Viceprovincia, della Cina del 1643," *ibid.*, 119, 25; A. S. Rosso, *Apostolic Legations to China* (South Pasadena, 1948), 92; J. Dehergne in MS, XVI (1957), 109.

L. Carrington Goodrich

LOU Liang 婁諒 (T. 克貞, H. 一齊), 1422-July 3, 1491, thinker, was a native of Shang-jao 上饒, in the prefecture of Kuang-hsin 廣信, Kiangsi, but his ancestors had originally lived in Hsin-yang 信陽, Honan. It is said that as a youth he devoted himself to study the Classics in order to pass the civil examinations. Although he tried to find a suitable teacher, he did not succeed until, after having acquired the *chü-jen* degree in 1453, he decided to visit Wu Yü-pi (*q. v.*), of whom he had heard much. In 1454 he traveled to Lin-ch'uan 臨川, Kiangsi, and was accepted as a disciple. Wu became impressed with Lou's intelligence and single-mindedness, while Lou, on his part, admired the older man for his learning and devotion to manual labor. According to Huang Tsung-hsi (ECCP), Wu Yü-pi was not in the habit of saying much to his disciples, but made an exception of Lou Liang. It is not known how long Lou remained with Wu. The sources tell us simply that he spent ten years or more after 1453 studying philosophy. In 1463 he set out for Peking, to take the *chin-shih* examinations, but traveled only as far as Hangchow, and then turned back. When asked for the reason, he explained that he had a premonition that there would be calamity awaiting him in Peking if he went. As it happened the examination halls did catch fire that year, snuffing out the lives of many candidates trapped inside. The following year, 1464, Lou finally went to Peking and took the examinations. He failed, but as his name appeared on the secondary list, he was given an assistant instructor's post in Chengtu, Szechwan. He resigned shortly afterward, however, returned to his native place, and devoted the rest of his life to writing and teaching.

Among his writings are the *Jih-lu* 日錄, probably his personal study notes, 40 *ch.*, the *San-li ting-o* 三禮定訛, 40 *ch.*, in which he takes the *Chou-li* to be the source of state ritual, the *I-li* as a book of family rites, and the *Li-chi* as a commentary on the other two texts. He also composed the *Ch'un-ch'iu pen-i* 春秋本義, 12 *p'ien* 篇, in which he explains the original meaning of the Spring and Autumn Annals without referring to the commentaries and the *Chu-ju fu-hui* 諸儒附會, 13 *p'ien*. Lou lived to the age of sixty-nine, dying content, on July 3, 1491, after remarking that both Chou Tun-i (1017-73) and Ch'eng Hao (1032-85) had died during the summer months. His disciples gave him the private posthumous title of Wen-su 文肅.

Lou Liang's son, Lou Hsing 性, rose to be director of a bureau in the ministry of War. He left a book entitled *Huang Ming cheng-yao* 皇明政要, 20 *ch.*, which outlines political events during the first five reigns of the Ming, that of Chien-wen excepted. This, arranged under forty topics, was completed in 1503. His other son, Lou Ch'en 忱 (T. 誠善, H. 冰溪), was a scholar who remained about ten years in an upper room of his house studying, and who had numerous disciples. His grand daughter married the prince of Ning, Chu Ch'en-hao (*see* Wang Shou-jen), but committed suicide when the latter failed in his rebellion against the emperor, Chu Hou-chao (*q. v.*), after having refused to listen to her counsel. On account of this connection with a rebel, Lou's family suffered imprisonment, and Lou's writings were eventually lost to posterity. It is interesting that the person who defeated Chu Ch'en-hao should be the philosopher-soldier, Wang Shou-jen, who had visited Lou Liang in Kuang-hsin in 1489, and drawn profit from discussions with him. Wang probably did not become Lou's disciple formally after the short meeting, but he was an acquaintance of Hsia Shang-p'u 夏尚樸 (cs 1511), a disciple of Lou. Hsia rose to be sub-director of the Court of the Imperial Stud in Nanking. He was a friend also of such other thinkers as Chan Jo-shui (*q. v.*) and Wei Chiao (*see* Cheng Jo-tseng). He is credited with the works *Chung-yung yü* 中庸語 and *Tung-yen wen-chi* 東巖文集.

Together with Hu Chü-jen and Ch'en Hsien-chang (*qq. v.*), Lou Liang is known as one of the principal disciples of Wu Yü-pi. As his writings are no longer extant, it is difficult to say much about his contributions to thought. According to the historical sources, especially according to Huang Tsung-hsi, Lou stressed the practice of inner reverence (ching 敬), and considered the recovery of the lost mind (*cf.* Legge, *Chinese Classics*, II/290) to be its starting point. This was also the doctrine which he left to posterity through Hsia Shang-p'u. Lou is also re-garded as important because he might have been instrumental in directing Wang Shou-jen back to Confucianism and the quest for sagehood. It must be pointed out, however, that Lou's personal interests went beyond the usual limits of the Con-fucian scholars. He was supposedly sym-pathetic to Ch'an Buddhist insights, re-garding simple persons, such as carriers of water and fuel, as men of Tao. Be-sides, he appeared to have parapsychic powers, including premonitions of his own approaching death. His fellow disciple, Hu Chü-jen, criticized both him and Ch'en Hsien-chang for their "unortho-dox" tendencies.

Bibliography

1/283/3a; 3/13/10a, 109/8b, 265/2b; 83/5/13b; Hu Chü-jen, *Chü-yeh lu* (TsSCC, lst ser.), 7/83; *Kuang-feng* 廣豐*-hsien chih* (1872), 8c/2a; *Kuang-hsin-fu chih* (1873), 9c/10b; TSCC (1885–88), XIV: 351, 4b, XXII: 172/4b; Juan Jun-ling (*see* Ch'en Hsien-chang), *Ch'en Po-sha hsien-sheng nien-p'u* in *Po-sha hsien-sheng chi-nien chi*, comp. by Ch'en Ying-yao (Hong Kong, 1952), 4; Lou Hsing, *Huang Ming cheng-yao* (Ming ed.), NLP microfilm, no. 291; Wang Shou-jen, *Wan Wen-ch'eng kung ch'üan-shu* (SPTK double-page lithog-raph ed., lst ser.); Wu Yü-pi, *K'ang-chai hsien-sheng wen-chi* (NLP microfilm, no. 952), 9/24; Lien-che Tu (Fang), "Lou-fei chih fu" 婁妃之父, *Chung-yang jih-pao* 中央日報, fu-k'an 副刊 (February 4, 1970).

Julia Ching and Huang P'ei

LU Chih 陸治 (T. 叔平, H. 包山), 1496–1576, a native of Wu-hsien (Soochow), was an essayist, poet, and painter of land-scapes and natural objects: flowers, birds, blossoming trees, etc. He was a student of the district school but failed in the higher examinations. Later he retired to a retreat in Chih-hsing-shan 支硎山, south-west of Wu-hsien, where he lived to the end of his days, tending his chrysanthemums, painting, and writing. From time to time acquaintances sought him out in his retreat, and to some he gave his paintings but reports have it that he refused to sell a single one. A close friend and perhaps at one time his tutor was Wen Cheng-ming (*q. v.*); Wen's calligraphy and poems appear on some of his works of art. (*Cf.* painting of Lake Shih below; Tomita and Ch'iu have translated Wen's poem into English.) Lu owed much as well to the masters of the 10th to 13th centuries. The notorious official Yen Sung (*q. v.*), whose possessions were confiscated by the gov-ernment at the time of Yen's trial for malfeasance in office, owned nine of Lu's hanging scrolls and one long hand scroll. The Palace Museum in Taiwan records in its collection twelve hanging scrolls (rang-ing in size from 26.3×61.7 cm. to 124.8×51.7 cm.), an album of ten paintings of flowers, and another album which contains, along with eleven specimens of calligraphy by Ts'ai Yü 蔡羽 (T. 九逵 H. 林屋山人, d. 1541), ten of Lu's paintings, mostly small landscapes, reproduced in 1934 under the title *Ming Lu Chih Ts'ai Yü shu-hua ho-pi* 明陸治蔡羽書畫合璧. Osvald Sirén hazards the judgment that Lu was at his best when working on a small scale. However that may be, his landscapes, large or small, are today par-ticularly prized, being composed with unusual skill. Lu was fond of using fresh colors such as earthen-red or Indian-red and emerald green.

According to Hsü Pang-ta 徐邦達, seventy-two of Lu's paintings have survived (O. Sirén lists eighty-two, fifty-one of which bear his signature). A considerable number of them carry dates, which seem to indicate that his productive period ran up to a year before his death, 1522 to 1575. Besides the Palace Museum collection and others on the Chinese mainland, there are several of Lu's paintings in Japan, Europe, Canada, and the United States. Two of the scenes represented he must have known particularly well: one is of his retreat (Chih-hsing-shan t'u), now in the Palace Museum, and the other is of Lake Shih 石湖, situated near Soochow, and depicts its islands, cottages, bridges, and boats; it is now in the Museum of Fine Arts, Boston. The Chinese government exhibited one of his paintings at the Panama Exposition (1915) and three at the International Exhibition of Chinese Art, London (1935-36).

Bibliography

5/115/96b; 40/50/2a; 65/6/7b; 86/14/3a; *Su-chou ming-hsien hua-hsiang chi* 蘇州名賢畫像記; *Chung-kuo li-tai ming-hua chi* 中國歷代名畫記, I (Peking, 1959), pt. 2, 59; Hsü Pang-ta, *Li-tai liu-ch'uan shu-hua tso-p'in pien-nien piao* 歷代流傳書畫作品編年表 (Shanghai, 1963), 69; *Shina nanka tai sei* 支那南畫大成; J. C. Ferguson, *Index of Artists*, 308b, 311b; Yonezawa Yoshiho, *Painting in the Ming Dynasty* (Tokyo, 1956), pl. 14; Osvald Sirén, *Chinese Painting*, VI: pl. 5, 249, 250 A & B, 251, VII: 213; *Catalogue of the Exhibition of Individualists and Eccentrics* (Toronto, 1963-64), 3-5, pl. 1; A. K. Ch'iu, K, Tomita, "Shih Hu (Stone Lake)," *Bull. of the Museum of Fine Arts*, Boston, XLIX (1951), 34; H. A. Giles, *History of Chinese Pictorial Art* (2d ed., rev. & enl., Shanghai, 1918), 189; A. Waley, *Index of Chinese Artists* (London, 1922), 65; Tokyo Kokuritsu hakubutsukan 東京國立博物館: *Min-Shin no kaiga* 明清の繪畫(Tokyo, 1964), 11, pls. 27, 28; E. J. Laing, *Chinese Painting in Chinese Publications, 1956-1968* (Ann Arbor, 1969), 178.

Chiang Yee

LU Hsi-hsing 陸西星 (T. 長庚, H. 方壺外史, 蘊空居士), 1520-*ca.* 1601, Confucian scholar, Taoist priest, Buddhist devotee, and the author of the popular piece of fiction *Feng-shen yen-i* 封神演義, 100 *ch.*, was a native of Hsing-hua 興化, northeast of Nanking. Facts about his life are little known and aroused scarcely any interest among scholars until about 1932 when the modern critic, Sun K'ai-ti (*see* Kuo Hsün), found in the bibliography of dramatic works, *Ch'uan-ch'i hui-k'ao* 傳奇彙考, that Lu Hsi-hsing wrote the *Feng-shen yen-i*; originally it was published anonymously but sometimes attributed to Hsü Chung-lin 許仲琳 of the early 17th century. In its history of Chinese literature published in 1959, the Department of Chinese Literature of Peking University listed Hsü as the author. Again, in 1963, the Academia Sinica in Peking brought out its version of a history of Chinese literature in which the author is recorded as unknown; in a footnote, however, Lu Hsi-hsing is referred to as possibly responsible, based upon a chance comment found in the *Ch'ü-hai tsung-mu t'i-yao* 曲海總目提要. After more than a decade devoted to collecting evidence, the undersigned is now confident that Lu is the author. [Editors' note: In the East Asian Library of Columbia University there is a lithographic edition of the *Nan-hua chen-ching fu-mo* 南華眞經副墨 (Shanghai, *ca.* 1915; text based on the edition of 1885) which was presented to the library by Hu Shih (BDRC) in October, 1958. It contains a few memoranda written by Dr. Hu on November 5, 1954, the day he bought the book in a New York bookstore "at a high price" (以重價買得). One of them reads as follows: "The author 陸西星 or 陸長庚 has been identified by modern research as the author of the popular novel 封神演義 or 封神榜. Hu Shih."]

Enough materials about Lu's life are available to give a short sketch here. Lu was born into a poor family, the son of a diviner and student of the Book of Changes. He was still a child when his father died, so he received his early education from his mother. He became a student in the district school and a close friend of his fellow townsman, Tsung Ch'en (*q.v.*). They frequently visited each other and went together several times to take the provincial examination at Nanking. Lu failed to qualify but Tsung became a provincial graduate in 1549 and a *chin-shih* in 1550. About 1553 or 1554 Tsung composed an essay in honor of Lu's mother (née Chang 張) on her sixtieth birthday, which tells something about Lu's early life. In 1560 Tsung died in Fukien while serving as surveillance vice commissioner in charge of education in that province. About this time, having failed in the provincial examinations for the ninth time, Lu decided to give up trying to enter the civil service; instead he joined the Taoist priesthood.

This was the Chia-ching period when the emperor himself, Chu Hou-ts'ung (*q. v.*) was an eager devotee of Taoist religious practices, priests of that religion being honored with titles as high as that of minister of Rites. The influence of their shrines, prosperous and influential throughout the Ming dynasty, reached full strength during Lu's lifetime. He probably hoped to rise in that community and so gain power and fame, but it seems that he was destined to limit his activities to literary pursuits and to writing on religious themes.

There were then two main sects of Taoism, the charm-dispensing Cheng-i 正一 (Orthodox One) sect headed by Chang T'ien-shih 張天師 (Heavenly Teacher Chang), said to be descended from Chang Ling of the second century, and the more subtle Ch'üan-chen 全眞 (Preservation of the True Self) sect founded in the late 12th century by Wang Che (1112–70; *see also* Lin Chao-en). The Ch'üan-chen sect, which stressed self-cultivation through training in controlled breathing (much as in Tantrism), abstinence, and renunciation of family life, taught the blending of the "three religions" Taoism, Buddhism,

and Confucianism. During the Jurchen Chin dynasty (1115–1234) and the Mongol Yüan dynasty (1260–1368), when north China was under foreign rule, alien rulers respected religious establishments which became the refuge of Chinese scholars. The Ch'üan-chen sect thus had a scholarly tradition. It was the priesthood of this sect which Lu joined about 1560.

Even less is known of Lu's life as a priest, except that he became a prolific writer. He probably made pilgrimages to places sacred to Taoism and assuredly visited the headquarters of the sect at the Po-yün-kuan 白雲觀 west of Peking. At times he stayed in his home district, for we know that he served as an editor of the local gazetteer, *Hsing-hua-hsien chih* 興化縣志, completed in 1591. In the meantime he produced a number of religious and philosophical works. Best remembered is his *Nan-hua chen-ching fu-mo*, a critical study of Chuang-tzu in 8 *chüan*, which he started to write in 1576. Engraved about 1578 and again in 1585 it won the admiration of the scholastic world of his day. Chiao Hung (ECCP) quoted it a number of times when he wrote the *Chuang-tzu i* 莊子翼 ; mention is made of it also both in the bibliographical treatise of the *Ming-shih* and in the *Ssu-k'u* catalogue. He wrote it chiefly to enable a Confucianist to understand the basic teaching of the Ch'üan-chen sect. In this work Lu included a number of extracts of Buddhist literature and made use of many Buddhist terms. He even proclaimed that "the sages and virtuous men of the three schools have but one and the same principle." In his opinion strict Confuciansists were, as he called them, chü-ju 局儒 (narrow-minded Confucianists). He is known also to have written eleven or twelve other books known as *Fang-hu wai-shih* 方壺外史 (An unofficial historian's accounts of the legendary Mt. Fang-hu). These four characters also formed one of his own sobriquets.

In his last years Lu wrote two treatises, *Leng-yen-ching shu chih* 楞嚴經述旨

and *Leng-yen-ching shuo yüeh* 說約, on the Tantric Buddhist work, the *Sūraṅgama sūtra*. He showed a deep understanding of Tantric Buddism which was probably one of the subjects taught in the Ch'üan-chen sect. Evidently Lu studied Buddhism quite seriously, for he also adopted the sobriquet Yün-k'ung chü-shih 蘊空居士, which may be translated: "a Buddhist devotee believing the Five Attributes of a man to be nonexistent." He seems to exemplify a Ch'üan-chen Taoist in robust health and length of years. As has been told, he edited his district's history about 1590 at the age of seventy. Now in his eighty-first year, in 1600, he took his manuscripts with him to Peking where he paid a visit to an old friend, the former magistrate (1568–71) of Hsing-hua, now minister of Personnel (1598–1604), Li Tai (*q.v.*). Lu apparently sought help from Li to finance the printing. After adding a preface to the *Leng-yen-ching shu chih* (March 5, 1601), Li wrote the incumbent prefects of Huai-an and Yangchow recommending that they sponsor the engraving of Lu's works. It is entirely possible that Li had performed some favors for these officials and was thus exacting repayment. Both officials were holding highly lucrative posts and could well afford the outlay required. By the same token Li was helping out an old friend without any expense to himself. It is not without interest that, in the preface to Lu's works on the *Sūraṅgama sūtra*, Li also praised Lu for his Taoist expositions, especially the *Nan-hua chen-ching fu-mo*. Li, in all likelihood, was a believer in Taoism himself.

In June, 1601, Lu wrote a preface to his own work on the *Leng-yen-ching* while on board a boat in T'ung-chou 通州, probably on his return trip by the Grand Canal. Incidentally, at the end of this preface he gave his age as eighty-two, from which the date of his birth is calculated. He probably did not live long after his return. He was laid to rest in his native place and to this day is honored by Taoists as one of their patriarchs.

The most important contribution of Lu Hsi-hsing is the long fictional work, *Feng-shen yen-i*, a story of fantasy and imagination about the conquest of the Shang dynasty by King Wu, the founder of the Chou dynasty, in the 12th century B. C. The story tells of the misrule of Chou, the last of the Shang kings, and the conduct of the war against him by King Wu's chief commander, Chiang Tzuya (also known as Lu Shang) under the name and title Chiang T'ai-kung. This general was worshiped during the T'ang and Sung dynasties by generals as their chief deity in the military temples, much as Confucius was in the civil temples. Because of the lack of factual records, when Chiang's story was told in the common people's legends, he was described as possessor of supernatural power enlisting the help of deities and fairies. After the Mongols discontinued the Chinese military temples and sent Chiang into oblivion, the tellers of his story began to treat him with little respect. The earliest extant story teller's prompt-book about the war of the 12th century B. C. is the *Wu-wang fa Chou p'ing-hua* 武王伐紂平話, printed not later than 1323. This is evidently the basic story which Lu Hsi-hsing expanded more than ten times into his *Feng-shen yen-i*, incorporating materials from other stories, such as the *Lieh-kuo chih chuan* 列國志傳, and adding episodes involving Buddhist and Taoist deities, also historical figures. The work ends with Chiang T'ai-kung rewarding his generals, and all the deities who came to help, with permanent positions in a pantheon which was a hodgepodge of all the popular cults and beliefs. One result of its publication was the popularization of the Ch'üan-chen teaching of the blending of Buddhist and Taoist principles in the material form of a mixture of their deities, with Buddhist images included in Taoist shrines and vice versa. The trend probably started as early as the 14th century, but Lu's romance certainly encouraged it.

The *Feng-shen yen-i* was first engraved probably shortly after Lu's death. It has always been published as an anonymous work. One edition appeared in Soochow bearing the editor's name, Hsü Chung-lin, and so for a time, about 1920 to 1960, some writers mistakenly attributed the authorship to Hsü.

Lu is known also for his calligraphy, painting, and poetry. Seven of his poems memorializing his deceased acquaintances have been preserved in the gazetteer of his native place, the *Hsing-hua-hsien chih*. One poem was in memory of his fellow townsman, Li Ch'un-fang (*q.v.*), who rose to be a grand secretary. Two others among those remembered were his close friend Tsung Ch'en and a nephew Lu Lü 陸律 (T. 子和, H. 從吾, *kung-sheng* 1564). The latter wrote a preface to the *Nan-hua chen-ching fu-mo* in 1578.

Lu Hsi-hsing's younger brother, Lu Yüan-po 陸原博 (T. 約之), was the compiler of an anthology of local poets, entitled *Ch'u-yang ming-hsien shih-hsüan* 楚陽名賢詩選, 2 *ch.*; the anthology *Ch'u-yang shih-i* 逸, credited to Lu Hsi-hsing in the local gazetteer, seems to be a supplement.

Bibliography

1/98/19b, 287/16a; *Hsing-hua-hsien chih* (1852), 6/5/11a, 8/6/3a; *Tsung Tzu-hsiang chi* 宗子相集 (1608); Chung-kuo k'o-hsüeh-yüan, *Chung-kuo wen-hsüeh shih* (Peking, 1963), III, 288; Yoshioka Giho, *Dōkyō no kenkyū* 道教の研究, Kyoto, 1952; for detailed bibliographical references *see* Liu Ts'un-yan, *Buddhist and Taoist Influences on Chinese Novels, I, The Authorship of the Feng Shen Yen I* (Wiesbaden, 1962), 118, 260.

Liu Ts'un-yan

LU Kuang 陸廣 (T. 季弘, H. 天游), a painter who flourished in the middle of the 14th century, was a native of Soochow. Little is known about him, although from scattered sources one learns that he seems to have led a long life, spending some fifty years wandering around many parts of China and visiting a number of famous mountains. Recorded dates and colophons on his paintings fall mostly into the 1350s and 1360s.

In spite of the fact that he was a native of Soochow during the period when that city was known for its distinction in arts and letters, he seems to have had little contact with the literati there. In fact, his efforts as a painter were apparently little appreciated until the last decades of the Ming when a change of taste in painting developed. Perhaps this obscurity about his life is due partly to his having lived outside of Soochow much of the time and partly to the fact that few of his works were known.

His art began to be valued only after the theories of art developed by Mo Shih-lung (*q.v.*) and Tung Ch'i-ch'ang (ECCP) had gained general acceptance. Consequently, all the major statements characterizing this painting were made by late Ming critics. Li Jih-hua (*q.v.*) writes: "Lu T'ien-yu stood half way between Yu-wen 幼文 (Hsü Pen, *q.v.*) and Yün-hsi 雲西 (Ts'ao Chih-po, 1272-1355), with feelings of loneliness and desolation as his main expression. It is difficult to get from him broad pieces with powerful brushwork." Tung Ch'i-ch'ang also points in the same direction: "Both Lu T'ien-yu and Hsü Yu-wen followed Huang Kung-wang" (1269-1354). Another critic reports that his paintings derived from Wang Meng (*q.v.*). His brushwork is described as having an antique spirit and his use of ink characterized as quite distinctive. The tree branches that he depicts are said to show the manner of "dancing pheasants and startled snakes."

Only some eight paintings attributed to him are extant. Among them, the most convincing in style and in related documentation are three: "Tan-t'ai ch'un shang" 丹台春賞 (Enjoying spring in the Tan-t'ai mountains), "Tan-t'ai ch'un hsiao 曉 (Dawn over the Tan-t'ai mountains), and "Shan-fang ch'iu chi" 山房秋霽 (Mountain pavilion in the autumn). All three are hanging scrolls painted in ink on paper, each with a poem written by the artist himself in formal manner. Their style has the simplicity and freedom of Huang Kung-wang, but their compositions seem to have derived from some Northern Sung painters, similar to those in the late works of Ts'ao Chih-po—mountains in vertical formations with buildings and pavilions nestled in their midst. The direct source of his compositions is probably the eleventh-century artist Yen Wen-kuei (d. *ca.* 1020), well known for this kind of composition. In his colophons on a hand-scroll attributed to Yen Wen-kuei, formerly in the Palace collection, Lu Kuang expresses his admiration and indebtedness to this Sung painter.

The combination of Northern Sung compositions of Yen Wen-kuei and the late Yüan style of Huang Kung-wang in his works is probably the main reason why he was not much appreciated in his own lifetime, but highly valued later when literati painters and critics sought to embrace both the monumentality of Northern Sung and the freedom and individuality of late Yüan painters. Thus he holds a position in the history of late Yüan painting similar to that of Ts'ao Chih-po and Hsü Pen, not so inventive as the Four Masters of late Yüan, but achieving a blending of Northern Sung and his own time in a happy union.

Another painting, "Hsien-shan lou kuan" 仙山樓觀 (Towers and pavilions on the mountains of Immortals), in the National Palace Museum, Taipei, is a painting of much larger dimension on silk, with an inscription by the artist indicating that it was painted in the "fourth year of T'ien-li," a date that is nonexistent. In colophons of both Li Jih-hua and Tung Ch'i-ch'ang, the painting is said to have been divided into two pieces but joined together again after their discovery by these connoisseurs. In style it does not seem to belong to the group mentioned above. There is also doubt about this painting in various late Ming and Ch'ing catalogues. Other attributions probably not of genuine quality include: "Hsi-t'ing shan-se" 溪亭山色 (Mountain colors as seen from the Hsi pavilion) in *Gems of Chinese Painting* (Shanghai, 1955, I, 14); "Shan-shui" 山水 (Landscape) in *Shen-chou kuo kuang chi* 神州國光集 (Vol. VI); "Wu jui t'u" 五瑞圖 (Five auspicious plants)" in *Ku-kung shu-hua chi* 故宮書畫集 (Vol. XVI); and "River landscape," in *Nansō Ihatsu* 南宗衣鉢 (Vol. IV).

Bibliography

Hsi Shih-ch'en 席世臣, *Yüan shih hsüan kuei chi* 元詩選癸集, 辛上 /21a; *Hua shih hui yao* 畫史會要, 58/4; *Soochow-fu chih* (1823), 105/7a; Wang K'o-yü, *Shan-hu wang*, 9/18, 19/4, 19/28; Li Jih-hua, *Tzu-t'ao-hsüan tso-cho*; Ts'ao Ch'en 曹臣, *She hua lu* 舌華錄 (in *Li-tai hsiao-shuo pi-chi hsüan* [*Ming*] 歷代小說筆記選(明) I [Hong Kong, 1958], 179); Chou Liang-kung(ECCP), *Shu ying* (Shanghai, 1957), 101; Osvald Sirén, *Chinese Painting*, IV (New York, 1958), 72 and VI, pls. 83B and 138A; *Ku-kung shu-hua chi* 故官書畫集, VIII; *Tō Sō Gen Min Meiga Taikan* 唐宋元明名畫大觀 (Tokyo, 1929), pl. 163; *Ch'ing-kung ts'ang Yen Wen-kuei ch'iu shan hsiao ssu chüan*, 清宮藏燕文貴秋山蕭寺卷, Shanghai (no date).

Chu-tsing Li

LU Nan 盧柟 (T. 少楩, 次楩, 仲木, H. 浮丘山人), died *ca.* 1560, poet and eccentric man of letters, was a native of Chün-hsien 濬縣, a district at that time under the jurisdiction of Pei-Chihli, but later made a part of the province of Honan. The Lu family, which was rich in land does not seem to have been on cordial terms with the local people. This was not an uncommon phenomenon in Ming times, the rich and the powerful showing scant compassion for the poor, who reciprocated with dislike, mounting occasionally to violence. His literary talent, together with his family wealth, perhaps made Lu Nan unusually arrogant and disagreeable, especially after he failed to pass the higher civil examinations. He prided himself, furthermore, on his capacity for strong drink, and went beyond all bounds in his denunciation and ranting when intoxicated. Thereby hangs the tale of his unhappy life; after surviving some twelve years of imprisonment, Lu found his family wealth gone, his parents and sons all dead, only his wife and daughter still living.

After becoming a *hsiu-ts'ai*, Lu Nan made several unsuccessful attempts to pass the provincial examinations. Around 1536 he purchased a *chien-sheng* degree, went to Peking, and enrolled in the National University. Records give no clue as to how long he remained in the capital, or when he returned home. It was in Peking that he made the acquaintance of Hsieh Chen (*see* Hsü Chung-hsing) another well-known poet with neither degree nor office who later contributed greatly to obtaining his release from prison. Lu Nan's trouble began in 1540 with the homicide case of Chang Kao 張果, one of his hired, or bonded, farm hands. One day Lu Nan discovered that Chang had stolen wheat from his farm and apparently had him beaten severely. A few days later Chang died in a house demolished in a rain storm. Chang's mother sued Lu, but Lu insisted that Chang's death was caused by the collapse of the house. The magistrate, however, ruled for the impoverished woman. Lu was thrown into prison, tortured, and sentenced to death.

Some people believed that the magistrate held a grudge against Lu, and seized this opportunity to take vengeance. The story goes that once the magistrate made an appointment to visit Lu's home, but was delayed and unable to get there until very late. Elaborately prepared for the occasion, Lu finally lost patience after long waiting, and proceeded to get drunk. When the magistrate arrived, Lu was already asleep, improperly attired, and in no condition to receive his guest, much less entertain him. The magistrate felt insulted and left immediately in a pet. To make the situation worse, some people also informed the magistrate that Lu Nan

had spoken unfavorably about the official's literary ability. The magistrate of Chün-hsien from 1539 to 1543, according to the *Ta-ming-fu chih* 大名府志 was Chiang Tsung-lu 蔣宗魯, a *chin-shih* of 1538, of military registration from Kweichow, who later was promoted to censorial posts in Peking. A censor at the capital could exercise great influence over the local officials in the provinces. For this reason, in spite of Lu Nan's wealth and repeated appeals, he was unsuccessful in having the case reopened.

In prison Lu Nan continued to compose poetry and prose, and to write letters, mostly to mourn his misfortune and to tell his side of the case, Four fu 賦 (poetic prose in irregular meters) of his came to the attention of the prince of Chao 趙王, Chu Hou-yü 朱厚煜 (H. 枕易道人, d. 1560, enf. in Honan). The prince, a scholar himself, impressed by his writings, ordered them printed. There is little doubt that Hsieh Chen must have been responsible, since he was not only one of the literary figures retained by the prince of Chao, but also had expressed concern over Lu Nan's fate. It seems that Hsieh then took these printed copies to Peking, where Lu Nan's case became widely known. In pleading for Lu, Hsieh declared that if the literati could not even save a Lu Nan of their own time, they had better not lament any more over the ill fate of Ch'ü Yüan, an ancient poet.

In 1548 a courageous and resourceful man, Lu Kuang-tsu 陸光祖 (T. 與繩, H. 五臺, 1521–97, cs 1547, Pth. 莊簡), was appointed magistrate of Chün-hsien. He had heard about Lu Nan's case in Peking. After assuming office, he reexamined the records, obtained and prepared the necessary official communications, reversed the previous decision, and freed Lu from prison. Some sources indicate that in his first meeting with the new magistrate, while still in prison garb, Lu demanded the proper seat for a guest, when he was asked by his benefactor to sit down.

During the few years immediately following his release, Lu was perhaps a frequent visitor of Chang Chia-yin (*q. v.*), the magistrate (1552–55) of the neighboring district of Hua-hsien 滑縣. Late in 1555, Lu Nan went to Honan to visit the prince of Chao, who treated him with honor and bestowed on him monetary and other gifts. His misfortune, however, had not changed his way of life; he still spent money freely, drank excessively, and became arrogant and disagreeable under the influence of liquor.

Later he went to Nanking, where his benefactor Lu Kuang-tsu was officiating as a bureau secretary in the ministry of Revenue. This afforded him an opportunity to make trips to various scenic places in the lower Yangtze region. Still due to his temperament no one seemed to be able to help him get employment. It is not clear when or where he died. According to Wang Shih-chen (*q.v.*), his death followed a three-day drinking spree at the time that Wang was in custody following the execution of his father. As the execution took place in 1560, Lu's death must have occurred at about the same time.

The collected literary works of Lu Nan entitled *Mieh-meng chi* 蠛蠓集, 5 *ch.* were first printed in 1574, and reprinted in 1602. Some of his fu and poems had been printed separately earlier. The first edition bears prefaces by Chang Chia-yin dated 1574, by Wan Kung 萬恭 (T. 肅卿, H. 兩溪, 1515–91, cs 1544), and by Lu himself dated 1543. Wang Shih-chen wrote a preface to a 3 *chüan* collection of Lu's works entitled *Lu Tz'u-pien chi* 次楩集. A drama of mediocre quality, the *Hsiang tang-jan* 想當然, attributed to Lu, was apparently by an early Ch'ing writer (*see* T'an Yüan-ch'un). A superb narrative by Lu Nan on Chang Chia-yin's capture of two daring robbers while he was serving as magistrate of Hua-hsien, is entitled *Hua-hsien ch'in-tao chi* 擒盜記. It is not included in the *Mieh-meng chi* but is preserved by Yao Shih-lin (*q. v.*) in his *Chien-chih pien*. The plot, the suspense,

and the vivid description, although based on a real occurrence, and not professing to be fiction, can match the best of Ming short stories. The story of Lu Nan's own life too was fictionalized and became known as "Lu t'ai-hsüeh shih-chiu ao kung-hou 太學詩酒傲公侯 (Lu the university student, a talented poet, and fond of liquor, refuses to humble himself before men of high position). It constitutes the twenty-ninth chapter of the collection of short stories *Hsing-shih heng-yen* (*see* Feng Meng-lung). Some years later it was selected for inclusion in the widely popular collection *Chin-ku ch'i-kuan* 今古奇觀. This story has been translated into German (by Walter Strzoda, *Die gelben Orangen der Prinzessin Dschau*, München, 1922).

In the story most characters appear under their real names, except the magistrate who sentenced Lu Nan and the two farm hands, who are given fictitious names. This piece of fiction elaborates greatly on Lu's garden estate, and also provides the dead man with a moderately attractive widow and a brother. To be in accord with the popular beliefs of the time, the story concludes with a hint that Lu Nan became an immortal. Otherwise the tale is rather close to the written records. To this reader, nevertheless, it seems strange that the story omits Hsieh Chen, Lu's prime benefactor. Because of the absence of Hsieh, the episode of Lu's visit to the prince of Chao is also omitted.

Bibliography

1/287/14a; 5/115/69a; 64/己4/1a; 84/丁上/51a, 丁下/75a; *Huang Ming wen-hai* (microfilm), biography of Lu Kuang-tsu; *Ta-ming-fu chih* (1853), 1/30b, 15/79b; *Hua-hsien chih* (1930), 14/21b (*see also Chin-shih lu* 金石錄, *I-wen lu* 藝文錄); Wang Shih-chen, *Yen-chou shan-jen ssu-pu kao* (1577), 64/9a, 83/10b; Yao Shih-lin, *Chien-chih pien* (*Yen-i chih-lin* 鹽邑志林 ed.), 上/33a, 下/5b; Fu Hsi-hua 傅惜華, *Ming-tai ch'uan-ch'i ch'üan-mu* 明代傳奇全目 (Peking, 1959), 358.

Lienche Tu Fang

LU Ping 陸炳 (T. 文孚), 1510-December 27, 1560, Commander of the Embroidered-uniform Guard, was born in An-lu 安陸, Hukuang, but his ancestral home was P'ing-hu 平湖, Chekiang. His grandfather Lu Ch'ih 墀, as an army scribe, was attached to the Embroidered-uniform Guard division in Peking. In 1494 as a sergeant in the bodyguard of Chu Yu-yüan, prince of Hsing (*see* Emperor Chu Hou-ts'ung) accompanying him to his estate at An-lu, Lu Ch'ih served the prince well. Later his son, Lu Sung 松 (d. 1536), became a member of the entourage of the future emperor, first at An-lu and, after the latter's ascent to the throne, in Peking; he rose to the rank of an assistant commander of the Embroidered-uniform Guard. One source suggests that Lu Sung's wife also served as the wet nurse of the future emperor.

A son of Lu Sung, Lu Ping represented the third generation in the service of the Chia-ching emperor's branch of the imperial family. He did not rely on that relationship to secure an office but showed his ambition by competing in the military examinations, becoming a military *chü-jen* in 1529. He was first made an assistant chiliarch commander in the Embroidered-uniform Guard, and a few years later on his father's death succeeded to the rank of assistant commander. It was not until 1539, however, during an imperial trip to the south, that Lu Ping received special notice from the emperor; this led to his rise in power, position, and exceptional imperial favors throughout his life.

In the spring of 1539 the emperor left Peking for a trip to An-lu, or Ch'eng-t'ien-fu 承天府 as it was called then, to visit his father's tomb. While the imperial party was stopping over one night at Wei-hui 衞輝, Honan, on March 18, a serious fire broke out in the emperor's lodging. It was said that in the sudden turmoil the emperor was left alone to face an ugly situation, and it was Lu Ping who rescued him and carried him to safety. Soon afterward Lu Ping was promoted to be a commander of the Embroidered-uniform Guard.

When Ch'en Yin 陳寅 (T. 敬夫, 1495-1549), commander in charge, retired early in 1545, Lu Ping was given full responsibility for the Embroidered-uniform Guard with the rank of a regional vice commander. In rapid succession he rose in rank first to assistant commissioner and then to vice commissioner of the central military commission. When he was impeached for causing disturbance to the populace and involvement in salt smuggling, the emperor chose not to pursue the matter. For his part in defending the capital against the threat of invasion of Altan-qaγan (*q.v.*) in 1550, he was elevated to the rank of commissioner, and in the following year appointed grand guardian to the heir apparent. For informing on Ch'iu Luan (*q.v.*) he was made junior guardian and concurrently grand tutor to the heir apparent with an additional annual official stipend of an earl in 1553. A year later, on the completion of the construction of the outer city wall of Peking, the emperor promoted him to be grand guardian with the additional privilege of having the rank of hereditary centurion in the Embroidered-uniform Guard for one of his descendants. Further imperial favors were also bestowed, such as permission to use a sedan chair (January, 1555), and, though a military officer, to sit among the high civil officials at the feast given in 1556 to the new *chin-shih* who had passed the civil examination in that year. Shortly before his death, he and Yen Sung (*q.v.*) headed the list of officials who were rewarded for their part in assisting the emperor in the performance of state affairs.

Occupying a powerful and feared position, close to and trusted by the emperor, Lu Ping must have taken part in many court intrigues and power struggles in the politics of the Chia-ching period, which historians failed to record. From all indications he was good at infighting. In 1547 on the death of Hsia Yen and Tseng Hsien (*qq.v.*) Lu Ping sided with Ch'iu Luan. Five years later, in bringing about the downfall of Ch'iu Luan, he joined forces with Yen Sung. By 1558 Lu Ping was already leaning more to the side of Hsü Chieh (*q.v.*), which induced Yen to become suspicious of him. We may surmise, therefore, that, had he lived a few years longer, he might have emerged again on the victorious side when the Yen father and son came to their tragic and disgraceful end.

When he died he was honored with the designation of earl of Chung-ch'eng 忠誠伯 and granted the posthumous title Wu-hui 武惠; ten years later, under a new reign, he was impeached by a censor. As a result his family property was confiscated, and his younger brother and sons were cashiered.

Lu Ping is described as tall, handsome, long-legged, and ruddy in complexion, and is portrayed as an able, thoughtful, and shrewd person. In his lifetime, he amassed tremendous wealth including material things for pleasure and real property in Peking and in other cities such as Yangchow, Chia-hsing 嘉興, Nanchang, and An-lu. As head of an organization of unlimited police power and secret service activities, he brought to many individuals bankruptcy, suffering, and death. Yet he was unusually kind to intellectuals and upright officials in comparison with previous and later powerful commanders of the Embroidered-uniform Guard during the Ming dynasty. Among other things, he was said to have used lighter flogging sticks. When in 1559 the celebrated general Yü Ta-yu (*q.v.*) was unjustly brought to Peking to be imprisoned, Lu Ping was credited with securing his release. It is to be noted, furthermore, that the Embroidered-uniform Guard is almost always mentioned together with the eunuchs, as both groups were in the emperor's personal service, both operated prisons, and both spied on people and officials. Of the two, the eunuchs generally had the upper hand, perhaps because they were even closer to the emperor. Nevertheless, during Lu Ping's time he was definitely in a stronger position than the eunuchs. In 1557 he had impeached the eunuch Li Pin 李彬 for grand larceny of millions of taels from the salt administration. As a result Li was put in the Embroidered-uniform Guard prison and sentenced to death.

Li Yü 李玉 (T. 玄玉, native of Soochow), a dramatist of the Ming-Ch'ing transitional period, wrote a lyric play entitled *I-feng-hsüeh* 一捧雪, which was later adapted as a Peking opera. As the judge in this play, Lu Ping's name has become widely known among the common people.

Bibliography

1/95/1a, 115/1a, 307/19a; 5/109/11a, 13a; KC (1958), ch. 52–63; Wang Shih-chen, *Chin-i chih*, in Shen Chieh-fu, ed., *Chi-lu hui-pien*; Yen Sung, *Ch'ien-shan-t'ang chi* (1806), 36/8a; Hsia Hsieh 夏燮, *Ming-t'ung-chien* 明通鑑 (Shanghai, 1959), 2407, 2411; Chao Ching-shen 趙景深, *Hsi-ch'ü pi-t'an* 戲曲筆談 (Shanghai, 1962), 75.

Lienche Tu Fang

LU Shen 陸深 (T. 子淵, H. 儼山), September 16, 1477-August 14, 1544, scholar-official and man of letters, was a native of Shanghai in the prefecture of Sung-chiang 松江. Early in the 12th century the Lu family, originally from Kaifeng, moved to Sung-chiang, and in time became one of the wealthiest in that area. During the rebel uprising of the 1360s, Lu Yü-ch'ing 餘慶 (d. 1384), Lu Shen's great-great-grandfather, once witnessed a robbery but was unable to prevent the victim from being harmed; hence the son of the latter bore him a grudge. After the enthronement of Chu Yüan-chang, this man brought the case before the court in Nanking; acting on his charges, the authorities arrested the culprit and indicted Lu Yü-ch'ing for his negligence, sentencing him to exile. Under the law, an offender receiving this sentence was required to be accompanied by two members of his family as guarantors; but first he was obliged to perform hard labor in a limestone mine for a hundred twenty days. Lu Yü-ch'ing chose his two sons-in-law in lieu of his own son who was still a child; and, having completed his term of hard labor in a locality twenty *li* from Nanking, proceeded to the capital to await further instruction. According to regulation, a convict was required to pay his own travel expenses and those of his companions; at that juncture he ran out of funds, and his sons-in-law, reluctant to spend money on their ill-fated father-in-law, deserted him. When Lu Yü-ch'ing discovered that his companions had vanished, he was in great distress, for it was a serious breach of the law for a convict to lose his guarantors—an offense which would involve his own children. Finding no other way to spare his family, Lu drowned himself, as the law required that if a convict died before reaching his destination, his children would not be required to complete the unfulfilled obligation of the father.

At the time of Lu Yü-ch'ing's suicide, Lu Shen's great-grandfather was only six years old; thirty-three years later he married the daughter of a wealthy man in Shanghai, settled in that district, and gradually his descendants became very prosperous.

A precocious child, Lu Shen won a name for his literary talents in his youth. Graduating as *chü-jen* in 1501, he set out for Peking in the following year but failed in the metropolitan examination because his exegesis of the Classics was unacceptable to the examiners. He then entered the National University at Nanking where he made a marked impression on the senior officials in charge, notably Chang Mou and Lo Ch'in-shun (*qq.v.*). Early in 1505 Lu Shen achieved the final degree and was immediately appointed a Hanlin bachelor. The senior members of the Grand Secretariat, such as Liu Chien, Li Tung-yang, and Hsieh Ch'ien (*qq.v.*), we are told, came to think well of his ability. In November, 1507, he was promoted to compiler and served in this capacity until his mother's death a year later. During the mourning period, the grand eunuch Liu Chin (*q.v.*) was in power; in his dislike for members of the Hanlin Academy, Liu had several of them banished from office. Lu was demoted (June, 1509) to be a secretary of the bureau of provisions in the ministry of Rites at Nanking, but he did not take office under the pretext of the mourning requirement. A year later, shortly after Liu Chin's downfall, he was reinstated in his former post; in June, 1512, he was named an attendant at the emperor's classical lessons. A month later he was sent as an envoy to Jao-chou 饒州, Kiangsi, for the investment as princess of the wife of Chu Yu-ch'i 朱祐棨 (the 4th prince of Huai 淮, successor to the princedom in 1505, d. 1524). He kept a diary of his trip entitled *Feng Huai jih-chi* 封淮日記. Arriving in Hangchow on his return journey, Lu was bothered by throat trouble; so he asked for permission to return home and take a prolonged rest. Resuming his duties early in 1516, he was put in charge of the palace examinations and concurrently served as tutor to the eunuchs. In September, 1518, he received promotion to be the director of studies at the National University, but reliquished the office following his father's death in April, 1521. Lu remained at home for the next few years to recuperate from his chronic throat complaint; he erected five rock formations in the vicinity of his residence and adopted the sobriquet Yen-shan 儼山.

Lu Shen was recalled in June, 1528, to be the chancellor of the National University, and occasionally served as expositor of the Classics. In April, 1529, an incident occurred as he was presenting a lecture on Mencius before Emperor Chu Hou-ts'ung (*q.v.*), which caused his removal from office. Before this, Lu had followed the custom of submitting the text to the Grand Secretariat for approval; later he discovered that the contents had been altered by Grand Secretary Kuei O (*q.v.*). Following his presentation Lu seized the occasion to memorialize the emperor, pointing out that it was unprecedented for an expositor's lecture to be altered by a Grand Secretary. The emperor was not disturbed, but it was a violation of the procedure for an expostor to address the emperor on the occasion of presenting a lecture. Lu subsequently submitted a memorial pleading guilty; acting on the recommendation of the ministry of Personnel, the emperor demoted him to be the prefect of Yen-p'ing 延平, Fukien. Lu assumed his duty in September. He left a diary of his trip entitled *Nan-ch'ien* 南遷 *jih-chi*, and recorded his experiences there in a miscellany entitled *Hsi-shan yü-hua* 谿山餘話, 1 *ch.* A month later, he received promotion to be the surveillance vice commissioner of Shansi in control of school administration, a charge he assumed in May, 1530. In this year he composed another miscellany dealing with the events and personalities of the early years of the dynasty, entitled (*Ho Fen*) *Yen-hsien lu* (河汾) 燕閒錄, 1 *ch.* The subjects of discussion ranged from quadruplets to the origins of tea and coal. Before long, however, he clashed with the local prefect over the punishment of a student; they brought the case before the Censorate, whereupon both were relieved of duty pending an investigation. Lu then left for home and did not return until after he was held to be innocent (May, 1532). Again he recorded in lively fashion his experiences en route in a miscellany entitled *T'ing-ts'an lu* 停驂錄, with a supplement called *Hsü* 續 *T'ing-ts'an lu* which includes also comments on national affairs. In October Lu was transferred to a similar position in Chekiang, being promoted in February, 1533, to be the administration vice commissioner of Kiangsi, where in October he became the junior administration commissioner. In this year he composed a miscellany of jottings on Kiangsi and the history of the early years of the dynasty, known as *Yü-chang tsa-ch'ao* 豫章雜抄.

Early in 1535 Lu Shen was transferred to Szechwan as the administration vice commissioner. In May the tribesmen of Mao-chou 茂州 (in western Szechwan) staged an uprising; whereupon the court appointed Chu Wan (*q.v.*) to command an expeditionary force against the rebels. Lu then sent a letter to the deputy regional commander, pointing out the nature of the uprising, and admonished him to adopt a cautious and flexible policy. He proposed the garrisoning of troops on the spot to keep track of the rebels, but favored persuasion rather than the use of arms. It does not seem, however, that his recommendation was adopted, for the rebellious tribesmen were crushed by force in the following month. In this year Lu composed several collections, one of which was an account of his experience in Szechwan, called *Shu-tu* 蜀都 *tsa-ch'ao*. Early in 1536 Lu received promotion to direct the Court of Imperial Sacrifices, returning to the capital after serving for seven years in the provinces.

Two years later Lu Shen began serving concurrently as senior expositor of the Hanlin Academy, returning to the post in which he had officiated two decades earlier. In subsequent years he accompanied Emperor Chu Hou-ts'ung on several occasions when the latter visited the imperial tombs. In March, 1539, as newly appointed grand supervisor of imperial instruction, he joined the entourage when the emperor went to the tomb of his father in Ch'eng-t'ien 承天, Hukuang. Lu wrote an account in two parts of the journey entitled (*Sheng-chia*) *nan-hsün jih-lu* (聖駕) 南巡日錄 and *Ta-chia pei-huan lu* 大駕北還錄 covering the entire trip from March to May. By this time in poor health, Lu decided to retire. He made his first attempt in August when there was a general review of the officials who had completed six years of service, but the emperor ignored his plea. In March, 1540, on the occasion of a natural disaster, he submitted a similar request, but the emperor asked him to remain. Finally in May, 1541, when a fire broke out in the imperial temple, he asked again; this time the emperor approved. Lu then returned home in August, and devoted his remaining years to promoting the welfare of his townsmen. He spent considerable sums in constructing a bridge to facilitate communications and in improving the irrigation system. Before long, however, he contracted malaria, and his health deteriorated. He died in August, 1544, at the age of sixty-seven, a month after the death of his wife, née Mei 梅. He received the canonized name Wen-yü 文裕 and the posthumous title of vice minister of Rites. It is of interest to note that one of his chief biographers was Yen Sung (*q.v.*). They both qualified for the *chin-shih* in the same year and both were selected to enter the Hanlin Academy. In later years they corresponded, exchanged poems and essays, and visited in each other's homes.

A belle-lettrist of note, Lu Shen was a prolific writer, a skillful calligrapher, and a connoisseur of antiques. His collection of writings, entitled *Lu Wen-yü kung chi* 文裕公集, or *Yen-shan wen* 文-*chi*, 100 *ch.*, *wai-chi* 外集, 40 *ch.*, was edited and engraved by his son Lu Chi (*see below*) in 1545; it included a preface by Hsü Chieh (*q.v.*). A supplement, *Lu Wen-yü kung hsü* 續-*chi*, 10 *ch.*, also compiled by Lu Chi, was printed in 1551, with a preface by his fellow townsman, T'ang Chin 唐錦 (T. 士絧, H. 龍江, 1475-1554, cs 1496). Copies of the original Chia-ching edition are held by several major libraries. Separate editions of the above are also available. Another edition of Lu Shen's writings, entitled *Lu Wen-yü kung hsiang-yüan* 向遠 *chi*, 25 *ch.*, containing those essays written during his journeys, is available in the Naikaku Bunko.

Lu Shen's writing covers wide-ranging subjects, including national affairs, eminent personalities, social conditions, phenomenal events, antiques, literature and the arts, and other miscellanea. These add valuable information about the earlier years of the dynasty and the events of his own time. In additon to his diaries,

the following titles are particularly important: *Chin-t'ai chi-wen* 金臺紀聞, 1 *ch.*, *Yü-t'ang man-pi* 玉堂漫筆, accounts of his experiences in the Hanlin Academy during the periods 1505-8, and 1538-41, and *P'ing Hu lu* 平胡錄, a narrative of the rebel uprisings of the 1360s and Chu Yüan-chang's victory over the Mongols. Lu Shen's ability as historian is also revealed in the *Shih-t'ung hui-yao* 史通會要, 3 *ch.* (completed in 1532), a collection of selected sections of and critical remarks about the famous historical work by Liu Chih-chi (661-721), one of the most important contributions on the book. Lu's skill as calligrapher evoked the admiration of Wang Shih-chen (*q.v.*); he also left a collection of comments on calligraphy and biographies of calligraphers of the past entitled *Shu-chi* 書輯, 3 *ch.*, with a preface of 1508. His collection of antiques may be appreciated by the catalogue he prepared: *Ku ch'i-ch'i lu* 古奇器錄, written in the same year. All these titles are included in the *Yen-shan wai-chi*. Lu likewise reprinted (1542) the *Tou-chen lun* 豆(痘)疹論, 2 *ch.*, by a Sung physician, Wen-jen Kuei 聞人規, whose postscript is dated 1232. The reason for this was the death by smallpox of several of Lu's children and grandchildren. Among his literary remains are several obituary pieces lamenting their early loss. In his preface to Wen-jen's work Lu Shen makes two interesting comments: 1) In ancient Chinese medical works the disease of smallpox was not recorded until toward the latter part of the Han dynasty. It was said that this terrible malady was carried back by the expeditionary army after suppressing the Ch'iang 羌 tribes (Tibetans) in the southwest. Was it true then that Chinese in ancient times never suffered from smallpox? 2) It was also observed that only when the Mongols came near the Great Wall did smallpox cause death to many of them. Could the difference between a cold and dry climate, and a hot and humid one be a factor in its spread? Lu then surmised that, since the climate south of the Yangtze was of the latter sort, perhaps it might be favorable for its spread. [Editors' note: On the outbreak of an undetermined pestilence in the first two centuries A. D., possibly as a result of contacts with people of south and central Asia, see Arthur Waley, "Life under the Han Dynasty," *History Today*, February, 1953, page 93 and F. Hirth, *China and the Roman Orient* (Leipsic & Munich, 1885), 175 n.]

Of Lu Shen's thirteen children only two grew to adulthood, Lu Chi 楫 (T. 思豫, H. 小山, 1515–52), and a daughter. The former also made a mark in literature and scholarship. Early in 1539, at the age of twenty-four, he received the yin privilege to become a student in the National University. It does not seem, however, that he ever held an official appointment; instead, he spent most of his years in literary pursuits. He edited a collection of short stories and miscellanies known as *Ku-chin shuo-hai* 古今說海, 32 *ts'e*, with a preface by T'ang Chin dated 1554, which enjoyed considerable popularity. Copies of the original Chia-ching edition are extant. His collection of writings, *Chien-hsia-t'ang kao* 兼葭堂稿, 8 *ch.*, which includes essays, poems, and jottings on the events of the Ming dynasty from the early years down to his time, was printed after his death and still survives. An abridged version of the latter, entitled *Chien-hsia-t'ang tsa-chu* 雜著, is included in the *Chi-lu hui-pien*, edited by Shen Chieh-fu (*q.v.*).

Lu Chi's wife bore him four sons, but all of them died young. In March, 1544, on his deathbed, Lu Shen proposed to Lu Chi that he adopt the son of his nephew as heir. Lu Chi agreed and the boy took the name Lu Yen 郯 (T. 承道, H. 三山). When he reached manhood, Lu Yen, through the yin privilege, became a chief clerk in the Censorate. In the later years of the Wan-li period, he served as prefect of Shih-ch'ien 石阡, Kweichow, and distinguished himself in the suppression of the rebellious Miao 苗 tribesmen. He had two sons, both of whom were

well-versed in letters and calligraphy, and earned the commendation of the distinguished painter Tung Ch'i-chang (ECCP).

Bibliography

1/286/21a; 5/18/42a; 40/28/14b; 43/3/1a; 64/丁 12/2b; 84/丙/33b; MSL (1964), Hsiao-tsung, 4207, Wu-tsung (1965), 770, 1153, 1455, Shih-tsung (1965), ch. 82–288; *Sung-chiang-fu chih*, (preface 1631, Tokyo microfilm), 39/18b, 46/56a, 48/43a, 55/59a; *Shanghai-hsien chih* (1871), 18/41a; Lu Shu-sheng 樹聲 (cs 1541), *Lu Wen-ting kung chi* 文定公集 (NCL microfilm), 5/3a; T'ang Chin, *Lung-chiang chi* 龍江集 (NLP microfilm, no. 899), 12/1a; Lu Shen, *Yen-shan wen-chi* (preface 1546); *id.*, *Yen-shan wai-chi* (NLP microfilm, no. 196); *Huang Ming wen-hai* (microfilm), 2/7/7, 9; Masuda Tsuneo增井經夫, "Mindai shitō gaku"明代史通學, *Tōhōgaku*東方學 15 (December, 1957), 12; W. Franke, *Sources*, 2.3.10, 7.1, 9.5.1; Ping-ti Ho, *The Ladder of Success in Imperial China* (New York, 1962), 66.

Hok-lam Chan

LU T'ang 盧鏜 (T. 子鳴), *ca.* 1520-*ca.* 1570), army officer, was a native of Ju-ning 汝寧 Guard, Honan. Inheriting a minor military rank from his father he served with varying success as regional commander in Nan-Chihli, Chekiang, and Fukien. Lu being purely a military leader with no political ambition, his career was not only determined by the numerous campaigns he conducted against the pirates and unruly Chinese merchants, but was also strongly bound up with the fate of the governor or supreme commander under whom he served. He was considered one of the most capable and daring officers of his time, and his son, Lu Hsiang 相, was also an active military officer.

While serving as regional commander of Fukien, Lu T'ang gained the confidence of the governor, Chu Wan (*q. v.*). In April/May, 1548, Lu, together with the surveillance vice commissioner, K'o Ch'iao 柯喬 (T. 遷之, cs 1529), launched the decisive blow against the pirate stronghold Shuang-hsü-kang 雙嶼港, off the coast of Ting-hai, Chekiang. In September,

1549, he arrested Li Kuang-t'ou 李光頭 and the Shuang-hsü band at Tsou-ma-ch'i 走馬溪, Fukien. Without authorization Chu Wan ordered Lu to have the captives executed. It turned out, however, that some of the victims were not pirates, but merchants from Malacca.

[Editors' note: Gaspar da Cruz (q. v.), in his narrative of sixteenth-century China, has a somewhat different version of the Tsou-ma-ch'i episode. In Chu's account two hundred thirty-nine people are listed, eleven of them white barbarians, their names being given in phoneticized form. No mention is made of the fact that they were Portuguese and that the coastal pirates and the captives, whom Lu reportedly put to death, according to Chinese sources, were Chinese agents of the Portuguese merchants who attempted to smuggle goods ashore for trade. The Portuguese lived to tell the tale. Lu T'ang's name is rendered as Luthissi.]

As a result, accusations were leveled against both of them. Chu committed suicide and Lu might have been condemned to death but for the intervention of Wang Yü (see Wang Shih-chen) who succeeded Chu Wan as governor of Chekiang. Shortly afterwards Lu was released from prison and late in 1551 resumed his post in Fukien. In 1554 he lost several campaigns against the pirates off the coast of Chekiang and together with Wang Yü was dismissed from office, but a short time later was reinstated as local commander of the general administration circuit of east Chekiang. Serving now under Chang Ching (q.v.), he was put in command of Miao 苗 contingents from Pao-ching 保靖, Hukuang. Together with Generals Yü Ta-yu (q.v.) and T'ang K'o-k'uan 湯克寬 (native of P'ei-chou-wei 邳州衞 in Nan-Chihli, d. 1576), he won his second great victory (May, 1555) over a large body of coastal pirates at Wang-chiang-ching 王江涇 in Chekiang. In September he succeeded in capturing Lin Pi-ch'uan 林碧川, a notorious pirate chief. The next year Lu served under Hu Tsung-hsien (q.v.),

governor of Chekiang. Lu took an active part in Hu's plan to capture the most powerful and most cunning of all pirates and illegal overseas merchants, Wang Chih 王 (汪) 直. In 1557 they caught Wang and two years later (December, 1559) put him to death. Early in this year renewed pirate activity was reported from the lower Yangtze and T'ang Shun-chih (q.v.), in his capacity as vice director of the bureau of operations, memorialized the court to have Lu transferred to the scene. Since Lu was able only to oust the pirates from the mainland without successfully annihilating them, Li Sui (see Li Ts'ai) accused him of neglecting his duty. Having just become assistant commissioner-in-chief, Lu as regional commander of Nan-Chihli and Chekiang was demoted but remained in office. Through the influence of T'ang Shun-chih, however, he was soon rehabilitated. For his success in capturing Wang Chih, he was finally promoted to the rank of vice commissioner-in-chief of the central military commission.

In December, 1562, Hu Tsung-hsien was charged with corruption and arrested. Lu, being Hu's protégé, was also involved. Somehow he managed to escape punishment and, stripped of his commissions, returned home. Little information is available on his later activities. As a military officer, according to T'ang Shun-chih, Lu was a seasoned campaigner and skilled in strategy, but his weakness lay in the timidity he showed when confronting the enemy. This might probably account for the several setbacks in his military career. Lu left a record on the coastal defense in Chekiang entitled Che-yang shao-shou ts'e 浙洋哨守册, fragments of which are now preserved in the Ch'ou-hai t'u-pien of Cheng Jo-tseng (q.v.).

Bibliography

1/212/8b; 3/196/7b; Che-chiang t'ung-chih (1899), 148/20a; MSL (1940) Chia-ching, 347/6a, 363/6b, 410/6a, 517/2a; KC (1958), 3732, 3753; Chu Wan, P'i-yü tsa-chi, chüan 2, 4; Cheng Jo-tseng,

Ch'ou-hai t'u-pien (1562), *ch.* 4, 5, 8, 9; T'ang Shun-chih, *T'ang Ching-chou wen-chi, wai-chi* 外集 (SPTK), ch. 2, 3; C. R. Boxer (ed.), *South China in the Sixteenth Century* (London, 1953), 194; Li Hsien-chang 李獻章, "Kasei nenkan ni okeru Sekkai no shishō oyobi hakushu Ō jiki gyoseki kō" 嘉靖年間における浙海の私商及び舶主王直行蹟考, *Shigaku* 史學, 34 (1961), 45, 163.

Bodo Wiethoff

LÜ Chi 呂紀 (T. 廷振, H. 樂愚, or 漁), fl. late 15th century, a native of Yin-hsien 鄞, Chekiang, was a court painter of note during the period of Emperor Chu Yu-t'ang (*q.v.*). Although he studied the work of a number of Sung masters, perhaps the dominant influence on his own craft was the flower and bird paintings of Pien Wen-chin (*q.v.*), a genre in which he too came to excel. As his talents became known he, together with Lin Liang (*q.v.*), was summoned to Peking and installed in the Jen-chih palace 仁智殿. Here Lü was much favored by the emperor, who gave him the title of a commander of the Embroi-dered-uniform Guard. The story is told that some of the paintings executed for the emperor contained didactic suggestions. Whether true or not, the ones that have come down to modern times seem to be straightforward illustrations of fauna and flora in picturesque settings, some-times rich in color. Although he is cred-ited with paintings of landscapes and of human figures in conventional arrange-ments, not one of these seems to have survived. Particularly well known are his paintings of domestic birds and waterfowl. Osvald Sirén makes the suggestion that he may have run "a large workshop and employed assistants of various grades of merit to meet the demands for decorative bird and flower paintings, commonly used as gifts on New Year's Day or on other festival occasions." This may account for the unevenness in quality of some assigned to his name. They were nonetheless highly popular in their day. It is reported that Yen Shih-fan and his father Yen Sung (*q.v.*), for example, who could af-ford every luxury, owned 115 hanging scrolls of flower-and-bird paintings by Lü Chi. Today fifty-one of Lü's paintings are known, according to Sirén. Of these twenty-nine bear his signature, and seven are marked "attributed to." The collection of the Palace Museum, Taiwan, includes twelve; the others are scattered about in collections in China, Japan, Europe, and North America. Hsü Pang-ta (*see* Lu Chih) records only one that bears a date, 1489. Two other dated scrolls in which Lü Chi had a hand are paintings of gar-den parties held in Peking. In the first (1499) Lü Chi was responsible for de-picting the birds; in the second (1503) he painted both figures and scenery (*see* Chou Ching and Li Tung-yang). The Chi-nese government must have considered them highly representative of the art for it sent paintings by Lü Chi to the Panama Exhibition (1915), to the International Exhibition in London (1935–36), and to the series of exhibitions in the United States museums (1961–62). A number of these have been reproduced in albums and general works on Chinese art; one even appeared in an issue of *Time* (May 6, 1957). The library of the Vatican also houses a print made from an engraving of a painting of storks by Lü. As to the paintings which exist, almost all are ver-tical hanging scrolls of good size. (Those preserved in the Palace Museum range from 107.4 × 54.5 cm. to 203.4 × 110.6 cm.)

In the development of the technique of painting flora and fauna, it seems that before the 14th century artists generally executed paintings of album size, seldom large scrolls. By the 15th century the style had developed to bigger composi-tions with freer brushwork. This is evident from the existing examples of Lü Chi's oeuvre. Moreover he evidently worked out his compositions with care and used light colors with skillful washes to produce a misty effect and poetic feeling. Another interesting fact is that probably in his day painting on folding fans was not yet in vogue for there is no record of a single example of his of that type.

Bibliography

65/3/3a; Ho Ch'iao-yüan, *Ming-shan ts'ang*, 藝妙記/4b; Chiang Shao-shu 姜紹書 (17th c.), *Wu-sheng shih shih* 無聲詩史(Shanghai, 1963), 2/19a; *Ku-kung shu-hua chi* 故宮書畫集, nos. 2, 6, 10, 11, 19, 33, 36, 37(October, 1930–October, 1933); *Ku-kung ming-hua san-pai chung* 名畫三百種 (Tai-chung, 1959), 217; *Chung-kuo li-tai ming-hua chi* 歷代名畫集,.I (Peking, 1959), pt. 2, nos. 16–19; Hsü Pang-ta, *Li-tai liu-ch'uan shu-hua tso-p'in pien-nien piao* 流傳書畫作品編年表 (Shanghai, 1963), 52; *Ming hua lu* 明畫錄 (TsSCC ed.), # 1658, 6/60; *Yin-hsien chih* (1877), 45/10b; J. C. Ferguson, *Index of Artists* (Nanking, 1934), 109a; Yonezawa Yoshiho, *Painting in the Ming Dynasty* (Tokyo, 1956), pl. 5; *Catalogue of Chinese Art Treasures* (1961–62), #93; E. A. Strehlneek, *Chinese Pictorial Art* (Shanghai, 1914), 174; O. Sirén, *A History of Later Chinese Painting*, I (1938), 223; *id.*, *Chinese Painting*, IV (1956–58), 142, VI, pls. 164, 165, VII, 216; P. Pelliot, TP, 21 (1922), 349; F. Hirth, *Scraps from a Collector's Notebook* (Leiden, 1905), pl. 2; H. A. Giles, *History of Chinese Pictorial Art* (2d ed. rev. and enl., Shanghai, 1918), 182; A. Waley, *Index of Chinese Artists* (London, 1922), 64.

Chiang Yee

LÜ K'un 呂坤 (T. 叔簡, H. 新吾, 抱獨居士, 沙隨先生), October 24, 1536–July 29, 1618, scholar, official, was a native of Ning-ling 寧陵, Honan, where his family had registered in the artisan category under the surname Li 李. According to a legend, his ancestor, an indigent gardener, provided some important information to the Ming troops about the year 1368 and was awarded a patent exempting him from a commoner's services. On the patent the surname was inadvertently written as Li, so the family was subsequently known by that name for over two hundred years. Lü K'un took the civil examinations under the name Li K'un. A *chü-jen* of 1561, he failed three times before finally passing the metropolitan examination (1571). His mother's illness and her subsequent death prevented his taking the palace examination for the *chin-shih* until 1574. It was only after that, at the age of thirty-nine, that he obtained official permission to restore the family name to Lü.

Throughout his education, official life, and retirement, Lü K'un seems to have sought consciously to embody the Confucian ideals of personal rectitude and official responsibility. At his first post, as magistrate of Hsiang-yüan 襄垣, Shansi, from 1574 to 1576, he gained such a reputation for ability and conduct that the governor made a special request to Peking to have him transferred to the difficult magistracy of Tatung. Here too Lü served meritoriously, once refusing to heed a high official's intervention in a judicial case, thus gaining that official's respect and recommendation. In 1578 before his term of office expired he was promoted to be a secretary in the ministry of Personnel. In both Hsiang-yüan and Tatung the people showed their appreciation by having a shrine erected in his honor. His unusual success may be attributed to many factors. He came from a family owning some two thousand *mou* of farm land which, in combination with his own frugal habits, enabled him to live in comfort and resist financial temptation. Lü was a man of integrity and insisted on strict discipline and the maintenance of law and order. By now he was completely mature, having had a long period of preparation. Whatever steps he took later in office he had probably considered well beforehand. He was determined to achieve a reputation as an official who, while executing the duties required by government regulation, always kept in mind interests of the common people, treating them fairly and with compassion. Perhaps the main factor in reaching his goal was the time of his service, namely, the period of reformation in government under Chang Chü-cheng (*q.v.*), when efficiency and ability counted.

In the ministry of Personnel Lü K'un served nine years (1578-87), rising from secretary to bureau director. The fact that he survived unscathed the purge after Chang Chü-cheng's death in 1582 indicates possibly that he was both astute in dealing with people and genuinely impartial in the matter of appointments. In any case in 1587 he was made an administration vice commissioner of Shantung with assignment as intendant of the Tsinan circuit. Thereafter he served as surveillance commissioner of Shansi (1589-91), administration commissioner of Shensi (1591), and governor of Shansi (1592-94). In all these provinces, in addition to official duties, he worked for the better maintenance of local granaries and the establishment of institutions for the relief of the poor, aged, and disabled. For those among the last who were not too young nor too old he prescribed training in skills like basketry or the braiding of mats. Especially compassionate towards the blind, since his mother suffered for years from loss of sight, Lü ordered the officials of each city to train the blind in a profession such as music, singing, storytelling, and fortunetelling. Although he did not believe in the last himself he compiled a simple textbook from which the younger people among the blind might be orally taught. One might speculate that the custom of addressing a blind fortuneteller respectfully as "hsien-sheng" started at that time.

Perhaps also in memory of his mother Lü compiled an illustrated primer for the instruction of women, entitled *Kuei-fan t'u-shuo* 閨範圖說, 4 *ch.*, published in 1590. The book became widely acclaimed and went through several reprintings. It is said that one copy found its way to the desk of the emperor, a collector of fiction and illustrated books, and was passed on to the favorite imperial concubine, Cheng Kuei-fei (*q.v.*). On her suggestion her brother had the book reprinted with a supplement bearing her name, apparently without consulting Lü; at least so Lü asserted. Later this book became the subject of a dispute in court politics and affected his career. At

the time, however, it enhanced his reputation as a teacher of morals for he was already well known as a promoter of ethical behavior for officials.

On the assumption of each provincial post, he had issued to his subordinates an exhortation which he called a yüeh 約 (agreement or promise). These documents circulated under the title of Ming-chih 明職 (on the duties of provincial officials), Hsiang-chia yüeh 鄉甲約 (local sub-official personnel), Feng-hsien yüeh 風憲約 (surveillance officials and the provincial censor), Yü-cheng 獄政 (officials in charge of prisons and convicts), and Tu-fu yüeh 督撫約 (governors and governors-general). In 1598 these were brought together and printed under the collective title *Lü-kung shih-cheng lu* 呂公實政錄 (Lü's writings on effective service), 10 *ch.* In the Ch'ing dynasty this work came to be regarded as a handbook for provincial administrators and circulated after some abridgment and adaptation under the title *Shih-cheng lu,* 7 *ch.*

Meanwhile Lü's official career, at first quite promising, was cut short on account of his outspokenness. In 1592 he was recalled to Peking as an assistant censor-in-chief. In the same year he was promoted to vice censor-in-chief and in 1594 to vice minister of Justice. He fell ill several times in 1595 and 1596, but his requests for retirement were refused. This was a difficult period for conscientious officials at the court, as the emperor Chu I-chün (*q.v.*) developed arrogant and irresponsible habits. In order to exact more money for his privy purse the emperor began to entrust eunuchs with missions and functions, sometimes outside the existing government organization, frequently with supervising power over the officials and almost always in conflict with the rights and privileges of the people. In May, 1597, Lü submitted a long memorial of some eight thousand words enumerating the evil practices at court, pointing out the signs of danger and restiveness throughout the empire—which Lü attributed to the greed, malice, callousness, and other failings of the emperor himself— and exhorting the emperor to reform. The document known as Yu-wei·shu 憂危疏 (memorial on impending disasters), reached the emperor but was laid aside without comment. Indirectly, however, the emperor showed his displeasure. Within half a month Lü was accused by a supervising censor of dereliction of duty and was "permitted to retire because of illness." When another supervising censor accused a grand secretary of forcing Lü out of government service, the emperor confessed that he himself was responsible for Lü's ousting—an unusual revelation by the emperor on the part he played in court affairs during his reign.

Even in retirement Lü was at first not permitted to live undisturbed. Early in 1598 an anonymous circular appeared in Peking, attacking him for his alleged part in the intrigue which favored the choice of the emperor's third son, Chu Ch'ang-hsün (see Cheng Kuei-fei), as heir apparent rather than the eldest son, Chu Ch'ang-lo (ECCP). Chu Ch'ang-hsün's mother was the emperor's favorite consort whose edition of Lü's book on female exemplars was shown as evidence against Lü. The circular bore the title Yu-wei hung-i 竑議, meaning a discussion of Lü's memorial, the Yu-wei shu. Lü submitted a memorial in April, 1598, declaring his innocence and asking for an investigation; the emperor upon its receipt remarked that he wanted no more vexatious protestations. Late in 1603 another anonymous circular on the same subject appeared, entitled Hsü 續 Yu-wei hung-i (further discussion on the Yu-wei shu; see Kuo Cheng-yü). This time Lü remained silent, for he knew that the emperor had a stubborn trait and would neither relent nor reform. (When Lü died in 1618, the emperor granted only the usual allowances for his burial, but in 1621 he received posthumously the higher rank of a minister of Justice.)

During the twenty-one years at home (1597–1618) Lü K'un always made himself available to the authorities for possible assistance in public works. In anticipation of the rebellions and civil wars that were to start barely ten years after his death, he directed the rebuilding of the city walls at his native place. He records the event in his Hsiu-ch'eng shu 修城書. He wrote a book in 1607 on city defense and weaponry for use against rebel attacks, to which he gave the title Chiu-ming shu 救命書 (A handbook on saving one's life). He had tried his best to warn the emperor and the officials that farmers and weavers, the country's chief producers, should be well treated; else disaster would surely befall. Now he could do no more than leave a book which told his neighbors how to save their lives, even though as he predicted in his preface he knew it was of no avail and that some day they would regret having paid no heed. The city of Ning-ling fell to the rebels in 1642 without a fight. A copy of the Chiu-ming shu printed in 1614 is in the Columbia university Library. The Chih-hai (ECCP, p. 36) includes another edition in 2 chüan with illustrated treatises on weapons, probably added by a later editor.

He also edited his essays and poems in his retirement and printed them in 1617 under the title Ch'ü-wei-chai wen-chi 去僞齋文集, 10 ch. This work was reprinted by a grandson in 1674. It met with some criticism in the 18th century for certain of its comments about developments on the frontier in 1588–90. This did not prevent the Ssu-k'u editors from expressing appreciation both of the author and of his work, although they failed to include the latter in the Imperial Library. Original unexpurgated texts have survived; one is in the Columbia University library. At about the same time (1674) all of his works then available were reissued under the collective title Lü Hsin-wu ch'üan-shu 新吾全書 consisting of twenty-two items in a total of 58 ch. The Shih-cheng lu is listed as 7 ch. in this collection, indicating that the part on the duties of governors and governors-general had been deleted. Among other titles may be mentioned the following: a work on measles *Chen-k'o* 疹科; a primer in rhyme for boys and girls by his father, Lü Te-sheng 得勝 (d. 1568), entitled *Hsiao-er yü* 小兒語 with Lü K'un's supplements *Hsü hsiao-er yü*; annotations of a Taoist work, *Yin-fu-ching chu* 陰符經注; a lexicon arranged by rhyme *Chiao-t'ai-yün* 交泰韻, and a collection of philosophical and ethical observations entitled *Shen-yin-yü* 呻吟語, 6 *ch*. The last mentioned work, first printed in 1593 in 4 *chüan*(?) originally, has been reprinted several times, and quoted in many anthologies. An abridged version, *Shen-yin-yü-chai* 摘, 2 *ch*., is said to have been edited by Lü K'un himself in his last years. It was printed in 1616 by his son, Lü Chih-wei 知畏, who added a supplement. Although ten titles by Lü K'un are mentioned in the *Ssu-k'u* catalogue, only the *Shen-yin-yü-chai* was copied into the Imperial Library about 1780, partly because it represented the author's own selections. The *Shen-yin-yü* in 6 *chüan* was reprinted in 1687 by Lu Lung-chi (ECCP) who added a *chüan* of critical notes, *chih-i* 質疑. In the meantime several editions of *Shen-yin-yü* reached Japan. One Japanese scholar of the Wang Yang-ming school, Ōshio Chū sai 大鹽中齋 (1793–1837), in a letter to Satō Issai 佐藤一齋 (1772–1859), mentioned how he was inspired by Lü's work. In 1860 the Japanese government reprinted the Lu Lung-chi edition of *Shen-yin-yü*, giving it the title *Ryo Shin-go sensei goroku* 呂新吾先生語錄, which seems to have been ignored by the public probably due to the shift of interest to Western studies at that time. In 1955 there appeared a complete translation by Kōda Rentarō 公田連太郎 (1874–1963), entitled *Shingingo*, which went through a second edition in 1963.

One passage in the book lamenting the decay of law and order of his day may be of interest today. A part of it reads, "Now at court the bureaucrats look down" on the ministers; on the frontier the soldiers disrespect their commanders; at home sons and their wives neglect their parents; in school the students are insolent toward their teachers. and lower classmen dispute their seniors; and in communities the lower and younger abuse their superiors and elders. All indulge in avarice and recalcitrance. ignoring manners and law. Such deterioration should have been checked but has been permitted to grow. It can lead only to rebellions and the fall of government. The tendency is already too serious to check, yet the idiots keep on making it worse. What's to be done!" His worries for late Ming China seem still applicable centuries later.

Lü K'un declared that in philosophy he belonged to no school or sect but was an independent thinker, saying 我只是我, "I am just myself." He was rather pragmatically and materialistically inclined. In his opinion the neo-Confucian writings at best were unlikely to have real effect on those responsible for the durability of the state or the sustenance and rectitude of the people, and he thought they should merely be filed away. He considered the Confucian theory, heaven's will manifesting itself in omens and disasters, as unfounded and harmful, for it allowed a person holding it, especially an emperor, to shift the blame for catastrophes to heaven and to neglect self-criticism. In this respect his thinking was close to that of Liu Tsung-yüan (773–819). In 1962 a selection of Lü's writing appeared in Peking under the title *Lü K'un che-hsüeh hsüan-chi* 哲學選集.

Like his older contemporaries, Chang Chü-cheng and Hai Jui (*q.v.*). Lü K'un laid stress on fairness and integrity in the enforcement of the law, based on an understanding of human nature, to achieve the smooth functioning of government for the benefit of all, the emperor, the nobility, and the people. He frequently commented that the main idea guiding an official in his dealings with the people should be compassion. In his opinion desires are a part of human nature and so he was opposed to the neo-Confucianists who considered desires evil. The law is drawn up to prevent the conflict of desires by defining the limit of each one's share or lot. This should be applied to everybody, including the emperor, he averred. He rebelled against some of the regulations on family relationship and rites as prescribed by Chu Hsi (1130–1200) and other neo-Confucianists, enumerating the practices he considered contrary to natural alliance (忠) and sincerity (信). This he did in a work entitled *Chia-li-i* 家禮疑 which. however. was regarded by later editors as too unconventional; they changed its title to a less obtrusive one, *Ssu-li i* 四禮疑, 5 *ch.*

Before he died he burned those of his writings which he held to be unacceptable to his contemporaries. One of the manuscripts he destroyed was a work to be entitled *Kang-mu shih-cheng* 綱目是正, exposing the objectionable passages in the chronicle *T'ung-chien* 通鑑 *kang-mu*, usually attributed to Chu Hsi. In the preface to the *Kang-mu shih-cheng*, the only part of the work that remains, Lü wrote that after forty years of study he had come to the conclusion that the chronicle was not the work of Chu Hsi; it contained. too many mistakes in judgment to be considered the product of a sage. To many of the rules of conduct which the Sung scholars propagated, Lü raised questions or objections. He forbade his family to solicit eulogies about him after his death or to have any religious ceremonies. He wrote his own epitaph in which he made an estimate of his character. Here is a summary of his confessions: he maintained that he was straightforward and strict, and that he enjoyed his reputation for incorruptibility because his love of being an official overcame his love for money, because he was constrained by the fear of being caught and punished, and because he desired to have the distinction of being unconcerned about making a name. This unusual autobio-

graphical epitaph was included in his collected works and reprinted in the *Lü K'un che-hsüeh hsüan-chi*. In 1826 the tablet of Lü K'un was admitted to the Temple of Confucius.

Bibliography

1/226/11a; 3/210/9b; 83/54/11a; KC (1958), 5122; MSL (1940), Shen-tsung, 309/1b, 312/12a, 320/5a, 572/12b; Liu Jo-yü, *Cho-chung chih*, 1/12a; Lü K'un, *Ch'ü-wei-chai wen-chi*; *Huang Ming ching-shih wen-pien*, chüan 415–16; Ku Ying-t'ai (ECCP), *Ming-ch'ao chi-shih pen-mo*, 67/9b, 12b; T'ao Hsi-sheng (BDRC), *Chung-kuo cheng-chih ssu-hsiang shih* 中國政治思想史, IV (Taipei, 1964), 242; Hou Wai-lu 侯外廬, *Chung-kuo ssu-hsiang t'ung-shih* 思想通史, IV (1960), 940; *Chung-kuo che-hsüeh shih tzu-liao hsüan-chi* 哲學史資料選集, Sung-Yüan-Ming, II (Peking, 1962), 600; Chu Chieh-fan 朱介凡, "Lü K'un ti 的 *Hsiao-er-yü*," in *Ta-lu tsa-chih*, XIX (1959), 191, 215; Cheng Lien 鄭廉, *Yü-pien chi-lüeh* 豫變紀略 (三怡堂 ed. 1922), 4/13b; SK (1930), 179/6a; Yao Chin-yüan, *Chin-hui ch'ou-hui shu-mu* (1883), 18b; *Lü K'un che-hsüeh hsüan-chi*, Peking, 1962; Kōda Rentarō (tr.), *Shingingo* (1963), 299; Sun Ch'i-feng (ECCP), *Li-hsüeh tsung-chuan* 理學宗傳 (1880), 23/1a; Shen Te-fu, *Yeh-hu pien* (1959), 474, 873; W. Franke, *Sources*, 5.7.27, 6.2.13; T. Watters, *A Guide to the Tablets in a Temple of Confucius* (1879), 218; John K. Skryock, *The Origin and Development of the State Cult of Confucius* (New York, 1932), 259.

Chaoying Fang

LÜ Nan 呂柟 (T. 仲木, H. 涇野), May 12, 1479-August 11, 1542, thinker and official, was a native of Kao-ling 高陵, Shensi. A disciple of Hsüeh Ching-chih (*see* Hsüeh Hsüan), Lü Nan attracted quite early the attention of the directors of education, especially Yang I-ch'ing (*q. v.*). He passed the provincial examination in 1501, but failed twice in the metropolitan. Meanwhile, he became a student in the National University, where he took part in the philosophical and ethical discussions, and was noted for his strict observance of the rules of conduct. It is said that in 1505, when the students assembled to mourn the death of the emperor, Chu Yu-t'ang (*q. v.*), and everyone was supposed only to cry out on command, Lü wept with genuine emotion. In 1508 he passed the metropolitan examination under Chan Jo-shui (*q. v.*), topped the *chin-shih* list as the *chuang-yüan*, and was appointed a first class Hanlin compiler. At that time the powerful eunuch, Liu Chin (*q. v.*), also a native of Shensi, was known to be partial to all northerners, especially his fellow provincials, but Lü was so well known for his integrity and his ability as a writer that his success in examinations did not cause any suspicion of favoritism. This was in sharp contrast to the scandal in connection with the son of Chiao Fang (*q. v.*), the fourth on the same *chin-shih* list. Reportedly Lü returned the gifts from Liu Chin and maintained a scrupulous distance from him. In 1510 Lü submitted a memorial advising the emperor, Chu Hou-chao (*q. v.*), to listen to classical lectures and attend to his governmental duties, and in this way hoped to steer the emperor away from his eunuch companions. Perhaps apprehensive of the eunuchs' wrath, Lü took leave and returned home, and so was not affected when, at the fall of Liu Chin, some officials from Shensi suffered punishment and disgrace.

In 1512 Lü was summoned to his previous office in the capital. When fire broke out in the palace precincts (1514), Lü once more submitted a memorial giving detailed advice, urging the emperor to reform his conduct and to attend more seriously to the business of government. As this yielded no result, he begged for sick leave, and returned home for seven years, during which his father died (1516). After the accession to the throne of Chu Hou-ts'ung (1521), Lü resumed his former post. By this time, his literary fame had spread far and wide. The Korean government even submitted a memorial to the court, praising Lü's talents, and asking for his writings. In 1523 he served as an associate at the metropolitan examination. In these days, there was much opposition at the capital to the philosophy of Wang Shou-

jen (*q. v.*). Lü Nan did his best to prevent the issuance of a formal order prohibiting Wang's teachings. When, in the following year, the emperor awarded his deceased father additional honors (*see* Chang Fu-ching), Lü remonstrated in a long memorial which brought about his imprisonment. A fellow inmate was Tsou Shou-i (*q. v.*), a disciple of Wang Shou-jen who only a few days previously had made a similar move, and was now on trial. Both, however, won wide praise for their courage. Lü Nan received a demotion to the assistant magistracy of Hsieh-chou 解州, Shansi, where he remained three years, improving the local administration, promoting moral education through community compacts (hsiang-yüeh 鄉約) and the establishment of the Hsieh-liang 解梁 Academy, and erecting a shrine in honor of Ssu-ma Kuang (1019-86). He was transferred next to Nanking as director of the bureau of evaluations in the ministry of Personnel (1527). Remaining there for eight years, he served in various capacities, including those of chief minister of the Seal Office, and vice minister of the Court of Imperial Sacrifices. Together with his mentor, Chan Jo-shui, he presided at numerous public lectures, attracting large audiences of interested scholars. His circle of friends included such men as Ku Lin (*see* Yüan Chiung) and Tsou Shou-i, who had also been transferred to Nanking. In 1535 he was appointed chancellor of the National University in Peking, but a year later was sent back to Nanking as vice minister of Rites. In 1537 he used his influence to protect Chan Jo-shui from being attacked as a teacher of "false learning." Two years later, on learning of the emperor's proposed visit to the grave of his deceased father in Hukuang, Lü submitted several memorials counseling the emperor to refrain from the costly adventure. The emperor ignored them, and proceeded to Hukuang (March 1539). After returning to Peking in May, he held audiences to receive congratulations from the officials.

Lü represented the courtiers of Nanking in presenting their felicitations. On the way north he saw the devastation of some areas in Honan where the imperial procession had passed through. There were still exposed corpses of people who had starved to death. These he ordered local officials to inter. His warnings proved prophetic, and he went to Peking with a heavy heart. Just then the main audience hall suffered some damage from a bolt of lightning, and higher officials were supposed to regard this sign as due to their own malfeasance or incompetence. Lü took the occasion to ask for retirement and it was granted. He returned home for the last time, and devoted himself to the instruction of disciples in the Pei-ch'üan ching-she 北泉精舍 one; was Lü Ch'ien 呂潛 (T. 時見, H. 愧軒, 1517–78), native of Shensi. He died four years later, at the age of sixty-three. In 1567 he received posthumously the title of minister of Rites, and was canonized as Wen-chien 文簡.

As a thinker, Lü Nan was brought up through the instruction of Hsüeh Ching-chih and in the teaching of Hsüeh Hsüan, a devoted adherent of the philosophy of Ch'eng I (1033–1107) and Chu Hsi (1130–1200). He interpreted the doctrine of "investigation of things" in terms of "exhausting the principles (li 理) of things," and also believed that knowledge should precede action. In his own life, he moved from the extensive study of the Classics to the moral cultivation of the person. He did not approve of Wang Shou-jen's doctrine of the extension of liang-chih, but made a special effort to understand it, even going to T'ai-chou to visit Wang Shou-jen's disciple, Wang Ken (q. v.). Lü was a tireless and devoted teacher, careful in cultivating the individual talents of his disciples. He came to be acclaimed as the foremost philosopher of northwest China since the time of Chang Tsai (1020–77). The editors of the Ming-shih make the comment that, at a time when scholars had become follow-ers either of Wang Shou-jen or of Chan Jo-shui, only Lü Nan and Lo Ch'in-shun (q. v.) remained faithful to the teachings of Ch'eng I and Chu Hsi.

Lü Nan left voluminous writings: essays, poems, commentaries on the Confucian Classics and on the Sung philosophers, official documents, and local gazetteers which he helped to compile. The Lü Ching-yeh 涇野 hsien-sheng wen-chi 文集 is extant, in 36 and 38 chüan. The latter version was published in 1832, with a preface dated 1592; chüan 31 contains a dozen or more of his memorials. There is also a supplement, the Hsü-k'o 續刻 Lü Ching-yeh hsien-sheng wen-chi, 8 ch., which includes the biography of Lü Nan by Feng Ts'ung-wu (q. v.). It too was republished in 1832. According to the editors of the Ssu-k'u, the following of Lü's lectures and recorded sayings on the Classics have been published: Chou-i shuo-i 周易說翼, 3 ch. (1539 preface); Shang-shu shuo-yao 尚書說要, 5 ch.; Mao-shih shuo-hsü 毛詩說序, 6 ch.; Li-wen 禮問, 2 ch.; Ch'un-ch'iu shuo-chih 春秋說志, 5 ch.; Ssu-shu yin-wen 四書因問, 6 ch. Some of these may have disappeared, but the last was included in the Imperial Library. A copy in 1 chüan is reportedly in the Jimben Library, Kyoto. Also included in the Ssu-k'u is the Ching-yeh tzu nei-p'ien 子內篇, 27 ch. Lü's works on the Sung philosophers include Chou-tzu ch'ao-shih 周子鈔釋, 3 ch., Chang-tzu 張子 ch'ao-shih, 6 ch., Er-Ch'eng-tzu 二程子 ch'ao-shih, 10 ch., and Chu-tzu 朱子 ch'ao-shih, 2 ch. Most of these give well selected passages from the philosophers, as well as Lü Nan's explanations. The Chu-tzu ch'ao-shih is, of course, too short to do any justice to the philosopher Chu Hsi. Lü Nan also helped to compile the local records, the Hsieh-chou chih (1525), the Yang-wu-hsien 陽武 縣 chih (in Honan, 1526), and the Kao-ling chih (1541); copies of the first two are exceedingly rare but are known to exist. Lü paid more than usual attention to his prose style. He was allegedly influenced in this respect by his contemporary, Li Meng-yang (q. v.).

Bibliography

3/264/5b; 5/37/21a; 7/28/11b; 16/45/26b; 32/104
/9a; 40/33/1a; 42/61/17a; 61/114/1a; 63/22/4a;
83/8/1a; *Ming-shih* (Taiwan ed.), 16/111, 282/
3183; MSL (1965), Wu-tsung, 0868, Shih-tsung,
0465, 0986; SK (1930), 7/5a, 13/4a, 17/3a, 25/
8a, 30/3a, 36/4a, 93/4b,   176/8a; Lü Nan, *Lü
Ching-yeh hsien-sheng wen-chi* (1832); id., *Hsü-k'o
Lü Ching-yeh hsien-sheng wen-chi* (1832); *Kao-
ling-hsien hsü-chih* 續志 (1884), 5/2b; *Ch'ung-hsiu
重修 Ching-yang* 涇陽 *-hsien hsü-chih*   (1911), 12/
16b; W. Franke, *Sources*, 5.5.22.

Julia Ching

LÜ T'iao-yang 呂調陽 (T. 和卿, H. 豫所),
1516-January 16, 1580, scholar-official, who
rose to be a grand secretary, was a native
of Lin-kuei 臨桂-hsien, prefectural city of
Kuei-lin 桂林, Kwangsi. His ancestors hailed
from Ta-yeh 大冶 in the prefecture of
Wuchang, but shortly after the beginning of the Ming dynasty the family, serving in the wei-so, were often stationed at
Kuei-lin. His great-grandfather eventually settled there. His grandfather,
ashamed of his military background, enrolled in the local school but died early.
His father, Lü Chang 璋 (T. 古愚子),
also went to school, became a *kung-sheng*,
and was eventually made the magistrate
of Hsü-wen 徐聞 in the prefecture of
Lei-chou 雷州, Kwangtung. He encouraged
Lü T'iao-yang to follow in his footsteps.
At the age of eighteen Lü succeeded in
qualifying for the *chü-jen* (1534), but did
not immediately go to Peking to take the
metropolitan examinations. Instead, he
married and accompanied his father to
Hsü-wen, and from there went north to
enroll at the National University; he likewise studied for three years under Ch'eng
Wen-te 程文德 (T. 舜敷, H. 松溪, cs 1529,
1497-1559, Pth. 文恭), a well-known follower of Wang Shou-jen (*q.v.*). After ten
years he decided to try for the *chin-shih*.
On his second attempt he attained second
place in the examinations of 1550, and
was given an appointment as compiler
in the Hanlin Academy. His service there
was interrupted in 1557, when he had to
hasten home to attend his father's obsequies, and again in 1559 his mother's.
Three years later he paid his respects at
the graves of his distant ancestors in Ta-
yeh before returning to the capital.

Lü became director of studies at the
National University in 1563 and two years
later grand counselor 諭德 of the directory of instruction and concurrently reader-in-waiting in the Hanlin Academy. His
political career took a sudden upward turn
in a succession of promotions with the
start of the Lung-ch'ing reign. First he
was appointed chancellor of the National
University in Nanking in mid-1567, and
three months later he was transferred to
the chancellorship of the National University in Peking, and became junior vice
minister of Rites in Nanking at the end
of the year. The following year he was
back in Peking as right vice minister of
Rites and concurrently Hanlin chancellor.
In 1569 he was shifted to the ministry of
Personnel, holding the same titles, and a
year later was promoted to be senior vice
minister of Personnel and put in charge of
the supervisorate of imperial instruction.
His lectures are said to have made an impression on Emperor Chu Tsai-hou (*q.v.*).
In 1571 he and Chang Chü-cheng (*q.v.*) were
put in charge of the metropolitan examinations, and Lü was ordered to instruct
newly recruited Hanlin bachelors. A year
later he became the minister of Rites.

The premature death of the emperor
brought further political advantage to Lü.
Perhaps because he appeared as a learned
and honest official rather than an overly
ambitious man, he was selected to enter
the Grand Secretariat at the instance of
Chang Chü-cheng with whom he was to
serve for the next six years. As Chang
assumed all the decision-making power,
Lü spent much of his time in literary
activity as Chang had intended. He helped
prepare both the *Mu-tsung shih-lu* (completed July, 1574) and the *Shih-tsung shih-
lu* (completed September, 1577). Wu Kuo-
lun (*q.v.*), who wrote the record of his
career 行狀, considered the *Shih-tsung*

shih-lu largely Lü's work and praised him highly as a historian. Tung Ch'i-ch'ang (ECCP), however, disagreed, considering some of his remarks about certain officials (Hu Tsung-hsien and T'ang Shun-chih, *qq.v.*), for example, derogatory and unfair. On the completion of both works, Lü and other editors received appropriate rewards. Lü also took part in compiling the *Ti-chien t'u-shuo* (*see* Chang Chü-cheng), an illustrated discussion of the imperial rulers of the past, which was submitted to the emperor (then hardly ten years of age) on January 20, 1573, to be used as his textbook. The editors of the *Ssu-k'u* catalogue consign it to the list of books to be noticed but not to be included in the Imperial Library. There are several copies both in Taiwan and in Japan; the Library of Congress copy is incomplete. Before he left office, Lü was also (1576) put in charge of the revision of the *Ta Ming hui-tien* (*see* Shen Shih-hsing) at the request of Chang Chü-cheng.

In 1577 Lü almost got the chance to become chief grand secretary because of the death of Chang Chü-cheng's father, the rule requiring an official to observe three years of mourning (actually 27 months). In fact, only three days after the news had reached Chang, Lü began to assume the role of a chief grand secretary. This step reportedly infuriated Chang. According to the *Kuo-ch'üeh* (*see* T'an Ch'ien), it was the reason for Chang's determination not to take the mourning leave for fear of losing his power. As Chang managed to have his way, Lü began to feel uneasy, for the emperor instructed Lü later to continue to perform the routine tasks but to leave important affairs for the chief grand secretary (*i.e.*, Chang Chü-cheng) to decide. As a result Lü requested retirement on grounds of ill health, and the request was eventually granted after ten attempts. He died a year and a half later at the age of sixty-three, and was given posthumously the title of grand guardian, and the name Wen-chien 文簡. Parenthetically one may

note that neither the *Ming-shih kao* nor the *Ming-shih* accords him a biography; this is true too of the *T'u-shu chi-ch'eng*. One must find the basic sources for his life in epitaphs and records written by his contemporaries. It is of interest to note that Chang Chü-cheng wrote his tomb inscription.

Lü T'iao-yang had one son, Lü Hsing-chou 興周 (T. 渭南), who became a *chin-shih* in 1577, the same year in which a son of Chang Chü-cheng took second place. Because Chang Chü-cheng and Lü T'iao-yang were grand secretaries, this fact naturally provoked unfavorable comment. But there seems to be no evidence of favoritism on the part of the examiners. Lü Hsing-chou received an appointment as director of an office in the ministry of Rites and rose to be sub-prefect of Nanking before retiring for reasons of health.

Bibliography

4/10/8b; 5/17/118a; 32/113/11b; *Ming-shih* (Taiwan ed.), 136, 726, 752, 2480, 2520, 2535, 2632, 2658; MSL (1965), Mu-tsung, 0061, 1652, 1665, Shen-tsung (1966), 0290, 1369, 1436, 1544, 1563, 1652; KC (1958), *ch.* 65–71; *Lin-kuei-hsien chih* (1905), 4/3b, 10b, 19/3b, 27/47b, 28/20a; SK (1930), 90/1a; NCL *Catalogue of Rare Books*, 404; Naikaku Bunko *Catalogue*, 100; L. of C. *Catalogue of Rare Books*, 441; Wu Kuo-lun, *Chan-ch'ui-tung-kao* (Ming ed.), 46/7b; *Chan-ch'ui-tung hsü 續-kao*, 1/14b; T'u Lung, *Pai-yü chi* (Ming ed.), 17/9b; Chang Chü-cheng, *Chang T'ai-yüeh wen-chi* (Ming ed.), 13/1; W. Franke, *Sources*, 1.1.9, 10.

L. Carrington Goodrich and Angela Hsi

LÜ Wei-ch'i 呂維祺 (T. 介孺, H. 豫石, 明德, Pth. 忠節), August 23, 1587-March 2, 1641, conscientious official, writer, and philanthropist, was a native of Hsin-an 新安, some thirty miles west of Loyang, Honan. His family was registered under the category of artisan. Having lost his mother at the age of five, he was brought up by his grandmother and later his stepmother. His father, Lü K'ung-hsüeh 孔學

(T. 尙文, H. 紹中, d. 1635), a clerk in the district office who raised his family from poverty to moderate means, was a strict disciplinarian so far as the son's schooling and social behavior were concerned. At fifteen Lü Wei-ch'i was admitted to the district school. Qualifying as *chü-jen* in 1612 and as *chin-shih* a year later, he received an appointment as prefectural judge of Yen-chou 兗州, Shantung, where he served five years (1614-19). In this position he put into effect the pao-chia 保甲 system, thus thwarting the rebellious plans of the White Lotus sect in the area (*see* Hsü Hung-ju). The people in gratitude erected shrines in his honor. In 1615 he was invited to serve as an assistant examiner in the provincial examination of Shensi and, in 1618, in the same capacity in Shantung. During a famine in 1616 he contributed from his own property to relief. When transferred (1619) to the ministry of Personnel, he served conscientiously, rising from secretary to vice director and then director of a bureau.

In September, 1620, when Lü learned that the youthful heir apparent, Chu Yu-chiao (ECCP), was about to make an excursion to the southern part of Peking two days before enthronement, he persuaded the grand secretaries to protest. He also wrote a memorial to the heir apparent warning him against the influence of the eunuchs, and urged him to confer with the grand secretaries on matters of state and to punish those allegedly responsible for the sudden death of the preceding emperor, Chu Ch'ang-lo (ECCP).

Early in 1621 Lü was granted temporary leave to be with his father at Hsin-an. In 1622 he established the academy, Chih-ch'üan shu-yüan 芝泉書院, where he lectured on Confucian tenets and tested the students in their writing of essays. A year later he built a shrine in the academy in memory of seven local neo-Confucianists, including the Ch'eng brothers of the 11th century, and the Ming scholars Ts'ao Tuan (*q.v.*) and

Meng Hua-li (*see* Ku Hsien-ch'eng). Apparently his activities at Hsin-an and Lo-yang were in accord with the national movement of the Tung-lin party (*see* Ku Hsien-ch'eng) and were considered as such by the eunuch party under Wei Chung-hsien (ECCP). In 1626, when Wei came to feel so secure in his position as imperial favorite that he even promoted a campaign to have temples in his honor erected throughout the land, Lü, learning that one was about to go up in the capital of his own province, Kaifeng, protested and tried to dissuade people from contributing. For this he was cashiered and prevented from being recalled to service, and his academy was named for destruction as were academies everywhere, but it was saved because of the shrine to the seven worthies.

After the death of Chu Yu-chiao, Lü came back into favor and expressed his feelings in a number of poems about reentering political life. In 1628 he received an appointment as chief minister of the seal office, and then transferred to the office of vice minister of the Court of Imperial Sacrifices. In this latter capacity he acted primarily as overseer of the Ssu-i kuan 四夷館 (College of Translators; *see* Cheng Ho). As overseer Lü revised and published (1630) a collection of documents on the college, which he entitled *Tseng-ting kuan-tse* 增定館則. This work, which derives from an earlier, compilation (1543) by Kuo Yün 郭鋆 (T. 允重, cs 1532), augmented (1613) by Hung Wen-heng 洪文衡 (T. 平仲, cs 1589), includes edicts and memorials concerning the college, details about its establishment, appointments of students, regulation of officials, salaries and allowances, expenses, petitions, communications, rules, and notices. Long thought lost in China, a copy of the 1688 edition was discovered in Japan and republished in 1928 by the University of Kyoto, with a preface by Haneda Tōru 羽田亨, under the title *Ssu-i 譯kuan-tse.* Later a facsimile reproduction of the 1688 edition was included in the

third series of *Hsüan-lan-t'ang ts'ung-shu*
(comp. by Cheng Chen-to, BDRC). In
the same year (1628) Lü was appointed
to serve in Nanking as second vice minister of Revenue and assistant censor-in-
chief, being put in charge of the grain
supply. At the same time he took office
the Yangtze valley granaries were empty
due to arrears in taxes, bribing of tax
officials, and heavy borrowing from them
by the government. He memorialized the
throne setting forth these facts and suggesting measures to collect taxes in arrears and to prevent misappropriations in
the future. The emperor approved. Lü
then established a rigid scheme of accounting and auditing and hastened the
recovery of sizable debts rather than minor
ones. He also decreased the percentage
of surtax on grain, allowing payment in
wet, unsifted rice in order to encourage
people to settle their tax debts more
promptly. By introducing reforms at the
local mints he increased tenfold the profits
from casting copper coins. He also rebuilt
the dilapidated granaries at Nanking and
in three years managed to have them
filled.

When in 1631 eunuchs were sent
out as grand defenders, Lü remonstrated
in blunt language to the throne. He also
revealed the bad effects of placing a customs barrier at Wu-hu 蕪湖 (Anhwei),
but his advice was ignored. Through his
reforms for the public weal he had antagonized many eunuchs and bureaucrats.
Then in 1633 he became minister of War
in Nanking. The rebellion led by Li Tzu-
ch'eng and Chang Hsien-chung (both in
ECCP) was, though still disorganized, a
serious threat, spreading from Honan in
all directions, including the region northwest of Nanking. Lü asked (February,
1634) that every effort be made to prevent the rebels from seizing the ancestral
tombs of the dynasty in Feng-yang 鳳陽
prefecture. Early in 1635, the rebels were
reported to be moving toward the area.
Lü dispatched local commanders there
and also strengthened the defenses at

Nanking. Feng-yang surrendered and the
ancestral tombs were destroyed. In March,
1635, when he was criticized by his detractors as responsible for these disasters, he
was dismissed. Before he left Nanking he
composed an appeal to the spirit of the
founder of the dynasty, protesting the injustice of his dismissal and enumerating his
achievements. He then joined his father at
Loyang, where he opened a second neo-Confucian school, the I-lo society 伊洛會. After
his father died in September, 1635, Lü completed his studies on the *Hsiao-ching* 孝經
(Classic of filial piety), consisting of the
Hsiao-ching pen-i 本義, 2 *ch.*, *Hsiao-ching
ta-ch'üan* 大全, 28 *ch.*, and *Hsiao-ching huo-
wen* 或問, 3 *ch.*, which he submitted to
the throne in 1639. In matters of morality
and ceremony he was dogmatic, believing
that excesses were at the root of the
social problems of his day.

A famine struck Loyang in 1637,
causing unrest among civilians and troops.
Lü appealed to the prince of Fu, Chu
Ch'ang-hsün (*see* Cheng Kuei-fei) who
resided at Loyang, to make his private
granaries available for public distribution.
The prince declined, but Lü opened his
own stores to relieve the refugees. He
also took the initiative in organizing help
on a larger scale. As a result of these
efforts he was restored to office.

The rebellion, after setbacks in 1638,
gathered new strength in Honan. In the
beginning of 1641 the rebel forces attacked Loyang. Lü was in charge of the
defense of the north gate. When the
officers in control of other parts of the
city capitulated and let the rebels in, Lü,
though offered several opportunities to
flee in return for his generous famine
relief, chose to remain. The rebels plundered the prince's home, distributed his
riches, and took him captive. He and Lü
encountered each other as prisoners, and
Lü admonished the prince about his royal
obligations and advised him not to bow to
the enemy. Taken to the Chou Kung 周公
temple, Lü was beheaded and the prince
executed on the same day. Lü was award-

ed the posthumous title of junior guardian of the heir apparent and later granted the rank of grand tutor at Nanking by the prince, Chu Yu-sung (ECCP).

Lü was responsible for a number of books besides those mentioned above. The editors of the *Ssu-k'u* catalogue cite four but included none in the Imperial Library. One of these, the *Ming-te-t'ang wen-chi* 文集 in 26 *chüan* (known also as *Shen-tu-t'ang* 慎獨堂 *chi*), is a collection of his prose (17 *ch.*), poems (3 *ch.*), guild regulations (2 *ch.*), and records of conversations (4 *ch.*), completed in 1640 but not published until 1668; this drew the attention of the censorial board a century later, and was ordered partially expunged. A son 1663 added a few leaves written by a friend on his father's success in dealing with the rebels in 1640. A collection of his memorials, entitled *Nan yü tsou-i* 南庾奏議, 8 *ch.*, published in the Ch'ung-chen period, is in the National Library, Peking. A large work which Lü compiled on rhymes, *Yin-yün jih-yüeh teng* 音韻日月燈, 64 *ch.* (70 according to the *Ssu-k'u* catalogue), printed in the same years, is preserved in the Library of Congress. Finally one may cite his *Sheng-hsien hsiang tsan* 聖賢像贊, 4 *ts'e*, printed in 1632 (a copy of which is in the Columbia University Library), which contains brief notices with portraits of some of the sages of the past, from Confucius to his own times. It is a catholic selection: Chu Hsi (1130–1200) is included and so too are Lu Chiu-yüan (1139–92) and Wang Shoujen (*q.v.*), Other representatives of Ming thought are Hsüeh Hsüan, Ch'en Hsienchang, and Hu Chü-jen (*qq.v.*).

Lü Wei-ch'i's younger brother, Lü Wei-chieh 祐 (T. 泰孺), a student in the National University, served for a term as magistrate of Lo-p'ing 羅平, Yunnan, then resigned and returned home. When rebels took Hsin-an in 1643, he refused to submit and was put to death.

Bibliography

1/264/6a; 3/251/5a; 41/1/12a; 64/辛 2/19b; 77/ 10/4a; 83/54/14a; KC (1958), 5627, 5690, 5885; TSCC(1885–88), XI: 748/43/1a, XIV: 406/2/22a; Huang Chi-ch'ang 黃基昌 *et al.*, *Lü Ming-te hsien-sheng nien-p'u* 年譜 (1663); Wu Wei-yeh (ECCP), *Mei-ts'un chia-ts'ang kao*, 41/3a; Ch'en Chi-sheng 陳濟生, *T'ien-ch'i Ch'ung-chen liang-ch'ao i-shih hsiao chuan* 兩朝遺詩小傳 (Shun-chih ed.), *ts'e*, 3/15a; *Lü Ming-te hsien-sheng wen-chi* 文集 (1668); *Hsin-an-hsien chih* (1914), 11/6b, 12/32b, 36b, 52a, 58a, 69a, 13/11a, 53a, 56a, *i-wen*, 6/52a; SK (1930), 25/9b, 44/4b, 96/10b, 180/2a; Sun Tien-ch'i (1957), 103; L. of C. *Catalogue of Rare Books*, 86; Kanda Kiichirō 神田喜一郎, *Shirin* 史林, 12:4 (October, 1927); Haneda Tōru, ed., *Ssu-i kuan-tse* (Kyoto, 1928); Norman Wild, "Materials for the Study of the Ssu I Kuan," BSOAS, 11 (1943–46), 617; Paul Pelliot, TP, 26 (1929), 53; *id.*, TP, 38 (1948), 225; Li Yen 李棪, *Tung-lin tang-chi k'ao* 東林黨籍考 (1957), 10, 178.

Søren Egerod

LÜ Yüan 呂原 (T. 逢原), July 21, 1418- December 18, 1462, official and scholar, was a native of Hsiu-shui 秀水, Chia-hsing prefecture 嘉興府, Chekiang. His father, Lü Ssu-fang 嗣芳, acted for a time as an instructor in the department school of Wan-ch'üan 萬泉, Shansi, and his elder brother, Lü Pen 本, served as assistant instructor in the department school of Ching-chou 景州, Pei-Chihli. While living a retired life at Ching-chou, his father passed away; subsequently his elder brother also died. As his family was poor and unable to take their remains home for burial, both coffins were placed in temporary shelters at Ching-chou. About 1437 he and his mother, née Ku 顧 returned to Hsiu-shui, their poverty more exigent than before.

Lü Yüan was an intelligent boy and a good student. By the age of nine, he began to show signs of becoming an avid reader. One day, after his return to Hsiu-shui from Ching-chou, one of his compositions came to the attention of the prefect of Chia-hsing, Huang Mou 黃懋 (T. 子勉, cs 1415). This led to his being appointed a supplementary licentiate and sent to the prefectural school for further study. In the provincial examination of Chekiang in 1441, he headed the list and came out second in the *chin-shih* tests the following year, and was made a Hanlin compiler.

The grand secretaries, Yang P'u and Yang Shih-ch'i (*q.v.*), found his services sufficiently valuable to appoint him (1447) together with several others, such as Liu Yen and Shang Lu (*qq.v.*), as lecturers, and had them study how to draft imperial decrees. Some four years later, Lü rose to be sub-expositor-in-waiting. In 1452 he became secretary in the directory of instruction, concurrently holding his previous post, while Ni Ch'ien (*q.v.*) was made another secretary and also sub-expositor-in-waiting; both of them, among other things, were ordered to teach certain eunuchs. One day during the same year, Emperor Chu Ch'i-yü (*q.v.*) asked Ni Ch'ien to explain a certain passage in the Odes and Lü Yüan to explain a passage in the Document of History. Their replies impressing him favorably, the emperor accorded both promotions.

As soon as Emperor Chu Ch'i-chen (*q.v.*) resumed control of the government in February, 1457, Lü entered the office of transmission, while still holding the post of expositor-in-waiting. On June 29 of the same year, the second day after Grand Secretary Hsü Yu-chen and Hanlin Chancellor Li Hsien (*qq.v.*) were put in jail—both, while serving at the Nei-ko, having fallen victims to a slander—, Lü was ordered to enter the Wen-yüan Hall 文淵閣 to participate in the management of the confidential affairs of state.

At that time General Shih Heng and the eunuch Ts'ao Chi-hsiang (*qq.v.*) were riding high and had become abusive in their power; nevertheless they respected Lü Yüan. Noticing that he wore a blue robe to court, Shih Heng once smiled and said: "I should like to change your robe to a purple one"—the assumption being a promotion. Lü, however, paid no attention. A few days later, Lü and Hanlin Compiler Yüeh Cheng (*see* Li Tung-yang), then

also serving in the Grand Secretariat, memorialized the throne, drawing attention to the faults of Shih Heng and Ts'ao Chi-hsiang; but the memorandum evoked no response.

Later, because of a fire within the Ch'eng-t'ien gate 承天門 on the night of July 25, 1457, Lü Yüan and Yüeh Cheng were told to draft a decree of self-reproach for the emperor. At the time this decree was issued, however, Ts'ao Chi-hsiang and Shih Heng reported to the emperor that a number of the words in the decree mocked His Majesty. The emperor was incensed. He promptly summoned Lü and Yüeh to his presence and said harshly: "You have been rude to me; I know Yüeh Cheng often displays crude manners, but Lü Yüan is usually respectful; why do you join him in this show of disrespect?" Consequently on the 30th of the same month, Yüeh was reduced to vice magistrate of Ch'in-chou 欽州, Kwangtung, while Lü was allowed to remain in office.

On the 29th of that month, Li Hsien was restored to his position, reentering the Nei-ko to direct state business; about two months later P'eng Shih (*q.v.*) was also ordered to serve with the rank of vice minister of the Court of Imperial Sacrifices and concurrent reader-in-waiting of the Hanlin Academy. Lü, P'eng, and Li, who was the senior in rank at the Grand Secretariat, were on friendly terms. Versed in the ways of the world, Li Hsien was quick in judgment; Lü Yüan, staid and grave in character, was accustomed to show fairness without favor. Because of these three ministers' efforts and cooperation, the affairs of state were put in generally good order, though at the same time several unworthy officials remained in power.

Lü became Hanlin chancellor on January 4, 1458. Besides serving at the Nei-ko, he was ordered in 1460 to take charge of the metropolitan examination conducted by the ministry of Rites, and a few months later was made one of the editors of the compila-

tion entitled *Ta-Ming i-t'ung-chih* 大明一
統志 (official geography of the Ming empire), 90 *ch.*, published in 1461, of which
Li Hsien was made the general editor
and P'eng Shih an associate. This was by
no means an original work, being based
almost entirely on the *Huan-yü t'ung-chih*
寰宇通志, 119 *ch.*, edited by Ch'en Hsün
陳循 (T. 德遵, H. 芳州, 1385-1462, optimus of 1415), presented to the preceding
emperor in 1456. P'eng Shih was the only
one to serve on both editorial boards. The
principal addition he and the other
editors of the second work made was the
inclusion of maps. Several copies of the
original edition survive, two examples
being at the Library of Congress and
at Columbia University.

Early in 1462, his mother became ill.
Grieving greatly, Lü often prepared medicine for her and attended her in person.
About September of the same year she
died; it is said that Lü touched no food
for three days. Although he asked the
emperor to allow him to return home to
bury his mother and remain to complete
the period of mourning for her, the
emperor, being in need of his services,
ordered him to come back to the capital
as soon as his mother had been laid
to rest. Escorting his mother's coffin
he promptly left Peking for Chekiang by
water, going by way of Ching-chou so as
to pick up his father's remains as well.
When he started out, he was somewhat
rotund but his grief and the rigors of
the journey made him lose weight, and
his health rapidly declined. On his arrival
at Hsiu-shui, he became ill and was soon
a shadow of his former self. He died the
same year aged only forty-four. Posthumously given the official title of left vice
minister of Rites, he was canonized as
Wen-i 文懿 (literary and virtuous).

Lü was a kindly man, known for his
sobriety and correct behavior. Being a
man of few desires, he practiced economy;
when he returned home he had only a
few suits of clothes in his baggage. He
was the author of a book entitled *Chieh-
hsien chi* 介軒集 or *Chieh-an* 菴 *chi* in 12
chüan. One edition compiled by Wang
Hung 王洪 (cj 1468), also in 12 *chüan*,
entitled *Lü-wen-i-kung ch'üan-chi* 公全集
(the complete works of Lü Yüan), is
still preserved in the Seikado Bunko, Tokyo. The National Central Library, Taipei,
has an incomplete copy in 8 *chüan* (*chüan*
2 to 5 missing).

Lü Yüan's wife, née Hsü 徐, was accorded the title of I-jen 宜人 (graceful
lady). They had two sons: Lü Ch'ang 戇
(T. 秉之) and Lü Hui 蕙. The former
was made a student of the National University by imperial favor and served in
the central drafting office. He qualified
for the *chü-jen* in 1471. Immediately thereafter, he received the appointment of
director of the bureau of receptions in
the ministry of Rites, and was subsequently raised to be vice minister of the
Court of the Imperial Stud in Nanking.
According to the usual practice, the number of horses maintained by the court
was kept secret. As a result, the registration of mounts was often incorrect,
sometimes even lacking. As soon as Lü
Ch'ang began his service, he suggested
that a census of them be carefully made
every three years. This was promptly
carried out and observed for a long time.
He was later elevated to be minister of
the Court of Imperial Sacrifices. At the
beginning of the Cheng-te period, he
retired from office and returned to his
native place. He wrote a book called
Chiu-po shan-fang kao 九柏山房稿 in 6
chüan; but it seems to be no longer extant.

Bibliography

1/176/6a; 3/159/13b; 4/7/7a; 5/13/53a; 6/1/28a,
5/8b, 7/3b, 12/5b, 27a, 15/27b, 30b, 20/29b, 24/
19a; 7/7/12a; 8/24/28a; 9/后 8/10a; 14/3/20b;
19/6/1a; 40/20/10b; 61/121/1a; 63/10/66a; 64/乙
17/8a; 86/7/7b; *Chia-hsing-fu chih* (1878), 45/11a,
52/1a, 81/37b; MSL (1964), Ying-tsung 6107,
6547, 6740; KC (1958), 2060, 2099, 2119;
Seikado library *Catalogue of Chinese Books* 靜嘉
堂文庫漢籍分類目錄 (Tokyo, 1930), 719; *Kuo-li
chung-yang t'u-shu-kuan shan-pen shu-mu* 國立中央
圖書館善本書目, II (Hong Kong, 1958), 111;

Ming-shih i-wen-chih pu-pien 補編 (Peking, 1959), 96; W. Franke, *Sources*, 8.1.1, 2; L.Carrington Goodrich, "Geographical Additions of the XIV and XV Centuries," MS, 15 (1956), 203; L. of C. *Catalogue of Rare Books* (1957), 326.

Chou Tao-chi

LUNG-ch'i 隆琦, better known by his *tzu* Yin-yüan 隱元, and in Japan as Ingen Ryūki, November 4, 1592-1673, was a Ch'an monk who became the founder of the Ōbaku sect 黃檗宗 in Japan. He was born into a Lin 林 family of Fu-ch'ing 福清, Fukien. After several years of wandering he decided to become a Buddhist monk and in 1620 was tonsured at the monastery, Wan-fu-ssu 萬福寺, on Mt. Huang-po 黃檗山 in his native district. Since its founding in the seventh century this monastery had flourished and become the center of the Huang-po branch of Ch'an Buddhism. In 1555 many buildings were destroyed during the invasion by Japanese pirates. By 1614 the monastery was to a large extent restored, partly with funds contributed by Emperor Chu I-chün (*q.v.*). After being ordained, Lung-ch'i traveled to Chekiang in an effort to raise more funds and in search of enlightenment from learned monks. In 1624 he began to study under Yüan-wu 圓悟 (T. 密雲, 1566-1642), the abbot at Chin-su-ssu 金粟寺 in Hai-yen 海鹽, Chekiang. It so happened that Yüan-wu was invited (1630) to preside at Wan-fu-ssu and Lung-ch'i accompanied him. Yüan-wu stayed only half a year but Lung-ch'i remained. In 1633 when the new abbot, T'ung-jung (*see* Han-shih), came to Wan-fu-ssu, he valued Lung-ch'i, appointing him hsi-t'ang 西堂 (second deputy abbot) and then shou-tso 首座 (first deputy abbot). In 1637 Lung-ch'i succeeded as abbot and devoted himself to the reconstruction of the temple and the improvement of its economic well-being. He sent many monks out to collect contributions. After four years the work of reconstruction was almost complete, and the temple's finances greatly improved. The monks reportedly numbered five hundred or more. During this period Lung-ch'i wrote the *Huang-po yü-lu* 語錄, 2 *ch.*, published in 1642, a collection of his discourses. It was this book which brought his name and beliefs to the attention of the Japanese.

When Lung-ch'i was sixty-two, he received an urgent invitation to come to Japan from Itsuzen 逸然, the chief monk of Kōfuku-ji 興福寺 in Nagasaki, a monastery established by Chinese merchants and sailors. They had their own temples such as Kōfuku, Sūfuku 崇福, and Fukusei 福濟, and often invited monks from China to serve in them. Since Sūfuku happened to lack an abbot, the Chinese community invited Yeh-lan 也懶 (Feng-shan Hsing-kuei 鳳山性圭), one of Yin-yüan's disciples at Wan-fu-ssu. Yeh-lan accepted and started for Japan, but lost his life in a storm at sea. They next asked Itsuzen to invite his master. At first Lung-ch'i declined, but finally, moved by Itsuzen's persuasiveness, he consented. Promising his fellow monks that he would return in three years he left Mt. Huang-po, accompanied by thirty disciples.

Arriving safely in Nagasaki (in 1654) he was installed in Kōfuku-ji. The news that a learned priest had come from China caused a sensation among not only the overseas Chinese but also those Japanese Zen (=Ch'an) monks who were drawn to the Chinese way of Dhyāna and to Chinese culture. When Lung-ch'i preached at Kōfuku-ji three months after his arrival, over a hundred Chinese and Japanese monks gathered to hear him; Kōfuku-ji seemed overnight to have changed from an insignificant Chinese shrine to an important Zen temple. Among the Japanese there were two monks, Ryūkei 龍溪 and Chikujin 竺仁 of Myōshin-ji 妙心寺 in Kyoto, who were so impressed they wanted to invite Lung-ch'i to their own monastery. Running into opposition from their fellow monks, however, they decided instead to invite him to Fumon-ji 普門寺 in Osaka.

It so happened that Lung-ch'i had reached Japan just thirteen years after the Tokugawa government, considering itself threatened by the Christian church and European expansionism, adopted a policy of national isolation (1641). Under such circumstances, to invite a Chinese monk to a Japanese temple was almost impossible of fulfillment. Ryūkei and Chikujin first approached Itakura Shigemune 板倉重宗, chief of police of Kyoto, and, after gaining his consent, went on to Edo to appeal to the retainers Sakai Tadakatsu 酒井忠勝 and Matsudaira Nobutsuna 松平信綱. Acting on their favorable report, the shōgun Ietsuna 家綱 (r. 1651-80) gave Ryūkei and Chikujin the required permission. Even at Fumon-ji, however, Lung-ch'i found himself restricted, unable to see Japanese people. Whenever he went outside the temple precincts Ryūkei, Chikujin, or some other Japanese monks of importance kept him under surveillance. Gradually, however, the restrictions were relaxed, especially after Itakure Shigemune met the Chinese monk and, impressed by his worthiness, allowed the Japanese to see him. Once this became known the curiosity of the people in the neighborhood was aroused and hundreds of them poured into the temple.

After three years in Japan, Lung-ch'i made plans to return home. To prevent this, Ryūkei besought Ietsuna to give Lung-ch'i a temple of his own and some land. Moved by this appeal, the shōgun invited him to Edo, and the following year presented him with a piece of property in Uji 宇治, and gave him permission to build a temple where he might propagate his faith. Thus dissuaded, he devoted himself to making his school popular in Japan. He put up a Chinese style monastery in Uji, which he named Ōbakuzan Manpuku-ji 黃檗山萬福寺 after his one-time seat in China.

As the school of Lung-ch'i was a branch of the Rinzai sect 臨濟宗 it was not fundamentally different. Nevertheless the Japanese called it the Ōbaku sect to distinguish it from the main sect. Actually it did seem different to the Japanese, as the rules of the temple and its ways of training monks were Chinese. One genuine difference was that it paid more attention to the act of saying prayers to the Buddha. It was not just Lung-ch'i and his followers who followed this practice; many other members of the Ch'an sect in China in his time did the same. As the Rinzai sect had been imported to Japan during the Sung dynasty, its followers made a practice of self-reliance, and rejected the custom of praying to the Buddha as reflecting an attitude of dependence on others. As a consequence, Japanese monks of the Rinzai sect had no desire to see the school of Lung-ch'i grow in influence. Those of the Myōshin-ji especially disliked and denounced him. For this reason Ryūkei left Myōshin temple and adhered to Lung-ch'i's teachings and practices. Instead of being weakened by the attacks, the Chinese school gained in popularity and a number of Rinzai temples came under the influence of Ōbaku shū.

In 1664, after being abbot of Mapuku-ji for three years, Lung-ch'i retired to live in a structure called Shōindō 松隱堂 in the same temple. Even so, many people came to see him. When at leisure he wrote a number of poems which were later collected into book form; he also enjoyed journeying to other monasteries. In 1671, at the age of eighty *sui*, he wrote out ten exhortations entitled *Yoshoku go* 預囑語 for the younger monks. The following year he ordered one of his Chinese disciples, Kao-ch'üan 高泉 (Kōsen in Japanese), to codify the rules of Ōbaku shū; these rules were made into a book entitled *Ōbaku shingi* 清規. At this point Lung-ch'i felt that his work was done. In 1673 he fell ill. One of his supporters, Gomizunoo Jōkō 後水尾上皇 (1597-1680, abdicated 1629), the former emperor, sent a special messenger several times to visit him. Learning that he was weakening, the one-time emperor con-

ferred on him the exalted title of Daikō-
fushōkokushi 大光普照國師. A little later
Lung-ch'i breathed his last, aged eighty-
one. A portrait of him, preserved in the
Manpuku-ji, is reproduced in *Ingen* (frontispiece), and illustrations of the temple
buildings appear in *Bukkyō Daijiten* 佛教
大辭典. The *Shinsan zenseki mokuroku*
新纂禪籍目錄 (1962) lists some one hundred titles either by or about Ingen Ryūki, including a life chronology, *Fushōkokushi nenpu* 年譜 and a tombstone inscription by Tu Li-te (1611-91, ECCP).

[Editors' Note: The sayings of Lung-
ch'i suggest that his teaching laid stress
on plain living and self-cultivation. His
talents and achievements were also manifested in organizational and managerial
work. When the Manpuku-ji of Uji was
opened it attracted some five hundred
monks. Today it is famous for its Chinese
style of architecture, the Ōbaku edition
of the *Tripiṭaka*, and the hundreds of
temples under its control. It is recorded
that most of its first twenty-one abbots
were Chinese. The vegetarian cuisine in
its neighborhood has a Chinese origin.
(There is even a bean named after Lung-
ch'i, the ingen mame.) In 1917 the Japanese honored him with the posthumous
name Shinkō daishi 眞空大師. According to Liang Jung-jo, the influence of
Lung-ch'i in Japan was manifested not
only in Ch'an Buddhism and architecture
but also in the fields of painting, calligraphy, sculpture, medicine, printing, and
social welfare. Several of his disciples
who accompanied him to Japan in 1654
were artists and experts in agriculture.
There was also the physican and calligrapher, Tai Li 戴笠 (T. 曼公, 1596-1672),
a native of Hangchow who had lived in
Nagasaki for a year before Lung-ch'i
arrived. After studying under Lung-ch'i
for several months, Tai was tonsured late
in 1654 under the name Hsing-i 性易. He
became well known in Japan by his courtesy name, Dokuritsu 獨立. He is often
mistaken for his namesake, the historian
Tai Li (T. 耘野, 1614-82) of Wu-chiang
吳江, near Soochow, and author of several books on the history of the late Ming
era.]

Bibliography

Liang Jung-jo 梁容若, "Yin-yüan Lung-ch'i yü
Jih-pen wen-hua" 與日本文化, *Ta-lu tsa-chih*, 8:12
(June 30, 1954), 360; *id.*, "Ming-chi liang Tai
Li shih-chi k'ao" 明季兩戴笠事蹟考, *ibid.*, 1:8
(October, 1955), 227: Akamatsu Fumyō 赤松普
明, *Ōbaku shu kōyō* 黃檗宗綱要, Tokyo, 1934;
Washio Junkei 鷲尾順敬, *Nihon zenshūshi no kenkyū* 日本禪宗史の研究 (1945), 368: Mochizuki
Shinkō 望月信亨, *Bukkyō daijiten* (Tokyo, 1936),
4762, 4987;Ōno Tatsunosuke 大野達之助, *Nihon
bukkyō shisō shi* 日本佛教思想史 (Tokyo, 1957),
260: Hirakubo Akira 平久保章, *Ingen*, Tokyo,
1962: Dōbata Yoshihide 道端良秀, *Chūgoku bukkyō shi* 中國佛教史 (Kyoto, 1965), 216.

Toyoko Chen